116th Edition

Statistical Abstract of the United States 1996

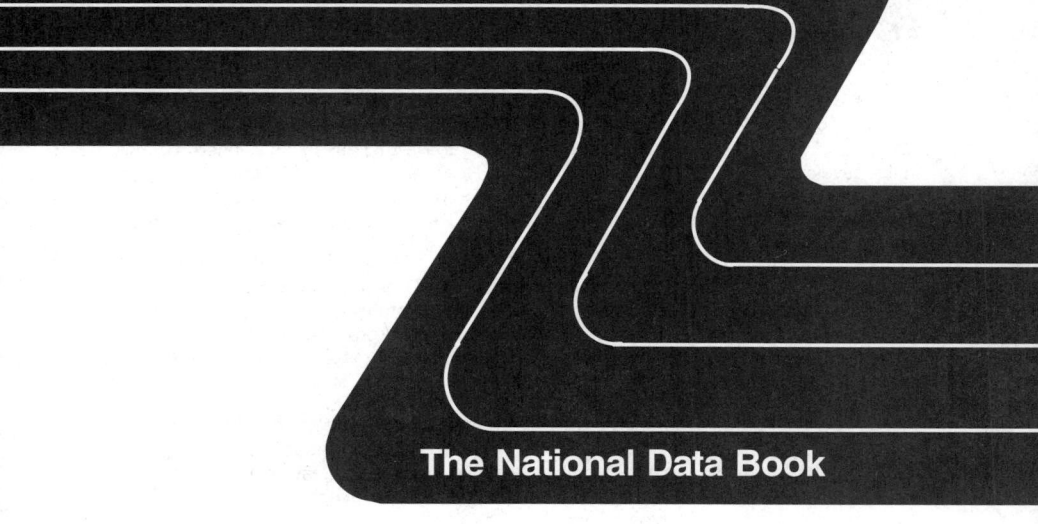

The National Data Book

Issued October 1996

U.S. Department of Commerce
Michael Kantor, Secretary

Economics and Statistics Administration
Everett M. Ehrlich, Under Secretary
for Economic Affairs

BUREAU OF THE CENSUS
Martha Farnsworth Riche, Director

ECONOMICS
AND STATISTICS
ADMINISTRATION

Economics and Statistics Administration

Everett M. Ehrlich, Under Secretary for Economic Affairs

BUREAU OF THE CENSUS

Martha Farnsworth Riche, Director
Bryant Benton, Deputy Director

ADMINISTRATIVE AND CUSTOMER SERVICES DIVISION
Walter C. Odom, Chief

Acknowledgments

Lars B. Johanson, Chief, Statistical Abstract Section, was responsible for the supervision and coordination of this volume under the general direction of **Glenn W. King**, Chief, Statistical Compendia Branch. Assisting in the research and analytical phases of assigned sections and in the developmental aspects of new tables were **Rosemary E. Clark**, **Edward C. Jagers,** and **David J. Fleck**. **Geraldine W. Blackburn** provided primary editorial assistance. Other editorial assistance was rendered by **Catherine Crusan**, **Patricia S. Lancaster**, **Catherine Lavender**, and **Joyce Mori**.

The staff of the Administrative and Customer Services Division, **Walter C. Odom**, Chief, performed publication planning, editorial review, design, composition, and printing planning and procurement. **Patricia Heiston**, assisted by **Gloria Davis**, provided publication coordination and editing. **Janet Sweeney** provided design and graphics services, and **Diane Oliff-Michael** provided printing services.

The cooperation of many contributors to this volume is gratefully acknowledged. The source note below each table credits the various government and private agencies which have collaborated in furnishing information for the **Statistical Abstract**. In a few instances, contributors have requested that their data be designated as subject to copyright restrictions, as indicated in the source notes to the tables affected. Permission to use copyright material should be obtained directly from the copyright owner.

Library of Congress Card No. 4–18089

SUGGESTED CITATION

U.S. Bureau of the Census, *Statistical Abstract of the United States: 1996* (116th edition.) Washington, DC, 1996

For sale by the U.S. Government Printing Office
Superintendent of Documents, Mail Stop: SSOP, Washington, DC 20402-9328
ISBN 0-16-048837-0

Preface

The *Statistical Abstract of the United States,* published since 1878, is the standard summary of statistics on the social, political, and economic organization of the United States. It is designed to serve as a convenient volume for statistical reference and as a guide to other statistical publications and sources. The latter function is served by the introductory text to each section, the source note appearing below each table, and Appendix I, which comprises the Guide to Sources of Statistics, the Guide to State Statistical Abstracts, and the Guide to Foreign Statistical Abstracts.

This volume includes a selection of data from many statistical publications, both government and private. Publications cited as sources usually contain additional statistical detail and more comprehensive discussions of definitions and concepts than can be presented here. Data not available in publications issued by the contributing agency but obtained from unpublished records are identified in the source notes as "unpublished data." More information on the subjects covered in the tables so noted may generally be obtained from the source.

Except as indicated, figures are for the United States as presently constituted. Although emphasis in the *Statistical Abstract* is primarily given to national data, many tables present data for regions and individual States and a smaller number for metropolitan areas and cities. Appendix II, Metropolitan Area Concepts and Components, presents explanatory text, a complete current listing and population data for metropolitan statistical areas (MSA's), the primary metropolitan statistical areas (PMSA's), and the consolidated metropolitan statistical areas (CMSA's) defined as of July 1, 1995. Table 43 in section 1 presents selected population characteristics for MSA's with population of 250,000 or more. Statistics for the Commonwealth of Puerto Rico and for outlying areas of the United States are included in many State tables and are supplemented by information in section 29. Additional information for States, cities, counties, metropolitan areas, and other small units, as well as more

historical data, are available in various supplements to the *Abstract* (see inside back cover).

Changes in this edition—The effects of the Federal Government shutdowns and weather related closings can be seen in this edition of the *Abstract.* Due to the need to go to print during the 1996 fiscal year, we were unable to update several data series. These include some series concerning national defense, flow of funds accounts, agriculture, and forestry and fisheries. We did concentrate on updating those statistics our respondents to the 1994 user questionnaire indicated are frequently used. These include our sections covering population, vital statistics, health, education, labor force, and income. In addition, we were able to incorporate throughout the book the historical revisions made to the Gross Domestic Product data series. For those statistics we are not able to update this year, we plan to update them for the 1997 edition.

We have also limited the number of new tables introduced in this edition. Typically, we introduce somewhere between 80 and 100 new tables in each edition. To lessen processing time further, we have included 33 new tables. These cover such topics as household projections, crime victims, profile of college faculty, labor force projections, building vacancy rates, merchandise line sales, and world food production. See Appendix VI, pp. 968 and 969 for a complete list of new tables.

Statistics in this edition are generally for the most recent year or period available by spring 1996. Each year almost 1,500 tables and charts are reviewed and evaluated; new tables and charts of current interest are added, continuing series are updated, and less timely data are condensed or eliminated. Text notes and appendices are revised as appropriate.

USA Statistics in Brief, 1996, a pocket-size pamphlet highlighting many statistical series in the *Abstract,* is available separately. Single copies can be obtained free from U.S. Bureau of the Census, Customer Services, Washington, DC 20233 (telephone 301-457-4100).

Historical statistics—Specific headnote references in this *Abstract* link many tables to earlier data shown in *Historical Statistics of the United States, Colonial Times to 1970.* (See Appendix IV, pp. 963 and 964.)

Statistics for States and metropolitan areas—Data for States and metro areas may also be found in the *State and Metropolitan Area Data Book, 1991.*

Statistical reliability and responsibility—The contents of this volume were taken from many sources. All data from either censuses and surveys or from administrative records are subject to error arising from a number of factors: Sampling variability (for statistics based on samples), reporting errors in the data for individual units, incomplete coverage, nonresponse, imputations, and processing error. (See also Appendix III, pp. 946-962.) The Bureau of the Census cannot accept the responsibility for the accuracy or limitations of the data presented here, other than those for which it collects. The responsibility for selection of the material and for proper presentation, however, rests with the Bureau.

For additional information on data presented—Please consult the source publications available in local libraries or write to the agency indicated in the source notes. Write to the Bureau of the Census only if it is cited as the source.

Suggestions and comments—Users of the *Statistical Abstract* and its supplements (see inside back cover) are urged to make their data needs known for consideration in planning future editions. Suggestions and comments for improving coverage and presentation of data should be sent to the Director, U.S. Bureau of the Census, Washington, DC 20233.

Contents

[Numbers following subjects are page numbers]

Contents

Weights and Measurements Conversions

APPROXIMATE CONVERSION MEASURES

[For assistance on metric usage, call or write the Office of Metric Programs, U.S. Department of Commerce, Washington, DC 20230 (301-975-3690)]

Symbol	When you know conventional	Multiply by	To find metric	Symbol
in	inch	2.54	centimeter	cm
ft	foot	30.48	centimeter	cm
yd	yard	0.91	meter	m
mi	mile	1.61	kilometer	km
in^2	square inch	6.45	square centimeter	cm^2
ft^2	square foot	0.09	square meter	m^2
yd^2	square yard	0.84	square meter	m^2
mi^2	square mile	2.59	square kilometer	km^2
	acre	0.41	hectare	ha
oz	ounce [1]	28.35	gram	g
lb	pound[1]	.45	kilograms	kg
oz (troy)	ounce [2]	31.10	gram	g
	short ton (2,000 lbs)	0.91	metric ton	t
	long ton (2,240 lbs)	1.02	metric ton	t
fl oz	fluid ounce	29.57	milliliter	mL
c	cup	0.24	liter	L
pt	pint	0.47	liter	L
qt	quart	0.95	liter	L
gal	gallon	3.78	liter	L
ft^3	cubic foot	0.03	cubic meter	m^3
yd^3	cubic yard	0.76	cubic meter	m^3
F	degrees Fahrenheit (subtract 32)	0.55	degrees Celsius	C

Symbol	When you know metric	Multiply by	To find conventional	Symbol
cm	centimeter	0.39	inch	in
cm	centimeter	0.33	foot	ft
m	meter	1.09	yard	yd
km	kilometer	0.62	mile	mi
cm^2	square centimeter	0.15	square inch	in^2
m^2	square meter	10.76	square foot	ft^2
m^2	square meter	1.20	square yard	yd^2
km^2	square kilometer	0.39	square mile	mi^2
ha	hectare	2.47	acre	
g	gram	.035	ounce [1]	oz
kg	kilogram	2.21	pounds	lb^1
g	gram	.032	ounce [2]	oz (troy)
t	metric ton	1.10	short ton (2,000 lbs)	
t	metric ton	0.98	long ton (2,240 lbs)	
mL	milliliter	0.03	fluid ounce	fl oz
L	liter	4.24	cup	c
L	liter	2.13	pint (liquid)	pt
L	liter	1.05	quart (liquid)	qt
L	liter	0.26	gallon	gal
m^3	cubic meter	35.32	cubic foot	ft^3
m^3	cubic meter	1.32	cubic yard	yd^3
C	degrees Celsius	1.80	degrees Fahrenheit (after subtracting 32)	F

[1] For weighing ordinary commodities. [2] For weighing precious metals, jewels, etc.

Example of table structure:
State and Local Government Retirement Systems—
Beneficiaries and Finances: 1980 to 1991

[In millions of dollars, except as indicated. For fiscal years closed during the 12 months ending June 30]

| YEAR AND LEVEL OF GOVERNMENT | Number of beneficiaries (1,000) | RECEIPTS | | | | | | BENEFITS AND WITHDRAWALS | | | Cash and security holdings |
| | | Total | Employee contributions | Government contributions | | Earnings on investments | Total | Benefits | Withdrawals | |
				State	Local					
1980: All systems	(NA)	37,313	6,466	7,581	9,951	13,315	14,008	12,207	1,801	185,226
State-administered . . .	(NA)	28,603	5,285	7,399	5,611	10,308	10,257	8,809	1,448	144,682
Locally administered . .	(NA)	8,710	1,180	181	4,340	3,008	3,752	3,399	353	40,544
1985: All systems	3,378	71,411	9,468	12,227	15,170	34,546	24,413	21,999	2,414	374,433
State-administered . . .	2,661	55,960	7,901	11,976	8,944	27,139	18,230	16,183	2,047	296,951
Locally administered . .	716	15,451	1,567	251	6,226	7,407	6,183	5,816	367	77,481
1990: All systems	4,026	111,339	13,853	13,994	18,583	64,907	38,396	35,966	2,430	703,772
State-administered . . .	3,232	89,162	11,648	13,964	11,538	52,012	29,603	27,562	2,041	565,641
Locally administered . .	794	22,177	2,205	32	7,045	12,895	8,793	8,404	389	138,131
1991: All systems	4,179	108,240	16,268	14,473	18,691	58,808	42,028	39,421	2,607	783,405
State-administered . . .	3,357	85,576	12,563	14,455	11,553	47,006	32,323	30,167	2,156	630,551
Locally administered . .	822	22,664	3,705	18	7,138	11,803	9,706	9,255	451	152,854

NA Not available.
Source: U.S. Bureau of the Census, *Finances of Employee-Retirement Systems of State and Local Governments*, series GF, No. 2, annual.

Headnotes immediately below table titles provide information important for correct interpretation or evaluation of the table as a whole or for a major segment of it.

Footnotes below the bottom rule of tables give information relating to specific items or figures within the table.

Unit indicators show the *specified quantities* in which data items are presented. They are used for two primary reasons. Sometimes data are not available in absolute form and are estimates (as in the case of many surveys). In other cases we round the numbers in order to save space to show more data, as in the case above.

EXAMPLES OF UNIT INDICATOR INTERPRETATION FROM TABLE

Year	Item	Unit Indicator	Number shown	Multiplier
1991	Beneficiaries	Thousands	4,179	1,000
1991	Receipts	$ Millions	108,240	1,000,000

To Determine the Figure it Is Necessary to Multiply the Number Shown by the Unit Indicator:
Beneficiaries = 4,179 * 1,000 or 4,179,000 (over 4 million).
Receipts = 108,240 * 1,000,000 or 108,240,000,000 (over 108 billion).

When a table presents data with more than one unit indicator, they are found in the headnotes and column headings (shown above), spanner (table 53), stub (table 76), or unit column (table 75). When the data in a table are shown in the same unit indicator, it is shown in boldface as the first part of the headnote (table 2). If no unit indicator is shown, data presented are in absolute form (table 1).

Heavy vertical rules are used to separate independent sections of a table, as shown above, or in tables where the stub is continued into one or more additional columns (table 4).

Averages. An average is a single number or value that is often used to represent the "typical value" of a group of numbers. It is regarded as a measure of "location" or "central tendency" of a group of numbers.

The *arithmetic mean* is the type of average used most frequently. It is derived by summing the individual item values of a particular group and dividing the total by the number of items. The arithmetic mean is often referred to as simply the "mean" or "average."

The *median* of a group of numbers is the middle number or value when each item in the group is arranged according to size (lowest to highest or visa versa); it generally has the same number of items above it as well as below it. If there is an even number if items in the group, the median is taken to be the average of the two middle numbers.

Per capita (or per person) quantities. A per capita figure represents an average computed for every person in a specified group (or population). It is derived by taking the total for an item (such as income, taxes, or retail sales) and dividing it by the number of persons in the specified population.

Index numbers. An index number is the measure of difference or change, usually expressed as a percent, relating one quantity (the variable) of a specified kind to another quantity of the same kind. Index numbers are widely used to express changes in prices over periods of time but may also be used to express differences between related subjects for a single point in time.

To compute a price index, a base year or period is selected. The base year price (of the commodity or service) is then designated as the base or reference price to which the prices for other years or periods are related. Many price indexes use the year 1982 as the base year; in tables this is shown as "1982=100". A method of expressing the price relationship is: The price of a set of one or more items for a related year (e.g. 1990) **divided by** the price of the same set of items for the base year (e.g. 1982). The result multiplied by 100 provides the index number. When 100 is subtracted from the index number, the result equals the percent change in price from the base year.

Average annual percent change. Unless otherwise stated in the *Abstract* (as in Section 1, Population), average annual percent change is computed by use of a *compound interest formula*. This formula assumes that the rate of change is constant throughout a specified compounding period (one year for average annual rates of change). The formula is similar to that used to compute the balance of a savings account which receives compound interest. According to this formula, at the end of a compounding period the amount of accrued change (e.g. school enrollment or bank interest) is added to the amount which existed at the beginning the period. As a result, over time (e.g., with each year or quarter), the same rate of change is applied to a larger and larger figure.

The *exponential formula,* which is based on continuous compounding, is often used to measure population change. It is preferred by population experts because they view population and population-related subjects as changing without interruption, ever ongoing. Both exponential and compound interest formulas assume a constant rate of change. The former, however, applies the amount of change continuously to the base rather than at the end of each compounding period. When the average annual rates are small (e.g., less than 5 percent) both formulas give virtually the same results. For an explanation

of these two formulas as they relate to population, see U.S. Bureau of the Census, *The Methods and Materials of Demography,* vol. 2, 3d printing (rev.), 1975, pp. 372-381.

Current and constant dollars. Statistics in some tables in a number of sections are expressed in both current and constant dollars (see, for example, table 699 in section 14). Current dollar figures reflect actual prices or costs prevailing during the specified year(s). Constant dollar figures are estimates representing an effort to remove the effects of price changes from statistical series reported in dollar terms. In general, constant dollar series are derived by dividing current dollar estimates by the appropriate price index for the appropriate period (for example, the Consumer Price Index). The result is a series as it would presumably exist if prices were the same throughout, as in the base year—in other words as if the dollar had constant purchasing power. Any changes in this constant dollar series would reflect only changes in real volume of output, income, expenditures, or other measure.

Explanation of Symbols:

The following symbols, used in the tables throughout this book, are explained in condensed form in footnotes to the tables where they appear:

- Represents zero or rounds to less than half the unit of measurement shown.

B Base figure too small to meet statistical standards for reliability of a derived figure.

D Figure withheld to avoid disclosure pertaining to a specific organization or individual.

NA Data not enumerated, tabulated, or otherwise available separately.

NS Percent change irrelevant or insignificant.

S Figure does not meet publication standards for reasons other than that covered by symbol B, above.

X Figure not applicable because column heading and stub line make entry impossible, absurd, or meaningless.

Z Entry would amount to less than half the unit of measurement shown.

In many tables, details will not add to the totals shown because of rounding.

Telephone Contacts List

To help *Abstract* users find more data and information about statistical publications, we are issuing this list of contacts for Federal agencies with major statistical programs. The intent is to give a single, first-contact point-of-entry for users of statistics. These agencies will provide general information on their statistical programs and publications, as well as specific information on how to order their publications. For the first time, we are also including the Internet (World Wide Web) addresses for many of these agencies.

Executive Office of the President

Office of Management and Budget
Administrator
Office of Information and Regulatory Affairs
Office of Management and Budget
Washington, DC 20503
Information: 202-395-3000
Publications: 202-395-7332
Internet address:
http://www.whitehouse.gov/fsbr/ssbr.html
and
http://www.whitehouse.gov/fsbr/esbr.html

Department of Agriculture

Economic Research Service
Research Support & Training Branch
U.S. Department of Agriculture
Room 110
1301 New York Ave., N.W.
Washington, DC 20005-4788
Information and Publications: 202-219-0515
Internet address: http://www.econ.ag.gov/

National Agricultural Statistics Service
National Agricultural Statistics Service
U.S. Department of Agriculture
14th St. and Independence Ave., S.W.
Washington, DC 20250
Information hotline: 1-800-727-9540
Internet address: http://www.usda.gov/nass/

Department of Commerce

Bureau of the Census
Customer Services Branch
Bureau of the Census
U.S. Department of Commerce
Washington, DC 20233
Information and Publications: 301-457-4100
Internet address: http://www.census.gov/

Bureau of Economic Analysis
Current Business Analysis Division, BE-53
Bureau of Economic Analysis
U.S. Department of Commerce
Washington, DC 20230
Information and Publications: 202-606-9900
Internet address: http://www.bea.doc.gov/

Department of Commerce —Con.
International Trade Administration
Trade Statistics Division
Office of Trade and Investment Analysis
International Trade Administration
Room 2814 B
U.S. Department of Commerce
Washington, DC 20230
Information and Publications: 202-482-2185

National Oceanic and Atmospheric Administration
National Oceanic and Atmospheric Administration Library
U.S. Department of Commerce
1315 East-West Highway 2nd Floor
Silver Spring MD 20910
Library: 301-713-2600
Internet address: http://www.noaa.gov/

Department of Defense
Department of Defense
Office of the Assistant to the Secretary of Defense (Public Affairs)
Room 1E794
Attention: Directorate for Public Correspondence
1400 Defense Pentagon
Washington, DC 20301-1400
Information: 703-697-5737
Internet address:
http://web1.whs.osd.mil/mmid/mmidhome.htm

Department of Education

Office of Information Services
Statistical Information Office
U.S. Department of Education
555 New Jersey Ave., N.W.
Washington, DC 20208-5641
Information and Publications: 1-800-424-1616
Internet address: http://www.ed.gov/NCES/

Department of Energy

Energy Information Administration
National Energy Information Center
U.S. Department of Energy
1000 Independence Ave., SW
1F048, EI-231
Washington, DC 20585
Information and Publications: 202-586-8800
Internet address: http://www.eia.doe.gov/

Department of Health and Human Services

Health Resources and Services Administration

Health Resources and Services
Administration
HRSA Office of Communications
5600 Fishers Lane, Room 14-45
Rockville, MD 20857
Publications: 301-443-2086
Internet address: http://www.hrsa.dhhs.gov/

*Substance Abuse Mental Health Services
Administration*

U.S. Department of Health and Human
Services
5600 Fishers Lane
Room 12C105
Rockville, MD 20857
Information: 301-443-4795
Publications: 1-800-729-6686
Internet address: http://www.samhsa.gov/

Centers for Disease Control and Prevention

Office of Information
Centers for Disease Control
21600 Clifton Road, N.E.
Atlanta, GA 30333
Public Inquiries: 404-639-3534
Internet address:
  http://www.cdc.gov/cdc.html

Health Care Financing Administration

Office of Public Affairs
Health Care Financing Administration
U.S. Department of Health and Human
Services
Room 403B, Humphrey Building
200 Independence Ave., S.W.
Washington, DC 20201
Media Relations: 202-690-6145
Internet address: http://www.hcfa.gov/

National Center for Health Statistics

Scientific and Technical Information Branch
National Center for Health Statistics
U.S. Department of Health and Human
Services
6525 Belcrest Rd. Rm. 1064
Hyattsville, MD 20782
Information and Publications: 301-436-8500
Internet address:
  http://www.cdc.gov/nchswww/nchshome.htm

Social Security Administration

Publications Staff
Office of Research and Statistics
Social Security Administration
U.S. Department of Health and Human
Services
Van Ness Centre, Room 209
4301 Connecticut Ave., N.W.
Washington, DC 20008
Information and Publications: 202-282-7138
Internet address:
  http://www.ssa.gov/statistics/ores_home.
  html

Department of Housing and Urban Development

*Assistant Secretary for Community Planning
and Development*

Office of the Assistant Secretary for
Community Planning and Development
U.S. Department of Housing and Urban
Development
451 7th St., S.W.
Washington, DC 20410-0555
Information: 202-708-2690
Publications: 1-800-245-2691
Internet address: http://www.huduser.org/

Department of the Interior

Bureau of Mines

Office of Public Information
Bureau of Mines
U.S. Department of the Interior
810 7th St., N.W.
Washington, DC 20241
Information: 202-501-9649
Publications: 202-501-9757

Geological Survey

Earth Science Information Center
Geological Survey
U.S. Department of the Interior
507 National Center
Reston, VA 22092
Information and Publications:
  703-648-6045
Internet address for minerals:
  http://minerals.er.usgs.gov:80/minerals/
Internet address for other USGS materials:
  http://www.usgs.gov/

Department of Justice

Bureau of Justice Statistics

Statistics Division
Bureau of Justice Statistics
U.S. Department of Justice
1110 Vermont Ave., NW, 10th Floor
Washington, DC 20005
Information and Publications: 202-307-6100
Internet address:
  http://www.ojp.usdoj.gov/bjs/

*National Criminal Justice Reference
Service*

Box 6000
Rockville, MD 20850
Information and Publications: 301-251-5500
Publications: 1-800-732-3277

Federal Bureau of Investigation

National Crime Information Center
Federal Bureau of Investigation
U.S. Department of Justice
935 Pennsylvania Ave., N.W.
Washington, DC 20535
Information and Publications: 202-324-3691
Publications: 202-324-5343
Internet address: http://www.fbi.gov/

Department of Justice —Con.
Immigration and Naturalization Service

Statistics Branch
Immigration and Naturalization Service
U.S. Department of Justice
425 I St., NW, Rm. 5309
Washington, DC 20536
Information and Publications:
 202-305-1613
Internet address:
 http://www.usdoj.gov/ins/ins.html

Department of Labor

Bureau of Labor Statistics

Office of Publications and Information
 Services
Bureau of Labor Statistics
U.S. Department of Labor
441 G St., N.W., Room 2831A
Washington, DC 20212
Information and Publications:
 202-606-7828
Internet address: http://stats.bls.gov/

*Employment and Training
Administration*

Office of Public Information
Employment and Training
 Administration
U.S. Department of Labor
200 Constitution Ave., N.W.,
 Room S4206
Washington, DC 20210
Information and Publications:
 202-219-6871
Internet address: http://www.doleta.gov/

Department of Transportation

Federal Aviation Administration

Public Inquiry Center
APA 200
Federal Aviation Administration
U.S. Department of Transportation
800 Independence Ave., S.W.
Washington, DC 20591
Information and Publications:
 202-267-3484
Internet address: http://www.faa.gov/

Bureau of Transportation Statistics
Internet address: http://www.bts.gov/

Federal Highway Administration

Office of Public Affairs
Federal Highway Administration
U.S. Department of Transportation
400 7th St., S.W.
Washington, DC 20590
Information: 202-366-0660

Department of Transportation —Con.
National Highway Traffic Safety Administration

Office of Public Affairs
National Highway Traffic Safety
 Administration
U.S. Department of Transportation
400 7th St., S.W.
Washington, DC 20590
Information: 202-366-9550
Publications: 202-366-2588
Internet address: http://www.nhtsa.dot.gov/

Department of the Treasury
Internal Revenue Service

Statistics of Income Division
Internal Revenue Service
U.S. Department of the Treasury
P.O. Box 2608
Washington, DC 20013
Information and Publications: 202-874-0410
Internet address:
 http://www.irs.ustreas.gov/prod/taxstats/index.html

Department of Veterans Affairs
Department of Veterans Affairs

Office of Public Affairs
Department of Veterans Affairs
810 Vermont Ave., N.W.
Washington, DC 20420
Information: 202-273-5700

Independent Agencies
Environmental Protection Agency

Public Information Center, Rm. MC3406
Environmental Protection Agency
401 M St., S.W.
Washington, DC 20460
Information: 202-260-2080
Internet address: http://www.epa.gov/

Federal Reserve Board

Division of Research and Statistics
Federal Reserve Board
Washington, DC 20551
Information: 202-452-3301
Publications: 202-452-3245
Internet address: http://www.bog.frb.fed.us/

National Science Foundation

Office of Legislative and Public Affairs
National Science Foundation
4201 Wilson Boulevard.
Arlington Virginia 22230
Information: 703-306-1234
Publications: 703-306-1130
Internet address:
 http://www.nsf.gov:80/sbe/srs/stats.htm

Securities and Exchange Commission

Office of Public Affairs
Securities and Exchange Commission
450 5th St., N.W.
Washington, DC 20549
Information: 202-942-0020
Publications: 202-942-4040
Internet address: http://www.sec.gov/

Population

This section presents statistics on the growth, distribution, and characteristics of the U.S. population. The principal source of these data is the Bureau of the Census, which conducts a decennial census of population, a monthly population survey, a program of population estimates and projections, and a number of other periodic surveys relating to population characteristics. For a list of relevant publications, see the Guide to Sources of Statistics in Appendix I.

Decennial censuses—The U.S. Constitution provides for a census of the population every 10 years, primarily to establish a basis for apportionment of members of the House of Representatives among the States. For over a century after the first census in 1790, the census organization was a temporary one, created only for each decennial census. In 1902, the Bureau of the Census was established as a permanent Federal agency, responsible for enumerating the population and also for compiling statistics on other subjects.

Historically the census of population has been a complete count. That is, an attempt is made to account for every person, for each person's residence, and for other characteristics (sex, age, family relationships, etc.). Since the 1940 census, in addition to the complete count information, some data have been obtained from representative samples of the population. In the 1990 census, variable sampling rates were employed. For most of the country, 1 in every 6 households (about 17 percent) received the long form or sample questionnaire; in governmental units estimated to have fewer than 2,500 inhabitants, every other household (50 percent) received the sample questionnaire to enhance the reliability of sample data for small areas. Exact agreement is not to be expected between sample data and the complete census count. Sample data may be used with confidence where large numbers are involved and assumed to indicate trends and relationships where small numbers are involved.

In Brief	
Total population, 1995	263 million
Northeast	*20%*
Midwest	*24%*
South	*35%*
West	*22%*
Total households, 1995	99 million
One-person households	*25%*

Census data presented here have not been adjusted for underenumeration. Results from the evaluation program for the 1990 census indicate that the overall national undercount was between 1 and 2 percent - the estimate from the Post Enumeration Survey (PES) was 1.6 percent and the estimate from Demographic Analysis (DA) was 1.8 percent. Both the PES and DA estimates show disproportionately high undercounts for some demographic groups. For example, the PES estimates of percent net undercount for Blacks (4.4 percent), Hispanics (5.0 percent), and American Indians (4.5 percent) were higher than the estimated undercount of non-Hispanic whites (0.7 percent). Historical DA estimates demonstrate that the overall undercount rate in the census has declined significantly over the past 50 years (from an estimated 5.4 percent in 1940 to 1.8 percent in 1990), yet the undercount of Blacks has remained disproportionately high.

Current Population Survey (CPS)— This is a monthly nationwide survey of a scientifically selected sample representing the noninstitutional civilian population. The sample is located in 754 areas comprising 2,121 counties, independent cities, and minor civil divisions with coverage in every State and the District of Columbia and is subject to sampling error. At the present time, about 50,000 occupied households are eligible for interview every month; of these between 4 and 5 percent are, for various reasons, unavailable for interview.

While the primary purpose of the CPS is to obtain monthly statistics on the labor force, it also serves as a vehicle for inquiries on other subjects. Using CPS data, the Bureau issues a series of publications under the general title of *Current Population Reports*, which cover population characteristics (P20), consumer income (P60), special studies (P23), and other topics.

Estimates of population characteristics based on the CPS will not agree with the counts from the census because the CPS and the census use different procedures for collecting and processing the data for racial groups, the Hispanic population, and other topics. Caution should also be used when comparing estimates for various years because of the periodic introduction of changes into the CPS. Beginning in January 1994, a number of changes were introduced into the CPS that effect all data comparisons with prior years. These changes include the results of a major redesign of the survey questionnaire and collection methodology and the introduction of 1990 census population controls, adjusted for the estimated undercount. This change in population controls had relatively little impact on derived measures such as means, medians, and percent distribution, but did have a significant impact on levels.

Population estimates and projections— National population estimates are derived by using decennial census data as benchmarks and data available from various agencies as follows: Births and deaths (National Center for Health Statistics); immigrants (Immigration and Naturalization Service); Armed Forces (Department of Defense and Department of Transportation); net movement between Puerto Rico and the U.S. mainland (Puerto Rico Planning Board); and Federal employees abroad (Office of Personnel Management and Department of Defense). Estimates for States and smaller areas are based on data series such as births and deaths, school statistics from State departments of education and parochial school systems, and Federal income tax returns. These estimates contain estimated emigration of 222,000 per year since 1980 and net undocumented immigration of 225,000 per year.

Data for the population by age for April 1, 1990, (shown in tables 14, 21, and 23) are modified counts. The review of detailed 1990 information indicated that respondents tended to provide their age as of the date of completion of the questionnaire, not their age as of April 1, 1990. In addition, there may have been a tendency for respondents to round up their age if they were close to having a birthday. A detailed explanation of the age modification procedure appears in 1990 Census of Population and Housing Data Paper Listing (CPH-L-74).

Population estimates and projections are published in the P25 series of *Current Population Reports*. These estimates and projections are generally consistent with official decennial census figures and do not reflect the amount of estimated census underenumeration. However, these estimates and projections by race have been modified and are not comparable to the census race categories (see section below under "race"). For details on methodology, see the sources cited below the individual tables.

The population projections for States, by single year of age, sex, race, and Hispanic origin prepared for July 1, 1993 to 2020 use the cohort-component method. This method requires separate assumptions for each component of population change: births, deaths, internal migration, and international migration. These components are produced and refined using various administrative records and census distributions. State estimates for 1992 are the starting points for these projections which are consistent with the national projections reported in the U.S. Bureau of the Census, *Current Population Reports*, series P25-1104. The four series of projections (see table 36) are based on different internal migration assumptions: 1) Series A, is the preferred series model and uses State-to-State migration observed from 1975-76 through 1991-92; 2) Series B, the economic model, uses the Bureau of Economic Analysis employment projections; 3) Series C, the floating mean model, is the mean of the n most recent years for the n-th projection year; and 4) Series D, is the zero net internal migration assumption.

Immigration—The principal source of immigration data is the *Statistical Yearbook of the Immigration and Naturalization Service*, published annually by the Immigration and Naturalization Service (INS), a unit of the Department of Justice. Immigration statistics are prepared from entry visas and change of immigration status forms. Immigrants are aliens admitted for legal permanent residence in the United States. The procedures for admission depend on whether the alien is residing inside or outside the United States at the time of application for permanent residence. Eligible aliens residing outside the United States are issued immigrant visas by the U.S. Department of State. Eligible aliens residing in the United States are allowed to change their status from temporary to permanent residence at INS district offices. The category, immigrant, includes persons who may have entered the United States as nonimmigrants or refugees, but who subsequently changed their status to that of a permanent resident. Nonresident aliens admitted to the United States for a temporary period are nonimmigrants (tables 7 and 430). Refugees are considered nonimmigrants when initially admitted into the United States, but are not included in nonimmigrant admission data. A refugee is any person who is outside his or her country of nationality who is unable or unwilling to return to that country because of persecution or a well-founded fear of persecution.

U.S. immigration law gives preferential immigration status to aliens who are related to certain U.S. citizens or legal permanent residents, aliens with needed job skills, or aliens who qualify as refugees. Immigration to the United States can be divided into two general categories: (1) those subject to the annual worldwide limitation, and (2) those exempt from it. The Immigration Act of 1990 established major revisions in the numerical limits and preference system regulating legal immigration. The numerical limits are imposed on visas issued and not on admissions. The maximum number of visas allowed to be issued under the preference categories in 1994 was 369,213—226,000 for family-sponsored immigrants and 143,213 for employment-based immigrants. There are nine categories among which the family-sponsored and employment-based immigrant visas are distributed, beginning in fiscal year 1992. The family-sponsored preferences are based on the alien's relationship with a U.S. citizen or legal permanent resident (see table 6). The employment-based preferences are 1) priority workers (persons of extraordinary ability, outstanding professors and researchers, and certain multinational executives and managers); 2) professionals with advanced degrees or aliens with exceptional ability; 3) skilled workers, professionals without advanced degrees, and needed unskilled workers; 4) special immigrants; and 5) employment creation immigrants (investors). Within the overall limitations the per-country limit for independent countries is set to 7 percent of the total family-sponsored and employment-based limits, while dependent areas are limited to two percent of the total. The 1994 limit allowed no more than 25,845 preference visas for any independent country and 7,384 for any dependency. Those exempt from the worldwide limitation include immediate relatives of U.S. citizens, refugees and asylees adjusting to permanent residence, and other various classes of special immigrants (see table 6).

The Refugee Act of 1980, effective April 1, 1980, provides for a uniform admission procedure for refugees of all countries, based on the United Nations' definition of refugees. Authorized admission ceilings are set annually by the President in consultation with Congress. After one year of residence in the United States, refugees are eligible for immigrant status.

The Immigration Reform and Control Act of 1986 (IRCA) allows two groups of illegal aliens to become temporary and then permanent residents of the United States: aliens who have been in the United States unlawfully since January 1, 1982, (legalization applicants), and aliens who were employed in seasonal agricultural work for a minimum period of time (Special Agricultural Worker (SAW) applicants). The application period for temporary residency for legalization applicants began on May 5, 1987, and ended on May 4, 1988, while the application period for SAW applicants began on June 1, 1987, and ended on November 30, 1988. Legalization applicants became eligible for permanent residence beginning in fiscal year 1989. Beginning 1989 immigrant data include temporary residents who were granted permanent residence under the legalization program of IRCA.

Metropolitan Areas (MA's)—The general concept of a metropolitan area is one of a core area containing a large population nucleus, together with adjacent communities that have a high degree of social and economic integration with that core. Metropolitan statistical areas (MSA's), consolidated metropolitan statistical areas (CMSA's), and primary metropolitan statistical areas (PMSA's) are defined by the Office of Management and Budget (OMB) as a standard for Federal agencies in the preparation and publication of statistics relating to metropolitan areas. The entire territory of the United States is classified as metropolitan (inside MSA's or CMSA's—PMSA's are components of CMSA's) or nonmetropolitan (outside MSA's or CMSA's). MSA's, CMSA's, and PMSA's are defined in terms of entire counties except in New England, where the definitions are in terms of cities and towns. The OMB also defines New England County Metropolitan Areas (NECMA's) which are county-based alternatives to the MSA's and CMSA's in the six New England States. From time to time, new MA's are created and the boundaries of others change. As a result, data for MA's over time may not be comparable and the analysis of historical trends must be made cautiously. For descriptive details and a listing of titles and components of MA's, see Appendix II.

Urban and rural—According to the 1990 census definition, the urban population comprises all persons living in (a) places of 2,500 or more inhabitants incorporated as cities, villages, boroughs (except in Alaska and New York), and towns (except in the New England States, New York, and Wisconsin), but excluding those persons living in the rural portions of extended cities (places with low population density in one or more large parts of their area); (b) census designated places (previously termed unincorporated) of 2,500 or more inhabitants; and (c) other territory,

incorporated or unincorporated, included in urbanized areas. An urbanized area comprises one or more places and the adjacent densely settled surrounding territory that together have a minimum population of 50,000 persons. In all definitions, the population not classified as urban constitutes the rural population

Residence—In determining residence, the Bureau of the Census counts each person as an inhabitant of a usual place of residence (i.e., the place where one usually lives and sleeps). While this place is not necessarily a person's legal residence or voting residence, the use of these different bases of classification would produce the same results in the vast majority of cases.

Race—The Bureau of the Census collects and publishes racial statistics as outlined in Statistical Policy Directive No. 15 issued by the U.S. Office of Management and Budget. This directive provides standards on ethnic and racial categories for statistical reporting to be used by all Federal agencies. According to the directive, the basic racial categories are American Indian or Alaska Native, Asian or Pacific Islander, Black, and White. (The directive identifies Hispanic origin as an ethnicity.) The concept of race the Bureau of the Census uses reflects self-identification by respondents; that is the individual's perception of his/her racial identity. The concept is not intended to reflect any biological or anthropological definition. Although the Bureau of the Census adheres to the overall guidelines of Directive No. 15, it recognizes that there are persons who do not identify with a specific racial group. The 1990 census race question includes an "Other race" category with provisions for a write-in entry. Furthermore, the Bureau of the Census recognizes that the categories of the race item include both racial and national origin or socio-cultural groups.

Differences between the 1990 census and earlier censuses affect the comparability of data for certain racial groups and American Indian tribes. The lack of comparability is due to changes in the way some respondents reported their race as well as changes in 1990 census procedures related to the racial classification. (For a fuller explanation, see *1990 Census of Population, Volume I,*

General Population Characteristics (1990 CP-1).)

Data for the population by race for April 1, 1990, (shown in tables 12, 13, 18, 19, 21, and 23) are modified counts and are not comparable to the 1990 census race categories. These numbers were computed using 1990 census data by race which had been modified to be consistent with the guidelines in Federal Statistical Directive No. 15 issued by the Office of Management and Budget. A detailed explanation of the race modification procedure appears in 1990 Census of Population and Housing Data Paper Listing (CPH-L-74).

In the CPS and other household sample surveys in which data are obtained through personal interview, respondents are asked to classify their race as: (1) White, (2) Black, (3) American Indian, Aleut, or Eskimo, or (4) Asian or Pacific Islander. The procedures for classifying persons of mixed races who could not provide a single response to the race question are generally similar to those used in the census.

Hispanic population—In the 1990 census, the Bureau of the Census collected data on the Hispanic origin population in the United States by using a self-identification question. Persons of Spanish/Hispanic origin are those who classified themselves in one of the specific Hispanic origin categories listed on the questionnaire—Mexican, Puerto Rican, Cuban, or Other Spanish/Hispanic origin. Both in 1980 and 1990, the Hispanic origin question contained prelisted categories for the largest Hispanic origin groups—Mexican, Puerto Rican, and Cuban as well as for the residual category Other Spanish/Hispanic. The 1990 Hispanic origin question differed from the 1980 question in that in 1990, unlike in 1980, the question contained a write-in line for the subgroups. Another difference between the 1980 and 1990 Hispanic origin question is that in 1980 the wording of the Hispanic origin question read: "Is this person of Spanish/Hispanic origin or descent?" while in 1990 the word "descent" was dropped from the question. Persons of Hispanic origin may be of any race.

In the CPS information on Hispanic persons is gathered by using a self-identification question. Persons classify themselves in one of the Hispanic categories in response to the question: "What is the origin or descent of each person in this household?" Hispanic persons in the CPS are persons who report themselves as Mexican-American, Chicano, Mexican, Puerto Rican, Cuban, Central or South American (Spanish countries), or other Hispanic origin.

Nativity—The native population consists of all persons born in the United States, Puerto Rico, or an outlying area of the United States. It also includes persons born at sea or in a foreign country who have at least one American parent. All others are classified as "foreign born."

Mobility status—The U.S. population is classified according to mobility status on the basis of a comparison between the place of residence of each individual at the time of the survey or census and the place of residence at a specified earlier date. Nonmovers are all persons who were living in the same house or apartment at the end of the period as at the beginning of the period. Movers are all persons who were living in a different house at the end of the period from that in which they were living at the beginning of the period. Movers from abroad include all persons, either citizens or aliens, whose place of residence was outside the United States at the beginning of the period; that is, in Puerto Rico, an outlying area under the jurisdiction of the United States, or a foreign country.

Living arrangements—Living arrangements refer to residency in households or in group quarters. A "household" comprises all persons who occupy a "housing unit," that is, a house, an apartment or other group of rooms, or a single room that constitutes "separate living quarters." A household includes the related family members and all the unrelated persons, if any, such as lodgers, foster children, wards, or employees who share the housing unit. A person living alone or a group of unrelated persons sharing the same housing unit is also counted as a household. See text, section 25, Construction and Housing, for definition of housing unit.

All persons not living in households are classified as living in group quarters. These individuals may be institutionalized, e.g., under care or custody in juvenile facilities, jails, correctional facilities, hospitals, or nursing homes; or they may be residents in noninstitutional group quarters such as college dormitories, military barracks, or rooming houses (see table 85).

Householder—The householder is the first adult household member listed on the questionnaire. The instructions call for listing first the person (or one of the persons) in whose name the home is owned or rented. If a home is owned or rented jointly by a married couple, either the husband or the wife may be listed first. Prior to 1980, the husband was always considered the household head (householder) in married-couple households.

Family—The term "family" refers to a group of two or more persons related by birth, marriage, or adoption and residing together in a household. A family includes among its members the householder.

Subfamily—A subfamily consists of a married couple and their children, if any, or one parent with one or more never-married children under 18 years old living in a household. Subfamilies are divided into "related" and "unrelated" subfamilies. A related subfamily is related to, but does not include, the householder. Members of a related subfamily are also members of the family with whom they live. The number of related subfamilies, therefore, is not included in the count of families. An unrelated subfamily may include persons such as guests, lodgers, or resident employees and their spouses and/or children; none of whom is related to the householder.

Married couple—A "married couple" is defined as a husband and wife living together in the same household, with or without children and other relatives.

Unrelated individuals—"Unrelated individuals" are persons (other than inmates of institutions) who are not members of families or subfamilies.

Secondary individuals—Secondary individuals are persons of any age who reside in a household, but are not related to the householder (except unrelated subfamily members). Persons who reside in group quarters are also secondary individuals. Examples of a secondary individual include (1) a guest, partner, roommate, or resident employee; (2) a foster child; or (3) a person residing in a rooming house, a halfway house, staff quarters at a hospital, or other type of group quarters.

Statistical reliability—For a discussion of statistical collection and estimation, sampling procedures, and measures of statistical reliability applicable to Census Bureau data, see Appendix III.

Historical statistics—Tabular headnotes provide cross-references, where applicable, to *Historical Statistics of the United States, Colonial Times to 1970.* See Appendix IV.

Figure 1.1
**Ten Fastest Growing States,
Percent Population Change: 1990 to 1995**

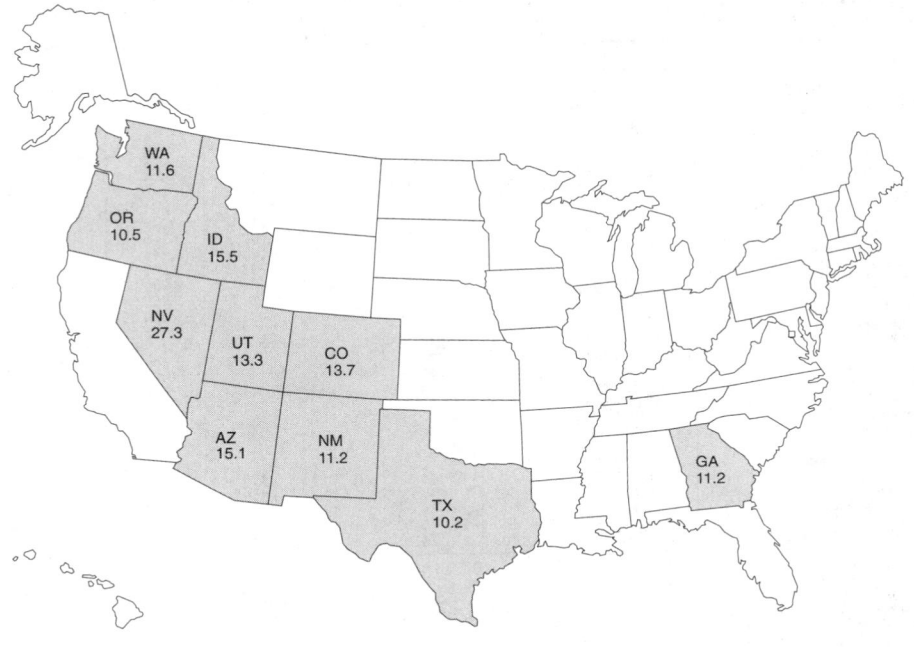

Source: Charts prepared by U.S. Bureau of the Census. For data, see table 28.

Figure 1.2
**Resident Population, by Hispanic
Origin Status: 1990 and 2000**

Non-Hispanic
White
Black
American Indian, Eskimo, Aleut
Asian, Pacific Islander

Hispanic origin[1]

Percent

[1] Persons of Hispanic origin may be of any race.
Source: Charts prepared by U.S. Bureau of the Census. For data, see table 19.

No. 1. Population and Area: 1790 to 1990

[Area figures represent area on indicated date including in some cases considerable areas not then organized or settled, and not covered by the census. Total area figures for 1790 to 1970 have been recalculated on the basis of the remeasurement of States and counties for the 1980 census, but not on the basis of the 1990 census. The land and water area figures for past censuses have not been adjusted and are not strictly comparable with the total area data for comparable dates because the land areas were derived from different base data, and these values are known to have changed with the construction of reservoirs, draining of lakes, etc. Density figures are based on land area measurements as reported in earlier censuses]

CENSUS DATE	RESIDENT POPULATION				AREA (square miles)		
	Number	Per square mile of land area	Increase over preceding census		Total	Land	Water
			Number	Percent			
CONTERMINOUS U.S. [1]							
1790 (Aug. 2)	3,929,214	4.5	(X)	(X)	891,364	864,746	24,065
1800 (Aug. 4)	5,308,483	6.1	1,379,269	35.1	891,364	864,746	24,065
1810 (Aug. 6)	7,239,881	4.3	1,931,398	36.4	1,722,685	1,681,828	34,175
1820 (Aug. 7)	9,638,453	5.5	2,398,572	33.1	1,792,552	1,749,462	38,544
1830 (June 1)	12,866,020	7.4	3,227,567	33.5	1,792,552	1,749,462	38,544
1840 (June 1)	17,069,453	9.8	4,203,433	32.7	1,792,552	1,749,462	38,544
1850 (June 1)	23,191,876	7.9	6,122,423	35.9	2,991,655	2,940,042	52,705
1860 (June 1)	[2]31,443,321	10.6	8,251,445	35.6	3,021,295	2,969,640	52,747
1870 (June 1)	[2]39,818,449	[2]13.4	8,375,128	26.6	3,021,295	2,969,640	52,747
1880 (June 1)	50,155,783	16.9	10,337,334	26.0	3,021,295	2,969,640	52,747
1890 (June 1)	62,947,714	21.2	12,791,931	25.5	3,021,295	2,969,640	52,747
1900 (June 1)	75,994,575	25.6	13,046,861	20.7	3,021,295	2,969,834	52,553
1910 (Apr. 15)	91,972,266	31.0	15,977,691	21.0	3,021,295	2,969,565	52,822
1920 (Jan. 1)	105,710,620	35.6	13,738,354	14.9	3,021,295	2,969,451	52,936
1930 (Apr. 1)	122,775,046	41.2	17,064,426	16.1	3,021,295	2,977,128	45,259
1940 (Apr. 1)	131,669,275	44.2	8,894,229	7.2	3,021,295	2,977,128	45,259
1950 (Apr. 1)	150,697,361	50.7	19,028,086	14.5	3,021,295	2,974,726	47,661
1960 (Apr. 1)	178,464,236	60.1	27,766,875	18.4	3,021,295	2,968,054	54,207
UNITED STATES							
1950 (Apr. 1)	151,325,798	42.6	19,161,229	14.5	3,618,770	3,552,206	63,005
1960 (Apr. 1)	179,323,175	50.6	27,997,377	18.5	3,618,770	3,540,911	74,212
1970 (Apr. 1)	[3]203,302,031	[3]57.4	23,978,856	13.4	3,618,770	[3]3,540,023	[3]78,444
1980 (Apr. 1)	[4]226,542,199	64.0	23,240,168	11.4	3,618,770	3,539,289	79,481
1990 (Apr. 1)	[5]248,718,301	70.3	22,176,102	9.8	[6]3,717,796	[6]3,536,278	[6][7]181,518

X Not applicable.   [1] Excludes Alaska and Hawaii.   [2] Revised to include adjustments for underenumeration in southern States; unrevised number is 38,558,371 (13.0 per square mile).   [3] Figures corrected after 1970 final reports were issued. [4] Total population count has been revised since the 1980 census publications. Numbers by age, race, Hispanic origin, and sex have not been corrected.   [5] The April 1, 1990, census count includes count resolution corrections processed through December 1995, and does not include adjustments for census coverage errors.   [6] Data reflect corrections made after publication of the results. [7] Comprises Great Lakes, inland, and coastal water. Data for prior years cover inland water only. For further explanation, see table 362.

Source: U.S. Bureau of the Census, *1990 Census of Population and Housing, Population and Housing Unit Counts* (CPH-2); 1990 Census of Population and Housing Listing (1990 CPH-L-157); and unpublished data.

No. 2. Population: 1950 to 1995

[In thousands, except percent. Estimates as of July 1. Total population includes Armed Forces abroad; civilian population excludes Armed Forces. For basis of estimates, see text, section 1. See also *Historical Statistics, Colonial Times to 1970*, series A 6-8]

YEAR	TOTAL		Resident population	Civilian population	YEAR	TOTAL		Resident population	Civilian population
	Population	Percent change				Population	Percent change		
1950	152,271	(X)	151,868	150,790	1973	211,909	0.96	211,357	209,600
1951	154,878	1.71	153,982	151,599	1974	213,854	0.92	213,342	211,636
1952	157,553	1.73	156,393	153,892	1975	215,973	0.99	215,465	213,789
1953	160,184	1.67	158,956	156,595	1976	218,035	0.95	217,563	215,894
1954	163,026	1.77	161,884	159,695	1977	220,239	1.01	219,760	218,106
1955	165,931	1.78	165,069	162,967	1978	222,585	1.06	222,095	220,467
1956	168,903	1.79	168,088	166,055	1979	225,055	1.11	224,567	222,969
1957	171,984	1.82	171,187	169,110	1980	227,726	1.19	227,225	225,621
1958	174,882	1.68	174,149	172,226	1981	229,966	0.98	229,466	227,818
1959	177,830	1.69	177,135	175,277	1982	232,188	0.97	231,664	229,995
1960	180,671	1.60	179,979	178,140	1983	234,307	0.91	233,792	232,097
1961	183,691	1.67	182,992	181,143	1984	236,348	0.87	235,825	234,110
1962	186,538	1.55	185,771	183,677	1985	238,466	0.90	237,924	236,219
1963	189,242	1.45	188,483	186,493	1986	240,651	0.92	240,133	238,412
1964	191,889	1.40	191,141	189,141	1987	242,804	0.89	242,289	240,550
1965	194,303	1.26	193,526	191,605	1988	245,021	0.91	244,499	242,817
1966	196,560	1.16	195,576	193,420	1989	247,342	0.95	246,819	245,131
1967	198,712	1.09	197,457	195,264	1990	249,913	1.04	249,403	247,763
1968	200,706	1.00	199,399	197,113	1991	252,650	1.10	252,138	250,527
1969	202,677	0.98	201,385	199,145	1992	255,419	1.10	255,039	253,454
1970	205,052	1.17	203,984	201,895	1993	258,137	1.06	257,800	256,328
1971	207,661	1.27	206,827	204,866	1994	260,660	0.98	260,350	258,940
1972	209,896	1.08	209,284	207,511	1995	263,034	0.91	262,755	261,407

X Not applicable.

Source: U.S. Bureau of the Census, *Current Population Reports*, P25-1045 and P25-1126 and Population Paper Listings PPL-41.

No. 3. Resident Population Projections: 1996 to 2050

[**In thousands**. As of **July 1**. Each series shown assumes middle levels of fertility, life expectancy, and net immigration unless otherwise specified. Middle level components are shown in footnote 1]

YEAR	Middle series [1]	Lowest series [2]	Highest series [3]	FERTILITY		LIFE EXPECTANCY		NET IMMIGRATION	
				Low	High	Low	High	Low	High
1996	265,253	264,869	265,646	265,143	265,350	265,186	265,330	265,046	265,472
1997	267,645	266,733	268,577	267,389	267,872	267,512	267,796	267,122	268,198
1998	270,002	268,396	271,647	269,565	270,392	269,783	270,250	269,050	271,008
1999	272,330	269,861	274,865	271,678	272,915	272,006	272,697	270,835	273,910
2000	274,634	271,237	278,129	273,731	275,448	274,185	275,141	272,581	276,802
2005	285,981	276,990	295,318	283,299	288,471	284,647	287,467	280,949	291,287
2010	297,716	281,468	314,571	292,303	302,893	294,986	300,482	289,423	306,444
2015	310,134	285,472	335,597	301,444	318,595	305,539	314,376	298,356	322,508
2020	322,742	288,807	357,702	310,429	334,889	315,885	328,698	307,290	338,955
2025	335,050	290,789	380,781	318,575	351,554	325,530	343,023	315,709	355,318
2030	346,899	291,070	405,089	325,517	368,732	334,331	357,227	323,414	371,480
2040	369,980	287,685	458,444	336,407	405,660	350,592	385,898	337,416	403,986
2050	393,931	282,524	518,903	345,352	447,502	367,913	415,908	351,354	438,299

[1] Ultimate total fertility rate = 2,245; life expectancy in 2050 = 82.0 years; and annual net immigration = 820,000. These are middle level assumptions. For explanation of total fertility rate; see headnote, table 94.   [2] Ultimate total fertility rate = 1,910; life expectancy in 2050 = 74.8 years; and annual net immigration = 300,000. These are lowest level assumptions.   [3] Ultimate total fertility rate = 2,580; life expectancy in 2050 = 89.4 years; and annual net immigration = 1,370,000. These are highest level assumptions.

Source: U.S. Bureau of the Census, *Current Population Reports*, P25-1130.

No. 4. Components of Population Change, 1980 to 1995, and Projections, 1996 to 2050

[Resident population. The estimates prior to 1990 are consistent with the original 1990 census count of 248,709,873. Starting with 1990, estimates reflect the revised April 1, 1990, census count of 248,718,291 which includes count resolution corrections processed through March 1994, and does not include adjustments for coverage errors]

YEAR	Popula-tion at start of period (1,000)	TOTAL (Jan. 1-Dec. 31)						RATE PER 1,000 MIDYEAR POPULATION				
		Net increase [1]		Natural increase		Net migra-tion [3]		Net growth rate [1]	Natural increase		Net migra-tion [3]
		Total (1,000)	Per-cent [2]	Births (1,000)	Deaths (1,000)	(1,000)			Birth rate	Death rate	
1980 [4]	226,546	1,900	0.8	2,743	1,463	724		11.1	16.0	8.6	4.2
1981	228,446	2,200	1.0	3,629	1,978	690		9.6	15.8	8.6	3.0
1982	230,645	2,157	0.9	3,681	1,975	595		9.3	15.9	8.5	2.6
1983	232,803	2,066	0.9	3,639	2,019	592		8.8	15.6	8.6	2.5
1984	234,868	2,070	0.9	3,669	2,039	589		8.8	15.6	8.6	2.5
1985	236,938	2,171	0.9	3,761	2,086	649		9.1	15.8	8.8	2.7
1986	239,109	2,158	0.9	3,757	2,105	661		9.0	15.6	8.8	2.8
1987	241,267	2,195	0.9	3,809	2,123	666		9.1	15.7	8.8	2.7
1988	243,462	2,243	0.9	3,910	2,168	662		9.2	16.0	8.9	2.7
1989 [5]	245,705	2,438	1.0	4,041	2,150	712		9.9	16.4	8.7	2.9
1990 [5]	248,143	2,571	1.0	4,148	2,155	[6]578		10.3	16.6	8.6	[6]2.3
1991	250,681	2,940	1.2	4,111	2,170	[6]999		11.7	16.3	8.6	[6]4.0
1992	253,621	2,907	1.1	4,065	2,176	1,018		11.4	15.9	8.5	4.0
1993	256,529	2,612	1.0	4,000	2,269	880		10.1	15.5	8.8	3.4
1994	259,141	2,485	1.0	3,979	2,286	792		9.5	15.3	8.8	3.0
1995	261,626	2,397	0.9	3,961	2,329	764		9.1	15.1	8.9	2.9
PROJECTIONS [7]											
1996	264,037	2,412	0.9	3,921	2,329	820		9.1	14.8	8.8	3.1
1997	266,449	2,374	0.9	3,907	2,353	820		8.9	14.6	8.8	3.1
1998	268,823	2,342	0.9	3,899	2,377	820		8.7	14.4	8.8	3.0
1999	271,166	2,316	0.9	3,896	2,401	820		8.5	14.3	8.8	3.0
2000	273,482	2,294	0.8	3,899	2,425	820		8.4	14.2	8.8	3.0
2005	284,847	2,278	0.8	4,001	2,543	820		8.0	14.0	8.9	2.9
2010	296,511	2,426	0.8	4,243	2,638	820		8.1	14.3	8.9	2.8
2015	308,875	2,521	0.8	4,450	2,749	820		8.1	14.3	8.9	2.6
2020	321,487	2,504	0.8	4,579	2,895	820		7.8	14.2	9.0	2.5
2025	333,838	2,414	0.7	4,679	3,085	820		7.2	14.0	9.2	2.4
2030	345,730	2,333	0.7	4,822	3,309	820		6.7	13.9	9.5	2.4
2040	368,823	2,319	0.6	5,248	3,749	820		6.3	14.2	10.1	2.2
2050	392,681	2,517	0.6	5,672	3,975	820		6.4	14.4	10.1	2.1

[1] Prior to April 1, 1990, includes "error of closure" (the amount necessary to make the components of change add to the net change between censuses), for which figures are not shown separately.   [2] Percent of population at beginning of period.   [3] Covers net international migration and movement of Armed Forces, federally affiliated civilian citizens, and their dependents.   [4] Data are for period April 1 to December 31.   [5] Net change for 1990 excludes "error of closure" for the three months prior to the April 1 census date. Therefore, it may not equal the difference between the populations at the beginning of 1990 and 1991.   [6] Data reflect movement of Armed Forces due to the Gulf War.   [7] Based on middle series of assumptions. See footnote 1, table 3.

Source: U.S. Bureau of the Census, *Current Population Reports*, P25-1095 and P25-1130; and Population Paper Listings PPL-41.

No. 5. Immigration: 1901 to 1994

[In thousands, except rate. For fiscal years ending in year shown ; see text, section 9. For definition of immigrants, see text, section 1. Data represent immigrants admitted. Rates based on Bureau of the Census estimates as of July 1 for resident population through 1929, and for total population thereafter (excluding Alaska and Hawaii prior to 1959). See also *Historical Statistics, Colonial Times to 1970*, series C 89]

PERIOD	Number	Rate [1]	YEAR	Number	Rate [1]
1901 to 1910.	8,795	10.4	1980.	531	2.3
1911 to 1920.	5,736	5.7	1985.	570	2.4
1921 to 1930.	4,107	3.5	1987.	602	2.5
1931 to 1940.	528	0.4	1988 [2].	643	2.6
1941 to 1950.	1,035	0.7	1989 [2].	1,091	4.4
1951 to 1960.	2,515	1.5	1990 [2].	1,536	6.1
1961 to 1970.	3,322	1.7	1991 [2].	1,827	7.2
1971 to 1980.	4,493	2.1	1992 [2].	974	3.8
1981 to 1990.	7,338	3.1	1993 [2].	904	3.5
1991 to 1994.	4,510	4.4	1994 [2].	804	3.1

[1] Annual rate per 1,000 U.S. population. Rate computed by dividing sum of annual immigration totals by sum of annual U.S. population totals for same number of years.   [2] Includes persons who were granted permanent residence under the legalization program of the Immigration Reform and Control Act of 1986.

Source: U.S. Immigration and Naturalization Service, *Statistical Yearbook*, annual.

No. 6. Immigrants Admitted, by Class of Admission: 1980 to 1994

[For fiscal year ending September 30. For definition of immigrants, see text, section 1. See also *Historical Statistics, Colonial Times to 1970*, series C 143-157]

CLASS OF ADMISSION	1980	1990	1991	1992	1993	1994
Immigrants, total.	**530,639**	**1,536,483**	**1,827,167**	**973,977**	**904,292**	**804,416**
New arrivals.	339,355	435,729	443,107	511,769	536,294	490,429
Adjustments	191,284	1,100,754	1,384,060	462,208	367,998	313,987
Preference immigrants, total	264,367	272,742	275,613	329,321	373,788	335,252
Family-sponsored immigrants, total.	216,856	214,550	216,088	213,123	226,776	211,961
Unmarried sons/daughters of U.S. citizens and their children.	5,668	15,861	15,385	12,486	12,819	13,181
Spouses, unmarried sons/daughters of alien residents, and their children	110,269	107,686	110,126	118,247	128,308	115,000
Married sons/daughters of U.S. citizens [1].	10,752	26,751	27,115	22,195	23,385	22,191
Brothers or sisters of U.S. citizens [1]	90,167	64,252	63,462	60,195	62,264	61,589
Employment-based immigrants, total.	47,511	58,192	59,525	116,198	147,012	123,291
Priority workers [1]	(X)	(X)	(X)	5,456	21,114	21,053
Professionals with advanced degrees [1]	(X)	(X)	(X)	58,401	29,468	14,432
Skilled workers, professionals, unskilled workers [1].	(X)	(X)	(X)	47,568	87,689	76,956
Special immigrants [1].	3,142	4,463	4,576	4,063	8,158	10,406
Employment creation [1]	(X)	(X)	(X)	59	583	444
Professional or highly skilled immigrants [1][2] . . .	18,583	26,546	27,748	340	(X)	(X)
Needed skilled or unskilled workers [1][2]	25,786	27,183	27,201	311	(X)	(X)
Immediate relatives.	157,743	231,680	237,103	235,484	255,059	249,764
Spouses of U.S. citizens.	96,854	125,426	125,397	128,396	145,843	145,247
Children of U.S. citizens	27,207	46,065	48,130	42,324	46,788	48,147
Orphans.	5,139	7,088	9,008	6,536	7,348	8,200
Parents of U.S. citizens	33,682	60,189	63,576	64,764	62,428	56,370
Refugees and asylees.	88,057	97,364	139,079	117,037	127,343	121,434
Cuban Refugee Act, Nov. 1966	6,021	5,730	5,486	5,365	6,976	8,316
Indochinese Refugee Act, Oct. 1977.	22,497	33	22	29	24	11
Refugee-Parolee Act, Oct. 1978	46,058	153	69	82	53	20
Asylees, Refugee Act of 1980	1,250	4,937	22,664	10,658	11,804	5,983
Refugees, Refugee Act of 1980	(X)	86,511	110,838	100,902	108,486	107,104
Other refugees	12,231	-	-	1	-	-
Other immigrants	20,472	934,697	1,175,372	292,135	148,102	97,966
Children born abroad to resident aliens or subsequent to issuance of visa	4,059	2,630	2,516	2,116	2,030	2,109
Diversity Programs [3]	(X)	29,161	22,070	36,348	33,468	41,056
Amerasians (P.L. 100-202) [4]	(X)	13,059	16,010	17,253	11,116	2,822
Immigration Reform and Control Act of 1986 legalization adjustments.	(X)	880,372	1,123,162	163,342	24,278	6,022
Legalization dependents [5].	(X)	(X)	(X)	52,272	55,344	34,074
Other	16,413	9,475	11,614	20,804	21,866	11,883

- Represents zero.   X Not applicable.   [1] Includes spouses and children.   [2] Category was eliminated in 1992 by the Immigration Act of 1990.   [3] Includes categories of immigrants admitted under three laws intended to diversify immigration: P.L. 99-603, P.L. 100-658, and P.L. 101-649.   [4] Under Public Law 100-202, Amerasians are aliens born in Vietnam between January 1, 1962, and January 1, 1976, who were fathered by U.S. citizens.   [5] Spouses and children of persons granted permanent resident status under provisions of the Immigration Reform and Control Act of 1986.

Source: U.S. Immigration and Naturalization Service, *Statistical Yearbook*, annual.

No. 7. Nonimmigrants Admitted, by Class of Admission: 1985 to 1994

[In thousands, except as noted. **For fiscal years ending Sept. 30;** see text, section 9. Nonimmigrants are nonresident aliens (non-U.S. citizens) admitted to the United States for a temporary period. Excluded are border crossers, crewmen, and insular travelers. See also *Historical Statistics, Colonial Times to 1970*, series C 149-157]

CLASS OF ADMISSION	1985	1988	1989	1990	1991	1992	1993	1994
Nonimmigrants [1]	9,540	14,592	16,145	17,574	18,963	20,794	21,566	22,119
Temporary visitors, total	8,405	13,197	14,667	16,080	17,386	19,238	19,879	20,319
For pleasure	6,609	10,821	12,115	13,418	14,734	16,450	16,918	17,155
For business	1,797	2,376	2,553	2,661	2,652	2,788	2,961	3,164
Transit aliens [2]	237	299	293	306	364	346	331	331
Foreign government officials [3]	90	99	102	97	98	103	102	105
Treaty traders and investors [3]	97	126	140	148	155	152	145	141
Students [3]	286	338	361	355	314	275	403	428
Representatives to international organizations [3]	57	59	61	61	64	70	73	75
Temporary workers and trainees [4]	75	113	139	140	161	163	163	186
Registered nurses [5]	(X)	(X)	(X)	(X)	1	7	7	6
Specialty occupations [6]	(X)	(X)	(X)	(X)	117	110	93	106
Workers of distinguished merit or ability [7]	47	78	90	100	(X)	(X)	(X)	(X)
Performing services unavailable in U.S.	25	33	47	36	40	34	29	29
North America Free-Trade Agreement [8]	(X)	(X)	3	5	8	13	17	25
Spouses and children of workers and trainees [9]	13	20	24	29	35	41	42	49
Representatives of foreign information media [3]	17	22	21	20	21	22	21	28
Exchange visitors [3]	141	203	217	215	224	232	239	259
NATO officials [3]	8	9	9	8	9	9	9	9
Fiances(ees) of U.S. citizens [10]	8	7	7	7	8	9	9	9
Intracompany transferees [3]	107	102	101	103	113	121	132	154
Parolees [11]	64	95	107	90	127	137	124	111
Refugees	68	80	101	110	100	123	113	114

X Not applicable. [1] Includes nonimmigrants whose class of admission is unknown. [2] Includes foreign government officials and their spouses and (unmarried minor or dependent) children, in transit. [3] Includes spouses and children. [4] Includes other classes of admission, not shown separately. [5] Entries began October 1, 1990 (fiscal year 1991). Data for fiscal year 1991 are underreported; an unknown number of H1A entries were counted as H1B entries. [6] Prior to October 1, 1991 (fiscal year 1992), H1B entries were termed "Distinguished merit or ability." Data for fiscal year 1991 are overreported; an unknown number of H1A entries were counted as H1B entries. [7] Beginning 1992, as a result of the Immigration Act of 1990, the existing temporary worker and trainee classes of admission have been revised and new worker classes have been created. [8] Entries under the U.S.-Canada Free Trade Agreement began in January 1989 and under the North American Free Trade Agreement (NAFTA) in January 1994. [9] Includes spouses and children under NAFTA. [10] Includes children of fiances(ees) of U.S. citizens. [11] Aliens allowed to enter the United States for a temporary period of time on emergency conditions or when the entry is determined to be in the public interest (e.g., witness in court).

No. 8. Immigrants, by Country of Birth: 1971 to 1994

[In thousands. **For fiscal years ending in year shown;** see text, section 9. For definition of immigrants, see text, section 1]

COUNTRY OF BIRTH	1971-80, total	1981-90, total	1991-93, total	1994	COUNTRY OF BIRTH	1971-80, total	1981-90, total	1991-93, total	1994
All countries [1]	4,493.3	7,338.1	3,705.4	804.4	Syria	13.3	20.6	8.7	2.4
Europe [1]	801.3	705.6	438.9	160.9	Taiwan	[3]	[3]	43.9	10.0
France	17.8	23.1	8.6	2.7	Thailand	44.1	64.4	21.1	5.5
Germany	66.0	70.1	23.7	7.0	Turkey	18.6	20.9	7.2	1.8
Greece	93.7	29.1	5.8	1.4	Vietnam	179.7	401.4	192.7	41.3
Ireland	14.1	32.8	30.6	17.3	**North America** [1]	1,645.0	3,125.0	1,896.4	272.2
Italy	130.1	32.9	7.7	2.3	Canada	114.8	119.2	45.9	16.1
Poland	43.6	97.4	72.5	28.0	Mexico	637.2	1,653.3	1,286.5	111.4
Portugal	104.5	40.0	9.4	2.2	Caribbean [1]	759.8	892.7	337.0	104.8
Romania	17.5	38.9	20.2	3.4	Barbados	20.9	17.4	3.7	0.9
Soviet Union, former [2]	43.2	84.0	159.2	63.4	Cuba	276.8	159.2	35.8	14.7
Armenia	(NA)	(NA)	(NA)	4.0	Dominican				
Azerbaijan	(NA)	(NA)	(NA)	3.8	Republic	148.0	251.8	128.8	51.2
Belarus	(NA)	(NA)	(NA)	5.4	Haiti	58.7	140.2	68.6	13.3
Moldova	(NA)	(NA)	(NA)	2.3	Jamaica	142.0	213.8	60.0	14.3
Russia	(NA)	(NA)	(NA)	15.2	Trinidad and				
Ukraine	(NA)	(NA)	(NA)	21.0	Tobago	61.8	39.5	22.0	6.3
Uzbekistan	(NA)	(NA)	(NA)	3.4	Central America [1]	132.4	458.7	226.8	39.9
Spain	30.0	15.8	4.9	1.4	El Salvador	34.4	214.6	100.4	17.6
United Kingdom	123.5	142.1	52.7	16.3	Guatemala	25.6	87.9	47.9	7.4
Yugoslavia	42.1	19.2	8.1	3.4	Honduras	17.2	49.5	25.3	5.3
Asia [1]	1,633.8	2,817.4	1,073.5	292.6	Nicaragua	13.0	44.1	33.9	5.3
Bangladesh	(NA)	15.2	17.7	3.4	Panama	22.7	29.0	9.7	2.4
Cambodia	8.4	116.6	7.5	1.4	**South America** [1]	284.4	455.9	189.2	47.4
China	[3]202.5	[3]388.8	137.5	54.0	Argentina	25.1	25.7	10.6	2.3
Hong Kong	47.5	63.0	30.0	7.7	Brazil	13.7	23.7	17.5	4.5
India	176.8	261.9	121.9	34.9	Chile	17.6	23.4	6.6	1.6
Iran	46.2	154.8	47.6	11.4	Colombia	77.6	124.4	45.7	10.8
Iraq	23.4	19.6	9.7	6.0	Ecuador	50.2	56.0	24.6	5.9
Israel	26.6	36.3	13.8	3.4	Guyana	47.5	95.4	29.1	7.7
Japan	47.9	43.2	23.0	6.1	Peru	29.1	64.4	36.6	9.2
Jordan	29.6	32.6	13.0	4.0	**Africa** [1]	91.5	192.3	91.0	26.7
Korea	272.0	338.8	63.9	16.0	Egypt	25.5	31.4	12.7	3.4
Laos	22.6	145.6	25.9	5.1	Ethiopia	(NA)	27.2	15.0	3.9
Lebanon	33.8	41.6	17.3	4.3	Ghana	(NA)	14.9	6.8	1.5
Pakistan	31.2	61.3	39.5	8.7	Nigeria	8.8	35.3	16.9	4.0
Philippines	360.2	495.3	188.1	53.5	Other countries [4]	37.3	41.9	16.4	4.6

NA Not available. [1] Includes countries not shown separately. [2] Includes other republics and unknown republics, not shown separately. [3] Data for Taiwan included with China. [4] Includes Australia, New Zealand, and unknown countries.
Source of tables 7 and 8: U.S. Immigration and Naturalization Service, *Statistical Yearbook*, annual; and releases.

No. 9. Immigrants Admitted as Permanent Residents Under Refugee Acts, by Country of Birth: 1971 to 1994

[For fiscal years ending in year shown; see text, section 9. Covers immigrants who were allowed to enter the United States under 1953 Refugee Relief Act and later acts; Hungarian parolees under July 1958 Act; refugee-escapee parolees under July 1960 Act; conditional entries by refugees under Oct. 1965 Act; Cuban parolees under Nov. 1966 Act; beginning 1978, Indochina refugees under Act of Oct. 1977; beginning 1980, refugee-parolees under the Act of Oct. 1978, and asylees under the Act of March 1980; and beginning 1981 refugees under the Act of March 1980]

COUNTRY OF BIRTH	1971-80, total	1981-90, total	1991-93, total	1994	COUNTRY OF BIRTH	1971-80, total	1981-90, total	1991-93, total	1994
Total	539,447	1,013,620	383,459	121,434	Cambodia	7,739	114,064	5,053	557
Europe [1]	71,858	155,512	158,862	54,978	China [3]	13,760	7,928	2,673	774
Albania	395	353	1,812	733	Hong Kong.....	3,468	1,916	358	82
Bulgaria.......	1,238	1,197	1,176	138	Iran..........	364	46,773	15,483	2,186
Czechoslovakia..	3,646	8,204	1,097	41	Iraq..........	6,851	7,540	2,414	4,400
Greece	478	1,408	194	65	Laos..........	21,690	142,964	23,700	4,482
Hungary	4,358	4,942	1,126	37	Philippines	216	3,403	592	103
Poland	5,882	33,889	6,448	334	Syria..........	1,336	2,145	463	34
Romania	6,812	29,798	12,901	1,199	Thailand	1,241	30,259	11,375	3,076
Soviet Union,					Turkey........	1,193	1,896	204	156
former [2]	31,309	72,306	130,955	50,756	Vietnam......	150,266	324,453	83,947	27,318
Azerbaijan ...	(NA)	(NA)	(NA)	2,668	North America [1] ..	252,633	121,840	53,205	14,204
Belarus	(NA)	(NA)	(NA)	5,156	Cuba.........	251,514	113,367	29,475	11,998
Moldova.....	(NA)	(NA)	(NA)	2,154	El Salvador	45	1,383	2,803	275
Russia	(NA)	(NA)	(NA)	10,359	Nicaragua	36	5,590	18,793	6
Ukraine	(NA)	(NA)	(NA)	19,366	South America ...	1,244	1,976	1,223	383
Uzbekistan ...	(NA)	(NA)	(NA)	3,211	Africa [1]	2,991	22,149	15,155	6,078
Spain	5,317	736	183	55	Egypt	1,473	426	105	37
Yugoslavia ...	11,297	324	201	506	Ethiopia.......	1,307	18,542	10,532	2,530
Asia [1].........	210,683	712,092	154,967	45,768	Other..........	38	51	47	23
Afghanistan	542	22,946	6,415	1,665					

NA Not available.   [1] Includes other countries, not shown separately.   [2] Includes other republics and unknown republics, not shown separately.   [3] Includes Taiwan.

Source: U.S. Immigration and Naturalization Service, *Statistical Yearbook,* annual; and releases.

No. 10. Estimated Undocumented Immigrants, by Selected States and Countries of Origin: 1992 and 1994

[In thousands. The ranges of estimates supplied by the Bureau of the Census represent indicators of magnitude which the Bureau believes is responsive to the inherent uncertainty in the assumptions underlying these estimates. The Census indicators are the results of applying three calculated percent distributions to two national estimates of the undocumented population. The three percent distributions by State are based on: (1) an average between the number of undocumented immigrants by State included in the 1980 census and of the number of legalization applicants by State produced by the Immigration Reform and Control Act (IRCA) of 1986; (2) the number of undocumented immigrants by State estimated by the Immigration and Naturalization Service (INS); and (3) the number of foreign born non-citizens by State counted in the 1990 census. The figures supplied by INS are based on estimates of illegal immigrant population who established residence in the United States before 1982 and did not legalize under IRCA and annual estimates of the number of persons who enter surreptitiously across land borders and nonimmigrant overstays who established residence here during the 1982 to 1992 period. The estimates for each country were distributed to States by INS based on U.S. residence pattern of each country's total number of applicants for legalization under IRCA]

STATE	BUREAU OF THE CENSUS ESTIMATES, 1994 Low	BUREAU OF THE CENSUS ESTIMATES, 1994 High	INS estimates, Oct. 1992	COUNTRY	INS estimates, Oct. 1992
United States, total [1]	3,500	4,000	3,379	Total [1].................	3,379
California	1,321	1,784	1,441	Mexico	1,321
New York	462	539	449	El Salvador	327
Texas....................	300	427	357	Guatemala...............	129
Florida	243	385	322	Canada	97
Illinois	157	225	176	Poland	91
New Jersey...............	98	168	116	Philippines...............	90
Massachusetts.............	42	106	45	Haiti	88
Arizona...................	50	68	57	Bahamas, The	71
Maryland	29	63	27	Nicaragua	68
Virginia..................	37	63	35	Italy	67
Washington...............	32	59	30	Honduras................	61
Michigan.................	10	53	(NA)	Colombia................	59
Pennsylvania..............	15	51	18	Ecuador	45
Connecticut...............	13	46	15	Jamaica.................	42
Georgia	29	36	28	Dominican Republic.........	40
Ohio	7	36	(NA)	Trinidad & Tobago..........	39
Colorado.................	22	29	22	Ireland..................	36
Oregon..................	21	27	20	Portugal	31
Hawaii	4	25	(NA)	Pakistan	30
New Mexico	14	25	19	India	28

NA Not available.   [1] Includes other States and countries not shown separately.

Source: U.S. Bureau of the Census, *"Illustrative Ranges of the Distribution of Undocumented Immigrants by State"* by Edward W. Fernandez and J. Gregory Robinson, *Technical Working Paper No. 8, October 1994*; and U.S. Immigration and Naturalization Service, *1993 Statistical Yearbook of the Immigration and Naturalization Service.*

No. 11. Immigrants Admitted, by Leading Country of Birth and State: 1994

[For year ending September 30. For definition of immigrants, see text, section 1]

REGION, DIVISION, AND STATE	Total [1]	Mexico	Soviet Union	China	Philippines	Vietnam	Dominican Republic	India	Poland
U.S. [2]	804,416	111,398	63,420	53,985	53,535	41,345	51,189	34,921	28,048
Northeast......	242,365	2,473	27,721	18,474	7,912	4,473	37,535	11,863	13,297
N.E.........	37,957	222	3,518	2,934	629	1,874	3,532	1,400	2,278
ME	829	11	47	60	45	39	2	26	17
NH	1,144	8	64	93	47	112	63	56	10
VT........	658	3	60	61	15	63	1	20	6
MA	22,882	86	2,438	1,995	259	1,366	2,581	805	672
RI........	2,907	24	250	174	54	17	636	41	114
CT	9,537	90	659	551	209	277	249	452	1,459
M.A	204,408	2,251	24,203	15,540	7,283	2,599	34,003	10,463	11,019
NY	144,354	1,310	19,618	11,745	3,878	995	28,250	5,338	6,733
NJ........	44,083	385	1,993	2,174	2,945	564	5,384	3,782	3,751
PA........	15,971	556	2,592	1,621	460	1,040	369	1,343	535
Midwest	92,690	10,960	8,625	5,589	4,310	4,725	315	6,632	12,390
E.N.C	73,365	9,315	6,695	4,001	3,655	1,857	279	5,792	12,271
OH	9,184	134	1,743	872	319	331	33	800	211
IN	3,725	401	329	375	182	164	19	365	115
IL	42,400	7,900	2,970	1,684	2,539	734	119	3,241	11,165
MI........	12,728	413	968	663	456	531	83	1,085	656
WI........	5,328	467	685	407	159	97	25	301	124
W.N.C.......	19,325	1,645	1,930	1,588	655	2,868	36	840	119
MN	7,098	207	762	448	157	806	14	183	49
IA	2,163	233	124	237	61	453	3	135	14
MO	4,362	195	554	464	243	601	6	295	29
ND	635	11	89	40	20	91	-	26	1
SD	570	13	66	26	19	18	-	13	4
NE	1,595	295	156	137	47	377	5	62	15
KS	2,902	691	179	236	108	522	8	126	7
South.......	184,148	31,658	6,245	8,336	6,769	12,734	3,196	8,008	1,306
S.A.........	112,569	3,597	4,939	5,120	4,208	6,322	2,997	4,468	1,058
DE	984	56	44	142	52	9	8	76	16
MD	15,937	163	2,144	1,620	752	656	233	1,058	117
DC	3,204	27	87	223	109	243	138	63	2
VA........	15,342	253	613	971	1,119	1,594	70	928	85
WV	663	10	8	103	56	9	2	62	8
NC	6,204	477	245	468	209	855	32	426	53
SC	2,110	61	51	200	149	171	4	173	73
GA	10,032	665	630	522	288	1,602	4	649	156
FL........	58,093	1,885	1,117	871	1,474	1,183	2,463	1,033	548
E.S.C	8,296	311	343	791	371	807	23	833	56
KY	2,036	60	118	203	78	211	4	209	15
TN	3,608	122	166	291	144	354	9	290	31
AL........	1,837	95	54	200	83	142	6	290	31
MS	815	34	5	97	66	100	4	112	-
W.S.C	63,283	27,750	963	2,425	2,190	5,605	176	2,707	192
AR	1,031	142	21	70	85	136	1	53	7
LA	3,366	80	35	225	155	650	57	206	21
OK	2,728	513	34	198	117	527	4	194	13
TX	56,158	27,015	873	1,932	1,833	4,292	114	2,254	151
West	270,464	66,226	20,827	21,449	32,350	19,383	220	8,396	1,054
Mountain.....	28,127	10,001	1,562	1,932	1,655	1,493	48	625	257
MT	447	10	48	34	25	5	-	5	2
ID	1,559	737	98	94	68	72	1	8	15
WY	217	36	-	18	16	-	-	4	2
CO	6,825	1,931	730	371	212	508	3	139	106
NM	2,936	1,674	60	157	81	89	1	96	15
AZ........	9,141	4,340	308	653	374	432	17	237	69
UT........	2,951	322	260	291	106	270	10	68	22
NV	4,051	951	58	314	773	117	16	68	26
Pacific	242,337	56,225	19,265	19,517	30,695	17,890	172	7,771	797
WA	18,180	2,573	3,340	842	1,781	2,607	11	475	128
OR	6,784	1,472	1,262	421	313	733	3	161	35
CA	208,498	52,088	14,542	17,447	23,942	14,162	120	7,085	598
AK	1,129	45	97	64	330	35	-	13	35
HI	7,746	47	24	743	4,329	353	-	37	1

- Represents zero. [1] Includes other countries, not shown separately. [2] Includes Guam, Puerto Rico, Northern Mariana Islands, Virgin Islands, and other or unknown areas not shown separately.

Source: U.S. Immigration and Naturalization Service, *Statistical Yearbook,* annual.

No. 12. Resident Population—Selected Characteristics, 1790 to 1995, and Projections, 2000 to 2050

[**In thousands**. See also *Historical Statistics, Colonial Times to 1970*, series A 73-81 and A 143-149]

| DATE | SEX | | RACE | | | | | Hispanic origin [1] |
	Male	Female	White	Black	Other Total	American Indian, Eskimo, Aleut	Asian and Pacific Islanders	
1790 (Aug. 2) [2]	(NA)	(NA)	3,172	757	(NA)	(NA)	(NA)	(NA)
1800 (Aug. 4) [2]	(NA)	(NA)	4,306	1,002	(NA)	(NA)	(NA)	(NA)
1850 (June 1) [2]	11,838	11,354	19,553	3,639	(NA)	(NA)	(NA)	(NA)
1900 (June 1) [2]	38,816	37,178	66,809	8,834	351	(NA)	(NA)	(NA)
1910 (Apr. 15) [2]	47,332	44,640	81,732	9,828	413	(NA)	(NA)	(NA)
1920 (Jan. 1) [2]	53,900	51,810	94,821	10,463	427	(NA)	(NA)	(NA)
1930 (Apr. 1) [2]	62,137	60,638	110,287	11,891	597	(NA)	(NA)	(NA)
1940 (Apr. 1) [2]	66,062	65,608	118,215	12,866	589	(NA)	(NA)	(NA)
1950 (Apr. 1) [2]	74,833	75,864	134,942	15,042	713	(NA)	(NA)	(NA)
1950 (Apr. 1)	75,187	76,139	135,150	15,045	1,131	(NA)	(NA)	(NA)
1960 (Apr. 1)	88,331	90,992	158,832	18,872	1,620	(NA)	(NA)	(NA)
1970 (Apr. 1) [3]	98,926	104,309	178,098	22,581	2,557	(NA)	(NA)	(NA)
1980 (Apr. 1) [4][5]	110,053	116,493	194,713	26,683	5,150	1,420	3,729	14,609
1990 (Apr. 1) [4][6]	121,244	127,474	208,710	30,486	9,523	2,065	7,458	22,354
1991 (July 1) [7]	122,951	129,187	211,017	31,110	10,011	2,107	7,904	23,381
1992 (July 1) [7]	124,436	130,603	212,957	31,659	10,423	2,142	8,280	24,272
1993 (July 1) [7]	125,812	131,988	214,805	32,174	10,821	2,177	8,644	25,198
1994 (July 1) [7]	127,085	133,265	216,496	32,669	11,184	2,210	8,974	26,099
1995 (July 1) [7]	128,314	134,441	218,085	33,141	11,529	2,242	9,287	26,994
2000 (July 1) [8]	134,181	140,453	225,532	35,454	13,647	2,402	11,245	31,366
2005 (July 1) [8]	139,785	146,196	232,463	37,734	15,784	2,572	13,212	36,057
2010 (July 1) [8]	145,584	152,132	239,588	40,109	18,019	2,754	15,265	41,139
2015 (July 1) [8]	151,750	158,383	247,193	42,586	20,355	2,941	17,413	46,705
2020 (July 1) [8]	158,021	164,721	254,887	45,075	22,780	3,129	19,651	52,652
2025 (July 1) [8]	164,119	170,931	262,227	47,539	25,284	3,319	21,965	58,930
2050 (July 1) [8]	193,234	200,696	294,615	60,592	38,724	4,371	34,352	96,508

NA Not available.   [1] Persons of Hispanic origin may be of any race.   [2] Excludes Alaska and Hawaii.   [3] The revised 1970 resident population count is 203,302,031; which incorporates changes due to errors found after tabulations were completed. The race and sex data shown here reflect the official 1970 census count.   [4] The race data shown have been modified; see text, section 1, for explanation.   [5] See footnote 4, table 1.   [6] The April 1, 1990, census count (248,718,291) includes count resolution corrections processed through March 1994 and does not include adjustments for census coverage errors.   [7] Estimated.   [8] Middle series projection; see table 3.

No. 13. Resident Population Characteristics—Percent Distribution and Median Age, 1850 to 1995, and Projections, 2000 to 2050

[**In percent, except as indicated**. For definition of median, see Guide to Tabular Presentation]

| DATE | SEX | | RACE | | | Hispanic origin [1] | Median age (years) |
	Male	Female	White	Black	Other		
1850 (June 1) [2]	51.0	49.0	84.3	15.7	(NA)	(NA)	18.9
1900 (June 1) [2]	51.1	48.9	87.9	11.6	0.5	(NA)	22.9
1910 (Apr. 15) [2]	51.5	48.5	88.9	10.7	0.4	(NA)	24.1
1920 (Jan. 1) [2]	51.0	49.0	89.7	9.9	0.4	(NA)	25.3
1930 (Apr. 1) [2]	50.6	49.4	89.8	9.7	0.5	(NA)	26.4
1940 (Apr. 1) [2]	50.2	49.8	89.8	9.8	0.4	(NA)	29.0
1950 (Apr. 1) [2]	49.7	50.3	89.5	10.0	0.5	(NA)	30.2
1950 (Apr. 1)	49.7	50.3	89.3	9.9	0.7	(NA)	30.2
1960 (Apr. 1)	49.3	50.7	88.6	10.5	0.9	(NA)	29.5
1970 (Apr. 1)	48.7	51.3	87.6	11.1	1.3	(NA)	28.0
1980 (Apr. 1) [3][4]	48.6	51.4	85.9	11.8	2.3	6.4	30.0
1990 (Apr. 1) [3][5]	48.7	51.3	83.9	12.3	3.8	9.0	32.8
1991 (July 1) [6]	48.8	51.2	83.7	12.3	4.0	9.3	33.1
1992 (July 1) [6]	48.8	51.2	83.5	12.4	4.1	9.5	33.4
1993 (July 1) [6]	48.8	51.2	83.3	12.5	4.2	9.8	33.7
1994 (July 1) [6]	48.8	51.2	83.2	12.5	4.3	10.0	34.0
1995 (July 1) [6]	48.8	51.2	83.0	12.6	4.4	10.3	34.3
2000 (July 1) [7]	48.9	51.1	82.1	12.9	5.0	11.4	35.7
2025 (July 1) [7]	49.0	51.0	78.3	14.2	7.5	17.6	38.0
2050 (July 1) [7]	49.1	50.9	74.8	15.4	9.8	24.5	38.1

NA Not available.   [1] Persons of Hispanic origin may be of any race.   [2] Excludes Alaska and Hawaii.   [3] The race data shown have been modified; see text, section 1 for explanation.   [4] See footnote 4, table 1.   [5] See footnote 6, table 12.   [6] Estimated.   [7] Middle series projection; see table 3.

Source of tables 12 and 13: U.S. Bureau of the Census, *U.S. Census of Population: 1940*, vol. II, part 1, and vol. IV, part 1; *1950*, vol. II, part 1; *1960*, vol. I, part 1; *1970*, vol. I, part B; *Current Population Reports*, P25-1095 and P25-1130; Population Paper Listings PPL-41; and unpublished data.

No. 14. Resident Population, by Age and Sex: 1970 to 1995

[In thousands, except as indicated. 1970, 1980, and 1990 data are enumerated population as of April 1; data for other years are estimated population as of July 1. Excludes Armed Forces overseas. For definition of median, see Guide to Tabular Presentation. See also Historical Statistics, Colonial Times to 1970, series A119-134]

YEAR AND SEX	Total, all years	Under 5 years	5-9 years	10-14 years	15-19 years	20-24 years	25-29 years	30-34 years	35-39 years	40-44 years	45-49 years	50-54 years	55-59 years	60-64 years	65-74 years	75-84 years	85 years and over	5-13 years	14-17 years	18-24 years	Median age (yr.)
1970, total [1]	203,235	17,163	19,969	20,804	19,084	16,383	13,486	11,437	11,113	11,988	12,124	11,111	9,979	8,623	12,443	6,122	1,408	36,675	15,851	23,714	28.0
Male	98,926	8,750	10,175	10,598	9,641	7,925	6,626	5,599	5,416	5,823	5,855	5,351	4,769	4,030	5,440	2,437	489	18,687	8,069	11,583	26.8
Female	104,309	8,413	9,794	10,206	9,443	8,458	6,859	5,838	5,697	6,166	6,269	5,759	5,210	4,593	7,002	3,684	919	17,987	7,782	12,131	29.3
1980, total [2]	226,546	16,348	16,700	18,242	21,168	21,319	19,521	17,561	13,965	11,669	11,090	11,710	11,615	10,088	15,581	7,729	2,240	31,159	16,247	30,022	30.0
Male	110,053	8,362	8,539	9,316	10,755	10,663	9,705	8,677	6,862	5,708	5,388	5,621	5,482	4,670	6,757	2,867	682	15,923	8,298	15,054	28.8
Female	116,493	7,986	8,161	8,926	10,413	10,655	9,816	8,884	7,104	5,961	5,702	6,089	6,133	5,418	8,824	4,862	1,559	15,237	7,950	14,969	31.3
1981, total	229,466	16,893	16,060	18,300	20,541	21,663	20,169	18,731	14,366	12,028	10,985	11,595	11,554	10,359	15,890	7,982	2,349	30,711	15,609	30,245	30.3
1982, total	231,664	17,228	15,958	18,145	19,962	21,682	20,704	18,714	15,566	12,464	11,011	11,414	11,463	10,567	16,147	8,203	2,437	30,528	15,057	30,162	30.5
1983, total	233,792	17,547	16,053	17,869	19,388	21,632	21,141	19,067	16,117	13,150	11,201	11,155	11,457	10,655	16,414	8,429	2,518	30,279	14,740	29,922	30.8
1984, total	235,825	17,695	16,533	17,450	18,931	21,529	21,459	19,503	16,867	13,636	11,429	10,957	11,352	10,803	16,626	8,656	2,595	30,062	14,725	29,461	31.1
1985, total	237,924	17,842	16,665	17,027	18,727	21,265	21,671	20,025	17,604	14,087	11,606	10,854	11,229	10,906	16,858	8,890	2,667	30,078	14,824	28,902	31.4
1986, total	240,133	17,963	17,098	16,474	18,813	20,744	21,893	20,479	18,611	14,398	11,878	10,781	11,135	10,859	17,137	9,129	2,742	29,893	14,888	28,227	31.7
1987, total	242,289	18,052	17,430	16,377	18,698	20,192	21,857	20,984	18,619	15,608	12,294	10,802	10,968	10,783	17,426	9,376	2,823	30,502	14,502	27,694	32.0
1988, total	244,499	18,195	17,759	16,496	18,496	19,655	21,739	21,391	18,993	16,188	12,954	10,995	10,722	10,791	17,626	9,612	2,885	31,028	14,023	27,356	32.3
1989, total	246,819	18,508	17,917	16,797	18,133	19,258	21,580	21,676	19,455	16,919	13,441	11,212	10,534	10,707	17,864	9,850	2,968	31,413	13,536	27,156	32.6
1990, total [3]	248,718	18,757	18,035	17,060	17,886	19,135	21,328	21,833	19,846	17,589	13,744	11,313	10,487	10,625	18,046	10,012	3,022	31,826	13,340	26,950	32.8
Male	121,244	9,599	9,232	8,739	9,175	9,743	10,703	10,862	9,834	8,677	6,739	5,493	5,008	4,947	7,907	3,745	841	16,295	6,857	13,738	31.6
Female	127,474	9,158	8,803	8,322	8,711	9,391	10,625	10,971	10,012	8,912	7,004	5,820	5,479	5,679	10,139	6,267	2,180	15,532	6,482	13,212	34.0
1991, total	252,138	19,198	18,238	17,668	17,187	19,176	20,737	22,152	20,513	18,755	14,096	11,647	10,422	10,584	18,274	10,311	3,178	32,498	13,420	26,351	33.1
1992, total	255,039	19,506	18,357	18,098	17,102	19,066	20,191	22,242	21,072	18,796	15,355	12,054	10,485	10,443	18,450	10,526	3,294	33,012	13,654	25,957	33.4
1993, total	257,800	19,689	18,536	18,522	17,270	18,783	19,646	22,240	21,571	19,190	15,927	12,726	10,680	10,243	18,641	10,722	3,415	33,498	13,929	25,684	33.7
1994, total	260,350	19,734	18,868	18,753	17,618	18,349	19,205	22,164	21,938	19,688	16,674	13,190	10,933	10,083	18,713	10,920	3,518	33,873	14,426	25,289	34.0
1995, total	262,755	19,591	19,220	18,915	18,065	17,882	19,005	21,868	22,249	20,219	17,449	13,630	11,085	10,046	18,759	11,145	3,628	34,384	14,765	24,932	34.3
Male	128,314	10,025	9,843	9,685	9,265	9,087	9,530	10,902	11,071	9,990	8,560	6,622	5,317	4,727	8,342	4,330	1,017	17,606	7,585	12,689	33.1
Female	134,441	9,566	9,377	9,229	8,799	8,795	9,476	10,966	11,178	10,228	8,889	7,008	5,767	5,320	10,417	6,815	2,611	16,777	7,180	12,243	35.4
Percent:																					
1970	100.0	8.4	9.8	10.2	9.4	8.1	6.6	5.6	5.5	5.9	6.0	5.5	4.9	4.2	6.1	3.0	0.7	18.0	7.8	11.7	(X)
1980 [2]	100.0	7.2	7.4	8.1	9.3	9.4	8.6	7.8	6.2	5.2	4.9	5.1	5.1	4.5	6.9	3.4	1.0	13.8	7.2	13.3	(X)
1990 [3]	100.0	7.5	7.3	6.9	7.2	7.7	8.6	8.8	8.0	7.1	5.5	4.5	4.2	4.3	7.3	4.0	1.2	12.8	5.4	10.8	(X)
1995	100.0	7.5	7.3	7.2	6.9	6.8	7.2	8.3	8.5	7.8	6.6	5.2	4.2	3.8	7.1	4.2	1.4	13.1	5.6	9.5	(X)
Male	100.0	7.8	7.7	7.5	7.2	7.1	7.4	8.5	8.6	7.8	6.7	5.2	4.1	3.7	6.5	3.4	0.8	13.7	5.9	9.9	(X)
Female	100.0	7.1	7.0	6.9	6.5	7.0	7.0	8.2	8.3	7.6	6.6	5.2	4.3	4.0	7.7	5.1	1.9	12.5	5.3	9.1	(X)

X Not applicable. [1] Official count. The revised 1970 resident population count is 203,302,031; the difference of 66,733 is due to errors found after release of the official series. [2] See footnote 4, table 1. [3] The data shown have been deleted from the official 1990 census counts. See text, section 1, for explanation. The April 1, 1990, census count (248,718,291) includes count resolution corrections processed through March 1994 and does not include adjustments for census coverage errors.

Source: U.S. Bureau of the Census, Current Population Reports, P25-917; and Population Paper Listings 21 and 41.

Population

No. 15. Ratio of Males to Females, by Age Group, 1950 to 1995, and Projections, 2000 and 2025

[Number of males per 100 females. Total resident population]

AGE	1950 (Apr. 1)	1960 (Apr. 1)	1970 (Apr. 1)	1980 (Apr. 1)	1990 [1] (Apr. 1)	1995 (July 1)	PROJECTIONS [2] 2000 (July 1)	PROJECTIONS [2] 2025 (July 1)
All ages.......	98.6	97.1	94.8	94.5	95.1	95.4	95.5	96.0
Under 14 years	103.7	103.4	103.9	104.6	104.9	104.9	104.8	105.1
14 to 24 years	98.2	98.7	98.7	101.9	104.6	104.4	104.1	104.2
25 to 44 years	96.4	95.7	95.5	97.4	98.9	99.2	98.9	97.7
45 to 64 years	100.1	95.7	91.6	90.7	92.5	93.5	93.8	93.5
65 years and over....	89.6	82.8	72.1	67.6	67.2	69.0	70.4	82.9

[1] The April 1, 1990, census count (248,718,291) includes count resolution corrections processed through March 1994, and does not include adjustments for census coverage errors. [2] Middle series projections; see table 3.

Source: U.S. Bureau of the Census, *U.S. Census of Population: 1950*, vol. II, part 1; *1960*, vol. I, part 1; *1970*, vol. I, part B; *Current Population Reports*, P25-1095 and P25-1130; Population Paper Listings PPL-41; and unpublished data.

No. 16. Resident Population, by Sex and Age: 1995

[In thousands, except as indicated. As of July 1. For derivation of estimates, see text, section 1]

AGE	Total	Male	Female	AGE	Total	Male	Female
Total	262,755	128,314	134,441	43 yrs. old	3,884	1,910	1,974
				44 yrs. old	3,857	1,911	1,946
Under 5 yrs. old	19,591	10,025	9,566	45 to 49 yrs. old	17,449	8,560	8,889
Under 1 yr. old	3,848	1,970	1,878	45 yrs. old	3,741	1,844	1,896
1 yr. old	3,840	1,964	1,876	46 yrs. old	3,557	1,746	1,812
2 yrs. old	3,882	1,990	1,892	47 yrs. old	3,586	1,755	1,831
3 yrs. old	3,965	2,026	1,939	48 yrs. old	3,658	1,792	1,866
4 yrs. old	4,056	2,075	1,981	49 yrs. old	2,907	1,423	1,484
5 to 9 yrs. old	19,220	9,843	9,377	50 to 54 yrs. old	13,630	6,622	7,008
5 yrs. old	4,039	2,069	1,970	50 yrs. old	2,890	1,409	1,481
6 yrs. old	3,888	1,991	1,897	51 yrs. old	2,782	1,353	1,429
7 yrs. old	3,810	1,949	1,861	52 yrs. old	2,914	1,418	1,496
8 yrs. old	3,616	1,851	1,765	53 yrs. old	2,568	1,244	1,324
9 yrs. old	3,867	1,983	1,883	54 yrs. old	2,476	1,198	1,278
10 to 14 yrs. old	18,915	9,685	9,229	55 to 59 yrs. old	11,085	5,317	5,767
10 yrs. old	3,869	1,985	1,884	55 yrs. old	2,312	1,113	1,199
11 yrs. old	3,705	1,897	1,808	56 yrs. old	2,316	1,112	1,203
12 yrs. old	3,778	1,932	1,846	57 yrs. old	2,291	1,099	1,192
13 yrs. old	3,811	1,949	1,863	58 yrs. old	2,029	970	1,058
14 yrs. old	3,751	1,922	1,829	59 yrs. old	2,137	1,023	1,115
15 to 19 yrs. old	18,065	9,265	8,799	60 to 64 yrs. old	10,046	4,727	5,320
15 yrs. old	3,790	1,944	1,846	60 yrs. old	2,111	997	1,114
16 yrs. old	3,627	1,866	1,761	61 yrs. old	1,934	918	1,016
17 yrs. old	3,597	1,853	1,744	62 yrs. old	1,939	912	1,027
18 yrs. old	3,506	1,794	1,712	63 yrs. old	1,968	926	1,042
19 yrs. old	3,544	1,808	1,736	64 yrs. old	2,095	975	1,120
20 to 24 yrs. old	17,882	9,087	8,795	65 to 69 yrs. old	9,928	4,506	5,422
20 yrs. old	3,564	1,821	1,743	65 yrs. old	2,067	959	1,108
21 yrs. old	3,418	1,745	1,673	66 yrs. old	2,010	923	1,087
22 yrs. old	3,402	1,731	1,671	67 yrs. old	2,041	930	1,110
23 yrs. old	3,575	1,812	1,763	68 yrs. old	1,913	856	1,056
24 yrs. old	3,924	1,978	1,945	69 yrs. old	1,897	837	1,060
25 to 29 yrs. old	19,005	9,530	9,476	70 to 74 yrs. old	8,831	3,836	4,995
25 yrs. old	3,878	1,953	1,925	70 yrs. old	1,884	829	1,055
26 yrs. old	3,749	1,880	1,869	71 yrs. old	1,822	797	1,025
27 yrs. old	3,719	1,866	1,853	72 yrs. old	1,762	769	993
28 yrs. old	3,594	1,797	1,797	73 yrs. old	1,712	736	976
29 yrs. old	4,065	2,035	2,031	74 yrs. old	1,652	705	947
30 to 34 yrs. old	21,868	10,902	10,966	75 to 79 yrs. old	6,681	2,720	3,961
30 yrs. old	4,210	2,100	2,111	75 yrs. old	1,512	635	877
31 yrs. old	4,270	2,129	2,141	76 yrs. old	1,405	583	821
32 yrs. old	4,358	2,172	2,187	77 yrs. old	1,312	532	780
33 yrs. old	4,427	2,201	2,226	78 yrs. old	1,264	504	760
34 yrs. old	4,602	2,301	2,301	79 yrs. old	1,189	466	723
35 to 39 yrs. old	22,249	11,071	11,178	80 to 84 yrs. old	4,464	1,609	2,854
35 yrs. old	4,594	2,293	2,301	80 yrs. old	1,076	409	668
36 yrs. old	4,432	2,203	2,228	81 yrs. old	976	361	616
37 yrs. old	4,490	2,233	2,257	82 yrs. old	895	321	574
38 yrs. old	4,220	2,095	2,125	83 yrs. old	801	280	521
39 yrs. old	4,514	2,248	2,267	84 yrs. old	715	239	476
40 to 44 yrs. old	20,219	9,990	10,228	85 to 89 yrs. old	2,321	707	1,614
40 yrs. old	4,343	2,154	2,188	90 to 94 yrs. old	991	247	744
41 yrs. old	4,131	2,039	2,092	95 to 99 yrs. old	263	54	210
42 yrs. old	4,004	1,976	2,028	100 yrs. old and over...	53	9	44
				Median age (yr.)	34.3	33.1	35.4

Source: U.S. Bureau of the Census, Population Paper Listings PPL-41.

No. 17. Resident Population Projections, by Age and Sex: 1996 to 2050

[In thousands, except as indicated. As of July. See headnote, table 3]

YEAR	Total	Under 5 years	5 to 13 years	14 to 17 years	18 to 24 years	25 to 34 years	35 to 44 years	45 to 54 years	55 to 64 years	65 to 74 years	75 to 84 years	85 years and over
TOTAL												
Lowest series:												
1996	264,869	19,282	34,781	15,150	24,573	40,325	43,283	32,320	21,341	18,663	11,419	3,731
1997	266,733	18,945	35,138	15,420	24,584	39,500	43,858	33,542	21,772	18,465	11,680	3,831
1998	268,396	18,626	35,487	15,428	24,972	38,530	44,257	34,432	22,585	18,286	11,851	3,943
1999	269,861	18,295	35,658	15,547	25,423	37,518	44,450	35,580	23,260	18,068	12,019	4,044
2000	271,237	17,943	35,790	15,602	25,876	36,740	44,364	36,840	23,798	17,974	12,162	4,148
2005	276,990	16,896	34,366	16,667	27,491	35,095	41,365	40,992	29,145	17,943	12,465	4,566
2010	281,468	16,563	31,950	16,319	29,050	36,393	37,049	42,589	34,393	20,245	11,912	5,005
2020	288,807	17,168	30,998	14,331	26,671	40,067	36,640	35,487	39,642	29,219	13,598	4,987
2030	291,070	16,450	31,454	14,631	25,111	36,312	40,222	35,075	32,948	33,483	19,610	5,776
2040	287,685	16,200	30,164	14,405	25,849	35,018	36,489	38,475	32,631	27,827	22,376	8,250
2050	282,524	16,330	30,124	13,925	24,810	35,604	35,185	34,868	35,747	27,700	18,588	9,642
Middle series:												
1996	265,253	19,403	34,809	15,167	24,616	40,374	43,311	32,341	21,360	18,685	11,440	3,747
1997	267,645	19,229	35,206	15,463	24,690	39,624	43,930	33,591	21,816	18,511	11,723	3,862
1998	270,002	19,117	35,609	15,503	25,160	38,757	44,389	34,520	22,662	18,365	11,925	3,996
1999	272,330	19,041	35,846	15,661	25,710	37,876	44,661	35,717	23,378	18,186	12,129	4,124
2000	274,634	18,987	36,043	15,752	26,258	37,233	44,659	37,030	23,962	18,136	12,315	4,259
2005	285,981	19,127	35,850	16,986	28,268	36,306	42,165	41,507	29,606	18,369	12,898	4,899
2010	297,716	20,012	35,605	16,894	30,138	38,292	38,521	43,564	35,283	21,057	12,680	5,671
2020	322,742	21,979	38,660	16,965	29,919	42,934	39,612	37,740	41,714	31,385	15,375	6,460
2030	346,899	23,066	41,589	18,788	31,826	42,744	44,263	38,897	36,348	37,406	23,517	8,455
2040	369,980	24,980	43,993	19,844	34,570	45,932	44,159	43,530	37,739	33,013	28,668	13,552
2050	393,931	27,106	47,804	21,207	36,333	49,365	47,393	43,494	42,368	34,731	25,905	18,223
Highest series:												
1996	265,646	19,510	34,838	15,186	24,660	40,429	43,349	32,362	21,376	18,704	11,465	3,766
1997	268,577	19,483	35,277	15,507	24,798	39,761	44,024	33,644	21,853	18,552	11,775	3,902
1998	271,647	19,563	35,735	15,581	25,352	39,004	44,561	34,615	22,728	18,434	12,011	4,063
1999	274,865	19,726	36,039	15,780	26,004	38,264	44,932	35,868	23,482	18,290	12,257	4,225
2000	278,129	19,955	36,300	15,909	26,651	37,766	45,038	37,241	24,105	18,276	12,490	4,399
2005	295,318	21,350	37,266	17,318	29,064	37,599	43,197	42,119	29,997	18,723	13,367	5,317
2010	314,571	23,649	39,195	17,467	31,248	40,275	40,302	44,738	36,018	21,696	13,465	6,518
2020	357,702	27,273	46,855	19,641	33,084	45,836	42,878	40,263	43,473	32,937	17,007	8,456
2030	405,089	30,818	52,876	23,276	38,886	49,091	48,519	42,895	39,398	40,270	26,861	12,198
2040	458,444	35,901	60,446	26,000	44,069	57,362	51,925	48,560	42,258	37,096	33,907	20,920
2050	518,903	41,213	70,000	30,005	49,683	64,279	60,324	51,967	47,950	40,319	32,070	31,093
MALE (middle series)												
1996	129,522	9,927	17,823	7,790	12,516	20,165	21,490	15,798	10,162	8,323	4,478	1,049
1997	130,712	9,839	18,024	7,941	12,550	19,774	21,808	16,409	10,390	8,266	4,621	1,089
1998	131,883	9,780	18,232	7,961	12,787	19,325	22,044	16,860	10,805	8,224	4,730	1,134
1999	133,039	9,740	18,355	8,042	13,063	18,869	22,184	17,446	11,150	8,171	4,839	1,179
2000	134,181	9,712	18,454	8,090	13,338	18,535	22,181	18,092	11,433	8,180	4,937	1,228
2005	139,785	9,786	18,353	8,724	14,359	18,014	20,891	20,304	14,166	8,408	5,306	1,473
2010	145,584	10,243	18,232	8,679	15,313	18,990	18,993	21,325	16,922	9,752	5,363	1,771
2020	158,021	11,259	19,813	8,718	15,201	21,319	19,466	18,347	20,120	14,791	6,845	2,141
2030	169,950	11,813	21,311	9,653	16,171	21,214	21,775	18,854	17,441	17,878	10,819	3,021
2040	181,261	12,788	22,534	10,192	17,563	22,808	21,723	21,139	18,093	15,796	13,522	5,103
2050	193,234	13,877	24,488	10,893	18,462	24,533	23,352	21,150	20,403	16,699	12,342	7,036
FEMALE (middle series)												
1996	135,731	9,476	16,986	7,377	12,100	20,209	21,820	16,543	11,198	10,362	6,962	2,697
1997	136,933	9,389	17,182	7,522	12,139	19,850	22,122	17,182	11,426	10,246	7,102	2,773
1998	138,119	9,336	17,377	7,542	12,373	19,432	22,345	17,659	11,857	10,141	7,194	2,862
1999	139,291	9,302	17,492	7,619	12,647	19,007	22,476	18,271	12,228	10,015	7,290	2,945
2000	140,453	9,274	17,589	7,662	12,920	18,699	22,478	18,938	12,529	9,956	7,377	3,031
2005	146,196	9,341	17,498	8,262	13,909	18,291	21,273	21,203	15,440	9,961	7,592	3,426
2010	152,132	9,768	17,373	8,215	14,824	19,301	19,527	22,240	18,362	11,305	7,317	3,899
2020	164,721	10,719	18,847	8,247	14,717	21,615	20,146	19,393	21,594	16,594	8,530	4,319
2030	176,949	11,253	20,278	9,135	15,655	21,529	22,488	20,044	18,907	19,529	12,699	5,433
2040	188,719	12,192	21,459	9,652	17,006	23,125	22,436	22,391	19,646	17,216	15,146	8,449
2050	200,696	13,229	23,316	10,314	17,871	24,832	24,041	22,344	21,965	18,032	13,563	11,188
PERCENT DISTRIBUTION (middle series)												
2000	100.0	6.9	13.1	5.7	9.6	13.6	16.3	13.5	8.7	6.6	4.5	1.6
2005	100.0	6.7	12.5	5.9	9.9	12.7	14.7	14.5	10.4	6.4	4.5	1.7
2010	100.0	6.7	12.0	5.7	10.1	12.9	12.9	14.6	11.9	7.1	4.3	1.9
2020	100.0	6.8	12.0	5.3	9.3	13.3	12.3	11.7	12.9	9.7	4.8	2.0
2050	100.0	6.9	12.1	5.4	9.2	12.5	12.0	11.0	10.8	8.8	6.6	4.6

Source: U.S. Bureau of the Census, *Current Population Reports*, P25-1130.

No. 18. Resident Population, by Race, 1980 to 1995, and Projections, 1996 to 2050

[In thousands, except as indicated. As of July, except as indicated. These data are consistent with the 1980 and 1990 decennial enumerations and have been modified from the official census counts; see text, section 1, for explanation. See headnote, table 3]

YEAR	Total	White	Black	American Indian, Eskimo, Aleut	Asian, Pacific Islander
1980 (April) [1]	226,546	194,713	26,683	1,420	3,729
1981	229,466	196,635	27,133	1,483	4,214
1982	231,664	198,037	27,508	1,537	4,581
1983	233,792	199,420	27,867	1,596	4,909
1984	235,825	200,708	28,212	1,656	5,249
1985	237,924	202,031	28,569	1,718	5,606
1986	240,133	203,430	28,942	1,783	5,978
1987	242,289	204,770	29,325	1,851	6,343
1988	244,499	206,129	29,723	1,923	6,724
1989	246,819	207,540	30,143	2,001	7,134
1990 (April) [2]	248,718	208,710	30,486	2,065	7,458
1991	252,138	211,017	31,110	2,107	7,904
1992	255,039	212,957	31,659	2,142	8,280
1993	257,800	214,805	32,174	2,177	8,644
1994	260,350	216,496	32,669	2,210	8,974
1995	262,755	218,085	33,141	2,242	9,287
PROJECTIONS					
Lowest series:					
1996	264,869	219,361	33,569	2,271	9,668
1997	266,733	220,507	33,973	2,300	9,953
1998	268,396	221,501	34,357	2,328	10,211
1999	269,861	222,346	34,721	2,355	10,440
2000	271,237	223,114	35,074	2,382	10,667
2005	276,990	226,006	36,695	2,514	11,774
2010	281,468	227,841	38,139	2,642	12,845
2020	288,807	230,202	40,709	2,881	15,015
2030	291,070	228,310	42,519	3,080	17,161
2040	287,685	221,671	43,674	3,247	19,092
2050	282,524	213,782	44,477	3,383	20,882
Middle series:					
1996	265,253	219,641	33,611	2,273	9,728
1997	267,645	221,163	34,075	2,305	10,102
1998	270,002	222,648	34,537	2,337	10,480
1999	272,330	224,103	34,997	2,369	10,861
2000	274,634	225,532	35,454	2,402	11,245
2005	285,981	232,463	37,734	2,572	13,212
2010	297,716	239,588	40,109	2,754	15,265
2020	322,742	254,887	45,075	3,129	19,651
2030	346,899	269,046	50,001	3,515	24,337
2040	369,980	281,720	55,094	3,932	29,235
2050	393,931	294,615	60,592	4,371	34,352
Highest series:					
1996	265,646	219,916	33,666	2,275	9,789
1997	268,577	221,809	34,200	2,310	10,257
1998	271,647	223,785	34,755	2,346	10,761
1999	274,865	225,848	35,332	2,383	11,302
2000	278,129	227,937	35,919	2,421	11,851
2005	295,318	238,906	39,050	2,627	14,735
2010	314,571	251,262	42,590	2,860	17,859
2020	357,702	279,139	50,490	3,365	24,709
2030	405,089	309,404	59,449	3,934	32,302
2040	458,444	343,201	69,844	4,609	40,790
2050	518,903	381,505	81,815	5,384	50,199
PERCENT DISTRIBUTION					
Middle series:					
2000	100.0	82.1	12.9	0.9	4.1
2010	100.0	80.5	13.5	0.9	5.1
2020	100.0	79.0	14.0	1.0	6.1
2030	100.0	77.6	14.4	1.0	7.0
2040	100.0	76.1	14.9	1.1	7.9
2050	100.0	74.8	15.4	1.1	8.7
PERCENT CHANGE (middle series)					
2000-2010	8.4	6.2	13.1	14.6	35.8
2010-2020	8.4	6.4	12.4	13.6	28.7
2020-2030	7.5	5.6	10.9	12.3	23.8
2030-2040	6.7	4.7	10.2	11.8	20.1
2040-2050	6.5	4.6	10.0	11.2	17.5

[1] See footnote 4, table 1.   [2] The April 1, 1990, census count (248,718,291) includes count resolution corrections processed through March 1994 and does not include adjustments for census coverage errors.

Source: U.S. Bureau of the Census, *Current Population Reports*, P25-1095 and P25-1130; and Population Paper Listing 41.

No. 19. Resident Population, by Hispanic Origin Status, 1980 to 1995, and Projections, 1996 to 2050

[**In thousands, except as indicated.** As of **July**, except as indicated. These data are consistent with the 1980 and 1990 decennial enumerations and have been modified from the official census counts; see text, section 1, for explanation. See headnote, table 3. Minus sign (-) indicates decrease]

YEAR	Total	Hispanic origin [1]	NOT OF HISPANIC ORIGIN			
			White	Black	American Indian, Eskimo, Aleut	Asian, Pacific Islander
1980 (April) [2]	226,546	14,609	180,906	26,142	1,326	3,563
1981	229,466	15,560	181,974	26,532	1,377	4,022
1982	231,664	16,240	182,782	26,856	1,420	4,367
1983	233,792	16,935	183,561	27,159	1,466	4,671
1984	235,825	17,640	184,243	27,444	1,512	4,986
1985	237,924	18,368	184,945	27,738	1,558	5,315
1986	240,133	19,154	185,678	28,040	1,606	5,655
1987	242,289	19,946	186,353	28,351	1,654	5,985
1988	244,499	20,786	187,012	28,669	1,703	6,329
1989	246,819	21,648	187,713	29,005	1,755	6,698
1990 (April) [3]	248,718	22,354	188,306	29,275	1,796	6,988
1991	252,138	23,381	189,692	29,825	1,829	7,411
1992	255,039	24,227	190,832	30,310	1,856	7,768
1993	257,800	25,198	191,852	30,757	1,882	8,112
1994	260,350	26,099	192,735	31,187	1,907	8,421
1995	262,755	26,994	193,523	31,591	1,931	8,715
PROJECTIONS						
Lowest series:						
1996	264,869	27,704	194,162	31,965	1,954	9,084
1997	266,733	28,431	194,657	32,314	1,977	9,354
1998	268,396	29,115	195,037	32,647	1,999	9,598
1999	269,861	29,757	195,307	32,962	2,020	9,815
2000	271,237	30,393	195,505	33,267	2,041	10,030
2005	276,990	33,527	195,589	34,652	2,145	11,077
2010	281,468	36,652	194,628	35,856	2,243	12,088
2020	288,807	43,287	191,047	37,913	2,424	14,136
2030	291,070	49,834	183,295	39,202	2,573	16,166
2040	287,685	56,104	171,054	39,841	2,695	17,991
2050	282,524	62,230	157,701	40,118	2,793	19,683
Middle series:						
1996	265,253	27,804	194,353	31,999	1,956	9,141
1997	267,645	28,680	195,091	32,396	1,980	9,497
1998	270,002	29,566	195,786	32,789	2,005	9,856
1999	272,330	30,461	196,441	33,180	2,029	10,219
2000	274,634	31,366	197,061	33,568	2,054	10,584
2005	285,981	36,057	199,802	35,485	2,183	12,454
2010	297,716	41,139	202,390	37,466	2,320	14,402
2020	322,742	52,652	207,393	41,538	2,601	18,557
2030	346,899	65,570	209,998	45,448	2,891	22,993
2040	369,980	80,164	209,621	49,379	3,203	27,614
2050	393,931	96,508	207,901	53,555	3,534	32,432
Highest series:						
1996	265,646	27,904	194,539	32,045	1,957	9,200
1997	268,577	28,931	195,516	32,501	1,983	9,646
1998	271,647	30,019	196,521	32,971	2,010	10,127
1999	274,865	31,172	197,556	33,457	2,038	10,642
2000	278,129	32,350	198,594	33,952	2,066	11,166
2005	295,318	38,648	203,949	36,589	2,218	13,914
2010	314,571	45,760	209,963	39,572	2,391	16,885
2020	357,702	62,279	223,082	46,183	2,765	23,392
2030	405,089	81,803	235,898	53,604	3,192	30,593
2040	458,444	105,274	248,715	62,132	3,703	38,620
2050	518,903	133,106	262,140	71,863	4,295	47,498
PERCENT DISTRIBUTION						
Middle series:						
2000	100.0	11.4	71.8	12.2	0.7	3.9
2010	100.0	13.8	68.0	12.6	0.8	4.8
2020	100.0	16.3	64.3	12.9	0.8	5.7
2030	100.0	18.9	60.5	13.1	0.8	6.6
2040	100.0	21.7	56.7	13.3	0.9	7.5
2050	100.0	24.5	52.8	13.6	0.9	8.2
PERCENT CHANGE (middle series)						
2000-2010	8.4	31.2	2.7	11.6	12.9	36.1
2010-2020	8.4	28.0	2.5	10.9	12.1	28.9
2020-2030	7.5	24.5	1.3	9.4	11.1	23.9
2030-2040	6.7	22.3	-0.2	8.6	10.8	20.1
2040-2050	6.5	20.4	-0.8	8.5	10.3	17.4

[1] Persons of Hispanic origin may be of any race.   [2] See footnote 4, table 1.   [3] The April 1, 1990, census count (248,718,291) includes count resolution corrections processed through March 1994 and does not include adjustments for census coverage errors.

Source: U.S. Bureau of the Census, *Current Population Reports*, P25-1095 and P25-1130; and Population Paper Listing 41.

No. 20. Components of Population Change, by Race and Hispanic Origin, 1990 to 1995, and Projections, 2000

[The April 1, 1990, census count (248,718,291) includes count resolution corrections processed through March 1994 and does not include adjustments for census coverage errors]

| YEAR | Popula-tion at start of period (1,000) | TOTAL (Jan. 1-Dec. 31) | | | | | RATE PER 1,000 MIDYEAR POPULATION | | | |
| | | Net increase [1] | | Natural increase | | Net migra-tion [3] (1,000) | Net growth rate [1] | Natural increase | | Net migra-tion [3] |
		Total (1,000)	Per-cent [2]	Births (1,000)	Deaths (1,000)			Birth rate	Death rate	
WHITE										
1990	208,376	1,711	0.8	3,265	1,860	[4]306	8.2	15.6	8.9	[4]1.5
1991	210,045	1,968	0.9	3,241	1,869	[4]595	9.3	15.4	8.9	[4]2.8
1992	212,013	1,953	0.9	3,202	1,874	625	9.2	15.0	8.8	2.9
1993	213,966	1,736	0.8	3,150	1,951	538	8.1	14.7	9.1	2.5
1994	215,702	1,654	0.8	3,112	1,965	508	7.6	14.4	9.1	2.3
1995	217,356	1,560	0.7	3,083	2,001	478	7.2	14.1	9.2	2.2
2000, proj. [5]	224,818	1,419	0.6	2,986	2,058	491	6.3	13.2	9.1	2.2
BLACK										
1990	30,377	453	1.5	692	266	[4]27	14.8	22.6	8.7	[4]0.9
1991	30,817	581	1.9	683	270	[4]168	18.7	21.9	8.7	[4]5.4
1992	31,398	541	1.7	674	269	136	17.1	21.3	8.5	4.3
1993	31,939	490	1.5	659	282	113	15.2	20.5	8.8	3.5
1994	32,429	486	1.5	669	283	101	14.9	20.5	8.7	3.1
1995	32,915	473	1.4	673	288	89	14.3	20.3	8.7	2.7
2000, proj. [5]	35,225	457	1.3	685	319	90	12.9	19.3	9.0	2.6
AMERICAN INDIAN, ESKIMO, ALEUT										
1990	2,044	35	1.7	42	8	[4]1	16.7	20.1	4.1	[4]0.6
1991	2,089	35	1.7	39	9	[4]5	16.6	18.4	4.1	[4]2.3
1992	2,125	36	1.7	39	9	5	16.7	18.4	4.2	2.5
1993	2,160	34	1.6	39	10	5	15.6	17.8	4.4	2.2
1994	2,194	32	1.5	39	11	4	14.6	17.9	5.0	1.7
1995	2,226	32	1.4	40	11	4	14.4	17.9	5.0	1.6
2000, proj. [5]	2,386	33	1.4	42	13	4	13.7	17.3	5.2	1.6
ASIAN, PACIFIC ISLANDER										
1990	7,345	372	5.1	149	21	[4]244	49.3	19.8	2.7	[4]32.3
1991	7,729	356	4.6	148	22	[4]230	45.0	18.7	2.8	[4]29.1
1992	8,085	378	4.7	150	24	252	45.7	18.1	2.9	30.4
1993	8,464	352	4.2	153	25	225	40.8	17.7	2.9	26.0
1994	8,816	312	3.5	159	26	179	34.8	17.7	2.9	20.0
1995	9,128	331	3.6	165	28	194	35.6	17.8	3.0	20.8
2000, proj. [5]	11,053	386	3.5	186	36	235	34.3	16.6	3.2	20.9
HISPANIC ORIGIN [6]										
1990	22,122	803	3.6	595	84	[4]292	35.6	26.4	3.7	[4]12.9
1991	22,969	841	3.7	628	85	[4]299	36.0	26.8	3.6	[4]12.8
1992	23,810	916	3.8	649	87	354	37.7	26.7	3.6	14.6
1993	24,727	915	3.7	661	93	347	36.3	26.2	3.7	13.8
1994	25,641	905	3.5	669	97	332	34.7	25.6	3.7	12.7
1995	26,546	920	3.5	685	102	337	34.1	25.4	3.8	12.5
2000, proj. [5]	30,913	910	2.9	683	123	350	29.0	21.8	3.9	11.2
WHITE, NON-HISPANIC										
1990	188,160	989	0.5	2,720	1,782	[4]52	5.2	14.4	9.4	[4]0.3
1991	189,088	1,213	0.6	2,667	1,790	[4]336	6.4	14.1	9.4	[4]1.8
1992	190,301	1,132	0.6	2,609	1,794	317	5.9	13.7	9.4	1.7
1993	191,434	917	0.5	2,546	1,865	236	4.8	13.3	9.7	1.2
1994	192,350	845	0.4	2,500	1,876	220	4.4	13.0	9.7	1.1
1995	193,195	737	0.4	2,459	1,908	186	3.8	12.7	9.9	1.0
2000, proj. [5]	196,751	605	0.3	2,365	1,946	186	3.1	12.0	9.9	0.9
BLACK, NON-HISPANIC										
1990	29,191	397	1.4	659	262	[4]-	13.5	22.4	8.9	[4]-
1991	29,562	522	1.8	646	265	[4]140	17.5	21.7	8.9	[4]4.7
1992	30,084	473	1.6	636	265	102	15.6	21.0	8.7	3.4
1993	30,557	423	1.4	620	277	80	13.7	20.2	9.0	2.6
1994	30,980	419	1.4	629	278	68	13.4	20.2	8.9	2.2
1995	31,399	404	1.3	632	283	55	12.8	20.0	9.0	1.8
2000, proj. [5]	33,374	387	1.2	641	312	57	11.5	19.1	9.3	1.7

- Represents or rounds to zero.   [1] Net change for 1990 excludes "error of closure" for the three months prior to the April 1 census date. Therefore, it may not equal the difference between the populations at the beginning of 1990 and 1991.   [2] Percent of population at beginning of period.   [3] Covers net international migration and movement of Armed Forces, federally affiliated civilian citizens, and their dependents.   [4] Data reflect movement of Armed Forces due to the Gulf War.   [5] Based on middle series of assumptions. See footnote 1, table 3.   [6] Persons of Hispanic origin may be of any race.

Source: U.S. Bureau of the Census, *Current Population Reports*, P25-1130; and Population Paper Listing 41.

No. 21. Resident Population, by Age and Race: 1980 to 1995

[In thousands, except percent. As of April, except 1995 as of July. See headnote, table 18 and, for 1980 data, footnote 4, table 1]

YEAR, SEX, AND RACE	Total, all years	Under 5 years	5-9 years	10-14 years	15-19 years	20-24 years	25-29 years	30-34 years	35-39 years	40-44 years	45-49 years	50-54 years	55-59 years	60-64 years	65-74 years	75-84 years	85 years and over	5-13 years	14-17 years	18-24 years
ALL RACES																				
1980	226,546	16,348	16,700	18,242	21,168	21,319	19,521	17,561	13,965	11,669	11,090	11,710	11,615	10,088	15,581	7,729	2,240	31,159	16,247	30,022
1990 [1]	248,718	18,757	18,035	17,060	17,886	19,135	21,328	21,833	19,846	17,589	13,744	11,313	10,487	10,625	18,046	10,012	3,022	31,826	13,340	26,950
1995	262,755	19,591	19,220	18,915	18,065	19,087	19,005	21,868	22,249	20,219	17,449	13,630	11,085	10,046	18,759	11,145	3,628	34,384	14,765	24,932
Male	128,314	10,025	9,843	9,685	9,265	9,087	9,530	10,902	11,071	9,990	8,560	6,622	5,317	4,727	8,342	4,330	1,017	17,606	7,585	12,689
Female	134,441	9,566	9,377	9,229	8,799	8,795	9,476	10,966	11,178	10,228	8,889	7,008	5,767	5,320	10,417	6,815	2,611	16,777	7,180	12,243
WHITE																				
1980	194,713	13,414	13,717	15,095	17,681	18,072	16,658	15,157	12,122	10,110	9,693	10,360	10,394	9,078	14,045	7,057	2,060	25,692	13,491	25,381
1990 [1]	208,710	14,960	15,237	13,670	14,354	15,640	17,638	18,190	16,652	15,001	11,826	9,744	9,131	9,381	16,175	9,085	2,761	25,557	10,664	21,946
1995	218,085	15,040	15,236	15,040	14,362	14,317	15,403	17,984	18,458	16,930	14,858	11,725	9,541	8,724	16,644	10,108	3,303	27,300	11,712	19,944
Male	106,994	7,924	7,818	7,721	7,390	7,324	7,796	9,062	9,282	8,461	7,370	5,754	4,626	4,152	7,455	3,940	919	14,010	6,032	10,211
Female	111,092	7,527	7,418	7,319	6,972	6,993	7,607	8,922	9,176	8,469	7,488	5,971	4,915	4,571	9,189	6,168	2,385	13,290	5,680	9,733
BLACK																				
1980	26,683	2,459	2,509	2,691	3,007	2,749	2,342	1,904	1,469	1,260	1,150	1,135	1,041	874	1,344	588	159	4,628	2,380	3,948
1990 [1]	30,486	2,939	2,711	2,629	2,715	2,656	2,780	2,718	2,360	1,882	1,413	1,178	1,041	972	1,498	772	223	4,838	2,056	3,818
1995	33,141	3,100	3,025	2,877	2,822	2,638	2,594	2,825	2,788	2,390	1,855	1,381	1,138	988	1,617	828	274	5,328	2,303	3,730
Male	15,721	1,570	1,535	1,460	1,430	1,299	1,240	1,325	1,307	1,109	846	620	500	425	674	302	79	2,703	1,173	1,848
Female	17,420	1,530	1,491	1,417	1,392	1,338	1,355	1,500	1,481	1,282	1,008	761	638	563	943	526	195	2,625	1,130	1,882
AMERICAN INDIAN, ESKIMO, ALEUT																				
1980	1,420	149	147	156	170	149	125	107	84	69	58	52	45	34	48	21	6	270	136	216
1990 [1]	2,065	220	209	197	191	179	188	181	157	132	99	79	64	53	73	34	9	368	151	257
1995	2,242	207	228	234	201	185	180	186	177	156	125	93	72	58	84	41	15	414	175	258
Male	1,110	105	116	118	101	95	93	93	87	75	61	45	34	27	38	17	5	210	88	131
Female	1,132	103	111	115	100	90	87	93	90	80	64	49	38	31	46	25	10	204	86	127
ASIAN, PACIFIC ISLANDER																				
1980	3,729	326	328	300	310	349	396	393	291	230	188	163	135	101	143	63	15	570	239	478
1990 [1]	7,458	638	612	564	626	661	722	745	678	574	405	312	252	220	300	122	29	1,063	469	930
1995	9,287	833	731	764	680	743	828	872	825	743	611	430	334	276	414	167	36	1,341	576	1,001
Male	4,489	426	374	387	343	369	401	422	395	346	282	203	158	122	176	72	14	683	292	499
Female	4,797	407	356	377	336	373	427	450	431	398	329	227	176	154	238	96	22	658	284	502
PERCENT																				
Total, **1995**	100.0	7.5	7.3	7.2	6.9	6.8	7.2	8.3	8.5	7.7	6.6	5.2	4.2	3.8	7.1	4.2	1.4	13.1	5.6	9.5
White	100.0	7.1	7.0	6.9	6.6	6.6	7.1	8.2	8.5	7.8	6.8	5.4	4.4	4.0	7.6	4.6	1.5	12.5	5.4	9.1
Black	100.0	9.4	9.1	8.7	8.5	8.0	7.8	8.5	8.4	7.2	5.6	4.2	3.4	3.0	4.9	2.5	0.8	16.1	6.9	11.3
American Indian, Eskimo, Aleut	100.0	9.3	10.1	10.4	9.0	8.2	8.0	8.3	7.9	6.9	5.6	4.2	3.2	2.6	3.8	1.8	0.7	18.5	7.8	11.5
Asian, Pacific Islander	100.0	9.0	7.9	8.2	7.3	8.0	8.9	9.4	8.9	8.0	6.6	4.6	3.6	3.0	4.5	1.8	0.4	14.4	6.2	10.8

[1] The April 1, 1990, census count (248,718,291) includes count resolution corrections processed through March 1994, and does not include adjustments for census coverage errors.

Source: U.S. Bureau of the Census, Current Population Reports, P25-1095; and Population Paper Listing 41.

Population

No. 22. Resident Population, by Race, Hispanic Origin, and Single Years of Age: 1995

[**In thousands, except as indicated**. As of **July 1**. Resident population. For derivation of estimates, see text, section 1]

AGE	Total	RACE				Hispanic origin [1]	NOT OF HISPANIC ORIGIN			
		White	Black	American Indian, Eskimo, Aleut	Asian, Pacific Islander		White	Black	American Indian, Eskimo, Aleut	Asian, Pacific Islander
Total	**262,755**	**218,085**	**33,141**	**2,242**	**9,287**	**26,994**	**193,523**	**31,591**	**1,931**	**8,715**
Under 5 yrs. old . .	19,591	15,451	3,100	207	833	3,212	12,518	2,918	175	769
Under 1 yr. old .	3,848	3,015	621	42	170	660	2,412	584	35	157
1 yr. old	3,840	3,028	608	40	165	648	2,436	571	34	152
2 yrs. old	3,882	3,067	611	41	163	641	2,482	574	34	150
3 yrs. old	3,965	3,137	619	42	168	642	2,550	583	35	155
4 yrs. old	4,056	3,205	642	42	167	621	2,638	606	36	155
5-9 yrs. old.	19,220	15,237	3,025	228	731	2,661	12,830	2,866	191	673
5 yrs. old	4,039	3,198	641	47	153	583	2,670	606	40	141
6 yrs. old	3,888	3,071	625	46	146	543	2,580	592	39	134
7 yrs. old	3,810	3,016	602	45	146	530	2,537	570	38	134
8 yrs. old	3,616	2,876	561	43	137	488	2,434	532	36	126
9 yrs. old	3,867	3,075	597	46	149	516	2,609	566	39	137
10-14 yrs. old. . . .	18,915	15,040	2,877	234	764	2,428	12,841	2,739	198	709
10 yrs. old	3,869	3,084	588	46	151	502	2,629	559	39	140
11 yrs. old	3,705	2,952	559	45	148	481	2,516	532	38	138
12 yrs. old	3,778	2,998	576	48	156	486	2,558	549	41	145
13 yrs. old	3,811	3,030	580	47	155	479	2,596	552	40	144
14 yrs. old	3,751	2,976	574	47	154	479	2,542	547	40	143
15-19 yrs. old. . . .	18,065	14,362	2,822	201	680	2,278	12,293	2,690	171	632
15 yrs. old	3,790	2,994	602	45	148	469	2,569	575	39	138
16 yrs. old	3,627	2,877	570	42	138	450	2,469	544	36	128
17 yrs. old	3,597	2,865	557	40	135	454	2,452	531	35	126
18 yrs. old	3,506	2,797	548	36	125	443	2,394	523	31	116
19 yrs. old	3,544	2,829	545	37	133	462	2,408	518	32	124
20-24 yrs. old. . . .	17,882	14,317	2,638	185	743	2,334	12,191	2,508	158	691
20 yrs. old	3,564	2,856	538	36	135	463	2,433	512	31	125
21 yrs. old	3,418	2,725	516	36	141	450	2,314	491	31	132
22 yrs. old	3,402	2,715	507	36	144	459	2,296	482	31	135
23 yrs. old	3,575	2,860	524	37	153	461	2,441	499	32	142
24 yrs. old	3,924	3,161	553	40	169	500	2,708	525	34	157
25-29 yrs. old. . . .	19,005	15,403	2,594	180	828	2,500	13,136	2,449	151	770
25 yrs. old	3,878	3,143	527	39	170	495	2,694	499	33	158
26 yrs. old	3,749	3,048	499	36	166	494	2,600	471	30	154
27 yrs. old	3,719	3,009	510	35	165	498	2,557	481	29	153
28 yrs. old	3,594	2,928	483	33	151	479	2,493	455	27	140
29 yrs. old	4,065	3,275	575	37	177	534	2,792	543	31	165
30-34 yrs. old. . . .	21,868	17,984	2,825	186	872	2,533	15,683	2,677	157	818
30 yrs. old	4,210	3,435	567	37	172	527	2,956	535	31	161
31 yrs. old	4,270	3,501	558	37	174	511	3,037	528	31	163
32 yrs. old	4,358	3,584	559	37	179	510	3,121	529	32	168
33 yrs. old	4,427	3,664	559	37	167	482	3,225	531	31	157
34 yrs. old	4,602	3,801	583	38	180	503	3,343	554	33	169
35-39 yrs. old. . . .	22,249	18,458	2,788	177	825	2,156	16,504	2,658	152	779
35 yrs. old	4,594	3,796	585	38	175	475	3,365	557	32	165
36 yrs. old	4,432	3,681	553	35	163	438	3,283	527	30	154
37 yrs. old	4,490	3,729	560	36	166	433	3,336	533	31	156
38 yrs. old	4,220	3,516	520	33	151	389	3,163	497	28	143
39 yrs. old	4,514	3,737	570	36	171	421	3,356	544	31	162
40-44 yrs. old. . . .	20,219	16,930	2,390	156	743	1,725	15,367	2,287	136	705
40 yrs. old	4,343	3,614	533	34	162	391	3,260	509	29	153
41 yrs. old	4,131	3,456	490	33	153	355	3,135	469	28	144
42 yrs. old	4,004	3,364	462	31	148	342	3,053	442	27	140
43 yrs. old	3,884	3,256	452	31	145	315	2,972	433	27	137
44 yrs. old	3,857	3,239	454	27	136	322	2,947	435	24	129

See footnotes at end of table.

No. 22. Resident Population, by Race, Hispanic Origin, and Single Years of Age: 1995—Continued

[See headnote, page 22]

AGE	Total	RACE				Hispanic origin [1]	NOT OF HISPANIC ORIGIN			
		White	Black	American Indian, Eskimo, Aleut	Asian, Pacific Islander		White	Black	American Indian, Eskimo, Aleut	Asian, Pacific Islander
45-49 yrs. old	17,449	14,858	1,855	125	611	1,311	13,666	1,779	111	582
45 yrs. old	3,741	3,144	433	27	137	297	2,874	415	24	130
46 yrs. old	3,557	3,018	388	25	127	271	2,771	372	22	121
47 yrs. old	3,586	3,044	387	26	128	262	2,806	372	24	122
48 yrs. old	3,658	3,191	335	23	109	247	2,965	321	21	104
49 yrs. old	2,907	2,461	312	23	111	233	2,249	298	21	105
50-54 yrs. old	13,630	11,725	1,381	93	430	961	10,848	1,326	84	410
50 yrs. old	2,890	2,467	302	21	100	217	2,269	290	19	96
51 yrs. old	2,782	2,394	280	19	89	197	2,214	269	18	84
52 yrs. old	2,914	2,537	274	19	84	195	2,359	263	17	80
53 yrs. old	2,568	2,205	268	17	78	176	2,045	257	16	74
54 yrs. old	2,476	2,122	258	17	80	175	1,962	247	16	76
55-59 yrs. old	11,085	9,541	1,138	72	334	762	8,844	1,095	65	319
55 yrs. old	2,312	1,967	254	16	75	163	1,819	244	14	71
56 yrs. old	2,316	1,996	236	15	68	160	1,850	227	13	65
57 yrs. old	2,291	1,969	239	15	68	155	1,827	230	14	65
58 yrs. old	2,029	1,763	195	13	59	138	1,636	187	11	56
59 yrs. old	2,137	1,845	214	14	64	145	1,712	206	13	62
60-64 yrs. old	10,046	8,724	988	58	276	634	8,141	954	53	264
60 yrs. old	2,111	1,832	206	13	59	141	1,703	199	12	56
61 yrs. old	1,934	1,678	189	12	55	125	1,563	183	11	53
62 yrs. old	1,939	1,672	199	12	56	122	1,561	192	11	53
63 yrs. old	1,968	1,717	188	11	51	119	1,608	182	10	49
64 yrs. old	2,095	1,823	205	11	55	127	1,707	198	10	53
65-69 yrs. old	9,928	8,726	920	47	235	542	8,226	891	43	226
65 yrs. old	2,067	1,799	205	11	53	121	1,688	198	10	51
66 yrs. old	2,010	1,761	192	10	48	114	1,656	185	9	46
67 yrs. old	2,041	1,796	189	9	47	110	1,694	183	8	45
68 yrs. old	1,913	1,691	169	9	44	99	1,600	164	8	42
69 yrs. old	1,897	1,679	165	9	44	97	1,590	160	8	42
70-74 yrs. old	8,831	7,918	697	37	179	404	7,543	678	34	172
70 yrs. old	1,884	1,677	157	8	41	92	1,592	152	8	39
71 yrs. old	1,822	1,634	143	8	38	87	1,553	139	7	36
72 yrs. old	1,762	1,578	138	8	38	82	1,502	134	7	37
73 yrs. old	1,712	1,543	130	7	32	74	1,474	127	6	31
74 yrs. old	1,652	1,487	129	7	30	70	1,422	125	6	29
75-79 yrs. old	6,681	6,039	510	25	107	255	5,802	497	23	103
75 yrs. old	1,512	1,358	122	6	27	62	1,300	119	5	26
76 yrs. old	1,405	1,272	105	5	23	54	1,221	102	5	22
77 yrs. old	1,312	1,189	97	5	20	49	1,143	95	5	20
78 yrs. old	1,264	1,146	94	5	19	46	1,104	92	4	18
79 yrs. old	1,189	1,074	91	5	19	44	1,034	89	4	18
80-84 yrs. old	4,464	4,069	318	16	60	169	3,911	311	15	58
80 yrs. old	1,076	981	76	4	15	40	943	75	4	15
81 yrs. old	976	890	70	4	13	37	856	68	3	12
82 yrs. old	895	815	65	3	12	34	783	63	3	11
83 yrs. old	801	734	54	3	10	30	706	52	3	10
84 yrs. old	715	649	54	3	10	28	623	53	3	9
85-89 yrs. old	2,321	2,125	164	9	23	83	2,046	161	8	22
90-94 yrs. old	991	897	81	5	9	36	863	80	4	8
95-99 yrs. old	263	237	22	1	3	9	229	22	1	3
100 yrs. old and over	53	45	7	1	1	2	43	7	-	1
Median age (yr.) . .	34.3	35.3	29.2	26.8	30.4	26.2	36.6	29.3	27.3	30.7

- Represents or rounds to zero.   [1] Persons of Hispanic origin may be of any race.

Source: U.S. Bureau of the Census, Population Paper Listing 41.

No. 23. Resident Population, by Age and Hispanic Origin: 1980 to 1995

[In thousands, except percent. As of April, except 1995 as of July. See headnote, table 18 and, for 1980 data, footnote 4, table 1. Hispanic persons may be of any race]

YEAR AND SEX	Total, all years	Under 5 years	5-9 years	10-14 years	15-19 years	20-24 years	25-29 years	30-34 years	35-39 years	40-44 years	45-49 years	50-54 years	55-59 years	60-64 years	65-74 years	75-84 years	85 years and over	5-13 years	14-17 years	18-24 years
HISPANIC ORIGIN																				
1980 [1]	14,609	1,663	1,537	1,475	1,606	1,586	1,376	1,129	854	712	622	564	454	321	457	203	49	2,715	1,251	2,240
1990 [1]	22,354	2,467	2,178	1,989	2,085	2,320	2,337	2,045	1,642	1,276	936	750	633	550	715	340	91	3,782	1,574	3,215
1995	26,994	3,212	2,661	2,428	2,278	2,334	2,500	2,533	2,156	1,725	1,311	961	762	634	946	424	130	4,609	1,852	3,239
Male	13,676	1,644	1,361	1,239	1,168	1,229	1,341	1,333	1,110	867	644	461	359	293	419	164	43	2,355	950	1,692
Female	13,318	1,568	1,300	1,189	1,110	1,104	1,159	1,200	1,045	858	667	500	402	341	528	260	87	2,254	902	1,546
NON-HISPANIC WHITE																				
1980 [1]	180,906	11,842	12,262	13,703	16,166	16,574	15,358	14,091	11,315	9,437	9,104	9,824	9,963	8,775	13,614	6,863	2,014	23,126	12,313	23,267
1990 [1]	188,306	12,721	12,516	11,854	12,450	13,524	15,508	16,331	15,162	13,839	10,971	9,057	8,548	8,872	15,511	8,767	2,675	22,106	9,224	19,014
1995	193,523	12,518	12,830	12,841	12,293	12,191	13,136	15,683	16,504	15,367	13,666	10,848	8,844	8,141	15,769	9,713	3,180	23,129	10,033	16,993
Male	94,540	6,423	6,588	6,598	6,328	6,201	6,577	7,849	8,275	7,675	6,784	5,333	4,296	3,882	7,067	3,786	878	11,879	5,171	8,666
Female	98,983	6,095	6,242	6,243	5,965	5,990	6,559	7,834	8,229	7,692	6,881	5,516	4,548	4,259	8,703	5,926	2,302	11,250	4,862	8,328
BLACK																				
1980 [1]	26,142	2,399	2,455	2,635	2,944	2,689	2,292	1,865	1,438	1,233	1,127	1,114	1,024	861	1,327	582	157	4,530	2,331	3,862
1990 [1]	29,275	2,798	2,596	2,525	2,605	2,528	2,650	2,601	2,265	1,811	1,362	1,138	1,008	945	1,465	758	219	4,638	1,975	3,642
1995	31,591	2,918	2,866	2,739	2,690	2,508	2,449	2,677	2,658	2,287	1,779	1,326	1,095	954	1,569	808	270	5,057	2,197	3,549
Male	14,941	1,477	1,452	1,389	1,363	1,234	1,164	1,248	1,240	1,056	809	594	480	410	653	295	78	2,564	1,118	1,756
Female	16,651	1,441	1,413	1,350	1,328	1,275	1,285	1,429	1,418	1,231	970	733	615	544	916	514	192	2,494	1,079	1,793
AMERICAN INDIAN, ESKIMO, ALEUT																				
1980 [1]	1,326	136	135	145	158	138	116	100	79	66	55	49	43	32	46	20	6	249	127	199
1990 [1]	1,796	185	179	170	165	151	160	156	138	117	90	72	58	48	68	31	9	316	131	217
1995	1,931	175	191	198	171	158	151	157	152	136	111	84	65	53	77	39	14	349	149	220
Male	950	88	97	100	86	80	77	78	74	65	54	40	31	25	34	15	5	177	75	112
Female	982	87	94	98	85	78	74	80	78	70	57	44	35	28	42	23	10	172	74	109
ASIAN, PACIFIC ISLANDER																				
1980 [1]	3,563	308	311	285	294	332	378	376	279	221	182	158	131	98	136	60	14	540	226	455
1990 [1]	6,988	586	566	522	581	612	673	700	640	545	384	297	240	210	287	116	27	983	436	862
1995	8,715	769	673	709	632	691	770	818	779	705	582	410	319	264	398	161	34	1,239	535	931
Male	4,207	393	345	359	319	343	371	395	372	327	269	194	151	117	169	69	13	631	271	464
Female	4,508	376	328	350	312	348	399	423	407	378	314	216	168	148	229	92	21	608	263	468
1995, PERCENT																				
Hispanic origin	100.0	11.9	9.9	9.0	8.4	8.6	9.3	9.4	8.0	6.4	4.9	3.6	2.8	2.3	3.5	1.6	0.5	17.1	6.9	12.0
Non-Hispanic:																				
White	100.0	6.5	6.6	6.6	6.4	6.3	6.8	8.1	8.5	7.9	7.1	5.6	4.6	4.2	8.1	5.0	1.6	12.0	5.2	8.8
Black	100.0	9.2	9.1	8.7	8.5	7.9	7.8	8.5	8.4	7.2	5.6	4.2	3.5	3.0	5.0	2.6	0.9	16.0	7.0	11.2
American Indian, Eskimo, Aleut	100.0	9.1	9.9	10.3	8.9	8.2	7.8	8.1	7.9	7.0	5.7	4.4	3.4	2.7	4.0	2.0	0.7	18.1	7.7	11.4
Asian, Pacific Islander	100.0	8.8	7.7	8.1	7.3	7.9	8.8	9.4	8.9	8.1	6.7	4.7	3.7	3.0	4.6	1.8	0.4	14.2	6.1	10.7

[1] The April 1, 1990, census count (248,718,291) includes count resolution corrections processed through March 1994 and does not include adjustments for census coverage errors.

Source: U.S. Bureau of the Census, Current Population Reports, P25-1095; and Population Paper Listings 21 and 41.

No. 24. Projections of Resident Population, by Age, Sex, and Race: 2000 to 2025

[As of **July 1**. Data are for middle series; for assumptions, see table 3]

AGE, SEX, AND RACE	POPULATION (1,000)				PERCENT DISTRIBUTION			
	2000	2005	2010	2025	2000	2005	2010	2025
Total	**274,634**	**285,981**	**297,716**	**335,050**	**100.0**	**100.0**	**100.0**	**100.0**
Under 5 years old	18,987	19,127	20,012	22,498	6.9	6.7	6.7	6.7
5 to 13 years old	36,043	35,850	35,605	40,413	13.1	12.5	12.0	12.1
14 to 17 years old	15,752	16,986	16,894	17,872	5.7	5.9	5.7	5.3
18 to 24 years old	26,258	28,268	30,138	30,372	9.6	9.9	10.1	9.1
25 to 34 years old	37,233	36,306	38,292	43,119	13.6	12.7	12.9	12.9
35 to 44 years old	44,659	42,165	38,521	42,391	16.3	14.7	12.9	12.7
45 to 54 years old	37,030	41,507	43,564	36,890	13.5	14.5	14.6	11.0
55 to 64 years old	23,962	29,606	35,283	39,542	8.7	10.4	11.9	11.8
65 to 74 years old	18,136	18,369	21,057	35,425	6.6	6.4	7.1	10.6
75 to 84 years old	12,315	12,898	12,680	19,481	4.5	4.5	4.3	5.8
85 years old and over	4,259	4,899	5,671	7,046	1.6	1.7	1.9	2.1
Male	134,181	139,785	145,584	164,119	48.9	48.9	48.9	49.0
Female	140,453	146,196	152,132	170,931	51.1	51.1	51.1	51.0
White, total	**225,532**	**232,463**	**239,588**	**262,227**	**100.0**	**100.0**	**100.0**	**100.0**
Under 5 years old	14,724	14,618	15,142	16,630	6.5	6.3	6.3	6.3
5 to 13 years old	28,254	27,716	27,087	29,949	12.5	11.9	11.3	11.4
14 to 17 years old	12,412	13,177	12,951	13,166	5.5	5.7	5.4	5.0
18 to 24 years old	20,852	22,306	23,489	22,702	9.2	9.6	9.8	8.7
25 to 34 years old	29,837	28,705	30,099	32,831	13.2	12.3	12.6	12.5
35 to 44 years old	36,762	34,201	30,646	32,869	16.3	14.7	12.8	12.5
45 to 54 years old	31,247	34,574	35,911	29,010	13.9	14.9	15.0	11.1
55 to 64 years old	20,600	25,334	29,845	32,246	9.1	10.9	12.5	12.3
65 to 74 years old	15,846	15,844	18,101	29,733	7.0	6.8	7.6	11.3
75 to 84 years old	11,131	11,553	11,208	16,969	4.9	5.0	4.7	6.5
85 years old and over	3,866	4,434	5,108	6,122	1.7	1.9	2.1	2.3
Male	110,799	114,350	118,000	129,596	49.1	49.2	49.3	49.4
Female	114,734	118,113	121,588	132,631	50.9	50.8	50.7	50.6
Black, total	**35,454**	**37,734**	**40,109**	**47,539**	**100.0**	**100.0**	**100.0**	**100.0**
Under 5 years old	3,127	3,244	3,454	3,964	8.8	8.6	8.6	8.3
5 to 13 years old	5,727	5,813	5,962	6,990	16.2	15.4	14.9	14.7
14 to 17 years old	2,414	2,735	2,737	3,104	6.8	7.2	6.8	6.5
18 to 24 years old	3,966	4,233	4,674	5,053	11.2	11.2	11.7	10.6
25 to 34 years old	5,172	5,212	5,489	6,514	14.6	13.8	13.7	13.7
35 to 44 years old	5,649	5,499	5,236	6,017	15.9	14.6	13.1	12.7
45 to 54 years old	4,111	4,909	5,326	5,007	11.6	13.0	13.3	10.5
55 to 64 years old	2,406	2,995	3,801	4,865	6.8	7.9	9.5	10.2
65 to 74 years old	1,675	1,781	2,033	3,901	4.7	4.7	5.1	8.2
75 to 84 years old	890	959	1,002	1,582	2.5	2.5	2.5	3.3
85 years old and over	317	354	396	541	0.9	0.9	1.0	1.1
Male	16,811	17,874	18,981	22,473	47.4	47.4	47.3	47.3
Female	18,643	19,860	21,129	25,066	52.6	52.6	52.7	52.7
American Indian, Eskimo, Aleut, total	**2,402**	**2,572**	**2,754**	**3,319**	**100.0**	**100.0**	**100.0**	**100.0**
Under 5 years old	210	226	245	275	8.7	8.8	8.9	8.3
5 to 13 years old	418	409	429	516	17.4	15.9	15.6	15.5
14 to 17 years old	196	210	197	240	8.2	8.2	7.2	7.2
18 to 24 years old	283	323	342	368	11.8	12.5	12.4	11.1
25 to 34 years old	361	376	421	475	15.0	14.6	15.3	14.3
35 to 44 years old	354	351	349	459	14.8	13.7	12.7	13.8
45 to 54 years old	263	300	321	333	11.0	11.7	11.7	10.0
55 to 64 years old	152	186	225	276	6.3	7.2	8.2	8.3
65 to 74 years old	93	104	122	210	3.9	4.1	4.4	6.3
75 to 84 years old	51	59	65	109	2.1	2.3	2.4	3.3
85 years old and over	22	28	36	59	0.9	1.1	1.3	1.8
Male	1,185	1,266	1,354	1,629	49.3	49.2	49.2	49.1
Female	1,217	1,306	1,400	1,690	50.7	50.8	50.8	50.9
Asian, Pacific Islander, total	**11,245**	**13,212**	**15,265**	**21,965**	**100.0**	**100.0**	**100.0**	**100.0**
Under 5 years old	926	1,040	1,170	1,628	8.2	7.9	7.7	7.4
5 to 13 years old	1,644	1,912	2,126	2,958	14.6	14.5	13.9	13.5
14 to 17 years old	729	864	1,008	1,362	6.5	6.5	6.6	6.2
18 to 24 years old	1,158	1,405	1,633	2,250	10.3	10.6	10.7	10.2
25 to 34 years old	1,863	2,012	2,283	3,300	16.6	15.2	15.0	15.0
35 to 44 years old	1,894	2,114	2,290	3,046	16.8	16.0	15.0	13.9
45 to 54 years old	1,409	1,724	2,006	2,539	12.5	13.1	13.1	11.6
55 to 64 years old	804	1,091	1,412	2,155	7.1	8.3	9.3	9.8
65 to 74 years old	522	640	802	1,581	4.6	4.8	5.3	7.2
75 to 84 years old	242	327	406	821	2.2	2.5	2.7	3.7
85 years old and over	55	83	130	324	0.5	0.6	0.9	1.5
Male	5,386	6,295	7,250	10,421	47.9	47.6	47.5	47.4
Female	5,859	6,918	8,015	11,543	52.1	52.4	52.5	52.6

Source: U.S. Bureau of the Census, *Current Population Reports*, P25-1130.

Population

No. 25. Projections of Hispanic and Non-Hispanic Populations, by Age and Sex: 2000 to 2025

[As of **July 1**. Resident population. Data are for middle series; for assumptions, see table 3]

AGE AND SEX	POPULATION (1,000)				PERCENT DISTRIBUTION			
	2000	2005	2010	2025	2000	2005	2010	2025
Hispanic origin, total [1]	**31,366**	**36,057**	**41,139**	**58,930**	**100.0**	**100.0**	**100.0**	**100.0**
Under 5 years old	3,203	3,580	4,080	5,662	10.2	9.9	9.9	9.6
5 to 13 years old	5,651	6,215	6,654	9,479	18.0	17.2	16.2	16.1
14 to 17 years old	2,179	2,672	3,007	3,944	6.9	7.4	7.3	6.7
18 to 24 years old	3,679	4,270	5,101	6,560	11.7	11.8	12.4	11.1
25 to 34 years old	5,181	5,414	6,059	8,748	16.5	15.0	14.7	14.8
35 to 44 years old	4,836	5,421	5,562	7,345	15.4	15.0	13.5	12.5
45 to 54 years old	3,049	3,927	4,833	5,791	9.7	10.9	11.7	9.8
55 to 64 years old	1,717	2,260	2,997	5,272	5.5	6.3	7.3	8.9
65 to 74 years old	1,120	1,308	1,606	3,595	3.6	3.6	3.9	6.1
75 to 84 years old	568	748	896	1,771	1.8	2.1	2.2	3.0
85 years old and over	183	242	345	763	0.6	0.7	0.8	1.3
Male	15,799	18,082	20,557	29,276	50.4	50.1	50.0	49.7
Female	15,566	17,975	20,582	29,654	49.6	49.9	50.0	50.3
Non-Hispanic White, total	**197,061**	**199,802**	**202,390**	**209,117**	**100.0**	**100.0**	**100.0**	**100.0**
Under 5 years old	11,807	11,367	11,445	11,510	6.0	5.7	5.7	5.5
5 to 13 years old	23,125	22,072	21,063	21,396	11.7	11.0	10.4	10.2
14 to 17 years old	10,444	10,769	10,230	9,622	5.3	5.4	5.1	4.6
18 to 24 years old	17,510	18,443	18,880	16,785	8.9	9.2	9.3	8.0
25 to 34 years old	25,144	23,806	24,631	24,935	12.8	11.9	12.2	11.9
35 to 44 years old	32,382	29,299	25,628	26,278	16.4	14.7	12.7	12.6
45 to 54 years old	28,485	31,024	31,541	23,797	14.5	15.5	15.6	11.4
55 to 64 years old	19,039	23,285	27,137	27,490	9.7	11.7	13.4	13.1
65 to 74 years old	14,825	14,660	16,653	26,504	7.5	7.3	8.2	12.7
75 to 84 years old	10,607	10,868	10,394	15,373	5.4	5.4	5.1	7.4
85 years old and over	3,694	4,209	4,788	5,428	1.9	2.1	2.4	2.6
Male	96,438	97,946	99,381	103,169	48.9	49.0	49.1	49.3
Female	100,624	101,856	103,009	105,948	51.1	51.0	50.9	50.7
Non-Hispanic Black, total	**33,568**	**35,485**	**37,466**	**43,511**	**100.0**	**100.0**	**100.0**	**100.0**
Under 5 years old	2,929	3,016	3,187	3,571	8.7	8.5	8.5	8.2
5 to 13 years old	5,391	5,430	5,531	6,339	16.1	15.3	14.8	14.6
14 to 17 years old	2,285	2,568	2,547	2,831	6.8	7.2	6.8	6.5
18 to 24 years old	3,751	3,975	4,354	4,609	11.2	11.2	11.6	10.6
25 to 34 years old	4,863	4,883	5,111	5,942	14.5	13.8	13.6	13.7
35 to 44 years old	5,347	5,154	4,877	5,521	15.9	14.5	13.0	12.7
45 to 54 years old	3,922	4,654	5,008	4,613	11.7	13.1	13.4	10.6
55 to 64 years old	2,301	2,850	3,601	4,498	6.9	8.0	9.6	10.3
65 to 74 years old	1,608	1,695	1,921	3,634	4.8	4.8	5.1	8.4
75 to 84 years old	862	919	947	1,457	2.6	2.6	2.5	3.3
85 years old and over	310	344	381	496	0.9	1.0	1.0	1.1
Male	15,871	16,760	17,676	20,494	47.3	47.2	47.2	47.1
Female	17,697	18,725	19,790	23,017	52.7	52.8	52.8	52.9
Non-Hispanic American Indian, Eskimo, Aleut, total	**2,054**	**2,183**	**2,320**	**2,744**	**100.0**	**100.0**	**100.0**	**100.0**
Under 5 years old	180	192	206	229	8.8	8.8	8.9	8.4
5 to 13 years old	352	347	364	429	17.1	15.9	15.7	15.6
14 to 17 years old	165	175	166	198	8.0	8.0	7.1	7.2
18 to 24 years old	239	268	282	304	11.6	12.3	12.1	11.1
25 to 34 years old	303	316	349	390	14.7	14.5	15.0	14.2
35 to 44 years old	301	293	290	372	14.7	13.4	12.5	13.6
45 to 54 years old	231	259	272	275	11.2	11.8	11.7	10.0
55 to 64 years old	136	164	195	227	6.6	7.5	8.4	8.3
65 to 74 years old	82	91	106	176	4.0	4.2	4.6	6.4
75 to 84 years old	46	52	57	92	2.2	2.4	2.4	3.4
85 years old and over	21	27	34	52	1.0	1.2	1.4	1.9
Male	1,008	1,070	1,136	1,342	49.1	49.0	48.9	48.9
Female	1,046	1,113	1,184	1,401	50.9	51.0	51.1	51.1
Non-Hispanic Asian, Pacific Islander, total	**10,584**	**12,454**	**14,402**	**20,748**	**100.0**	**100.0**	**100.0**	**100.0**
Under 5 years old	867	973	1,093	1,526	8.2	7.8	7.6	7.4
5 to 13 years old	1,524	1,787	1,993	2,770	14.4	14.4	13.8	13.4
14 to 17 years old	680	803	944	1,277	6.4	6.4	6.6	6.2
18 to 24 years old	1,080	1,311	1,521	2,114	10.2	10.5	10.6	10.2
25 to 34 years old	1,744	1,887	2,141	3,104	16.5	15.2	14.9	15.0
35 to 44 years old	1,793	1,998	2,165	2,876	16.9	16.0	15.0	13.9
45 to 54 years old	1,344	1,644	1,910	2,415	12.7	13.2	13.3	11.6
55 to 64 years old	770	1,046	1,354	2,055	7.3	8.4	9.4	9.9
65 to 74 years old	500	615	771	1,516	4.7	4.9	5.4	7.3
75 to 84 years old	231	311	387	787	2.2	2.5	2.7	3.8
85 years old and over	51	78	123	308	0.5	0.6	0.9	1.5
Male	5,065	5,928	6,835	9,838	47.9	47.6	47.5	47.4
Female	5,520	6,526	7,567	10,910	52.1	52.4	52.5	52.6

[1] Persons of Hispanic origin may be of any race.

Source: U.S. Bureau of the Census, *Current Population Reports*, P25-1130.

No. 26. Centers of Population: 1790 to 1990

[Prior to 1960, excludes Alaska and Hawaii. The median center is located at the intersection of two median lines, a north-south line constructed so that half of the nation's population lives east and half lives west of it, and an east-west line selected so that half of the Nation's population lives north and half lives south of it. The mean center of population is that point at which an imaginary, flat, weightless, and rigid map of the United States would balance if weights of identical value were placed on it so that each weight represented the location of one person on the date of the census]

YEAR	MEDIAN CENTER		MEAN CENTER		
	Latitude-N	Longitude-W	Latitude-N	Longitude-W	Approximate location
1790 (August 2)	(NA)	(NA)	39 16 30	76 11 12	In Kent County, MD, 23 miles E of Baltimore, MD
1850 (June 1) ..	(NA)	(NA)	38 59 00	81 19 00	In Wirt County, WV, 23 miles SE of Parkersburg, WV[1]
1900 (June 1) ..	40 03 32	84 49 01	39 09 36	85 48 54	In Bartholomew County, IN, 6 miles SE of Columbus, IN
1950 (April 1)...	40 00 12	84 56 51	38 50 21	88 09 33	In Richland County, IL, 8 miles NNW of Olney, IL
1960 (April 1)...	39 56 25	85 16 60	38 35 58	89 12 35	In Clinton County, IL, 6.5 miles NW of Centralia, IL
1970 (April 1)...	39 47 43	85 31 43	38 27 47	89 42 22	In St. Clair Country, IL, 5.3 miles ESE of Mascoutah, IL
1980 (April 1)...	39 18 60	86 08 15	38 08 13	90 34 26	In Jefferson Country, MO, .25 mile W of DeSoto, MO
1990 (April 1)...	38 57 55	86 31 53	37 52 20	91 12 55	In Crawford Country, MO, 10 miles SE of Steelville, MO

NA Not available. [1] West Virginia was set off from Virginia, Dec. 31, 1862, and admitted as a State, June 19, 1863.

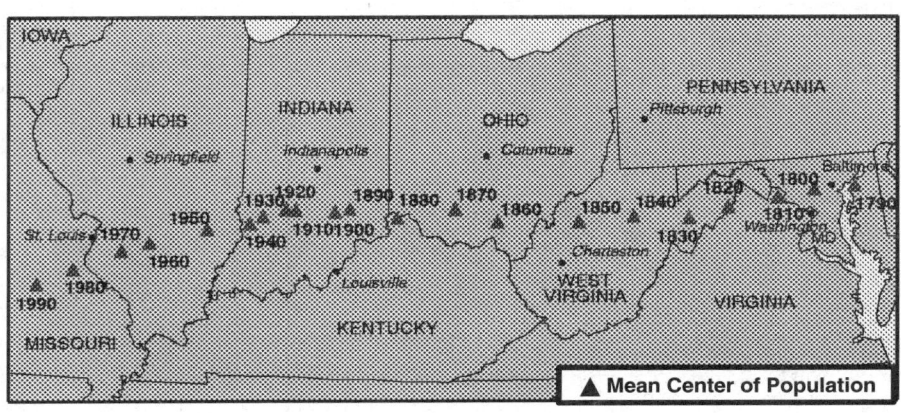

Source: U.S. Bureau of the Census, *1990 Census of Population and Housing, Population and Housing Unit Counts, United States* (1990 CPH-2-1).

No. 27. Resident Population—States: 1970 to 1995

[**In thousands**. As of July 1; except **1970, 1980, and 1990**, as of **April 1**. Insofar as possible, population shown for all years is that of present area of State. See *Historical Statistics, Colonial Times to 1970*, series A 172, for population by regions, and A 195 for population by States]

REGION, DIVISION, AND STATE	1970	1980 [1]	1985	1988	1989	1990 [2]	1991	1992	1993	1994	1995
U.S.	203,302	226,546	237,924	244,499	246,819	248,718	252,138	255,039	257,800	260,350	262,755
Northeast	49,061	49,135	49,869	50,584	50,757	50,811	50,959	51,097	51,275	51,382	51,466
N.E.	11,848	12,348	12,741	13,085	13,182	13,207	13,208	13,201	13,232	13,265	13,312
ME	994	1,125	1,163	1,204	1,220	1,228	1,236	1,236	1,239	1,239	1,241
NH	738	921	997	1,083	1,105	1,109	1,108	1,114	1,123	1,135	1,148
VT	445	511	530	550	558	563	569	572	576	580	585
MA	5,689	5,737	5,881	5,980	6,015	6,016	6,001	5,999	6,018	6,041	6,074
RI	950	947	969	996	1,001	1,003	1,004	1,001	999	994	990
CT	3,032	3,108	3,201	3,272	3,283	3,287	3,291	3,279	3,278	3,275	3,275
M.A	37,213	36,787	37,128	37,499	37,575	37,604	37,751	37,895	38,044	38,117	38,153
NY	18,241	17,558	17,792	17,941	17,983	17,991	18,039	18,094	18,153	18,153	18,136
NJ	7,171	7,365	7,566	7,712	7,726	7,730	7,766	7,811	7,859	7,903	7,945
PA	11,801	11,864	11,771	11,846	11,866	11,883	11,947	11,990	12,031	12,062	12,072
Midwest	56,589	58,866	58,820	59,254	59,468	59,669	60,173	60,622	61,040	61,408	61,804
E.N.C	40,262	41,682	41,418	41,721	41,873	42,009	42,377	42,685	42,960	43,193	43,456
OH	10,657	10,798	10,735	10,799	10,829	10,847	10,931	11,002	11,061	11,104	11,151
IN	5,195	5,490	5,459	5,492	5,524	5,544	5,604	5,653	5,707	5,755	5,803
IL	11,110	11,427	11,400	11,390	11,410	11,431	11,525	11,611	11,690	11,759	11,830
MI	8,882	9,262	9,076	9,218	9,253	9,295	9,369	9,422	9,457	9,492	9,549
WI	4,418	4,706	4,748	4,822	4,857	4,892	4,949	4,997	5,044	5,083	5,123
W.N.C	16,327	17,183	17,402	17,533	17,595	17,660	17,796	17,937	18,080	18,215	18,348
MN	3,806	4,076	4,184	4,296	4,338	4,376	4,429	4,474	4,524	4,568	4,610
IA	2,825	2,914	2,830	2,768	2,771	2,777	2,791	2,808	2,822	2,831	2,842
MO	4,678	4,917	5,000	5,082	5,096	5,117	5,157	5,192	5,235	5,279	5,324
ND	618	653	677	655	646	639	634	635	637	639	641
SD	666	691	698	698	697	696	702	709	717	723	729
NE	1,485	1,570	1,585	1,571	1,575	1,578	1,591	1,604	1,614	1,624	1,637
KS	2,249	2,364	2,427	2,462	2,473	2,478	2,491	2,515	2,532	2,551	2,565
South	62,812	75,372	81,409	83,890	84,700	85,454	86,928	88,166	89,426	90,712	91,890
S.A.	30,678	36,959	40,159	42,318	43,008	43,571	44,443	45,088	45,725	46,378	46,995
DE	548	594	618	648	658	666	680	690	699	708	717
MD	3,924	4,217	4,413	4,658	4,727	4,781	4,859	4,909	4,952	5,000	5,042
DC	757	638	635	630	624	607	594	586	578	567	554
VA	4,651	5,347	5,715	6,037	6,120	6,189	6,287	6,389	6,475	6,551	6,618
WV	1,744	1,950	1,907	1,830	1,807	1,793	1,799	1,807	1,818	1,824	1,828
NC	5,084	5,882	6,254	6,481	6,565	6,632	6,751	6,837	6,953	7,070	7,195
SC	2,591	3,122	3,303	3,412	3,457	3,486	3,555	3,594	3,627	3,643	3,673
GA	4,588	5,463	5,963	6,316	6,411	6,478	6,624	6,764	6,901	7,058	7,201
FL	6,791	9,746	11,351	12,306	12,638	12,938	13,294	13,512	13,722	13,958	14,166
E.S.C	12,808	14,666	14,971	15,107	15,136	15,180	15,343	15,515	15,706	15,895	16,066
KY	3,221	3,661	3,695	3,680	3,677	3,687	3,715	3,752	3,793	3,828	3,860
TN	3,926	4,591	4,715	4,822	4,854	4,877	4,950	5,020	5,093	5,176	5,256
AL	3,444	3,894	3,973	4,024	4,030	4,040	4,087	4,131	4,181	4,220	4,253
MS	2,217	2,521	2,588	2,580	2,574	2,575	2,592	2,612	2,639	2,670	2,697
W.S.C	19,326	23,747	26,279	26,466	26,556	26,703	27,141	27,562	27,995	28,440	28,828
AR	1,923	2,286	2,327	2,343	2,346	2,351	2,371	2,395	2,425	2,453	2,484
LA	3,645	4,206	4,408	4,289	4,253	4,220	4,241	4,273	4,289	4,316	4,342
OK	2,559	3,025	3,271	3,167	3,150	3,146	3,168	3,207	3,232	3,257	3,278
TX	11,199	14,229	16,273	16,667	16,807	16,986	17,362	17,687	18,049	18,413	18,724
West	34,838	43,172	47,827	50,770	51,894	52,784	54,078	55,155	56,059	56,848	57,596
Mountain	8,289	11,373	12,741	13,303	13,498	13,659	14,022	14,380	14,785	15,233	15,645
MT	694	787	822	800	800	799	808	823	841	856	870
ID	713	944	994	986	994	1,007	1,039	1,066	1,101	1,134	1,163
WY	332	470	500	465	458	454	458	464	470	476	480
CO	2,210	2,890	3,209	3,262	3,276	3,294	3,371	3,465	3,568	3,662	3,747
NM	1,017	1,303	1,438	1,490	1,504	1,515	1,547	1,581	1,616	1,655	1,685
AZ	1,775	2,718	3,184	3,535	3,622	3,665	3,747	3,835	3,944	4,079	4,218
UT	1,059	1,461	1,643	1,689	1,706	1,723	1,767	1,811	1,860	1,909	1,951
NV	489	800	951	1,075	1,137	1,202	1,285	1,333	1,385	1,462	1,530
Pacific	26,549	31,800	35,086	37,467	38,397	39,125	40,056	40,775	41,274	41,615	41,951
WA	3,413	4,132	4,400	4,640	4,746	4,867	5,018	5,146	5,255	5,338	5,431
OR	2,092	2,633	2,673	2,741	2,791	2,842	2,919	2,974	3,035	3,087	3,141
CA	19,971	23,668	26,441	28,464	29,218	29,758	30,416	30,914	31,220	31,408	31,589
AK	303	402	532	542	547	550	569	587	598	603	604
HI	770	965	1,040	1,080	1,095	1,108	1,134	1,153	1,166	1,178	1,187

[1] See footnote 4, table 1. [2] The April 1, 1990, census counts include count resolution corrections processed through March 1994 and do not include adjustments for census coverage errors.

Source: U.S. Bureau of the Census, *1990 Census of Population and Housing, Population and Housing Unit Counts* (CPH-2); *Current Population Reports*, P25-1106; press release CB96-10; and unpublished data.

No. 28. State Population—Rank, Percent Change, and Population Density: 1970 to 1995

[As of **April 1**, except **1995**, as of **July 1**. For area figures of States, see table 362. Minus sign (-) indicates decrease. See *Historical Statistics, Colonial Times to 1970*, series A 197]

REGION, DIVISION, AND STATE	RANK				PERCENT CHANGE			POPULATION PER SQ. MILE OF LAND AREA [1]	
	1970	1980	1990	1995	1970-80	1980-90	1990-95	1970	1995
U.S.	(X)	(X)	(X)	(X)	11.4	9.8	5.6	57.5	74.3
Northeast	(X)	(X)	(X)	(X)	0.2	3.4	1.3	302.3	317.2
N.E.	(X)	(X)	(X)	(X)	4.2	6.9	0.8	188.6	211.9
ME	38	38	38	39	13.2	9.1	1.1	32.2	40.2
NH	41	42	40	42	24.8	20.5	3.5	82.2	128.0
VT.	48	48	48	49	15.0	10.0	3.9	48.1	63.2
MA	10	11	13	13	0.8	4.9	0.9	725.8	774.9
RI	39	40	43	43	-0.3	5.9	-1.4	908.8	947.2
CT	24	25	27	28	2.5	5.8	-0.4	625.8	675.9
M.A	(X)	(X)	(X)	(X)	-1.1	2.2	1.5	374.1	383.6
NY	2	2	2	3	-3.7	2.5	0.8	386.3	384.0
NJ.	8	9	9	9	2.7	5.0	2.8	966.6	1,070.9
PA.	3	4	5	5	0.5	0.2	1.6	263.3	269.3
Midwest	(X)	(X)	(X)	(X)	4.0	1.4	3.6	75.3	82.2
E.N.C	(X)	(X)	(X)	(X)	3.5	0.8	3.4	165.3	178.4
OH	6	6	7	7	1.3	0.5	2.8	260.2	272.3
IN	11	12	14	14	5.7	1.0	4.7	144.8	161.8
IL	5	5	6	6	2.8	(Z)	3.5	199.9	212.8
MI	7	8	8	8	4.3	0.4	2.7	156.3	168.1
WI.	16	16	16	18	6.5	4.0	4.7	81.3	94.3
W.N.C	(X)	(X)	(X)	(X)	5.2	2.8	3.9	32.1	36.1
MN	19	21	20	20	7.1	7.4	5.3	47.8	57.9
IA	25	27	30	30	3.1	-4.7	2.3	50.6	50.9
MO	13	15	15	16	5.1	4.1	4.0	67.9	77.3
ND	45	46	47	47	5.7	-2.1	0.4	9.0	9.3
SD	44	45	45	45	3.7	0.8	4.7	8.8	9.6
NE	35	35	36	37	5.7	0.5	3.7	19.3	21.3
KS	28	32	32	32	5.1	4.8	3.5	27.5	31.4
South.	(X)	(X)	(X)	(X)	20.0	13.4	7.5	72.1	105.5
S.A.	(X)	(X)	(X)	(X)	20.5	17.9	7.9	115.2	176.5
DE	46	47	46	46	8.4	12.1	7.7	280.4	366.9
MD	18	18	19	19	7.5	13.4	5.5	401.4	515.9
DC	(X)	(X)	(X)	(X)	-15.6	-4.9	-8.7	12,404.4	9,086.2
VA.	14	14	12	12	14.9	15.8	6.9	117.5	167.1
WV	34	34	34	35	11.8	-8.0	1.9	72.4	75.9
NC	12	10	10	11	15.7	12.8	8.5	104.4	147.7
SC	26	24	25	26	20.5	11.7	5.4	86.0	122.0
GA	15	13	11	10	19.1	18.6	11.2	79.2	124.3
FL.	9	7	4	4	43.5	32.7	9.5	125.8	262.3
E.S.C	(X)	(X)	(X)	(X)	14.5	3.5	5.8	71.7	89.9
KY	23	23	23	24	13.7	0.7	4.7	81.1	97.2
TN	17	17	17	17	16.9	6.2	7.8	95.2	127.5
AL.	21	22	22	22	13.1	3.8	5.3	67.9	83.8
MS	29	31	31	31	13.7	2.2	4.7	47.3	57.5
W.S.C	(X)	(X)	(X)	(X)	22.9	12.5	8.0	45.3	67.6
AR	32	33	33	33	18.9	2.8	5.7	36.9	47.7
LA.	20	19	21	21	15.4	0.3	2.9	83.7	99.7
OK	27	26	28	27	18.2	4.0	4.2	37.3	47.7
TX.	4	3	3	2	27.1	19.4	10.2	42.8	71.5
West	(X)	(X)	(X)	(X)	23.9	22.3	9.1	19.9	32.9
Mountain.	(X)	(X)	(X)	(X)	37.2	20.1	14.5	9.7	18.3
MT	43	44	44	44	13.3	1.6	8.9	4.8	6.0
ID	42	41	42	41	32.4	6.6	15.5	8.6	14.1
WY	49	49	50	50	41.3	-3.4	5.9	3.4	4.9
CO	30	28	26	25	30.8	14.0	13.7	21.3	36.1
NM	37	37	37	36	28.1	16.2	11.2	8.4	13.9
AZ.	33	29	24	23	53.1	34.9	15.1	15.6	37.1
UT	36	36	35	34	37.9	17.9	13.3	12.9	23.7
NV	47	43	39	38	63.8	50.1	27.3	4.5	13.9
Pacific	(X)	(X)	(X)	(X)	19.8	23.0	7.2	29.7	46.9
WA	22	20	18	15	21.1	17.8	11.6	51.3	81.6
OR	31	30	29	29	25.9	7.9	10.5	21.8	32.7
CA	1	1	1	1	18.5	25.7	6.2	128.0	202.5
AK	50	50	49	48	32.8	36.9	9.7	0.5	1.1
HI	40	39	41	40	25.3	14.9	7.1	119.9	184.8

X Not applicable.   Z Less than 0.5 percent.   [1] Persons per square mile were calculated on the basis of land area data from the 1990 census.

Source: U.S. Bureau of the Census, *1990 Census of Population and Housing, Population and Housing Unit Counts* (CPH-2); and press release CB96-10.

No. 29. Components of Population Change—States: 1990 to 1995

[In thousands, except percent. Covers period **April 1, 1990, to July 1, 1995**]

REGION, DIVISION, AND STATE	NET CHANGE, 1990-95		Births	Deaths	NET MOVEMENT FROM ABROAD		Net domestic migration	Residual change [1]
	Number	Percent			International migration	Federal U.S. citizen		
United States . . .	14,037	5.6	21,260	11,652	3,966	462	-	-
Northeast.	**655**	**1.3**	**3,971**	**2,523**	**969**	**26**	**-1,768**	**-22**
New England	**105**	**0.8**	**987**	**617**	**137**	**10**	**-406**	**-6**
Maine	13	1.1	83	60	3	2	-15	1
New Hampshire. . . .	39	3.5	83	46	5	-	-5	-1
Vermont.	22	3.9	41	25	3	-	3	1
Massachusetts	57	0.9	456	286	83	3	-194	-5
Rhode Island	-14	-1.4	75	50	7	2	-46	-1
Connecticut	-12	-0.4	250	151	37	3	-149	-3
Middle Atlantic	**549**	**1.5**	**2,984**	**1,906**	**832**	**17**	**-1,362**	**-16**
New York	145	0.8	1,503	874	575	10	-1,053	-16
New Jersey	215	2.8	625	375	194	4	-235	-1
Pennsylvania	189	1.6	856	656	63	3	-75	-1
Midwest.	**2,135**	**3.6**	**4,799**	**2,885**	**433**	**36**	**-261**	**13**
East North Central. . .	**1,447**	**3.4**	**3,427**	**2,013**	**359**	**16**	**-353**	**12**
Ohio	303	2.8	848	533	35	3	-52	2
Indiana	259	4.7	443	269	14	1	66	4
Illinois	399	3.5	1,010	553	231	9	-298	2
Michigan	254	2.7	756	426	60	2	-139	2
Wisconsin	231	4.7	370	230	18	-	71	2
West North Central . .	**687**	**3.9**	**1,372**	**873**	**74**	**20**	**93**	**2**
Minnesota	234	5.3	346	189	24	1	53	-1
Iowa	65	2.3	201	145	8	-	1	-
Missouri.	207	4.0	401	275	19	5	57	1
North Dakota	3	0.4	46	30	2	3	-18	-
South Dakota	33	4.7	57	35	2	2	8	-
Nebraska.	59	3.7	124	78	6	3	3	1
Kansas	88	3.5	198	120	12	7	-10	1
South	**6,435**	**7.5**	**7,281**	**4,150**	**916**	**249**	**2,097**	**43**
South Atlantic.	**3,424**	**7.9**	**3,575**	**2,167**	**486**	**168**	**1,343**	**19**
Delaware	51	7.7	57	32	4	1	20	1
Maryland	262	5.5	405	209	65	13	-14	2
District of Columbia .	-53	-8.7	57	38	16	2	-89	-1
Virginia	429	6.9	507	267	71	53	61	4
West Virginia	35	1.9	116	105	2	-	20	1
North Carolina.	563	8.5	540	320	23	32	283	4
South Carolina	187	5.4	291	164	7	15	35	3
Georgia	723	11.2	585	286	42	21	357	5
Florida.	1,227	9.5	1,017	746	256	29	672	-
East South Central . .	**887**	**5.8**	**1,220**	**793**	**32**	**25**	**394**	**9**
Kentucky	173	4.7	281	189	8	8	63	3
Tennessee	379	7.8	388	253	14	6	223	1
Alabama	213	5.3	327	214	7	6	84	2
Mississippi	122	4.7	224	137	3	5	24	2
West South Central . .	**2,125**	**8.0**	**2,486**	**1,190**	**399**	**56**	**360**	**15**
Arkansas	133	5.7	183	135	4	2	79	1
Louisiana	122	2.9	370	202	12	8	-68	2
Oklahoma	132	4.2	247	164	11	9	27	2
Texas	1,738	10.2	1,686	688	372	37	321	10
West	**4,812**	**9.1**	**5,210**	**2,095**	**1,648**	**151**	**-68**	**-34**
Mountain	**1,986**	**14.5**	**1,295**	**554**	**138**	**32**	**1,060**	**14**
Montana	71	8.9	60	38	2	1	46	1
Idaho	157	15.5	91	42	7	1	99	1
Wyoming	27	5.9	35	18	1	1	6	1
Colorado	452	13.7	284	121	29	12	245	2
New Mexico	170	11.2	146	60	18	5	60	1
Arizona	553	15.1	365	167	50	7	293	4
Utah	229	13.3	196	52	11	2	71	2
Nevada	328	27.3	118	55	19	3	240	3
Pacific	**2,826**	**7.2**	**3,915**	**1,540**	**1,510**	**119**	**-1,129**	**-48**
Washington	564	11.6	413	204	64	17	277	-2
Oregon	298	10.5	222	139	28	1	187	-1
California	1,831	6.2	3,116	1,148	1,380	77	-1,548	-46
Alaska.	54	9.7	60	12	5	7	-7	1
Hawaii.	79	7.1	104	38	33	17	-38	-

- Represents or rounds to zero.　[1] The residual is the effect of national controls on subnational estimates. It is the difference between the implementation of the national estimates model and the county/State estimates model.

Source: U.S. Bureau of the Census, unpublished data.

No. 30. U.S. Resident Population, by Region and Division: 1960 to 1995

[As of **April 1**; except **1985** and **1995**, as of **July 1**. For composition of divisions, see table 27]

REGION AND DIVISION	POPULATION (millions)						PERCENT DISTRIBUTION					
	1960	1970	1980	1985	1990	1995	1960	1970	1980	1985	1990	1995
United States.	179.3	203.3	226.5	237.9	248.7	262.8	100.0	100.0	100.0	100.0	100.0	100.0
Northeast	44.7	49.1	49.1	49.9	50.8	51.5	24.9	24.1	21.7	21.0	20.4	19.6
New England	10.5	11.8	12.3	12.7	13.2	13.3	5.9	5.8	5.5	5.4	5.3	5.1
Middle Atlantic	34.2	37.2	36.8	37.1	37.6	38.2	19.1	18.3	16.2	15.6	15.1	14.5
Midwest	51.6	56.6	58.9	58.8	59.7	61.8	28.8	27.8	26.0	24.7	24.0	23.5
East North Central . . .	36.2	40.3	41.7	41.4	42.0	43.5	20.2	19.8	18.4	17.4	16.9	16.5
West North Central . . .	15.4	16.3	17.2	17.4	17.7	18.3	8.6	8.0	7.6	7.3	7.1	7.0
South	55.0	62.8	75.4	81.4	85.5	91.9	30.7	30.9	33.3	34.2	34.4	35.0
South Atlantic.	26.0	30.7	37.0	40.2	43.6	47.0	14.5	15.1	16.3	16.9	17.5	17.9
East South Central . . .	12.1	12.8	14.7	15.0	15.2	16.1	6.7	6.3	6.5	6.3	6.1	6.1
West South Central . . .	17.0	19.3	23.7	26.3	26.7	28.8	9.5	9.5	10.5	11.0	10.7	11.0
West	28.1	34.8	43.2	47.8	52.8	57.6	15.6	17.1	19.1	20.1	21.2	21.9
Mountain	6.9	8.3	11.4	12.7	13.7	15.6	3.8	4.1	5.0	5.4	5.5	6.0
Pacific	21.2	26.5	31.8	35.1	39.1	42.0	11.8	13.1	14.0	14.7	15.7	16.0

Source: U.S. Bureau of the Census, *1990 Census of Population and Housing, Population and Housing Unit Counts* (CPH-2); and press release CB96-10.

No. 31. Resident Population, by Region, Race, and Hispanic Origin: 1990

[As of **April 1**. For composition of regions, see table 27]

RACE AND HISPANIC ORIGIN	POPULATION (1,000)					PERCENT DISTRIBUTION				
	United States	North-east	Midwest	South	West	United States	North-east	Midwest	South	West
Total.	248,710	50,809	59,669	85,446	52,786	100.0	20.4	24.0	34.4	21.2
White.	199,686	42,069	52,018	65,582	40,017	100.0	21.1	26.0	32.8	20.0
Black.	29,986	5,613	5,716	15,829	2,828	100.0	18.7	19.1	52.8	9.4
American Indian, Eskimo, Aleut	1,959	125	338	563	933	100.0	6.4	17.2	28.7	47.6
American Indian.	1,878	122	334	557	866	100.0	6.5	17.8	29.7	46.1
Eskimo.	57	2	2	3	51	100.0	2.9	3.5	4.9	88.8
Aleut	24	2	2	3	17	100.0	8.1	8.1	11.5	72.3
Asian or Pacific Islander . .	7,274	1,335	768	1,122	4,048	100.0	18.4	10.6	15.4	55.7
Chinese	1,645	445	133	204	863	100.0	27.0	8.1	12.4	52.4
Filipino	1,407	143	113	159	991	100.0	10.2	8.1	11.3	70.5
Japanese	848	74	63	67	643	100.0	8.8	7.5	7.9	75.9
Asian Indian	815	285	146	196	189	100.0	35.0	17.9	24.0	23.1
Korean	799	182	109	153	355	100.0	22.8	13.7	19.2	44.4
Vietnamese	615	61	52	169	334	100.0	9.8	8.5	27.4	54.3
Laotian.	149	16	28	29	76	100.0	10.7	18.6	19.6	51.0
Cambodian	147	30	13	19	85	100.0	20.5	8.8	13.1	57.7
Thai	91	12	13	24	43	100.0	12.9	14.2	26.0	46.8
Hmong	90	2	37	2	50	100.0	1.9	41.3	1.8	55.0
Pakistani.	81	28	15	22	17	100.0	34.3	18.9	26.5	20.4
Hawaiian.	211	4	6	12	189	100.0	2.0	2.6	5.8	89.6
Samoan	63	2	2	4	55	100.0	2.4	3.6	6.4	87.6
Guamanian	49	4	3	8	34	100.0	7.3	6.4	16.8	69.5
Other Asian or Pacific Islander	263	49	34	54	126	100.0	18.6	12.9	20.5	48.0
Other races	9,805	1,667	829	2,350	4,960	100.0	17.0	8.5	24.0	50.6
Hispanic origin [1]	22,354	3,754	1,727	6,767	10,106	100.0	16.8	7.7	30.3	45.2
Mexican	13,496	175	1,153	4,344	7,824	100.0	1.3	8.5	32.2	58.0
Puerto Rican	2,728	1,872	258	406	192	100.0	68.6	9.4	14.9	7.0
Cuban	1,044	184	37	735	88	100.0	17.6	3.5	70.5	8.5
Other Hispanic.	5,086	1,524	279	1,282	2,002	100.0	30.0	5.5	25.2	39.4
Not of Hispanic origin	226,356	47,055	57,942	78,679	42,680	100.0	20.8	25.6	34.8	18.9

[1] Persons of Hispanic origin may be of any race.

Source: U.S. Bureau of the Census, *1990 Census of Population, General Population Characteristics, United States* (CP-1-1).

No. 32. Annual Inmigration, Outmigration, and Net Migration for Regions: 1980 to 1994

[In thousands. As of **March**. For persons 1 year old and over. Excludes members of the Armed Forces except those living off post or with their families on post. Based on Current Population Survey; see text, section 1, and Appendix III. For composition of regions, see table 27. Minus sign (-) indicates net outmigration]

PERIOD	North-east	Mid-west	South	West	PERIOD	North-east	Mid-west	South	West
1980-81: Inmigrants	464	650	1,377	871	**1990-91:** Inmigrants	346	782	1,421	835
Outmigrants	706	1,056	890	710	Outmigrants	932	797	987	668
Net internal migration	-242	-406	487	161	Net internal migration	-585	-15	433	167
Movers from abroad	207	180	412	514	Movers from abroad	209	208	351	617
Net migration	-35	-226	899	675	Net migration	-376	193	784	784
1985-86: Inmigrants	502	1,011	1,355	910	**1991-92:** Inmigrants	409	816	1,305	755
Outmigrants	752	996	1,320	710	Outmigrants	701	878	1,081	626
Net internal migration	-250	15	35	200	Net internal migration	-292	-62	224	129
Movers from abroad	198	158	342	502	Movers from abroad	255	175	383	442
Net migration	-52	173	377	702	Net migration	-37	113	607	571
1986-87: Inmigrants	398	858	1,374	916	**1992-93:** Inmigrants	313	841	1,145	769
Outmigrants	732	969	1,095	750	Outmigrants	647	608	1,044	770
Net internal migration	-334	-111	279	166	Net internal migration	-334	233	101	-1
Movers from abroad	214	193	277	458	Movers from abroad	230	198	513	364
Net migration	-120	82	556	624	Net migration	-104	431	614	363
1987-88: Inmigrants	430	715	1,338	613	**1993-94:**				
Outmigrants	671	818	886	721	Total inmigrants	348	706	1,336	746
Net internal migration	-241	-103	452	-108	From Northeast	(X)	84	449	143
Movers from abroad	261	146	414	379	From Midwest	53	(X)	468	215
Net migration	20	43	866	271	From South	201	371	(X)	388
1988-89: Inmigrants	370	777	1,318	791	From West	93	251	419	(X)
Outmigrants	714	703	1,071	637	Total outmigrants	676	737	960	763
Net internal migration	-344	74	247	154	To Northeast	(X)	53	201	93
Movers from abroad	292	170	375	629	To Midwest	84	(X)	371	251
Net migration	-52	244	622	783	To South	449	468	(X)	419
1989-90: Inmigrants	461	908	1,428	964	To West	143	215	388	(X)
Outmigrants	758	1,024	1,198	781	Net internal migration	-328	-31	376	-17
Net internal migration	-297	-116	230	183	Movers from abroad	267	132	451	396
Movers from abroad	328	169	500	562	Net migration	-61	101	827	379
Net migration	30	53	730	745					

X Not applicable.

Source: U.S. Bureau of the Census, *Current Population Reports*, P20-485, and earlier reports.

No. 33. Mobility Status of the Population, by Selected Characteristics: 1980 to 1994

[As of **March**. For persons 1 year old and over. Excludes members of the Armed Forces except those living off post or with their families on post. Based on Current Population Survey; see text, section 1, and Appendix III. For composition of regions, see table 27]

MOBILITY PERIOD, AGE, AND REGION	Total (1,000)	PERCENT DISTRIBUTION						Movers from abroad
		Non-movers	Movers (different house in United States)					
			Total	Same county	Different county			
					Total	Same State	Different State	
1980-81	221,641	83	17	10	6	3	3	1
1985-86	232,998	82	18	11	7	4	3	1
1990-91	244,884	83	16	10	6	3	3	1
1991-92	247,380	83	17	11	6	3	3	1
1992-93	250,210	83	16	11	6	3	3	1
1993-94, total	**255,774**	83	17	10	6	3	3	1
1 to 4 years old	16,477	78	22	15	7	4	3	1
5 to 9 years old	19,365	83	17	11	6	3	3	(Z)
10 to 14 years old	19,152	87	13	9	4	2	2	(Z)
15 to 19 years old	17,722	82	17	11	6	3	3	1
20 to 24 years old	18,559	64	34	22	12	7	5	1
25 to 29 years old	19,622	69	30	19	11	6	5	1
30 to 44 years old	63,843	82	17	11	6	4	3	1
45 to 64 years old	50,257	91	9	5	3	2	2	(Z)
65 to 74 years old	18,085	94	6	3	3	1	1	(Z)
75 to 84 years old	9,858	95	5	3	2	1	1	(Z)
85 years old and over	2,835	94	6	3	3	1	1	(Z)
Northeast	50,816	88	11	7	4	2	2	1
Midwest	60,295	84	16	10	6	3	2	(Z)
South	88,493	82	18	11	7	4	4	1
West	56,170	80	20	13	6	3	3	1

Z Less than 0.5 percent.

Source: U.S. Bureau of the Census, *Current Population Reports*, P20-485.

No. 34. Resident Population, by Age and State: 1995

[In thousands, except percent. As of July 1. Includes Armed Forces stationed in area. See text, section 1, for basis of estimates. See *Historical Statistics, Colonial Times to 1970*, series A 204-209 for decennial census data]

REGION, DIVISION, AND STATE	Total	Under 5 years	5 to 17 years	18 to 24 years	25 to 34 years	35 to 44 years	45 to 54 years	55 to 64 years	65 to 74 years	75 to 84 years	85 years and over	Percent 65 years and over
U.S.	262,755	19,591	49,149	24,932	40,873	42,468	31,079	21,131	18,759	11,145	3,628	12.8
Northeast . . .	51,466	3,617	9,006	4,536	8,077	8,373	6,260	4,302	4,029	2,450	813	14.2
N.E.	13,312	896	2,318	1,159	2,188	2,221	1,623	1,045	1,004	637	222	14.0
ME	1,241	75	230	113	180	212	156	103	95	57	21	13.9
NH	1,148	76	219	96	189	208	140	83	76	45	15	11.9
VT.	585	37	110	54	88	104	76	46	39	23	9	12.0
MA	6,074	413	1,019	536	1,053	992	728	471	461	296	104	14.2
RI	990	68	170	90	160	158	113	75	84	54	18	15.7
CT	3,275	228	570	269	517	546	410	267	250	163	54	14.3
M.A	38,153	2,721	6,688	3,378	5,889	6,152	4,638	3,257	3,026	1,813	592	14.2
NY	18,136	1,360	3,177	1,636	2,918	2,891	2,196	1,534	1,349	798	277	13.4
NJ.	7,945	577	1,386	672	1,231	1,325	993	670	613	364	114	13.7
PA.	12,072	784	2,125	1,070	1,740	1,936	1,448	1,053	1,064	651	201	15.9
Midwest	61,804	4,393	11,817	5,884	9,269	10,000	7,285	5,062	4,418	2,732	944	13.1
E.N.C	43,456	3,128	8,217	4,157	6,596	7,056	5,170	3,560	3,099	1,863	610	12.8
OH	11,151	773	2,087	1,063	1,657	1,801	1,336	944	842	492	157	13.4
IN	5,803	408	1,079	582	877	938	700	486	411	242	81	12.6
IL	11,830	921	2,205	1,115	1,855	1,911	1,387	952	813	504	167	12.5
MI	9,549	683	1,837	918	1,447	1,570	1,150	763	670	390	122	12.4
WI.	5,123	344	1,009	480	760	836	598	414	363	236	84	13.3
W.N.C	18,348	1,265	3,600	1,727	2,672	2,945	2,115	1,502	1,319	869	333	13.7
MN	4,610	321	925	415	709	777	536	353	297	199	76	12.4
IA	2,842	184	541	272	391	443	331	248	221	152	59	15.2
MO	5,324	369	1,012	497	786	841	625	452	399	249	92	13.9
ND	641	42	129	66	89	101	69	53	46	34	13	14.5
SD	729	52	154	72	97	112	78	59	54	37	14	14.4
NE	1,637	114	329	159	228	259	185	134	118	78	32	13.9
KS	2,565	183	510	246	372	411	289	203	183	120	47	13.7
South.	91,890	6,782	17,148	9,008	14,192	14,621	10,890	7,565	6,642	3,832	1,209	12.7
S.A.	46,995	3,325	8,313	4,382	7,425	7,550	5,648	3,907	3,671	2,128	645	13.7
DE	717	52	127	66	121	118	84	58	54	28	9	12.6
MD	5,042	368	904	432	860	880	636	391	332	183	57	11.3
DC	554	40	75	52	111	89	65	45	43	25	9	13.9
VA.	6,618	464	1,149	658	1,131	1,121	835	524	428	237	72	11.1
WV	1,828	106	315	190	235	287	236	178	158	92	29	15.3
NC	7,195	514	1,285	715	1,153	1,148	872	609	523	289	87	12.5
SC	3,673	263	682	383	571	582	446	305	261	139	40	12.0
GA	7,201	551	1,372	728	1,217	1,200	874	541	412	234	72	10.0
FL.	14,166	968	2,403	1,158	2,026	2,125	1,600	1,255	1,459	901	271	18.6
E.S.C	16,066	1,136	2,989	1,660	2,394	2,520	1,943	1,396	1,144	666	218	12.6
KY	3,860	261	712	400	574	616	474	338	275	160	52	12.6
TN	5,256	365	945	516	805	845	660	462	373	215	70	12.5
AL.	4,253	301	779	442	632	661	511	375	312	182	58	13.0
MS	2,697	209	553	302	383	398	298	222	184	110	37	12.3
W.S.C	28,828	2,321	5,846	2,966	4,373	4,551	3,299	2,262	1,827	1,037	346	11.1
AR	2,484	173	477	249	344	364	296	223	196	123	41	14.5
LA.	4,342	336	903	458	631	672	496	351	285	159	50	11.4
OK	3,278	230	648	329	453	498	388	289	242	148	53	13.5
TX.	18,724	1,582	3,819	1,930	2,945	3,016	2,119	1,398	1,104	608	203	10.2
West	57,596	4,799	11,177	5,504	9,336	9,473	6,644	4,202	3,670	2,131	662	11.2
Mountain. .	15,645	1,245	3,223	1,547	2,294	2,517	1,830	1,222	1,018	576	172	11.3
MT	870	57	179	83	104	145	111	77	61	40	13	13.1
ID	1,163	89	258	125	149	181	135	93	72	46	14	11.4
WY	480	32	104	50	58	82	60	40	31	17	6	11.1
CO	3,747	269	712	350	572	681	488	298	216	119	40	10.0
NM	1,685	138	362	167	235	270	195	135	107	58	18	10.9
AZ.	4,218	356	837	397	638	638	465	326	323	186	51	13.3
UT	1,951	184	491	247	285	268	184	121	96	58	18	8.8
NV	1,530	119	279	128	253	251	192	133	112	52	12	11.4
Pacific . . .	41,951	3,554	7,954	3,957	7,041	6,956	4,814	2,980	2,652	1,555	489	11.2
WA	5,431	386	1,033	498	843	951	684	410	345	215	68	11.6
OR	3,141	210	587	281	439	533	409	255	230	149	47	13.6
CA	31,589	2,810	5,984	3,000	5,491	5,157	3,501	2,184	1,967	1,137	359	11.0
AK	604	53	136	62	91	116	77	38	20	8	2	4.9
HI	1,187	96	213	115	178	198	143	93	90	47	13	12.6

Source: U.S. Bureau of the Census, press release CB96-88.

No. 35. Resident Population by Race, Hispanic Origin, and State: 1992

[In thousands. As of July 1. These estimates are consistent with press release CB95-166, issued September 20, 1995, and with State-level data released in PPL-3 and PE-12 and national-level data released in PPL-8. Consequently the estimates shown in this table are not consistent with subsequently released State estimates. These estimates are developed using a cohort-component method whereby each component of population change - births, deaths, domestic migration, and international migration is estimated separately for each birth cohort by sex and race]

REGION, DIVISION, AND STATE	Total	RACE					NOT OF HISPANIC ORIGIN			
		White	Black	American Indian; Eskimo, Aleut	Asian, Pacific Islander	Hispanic origin [1]	White	Black	American Indian, Eskimo, Aleut	Asian, Pacific Islander
U.S.	255,078	212,919	31,650	2,145	8,364	24,268	190,789	30,306	1,858	7,856
Northeast.	51,121	43,410	6,048	136	1,528	4,038	40,196	5,323	107	1,458
N.E	13,196	12,204	694	35	263	615	11,694	604	30	253
ME	1,236	1,217	5	6	8	7	1,211	5	6	7
NH	1,115	1,096	7	2	10	12	1,086	6	2	10
VT	571	564	2	2	4	4	560	2	2	4
MA	5,993	5,469	347	13	163	314	5,221	289	11	158
RI	1,001	932	45	4	20	51	892	36	4	19
CT	3,279	2,926	288	7	58	228	2,724	266	6	55
M.A	37,925	31,205	5,354	101	1,265	3,423	28,503	4,718	77	1,204
NY	18,109	14,134	3,118	68	790	2,362	12,343	2,605	51	749
NJ	7,820	6,385	1,101	17	317	807	5,685	1,012	13	303
PA	11,995	10,687	1,134	16	159	254	10,474	1,101	14	152
Midwest.	60,639	53,454	5,955	358	873	1,868	51,742	5,864	330	836
E.N.C	42,719	36,901	5,012	160	647	1,548	35,474	4,937	142	618
OH	11,021	9,692	1,206	21	102	149	9,559	1,194	19	99
IN	5,658	5,153	450	13	42	106	5,056	444	12	40
IL	11,613	9,511	1,756	25	322	975	8,597	1,719	18	304
MI	9,434	7,920	1,337	58	119	215	7,728	1,322	53	115
WI	4,993	4,625	263	42	62	102	4,534	257	40	60
W.N.C	17,920	16,553	943	198	226	320	16,267	927	187	218
MN	4,468	4,215	109	53	91	62	4,162	105	51	89
IA	2,803	2,714	52	8	29	37	2,680	50	7	28
MO	5,191	4,558	565	20	48	66	4,499	561	19	46
ND	634	599	4	27	4	5	594	4	27	4
SD	708	648	4	53	4	6	644	4	52	4
NE	1,601	1,513	60	13	15	42	1,474	58	12	14
KS	2,515	2,306	150	23	36	101	2,215	146	20	34
South	88,185	69,693	16,574	595	1,322	7,367	62,725	16,303	545	1,243
S.A	45,092	34,760	9,404	184	743	2,359	32,613	9,245	171	705
DE	691	557	121	2	11	18	542	119	2	11
MD	4,917	3,482	1,262	14	160	143	3,365	1,243	12	154
DC	585	185	384	1	16	35	159	378	1	12
VA	6,394	4,964	1,228	17	186	178	4,809	1,213	15	179
WV	1,809	1,741	57	2	8	9	1,733	56	2	8
NC	6,836	5,178	1,514	84	61	84	5,108	1,503	82	58
SC	3,603	2,489	1,080	8	25	35	2,461	1,075	8	24
GA	6,773	4,811	1,856	15	92	124	4,706	1,842	13	88
FL	13,483	11,354	1,903	41	184	1,733	9,730	1,815	35	170
E.S.C	15,532	12,329	3,067	41	95	105	12,242	3,054	40	92
KY	3,754	3,460	269	6	20	23	3,440	267	5	19
TN	5,025	4,170	808	11	36	38	4,138	804	10	35
AL	4,138	3,044	1,053	16	25	27	3,022	1,049	16	24
MS	2,615	1,655	937	9	14	17	1,642	934	8	14
W.S.C	27,561	22,604	4,103	370	484	4,903	17,871	4,005	335	447
AR	2,394	1,986	381	13	14	22	1,966	380	13	14
LA	4,279	2,876	1,337	19	47	98	2,792	1,327	17	44
OK	3,205	2,660	246	261	39	94	2,584	241	251	36
TX	17,683	15,083	2,139	77	385	4,689	10,529	2,057	54	353
West	55,133	46,362	3,074	1,056	4,641	10,995	36,126	2,816	876	4,319
Mountain . . .	14,379	13,168	424	528	260	2,164	11,123	385	472	236
MT	822	766	3	49	5	13	754	2	48	5
ID	1,066	1,036	4	15	11	59	981	3	13	10
WY	465	448	4	10	3	27	422	3	9	3
CO	3,465	3,216	147	33	70	457	2,784	136	23	64
NM	1,582	1,384	36	144	18	614	790	29	134	15
AZ	3,832	3,415	125	226	67	751	2,710	111	201	59
UT	1,811	1,731	13	27	39	94	1,644	12	24	37
NV	1,336	1,173	92	23	48	149	1,037	87	20	44
Pacific	40,753	33,194	2,650	528	4,381	8,831	25,003	2,431	404	4,084
WA	5,143	4,636	165	93	249	242	4,424	157	83	237
OR	2,972	2,797	51	42	81	127	2,681	48	38	78
CA	30,895	24,924	2,381	295	3,295	8,353	17,112	2,176	190	3,064
AK	588	450	24	91	23	20	434	23	89	21
HI	1,156	387	29	6	733	90	351	27	4	683

[1] Persons of Hispanic origin may be of any race.

Source: U.S. Bureau of the Census, Internet sites http:>ww.census.gov/population/estimate-extract/state/intnttbl1.tbl and http://www.census.gov/population/estimate-extract/state/intnttbl2.tbl (accessed 15 March 1996).

No. 36. State Population Projections: 2000 to 2010

[**In thousands**. As of July 1. Series A, B, C, and D reflect different interstate migration assumptions. Series A is the preferred series model. For explanation of methodology, see text, section 1]

REGION, DIVISION, AND STATE	Series A			Series B			Series C			Series D		
	2000	2005	2010	2000	2005	2010	2000	2005	2010	2000	2005	2010
U.S	276,242	288,283	300,430	276,242	288,283	300,431	276,239	288,287	300,431	276,239	288,286	300,430
Northeast.....	51,884	52,472	53,301	53,210	54,151	55,102	52,329	53,279	54,225	54,582	56,418	58,183
N.E	13,216	13,406	13,755	14,025	14,408	14,785	13,507	13,868	14,212	13,996	14,392	14,751
ME	1,240	1,265	1,309	1,323	1,367	1,413	1,288	1,332	1,375	1,270	1,286	1,300
NH	1,165	1,215	1,280	1,274	1,355	1,429	1,204	1,281	1,350	1,163	1,186	1,207
VT	592	607	623	623	649	675	605	625	644	596	609	620
MA	5,950	5,991	6,097	6,254	6,372	6,495	6,032	6,140	6,249	6,401	6,605	6,785
RI.	998	1,009	1,034	1,060	1,087	1,115	1,022	1,047	1,072	1,065	1,096	1,126
CT	3,271	3,319	3,412	3,491	3,578	3,658	3,356	3,443	3,522	3,501	3,610	3,713
M.A	38,668	39,066	39,546	39,185	39,743	40,317	38,822	39,411	40,013	40,586	42,026	43,432
NY	18,237	18,348	18,546	18,504	18,666	18,856	18,321	18,547	18,799	19,838	20,808	21,761
NJ	8,135	8,338	8,562	8,267	8,482	8,681	8,165	8,431	8,677	8,413	8,746	9,075
PA	12,296	12,380	12,438	12,414	12,595	12,780	12,336	12,433	12,537	12,335	12,472	12,596
Midwest......	63,836	65,193	66,333	62,610	63,709	64,953	63,664	64,798	65,982	64,075	65,900	67,716
E.N.C......	44,806	45,620	46,259	44,013	44,717	45,506	44,769	45,495	46,242	45,220	46,528	47,805
OH	11,453	11,587	11,659	11,238	11,361	11,500	11,430	11,544	11,661	11,479	11,705	11,913
IN	6,045	6,190	6,286	5,922	6,066	6,212	6,032	6,155	6,274	5,929	6,065	6,187
IL	12,168	12,417	12,652	11,974	12,180	12,424	12,153	12,378	12,621	12,533	13,035	13,541
MI.	9,759	9,898	10,033	9,614	9,698	9,803	9,826	9,992	10,160	10,040	10,356	10,666
WI	5,381	5,528	5,629	5,265	5,412	5,567	5,328	5,426	5,526	5,239	5,367	5,498
W.N.C......	19,030	19,573	20,074	18,597	18,992	19,447	18,895	19,303	19,740	18,855	19,372	19,911
MN	4,824	4,986	5,127	4,733	4,873	5,020	4,814	4,955	5,096	4,756	4,909	5,068
IA	2,930	2,965	2,981	2,867	2,902	2,946	2,885	2,872	2,868	2,912	2,971	3,032
MO	5,437	5,592	5,760	5,313	5,392	5,489	5,459	5,622	5,788	5,406	5,521	5,638
ND	643	657	676	633	635	642	622	621	626	663	680	698
SD	770	796	815	737	757	781	750	766	786	749	776	805
NE	1,704	1,752	1,793	1,660	1,697	1,742	1,681	1,706	1,734	1,680	1,725	1,773
KS	2,722	2,825	2,922	2,654	2,736	2,827	2,684	2,761	2,842	2,689	2,790	2,897
South	97,244	102,364	107,385	96,576	101,382	106,120	96,931	101,911	106,852	94,503	98,001	101,445
S.A	50,005	52,708	55,321	50,015	52,762	55,422	50,517	53,667	56,737	48,004	49,521	50,976
DE	759	789	815	757	795	834	770	810	850	727	743	758
MD	5,322	5,548	5,782	5,334	5,552	5,762	5,420	5,718	6,008	5,334	5,553	5,763
DC	537	547	577	545	539	545	549	564	584	640	669	697
VA	7,048	7,398	7,728	7,060	7,423	7,760	7,106	7,515	7,902	6,854	7,097	7,318
WV	1,840	1,844	1,842	1,811	1,815	1,827	1,783	1,746	1,720	1,830	1,836	1,835
NC	7,617	8,002	8,341	7,588	8,009	8,416	7,616	8,040	8,455	7,169	7,314	7,438
SC	3,932	4,122	4,311	3,924	4,107	4,287	3,976	4,178	4,378	3,808	3,908	3,998
GA	7,637	8,111	8,553	7,678	8,188	8,679	7,664	8,206	8,732	7,249	7,510	7,758
FL	15,313	16,347	17,372	15,318	16,334	17,312	15,633	16,890	18,108	14,393	14,891	15,411
E.S.C	16,762	17,383	17,941	16,357	16,868	17,412	16,633	17,163	17,697	16,252	16,622	16,962
KY	3,989	4,086	4,160	3,883	3,962	4,050	3,927	3,984	4,046	3,913	3,993	4,064
TN	5,538	5,791	6,007	5,399	5,626	5,857	5,513	5,750	5,980	5,222	5,313	5,392
AL	4,485	4,674	4,856	4,375	4,521	4,677	4,471	4,644	4,818	4,357	4,472	4,580
MS	2,750	2,832	2,918	2,700	2,759	2,828	2,722	2,785	2,853	2,760	2,844	2,926
W.S.C......	30,477	32,273	34,123	30,204	31,752	33,286	29,781	31,081	32,418	30,247	31,858	33,507
AR	2,578	2,679	2,782	2,557	2,653	2,751	2,546	2,629	2,716	2,489	2,540	2,592
LA	4,478	4,627	4,808	4,424	4,509	4,604	4,343	4,398	4,471	4,592	4,769	4,947
OK	3,382	3,520	3,683	3,366	3,469	3,578	3,259	3,294	3,352	3,353	3,438	3,524
TX	20,039	21,447	22,850	19,857	21,121	22,353	19,633	20,760	21,879	19,813	21,111	22,444
West	63,278	68,254	73,411	63,846	69,041	74,256	63,315	68,299	73,372	63,079	67,967	73,086
Mountain ...	16,890	18,087	19,093	16,339	17,486	18,625	16,391	17,357	18,331	15,718	16,526	17,359
MT	920	962	996	894	941	993	867	880	899	859	882	906
ID	1,290	1,385	1,454	1,200	1,285	1,373	1,229	1,281	1,335	1,158	1,219	1,282
WY	522	559	596	512	541	571	467	485	491	495	514	534
CO	4,059	4,309	4,494	3,957	4,224	4,477	3,851	4,017	4,183	3,729	3,867	4,000
NM	1,823	1,956	2,082	1,780	1,894	2,005	1,776	1,892	2,009	1,737	1,836	1,939
AZ	4,437	4,763	5,074	4,320	4,604	4,891	4,404	4,772	5,136	4,201	4,417	4,645
UT	2,148	2,318	2,462	2,079	2,244	2,413	2,063	2,177	2,294	2,076	2,254	2,442
NV	1,691	1,835	1,935	1,597	1,753	1,902	1,718	1,853	1,984	1,463	1,537	1,611
Pacific	46,388	50,167	54,318	47,507	51,555	55,631	46,924	50,942	55,041	47,361	51,441	55,727
WA	6,070	6,570	7,025	6,025	6,564	7,087	6,054	6,477	6,898	5,539	5,770	6,005
OR	3,404	3,645	3,876	3,340	3,573	3,812	3,396	3,571	3,753	3,151	3,253	3,360
CA	34,888	37,771	41,085	36,062	39,138	42,255	35,490	38,749	42,075	36,689	40,288	44,076
AK	699	745	781	732	809	880	658	706	754	666	716	769
HI.	1,327	1,436	1,551	1,348	1,471	1,597	1,326	1,439	1,561	1,316	1,414	1,517

Source: U.S. Bureau of the Census, *Current Population Reports*, series P25-1111.

No. 37. Population Projections, by Age—States: 2000 to 2010

[In thousands. As of July 1. Data shown are for series A, the preferred series model; for explanation of methodology, see text, section 1]

REGION, DIVISION, AND STATE	UNDER 18 YEARS			18 TO 44 YEARS			45 TO 64 YEARS			65 YEARS AND OVER		
	2000	2005	2010	2000	2005	2010	2000	2005	2010	2000	2005	2010
U.S........	71,789	73,120	73,619	109,274	108,106	108,058	59,860	70,087	78,651	35,324	36,965	40,099
Northeast........	12,801	12,669	12,326	20,069	19,240	18,912	11,711	13,266	14,465	7,304	7,298	7,597
N.E	3,191	3,126	3,045	5,154	4,946	4,902	3,018	3,474	3,830	1,853	1,863	1,977
ME	294	287	286	477	461	458	294	339	375	175	179	191
NH	288	286	285	464	454	457	273	328	372	141	148	165
VT	149	147	146	235	230	228	135	155	167	72	75	82
MA	1,420	1,378	1,317	2,358	2,255	2,226	1,329	1,520	1,672	842	838	881
RI	237	232	227	387	371	368	223	259	286	151	148	153
CT	803	796	784	1,233	1,175	1,165	764	873	958	472	475	505
M.A	9,610	9,543	9,281	14,915	14,294	14,010	8,693	9,792	10,635	5,451	5,435	5,620
NY	4,611	4,566	4,439	7,143	6,851	6,735	4,058	4,499	4,846	2,426	2,431	2,525
NJ	2,047	2,080	2,051	3,121	3,005	2,972	1,854	2,125	2,348	1,112	1,128	1,192
PA	2,952	2,897	2,791	4,651	4,438	4,303	2,781	3,168	3,441	1,913	1,876	1,903
Midwest........	16,593	16,537	16,340	25,095	24,354	23,799	13,784	15,791	17,282	8,369	8,508	8,912
E.N.C..........	11,665	11,646	11,467	17,676	17,075	16,660	9,711	11,058	12,035	5,755	5,840	6,097
OH	2,891	2,855	2,778	4,483	4,298	4,159	2,532	2,867	3,103	1,547	1,567	1,618
IN	1,550	1,559	1,534	2,409	2,338	2,278	1,314	1,499	1,636	772	793	836
IL	3,206	3,228	3,198	4,857	4,714	4,640	2,592	2,949	3,225	1,513	1,526	1,589
MI	2,635	2,642	2,621	3,802	3,646	3,569	2,112	2,388	2,567	1,211	1,222	1,278
WI	1,383	1,362	1,336	2,125	2,079	2,014	1,161	1,355	1,504	712	732	776
W.N.C.........	4,928	4,891	4,873	7,419	7,279	7,139	4,073	4,733	5,247	2,614	2,668	2,815
MN	1,254	1,235	1,225	1,930	1,894	1,849	1,038	1,225	1,370	602	630	683
IA	736	721	705	1,128	1,097	1,061	627	708	767	439	439	449
MO	1,381	1,375	1,371	2,090	2,040	2,006	1,197	1,389	1,546	769	789	837
ND	164	160	163	254	251	250	133	154	170	94	91	93
SD	216	217	218	292	289	284	155	182	203	107	108	111
NE	452	450	448	663	657	649	354	407	447	236	238	248
KS	725	733	743	1,062	1,051	1,040	569	668	744	367	373	394
South	24,901	25,459	25,688	38,346	38,075	37,992	21,274	25,209	28,647	12,724	13,619	15,055
S.A	12,217	12,482	12,505	19,402	19,196	19,107	11,255	13,330	15,148	7,130	7,698	8,559
DE	191	194	193	305	299	295	164	191	214	99	104	113
MD	1,405	1,441	1,453	2,124	2,084	2,077	1,192	1,386	1,551	602	636	701
DC	99	99	102	248	250	261	117	128	142	73	71	72
VA	1,745	1,781	1,780	2,923	2,895	2,879	1,576	1,855	2,101	803	865	967
WV	425	420	406	703	667	642	434	482	514	277	275	280
NC	1,862	1,900	1,879	3,045	3,006	2,978	1,713	2,017	2,284	997	1,080	1,199
SC	1,013	1,034	1,036	1,570	1,552	1,548	867	1,018	1,152	481	518	575
GA	2,030	2,101	2,125	3,153	3,154	3,161	1,656	1,981	2,269	798	876	998
FL	3,447	3,512	3,531	5,331	5,289	5,266	3,536	4,272	4,921	3,000	3,273	3,654
E.S.C.........	4,275	4,330	4,305	6,606	6,468	6,352	3,714	4,310	4,824	2,167	2,277	2,459
KY	996	998	982	1,594	1,541	1,490	890	1,021	1,125	509	528	563
TN	1,343	1,358	1,343	2,209	2,183	2,151	1,269	1,485	1,674	717	764	839
AL	1,183	1,221	1,233	1,736	1,705	1,691	975	1,128	1,264	591	620	667
MS	753	753	747	1,067	1,039	1,020	580	676	761	350	365	390
W.S.C.........	8,409	8,647	8,878	12,338	12,411	12,533	6,305	7,569	8,675	3,427	3,644	4,037
AR	657	662	661	960	944	927	578	673	758	383	400	436
LA	1,247	1,257	1,282	1,792	1,766	1,766	925	1,073	1,195	515	529	565
OK	875	883	900	1,314	1,307	1,312	739	863	969	454	467	502
TX	5,630	5,845	6,035	8,272	8,394	8,528	4,063	4,960	5,753	2,075	2,248	2,534
West	17,494	18,455	19,265	25,764	26,437	27,355	13,091	15,821	18,257	6,927	7,540	8,535
Mountain	4,690	4,872	4,967	6,770	6,874	6,919	3,503	4,240	4,847	1,924	2,099	2,362
MT	242	247	250	356	357	357	203	236	260	117	121	130
ID	373	390	396	512	524	526	262	316	360	143	154	172
WY	145	153	162	218	226	235	108	129	144	51	51	54
CO	1,037	1,055	1,054	1,722	1,735	1,728	885	1,063	1,198	415	455	514
NM	540	568	588	705	718	734	374	449	515	204	222	247
AZ	1,213	1,260	1,281	1,673	1,687	1,705	927	1,129	1,305	623	688	783
UT	723	766	800	882	912	928	356	435	504	188	204	230
NV	417	433	436	702	715	706	388	483	561	183	204	232
Pacific	12,804	13,583	14,298	18,994	19,563	20,436	9,588	11,581	13,410	5,003	5,441	6,173
WA	1,589	1,663	1,712	2,464	2,533	2,589	1,342	1,642	1,888	675	732	836
OR	869	912	945	1,328	1,364	1,400	773	914	1,026	434	456	504
CA	9,779	10,406	11,008	14,327	14,753	15,494	7,077	8,563	9,978	3,704	4,048	4,605
AK	221	231	239	319	331	342	129	149	163	31	34	38
HI	346	371	394	556	582	611	267	313	355	159	171	190

Source: U.S. Bureau of the Census, *Current Population Reports*, series P25-1111.

No. 38. Population Projections, by Race and Hispanic Origin Status—States: 2000 and 2010

[**In thousands**. As of **July 1**. Data shown are for series A, the preferred series model; for explanation of methodology, see text, section 1. Persons of Hispanic origin may be of any race]

REGION, DIVISION, AND STATE	WHITE		BLACK		AMERICAN INDIAN, ESKIMO, ALEUT		ASIAN, PACIFIC ISLANDER		HISPANIC ORIGIN		NOT OF HISPANIC ORIGIN	
	2000	2010	2000	2010	2000	2010	2000	2010	2000	2010	2000	2010
U.S	**226,268**	**240,293**	**35,475**	**40,227**	**2,382**	**2,718**	**12,121**	**17,188**	**31,164**	**40,526**	**245,078**	**259,904**
Northeast.	**43,218**	**43,268**	**6,570**	**7,267**	**108**	**98**	**1,989**	**2,669**	**4,690**	**5,559**	**47,194**	**47,742**
N.E	**12,120**	**12,408**	**718**	**810**	**31**	**31**	**348**	**506**	**796**	**1,035**	**12,420**	**12,720**
ME	1,220	1,283	5	5	6	6	9	14	11	15	1,229	1,294
NH	1,137	1,236	8	10	3	3	18	31	16	24	1,149	1,256
VT	582	609	3	4	2	2	5	9	5	8	587	615
MA	5,373	5,387	352	393	10	10	215	307	394	510	5,556	5,587
RI	917	933	46	51	4	4	31	46	70	95	928	939
CT	2,891	2,960	304	347	6	6	70	99	300	383	2,971	3,029
M.A	**31,098**	**30,860**	**5,852**	**6,457**	**77**	**67**	**1,641**	**2,163**	**3,894**	**4,524**	**34,774**	**35,022**
NY	13,819	13,542	3,391	3,705	50	43	977	1,257	2,498	2,750	15,739	15,796
NJ	6,445	6,526	1,242	1,434	13	11	435	591	1,037	1,287	7,098	7,275
PA	10,834	10,792	1,219	1,318	14	13	229	315	359	487	11,937	11,951
Midwest.	**55,391**	**56,441**	**6,689**	**7,526**	**411**	**460**	**1,345**	**1,900**	**2,479**	**3,284**	**61,357**	**63,049**
E.N.C	**38,006**	**38,350**	**5,653**	**6,379**	**170**	**174**	**976**	**1,354**	**2,037**	**2,683**	**42,769**	**43,576**
OH	9,943	9,948	1,335	1,483	22	22	152	206	201	268	11,252	11,391
IN	5,444	5,587	514	582	15	15	72	102	145	197	5,900	6,089
IL	9,713	9,801	1,957	2,181	22	21	476	648	1,264	1,643	10,904	11,009
MI	8,000	7,979	1,520	1,737	63	64	176	253	283	375	9,476	9,658
WI	4,906	5,035	327	396	48	52	100	145	144	200	5,237	5,429
W.N.C.	**17,385**	**18,091**	**1,036**	**1,147**	**241**	**286**	**369**	**546**	**442**	**601**	**18,588**	**19,473**
MN	4,498	4,699	111	122	64	74	151	232	83	116	4,741	5,011
IA	2,816	2,841	65	78	8	8	41	53	56	75	2,874	2,906
MO	4,737	4,970	609	664	20	21	72	105	82	108	5,355	5,652
ND	601	622	4	5	31	37	7	11	6	8	637	668
SD	685	702	4	4	74	97	7	11	9	11	761	804
NE	1,598	1,669	69	76	15	16	22	31	67	93	1,637	1,700
KS	2,450	2,588	174	198	29	33	69	103	139	190	2,583	2,732
South	**75,813**	**82,386**	**18,708**	**21,297**	**630**	**677**	**2,094**	**3,024**	**9,752**	**12,944**	**87,492**	**94,441**
S.A	**37,772**	**40,805**	**10,868**	**12,615**	**194**	**208**	**1,173**	**1,691**	**3,166**	**4,316**	**46,839**	**51,005**
DE	589	603	149	181	3	3	18	28	28	39	731	776
MD	3,546	3,631	1,514	1,776	13	14	249	361	188	248	5,134	5,534
DC	176	195	349	365	1	1	12	16	29	32	508	545
VA	5,367	5,743	1,391	1,592	15	15	275	378	228	308	6,820	7,420
WV	1,770	1,768	53	50	3	3	14	20	12	16	1,828	1,826
NC	5,682	6,125	1,715	1,916	98	109	123	190	123	167	7,494	8,174
SC	2,677	2,902	1,207	1,344	9	9	39	56	49	67	3,883	4,244
GA	5,346	5,857	2,139	2,485	12	12	140	199	176	237	7,461	8,316
FL	12,619	13,981	2,351	2,906	40	42	303	443	2,333	3,202	12,980	14,170
E.S.C	**13,231**	**14,042**	**3,331**	**3,634**	**45**	**46**	**155**	**219**	**132**	**176**	**16,630**	**17,765**
KY	3,646	3,769	307	345	6	6	30	40	26	34	3,963	4,126
TN	4,563	4,899	905	1,014	11	11	59	83	51	67	5,487	5,940
AL	3,284	3,529	1,139	1,243	18	19	44	65	35	49	4,450	4,807
MS	1,738	1,845	980	1,032	10	10	22	31	20	26	2,730	2,892
W.S.C	**24,810**	**27,539**	**4,509**	**5,048**	**391**	**423**	**766**	**1,114**	**6,454**	**8,452**	**24,023**	**25,671**
AR	2,139	2,311	395	412	17	18	27	41	33	44	2,545	2,738
LA	2,953	3,119	1,427	1,550	19	20	78	119	124	154	4,354	4,654
OK	2,770	2,979	251	269	290	320	71	115	124	160	3,258	3,523
TX	16,948	19,130	2,436	2,817	65	65	590	839	6,173	8,094	13,866	14,756
West	**51,846**	**58,198**	**3,508**	**4,137**	**1,233**	**1,483**	**6,693**	**9,595**	**14,243**	**18,739**	**49,035**	**54,672**
Mountain . . .	**15,248**	**16,974**	**485**	**556**	**669**	**818**	**490**	**748**	**2,945**	**3,954**	**13,945**	**15,139**
MT	847	908	2	3	62	74	8	12	17	22	903	974
ID	1,242	1,392	6	8	21	24	21	31	95	138	1,195	1,316
WY	498	564	5	5	14	17	6	9	36	45	486	551
CO	3,733	4,090	174	200	36	38	117	166	595	771	3,464	3,723
NM	1,574	1,760	33	35	181	231	35	56	792	1,024	1,031	1,058
AZ	3,894	4,379	131	143	285	348	127	204	1,019	1,382	3,418	3,692
UT	2,017	2,272	16	18	39	50	77	122	127	170	2,021	2,292
NV	1,443	1,609	118	144	31	36	99	148	264	402	1,427	1,533
Pacific	**36,598**	**41,224**	**3,023**	**3,581**	**564**	**665**	**6,203**	**8,847**	**11,298**	**14,785**	**35,090**	**39,533**
WA	5,360	6,071	174	187	112	131	424	635	368	526	5,702	6,499
OR	3,139	3,508	60	70	52	60	153	238	189	265	3,215	3,611
CA	26,987	30,357	2,719	3,245	276	314	4,906	7,169	10,584	13,775	24,304	27,310
AK	516	543	28	29	116	150	39	59	26	33	673	748
HI	596	745	42	50	8	10	681	746	131	186	1,196	1,365

Source: U.S. Bureau of the Census, *Current Population Reports*, series P25-1111.

No. 39. Population in Coastal Counties: 1960 to 1994

[Enumerated population as of **April 1**, except as indicated. Areas as defined by U.S. National Oceanic and Atmospheric Agency, 1992. Covers 672 counties and equivalent areas with at least 15 percent of their land area either in a coastal watershed (drainage area) or in a coastal cataloging unit (a coastal area between watersheds)]

| YEAR | Total | COUNTIES IN COASTAL REGIONS | | | | | Balance of United States |
		Total	Atlantic	Gulf of Mexico	Great Lakes	Pacific	
Land area, 1990 (1,000 sq. mi.)	3,536	888	148	114	115	510	2,649
POPULATION							
1960 (mil.).	179.3	94.5	44.5	8.4	23.7	17.9	84.8
1970 (mil.).	203.3	110.0	51.1	10.0	26.0	22.8	93.3
1980 (mil.).	226.5	119.8	53.7	13.1	26.0	27.0	106.7
1990 (mil.).	248.7	133.4	59.0	15.2	25.9	33.2	115.3
1994 (July 1)(mil.).	260.3	138.5	60.7	16.3	26.4	35.1	121.8
1960 (percent).	100	53	25	5	14	10	47
1970 (percent).	100	54	25	5	13	11	46
1980 (percent).	100	53	24	6	11	12	47
1990 (percent).	100	54	24	6	10	13	46
1994 (July 1)(percent).	100	53	23	6	10	13	47

Source: U.S. Bureau of the Census, *U.S. Census of Population: 1960* and *1970; 1980 Census of Population*, vol. 1, chapter A (PC80-1-A-1), *U.S. Summary; 1990 Census of Population and Housing* (CPH1); and unpublished data.

No. 40. Metropolitan and Nonmetropolitan Area Population: 1970 to 1994

[As of **April 1**, except **1994**, as of **July 1**. Data exclude Puerto Rico. Metropolitan areas are as defined by U.S. Office of Management and Budget as of year shown, except as noted]

| ITEM | 1970 | 1980 [1] (SMSA's) | MSA's AND CMSA's [2] | | |
			1980	1990	1994
Metropolitan areas: Number of areas	243	318	271	271	271
Population (1,000).	139,480	169,431	177,143	198,023	207,654
Percent change over previous year shown . .	[3]23.6	21.5	(X)	11.8	4.9
Percent of total U.S. population	68.6	74.8	78.2	79.6	79.8
Land area, percent of U.S. land area	10.9	16.0	19.8	19.8	19.8
Nonmetropolitan areas, population (1,000)	63,822	57,115	49,399	50,696	52,687

X Not applicable.　[1] SMSA=standard metropolitan statistical area. Areas are as defined June 30, 1981.　[2] Areas are as defined June 30, 1995.　[3] Percent change from 1960.

Source: U.S. Bureau of the Census, *U.S. Census of Population: 1970; 1990 Census of Population and Housing, Supplementary Reports, Metropolitan Areas as Defined by the Office of Management and Budget, June 30, 1993* (1990 CPH-S-1-1); *1990 Census of Population and Housing, Population and Housing Unit Counts* (CPH-2-1); Population Paper Listings PPL-27; and unpublished data.

No. 41. Number and Population of Metropolitan Areas, by Population Size-Class in 1990: 1990 and 1994

[As of **April 1** for 1990 and as of July for 1994. Data exclude Puerto Rico. CMSA=consolidated metropolitan statistical area. MSA=metropolitan statistical area. PMSA=primary metropolitan statistical area. Areas are as defined by U.S. Office of Management and Budget, June 30, 1995. For area definitions, see Appendix II]

| LEVEL AND POPULATION SIZE-CLASS OF METROPOLITAN AREA IN 1990 | CMSA's AND MSA's | | | | MSA's AND PMSA's | | | |
| | Number, 1990 | Population, 1990 (mil.) | Population, 1994 | | Number, 1994 | Population, 1994 | | |
			Total (mil.)	Percent in each class		Total (mil.)	Percent in each class	
Total, all metropolitan areas . . .	271	198.0	207.7	100	326	207.7	100	
Level A (1,000,000 or more).	40	132.9	138.7	67	51	123.9	60	
2,500,000 or more	15	94.1	97.9	47	13	60.5	29	
1,000,000 to 2,499,999	25	38.8	40.8	20	38	63.4	31	
Level B (250,000 to 999,999)	96	46.4	49.2	24	119	60.2	29	
500,000 to 999,999.	33	24.3	25.9	12	41	31.2	15	
250,000 to 499,999	63	22.0	23.3	11	78	29.0	14	
Level C (100,000 to 249,999)	111	16.6	17.6	8	131	21.3	10	
Level D (less than 100,000)	24	2.1	2.1	1	25	2.2	1	

Source: U.S. Bureau of the Census, *1990 Census of Population and Housing, Supplementary Reports, Metropolitan Areas as Defined by the Office of Management and Budget, June 30, 1993,* (1990 CPH-S-1-1); and *1990 Census of Population and Housing, Population and Housing Unit Counts* (CPH-2-1); and Population Paper Listings PPL-27.

No. 42. Metropolitan and Nonmetropolitan Population—States: 1980 to 1994

[As of April 1, except 1994, as of July. Metropolitan refers to 253 metropolitan statistical areas and 18 consolidated metropolitan statistical areas as defined by U.S. Office of Management and Budget, June 30, 1995; nonmetropolitan is the area outside metropolitan areas; see Appendix II. Minus sign (-) indicates decrease]

REGION, DIVISION, AND STATE	METROPOLITAN POPULATION						NONMETROPOLITAN POPULATION					
	Total (1,000)			Percent change, 1990-94	Percent of State		Total (1,000)			Percent change, 1990-94	Percent of State	
	1980	1990	1994		1990	1994	1980	1990	1994		1990	1994
U.S.	177,143	198,023	207,654	4.9	79.6	79.8	49,399	50,696	52,687	3.9	20.4	20.2
Northeast ..	44,047	45,457	45,931	1.0	89.5	89.4	5,090	5,354	5,464	2.1	10.5	10.6
N.E.	10,470	11,127	11,155	0.3	84.2	84.1	1,878	2,080	2,116	1.7	15.8	15.9
ME....	405	443	445	0.5	36.1	35.9	721	785	795	1.3	63.9	64.1
NH....	535	659	677	2.8	59.4	59.6	386	450	460	2.0	40.6	40.4
VT	133	152	158	4.3	26.9	27.2	378	411	422	2.6	73.1	72.8
MA....	5,530	5,788	5,807	0.3	96.2	96.1	207	229	234	2.4	3.8	3.9
RI	886	938	935	-0.4	93.5	93.8	61	65	62	-5.1	6.5	6.2
CT	2,982	3,148	3,133	-0.5	95.8	95.7	126	140	142	2.0	4.2	4.3
M.A.	33,576	34,330	34,777	1.3	91.3	91.2	3,212	3,274	3,349	2.3	8.7	8.8
NY	16,144	16,516	16,666	0.9	91.8	91.7	1,414	1,475	1,503	1.9	8.2	8.3
NJ	7,365	7,730	7,904	2.2	100.0	100.0	(X)	(X)	(X)	(X)	(X)	(X)
PA	10,067	10,084	10,206	1.2	84.9	84.7	1,798	1,799	1,846	2.6	15.1	15.3
Midwest ...	42,557	43,691	45,049	3.1	73.2	73.4	16,310	15,978	16,345	2.3	26.8	26.6
E.N.C. ...	33,031	33,391	34,308	2.7	79.5	79.4	8,652	8,618	8,876	3.0	20.5	20.6
OH....	8,791	8,826	9,016	2.2	81.4	81.2	2,007	2,021	2,086	3.2	18.6	18.8
IN	3,885	3,962	4,124	4.1	71.5	71.7	1,605	1,582	1,628	2.9	28.5	28.3
IL.....	9,461	9,574	9,879	3.2	83.8	84.1	1,967	1,857	1,873	0.9	16.2	15.9
MI	7,719	7,698	7,837	1.8	82.8	82.5	1,543	1,598	1,659	3.9	17.2	17.5
WI	3,176	3,331	3,452	3.6	68.1	67.9	1,530	1,561	1,630	4.4	31.9	32.1
W.N.C ...	9,526	10,300	10,741	4.3	58.3	59.0	7,658	7,360	7,470	1.5	41.7	41.0
MN....	2,674	3,011	3,172	5.3	68.8	69.4	1,402	1,364	1,395	2.3	31.2	30.6
IA.....	1,198	1,200	1,246	3.8	43.2	44.0	1,716	1,577	1,584	0.4	56.8	56.0
MO....	3,314	3,491	3,591	2.9	68.2	68.1	1,603	1,626	1,686	3.7	31.8	31.9
ND....	234	257	269	4.5	40.3	42.1	418	381	369	-3.2	59.7	57.9
SD....	194	221	238	8.0	31.7	33.0	497	475	483	1.6	68.3	67.0
NE....	728	787	823	4.5	49.9	50.7	842	791	800	1.1	50.1	49.3
KS....	1,184	1,333	1,402	5.2	53.8	54.9	1,180	1,145	1,152	0.7	46.2	45.1
South	53,724	63,194	67,581	6.9	74.0	74.5	21,643	22,260	23,111	3.8	26.0	25.5
S.A.	28,226	34,298	36,684	7.0	78.7	79.1	8,732	9,274	9,715	4.8	21.3	20.9
DE....	496	553	584	5.7	83.0	82.7	98	113	122	7.9	17.0	17.3
MD....	3,920	4,438	4,641	4.6	92.8	92.7	297	343	365	6.6	7.2	7.3
DC....	638	607	570	-6.6	100.0	100.0	(X)	(X)	(X)	(X)	(X)	(X)
VA....	3,966	4,775	5,091	6.6	77.2	77.7	1,381	1,414	1,461	3.3	22.8	22.3
WV....	796	748	762	1.9	41.7	41.8	1,155	1,045	1,060	1.4	58.3	58.2
NC....	3,749	4,380	4,708	7.5	66.0	66.6	2,131	2,253	2,362	4.9	34.0	33.4
SC....	2,114	2,422	2,555	5.5	69.5	69.7	1,006	1,064	1,109	4.2	30.5	30.3
GA....	3,507	4,351	4,804	10.4	67.2	68.1	1,956	2,127	2,251	5.8	32.8	31.9
FL....	9,039	12,024	12,970	7.9	92.9	93.0	708	915	982	7.4	7.1	7.0
E.S.C.	8,147	8,662	9,139	5.5	57.1	57.5	6,519	6,518	6,751	3.6	42.9	42.5
KY	1,735	1,780	1,848	3.8	48.3	48.3	1,925	1,907	1,979	3.8	51.7	51.7
TN	3,045	3,298	3,509	6.4	67.6	67.8	1,546	1,579	1,666	5.5	32.4	32.2
AL....	2,560	2,710	2,847	5.1	67.1	67.5	1,334	1,331	1,371	3.1	32.9	32.5
MS....	806	874	935	6.9	34.0	35.0	1,715	1,701	1,734	2.0	66.0	65.0
W.S.C. ...	17,351	20,235	21,758	7.5	75.8	76.6	6,392	6,468	6,646	2.8	24.2	23.4
AR....	963	1,040	1,103	6.1	44.2	45.0	1,323	1,311	1,350	3.0	55.8	55.0
LA....	3,125	3,160	3,240	2.6	74.9	75.1	1,082	1,061	1,075	1.3	25.1	24.9
OK....	1,724	1,870	1,960	4.8	59.4	60.2	1,301	1,276	1,298	1.7	40.6	39.8
TX	11,539	14,166	15,455	9.1	83.4	84.1	2,686	2,821	2,923	3.6	16.6	15.9
West	36,816	45,680	49,093	7.5	86.5	86.3	6,356	7,104	7,766	9.3	13.5	13.7
Mountain .	7,806	9,800	10,987	12.1	71.7	72.2	3,566	3,859	4,228	9.5	28.3	27.8
MT	189	191	204	6.7	23.9	23.8	598	608	652	7.3	76.1	76.2
ID	257	296	348	17.6	29.4	30.7	687	711	785	10.5	70.6	69.3
WY....	141	134	142	5.6	29.6	29.8	329	319	334	4.6	70.4	70.2
CO....	2,408	2,779	3,086	11.0	84.4	84.4	482	515	570	10.6	15.6	15.6
NM....	675	842	932	10.7	55.6	56.4	628	673	722	7.2	44.4	43.6
AZ	2,339	3,202	3,557	11.1	87.4	87.3	378	463	518	11.9	12.6	12.7
UT	1,132	1,341	1,475	10.0	77.8	77.3	329	382	433	13.3	22.2	22.7
NV	666	1,014	1,243	22.6	84.4	85.3	135	188	214	13.9	15.6	14.7
Pacific ...	29,010	35,881	38,106	6.2	91.7	91.5	2,790	3,245	3,539	9.0	8.3	8.5
WA....	3,366	4,036	4,428	9.7	82.9	82.9	766	830	915	10.2	17.1	17.1
OR....	1,799	1,985	2,162	8.9	69.8	70.1	834	858	924	7.8	30.2	29.9
CA....	22,907	28,797	30,388	5.5	96.8	96.7	760	961	1,043	8.4	3.2	3.3
AK....	174	226	254	12.1	41.1	41.8	227	324	353	8.9	58.9	58.2
HI	763	836	874	4.6	75.5	74.2	202	272	304	11.9	24.5	25.8

X Not applicable.

Source: U.S. Bureau of the Census, 1990 Census of Population and Housing, Supplementary Reports, Metropolitan Areas as Defined by the Office of Management and Budget, June 30, 1993, (1990 CPH-S-1-1); 1990 Census of Population and Housing, Population and Housing Unit Counts (CPH-2-1); Current Population Reports, P25-1127; and Population Paper Listings PPL-27.

Population

No. 43. Large Metropolitan Areas—Population: 1980 to 1994

[**In thousands, except percent**. As of **April 1**, except as noted. Covers 18 consolidated metropolitan statistical areas (CMSA's), their 73 component primary metropolitan statistical areas (PMSA's), and the remaining 121 MSA's with 250,000 and over population in 1994 as defined by the U.S. Office of Management and Budget as of June 30, 1995. For definitions and components of all MA's and population of NECMA's (New England County Metropolitan Areas), see Appendix II. Minus sign (-) indicates decrease]

METROPOLITAN AREA	1980	1990 [1]	1991 (July)	1992 (July)	1993 (July)	1994 (July)	PERCENT CHANGE 1980-90	PERCENT CHANGE 1990-94
Albany-Schenectady-Troy, NY MSA.	825	862	869	872	874	875	4.5	1.6
Albuquerque, NM MSA.	485	589	602	616	630	646	21.4	9.6
Allentown-Bethlehem-Easton, PA MSA.	551	595	602	606	609	612	8.0	2.8
Anchorage, AK MSA	174	226	235	246	250	254	29.8	12.1
Appleton-Oshkosh-Neenah, WI MSA.	291	315	320	324	329	332	8.2	5.4
Atlanta, GA MSA	2,233	2,960	3,054	3,135	3,229	3,331	32.5	12.6
Augusta-Aiken, GA-SC MSA	363	415	430	443	444	448	14.2	8.0
Austin-San Marcos, TX MSA	585	846	873	900	932	964	44.6	13.9
Bakersfield, CA MSA	403	545	571	588	600	609	35.2	11.8
Baton Rouge, LA MSA	494	528	537	546	553	558	6.9	5.7
Beaumont-Port Arthur, TX MSA	373	361	366	369	372	373	-3.2	3.2
Biloxi-Gulfport-Pascagoula, MS MSA.	300	312	316	323	330	339	4.1	8.6
Binghamton, NY MSA.	263	264	265	266	264	262	0.4	-1.0
Birmingham, AL MSA	815	840	849	856	865	872	3.0	3.8
Boise City, ID MSA	257	296	310	320	334	348	15.2	17.6
Boston-Worcester-Lawrence, MA-NH-ME-CT CMSA .	5,122	5,455	5,439	5,443	5,468	5,497	6.5	0.8
Boston, MA-NH PMSA	3,149	3,228	3,216	3,215	3,226	3,240	2.5	0.4
Brockton, MA PMSA	225	236	236	236	238	239	5.1	1.1
Fitchburg-Leominster, MA PMSA	125	138	137	137	136	136	10.5	-1.6
Lawrence, MA-NH PMSA.	298	353	356	358	361	364	18.4	3.2
Lowell, MA-NH PMSA	249	281	281	282	284	285	12.5	1.6
Manchester, NH PMSA	146	174	174	175	176	177	18.9	2.1
Nashua, NH PMSA.	134	168	169	171	173	176	25.4	4.5
New Bedford, MA PMSA	167	176	175	173	173	172	5.4	-1.9
Portsmouth-Rochester, NH-ME PMSA	189	223	217	218	220	222	18.0	-0.6
Worcester, MA-CT PMSA.	439	478	477	478	482	485	8.9	1.4
Brownsville-Harlingen-San Benito, TX MSA	210	260	270	279	291	300	24.0	15.2
Buffalo-Niagara Falls, NY MSA.	1,243	1,189	1,192	1,193	1,192	1,189	-4.3	-
Canton-Massillon, OH MSA	404	394	397	399	401	402	-2.6	2.1
Charleston-North Charleston, SC MSA	430	507	523	527	526	522	17.8	3.0
Charleston, WV MSA	270	250	251	253	254	255	-7.1	1.7
Charlotte-Gastonia-Rock Hill, NC-SC MSA	971	1,162	1,192	1,210	1,234	1,260	19.6	8.5
Chattanooga, TN-GA MSA.	418	424	428	430	435	439	1.6	3.5
Chicago-Gary-Kenosha, IL-IN-WI CMSA	8,115	8,240	8,326	8,400	8,466	8,527	1.5	3.5
Chicago, IL PMSA	7,246	7,411	7,486	7,553	7,612	7,668	2.3	3.5
Gary, IN PMSA	643	605	611	614	617	620	-5.9	2.5
Kankakee, IL PMSA	103	96	98	99	100	101	-6.5	5.2
Kenosha, WI PMSA	123	128	132	134	136	138	4.1	7.5
Cincinnati-Hamilton, OH-KY-IN CMSA	1,726	1,818	1,843	1,862	1,881	1,894	5.3	4.2
Cincinnati, OH-KY-IN PMSA.	1,468	1,526	1,544	1,558	1,572	1,581	4.0	3.6
Hamilton-Middletown, OH PMSA.	259	291	299	304	309	313	12.6	7.3
Cleveland-Akron, OH CMSA	2,938	2,860	2,874	2,887	2,894	2,899	-2.7	1.4
Akron, OH PMSA	660	658	664	668	673	677	-0.4	2.9
Cleveland-Lorain-Elyria, OH PMSA	2,278	2,202	2,211	2,219	2,221	2,222	-3.3	0.9
Colorado Springs, CO MSA.	309	397	404	421	435	452	28.3	14.0
Columbia, SC MSA	410	454	465	471	480	486	10.7	7.1
Columbus, GA-AL MSA	255	261	260	270	271	274	2.4	5.1
Columbus, OH MSA.	1,214	1,345	1,371	1,391	1,409	1,423	10.8	5.8
Corpus Christi, TX MSA	326	350	356	361	369	376	7.3	7.4
Dallas-Fort Worth, TX CMSA.	3,046	4,037	4,139	4,207	4,279	4,362	32.5	8.1
Dallas, TX PMSA	2,055	2,676	2,742	2,790	2,844	2,898	30.2	8.3
Fort Worth-Arlington, TX PMSA.	991	1,361	1,397	1,417	1,435	1,464	37.4	7.6
Davenport-Moline-Rock Island, IA-IL MSA	385	351	354	357	357	358	-8.8	2.0
Dayton-Springfield, OH MSA	942	951	956	959	959	956	1.0	0.5
Daytona Beach, FL MSA.	270	399	414	423	432	440	48.1	10.3
Denver-Boulder-Greeley, CO CMSA	1,742	1,980	2,029	2,088	2,146	2,190	13.7	10.6
Boulder-Longmont, CO PMSA	190	225	231	238	244	250	18.8	10.8
Denver, CO PMSA.	1,429	1,623	1,664	1,714	1,762	1,796	13.6	10.7
Greeley, CO PMSA.	123	132	134	136	140	144	6.8	9.3
Des Moines, IA MSA	368	393	400	406	412	416	6.9	6.0
Detroit-Ann Arbor-Flint, MI CMSA	5,293	5,187	5,215	5,236	5,246	5,256	-2.0	1.3
Ann Arbor, MI PMSA.	455	490	498	504	509	515	7.7	5.1
Detroit, MI PMSA	4,388	4,267	4,285	4,299	4,304	4,307	-2.8	0.9
Flint, MI PMSA.	450	430	432	432	433	433	-4.4	0.7
El Paso, TX MSA.	480	592	613	628	647	665	23.3	12.4
Erie, PA MSA	280	276	278	279	280	280	-1.5	1.7
Eugene-Springfield, OR MSA.	275	283	288	291	295	299	2.8	5.7
Evansville-Henderson, IN-KY MSA	276	279	281	283	285	287	1.0	2.7
Fayetteville, NC MSA	247	275	278	277	284	286	11.1	4.2
Fort Myers-Cape Coral, FL MSA.	205	335	347	353	359	367	63.3	9.6
Fort Pierce-Port St. Lucie, FL MSA	151	251	261	266	272	278	66.1	10.8
Fort Wayne, IN MSA	445	456	460	463	466	469	2.6	2.8
Fresno, CA MSA	578	756	785	805	823	835	30.8	10.5

See footnotes at end of table.

No. 43. Metropolitan Areas—Population: 1980 to 1994—Continued

[See headnote, page 40]

METROPOLITAN AREA	1980	1990 [1]	1991 (July)	1992 (July)	1993 (July)	1994 (July)	PERCENT CHANGE 1980-90	1990-94
Grand Rapids-Muskegon-Holland, MI MSA........	841	938	954	964	974	985	11.5	5.0
Greensboro—Winston-Salem—High Point, NC MSA .	951	1,050	1,066	1,078	1,092	1,107	10.5	5.4
Greenville-Spartanburg-Anderson, SC MSA	744	831	843	852	862	873	11.6	5.2
Harrisburg-Lebanon-Carlisle, PA MSA	556	588	596	601	605	610	5.7	3.7
Hartford, CT MSA	1,081	1,158	1,159	1,156	1,154	1,151	7.1	-0.5
Hickory-Morganton, NC MSA..................	270	292	296	298	302	306	8.1	4.6
Honolulu, HI MSA	763	836	849	861	867	874	9.7	4.6
Houston-Galveston-Brazoria, TX CMSA..........	3,118	3,731	3,854	3,950	4,028	4,099	19.6	9.9
Brazoria, TX PMSA......................	170	192	199	203	207	212	13.0	10.3
Galveston-Texas City, TX PMSA	196	217	223	227	232	235	11.1	8.0
Houston, TX PMSA.......................	2,753	3,322	3,433	3,520	3,589	3,653	20.7	10.0
Huntington-Ashland, WV-KY-OH MSA	336	313	314	315	316	316	-7.1	1.3
Huntsville, AL MSA	243	293	300	307	314	316	20.6	7.9
Indianapolis, IN MSA	1,306	1,380	1,406	1,424	1,443	1,462	5.7	5.9
Jackson, MS MSA...........................	362	395	399	404	407	412	9.2	4.2
Jacksonville, FL MSA........................	722	907	931	950	962	972	25.5	7.2
Johnson City-Kingsport-Bristol, TN-VA MSA	434	436	440	444	448	451	0.6	3.3
Kalamazoo-Battle Creek, MI MSA..............	421	429	433	436	440	443	2.1	3.1
Kansas City, MO-KS MSA....................	1,449	1,583	1,601	1,614	1,631	1,647	9.2	4.1
Killeen-Temple, TX MSA.....................	215	255	251	255	269	287	19.0	12.5
Knoxville, TN MSA..........................	546	586	598	610	620	631	7.2	7.7
Lafayette, LA MSA..........................	331	345	349	353	358	361	4.3	4.7
Lakeland-Winter Haven, FL MSA	322	405	413	419	423	430	26.0	6.0
Lancaster, PA MSA	362	423	430	434	439	443	16.7	4.7
Lansing-East Lansing, MI MSA.................	420	433	436	436	436	436	3.1	0.8
Las Vegas, NV-AZ MSA	528	853	927	967	1,010	1,076	61.5	26.2
Lexington, KY MSA	371	406	413	419	426	431	9.4	6.1
Little Rock-North Little Rock, AR MSA	474	513	519	525	533	538	8.1	4.8
Los Angeles-Riverside-Orange County, CA CMSA ...	11,498	14,532	14,823	15,063	15,210	15,302	26.4	5.3
Los Angeles-Long Beach, CA PMSA	7,477	8,863	8,960	9,068	9,134	9,150	18.5	3.2
Orange County, CA PMSA	1,933	2,411	2,447	2,486	2,515	2,543	24.7	5.5
Riverside-San Bernardino, CA PMSA..........	1,558	2,589	2,739	2,823	2,867	2,907	66.1	12.3
Ventura, CA PMSA.......................	529	669	677	687	694	703	26.4	5.0
Louisville, KY-IN MSA........................	954	949	958	966	974	981	-0.5	3.4
Macon, GA MSA	273	291	295	298	303	307	6.6	5.6
Madison, WI MSA	324	367	375	380	386	390	13.5	6.3
McAllen-Edinburg-Mission, TX MSA	283	384	402	421	443	461	35.4	20.2
Melbourne-Titusville-Palm Bay, FL MSA.........	273	399	415	425	436	443	46.2	11.2
Memphis, TN-AR-MS MSA	939	1,007	1,021	1,032	1,042	1,056	7.3	4.8
Miami-Fort Lauderdale, FL CMSA.............	2,644	3,193	3,266	3,317	3,354	3,408	20.8	6.7
Fort Lauderdale, FL PMSA.................	1,018	1,256	1,288	1,311	1,351	1,383	23.3	10.2
Miami, FL PMSA	1,626	1,937	1,978	2,006	2,003	2,025	19.2	4.5
Milwaukee-Racine, WI CMSA.................	1,570	1,607	1,620	1,629	1,634	1,637	2.4	1.9
Milwaukee-Waukesha, WI PMSA.............	1,397	1,432	1,443	1,450	1,454	1,456	2.5	1.6
Racine, WI PMSA........................	173	175	178	179	180	182	1.1	3.8
Minneapolis-St. Paul, MN-WI MSA	2,198	2,539	2,582	2,617	2,655	2,688	15.5	5.9
Mobile, AL MSA............................	444	477	485	494	505	512	7.5	7.4
Modesto, CA MSA..........................	266	371	386	395	402	407	39.3	9.8
Montgomery, AL MSA.......................	273	293	298	302	307	312	7.3	6.7
Nashville, TN MSA..........................	851	985	1,003	1,022	1,045	1,070	15.8	8.6
New London-Norwich, CT-RI MSA	273	291	290	284	284	285	6.5	-2.0
New Orleans, LA MSA	1,304	1,285	1,290	1,299	1,304	1,309	-1.5	1.8
New York-Northern New Jersey-Long Island, NY-NJ-CT-PA CMSA...................	18,906	19,550	19,586	19,652	19,738	19,796	3.4	1.3
Bergen-Passaic, NJ PMSA.................	1,293	1,279	1,282	1,290	1,298	1,304	-1.1	2.0
Bridgeport, CT PMSA	439	444	444	443	443	443	1.2	-0.2
Danbury, CT PMSA	175	194	195	196	198	199	10.3	2.7
Dutchess County, NY PMSA................	245	259	261	263	263	261	5.9	0.8
Jersey City, NJ PMSA....................	557	553	553	553	553	552	-0.7	-0.1
Middlesex-Somerset-Hunterdon, NJ PMSA	886	1,020	1,031	1,044	1,057	1,069	15.1	4.8
Monmouth-Ocean, NJ PMSA	849	986	998	1,010	1,023	1,035	16.1	4.9
Nassau-Suffolk, NY PMSA.................	2,606	2,609	2,617	2,631	2,643	2,652	0.1	1.6
New Haven-Meriden, CT PMSA	500	530	529	527	525	523	5.9	-1.4
New York, NY PMSA.....................	8,275	8,547	8,538	8,546	8,574	8,586	3.3	0.5
Newark, NJ PMSA	1,964	1,916	1,915	1,921	1,929	1,934	-2.4	0.9
Newburgh, NY-PA PMSA..................	278	336	343	348	353	356	20.8	6.1
Stamford-Norwalk, CT PMSA	326	330	331	330	331	332	1.3	0.6
Trenton, NJ PMSA	308	326	327	327	329	329	5.8	1.1
Waterbury, CT PMSA	205	222	223	222	222	221	8.1	-0.2
Norfolk-Virginia Beach-Newport News, VA-NC MSA ..	1,201	1,445	1,463	1,496	1,514	1,529	20.3	5.8
Oklahoma City, OK MSA.....................	861	959	969	982	996	1,007	11.4	5.1
Omaha, NE-IA MSA.........................	605	640	649	656	658	663	5.6	3.6
Orlando, FL MSA...........................	805	1,225	1,275	1,303	1,334	1,361	52.2	11.2
Pensacola, FL MSA.........................	290	344	352	360	365	371	18.9	7.7
Peoria-Pekin, IL MSA.......................	366	339	342	343	343	344	-7.3	1.3

See footnotes at end of table.

Population

No. 43. Metropolitan Areas—Population: 1980 to 1994—Continued

[See headnote, page 40]

METROPOLITAN AREA	1980	1990 [1]	1991 (July)	1992 (July)	1993 (July)	1994 (July)	PERCENT CHANGE 1980-90	PERCENT CHANGE 1990-94
Philadelphia-Wilmington-Atlantic City, PA-NJ-DE-MD CMSA	5,649	5,893	5,916	5,928	5,942	5,959	4.3	1.1
Atlantic-Cape May, NJ PMSA	276	319	324	327	328	330	15.6	3.3
Philadelphia, PA-NJ PMSA	4,781	4,922	4,930	4,933	4,940	4,949	2.9	0.5
Vineland-Millville-Bridgeton, NJ PMSA	133	138	139	139	139	139	3.9	0.5
Wilmington-Newark, DE-MD PMSA	459	513	523	529	535	541	11.9	5.5
Phoenix-Mesa, AZ MSA	1,600	2,238	2,285	2,333	2,392	2,473	39.9	10.5
Pittsburgh, PA MSA	2,571	2,395	2,399	2,405	2,407	2,402	-6.9	0.3
Portland-Salem, OR-WA CMSA	1,584	1,793	1,857	1,899	1,944	1,982	13.3	10.5
Portland-Vancouver, OR-WA PMSA	1,334	1,515	1,571	1,607	1,645	1,676	13.6	10.6
Salem, OR PMSA	250	278	286	293	300	306	11.3	10.0
Providence-Fall River-Warwick, RI-MA MSA	1,077	1,134	1,134	1,132	1,131	1,129	5.4	-0.5
Provo-Orem, UT MSA	218	264	269	276	283	291	20.9	10.4
Raleigh-Durham-Chapel Hill, NC MSA	665	858	888	911	938	965	29.1	12.4
Reading, PA MSA	313	337	341	343	346	348	7.7	3.3
Reno, NV MSA	194	255	262	268	275	283	31.5	11.1
Richmond-Petersburg, VA MSA	761	866	880	894	906	917	13.7	5.9
Rochester, NY MSA	1,031	1,062	1,072	1,082	1,089	1,091	3.1	2.6
Rockford, IL MSA	326	330	336	340	343	347	1.2	5.2
Sacramento-Yolo, CA CMSA	1,100	1,481	1,538	1,561	1,576	1,588	34.7	7.2
Sacramento, CA PMSA	986	1,340	1,395	1,416	1,431	1,441	35.8	7.6
Yolo, CA PMSA	113	141	143	145	146	146	24.6	3.7
Saginaw-Bay City-Midland, MI MSA	422	399	401	402	403	402	-5.3	0.7
St. Louis, MO-IL MSA	2,414	2,492	2,508	2,516	2,528	2,536	3.2	1.8
Salinas, CA MSA	290	356	363	369	366	352	22.5	-1.0
Salt Lake City-Ogden, UT MSA	910	1,072	1,100	1,127	1,154	1,178	17.8	9.9
San Antonio, TX MSA	1,089	1,325	1,349	1,377	1,407	1,437	21.7	8.5
San Diego, CA MSA	1,862	2,498	2,556	2,602	2,612	2,632	34.2	5.4
San Francisco-Oakland-San Jose, CA CMSA	5,368	6,250	6,335	6,410	6,469	6,513	16.4	4.2
Oakland, CA PMSA	1,762	2,080	2,117	2,148	2,169	2,182	18.1	4.9
San Francisco, CA PMSA	1,489	1,604	1,614	1,626	1,638	1,646	7.7	2.6
San Jose, CA PMSA	1,295	1,498	1,511	1,528	1,544	1,557	15.6	4.0
Santa Cruz-Watsonville, CA PMSA	188	230	229	231	233	235	22.1	2.3
Santa Rosa, CA PMSA	300	388	397	403	406	410	29.5	5.7
Vallejo-Fairfield-Napa, CA PMSA	334	450	467	474	479	483	34.6	7.2
Santa Barbara-Santa Maria-Lompoc, CA MSA	299	370	374	377	378	380	23.7	2.9
Sarasota-Bradenton, FL MSA	351	489	501	504	510	518	39.6	5.8
Savannah, GA MSA	231	258	262	267	272	276	11.8	6.9
Scranton—Wilkes-Barre—Hazleton, PA MSA	659	639	640	640	639	637	-3.2	-0.2
Seattle-Tacoma-Bremerton, WA CMSA	2,409	2,970	3,057	3,132	3,189	3,226	23.3	8.6
Bremerton, WA PMSA	147	190	200	211	215	220	28.9	16.2
Olympia, WA PMSA	124	161	170	177	183	187	29.8	16.1
Seattle-Bellevue-Everett, WA PMSA	1,652	2,033	2,082	2,125	2,159	2,180	23.1	7.2
Tacoma, WA PMSA	486	586	605	620	632	638	20.7	8.9
Shreveport-Bossier City, LA MSA	377	376	373	374	377	378	-0.1	0.5
South Bend, IN MSA	242	247	249	251	253	255	2.2	3.4
Spokane, WA MSA	342	361	372	382	391	396	5.7	9.6
Springfield, MO MSA	228	264	270	276	282	289	15.9	9.3
Springfield, MA MSA	570	588	585	583	582	580	3.2	-1.4
Stockton-Lodi, CA MSA	347	481	495	504	511	518	38.4	7.8
Syracuse, NY MSA	723	742	749	752	755	754	2.7	1.6
Tallahassee, FL MSA	190	234	240	245	250	253	22.7	8.5
Tampa-St. Petersburg-Clearwater, FL MSA	1,614	2,068	2,101	2,117	2,137	2,157	28.2	4.3
Toledo, OH MSA	617	614	614	614	614	614	-0.4	-
Tucson, AZ MSA	531	667	676	692	710	732	25.5	9.7
Tulsa, OK MSA	657	709	721	730	738	743	7.9	4.8
Utica-Rome, NY MSA	320	317	319	319	318	316	-1.1	-0.1
Visalia-Tulare-Porterville, CA MSA	246	312	323	331	338	343	26.9	10.0
Washington-Baltimore, DC-MD-VA-WV CMSA	5,791	6,726	6,829	6,908	6,980	7,051	16.2	4.8
Baltimore, MD PMSA	2,199	2,382	2,412	2,430	2,444	2,458	8.3	3.2
Hagerstown, MD PMSA	113	121	124	125	126	127	7.3	4.3
Washington, DC-MD-VA-WV PMSA	3,478	4,223	4,293	4,353	4,410	4,466	21.4	5.8
West Palm Beach-Boca Raton, FL MSA	577	864	890	909	932	955	49.7	10.5
Wichita, KS MSA	442	485	492	500	505	507	9.7	4.4
York, PA MSA	313	340	345	350	354	358	8.5	5.4
Youngstown-Warren, OH MSA	645	601	603	605	605	604	-6.8	0.5

- Represents or rounds to zero.   [1] The April 1, 1990, census count includes count resolution corrections processed through March 1994, and does not include adjustments for census coverage errors.

Source: U.S. Bureau of the Census, *1990 Census of Population and Housing, Supplementary Reports, Metropolitan Areas as Defined by the Office of Management and Budget, June 30, 1993* (CPH-S-1-1); *1990 Census of Population and Housing, Population and Housing Unit Counts* (CPH-2-1); computer diskette PE-23; and unpublished data.

No. 44. Urban and Rural Population, 1960 to 1990, and by State, 1990

[In thousands, except percent. As of April 1. Resident population]

REGION, DIVISION, AND STATE	Total	URBAN Number	URBAN Percent	Rural	REGION, DIVISION, AND STATE	Total	URBAN Number	URBAN Percent	Rural
1960	179,323	125,269	69.9	54,054	MD	4,781	3,888	81.3	893
1970	[1]203,212	149,647	73.6	53,565	DC	607	607	100.0	-
1980	[2]226,546	167,051	73.7	59,495	VA	6,187	4,293	69.4	1,894
1990, total .	[2]248,710	187,053	75.2	61,656	WV	1,793	648	36.1	1,145
Northeast.....	50,809	40,092	78.9	10,717	NC	6,629	3,338	50.4	3,291
N.E	13,207	9,829	74.4	3,378	SC	3,487	1,905	54.6	1,581
ME	1,228	548	44.6	680	GA	6,478	4,097	63.2	2,381
NH	1,109	566	51.0	544	FL	12,938	10,967	84.8	1,971
VT	563	181	32.2	382	E.S.C	15,176	8,531	56.2	6,646
MA	6,016	5,070	84.3	947	KY	3,685	1,910	51.8	1,775
RI	1,003	863	86.0	140	TN	4,877	2,970	60.9	1,907
CT	3,287	2,602	79.1	686	AL	4,041	2,440	60.4	1,601
M.A	37,602	30,263	80.5	7,340	MS	2,573	1,211	47.1	1,362
NY	17,990	15,164	84.3	2,826	W.S.C	26,703	19,894	74.5	6,808
NJ	7,730	6,910	89.4	820	AR	2,351	1,258	53.5	1,093
PA	11,882	8,188	68.9	3,693	LA	4,220	2,872	68.1	1,348
Midwest......	59,669	42,774	71.7	16,894	OK	3,146	2,130	67.7	1,015
E.N.C	42,009	31,074	74.0	10,935	TX	16,987	13,635	80.3	3,352
OH	10,847	8,039	74.1	2,808	West	52,786	45,531	86.3	7,255
IN	5,544	3,598	64.9	1,946	Mountain ...	13,659	10,881	79.7	2,777
IL	11,431	9,669	84.6	1,762	MT	799	420	52.5	379
MI	9,295	6,556	70.5	2,739	ID	1,007	578	57.4	429
WI	4,892	3,212	65.7	1,680	WY	454	295	65.0	159
W.N.C	17,660	11,700	66.3	5,959	CO	3,294	2,716	82.4	579
MN	4,375	3,056	69.9	1,319	NM	1,515	1,106	73.0	409
IA	2,777	1,683	60.6	1,094	AZ	3,665	3,207	87.5	458
MO	5,117	3,516	68.7	1,601	UT	1,723	1,499	87.0	224
ND	639	340	53.3	298	NV	1,202	1,061	88.3	140
SD	696	348	50.0	348	Pacific	39,127	34,650	88.6	4,477
NE	1,578	1,044	66.1	534	WA	4,867	3,718	76.4	1,149
KS	2,478	1,713	69.1	765	OR	2,842	2,003	70.5	839
South	85,446	58,656	68.6	26,790	CA	29,760	27,571	92.6	2,189
S.A	43,567	30,231	69.4	13,336	AK	550	371	67.5	179
DE	666	487	73.0	180	HI	1,108	986	89.0	122

- Represents zero. [1] The revised 1970 resident population count is 203,302,031; which incorporates changes due to errors found after tabulations were completed. [2] Total population count has been revised since the 1980 and 1990 censuses publications to 226,542,199 and 248,718,301, respectively.

Source: U.S. Bureau of the Census, *1990 Census of Population and Housing, Population and Housing Unit Counts* (1990 CPH-2).

No. 45. Incorporated Places, by Population Size: 1970 to 1994

POPULATION SIZE	NUMBER OF INCORPORATED PLACES				POPULATION (mil.)				PERCENT OF TOTAL			
	1970	1980	1990	1994	1970	1980	1990	1994	1970	1980	1990	1994
Total	18,666	19,097	19,262	19,314	131.9	140.3	152.9	160.7	100.0	100.0	100.0	100.0
1,000,000 or more ...	6	6	8	8	18.8	17.5	20.0	20.0	14.2	12.5	13.0	12.4
500,000 to 999,999 ...	20	16	15	16	13.0	10.9	10.1	10.8	9.8	7.8	6.6	6.7
250,000 to 499,999 ...	30	33	41	41	10.5	11.8	14.2	14.8	7.9	8.4	9.3	9.2
100,000 to 249,999 ...	97	114	131	144	13.9	16.6	19.1	21.1	10.5	11.8	12.5	13.1
50,000 to 99,999	232	250	309	343	16.2	17.6	21.2	23.4	12.2	12.3	13.9	14.6
25,000 to 49,999	455	526	567	588	15.7	18.4	20.0	20.6	11.9	13.1	13.0	12.8
10,000 to 24,999	1,127	1,260	1,290	1,372	17.6	19.8	20.3	21.5	13.3	14.1	13.3	13.4
Under 10,000	16,699	16,892	16,901	16,802	26.4	28.0	28.2	28.6	20.0	20.0	18.4	17.8

Source: U..S. Bureau of the Census, *Census of Population: 1970* and *1980*, vol. I, *1990 Census of Population and Housing, Population and Housing Unit Counts* (CPH-2-1); computer diskette PE-28; and unpublished data.

No. 46. Cities With 100,000 or More Inhabitants in 1994—Population, 1980 to 1994, and Land Area, 1990

[Population: As of April 1; except 1994, as of July 1. Data refer to boundaries in effect on January 1, 1990. Minus sign (-) indicates decrease]

CITY	1980, total (1,000)	POPULATION 1990					POPULATION 1994			Land area, 1990 (square miles)
		Total (1,000)	Percent—				Total (1,000)	Rank	Percent change, 1990-94	
			Black	American Indian, Eskimo, Aleut	Asian, Pacific Islander	His- panic [1]				
Abilene, TX	98	107	7.0	0.4	1.3	15.5	110	182	3.1	103.1
Akron, OH	237	223	24.5	0.3	1.2	0.7	222	75	-0.5	62.2
Albany, NY	102	100	20.6	0.3	2.3	3.1	105	195	4.8	21.4
Albuquerque, NM	332	385	3.0	3.0	1.7	34.5	412	36	7.1	132.2
Alexandria, VA	103	111	21.9	0.3	4.2	9.7	113	174	1.5	15.3
Allentown, PA	104	105	5.0	0.2	1.3	11.7	105	193	(Z)	17.7
Amarillo, TX	149	158	6.0	0.8	1.9	14.7	165	110	4.7	87.9
Anaheim, CA	219	266	2.5	0.5	9.4	31.4	282	58	5.9	44.3
Anchorage, AK	174	226	6.4	6.4	4.8	4.1	254	64	12.1	1,697.6
Ann Arbor, MI	108	110	9.0	0.4	7.7	2.6	109	186	-0.7	25.9
Arlington, TX [2]	160	262	8.4	0.5	3.9	8.9	287	56	9.6	93.0
Arlington, VA [2]	153	171	10.5	0.3	6.8	13.5	175	105	2.2	25.9
Atlanta, GA	425	394	67.1	0.1	0.9	1.9	396	37	0.5	131.8
Aurora, CO	159	222	11.4	0.6	3.8	6.6	251	65	12.9	132.5
Aurora, IL	81	100	11.9	0.2	1.3	23.0	112	176	12.8	33.5
Austin, TX	346	466	12.4	0.4	3.0	23.0	514	23	10.4	217.8
Bakersfield, CA	106	175	9.4	1.1	3.6	20.5	191	89	9.2	91.8
Baltimore, MD	787	736	59.2	0.3	1.1	1.0	703	14	-4.5	80.8
Baton Rouge, LA	220	220	43.9	0.1	1.7	1.6	227	72	3.6	73.9
Beaumont, TX	118	114	41.3	0.2	1.7	4.3	115	168	0.6	80.1
Birmingham, AL	284	265	63.3	0.1	0.6	(Z)	265	61	-0.3	148.5
Boise City, ID	102	126	0.6	0.6	1.6	2.7	146	126	16.3	46.1
Boston, MA	563	574	25.6	0.3	5.3	10.8	548	21	-4.6	48.4
Bridgeport, CT	143	142	26.6	0.3	2.3	26.5	133	144	-6.2	16.0
Brownsville, TX	85	99	0.2	0.1	0.3	90.1	113	173	14.1	27.9
Buffalo, NY	358	328	30.7	0.8	1.0	4.9	313	53	-4.6	40.6
Cedar Rapids, IA	110	109	2.9	0.2	1.0	1.1	113	172	4.3	53.5
Chandler, AZ	30	90	2.6	1.2	2.4	17.3	119	159	32.7	47.6
Charlotte, NC	315	396	31.8	0.4	1.8	1.4	438	32	10.6	174.3
Chattanooga, TN	170	152	33.7	0.2	1.0	0.6	152	118	-0.1	118.4
Chesapeake, VA	114	152	27.4	0.3	1.2	1.3	181	98	18.8	340.7
Chicago, IL	3,005	2,784	39.1	0.3	3.7	19.6	2,732	3	-1.9	227.2
Chula Vista, CA	84	135	4.6	0.6	8.9	37.3	149	122	10.4	29.0
Cincinnati, OH	385	364	37.9	0.2	1.1	0.7	358	46	-1.6	77.2
Cleveland, OH	574	506	46.6	0.3	1.0	4.6	493	26	-2.5	77.0
Colorado Springs, CO	215	280	7.0	0.8	2.4	9.1	316	51	12.9	183.2
Columbia, SC [3]	101	103	43.7	0.3	1.4	2.0	104	197	0.6	117.1
Columbus, GA [3]	169	179	38.1	0.3	1.4	3.0	186	92	4.4	216.1
Columbus, OH	565	633	22.6	0.2	2.4	1.1	636	16	0.5	190.9
Concord, CA	104	111	2.4	0.7	8.7	11.5	112	177	0.5	29.5
Corpus Christi, TX	232	257	4.8	0.4	0.9	50.4	275	59	7.0	135.0
Dallas, TX	905	1,008	29.5	0.5	2.2	20.9	1,023	8	1.5	342.4
Dayton, OH	194	182	40.4	0.2	0.6	0.7	179	100	-1.9	55.0
Denver, CO	493	468	12.8	1.2	2.4	23.0	494	25	5.5	153.3
Des Moines, IA	191	193	7.1	0.4	2.4	2.4	194	86	0.4	75.3
Detroit, MI	1,203	1,028	75.7	0.4	0.8	2.8	992	10	-3.5	138.7
Durham, NC	101	137	45.7	0.2	2.0	1.2	143	131	5.0	69.3
Elizabeth, NJ	106	110	19.8	0.3	2.7	39.1	106	190	-3.4	12.3
El Monte, CA	79	106	1.0	0.6	11.8	72.5	105	196	-1.4	9.5
El Paso, TX	425	515	3.4	0.4	1.2	69.0	579	19	12.4	245.4
Erie, PA	119	109	12.0	0.2	0.5	2.4	108	187	-0.3	22.0
Escondido, CA	64	109	1.5	0.8	3.7	23.4	116	165	7.1	35.6
Eugene, OR	106	113	1.3	0.9	3.5	2.7	118	161	4.8	38.0
Evansville, IN	130	126	9.5	0.2	0.6	0.6	129	145	2.5	40.7
Flint, MI	160	141	47.9	0.7	0.5	2.9	138	140	-2.0	33.8
Fontana, CA	37	88	8.7	0.9	4.5	36.1	104	198	18.5	35.6
Fort Lauderdale, FL	153	149	28.1	0.2	0.9	7.2	163	112	9.1	31.4
Fort Wayne, IN	172	184	16.7	0.3	1.0	2.7	183	95	-0.5	62.7
Fort Worth, TX	385	448	22.0	0.4	2.0	19.5	452	29	0.9	281.1
Fremont, CA	132	173	3.8	0.7	19.4	13.3	184	93	5.9	77.0
Fresno, CA	217	354	8.3	1.1	12.5	29.9	387	38	9.2	99.1
Fullerton, CA	102	114	2.2	0.5	12.2	21.3	117	163	2.4	22.1
Garden Grove, CA	123	143	1.5	0.6	20.5	23.5	148	124	3.5	17.9
Garland, TX	139	181	8.9	0.5	4.5	11.6	194	84	7.5	57.3
Gary, IN	152	117	80.6	0.2	0.2	5.7	114	170	-2.0	50.2
Glendale, AZ	97	148	3.0	0.9	2.1	15.5	168	108	13.9	52.2
Glendale, CA	139	180	1.3	0.3	14.1	21.0	178	101	-0.9	30.6
Grand Prairie, TX	71	100	9.7	0.8	3.0	20.5	109	185	9.3	68.5
Grand Rapids, MI	182	189	18.5	0.8	1.1	5.0	190	90	0.7	44.3
Green Bay, WI	88	96	0.5	2.5	2.3	1.1	103	203	6.5	43.8
Greensboro, NC	156	184	33.9	0.5	1.4	1.0	196	80	6.7	79.8

See footnotes at end of table.

No. 46. Cities With 100,000 or More Inhabitants in 1994—Population, 1980 to 1994, and Land Area, 1990—Continued

[See headnote, p. 44]

		POPULATION								Land area, 1990 (square miles)
		1990						1994		
CITY	1980, total (1,000)	Total (1,000)	Percent—				Total (1,000)	Rank	Per-cent change, 1990-94	
			Black	American Indian, Eskimo, Aleut	Asian, Pacific Islander	His-panic [1]				
Hampton, VA	123	134	38.9	0.3	1.7	2.0	140	136	4.3	51.8
Hartford, CT	136	140	38.9	0.3	1.4	31.6	124	151	-11.1	17.3
Hayward, CA	94	111	9.8	1.0	15.5	23.9	116	167	3.8	43.5
Henderson, NV	24	65	2.7	1.0	2.0	8.1	102	205	57.0	71.5
Hialeah, FL	145	188	1.9	0.1	0.5	87.6	194	85	3.3	19.2
Hollywood, FL	121	122	8.5	0.2	1.3	11.9	125	150	2.7	27.3
Honolulu, HI [4]	365	377	1.3	0.3	70.5	4.6	386	39	2.3	85.7
Houston, TX	1,595	1,631	28.1	0.3	4.1	27.6	1,702	4	4.4	539.9
Huntington Beach, CA	171	182	0.9	0.6	8.3	11.2	189	91	4.2	26.4
Huntsville, AL	143	160	24.4	0.5	2.1	1.2	160	113	0.3	164.4
Independence, MO	112	112	1.4	0.6	1.0	2.0	112	178	-0.6	78.2
Indianapolis, IN [3]	701	731	22.6	0.2	0.9	1.1	752	12	2.9	361.7
Inglewood, CA	94	110	51.9	0.4	2.5	38.5	110	181	0.4	9.2
Irvine, CA	62	110	1.8	0.2	18.1	6.3	126	148	13.9	42.3
Irving, TX	110	155	7.5	0.6	4.6	16.3	165	111	6.4	67.6
Jackson, MS	203	197	55.7	0.1	0.5	0.4	193	87	-1.8	109.0
Jacksonville, FL [3]	541	635	25.2	0.3	1.9	2.6	665	15	4.7	758.7
Jersey City, NJ	224	229	29.7	0.3	11.4	24.2	226	73	-1.1	14.9
Kansas City, KS	161	150	29.3	0.7	1.2	7.1	143	133	-4.8	107.8
Kansas City, MO	448	435	29.6	0.5	1.2	3.9	444	31	2.1	311.5
Knoxville, TN	175	165	15.8	0.2	1.0	0.7	169	107	2.6	77.2
Lafayette, LA	81	97	27.2	0.2	1.3	1.7	102	204	5.0	40.9
Lakewood, CO	114	126	1.0	0.7	1.9	9.1	126	147	-0.4	40.8
Lancaster, CA	48	97	7.4	0.9	3.7	15.2	119	160	22.5	88.8
Lansing, MI	130	127	18.6	1.0	1.8	7.9	120	156	-6.1	33.9
Laredo, TX	91	123	0.1	0.2	0.4	93.9	150	120	22.0	32.9
Las Vegas, NV	165	258	11.4	0.9	3.6	12.5	328	49	27.0	83.3
Lexington-Fayette, KY	204	225	13.4	0.2	1.6	1.1	238	69	5.4	284.5
Lincoln, NE	172	192	2.4	0.6	1.7	2.0	203	77	5.8	63.3
Little Rock, AR	159	176	34.0	0.3	0.9	0.8	178	102	1.4	102.9
Livonia, MI	105	101	0.3	0.2	1.3	1.3	100	209	-0.4	35.7
Long Beach, CA	361	429	13.7	0.6	13.6	23.6	434	34	1.1	50.0
Los Angeles, CA	2,969	3,486	14.0	0.5	9.8	39.9	3,449	2	-1.1	469.3
Louisville, KY	299	270	29.7	0.2	0.7	0.7	270	60	0.3	62.1
Lubbock, TX	174	186	8.6	0.3	1.4	22.5	194	83	4.4	104.1
Macon, GA	117	107	52.2	0.1	0.4	0.6	109	183	1.7	47.9
Madison, WI	171	191	4.2	0.4	3.9	2.0	195	82	2.0	57.8
Memphis, TN	646	619	54.8	0.2	0.8	0.7	614	18	-0.7	256.0
Mesa, AZ	152	289	1.9	1.0	1.5	10.9	314	52	8.5	108.6
Mesquite, TX	67	101	5.8	0.5	2.6	8.8	114	171	12.0	42.8
Miami, FL	347	359	27.4	0.2	0.6	62.5	373	42	4.0	35.6
Milwaukee, WI	636	628	30.5	0.9	1.9	6.3	617	17	-1.8	96.1
Minneapolis, MN	371	368	13.0	3.3	4.3	2.1	355	47	-3.7	54.9
Mobile, AL	200	196	38.9	0.2	1.0	1.0	204	76	4.2	118.0
Modesto, CA	107	165	2.7	1.0	7.9	16.3	195	81	4.2	30.2
Montgomery, AL	178	188	42.3	0.2	0.7	0.8	176	104	7.0	135.0
Moreno Valley, CA	(5)	119	13.8	0.7	6.6	22.9	139	137	17.3	49.1
Naperville, IL	43	86	2.1	0.1	4.8	1.8	101	206	17.9	27.9
Nashville-Davidson, TN [3]	456	488	24.3	0.2	1.4	0.9	505	24	3.3	473.3
Newark, NJ	329	275	58.5	0.2	1.2	26.1	259	63	-6.0	23.8
New Haven, CT	126	130	36.1	0.3	2.4	13.2	120	155	-8.3	18.9
New Orleans, LA	558	497	61.9	0.2	1.9	3.5	484	27	-2.6	180.6
Newport News, VA	145	171	33.6	0.3	2.3	2.8	179	99	4.5	68.3
New York, NY	7,072	7,323	28.7	0.4	7.0	24.4	7,333	1	0.1	308.9
Norfolk, VA	267	261	39.1	0.4	2.6	2.9	241	67	-7.6	53.8
Norwalk, CA	85	94	3.2	0.9	12.4	47.9	101	207	6.9	9.8
Oakland, CA	339	372	43.9	0.6	14.8	13.9	367	44	-1.4	56.1
Oceanside, CA	77	128	7.9	0.7	6.1	22.6	146	125	14.2	40.7
Oklahoma City, OK	404	445	16.0	4.2	2.4	5.0	463	28	4.2	608.2
Omaha, NE	314	336	13.1	0.7	1.0	3.1	345	48	2.8	100.6
Ontario, CA	89	133	7.3	0.7	3.9	41.7	135	141	1.2	36.7
Orange, CA	91	111	1.4	0.5	7.9	22.8	117	164	5.5	23.3
Orlando, FL	128	165	26.9	0.3	1.6	8.7	177	103	7.5	67.3
Overland Park, KS	82	112	1.8	0.3	1.9	2.0	125	149	12.0	55.7
Oxnard, CA	108	143	5.2	0.8	8.6	54.4	146	127	2.3	24.4
Palmdale, CA	12	70	6.4	0.9	4.4	22.0	103	201	47.2	77.6
Pasadena, CA	118	132	19.0	0.4	8.1	27.3	134	142	2.0	23.0
Pasadena, TX	113	120	1.0	0.5	1.6	28.8	129	146	8.1	43.8
Paterson, NJ	138	141	36.0	0.3	1.4	41.0	138	138	-1.8	8.4
Peoria, IL	124	114	20.9	0.2	1.7	1.6	113	175	-0.6	40.9
Philadelphia, PA	1,688	1,586	39.9	0.2	2.7	5.6	1,524	5	-3.9	135.1
Phoenix, AZ	790	984	5.2	1.9	1.7	20.0	1,049	7	6.6	419.9
Pittsburgh, PA	424	370	25.8	0.2	1.6	0.9	359	45	-3.0	55.6

See footnotes at end of table.

Population

No. 46. Cities With 100,000 or More Inhabitants in 1994—Population, 1980 to 1994, and Land Area, 1990—Continued

[See headnote, p. 44]

CITY	1980, total (1,000)	POPULATION 1990 Total (1,000)	Percent— Black	Percent— American Indian, Eskimo, Aleut	Percent— Asian, Pacific Islander	Percent— Hispanic [1]	1994 Total (1,000)	1994 Rank	Percent change, 1990-94	Land area, 1990 (square miles)
Plano, TX	72	128	4.1	0.3	4.0	6.2	157	115	23.1	66.2
Pomona, CA	93	132	14.4	0.6	6.7	51.3	144	130	9.2	22.8
Portland, OR	368	439	7.7	1.2	5.3	3.2	451	30	2.7	124.7
Portsmouth, VA	105	104	47.3	0.3	0.8	1.3	103	200	-0.4	33.1
Providence, RI	157	161	14.8	0.9	5.9	15.5	151	119	-6.3	18.5
Pueblo, CO	102	99	2.2	0.8	0.6	39.5	100	208	1.9	35.9
Raleigh, NC	150	212	27.6	0.3	2.5	1.4	237	70	11.6	88.1
Rancho Cucamonga, CA	55	101	5.9	0.6	5.4	20.0	115	169	13.2	37.8
Reno, NV	101	134	2.9	1.4	4.9	11.1	145	128	8.4	57.5
Richmond, VA	219	203	55.2	0.2	0.9	0.9	201	78	-0.8	60.1
Riverside, CA	171	227	7.4	0.8	5.2	26.0	242	66	6.7	77.7
Rochester, NY	242	230	31.5	0.5	1.8	8.7	231	71	0.4	35.8
Rockford, IL	140	140	15.0	0.3	1.5	4.2	143	132	2.3	45.0
Sacramento, CA	276	369	15.3	1.2	15.0	16.2	374	41	1.2	96.3
St. Louis, MO	453	397	47.5	0.2	0.9	1.3	368	43	-7.2	61.9
St. Paul, MN	270	272	7.4	1.4	7.1	4.2	262	62	-3.7	52.8
St. Petersburg, FL	239	240	19.6	0.2	1.7	2.6	239	68	-0.7	59.2
Salem, OR	89	108	1.5	1.6	2.4	6.1	116	166	7.5	41.5
Salinas, CA	80	109	3.0	0.9	8.1	50.6	120	154	10.1	18.6
Salt Lake City, UT	163	160	1.7	1.6	4.7	9.7	172	106	7.5	109.0
San Antonio, TX	786	935	7.0	0.4	1.1	55.6	999	9	6.8	333.0
San Bernardino, CA	119	164	16.0	1.0	4.0	34.6	182	97	10.7	55.1
San Diego, CA	876	1,111	9.4	0.6	11.8	20.7	1,152	6	3.7	324.0
San Francisco, CA	679	724	10.9	0.5	29.1	13.9	735	13	1.5	46.7
San Jose, CA	629	782	4.7	0.7	19.5	26.6	817	11	4.4	171.3
Santa Ana, CA	204	294	2.6	0.5	9.7	65.2	291	55	-1.0	27.1
Santa Clarita, CA	([5])	118	1.5	0.6	4.2	13.4	124	152	4.7	40.5
Santa Rosa, CA	83	113	1.8	1.2	3.4	9.5	117	162	3.3	33.7
Savannah, GA	142	138	51.3	0.2	1.1	1.4	141	135	2.0	62.6
Scottsdale, AZ	89	130	0.8	0.6	1.2	4.8	152	117	17.2	184.4
Seattle, WA	494	516	10.1	1.4	11.8	3.6	521	22	0.9	83.9
Shreveport, LA	206	199	44.8	0.2	0.5	1.1	197	79	-0.8	98.6
Simi Valley, CA	78	100	1.5	0.6	5.5	12.7	107	189	6.7	33.0
Sioux Falls, SD	81	101	0.7	1.6	0.7	0.6	109	184	8.3	45.1
South Bend, IN	110	106	20.9	0.4	0.9	3.4	105	194	-0.4	36.4
Spokane, WA	171	177	1.9	2.0	2.1	2.1	193	88	8.8	55.9
Springfield, IL	100	105	13.0	0.2	1.0	0.8	106	191	0.5	42.5
Springfield, MA	152	157	19.2	0.2	1.0	16.9	149	123	-5.0	32.1
Springfield, MO	133	140	2.5	0.7	0.9	1.0	150	121	6.6	68.0
Stamford, CT	102	108	17.8	0.1	2.6	9.8	107	188	-0.8	37.7
Sterling Heights, MI	109	118	0.4	0.2	2.9	1.1	120	158	1.4	36.6
Stockton, CA	150	211	9.6	1.0	22.8	25.0	223	74	5.5	52.6
Sunnyvale, CA	107	117	3.4	0.5	19.3	13.2	120	157	1.9	21.9
Syracuse, NY	170	164	20.3	1.3	2.2	2.9	160	114	-2.4	25.1
Tacoma, WA	159	177	11.4	2.0	6.9	3.8	183	96	3.6	48.0
Tallahassee, FL	82	125	29.1	0.2	1.8	3.0	134	143	7.2	63.3
Tampa, FL	272	280	25.0	0.3	1.4	15.0	286	57	2.0	108.7
Tempe, AZ	107	142	3.2	1.3	4.1	10.9	144	129	1.6	39.5
Thousand Oaks, CA	77	104	1.2	0.4	4.8	9.6	111	180	6.3	49.6
Toledo, OH	355	333	19.7	0.3	1.0	4.0	323	50	-3.1	80.6
Topeka, KS	119	120	10.6	1.3	0.8	5.8	121	153	0.6	55.2
Torrance, CA	130	133	1.5	0.4	21.9	10.1	138	139	3.8	20.5
Tucson, AZ	331	409	4.3	1.6	2.2	29.3	435	33	6.4	156.3
Tulsa, OK	361	367	13.6	4.7	1.4	2.6	375	40	2.1	183.5
Vallejo, CA	80	109	21.2	0.7	23.0	10.8	111	179	2.1	30.2
Virginia Beach, VA	262	393	13.9	0.4	4.3	3.1	430	35	9.5	248.3
Waco, TX	101	104	23.1	0.3	0.9	16.3	106	192	2.2	75.8
Warren, MI	161	145	0.7	0.5	1.3	1.1	143	134	-1.5	34.3
Washington, DC	638	607	65.8	0.2	1.8	5.4	567	20	-6.6	61.4
Waterbury, CT	103	109	13.0	0.3	0.7	13.4	104	199	-5.0	28.6
West Covina, CA	80	96	8.5	0.5	17.2	34.6	103	202	7.3	16.2
Wichita, KS	280	304	11.3	1.2	2.6	5.0	310	54	2.0	115.1
Winston-Salem, NC	132	151	39.3	0.2	0.8	0.9	155	116	2.8	71.1
Worcester, MA	162	170	4.5	0.3	2.8	9.6	165	109	-2.6	37.6
Yonkers, NY	195	188	14.1	0.2	3.0	16.7	183	94	-2.4	18.1

Z Less than .05 percent. [1] Hispanic persons may be of any race. [2] Data are for Arlington CDP (census designated place) which is not incorporated as a city but is recognized for census purposes as a large urban place. Arlington CDP is coextensive with Arlington County. [3] Represents the portion of a consolidated city that is not within one or more separately incorporated places. [4] The population shown in this table is for the CDP; the 1990 census population for the City and County of Honolulu is 836,231. [5] Not incorporated.

Source: U.S. Bureau of the Census, *1980 Census of Population*, vol. 1, chapters A and B; *1990 Census of Population and Housing, Population and Housing Unit Counts*, (CPH-2) and *General Population Characteristics*, (CP-1); and Internet site http://www.census.gov/ftp/pub/population/www/ (accessed 15 March 1996).

No. 47. Population 65 Years Old and Over, by Age Group and Sex, 1980 to 1995, and Projections, 2000

[As of **April**, except **1995** and **2000**, as of **July**. Projection based on middle series, see table 3]

AGE GROUP AND SEX	NUMBER (1,000)				PERCENT DISTRIBUTION			
	1980	1990 [1]	1995	2000, proj.	1980	1990 [1]	1995	2000, proj.
Persons 65 yrs. and over	25,549	31,080	33,532	34,709	100	100	100	100
65 to 69 years old	8,782	10,066	9,928	9,410	34	32	30	27
70 to 74 years old	6,798	7,980	8,831	8,726	27	26	26	25
75 to 79 years old	4,794	6,103	6,681	7,415	19	20	20	21
80 to 84 years old	2,935	3,909	4,464	4,900	12	13	13	14
85 years old and over	2,240	3,022	3,628	4,259	9	10	11	12
Males, 65 yrs. and over..........	10,305	12,493	13,689	14,346	100	100	100	100
65 to 69 years old...............	3,903	4,508	4,506	4,321	38	36	33	30
70 to 74 years old...............	2,854	3,399	3,836	3,859	28	27	28	27
75 to 79 years old...............	1,848	2,389	2,720	3,092	18	19	20	22
80 to 84 years old...............	1,019	1,356	1,609	1,846	10	11	12	13
85 years old and over	682	841	1,017	1,228	7	7	7	9
Females, 65 yrs. and over	15,245	18,587	19,844	20,364	100	100	100	100
65 to 69 years old...............	4,880	5,558	5,422	5,089	32	30	27	25
70 to 74 years old...............	3,945	4,580	4,995	4,867	26	25	25	24
75 to 79 years old...............	2,946	3,714	3,961	4,323	19	20	20	21
80 to 84 years old...............	1,916	2,553	2,854	3,055	13	14	14	15
85 years old and over	1,559	2,180	2,611	3,031	10	12	13	15

[1] The April 1, 1990, census count (248,718,291) includes count resolution corrections processed through March 1994, and does not include adjustments for census coverage errors.

Source: U.S. Bureau of the Census, *Current Population Reports*, P25-1095 and P25-1130; and Population Paper Listing 41.

No. 48. Persons 65 Years Old and Over—Characteristics, by Sex: 1980 to 1995

[As of **March, except as noted.** Covers civilian noninstitutional population. See headnote, table 49]

CHARACTERISTIC	TOTAL				MALE				FEMALE			
	1980	1985	1990	1995	1980	1985	1990	1995	1980	1985	1990	1995
Total [1] (million)	24.2	26.8	29.6	31.3	9.9	11.0	12.3	13.0	14.2	15.8	17.2	18.3
White (million)	21.9	24.2	26.5	28.0	9.0	9.9	11.0	11.7	12.9	14.3	15.4	16.3
Black (million)	2.0	2.2	2.5	2.6	0.8	0.9	1.0	1.0	1.2	1.3	1.5	1.6
Percent below poverty level [2]	15.2	12.4	11.4	11.7	11.1	8.7	7.8	7.2	17.9	15.0	13.9	14.9
PERCENT DISTRIBUTION												
Marital status:												
Single......................	5.5	5.2	4.6	4.2	4.9	5.3	4.2	4.2	5.9	5.1	4.9	4.2
Married.....................	55.4	55.2	56.1	56.9	78.0	77.2	76.5	77.0	39.5	39.9	41.4	42.5
Spouse present.............	53.6	53.4	54.1	54.7	76.1	75.0	74.2	74.5	37.9	38.3	39.7	40.6
Spouse absent	1.8	1.8	2.0	2.2	1.9	2.2	2.3	2.5	1.7	1.6	1.7	1.9
Widowed....................	35.7	35.6	34.2	33.2	13.5	13.8	14.2	13.5	51.2	50.7	48.6	47.3
Divorced	3.5	4.0	5.0	5.7	3.6	3.7	5.0	5.2	3.4	4.3	5.1	6.0
Family status:												
In families [3]	67.6	67.3	66.7	66.6	83.0	82.4	81.9	80.6	56.8	56.7	55.8	56.7
Nonfamily householders.........	31.2	31.1	31.9	32.4	15.7	15.4	16.6	18.4	42.0	42.1	42.8	42.4
Secondary individuals	1.2	1.6	1.4	1.0	1.3	2.2	1.5	1.0	1.1	1.1	1.4	0.9
Living arrangements:												
Living in household	99.8	99.6	99.7	99.9	99.9	99.5	99.9	100.0	99.7	99.6	99.5	99.9
Living alone	30.3	30.2	31.0	31.5	14.9	14.7	15.7	17.3	41.0	41.1	42.0	41.7
Spouse present.............	53.6	53.4	54.1	54.7	76.1	75.0	74.3	74.5	37.9	38.3	39.7	40.6
Living with someone else	15.9	15.9	14.6	13.7	8.9	9.8	9.9	8.1	20.8	20.2	17.8	17.6
Not in household [4]	0.2	0.4	0.3	0.1	0.1	0.5	0.1	-	0.3	0.4	0.5	0.1
Years of school completed:												
8 years or less...............	43.1	35.4	28.5	21.0	45.3	37.2	30.0	22.0	41.6	34.1	27.5	20.3
1 to 3 years of high school	16.2	16.5	16.1	[5]15.2	15.2	15.5	15.7	[5]14.5	16.7	17.0	16.4	[5]15.6
4 years of high school	24.0	29.0	32.9	[6]33.8	21.4	26.4	29.0	[6]29.2	25.8	30.7	35.6	[6]37.1
1 to 3 years of college	8.2	9.8	10.9	[7]17.1	7.5	9.1	10.8	[7]17.1	8.6	10.3	11.0	[7]17.0
4 years or more of college	8.6	9.4	11.6	[8]13.0	10.3	11.5	14.5	[8]17.2	7.4	8.0	9.5	[8]9.9
Labor force participation: [9]												
Employed	12.2	10.4	11.5	11.7	18.4	15.3	15.9	16.1	7.8	7.0	8.4	8.5
Unemployed	0.4	0.3	0.4	0.5	0.6	0.5	0.5	0.7	0.3	0.2	0.3	0.3
Not in labor force	87.5	89.2	88.1	87.9	81.0	84.2	83.6	83.2	91.9	92.7	91.3	91.2

- Represents zero. [1] Includes other races, not shown separately. [2] Poverty status based on income in preceding year. [3] Excludes those living in unrelated subfamilies. [4] In group quarters other than institutions. [5] Represents those who completed ninth to twelfth grade, but have no high school diploma. [6] High school graduate. [7] Some college or associate degree. [8] Bachelor's or advanced degree. [9] Annual averages of monthly figures. Source: U.S. Bureau of Labor Statistics, *Employment and Earnings*, January issues. Data beginning 1994 not directly comparable with earlier years. See text, section 13, and February 1994 and March 1996 issues of *Employment and Earnings*.

Source: Except as noted, U.S. Bureau of the Census, *Current Population Reports*, P20-450, and earlier reports; P60-189; and unpublished data.

No. 49. Social and Economic Characteristics of the White and Black Populations: 1980 to 1995

[As of **March, except labor force status, annual average.** Excludes members of Armed Forces except those living off post or with their families on post. Data for 1980 and 1990 are based on 1980 census population controls; 1995 data based on 1990 census population controls. Based on Current Population Survey; see text, section 1, and Appendix III]

CHARACTERISTIC	NUMBER (1,000)						PERCENT DISTRIBUTION			
	White			Black			White		Black	
	1980	1990	1995	1980	1990	1995	1980	1995	1980	1995
Total persons	191,905	206,983	216,751	26,033	30,392	33,531	100.0	100.0	100.0	100.0
Under 5 years old	13,307	15,161	15,915	2,444	2,932	3,342	6.9	7.3	9.4	10.0
5 to 14 years old	28,828	28,405	30,786	5,190	5,546	6,268	15.0	14.2	19.9	18.7
15 to 44 years old	88,570	96,656	97,876	12,247	14,660	16,101	46.2	45.2	47.0	48.0
45 to 64 years old	39,302	40,282	44,189	4,112	4,766	5,264	20.5	20.4	15.8	15.7
65 years old and over.	21,898	26,479	27,985	2,040	2,487	2,557	11.4	12.9	7.8	7.6
YEARS OF SCHOOL COMPLETED										
Persons 25 years old and over	114,763	134,687	141,113	12,927	16,751	18,457	100.0	100.0	100.0	100.0
Elementary: 0 to 8 years	18,739	14,131	11,101	3,559	2,701	1,800	16.3	7.9	27.5	9.8
High school: 1 to 3 years	15,064	14,080	[1]12,882	2,748	2,969	[1]3,041	13.1	[1]9.1	21.3	[1]16.5
4 years	43,149	52,449	[2]47,986	3,980	6,239	[2]6,686	37.6	[2]34.0	30.8	[2]36.2
College: 1 to 3 years	17,350	24,350	[3]35,321	1,618	2,952	[3]4,486	15.1	[3]25.0	12.5	[3]24.3
4 years or more.	20,460	29,677	[4]33,824	1,024	1,890	[4]2,444	17.8	[4]24.0	7.9	[4]13.2
LABOR FORCE STATUS [5]										
Civilians 16 years old and over	146,122	160,415	166,914	17,824	21,300	23,246	100.0	100.0	100.0	100.0
Civilian labor force	93,600	107,177	111,950	10,865	13,493	14,817	64.1	67.1	61.0	63.7
Employed	87,715	102,087	106,490	9,313	11,966	13,279	60.0	63.8	52.2	57.1
Unemployed	5,884	5,091	5,459	1,553	1,527	1,538	4.0	3.3	8.7	6.6
Unemployment rate [6]	6.3	4.7	4.9	14.3	11.3	10.4	(X)	(X)	(X)	(X)
Not in labor force	52,523	53,237	54,965	6,959	7,808	8,429	35.9	32.9	39.0	36.3
FAMILY TYPE										
Total families . . . . [7] . . .	52,243	56,590	58,437	6,184	7,470	8,093	100.0	100.0	100.0	100.0
With own children [7] . . .	26,474	26,718	27,951	3,820	4,378	4,682	50.7	47.8	61.8	57.9
Married couple	44,751	46,981	47,899	3,433	3,750	3,842	85.7	82.0	55.5	47.5
With own children [7].	22,415	21,579	22,005	1,927	1,972	1,926	42.9	37.7	31.2	23.8
Female householder, no spouse present . . [7]	6,052	7,306	8,031	2,495	3,275	3,716	11.6	13.7	40.3	45.9
With own children [7].	3,558	4,199	4,841	1,793	2,232	2,489	6.8	8.3	29.0	30.8
Male householder, no spouse present . . [7]	1,441	2,303	2,507	256	446	536	2.8	4.3	4.1	6.6
With own children [7].	500	939	1,105	99	173	267	1.0	1.9	1.6	3.3
FAMILY INCOME IN PREVIOUS YEAR IN CONSTANT (1994) DOLLARS										
Total families	52,243	56,590	58,444	6,184	7,470	8,093	100.0	100.0	100.0	100.0
Less than $5,000	888	1,188	1,344	383	650	664	1.7	2.3	6.2	8.2
$5,000 to $9,999	1,985	2,150	2,630	816	949	1,036	3.8	4.5	13.2	12.8
$10,000 to $14,999	2,978	3,226	3,624	798	859	906	5.7	6.2	12.9	11.2
$15,000 to $24,999	7,680	7,640	8,533	1,323	1,397	1,489	14.7	14.6	21.4	18.4
$25,000 to $34,999	7,889	7,979	8,474	878	979	1,093	15.1	14.5	14.2	13.5
$35,000–$49,999	11,755	11,261	10,812	940	1,128	1,198	22.5	18.5	15.2	14.8
$50,000 or more	19,121	23,145	23,027	1,039	1,501	1,716	36.6	39.4	16.8	21.2
Median income (dol.) [8]	40,933	42,996	40,884	23,179	24,153	24,698	(X)	(X)	(X)	(X)
Families below poverty level [9] .	3,581	4,409	5,312	1,722	2,077	2,212	6.9	9.1	27.8	27.3
Persons below poverty level [9] .	17,214	20,785	25,379	8,050	9,302	10,196	9.0	11.7	31.0	30.6
HOUSING TENURE										
Total occupied units	70,766	80,163	83,737	8,586	10,486	11,655	100.0	100.0	100.0	100.0
Owner-occupied	49,913	54,094	57,449	4,173	4,445	4,888	70.5	68.6	48.6	41.9
Renter-occupied	19,581	24,685	24,793	4,257	5,862	6,547	27.7	29.6	49.6	56.2
No cash rent.	1,272	1,384	1,494	156	178	220	1.8	1.8	1.8	1.9

X Not applicable.   [1] Represents those who completed ninth to twelfth grade, but have no high school diploma.   [2] High school graduate.   [3] Some college or associate degree.   [4] Bachelor's or advanced degree.   [5] Source: U.S. Bureau of Labor Statistics, *Employment and Earnings,* January issues. Data beginning 1994 not directly comparable with earlier years. See text, section 13, and February 1994 and March 1996 issues of *Employment and Earnings.*   [6] Total unemployment as percent of civilian labor force.   [7] Children under 18 years old.   [8] For definition of median, see Guide to Tabular Presentation.   [9] For explanation of poverty level, see text, section 14.

Source: Except as noted, U.S. Bureau of the Census *Current Population Reports,* P20-448, and earlier reports; P60-189; and Internet site http://www.census.gov/population/socdemo/race/black/black.html.

No. 50. Social and Economic Characteristics of the Asian and Pacific Islander Population: 1990 and 1995

[As of **March**. Excludes members of Armed Forces except those living off post or with their families on post. Data for 1990 are based on 1980 census population controls; 1995 data are based on 1990 census population controls. The independent estimate of 9.3 million for the Asian and Pacific Islander population differs substantially from the March 1995 Current Population Survey (CPS) estimate of 6.7 million for this population. The CPS estimate, based on a sample, is subject to both sampling and nonsampling errors. It is not controlled to independent estimates for this population. Estimates may differ because of different data collection and estimation procedures and sampling error. However, distributions of characteristics for the Asian and Pacific Islander population in the March 1995 CPS appear reasonable when compared to the 1990 census distribution. When comparing data for the Asian and Pacific Islander population for previous years, caution should be used. Based on Current Population Survey; see text, section 1, and Appendix III]

CHARACTERISTIC	NUMBER (1,000)		PERCENT DISTRIBUTION	
	1990	1995	1990	1995
Total persons	**6,679**	**6,656**	**100.0**	**100.0**
Under 5 years old	602	440	9.0	6.6
5 to 14 years old	1,112	981	16.6	14.7
15 to 44 years old	3,345	3,439	50.1	51.7
45 to 64 years old	1,155	1,283	17.3	19.3
65 years old and over	465	513	7.0	7.7
YEARS OF SCHOOL COMPLETED				
Persons 25 years old and over	**3,961**	**4,200**	**100.0**	**100.0**
Elementary: 0 to 8 years	543	418	13.7	10.0
High school: 1 to 3 years	234	[1]269	5.9	[1]6.4
4 years	1,038	[2]995	26.2	[2]23.7
College: 1 to 3 years	568	[3]913	14.3	[3]21.7
4 years or more	1,578	[4]1,605	39.9	[4]38.2
LABOR FORCE STATUS [5]				
Civilians 16 years old and over	**4,849**	**5,083**	**100.0**	**100.0**
Civilian labor force	3,216	3,288	66.3	64.7
Employed	3,079	3,125	63.5	61.5
Unemployed	136	163	2.8	3.2
Unemployment rate [6]	4.2	5.0	(X)	(X)
Not in labor force	1,634	1,795	33.7	35.3
FAMILY TYPE				
Total families	**1,531**	**1,588**	**100.0**	**100.0**
Married couple	1,256	1,290	82.1	81.2
Female householder, no spouse present	188	200	12.3	12.6
Male householder, no spouse present	86	98	5.6	6.2
FAMILY INCOME IN PREVIOUS YEAR IN CONSTANT (**1994**) DOLLARS				
Total families	**1,531**	**1,588**	**100.0**	**100.0**
Less than $5,000	(NA)	59	(NA)	3.7
$5,000 to $9,999	(NA)	85	(NA)	5.4
$10,000 to $14,999	(NA)	100	(NA)	6.3
$15,000 to $24,999	(NA)	162	(NA)	10.2
$25,000 to $34,999	(NA)	199	(NA)	12.5
$35,000 to $49,999	(NA)	249	(NA)	15.7
$50,000 or more	(NA)	734	(NA)	46.2
Median income [7]	50,490	46,106	(X)	(X)
Families below poverty level [8]	182	208	11.9	13.1
Persons below poverty level [8]	939	974	14.1	14.6
HOUSING TENURE				
Total occupied units	**1,988**	**2,040**	**100.0**	**100.0**
Owner-occupied	977	1,012	49.1	49.6
Renter-occupied	982	997	49.4	48.9
No cash rent	30	31	1.5	1.5

NA Not available.   X Not applicable.   [1] Represents those who completed ninth to twelfth grade, but have no high school diploma.   [2] High school graduate.   [3] Some college or associate degree.   [4] Bachelor's or advanced degree.   [5] Data beginning 1994 not directly comparable with earlier years. See text, section 14.   [6] Total unemployment as percent of civilian labor force.   [7] For definition of median, see Guide to Tabular Presentation.   [8] For explanation of poverty level, see text, section 14.

Source: U.S. Bureau of the Census, *Current Population Reports*, P20-459; and unpublished data.

No. 51. Population Living on Selected Reservations and Trust Lands and American Indian Tribes With 10,000 or More American Indians: 1990

[As of **April**]

RESERVATION AND TRUST LANDS WITH 5,000 OR MORE AMERICAN INDIANS, ESKIMOS, AND ALEUTS	Total popula- tion	AMERICAN INDIANS, ESKIMOS, ALEUTS		AMERICAN INDIAN TRIBE	Number	Percent distri- bution
		Number	Percent of total			
All reservation and trust lands	**808,163**	**437,431**	**54.1**	**American Indian population, total [2]**	**1,878,285**	**100.0**
Navajo and Trust Lands, AZ-NM-UT.	148,451	143,405	96.6	Cherokee	308,132	16.4
Pine Ridge and Trust Lands, NE-SD	12,215	11,182	91.5	Navajo	219,198	11.7
				Chippewa	103,826	5.5
Fort Apache, AZ.	10,394	9,825	94.5	Sioux [3]	103,255	5.5
Gila River, AZ	9,540	9,116	95.6	Choctaw.	82,299	4.4
Papago, AZ.	8,730	8,480	97.1	Pueblo	52,939	2.8
Rosebud and Trust Lands, SD.	9,696	8,043	83.0	Apache [4]	50,051	2.7
				Iroquois [4]	49,038	2.6
San Carlos, AZ	7,294	7,110	97.5	Lumbee	48,444	2.6
				Creek.	43,550	2.3
Zuni Pueblo, AZ-NM	7,412	7,073	95.4	Blackfoot	32,234	1.7
Hopi and Trust Lands, AZ . . .	7,360	7,061	95.9	Canadian and Latin American. .	22,379	1.2
Blackfeet, MT	8,549	7,025	82.2	Chickasaw	20,631	1.1
Turtle Mountain and Trust Lands, ND-SD	7,106	6,772	95.3	Potawatomi [4]	16,763	0.9
				Tohono O'Odham	16,041	0.9
Yakima and Trust Lands, WA . .	27,668	6,307	22.8	Pima	14,431	0.8
				Tlingit.	13,925	0.7
Osage, OK [1]	41,645	6,161	14.8	Seminole	13,797	0.7
Fort Peck, MT	10,595	5,782	54.6	Alaskan Athabaskans	13,738	0.7
Wind River, WY	21,851	5,676	26.0	Cheyenne	11,456	0.6
Eastern Cherokee, NC	6,527	5,388	82.5	Comanche	11,322	0.6
Flathead, MT.	21,259	5,130	24.1	Paiute	11,142	0.6
Cheyenne River, SD	7,743	5,100	65.9	Puget Sound Salish	10,246	0.5

[1] The Osage Reservation is coextensive with Osage County. Data shown for the reservation are for the entire reservation. [2] Includes other American Indian tribes, not shown separately. [3] Any entry with the spelling "Siouan" was miscoded to Sioux in North Carolina. [4] Reporting and/or processing problems have affected the data for this tribe.
Source: U.S. Bureau of the Census, *1990 Census of Population, General Population Characteristics, American Indian and Alaska Native Areas* (CP-1-1A); and press releases CB91-232 and CB92-244.

No. 52. Social and Economic Characteristics of the American Indian Population: 1990

[**As of April**. Based on a sample and subject to sampling variability]

CHARACTERISTIC	American Indian, total [1]	Chero- kee	Navajo	Sioux [2]	Chip- pewa	Choctaw	Pueblo	Apache	Iro- quois [3]	Lumbee
Total persons	**1,937,391**	**369,035**	**225,298**	**107,321**	**105,988**	**86,231**	**55,330**	**53,330**	**52,557**	**50,888**
Percent under 5 years old	9.7	6.3	13.6	12.3	10.3	8.2	10.3	10.2	8.1	8.3
Percent 18 years old and over .	65.8	73.3	57.7	60.0	64.0	68.8	64.2	64.7	71.1	66.2
Percent 65 years old and over .	5.9	7.2	4.6	4.4	4.7	8.0	5.8	3.4	6.7	5.6
EDUCATIONAL ATTAINMENT										
Persons 25 years old and over	1,040,955	229,231	100,594	51,014	54,804	49,128	28,597	27,717	30,882	27,343
Percent high school graduates or higher.	65.6	68.2	51.0	69.7	69.7	70.3	71.5	63.8	71.9	51.6
Percent bachelor's degree or higher	9.4	11.1	4.5	8.9	8.2	13.3	7.3	6.9	11.3	9.4
FAMILY TYPE										
Total families	449,281	98,610	44,845	22,669	25,077	21,856	11,825	12,314	12,988	12,650
Percent distribution:										
Married couple.	65.8	73.1	61.1	54.2	58.4	75.2	61.2	66.9	67.5	68.5
Female householder, no spouse present	26.2	20.8	28.6	36.0	33.1	20.0	29.2	24.7	25.5	23.9
Male householder, no spouse present	8.0	6.1	10.3	9.8	8.5	4.8	9.6	8.4	7.0	7.6
INCOME IN 1989										
Median family (dol.) [4]	21,619	24,907	13,940	16,525	20,249	24,467	19,845	19,690	27,025	23,934
Median household (dol.) [4]	19,900	21,922	12,817	15,611	18,801	21,640	19,097	18,484	23,460	21,708
Per capita (dol.).	8,284	10,469	4,788	6,508	7,777	9,463	6,679	7,271	10,568	8,625
Families below poverty level [5] .	122,237	19,100	21,204	8,939	7,814	4,347	3,691	3,913	2,249	2,554
Percent below poverty level .	27.2	19.4	47.3	39.4	31.2	19.9	31.2	31.8	17.3	20.2
Persons below poverty level [5] .	585,273	79,271	107,526	45,658	35,231	19,453	17,981	19,246	10,253	10,966
Percent below poverty level .	31.2	22.0	48.8	44.4	34.3	23.0	33.2	37.5	20.1	22.1

[1] Includes other American Indian tribes not shown separately. [2] Any entry with the spelling "Siouan" was miscoded to Sioux in North Carolina. [3] Reporting and/or processing problems have affected the data for this tribe. [4] For definition of median, see Guide to Tabular Presentation. [5] For explanation of poverty level, see text, section 14.
Source: U.S. Bureau of the Census, *1990 Census of Population, Characteristics of American Indians by Tribe and Language*, 1990 CP-3-7.

No. 53. Social and Economic Characteristics of the Hispanic Population: 1995

[As of March, except labor force status, annual average. Excludes members of the Armed Forces except those living off post or with their families on post. Based on Current Population Survey; see text, section 1, and Appendix III]

CHARACTERISTIC	NUMBER (1,000)						PERCENT DISTRIBUTION					
	His-panic, total	Mexi-can	Puer-to Rican	Cuban	Cen-tral and South Amer-ican	Other His-panic	His-panic, total	Mexi-can	Puer-to Rican	Cuban	Cen-tral and South Amer-ican	Other His-panic
Total persons	27,521	17,982	2,730	1,156	3,686	1,967	100.0	100.0	100.0	100.0	100.0	100.0
Under 5 years old	3,318	2,413	272	68	360	205	12.1	13.4	10.0	5.9	9.8	10.4
5 to 14 years old	5,215	3,611	539	131	577	356	18.9	20.1	19.7	11.3	15.7	18.1
15 to 44 years old.	13,894	9,049	1,323	486	2,102	933	50.5	50.3	48.5	42.0	57.0	47.4
45 to 64 years old.	3,666	2,127	466	265	489	320	13.3	11.8	17.1	22.9	13.3	16.3
65 years old and over	1,428	781	130	207	159	154	5.2	4.3	4.8	17.9	4.3	7.8
EDUCATIONAL ATTAINMENT												
Persons 25 years old and over	14,171	8,737	1,437	820	2,082	1,095	100.0	100.0	100.0	100.0	100.0	100.0
High school graduate or higher	7,563	4,067	880	531	1,337	749	53.4	46.5	61.3	64.7	64.2	68.4
Bachelor's degree or higher . .	1,312	572	153	158	272	156	9.3	6.5	10.7	19.3	13.1	14.2
LABOR FORCE STATUS [1]												
Civilians 16 years old and over	18,629	11,609	1,896	1,019	2,686	1,419	100.0	100.0	100.0	100.0	100.0	100.0
Civilian labor force	12,267	7,765	1,098	613	1,885	906	65.8	66.9	57.9	60.2	70.2	63.8
Employed.	11,127	7,016	974	568	1,734	835	59.7	60.4	51.4	55.7	64.6	58.8
Unemployed	1,140	750	123	45	150	72	6.1	6.5	6.5	4.4	5.6	5.1
Unemployment rate [2] . . .	9.3	9.7	11.2	7.4	8.0	7.9	(X)	(X)	(X)	(X)	(X)	(X)
Not in labor force	6,362	3,844	798	406	802	512	34.2	33.1	42.1	39.8	29.9	36.1
FAMILY TYPE												
Total families	6,200	3,847	729	315	817	491	100.0	100.0	100.0	100.0	100.0	100.0
Married couple	4,235	2,745	386	235	541	328	68.3	71.4	52.9	74.6	66.1	66.8
Female householder, no spouse present.	1,485	766	300	67	208	145	24.0	19.9	41.2	21.3	25.4	29.5
Male householder, no spouse present.	479	336	43	13	69	18	7.7	8.7	5.9	4.0	8.5	3.7
FAMILY INCOME IN 1994												
Total families	6,200	3,847	729	315	817	491	100.0	100.0	100.0	100.0	100.0	100.0
Less than $5,000	375	232	54	14	45	30	6.0	6.0	7.4	4.4	5.6	6.0
$5,000 to $9,999	730	446	136	27	73	49	11.8	11.6	18.6	8.5	8.9	9.9
$10,000 to $14,999.	779	517	97	24	92	50	12.6	13.4	13.3	7.5	11.3	10.1
$15,000 to $24,999.	1,301	844	122	68	180	88	21.0	21.9	16.7	21.5	22.0	17.9
$25,000 to $34,999.	923	583	92	46	133	68	14.9	15.2	12.6	14.5	16.3	13.9
$35,000 to $49,999.	924	575	80	38	139	92	14.9	14.9	10.9	12.0	17.1	18.7
$50,000 or more.	1,168	650	149	100	154	115	18.8	16.9	20.4	31.7	18.8	23.4
Median income (dol.) [3]	24,313	23,609	20,929	30,584	26,558	28,658	(X)	(X)	(X)	(X)	(X)	(X)
Families below poverty level [4].	1,724	1,138	242	43	196	105	27.8	29.6	33.2	13.6	23.9	21.4
Persons below poverty level [4].	8,416	5,781	981	205	949	500	30.7	32.3	36.0	17.8	25.8	25.5
HOUSING TENURE												
Total occupied units . . .	7,735	4,653	935	451	1,040	656	100.0	100.0	100.0	100.0	100.0	100.0
Owner-occupied	3,278	2,145	268	236	304	325	42.4	46.1	28.7	52.3	29.2	49.6
Renter-occupied [5]	4,457	2,508	667	215	736	331	57.6	53.9	71.3	47.7	70.8	50.4

X Not applicable.   [1] Source: U.S. Bureau of Labor Statistics, *Employment and Earnings*, January 1996.   [2] Total unemployment as percent of civilian labor force.   [3] For definition of median, see Guide to Tabular Presentation.   [4] For explanation of poverty level, see text, section 14.   [5] Includes no cash rent.

Source: Except as noted, U.S. Bureau of the Census, unpublished data.

No. 54. Native and Foreign-Born Population, by Place of Birth: 1920 to 1990

[**In thousands, except percent**. Beginning 1950, data are based on a sample from the census; for details, see text, section 1. See source for sampling variability. See also *Historical Statistics, Colonial Times to 1970*, series C 1-10]

YEAR	Total popula-tion	NATIVE POPULATION						FOREIGN-BORN	
		Total	Born in State of resi-dence	Born in other States	State of birth not reported	Born in outlying areas [1]	Born abroad or at sea of American parents	Number	Percent of total population
1920	105,711	91,790	71,071	20,274	314	38	93	13,921	13.2
1930	122,775	108,571	82,678	25,388	238	136	131	14,204	11.6
1940	131,669	120,074	92,610	26,906	280	157	122	11,595	8.8
1950	150,216	139,869	102,788	35,284	1,370	330	96	10,347	6.9
1960	178,467	168,806	118,802	44,264	4,526	817	397	9,661	5.4
1970	203,194	193,454	131,296	51,659	8,882	873	744	9,740	4.8
1980	226,546	212,466	144,871	65,452	(NA)	1,088	1,055	14,080	6.2
1990	248,710	228,943	153,685	72,011	(NA)	1,382	1,864	19,767	7.9

NA Not available.　　[1] 1920-50, includes Alaska and Hawaii. Includes Puerto Rico.

Source: U.S. Bureau of the Census, *1970 Census of Population*, vol. II, PC(2)-2A; and *1990 Census of Population Listing* (1990CPH-L-121).

No. 55. Native and Foreign-Born Populations by Selected Characteristics: 1994

[**In thousands, except as indicated**. The foreign-born population includes some undocumented immigrants, refugees, and temporary residents such as students and temporary workers as well as legally-admitted immigrants. Based on Current Population Survey; see text, section 1 and Appendix III]

CHARACTERISTIC	Native popula-tion	FOREIGN-BORN POPULATION						
		Total [1]	Year of entry				Country of birth	
			Before 1970	1970 to 1979	1980 to 1989	1990 to 1994	Mexico	Philip-pines
Total	237,184	22,568	4,974	4,781	8,311	4,502	6,264	1,033
Under 5 years old	20,160	298	(X)	(X)	24	274	136	4
5 to 17 years old	47,118	2,190	(X)	88	1,203	899	819	87
18 to 24 years old	22,839	2,636	1	533	1,196	904	1,087	87
25 to 29 years old	17,034	2,592	106	402	1,410	673	1,026	107
30 to 34 years old	19,643	2,677	251	578	1,324	524	851	107
35 to 44 years old	37,006	4,522	662	1,528	1,757	575	1,159	257
45 to 64 years old	45,245	5,014	2,088	1,359	1,069	498	900	280
65 years old and over	28,139	2,640	1,864	293	328	154	287	105
Male	115,782	11,132	2,165	2,318	4,381	2,269	3,404	468
Female	121,402	11,436	2,810	2,463	3,930	2,233	2,860	565
White	199,793	15,428	4,313	3,058	5,190	2,867	5,796	42
Black	31,443	1,596	200	342	738	317	26	11
Asian or Pacific Islander	2,813	4,630	386	1,176	1,992	1,076	4	971
Hispanic origin [2]	16,376	10,270	1,560	2,334	4,404	1,971	6,126	28
EDUCATIONAL ATTAINMENT								
Persons 25 years old and over	147,067	17,445	4,972	4,161	5,887	2,423	4,222	856
Not high school graduate	25,166	6,274	1,590	1,574	2,302	807	3,006	111
High school grad/some college	89,382	7,147	2,402	1,667	2,245	831	1,026	352
Bachelor's degree	21,660	2,596	588	620	882	506	136	339
Graduate or professional degree	10,859	1,428	392	300	458	279	54	54
LABOR FORCE STATUS								
Persons 16 years old and over [3]	176,607	20,559	4,974	4,748	7,334	3,504	5,477	958
In the civilian labor force	116,281	12,883	2,482	3,360	5,100	1,939	3,631	686
Employed	108,402	11,706	2,342	3,077	4,583	1,703	3,227	641
Unemployed	7,880	1,176	140	283	517	236	404	45
Not in the labor force	59,411	7,635	2,485	1,363	2,223	1,565	1,842	254
INCOME IN 1993								
Persons 16 years old and over	176,607	20,559	4,974	4,748	7,334	3,504	5,477	958
Without income	10,540	2,802	210	504	1,144	943	1,117	89
With income	166,067	17,757	4,764	4,244	6,190	2,561	4,360	869
$1 to $9,999 or loss	57,416	7,283	1,759	1,478	2,614	1,429	2,093	225
$10,000 to $19,999	39,905	4,909	1,197	1,208	1,887	615	1,501	211
$20,000 to $34,999	36,994	3,067	938	825	1,001	303	565	238
$35,000 to $49,999	17,122	1,252	400	376	392	83	127	109
$50,000 or more	14,629	1,248	471	356	293	129	74	86
Median income (dollars)	15,876	12,179	14,473	15,121	11,580	8,393	(NA)	(NA)
POVERTY STATUS [4]								
In poverty	34,086	5,179	535	778	2,195	1,672	2,248	40
Not in poverty	202,659	17,355	4,440	4,004	6,106	2,805	4,004	991

NA Not available.　　X Not applicable.　　[1] Includes other countries, not shown separately.　　[2] Persons of Hispanic origin may be of any race.　　[3] Includes persons in Armed Forces, not shown separately.　　[4] Persons for whom poverty status is determined.

Source: U.S. Bureau of the Census, *Current Population Reports*, P20-486 and Internet site http://www.census.gov/ftp/pub/population/www/ (accessed 5 March 1996).

No. 56. Population, by Selected Ancestry Group and Region: 1990

[As of **April 1**. Covers persons who reported single and multiple ancestry groups. Persons who reported a multiple ancestry group may be included in more than one category. Major classifications of ancestry groups do not represent strict geographic or cultural definitions. Based on a sample and subject to sampling variability; see text, section 1]

ANCESTRY GROUP	Total (1,000)	PERCENT DISTRIBUTION, BY REGION				ANCESTRY GROUP	Total (1,000)	PERCENT DISTRIBUTION, BY REGION			
		North-east	Mid-west	South	West			North-east	Mid-west	South	West
European: [1]						Central & South					
Austrian	865	38	21	19	22	America [3]					
British.	1,119	17	18	39	26	and Spain:					
Croatian	544	21	43	20	16	Cuban	860	18	3	69	9
Czech	1,296	10	52	22	16	Dominican. . . .	506	86	1	10	2
Danish	1,635	9	34	12	45	Hispanic [4] . . .	1,113	13	6	31	50
Dutch.	6,227	16	34	29	21	Mexican	11,587	1	9	33	57
English.	32,652	18	22	35	25	Puerto Rican . .	1,955	66	11	15	8
European	467	14	17	31	39	Salvadoran . . .	499	13	2	23	62
Finnish [2]	659	14	47	11	27	Spanish	2,024	16	8	30	45
French [2]	10,321	26	26	29	20	West Indian: [1]					
German	57,947	17	39	25	19	Jamaican	435	59	5	31	6
Greek.	1,110	37	23	21	19	Asia:					
Hungarian. . . .	1,582	36	32	17	16	Asian Indian . .	570	32	19	26	24
Irish.	38,736	24	25	33	17	Chinese	1,505	25	8	12	55
Italian.	14,665	51	17	17	15	Filipino	1,451	10	9	13	68
Lithuanian. . . .	812	43	28	16	13	Japanese	1,005	9	8	11	72
Norwegian. . . .	3,869	6	52	10	33	Korean	837	22	14	20	44
Polish.	9,366	37	37	15	11	Vietnamese. . .	536	9	8	28	54
Portuguese . . .	1,153	49	3	8	41						
Russian	2,953	44	16	18	22	North America:					
Scandinavian. .	679	8	33	15	45	Acadian/Cajun .	668	1	2	91	5
Scotch-Irish. . .	5,618	14	19	47	20	Afro-American .	23,777	15	21	54	10
Scottish	5,394	20	21	33	26	American Indian	8,708	9	22	47	23
Slovak	1,883	40	34	14	11	American	12,396	10	18	61	11
Swedish	4,681	14	40	14	32	Canadian	550	34	18	21	28
Swiss.	1,045	16	36	17	30	French Canadian	2,167	45	20	20	15
Ukrainian	741	51	22	14	13	United States. .	644	16	18	53	13
Welsh.	2,034	22	24	27	27	White	1,800	7	13	53	28
Yugoslavian. . .	258	23	28	12	37						

[1] Non-Hispanic groups. [2] Excludes French Basque. [3] Hispanic groups. [4] A general type of response which may encompass several ancestry groups.

Source: U.S. Bureau of the Census, *1990 Census of Population, Supplementary Reports, Detailed Ancestry Groups for States* (1990 CP-S-1-2).

No. 57. Persons Speaking a Language Other Than English at Home, by Age and Language: 1990

[As of **April**. Based on a sample and subject to sampling variability]

AGE GROUP AND LANGUAGE SPOKEN AT HOME	Persons who speak language (1,000)	Percent who speak English less than "very well"	LANGUAGE	Persons, 5 years old and over who speak language (1,000)
Persons 5 years old and over	230,446	(X)	Speak only English	198,601
Speak only English.	198,601	(X)	Spanish.	17,339
Speak other language.	31,845	43.9	French	1,702
Speak Spanish or Spanish Creole	17,345	47.9	German	1,547
Speak Asian or Pacific Island language. .	4,472	54.1	Italian	1,309
Speak other language	10,028	32.4	Chinese.	1,249
			Tagalog.	843
Persons 5 to 17 years old	45,342	(X)	Polish	723
Speak only English.	39,020	(X)	Korean	626
Speak other language.	6,323	37.8	Vietnamese	507
Speak Spanish or Spanish Creole	4,168	39.3	Portuguese	430
Speak Asian or Pacific Island language. .	816	44.2	Japanese.	428
Speak other language	1,340	29.2	Greek	388
			Arabic	355
Persons 18 to 64 years old	153,908	(X)	Hindi (Urdu)	331
Speak only English.	132,200	(X)	Russian	242
Speak other language.	21,708	45.1	Yiddish	213
Speak Spanish or Spanish Creole	12,121	49.6	Thai (Laotian)	206
Speak Asian or Pacific Island language. .	3,301	54.7	Persian	202
Speak other language	6,286	31.4	French Creole.	188
			Armenian.	150
Persons 65 years old and over	31,195	(X)	Navaho	149
Speak only English.	27,381	(X)	Hungarian	148
Speak other language.	3,814	47.2	Hebrew	144
Speak Spanish or Spanish Creole	1,057	62.3	Dutch	143
Speak Asian or Pacific Island language. .	355	72.0	Mon-Khmer (Cambodian) . . .	127
Speak other language	2,402	36.9	Gujarathi	102

X Not applicable.

Source: U.S. Bureau of the Census, *1990 Census of Population and Housing Data Paper Listing* (CPH-L-133); and Summary Tape File 3C.

No. 58. Marital Status of the Population, by Sex, Race, and Hispanic Origin: 1970 to 1995

[In millions, except percent. As of **March, except as noted. Persons 18 years old and over**. Excludes members of Armed Forces except those living off post or with their families on post. Except as noted, based on Current Population Survey, see text, section 1, and Appendix III. See *Historical Statistics, Colonial Times to 1970,* series A 160-171, for decennial data]

MARITAL STATUS, RACE, AND HISPANIC ORIGIN	TOTAL				MALE				FEMALE			
	1970	1980	1990	1995	1970	1980	1990	1995	1970	1980	1990	1995
Total [1]	132.5	159.5	181.8	191.6	62.5	75.7	86.9	92.0	70.0	83.8	95.0	99.6
Never married	21.4	32.3	40.4	43.9	11.8	18.0	22.4	24.6	9.6	14.3	17.9	19.3
Married	95.0	104.6	112.6	116.7	47.1	51.8	55.8	57.7	47.9	52.8	56.7	58.9
Widowed	11.8	12.7	13.8	13.4	2.1	2.0	2.3	2.3	9.7	10.8	11.5	11.1
Divorced	4.3	9.9	15.1	17.6	1.6	3.9	6.3	7.4	2.7	6.0	8.8	10.3
Percent of total	100.0	100.0	100.0	100.0	100.0	100.0	100.0	100.0	100.0	100.0	100.0	100.0
Never married	16.2	20.3	22.2	22.9	18.9	23.8	25.8	26.8	13.7	17.1	18.9	19.4
Married	71.7	65.5	61.9	60.9	75.3	68.4	64.3	62.7	68.5	63.0	59.7	59.2
Widowed	8.9	8.0	7.6	7.0	3.3	2.6	2.7	2.5	13.9	12.8	12.1	11.1
Divorced	3.2	6.2	8.3	9.2	2.5	5.2	7.2	8.0	3.9	7.1	9.3	10.3
Percent standardized for age: [2]												
Never married	14.1	16.5	20.6	22.4	16.5	18.7	23.3	25.3	12.1	14.5	18.2	19.7
Married	74.2	69.3	63.7	62.0	77.6	72.9	66.5	64.1	70.8	65.9	61.2	60.1
Widowed	8.3	7.6	6.9	6.1	3.3	2.7	2.7	2.4	13.0	12.1	10.8	9.6
Divorced	3.4	6.6	8.7	9.4	2.6	5.6	7.6	8.2	4.1	7.6	9.8	10.6
White, total	118.2	139.5	155.5	161.3	55.9	66.7	74.8	78.1	62.2	72.8	80.6	83.2
Never married	18.4	26.4	31.6	33.2	10.2	15.0	18.0	19.2	8.2	11.4	13.6	14.0
Married	85.8	93.8	99.5	102.0	42.7	46.7	49.5	50.6	43.1	47.1	49.9	51.3
Widowed	10.3	10.9	11.7	11.3	1.7	1.6	1.9	1.9	8.6	9.3	9.8	9.4
Divorced	3.7	8.3	12.6	14.8	1.3	3.4	5.4	6.3	2.3	5.0	7.3	8.4
Percent of total	100.0	100.0	100.0	100.0	100.0	100.0	100.0	100.0	100.0	100.0	100.0	100.0
Never married	15.6	18.9	20.3	20.6	18.2	22.5	24.1	24.6	13.2	15.7	16.9	16.9
Married	72.6	67.2	64.0	63.2	76.3	70.0	66.2	64.9	69.3	64.7	61.9	61.7
Widowed	8.7	7.8	7.5	7.0	3.1	2.5	2.6	2.5	13.8	12.8	12.2	11.3
Divorced	3.1	6.0	8.1	9.1	2.4	5.0	7.2	8.1	3.8	6.8	9.0	10.1
Black, total	13.0	16.6	20.3	22.1	5.9	7.4	9.1	9.9	7.1	9.2	11.2	12.2
Never married	2.7	5.1	7.1	8.5	1.4	2.5	3.5	4.1	1.2	2.5	3.6	4.4
Married	8.3	8.5	9.3	9.6	3.9	4.1	4.5	4.6	4.4	4.5	4.8	4.9
Widowed	1.4	1.6	1.7	1.7	0.3	0.3	0.3	0.3	1.1	1.3	1.4	1.4
Divorced	0.6	1.4	2.1	2.4	0.2	0.5	0.8	0.8	0.4	0.9	1.3	1.5
Percent of total	100.0	100.0	100.0	100.0	100.0	100.0	100.0	100.0	100.0	100.0	100.0	100.0
Never married	20.6	30.5	35.1	38.4	24.3	34.3	38.4	41.7	17.4	27.4	32.5	35.8
Married	64.1	51.4	45.8	43.2	66.9	54.6	49.2	46.7	61.7	48.7	43.0	40.4
Widowed	11.0	9.8	8.5	7.6	5.2	4.2	3.7	3.1	15.8	14.3	12.4	11.3
Divorced	4.4	8.4	10.6	10.7	3.6	7.0	8.8	8.5	5.0	9.5	12.0	12.5
Hispanic, [3] **total . . . . .**	5.1	7.9	13.6	17.6	2.4	3.8	6.7	8.8	2.6	4.1	6.8	8.8
Never married	0.9	1.9	3.7	5.0	0.5	1.0	2.2	3.0	0.4	0.9	1.5	2.1
Married	3.6	5.2	8.4	10.4	1.8	2.5	4.1	5.1	1.8	2.6	4.3	5.3
Widowed	0.3	0.4	0.5	0.7	0.1	0.1	0.1	0.2	0.2	0.3	0.4	0.6
Divorced	0.2	0.5	1.0	1.4	0.1	0.2	0.4	0.6	0.1	0.3	0.6	0.8
Percent of total	100.0	100.0	100.0	100.0	100.0	100.0	100.0	100.0	100.0	100.0	100.0	100.0
Never married	18.6	24.1	27.2	28.6	21.2	27.3	32.1	33.8	16.2	21.1	22.5	23.5
Married	71.8	65.6	61.7	59.3	73.8	67.1	60.9	57.9	70.0	64.3	62.4	60.7
Widowed	5.6	4.4	4.0	4.2	2.3	1.6	1.5	1.8	8.7	7.1	6.5	6.6
Divorced	3.9	5.8	7.0	7.9	2.7	4.0	5.5	6.6	5.1	7.6	8.5	9.2

[1] Includes persons of other races, not shown separately. [2] 1960 age distribution used as standard; standardization improves comparability over time by removing effects of changes in age distribution of population. [3] Hispanic persons may be of any race. 1970 data as of April and based on census.

Source: U.S. Bureau of the Census, *1970 Census of Population,* vol. I, part 1, and *Current Population Reports,* P20-450, and earlier reports; and unpublished data.

No. 59. Marital Status of the Population, by Sex and Age: 1995

[As of **March. Persons 18 years old and over.** Excludes members of Armed Forces except those living off post or with their families on post. Based on Current Population Survey; see text, section 1, and Appendix III. See *Historical Statistics, Colonial Times to 1970,* series A 160-171, for decennial census data]

SEX AND AGE	NUMBER OF PERSONS (1,000)					PERCENT DISTRIBUTION				
	Total	Never married	Mar-ried	Wid-owed	Di-vorced	Total	Never married	Mar-ried	Wid-owed	Di-vorced
Male	**92,008**	**24,628**	**57,730**	**2,282**	**7,367**	**100.0**	**26.8**	**62.7**	**2.5**	**8.0**
18 to 19 years old	3,522	3,441	80	-	-	100.0	97.7	2.3	-	-
20 to 24 years old	9,023	7,285	1,638	-	100	100.0	80.7	18.2	-	1.1
25 to 29 years old	9,689	4,944	4,337	6	401	100.0	51.0	44.8	0.1	4.1
30 to 34 years old	10,900	3,075	6,887	11	927	100.0	28.2	63.2	0.1	8.5
35 to 39 years old	11,041	2,241	7,561	35	1,204	100.0	20.3	68.5	0.3	10.9
40 to 44 years old	9,931	1,390	7,260	46	1,234	100.0	14.0	73.1	0.5	12.4
45 to 54 years old	15,022	1,214	11,848	153	1,807	100.0	8.1	78.9	1.0	12.0
55 to 64 years old	9,878	494	8,097	275	1,011	100.0	5.0	82.0	2.8	10.2
65 to 74 years old	8,097	342	6,549	693	513	100.0	4.2	80.9	8.6	6.3
75 years old and over . . .	4,906	201	3,474	1,062	168	100.0	4.1	70.8	21.6	3.4
Female	**99,588**	**19,312**	**58,931**	**11,080**	**10,266**	**100.0**	**19.4**	**59.2**	**11.1**	**10.3**
18 to 19 years old	3,494	3,202	277	2	13	100.0	91.6	7.9	0.1	0.4
20 to 24 years old	9,119	6,087	2,769	17	247	100.0	66.8	30.4	0.2	2.7
25 to 29 years old	9,712	3,429	5,576	17	689	100.0	35.3	57.4	0.2	7.1
30 to 34 years old	11,088	2,111	7,758	69	1,150	100.0	19.0	70.0	0.6	10.4
35 to 39 years old	11,200	1,408	8,103	120	1,569	100.0	12.6	72.3	1.1	14.0
40 to 44 years old	10,163	881	7,519	159	1,604	100.0	8.7	74.0	1.6	15.8
45 to 54 years old	15,672	959	11,617	655	2,441	100.0	6.1	74.1	4.2	15.6
55 to 64 years old	10,878	467	7,543	1,405	1,463	100.0	4.3	69.3	12.9	13.4
65 to 74 years old	10,117	408	5,571	3,352	786	100.0	4.0	55.1	33.1	7.8
75 years old and over . . .	8,147	360	2,196	5,284	305	100.0	4.4	27.0	64.9	3.7

- Represents or rounds to zero.

Source: U.S. Bureau of the Census, unpublished data.

No. 60. Marital Status of the Population—Projections, by Age and Sex: 2000 and 2010

[These numbers are based on the 1990 census, as enumerated, with modifications for age and race, and household estimates from 1991 to 1994, and are projected forward using alternative marital status and household-type proportions. Series 1, shown here, is based on a time series model and is the preferred projection. For series 1, assumptions about future changes in family and household situation extend trends of the past 30 years]

CHARACTERISTIC	NUMBER (1,000)		PERCENT DISTRIBUTION		CHARACTERISTIC	NUMBER (1,000)		PERCENT DISTRIBUTION	
	2000	2010	2000	2010		2000	2010	2000	2010
Population 18 years and over	203,852	225,206	100.0	100.0	55 to 64 years old	23,962	35,283	100.0	100.0
Never married (single) . .	44,459	50,747	21.8	22.5	Never married (single) .	1,254	1,905	5.2	5.4
Ever married	159,393	174,459	78.2	77.5	Ever married	22,707	33,379	94.8	94.6
Married, spouse present	111,408	119,016	54.7	52.8	Married, spouse present	16,424	23,360	68.5	66.2
Other	47,985	55,443	23.5	24.6	Other	6,283	10,019	26.2	28.4
18 to 24 years old	26,258	30,138	100.0	100.0	65 to 74 years old	18,136	21,057	100.0	100.0
Never married (single) .	20,917	24,429	79.7	81.1	Never married (single) .	825	899	4.5	4.3
Ever married	5,341	5,708	20.3	18.9	Ever married	17,311	20,159	95.5	95.7
Married, spouse present	3,750	4,003	14.3	13.3	Married, spouse present	11,309	13,305	62.4	63.2
Other	1,591	1,705	6.1	5.7	Other	6,002	6,854	33.1	32.5
25 to 34 years old	37,233	38,292	100.0	100.0	75 years and over	16,574	18,351	100.0	100.0
Never married (single) .	12,288	14,006	33.0	36.6	Never married (single) .	943	1,012	5.7	5.5
Ever married	24,946	24,286	67.0	63.4	Ever married	15,631	17,339	94.3	94.5
Married, spouse present	18,967	18,115	50.9	47.3	Married, spouse present	6,293	7,394	38.0	40.3
Other	5,979	6,171	16.1	16.1	Other	9,338	9,944	56.3	54.2
35 to 44 years old	44,659	38,521	100.0	100.0	Females, 18 years and over	105,927	116,776	100.0	100.0
Never married (single) .	5,886	5,660	13.2	14.7	Never married (single) .	19,955	22,904	18.8	19.6
Ever married	38,774	32,860	86.8	85.3	Ever married	85,972	93,872	81.2	80.4
Married, spouse present	28,930	23,628	64.8	61.3	Married, spouse present	55,682	59,485	52.6	50.9
Other	9,844	9,233	22.0	24.0	Other	30,290	34,387	28.6	29.4
45 to 54 years old	37,030	43,564	100.0	100.0	Males, 18 years and over	97,925	108,430	100.0	100.0
Never married (single) .	2,346	2,836	6.3	6.5	Never married (single) .	24,504	27,843	25.0	25.7
Ever married	34,684	40,729	93.7	93.5	Ever married	73,421	80,587	75.0	74.3
Married, spouse present	25,736	29,212	69.5	67.1	Married, spouse present	55,726	59,531	56.9	54.9
Other	8,948	11,517	24.2	26.4	Other	17,695	21,056	18.1	19.4

Source: U.S. Bureau of the Census, *Current Population Reports,* P25-1129.

Population

No. 61. Unmarried Couples, by Selected Characteristics: 1970 to 1995

[**In thousands**. As of **March**. An "unmarried couple" is two unrelated adults of the opposite sex sharing the same household. See headnote, table 66]

PRESENCE OF CHILDREN AND AGE OF HOUSEHOLDER	1970	1980	1985	1990	1995
Unmarried couples, total.	523	1,589	1,983	2,856	3,668
No children under 15 years old.	327	1,159	1,380	1,966	2,349
Some children under 15 years old.	196	431	603	891	1,319
Under 25 years old.	55	411	425	596	742
25 to 44 years old	103	837	1,203	1,775	2,188
45 to 64 years old	186	221	239	358	558
65 years old and over.	178	119	116	127	180

Source: U.S. Bureau of the Census, *Current Population Reports*, P20-450 and earlier reports; and unpublished data.

No. 62. Married Couples of Same or Mixed Races and Origins: 1970 to 1995

[**In thousands**. As of **March, except as noted. Persons 15 years old and over.** Persons of Hispanic origin may be of any race. Except as noted, based on Current Population Survey; see headnote, table 66]

RACE AND ORIGIN OF SPOUSES	1970 [1]	1980	1990	1995
Married couples, total	**44,598**	**49,714**	**53,256**	**54,937**
RACE				
Same race couples	43,922	48,264	50,889	51,733
White/White.	40,578	44,910	47,202	48,030
Black/Black	3,344	3,354	3,687	3,703
Interracial couples	310	651	964	1,392
Black/White.	65	167	211	328
Black husband/White wife.	41	122	150	206
White husband/Black wife.	24	45	61	122
White/other race [2]	233	450	720	988
Black/other race [2]	12	34	33	76
All other couples [2]	366	799	1,401	1,811
HISPANIC ORIGIN				
Hispanic/Hispanic	1,368	1,906	3,085	3,857
Hispanic/other origin (not Hispanic).	584	891	1,193	1,434
All other couples (not of Hispanic origin)	42,645	46,917	48,979	49,646

[1] As of April and based on Census of Population.   [2] Excluding White and Black.

Source: U.S. Bureau of the Census, *Current Population Reports*, P20-450, and earlier reports; and unpublished data.

No. 63. Householder and Marital Status of Population, 15 Years Old and Over: 1995

[**In thousands**. As of **March**. See headnote, table 66]

HOUSEHOLDER AND MARITAL STATUS	Total, 15 yrs. and over	MALE					FEMALE				
		Total [1]	20 to 24 years	25 to 44 years	45 to 64 years	65 yr. and over	Total [1]	20 to 24 years	25 to 44 years	45 to 64 years	65 yr. and over
Total persons	**202,732**	**97,704**	**9,023**	**41,561**	**24,900**	**13,003**	**105,028**	**9,119**	**42,163**	**26,550**	**18,264**
Householder.	99,087	61,779	2,468	27,636	20,329	11,116	37,308	2,476	14,757	9,495	10,267
Never married	15,874	7,848	1,318	4,833	1,074	438	8,026	1,728	4,375	1,046	613
Married, spouse present .	53,865	45,331	1,064	19,703	16,212	8,313	8,534	489	4,538	2,493	972
Married, spouse absent. .	4,720	1,668	48	817	535	262	3,052	161	1,679	926	282
Widowed	11,456	1,947	-	70	349	1,529	9,509	7	298	1,769	7,434
Divorced.	13,174	4,986	39	2,212	2,159	575	8,188	91	3,867	3,259	965
Not householder	103,645	35,925	6,555	13,924	4,570	1,887	67,720	6,643	27,405	17,054	7,997
Never married	39,105	22,438	5,967	6,818	636	105	16,667	4,359	3,454	380	155
Married, spouse present .	56,023	9,613	442	4,783	2,970	1,379	46,410	1,969	22,207	15,536	6,448
Married, spouse absent. .	2,126	1,139	85	740	227	68	988	150	534	204	65
Widowed	1,911	337	-	30	79	226	1,573	10	67	291	1,202
Divorced.	4,480	2,398	61	1,554	659	107	2,082	156	1,145	644	127

- Represents or rounds to zero.   [1] Includes 15 to 19 year olds.

Source: U.S. Bureau of the Census, unpublished data.

No. 64. Living Arrangements of Persons 15 Years Old and Over, by Selected Characteristics: 1995

[As of **March.** Based on Current Population Survey which includes members of Armed Forces living off post or with families on post, but excludes other Armed Forces; see text, section 1, and Appendix III]

AGE AND SEX	ALL RACES [1]					WHITE PERSONS PERCENT LIVING—			BLACK PERSONS PERCENT LIVING—		
	Total (1,000)	Percent living—				Alone	With spouse	With other rela- tives	Alone	With spouse	With other rela- tives
		Alone	With spouse	With other rela- tives	With non- rela- tives						
Total	**202,732**	**12**	**54**	**27**	**7**	**12**	**57**	**24**	**13**	**33**	**48**
15 to 19 years old.	18,152	1	2	93	4	1	2	93	-	-	97
20 to 24 years old.	18,142	6	22	55	17	6	24	51	6	9	75
25 to 34 years old.	41,388	9	55	24	12	9	59	21	10	33	47
35 to 44 years old.	42,335	9	67	18	6	8	71	15	11	42	40
45 to 54 years old.	30,693	11	72	13	4	10	75	11	17	50	28
55 to 64 years old.	20,755	15	72	10	3	14	75	8	21	50	24
65 years old and over	31,267	32	55	12	2	32	56	10	34	37	26
65 to 74 years old	18,214	24	64	10	2	24	66	8	29	43	23
75 years old and over . .	13,053	42	41	15	2	43	43	13	40	27	30
Male	**97,704**	**10**	**56**	**25**	**8**	**10**	**59**	**23**	**13**	**37**	**42**
15 to 19 years old.	9,218	1	1	94	4	1	1	94	-	-	97
20 to 24 years old.	9,023	6	17	58	19	7	18	55	6	7	75
25 to 34 years old.	20,589	11	51	23	15	11	54	21	12	35	39
35 to 44 years old.	20,972	11	67	15	8	10	69	12	14	45	32
45 to 54 years old.	15,022	11	76	8	5	10	77	8	19	57	16
55 to 64 years old.	9,878	12	79	6	4	11	81	5	18	63	12
65 years old and over	13,003	17	75	6	2	17	76	5	23	56	17
65 to 74 years old	8,097	14	78	5	2	14	80	4	21	58	14
75 years old and over . .	4,906	23	68	7	1	23	70	6	26	51	21
Female	**105,028**	**14**	**52**	**28**	**5**	**14**	**56**	**25**	**13**	**29**	**53**
15 to 19 years old.	8,934	1	3	92	4	-	4	91	1	-	97
20 to 24 years old.	9,119	6	27	51	16	6	30	47	6	11	76
25 to 34 years old.	20,800	7	59	26	9	7	63	20	8	32	54
35 to 44 years old.	21,363	7	68	22	4	6	72	18	9	39	47
45 to 54 years old.	15,672	11	69	17	3	10	73	13	15	44	38
55 to 64 years old.	10,878	18	66	14	2	17	69	12	23	40	33
65 years old and over	18,264	42	41	16	2	42	42	14	41	25	32
65 to 74 years old	10,117	32	53	13	1	32	55	11	35	33	30
75 years old and over . .	8,147	54	25	19	2	55	26	17	48	14	35

- Represents or rounds to zero.   [1] Includes other races not shown separately.

Source: U.S. Bureau of the Census, unpublished data.

No. 65. Living Arrangements of Young Adults: 1970 to 1995

[**1970** and **1980**, as of **April.** Beginning **1985**, as of **March** and based on Current Population Survey, see headnote, table 64]

LIVING ARRANGEMENTS AND SEX	PERSONS 18 TO 24 YEARS OLD					PERSONS 25 TO 34 YEARS OLD				
	1970	1980	1985	1990	1995	1970	1980	1985	1990	1995
Total (1,000)	**22,357**	**29,122**	**27,844**	**25,310**	**25,158**	**24,566**	**36,796**	**40,857**	**43,240**	**41,389**
Percent distribution:										
Child of householder [1]	47	48	54	53	53	8	9	11	12	12
Family householder or spouse . . .	38	29	24	22	21	83	72	68	65	63
Nonfamily householder.	5	10	8	9	9	5	12	13	13	13
Other	10	13	14	16	17	4	7	9	11	13
Male (1,000)	**10,398**	**14,278**	**13,695**	**12,450**	**12,545**	**11,929**	**18,107**	**20,184**	**21,462**	**20,589**
Percent distribution:										
Child of householder [1]	54	54	60	58	58	10	11	13	15	15
Family householder or spouse . . .	30	21	16	15	13	79	66	60	56	53
Nonfamily householder.	5	11	10	10	10	7	15	16	16	16
Other	10	13	14	17	18	5	8	11	13	15
Female (1,000)	**11,959**	**14,844**	**14,149**	**12,860**	**12,613**	**12,637**	**18,689**	**20,673**	**21,779**	**20,800**
Percent distribution:										
Child of householder [1]	41	43	48	48	47	7	7	8	8	8
Family householder or spouse . . .	45	36	32	30	28	86	78	76	73	72
Nonfamily householder.	4	8	7	8	9	4	9	10	10	10
Other	10	13	13	15	16	4	6	7	9	10

[1] Includes unmarried college students living in dormitories.

Source: U.S. Bureau of the Census, *1970* and *1980 Census of Population*, PC(2)-4B and *Current Population Reports*, P20-410 and P20-450; and unpublished data.

No. 66. Households, Families, Subfamilies, Married Couples, and Unrelated Individuals: 1960 to 1995

[In thousands, except as indicated. As of March. Based on Current Population Survey; includes members of Armed Forces living off post or with their families on post, but excludes all other members of Armed Forces; see text, section 1, and Appendix III. For definition of terms, see text, section 1. Minus sign (-) indicates decrease. See also *Historical Statistics, Colonial Times to 1970*, series A 288-319]

TYPE OF UNIT	1960	1970	1975	1980	1985	1990	1994	1995	PERCENT CHANGE		
									1970-80	1980-90	1990-95
Households	52,799	63,401	71,120	80,776	86,789	93,347	97,107	98,990	27	16	6
Average size	3.33	3.14	2.94	2.76	2.69	2.63	2.67	2.65	(X)	(X)	(X)
Family households	44,905	51,456	55,563	59,550	62,706	66,090	68,490	69,305	16	11	5
Married couple . . . ₁	39,254	44,728	46,951	49,112	50,350	52,317	53,171	53,858	10	7	3
Male householder [1] . ₁	1,228	1,228	1,485	1,733	2,228	2,884	2,913	3,226	41	66	12
Female householder [1]	4,422	5,500	7,127	8,705	10,129	10,890	12,406	12,220	58	25	12
Nonfamily households	7,895	11,945	15,557	21,226	24,082	27,257	28,617	29,686	78	28	9
Male householder	2,716	4,063	5,912	8,807	10,114	11,606	12,462	13,190	117	32	14
Female householder	5,179	7,882	9,645	12,419	13,968	15,651	16,155	16,496	58	26	5
One person	6,896	10,851	13,939	18,296	20,602	22,999	23,611	24,732	69	26	8
Families	45,111	51,586	55,712	59,550	62,706	66,090	68,490	69,305	15	11	5
Average size	3.67	3.58	3.42	3.29	3.23	3.17	3.20	3.20	(X)	(X)	(X)
Married couple . . . ₁	39,329	44,755	46,971	49,112	50,350	52,317	53,171	53,858	10	7	3
Male householder [1]	1,275	1,239	1,499	1,733	2,228	2,884	2,913	3,226	40	66	12
Female householder [1]	4,507	5,591	7,242	8,705	10,129	10,890	12,406	12,220	56	25	12
Unrelated subfamilies	207	130	149	360	526	534	716	674	177	48	26
Married couple	75	27	20	20	46	68	66	64	(B)	(B)	(B)
Male reference persons [1] . ₁ .	47	11	14	36	85	45	78	59	(B)	(B)	(B)
Female reference persons [1] . .	85	91	115	304	395	421	571	550	234	39	31
Related subfamilies	1,514	1,150	1,349	1,150	2,228	2,403	2,813	2,878	-	109	20
Married couple	871	617	576	582	719	871	1,014	1,015	-6	50	17
Father-child [1]	115	48	69	54	116	153	164	195	(B)	(B)	27
Mother-child [1]	528	484	705	512	1,392	1,378	1,636	1,668	6	169	21
Married couples	40,200	45,373	47,547	49,714	51,114	53,256	54,251	54,937	10	7	3
With own household	39,254	44,728	46,951	49,112	50,350	52,317	53,171	53,858	10	7	3
Without own household	946	645	596	602	764	939	1,080	1,079	-7	56	15
Percent without	2.4	1.4	1.3	1.2	1.5	1.8	2.0	2.0	(X)	(X)	(X)
Unrelated individuals	11,092	14,988	19,100	26,426	30,518	35,384	38,469	39,048	76	34	10
Nonfamily householders	7,895	11,945	15,557	21,226	24,082	27,257	28,617	29,686	78	28	9
Secondary individuals	3,198	3,043	3,543	5,200	6,436	8,127	9,852	9,362	71	56	15
Male	1,746	1,631	2,087	3,006	3,743	4,711	5,892	5,442	84	57	16
Female	1,451	1,412	1,456	2,194	2,693	3,416	3,961	3,920	55	56	15

- Represents or rounds to zero.   B Not shown; base less than 75,000.   X Not applicable.   [1] No spouse present.
Source: U.S. Bureau of the Census, *Current Population Reports*, P20-483 and unpublished data.

No. 67. Households—Projections, by Type of Household: 1996 to 2010

[In thousands. These numbers are based on the 1990 census, as enumerated, with modifications for age and race, and household estimates from 1991 to 1994, and are projected forward using alternative marital status and household-type proportions. Series 2 reflects the consequences of projected changes in the age/sex structure of the population only assuming no change from the composition in 1990 of the proportion maintaining households for specific types by age and sex. For details of assumptions for series 1 and 3, see tables 71 and 72]

TYPE OF HOUSEHOLD	1996	1997	1998	1999	2000	2005	2010
TOTAL HOUSEHOLDS							
Series 1	98,857	99,965	101,043	102,119	103,246	108,819	114,825
Series 2	98,801	99,880	100,924	101,966	103,058	108,426	114,200
Series 3	98,641	99,680	100,684	101,683	102,734	107,892	113,426
TYPE OF HOUSEHOLD (Series 1)							
Total	98,857	99,965	101,043	102,119	103,246	108,819	114,825
Family households	69,090	69,761	70,387	71,015	71,669	74,733	77,895
Married couple	53,893	54,319	54,707	55,092	55,496	57,371	59,308
Female householder, no spouse present . .	11,607	11,774	11,935	12,101	12,272	13,084	13,927
Male householder, no spouse present	3,590	3,668	3,745	3,822	3,901	4,278	4,660
With children under 18	32,806	32,951	33,001	33,058	33,117	32,699	32,203
Married couple	24,720	24,770	24,740	24,713	24,686	23,958	23,126
Female householder, no spouse present .	6,507	6,571	6,624	6,679	6,737	6,944	7,189
Male householder, no spouse present . .	1,578	1,610	1,638	1,666	1,694	1,797	1,888
Without children under 18	36,284	36,810	37,386	37,957	38,552	42,034	45,692
Married couple	29,173	29,549	29,968	30,378	30,810	33,413	36,182
Female householder, no spouse present .	5,099	5,202	5,311	5,422	5,535	6,140	6,738
Male householder, no spouse present . .	2,012	2,058	2,107	2,157	2,208	2,481	2,772
Nonfamily households	29,767	30,204	30,656	31,104	31,577	34,086	36,931
Female householder, total	16,269	16,464	16,671	16,875	17,095	18,301	19,702
Living alone [1]	14,304	14,480	14,664	14,844	15,035	16,093	17,327
Male householder, total	13,497	13,741	13,985	14,228	14,482	15,784	17,229
Living alone [1]	10,382	10,587	10,789	10,989	11,195	12,244	13,400

[1] These counts cover individuals 15 years of age or older.
Source: U.S. Bureau of the Census, *Current Population Reports*, P25-1129.

No. 68. Households, 1980 to 1995, and Persons in Households, 1995, by Type of Household and Presence of Children

[As of **March.** Based on Current Population Survey; see headnote, table 66]

TYPE OF HOUSEHOLD AND PRESENCE OF CHILDREN	HOUSEHOLDS					PERSONS IN HOUSEHOLDS, 1995		Persons per house-hold, 1995
	Number (1,000)			Percent distribution		Num-ber (1,000)	Percent distribu-tion	
	1980	1990	1995	1990	1995			
Total households	80,776	93,347	98,990	100	100	261,950	100	2.65
Family households	59,550	66,090	69,305	71	70	225,156	86	3.25
With own children under 18.	31,022	32,289	34,296	35	35	135,344	52	3.95
Without own children under 18.	28,528	33,801	35,009	36	35	89,812	34	2.57
Married couple family.	49,112	52,317	53,858	56	54	175,913	67	3.27
With own children under 18.	24,961	24,537	25,241	26	25	105,498	40	4.18
Without own children under 18.	24,151	27,780	28,617	30	29	70,415	27	2.46
Male householder, no spouse present. . .	1,733	2,884	3,226	3	3	10,294	4	3.19
With own children under 18.	616	1,153	1,440	1	1	4,813	2	3.34
Without own children under 18.	1,117	1,731	1,786	2	2	5,481	2	3.07
Female householder, no spouse present .	8,705	10,890	12,220	12	12	38,949	15	3.19
With own children under 18.	5,445	6,599	7,615	7	8	25,032	10	3.29
Without own children under 18.	3,261	4,290	4,606	5	5	13,917	5	3.02
Nonfamily households.	21,226	27,257	29,686	29	30	36,794	14	1.24
Living alone	18,296	22,999	24,732	25	25	24,732	9	1.00
Male householder	8,807	11,606	13,190	12	13	17,873	7	1.36
Living alone	6,966	9,049	10,140	10	10	10,140	4	1.00
Female householder	12,419	15,651	16,496	17	17	18,921	7	1.15
Living alone	11,330	13,950	14,592	15	15	14,592	6	1.00

Source: U.S. Bureau of the Census, *Current Population Reports*, P20-447, and earlier reports; and unpublished data.

No. 69. Household Characteristics, by Type of Household: 1995

[As of **March**. Based on Current Population Survey; see headnote, table 66. For composition of regions, see table 27]

CHARACTERISTIC	NUMBER OF HOUSEHOLDS (1,000)					PERCENT DISTRIBUTION				
	Total	Family households			Non-family house-holds	Total	Family households			Non-family house-holds
		Total [1]	Married couple	Female house-holder [2]			Total [1]	Married couple	Female house-holder [2]	
Total	98,990	69,305	53,858	12,220	29,686	100	100	100	100	100
Age of householder:										
15 to 24 years old.	5,444	3,079	1,632	1,124	2,365	5	4	3	9	8
25 to 29 years old.	8,400	5,575	3,959	1,234	2,825	8	8	7	10	10
30 to 34 years old.	11,052	8,502	6,357	1,731	2,551	11	12	12	14	9
35 to 44 years old.	22,914	18,273	13,919	3,502	4,641	23	26	26	29	16
45 to 54 years old.	17,590	13,746	11,153	2,037	3,845	18	20	21	17	13
55 to 64 years old.	12,224	8,894	7,552	1,056	3,330	12	13	14	9	11
65 to 74 years old.	11,803	7,268	6,169	853	4,535	12	10	11	7	15
75 years old and over	9,562	3,969	3,117	683	5,593	10	6	6	6	19
Region:										
Northeast	19,593	13,482	10,336	2,515	6,111	20	19	19	21	21
Midwest	23,683	16,264	12,836	2,754	7,418	24	23	24	23	25
South	34,766	24,871	19,201	4,590	9,895	35	36	36	38	33
West.	20,948	14,687	11,485	2,363	6,261	21	21	21	19	21
Size of household:										
One person	24,732	(X)	(X)	(X)	24,732	25	(X)	(X)	(X)	83
Two persons	31,834	27,875	21,366	5,065	3,959	32	40	40	41	13
Three persons	16,827	16,212	11,485	3,809	614	17	23	21	31	2
Four persons	15,321	15,056	12,741	1,837	265	15	22	24	15	1
Five persons	6,616	6,530	5,433	904	86	7	9	10	7	(Z)
Six persons	2,279	2,260	1,823	337	19	2	3	3	3	(Z)
Seven persons or more . . .	1,382	1,372	1,010	269	10	1	2	2	2	(Z)
Marital status of householder:										
Never married (single)	15,802	4,421	(X)	3,240	11,381	16	6	(X)	27	38
Married, spouse present. . .	53,858	53,858	53,858	(X)	(X)	54	78	100	(X)	(X)
Married, spouse absent . . .	4,708	2,645	(X)	2,160	2,063	5	4	(X)	18	7
Widowed.	11,450	2,715	(X)	2,283	8,734	12	4	(X)	19	29
Divorced	13,174	5,666	(X)	4,537	7,508	13	8	(X)	37	25
Tenure:										
Owner occupied	64,045	49,970	42,780	5,440	14,075	65	72	79	45	47
Renter occupied	34,946	19,335	11,078	6,781	15,611	35	28	21	55	53

X Not applicable.   Z Less than 0.5 percent.   [1] Includes male householder, no spouse present.   [2] No spouse present.

Source: U.S. Bureau of the Census, unpublished data.

No. 70. Households, by Age of Householder and Size of Household: 1970 to 1995

[**In millions**. As of **March**. Based on Current Population Survey; see headnote, table 66. See also *Historical Statistics, Colonial Times to 1970*, series A 335-349]

AGE OF HOUSEHOLDER AND SIZE OF HOUSEHOLD	1970	1975	1980	1985	1990	1995 Total [1]	White	Black	His-panic [2]
Total	63.4	71.1	80.8	86.8	93.3	99.0	83.7	11.7	7.7
Age of householder: [3]									
15 to 24 years old [3]	4.4	5.8	6.6	5.4	5.1	5.4	4.4	0.8	0.7
25 to 29 years old	6.1	7.8	9.3	9.6	9.4	8.4	6.8	1.2	1.0
30 to 34 years old	5.6	7.1	9.3	10.4	11.0	11.1	9.1	1.5	1.2
35 to 44 years old	11.8	11.9	14.0	17.5	20.6	22.9	19.0	3.0	1.9
45 to 54 years old	12.2	12.9	12.7	12.6	14.5	17.6	14.8	2.0	1.2
55 to 64 years old	10.8	11.3	12.5	13.1	12.5	12.2	10.6	1.3	0.8
65 to 74 years old	7.7	8.9	10.1	10.9	11.7	11.8	10.5	1.1	0.6
75 years old and over	4.8	5.4	6.4	7.3	8.4	9.6	8.7	0.7	0.3
One person	10.9	13.9	18.3	20.6	23.0	24.7	21.0	3.1	1.2
Male	3.5	4.9	7.0	7.9	9.0	10.1	8.5	1.4	0.5
Female	7.3	9.0	11.3	12.7	14.0	14.6	12.5	1.7	0.6
Two persons	18.3	21.8	25.3	27.4	30.1	31.8	28.0	3.0	1.7
Three persons	10.9	12.4	14.1	15.5	16.1	16.8	13.9	2.2	1.5
Four persons	10.0	11.1	12.7	13.6	14.5	15.3	12.8	1.7	1.6
Five persons	6.5	6.4	6.1	6.1	6.2	6.6	5.3	0.9	1.0
Six persons	3.5	3.1	2.5	2.3	2.1	2.3	1.8	0.4	0.5
Seven persons or more	3.2	2.5	1.8	1.3	1.3	1.4	0.9	0.3	0.4

[1] Includes other races, not shown separately.   [2] Hispanic persons may be of any race.   [3] 1970 and 1975, persons 14 to 24 years old.

Source: U.S. Bureau of the Census, *Current Population Reports*, P20-447, and earlier reports; and unpublished data.

No. 71. Households—Projections, by Age of Householder: 1996 to 2010

[**In thousands**. These numbers are based on the **1990** census, as enumerated, with modifications for age and race, and household estimates from **1991** to **1994**, and are projected forward using alternative marital status and household-type proportions. Series 1, shown here, is based on a time series model and is the preferred projection. For series 1, assumptions about future changes in family and household situation extend trends of the past 30 years]

AGE OF HOUSEHOLDER	1996	1997	1998	1999	2000	2005	2010
Households, total	98,857	99,965	101,043	102,119	103,246	108,819	114,825
Under 25 years old	4,712	4,700	4,758	4,854	4,966	5,399	5,724
25 to 34 years old	18,528	18,159	17,746	17,336	17,045	16,547	17,426
35 to 44 years old	23,183	23,517	23,767	23,916	23,914	22,560	20,581
45 to 54 years old	18,449	19,179	19,727	20,434	21,210	23,924	25,283
55 to 64 years old	12,464	12,735	13,237	13,658	14,002	17,331	20,693
65 to 74 years old	11,797	11,682	11,588	11,475	11,446	11,597	13,298
75 years and over	9,723	9,993	10,221	10,447	10,663	11,462	11,821

Source: U.S. Bureau of the Census, *Current Population Reports*, P25-1129.

No. 72. Households—Projections, by Race and Hispanic Origin of Householder: 1996 to 2010

[**In thousands**. These numbers are based on the **1990** census, as enumerated, with modifications for age and race, and household estimates from **1991** to **1994**, and are projected forward using alternative marital status and household-type proportions. Race and Hispanic origin of householders were not tabulated for either series 1 or series 2. Series 3, shown here, reflects the consequences of projected change in both the age/sex structure and race/origin composition of the population. Current patterns of family and householdership are assumed to remain at their **1990** proportions]

CHARACTERISTIC OF HOUSEHOLDER	1996	1997	1998	1999	2000	2005	2010
Households, total	98,641	99,680	100,684	101,683	102,734	107,892	113,426
White	83,870	84,586	85,271	85,952	86,676	90,204	94,010
Black	11,354	11,556	11,753	11,948	12,149	13,137	14,185
American Indian, Eskimo, Aleut	700	713	727	740	754	827	906
Asian, Pacific Islander	2,717	2,824	2,933	3,043	3,155	3,724	4,324
Hispanic origin [1]	7,643	7,917	8,195	8,474	8,761	10,236	11,866

[1] Persons of Hispanic origin may be of any race.

Source: U.S. Bureau of the Census, *Current Population Reports*, P25-1129.

No. 73. Households—States: 1980 to 1994

[As of **April 1**, except **beginning 1991**, as of **July 1**. Minus sign (-) indicates decrease]

REGION, DIVISION, AND STATE	NUMBER (1,000)							PERCENT CHANGE		PERSONS PER HOUSEHOLD		
						1994						
	1980	1990	1991	1992	1993	Total	Householder 65 yrs. and over	1980-90	1990-94	1980	1990	1994
U.S.	80,390	91,946	93,183	94,652	95,335	95,946	20,876	14.4	4.4	2.75	2.63	2.64
Northeast . .	17,471	18,873	18,964	19,092	19,067	19,045	4,506	8.0	0.9	2.74	2.61	2.62
N.E	4,362	4,943	4,961	4,987	4,980	4,980	1,142	13.3	0.8	2.74	2.58	2.58
ME. . . .	395	465	471	474	475	474	108	17.7	2.0	2.75	2.56	2.54
NH. . . .	323	411	413	417	419	424	83	27.1	3.0	2.75	2.62	2.61
VT	178	211	214	217	219	220	44	18.1	4.6	2.75	2.57	2.54
MA. . . .	2,033	2,247	2,250	2,263	2,262	2,265	528	10.5	0.8	2.72	2.58	2.57
RI	339	378	379	380	377	374	96	11.6	-1.1	2.70	2.55	2.57
CT	1,094	1,230	1,234	1,235	1,228	1,222	283	12.5	-0.7	2.76	2.59	2.60
M.A	13,109	13,930	14,003	14,106	14,087	14,065	3,364	6.3	1.0	2.74	2.62	2.64
NY	6,340	6,639	6,662	6,703	6,689	6,669	1,494	4.7	0.4	2.70	2.63	2.64
NJ	2,549	2,795	2,812	2,839	2,839	2,845	659	9.7	1.8	2.84	2.70	2.72
PA	4,220	4,496	4,529	4,564	4,559	4,551	1,211	6.5	1.2	2.74	2.57	2.57
Midwest . . .	20,859	22,317	22,543	22,818	22,893	22,937	5,156	7.0	2.8	2.75	2.60	2.61
E.N.C. . . .	14,654	15,597	15,776	15,970	16,021	16,051	3,539	6.4	2.9	2.78	2.63	2.62
OH. . . .	3,834	4,088	4,135	4,181	4,189	4,190	949	6.6	2.5	2.76	2.59	2.59
IN	1,927	2,065	2,102	2,133	2,149	2,161	470	7.2	4.6	2.77	2.61	2.59
IL	4,045	4,202	4,243	4,291	4,301	4,308	936	3.9	2.5	2.76	2.65	2.66
MI	3,195	3,419	3,454	3,496	3,498	3,502	754	7.0	2.4	2.84	2.66	2.65
WI	1,652	1,822	1,842	1,869	1,883	1,890	430	10.3	3.7	2.77	2.61	2.62
W.N.C . . .	6,205	6,720	6,767	6,848	6,872	6,886	1,617	8.3	2.5	2.68	2.55	2.57
MN. . . .	1,445	1,648	1,667	1,689	1,702	1,711	362	14.0	3.8	2.74	2.58	2.60
IA. . . .	1,053	1,064	1,069	1,083	1,084	1,082	277	1.1	1.6	2.68	2.52	2.52
MO. . . .	1,793	1,961	1,976	1,996	2,002	2,008	478	9.4	2.4	2.67	2.53	2.56
ND. . . .	228	241	240	242	242	241	60	5.8	0.2	2.75	2.55	2.54
SD	243	259	260	263	264	265	68	6.8	2.1	2.74	2.59	2.63
NE	571	602	606	614	614	614	147	5.4	2.0	2.66	2.54	2.56
KS	872	945	948	961	964	966	225	8.3	2.2	2.62	2.53	2.56
South	26,486	31,821	32,376	32,976	33,342	33,713	7,325	20.1	5.9	2.77	2.61	2.62
S.A	13,160	16,502	16,826	17,149	17,331	17,530	3,970	25.4	6.2	2.73	2.56	2.58
DE	207	247	253	258	262	264	56	19.5	6.8	2.79	2.61	2.59
MD. . . .	1,461	1,749	1,778	1,807	1,818	1,831	344	19.7	4.7	2.82	2.67	2.67
DC. . . .	253	250	247	245	242	237	51	-1.4	-5.2	2.40	2.26	2.24
VA. . . .	1,863	2,292	2,333	2,384	2,413	2,439	453	23.0	6.4	2.77	2.61	2.60
WV. . . .	686	689	696	703	705	705	188	0.3	2.4	2.79	2.55	2.53
NC. . . .	2,043	2,517	2,566	2,608	2,641	2,679	566	23.2	6.4	2.78	2.54	2.55
SC	1,030	1,258	1,292	1,313	1,325	1,337	280	22.1	6.3	2.93	2.68	2.66
GA. . . .	1,872	2,366	2,425	2,488	2,531	2,581	451	26.4	9.1	2.84	2.66	2.67
FL	3,744	5,135	5,236	5,341	5,393	5,456	1,581	37.1	6.3	2.55	2.46	2.50
E.S.C. . . .	5,051	5,652	5,743	5,832	5,886	5,938	1,328	11.9	5.1	2.83	2.62	2.61
KY	1,263	1,380	1,398	1,418	1,431	1,440	321	9.2	4.3	2.82	2.60	2.59
TN	1,619	1,854	1,887	1,921	1,942	1,966	424	14.5	6.0	2.77	2.56	2.57
AL	1,342	1,507	1,533	1,558	1,573	1,583	363	12.3	5.1	2.84	2.62	2.61
MS. . . .	827	911	925	934	941	949	221	10.2	4.2	2.97	2.75	2.74
W.S.C . . .	8,276	9,667	9,807	9,996	10,124	10,245	2,027	16.8	6.0	2.80	2.69	2.71
AR	816	891	899	910	919	927	235	9.2	4.0	2.74	2.57	2.58
LA	1,412	1,499	1,514	1,534	1,538	1,543	321	6.2	2.9	2.91	2.74	2.72
OK. . . .	1,119	1,206	1,211	1,229	1,234	1,236	288	7.8	2.5	2.62	2.53	2.56
TX	4,929	6,071	6,183	6,322	6,433	6,539	1,184	23.2	7.7	2.82	2.73	2.75
West	15,574	18,935	19,300	19,765	20,033	20,251	3,889	21.6	6.9	2.71	2.72	2.74
Mountain .	3,986	5,033	5,151	5,303	5,433	5,574	1,092	26.3	10.7	2.79	2.65	2.68
MT	284	306	309	315	321	325	73	7.9	6.1	2.70	2.53	2.56
ID	324	361	372	384	395	405	84	11.3	12.2	2.85	2.73	2.75
WY. . . .	166	169	170	174	176	178	34	1.9	5.3	2.78	2.63	2.62
CO. . . .	1,061	1,282	1,306	1,348	1,386	1,417	234	20.8	10.5	2.65	2.51	2.52
NM. . . .	441	543	553	568	577	587	116	22.9	8.1	2.90	2.74	2.77
AZ	957	1,369	1,390	1,429	1,461	1,503	340	43.0	9.8	2.79	2.62	2.66
UT	449	537	553	571	585	599	107	19.8	11.6	3.20	3.15	3.13
NV	304	466	496	516	532	560	102	53.2	20.1	2.59	2.53	2.56
Pacific. . .	11,587	13,902	14,149	14,462	14,600	14,677	2,798	20.0	5.6	2.68	2.74	2.77
WA. . . .	1,541	1,872	1,922	1,977	2,018	2,042	391	21.5	9.1	2.61	2.53	2.56
OR. . . .	992	1,103	1,130	1,156	1,178	1,195	267	11.3	8.3	2.60	2.52	2.53
CA. . . .	8,630	10,381	10,536	10,752	10,821	10,850	2,042	20.3	4.5	2.68	2.79	2.83
AK	131	189	194	202	206	208	17	43.7	10.3	2.93	2.80	2.81
HI	294	356	367	375	378	381	81	21.2	7.1	3.15	3.01	2.99

Source: U.S. Bureau of the Census, *1980 Census of Population*, vol. 1, chapter B; *1990 Census of Population, General Population Characteristics, United States* (1990 CP-1-1); and unpublished data.

No. 74. Family and Nonfamily Households, by Race, Hispanic Origin, and Type: 1970 to 1995

[As of **March**, except as noted. Based on Current Population Survey, except as noted; see headnote, table 66. See also *Historical Statistics, Colonial Times to 1970*, series A 292-295 and A 320-334]

RACE, HISPANIC ORIGIN, AND TYPE	NUMBER (1,000)					PERCENT DISTRIBUTION				
	1970	1980	1985	1990	1995	1970	1980	1985	1990	1995
TOTAL HOUSEHOLDS										
Total [1]	63,401	80,776	86,789	93,347	98,990	100	100	100	100	100
White	56,602	70,766	75,328	80,163	83,737	89	88	87	86	85
Black	6,223	8,586	9,480	10,486	11,655	10	11	11	11	12
Hispanic [2]	2,303	3,684	4,883	5,933	7,735	4	5	6	6	8
FAMILY HOUSEHOLDS										
White, total	46,166	52,243	54,400	56,590	58,437	100	100	100	100	100
Married couple	41,029	44,751	45,643	46,981	47,899	89	86	84	83	82
Male householder [3]	1,038	1,441	1,816	2,303	2,507	2	3	3	4	4
Female householder [3]	4,099	6,052	6,941	7,306	8,031	9	12	13	13	14
Black, total	4,856	6,184	6,778	7,470	8,093	100	100	100	100	100
Married couple	3,317	3,433	3,469	3,750	3,842	68	56	51	50	47
Male householder [3]	181	256	344	446	536	4	4	5	6	7
Female householder [3]	1,358	2,495	2,964	3,275	3,716	28	40	44	44	46
Asian or Pacific Islander, total [4]	(NA)	818	(NA)	1,531	1,588	(NA)	100	(NA)	100	100
Married couple	(NA)	691	(NA)	1,256	1,290	(NA)	84	(NA)	82	81
Male householder [3]	(NA)	39	(NA)	86	98	(NA)	5	(NA)	6	6
Female householder [3]	(NA)	88	(NA)	188	200	(NA)	11	(NA)	12	13
Hispanic, total [2]	2,004	3,029	3,939	4,840	6,200	100	100	100	100	100
Married couple	1,615	2,282	2,824	3,395	4,235	81	75	72	70	68
Male householder [3]	82	138	210	329	479	4	5	5	7	8
Female householder [3]	307	610	905	1,116	1,485	15	20	23	23	24
NONFAMILY HOUSEHOLDS										
White, total	10,436	18,522	20,928	23,573	25,300	100	100	100	100	100
Male householder	3,406	7,499	8,608	9,951	11,093	33	40	41	42	44
Female householder	7,030	11,023	12,320	13,622	14,207	67	60	59	58	56
Black, total	1,367	2,402	2,703	3,015	3,562	100	100	100	100	100
Male householder	564	1,146	1,244	1,313	1,653	41	48	46	44	46
Female householder	803	1,256	1,459	1,702	1,909	59	52	54	56	54
Hispanic, total [2]	299	654	944	1,093	1,535	100	100	100	100	100
Male householder	150	365	509	587	790	50	56	54	54	51
Female householder	148	289	435	506	745	49	44	46	46	49

NA Not available.   [1] Includes other races not shown separately.   [2] Hispanic persons may be of any race. 1970 data as of April.   [3] No spouse present.   [4] 1980 data as of April and are from 1980 Census of Population.
Source: U.S. Bureau of the Census, *Census of Population: 1970, Persons of Spanish Origin*, PC(2)-1C; and *Current Population Reports*, P20-447, and earlier reports; and unpublished data.

No. 75. Family Groups with Children Under 18 Years Old, by Race and Hispanic Origin: 1970 to 1995

[As of **March**. Family groups comprise family households, related subfamilies, and unrelated subfamilies. Excludes members of Armed Forces except those living off post or with their families on post. Based on Current Population Survey; see text, section 1, and Appendix III]

RACE AND HISPANIC ORIGIN OF HOUSEHOLDER OR REFERENCE PERSON	NUMBER (1,000)				PERCENT DISTRIBUTION			
	1970	1980	1990	1995	1970	1980	1990	1995
All races, total [1]	29,631	32,150	34,670	37,168	100	100	100	100
Two-parent family groups	25,823	25,231	24,921	25,640	87	79	72	69
One-parent family groups	3,808	6,920	9,749	11,528	13	22	28	31
Maintained by mother	3,415	6,230	8,398	9,834	12	19	24	26
Maintained by father	393	690	1,351	1,694	1	2	4	5
White, total	26,115	27,294	28,294	29,846	100	100	100	100
Two-parent family groups	23,477	22,628	21,905	22,320	90	83	77	75
One-parent family groups	2,638	4,664	6,389	7,525	10	17	23	25
Maintained by mother	2,330	4,122	5,310	6,239	9	15	19	21
Maintained by father	307	542	1,079	1,286	1	2	4	4
Black, total	3,219	4,074	5,087	5,491	100	100	100	100
Two-parent family groups	2,071	1,961	2,006	1,962	64	48	39	36
One-parent family groups	1,148	2,114	3,081	3,529	36	52	61	64
Maintained by mother	1,063	1,984	2,860	3,197	33	49	56	58
Maintained by father	85	129	221	332	3	3	4	6
Hispanic, total [2]	(NA)	2,194	3,429	4,527	(NA)	100	100	100
Two-parent family groups	(NA)	1,626	2,289	2,879	(NA)	74	67	64
One-parent family groups	(NA)	568	1,140	1,647	(NA)	26	33	36
Maintained by mother	(NA)	526	1,003	1,404	(NA)	24	29	31
Maintained by father	(NA)	42	138	243	(NA)	2	4	5

NA Not available.   [1] Includes other races, not shown separately.   [2] Hispanic persons may be of any race.
Source: U.S. Bureau of the Census, *Current Population Reports*, P20-447, and earlier reports; and unpublished data.

No. 76. Family Groups With Children Under 18 Years Old, by Type, Race and Hispanic Origin: 1995

[As of **March**. Excludes members of Armed Forces except those living off post or with their families on post. Based on Current Population Survey; see text, section 1, and Appendix III]

RACE AND HISPANIC ORIGIN OF HOUSEHOLDER OR REFERENCE PERSON	NUMBER (1,000)					PERCENT DISTRIBUTION				
	Total	Family house-holds	Subfamilies			Total	Family house-holds	Subfamilies		
			Total	Related	Unre-lated			Total	Related	Unre-lated
All races, total [1]	37,168	34,296	2,872	2,241	631	100	100	100	100	100
Two-parent family groups	25,640	25,241	399	377	22	69	74	14	17	3
One-parent family groups	11,528	9,055	2,473	1,863	609	31	26	86	83	97
Maintained by mother.	9,834	7,615	2,219	1,668	550	26	22	77	74	87
Maintained by father.	1,694	1,440	254	195	59	5	4	9	9	9
White, total.	29,846	27,951	1,895	1,371	524	100	100	100	100	100
Two-parent family groups	22,320	22,005	315	296	20	75	79	17	22	4
One-parent family groups	7,525	5,946	1,579	1,075	504	25	21	83	78	96
Maintained by mother.	6,239	4,841	1,398	940	458	21	17	74	69	87
Maintained by father.	1,286	1,105	181	135	46	4	4	10	10	9
Black, total.	5,491	4,682	809	729	80	100	100	100	100	100
Two-parent family groups	1,962	1,926	36	34	2	36	41	4	5	3
One-parent family groups	3,529	2,756	773	694	79	64	59	96	95	99
Maintained by mother.	3,197	2,489	708	642	66	58	53	88	88	83
Maintained by father.	332	267	65	52	13	6	6	8	7	16
Hispanic, total [2]	4,527	3,984	543	448	95	100	100	100	100	100
Two-parent family groups	2,879	2,743	136	123	13	64	69	25	27	14
One-parent family groups	1,647	1,240	407	325	82	36	31	75	73	86
Maintained by mother.	1,404	1,048	356	277	79	31	26	66	62	83
Maintained by father.	243	192	51	48	3	5	5	9	11	3

[1] Includes other races, not shown separately. [2] Hispanic persons may be of any race.

Source: U.S. Bureau of the Census, unpublished data.

No. 77. Families, by Size and Presence of Children: 1980 to 1995

[In thousands, except as indicated. As of **March**. Excludes members of Armed Forces except those living off post or with their families on post. Based on Current Population Survey; see text, section 1, and Appendix III. For definition of families, see text, section 1]

CHARACTERISTIC	NUMBER				PERCENT DISTRIBUTION			
	1980	1985	1990	1995	1980	1985	1990	1995
Total.	59,550	62,706	66,090	69,305	100	100	100	100
Size of family:								
Two persons	23,461	25,349	27,606	29,176	39	40	42	42
Three persons	13,603	14,804	15,353	15,903	23	24	23	23
Four persons	12,372	13,259	14,026	14,624	21	21	21	21
Five persons	5,930	5,894	5,938	6,283	10	9	9	9
Six persons	2,461	2,175	1,997	2,106	4	4	3	3
Seven or more persons . .	1,723	1,225	1,170	1,213	3	2	2	2
Average per family	3.29	3.23	3.17	3.19	(X)	(X)	(X)	(X)
Own children under age 18:								
None	28,528	31,594	33,801	35,009	48	50	51	51
One	12,443	13,108	13,530	14,088	21	21	20	20
Two	11,470	11,645	12,263	13,213	19	19	19	19
Three	4,674	4,486	4,650	5,044	8	7	7	7
Four or more	2,435	1,873	1,846	1,951	4	3	3	3
Own children under age 6:								
None	46,063	48,505	50,905	53,695	77	77	77	77
One	9,441	9,677	10,304	10,733	16	15	16	15
Two or more	4,047	4,525	4,882	4,876	7	7	7	7

X Not applicable.

Source: U.S. Bureau of the Census, *Current Population Reports*, P20-447, and earlier reports; and unpublished data.

No. 78. Families, by Number of Own Children Under 18 Years Old: 1970 to 1995

[Except as noted, as of **March** and based on Current Population Survey; see headnote, table 77. See also *Historical Statistics, Colonial Times to 1970*, series A 353-358]

RACE, HISPANIC ORIGIN, AND YEAR	NUMBER OF FAMILIES (1,000)					PERCENT DISTRIBUTION				
	Total	No chil-dren	One child	Two chil-dren	Three or more chil-dren	Total	No chil-dren	One child	Two chil-dren	Three or more chil-dren
ALL FAMILIES [1]										
1970	51,586	22,774	9,398	8,969	10,445	100	44	18	17	20
1980	59,550	28,528	12,443	11,470	7,109	100	48	21	19	12
1985	62,706	31,594	13,108	11,645	6,359	100	50	21	19	10
1990	66,090	33,801	13,530	12,263	6,496	100	51	20	19	10
1995	69,305	35,009	14,088	13,213	6,995	100	51	20	19	10
Married couple	53,858	28,617	9,564	10,358	5,319	100	53	18	19	10
Male householder [2]	3,226	1,786	891	405	144	100	55	28	13	4
Female householder [2]	12,220	4,606	3,633	2,450	1,531	100	38	30	20	13
WHITE FAMILIES										
1970	46,261	20,719	8,437	8,174	8,931	100	45	18	18	19
1980	52,243	25,769	10,727	9,977	5,769	100	49	21	19	11
1985	54,400	28,169	11,174	9,937	5,120	100	52	21	18	9
1990	56,590	29,872	11,186	10,342	5,191	100	53	20	18	9
1995	58,437	30,486	11,491	10,983	5,478	100	52	20	19	9
BLACK FAMILIES										
1970	4,887	1,903	858	726	1,401	100	39	18	15	29
1980	6,184	2,364	1,449	1,235	1,136	100	38	23	20	18
1985	6,778	2,887	1,579	1,330	982	100	43	23	20	15
1990	7,470	3,093	1,894	1,433	1,049	100	41	25	19	14
1995	8,093	3,411	1,971	1,593	1,117	100	42	24	20	14
HISPANIC FAMILIES [3]										
1970	2,004	597	390	388	629	100	30	20	19	31
1980	3,029	946	680	698	706	100	31	22	23	23
1985	3,939	1,337	904	865	833	100	34	23	22	21
1990	4,840	1,790	1,095	1,036	919	100	37	23	21	19
1995	6,200	2,216	1,408	1,406	1,171	100	36	23	23	19

[1] Includes other races, not shown separately. [2] No spouse present. [3] Hispanic persons may be of any race. 1970 Hispanic data as of April and based on Census of Population.

Source: U.S. Bureau of the Census, *U.S. Census of Population, 1970* (PC-2-4A), and *Current Population Reports*, P20-447, and earlier reports; and unpublished data.

No. 79. Female Family Householders With No Spouse Present—Characteristics, by Race and Hispanic Origin: 1980 to 1995

[As of **March**. Covers persons 15 years old and over. Based on Current Population Survey; see headnote, table 77]

CHARACTERISTIC	Unit	WHITE			BLACK			HISPANIC ORIGIN [1]		
		1980	1990	1995	1980	1990	1995	1980	1990	1995
Female family householder	1,000	**6,052**	**7,306**	**8,031**	**2,495**	**3,275**	**3,716**	**610**	**1,116**	**1,485**
Marital status:										
Never married (single)	Percent ...	11	15	19	27	39	42	23	27	31
Married, spouse absent	Percent ...	17	16	17	29	21	19	32	29	26
Widowed	Percent ...	33	26	21	22	17	14	15	16	14
Divorced	Percent ...	40	43	43	22	23	25	30	29	29
Presence of children under age 18:										
No own children	Percent ...	41	43	40	28	32	33	25	33	29
With own children	Percent ...	59	58	60	72	68	67	75	67	71
One child	Percent ...	28	30	31	26	30	28	28	25	28
Two children	Percent ...	20	19	20	23	22	21	23	22	22
Three children	Percent ...	7	7	7	11	9	11	15	13	13
Four or more children	Percent ...	3	2	3	11	7	7	9	6	8
Children per family	Number ...	1.03	0.95	1.02	1.51	1.26	1.27	1.56	1.37	1.50

[1] Persons of Hispanic origin may be of any race.

Source: U.S. Bureau of the Census, *Current Population Reports*, P20-447, and earlier reports; and unpublished data.

No. 80. Family Households With Own Children Under Age 18, by Type of Family, 1980 to 1995, and by Age of Householder, 1995

[As of **March**. Excludes members of Armed Forces except those living off post or with their families on post. Based on Current Population Survey; see text, section 1, and Appendix III]

FAMILY TYPE	1980	1990	1995 Total	15 to 24 years old	25 to 34 years old	35 to 44 years old	45 to 54 years old	55 to 64 years old	65 years old and over
NUMBER (1,000)									
Family households with children...	31,022	32,289	34,296	1,969	10,763	14,922	5,752	743	147
Married couple	24,961	24,537	25,241	899	7,528	11,383	4,712	602	118
Male householder [1]	616	1,153	1,440	106	466	556	243	53	16
Female householder [1]	5,445	6,599	7,615	963	2,769	2,983	798	88	13
PERCENT DISTRIBUTION									
Family households with children...	100	100	100	100	100	100	100	100	100
Married couple	81	76	74	46	70	76	82	81	80
Male householder [1]	2	4	4	5	4	4	4	7	11
Female householder [1]	18	20	22	49	26	20	14	12	9
HOUSEHOLDS WITH CHILDREN, AS A PERCENT OF ALL FAMILY HOUSEHOLDS, BY TYPE									
Family households with children, total	52	49	49	64	76	82	42	8	1
Married couple	51	47	47	55	73	82	42	8	1
Male householder [1]	36	40	45	33	59	65	44	19	4
Female householder [1]	63	61	62	86	93	85	39	8	1

[1] No spouse present.

Source: U.S. Bureau of the Census, *Current Population Reports*, P20-447, and earlier reports; and unpublished data.

No. 81. Children Under 18 Years Old, by Presence of Parents: 1970 to 1995

[As of **March**. Excludes persons under 18 years old who maintained households or family groups. Based on Current Population Survey; see headnote, table 77]

RACE, HISPANIC ORIGIN, AND YEAR	Number (1,000)	PERCENT LIVING WITH— Both parents	Mother only Total	Divorced	Married, spouse absent	Never married	Wid-owed	Father only	Neither parent
ALL RACES [1]									
1970	69,162	85	11	3	5	1	2	1	3
1980	63,427	77	18	8	6	3	2	2	4
1985	62,475	74	21	9	5	6	2	3	3
1990	64,137	73	22	8	5	7	2	3	3
1995	70,254	69	23	9	6	8	1	4	4
WHITE									
1970	58,790	90	8	3	3	(Z)	2	1	2
1980	52,242	83	14	7	4	1	2	2	2
1985	50,836	80	16	8	4	2	1	2	2
1990	51,390	79	16	8	4	3	1	3	2
1995	55,327	76	18	8	5	4	1	3	3
BLACK									
1970	9,422	59	30	5	16	4	4	2	10
1980	9,375	42	44	11	16	13	4	2	12
1985	9,479	40	51	11	12	25	3	3	7
1990	10,018	38	51	10	12	27	2	4	8
1995	11,301	33	52	11	11	29	2	4	11
HISPANIC [2]									
1970	[3]4,006	78	(NA)	(NA)	(NA)	(NA)	(NA)	(NA)	(NA)
1980	5,459	75	20	6	8	4	2	2	4
1985	6,057	68	27	7	11	7	2	2	3
1990	7,174	67	27	7	10	8	2	3	3
1995	9,843	63	28	8	9	10	1	4	4

NA Not available.   Z Less than 0.5 percent.   [1] Includes other races not shown separately.   [2] Hispanic persons may be of any race.   [3] All persons under 18 years old.

Source: U.S. Bureau of the Census, *Current Population Reports*, P20-450, and earlier reports; and unpublished data.

No. 82. Living Arrangements of Children Under 18 Years Old Living With One or Both Parents: 1995

[In thousands. As of March. Covers only those persons under 18 years old who are living with one or both parents. Characteristics are shown for the householder or reference person in married-couple situations. See also headnote, table 77]

CHARACTERISTIC OF PARENT	ALL RACES [1] Total	Living with—Both parents	Mother only	Father only	WHITE Total	Living with—Both parents	Mother only	Father only	BLACK Total	Living with—Both parents	Mother only	Father only	HISPANIC [2] Total	Living with—Both parents	Mother only	Father only
Children under 18 years old	**67,214**	**48,276**	**16,477**	**2,461**	**53,665**	**41,946**	**9,827**	**1,892**	**10,085**	**3,746**	**5,881**	**458**	**9,405**	**6,191**	**2,798**	**417**
Age:																
15 to 24 years old	4,094	1,374	2,552	170	2,635	1,219	1,289	126	1,256	78	1,140	38	876	365	459	52
25 to 29 years old	7,751	4,628	2,753	370	5,723	3,905	1,537	281	1,630	478	1,088	64	1,525	960	490	76
30 to 34 years old	14,531	10,139	3,908	484	11,377	8,732	2,295	349	2,487	939	1,435	113	2,142	1,403	647	92
35 to 39 years old	17,459	13,060	3,857	541	14,402	11,521	2,473	407	2,233	923	1,197	113	2,194	1,456	670	68
40 to 44 years old	13,072	10,541	2,094	437	11,028	9,307	1,377	343	1,370	666	633	71	1,444	1,042	334	69
45 to 54 years old	9,018	7,488	1,176	353	7,476	6,387	777	312	915	551	332	32	1,026	814	165	46
55 to 64 years old	1,091	894	114	82	876	742	72	62	150	93	39	17	163	127	31	5
65 years old and over	199	152	24	23	149	132	6	10	44	17	15	11	35	24	2	9
Educational attainment:																
Less than 9th grade	4,174	3,009	1,030	135	3,283	2,429	750	105	280	98	169	14	2,781	2,012	692	78
9th to 12th grade, no diploma	7,776	3,876	3,453	447	5,239	3,254	1,668	316	2,108	381	1,608	120	2,015	1,107	790	118
High school graduate [3]	21,807	14,757	6,037	1,012	17,164	12,714	3,670	780	3,841	1,490	2,165	187	2,417	1,511	772	133
Some college, no degree or associate degree	18,040	12,848	4,623	570	14,414	11,188	2,773	453	2,862	1,144	1,626	91	1,591	1,030	483	78
Bachelor's degree	9,822	8,665	963	194	8,570	7,737	672	161	758	476	252	30	377	334	38	5
Graduate or professional degree	5,594	5,120	372	102	4,995	4,624	294	77	236	158	61	17	225	196	23	6
Employment status: [4]																
In the civilian labor force	55,405	42,724	10,545	2,135	45,902	37,508	6,694	1,700	6,868	3,135	3,387	345	7,059	5,326	1,377	357
Employed	51,946	40,915	9,082	1,949	43,510	36,030	5,921	1,559	6,039	2,960	2,763	316	6,310	4,915	1,073	322
Both parents employed	27,938	27,938	(X)	(X)	24,508	24,508	(X)	(X)	2,227	2,227	(X)	(X)	2,450	2,450	(X)	(X)
Unemployed	3,459	1,810	1,463	186	2,392	1,478	773	141	829	175	624	29	750	411	304	35
Not in the labor force	10,838	4,609	5,923	306	7,056	3,751	3,128	178	3,038	436	2,489	113	2,293	812	1,421	60
Family income:																
Under $5,000	3,291	629	2,513	149	1,855	462	1,297	96	1,212	58	1,108	44	728	191	488	49
$5,000 to $9,999	5,349	1,378	3,728	244	3,258	1,135	1,959	165	1,796	130	1,597	69	1,320	477	793	51
$10,000 to $14,999	5,069	2,185	2,541	343	3,453	1,717	1,487	249	1,282	273	936	72	1,324	711	553	61
$15,000 to $24,999	9,151	5,526	3,046	579	6,995	4,653	1,896	445	1,625	532	995	98	2,040	1,472	455	113
$25,000 to $29,999	4,258	3,072	992	194	3,408	2,563	690	155	650	344	271	34	653	528	108	16
$30,000 to $39,999	8,907	6,963	1,591	352	7,448	6,028	1,127	293	997	562	387	47	1,154	927	164	63
$40,000 to $49,999	7,643	6,605	850	188	6,567	5,830	579	158	768	529	222	17	756	631	109	16
$50,000 and over	23,546	21,917	1,217	411	20,680	19,557	792	332	1,755	1,317	362	75	1,430	1,254	129	47
Tenure: [5]																
Owned	42,406	35,588	5,558	1,261	37,154	32,084	4,001	1,069	3,552	2,090	1,317	144	3,846	3,092	608	146
Rented	24,808	12,688	10,920	1,200	16,511	9,862	5,826	823	6,534	1,657	4,563	314	5,559	3,098	2,190	270

X Not applicable.　[1] Includes other races, not shown separately.　[2] Persons of Hispanic origin may be of any race.　[3] Includes equivalency.　[4] Excludes children whose parent is in the Armed Forces.　[5] Refers to the tenure of the householder (who may or may not be the child's parent).

Source: U.S. Bureau of the Census, unpublished data.

No. 83. Nonfamily Households, by Sex and Age of Householder: 1980 to 1995

[In thousands. As of March. See headnote, table 77]

ITEM	MALE HOUSEHOLDER					FEMALE HOUSEHOLDER				
	Total	15 to 24 yr. old	25 to 44 yr. old	45 to 64 yr. old	65 yr. old and over	Total	15 to 24 yr. old	25 to 44 yr. old	45 to 64 yr. old	65 yr. old and over
1980, total	**8,807**	**1,567**	**3,854**	**1,822**	**1,565**	**12,419**	**1,189**	**2,198**	**3,048**	**5,983**
One person (living alone).	6,966	947	2,920	1,613	1,486	11,330	779	1,809	2,901	5,842
Nonrelatives present. . . .	1,841	620	934	209	79	1,089	410	389	147	141
1990, total	**11,606**	**1,236**	**5,780**	**2,536**	**2,053**	**15,651**	**1,032**	**3,697**	**3,545**	**7,377**
One person (living alone).	9,049	674	4,231	2,203	1,943	13,950	536	2,881	3,300	7,233
Nonrelatives present. . . .	2,557	560	1,551	334	112	1,701	497	817	245	143
Never married	5,844	1,175	3,689	696	285	4,382	976	2,406	510	491
Married [1]	1,117	28	513	391	187	794	15	261	320	198
Widowed	1,417	-	29	221	1,166	7,428	4	52	1,333	6,038
Divorced.	3,228	33	1,550	1,229	416	3,046	37	977	1,382	649
1995, total	**13,190**	**1,258**	**6,273**	**3,270**	**2,388**	**16,496**	**1,108**	**3,744**	**3,904**	**7,741**
One person (living alone).	10,140	623	4,477	2,787	2,253	14,592	572	2,839	3,589	7,591
Nonrelatives present. . . .	3,050	635	1,796	483	135	1,904	536	904	315	150
Single (Never married) . .	6,644	1,185	4,115	953	389	4,737	1,046	2,436	749	505
Married [1]	1,175	37	547	378	212	888	31	288	347	222
Widowed	1,514	-	22	238	1,256	7,220	3	74	952	6,191
Divorced.	3,857	35	1,587	1,703	530	3,651	27	946	1,855	823

- Represents or rounds to zero.   [1] No spouse present.

Source: U.S. Bureau of the Census, *Current Population Reports*, P20-450, and earlier reports; and unpublished data.

No. 84. Persons Living Alone, by Sex and Age: 1970 to 1995

[As of March. Based on Current Population Survey; see headnote, table 77]

SEX AND AGE	NUMBER OF PERSONS (1,000)					PERCENT DISTRIBUTION				
	1970	1980	1985	1990	1995	1970	1980	1985	1990	1995
Both sexes	**10,851**	**18,296**	**20,602**	**22,999**	**24,732**	**100**	**100**	**100**	**100**	**100**
15 to 24 years old [1]	556	1,726	1,324	1,210	1,196	5	9	6	5	5
25 to 34 years old	[2]1,604	[2]4,729	3,905	3,972	3,653	[2]15	[2]26	19	17	15
35 to 44 years old	[2]	[2]	2,322	3,138	3,663	[2]	[2]	11	14	15
45 to 64 years old	3,622	4,514	4,939	5,502	6,377	33	25	24	24	26
65 to 74 years old	2,815	3,851	4,130	4,350	4,374	26	21	20	19	18
75 years old and over	2,256	3,477	3,982	4,825	5,470	21	19	19	21	22
Male	**3,532**	**6,966**	**7,922**	**9,049**	**10,140**	**33**	**38**	**39**	**39**	**41**
15 to 24 years old [1]	274	947	750	674	623	3	5	4	3	3
25 to 34 years old	[2]933	[2]2,920	2,307	2,395	2,213	[2]9	[2]16	11	10	9
35 to 44 years old	[2]	[2]	1,406	1,836	2,263	[2]	[2]	7	8	9
45 to 64 years old	1,152	1,613	1,845	2,203	2,787	11	9	9	10	11
65 to 74 years old	611	775	868	1,042	1,134	6	4	4	5	5
75 years old and over	563	711	746	901	1,120	5	4	4	4	5
Female	**7,319**	**11,330**	**12,680**	**13,950**	**14,592**	**68**	**62**	**62**	**61**	**59**
15 to 24 years old [1]	282	779	573	536	572	3	4	3	2	2
25 to 34 years old	[2]671	[2]1,809	1,598	1,578	1,440	[2]6	[2]10	8	7	6
35 to 44 years old	[2]	[2]	916	1,303	1,399	[2]	[2]	4	6	6
45 to 64 years old	2,470	2,901	3,095	3,300	3,589	23	16	15	14	15
65 to 74 years old	2,204	3,076	3,262	3,309	3,240	20	17	16	14	13
75 years old and over	1,693	2,766	3,236	3,924	4,351	16	15	16	17	18

[1] 1970, persons 14 to 24 years old.   [2] Data for persons 35 to 44 years old included with persons 25 to 34 years old.

Source: U.S. Bureau of the Census, *Current Population Reports*, P20-450, and earlier reports; and unpublished data.

No. 85. Population in Institutions and Other Group Quarters, by Type of Group Quarters and State: 1990

[As of **April** 1. See text, section 1, and Appendix III. See *Historical Statistics, Colonial Times to 1970*, series A 359-371, for inmates of institutions]

REGION, DIVISION, AND STATE	Group quarters population, total[1]	INSTITUTIONALIZED PERSONS Total[2]	Nursing homes	College dormitories
U.S. ...	6,697,744	3,334,018	1,772,032	1,953,558
Northeast..	1,510,088	713,335	399,329	540,689
N.E	445,031	179,333	119,646	198,866
ME ...	37,169	14,136	9,855	14,118
NH ...	32,151	11,466	8,202	17,025
VT ...	21,642	6,161	4,809	13,435
MA ...	214,307	84,345	55,662	100,487
RI ...	38,595	14,801	10,156	18,898
CT ...	101,167	48,424	30,962	34,903
M.A	1,065,057	534,002	279,683	341,823
NY ...	545,265	267,122	126,175	165,925
NJ ...	171,368	92,670	47,054	43,711
PA ...	348,424	174,210	106,454	132,187
Midwest...	1,598,620	852,419	544,650	557,270
E.N.C. ...	1,055,689	568,050	346,243	369,009
OH ...	261,451	152,331	93,769	88,785
IN ...	161,992	81,686	50,845	70,873
IL ...	286,956	149,842	93,662	86,777
MI ...	211,692	112,903	57,622	73,093
WI ...	133,598	71,288	50,345	49,481
W.N.C. ...	542,931	284,369	198,407	188,261
MN ...	117,621	63,279	47,051	39,280
IA ...	99,520	47,841	36,455	43,093
MO ...	145,397	80,854	52,060	44,033
ND ...	24,234	10,574	8,159	10,377
SD ...	25,841	13,305	9,356	9,306
NE ...	47,553	25,620	19,171	16,692
KS ...	82,765	42,896	26,155	25,480
South	2,294,420	1,145,986	558,382	615,791
S.A.	1,243,962	577,690	270,930	322,299
DE ...	20,071	8,662	4,596	8,806
MD ...	113,856	62,760	26,884	30,892
DC ...	41,717	14,070	7,008	16,126
VA ...	209,300	84,292	37,762	61,943
WV ...	36,911	19,469	12,591	15,083
NC ...	224,470	83,400	47,014	71,266
SC ...	116,543	44,134	18,228	35,488
GA ...	173,633	87,266	36,549	39,723
FL ...	307,461	173,637	80,298	42,972
E.S.C ...	392,424	194,314	102,900	131,846
KY ...	101,176	47,609	27,874	30,600
TN ...	129,129	65,389	35,192	43,683
AL ...	92,402	51,583	24,031	28,859
MS ...	69,717	29,733	15,803	28,704
W.S.C ...	658,034	373,982	184,552	161,646
AR ...	58,332	34,223	21,809	16,775
LA ...	112,578	67,276	32,072	27,990
OK ...	93,677	51,211	29,666	24,924
TX ...	393,447	221,272	101,005	91,957
West	1,294,616	622,278	269,671	239,808
Mountain	297,687	144,834	65,842	77,782
MT ...	23,747	11,125	7,764	6,195
ID ...	21,490	10,478	6,318	6,676
WY ...	10,240	5,434	2,679	3,414
CO ...	79,472	35,976	18,506	22,749
NM ...	28,807	14,024	6,276	8,333
AZ ...	80,683	41,508	14,472	18,459
UT ...	29,048	12,739	6,222	10,156
NV ...	24,200	13,550	3,605	1,800
Pacific ..	996,929	477,444	203,829	162,026
WA ...	120,531	55,313	32,840	27,908
OR ...	66,205	33,378	18,200	18,970
CA ...	751,860	376,374	148,362	108,880
AK ...	20,701	4,574	1,202	1,310
HI ...	37,632	7,805	3,225	4,958

[1] Includes persons in other types of group quarters not shown separately. [2] Includes other institutionalized persons not shown separately.

Source: U.S. Bureau of the Census, *1990 Census of Population, General Population Characteristics* (CP-1).

No. 86. Religious Congregations—Summary: 1991

[Excludes Alaska and Hawaii. A religious congregation is a community of people who meet together for worship, for fellowship, and for service to their members and the larger communities in which they live. Excludes informal congregational groups that did not have an official meeting place, denominational organizations, religious charities, and religiously-owned or -affiliated institutions. Based on a sample survey of 1,003 congregations with telephones conducted by the source; for details, see source]

SIZE OF CONGREGATION	Number of congregations	AREAS OF ACTIVITY	Percent of all congregations providing support or service[4]	SOURCE OF REVENUE OR TYPE OF EXPENDITURE	Amount (mil. dol.)
Total	[1]257,648	Human services.....	91.7	**Revenues, total[9]**.........	**48,412**
Fewer than 100 members ..	[2]52,065	Recreation[5]........	72.6	Individual giving..............	39,223
100-199 members	[3]70,464	Marriage counseling....	70.5	Fees, charges for services.......	1,851
200-299 members	39,553	Family counseling	61.8	School tuition	1,352
300-399 members	23,521	Meal services[6]......	50.1		
400-499 members	16,051	Single adults programs..	46.5	**Expenditures, total**	**47,648**
500-999 members	31,826	Health	89.5	Current operating[9]	34,183
1,000-1,999 members.....	15,451	Visitation and support[7] .	87.4	Wages, salaries.............	16,532
2,000 or more members ...	8,717	Alcohol/drug prevention.	47.3	Fringe benefits..............	3,696
		International	73.9	Supplies, services............	10,400
Fewer than 100 nonmembers..	136,513	Relief abroad	61.5	Donations[9]................	6,626
100-199 nonmembers.....	63,956	Education &/or health...	39.0	Within denomination	4,655
200-299 nonmembers.....	20,883	Public benefit	62.2	To other organizations	1,317
300-499 nonmembers ...	12,150	Abortion activities[8]	41.8	Construction, capital improvements[10].	5,051
500 or more nonmembers ..	19,804	Education.........	53.3	Savings	1,788

[1] Includes those who don't know or did not answer. [2] Includes churches with fewer than 100 nonmembers. [3] Includes churches with fewer than 100 members but with 100 or more nonmembers. [4] Congregations could give multiple responses. [5] Includes camp programs and other youth programs. [6] Includes food kitchens. [7] Programs for sick and shut-ins. [8] Pro-life or pro-choice. [9] Includes other items, not shown separately. [10] Includes acquisition of real property.

Source: INDEPENDENT SECTOR, Washington, DC, *From Belief to Commitment: The Community Service Activities and Finances of Religious Congregations in the United States, 1993 Edition* (copyright).

No. 87. Religious Bodies—Selected Data

[Includes the self-reported membership of religious bodies with 60,000 or more as reported to the Yearbook of American and Canadian Churches. Groups may be excluded if they do not supply information. The data are not standardized so comparisons between groups are difficult. The definition of "church member" is determined by the religious body]

RELIGIOUS BODY	Year reported	Churches reported	Member-ship (1,000)	Pastors serving parishes [1]
African Methodist Episcopal Church [2]	1991	8,000	3,500	(NA)
African Methodist Episcopal Zion Church	1994	3,098	1,231	2,571
American Baptist Association	1986	1,705	250	1,740
American Baptist Churches in the U.S.A.	1994	5,686	1,508	4,359
Antiochian Orthodox Christian Archdiocese of North America, The. . . .	1994	184	300	200
Armenian Apostolic Church of America	1992	32	150	20
Assemblies of God	1994	11,764	2,325	17,486
Baptist Bible Fellowship International, The	1994	3,600	1,500	(NA)
Baptist General Conference	1994	813	135	813
Baptist Missionary Association of America	1994	1,360	230	1,225
Buddhist [3]	1990	(NA)	401	(NA)
Christian and Missionary Alliance, The	1993	1,943	302	1,610
Christian Brethren (a.k.a. Plymouth Brethren)	1984	1,150	98	500
Christian Church (Disciples of Christ)	1994	3,933	938	3,938
Christian Churches and Churches of Christ	1988	5,579	1,071	5,525
Christian Congregation, Inc., The	1994	1,437	112	1,431
Christian Methodist Episcopal Church	1983	2,340	719	(NA)
Christian Reformed Church in North America	1995	737	211	666
Church of God (Anderson, IN)	1993	2,314	216	2,132
Church of God (Cleveland, TN)	1994	5,918	723	2,400
Church of God in Christ, The	1991	15,300	5,500	28,988
Church of God of Prophecy, The	1994	2,005	71	8,791
Church of Jesus Christ of Latter-day Saints, The	1994	10,218	4,613	30,654
Church of the Brethren	1994	1,127	144	831
Church of the Nazarene	1994	5,156	598	4,474
Churches of Christ	1994	13,013	1,651	10,000
Conservative Baptist Association of America	1992	1,084	200	(NA)
Coptic Orthodox Church	1992	85	180	65
Cumberland Presbyterian Church	1994	772	90	(NA)
Diocese of the Armenian Church of America	1991	72	414	49
Episcopal Church, The	1993	7,388	2,505	8,004
Evangelical Covenant Church, The	1993	597	90	551
Evangelical Free Church of America	1995	1,213	227	1,920
Evangelical Lutheran Church in America	1994	10,973	5,199	9,826
Free Methodist Church of North America	1993	1,050	75	923
General Association of Regular Baptist Churches	1994	1,458	136	(NA)
General Baptists (General Association of)	1990	876	74	1,384
Grace Gospel Fellowship	1992	128	60	160
Greek Orthodox Archdiocese of North and South America	1977	535	1,950	(NA)
Hindu [3]	1990	(NA)	227	(NA)
Independent Fundamental Churches of America	1994	607	70	737
International Church of the Foursquare Gospel	1994	1,710	223	(NA)
International Council of Community Churches	1994	423	500	560
International Pentecostal Holiness Church	1994	1,645	150	(NA)
Jehovah's Witnesses	1994	1,037	946	(NA)
Jewish [3]	1990	(NA)	3,137	(NA)
Lutheran Church - Missouri Synod, The	1994	6,148	2,597	5,556
Mennonite Church	1994	1,099	96	1,364
Muslim / Islamic [3]	1990	(NA)	527	(NA)
National Association of Congregational Christian Churches	1994	424	70	400
National Association of Free Will Baptists	1994	2,496	208	2,800
National Baptist Convention of America, Inc.	1987	2,500	3,500	8,000
National Baptist Convention, U.S.A., Inc	1992	33,000	8,200	32,832
National Missionary Baptist Convention of America	1992	(NA)	2,500	(NA)
Old Order Amish Church	1993	898	81	3,592
Orthodox Church in America	1995	600	2,000	650
Pentecostal Assemblies of the World	1994	1,760	1,000	4,262
Pentecostal Church of God, Inc.	1994	1,209	113	(NA)
Polish National Catholic Church of North America	1960	162	282	(NA)
Presbyterian Church in America	1994	1,263	258	1,465
Presbyterian Church (U.S.A.)	1994	11,399	3,698	9,683
Progressive National Baptist Convention, Inc.	1994	2,000	2,500	(NA)
Reformed Church in America	1994	915	309	736
Reorganized Church of Jesus Christ of Latter-day Saints	1992	1,001	150	(NA)
Roman Catholic Church, The	1994	19,723	60,191	(NA)
Romanian Orthodox Episcopate of America	1994	37	65	37
Salvation Army, The	1994	1,222	443	3,642
Serbian Orthodox Church in the U.S.A. and Canada	1986	68	67	60
Seventh-day Adventist Church	1994	4,303	775	2,374
Southern Baptist Convention	1994	39,863	15,614	38,732
Unitarian Universalist [3]	1990	(NA)	502	(NA)
United Church of Christ	1994	6,180	1,501	4,443
United Methodist Church, The	1994	36,559	8,584	19,880
United Pentecostal Church International	1994	3,730	550	(NA)
Wesleyan Church (USA), The	1994	1,609	117	1,782
Wisconsin Evangelical Lutheran Synod	1994	1,251	415	1,213

NA Not available.   [1] Does not include retired clergy or clergy not working with congregations.   [2] Figures obtained from the Directory of African American Religious Bodies, 1991.   [3] Figures obtained from the National Survey of Religious Identification, a survey conducted by the City University of New York in 1990 and published in One Nation Under God: Religion in Contemporary American Society, by Barry Kosmin and Seymour Lachman (1993).

Source: Kenneth B. Bedell, editor, Yearbook of American and Canadian Churches, annual (copyright).

No. 88. Religious Preference, Church Membership, and Attendance: 1967 to 1994

[In percent. Covers civilian noninstitutional population, 18 years old and over. Data represent averages of the combined results of several surveys during year or period indicated. Data are subject to sampling variability, see source]

YEAR	RELIGIOUS PREFERENCE					Church/ synagogue members	Persons attending church/ synagogue[1]	AGE AND REGION	Church/ synagogue members, 1994
	Protestant	Catholic	Jewish	Other	None				
1967	67	25	3	3	2	[2]73	43	18-29 years old....	61
1975	62	27	2	4	6	71	41	30-49 years old....	65
1980	61	28	2	2	7	69	40	50 years and over..	77
1985	57	28	2	4	9	71	42	East [4]	68
1990	56	25	2	6	11	65	40	Midwest [5]	72
1993	57	26	1	8	[3]8	68	40	South [6]	75
1994	60	24	2	6	[3]8	68	42	West [7]..........	55

[1] Persons who attended a church or synagogue in the last seven days. [2] 1965 data. [3] Includes those respondents who did not designate. [4] ME, NH, RI, NY, CT, VT, MA, NJ, PA, WV, DE, MD, and DC. [5] OH, IN, IL, MI, MN, WI, IA, ND, SD, KS, NE, and MO. [6] KY, TN, VA, NC, SC, GA, FL, AL, MS, TX, AR, OK, and LA. [7] AZ, NM, CO, NV, MT, ID, WY, UT, CA, WA, OR, AK, and HI.

Source: Princeton Religion Research Center, Princeton, NJ, "Emerging Trends," periodical. Based on surveys conducted by The Gallup Organization, Inc.

No. 89. Christian Church Adherents, 1990, and Jewish Population, 1994—States

[Christian church adherents were defined as "all members, including full members, their children and the estimated number of other regular participants who are not considered as communicant, confirmed or full members." Data on Christian church adherents are based on reports of 133 church groupings and exclude 34 church bodies that reported more than 100,000 members to the Yearbook of American and Canadian Churches. The Jewish population includes Jews who define themselves as Jewish by religion as well as those who define themselves as Jewish in cultural terms. Data on Jewish population are based primarily on a compilation of individual estimates made by local Jewish federations. Additionally, most large communities have completed Jewish demographic surveys from which the Jewish population can be determined]

REGION, DIVISION, AND STATE	CHRISTIAN ADHERENTS, 1990		JEWISH POPULATION, 1994		REGION, DIVISION, AND STATE	CHRISTIAN ADHERENTS, 1990		JEWISH POPULATION, 1994	
	Number (1,000)	Percent of population[1]	Number (1,000)	Percent of population[1]		Number (1,000)	Percent of population[1]	Number (1,000)	Percent of population[1]
U.S.. .	131,084	52.7	5,880	2.3	DC ..	349	57.5	26	4.4
Northeast.	28,692	56.5	2,816	5.5	VA...	2,898	46.8	69	1.1
N.E....	7,456	56.5	404	3.1	WV ..	740	41.3	2	0.1
ME ..	439	35.8	8	0.6	NC ..	3,962	59.8	22	0.3
NH ..	431	38.9	10	0.8	SC ..	2,149	61.6	9	0.2
VT..	232	41.2	6	0.9	GA ..	3,659	56.5	75	1.1
MA ..	3,666	60.9	268	4.5	FL...	5,106	39.5	638	4.7
RI ..	754	75.1	16	1.6	E.S.C ..	9,844	64.9	40	0.3
CT ..	1,935	58.9	98	3.0	KY ..	2,216	60.1	11	0.3
M.A ...	21,235	56.5	2,412	6.3	TN ..	2,966	60.8	18	0.3
NY ...	9,970	55.4	1,645	9.0	AL..	2,858	70.7	9	0.2
NJ...	4,305	55.7	436	5.5	MS ..	1,804	70.1	1	0.1
PA...	6,961	58.6	331	2.7	W.S.C..	17,267	64.7	133	0.5
Midwest..	32,882	55.1	688	1.1	AR ..	1,423	60.5	2	0.1
E.N.C ..	22,220	52.9	556	1.3	LA..	2,959	70.1	17	0.4
OH ..	5,307	48.9	128	1.2	OK ..	2,097	66.7	6	0.2
IN ...	2,617	47.2	18	0.3	TX ..	10,787	63.5	109	0.6
IL ...	6,591	57.7	268	2.3	West	21,141	40.1	1,143	2.0
MI ...	4,580	49.3	107	1.1	Mt	6,434	47.1	158	1.1
WI...	3,125	63.9	35	0.7	MT ..	341	42.7	1	0.1
W.N.C..	10,662	60.4	132	0.7	ID ...	507	50.4	(Z)	0.1
MN ..	2,807	64.2	42	0.9	WY ..	216	47.6	(Z)	0.1
IA ...	1,675	60.3	6	0.2	CO ..	1,244	37.8	52	1.4
MO ..	2,883	56.3	62	1.2	NM ..	883	58.3	9	0.5
ND ..	484	75.8	1	0.1	AZ..	1,505	41.1	72	1.8
SD ..	474	68.1	(Z)	0.1	UT ..	1,371	79.6	3	0.2
NE ..	1,000	63.4	7	0.4	NV ..	366	30.5	21	1.5
KS ..	1,341	54.1	14	0.6	Pac	14,707	37.6	985	2.4
South.	48,370	56.6	1,233	1.4	WA ..	1,580	32.5	34	0.6
S.A....	21,258	48.8	1,061	2.3	OR ..	903	31.8	20	0.6
DE ..	297	44.6	9	1.4	CA ..	11,665	39.2	922	3.0
MD ..	2,101	43.9	212	4.3	AK ..	175	31.8	3	0.5
					HI ...	384	34.6	7	0.6

Z Fewer than 500. [1] Based on U.S. Bureau of the Census data for resident population enumerated as of April 1, 1990, and estimated as of July 1, 1994.

Source: Christian church adherents—M. Bradley; N. Green, Jr.; D. Jones; M. Lynn; and L. McNeil; Churches and Church Membership in the United States 1990, Glenmary Research Center, Atlanta, GA, 1992 (copyright); Jewish population—American Jewish Committee, New York, NY, American Jewish Year Book, 1994 (copyright).

Vital Statistics

This section presents vital statistics data on births, deaths, abortions, fetal deaths, fertility, life expectancy, marriages, and divorces. Vital statistics are compiled for the country as a whole by the National Center for Health Statistics (NCHS) and published in its annual report, *Vital Statistics of the United States,* in certain reports of the *Vital and Health Statistics* series, and in the *Monthly Vital Statistics Report.* Reports in this field are also issued by the various State bureaus of vital statistics. Data on fertility, on age of persons at first marriage, and on marital status and marital history are compiled by the Bureau of the Census from its Current Population Survey (CPS; see text, section 1) and published in *Current Population Reports,* P20 series. Data on abortions are published by the Alan Guttmacher Institute, New York, NY, in selected issues of *Family Planning Perspectives.*

Registration of vital events—The registration of births, deaths, fetal deaths, and other vital events in the United States is primarily a State and local function. The civil laws of every State provide for a continuous and permanent birth- and death-registration system. Many States also provide for marriage- and divorce-registration systems. Vital events occurring to U.S. residents outside the United States are not included in the data.

Births and deaths—The live-birth, death, and fetal-death statistics prepared by NCHS are based on vital records filed in the registration offices of all States, of New York City, and of the District of Columbia. The annual collection of death statistics on a national basis began in 1900 with a national death-registration area of 10 States and the District of Columbia; a similar annual collection of birth statistics for a national birth-registration area began in 1915, also with 10 reporting States and the District of Columbia. Since 1933, the birth- and death-registration areas have comprised the entire United States, including Alaska (beginning 1959) and Hawaii (beginning 1960). National statistics on fetal

In Brief	
	1994
Births	*3,979,000*
Deaths	*2,286,000*
Marriages	*2,362,000*
Divorces	*1,191,000*

Acquired Immunodeficiency Syndrome deaths; thru 1995:

All ages	*305,843*
13 to 29 years old	*53,632*
30 to 39 years old	*138,660*
40 to 49 years old	*77,425*
50 to 59 years old	*25,383*
60 years old and over	*10,743*

deaths were first compiled for 1918 and annually since 1922.

Prior to 1951, birth statistics came from a complete count of records received in the Public Health Service (now received in NCHS). From 1951 through 1971, they were based on a 50-percent sample of all registered births (except for a complete count in 1955 and a 20- to 50-percent sample in 1967). Beginning in 1972, they have been based on a complete count for States participating in the Vital Statistics Cooperative Program (VSCP) (for details, see the technical appendix in *Vital Statistics of the United States*) and on a 50-percent sample of all other areas. Beginning 1986 all reporting areas participated in the VSCP. Mortality data have been based on a complete count of records for each area (except for a 50-percent sample in 1972). Beginning in 1970, births to, and deaths of nonresident aliens of the United States and U.S. citizens outside the United States have been excluded from the data. Fetal deaths and deaths among Armed Forces abroad are excluded. Data based on samples are subject to sampling error; for details, see annual issues of *Vital Statistics of the United States.*

Mortality statistics by cause of death are compiled in accordance with World Health Organization regulations according to the *International Classification of Diseases* (ICD). The ICD is revised approximately every 10 years. The ninth revision of the ICD was employed beginning in 1979. Deaths for prior years were classified according to the revision of the ICD in use at the time. Each revision of the ICD introduces a number of discontinuities in mortality statistics; for a discussion of those between the eighth and ninth revisions of the ICD, see *Monthly Vital Statistics Report,* vol. 28, No. 11, supplement.

Some of the tables present age-adjusted death rates in addition to crude death rates. Age-adjusted death rates shown in this section were prepared using the direct method, in which age-specific death rates for a population of interest are applied to a standard population distributed by age. Age adjustment eliminates the differences in observed rates between points in time or among compared population groups that result from age differences in population composition.

Abortions—The U.S. Centers for Disease Control (CDC) collects data on abortions annually from States which have a central health agency with a statewide reporting system. The Alan Guttmacher Institute, New York, NY, also issues data on the number of abortions based on its own surveys of hospitals and physicians. The Guttmacher Institute also publishes data on the characteristics of abortions after adjusting CDC data for changes in the number of States reporting each year.

Fertility and life expectancy—The total fertility rate, defined as the number of births that 1,000 women would have in their lifetime if, at each year of age, they experienced the birth rates occurring in the specified year, is compiled and published by NCHS. Other data relating to social and medical factors which affect fertility rates, such as contraceptive use and birth expectations, are collected and made available by both NCHS and the Bureau of the Census. NCHS figures are based on information in birth and fetal death certificates and on the periodic National Surveys of Family Growth; Bureau of the Census data are based on decennial censuses and the CPS.

Data on life expectancy, the average remaining lifetime in years for persons who attain a given age, are computed and published by NCHS. For details, see the technical appendix in *Vital Statistics of the United States.*

Marriage and divorce—The compilation of nationwide statistics on marriages and divorces in the United States began in 1887-88 when the National Office of Vital Statistics prepared estimates for the years 1867-86. Although periodic updates took place after 1888, marriage and divorce statistics were not collected and published annually until 1944 by that Office. In 1957 and 1958, respectively, the same Office established marriage- and divorce-registration areas. Beginning in 1957, the marriage-registration area comprised 30 States, plus Alaska, Hawaii, Puerto Rico, and the Virgin Islands; it currently includes 42 States and the District of Columbia. The divorce-registration area, starting in 1958 with 14 States, Alaska, Hawaii, and the Virgin Islands, currently includes a total of 31 States and the Virgin Islands. Procedures for estimating the number of marriages and divorces in the registration States are discussed in *Vital Statistics of the United States,* vol. III— *Marriage and Divorce.* Total counts of events for registration and nonregistration States are gathered by collecting already summarized data on marriages and divorces reported by State offices of vital statistics and by county offices of registration.

Another important source of data on marriage and divorce trends in the United States is the March supplement to the Current Population Survey conducted by the Bureau of the Census. For information on marital status, see section 1.

Vital statistics rates—Except as noted, vital statistics rates computed by NCHS are based on decennial census population figures as of April 1 for 1940, 1950, 1960, 1970, 1980, and 1990; and on midyear population figures for other years, as estimated by the Bureau of the Census (see text, section 1).

Race—Data by race for births, deaths, marriages, and divorces from NCHS are based on information contained in the certificates of registration. The Census Bureau's Current Population Survey obtains information on race by asking respondents to classify their race as: (1) White, (2) Black, (3) American Indian, Eskimo, or Aleut, or (4) Asian or Pacific Islander.

Figure 2.1
Distribution of AIDS Deaths, by Age: 1982 Through 1995

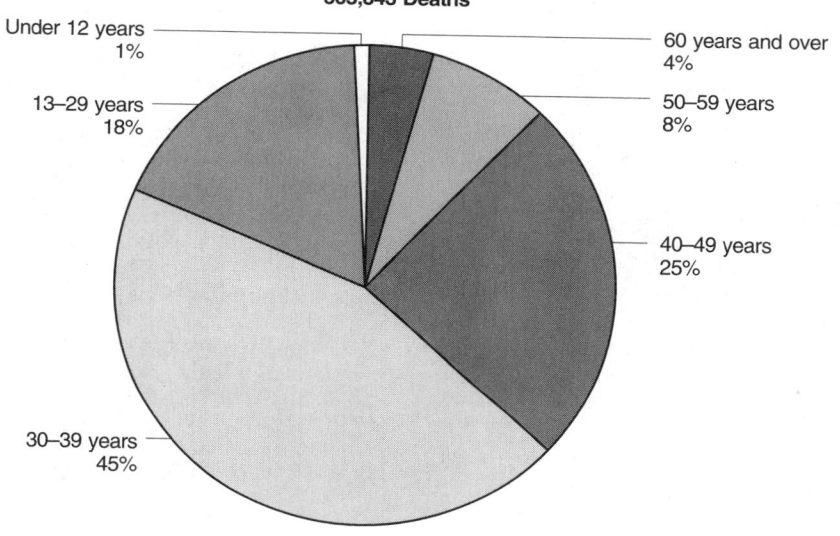

305,843 Deaths

Under 12 years
1%

60 years and over
4%

13–29 years
18%

50–59 years
8%

40–49 years
25%

30–39 years
45%

Source: Chart prepared by U.S. Bureau of the Census. For data, see table 134.

Figure 2.2
Births to Teenage Mothers as a Percent
of Total Births, by Race: 1993

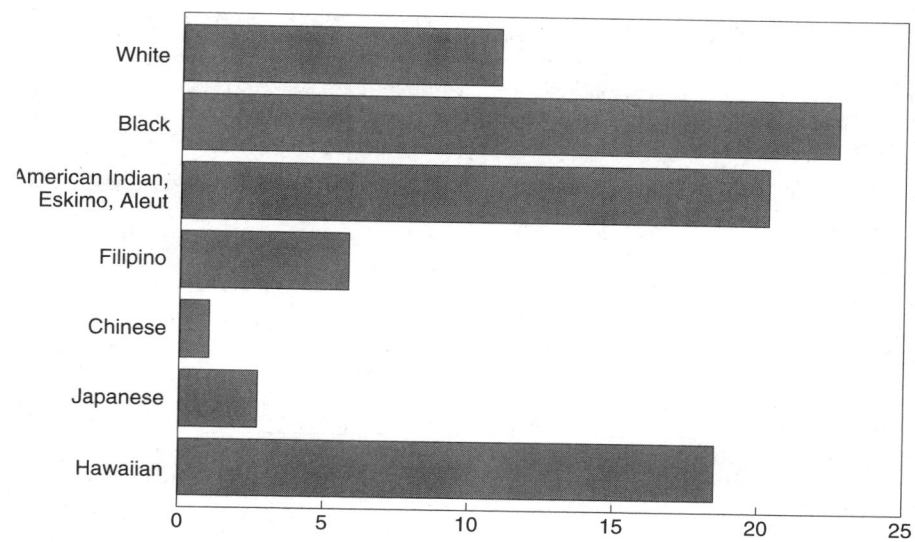

Source: Chart prepared by U.S. Bureau of the Census. For data, see table 91.

No. 90. Live Births, Deaths, Marriages, and Divorces: 1950 to 1994

[Prior to 1960, excludes Alaska and Hawaii. Beginning 1970, excludes births to, and deaths of nonresidents of the United States. See Appendix III. See also *Historical Statistics, Colonial Times to 1970*, series B 1-5, B 142, B 167, and B 216]

YEAR	NUMBER (1,000)					RATE PER 1,000 POPULATION				
	Births [1]	Deaths		Mar-riages [3]	Divor-ces [4]	Births [1]	Deaths		Mar-riages [3]	Divor-ces [4]
		Total	Infant [2]				Total	Infant [2]		
1950	3,632	1,452	104	1,667	385	24.1	9.6	29.2	11.1	2.6
1955	4,097	1,529	107	1,531	377	25.0	9.3	26.4	9.3	2.3
1957	4,300	1,633	112	1,518	381	25.3	9.6	26.3	8.9	2.2
1960	4,258	1,712	111	1,523	393	23.7	9.5	26.0	8.5	2.2
1965	3,760	1,828	93	1,800	479	19.4	9.4	24.7	9.3	2.5
1970	3,731	1,921	75	2,159	708	18.4	9.5	20.0	10.6	3.5
1971	3,556	1,928	68	2,190	773	17.2	9.3	19.1	10.6	3.7
1972	3,258	1,964	60	2,282	845	15.6	9.4	18.5	10.9	4.0
1973	3,137	1,973	56	2,284	915	14.8	9.3	17.7	10.8	4.3
1974	3,160	1,934	53	2,230	977	14.8	9.1	16.7	10.5	4.6
1975	3,144	1,893	51	2,153	1,036	14.6	8.8	16.1	10.0	4.8
1976	3,168	1,909	48	2,155	1,083	14.6	8.8	15.2	9.9	5.0
1977	3,327	1,900	47	2,178	1,091	15.1	8.6	14.1	9.9	5.0
1978	3,333	1,928	46	2,282	1,130	15.0	8.7	13.8	10.3	5.1
1979	3,494	1,914	46	2,331	1,181	15.6	8.5	13.1	10.4	5.3
1980	3,612	1,990	46	2,390	1,189	15.9	8.8	12.6	10.6	5.2
1981	3,629	1,978	43	2,422	1,213	15.8	8.6	11.9	10.6	5.3
1982	3,681	1,975	42	2,456	1,170	15.9	8.5	11.5	10.6	5.1
1983	3,639	2,019	41	2,446	1,158	15.6	8.6	11.2	10.5	5.0
1984	3,669	2,039	40	2,477	1,169	15.6	8.6	10.8	10.5	5.0
1985	3,761	2,086	40	2,413	1,190	15.8	8.8	10.6	10.1	5.0
1986	3,757	2,105	39	2,407	1,178	15.6	8.8	10.4	10.0	4.9
1987	3,809	2,123	38	2,403	1,166	15.7	8.8	10.1	9.9	4.8
1988	3,910	2,168	39	2,396	1,167	16.0	8.9	10.0	9.8	4.8
1989	4,041	2,150	40	2,403	1,157	16.4	8.7	9.8	9.7	4.7
1990	4,158	2,148	38	2,443	1,182	16.7	8.6	9.2	9.8	4.7
1991	4,111	2,170	37	2,371	1,187	16.3	8.6	8.9	9.4	4.7
1992	4,065	2,176	35	2,362	1,215	15.9	8.5	8.5	9.3	4.8
1993	4,000	2,269	33	2,334	1,187	15.5	8.8	8.4	9.0	4.6
1994	[5]3,979	[5]2,286	[5]31	[5]2,362	[5]1,191	[5]15.0	[5]8.8	[5]7.9	[5]9.1	[5]4.6

[1] Prior to 1960, data adjusted for underregistration.   [2] Infants under 1 year, excluding fetal deaths; rates per 1,000 registered live births.   [3] Includes estimates for some States through 1965 and also for 1976 and 1977 and marriage licenses for some States for all years except 1973 and 1975. Beginning 1978, includes nonlicensed marriages in California.   [4] Includes reported annulments and some estimated State figures for all years.   [5] Preliminary.

Source: U.S. National Center for Health Statistics, *Vital Statistics of the United States*, annual, *Monthly Vital Statistics Report*; and unpublished data.

No. 91. Live Births, by Race and Type of Hispanic Origin—Selected Characteristics: 1990 and 1993

[Represents registered births. Excludes births to nonresidents of the United States. Data are based on race of mother and Hispanic origin of mother. Hispanic origin data are available from 48 States and DC in 1990]

RACE AND HISPANIC ORIGIN	NUMBER OF BIRTHS (1,000)		BIRTHS TO TEENAGE MOTHERS, PERCENT OF TOTAL		BIRTHS TO UNMARRIED MOTHERS, PERCENT OF TOTAL		PERCENT OF MOTHERS BEGINNING PRENATAL CARE DURING—				PERCENT OF BIRTHS WITH LOW BIRTH WEIGHT [1]	
							First trimester		Third trimester or no care			
	1990	1993	1990	1993	1990	1993	1990	1993	1990	1993	1990	1993
Total	4,158	4,000	12.8	12.8	26.6	31.0	74.2	78.9	6.0	4.8	7.0	7.2
White	3,290	3,150	10.9	11.0	16.9	23.6	77.7	81.8	4.9	3.9	5.7	6.0
Black	684	659	23.1	22.7	66.7	68.7	60.7	66.0	10.9	9.0	13.3	13.3
American Indian, Eskimo, Aleut	39	39	19.5	20.3	53.6	55.8	57.9	63.4	12.9	10.3	6.1	6.4
Asian and Pacific Islander [2]	142	153	5.7	5.7	(NA)	15.7	(NA)	77.6	(NA)	4.6	(NA)	6.6
Filipino	26	30	6.1	5.8	15.9	17.7	77.1	79.3	4.5	4.0	7.3	7.0
Chinese	23	26	1.2	1.0	5.0	6.7	81.3	84.6	3.4	2.9	4.7	4.9
Japanese	9	9	2.9	2.9	9.6	10.0	87.0	87.2	2.9	2.8	6.2	6.5
Hawaiian	6	6	18.4	18.5	45.0	47.8	65.8	70.6	8.7	6.7	7.2	6.8
Hispanic origin [3]	595	654	16.8	17.4	36.7	40.0	60.2	66.6	12.0	8.8	6.1	6.2
Mexican	386	444	17.7	18.2	33.3	37.0	57.8	64.8	13.2	9.7	5.5	5.8
Puerto Rican	59	58	21.7	22.3	55.9	59.4	63.5	70.0	10.6	7.1	9.0	9.2
Cuban	11	12	7.7	6.8	18.2	21.0	84.8	88.9	2.8	1.8	5.7	6.2
Central and South American	83	92	9.0	10.0	41.2	45.2	61.5	68.7	10.9	7.3	5.8	5.9

NA Not available.   [1] Births less than 2,500 grams (5 lb.-8 oz.).   [2] Includes other races not shown separately.   [3] Hispanic persons may be of any race. Includes other types, not shown separately.

Source: U.S. National Center for Health Statistics, *Vital Statistics of the United States*, annual, *Monthly Vital Statistics Report*, and unpublished data.

No. 92. Births and Birth Rates: 1970 to 1993

[Births in thousands. Beginning 1980, births by race of child. Excludes births to nonresidents of the United States. For population bases used to derive these data, see text, section 2, and Appendix III. See also *Historical Statistics, Colonial Times to 1970*, series B 1, B 5-10, and B 12-20]

ITEM	1970	1980	1985	1986	1987	1988	1989	1990	1991	1992	1993
Live births [1]	3,731	3,612	3,761	3,757	3,809	3,910	4,041	4,158	4,111	4,065	4,000
White.	3,091	2,936	3,038	3,019	3,044	3,102	3,192	3,290	3,241	3,202	3,150
Black.	572	568	582	593	611	639	673	684	683	674	659
American Indian.	26	29	34	34	35	37	39	39	39	39	39
Asian or Pacific Islander	(NA)	74	105	108	117	129	133	142	145	150	153
Male	1,915	1,853	1,928	1,925	1,951	2,002	2,069	2,129	2,102	2,082	2,049
Female.	1,816	1,760	1,833	1,832	1,858	1,907	1,971	2,029	2,009	1,983	1,951
Males per 100 females.	106	105	105	105	105	105	105	105	105	105	105
Age of mother:											
Under 20 years old	656	562	478	472	473	489	518	533	532	518	501
20 to 24 years old.	1,419	1,226	1,141	1,102	1,076	1,067	1,078	1,094	1,090	1,070	1,038
25 to 29 years old.	995	1,108	1,201	1,200	1,216	1,239	1,263	1,277	1,220	1,179	1,129
30 to 34 years old.	428	550	696	721	761	804	842	886	885	895	901
35 to 39 years old.	180	141	214	230	248	270	294	318	331	345	357
40 years old or more	53	24	29	31	36	41	46	50	54	58	61
Age of father:											
Under 20 years old	189	137	108	105	105	111	120	129	130	129	(NA)
20 to 24 years old.	1,015	803	685	651	627	617	613	628	625	621	(NA)
25 to 29 years old.	1,085	1,082	1,081	1,059	1,053	1,055	1,056	1,060	1,007	969	(NA)
30 to 34 years old.	599	739	837	845	872	904	922	955	940	940	(NA)
35 to 39 years old.	298	275	381	398	413	431	451	474	478	488	(NA)
40 years old or more	214	139	167	174	191	205	221	231	236	242	(NA)
Age not stated	330	437	502	524	549	585	659	681	696	677	(NA)
Birth rate per 1,000 population	18.4	15.9	15.8	15.6	15.7	16.0	16.4	16.7	16.3	15.9	15.5
White.	17.4	15.1	15.0	14.8	14.9	15.0	15.4	15.8	15.4	15.0	14.7
Black.	25.3	21.3	20.4	20.5	20.8	21.5	22.3	22.4	21.9	21.3	20.5
American Indian.	(NA)	20.7	19.8	19.2	19.1	19.3	19.7	18.9	18.3	18.4	17.8
Asian or Pacific Islander	(NA)	19.9	18.7	18.0	18.4	19.2	18.7	19.0	18.2	18.0	17.7
Male	19.4	16.8	16.7	16.5	16.5	16.8	17.2	17.6	17.1	16.7	(NA)
Female.	17.4	15.1	15.0	14.9	14.9	15.2	15.6	15.9	15.6	15.2	(NA)
Plural birth ratio [2]	(NA)	19.3	21.0	21.6	22.0	22.4	23.0	23.3	23.9	24.4	25.2
White.	(NA)	18.5	20.4	21.2	21.6	22.0	22.5	22.9	23.4	24.0	24.9
Black.	(NA)	24.1	25.3	24.9	25.4	25.8	26.9	27.0	27.8	28.2	28.7
Fertility rate per 1,000 women [3]	87.9	68.4	66.2	65.4	65.7	67.2	69.2	70.9	69.6	68.9	67.6
White [3].	84.1	64.8	64.1	63.1	63.3	64.5	66.4	68.3	67.0	66.5	65.4
Black [3].	115.4	84.7	78.8	78.9	80.1	82.6	86.2	86.8	85.2	83.2	80.5
American Indian [3].	(NA)	82.7	78.6	75.9	75.6	76.8	79.0	76.2	75.1	75.4	73.4
Asian or Pacific Islander [3]	(NA)	73.2	68.4	66.0	67.1	70.2	68.2	69.6	67.6	67.2	66.7
Age of mother:											
10 to 14 years old.	1.2	1.1	1.2	1.3	1.3	1.3	1.4	1.4	1.4	1.4	1.4
15 to 19 years old.	68.3	53.0	51.0	50.2	50.6	53.0	57.3	59.9	62.1	60.7	59.6
20 to 24 years old.	167.8	115.1	108.3	107.4	107.9	110.2	113.8	116.5	115.7	114.6	112.6
25 to 29 years old.	145.1	112.9	111.0	109.8	111.6	114.4	117.6	120.2	118.2	117.4	115.5
30 to 34 years old.	73.3	61.9	69.1	70.1	72.1	74.8	77.4	80.8	79.5	80.2	80.8
35 to 39 years old.	31.7	19.8	24.0	24.4	26.3	28.1	29.9	31.7	32.0	32.5	32.9
40 to 44 years old.	8.1	3.9	4.0	4.1	4.4	4.8	5.2	5.5	5.5	5.9	6.1
45 to 49 years old.	0.5	0.2	0.2	0.2	0.2	0.2	0.2	0.2	0.2	0.3	0.3

NA Not available.   [1] Includes other races not shown separately.   [2] Number of multiple births per 1,000 live births.   [3] Per 1,000 women, 15 to 44 years old in specified group. The rate for *age of mother 45 to 49 years old* computed by relating births to mothers 45 years old and over to women 45 to 49 years old.

Source: U.S. National Center for Health Statistics, *Vital Statistics of the United States*, annual; *Monthly Vital Statistics Report*; and unpublished data.

Vital Statistics

No. 93. Live Births, by State: 1993

[Number of births, except rate. Registered births. Excludes births to nonresidents of the United States. By race of mother. See Appendix III]

DIVISION AND STATE	All races [1]	WHITE		BLACK		Hispanic [2]	Birth rate [3]	Fertility rate [4]
		Total	Non-Hispanic	Total	Non-Hispanic			
United States	4,000,240	3,149,833	2,472,031	658,875	641,273	654,418	15.5	67.6
Northeast	744,142	591,870	489,276	123,284	112,394	91,348	(NA)	(NA)
New England	183,302	161,862	142,022	15,662	13,149	15,549	(NA)	(NA)
Maine.	15,065	14,779	14,340	57	54	107	12.2	53.3
New Hampshire	15,436	15,149	12,795	109	83	190	13.7	57.6
Vermont	7,457	7,346	6,940	29	28	25	13.0	55.1
Massachusetts.	84,668	72,845	65,659	8,356	6,860	8,252	14.1	59.5
Rhode Island	13,976	12,204	9,624	1,151	925	1,594	14.0	60.9
Connecticut	46,700	39,539	32,664	5,960	5,199	5,381	14.2	62.7
Middle Atlantic.	560,840	430,008	347,254	107,622	99,245	75,799	(NA)	(NA)
New York	282,392	208,093	147,516	60,083	53,848	51,847	15.6	67.2
New Jersey	117,686	88,852	72,747	23,128	21,384	17,650	15.0	65.8
Pennsylvania	160,762	133,063	126,991	24,411	24,013	6,302	13.4	60.6
Midwest	900,918	742,533	683,085	134,815	133,153	47,559	(NA)	(NA)
East North Central	643,152	516,377	471,151	113,224	112,313	39,960	(NA)	(NA)
Ohio.	158,793	131,439	128,656	25,458	25,321	2,655	14.4	62.7
Indiana	83,949	73,713	71,507	9,374	9,341	2,131	14.7	63.6
Illinois.	190,788	142,175	113,842	42,900	42,573	28,610	16.3	71.1
Michigan	139,855	109,182	99,426	28,312	27,950	4,389	14.8	63.6
Wisconsin	69,767	59,868	57,720	7,180	7,128	2,175	13.8	61.2
West North Central	257,766	226,156	211,934	21,591	20,840	7,599	(NA)	(NA)
Minnesota	64,648	58,302	50,870	2,828	2,163	1,560	14.3	62.4
Iowa.	37,826	35,972	35,004	1,092	1,084	967	13.4	61.8
Missouri	75,253	61,045	59,912	13,007	12,974	1,150	14.4	64.3
North Dakota	8,690	7,742	7,544	89	88	122	13.6	63.1
South Dakota.	10,719	8,827	8,721	77	76	122	15.0	70.4
Nebraska	23,224	21,233	19,621	1,260	1,251	1,261	14.4	65.1
Kansas	37,406	33,035	30,262	3,238	3,204	2,417	14.8	66.9
South	1,373,149	996,853	816,415	342,223	339,187	183,559	(NA)	(NA)
South Atlantic	671,272	460,462	416,433	194,084	191,563	46,808	(NA)	(NA)
Delaware	10,568	7,943	7,510	2,411	2,363	472	15.1	64.1
Maryland.	74,988	46,812	44,519	24,658	23,967	2,996	15.1	62.8
Dist. of Columbia	10,629	1,595	1,355	8,500	8,154	930	18.4	70.8
Virginia	94,944	68,345	64,359	23,334	23,170	4,135	14.7	60.8
West Virginia	21,792	20,834	20,771	818	815	81	12.0	54.0
North Carolina	101,357	68,998	66,506	29,487	29,435	2,560	14.6	62.6
South Carolina	53,835	32,690	32,116	20,520	20,482	617	14.8	62.8
Georgia	110,622	68,759	65,281	39,873	39,707	3,467	16.0	65.7
Florida	192,537	144,486	114,016	44,483	43,470	31,550	14.0	67.0
East South Central	229,872	163,531	161,761	63,955	63,856	1,745	(NA)	(NA)
Kentucky.	53,000	47,674	47,266	4,840	4,822	401	14.0	60.3
Tennessee	73,017	54,609	53,896	17,578	17,550	694	14.3	61.9
Alabama	61,706	39,990	39,508	21,116	21,067	509	14.8	63.9
Mississippi.	42,149	21,258	21,091	20,421	20,417	141	16.0	69.2
West South Central . . .	472,005	372,860	238,221	84,184	83,768	135,006	(NA)	(NA)
Arkansas	34,289	25,986	25,403	7,848	7,822	579	14.1	64.6
Louisiana	69,402	38,528	37,658	29,698	29,633	1,001	16.2	69.1
Oklahoma	46,243	36,135	34,074	4,944	4,896	2,133	14.3	65.4
Texas	322,071	272,211	141,086	41,694	41,417	131,293	17.9	76.1
West.	982,031	818,577	483,255	58,553	56,539	331,952	(NA)	(NA)
Mountain	245,820	219,379	163,603	8,333	7,944	55,298	(NA)	(NA)
Montana	11,365	9,986	9,445	48	34	190	13.5	63.1
Idaho	17,440	16,891	15,044	46	44	1,850	15.8	72.1
Wyoming.	6,555	6,190	5,713	61	60	488	14.0	62.7
Colorado.	54,022	49,256	39,156	2,939	2,849	10,268	15.2	64.2
New Mexico.	27,852	23,082	10,155	561	525	13,054	17.2	76.6
Arizona.	69,056	59,701	36,517	2,403	2,272	22,579	17.5	79.7
Utah.	37,127	35,198	32,834	278	202	2,456	20.0	85.9
Nevada.	22,403	19,075	14,739	1,997	1,958	4,413	16.2	73.1
Pacific.	736,211	599,198	319,652	50,220	48,595	276,654	(NA)	(NA)
Washington	78,645	68,921	59,636	3,145	3,036	7,708	15.0	64.6
Oregon.	41,576	38,703	34,726	893	890	4,002	13.7	61.5
California	585,324	478,472	213,326	44,973	43,497	262,313	18.8	80.5
Alaska	11,073	7,508	7,106	585	570	439	18.5	77.9
Hawaii	19,593	5,594	4,858	624	602	2,192	16.8	74.8

NA Not available.   [1] Includes other races not shown separately.   [2] Persons of Hispanic origin may be of any race. Births by Hispanic origin of mother.   [3] Per 1,000 estimated population.   [4] Per 1,000 women aged 15-44 years estimated.

Source: U.S. National Center for Health Statistics, *Vital Statistics of the United States*, annual, and *Monthly Vital Statistics Report*.

No. 94. Total Fertility Rate and Intrinsic Rate of Natural Increase: 1960 to 1993

[Based on race of child and registered births only, thru 1979. Beginning 1980, based on race of mother. Beginning 1970, excludes births to nonresidents of United States. The *total fertility rate* is the number of births that 1,000 women would have in their lifetime if, at each year of age, they experienced the birth rates occurring in the specified year. A total fertility rate of 2,110 represents "replacement level" fertility for the total population under current mortality conditions (assuming no net immigration). The *intrinsic rate of natural increase* is the rate that would eventually prevail if a population were to experience, at each year of age, the birth rates and death rates occurring in the specified year and if those rates remained unchanged over a long period of time. Minus sign (-) indicates decrease. See also Appendix III and *Historical Statistics, Colonial Times to 1970*, series B 11]

ANNUAL AVERAGE AND YEAR	TOTAL FERTILITY RATE			INTRINSIC RATE			ANNUAL AVERAGE AND YEAR	TOTAL FERTILITY RATE			INTRINSIC RATE		
	Total	White	Black and other	Total	White	Black and other		Total	White	Black and other	Total	White	Black and other
1960-64 . . .	3,449	3,326	4,326	18.6	17.1	27.7	1979	1,808	1,716	2,310	-5.7	-7.7	3.8
1965-69 . . .	2,622	2,512	3,362	8.2	6.4	18.6	1980	1,840	1,773	2,177	-5.1	-7.0	4.0
1970-74 . . .	2,094	1,997	2,680	-0.7	-2.5	9.1	1981	1,812	1,748	2,118	-5.6	-7.4	3.0
1975-79 . . .	1,774	1,685	2,270	-6.6	-8.5	3.0	1982	1,828	1,767	2,107	-5.2	-7.0	3.0
1980-84 . . .	1,819	1,731	2,262	-5.4	-7.3	3.0	1983	1,799	1,741	2,066	-5.8	-7.5	2.2
1985-88 . . .	1,870	1,769	2,339	-4.2	-6.3	4.3	1984	1,807	1,749	2,071	-5.6	-7.3	2.1
1970	2,480	2,385	3,067	6.0	4.5	14.4	1985	1,844	1,787	2,109	-4.8	-6.5	2.7
1971	2,267	2,161	2,920	2.6	0.8	12.6	1986	1,838	1,776	2,136	-4.9	-6.7	2.8
1972	2,010	1,907	2,628	-2.0	-3.9	8.6	1987	1,872	1,805	2,198	-4.1	-6.1	4.0
1973	1,879	1,783	2,443	-4.5	-6.5	5.7	1988	1,934	1,857	2,298	-2.9	-5.1	5.7
1974	1,835	1,749	2,339	-5.4	-7.2	4.0	1989	2,014	1,931	2,433	-1.4	-3.6	7.4
1975	1,774	1,686	2,276	-6.7	-8.6	3.0	1990	2,081	2,003	2,480	-0.1	-2.3	8.3
1976	1,738	1,652	2,223	-7.4	-9.3	2.1	1991	2,073	1,996	2,480	-0.2	-2.4	8.2
1977	1,790	1,703	2,279	-6.2	-8.1	3.2	1992	2,065	1,994	2,442	-0.4	-2.5	7.5
1978	1,760	1,668	2,265	-6.8	-8.8	2.9	1993	2,046	1,982	2,385	-0.7	-1.9	3.7

Source: U.S. National Center for Health Statistics, *Vital Statistics of the United States*, annual; and unpublished data.

No. 95. Projected Fertility Rates, by Race and Age Group: 1995 and 2010

[For definition of total fertility rate, see headnote, table 94. Birth rates represent live births per 1,000 women in age group indicated. Projections are based on middle fertility assumptions. For explanations of methodology, see text, section 1]

AGE GROUP	ALL RACES [1]		WHITE		BLACK		AMERICAN INDIAN, ESKIMO, ALEUT		ASIAN AND PACIFIC ISLANDERS		HISPANIC [1]	
	1995	2010	1995	2010	1995	2010	1995	2010	1995	2010	1995	2010
Total fertility rate . .	2,055	2,108	1,984	2,046	2,427	2,438	2,151	2,159	1,953	1,954	2,977	2,777
Birth rates:												
10 to 14 years old. . . .	1.4	1.6	0.8	0.9	4.8	4.8	1.7	1.7	0.8	0.8	2.6	2.3
15 to 19 years old. . . .	59.4	63.6	50.7	56.0	109.6	111.5	78.7	81.8	28.5	28.7	103.7	95.8
20 to 24 years old. . . .	115.4	118.2	108.9	112.6	157.4	158.7	143.3	143.7	80.3	79.5	184.1	172.6
25 to 29 years old. . . .	117.8	119.5	118.7	120.7	112.0	113.1	108.3	109.0	121.6	121.7	152.4	143.7
30 to 34 years old. . . .	78.9	81.0	80.0	82.0	66.6	67.8	61.7	62.9	100.9	101.1	96.7	91.5
35 to 39 years old. . . .	31.6	32.1	31.5	31.7	27.8	27.7	27.4	27.4	47.9	47.3	45.3	40.5
40 to 44 years old. . . .	5.6	5.9	5.4	5.6	5.4	5.3	6.0	6.0	10.4	10.3	10.8	8.5
45 to 49 years old. . . .	0.3	0.3	0.2	0.2	0.3	0.2	0.3	0.3	1.0	1.0	0.6	0.5

[1] Persons of Hispanic origin may be of any race.

Source: U.S. Bureau of the Census, *Current Population Reports*, P25-1130.

No. 96. Birth Rates, by Live-Birth Order and Race: 1970 to 1993

[**Births per 1,000 women 15 to 44 years old in specified racial group.** Live-birth order refers to number of children born alive. Figures for births of order not stated are distributed. See also headnote, table 92, and *Historical Statistics, Colonial Times to 1970*, series B 20-27]

LIVE-BIRTH ORDER	ALL RACES [1]					WHITE					BLACK				
	1970	1980	1990	1992	1993	1970	1980	1990	1992	1993	1970	1980	1990	1992	1993
Total	87.9	68.4	70.9	68.9	67.6	84.1	65.6	68.3	66.5	65.4	115.4	84.9	86.8	83.2	80.5
First birth	34.2	29.5	29.0	27.8	27.5	32.9	28.8	28.4	27.3	27.0	43.3	33.7	32.4	30.6	30.2
Second birth	24.2	21.8	22.8	22.3	21.9	23.7	21.3	22.4	22.0	21.7	27.1	24.7	25.6	24.3	23.4
Third birth.	13.6	10.3	11.7	11.3	11.0	13.3	9.6	11.1	10.8	10.5	16.1	14.0	15.6	15.0	14.1
Fourth birth	7.2	3.9	4.5	4.4	4.3	6.8	3.4	4.0	4.0	3.9	10.0	6.5	7.4	7.2	6.9
Fifth birth	3.8	1.5	1.7	1.7	1.6	3.4	1.3	1.4	1.4	1.4	6.4	2.9	3.2	3.3	3.1
Sixth and seventh	3.2	1.0	1.0	1.0	1.0	2.7	0.8	0.8	0.8	0.8	7.0	2.1	2.0	2.2	2.2
Eighth and over	1.8	0.4	0.3	0.3	0.3	1.2	0.3	0.2	0.2	0.2	5.6	0.9	0.5	0.6	0.7

[1] Includes other races not shown separately.

Source: U.S. National Center for Health Statistics, *Vital Statistics of the United States*, annual; and *Monthly Vital Statistics Reports*.

Vital Statistics

No. 97. Births to Teens, Unmarried Mothers, and Prenatal Care: 1985 to 1992

[Represents registered births. See headnote, table 91]

CHARACTERISTIC	1985	1987	1988	1989	1990	1991	1992
Births to teenage mothers, total.	**12.7**	**12.4**	**12.5**	**12.8**	**12.8**	**12.9**	**12.7**
White	10.8	10.4	10.5	10.7	10.9	11.0	10.9
Black	23.0	22.6	22.7	23.1	23.1	23.1	22.7
American Indian, Eskimo, Aleut	19.1	18.9	18.4	18.8	19.5	20.3	20.0
Asian and Pacific Islander [1]	5.5	5.5	5.7	6.1	5.7	5.8	5.6
Filipino	5.8	6.0	6.2	6.4	6.1	6.1	5.6
Chinese.	1.1	1.1	1.1	1.2	1.2	1.1	1.0
Japanese.	2.9	2.7	2.8	2.9	2.9	2.7	2.6
Hawaiian	15.9	15.4	15.4	16.4	18.4	18.1	18.4
Hispanic origin [2]	16.5	16.3	16.4	16.7	16.8	17.2	17.1
Mexican.	17.5	17.3	17.3	17.4	17.7	18.1	18.0
Puerto Rican	20.9	20.5	21.4	21.9	21.7	21.7	21.4
Cuban.	7.1	6.2	6.1	7.0	7.7	7.1	7.1
Central and South American	8.2	8.0	8.1	8.6	9.0	9.4	9.6
Percent births to unmarried mothers . .	**22.0**	**24.5**	**25.7**	**27.1**	**26.6**	**28.0**	**30.1**
White	14.5	16.7	17.7	19.0	16.9	18.0	22.6
Black	60.1	62.2	63.5	64.5	66.7	68.2	68.1
American Indian, Eskimo, Aleut	40.7	44.9	45.6	NA	53.6	55.3	55.3
Asian and Pacific Islander [1]	10.1	11.5	12.0	NA	(NA)	(NA)	14.7
Filipino	12.1	13.4	14.5	NA	15.9	16.8	16.8
Chinese.	3.7	4.9	4.3	NA	5.0	5.5	6.1
Japanese.	7.9	8.0	8.6	NA	9.6	9.8	9.8
Hawaiian	(NA)	35.0	35.9	NA	45.0	45.0	45.7
Hispanic origin [2]	29.5	32.6	34.0	35.5	36.7	38.5	39.1
Mexican.	25.7	28.9	30.6	31.7	33.3	35.3	36.3
Puerto Rican	51.1	53.0	53.3	55.2	55.9	57.5	57.5
Cuban.	16.1	16.1	16.3	17.5	18.2	19.5	20.2
Central and South American	34.9	37.1	36.4	38.9	41.2	43.1	43.9
Percent of mothers beginning							
prenatal care 1st trimester	**76.2**	**74.4**	**75.9**	**75.5**	**74.2**	**76.2**	**77.7**
White	79.4	77.9	79.4	79.0	77.7	79.5	80.8
Black	61.8	59.3	61.1	60.4	60.7	61.9	63.9
American Indian, Eskimo, Aleut	60.3	(NA)	(NA)	60.5	57.9	59.9	62.1
Asian and Pacific Islander [1]	75.0	(NA)	(NA)	75.6	(NA)	(NA)	76.6
Filipino	77.2	(NA)	(NA)	78.0	77.1	77.1	78.7
Chinese.	82.4	(NA)	(NA)	81.9	81.3	82.3	83.8
Japanese.	85.8	(NA)	(NA)	86.7	87.0	87.7	88.2
Hawaiian	(NA)	(NA)	(NA)	69.7	65.8	68.1	69.9
Hispanic origin [2]	61.2	61.0	61.3	59.5	60.2	61.0	64.2
Mexican.	59.9	60.0	58.3	56.7	57.8	58.7	62.1
Puerto Rican	58.3	57.4	63.2	62.7	63.5	65.0	67.8
Cuban.	82.5	83.1	83.4	83.2	84.8	85.4	86.8
Central and South American	60.6	59.1	62.8	60.8	61.5	63.4	66.8
Percent of mothers beginning							
prenatal care 3d trimester or no care . .	**5.7**	**6.0**	**6.1**	**6.4**	**6.0**	**5.8**	**5.2**
White	4.7	4.9	5.0	5.2	4.9	4.7	4.2
Black	10.0	10.7	10.9	11.7	10.9	10.7	9.9
American Indian, Eskimo, Aleut	11.5	(NA)	(NA)	11.9	12.9	12.2	11.0
Asian and Pacific Islander [1]	6.1	(NA)	(NA)	5.8	(NA)	(NA)	4.9
Filipino	4.6	(NA)	(NA)	4.6	4.5	5.0	4.3
Chinese.	4.2	(NA)	(NA)	3.5	3.4	3.4	2.9
Japanese.	2.6	(NA)	(NA)	2.6	2.9	2.5	2.4
Hawaiian	(NA)	(NA)	(NA)	7.6	8.7	7.5	7.0
Hispanic origin [2]	12.5	12.7	12.1	13.0	12.0	11.0	9.5
Mexican.	12.9	13.0	13.9	14.6	13.2	12.2	10.5
Puerto Rican	15.5	17.1	10.2	11.3	10.6	9.1	8.0
Cuban.	3.7	3.9	3.6	4.0	2.8	2.4	2.1
Central and South American	12.5	13.5	9.9	11.9	10.9	9.5	7.9
Percent of births with low birth weight [3].	**6.8**	**6.9**	**6.9**	**7.0**	**7.0**	**7.1**	**7.1**
White	5.6	5.7	5.6	5.7	5.7	5.8	5.8
Black	12.4	12.7	13.0	13.2	13.3	13.6	13.3
American Indian, Eskimo, Aleut	5.9	6.2	6.1	6.4	6.1	6.2	6.2
Asian and Pacific Islander [1]	6.1	6.4	6.3	6.9	(NA)	(NA)	6.6
Filipino	6.9	7.3	7.1	7.3	7.3	7.3	7.4
Chinese.	5.0	5.0	4.7	5.0	4.7	5.1	5.0
Japanese.	5.9	6.3	6.2	6.4	6.2	5.9	7.0
Hawaiian	6.4	6.6	6.8	7.2	7.2	6.7	6.9
Hispanic origin [2]	6.2	6.2	6.2	6.2	6.1	6.1	6.1
Mexican.	5.8	5.7	5.6	5.6	5.5	5.6	5.6
Puerto Rican	8.7	9.3	9.4	9.5	9.0	9.4	9.2
Cuban.	6.0	5.9	5.9	5.8	5.7	5.6	6.1
Central and South American	5.7	5.7	5.6	5.8	5.8	5.9	5.8

NA Not available. [1] Includes other races not shown separately. [2] Hispanic persons may be of any race. Includes other types, not shown separately. [3] Births less than 2,500 grams (5 lb.-8 oz.).

Source: U.S. National Center for Health Statistics, *Vital Statistics of the United States*, annual, *Monthly Vital Statistics Report*, and unpublished data.

No. 98. Births to Unmarried Women, by Race of Child and Age of Mother: 1970 to 1993

[Excludes births to nonresidents of United States. Data for **1970** include estimates for States in which marital status data were not reported. Beginning in **1980**, marital status is inferred from a comparison of the child's and parents' surnames on the birth certificate for those States that do not report on marital status. No estimates included for misstatements on birth records or failures to register births. See also Appendix III and *Historical Statistics, Colonial Times to 1970*, series B 28-35]

RACE OF CHILD AND AGE OF MOTHER	1970	1980	1990	1992	1993	RACE OF CHILD AND AGE OF MOTHER	1970	1980	1990	1992	1993
NUMBER (1,000)						20 to 24 years	31.8	35.6	34.7	35.6	35.4
Total live births[1]	399	666	1,165	1,225	1,240	25 to 29 years	10.2	15.0	19.7	19.1	18.9
White	175	320	647	722	742	30 to 34 years	4.8	6.2	10.1	10.4	10.7
Black	215	326	473	459	452	35 years and over	3.1	2.4	4.5	5.1	5.4
Under 15 years old . . .	10	9	11	11	11	AS PERCENT OF ALL BIRTHS IN RACIAL GROUPS					
15 to 19 years old	190	263	350	354	357						
20 to 24 years old	127	237	404	436	439	**Total** [1]	10.7	18.4	28.0	30.1	31.0
25 to 29 years old	41	100	230	233	234	White	5.7	11.0	20.1	22.6	23.6
30 to 34 years old . . .	19	41	118	128	132	Black	37.6	55.2	65.2	68.1	68.7
35 years old and over .	12	16	53	63	67	BIRTH RATE [2]					
PERCENT DISTRIBUTION						**Total** [1]	26.4	29.4	43.8	45.2	45.3
						White [3]	13.9	17.6	31.8	35.2	35.9
Total [1]	100.0	100.0	100.0	100.0	100.0	Black [3]	95.5	82.9	93.9	86.5	84.0
White	43.9	48.1	55.6	58.9	59.8	15 to 19 years	22.4	27.6	42.5	44.6	44.5
Black	54.0	48.9	40.6	37.5	36.5	20 to 24 years	38.4	40.9	65.1	68.5	69.2
Under 15 years	2.4	1.4	0.9	0.9	0.9	25 to 29 years	37.0	34.0	56.0	56.5	57.1
15 to 19 years	47.8	39.5	30.0	28.9	28.8	30 to 34 years	27.1	21.1	37.6	37.9	38.5

[1] Includes other races not shown separately. [2] Rate per 1,000 unmarried women (never-married, widowed, and divorced) estimated as of July 1. [3] Covers women aged 15 to 44 years.

Source: U.S. National Center for Health Statistics, *Vital Statistics of the United States*, annual; *Monthly Vital Statistics Report*; and unpublished data.

No. 99. Low Birth Weight and Births to Teenage Mothers and to Unmarried Women—States: 1980 and 1993

[Represents registered births. Excludes births to nonresidents of the United States. Based on 100 percent of births in all States and the District of Columbia. See Appendix III]

DIVISION AND STATE	PERCENT OF BIRTHS WITH LOW BIRTH WEIGHT[1]		BIRTHS TO TEENAGE MOTHERS, PERCENT OF TOTAL		BIRTHS TO UNMAR-RIED WOMEN, PERCENT OF TOTAL		DIVISION AND STATE	PERCENT OF BIRTHS WITH LOW BIRTH WEIGHT[1]		BIRTHS TO TEENAGE MOTHERS, PERCENT OF TOTAL		BIRTHS TO UNMAR-RIED WOMEN, PERCENT OF TOTAL	
	1980	1993	1980	1993	1980	1993		1980	1993	1980	1993	1980	1993
U.S..	6.8	7.2	15.6	12.8	18.4	31.0	VA	7.5	7.3	15.5	10.9	19.2	29.0
N.E.	6.2	(NA)	11.6	(NA)	15.5	(NA)	WV	6.7	7.2	20.1	17.6	13.1	29.0
ME	6.5	5.4	15.3	10.1	13.9	27.0	NC	7.9	8.6	19.2	15.3	19.0	32.1
NH	5.4	5.0	10.7	6.8	11.0	20.6	SC	8.6	9.3	19.8	16.2	23.0	36.0
VT	5.9	5.7	13.0	8.7	13.7	24.2	GA	8.6	8.7	20.7	16.1	23.2	35.8
MA	6.1	6.2	10.7	7.8	15.7	26.4	FL	7.6	7.5	18.2	13.4	23.0	35.0
RI	6.3	6.5	12.3	10.4	15.7	31.7	E.S.C.	7.8	(NA)	21.0	(NA)	20.9	(NA)
CT	6.7	6.9	11.4	8.0	[2]17.9	29.8	KY	6.8	7.1	21.1	16.8	15.1	27.2
M.A.	7.1	(NA)	12.6	(NA)	21.3	(NA)	TN	8.0	8.8	19.9	16.9	19.9	33.6
NY	7.4	7.7	11.8	9.3	[2]23.8	37.2	AL	7.9	8.7	20.6	17.8	22.2	33.5
NJ	7.2	7.6	12.3	7.9	21.1	27.1	MS	8.7	10.1	23.2	21.7	28.0	44.4
PA	6.5	7.4	13.9	10.5	17.7	32.2	W.S.C.	7.3	(NA)	19.1	(NA)	15.8	(NA)
E.N.C.	6.7	(NA)	15.2	(NA)	18.0	(NA)	AR	7.6	8.2	21.6	19.4	20.5	31.7
OH	6.8	7.5	15.7	13.6	[2]17.8	33.0	LA	8.6	9.3	20.1	18.7	23.4	42.0
IN	6.3	7.0	17.3	14.1	15.5	30.8	OK	6.8	6.7	19.6	17.2	[2]14.0	29.1
IL	7.2	8.1	15.7	12.8	22.5	34.1	TX	6.9	7.1	18.3	16.1	[2]13.3	17.0
MI	6.9	7.6	14.0	12.6	[2]16.2	26.0	Mountain	6.6	(NA)	14.3	(NA)	[2]12.7	(NA)
WI	5.4	6.1	12.3	10.4	13.9	27.1	MT	5.6	6.0	12.4	12.5	[2]12.5	27.3
W.N.C.	5.7	(NA)	13.5	(NA)	13.1	(NA)	ID	5.3	5.3	13.1	13.4	7.9	18.7
MN	5.1	5.5	10.4	8.2	11.4	23.4	WY	7.3	7.3	15.5	14.0	8.2	25.8
IA	5.0	5.7	12.5	10.7	10.3	24.6	CO	8.2	8.4	13.3	11.9	13.0	24.8
MO	6.6	7.5	16.9	14.2	17.6	32.4	NM	7.6	7.3	18.2	17.8	16.1	41.4
ND	4.9	5.3	10.9	9.6	9.2	23.0	AZ	6.2	6.7	16.5	15.1	18.7	37.9
SD	5.1	5.5	13.5	11.1	13.4	27.7	UT	5.2	5.9	11.0	10.8	6.2	15.5
NE	5.6	5.9	12.1	10.1	11.6	23.5	NV	6.6	7.4	15.4	13.3	[2]13.5	34.0
KS	5.8	6.6	15.0	12.9	12.3	25.9	Pacific	5.8	(NA)	13.6	(NA)	19.6	(NA)
S.A.	8.0	(NA)	18.3	(NA)	22.2	(NA)	WA	5.1	5.2	12.5	11.0	13.6	26.3
DE	7.7	7.8	16.7	12.5	24.2	33.8	OR	4.9	5.2	13.3	12.4	14.8	28.2
MD	8.2	8.5	14.8	10.0	[2]25.2	32.5	CA	5.9	6.0	13.9	12.0	[2]21.4	35.3
DC	12.8	14.6	20.7	17.4	56.5	67.8	AK	5.4	4.9	11.8	10.8	15.1	28.0
							HI	7.1	6.8	11.5	10.1	17.6	27.2

NA Not available. [1] Less than 2,500 grams (5 pounds-8 ounces). [2] Marital status of mother is inferred.

Source: U.S. National Center for Health Statistics, *Vital Statistics of the United States*, annual; and *Monthly Vital Statistics Report*.

Vital Statistics

No. 100. Live Births, by Place of Delivery, Median and Low Birth Weight, and Prenatal Care: 1970 to 1993

[Represents registered births. Excludes births to nonresidents of the United States. For total number of births, see table 92. See Appendix III]

YEAR	BIRTHS ATTENDED (1,000)			MEDIAN BIRTH WEIGHT [3]			PERCENT OF BIRTHS WITH LOW BIRTH WEIGHT [5]			PERCENT OF BIRTHS BY PERIOD IN WHICH PRENATAL CARE BEGAN	
	In hos-pital [1]	Not in hospital		Total [4]	White	Black	Total [3]	White	Black	1st tri-mester	3d tri-mester or no prenatal care
		Physi-cian	Mid-wife and other [2]								
1970	3,708	5	18	7 lb.-4 oz. . .	7 lb.-5 oz. . .	6 lb.-14 oz. . .	7.9	6.8	13.9	68.0	7.9
1980	3,576	12	24	7 lb.-7 oz. . .	7 lb.-8 oz. . .	7 lb.-0 oz. . .	6.8	5.7	12.5	76.3	5.1
1990	4,110	14	21	7 lb.-7 oz. . .	7 lb.-8 oz. . .	7 lb.-0 oz. . .	7.0	5.7	13.3	74.2	6.0
1993	3,959	8	20	7 lb.-7 oz. . .	7 lb.-8 oz. . .	7 lb.-0 oz. . .	7.2	6.0	13.3	78.9	4.8

[1] Includes all births in hospitals or institutions and in clinics. [2] Includes births with attendant not specified. [3] Beginning 1990, median birth weight based on race of mother; prior to 1989, based on race of child. [4] Includes other races not shown separately. [5] For 1970, births of 2,500 grams (5 lb.-8 oz.) or less at birth; thereafter, less than 2,500 grams.

No. 101. Cesarean Section Deliveries, by Age of Mother: 1990 to 1993

AGE OF MOTHER	1990	1991	1992	1993
Number of cesarean deliveries, total (1,000)	**945**	**905**	**921**	**917**
Rate: Mothers, all ages [1]	23.5	22.6	22.3	22.8
Under 20 years old	16.6	16.4	17.5	15.6
20 to 24 years old	21.0	19.9	21.4	19.9
25 to 29 years old	23.3	23.3	23.2	23.0
30 to 34 years old	27.8	25.7	27.1	26.3
35 years and over	31.4	29.4	30.1	30.3

[1] Cesarean rates are the number of cesarean deliveries per 100 total deliveries for specified category.

No. 102. Live Births and Births to Teenage Mothers—20 Largest Metropolitan Areas: 1993

[Excludes births to and deaths of nonresidents of the United States. Data are by place of residence. Metropolitan statistical areas (MSA's), consolidated metropolitan statistical areas (CMSA's), and New England County Metropolitan Areas (NECMA's) are defined by the U.S. Office of Management and Budget as of June 30, 1990. See Appendix II for definitions and components]

METROPOLITAN AREA	ALL BIRTHS		BIRTHS TO TEENAGE MOTHERS	
	Number	Rate per 1,000 population	Number of teen births	Percent of total births
New York-Northern New Jersey-Long Island, NY-NJ-CT-PA	290,532	16	22,950	8
Los Angeles-Anaheim-Riverside, CA CMSA	310,792	20	36,390	12
Chicago-Gary-Lake County, IL-IN-WI CMSA	146,678	18	17,688	12
Washington, DC-MD-VA MSA	66,625	16	5,262	8
San Francisco-Oakland-San Jose, CA CMSA	101,011	16	8,753	9
Philadelphia-Wilmington-Trenton, PA-NJ-DE-MD CMSA.	89,732	15	9,609	11
Boston-Lawerence-Salem-Lowell-Brockton, MA NECMA	54,291	14	3,402	6
Detroit-Ann Arbor, MI CMSA.	72,354	15	8,347	12
Dallas-Fort Worth, TX CMSA	73,645	18	9,788	13
Houston-Galveston-Brazoria, TX CMSA	74,277	19	10,226	14
Miami-Fort Lauderdale, FL CMSA	52,393	16	5,476	10
Seattle-Tacoma, WA CMSA	40,565	15	3,458	9
Atlanta, GA MSA	51,280	17	5,955	12
Cleveland-Akron-Lorain, OH CMSA	40,822	15	4,891	12
Minneapolis-St.Paul, MN-WI MSA	40,314	16	2,972	7
San Diego, CA MSA	48,935	19	5,207	11
St. Louis, MO-IL MSA	38,042	15	4,953	13
Pittsburgh-Beaver Valley, PA CMSA.	27,177	12	2,548	9
Phoenix, AZ MSA.	40,406	18	5,643	14
Tampa-St. Petersburg-Clearwater, FL MSA	27,658	13	3,653	13
Baltimore, MD MSA	36,237	15	4,028	11
Denver-Boulder, CO CMSA	31,139	16	3,330	11
Cincinnati-Hamilton, OH-KY-IN CMSA	27,104	15	3,611	13
Milwaukee-Racine, WI CMSA	25,099	15	3,235	13
Kansas City, MO-KS MSA	24,787	15	3,011	12

Source of tables 100-102: U.S. National Center for Health Statistics, Vital Statistics of the United States, annual; and unpublished data.

No. 103. Women Who Have Had a Child in the Last Year, by Age: 1980 to 1994

[See headnote, table 104]

AGE OF MOTHER	WOMEN WHO HAD A CHILD IN LAST YEAR (1,000)			TOTAL BIRTHS PER 1,000 WOMEN			FIRST BIRTHS PER 1,000 WOMEN		
	1980	1990	1994	1980	1990	1994	1980	1990	1994
Total	3,247	3,913	3,890	71.1	67.0	64.7	28.5	26.4	27.4
15 to 29 years old [1] . .	2,476	2,568	2,389	103.7	90.8	85.6	48.6	43.2	46.3
15 to 19 years old . .	(NA)	338	397	(NA)	39.8	45.2	(NA)	30.1	36.3
20 to 24 years old [2] . .	1,396	1,038	938	96.6	113.4	100.7	(NA)	51.8	58.4
25 to 29 years old . .	1,081	1,192	1,054	114.8	112.1	107.7	(NA)	46.2	43.9
30 to 44 years old	770	1,346	1,501	35.4	44.7	46.6	6.3	10.6	11.0
30 to 34 years old . .	519	892	1,006	60.0	80.4	90.4	(NA)	21.9	23.0
35 to 39 years old . .	192	377	399	26.9	37.3	36.0	(NA)	6.5	7.3
40 to 44 years old . .	59	77	95	9.9	8.6	9.6	(NA)	1.2	1.8

NA Not available.   [1] For 1980-88, 18 to 29 years old.   [2] For 1980-88, 18 to 24 years old.

Source: U.S. Bureau of the Census, *Current Population Reports,* P20-375, P20-454 and P20-482.

No. 104. Characteristics of Women Who Have Had a Child in the Last Year: 1994

[As of **June.** Covers civilian noninstitutional population. Since the number of women who had a birth during the 12-month period was tabulated and not the actual numbers of births, some small underestimation of fertility for this period may exist due to the omission of: (1) Multiple births, (2) Two or more live births spaced within the 12-month period (the woman is counted only once), (3) Women who had births in the period and who did not survive to the survey date, (4) Women who were in institutions and therefore not in the survey universe. These losses may be somewhat offset by the inclusion in the CPS of births to immigrants who did not have their children born in the United States and births to nonresident women. These births would not have been recorded in the vital registration system. Based on Current Population Survey (CPS); see text, section 1, and Appendix III]

CHARACTERISTIC	TOTAL, 15 TO 44 YEARS OLD			15 TO 29 YEARS OLD			30 TO 44 YEARS OLD		
	Num-ber of women (1,000)	Women who have had a child in the last year		Num-ber of women (1,000)	Women who have had a child in the last year		Num-ber of women (1,000)	Women who have had a child in the last year	
		Total births per 1,000 women	First births per 1,000 women		Total births per 1,000 women	First births per 1,000 women		Total births per 1,000 women	First births per 1,000 women
Total [1]	60,088	64.7	27.4	27,893	85.6	46.3	32,195	46.6	11.0
White.	48,531	64.0	28.3	22,104	83.8	47.3	26,427	47.5	12.3
Black.	8,524	66.5	24.3	4,269	98.3	44.1	4,255	34.6	4.4
Hispanic [2]	6,492	99.2	42.4	3,469	129.6	65.2	3,023	64.4	16.2
Currently married.	31,659	91.1	35.1	8,917	174.3	88.9	22,742	58.4	14.0
Married, spouse present	29,218	94.0	36.5	8,053	182.3	94.4	21,165	60.5	14.5
Married, spouse absent [3]	2,441	55.4	17.9	864	100.4	38.4	1,576	30.8	6.7
Widowed or divorced	5,697	20.1	4.3	948	59.8	21.1	4,749	12.2	1.0
Never married.	22,733	39.2	22.5	18,028	43.1	26.6	4,705	24.3	6.8
Educational attainment:									
Less than high school	12,369	67.3	28.3	8,732	76.4	38.0	3,637	45.5	5.2
High school, 4 years	18,543	70.3	28.1	7,426	116.7	60.0	11,117	39.3	6.9
College: 1 or more years	29,176	60.1	26.6	11,735	72.9	44.0	17,441	51.5	14.9
No degree	12,672	53.6	23.3	6,448	68.6	39.3	6,224	38.0	6.7
Associate degree	4,756	63.4	29.1	1,536	112.2	73.6	3,221	40.2	7.9
Bachelor's degree	8,850	70.3	31.4	3,291	65.6	40.8	5,559	73.1	25.8
Grad. or prof. degree	2,897	52.2	22.1	459	53.4	32.1	2,438	52.0	20.2
Labor force status:									
Employed	39,644	46.3	21.8	16,690	60.4	37.1	22,954	36.0	10.7
Unemployed	3,352	69.2	31.9	2,199	91.0	48.4	1,153	27.4	0.3
Not in labor force	17,092	106.7	39.6	9,003	131.0	63.0	8,089	79.5	13.5
Occupation of employed women:									
Managerial-professional	10,880	51.0	23.9	3,190	66.1	42.0	7,690	44.7	16.4
Tech., sales, admin. support	16,903	42.9	21.4	7,781	55.0	36.3	9,122	32.7	8.7
Service workers	7,544	47.5	21.2	4,042	60.1	33.3	3,502	33.0	7.1
Farming, forestry, and fishing	469	37.2	25.4	215	53.0	53.0	255	23.8	2.2
Precision prod., craft, repair	831	55.5	30.2	261	106.2	71.9	570	32.2	11.1
Operators, fabricators, laborers	3,016	44.0	14.9	1,202	73.5	30.9	1,815	24.4	4.4
Family income: Under $10,000	7,555	89.0	34.9	4,282	123.3	57.4	3,273	44.2	5.5
$10,000 to $19,999	8,956	73.7	28.7	4,897	98.8	48.9	4,059	43.4	4.3
$20,000 to $24,999	4,758	76.8	34.6	2,394	111.2	55.6	2,364	41.9	13.3
$25,000 to $29,999	4,593	62.6	28.8	2,310	90.1	52.4	2,283	34.7	4.9
$30,000 to $34,999	4,341	62.2	23.0	1,963	77.6	43.9	2,378	49.4	5.8
$35,000 to $49,999	10,239	58.0	26.9	4,324	78.5	47.9	5,915	43.0	11.6
$50,000 to $74,999	9,571	54.4	24.8	3,715	58.2	40.1	5,856	52.0	15.1
$75,000 and over	6,494	48.8	17.9	2,468	29.2	14.5	4,026	60.8	20.0

[1] Includes women of other races and women with family income not reported, not shown separately.   [2] Persons of Hispanic origin may be of any race.   [3] Includes separated women.

Source: U.S. Bureau of the Census, *Current Population Reports,* P20-375, P20-454 and P20-482.

No. 105. Women Who Have Had a Child in the Last Year, by Age and Labor Force Status: 1980 to 1994

[See headnote, table 104]

YEAR	TOTAL, 18 TO 44 YEARS OLD			18 TO 29 YEARS OLD			30 TO 44 YEARS OLD		
	Number (1,000)	In the labor force		Number (1,000)	In the labor force		Number (1,000)	In the labor force	
		Number (1,000)	Percent		Number (1,000)	Percent		Number (1,000)	Percent
1980	3,247	1,233	38	2,476	947	38	770	287	37
1981	3,381	1,411	42	2,499	1,004	40	881	407	46
1982	3,433	1,508	44	2,445	1,040	43	988	469	48
1983	3,625	1,563	43	2,682	1,138	42	942	425	45
1984	3,311	1,547	47	2,375	1,058	45	936	489	52
1985	3,497	1,691	48	2,512	1,204	48	984	488	50
1986	3,625	1,805	50	2,452	1,185	48	1,174	620	53
1987	3,701	1,881	51	2,521	1,258	50	1,180	623	53
1988	3,667	1,866	51	2,384	1,177	49	1,283	688	54
1990 [1]	3,913	2,068	53	2,568	1,275	50	1,346	793	59
1992 [1]	3,688	1,985	54	2,346	1,182	50	1,342	802	60
1994 [1]	3,890	2,066	53	2,389	1,209	51	1,501	857	57

[1] Lower age limit is 15 years old.
Source: U.S. Bureau of the Census, *Current Population Reports*, P20-482.

No. 106. Childless Women and Children Ever Born, by Race, Age, and Marital Status: 1994

[See headnote, table 104]

CHARACTERISTIC	Total number of women (1,000)	WOMEN BY NUMBER OF CHILDREN EVER BORN (percent)				CHILDREN EVER BORN	
		Total	None	One	Two or more	Total number (1,000)	Per 1,000 women
ALL RACES [1]							
Women ever married	37,355	100	19.1	22.5	58.5	65,954	1,766
15 to 19 years old	393	100	49.2	43.5	7.2	230	584
20 to 24 years old	3,189	100	37.4	36.4	26.2	3,120	978
25 to 29 years old	6,283	100	28.9	29.0	42.2	8,420	1,340
30 to 34 years old	8,898	100	17.5	22.8	59.7	15,912	1,788
35 to 39 years old	9,584	100	13.3	17.0	69.7	19,408	2,025
40 to 44 years old	9,009	100	12.1	17.6	70.3	18,863	2,094
Women never married	22,733	100	79.8	10.3	9.9	8,690	382
15 to 19 years old	8,405	100	93.5	5.2	1.3	683	81
20 to 24 years old	6,121	100	79.8	12.9	7.4	1,930	315
25 to 29 years old	3,502	100	70.0	13.0	17.1	2,121	606
30 to 34 years old	2,233	100	61.4	14.1	24.4	1,924	862
35 to 39 years old	1,509	100	59.9	15.5	24.5	1,302	863
40 to 44 years old	963	100	68.4	12.6	18.9	730	758
WHITE							
Women ever married	31,863	100	19.6	22.4	58.0	55,152	1,731
15 to 19 years old	346	100	46.4	46.9	6.7	210	607
20 to 24 years old	2,762	100	37.7	36.5	25.9	2,667	966
25 to 29 years old	5,367	100	29.5	28.5	42.1	7,072	1,318
30 to 34 years old	7,643	100	18.0	22.7	59.3	13,350	1,747
35 to 39 years old	8,155	100	13.9	17.0	69.1	16,229	1,990
40 to 44 years old	7,591	100	12.5	17.1	70.4	15,624	2,058
Women never married	16,668	100	87.1	7.9	5.0	3,523	211
15 to 19 years old	6,560	100	95.4	3.8	0.8	377	57
20 to 24 years old	4,589	100	85.4	10.6	4.0	935	204
25 to 29 years old	2,481	100	79.6	10.6	9.7	886	357
30 to 34 years old	1,453	100	76.6	10.3	13.1	649	447
35 to 39 years old	927	100	76.6	11.2	12.2	401	433
40 to 44 years old	659	100	81.9	8.3	9.8	275	418
BLACK							
Women ever married	3,669	100	13.6	24.8	61.7	7,496	2,043
15 to 19 years old	22	100	(B)	(B)	(B)	13	(B)
20 to 24 years old	261	100	26.8	41.1	32.1	319	1,222
25 to 29 years old	618	100	22.2	31.5	46.3	956	1,548
30 to 34 years old	829	100	13.4	25.1	61.4	1,757	2,120
35 to 39 years old	948	100	7.7	18.3	73.9	2,141	2,259
40 to 44 years old	991	100	9.4	22.3	68.3	2,310	2,330
Women never married	4,855	100	53.8	19.4	26.8	4,743	977
15 to 19 years old	1,395	100	85.1	11.7	3.2	259	186
20 to 24 years old	1,154	100	55.2	23.3	21.5	921	798
25 to 29 years old	818	100	40.2	21.1	38.8	1,109	1,354
30 to 34 years old	695	100	30.0	21.7	48.4	1,189	1,712
35 to 39 years old	530	100	31.0	23.7	45.4	821	1,551
40 to 44 years old	263	100	32.5	24.0	43.5	443	1,685

B Base figure too small to meet statistical standards for reliability.   [1] Includes other races, not shown separately.
Source: U.S. Bureau of the Census, *Current Population Reports*, series P20-482.

No. 107. Lifetime Births Expected per 1,000 Wives: 1971 to 1992

[See headnote, table 104]

YEAR	LIFETIME BIRTHS TO ALL WIVES [1] AGED—			LIFETIME BIRTHS TO WHITE WIVES AGED—			LIFETIME BIRTHS TO BLACK WIVES AGED—			LIFETIME BIRTHS TO HISPANIC [2] WIVES AGED—		
	18 to 24 yrs. old	25 to 29 yrs. old	30 to 34 yrs. old	18 to 24 yrs. old	25 to 29 yrs. old	30 to 34 yrs. old	18 to 24 yrs. old	25 to 29 yrs. old	30 to 34 yrs. old	18 to 24 yrs. old	25 to 29 yrs. old	30 to 34 yrs. old
1971....	2,375	2,619	2,989	2,353	2,577	2,936	2,623	3,112	3,714	(NA)	(NA)	(NA)
1975....	2,173	2,260	2,610	2,147	2,233	2,564	2,489	2,587	3,212	2,223	2,607	3,238
1980....	2,134	2,166	2,248	2,130	2,146	2,223	2,155	2,426	2,522	2,428	2,495	2,909
1985....	2,183	2,236	2,167	2,177	2,227	2,139	2,242	2,259	2,521	2,367	2,628	2,712
1990....	2,244	2,285	2,277	2,218	2,272	2,257	2,509	2,443	2,579	2,404	2,482	2,824
1992....	2,279	2,271	2,218	2,274	2,259	2,208	2,353	2,389	2,362	2,511	2,437	2,600

NA Not available.   [1] Includes other races not shown separately.   [2] Persons of Hispanic origin may be of any race.

No. 108. Lifetime Births Expected by Women, 18 to 34 Years Old, by Selected Characteristics: 1992

[As of **June.** Covers women in the civilian noninstitutional population. Based on Current Population Survey; see text, section 1, and Appendix III]

CHARACTERISTIC	Women reporting on birth expectations (1,000)	RATE PER 1,000 WOMEN			PERCENTAGE EXPECTING—	
		Births to date	Future births expected	Lifetime births expected	No lifetime births	No future births
Total [1]	24,223	1,135	963	2,098	9.3	48.3
White.....................	20,141	1,077	1,014	2,091	9.3	46.1
Black	3,217	1,508	628	2,136	9.3	63.4
Hispanic [2]................	2,357	1,493	838	2,331	5.7	51.4
Not a high school graduate	3,599	1,776	616	2,393	7.6	63.8
High school, 4 years..............	8,760	1,325	718	2,043	9.0	57.9
College: 1 or more years..........	11,864	800	1,249	2,049	10.0	36.5
Some college, no degree	5,871	848	1,216	2,064	10.0	39.2
Associate degree	1,731	1,020	1,018	2,038	8.9	43.4
Bachelor's degree.............	3,466	663	1,380	2,043	10.3	31.0
Graduate or professional degree ...	795	563	1,427	1,990	12.0	26.0
In labor force.................	17,834	929	1,069	1,998	10.5	44.1
Employed	16,130	903	1,077	1,980	10.7	43.6
Unemployed	1,705	1,176	991	2,167	8.4	49.3
Not in labor force	6,389	1,710	667	2,377	6.0	60.1
Managerial and professional........	3,760	725	1,232	1,957	11.3	36.8
Technical, sales, and admin. support ..	7,511	835	1,126	1,962	10.2	41.0
Service workers...............	3,127	1,097	974	2,071	9.5	48.2
Farming, forestry, and fishing	198	1,426	972	2,398	14.1	55.5
Precision production, craft, and repair .	299	1,135	714	1,849	12.7	59.5
Operators, fabricators, and laborers...	1,235	1,223	675	1,897	13.5	62.4

[1] Includes other races not shown separately.   [2] Persons of Hispanic origin may be of any race.
Source of tables 107 and 108: U.S. Bureau of the Census, *Current Population Reports*, series P20-470.

No. 109. Pregnancies, Number and Outcome: 1976 to 1992

[**Live births:** source of data is statistics of registered births published annually by National Center for Health Statistics (NCHS). **induced abortions:** derived from published reports by the Alan Guttmacher Institute. **Fetal losses:** based on the National Survey of Family Growth conducted by NCHS]

YEAR	NUMBER (1,000)				RATE PER 1,000 WOMEN, 15 TO 44 YEARS OLD			
	Total	Live births	Induced abortions	Fetal losses	Total	Live births	Induced abortions	Fetal losses
1976.........	5,002	3,168	1,179	655	102.7	65.0	24.2	13.4
1977.........	5,331	3,327	1,317	687	107.0	66.8	26.4	13.8
1978.........	5,433	3,333	1,410	690	106.7	65.5	27.7	13.5
1979.........	5,714	3,494	1,498	722	109.9	67.2	28.8	13.9
1980.........	5,912	3,612	1,554	746	111.9	68.4	29.4	14.1
1981.........	5,958	3,629	1,577	751	110.5	67.3	29.3	13.9
1982.........	6,024	3,681	1,574	769	110.1	67.3	28.8	14.1
1983.........	5,977	3,639	1,575	763	108.0	65.7	28.5	13.8
1984.........	6,019	3,669	1,577	773	107.4	65.5	28.1	13.8
1985.........	6,144	3,761	1,589	795	108.3	66.3	28.0	14.0
1986.........	6,129	3,757	1,574	798	106.7	65.4	27.4	13.9
1987.........	6,183	3,809	1,559	815	106.8	65.8	26.9	14.1
1988.........	6,341	3,910	1,591	840	109.1	67.3	27.4	14.5
1989.........	6,480	4,041	1,567	873	111.0	69.2	26.8	15.0
1990.........	6,668	4,158	1,609	902	113.8	70.9	27.4	15.4
1991.........	6,563	4,111	1,557	896	111.1	69.6	26.3	15.2
1992.........	6,484	4,065	1,529	890	109.9	68.9	25.9	15.1

Source: U.S. National Center for Health Statistics, *Monthly Vital Statistics Report,* vol. 41, No. 6, Supplement.

No. 110. Pregnancies, by Outcome, Age of Woman, and Race: 1991

[See headnote, table 109]

ITEM	Total	Under 15 years old	15 to 19 years old	20 to 24 years old	25 to 29 years old	30 to 34 years old	35 to 39 years old	40 years old and over
PREGNANCIES								
Non-Hispanic:								
White, pregnancies	3,964	8	489	1,007	1,145	884	368	63
Live births	2,635	3	250	637	834	640	235	36
Induced abortions	774	4	164	264	163	106	58	16
Fetal losses	556	1	75	107	148	138	76	11
Black, pregnancies	1,344	14	272	439	320	202	81	15
Live births	673	6	149	216	160	98	37	6
Induced abortions	507	7	101	178	119	67	29	7
Fetal losses	164	1	22	45	41	37	15	3
Hispanic:								
Pregnancies.	965	5	177	306	250	149	64	14
Live births	623	2	105	199	170	100	39	8
Induced abortions	208	1	40	73	50	28	13	4
Fetal losses	134	1	32	33	30	22	12	2
RATE PER 1,000 WOMEN								
Non-Hispanic:								
White, pregnancies	91.8	1.3	84.7	151.4	154.7	107.6	47.3	8.6
Live births	61.0	0.5	43.4	95.7	112.7	77.9	30.2	4.8
Induced abortions	17.9	0.7	28.4	39.6	22.0	12.9	7.4	2.2
Fetal losses	12.9	0.2	13.0	16.0	20.0	16.8	9.7	1.6
Black, pregnancies	174.8	11.0	216.7	337.2	232.3	142.7	63.9	14.4
Live births	87.6	4.9	118.9	166.1	116.3	69.3	28.9	5.7
Induced abortions	65.9	5.1	80.5	136.4	86.3	47.1	23.0	6.2
Fetal losses	21.3	0.9	17.2	34.7	29.7	26.3	12.1	2.4
Hispanic:								
Pregnancies.	167.4	4.8	180.2	285.6	224.3	143.9	74.8	19.8
Live births	108.1	2.4	106.7	186.3	152.8	96.1	44.9	11.1
Induced abortions	36.2	1.4	40.4	68.1	44.4	27.1	15.5	5.2
Fetal losses	23.2	1.0	33.1	31.2	27.1	20.7	14.4	3.6

Source: U.S. National Center for Health Statistics, *Monthly Vital Statistics Report*, vol. 43, No. 12.

No. 111. Contraceptive Use by Women, 15 to 44 Years Old: 1990

[Based on samples of the female population of of the United States; see source for details. See Appendix III]

CONTRACEPTIVE STATUS AND METHOD	All women [1]	AGE			RACE			MARITAL STATUS		
		15-24 years	25-34 years	35-44 years	Non-Hispanic		His-panic	Never married	Cur-rently married	For-merly married
					White	Black				
All women (1,000).	58,381	17,637	21,728	19,016	42,968	7,510	5,500	20,788	30,561	7,033
PERCENT DISTRIBUTION										
Sterile.	32.1	3.8	26.4	64.6	32.9	34.0	27.5	7.1	46.0	45.2
Surgically sterile . . . . [2]	30.2	3.1	24.8	61.1	31.2	31.4	23.9	5.7	43.9	42.3
Noncontraceptively sterile [2] .	5.2	0.3	2.7	12.5	5.4	6.5	3.2	1.1	6.6	10.9
Contraceptively sterile [3]	25.0	2.8	22.1	48.6	25.8	24.9	20.7	4.6	37.3	31.4
Nonsurgically sterile [4]	1.9	0.7	1.6	3.5	1.7	2.6	3.6	1.4	2.1	2.9
Pregnant, postpartum	5.4	7.0	7.9	1.2	5.2	5.5	7.7	3.4	7.3	3.1
Seeking pregnancy	4.0	1.8	7.6	2.0	3.7	4.7	5.1	1.1	6.6	1.5
Other nonusers	24.2	46.4	17.1	12.0	23.6	22.1	28.3	50.0	6.6	24.4
Never had intercourse	9.4	26.4	2.8	1.3	8.7	7.0	16.4	26.4	-	-
No intercourse in last month . .	7.0	7.7	7.1	6.4	7.2	7.5	5.1	12.5	0.6	18.9
Had intercourse in last month .	7.8	12.3	7.2	4.3	7.7	7.6	6.8	11.1	6.0	5.5
Nonsurgical contraceptors	34.3	41.2	41.3	20.1	34.6	33.8	31.7	38.5	33.3	25.8
Pill	16.9	23.9	22.0	4.7	17.3	16.7	16.4	21.7	14.5	12.8
IUD.	0.8	0.2	0.4	1.8	0.8	0.8	1.0	0.4	1.0	1.4
Diaphragm	1.7	0.2	2.3	2.4	1.8	1.0	0.8	0.3	2.9	0.5
Condom	10.5	13.9	11.0	6.7	10.3	11.4	8.9	13.0	9.9	5.6
Periodic abstinence	1.6	1.0	2.0	1.6	1.6	0.7	1.9	0.8	2.4	0.4
Natural family planning	0.2	0.1	0.4	0.2	0.2	-	-	-	0.4	-
Withdrawal	0.6	0.6	0.6	0.5	0.6	0.4	0.4	0.7	0.5	0.1
Other methods [5]	2.3	1.4	3.0	2.4	2.2	2.8	2.3	1.6	2.1	5.0

- Represents or rounds to zero. [1] Includes other races, not shown separately. [2] Persons who had sterilizing operation and who gave as one reason that they had medical problems with their female organs. [3] Includes all other sterilization operations, and sterilization of the husband or current partner. [4] Persons sterile from illness, accident, or congenital conditions. [5] Douche, suppository, and less frequently used methods.

Source: U.S. National Center for Health Statistics, *Advance Data from Vital and Health Statistics*, No. 182.

No. 112. Live Births—Mothers Who Smoked During Pregnancy, According to Educational Attainment and Race of Mother: 1993

[In thousands, except percents. Excludes California, Indiana, New York, and South Dakota, which did not require reporting of tobacco use during pregnancy]

SMOKING MEASURE AND RACE OF MOTHER	Total	YEARS OF SCHOOL COMPLETED BY MOTHER					
		0-8 years	9-11 years	12 years	13-15 years	16 years or more	Not stated
All races¹	3,038	143	500	1,100	655	598	42
White	2,381	115	339	843	526	528	29
Black	544	20	144	221	108	42	9
Percent: Smoker¹	15.8	15.2	29.0	19.3	11.3	3.1	15.6
White	16.8	16.6	34.0	21.3	12.0	3.2	16.3
Black	12.7	10.2	18.2	12.6	9.0	4.1	17.2
All races¹: Smoker	100.0	100.0	100.0	100.0	100.0	100.0	100.0
10 cigarettes or less	62.7	57.2	61.6	62.3	65.5	71.5	64.2
11-20 cigarettes	32.1	34.5	32.6	32.9	30.2	25.2	30.8
21 cigarettes or more	5.2	8.3	5.8	4.9	4.3	3.3	5.0
White: Smoker	100.0	100.0	100.0	100.0	100.0	100.0	100.0
10 cigarettes or less	59.7	54.9	57.7	59.3	63.2	70.2	60.0
11-20 cigarettes	34.6	36.2	35.8	35.4	32.1	26.3	34.3
21 cigarettes or more	5.7	8.8	6.5	5.3	4.7	3.6	5.7
Black: Smoker	100.0	100.0	100.0	100.0	100.0	100.0	100.0
10 cigarettes or less	78.3	75.1	76.8	79.5	79.3	82.3	76.1
11-20 cigarettes	19.1	20.4	20.1	18.3	18.8	16.5	20.8
21 cigarettes or more	2.6	4.6	3.1	2.2	1.9	(B)	3.1

B Base data too small to meet statistical standards for reliability of a derived figure.   ¹ Includes races other than White and Black.

Source: U.S. National Center for Health Statistics, *Monthly Vital Statistics Reports.*

No. 113. Percent Low Birthweight, by Smoking Status, Age, and Race of Mother: 1993

[Low birthweight is defined as weight of less than 2,500 grams (5 lb. 8 oz.). Excludes California, Indiana, New York, and South Dakota, which did not require reporting of tobacco use during pregnancy]

SMOKING STATUS AND RACE OF MOTHER	All ages	Under 15 years	15-19 years			20-24 years	25-29 years	30-34 years	35-39 years	40-49 years
			Total	15-17 years	18-19 years					
All races¹	7.4	13.8	9.6	10.5	9.0	7.5	6.5	6.8	8.0	9.0
Smoker	11.8	14.7	10.8	11.4	10.5	10.4	11.5	13.6	16.1	17.8
Nonsmoker	6.6	13.8	9.3	10.3	8.6	6.8	5.6	5.7	6.8	7.9
Not stated	9.2	14.2	11.8	12.9	11.1	9.0	8.2	8.7	9.9	10.3
White	6.1	10.8	7.9	8.6	7.5	6.1	5.4	5.7	6.8	7.7
Smoker	10.1	14.0	10.3	11.0	9.9	9.2	9.4	10.9	13.3	14.7
Nonsmoker	5.2	10.3	7.1	7.9	6.6	5.2	4.6	4.9	5.9	6.9
Not stated	7.6	(B)	9.7	10.9	9.1	7.8	6.6	7.4	8.2	9.5
Black	13.4	16.1	13.4	13.9	13.0	12.3	13.2	14.8	16.6	17.4
Smoker	22.6	19.6	17.2	17.1	17.3	18.8	23.2	26.3	27.8	30.4
Nonsmoker	12.0	15.9	13.1	13.7	12.6	11.4	11.2	11.8	13.6	14.6
Not stated	16.9	(B)	17.5	17.5	17.4	13.9	16.9	18.4	23.7	22.7

B Base data too small to meet statistical standards for reliability of a derived figure.   ¹ Includes races other than White and Black.

Source: U.S. National Center for Health Statistics, *Monthly Vital Reports.*

No. 114. Live Births—Drinking Status of Mother Who Drank During Pregnancy, According to Age and Race of Mother: 1993

[In thousands, except percents. Excludes California, New York, and South Dakota, which did not require reporting of alcohol abuse during pregnancy]

DRINKING STATUS, DRINKING MEASURE, AND RACE OF MOTHER	All ages	Under 15 years	15-19 years			20-24 years	25-29 years	30-34 years	35-39 years	40-49 years
			Total	15-17 years	18-19 years					
All races¹, total	3,121.8	10.3	405.7	153.8	251.9	827.2	879.0	691.6	264.9	43.1
Drinker	63.8	0.1	4.4	1.5	2.9	13.4	17.7	18.5	8.4	1.3
Nondrinker	2,999.2	10.1	394.3	149.7	244.6	799.1	845.2	659.2	250.6	40.7
Not stated	58.8	0.2	7.1	2.6	4.4	14.6	16.1	13.9	5.9	1.1
White, total	2,454.4	4.3	268.2	93.7	174.4	620.7	721.6	583.7	220.9	35.1
Drinker	44.8	(Z)	3.0	1.0	2.0	8.9	11.8	13.6	6.4	1.0
Nondrinker	2,363.8	4.1	260.3	91.1	169.2	601.0	697.0	558.6	209.6	33.2
Not stated	45.9	0.1	4.9	1.7	3.2	10.9	12.8	11.5	4.9	0.9
Black, total	553.7	5.8	126.0	55.7	70.3	180.0	124.1	80.2	32.0	5.5
Drinker	16.6	(Z)	1.0	0.4	0.7	3.8	5.3	4.4	1.8	0.3
Nondrinker	527.3	5.7	123.1	54.6	68.5	173.2	116.3	74.1	29.6	5.2
Not stated	9.8	0.1	1.9	0.8	1.1	3.0	2.5	1.7	0.7	0.1
Percent: Drinker¹	2.1	0.8	1.1	1.0	1.2	1.7	2.1	2.7	3.2	3.2
White	1.9	1.2	1.1	1.1	1.2	1.5	1.7	2.4	3.0	3.0
Black	3.1	0.5	0.8	0.6	1.0	2.2	4.3	5.6	5.6	5.1

Z Less than 50.   ¹ Includes races other than White or Black.

Source: U.S. National Center for Health Statistics, *Monthly Vital Statistics Reports.*

No. 115. Abortions—Number, Rate, and Ratio, by Race: 1975 to 1992

YEAR	ALL RACES				WHITE				BLACK AND OTHER			
	Women 15-44 years old (1,000)	Abortions			Women 15-44 years old (1,000)	Abortions			Women 15-44 years old (1,000)	Abortions		
		Num-ber (1,000)	Rate per 1,000 women	Ratio per 1,000 live births [1]		Num-ber (1,000)	Rate per 1,000 women	Ratio per 1,000 live births [1]		Num-ber (1,000)	Rate per 1,000 women	Ratio per 1,000 live births [1]
1975 ..	47,606	1,034	21.7	331	40,857	701	17.2	276	6,749	333	49.3	565
1979 ..	52,016	1,498	28.8	420	44,266	1,062	24.0	373	7,750	435	56.2	625
1980 ..	53,048	1,554	29.3	428	44,942	1,094	24.3	376	8,106	460	56.5	642
1981 ..	53,901	1,577	29.3	430	45,494	1,108	24.3	377	8,407	470	55.9	645
1982 [2] .	54,679	1,574	28.8	428	46,049	1,095	23.8	373	8,630	479	55.5	646
1983 [2] .	55,340	1,575	28.5	436	46,506	1,084	23.3	376	8,834	491	55.5	670
1984 ..	56,061	1,577	28.1	423	47,023	1,087	23.1	366	9,038	491	54.3	646
1985 ..	56,754	1,589	28.0	422	47,512	1,076	22.6	360	9,242	513	55.5	659
1986 [2] .	57,483	1,574	27.4	416	48,010	1,045	21.8	350	9,473	529	55.9	661
1987 ..	57,964	1,559	27.1	405	48,288	1,017	21.1	338	9,676	542	56.0	648
1988 [2] .	58,192	1,591	27.3	401	48,325	1,026	21.2	333	9,867	565	57.3	638
1989 [2] .	58,365	1,567	26.8	380	48,104	1,006	20.9	309	10,261	561	54.7	650
1990 [2] .	58,700	1,609	27.4	389	48,224	1,039	21.5	318	10,476	570	54.4	655
1991 ..	59,080	1,557	26.3	379	48,406	982	20.3	303	10,674	574	53.8	661
1992 ..	59,020	1,529	25.9	379	(NA)	(NA)	(NA)	(NA)	(NA)	(NA)	(NA)	(NA)

NA Not available.　[1] Live births are those which occurred from July 1 of year shown through June 30 of the following year (to match time of conception with abortions). Births are classified by race of child 1972-1988, and by race of mother after 1988.　[2] Total numbers of abortions in 1983 and 1986 have been estimated by interpolation; 1989 and 1990 have been estimated using trends in CDC data.

No. 116. Abortions, by Selected Characteristics: 1985 to 1991

[Number of abortions from surveys conducted by source; characteristics from the U.S. Centers for Disease Control's (CDC) annual abortion surveillance summaries, with adjustments for changes in States reporting data to the CDC each year]

CHARACTERISTIC	NUMBER (1,000)			PERCENT DISTRIBUTION			ABORTION RATIO [1]		
	1985	1990 [1]	1991	1985	1990 [1]	1991	1985	1990 [1]	1991
Total abortions	1,589	1,609	1,557	100	100	100	297	280	275
Age of woman:									
Less than 15 years old	17	13	12	1	1	1	624	515	502
15 to 19 years old	399	351	314	25	22	20	462	403	379
20 to 24 years old	548	532	533	35	33	34	328	328	330
25 to 29 years old	336	360	348	21	22	22	219	224	224
30 to 34 years old	181	216	213	11	13	14	203	196	192
35 to 39 years old	87	108	107	5	7	7	280	249	241
40 years old and over.	21	29	29	1	2	2	409	354	339
Race of woman:									
White.	1,076	1,039	982	68	65	63	265	241	233
Black and other	513	570	574	32	35	37	397	396	398
Marital status of woman:									
Married	281	284	271	18	18	17	88	88	86
Unmarried	1,307	1,325	1,285	82	82	83	605	527	512
Number of prior live births:									
None.	872	780	724	55	49	46	358	316	303
One.	349	396	398	22	25	26	219	230	231
Two	240	280	281	15	17	18	288	292	294
Three	85	102	105	5	6	7	281	279	285
Four or more	43	50	50	3	3	3	230	223	218
Number of prior induced abortions:									
None	944	891	840	60	55	54	(NA)	(NA)	(NA)
One.	416	443	437	26	28	28	(NA)	(NA)	(NA)
Two or more	228	275	279	14	17	18	(NA)	(NA)	(NA)
Weeks of gestation: [2]									
Less than 9 weeks.	779	817	805	49	51	52	(NA)	(NA)	(NA)
9 to 10 weeks	425	418	399	27	26	26	(NA)	(NA)	(NA)
11 to 12 weeks	211	199	188	13	12	12	(NA)	(NA)	(NA)
13 weeks or more	173	175	164	11	11	11	(NA)	(NA)	(NA)

NA Not available.　[1] Number of abortions per 1,000 abortions and live births. Live births are those which occurred from July 1 of year shown through June 30 of the following year (to match time of conception with abortions).　[2] Beginning 1985, data not exactly comparable with prior years because of a change in the method of calculation.

Source of tables 115 and 116: S.K. Henshaw and J. Van Vort, eds., *Abortion Factbook, 1992 Edition: Readings, Trends, and State and Local Data to 1988*, The Alan Guttmacher Institute, New York, NY, 1992 (copyright); S.K. Henshaw and J. Van Vort, *Abortion Services in the United States, 1991 and 1992; Family Perspectives, 26:100, 1994;* and unpublished data.

No. 117. Abortions—Number, Rate, and Abortion/Live Birth Ratio, by State: 1980 to 1992

[Number of abortions from surveys of hospitals, clinics, and physicians identified as providers of abortion services conducted by The Alan Guttmacher Institute. Abortion rates are computed per 1,000 women 15 to 44 years of age on July 1 of specified year; abortion ratios are computed as the number of abortions per 1,000 live births from July 1 of year shown to June 30 of following year, by State of occurrence]

DIVISION, REGION, AND STATE	NUMBER OF ABORTIONS (1,000)			RATE PER 1,000 WOMEN, 15 TO 44 YEARS OLD			RATIO: ABORTIONS PER 1,000 LIVE BIRTHS		
	1980	1985	1992	1980	1985	1992	1980	1985	1992
United States	1,554	1,589	1,529	29.3	28.0	25.9	428	422	379
Northeast	396	407	379	34.9	(NA)	32.1	604	(NA)	506
New England	84	85	78	28.9	28.6	25.2	530	504	429
Maine	5	5	4	18.6	18.6	14.7	289	308	282
New Hampshire	5	7	4	21.1	29.0	14.6	347	419	269
Vermont	4	3	3	30.4	26.2	21.2	466	448	393
Massachusetts	46	40	41	33.5	29.3	28.4	609	533	472
Rhode Island	7	8	7	30.7	35.5	30.0	529	572	461
Connecticut	19	22	20	25.6	29.3	26.2	561	550	444
Middle Atlantic	312	322	300	37.0	37.6	34.6	627	607	530
New York	188	195	195	45.8	47.4	46.2	780	746	694
New Jersey	56	69	55	32.8	39.6	31.0	591	672	460
Pennsylvania	69	57	50	26.1	21.3	18.6	423	348	302
Midwest	318	289	262	23.3	(NA)	18.9	336	(NA)	287
East North Central	243	221	205	24.9	22.1	20.7	369	356	313
Ohio	67	57	50	26.8	22.4	19.5	397	357	294
Indiana	20	16	16	15.3	12.2	12.0	227	202	185
Illinois	69	65	68	25.9	23.8	25.4	374	372	361
Michigan	65	64	56	29.7	28.7	25.2	457	486	393
Wisconsin	22	18	15	20.1	15.7	13.6	292	246	223
West North Central	75	68	57	19.2	16.7	14.3	260	252	221
Minnesota	20	17	16	20.7	16.6	15.6	288	257	251
Iowa	9	10	7	14.3	15.0	11.4	195	248	185
Missouri	22	20	14	19.4	17.3	11.6	273	261	175
North Dakota	3	3	1	21.5	18.5	10.7	235	230	149
South Dakota	1	2	1	9.0	10.6	6.8	103	140	92
Nebraska	6	7	6	17.9	18.2	15.7	227	268	246
Kansas	14	10	13	25.6	18.2	22.4	343	264	353
South	457	453	450	25.9	(NA)	22.0	369	(NA)	323
South Atlantic	255	257	269	29.4	27.1	25.9	462	429	397
Delaware	4	5	6	25.9	30.9	35.2	395	451	502
Maryland	31	30	31	29.2	26.9	26.4	571	480	454
District of Columbia	29	24	21	168.3	145.9	138.4	1,569	1,186	1,104
Virginia	32	34	35	24.2	24.0	22.7	417	412	373
West Virginia	3	5	3	6.9	10.1	7.7	104	185	134
North Carolina	32	34	36	22.8	22.6	22.4	377	379	357
South Carolina	14	11	12	18.2	13.7	14.2	274	228	229
Georgia	38	38	40	28.4	26.1	24.0	395	397	350
Florida	74	77	85	35.5	31.8	30.0	547	465	438
East South Central	65	57	54	19.2	15.8	14.9	271	258	228
Kentucky	13	10	10	15.1	11.0	11.4	215	189	191
Tennessee	26	22	19	23.6	19.1	16.2	352	315	243
Alabama	21	19	17	23.1	20.2	18.2	331	333	277
Mississippi	6	6	8	10.6	9.7	12.4	132	142	176
West South Central	137	139	127	24.5	21.8	19.6	308	290	266
Arkansas	6	5	7	12.3	10.1	13.5	173	159	213
Louisiana	18	19	14	17.6	17.4	13.4	218	240	195
Oklahoma	11	13	9	16.4	17.1	12.5	221	269	193
Texas	102	101	97	30.0	25.5	23.1	367	320	297
West	383	440	438	36.8	(NA)	34.1	486	(NA)	446
Mountain	68	75	70	25.0	23.6	21.0	302	316	280
Montana	4	4	3	20.1	19.0	18.2	265	288	298
Idaho	3	3	2	12.7	11.1	7.2	141	155	97
Wyoming	1	1	-	9.5	7.9	4.3	107	125	74
Colorado	23	24	20	31.4	28.8	23.6	447	438	362
New Mexico	8	6	6	27.0	17.4	17.7	358	219	228
Arizona	16	22	21	25.0	29.9	24.1	310	373	295
Utah	4	4	4	12.3	11.1	9.3	97	116	104
Nevada	9	10	13	46.6	40.5	44.2	697	641	591
Pacific	315	365	368	41.0	42.8	38.7	561	594	501
Washington	37	31	33	37.5	28.0	27.7	522	458	447
Oregon	18	15	16	28.3	22.3	23.9	396	374	372
California	250	304	304	43.7	47.9	42.1	598	640	519
Alaska	2	4	2	17.9	27.7	16.5	196	283	222
Hawaii	8	11	12	34.4	43.7	46.0	441	611	617

- Represents zero.   NA Not available.

Source: S.K. Henshaw and J. Van Vort, eds., *Abortion Factbook, 1992 Edition: Readings, Trends, and State and Local Data to 1988*, The Alan Guttmacher Institute, New York, NY, 1992 (copyright); S.K. Henshaw and J. Van Vort, *Abortion Services in the United States, 1991 and 1992, Family Planning Perspectives, 26:100, 1994;* and unpublished data.

No. 118. Expectation of Life at Birth, 1970 to 1994, and Projections, 1995 to 2010

[**In years.** Excludes deaths of nonresidents of the United States. See also *Historical Statistics, Colonial Times to 1970*, series B 107-115]

YEAR	TOTAL			WHITE			BLACK AND OTHER			BLACK		
	Total	Male	Female	Total	Male	Female	Total	Male	Female	Total	Male	Female
1970.	70.8	67.1	74.7	71.7	68.0	75.6	65.3	61.3	69.4	64.1	60.0	68.3
1975.	72.6	68.8	76.6	73.4	69.5	77.3	68.0	63.7	72.4	66.8	62.4	71.3
1980.	73.7	70.0	77.4	74.4	70.7	78.1	69.5	65.3	73.6	68.1	63.8	72.5
1982.	74.5	70.8	78.1	75.1	71.5	78.7	70.9	66.8	74.9	69.4	65.1	73.6
1983.	74.6	71.0	78.1	75.2	71.6	78.7	70.9	67.0	74.7	69.4	65.2	73.5
1984.	74.7	71.1	78.2	75.3	71.8	78.7	71.1	67.2	74.9	69.5	65.3	73.6
1985.	74.7	71.1	78.2	75.3	71.8	78.7	71.0	67.0	74.8	69.3	65.0	73.4
1986.	74.7	71.2	78.2	75.4	71.9	78.8	70.9	66.8	74.9	69.1	64.8	73.4
1987.	74.9	71.4	78.3	75.6	72.1	78.9	71.0	66.9	75.0	69.1	64.7	73.4
1988.	74.9	71.4	78.3	75.6	72.2	78.9	70.8	66.7	74.8	68.9	64.4	73.2
1989.	75.1	71.7	78.5	75.9	72.5	79.2	70.9	66.7	74.9	68.8	64.3	73.3
1990.	75.4	71.8	78.8	76.1	72.7	79.4	71.2	67.0	75.2	69.1	64.5	73.6
1991.	75.5	72.0	78.9	76.3	72.9	79.6	71.5	67.3	75.5	69.3	64.6	73.8
1992.	75.8	72.3	79.1	76.5	73.2	79.8	71.8	67.7	75.7	69.6	65.0	73.9
1993.	75.5	72.2	78.8	76.3	73.1	79.5	71.5	67.3	75.5	69.2	64.6	73.7
1994.	75.7	72.3	79.0	76.4	73.2	79.6	71.7	67.5	75.8	69.6	64.9	74.1
Projections: [1] 1995 . . .	76.3	72.5	79.3	77.0	73.6	80.1	72.5	68.2	76.8	70.3	64.8	74.5
2000 . . .	76.7	73.0	79.7	77.6	74.2	80.5	72.9	68.3	77.5	70.2	64.6	74.7
2005 . . .	77.3	73.5	80.2	78.2	74.7	81.0	73.6	69.1	78.1	70.7	64.5	75.0
2010 . . .	77.9	74.1	80.6	78.8	75.5	81.6	74.3	69.9	78.7	71.3	65.1	75.5

[1] Based on middle mortality assumptions; for details, see source. Source: U.S. Bureau of the Census, *Current Population Reports*, P25-1104.

Source: Except as noted, U.S. National Center for Health Statistics, *Vital Statistics of the United States,* annual, and *Monthly Vital Statistics Reports.*

No. 119. Selected Life Table Values: 1979 to 1993

[See also *Historical Statistics, Colonial Times to 1970,* series B 116-125]

AGE AND SEX	TOTAL [1]			WHITE			BLACK		
	1979-1981	1990	1993	1979-1981	1990	1993	1979-1981	1990	1993
AVERAGE EXPECTATION OF LIFE IN YEARS									
At birth: Male.	70.1	71.8	72.2	70.8	72.7	73.1	64.1	64.5	64.6
Female	77.6	78.8	78.8	78.2	79.4	79.5	72.9	73.6	73.7
Age 20: Male.	51.9	53.3	53.5	52.5	54.0	54.2	46.4	46.7	46.8
Female	59.0	59.8	59.8	59.4	60.3	60.3	54.9	55.3	55.3
Age 40: Male.	33.6	35.1	35.4	34.0	35.6	35.9	29.5	30.1	30.2
Female	39.8	40.6	40.6	40.2	41.0	41.0	36.3	36.8	36.9
Age 50: Male.	25.0	26.4	26.7	25.3	26.7	27.0	22.0	22.5	22.8
Female	30.7	31.3	31.4	31.0	31.6	31.7	27.8	28.2	28.3
Age 65: Male.	14.2	15.1	15.3	14.3	15.2	15.4	13.3	13.2	13.4
Female	18.4	18.9	18.9	18.6	19.1	19.0	17.1	17.2	17.1
EXPECTED DEATHS PER 1,000 ALIVE AT SPECIFIED AGE [2]									
At birth: Male.	13.9	10.3	9.2	12.3	8.6	7.6	23.0	19.7	18.3
Female	11.2	8.2	7.4	9.7	6.6	6.0	19.3	16.3	14.6
Age 20: Male.	1.8	1.6	1.5	1.8	1.4	1.3	2.2	2.7	3.1
Female	0.6	0.5	0.5	0.6	0.5	0.5	0.7	0.7	0.7
Age 40: Male.	3.0	3.1	3.2	2.6	2.7	2.7	6.9	7.1	6.7
Female	1.6	1.4	1.4	1.4	1.2	1.2	3.2	3.1	3.1
Age 50: Male.	7.8	6.2	5.5	7.1	5.6	5.0	14.9	12.8	10.3
Female	4.2	3.5	3.2	3.8	3.2	2.9	7.7	6.6	5.9
Age 65: Male.	28.2	12.9	17.4	27.4	23.0	17.3	38.5	36.8	19.9
Female	14.3	13.5	11.4	13.6	12.8	11.1	21.6	21.4	15.2
NUMBER SURVIVING TO SPECIFIED AGE PER 1,000 BORN ALIVE									
Age 20: Male.	973	979	980	975	981	983	961	963	963
Female	982	986	987	984	988	989	972	976	977
Age 40: Male.	933	938	938	940	946	947	885	880	878
Female	965	971	971	969	975	976	941	944	944
Age 50: Male.	890	899	899	901	912	912	801	801	797
Female	941	950	950	947	957	957	896	904	902
Age 65: Male.	706	741	746	724	760	766	551	571	573
Female	835	851	854	848	864	866	733	751	757

[1] Includes other races not shown separately. [2] See footnote 1, table 116.

Source: U.S. National Center for Health Statistics, *U.S. Life Tables and Actuarial Tables, 1959-61, 1969-71, and 1979-81; Vital Statistics of the United States,* annual; and unpublished data.

No. 120. Expectation of Life and Expected Deaths, by Race, Sex, and Age: 1993

AGE IN 1990 (years)	EXPECTATION OF LIFE IN YEARS					EXPECTED DEATHS PER 1,000 ALIVE AT SPECIFIED AGE [1]				
	Total	White		Black		Total	White		Black	
		Male	Female	Male	Female		Male	Female	Male	Female
At birth	75.5	73.1	79.5	64.6	73.7	8.35	7.55	6.03	18.27	14.64
1	75.2	72.6	79.0	64.8	73.8	0.63	0.63	0.46	1.24	0.87
2	74.2	71.7	78.0	63.9	72.9	0.47	0.45	0.35	0.87	0.73
3	73.3	70.7	77.0	62.9	71.9	0.36	0.34	0.28	0.63	0.61
4	72.3	69.7	76.1	62.0	71.0	0.30	0.27	0.23	0.50	0.50
5	71.3	68.8	75.1	61.0	70.0	0.26	0.24	0.20	0.43	0.42
6	70.3	67.8	74.1	60.0	69.0	0.23	0.23	0.18	0.38	0.35
7	69.3	66.8	73.1	59.0	68.0	0.21	0.22	0.16	0.34	0.30
8	68.4	65.8	72.1	58.1	67.1	0.19	0.20	0.15	0.29	0.27
9	67.4	64.8	71.1	57.1	66.1	0.16	0.17	0.14	0.21	0.24
10	66.4	63.8	70.1	56.1	65.1	0.14	0.15	0.12	0.16	0.23
11	65.4	62.8	69.1	55.1	64.1	0.15	0.15	0.13	0.17	0.23
12	64.4	61.8	68.2	54.1	63.1	0.20	0.22	0.15	0.31	0.24
13	63.4	60.9	67.2	53.1	62.1	0.31	0.36	0.20	0.61	0.28
14	62.4	59.9	66.2	52.2	61.2	0.45	0.55	0.27	1.03	0.33
15	61.5	58.9	65.2	51.2	60.2	0.62	0.76	0.35	1.50	0.39
16	60.5	58.0	64.2	50.3	59.2	0.77	0.96	0.43	1.95	0.45
17	59.5	57.0	63.2	49.4	58.2	0.90	1.12	0.47	2.33	0.52
18	58.6	56.1	62.3	48.5	57.3	0.97	1.20	0.48	2.63	0.59
19	57.7	55.1	61.3	47.7	56.3	1.00	1.24	0.47	2.85	0.66
20	56.7	54.2	60.3	46.8	55.3	1.02	1.28	0.45	3.07	0.74
21	55.8	53.3	59.4	45.9	54.4	1.05	1.32	0.43	3.30	0.83
22	54.8	52.4	58.4	45.1	53.4	1.08	1.35	0.43	3.44	0.91
23	53.9	51.4	57.4	44.3	52.5	1.10	1.37	0.43	3.49	0.99
24	52.9	50.5	56.4	43.4	51.5	1.11	1.39	0.45	3.47	1.06
25	52.1	49.6	55.5	42.6	50.6	1.13	1.41	0.47	3.42	1.15
26	51.1	48.6	54.5	41.7	49.6	1.14	1.42	0.49	3.39	1.23
27	50.1	47.7	53.5	40.9	48.7	1.18	1.46	0.52	3.43	1.32
28	49.2	46.8	52.5	40.0	47.8	1.23	1.54	0.55	3.56	1.41
29	48.3	45.9	51.6	39.2	46.8	1.31	1.65	0.58	3.78	1.51
30	47.3	44.9	50.6	38.3	45.9	1.39	1.77	0.61	4.01	1.61
31	46.4	44.0	49.6	37.5	45.0	1.47	1.88	0.65	4.24	1.72
32	45.5	43.1	48.7	36.7	44.1	1.55	1.98	0.70	4.47	1.84
33	44.5	42.2	47.7	35.8	43.2	1.63	2.07	0.74	4.68	1.99
34	43.6	41.3	46.7	35.0	42.2	1.71	2.15	0.79	4.90	2.14
35	42.7	40.4	45.8	34.2	41.3	1.80	2.22	0.85	5.11	2.32
36	41.8	39.5	44.8	33.4	40.4	1.89	2.31	0.91	5.35	2.49
37	40.8	38.6	43.9	32.6	39.5	1.99	2.41	0.97	5.62	2.66
38	39.9	37.7	42.9	31.8	38.6	2.08	2.50	1.04	5.94	2.80
39	39.0	36.8	41.9	31.0	37.8	2.18	2.61	1.11	6.29	2.93
40	38.1	35.9	41.0	30.2	36.9	2.30	2.73	1.19	6.67	3.06
41	37.2	35.0	40.0	29.5	36.0	2.43	2.86	1.28	7.05	3.22
42	36.3	34.1	39.1	28.7	35.1	2.56	3.00	1.38	7.39	3.40
43	35.4	33.2	38.1	27.9	34.2	2.69	3.14	1.51	7.68	3.63
44	34.5	32.3	37.2	27.2	33.4	2.84	3.29	1.66	7.93	3.90
45	33.6	31.4	36.3	26.4	32.5	3.01	3.46	1.82	8.18	4.19
46	32.7	30.5	35.3	25.7	31.7	3.20	3.67	2.01	8.47	4.49
47	31.8	29.6	34.4	24.9	30.8	3.43	3.92	2.21	8.82	4.81
48	30.9	28.7	33.5	24.2	30.0	3.70	4.22	2.42	9.26	5.15
49	30.0	27.9	32.6	23.5	29.1	4.00	4.57	2.66	9.77	5.50
50	29.2	27.0	31.7	22.8	28.3	4.35	4.97	2.92	10.31	5.87
51	28.3	26.2	30.7	22.0	27.5	4.73	5.41	3.21	10.86	6.27
52	27.4	25.3	29.9	21.4	26.7	5.14	5.90	3.54	11.46	6.71
53	26.6	24.5	29.0	20.7	25.9	5.61	6.44	3.90	12.12	7.20
54	25.7	23.6	28.1	20.0	25.1	6.12	7.04	4.30	12.83	7.73
55	24.9	22.8	27.2	19.3	24.3	6.66	7.67	4.72	13.57	8.29
56	24.1	22.0	26.3	18.7	23.5	7.24	8.35	5.18	14.30	8.87
57	23.3	21.2	25.5	18.0	22.8	7.88	9.12	5.69	15.03	9.47
58	22.5	20.5	24.6	17.4	22.0	8.59	9.99	6.26	15.72	10.09
59	21.7	19.7	23.8	16.8	21.3	9.34	10.93	6.89	16.39	10.74
60	20.9	18.9	23.0	16.2	20.6	10.14	11.91	7.56	17.07	11.41
61	20.2	18.2	22.2	15.6	19.8	10.96	12.92	8.25	17.74	12.11
62	19.5	17.5	21.4	15.1	19.1	11.80	13.96	8.96	18.36	12.84
63	18.7	16.8	20.6	14.5	18.4	12.64	15.03	9.65	18.93	13.61
64	18.0	16.1	19.8	13.9	17.8	13.48	16.13	10.35	19.45	14.41
65	17.3	15.4	19.0	13.4	17.1	14.35	17.25	11.08	19.90	15.21
70	14.0	12.3	15.3	10.8	13.9	19.21	22.58	15.84	23.18	19.91
75	10.9	9.5	12.0	8.7	11.1	24.52	27.91	21.99	23.31	23.41
80	8.3	7.1	8.9	6.7	8.5	29.38	31.35	29.20	21.69	26.60
85 and over	6.0	5.2	6.4	5.0	6.3	324.28	239.75	425.13	131.98	300.96

[1] Based on the proportion of the cohort who are alive at the beginning of an indicated age interval who will die before reaching the end of that interval. For example, out of every 1,000 people alive and exactly 50 years old at the beginning of the period, between 4 and 5 (4.86) will die before reaching their 51st birthdays.

Source: U.S. National Center for Health Statistics, *Vital Statistics of the United States,* annual; and unpublished data.

No. 121. Deaths and Death Rates, by Sex and Race: 1970 to 1994

[Rates are per 1,000 population for specified groups. Excludes deaths of nonresidents of the United States and fetal deaths. For explanation of age-adjustment, see text, section 2. The standard population for this table is the total population of the United States enumerated in 1940. See Appendix III. See also *Historical Statistics, Colonial Times to 1970*, series B 167-173 and B 181-192]

SEX AND RACE	1970	1980	1985	1986	1987	1988	1989	1990	1991	1992	1993	1994
Deaths [1] (1,000)	**1,921**	**1,990**	**2,086**	**2,105**	**2,123**	**2,168**	**2,150**	**2,148**	**2,170**	**2,176**	**2,269**	**2,286**
Male [1] (1,000)	1,078	1,075	1,098	1,104	1,108	1,126	1,114	1,113	1,122	1,122	1,162	1,167
Female [1] (1,000)	843	915	989	1,001	1,015	1,042	1,036	1,035	1,048	1,053	1,107	1,118
White (1,000)	1,682	1,739	1,819	1,831	1,843	1,877	1,854	1,853	1,869	1,874	1,951	1,966
Male (1,000)	942	934	950	953	953	965	951	951	956	957	988	992
Female (1,000)	740	805	869	879	890	911	903	902	912	917	963	974
Black (1,000)	226	233	244	250	255	264	268	266	270	269	282	283
Male (1,000)	128	130	134	137	140	144	146	146	147	147	154	154
Female (1,000)	98	103	111	113	115	120	121	120	122	123	129	129
Death rates [1]	**9.5**	**8.8**	**8.8**	**8.8**	**8.8**	**8.8**	**8.7**	**8.6**	**8.6**	**8.6**	**8.5**	**8.8**
Male [1]	10.9	9.8	9.5	9.4	9.4	9.5	9.3	9.2	9.1	9.0	9.2	9.2
Female [1]	8.1	7.9	8.1	8.1	8.2	8.3	8.2	8.1	8.1	8.1	8.4	8.4
White	9.5	8.9	9.0	9.0	9.0	9.1	8.9	8.9	8.9	8.8	9.1	9.1
Male	10.9	9.8	9.6	9.6	9.5	9.6	9.4	9.3	9.3	9.2	9.4	9.3
Female	8.1	8.1	8.4	8.4	8.5	8.7	8.5	8.5	8.5	8.4	8.8	8.8
Black	10.0	8.8	8.5	8.6	8.7	8.9	8.9	8.8	8.6	8.5	8.8	8.7
Male	11.9	10.3	9.9	10.0	10.1	10.3	10.3	10.1	10.0	9.8	10.1	9.9
Female	8.3	7.3	7.3	7.4	7.5	7.6	7.6	7.5	7.4	7.4	7.6	7.5
Age-adjusted death rates [1]	**7.1**	**5.9**	**5.5**	**5.4**	**5.4**	**5.4**	**5.3**	**5.2**	**5.1**	**5.0**	**5.1**	**5.1**
Male [1]	9.3	7.8	7.2	7.2	7.1	7.1	6.9	6.8	6.7	6.6	6.6	6.6
Female [1]	5.3	4.3	4.1	4.1	4.0	4.1	4.0	3.9	3.9	3.8	3.9	3.8
White	6.8	5.6	5.2	5.2	5.1	5.1	5.0	4.9	4.9	4.8	4.9	4.8
Male	8.9	7.5	6.9	6.8	6.7	6.7	6.5	6.4	6.3	6.2	6.3	6.2
Female	5.0	4.1	3.9	3.9	3.8	3.9	3.8	3.7	3.7	3.6	3.7	3.6
Black	10.4	8.4	7.9	8.0	8.0	8.1	8.1	7.9	7.8	7.7	7.9	7.7
Male	13.2	11.1	10.5	10.6	10.6	10.8	10.8	10.6	10.5	10.3	10.5	10.3
Female	8.1	6.3	5.9	5.9	5.9	6.0	5.9	5.8	5.8	5.7	5.8	5.7

[1] Includes other races, not shown separately.

Source: U.S. National Center for Health Statistics, *Vital Statistics of the United States*, annual; and *Monthly Vital Statistics Report*.

No. 122. Death Rates, by Age, Sex, and Race: 1970 to 1994

[Number of deaths per 100,000 population in specified group. See headnote, table 121]

SEX, YEAR, AND RACE	All ages [1]	Under 1 yr. old	1-4 yr. old	5-14 yr. old	15-24 yr. old	25-34 yr. old	35-44 yr. old	45-54 yr. old	55-64 yr. old	65-74 yr. old	75-84 yr. old	85 yr. old and over
MALE [2]												
1970	1,090	2,410	93	51	189	215	403	959	2,283	4,874	10,010	17,822
1980	977	1,429	73	37	172	196	299	767	1,815	4,105	8,817	18,801
1990	918	1,083	52	29	147	204	310	610	1,553	3,492	7,889	18,057
1993	924	946	50	27	146	209	329	596	1,480	3,395	7,653	18,257
1994	919	899	52	26	151	207	337	585	1,467	3,347	7,490	17,936
White: 1970	1,087	2,113	84	48	171	177	344	883	2,203	4,810	10,099	18,552
1980	983	1,230	66	35	167	171	257	699	1,729	4,036	8,830	19,097
1990	931	896	46	26	131	176	268	549	1,467	3,398	7,845	18,268
1993	939	773	43	25	123	181	283	534	1,395	3,307	7,597	18,443
1994	934	732	44	23	130	179	289	523	1,382	3,261	7,434	18,127
Black: 1970	1,187	4,299	151	67	321	560	957	1,778	3,257	5,803	9,455	12,222
1980	1,034	2,587	111	47	209	407	690	1,480	2,873	5,131	9,232	16,099
1990	1,008	2,112	86	41	252	431	700	1,261	2,618	4,946	9,130	16,955
1993	1,006	1,922	86	41	289	429	730	1,266	2,518	4,791	9,013	17,033
1994	994	1,831	87	43	274	411	759	1,227	2,460	4,717	8,915	16,645
FEMALE [2]												
1970	808	1,864	75	32	68	102	231	517	1,099	2,580	6,678	15,518
1980	785	1,142	55	24	58	76	159	413	934	2,145	5,440	14,747
1990	812	856	41	19	49	74	138	343	879	1,991	4,883	14,274
1993	839	759	40	19	49	76	144	330	861	2,001	4,899	14,417
1994	839	719	37	19	47	76	144	326	843	1,989	4,921	14,301
White: 1970	813	1,615	66	30	62	84	193	463	1,015	2,471	6,699	15,980
1980	806	963	49	23	56	65	138	373	876	2,067	5,402	14,980
1990	847	690	36	18	46	62	117	309	823	1,924	4,839	14,401
1993	879	618	34	17	44	63	120	297	811	1,938	4,845	14,558
1994	883	608	31	17	43	63	120	291	789	1,929	4,878	14,460
Black: 1970	829	3,369	129	44	112	231	533	1,044	1,986	3,861	6,692	10,707
1980	733	2,124	84	31	71	150	324	768	1,561	3,057	6,212	12,367
1990	748	1,736	68	28	69	160	299	639	1,453	2,866	5,688	13,310
1993	760	1,543	72	30	73	165	317	632	1,364	2,857	5,887	13,351
1994	750	1,308	74	27	68	158	320	630	1,358	2,827	5,806	13,138

[1] Includes unknown age. [2] Includes other races not shown separately.

Source: U.S. National Center for Health Statistics, *Vital Statistics of the United States*, annual; *Monthly Vital Statistics Report*; and unpublished data.

No. 123. Deaths and Death Rates, by State: 1980 to 1994

[By State of residence. Excludes deaths of nonresidents of the United States, except as noted. Caution should be used in comparing death rates by State; rates are affected by the population composition of the area. See also Appendix III]

DIVISION AND STATE	NUMBER OF DEATHS (1,000)							RATE PER 1,000 POPULATION [2]						
	1980	1985	1990	1991	1992	1993	1994 prel. [1]	1980	1985	1990	1991	1992	1993	1994 prel. [1]
United States..	1,990	2,086	2,148	2,165	2,176	2,269	2,286	8.8	8.8	8.6	8.6	8.5	8.8	8.8
New England	115	118	115	112	116	120	117	9.3	9.3	8.7	8.5	8.8	9.1	8.8
Maine	11	11	11	11	11	12	11	9.6	9.8	9.0	8.9	9.0	9.3	9.2
New Hampshire . .	8	8	8	9	9	9	9	8.3	8.5	7.7	7.7	7.7	7.9	7.8
Vermont	5	5	5	5	5	5	5	9.0	8.8	8.2	8.0	8.4	8.5	7.9
Massachusetts . . .	55	56	53	51	54	56	55	9.6	9.5	8.8	8.6	9.0	9.4	9.0
Rhode Island	9	10	10	9	9	10	9	9.8	10.0	9.5	9.2	9.5	9.7	9.4
Connecticut	27	28	28	28	28	29	29	8.8	8.8	8.4	8.4	8.6	8.9	8.7
Middle Atlantic	365	367	361	360	361	370	369	9.9	9.9	9.6	9.5	9.5	9.7	9.7
New York	173	172	169	167	166	171	168	9.8	9.7	9.4	9.2	9.2	9.4	9.2
New Jersey	69	71	70	70	71	73	73	9.4	9.4	9.1	9.0	9.1	9.2	9.2
Pennsylvania	124	124	122	124	124	126	128	10.4	10.5	10.3	10.3	10.3	10.5	10.6
East North Central .	365	370	373	379	373	389	395	8.8	8.9	8.9	8.9	8.7	9.0	9.1
Ohio	98	99	99	99	99	103	106	9.1	9.2	9.1	9.1	9.0	9.1	9.5
Indiana	47	48	50	52	50	52	53	8.6	8.8	8.9	9.2	8.8	9.1	9.3
Illinois	103	102	103	105	102	107	108	9.0	9.0	9.0	9.1	8.8	9.2	9.2
Michigan	75	79	79	80	79	83	83	8.1	8.7	8.5	8.5	8.4	8.7	8.8
Wisconsin	41	41	43	44	42	45	45	8.7	8.7	8.7	8.8	8.5	8.7	8.8
West North Central .	159	162	161	164	162	169	170	9.2	9.3	9.1	9.2	9.0	9.6	9.3
Minnesota	33	35	35	35	35	36	36	8.2	8.3	7.9	8.0	7.8	8.0	8.0
Iowa	27	28	27	26	27	28	26	9.3	9.8	9.7	9.3	9.5	9.9	9.3
Missouri	50	50	50	53	51	54	56	10.1	10.1	9.8	10.4	9.8	10.8	10.6
North Dakota . . .	6	6	6	6	6	6	6	8.6	8.3	8.9	8.9	9.0	9.3	9.6
South Dakota	7	7	6	7	7	7	7	9.5	9.5	9.1	9.4	9.5	9.6	9.5
Nebraska	14	15	15	15	15	15	15	9.2	9.4	9.4	9.2	9.2	9.6	9.1
Kansas	22	22	22	23	22	24	24	9.3	9.1	9.0	9.0	8.8	9.2	9.2
South Atlantic	330	364	392	397	404	423	429	8.9	9.1	9.0	8.9	9.0	9.3	9.2
Delaware	5	5	6	6	6	6	6	8.5	8.9	8.7	8.6	8.6	8.7	8.8
Maryland	34	37	38	38	39	40	41	8.1	8.3	8.0	7.8	7.9	8.7	8.1
Dist. of Col.	7	7	7	7	7	7	7	11.1	11.0	12.0	11.7	12.1	11.6	12.1
Virginia	43	45	48	49	49	52	54	8.0	7.9	7.8	7.8	7.7	8.0	8.2
West Virginia	19	19	19	20	20	20	20	9.9	10.2	10.8	11.0	10.9	11.0	11.1
North Carolina . . .	48	53	57	59	60	62	65	8.2	8.5	8.6	8.7	8.7	9.0	9.1
South Carolina . . .	25	27	30	30	31	32	32	8.1	8.2	8.5	8.4	8.5	8.6	8.6
Georgia	44	49	52	53	53	56	56	8.1	8.2	8.0	8.0	7.8	8.1	8.0
Florida	105	121	134	135	140	147	148	10.7	10.7	10.4	10.2	10.4	10.7	10.6
East South Central .	134	140	146	144	146	154	156	9.1	9.4	9.6	9.4	9.4	9.8	9.8
Kentucky	34	35	35	35	35	37	37	9.2	9.4	9.5	9.5	9.3	9.7	9.8
Tennessee	41	43	46	45	47	49	50	8.9	9.2	9.5	9.2	9.3	9.7	9.6
Alabama	36	38	39	38	39	41	42	9.1	9.5	9.7	9.3	9.5	9.9	10.0
Mississippi	24	25	25	26	25	26	27	9.4	9.5	9.8	9.9	9.7	10.1	10.1
West South Central.	195	209	218	222	222	233	237	8.2	8.0	8.2	8.2	8.1	8.4	8.4
Arkansas	23	24	25	24	25	27	27	9.9	10.4	10.5	10.2	10.4	10.9	10.9
Louisiana	36	37	38	38	38	40	40	8.5	8.4	8.9	9.0	8.8	9.3	9.4
Oklahoma	28	30	30	30	31	32	32	9.3	9.1	9.7	9.6	9.5	10.1	10.0
Texas	108	118	125	129	129	135	138	7.6	7.3	7.4	7.4	7.3	7.5	7.5
Mountain	80	88	97	99	103	110	113	7.0	6.9	7.1	7.1	7.2	7.3	7.4
Montana	7	7	7	7	7	7	7	8.5	8.2	8.6	8.7	8.6	8.9	8.6
Idaho	7	7	7	8	8	8	9	7.2	7.2	7.4	7.5	7.4	7.6	7.5
Wyoming	3	3	3	3	3	3	4	6.9	6.6	7.1	6.9	7.1	7.5	7.4
Colorado	19	20	22	22	22	24	24	6.6	6.3	6.6	6.6	6.5	6.7	6.7
New Mexico	9	10	11	11	11	12	12	7.0	6.8	7.0	7.2	7.1	7.3	7.4
Arizona	21	25	29	29	31	33	35	7.9	7.7	7.9	7.8	8.1	8.2	8.5
Utah	8	9	9	9	10	10	11	5.6	5.5	5.3	5.2	5.4	5.5	5.5
Nevada	6	7	9	9	10	11	12	7.4	7.6	7.8	7.2	7.7	7.8	8.1
Pacific	247	268	286	290	289	300	301	7.8	7.6	7.3	7.3	7.1	7.2	7.2
Washington	32	35	37	38	38	40	40	7.7	7.8	7.6	7.5	7.4	8.0	7.4
Oregon	22	24	25	25	26	28	27	8.3	8.9	8.8	8.6	8.7	9.0	8.8
California	187	202	214	219	216	222	224	7.9	7.6	7.2	7.2	7.0	7.0	7.1
Alaska	2	2	2	2	2	2	2	4.3	3.9	4.0	3.8	3.9	3.8	4.0
Hawaii	5	6	7	7	7	7	7	5.2	5.6	6.1	5.9	6.0	6.2	6.1

[1] Includes deaths of nonresidents. [2] Rates based on enumerated resident population as of April 1 for 1980; and 1990; estimated resident population as of July 1 for all other years.

Source: U.S. National Center for Health Statistics, Vital Statistics of the United States, annual; and Monthly Vital Statistics Report.

No. 124. Infant, Maternal, and Neonatal Mortality Rates and Fetal Mortality Ratios, by Race: 1970 to 1993

[Deaths per 1,000 live births, except as noted. Excludes deaths of nonresidents of U.S. Beginning 1980, race for live births tabulated according to race of mother, for infant and neonatal mortality rates. Beginning 1989, race for live births tabulated according to race of mother, for maternal mortality rates and mortality rates. See also Appendix III and *Historical Statistics, Colonial Times to 1970*, series B 136-147]

ITEM	1970	1980	1983	1984	1985	1986	1987	1988	1989	1990	1991	1992	1993
Infant deaths [1]	20.0	12.6	11.2	10.8	10.6	10.4	10.1	10.0	9.8	9.2	8.9	8.5	8.4
White	17.8	10.9	9.6	9.3	9.2	8.8	8.5	8.4	8.1	7.6	7.3	6.9	6.8
Black and other	30.9	20.2	17.8	17.1	16.8	16.7	16.5	16.1	16.3	15.5	15.1	14.4	14.1
Black.	32.6	22.2	20.0	19.2	19.0	18.9	18.8	18.5	18.6	18.0	17.6	16.8	16.5
Maternal deaths [2]	21.5	9.2	8.0	7.8	7.8	7.2	6.6	8.4	7.9	8.2	7.9	7.8	(NA)
White	14.4	6.7	5.9	5.4	5.2	4.9	5.1	5.9	5.6	5.4	5.8	5.0	(NA)
Black and other	55.9	19.8	16.3	16.9	18.1	16.0	12.0	17.4	16.5	19.1	15.6	18.2	(NA)
Black.	59.8	21.5	18.3	19.7	20.4	18.8	14.2	19.5	18.4	22.4	18.3	20.8	(NA)
Fetal deaths [3]	14.2	9.2	8.5	8.2	7.9	7.7	7.7	7.5	7.5	7.5	7.3	7.4	(NA)
White	12.4	8.2	7.5	7.4	7.0	6.8	6.7	6.4	6.4	6.4	6.2	6.3	(NA)
Black and other	22.6	13.4	12.4	11.5	11.3	11.2	11.5	11.4	11.7	11.9	11.4	11.7	(NA)
Neonatal deaths [4]	15.1	8.5	7.3	7.0	7.0	6.7	6.5	6.3	6.2	5.8	5.6	5.4	5.3
White	13.8	7.4	6.3	6.1	6.0	5.7	5.4	5.3	5.1	4.8	4.5	4.3	4.3
Black and other	21.4	13.2	11.4	10.9	11.0	10.8	10.7	10.3	10.3	9.9	9.5	9.2	9.0
Black.	22.8	14.6	12.9	12.3	12.6	12.3	12.3	12.1	11.9	11.6	11.2	10.8	10.7

NA Not available. [1] Represents deaths of infants under 1 year old, exclusive of fetal deaths. [2] Per 100,000 live births from deliveries and complications of pregnancy, childbirth, and the puerperium. Beginning 1979, deaths are classified according to the ninth revision of the *International Classification of Diseases;* earlier years classified according to the revision in use at the time; see text, section 2. [3] Includes only those deaths with stated or presumed period of gestation of 20 weeks or more. [4] Represents deaths of infants under 28 days old, exclusive of fetal deaths.

No. 125. Fetal and Infant Deaths—Number and Percent Distribution: 1970 to 1992

[State requirements for reporting of fetal deaths vary. Most States require reporting of fetal dea more. There is substantial evidence that not all fetal deaths for which reporting is required are reported. For details of methodology, see Appendix III and source]

YEAR	NUMBER						PERCENT DISTRIBUTION					
	Total	Fetal deaths		Infant deaths			Total	Fetal deaths		Infant deaths		
		Early [1]	Late [2]	Neonatal		Post-neo-natal [5]		Early [1]	Late [2]	Neonatal		Post-neo-natal [5]
				Early [3]	Late [4]					Early [3]	Late [4]	
1970	127,628	17,170	35,791	50,821	5,458	18,388	100.0	13.5	28.0	39.8	4.3	14.4
1980	78,879	10,754	22,599	25,492	5,126	14,908	100.0	13.6	28.7	32.3	6.5	18.9
1981	75,901	11,126	21,470	24,384	4,737	14,184	100.0	14.7	28.3	32.1	6.2	18.7
1982	75,095	11,028	21,666	23,706	4,629	14,066	100.0	14.7	28.9	31.6	6.2	18.7
1983	71,379	10,933	19,819	22,315	4,192	14,120	100.0	15.3	27.8	31.3	5.9	19.8
1984	69,679	10,963	19,136	21,566	4,125	13,889	100.0	15.7	27.5	31.0	5.9	19.9
1985	69,691	10,958	18,703	21,865	4,314	13,851	100.0	15.7	26.8	31.4	6.2	19.9
1986	67,863	11,100	17,872	21,053	4,159	13,679	100.0	16.4	26.3	31.0	6.1	20.2
1987	67,757	11,656	17,693	20,471	4,156	13,781	100.0	17.2	26.1	30.2	6.1	20.3
1988	68,352	11,833	17,609	20,471	4,219	14,220	100.0	17.3	25.8	29.9	6.2	20.8
1989	70,124	12,397	18,072	20,796	4,372	14,487	100.0	17.7	25.8	29.7	6.2	20.7
1990	67,696	12,554	16,791	20,020	4,289	14,042	100.0	18.5	24.8	29.6	6.3	20.7
1991	65,000	12,310	15,924	18,916	4,062	13,788	100.0	18.9	24.5	29.1	6.2	21.2
1992	63,153	12,704	15,821	17,798	4,051	12,779	100.0	20.1	25.1	28.2	6.4	21.8

[1] 20-27 weeks gestation. [2] 28 weeks or more gestation. [3] Less than 7 days. [4] 7-27 days. [5] 28 days-11 months.

No. 126. Infant Deaths and Infant Mortality Rates, by Cause of Death: 1980 to 1993

[Excludes deaths of nonresidents of the United States. Deaths classified according to ninth revision of *International Classification of Diseases*. See also Appendix III]

CAUSE OF DEATH	NUMBER			PERCENT DISTRIBUTION			INFANT MORTALITY RATE [1]		
	1980	1990	1993	1980	1990	1993	1980	1990	1993
Total	45,526	38,351	33,466	100	100	100	12.6	9.2	8.4
Congenital anomalies.	9,220	8,239	7,129	20	21	21	2.6	2.0	1.8
Sudden infant death syndrome	5,510	5,417	4,669	12	14	14	1.5	1.3	1.2
Respiratory distress syndrome.	4,989	2,850	1,815	11	7	5	1.4	0.7	0.5
Disorders relating to short gestation and unspecified low birth weight.	3,648	4,013	4,310	8	10	13	1.0	1.0	1.1
Newborn affected by maternal complications of pregnancy	1,572	1,655	1,343	4	4	4	0.4	0.4	0.3
Intrauterine hypoxia and birth asphyxia . .	1,497	762	549	3	2	2	0.4	0.2	0.1
Infections specific to the perinatal period	971	875	772	2	2	2	0.3	0.2	0.2
Accidents and adverse effects	1,166	930	898	3	2	3	0.3	0.2	0.2
Newborn affected by complications of placenta, cord, and membranes	985	975	994	2	3	3	0.3	0.2	0.2
Pneumonia and influenza	1,012	634	530	2	2	2	0.3	0.2	0.1
All other causes	14,956	12,001	10,457	33	31	31	4.1	2.9	2.6

[1] Deaths of infants under 1 year old per 1,000 live births.
Sources of tables 124-126: U.S. National Center for Health Statistics, *Vital Statistics of the United States,* annual, and *Monthly Vital Statistics Report;* and unpublished data.

No. 127. Infant Mortality Rates, by Race—States: 1980 to 1993

[**Deaths per 1,000 live births, by place of residence.** Represents deaths of infants under 1 year old, exclusive of fetal deaths. Excludes deaths of nonresidents of the United States. See Appendix III and *Historical Statistics, Colonial Times to 1970*, series B 143-147, for U.S. totals]

DIVI-SION AND STATE	TOTAL [1]			WHITE		BLACK		DIVI-SION AND STATE	TOTAL [1]			WHITE		BLACK	
	1980	1990	1993	1990	1993	1990	1993		1980	1990	1993	1990	1993	1990	1993
U.S	12.6	9.2	8.4	7.7	6.8	18.0	16.5	VA...	13.6	10.2	8.7	7.5	6.7	19.5	14.9
								WV..	11.8	9.9	8.6	9.6	8.1	(NA)	(NA)
N.E....	10.5	7.2	6.5	6.8	6.0	14.0	13.1	NC...	14.5	10.6	10.5	8.3	7.7	16.5	17.1
ME..	9.2	6.2	6.8	6.2	6.9	(NA)	(NA)	SC...	15.6	11.7	10.1	8.3	6.7	17.3	15.7
NH...	9.9	7.1	5.6	7.2	5.7	[2](NA)	(NA)	GA...	14.5	12.4	10.4	9.1	7.2	18.3	16.3
VT...	10.7	6.4	6.7	6.5	6.7	(NA)	(NA)	FL...	14.6	9.6	8.6	7.6	6.6	16.8	15.3
MA..	10.5	7.0	6.2	6.7	5.7	11.9	11.4	**E.S.C..**	14.5	10.4	9.7	8.1	7.5	16.4	15.7
RI...	11.0	8.1	7.3	8.3	7.1	[2](NA)	(NA)	KY...	12.9	8.5	8.2	8.0	7.6	14.3	14.3
CT...	11.2	7.9	7.1	6.6	5.8	17.6	15.6	TN...	13.5	10.3	9.4	8.0	6.7	17.9	17.9
M.A...	12.8	9.5	8.4	7.5	6.5	18.7	16.8	AL...	15.1	10.8	10.3	8.3	7.9	16.0	15.1
NY...	12.5	9.6	8.4	7.7	6.6	18.1	15.4	MS...	17.0	12.1	11.5	8.5	8.4	16.2	14.7
NJ...	12.5	9.0	8.3	6.8	6.1	18.4	17.5	**W.S.C..**	12.7	8.7	8.3	7.4	7.0	15.3	14.9
PA...	13.2	9.6	8.6	7.8	6.6	20.5	19.7	AR...	12.7	9.2	10.0	8.0	9.1	13.9	13.4
E.N.C..	13.0	10.1	9.3	8.0	7.4	21.0	18.7	LA...	14.3	11.1	10.8	7.3	7.4	16.7	15.6
OH..	12.8	9.8	9.2	8.2	7.6	19.5	17.9	OK...	12.7	9.2	8.8	9.4	8.3	14.3	16.4
IN...	11.9	9.6	9.2	8.9	8.0	17.4	18.3	TX...	12.2	8.1	7.5	7.1	6.5	14.7	14.6
IL...	14.8	10.7	9.9	7.7	7.1	22.4	19.6	**Mt.....**	11.0	8.6	7.4	8.3	6.9	18.5	18.0
MI...	12.8	10.7	9.5	7.9	7.1	21.6	18.8	MT...	12.4	9.0	7.4	8.6	6.9	(NA)	(NA)
WI...	10.3	8.2	7.9	7.2	7.0	19.0	16.0	ID...	10.7	8.7	7.2	8.7	7.0	(NA)	(NA)
W.N.C..	11.3	8.4	8.1	7.5	7.2	18.9	17.1	WY..	9.8	8.6	7.9	8.8	7.9	[2](NA)	(NA)
MN..	10.0	7.3	7.5	6.7	7.1	23.7	14.1	CO...	10.1	8.8	7.9	8.4	7.4	19.4	17.0
IA...	11.8	8.1	6.9	7.8	6.4	21.9	22.9	NM..	11.5	9.0	8.4	9.3	7.3	[2](NA)	(NA)
MO..	12.4	9.4	8.4	7.8	7.1	18.2	14.8	AZ...	12.4	8.8	7.6	8.2	6.0	20.6	22.1
ND...	12.1	8.0	7.9	7.9	7.9	[2](NA)	(NA)	UT...	10.4	7.5	6.0	7.4	6.0	[2](NA)	(NA)
SD...	10.9	10.1	9.5	8.6	7.6	(NA)	(NA)	NV...	10.7	8.4	6.7	8.1	6.2	14.2	14.0
NE...	11.5	8.3	9.1	7.2	8.3	18.9	26.2	**Pac....**	11.2	7.9	6.8	7.6	6.3	17.1	15.8
KS...	10.4	8.4	8.8	7.7	7.5	17.7	23.5	WA..	11.8	7.8	6.4	7.6	6.0	20.6	17.8
S.A....	14.5	10.7	9.6	8.0	6.9	17.9	16.4	OR...	12.2	8.3	7.2	8.1	7.0	[2](NA)	(NA)
DE...	13.9	10.1	8.8	7.3	5.7	20.1	19.9	CA...	11.1	7.9	6.8	7.6	6.3	16.8	15.6
MD...	14.0	9.5	9.8	6.5	6.3	17.1	17.6	AK...	12.3	10.5	8.2	8.5	6.3	[2](NA)	(NA)
DC...	25.0	20.7	17.4	[2]12.1	(NA)	24.6	20.6	HI...	10.3	6.7	7.2	5.1	3.8	[2](NA)	(NA)

NA Not available.   [1] Includes other races, not shown separately.   [2] Based on a frequency of less than 20 infant deaths.
Source: U.S. National Center for Health Statistics, *Vital Statistics of the United States*, annual; and unpublished data.

No. 128. Age-Adjusted Death Rates, by Selected Causes: 1980 to 1993

[**Rates per 100,000 population.** For explanation of age-adjustment see text, section 2. The standard population for this table is the total population of the United States enumerated in 1940. See also headnote, table 125]

CAUSE OF DEATH	1980	1990	1993	CAUSE OF DEATH	1980	1990	1993
All causes.................	585.8	520.2	513.3	Pneumonia and influenza	12.9	14.0	13.5
				Pneumonia..................	12.4	13.7	13.3
Major cardiovascular diseases	256.0	189.8	181.8	Influenza...................	0.5	0.3	0.2
Diseases of heart...............	202.0	152.0	145.3				
Rheumatic fever and rheumatic heart disease	2.6	1.5	1.3	Diabetes mellitus...............	10.1	11.7	12.4
Hypertensive heart disease [1].....	6.8	5.3	4.9	Suicide	11.4	11.5	11.3
Ischemic heart disease	149.8	102.6	94.9	Chronic liver disease and cirrhosis	12.2	8.6	7.9
Other diseases of endocardium ...	2.0	2.5	2.6	Nephritis, nephrotic syndrome, and nephrosis	4.5	4.3	4.5
All other forms of heart disease ...	40.8	40.1	41.1	Homicide and legal intervention	10.8	10.2	10.7
Hypertension [1]...............	2.0	1.9	2.2				
Cerebrovascular diseases	40.8	27.7	26.5	Septicemia..................	2.6	4.1	4.1
Atherosclerosis	5.7	2.7	2.4	Other infectious and parasitic diseases .	1.8	12.0	15.9
Other....................	5.5	5.4	5.4	Benign neoplasms [4]............	2.0	1.7	1.7
Malignancies [2]	132.8	135.0	132.6	Ulcer of stomach and duodenum	1.7	1.3	1.2
Of respiratory and intrathoracic organs	36.4	41.4	40.8	Hernia of abdominal cavity and intestinal obstruction [5]...........	1.4	1.1	1.0
Of digestive organs and peritoneum..	33.0	30.2	29.5	Anemias....................	0.9	0.9	0.9
Of genital organs	13.6	13.6	13.2	Cholelithiasis and other disorders of gallbladder	0.8	0.6	0.5
Of breast	12.5	12.7	11.8	Nutritional deficiencies	0.5	0.5	0.9
Of urinary organs	5.2	5.1	5.0	Infections of kidney	0.7	0.2	0.2
Leukemia	5.4	5.0	4.9	Tuberculosis.................	0.6	0.5	0.4
Accidents and adverse effects	42.3	32.5	30.3	Meningitis..................	0.6	0.3	0.3
Motor vehicle...............	22.9	18.5	16.0	Viral hepatitis	0.3	0.5	0.8
All other	19.5	14.0	14.4	Acute bronchitis and bronchiolitis	0.2	0.1	0.1
Chronic obstructive pulmonary diseases and allied conditions [3]...........	15.9	19.7	21.4	Hyperplasia of prostate...........	0.2	0.1	0.1
Bronchitis, chronic and unspecified ..	1.0	0.8	0.8	Symptoms, signs, and ill-defined conditions..................	9.8	7.3	7.4
Emphysema.................	4.0	3.7	3.9	All other causes................	36.8	38.4	39.7
Asthma....................	1.0	1.4	1.4				
Other.....................	9.9	13.7	15.2				

[1] With or without renal disease.   [2] Includes other types of malignancies not shown separately.   [3] Prior to 1980, data are shown for bronchitis, emphysema, and asthma.   [4] Includes neoplasms of unspecified nature; beginning 1980, also includes carcinoma in situ.   [5] Without mention of hernia.
Source: U.S. National Center for Health Statistics, *Vital Statistics of the United States*, annual; *Monthly Vital Statistics Reports*; and unpublished data.

No. 129. Deaths and Death Rates, by Selected Causes: 1970 to 1994

[Excludes deaths of nonresidents of the United States, except as noted. Beginning 1980, deaths classified according to ninth revision of *International Classification of Diseases;* for earlier years, classified according to revision in use at that time. See also Appendix III and *Historical Statistics, Colonial Times to 1970,* series B 149-166]

CAUSE OF DEATH	DEATHS (1,000)					CRUDE DEATH RATE PER 100,000 POPULATION [2]				
	1970	1980	1990	1993 [1]	1994 [1]	1970	1980	1990	1993 [1]	1994 [1]
All causes	**1,921.0**	**1,989.8**	**2,148.5**	**2,268.6**	**2,286.0**	**945.3**	**878.3**	**863.8**	**880.0**	**876.9**
Major cardiovascular diseases	1,008.0	988.5	916.0	948.1	945.2	496.0	436.4	368.3	367.8	362.6
Diseases of heart	735.5	761.1	720.1	743.5	734.1	362.0	336.0	289.5	288.4	281.6
Percent of total	38.3	38.3	33.5	32.8	32.1	38.3	38.3	33.5	32.8	32.1
Rheumatic fever and rheumatic heart disease	14.9	7.8	6.0	5.7	5.5	7.3	3.5	2.4	2.2	2.1
Hypertensive heart disease [3]	15.0	24.8	23.4	23.0	23.8	7.4	10.9	9.5	8.9	9.1
Ischemic heart disease	666.7	565.8	489.2	490.1	487.5	328.1	249.7	196.7	190.1	187.0
Other diseases of endocardium . . .	6.7	7.2	13.0	15.2	14.5	3.3	3.2	5.2	5.9	5.6
All other forms of heart disease . . .	32.3	155.5	188.4	207.0	200.1	15.9	68.7	75.8	80.3	76.8
Hypertension [3]	8.3	7.8	9.2	11.2	11.7	4.1	3.5	3.7	4.4	4.5
Cerebrovascular diseases	207.2	170.2	144.1	150.1	154.4	101.9	75.1	57.9	58.2	59.2
Atherosclerosis	31.7	29.4	18.0	17.3	18.0	15.6	13.0	7.3	6.7	6.9
Other	25.3	20.0	24.6	26.0	27.1	12.5	8.8	9.9	10.1	10.4
Malignancies [4]	330.7	416.5	505.3	529.9	536.9	162.8	183.9	203.2	205.6	206.0
Percent of total	17.2	20.9	23.5	23.4	23.5	17.2	20.9	23.5	23.4	23.5
Of respiratory and intrathoracic organs	69.5	108.5	146.4	154.2	154.3	34.2	47.9	58.9	59.8	59.2
Of digestive organs and peritoneum	94.7	110.6	120.8	124.5	127.2	46.6	48.8	48.6	48.3	48.8
Of genital organs	41.2	46.4	57.5	60.4	62.1	20.3	20.5	23.1	23.4	23.8
Of breast	29.9	35.9	43.7	43.9	43.3	14.7	15.8	17.6	17.0	16.6
Of urinary organs	15.5	17.8	20.7	21.8	22.0	7.6	7.9	8.3	8.4	8.4
Leukemia	14.5	16.5	18.6	19.5	20.1	7.1	7.3	7.5	7.6	7.7
Accidents and adverse effects	114.6	105.7	92.0	90.5	90.1	56.4	46.7	37.0	35.1	34.6
Motor vehicle	54.6	53.2	46.8	41.9	42.2	26.9	23.5	18.8	16.3	16.2
All other	60.0	52.5	45.2	48.6	48.0	29.5	23.3	18.2	18.9	18.4
Chronic obstructive pulmonary diseases and allied conditions [5]	30.9	56.1	86.7	101.1	101.9	15.2	24.7	34.9	39.2	39.1
Bronchitis, chronic and unspecified . .	5.8	3.7	3.6	3.8	3.6	2.9	1.6	1.4	1.5	1.4
Emphysema	22.7	13.9	15.7	17.6	17.3	11.2	6.1	6.3	6.8	6.6
Asthma.	2.3	2.9	4.8	5.2	5.7	1.1	1.3	1.9	2.0	2.2
Other	([6])	35.6	62.6	74.5	75.3	([6])	15.7	25.2	28.9	28.9
Pneumonia and influenza	62.7	54.6	79.5	82.8	82.1	30.9	24.1	32.0	32.1	31.5
Pneumonia	59.0	51.9	77.4	81.8	80.8	29.0	22.9	31.1	31.7	31.0
Influenza	3.7	2.7	2.1	1.0	1.3	1.8	1.2	0.8	0.4	0.5
Diabetes mellitus	38.3	34.9	47.7	53.9	55.4	18.9	15.4	19.2	20.9	21.2
Suicide	23.5	26.9	30.9	31.1	32.4	11.6	11.9	12.4	12.1	12.4
Chronic liver disease and cirrhosis	31.4	30.6	25.8	25.2	25.7	15.5	13.5	10.4	9.8	9.9
Other infectious and parasitic diseases . .	6.9	5.1	32.2	44.4	48.5	3.4	2.2	13.0	17.2	18.6
Homicide and legal intervention	16.8	24.3	24.9	26.0	23.7	8.3	10.7	10.0	10.1	9.1
Nephritis, nephrotic syndrome, and nephrosis	8.9	16.8	20.8	23.3	23.6	4.4	7.4	8.3	9.0	9.1
Septicemia	3.5	9.4	19.2	20.6	19.9	1.7	4.2	7.7	8.0	7.6
Certain conditions originating in the perinatal period	43.2	22.9	17.7	15.1	14.1	21.3	10.1	7.1	5.9	5.4
Congenital anomalies	16.8	13.9	13.1	12.4	11.9	8.3	6.2	5.3	4.8	4.6
Benign neoplasms [7]	4.8	6.2	6.8	7.4	7.0	2.4	2.7	2.7	2.9	2.7
Ulcer of stomach and duodenum	8.6	6.1	6.2	5.9	6.0	4.2	0.0	2.5	2.3	2.3
Hernia of abdominal cavity and intestinal obstruction [8]	7.2	5.4	5.8	5.9	6.0	3.6	2.4	2.3	2.3	2.3
Anemias.	3.4	3.2	4.1	4.3	4.2	1.7	1.4	1.6	1.7	1.6
Cholelithiasis and other disorders of gall bladder.	4.0	3.3	3.0	2.8	2.6	2.0	1.5	1.2	1.1	1.0
Nutritional deficiencies	2.5	2.4	3.0	3.5	3.2	1.2	1.0	1.2	1.3	1.2
Tuberculosis	5.2	2.0	1.8	1.6	1.6	2.6	0.9	0.7	0.6	0.6
Infections of kidney	8.2	2.7	1.3	1.0	1.0	4.0	1.2	0.5	0.4	0.4
Viral hepatitis	1.0	0.8	1.6	2.5	2.8	0.5	0.4	0.6	1.0	1.1
Meningitis.	1.7	1.4	1.0	0.8	0.9	0.8	0.6	0.4	0.3	0.4
Acute bronchitis and bronchiolitis	1.3	0.6	0.6	0.7	0.5	0.6	0.3	0.3	0.3	0.2
Hyperplasia of prostate	2.2	0.8	0.5	0.4	0.5	1.1	0.3	0.2	0.2	0.2
Symptoms, signs, and ill-defined conditions	25.8	28.8	24.1	26.5	26.6	12.7	12.7	9.7	10.3	10.2
All other causes.	108.8	120.0	172.9	195.6	206.1	53.5	53.0	69.5	75.9	79.1

[1] Based on a 10-percent sample of deaths. Includes deaths of nonresidents.　[2] 1970, 1980, and 1990 based on resident population enumerated as of April 1. Other years based on resident population estimated as of July 1.　[3] With or without renal disease.　[4] Includes other types of malignancies not shown separately.　[5] Prior to 1980, data are shown for bronchitis, emphysema, and asthma.　[6] Included in "all other causes." Comparable data not available separately.　[7] Includes neoplasms of unspecified nature; beginning 1980 also includes carcinoma in situ.　[8] Without mention of hernia.

Source: U.S. National Center for Health Statistics, *Vital Statistics of the United States,* annual; *Monthly Vital Statistics Report;* and unpublished data.

No. 130. Deaths, by Selected Causes and Selected Characteristics: 1993

[In thousands. Excludes deaths of nonresidents of the U.S. Deaths classified according to ninth revision of *International Classification of Diseases*. See also Appendix III]

AGE, SEX, AND RACE	Total [1]	Heart disease	Cancer	Accidents and adverse effects	Cerebrovascular diseases	Chronic obstructive pulmonary diseases [2]	Pneumonia, flu	Suicide	Chronic liver disease, cirrhosis	Diabetes mellitus	Homicide and legal intervention
ALL RACES [3]											
Both sexes, total [4]	2,268.6	743.5	529.9	90.5	150.1	101.1	82.8	31.1	25.2	53.9	26.0
Under 1 year old	33.5	0.7	0.1	0.9	0.2	0.1	0.5	-	(Z)	(Z)	0.3
1 to 4 years old	7.1	0.3	0.5	2.6	(Z)	0.1	0.2	-	(Z)	(Z)	0.5
5 to 14 years old	8.7	0.3	1.1	3.5	0.1	0.1	0.1	-	(Z)	(Z)	0.7
15 to 24 years old	35.5	1.0	1.7	14.0	0.2	0.2	0.3	0.3	(Z)	(Z)	8.4
25 to 34 years old	59.6	3.5	5.1	14.0	0.8	0.3	0.7	4.8	0.7	0.1	7.3
35 to 44 years old	96.0	13.1	16.8	13.3	2.5	0.7	1.6	6.3	3.8	0.6	4.5
45 to 54 years old	131.8	32.7	42.4	8.0	5.1	2.5	1.9	6.2	4.7	1.7	2.1
55 to 64 years old	241.6	72.0	90.7	6.4	9.6	10.7	3.7	4.2	5.6	3.4	1.0
65 to 74 years old	487.8	158.1	163.3	8.1	25.3	31.3	10.8	3.1	6.1	7.5	0.7
75 to 84 years old	638.0	234.0	146.5	10.7	51.4	38.3	25.9	3.0	3.5	15.0	0.4
85 years old and over	528.4	227.6	61.7	9.0	54.9	16.9	37.2	2.4	0.7	16.3	0.1
Male, total [4]	1,161.8	367.5	279.4	60.1	59.0	54.4	38.0	25.0	16.3	23.4	20.3
Under 1 year old	19.0	0.4	0.1	0.5	0.1	(Z)	0.3	-	(Z)	(Z)	0.2
1 to 4 years old	4.0	0.2	0.3	1.5	(Z)	(Z)	0.1	-	(Z)	(Z)	0.3
5 to 14 years old	5.2	0.1	0.6	2.2	(Z)	0.1	0.1	0.2	(Z)	(Z)	0.4
15 to 24 years old	26.9	0.6	1.0	10.6	0.1	0.1	0.1	4.1	0.0	0.1	7.2
25 to 34 years old	43.7	2.4	2.5	10.9	0.4	0.1	0.4	5.2	0.5	0.3	5.7
35 to 44 years old	66.4	9.6	7.7	10.2	1.4	0.4	1.0	4.8	2.7	1.0	3.5
45 to 54 years old	83.4	24.2	21.1	5.9	2.7	1.3	1.2	3.1	3.5	1.9	1.6
55 to 64 years old	146.9	49.6	50.4	4.4	5.2	5.8	2.2	2.4	3.8	3.8	0.7
65 to 74 years old	279.6	96.8	91.7	4.9	13.0	17.2	6.4	2.4	3.7	7.0	0.4
75 to 84 years old	313.6	114.3	77.2	5.5	21.5	21.0	13.2	2.0	1.7	6.6	0.2
85 years old and over	172.8	69.4	26.8	3.5	14.6	8.4	12.9	0.6	0.3	2.7	0.1
Female, total [4]	1,106.8	376.0	250.5	30.4	91.1	46.7	44.8	6.1	8.9	30.5	5.7
Under 1 year old	14.5	0.3	(Z)	0.4	0.1	(Z)	0.2	-	(Z)	(Z)	0.2
1 to 4 years old	3.1	0.1	0.2	1.0	(Z)	(Z)	0.1	-	(Z)	(Z)	0.2
5 to 14 years old	3.5	0.2	0.5	1.2	(Z)	0.1	0.1	0.1	(Z)	(Z)	0.2
15 to 24 years old	8.6	0.4	0.7	3.4	0.1	0.1	0.1	0.7	(Z)	(Z)	1.2
25 to 34 years old	16.0	1.2	2.6	3.1	0.4	0.2	0.3	1.1	0.2	0.1	1.6
35 to 44 years old	29.6	3.5	9.1	3.1	1.2	0.4	0.5	1.3	1.0	0.7	1.1
45 to 54 years old	48.4	8.5	21.3	2.1	2.3	1.2	0.7	1.0	1.3	0.7	0.5
55 to 64 years old	94.7	22.5	40.3	2.0	4.4	4.9	1.5	1.0	1.8	1.5	0.2
65 to 74 years old	208.2	61.3	71.6	3.3	12.3	14.1	4.4	0.7	2.4	3.7	0.3
75 to 84 years old	324.5	119.8	69.3	5.2	29.9	17.3	12.6	0.6	1.7	8.0	0.2
85 years old and over	355.7	158.2	34.9	5.5	40.3	8.5	24.3	0.1	0.4	9.7	0.1
WHITE											
Both sexes, total [4]	1,951.4	655.4	461.9	75.2	130.0	93.6	73.7	28.0	21.3	43.5	12.3
Under 1 year old	21.5	0.4	0.1	0.6	0.2	(Z)	0.3	-	(Z)	(Z)	0.2
1 to 4 years old	4.8	0.2	0.4	1.8	(Z)	(Z)	0.1	-	(Z)	(Z)	0.2
5 to 14 years old	6.3	0.2	0.9	2.5	0.1	0.1	0.1	0.3	(Z)	(Z)	0.3
15 to 24 years old	24.5	0.6	1.4	11.6	0.2	0.1	0.2	4.0	(Z)	0.1	3.1
25 to 34 years old	68.8	2.4	4.0	11.5	0.5	0.2	0.5	5.4	0.5	0.4	3.3
35 to 44 years old	101.9	25.3	34.4	10.5	1.6	0.5	1.0	5.6	2.8	1.2	2.3
45 to 54 years old	198.2	58.6	76.7	6.5	3.4	2.0	1.4	3.9	3.7	2.5	1.3
55 to 64 years old	422.8	136.6	143.3	5.3	7.1	9.5	2.9	2.9	4.8	5.5	0.6
65 to 74 years old	574.0	211.1	131.7	7.0	20.8	29.0	9.2	2.9	5.5	11.9	0.5
75 to 84 years old	486.2	210.4	55.8	9.7	45.6	36.2	23.4	2.3	3.3	13.8	0.3
85 years old and over	486.2	210.4	55.8	8.3	50.6	16.0	34.7	0.8	0.7	8.0	0.1
BLACK											
Both sexes, total [4]	282.2	79.0	59.9	12.7	17.6	6.4	7.7	2.3	3.2	9.4	12.9
Under 1 year old	10.9	0.2	(Z)	0.3	(Z)	(Z)	0.2	-	(Z)	-	0.1
1 to 4 years old	2.0	0.1	0.1	0.7	(Z)	(Z)	0.1	-	(Z)	(Z)	0.2
5 to 14 years old	2.0	0.1	0.2	0.8	(Z)	0.1	(Z)	(Z)	(Z)	(Z)	0.3
15 to 24 years old	9.7	0.3	0.3	1.9	(Z)	0.1	0.1	0.6	(Z)	(Z)	5.1
25 to 34 years old	15.9	1.1	0.9	2.1	0.2	0.1	0.2	0.6	0.1	0.2	3.8
35 to 44 years old	24.9	3.5	3.0	2.4	0.8	0.3	0.5	0.4	0.8	0.5	2.1
45 to 54 years old	26.9	6.7	7.0	1.3	1.5	0.4	0.5	0.2	0.8	0.9	0.7
55 to 64 years old	38.6	12.2	12.3	1.0	2.3	1.0	0.7	0.1	0.7	1.7	0.3
65 to 74 years old	57.9	19.4	17.8	1.0	4.0	1.9	1.4	0.1	0.5	2.8	0.2
75 to 84 years old	56.3	20.3	13.1	0.8	5.0	1.8	2.1	0.1	0.2	2.3	0.1
85 years old and over	37.0	15.2	5.2	0.6	3.7	0.7	2.0	(Z)	(Z)	1.1	(Z)

- Represents zero. Z Fewer than 50. [1] Includes other causes not shown separately. [2] Includes allied conditions. [3] Includes other races not shown separately. [4] Includes those deaths with age not stated.

Source: U.S. National Center for Health Statistics, *Vital Statistics of the United States*, annual.

No. 131. Deaths, by Age and Leading Cause: 1993

[Excludes deaths of nonresidents of the United States. Deaths classified according to ninth revision of *International Classification of Diseases.* See also Appendix III and *Historical Statistics, Colonial Times to 1970,* series B 149-166]

AGE AND LEADING CAUSE OF DEATH	NUMBER OF DEATHS			DEATH RATE PER 100,000 POPULATION		
	Total	Male	Female	Total	Male	Female
All ages [1]	**2,268,553**	**1,161,797**	**1,106,756**	**880.0**	**923.5**	**838.6**
Leading causes of death:						
Heart disease	743,460	367,479	375,981	288.4	292.1	284.9
Malignant neoplasms (cancer)	529,904	279,375	250,529	205.6	222.1	189.8
Cerebrovascular disease (stroke)	150,108	59,048	91,060	58.2	46.9	69.0
Chronic obstructive pulmonary disease	101,077	54,371	46,706	39.2	43.2	35.4
Accidents	90,523	60,117	30,406	35.1	47.8	23.0
Pneumonia	82,820	37,996	44,824	32.1	30.2	34.0
Diabetes	53,894	23,430	30,464	20.9	18.6	23.1
HIV infection [2]	37,267	32,093	5,174	14.5	25.5	(NA)
Suicide	31,102	25,007	6,095	12.1	19.9	4.6
Homicide and legal intervention	26,009	20,290	5,719	10.1	16.1	4.3
1 TO 4 YEARS OLD						
All causes	**7,066**	**3,992**	**3,074**	**44.8**	**49.5**	**39.9**
Leading causes of death:						
Accidents	2,590	1,545	1,045	16.4	19.1	13.6
Congenital anomalies	804	388	416	5.1	4.8	5.4
Malignant neoplasms (cancer)	522	301	221	3.3	3.7	2.9
Homicide and legal intervention	464	274	190	2.9	3.4	2.5
Heart disease	296	164	132	1.9	2.0	1.7
Pneumonia and influenza	182	93	89	1.2	1.2	1.2
HIV infection [2]	204	104	100	1.3	1.3	1.3
5 TO 14 YEARS OLD						
All causes	**8,658**	**5,207**	**3,451**	**23.4**	**27.4**	**19.1**
Leading causes of death:						
Accidents	3,466	2,247	1,219	9.4	11.8	6.7
Malignant neoplasms (cancer)	1,089	621	468	2.9	3.3	2.6
Congenital anomalies	485	264	221	1.3	1.4	1.2
Suicide	321	233	88	0.9	1.2	0.5
Homicide and legal intervention	656	408	248	1.8	2.2	1.4
Heart disease	303	149	154	0.8	0.8	0.9
Pneumonia and influenza	135	72	63	0.4	0.4	0.3
HIV infections [2]	155	78	77	0.4	0.4	0.4
15 TO 24 YEARS OLD						
All causes	**35,483**	**26,906**	**8,577**	**98.5**	**146.2**	**48.6**
Leading causes of death:						
Accidents	13,966	10,601	3,365	38.8	57.6	19.1
Homicide and legal intervention	8,424	7,206	1,218	23.4	39.2	6.9
Suicide	4,849	4,119	730	13.5	22.4	4.1
Malignant neoplasms (cancer)	1,738	1,013	725	4.8	5.5	4.1
Cerebrovascular disease (stroke)	208	94	114	0.6	0.5	0.6
Chronic obstructive pulmonary disease	206	128	78	0.6	0.7	0.4
Congenital anomalies	472	277	195	1.3	1.5	1.1
Heart disease	981	627	354	2.7	3.4	2.0
Pneumonia and influenza	251	127	124	0.7	0.7	0.7
HIV infection [2]	609	414	195	1.7	2.3	1.1
25 TO 44 YEARS OLD						
All causes	**156,683**	**110,082**	**45,601**	**188.3**	**267.5**	**109.8**
Leading causes of death:						
Accidents	27,277	21,068	6,209	33.0	51.2	15.0
Malignant neoplasms (cancer)	21,834	10,180	11,654	26.4	24.7	28.1
Cerebrovascular disease (stroke)	3,316	1,785	1,531	4.0	4.3	3.7
HIV infection [2]	27,228	23,460	3,768	32.9	57.0	9.1
Heart disease	16,660	11,933	4,727	20.2	29.0	11.4
Pneumonia and influenza	2,275	1,434	841	2.8	3.5	2.0
Diabetes	2,299	1,343	956	1.4	3.3	2.3
Homicide and legal intervention	11,815	9,162	2,653	14.3	22.3	6.4
Suicide	12,477	10,060	2,417	15.1	24.4	5.8
45 TO 64 YEARS OLD						
All causes	**373,396**	**230,354**	**143,042**	**753.1**	**962.7**	**557.6**
Leading causes of death:						
Malignant neoplasms (cancer)	133,057	71,462	61,595	268.4	298.7	240.1
Heart disease	104,722	73,750	30,972	211.2	308.2	120.7
Pneumonia and influenza	5,583	3,388	2,195	11.3	14.2	8.6
HIV infection [2]	8,330	7,472	858	16.8	31.2	(NA)
Cerebrovascular (stroke)	14,682	7,958	6,724	29.6	33.3	26.2
Accidents	14,434	10,265	4,169	29.1	42.9	16.3
Chronic obstructive pulmonary disease	13,165	7,099	6,066	26.6	29.7	23.6
Chronic liver disease and cirrhosis	10,316	7,247	3,069	20.8	30.3	12.0
Diabetes	10,927	5,701	5,226	22.0	23.8	20.4
Suicide	7,229	5,506	1,723	14.6	23.0	6.7
65 YEARS OLD AND OVER						
All causes	**1,654,294**	**765,943**	**888,351**	**5,047.7**	**5,767.8**	**4,557.1**
Leading causes of death:						
Heart disease	619,755	280,443	339,312	1,891.0	2,111.8	1,740.6
Malignant neoplasms (cancer)	317,549	195,730	175,819	1,133.7	1,473.9	901.9
Cerebrovascular (stroke)	131,551	49,013	82,538	401.4	369.1	423.4
Chronic obstructive pulmonary disease	86,425	46,504	39,921	263.7	350.2	204.8
Pneumonia and influenza	73,853	32,564	41,289	225.3	245.2	211.8
Diabetes	40,502	16,301	24,201	123.6	122.8	124.1
Accidents	27,784	13,791	13,993	84.8	103.9	71.8

NA Not available.   [1] Includes those deaths with age not stated.   [2] Human immunodeficiency virus.
Source: U.S. National Center for Health Statistics, *Vital Statistics of the United States,* annual; and unpublished data.

No. 132. Death Rates, by Leading Causes and Age: 1980 to 1993

[Deaths per 100,000 population in specified group. Except as noted, excludes deaths of nonresidents of the United States. See text, section 2]

YEAR, RACE, AND AGE	Total [1]	Heart disease	Malignant neoplasms	Accidents and adverse effects	Cerebrovascular diseases	Chronic obstructive pulmonary diseases [2]	Pneumonia, flu	Suicide	Chronic liver disease, cirrhosis	Diabetes mellitus	Homicide and legal intervention
ALL RACES [3]											
Both sexes:											
1980, age-adjusted. . .	585.8	336.0	183.9	46.7	75.1	24.7	24.1	11.9	13.5	15.4	10.7
1990, age-adjusted. . .	520.2	289.5	203.2	37.0	57.9	34.9	32.0	12.4	10.4	19.2	10.0
1992, age adjusted. . .	504.5	281.4	204.1	34.0	56.4	36.0	29.7	12.0	9.9	19.6	10.0
1993, age adjusted. . .	513.3	288.4	205.6	35.1	58.2	39.2	32.1	12.1	9.8	20.9	10.1
15 to 24 years old. .	(NA)	2.7	4.8	38.8	0.6	0.6	0.7	13.5	0.1	0.3	23.4
25 to 34 years old. .	(NA)	8.5	12.1	33.5	1.9	0.7	1.7	15.1	1.7	1.4	17.4
35 to 44 years old. .	(NA)	32.2	41.1	32.5	6.2	1.8	3.8	15.1	9.2	4.2	11.1
45 to 54 years old. .	(NA)	114.0	147.9	28.0	17.6	8.7	6.6	14.5	16.4	12.0	7.2
55 to 64 years old. .	(NA)	344.3	433.4	30.6	46.0	51.0	17.7	14.6	26.8	35.7	4.7
65 to 74 years old. .	(NA)	848.2	876.1	43.6	135.8	167.8	58.1	16.3	32.7	80.4	3.7
75 to 84 years old. .	(NA)	2,182.9	1,366.9	99.5	479.1	357.3	241.2	22.3	32.6	152.3	3.5
85 years old and over	(NA)	6,668.9	1,807.7	263.5	1607.7	493.9	1,089.0	22.8	21.7	269.4	4.1
Male:											
1980, age-adjusted . . .	777.2	368.6	205.3	67.4	63.6	35.1	25.1	18.6	18.0	13.0	17.3
1990, age-adjusted . . .	680.2	297.6	221.3	51.1	46.8	40.8	30.4	20.4	13.7	16.7	16.2
1992, age-adjusted . . .	656.0	287.2	220.8	46.5	45.5	40.5	28.5	19.6	13.2	17.4	16.2
1993, age-adjusted . . .	664.9	292.1	222.1	47.8	46.9	43.2	30.2	19.9	12.9	18.6	16.1
15 to 24 years old . . .	(NA)	3.4	5.5	57.6	0.5	0.7	0.7	22.4	0.1	0.4	39.2
25 to 34 years old . . .	(NA)	11.3	11.9	51.9	2.0	0.6	2.0	24.9	2.3	1.5	27.2
35 to 44 years old . . .	(NA)	47.4	38.0	50.5	6.8	1.8	5.0	24.0	13.5	5.0	17.2
45 to 54 years old . . .	(NA)	172.8	150.7	42.2	19.6	9.5	8.3	22.4	24.6	13.7	11.4
55 to 64 years old . . .	(NA)	499.2	507.4	43.9	52.5	58.1	22.4	23.9	38.2	38.1	7.4
65 to 74 years old . . .	(NA)	1,175.3	1,113.3	59.0	157.4	208.4	78.1	29.4	44.8	85.1	5.3
75 to 84 years old . . .	(NA)	2,788.7	1,885.4	133.2	523.7	512.1	323.0	48.9	42.6	161.5	4.5
85 years old and over .	(NA)	7,331.9	2,830.7	366.9	1,541.9	883.1	1,363.4	68.3	34.2	282.2	5.7
Female:											
1980, age-adjusted	432.6	305.1	163.6	27.1	86.1	15.0	23.2	5.5	9.3	17.6	4.5
1990, age-adjusted	390.6	281.8	186.0	23.6	68.6	29.2	33.4	4.8	7.2	21.5	4.2
1992, age-adjusted	380.3	275.8	188.2	22.1	66.7	31.8	30.8	4.6	6.7	21.7	4.1
1993, age-adjusted	388.3	284.9	189.8	23.0	69.0	35.4	34.0	4.6	6.8	23.1	4.3
15 to 24 years old . . .	(NA)	2.0	4.1	19.1	0.6	0.4	0.7	4.1	(NA)	0.3	6.9
25 to 34 years old . . .	(NA)	5.6	12.3	15.0	1.8	0.8	1.4	5.2	1.2	1.3	7.6
35 to 44 years old . . .	(NA)	17.2	44.1	14.9	5.6	1.8	2.6	6.5	5.0	3.3	5.2
45 to 54 years old . . .	(NA)	57.9	145.2	14.5	15.8	8.0	4.9	7.1	8.5	10.5	3.1
55 to 64 years old . . .	(NA)	204.5	366.7	18.6	40.1	44.6	13.4	6.3	16.5	33.6	2.2
65 to 74 years old . . .	(NA)	589.3	688.4	31.4	118.7	135.6	42.2	5.9	23.1	76.6	2.5
75 to 84 years old . . .	(NA)	1,808.2	1,046.1	78.6	451.6	261.5	190.6	5.8	26.3	146.5	3.0
85 years old and over .	(NA)	6,414.6	1,415.3	223.8	1,632.9	344.6	983.7	5.4	16.9	264.5	3.4
WHITE											
Both sexes:											
1980, age-adjusted. . .	559.4	350.8	189.0	46.3	76.3	26.9	24.8	12.7	13.0	14.8	7.0
1990, age-adjusted. . .	492.8	305.4	211.6	36.9	59.7	38.4	33.9	13.5	10.3	18.5	5.8
1992, age-adjusted. . .	477.5	297.5	213.5	34.0	58.4	40.0	31.7	13.0	10.0	19.0	5.9
1993, age-adjusted. . .	485.1	305.1	215.1	35.0	60.5	43.6	34.3	13.1	9.9	20.2	5.7
Male:											
1980, age-adjusted	745.3	384.0	208.7	66.3	63.3	37.9	25.1	19.9	17.3	12.8	10.9
1990, age-adjusted	644.3	312.7	227.7	50.3	47.0	44.3	31.4	22.0	13.6	16.5	9.0
1992, age-adjusted	620.9	302.4	228.6	45.9	46.1	44.4	29.7	21.2	13.3	17.2	9.1
1993, age-adjusted	627.5	307.6	229.8	47.0	47.7	47.3	31.5	21.4	13.1	18.3	8.6
Female:											
1980, age-adjusted	411.1	319.2	170.3	27.2	88.8	16.4	24.6	5.9	8.8	16.8	3.2
1990, age-adjusted	369.9	298.4	196.1	24.0	71.8	32.8	36.3	5.3	7.1	20.5	2.8
1992, age-adjusted	359.9	292.9	199.0	22.6	70.3	35.8	33.6	5.1	6.8	20.7	2.8
1993, age-adjusted	367.7	302.8	200.9	23.5	72.8	40.0	37.0	5.0	6.9	22.1	3.0
BLACK											
Both sexes:											
1980, age-adjusted. . .	842.5	274.0	169.1	50.6	75.6	12.7	21.2	6.0	18.0	20.8	38.6
1990, age-adjusted. . .	789.2	246.4	187.2	40.7	57.1	18.6	24.8	6.9	12.3	26.6	39.8
1992, age-adjusted. . .	767.5	238.8	184.5	37.3	53.8	18.5	22.3	6.8	10.5	27.3	38.9
1993, age-adjusted. . .	785.2	245.5	186.1	39.5	54.6	20.0	24.0	7.0	10.0	29.1	40.2
Male:											
1980, age-adjusted	1,112.8	301.0	205.5	77.1	73.1	19.3	26.9	10.3	24.0	16.0	66.6
1990, age-adjusted	1,061.3	256.8	221.9	60.7	53.1	25.2	28.9	12.0	16.6	21.1	69.2
1992, age-adjusted	1,026.9	246.9	214.4	54.9	49.5	23.8	25.5	12.0	14.5	21.8	67.5
1993, age-adjusted	1,052.2	251.4	216.8	58.3	49.8	25.7	26.6	12.5	13.8	23.9	69.7
Female:											
1980, age-adjusted	631.1	249.7	136.5	26.9	77.9	6.8	16.1	2.2	12.6	25.2	13.5
1990, age-adjusted	581.6	237.0	156.1	22.8	60.7	12.6	21.2	2.3	8.5	31.5	13.5
1992, age-adjusted	568.4	231.6	157.6	21.5	57.8	13.7	19.5	2.0	6.8	32.3	13.1
1993, age-adjusted	578.8	240.2	158.4	22.5	58.8	14.9	21.7	2.1	6.7	33.9	13.6

NA Not available. [1] Includes other causes not shown separately. [2] Includes allied conditions. [3] Includes other races not shown separately.

Source: U.S. National Center for Health Statistics, *Vital Statistics of the United States*, annual; and *Monthly Vital Statistics Report*.

No. 133. Death Rates, by Leading Cause—States: 1993

[**Deaths per 100,000 resident population enumerated as of April 1.** By place of residence. Excludes nonresidents of the United States. Causes of death classified according to ninth revisions of *International Classification of Diseases*]

DIVISION AND STATE	Total[1]	Heart disease	Cancer	Cerebro-vascular diseases[2]	Accidents and adverse effects	Motor vehicle accidents	Chronic obstructive pulmonary diseases[2]	Diabetes mellitus	HIV[3]	Suicide	Homicide
U.S.	**880.0**	**288.4**	**205.6**	**58.2**	**35.1**	**16.3**	**39.2**	**20.9**	**14.5**	**12.1**	**10.1**
Northeast:											
N.E.	**906.4**	**294.4**	**226.2**	**57.1**	**25.7**	**10.6**	**38.8**	**21.2**	**11.7**	**9.6**	**4.3**
ME	943.3	298.2	244.8	60.7	31.4	14.8	49.4	22.7	5.9	14.6	1.7
NH	787.7	252.7	210.7	56.7	23.0	9.9	36.9	20.6	3.3	12.8	2.3
VT	861.1	272.9	197.5	55.6	39.6	17.0	44.1	23.5	4.5	16.0	(NA)
MA	924.5	292.7	232.6	56.1	22.4	9.1	38.7	22.2	12.9	7.8	4.1
RI	979.0	341.7	236.7	64.0	21.6	8.5	43.1	24.2	10.4	9.0	4.5
CT	885.8	299.8	214.8	56.0	29.6	11.3	33.6	17.6	16.3	9.2	6.4
M.A.......	**973.7**	**353.2**	**228.7**	**53.2**	**30.2**	**11.7**	**36.9**	**22.5**	**26.5**	**8.8**	**9.8**
NY	943.3	365.8	211.7	46.6	28.2	10.8	33.8	17.2	37.4	7.6	13.5
NJ	925.1	304.4	232.9	49.9	27.2	10.6	34.1	27.5	28.0	7.1	5.5
PA	1,051.3	366.1	251.7	65.4	35.1	13.6	43.3	27.5	9.1	11.7	7.1
Midwest:											
E.N.C......	**906.2**	**306.8**	**214.8**	**60.7**	**31.9**	**14.5**	**39.4**	**23.7**	**7.6**	**11.0**	**8.6**
OH	928.4	317.7	225.4	56.7	30.3	13.5	43.1	27.5	6.3	10.4	5.5
IN	916.8	306.9	214.8	66.7	33.1	16.5	43.4	24.0	5.2	12.8	7.1
IL	917.3	306.9	216.2	61.2	33.4	13.5	37.0	21.6	11.2	9.9	12.2
MI	872.9	302.6	203.5	56.1	30.3	15.4	36.6	22.3	7.4	11.5	11.0
WI	882.3	290.5	209.3	69.9	33.8	14.9	37.6	21.9	5.1	11.7	4.6
W.N.C......	**937.0**	**310.5**	**212.5**	**70.1**	**37.8**	**16.7**	**43.8**	**20.5**	**4.9**	**12.1**	**6.2**
MN	805.6	232.7	186.3	67.2	33.8	13.4	36.5	16.9	4.5	11.0	3.2
IA	991.5	345.8	229.7	74.0	36.5	16.6	47.0	21.2	2.6	11.3	2.2
MO	1,026.6	358.4	231.7	71.8	41.0	18.4	47.0	23.0	8.1	12.8	11.5
ND	914.8	305.3	211.9	68.9	35.7	14.6	34.6	28.7	(NA)	12.4	3.3
SD	947.1	315.2	212.0	67.9	45.4	19.6	49.0	22.8	(NA)	16.3	4.0
NE	931.4	313.0	207.3	70.4	38.1	16.9	46.8	17.5	2.7	10.6	3.7
KS	932.2	309.6	204.0	68.5	38.1	18.5	45.4	20.2	4.6	13.3	7.8
South:											
S.A.	**924.6**	**293.6**	**218.8**	**62.2**	**37.5**	**18.5**	**41.3**	**22.0**	**18.5**	**13.1**	**11.6**
DE	880.5	276.2	230.8	46.8	35.8	14.5	38.9	26.9	15.3	13.5	5.3
MD	814.3	244.8	199.6	45.6	27.8	13.5	31.1	25.4	20.2	10.7	13.4
DC	1,241.8	314.8	253.7	57.7	36.3	12.1	28.1	34.5	101.2	7.4	72.4
VA	796.2	247.2	191.9	56.7	31.9	13.6	34.1	16.1	10.5	12.1	8.7
WV	1,122.1	395.2	260.0	66.6	46.0	24.1	60.3	30.6	3.4	14.8	7.7
NC	898.8	275.6	207.3	69.0	40.6	20.2	40.7	22.6	11.6	11.3	12.4
SC	880.5	273.1	196.6	70.9	44.8	23.1	36.1	24.1	12.7	13.5	11.3
GA	812.8	251.6	178.0	55.6	40.9	20.6	34.1	16.3	18.1	12.4	12.2
FL	1,068.8	356.0	263.1	68.8	37.6	19.4	51.9	23.8	25.5	15.5	10.1
E.S.C......	**979.0**	**327.3**	**219.6**	**68.9**	**50.3**	**25.8**	**42.5**	**21.2**	**6.7**	**13.2**	**12.0**
KY	971.8	324.6	230.7	65.0	45.9	23.3	47.8	23.3	3.7	13.8	6.5
TN	966.8	314.3	217.0	73.8	48.1	23.5	42.8	21.7	7.8	13.2	11.2
AL	987.2	324.3	218.3	67.5	51.1	26.5	40.3	20.5	7.5	13.2	13.9
MS	1,000.0	361.3	210.5	67.4	59.5	32.9	38.1	18.5	7.3	12.4	18.6
W.S.C......	**833.8**	**264.3**	**190.1**	**56.7**	**38.3**	**19.4**	**36.3**	**25.4**	**12.6**	**12.9**	**13.6**
AR	1,093.7	355.0	246.3	92.5	48.0	24.6	48.5	23.4	5.1	13.1	12.3
LA	922.8	293.0	212.8	56.2	44.1	21.2	33.0	34.1	14.7	12.4	21.3
OK	1,002.9	352.5	217.7	68.8	44.9	21.9	47.7	19.5	6.5	15.2	9.8
TX	747.2	229.4	172.1	49.9	34.5	17.8	33.3	24.6	14.2	12.6	12.6
West:											
Mountain ...	**743.0**	**210.0**	**167.8**	**47.9**	**39.9**	**19.7**	**44.1**	**16.7**	**8.2**	**18.0**	**7.2**
MT	888.5	251.1	206.9	63.0	47.2	22.1	57.7	22.5	(NA)	18.4	4.5
ID	762.9	223.0	169.8	59.4	45.2	22.5	42.4	15.5	3.3	17.2	3.2
WY	743.0	210.1	163.1	54.5	46.2	23.0	52.8	16.8	(NA)	22.4	(NA)
CO	666.4	172.0	149.7	45.3	34.0	16.8	42.6	12.9	10.8	17.0	5.8
NM	726.1	185.3	157.2	39.9	53.5	25.3	42.9	24.6	7.2	17.8	10.1
AZ	844.7	255.9	195.3	52.6	41.5	20.2	49.1	16.8	10.5	18.4	9.5
UT	562.7	158.3	110.9	38.6	34.8	18.1	22.0	18.2	4.0	14.0	3.7
NV	808.5	240.4	201.7	41.9	31.1	16.1	55.4	12.4	11.7	23.4	11.5
Pacific	**726.3**	**221.6**	**169.0**	**51.7**	**32.5**	**14.4**	**35.9**	**13.7**	**17.6**	**12.7**	**11.7**
WA	769.6	225.7	187.2	60.3	32.8	13.9	42.0	17.8	10.1	13.1	5.4
OR	909.5	252.7	217.2	72.1	41.0	16.9	51.4	20.7	8.9	15.3	4.8
CA	711.1	221.7	163.4	49.0	31.4	14.3	34.2	12.4	20.2	12.4	13.8
AK	398.6	82.8	94.8	19.2	56.4	18.4	16.6	9.9	4.3	16.2	7.2
HI	628.8	191.2	149.7	47.3	25.6	11.7	22.3	15.6	10.0	10.3	3.1

NA Not available.   [1] Includes other causes not shown separately.   [2] Includes allied conditions.   [3] Human immunodeficiency virus.

Source: U.S. National Center for Health Statistics, *Monthly Vital Statistics Report;* and unpublished data.

No. 134. Acquired Immunodeficiency Syndrome (AIDS) Deaths, by Selected Characteristics: Thru 1995

[Data are shown by year of death and are subject to substantial retrospective changes. For data on AIDS cases reported, see table 217. Based on reporting by State health departments]

CHARACTERISTIC	NUMBER									PERCENT DISTRIBUTION	
	Total cases	1985 and before [1]	1989	1990	1991	1992	1993	1994	1995	1995	1993 -1995
Total [2]	305,843	12,493	26,355	29,934	34,651	38,813	41,077	43,975	31,256	100.0	100.0
Age:											
13 to 29 years old. . . .	53,632	2,558	4,924	5,427	6,059	6,481	6,815	6,930	5,105	16.3	16.2
30 to 39 years old. . . .	138,660	5,714	12,056	13,695	15,582	17,437	18,548	20,037	14,083	45.1	45.3
40 to 49 years old. . . .	77,425	2,726	6,205	7,329	8,943	10,339	10,975	11,921	8,543	27.3	27.0
50 to 59 years old. . . .	25,383	1,104	2,218	2,433	2,822	3,175	3,389	3,721	2,572	8.2	8.3
60 years old and over .	10,743	391	952	1,050	1,245	1,381	1,350	1,366	953	3.0	3.2
Sex:											
Male.	268,987	11553	23,742	26,752	30,725	34,072	35,551	37,360	26,375	84.4	85.4
Female	36,856	940	2,613	3,182	3,926	4,741	5,526	6,615	4,881	15.6	14.6
Race/ethnicity:											
White	159,292	7,267	14,481	16,517	18,693	19,982	20,376	20,733	14,389	46.0	47.7
Black	100,167	3,424	7,950	9,010	10,722	12,839	14,420	16,294	11,879	38.0	36.6
Hispanic	43,154	1,719	3,656	4,120	4,851	5,578	5,820	6,421	4,574	14.6	14.5
Other/unknown	3,230	83	268	287	385	414	461	527	414	1.3	1.2

Z Less than 0.5 percent.   [1] Includes deaths prior to 1982.   [2] Includes other race/ethnicity groups not shown separately.

Source: U.S. Centers for Disease Control, *Surveillance Report*, annual.

No. 135. Death Rates From Heart Disease, by Sex and Age: 1970 to 1993

[Deaths per 100,000 population in specified age groups. Excludes deaths of nonresidents of the United States. Beginning 1980, deaths classified according to the ninth revision of the *International Classification of Diseases*. For earlier years, classified according to the revision in use at the time; see text, section 2. See Appendix III]

AGE AT DEATH AND SELECTED TYPE OF HEART DISEASE	MALE					FEMALE				
	1970	1980	1990	1992	1993	1970	1980	1990	1992	1993
Total U.S. rate [1]	422.5	368.6	297.6	287.2	292.1	304.5	305.1	281.8	275.8	284.9
25 to 34 years old	15.2	11.4	10.3	10.7	11.3	7.7	5.3	5.0	5.4	5.6
35 to 44 years old	103.2	68.7	48.1	47.8	47.4	32.2	21.4	15.1	16.1	17.2
45 to 54 years old	376.4	282.6	183.0	173.7	172.8	109.9	84.5	61.0	58.1	57.9
55 to 64 years old	987.2	746.8	537.3	503.9	499.2	351.6	272.1	215.7	204.9	204.5
65 to 74 years old	2,170.3	1,728.0	1,250.0	1,178.8	1,175.3	1,082.7	828.6	616.8	587.8	589.3
75 to 84 years old	4,534.8	3,834.3	2,968.2	2,754.0	2,754.1	3,120.8	2,497.0	1,893.8	1,776.2	1,808.2
85 years old and over	8,426.2	8,752.7	7,418.4	7,156.5	7,331.9	7,591.8	7,350.5	6,478.1	6,263.1	6,414.6
Persons 45 to 54 years old:										
Ischemic heart.	338.0	217.3	123.8	114.9	112.0	84.0	52.2	33.6	31.6	30.8
Rheumatic heart . [2]	11.4	3.1	1.1	1.2	0.9	10.6	4.3	1.9	1.6	1.7
Hypertensive heart [2].	4.6	8.3	7.6	7.6	(NA)	4.0	5.5	4.3	4.1	(NA)
Persons 55 to 64 years old:										
Ischemic heart.	904.6	581.1	375.4	345.1	337.9	299.1	189.0	135.4	126.7	124.5
Rheumatic heart . [2]	21.5	6.2	3.4	2.6	2.7	20.8	9.2	4.7	4.3	3.9
Hypertensive heart [2].	11.7	21.8	18.1	18.9	(NA)	9.1	13.3	10.9	11.4	(NA)
Persons 65 to 74 years old:										
Ischemic heart.	2,010.0	1,355.5	898.5	837.5	823.7	978.0	605.3	415.2	387.9	383.6
Rheumatic heart . [2]	31.9	11.8	7.1	5.7	6.0	30.2	18.6	10.5	9.9	9.7
Hypertensive heart [2].	30.6	44.3	33.2	32.5	(NA)	24.8	36.2	25.9	24.5	(NA)
Persons 75 to 84 years old:										
Ischemic heart.	4,222.7	2,953.7	2,129.6	1,961.2	1,962.7	2,866.3	1,842.7	1,287.6	1,186.1	1,188.3
Rheumatic heart . [2]	34.8	16.7	12.3	12.1	12.4	34.3	25.4	22.5	20.7	19.6
Hypertensive heart [2].	80.8	90.7	67.9	64.8	(NA)	83.9	101.1	69.7	66.9	(NA)
Persons 85 years old and over:										
Ischemic heart.	7,781.5	6,501.6	5,120.7	4,878.3	4,920.7	6,951.5	5,280.6	4,257.8	4,056.4	4,097.6
Rheumatic heart . [2]	34.7	19.5	18.7	19.9	24.6	39.2	25.8	33.3	30.0	31.3
Hypertensive heart [2].	182.0	180.3	154.3	157.8	(NA)	223.5	250.8	212.1	216.4	(NA)

NA Not available.   [1] Includes persons under 25 years old not shown separately.   [2] With or without renal disease.

Source: U.S. National Center for Health Statistics, *Vital Statistics of the United States,* annual; and unpublished data.

No. 136. Death Rates From Cancer, by Sex and Age: 1970 to 1993

[**Deaths per 100,000 population in the specified age groups.** See headnote, table 135]

AGE AT DEATH AND SELECTED TYPE OF CANCER	MALE					FEMALE				
	1970	1980	1990	1992	1993	1970	1980	1990	1992	1993
Total [1]	182.1	205.3	221.3	220.8	222.1	144.4	163.6	186.0	188.2	189.8
25 to 34 years	16.3	13.4	12.6	12.1	11.9	16.7	14.0	12.6	12.9	12.3
35 to 44 years	53.0	44.0	38.5	38.1	38.0	65.6	53.1	48.1	46.5	44.1
45 to 54 years	183.5	188.7	162.5	153.8	150.7	181.5	171.8	155.5	147.0	145.2
55 to 64 years	511.8	520.8	532.9	513.4	507.4	343.2	361.7	375.2	369.7	366.7
65 to 74 years	1,006.8	1,093.2	1,122.2	1,111.1	1,113.3	557.9	607.1	677.4	686.5	688.4
75 to 84 years	1,588.3	1,790.5	1,914.4	1,882.7	1,885.4	891.9	903.1	1,010.3	1,025.6	1,046.1
85 years old and over	1,720.8	2,369.5	2,739.9	2,802.3	2,830.7	1,096.7	1,255.7	1,372.1	1,393.9	1,415.3
Persons, 35 to 44 years old:										
Respiratory, intrathoracic	17.0	12.6	9.1	8.6	8.3	6.5	6.8	5.4	5.6	5.0
Digestive organs, peritoneum . .	11.4	9.5	8.9	9.1	9.1	8.6	6.5	5.5	5.7	5.5
Breast.	0.1	-	(B)	0.0	(B)	20.4	17.9	17.8	16.1	15.2
Genital organs	1.4	0.7	0.6	0.6	0.6	13.6	8.3	7.3	7.3	6.8
Lymphatic and hematopoietic tissues, excl. leukemia	5.6	4.3	4.5	4.9	4.7	3.2	2.4	2.1	2.2	2.0
Urinary organs	1.9	1.4	1.5	1.4	1.5	1.0	0.6	0.6	0.7	0.7
Lip, oral cavity, and pharynx . . .	1.7	1.8	1.3	1.2	1.3	0.7	0.5	0.3	0.4	0.4
Leukemia	3.4	3.2	2.5	2.5	2.5	2.8	2.6	2.2	1.8	2.0
Persons, 45 to 54 years old:										
Respiratory, intrathoracic	72.1	79.8	63.0	57.7	54.6	22.2	34.8	35.3	32.5	31.6
Digestive organs, peritoneum . .	45.9	44.3	40.4	37.6	37.6	32.5	27.8	23.3	21.6	21.5
Breast.	0.4	0.2	0.3	0.2	0.3	52.6	48.1	45.4	42.8	42.0
Genital organs	3.4	3.4	2.9	2.7	2.7	34.4	24.1	19.4	18.2	17.9
Lymphatic and hematopoietic tissues, excl. leukemia	12.8	10.2	10.9	10.8	10.3	8.3	6.6	6.0	6.1	6.0
Urinary organs	8.0	7.4	7.2	7.4	7.4	3.5	3.3	2.9	2.8	3.0
Lip, oral cavity, and pharynx . . .	7.9	8.2	5.9	5.5	6.0	2.8	2.6	1.6	1.6	1.7
Leukemia	6.6	6.2	5.6	5.2	5.2	4.9	4.4	4.1	4.0	3.9
Persons, 55 to 64 years old:										
Respiratory, intrathoracic	202.3	223.8	232.6	217.0	216.0	38.9	74.5	107.6	108.4	107.3
Digestive organs, peritoneum . .	139.0	129.3	124.0	122.0	122.0	86.0	79.1	69.3	67.8	67.9
Breast.	0.6	0.7	0.6	0.5	0.7	77.6	80.5	78.6	73.6	72.2
Genital organs	22.8	23.5	27.9	26.6	24.9	58.2	46.8	40.1	39.2	38.1
Lymphatic and hematopoietic tissues, excl. leukemia	27.1	24.4	27.2	26.5	26.1	17.7	16.8	16.7	17.3	18.4
Urinary organs	26.4	22.9	23.5	23.1	22.3	9.4	8.9	8.8	9.1	8.4
Lip, oral cavity, and pharynx . . .	20.1	17.9	16.2	14.8	14.2	6.2	6.0	4.7	4.4	4.3
Leukemia	15.4	14.7	14.7	14.9	14.7	9.0	9.3	8.8	9.0	8.7
Persons, 65 to 74 years old:										
Respiratory, intrathoracic	340.7	422.0	447.3	439.8	441.2	45.6	106.1	181.7	195.3	199.2
Digestive organs, peritoneum . .	293.3	284.1	267.4	263.6	259.6	185.8	173.6	153.0	148.4	151.8
Breast.	1.4	1.1	1.1	1.1	1.1	93.8	101.1	111.7	109.3	105.7
Genital organs	103.7	107.6	123.5	122.0	117.9	85.6	73.6	71.0	70.5	67.0
Lymphatic and hematopoietic tissues, excl. leukemia	50.3	48.1	56.8	58.7	59.0	34.6	34.4	39.5	41.0	42.5
Urinary organs	60.3	56.9	50.7	51.2	53.3	20.1	19.7	19.8	19.8	19.5
Lip, oral cavity, and pharynx . . .	26.8	25.4	21.5	20.3	20.1	6.7	8.8	8.3	7.8	7.5
Leukemia	35.3	35.3	36.0	36.1	36.7	19.3	18.7	18.8	19.0	19.1
Persons, 75 to 84 years old:										
Respiratory, intrathoracic	354.2	511.5	594.4	587.5	384.8	56.5	98.0	194.5	216.0	226.3
Digestive organs, peritoneum . .	507.5	496.6	468.0	444.0	441.7	353.3	326.3	293.3	288.7	287.7
Breast.	2.7	2.1	1.6	2.0	2.3	127.4	126.4	146.3	140.8	146.4
Genital organs	299.4	315.4	358.5	355.7	356.6	104.9	95.7	95.3	97.2	97.4
Lymphatic and hematopoietic tissues, excl. leukemia	74.0	80.0	104.5	106.5	107.8	49.4	57.8	71.2	74.6	78.4
Urinary organs	112.2	112.4	107.5	104.5	103.4	44.0	37.4	38.5	40.0	38.0
Lip, oral cavity, and pharynx . . .	36.6	31.4	26.1	23.3	24.6	10.8	10.9	11.6	10.9	10.4
Leukemia	68.3	71.5	71.9	72.3	71.4	39.6	38.5	38.8	38.0	37.8
Persons, 85 years old and over:										
Respiratory, intrathoracic	215.3	386.3	538.0	545.4	559.7	56.5	96.3	142.8	160.8	173.9
Digestive organs, peritoneum . .	583.7	705.8	699.5	683.8	668.5	465.0	504.3	497.6	495.7	487.0
Breast.	2.9	2.6	2.4	4.4	5.1	157.1	169.3	196.8	195.5	206.0
Genital organs	434.2	612.3	750.0	808.3	842.2	107.3	115.9	115.6	115.8	114.4
Lymphatic and hematopoietic tissues, excl. leukemia	58.1	93.2	140.5	138.9	145.6	41.7	63.0	90.0	92.5	95.5
Urinary organs	140.5	177.0	186.3	192.9	190.3	59.9	63.8	68.5	69.6	64.5
Lip, oral cavity, and pharynx . . .	47.0	40.2	37.4	32.8	31.1	19.2	16.0	17.5	16.9	16.8
Leukemia	83.3	117.1	116.0	116.8	115.6	50.9	61.1	65.0	67.7	68.2

- Represents zero.   B Base figure too small to meet statistical standards for reliability of a derived figure.   [1] Includes persons under 25 years of age and malignant neoplasms of other and unspecified sites, not shown separately.

Source: U.S. National Center for Health Statistics, *Vital Statistics of the United States,* annual; and unpublished data.

No. 137. Death Rates From Accidents and Violence, by Race and Sex: 1980 to 1993

[Rates are per 100,000 population. Excludes deaths of nonresidents of the United States. Beginning 1980, deaths classified according to the ninth revision of the *International Classification of Diseases*. For earlier years, classified according to the revisions in use at the time; see text, section 2. See Appendix III]

CAUSE OF DEATH AND AGE	WHITE						BLACK					
	Male			Female			Male			Female		
	1980	1990	1993	1980	1990	1993	1980	1990	1993	1980	1990	1993
Total [1]	97.1	81.2	77.0	36.3	32.1	31.5	154.0	142.0	140.6	42.6	38.6	38.2
Motor vehicle accidents	35.9	26.1	22.7	12.8	11.4	10.3	31.1	28.1	24.6	8.3	9.4	8.7
All other accidents	30.4	23.6	24.3	14.4	12.4	13.2	46.0	32.7	33.7	18.6	13.4	13.8
Suicide	19.9	22.0	21.4	5.9	5.3	5.0	10.3	12.0	12.5	2.2	2.3	2.1
Homicide	10.9	9.0	8.6	3.2	2.8	3.0	66.6	69.2	69.7	13.5	13.5	13.6
15 to 24 years old	138.6	107.3	99.1	37.3	30.5	28.2	162.0	208.0	242.2	35.0	34.9	39.9
25 to 34 years old	118.4	97.4	92.0	29.0	26.0	24.8	256.9	218.1	197.3	49.4	48.1	46.2
35 to 44 years old	94.1	82.3	82.9	29.2	24.4	24.9	218.1	176.6	169.9	43.2	38.5	40.1
45 to 54 years old	90.8	73.5	70.5	31.8	25.3	24.3	207.3	138.5	137.2	40.2	30.7	28.7
55 to 64 years old	92.3	79.5	71.7	33.8	29.4	26.7	188.5	129.9	112.1	47.3	36.1	31.9
65 years old and over	163.9	150.7	157.1	87.2	80.1	78.6	215.8	175.5	164.3	102.9	81.6	70.8
65 to 74 years old	116.7	99.7	91.1	46.4	40.5	39.0	182.2	141.8	136.3	68.7	50.4	47.1
75 to 84 years old	209.2	195.7	187.3	101.5	89.4	87.1	261.4	206.1	185.9	137.5	95.8	94.9
85 years old and over	438.5	428.3	449.1	268.1	232.4	236.2	379.2	359.1	399.2	235.7	213.0	190.3

[1] Includes persons under 15 years old, not shown separately.

No. 138. Deaths and Death Rates From Accidents, by Type: 1970 to 1993

[See headnote, table 137 and Appendix III. See also *Historical Statistics, Colonial Times to 1970*, series B 163-165]

TYPE OF ACCIDENT	DEATHS (number)					RATE PER 100,000 POPULATION				
	1970	1980	1990	1992	1993	1970	1980	1990	1992	1993
Total	114,638	105,718	91,983	86,777	90,523	56.4	46.7	37.0	34.0	35.1
Motor vehicle accidents	54,633	53,172	46,814	40,982	41,893	26.9	23.5	18.8	16.1	16.3
Traffic	53,493	51,930	45,827	39,985	40,899	26.3	22.9	18.4	15.7	15.9
Nontraffic	1,140	1,242	987	997	994	0.6	0.5	0.4	0.4	0.4
Water-transport accidents	1,651	1,429	923	837	763	0.8	0.6	0.4	0.3	0.3
Air and space transport accidents . .	1,612	1,494	941	1,094	859	0.8	0.7	0.4	0.4	0.3
Railway accidents	852	632	663	642	670	0.4	0.3	0.3	0.3	0.3
Accidental falls	16,926	13,294	12,313	12,646	13,141	8.3	5.9	5.0	5.0	5.1
Fall from one level to another. . . .	4,798	3,743	3,194	3,091	3,160	2.4	1.7	1.3	1.2	1.2
Fall on the same level.	828	415	499	483	529	0.4	0.2	0.2	0.2	0.2
Fracture, cause unspecified, and other unspecified falls	11,300	9,136	8,620	9,072	9,452	5.6	4.0	3.5	3.6	3.7
Accidental drowning.	6,391	6,043	3,979	3,524	3,807	3.1	2.7	1.6	1.4	1.5
Accidents caused by—										
Fires and flames	6,718	5,822	4,175	3,958	3,900	3.3	2.6	1.7	1.6	1.5
Firearms.	2,406	1,955	1,416	1,409	1,521	1.2	0.9	0.6	0.6	0.6
Electric current	1,140	1,095	670	525	548	0.6	0.5	0.3	0.2	0.2
Accidental poisoning by—										
Drugs and medicines	2,505	2,492	4,506	5,951	7,382	1.2	1.1	1.8	2.3	2.9
Other solid and liquid substances .	1,174	597	549	498	495	0.6	0.3	0.2	0.2	0.2
Gases and vapors	1,620	1,242	748	633	660	0.8	0.5	0.3	0.2	0.3
Complications due to medical procedures.	3,581	2437	2,669	2,669	2,724	1.8	1.1	1.1	1.0	1.1
Inhalation and ingestion of objects . .	2,753	3,249	3,303	3,128	3,160	1.4	1.5	1.3	1.2	1.2

No. 139. Suicides, by Sex and Method Used: 1970 to 1993

[Excludes deaths of nonresidents of the United States. Beginning 1979, deaths classified according to the ninth revision of the *International Classification of Diseases*. For earlier years, classified according to the revision in use at the time; see text, section 2. See also *Historical Statistics, Colonial Times to 1970*, series H 979-986]

METHOD	MALE						FEMALE					
	1970	1980	1985	1990	1992	1993	1970	1980	1985	1990	1992	1993
Total	16,629	20,505	23,145	24,724	24,457	25,007	6,851	6,364	6,308	6,182	6,027	6,095
Firearms [1]	9,704	12,937	14,809	16,285	15,802	16,381	2,068	2,459	2,554	2,600	2,367	2,559
Percent of total . .	58	63	64	66	65	66	30	39	41	42	39	39
Poisoning [2]	3,299	2,997	3,319	3,221	3,690	3,569	3,285	2,456	2,385	2,203	2,233	2,110
Hanging and strangulation [3]. . .	2,422	2,997	3,532	3,688	3,822	3,824	831	694	732	756	856	803
Other [4]	1,204	1,574	1,485	1,530	1,571	1,641	667	755	637	623	571	623

[1] Includes explosives in 1970. [2] Includes solids, liquids, and gases. [3] Includes suffocation. [4] Beginning 1980, includes explosives.

Source of tables 137-139: U.S. National Center for Health Statistics, *Vital Statistics of the United States*, annual; and unpublished data.

No. 140. Suicide Rates, by Sex, Race, and Age Group: 1980 to 1993

[See headnote, tables 132 and 137]

AGE	TOTAL [1]			MALE						FEMALE					
				White			Black			White			Black		
	1980	1990	1993	1980	1990	1993	1980	1990	1993	1980	1990	1993	1980	1990	1993
All ages [2]......	11.9	12.4	12.1	19.9	22.0	21.4	10.3	12.0	12.5	5.9	5.3	5.0	2.2	2.3	2.1
10 to 14 years old....	0.8	1.5	1.7	1.4	2.3	2.4	0.5	1.6	2.3	0.3	0.9	1.0	0.1	(B)	(B)
15 to 19 years old....	8.5	11.1	10.9	15.0	19.3	18.5	5.6	11.5	14.4	3.3	4.0	4.2	1.6	1.9	(B)
20 to 24 years old....	16.1	15.1	15.8	27.8	26.8	27.4	20.0	19.0	25.9	5.9	4.4	4.4	3.1	2.6	3.9
25 to 34 years old....	16.0	15.2	15.1	25.6	25.6	25.9	21.8	21.9	21.5	7.5	6.0	5.5	4.1	3.7	3.1
35 to 44 years old....	15.4	15.3	15.1	23.5	25.3	25.5	15.6	16.9	16.2	9.1	7.4	7.1	4.6	4.0	3.0
45 to 54 years old....	15.9	14.8	14.5	24.2	24.8	23.9	12.0	14.8	14.1	10.2	7.5	7.8	2.8	3.2	2.2
55 to 64 years old....	15.9	16.0	14.6	25.8	27.5	25.7	11.7	10.8	9.7	9.1	8.0	6.8	2.3	2.6	2.6
65 to 74 years over...	16.9	17.9	16.3	32.5	34.2	31.4	11.1	14.7	11.7	7.0	7.2	6.2	1.7	2.6	2.2
75 to 84 years over...	19.1	24.9	22.3	45.5	60.2	52.1	10.5	14.4	16.3	5.7	6.7	6.1	1.4	(B)	(B)
85 years and over....	19.2	22.2	22.8	52.8	70.3	73.6	18.9	(B)	(B)	5.8	5.4	5.4	0.1	(B)	(B)

B Base figure too small to meet statistical standards for reliability of a derived figure. [1] Includes other races not shown separately. [2] Includes other age groups not shown separately.

Source: U.S. National Center for Health Statistics, *Monthly Vital Statistics Report;* and unpublished data.

No. 141. Firearm Mortality Among Children, Youth, and Young Adults, 1 to 34 Years Old: 1992

[**Death rate per 100,000 population.** Deaths classified according to the ninth revision of the *International Classification of Diseases*]

ITEM	Under 5 years old	5 to 9 years old	10 to 14 years old	15 to 19 years old	20 to 24 years old	25 to 29 years old	30 to 34 years old
MALE							
Firearms:							
Total:							
White...............	0.5	0.5	4.6	29.1	34.6	29.0	26.0
Black...............	1.4	1.5	11.5	140.5	184.3	129.4	94.8
Accidents:							
White...............	0.1	0.3	1.6	2.9	1.6	1.0	0.8
Black...............	0.2	0.6	2.0	6.3	4.7	2.2	1.2
Suicide:							
White...............	(X)	(X)	1.5	13.6	17.7	15.3	14.9
Black...............	(X)	(X)	1.1	9.0	14.4	13.4	10.5
Homicide:							
White...............	0.3	0.3	1.4	11.8	14.9	12.3	10.1
Black...............	1.1	0.9	8.2	123.6	164.4	113.4	82.9
FEMALE							
Firearms:							
Total:							
White...............	0.4	0.3	1.0	4.6	5.1	4.9	5.5
Black...............	1.5	0.5	3.0	12.7	17.7	16.5	13.9
Accidents:							
White...............	0.1	0.1	0.1	0.2	0.2	0.1	0.1
Black...............	0.4	0.1	0.2	0.2	(X)	0.1	0.1
Suicide:							
White...............	(X)	(X)	0.4	2.1	2.0	2.4	2.8
Black...............	(X)	(X)	0.1	0.8	0.7	1.9	0.7
Homicide:							
White...............	0.3	0.2	0.5	2.2	2.7	2.3	2.4
Black...............	1.1	0.4	2.7	11.2	16.8	14.4	13.1

X Not applicable.

Source: U.S. National Center for Health Statistics, *Advance Data from Vital and Health Statistics,* No. 231.

No. 142. Deaths and Death Rates for Injury by Firearms, by Race and Sex: 1980 to 1993

[Age-adjusted rates per 100,000]

| YEAR | ALL RACES | | | WHITE | | | BLACK AND OTHER | | | | | |
| | Both sexes | Male | Female | Both sexes | Male | Female | Total | | | Black | | |
							Both sexes	Male	Female	Both sexes	Male	Female
NUMBER												
1980	33,780	28,322	5,458	24,849	20,714	4,135	8,931	7,608	1,323	8,505	7,265	1,240
1985	31,566	26,382	5,184	24,507	20,389	4,118	7,059	5,993	1,066	6,565	5,584	981
1990	37,155	31,736	5,419	26,299	22,249	4,050	10,856	9,487	1,369	10,175	8,922	1,253
1991	38,317	32,882	5,435	26,455	22,448	4,007	11,862	10,434	1,428	11,025	9,733	1,292
1992	37,776	32,425	5,351	26,120	22,208	3,912	11,656	10,217	1,439	10,906	9,581	1,325
1993	39,595	33,711	5,884	26,948	22,608	4,268	12,647	11,031	1,616	11,763	10,310	1,453
RATE [1]												
1980	14.8	25.3	4.8	12.4	21.1	4.2	29.1	53.0	8.1	33.5	61.8	9.1
1985	12.7	21.8	4.2	11.4	19.4	3.9	19.7	35.4	5.7	23.2	42.2	6.5
1990	14.6	25.4	4.2	11.9	20.5	3.7	26.9	48.9	6.5	33.4	61.5	7.8
1991	15.2	26.4	4.2	12.0	20.7	3.7	29.0	52.9	6.6	35.9	66.4	8.0
1992	14.9	25.9	4.1	11.8	20.4	3.6	28.0	50.9	6.6	35.1	64.5	8.0
1993	15.6	26.9	4.6	12.2	20.7	3.9	30.1	54.4	7.3	37.6	68.8	8.8

[1] Age-adjusted death rate. For method of computation see source.

No. 143. Deaths and Death Rates for Drug-Induced Causes, by Race and Sex: 1980 to 1993

[Age-adjusted rates per 100,000]

| YEAR | ALL RACES | | | WHITE | | | BLACK AND OTHER | | | | | |
| | Both sexes | Male | Female | Both sexes | Male | Female | Total | | | Black | | |
							Both sexes	Male	Female	Both sexes	Male	Female
NUMBER												
1980	6,900	3,771	3,129	5,814	3,088	2,726	1,086	683	403	1,006	648	358
1985	8,663	5,342	3,321	6,946	4,172	2,774	1,717	1,170	547	1,600	1,107	493
1990	9,463	5,897	3,566	7,603	4,646	2,957	1,860	1,251	609	1,703	1,155	548
1991	10,388	6,593	3,795	8,204	5,129	3,075	2,184	1,464	720	2,037	1,385	652
1992	11,703	7,766	3,937	9,360	6,124	3,236	2,343	1,642	701	2,037	1,385	652
1993	13,275	9,052	4,223	10,394	7,005	3,389	2,881	2,047	834	2,688	1,924	764
RATE [1]												
1980	3.0	3.4	2.6	2.9	3.2	2.6	3.7	4.9	2.5	4.1	5.8	2.7
1985	3.5	4.5	2.6	3.3	4.0	2.5	4.9	7.2	2.9	5.9	8.9	3.3
1990	3.6	4.6	2.6	3.3	4.2	2.5	4.6	6.7	2.8	5.7	8.4	3.4
1991	3.8	5.0	2.7	3.6	4.6	2.6	5.2	7.5	3.2	6.6	9.7	3.9
1992	4.3	5.9	2.8	4.1	5.5	2.7	5.5	8.3	3.1	6.6	9.7	3.9
1993	4.8	6.8	3.0	4.5	6.2	2.8	6.6	10.0	3.6	8.3	13.0	4.4

[1] Age-adjusted death rate. For method of computation see source.

No. 144. Deaths and Death Rates for Alcohol-Induced Causes, by Race and Sex: 1980 to 1993

[Age-adjusted rates per 100,000]

| YEAR | ALL RACES | | | WHITE | | | BLACK AND OTHER | | | | | |
| | Both sexes | Male | Female | Both sexes | Male | Female | Total | | | Black | | |
							Both sexes	Male	Female	Both sexes	Male	Female
NUMBER												
1980	19,765	14,447	5,318	14,815	10,936	3,879	4,950	3,511	1,439	4,451	3,170	1,281
1985	17,741	13,216	4,525	13,216	9,922	3,294	4,525	3,294	1,231	4,114	3,030	1,084
1990	19,757	14,842	4,915	14,904	11,334	3,570	4,853	3,508	1,345	4,337	3,172	1,165
1991	19,233	14,467	4,766	14,825	11,286	3,539	4,408	3,181	1,227	3,883	2,816	1,067
1992	19,568	14,926	4,642	15,143	11,701	3,442	4,425	3,225	1,200	3,809	2,800	1,009
1993	19,557	14,873	4,684	15,293	11,716	3,577	4,264	3,157	1,107	3,663	2,759	904
RATE [1]												
1980	8.4	13.0	4.3	6.9	10.8	3.5	18.8	29.5	10.0	20.4	32.4	10.6
1985	7.0	11.0	3.4	5.8	9.2	2.8	14.6	23.5	7.2	16.8	27.7	8.0
1990	7.2	11.4	3.4	6.2	9.9	2.8	13.6	22.0	6.8	16.1	26.6	7.7
1991	6.8	10.9	3.2	6.0	9.7	2.7	11.8	19.2	5.9	13.9	22.9	6.8
1992	6.8	11.0	3.1	6.1	9.9	2.6	11.6	18.9	5.6	13.4	22.3	6.3
1993	6.7	10.8	3.0	6.1	9.7	2.7	10.8	17.8	5.0	12.5	21.3	5.5

[1] Age-adjusted death rate. For method of computation see source.

Source of tables 142-144: U.S. National Center for Health Statistics, *Monthly Vital Statistics Reports*.

No. 145. Deaths—Life Years Lost and Mortality Costs, by Age, Sex, and Cause: 1992

[**Life years lost:** Number of years person would have lived in absence of death. **Mortality cost:** value of lifetime earnings lost by persons who die prematurely, discounted at 6 percent]

CHARACTER-ISTIC	Number of deaths (1,000)	LIFE YEARS LOST [1]		MORTALITY COST [2]		CHARACTER-ISTIC	Number of deaths (1,000)	LIFE YEARS LOST [1]		MORTALITY COST [2]	
		Total (1,000)	Per death	Total (mil.)	Per death			Total (1,000)	Per death	Total (mil.)	Per death
Total.....	**2,176**	**36,707**	**17**	**312,198**	**143,530**	Heart disease .	358	4,722	13	38,714	108,278
Under 5 yrs. . .	41	3,096	75	20,796	502,421	Cancer......	275	4,097	15	36,174	131,618
5-14 yrs......	8	554	68	5,505	671,889	Cerebrovas-					
15-24 yrs.....	35	1,963	57	30,164	873,096	cular diseases	57	672	12	4,941	87,233
25-44 yrs.....	150	6,338	42	117,657	785,580	Injuries......	58	2,077	36	34,028	588,094
45-64 yrs.....	366	9,011	25	101,882	278,350	Other........	375	8,399	22	105,947	282,190
65 yrs. and over	1,575	15,745	10	36,194	22,977						
Heart disease .	718	8,959	12	54,081	75,352	**Female . . .**	**1,053**	**16,741**	**16**	**92,394**	**87,730**
Cancer......	521	8,544	16	63,901	122,749	Under 5 yrs. . .	18	1,420	79	8,011	444,126
Cerebrovas-						5-14 yrs......	3	224	72	1,819	584,186
cular diseases	144	1,680	12	8,768	60,984	15-24 yrs.....	8	517	62	6,033	723,352
Injuries......	87	3,007	35	42,823	493,485	25-44 yrs.....	44	2,019	46	26,678	607,969
Other........	707	14,517	21	142,626	201,797	45-64 yrs.....	140	3,823	27	32,490	232,285
Male.....	**1,122**	**19,966**	**18**	**219,804**	**195,907**	65 yrs. and over	840	8,738	10	17,363	20,672
Under 5 yrs. . .	23	1,676	72	12,785	547,446	Heart disease .	360	4,237	12	15,366	42,665
5-14 yrs......	5	330	65	3,686	725,633	Cancer......	246	4,448	18	27,727	112,830
15-24 yrs.....	26	1,446	55	24,130	920,756	Cerebrovas-					
25-44 yrs.....	106	4,319	41	90,979	859,182	cular diseases	87	1,009	12	3,826	43,917
45-64 yrs.....	226	5,188	23	69,392	306,841	Injuries......	29	930	32	8,795	304,162
65 yrs. and over	735	7,007	10	18,832	25,611	Other........	331	6,118	18	36,679	110,701

[1] Based on life expectancy at year of death. [2] Cost estimates based on the person's age, sex, life expectancy at the time of death, labor force participation rates, annual earnings, value of homemaking services, and a 6-percent discount rate by which to convert to present worth the potential aggregate earnings lost over the years.

Source: Institute for Health and Aging, University of California, San Francisco, CA, unpublished data.

No. 146. Marriages and Divorces: 1970 to 1994

[See also *Historical Statistics, Colonial Times to 1970,* series B 214-217]

YEAR	MARRIAGES [1]							DIVORCES AND ANNULMENTS		
	Number (1,000)	Rate per 1,000 population						Number (1,000)	Rate per 1,000 population	
		Total	Men, 15 yrs. old and over	Women, 15 yrs. old and over	Unmarried women				Total	Married women, 15 yrs. old and over
					15 yrs. old and over	15 to 44 yrs. old				
1970	2,159	10.6	31.1	28.4	76.5	140.2		708	3.5	14.9
1975	2,153	10.0	27.9	25.6	66.9	118.5		1,036	4.8	20.3
1980	2,390	10.6	28.5	26.1	61.4	102.6		1,189	5.2	22.6
1983	2,446	10.5	28.0	25.7	59.9	99.3		1,158	5.0	21.3
1984	2,477	10.5	28.0	25.8	59.5	99.0		1,169	5.0	21.5
1985	2,413	10.1	27.0	24.9	57.0	94.9		1,190	5.0	21.7
1986	2,407	10.0	26.6	24.5	56.2	93.9		1,178	4.9	21.2
1987	2,403	9.9	26.3	24.3	55.7	92.4		1,166	4.8	20.8
1988	2,396	9.8	26.0	24.0	54.6	91.0		1,167	4.8	20.7
1989	2,403	9.7	25.8	23.9	54.2	91.2		1,157	4.7	20.4
1990	2,443	9.8	26.0	24.1	54.5	91.3		1,182	4.7	20.9
1991	2,371	9.4	(NA)	(NA)	54.2	86.8		1,189	4.7	20.9
1992	2,362	9.3	(NA)	(NA)	53.3	88.2		1,215	4.8	21.2
1993	2,334	9.0	(NA)	(NA)	52.3	86.8		1,187	4.6	20.5
1994	2,362	9.1	(NA)	(NA)	51.5	84.0		1,191	4.6	20.5

NA Not available. [1] Beginning 1980, includes nonlicensed marriages registered in California.

No. 147. Percent Distribution of Marriages, by Marriage Order: 1970 to 1988

[Excludes marriages with marriage order not stated. See headnote, table 149]

MARRIAGE ORDER	1970	1980	1981	1982	1983	1984	1985	1986	1987	1988
Total.........................	100.0	100.0	100.0	100.0	100.0	100.0	100.0	100.0	100.0	100.0
First marriage of bride and groom	68.6	56.2	54.7	54.8	54.4	54.4	54.3	53.9	53.9	54.1
First marriage of bride, remarriage of groom . . .	7.6	11.3	11.8	11.6	11.6	11.5	11.5	11.3	11.3	11.1
Remarriage of bride, first marriage of groom . . .	7.3	9.8	10.1	10.3	10.5	10.7	10.9	11.2	11.3	11.4
Remarriage of bride and groom	16.5	22.7	23.4	23.3	23.5	23.4	23.4	23.6	23.5	23.4

Source of tables 146 and 147: U.S. National Center for Health Statistics, *Vital Statistics of the United States,* annual; *Monthly Vital Statistics Report;* and unpublished data.

No. 148. Percent Distribution of Marriages, by Age, Sex, and Previous Marital Status: 1980 to 1990

[Data cover marriage registraction area; see text, section 2. Based on a sample and subject to sampling variability; for details, see source]

SEX AND PREVIOUS MARITAL STATUS	Total	Under 20 years old	20-24 years old	25-29 years old	30-34 years old	35-44 years old	45-64 years old	65 years old and over
WOMEN								
All marriages: [1]								
1980	100.0	21.1	37.1	18.7	9.3	7.8	5.0	1.0
1990	100.0	10.6	29.3	24.6	14.2	13.9	6.1	1.0
First marriages: [2]								
1980	100.0	30.4	47.3	16.0	4.0	1.6	0.6	0.1
1990	100.0	16.6	40.8	27.2	10.1	4.5	0.7	0.1
Remarriages: [2] [3]								
1980	100.0	1.7	15.3	24.4	20.6	20.8	14.3	2.9
1990	100.0	0.6	8.0	19.9	21.7	31.3	16.0	2.7
Previously divorced: [4] 1980	100.0	1.7	16.7	26.7	22.5	21.6	10.0	0.6
1990	100.0	0.6	8.6	20.9	23.0	32.5	13.6	0.6
MEN								
All marriages: [1]								
1980	100.0	8.5	35.7	23.8	12.3	10.5	7.4	1.8
1990	100.0	4.3	24.7	27.1	16.6	16.4	9.1	1.9
First marriages: [2]								
1980	100.0	12.7	50.0	25.7	7.5	2.9	1.1	0.1
1990	100.0	6.6	36.0	34.3	14.8	7.1	1.1	0.1
Remarriages: [2] [3]								
1980	100.0	0.2	7.2	20.1	21.9	25.6	20.0	5.1
1990	100.0	0.1	3.6	13.8	19.9	33.8	23.8	5.1
Previously divorced: [4] 1980	100.0	0.2	7.7	21.7	24.1	27.7	17.3	1.4
1990	100.0	0.1	3.8	14.8	21.2	35.8	22.6	1.7

[1] Includes marriage order not stated.   [2] Excludes data for Iowa.   [3] Includes remarriages of previously widowed.
[4] Excludes remarriages in Michigan, Ohio, and South Carolina.

No. 149. Marriage Rates and Median Age of Bride and Groom, by Previous Marital Status: 1970 to 1990

[Data cover marriage registration area; see text, section 2. Figures for previously divorced and previously widowed exclude data for Michigan and Ohio for all years, for South Carolina beginning 1975, and for the District Columbia for 1970. Based on a sample and subject to sampling variability; for details, see source. For definition of median, Guide to Tabular Presentation. See also *Historical Statistics, Colonial Times to 1970*, series A 158-159]

YEAR	MARRIAGE RATES [1]						MEDIAN AGE AT MARRIAGE (years)					
	Women			Men			Women			Men		
	Single	Divorced	Widowed	Single	Divorced	Widowed	First marriage	Remarriage		First marriage	Remarriage	
								Divorced	Widowed		Divorced	Widowed
1970	93.4	123.3	10.2	80.4	204.5	40.6	20.6	30.1	51.2	22.5	34.5	58.7
1975	75.9	117.2	8.3	61.5	189.8	40.4	20.8	30.2	52.4	22.7	33.6	59.4
1980	66.0	91.3	6.7	54.7	142.1	32.2	21.8	31.0	53.6	23.6	34.0	61.2
1985	61.5	81.8	5.7	50.1	121.6	27.7	23.0	32.8	54.6	24.8	36.1	62.7
1986	59.7	79.5	5.5	49.1	117.8	26.8	23.3	33.1	54.3	25.1	36.6	62.9
1987	58.9	80.7	5.4	48.8	115.7	26.1	23.6	33.3	53.9	25.3	36.7	62.8
1988	58.4	78.6	5.3	48.3	109.7	25.1	23.7	33.6	53.9	25.5	37.0	63.0
1989	58.7	75.6	5.1	48.2	105.6	24.5	23.9	34.0	53.8	25.9	37.3	62.9
1990	57.7	76.2	5.2	47.0	105.9	23.8	24.0	34.2	54.0	25.9	37.4	63.1

[1] Rate per 1,000 population 15 years old and over in specified group.

No. 150. Divorces and Annulments—Duration of Marriage, Age at Divorce, and Children Involved: 1970 to 1990

[Data cover divorce-registration area; see text, section 2. Based on a sample and subject to sampling variability; for details, see source. Median age computed on data by single years of age. See also *Historical Statistics, Colonial Times to 1970*, series B 21]

DURATION OF MARRIAGE, AGE AT DIVORCE, AND CHILDREN INVOLVED	1970	1975	1980	1983	1984	1985	1986	1987	1988	1989	1990
Median duration of marriage (years)	6.7	6.5	6.8	7.0	6.9	6.8	6.9	7.0	7.1	7.2	7.2
Median age at divorce:											
Men (years)	32.9	32.2	32.7	34.0	34.3	34.4	34.6	34.9	35.1	35.4	35.6
Women (years)	29.8	29.5	30.3	31.5	31.7	31.9	32.1	32.5	32.6	32.9	33.2
Estimated number of children involved in (1,000)	870	1,123	1,174	1,091	1,081	1,091	1,064	1,038	1,044	1,063	1,075
Avg. number of children per decree	1.22	1.08	0.98	0.94	0.92	0.92	0.90	0.89	0.89	0.91	0.90
Rate per 1,000 children under 18 years of	12.5	16.7	17.3	17.4	17.2	17.3	16.8	16.3	16.4	16.8	16.8

Source of tables 148-150: U.S. National Center for Health Statistics of the United States, *Vital Statistics of the United States*, annual, *Monthly Vital Statistics Report;* and unpublished data.

No. 151. First Marriage Dissolution and Years Until Remarriage for Women, by Race and Hispanic Origin: 1988

[For women 15 to 44 years old. Based on 1988 National Survey of Family Growth; see Appendix III. Marriage dissolution includes death of spouse, separation because of marital discord, and divorce]

ITEM	Number (1,000)	YEARS UNTIL REMARRIAGE (cumulative percent)					
		All	1	2	3	4	5
ALL RACES [1]							
Year of dissolution of first marriage:							
All years	11,577	56.8	20.6	32.8	40.7	46.2	49.7
1980-84	3,504	47.5	16.3	28.1	36.4	[2]41.1	[2]45.4
1975-79	3,235	65.3	21.9	36.0	44.7	52.7	55.4
1970-74	1,887	83.2	24.9	38.6	47.9	56.4	61.2
1965-69	1,013	89.9	32.6	48.7	60.2	65.0	72.8
WHITE							
Year of dissolution of first marriage:							
All years	10,103	59.9	21.9	35.2	43.5	49.4	53.0
1980-84	3,030	51.4	18.2	31.1	40.3	[2]45.2	[2]49.8
1975-79	2,839	69.5	23.2	38.5	46.9	55.6	58.4
1970-74	1,622	87.5	24.9	39.8	49.8	59.3	64.3
1965-69	893	91.0	34.7	52.3	64.9	69.3	76.9
BLACK							
Year of dissolution of first marriage:							
All years	1,166	34.0	10.9	16.5	19.6	22.7	25.0
1980-84	380	19.7	[3]4.7	[3]10.6	[3]12.9	[2]14.8	[2]14.8
1975-79	301	32.3	[3]11.4	[3]15.6	18.5	22.2	24.9
1970-74	227	59.0	22.3	29.4	35.3	38.7	42.3
1965-69	98	81.2	[3]20.9	[3]27.3	[3]31.3	40.8	52.1
Hispanic, [4] all years	942	44.7	12.5	16.6	22.7	27.8	29.9

[1] Includes other races.   [2] The percent having remarried is biased downward because the women had not completed the indicated number of years since dissolution of first marriage at the time of the survey.   [3] Figure does not meet standard of reliability or precision.   [4] Hispanic persons may be of any race.
Source: National Center for Health Statistics, *Advance Data from Vital and Health Statistics,* No. 194.

No. 152. Marriage Experience for Women, by Age and Race: 1980 and 1990

[**In percent.** As of **June.** Based on Current Population Survey; see text, section 1]

MARITAL STATUS AND AGE	ALL RACES		WHITE		BLACK		HISPANIC [1]	
	1980	1990	1980	1990	1980	1990	1980	1990
EVER MARRIED								
20 to 24 years old	49.5	38.5	52.2	41.3	33.3	23.5	55.4	45.8
25 to 29 years old	78.6	69.0	81.0	73.2	62.3	45.0	80.2	69.6
30 to 34 years old	89.9	82.2	91.6	85.6	77.9	61.1	88.3	83.0
35 to 39 years old	94.3	89.4	95.3	91.4	87.4	74.9	91.2	88.9
40 to 44 years old	95.1	92.0	95.8	93.4	89.7	82.1	94.2	92.8
45 to 49 years old	95.9	94.4	96.4	95.1	92.5	89.7	94.4	91.7
50 to 54 years old	95.3	95.5	95.8	96.1	92.1	91.9	95.0	91.8
DIVORCED AFTER FIRST MARRIAGE								
20 to 24 years old	14.2	12.5	14.7	12.8	10.5	9.6	9.4	6.8
25 to 29 years old	20.7	19.2	21.0	19.8	20.2	17.8	13.9	13.5
30 to 34 years old	26.2	28.1	25.8	28.6	31.4	26.6	21.1	19.9
35 to 39 years old	27.2	34.1	26.7	34.6	32.9	35.8	21.9	29.7
40 to 44 years old	26.1	35.8	25.5	35.2	33.7	45.1	19.7	26.6
45 to 49 years old	23.1	35.2	22.7	35.5	29.0	39.8	23.9	24.6
50 to 54 years old	21.8	29.5	21.0	28.5	29.0	39.2	22.5	22.9
REMARRIED AFTER DIVORCE								
20 to 24 years old	45.5	38.1	47.0	39.3	(B)	(B)	(B)	(B)
25 to 29 years old	53.4	51.8	56.4	52.8	27.9	44.4	(B)	49.5
30 to 34 years old	60.9	59.6	63.3	61.4	42.0	42.0	58.3	45.9
35 to 39 years old	64.9	65.0	66.9	66.5	50.6	54.0	45.2	51.2
40 to 44 years old	67.4	67.1	68.6	69.5	58.4	50.3	(B)	53.9
45 to 49 years old	69.2	65.9	70.4	67.2	62.7	55.0	(B)	51.0
50 to 54 years old	72.0	63.0	72.6	65.4	72.7	50.2	(B)	62.2
REDIVORCED AFTER REMARRIAGE								
20 to 24 years old	8.5	13.1	(NA)	(NA)	(NA)	(NA)	(NA)	(NA)
25 to 29 years old	15.6	17.8	(NA)	(NA)	(NA)	(NA)	(NA)	(NA)
30 to 34 years old	19.1	22.7	(NA)	(NA)	(NA)	(NA)	(NA)	(NA)
35 to 39 years old	24.7	28.5	(NA)	(NA)	(NA)	(NA)	(NA)	(NA)
40 to 44 years old	28.4	30.6	(NA)	(NA)	(NA)	(NA)	(NA)	(NA)
45 to 49 years old	25.1	36.4	(NA)	(NA)	(NA)	(NA)	(NA)	(NA)
50 to 54 years old	29.0	34.5	(NA)	(NA)	(NA)	(NA)	(NA)	(NA)

B Base is less than 75,000.   NA Not available.   [1] Persons of Hispanic origin may be of any race.
Source: U.S. Bureau of the Census, *Current Population Reports,* P23-180.

No. 153. Marriages and Divorces—Number and Rate, by State: 1980 to 1994

[By place of occurrence]

DIVISION AND STATE	MARRIAGES [1] Number (1,000)			Rate per 1,000 population [2]			DIVORCES [3] Number (1,000)			Rate per 1,000 population [2]		
	1980	1985	1994	1980	1985	1994	1980	1985	1994	1980	1985	1994
U.S.	2,390.3	2,412.6	[4]2,362.0	10.6	10.1	9.1	1,189.0	[5]1,190.0	1,191.0	5.2	[5]5.0	4.6
New England	106.3	114.3	105.1	8.6	9.0	7.9	49.0	49.9	39.7	4.0	3.9	3.0
Maine	12.0	12.2	10.9	10.7	10.5	8.8	6.2	6.1	5.4	5.5	5.2	4.4
New Hampshire	9.3	11.4	9.8	10.0	11.4	8.6	5.3	4.9	5.0	5.7	4.9	4.4
Vermont	5.2	5.5	5.8	10.2	10.4	10.1	2.6	2.4	2.3	5.1	4.4	4.0
Massachusetts	46.3	49.8	49.7	8.1	8.6	8.2	17.9	21.6	14.5	3.1	3.7	2.4
Rhode Island	7.5	8.0	7.0	7.9	8.3	7.0	3.6	3.7	3.2	3.8	3.8	3.2
Connecticut	26.0	27.3	21.9	8.4	8.6	6.7	13.5	11.2	9.1	4.3	3.5	2.8
Middle Atlantic	294.0	314.3	277.9	8.0	8.5	7.3	124.7	137.1	123.1	3.4	3.7	3.2
New York	144.5	164.0	149.6	8.2	9.2	8.2	62.0	67.6	59.2	3.5	3.8	3.3
New Jersey	55.8	61.2	52.8	7.6	8.1	6.7	27.8	29.3	23.9	3.8	3.9	3.0
Pennsylvania	93.7	89.1	75.5	7.9	7.5	6.3	34.9	40.2	40.0	2.9	3.4	3.3
East North Central	395.5	[6]362.2	342.9	9.5	[6]8.7	7.9	212.4	[6]192.6	[7]149.6	5.1	[6]4.6	4.0
Ohio	99.8	[6]94.4	92.8	9.2	[6]8.8	8.4	58.8	[6]53.0	50.0	5.4	[6]4.9	4.5
Indiana	57.9	51.1	50.3	10.5	9.3	8.7	40.0	[8]35.3	(NA)	7.3	[8]6.4	(NA)
Illinois	109.8	97.7	92.7	9.6	8.5	7.9	51.0	48.9	43.4	4.5	4.2	3.7
Michigan	86.9	79.0	70.8	9.4	8.7	7.5	45.0	38.8	38.7	4.9	4.3	4.1
Wisconsin	41.1	40.0	36.4	8.7	8.4	7.2	17.5	16.6	17.5	3.7	3.5	3.4
West North Central	173.7	158.3	145.0	10.1	9.0	8.0	79.6	74.3	77.3	4.6	4.2	4.2
Minnesota	37.6	35.1	32.5	9.2	8.4	7.1	15.4	14.8	16.2	3.8	3.5	3.6
Iowa	27.5	24.6	22.7	9.4	8.5	8.0	11.9	10.5	10.9	4.1	3.7	3.9
Missouri	54.6	49.5	44.2	11.1	9.8	8.4	27.6	25.0	26.3	5.6	5.0	5.0
North Dakota	6.1	5.4	4.8	9.3	7.9	7.5	2.1	2.3	2.2	3.3	3.4	3.4
South Dakota	8.8	7.8	7.4	12.7	11.0	10.3	2.8	2.6	3.0	4.1	3.6	4.2
Nebraska	14.2	12.7	12.3	9.1	7.9	7.6	6.4	6.4	6.5	4.1	4.0	4.0
Kansas	24.8	23.3	20.9	10.5	9.5	8.2	13.4	12.8	12.1	5.7	5.2	4.7
South Atlantic	413.1	438.8	442.5	11.2	10.9	9.5	206.3	210.5	233.8	5.6	5.2	5.0
Delaware	4.4	5.4	5.0	7.5	8.6	7.2	2.3	3.0	3.4	3.9	4.8	4.8
Maryland	46.3	46.1	43.4	11.0	10.5	8.7	17.5	16.2	17.4	4.1	3.7	3.5
Dist. of Columbia	5.2	5.0	3.6	8.1	8.1	6.3	4.7	2.7	2.2	7.3	4.3	3.9
Virginia	60.2	66.5	69.3	11.3	11.7	10.6	23.6	24.1	30.0	4.4	4.2	4.6
West Virginia	17.4	14.6	10.9	8.9	7.5	6.0	10.3	9.9	9.2	5.3	5.1	5.0
North Carolina	46.7	50.5	51.9	7.9	8.1	7.3	28.1	30.2	36.3	4.8	4.8	5.1
South Carolina	53.9	52.8	50.9	17.3	15.8	13.9	13.6	13.5	15.3	4.4	4.0	4.2
Georgia	70.6	72.3	62.9	12.9	12.1	8.9	34.7	33.4	37.0	6.4	5.6	5.2
Florida	108.3	125.5	144.5	11.1	11.0	10.4	71.6	77.5	83.0	7.3	6.8	5.9
East South Central	[6]168.8	171.8	189.9	11.5	11.4	12.0	87.5	[6]86.2	97.7	6.0	[6]5.7	6.1
Kentucky	[6]32.7	46.0	47.3	8.9	12.3	12.4	16.7	18.3	22.2	4.6	4.9	5.8
Tennessee	59.2	55.0	80.0	12.9	11.5	15.5	30.2	29.9	34.2	6.6	6.3	6.6
Alabama	49.0	46.1	40.2	12.6	11.5	9.5	26.7	25.0	26.1	6.9	6.2	6.2
Mississippi	27.9	24.8	22.4	11.1	9.5	8.4	13.8	[10]13.0	15.2	5.5	[10]5.0	5.7
West South Central	298.2	308.6	299.4	12.6	11.6	10.5	155.0	160.9	138.4	6.5	(NA)	[7]5.7
Arkansas	26.5	31.7	38.2	11.6	13.4	15.6	15.9	[6]16.5	17.4	6.9	[6]7.0	7.1
Louisiana	43.5	39.4	41.8	10.3	8.8	9.7	18.1	17.6	-	4.3	(NA)	(NA)
Oklahoma	46.5	35.9	29.3	15.4	10.9	9.0	24.2	26.4	21.9	8.0	8.0	6.7
Texas	181.8	201.6	190.3	12.8	12.3	10.4	96.8	100.4	99.1	6.8	6.1	5.4
Mountain	241.7	233.7	270.8	21.3	18.3	17.8	86.1	89.9	88.8	7.6	7.0	5.8
Montana	8.3	7.2	6.9	10.6	8.7	8.1	4.9	4.3	4.2	6.3	5.2	4.9
Idaho	13.4	12.3	15.2	14.2	12.2	13.4	6.6	6.2	7.1	7.0	6.2	6.2
Wyoming	6.9	5.4	4.8	14.6	10.6	10.1	4.0	3.8	3.1	8.5	7.5	6.5
Colorado	34.9	33.6	34.4	12.1	10.4	9.4	18.6	19.2	18.8	6.4	5.9	5.1
New Mexico	16.6	[9]15.5	12.2	12.8	[9]10.7	7.4	10.4	[10]13.2	9.9	8.0	[10]9.1	6.0
Arizona	30.2	35.7	36.7	11.1	11.2	9.0	19.9	21.2	23.7	7.3	6.6	5.8
Utah	17.0	17.5	20.3	11.6	10.6	10.7	7.8	8.8	9.0	5.3	5.3	4.7
Nevada	114.3	106.5	140.3	142.8	113.7	96.3	13.8	13.3	13.1	17.3	14.2	9.0
Pacific	298.8	310.6	295.1	9.4	8.9	7.1	187.9	188.5	54.6	5.9	5.4	5.3
Washington	47.7	43.8	43.6	11.6	9.9	8.2	28.6	26.3	30.0	6.9	6.0	5.6
Oregon	23.0	22.4	25.2	8.7	8.3	8.2	17.8	15.7	16.3	6.7	5.9	5.3
California [11]	210.9	222.8	202.8	8.9	8.5	6.5	133.5	[12]137.5	-	5.6	[12]5.2	(NA)
Alaska	5.4	6.2	5.6	13.3	11.8	9.2	3.5	4.0	3.4	8.8	7.7	5.5
Hawaii	11.9	15.4	17.9	12.3	14.7	15.2	4.4	4.9	5.0	4.6	4.6	4.2

- Represents or rounds to zero. NA Not available. [1] Data are counts of marriages performed, except as noted. [2] Based on total population residing in area; population enumerated as of April 1 for 1980; estimated as of July 1 for all other years. [3] Includes annulments. [4] Estimate for U.S. is based on monthly reports adjusted for observed differences from final monthly figures. State figures are not adjusted in this manner. [5] Estimated. [6] Data are incomplete. [7] Excludes figures for States shown below as not available. [8] Includes divorce petitions filed for some counties. [9] Premarital health forms issued. [10] Divorce petitions filed. [11] Marriage data include nonlicensed marriages registered. [12] Data include legal separations.

Source: U.S. National Center for Health Statistics, *Vital Statistics of the United States*, annual; and *Monthly Vital Statistics Reports*.

Figure 3.1
**Personal Health Care Expenditures per Capita:
1970 to 1994**

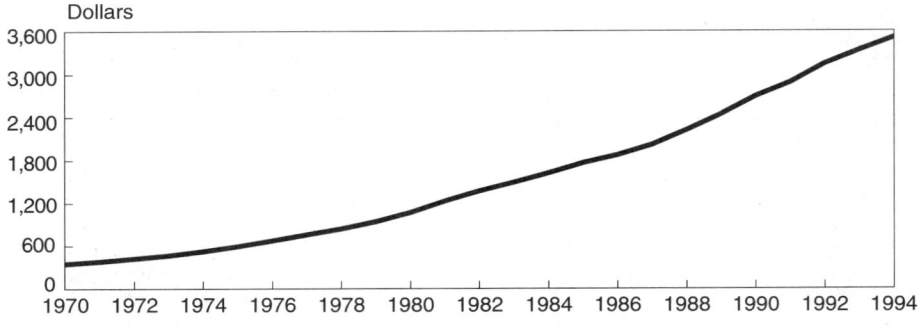

Source: Charts prepared by U.S. Bureau of the Census.
For data, see table 154.

Figure 3.2
**Consumer Price Indexes—
Medical Services: 1970 to 1995**

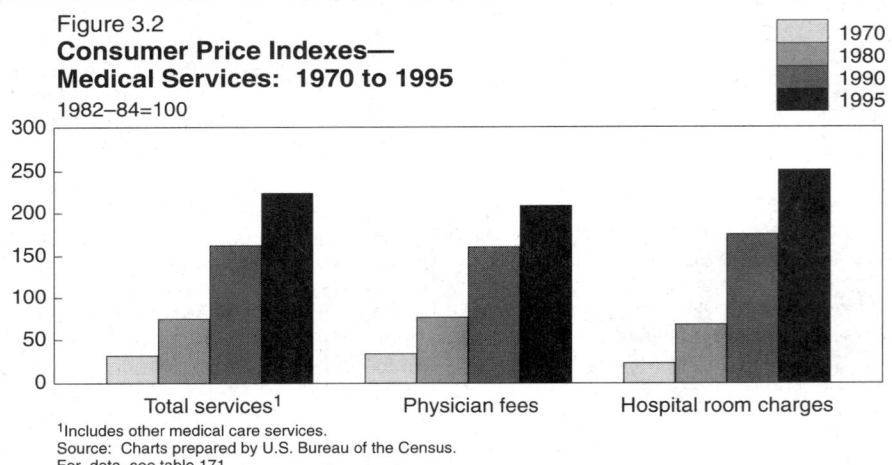

1Includes other medical care services.
Source: Charts prepared by U.S. Bureau of the Census.
For data, see table 171.

Figure 3.3
**Per Capita Food Consumption,
by Selected Products: 1970 to 1994**

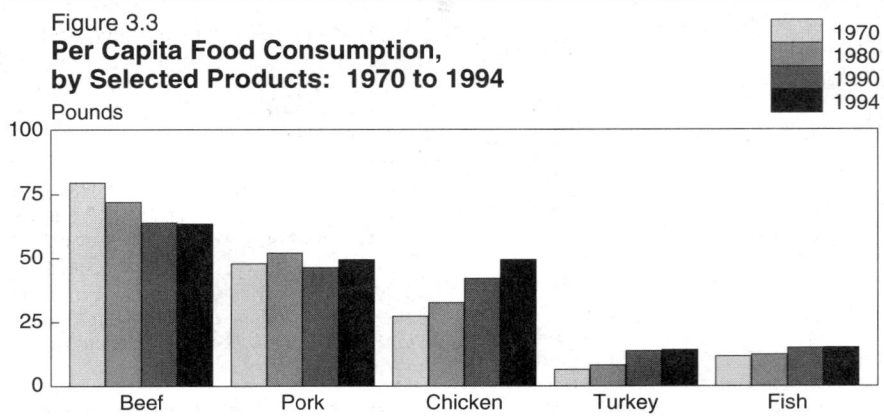

Source: Charts prepared by U.S. Bureau of the Census.
For data, see table 226.

Health and Nutrition

This section presents statistics on health expenditures and insurance coverage, including Medicare and Medicaid, medical personnel, hospitals, nursing homes and other care facilities, incidence of acute and prevalence of chronic conditions, nutritional intake of the population, and food consumption. Summary statistics showing recent trends on health care and discussions of selected health issues are published annually by the U.S. National Center for Health Statistics (NCHS) in *Health, United States*. Data on national health expenditures, medical costs, and insurance coverage are compiled by the U.S. Health Care Financing Administration (HCFA) and appear in the quarterly *Health Care Financing Review* and in the *Annual Medicare Program Statistics* series. Statistics on health insurance are also collected by NCHS and are published in series 10 of *Vital and Health Statistics*. The Census Bureau also publishes data on insurance coverage in *Current Population Reports*, series P70. Statistics on health facilities are collected by NCHS and are published in series 14 of *Vital and Health Statistics*. Statistics on hospitals are published annually by the American Hospital Association, Chicago, IL, in *Hospital STAT*. Primary sources for data on nutrition are the quarterly *National Food Review* and the annual *Food Consumption, Prices, and Expenditures*, both issued by the U.S. Department of Agriculture. NCHS also conducts periodic surveys of nutrient levels in the population, including estimates of food and nutrient intake, overweight and obesity, hypercholesterolemia, hypertension, and clinical signs of malnutrition.

National health expenditures—HCFA compiles estimates of national health expenditures (NHE) to measure spending for health care in the United States. With the publication of the 1988 estimates, major revisions to the NHE back to 1960 have been incorporated into the accounts.
The NHE accounts are structured to show spending by type of expenditure (i.e., hospital care, physician care, dental care, and other professional care; home health; drugs and other medical nondurables; vision products and other medical durables; nursing home care and other

In Brief	
In 1994:	
40 million with no health insurance.	
Hospital surgeries— percent outpatient:	
1980	16%
1994	57%
Per capita consumption of chicken:	
1980	33 pounds
1994	50 pounds

personal health expenditures; plus nonpersonal health expenditures for such items as public health, research, construction of medical facilities, and administration) and by source of funding (e.g., private health insurance, out-of-pocket payments, and a range of public programs including Medicare, Medicaid, and those operated by the Department of Veterans Affairs (VA)).

In all cases except private insurance (HCFA conducts its own survey of part of the health insurance industry), data used to estimate health expenditures come from existing sources which are tabulated for other purposes. The type of expenditure estimates rely upon statistics produced by such groups as the American Hospital Association, the Internal Revenue Service, the Department of Commerce, and the Department of Health and Human Services (HHS). Source of funding estimates are constructed using administrative and statistical records from the Medicare and Medicaid programs, the Department of Defense and VA medical programs, the Social Security Administration, Census Bureau's *Governmental Finances*, State and local governments, other HHS agencies, and other nongovernment sources. Detailed descriptions of sources and methods, along with the most recent analysis of health care expenditure estimates, are published in the *Health Care Financing Review's* annual article on national health expenditures.

Medicare and Medicaid—Since July 1966, the Federal Medicare program has provided two coordinated plans for nearly all people age 65 and over: (1) A hospital insurance plan which covers hospital and related services and (2) a voluntary supplementary medical insurance plan, financed partially by monthly premiums paid by participants, which partly covers physicians' and related medical services. Such insurance also applies, since July 1973, to disabled beneficiaries of any age after 24 months of entitlement to cash benefits under the social security or railroad retirement programs and to persons with end stage renal disease.

Under Medicaid, all States offer basic health services to certain very poor people: Individuals who are pregnant, aged, disabled or blind, and families with dependent children. Medicaid eligibility is automatic for almost all cash welfare recipients in these States. Thirty-nine States also extend Medicaid to certain other persons who qualify, except for incomes above regular eligibility levels; those persons include those who have medical expenses which, when subtracted from their income, spend down to a State "medically needy" level or those who meet the higher "medically needy" income restrictions. Within Federal guidelines, each State determines its own Medicaid eligibility criteria and the health services to be provided under Medicaid. The cost of providing Medicaid services is jointly shared by the Federal Government and the States.

Health resources—Hospital statistics based on data from the American Hospital Association's yearly survey are published annually in *Hospital Statistics,* and cover all hospitals accepted for registration by the Association. To be accepted for registration, a hospital must meet certain requirements relating to number of beds, construction, equipment, medical and nursing staff, patient care, clinical records, surgical and obstetrical facilities, diagnostic and treatment facilities, laboratory services, etc. Data obtained from NCHS cover all U.S. hospitals which meet certain criteria for inclusion. The criteria are published in *Vital and Health Statistics* reports, series 13. NCHS defines a hospital as a non-Federal short-term general or special facility with six or more inpatient beds with an average stay of less than 60 days.

Statistics on the demographic characteristics of persons employed in the health occupations are compiled by the U.S. Bureau of Labor Statistics and reported in *Employment and Earnings* (monthly) (see table 637, section 13). Data based on surveys of health personnel and utilization of health facilities providing long-term care, ambulatory care, and hospital care are presented in NCHS series 13 and series 14, *Data on Health Resources Utilization* and *Data on Health Resources: Manpower and Facilities.* Statistics on patient visits to health care providers, as reported in health interviews, appear in NCHS series 10, *National Health Interview Survey Data.*

The HCFA's *Health Care Financing Review* and *Health Care Financing Program Statistics* present data for hospitals and nursing homes as well as extended care facilities and home health agencies. These data are based on records of the Medicare program and differ from those of other sources because they are limited to facilities meeting Federal eligibility standards for participation in Medicare.

Data on patients in hospitals for the mentally ill and on mental health facilities are collected by the National Institute of Mental Health (NIMH) and appear in *Mental Health, U.S.,* the *Mental Health Statistics* reports, (series CN), and the Mental Health Statistical Note series.

Disability and illness—General health statistics, including morbidity, disability, injuries, preventive care, and findings from physiological testing are collected by NCHS in its National Health Interview Survey and its National Health and Nutrition Examination Surveys and appear in *Vital and Health Statistics,* series 10 and 11, respectively. The Department of Labor compiles statistics on industrial injuries (see section 13). Annual incidence data on notifiable diseases are compiled by the Public Health Service (PHS) at its Centers for Disease Control and Prevention in Atlanta, Georgia, and are published as a supplement to its *Morbidity and Mortality Weekly Report.* The list of diseases is revised annually and includes those which, by mutual agreement of the States and PHS, are communicable diseases of national importance.

Nutrition—Statistics on annual per capita consumption of food and its nutrient value are estimated by the U.S. Department of Agriculture and published quarterly in *National Food Review.* Historical data can be found in *Food Consumption, Prices, and Expenditures,* issued annually.

Statistics on food insufficiency and food and nutrient intake are collected by NCHS to estimate the nation's population diet. NCHS also collects physical examination data to assess the population's nutritional status, including growth, overweight/obesity, nutritional deficiencies, and prevalence of nutrition-related conditions, such as hypertension, hypercholesterolemia, and diabetes.

Statistical reliability—For discussion of statistical collection, estimation, and sampling procedures and measures of reliability applicable to data from NCHS and HCFA, see Appendix III.

Historical statistics—Tabular headnotes provide cross-references, where applicable, to *Historical Statistics of the United States, Colonial Times to 1970.* See Appendix IV.

No. 154. National Health Expenditures: 1960 to 1994

[Includes Puerto Rico and outlying areas]

YEAR	TOTAL[1]			HEALTH SERVICES AND SUPPLIES						
				Private				Public		
					Out-of-pocket payments				Medical payments	
	Total (bil.dol.)	Per capita (dol.)	Percent of GDP[2]	Total[3] (bil.dol.)	Total (bil.dol.)	Percent of total private	Insurance premiums[4] (bil.dol.)	Total (bil.dol.)	Medicare (bil. dol.)	Public assistance (bil. dol.)
1960	26.9	141	5.1	19.5	13.1	67.2	5.9	5.7	(X)	0.5
1965	41.1	202	5.7	29.4	18.5	62.9	10.0	8.3	(X)	1.7
1970	73.2	341	7.1	43.0	24.9	57.9	16.3	24.9	7.7	6.3
1971	81.0	373	7.2	46.9	26.4	56.3	18.6	28.1	8.5	7.7
1972	90.9	415	7.4	52.5	29.0	55.2	21.3	31.8	9.4	8.9
1973	100.8	456	7.3	58.2	32.0	55.0	23.9	35.9	10.8	10.2
1974	114.3	513	7.6	64.3	34.8	54.1	26.8	42.7	13.5	11.9
1975	130.7	582	8.0	72.3	38.1	52.7	31.3	50.1	16.4	14.5
1976	149.9	662	8.2	83.8	41.9	50.0	37.9	56.7	19.8	16.4
1977	170.4	746	8.4	96.6	46.4	48.0	45.9	64.5	23.0	18.8
1978	190.6	827	8.3	107.4	49.7	46.3	52.5	73.3	26.8	20.9
1979	215.2	924	8.4	121.2	54.3	44.8	60.9	83.7	31.0	24.0
1980	247.2	1,052	8.9	138.0	60.3	43.7	69.7	97.6	37.5	28.0
1981	286.9	1,208	9.2	160.3	68.5	42.7	82.1	113.4	44.9	32.6
1982	322.9	1,346	10.0	181.8	75.5	41.5	95.3	126.4	52.5	34.6
1983	355.2	1,467	10.1	200.3	82.3	41.1	106.1	138.9	59.8	38.0
1984	389.7	1,594	10.0	222.4	90.8	40.8	118.8	150.9	66.5	41.1
1985	428.2	1,735	10.2	247.4	100.6	40.7	132.3	164.4	72.2	44.4
1986	460.9	1,849	10.4	264.4	108.0	40.8	140.1	179.7	76.9	49.0
1987	500.1	1,987	10.7	285.7	116.0	40.6	152.1	196.1	82.6	54.0
1988	559.6	2,201	11.1	324.5	129.2	39.8	175.1	213.9	90.4	58.9
1989	622.0	2,422	11.4	360.8	136.2	37.7	203.8	239.0	102.5	66.4
1990	697.5	2,688	12.1	402.9	148.4	36.8	232.4	270.0	112.1	80.4
1991	761.3	2,902	12.9	430.9	155.1	36.0	251.9	305.5	123.0	99.2
1992	833.6	3,144	13.3	465.9	164.4	35.3	276.6	340.1	138.7	112.4
1993	892.3	3,331	13.6	493.1	169.4	34.4	296.5	370.0	151.7	124.4
1994	949.4	3,510	13.7	517.1	174.9	33.8	313.3	402.2	169.2	134.8

X Not applicable. [1] Includes medical research and medical facilities construction. [2] GDP=Gross domestic product; see table 687. [3] Includes other sources of funds not shown separately. [4] See footnote 2, table 155.

Source: U. S. Health Care Financing Administration, *Health Care Financing Review,* spring 1996.

No. 155. National Health Expenditures, by Type: 1980 to 1994

[In millions of dollars, except percent. Includes Puerto Rico and outlying areas. See also *Historical Statistics, Colonial Times to 1970*, series B 248-261]

TYPE OF EXPENDITURE	1980	1985	1989	1990	1991	1992	1993	1994
Total	**247,245**	**428,204**	**622,027**	**697,453**	**761,258**	**833,559**	**892,267**	**949,419**
Annual percent change [1]	14.9	9.9	11.2	12.1	9.1	9.5	7.0	6.4
Private expenditures	**142,463**	**253,903**	**369,844**	**413,145**	**440,978**	**477,024**	**505,086**	**528,584**
Health services and supplies	138,010	247,403	360,792	402,897	430,854	465,898	493,052	517,056
Out-of-pocket payments	60,254	100,595	136,186	148,390	155,098	164,382	169,376	174,879
Insurance premiums [2]	69,728	132,254	203,761	232,436	251,851	276,596	296,469	313,268
Other	8,028	14,554	20,846	22,071	23,905	24,920	27,207	28,909
Medical research	292	538	882	960	1,090	1,183	1,215	1,276
Medical facilities construction	4,161	5,962	8,170	9,288	9,034	9,942	10,819	10,252
Public expenditures	**104,782**	**174,301**	**252,183**	**284,309**	**320,279**	**356,535**	**387,181**	**420,835**
Percent Federal of public	68.7	70.7	69.3	68.9	70.1	71.5	71.9	72.1
Health services and supplies	97,599	164,430	239,012	270,033	305,469	340,100	370,036	402,163
Medicare [3]	37,519	72,186	102,484	112,091	122,986	138,723	151,717	169,246
Public assistance medical payments [4]	28,033	44,439	66,388	80,395	99,235	112,396	124,408	134,765
Temporary disability insurance [5]	52	51	64	62	66	70	54	53
Workers' compensation (medical) [5]	5,141	7,971	14,298	16,067	17,163	18,983	18,910	18,903
Defense Dept. hospital, medical	4,350	7,498	10,319	11,579	12,849	12,886	13,406	13,156
Maternal, child health programs	892	1,262	1,795	1,892	2,014	2,119	2,194	2,286
Public health activities	6,732	11,618	18,060	19,613	21,408	23,417	25,675	28,849
Veterans' hospital, medical care	5,934	8,713	10,640	11,424	12,366	13,205	14,267	15,140
Medical vocational rehabilitation	298	401	523	555	595	635	619	705
State and local hospitals [6]	5,589	7,030	10,583	11,346	11,030	11,134	11,841	11,784
Other [7]	3,059	3,263	3,859	5,009	5,758	6,531	6,944	7,277
Medical research	5,169	7,302	10,377	11,254	11,827	12,995	13,278	14,650
Medical facilities construction	2,014	2,569	2,793	3,022	2,983	3,440	3,866	4,021

[1] Change from immediate prior year. For explanation of average annual percent change, see Guide to Tabular Presentation. [2] Covers insurance benefits and amount retained by insurance companies for expenses, additions to reserves, and profits (net cost of insurance). [3] Represents expenditures for benefits and administrative cost from Federal hospital and medical insurance trust funds under old-age, survivors, disability, and health insurance programs; see text, section 12. [4] Payments made directly to suppliers of medical care (primarily Medicaid). [5] Includes medical benefits paid under public law by private insurance carriers and self-insurers. [6] Expenditures not offset by other revenues. [7] Covers expenditures for Alcohol, Drug Abuse, and Mental Health Administration; Indian Health Service; school health and other programs.

Source: U.S. Health Care Financing Administration, *Health Care Financing Review*, spring 1996.

No. 156. National Health Expenditures, by Object: 1980 to 1994

[In billions of dollars. Includes Puerto Rico and outlying areas. See also *Historical Statistics, Colonial Times to 1970*, series B 221-235]

OBJECT OF EXPENDITURE	1980	1985	1989	1990	1991	1992	1993	1994
Total	**247.2**	**428.2**	**622.0**	**697.5**	**761.3**	**833.6**	**892.3**	**949.4**
Spent by—								
Consumers	130.0	232.8	339.9	380.8	406.9	441.0	465.8	488.1
Government	104.8	174.3	252.2	284.3	320.3	356.5	387.2	420.8
Other [1]	12.5	21.1	29.9	32.3	34.0	36.0	39.2	40.4
Spent for—								
Health services and supplies	235.6	411.8	599.8	672.9	736.3	806.0	863.1	919.2
Personal health care expenses	217.0	376.4	550.1	614.7	676.2	739.8	786.5	831.7
Hospital care	102.7	168.3	231.6	256.4	282.3	305.3	324.2	338.5
Physician services	45.2	83.6	131.3	146.3	158.6	174.7	181.1	189.4
Dental services	13.3	21.7	29.5	31.6	33.3	37.0	39.2	42.2
Other professional services [2]	6.4	16.6	29.8	34.7	38.3	42.1	46.3	49.6
Home health care	2.4	5.6	10.2	13.1	16.1	19.6	23.0	26.2
Drugs/other medical nondurables [5]	21.6	37.1	53.7	59.9	65.6	71.3	75.2	78.6
Vision products/other med. durables [3]	3.8	6.7	9.6	10.5	11.2	11.9	12.6	13.1
Nursing home care	17.6	30.7	44.9	50.9	57.2	62.3	67.0	72.3
Other health services	4.0	6.1	9.5	11.2	13.6	15.6	17.8	21.8
Net cost of insurance and admin. [4]	11.8	23.8	31.6	38.6	38.7	42.8	51.0	58.7
Government public health activities	6.7	11.6	18.1	19.6	21.4	23.4	25.7	28.8
Medical research	5.5	7.8	11.3	12.2	12.9	14.2	14.5	15.9
Medical facilities construction	6.2	8.5	11.0	12.3	12.0	13.4	14.7	14.3

[1] Includes nonpatient revenues, privately funded construction, and industrial input. [2] Includes services of registered and practical nurses in private duty, podiatrists, optometrists, physical therapists, clinical psychologists, chiropractors, naturopaths, and Christian Science practitioners. [3] Includes expenditures for eyeglasses, hearing aids, orthopedic appliances, artificial limbs, crutches, wheelchairs, etc. [4] Includes administrative expenses of federally financed health programs.

Source: U.S. Health Care Financing Administration, *Health Care Financing Review*, spring 1996.

No. 157. Per Capita Personal Health Care Expenditures, by State of Residence: 1991

[In dollars. For calendar year. Based on resident population estimated as of July 1]

STATE OF RESIDENCE	Total	Hospital services	Physi-cian serv-ices [1]	Home health care [2]	Nursing home care [2]	Other profes-sional serv-ices [3]	Dental services	Medical durables	Drugs and other non-durables	Other personal health care
United States . . .	2,648	1,109	596	66	227	160	126	45	266	54
Alabama.	2,554	1,111	613	91	148	130	94	37	272	60
Alaska	2,431	1,121	493	5	88	174	170	40	249	93
Arizona.	2,382	927	654	48	122	159	118	51	256	48
Arkansas	2,347	1,023	550	41	207	115	90	27	257	37
California	2,653	996	800	37	117	186	164	45	264	44
Colorado.	2,447	980	583	37	165	173	143	55	231	79
Connecticut.	3,298	1,208	706	92	479	185	186	54	282	107
Delaware	2,852	1,192	620	57	284	176	124	46	279	73
District of Columbia .	4,693	2,492	810	62	351	327	138	53	284	176
Florida	2,897	1,129	726	121	193	201	127	56	295	49
Georgia	2,508	1,090	583	68	133	147	110	43	277	59
Hawaii	2,592	1,066	605	16	148	151	156	47	328	75
Idaho	2,037	849	473	28	152	111	136	35	215	39
Illinois	2,698	1,237	569	50	235	146	120	43	257	41
Indiana.	2,470	1,051	509	34	295	146	98	45	255	37
Iowa	2,486	1,095	488	35	285	142	112	52	242	35
Kansas.	2,542	1,085	561	37	254	157	115	39	251	42
Kentucky	2,419	1,069	481	67	201	144	84	37	287	49
Louisiana	2,589	1,210	534	45	219	136	86	38	271	50
Maine.	2,453	1,015	449	60	316	144	114	37	248	71
Maryland	2,793	1,154	674	51	201	151	137	49	322	53
Massachusetts.	3,333	1,414	625	102	425	198	148	40	301	80
Michigan.	2,607	1,133	557	58	186	155	143	45	285	44
Minnesota.	2,580	926	597	66	361	161	122	47	232	69
Mississippi	2,162	1,017	431	87	142	98	70	25	250	41
Missouri	2,511	1,176	472	47	235	146	97	45	249	45
Montana.	2,274	984	434	45	203	158	111	42	227	71
Nebraska	2,332	1,045	444	33	257	110	104	47	240	52
Nevada	2,342	882	681	49	102	161	125	43	262	38
New Hampshire	2,505	1,012	528	48	206	190	134	37	261	87
New Jersey.	2,900	1,200	644	69	241	191	158	46	287	63
New Mexico	2,185	1,052	426	27	121	136	92	42	228	62
New York	3,255	1,372	571	183	444	165	137	57	259	68
North Carolina	2,245	973	468	54	186	122	99	37	264	44
North Dakota.	2,514	1,068	526	18	350	114	96	41	231	69
Ohio	2,668	1,133	594	45	294	145	110	44	268	36
Oklahoma.	2,295	999	492	38	215	123	98	41	248	42
Oregon.	2,267	820	560	29	215	141	166	29	229	80
Pennsylvania.	2,941	1,332	581	52	299	191	124	42	270	52
Rhode Island.	2,937	1,195	534	68	385	193	137	37	288	101
South Carolina.	2,238	1,071	436	37	150	109	96	30	245	64
South Dakota	2,393	1,123	430	11	269	149	96	39	209	66
Tennessee	2,579	1,130	526	113	174	174	96	35	291	40
Texas.	2,345	999	525	56	152	154	95	46	258	60
Utah	1,904	783	431	32	133	95	121	54	211	44
Vermont	2,367	921	444	61	247	171	125	41	256	101
Virginia.	2,363	1,016	550	42	138	124	117	43	282	49
Washington.	2,508	902	625	52	207	177	186	43	254	63
West Virginia	2,539	1,185	519	53	178	138	79	43	290	56
Wisconsin.	2,568	1,001	575	57	310	145	135	46	234	65
Wyoming	2,229	1,042	425	26	143	137	115	40	219	82

[1] Includes independent laboratory services. [2] Services provided by free-standing facilities. [3] Includes expenditures for end stage renal disease in free-standing facilities.

Source: U.S. Health Care Financing Administration, Office of the Actuary. Estimates prepared by the Office of National Health Statistics.

No. 158. Health Services and Supplies—Per Capita Consumer Expenditures, by Object: 1980 to 1994

[In dollars, except percent. Based on Social Security Administration estimates of total U.S. population as of July 1, including Armed Forces and Federal employees abroad and civilian population of outlying areas. Excludes research and construction. See also *Historical Statistics, Colonial Times to 1970*, series B 222-232]

OBJECT OF EXPENDITURE	1980	1985	1988	1989	1990	1991	1992	1993	1994
Total, national	**1,002**	**1,668**	**2,118**	**2,336**	**2,593**	**2,807**	**3,040**	**3,222**	**3,398**
Annual percent change [1]	13.9	9.3	10.6	10.3	11.0	8.3	8.3	6.0	5.5
Hospital care	437	682	832	902	988	1,076	1,151	1,210	1,251
Physicians' services	192	339	467	511	564	605	659	676	700
Dentists' services	57	88	108	115	122	127	140	146	156
Other professional services [2]	27	67	105	116	134	146	159	173	183
Home health care	10	23	33	40	51	61	74	86	97
Drugs and other medical nondurables [2]	92	150	193	209	231	250	269	281	290
Vision products and other medical durables [2]	16	27	35	37	40	43	45	47	49
Nursing home care	75	124	156	175	196	218	235	250	267
Other health services	17	25	34	37	43	52	59	67	81
Net cost of insurance and administration [2]	50	96	93	123	149	148	161	190	217
Government public health activities	29	47	61	70	76	82	88	96	107
Total, private consumer [3]	**553**	**943**	**1,197**	**1,324**	**1,467**	**1,551**	**1,663**	**1,739**	**1,805**
Hospital care	178	274	337	370	402	425	439	459	464
Physicians' services	135	234	318	346	380	408	450	457	464
Dentists' services	54	85	105	112	118	123	134	139	149
Other professional services [2]	19	50	79	86	98	105	114	122	128
Home health care	4	8	16	19	23	26	30	32	35
Drugs and other medical nondurables [2]	85	138	175	188	206	221	238	246	254
Vision products and other medical durables [2]	14	21	27	28	30	30	31	31	32
Nursing home care	32	58	75	80	93	97	100	102	107
Net cost of insurance	33	75	66	94	118	117	128	150	172

[1] Change from immediate prior year. [2] See footnotes for corresponding objects in table 156. [3] Represents out-of-pocket payments and private health insurance.

Source: U.S. Health Care Financing Administration, *Health Care Financing Review*, spring 1996.

No. 159. Government Expenditures for Health Services and Supplies: 1994

[In millions of dollars. Includes Puerto Rico and outlying areas. Excludes medical research and construction]

TYPE OF SERVICE	Total [1]	Federal	State and local	Medi- care [2] (OASDHI)	Public assis- tance [3]	OTHER HEALTH SERVICES		
						Veterans	Defense Dept. [4]	Workers' compensa- tion [5]
Total [1]	402,163	290,321	111,843	169,246	134,765	15,140	13,156	18,903
Hospital care	199,568	162,737	36,831	101,645	52,734	12,430	10,292	8,447
Physician services	60,870	48,597	12,273	38,102	13,747	141	1,640	6,437
Nursing home care	41,845	26,956	14,890	5,923	34,383	1,539	-	-
Drugs and other medical nondurables	9,999	5,151	4,848	-	9,419	13	176	348
Administration	11,531	6,609	4,921	3,120	6,375	58	193	1,518
Public health activities	28,849	3,750	25,099	-	-	-	-	-

- Represents zero. [1] Includes other items not shown separately. [2] Covers hospital and medical insurance payments and administrative costs under old-age, survivors, disability, and health insurance program. [3] Covers Medicaid and other medical public assistance. Excludes funds paid into Medicare trust fund by States to cover premiums for public assistance recipients and medically indigent persons. [4] Includes care for retirees and military dependents. [5] Medical benefits.

Source: U.S. Health Care Financing Administration, *Health Care Financing Review*, spring 1996.

No. 160. Expenditures for Health Services and Supplies, by Type of Payer: 1980 to 1994

[In billions of dollars]

TYPE OF PAYER	1980	1985	1987	1988	1989	1990	1991	1992	1993	1994
Total expenditures	**235.6**	**411.8**	**481.8**	**536.3**	**599.8**	**672.9**	**736.3**	**806.0**	**863.1**	**919.2**
Private	158.4	282.2	330.3	371.5	411.0	450.8	481.9	520.1	544.2	577.3
Business	61.7	108.6	129.4	144.0	165.4	185.8	198.2	215.9	226.8	241.3
Share of private health insurance premiums	45.3	79.1	92.8	104.1	121.4	138.4	146.6	160.4	170.0	179.5
Households [1]	89.5	160.5	185.0	209.2	226.8	245.3	262.2	281.9	292.9	310.1
Share of private health insurance premiums	14.6	30.7	33.5	40.1	45.8	51.3	57.4	63.6	68.2	70.6
Out-of-pocket spending	60.3	100.6	116.0	129.2	136.2	148.4	155.1	164.4	169.4	174.9
Nonpatient revenues [2]	7.2	13.1	15.9	18.3	18.8	19.8	21.5	22.3	24.4	25.9
Public	77.3	129.6	151.5	166.8	188.9	222.1	254.4	285.9	318.9	342.0
Federal government	42.4	68.4	76.3	84.1	96.3	115.1	136.2	159.7	181.1	190.6
State/local government	34.8	61.2	76.2	82.7	82.5	107.0	118.2	126.2	137.8	151.3

[1] Includes other items not shown separately. [2] Includes philanthropy.

Source: U.S. Health Care Financing Administration, *Health Care Financing Review*, spring 1996.

No. 161. Personal Health Care—Third Party Payments and Private Consumer Expenditures: 1980 to 1994

[In billions of dollars, except percent. See headnote, table 162]

ITEM	1980	1985	1988	1989	1990	1991	1992	1993	1994
Personal health care expenditures.......	217.0	376.4	499.3	550.1	614.7	676.2	739.8	786.5	831.7
Third party payments, total	**156.8**	**275.8**	**370.1**	**413.9**	**466.3**	**521.1**	**575.4**	**617.1**	**656.8**
Percent of personal health care	72.2	73.3	74.1	75.2	75.9	77.1	77.8	78.5	79.0
Private insurance payments	62.0	113.8	158.2	179.5	201.8	221.2	242.7	256.4	266.8
Government expenditures...........	87.0	148.0	192.1	214.1	243.0	276.6	308.3	334.1	361.8
Other [1]	7.8	14.1	19.7	20.3	21.5	23.3	24.3	26.6	28.2
Private consumer expenditures [2]	**122.2**	**214.4**	**287.4**	**315.7**	**350.2**	**376.3**	**407.1**	**425.8**	**441.6**
Percent met by private insurance	50.7	53.1	55.1	56.9	57.6	58.8	59.6	60.2	60.4
Hospital care	46.8	75.8	96.8	105.8	115.0	123.2	128.5	136.2	138.9
Percent met by private insurance	87.2	87.0	87.9	89.8	90.1	89.9	90.9	91.9	92.2
Physicians' services	32.1	59.1	83.1	91.4	101.4	109.4	121.9	125.1	128.5
Percent met by private insurance	53.9	57.8	60.2	62.1	64.1	66.7	68.2	69.7	71.4

[1] Includes nonpatient revenues and industrial inplant health services. [2] Includes expenditures not shown separately. Represents out-of-pocket payments and private health insurance benefits. Excludes net cost of insurance.

Source: U.S. Health Care Financing Administration, *Health Care Financing Review,* spring 1996.

No. 162. Personal Health Care Expenditures, by Object and Source of Payment: 1994

[In millions of dollars, except as indicated. Includes Puerto Rico and outlying areas. Covers all expenditures for health services and supplies, except net cost of insurance and administration, government public health activities, and expenditures of philanthropic agencies for fund raising activities]

OBJECT OF PAYMENT	Total	Out of pocket payments	THIRD PARTY PAYMENTS				Private pay- ments [2]
			Total	Private health insurance	Govern- ment	Other [1]	
Total	**831,675**	**174,879**	**656,795**	**266,765**	**361,784**	**28,247**	**469,891**
Hospital care...................	338,511	9,799	328,712	115,708	199,568	13,436	138,943
Physicians' services	189,391	35,844	153,547	89,647	60,870	3,030	128,521
Dentists' services..............	42,185	20,479	21,706	19,785	1,756	166	40,429
Other professional services [3]	49,628	19,458	30,170	15,207	11,243	3,720	38,385
Home health care...............	26,158	6,101	20,056	3,394	13,170	3,493	12,988
Drugs/other medical nondurables [3]	78,577	48,606	29,971	19,972	9,999	-	68,579
Vision products/other med. durables [3]	13,134	7,747	5,387	850	4,537	-	8,597
Nursing home care..............	72,253	26,846	45,407	2,202	41,845	1,360	30,408
Other health services............	21,838	-	21,838	-	18,796	3,042	3,042

- Represents zero. [1] Includes nonpatient revenues and industrial plant. [2] Covers out-of-pocket payments, private health insurance, and other. [3] See footnotes for corresponding items on table 156.

Source: U.S. Health Care Financing Administration, *Health Care Financing Review,* spring 1996.

No. 163. Medicare Enrollees and Expenditures: 1970 to 1994

[In millions. Enrollment as of July 1. Includes Puerto Rico and outlying areas and enrollees in foreign countries and unknown place of residence]

ITEM	1970	1980	1985	1990	1991	1992	1993	1994
ENROLLEES								
Total	**20.5**	**28.5**	**31.1**	**34.2**	**34.9**	**35.6**	**36.3**	**36.9**
Hospital insurance	20.4	28.1	30.6	33.7	34.4	35.2	35.9	36.5
Supplementary medical insurance ..	19.6	27.4	30.0	32.6	33.2	33.9	34.6	35.2
EXPENDITURES								
Total	**7,493**	**36,802**	**72,294**	**110,984**	**121,447**	**135,845**	**150,370**	**164,862**
Hospital insurance [1]	5,281	25,557	48,414	66,997	72,570	85,015	94,391	104,545
Inpatient hospital.............	4,827	24,116	44,940	59,451	62,777	71,147	76,402	81,229
Skilled nursing facility.........	246	395	548	2,575	2,652	4,119	5,780	7,516
Home health agency	51	540	1,913	3,666	5,327	7,579	10,049	12,862
Hospice	-	-	43	358	561	846	1,059	1,486
Supplementary medical insurance [1] .	2,212	11,245	23,880	43,987	48,877	50,830	55,979	60,317
Physician	1,790	8,187	17,312	29,609	32,313	32,473	35,282	37,435
Outpatient hospital...........	114	1,897	4,319	8,482	9,783	10,894	11,539	13,497
Home health agency	34	234	38	74	65	79	112	144
Group practice prepayment	26	203	720	2,827	3,531	3,942	5,002	5,465
Independent laboratory........	11	114	558	1,476	1,644	1,876	2,044	2,077

- Represents zero. [1] Includes administrative expenses and, for hospital insurance, peer review activity, not shown separately.

Source: U.S. Health Care Financing Administration, Office of the Actuary.

No. 164. Medicare—Persons Served and Reimbursements: 1990 to 1994

[Persons served are enrollees who use covered services, incurred expenses greater than the applicable deductible amounts and for whom Medicare paid benefits. Reimbursements are amounts paid to providers for covered services. Excluded are retroactive adjustments resulting from end of fiscal year cost settlements and certain lump-sum interim payments. Also excluded are beneficiary (or third party payor) liabilities for applicable deductibles, coinsurance amounts, and charges for noncovered services. Includes data for enrollees living in outlying territories and foreign countries]

TYPE OF COVERAGE AND SERVICE	Unit	PERSONS 65 YEARS OLD AND OVER			DISABLED PERSONS [1]		
		1990	1993	1994	1990	1993	1994
Persons served, total [2]	1,000 . .	24,809	26,793	27,223	2,390	2,888	3,126
Hospital insurance [2]	1,000 . .	6,367	6,912	7,043	680	812	879
Inpatient hospital	1,000 . .	5,906	6,109	6,157	644	748	803
Skilled-nursing services	1,000 . .	615	875	1,026	23	33	42
Home health services	1,000 . .	1,818	2,669	2,938	122	199	237
Supplementary medical insurance [2]	1,000 . .	24,687	26,657	27,075	2,365	2,858	3,094
Physicians' and other medical							
services.	1,000 . .	24,193	26,169	26,476	2,249	2,744	2,986
Outpatient services	1,000 . .	14,055	16,496	16,989	1,496	1,936	2,097
Home health services	1,000 . .	38	37	37	-	-	-
Persons served per 1,000 enrollees, total [2].	Rate . .	802	825	830	734	751	755
Hospital insurance [2]	Rate. . .	209	216	217	209	211	213
Inpatient hospital	Rate. . .	194	191	190	198	195	194
Skilled-nursing services	Rate. . .	20	27	32	7	9	10
Home health services	Rate. . .	60	83	91	38	52	57
Supplementary medical insurance [2].	Rate. . .	832	856	861	804	825	831
Physicians' and other medical							
services.	Rate. . .	815	840	842	764	792	803
Outpatient services	Rate. . .	474	530	540	508	559	564
Home health services	Rate. . .	1	1	1	-	-	-
Reimbursements, total	**Mil. dol**	**88,778**	**114,247**	**129,033**	**11,239**	**15,850**	**18,818**
Per person served	Dollars .	3,578	4,264	4,740	4,703	5,488	6,021
Hospital insurance	Mil. dol .	54,244	72,958	83,072	6,694	9,479	11,501
Inpatient hospital	Mil. dol .	48,952	59,906	65,722	6,346	8,566	10,230
Skilled-nursing services	Mil. dol .	1,886	4,136	5,735	85	175	258
Home health services	Mil. dol .	3,406	8,916	11,614	264	738	1,013
Supplementary medical insurance	Mil. dol .	34,533	41,289	45,961	4,545	6,371	7,317
Physicians' and other medical							
services.	Mil. dol .	27,379	31,258	34,408	2,831	3,693	4,321
Outpatient services	Mil. dol .	7,077	9,899	11,395	1,714	2,678	2,996
Home health services	Mil. dol .	78	131	158	-	-	-

  - Represents or rounds to zero.   [1] Age under 65; includes persons enrolled because of end-stage renal disease (ESRD) only. [2] Persons are counted once for each type of covered service used, but are not double counted in totals.

    Source: U.S. Health Care Financing Administration, *Medicare Program Statistics,* annual; and unpublished data.

No. 165. Medicare—Utilization and Charges: 1980 to 1994

[**Fiscal year data, except as indicated.** Data reflect date expense was incurred based on bills submitted for payment and recorded in Health Care Financing Administration central records through June 1995. Includes Puerto Rico, Virgin Islands, Guam, other outlying areas, and enrollees in foreign countries]

ITEM	Unit	PERSONS 65 YEARS OLD AND OVER				DISABLED PERSONS [1]			
		1980	1985	1990	1994	1980	1985	1990	1994
Hospital inpatient care:									
Admissions [2]	1,000. . .	9,258	9,751	9,216	10,399	1,271	1,319	1,257	1,418
Per 1,000 enrollees [3] . . .	Rate . . .	369	352	309	317	429	454	396	343
Covered days of care	Millions .	98	80	82	79	13	11	11	11
Per 1,000 enrollees [3] . . .	Rate . . .	3,885	2,882	2,702	2,408	4,549	3,739	3,464	2,660
Per admission.	Days . . .	10.5	8.2	8.9	7.6	10.6	8.2	8.8	7.8
Hospital covered charges . .	Mil. dol . .	28,615	49,236	90,846	133,591	4,087	6,582	11,910	18,217
Per covered day	Dollars. .	293	617	1,104	1,691	303	606	1,083	1,656
Percent of covered									
charges reimbursed [4] . .	Percent .	70.0	65.6	47.5	48.9	68.6	64.4	46.5	48.9
Physician allowed charges [5] . .	Mil. dol . .	9,011	17,743	30,447	38,151	1,112	1,823	2,907	5,202
Percent reimbursed	Percent .	78.0	78.8	77.0	76.2	78.7	78.7	75.7	76.2

   [1] Disabled persons under age 65 and persons enrolled solely because of end-stage renal disease.   [2] Beginning 1990, represents number of discharges and includes pass-through amounts, except for kidney acquisition.   [3] Based on Hospital Insurance (HI) enrollment as of July 1.   [4] Prior to 1990, billing reimbursements exclude: (1) PPS pass-through amounts for capital, direct medical education, kidney acquisitions, and bad debts by Medicare patients; (2) certain lump-sum interim payments. All years exclude retroactive adjustments resulting from end-of-fiscal year cost reports.   [5] Calendar year data.

    Source: U.S. Health Care Financing Administration, unpublished data.

No. 166. Medicare—Summary, by State and Other Areas: 1993 and 1994

STATE AND AREA	1993 Enroll-ment [1] (1,000)	1993 Pay-ments [2] (mil. dol.)	1994 Enroll-ment [1] (1,000)	1994 Pay-ments [2] (mil. dol.)	STATE AND AREA	1993 Enroll-ment [1] (1,000)	1993 Pay-ments [2] (mil. dol.)	1994 Enroll-ment [1] (1,000)	1994 Pay-ments [2] (mil. dol.)
All areas ..	36,271	142,934	36,893	159,345	MO	814	3,122	823	3,352
U.S....	35,497	142,211	36,102	158,517	MT	125	370	128	396
AL	618	2,461	630	2,717	NE	245	689	247	758
AK	30	97	32	111	NV	170	664	182	810
AZ	554	2,178	577	2,483	NH	148	462	152	530
AR	410	1,306	416	1,455	NJ	1,144	4,749	1,158	5,188
CA	3,504	16,488	3,562	18,938	NM	198	557	205	596
CO	396	1,430	409	1,635	NY	2,594	11,448	2,618	12,565
CT	491	2,053	497	2,314	NC	971	3,242	999	3,679
DE	96	368	98	452	ND	102	347	102	373
DC	78	1,112	79	1,135	OH	1,626	6,086	1,646	6,513
FL	2,494	11,722	2,554	13,733	OK	473	1,547	479	1,793
GA	791	3,302	811	3,629	OR	452	1,444	460	1,589
HI	141	473	146	532	PA	2,039	9,271	2,055	10,066
ID	142	342	146	401	RI	165	628	166	703
IL	1,593	6,136	1,606	6,617	SC	481	1,440	495	1,697
IN	803	2,877	813	3,153	SD	115	331	116	357
IA	469	1,305	472	1,407	TN	738	3,252	753	3,664
KS	376	1,350	380	1,536	TX	1,973	8,007	2,024	9,386
KY	565	1,959	575	2,177	UT	177	591	182	630
LA	563	2,607	572	2,953	VT	79	228	81	250
ME	194	561	198	625	VA	779	2,420	798	2,700
MD	578	2,470	591	2,707	WA	658	2,167	671	2,277
MA	911	4,487	923	4,958	WV	322	1,017	325	1,100
MI	1,309	5,171	1,329	5,634	WI	745	2,305	753	2,436
MN	615	2,106	623	2,172	WY	57	139	59	159
MS	384	1,328	390	1,477	PR	457	709	467	801
					Other areas .	317	13	324	27

[1] Hospital and/or medical insurance enrollment as of September.   [2] Benefit payments for all areas represent 100% fee for service experience and actual HMO expenditures through the fiscal year and relate to the State of the provider.

Source: U.S. Health Care Financing Administration, unpublished data.

No. 167. Medicaid—Summary, by State and Other Areas: 1993 and 1994

[Data are for fiscal years]

STATE AND AREA	1993 Recipi-ents [1] (1,000)	1993 Pay-ments [2] (mil. dol.)	1994 Recipi-ents [1] (1,000)	1994 Pay-ments [2] (mil. dol.)	STATE AND AREA	1993 Recipi-ents [1] (1,000)	1993 Pay-ments [2] (mil. dol.)	1994 Recipi-ents [1] (1,000)	1994 Pay-ments [2] (mil. dol.)
All areas ..	33,432	101,709	35,053	108,270	MO	609	1,548	669	1,809
U.S....	32,664	101,547	34,110	108,029	MT	89	287	96	303
AL	522	1,192	544	1,312	NE	165	553	164	593
AK	65	217	69	243	NV	88	301	95	307
AZ	404	212	510	199	NH	79	380	86	389
AR	339	998	340	1,253	NJ	794	3,485	790	3,612
CA	4,834	9,650	5,008	9,988	NM	241	543	268	638
CO	281	911	289	952	NY	2,742	17,557	2,908	18,731
CT	334	1,825	354	1,943	NC	898	2,452	985	2,685
DE	69	252	75	277	ND	62	273	63	284
DC	120	555	127	550	OH	1,491	4,667	1,523	4,995
FL	1,745	4,131	1,727	4,266	OK	387	1,043	391	974
GA	955	2,441	1,085	2,845	OR	325	831	411	1,036
HI	110	293	121	338	PA	1,223	3,886	1,255	4,224
ID	100	301	110	331	RI	191	710	115	685
IL	1,396	4,625	1,441	4,826	SC	470	1,249	486	1,396
IN	565	2,354	605	2,250	SD	70	264	72	284
IA	289	896	303	982	TN	909	1,977	939	1,965
KS	243	702	252	782	TX	2,308	5,575	2,514	6,141
KY	618	1,707	638	1,779	UT	148	408	157	451
LA	751	2,873	778	2,684	VT	81	235	94	259
ME	169	713	177	807	VA	576	1,623	643	1,723
MD	445	1,721	415	1,875	WA	633	1,537	668	1,574
MA	765	2,726	710	3,052	WV	347	1,056	367	1,107
MI	1,172	3,077	1,187	3,274	WI	471	1,786	474	1,830
MN	425	1,930	426	1,982	WY	46	125	51	157
MS	504	896	537	1,090	PR	757	158	927	233
					Virgin Islands	11	4	16	8

[1] Persons who had payments made on their behalf at any time during the fiscal year.   [2] Payments are for fiscal year and reflect Federal and state contribution payments. Data exclude disproportionate hospital share payments.

Source: U.S. Health Care Financing Administration, unpublished data.

No. 168. Medicaid—Selected Utilization Measures: 1975 to 1993

[In thousands. For fiscal years ending in year shown. Includes Virgin Islands. See text, section 3]

MEASURE	1975	1980	1985	1989	1990	1991	1992	1993
General hospitals:								
Recipients discharged	2,336	2,255	2,390	2,701	3,261	3,638	3,866	4,050
Total days of care	22,941	24,089	29,562	22,754	27,471	28,998	29,921	31,216
Nursing facilities: [1]								
Total recipients	1,212	1,395	1,375	1,438	1,461	1,500	1,573	1,610
Total days of care	199,715	273,497	277,996	367,228	360,044	387,621	408,191	416,200
Intermediate care facilities: [2]								
Total recipients	69	121	147	147	146	146	151	149
Total days of care	9,060	250,124	47,324	50,276	49,730	50,223	53,538	51,716

[1] Includes skilled nursing facilities and intermediate care facilities for all other than the mentally retarded.　　[2] Mentally retarded.

Source: U.S. Health Care Financing Administration, Bureau of Data Management and Strategy, Division of Program Systems, *Statistical Report on Medical Care: Eligibles, Recipients, Payments, and Services.*

No. 169. Medicaid—Selected Characteristics of Persons Covered: 1988 to 1994

[In thousands, except percent. Represents number of persons as of March of following year who were enrolled at any time in year shown. Person did not have to receive medical care paid for by Medicaid in order to be counted. See headnote, table 578]

POVERTY STATUS	1988	1990	1994 Total [1]	White	Black	His- panic [2]	Under 18 years old	18-44 years old	45-64 years old	65 years and over
Persons covered, total	20,674	24,160	31,401	20,347	8,896	6,174	15,888	9,845	2,794	2,875
Below poverty level.	13,185	15,175	17,578	10,308	6,151	4,011	9,778	5,384	1,366	1,050
Above poverty level	7,489	8,985	13,823	10,039	2,731	2,163	6,110	4,461	1,428	1,825
Percent of population										
covered	8.5	9.7	12.0	9.4	26.7	22.5	22.7	9.0	5.4	9.2
Below poverty level.	41.5	45.2	46.2	40.6	60.3	47.7	64.0	37.2	29.4	28.7
Above poverty level	3.5	4.2	6.2	5.3	11.9	11.4	11.2	4.7	3.1	6.6

[1] Includes other races not shown separately.　　[2] Persons of Hispanic origin may be of any race.

Source: U.S. Bureau of the Census, *Current Population Reports,* P60-189, earlier reports; and unpublished data.

No. 170. Medicaid—Recipients and Payments: 1980 to 1994

[For fiscal year ending in year shown; see text, section 10. Includes Puerto Rico and outlying areas. Medical vendor payments are those made directly to suppliers of medical care]

BASIS OF ELIGIBILITY AND TYPE OF SERVICE	RECIPIENTS (1,000)					PAYMENTS (mil. dol.)				
	1980	1985	1990	1993	1994	1980	1985	1990	1993	1994
Total [1]	21,605	21,814	25,255	33,432	35,053	23,311	37,508	64,859	101,709	108,270
Age 65 and over	3,440	3,061	3,202	3,863	4,035	8,739	14,096	21,508	31,554	33,618
Blindness	92	80	83	84	86	124	249	434	589	644
Disabled [2]	2,819	2,937	3,635	4,932	5,372	7,497	13,203	23,969	38,065	41,654
AFDC [3] program	14,210	15,275	17,230	23,790	24,780	6,354	9,160	17,690	30,109	30,887
Other and unknown	1,499	1,214	1,105	763	779	596	798	1,257	1,391	1,467
Inpatient services in—										
General hospital	3,680	3,434	4,593	5,894	5,866	6,412	9,453	16,674	25,734	26,180
Mental hospital	66	60	92	75	85	775	1,192	1,714	2,161	2,057
Intermediate care facilities:										
Mentally retarded	121	147	147	149	159	1,989	4,731	7,354	8,831	8,347
Nursing facility services [4]	1,398	1,375	1,461	1,610	1,639	7,887	11,587	17,693	25,431	27,095
Physicians	13,765	14,387	17,078	23,746	24,267	1,875	2,346	4,018	6,952	7,189
Dental	4,652	4,672	4,552	6,174	6,352	462	458	593	961	969
Other practitioner	3,234	3,357	3,873	5,229	5,409	198	251	372	937	1,040
Outpatient hospital	9,705	10,072	12,370	16,436	16,567	1,101	1,789	3,324	6,215	6,342
Clinic	1,531	2,121	2,804	4,839	5,258	320	714	1,688	3,457	3,747
Laboratory [5]	3,212	6,354	8,959	12,970	13,412	121	337	721	1,137	1,176
Home health	392	535	719	1,067	1,293	332	1,120	3,404	5,601	7,042
Prescribed drugs	13,707	13,921	17,294	23,901	24,470	1,318	2,315	4,420	7,970	8,875
Family planning	1,129	1,636	1,752	2,538	2,566	81	195	265	538	516

[1] Recipient data do not add due to small number of recipients that are reported in more than one category. Includes recipients of, and payments for, other care not shown separately.　　[2] Permanently and totally.　　[3] Aid to families with dependent children.　　[4] Nursing facility services includes skilled nursing facility services and intermediate care facility services for all other than the mentally retarded.　　[5] Includes radiological services.

Source: U.S. Health Care Financing Administration, *Health Care Financing Review,* quarterly.

No. 171. Consumer Price Indexes of Medical Care Prices: 1970 to 1995

[1982-1984=100. Indexes are annual averages of monthly data based on components of consumer price index for all urban consumers; for explanation, see text, section 15. See *Historical Statistics, Colonial Times to 1970,* series B 262-272 for similar data]

YEAR	Medical care	MEDICAL CARE SERVICES					Medical care commodities [2]	ANNUAL PERCENT CHANGE [3]					Medical care commodities [2]
		Total [1]	Professional services			Hospital room		Medical care	Medical care services				
			Total [1]	Physicians	Dental				Total [1]	Physicians	Dental	Hospital room	
1970	34.0	32.3	37.0	34.5	39.2	23.6	46.5	6.6	7.0	7.5	5.7	12.9	2.4
1975	47.5	46.6	50.8	48.1	53.2	38.3	53.3	12.0	12.6	12.1	10.4	17.1	8.3
1980	74.9	74.8	77.9	76.5	78.9	68.0	75.4	11.0	11.3	10.5	11.9	13.1	9.3
1985	113.5	113.2	113.5	113.3	114.2	115.4	115.2	6.3	6.1	5.9	6.2	5.9	7.2
1988	138.6	138.3	137.5	139.8	137.5	143.3	139.9	6.5	6.4	7.2	6.8	9.3	6.8
1989	149.3	148.9	146.4	150.1	146.1	158.1	150.8	7.7	7.7	7.4	6.3	10.3	7.8
1990	162.8	162.7	156.1	160.8	155.8	175.4	163.4	9.0	9.3	7.1	6.6	10.9	8.4
1991	177.0	177.1	165.7	170.5	167.4	191.9	176.8	8.7	8.9	6.0	7.4	9.4	8.2
1992	190.1	190.5	175.8	181.2	178.7	208.7	188.1	7.4	7.6	6.3	6.8	8.8	6.4
1993	201.4	202.9	184.7	191.3	188.1	226.4	195.0	5.9	6.5	5.6	5.3	8.5	3.7
1994	211.0	213.4	192.5	199.8	197.1	239.2	200.7	4.8	5.2	4.4	4.8	5.7	2.9
1995	220.5	224.2	201.0	208.8	206.8	251.2	204.5	4.5	5.1	4.5	4.9	5.0	1.9

[1] Includes other services not shown separately.   [2] Prior to 1980, covers drugs and prescriptions only.   [3] Percent change from the immediate prior year.

Source: U.S. Bureau of Labor Statistics, *CPI Detailed Report,* January 1996; and unpublished data.

No. 172. Average Annual Expenditures per Consumer Unit for Health Care: 1985 to 1994

[In dollars, except percent. See text, section 14, and headnote, table 704. For composition of regions, see table 27]

ITEM	HEALTH CARE, TOTAL		Health insurance	Medical services	Drugs and medical supplies [1]	PERCENT DISTRIBUTION		
	Amount	Percent of total expenditures				Health insurance	Medical services	Drugs and medical supplies [1]
1985	1,108	4.7	375	496	238	33.8	44.8	21.5
1988	1,298	5.0	474	529	294	36.5	40.8	22.7
1989	1,407	5.1	537	542	327	38.2	38.5	23.2
1990	1,480	5.2	581	562	337	39.3	38.0	22.8
1991	1,554	5.2	656	555	344	42.2	35.7	22.1
1992	1,634	5.5	725	533	375	44.4	32.6	22.9
1993	1,776	5.8	800	574	402	45.0	32.3	22.6
1994	**1,755**	**5.5**	**815**	**571**	**369**	**46.4**	**32.5**	**21.0**
Age of reference person:								
Under 25 years old.	505	2.7	186	218	102	36.8	43.2	20.2
25 to 34 years old	1,086	3.6	479	407	199	44.1	37.5	18.3
35 to 44 years old	1,616	4.3	689	627	299	42.6	38.8	18.5
45 to 54 years old	1,855	4.5	772	673	410	41.6	36.3	22.1
55 to 64 years old	2,144	6.4	895	791	459	41.7	36.9	21.4
65 to 74 years old	2,592	10.3	1,467	539	586	56.6	20.8	22.6
75 years old and over.	2,787	14.4	1,496	639	653	53.7	22.9	23.4
Origin of reference person: Hispanic . . .	1,061	4.0	477	397	187	45.0	37.4	17.6
Non-Hispanic.	1,811	5.6	843	585	384	46.5	32.3	21.2
Black	928	4.2	481	213	234	51.8	23.0	25.2
Other	1,920	5.7	887	631	402	46.2	32.9	20.9
Region of residence:								
Northeast	1,679	5.2	816	548	315	48.6	32.6	18.8
Midwest	1,698	5.6	806	507	386	47.5	29.9	22.7
South.	1,854	6.2	868	578	408	46.8	31.2	22.0
West	1,737	4.9	740	661	336	42.6	38.1	19.3
Size of consumer unit:								
One person.	1,178	6.1	546	363	269	46.3	30.8	22.8
Two or more persons	1,984	5.4	922	654	408	46.5	33.0	20.6
Two persons	2,171	6.6	1,056	635	480	48.6	29.2	22.1
Three persons	1,801	4.9	806	619	376	44.8	34.4	20.9
Four persons	1,865	4.5	848	670	348	45.5	35.9	18.7
Five persons or more	1,859	4.6	793	742	325	42.7	39.9	17.5
Income before taxes:								
Complete income reporters [2]	1,768	5.4	818	567	382	46.3	32.1	21.6
Quintiles of income:								
Lowest 20 percent.	1,114	7.9	564	266	283	50.6	23.9	25.4
Second 20 percent	1,607	7.7	816	417	374	50.8	25.9	23.3
Third 20 percent	1,653	5.8	771	509	374	46.6	30.8	22.6
Fourth 20 percent	2,008	5.1	895	710	403	44.6	35.4	20.1
Highest 20 percent	2,455	4.0	1,044	933	477	42.5	38.0	19.4
Incomplete reporters of income.	1,702	6.3	796	591	314	46.8	34.7	18.4

[1] Includes prescription and nonprescription drugs.   [2] A complete reporter is a consumer unit providing values for at least one of the major sources of income.

Source: Bureau of Labor Statistics, *Consumer Expenditure Survey,* annual.

No. 173. Health Insurance Coverage Status, by Selected Characteristics: 1987 to 1994

[Persons as of following year for coverage in the year shown. Government health insurance includes Medicare, Medicaid, and military plans. Based on Current Population Survey; see text, section 1, and Appendix III]

CHARACTERISTIC	Total persons	NUMBER (mil.)						PERCENT			
		Covered by private or Government health insurance					Not covered by health insurance	Covered by private or Government health insurance			Not covered by health insurance
		Total [1]	Private		Government			Total [1]	Private	Medi-caid	
			Total	Group health [2]	Medi-care	Medi-caid					
1987	241.2	210.2	182.2	149.7	30.5	20.2	31.0	87.1	75.5	8.4	12.9
1988	243.7	211.0	182.0	150.9	30.9	20.7	32.7	86.6	74.7	8.5	13.4
1989	246.2	212.8	183.6	151.6	31.5	21.2	33.4	86.4	74.6	8.6	13.6
1990	248.9	214.2	182.1	150.2	32.3	24.3	34.7	86.1	73.2	9.7	13.9
1991	251.4	216.0	181.4	150.1	32.9	26.9	35.4	85.9	72.1	10.7	14.1
1992 [3]	256.8	218.2	181.5	148.8	33.2	29.4	38.6	85.0	70.7	11.5	15.0
1993 [3]	259.8	220.0	182.4	148.3	33.1	31.7	39.7	84.7	70.2	12.2	15.3
1994, total [3] [4] . .	**262.1**	**222.4**	**184.3**	**159.6**	**33.9**	**31.6**	**39.7**	**84.8**	**70.3**	**12.1**	**15.2**
Sex: Male	128.1	106.8	90.4	79.7	14.5	13.2	21.3	83.4	70.6	10.3	16.6
Female	134.0	115.6	93.9	79.9	19.4	18.4	18.4	86.3	70.0	13.7	13.7
Race: White	216.8	186.4	160.4	138.0	30.0	20.5	30.3	86.0	74.0	9.4	14.0
Black	33.5	26.9	17.1	15.6	3.2	9.0	6.6	80.3	51.1	26.9	19.7
Hispanic origin [5]	27.5	18.2	11.7	10.7	1.7	6.2	9.3	66.3	42.7	22.6	33.7
Age: Under 18 years.	70.5	60.5	46.3	43.0	0.2	16.1	10.0	85.8	65.6	22.9	14.2
18 to 24 years . . .	25.2	18.4	15.5	12.9	0.1	3.2	6.7	73.3	61.7	12.6	26.7
25 to 34 years . . .	41.4	32.3	28.4	26.4	0.4	3.7	9.1	78.0	68.6	9.1	22.0
35 to 44 years . . .	42.3	35.6	32.2	30.0	0.7	2.9	6.8	84.0	76.2	6.9	16.0
45 to 54 years . . .	30.7	26.8	24.9	22.9	0.8	1.5	3.9	87.2	81.0	4.9	12.8
55 to 64 years . . .	20.8	17.9	15.7	13.5	1.5	1.3	2.9	86.1	75.8	6.2	13.9
65 years and over.	31.3	31.0	21.3	11.1	30.2	2.9	0.3	99.1	68.0	9.2	0.9

[1] Includes other Government insurance, not shown separately. Persons with coverage counted only once in total, even though they may have been covered by more that one type of policy.   [2] Related to employment of self or other family members. [3] Beginning 1992, data based on 1990 census adjusted population controls.   [4] Includes other races not shown separately. [5] Persons of Hispanic origin may be of any race.

Source: U.S. Bureau of the Census, March Supplement to the Current Population Survey, unpublished data.

No. 174. Persons Not Covered by Health Insurance, by State: 1994

[**In percent.** Based on the Current Population Survey and subject to sampling error; see text, section 1, and Appendix III]

STATE	1994	STATE	1994
United States	**15.2**	Missouri	12.2
Alabama	19.2	Montana	13.6
Alaska.	13.3	Nebraska.	10.7
Arizona	20.2	Nevada.	15.7
Arkansas	17.4	New Hampshire	11.9
California.	21.1	New Jersey.	13.0
Colorado	12.4	New Mexico.	23.1
Connecticut	10.4	New York.	16.0
Delaware.	13.5	North Carolina	13.3
District of Columbia	16.4	North Dakota	8.4
Florida	17.2	Ohio	11.0
Georgia.	16.2	Oklahoma	17.8
Hawaii.	9.2	Oregon	13.1
Idaho	14.0	Pennsylvania	10.6
Illinois	11.4	Rhode Island	11.5
Indiana	10.5	South Carolina	14.2
Iowa.	9.7	South Dakota	10.0
Kansas	12.9	Tennessee	10.2
Kentucky	15.2	Texas	24.2
Louisiana.	19.2	Utah	11.5
Maine	13.1	Vermont	8.6
Maryland	12.6	Virginia	12.0
Massachusetts	12.5	Washington	12.7
Michigan	10.8	West Virginia	16.2
Minnesota	9.5	Wisconsin	8.9
Mississippi	17.8	Wyoming	15.4

Source: U.S. Bureau of the Census, *Current Population Reports,* series P60-190.

No. 175. Health Insurance Coverage, by Selected Characteristic: 1992-94

[Data represent persons covered by Government or private health insurance coverage during a 28-month period, beginning early 1992. Based on Survey of Income and Program Participation. See text, section 14]

CHARACTERISTIC	All persons (mil.)	COVERED BY INSURANCE (mil.)				PERCENT COVERED BY INSURANCE			
		Government or private			Private for entire period	Government or private			Private for entire period
		For entire period	For part of the period	No coverage		For entire period	For part of the period	No coverage	
Total	246.2	179.6	54.7	11.9	151.1	73.0	22.2	4.8	61.4
Under 18 years old.	68.1	47.7	17.6	2.8	39.1	70.0	25.9	4.1	57.3
18 to 21 years old	24.3	11.8	10.9	1.7	10.2	48.5	44.6	6.9	42.0
25 to 34 years old	41.9	27.7	11.4	2.9	25.2	66.1	27.1	6.8	60.1
35 to 44 years old	39.2	29.9	7.1	2.2	28.0	76.4	18.0	5.6	71.5
45 to 64 years old	46.3	36.4	7.6	2.3	32.8	78.6	16.4	5.0	70.7
65 years old and over . . .	26.4	26.1	-	0.2	15.8	99.1	-	0.8	60.1
Male	119.3	84.6	27.9	6.8	73.4	70.9	23.4	5.7	61.5
Female.	126.8	95.0	26.9	5.0	77.7	74.9	21.2	3.9	61.2
White.	205.6	153.2	43.1	9.3	133.7	74.5	21.0	4.5	65.0
Black	31.0	19.8	9.3	1.8	11.9	64.1	30.1	5.9	38.6
Hispanic [1]	23.2	11.8	8.9	2.6	8.0	50.7	38.2	11.1	34.4
Residence:									
Northeast	49.2	38.6	9.1	1.6	32.2	78.3	18.6	3.2	65.4
Midwest	63.9	49.5	12.1	2.3	43.3	77.4	19.0	3.6	67.9
South	84.4	58.0	21.0	5.4	47.7	68.7	24.8	6.4	56.6
West.	48.7	33.6	12.5	2.6	27.8	69.0	25.7	5.3	57.1
Educational attainment: [2]									
High school	35.4	23.9	8.3	3.2	13.8	67.6	23.4	9.0	38.9
High school, no college	67.4	48.2	15.4	3.9	42.0	71.4	22.8	5.8	62.2
College, 1+ years	75.2	59.8	13.4	1.9	56.3	79.6	17.9	2.6	74.8
Work-status: [3] Worked entire 28 months—									
Full time.	57.3	49.5	(NA)	(NA)	49.0	86.5	(NA)	(NA)	85.5
Part time	5.6	4.1	(NA)	(NA)	3.9	73.5	(NA)	(NA)	69.6
Had at least one work interruption	75.8	44.0	(NA)	(NA)	36.0	58.1	(NA)	(NA)	47.5

- Represents or rounds to zero.   NA Not available.   [1] Persons of Hispanic origin may be of any race.   [2] For persons 18 years old and over.   [3] For wage and salary workers.

Source: U.S. Bureau of the Census, Internet site http://www.census.gov/hhes/www/hlth9293.html (accessed 28 June 1996).

No. 176. Health Maintenance Organizations (HMO's): 1980 to 1995

[As of June 30, except as noted. Under the Health Maintenance Organization Act, an HMO must have four characteristics: (1) an organized system for providing health care in a geographic area, for which the HMO is responsible for providing or otherwise assuring its delivery; (2) an agreed upon set of basic and supplemental health maintenance and treatment services; (3) a voluntarily enrolled group of people; and (4) community rating. A staff HMO delivers services through a physician group controlled by the HMO unit. A group HMO contracts with one or more medical groups to provide services to members and generally provides all services except hospital care under one roof. A network HMO provides comprehensive health services to members in two or more distinct geographic areas. Individual practice association (IPA) HMO contracts with a physician organization that in turn contracts with individual physicians. IPA physicians provide care to HMO members from their private offices and continue to see their fee-for-service patients. An open-ended product line allows enrollees to receive services from health care providers outside the HMO network for additional out-of-pocket fee (typically a deductible and coinsurance are imposed)]

TYPE OF PRACTICE AND SIZE	1980	1985	1989 (July 1)	1990 (July 1)	1991 (July 1)	1992 (July 1)	1993 (July 1)	1994 (July 1)	1995 (Jan. 31)
NUMBER OF PLANS									
Total	236	393	[1]590	[1]556	[1]559	[1]559	[1]540	[1]547	[1]550
Staff	63	55	60	50	46	41	37	26	22
Group	76	71	66	62	55	54	53	46	42
Network.	(NA)	86	93	82	68	61	42	41	43
I.P.A	97	181	371	350	349	342	320	323	323
Mixed	(NA)	(NA)	(NA)	12	41	61	(NA)	(NA)	(NA)
ENROLLMENT (1,000)									
Total	9,100	18,894	[2]32,493	[2]33,622	[2]35,052	[2]37,199	[2]39,783	[2]43,443	[2]46,182
Staff	1,673	2,686	3,997	3,577	3,425	2,332	1,757	1,377	728
Group	5,732	6,488	9,177	9,535	9,471	9,600	9,877	8,978	9,185
Network.	(NA)	5,073	5,719	5,874	4,077	3,762	2,939	2,659	2,964
I.P.A	1,694	4,646	13,598	13,879	13,984	15,124	15,360	16,382	17,373
Mixed	(NA)	(NA)	(NA)	755	4,096	6,382	(NA)	(NA)	(NA)
HMO'S WITH OPEN-ENDED PRODUCT LINE									
Number of plans.	(X)	(X)	78	96	157	178	241	306	307
Enrollment (1,000)	(X)	(X)	703	1,041	1,430	1,643	2,302	3,227	4,081

NA Not available.   X Not applicable.   [1] Includes HMO's containing only open-ended members.   [2] Excludes enrollees participating in open-ended plans.

Source: Interstudy, Minneapolis, MN, The InterStudy Competitive Edge, 1995, vol. 5, No. 2, and earlier publications (copyright); and Group Health Association of America, Inc., Washington, DC, National Directory of HMO's, annual.

No. 177. Employment in the Health Service Industries: 1980 to 1995

[In thousands. See headnote table 654]

INDUSTRY	1987 SIC code [1]	1980	1985	1990	1993	1994	1995
Health services [2]	80	5,278	6,293	7,814	8,756	8,992	9,257
Offices and clinics of MD's	801	802	1,028	1,338	1,506	1,545	1,606
Offices and clinics of Dentist's	802	(NA)	439	513	556	574	597
Offices and clinics of other practitioners	804	96	165	277	353	378	407
Nursing and personal care facilities	805	997	1,198	1,415	1,585	1,649	1,693
Skilled nursing care facilities	8051	(NA)	791	989	1,147	1,221	1,252
Intermediate care facilities	8052	(NA)	(NA)	200	215	206	213
Other, n.e.c. [3]	8059	(NA)	(NA)	227	224	222	229
Hospitals	806	2,750	2,997	3,549	3,779	3,763	3,784
General medical and surgical hospitals	8062	(NA)	2,811	3,268	3,475	3,459	3,484
Psychiatric hospitals	8063	(NA)	59	104	99	97	91
Specialty hospitals, exc. psychiatric	8069	(NA)	126	176	205	207	208
Medical and dental laboratories	807	(NA)	119	166	187	189	193
Home health care services	808	(NA)	(NA)	291	469	559	626

NA Not available.   [1] Based on the 1987 Standard Industrial Classification code; see text, section 13.   [2] Includes other industries not shown separately.   [3] N.e.c. means not elsewhere classified.

Source: U.S. Bureau of Labor Statistics, Bulletins 2445 and 2481, and *Employment and Earnings,* March and June issues.

No. 178. Annual Receipts/Revenue for the Health Service Industries: 1989 to 1994

[In millions of dollars. Unless otherwise noted, receipts estimates are obtained from a sample of employer and nonemployer firms. Revenue estimates are obtained from a sample of employer firms only]

INDUSTRY	1987 SIC code [1]	1989	1990	1991	1992	1993	1994
TAXABLE FIRMS—RECEIPTS							
Health services [2]	80	241,558	271,212	293,907	321,653	337,946	356,471
Offices and clinics of MD's	801	117,213	128,871	138,576	151,824	155,212	161,589
Offices and clinics of dentist's	802	29,297	31,502	33,279	36,939	39,156	42,108
Offices and clinics of doctor's of osteopathy	803	2,833	3,254	3,584	4,008	4,086	4,204
Offices and clinics of other practitioners [2]	804	17,084	20,139	21,449	23,893	25,649	26,340
Offices and clinics of chiropractors	8041	5,005	5,467	5,647	6,555	7,122	7,160
Offices and clinics of optometrists	8042	4,296	4,799	5,028	5,333	5,686	5,958
Offices and clinics of podiatrists	8043	(NA)	1,811	1,957	2,102	2,221	2,321
Nursing and personal care facilities	805	25,753	30,162	32,862	34,743	37,414	39,554
Hospitals [3]	806	23,495	26,487	28,807	31,083	32,894	34,103
General medical and surgical hospitals [3]	8062	(NA)	20,442	22,220	24,162	26,070	26,658
Psychiatric hospitals [3]	8063	(NA)	4,129	4,402	4,396	3,935	4,126
Specialty hospitals, except psychiatric [3]	8069	(NA)	1,916	2,185	2,525	2,889	3,319
Medical and dental laboratories	807	10,336	12,033	13,567	15,172	16,341	18,057
Medical laboratories	8071	8,470	9,996	11,458	12,882	13,983	15,589
Dental laboratories	8072	1,866	2,037	2,109	2,290	2,358	2,468
Home health care services	808	(NA)	7,556	9,129	11,208	12,973	14,916
Miscellaneous allied services, n.e.c. [2][4]	809	9,952	11,208	12,654	12,783	14,221	15,599
Kidney dialysis centers	8092	(NA)	1,451	1,717	2,140	2,480	2,925
Specialty outpatient facilities, n.e.c. [4]	8093	(NA)	5,326	6,508	6,476	6,867	7,663
TAX EXEMPT FIRMS—REVENUE [3]							
Selected health services [2]	805, 6, 8, 9	(NA)	267,858	298,168	324,416	343,916	360,492
Offices and clinics of doctors of medicine	801	(NA)	12,888	14,744	16,548	19,126	20,662
Nursing and personal care facilities	805	10,573	12,132	13,628	15,221	16,618	17,951
Hospitals	806	(NA)	233,615	259,188	279,736	293,255	304,809
General medical and surgical hospitals	8062	(NA)	210,503	234,056	254,391	266,997	277,468
Psychiatric hospitals	8063	(NA)	11,008	11,461	10,933	11,141	11,605
Specialty hospitals, exc. psychiatric	8069	(NA)	12,104	13,671	14,412	15,117	15,736
Home health care services	808	(NA)	3,874	4,624	5,714	6,827	7,944
Miscellaneous allied services, n.e.c. [2][4]	809	(NA)	5,285	5,915	7,123	8,010	9,040
Kidney dialysis centers	8092	(NA)	305	357	400	455	510
Specialty outpatient facilities, n.e.c. [4]	8093	(NA)	3,519	3,834	4,437	4,720	5,285

NA Not available.   [1] Based on the 1987 Standard Industrial Classification code; see text, section 13.   [2] Includes other industries not shown separately.   [3] Estimates are obtained from a sample of employer firms only.   [4] N.e.c. means not elsewhere classified.

Source: U.S. Bureau of the Census, *Current Business Reports, Service Annual Survey: 1994,* BS/94.

No. 179. Physicians, by Selected Activity: 1970 to 1994

[In thousands. Through 1985, as of Dec. 31; thereafter as of Jan. 1, except as noted. Includes Puerto Rico and outlying areas. See also Historical Statistics, Colonial Times to 1970, series B 275-280]

ACTIVITY	1970	1980	1985	1990	1992	1993	1994
Doctors of medicine, total	334.0	467.7	552.7	615.4	653.1	670.3	684.4
Professionally active	311.2	435.5	511.1	560.0	594.7	605.7	619.8
Place of medical education:							
U.S. medical graduates	256.8	343.6	398.4	437.2	460.4	466.6	475.0
Foreign medical graduates [1]	54.4	91.8	112.7	122.8	134.3	139.1	144.8
Sex: Male	289.8	386.7	436.3	463.9	484.6	488.5	494.9
Female	21.4	48.7	74.8	96.1	110.1	117.2	124.9
Active Non-Federal	281.7	417.7	489.5	539.5	575.5	584.0	597.3
Patient care	255.0	361.9	431.5	487.8	520.2	531.7	543.2
Office-based practice	188.9	271.3	329.0	359.9	387.9	398.8	407.0
General and family practice	50.8	47.8	53.9	57.6	58.6	58.1	58.2
Cardiovascular diseases	3.9	6.7	9.1	10.7	11.4	12.1	12.9
Dermatology	2.9	4.4	5.3	6.0	6.3	6.5	6.7
Gastroenterology	1.1	2.7	4.1	5.2	5.7	6.3	6.7
Internal medicine	23.0	40.5	52.7	57.8	65.1	67.3	67.9
Pediatrics	10.3	17.4	22.4	26.5	29.0	30.8	31.5
Pulmonary diseases	0.8	2.0	3.0	3.7	4.0	4.4	4.6
General surgery	18.1	22.4	24.7	24.5	24.9	24.3	24.2
Obstetrics and gynecology	13.8	19.5	23.5	25.5	27.1	27.6	28.2
Ophthalmology	7.6	10.6	12.2	13.1	13.7	13.9	14.3
Orthopedic surgery	6.5	10.7	13.0	14.2	15.8	16.3	16.6
Otolaryngology	3.9	5.3	5.8	6.4	6.6	6.7	6.9
Plastic surgery	1.2	2.4	3.3	3.8	4.0	4.1	4.3
Urological surgery	4.3	6.2	7.1	7.4	7.7	7.8	7.8
Anesthesiology	7.4	11.3	15.3	17.8	20.0	20.6	22.0
Diagnostic radiology	0.9	4.2	7.7	9.8	10.9	11.9	12.1
Emergency medicine	(NA)	(NA)	(NA)	8.4	9.4	9.8	10.6
Neurology	1.2	3.2	4.7	5.6	6.3	6.8	7.1
Pathology, anatomical/clinical	3.0	6.0	6.9	7.3	7.9	8.5	8.7
Psychiatry	10.1	15.9	18.5	20.0	21.8	22.3	22.6
Other specialty	18.2	31.9	35.8	28.8	31.7	32.4	33.2
Hospital-based practice	66.1	90.6	102.5	127.9	132.3	132.9	136.1
Clinical fellows	(NA)	(NA)	(NA)	8.2	6.8	5.9	4.7
Residents and interns	45.8	59.6	72.2	81.7	85.4	83.1	86.8
Full-time hospital staff	20.3	31.0	30.3	38.0	40.1	43.9	44.6
Other professional activity [2]	26.3	35.2	44.0	39.0	38.7	37.7	39.9
Not classified [3]	0.4	20.6	14.0	12.7	16.6	14.7	14.3
Federal	29.5	17.8	21.6	20.5	19.2	21.7	22.5
Patient care	23.5	14.6	17.3	16.1	15.0	18.8	19.3
Office-based practice	3.5	0.7	1.2	1.1	1.5	0.1	-
Hospital-based practice	20.0	13.9	16.1	15.0	13.5	18.7	19.3
Other professional activity [2]	6.0	3.2	4.3	4.4	4.2	2.9	3.2
Inactive/unknown address	22.8	32.1	41.6	55.4	58.4	64.7	64.7
Doctors of osteopathy [4]	14.3	18.8	24.0	30.9	33.5	33.4	35.0
Medical and osteopathic schools [5]	110	141	142	141	141	142	143
Students [5]	42.6	70.1	73.2	72.0	73.5	74.5	(NA)
Graduates [5]	8.8	16.2	17.8	16.9	17.1	17.1	(NA)

- Represents zero. NA Not available. [1] Foreign medical graduates received their medical education in schools outside the United States and Canada. [2] Includes medical teaching, administration, research, and other. [3] Not classified established in 1970; however, complete data not available until 1972. [4] As of July. Total DO's. Source: American Osteopathic Association, Chicago, IL. [5] Number of schools and students as of fall; graduates for academic year ending in year shown. Based on data from annual surveys conducted by the Association of American Medical Colleges and the American Association of Colleges of Osteopathic Medicine.

Source: Except as noted, American Medical Association, Chicago, IL, Physician Characteristics and Distribution in the U.S., annual (copyright).

No. 180. Dentists and Nurses: 1970 to 1994

[As of end of year, except as noted. Excludes Puerto Rico and outlying areas. See also Historical Statistics, Colonial Times to 1970, series B 281-290]

ITEM	Unit	1970	1975	1980	1985	1990	1991	1992	1993	1994
Dentists, number [1]	1,000	116	127	141	156	[2]173	179	183	187	190
Active (exc. in Federal service) [3]	1,000	96	107	121	136	147	149	152	154	157
Rate per 100,000 population [4]	Rate	47	50	53	57	59	59	60	60	61
Dental schools [5]	Number	53	59	60	60	56	55	55	54	54
Students [5]	1,000	16.6	20.8	22.8	19.6	16.0	15.9	16.0	16.3	16.4
Graduates [5]	1,000	3.7	5.0	5.3	5.4	4.2	4.0	3.9	3.8	3.9
Nurses, number (active registered) [6]	1,000	750	961	1,273	1,538	1,790	1,853	1,907	1,978	2,044
Rate per 100,000 population [4]	Rate	368	446	560	644	713	730	755	774	793
Nursing programs [6]	Number	1,343	1,360	1,385	1,473	1,470	1,484	1,484	1,493	1,501
Students [6]	1,000	165	250	231	218	221	238	258	270	268
Graduates [6]	1,000	44	75	76	82	66	72	81	88	95

[1] Includes current year's graduates. [2] Revised since originally published. [3] Source: American Dental Association, Bureau of Economic and Behavioral Research, Master Membership file and periodic censuses. [4] Based on Bureau of Census estimated resident population as of July 1. Estimates reflect revisions based on the 1990 Census of Population. [5] Number of schools and students as of fall; graduates for academic year ending in year shown. Based on data from the American Dental Association, Council on Dental Education, Annual Report on Dental Education. [6] Number of programs and students are as of October 15 and number of graduates are for academic year ending in year shown; from National League for Nursing, NLN Data Book, annual issues and State-Approved Schools of Nursing, RN, annual issues.

Source: Except as noted, U.S. Dept. of Health and Human Services, Health Resources and Services Administration, unpublished data. Prior to 1980, data were published by U.S. National Center for Health Statistics in Health Resources Statistics, annual.

No. 181. Active Non-Federal Physicians and Nurses, by State: 1994

[**Nurses as of December; Physicians as of Jan. 1.** Excludes doctors of osteopathy, Federally employed persons, and physicians with addresses unknown. Includes all physicians not classified according to activity status]

STATE	PHYSICIANS Total	PHYSICIANS Rate [1]	NURSES Total	NURSES Rate [1]	STATE	PHYSICIANS Total	PHYSICIANS Rate [1]	NURSES Total	NURSES Rate [1]
United States. .	589,906	230	2,044,000	789	Missouri	11,131	213	42,000	798
Alabama	7,294	175	33,400	795	Montana	1,434	171	6,200	728
Alaska	820	143	3,600	621	Nebraska	3,073	192	14,700	911
Arizona	7,874	201	30,800	759	Nevada	2,194	159	8,800	606
Arkansas	4,027	166	18,500	756	New Hampshire	2,383	212	11,100	978
California	74,540	241	181,900	583	New Jersey	21,137	269	71,700	909
Colorado	7,960	226	30,500	842	New Mexico	3,144	196	12,400	756
Connecticut	10,633	325	31,500	965	New York	62,182	343	170,700	942
Delaware	1,488	214	6,200	882	North Carolina	14,073	205	55,800	801
District of Columbia . .	3,662	641	8,000	1,428	North Dakota	1,209	192	6,400	1,014
Florida	29,817	219	104,400	752	Ohio	23,509	213	99,800	900
Georgia	12,801	187	48,400	693	Oklahoma	4,965	155	18,300	567
Hawaii	2,732	245	9,400	835	Oregon	6,434	212	24,400	791
Idaho	1,489	136	6,700	593	Pennsylvania	31,505	262	125,500	1,041
Illinois	27,388	235	98,600	840	Rhode Island	2,758	278	9,600	970
Indiana	9,882	173	44,000	765	South Carolina	6,401	179	22,600	628
Iowa	4,525	160	29,000	1,025	South Dakota	1,139	160	7,200	1,002
Kansas	4,728	188	21,500	851	Tennessee	11,045	218	40,900	793
Kentucky	6,959	185	31,100	818	Texas	32,896	183	101,900	557
Louisiana	8,964	210	27,800	647	Utah	3,525	190	11,300	594
Maine	2,414	196	11,600	939	Vermont	1,529	266	5,500	948
Maryland	16,744	341	42,000	847	Virginia	13,882	220	48,100	753
Massachusetts	22,397	373	70,100	1,162	Washington	11,679	225	44,300	838
Michigan	18,896	200	72,500	764	West Virginia	3,454	190	13,900	762
Minnesota	10,714	237	44,900	984	Wisconsin	10,349	205	45,100	887
Mississippi	3,470	132	16,300	614	Wyoming	658	141	3,500	741

[1] Per 100,000 civilian population. Based on U.S. Bureau of the Census estimates as of July 1, 1994, for nurses, and July 1, 1993 for physicians.

Source: Physicians: American Medical Association, Chicago, IL, *Physician Characteristics and Distribution in the U.S.*, annual (copyright); Nurses: U.S. Dept. of Health and Human Services, Health Resources and Services Administration, unpublished data.

No. 182. Physician and Dental Contacts, by Patient Characteristics: 1970 to 1994

[See headnote, table 208. Based on National Health Interview Survey; see Appendix III]

TYPE OF VISIT AND YEAR	TOTAL VISITS (mil.) Sex Male	TOTAL VISITS (mil.) Sex Female	TOTAL VISITS (mil.) Race [1] White	TOTAL VISITS (mil.) Race [1] Black	VISITS PER PERSON PER YEAR Sex Male	VISITS PER PERSON PER YEAR Sex Female	VISITS PER PERSON PER YEAR Race [1] White	VISITS PER PERSON PER YEAR Race [1] Black	Age (years) Under 5	Age (years) 5 to 17	Age (years) 18 to 24	Age (years) 25 to 44	Age (years) 45 to 64	Age (years) 65 and over
PHYSICIANS														
1970	396	531	832	87	4.1	5.1	4.8	3.9	[2]5.9	[3]2.9	[4]4.6	4.6	5.2	6.3
1980	426	610	903	115	4.0	5.4	4.8	4.5	[2]6.7	[3]3.2	[4]4.0	4.6	5.1	6.4
1983	470	694	1,018	126	4.3	5.8	5.2	4.6	[2]6.5	[3]3.2	[4]4.0	4.7	5.8	7.6
1985	498	733	1,074	132	4.4	6.1	5.4	4.7	[2]6.3	[3]3.1	[4]4.2	4.9	6.1	8.3
1986	515	756	1,110	131	4.5	6.2	5.5	4.6	6.3	3.3	4.2	4.7	6.6	9.1
1987	523	765	1,118	140	4.5	6.2	5.5	4.9	6.7	3.3	4.4	4.8	6.4	8.9
1988	530	774	1,139	136	4.5	6.2	5.6	4.6	7.0	3.4	3.8	5.1	6.1	8.7
1989	552	771	1,148	140	4.7	6.1	5.6	4.7	6.7	3.5	3.9	5.1	6.1	8.9
1990	558	806	1,178	148	4.7	6.4	5.7	4.9	6.9	3.2	4.3	5.1	6.4	9.2
1991	589	842	1,243	152	4.9	6.6	6.0	4.9	7.1	3.4	3.9	5.1	6.6	10.4
1992	624	889	1,286	181	5.1	6.9	6.1	5.8	6.9	3.5	4.1	5.4	7.2	10.6
1993	634	917	1,314	183	5.1	7.0	6.2	5.7	7.2	3.6	4.0	5.4	7.1	10.9
1994	652	930	1,350	179	5.2	7.0	6.3	5.4	6.8	3.5	3.9	5.5	7.3	11.3
DENTISTS														
1970	133	171	283	17	1.4	1.7	1.6	0.8	[2]0.5	[3]1.9	[4]1.8	1.7	1.5	1.1
1980	158	207	333	26	1.5	1.8	1.8	1.0	[2]0.5	[3]2.3	[4]1.6	1.7	1.8	1.4
1983	183	239	382	31	1.6	2.0	1.9	1.1	[2]0.5	[3]2.6	[4]1.6	1.9	2.0	1.5
1986	210	256	416	37	1.9	2.2	2.1	1.4	0.7	2.4	1.7	2.0	2.2	2.1
1989	221	271	441	34	1.9	2.2	2.2	1.2	0.5	2.4	1.6	2.0	2.4	2.0

[1] See footnote 2, table 208.   [2] Under 6 years.   [3] 6 to 17 years.   [4] 17 to 24 years.

Source: U.S. National Center for Health Statistics, *Vital and Health Statistics*, series 10, No. 193, and earlier reports; and unpublished data.

No. 183. Visits to Office Based Physicians: 1994

[Based on the 1994 National Ambulatory Care Survey and subject to sampling error; see source for details]

CHARACTERISTIC	Number of visits (1,000)	Percent distri- bution	Visits per person per year	CHARACTERISTIC	Number of visits (1,000)	Percent distri- bution	Visits per person per year
All visits	681,457	100.0	2.6	New problem.	141,655	20.8	(X)
Age:				New patient	112,158	16.5	(X)
Under 15 years old	124,421	18.3	2.1				
15 to 24 years old	60,722	8.9	1.7	Expected source of payment: [1]			
25 to 44 years old	184,143	27.0	2.2	Private/commercial insurance .	265,972	39.0	(X)
45 to 64 years old	149,038	21.9	3.0	Medicaid	66,686	9.8	(X)
65 to 74 years old	87,461	12.8	4.8	HMO/other prepaid	146,243	21.5	(X)
75 years old and over	75,674	11.1	5.9	Patient paid	84,162	12.4	(X)
Sex:				Medicare	148,827	21.8	(X)
Male	273,409	40.1	2.2	Other government	14,267	2.1	(X)
Female	408,049	59.9	3.1	No charge	8,048	1.2	(X)
Race:				Other/unknown	37,320	5.5	(X)
White	597,091	87.6	2.8	Disposition: [1]			
Black	57,723	8.5	1.7	Return to at specified time . . .	433,430	63.6	(X)
Asian/Pacific Islander	24,965	3.7	(NA)	Return if needed	154,609	22.7	(X)
American Indian/Eskimo/Aleut .	1,678	0.2	(NA)	No followup	56,636	8.3	(X)
Visit status:				Telephone followup	22,809	3.3	(X)
Old patient	569,299	83.5	(X)	Referred to other physician . . .	29,741	4.4	(X)
Old problem	427,644	62.8	(X)	Admit to hospital	5,123	0.8	(X)
				Return to referring physician . .	9,159	1.3	(X)
				Other	12,409	1.8	(X)

NA Not available.   X Not applicable.   [1] More than one reported source of payment or disposition may be reported.

Source: U.S. National Center for Health Statistics, *Advafnce Data*, No. 273, April 16, 1996.

No. 184. Medical Practice Characteristics, by Selected Specialty: 1985 to 1993

[**Dollar figures in thousands.** Based on a sample telephone survey of 4,000 non-Federal office and hospital based patient care physicians, excluding residents, with a response rate of 69.1% in 1990, 66.7% in 1991, 64.4% in 1992, and 64.6% in 1993. For details see source. For definition of mean, see Guide to Tabular Presentation]

SPECIALTY	1985	1988	1989	1990	1991	1992	1993
MEAN PATIENT VISITS PER WEEK							
All physicians [1]	117.1	121.1	121.6	120.9	118.4	114.8	112.4
General/Family practice	138.1	145.6	143.0	146.0	144.4	138.4	137.0
Internal medicine	105.2	113.0	117.9	112.0	110.7	109.4	105.3
Surgery	108.2	105.0	107.7	107.6	106.9	101.6	98.3
Pediatrics	130.8	135.1	138.1	134.0	133.5	126.9	130.9
Obstetrics/Gynecology	112.0	118.9	115.6	120.0	112.2	110.5	111.0
MEAN HOURS IN PATIENT CARE PER WEEK							
All physicians [1]	51.3	53.1	53.3	53.3	53.3	52.9	52.9
General/Family practice	53.6	54.4	54.4	55.0	54.7	53.1	54.0
Internal medicine	52.4	56.2	56.8	55.7	56.3	55.5	56.0
Surgery	51.2	53.8	53.3	53.1	53.4	53.0	54.3
Pediatrics	50.6	52.5	53.4	52.4	52.4	52.6	53.8
Obstetrics/Gynecology	56.9	59.4	59.0	60.4	59.5	58.8	58.9
MEAN NET INCOME							
All physicians [1]	112.2	144.7	155.8	164.3	170.6	181.7	189.3
General/Family practice	77.9	94.6	95.9	102.7	111.5	114.4	116.8
Internal medicine	102.0	130.9	146.5	152.5	149.6	162.1	180.8
Surgery	155.0	207.5	220.5	236.4	233.8	250.5	262.7
Pediatrics	76.2	94.9	104.7	106.5	119.3	123.9	135.4
Obstetrics/Gynecology	124.3	180.7	194.3	207.3	221.8	220.7	221.9
MEAN PROFESSIONAL EXPENSES							
All physicians [1]	102.7	140.8	148.4	150.0	168.4	183.4	182.2
General/Family practice	96.5	122.3	128.5	134.5	146.4	162.9	162.4
Internal medicine	90.0	136.3	139.1	139.2	159.0	174.1	185.2
Surgery	135.7	188.2	203.2	201.0	215.6	245.1	245.9
Pediatrics	87.3	115.3	132.5	138.0	145.4	173.7	167.4
Obstetrics/Gynecology	131.9	189.6	197.4	212.6	236.2	239.7	238.1
MEAN LIABILITY PREMIUM							
All physicians [1]	10.5	15.9	15.5	14.5	14.9	13.8	14.4
General/Family practice	6.8	9.4	9.0	7.8	8.1	8.2	7.9
Internal medicine	5.8	9.0	8.2	9.2	8.0	8.6	9.0
Surgery	16.6	26.5	25.8	22.8	22.5	20.9	22.7
Pediatrics	4.7	9.3	7.8	7.8	8.4	7.7	8.6
Obstetrics/Gynecology	23.5	35.3	37.0	34.3	34.9	34.4	33.7

[1] Includes other specialties not shown separately.

Source: American Medical Association, Chicago IL, *Socioeconomic Characteristics of Medical Practice*, annual (copyright).

No. 185. Hospital Registered Nursing Personnel—Summary: 1992

[In percent, except as indicated. Based on a sample of 5,417 U.S. short term acute care hospitals registered and unregistered by the American Hospital Association, with a response rate of 50.2 percent. For details see source. For an explanation of mean, see Guide to Tabular Presentation]

CHARACTERISTIC	1992	CHARACTERISTIC	1992
Full-time registered nurses per hospital (mean) [1] . . .	112.7	Registered nurse, full time:	
		Lowest mean hourly wage paid	13.96
LENGTH OF EMPLOYMENT AT HOSPITAL [2]		Highest mean hourly wage paid	19.71
		Mean hourly wage paid.	16.92
Full-time: Less than 1 year	15.5		
1 year to less than 2 years	14.3	HOSPITAL STAFFING MECHANISMS [4]	
2 years to less than 5 years.	25.0		
5 years or more.	45.2	Per-diem	41.2
		Float-pool [5]	27.3
Part-time: Less than 1 year.	13.1	On-call	11.1
1 year to less than 2 years	13.1	Temporary nursing service	16.7
2 years to less than 5 years.	25.2	Other	3.7
5 years or more.	48.7		
		HOSPITAL POSITION SCHEDULES [6]	
EDUCATIONAL ATTAINMENT [3]			
		Days only	32.6
Associate degree in nursing	39.4	Evenings only.	17.1
Nursing diploma	27.7	Nights only.	18.6
Baccalaureate degree in nursing	31.0	Shifts: Day/evening	11.1
Master's degree in nursing or higher.	2.0	Day/night	6.1
		Evening/night	4.2
SALARY/WAGES (dol. per hr.) [2]		Rotate all	10.3
Full-time head nurse:		HOSPITAL BARGAINING STATUS	
Lowest mean annual salary paid.	17.57		
Highest mean annual salary paid	22.59	Organized for the purpose of collective bargaining. . .	15.8

[1] Source: American Hospital Association, Chicago, IL, 1991 Human Resource Survey.   [2] Full time: at least 35 hours worked per week. Part time: less than 35 hours worked per week.   [3] Full time only.   [4] Percent of positions with each mechanism. [5] In-house nursing staff personnel routinely assigned schedules who work different units in the institution according to the demands of variable patient volume and acuity levels.   [6] Percent of positions.

Source: Except as indicated, American Hospital Association, Chicago, IL, *Report of the Hospital Nursing Personnel Survey, 1992* (copyright).

No. 186. Hospitals and Nursing Homes—Summary Characteristics: 1971 to 1993

[Except as indicated, based on National Master Facility Inventory]

YEAR AND TYPE OF FACILITY	Total	FACILITIES UNDER—			FACILITIES WITH—			Resi-dents [2] (1,000)	Full-time employ-ees (1,000)
		Gov't. control	Propri-etary control	Non-profit control	Fewer than 25 beds [1]	25-74 beds	75 or more beds		
1971: All facilities . . . . [3]	29,682	4,178	18,091	7,413	8,902	10,959	9,821	2,262	3,007
Nursing homes [3]	22,004	1,368	17,049	3,587	8,266	8,259	5,479	1,076	568
Hospitals	7,678	2,810	1,042	3,826	636	2,700	4,342	1,186	2,439
1980: All facilities . . . . [3][4]	30,116	3,498	19,611	7,007	8,852	8,573	12,691	2,427	3,919
Nursing homes [3][4]	23,065	936	18,669	3,460	8,498	6,362	8,205	1,396	[5] 798
Hospitals	7,051	2,562	942	3,547	354	2,211	4,486	1,031	3,121
1986: All facilities . . . . [6]	32,600	3,275	21,399	7,926	9,903	8,755	13,942	2,427	(NA)
All hospitals [6]	6,954	2,230	1,176	3,548	290	2,150	4,514	874	3,241
General	5,956	1,871	829	3,256	259	1,849	3,848	690	2,871
Psychiatric	584	267	218	99	12	140	432	139	248
Chronic	44	30	4	10	-	6	38	13	21
Tuberculosis	4	3	-	1	-	1	3	(Z)	1
Nursing homes [3]	25,646	1,045	20,223	4,378	9,613	6,605	9,428	1,553	(NA)
1990: All hospitals [6]	6,779	2,145	1,203	3,431	326	2,077	4,376	840	3,562
General.	5,611	1,788	711	3,112	290	1,690	3,631	673	3,168
Psychiatric.	734	272	350	112	17	211	506	128	262
Chronic.	34	27	2	5	-	6	28	10	18
Tuberculosis	1	3	-	1	-	1	3	(Z)	1
1993: All hospitals [6]	6,580	2,046	1,167	3,367	310	2,010	4,260	781	3,783
General.	5,403	1,697	660	3,046	260	1,586	3,557	634	3,401
Psychiatric.	737	266	358	113	24	242	471	107	231
Chronic.	26	21	1	4	1	3	22	9	16
Tuberculosis	4	3	-	1	-	2	2	(Z)	1

- Represents zero.   NA Not available.   Z Fewer that 500.   [1] For hospitals, minimum of six beds; for nursing homes, minimum of three beds.   [2] Number of residents as of date of interview.   [3] See footnotes 1, 3, and 4, table 204.   [4] Includes 1978 data for Alaska and South Dakota.   [5] Estimated.   [6] Includes types not shown separately. Based on data from the American Hospital Association.

Source: U.S. National Center for Health Statistics, *Health Resources Statistics, 1971;* and unpublished data.

No. 187. Hospitals—Summary Characteristics: 1972 to 1994

[Covers hospitals accepted for registration by the American Hospital Association; see text, section 3. Short-term hospitals have an average patient stay of less than 30 days; long-term, an average stay of longer duration. Special hospitals include obstetrics and gynecology; eye, ear, nose, and throat; rehabilitation; orthopedic; and chronic and other special hospitals except psychiatric, tuberculosis, alcoholism, and chemical dependency hospitals. See also *Historical Statistics, Colonial Times to 1970*, series B 305-318, B 331-344, and B 413-422]

ITEM	1972	1980	1985	1989	1990	1991	1992	1993	1994
Number:									
All hospitals	7,061	6,965	6,872	6,720	6,649	6,634	6,539	6,467	6,374
With 100 beds or more	2,710	3,755	3,805	3,650	3,620	3,611	3,572	3,558	3,492
Non-Federal [1]	6,660	6,606	6,529	6,380	6,312	6,300	6,214	6,151	6,067
Community hospitals [2]	5,746	5,830	5,732	5,455	5,384	5,342	5,292	5,261	5,229
Nongovernmental nonprofit	3,301	3,322	3,349	3,220	3,191	3,175	3,173	3,154	3,139
For profit	738	730	805	769	749	738	723	717	719
State and local government	1,707	1,778	1,578	1,466	1,444	1,429	1,396	1,390	1,371
Long-term general and special	216	157	128	138	131	126	115	117	110
Psychiatric	529	534	610	741	757	800	774	741	696
Tuberculosis	72	11	7	4	4	4	4	4	5
Federal	401	359	343	340	337	334	325	316	307
Beds (1,000):									
All hospitals [3]	1,550	1,365	1,309	1,224	1,211	1,197	1,174	1,158	1,128
Rate per 1,000 population [4]	7.4	6.0	5.5	5.0	4.9	4.7	4.6	4.5	4.3
Beds per hospital	220	196	190	182	182	180	180	179	177
Non-Federal [1]	1,407	1,248	1,197	1,124	1,113	1,101	1,085	1,071	1,044
Community hospitals [2]	879	988	1,001	933	928	924	921	916	902
Rate per 1,000 population [4]	4.2	4.3	4.2	3.8	3.7	3.7	3.6	3.6	3.6
Nongovernmental nonprofit	617	692	707	660	657	656	656	649	637
For profit	57	87	104	103	102	100	99	99	101
State and local government	205	209	189	170	169	168	167	169	164
Long-term general and special	54	39	31	27	25	25	23	21	19
Psychiatric	457	215	169	160	158	150	139	131	121
Tuberculosis	13	2	1	(Z)	(Z)	(Z)	(Z)	(Z)	1
Federal	143	117	112	100	98	95	89	87	84
Occupancy rate: [5]									
All hospitals	78.0	77.7	69.5	69.7	69.7	69.1	68.7	67.6	66.1
Non-Federal [1]	78.0	77.4	68.9	69.3	69.4	68.8	68.0	66.9	65.4
Community hospitals [2]	75.4	75.6	64.8	66.2	66.7	66.1	65.6	64.6	62.9
Nongovernmental nonprofit	77.5	78.2	67.2	68.8	69.3	68.6	67.9	66.7	64.8
For profit	68.7	65.2	52.2	51.6	52.6	52.5	52.0	51.1	50.1
State and local government	71.0	71.1	62.9	64.9	65.3	64.4	64.7	64.5	63.5
Long-term general and special	83.0	85.9	88.5	86.6	85.9	84.9	84.5	83.8	82.9
Psychiatric	82.8	85.2	87.0	84.6	82.5	82.4	81.4	80.1	80.3
Tuberculosis	61.2	67.0	64.1	69.3	66.4	76.6	82.9	84.8	80.7
Federal	80.0	80.1	76.3	73.7	73.3	72.8	77.3	76.8	74.9
Expenses (bil. dol.): [6]									
All hospitals	32.7	91.9	153.3	214.9	234.9	258.5	282.5	301.5	310.8
Non-Federal [1]	30.0	84.0	141.0	199.8	219.6	241.7	264.3	281.9	290.8
Community hospitals [2]	25.5	76.9	130.5	184.9	203.7	225.0	248.1	266.1	275.8
Nongovernmental nonprofit	18.4	55.8	96.1	136.9	150.7	166.8	183.8	197.2	204.2
For profit	1.4	5.8	11.5	17.2	18.8	20.5	22.5	23.1	23.4
State and local government	5.7	15.2	22.9	30.8	34.2	37.7	41.8	45.8	48.1
Long-term general and special	0.7	1.2	1.9	2.5	2.7	2.9	2.7	2.7	2.3
Psychiatric	3.1	5.8	8.3	12.0	12.9	13.5	13.2	12.7	12.3
Tuberculosis	0.1	0.1	0.1	(Z)	0.1	(Z)	(Z)	0.1	0.1
Federal	3.1	7.9	12.3	15.1	15.2	16.8	18.2	19.6	20.0
Personnel (1,000): [7]									
All hospitals	2,671	3,492	3,625	3,937	4,063	4,165	4,236	4,289	4,270
Non-Federal [1]	2,439	3,213	3,326	3,648	3,760	3,864	3,929	3,970	3,969
Community hospitals [2]	2,051	2,873	2,997	3,303	3,420	3,535	3,620	3,677	3,692
Nongovernmental nonprofit	1,473	2,086	2,216	2,454	2,533	2,624	2,692	2,711	2,719
For profit	105	189	221	261	273	281	285	289	302
State and local government	473	598	561	589	614	630	643	676	672
Long-term general and special	63	56	58	56	55	55	49	45	38
Psychiatric	307	275	263	284	280	269	256	242	233
Tuberculosis	12	3	2	1	1	1	1	1	1
Federal	232	279	299	288	303	301	306	320	301
Personnel per 100 patients [7]	221	329	398	462	482	504	525	548	573
Outpatient visits (mil.)	219.2	263.0	282.1	352.2	368.2	387.7	417.9	435.7	453.6
Emergency	60.1	82.0	80.1	89.9	92.8	93.5	95.8	97.4	96.0
Closures	(NA)	73	59	80	63	67	60	83	40

NA Not available.   Z Less than 500 beds, $50 million, or 0.5 percent.   [1] Short term (average length of stay less than 30 days) general and special (e.g., obstetrics and gynecology); eye, ear, nose and throat; rehabilitation etc. except psychiatric, tuberculosis, alcoholism and chemical dependency). Includes hospital units of institutions.   [2] Excludes hospital units of institutions.   [3] Beginning 1989, number of beds at end of reporting period; prior years, average number in 12 month period.   [4] Based on Bureau of the Census estimated resident population as of July 1. Estimates reflect revisions based on the 1990 Census of Population.   [5] Ratio of average daily census to every 100 beds.   [6] Excludes new construction.   [7] Includes full-time equivalents of part-time personnel.

Source: American Hospital Association, Chicago, IL, *Hospital Stat, 1995-96*, and prior years (previously called *Hospital Statistics*) (copyright).

Health and Nutrition

No. 188. Community Hospitals—States and Puerto Rico: 1994

[For definition of community hospitals see footnotes 1 and 2, table 187. See also *Historical Statistics, Colonial Times to 1970*, series B 305-308 and B 359-362 for data on all hospitals]

REGION, DIVISION, AND STATE OR OTHER AREA	Number of hospitals	Beds (1,000)	Patients admitted (1,000)	Average daily census [1] (1,000)	Occupancy rate [2] (percent)	Personnel [3] (1,000)	Outpatient visits (mil.)
United States	5,229	902.1	30,718.1	567.8	62.9	3,692.3	382.9
Northeast	778	198.9	6,799.1	148.5	74.6	874.7	97.6
New England	225	41.3	1,563.5	28.9	69.9	205.9	23.9
Maine.	39	4.2	143.2	2.8	66.4	18.1	2.2
New Hampshire	28	3.3	109.5	2.2	64.7	14.3	1.8
Vermont	15	1.9	57.1	1.3	67.9	7.0	0.9
Massachusetts.	95	19.9	781.5	13.6	68.3	108.4	12.4
Rhode Island	11	2.7	121.9	2.1	75.3	14.4	1.3
Connecticut	37	9.2	350.3	7.0	75.7	43.8	5.4
Middle Atlantic	553	157.6	5,235.6	119.6	75.9	668.8	73.7
New York	229	76.6	2,371.0	62.5	81.5	331.6	37.4
New Jersey	94	30.6	1,085.7	22.3	72.9	122.1	11.6
Pennsylvania	230	50.4	1,779.0	34.8	69.1	215.1	24.7
Midwest	1,513	234.1	7,417.4	140.2	59.9	933.8	106.5
East North Central	804	151.6	5,206.9	91.8	60.5	649.9	77.9
Ohio.	187	40.1	1,375.0	23.3	58.0	172.7	20.2
Indiana	114	19.9	699.9	11.6	58.3	88.0	11.6
Illinois.	207	43.2	1,462.5	26.0	60.2	179.5	20.2
Michigan	169	31.3	1,101.0	20.2	64.6	144.3	18.1
Wisconsin	127	17.1	568.4	10.7	62.7	65.4	7.8
West North Central	709	82.5	2,210.5	48.4	58.7	283.9	28.6
Minnesota	143	18.1	492.4	11.5	63.3	56.1	5.5
Iowa	116	13.0	355.3	7.3	56.3	45.4	5.6
Missouri	129	23.0	710.4	13.4	58.2	96.1	9.6
North Dakota	46	4.4	90.3	2.8	63.8	12.8	1.0
South Dakota.	50	4.4	96.3	2.7	60.8	10.8	1.0
Nebraska	91	8.5	176.4	4.8	57.1	27.1	2.3
Kansas	134	11.1	289.6	5.9	53.4	35.7	3.7
South	1,977	326.8	11,141.6	195.5	59.8	1283.8	109.6
South Atlantic	784	158.5	5,553.6	100.0	63.1	635.1	54.7
Delaware	8	1.8	79.5	1.5	83.4	10.3	1.2
Maryland.	49	12.9	556.6	9.1	71.0	59.4	4.5
District of Columbia. . .	12	4.0	156.7	3.0	74.3	20.6	1.2
Virginia	96	19.3	691.2	11.8	61.3	75.1	6.9
West Virginia	58	8.1	272.4	5.0	61.1	30.5	3.7
North Carolina	119	23.1	807.6	15.7	67.7	98.7	8.3
South Carolina	67	11.5	400.3	7.6	65.7	47.4	4.2
Georgia	157	26.4	853.2	16.3	61.9	98.5	9.0
Florida	218	51.4	1,736.2	30.0	58.5	194.6	15.5
East South Central	443	68.1	2,273.1	40.8	60.0	245.8	20.9
Kentucky.	105	15.5	524.0	9.4	60.6	56.4	5.3
Tennessee	126	21.9	742.1	13.2	59.9	84.4	7.0
Alabama	114	18.1	628.5	10.8	59.5	65.0	5.7
Mississippi.	98	12.5	378.6	7.5	60.0	40.1	2.9
West South Central . . .	750	100.1	3,314.8	54.7	54.6	402.9	33.9
Arkansas	86	10.2	339.8	5.9	57.5	36.4	3.2
Louisiana	132	18.9	611.0	10.7	56.3	75.5	7.2
Oklahoma	110	11.6	364.7	6.2	54.0	46.8	3.1
Texas	422	59.4	1,999.3	31.9	53.7	244.2	20.4
West.	961	142.3	5,360.1	83.6	58.7	599.9	69.2
Mountain	348	41.6	1,443.6	23.7	57.0	163.3	19.1
Montana	53	4.2	100.3	2.9	67.7	11.9	1.4
Idaho	41	3.4	104.1	1.9	54.0	11.0	1.7
Wyoming.	25	2.2	44.0	1.1	48.6	5.8	0.7
Colorado.	69	9.7	334.2	5.7	58.6	42.6	5.0
New Mexico.	37	4.1	152.0	2.2	53.3	18.9	2.5
Arizona.	60	9.9	411.0	5.6	56.5	40.8	3.7
Utah.	42	4.3	165.2	2.1	49.8	19.6	2.7
Nevada.	21	3.7	132.9	2.3	62.8	12.7	1.4
Pacific.	613	100.7	3,916.5	59.9	59.4	436.6	50.2
Washington	88	11.4	477.4	6.4	56.0	54.9	7.6
Oregon.	63	7.2	283.3	4.0	55.0	32.5	5.0
California	427	78.0	3,020.9	46.5	59.7	330.7	34.8
Alaska	16	1.3	36.9	0.6	51.8	4.8	0.7
Hawaii	19	2.9	97.9	2.3	80.5	13.7	2.1
Puerto Rico	50	8	400.0	5.6	70.0	28.4	3.8

[1] Inpatients receiving treatment each day; excludes newborn.   [2] Ratio of average daily census to every 100 beds.
[3] Includes full-time equivalents of part-time personnel.

Source: American Hospital Association, Chicago, IL, *Hospital Stat, 1995-96* (previously called *Hospital Statistics*) (copyright).

No. 189. Hospital Use Rates, by Type of Hospital: 1972 to 1994

[See also *Historical Statistics, Colonial Times to 1970*, series B 384-387]

TYPE OF HOSPITAL	1972	1980	1985	1990	1991	1992	1993	1994
Community hospitals: [1]								
Admissions per 1,000 population [2]	147	159	141	125	123	122	119	118
Admissions per bed.	35	37	33	34	34	34	33	34
Average length of stay [3] (days)	7.9	7.6	7.1	7.2	7.2	7.1	7.0	6.7
Outpatient visits per admission	1.8	5.6	6.5	9.7	10.4	11.2	11.9	12.5
Outpatient visits per 1,000 population [2]	777	890	919	1,208	1,277	1,367	1,423	1,471
Surgical operations (million)	14.8	18.8	20.1	21.9	22.4	22.9	22.8	23.0
Number per admission	0.5	0.5	0.6	0.7	0.7	0.7	0.7	0.7
Non-Federal psychiatric:								
Admissions per 1,000 population [2]	2.8	2.5	2.5	2.9	2.9	2.9	2.9	2.9
Days in hospital per 1,000 population [2]	661	295	224	190	179	162	149	136

[1] For definition of community hospitals, see footnotes 1 and 2, table 187.   [2] Based on Bureau of the Census estimated resident population as of July 1. Estimates reflect revisions based on the 1990 Census of Population.   [3] Number of inpatient days divided by number of admissions.

Source: American Hospital Association, Chicago, IL, *Hospital Stat, 1995-96*, and prior years (previously called *Hospital Statistics*) (copyright).

No. 190. Average Cost to Community Hospitals per Patient: 1970 to 1994

[In dollars, except percent. Covers non-Federal short-term general or special hospitals (excluding psychiatric or tuberculosis hospitals and, beginning 1975, hospital units of institutions). Total cost per patient based on total hospital expenses (payroll, employee benefits, professional fees, supplies, etc.). Data have been adjusted for outpatient visits]

TYPE OF EXPENSE AND HOSPITAL	1970	1975	1980	1985	1989	1990	1991	1992	1993	1994
Average cost per day, total.	74	134	245	460	637	687	752	820	881	931
Annual percent change [1]	12.7	17.5	12.9	11.9	8.7	7.8	9.5	9.0	7.4	5.7
Nongovernmental nonprofit	75	133	246	463	642	692	758	828	898	950
For profit.	71	133	257	500	708	752	820	889	914	924
State and local government	71	136	239	433	582	634	696	754	800	859
Average cost per stay, total	605	1,030	1,851	3,245	4,588	4,947	5,360	5,794	6,132	6,230
Nongovernmental nonprofit	615	1,040	1,902	3,307	4,649	5,001	5,393	5,809	6,178	6,257
For profit.	486	876	1,676	3,033	4,406	4,727	5,134	5,548	5,643	5,529
State and local government	614	1,031	1,750	3,106	4,430	4,838	5,340	5,871	6,206	6,513

[1] Change from immediate prior year, except 1970, average annual change from 1965. For explanation of average annual change, see Guide to Tabular Presentation.

Source: American Hospital Association, Chicago, IL, *Hospital Stat, 1995-96*, and prior years (previously called *Hospital Statistics*) (copyright).

No. 191. Average Cost to Community Hospitals per Patient, by State: 1990 to 1994

[In dollars. See headnote, table 190]

STATE	AVERAGE COST PER DAY			AVERAGE COST PER STAY			STATE	AVERAGE COST PER DAY			AVERAGE COST PER STAY		
	1990	1993	1994	1990	1993	1994		1990	1993	1994	1990	1993	1994
U.S. . . .	687	881	931	4,947	6,132	6,230	MO	679	863	915	5,022	6,161	6,249
AL	588	775	781	4,175	5,229	4,895	MT	405	481	470	3,973	4,953	4,965
AK	1,070	1,136	1,263	6,249	7,594	8,168	NE	490	626	606	4,675	6,024	6,006
AZ	867	1,091	1,091	4,877	5,528	5,375	NV	854	900	1,016	5,511	6,796	6,526
AR	534	678	724	3,730	4,585	4,514	NH	671	976	825	4,544	6,964	5,978
CA	939	1,221	1,301	5,709	6,918	7,252	NJ	613	829	934	4,573	6,540	6,933
CO	725	961	993	5,209	6,212	6,241	NM	734	1,046	1,047	4,172	5,600	5,564
CT	825	1,058	1,121	6,238	7,478	7,835	NY	641	784	854	6,397	7,716	8,127
DE	771	1,028	1,042	5,112	7,307	7,303	NC	595	763	806	4,408	5,571	5,701
DC	995	1,201	1,304	7,876	8,594	9,021	ND	427	507	515	4,468	5,403	5,547
FL	769	940	975	5,312	6,169	6,106	OH	720	940	1,008	4,801	5,923	6,103
GA	630	775	797	4,303	5,554	5,621	OK	632	797	848	4,302	5,093	5,291
HI	638	823	958	6,048	7,633	8,428	OR	800	1,053	1,077	4,432	5,309	5,492
ID	547	659	679	3,701	4,635	4,448	PA	662	861	892	5,120	6,564	6,332
IL	717	912	988	5,253	6,318	6,372	RI	663	885	970	4,839	5,672	5,984
IN	667	898	955	4,390	5,677	5,715	SC	590	838	876	4,168	5,955	6,056
IA	495	612	672	4,135	4,980	5,077	SD	391	506	470	3,905	5,052	4,797
KS	532	666	715	4,161	5,108	5,240	TN	633	859	870	4,340	5,798	5,621
KY	563	703	748	3,762	4,749	4,873	TX	752	1,010	1,055	4,663	6,021	6,051
LA	701	875	929	4,575	5,781	5,916	UT	832	1,081	1,115	4,409	5,314	5,378
ME	574	738	802	4,604	5,543	5,685	VT	598	676	651	4,343	5,241	5,400
MD	678	889	981	4,640	5,632	5,833	VA	635	830	885	4,408	5,504	5,518
MA	788	1,036	1,131	5,709	6,843	7,018	WA	817	1,143	1,206	4,519	5,792	5,909
MI	716	902	929	5,358	6,147	6,169	WV	565	701	727	3,918	4,712	4,839
MN	536	652	695	4,782	5,867	6,029	WI	554	744	802	4,083	5,348	5,536
MS	439	555	584	3,116	4,053	4,235	WY	462	537	504	3,990	4,706	4,639

Source: American Hospital Association, Chicago, IL, *Hospital Stat, 1995-96*, and prior years (previously called *Hospital Statistics*) (copyright).

No. 192. Facilities and Services Provided by Community Hospitals: 1993

[Community hospitals are non-Federal short-stay (average length stay fewer than 30 days) excluding hospital units of institutions. Data are for hospitals responding to that portion of the questionnaire 4,845 of a total of 5,261 community hospitals in 1993]

SERVICE	Hospi-tals with service	Percent of total	SERVICE	Hospi-tals with service	Percent of total
Adult day care program.	362	7.5	Outpatient surgery services	4,541	93.7
Alzheimer's diagnostic/assessment	475	9.8	Patient representative services.	2,739	56.5
Angioplasty.	1,055	21.8	Psychiatric services:		
Alcoholism/chemical dependency			Emergency	1,694	35.0
outpatient services	1,025	21.2	Outpatient.	1,130	23.3
Birthing rooms.	3,228	66.6	Radiation therapy:		
Blood bank.	3,382	69.8	X-ray	967	20.0
Cardiac catheterization	1,610	33.2	Megavoltage (mil. volts).	1,006	20.8
Cardiac rehabilitation	2,374	49.0	Radio-active implants	1,231	25.4
Computed tomographic (CT) scanner . .	3,750	77.4	Radio isotope facilities:		
Emergency department.	4,460	92.1	Diagnostic.	2,988	61.7
Extracorporeal shock wave			Therapeutic.	1,288	26.6
lithotripter	516	10.7	Rehabilitation outpatient		
Genetic counseling services.	501	10.3	department	2,802	57.8
Geriatric services.	3,147	65.0	Reproductive health services	2,130	44.0
Hemodialysis	1,358	28.0	Therapy services:		
Histopathology laboratory	3,105	64.1	Occupational therapy services	2,688	55.5
Home health services.	2,047	42.2	Physical therapy services.	4,143	85.5
Hospice	964	19.9	Recreational therapy services.	1,751	36.1
Hospital auxiliary	3,861	79.7	Respiratory therapy services.	4,420	91.2
AIDS inpatient care	3,564	73.6	Trauma center.	810	16.7
AIDS outpatient care	326	6.7	Ultrasound	4,115	84.9
Magnetic resonance imaging (MRI). . . .	1,507	31.1	Volunteer services department	3,356	69.3
Open-heart surgery facilities	908	18.7	Women's center	1,364	28.2

Source: American Hospital Association, Chicago, IL, *Hospital Statistics*, 1994-95, and the *1993 Annual Survey of Hospitals* (copyright).

No. 193. Hospital Utilization Rates: 1970 to 1993

[Represents estimates of inpatients discharged from noninstitutional, short-stay hospitals, exclusive of Federal hospitals. Excludes newborn infants. Based on sample data collected from the National Hospital Discharge Survey, a sample survey of hospital records of patients discharged in year shown; subject to sampling variability. For composition of regions, see table 27]

SELECTED CHARACTERISTIC	Patients dis-charged (1,000)	PATIENTS DISCHARGED PER 1,000 PERSONS [1]			DAYS OF CARE PER 1,000 PERSONS [1]			AVERAGE STAY (days)		
		Total	Male	Female	Total	Male	Female	Total	Male	Female
1970	29,127	144	118	169	1,122	982	1,251	8.0	8.7	7.6
1980	37,832	168	139	194	1,217	1,068	1,356	7.3	7.7	7.0
1985	35,056	148	124	171	954	849	1,053	6.5	6.9	6.2
1986	34,256	143	121	164	913	817	1,003	6.4	6.8	6.1
1987 [2]	33,387	138	116	159	889	806	968	6.4	6.9	6.1
1988 [2]	31,146	128	107	147	834	757	907	6.5	7.1	6.2
1989 [2]	30,947	126	105	145	815	741	884	6.5	7.0	6.1
1990 [2]	30,788	124	102	144	792	704	875	6.4	6.9	6.1
1991 [2]	31,098	124	103	144	795	715	869	6.4	7.0	6.0
1992 [2]	30,951	122	101	142	751	680	818	6.2	6.7	5.8
1993, [2] total	**30,825**	**120**	**98**	**141**	**720**	**644**	**792**	**6.0**	**6.5**	**5.6**
Age:										
Under 1 year old	710	181	206	156	1,155	1,265	1,041	6.4	6.1	6.7
1 to 4 years old	654	41	46	37	163	169	157	3.9	3.7	4.3
5 to 14 years old	777	21	22	20	108	110	105	5.1	5.1	5.2
15 to 24 years old	3,088	87	37	138	309	204	416	3.5	5.5	3.0
25 to 34 years old	4,655	113	53	171	446	313	575	4.0	5.9	3.4
35 to 44 years old	3,457	85	72	99	431	424	438	5.1	5.9	4.4
45 to 64 years old	6,283	127	132	123	785	831	742	6.2	6.3	6.1
65 to 74 years old	4,890	262	284	245	1,927	2,033	1,844	7.4	7.2	7.5
75 years old and over. . .	6,310	446	476	430	3,665	3,764	3,609	8.2	7.9	8.4
Region:										
Northeast	6,965	136	119	152	952	876	1,023	7.0	7.4	6.7
Midwest	7,097	116	98	134	706	638	771	6.1	6.5	5.8
South	11,580	131	104	156	749	658	834	5.7	6.3	5.4
West	5,183	93	72	114	473	419	527	5.1	5.8	4.6

[1] Based on Bureau of the Census estimated civilian population as of July 1. Estimates for 1980-90 do not reflect revisions based on the 1990 Census of Population. [2] Comparisons beginning 1988 with data for earlier years should be made with caution as estimates of change may reflect improvements in the design rather than true changes in hospital use.

Source: U.S. National Center for Health Statistics, *Vital and Health Statistics*, series 13; and unpublished data.

No. 194. Hospital Outpatient Department Visits: 1994

[An outpatient department is a hospital facility where nonurgent ambulatory care is provided under the supervision of a physician. Data exclude clinics where only ancillary services, such as radiology, are provided. Based on the 1994 National Hospital Ambulatory Care Surveys and subject to sampling error; see source for details]

CHARACTERISTIC	Number of visits (1,000)	Percent distribution	Visits per 100 persons	CHARACTERISTIC	Number of visits (1,000)	Percent distribution	Visits per 100 persons
All visits	**66,345**	**100.0**	**25.6**	New patient	14,165	21.4	(X)
Age:				Expected source of payment: [1]			
Under 15 years old	13,516	20.4	22.9	Medicaid	20,029	30.2	(X)
15 to 24 years old	7,834	11.8	21.7	Private/commercial insurance	18,411	27.8	(X)
25 to 44 years old	19,815	29.9	23.9	Medicare	11,867	17.9	(X)
45 to 64 years old	14,306	21.6	28.4	Patient paid	7,323	11.0	(X)
65 to 74 years old	5,955	9.0	32.6	HMO/other prepaid	7,680	11.6	(X)
75 years old and over	4,920	7.4	38.5	Other government	2,342	3.5	(X)
Sex:				No charge	923	1.4	(X)
Male	25,746	38.8	20.4	Other and unknown	6,080	9.2	(X)
Female	40,599	61.2	30.5	Disposition: [1]			
Race:				Return to clinic:			
White	49,701	74.9	23.2	By appointment	42,821	64.5	(X)
Black	15,132	22.8	45.8	As needed	13,135	19.8	(X)
Asian/Pacific Islander	1,283	1.9	(NA)	Refer to other clinic/physician	5,045	7.6	(X)
American Indian/Eskimo/Aleut. .	228	0.3	(NA)	Return to referring physician. . .	2,004	3.0	(X)
Visit status:				No followup	4,122	6.2	(X)
Old patient	52,180	78.7	(X)	Telephone followup	2,044	3.1	(X)
Old problem	42,258	63.7	(X)	Admit to hospital	938	1.4	(X)
New problem	9,922	15.0	(X)	Other	1,659	2.5	(X)

NA Not available.   X Not applicable.   [1] More than one reported source of payment or disposition may be reported.

Source: U.S. National Center for Health Statistics, *Advance Data*, No. 276, June 11, 1996.

No. 195. Hospital Emergency Room Visits: 1994

[An emergency room is a hospital facility staffed by physicians for the provision of providing outpatient services to patients whose conditions require immediate attention and is staffed 24 hours a day. Data are for non-Federal short stay, or general hospitals. Based on the 1994 National Hospital Ambulatory Care Survey and subject to sampling error; see source for details]

CHARACTERISTIC	NUMBER OF VISITS (1,000)				VISITS PER 100 PERSONS			
	Total	Urgent [1]	Nonurgent	Injury-related	Total	Urgent [1]	Nonurgent	Injury-related
All visits [2]	**93,402**	**44,091**	**49,311**	**39,640**	**36.0**	**17.0**	**19.0**	**15.6**
Age:								
Under 15 years old	23,751	9,985	13,766	9,839	40.2	16.9	23.3	16.6
15 to 24 years old	15,411	6,532	8,879	7,632	42.7	18.1	24.5	21.1
25 to 44 years old	28,219	12,241	15,978	13,250	34.0	14.8	19.3	16.0
45 to 64 years old	13,011	6,949	6,062	5,105	25.8	13.8	12.0	10.1
65 to 74 years old	5,797	3,576	2,221	1,586	30.3	19.6	10.7	8.7
75 years old and over	7,214	4,808	2,406	2,229	56.5	37.6	18.8	17.5
Sex:								
Male	44,666	21,622	23,044	21,776	35.3	17.1	18.2	17.6
Female	48,736	22,469	26,267	17,863	36.6	16.9	19.7	13.7
Race:								
White	72,337	34,839	37,498	31,857	33.7	16.2	17.5	14.9
Black	18,603	8,158	10,445	6,842	56.3	24.7	31.6	20.7

[1] Patient requires immediate attention.   [2] Includes other races, not shown separately.

Source: U.S. National Center for Health Statistics, *Advance Data*, No. 275, May 17, 1996.

No. 196. Hospital Discharges and Days of Care: 1993

[See headnote, table 193]

AGE AND FIRST-LISTED DIAGNOSIS	DISCHARGES Number (1,000)	DISCHARGES Per 1,000 persons [1]	Days of care per 1,000 persons [1]	Average stay (days)	AGE AND FIRST-LISTED DIAGNOSIS	DISCHARGES Number (1,000)	DISCHARGES Per 1,000 persons [1]	Days of care per 1,000 persons [1]	Average stay (days)
MALE					FEMALE				
All ages [2]	12,262	98.4	643.5	6.5	**All ages [2]**	18,563	140.8	792.1	5.6
Diseases of heart	2,078	16.7	100.7	6.0	Delivery	4,015	30.5	74.1	2.4
Malignant neoplasms	690	5.5	47.2	8.5	Diseases of heart	1,873	14.2	93.4	6.6
Pneumonia, all forms	598	4.8	36.3	7.6	Malignant neoplasms	792	6.0	46.3	7.7
Psychoses	500	4.0	46.5	11.6	Pneumonia, all forms	586	4.4	35.7	8.0
Fractures, all sites	440	3.5	23.7	6.7	Psychoses	554	4.2	51.8	12.3
Under 15 years [2]	1,193	41.1	206.2	5.0	Under 15 years [2]	948	34.2	184.2	5.4
Acute respiratory infection	136	4.7	15.0	3.2	Acute respiratory infection	86	3.1	10.3	3.3
Pneumonia, all forms	126	4.3	18.7	4.3	Pneumonia, all forms	83	3.0	16.3	5.4
Bronchitis, emphysema [3]	105	3.6	11.3	3.1	Bronchitis, emphysema [3]	63	2.3	8.6	3.8
Congenital anomalies	64	2.2	14.2	6.5	Noninfectious enteritis [4]	43	1.5	3.7	2.4
Fractures, all sites	45	1.5	6.4	4.2	Congenital anomalies	42	1.5	12.5	8.4
15 to 44 years [2]	3,179	54.5	317.8	5.8	15 to 44 years [2]	8,021	136.0	479.9	3.5
Psychoses	296	5.1	56.1	11.1	Delivery	4,001	67.8	164.9	2.4
Fractures, all sites	216	3.7	20.5	5.5	Psycoses	268	4.5	49.0	10.8
Diseases of heart	161	2.8	12.7	4.6	Benign neoplasms	152	2.6	8.9	3.4
Alcohol dependence syndrome	130	2.2	17.9	8.0	Cholelithiasis	136	2.3	7.1	3.1
Intervertebral disk disorders	130	2.2	7.4	3.3	Pregnancy w/abortive outcome	132	2.2	4.4	2.0
45 to 64 years [2]	3,143	131.5	831.0	6.3	45 to 64 years [2]	3,141	122.5	742.2	6.1
Diseases of heart	743	31.1	169.6	5.5	Diseases of heart	423	16.5	91.4	5.5
Malignant neoplasms	201	8.4	74.2	8.8	Malignant neoplasms	258	10.1	75.0	7.4
Psychoses	115	4.8	57.1	11.8	Psychoses	122	4.7	61.2	12.9
Pneumonia, all forms	97	4.0	29.2	7.2	Bronchitis, emphysema [3]	111	4.3	26.9	6.2
Cerebrovascular disease	96	4.0	33.1	8.3	Benign neoplasms	105	4.1	16.8	4.1
65 years old and older [2]	4,748	357.2	2,691.2	7.5	65 years old and older [2]	6,453	330.9	2,666.0	8.1
Diseases of heart	1,167	87.8	580.1	6.6	Diseases of heart	1,362	69.9	489.1	7.0
Malignant neoplasms	409	30.8	265.8	8.6	Malignant neoplasms	402	20.6	176.2	8.6
Pneumonia, all forms	307	23.1	208.9	9.0	Fractures, all sites	381	19.5	182.0	9.3
Cerebrovascular disease	268	20.2	162.3	8.0	Cerebrovascular disease	362	18.5	161.2	8.7
Hyperplasia of prostate	140	10.5	41.5	3.9	Pneumonia, all forms	335	17.2	159.6	9.3

[1] See footnote 1, table 193.   [2] Includes other first-listed diagnoses not shown separately.   [3] Includes asthma.   [4] Includes colitis.

Source: U.S. National Center for Health Statistics, *Health, United States,* 1994; and unpublished data.

No. 197. Outpatient Surgery Performed in Hospitals: 1980 to 1994

TYPE OF HOSPITAL	1980	1985	1988	1989	1990	1991	1992	1993	1994
OUTPATIENT SURGERIES (1,000)									
All hospitals	3,198	7,309	10,586	10,953	11,678	12,209	12,849	13,098	13,612
Ownership:									
Non-Federal hospitals	3,063	6,984	10,038	10,362	11,085	11,724	12,316	12,641	13,167
Community hospitals [1]	3,054	6,951	10,028	10,351	11,070	11,712	12,308	12,624	13,155
Nongovernmental nonprofit	2,416	5,392	7,577	7,834	8,389	8,989	9,500	9,685	10,045
Federal hospitals	135	325	548	591	593	486	533	457	445
Size of hospital: 6 to 99 beds	354	752	1,229	1,241	1,303	1,366	1,464	1,473	1,588
100 to 199 beds	571	1,502	2,252	2,360	2,498	2,636	2,824	2,927	3,042
200 to 299 beds	630	1,521	2,297	2,383	2,543	2,695	2,790	2,906	3,072
300 to 499 beds	977	2,069	2,845	2,920	3,172	3,293	3,340	3,424	3,421
500 beds or more	666	1,465	1,963	2,049	2,162	2,220	2,431	2,368	2,489
OUTPATIENT SURGERIES AS PERCENT OF TOTAL									
All hospitals	16.4	34.5	47.0	48.7	50.6	52.1	53.6	54.9	56.9
Ownership:									
Non-Federal hospitals	16.3	34.5	46.8	48.5	50.5	52.3	53.8	55.4	57.2
Community hospitals [1]	16.3	34.6	46.8	48.5	50.5	52.3	53.8	55.4	57.2
Nongovernmental nonprofit	17.1	35.5	47.0	48.6	50.7	52.5	54.0	55.7	57.4
Federal hospitals	18.6	33.9	49.7	51.5	51.8	47.8	49.3	45.4	48.7
Size of hospital: 6 to 99 beds	17.9	36.5	52.8	54.1	56.2	58.7	61.1	62.5	65.0
100 to 199 beds	15.4	36.3	50.3	52.3	55.0	56.3	58.3	59.4	61.7
200 to 299 beds	16.7	36.4	49.2	50.7	52.9	54.6	55.3	57.2	58.8
300 to 499 beds	17.2	34.4	46.5	48.0	48.8	50.6	51.9	53.2	54.2
500 beds or more	15.1	30.4	39.6	41.6	43.9	44.4	46.5	46.9	49.7

[1] For definition of community hospital, see footnotes 1 and 2, table 187.

Source: American Hospital Association, Chicago, IL, *Hospital Stat, 1995-96,* and prior years (previously called *Hospital Statistics*) (copyright); and unpublished data from the Annual Survey of Hospitals.

No. 198. Procedures for Inpatients Discharged From Short-Stay Hospitals: 1980 to 1993

[Excludes newborn infants and discharges from Federal hospitals. See headnote, table 193]

SEX AND TYPE OF PROCEDURE	NUMBER OF PROCEDURES (1,000)				RATE PER 1,000 POPULATION [2]			
	1980	1985	1990 [1]	1993 [1]	1980	1985	1990 [1]	1993 [1]
Surgical procedures, total [3] [4]	**24,494**	**24,799**	**23,051**	**22,767**	**108.6**	**104.6**	**92.4**	**88.8**
MALE								
Total [3] [4]	**8,505**	**8,805**	**8,538**	**8,355**	**78.1**	**76.8**	**70.6**	**67.1**
Cardiac catheterization	228	439	620	613	2.1	3.8	5.1	4.9
Prostatectomy	335	367	364	317	3.1	3.2	3.0	2.5
Reduction of fracture [5]	325	339	300	294	3.0	3.0	2.5	2.4
Repair of inguinal hernia	483	370	181	96	4.4	3.2	1.5	0.8
FEMALE								
Total [3] [4]	**15,989**	**15,994**	**14,513**	**14,411**	**137.1**	**130.6**	**113.0**	**109.3**
Procedures to assist delivery [4]	2,391	2,494	2,491	2,428	20.5	20.4	19.4	18.4
Cesarean section	619	877	945	917	5.3	7.2	7.4	7.0
Repair of current obstetric laceration	355	548	795	860	3.0	4.5	6.2	6.5
Hysterectomy	649	670	591	562	5.6	5.5	4.6	4.3
Diagnostic and other nonsurgical procedures [4] [6]	**6,918**	**11,961**	**17,455**	**18,842**	**30.7**	**50.5**	**70.0**	**73.5**
MALE								
Total [4] [6]	**3,386**	**5,889**	**7,378**	**7,787**	**31.1**	**51.4**	**61.0**	**62.5**
Angiocardiography and arteriography [7]	355	693	1,051	1,024	3.3	6.0	8.7	8.2
CAT scan [8]	152	671	736	565	1.4	5.9	6.1	4.5
FEMALE								
Total [4] [6]	**3,532**	**6,072**	**10,077**	**11,055**	**30.3**	**49.6**	**78.5**	**83.8**
Diagnostic ultrasound	204	756	941	848	1.7	6.2	7.3	6.4
CAT scan [8]	154	707	770	594	1.3	5.8	6.0	4.5

[1] Comparisons beginning 1990 with data for earlier years should be made with caution as estimates of change may reflect improvements in the design rather than true changes in hospital use. [2] Based on Bureau of the Census estimated civilian population as of July 1. Population estimates for the 1980's do not reflect revised estimates based on the 1990 Census of Population. [3] Includes other types of surgical procedures not shown separately. [4] Beginning in 1990, the definition of some surgical and diagnostic and other nonsurgical procedures was revised, causing a discontinuity in the trends for some totals. [5] Excluding skull, nose, and jaw. [6] Includes other nonsurgical procedures not shown separately. [7] Using contrast material. [8] Computerized axial tomography.
Source: U.S. National Center for Health Statistics, *Vital and Health Statistics*, series 13; and unpublished data.

No. 199. Hospital Discharges—Principal Source of Expected Payment: 1993

[See headnote, table 193]

CHARACTERISTIC	Total discharges [1] (1,000)	PRINCIPAL SOURCE OF EXPECTED PAYMENT—PERCENT DISTRIBUTION							
		Private insurance	Government				Self-pay	No charge	Other [2]
			Medicare	Medicaid	Worker's compensation	Other			
AGE									
All ages	**30,825**	**33.9**	**37.8**	**14.7**	**1.3**	**1.8**	**4.9**	**0.4**	**3.0**
Under 15 years old . . .	2,141	42.2	1.4	40.0	(X)	3.0	5.6	1.4	4.0
15 to 44 years old. . . .	11,200	49.4	4.6	25.2	2.1	2.7	8.3	0.6	4.4
45 to 64 years old. . . .	6,283	55.4	15.9	11.2	2.0	2.3	6.3	0.5	4.1
65 years old and over .	11,201	4.8	90.3	1.3	0.2	0.3	0.5	([3])	0.8
SEX									
Male, all ages	**12,262**	**31.4**	**41.9**	**10.9**	**2.0**	**1.9**	**5.8**	**0.5**	**3.1**
Under 15 years old . . .	1,193	42.2	0.9	41.1	(X)	2.8	5.4	1.4	4.1
15 to 44 years old. . . .	3,179	43.5	9.4	15.8	4.8	3.5	12.9	1.0	5.1
45 to 64 years old. . . .	3,143	53.9	18.4	9.4	2.4	2.3	6.4	0.5	4.2
65 years old and over .	4,748	5.7	89.4	1.1	0.3	0.4	0.6	([3])	0.8
Female, all ages . .	**18,563**	**35.5**	**35.1**	**17.2**	**0.8**	**1.7**	**4.3**	**0.3**	**2.9**
Under 15 years old . . .	948	42.2	2.0	38.5	(X)	3.2	5.7	1.4	3.9
15 to 44 years old. . . .	8,021	51.7	2.7	28.9	1.0	2.4	6.5	0.4	4.1
45 to 64 years old. . . .	3,141	56.9	13.3	12.9	1.6	2.3	6.2	0.5	4.0
65 years old and over .	6,453	4.0	90.9	1.5	0.2	0.2	0.5	([3])	0.8
RACE									
White	20,101	36.5	41.5	9.6	1.2	1.4	4.2	0.3	3.1
All other	4,912	25.4	25.7	31.6	0.8	2.9	6.8	1.1	3.4
Not stated	5,812	32.0	35.4	17.9	1.8	2.2	5.7	([3])	2.5
REGION									
Northeast	6,965	33.5	38.6	14.7	1.0	0.8	4.7	0.4	3.6
Midwest	7,097	34.9	42.0	12.2	0.7	1.9	4.1	0.3	2.5
South	11,580	33.7	38.0	13.7	1.8	2.3	6.0	0.6	1.4
West	5,183	33.6	30.7	20.4	1.2	1.8	3.8	([3])	6.6

X Not applicable. [1] Includes discharges for whom expected source of payment was unknown. [2] Includes all other nonprofit source of payment such as church, welfare, or United Way. [3] Figure does not meet standards of reliability or precision.
Source: U.S. National Center for Health Statistics, unpublished data.

No. 200. Organ Transplants and Grafts: 1981 to 1995

[**As of end of year.** Based on reports of procurement programs and transplant centers in the United States, except as noted]

PROCEDURE	NUMBER OF PROCEDURES							NUMBER OF CENTERS		Number of people waiting, 1995	1-year survival rates, 1994 (percent)
	1981	1985	1990	1992	1993	1994	1995	1987	1994		
Transplant:											
Heart	62	719	1,998	2,172	2,298	2,340	1,952	104	165	3,468	84.3
Liver	26	602	2,534	3,059	3,440	3,652	3,229	45	117	5,691	82.9
Kidney	4,883	7,695	9,433	10,210	10,361	10,644	9,004	200	248	31,045	95.0
Heart-lung	5	30	52	48	61	70	63	23	92	208	75.8
Lung	-	2	187	535	669	722	727	(NA)	85	1,923	(NA)
Pancreas/Islet cell	(NA)	130	529	557	[1]113	[1]95	[1]89	31	116	285	(NA)
Cornea grafts [2] . . .	15,500	26,300	40,631	42,337	40,215	43,743	(NA)	[3]103	[3]115	(NA)	(NA)
Bone grafts	(NA)	(NA)	350,000	350,000	(NA)	(NA)	(NA)	(NA)	(NA)	(NA)	(NA)
Skin grafts	(NA)	(NA)	5,500	5,500	(NA)	(NA)	(NA)	(NA)	(NA)	(NA)	(NA)

- Represents zero. NA Not available. [1] Pancreas only. [2] 1981 through 1992, number of procedures and eye banks include Canada. [3] Eye banks.

Source: Transplants: through 1992, U.S. Department of Health and Human Services, Public Health Service, Division of Organ Transplantation; beginning 1993, United Network for Organ Sharing, Richmond, VA; American Association of Tissue Banks, Mclean, VA; and Eye Bank Association of America, Washington, DC; and unpublished data.

No. 201. Home Health and Hospice Care Patients, by Selected Characteristics: 1994

[See headnote, table 203]

ITEM	CURRENT PATIENTS [1]			DISCHARGES [2]		
	Total	Home health agency	Hospice	Total	Home health agency	Hospice
Total (1,000)	1,950.3	1,889.4	61.0	5,600.2	5,272.2	328.0
PERCENT DISTRIBUTION						
Age:						
Under 45 years old	12.6	12.7	9.0	14.3	14.9	6.2
45-54 years old	4.4	4.4	6.3	5.3	5.2	6.9
55-64 years old	10.1	9.9	15.6	7.8	7.4	13.9
65 years old and over	72.8	73.0	69.1	72.6	72.5	73.0
65-69 years old	9.3	9.3	9.5	9.4	9.2	11.6
70-74 years old	12.6	12.6	13.8	14.6	14.5	16.2
75-79 years old	14.9	15.0	12.3	16.4	16.5	15.5
80-84 years old	15.9	15.9	16.5	18.1	18.5	12.4
85 years old and over	20.1	20.2	16.9	14.1	13.9	17.4
Sex:						
Male	32.8	32.5	44.7	41.0	40.3	52.3
Female	67.2	67.5	55.3	59.0	59.7	47.7
Race:						
White	63.8	63.3	80.8	66.8	66.0	79.4
Black	15.6	15.9	7.2	8.6	8.6	7.3
Other or unknown	20.6	20.8	12.0	24.7	25.4	13.3
Marital status: [3]						
Married	31.2	30.6	48.4	38.3	37.7	48.9
Widowed	36.0	36.2	30.6	30.6	30.7	29.7
Divorced or separated	4.8	4.7	6.0	4.7	4.6	5.5
Never married	16.5	16.7	11.4	14.9	15.2	9.2
Unknown	11.5	11.7	3.7	11.5	11.8	6.8

[1] Patients on the rolls of the agency as of midnight the day prior to the survey. [2] Patients removed from the rolls of the agency during the 12 months prior to the day of the survey. A patient could be included more than once if the individual had more than one episode of care during the year. [3] For current patients, marital status at admission; for discharged patients, status at time of discharge.

Source: U.S. National Center for Health Statistics, *Advance Data*, No. 274, April 24, 1996.

No. 202. Elderly Home Health Patients: 1994

[Covers the civilian noninstitutionalized population 65 years old and over who are home health care patients. Home health care is provided to individuals and families in their place of residence. Based on the 1994 National Home and Hospice Care Survey]

ITEM	CURRENT PATIENTS [1] Number (1,000)	Per-cent	DIS-CHARGES [2] Number (1,000)	Per-cent	ITEM	CURRENT PATIENTS [1] Number (1,000)	Per-cent	DIS-CHARGES [2] Number (1,000)	Per-cent
Total 65 years old and over	**1,379.8**	**100.0**	**3,826.5**	**100.0**	Services rendered last billing period:				
Received help with—					Skilled nursing	1,122.4	81.3	3,302.8	86.3
Bathing or showering..	746.6	54.1	1,580.1	41.3	Personal care	585.5	42.4	1,176.7	30.8
Dressing	632.4	45.8	1,307.7	34.2	Social services	124.6	9.0	368.4	9.6
Eating	127.1	9.2	223.3	5.8	Counseling	48.3	3.5	165.7	4.3
Transferring in/out of a bed or chair	436.3	31.6	1,048.0	27.4	Medications	74.3	5.4	190.2	5.0
Using the toilet	336.6	24.4	759.7	19.9	Physical therapy	232.3	16.8	933.9	24.4
Doing light housework	564.4	40.9	918.4	24.0	Homemaker/companion services	322.2	23.4	612.4	16.0
Managing money	27.4	2.0	40.4	1.1	Referral services	20.8	1.5	66.4	1.7
Shopping for groceries or clothes	252.5	18.3	454.1	11.9	Dietary and nutrition services	44.1	3.2	76.0	2.0
Using the telephone	47.0	3.4	40.6	1.1	Physician services	16.2	1.2	48.9	1.3
Preparing meals	351.4	25.5	728.8	19.0	High tech care	13.9	1.0	39.8	1.0
Taking medications	340.4	24.7	755.6	19.7	Occupational/vocational therapy	39.0	2.8	164.2	4.3
Primary source of payment of last billing:					Speech therapy/audiology	17.0	1.2	46.9	1.2
Private insurance	26.2	1.9	315.5	8.2					
Own income	63.1	4.6	116.1	3.0					
Medicare	1,004.6	72.8	3,068.5	80.2					
Medicaid	120.5	8.7	108.9	2.8					

[1] Patients on the rolls of the agency as of midnight the day prior to the survey. [2] Patients removed from the rolls of the agency during the 12 months prior to the day of the survey. A patient could be included more than once if the individual had more than one episode of care during the year.

Source: U.S. National Center for Health Statistics, unpublished data.

No. 203. Home Health and Hospice Care Agencies, by Selected Characteristics: 1994

[In percent, except total in thousands. Based on the 1994 National Home and Hospice Care Survey. Home health care is provided to individuals and families in their place of residence. Hospice care is available in both the home and inpatient settings. Agencies which provide both types of care are classified according to how the majority of their patients are cared for. See source for details. For composition of regions, see table 27]

ITEM	AGENCIES Total	Home health agency	Hospice	CURRENT PATIENTS [1] Total	Home health agency	Hospice	DISCHARGES [2] Total	Home health agency	Hospice
Total (1,000)	**10.9**	**9.8**	**1.1**	**1,950.3**	**1,889.4**	**61.0**	**5,600.2**	**5,272.2**	**328.0**
PERCENT DISTRIBUTION									
Ownership:									
Proprietary	40.2	43.8	7.3	29.7	30.3	11.0	26.9	28.0	10.2
Voluntary nonprofit	42.0	36.8	90.4	59.8	59.0	86.3	66.6	65.4	87.0
Government and other	17.8	19.5	2.3	10.5	10.7	2.7	6.4	6.7	2.8
Certification:									
Medicare	79.4	80.0	69.2	88.1	87.9	84.3	94.9	95.1	87.6
Medicaid	38.0	79.4	59.9	87.9	87.9	80.8	91.5	91.5	85.3
Region:									
Northeast	18.0	18.1	16.9	33.4	33.7	25.2	36.9	37.1	33.5
Midwest	26.8	26.8	27.0	19.5	19.4	23.4	20.4	20.2	22.4
South	41.1	41.7	35.9	34.0	34.0	34.2	26.8	26.7	29.8
West	14.0	13.3	20.3	13.1	12.9	17.2	15.9	16.0	14.3

[1] Patients on the rolls of the agency as of midnight the day prior to the survey. [2] Patients removed from the rolls of the agency during the 12 months prior to the day of the survey. A patient could be included more than once if the individual had more than one episode of care during the year.

Source: U.S. National Center for Health Statistics, Advance Data, No. 274, April 24, 1996.

No. 204. Nursing and Related Care Facilities: 1971 to 1994

ITEM	Unit	1971	1976	1978	1980	1982	1986	1991	1994
Nursing and related care: [1]									
Facilities	Number .	22,004	20,468	[2]18,722	[3]23,065	[4]25,849	[4]25,646	[4]33,006	(NA)
Beds	1,000. . .	1,202	1,415	[2]1,349	[3]1,537	[4]1,642	[4]1,707	[4]1,921	(NA)
Resident patients	1,000. . .	1,076	1,293	[2]1,240	[3]1,396	[4]1,493	[4]1,553	[4]1,729	(NA)
Employees, full-time. . . .	1,000. . .	568	653	[2]664	[3]798	(NA)	(NA)	(NA)	(NA)
Per 1,000 patients . . .	Rate . . .	528	505	[2]535	[3]571	(NA)	(NA)	(NA)	(NA)
Skilled nursing facilities [5] . .	Number .	4,277	3,922	4,745	5,052	5,408	6,897	9,674	12,265
Beds	1,000. . .	307	309	408	436	488	(NA)	567	639
Per 1,000 Medicare									
enrollees [6]	Rate . . .	15.1	13.7	17.3	17.7	19.1	(NA)	15.3	17.4

NA Not available.   [1] Covers nursing homes with three beds or more and all other places providing some form of nursing, personal, or domiciliary care; standards vary widely among States. Includes skilled nursing facilities. 1971-1982 based on National Master Facility Inventory. Some changes in data beginning 1976 may be due to dependence on State collection. 1986 data based on the 1986 Inventory of Long Term Care Places. Data may not be strictly comparable with previous years. 1991 based on National Health Provider Inventory; excludes board and care homes for the mentally retarded.   [2] Includes 1976 data for California, District of Columbia, New York, and North Carolina.   [3] Excludes hospital-based nursing homes and includes 1978 data for Alaska and South Dakota.   [4] Excludes hospital-based nursing homes.   [5] Source: Through 1976, U.S. Social Security Administration, *Health Insurance Statistics* and unpublished data. Beginning 1978, U.S. Health Care Financing Administration, *Medicare Participating Providers and Suppliers of Health Services, 1980;* and unpublished data. Covers facilities and beds certified for participation under Medicare as of midyear. Includes facilities which have transfer agreements with one or more participating hospitals, and are engaged primarily in providing skilled nursing care and related services for the rehabilitation of injured, disabled, or sick persons.   [6] Based on number of aged persons residing in United States who were enrolled in the Medicare hospital insurance program as of July 1 of year stated.

Source: Except as noted, U.S. National Center for Health Statistics, *Health Resources Statistics,* annual through 1976 and 1978; 1982, 1986, and 1991, *Advance Data from Vital and Health Statistics,* No. 111, No. 147, and No. 244; and unpublished data.

No. 205. Nursing and Related Care Facilities, by Selected Characteristics: 1991

[Excludes hospital-based nursing homes which numbered 767 with 51,897 residents in 1991. Based on the National Health Provider Inventor. For composition of regions, see table 27]

CHARACTERISTIC	TOTAL FACILITIES				NURSING HOMES [1]				BOARD AND CARE HOMES [2]			
	Homes	Beds (1,000)	Average number of beds	Occupancy rate	Homes	Beds (1,000)	Average number of beds	Occupancy rate	Homes	Beds (1,000)	Average number of beds	Occupancy rate
Total	33,006	1,920	58	90.0	14,744	1,558	106	91.5	18,262	362	20	83.6
REGION												
Northeast	5,834	414	71	93.5	2,654	328	124	95.3	3,180	86	27	86.6
Midwest	9,142	583	64	89.7	5,137	519	101	90.3	4,005	64	16	84.7
South	9,499	608	64	89.7	4,708	502	107	91.2	4,791	106	22	83.0
West	8,531	315	37	86.8	2,245	209	93	89.6	6,286	106	17	81.3
OWNERSHIP												
Government.	1,570	113	72	92.3	725	100	138	93.5	845	13	16	83.8
Proprietary.	24,256	1,347	56	89.1	10,522	1,086	103	90.7	13,734	262	19	82.6
Nonprofit.	7,180	459	64	92.2	3,497	372	106	93.5	3,683	87	24	86.8
SIZE												
Fewer than 10 beds . .	10,025	53	5	83.9	165	1	5	81.6	9,860	52	5	83.9
10 to 24 beds	5,281	82	15	85.5	398	7	18	88.5	4,883	74	15	85.2
25 to 49 beds	3,381	124	37	87.9	1,590	61	39	91.1	1,791	62	35	84.9
50 to 74 beds	3,792	229	60	90.9	3,050	184	60	92.1	742	44	60	85.8
75 to 99 beds	2,795	245	88	90.2	2,401	211	88	91.2	394	34	86	83.6
100 to 199 beds	6,497	854	132	90.8	6,028	792	131	91.5	469	62	132	81.9
200 to 299 beds	942	218	231	90.1	847	196	231	91.3	95	22	228	79.0
300 to 499 beds	248	89	358	89.5	224	80	359	91.0	24	8	347	75.5
500 beds or more . . .	45	28	618	94.7	41	25	608	96.6	4	3	721	78.8

[1] These facilities have three or more beds.   [2] These facilities offer no nursing services and provide only personal care or supervisory care. Excludes board and care homes for the mentally retarded.

Source: U.S. National Center for Health Statistics, *Advance Data From Vital and Health Statistics,* No. 244; and unpublished data.

No. 206. Residential Facilities for Persons with Mental Retardation: 1970 to 1993

[For years ending **June 30.** Persons with mental retardation refers to those who have been so designated by State governments in the process of placing them into residential facilities]

ITEM	STATE OPERATED FACILITIES [1]					PRIVATE FACILITIES [3]			
	1970	1980 [2]	1985 [2]	1990 [2]	1993 [2]	1977	1982	1990	1993
Number of facilities [4]	190	394	881	1,321	1,765	10,219	14,605	41,588	58,790
Residents beginning of year	189,956	148,734	117,101	94,625	73,856	(NA)	(NA)	(NA)	(NA)
Admissions [5]	14,985	14,064	7,713	5,548	4,700	22,363	22,431	(NA)	(NA)
Deaths in institutions	3,496	2,142	1,537	1,100	1,167	891	920	(NA)	(NA)
Live releases [6]	14,702	16,225	10,310	7,620	7,258	12,384	12,999	(NA)	(NA)
Residents end of year	186,743	140,230	112,183	91,640	69,760	89,120	115,032	188,902	229,279
Rate per 100,000 population [7]	92.5	62.2	47.5	34.7	31.9	40.9	50.0	76.0	89.6
Average daily residents	187,897	136,304	111,791	92,729	71,477	(NA)	(NA)	(NA)	(NA)
Maintenance expenditures per day per average daily resident (dollars) [8]	13	68	122	196	225	[9]19	[9]37	(NA)	(NA)

NA Not available. [1] Data as submitted by many State agencies; figures reflect some estimates. Resident patients at the end of a year do not equal the number at the beginning of a succeeding year. Includes estimates for underreporting. [2] Includes data for 142 facilities in 1980, 121 facilities in 1985, 108 in 1990, and 110 in 1993 operated as mental hospitals or other facilities and which have residents with mental retardation. The average daily number of residents with mental retardation in these facilities was 8,240 in 1980, 5,602 in 1985, 1,487 in 1990, and 1,515 in 1993. [3] A privately-operated living quarter which provides 24-hour, 7-days-a-week responsibility for room, board, and supervision of mentally retarded persons. Excludes single-family homes providing services to a relative; and nursing homes, boarding homes, and foster homes not formally licensed or contracted as mental retardation service providers. [4] Beginning 1985, reflects the development of a large number of community based State-operated facilities which were developed in the early 1980's. [5] Includes readmissions and excludes transfers. Excludes people entering newly opened facilities. [6] 1970, represents excess of residents released alive from facility over those returning to facility. Beginning 1980, total live releases. [7] Based on Bureau of the Census estimated civilian population as of July 1. Estimates reflect revisions based on 1990 Census of Population. [8] Reporting facilities only; includes salaries and wages, purchased provisions, fuel, light, water, etc. [9] Represents average daily reimbursement rate per resident.

Source: 1970 State-operated facilities: U.S. Office of Human Development Services, *Residents in Public Institutions for the Mentally Retarded*, annual, and unpublished data; later State-operated facilities and private facilities: Center for Residential Services and Community Living (CRSCL), Institute on Community Integration, UAP, University of Minnesota, Minneapolis, MN, Magan, Blake, Prouty, and Larkin, Report No. 40, and earlier reports and unpublished data.

No. 207. Mental Health Facilities—Summary, by Type of Facility: 1992

[Facilities, beds and inpatients as of year-end; other data are for calendar year or fiscal year ending in a month other than December since facilities are permitted to report on either a calendar or fiscal year basis. Excludes private psychiatric office practice and psychiatric service modes of all types in hospitals or outpatient clinics of Federal agencies other than U.S. Dept. of Veterans Affairs. Excludes data from Puerto Rico, Virgin Islands, Guam, and other territories]

TYPE OF FACILITY	Number of facilities	INPATIENT BEDS		INPATIENTS		Average daily inpatients (1,000)	Inpatient care episodes [2] (1,000)	EXPENDITURES		Patient care staff [4] 1,000
		Total (1,000)	Rate [1]	Total (1,000)	Rate [1]			Total (mil. dol.)	Per capita [3] (dol.)	
Total	5,498	271.1	108.0	215.5	85.8	216.9	1,942	28,382	111.4	432.2
Mental hospitals:										
State and county	273	93.1	36.7	83.4	32.9	83.9	93.8	7,970	31.3	110.9
Private [5]	972	73.8	29.1	51.8	20.4	52.7	495.3	6,086	23.9	99.7
General hospitals [6]	1,616	52.1	21.3	35.6	14.6	36.3	987.6	5,193	20.4	72.9
Veterans Administration [7]	162	22.5	9.2	18.5	7.6	18.1	198.9	1,530	6.0	20.8
Free-standing psychiatric outpatient clinics [8]	862	(X)	(X)	(X)	(X)	(X)	(X)	821	3.2	13.2
Other [9]	1,613	29.6	11.7	26.2	10.3	25.9	166.7	6,782	26.6	114.7

X Not applicable. [1] Rate per 100,000 population. Based on Bureau of the Census estimated civilian population as of July 1. [2] "Inpatient care episodes" is defined as the number of residents in inpatient facilities at the beginning of the year plus the total additions to inpatient facilities during the year. [3] Based on Bureau of the Census estimated civilian population as of July 1. [4] Full-time equivalent. [5] Non-Federal. [6] Includes residential treatment centers for emotionally disturbed children. [7] Includes U.S. Department of Veterans Affairs (VA) neuropsychiatric hospitals, VA general hospitals with separate psychiatric settings and VA freestanding psychiatric outpatient clinics. [8] Includes mental health facilities which provide only psychiatric outpatient services. [9] Includes other multiservice mental health facilities with two or more settings, which are not elsewhere classified, as well as freestanding partial care facilities which only provide psychiatric partial care services. Number of facilities, expenditures, and staff data also include freestanding psychiatric partial care facilities.

Source: U.S. Substance Abuse and Mental Health Services Administration, Center for Mental Health Services, unpublished data.

No. 208. Days of Disability, by Type and Selected Characteristics: 1970 to 1994

[Covers civilian noninstitutional population. Beginning 1985, the levels of estimates may not be comparable to estimates for 1970-1980 because the later data are based on a revised questionnaire and field procedures; for further information, see source. Based on National Health Interview Survey; see Appendix III. For composition of regions, see table 27]

ITEM	TOTAL DAYS OF DISABILITY (millions)						DAYS PER PERSON					
	1970	1980	1985	1990	1993	1994	1970	1980	1985	1990	1993	1994
Restricted-activity days [1] . .	2,913	4,165	3,453	3,669	4,346	4,143	14.6	19.1	14.8	14.9	17.1	16.0
Male	1,273	1,802	1,442	1,558	1,844	1,723	13.2	17.1	12.8	13.1	14.9	13.6
Female	1,640	2,363	2,011	2,111	2,502	2,420	15.8	21.0	16.6	16.7	19.2	18.2
White [2]	2,526	3,518	2,899	3,057	3,598	3,375	14.4	18.7	14.5	14.8	17.0	15.7
Black [2]	365	580	489	536	616	608	16.2	22.7	17.4	17.7	19.2	18.4
Under 65 years	2,331	3,228	2,557	2,734	3,289	3,070	12.9	16.6	12.4	12.6	14.7	13.4
65 years and over	582	937	895	936	1,057	1,073	30.7	39.2	33.1	31.4	33.8	34.6
Northeast	709	862	689	656	798	803	14.5	17.9	13.8	13.2	15.9	15.9
Midwest	691	989	744	836	978	879	12.4	17.2	12.7	14.0	15.8	13.9
South	996	1,415	1,308	1,404	1,564	1,443	15.9	19.8	16.3	16.7	18.3	16.4
West	518	899	712	773	1,006	1,017	15.6	22.0	15.7	14.8	17.7	17.6
Family income:												
Under $10,000	(NA)	(NA)	893	662	741	681	(NA)	(NA)	25.8	27.3	30.2	29.1
$10,000 to $19,999 . . .	(NA)	(NA)	781	758	857	801	(NA)	(NA)	16.7	19.1	22.3	21.5
$20,000 to $34,999 . . .	(NA)	(NA)	791	715	849	825	(NA)	(NA)	12.1	13.5	15.2	15.2
$35,000 or more	(NA)	(NA)	568	912	1,086	1,051	(NA)	(NA)	9.9	10.3	11.2	10.5
Bed-disability days [3]	1,222	1,520	1,436	1,521	1,708	1,603	6.1	7.0	6.1	6.2	6.7	6.2
Male	503	616	583	625	688	623	5.2	5.9	5.2	5.2	5.6	4.9
Female	720	904	852	896	1,020	980	6.9	8.0	7.1	7.1	7.8	7.4
Under 65 years	959	1,190	1,064	1,115	1,286	1,155	5.3	6.1	5.1	5.2	5.8	5.1
65 years and over	263	330	371	406	422	448	13.8	13.8	13.7	13.6	13.5	14.4
Work-loss days [4]	417	485	575	621	666	642	5.4	5.0	5.3	5.3	5.6	5.2
Male	243	271	287	303	315	311	5.0	4.9	4.8	4.7	4.8	4.6
Female	175	215	288	319	351	332	5.9	5.1	6.0	5.9	6.4	5.9
School-loss days [5]	222	204	217	212	250	225	4.9	5.3	4.8	4.6	5.3	4.5
Male	108	95	100	100	121	104	4.7	4.8	4.4	4.3	5.0	4.1
Female	114	109	117	112	129	121	5.1	5.7	5.3	5.0	5.5	5.0

NA Not available.   [1] A day when a person cuts down on his activities for more than half a day because of illness or injury. Includes bed-disability, work-loss, and school-loss days. Total includes other races and unknown income, not shown separately.   [2] Beginning 1980, race was determined by asking the household respondent to report his race. In earlier years the racial classification of respondents was determined by interviewer observation.   [3] A day when a person stayed in bed more than half a day because of illness or injury. Includes those work-loss and school-loss days actually spent in bed.   [4] A day when a person lost more than half a workday because of illness or injury. Computed for persons 17 years of age and over (beginning 1985, 18 years of age and over) in the currently employed population, defined as those who were working or had a job or business from which they were not on layoff during the 2-week period preceding the week of interview.   [5] Child's loss of more than half a school day because of illness or injury. Computed for children 6-16 years of age. Beginning 1985, children 5-17 years old.

Source: U.S. National Center for Health Statistics, *Vital and Health Statistics*, series 10, No. 193; and earlier reports and unpublished data.

No. 209. Costs of Unintentional Injuries: 1994

[Covers costs of deaths or disabling injuries together with vehicle accidents and fires]

COST	AMOUNT (bil. dol.)					PERCENT DISTRIBUTION				
	Total [1]	Motor vehicle	Work	Home	Other	Total [1]	Motor vehicle	Work	Home	Other
Total	440.9	176.5	120.7	94.3	63.2	100.0	100.0	100.0	100.0	100.0
Wage and productivity losses [2]	227.0	66.4	60.9	59.9	43.0	51.5	37.6	50.5	63.5	68.0
Medical expense	77.8	23.0	21.1	21.8	13.1	17.6	13.0	17.5	23.1	20.7
Administrative expenses [3]	70.1	45.9	23.7	4.2	3.3	15.9	26.0	19.6	4.5	5.2
Motor vehicle damage	39.1	39.1	2.0	(NA)	(NA)	8.9	22.2	1.7	(NA)	(NA)
Employer cost [4]	18.7	2.1	10.6	3.6	2.8	4.2	1.2	8.8	3.8	4.4
Fire loss	8.2	(NA)	2.4	4.8	1.0	1.9	(NA)	2.0	5.1	1.6

NA Not available.   [1] Excludes duplication between work and motor vehicle ($13.8 billion) in 1994.   [2] Actual loss of wages and household production, and the present value of future earnings lost.   [3] Includes the administrative cost of public and private insurance, and police and legal costs.   [4] Estimate of the uninsured costs incurred by employers, representing the money value of time lost by noninjured workers.

Source: National Safety Council, Itasca, IL, *Accident Facts, 1995* (copyright).

No. 210. Injuries Associated With Consumer Products: 1992 and 1993

[For products associated with more than 16,600 injuries in 1992. Estimates calculated from a representative sample of hospitals with emergency treatment departments in the United States. Data are estimates of the number of emergency room treated cases nationwide associated with various products. Product involvement does not necessarily mean the product caused the accident. Products were selected from the U.S. Consumer Product Safety Commission's National Electronic Injury Surveillance System]

PRODUCT	1992	1993	PRODUCT	1992	1993
Home maintenance:			General household appliances:		
Noncaustic cleaning equip. [1]	26,654	27,184	Cooking ranges, ovens, etc	53,401	51,243
Cleaning agents (except soap)	43,758	42,426	Irons, clothes steamers	17,266	17,888
Paints, solvents, lubricants	23,383	21,071	Refrigerators, freezers	35,895	33,895
Misc. household chemicals	24,679	23,709	Washers, dryers	22,590	22,786
Home workshop equipment:			Misc. household appliances	34,941	31,314
Power home tools, except saws	31,742	30,200			
Power home workshop saws	97,606	89,177	Heating, cooling equipment: [4]		
Welding, soldering, cutting tools	20,686	23,678	Chimneys, fireplaces	26,664	23,256
Workshop manual tools	125,780	122,221	Fans (except stove)	17,050	20,661
Misc. workshop equipment	46,407	44,797	Heating stoves, space heaters	37,805	31,005
Household packaging and containers:			Pipes, heating and plumbing	23,216	23,335
Cans, other containers	239,521	238,081	Home entertainment equipment:		
Glass bottles, jars	63,170	62,342	Pet supplies, equipment	26,703	(NA)
Paper, cardboard, plastic products	47,495	46,358	Sound recording equip [5]	46,022	43,898
Housewares:			Television sets, stands	42,000	42,988
Cookware, pots, pans	36,700	31,110	Personal use items:		
Cutlery, knives, unpowered	468,587	460,248	Cigarettes, lighters, fuels	23,547	20,737
Drinking glasses	130,200	127,111	Clothing	142,457	148,136
Scissors	34,602	29,381	Grooming devices	31,991	32,918
Small kitchen appliances	43,453	38,789	Jewelry	55,142	55,677
Tableware and accessories	120,940	110,526	Paper money, coins	30,274	28,592
Misc. housewares	61,201	60,789	Pencils, pens, other desk supplies	49,226	46,376
Home furnishing: [2]			Razors, shavers, razor blades	43,365	44,147
Bathtub, shower structures	166,327	161,673	Sewing equipment	29,814	(NA)
Beds, mattresses, pillows	400,732	395,268			
Carpets, rugs	112,763	127,341	Yard and garden equipment:		
Chairs, sofas, sofa beds	413,759	407,472	Chains and saws	38,692	40,149
Desks, cabinets, shelves, racks	228,676	223,309	Hand garden tools	36,374	44,835
Electric fixtures, lamps, equipment	54,097	58,213	Hatchets, axes	16,760	16,929
Ladders, stools	189,210	189,596	Lawn garden care equipment	51,324	62,708
Mirrors, mirror glass	24,928	20,261	Lawn mowers	85,202	78,553
Sinks, toilets	61,281	60,557	Other power lawn equipment	21,598	24,929
Tables	345,271	329,573			
Other misc. accessories	57,555	59,030	Sports and recreation equipment:		
			Bicycles, accessories	649,536	603,946
Home structures, construction: [3]			Exercise equipment	95,127	91,238
Cabinets or door hardware	24,876	25,908	Mopeds, minibikes, ATV's [6]	132,271	122,615
Ceilings, walls, inside panels	262,572	262,316	Nonpowder guns, BB's, pellets	34,552	29,502
Counters, counter tops	36,888	36,896	Playground equipment	290,382	268,915
Fences	123,014	126,714	Skateboards	44,068	27,718
Glass doors, windows, panels	216,193	215,284	Toboggans, sleds, snow disks, etc	43,273	59,698
Handrails, railings, banisters	42,965	42,876	Trampolines	43,665	46,215
Nails, carpet tacks, etc	239,711	233,507	Miscellaneous products:		
Nonglass doors, panels	357,149	349,080	Dollies, carts	45,257	46,549
Porches, open side floors, etc	129,152	131,475	Gasoline and diesel fuels	19,205	20,386
Stairs, ramps, landings, floors	1,879,029	1,912,743	Nursery equipment	117,732	110,498
Window, door sills, frames	60,147	59,146	Toys	177,061	164,379
Misc. construction materials	95,147	88,684			

NA Not available. [1] Includes detergent. [2] Includes accessories. [3] Includes materials. [4] Includes ventilating equipment. [5] Includes reproducing equipment. [6] All-terrain vehicles.

Source: National Safety Council, Itasca, IL, *Accident Facts,* annual (copyright).

No. 211. Injuries, by Sex: 1970 to 1993

[Covers civilian noninstitutional population and comprises incidents leading to restricted activity and/or medical attention. Beginning 1983, data not strictly comparable with other years. See headnote, table 208. Based on National Health Interview Survey; see Appendix III]

YEAR	INJURIES (mil.)			RATE PER 100 POPULATION			YEAR	INJURIES (mil.)			RATE PER 100 POPULATION		
	Total	Male	Female	Total	Male	Female		Total	Male	Female	Total	Male	Female
1970	56.0	31.8	24.2	28.0	33.0	23.3	1987	62.1	33.6	28.4	26.0	29.1	23.1
1975	71.9	39.4	32.5	34.4	39.1	30.0	1988	59.2	32.4	26.8	24.6	27.7	21.6
1980	68.1	39.0	29.1	31.2	37.1	25.8	1989	58.0	31.7	26.3	23.8	26.9	20.9
1983	61.1	33.0	28.1	26.6	29.8	23.7	1990	60.1	33.6	26.6	24.4	28.1	21.0
1984	61.1	33.7	27.4	26.4	30.1	22.9	1991	59.7	32.2	27.5	24.0	26.7	21.5
1985	62.6	34.6	28.0	26.8	30.6	23.1	1992	59.6	32.8	26.8	23.7	26.8	20.7
1986	62.4	34.0	28.4	26.4	29.8	23.3	1993	62.1	33.4	28.7	24.4	27.0	22.0

Source: U.S. National Center for Health Statistics, *Vital and Health Statistics,* series 10, No. 190, and earlier reports; and unpublished data.

No. 212. Injuries, by Age and Condition: 1993

[See headnote, table 211]

AGE AND TYPE	INJURIES (mil.)			RATE PER 100 POPULATION		
	Total	Male	Female	Total	Male	Female
Total [1]	62.1	33.4	28.7	24.4	27.0	22.0
Under 5 years	5.0	2.7	2.2	24.9	26.6	23.1
5 to 17 years	12.5	7.6	4.9	26.2	31.0	21.2
18 to 44 years	29.1	16.7	12.4	27.5	32.0	23.2
45 years and over.	15.6	6.5	9.1	19.2	17.4	20.7
Fractures [2]	7.9	4.3	3.6	3.1	3.5	2.8
Sprains and strains.	14.2	7.4	6.8	5.6	6.0	5.2
Open wounds and lacerations.	12.5	8.6	3.9	4.9	7.0	3.0
Contusions [3]	12.1	6.2	5.9	4.8	5.0	4.5
Other	15.4	6.8	8.5	6.1	5.5	6.5

[1] Includes unknown place of accident not shown separately.　　[2] Includes dislocations.　　[3] Includes superficial injuries.

Source: U.S. National Center for Health Statistics, *Vital and Health Statistics,* series 10, No. 190, and earlier reports; and unpublished data.

No. 213. Persons With Disabilities: 1991-92

[Covers the civilian noninstitutional resident population 15 years old and over and members of the Armed Forces living off post or with their families on post. The criteria for presence of disability varied by age. In general, a disability is considered a reduced ability to perform tasks one would normally do at a given stage in life. Based on the Survey of Income and Program Participation; for details, see source]

CHARACTERISTIC	PERSONS (1,000)			PERCENT DISTRIBUTION		
	Total	Male	Female	Total	Male	Female
Total 15 years old and over	**195,729**	**93,985**	**101,744**	**100.0**	**100.0**	**100.0**
With a disability	46,023	21,040	24,982	23.5	22.4	24.6
Severe	23,588	9,593	13,995	12.1	10.2	13.8
Not severe	22,435	11,447	10,987	11.5	12.2	10.8
With functional limitations	34,163	14,774	19,389	17.5	15.7	19.1
Has difficulty—						
Seeing words and letters	9,685	4,006	5,679	5.0	4.3	5.6
Hearing normal conversation.	10,928	6,421	4,506	5.6	6.8	4.4
Having speech understood	2,284	1,316	968	1.2	1.4	1.0
Lifting or carrying 10 lbs.	16,205	5,218	10,987	8.3	5.6	10.8
Climbing stairs without resting	17,469	6,465	11,003	8.9	6.9	10.8
Walking three city blocks	17,319	6,653	10,665	8.9	7.1	10.5
Is unable to—						
See words and letters	1,590	661	929	0.8	0.7	0.9
Hear normal conversation.	924	529	396	0.5	0.6	0.4
Have speech understood	237	141	95	0.1	0.2	0.1
Lift or carry 10 lbs.	7,734	2,375	5,359	4.0	2.5	5.3
Climb stairs without resting	9,116	3,277	5,839	4.7	3.5	5.7
Walk three city blocks	8,972	3,236	5,736	4.6	3.4	5.6
With limitations of activities of daily living	7,919	3,013	4,907	4.1	3.2	4.8
Has difficulty—						
Getting around inside the house.	3,664	1,376	2,288	1.9	1.5	2.3
Getting in/out of bed or a chair	5,280	2,006	3,274	2.7	2.1	3.2
Taking a bath or shower.	4,501	1,550	2,951	2.3	1.7	2.9
Dressing	3,234	1,262	1,971	1.7	1.3	1.9
Eating.	1,077	437	640	0.6	0.5	0.6
Getting to or using the toilet	2,084	767	1,317	1.1	0.8	1.3
Needs personal assistance with—						
Getting around inside the house.	1,706	698	1,008	0.9	0.7	1.0
Getting in/out of bed or a chair	2,022	796	1,227	1.0	0.9	1.2
Taking a bath or shower.	2,718	1,028	1,691	1.4	1.1	1.7
Dressing	2,060	866	1,193	1.1	0.9	1.2
Eating.	487	226	261	0.3	0.2	0.3
Getting to or using the toilet	1,157	477	680	0.6	0.5	0.7
With limitations of instrumental activities of daily living	11,694	4,601	7,093	6.0	4.9	7.0
Has difficulty—						
Going outside the home	7,809	2,759	5,050	4.0	2.9	5.0
Keeping track of money and bills	3,901	1,621	2,280	2.0	1.7	2.2
Preparing meals	4,530	1,699	2,831	2.3	1.8	2.8
Doing light housework	6,313	2,191	4,122	3.2	2.3	4.1
Using the telephone.	3,130	1,749	1,381	1.6	1.9	1.4
Needs personal assistance with—						
Going outside the home	6,011	2,017	3,994	3.1	2.2	3.9
Keeping track of money and bills	3,425	1,460	1,965	1.8	1.6	1.9
Preparing meals	3,685	1,447	2,238	1.9	1.5	2.2
Doing light housework	4,745	1,626	3,119	2.4	1.7	3.1
Using the telephone.	933	509	424	0.5	0.5	0.4

Source: U.S. Bureau of the Census, *Current Population Reports,* P70-33.

No. 214. Children Immunized Against Specified Diseases: 1991 to 1994

[In percent. Covers civilian noninstitutionalized population ages 19 months to 35 months. Based on estimates from the National Health Interview Survey. Excludes respondents with unknown or missing information. See Appendix III]

VACCINATION	1991, total	1992, total	1993, total	1994 Total	1994 White	1994 Black	1994 Other
Diphtheria-tetanus-pertussis (DPT)/ diphtheria-tetanus:							
3+ doses	68.8	83.0	88.2	89.5	90.5	84.7	88.2
4+ doses	43.3	59.0	72.1	70.0	70.7	64.2	77.4
Polio: 3+ doses	53.2	72.4	78.9	79.1	80.1	72.9	82.1
Hib [1]: 3+ doses	1.7	28.2	55.0	75.2	76.7	67.8	72.6
Hepatitis B: 3+ doses	(NA)	(NA)	16.3	34.8	34.1	36.9	39.9
Measles containing	82.0	82.5	84.1	90.2	91.6	85.8	81.1
3 DPT/3 polio/1 MMR [2]	50.0	68.7	74.5	77.1	78.5	69.9	76.5
4 DPT/3 polio/1 MMR [2][3]	37.0	55.3	67.1	67.3	68.3	60.5	72.2

NA Not available. [1] Haemophilus B. [2] Measles, measles/rubella, measles/mumps, and measles/mumps/rubella. [3] Up-to-date for age.

Source: U.S. Centers for Disease Control and Prevention, Atlanta, GA, the National Health Interview Survey.

No. 215. Specified Reportable Diseases—Cases Reported: 1970 to 1994

[Figures should be interpreted with caution. Although reporting of some of these diseases is incomplete, the figures are of value in indicating trends of disease incidence. Includes cases imported from outside the United States. See *Historical Statistics, Colonial Times to 1970*, series B 291-303, for related data]

DISEASE	1970	1980	1985	1989	1990	1991	1992	1993	1994
AIDS [1]	(NA)	(NA)	8,249	33,722	41,595	43,672	45,472	103,533	78,279
Amebiasis	2,888	5,271	4,433	3,217	3,328	2,989	2,942	2,970	2,983
Aseptic meningitis	6,480	8,028	10,619	10,274	11,852	14,526	12,223	12,848	8,932
Botulism [2]	12	89	122	89	92	114	91	97	143
Brucellosis (undulant fever)	213	183	153	95	85	104	105	120	119
Chickenpox (1,000)	[3]	190.9	178.2	185.4	173.1	147.1	158.4	134.7	151.2
Diphtheria	435	3	3	3	4	5	4	-	2
Encephalitis:									
Primary infectious [4]	1,580	1,362	1,376	981	1,341	1,021	774	919	717
Post infectious [4]	370	40	161	88	105	82	129	170	143
Escherichia coli 0157:H7	[3]	[3]	[3]	[3]	[3]	[3]	[3]	[3]	1,420
Haemophilus influenza	[3]	[3]	[3]	[3]	[3]	2,764	1,412	1,419	1,174
Hepatitis: B (serum) (1,000)	8.3	19.0	26.6	23.4	21.1	18.0	16.1	13.4	12.5
A (infectious) (1,000)	56.8	29.1	23.2	35.8	31.4	24.4	23.1	24.2	29.8
Unspecified (1,000)	[3]	11.9	5.5	2.3	1.7	1.3	0.9	0.6	0.4
Non-A, non-B (1,000) [5]	[3]	[3]	4.2	2.5	2.6	3.6	6.0	4.8	4.4
Legionellosis	[3]	[3]	830	1,190	1,370	1,317	1,339	1,280	1,615
Leprosy (Hansen disease)	129	223	361	163	198	154	172	187	136
Leptospirosis	47	85	57	93	77	58	54	51	38
Lyme disease	[3]	[3]	[3]	[3]	[3]	9,465	9,895	8,257	13,043
Malaria	3,051	2,062	1,049	1,277	1,292	1,278	1,087	1,411	1,229
Measles (1,000)	47.4	13.5	2.8	18.2	27.8	9.6	2.2	0.3	1.0
Meningococcal infections	2,505	2,840	2,479	2,727	2,451	2,130	2,134	2,637	2,886
Mumps (1,000)	105.0	8.6	3.0	5.7	5.3	4.3	2.6	1.7	1.5
Pertussis [6] (1,000)	4.2	1.7	3.6	4.2	4.6	2.7	4.1	6.6	4.6
Plague	13	18	17	4	2	11	13	10	17
Poliomyelitis, acute [7]	33	9	7	9	6	9	6	3	-
Psittacosis	35	124	119	116	113	94	92	60	38
Rabies, animal	3,224	6,421	5,565	4,724	4,826	6,910	8,589	9,377	8,147
Rabies, human	3	-	1	1	1	3	1	3	6
Rheumatic fever, acute [8]	3,227	432	90	144	108	127	75	112	112
Rubella [9] (1,000)	56.6	3.9	0.6	0.4	1.1	1.4	0.2	0.2	0.2
Salmonellosis [10] (1,000)	22.1	33.7	65.3	47.8	48.6	48.2	40.9	41.6	43.3
Shigellosis [11] (1,000)	13.8	19.0	17.1	25.0	27.1	23.5	23.9	32.2	29.8
Tetanus	148	95	83	53	64	57	45	48	51
Toxic-shock syndrome	[3]	[3]	384	400	322	280	244	212	192
Trichinosis	109	131	61	30	129	62	41	16	32
Tuberculosis [12] (1,000)	37.1	27.7	22.2	23.5	25.7	26.3	26.7	25.3	24.4
Tularemia	172	234	177	152	152	193	159	132	96
Typhoid fever	346	510	402	460	552	501	414	440	441
Typhus fever:									
Flea-borne (endemic-murine)	27	81	37	41	50	43	28	25	[3]
Tick-borne (Rocky Mt. spotted fever)	380	1,163	714	623	651	628	502	456	465
Sexually transmitted diseases:									
Gonorrhea (1,000)	600	1,004	911	733	690	620	501	440	418
Syphilis (1,000)	91	69	68	111	134	129	113	101	82
Other (1,000)	2.2	1.0	2.3	4.9	4.6	4.0	2.2	1.7	1.0

- Represents zero. NA Not available. [1] Acquired immunodeficiency syndrome was not a notifiable disease until 1984. Figures are shown for years in which cases were reported to the CDC. Beginning 1993, based on revised classification system and expanded surveillance case definition. [2] Beginning in 1980, includes foodborne, infant, wound, and unspecified cases. [3] Disease was not notifiable. [4] Beginning 1980, reported data reflect new diagnostic categories. [5] Includes some persons positive for antibody to hepatitis C virus who do not have hepatitis. [6] Whooping cough. [7] Revised. Data subject to annual revisions. [8] Based on reports from States: 38 in 1970, 37 in 1980, 31 in 1985, 28 in 1989, 30 in 1990, 23 in 1991, 26 in 1992 and 1993, and 27 in 1994. [9] German measles. [10] Excludes typhoid fever. [11] Bacillary dysentery. [12] Newly reported active cases. New diagnostic standards introduced in 1980.

Source: U.S. Centers for Disease Control and Prevention, Atlanta, GA, *Summary of Notifiable Diseases, United States, Morbidity and Mortality Weekly Report*, vol. 43, No. 53, October 6, 1995.

No. 216. Selected Measures of Hospital Utilization for Patients Discharged With the Diagnosis of Human Immunodeficiency Virus (HIV): 1985 to 1993

[See headnote, table 193]

MEASURE OF UTILIZATION	Unit	1985	1989	1990	1991	1992	1993
Number of patients discharged [1]	1,000....	23	140	146	165	194	225
Rate of patient discharges [2]	Rate	1.0	5.7	5.9	6.6	7.6	8.8
Number of days of care	1,000....	387	1,731	2,188	2,108	2,136	2,561
Rate of days of care [2]	Rate	16.3	70.2	87.7	84.1	84.3	99.9
Average length of stay [3]	Days	17.1	12.4	14.9	12.8	11.0	11.4

[1] Comparisons beginning 1989 with data for earlier years should be made with caution as estimates of change may reflect improvements in the 1988 design rather than true changes in hospital use.   [2] Per 10,000 population. Based on Bureau of the Census estimated civilian population as of July 1. Population estimates for the 1980's do not reflect revised estimates based on the 1990 Census of Population.   [3] For similar data on all patients, see table 193.

Source: National Center for Health Statistics, *Vital and Health Statistics,* series 13.

No. 217. AIDS Cases Reported, by Patient Characteristic: 1981 to 1995

[**Provisional.** For cases reported in the year shown. For data on AIDS deaths, see table 134. Data are subject to retrospective changes and may differ from those data in table 215]

CHARACTERISTIC	Total	1981-1986	1987	1988	1989	1990	1991	1992	1993	1994	1995
Total [1]	496,896	28,358	21,478	30,657	33,559	41,639	43,653	45,839	102,605	77,561	71,547
Age:											
Under 5 years old ..	5,236	350	269	440	484	583	522	613	674	747	554
5 to 12 years old ...	1,365	50	55	124	101	142	145	137	198	220	193
13 to 29 years old ..	91,043	6,041	4,407	6,306	6,758	8,160	7,902	8,011	18,801	13,045	11,612
30 to 39 years old ..	225,428	13,233	9,773	14,105	15,469	18,844	19,875	20,601	46,574	34,966	31,988
40 to 49 years old ..	123,035	5,888	4,666	6,532	7,327	9,731	10,630	11,599	26,396	20,617	19,649
50 to 59 years old ..	36,752	2,107	1,595	2,134	2,418	2,929	3,243	3,432	7,385	5,905	5,604
Over 60 years old ..	14,037	689	713	1,016	1,002	1,250	1,336	1,446	2,577	2,061	1,947
Sex:											
Male	425,295	26,222	19,643	27,375	29,921	36,766	37,997	39,507	86,173	63,684	58,007
Female	71,601	2,136	1,835	3,282	3,638	4,873	5,656	6,332	16,432	13,877	13,540
Race/ethnic group:											
White [2]	243,002	16,851	13,239	17,029	18,571	22,327	22,125	22,455	47,762	32,928	29,715
Black [2]	174,562	7,364	5,429	9,123	10,254	13,200	14,638	16,053	38,072	31,103	29,326
Hispanic	73,721	3,941	2,601	4,232	4,364	5,669	6,417	6,771	15,529	12,620	11,577
Other/unknown	5,611	202	209	273	370	443	473	560	1,242	910	929
Leading States: [3]											
New York	94,751	9,093	4,001	6,916	5,956	8,288	8,072	8,241	17,056	14,729	12,399
California	88,933	5,978	5,177	5,684	6,432	7,359	7,689	8,819	18,529	12,132	11,134
Florida	51,838	2,093	1,631	2,650	3,446	4,011	5,456	5,074	10,896	8,522	8,059
Texas	35,114	1,778	1,665	2,212	2,382	3,317	3,049	2,923	7,464	5,847	4,477
New Jersey	29,327	1,734	1,514	2,460	2,228	2,447	2,281	2,019	5,363	4,872	4,409
Illinois	16,411	691	629	983	1,119	1,266	1,608	1,881	2,952	3,062	2,220
Pennsylvania	15,089	638	665	850	1,071	1,222	1,231	1,349	3,176	2,510	2,377
Georgia	14,549	589	517	841	1,097	1,229	1,463	1,411	2,845	2,266	2,291
Maryland	13,066	419	456	549	711	987	970	1,199	2,514	2,686	2,575
Massachusetts	10,664	582	454	708	749	838	959	859	2,686	1,382	1,447
District of Columbia .	8,157	522	466	503	495	733	711	710	1,588	1,400	1,029
Virginia	7,916	332	244	351	397	746	680	780	1,621	1,155	1,610
Louisiana	7,666	342	334	402	506	702	827	819	1,417	1,230	1,087
Ohio	7,630	309	342	504	492	693	632	787	1,568	1,193	1,110
Michigan	7,426	256	212	455	505	579	638	749	1,810	1,021	1,201
Connecticut	7,410	347	255	413	432	427	566	650	1,755	913	1,652
Washington	6,807	343	324	341	524	749	582	564	1,559	929	892
North Carolina	6,420	171	209	277	446	571	602	585	1,371	1,188	1,000
Missouri	6,405	155	240	408	441	579	657	709	1,718	707	791
South Carolina	5,400	113	84	174	325	374	348	394	1,461	1,151	976
Colorado	5,238	292	226	324	388	365	431	404	1,323	812	673
Tennessee	4,712	97	73	329	266	340	353	408	1,198	751	897
Arizona	4,455	155	215	276	323	317	284	381	1,216	610	678
Indiana	3,832	126	133	78	397	294	316	398	944	617	529
Alabama	3,663	71	154	212	216	239	376	440	731	582	642
Oregon	3,400	113	165	176	227	336	257	288	774	605	459
Minnesota	2,709	155	130	167	176	203	214	217	659	419	369
Nevada	2,648	54	88	119	177	189	261	249	634	384	493
Wisconsin	2,521	76	96	115	130	212	213	230	726	373	350
Oklahoma	2,459	84	109	152	168	206	188	268	721	268	295
Mississippi	2,414	39	50	126	144	289	198	256	441	429	442
Arkansas	1,890	38	49	78	76	211	197	277	402	285	277
Kentucky	1,826	63	50	90	115	192	164	215	321	318	298
Percent of total ..	97.2	98.2	97.6	97.6	97.0	97.3	97.3	97.2	96.9	97.1	96.6

[1] Includes other states, not shown separately and persons whose residence is unknown.   [2] Non-Hispanic.   [3] States with at least 1,800 total cases reported through 1995.

Source: U.S. Centers for Disease Control and Prevention, Atlanta, GA, unpublished data.

No. 218. Acute Conditions, by Type: 1970 to 1994

[Covers civilian noninstitutional population. Estimates include only acute conditions which were medically attended or caused at least 1 day of restricted activity. Based on National Health Interview Survey; see Appendix III. See headnote, table 208. For composition of regions, see table 27]

YEAR AND CHARACTERISTIC	NUMBER OF CONDITIONS (mil.)					RATE PER 100 POPULATION				
	Infective and parasitic	Respiratory		Diges-tive system	Injuries	Infective and parasitic	Respiratory		Diges-tive system	Injuries
		Common cold	Influ-enza				Common cold	Influ-enza		
1970	48.2	(NA)	(NA)	23.0	59.2	24.1	(NA)	(NA)	11.5	29.6
1975	47.6	(NA)	(NA)	21.6	76.2	22.8	(NA)	(NA)	10.3	36.4
1980	53.6	(NA)	(NA)	24.9	72.7	24.6	(NA)	(NA)	11.4	33.4
1985	47.8	(NA)	(NA)	16.3	64.0	20.5	(NA)	(NA)	7.0	27.4
1990	51.7	61.5	106.8	13.0	60.1	21.0	25.0	43.4	5.3	24.4
1992	56.2	64.6	107.3	17.6	59.6	22.4	25.7	42.7	7.0	23.7
1993	54.3	68.2	132.6	16.1	62.1	21.3	26.8	52.2	6.3	24.4
1994, total [1]	**54.2**	**66.0**	**90.4**	**15.9**	**61.9**	**20.9**	**25.4**	**34.8**	**6.1**	**23.8**
Under 5 years old.	11.2	14.0	7.6	2.2	5.2	54.7	68.5	37.3	10.5	25.6
5 to 17 years old	20.8	14.6	22.9	4.1	12.9	41.9	29.4	46.3	8.3	26.0
18 to 24 years old	4.7	6.6	9.8	1.9	8.3	18.5	26.1	38.7	7.4	32.7
25 to 44 years old	12.1	18.6	31.4	3.9	20.7	14.6	22.4	37.8	4.7	25.0
45 to 64 years old	3.9	8.4	13.1	2.1	8.7	7.7	16.6	25.9	4.1	17.2
65 years old and over . . .	1.6	3.8	5.7	1.7	6.1	5.2	12.3	18.3	5.6	19.6
Male	23.8	30.3	43.2	6.9	32.6	18.8	24.0	34.1	5.5	25.8
Female.	30.4	35.7	47.3	9.0	29.2	22.8	26.8	35.5	6.7	22.0
White	46.4	52.2	78.3	12.1	53.1	21.6	24.3	36.5	5.7	24.8
Black	6.7	9.7	7.7	2.9	6.8	20.2	29.3	23.2	8.9	20.6
Northeast	12.4	14.9	13.2	2.6	10.2	24.5	29.4	26.0	5.2	20.2
Midwest	10.5	14.8	26.9	3.3	15.9	16.6	23.3	42.5	5.2	25.2
South.	21.5	17.1	22.0	5.9	20.8	24.4	19.4	25.0	6.7	23.6
West	9.8	19.2	28.3	4.1	14.9	17.0	33.3	49.1	7.0	25.8
Family income:										
Under $10,000	3.8	8.0	8.9	2.4	7.9	16.2	34.4	38.0	10.1	33.9
$10,000 to $19,999. . .	6.9	9.7	11.7	3.0	9.3	18.4	26.0	31.3	8.0	25.1
$20,000 to $34,999. . .	11.2	13.6	20.8	3.1	12.5	20.7	25.1	38.5	5.7	23.0
$35,000 or more.	24.6	25.5	38.1	5.1	22.1	24.6	25.4	38.0	5.1	22.0

NA Not available.   [1] Includes other races and unknown income not shown separately.

Source: U.S. National Center for Health Statistics, *Vital and Health Statistics*, series 10, No. 193, and earlier reports; and unpublished data.

No. 219. Prevalence of Selected Chronic Conditions, by Age and Sex: 1994

[Covers civilian noninstitutional population. Conditions classified according to ninth revision of International Classification of Diseases. Based on National Health Interview Survey; see Appendix III. See headnote, table 208]

CHRONIC CONDITION	Condi-tions (1,000)	RATE [1]							
		Male				Female			
		Under 45 years old	45 to 64 years old	65 to 74 years old	75 years old and over	Under 45 years old	45 to 64 years old	65 to 74 years old	75 years old and over
Arthritis.	33,446	27.4	176.8	430.8	424.9	38.2	297.0	513.6	604.4
Dermatitis, including eczema	9,192	29.3	21.8	25.3	[2]17.6	43.6	44.6	38.6	40.2
Trouble with—									
Dry (itching) skin.	6,166	17.1	29.6	36.6	46.7	20.5	36.1	30.8	40.5
Ingrown nails	5,987	16.0	32.1	40.9	38.8	16.4	29.7	52.9	61.4
Corns and calluses	4,356	6.9	25.3	21.0	[2]17.8	12.2	32.5	46.5	58.1
Visual impairments	8,601	29.5	52.7	78.4	113.7	12.9	38.0	48.0	110.7
Cataracts	6,473	2.5	12.3	79.0	214.7	2.5	21.9	140.0	259.2
Hearing impairments.	22,400	43.2	191.9	298.8	447.1	30.4	87.5	183.3	307.8
Tinnitus	7,033	11.6	60.4	118.1	106.6	9.8	33.2	67.7	79.9
Deformities or orthopedic									
impairments.	31,068	93.5	166.7	144.4	169.3	101.3	173.2	161.8	189.9
Ulcer	4,447	11.3	27.4	27.1	[2]30.9	13.3	23.3	42.8	22.3
Hernia of abdominal cavity.	4,778	7.8	31.2	54.7	55.6	5.8	31.3	70.0	72.3
Frequent indigestion	6,957	20.5	42.8	44.6	51.5	18.9	39.0	41.0	45.3
Frequent constipation	4,040	4.3	6.8	[2]13.8	60.2	15.1	17.3	47.3	102.2
Diabetes.	7,766	7.3	63.3	102.4	115.6	8.9	63.0	101.0	91.8
Migraine	11,256	22.0	24.2	[2]17.1	[2]5.2	67.1	78.9	29.9	26.2
Heart conditions.	22,279	27.0	162.0	319.3	429.9	33.1	111.0	250.8	361.4
High blood pressure									
(Hypertension)	28,236	31.9	220.0	307.7	339.2	32.4	224.5	378.7	417.5
Varicose veins of lower									
extremities.	7,260	3.7	17.8	32.5	58.5	23.3	81.0	109.0	83.8
Hemorrhoids	9,321	19.1	68.7	51.0	66.6	29.0	55.8	70.2	58.6
Chronic bronchitis.	14,021	43.6	43.8	41.7	68.0	56.5	82.7	79.0	51.7
Asthma	14,562	57.1	32.3	39.3	70.3	60.0	68.0	62.8	34.1
Hay fever, allergic rhinitis without									
asthma	26,146	98.0	107.3	79.6	56.6	99.2	133.4	92.2	78.8
Chronic sinusitis.	34,902	101.9	147.5	118.2	113.9	135.5	210.2	175.5	176.1

[1] Conditions per 1,000 persons.   [2] Figure does not meet standards of reliability or precision.

Source: U.S. National Center for Health Statistics, *Vital and Health Statistics*, series 10, No. 193, and earlier reports; and unpublished data.

No. 220. Substance Abuse Treatment Services: 1993

[As of **September 30.** Based on the National Drug and Alcoholism Treatment Unit Survey (NDATUS), a census of all known drug abuse and alcoholism treatment facilities in the United States. Data collected in cooperation with State agencies which defined what constitutes a facility for reporting purposes]

TYPE OF CARE AND LOCATION	Service locations reporting [1]	All clients	Drug abuse clients only	Alcoholism clients only	Clients with both problems	Clients with a drug problem [2]	Clients with an alcohol problem [3]
Total	11,496	944,208	235,953	325,952	382,303	618,256	708,255
TYPE OF CARE							
Detoxification: [4] Hospital inpatient . .	960	7,335	1,166	2,322	3,847	5,013	6,169
Free-standing residential	593	6,608	1,171	2,440	2,997	4,168	5,437
Rehab/residential: [5]							
Hospital inpatient	873	14,383	1,752	4,691	7,940	9,692	12,631
Short-term—30 days or less	815	16,365	2,616	4,489	9,260	11,876	13,749
Long-term—over 30 days	2,413	76,370	18,639	11,232	46,499	65,138	57,731
Ambulatory: [6] Outpatient	7,460	735,242	191,311	276,870	267,061	458,372	543,931
Intensive outpatient [7]	2,961	81,244	14,142	23,555	43,547	57,689	67,102
Detoxification [8]	330	6,661	5,156	353	1,152	6,308	1,505
UNIT LOCATION							
Community mental health care	1,413	140,685	30,490	58,194	52,001	82,491	110,195
Free-standing nonresidential facility . . .	5,034	503,429	140,426	190,154	172,849	313,275	363,003
Hospital [9]	1,766	118,540	27,167	35,020	56,353	83,520	91,373
Correctional facility	310	38,260	5,143	3,884	29,233	34,376	33,117
Halfway house	955	24,343	2,984	7,351	14,008	16,992	21,359
Other residential facility	1,526	70,276	19,429	15,621	35,226	54,655	50,847
Other site	180	11,190	2,796	3,252	5,142	7,938	8,394
Multiple sites	155	27,671	5,255	9,306	13,110	18,365	22,416
Unknown	157	9,814	2,263	3,170	4,381	6,644	7,551

[1] Some units provide more than one type of treatment but are counted only once in the total.   [2] The sum of clients with a drug problem and clients with both diagnoses.   [3] The sum of clients with an alcohol problem and clients with both diagnoses.   [4] 24 hour care for the withdrawal and transition to ongoing treatment.   [5] Other than detoxification. Provides treatment services for dependency.   [6] Ambulatory care provides care in a nonresidential setting.   [7] "Intensive" outpatient involves at least 2 hours of treatment a day for 3 or more days a week.   [8] Less than 24 hour care.   [9] Includes general hospitals, alcoholism hospitals, mental/psychiatric hospitals, and other specialized hospitals.

Source: U.S. Substance Abuse and Mental Health Services Administration and U.S. Institute on Alcohol Abuse and Alcoholism, *1993 National Drug and Alcoholism Treatment Unit Survey: Final Report.*

No. 221. Drug Use, by Type of Drug and Age Group: 1974 to 1994

[**In percent.** Current users are those who used drugs at least once within month prior to this study. Based on national samples of respondents residing in households. Subject to sampling variability; see source]

AGE AND TYPE OF DRUG	EVER USED					CURRENT USER				
	1974	1979	1985	1988	1994	1974	1979	1985	1988	1994
12 TO 17 YEARS OLD										
Marijuana	23.0	30.8	23.2	17.4	16.0	12.0	16.8	11.9	6.4	7.3
Cocaine	3.6	5.5	4.8	3.4	1.3	1.0	1.4	1.4	1.1	0.4
Inhalants	8.5	9.9	9.6	8.8	6.2	0.7	3.9	3.7	2.0	2.0
Hallucinogens	6.0	7.2	3.2	3.5	4.0	1.3	2.2	1.2	0.8	1.2
Heroin	1.0	0.5	0.4	0.6	0.4	(B)	0.1	0.1	0.1	(B)
Stimulants [1]	5.0	3.5	5.5	4.2	2.6	1.0	1.1	1.6	1.2	0.4
Sedatives [1]	5.0	3.2	4.1	2.3	3.2	1.0	1.2	1.0	0.6	0.3
Tranquilizers [1]	3.0	4.1	4.9	2.0	2.0	1.0	0.6	0.6	0.2	0.2
Analgesics [1]	(NA)	3.2	6.0	4.1	4.7	(NA)	0.6	1.7	0.9	1.3
Alcohol	54.0	69.9	55.4	50.2	41.2	34.0	37.3	31.0	25.2	16.3
Cigarettes	52.0	54.0	45.3	42.3	33.5	25.0	12.0	15.3	11.8	9.8
18 TO 25 YEARS OLD										
Marijuana	52.7	68.1	59.4	56.4	43.4	25.2	35.3	21.9	15.5	12.2
Cocaine	12.7	27.3	24.4	19.7	9.6	3.1	9.2	7.5	4.5	1.0
Inhalants	9.2	16.3	13.0	12.5	8.3	(B)	2.3	0.8	1.7	0.9
Hallucinogens	16.6	24.9	11.6	13.8	11.7	2.5	4.4	1.8	1.9	1.5
Heroin	4.5	3.4	1.3	0.3	0.2	(B)	0.3	0.3	0.1	0.1
Stimulants [1]	17.0	18.0	17.5	11.3	5.3	3.7	3.5	3.8	2.4	0.3
Sedatives [1]	15.0	16.9	11.8	5.5	1.9	1.6	2.8	1.6	0.9	0.3
Tranquilizers [1]	10.0	15.7	12.6	7.8	4.5	1.2	2.2	1.6	1.0	0.4
Analgesics [1]	(NA)	11.6	11.5	9.4	7.1	(NA)	0.9	2.0	1.5	0.7
Alcohol	81.6	95.1	92.0	90.3	86.8	69.3	75.7	70.7	65.3	63.8
Cigarettes	68.8	82.9	75.2	74.9	68.6	48.8	42.6	36.6	35.2	26.5
26 YEARS OLD AND OVER										
Marijuana	9.9	19.8	26.6	30.7	35.0	2.0	6.1	6.0	3.9	3.0
Cocaine	0.9	4.4	9.2	9.9	10.9	(B)	0.9	1.9	0.9	0.6
Inhalants	1.2	4.0	5.3	3.9	4.4	(B)	0.7	0.5	0.2	0.5
Hallucinogens	1.3	4.5	6.0	6.6	8.0	(B)	0.1	(B)	(B)	-
Heroin	0.5	1.0	1.1	1.1	1.3	(B)	(B)	(B)	(B)	(B)
Stimulants [1]	3.0	5.9	7.9	6.6	6.0	(B)	0.5	0.7	0.5	0.1
Sedatives [1]	2.0	3.6	5.6	3.3	3.9	(B)	0.4	0.6	0.3	-
Tranquilizers [1]	2.0	3.2	7.8	4.5	4.3	(B)	0.3	1.0	0.6	0.1
Analgesics [1]	(NA)	2.8	5.9	4.5	4.7	(NA)	0.1	0.9	0.4	0.4
Alcohol	73.2	91.5	89.2	88.6	91.0	54.5	61.5	59.8	54.8	55.6
Cigarettes	65.4	83.2	80.6	79.6	76.8	39.1	37.2	32.7	29.8	24.7

- Represents zero.   B Base too small to meet statistical standards for reliability of a derived figure.   NA Not available.
[1] Nonmedical use; does not include over-the-counter drugs.

Source: U.S. Substance Abuse and Mental Health Services Administration, *National Household Survey on Drug Abuse,* annual.

No. 222. Current Cigarette Smoking: 1965 to 1993

[**In percent.** Prior to 1992, a current smoker is a person who has smoked at least 100 cigarettes and who now smokes. Beginning 1992, definition includes persons who smoke only "some days." Excludes unknown smoking status. Based on the National Health Interview Survey; for details, see Appendix III]

SEX, AGE, AND RACE	1965	1974	1979	1983	1985	1987	1990	1992	1993
Total smokers, 18 years old and over	**42.4**	**37.1**	**33.5**	**32.1**	**30.1**	**28.8**	**25.5**	**26.5**	**25.0**
Male, total	51.9	43.1	37.5	35.1	32.6	31.2	28.4	28.6	27.7
18 to 24 years	54.1	42.1	35.0	32.9	28.0	28.2	26.6	28.0	28.8
25 to 34 years	60.7	50.5	43.9	38.8	38.2	34.8	31.6	32.8	30.2
35 to 44 years	58.2	51.0	41.8	41.0	37.6	36.6	34.5	32.9	32.0
45 to 64 years	51.9	42.6	39.3	35.9	33.4	33.5	29.3	28.6	29.2
65 years and over	28.5	24.8	20.9	22.0	19.6	17.2	14.6	16.1	13.5
White, total	51.1	41.9	36.8	34.5	31.7	30.5	28.0	28.2	27.0
18 to 24 years	53.0	40.8	34.3	32.5	28.4	29.2	27.4	30.0	30.4
25 to 34 years	60.1	49.5	43.6	38.6	37.3	33.8	31.6	33.5	29.9
35 to 44 years	57.3	50.1	41.3	40.8	36.6	36.2	33.5	30.9	31.2
45 to 64 years	51.3	41.2	38.3	35.0	32.1	32.4	28.7	28.1	27.8
65 years and over	27.7	24.3	20.5	20.6	18.9	16.0	13.7	14.9	12.5
Black, total	60.4	54.3	44.1	40.6	39.9	39.0	32.5	32.2	32.7
18 to 24 years	62.8	54.9	40.2	34.2	27.2	24.9	21.3	16.2	19.9
25 to 34 years	68.4	58.5	47.5	39.9	45.6	44.9	33.8	29.5	30.7
35 to 44 years	67.3	61.5	48.6	45.5	45.0	44.0	42.0	47.5	36.9
45 to 64 years	57.9	57.8	50.0	44.8	46.1	44.3	36.7	35.4	42.4
65 years and over	36.4	29.7	26.2	38.9	27.7	30.3	21.5	28.3	27.9
Female, total	33.9	32.1	29.9	29.5	27.9	26.5	22.8	24.6	22.5
18 to 24 years	38.1	34.1	33.8	35.5	30.4	26.1	22.5	24.9	22.9
25 to 34 years	43.7	38.8	33.7	32.6	32.0	31.8	28.2	30.1	27.3
35 to 44 years	43.7	39.8	37.0	33.8	31.5	29.6	24.8	27.3	27.4
45 to 64 years	32.0	33.4	30.7	31.0	29.9	28.6	24.8	26.1	23.0
65 years and over	9.6	12.0	13.2	13.1	13.5	13.7	11.5	12.4	10.5
White, total	34.0	31.7	30.1	29.4	27.7	26.7	23.4	25.1	23.1
18 to 24 years	38.4	34.0	34.5	36.5	31.8	27.8	25.4	28.5	26.8
25 to 34 years	43.4	38.6	34.1	32.2	32.0	31.9	28.5	31.5	28.4
35 to 44 years	43.9	39.3	37.2	34.8	31.0	29.2	25.0	27.6	27.3
45 to 64 years	32.7	33.0	30.6	30.6	29.7	29.0	25.4	25.8	23.4
65 years and over	9.8	12.3	13.8	13.2	13.3	13.9	11.5	12.6	10.5
Black, total	33.7	36.4	31.1	32.2	31.0	28.0	21.2	24.2	20.8
18 to 24 years	37.1	35.6	31.8	32.0	23.7	20.4	10.0	10.3	8.2
25 to 34 years	47.8	42.2	35.2	38.0	36.2	35.8	29.1	26.9	24.7
35 to 44 years	42.8	46.4	37.7	32.7	40.2	35.3	25.5	32.4	31.5
45 to 64 years	25.7	38.9	34.2	36.3	33.4	28.4	22.6	30.9	21.3
65 years and over	7.1	8.9	8.5	13.1	14.5	11.7	11.1	11.1	10.2

Source: U.S. National Center for Health Statistics, *Health, United States, 1994.*

No. 223. Cancer—Estimated New Cases, 1996, and Survival Rates, 1974-77 to 1986-91

[The 5-year relative survival rate, which is derived by adjusting the observed survival rate for expected mortality, represents the liklihood that a person will not die from causes directly related to their cancer within 5 years. Survival data shown are based on those patients diagnosed while residents of an area listed below during the time periods shown. Data are based on information collected as part of the National Cancer Institute's Surveillance, Epidemiology and End Results (SEER) program, a collection of population-based registries in Connecticut, New Mexico, Utah, Iowa, Hawaii, Atlanta, Detroit, Seattle-Puget Sound, and San Francisco-Oakland]

SITE	ESTIMATED NEW CASES, [1] 1996 (1,000)			5-YEAR RELATIVE SURVIVAL RATES (percent)							
				White				Black			
	Total	Male	Fe-male	1974 -77	1978 -81	1982 -85	1986 -91	1974 -77	1978 -81	1982 -85	1986 -91
All sites [2]	**1,359**	**764**	**595**	**52.2**	**53.2**	**55.6**	**60.6**	**40.3**	**40.7**	**41.2**	**44.9**
Lung	177	99	78	12.6	13.4	14.0	13.7	11.2	11.8	11.4	10.8
Breast [3]	186	1	184	75.1	75.8	79.2	84.3	62.9	64.0	64.2	69.0
Colon and rectum	134	68	66	50.2	53.4	57.7	61.7	45.4	45.9	47.3	52.4
Prostate	317	317	(X)	68.5	73.5	76.8	87.2	59.6	63.1	64.0	71.0
Bladder	53	38	15	73.8	77.9	79.1	82.1	49.4	57.2	58.5	58.6
Corpus uteri	34	(X)	34	88.8	84.9	85.1	85.7	61.4	55.4	55.7	57.3
Non-Hodgkin's lymphoma [4]	53	30	23	47.5	50.4	53.9	51.5	48.0	50.9	46.8	44.7
Oral cavity and pharynx	29	20	9	54.3	55.6	55.0	54.7	36.5	34.4	32.8	33.0
Leukemia [4]	28	15	12	35.8	38.1	40.5	41.2	31.9	30.8	32.9	32.4
Melanoma of skin	38	22	16	80.7	81.9	84.6	86.7	59.6	52.9	78.6	70.0
Pancreas	26	12	14	2.4	2.7	2.9	3.4	2.4	5.4	4.6	4.8
Kidney	31	19	12	50.1	52.2	54.8	58.7	49.5	55.8	52.5	53.5
Stomach	23	14	9	14.5	16.4	16.6	18.7	15.9	16.9	19.0	19.9
Ovary	27	(X)	27	36.8	38.2	39.7	44.0	40.1	39.0	40.7	38.0
Cervix uteri [5]	16	(X)	16	69.4	68.7	69.1	71.0	64.0	59.9	60.4	56.3

X Not applicable. [1] Estimates provided by American Cancer Society are based on rates from the National Cancer Institute's SEER program. [2] Includes other sites not shown separately. [3] Survival rates for female only. [4] All types combined. [5] Invasive cancer only.

Source: U.S. National Institutes of Health, National Cancer Institute, *Cancer Statistics Review,* annual.

No. 224. Personal Health Practices, by Selected Characteristic: 1990

[In percent, except total persons. For persons 18 years of age and over. Based on the National Health Interview Survey and subject to sampling error; for details see source and Appendix III]

CHARACTERISTIC	Total persons (1,000)	Eats break-fast [1]	Rarely snacks	Exercised regularly [2]	Had two or more drinks on any day [3]	Current smoker	20 percent or more above weight [4]
All persons [5]	181,447	56.4	25.5	40.7	5.5	25.5	27.5
Sex: Male	86,278	54.6	25.6	44.0	9.7	28.4	29.6
Female	95,169	58.0	25.4	37.7	1.7	22.8	25.6
Race: White	155,301	57.8	25.8	41.5	5.8	25.6	26.7
Black	20,248	46.9	22.7	34.3	4.3	26.2	38.0
Hispanic origin: Hispanic	14,314	52.5	29.3	34.9	4.6	23.0	27.6
Non-Hispanic	166,599	56.7	25.2	41.2	5.6	25.7	27.5
Marital status:							
Currently married	117,413	57.8	25.3	39.4	5.3	24.6	29.2
Formerly married	30,439	61.5	31.2	34.3	5.3	30.3	29.1
Never married	33,413	46.9	20.9	51.3	6.6	24.3	19.8
Education level:							
Less than 12 years	38,367	58.6	27.8	25.9	5.1	31.8	32.7
12 years	69,405	52.6	24.3	37.0	5.9	29.6	28.6
More than 12 years	73,244	58.8	25.5	52.1	5.4	18.3	23.8
Income: Less than $10,000	18,469	54.1	27.6	32.9	4.8	31.6	29.3
$10,000 to $19,999	30,452	56.6	25.9	32.3	4.9	29.8	28.5
$20,000 to $34,999	40,216	55.2	25.1	40.5	5.8	26.9	28.2
$35,000 to $49,999	29,795	53.7	23.8	46.1	5.6	23.4	27.8
$50,000 or more	36,199	57.2	25.8	51.7	6.7	19.3	24.9

[1] Almost every day.   [2] Or played sports regularly.   [3] On average per day in the past 2 weeks.   [4] Above desirable weight. Based on 1983 Metropolitan Life Insurance Company standards. Height and weight data are self-reported.   [5] Includes persons whose characteristics are unknown.

Source: U.S. National Center for Health Statistics, *Health Promotion and Disease Prevention: United States, 1990, Vital and Health Statistics*, series 10, No. 185.

No. 225. Nutrition—Nutrients in Foods Available for Civilian Consumption per Capita per Day: 1950 to 1990

[Computed by the Center for Nutrition Policy and Promotion (CNPP). Based on Economic Research Service (ERS) estimates of per capita quantities of food available for consumption from "Food Consumption, Prices, and, Expenditures," on imputed consumption data for foods no longer reported by ERS, and on CNPP estimates of quantities of produce from home gardens. Food supply estimates do not reflect loss of food or nutrients from further marketing or home processing. Enrichment and fortification levels of iron, thiamin, riboflavin, niacin, vitamin A, vitamin B_6, vitamin B_{12}, and ascorbic acid are included. See *Historical Statistics, Colonial Times to 1970*, series G 851-856 for related details]

NUTRIENT	Unit	1950-59	1960-69	1970-79	1980-89	1990
Food energy	Calories	3,100	3,200	3,300	3,500	3,700
Carbohydrate	Grams	382	374	388	416	452
Protein	Grams	93	96	99	101	105
Total fat [1]	Grams	141	150	158	165	165
Saturated	Grams	60	62	59	60	59
Monounsaturated	Grams	57	61	64	66	67
Polyunsaturated	Grams	18	22	28	32	32
Cholesterol	Milligrams	510	490	460	440	410
Vitamin A	Micrograms RE [2]	1,310	1,320	1,520	1,460	1,420
Carotenes	Micrograms RE [2]	420	410	570	580	620
Vitamin E	Milligrams α-TE [3]	11.7	12.4	13.6	14.7	15.7
Vitamin C	Milligrams	101	96	110	113	110
Thiamin	Milligrams	1.9	1.9	2.2	2.4	2.5
Riboflavin	Milligrams	2.4	2.3	2.4	2.5	2.6
Niacin	Milligrams	19.9	21.3	24.4	26.7	27.9
Vitamin B_6	Milligrams	1.9	1.9	2.1	2.1	2.2
Folacin	Micrograms	292	275	287	294	296
Vitamin B_{12}	Micrograms	9.2	9.8	10.1	9.2	8.7
Calcium	Milligrams	940	890	870	880	920
Phosphorus	Milligrams	1,460	1,460	1,480	1,530	1,600
Magnesium	Milligrams	330	320	320	330	350
Iron	Milligrams	14.1	14.5	18.7	17.8	19.3
Zinc	Milligrams	11.8	12.2	12.6	12.6	12.7
Copper	Milligrams	1.6	1.6	1.6	1.7	1.7
Potassium	Milligrams	3,630	3,500	3,480	3,480	3,540

[1] Includes other types of fat not shown separately.   [2] Retinol equivalents.   [3] Alpha-Tocopherol equivalents.

Source: U.S. Dept. of Agriculture, Center for Nutrition Policy and Promotion. Data published by Economic Research Service in *Food Consumption, Prices, and Expenditures*, annual.

No. 226. Per Capita Consumption of Major Food Commodities: 1970 to 1994

[In pounds, retail weight except as indicated. Consumption represents the residual after exports, nonfood use and ending stocks are subtracted from the sum of beginning stocks, domestic production, and imports. Based on Bureau of the Census estimated population. Estimates reflect revisions based on the 1990 Census of Population. For similar but unrevised data, see *Historical Statistics, Colonial Times to 1970*, series G 881-915]

COMMODITY	1970	1975	1980	1985	1990	1992	1993	1994
Red meat, total (boneless, trimmed weight) [1][2]	131.7	125.8	126.4	124.9	112.3	114.1	112.1	114.8
Beef	79.6	83.0	72.1	74.6	64.0	62.8	61.5	63.6
Veal	2.0	2.8	1.3	1.5	0.9	0.8	0.8	0.8
Lamb and mutton	2.1	1.3	1.0	1.1	1.0	1.0	1.0	0.9
Pork (excluding lard)	48.0	38.7	52.1	47.7	46.4	49.5	48.9	49.5
Fish and shellfish (edible weight) [3]	11.7	12.1	12.4	15.0	15.0	14.7	14.9	15.1
Fresh and frozen	6.9	7.5	7.8	9.7	9.6	9.8	10.1	10.3
Canned	4.4	4.2	4.3	5.0	5.1	4.6	4.5	4.5
Tuna	2.5	2.8	3.0	3.3	3.7	3.5	3.5	3.3
Cured	0.4	0.4	0.3	0.3	0.3	0.3	0.3	0.3
Poultry products: (boneless weight) [2][4]	33.8	32.9	40.8	45.5	56.3	60.9	62.6	63.7
Chicken	27.4	26.4	32.7	36.4	42.5	46.7	48.5	49.5
Turkey	6.4	6.5	8.1	9.1	13.8	14.2	14.1	14.2
Eggs (farm weight) (number)	308.9	276.0	271.1	254.7	234.3	235.0	235.5	237.6
Dairy products:								
Total (milk equivalent, milkfat basis) [5]	563.8	539.1	543.2	593.7	568.5	565.8	574.1	586.2
Fluid milk and cream [6]	275.1	261.4	245.6	241.0	233.4	230.9	226.8	225.7
Beverage milks	269.1	254.0	237.4	229.7	221.7	218.6	214.3	213.0
Plain whole milk	213.5	174.9	141.7	119.7	87.6	81.4	77.8	75.8
Plain lowfat milk	29.8	53.2	70.1	83.3	98.3	99.4	97.1	95.6
Plain skim milk	11.6	11.5	11.6	12.6	22.9	25.0	26.7	28.8
Flavored whole milk	5.6	6.3	4.7	3.7	2.8	2.7	2.7	2.7
Flavored lowfat and skim milks	3.0	3.3	5.3	6.0	6.6	6.9	6.9	7.1
Buttermilk	5.5	4.7	4.1	4.4	3.5	3.2	3.0	2.9
Yogurt (excl. frozen)	0.8	2.1	2.6	4.1	4.1	4.3	4.4	4.7
Cream [7]	3.8	3.3	3.4	4.4	4.6	4.8	4.9	4.9
Sour cream and dip	1.1	1.6	1.8	2.3	2.5	2.7	2.7	2.7
Condensed and evaporated milk:								
Whole milk	7.0	5.1	3.8	3.6	3.2	3.3	3.0	3.2
Skim milk	5.0	3.5	3.3	3.8	4.8	5.2	5.2	4.8
Cheese [8]	11.4	14.3	17.5	22.5	24.6	26.0	26.3	26.8
American	7.0	8.2	9.6	12.2	11.1	11.3	11.4	11.6
Cheddar	5.8	6.0	6.9	9.8	9.0	9.2	9.1	9.1
Italian [9]	2.1	3.2	4.4	6.5	9.0	10.0	9.8	10.3
Mozzarella	1.2	2.1	3.0	4.6	6.9	7.7	7.6	7.9
Other [9]	2.3	2.9	3.4	3.9	4.5	4.7	5.0	5.0
Swiss	0.9	1.1	1.3	1.3	1.4	1.2	1.2	1.2
Cream and Neufchatel	0.6	0.7	1.0	1.2	1.7	2.0	2.1	2.2
Cottage cheese	5.2	4.6	4.5	4.1	3.4	3.1	2.9	2.8
Ice cream	17.8	18.6	17.5	18.1	15.8	16.3	16.1	16.1
Ice milk	7.7	7.6	7.1	6.9	7.7	7.1	6.9	7.6
Fats and oils:								
Total, fat content only [10]	52.6	52.6	57.2	64.3	62.2	65.7	68.4	66.9
Butter (product weight)	5.4	4.7	4.5	4.9	4.4	4.4	4.7	4.8
Margarine (product weight)	10.8	11.0	11.3	10.8	10.9	11.0	11.1	9.9
Lard (direct use)	4.6	3.2	2.6	1.8	1.9	1.7	1.6	1.7
Edible tallow (direct use)	(NA)	(NA)	1.1	1.9	0.6	2.4	2.2	3.3
Shortening	17.3	17.0	18.2	22.9	22.2	22.4	25.1	24.1
Salad and cooking oils	15.4	17.9	21.2	23.5	24.2	25.6	25.1	24.3
Other edible fats and oils	2.3	2.0	1.5	1.6	1.2	1.4	1.7	1.6
Flour and cereal products	135.3	139.1	144.7	156.3	184.7	190.8	195.8	198.7
Wheat flour [11]	110.9	114.5	116.9	124.6	135.6	138.8	143.3	144.5
Rye flour	1.2	1.0	0.7	0.7	0.6	0.6	0.6	0.6
Rice, milled	6.7	7.6	9.4	9.0	16.3	17.5	17.6	19.0
Corn products	11.1	10.8	12.9	17.1	22.1	23.2	23.5	23.7
Oat products	4.7	4.4	3.9	4.0	8.7	9.0	9.2	9.2
Barley products	1.0	0.9	1.0	1.0	1.4	1.7	1.7	1.7
Caloric sweeteners, total [12]	122.3	118.0	123.0	128.8	137.0	141.2	144.4	147.6
Sugar, refined cane and beet	101.8	89.2	83.6	62.7	64.4	64.6	64.3	65.0
Corn sweeteners (dry weight)	19.1	27.4	38.2	64.8	71.2	75.3	78.7	81.3
Other:								
Cocoa beans	3.9	3.2	3.4	4.6	5.4	5.7	5.5	5.1
Coffee (green beans)	13.6	12.2	10.3	10.5	10.3	10.0	9.1	8.2
Peanuts (shelled)	5.5	6.0	4.8	6.3	6.0	6.2	6.0	5.8
Tree nuts (shelled)	1.7	1.9	1.8	2.5	2.4	2.2	2.2	2.3

NA Not available.   [1] Excludes edible offals.   [2] Excludes shipments to Puerto Rico and the other U.S. possessions.
[3] Excludes consumption from recreational fishing, approximately 3 to 4 pounds per capita.   [4] Includes backs, necks, skin, and giblets.   [5] Includes other products, not shown separately.   [6] Fluid milk figures are aggregates of commercial sales and milk produced and consumed on farms.   [7] Heavy cream, light cream, and half and half.   [8] Excludes cottage, pot, and baker's cheese.   [9] Includes other cheeses not shown separately.   [10] The fat content of butter and margarine is 80 percent of product weight.   [11] White, whole wheat, semolina, and durum flour.   [12] Dry weight. Includes edible syrups (maple, molasses, etc.) and honey not shown separately.

Source: U.S. Department of Agriculture, Economic Research Service, *Food Consumption, Prices, and Expenditures, 1996:* Annual Data, 1970-1994. Statistical Bulletin No. 928, April 1, 1996.

No. 227. Per Capita Utilization of Selected Commercially Produced Fresh Fruits and Vegetables: 1970 to 1994

[**In pounds, farm weight.** Domestic food use of fresh fruits and vegetables reflects the fresh-market share of commodity production plus imports and minus exports. All data are on a calendar year basis except for citrus fruits, October or November; apples, August; grapes and pears, July. See headnote, table 226]

COMMODITY	1970	1975	1980	1985	1990	1991	1992	1993	1994
Fresh fruits, total	101.2	101.8	104.8	110.6	116.5	113.2	123.6	124.9	126.7
Noncitrus	72.4	72.8	78.8	89.2	95.2	94.1	99.3	99.0	101.7
Bananas	17.4	17.6	20.8	23.5	24.4	25.1	27.3	26.8	28.1
Apples	17.0	19.5	19.2	17.3	19.6	18.2	19.2	19.2	19.5
Grapes	2.9	3.6	4.0	6.8	7.9	7.3	7.2	7.0	7.3
Nectarines and peaches	5.8	5.0	7.1	5.5	5.5	6.4	6.0	6.0	5.5
Pears	1.9	2.7	2.6	2.8	3.2	3.2	3.1	3.4	3.5
Strawberries	1.7	1.8	2.0	3.0	3.2	3.6	3.6	3.6	4.0
Pineapples	0.7	1.0	1.5	1.5	2.1	1.9	2.0	2.1	2.0
Plums and prunes	1.5	1.3	1.5	1.4	1.5	1.4	1.8	1.3	1.6
Selected melons	21.6	17.7	17.9	24.1	24.6	23.4	25.4	25.0	26.1
Watermelons	13.5	11.4	10.7	13.5	13.3	12.8	14.8	14.6	15.5
Cantaloups	7.2	5.2	5.8	8.5	9.2	8.7	8.5	8.7	8.8
Honeydews	0.9	1.1	1.4	2.1	2.1	1.9	2.1	1.7	1.8
Other [1]	1.9	2.6	2.2	3.3	3.2	3.6	3.7	4.6	4.1
Citrus	28.9	29.0	26.1	21.5	21.4	19.1	24.4	26.0	24.9
Oranges	16.2	15.9	14.3	11.6	12.4	8.5	12.9	14.3	13.1
Grapefruit	8.2	8.4	7.3	5.5	4.4	5.9	5.9	6.2	6.1
Other [2]	4.5	4.7	4.5	4.4	4.6	4.7	5.6	5.6	5.7
Selected fresh vegetables	85.4	88.4	92.5	102.7	113.9	110.9	116.1	116.2	113.9
Asparagus	0.4	0.4	0.3	0.5	0.6	0.6	0.6	0.6	0.6
Broccoli	0.5	1.0	1.4	2.6	3.4	3.1	3.4	2.9	2.8
Cabbage	8.8	9.1	8.1	8.8	8.8	8.5	8.9	9.7	9.7
Carrots	6.0	6.4	6.2	6.5	8.3	7.7	8.3	8.2	7.9
Cauliflower	0.7	0.9	1.1	1.8	2.2	2.0	1.8	1.7	1.4
Celery	7.3	6.9	7.4	6.9	7.2	6.8	7.4	7.1	6.8
Corn	7.8	7.8	6.5	6.4	6.7	5.9	6.9	7.0	7.9
Cucumbers	2.8	2.8	3.9	4.4	4.7	4.6	5.0	5.3	5.3
Iceberg lettuce	22.4	23.5	25.6	23.7	27.8	26.1	25.9	24.6	22.5
Onions	10.1	10.5	11.4	13.6	15.1	15.7	16.2	16.0	16.3
Snap beans	1.5	1.4	1.3	1.3	1.1	1.1	1.5	1.5	1.5
Green peppers	2.2	2.5	2.9	3.8	4.5	5.1	5.7	6.2	6.6
Tomatoes	12.1	12.0	12.8	14.9	15.5	15.4	15.5	16.0	15.7
Other fresh vegetables [3]	2.8	3.2	3.6	7.5	8.0	8.3	9.0	9.4	8.9
Potatoes	121.7	121.9	114.7	122.4	127.7	130.4	132.4	137.1	141.0
Fresh	61.8	52.6	51.1	46.3	45.8	46.4	48.9	49.9	50.2
For freezing	28.5	37.1	35.4	45.4	50.2	51.3	51.0	54.5	57.8
For chips/shoestrings	17.4	15.5	16.5	17.6	17.0	17.3	17.5	17.6	17.5
For dehydrating	12.0	14.7	9.8	11.2	12.8	13.7	13.2	13.4	13.8
For canning	2.0	2.0	1.9	1.9	1.9	1.7	1.8	1.7	1.7
Sweet potatoes [4]	5.4	5.4	4.4	5.4	4.6	4.0	4.3	3.9	4.7
Mushrooms	1.3	1.9	2.7	3.6	3.7	3.7	3.7	3.7	3.8
For fresh	0.3	0.7	1.2	1.8	2.0	1.9	2.0	2.0	2.0
For processing	1.0	1.2	1.5	1.8	1.7	1.8	1.7	1.7	1.8

[1] Includes apricots, avocados, cherries, cranberries, kiwifruit, mangos, and papayas.   [2] Includes tangerines, tangelos, lemons, and limes.   [3] Includes artichokes, Brussels sprouts, eggplant, escarole/endive, garlic, romaine and leaf lettuce (after 1984), radishes, and spinach.   [4] Fresh and processed.

No. 228. Per Capita Consumption of Selected Beverages, by Type: 1970 to 1994

[**In gallons.** See headnote, table 226]

COMMODITY	1970	1975	1980	1985	1990	1991	1992	1993	1994
Nonalcoholic [1]	101.5	103.2	106.3	109.1	126.4	129.7	128.5	129.8	130.4
Milk (plain and flavored)	31.3	29.5	27.6	26.7	25.7	25.7	25.4	24.9	24.7
Whole	25.5	21.1	17.0	14.3	10.5	10.2	9.8	9.4	9.1
Lowfat	4.4	7.1	9.2	10.9	12.6	12.7	12.7	12.4	12.2
Skim	1.3	1.3	1.3	1.5	2.6	2.8	2.9	3.1	3.3
Tea	6.8	7.5	7.3	7.1	6.7	6.8	7.0	7.0	7.0
Coffee	33.4	31.4	26.7	27.4	26.9	26.8	25.9	23.5	21.1
Bottled water	(NA)	(NA)	2.4	4.5	8.0	8.0	8.2	9.4	10.5
Soft drinks	24.3	28.2	35.1	35.7	46.3	47.9	48.5	50.2	52.2
Diet	2.1	3.2	5.1	7.1	10.7	11.7	11.6	11.7	11.9
Regular	22.2	25.0	29.9	28.7	35.6	36.3	36.9	38.5	40.3
Selected fruit juices	5.7	6.6	7.2	7.7	6.9	7.9	7.3	8.4	8.6
Fruit drinks, cocktails, and ades	(NA)	(NA)	(NA)	(NA)	5.8	6.4	6.0	6.0	5.7
Canned iced tea	(NA)	(NA)	(NA)	(NA)	0.1	0.2	0.2	0.4	0.6
Alcoholic (adult population)	35.7	39.7	42.8	40.7	40.0	37.8	37.3	36.7	36.4
Beer	30.6	33.9	36.6	34.6	34.9	33.2	32.6	32.3	32.0
Wine [2]	2.2	2.7	3.2	3.5	2.9	2.7	2.7	2.5	2.5
Distilled spirits	3.0	3.1	3.0	2.6	2.2	2.0	2.0	1.9	1.8

NA Not available.   [1] Excludes vegetable juices.   [2] Beginning 1985, incudes wine coolers.

Source of tables 227 and 228: U.S. Department of Agriculture, Economic Research Service, *Food Consumption, Prices, and Expenditures, 1996: Annual Data, 1970-1994*. Statistical Bulletin No. 928, April 1, 1996.

No. 229. Cumulative Percent Distribution of Population, by Height and Sex: 1976-80

[For persons 18 to 74 years old. Height was measured without shoes. Based on sample and subject to sampling variability; see source]

HEIGHT	MALES						FEMALES					
	18-24 years	25-34 years	35-44 years	45-54 years	55-64 years	65-74 years	18-24 years	25-34 years	35-44 years	45-54 years	55-64 years	65-74 years
Percent under—												
4'8"	-	-	-	-	-	-	-	-	-	-	-	-
4'9"	-	-	-	-	-	-	0.05	-	0.10	0.28	0.46	1.04
4'10"	-	-	-	-	-	-	0.43	0.23	0.34	0.35	1.07	2.27
4'11"	-	-	-	-	-	-	0.94	0.64	0.95	1.22	3.02	4.23
5'	0.18	0.05	0.27	-	0.27	0.24	2.22	1.65	1.94	4.20	6.43	9.33
							4.22	3.65	4.56	8.88	11.40	17.20
5'1"	0.18	0.31	0.34	0.19	0.72	1.22	9.13	8.60	7.75	16.16	19.70	29.00
5'2"	0.34	0.42	0.87	0.70	0.92	2.66	17.75	19.11	18.24	27.68	31.71	44.34
5'3"	0.61	0.54	2.07	1.50	2.78	5.97	29.06	32.96	33.11	39.83	45.87	59.15
5'4"	2.37	1.55	3.68	2.55	5.28	10.53	41.81	47.43	49.90	57.21	63.89	76.44
5'5"	3.85	4.36	6.36	5.72	9.29	18.31	58.09	61.36	63.88	70.47	77.44	86.97
5'6"	8.24	9.51	12.39	11.39	17.54	29.42	74.76	74.92	78.07	84.64	88.91	94.63
5'7"	16.18	15.25	17.63	21.24	29.10	41.63	85.37	85.65	87.95	91.21	94.56	97.86
5'8"	26.68	26.69	26.40	33.56	43.53	57.75	92.30	93.28	93.43	96.28	97.70	99.20
5'9"	38.89	39.68	42.52	50.39	58.21	69.96	96.23	97.19	97.18	98.17	99.36	99.81
5'10"	53.66	55.35	57.01	63.38	71.51	81.95	98.34	99.49	99.19	99.58	99.78	99.92
5'11"	68.25	69.67	70.70	76.94	83.09	89.59	99.38	99.68	99.39	99.84	99.81	100.00
6'	80.14	81.58	81.15	85.83	90.99	94.52	100.00	100.00	100.00	100.00	100.00	100.00
6'1"	88.54	89.95	90.04	93.43	96.28	97.82	100.00	100.00	100.00	100.00	100.00	100.00
6'2"	92.74	95.57	95.05	98.01	97.66	99.17	100.00	100.00	100.00	100.00	100.00	100.00
6'3"	96.17	97.98	97.82	99.35	98.90	99.86	100.00	100.00	100.00	100.00	100.00	100.00
6'4"	98.40	99.23	99.19	99.70	99.79	100.00	100.00	100.00	100.00	100.00	100.00	100.00

- Represents or rounds to zero.

Source: U.S. National Center for Health Statistics, *Vital and Health Statistics*, series 11, No. 238.

No. 230. Cumulative Percent Distribution of Population, by Weight and Sex: 1976-80

[For persons 18 to 74 years old. Weight measured includes clothes weight, estimated as ranging from .20 pounds to .62 pounds. Based on sample and subject to sampling variability; see source]

WEIGHT	MALES						FEMALES					
	18-24 years	25-34 years	35-44 years	45-54 years	55-64 years	65-74 years	18-24 years	25-34 years	35-44 years	45-54 years	55-64 years	65-74 years
Percent under—												
90 pounds . . .	-	-	-	-	-	-	0.7	0.4	0.1	0.7	0.5	0.5
100 pounds . .	0.2	-	-	-	0.1	0.5	3.6	3.3	1.7	2.4	2.1	3.1
110 pounds . .	0.6	0.2	0.7	-	0.7	1.4	12.7	10.7	6.1	6.9	6.9	8.4
120 pounds . .	2.3	1.0	1.3	1.3	1.4	5.0	30.6	25.6	17.8	17.0	15.7	17.3
130 pounds . .	7.7	4.1	4.3	3.2	4.1	10.5	52.7	41.3	32.3	29.0	29.0	29.5
140 pounds . .	20.4	10.9	8.1	7.6	9.5	18.5	69.7	59.1	50.4	44.5	43.4	45.3
150 pounds . .	35.9	21.8	15.5	17.1	19.5	30.3	80.8	71.7	63.6	56.7	56.9	60.4
160 pounds . .	52.4	35.1	26.7	27.2	32.3	44.7	86.8	79.1	73.0	69.3	67.8	73.3
170 pounds . .	66.7	48.0	41.2	43.4	47.9	57.7	91.7	84.2	80.2	77.3	77.4	81.3
180 pounds . .	78.7	62.1	54.9	57.6	62.5	71.9	94.2	88.6	84.5	84.3	83.8	86.9
190 pounds . .	86.2	77.5	68.4	68.7	75.8	82.0	96.2	91.3	88.8	89.1	88.7	91.5
200 pounds . .	90.3	84.6	79.2	77.4	85.2	89.0	97.5	94.1	91.9	92.5	92.5	94.6
210 pounds . .	93.3	90.1	85.8	85.7	90.6	94.2	97.8	95.4	94.0	94.6	95.3	96.4
220 pounds . .	95.2	93.5	91.0	90.7	93.4	96.4	98.4	96.9	95.2	96.1	96.7	97.4
230 pounds . .	97.0	95.4	94.9	94.6	96.3	98.2	98.7	97.8	96.5	97.2	97.6	98.0
240 pounds . .	98.8	96.5	97.3	96.9	98.1	99.2	99.0	98.7	97.5	97.8	98.2	98.8
250 pounds . .	99.2	97.8	98.8	98.4	98.4	99.6	99.2	98.9	98.5	98.7	98.9	99.3
260 pounds . .	100.0	100.0	100.0	100.0	100.0	100.0	99.6	99.2	99.0	99.1	99.4	99.7
270 pounds . .	100.0	100.0	100.0	100.0	100.0	100.0	100.0	99.3	99.3	99.3	99.5	99.8
280 pounds . .	100.0	100.0	100.0	100.0	100.0	100.0	100.0	99.4	99.7	99.3	99.7	99.8

- Represents or rounds to zero.

Source: U.S. National Center for Health Statistics, *Vital and Health Statistics*, series 11, No. 238.

Figure 4.1
**Educational Attainment by Race and Hispanic Origin:
1960 to 1995**
(For persons 25 years old and over)

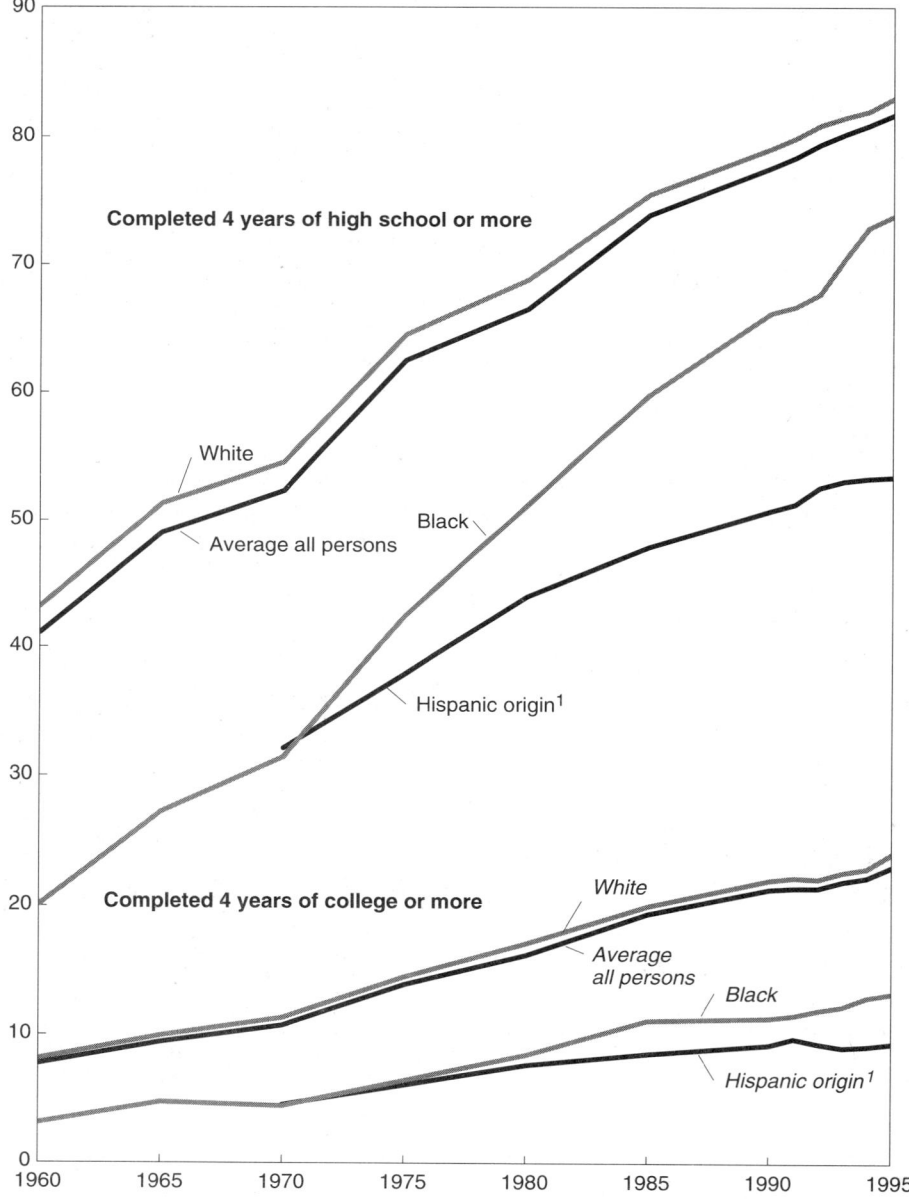

Education

This section presents data primarily concerning formal education as a whole, at various levels, and for public and private schools. Data shown relate to the school-age population and school enrollment, educational attainment, education personnel, and financial aspects of education. In addition, data are shown for libraries, computer usage in schools, and adult education. The chief sources are the decennial census of population and the Current Population Survey (CPS), both conducted by the Bureau of the Census (see text, section 1); annual, biennial, and other periodic surveys conducted by the National Center for Education Statistics, a part of the U.S. Department of Education; and surveys conducted by the National Education Association.

The censuses of population have included data on school enrollment since 1840 and on educational attainment since 1940. The CPS has reported on school enrollment annually since 1945 and on educational attainment periodically since 1947.

The National Center for Education Statistics is continuing the pattern of statistical studies and surveys conducted by the U.S. Office of Education since 1870. The annual *Digest of Education Statistics* provides summary data on pupils, staff, finances, including government expenditures, and organization at the elementary, secondary, and higher education levels. It is also a primary source for detailed information on Federal funds for education, projections of enrollment, graduates, and teachers. *The Condition of Education,* issued annually, presents a summary of information on education of particular interest to policymakers.

Other sources of data include special studies by the National Center for Education Statistics and annual or biennial reports of education agencies in individual States. The census of governments, conducted by the Bureau of the Census every 5 years (for the years ending in "2" and "7"), provides data on school district

In Brief

The enrollment rate of 3 to 5 year olds in preprimary school:

1970	*37 percent*
1994	*61 percent*

Persons 25 years old and over completing college:

1970	*11 percent*
1995	*23 percent*

Elementary and secondary schools with microcomputers:

1985	*78 percent*
1994	*97 percent*

finances and State and local government expenditures for education. Reports published by the Bureau of Labor Statistics contain data relating civilian labor force experience to educational attainment (see also tables 617, 618, 640, 648, and 649 in section 13).

Types and sources of data—The statistics in this section are of two general types. One type, exemplified by data from the Bureau of the Census, is based on direct interviews with individuals to obtain information about their own and their family members' education. Data of this type relate to school enrollment and level of education attained, classified by age, sex, and other characteristics of the population. The school enrollment statistics reflect attendance or enrollment in any regular school within a given period; educational attainment statistics reflect the highest grade completed by an individual or, beginning in 1992, the highest diploma or degree received.

For enrollment data starting in October 1994, the CPS used 1990 census population controls plus adjustments for undercount. Also the survey changed from paper to computer assisted technology; for years 1981 through 1993, 1980 population controls were used; 1971 through 1980, 1970 census population controls had been used. These changes had little impact on summary measures (e.g., medians) and proportional measures (e.g., enrollment rates); however, use of the controls may have significant impact on absolute numbers.

Beginning with data for 1986, a new edit and tabulation package for school enrollment has been introduced. In 1988, a new edit and tabulation package was introduced for educational attainment data.

The second type, generally exemplified by data from the National Center for Education Statistics and the National Education Association, is based on reports from administrators of educational institutions and of State and local agencies having jurisdiction over education. Data of this type relate to enrollment, attendance, staff, and finances for the Nation, individual States, and local areas.

Unlike the National Center for Education Statistics, the Census Bureau does not regularly include specialized vocational, trade, business, or correspondence schools in its surveys. The National Center for Education Statistics includes nursery schools and kindergartens that are part of regular grade schools in their enrollment figures. The Census Bureau includes all nursery schools and kindergartens. At the higher education level, the statistics of both agencies are concerned with institutions granting degrees or offering work acceptable for degree-credit, such as junior colleges.

School attendance—All States require that children attend school. While State laws vary as to the ages and circumstances of compulsory attendance, generally they require that formal schooling begin by age 6 and continue to age 16.

Schools—The National Center for Education Statistics defines a *school* as "a division of the school system consisting of students composing one or more grade groups or other identifiable groups, organized as one unit with one or more teachers to give instruction of a defined type, and housed in a school plant of one or more buildings. More than one school may be housed in one school plant, as is the case when the elementary and secondary programs are housed in the same school plant."

Regular schools are those which advance a person toward a diploma or degree. They include public and private nursery schools, kindergartens, graded schools, colleges, universities, and professional schools.

Public schools are schools controlled and supported by local, State, or Federal governmental agencies; *private* schools are those controlled and supported mainly by religious organizations or by private persons or organizations.

The Bureau of the Census defines *elementary* schools as including grades 1 through 8; *high* schools as including grades 9 through 12; and *colleges* as including junior or community colleges, regular 4-year colleges, and universities and graduate or professional schools. Statistics reported by the National Center for Education Statistics and the National Education Association by type of organization, such as elementary level and secondary level, may not be strictly comparable with those from the Bureau of the Census because the grades included at the two levels vary, depending on the level assigned to the middle or junior high school by the local school systems.

School year—Except as otherwise indicated in the tables, data refer to the school year which, for elementary and secondary schools, generally begins in September of the preceding year and ends in June of the year stated. For the most part, statistics concerning school finances are for a 12-month period, usually July 1 to June 30. Enrollment data generally refer to a specific point in time, such as fall, as indicated in the tables.

Statistical reliability—For a discussion of statistical collection, estimation, and sampling procedures and measures of statistical reliability applicable to Census Bureau and the National Center for Education Statistics data, see Appendix III.

Historical statistics—Tabular headnotes provide cross-references, where applicable, to *Historical Statistics of the United States, Colonial Times to 1970*. See Appendix IV.

No. 231. School Enrollment: 1965 to 2006

[In thousands. As of fall. See *Historical Statistics, Colonial Times to 1970,* series H 421-429]

ITEM AND YEAR	TOTAL		K THROUGH GRADE 8		GRADES 9 THROUGH 12		COLLEGE	
	Public	Private	Public	Private	Public	Private	Public	Private
1965	46,143	8,251	30,563	4,900	11,610	1,400	3,970	1,951
1970	52,322	7,516	32,558	4,052	13,336	1,311	6,428	2,153
1975	53,654	7,350	30,515	3,700	14,304	1,300	8,835	2,153
1980	50,335	7,971	27,647	3,992	13,231	1,339	9,457	2,640
1981	49,691	8,225	27,280	4,100	12,764	1,400	9,647	2,725
1982	49,262	8,330	27,161	4,200	12,405	1,400	9,696	2,730
1983	48,935	8,497	26,981	4,315	12,271	1,400	9,683	2,782
1984	48,686	8,465	26,905	4,300	12,304	1,400	9,477	2,765
1985	48,901	8,325	27,034	4,195	12,388	1,362	9,479	2,768
1986	49,467	8,242	27,420	4,116	12,333	1,336	9,714	2,790
1987	49,982	8,272	27,933	4,232	12,076	1,247	9,973	2,793
1988	50,349	8,136	28,501	4,036	11,687	1,206	10,161	2,894
1989	51,120	8,316	29,152	4,162	11,390	1,193	10,578	2,961
1990	52,061	8,206	29,878	4,095	11,338	1,137	10,845	2,974
1991	53,357	8,248	30,506	4,074	11,541	1,125	11,310	3,049
1992	54,200	8,478	31,081	4,212	11,735	1,163	11,385	3,103
1993, prel.	54,665	8,587	31,515	4,280	11,961	1,191	11,189	3,116
1994, prel.	55,364	8,741	31,864	4,360	12,366	1,236	11,134	3,145
1995, proj.	56,184	8,801	32,383	4,431	12,693	1,269	11,108	3,101
1996, proj.	57,140	8,942	32,837	4,493	13,049	1,304	11,254	3,145
1997, proj.	57,930	9,067	33,226	4,547	13,299	1,329	11,405	3,191
1998, proj.	58,615	9,192	33,522	4,587	13,466	1,346	11,627	3,259
1999, proj.	59,251	9,319	33,692	4,610	13,673	1,367	11,886	3,342
2000, proj.	59,747	9,418	33,852	4,632	13,804	1,380	12,091	3,406
2001, proj.	60,116	9,488	34,029	4,656	13,862	1,386	12,225	3,446
2002, proj.	60,421	9,545	34,098	4,666	14,004	1,400	12,319	3,479
2003, proj.	60,654	9,589	34,065	4,661	14,169	1,416	12,420	3,512
2004, proj.	60,896	9,631	33,882	4,636	14,483	1,448	12,531	3,547
2005, proj.	61,144	9,672	33,680	4,609	14,818	1,481	12,646	3,582
2006, proj.	61,296	9,707	33,507	4,585	15,021	1,501	12,768	3,621

Source: U.S. National Center for Education Statistics, *Digest of Education Statistics,* annual, and *Projections of Education Statistics,* annual.

No. 232. School Expenditures, by Type of Control and Level of Instruction in Constant (1993-94) Dollars: 1960 to 1995

[In millions of dollars. For school years ending in year shown. Total expenditures for public elementary and secondary schools include current expenditures, interest on school debt and capital outlay. Data deflated by the Consumer Price Index, wage earners, and clerical workers through 1975; thereafter, all urban consumers, on a school year basis (supplied by the National Center for Education Statistics). See also Appendix III. See *Historical Statistics, Colonial Times to 1970,* series H 494, 499, and 500 for related but not comparable data, and H 513-519 for private schools]

YEAR	Total	ELEMENTARY AND SECONDARY SCHOOLS			COLLEGES AND UNIVERSITIES		
		Total	Public	Private [1]	Total	Public	Private [1]
1960	118,735	83,169	77,695	5,474	35,566	19,426	16,140
1970	264,987	167,152	157,475	9,677	97,835	62,838	34,997
1975	306,775	194,363	183,070	11,293	112,413	76,131	36,282
1980	311,948	194,298	180,738	13,561	117,649	78,038	39,611
1983	315,944	191,765	176,421	15,344	124,178	80,949	43,230
1984	328,393	199,681	183,161	16,520	128,712	83,499	45,213
1985	342,373	206,537	189,395	17,142	135,836	88,069	47,767
1986	362,106	217,410	199,673	17,737	144,696	94,151	50,544
1987	383,803	230,302	211,505	18,798	153,501	97,999	55,501
1988	395,544	237,294	217,982	19,312	158,250	100,799	57,451
1989	418,510	252,612	232,826	19,786	165,898	105,094	60,805
1990	439,000	265,630	244,672	20,958	173,371	110,994	62,378
1991	450,552	271,793	250,502	21,291	178,758	114,025	64,733
1992, prel.	459,258	276,402	255,032	21,371	182,856	115,344	67,512
1993, est.	469,815	282,492	260,435	22,057	187,422	118,461	68,961
1994, est	486,100	294,600	272,000	22,600	191,500	120,900	70,600
1995, est.	494,137	298,932	275,989	22,942	195,205	123,072	72,132

[1] Estimated.

Source: U.S. National Center for Education Statistics, *Digest Education Statistics,* annual.

No. 233. School Enrollment, Faculty, Graduates, and Finances, With Projections: 1985 to 2005

[As of **fall, except as indicated**]

ITEM	Unit	1985	1990	1994, prel.	1995, prel.	2000, proj.	2003, proj.	2005, proj.
ELEMENTARY AND SECONDARY SCHOOLS								
School enrollment: Total	1,000...	44,979	46,448	49,826	50,776	53,668	54,312	54,587
Kindergarten through grade 8	1,000...	31,229	33,973	36,225	36,814	38,484	38,726	38,289
Grades 9 through 12	1,000...	13,750	12,475	13,602	13,962	15,184	15,586	16,299
Public, total	1,000...	39,422	41,217	44,230	45,076	47,656	48,234	48,497
Kindergarten through grade 8	1,000...	27,034	29,878	31,864	32,383	33,852	34,065	33,680
Grades 9 through 12	1,000...	12,388	11,338	12,366	12,693	13,804	14,169	14,818
Private, total	1,000...	5,557	5,232	5,596	5,700	6,012	6,078	6,090
Kindergarten through grade 8	1,000...	4,195	4,095	4,360	4,431	4,632	4,661	4,609
Grades 9 through 12	1,000...	1,362	1,137	1,236	1,269	1,380	1,416	1,481
Enrollment rate:								
5 and 6 year olds	Percent .	96.1	96.5	96.7	(NA)	(NA)	(NA)	(NA)
7 to 13 year olds	Percent .	99.2	99.6	99.3	(NA)	(NA)	(NA)	(NA)
14 to 17 year olds	Percent .	94.9	95.8	96.6	(NA)	(NA)	(NA)	(NA)
Classroom teachers: Total [1]	1,000...	2,549	2,753	2,915	3,017	3,239	3,334	3,403
Public, total	1,000...	2,206	2,398	2,547	2,631	2,826	2,910	2,971
Private, total	1,000...	343	355	368	386	413	424	432
High school graduates, total [2]	1,000...	2,643	2,503	2,505	2,564	2,873	2,981	3,051
Public	1,000...	2,383	2,235	2,300	2,321	2,631	2,739	2,710
Public schools: [2]								
Average daily attendance (ADA)	1,000...	36,523	38,427	41,034	41,819	44,213	44,749	44,993
Constant (**1993-94**) dollars:								
Teachers' average salary	Dol..	33,867	36,126	35,908	36,343	37,717	37,982	38,182
Current school expenditures	Bil. dol .	184	221	244	253	293	310	321
HIGHER EDUCATION								
Enrollment, total	1,000...	12,247	13,819	14,279	14,210	15,497	15,932	16,229
Male	1,000...	5,818	6,284	6,372	6,381	6,985	7,194	7,304
Full-time	1,000...	3,608	3,808	3,855	3,903	4,458	4,654	4,753
Part-time	1,000...	2,211	2,476	2,517	2,478	2,526	2,540	2,551
Female	1,000...	6,429	7,535	7,907	7,829	8,512	8,738	8,925
Full-time	1,000...	3,468	4,013	4,283	4,161	4,713	4,901	5,047
Part-time	1,000...	2,961	3,521	3,624	3,668	3,799	3,837	3,878
Public	1,000...	9,479	10,845	11,133	11,108	12,091	12,420	12,646
Four-year institutions	1,000...	5,210	5,848	5,825	5,881	6,456	6,671	6,810
Two-year institutions	1,000...	4,270	4,996	5,308	5,227	5,635	5,749	5,836
Private	1,000...	2,768	2,974	3,145	3,102	3,406	3,512	3,582
Four-year institutions	1,000...	2,506	2,730	2,924	2,861	3,137	3,236	3,301
Two-year institutions	1,000...	261	244	221	241	269	276	281
Undergraduate	1,000...	10,597	11,959	12,263	12,171	13,336	13,757	14,035
Graduate	1,000...	1,376	1,586	1,721	1,736	1,826	1,834	1,847
First-time professional	1,000...	274	273	295	303	335	341	346
Full-time equivalent	1,000...	8,943	9,983	10,348	10,286	11,457	11,860	12,123
Public	1,000...	6,668	7,558	7,784	7,761	8,638	8,936	9,132
Private	1,000...	2,276	2,425	2,564	2,525	2,819	2,924	2,991
Faculty, total	1,000...	715	817	826	833	894	(NA)	(NA)
Public	1,000...	503	574	577	581	626	(NA)	(NA)
Private	1,000...	212	244	249	252	268	(NA)	(NA)
Degrees conferred, total [2]	1,000...	1,830	2,025	2,247	2,259	2,325	2,451	2,497
Associate's	1,000...	446	482	530	534	549	576	584
Bachelor's	1,000...	988	1,095	1,192	1,195	1,211	1,288	1,316
Master's	1,000...	289	337	405	409	435	452	462
Doctorate's	1,000...	34	39	43	43	46	44	43
First-professional	1,000...	74	72	77	78	84	90	92

NA Not available.   [1] Full-time equivalents.   [2] For school year ending June the following year.

Source: U.S. National Center for Education Statistics, *Digest of Education Statistics*, annual, and *Projections of Educational Statistics*, annual.

No. 234. Federal Funds for Education and Related Programs: 1993 to 1995

[In millions of dollars, except percent. For fiscal years ending in September. Figures represent on-budget funds]

LEVEL, AGENCY, AND PROGRAM	1993	1994	1995[1]
Total, all programs	**67,740.6**	**63,800.3**	**73,828.1**
Percent of Federal budget outlays	4.8	4.4	4.9
Elementary/secondary education programs	**30,834.3**	**32,305.6**	**35,197.8**
Department of Education[2]	13,059.0	13,769.2	15,378.6
Grants for the disadvantaged[3]	6,615.0	6,845.7	7,032.2
School improvement programs	2,032.6	1,470.0	1,588.8
Indian Education	99.9	79.1	82.8
Education for the handicapped	2,564.1	2,980.3	3,611.7
Vocational and adult education	190.4	1,340.8	1,543.8
Department of Agriculture[2]	7,154.5	7,604.5	8,169.5
Child nutrition programs	6,596.6	7,043.7	7,644.8
Agricultural Marketing Service— commodities[4]	389.9	400.0	400.0
Department of Defense[2]	1,259.4	1,210.2	1,225.9
Overseas dependents schools	895.7	849.6	845.3
Section VI schools[5]	279.6	265.0	261.0
Department of Energy[2]	6.3	11.6	11.5
Department of Health and Human Services	4,114.5	4,669.2	5,090.2
Head Start	2,776.3	3,215.9	3,534.0
Social security student benefits	601.7	614.3	619.2
Department of the Interior[2]	536.5	485.8	493.6
Mineral Leasing Act and other funds	143.8	61.5	57.0
Indian Education	391.8	423.6	435.9
Department of Justice	107.9	112.4	138.8
Inmate programs	106.1	111.2	135.3
Department of Labor	4,241.0	4,011.2	4,299.5
Job Corps	949.3	964.2	1,042.4
Department of Veterans Affairs	222.6	335.9	310.4
Vocational rehab for disabled veterans	216.3	265.6	296.6
Other agencies and programs[2]	132.8	95.6	79.8
Higher education programs[2]	**17,844.0**	**11,383.8**	**17,690.1**
Department of Education[2]	14,660.7	8,081.4	14,061.3
Student financial assistance	7,678.3	7,118.0	7,264.8
Federal Family Education Loans[2]	5,554.9	-280.3	4,742.5
Department of Agriculture	32.7	25.5	25.5
Department of Defense	696.8	679.0	727.3
Tuition assistance for military personnel[6]	123.4	130.2	133.0
Service academies[6]	128.0	141.5	157.0
Senior ROTC	184.1	195.3	208.9
Professional development education	261.3	212.0	228.4
Department of Energy[2]	17.7	18.0	17.0

LEVEL, AGENCY, AND PROGRAM	1993	1994	1995[1]
Department of Health and Human Services[2]	720.9	795.9	826.4
Health professions training programs	299.8	305.5	313.0
National Health Service Corps scholarships[7]	33.3	79.3	80.1
National Institutes of Health training grants[7]	350.8	372.7	381.3
Department of the Interior[2]	132.9	156.7	157.9
Shared revenues, Mineral Leasing Act and other receipts—estimated education share	61.6	79.8	81.7
Indian programs	71.4	76.9	76.2
Department of Transportation	57.6	56.6	57.1
Department of Veterans Affairs[2]	920.0	1,043.7	1,218.8
Other agencies and programs[2]	604.7	527.0	598.8
Post-Vietnam veterans	65.9	48.1	35.4
All-volunteer-force educational assistance	745.8	887.0	1,075.0
National Endowment for the Humanities	57.8	58.4	58.0
National Science Foundation	246.6	225.2	265.1
United States Information Agency	256.1	200.4	234.3
Other education programs[2]	**4,107.2**	**4,484.0**	**5,014.4**
Department of Education[2]	2,526.4	2,796.0	3,177.1
Administration	353.5	403.9	465.1
Libraries	181.2	142.2	150.2
Rehabilitative services and handicapped research	1,983.8	2,244.2	2,554.1
Department of Agriculture	443.7	426.3	430.7
Department of Health and Human Services	96.9	107.9	125.2
Department of Justice	37.0	34.1	27.8
Department of State	58.8	46.6	46.7
Department of the Treasury	56.8	62.0	63.9
Other agencies and programs[2]	887.7	1,010.8	1,143.1
Agency for International Development	215.2	242.0	207.7
Library of Congress	311.5	312.7	337.4
National Endowment for the Arts	2.8	2.2	2.1
National Endowment for the Humanities	100.8	99.1	100.0
Research programs at universities and related institutions[2]	**14,955.1**	**15,627.0**	**15,925.8**
Department of Agriculture	436.2	453.5	424.4
Department of Defense	2,002.6	2,105.0	1,791.3
Department of Energy	2,763.5	2,705.1	2,579.8
Department of Health and Human Services	5,953.0	6,368.6	6,639.9
National Aeronautics and Space Administration	1,367.5	1,548.5	1,808.2
National Science Foundation	1,833.6	1,800.7	1,966.0

[1] Estimated. [2] Includes other programs and agencies, not shown separately. [3] Starting in 1994, the Special Milk Program was included in the Child Nutrition Program. [4] Purchased under Section 32 of the Act of August 1935 for use in child nutrition programs. [5] Program provides for the education of dependents of federal employees residing on federal property where free public education is unavailable in the nearby community. [6] Instructional costs only including academics, audiovisual, academic computer center, faculty training, military training, physical education, and libraries. [7] Beginning 1992, includes alcohol, drug abuse, and mental health training programs.

Source: U.S. National Center for Education Statistics, Digest of Education Statistics, 1995.

No. 235. School Expenditures, by Source of Funds in Constant (1992-93) Dollars: 1980 to 1993

[In billions of dollars. For school years ending in year shown. Includes nursery, kindergarten, and special programs when provided by school system. Data are deflated by the Consumer Price Index for all urban consumers, on a school year basis (supplied by the U.S. National Center for Education Statistics). Distribution by source of funds is estimated]

SOURCE OF FUNDS AND CONTROL OF SCHOOL	1980	1985	1986	1987	1988	1989	1990	1991	1992	1993
Total	**304.0**	**333.8**	**353.0**	**374.1**	**385.6**	**408.0**	**427.9**	**439.2**	**447.7**	**458.0**
Federal	34.7	28.7	30.8	32.3	32.9	34.1	35.5	36.3	38.4	40.1
State	118.0	129.5	137.9	145.0	148.9	153.1	159.4	161.3	159.9	159.9
Local	79.5	85.3	88.9	94.0	97.6	108.4	109.8	112.3	114.9	118.3
All other	71.8	90.2	95.4	102.6	106.3	112.4	123.2	129.3	134.5	139.8
Public	252.3	270.5	286.4	301.8	310.8	329.4	346.7	355.4	361.0	369.3
Federal	27.2	21.3	22.7	23.1	23.6	24.6	25.7	26.5	28.3	30.1
State	117.3	128.7	137.0	143.9	147.5	151.6	157.8	160.0	158.3	158.3
Local	79.1	85.0	88.7	93.7	97.2	108.0	109.3	111.7	114.5	117.8
All other	28.6	35.4	38.1	41.0	42.6	45.3	53.8	57.2	60.0	63.1
Private	51.8	63.3	66.5	72.4	74.8	78.6	81.3	83.9	86.6	88.7
Federal	7.5	7.4	8.1	9.2	9.4	9.5	9.7	9.8	10.1	10.0
State and local	1.1	1.2	1.2	1.5	1.8	2.0	2.0	1.8	2.1	2.0
All other	43.1	54.7	57.1	61.6	63.7	67.2	69.6	72.3	74.5	76.7
Elementary and secondary	**189.5**	**201.3**	**211.9**	**224.5**	**231.3**	**246.3**	**259.0**	**264.9**	**269.4**	**275.3**
Federal	17.3	12.3	13.0	13.2	13.4	14.1	14.6	15.1	16.4	17.6
State	82.1	90.0	95.7	102.1	104.8	108.1	112.8	115.2	115.3	115.8
Local	76.4	81.9	85.4	90.2	93.6	104.2	105.4	107.7	110.3	113.5
All other	13.8	17.2	17.8	19.0	19.4	20.0	26.2	27.0	27.4	28.3
Public	176.2	184.6	194.6	206.2	212.5	227.0	238.5	244.1	248.6	253.9
Federal	17.3	12.3	13.0	13.2	13.4	14.1	14.6	15.1	16.4	17.6
State	82.1	90.0	95.7	102.1	104.8	108.1	112.8	115.2	115.3	115.8
Local	76.4	81.9	85.4	90.2	93.6	104.2	105.4	107.7	110.3	113.5
All other [1]	0.6	0.5	0.5	0.6	0.6	0.7	5.7	6.3	6.6	6.9
Private	13.2	16.7	17.3	18.3	18.8	19.3	20.4	20.8	20.8	21.5
Higher education	**114.7**	**132.5**	**141.1**	**149.7**	**154.3**	**161.7**	**169.0**	**174.2**	**178.2**	**182.7**
Federal	17.4	16.4	17.8	19.1	19.4	20.0	20.9	21.2	22.0	22.5
State	36.0	39.6	42.2	42.9	44.0	45.0	46.7	46.2	44.7	44.0
Local	3.1	3.4	3.5	3.8	3.9	4.2	4.4	4.6	4.5	4.7
All other	58.0	72.9	77.4	83.7	86.9	92.4	97.1	102.3	107.0	111.4
Public	76.0	85.8	91.8	95.6	98.3	102.4	108.2	111.1	112.4	115.5
Federal	9.9	9.0	9.7	9.9	10.1	10.5	11.1	11.4	11.9	12.4
State	35.2	38.7	41.3	41.8	42.9	43.5	45.1	44.8	43.0	42.5
Local	2.8	3.1	3.3	3.5	3.6	3.8	3.9	4.2	4.1	4.3
All other	28.1	34.9	37.6	40.4	42.0	44.6	47.9	50.8	53.4	56.2
Private	38.6	46.6	49.2	54.1	56.0	59.3	60.8	63.1	65.8	67.2
Federal	7.5	7.4	8.1	9.2	9.4	9.5	9.7	9.8	10.1	10.0
State and local	1.1	1.2	1.2	1.5	1.8	2.0	2.0	1.8	2.1	2.0
All other	29.9	38.0	39.8	43.3	44.9	47.7	49.2	51.5	53.7	55.2

[1] Beginning in 1989-90, includes all fees for transportation, books, and food services.

Source: U.S. National Center for Education Statistics, *Digest of Education Statistics*, annual.

No. 236. Enrollment in Public and Private Schools, by Control and Level, With Projections: 1970 to 2005

[In thousands. As of fall. Data are for regular day schools and exclude independent nursery schools and kindergartens, residential schools for exceptional children, subcollegiate departments of colleges, Federal schools for Indians, and federally operated schools on Federal installations College data include degree-credit and nondegree-credit enrollment]

CONTROL OF SCHOOL AND LEVEL	1970	1980	1985	1990	1993, prel.	1994, prel.	1995, proj.	2000, proj.	2003, proj.	2004, proj.	2005, proj.
Total	59,838	58,305	57,226	60,267	63,253	64,106	64,986	69,165	70,243	70,527	70,816
Public	52,322	50,335	48,901	52,061	54,665	55,364	56,184	59,747	60,654	60,896	61,144
Private	7,516	7,971	8,325	8,206	8,587	8,741	8,801	9,418	9,589	9,631	9,672
Kindergarten through 8	36,610	31,639	31,229	33,973	35,796	36,225	36,814	38,484	38,726	38,518	38,289
Public	32,558	27,647	27,034	29,878	31,515	31,864	32,383	33,852	34,065	33,882	33,680
Private	4,052	3,992	4,195	4,095	4,280	4,360	4,431	4,632	4,661	4,636	4,609
Grades 9 through 12	14,647	14,570	13,750	12,475	13,152	13,602	13,962	15,184	15,585	15,931	16,299
Public	13,336	13,231	12,388	11,338	11,961	12,366	12,693	13,804	14,169	14,483	14,818
Private	1,311	1,339	1,362	1,137	1,191	1,236	1,269	1,380	1,416	1,448	1,481
College	8,581	12,097	12,247	13,820	14,305	14,279	14,210	15,497	15,932	16,078	16,229
Public	6,428	9,457	9,479	10,845	11,189	11,134	11,108	12,091	12,420	12,531	12,646
Private	2,153	2,640	2,768	2,975	3,116	3,145	3,101	3,406	3,512	3,547	3,582

Source: U.S. National Center for Education Statistics, *Digest of Education Statistics*, annual; *Projections of Education Statistics*, annual; and unpublished data.

No. 237. School Enrollment, by Age: 1970 to 1994

[As of **October.** Covers civilian noninstitutional population enrolled in nursery school and above. Based on Current Population Survey, see text, section 1. See *Historical Statistics, Colonial Times to 1970*, series H 442-476 for enrollment 5-34 years old]

AGE	1970	1980	1985	1988	1989	1990	1991	1992	1993	1994
ENROLLMENT										
Total 3 to 34 years old......	60,357	57,348	58,013	58,846	59,235	60,588	61,276	62,084	62,730	66,427
3 and 4 years old......	1,461	2,280	2,801	2,797	2,898	3,292	3,068	3,063	3,275	3,917
5 and 6 years old......	7,000	5,853	6,697	7,044	6,990	7,207	7,178	7,252	7,298	7,752
7 to 13 years old......	28,943	23,751	22,849	24,044	24,431	25,016	25,445	25,768	26,110	26,768
14 and 15 years old....	7,869	7,282	7,362	6,481	6,493	6,555	6,634	6,861	7,011	7,519
16 and 17 years old....	6,927	7,129	6,654	6,561	6,254	6,098	6,155	6,272	6,339	6,895
18 and 19 years old....	3,322	3,788	3,716	4,059	4,125	4,044	3,969	4,012	4,063	4,180
20 and 21 years old....	1,949	2,515	2,708	2,724	2,630	2,852	3,041	3,027	2,810	3,133
22 to 24 years old.....	1,410	1,931	2,068	2,092	2,207	2,231	2,365	2,577	2,579	2,724
25 to 29 years old.....	1,011	1,714	1,942	1,773	1,960	2,013	2,045	1,907	1,942	2,070
30 to 34 years old.....	466	1,105	1,218	1,271	1,248	1,281	1,377	1,344	1,303	1,468
35 years old and over.......	(NA)	1,290	1,766	2,270	2,230	2,439	2,620	2,473	2,634	2,845
ENROLLMENT RATE										
Total 3 to 34 years old......	56.4	49.7	48.3	48.7	49.1	50.2	50.7	51.4	51.8	53.3
3 and 4 years old......	20.5	36.7	38.9	38.2	39.1	44.4	40.5	39.7	40.4	47.3
5 and 6 years old......	89.5	95.7	96.1	96.0	95.2	96.5	95.4	95.5	95.4	96.7
7 to 13 years old......	99.2	99.3	99.2	99.7	99.3	99.6	99.7	99.4	99.5	99.3
14 and 15 years old....	98.1	98.2	98.1	98.9	98.8	99.0	98.8	99.1	98.9	98.8
16 and 17 years old....	90.0	89.0	91.7	91.6	92.7	92.5	93.3	94.1	94.0	94.4
18 and 19 years old....	47.7	46.4	51.6	55.7	56.0	57.3	59.6	61.4	61.6	60.2
20 and 21 years old....	31.9	31.0	35.3	39.1	38.5	39.7	42.0	44.0	42.7	44.9
22 to 24 years old.....	14.9	16.3	16.9	18.3	19.9	21.0	22.2	23.7	23.6	24.1
25 to 29 years old.....	7.5	9.3	9.2	8.3	9.3	9.7	10.2	9.8	10.2	10.8
30 to 34 years old.....	4.2	6.4	6.1	3.9	5.7	5.8	6.2	6.1	5.9	6.7
35 years old and over.......	(NA)	1.4	1.6	2.1	2.0	2.1	2.2	2.1	2.2	2.3

NA Not available.

Source: U.S. Bureau of the Census, *Current Population Reports*, P20-487; and earlier reports.

No. 238. School Enrollment, by Race, Hispanic Origin, and Age: 1980 to 1994

[See headnote, table 237]

AGE	WHITE			BLACK			HISPANIC ORIGIN [1]		
	1980	1990	1994	1980	1990	1994	1980	1990	1994
ENROLLMENT									
Total 3 to 34 years old	47,673	48,899	52,482	8,251	8,854	10,337	4,263	6,073	7,947
3 and 4 years old..........	1,844	2,700	3,059	371	452	697	172	249	376
5 and 6 years old..........	4,781	5,750	6,052	904	1,129	1,296	491	835	1,065
7 to 13 years old..........	19,585	20,076	21,152	3,598	3,832	4,230	2,009	2,794	3,508
14 and 15 years old........	6,038	5,265	5,909	1,088	1,023	1,220	568	739	904
16 and 17 years old........	5,937	4,858	5,421	1,047	962	1,151	454	592	784
18 and 19 years old........	3,199	3,271	3,386	494	596	549	226	329	475
20 and 21 years old........	2,206	2,402	2,532	242	305	371	111	213	252
22 to 24 years old..........	1,669	1,781	2,149	196	274	356	93	121	240
25 to 29 years old..........	1,473	1,706	1,625	187	162	264	84	130	197
30 to 34 years old..........	942	1,090	1,197	124	119	203	54	72	146
35 years old and over....	1,104	2,096	2,340	186	238	365	(NA)	145	236
ENROLLMENT RATE									
Total 3 to 34 years old	48.9	49.5	52.6	53.9	51.9	56.4	49.8	47.4	49.0
3 and 4 years old..........	36.3	44.9	47.0	38.2	41.6	51.9	28.5	29.8	30.8
5 and 6 years old..........	95.8	96.5	96.6	95.4	96.3	97.2	94.5	94.8	96.1
7 to 13 years old..........	99.2	99.6	99.3	99.4	99.8	99.6	99.2	99.4	99.3
14 and 15 years old........	98.3	99.1	98.7	97.9	99.2	99.2	94.3	99.0	96.1
16 and 17 years old........	88.6	92.5	94.3	90.6	91.7	95.4	81.8	85.4	88.3
18 and 19 years old........	46.3	57.1	60.9	45.7	55.2	54	37.8	44.1	51.4
20 and 21 years old........	31.9	41.0	46.2	23.4	28.4	34.9	19.5	27.2	24.9
22 to 24 years old..........	16.4	20.2	23.5	13.6	20.0	22.6	11.7	9.9	15.1
25 to 29 years old..........	9.2	9.9	10.4	8.8	6.1	10.5	6.9	6.3	8.1
30 to 34 years old..........	6.3	5.9	6.6	6.8	4.4	7.2	5.1	3.6	5.7
35 years old and over....	1.3	2.1	2.2	1.8	2.1	2.9	(NA)	2.1	2.7

NA Not available.   [1] Persons of Hispanic origin may be of any race.

Source: U.S. Bureau of the Census, *Current Population Reports*, P20-487; and earlier reports.

No. 239 Enrollment in Public and Private Schools: 1960 to 1994

[In millions, except percent. As of **October.** For civilian noninstitutional population. For **1960,** 5 to 34 years old; for **1970 to 1985,** 3 to 34 years old; **beginning 1986,** for 3 years old and over]

YEAR	PUBLIC						PRIVATE					
	Total	Nur-sery	Kinder-garten	Ele-mentary	High School	College	Total	Nur-sery	Kinder-garten	Ele-mentary	High School	College
1960	39.0	(NA)	(¹)	27.5	9.2	2.3	7.2	(NA)	(¹)	4.9	1.0	1.3
1970	52.2	0.3	2.6	30.0	13.5	5.7	8.1	0.8	0.5	3.9	1.2	1.7
1975	52.8	0.6	2.9	27.2	14.5	7.7	8.2	1.2	0.5	3.3	1.2	2.0
1977	51.6	0.6	2.7	26.0	14.5	7.9	8.4	1.1	0.5	3.3	1.2	2.3
1978	50.0	0.6	2.5	25.3	14.2	7.4	8.6	1.2	0.5	3.2	1.2	2.4
1979	50.0	0.6	2.6	24.8	14.0	7.7	8.2	1.2	0.4	3.1	1.1	2.3
1980	(NA)	0.6	2.7	24.4	(NA)	(NA)	(NA)	1.4	0.5	3.1	(NA)	(NA)
1981	49.7	0.7	2.6	24.8	13.5	8.2	8.7	1.4	0.5	3.0	1.1	2.6
1982	49.2	0.7	2.7	24.4	13.0	8.4	8.2	1.4	0.6	3.0	1.1	2.6
1983	48.7	0.8	2.7	24.2	12.8	8.2	9.0	1.5	0.7	3.0	1.2	2.6
1984	49.0	0.8	3.0	24.1	12.7	8.5	8.3	1.6	0.5	2.7	1.1	2.4
1985 ²	49.0	0.9	3.2	23.8	12.8	8.4	9.0	1.6	0.6	3.1	1.2	2.5
1986 ²	51.2	0.8	3.4	24.2	13.0	9.8	9.4	1.7	0.6	3.0	1.2	2.9
1987 ²	51.7	0.8	3.4	24.8	12.7	10.0	8.9	1.7	0.6	2.8	1.1	2.8
1988 ²	52.2	0.9	3.4	25.5	12.2	10.3	8.9	1.8	0.5	2.8	1.0	2.8
1989 ²	52.5	0.9	3.3	25.9	12.1	10.3	8.9	1.9	0.6	2.7	0.8	2.9
1990 ²	53.8	1.2	3.3	26.6	11.9	10.7	9.2	2.2	0.6	2.7	0.9	2.9
1991 ²	54.5	1.1	3.5	26.6	12.2	11.1	9.4	1.8	0.6	3.0	1.0	3.0
1992 ²	55.0	1.1	3.5	27.1	12.3	11.1	9.4	1.8	0.6	3.1	1.0	3.0
1993 ²	56.0	1.2	3.5	27.7	12.6	10.9	9.4	1.8	0.7	2.9	1.0	3.0
1994 ²	58.6	1.9	3.3	28.1	13.5	11.7	10.7	2.3	0.6	3.4	1.1	3.3
Percent White:												
1960.	85.7	(NA)	(¹)	84.3	88.2	92.2	95.7	(NA)	(¹)	95.3	96.7	96.3
1970.	84.5	59.5	84.4	83.1	85.6	90.7	93.4	91.1	88.2	94.1	96.1	92.8
1980.	(NA)	68.2	80.7	80.9	(NA)	(NA)	(NA)	89.0	87.0	90.7	(NA)	(NA)
1990.	79.8	71.7	78.3	78.9	79.2	84.1	87.4	89.6	83.2	88.2	89.4	85.0
1992.	79.2	71.5	77.8	78.4	78.6	83.1	86.7	89.0	84.9	87.6	87.5	84.5
1993.	78.9	68.5	76.6	78.4	78.3	82.5	85.3	89.7	86.9	87.0	83.1	81.4
1994.	77.9	68.6	76.4	77.4	77.8	80.4	85.4	88.2	86.2	85.3	85.2	80.4

NA Not available. ¹ Included in elementary school. ² See table 282 for college enrollment 35 years old and over. Also data beginning 1986 based on a revised edit and tabulation package.

Source: U.S. Bureau of the Census, *Current Population Reports,* P20-487; and earlier reports.

No. 240. School Enrollment, by Sex and Level: 1960 to 1994

[In millions. As of **Oct.** For the civilian noninstitutional population. For **1960,** persons 5 to 34 years old; **1970-1979,** 3 to 34 years old; **beginning 1980,** 3 years old and over. Elementary includes kindergarten and grades 1-8; high school, grades 9-12; and college, 2-year and 4-year colleges, universities, and graduate and professional schools. Data for college represent degree-credit enrollment]

YEAR	ALL LEVELS ¹			ELEMENTARY			HIGH SCHOOL			COLLEGE		
	Total	Male	Female	Total	Male	Female	Total	Male	Female	Total	Male	Female
1960	46.3	24.2	22.0	32.4	16.7	15.7	10.2	5.2	5.1	3.6	2.3	1.2
1970	60.4	31.4	28.9	37.1	19.0	18.1	14.7	7.4	7.3	7.4	4.4	3.0
1975	61.0	31.6	29.4	33.8	17.3	16.5	15.7	8.0	7.7	9.7	5.3	4.4
1977	60.0	30.8	29.2	32.4	16.6	15.8	15.8	8.0	7.7	10.2	5.4	4.8
1978	58.6	30.1	28.6	31.5	16.1	15.3	15.5	7.8	7.6	9.8	5.1	4.7
1979	57.9	29.5	28.3	30.9	15.9	15.0	15.1	7.7	7.4	10.0	5.0	5.0
1980 ²	58.6	29.6	29.1	30.6	15.8	14.9	14.6	7.3	7.3	11.4	5.4	6.0
1981 ²	58.4	29.5	28.9	30.1	15.5	14.7	14.4	7.3	7.1	11.8	5.6	6.2
1981 ³	59.9	30.3	29.6	31.0	15.9	15.0	14.7	7.5	7.3	12.1	5.8	6.3
1982 ²	59.4	30.0	29.4	30.7	15.8	14.9	14.2	7.2	7.0	12.3	5.9	6.4
1983 ²	59.3	30.1	29.2	30.6	15.7	14.8	14.1	7.1	7.0	12.4	6.0	6.3
1984	58.9	29.9	29.0	30.3	15.6	14.7	13.9	7.1	6.8	12.3	6.0	6.3
1985	59.8	30.0	29.7	30.7	15.7	15.0	14.1	7.2	6.9	12.5	5.9	6.6
1986	60.1	30.4	29.7	31.1	16.1	15.0	14.0	7.1	6.9	12.4	5.8	6.6
1986 ⁴	60.5	30.6	30.0	31.1	16.1	15.0	14.2	7.2	7.0	12.7	6.0	6.7
1987	60.6	30.7	29.9	31.6	16.3	15.3	13.8	7.0	6.8	12.7	6.0	6.7
1988	61.1	30.7	30.5	32.2	16.6	15.6	13.2	6.7	6.4	13.1	5.9	7.2
1989	61.5	30.8	30.7	32.5	16.7	15.8	12.9	6.6	6.3	13.2	6.0	7.2
1990	63.0	31.5	31.5	33.2	17.1	16.0	12.8	6.5	6.4	13.6	6.2	7.4
1991	63.9	32.1	31.8	33.8	17.3	16.4	13.1	6.8	6.4	14.1	6.4	7.6
1992	64.6	32.2	32.3	34.3	17.7	16.6	13.3	6.8	6.5	14.0	6.2	7.8
1993	65.4	32.9	32.5	34.8	17.9	16.9	13.6	7.0	6.6	13.9	6.3	7.6
1994	69.3	34.6	34.6	35.4	18.2	17.2	14.6	7.4	7.2	15.0	6.8	8.2

¹ Beginning 1970, includes nursery schools, not shown separately. ² Based on 1970 population controls. ³ Based on 1980 population controls. ⁴ Revised. Data beginning 1986, based on a revised edit and tabulation package.

Source: U.S. Bureau of the Census, *Current Population Reports,* P20-487; and earlier reports.

No. 241. Educational Attainment, by Race and Hispanic Origin: 1960 to 1995

[In percent. For persons 25 years old and over. 1960, 1970, and 1980 as of April 1 and based on sample data from the censuses of population. Other years as of March and based on the Current Population Survey; see text, section 1, and Appendix III. See table 242 for data by sex]

YEAR	Total [1]	White	Black	Asian and Pacific Islander	HISPANIC [2] Total [3]	Mexican	Puerto Rican	Cuban
COMPLETED 4 YEARS OF HIGH SCHOOL OR MORE								
1960	41.1	43.2	20.1	(NA)	(NA)	(NA)	(NA)	(NA)
1965	49.0	51.3	27.2	(NA)	(NA)	(NA)	(NA)	(NA)
1970	52.3	54.5	31.4	(NA)	32.1	24.2	23.4	43.9
1975	62.5	64.5	42.5	(NA)	37.9	31.0	28.7	51.7
1980	66.5	68.8	51.2	(NA)	44.0	37.6	40.1	55.3
1985	73.9	75.5	59.8	(NA)	47.9	41.9	46.3	51.1
1990	77.6	79.1	66.2	80.4	50.8	44.1	55.5	63.5
1993 [4]	80.2	81.5	70.4	(NA)	53.1	46.2	59.8	62.1
1994 [4]	80.9	82.0	72.9	(NA)	53.3	46.7	59.4	64.1
1995 [4]	81.7	83.0	73.8	(NA)	53.4	(NA)	(NA)	(NA)
COMPLETED 4 YEARS OF COLLEGE OR MORE								
1960	7.7	8.1	3.1	(NA)	(NA)	(NA)	(NA)	(NA)
1965	9.4	9.9	4.7	(NA)	(NA)	(NA)	(NA)	(NA)
1970	10.7	11.3	4.4	(NA)	(NA)	(NA)	(NA)	(NA)
1975	13.9	14.5	6.4	(NA)	4.5	2.5	2.2	11.1
1980	16.2	17.1	8.4	(NA)	7.6	4.9	5.6	16.2
1985	19.4	20.0	11.1	(NA)	8.5	5.5	7.0	13.7
1990	21.3	22.0	11.3	39.9	9.2	5.4	9.7	20.2
1993 [4]	21.9	22.6	12.2	(NA)	9.0	5.9	8.0	16.5
1994 [4]	22.2	22.9	12.9	(NA)	9.1	6.3	9.7	16.2
1995 [4]	23.0	24.0	13.2	(NA)	9.3	(NA)	(NA)	(NA)

NA Not available. [1] Includes other races, not shown separately. [2] Persons of Hispanic origin may be of any race. [3] Includes persons of other Hispanic origin, not shown separately. [4] Beginning 1993, persons high school graduates and those with a BA degree or higher.

Source: U.S. Bureau of the Census, *U.S. Census of Population, U.S. Summary*, PC80-1-C1 and *Current Population Reports* P20-455, P20-459, P20-462, P20-465RV, P20-475; and unpublished data.

No. 242. Educational Attainment, by Race, Hispanic Origin, and Sex: 1960 to 1995

[In percent. For persons 25 years old and over. 1960, 1970 and 1980 as of April 1 and based on sample data from the censuses of population. Other years as of March and based on the Current Population Survey; see text, section 1, and Appendix III. See table 241 for totals for both sexes]

YEAR	ALL RACES [1] Male	Female	WHITE Male	Female	BLACK Male	Female	ASIAN AND PACIFIC ISLANDER Male	Female	HISPANIC [2] Male	Female
COMPLETED 4 YEARS OF HIGH SCHOOL OR MORE										
1960	39.5	42.5	41.6	44.7	18.2	21.8	(NA)	(NA)	(NA)	(NA)
1965	48.0	49.9	50.2	52.2	25.8	28.4	(NA)	(NA)	(NA)	(NA)
1970	51.9	52.8	54.0	55.0	30.1	32.5	(NA)	(NA)	37.9	34.2
1975	63.1	62.1	65.0	64.1	41.6	43.3	(NA)	(NA)	39.5	36.7
1980	67.3	65.8	69.6	68.1	50.8	51.5	(NA)	(NA)	67.3	65.8
1985	74.4	73.5	76.0	75.1	58.4	60.8	(NA)	(NA)	48.5	47.4
1990	77.7	77.5	79.1	79.0	65.8	66.5	84.0	77.2	50.3	51.3
1993 [3]	80.5	80.0	81.8	81.3	69.6	71.1	(NA)	(NA)	52.9	53.2
1994 [3]	81.0	80.7	82.1	81.9	71.7	73.8	(NA)	(NA)	53.4	53.2
1995 [3]	81.7	81.6	83.0	83.0	73.4	74.1	(NA)	(NA)	52.9	53.8
COMPLETED 4 YEARS OF COLLEGE OR MORE										
1960	9.7	5.8	10.3	6.0	2.8	3.3	(NA)	(NA)	(NA)	(NA)
1965	12.0	7.1	12.7	7.3	4.9	4.5	(NA)	(NA)	(NA)	(NA)
1970	13.5	8.1	14.4	8.4	4.2	4.6	(NA)	(NA)	7.8	4.3
1975	17.6	10.6	18.4	11.0	6.7	6.2	(NA)	(NA)	8.3	4.6
1980	20.1	12.8	21.3	13.3	8.4	8.3	(NA)	(NA)	9.4	6.0
1985	23.1	16.0	24.0	16.3	11.2	11.0	(NA)	(NA)	9.7	7.3
1990	24.4	18.4	25.3	19.0	11.9	10.8	44.9	35.4	9.8	8.7
1993 [3]	24.8	19.2	25.7	19.7	11.9	12.4	(NA)	(NA)	9.5	8.5
1994 [3]	25.1	19.6	26.1	20.0	12.8	13.0	(NA)	(NA)	9.6	8.6
1995 [3]	26.0	20.2	27.2	21.0	13.6	12.9	(NA)	(NA)	10.1	8.4

NA Not available. [1] Includes other races, not shown separately. [2] Persons of Hispanic origin may be of any race. [3] Beginning 1993, persons high school graduates and those with a BA degree or higher.

Source: U.S. Bureau of the Census, *U.S. Census of Population, 1960, 1970, and 1980, vol.1;* and *Current Population Reports* P20-459, P20-462, P20-475; and unpublished data.

No. 243. Educational Attainment, by Selected Characteristic: 1995

[For persons 25 years old and over. As of **March.** Based on Current Population Survey; see text, section 1, and Appendix III. For composition of regions, see table 27]

CHARACTERISTIC	Population (1,000)	PERCENT OF POPULATION—HIGHEST LEVEL					
		Not a high school graduate	High school graduate	Some college, but no degree	Associate's degree [1]	Bachelor's degree	Advanced degree
Total persons	166,438	18.3	33.9	17.6	7.1	15.2	7.8
Age:							
25 to 34 years old.	41,388	12.9	34.0	19.6	8.6	19.5	5.5
35 to 44 years old.	42,335	11.6	33.3	19.4	9.0	17.4	9.2
45 to 54 years old.	30,693	13.7	32.5	18.0	7.7	16.4	11.6
55 to 64 years old.	20,755	22.8	37.3	15.6	5.2	10.9	8.1
65 to 74 years old.	18,214	31.1	36.4	14.4	3.9	9.0	5.2
75 years old or over	13,053	43.2	30.2	12.4	2.9	7.1	4.1
Sex: Male	79,463	18.3	31.9	17.4	6.5	16.5	9.4
Female	86,975	18.4	35.7	17.9	7.8	14.0	6.2
Race: White	141,113	17.0	34.0	17.7	7.3	15.8	8.2
Black	18,457	26.2	36.2	18.0	6.3	9.6	3.7
Other	6,869	24.6	25.9	14.7	6.3	18.8	9.7
Hispanic origin: Hispanic	14,171	46.6	26.3	13.2	4.6	6.5	2.7
Non-Hispanic	152,267	15.7	34.6	18.0	7.4	16.0	8.2
Region: Northeast	33,580	16.6	37.2	13.3	6.7	16.4	9.9
Midwest	38,534	16.1	37.5	17.4	7.4	14.8	6.9
South	58,380	21.6	32.9	17.8	6.5	14.1	7.0
West.	35,945	17.0	28.7	21.7	8.4	16.3	7.9
Marital status:							
Never married	23,926	16.7	31.1	17.1	6.9	19.7	8.4
Married spouse present	105,558	15.4	34.2	17.7	7.5	16.3	8.8
Married spouse absent	6,339	31.2	32.8	17.7	6.0	8.6	3.7
Separated	4,546	28.9	35.5	18.8	6.1	7.8	2.8
Widowed.	13,343	40.9	33.3	12.6	3.8	6.4	2.9
Divorced	17,273	16.0	36.9	21.7	8.0	11.4	5.9
Civilian labor force status:							
Employed	105,163	10.6	33.0	19.1	8.6	18.8	9.9
Unemployed	5,193	22.6	36.1	19.5	6.6	10.6	4.6
Not in the labor force.	55,309	32.9	35.6	14.5	4.3	8.9	3.8

[1] Includes vocational degrees.

Source: U.S. Bureau of the Census, *Current Population Reports*, P20-476; and unpublished data.

No. 244. Mean Monthly Income, by Highest Degree Earned: 1993

[For persons 18 years old and over. Based on the Survey of Income and Program Participation; see source for details]

CHARACTERISTIC	Total persons	LEVEL OF HIGHEST DEGREE								
		Not a high school graduate	High school graduate only	Some college, no degree	Vocational	Associate's	Bachelor's	Master's	Professional	Doctorate
MEAN MONTHLY INCOME [1] (dol.)										
All persons [2]	1,687	906	1,380	1,579	1,736	1,985	2,625	3,411	5,534	4,328
Age: 18 to 24 years old . .	709	459	783	610	1,017	912	1,128	1,351	1,295	(B)
25 to 34 years old. . . .	1,622	936	1,310	1,610	1,643	1,760	2,341	2,648	3,515	3,465
35 to 44 years old. . . .	2,082	1,032	1,603	1,936	2,030	2,145	2,891	3,180	6,537	4,032
45 to 54 years old. . . .	2,302	1,096	1,711	2,484	1,990	2,534	3,345	3,983	6,606	5,267
55 to 64 years old. . . .	1,922	1,045	1,535	1,974	1,731	2,969	3,397	4,462	6,921	4,246
65 years old and over .	1,329	878	1,217	1,648	1,516	1,697	2,324	3,163	3,820	3,639
Sex: Male	2,230	1,211	1,812	2,045	2,318	2,561	3,430	4,298	6,312	4,421
Female	1,186	621	1,008	1,139	1,373	1,544	1,809	2,505	3,530	4,020
Race: White	1,756	951	1,422	1,649	1,768	2,021	2,682	3,478	5,590	4,449
Black	1,192	713	1,071	1,222	1,428	1,746	2,333	2,834	3,445	3,778
Hispanic [3]	1,126	786	1,106	1,239	1,329	2,069	2,186	2,605	2,317	2,677

B Base figure too small to meet statistical standards for reliability of a derived figure.   [1] For definition of mean, see Guide to Tabular Presentation.   [2] Includes other races, not shown separately.   [3] Persons of Hispanic origin may be of any race.

Source: U.S. Bureau of the Census, *Current Population Reports*, P70-51; unpublished data.

No. 245. Educational Attainment—States: 1990

[As of **April 1**. **For persons 25 years old and over, except as indicated.** Based on the 1990 Census of Population; see text, section 1, and Appendix III]

STATE	Population (1,000)	PERCENT OF POPULATION—HIGHEST LEVEL						Drop-outs[1] (percent)
		Not a high school graduate	High school graduate	Some college, but no degree	Associate's degree	Bachelor's degree	Advanced degree	
United States	158,868	24.8	30.0	18.7	6.2	13.1	7.2	11.2
Alabama.	2,546	33.1	29.4	16.8	5.0	10.1	5.5	12.6
Alaska	323	13.4	28.7	27.6	7.2	15.0	8.0	10.9
Arizona.	2,301	21.3	26.1	25.4	6.8	13.3	7.0	14.4
Arkansas	1,496	33.7	32.7	16.6	3.7	8.9	4.5	11.4
California	18,695	23.8	22.3	22.6	7.9	15.3	8.1	14.2
Colorado.	2,107	15.6	26.5	24.0	6.9	18.0	9.0	9.8
Connecticut.	2,199	20.8	29.5	15.9	6.6	16.2	11.0	9.0
Delaware	428	22.5	32.7	16.9	6.5	13.7	7.7	10.4
District of Columbia	409	26.9	21.2	15.6	3.1	16.1	17.2	13.9
Florida	8,887	25.6	30.1	19.4	6.6	12.0	6.3	14.3
Georgia	4,023	29.1	29.6	17.0	5.0	12.9	6.4	14.1
Hawaii	710	19.9	28.7	20.1	8.3	15.8	7.1	7.5
Idaho.	601	20.3	30.4	24.2	7.5	12.4	5.3	10.4
Illinois.	7,294	23.8	30.0	19.4	5.8	13.6	7.5	10.6
Indiana.	3,489	24.4	38.2	16.6	5.3	9.2	6.4	11.4
Iowa	1,777	19.9	38.5	17.0	7.7	11.7	5.2	6.6
Kansas.	1,566	18.7	32.8	21.9	5.4	14.1	7.0	8.7
Kentucky	2,334	35.4	31.8	15.2	4.1	8.1	5.5	13.3
Louisiana	2,537	31.7	31.7	17.2	3.3	10.5	5.6	12.5
Maine.	796	21.2	37.1	16.1	6.9	12.7	6.1	8.3
Maryland	3,123	21.6	28.1	18.6	5.2	15.6	10.9	10.9
Massachusetts.	3,962	20.0	29.7	15.8	7.2	16.6	10.6	8.5
Michigan.	5,843	23.2	32.3	20.4	6.7	10.9	6.4	10.0
Minnesota.	2,771	17.6	33.0	19.0	8.6	15.6	6.3	6.4
Mississippi	1,539	35.7	27.5	16.9	5.2	9.7	5.1	11.8
Missouri	3,292	26.1	33.1	18.4	4.5	11.7	6.1	11.4
Montana	508	19.0	33.5	22.1	5.6	14.1	5.7	8.1
Nebraska	996	18.2	34.7	21.1	7.1	13.1	5.9	7.0
Nevada	790	21.2	31.5	25.8	6.2	10.1	5.2	15.2
New Hampshire	714	17.8	31.7	18.0	8.1	16.4	7.9	9.4
New Jersey.	5,166	23.3	31.1	15.5	5.2	16.0	8.8	9.6
New Mexico	923	24.9	28.7	20.9	5.0	12.1	8.3	11.7
New York	11,819	25.2	29.5	15.7	6.5	13.2	9.9	9.9
North Carolina	4,253	30.0	29.0	16.8	6.8	12.0	5.4	12.5
North Dakota.	397	23.3	28.0	20.5	10.0	13.5	4.5	4.6
Ohio	6,925	24.3	36.3	17.0	5.3	11.1	5.9	8.9
Oklahoma.	1,995	25.4	30.5	21.3	5.0	11.8	6.0	10.4
Oregon.	1,855	18.5	28.9	25.0	6.9	13.6	7.0	11.8
Pennsylvania.	7,873	25.3	38.6	12.9	5.2	11.3	6.6	9.1
Rhode Island.	659	28.0	29.5	15.0	6.3	13.5	7.8	11.1
South Carolina.	2,168	31.7	29.5	15.8	6.3	11.2	5.4	11.7
South Dakota	431	22.9	33.7	18.8	7.4	12.3	4.9	7.7
Tennessee	3,139	32.9	30.0	16.9	4.2	10.5	5.4	13.4
Texas	10,311	27.9	25.6	21.1	5.2	13.9	6.5	12.9
Utah	897	14.9	27.2	27.9	7.8	15.4	6.8	8.7
Vermont	357	19.2	34.6	14.7	7.2	15.4	8.9	8.0
Virginia.	3,975	24.8	26.6	18.5	5.5	15.4	9.1	10.0
Washington.	3,126	16.2	27.9	25.0	7.9	15.9	7.0	10.6
West Virginia	1,172	34.0	36.6	13.2	3.8	7.5	4.8	10.9
Wisconsin	3,094	21.4	37.1	16.7	7.1	12.1	5.6	7.1
Wyoming	278	17.0	33.2	24.2	6.9	13.1	5.7	6.9

[1] For persons 16 to 19 years old. A dropout is a person who is not in regular school and who has not completed the 12th grade or received a general equivalency degree.

Source: U.S. Bureau of the Census, *1990 Census of Population*, CPH-L-96.

No. 246. Preprimary School Enrollment—Summary: 1970 to 1994

[As of **October**. Civilian noninstitutional population. Includes public and nonpublic nursery school and kindergarten programs. Excludes 5 year olds enrolled in elementary school. Based on Current Population Survey; see text, section 1]

ITEM	1970	1975	1980	1985	1990	1991	1992	1993	1994
NUMBER OF CHILDREN (1,000)									
Population, 3 to 5 years old	**10,949**	**10,183**	**9,284**	**10,733**	**11,207**	**11,370**	**11,544**	**11,954**	**12,328**
Total enrolled [1]	**4,104**	**4,954**	**4,878**	**5,865**	**6,659**	**6,334**	**6,403**	**6,581**	**7,514**
Nursery	1,094	1,745	1,981	2,477	3,378	2,824	2,857	2,984	4,162
Public	332	570	628	846	1,202	996	1,074	1,204	1,848
Private	762	1,174	1,353	1,631	2,177	1,827	1,784	1,779	2,314
Kindergarten	3,010	3,211	2,897	3,388	3,281	3,510	3,546	3,597	3,352
Public	2,498	2,682	2,438	2,847	2,767	2,968	2,996	3,020	2,819
Private	511	528	459	541	513	543	550	577	534
White	3,443	4,105	3,994	4,757	5,389	5,104	5,137	5,224	5,889
Black	586	731	725	919	964	928	966	1,011	1,289
Hispanic [2]	(NA)	(NA)	370	496	642	675	728	657	851
3 years old	454	683	857	1,035	1,205	1,075	1,081	1,097	1,385
4 years old	1,007	1,418	1,423	1,765	2,086	1,993	1,982	2,179	2,532
5 years old	2,643	2,852	2,598	3,065	3,367	3,266	3,340	3,306	3,597
ENROLLMENT RATE									
Total enrolled [1]	**37.5**	**48.6**	**52.5**	**54.6**	**59.4**	**55.7**	**55.5**	**55.1**	**61.0**
White	37.8	48.6	52.7	54.7	59.7	56.2	55.8	55.7	60.9
Black	34.9	48.1	51.8	55.8	57.8	53.1	55.1	52.7	64.2
Hispanic [2]	(NA)	(NA)	43.3	43.3	49.0	46.4	48.4	43.9	47.7
3 years old	12.9	21.5	27.3	28.8	32.6	28.2	27.7	27.1	33.9
4 years old	27.8	40.5	46.3	49.1	56.0	53.0	52.1	53.9	60.3
5 years old	69.3	81.3	84.7	86.5	88.8	86.0	87.2	85.7	88.9

NA Not available.   [1] Includes races not shown separately.   [2] Persons of Hispanic origin may be of any race. The method of identifying Hispanic children was changed in 1980 from allocation based on status of mother to status reported for each child. The number of Hispanic children using the new method is larger.

Source: U.S. Bureau of the Census, *Current Population Reports*, P20-487.

No. 247. School Enrollment of 3 to 5 Year Olds, by Education and Labor Force Status of Mother and Family Income: 1994

[**In thousands**. As of **October**. Civilian noninstitutional population. Based on Current Population Survey; see text, section 1]

CHARACTERISTIC	Total popula-tion [1]	ENROLLED IN NURSERY SCHOOL			ENROLLED IN KINDERGARTEN			Enrolled in elementary school
		Total	Public	Private	Total	Public	Private	
NUMBER								
Total children 3 to 5 years old	**12,328**	**4,162**	**1,848**	**2,314**	**3,352**	**2,819**	**534**	**247**
3 and 4 year olds	8,283	3,608	1,489	2,119	309	217	91	-
5 year olds	4,044	553	359	194	3,044	2,601	442	247
Education of mother:								
Children living with mother	11,504	3,889	1,668	2,221	3,145	2,638	506	216
Elementary: 0 to 8 years	591	97	94	2	156	148	8	16
High school: 1-3 years	1,319	310	248	62	337	328	9	25
High school graduate	3,981	1,168	618	549	1,072	937	135	76
College: Less than a BA degree	3,353	1,249	515	734	976	796	180	67
BA degree or higher	2,261	1,066	193	873	603	429	174	34
Labor force status of mother:								
Children living with mother	11,504	3,889	1,668	2,221	3,145	2,638	506	216
Mother in the labor force	7,041	2,582	1,030	1,552	1,966	1,598	368	149
Employed	6,503	2,414	906	1,508	1,820	1,459	361	140
Full-time	4,472	1,587	627	959	1,242	1,017	226	101
Part-time	2,031	827	278	549	577	442	135	39
Unemployed	539	168	124	44	146	139	7	9
Mother not in the labor force	4,463	1,307	638	669	1,179	1,040	138	67
Children not living with mother	824	273	180	93	208	180	28	31
Family income:								
Less than $10,000	2,157	630	539	90	615	579	36	51
$10,000 to 14,999	1,153	317	231	86	325	295	30	24
$15,000 to 19,999	749	210	122	88	160	145	15	16
$20,000 to 24,999	871	259	166	93	211	187	24	19
$25,000 to 29,999	875	264	118	146	232	209	24	14
$30,000 to 34,999	850	278	109	169	232	185	46	8
$35,000 to 39,999	802	246	95	151	225	180	46	15
$40,000 to 49,999	1,130	408	124	283	310	256	54	32
$50,000 to 74,999	1,800	749	159	590	503	394	109	34
$75,000 and over	1,257	624	99	526	331	218	113	30
Not reported	684	178	86	92	207	171	36	5

- Represents zero.   [1] Includes those not enrolled, not shown separately.

Source: U.S. Bureau of the Census, *Current Population Reports*, P20-487.

No. 248. Public Elementary and Secondary Schools—Summary: 1980 to 1995

[For school year ending in year shown, except as indicated. Data are estimates]

ITEM	Unit	1980	1985	1990	1992	1993	1994	1995
School districts, total.	Number .	16,044	15,812	15,552	15,360	15,212	15,052	(NA)
ENROLLMENT								
Population 5-17 years old [1]	1,000. . .	48,041	44,787	44,949	45,918	46,667	47,427	48,299
Percent of resident population	Percent .	21.4	19.0	18.2	18.2	18.3	18.4	18.6
Fall enrollment [2].	1,000. . .	41,778	39,354	40,527	41,956	42,660	43,303	43,934
Percent of population 5-17 years old [3]	Percent .	87.0	87.9	90.2	91.4	91.4	91.3	91.0
Elementary [3]	1,000. . .	24,397	23,830	26,253	27,432	27,858	28,212	28,478
Secondary [4].	1,000. . .	17,381	15,524	14,274	14,524	14,802	15,091	15,455
Average daily:								
Attendance (ADA).	1,000. . .	38,411	36,530	37,573	38,927	39,605	40,079	40,768
High school graduates	1,000. . .	2,762	2,424	2,327	2,237	2,248	2,241	2,282
INSTRUCTIONAL STAFF								
Total [5]	1,000. . .	2,521	2,473	2,685	2,763	2,811	2,860	2,902
Classroom teachers.	1,000. . .	2,211	2,175	2,362	2,428	2,466	2,507	2,547
Average salaries:								
Instructional staff.	Dollar . .	16,715	24,666	32,638	35,552	36,454	37,383	38,501
Classroom teachers.	Dollar . .	15,970	23,600	31,367	34,063	35,029	35,819	36,802
REVENUES								
Revenue receipts	Mil. dol. .	97,635	141,013	208,656	234,924	247,706	255,769	270,876
Federal.	Mil. dol. .	9,020	9,533	13,184	15,704	17,521	18,423	18,858
State	Mil. dol. .	47,929	69,107	100,787	111,348	115,855	117,646	129,456
Local	Mil. dol. .	40,686	62,373	94,685	107,871	114,330	119,700	122,561
Percent of total:								
Federal.	Percent .	9.2	6.8	6.3	6.7	7.1	7.2	7.0
State	Percent .	49.1	49.0	48.3	47.4	46.8	46.0	47.8
Local	Percent .	41.7	44.2	45.4	45.9	46.2	46.8	45.2
EXPENDITURES								
Total	Mil. dol. .	96,105	139,382	209,698	236,750	248,564	260,179	274,603
Current expenditures (day schools)	Mil. dol. .	85,661	127,230	186,583	208,352	218,944	229,129	240,816
Other current expenditures [6]	Mil. dol. .	1,859	2,109	3,341	4,611	5,142	5,664	5,592
Capital outlay.	Mil. dol. .	6,504	7,529	16,012	18,870	18,770	19,610	21,269
Interest on school debt	Mil. dol. .	2,081	2,514	3,762	4,918	5,707	5,775	6,925
Percent of total:								
Current expenditures (day schools)	Percent .	89.1	91.3	89.0	88.0	88.1	88.1	87.7
Other current expenditures [6]	Percent .	1.9	1.5	1.6	2.0	2.1	2.2	2.0
Capital outlay.	Percent .	6.8	5.4	7.6	8.0	7.6	7.5	7.7
Interest on school debt	Percent .	2.2	1.8	1.8	2.1	2.3	2.2	2.5
In current dollars:								
Revenue receipts per pupil enrolled.	Dollar . .	2,337	3,583	5,149	5,599	5,807	5,907	6,166
Current expenditures per pupil enrolled.	Dollar . .	2,050	3,233	4,604	4,966	5,132	5,291	5,481
In constant **(1995)** dollars: [7]								
Revenue receipts per pupil enrolled.	Dollar . .	4,529	5,094	6,097	6,094	6,128	6,076	6,166
Current expenditures per pupil enrolled.	Dollar . .	3,974	4,596	5,452	5,404	5,417	5,443	5,481

NA Not available.   [1] Estimated resident population as of July 1 of the previous year. Estimates reflect revisions based on the 1990 Census of Population.   [2] Fall enrollment of the previous year.   [3] Kindergarten through grade 6.   [4] Grades 7 through 12.   [5] Full-time equivalent.   [6] Current expenses for summer schools, adult education, post-high school vocational education, personnel retraining, etc., when operated by local school districts and not part of regular public elementary and secondary day-school program.   [7] Compiled by U.S. Bureau of the Census. Deflated by the Consumer Price Index, all urban consumers (for school year) supplied by U.S. National Center for Education Statistics.

Source: Except as noted, National Education Association, Washington, DC, *Estimates of School Statistics*, annual (copyright); *Rankings of the States*, annual (copyright); and unpublished data.

No. 249. Elementary and Secondary Schools—Teachers and Pupil-Teacher Ratios With Projections: 1960 to 1995

[In thousands, except ratios. As of fall. Data are for full-time equivalents. Schools are classified by type of organization, rather than by grade group; elementary includes kindergarten and secondary includes junior high]

ITEM	TOTAL			PUBLIC			PRIVATE		
	Total	Elemen-tary	Second-ary	Total	Elemen-tary	Second-ary	Total	Elemen-tary	Second-ary
Number of teachers:									
1960	1,600	991	609	1,408	858	550	192	133	59
1965	1,933	1,112	822	1,710	965	746	223	147	76
1970	2,292	1,283	1,009	2,059	1,130	929	233	153	80
1975	2,453	1,353	1,100	2,198	1,181	1,017	255	172	83
1980	2,485	1,401	1,084	2,184	1,189	995	301	212	89
1985	2,549	1,483	1,066	2,206	1,237	969	343	246	97
1986	2,592	1,521	1,071	2,244	1,271	973	348	250	98
1987	2,632	1,564	1,068	2,279	1,307	973	353	257	95
1988	2,668	1,604	1,064	2,323	1,353	970	345	251	94
1989	2,679	1,622	1,057	2,357	1,387	970	322	235	87
1990	2,753	1,680	1,073	2,398	1,426	972	355	254	101
1991	2,787	1,713	1,074	2,432	1,459	973	355	254	101
1992	2,822	1,743	1,079	2,459	1,483	976	363	260	103
1993, prel.	2,871	1,772	1,099	2,505	1,510	995	366	262	104
1994, prel.	2,915	1,754	1,163	2,547	1,495	1,053	368	259	110
1995, proj.	2,971	1,784	1,187	2,595	1,520	1,075	375	264	112
Pupil-teacher ratio:									
1960	26.4	29.4	21.4	25.8	28.4	21.7	30.7	36.1	18.6
1965	25.1	28.4	20.6	24.7	27.6	20.8	28.3	33.3	18.4
1970	22.4	24.6	19.5	22.3	24.3	19.8	23.0	26.5	16.4
1975	20.3	21.7	18.6	20.4	21.7	18.8	19.6	21.5	15.7
1980	18.6	20.1	16.6	18.7	20.4	16.8	17.7	18.8	15.0
1985	17.6	19.1	15.6	17.9	19.5	15.8	16.2	17.1	14.0
1986	17.4	18.8	15.5	17.7	19.3	15.7	15.7	16.5	13.6
1987	17.3	18.8	15.0	17.6	19.3	15.2	15.5	16.4	13.1
1988	17.0	18.6	14.7	17.3	19.0	14.9	15.2	16.1	12.8
1989	17.1	18.8	14.5	17.2	19.0	14.6	16.6	17.7	13.7
1990	16.9	18.5	14.3	17.2	19.0	14.6	14.7	16.1	11.3
1991	17.0	18.6	14.3	17.3	19.0	14.7	14.6	16.0	11.1
1992	17.1	18.5	14.7	17.4	18.9	15.1	14.8	16.2	11.3
1993, prel.	17.0	18.4	14.8	17.4	18.8	15.2	14.9	16.3	11.5
1994, prel.	17.0	18.7	14.5	17.3	19.0	14.9	15.2	16.8	11.2
1995, proj.	17.1	18.7	14.6	17.4	19.1	14.9	15.1	16.7	11.3

Source: U.S. National Center for Education Statistics, *Digest of Education Statistics,* annual.

No. 250. Public Elementary and Secondary Schools, by Type and Size of School: 1993-94

[Data reported by schools, rather than school districts]

ENROLLMENT SIZE OF SCHOOL	NUMBER OF SCHOOLS					ENROLLMENT (1,000)				
	Total	Ele-men-tary [1]	Second-ary [2]	Com-bined [3]	Other [4]	Total	Ele-men-tary [1]	Second-ary [2]	Com-bined [3]	Other [4]
Total.	85,393	60,052	20,059	2,674	2,608	43,278	28,096	13,933	1,118	132
PERCENT DISTRIBUTION [5]										
Total.	100.0	100.0	100.0	100.0	100.0	100.0	100.0	100.0	100.0	100.0
Under 100 students	8.7	5.9	12.5	28.7	55.4	0.8	0.6	0.9	3.0	14.8
100 to 199 students	9.9	9.3	10.8	13.8	19.9	2.9	3.0	2.3	4.8	17.9
200 to 299 students	11.5	12.5	8.7	10.2	10.8	5.6	6.8	3.1	6.0	16.6
300 to 399 students	13.7	15.9	7.8	8.0	6.0	9.2	11.9	3.9	6.7	13.2
400 to 499 students	13.5	16.1	7.2	7.1	2.6	11.8	15.4	4.7	7.7	7.4
500 to 599 students	11.7	13.6	7.0	7.0	1.6	12.4	16.0	5.6	9.2	5.3
600 to 699 students	8.8	9.8	6.4	5.8	1.2	11.0	13.5	6.0	9.0	4.9
700 to 799 students	6.1	6.4	5.6	4.3	0.4	8.8	10.2	6.0	7.6	1.7
800 to 999 students	7.2	6.6	9.4	5.9	0.8	12.3	12.5	12.1	12.6	4.6
1,000 to 1,499 students . . .	6.1	3.5	13.9	6.3	1.1	14.0	8.7	24.5	17.9	8.1
1,500 to 1,999 students . . .	1.8	0.3	6.4	1.8	0.1	6.0	1.2	15.8	7.3	1.4
2,000 to 2,999 students . . .	0.9	(Z)	3.6	0.9	0.1	4.2	0.2	12.3	5.3	1.8
3,000 or more students. . . .	0.1	(Z)	0.5	0.2	-	1.0	(Z)	2.8	2.8	-
Average enrollment [5]	(X)	(X)	(X)	(X)	(X)	518	468	695	418	158

- Represents zero. X Not applicable. Z Less than .05 percent. [1] Includes schools beginning with grade 6 or below and with no grade higher than 8. [2] Includes schools with no grade lower than 7. [3] Includes schools with both elementary and secondary grades. [4] Includes special education, alternative, and other schools not classified by grade span. [5] Data for those schools reporting enrollment.

Source: U.S. National Center for Education Statistics, *Digest of Education Statistics,* annual.

No. 251. Public Elementary and Secondary School Enrollment, by State: 1980 to 1994

[**In thousands, except rate**. As of **fall**. Includes unclassified students]

STATE	ENROLLMENT K through Grade 8 [1]				ENROLLMENT Grades 9 through 12				ENROLLMENT RATE [2]				
	1980	1985	1990	1993, prel.	1980	1985	1990	1993, prel.	1980	1985	1990	1993, prel.	1994, est.
U.S.	27,647	27,034	29,878	31,515	13,231	12,388	11,338	11,961	86.2	87.7	91.3	91.7	91.2
AL.	528	517	527	536	231	213	195	199	87.6	89.6	93.3	95.3	94.3
AK.	60	77	85	94	26	30	29	32	94.0	99.4	97.4	95.4	90.3
AZ.	357	386	479	526	157	162	161	183	88.9	90.8	93.3	93.1	99.6
AR.	310	304	314	318	138	130	123	127	90.3	91.8	95.9	95.7	92.3
CA.	2,730	2,927	3,615	3,904	1,347	1,329	1,336	1,424	87.1	89.5	92.8	92.9	91.4
CO	374	379	420	460	172	172	154	165	92.2	92.7	94.6	92.3	91.5
CT.	364	321	347	369	168	141	122	128	83.3	83.4	90.2	91.1	90.4
DE.	62	63	73	77	37	30	27	29	79.5	80.1	87.4	86.5	86.3
DC	71	62	61	61	29	25	19	19	91.8	96.8	100.9	107.6	106.0
FL.	1,042	1,086	1,370	1,515	468	476	492	526	84.4	86.7	92.6	91.5	91.7
GA	742	757	849	910	327	323	303	325	86.8	88.2	93.6	94.4	94.6
HI.	110	113	123	132	55	51	49	49	83.4	84.2	87.6	88.0	87.6
ID.	144	149	160	167	59	59	61	70	95.4	93.6	96.9	96.6	95.5
IL.	1,335	1,246	1,310	1,356	649	580	512	537	82.6	83.3	86.9	88.3	88.5
IN.	708	654	676	679	347	312	279	287	88.0	88.4	90.4	91.4	91.2
IA.	351	324	345	348	183	161	139	151	88.4	89.1	92.1	93.0	92.1
KS.	283	286	320	330	133	125	117	128	88.7	91.0	92.6	92.1	91.0
KY.	464	449	459	467	206	195	177	188	83.7	85.8	90.5	92.9	92.5
LA.	544	573	586	587	234	215	199	213	80.2	83.9	88.2	89.6	87.1
ME	153	142	155	157	70	64	60	60	91.6	93.3	96.5	96.0	94.5
MD	493	446	527	569	258	225	188	203	83.9	84.9	89.1	89.4	89.5
MA	676	559	604	646	346	285	230	232	88.6	86.3	88.8	89.7	89.7
MI.	1,227	1,086	1,145	1,160	570	517	440	439	86.9	87.8	90.3	89.0	87.9
MN	482	468	546	577	272	237	211	233	87.2	89.4	91.2	90.7	90.5
MS	330	330	372	369	147	141	131	137	79.6	81.0	91.3	92.8	91.7
MO	567	544	588	632	277	251	228	244	83.8	84.9	86.5	89.0	85.9
MT	106	108	111	117	50	46	42	46	92.9	93.8	93.8	93.7	92.0
NE.	189	184	198	203	91	82	76	82	86.6	87.7	88.7	88.8	87.9
NV.	101	107	150	175	49	48	51	61	93.4	93.3	98.7	95.9	96.0
NH	112	107	126	136	55	54	46	49	85.3	87.5	89.1	90.0	88.1
NJ.	820	740	784	844	426	376	306	308	81.5	82.9	86.1	86.8	86.9
NM	186	187	208	226	85	90	94	96	89.5	91.6	94.3	92.9	88.2
NY.	1,838	1,703	1,828	1,921	1,033	918	770	813	80.8	82.3	86.6	88.4	89.2
NC	786	749	783	828	343	337	304	305	90.1	91.2	94.8	93.3	92.0
ND	77	84	85	84	40	35	33	35	85.9	89.2	92.8	93.1	92.6
OH	1,312	1,206	1,258	1,290	645	588	514	517	84.8	85.6	88.0	88.2	88.2
OK	399	414	425	441	179	178	154	163	92.9	94.3	95.1	95.4	95.1
OR	319	305	340	368	145	142	132	148	88.5	89.7	90.7	91.6	91.0
PA	1,231	1,093	1,172	1,233	678	591	496	511	80.4	80.3	83.6	84.4	84.8
RI.	98	90	102	107	51	44	37	39	80.1	81.2	87.3	88.3	87.4
SC.	426	424	452	467	193	183	170	177	88.1	89.6	94.0	95.8	94.6
SD.	86	88	95	102	42	37	34	41	87.4	90.7	89.7	94.0	92.9
TN.	602	575	598	630	252	239	226	237	87.8	88.3	93.5	95.1	93.0
TX.	2,049	2,261	2,511	2,681	851	871	872	927	92.4	93.2	98.4	98.6	98.3
UT.	250	299	325	330	93	105	122	141	98.2	96.3	97.7	97.8	96.1
VT.	66	63	71	75	29	27	25	28	87.9	89.3	93.9	96.9	99.6
VA.	703	665	728	767	307	303	270	278	90.7	94.0	94.2	93.8	93.4
WA	515	507	613	660	242	243	227	256	91.7	92.2	94.0	92.5	92.2
WV	270	249	224	216	113	109	98	99	92.6	92.2	95.7	97.3	96.5
WI	528	501	566	596	303	267	232	248	82.1	83.8	86.0	86.0	86.0
WY	70	74	71	71	28	29	27	29	97.3	97.0	97.3	98.0	97.2

[1] Data include a small number of pre-kindergarten students.   [2] Percent of persons 5-17 years old. Based on enumerated resident population as of April 1, 1980, and 1990, and estimated resident population as of July 1 for other years. Data not adjusted for revisions based on the 1990 Census of Population.

Source: U.S. National Center for Education Statistics, *Digest of Education Statistics*, annual.

No. 252. Public Elementary and Secondary School Enrollment, by Grade: 1960 to 1993

[In thousands. 1960, for school year; thereafter, as of **fall** of year. Beginning 1970, kindergarten includes nursery schools. For 1960, enrollment figures are prorated and 12th grade includes postgraduates. See also *Historical Statistics, Colonial Times to 1970,* series H 420-424]

GRADE	1960	1970	1975	1980	1985	1987	1988	1989	1990	1991	1992	1993, prel.
Pupils enrolled	**36,087**	**45,894**	**44,819**	**40,877**	**39,422**	**40,008**	**40,189**	**40,543**	**41,217**	**42,047**	**42,816**	**43,476**
Kindergarten and grades 1 to 8.	27,602	32,558	30,515	27,647	27,034	27,933	28,501	29,152	29,878	30,506	31,081	31,515
Kindergarten	1,923	2,564	2,971	2,689	3,192	3,388	3,433	3,486	3,610	3,686	3,810	3,934
First	3,733	3,817	3,238	2,894	3,239	3,407	3,460	3,485	3,499	3,556	3,542	3,529
Second	3,436	3,654	3,027	2,800	2,941	3,173	3,223	3,289	3,327	3,360	3,431	3,429
Third.	3,302	3,663	3,038	2,893	2,895	3,046	3,167	3,235	3,297	3,334	3,361	3,437
Fourth.	3,146	3,675	3,112	3,107	2,771	2,938	3,051	3,182	3,248	3,315	3,342	3,361
Fifth	3,118	3,635	3,281	3,130	2,776	2,901	2,945	3,067	3,197	3,268	3,325	3,350
Sixth.	3,070	3,598	3,476	3,038	2,789	2,811	2,937	2,987	3,110	3,239	3,303	3,356
Seventh	3,173	3,662	3,619	3,085	2,938	2,910	2,905	3,027	3,067	3,181	3,299	3,355
Eighth.	2,701	3,601	3,636	3,086	2,982	2,839	2,853	2,853	2,979	3,020	3,129	3,249
Unclassified [1]. . . .	(X)	690	1,116	924	511	520	527	540	543	545	539	515
Grades 9 to 12	8,485	13,336	14,304	13,231	12,388	12,076	11,687	11,390	11,338	11,541	11,735	11,961
Ninth	2,412	3,654	3,879	3,377	3,377	3,143	3,106	3,141	3,169	3,313	3,352	3,487
Tenth	2,258	3,458	3,723	3,368	3,230	3,020	2,895	2,868	2,896	2,915	3,027	3,050
Eleventh	2,063	3,128	3,354	3,195	2,866	2,936	2,749	2,629	2,612	2,645	2,656	2,751
Twelfth	1,752	2,775	2,986	2,925	2,550	2,681	2,650	2,650	2,473	2,381	2,392	2,431	2,424
Unclassified [1]. . . .	(X)	321	362	366	303	296	288	279	282	275	269	248

X Not applicable.   [1] Includes ungraded and special education.

Source: U.S. National Center for Education Statistics, *Digest of Education Statistics,* annual.

No. 253. Public Elementary and Secondary School Teachers—Selected Characteristics: 1993-94

[**For school year.** Based on survey and subject to sampling error; for details, see source. Excludes prekindergarten teachers. See table 268 for similar data on private school teachers]

CHARACTERISTIC	Unit	AGE				SEX		RACE/ETHNICITY		
		Under 30 years old	30 to 39 years old	40 to 49 years old	Over 50 years old	Male	Female	White [1]	Black [1]	Hispanic
Total teachers [2].	**1,000 . . .**	**479**	**762**	**981**	**339**	**694**	**1,867**	**2,217**	**188**	**109**
Highest degree held:										
Bachelor's.	Percent .	76.3	52.8	43.1	41.4	46.2	54.1	51.8	48.4	62.8
Master's	Percent .	21.5	42.0	49.6	48.8	45.7	40.6	42.5	44.6	29.8
Education specialist	Percent .	1.5	4.0	5.8	6.7	5.1	4.4	4.4	5.4	4.6
Doctorate	Percent .	0.1	0.5	0.8	1.9	1.3	0.5	0.7	0.9	1.4
Full-time teaching experience:										
Less than 3 years.	Percent .	33.9	7.0	3.0	1.0	8.9	10.0	9.4	8.5	16.7
3 to 9 years.	Percent .	61.8	28.5	12.2	5.8	21.6	26.9	25.5	20.9	32.1
10 to 20 years	Percent .	4.3	62.3	33.5	21.8	29.9	37.0	35.2	35.6	34.1
20 years or more	Percent .	(X)	2.2	51.3	71.5	39.6	26.1	30.0	35.3	17.1
Full-time teachers	1,000 . . .	440	685	902	314	643	1,697	2,012	182	103
Earned income	Dol.	27,974	33,448	39,586	41,951	39,591	34,536	36,000	35,548	34,837
Salary.	Dol.	25,966	31,737	37,803	40,414	36,182	33,384	34,221	33,889	32,996
Supplemental contract during school year:										
Teachers receiving	1,000 . . .	193	242	301	79	349	467	723	49	32
Salary	Dol.	1,930	2,146	2,115	2,064	2,922	1,442	2,067	2,325	1,930
Supplemental contract during summer:										
Teachers receiving	1,000 . . .	92	121	151	38	147	254	328	41	24
Salary.	Dol.	1,880	1,891	2,273	2,290	2,530	1,803	2,015	2,221	2,477
Teachers with nonschool employment:										
Teaching/tutoring	1,000 . . .	20	33	49	16	37	81	100	11	6
Education related	1,000 . . .	15	25	31	9	39	41	69	5	4
Not education related	1,000 . . .	46	67	97	28	124	113	208	16	7

X Not applicable.   [1] Non-Hispanic.   [2] Includes teachers with no degrees and associates degrees, not shown separately.

Source: U.S. National Center for Education Statistics, *Digest of Education Statistics,* 1995.

No. 254. Public Elementary and Secondary Schools—Number and Average Salary of Classroom Teachers, 1960 to 1995, and by State, 1995

[Estimates for school year ending in **June** of year shown. Schools classified by type of organization rather than by grade-group; elementary includes kindergarten]

YEAR AND STATE	TEACHERS [1] (1,000)			AVG. SALARY ($1,000)			YEAR AND STATE	TEACHERS [1] (1,000)			AVG. SALARY ($1,000)		
	Total	Elementary	Secondary	All teachers	Elementary	Secondary		Total	Elementary	Secondary	All teachers	Elementary	Secondary
1960	1,355	834	521	5.0	4.8	5.3	LA	47.3	33.2	14.1	26.5	26.5	26.5
1970	2,008	1,109	899	8.6	8.4	8.9	ME......	14.8	9.5	5.4	32.0	31.5	33.1
1975	2,171	1,169	1,001	11.7	11.3	12.0	MD......	45.3	25.5	19.8	40.7	39.6	41.8
1980	2,211	1,206	1,005	16.0	15.6	16.5	MA......	60.5	26.0	34.5	42.2	42.2	42.2
1985	2,175	1,212	963	23.6	23.2	24.2	MI	68.7	48.3	20.4	47.4	47.4	47.4
1986	2,215	1,242	973	25.2	24.7	25.8	MN......	47.6	24.2	23.4	35.9	35.7	36.2
1987	2,249	1,274	975	26.6	26.1	27.2	MS......	29.1	16.0	13.1	26.8	26.4	27.4
1988	2,282	1,308	974	28.0	27.5	28.8	MO	56.5	29.6	26.9	31.2	30.4	32.1
1989	2,324	1,354	970	29.6	29.0	30.2	MT......	10.1	7.0	3.1	28.8	28.5	29.5
1990	2,362	1,390	972	31.4	30.8	32.0	NE......	19.6	11.2	8.3	30.9	30.9	30.9
1991	2,409	1,435	974	33.1	32.5	33.9	NV......	13.2	7.6	5.7	34.8	34.4	35.5
1992	2,428	1,466	963	34.1	33.5	34.8	NH......	12.3	8.3	4.0	34.7	34.7	34.7
1993	2,466	1,496	970	35.0	34.3	35.9	NJ......	85.3	54.7	30.6	46.1	45.1	47.9
1994	2,507	1,517	990	35.8	35.3	36.7	NM......	18.5	13.0	5.5	28.5	27.6	28.4
1995, U.S.	**2,547**	**1,535**	**1,012**	**36.8**	**36.3**	**37.6**	NY......	190.4	94.8	95.6	47.6	46.1	49.1
AL......	43.4	23.8	19.6	31.1	31.1	31.1	NC......	70.7	44.4	26.3	30.8	30.7	31.0
AK......	7.2	4.6	2.5	48.0	48.0	48.0	ND......	7.8	5.0	2.8	26.3	26.4	26.2
AZ......	38.7	29.8	8.9	32.2	32.2	32.2	OH......	104.8	69.7	35.1	36.8	36.3	37.7
AR......	26.6	13.0	13.6	28.9	28.1	29.7	OK......	39.3	20.8	18.5	28.2	27.5	28.9
CA......	221.7	162.8	58.9	41.1	40.6	42.7	OR......	27.0	17.1	9.9	38.6	38.2	39.4
CO......	34.9	17.7	17.2	34.6	34.2	35.0	PA......	103.0	53.1	49.9	44.5	43.8	45.2
CT......	35.6	25.4	10.1	50.0	49.6	51.6	RI	10.1	5.5	4.6	40.7	40.7	40.8
DE......	6.4	3.2	3.2	39.1	38.6	39.6	SC......	38.7	26.5	12.2	30.3	30.0	30.9
DC......	5.9	3.6	2.3	43.7	44.2	45.0	SD......	8.9	6.2	2.7	26.0	25.7	25.9
FL......	119.3	65.6	53.7	32.6	32.6	32.6	TN......	48.5	34.6	13.9	32.5	32.4	33.6
GA......	77.9	56.6	21.3	32.6	32.6	32.6	TX......	234.2	123.1	111.1	31.2	30.5	32.0
HI	10.7	6.0	4.7	38.5	38.5	38.5	UT......	19.9	10.8	9.1	29.1	29.4	29.1
ID......	12.6	6.5	6.1	29.8	29.7	29.9	VT......	7.4	3.8	3.7	35.4	35.4	35.5
IL......	112.7	78.8	33.8	39.4	37.7	43.5	VA......	70.5	42.6	27.9	34.0	33.0	35.5
IN......	55.2	29.6	25.6	36.8	36.8	36.8	WA	46.3	27.1	19.3	36.2	35.9	36.5
IA	31.9	14.9	17.0	31.5	30.5	32.4	WV	20.9	12.1	8.8	31.9	31.6	32.4
KS......	30.6	16.5	14.1	34.7	34.7	34.7	WI	55.9	36.7	19.2	37.7	37.2	39.1
KY......	35.9	25.3	10.6	32.3	31.5	33.9	WY.....	6.7	3.4	3.3	31.3	31.2	31.4

[1] Full-time equivalent.

Source: National Education Association, Washington, DC, *Estimates of School Statistics, 1994-95,* and earlier issues. (Copyright by the National Education Association. All rights reserved.)

No. 255. Average Starting Salaries of Public School Teachers Compared With Salaries in Private Industry, by Selected Position: 1975 to 1993

[Except as noted, salaries represent what corporations plan to offer graduates graduating in the year shown with bachelors' degrees. Based on a survey of approximately 200 companies]

ITEM AND POSITION	1975	1980	1985	1988	1989	1990	1991	1992	1993
SALARIES (dollars)									
Teachers [1]	8,233	10,764	15,460	19,400	(NA)	20,486	21,481	22,171	22,505
College graduates:									
Engineering	12,744	20,136	26,880	29,856	30,852	32,304	34,236	34,620	35,004
Accounting	11,880	15,720	20,628	25,140	25,908	27,408	27,924	28,404	28,020
Sales—marketing	10,344	15,936	20,616	23,484	27,768	27,828	26,580	26,532	28,536
Business administration ...	9,768	14,100	19,986	23,880	25,908	26,496	26,256	27,156	27,564
Liberal arts [2]	9,312	13,296	18,828	23,508	25,608	26,364	25,560	27,324	27,216
Chemistry	11,904	17,124	24,216	27,108	27,552	29,088	29,700	30,360	30,456
Mathematics—statistics ...	10,980	17,604	22,704	25,548	28,416	28,944	29,244	29,472	30,756
Economics—finance	10,212	14,472	20,964	23,928	25,812	26,712	26,424	27,708	28,584
Computer science	(NA)	17,712	24,156	26,904	28,608	29,100	30,924	30,888	31,164
INDEX (1975=100)									
Teachers [1]	100	131	187	236	(NA)	249	261	269	273
College graduates:									
Engineering	100	158	211	234	242	253	268	271	275
Accounting	100	132	174	212	218	230	235	239	236
Sales—marketing	100	154	199	227	268	269	257	256	276
Business administration ...	100	144	204	244	259	271	268	278	282
Liberal arts [2]	100	143	202	252	275	283	274	293	292
Chemistry	100	144	203	228	231	244	249	255	256
Mathematics—statistics ...	100	160	207	233	258	263	266	268	280
Economics—finance	100	142	205	234	252	261	258	271	280
Computer science [3]......	(NA)	125	171	190	202	205	218	217	218

NA Not available. [1] Estimate. Minimum mean salary. Source: National Education Association, Washington, DC, unpublished data. [2] Excludes Chemistry, Mathematics, Economics, and Computer Science. [3] Computer science index (1978=100).

Source: Except as noted, Northwestern University Placement Center, Evanston, IL, *The Northwestern University Lindquist-Endicott Report* (copyright).

No. 256. Average Salary and Wages Paid in Public School Systems: 1975 to 1996

[In dollars. For school year ending in year shown. Data reported by a stratified sample of school systems enrolling 300 or more pupils. Data represent unweighted means of average salaries paid school personnel reported by each school system]

POSITION	1975	1980	1985	1990	1992	1993	1994	1995	1996
ANNUAL SALARY									
Central office administrators:									
Superintendent (contract salary) . . .	30,338	39,344	56,954	75,425	83,342	85,120	87,717	90,198	94,229
Deputy/assoc. superintendent	30,074	37,440	52,877	69,623	76,796	77,057	78,672	81,266	84,077
Assistant superintendent	26,460	33,452	48,003	62,698	69,315	70,525	72,701	75,236	77,007
Administrators for—									
Finance and business	21,850	27,147	40,344	52,354	57,036	57,864	59,997	61,323	63,840
Instructional services	22,608	29,790	43,452	56,359	62,102	62,508	64,676	66,767	68,463
Public relations/information	21,470	24,021	35,287	44,926	50,625	50,622	52,366	53,263	53,860
Staff personnel services	21,470	29,623	44,182	56,344	62,269	62,162	63,690	65,819	67,760
Subject area supervisors	18,601	23,974	34,422	45,929	50,580	51,407	52,837	54,534	56,145
School building administrators:									
Principals:									
Elementary.	19,061	25,165	36,452	48,431	53,856	54,905	56,906	58,589	60,922
Junior high/middle	21,136	27,625	39,650	52,163	57,504	58,620	60,651	62,311	64,452
Senior high.	22,894	29,207	42,094	55,722	61,768	63,054	64,993	66,596	69,277
Assistant principals:									
Elementary.	15,968	20,708	30,496	40,916	45,558	45,377	47,057	48,491	50,537
Junior high/middle	17,868	23,507	33,793	44,570	48,956	49,925	51,518	52,942	54,355
Senior high.	18,939	24,816	35,491	46,486	51,318	52,348	54,170	55,556	57,555
Classroom teachers.	11,507	15,913	23,587	31,278	34,565	35,291	36,531	37,264	38,706
Auxiliary professional personnel:									
Counselors	14,479	18,847	27,593	35,979	39,563	40,413	41,355	42,486	44,073
Librarians	12,546	16,764	24,981	33,469	37,227	37,945	39,319	40,418	41,761
School nurses	10,673	13,788	19,944	26,090	28,721	29,555	30,630	31,066	32,786
Secretarial/clerical personnel:									
Central office:									
Secretaries/stenographers.	7,318	10,331	15,343	20,238	22,309	22,770	23,495	23,935	24,809
Accounting/payroll clerks.	7,588	10,479	15,421	20,088	22,215	22,605	23,275	24,042	25,009
Clerk-typists	6,089	8,359	12,481	16,125	17,646	17,772	18,296	18,674	19,447
School building level:									
Secretaries/stenographers.	6,046	8,348	12,504	16,184	17,784	18,104	18,692	19,170	20,076
Library clerks	5,052	6,778	9,911	12,151	13,347	13,311	13,809	14,381	14,791
HOURLY WAGE RATE									
Other support personnel:									
Teacher aides:									
Instructional	2.91	4.06	5.89	7.43	8.15	8.31	8.50	8.77	9.04
Noninstructional	2.81	3.89	5.60	7.08	7.70	7.82	8.14	8.29	8.52
Custodians	3.54	4.88	6.90	8.54	9.35	9.51	9.76	10.05	10.35
Cafeteria workers	2.61	3.78	5.42	6.77	7.39	7.56	7.72	7.89	8.15
Bus drivers	3.75	5.21	7.27	9.21	10.04	10.15	10.35	10.69	11.04

Source: Educational Research Service, Arlington, VA, *National Survey of Salaries and Wages in Public Schools,* annual, vols. 2 and 3. (All rights reserved. Copyright.)

No. 257. Public School Employment: 1982 and 1994

[In thousands. Covers full-time employment. Excludes Hawaii. 1982 also excludes District of Columbia and New Jersey. 1982 based on sample survey of school districts with 250 or more students. 1994 based on sample survey of school districts with 100 or more employees; see source for sampling variability]

OCCUPATION	1982					1994				
	Total	Male	Female	White [1]	Black [1]	Total	Male	Female	White [1]	Black [1]
All occupations	**3,082**	**1,063**	**2,019**	**2,498**	**432**	**3,518**	**967**	**2,551**	**2,749**	**506**
Officials, administrators	41	31	10	36	3	45	27	18	38	5
Principals and assistant										
principals.	90	72	19	76	11	97	55	42	75	15
Classroom teachers [2]	1,680	534	1,146	1,435	186	1,948	500	1,448	1,637	205
Elementary schools	798	129	669	667	98	947	119	828	783	105
Secondary schools	706	363	343	619	67	753	327	425	645	73
Other professional staff	235	91	144	193	35	258	61	197	213	31
Teachers aides [3]	215	14	200	146	45	371	62	309	235	80
Clerical, secretarial staff	210	4	206	177	19	240	6	234	186	28
Service workers [4]	611	316	295	434	132	558	256	302	364	141

[1] Excludes individuals of Hispanic origin.   [2] Includes other classroom teachers, not shown separately.   [3] Includes technicians.   [4] Includes craftworkers and laborers.

Source: U.S. Equal Employment Opportunity Commission, *Elementary-Secondary Staff Information (EEO-5),* biennial.

No. 258. Public Elementary and Secondary School Price Indexes: 1975 to 1994

[1983=100. For years ending **June 30**. Reflects prices paid by public elementary-secondary schools. For explanation of average annual percent change, see Guide to Tabular Presentation]

YEAR	Index, total	PERSONNEL COMPENSATION				CONTRACTED SERVICES, SUPPLIES AND EQUIPMENT							
		Total	Professional salaries	Nonprofessional salaries	Fringe benefits	Total	Services	Supplies and materials	Equipment replacement	Library materials and textbooks	Utilities	Fixed costs
1975 . .	52.7	53.4	56.0	55.6	40.9	50.4	55.7	58.0	53.7	53.8	34.5	45.2
1980 . .	76.6	75.9	76.7	77.8	71.0	79.2	77.4	85.9	79.6	82.1	71.1	77.9
1982 . .	93.7	92.6	92.8	94.4	90.3	97.8	94.6	101.1	95.5	91.6	102.3	94.1
1983 . .	100.0	100.0	100.0	100.0	100.0	100.0	100.0	100.0	100.0	100.0	100.0	100.0
1984 . .	105.0	106.0	105.8	104.5	108.3	101.4	105.6	99.5	103.4	107.3	94.1	104.5
1985 . .	111.9	113.7	113.4	111.3	117.1	105.1	111.1	103.3	107.2	113.0	93.0	109.9
1986 . .	118.4	121.1	121.4	117.6	123.3	108.0	117.1	102.8	109.3	121.2	93.5	115.2
1987 . .	123.0	127.4	128.3	121.9	128.8	106.3	118.7	101.8	112.9	129.1	75.1	121.6
1988 . .	129.7	134.5	135.5	127.5	137.0	111.2	123.6	106.0	113.4	145.1	78.0	127.2
1989 . .	136.1	141.6	142.2	133.3	147.0	115.4	128.8	112.5	116.0	151.4	75.0	133.3
1990 . .	144.1	150.0	150.1	139.4	159.3	121.8	134.2	119.4	121.2	176.0	77.6	139.0
1991 . .	152.2	158.3	158.1	146.5	169.8	129.3	139.9	123.0	125.7	196.2	92.6	143.6
1992 . .	158.2	165.4	165.8	152.4	175.8	130.8	143.5	122.2	128.5	204.6	90.7	147.4
1993 . .	161.8	169.6	169.2	155.1	184.4	132.3	145.5	121.5	131.8	211.1	90.0	152.3
1994 . .	166.8	175.1	175.1	159.3	189.9	135.0	148.4	122.3	135.4	224.3	90.2	157.1

Source: Research Associates of Washington, Washington, DC, *Inflation Measures for Schools, Colleges, and Libraries*, annual (copyright).

No. 259. Finances of Public Elementary and Secondary School Systems, by Enrollment-Size Group: 1990-91

[**In millions of dollars, except as indicated.** Data are estimates subject to sampling variability. For details, see source. See also Appendix III]

ITEM	All school systems	ENROLLMENT SIZE						
		50,000 or more	25,000 to 49,999	15,000 to 24,999	7,500 to 14,999	5,000 to 7,499	3,000 to 4,999	Under 3,000
Enrollment, fall (1,000)	41,255	7,548	4,301	3,746	6,235	3,773	4,764	10,888
General revenue [1]	224,226	42,858	21,680	18,243	31,591	19,421	25,419	65,014
Intergovernmental	122,415	23,839	12,630	10,847	17,038	9,713	12,112	36,236
From Federal government	1,352	284	100	75	150	107	116	520
From States	118,050	23,356	12,193	10,532	16,523	9,367	11,633	34,445
Federal aid distributed by State governments	11,983	3,071	1,273	979	1,541	913	1,108	3,099
From local governments.	3,013	199	337	239	364	239	363	1,271
From own sources	101,811	19,019	9,050	7,396	14,553	9,708	13,306	28,778
Taxes	69,147	9,283	6,152	5,072	10,017	7,149	9,713	21,759
Property	67,383	8,900	5,962	4,997	9,765	6,963	9,451	21,344
Contribution from parent government	19,135	7,548	1,541	1,046	2,464	1,355	1,995	3,186
Charges and miscellaneous	13,529	2,189	1,356	1,277	2,072	1,203	1,598	3,833
Current charges	6,353	1,168	646	579	959	560	731	1,711
School lunch sales	3,639	485	357	322	584	370	478	1,042
Interest earnings	3,584	527	352	324	529	335	428	1,089
Other	3,592	493	359	375	584	309	439	1,033
Employee-retirement revenue	1,007	793	203	11	-	(Z)	-	-
General expenditure [1]	226,803	43,962	22,310	18,601	32,088	19,568	25,730	64,544
Intergovernmental	604	24	31	53	107	64	99	226
Direct.	226,199	43,938	22,279	18,548	31,981	19,503	25,632	64,318
Current operation	203,735	40,010	19,715	16,418	28,559	17,679	22,989	58,364
Salaries and wages	131,966	26,590	13,417	11,203	19,155	11,751	15,147	34,703
Capital outlay.	18,607	3,322	2,131	1,769	2,811	1,489	2,149	4,936
Construction.	11,153	1,944	1,184	1,079	1,783	874	1,383	2,906
Interest on debt	3,857	606	433	360	611	336	493	1,018
Employee-retirement expenditure	324	198	120	5	-	(Z)	-	-
Debt outstanding [2]	63,669	11,110	6,660	5,769	9,820	5,404	8,190	16,716
Long-term.	60,521	11,043	6,519	5,664	9,279	5,105	7,559	15,351
Short-term	3,148	67	141	104	541	298	632	1,365
Long-term debt issued	12,806	2,251	1,460	1,245	2,076	1,008	1,510	3,257
Long-term debt retired	5,777	854	647	479	869	574	765	1,590
Cash and security holdings	50,909	10,177	6,016	3,649	5,854	3,734	5,060	16,419
Employee-retirement holdings	6,278	4,385	1,792	101	-	(Z)	-	(Z)

- Represents zero.   Z Less than $500,000.   [1] Excludes interschool system transactions.   [2] As of end of fiscal year.

Source: U.S. Bureau of the Census, *Public Education Finances: 1990-91*, GF/91-10.

No. 260. Public Elementary and Secondary Estimated Finances, 1970 to 1995, and by State, 1995

[In millions of dollars, except as noted. For school years ending in June of year shown]

	RECEIPTS					EXPENDITURES				
		Revenue receipts						Current expenditures		
YEAR AND STATE	Total	Total	Source			Non-revenue receipts [1]	Total [2]	Per capita [3] (dol.)	Elementary and secondary day schools	Average per pupil in ADA [4]	
			Federal	State	Local					Amount (dol.)	Rank
1970	41,621	38,192	2,767	15,628	19,797	3,429	39,091	194	32,683	773	(X)
1975	66,319	63,047	5,089	27,472	30,486	3,273	62,340	292	53,333	1,286	(X)
1980	101,724	97,635	9,020	47,929	40,686	4,089	96,105	428	85,661	2,230	(X)
1985	146,976	141,013	9,533	69,107	62,373	5,963	139,382	591	127,230	3,483	(X)
1990	218,126	208,656	13,184	100,787	94,685	9,469	209,698	850	186,583	4,966	(X)
1992	254,510	234,924	15,704	111,348	107,871	19,586	236,750	939	208,352	5,352	(X)
1993	268,823	247,706	17,521	115,855	114,330	21,118	248,564	975	218,944	5,528	(X)
1995, total .	**286,025**	**270,876**	**18,858**	**129,456**	**122,561**	**15,150**	**274,603**	**1,055**	**240,816**	**5,907**	**(X)**
Alabama.......	3,265	3,146	356	2,181	609	120	3,486	826	3,078	4,458	45
Alaska........	1,183	1,059	133	673	253	124	1,163	1,929	1,065	9,934	1
Arizona.......	4,201	3,714	326	1,566	1,822	488	3,899	956	2,923	4,252	49
Arkansas......	2,236	2,060	182	1,326	551	176	2,062	840	1,775	4,257	48
California......	29,492	28,692	2,619	15,648	10,424	800	28,176	897	24,919	4,731	41
Colorado.......	3,708	3,480	194	1,552	1,733	228	3,907	1,067	3,267	5,500	30
Connecticut.....	4,462	4,459	216	1,743	2,500	3	4,462	1,363	4,102	8,503	4
Delaware.......	822	774	67	502	205	48	780	1,102	709	7,172	10
District of Columbia......	595	589	83	-	506	6	616	1,087	572	8,211	5
Florida	13,502	12,804	971	6,286	5,547	698	13,747	985	11,017	5,717	25
Georgia	7,310	7,087	512	3,649	2,925	224	7,222	1,023	6,335	5,396	33
Hawaii	1,192	1,192	87	1,079	26	-	1,173	996	1,046	6,159	17
Idaho	1,112	1,086	80	670	335	27	1,112	980	979	4,330	47
Illinois........	12,894	11,794	1,081	3,792	6,921	1,100	10,719	912	9,119	5,259	35
Indiana........	6,359	6,156	310	3,232	2,614	203	6,293	1,094	5,342	6,033	20
Iowa	3,168	2,813	148	1,376	1,289	355	3,314	1,171	2,612	5,560	29
Kansas........	2,991	2,730	152	1,597	980	261	2,673	1,048	2,383	5,761	24
Kentucky.......	3,717	3,463	319	2,318	825	254	3,507	916	3,228	5,611	28
Louisiana	4,101	3,790	458	1,999	1,332	311	3,733	865	3,397	4,705	42
Maine.........	1,376	1,335	92	643	601	41	1,376	1,110	1,284	6,410	15
Maryland.......	5,497	5,236	271	2,044	2,921	261	5,452	1,090	4,913	6,719	13
Massachusetts ...	6,531	6,515	349	2,410	3,757	16	6,370	1,054	6,019	7,341	8
Michigan.......	12,368	11,680	314	7,996	3,370	688	12,002	1,264	10,334	6,929	12
Minnesota	6,641	5,666	253	2,796	2,617	975	5,682	1,244	4,570	6,033	20
Mississippi......	2,275	2,145	321	1,200	624	130	2,187	819	1,942	4,123	50
Missouri	5,069	4,817	313	1,820	2,683	252	4,646	880	3,935	4,972	37
Montana	932	916	91	449	375	16	952	1,111	863	5,831	22
Nebraska	1,502	1,483	70	576	838	19	1,593	981	1,441	5,384	34
Nevada........	1,427	1,320	66	443	811	107	1,403	960	1,177	5,126	36
New Hampshire ..	1,224	1,208	38	94	1,076	17	1,149	1,012	1,061	6,127	18
New Jersey.....	11,705	11,607	423	4,680	6,504	99	11,272	1,426	10,791	9,860	2
New Mexico.....	2,106	1,888	190	1,247	451	219	1,911	1,155	1,473	5,423	31
New York	27,302	25,107	1,503	9,829	13,775	2,195	25,945	1,429	23,295	9,448	3
North Carolina ...	6,086	5,926	506	3,899	1,521	160	5,759	815	5,312	4,951	38
North Dakota	626	597	72	256	268	29	569	890	525	4,603	43
Ohio..........	11,479	10,432	674	4,381	5,377	1,048	11,192	1,008	9,460	5,620	27
Oklahoma......	3,039	2,820	262	1,768	789	219	2,952	907	2,498	4,381	46
Oregon........	3,384	2,970	214	1,478	1,278	414	3,452	1,118	2,975	6,250	16
Pennsylvania	13,716	13,687	760	5,784	7,142	30	12,367	1,025	11,686	7,196	9
Rhode Island	1,061	1,061	44	435	582	-	1,036	1,042	1,002	7,356	7
South Carolina ...	3,594	3,308	311	1,533	1,464	286	3,287	902	2,891	4,931	39
South Dakota....	712	690	69	180	441	22	695	962	618	4,838	40
Tennessee......	3,909	3,824	347	1,907	1,570	85	3,829	740	3,667	4,544	44
Texas	21,584	20,488	1,692	8,902	9,894	1,095	21,120	1,147	18,373	5,416	32
Utah..........	2,100	1,927	133	1,054	739	174	2,146	1,125	1,623	3,668	51
Vermont	769	746	37	229	480	22	734	1,264	671	7,372	6
Virginia	6,093	6,023	326	2,132	3,565	70	6,435	982	5,625	5,664	26
Washington.....	6,301	5,876	358	4,121	1,398	425	6,316	1,183	5,087	5,811	23
West Virginia	2,115	2,072	161	1,212	699	43	2,088	1,145	1,874	6,521	14
Wisconsin	6,498	5,989	262	2,460	3,267	509	6,009	1,182	5,395	7,001	11
Wyoming......	693	634	42	304	287	59	628	1,320	569	6,070	19

- Represents or rounds to zero.   X Not applicable.   [1] Amount received by local education agencies from the sales of bonds and real property and equipment, loans, and proceeds from insurance adjustments.   [2] Includes interest on school debt and other current expenditures not shown separately.   [3] Based on Bureau of the Census estimated resident population, as of July 1, the previous year. Estimates reflect revisions based on the 1990 Census of Population.   [4] Average daily attendance.

Source: National Education Association, Washington, DC, *Estimates of School Statistics*, annual (copyright); and unpublished data.

No. 261. Microcomputers for Student Instruction in Elementary and Secondary Schools: 1985 and 1994

[As of **fall for public schools; as of midwinter for private schools.** Public school data based on surveys of every school district and all public schools. Private school data based on surveys of all Catholic and private schools. For details, see source]

LEVEL	1984-85				1993-94			
	Total schools	Percent with micros	Number of micros [1]	Students per micro	Total schools	Percent with micros	Number of micros [1]	Students per micro
U.S. total	105,509	77.7	631,983	62.7	105,763	97.5	4,470,573	11.0
Public schools, total	81,100	85.1	569,825	63.5	83,435	98.6	4,079,260	10.8
Elementary	50,967	82.2	215,393	79.3	50,033	98.7	1,863,499	12.1
Middle/junior high	9,791	93.1	100,331	61.2	12,181	99.6	717,298	11.1
Senior high	15,152	94.6	228,726	51.5	14,322	99.5	1,237,086	9.0
K-12/other	5,190	70.3	25,375	45.8	6,899	86.8	261,377	9.6
Catholic schools, total	9,463	63.4	28,427	73.5	8,345	97.9	197,944	13.0
Elementary	7,831	56.4	15,863	85.1	6,940	97.9	137,275	14.0
Secondary	1,481	87.0	12,147	57.8	1,255	97.9	56,443	10.7
K-12/other	151	46.4	417	(NA)	150	96.2	4,226	10.4
Other private schools, total. . .	14,946	46.4	33,731	40.5	13,983	85.7	193,369	11.9
Elementary	8,226	45.1	13,400	42.7	7,118	85.9	77,363	13.2
Secondary	950	82.7	6,266	40.1	1,039	86.3	26,339	8.1
K-12/other	5,770	42.4	14,065	(NA)	5,826	85.1	89,666	11.8

NA Not available.   [1] Includes estimates for schools not reporting number of micros.

Source: Market Data Retrieval, Shelton, CT, unpublished data.

No. 262. Instructional Use of Computers in Elementary and Secondary Schools: 1985 to 1992

[Includes microcomputers and terminals used by students or teachers. Based on stratified, probability sample of 1,416 public, private, and parochial schools surveyed in spring 1989, and 571 surveyed in spring 1992. Represents all elementary and secondary schools in the United States, except preschools and those that have no grade 5 or higher]

ITEM	Unit	Total, 1985	Total, 1989	1992, BY GRADE LEVEL			
				Total	Grade 5	Grade 8	Grade 11
ALL SCHOOLS							
Computers used for instruction	1,000 . .	1,034	2,355	3,536	1,485	874	1,177
Schools using computers	Percent .	86	96	100	100	100	100
Schools with 15 or more computers	Percent .	24	57	80	77	75	96
SCHOOLS USING COMPUTERS FOR INSTRUCTION							
Mean [1] number of computers	Number.	10	26	37	28	31	65
Median [1]	Number.	8	19	25	23	24	47
Students per computer, median [1]	Number.	42	20	14	15	14	10
Percent of all instructional computers in—							
Classrooms.	Percent .	37	36	37	41	28	33
Computer labs.	Percent .	49	50	50	47	58	52
Other locations	Percent .	14	14	13	12	14	15
Percent of all instructional computers used—							
Usually every day	Percent .	(NA)	71	(NA)	(NA)	(NA)	(NA)
Less than every week or not used at all	Percent .	(NA)	10	(NA)	(NA)	(NA)	(NA)
Median hours of use per week (in rooms with greatest number of computers) [1]	Number.	17	20	20	20	18	22
Percent of all student computer use: [2]							
Learning math.	Percent .	(NA)	14	15	18	12	7
Word processing (how to use)	Percent .	(NA)	14	14	12	16	17
Keyboarding (how to)	Percent .	(NA)	13	14	13	15	14
Learning English	Percent .	(NA)	13	13	17	10	7
Programming	Percent .	(NA)	8	5	3	7	8
Recreational use	Percent .	(NA)	8	9	10	10	6
Tools, e.g., spreadsheets.	Percent .	(NA)	7	6	4	8	12
Learning science	Percent .	(NA)	6	7	8	7	6
Learning social studies	Percent .	(NA)	5	7	9	6	3
Business education [3]	Percent .	(NA)	5	4	3	3	10
Industrial arts	Percent .	(NA)	3	2	1	3	6
Fine arts.	Percent .	(NA)	2	2	2	2	2
Learning foreign languages	Percent .	(NA)	1	1	-	1	2
Other.	Percent .	(NA)	1	1	1	1	-

- Represents zero.   NA Not available.   [1] For definition of mean and median, see Guide to Tabular Presentation.   [2] Estimates supplied by each school's technology coordinator.   [3] Other than keyboarding or word processing instruction.

Source: University of Minnesota, Minneapolis, MN, Department of Sociology, IEA Computers in Education Study.

Education

No. 263. Student Use of Computers: 1984 and 1993

[**In percent.** As of **October.** Based on the Current Population Survey and subject to sampling error; see Appendix III and source]

CHARACTERISTIC	1984, total	1993					
		Total	Prekinder-garten and kinder-garden	Grades 1-8	Grades 9-12	1st to 4th year of college	5th or later year of college
USING COMPUTERS AT SCHOOL							
Total	27.3	59.0	26.2	68.9	58.2	55.2	52.1
Sex:							
Male	29.0	59.4	25.9	69.5	56.5	57.5	56.7
Female	25.5	58.7	26.5	68.4	60.0	53.3	47.8
Race/ethnicity:							
White [1]	30.0	61.6	29.4	73.7	59.9	54.9	49.8
Black [1]	16.8	51.5	16.5	56.5	54.5	56.9	57.9
Hispanic	18.6	52.3	19.2	58.4	54.1	51.9	53.7
Other	28.6	59.0	23.5	65.7	57.3	60.9	69.4
Household income:							
Less than $5,000	18.7	51.2	19.6	55.0	50.6	61.7	66.7
$5,000 to $9,999	21.0	53.3	24.4	60.3	51.9	53.9	56.2
$10,000 to $14,999	22.4	56.4	20.1	64.7	56.7	50.7	76.1
$15,000 to $19,999	25.9	58.1	23.8	67.5	57.4	51.2	58.5
$20,000 to $24,999	26.7	56.4	23.7	64.3	53.0	57.4	52.4
$25,000 to $29,999	30.5	60.0	28.0	70.1	60.3	51.5	58.0
$30,000 to $34,999	30.5	59.1	23.7	69.6	59.7	51.7	45.3
$35,000 to $39,999	32.3	60.7	27.1	72.1	61.7	49.2	47.9
$40,000 to $49,999	32.8	59.3	28.5	70.3	57.2	53.9	48.6
$50,000 to $74,999	35.5	62.6	28.6	75.6	61.5	57.4	44.2
$75,000 or more	36.0	64.6	33.5	78.7	62.5	60.9	47.7
Control of school:							
Public	27.4	60.2	30.1	68.6	58.1	53.9	54.1
Private	26.5	52.1	18.7	72.5	60.7	60.7	48.0
USING COMPUTERS AT HOME							
Total	11.5	27.0	15.6	24.7	28.7	32.8	52.6
Sex:							
Male	14.0	27.4	15.1	24.8	28.2	36.6	56.1
Female	9.0	26.6	16.1	24.6	29.2	29.7	49.5
Race/ethnicity:							
White [1]	13.7	32.8	19.4	31.4	35.9	36.0	53.6
Black [1]	4.9	10.9	4.2	9.0	10.4	19.4	48.1
Hispanic	3.6	10.4	5.7	7.5	9.8	22.0	52.2
Other	9.0	28.7	17.0	23.2	37.0	33.0	47.1
Household income:							
Less than $5,000	2.9	9.7	1.1	4.1	6.8	25.6	45.2
$5,000 to $9,999	3.2	8.0	0.9	4.5	5.3	21.3	45.6
$10,000 to $14,999	5.0	11.4	4.6	6.4	8.7	29.8	50.0
$15,000 to $19,999	7.5	15.1	6.9	10.9	14.1	28.9	43.0
$20,000 to $24,999	9.9	16.8	7.4	13.1	17.9	27.7	49.6
$25,000 to $29,999	12.8	21.1	12.3	19.3	22.0	26.1	47.0
$30,000 to $34,999	15.8	24.1	18.7	20.5	29.1	26.4	44.4
$35,000 to $39,999	19.4	27.1	13.0	26.3	28.1	32.7	52.7
$40,000 to $49,999	20.4	32.2	21.6	32.9	33.9	32.5	45.9
$50,000 to $74,999	24.2	43.0	25.5	45.3	46.4	40.1	58.2
$75,000 or more	22.1	56.1	38.2	62.3	61.0	47.0	64.7
Control of school:							
Public	11.2	25.3	12.1	23.0	27.2	31.9	50.0
Private	13.8	37.4	22.4	41.5	47.2	36.9	57.7
USING COMPUTERS AT HOME FOR SCHOOL WORK							
Total	4.6	14.9	0.6	10.8	20.9	23.1	36.6
Sex:							
Male	5.9	14.8	0.9	10.1	20.5	26.3	40.3
Female	3.3	15.0	0.4	11.5	21.4	20.5	33.2
Race/ethnicity:							
White [1]	5.4	18.2	0.8	13.8	26.5	25.7	37.8
Black [1]	2.3	5.7	(NA)	4.0	6.9	11.5	30.1
Hispanic	1.4	5.6	(NA)	2.9	6.7	15.9	36.8
Other	3.8	16.0	1.1	9.3	27.0	23.7	29.2
Household income:							
Less than $5,000	1.0	6.7	(NA)	2.5	4.0	18.7	36.0
$5,000 to $9,999	1.5	4.8	(NA)	1.1	3.6	16.1	35.5
$10,000 to $14,999	1.9	7.3	(NA)	2.6	5.6	25.9	34.6
$15,000 to $19,999	3.0	8.6	0.4	4.7	10.8	18.7	31.0
$20,000 to $24,999	3.1	9.8	0.7	5.1	12.6	22.9	35.0
$25,000 to $29,999	5.1	10.4	1.1	6.3	13.4	19.5	34.9
$30,000 to $34,999	4.9	13.0	0.8	8.1	21.9	18.0	35.1
$35,000 to $39,999	7.1	15.4	0.8	12.4	21.0	22.6	37.2
$40,000 to $49,999	9.2	17.1	1.1	14.7	24.2	22.2	32.1
$50,000 to $74,999	11.5	23.2	1.0	19.7	35.0	27.0	38.2
$75,000 or more	9.8	30.4	0.8	29.4	45.2	30.6	41.5
Control of school:							
Public	4.5	14.2	0.5	10.1	19.8	22.7	34.7
Private	5.4	18.8	1.0	17.8	35.4	24.8	40.1

NA Not available.   [1] Non-Hispanic.
Source: U.S. National Center for Education Statistics, *Digest of Education Statistics,* 1994.

No. 264. Technology in Public Schools: 1992 to 1995

[**For school year ending in year shown.** Based on surveys of school districts conducted in the spring and summer of the school year. For details, see source]

TECHNOLOGY	NUMBER				PERCENT OF TOTAL	
	1992	1993	1994	1995	1992	1995
Schools with interactive videodisk						
players [1]	6,502	11,729	19,189	23,112	8	27
Elementary [2]	2,921	5,986	10,043	12,326	6	24
Junior high [3]	1,258	2,386	3,844	4,672	10	34
Senior high [4]	2,106	3,129	5,026	5,805	14	34
Students represented (1,000)	5,781	9,064	13,434	16,060	14	36
Schools with modems [1]	13,597	18,471	24,277	28,275	16	34
Elementary [2]	5,831	8,492	11,679	14,782	11	29
Junior high [3]	2,608	3,431	4,531	5,393	20	39
Senior high [4]	5,001	6,371	7,853	8,620	30	51
Students represented (1,000)	10,717	13,382	16,476	19,326	25	43
Schools with networks [1]	4,184	11,657	19,272	23,402	5	28
Elementary [2]	1,583	4,683	8,477	11,155	3	22
Junior high [3]	776	2,030	3,611	4,425	6	32
Senior high [4]	1,736	4,895	7,104	8,042	10	48
Students represented (1,000)	3,754	8,043	12,713	15,160	9	34
Schools with CD-ROM's [1]	5,706	11,021	24,526	31,501	7	37
Elementary [2]	1,897	4,457	11,794	16,816	4	33
Junior high [3]	1,231	2,326	4,874	6,170	9	45
Senior high [4]	2,543	4,168	7,724	9,063	15	54
Students represented (1,000)	5,298	8,534	15,576	19,501	12	44
Schools with satellite dishes [1]	1,129	8,812	12,580	14,290	1	17
Elementary [2]	351	2,988	4,269	5,154	1	10
Junior high [3]	166	1,503	2,497	3,004	1	22
Senior high [4]	606	4,292	5,770	6,263	4	37
Students represented (1,000)	1,906	4,668	6,740	7,946	4	18
Schools with cable [1]	(NA)	47,745	58,652	62,593	(NA)	74
Elementary [2]	(NA)	27,923	35,325	37,730	(NA)	73
Junior high [3]	(NA)	9,266	10,696	11,416	(NA)	83
Senior high [4]	(NA)	10,296	12,198	13,089	(NA)	78
Students represented (1,000)	(NA)	27,324	33,510	35,770	(NA)	80

NA Not available. [1] Includes schools for special education and adult education, not shown separately. [2] Includes K-12, preschool, preschool through 3, K-6, and K-8. [3] Includes schools with grade spans of 4-8, 7-8, and 7-9. [4] Includes 7-12, 9-12, 10-12, vocational technical, and alternative high schools.

Source: Quality Education Data, Inc., Denver, CO, *Technology in Public Schools*, annual.

No. 265. Children and Youth with Disabilities Served by Selected Programs: 1989 to 1994

[**For school year ending in year shown.** Excludes outlying areas. For persons age 6 to 21 years old served under IDEA (Individuals with Disabilities Act), Part B and Chapter 1 of ESEA (Elementary and Secondary Education Act), SOP (State Operated Program)]

ITEM	1989	1990	1991	1992	1993	1994
All Conditions (1,000)	4,173.5	4,219.5	4,320.3	4,459.2	4,586.2	4,730.4
PERCENT DISTRIBUTION						
Learning disabilities	47.8	48.6	49.3	50.1	51.3	50.9
Speech impairments	23.1	23.1	22.8	22.3	21.7	21.4
Mental retardation	13.8	13.0	12.4	12.0	11.3	11.3
Emotional disturbance	8.9	9.0	9.0	8.9	8.7	8.7
Hearing impairments	1.4	1.3	1.3	1.3	1.3	1.3
Orthopedically impairments	1.1	1.1	1.1	1.1	1.1	1.2
Other health impairments	1.2	1.2	1.3	1.3	1.4	1.7
Visually impaired	0.5	0.5	0.5	0.5	0.5	0.5
Multiple disabilities	2.0	2.0	2.2	2.2	2.2	2.3
Deaf-blind	(Z)	(Z)	(Z)	(Z)	(Z)	(Z)
Autism	(NA)	(NA)	(NA)	0.1	0.3	0.4
Traumatic brain injury	(NA)	(NA)	(NA)	(Z)	0.1	0.1

Z less than .05 percent. NA Not available.

Source: U.S. Department of Education, Office of Special Education Programs, Data Analysis System (DANS).

No. 266. Children and Youth With Disabilities, by Age and Educational Environment: 1992

[For school year ending in year shown. Covers children 3 to 21 served under IDEA, Part B and Chapter 1 of ESEA (SOP); see headnote, table 265]

ENVIRONMENT	NUMBER (1,000)					PERCENT DISTRIBUTION			
	Total	3-5 years old	6-11 years old	12-17 years old	18-21 years	3-5 years old	6-11 years old	12-17 years old	18-21 years old
Total.	4,810.7	372.9	2,326.1	1,885.5	226.3	100.0	100.0	100.0	100.0
Regular class [1]	1,731.8	173.2	1,072.6	443.9	42.1	46.5	46.1	23.5	18.6
Resource room [2]	1,648.0	41.4	717.8	811.4	77.5	11.1	30.9	43.0	34.2
Separate class [3]	1,149.3	108.4	459.1	510.3	71.6	29.1	19.7	27.1	31.6
Separate school facility:									
Public	128.4	18.0	36.8	53.9	19.7	4.8	1.6	2.9	8.7
Private	88.2	26.3	27.1	28.9	6.0	7.0	1.2	1.5	2.7
Separate residential facility:									
Public	28.9	0.9	5.8	16.6	5.5	0.2	0.2	0.9	2.4
Private	11.6	0.3	2.1	7.2	2.1	0.1	0.1	0.4	0.9
Correctional facility [4]	10.4	(NA)	(NA)	(NA)	(NA)	(NA)	(NA)	(NA)	(NA)
Home/hospital	24.4	4.4	4.8	13.2	2.0	1.2	0.2	0.7	0.9

NA Not available. [1] Receives special education and related services outside the regular classroom for less than 21 percent of the school day. [2] Receives special education and related services outside the regular classroom between 21 and 60 percent of the school day. [3] Receives special education and related services outside the regular classroom for more than 60 percent of the school day. [4] Students in correctional facilities are also distributed by type environment, but not duplicated in the total.
Source: U.S. Department of Education, Office of Special Education Programs, Data Analysis System (DANS).

No. 267. Catholic Elementary and Secondary Schools: 1960 to 1994

[As of **October 1**. Regular sessions only. See also *Historical Statistics, Colonial Times to 1970*, series H 535-544]

ITEM	Unit	1960	1970	1975	1980	1985	1990	1991	1992	1993	1994
Elementary schools. . .	Number	10,501	9,362	8,340	8,043	7,806	7,291	7,239	7,174	7,114	7,055
Pupils enrolled	1,000. .	4,373	3,359	2,525	2,269	2,057	1,884	1,964	1,984	1,992	2,004
Teachers, total [1] . . .	1,000. .	108	112	99	97	97	91	109	110	112	118
Religious	1,000. .	79	52	35	25	18	11	12	11	12	11
Lay	1,000. .	29	60	64	72	79	80	96	98	100	107
Secondary schools . . .	Number	2,392	1,981	1,653	1,516	1,430	1,296	1,269	1,249	1,231	1,238
Pupils enrolled	1,000. .	880	1,008	890	837	762	592	587	584	585	615
Teachers, total [1] . . .	1,000. .	44	54	50	49	50	40	44	45	45	47
Religious	1,000. .	33	28	20	14	11	6	6	6	7	6
Lay	1,000. .	11	26	30	35	39	34	37	38	38	40

[1] Beginning 1991, includes part-time teachers.
Source: National Catholic Educational Association, (NCEA) Washington, DC; from the NCEA Data Bank—*U.S. Catholic Schools l967-1968*, (copyright) and *U.S. Catholic Elementary and Secondary Schools 1994-1995 Annual Statistical Report on Schools, Enrollment & Staffing*, NCEA, annual (copyright); and NCEA/Ganley's *Catholic Schools in America*, 1995 edition, annual (copyright).

No. 268. Private Elementary and Secondary School Teachers—Selected Characteristics: 1993-94

[For school year. Based on survey and subject to sampling error; for details, see source. See table 253 for similar data on public school teachers]

CHARACTERISTIC	Unit	AGE				SEX		RACE/ETHNICITY		
		Under 30 years old	30 to 39 years old	40 to 49 years old	Over 50 years old	Male	Female	White [1]	Black [1]	His-panic
Total teachers [2] . . .	1,000. . .	102	109	116	52	93	285	348	12	12
Highest degree held:										
Bachelor's	Percent .	74.5	57.7	53.1	44.0	47.3	62.8	59.4	55.8	57.4
Master's	Percent .	14.9	31.0	35.9	43.3	40.6	26.3	30.2	26.4	19.9
Education specialist .	Percent .	1.7	3.1	3.4	3.7	2.6	3.0	2.6	4.8	4.4
Doctorate	Percent .	0.5	1.6	2.2	3.0	4.3	0.8	1.6	1.0	2.3
Full-time teaching experience:										
Less than 3 years . .	Percent .	42.9	19.1	9.5	6.6	21.7	20.6	20.4	26.9	25.5
3 to 9 years	Percent .	54.3	35.3	25.2	10.2	28.2	35.8	33.6	34.9	41.8
10 to 20 years.	Percent .	2.7	44.6	42.1	22.9	28.7	29.9	30.0	27.9	21.6
20 years or more . .	Percent .	(Z)	1.0	23.2	60.3	21.4	13.7	16.0	10.3	11.1
Full-time teachers	1,000. . .	87	83	92	40	72	230	278	9	10
Earned income	Dol.	19,776	23,700	25,225	26,437	28,948	21,657	23,415	22,532	22,013
Salary	Dol.	18,052	22,193	23,999	25,362	26,120	20,669	22,000	20,796	20,672

Z Less than .05 percent. [1] Non-Hispanic. [2] Includes teachers with no degrees and associates degrees, not shown separately.
Source: U.S. National Center for Education Statistics, *Digest of Education Statistics*, 1995.

No. 269. Private Elementary and Secondary Schools—Enrollment and Tuition, by Orientation: 1993-94

[For school year ending in year shown. Based on survey and subject to sampling error; for details see source]

CHARACTERISTIC	ENROLLMENT (1,000)				SCHOOLS			
	Total	Catholic	Other religious	Non-sectarian	Total	Catholic	Other religious	Non-sectarian
Total	4,970.6	2,516.1	1,686.1	768.5	26,093	8,351	12,180	5,563
School enrollment:								
Less than 150 students	890.3	168.2	509.0	213.1	14,155	1,572	8,499	4,084
150 to 299 students.	1,482.2	853.1	467.7	161.3	6,820	3,815	2,232	773
300 to 499 students.	1,243.6	719.0	359.3	165.3	3,272	1,885	973	414
500 to 749 students.	736.1	432.6	196.8	106.7	1,228	729	327	172
750 or more students.	618.5	343.2	153.3	122.0	619	350	149	120
Percent minority students:								
Less than 5 percent.	1,855.4	876.6	774.1	204.7	10,750	3,152	6,137	1,461
5 percent, less than 20 percent	1,620.4	761.7	502.8	355.8	7,482	2,376	3,070	2,036
20 percent, less than 50 percent	704.4	375.8	189.6	139.0	3,785	1,095	1,395	1,295
50 percent or more	790.5	502.0	219.6	68.9	4,076	1,727	1,578	771
Average annual tuition (dol.):								
Total	(X)	(X)	(X)	(X)	3,116	2,178	2,915	6,631
Elementary	(X)	(X)	(X)	(X)	2,138	1,628	2,606	4,693
Secondary	(X)	(X)	(X)	(X)	4,578	3,643	5,261	9,525
Combined.	(X)	(X)	(X)	(X)	4,266	4,153	2,831	7,056

X Not applicable.

Source: U.S. National Center for Education Statistics, *Digest of Education Statistics*, 1995.

No. 270. High School Dropouts, by Race and Hispanic Origin: 1973 to 1994

[In percent. As of October]

ITEM	1973	1975	1980	1985	1987 [1]	1988	1989	1990	1991	1992	1993	1994
EVENT DROPOUTS [2]												
Total [3]	6.3	5.8	6.0	5.2	4.1	4.8	4.5	4.0	4.0	4.3	4.2	5.0
White.	5.7	5.4	5.6	4.8	3.7	4.7	3.9	3.8	3.7	4.1	4.1	4.7
Male.	6.1	5.0	6.4	4.9	4.1	5.1	4.1	4.1	3.6	3.8	4.1	4.6
Female	5.3	5.8	4.9	4.7	3.4	4.3	3.8	3.5	3.8	4.4	4.1	4.9
Black	10.1	8.7	8.3	7.7	6.4	6.3	7.7	5.1	6.2	4.9	5.4	6.2
Male.	12.0	8.3	8.0	8.3	6.2	6.7	6.9	4.1	5.5	3.3	5.7	6.5
Female	8.4	9.0	8.5	7.2	6.4	6.0	8.6	6.0	7.0	6.7	5.0	5.7
Hispanic [4]	10.0	10.9	11.5	9.7	5.6	10.5	7.7	8.0	7.3	7.9	5.4	9.2
Male.	7.9	10.1	16.9	9.3	5.0	12.3	7.6	8.7	10.4	5.8	5.7	8.4
Female	12.0	11.6	6.9	9.8	6.2	8.4	7.7	7.2	4.8	8.6	5.0	10.1
STATUS DROPOUTS [5]												
Total [3]	15.7	15.6	15.6	13.9	14.5	14.6	14.4	13.6	14.2	12.7	12.7	13.3
White.	14.2	13.9	14.4	13.5	14.2	14.2	14.1	13.5	14.2	12.2	12.2	12.7
Male.	13.8	13.5	15.7	14.7	15.1	15.4	15.4	14.2	15.4	13.3	13.0	13.6
Female	14.5	14.2	13.2	12.3	13.2	13.0	12.8	12.8	13.1	11.1	11.5	11.7
Black	26.5	27.3	23.5	17.6	17.0	17.7	16.4	15.1	15.6	16.3	16.4	15.5
Male.	25.9	27.8	26.0	18.8	18.7	18.9	18.6	13.6	15.4	15.5	15.6	17.5
Female	27.1	26.9	21.5	16.6	15.4	16.6	14.5	16.2	15.8	17.1	17.2	13.7
Hispanic [4]	38.9	34.9	40.3	31.5	32.8	39.6	37.7	37.3	39.6	33.9	32.7	34.7
Male.	36.5	32.6	42.6	35.8	34.5	40.2	40.3	39.8	44.4	38.4	34.7	36.1
Female	41.3	36.8	38.1	27.0	30.8	38.8	35.0	34.5	34.5	29.6	31.0	33.1

[1] Beginning 1987 reflects new editing procedures for cases with missing data on school enrollment.   [2] Percent of students who drop out in a single year without completing high school. For grades 10 to 12.   [3] Includes other races, not shown separately.   [4] Persons of Hispanic origin may be of any race.   [5] Percent of the population who have not completed high school and are not enrolled, regardless of when they dropped out. For persons 18 to 24 years old.

Source: U.S. Bureau of the Census, *Current Population Reports*, P20-487.

No. 271. High School Dropouts by Age, Race, and Hispanic Origin: 1970 to 1994

[As of **October. For persons 14 to 24 years old.** See table 273 for definition of dropouts]

AGE AND RACE	NUMBER OF DROPOUTS (1,000)					PERCENT OF POPULATION				
	1970	1980	1985	1990	1994	1970	1980	1985	1990	1994
Total dropouts [1][2]	4,670	5,212	4,456	3,854	3820	12.2	12.0	10.6	10.1	9.5
16 to 17 years	617	709	505	418	362	8.0	8.8	7.0	6.3	4.9
18 to 21 years	2,138	2,578	2,095	1,921	1903	16.4	15.8	14.1	13.4	13.7
22 to 24 years	1,770	1,798	1,724	1,458	1462	18.7	15.2	14.1	13.8	12.9
White [2]	3,577	4,169	3,583	3,127	2910	10.8	11.3	10.3	10.1	9.1
16 to 17 years	485	619	424	334	282	7.3	9.2	7.1	6.4	4.9
18 to 21 years	1,618	2,032	1,678	1,516	1411	14.3	14.7	13.6	13.1	12.8
22 to 24 years	1,356	1,416	1,372	1,235	1142	16.3	14.0	13.3	14.0	12.5
Black [2]	1,047	934	748	611	629	22.2	16.0	12.6	10.9	10.3
16 to 17 years	125	80	70	73	51	12.8	6.9	6.5	6.9	4.2
18 to 21 years	500	486	376	345	367	30.5	23.0	17.5	16.0	17.6
22 to 24 years	397	346	279	185	201	37.8	24.0	17.8	13.5	12.7
Hispanic [2][3]	(NA)	919	820	1,122	1359	(NA)	29.5	23.3	26.8	25.4
16 to 17 years	(NA)	92	97	89	98	(NA)	16.6	14.6	12.9	11.0
18 to 21 years	(NA)	470	335	502	608	(NA)	40.3	29.3	32.9	31.4
22 to 24 years	(NA)	323	365	523	616	(NA)	40.6	33.9	42.8	38.8

NA Not available.   [1] Includes other groups not shown separately.   [2] Includes persons 14 to 15 years, not shown separately. [3] Persons of Hispanic origin may be of any race.

Source: U.S. Bureau of the Census, *Current Population Reports*, P20-487; and earlier reports.

No. 272. Enrollment Status, by Race, Hispanic Origin, and Sex: 1975 and 1994

[As of **October. For persons 18 to 21 years old.** For the civilian noninstitutional population. Based on the Current Population Survey; see text, section 1 and Appendix III]

CHARACTERISTIC	TOTAL PERSONS 18 TO 21 YEARS OLD (1,000)		PERCENT DISTRIBUTION							
			Enrolled in high school		High school graduates				Not high school graduates	
					Total		In college			
	1975	1994	1975	1994	1975	1994	1975	1994	1975	1994
Total [1]	15,693	13,927	5.7	8.7	78.0	77.5	33.5	43.6	16.3	13.7
White	13,448	11,038	4.7	7.9	80.6	79.2	34.6	45.5	14.7	12.8
Black	1,997	2,081	12.5	12.4	60.4	69.7	24.9	31.6	27.0	17.6
Hispanic [2]	899	1,937	12.0	13.7	57.2	54.6	24.4	23.5	30.8	31.4
Male [1]	7,584	6,923	7.4	10.5	76.6	74.5	35.4	40.9	15.9	14.8
White	6,545	5,523	6.2	9.7	79.7	76.3	36.9	42.6	14.1	13.8
Black	911	1,009	15.9	14.1	55.0	65.3	23.9	29.0	29.0	20.2
Hispanic [2]	416	1,009	17.3	16.7	54.6	50.0	25.2	20.2	27.9	32.8
Female [1]	8,109	7,003	4.2	6.9	79.2	80.4	31.8	46.4	16.6	12.5
White	6,903	5,515	3.2	6.1	81.4	82.0	32.4	48.5	15.3	11.7
Black	1,085	1,072	9.7	10.8	65.0	73.9	25.8	34.0	25.4	15.2
Hispanic [2]	484	928	7.6	10.7	59.3	59.5	23.6	27.0	33.1	29.8

[1] Includes other races not shown separately.   [2] Persons of Hispanic origin may be of any race.

Source: U.S. Bureau of the Census, *Current Population Reports*, P20-487; and earlier reports.

No. 273. Employment Status of High School Graduates and School Dropouts: 1980 to 1993

[**In thousands, except percent**. As of **October.** For civilian noninstitutional population 16 to 24 years old. Based on Current Population Survey; see text, section 1, and Appendix III]

EMPLOYMENT STATUS, SEX, AND RACE	GRADUATES [1]				DROPOUTS [2]			
	1980	1985	1990	1993	1980	1985	1990	1993
Civilian population	11,622	10,381	8,370	6,819	5,254	4,323	3,800	3,390
In labor force	9,795	8,825	7,107	5,652	3,549	2,920	2,506	2,084
Percent of population	84.3	85.0	84.9	82.9	67.5	67.5	66.0	61.5
Employed	8,567	7,707	6,279	4,969	2,651	2,165	1,993	1,658
Percent of labor force	87.5	87.3	88.3	87.9	74.7	74.1	79.5	79.6
Unemployed	1,228	1,118	828	683	898	755	513	426
Unemployment rate, total [3]	12.5	12.7	11.7	12.1	25.3	25.9	20.5	20.4
Male	13.5	12.5	11.1	12.2	23.5	23.9	18.8	17.5
Female	11.5	12.9	12.3	11.9	28.7	29.8	23.5	26.8
White	10.8	9.8	9.0	10.6	21.6	23.6	17.0	18.3
Black	26.1	29.4	26.0	21.1	43.9	41.5	43.3	34.4
Not in labor force	1,827	1,556	1,262	1,167	1,705	1,403	1,294	1,305
Percent of population	15.7	15.0	15.1	17.1	32.5	32.5	34.1	38.5

[1] For persons not enrolled in college who have completed 4 years of high school only.   [2] For persons not in regular school and who have not completed the 12th grade nor received a general equivalency degree.   [3] Includes other races not shown separately.

Source: U.S. Bureau of Labor Statistics, Bulletin 2307, *News*, USDL 94-252, May 20, 1994; and unpublished data.

No. 274. Scholastic Assessment Test (SAT) Scores and Characteristics of College-Bound Seniors: 1967 to 1995

[For school year ending in year shown. Data are for the SAT I: Reasoning Tests. Prior to 1994, named Scholastic Aptitude Test]

TYPE OF TEST AND CHARACTERISTIC	Unit	1967	1970	1975	1980	1985	1990	1992	1993	1994	1995
TEST SCORES [1]											
Verbal, total [2]	Point . . .	466	460	434	424	431	424	423	424	423	428
Male	Point . . .	463	459	437	428	437	429	428	428	425	429
Female	Point . . .	468	461	431	420	425	419	419	420	421	426
Math, total [2]	Point . . .	492	488	472	466	475	476	476	478	479	482
Male	Point . . .	514	509	495	491	499	499	499	502	501	503
Female	Point . . .	467	465	449	443	452	455	456	457	460	463
PARTICIPANTS											
Total	1,000 . . .	(NA)	(NA)	996	992	977	1,026	1,034	1,044	1,050	1,068
Male	Percent .	(NA)	(NA)	49.9	48.2	48.3	47.8	47.6	47.4	46.9	46.4
White	Percent .	(NA)	(NA)	86.0	82.1	81.0	73.0	71.5	70.4	69.4	69.2
Black	Percent .	(NA)	(NA)	7.9	9.1	7.5	10.0	10.4	10.8	10.8	10.7
Obtaining scores [1] of—											
600 or above:											
Verbal	Percent .	(NA)	(NA)	7.9	7.2	7.9	7.4	7.3	7.8	7.6	8.3
Math	Percent .	(NA)	(NA)	15.6	15.1	17.1	18.4	18.1	18.8	18.9	21.5
Below 400:											
Verbal	Percent .	(NA)	(NA)	37.8	41.8	39.4	41.2	41.3	41.3	42.3	40.2
Math	Percent .	(NA)	(NA)	28.5	30.2	28.2	28.4	28.2	27.7	27.0	28.4
Selected intended area of study:											
Business and commerce	Percent .	(NA)	(NA)	11.5	18.6	21.0	21.0	16.8	15.0	13.8	13.3
Engineering	Percent .	(NA)	(NA)	6.7	11.1	11.7	10.0	10.5	10.2	9.4	8.8
Social science	Percent .	(NA)	(NA)	7.7	7.8	7.5	13.0	12.1	12.2	12.1	11.6
Education	Percent .	(NA)	(NA)	9.1	6.1	4.7	7.0	8.1	8.0	8.0	8.1
SAT average [1] by high school rank:											
Top tenth	Point . . .	(NA)	(NA)	(NA)	539	547	549	549	550	549	556
Second tenth	Point . . .	(NA)	(NA)	(NA)	470	482	481	480	481	481	485
Second fifth	Point . . .	(NA)	(NA)	(NA)	431	442	438	438	439	439	441
Third fifth	Point . . .	(NA)	(NA)	(NA)	386	396	392	392	393	394	394

NA Not available. [1] Minimum score 200; maximum score, 800. [2] 1967 and 1970 are estimates based on total number of persons taking SAT.

Source: College Entrance Examination Board, New York, NY, *National College-Bound Senior*, annual (copyright).

No. 275. American College Testing (ACT) Program Scores and Characteristics of College-Bound Students: 1967 to 1995

[For academic year ending in year shown. Except as indicated, test scores and characteristics of college-bound students. Through 1985, data based on 10 percent sample; thereafter, based on all ACT tested seniors]

TYPE OF TEST AND CHARACTERISTIC	Unit	1967	1970	1975	1980	1985	1990 [1]	1992 [1]	1993 [1]	1994 [1]	1995 [1]
TEST SCORES [2]											
Composite	Point . . .	19.9	18.6	18.5	18.5	18.6	20.6	20.6	20.7	20.8	20.8
Male	Point . . .	20.3	19.5	19.3	19.3	19.4	21.0	20.9	21.0	20.9	21.0
Female	Point . . .	19.4	17.8	17.9	17.8	17.9	20.3	20.5	20.5	20.7	20.7
English	Point . . .	18.5	17.7	17.9	17.8	18.1	20.5	20.2	20.3	20.3	20.2
Male	Point . . .	17.6	17.1	17.3	17.3	17.6	20.1	19.8	19.8	19.8	19.8
Female	Point . . .	19.4	18.3	18.3	18.2	18.6	20.9	20.6	20.6	20.7	20.6
Math	Point . . .	20.0	17.6	17.4	17.3	17.2	19.9	20.0	20.1	20.2	20.2
Male	Point . . .	21.1	19.3	18.9	18.9	18.6	20.7	20.7	20.8	20.8	20.9
Female	Point . . .	18.8	16.2	16.2	16.0	16.0	19.3	19.5	19.6	19.6	19.7
Reading [3]	Point . . .	19.7	17.4	17.2	17.2	17.4	(NA)	21.1	21.2	21.2	21.3
Male	Point . . .	20.3	18.7	18.2	18.3	18.3	(NA)	21.1	21.2	21.1	21.1
Female	Point . . .	19.0	16.4	16.4	16.4	16.6	(NA)	21.1	21.2	21.4	21.4
Science reasoning [4]	Point . . .	20.8	21.1	21.1	21.0	21.2	(NA)	20.7	20.8	20.9	21.0
Male	Point . . .	21.6	22.4	22.4	22.3	22.6	(NA)	21.4	21.5	21.6	21.6
Female	Point . . .	20.0	20.0	20.0	20.0	20.0	(NA)	20.1	20.3	20.4	20.5
PARTICIPANTS [5]											
Total	1,000 . . .	788	714	822	836	739	817	832	876	892	945
Male	Percent .	52	46	45	45	46	46	45	45	45	44
White	Percent .	(NA)	77	83	83	82	79	80	80	79	80
Black	Percent .	4	7	8	8	8	9	9	9	9	9
Obtaining composite scores [6] of— 27 or above	Percent .	14	14	13	13	14	12	12	12	13	13
18 or below	Percent .	21	33	33	33	32	35	35	35	34	34
Planned educational major:											
Business [7]	Percent .	18	21	20	19	21	20	17	15	14	14
Engineering	Percent .	8	6	8	10	9	9	11	10	9	9
Social science [8]	Percent .	10	9	6	6	7	10	10	10	9	9
Education	Percent .	16	12	9	7	6	8	9	9	10	9

NA Not available. [1] Beginning 1990, not comparable with previous years because a new version of the ACT was introduced. Estimated average composite scores for prior years: 1989, 20.6; 1988, 1987, and 1986, 20.8. [2] Minimum score, 1; maximum score, 36. [3] Prior to 1990, social studies; data not comparable with previous years. [4] Prior to 1990, natural sciences; data not comparable with previous years. [5] Beginning 1985, data are for seniors who graduated in year shown and had taken the ACT in their junior or senior years. [6] Prior to 1990, 26 or above and 15 or below. [7] Includes political and persuasive (e.g. sales) fields through 1975; thereafter, business and commerce. [8] Includes religion through 1975.

Source: The American College Testing Program, Iowa City, IA, *High School Profile Report*, annual.

No. 276. Proficiency Test Scores for Selected Subjects, by Characteristic: 1977 to 1992

[Based on The National Assessment of Educational Progress Tests which are administered to a representative sample of students in public and private schools. Test scores can range from 0 to 500. For details, see source]

TEST AND YEAR	Total	SEX		RACE		His-panic origin	PARENTAL EDUCATION				
		Male	Fe-male	White [1]	Black [1]		Less than high school	High school	More than high school		
									Total	Some college	College graduate
READING											
9 year olds:											
1979-80	215	210	220	221	189	190	194	213	226	(NA)	(NA)
1983-84	211	208	214	218	186	187	195	209	223	(NA)	(NA)
1987-88	212	208	216	218	189	194	193	211	220	(NA)	(NA)
1989-90	209	204	215	217	182	189	193	209	218	(NA)	(NA)
1991-92	211	206	215	218	185	192	195	207	220	(NA)	(NA)
13 year olds:											
1979-80	259	254	263	264	233	237	239	254	271	(NA)	(NA)
1983-84	257	253	262	263	236	240	240	253	268	(NA)	(NA)
1987-88	258	252	263	261	243	240	247	253	265	(NA)	(NA)
1989-90	257	251	263	262	242	238	241	251	267	(NA)	(NA)
1991-92	260	254	265	266	238	239	239	252	270	(NA)	(NA)
17 year olds:											
1979-80	286	282	289	293	243	261	262	278	290	(NA)	(NA)
1983-84	289	284	294	295	264	268	269	281	301	(NA)	(NA)
1987-88	290	286	294	295	274	271	267	282	300	(NA)	(NA)
1989-90	290	284	297	297	267	275	270	283	300	(NA)	(NA)
1991-92	290	284	296	297	261	271	271	281	299	(NA)	(NA)
WRITING [2]											
4th graders:											
1983-84	204	201	208	211	182	189	179	192	217	208	218
1987-88	206	199	213	215	173	190	194	199	212	211	212
1989-90	202	195	209	211	171	184	186	197	210	214	209
1991-92	207	198	216	217	175	189	191	202	212	201	214
8th graders:											
1983-84	267	258	276	272	247	247	258	261	276	271	278
1987-88	264	254	274	269	246	250	254	258	271	275	271
1989-90	257	246	268	262	239	246	246	253	265	267	265
1991-92	274	264	285	279	258	265	258	268	283	280	284
11th graders:											
1983-84	290	281	299	297	270	259	274	284	299	298	300
1987-88	291	282	299	296	275	274	276	285	298	296	299
1989-90	287	276	298	293	268	277	268	278	296	292	298
1991-92	287	279	296	294	263	274	271	278	295	292	296
MATHEMATICS											
9 year olds:											
1977-78	219	217	220	224	192	203	200	219	231	230	231
1985-86	222	222	222	227	202	205	201	218	231	229	231
1989-90	230	229	230	235	208	214	210	226	237	236	238
1991-92	230	231	228	235	208	212	217	222	236	237	236
13 year olds:											
1977-78	264	264	265	272	230	238	245	263	280	273	284
1985-86	269	270	268	274	249	254	252	263	278	274	280
1989-90	270	271	270	276	249	255	253	263	279	277	280
1991-92	273	274	272	279	250	259	256	263	281	278	283
17 year olds:											
1977-78	300	304	297	306	268	276	280	294	313	305	317
1985-86	302	305	299	308	279	283	279	293	310	305	314
1989-90	305	306	303	310	289	284	285	294	313	308	316
1991-92	307	309	305	312	286	292	286	298	313	308	316
SCIENCE											
9 year olds:											
1976-77	220	221	218	230	175	192	199	223	233	237	232
1985-86	224	230	221	232	196	199	204	220	235	236	235
1989-90	229	235	227	238	196	206	210	226	236	238	236
1991-92	231	235	227	239	200	205	217	222	238	237	239
13 year olds:											
1976-77	247	251	244	256	208	213	224	245	264	260	266
1985-86	251	256	247	259	222	226	229	245	262	258	264
1989-90	255	259	252	264	226	232	233	247	266	263	268
1991-92	258	260	256	267	224	238	234	246	268	266	269
17 year olds:											
1976-77	290	297	282	298	240	262	265	284	304	296	309
1985-86	289	295	282	298	253	259	258	277	300	295	304
1989-90	290	296	285	301	253	262	261	276	302	297	306
1991-92	294	299	289	304	256	270	262	280	304	296	308

NA Not available.   [1] Non-Hispanic. [2] Writing scores revised from previous years; previous writing scores were recorded on a 0 to 400 rather than 0 to 500 scale.

Source: U.S. National Center for Education Statistics, *NAEP Trends in Academic Progress*, Report No. 23-TR01, July 1994.

No. 277. Public High School Graduates, by State: 1980 to 1995

[In thousands. For school year ending in year shown]

STATE	1980	1985	1988	1989	1990	1991	1992	1993	1994, est.	1995, est.
U.S.....	2,747.7	2,414.0	2,500.2	2,458.8	2,320.3	2,234.9	2,226.0	2,233.2	2,224.8	2,299.7
AL.......	45.2	40.0	43.8	43.4	40.5	39.0	38.7	36.0	34.4	37.1
AK.......	5.2	5.2	5.9	5.6	5.4	5.5	5.5	5.5	5.8	5.9
AZ.......	28.6	27.9	29.8	31.9	32.1	31.3	31.3	31.7	30.1	31.2
AR.......	29.1	26.3	27.8	27.9	26.5	25.7	25.8	25.7	24.8	25.8
CA.......	249.2	225.4	249.6	244.6	236.3	234.2	244.6	249.3	258.0	262.0
CO.......	36.8	32.3	36.0	35.5	33.0	31.3	31.1	31.8	32.3	33.1
CT.......	37.7	32.1	32.4	30.9	27.9	27.3	27.1	26.8	26.8	26.8
DE.......	7.6	5.9	6.0	6.1	5.6	5.2	5.3	5.5	5.2	5.2
DC.......	5.0	3.9	3.9	3.6	3.6	3.4	3.4	3.1	2.9	3.1
FL.......	87.3	81.1	89.2	90.8	88.9	87.4	93.7	89.4	88.0	90.3
GA.......	61.6	58.7	61.8	61.9	56.6	60.1	57.7	57.6	58.3	57.8
HI.......	11.5	10.1	10.6	10.4	10.3	9.0	9.2	8.9	9.9	9.9
ID.......	13.2	12.1	12.4	12.5	12.0	12.0	12.7	13.0	13.3	13.9
IL.......	135.6	117.0	119.1	116.7	108.1	103.3	102.7	103.6	102.1	105.8
IN.......	73.1	63.3	64.0	63.6	60.0	57.9	56.6	57.6	55.1	59.0
IA.......	43.4	36.1	35.2	34.3	31.8	28.6	29.2	30.7	30.2	31.7
KS.......	30.9	26.0	27.0	26.8	25.4	24.4	24.1	24.7	25.1	26.1
KY.......	41.2	38.0	39.5	38.9	38.0	35.8	33.9	36.4	34.1	36.4
LA.......	46.3	39.7	39.1	37.2	36.1	33.5	32.2	33.7	34.5	36.0
ME.......	15.4	13.9	13.8	13.9	13.8	13.2	13.2	12.1	12.4	13.0
MD.......	54.3	48.3	47.2	45.8	41.6	39.0	39.7	39.5	39.1	41.4
MA.......	73.8	63.4	59.5	57.3	55.9	50.2	50.3	48.3	47.4	48.3
MI.......	124.3	105.9	106.2	101.8	93.8	88.2	87.8	85.3	83.6	88.5
MN.......	64.9	53.4	54.6	53.1	49.1	46.5	46.2	48.0	48.6	50.9
MS.......	27.6	25.3	27.9	24.2	25.2	23.7	22.9	23.6	23.4	23.1
MO.......	62.3	51.3	51.3	52.0	49.0	46.9	46.6	46.9	46.5	46.9
MT.......	12.1	10.0	10.3	10.5	9.4	9.0	9.0	9.4	9.6	10.0
NE.......	22.4	18.0	18.3	18.7	17.7	16.5	17.1	17.6	17.1	19.9
NV.......	8.5	8.6	9.4	9.5	9.5	9.4	8.8	9.0	9.5	10.0
NH.......	11.7	11.1	11.7	11.3	10.8	10.1	10.3	10.1	9.4	9.3
NJ.......	94.6	81.5	80.9	76.3	69.8	67.0	66.7	67.1	66.1	65.8
NM.......	18.4	15.6	15.9	15.5	14.9	15.2	14.8	15.2	14.9	15.1
NY.......	204.1	166.8	165.4	154.6	143.3	133.6	134.6	133.0	133.2	135.5
NC.......	70.9	67.2	67.8	70.0	64.8	62.8	61.2	60.5	57.5	59.7
ND.......	9.9	8.1	8.4	8.1	7.7	7.6	7.4	7.3	7.3	7.5
OH.......	144.2	122.3	124.5	125.0	114.5	107.5	104.5	109.2	107.7	110.1
OK.......	39.3	34.6	36.1	36.8	35.6	33.0	32.7	30.5	28.9	31.3
OR.......	29.9	26.9	28.1	26.9	25.5	24.6	25.3	26.3	26.5	27.5
PA.......	146.5	127.2	124.4	118.9	110.5	104.8	103.9	103.7	103.1	107.2
RI.......	10.9	9.2	8.9	8.6	7.8	7.7	7.9	7.6	7.5	7.8
SC.......	38.7	34.5	36.1	37.0	32.5	33.0	30.7	31.3	32.4	33.9
SD.......	10.7	8.2	8.4	8.2	7.7	7.1	7.3	8.0	8.6	8.6
TN.......	49.8	43.3	47.9	48.6	46.1	44.8	45.1	44.2	44.2	45.4
TX.......	171.4	159.2	171.4	177.0	172.5	174.3	162.3	160.5	160.1	162.4
UT.......	20.0	19.9	22.2	22.9	21.2	22.2	23.5	24.2	27.7	29.2
VT.......	6.7	5.8	6.2	6.0	6.1	5.2	5.2	5.2	5.1	5.7
VA.......	66.6	61.0	65.7	65.0	60.6	58.4	57.3	56.9	54.1	58.5
WA.......	50.4	45.4	51.8	48.9	45.9	42.5	44.4	45.3	47.9	49.6
WV.......	23.4	22.3	22.4	22.9	21.9	21.1	20.1	20.2	20.3	20.8
WI.......	69.3	58.9	58.4	55.0	52.0	49.3	48.6	50.0	48.4	53.5
WY.......	6.1	5.7	6.1	6.1	5.8	5.7	5.8	5.8	5.8	6.3

Source: U.S. National Center for Education Statistics, *Digest of Education Statistics*, annual.

No. 278. General Educational Development (GED) Credentials Issued: 1974 to 1994

[Includes outlying areas]

YEAR	GED's issued (1,000)	PERCENT DISTRIBUTION BY AGE OF TEST TAKER				
		Under 19 years old	20 to 24 years old	25 to 29 years old	30 to 34 years old	35 years old or over
1974	295	35	27	13	9	17
1975	342	33	26	14	9	18
1980	488	37	27	13	8	15
1985	427	33	26	15	10	16
1986	439	33	26	15	10	16
1987	458	33	24	15	10	18
1988	421	36	23	14	10	17
1989	364	36	24	13	10	16
1990	419	35	25	14	10	17
1991	471	33	27	14	10	17
1992	465	32	28	13	11	16
1993	476	33	27	14	11	16
1994	498	35	26	13	10	16

Source: U.S. National Center for Education Statistics, *Digest of Education Statistics*, 1995.

279. College Enrollment of Recent High School Graduates: 1960 to 1994

[For persons 16 to 24 who graduated from high school in the preceeding 12 months. Includes persons receiving GED's. Based on surveys and subject to sampling error]

YEAR	NUMBER OF HIGH SCHOOL GRADUATES (1,000)					PERCENT ENROLLED IN COLLEGE [2]				
	Total [1]	Male	Female	White	Black	Total [1]	Male	Female	White	Black
1960	1,679	756	923	1,565	(NA)	45.1	54.0	37.9	45.8	(NA)
1961	1,763	790	973	1,612	(NA)	48.0	56.3	41.3	49.5	(NA)
1962	1,838	872	966	1,660	(NA)	49.0	55.0	43.5	50.6	(NA)
1963	1,741	794	947	1,615	(NA)	45.0	52.3	39.0	45.6	(NA)
1964	2,145	997	1,148	1,964	(NA)	48.3	57.2	40.7	49.2	(NA)
1965	2,659	1,254	1,405	2,417	(NA)	50.9	57.3	45.3	51.7	(NA)
1966	2,612	1,207	1,405	2,403	(NA)	50.1	58.7	42.7	51.7	(NA)
1967	2,525	1,142	1,383	2,267	(NA)	51.9	57.6	47.2	53.0	(NA)
1968	2,606	1,184	1,422	2,303	(NA)	55.4	63.2	48.9	56.6	(NA)
1969	2,842	1,352	1,490	2,538	(NA)	53.3	60.1	47.2	55.2	(NA)
1970	2,757	1,343	1,414	2,461	(NA)	51.8	55.2	48.5	52.0	(NA)
1971	2,872	1,369	1,503	2,596	(NA)	53.4	57.6	49.7	54.0	(NA)
1972	2,961	1,420	1,541	2,614	(NA)	49.2	52.7	45.9	49.4	(NA)
1973	3,059	1,458	1,601	2,707	(NA)	46.6	50.1	43.4	48.1	(NA)
1974	3,101	1,491	1,610	2,736	(NA)	47.5	49.4	45.8	47.1	(NA)
1975	3,186	1,513	1,673	2,825	(NA)	50.7	52.6	49.0	51.2	(NA)
1976	2,987	1,450	1,537	2,640	320	48.8	47.2	50.3	48.9	41.9
1977	3,140	1,482	1,658	2,768	335	50.6	52.2	49.3	50.7	49.6
1978	3,161	1,485	1,676	2,750	352	50.1	51.0	49.3	50.1	45.7
1979	3,160	1,474	1,686	2,776	324	49.3	50.4	48.4	49.6	45.4
1980	3,089	1,500	1,589	2,682	361	49.3	46.7	51.8	49.9	41.8
1981	3,053	1,490	1,563	2,626	359	53.9	54.8	53.1	54.6	42.9
1982	3,100	1,508	1,592	2,644	384	50.6	49.0	52.1	52.0	36.5
1983	2,964	1,390	1,574	2,496	392	52.7	51.9	53.4	55.0	38.5
1984	3,012	1,429	1,583	2,514	438	55.2	56.0	54.5	57.9	40.2
1985	2,666	1,286	1,380	2,241	333	57.7	58.6	56.9	59.4	42.3
1986	2,786	1,331	1,455	2,307	386	53.8	55.9	51.9	56.0	36.5
1987	2,647	1,278	1,369	2,207	337	56.8	58.4	55.3	56.6	51.9
1988	2,673	1,334	1,339	2,187	382	58.9	57.0	60.8	60.7	45.0
1989	2,454	1,208	1,245	2,051	337	59.6	57.6	61.6	60.4	52.8
1990	2,355	1,169	1,185	1,921	341	59.9	57.8	62.0	61.5	46.3
1991	2,276	1,139	1,137	1,867	320	62.4	57.6	67.1	64.6	45.6
1992	2,398	1,216	1,182	1,900	353	61.7	59.6	63.8	63.4	47.9
1993	2,338	1,118	1,219	1,910	302	62.6	59.7	65.4	62.8	55.6
1994	2,517	1,244	1,273	2,065	318	61.9	60.6	63.2	63.6	50.9

NA Not available.   [1] Includes other races, not shown separately.   [2] As of October.

Source: U.S. Department of Education Statistics, *Digest of Education Statistics*, 1995.

No. 280. College Enrollment, by Sex and Attendance Status: 1983 to 1993

[As of **fall. In thousands**]

SEX AND AGE	1983		1988		1989		1991		1993, prel.	
	Total	Part time	Total	Part time	Total	Part time	Total	Part time	Total	Part time
Total	**12,465**	**5,204**	**13,055**	**5,619**	**13,539**	**5,878**	**14,359**	**6,244**	**14,305**	**6,178**
Male	6,024	2,264	6,002	2,340	6,190	2,450	6,502	2,573	6,427	2,537
14 to 17 years old	102	16	55	5	71	12	46	6	83	10
18 to 19 years old	1,256	158	1,290	132	1,342	113	1,217	121	1,224	138
20 to 21 years old	1,241	205	1,243	216	1,189	198	1,306	230	1,294	209
22 to 24 years old	1,158	382	1,106	378	1,090	367	1,214	378	1,260	392
25 to 29 years old	1,115	624	875	485	1,038	639	1,082	587	950	564
30 to 34 years old	570	384	617	456	603	439	664	475	661	484
35 years old and over	583	494	816	668	857	682	972	775	955	739
Female	6,441	2,940	7,053	3,278	7,349	3,428	7,857	3,672	7,877	3,641
14 to 17 years old	142	16	115	17	101	12	76	1	93	6
18 to 19 years old	1,496	179	1,536	195	1,515	184	1,496	185	1,416	172
20 to 21 years old	1,125	204	1,278	218	1,253	213	1,462	239	1,414	279
22 to 24 years old	884	378	932	403	1,104	470	1,072	412	1,263	493
25 to 29 years old	947	658	932	633	1,052	732	1,053	679	1,058	689
30 to 34 years old	721	553	698	499	750	563	804	593	811	575
35 years old and over	1,126	953	1,563	1,313	1,574	1,253	1,895	1,564	1,824	1,427

Source: U.S. National Center for Education Statistics, *Digest of Education Statistics*, annual.

No. 281. College Enrollment, by Selected Characteristics: 1978 to 1994

[In thousands. As of fall. Totals may differ from other tables because of adjustments to underreported and nonreported racial/ethnic data. Nonresident alien students are not distributed among racial/ethnic groups]

CHARACTERISTIC	1978	1980	1988	1990	1991	1992	1993, prel.	1994, prel.
Total	**11,231.2**	**12,086.8**	**13,043.1**	**13,819.5**	**14,359.0**	**14,487.4**	**14,304.8**	**14,278.8**
Male	5,621.5	5,868.1	5,998.2	6,284.4	6,501.8	6,524.0	6,427.5	6,371.9
Female	5,609.6	6,218.7	7,044.9	7,535.1	7,857.1	7,963.4	7,877.4	7,906.9
Public	8,769.8	9,456.4	10,156.4	10,844.7	11,309.6	11,384.6	11,189.1	11,133.7
Private	2,461.4	2,630.4	2,886.7	2,974.8	3,049.4	3,102.8	3,115.7	3,145.1
2-year	4,028.8	4,521.4	4,868.1	5,240.1	5,651.9	5,722.4	5,565.9	5,529.7
4-year	7,202.4	7,565.4	8,175.0	8,579.4	8,707.1	8,763.9	8,738.9	8,749.1
Undergraduate	9,665.8	10,469.1	11,304.2	11,959.2	12,439.3	12,537.7	12,324.0	12,262.6
Graduate	1,310.4	1,340.9	1,471.9	1,586.2	1,639.1	1,668.7	1,688.4	1,721.5
First professional	255.0	276.8	267.1	274.1	280.5	280.9	292.4	294.7
White [1]	9,194.0	9,833.0	10,283.2	10,723.0	10,989.8	10,874.8	10,600.0	10,415.8
Male	4,613.1	4,772.9	4,711.6	4,861.3	4,962.2	4,884.3	4,755.0	4,645.6
Female	4,580.9	5,060.1	5,571.6	5,861.7	6,027.6	5,990.5	5,845.1	5,770.3
Public	7,136.1	7,656.1	7,963.8	8,385.4	8,622.2	8,493.2	8,226.6	8,045.1
Private	2,057.9	2,176.9	2,319.4	2,337.6	2,367.5	2,381.6	2,373.5	2,370.6
2-year	3,166.9	3,558.5	3,701.5	3,954.3	4,198.8	4,131.2	3,960.6	3,850.5
4-year	6,027.1	6,274.5	6,581.6	6,768.7	6,791.0	6,743.6	6,639.5	6,565.3
Undergraduate	7,870.6	8,480.7	8,906.7	9,272.6	9,507.7	9,386.8	9,100.4	8,904.9
Graduate	1,094.1	1,104.7	1,153.2	1,228.4	1,258.0	1,267.4	1,273.8	1,286.8
First professional	229.3	247.7	223.2	222.0	224.0	220.6	225.9	224.2
Black [1]	1,054.4	1,106.8	1,129.6	1,247.1	1,335.4	1,392.7	1,412.8	1,448.2
Male	453.3	463.7	442.7	484.7	517.0	536.8	543.7	549.6
Female	601.1	643.0	686.9	762.4	818.4	855.9	869.1	898.6
Public	839.5	876.1	881.1	976.5	1,053.4	1,100.4	1,114.3	1,144.1
Private	214.9	230.7	248.5	270.6	281.9	292.3	298.5	304.1
2-year	442.6	472.5	473.3	524.3	577.6	601.6	599.0	614.6
4-year	611.8	634.3	656.3	722.8	757.7	791.1	813.7	833.6
Undergraduate	966.5	1,018.8	1,038.8	1,147.2	1,229.3	1,280.5	1,290.4	1,316.9
Graduate	76.4	75.1	76.5	83.9	88.9	94.0	102.2	110.6
First professional	11.4	12.8	14.3	16.0	17.2	18.2	20.2	20.7
Hispanic	417.3	471.7	680.0	782.6	866.6	954.9	988.8	1,056.6
Male	212.5	231.6	310.3	354.0	390.5	427.7	441.2	469.0
Female	204.7	240.1	369.6	428.6	476.0	527.2	547.6	587.6
Public	362.5	406.2	586.9	671.4	742.1	822.2	851.3	909.7
Private	54.7	65.5	93.1	111.1	124.5	132.7	137.5	146.8
2-year	226.9	255.1	383.9	424.2	483.7	545.0	556.8	593.9
4-year	190.4	216.6	296.0	358.3	382.9	409.9	432.0	462.7
Undergraduate	384.0	433.1	631.2	724.6	804.2	887.7	918.1	979.3
Graduate	28.0	32.1	39.5	47.2	50.9	55.2	57.9	63.9
First professional	5.4	6.5	9.3	10.9	11.4	12.0	12.8	13.4
American Indian [1]	77.9	83.9	92.5	102.8	113.7	119.3	121.7	127.8
Male	36.8	37.8	39.1	43.1	47.6	50.2	51.2	53.2
Female	41.0	46.1	53.4	59.7	66.1	69.1	70.5	74.6
Public	68.5	74.2	81.1	90.4	100.2	103.3	106.4	111.2
Private	9.5	9.7	11.5	12.4	13.6	15.9	15.3	16.6
2-year	43.1	47.0	50.4	54.9	62.6	64.4	63.2	66.6
4-year	34.8	36.9	42.1	47.9	51.2	54.8	58.5	61.2
Undergraduate	71.9	77.9	85.9	95.5	105.8	110.9	112.7	117.8
Graduate	4.9	5.2	5.6	6.2	6.6	7.0	7.3	8.1
First professional	1.1	0.8	1.1	1.1	1.3	1.5	1.7	1.8
Asian [1]	235.1	286.4	496.7	572.5	637.2	696.9	724.4	773.9
Male	126.3	151.3	259.2	294.9	325.1	351.5	363.1	384.8
Female	108.7	135.2	237.5	277.6	312.0	345.5	361.3	389.1
Public	195.4	239.7	405.7	461.0	516.3	565.8	586.3	621.7
Private	39.6	46.7	91.0	111.6	120.9	131.1	138.2	152.2
2-year	97.2	124.3	199.3	215.2	255.7	289.5	295.0	312.1
4-year	137.8	162.1	297.4	357.3	381.5	407.4	429.4	461.8
Undergraduate	202.8	248.7	436.6	500.5	558.7	613.0	634.2	673.7
Graduate	27.5	31.6	45.7	53.2	57.6	61.5	65.2	72.6
First professional	4.8	6.1	14.4	18.8	20.8	22.5	25.0	27.6
Nonresident alien	252.6	305.0	361.2	391.5	416.4	447.7	457.1	456.5
Male	179.5	210.8	235.3	246.3	259.4	273.1	273.4	269.7
Female	73.1	94.2	125.9	145.2	157.0	174.6	183.7	186.8
Public	167.7	204.1	237.8	260.0	275.3	299.5	304.3	301.8
Private	84.8	100.8	123.3	131.5	141.0	148.1	152.7	154.7
2-year	52.0	64.1	59.6	67.1	73.5	90.6	91.2	91.9
4-year	200.5	240.9	301.5	324.4	342.8	357.0	365.9	364.5
Undergraduate	170.1	209.9	205.0	218.7	233.6	257.9	268.2	269.9
Graduate	79.5	92.2	151.4	167.3	177.0	183.6	182.0	179.5
First professional	3.0	2.9	4.7	5.4	5.8	6.2	6.9	7.0

[1] Non-Hispanic.
Source: U.S. National Center for Education Statistics, *Digest of Education Statistics*, annual.

No. 282. College Enrollment, by Sex, Age, Race, and Hispanic Origin: 1975 to 1994

[In thousands. As of October for the civilian noninstitutional population, 14 years old and over. Based on the Current Population Survey; see text, section 1, and Appendix III]

CHARACTERISTIC	1975	1980	1985	1987[1]	1988	1989	1990	1991	1992	1993	1994
Total[2]	10,880	11,387	12,524	12,719	13,116	13,180	13,621	14,057	14,035	13,898	15,022
Male[3]	5,911	5,430	5,906	6,030	5,950	5,950	6,192	6,439	6,192	6,324	6,764
18 to 24 years	3,693	3,604	3,749	3,867	3,770	3,717	3,922	3,954	3,912	3,994	4,152
25 to 34 years	1,521	1,325	1,464	1,421	1,395	1,443	1,412	1,605	1,392	1,406	1,589
35 years old and over . .	569	405	561	625	727	716	772	832	789	873	958
Female[3]	4,969	5,957	6,618	6,689	7,166	7,231	7,429	7,618	7,844	7,574	8,258
18 to 24 years	3,243	3,625	3,788	3,826	4,021	4,085	4,042	4,218	4,429	4,199	4,576
25 to 34 years	947	1,378	1,599	1,564	1,568	1,639	1,749	1,680	1,732	1,688	1,830
35 years old and over . .	614	802	1,100	1,176	1,452	1,396	1,546	1,636	1,575	1,616	1,766
White[3]	9,546	9,925	10,781	10,731	11,140	11,243	11,488	11,686	11,710	11,434	12,222
18 to 24 years	6,116	6,334	6,500	6,483	6,659	6,631	6,635	6,813	6,916	6,763	7,118
25 to 34 years	2,147	2,328	2,604	2,468	2,448	2,597	2,698	2,661	2,582	2,505	2,735
35 years old and over . .	1,031	1,051	1,448	1,584	1,896	1,868	2,023	2,107	2,053	2,068	2,267
Male	5,263	4,804	5,103	5,104	5,078	5,136	5,235	5,304	5,210	5,222	5,524
Female	4,284	5,121	5,679	5,627	6,063	6,107	6,253	6,382	6,499	6,212	6,698
Black[3]	1,099	1,163	1,263	1,351	1,321	1,287	1,393	1,477	1,424	1,545	1,800
18 to 24 years	665	688	734	823	752	835	894	828	886	861	1,001
25 to 34 years	248	289	295	341	330	275	258	373	302	386	440
35 years old and over . .	152	156	213	155	206	146	207	257	208	284	323
Male	523	476	552	587	494	480	587	629	527	636	745
Female	577	686	712	764	827	807	807	848	897	909	1,054
Hispanic origin[3][4]	411	443	580	739	747	754	748	830	918	995	1,187
18 to 24 years	295	315	375	455	450	453	435	516	586	602	662
25 to 34 years	103	118	189	204	191	170	168	196	214	249	312
35 years old and over . .	(NA)	(NA)	(NA)	73	93	114	130	109	102	129	205
Male	218	222	279	390	355	353	364	347	388	442	529
Female	193	221	299	349	391	401	384	483	530	553	659

NA Not available.　[1] Beginning 1987, based on a revised edit and tabulation package.　[2] Includes other races not shown separately.　[3] Includes persons 14 to 17 years old, not shown separately.　[4] Persons of Hispanic origin may be of any race.

Source: U.S. Bureau of the Census, *Current Population Reports*, P20-487; and earlier reports.

No. 283. College Population, by Selected Characteristics: 1987 and 1994

[In thousands, except percent. As of October. Based on the Current Population Survey. See text, section 1, and Appendix III]

CHARACTERISTIC	Total popula-tion	ENROLLED IN COLLEGE							
		Total	Type of school			Percent enrolled full time	Percent employed		
			2-year	4-year	Graduate school		Total	Full time	Part time
Total, 1987[1]	190,058	12,719	3,648	6,656	2,415	62.6	60.4	31.7	28.7
Male	90,610	6,030	1,522	3,356	1,152	67.2	60.6	31.7	28.9
Female	99,449	6,689	2,127	3,299	1,264	58.4	60.1	31.6	28.5
White	162,757	10,731	3,039	5,617	2,075	61.6	62.2	32.6	29.6
Black	21,520	1,351	422	748	181	66.3	50.5	28.6	21.9
Hispanic origin[2]	13,687	739	307	342	90	57.3	65.5	37.0	28.6
14 to 19 years old	21,410	3,284	1,111	2,172	1	88.1	44.0	7.6	36.4
20 and 21 years old	7,078	2,642	624	1,961	58	84.4	53.3	14.5	38.8
22 to 24 years old	11,712	2,006	457	1,055	494	67.2	62.5	29.8	32.7
25 to 34 years old	42,374	2,985	851	996	1,137	36.4	74.0	55.8	18.2
35 years and older	107,484	1,802	605	471	725	22.3	83.1	62.8	20.3
Total, 1994[1]	201,148	15,022	4,208	8,202	2,612	63.7	62.9	32.4	30.4
Male	96,565	6,764	1,704	3,823	1,238	67.8	63.5	33.7	29.8
Female	104,582	8,258	2,504	4,379	1,375	60.4	62.3	31.3	31.0
White	168,874	12,222	3,368	6,680	2,173	63.2	65.2	32.9	32.3
Black	23,594	1,800	582	1,002	216	63.7	54.6	34.3	20.3
Hispanic origin[2]	18,751	1,187	474	578	136	53.9	65.3	33.7	31.6
15 to 19 years old	17,971	3,201	1,063	2,130	9	89.1	45.5	8.1	37.3
20 and 21 years old	6,981	3,028	623	2,383	21	86.0	56.7	13.4	43.3
22 to 24 years old	11,327	2,650	621	1,478	551	69.1	65.7	29.2	36.4
25 to 34 years old	41,117	3,419	1,011	1,270	1,138	44.5	71.8	52.3	19.5
35 years and older	123,752	2,725	890	942	893	27.9	76.1	60.2	15.9

[1] Includes other races, not shown separately.　[2] Persons of Hispanic origin may be of any race.

Source: U.S. Bureau of the Census, *Current Population Reports*, P20-443 and and P20-487.

No. 284. Higher Education—Summary: 1970 to 1993

[Institutions, staff, and enrollment as of fall. Finances for fiscal year ending in the following year. Covers universities, colleges, professional schools, junior and teachers colleges, both publicly and privately controlled, regular session. Includes estimates for institutions not reporting. See also Appendix III, and *Historical Statistics, Colonial Times to 1970*, series H 680, H 690-692, H 699-705, and H 710]

ITEM	Unit	1970	1980	1985	1988	1989	1990	1991	1992, est.	1993, prel.
ALL INSTITUTIONS										
Number of institutions [1].	Number .	2,556	3,231	3,340	3,565	3,535	3,559	3,601	3,638	3,632
4-year.	Number .	1,665	1,957	2,029	2,129	2,127	2,141	2,157	2,169	2,190
2-year.	Number .	891	1,274	1,311	1,436	1,408	1,418	1,444	1,469	1,442
Instructional staff—										
(Lecturer or above) [2]	1,000. . .	474	686	715	804	824	817	826	834	825
Percent full time	Percent .	78	66	64	(NA)	64	61	65	(NA)	(NA)
Total enrollment [3]	1,000. . .	8,581	12,097	12,247	13,055	13,539	13,818	14,359	14,487	14,305
Male	1,000. . .	5,044	5,874	5,818	6,002	6,190	6,284	6,502	6,524	6,427
Female	1,000. . .	3,537	6,223	6,429	7,053	7,349	7,535	7,857	7,963	7,877
4-year institutions	1,000. . .	6,262	7,571	7,716	8,180	8,388	8,579	8,707	8,765	8,739
2-year institutions	1,000. . .	2,319	4,526	4,531	4,875	5,151	5,240	5,652	5,722	5,566
Full time	1,000. . .	5,816	7,098	7,075	7,437	7,661	7,821	8,115	8,162	8,128
Part time	1,000. . .	2,765	4,999	5,172	5,619	5,878	5,998	6,244	6,325	6,177
Public	1,000. . .	6,428	9,457	9,479	10,161	10,578	10,844	11,310	11,385	11,189
Private	1,000. . .	2,153	2,640	2,768	2,894	2,961	2,975	3,049	3,103	3,116
Undergraduate [4]	1,000. . .	7,376	10,475	10,597	11,317	11,743	11,959	12,439	12,538	12,324
Men.	1,000. . .	4,254	5,000	4,962	5,138	5,311	5,380	5,571	5,583	5,484
Women	1,000. . .	3,122	5,475	5,635	6,179	6,432	6,579	6,868	6,955	6,840
First-time freshmen.	1,000. . .	2,063	2,588	2,292	2,379	2,341	2,257	2,278	2,186	2,161
First professional.	1,000. . .	173	278	274	267	274	274	281	281	292
Men.	1,000. . .	159	199	180	167	168	167	170	169	173
Women	1,000. . .	15	78	94	100	105	107	111	112	120
Graduate [4].	1,000. . .	1,031	1,343	1,376	1,472	1,522	1,586	1,639	1,669	1,688
Men.	1,000. . .	630	675	677	697	710	737	761	772	771
Women	1,000. . .	400	670	700	774	811	849	878	896	917
Current funds revenues [5]. . . .	Mil. dol .	23,879	65,585	100,438	128,502	139,635	149,766	161,396	170,881	(NA)
Tuition and fees	Mil. dol. .	5,021	13,773	23,117	30,807	33,926	37,434	41,559	45,346	(NA)
Federal government.	Mil. dol. .	4,190	9,748	12,705	15,894	17,255	18,236	19,833	21,015	(NA)
State government	Mil. dol. .	6,503	20,106	29,912	36,031	38,349	39,481	40,587	41,248	(NA)
Auxiliary enterprises.	Mil. dol. .	3,125	7,287	10,674	12,856	13,938	14,903	15,759	16,663	(NA)
Plant funds [6]	Mil. dol. .	(NA)	4,774	7,713	(NA)	(NA)	(NA)	(NA)	(NA)	(NA)
Increase in fund balance [7] . . .	Mil. dol. .	498	2,793	7,239	(NA)	(NA)	(NA)	(NA)	(NA)	(NA)
Current funds expenditures [5] .	Mil. dol .	23,375	64,053	97,536	123,867	134,656	146,088	156,189	165,241	(NA)
Educational and general [8]. . .	Mil. dol. .	17,616	50,074	76,128	96,803	105,585	114,140	121,567	128,978	(NA)
Auxiliary enterprises [9]	Mil. dol. .	2,988	7,288	10,528	12,280	13,204	14,272	14,966	15,562	(NA)
Gross addition to plant value. . .	Mil. dol. .	4,165	6,471	10,149	13,638	17,107	19,672	(NA)	(NA)	(NA)
Value of plant.	Mil. dol. .	46,054	88,761	122,261	158,693	182,609	190,355	(NA)	(NA)	(NA)
Endowment (market value). . . .	Mil. dol. .	13,714	23,465	50,281	64,155	67,979	72,049	(NA)	(NA)	(NA)
2-YEAR INSTITUTIONS										
Number of institutions [1][10]. . .	Number .	891	1,274	1,311	1,436	1,408	1,418	1,444	1,469	1,442
Public	Number .	654	945	932	984	968	972	999	1,024	1,021
Private	Number .	237	329	379	452	440	446	445	445	421
Instructional staff—										
(Lecturer or above) [2]	1,000. . .	92	192	211	(NA)	241	(NA)	235	(NA)	(NA)
Enrollment [3][4].	1,000. . .	2,319	4,526	4,531	4,875	5,151	5,240	5,652	5,722	5,566
Public	1,000. . .	2,195	4,329	4,270	4,615	4,884	4,996	5,405	5,485	5,337
Private	1,000. . .	124	198	261	260	267	244	247	238	229
Male	1,000. . .	1,375	2,047	2,002	2,090	2,217	2,232	2,401	2,413	2,345
Female	1,000. . .	945	2,479	2,529	2,785	2,934	3,008	3,250	3,309	3,220
Current funds revenue [5]	Mil. dol .	2,504	8,505	12,293	15,387	16,777	18,021	19,695	20,805	(NA)
Tuition and fees	Mil. dol. .	413	1,618	2,618	3,376	3,623	4,029	4,649	5,218	(NA)
State government	Mil. dol. .	926	3,961	5,659	6,898	7,558	8,001	8,537	8,647	(NA)
Local government	Mil. dol. .	701	1,623	2,027	2,662	2,831	3,044	3,259	3,524	(NA)
Current funds expenditures . .	Mil. dol .	2,327	8,212	11,976	14,726	16,077	17,494	18,814	19,941	(NA)
Education and general [8]	Mil. dol. .	2,073	7,608	11,118	13,676	14,936	16,270	17,462	18,578	(NA)
Instruction.	Mil. dol. .	1,205	3,764	5,398	6,617	7,236	7,903	8,547	9,018	(NA)

NA Not available.   [1] Beginning 1980, number of institutions includes count of branch campuses. Due to revised survey procedures, data beginning 1988 are not comparable with previous years.   [2] Due to revised survey methods, data beginning 1988 not comparable with previous years.   [3] Beginning 1980, branch campuses counted according to actual status, e.g., 2-year branch in 2-year category; previously a 2-year branch included in university category.   [4] Includes unclassified students. (Students taking courses for credit, but are not candidates for degrees.)   [5] Includes items not shown separately.   [6] Annual net increase in plant funds.   [7] Includes endowment, and, beginning 1980, annuity and student loans.   [8] Data for 1970 are not strictly comparable with later years.   [9] Includes activities.   [10] Beginning 1980, includes schools accredited by the National Association of Trade and Technical Schools.

Source: U.S. National Center for Education Statistics, *Digest of Education Statistics*, annual; *Projections of Education Statistics*, annual; and unpublished data.

No. 285. Colleges—Number and Enrollment, by State: 1994

[Number of institutions beginning in academic year. Opening fall enrollment of resident and extension students attending full time or part time. Excludes students taking courses for credit by mail, radio, or TV, and students in branches of U.S. institutions operated in foreign countries. See Appendix III]

STATE	Number of institutions [1]	ENROLLMENT, prel. (1,000)										
		Total	Male	Female	Public	Private	Full time	White [2]	Minority enrollment			Non-resident alien
									Total [3]	Black [2]	Hispanic	
United States. .	**3,688**	**14,280**	**6,372**	**7,907**	**11,134**	**3,145**	**8,138**	**10,416**	**3,408**	**1,448**	**1,057**	**456**
Alabama.	80	230	102	127	207	23	152	168	57	52	2	5
Alaska	9	29	12	17	28	1	12	23	5	1	1	1
Arizona.	43	275	124	150	252	23	128	203	64	9	37	7
Arkansas	35	96	41	55	86	11	67	78	16	14	1	2
California	336	1,836	834	1,002	1,583	253	864	941	810	138	343	85
Colorado.	61	241	112	130	210	32	128	195	40	8	21	6
Connecticut.	43	160	69	91	102	58	82	129	25	12	8	5
Delaware	9	44	19	25	36	8	26	35	8	6	1	1
District of Columbia .	19	78	35	42	11	67	49	38	31	24	3	8
Florida	111	634	279	355	528	106	302	434	182	80	81	19
Georgia	119	309	135	174	244	65	203	214	87	75	4	8
Hawaii	16	64	29	35	52	13	35	17	42	2	2	6
Idaho	11	60	27	33	49	11	40	55	4	(Z)	2	1
Illinois	167	731	324	407	546	185	372	522	192	93	57	18
Indiana.	78	292	133	159	228	64	190	254	30	18	6	9
Iowa	60	172	78	94	122	50	121	153	12	5	3	7
Kansas	52	171	76	94	153	18	98	145	19	8	5	6
Kentucky	62	183	76	107	152	31	119	163	16	12	1	3
Louisiana	35	204	87	117	175	28	144	136	62	52	5	5
Maine.	33	57	23	34	39	18	32	54	2	(Z)	(Z)	1
Maryland	57	266	112	154	224	43	125	180	77	56	6	9
Massachusetts.	118	417	184	233	180	237	261	327	65	23	17	24
Michigan.	109	551	243	308	467	85	279	445	90	59	11	16
Minnesota.	109	289	131	158	227	62	162	249	33	7	15	7
Mississippi	46	121	52	69	108	12	90	82	37	35	1	2
Missouri	102	294	130	164	192	102	167	248	38	26	5	8
Montana	21	40	19	21	35	5	31	34	4	(Z)	(Z)	1
Nebraska	35	116	52	64	96	20	67	105	8	3	2	3
Nevada	10	64	28	36	63	1	21	50	12	3	4	2
New Hampshire	30	63	27	36	35	28	40	59	3	1	1	1
New Jersey.	61	336	147	189	272	63	173	235	89	39	29	11
New Mexico	35	102	44	58	97	5	51	58	42	3	31	2
New York	314	1,058	456	602	604	453	675	713	303	137	97	42
North Carolina	123	369	159	210	304	66	235	276	88	73	4	5
North Dakota.	20	40	20	20	37	4	32	35	3	(Z)	(Z)	2
Ohio	157	549	248	301	418	132	342	463	70	50	8	16
Oklahoma	46	185	84	101	162	23	110	142	35	14	4	8
Oregon.	44	164	77	87	141	23	92	139	19	3	5	7
Pennsylvania	218	611	278	333	343	269	386	515	79	47	11	17
Rhode Island.	13	75	34	41	39	35	47	64	8	3	2	2
South Carolina.	59	173	74	100	149	25	107	128	42	38	1	3
South Dakota	21	38	17	21	31	7	27	34	3	(Z)	(Z)	1
Tennessee	78	243	108	135	191	52	156	196	42	36	2	5
Texas.	178	955	443	511	843	111	514	602	326	94	186	27
Utah	16	146	73	73	109	38	96	132	9	1	4	6
Vermont	22	35	15	20	21	15	24	33	2	(Z)	(Z)	1
Virginia.	93	354	155	199	293	61	199	265	82	57	7	7
Washington	62	285	127	157	245	40	172	229	47	10	10	9
West Virginia.	28	88	39	49	76	12	61	81	5	3	(Z)	2
Wisconsin.	65	304	134	170	250	54	181	269	28	13	6	7
Wyoming	9	31	13	17	30	1	18	28	2	(Z)	1	1
U.S. military [4] . .	10	51	30	22	51	-	30	40	11	5	4	1

- Represents zero.   Z Fewer than 500.   [1] Branch campuses counted as separate institutions.   [2] Non-Hispanic.
[3] Includes other races not shown separately.   [4] Service schools.

Source: U.S. National Center for Education Statistics, *Digest of Education Statistics,* annual.

No. 286. Higher Education Price Indexes: 1965 to 1994

[1983=100. For years ending June 30. Reflects prices paid by colleges and universities]

YEAR	Index, total	PERSONNEL COMPENSATION				CONTRACTED SERVICES, SUPPLIES, AND EQUIPMENT					
		Total	Professional salaries	Nonprofessional salaries	Fringe benefits	Total	Services	Supplies and materials	Equipment	Library acquisitions	Utilities
1965 ..	29.8	30.5	34.9	31.0	13.0	27.6	35.8	33.8	36.0	19.3	15.7
1970 ..	39.5	42.1	47.7	38.8	24.7	31.9	42.8	37.6	41.9	25.7	16.3
1971 ..	42.1	44.8	50.1	41.8	28.0	34.1	45.1	39.0	43.5	30.8	18.0
1972 ..	44.3	47.1	52.0	44.9	31.1	36.0	47.8	39.8	45.1	34.9	19.2
1973 ..	46.7	49.8	54.3	47.6	34.7	37.6	49.9	41.1	46.5	37.7	20.2
1974 ..	49.9	52.8	57.2	50.6	38.6	41.4	52.2	46.5	49.4	41.6	24.8
1975 ..	54.3	56.3	60.3	54.6	42.9	48.5	56.8	58.0	58.3	46.7	31.8
1976 ..	57.8	60.0	63.5	59.0	47.8	51.3	59.1	60.7	61.7	52.1	34.4
1977 ..	61.5	63.5	66.4	63.1	52.8	55.7	62.6	63.8	64.8	56.8	40.5
1978 ..	65.7	67.6	69.9	68.1	58.4	60.2	66.6	66.6	69.3	63.2	45.9
1979 ..	70.5	72.4	74.1	73.4	64.5	65.1	71.2	71.7	74.7	70.0	50.3
1980 ..	77.5	78.4	79.4	80.2	72.6	75.0	77.0	84.6	81.6	77.8	64.1
1981 ..	85.8	85.8	86.3	87.7	81.8	85.9	85.2	95.6	89.6	85.9	79.7
1982 ..	93.9	93.5	93.7	94.6	91.5	94.9	94.2	100.4	96.4	93.5	92.4
1983 ..	100.0	100.0	100.0	100.0	100.0	100.0	100.0	100.0	100.0	100.0	100.0
1984 ..	104.8	105.3	104.7	105.1	108.3	103.2	105.5	99.7	102.3	105.2	102.4
1985 ..	110.7	112.0	111.4	109.0	117.7	106.9	110.2	103.0	104.8	111.7	105.2
1986 ..	116.2	118.7	118.2	112.8	127.7	108.8	114.6	102.6	107.2	121.4	102.9
1987 ..	120.7	125.4	125.0	116.2	137.4	106.6	117.5	99.0	108.9	132.9	90.8
1988 ..	126.0	131.6	130.9	120.3	147.1	109.5	122.4	101.1	120.5	140.3	87.5
1989 ..	132.6	139.5	138.8	124.9	158.8	112.4	127.6	108.3	115.1	153.1	85.2
1990 ..	140.7	148.2	147.6	129.9	171.4	118.6	133.7	114.3	119.6	166.3	90.0
1991 ..	148.1	156.5	155.6	135.0	184.5	123.1	139.7	116.4	123.3	179.4	92.2
1992 ..	153.2	162.3	160.8	140.0	193.9	126.1	143.5	115.2	126.3	193.2	93.2
1993 ..	157.9	167.5	165.1	143.7	204.3	129.3	149.0	113.2	128.6	204.9	94.5
1994 ..	163.2	173.3	170.3	147.7	214.3	133.2	152.2	114.3	130.8	218.0	98.4

Source: Research Associates of Washington, Washington, DC, *Inflation Measures for Schools, Colleges, and Libraries,* annual (copyright).

No. 287. Institutions of Higher Education—Finances: 1980 to 1993

[In millions of dollars. For fiscal years ending in year shown. For coverage, see headnote, table 284. See also Appendix III and *Historical Statistics, Colonial Times to 1970,* series H 729-738 and H 747-749]

ITEM	1980	1985	1989	1990	1991	1992	1993 Total	1993 Public	1993 Private
Current funds revenues	58,520	92,473	128,502	139,635	149,766	161,396	170,881	108,186	62,694
Tuition and fees	11,930	21,283	30,807	33,926	37,434	41,559	45,346	19,490	25,856
Federal government.	8,902	11,509	15,894	17,255	18,236	19,833	21,015	11,655	9,360
State government	18,378	27,583	36,031	38,349	39,481	40,587	41,248	39,790	1,458
Local government	1,588	2,387	3,364	3,640	3,931	4,160	4,445	4,041	404
Private gifts, grants, and con- tracts [1]	2,808	4,896	7,061	7,781	8,361	8,977	9,660	4,330	5,330
Endowment earnings [2]	1,177	2,096	2,914	3,144	3,269	3,442	3,628	668	2,960
Educational activities [2]	1,239	2,127	3,316	3,632	4,055	4,521	5,038	3,236	1,802
Auxiliary enterprises.	6,481	10,100	12,856	13,938	14,903	15,759	16,663	10,255	6,408
Hospitals [3]	(3)	7,475	11,991	13,217	15,150	17,240	18,124	11,791	6,333
Other funds revenues [4].	6,015	3,015	4,269	4,753	4,946	5,318	5,715	2,931	2,784
Current funds expenditures [5]	56,914	89,951	123,867	134,656	146,088	156,189	165,241	104,570	60,671
Educational and general	44,543	70,061	96,803	105,585	114,140	121,567	128,978	83,211	45,767
Instruction.	18,497	28,777	38,813	42,146	45,496	47,997	50,341	34,260	16,081
Institutional support	5,054	8,587	11,529	12,674	13,726	14,475	15,250	9,050	6,200
Research	5,099	7,552	11,432	12,506	13,444	14,262	15,291	10,605	4,686
Plant operation [6]	4,700	7,345	8,740	9,458	10,063	10,347	10,784	7,077	3,707
Academic support	3,876	6,074	8,904	9,438	10,051	10,577	11,073	7,613	3,460
Libraries	1,624	2,362	3,010	3,254	3,344	3,596	3,685	2,330	1,355
Student services	2,567	4,178	5,781	6,388	7,025	7,509	8,165	5,173	2,992
Scholarships and fellowships . . .	2,200	3,670	5,919	6,656	7,551	9,060	10,148	3,728	6,421
Unrestricted funds.	905	1,962	3,283	3,854	4,445	5,206	5,949	1,745	4,204
Restricted funds	1,296	1,709	2,636	2,802	3,106	3,854	4,199	1,982	2,217
Public service	1,817	2,861	4,227	4,690	5,076	5,489	5,935	4,563	1,372
Mandatory transfers	732	1,016	1,458	1,630	1,707	1,851	1,991	1,142	849
Auxiliary enterprises [5].	6,486	10,012	12,280	13,204	14,272	14,966	15,562	10,024	5,537
Hospitals [5]	4,757	8,010	11,825	12,679	14,326	16,104	17,050	11,101	5,949
Independent operations [5]	1,128	1,868	2,959	3,187	3,350	3,552	3,652	234	3,418

[1] Private grants represent nongovernmental revenue for sponsored research and other sponsored programs; includes private contracts. [2] Sales and service of educational departments only. [3] Included in other. [4] Includes sales and services of federally funded research and development centers, and others sources. [5] Includes mandatory transfers which are primarily current expenditures for plant. [6] Includes maintenance.

Source: U.S. National Center for Education Statistics, *Digest of Education Statistics,* annual.

No. 288. Major Federal Student Financial Assistance Programs: 1970 to 1993

[**For award years July 1 of year shown to the following June 30, except as indicated.** Funds utilized exclude operating costs, etc., and represent funds given to students]

PROGRAM	Unit	1970	1980	1985	1988	1989	1990	1991	1992	1993, est.
Pell Grants:										
Number of recipients...	1,000...	(X)	2,708	2,813	3,198	3,322	3,405	3,786	4,002	3,539
Funds utilized	Mil. dol..	(X)	2,387	3,597	4,476	4,778	4,935	5,793	6,176	5,683
Average grant	dollars ..	(X)	882	1,279	1,399	1,438	1,449	1,530	1,543	1,606
Supplemental Educational Opportunity Grants: [1]										
Number of recipients...	1,000...	253.4	716.5	686.0	678.8	727.6	761.2	881.3	976.3	908.0
Funds utilized	Mil. dol..	134	368	410	423	466	503	586	651	663
Average grant	dollars ..	527	513	598	621	641	661	665	667	730
College Work-Study:										
Number of recipients...	1,000...	425.0	819.1	728.4	672.7	676.7	687.4	697.3	714.4	813.0
Funds utilized [2]	Mil. dol..	200	660	656	625	664	727	760	780	813
Average annual earnings	dollars ..	470	806	901	930	980	1,059	1,090	1,097	1,000
Perkins Loans: [3]										
Number of recipients...	1,000...	452.0	813.4	700.9	692.1	695.9	660.2	654.2	669.0	571.0
Loan funds utilized [2] ...	Mil. dol..	241	694	703	874	903	870	868	868	720
Average loan..........	dollars ..	532	853	1,003	1,262	1,297	1,318	1,326	1,333	1,261
Loans in default [4].....	Mil. dol..	(NA)	612.0	690.0	749.8	741.1	727.5	744.7	569.3	(NA)
Default rate	Percent .	(NA)	11.6	8.3	7.3	6.8	6.2	6.0	12.2	(NA)
Federal Family Education Loans [5]										
Number of loans..	1,000...	1,017	2,905	3,833	4,513	4,713	4,493	4,818	5,130	5,647
Loan funds utilized [6] ...	Mil. dol..	1,015	6,200	8,913	11,816	12,466	12,291	13,500	14,749	17,863
Average loan........	dollars ..	998	2,135	2,374	2,618	2,645	2,734	2,804	2,875	3,163
Loans in default [7]....	Mil. dol..	(NA)	1,454	4,272	8,434	10,471	13,151	16,374	19,029	21,534
Default rate [8]........	Percent .	(NA)	10.1	9.0	9.2	9.7	10.4	11.6	11.6	11.1

NA Not available.   X Not applicable.   [1] For 1970, data represents Educational Opportunity Grants Program.   [2] Includes institutional matching funds.   [3] Formerly National Direct Student Loans.   [4] Loans in default represents all loans in institutions' portfolio.   [5] Formerly Guaranteed Student Loans. Beginning with 1985, data include activity under the Stafford program, the PLUS (Parent Loans for Undergraduate Students), FISL (Federally Insured Student Loans), and SLS (Supplemental Loans Students) programs.   [6] Represents dollar amount of commitments.   [7] As of September 30 of year shown. Data are cumulative.   [8] Cumulative dollar amount of default claims to lenders, minus cumulative collections as a percent of all loans that have ever gone into repayment.

Source: U.S. Dept. of Education, Office of Postsecondary Education, unpublished data.

No. 289. Finances of Public Colleges, 1990 to 1993, and by State, 1994

[**For academic years ending in year shown.** Data provided by the State higher education finance officers]

STATE	FTE [1] enrollment (1,000)	Appropriations for current operations [2] (mil. dol.)	Net tuition revenues (mil. dol.)[3]	STATE	FTE [1] enrollment (1,000)	Appropriations for current operations [2] (mil. dol.)	Net tuition revenues (mil. dol.)[3]
Total, 1990	7,883.0	33,857.6	11,310.2	Minnesota	170.6	792.2	347.6
Total, 1991	8,068.1	35,211.9	12,474.5	Mississippi..........	101.1	319.1	202.2
Total, 1992	8,291.2	35,027.9	14,188.0	Missouri	134.4	587.7	379.1
Total, 1993	8,362.5	35,272.3	15,770.0	Montana	29.7	102.9	56.8
				Nebraska	69.8	280.2	106.7
**Total, 1994 .... **	**8,386.3**	**36,579.0**	**16,763.9**	Nevada	34.9	171.1	36.0
Alabama	183.8	613.8	374.4	New Hampshire	28.7	75.7	130.6
Alaska	16.6	159.9	29.8	New Jersey	191.0	1,080.5	439.6
Arizona	162.2	664.6	293.9	New Mexico.........	71.1	376.0	88.7
Arkansas...........	74.1	310.3	141.0	New York	438.9	2,375.8	913.0
California...........	1,270.2	5,184.7	1,253.0	North Carolina	238.4	1,300.6	319.3
Colorado...........	137.6	426.4	384.2	North Dakota	31.6	118.8	62.1
Connecticut	60.9	401.8	192.8	Ohio..............	350.4	1,252.5	1,010.3
Delaware...........	26.5	111.2	139.9	Oklahoma	115.5	493.8	153.3
District of Columbia....	8.0	66.5	8.9	Oregon............	101.9	425.4	216.8
Florida	357.5	1,686.3	521.4	Pennsylvania	301.2	1,380.4	1,221.3
Georgia	202.6	969.3	330.0	Rhode Island	26.8	113.6	105.6
Hawaii	33.0	273.1	32.5	South Carolina	129.9	461.8	300.3
Idaho	38.8	192.9	35.7	South Dakota.......	22.9	79.6	52.6
Illinois............	375.6	1,674.1	442.3	Tennessee..........	155.7	663.1	269.1
Indiana	178.4	753.5	494.3	Texas	623.7	2,656.8	886.9
Iowa.............	103.9	517.6	263.1	Utah..............	77.9	328.7	124.0
Kansas............	107.5	460.3	192.3	Vermont	15.7	35.3	127.8
Kentucky...........	119.8	425.7	199.8	Virginia	223.2	756.3	603.7
Louisiana	135.0	444.7	315.6	Washington	186.7	857.0	258.9
Maine............	28.6	157.0	83.9	West Virginia	61.1	178.1	130.6
Maryland...........	163.0	653.4	441.0	Wisconsin	185.6	976.7	485.0
Massachusetts.......	122.0	538.8	314.5	Wyoming...........	21.6	138.5	33.6
Michigan...........	340.5	1,514.9	1,218.1				

[1] Full-time equivalent (FTE). Credit and noncredit program enrollment including summer session. Excludes medical enrollments.   [2] State and local appropriations. Includes aid to students attending in-State public institutions. Excludes sums for research, agriculture stations and cooperative extension, and hospitals and medical schools.   [3] Excludes appropriated aid to students attending in-State public institutions.

Source: Research Associates of Washington, Washington, DC, *State Profiles: Financing Public Higher Education*, annual (copyright).

No. 290. Institutions of Higher Education—Charges: 1985 to 1995

[In dollars. Estimated. **For the entire academic year ending in year shown.** Figures are average charges per full-time equivalent student. Room and board are based on full-time students]

ACADEMIC CONTROL AND YEAR	TUITION AND REQUIRED FEES [1]				BOARD RATES [2]				DORMITORY CHARGES			
	All institutions	2-yr. colleges	4-yr. colleges	Other 4-yr. schools	All institutions	2-yr. colleges	4-yr. colleges	Other 4-yr. schools	All institutions	2-yr. colleges	4-yr. colleges	Other 4-yr. schools
Public:												
1985.....	971	584	1,386	1,117	1,241	1,302	1,276	1,201	1,196	921	1,237	1,200
1987.....	1,106	660	1,651	1,248	1,398	1,349	1,464	1,348	1,301	979	1,355	1,295
1988.....	1,218	706	1,726	1,407	1,454	1,417	1,482	1,434	1,378	943	1,410	1,409
1989.....	1,285	730	1,846	1,515	1,533	1,488	1,576	1,504	1,457	965	1,483	1,506
1990.....	1,356	756	2,035	1,608	1,635	1,581	1,728	1,561	1,513	962	1,561	1,554
1991.....	1,454	824	2,159	1,707	1,691	1,594	1,767	1,641	1,612	1,050	1,658	1,655
1992.....	1,624	937	2,410	1,933	1,780	1,612	1,852	1,745	1,731	1,074	1,789	1,782
1993.....	1,782	1,025	2,604	2,192	1,841	1,668	1,982	1,761	1,756	1,106	1,856	1,787
1994.....	1,942	1,125	2,820	2,360	1,880	1,681	1,993	1,828	1,873	1,190	1,897	1,958
1995 [3]	2,057	1,194	2,982	2,507	1,947	1,716	2,107	1,863	1,959	1,239	1,993	2,041
Private:												
1985.....	5,315	3,485	6,843	5,135	1,462	1,294	1,647	1,405	1,426	1,424	1,753	1,309
1987.....	6,316	3,684	8,118	6,171	1,702	1,434	2,063	1,587	1,658	1,266	2,097	1,518
1988.....	6,988	4,161	8,771	6,574	1,775	1,537	2,060	1,687	1,748	1,380	2,244	1,593
1989.....	7,461	4,817	9,451	7,172	1,880	1,609	2,269	1,762	1,849	1,540	2,353	1,686
1990.....	8,174	5,196	10,348	7,778	1,948	1,811	2,339	1,823	1,923	1,663	2,411	1,774
1991.....	8,772	5,570	11,379	8,389	2,074	1,989	2,470	1,943	2,063	1,744	2,654	1,889
1992.....	9,434	5,752	12,192	9,053	2,252	2,090	2,727	2,098	2,221	1,789	2,860	2,038
1993.....	9,942	6,059	13,055	9,533	2,344	1,875	2,825	2,197	2,348	1,970	3,018	2,151
1994.....	10,572	6,370	13,874	10,100	2,434	1,970	2,946	2,278	2,490	2,067	3,277	2,261
1995 [3]	11,128	6,865	14,510	10,698	2,508	2,028	3,032	2,363	2,586	2,166	3,468	2,350

[1] For in-State students.   [2] Beginning 1987, rates reflect 20 meals per week, rather than meals served 7 days a week.
[3] Preliminary.

Source: U.S. National Center for Education Statistics, *Digest of Education Statistics,* annual.

No. 291. Voluntary Financial Support of Higher Education: 1970 to 1994

[**For school years ending in years shown; enrollment as of fall of preceding year.** Voluntary support, as defined in Gift Reporting Standards, excludes income from endowment and other invested funds as well as all support received from Federal, State, and local governments and their agencies and contract research]

ITEM	Unit	1970	1980	1985	1990	1991	1992	1993	1994
Estimated support, total [1] **.....**	**Mil. dol.**	**1,780**	**3,800**	**6,320**	**9,800**	**10,200**	**10,700**	**11,200**	**12,350**
Individuals...............	Mil. dol .	822	1,757	2,876	4,770	4,990	5,340	5,510	6,210
Alumni................	Mil. dol .	381	910	1,460	2,540	2,680	2,840	2,980	3,410
Business corporations	Mil. dol .	269	696	1,574	2,170	2,230	2,260	2,400	2,510
Foundations..............	Mil. dol .	434	903	1,175	1,920	2,030	2,090	2,200	2,540
Religious organizations	Mil. dol .	102	155	208	240	240	240	250	240
Current operations	Mil. dol .	960	2,250	3,800	5,440	5,830	6,100	6,300	6,710
Capital purposes...........	Mil. dol .	820	1,550	2,520	4,360	4,370	4,600	4,900	5,640
Enrollment, higher education...	1,000 . .	8,094	11,570	12,242	13,539	13,820	14,359	14,558	14,600
Support per student.........	Dollars .	220	328	516	724	738	745	769	846
In 1993-94 dollars	Dollars .	850	617	713	832	805	787	788	846
Expenditures, higher education .	Bil. dol .	24.7	62.5	98.3	151.8	165.8	176.5	186.7	198.6
Expenditures per student	Dollars .	3,052	5,402	8,030	11,212	11,997	12,292	12,825	13,603
In 1993-94 dollars	Dollars .	11,796	10,162	11,094	12,893	13,088	12,990	13,143	13,603
Institutions reporting support	Number.	1,045	1,019	1,114	1,056	1,046	1,060	1,106	992
Total support reported	**Mil. dol.**	**1,472**	**3,055**	**5,295**	**8,214**	**8,559**	**9,033**	**9,491**	**10,326**
Private 4-year institutions	Mil. dol .	1,154	2,178	3,522	5,072	5,262	5,360	5,767	6,103
Public 4-year institutions......	Mil. dol .	292	856	1,728	3,056	3,222	3,583	3,610	4,138
2-year colleges............	Mil. dol .	26	20	45	85	75	89	115	84

[1] Includes other contributions, not shown separately.

Source: Council for Aid to Education, New York, NY, *Voluntary Support of Education,* annual.

No. 292. Average Salaries for College Faculty Members: 1993 to 1995

[In thousands of dollars. **For academic year ending in year shown.** Figures are for 9 months teaching for full-time faculty members in 4-year institutions. Fringe benefits in 1993 averaged $11,500 in public institutions and $13,100 in private institutions, in 1994, $12,000 in public institutions and $13,900 in private ones and in 1995, $12,400 in public institutions and $14,300 in private ones]

TYPE OF CONTROL AND ACADEMIC RANK	1993	1994	1995	TYPE OF CONTROL AND ACADEMIC RANK	1993	1994	1995
Public: All ranks.............	46.0	47.3	49.1	Private: [1] All ranks...........	51.6	53.8	55.4
Professor	58.4	59.8	62.0	Professor	68.7	71.2	73.2
Associate professor	44.1	45.3	47.0	Associate professor	46.9	48.5	50.0
Assistant professor..........	37.0	38.0	39.2	Assistant professor..........	38.6	40.1	41.2
Instructor	27.8	28.8	29.6	Instructor	28.3	30.2	31.7

[1] Excludes church-related colleges and universities.

Source: American Association of University Professors, Washington, DC, *AAUP Annual Report on the Economic Status of the Profession.*

Education

No. 293. Instructional Faculty and Staff, by Selected Characteristics and Field: 1992

[**As of fall.** For full-time faculty and staff]

CHARACTERISTIC	Total (1,000) [1]	PERCENT DISTRIBUTION, BY FIELD								
		All fields [1]	Busi-ness	Educa-tion	Engi-neering	Fine arts	Health	Humani-ties	Natural sci-ences	Social sciences
Total	526	100.0	100.0	100.0	100.0	100.0	100.0	100.0	100.0	100.0
Age:										
under 30 years old . . .	8	1.4	1.2	1.1	1.3	1.3	1.1	1.6	1.5	0.8
30 to 34 years old	35	6.7	6.3	3.5	11.1	6.1	8.5	4.7	6.7	7.3
35 to 39 years old	66	12.6	13.5	7.8	13.2	13.0	16.2	9.5	13.9	12.9
40 to 44 years old	90	17.0	16.4	17.5	16.8	17.7	21.7	13.3	15.9	16.4
45 to 49 years old	97	18.5	20.9	19.6	14.7	18.4	19.3	20.0	17.1	17.8
50 to 54 years old	95	18.0	16.1	21.1	12.2	17.4	13.4	21.6	19.3	19.2
55 to 59 years old	67	12.7	11.9	14.2	15.0	14.1	9.5	14.6	13.3	12.3
60 to 64 years old	45	8.5	8.0	10.6	10.7	7.9	7.6	9.9	7.5	9.2
65 years old and over .	24	4.5	5.8	4.7	5.1	4.0	2.7	4.8	4.7	4.2
Sex:										
Male	355	67.5	69.8	49.9	94.1	67.8	50.6	59.1	80.3	73.2
Female	171	32.5	30.2	50.1	5.9	32.2	49.4	40.9	19.7	26.8
Race/ethnicity:										
White [2]	457	86.8	88.9	85.1	76.8	88.7	86.6	88.3	86.3	87.7
Black [2]	26	4.9	3.9	9.0	2.7	5.7	5.2	4.1	3.4	5.9
Hispanic	13	2.5	1.4	3.3	2.9	2.4	2.0	4.0	1.8	2.7
Asian	28	5.2	4.9	1.6	16.9	2.7	6.0	3.2	8.1	3.3
American Indian	3	0.5	1.0	1.0	0.7	0.5	0.2	0.5	0.3	0.5
Highest degree:										
Less than bachelor's . .	6	1.2	0.5	0.3	2.0	0.7	1.2	(Z)	0.2	0.1
Bachelor's	21	4.0	4.5	2.9	5.1	5.3	5.9	1.2	2.8	0.7
Master's	154	29.4	37.9	30.3	18.4	56.0	29.6	31.6	21.9	18.9
Professional	57	10.9	4.5	3.0	2.3	4.4	43.3	2.4	4.5	3.5
Doctorate	285	54.5	52.6	63.6	72.2	33.6	20.0	64.8	70.7	76.8
Rank:										
Full professor	161	30.6	24.9	24.6	36.9	32.3	21.5	33.3	37.3	37.2
Associate professor . . .	123	23.5	25.7	29.6	28.0	25.5	23.0	22.2	22.6	24.7
Assistant professor . . .	123	23.4	25.5	22.8	22.4	21.4	32.8	19.3	20.6	24.1
Instructor	73	13.9	16.5	13.2	10.4	10.1	16.6	14.8	11.6	7.9
Lecturer	12	2.2	1.3	2.5	0.9	2.9	2.3	3.8	1.8	1.7
Other	17	3.2	2.1	5.5	0.5	3.2	2.4	1.9	2.4	2.0
No rank	17	3.2	4.0	1.9	1.0	4.6	1.4	4.7	3.9	2.5

Z less than .05 percent.   [1] Includes other fields, not shown separately.

Source: U.S. National Center for Education Statistics, *Digest of Education Statistics,* 1995.

No. 294. Tenure Status of Full-Time College Faculty Members: 1995

[**In percent. For academic year ending in year shown.** Data are for those institutions of higher education reporting tenure status and are preliminary. Excludes schools with no tenure]

TYPE OF INSTITUTION AND CONTROL	Total faculty	ACADEMIC RANK						SEX	
		Profes-sor	Associate professor	Assistant professor	Instruc-tor	Lecturer	No academic rank	Male	Female
All institutions	64.3	96.0	82.2	16.8	7.4	1.5	75.9	71.3	50.3
4-year	62.5	96.2	82.1	13.9	3.9	1.5	22.8	70.2	45.3
University	66.6	97.4	87.0	7.5	2.7	1.3	3.7	74.0	45.7
Other 4-year . . .	59.9	95.3	78.9	17.2	4.2	1.7	31.2	67.5	45.1
2-year	73.3	93.4	84.0	48.5	18.4	0.3	79.9	78.2	67.1
Public institutions . . .	67.2	97.0	86.1	20.0	9.3	1.6	77.1	74.0	53.6
4-year	65.3	97.4	86.3	15.9	5.0	1.6	13.0	73.0	47.4
University	68.7	98.1	90.7	8.5	3.4	1.5	1.3	76.0	47.6
Other 4-year . . .	62.8	96.9	83.0	20.3	5.6	1.7	19.2	70.6	47.3
2-year	73.4	93.4	84.3	49.1	18.1	0.3	79.9	78.2	67.3
Private institutions . .	57.3	93.7	73.8	10.6	2.2	1.2	56.1	64.8	41.7
4-year	57.2	93.7	73.8	10.5	1.7	1.2	34.9	64.6	41.4
University	61.6	95.9	77.1	5.4	0.9	0.7	7.6	68.9	41.3
Other 4-year . . .	55.0	92.3	72.3	12.5	1.9	2.0	44.4	62.2	41.5
2-year	68.2	89.7	66.4	27.2	29.9	(NA)	80.4	75.8	57.3

NA Not available.

Source: U.S. National Center for Education Statistics, *Digest of Education Statistics,* annual.

No. 295. Higher Education Registrations in Foreign Languages: 1960 to 1990

[As of **fall**]

ITEM	1960	1968	1970	1974	1977	1980	1983	1986	1990
Registrations [1] (1,000)	[2]647.1	1,127.4	1,111.5	946.6	933.5	924.8	966.0	1,003.2	1,184.1
Index (1960=100)...............	100.0	174.2	171.8	146.3	144.3	142.9	149.3	155.0	183.0
By selected language (1,000):									
Spanish	178.7	364.9	389.2	362.2	376.7	379.4	386.2	411.3	533.9
French	228.8	388.1	359.3	253.1	246.1	248.4	270.1	275.3	272.5
German	146.1	216.3	202.6	152.1	135.4	126.9	128.2	121.0	133.3
Italian	11.1	30.4	34.2	33.0	33.3	34.8	38.7	40.9	49.7
Japanese	1.7	4.3	6.6	9.6	10.7	11.5	16.1	23.5	45.7
Russian	30.6	40.7	36.1	32.5	27.8	24.0	30.4	34.0	44.6
Latin......................	[2]25.7	35.0	27.6	25.2	24.4	25.0	24.2	25.0	28.2
Chinese	1.8	5.1	6.2	10.6	9.8	11.4	13.2	16.9	19.5
Ancient Greek	[2]12.7	19.3	16.7	24.4	25.8	22.1	19.4	17.6	16.4
Hebrew....................	3.8	10.2	16.6	22.4	19.4	19.4	18.2	15.6	13.0
Portuguese	1.0	4.0	5.1	5.1	5.0	4.9	4.4	5.1	6.2
Arabic....................	0.5	1.1	1.3	2.0	3.1	3.5	3.4	3.4	3.5
12 languages as percent of total .	99.3	99.3	99.1	98.5	98.3	98.5	98.6	98.6	98.5

[1] Includes other foreign languages, not shown separately.   [2] Estimated.

Source: Association of Departments of Foreign Languages, New York, NY, *ADFL Bulletin*, vol. 23, No. 3, and earlier issues (copyright).

No. 296. College Freshmen—Summary Characteristics: 1970 to 1994

[**In percent**. As of **fall** for first-time full-time freshmen. Based on sample survey and subject to sampling error; see source]

CHARACTERISTIC	1970	1980	1985	1989	1990	1991	1992	1993	1994
Sex: Male.............................	55	49	48	46	46	47	46	45	46
Female...........................	45	51	52	54	54	53	54	55	54
Applied to three or more colleges	[1]15	26	29	37	36	34	33	37	36
Average grade in high school:									
A- to A+	16	21	21	23	23	24	26	27	28
B- to B+.............................	58	60	59	59	58	57	57	57	56
C to C+..............................	27	19	20	17	19	19	17	16	15
D...................................	1	1	1	-	-	-	-	-	-
Political orientation:									
Liberal	34	20	21	22	23	24	24	25	23
Middle of the road......................	45	60	57	54	55	54	53	50	53
Conservative	17	17	19	21	20	19	19	21	21
Probable field of study:									
Arts and humanities	16	9	8	9	9	8	8	8	8
Biological sciences	4	4	4	4	4	4	5	6	7
Business............................	16	24	27	25	21	18	16	16	16
Education	11	7	7	9	10	9	10	10	10
Engineering..........................	9	12	11	10	8	10	9	9	8
Physical science......................	2	3	2	2	2	2	2	3	2
Social science	14	7	8	10	10	8	9	9	10
Professional..........................	(NA)	15	13	13	15	18	20	20	19
Technical............................	4	6	5	3	4	4	3	3	3
Data processing/computer programming	(NA)	2	2	1	1	1	1	1	1
Other [2]	(NA)	(NA)	16	15	16	17	17	17	17
Communications	(NA)	2	2	3	2	2	2	2	2
Computer science	(NA)	1	2	2	2	2	1	2	2
Recipient of financial aid:									
Pell grant...........................	(NA)	33	19	22	23	23	23	24	23
Supplemental educational opportunity grant.....	(NA)	8	5	6	7	7	6	6	6
State scholarship or grant.................	(NA)	16	14	15	16	13	14	14	16
College grant.........................	(NA)	13	19	20	22	22	24	24	26
Federal guaranteed student loan	(NA)	21	23	23	23	22	23	28	29
Perkins loan [3]	(NA)	9	6	2	8	7	8	8	9
College loan..........................	(NA)	4	4	8	6	5	6	6	8
College work-study grant	(NA)	15	10	10	10	11	12	12	13
Attitudes—agree or strongly agree:									
Activities of married women are best confined to home and family.......................	48	27	22	26	25	26	26	24	25
Capital punishment should be abolished	56	34	27	21	22	21	21	22	20
Legalize marijuana	38	39	22	17	19	21	23	28	32
There is too much concern for the rights of criminals	52	66	(NA)	69	(NA)	65	67	68	73
Abortion should be legalized...............	(NA)	54	55	65	65	63	64	62	60
Aspires to an advanced degree	49	49	51	60	61	60	55	65	66

- Represents or rounds to zero.   NA Not available.   [1] 1969 data.   [2] Includes other fields, not shown separately.
[3] National Direct Student Loan prior to 1990.

Source: The Higher Education Research Institute, University of California, Los Angeles, CA, *The American Freshman: National Norms*, annual.

No. 297. Foreign (Nonimmigrant) Student Enrollment in College: 1976 to 1995

[For **fall** of the previous year]

REGION OF ORIGIN	ENROLLMENT (1,000)									PERCENT ENROLLED IN—					
										Engineering		Science[1]		Business	
	1976	1980	1985	1990	1991	1992	1993	1994	1995	1980	1994	1980	1994	1980	1994
All regions . . .	179	286	342	387	408	420	439	449	453	25	18	8	9	16	20
Africa.	25	36	40	25	24	22	21	21	21	20	15	9	8	19	19
Nigeria	11	16	18	4	4	3	2	2	2	19	10	9	7	22	19
Asia [2].	97	165	200	245	263	277	291	294	292	32	21	8	10	16	20
China: Taiwan . . .	11	18	23	31	34	36	37	37	36	17	21	15	7	17	23
Hong Kong	12	10	10	11	13	13	14	14	13	22	16	9	5	26	31
India.	10	9	15	26	29	23	36	35	34	31	39	16	9	21	13
Indonesia	1	2	7	9	10	10	11	11	12	27	20	7	4	21	41
Iran	20	51	17	7	6	5	4	4	3	45	28	7	21	11	6
Japan.	7	12	13	30	37	42	43	44	45	7	4	5	3	19	21
Malaysia	2	4	22	14	14	13	13	14	14	13	30	14	3	22	32
Saudi Arabia	3	10	8	4	4	4	4	4	4	30	32	4	5	14	12
South Korea	3	5	16	22	23	26	29	31	34	17	13	11	9	15	16
Thailand	7	7	7	7	7	8	9	9	11	17	14	6	3	26	42
Europe.	14	23	33	46	50	54	58	62	65	15	11	9	9	14	22
Latin America [3]	30	42	49	48	48	43	43	45	47	20	15	8	7	14	23
Mexico	5	6	6	7	7	7	8	8	9	16	14	7	6	11	20
Venezuela	5	10	10	3	3	3	3	4	4	30	17	8	6	11	24
North America	10	16	16	19	19	20	22	23	23	8	6	6	6	13	11
Canada.	10	15	15	18	18	19	21	22	23	8	6	6	6	12	11
Oceania	3	4	4	4	4	4	4	4	4	5	5	7	6	16	16

[1] Physical and life sciences.　[2] Includes countries not shown separately.　[3] Includes Central America, Caribbean, and South America.

Source: Institute of International Education, New York, NY, *Open Doors*, annual (copyright).

No. 298. Salary Offers to Candidates for Degrees: 1990 to 1995

[**In dollars**. Data are average beginning salaries based on offers made by business, industrial, government, and nonprofit and educational employers to graduating students. Data from representative colleges throughout the United States]

FIELD OF STUDY	BACHELOR'S			MASTER'S [1]			DOCTOR'S		
	1990	1994	1995	1990	1994	1995	1990	1994	1995
Accounting	26,391	28,372	27,926	29,647	32,395	31,474	(NA)	(NA)	(NA)
Business, general [2]	23,529	25,102	25,711	36,175	38,792	39,293	(NA)	(NA)	(NA)
Marketing	23,543	24,584	25,400	35,440	45,999	40,899	(NA)	(NA)	(NA)
Engineering:									
Civil	28,136	29,809	30,618	32,336	34,987	34,600	44,481	51,200	42,323
Chemical.	35,122	39,204	39,880	37,862	40,457	41,757	50,524	57,803	57,299
Computer	31,490	33,842	34,941	35,748	39,056	40,889	50,526	62,000	59,280
Electrical	31,778	34,840	36,049	37,526	41,924	43,137	53,147	59,184	56,065
Mechanical	32,064	35,051	35,744	36,506	41,450	42,067	49,887	52,678	51,989
Nuclear [3].	31,750	33,603	38,531	36,728	36,500	45,167	(NA)	(NA)	(NA)
Petroleum	35,202	38,286	37,476	38,412	(NA)	43,517	(NA)	(NA)	(NA)
Engineering technology	29,318	30,509	31,663	(NA)	(NA)	(NA)	(NA)	(NA)	(NA)
Chemistry	27,494	28,128	29,340	32,320	36,392	38,000	45,356	49,455	52,907
Mathematics	27,032	28,221	30,271	30,069	30,552	35,570	42,775	49,154	52,057
Physics	28,002	28,117	31,996	31,480	31,800	37,835	41,486	54,469	53,660
Humanities	23,213	23,519	22,811	(NA)	(NA)	(NA)	(NA)	(NA)	(NA)
Social sciences [4]	21,627	23,023	24,010	(NA)	(NA)	(NA)	(NA)	(NA)	(NA)
Computer science	29,804	31,783	33,712	36,849	37,512	42,885	54,788	55,228	48,000

NA Not available.　[1] Candidates with 1 year or less of full-time nonmilitary employment.　[2] For master's degree, offers are after nontechnical undergraduate degree.　[3] Includes engineering physics.　[4] Excludes economics.

Source: National Association of Colleges and Employers, Bethlehem, PA, Salary Survey, *A Study of Beginning Offers*, annual (copyright).

No. 299. Time Spent Earning Bachelor's Degree, by Selected Characteristic: 1993

[As of **spring**. Based on Survey of Income and Program Participation; for details, see source]

CHARACTERISTIC	Total with bache-lor's degrees (1,000)	YEARS TO BA DEGREE FROM END OF HIGH SCHOOL						Mean dura-tion [1]
		Number (1,000)			Percent			
		4 years or less	5 years or less	6 years or less	4 years or less	5 years or less	6 years or less	
All persons	36,787	15,624	23,810	27,334	42.5	64.7	74.3	6.29
Male	19,351	7,321	11,695	13,827	37.8	60.4	71.5	6.28
Female	17,436	8,302	12,115	13,508	47.6	69.5	77.5	6.30
White	32,279	14,161	21,201	24,235	43.9	65.7	75.1	6.24
Male	17,258	6,717	10,537	12,411	38.9	61.1	71.9	6.22
Female	15,021	7,444	10,664	11,824	49.6	71.0	78.7	6.26
Black	2,314	713	1,258	1,473	30.8	54.4	63.7	7.19
Male	926	264	493	570	28.5	53.2	61.6	6.98
Female	1,388	448	764	904	32.3	55.0	65.1	7.33
Hispanic origin [2]	1,367	363	689	852	26.6	50.4	62.3	6.79
Male	693	187	308	407	27.0	44.4	58.7	7.06
Female	674	176	381	445	26.1	56.5	66.0	6.50
Field of Bachelor's degree: [3]								
Agriculture/Forestry	395	103	209	293	26.1	52.9	74.2	5.78
Biology	624	241	416	471	38.6	66.7	75.5	6.34
Business/Management	5,282	1,952	3,117	3,628	37.0	59.0	68.7	6.72
Economics	660	321	433	479	48.6	65.6	72.6	6.35
Education	3,613	1,522	2,338	2,658	42.1	64.7	73.6	7.03
Engineering	2,577	729	1,392	1,733	28.3	54.0	67.2	6.66
English/Journalism	1,137	553	743	854	48.6	65.3	75.1	6.28
Home Economics	337	177	262	284	52.5	77.7	84.3	4.71
Law	145	73	98	104	(B)	(B)	(B)	6.33
Liberal Arts/Humanities	2,188	894	1,413	1,592	40.9	64.6	72.8	6.44
Mathematics/Statistics	567	283	412	457	49.9	72.7	80.6	5.28
Medicine/Dentistry	142	39	74	104	(B)	(B)	(B)	6.32
Nursing/Pharmacy/Technical Health	1,626	498	914	1,092	30.6	56.2	67.2	7.10
Physical/Earth Sciences	614	194	362	470	31.6	59.0	76.5	6.25
Police Science/Law Enforcement	326	95	182	240	29.1	55.8	73.6	6.11
Psychology	815	328	555	619	40.2	68.1	76.0	6.02
Religion/Theology	138	52	66	71	(B)	(B)	(B)	7.64
Social Sciences	1,760	683	1,113	1,333	38.8	63.2	75.7	6.44
Vo-tech Studies	181	64	121	135	(B)	(B)	(B)	7.39
Other	1,816	735	1,082	1,302	40.5	59.6	71.7	6.63
Advanced degree	11,843	6,089	8,507	9,417	51.4	71.8	79.5	5.67

B Base is less than 200,000 persons.   [1] For definition of mean, see Guide to Tabular Presentation.   [2] Persons of Hispanic origin may be of any race.   [3] For persons whose highest degree is the BA.

Source: U.S. Bureau of the Census, unpublished data.

No. 300. Earned Degrees Conferred, by Level and Sex, With Projections: 1950 to 2006

[**In thousands, except percent**. Beginning 1960, includes Alaska and Hawaii. See *Historical Statistics, Colonial Times to 1970*, series H-751-763 for similar data. See also Appendix III]

YEAR ENDING	ALL DEGREES		ASSOCIATE'S		BACHELOR'S		MASTER'S		FIRST PROFES-SIONAL		DOCTOR'S	
	Total	Percent male	Male	Female	Male	Female	Male	Female	Male	Female	Male	Female
1950 [1]	497	75.7	(NA)	(NA)	329	103	41	17	(NA)	(NA)	6	1
1960 [1]	477	65.8	(NA)	(NA)	254	138	51	24	(NA)	(NA)	9	1
1965	660	61.5	(NA)	(NA)	282	212	81	40	27	1	15	2
1970	1,271	59.2	117	89	451	341	126	83	33	2	26	4
1975	1,666	56.0	191	169	505	418	162	131	49	7	27	7
1980	1,731	51.1	184	217	474	456	151	147	53	17	23	10
1985	1,828	49.3	203	252	483	497	143	143	50	25	22	11
1986	1,830	49.0	196	250	486	502	144	145	49	25	22	12
1987	1,823	48.4	191	245	481	510	141	148	47	25	22	12
1988	1,835	48.0	190	245	477	518	145	154	45	25	23	12
1989	1,873	47.3	186	250	483	535	149	161	45	26	23	13
1990	1,940	46.6	191	264	492	560	154	171	44	27	24	14
1991	2,025	45.8	199	283	504	590	156	181	44	28	25	15
1992	2,108	45.6	207	297	521	616	162	191	45	29	26	15
1993	2,167	45.5	212	303	533	632	169	200	45	30	26	16
1994, prel.	2,222	45.4	217	314	535	647	186	205	45	31	26	16
1995, proj.	2,247	45.3	216	314	535	657	195	210	45	32	27	16
2000, proj.	2,287	45.3	212	326	539	652	208	220	50	34	28	19
2004, proj.	2,451	44.6	222	354	580	708	212	240	55	36	24	21
2005, proj.	2,473	44.4	223	356	585	717	212	245	55	36	23	21
2006, proj.	2,497	44.2	224	360	591	725	212	250	55	37	22	21

NA Not available.   [1] First-professional degrees are included with bachelor's degrees.

Source: U.S. National Center for Education Statistics, *Digest of Education Statistics*, annual; and *Projections of Education Statistics to 2006*, annual.

No. 301. Degrees and Awards Earned Below Bachelor's, by Field: 1993

[Covers associate degrees and other awards based on postsecondary curriculums of less than 4 years in institutions of higher education]

FIELD OF STUDY	LESS THAN 1-YEAR AWARDS		1- TO LESS THAN 4-YEAR AWARDS		ASSOCIATE DEGREES	
	Total	Women	Total	Women	Total	Women
Total	70,922	35,941	146,859	86,031	514,756	302,792
Agriculture and natural resources	1,778	409	4,741	2,527	5,398	1,648
Architecture and related programs	2	2	56	48	372	253
Area, ethnic, and cultural studies	105	76	414	276	33	23
Biological/life sciences	116	31	20	11	1,435	847
Business management and administrative services	13,373	9,753	29,291	24,233	99,164	69,010
Communications and communications technologies	516	204	682	385	3,732	1,591
Computer and information sciences	1,859	919	4,594	2,529	9,196	4,655
Construction trades	1,497	90	4,062	203	1,653	72
Consumer and personal services	855	618	5,591	4,276	4,692	1,572
Education	510	379	954	848	9,315	6,284
Engineering and engineering technologies	2,330	326	8,607	872	38,799	3,999
English language and literature/letters	165	91	53	48	1,320	851
Foreign languages and literatures	339	218	27	23	511	358
Health professions and related sciences	23,278	16,638	38,933	32,892	86,237	73,266
Home economics and vocational home economics	3,214	2,096	7,512	6,493	6,914	6,259
Law and legal studies	866	724	2,447	1,974	8,028	7,069
Liberal/general studies and humanities	132	92	808	484	158,040	94,173
Library science	97	91	53	49	85	76
Mathematics	-	-	15	6	743	315
Mechanics and repairers	3,613	125	18,417	1,174	10,966	686
Multi/interdisciplinary studies	246	127	133	76	8,486	4,411
Parks, recreation, leisure, and fitness	29	21	126	67	717	288
Physical sciences	30	15	81	25	2,241	945
Precision production trades	2,552	397	7,408	1,075	9,204	1,811
Protective services	6,664	1,166	4,330	818	16,834	4,545
Psychology	33	23	47	38	1,237	955
Public administration and services	235	169	589	375	3,301	2,653
Social sciences and history	22	14	117	72	3,930	2,252
Theological studies, religion and philosophy	94	64	1,250	731	619	262
Transportation and material moving	5,525	598	437	70	2,210	360
Visual and performing arts	279	175	3,913	2,681	12,690	7,606
Undistributed and unclassified	567	290	1,151	652	6,654	3,697

- Represents zero.
Source: U.S. National Center for Education Statistics, *Digest of Education Statistics*, 1995.

No. 302. Bachelor's Degrees Earned, by Field: 1971 to 1993

FIELD OF STUDY	1971	1980	1985	1990	1993	PERCENT FEMALE	
						1971	1993
Total	839,730	929,417	979,477	1,051,344	1,165,178	43.4	54.3
Agriculture and natural resources	12,672	22,802	18,107	12,900	16,778	4.2	54.0
Architecture and environmental design	5,570	9,132	9,325	9,364	9,167	11.9	35.2
Area, ethnic and cultural studies	2,582	2,840	2,985	4,613	5,481	52.4	63.9
Biological sciences/life sciences	35,743	46,370	38,445	37,204	47,038	29.1	51.4
Business and management	114,729	184,867	232,636	248,698	256,842	9.1	47.2
Communications [1]	10,802	28,616	42,002	51,308	54,706	35.3	59.7
Computer and information sciences	2,388	11,154	38,878	27,257	24,200	13.6	28.1
Education	176,307	118,038	88,072	105,112	107,781	74.5	78.4
Engineering [1]	50,046	68,893	95,828	81,322	78,051	0.8	14.4
English language and literature/letters	64,342	32,541	33,218	47,519	56,133	65.6	65.7
Foreign languages	20,536	12,089	10,827	12,386	14,387	74.0	71.1
Health sciences	25,226	63,920	64,422	58,302	67,089	77.1	83.1
Home economics	11,167	18,411	15,157	14,491	15,100	97.3	89.2
Law	545	683	1,157	1,592	2,056	5.0	67.6
Liberal/general studies	7,481	23,196	21,818	27,985	33,456	33.6	60.3
Library and archival sciences	1,013	398	197	77	83	92.0	89.2
Mathematics	24,937	11,872	15,861	15,176	14,812	37.9	47.2
Military technologies	357	38	299	196	11	0.3	(Z)
Multi/interdisciplinary studies	6,286	11,277	12,978	16,267	23,955	22.8	62.8
Parks and recreation	1,621	5,753	4,725	4,582	9,859	34.7	50.5
Philosophy, religion, and theology	11,890	13,276	12,447	12,068	13,214	25.5	31.1
Physical sciences [1]	21,412	23,410	23,704	16,066	17,545	13.8	32.6
Protective services	2,045	15,015	12,510	15,354	20,902	9.2	37.7
Psychology	38,187	42,093	39,900	53,952	66,728	44.4	73.2
Public affairs	5,466	16,644	11,754	13,908	16,775	68.4	77.3
Social sciences [2]	155,324	103,662	91,570	118,083	135,703	36.8	45.8
Visual and performing arts	30,394	40,892	38,140	39,934	47,761	59.7	61.0
Unclassified	662	1,535	2,515	5,628	9,565	0.9	35.9

Z Less than .01 percent.   [1] Includes technologies.   [2] Includes history.
Source: U.S. National Center for Education Statistics, *Digest of Education Statistics*, annual.

No. 303. Master's and Doctorate's Degrees Earned, by Field: 1971 to 1993

LEVEL AND FIELD OF STUDY	1971	1980	1985	1990	1993	PERCENT FEMALE	
						1971	1993
MASTER'S DEGREES							
Total	**230,509**	**298,081**	**286,251**	**324,301**	**369,585**	**40.1**	**54.2**
Agriculture and natural resources	2,457	3,976	3,928	3,382	3,965	5.9	37.5
Architecture and related programs	1,705	3,139	3,275	3,499	3,808	13.8	37.6
Area, ethnic and cultural studies	1,032	852	904	1,212	1,523	38.3	51.9
Biological sciences/life sciences	5,728	6,510	5,059	4,869	4,756	33.6	50.7
Business management and administrative services	25,977	54,484	66,996	76,676	89,615	3.9	35.7
Communications and technologies	1,856	3,082	3,669	4,362	5,209	34.6	62.0
Computer and information sciences	1,588	3,647	7,101	9,677	10,163	10.3	27.1
Education	87,666	101,819	74,654	84,881	96,028	56.2	76.9
Engineering and engineering technologies	16,443	16,243	21,555	24,772	28,726	1.1	14.9
English language and literature/letters	10,686	6,189	5,187	6,567	7,790	60.6	65.8
Foreign languages	5,217	2,854	2,471	2,760	3,198	64.2	66.8
Health sciences	5,749	15,704	17,385	20,321	25,718	55.3	79.7
Home economics	1,452	2,690	2,375	2,100	2,479	93.9	83.0
Law and legal studies	955	1,817	1,796	1,888	2,197	4.8	32.6
Liberal arts and sciences, general studies and humanities	885	2,646	1,696	1,999	2,416	44.6	65.2
Library science	7,001	5,374	3,870	4,341	4,871	81.3	80.3
Mathematics	5,695	3,382	3,413	4,146	4,067	27.1	39.6
Military technologies	2	46	119	-	108	-	7.4
Multi/interdisciplinary studies	821	2,306	2,583	2,834	2,498	25.0	51.1
Parks and recreation	218	647	596	529	1,434	29.8	50.2
Philosophy, religion, and theology	4,036	5,126	5,602	6,265	6,410	27.1	38.0
Physical sciences and science technologies	6,367	5,219	5,796	5,449	5,366	13.3	29.0
Protective services	194	1,805	1,235	1,151	1,357	10.3	38.3
Psychology	5,717	9,938	9,891	10,730	10,957	40.6	72.4
Public administration and services	7,785	17,560	15,575	17,399	20,634	50.0	70.4
Social sciences [1]	16,539	12,176	10,503	11,634	13,471	28.5	43.1
Visual and performing arts	6,675	8,708	8,718	8,481	9,440	47.4	56.6
Unclassified	63	142	299	2,377	1,381	-	30.3
DOCTORATE'S DEGREES							
Total	**32,107**	**32,615**	**32,943**	**38,371**	**42,132**	**14.3**	**38.1**
Agriculture and natural resources	1,086	991	1,213	1,295	1,173	2.9	25.1
Architecture and related programs	36	79	89	103	148	8.3	29.1
Area, ethnic and cultural studies	144	151	140	131	178	16.7	49.4
Biological sciences/life sciences	3,645	3,636	3,432	3,844	4,435	16.3	39.9
Business management and administrative services	757	753	831	1,093	1,346	2.8	28.0
Communications and technologies	145	193	234	273	301	13.1	51.5
Computer and information sciences	128	240	248	627	805	2.3	14.4
Education	6,041	7,314	6,612	6,502	7,030	21.0	59.2
Engineering and engineering technology	3,638	2,507	3,230	4,981	5,843	0.6	9.6
English language and literature/letters	1,650	1,294	1,041	1,078	1,341	28.8	59.0
Foreign languages	988	755	635	724	830	34.6	57.2
Health sciences	466	786	1,199	1,536	1,767	16.5	57.4
Home economics	123	192	273	301	345	61.0	71.9
Law and legal studies	20	40	105	111	86	-	24.4
Liberal arts and sciences, general studies and humanities	32	192	112	63	81	31.3	53.1
Library science	39	73	87	42	77	28.2	66.2
Mathematics	1,249	763	734	966	1,189	7.6	23.8
Multi/interdisciplinary studies	59	209	219	272	196	6.8	41.3
Parks and recreation	2	21	36	35	108	50.0	30.6
Philosophy, religion, and theology	866	1,693	1,612	1,756	1,865	5.8	17.3
Physical sciences and science technologies	4,390	3,089	3,403	4,164	4,393	5.6	21.9
Protective services	1	18	33	38	32	-	28.1
Psychology	2,144	3,395	3,447	3,811	3,651	24.0	61.2
Public administration and services	174	342	431	508	459	24.1	53.2
Social sciences [1]	3,660	3,230	2,851	3,010	3,460	13.9	36.3
Visual and performing arts	621	655	696	849	882	22.2	45.8
Unclassified	3	4	-	258	111	-	16.2

- Represents zero.   [1] Includes history.

Source: U.S. National Center for Education Statistics, *Digest of Education Statistics,* annual.

No. 304. First Professional Degrees Earned in Selected Professions: 1960 to 1993

[First professional degrees include degrees which require at least 6 years of college work for completion (including at least 2 years of preprofessional training). See Appendix III]

TYPE OF DEGREE AND SEX OF RECIPIENT	1960	1970	1975	1980	1985	1989	1990	1991	1992	1993
Medicine (M.D.):										
Institutions conferring degrees	79	86	104	112	120	124	124	121	120	122
Degrees conferred, total	7,032	8,314	12,447	14,902	16,041	15,460	15,075	15,043	15,243	15,531
Percent to women	5.5	8.4	13.1	23.4	30.4	33.3	34.2	36.0	35.7	37.7
Dentistry (D.D.S. or D.M.D.):										
Institutions conferring degrees	45	48	52	58	59	58	57	55	52	55
Degrees conferred, total	3,247	3,718	4,773	5,258	5,339	4,265	4,100	3,699	3,593	3,605
Percent to women	0.8	0.9	3.1	13.3	20.7	26.8	30.9	32.1	32.3	33.9
Law (LL.B. or J.D.):										
Institutions conferring degrees	134	145	154	179	181	182	182	179	177	184
Degrees conferred, total	9,240	14,916	29,296	35,647	37,491	35,634	36,485	37,945	38,848	40,302
Percent to women	2.5	5.4	15.1	30.2	38.5	40.9	42.2	43.0	42.7	42.5
Theological (B.D., M.Div., M.H.L.):										
Institutions conferring degrees	(NA)	(NA)	(NA)	(NA)	(NA)	(NA)	(NA)	(NA)	(NA)	(NA)
Degrees conferred, total	(NA)	5,298	5,095	7,115	7,221	6,012	5,851	5,695	5,251	5,447
Percent to women	(NA)	2.3	6.8	13.8	18.5	22.8	24.8	23.4	23.3	24.8

NA Not available.

Source: U.S. National Center for Education Statistics, *Digest of Education Statistics*, annual.

No. 305. Degrees Earned, by Level and Race/Ethnicity: 1981 to 1993

[For **school year ending in year shown.** Data exclude some institutions not reporting field of study and are slight undercounts of degrees awarded]

LEVEL OF DEGREE AND RACE/ETHNICITY	TOTAL						PERCENT DISTRIBUTION	
	1981	1985	1990	1991	1992	1993	1981	1993
Associate's degrees, total	410,174	429,815	450,263	462,030	494,387	508,154	100.0	100.0
White, non-Hispanic	339,167	355,343	369,580	376,081	400,530	405,883	82.7	79.9
Black, non-Hispanic	35,330	35,791	35,327	37,657	39,411	42,340	8.6	8.3
Hispanic	17,800	19,407	22,195	24,251	26,905	29,991	4.3	5.9
Asian or Pacific Islander	8,650	9,914	13,482	13,725	15,596	16,632	2.1	3.3
American Indian/Alaskan Native	2,584	2,953	3,530	3,672	4,008	4,379	0.6	0.9
Nonresident alien	6,643	6,407	6,149	6,644	7,937	8,929	1.6	1.8
Bachelor's degrees, total	934,800	968,311	1,048,631	1,081,280	1,129,833	1,159,931	100.0	100.0
White, non-Hispanic	807,319	826,106	884,376	904,062	936,771	947,309	86.4	81.7
Black, non-Hispanic	60,673	57,473	61,063	65,341	72,326	77,872	6.5	6.7
Hispanic	21,832	25,874	32,844	36,612	40,761	45,376	2.3	3.9
Asian or Pacific Islander	18,794	25,395	39,248	41,618	46,720	51,463	2.0	4.4
American Indian/Alaskan Native	3,593	4,246	4,392	4,513	5,176	5,671	0.4	0.5
Nonresident alien	22,589	29,217	26,708	29,134	28,079	32,240	2.4	2.8
Master's degrees, total	294,183	280,421	322,465	328,645	348,682	368,701	100.0	100.0
White, non-Hispanic	241,216	223,628	251,690	255,281	268,371	278,829	82.0	75.6
Black, non-Hispanic	17,133	13,939	15,446	16,139	18,116	19,780	5.8	5.4
Hispanic	6,461	6,864	7,950	8,386	9,358	10,665	2.2	2.9
Asian or Pacific Islander	6,282	7,782	10,577	11,180	12,658	13,866	2.1	3.8
American Indian/Alaskan Native	1,034	1,256	1,101	1,136	1,273	1,407	0.4	0.4
Nonresident alien	22,057	26,952	35,701	36,523	38,906	44,154	7.5	12.0
Doctor's degrees, total	32,839	32,307	38,113	38,547	40,090	42,021	100.0	100.0
White, non-Hispanic	25,908	23,934	25,880	25,328	25,813	26,700	78.9	63.5
Black, non-Hispanic	1,265	1,154	1,153	1,211	1,223	1,352	3.9	3.2
Hispanic	456	677	788	732	811	827	1.4	2.0
Asian or Pacific Islander	877	1,106	1,235	1,459	1,559	1,582	2.7	3.8
American Indian/Alaskan Native	130	119	99	102	118	106	0.4	0.3
Nonresident alien	4,203	5,317	8,958	9,715	10,566	11,454	12.8	27.3
First-professional degrees, total	71,340	71,057	70,744	71,515	72,129	74,960	100.0	100.0
White, non-Hispanic	64,551	63,219	60,240	60,327	59,800	60,830	90.5	81.1
Black, non-Hispanic	2,931	3,029	3,410	3,575	3,560	4,100	4.1	5.5
Hispanic	1,541	1,884	2,427	2,527	2,766	2,984	2.2	4.0
Asian or Pacific Islander	1,456	1,816	3,362	3,755	4,455	5,160	2.0	6.9
American Indian/Alaskan Native	192	248	257	261	296	368	0.3	0.5
Nonresident alien	669	861	1,048	1,070	1,252	1,518	0.9	2.0

Source: U.S. National Center for Education Statistics, *Digest of Education Statistics*, annual.

No. 306. Libraries—Number, by Type: 1980 to 1993

TYPE	1980	1985	1990	1993	TYPE	1980	1985	1990	1993
Total [1]	31,564	32,323	34,613	36,445	Junior college . . .	1,191	1,188	1,233	1,255
					Colleges,				
United States . . .	28,638	29,843	30,761	32,414	universities	3,400	3,846	3,360	3,364
Public	8,717	8,849	9,060	9,097	Departmental .	1,489	1,824	1,454	1,455
Public branches . . .	5,936	6,330	5,833	6,215	Law,				
Special [2]	7,649	7,530	9,051	10,149	medicine,				
Medicine	1,674	1,667	1,861	1,925	religious . .	269	531	501	495
Religious	913	839	946	1,011	Government.	1,260	1,574	1,735	1,871
Law [3]	417	435	647	1,140	Armed Forces	485	526	489	463
Academic	4,591	5,034	4,593	4,619	Outlying areas . .	113	114	110	(NA)

NA Not available.   [1] Includes Canadian libraries, and libraries in regions administered by the United States, not shown separately. Data are exclusive of elementary and secondary school libraries. Law libraries with fewer than 10,000 volumes are included only if they specialize in a particular field.   [2] Includes other types of special libraries, not shown separately. Increase between 1985 and 1990 is due mainly to revised criteria for identifying special libraries and improved methods of counting.   [3] Increase beginning 1993 due to increased effort in identifying special libraries.

Source: R.R. Bowker Co., New York, NY, *The Bowker Annual: Library and Book Trade Almanac* and *American Library Directory*, annual. (Copyright by Reed Publishing (USA) Inc.)

No. 307. Public Libraries, Selected Characteristics: 1993

[Based on survey of public libraries. Data are for public libraries in the 50 States and the District of Columbia. The response rates for these items are between 95 and 100 percent]

POPULATION OF SERVICE AREA	NUMBER OF—		OPERATING INCOME			PAID STAFF [3]		Books and serial volumes (per capita)
	Public libraries	Stationary outlets [1]	Total (mil. dol.) [2]	Source (percent)		Total	Librar- ians with ALA- MLS [4]	
				State govern- ment	Local govern- ment			
Total	8,929	15,893	5,069	12.5	78.0	111,939	24,825	2.7
1,000,000 or more	22	856	717	12.5	74.1	14,174	3,860	2.3
500,000 to 999,000	50	1,051	811	18.5	73.7	15,372	3,988	2.5
250,000 to 499,999	100	1,066	630	12.3	80.8	12,872	3,197	2.2
100,000 to 249,999	296	1,869	779	10.0	81.7	17,412	3,899	2.2
50,000 to 99,999	507	1,610	660	12.7	79.5	14,855	3,297	2.4
25,000 to 49,999	866	1,640	606	11.5	79.3	14,211	3,054	2.8
10,000 to 24,999	1,645	2,135	531	10.1	79.7	12,855	2,535	3.4
5,000 to 9,999	1,506	1,678	203	11.1	75.8	5,527	723	4.2
2,500 to 4,999	1,321	1,361	76	7.1	74.8	2,460	191	5.2
1,000 to 2,499	1,639	1,649	44	5.6	70.1	1,625	68	7.5
Fewer than 1,000	977	978	12	8.7	66.2	576	13	13.2

[1] The sum of central and branches libraries. The total number of central libraries was 8,876; the total of branch libraries was 7,017.   [2] Includes income from the Federal Government (1.0%) and other sources (8.4%), not shown separately.   [3] Full-time equivalents.   [4] Librarians with master's degrees from a graduate library education program accredited by the American Library Association (ALA). Total librarians, including those without ALA-MLS, were 37,349.

Source: U.S. National Center for Education Statistics, *Public Libraries in the United States: 1993*.

No. 308. College and University Libraries—Summary: 1975 to 1992

[For school year ending in year shown, except enrollment as of fall of the prior year. Prior to 1982, includes outlying areas]

ITEM	1975	1979	1982	1985	1988	1990	1992
Number of libraries	2,972	3,122	3,104	3,322	3,438	3,274	3,274
Total enrollment (1,000)	10,322	11,392	12,372	12,242	12,767	13,539	14,359
COLLECTIONS (1,000)							
Number of volumes	447,059	519,895	567,826	631,727	706,504	717,042	749,429
Volumes added during year	23,242	21,608	19,507	20,658	21,907	19,003	20,982
Number of serial subscriptions	4,434	4,775	4,890	6,317	6,416	5,748	6,966
STAFF							
Total	56,836	58,416	58,476	58,476	67,251	69,359	67,166
Librarians and professional	23,530	23,676	23,816	21,822	25,115	26,101	26,341
OPERATING EXPENDITURES ($1,000)							
Total [1]	1,091,784	1,502,158	1,943,769	2,404,524	2,770,075	3,257,813	3,648,654
Salaries	592,568	824,438	1,081,894	1,156,138	1,451,551	1,693,813	1,889,368
Collection	327,904	450,180	561,199	750,282	891,281	1,040,928	1,197,293

[1] Includes other expenditures, not shown separately.

Source: U.S. National Center for Education Statistics, *Digest of Education Statistics*, 1995; and *Academic Libraries: 1990*, 1992.

No. 309. Participation in Adult Education: 1994-95

[For the civilian noninstitutional population 17 years old and over not enrolled full-time in elementary or secondary school at the time of the survey. Adult education is considered any enrollment in any educational activity at any time in the prior 12 months. Based on survey and subject to sampling error; source for details]

CHARACTERISTIC	Adult popu-lation (1,000)	PARTICIPANTS IN ADULT EDUCATION					
		Number taking adult ed. courses (1,000)	Percent of total	Reason for taking course (percent) [1]			
				Personal/ social	Advance on the job	Train for a new job	Complete degree or diploma
Total................	**189,543**	**76,261**	**40**	**44**	**54**	**11**	**10**
Age: 17 to 24 years old..........	22,407	10,539	47	39	33	21	19
25 to 34 years old.............	40,326	19,508	48	41	56	14	8
35 to 44 years old.............	42,304	20,814	49	40	64	10	9
45 to 54 years old.............	31,807	14,592	46	39	65	7	10
55 to 64 years old.............	21,824	6,117	28	52	54	4	6
65 years old and over.........	30,876	4,691	15	86	14	1	3
Sex: Male...................	90,256	34,450	38	34	60	10	10
Female...................	99,287	41,811	42	51	49	12	9
Race/ethnicity:							
White [2].................	144,587	59,982	41	44	57	10	9
Black [2].................	20,806	7,704	37	45	48	13	12
Hispanic.............	15,689	5,281	34	40	37	13	11
Other races [2]............	8,461	3,294	39	40	45	16	13
Marital status:							
Never married...........	38,627	17,094	44	37	44	20	15
Currently married..........	114,678	48,200	42	45	58	8	8
Other...................	36,238	10,967	30	48	52	9	8
Children under 18 in household:							
Yes....................	77,787	36,103	46	43	56	11	9
No.....................	111,756	40,158	36	44	52	11	10
Educational attainment:							
Up to 8th grade...........	12,808	1,283	10	52	20	8	9
9th to 12th grade..........	16,511	3,332	20	45	27	10	18
High school diploma or GED......	62,956	19,341	31	44	49	10	6
Vocational school after high school .	6,327	2,648	42	44	57	8	8
Some college.............	34,433	16,978	49	45	47	16	13
Associate's degree...........	9,975	5,601	56	39	64	9	9
Bachelor's or higher..........	46,535	27,078	58	43	65	9	9
Labor force status:							
Employed................	117,826	59,734	51	37	64	10	10
Unemployed..............	8,155	2,983	37	39	27	25	13
Not in the labor force..........	63,562	13,544	21	72	15	11	8
Occupation: [3]							
Professional..............	16,814	12,219	73	37	74	8	10
Executive, administrative and managerial................	12,500	7,070	57	37	76	8	10
Technical and related support.....	4,812	3,300	69	32	73	9	11
Sales workers.............	15,666	7,131	46	41	53	12	11
Administrative support [4]........	20,460	10,727	52	43	62	11	6
Service.................	17,355	8,238	47	37	51	14	12
Agriculture, forestry, and fishing....	1,908	500	26	40	49	6	12
Precision production, craft and repair...............	11,441	4,977	43	30	62	8	11
Machine operators, assemblers [5]...	8,309	2,515	30	28	58	10	9
Transportation and materials moving...............	4,488	1,295	29	35	60	13	12
Handlers, equipment cleaners, helpers and laborers..........	1,989	519	26	33	43	24	5
Nonclassifiable, undetermined.....	2,022	1,194	59	35	71	6	4
Household income:							
Under $10,000..............	30,198	6,883	23	48	25	20	12
$10,001 to $15,000...........	13,523	3,610	27	51	32	17	10
$15,001 to $20,000...........	13,116	4,176	32	45	38	15	12
$20,001 to $25,000...........	13,812	4,339	31	47	44	13	11
$25,001 to $30,000...........	16,386	6,208	38	45	46	13	11
$30,001 to $40,000...........	28,628	12,220	43	45	55	11	9
$40,001 to $50,000...........	20,446	9,567	47	41	61	10	8
$50,001 to $75,000...........	29,161	15,169	52	39	67	7	8
More than $75,000...........	24,274	14,089	58	43	64	7	9

[1] Reason for taking at least one course. Includes duplication. Excludes "to improve basic skills," cited by no more than 6 percent of participants.   [2] Non-Hispanic.   [3] For those employed in the 12 months prior to the interview. Excludes those participating exclusively in full-time credential programs.   [4] Includes clerical.   [5] Includes inspectors.

Source: U.S. Department of Education, National Center for Education Statistics, *1995 National Household Education Survey.*

Law Enforcement, Courts, and Prisons

This section presents data on crimes committed, victims of crimes, arrests, and data related to criminal violations and the criminal justice system. The major sources of these data are the Bureau of Justice Statistics (BJS), the Federal Bureau of Investigation (FBI), and the Administrative Office of the U.S. Courts. BJS issues several reports, including *Sourcebook of Criminal Justice Statistics, Criminal Victimization in the United States, Prisoners in State and Federal Institutions, Children in Custody, National Survey of Courts, Census of State Correctional Facilities* and *Survey of Prison Inmates, Census of Jails* and *Survey of Jail Inmates, Parole in the United States, Capital Punishment,* and the annual *Expenditure and Employment Data for the Criminal Justice System.* The Federal Bureau of Investigation's major annual report is *Crime in the United States,* which presents data on reported crimes as gathered from State and local law enforcement agencies.

Other major sources of these data include: *Annual Report of the Director* and *Federal Court Management Statistics* issued by the Administrative Office of the U.S. Courts; *Governmental Finances and Public Employment,* issued annually by the Bureau of the Census; and the *Statistical Report,* issued annually by the Federal Bureau of Prisons.

Legal jurisdiction and law enforcement—Law enforcement is, for the most part, a function of State and local officers and agencies. The U.S. Constitution reserves general police powers to the States. By act of Congress, Federal offenses include only offenses against the U.S. Government and against or by its employees while engaged in their official duties, and offenses which involve the crossing of State lines or an interference with interstate commerce. Excluding the military, there are 52 separate criminal law jurisdictions in the United States: 1 in each of the 50 States, 1 in the District of Columbia, and the Federal jurisdiction. Each of these has its own criminal law and procedure and its own law enforcement agencies. While the systems of law enforcement are

In Brief

In 1994, U.S. residents 12 years or older experienced 42 million crimes.

The Nation's prisons held a record 1,054,000 inmates at yearend 1994.

Over 1 million child victims in cases of substantiated maltreatment and neglect in 1994.

quite similar among the States, there are often substantial differences in the penalties for like offenses.

Law enforcement can be divided into three parts: Investigation of crimes and arrests of persons suspected of committing them; prosecution of those charged with crime; and the punishment or treatment of persons convicted of crime.

Crime—There are two major approaches taken in determining the extent of crime. One perspective is provided by the FBI through its Uniform Crime Reporting Program (UCR). The FBI receives monthly and annual reports from law enforcement agencies throughout the country, currently representing 98 percent of the national population. Each month, city police, sheriffs, and State police file reports on the number of index offenses that become known to them.

The FBI Crime Index offenses are as follows: *Murder and nonnegligent manslaughter,* is based on police investigations, as opposed to the determination of a medical examiner or judicial body, includes willful felonious homicides, and excludes attempts and assaults to kill, suicides, accidental deaths, justifiable homicides, and deaths caused by negligence; *forcible rape* includes forcible rapes and attempts; *robbery* includes stealing or taking anything of value by force or violence or threat of force or violence and includes attempted robbery; *aggravated assault* includes assault with intent to kill; *burglary* includes any unlawful entry to commit a felony or a theft and includes attempted burglary and burglary followed by larceny; *larceny* includes theft of property or articles of value without use of force and violence or fraud and excludes embezzlement, "con games," forgery, etc.; *motor vehicle theft* includes all cases where vehicles are driven away and abandoned, but excludes vehicles taken for temporary use and returned by the taker. Arson was added as the eighth Index offense in April 1979 following a Congressional mandate. *Arson* includes any willful or malicious burning or attempt to burn with or without intent to defraud, a dwelling house, public building, motor vehicle or aircraft, personal property of another, etc.

The monthly Uniform Crime Reports also contain data on crimes cleared by arrest and on characteristics of persons arrested for all criminal offenses. In summarizing and publishing crime data, the FBI depends primarily on the adherence to the established standards of reporting for statistical accuracy, presenting the data as information useful to persons concerned with the problem of crime and criminal-law enforcement.

National Crime Victimization Survey (NCVS)—A second perspective on crime is provided by this survey (formerly the National Crime Survey until August 1991) of the Bureau of Justice Statistics. Details about the crimes come directly from the victims. No attempt is made to validate the information against police records or any other source.

The NCVS measures rape, robbery, assault, household and personal larceny, burglary, and motor vehicle theft. The NCVS includes offenses reported to the police, as well as those not reported. Police reporting rates (percent of victimizations) varied by type of crime. In 1994, for instance, 32 percent of the rapes/sexual assaults were reported; 55 percent of the robberies; 40 percent of assaults; 33 percent of personal thefts; 51 percent of the household burglaries; and 78 percent of motor vehicle thefts.

Murder and kidnaping are not covered. Commercial burglary and robbery were dropped from the program during 1977. The so-called victimless crimes, such as drunkenness, drug abuse, and prostitution, also are excluded, as are crimes for which it is difficult to identify knowledgeable respondents or to locate data records.

Crimes of which the victim may not be aware also cannot be measured effectively. Buying stolen property may fall into this category, as may some instances of embezzlement. Attempted crimes of many types probably are under recorded for this reason. Events in which the victim has shown a willingness to participate in illegal activity also are excluded.

In any encounter involving a personal crime, more than one criminal act can be committed against an individual. For example; a rape may be associated with a robbery; or a household offense, such as a burglary, can escalate into something more serious in the event of a personal confrontation. In classifying the survey-measured crimes, each criminal incident has been counted only once—by the most serious act that took place during the incident and ranked in accordance with the seriousness classification system used by the Federal Bureau of Investigation. The order of seriousness for crimes against persons is as follows: Rape, robbery, assault, and larceny. Consequently, if a person were both robbed and assaulted, the event would be classified as robbery; if the victim suffered physical harm, the crime would be categorized as robbery with injury. Personal crimes take precedence over household offenses.

A *victimization,* basic measure of the occurrence of a crime, is a specific criminal act as it affects a single victim. The number of victimizations is determined by the number of victims of such acts. Victimization counts serve as key elements in computing rates of victimization. For crimes against persons, the rates are based on the total number of individuals age 12 and over or on a portion of that population sharing a particular characteristic or set of traits. As general indicators of the danger of having been victimized during the reference period, the rates are not sufficiently refined to represent true measures of risk for specific individuals or households.

An *incident* is a specific criminal act involving one or more victims; therefore, the number of incidents of personal crimes lower than that of victimizations.

A major redesign of the survey was recently implemented involving such changes as a new screening questionnaire, improved measurement of rape and sexual assault categories, improvements to measurement of domestic violence, changes in crime definitions, and increased automation through the use of computer-assisted telephone interviewing (CATI). The effects of the redesign show that the new methods elicit more reports of victimizations.

Courts—Statistics on criminal offenses and the outcome of prosecutions are incomplete for the country as a whole, although data are available for many States individually. The only national compilations of such statistics were made by the Bureau of the Census for 1932 to 1945 covering a maximum of 32 States and by the Bureau of Justice Statistics for 1986, 1988, 1990, and 1992 based on a nationally representative sample survey.

The bulk of civil and criminal litigation in the country is commenced and determined in the various State courts. Only when the U.S. Constitution and acts of Congress specifically confer jurisdiction upon the Federal courts may civil litigation be heard and decided by them. Generally, the Federal courts have jurisdiction over the following types of cases: Suits or proceedings by or against the United States; civil actions between private parties arising under the Constitution, laws, or treaties of the United States; civil actions between private litigants who are citizens of different States; civil cases involving admiralty, maritime, or prize jurisdiction; and all matters in bankruptcy.

There are several types of courts with varying degrees of legal jurisdiction. These jurisdictions include original, appellate, general, and limited or special. A *court of original jurisdiction* is one having the authority initially to try a case and pass judgment on the law and the facts; a *court of appellate jurisdiction* is one with the legal authority to review cases and hear appeals; a *court of general jurisdiction* is a trial court of unlimited original jurisdiction in civil and/or criminal cases, also called a "major trial court"; a *court of limited or special jurisdiction* is a trial court with legal authority over only a particular class of cases, such as probate, juvenile, or traffic cases.

The 94 Federal courts of original jurisdiction are known as the U.S. district courts. One or more of these courts is established in every State and one each in the District of Columbia, Puerto Rico, the Virgin Islands, the Northern Mariana Islands, and Guam. Appeals from the district courts are taken to intermediate appellate courts of which there are 13, known as U.S. courts of appeals and the United States Court of Appeals for the Federal Circuit. The Supreme Court of the United States is the final and highest appellate court in the Federal system of courts.

Juvenile offenders—For statistical purposes, the FBI and most States classify as juvenile offenders persons under the age of 18 years who have committed a crime or crimes.

Delinquency cases are all cases of youths referred to a juvenile court for violation of a law or ordinance or for seriously "antisocial" conduct. Several types of facilities are available for those adjudicated delinquent, ranging from the short-term physically unrestricted environment to the long-term very restrictive atmosphere.

Prisoners—Data on prisoners in Federal and State prisons and reformatories were collected annually by the Bureau of the Census until 1950, by the Federal Bureau of Prisons until 1971, transferred then to the Law Enforcement Assistance Administration and, in 1979, to the Bureau of Justice Statistics. Adults convicted of criminal activity may be given a prison or jail sentence. A *prison* is a confinement facility having custodial authority over adults sentenced to confinement of more than one year. A *jail* is a facility, usually operated by a local law enforcement agency, holding persons detained pending adjudication and/or persons committed after adjudication to 1 year or less. Nearly every State publishes annual data either for its whole prison system or for each separate State institution.

Statistical reliability—For discussion of statistical collection, estimation, and sampling procedures and measures of statistical reliability pertaining to the National Crime Victimization Survey and Uniform Crime Reporting Program, see Appendix III.

Historical statistics—Tabular headnotes provide cross-references, where applicable, to *Historical Statistics of the United States, Colonial Times to 1970*. See Appendix IV.

Figure 5.1
Violent and Property Crime Rates: 1980 to 1994

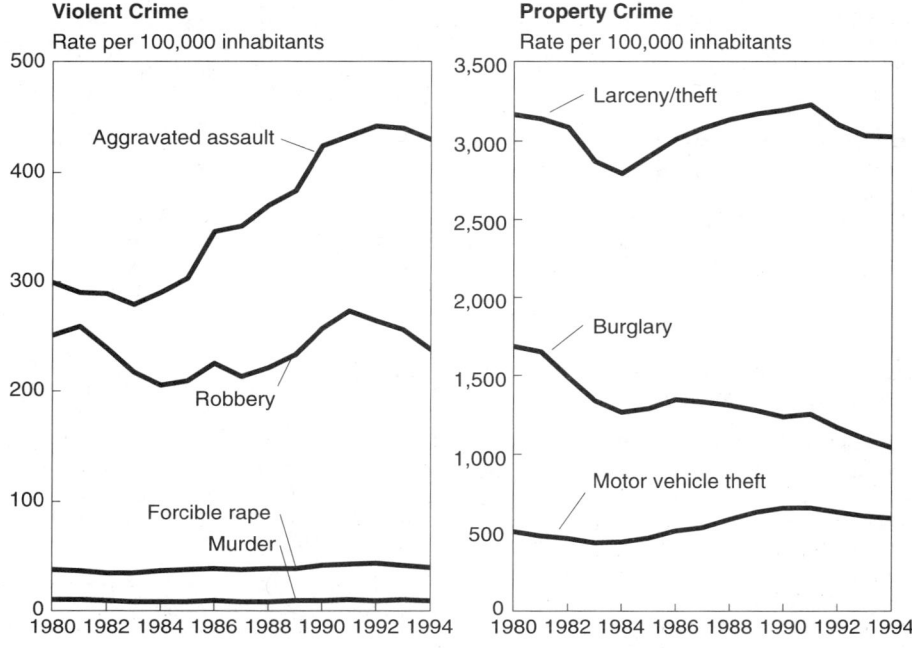

Source: Chart prepared by U.S. Bureau of the Census. For data, see table 310.

Figure 5.2
Child Abuse and Neglect Cases: 1994

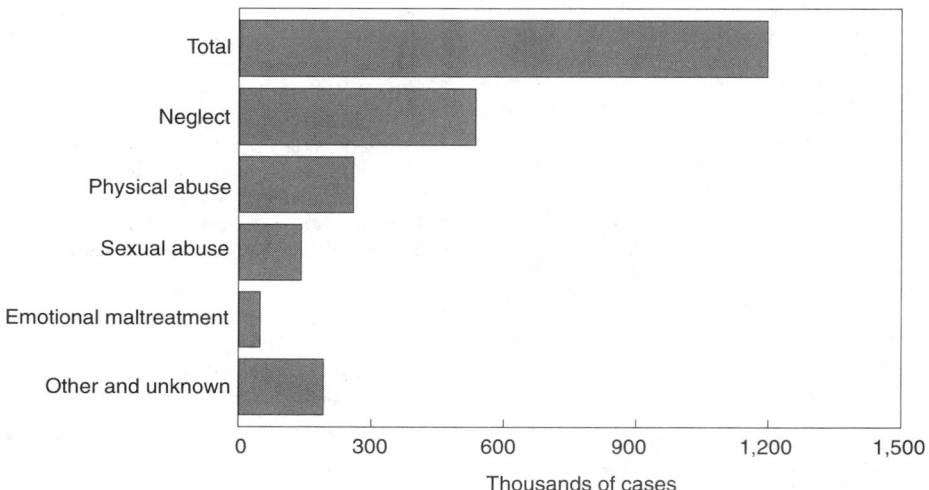

Note: More than one type of maltreatment may be substantiated per child. Therefore, items add up to more than the total shown.
Source: Chart prepared by U.S. Bureau of the Census. For data, see table 347.

No. 310. Crimes and Crime Rates, by Type: 1984 to 1994

[Data refer to offenses known to the police. Rates are based on Bureau of the Census estimated resident population as of **July 1, 1990, enumerated as of April 1.** See source for details. Minus sign (-) indicates decrease. For definitions of crimes, see text, section 5. See *Historical Statistics, Colonial Times to 1970*, series H 952-961 for related data]

ITEM AND YEAR	Total	VIOLENT CRIME					PROPERTY CRIME			
		Total	Murder [1]	Forcible rape	Rob-bery	Aggra-vated assault	Total	Burglary	Larceny—theft	Motor vehicle theft
Number of offenses (1,000):										
1984.	11,882	1,273	18.7	84.2	485	685	10,609	2,984	6,592	1,032
1985.	12,431	1,329	19.0	88.7	498	723	11,103	3,073	6,926	1,103
1986.	13,212	1,489	20.6	91.5	543	834	11,723	3,241	7,257	1,224
1987.	13,509	1,484	20.1	91.1	518	855	12,025	3,236	7,500	1,289
1988.	13,923	1,566	20.7	92.5	543	910	12,357	3,218	7,706	1,433
1989.	14,251	1,646	21.5	94.5	578	952	12,605	3,168	7,872	1,565
1990.	14,476	1,820	23.4	102.6	639	1,055	12,656	3,074	7,946	1,636
1991.	14,873	1,912	24.7	106.6	688	1,093	12,961	3,157	8,142	1,662
1992.	14,438	1,932	23.8	109.1	672	1,127	12,506	2,980	7,915	1,611
1993.	14,145	1,926	24.5	106.0	660	1,136	12,219	2,835	7,821	1,563
1994.	13,992	1,864	23.3	102.1	619	1,120	12,128	2,712	7,876	1,539
Percent change, number of offenses:										
1984 to 1994	17.8	46.4	24.6	21.3	27.6	63.5	14.3	-9.1	19.5	49.1
1991 to 1992	-3.0	1.0	-3.8	2.3	-2.4	3.0	-3.6	-5.9	-2.9	-3.2
1992 to 1993	-2.1	-0.3	2.9	-2.9	-1.8	0.8	-2.3	-5.1	-1.2	-3.1
1993 to 1994	-1.1	-3.3	-5.2	-3.8	-6.6	-1.4	-0.8	-4.5	0.7	-1.6
Rate per 100,000 population:										
1984.	5,031	539	7.9	35.7	205	290	4,492	1,264	2,791	437
1985.	5,207	557	7.9	37.1	209	303	4,651	1,287	2,901	462
1986.	5,480	618	8.6	37.9	225	346	4,863	1,345	3,010	508
1987.	5,550	610	8.3	37.4	213	351	4,940	1,330	3,081	529
1988.	5,664	637	8.4	37.6	221	370	5,027	1,309	3,135	583
1989.	5,741	663	8.7	38.1	233	383	5,078	1,276	3,171	630
1990.	5,820	732	9.4	41.2	257	424	5,089	1,236	3,195	658
1991.	5,898	758	9.8	42.3	273	433	5,140	1,252	3,229	659
1992.	5,660	758	9.3	42.8	264	442	4,903	1,168	3,103	631
1993.	5,484	747	9.5	41.1	256	440	4,738	1,099	3,032	606
1994.	5,374	716	9.0	39.2	238	430	4,658	1,042	3,025	591
Percent change, rate per 100,000 population:										
1984 to 1994	6.8	32.8	13.9	9.8	16.1	48.3	3.7	-17.6	8.4	35.2
1991 to 1992	-4.2	-	-5.4	1.2	-3.3	2.0	-4.8	-7.2	-4.1	-4.4
1992 to 1993	-3.2	-1.5	2.1	-4.1	-3.1	-0.5	-3.5	-6.3	-2.3	-4.1
1993 to 1994	-2.0	-4.3	-5.6	-4.8	-7.6	-2.3	-1.7	-5.5	-0.2	-2.5

- Represents zero.   [1] Includes nonnegligent manslaughter.

Source: U.S. Federal Bureau of Investigation, *Crime in the United States*, annual.

No. 311. Crimes and Crime Rates, by Type and Area: 1994

[**In thousands, except rate.** Rate per 100,000 population; see headnote, table 310. Estimated totals based on reports from city and rural law enforcement agencies representing 96 percent of the national population. For definitions of crimes, see text, section 5]

TYPE OF CRIME	UNITED STATES		METROPOLITAN AREAS [1]		OTHER CITIES		RURAL AREAS	
	Total	Rate	Total	Rate	Total	Rate	Total	Rate
Total.	13,992	5,374	12,209	5,894	1,134	5,318	648	2,034
Violent crime.	1,864	716	1,682	812	107	500	75	237
Murder and nonnegligent manslaughter	23	9	21	10	1	5	2	5
Forcible rape	102	39	85	41	8	39	8	26
Robbery.	619	238	598	288	16	75	5	17
Aggravated assault	1,120	430	978	472	81	382	60	189
Property crime.	12,128	4,658	10,527	5,082	1,028	4,818	573	1,797
Burglary.	2,712	1,042	2,305	1,113	206	965	202	632
Larceny-theft	7,876	3,025	6,770	3,268	773	3,623	333	1,046
Motor vehicle theft	1,539	591	1,452	701	49	230	38	119

[1] For definition, see Appendix II.

Source: U.S. Federal Bureau of Investigation, *Crime in the United States*, annual.

No. 312. Crime Rates, by State, 1992 to 1994, and by Type, 1994

[**Offenses known to the police per 100,000 population.** Based on Bureau of the Census estimated resident population as of July 1. For definitions of crimes, see text, section 5]

REGION, DIVISION, AND STATE	1992, total	1993, total	1994									
			Total	Violent crime					Property crime			
				Total	Mur-der [1]	Forci-ble rape	Rob-bery	Aggra-vated assault	Total	Bur-glary	Larce-ny—theft	Motor vehi-cle theft
United States . . .	5,660	5,483	5,374	716	9.0	39.2	238	430	4,658	1,042	3,025	591
Northeast.	4,837	4,613	4,345	662	7.1	26.5	291	337	3,682	804	2,280	599
New England	4,614	4,431	4,136	489	3.9	28.6	134	322	3,647	829	2,271	547
Maine	3,524	3,154	3,273	130	2.3	25.6	22	80	3,143	721	2,279	143
New Hampshire. . . .	3,081	2,905	2,741	117	1.4	35.8	27	53	2,624	464	1,958	203
Vermont.	3,410	3,972	3,250	97	1.0	27.6	12	56	3,153	737	2,268	149
Massachusetts	5,003	4,894	4,441	708	3.5	30.2	168	506	3,733	881	2,151	701
Rhode Island	4,578	4,499	4,119	376	4.1	27.4	87	257	3,744	913	2,311	520
Connecticut	5,053	4,560	4,548	456	6.6	24.6	188	237	4,093	890	2,587	616
Middle Atlantic	4,914	4,676	4,417	722	8.2	25.7	346	343	3,695	795	2,283	617
New York	5,858	5,551	5,071	966	11.1	25.9	477	452	4,105	906	2,490	709
New Jersey	5,064	4,801	4,661	614	5.0	24.9	288	296	4,047	912	2,475	660
Pennsylvania	3,393	3,271	3,272	427	5.9	26.1	187	208	2,845	552	1,844	449
Midwest.	4,975	4,806	4,816	601	7.5	42.9	200	350	4,215	886	2,869	460
East North Central. . .	5,136	4,953	4,951	657	8.4	44.2	231	373	4,295	898	2,889	508
Ohio	4,666	4,485	4,461	486	6.0	47.1	188	245	3,976	866	2,682	427
Indiana [2]	4,687	4,465	4,593	525	7.9	35.6	130	352	4,068	851	2,782	435
Illinois [2]	5,765	5,618	5,626	961	11.7	33.3	373	543	4,665	1,005	3,096	564
Michigan	5,611	5,453	5,445	766	9.8	70.8	229	457	4,679	967	3,056	656
Wisconsin	4,319	4,054	3,944	271	4.5	23.5	113	130	3,674	646	2,667	361
West North Central . .	4,594	4,454	4,496	468	5.3	39.8	128	295	4,027	858	2,822	347
Minnesota	4,591	4,386	4,341	359	3.2	59.7	118	179	3,982	792	2,876	314
Iowa	3,957	3,846	3,655	315	1.7	23.5	47	243	3,340	667	2,492	180
Missouri.	5,097	5,095	5,308	744	10.5	37.0	231	465	4,564	1,053	2,999	512
North Dakota	2,903	2,820	2,736	82	0.2	23.4	11	47	2,654	325	2,179	151
South Dakota	2,999	2,958	3,102	228	1.4	42.0	19	166	2,875	546	2,208	121
Nebraska	4,324	4,117	4,440	390	3.1	30.8	75	280	4,051	676	2,991	384
Kansas	5,320	4,975	4,894	479	5.8	37.1	120	316	4,415	1,121	2,955	339
South	6,155	5,983	5,848	769	10.7	43.4	221	494	5,080	1,206	3,329	545
South Atlantic.	6,428	6,334	6,257	830	10.1	41.2	254	524	5,427	1,271	3,570	585
Delaware	4,848	4,872	4,148	561	4.7	75.6	126	355	3,587	790	2,446	350
Maryland	6,225	6,107	6,123	948	11.6	40.7	403	493	5,175	1,043	3,368	763
Dist. of Columbia [3]. .	11,407	11,761	11,085	2,663	70.0	43.7	1,107	1,442	8,423	1,761	5,213	1,449
Virginia	4,299	4,116	4,048	358	8.7	28.5	133	188	3,690	639	2,772	279
West Virginia	2,610	2,533	2,528	216	5.4	20.3	42	148	2,313	586	1,547	180
North Carolina. . . .	5,802	5,652	5,625	655	10.9	33.0	181	430	4,970	1,473	3,196	302
South Carolina	5,893	5,903	6,001	1,031	9.6	54.3	186	780	4,970	1,274	3,337	360
Georgia	6,405	6,193	6,010	668	10.0	34.7	223	400	5,343	1,154	3,632	557
Florida.	8,358	8,351	8,250	1,147	8.3	52.3	329	757	7,103	1,701	4,491	912
East South Central . .	4,589	4,528	4,624	654	10.3	41.5	163	439	3,971	1,047	2,531	393
Kentucky	3,324	3,260	3,499	605	6.4	35.3	94	470	2,893	750	1,919	224
Tennessee	5,136	5,240	5,120	748	9.3	49.2	207	482	4,372	1,142	2,670	560
Alabama	5,268	4,879	4,903	684	11.9	35.2	171	465	4,219	1,044	2,843	332
Mississippi.	4,282	4,418	4,837	494	15.3	45.4	163	271	4,343	1,292	2,646	405
West South Central . .	6,589	6,228	5,866	732	12.0	48.1	199	473	5,134	1,188	3,382	564
Arkansas	4,762	4,811	4,799	595	12.0	41.9	129	413	4,204	1,097	2,792	315
Louisiana	6,546	6,847	6,671	982	19.8	44.6	267	650	5,689	1,279	3,803	608
Oklahoma	5,432	5,294	5,570	652	6.9	49.6	128	467	4,919	1,251	3,193	475
Texas	7,058	6,439	5,872	707	11.0	49.5	205	441	5,166	1,168	3,395	603
West	6,388	6,220	6,152	805	9.4	40.0	256	500	5,346	1,163	3,384	800
Mountain	6,012	5,929	6,097	581	7.3	42.2	130	402	5,516	1,105	3,830	581
Montana	4,596	4,790	5,019	177	3.3	27.2	33	114	4,842	722	3,834	286
Idaho	3,996	3,845	4,077	286	3.5	27.9	18	236	3,791	719	2,877	195
Wyoming	4,575	4,163	4,290	273	3.4	33.6	17	219	4,017	651	3,205	162
Colorado	5,959	5,527	5,318	510	5.4	43.2	107	354	4,809	926	3,490	393
New Mexico	6,434	6,266	6,188	889	10.7	52.4	141	685	5,299	1,327	3,467	505
Arizona	7,029	7,432	7,925	703	10.5	36.0	162	495	7,221	1,476	4,679	1,067
Utah	5,659	5,237	5,301	305	2.9	42.2	64	196	4,996	791	3,907	298
Nevada	6,204	6,180	6,677	1,002	11.7	68.7	352	569	5,676	1,355	3,562	759
Pacific	6,521	6,324	6,172	887	10.2	39.2	303	535	5,284	1,184	3,221	880
Washington	6,173	5,952	6,028	511	5.5	60.5	140	306	5,516	1,044	3,972	501
Oregon	5,821	5,766	6,296	521	4.9	43.2	138	334	5,776	1,101	3,970	705
California	6,679	6,457	6,174	1,013	11.8	34.9	357	609	5,161	1,223	2,958	981
Alaska.	5,570	5,568	5,708	766	6.3	69.0	146	545	4,942	800	3,601	540
Hawaii.	6,112	6,277	6,681	262	4.2	30.4	104	124	6,418	1,190	4,687	541

[1] Includes nonnegligent manslaughter. [2] Forcible rape figures for 1992 to 1994 were estimated using the national rate of forcible rapes when grouped by like agencies as figures submitted were not in accordance with national Uniform Crime Reporting program guidelines. [3] Includes offenses reported by the police at the National Zoo.

Source: U.S. Federal Bureau of Investigation, *Crime in the United States*, annual.

No. 313. Crime Rates, by Type—Selected Large Cities: 1994

[**Offenses known to the police per 100,000 population.** Based on Bureau of the Census estimated resident population as of July 1. For definitions of crimes, see text, section 5]

CITY RANKED BY POPULATION SIZE, 1994 [1]	Crime index, total	VIOLENT CRIME					PROPERTY CRIME			
		Total	Murder	Forcible rape	Robbery	Aggravated assault	Total	Burglary	Larceny—theft	Motor vehicle theft
New York, NY	7,226.1	1,860.9	21.3	36.3	988.8	814.5	5,365.1	1,204.6	2,859.9	1,300.7
Los Angeles, CA	7,840.0	2,059.0	23.8	43.8	868.0	1,123.4	5,781.0	1,226.2	3,120.5	1,434.3
Chicago, IL	(2)	(2)	33.1	(2)	1,210.5	1,440.9	7,314.9	1,563.6	4,323.4	1,427.9
Houston, TX	7,285.4	1,307.5	21.3	53.0	567.7	665.5	5,977.9	1,451.5	3,239.2	1,287.2
Philadelphia, PA	6,434.6	1,322.5	25.9	46.2	814.2	436.2	5,112.2	903.9	2,588.3	1,620.0
San Diego, CA	6,564.5	1,078.0	9.7	34.5	329.0	704.8	5,486.6	1,102.8	3,012.0	1,371.8
Phoenix, AZ	10,048.3	1,080.5	21.5	40.7	320.7	697.6	8,967.9	1,983.7	5,063.9	1,920.3
Dallas, TX	9,476.7	1,589.0	27.8	90.1	666.0	805.2	7,887.7	1,680.7	4,542.1	1,664.9
Detroit, MI	11,917.2	2,687.2	52.9	109.2	1,249.4	1,275.8	9,229.9	2,167.3	4,170.2	2,892.4
San Antonio, TX	8,768.8	647.2	19.4	56.5	278.1	293.1	8,121.6	1,642.4	5,491.5	987.7
Honolulu, HI	6,906.5	287.0	4.0	30.2	120.1	132.7	6,619.5	1,137.5	4,831.7	650.3
San Jose, CA	4,484.5	725.6	4.0	46.0	136.0	539.5	3,758.9	714.3	2,490.1	554.6
Las Vegas, NV	7,728.2	1,251.4	14.0	76.3	505.6	655.6	6,476.8	1,548.9	3,900.1	1,027.8
San Francisco, CA	8,341.8	1,461.4	12.3	39.4	893.2	516.5	6,880.4	1,086.2	4,547.0	1,247.2
Baltimore, MD	12,552.2	2,834.4	43.4	86.2	1,525.3	1,179.4	9,717.8	2,150.6	5,736.4	1,830.8
Jacksonville, FL	9,623.7	1,519.9	15.5	94.5	499.7	910.2	8,103.8	2,089.2	5,023.9	990.7
Columbus, OH	8,696.8	1,043.6	15.4	104.8	555.5	367.8	7,653.2	2,019.9	4,596.1	1,037.3
Milwaukee, WI	8,149.8	1,043.7	22.1	68.2	638.9	314.4	7,106.2	1,345.7	4,060.8	1,699.6
Memphis, TN	9,770.1	1,568.3	25.3	110.6	793.8	638.6	8,201.8	2,503.4	3,834.7	1,863.7
Washington, DC	11,077.9	2,662.6	70.0	43.7	1,107.2	1,441.8	8,415.3	1,760.9	5,205.8	1,448.6
El Paso, TX	7,159.6	950.0	7.8	41.2	192.2	708.8	6,209.7	756.7	4,762.2	690.7
Boston, MA	9,534.0	1,915.5	15.3	81.4	762.5	1,056.4	7,618.5	1,221.3	4,378.3	2,019.0
Seattle, WA	10,717.8	1,210.1	12.8	58.9	469.4	669.1	9,507.7	1,515.2	6,803.7	1,188.9
Charlotte, NC	9,686.0	1,726.7	16.5	66.4	514.7	1,129.2	7,959.3	1,958.9	5,400.8	599.5
Nashville-Davidson, TN	10,065.0	1,798.4	14.0	97.4	508.7	1,178.2	8,266.6	1,600.2	5,520.6	1,145.8
Austin, TX	7,941.0	635.0	7.2	48.7	301.4	277.7	7,306.0	1,377.2	5,160.1	768.7
Denver, CO	6,933.1	920.8	15.8	71.6	335.4	498.0	6,012.3	1,518.1	3,272.1	1,222.1
Cleveland, OH	7,456.1	1,529.7	26.1	148.0	775.1	580.6	5,926.4	1,581.7	2,554.4	1,790.3
New Orleans, LA	10,089.7	1,886.9	85.8	88.3	976.1	736.7	8,202.8	2,037.3	4,431.3	1,734.2
Fort Worth, TX	9,189.3	1,277.8	27.9	87.4	503.7	658.7	7,911.5	1,756.3	5,020.7	1,134.5
Portland, OR	11,815.7	1,902.1	10.8	86.4	506.2	1,298.7	9,913.6	1,727.8	6,125.0	2,060.8
Oklahoma City, OK	12,004.7	1,402.9	14.1	118.4	379.0	891.4	10,601.8	2,233.2	7,308.3	1,060.3
Long Beach, CA	7,530.3	1,416.7	17.9	37.4	767.3	594.1	6,113.6	1,453.0	3,057.0	1,603.6
Tucson, AZ	12,254.8	1,106.0	8.4	65.5	229.3	802.9	11,148.8	1,632.3	7,976.6	1,539.9
Kansas City, MO	12,551.4	2,435.3	32.3	111.6	848.8	1,442.5	10,116.2	2,723.4	5,718.4	1,674.4
Virginia Beach, VA	4,966.0	270.9	7.7	33.9	142.5	86.8	4,695.1	759.8	3,713.9	221.3
Atlanta, GA	16,118.5	3,571.0	46.4	102.6	1,299.4	2,122.5	12,547.5	2,951.3	7,511.6	2,084.6
St. Louis, MO	16,350.7	3,750.7	63.5	77.9	1,543.1	2,066.1	12,600.0	3,207.2	7,105.9	2,286.9
Sacramento, CA	10,326.7	1,206.3	15.9	44.7	588.5	557.2	9,120.4	2,073.7	4,775.4	2,271.4
Fresno, CA	12,041.1	1,620.0	22.0	50.2	734.3	813.5	10,421.1	2,001.5	4,871.2	3,548.4
Tulsa, OK	7,400.7	1,215.5	11.0	77.6	280.6	846.3	6,185.1	1,715.8	3,289.0	1,180.4
Miami, FL	17,177.0	3,413.6	30.5	58.2	1,537.2	1,787.7	13,763.4	2,967.8	8,064.9	2,730.7
Oakland, CA	10,633.0	2,193.9	36.9	85.1	1,021.1	1,050.8	8,439.1	1,850.4	4,688.0	1,900.7
Minneapolis, MN	11,167.0	1,907.6	16.7	155.9	928.7	806.3	9,259.4	2,387.6	5,738.1	1,133.7
Pittsburgh, PA	7,148.8	1,113.7	17.4	70.8	669.8	355.7	6,035.1	1,176.1	3,409.7	1,449.3
Cincinnati, OH	8,012.7	1,323.1	10.4	104.1	580.7	627.9	6,689.7	1,640.5	4,577.2	472.0
Toledo, OH	9,130.5	1,104.5	12.1	107.3	523.0	462.1	8,026.1	1,985.6	4,849.5	1,191.0
Buffalo, NY	9,552.2	2,124.2	27.7	86.3	1,007.8	1,002.3	7,428.0	2,247.2	3,774.6	1,406.2
Wichita, KS	9,208.3	742.2	13.3	70.7	334.8	323.4	8,466.1	2,053.2	5,328.9	1,083.9
Mesa, AZ	8,295.9	749.4	5.4	38.0	129.0	576.9	7,546.5	1,582.8	4,863.4	1,100.3
Colorado Springs, CO	6,667.6	481.5	4.5	73.0	128.5	275.5	6,186.0	971.7	4,865.1	349.2
Tampa, FL	17,481.0	3,482.6	21.0	101.1	1,146.4	2,214.1	13,998.4	2,964.1	7,297.5	3,736.8
Santa Ana, CA	6,023.1	1,050.8	25.3	27.3	604.4	393.8	4,972.3	836.8	2,864.0	1,271.6
Arlington, TX	7,253.1	852.0	6.3	50.2	228.1	567.4	6,401.1	1,210.1	4,325.1	865.9
Anaheim, CA	6,554.6	947.9	8.6	32.3	406.2	500.9	5,606.7	1,175.6	3,201.7	1,229.4
Corpus Christi, TX	9,817.6	856.3	4.7	64.3	177.7	609.7	8,961.3	1,534.2	6,939.8	487.2
Louisville, KY	6,430.5	1,004.7	18.8	51.4	473.0	461.4	5,425.8	1,593.5	2,945.3	887.1
St. Paul, MN	7,101.1	995.6	10.6	98.1	318.0	568.9	6,105.5	1,485.7	3,881.0	738.8
Newark, NJ	13,827.1	3,840.6	35.4	76.4	2,130.8	1,598.0	9,986.5	2,375.4	4,118.8	3,492.3
Birmingham, AL	12,191.8	2,444.8	49.8	100.7	730.7	1,563.6	9,746.9	2,392.4	6,009.7	1,344.8
Norfolk, VA	7,635.0	916.0	23.5	60.4	460.3	371.9	6,719.0	1,199.8	4,823.1	696.1
Anchorage, AK	7,356.9	976.9	8.7	78.1	287.4	602.8	6,380.0	897.2	4,619.0	863.7
Aurora, CO	7,813.9	1,448.0	5.9	58.1	246.4	1,137.5	6,365.9	1,193.7	4,667.9	504.3
St. Petersburg, FL	9,844.2	2,254.5	9.4	87.5	619.7	1,537.9	7,590.3	1,931.8	5,067.2	591.4
Riverside, CA	9,203.3	1,626.8	15.2	55.2	502.6	1,053.8	7,576.4	2,068.9	3,894.3	1,613.2
Lexington-Fayette, KY	6,799.7	980.4	9.7	48.9	294.4	627.5	5,819.3	1,300.9	4,235.8	282.6
Rochester, NY	9,613.2	1,154.3	26.4	61.7	710.0	356.3	8,458.8	2,272.5	5,272.9	913.4
Jersey City, NJ	8,119.4	1,865.1	16.0	32.0	969.6	847.5	6,254.2	1,854.8	2,803.6	1,595.9
Raleigh, NC	7,243.6	951.4	13.2	39.0	361.7	537.5	6,292.3	1,554.6	4,292.6	445.0
Baton Rouge, LA	14,052.4	2,449.7	28.2	79.4	648.7	1,693.3	11,602.6	2,362.8	7,254.8	1,985.0
Akron, OH	7,102.8	960.7	10.2	86.6	360.5	503.4	6,142.2	1,350.4	3,879.9	911.8
Stockton, CA	10,499.9	1,613.5	19.7	54.2	641.4	898.3	8,886.4	2,041.3	4,991.3	1,853.8

[1] Crime data were not available for Indianapolis, IN, and Albuquerque, NM, in 1994.   [2] The rates for forcible rape, violent crime, and crime index are not shown because the forcible rape figures were not in accordance with national Uniform Crime Reporting guidelines.

Source: U.S. Federal Bureau of Investigation, *Crime in the United States*, annual.

No. 314. Murder—Circumstances and Weapons Used or Cause of Death: 1980 to 1994

[Based solely on police investigation. For definition of murder, see text, section 5]

CHARACTERISTIC	1980	1990	1993	1994	CHARACTERISTIC	1980	1990	1993	1994
Murders, total	**21,860**	**20,273**	**23,180**	**22,084**	Other motives	20.6	19.4	21.7	23.1
Percent distribution	100.0	100.0	100.0	100.0	Unknown.	15.1	24.8	27.5	28.1
CIRCUMSTANCES					TYPE OF WEAPON OR CAUSE OF DEATH				
Felonies, total	17.7	20.8	19.2	18.4					
Robbery	10.8	9.2	9.9	9.4	Guns	62.4	64.3	69.6	70.0
Narcotics	1.7	6.7	5.6	5.6	Handguns	45.8	49.8	57.0	57.8
Sex offenses	1.5	1.1	0.7	0.6	Cutting or stabbing	19.3	17.4	12.8	12.7
Other felonies	3.7	3.7	3.0	2.8	Blunt objects [1]	5.0	5.4	4.4	4.1
Suspected felonies	6.7	0.7	0.6	0.6	Personal weapons [2] . . .	5.9	5.5	5.0	5.3
Argument, total.	39.9	34.4	30.9	29.8	Strangulations,				
Property or money. . .	2.6	2.5	1.9	1.8	asphyxiations	2.3	2.0	1.9	1.8
Romantic triangle . . .	2.3	2.0	1.9	1.7	Fire	1.3	1.4	0.9	0.9
Other arguments	35.0	29.8	27.1	26.3	All other [3]	3.8	4.0	5.4	5.2

[1] Refers to club, hammer, etc. [2] Hands, fists, feet, etc. [3] Includes poison, drowning, explosives, narcotics, and unknown.
Source: U.S. Federal Bureau of Investigation, *Crime in the United States*, annual.

No. 315. Murder Victims, by Age, Sex, and Race: 1994

AGE	Total	SEX			RACE			
		Male	Female	Unknown	White	Black	Other	Unknown
Total	**22,084**	**17,317**	**4,740**	**27**	**10,198**	**11,223**	**498**	**165**
Percent distribution	100.0	70.4	21.5	0.1	46.2	50.8	2.3	0.7
Under 18 yrs. old	2,521	1,847	674	-	1,115	1,311	84	11
18 yrs. old and over	19,179	15,186	3,988	5	8,898	9,770	409	102
Infant (under 1 yr. old).	257	150	107	-	150	97	7	3
1 to 4 yrs. old	470	263	207	-	241	214	13	2
5 to 9 yrs. old	138	62	76	-	80	54	4	-
10 to 14 yrs. old.	317	206	111	-	137	165	14	1
15 to 19 yrs. old	3,021	2,661	359	1	1,120	1,795	87	19
20 to 24 yrs. old	4,091	3,517	574	-	1,536	2,471	64	20
25 to 29 yrs. old.	3,236	2,629	605	2	1,355	1,809	61	11
30 to 34 yrs. old.	2,917	2,210	707	-	1,388	1,450	62	17
35 to 39 yrs. old	2,248	1,686	562	-	1,087	1,108	47	6
40 to 44 yrs. old	1,565	1,236	329	-	781	719	55	10
45 to 49 yrs. old	1,007	773	234	-	568	400	33	6
50 to 54 yrs. old	682	520	161	1	428	230	18	6
55 to 59 yrs. old	444	331	113	-	287	141	11	5
60 to 64 yrs. old	342	252	90	-	233	102	6	1
65 to 69 yrs. old	284	182	102	-	172	106	4	2
70 to 74 yrs. old	245	145	100	-	153	87	4	1
75 yrs. old and over	436	210	225	1	297	133	3	3
Age unknown	384	284	78	22	185	142	5	52

- Represents zero.
Source: U.S. Federal Bureau of Investigation, *Crime in the United States*, annual.

No. 316. Homicide Victims, by Race and Sex: 1970 to 1993

[**Rates per 100,000 resident population in specified group.** Excludes deaths to nonresidents of United States. Beginning 1980, deaths classified according to the ninth revision of the *International Classification of Diseases;* for earlier years, classified according to revision in use at the time; see text, section 2. See also *Historical Statistics, Colonial Times to 1970*, series H 971-978]

YEAR	HOMICIDE VICTIMS					HOMICIDE RATE [2]				
	Total [1]	White		Black		Total [1]	White		Black	
		Male	Female	Male	Female		Male	Female	Male	Female
1970	16,848	5,865	1,938	7,265	1,569	8.3	6.8	2.1	67.6	13.3
1980	24,278	10,381	3,177	8,385	1,898	10.7	10.9	3.2	66.6	13.5
1981	23,646	9,941	3,125	8,312	1,825	10.3	10.4	3.1	64.8	12.7
1982	22,358	9,260	3,179	7,730	1,743	9.6	9.6	3.1	59.1	12.0
1983	20,191	8,355	2,880	6,822	1,672	8.6	8.6	2.8	51.4	11.3
1984	19,796	8,171	2,956	6,563	1,677	8.4	8.3	2.9	48.7	11.2
1985	19,893	8,122	3,041	6,616	1,666	8.3	8.2	2.9	48.4	11.0
1986	21,731	8,567	3,123	7,634	1,861	9.0	8.6	3.0	55.0	12.1
1987	21,103	7,979	3,149	7,518	1,969	8.7	7.9	3.0	53.3	12.6
1988	22,032	7,994	3,072	8,314	2,089	9.0	7.9	2.9	58.0	13.2
1989	22,909	8,337	2,971	8,888	2,074	9.2	8.2	2.8	61.1	12.9
1990	24,932	9,147	3,006	9,981	2,163	10.0	9.0	2.8	69.2	13.5
1991	26,513	9,581	3,201	10,628	2,330	10.5	9.3	3.0	72.0	14.2
1992	25,488	9,456	3,012	10,131	2,187	10.0	9.1	2.8	67.5	13.1
1993	26,009	9,054	3,232	10,640	2,297	10.1	8.6	3.0	69.7	13.6

[1] Includes races not shown separately. [2] Rate based on enumerated population figures as of April 1 for 1970, 1980, and 1990; July 1 estimates for other years.
Source: U.S. National Center for Health Statistics, *Vital Statistics of the United States*, annual, and unpublished data.

No. 317. Forcible Rape—Number and Rate: 1970 to 1994

[For definition of rape, see text, section 5]

ITEM	1970	1980	1985	1988	1989	1990	1991	1992	1993	1994
NUMBER										
Total.	37,990	82,990	88,670	92,490	94,500	102,560	106,590	109,060	106,010	102,100
By force	26,888	63,599	71,060	75,441	78,411	86,541	91,522	93,825	92,360	89,193
Attempt.	11,102	19,391	17,610	17,049	16,089	16,019	15,068	15,235	13,650	12,907
RATE										
Per 100,000 population	18.7	36.8	37.1	37.6	38.1	41.2	42.3	42.8	41.1	39.2
Per 100,000 females	30.4	71.6	72.3	73.4	74.3	80.5	82.5	83.5	80.3	76.6
Per 100,000 females 12 years years old and over.	46.3	86.3	86.6	88.1	89.3	96.6	100.9	100.5	96.4	92.1
AVERAGE ANNUAL PERCENT CHANGE IN RATE [1]										
Per 100,000 population	(NA)	6.1	3.9	0.5	1.3	8.1	2.7	1.2	-4.0	-4.6
Per 100,000 females 12 years old and over.	(NA)	6.0	4.3	0.7	1.4	8.2	4.5	-0.4	-4.1	-4.5

NA Not available.   [1] Represents annual average from prior year shown except for 1980, from 1979; for 1985, from 1984; and for 1988, from 1987.

Source: U.S. Federal Bureau of Investigation, *Population-at-Risk Rates and Selected Crime Indicators,* annual.

No. 318. Robbery and Property Crimes, by Type and Selected Characteristic: 1980 to 1994

[For definition of crime, see text, section 5]

ITEM	NUMBER OF OFFENSES (1,000)				RATE PER 100,000 INHABITANTS				AVERAGE VALUE LOST (dol.)	
	1980	1990	1993	1994	1980	1990	1993	1994	1993	1994
Robbery, total [1] **. . . . .**	**566**	**639**	**660**	**620**	**251.1**	**257.0**	**255.8**	**237.7**	**815**	**801**
Type of crime:										
Street or highway	293	359	361	338	130.1	144.2	139.9	129.7	628	651
Commercial house	78	73	82	76	34.6	29.5	31.9	29.2	1,304	1,229
Gas station	23	18	15	13	10.4	7.1	6.0	5.2	515	450
Convenience store	38	39	35	32	17.0	15.6	13.5	12.2	449	387
Residence	60	62	68	67	26.8	25.1	26.3	25.9	1,104	1,041
Bank	8	9	12	9	3.8	3.8	4.6	3.4	3,308	3,551
Weapon used:										
Firearm.	228	234	280	257	101.3	94.1	108.4	98.8	(NA)	(NA)
Knife or cutting instrument	73	76	66	59	32.3	30.7	25.5	22.5	(NA)	(NA)
Other dangerous weapon	51	61	62	60	22.8	24.5	24.2	22.9	(NA)	(NA)
Strongarm	214	268	252	243	94.8	107.7	97.7	93.5	(NA)	(NA)
Burglary, total	**3,795**	**3,074**	**2,835**	**2,712**	**1,684.1**	**1,235.9**	**1,099.2**	**1,041.8**	**1,185**	**1,311**
Forcible entry	2,789	2,150	1,932	1,822	1,237.5	864.5	749.3	700.0	(NA)	(NA)
Unlawful entry	711	678	676	677	315.6	272.8	262.2	260.1	(NA)	(NA)
Attempted forcible entry.	295	245	226	213	131.0	98.7	87.7	81.7	(NA)	(NA)
Residence	2,525	2,033	1,884	1,814	1,120.6	817.4	730.5	696.7	1,189	1,296
Nonresidence	1,270	1,041	951	898	563.5	418.5	368.7	345.1	1,179	1,341
Occurred during the night	1,508	1,135	1,032	957	669.0	456.4	400.2	367.7	(NA)	(NA)
Occurred during the day	1,263	1,151	1,070	1,049	560.3	462.8	414.9	402.7	(NA)	(NA)
Larceny-theft, total.	**7,137**	**7,946**	**7,821**	**7,876**	**3,167.0**	**3,194.8**	**3,032.4**	**3,025.4**	**504**	**505**
Pocket picking.	85	81	73	64	37.9	32.4	28.2	24.5	411	428
Purse snatching.	107	82	68	60	47.5	32.8	26.5	23.2	341	279
Shoplifting.	773	1,291	1,201	1,178	343.0	519.1	465.6	452.4	109	133
From motor vehicles.	1,231	1,744	1,828	1,865	546.4	701.3	708.6	716.4	531	542
Motor vehicle accessories	1,366	1,185	1,091	1,014	606.2	476.3	423.0	389.4	303	312
Bicycles	715	443	478	496	317.5	178.2	185.5	190.7	241	252
From buildings.	1,187	1,118	1,029	1,027	526.9	449.4	399.0	394.3	831	851
From coin-operated machines. . . .	58	63	62	53	25.8	25.4	23.9	20.4	208	228
Other.	1,613	1,940	1,991	2,120	715.7	780.0	772.0	814.2	740	680
Motor vehicles, total [2] **. . . .**	**1,132**	**1,636**	**1,561**	**1,539**	**502.2**	**657.8**	**605.3**	**591.2**	**4,808**	**4,940**
Automobiles	845	1,304	1,236	1,216	374.8	524.3	479.2	467.2	(NA)	(NA)
Trucks and buses.	149	238	240	239	66.1	95.5	93.0	92.0	(NA)	(NA)

NA Not available.   [1] Includes other crimes not shown separately.   [2] Includes other types of motor vehicles not shown separately.

Source: U.S. Federal Bureau of Investigation, *Population-at-Risk Rates and Selected Crime Indicators,* annual.

No. 319. Criminal Victimizations and Victimization Rates: 1993 and 1994

[Based on National Crime Victimization Survey; see text, section 5, and Appendix III. The total population age 12 or older in 1993 was 211,524,770; in 1994 the population was 213,747,400]

TYPE OF CRIME	NUMBER OF VICTIMIZATIONS (1,000)		VICTIMIZATION RATES [1]	
	1993	1994	1993	1994
All crimes, total.............................	**43,547**	**42,359**	**(X)**	**(X)**
Personal crimes [2]............................	**11,365**	**11,349**	**53.7**	**53.1**
Crimes of violence.............................	10,848	10,860	51.3	50.8
Completed violence..........................	3,213	3,205	15.2	15.0
Attempted/threatened violence..................	7,635	7,654	36.1	35.8
Rape/sexual assault..........................	485	433	2.3	2.0
Rape/attempted rape.......................	313	316	1.5	1.5
Rape..................................	160	168	0.8	0.8
Attempted rape.........................	152	149	0.7	0.7
Sexual assault...........................	173	117	0.8	0.5
Robbery..................................	1,291	1,299	6.1	6.1
Completed/property taken....................	815	795	3.9	3.7
With injury...........................	274	288	1.3	1.3
Without injury........................	541	507	2.6	2.4
Attempted to take property..................	476	504	2.3	2.4
With injury...........................	96	122	0.5	0.6
Without injury........................	381	382	1.8	1.8
Assault...................................	9,072	9,128	42.9	42.7
Aggravated..............................	2,563	2,478	12.1	11.6
With injury...........................	713	679	3.4	3.2
Threatened with weapon....................	1,850	1,799	8.7	8.4
Simple.................................	6,509	6,650	30.8	31.1
With minor injury.......................	1,356	1,466	6.4	6.9
Without injury.........................	5,153	5,184	24.4	24.3
Personal theft [3]...........................	517	489	2.4	2.3
Property crimes.............................	**32,182**	**31,011**	**322.1**	**307.6**
Household burglary...........................	5,984	5,482	59.9	54.4
Completed..............................	4,824	4,573	48.3	45.4
Attempted forcible entry....................	1,160	910	11.6	9.0
Motor vehicle theft...........................	1,961	1,764	19.6	17.5
Completed..............................	1,291	1,172	12.9	11.6
Attempted..............................	670	591	6.7	5.9
Theft.....................................	24,238	23,765	242.6	235.7
Completed [4]............................	23,020	22,743	230.4	225.6
Attempted...............................	1,218	1,022	14.3	10.1

X Not applicable.   [1] Per 1,000 persons age 12 or older or per 1,000 households.   [2] The victimization survey cannot measure murder because of the inability to question the victim.   [3] Includes pocket picking, purse snatching, and attempted purse snatching.   [4] Includes thefts in which the amount taken was not ascertained. In 1993, this category accounted for 1,433,000 victimizations and in 1994, 1,241,000.

Source: U.S. Bureau of Justice Statistics, *Criminal Victimization 1994*, April 1996.

No. 320. Victimization Rates, by Type of Crime and Characteristic: 1994

[**Rate per 1,000 persons age 12 years or older**. Based on National Crime Victimization Survey; see text, section 5, and Appendix III]

CHARACTERISTIC	All crime	CRIMES OF VIOLENCE						Personal theft
		All crimes of violence	Rape/ sexual assault	Robbery	Assault			
					Total	Aggra- vated	Simple	
Total.....................	**53.1**	**50.8**	**2.0**	**6.1**	**42.7**	**11.6**	**31.1**	**2.3**
Male..........................	61.7	59.6	0.2	8.1	51.3	15.3	35.9	2.0
Female........................	45.1	42.5	3.7	4.1	34.7	8.1	26.6	2.5
12 to 15 yrs. old................	117.4	114.8	3.1	12.0	99.7	22.2	77.6	2.6
16 to 19 yrs. old................	125.9	121.7	5.1	11.8	104.8	33.7	71.1	4.2
20 to 24 yrs. old................	102.5	99.2	5.0	11.3	82.9	26.6	56.4	3.3
25 to 34 yrs. old................	63.2	60.9	2.9	7.5	50.6	13.7	36.9	2.3
35 to 49 yrs. old................	41.4	39.5	1.6	5.2	32.8	7.6	25.2	1.9
50 to 64 yrs. old................	16.8	15.1	0.2	2.3	12.6	3.3	9.3	1.7
65 yrs. old and over.............	7.2	5.1	0.1	1.4	3.6	1.2	2.4	2.1
White.........................	51.5	49.4	1.9	4.8	42.7	10.9	31.8	2.1
Black.........................	65.4	61.8	2.7	14.0	45.0	16.6	28.4	3.6
Other.........................	49.1	47.6	2.5	9.0	36.1	11.9	24.2	1.6
Hispanic......................	63.3	59.8	2.6	9.8	47.4	16.2	31.2	3.5
Non-Hispanic..................	51.9	49.8	2.0	5.6	42.1	11.1	31.0	2.1
Household income:								
Less than $7,500..............	88.3	83.6	6.7	11.1	65.8	20.5	45.3	4.7
$7,500-$14,999...............	60.8	58.6	3.3	7.1	48.1	13.8	34.3	2.2
$15,000-$24,999.............	51.7	49.9	2.3	5.9	41.7	13.2	28.5	1.8
$25,000-$34,999.............	51.3	49.3	1.2	4.6	43.5	11.3	32.3	2.0
$35,000-$49,999.............	49.3	46.8	0.9	4.8	41.1	10.1	31.0	2.6
$50,000-$74,999.............	47.6	46.1	0.8	4.2	41.1	9.5	31.6	1.5
$75,000 or more	42.7	40.0	0.9	4.5	34.6	8.0	26.5	2.7

Source: U.S. Bureau of Justice Statistics, *Criminal Victimization 1994*, April 1996.

No. 321. Victim-Offender Relationship in Crimes of Violence, by Characteristics of the Criminal Incident: 1994

[In percent. Covers only crimes of violence. Based on National Crime Victimization Survey; see text, section 5, and Appendix III]

CHARACTERISTICS OF INCIDENT	Total	Rape/ sexual assault	Robbery	ASSAULT Total	ASSAULT Aggra-vated[1]	ASSAULT Simple
Total.	**100%**	**100%**	**100%**	**100%**	**100%**	**100%**
Victim/offender relationship: [2]						
Relatives.	9	11	6	9	7	10
Well-known	23	35	13	24	21	25
Casual acquaintance.	15	21	3	16	12	18
Stranger	53	33	77	51	60	48
Time of day:						
6 a.m. to 6 p.m.	53	31	42	62	36	62
6 p.m. to midnight.	35	37	43	37	33	33
Midnight to 6 a.m..	12	32	15	1	32	5
Location of crime:						
At or near victim's home or lodging	26	37	24	26	25	26
Friend's/relative's/neighbor's home.	7	21	4	7	9	7
Commercial places	13	7	8	14	11	15
Parking lots/garages	8	6	12	7	9	7
School	13	3	4	15	7	18
Streets other than near victim's home. . .	20	8	37	18	26	15
Other [3]	13	17	10	13	12	13
Victim's activity:						
At work or traveling to or from work	22	8	16	23	21	24
School	13	5	7	14	8	16
Activities at home	22	38	17	22	19	23
Shopping/errands	4	2	11	3	4	3
Leisure activities away from home	23	32	21	23	28	21
Traveling.	10	6	20	9	12	7
Other	7	8	8	7	9	6
Distance from victim's home:						
Inside home or lodging	5	34	14	14	12	14
Near victim's home	16	10	13	15	16	15
1 mile or less.	24	12	29	21	22	21
5 miles or less	26	14	22	24	25	24
50 miles or less	24	23	19	22	20	22
More than 50 miles	5	6	4	4	5	4
Weapons:						
No weapons present	71	84	45	73	5	(X)
Weapons present	29	16	55	27	95	(X)
Firearm	12	6	31	10	35	(X)
Other type of weapon [4].	17	10	25	17	60	(X)

X Not applicable. [1] An aggravated assault is any assault in which an offender possesses or uses a weapon or inflicts serious injury. [2] Excludes "don't know" relationships. [3] Includes areas on public transportation or inside station, in apartment yard, park, field, playground, and other areas. [4] Includes knives, other sharp objects, blunt objects, and other types of weapons.

Source: U.S. Bureau of Justice Statistics, *Criminal Victimization 1994*, April 1996.

No. 322. Property Victimization Rates, by Characteristic: 1994

[Victimizations per 1,000 households. Based on National Crime Victimization Survey; see text, section 5, and Appendix III]

CHARACTERISTIC	Total	Burglary	Motor vehicle theft	Theft
Total.	**307.6**	**54.4**	**17.5**	**235.7**
Race:				
White.	301.9	51.7	15.6	234.6
Black.	341.3	70.8	26.6	243.8
Other.	334.9	64.3	34.1	236.5
Ethnicity:				
Hispanic.	425.5	71.0	39.9	314.5
Non-Hispanic.	298.0	53.1	15.6	229.3
Household income:				
Less than $7,500	295.8	78.6	13.9	203.2
$7,500-$14,999	296.6	65.4	15.2	216.0
$15,000-$24,999	307.0	60.5	16.3	230.2
$25,000-$34,999	307.1	50.9	20.0	236.3
$35,000-$49,999	325.8	51.6	17.0	257.2
$50,000-$74,999	356.3	39.6	20.7	296.0
$75,000 or more	356.6	40.9	17.7	297.9
Residence:				
Urban.	376.4	69.4	29.3	277.7
Suburban.	296.5	46.5	15.6	234.3
Rural.	246.4	49.6	6.9	189.8
Form of tenure:				
Home owned.	272.2	45.5	14.5	212.2
Home rented.	371.2	70.3	22.8	278.1

Source: U.S. Bureau of Justice Statistics, *Criminal Victimization 1994*, April 1996.

No. 323. Persons Arrested, by Charge and Race: 1994

[Represents arrests (not charges) reported by 10,693 agencies with a total 1994 population 208 million as estimated by FBI]

OFFENSE CHARGED	TOTAL ARRESTS (1,000)					PERCENT DISTRIBUTION				
	Total	White	Black	American Indian or Alaskan Native	Asian or Pacific Islander	Total	White	Black	American Indian or Alaskan Native	Asian or Pacific Islander
Total	11,880	7,921	3,712	127	120	100.0	66.7	31.2	1.1	1.0
Serious crimes [1]	2,388	1,467	866	23	32	100.0	61.4	36.3	1.0	1.3
Murder and nonnegligent manslaughter	19	8	10	-	-	100.0	41.7	56.4	0.7	1.2
Forcible rape	30	17	12	-	-	100.0	56.1	41.7	1.1	1.1
Robbery	147	55	89	1	2	100.0	37.5	60.8	0.5	1.2
Aggravated assault	450	265	176	4	5	100.0	58.9	39.2	0.9	1.0
Burglary	321	216	98	3	3	100.0	67.4	30.7	0.9	1.1
Larceny/theft	1,239	798	409	13	19	100.0	64.5	33.0	1.1	1.5
Motor vehicle theft	166	95	67	2	3	100.0	57.3	40.1	0.9	1.7
Arson	17	12	4	-	-	100.0	75.1	23.0	1.0	0.9
All other nonserious crimes:										
Other assaults	993	628	343	12	10	100.0	63.2	34.6	1.2	1.0
Forgery and counterfeiting	93	59	32	1	1	100.0	63.7	34.4	0.6	1.4
Fraud	331	206	121	2	3	100.0	62.2	36.5	0.5	0.8
Embezzlement	12	8	4	-	-	100.0	65.5	32.8	0.4	1.3
Stolen property—buying, receiving, possessing	135	78	55	1	1	100.0	57.7	40.5	0.7	1.1
Vandalism	260	194	59	3	3	100.0	74.8	22.8	1.1	1.3
Weapons; carrying, possessing, etc.	213	122	88	1	2	100.0	57.2	41.1	0.6	1.1
Prostitution and commercialized vice	87	54	31	-	2	100.0	62.1	35.6	0.6	1.8
Sex offenses (except forcible rape and prostitution)	82	63	18	1	1	100.0	76.2	21.6	1.1	1.1
Drug abuse violations	1,120	679	430	5	6	100.0	60.6	38.4	0.4	0.6
Gambling	16	8	7	-	1	100.0	49.5	45.7	0.3	4.5
Offenses against family and children	91	58	30	1	2	100.0	64.1	32.7	1.3	1.8
Driving under the influence	1,067	936	108	15	9	100.0	87.7	10.1	1.4	0.8
Liquor laws	427	356	58	10	3	100.0	83.4	13.5	2.4	0.7
Drunkenness	572	461	96	13	2	100.0	80.6	16.8	2.2	0.3
Disorderly conduct	602	392	199	8	3	100.0	65.1	33.1	1.2	0.6
Vagrancy	21	12	9	-	-	100.0	57.3	40.4	1.7	0.5
All other offenses (except traffic)	3,050	1,897	1,093	29	31	100.0	62.2	35.8	0.9	1.0
Suspicion	11	6	6	-	-	100.0	49.7	49.5	0.6	0.3
Curfew and loitering law violations	107	82	22	1	2	100.0	76.2	20.7	1.2	1.9
Runaways	202	156	38	2	6	100.0	77.3	19.0	0.8	2.8

- Represents zero.   [1] Includes arson.

Source: U.S. Federal Bureau of Investigation, Crime in the United States, annual.

No. 324. Juvenile Arrests for Selected Offenses: 1980 to 1994

[Juveniles are persons between the ages 10-17]

OFFENSE	1980	1985	1987	1988	1989	1990	1991	1992	1993	1994
Number of contributing agencies	8,178	11,263	10,616	10,077	10,502	10,765	10,148	11,058	10,277	10,693
Population covered (1,000)	169,439	206,269	202,337	192,275	199,098	204,543	189,962	217,754	213,705	208,035
NUMBER										
Violent crime, total	77,220	75,077	72,829	71,251	84,551	97,103	95,677	118,358	122,434	125,141
Murder	1,475	1,384	1,592	1,827	2,204	2,661	2,626	3,025	3,473	3,114
Forcible rape	3,668	5,073	4,909	4,278	4,691	4,971	4,766	5,451	5,490	4,873
Robbery	38,529	31,833	27,682	25,459	30,728	34,944	35,632	42,639	44,598	47,046
Aggravated assault	33,548	36,787	38,646	39,687	46,928	54,527	52,653	67,243	68,873	70,108
Weapon law violations	21,203	27,035	25,653	27,473	31,480	33,123	37,575	49,903	54,414	52,278
Drug abuse, total	86,685	78,660	71,716	72,303	86,757	66,300	58,603	73,232	90,618	124,931
Sale and manufacturing	13,004	14,846	18,718	23,174	33,652	24,575	22,929	25,331	27,635	32,746
Heroin/cocaine	1,318	2,851	9,315	14,914	19,760	15,194	15,011	17,881	18,716	20,327
Marijuana	8,876	8,646	5,922	4,811	6,781	4,372	3,579	4,853	6,144	8,812
Synthetic narcotics	465	414	1,189	846	701	346	570	663	455	465
Dangerous nonnarcotic drug	2,345	2,935	2,292	2,603	6,410	2,346	1,865	1,934	2,320	3,142
Possession	73,681	63,814	52,998	49,129	53,105	41,725	35,674	47,901	62,983	92,185
Heroin/cocaine	2,614	7,809	13,428	15,754	19,745	15,194	13,747	16,855	17,726	21,004
Marijuana	64,465	50,582	34,981	28,885	27,253	20,940	16,490	25,004	37,915	61,003
Synthetic narcotics	1,524	1,085	1,051	1,096	1,115	1,155	885	897	1,008	1,227
Dangerous nonnarcotic drug	5,078	4,338	3,538	3,394	4,992	4,436	4,552	5,145	6,334	8,951

Source: U.S. Federal Bureau of Investigation, Crime in the United States, annual.

No. 325. Persons Arrested, by Charge, Sex, and Age: 1994

[Represents arrests (not charges) reported by 10,698 agencies (reporting 12 months) with a total 1994 population of 208 million as estimated by FBI]

CHARGE	Total (1,000)	PERCENT DISTRIBUTION							
		Male	Under 15 years	Under 18 years	18-24 years	25-44 years	45-54 years	55-64 years	65 yr. and over
Total arrests.	11,912	80.0	6.6	18.6	26.7	46.9	5.6	1.6	0.7
Serious crimes [1]	2,391	76.6	12.6	30.9	24.9	38.3	4.0	1.2	0.7
Murder and nonnegligent									
manslaughter	19	89.5	2.0	16.4	40.1	34.8	4.2	1.5	0.7
Forcible rape	30	98.6	6.3	16.3	25.8	49.2	5.8	1.8	0.9
Robbery	147	90.9	9.2	32.1	32.3	33.8	1.6	0.3	0.1
Aggravated assault	451	83.3	5.2	15.6	26.0	50.2	5.7	0.8	0.8
Burglary [2]	321	89.7	14.9	36.2	26.7	34.4	2.2	0.4	0.1
Larceny—theft	1,240	66.8	15.1	33.4	22.7	37.2	4.4	1.4	0.9
Motor vehicle theft	167	87.4	13.1	44.0	27.8	26.1	1.6	0.3	0.1
Arson	17	83.6	36.7	54.0	14.1	24.4	3.8	1.1	0.5
All other nonserious crimes	9,520	80.9	5.1	15.6	27.1	49.0	6.0	1.7	0.7
Other assaults	995	81.3	7.3	17.3	23.8	51.4	5.4	1.5	0.6
Forgery and counterfeiting	93	64.6	1.0	7.6	31.9	55.4	4.4	0.9	0.3
Fraud	332	60.5	1.3	5.6	27.5	57.7	6.8	1.6	0.6
Embezzlement	12	57.1	0.8	6.7	32.8	48.9	6.4	1.6	0.6
Stolen property [3]	135	86.7	8.0	26.9	33.0	36.4	2.9	0.7	0.2
Vandalism	261	87.1	23.2	47.0	23.4	26.4	2.2	0.5	0.3
Weapons (carrying, etc.)	214	91.8	7.8	24.5	34.4	35.0	4.2	1.3	0.6
Prostitution and commercialized									
vice	87	38.5	0.1	1.2	21.3	70.3	5.0	1.4	0.6
Sex offenses [4]	82	91.8	9.2	17.6	18.6	48.7	9.0	3.9	2.3
Drug abuse violations	1,121	83.5	2.0	11.7	31.5	51.9	4.0	0.7	0.2
Gambling	16	84.5	1.5	9.3	20.5	43.7	13.5	8.3	3.7
Offenses against family and									
children	92	78.9	1.6	4.6	20.5	65.3	6.9	1.7	0.6
Driving under the influence	1,083	85.8	-	1.0	21.6	62.1	10.4	3.6	1.4
Liquor laws	428	80.4	2.4	22.2	49.9	22.4	3.7	1.4	0.5
Drunkenness	572	88.4	0.4	2.6	20.6	60.2	11.3	3.9	1.4
Disorderly conduct	603	79.1	8.2	22.9	29.4	41.1	4.6	1.4	0.6
Vagrancy	21	81.0	4.4	17.4	24.1	51.0	7.4	1.8	0.6
Suspicion	11	87.4	5.0	15.6	24.6	56.4	5.5	1.3	0.4
Curfew, loitering (juveniles)	107	71.5	30.1	100.5	(X)	(X)	(X)	(X)	(X)
Runaways (juveniles)	202	43.2	44.7	100.1	(X)	(X)	(X)	(X)	(X)
All other offenses, except traffic	3,053	82.1	3.3	11.3	28.8	51.9	5.8	1.6	0.6

- Represents zero.   X Not applicable.   [1] Includes arson arrests, a newly established index offense in 1979.   [2] Breaking or entering.   [3] Buying, receiving, possessing.   [4] Excludes forcible rape and prostitution, shown separately.

Source: U.S. Federal Bureau of Investigation, *Crime in the United States,* annual.

No. 326. Drug Use by Arrestees in Major U.S. Cities, by Type of Drug and Sex: 1994

[Percent testing positive]

CITY	MALE				FEMALE			
	Any drug [1]	Mari- juana	Cocaine	Heroin	Any drug [1]	Marijuana	Cocaine	Heroin
Atlanta, GA	69.4	24.7	57.3	2.5	72.4	14.9	62.4	3.7
Birmingham, AL	69.2	28.1	50.4	3.6	63.1	16.8	49.8	3.3
Chicago, IL	78.9	38.2	56.6	27.1	(NA)	(NA)	(NA)	(NA)
Cleveland, OH	65.9	27.5	47.9	2.7	81.6	15.7	73.8	4.5
Dallas, TX	57.4	32.7	34.9	3.0	63.4	22.5	46.1	7.3
Denver, CO	67.1	38.6	40.2	4.0	67.6	22.1	51.4	4.9
Detroit, MI	65.5	37.6	34.1	7.4	61.8	16.2	45.6	13.2
Fort Lauderdale, FL	58.1	29.4	40.8	1.1	62.4	18.4	52.0	2.6
Houston, TX	47.7	22.6	29.0	2.8	47.6	12.8	35.7	6.1
Indianapolis, IN	69.4	39.1	47.2	2.6	69.4	22.2	56.5	4.8
Los Angeles, CA	66.4	19.6	48.4	9.5	71.8	12.3	53.2	12.3
Manhattan, NY	82.0	24.2	67.9	18.9	89.6	15.4	80.5	30.2
Miami, FL	66.3	27.8	55.6	2.2	(NA)	(NA)	(NA)	(NA)
New Orleans, LA	63.3	28.5	46.7	4.7	31.9	7.3	24.9	2.4
Omaha, NE	59.2	44.2	25.8	2.4	58.4	28.3	34.5	1.8
Philadelphia, PA	76.1	32.3	54.2	14.4	75.5	18.3	61.1	18.1
Phoenix, AZ	64.8	28.8	28.4	6.4	66.8	21.8	36.0	12.4
Portland, OR	65.3	26.9	32.2	11.8	73.8	19.4	42.7	21.2
St. Louis, MO	73.5	36.4	50.2	10.9	75.5	14.7	68.6	8.2
San Antonio, TX	51.8	29.5	30.9	12.7	39.0	14.8	22.4	13.9
San Diego, CA	79.2	36.2	30.0	12.4	75.6	19.8	18.3	13.1
San Jose, CA	55.0	29.7	19.1	5.9	60.9	17.8	23.1	9.6
Washington, DC	63.8	30.2	38.1	9.1	67.4	10.5	55.4	12.8

NA Not available.   [1] Includes other drugs not shown separately.

Source: U.S. National Institute of Justice, *Drug Use Forecasting,* annual.

No. 327. Drug Arrest Rates for Drug Abuse Violations, 1980 to 1994, and by Region, 1994

[Rate per 100,000 inhabitants. Based on Bureau of the Census estimated resident population as of July 1, except 1980 and 1990, enumerated as of April 1. For composition of regions, see table 27]

OFFENSE	1980	1990	1992	1993	1994					
					Total	Region				
						North-east	Mid-west	South	West	
Drug arrest rate, total	256.0	435.3	418.1	437.2	510.5	600.5	332.1	434.5	675.5	
Sale and/or manufacture	57.9	139.0	131.6	129.8	136.5	224.2	92.4	102.8	145.1	
Heroin or cocaine [1]	10.8	93.7	85.9	84.1	85.7	179.9	30.8	67.6	73.3	
Marijuana.	28.4	26.4	27.1	27.1	29.5	36.0	25.9	24.5	34.3	
Synthetic or manufactured drugs	2.8	2.7	2.9	2.5	2.7	3.2	1.4	3.4	2.3	
Other dangerous nonnarcotic drugs . .	15.9	16.2	15.7	16.1	18.6	5.1	34.3	7.4	35.2	
Possession	198.1	296.3	286.4	307.4	374.0	376.3	239.7	331.6	530.4	
Heroin or cocaine [1]	22.2	144.4	136.8	136.1	154.6	194.2	60.1	135.5	217.5	
Marijuana.	146.2	104.9	106.5	120.6	152.1	165.0	134.3	168.9	129.4	
Synthetic or manufactured drugs	6.7	6.6	5.0	5.2	6.2	4.6	3.3	6.9	8.4	
Other dangerous nonnarcotic drugs . .	23.0	40.4	38.1	45.6	61.1	12.5	42.1	20.3	175.1	

[1] Includes other derivatives such as morphine, heroin, and codeine.

Source: U.S. Federal Bureau of Investigation, *Crime in the United States*, annual.

No. 328. Federal Drug Seizures, by Type of Drug: 1990 to 1994

[For fiscal years ending in year shown. Reflects the combined drug seizure effort of the Drug Enforcement Administration, the Federal Bureau of Investigation, the U.S. Customs Services within the jurisdiction of the United States as well as maritime seizures by the U.S. Coast Guard. Based on reports to the Federal-wide Drug Seizure System, which eliminates duplicate reporting of a seizure involving more than one Federal agency]

DRUG	1990	1991	1992	1993	1994, prel.
AMOUNTS (lbs.)					
Heroin	1,794	3,030	2,551	3,514	2,824
Cocaine	235,214	246,324	303,254	244,302	282,086
Marijuana	483,248	499,070	783,343	772,307	778,715
Hashish	17,062	178,211	4,048	26,060	1,616
PERCENT CHANGE					
Heroin	(NA)	68.9	-15.8	37.7	-19.6
Cocaine	(NA)	4.7	23.1	-19.4	15.5
Marijuana	(NA)	3.3	57.0	-1.4	0.8
Hashish	(NA)	944.5	-97.7	543.8	-93.8

NA Not available.

Source: U.S. Bureau of Justice Statistics, *Fact Sheet: Drug Data Summary*, July 1994, series NCJ-148213; and unpublished data.

No. 329. Drug Removals, Laboratory Seizures, and Persons Indicted, by DEA: 1985 to 1993

[Represents domestic drug removals. 1 kg=.454 lbs; du=dosage unit]

ITEM	Unit	1985	1988	1989	1990	1991	1992	1993
Domestic drug removals:								
Heroin.	kg	447	829	629	637	1,124	696	722
Cocaine	kg	18,129	57,113	82,438	73,635	57,080	78,211	60,666
Cannabis (Marijuana).	1,000 kg .	745	602	336	149	108	202	143
Dangerous drugs	mil. du . .	26	114	109	148	532	49	84
Clandestine laboratory seizures . .	Number .	338	810	852	549	408	335	286
Narcotic Title III intercepts	Number .	136	129	192	235	256	291	308
Asset removals:								
Total seizures.	$1,000 . .	246,344	671,290	975,884	1,106,827	956,960	879,058	679,550
DEA seizures	$1,000 . .	171,888	483,355	659,802	886,184	705,003	669,581	553,133
Seizures through inter-agency cooperation	$1,000 . .	74,456	187,936	316,082	220,643	251,957	209,478	126,416
Arrests.	Number .	15,727	23,994	25,718	23,082	23,025	24,386	21,442
Convictions	Number .	10,519	13,091	15,917	15,662	15,962	17,476	18,371

Source: Drug Enforcement Administration (DEA), *Annual Report*.

No. 330. Authorized Intercepts of Communication—Summary: 1980 to 1994

[Data for jurisdictions with statutes authorizing or approving interception of wire or oral communication]

ITEM	1980	1984	1985	1986	1987	1988	1989	1990	1991	1992	1993	1994
Jurisdictions: [1]												
With wiretap statutes	28	31	32	32	33	34	37	40	41	41	41	41
Reporting interceptions	22	24	22	24	22	23	25	25	23	23	23	18
Intercept applications authorized	564	801	784	754	673	738	763	872	856	919	976	1,154
Intercept installations	524	773	722	676	634	678	720	812	802	846	938	1,100
Federal	79	277	235	247	233	286	305	321	349	332	444	549
State	445	496	487	429	401	392	415	491	453	514	494	551
Intercepted communications,												
average [2]	1,058	1,209	1,320	1,328	1,299	1,251	1,656	1,487	1,584	1,861	1,801	2,139
Incriminating	315	298	275	253	230	316	337	321	290	347	364	373
Persons arrested [3]	1,871	2,393	2,469	2,410	2,226	2,486	2,804	2,057	2,364	2,685	2,428	2,852
Convictions [3]	259	649	660	761	506	543	706	420	605	607	413	772
Major offense specified:												
Gambling	199	186	206	189	135	126	111	116	98	66	96	86
Drugs	282	483	434	348	379	435	471	520	536	634	679	876
Homicide and assault	13	30	25	34	18	14	20	21	21	35	28	19
Other	70	102	119	183	141	163	161	204	201	184	173	173

[1] Jurisdictions include Federal Government, States, and District of Columbia.   [2] Average per authorized installation.
[3] Based on information received from intercepts installed in year shown; additional arrests/convictions will occur in subsequent years but are not shown here.

Source: Administrative Office of the U.S. Courts, *Report on Applications for Orders Authorizing or Approving the Interception of Wire, Oral or Electronic Communications* (Wiretap Report), annual.

No. 331. Aliens Expelled and Immigration Violations: 1980 to 1994

[For fiscal years ending in year shown. See text, section 9. See also *Historical Statistics, Colonial Times to 1970*, series C 144, C 149, and C 158-160]

ITEM	Unit	1980	1985	1988	1989	1990	1991	1992	1993	1994
Aliens expelled	1,000	737	1,062	934	860	1,045	1,091	1,144	1,280	1,068
Deported	1,000	17	21	23	30	26	28	38	37	40
Required to depart	1,000	719	1,041	911	830	1,019	1,063	1,106	1,243	1,029
Prosecutions disposed of	Number . .	14,863	17,688	18,360	18,580	20,079	18,882	14,655	19,650	15,348
Immigration violations	Number. . .	14,498	16,976	17,590	17,992	19,351	18,297	14,138	18,958	14,842
Nationality violations	Number. . .	365	712	770	588	728	585	517	692	506
Convictions.	Number . .	12,935	9,833	12,208	12,561	12,719	11,509	9,865	12,538	10,646
Immigration violations	Number. . .	12,678	9,635	11,929	12,379	12,515	11,392	9,766	12,252	10,486
Nationality violations	Number. . .	257	198	279	182	204	117	99	286	160

No. 332. Immigration Border Patrol and Investigation Activities: 1980 to 1994

[In thousands, except where indicated. For fiscal years ending in year shown. See text, section 9]

ITEM	Unit	1980	1985	1988	1989	1990	1991	1992	1993	1994
BORDER PATROL										
Border patrol agents:										
Authorized number	Number. . .	2,484	3,228	4,812	4,804	4,852	4,968	4,948	4,143	4,559
On duty	Number. . .	2,329	3,023	4,074	3,857	4,360	4,312	4,759	3,991	4,219
Border patrol obligations	Mil. dol. . . .	82.5	141.9	205.3	246.4	261.1	295.5	325.8	354.5	374.5
Persons apprehended [1]	1,000	766.6	1,272.4	980.5	906.5	1,123.2	1,152.7	1,221.9	1,281.7	1,046.6
Deportable aliens located [2] . .	1,000	759.4	1,262.4	971.1	893.0	1,103.4	1,132.9	1,199.6	1,263.5	1,031.7
Mexican	1,000	734.2	1,218.7	929.8	832.2	1,054.8	1,095.1	1,168.9	1,230.1	999.9
Canadian	1,000	5.3	5.9	4.3	5.3	5.7	6.7	6.2	5.2	3.4
Other	1,000	19.9	37.8	37.0	55.5	42.8	31.1	24.4	28.1	28.4
Number of seizures	Number. . .	1,920	7,827	6,643	10,789	17,275	14,261	11,391	10,995	9,134
Value of seizures	Mil. dol. . . .	116.1	122.0	721.2	1,212.7	843.6	950.2	1,247.9	1,383	1,598
Narcotics	Mil. dol. . . .	110.3	119.8	700.5	1,191.5	797.8	910.1	1,216.8	1,338	1,556
INVESTIGATIONS										
Deportable aliens located. . . .	1,000	150.9	83.9	37.0	61.1	64.1	63.6	57.4	60.4	61.6
Mexican	1,000	83.3	48.3	19.9	33.1	35.8	35.5	36.2	38.8	40.1
Canadian	1,000	1.5	1.1	0.4	0.5	0.4	0.5	0.4	0.4	0.5
Other	1,000	66.1	34.5	16.7	28.5	30.0	29.7	20.8	21.1	21.1

[1] Covers deportable aliens located and U.S. citizens engaged in smuggling or other immigration violations.   [2] Beginning 1988, includes apprehension by the antismuggling unit.

Source of tables 331 and 332: U.S. Immigration and Naturalization Service, *Statistical Yearbook*, annual; and unpublished data.

No. 333. Criminal Justice System—Direct and Intergovernment Expenditures and Employment, by Type of Activity and Level of Government: 1982 to 1992

LEVEL	DIRECT AND INTERGOVERNMENTAL EXPENDITURES (mil. dol.)				EMPLOYMENT (1,000)			
	Total	Police protection	Judicial and legal	Corrections	Total	Police protection	Judicial and legal	Corrections
All governments:								
1982	35,841.9	19,022.2	7,770.8	9,048.9	1,270.3	723.9	247.7	298.7
1983	39,680.2	20,648.2	8,620.6	10,411.4	1,313.8	733.1	261.4	319.3
1984	43,942.7	22,685.8	9,463.2	11,793.7	1,373.4	747.0	277.6	348.8
1985	48,563.1	24,399.4	10,628.8	13,534.9	1,422.7	757.0	293.0	372.7
1986	53,499.8	26,255.0	11,485.4	15,759.4	1,464.1	771.9	300.1	392.0
1987	58,871.3	28,767.6	12,555.0	17,548.8	1,525.0	792.8	312.3	419.8
1988	65,230.5	30,960.8	13,970.6	20,299.2	1,583.7	804.7	323.6	455.4
1989	70,949.5	32,794.2	15,588.7	22,566.6	1,636.9	811.5	336.9	488.5
1990	79,434.0	35,923.5	17,356.8	26,153.7	1,710.4	825.4	350.8	534.2
1991	87,566.8	38,971.2	19,298.4	29,297.2	1,760.6	837.0	362.2	561.3
1992	93,776.9	41,326.5	20,988.9	31,461.4	1,797.7	857.6	373.6	566.5
Federal Government:								
1982	4,458.0	2,527.0	1,390.0	541.0	94.6	55.9	28.6	10.0
1983	4,844.0	2,815.0	1,523.0	606.0	103.8	63.9	29.8	10.1
1984	5,868.0	3,396.0	1,785.0	687.0	106.9	65.2	31.2	10.5
1985	6,416.0	3,495.0	2,129.0	792.0	110.7	66.0	33.2	11.5
1986	6,595.0	3,643.0	2,090.0	862.0	112.4	66.7	33.6	12.1
1987	7,496.0	4,231.0	2,271.0	994.0	121.3	72.8	35.7	12.9
1988	8,851.0	4,954.0	2,639.0	1,258.0	130.4	78.8	37.8	13.9
1989	9,674.0	5,307.0	2,949.0	1,418.0	134.5	78.7	39.7	16.1
1990	12,798.0	5,666.0	5,398.0	1,734.0	139.8	77.6	43.3	18.9
1991	15,231.0	6,725.0	6,384.0	2,122.0	150.1	81.8	46.8	21.5
1992	17,423.0	7,400.0	7,377.0	2,646.0	162.2	87.6	50.8	23.8
State and local governments:								
1982	31,572.9	16,656.2	6,380.8	8,535.9	1,175.8	668.0	219.1	288.7
1983	34,836.2	17,903.2	7,097.6	9,835.4	1,210.0	669.2	231.6	309.2
1984	38,155.7	19,330.8	7,678.2	11,146.7	1,266.4	681.8	246.4	338.3
1985	42,284.1	20,969.4	8,499.8	12,814.9	1,312.1	691.0	259.9	361.2
1986	47,069.8	22,713.0	9,395.4	14,961.4	1,351.7	705.2	266.5	380.0
1987	51,640.3	24,731.6	10,284.0	16,624.8	1,403.7	720.0	276.7	407.0
1988	56,766.5	26,303.8	11,331.6	19,131.2	1,453.3	725.9	285.8	441.5
1989	61,745.5	27,842.2	12,639.7	21,263.6	1,502.3	732.8	297.1	472.4
1990	69,215.0	30,579.5	14,075.8	24,559.7	1,570.6	747.8	307.5	515.3
1991	75,460.8	32,801.2	15,303.4	27,356.2	1,610.5	755.2	315.4	539.9
1992	80,247.9	34,623.5	16,573.9	29,050.4	1,635.5	770.0	322.8	542.7

Source: U.S. Bureau of Justice Statistics, *Sourcebook of Criminal Justice Statistics—1994.*

No. 334. Number and Rate of Full-Time Sworn Police Officers in State and Local Law Enforcement Agencies: 1992

[In thousands, except "Rate"; rate is per 10,000 population and is based on U.S. Bureau of Census population estimates for April 1, 1992]

TOTAL	Number[1]	Rate	TYPE OF AGENCY			TOTAL	Number[1]	Rate	TYPE OF AGENCY		
			Local	State	Sheriff				Local	State	Sheriff
Total	604.0	24	373.1	53.0	136.5	MO	11.3	22	7.9	0.9	2.1
AL	8.8	21	5.6	0.6	1.9	MT	1.4	17	0.6	0.2	0.6
AK	1.1	18	0.7	0.3	-	NE	3.1	19	1.7	0.5	0.8
AZ	7.9	21	5.2	1.1	1.4	NV	3.1	23	1.8	0.3	0.8
AR	4.5	19	2.5	0.5	1.1	NH	2.1	19	1.7	0.3	0.1
CA	65.8	21	33.2	6.1	22.6	NJ	26.7	34	19.2	2.6	3.8
CO	8.7	25	4.8	0.5	3.0	NM	3.4	22	2.1	0.4	0.8
CT	7.6	23	6.1	0.9	0.4	NY	68.2	38	45.8	4.0	5.0
DE	1.6	23	0.9	0.5	-	NC	14.6	21	8.0	1.3	4.6
DC	5.2	89	4.9	-	-	ND	1.1	17	0.5	0.1	0.3
FL	32.9	24	18.0	1.6	11.8	OH	20.9	19	14.7	1.3	3.9
GA	16.8	25	9.4	0.8	5.9	OK	6.5	20	4.5	0.8	0.8
HI	2.8	24	2.7	-	-	OR	5.5	18	2.8	0.9	1.7
ID	2.2	20	0.9	0.2	1.0	PA	23.7	20	17.3	4.1	1.1
IL	35.7	31	25.0	2.0	7.8	RI	2.4	24	2.0	0.2	0.1
IN	10.0	18	6.0	1.1	2.4	SC	7.8	22	3.5	1.2	2.5
IO	4.7	17	2.9	0.4	1.2	SD	1.1	16	0.6	0.2	0.3
KS	5.6	22	3.2	0.6	1.5	TN	10.4	21	6.2	0.8	2.9
KY	6.1	16	3.8	1.0	1.0	TX	41.3	23	24.6	2.8	9.9
LA	15.0	35	5.5	0.7	8.2	UT	3.0	16	1.5	0.4	0.8
ME	2.3	18	1.4	0.3	0.4	VT	1.0	17	0.6	0.3	0.1
MD	12.6	26	8.3	1.7	1.3	VA	16.4	26	8.2	1.6	5.6
MA	16.0	27	12.1	2.1	1.3	WA	8.2	16	4.7	1.0	2.2
MI	19.6	21	13.0	2.0	4.0	WV	2.6	14	1.3	0.5	0.7
MN	7.4	16	4.6	0.5	1.9	WI	11.6	23	7.2	0.5	3.3
MS	4.7	18	2.7	0.5	1.1	WY	1.2	26	0.6	0.2	0.4

- Represents or rounds to zero.   [1] Includes special police.

Source: U.S. Bureau of Justice Statistics, *Sourcebook of Criminal Justice—1994.*

No. 335. General Purpose Law Enforcement Agencies—Number, Employment, and Expenditures: 1993

[Includes both full-time and part-time employees. State police data are based on the 49 main State police agencies; Hawaii does not have a State police agency. Expenditure data cover fiscal years ending in year stated]

TYPE OF AGENCY	Number of agencies[1]	NUMBER OF EMPLOYEES						Operating expenditures (bil. dol.)
			Full-time			Part-time		
		Total	Sworn	Civilian	Total	Sworn	Civilian	
NUMBER								
Total	17,120	828,435	622,913	205,522	87,875	42,890	44,985	41.9
Local police	12,361	474,072	373,554	100,518	58,146	28,186	29,960	24.3
Sheriff.	3,084	224,236	155,815	68,421	19,660	11,048	8,612	10.7
State police	49	76,972	51,874	25,098	845	228	617	4.2
Special police.	1,626	53,156	41,670	11,485	9,224	3,428	5,796	2.8
PERCENT								
Total.	100	100	100	100	100	100	100	100
Local police	72.2	57.2	60.0	48.9	66.2	65.7	66.6	58.0
Sheriff.	18.0	27.1	25.0	33.3	22.4	25.8	19.1	25.5
State police	0.3	9.3	8.3	12.2	1.0	0.5	1.4	10.0
Special police.	9.5	6.4	6.7	5.6	10.5	8.0	12.9	6.7

[1] The number of agencies reported here is the result of a weighted sample and not an exact enumeration.
Source: U.S. Bureau of Justice Statistics, *Local Police Departments, 1993*, April 1996.

No. 336. Federal Agencies Employing 500 or More Full-Time Officers With Authority to Carry Firearms and Make Arrests, by Function: 1993

[As of December]

AGENCY	Total	Police response and patrol	Criminal investigation and enforcement	Other
All agencies [1]	68,825	7,127	40,002	21,696
U.S. Customs Service.	10,120	43	10,077	-
Federal Bureau of Investigation	10,075	-	10,000	75
Federal Bureau of Prisons	9,984	-	-	9,984
Immigration and Naturalization Service. . . .	9,466	3,920	4,457	1,089
Administrative Office of the U.S. Courts . . .	3,763	-	-	3,763
Internal Revenue Service.	3,621	-	3,621	-
U.S. Postal Inspection Service	3,587	-	2,129	1,458
Drug Enforcement Administration	2,813	-	2,813	-
U.S. Secret Service	2,186	-	1,594	592
National Park Service	2,160	439	1,563	158
Ranger Activities Division	1,500	-	1,500	-
U.S. Park Police	660	439	63	158
U.S. Marshals Service.	2,153	-	-	2153
Bureau of Alcohol, Tobacco and Firearms. .	1,959	-	1,832	127
U.S. Capitol Police	1,080	122	41	917
Tennessee Valley Authority.	740	357	-	383
U.S. Forest Service	732	527	205	-
GSA - Federal Protective Services.	732	505	66	161
U.S. Fish and Wildlife Service.	620	397	223	-

- Represents or rounds to zero.   [1] Includes agencies not shown separately.
Source: U.S. Bureau of Justice Statistics, *Federal Law Enforcement Officers, 1993*.

No. 337. Law Enforcement Officers Killed and Assaulted: 1980 to 1994

[Covers officers killed feloniously and accidentally in line of duty; includes Federal officers. 1988 excludes Florida and Kentucky. For composition of regions, see table 27. See also *Historical Statistics, Colonial Times to 1970*, series H 987-998]

ITEM	1980	1985	1988	1989	1990	1991	1992	1993	1994
OFFICERS KILLED									
Total killed	165	148	155	145	132	123	129	129	138
Northeast	31	19	17	23	13	16	16	12	18
Midwest	23	23	18	22	20	26	15	27	29
South.	72	64	77	68	68	55	68	57	50
West	32	29	39	23	23	17	23	22	30
Puerto Rico.	6	10	-	8	8	8	7	11	6
Outlying areas, foreign countries	1	3	4	1	-	1	-	-	5
ASSAULTS									
Population (1,000) [1]	182,288	198,935	186,418	189,641	199,065	191,397	217,997	210,658	260,341
Number of—									
Agencies represented	9,235	9,906	8,866	9,213	9,483	9,263	10,682	9,809	10,626
Police officers.	345,554	389,808	369,743	380,232	412,314	405,069	460,430	454,105	480,343
Total assaulted	57,847	61,724	58,752	62,172	71,794	62,852	81,252	66,975	64,912
Firearm	3,295	2,793	2,759	3,154	3,662	3,532	4,455	4,002	3,168
Knife or cutting instrument . . .	1,653	1,715	1,367	1,379	1,641	1,493	2,095	1,574	1,513
Other dangerous weapon . . .	5,415	5,263	5,573	5,778	7,390	7,014	8,604	7,551	7,210
Hands, fists, feet, etc	47,484	51,953	49,053	51,861	59,101	50,813	66,098	53,848	53,021

- Represents zero.   [1] Represents the number of persons covered by agencies shown.
Source: U.S. Federal Bureau of Investigation, *Law Enforcement Officers Killed and Assaulted*, annual.

No. 338. Lawyers—Selected Characteristics: 1960 to 1991

[Data based on editions of Martindale-Hubbell Law Directory. Represents all persons who are members of the bar, including those in industries, educational institutions, etc., and those inactive or retired. See also *Historical Statistics, Colonial Times to 1970*, series H 1028-1062]

CHARACTERISTIC	1960	1970	1980	1985	1988	1991
All lawyers [1]	**285,933**	**355,242**	**542,205**	**655,191**	**723,189**	**805,872**
Lawyers reporting [2]	252,385	324,818	(X)	(X)	(X)	(X)
Male	245,897	315,715	498,019	569,649	606,768	646,495
Female.	6,488	9,103	44,185	85,542	116,421	159,377
Status in practice: [3]						
Government.	25,621	35,803	50,490	53,035	57,742	66,227
Federal	13,045	18,710	20,132	19,989	23,042	27,985
State.	4,316	9,293	30,358	33,046	34,700	38,242
City or county	8,260	7,800	([4])	([4])	([4])	([4])
Judicial [5].	8,180	10,349	19,160	21,677	19,547	21,536
Federal	599	878	2,611	3,003	2,846	3,119
State and county	5,301	7,548	16,549	18,674	16,701	18,417
City.	2,280	1,923	([4])	([4])	([4])	([4])
Private practice.	192,353	236,085	370,111	460,206	519,941	587,289
Individual	116,911	118,963	179,923	216,336	240,141	262,622
Partner	60,709	92,442	144,279	177,392	194,976	213,016
Associate [5].	14,733	24,680	45,908	66,478	84,824	111,651
Salaried	25,198	40,486	73,862	83,843	85,671	93,849
Private industry	22,533	33,593	54,626	63,622	66,627	71,022
Educational institutions . .	1,798	3,732	6,606	7,254	7,575	8,177
Other private employment	867	3,161	12,630	12,967	11,469	14,650
Inactive or retired	10,887	16,812	28,582	36,430	40,288	36,971

X Not applicable.   [1] 1960 to 1970 includes lawyers not reporting and an adjustment (subtraction) for duplications; 1980 to 1991, weighted to account for nonreporters and duplicate listings.   [2] 1960 and 1970 includes duplications; 1980, 1985, and figures are weighted to adjust for duplication of entries.   [3] 1960 and 1970, in cases where more than one subentry was applicable, the individual was tabulated in each. In 1980 and 1985 lawyers who were in both private practice and government service are coded in private practice.   [4] Data no longer available separately; included with category above.   [5] Associates are lawyers designated as such by their employers.

Source: American Bar Foundation, Chicago, IL, 1960 to 1970, *The 1971 Lawyer Statistical Report*, 1971 (copyright); 1980, *The Lawyer Statistical Report: A Statistical Profile of the U.S. Legal Profession in the 1980's*, 1985 (copyright); 1985 and 1988, *Supplement to The Lawyer Statistical Report: The U.S. Legal Profession in 1988*, 1991 and similar report for 1985; 1991 Lawyer Statistical Report: The U.S. Legal Profession in the 1990's, 1994 (copyright).

No. 339. U.S. Supreme Court—Cases Filed and Disposition: 1980 to 1994

[Statutory term of court begins first Monday in **October**. See *Historical Statistics, Colonial Times to 1970* series H 1063-1078, for related but not comparable data]

ACTION	1980	1985	1988	1989	1990	1991	1992	1993	1994
Total cases on docket	**5,144**	**5,158**	**5,657**	**5,746**	**6,316**	**6,770**	**7,245**	**7,786**	**8,100**
Appellate cases on docket	2,749	2,571	2,587	2,416	2,351	2,451	2,441	2,442	2,515
From prior term	527	400	446	384	365	365	379	342	377
Docketed during present term	2,222	2,171	2,141	2,032	1,986	2,086	2,062	2,100	2,138
Cases acted upon [1].	2,324	2,185	2,271	2,096	2,042	2,125	2,140	2,099	2,185
Granted review	167	166	130	103	114	103	83	78	83
Denied, dismissed, or withdrawn	1,999	1,863	1,973	1,881	1,802	1,914	1,920	1,947	2,016
Summarily decided	90	78	75	44	81	52	84	34	52
Cases not acted upon	425	386	316	320	309	326	301	343	330
Pauper cases on docket	2,371	2,577	3,056	3,316	3,951	4,307	4,792	5,332	5,574
Cases acted upon	2,027	2,189	2,638	2,891	3,436	3,768	4,261	4,621	4,983
Granted review	17	20	17	19	27	17	14	21	10
Denied, dismissed, or withdrawn	1,968	2,136	2,577	2,824	3,369	3,716	4,209	4,566	4,955
Summarily decided	32	24	32	35	28	22	25	30	14
Cases not acted upon	344	388	418	425	515	539	531	711	591
Original cases on docket	24	10	14	14	14	12	12	12	11
Cases disposed of during term	7	2	2	2	3	1	1	1	-
Total cases available									
for argument	**264**	**276**	**254**	**204**	**201**	**196**	**166**	**145**	**136**
Cases disposed of	162	175	173	147	131	130	120	105	97
Cases argued	154	171	170	146	125	127	116	99	94
Cases dismissed or remanded									
without argument	8	4	3	1	6	3	4	6	3
Cases remaining	102	101	81	57	70	66	46	40	39
Cases decided by signed opinion	144	161	156	143	121	120	111	93	91
Cases decided by per curiam opinion. . . .	8	10	12	3	4	3	4	6	3
Number of signed opinions.	123	146	133	129	112	107	107	84	82

- Represents zero.   [1] Includes cases granted review and carried over to next term, not shown separately.

Source: Office of the Clerk, Supreme Court of the United States, unpublished data.

No. 340. U.S. Courts of Appeals—Cases Commenced and Disposition: 1980 to 1995

[For years ending **June 30.** See also *Historical Statistics, Colonial Times to 1970*, series H 1079-1096]

ITEM	1980	1985	1989	1990	1991	1992	1993	1994	1995
Cases commenced [1]	23,200	33,360	39,734	40,898	42,033	46,032	49,770	48,815	49,671
Criminal	4,405	4,989	8,020	9,493	9,949	10,956	11,885	11,052	10,171
U.S. civil	4,654	6,744	6,349	6,626	6,663	7,113	7,758	7,518	7,761
Private civil	10,200	16,827	20,626	20,490	20,798	22,862	24,030	24,781	25,992
Administrative appeals. .	2,950	3,179	2,965	2,578	2,764	3,052	3,824	3,560	3,345
Cases terminated [1]	20,887	31,387	37,372	38,520	41,414	42,933	47,466	48,546	50,085
Criminal	3,993	4,892	6,297	7,509	9,198	9,830	11,043	11,519	11,320
U.S. civil	4,346	6,363	6,127	6,379	6,579	6,797	7,462	7,637	7,710
Private civil	8,942	15,743	20,313	20,369	20,698	21,628	23,437	23,943	25,574
Administrative appeals. .	2,643	2,760	2,914	2,582	3,148	2,801	3,464	3,480	3,254
Cases disposed of [2]	10,607	16,369	19,322	21,006	22,707	23,162	25,567	26,475	28,187
Affirmed or granted	8,017	12,286	15,240	16,629	17,988	18,463	20,604	21,371	22,825
Reversed or denied . . .	1,845	2,770	2,617	2,565	2,503	2,681	2,514	2,636	2,679
Other . . . . . , ...	745	1,313	1,465	1,812	2,216	2,018	2,449	2,468	2,683
Median months [3]	8.9	10.3	10.3	10.1	10.2	10.5	10.4	10.5	10.5

[1] Includes original proceedings and bankruptcy appeals not shown separately. [2] Terminated on the merits after hearing or submission. [3] Prior to 1985, the figure is from filing of complete record to final disposition; beginning 1985, figure is from filing notice of appeal to final disposition. For definition of median, see Guide to Tabular Presentation.

No. 341. U.S. District Courts—Civil and Criminal Cases: 1980 to 1995

[**In thousands, except percent.** For years ending **June 30.** See also *Historical Statistics, Colonial Times to 1970*, series H 1097-1111]

ITEM	1980	1985	1989	1990	1991	1992	1993	1994	1995
Civil cases: Commenced	168.8	273.7	233.5	217.9	207.7	226.9	228.6	236.0	239.0
Cases terminated [1]	155.0	268.6	234.6	213.4	211.7	239.6	225.2	228.9	226.1
No court action	68.7	129.4	64.3	51.6	44.6	51.4	44.0	40.5	37.0
Court action, total	86.2	139.2	170.4	161.8	166.5	187.6	181.2	188.4	189.1
Before pretrial	53.8	95.5	129.7	127.0	136.9	153.4	152.3	159.6	161.6
Pretrial	22.4	31.1	29.5	25.5	21.1	26.2	21.1	21.0	19.7
Trials	10.1	12.6	11.2	9.2	8.4	8.0	7.9	7.8	7.7
Percent reaching trial. . .	6.5	4.7	4.8	4.3	4.0	3.4	3.5	3.4	3.4
Criminal cases: Commenced [2] . . .	28.0	38.5	44.9	46.5	45.1	47.5	45.7	44.9	44.2
Defendants disposed of [3]	36.6	47.4	54.6	56.5	56.7	58.4	59.5	61.2	55.3
Not convicted	8.0	8.8	10.1	9.8	10.0	10.0	9.2	10.0	9.0
Convicted.	28.6	38.5	44.5	46.7	46.8	48.4	50.4	51.1	46.3
Imprisonment	13.2	18.7	24.9	27.8	29.2	31.1	34.2	34.5	31.7
Probation	11.1	14.4	15.0	14.2	13.8	13.1	12.6	12.8	11.5
Fine and other.	4.4	5.4	4.7	4.7	3.8	4.3	3.7	3.9	3.2

[1] Excludes land condemnation cases. [2] Excludes transfers. [3] Includes Guam, Virgin Islands, and Northern Mariana Islands; 1980 includes Canal Zone.

No. 342. U.S. District Courts—Civil Cases Commenced and Pending: 1992 to 1995

[For years ending **June 30**]

TYPE OF CASE	CASES COMMENCED				CASES PENDING			
	1992	1993	1994	1995	1992	1993	1994	1995
Cases total	**226,895**	**228,562**	**235,996**	**239,013**	**237,040**	**215,574**	**217,963**	**230,407**
Contract actions [1]	51,246	38,240	31,988	31,619	41,588	40,525	29,697	28,961
Recovery of overpayments [2] . . .	17,475	7,255	2,591	2,099	4,663	5,995	1,227	1,010
Real property actions	10,143	8,436	7,468	7,282	7,657	7,743	5,855	5,167
Tort actions	36,469	40,939	48,067	44,511	69,734	45,148	47,186	55,491
Personal injury	33,147	37,409	44,734	41,102	65,792	41,324	43,638	51,916
Personal injury product liability [1]	10,769	16,545	23,977	17,631	39,264	15,208	20,694	26,931
Asbestos	4,673	4,900	7,111	6,821	31,218	7,154	3,704	6,002
Other personal injury	22,378	20,864	20,757	23,471	26,528	26,116	22,944	24,985
Personal property damage	3,322	3,530	3,333	3,409	3,942	3,824	3,548	3,575
Actions under statutes [1]	128,921	140,811	148,344	155,495	117,538	121,964	135,020	140,607
Civil rights [1]	23,419	26,483	31,521	35,566	24,009	26,477	33,271	37,723
Employment	10,275	12,221	15,256	18,225	11,156	12,530	17,359	20,419
Bankruptcy suits	5,243	6,192	5,675	5,138	4,083	4,203	4,705	4,601
Commerce (ICC rates, etc.) . . .	2,475	1,475	1,228	613	1,189	1,238	693	467
Environmental matters	1,252	1,077	1,059	1,136	1,719	1,943	1,864	1,853
Prisoner petitions	46,452	52,454	56,283	62,597	37,259	39,512	45,417	48,255
Forfeiture and penalty	5,492	4,832	3,548	2,670	4,967	4,850	3,359	2,525
Labor laws.	15,800	16,174	15,800	15,030	12,778	13,026	12,346	12,078
Protected property rights [3]	5,670	6,202	7,051	6,990	5,296	5,281	5,963	6,095
Securities commodities and exchanges	1,998	1,875	1,742	1,870	4,555	3,983	3,130	3,058
Social Security laws	8,415	11,602	11,142	10,168	8,154	8,304	12,302	11,510
Tax suits	2,305	2,267	2,275	2,144	2,713	2,255	1,884	1,722
Freedom of information	439	425	566	481	465	498	502	506

[1] Includes other types not shown separately. [2] Includes enforcement of judgments in student loan cases, and overpayments of veterans benefits. [3] Includes copyright, patent, and trademark rights.

Source of tables 340-342: Administrative Office of the U.S. Courts, *Annual Report of the Director.*

No. 343. U.S. District Courts—Offenders Convicted and Sentenced to Prison, and Length of Sentence: 1994

MOST SERIOUS OFFENSE OF CONVICTION	Offenders convicted	Convicted offenders sentenced to prison	Length of sentence (mo.)	MOST SERIOUS OFFENSE OF CONVICTION	Offenders convicted	Convicted offenders sentenced to prison	Length of sentence (mo.)
Total [1]	48,678	31,586	60.9	Drug offenses [2]	17,722	14,835	80.1
				Possession	1,308	563	22.0
Violent offenses	2,927	2,443	88.2	Trafficking and			
Property offenses	13,201	6,466	25.1	manufacturing.....	16,414	14,272	82.5
Fraudulent offenses [2] .	9,466	4,967	20.7	Public-order offenses...	14,825	7,838	46.0
Embezzlement....	1,311	519	14.3	Regulatory offenses..	1,905	876	31.7
Fraud [3]	6,909	3,855	22.1	Other offenses	12,920	6,962	47.8
Forgery	536	197	16.8	Weapons	2,879	2,812	81.2
Other offenses [2]	3,735	1,499	39.9	Immigration......	2,588	2,243	19.9
Larceny	2,728	851	25.0	Tax law violations [4].	901	329	15.7

[1] Total may include offenders for whom offense category could not be determined   [2] Includes offenses not shown separately.   [3] Excludes tax fraud.   [4] Includes tax fraud.

Source: U.S. Bureau of Justice Statistics, *Federal Criminal Case Processing*, annual.

No. 344. Civil Jury Cases and Verdicts in Large Counties: 1992

[Based on the Civil Justice Survey of State Courts, **1992**. Tort cases are claims arising from personal injury or property damage caused by negligent or intentional act of another person or business. Contract cases arise in cases of all allegations of breach of contract. Real property cases involve any claim regarding the ownership of real property, excluding mortgage foreclosures, which are under contracts]

CASE TYPE	CIVIL CASES		JURY CIVIL CASES		Average award to plaintiff ($1,000)
	Number	Percent disposed by jury trial	Number	Cases with a plaintiff winner	
Total cases.....................	761,919	1.5	12,026	5,949	455
Tort cases.......................	377,421	2.3	9,532	4,584	408
Automobile	227,087	1.6	3,915	2,280	220
Premises liability................	65,372	3.3	1,991	845	232
Medical malpractice..............	18,396	6.4	1,370	403	1,484
Intentional tort	10,879	2.7	448	199	530
Product liability................	12,763	2.6	360	142	727
Toxic substance	6,045	2.8	287	202	526
Professional malpractice...........	6,827	3.2	187	92	1,057
Slander/libel...................	3,159	1.9	66	27	229
Other tort	26,891	2.6	909	393	391
Contract cases	365,263	0.7	2,217	1,322	620
Seller plaintiff.................	188,761	0.5	610	417	212
Buyer plaintiff.................	44,592	1.1	593	363	479
Fraud	15,917	2.0	317	173	678
Employment..................	8,064	4.0	311	170	1,462
Rental/lease..................	20,587	0.4	133	85	1,881
Mortgage foreclosure............	68,811	0.1	6	(NA)	(NA)
Other contract	18,531	1.3	246	113	280
Real property cases	19,235	2.1	277	43	325
Eminent domain	4,596	4.3	204	(NA)	(NA)
Other real property	14,640	1.4	74	(NA)	(NA)

NA Not available.

Source: U.S. Bureau of Justice Statistics, Special Report, *Civil Jury Cases and Verdicts in Large Counties*, 1992.

No. 345. Federal Prosecutions of Public Corruption: 1980 to 1994

[As of **Dec. 31.** Prosecution of persons who have corrupted public office in violation of Federal Criminal Statutes]

PROSECUTION STATUS	1980	1984	1985	1986	1987	1988	1989	1990	1991	1992	1993	1994
Total: [1] Indicted	727	931	1,157	1,208	1,276	1,274	1,348	1,176	1,452	1,189	1,371	1,165
Convicted	602	934	997	1,026	1,081	1,067	1,149	1,084	1,194	1,081	1,362	969
Awaiting trial............	213	269	256	246	368	288	375	300	346	380	403	332
Federal officials: Indicted	123	408	563	596	651	629	695	615	803	624	627	571
Convicted	131	429	470	523	545	529	610	583	665	532	595	488
Awaiting trial............	16	77	90	83	118	86	126	103	149	139	133	124
State officials: Indicted	72	58	79	88	102	66	71	96	115	84	113	99
Convicted	51	52	66	71	76	69	54	79	77	92	133	97
Awaiting trial............	28	21	20	24	26	14	18	28	42	24	39	17
Local officials: Indicted......	247	203	248	232	246	276	269	257	242	232	309	248
Convicted	168	196	221	207	204	229	201	225	180	211	272	202
Awaiting trial............	82	74	49	55	89	79	122	98	88	91	132	96

[1] Includes individuals who are neither public officials nor employees but who were involved with public officials or employees in violating the law, not shown separately.

Source: U.S. Department of Justice, *Federal Prosecutions of Corrupt Public Officials, 1970-1980* and *Report to Congress on the Activities and Operations of the Public Integrity Section*, annual.

No. 346. Delinquency Cases Disposed by Juvenile Courts, by Reason for Referral: 1983 to 1993

[In thousands. A delinquency offense is an act committed by a juvenile for which an adult could be prosecuted in a criminal court. Disposition of a case involves taking a definite action such as transferring the case to criminal court, dismissing the case, placing the youth placing the youth in a facility for delinquents, or such actions as fines, restitution, and community service]

REASON FOR REFERRAL	1983	1984	1985	1986	1987	1988	1989	1990	1991	1992	1993
All delinquency offense . .	1,030	1,034	1,112	1,150	1,155	1,170	1,212	1,299	1,407	1,460	1,490
Case rate [1]	38.3	38.7	42.2	43.9	44.5	45.7	47.8	51.0	53.9	54.7	54.6
Violent offenses	55	61	67	73	67	71	78	96	109	118	122
Criminal homicide	1	1	1	2	1	2	2	3	3	3	3
Forcible rape	3	3	4	5	4	4	4	4	5	5	6
Robbery	24	22	26	26	22	22	23	28	33	34	36
Aggravated assault	27	35	36	40	39	43	49	60	69	77	78
Property offenses	451	442	489	496	498	501	525	546	601	595	573
Burglary	145	129	139	140	131	129	131	143	155	156	150
Larceny	270	276	307	308	314	311	319	326	366	360	354
Motor vehicle theft	31	31	36	42	47	55	68	71	73	71	61
Arson	5	6	7	6	6	7	7	7	8	8	8
Delinquency offenses	524	530	555	583	590	599	610	657	696	746	795
Simple assault	81	73	92	95	100	104	110	125	137	152	166
Vandalism	64	69	84	84	83	81	83	97	111	117	117
Drug law violations	57	65	76	73	73	82	78	71	66	72	89
Obstruction of justice.	55	63	68	76	79	79	82	86	82	86	96
Other [2]	268	260	235	255	256	253	256	278	301	320	327

[1] Number of cases disposed per 1,000 youth (ages 10 to 17) at risk. [2] Includes such offenses as stolen property offenses, trespassing, weapons offenses, other sex offenses, liquor law violations, disorderly conduct, and miscellaneous offenses.

Source: National Center for Juvenile Justice, Pittsburgh, PA, *Juvenile Court Statistics,* annual.

No. 347. Child Abuse and Neglect Cases Substantiated and Indicated— Victim Characteristics: 1990 to 1994

[Based on reports alleging child abuse and neglect that were referred for investigation by the respective child protective services agency in each State. The reporting period may be either calendar or fiscal year. The majority of States provided duplicated counts. Also, varying number of States reported the various characteristics presented below. A substantiated case represents a type of investigation disposition that determines that there is sufficient evidence under State law to conclude that maltreatment occurred or that the child is at risk of maltreatment. An indicated case represents a type of disposition that concludes that there was a reason to suspect maltreatment had occurred]

ITEM	1990		1992		1993		1994	
	Number	Percent	Number	Percent	Number	Percent	Number	Percent
TYPES OF SUBSTANTIATED MALTREATMENT								
Victims, total [1]	761,153	(X)	1,054,456	(X)	1,067,231	100.0	1,197,133	100.0
Neglect	343,312	45.1	455,319	43.2	475,153	44.5	535,510	44.7
Physical abuse	188,960	24.8	213,726	20.3	233,487	21.9	258,320	21.6
Sexual abuse	120,732	15.9	130,739	12.4	139,817	13.1	139,980	11.7
Emotional maltreatment	46,315	6.1	49,527	4.7	48,288	4.5	47,610	4.0
Medical Neglect	(NA)	(NA)	25,503	2.4	23,009	2.2	25,018	2.1
Other and unknown	61,834	8.1	179,642	17.0	147,477	13.8	190,695	15.9
SEX OF VICTIM								
Victims, total	794,101	100.0	967,096	100.0	926,322	100.0	937,070	100.0
Male	357,367	45.0	430,347	44.5	413,277	44.6	437,485	46.7
Female	405,409	51.1	488,384	50.5	470,658	50.8	489,688	52.3
Unknown	31,325	3.9	48,365	5.0	42,387	4.6	9,897	1.1
AGE OF VICTIM								
Victims, total	807,965	100.0	964,529	100.0	926,674	100.0	901,487	100.0
1 year and younger	106,507	13.2	122,642	12.7	121,700	13.1	119,201	13.2
2 to 5 years old.	192,018	23.8	244,256	25.3	236,997	25.6	240,904	26.7
6 to 9 years old.	175,609	21.7	216,479	22.4	209,292	22.6	210,301	23.3
10 to 13 years old	150,507	18.6	183,341	19.0	177,581	19.2	172,777	19.2
14 to 17 years old	116,015	14.4	138,681	14.4	133,866	14.4	132,528	14.7
18 and over	5,464	0.7	7,377	0.8	6,799	0.7	6,791	0.8
Unknown	61,845	7.7	51,753	5.4	40,439	4.4	18,985	2.1
RACE/ETHNIC GROUP OF VICTIM [2]								
Victims, total	793,773	100.0	967,264	100.0	926,924	100.0	928,817	100.0
White	428,506	54.0	509,268	52.7	497,924	53.7	523,820	56.4
Black	198,365	25.0	242,500	25.1	229,724	24.8	245,472	26.4
Asian and Pacific Islander.	6,479	0.8	7,897	0.8	7,775	0.8	8,142	0.9
American Indian, Eskimo, and Aleut .	10,323	1.3	12,782	1.3	13,657	1.5	15,317	1.6
Other races	11,088	1.4	15,127	1.6	13,659	1.5	14,104	1.5
Hispanic origin	73,590	9.3	89,471	9.2	85,067	9.2	87,161	9.4
Unknown	65,422	8.2	90,219	9.3	79,118	8.5	34,801	3.7

X Not applicable. [1] More than one type of maltreatment may be substantiated per child. [2] Some States were unable to report on the number of Hispanic victims, thus it is probable that nationwide the percentage of Hispanic victims is higher.

Source: U.S. Department of Health and Human Services, National Center on Child Abuse and Neglect, National Child Abuse and Neglect Data System, *Child Maltreatment - 1994.*

No. 348. Child Abuse and Neglect Cases Reported and Investigated, by State: 1993 and 1994

[Based on reports alleging child abuse and neglect that were referred for investigation by the respective child protective services agency in each State. The reporting period may be either calendar or fiscal year. The majority of States were unable to provide unduplicated counts. Only nine jurisdictions (Alaska, Hawaii, Michigan, Montana, Ohio, Oregon, South Carolina, Vermont, and Washington) provided unduplicated counts of children subject of report. Excludes the Armed Forces]

STATE	1993				1994			
		Reports		Investigation disposition, number of children substantiated[2]		Reports		Investigation disposition, number of children substantiated[2]
	Population under 18 years old	Number of reports[1]	Number of children subject of a report		Population under 18 years old	Number of reports[1]	Number of children subject of a report	
United States . . .	67,135,000	1,938,164	2,893,410	1,009,289	68,024,000	1,978,519	2,935,470	1,011,628
Alabama	1,077,000	26,758	40,388	19,130	1,080,000	26,515	40,164	21,591
Alaska.	189,000	[3]9,920	9,920	6,917	192,000	[3]10,071	10,071	6,774
Arizona	1,070,000	29,747	51,068	30,729	1,139,000	28,275	48,722	29,531
Arkansas	635,000	17,489	25,624	10,336	640,000	18,429	18,429	7,915
California	8,594,000	342,537	455,526	161,612	8,677,000	352,059	449,177	159,031
Colorado	938,000	33,287	52,257	7,892	970,000	27,797	43,919	(NA)
Connecticut	775,000	17,871	27,710	23,069	788,000	24,038	37,043	27,618
Delaware	175,000	5,386	9,635	2,271	175,000	5,275	9,441	2,542
District of Columbia . . .	115,000	5,669	12,773	3,327	119,000	5,612	13,369	5,636
Florida.	3,169,000	105,468	161,686	81,982	3,262,000	108,943	164,945	77,101
Georgia	1,841,000	52,519	85,118	55,516	1,893,000	55,578	89,958	63,721
Hawaii.	299,000	[3]5,412	5,412	2,297	304,000	[3]5,944	5,944	2,380
Idaho	333,000	12,494	24,759	6,892	339,000	13,592	34,313	9,461
Illinois	3,068,000	72,101	126,960	43,519	3,083,000	77,289	140,651	53,056
Indiana	1,469,000	40,263	59,481	29,136	1,473,000	41,725	62,553	25,343
Iowa	734,000	20,866	30,776	8,834	729,000	21,210	31,240	9,172
Kansas	684,000	[3]24,797	24,797	12,327	690,000	[3]33,928	33,928	3,644
Kentucky	971,000	36,901	57,706	25,282	970,000	37,911	59,540	25,940
Louisiana.	1,243,000	27,218	46,170	15,253	1,235,000	28,094	44,901	15,015
Maine	307,000	4,286	9,567	4,955	306,000	4,010	8,902	4,769
Maryland	1,241,000	29,412	46,174	(NA)	1,263,000	25,908	40,934	(NA)
Massachusetts	1,393,000	31,833	51,941	24,186	1,424,000	33,844	56,178	23,964
Michigan	2,506,000	53,302	126,601	19,522	2,525,000	57,394	136,989	21,951
Minnesota	1,228,000	19,349	29,953	11,871	1,241,000	16,689	26,483	10,471
Mississippi	758,000	17,606	27,568	8,812	756,000	17,322	27,123	7,982
Missouri.	1,363,000	52,268	85,323	20,472	1,379,000	52,754	86,007	15,842
Montana	232,000	9,005	13,713	4,827	238,000	8,905	13,528	4,194
Nebraska.	439,000	8,439	17,481	5,726	442,000	8,405	17,508	4,514
Nevada	352,000	12,568	19,730	7,085	376,000	13,329	21,060	8,037
New Hampshire	283,000	6,225	7,234	928	292,000	6,118	9,666	1,043
New Jersey	1,896,000	[3]65,102	65,102	10,510	1,931,000	[3]65,954	65,954	9,519
New Mexico	481,000	[3]24,984	24,984	6,880	498,000	[3]24,933	24,933	7,356
New York.	4,468,000	139,468	230,916	59,311	4,511,000	128,111	210,997	54,993
North Carolina	1,704,000	58,376	92,739	29,809	1,756,000	59,135	95,144	30,013
North Dakota	172,000	4,884	8,252	4,010	172,000	4,518	7,753	3,617
Ohio	2,859,000	[3]93,144	147,106	51,850	2,854,000	96,747	156,635	61,806
Oklahoma	869,000	[3]26,349	26,349	8,359	880,000	[3]34,846	34,846	10,891
Oregon	782,000	25,227	39,604	(NA)	783,000	26,436	41,769	7,946
Pennsylvania	2,872,000	[3]24,909	24,909	7,814	2,898,000	[3]23,722	23,722	7,038
Rhode Island	235,000	8,278	13,065	3,130	240,000	8,862	14,303	3,207
South Carolina	952,000	21,227	40,147	11,263	952,000	21,656	40,461	11,628
South Dakota	208,000	[3]10,284	10,284	2,368	208,000	[3]10,156	10,156	1,923
Tennessee	1,269,000	[3]32,739	32,739	12,136	1,297,000	[3]34,714	34,714	12,175
Texas	5,183,000	110,973	177,328	58,304	5,301,000	110,742	173,644	55,266
Utah	665,000	16,168	27,485	10,976	672,000	17,125	29,112	10,430
Vermont	144,000	2,732	3,190	1,305	146,000	2,579	3,025	1,234
Virginia	1,588,000	36,257	55,937	14,066	1,603,000	36,431	56,331	10,264
Washington	1,393,000	40,075	55,689	41,602	1,408,000	41,050	57,100	44,197
West Virginia	434,000	12,932	20,302	(NA)	429,000	12,370	19,544	(NA)
Wisconsin	1,342,000	[3]49,152	49,152	19,189	1,347,000	[3]47,561	47,561	18,185
Wyoming.	138,000	3,908	5,080	1,702	138,000	3,908	5,080	1,702

NA Not available.   [1] Except as noted, reports are on incident/family based basis or based on number of reported incidents regardless of the number of children involved in the incidents.   [2] Type of investigation disposition that determines that there is sufficient evidence under State law to conclude that maltreatment occurred or that the child is at risk of maltreatment.   [3] Child-based report that enumerates each child who is a subject of a report.

Source: U.S. Department of Health and Human Services, National Center on Child Abuse and Neglect, National Child Abuse and Neglect Data System, *Child Maltreatment - 1994.*

No. 349. Jail Inmates, by Race and Detention Status: 1978 to 1994

[Excludes Federal and State prisons or other correctional institutions; institutions exclusively for juveniles; State-operated jails in Alaska, Connecticut, Delaware, Hawaii, Rhode Island, and Vermont; and other facilities which retain persons for less than 48 hours. As of June 30. For 1978 and 1988, data based on National Jail Census; for other years, based on sample survey and subject to sampling variability]

CHARACTERISTIC	1978	1985	1988	1989	1990	1991	1992	1993	1994
Total inmates [1]	158,394	256,615	343,569	395,553	405,320	426,479	444,584	459,804	490,442
Percent of rated capacity	65	94	101	108	104	101	99	97	97
Male	148,839	235,909	313,158	356,050	368,002	386,865	403,768	415,576	441,219
Female	9,555	19,077	30,411	37,253	37,318	39,614	40,816	44,228	49,223
White [2]	89,418	151,403	166,302	201,732	186,989	190,333	191,362	180,914	183,762
Black [2]	65,104	102,646	141,979	185,910	174,335	187,618	195,156	203,463	206,278
Other races [2]	3,872	2,566	3,932	7,911	5,321	5,391	5,831	6,178	7,344
Hispanic [3]	16,349	35,926	51,455	55,377	57,449	60,129	62,961	69,249	75,500
Non-Hispanic	142,045	220,689	292,114	340,176	347,871	366,350	381,623	387,555	414,942
Adult [4]	156,783	254,986	341,893	393,303	403,019	424,129	441,781	455,500	(NA)
Awaiting arraignment or trial	77,453	127,059	175,669	204,291	207,358	217,671	223,840	228,900	(NA)
Convicted	75,438	123,409	166,224	189,012	195,661	206,458	217,940	226,600	(NA)
Juvenile [5]	1,611	1,629	1,676	2,250	2,301	2,350	2,804	3,400	(NA)

NA Not available.   [1] For 1985, 1989-1994, includes juveniles not shown separately by sex, and for 1988 and 1990-1994 includes 31,356, 38,675, 43,138, 52,235, 66,249, and 93,058 persons, respectively, of unknown race not shown separately. [2] Beginning 1993, data represent White, non-hispanic and Black, non-hispanic and rounded to nearest 100.   [3] Hispanic persons may be of any race. Data for 1993 and 1994 are estimated and rounded to nearest 100.   [4] Includes inmates not classified by conviction status.   [5] Juveniles are persons whose age makes them initially subject to juvenile court authority although they are sometimes tried as adults in criminal court. In 1993, includes juveniles who were tried as adults. In 1994, includes all persons under age 18.
Source: U.S. Bureau of Justice Statistics, *Profile of Jail Inmates, 1978 and 1989; Jail Inmates,* annual; and *1988 Census of Local Jails.*

No. 350. Federal and State Prisoners: 1970 to 1994

[Based on Bureau of the Census estimated resident population, as of July 1. Prior to 1970, excludes State institutions in Alaska. Beginning 1980, includes all persons under jurisdiction of Federal and State authorities rather than those in the custody of such authorities. Represents inmates sentenced to maximum term of more than a year. See also *Historical Statistics, Colonial Times to 1970,* series H 1135-1140]

YEAR	PRESENT AT END OF YEAR						RECEIVED FROM COURTS					
	All institutions		Federal		State		All institutions		Federal		State	
	Number	Rate [1]	Number	Rate [1]	Number	Rate [1]	Number	Rate [1]	Number	Rate [1]	Number	Rate [1]
1970 ...	196,429	96.7	20,038	9.8	176,391	86.8	79,351	39.1	12,047	5.9	67,304	33.1
1975 ...	240,593	113.3	24,131	11.4	216,462	102.0	129,573	61.0	16,770	7.9	112,803	53.1
1980 ...	315,974	139.2	20,611	9.1	295,363	130.1	142,122	62.7	10,907	4.8	131,215	57.9
1985 ...	480,568	216.5	32,695	13.6	447,873	187.6	198,499	82.7	15,368	6.4	183,131	76.3
1986 ...	522,084	230.4	36,531	15.0	485,553	201.4	219,382	91.0	16,067	7.0	203,315	84.0
1987 ...	560,812	229.0	39,523	16.0	521,289	214.2	241,887	99.0	16,260	7.0	225,627	92.0
1988 ...	603,732	244.0	42,738	17.0	560,994	227.0	261,242	106.0	15,932	6.4	245,310	99.3
1989 ...	680,907	274.3	47,168	19.0	633,739	255.3	316,215	127.4	18,388	7.4	297,827	120.0
1990 ...	739,980	295.0	50,403	20.1	689,577	274.9	(NA)	(NA)	(NA)	(NA)	323,069	128.8
1991 ...	789,610	309.6	56,696	22.2	732,914	287.3	(NA)	(NA)	(NA)	(NA)	317,237	124.4
1992 ...	846,277	331.8	65,706	25.8	780,571	306.0	(NA)	(NA)	(NA)	(NA)	334,301	130.3
1993 ...	932,074	359.4	74,399	28.8	857,675	330.7	(NA)	(NA)	(NA)	(NA)	(NA)	(NA)
1994 ...	1,016,760	388.6	79,795	30.5	936,965	358.1	345,035	131.9	23,956	9.2	321,079	122.7

NA Not available.   [1] Rate per 100,000 estimated population.
Source: U.S. Bureau of Justice Statistics, *Prisoners in State and Federal Institutions on December 31,* annual, and *Correctional Populations in the United States,* annual.

No. 351. State Prison Inmates—Selected Characteristics: 1986 and 1991

[Based on a sample survey of about 13,986 inmates in 1991 and 13,711 inmates in 1986; subject to sampling variability]

CHARACTERISTIC	NUMBER		PERCENT OF PRISON INMATES		CHARACTERISTIC	NUMBER		PERCENT OF PRISON INMATES	
	1986	1991	1986	1991		1986	1991	1986	1991
Total [1]	450,416	711,643	100.0	100.0	Never married	241,707	389,302	53.7	55.3
					Married	91,492	127,389	20.3	18.1
Under 18 years old	2,057	4,552	0.5	0.6	Widowed	8,343	13,036	1.9	1.9
18 to 24 years old	120,384	151,328	26.7	21.3	Divorced	81,264	129,913	18.1	18.5
25 to 34 years old	205,817	325,429	45.7	45.7	Separated	26,985	44,095	6.0	6.3
35 to 44 years old	87,502	161,651	19.4	22.7	Years of school:				
45 to 54 years old	23,524	46,475	5.2	6.5	Less than 12 years	276,309	[2]290,722	61.6	[2]41.2
55 to 64 years old	8,267	16,997	1.8	2.4	12 years or more	172,386	415,451	38.4	58.8
65 years old and over	2,808	5,210	0.6	0.7	Pre-arrest employment status:				
Male	430,604	672,847	95.6	94.5	Employed	309,364	476,068	69.0	67.3
Female	19,812	38,796	4.4	5.5	Not employed	139,097	230,876	31.0	32.7
White	223,648	349,628	49.7	49.1	Looking for work	80,750	115,590	18.0	16.4
Black	211,021	336,920	46.9	47.3	Not looking for work	58,347	115,286	13.0	16.3
Other races	15,412	25,094	3.4	3.5					

[1] For 1986, includes data not reported for all characteristics except sex. For 1991, includes data not reported for marital status, re-arrest, employment status, and years of school.   [2] In 1991, the survey question was revised; therefore, the response may not be entirely comparable with 1986 and before.
Source: U.S. Bureau of Justice Statistics, *Profile of State Prison Inmates, 1986 Survey of State Prison Inmates, 1991.*

No. 352. State Prison Inmates Who Committed Crimes Against Children: 1991

[Based on a sample survey of about 13,986 inmates of State correctional facilities, subject to sampling variability]

OFFENSE	ALL PRISONERS		PRISONERS SERVING TIME FOR CRIMES AGAINST CHILDREN					
	Total	Percent distri- bution	Child victim- izers, total	Percent of all pris- oners	Percent distri- bution	Violet child victim- izers, total	Victims age 12 or younger	Victims age 13 to 17
All offenses	711,643	100.0	65,163	9.2	100.0	(NA)	(NA)	(NA)
Violent offenses	327,958	46.1	61,037	18.6	93.7	60,285	33,287	26,998
Homicide	87,479	12.3	5,792	6.6	8.9	5,792	3,006	2,787
Murder	74,693	10.5	4,677	6.3	7.2	4,677	2,279	2,399
Negligent manslaughter	12,786	1.8	1,115	8.7	1.7	1,115	727	388
Kidnaping	8,369	1.2	1,508	18.0	2.3	1,508	682	826
Rape and sexual assault	66,482	9.3	43,552	65.5	66.8	42,993	25,102	17,892
Forcible rape	22,797	3.2	8,908	39.1	13.7	8,908	3,893	5,015
Forcible sodomy	2,036	0.3	1,741	85.5	2.7	1,729	1,039	690
Statutory rape	1,162	0.2	1,102	94.8	1.7	984	611	373
Lewd acts with children	10,799	1.5	10,799	100.0	16.6	10,370	7,175	3,195
Other sexual assault	29,688	4.2	21,002	70.7	32.2	21,002	12,384	8,619
Robbery	104,136	14.6	3,772	3.6	5.8	3,656	1,051	2,605
Assault	59,275	8.3	6,058	10.2	9.3	6,035	3,215	2,818
Aggravated assault	55,549	7.8	3,933	7.1	6.0	3,933	1,623	2,309
Child abuse	1,717	0.2	1,717	100.0	2.6	1,694	1,513	181
Simple assault	2,009	0.3	408	20.3	0.6	408	79	328
Other violent	2,217	0.3	355	16.0	0.5	301	231	70
Nonviolent offenses	383,685	53.9	4,126	1.1	6.3	(NA)	(NA)	(NA)

NA Not available.

Source: U.S. Bureau of Justice Statistics, *Child Victimizers: Violent Offenders and Their Victims,* March 1996.

No. 353. Prisoners Under Jurisdiction of State and Federal Correctional Authorities— Summary, by State: 1980 to 1994

[For years ending December 31]

SEX, REGION, DIVISION, AND STATE	1980	1990	1993	1994		SEX, REGION, DIVISION, AND STATE	1980	1990	1993	1994	
				Total	Percent change, 1993- 1994					Total	Percent change, 1993- 1994
U.S.. . .	329,821	773,919	969,301	1,054,774	8.8	DE [1]	1,474	3,471	4,210	4,466	6.1
Male.	316,401	729,840	911,044	990,434	8.7	MD .	7,731	17,848	20,264	20,998	3.6
Female. . . .	13,420	44,079	58,257	64,340	10.4	DC [1] .	3,145	9,947	10,945	10,949	1.0
Federal. . .	24,363	65,526	89,587	95,034	6.1	VA. . .	8,920	17,593	22,850	26,968	18.0
State	305,458	708,393	879,714	959,740	9.1	WV . . .	1,805	1,565	1,805	1,930	6.9
						NC . .	15,513	18,411	21,892	23,648	8.0
Northeast. .	45,796	123,464	145,620	153,175	5.2	SC . .	7,862	17,319	18,704	18,999	1.6
N.E.	9,926	25,151	31,170	33,491	7.4	GA [2] .	12,178	22,411	27,783	33,425	20.3
ME . .	814	1,523	1,469	1,474	0.3	FL [2] .	20,735	44,387	53,048	57,168	7.8
NH . .	326	1,342	1,775	2,021	13.9	E.S.C . .	21,055	43,451	51,795	55,970	8.1
VT [1] .	480	1,049	1,223	1,301	6.4	KY . .	3,588	9,023	10,440	11,066	6.0
MA [2] .	3,185	8,345	10,229	11,396	11.4	TN . .	7,022	10,388	12,824	14,401	12.3
RI [1] .	813	2,392	2,783	2,919	4.9	AL. . .	6,543	15,665	18,624	19,573	5.1
CT [1] .	4,308	10,500	13,691	14,380	5.0	MS . .	3,902	8,375	9,907	10,930	10.3
M.A . . .	35,870	98,313	114,450	119,684	4.6	W.S.C. .	46,488	88,248	139,515	167,532	20.1
NY . .	21,815	54,895	64,569	66,750	3.4	AR . .	2,911	7,322	8,625	8,643	0.2
NJ. .	5,884	21,128	23,831	24,632	3.4	LA . .	8,889	18,599	22,468	24,063	7.1
PA. . .	8,171	22,290	26,050	28,302	8.6	OK . .	4,796	12,285	16,409	16,631	1.4
Midwest. .	66,211	145,894	173,277	184,508	6.5	TX [4] .	29,892	50,042	92,013	118,195	28.5
E.N.C. .	51,175	113,806	137,705	145,272	5.5	West	47,093	154,384	188,106	200,004	6.3
OH . .	13,489	31,822	40,641	43,074	6.0	Mt	13,141	37,433	45,347	50,005	10.3
IN [2] .	6,683	12,736	14,470	15,014	3.8	MT . .	739	1,425	1,541	1,764	14.5
IL [2] .	11,899	27,516	34,495	36,531	5.9	ID . .	817	1,961	2,606	2,811	7.9
MI [2] .	15,124	34,267	39,318	40,631	3.3	WY . .	534	1,110	1,129	1,217	7.8
WI. . .	3,980	7,465	8,781	10,022	14.1	CO . .	2,629	7,671	9,462	10,717	13.3
W.N.C. .	15,036	32,088	35,572	39,236	10.3	NM . .	1,279	3,187	3,498	3,712	6.1
MN . .	2,001	3,176	4,200	4,575	8.9	AZ [2] .	4,372	14,261	17,811	19,746	10.9
IA [2] .	2,481	3,967	4,898	5,437	11.0	UT . .	932	2,496	2,888	3,045	5.4
MO [3] .	5,726	14,943	16,178	17,898	10.6	NV . .	1,839	5,322	6,412	6,993	9.1
ND . .	253	483	498	536	7.6	Pac	33,952	116,951	142,759	149,999	5.1
SD . .	635	1,341	1,553	1,708	10.0	WA . .	4,399	7,995	10,419	10,833	4.0
NE . .	1,446	2,403	2,518	2,711	7.7	OR . .	3,177	6,492	6,657	6,936	5.8
KS . .	2,494	5,775	5,727	6,371	11.2	CA [2] .	24,569	97,309	119,951	125,605	4.7
South. . .	146,358	284,651	372,711	422,053	13.2	AK [1 2] .	822	2,622	2,703	3,292	21.8
S.A. . . .	78,815	152,952	181,401	198,551	9.5	HI [1] .	985	2,533	3,129	3,333	6.5

[1] Includes both jail and prison inmates (State has combined jail and prison system).   [2] Numbers are for custody rather than jurisdiction counts.   [3] Data are for custody counts until 1994 when jurisdiction counts are reported.   [4] Data are for custody counts until 1993 when jurisdiction counts are reported.

Source: U.S. Bureau of Justice Statistics, *Prisoners in 1994,* and earlier reports.

No. 354. Adults on Probation, in Jail or Prison, or on Parole: 1980 to 1993

[As of **December 31, except jail counts as of June 30**]

ITEM	Total [1]	Probation	Jail	Prison	Parole
1980	1,840,400	1,118,097	[2]182,288	319,598	220,438
1981	2,006,600	1,225,934	[2]195,085	360,029	225,539
1982	2,192,600	1,357,264	207,853	402,914	224,604
1983	2,475,100	1,582,947	221,815	423,898	246,440
1984	2,689,200	1,740,948	233,018	448,264	266,992
1985	3,011,400	1,968,712	254,986	487,593	300,203
1986	3,239,400	2,114,621	272,735	526,436	325,638
1987	3,459,600	2,247,158	294,092	562,814	355,505
1988	3,714,100	2,356,483	341,893	607,766	407,977
1989	4,055,600	2,522,125	393,303	683,367	456,803
1990	4,348,100	2,670,234	403,019	743,382	531,407
1991	4,536,200	2,729,322	424,129	792,535	590,198
1992 [3]	**4,763,200**	**2,811,611**	**441,781**	**851,205**	**658,601**
Sex:					
Male	4,050,900	2,257,900	401,100	804,200	587,700
Female	712,300	553,700	40,700	47,100	70,800
Race:					
White	2,682,200	1,689,500	233,000	411,800	347,800
Black	1,781,700	857,100	195,200	427,700	301,600
1993 [3]	**4,879,600**	**2,843,445**	[2]**455,500**	**909,186**	**671,470**
Sex:					
Male	4,161,000	2,286,700	411,500	857,900	604,900
Female	718,700	556,700	44,100	51,300	66,600
Race:					
White	2,834,700	1,830,500	239,000	435,200	330,000
Black	1,985,300	978,000	210,500	460,200	336,600
Other	59,400	34,600	6,100	13,800	4,900

[1] Totals may not add due to individuals having multiple correctional statuses. [2] Estimated. [3] Totals may not add due to rounding.

Source: U.S. Bureau of Justice Statistics, *Correctional Populations in the United States, annual.*

No. 355. Prisoners Under Sentence of Death: 1980 to 1994

[As of **December 31**. Excludes prisoners under sentence of death who remained within local correctional systems pending exhaustion of appellate process or who had not been committed to prison]

CHARACTERISTIC	1980	1984	1985	1986	1987	1988	1989	1990	1991	1992	1993	1994
Total [1]	**688**	**1,420**	**1,575**	**1,800**	**1,967**	**2,117**	**2,243**	**2,346**	**2,466**	**2,575**	**2,727**	**2,890**
White	418	806	896	1,013	1,128	1,235	1,308	1,368	1,450	1,508	1,575	1,645
Black and other	270	614	679	787	839	882	935	978	1,016	1,067	1,152	1,245
Under 20 years	11	11	13	19	10	11	6	8	14	12	13	19
20 to 24 years	173	215	212	217	222	195	191	168	179	188	211	231
25 to 34 years	334	702	804	872	969	1,048	1,080	1,110	1,087	1,078	1,066	1,088
35 to 54 years	186	453	531	639	744	823	917	1,006	1,129	1,212	1,330	1,449
55 years and over	10	24	31	34	39	47	56	64	73	85	96	103
Years of school completed:												
7 years or less	68	121	147	164	181	180	183	178	173	181	185	186
8 years	74	137	159	174	183	184	178	186	181	180	183	198
9 to 11 years	204	401	483	577	650	692	739	775	810	836	885	930
12 years	162	385	440	515	591	657	695	729	783	831	887	939
More than 12 years	43	110	127	143	168	180	192	209	222	232	244	255
Unknown	163	251	235	208	211	231	263	279	313	315	332	382
Marital status:												
Never married	268	570	655	772	856	898	956	998	1,071	1,132	1,222	1,320
Married	229	443	487	525	571	594	610	632	663	663	671	707
Divorced [2]	217	392	449	484	557	632	684	726	746	780	823	863
Time elapsed since sentencing:												
Less than 12 months	185	279	273	293	295	293	231	231	252	265	262	280
12 to 47 months	389	694	739	757	804	812	809	753	718	720	716	755
48 to 71 months	102	228	303	376	412	409	408	438	441	444	422	379
72 months and over	38	204	276	355	473	610	802	934	1,071	1,146	1,316	1,476
Legal status at arrest:												
Not under sentence [3]	384	739	861	992	1,123	1,207	1,301	1,345	1,415	1,476	1,562	1,662
Parole or probation [3]	115	279	350	409	480	545	585	578	615	702	754	800
Prison or escaped	45	84	81	82	91	93	94	128	102	101	102	103
Unknown	170	303	299	298	290	279	270	305	321	296	298	325

[1] For 1980 to 1993, revisions to the total number of prisoners were not carried to the characteristics except for race. [2] Includes persons married but separated, widows, widowers, and unknown. [3] Includes prisoners on mandatory conditional release, work release, leave, AWOL, or bail. Covers 24 prisoners in 1989, 28 in 1990, and 29 in 1991 and 1992.

Source: U.S. Bureau of Justice Statistics, *Capital Punishment, annual.*

No. 356. Movement of Prisoners Under Sentence of Death: 1980 to 1994

[Prisoners reported under sentence of death by civil authorities. The term "under sentence of death" begins when the court pronounces the first sentence of death for a capital offense]

STATUS	1980	1985	1986	1987	1988	1989	1990	1991	1992	1993	1994
Under sentence of death, Jan. 1 . . .	595	1,420	1,575	1,800	1,967	2,117	2,243	2,346	2,465	2,580	2,727
Received death sentence [1] [2]	203	281	297	299	296	251	244	266	265	282	306
White.	125	165	164	190	196	133	147	163	147	146	162
Black.	77	114	123	106	91	114	94	101	114	130	136
Dispositions other than executions . .	101	108	73	90	128	102	108	116	124	108	112
Executions.	-	18	18	25	11	16	23	14	31	38	31
Under sentence of death, Dec. 31 [1] [2]	688	1,575	1,800	1,967	2,117	2,243	2,346	2,466	2,575	2,727	2,890
White.	425	896	1,006	1,128	1,238	1,308	1,368	1,450	1,508	1,575	1,645
Black.	268	664	750	813	853	898	940	1,016	1,029	1,111	1,197

- Represents zero. [1] Includes races other than White or Black. [2] Revisions to total number of prisoners under death sentence not carried to this category.

Source: U.S. Bureau of Justice Statistics, *Capital Punishment,* annual.

No. 357. Prisoners Executed Under Civil Authority: 1930 to 1994

[Excludes executions by military authorities. The Army (including the Air Force) carried out 160 (148 between 1942 and 1950; 3 each in 1954, 1955, and 1957; and 1 each in 1958, 1959, and 1961). Of the total, 106 were executed for murder (including 21 involving rape), 53 for rape, and 1 for desertion. The Navy carried out no executions during the period. See also *Historical Statistics, Colonial Times to 1970,* series H 1155-1167]

YEAR OR PERIOD	Total [1]	White	Black	EXECUTED FOR MURDER			EXECUTED FOR RAPE			EXECUTED, OTHER OFFENSES [2]		
				Total [1]	White	Black	Total [1]	White	Black	Total [1]	White	Black
All years	4,116	1,907	2,165	3,591	1,820	1,734	455	48	405	70	39	31
1930 to 1939.	1,667	827	816	1,514	803	687	125	10	115	28	14	14
1940 to 1949.	1,284	490	781	1,064	458	595	200	19	179	20	13	7
1950 to 1959.	717	336	376	601	316	280	102	13	89	14	7	7
1960 to 1967.	191	98	93	155	87	68	28	6	22	8	5	3
1968 to 1976.	-	-	-	-	-	-	-	-	-	-	-	-
1977 to 1982.	6	5	1	6	5	6	-	-	-	-	-	-
1983	5	4	1	5	4	1	-	-	-	-	-	-
1984	21	13	8	21	13	8	-	-	-	-	-	-
1985	18	11	7	18	11	7	-	-	-	-	-	-
1986	18	11	7	18	11	7	-	-	-	-	-	-
1987	25	13	12	25	13	12	-	-	-	-	-	-
1988	11	6	5	11	6	5	-	-	-	-	-	-
1989	16	8	8	16	8	8	-	-	-	-	-	-
1990	23	16	7	23	16	7	-	-	-	-	-	-
1991	14	7	7	14	7	7	-	-	-	-	-	-
1992	31	19	11	31	19	11	-	-	-	-	-	-
1993	38	23	14	38	23	14	-	-	-	-	-	-
1994	31	20	11	31	20	11	-	-	-	-	-	-

- Represents zero. [1] Includes races other than White or Black. [2] Includes 25 armed robbery, 20 kidnapping, 11 burglary, 8 espionage (6 in 1942 and 2 in 1953), and 6 aggravated assault.

Source: Through 1978, U.S. Law Enforcement Assistance Administration; thereafter, U.S. Bureau of Justice Statistics, *Correctional Populations in the United States,* annual.

No. 358. Prisoners Under Sentence of Death and Executed Under Civil Authority, by States: 1977 to 1994

[Alaska, District of Columbia, Hawaii, Iowa, Maine, Massachusetts, Michigan, Minnesota, New York, North Dakota, Rhode Island, Vermont, West Virginia, and Wisconsin are jurisdictions without a death penalty]

STATE	1977 to 1994	1991	1992	1993	1994	STATE	1977 to 1994	1991	1992	1993	1994	STATE	1977 to 1994	1991	1992	1993	1994
U.S..	257	14	31	38	31	ID	1	-	-	-	1	NC . . .	6	1	1	-	1
						IL	2	-	-	-	1	OK . . .	3	-	2	-	-
AL . . .	10	-	2	-	-	IN . . .	3	-	-	-	1	SC . . .	4	1	-	-	-
AZ . . .	3	-	1	2	-	LA . . .	21	1	-	1	-	TX . . .	85	5	12	17	14
AR . . .	9	-	2	-	5	MD . . .	1	-	-	-	1	UT . . .	4	-	1	-	-
CA . . .	2	-	1	1	-	MS . . .	4	-	-	-	-	VA . . .	24	2	4	5	2
DE . . .	4	-	1	2	1	MO . . .	11	1	1	4	-	WA . . .	2	-	-	1	1
FL . . .	33	2	2	3	1	NE . . .	1	-	-	-	1	WY . . .	1	-	1	-	-
GA . . .	18	1	-	2	1	NV . . .	5	-	-	-	-						

- Represents zero.

Source: Through 1978, U.S. Law Enforcement Assistance Administration; thereafter, U.S. Bureau of Justice Statistics, *Capital Punishment,* annual.

No. 359. Fire Losses—Total and Per Capita: 1970 to 1994

[Includes allowance for uninsured and unreported losses but excludes losses to government property and forests. Represents incurred losses]

YEAR	Total (mil. dol.)	Per capita [1]	YEAR	Total (mil. dol.)	Per capita [1]	YEAR	Total (mil. dol.)	Per capita [1]
1970	2,328	11.41	1979	4,851	21.60	1988	9,626	39.11
1971	2,316	11.20	1980	5,579	24.56	1989	9,514	38.33
1972	2,304	11.01	1981	5,625	24.53	1990	9,495	38.26
1973	2,639	12.49	1982	5,894	25.61	1991	11,302	44.83
1974	3,190	14.95	1983	6,320	27.20	1992	13,588	48.24
1975	3,190	14.81	1984	7,602	32.35	1993	11,331	43.96
1976	3,558	16.35	1985	7,753	32.70	1994	12,333	47.97
1977	3,764	17.13	1986	8,488	35.21			
1978	4,008	18.05	1987	8,504	34.96			

[1] Based on Bureau of the Census estimated resident population as of July 1.
Source: Insurance Information Institute, New York, NY, *Insurance Facts*, annual.

No. 360. Fires—Number and Loss, by Type and Property Use: 1991 to 1994

[Based on annual sample survey of fire departments. No adjustments were made for unreported fires and losses. Property loss includes direct property loss only]

TYPE AND PROPERTY USE	NUMBER (1,000)				PROPERTY LOSS (mil. dol.)			
	1991	1992	1993	1994	1991	1992	1993	1994
Fires, total.	**2,041**	**1,965**	**1,953**	**2,054**	**9,467**	**8,295**	**8,546**	**8,151**
Structure	640	638	621	614	8,320	6,957	7,406	6,867
Outside of structure [1]	54	50	52	66	55	318	63	120
Brush and rubbish	806	743	732	795	-	-	-	-
Vehicle.	428	405	421	422	1,049	965	1,030	1,111
Other	113	129	127	157	43	55	47	53
Structure by property use:								
Public assembly	16	17	16	17	362	361	298	334
Educational	9	10	9	9	58	68	64	91
Institutional	12	12	10	11	28	35	30	20
Stores and offices	33	33	29	30	[2]931	[3]1,105	741	598
Residential.	478	472	470	451	[4]5,552	3,880	4,843	4,317
1-2 family units [5]	363	358	358	341	3,354	3,178	[6]4,111	3,537
Apartments.	102	101	100	97	609	597	653	678
Other residential [7]	13	13	12	13	89	105	79	102
Storage [8]	44	42	39	43	594	734	651	568
Industry, utility, defense [8] . .	19	19	19	19	605	597	623	758
Special structures	29	33	29	34	190	177	156	181

- Represents zero. [1] Includes outside storage, crops, timber, etc. [2] Includes one large store and office fire totaling $325 million. [3] Includes estimated loss of $567 involving 862 structures from the April 1992 civil disturbance in Los Angeles, CA. [4] Includes the Oakland, CA, fire which resulted in $1.5 billion in residential property damage. [5] Includes mobile homes. [6] Reflects wildfires that occurred in southern California in 1993 that resulted in $809 million in property damage. [7] Includes hotels and motels, college dormitories, boarding houses, etc. [8] Data underreported as some incidents were handled by private fire brigades or fixed suppression systems which do not report.
Source: National Fire Protection Association, Quincy, MA, "NFPA Reports on U.S. Fire Loss — 1994," *NFPA Journal*, September/October 1995, and prior issues (copyright 1995).

No. 361. Fires and Property Loss for Incendiary and Suspicious Fires and Civilian Fire Deaths and Injuries, by Selected Property Type: 1991 to 1994

[Based on sample survey of fire departments]

ITEM	1991	1992	1993	1994	ITEM	1991	1992	1993	1994
NUMBER (1,000)					CIVILIAN FIRE DEATHS				
Structure fires, total. . .	640	638	621	614	Deaths, total [2]	4,465	4,730	4,635	4,275
Structure fires of incendiary									
or suspicious origin	98	94	85	86	Residential property.	3,575	3,765	3,825	3,465
					One- and two-family				
Fires of incendiary origin .	62	58	54	53	dwellings	2,905	3,160	3,035	2,785
Fires of suspicious origin .	36	36	31	33	Apartments	595	545	685	640
					Vehicles	605	730	595	630
PROPERTY LOSS [1] (mil. dol.)					CIVILIAN FIRE INJURIES				
Structure fires, total. . .	8,320	6,957	7,406	6,867	Injuries, total [2]	29,375	28,700	30,475	27,250
Structure fires of incendiary					Residential property.	21,850	21,600	22,600	20,025
or suspicious origin	1,531	1,999	2,351	1,447	One- and two-family				
					dwellings	15,600	15,275	15,700	14,000
Fires of incendiary origin .	1,072	[3]1,493	[4]1,901	964	Apartments	5,675	5,825	6,300	5,475
Fires of suspicious origin .	459	506	450	483	Vehicles	3,050	3,000	2,675	2,625

[1] Direct property loss only. [2] Includes other not shown separately. [3] Includes estimated loss of $567 million from the April 1992 civil disturbance in Los Angeles, CA. [4] Includes fire losses that occurred during the wildfires in California and the World Trade Center bombing in New York city, which resulted in combined estimated losses of $1.039 billion.
Source: National Fire Protection Association, Quincy, MA, " NFPA Reports on U.S. Fire Loss — 1994", *NFPA Journal*, September/October 1995, and prior issues (copyright 1995).

Figure 6.1
National Air Pollutant Emissions: 1983 to 1994

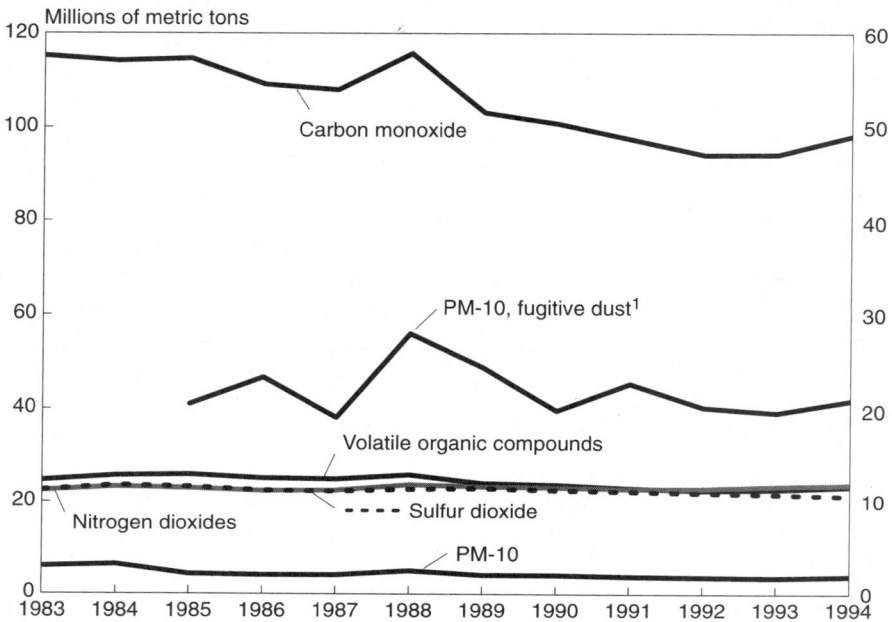

[1] PM-10=Particulate matter of less than ten microns. From sources such as agricultural tilling, construction, mining and quarrying, paved and unpaved roads, and wind erosion.
Source: Chart prepared by U.S. Bureau of the Census. For data, see table 374.

Figure 6.2
Toxic Releases—Top 10 Industries: 1993

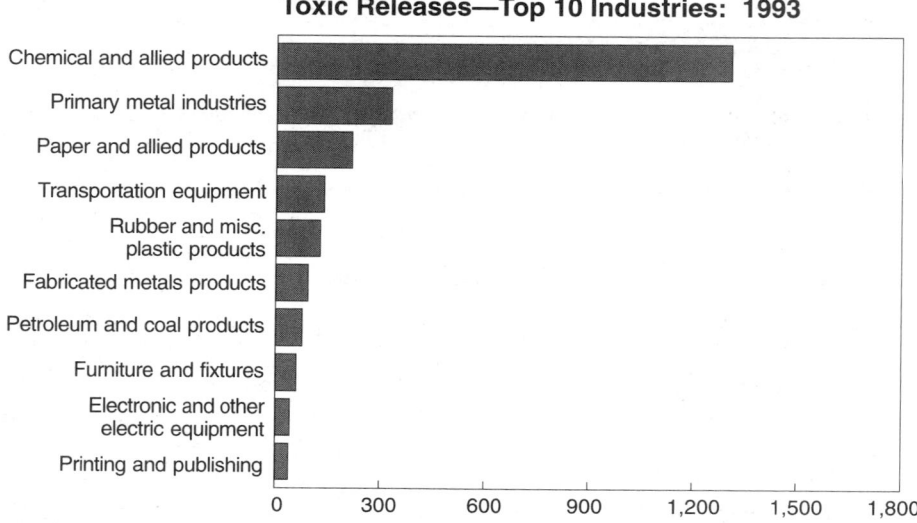

Source: Chart prepared by U.S. Bureau of the Census. For data, see table 379.

Geography and Environment

This section presents a variety of information on the physical environment of the United States, starting with basic area measurement data and ending with climatic data for selected weather stations around the country. The subjects covered between those points are mostly concerned with environmental trends, but include such related subjects as land use, water consumption, air pollutant emissions, toxic releases, oil spills, hazardous waste sites, threatened and endangered wildlife, and expenditures for pollution abatement and control.

The information in this section is selected from a wide range of Federal agencies that compile the data for various administrative or regulatory purposes, such as the Environmental Protection Agency, U.S. Geological Survey, National Oceanic and Atmospheric Administration, Soil Conservation Service, and General Services Administration. Other agencies include the Bureau of the Census, which presents nationwide area measurement information and the Bureau of Economic Analysis, which compiles data on pollution abatement and control expenditures.

Area—For the 1990 census, area measurements were calculated by computer based on the information contained in a single, consistent geographic data base, the TIGER^{TM} File (described below), rather than relying on historical, local, and manually calculated information. This especially affects water area figures reported in 1990; these had only included those bodies of water of least 40 acres and those streams with a width of at least one-eighth of a statute mile from 1940 to 1980. Water area figures for 1990 increased because the data reflected all water recorded in the Census Bureau's geographic data base including coastal, Great Lakes, and territorial waters.

Geography—The U.S. Geological Survey conducts investigations, surveys, and research in the fields of geography, geology, topography, geographic information systems, mineralogy, hydrology, and geothermal energy resources as

In Brief

The environmental industry generated $180 billion in revenues and employed 1.3 million workers in 1995.

There were 1,270 hazardous waste sites on the Superfund's National Priority List in 1995.

Emissions of CFC gases in the air down 52% between 1988 and 1994.

well as natural hazards. In cooperation with State and local agencies, the U.S. Geological Survey prepares and publishes topographic, land use/land cover, geologic, and hydrologic maps and digital data compilations. The U.S. Geological Survey provides United States cartographic data through the Earth Sciences Information Center, water resources data through the National Water Data Exchange (NAWDEX), and a variety of research and Open-File reports which are announced monthly in New Publications of the U.S. Geological Survey. In a joint project with the Census Bureau, the U.S. Geological Survey provided the basic information on geographic features for input into a national geographic and cartographic data base prepared by the Census Bureau, called the TIGER^{TM} (Topologically Integrated Geographic Encoding and Referencing) System.

Maps prepared by the Bureau of the Census show the names and boundaries of various types of legal and statistical entities, such as places, county subdivisions, and larger areas and are available as of the specific decennial census. An inventory is available for the 1990 census, both on computer tape and CD-ROM as the 1990 TIGER/GICS (Geographic Identification Code Scheme) and for the 1992 economic censuses in the *Geographic Reference Manual* (EC92-R-1). The Census Bureau maintains a current inventory of governmental units and their legal boundaries through its Boundary and Annexation Survey.

The TIGER™ System contains information on the legal and statistical entities used by the Census Bureau, as well as on both manmade and natural features, such as streets, roads, railroads, rivers, and lakes; information is available to the public in the form of machine-readable TIGER™ extract files.

An inventory of the Nation's land resources by type of use/cover was conducted by the Soil Conservation Service in 1982, 1987, and 1992. The results, published in the *1992 National Inventory of Land Resources*, cover all non-Federal land in Puerto Rico, the Virgin Islands, and the United States except Alaska.

Environment—The principal Federal agency responsible for pollution abatement and control activities is the Environmental Protection Agency (EPA). It is responsible for establishing and monitoring national air quality standards, water quality activities, solid and hazardous waste disposal, and control of toxic substances.

National Ambient Air Quality Standards (NAAQS) for suspended particulate matter, sulfur dioxide, photochemical oxidants, carbon monoxide, and nitrogen dioxide were originally set by the EPA in April 1971. Every 5 years, each of the NAAQS is reviewed and revised if new health or welfare data indicates that a change is necessary. The standard for photochemical oxidants, now called ozone, was revised in February 1979. Also, a new NAAQS for lead was promulgated in October 1978 and for suspended particulate matter in 1987. Table 363 gives some of the health-related standards for the six air pollutants having NAAQS. Responsibility for demonstrating compliance with or progress toward achieving these standards lies with the State agencies. In 1993, there were 1,508 non-Federal sampling stations for particulates, 692 for sulfur dioxide, 537 for carbon monoxide, 925 for ozone, 377 for nitrogen dioxide, and 430 for lead. Data from these State networks are periodically submitted to EPA's National Aerometric Information Retrieval System (AIRS) for summarization in annual reports on the nationwide status and trends in air quality; for details, see *National Air Quality and Emissions Trends Report, 1994*.

Pollution abatement and control expenditures—Data on expenditures for pollution abatement and control are compiled and published by the Bureau of Economic Analysis (BEA) and the U.S. Bureau of the Census. The BEA conducts surveys on national expenditures for pollution abatement and control and presents the data in its *Survey of Current Business*. The Bureau of the Census collects data on expenditures for pollution control activities for State and local governments and industry. Data on government expenditures are reported in an annual series of publications, *Government Finances*, which covers expenditures on sewage and sanitation outlays. Industry data are reported annually in *Current Industrial Reports*. The Council on Environmental Quality published some expenditure data in *Environmental Quality* along with other environmental indicator.

Climate—NOAA, through the National Weather Service and the National Environmental Satellite, Data and Information Service, is responsible for data on climate. NOAA maintains about 11,600 weather stations, of which over 3,000 produce autographic precipitation records, about 600 take hourly readings of a series of weather elements, and the remainder record data once a day. These data are reported monthly in the *Climatological Data* (published by State), and monthly and annually in the *Local Climatological Data* (published by location for major cities).

The normal climatological temperatures, precipitation, and degree days listed in this publication are derived for comparative purposes and are averages for the 30-year period, 1961-90. For stations that did not have continuous records for the entire 30 years from the same instrument site, the normals have been adjusted to provide representative values for the current location. The information in all other tables is based on data from the beginning of the record at that location through 1994, except as noted.

Historical statistics—Tabular headnotes provide cross-references, where applicable, to *Historical Statistics of the United States, Colonial Times to 1970*. See Appendix IV.

No. 362. Land and Water Area of States and Other Entities: 1990

[One square mile=2.59 square kilometers. Excludes territorial water, which was included in the 1993 edition of the *Statistical Abstract*. See *Historical Statistics of the United States, Colonial Times to 1970*, series A 210-263, for land area]

REGION, DIVISION, STATE, AND OTHER AREA	TOTAL AREA Sq. mi.	Sq. km.	LAND AREA Sq. mi.	Sq. km.	WATER AREA Total Sq. mi.	Sq. km.	Inland sq. mi.	Coastal sq. mi.	Great Lakes sq. mi.
United States	3,717,796	9,629,091	3,536,278	9,158,960	181,518	470,131	78,937	42,528	60,052
Northeast	176,917	458,215	162,274	420,289	14,643	37,926	6,444	3,549	4,650
New England	68,655	177,815	62,812	162,682	5,843	15,133	3,695	2,148	-
Maine.	33,741	87,388	30,865	79,939	2,876	7,449	2,263	613	-
New Hampshire	9,283	24,044	8,969	23,231	314	813	314	-	-
Vermont	9,615	24,903	9,249	23,956	366	947	366	-	-
Massachusetts	9,241	23,934	7,838	20,300	1,403	3,634	424	979	-
Rhode Island	1,231	3,189	1,045	2,707	186	482	168	18	-
Connecticut	5,544	14,358	4,845	12,550	698	1,808	161	538	-
Middle Atlantic	108,263	280,400	99,462	257,607	8,800	22,793	2,749	1,401	4,650
New York	53,989	139,833	47,224	122,310	6,766	17,523	1,888	976	3,901
New Jersey	8,215	21,277	7,419	19,215	796	2,062	371	425	-
Pennsylvania	46,058	119,291	44,820	116,083	1,239	3,208	490	-	749
Midwest	821,762	2,128,364	751,519	1,946,435	70,243	181,929	14,841	-	55,402
East North Central	301,369	780,547	243,539	630,766	57,830	149,781	4,974	-	52,856
Ohio.	44,828	116,103	40,953	106,067	3,875	10,036	376	-	3,499
Indiana	36,420	94,328	35,870	92,904	550	1,424	315	-	235
Illinois.	57,918	150,007	55,593	143,987	2,325	6,021	750	-	1,575
Michigan	96,705	250,465	56,809	147,136	39,895	103,329	1,704	-	38,192
Wisconsin	65,499	169,643	54,314	140,672	11,186	28,971	1,831	-	9,355
West North Central. . . .	520,393	1,347,817	507,980	1,315,669	12,412	32,148	9,866	-	2,546
Minnesota	86,943	225,182	79,617	206,207	7,326	18,975	4,780	-	2,546
Iowa.	56,276	145,754	55,875	144,716	401	1,038	401	-	-
Missouri	69,709	180,546	68,898	178,446	811	2,100	811	-	-
North Dakota	70,704	183,123	68,994	178,695	1,710	4,428	1,710	-	-
South Dakota.	77,121	199,744	75,896	196,571	1,225	3,174	1,225	-	-
Nebraska	77,358	200,358	76,878	199,113	481	1,245	481	-	-
Kansas	82,282	213,110	81,823	211,922	459	1,189	459	-	-
South	907,178	2,349,591	871,010	2,255,916	36,168	93,674	27,355	8,813	-
South Atlantic	284,085	735,780	266,160	689,355	17,925	46,426	12,557	5,368	-
Delaware	2,396	6,206	1,955	5,062	442	1,144	71	371	-
Maryland.	12,297	31,849	9,775	25,316	2,522	6,533	680	1,842	-
District of Columbia. . .	68	177	61	159	7	18	7	-	-
Virginia	42,326	109,625	39,598	102,558	2,729	7,067	1,000	1,728	-
West Virginia	24,231	62,759	24,087	62,384	145	375	145	-	-
North Carolina	52,672	136,421	48,718	126,180	3,954	10,241	3,954	-	-
South Carolina	31,189	80,779	30,111	77,988	1,078	2,791	1,006	72	-
Georgia	58,977	152,750	57,919	150,010	1,058	2,740	1,011	47	-
Florida	59,928	155,214	53,937	139,697	5,991	15,517	4,683	1,308	-
East South Central. . . .	183,080	474,176	178,616	462,615	4,464	11,561	3,355	1,109	-
Kentucky.	40,411	104,665	39,732	102,907	679	1,759	679	-	-
Tennessee	42,146	109,158	41,219	106,758	926	2,400	926	-	-
Alabama	52,237	135,293	50,750	131,443	1,486	3,850	968	519	-
Mississippi.	48,286	125,060	46,914	121,506	1,372	3,553	781	591	-
West South Central . . .	440,013	1,139,634	426,234	1,103,947	13,779	35,687	11,444	2,335	-
Arkansas	53,182	137,742	52,075	134,875	1,107	2,867	1,107	-	-
Louisiana	49,651	128,595	43,566	112,836	6,085	15,759	4,153	1,931	-
Oklahoma	69,903	181,048	68,679	177,877	1,224	3,171	1,224	-	-
Texas	267,277	692,248	261,914	678,358	5,363	13,890	4,959	404	-
West.	1,811,939	4,692,921	1,751,475	4,536,320	60,464	156,601	30,297	30,167	-
Mountain	863,613	2,236,757	856,121	2,217,354	7,492	19,404	7,492	-	-
Montana	147,046	380,849	145,556	376,991	1,490	3,859	1,490	-	-
Idaho	83,574	216,456	82,751	214,325	823	2,131	823	-	-
Wyoming.	97,818	253,349	97,105	251,501	714	1,848	714	-	-
Colorado.	104,100	269,618	103,729	268,658	371	960	371	-	-
New Mexico.	121,598	314,939	121,364	314,334	234	605	234	-	-
Arizona.	114,006	295,276	113,642	294,333	364	943	364	-	-
Utah.	84,904	219,902	82,168	212,815	2,736	7,086	2,736	-	-
Nevada.	110,567	286,367	109,806	284,396	761	1,971	761	-	-
Pacific.	948,326	2,456,164	895,354	2,318,967	52,972	137,197	22,805	30,167	-
Washington	70,637	182,949	66,581	172,445	4,055	10,503	1,545	2,511	-
Oregon.	97,132	251,571	96,002	248,646	1,129	2,925	1,050	80	-
California	158,869	411,470	155,973	403,971	2,895	7,499	2,674	222	-
Alaska	615,230	1,593,444	570,374	1,477,268	44,856	116,177	17,501	27,355	-
Hawaii	6,459	16,729	6,423	16,636	36	93	36	-	-
Other areas:									
Puerto Rico.	3,508	9,085	3,427	8,875	81	210	65	16	-
American Samoa	90	233	77	200	13	33	7	6	-
Guam	217	561	210	543	7	18	7	-	-
No. Mariana Islands	189	490	179	464	10	26	2	8	-
Palau.	241	624	177	458	64	165	40	24	-
Virgin Islands of the U.S .	171	443	134	346	37	96	17	20	-

- Represents or rounds to zero.

Source: U.S. Bureau of the Census, *1990 Census of Population and Housing*, series CPH-2; and unpublished data from the TIGER/Geographic Information Control System (TIGER/GICS)computer file.

No. 363. Area and Acquisition of the Federal Public Domain: 1781 to 1991

[In millions of acres. Areas of acquisitions are as computed in 1912, and do not agree with figures in square miles shown in table 362 which include later adjustments and reflect subsequent remeasurement. Excludes outlying areas of the United States amounting to 645,949 acres in 1978. See also *Historical Statistics, Colonial Times to 1970*, series J 3-6]

YEAR	Land area total [1]	YEAR	LAND AREA [1]			YEAR AND ACQUISITION	ACREAGE		
			Total	Public domain	Acquired		Total	Land	Inland water
1802 ...	200.0	1980 ...	719.5	648.0	71.5	**Aggregate**	**1,837.8**	**1,804.7**	**33.1**
1850 ...	1,200.0	1981 ...	730.8	668.7	62.2				
1880 ...	900.0	1982 ...	729.8	670.0	59.8	1781-1802 (State Cessions)	236.8	233.4	3.4
1912 ...	600.0	1983 ...	732.0	672.4	59.6	1803, Louisiana Purchase [2]	529.9	523.4	6.5
1946 ...	413.0	1984 ...	726.6	658.9	67.7	1819, Cession from Spain	46.1	43.3	2.8
1950 ...	412.0	1985 ...	726.7	656.2	70.5	Red River Basin [3]	29.6	29.1	0.5
1955 ...	407.9	1986 ...	727.1	662.7	64.4				
1959 ...	768.6	1987 ...	724.3	661.0	63.3	1846, Oregon Compromise	183.4	180.6	2.7
1960 ...	771.5	1988 ...	688.2	623.2	65.0	1848, Mexican Cession [2]	338.7	334.5	4.2
1965 ...	765.8	1989 ...	662.2	597.9	64.3	1850, Purchase from Texas	78.9	78.8	0.1
1970 ...	761.3	1990 ...	649.8	587.4	62.4	1853, Gadsden Purchase	19.0	19.0	(Z)
1975 ...	760.4	1991 ...	649.3	587.6	61.8	1867, Alaska Purchase	375.3	362.5	12.8
1976 ...	762.2								
1977 ...	741.5								
1978 ...	775.2								
1979 ...	744.1								

Z Less than 50,000.   [1] Owned by Federal Government. Comprises original public domain plus acquired lands. Estimated from imperfect data available for indicated years. Prior to 1959, excludes Alaska, and 1960, Hawaii. Source: Beginning 1955, U.S. General Services Administration, *Inventory Report on Real Property Owned by the United States Throughout the World*, annual.   [2] Data for Louisiana Purchase exclude areas eliminated by Treaty of 1819 with Spain. Such areas are included in figures for Mexican Cession.   [3] Represents drainage basin of Red River of the North, south of 49th parallel. Authorities differ as to method and date of its acquisition. Some hold it as part of the Louisiana Purchase; others, as acquired from Great Britain.

Source: Except as noted, U.S. Dept. of the Interior. Estimated area, Bureau of Land Management; all other data, Office of the Secretary, *Areas of Acquisitions to the Territory of the U.S.*, 1922.

No. 364. Total and Federally Owned Land, 1960 to 1993, and by State, 1993

[As of **end of fiscal year**; see text, section 9. Total land area figures are not comparable with those in table 362]

REGION, DIVISION, AND STATE	Total (1,000 acres)	Not owned by Federal Government (1,000 acres)	OWNED BY FEDERAL GOVERNMENT[1]		REGION, DIVISION, AND STATE	Total (1,000 acres)	Not owned by Federal Government (1,000 acres)	OWNED BY FEDERAL GOVERNMENT[1]	
			Acres (1,000)	Percent				Acres (1,000)	Percent
1960	2,273,407	1,501,894	771,512	33.9	**South ......**	561,238	539,896	21,342	3.8
1965	2,271,343	1,505,546	765,797	33.7	**S.A.**	171,325	161,040	10,285	6.0
1970	2,271,343	1,510,042	761,301	33.5	DE	1,266	1,237	29	2.3
1975	2,271,343	1,510,929	760,414	33.5	MD	6,319	6,131	188	3.0
1980	2,271,343	1,551,822	719,522	31.7	DC	39	30	9	24.1
1985	2,271,343	1,544,658	726,686	32.0	VA	25,496	23,683	1,813	7.1
1990	2,271,343	1,621,541	649,802	28.6	WV	15,411	14,388	1,022	6.6
1991	2,271,343	1,621,998	649,346	28.6	NC	31,403	29,397	2,005	6.4
1992	2,271,343	1,620,250	651,094	28.7	SC	19,374	18,630	744	3.8
1993, total	**2,271,343**	**1,621,021**	**650,322**	**28.6**	GA	37,295	35,799	1,497	4.0
Northeast....	**104,700**	**102,329**	**2,371**	**2.3**	FL	34,721	31,745	2,977	8.6
N.E.......	**40,401**	**39,035**	**1,366**	**3.4**	**E.S.C**	**115,141**	**110,658**	**4,483**	**3.9**
ME	19,848	19,684	163	0.8	KY	25,512	24,432	1,080	4.2
NH	5,769	5,034	735	12.7	TN	26,728	25,708	1,019	3.8
VT	5,937	5,579	358	6.0	AL	32,678	31,599	1,079	3.3
MA	5,035	4,938	97	1.9	MS	30,223	28,919	1,304	4.3
RI	677	672	5	0.7	**W.S.C.**	**274,772**	**268,198**	**6,574**	**2.4**
CT	3,135	3,127	8	0.3	AR	33,599	30,840	2,759	8.2
M.A	**64,299**	**63,294**	**1,005**	**1.6**	LA	28,868	28,046	822	2.8
NY	30,681	30,469	212	0.7	OK	44,088	43,371	716	1.6
NJ	4,813	4,651	162	3.4	TX	168,218	165,941	2,277	1.4
PA	28,804	28,173	631	2.2	**West ....**	**1,122,535**	**519,449**	**603,086**	**53.7**
Midwest	**482,870**	**459,347**	**23,523**	**4.9**	**Mountain. ...**	**548,449**	**283,611**	**264,837**	**48.3**
E.N.C	**156,679**	**146,785**	**9,894**	**6.3**	MT	93,271	67,204	26,067	27.9
OH	26,222	25,883	339	1.3	ID	52,933	20,328	32,605	61.6
IN	23,158	22,695	464	2.0	WY	62,343	31,888	30,455	48.9
IL	35,795	34,833	962	2.7	CO	66,486	42,400	24,086	36.2
MI	36,492	31,900	4,592	12.6	NM	77,766	51,513	26,253	33.8
WI	35,011	31,474	3,537	10.1	AZ	72,688	38,374	34,314	47.2
W.N.C.	**326,191**	**312,562**	**13,629**	**4.2**	UT	52,697	19,935	32,762	62.2
MN	51,206	45,828	5,377	10.5	NV	70,264	11,969	58,295	83.0
IA	35,860	35,524	336	0.9	**Pacfic .....**	**574,086**	**235,838**	**338,249**	**58.9**
MO	44,248	42,159	2,089	4.7	WA	42,694	30,603	12,091	28.3
ND	44,452	42,566	1,887	4.2	OR	61,599	29,300	32,298	52.4
SD	48,882	46,076	2,805	5.7	CA	100,207	54,997	45,210	45.1
NE	49,032	48,321	711	1.4	AK	365,482	117,483	247,999	67.9
KS	52,511	52,087	424	0.8	HI	4,106	3,455	650	15.8

[1] Excludes trust properties.

Source: U.S. General Services Administration, *Inventory Report on Real Property Owned by the United States Throughout the World*, annual.

No. 365. Land Cover/Use, by State: 1992

[**In thousands of acres.** Excludes Alaska and District of Columbia]

STATE	Total surface area [1]	Federal land	NONFEDERAL LAND							
			Total	Developed [2]	Rural					
					Total	Crop-land	Pasture land	Range-land	Forest land	Minor cover/use
Total	**1,940,011**	**407,989**	**1,483,126**	**92,352**	**1,390,774**	**382,317**	**125,927**	**398,949**	**394,958**	**88,624**
United States	1,937,678	407,899	1,480,916	91,946	1,388,970	381,950	125,215	398,803	394,437	88,565
Alabama	33,091	921	31,192	2,046	29,147	3,147	3,760	67	20,968	1,205
Arizona	72,960	30,280	42,408	1,404	41,004	1,198	76	32,227	4,718	2,785
Arkansas	34,040	3,207	29,803	1,322	28,480	7,730	5,727	159	14,267	598
California	101,572	46,792	52,892	5,001	47,892	10,052	1,161	17,140	14,794	4,746
Colorado	66,618	23,923	42,240	1,694	40,547	8,940	1,256	23,537	3,755	3,059
Connecticut	3,212	15	3,054	816	2,238	229	110	-	1,760	140
Delaware	1,309	33	1,213	205	1,008	499	26	-	353	130
Florida	37,545	3,791	30,406	4,645	25,761	2,997	4,373	3,467	12,378	2,545
Georgia	37,702	2,087	34,599	3,077	31,523	5,173	3,075	-	21,714	1,560
Hawaii	4,093	432	3,621	170	3,451	274	88	925	1,483	680
Idaho	53,481	33,298	19,521	587	18,934	5,600	1,243	6,668	4,024	1,399
Illinois	36,061	521	34,766	3,094	31,672	24,100	2,764	-	3,419	1,390
Indiana	23,159	487	22,287	2,095	20,193	13,513	1,866	-	3,626	1,188
Iowa	36,016	184	35,363	1,779	33,584	24,988	3,712	-	1,931	2,953
Kansas	52,658	606	51,488	1,997	49,491	26,565	2,306	15,723	1,331	3,565
Kentucky	25,862	1,201	23,985	1,653	22,332	5,092	5,859	-	10,312	1,069
Louisiana	30,561	1,264	26,373	1,764	24,609	5,972	2,269	227	12,961	3,181
Maine	21,290	164	19,517	697	18,820	448	111	-	17,557	705
Maryland	6,695	167	6,034	1,095	4,939	1,673	545	-	2,364	356
Massachusetts	5,302	89	4,839	1,309	3,530	272	170	-	2,778	310
Michigan	37,457	3,166	33,040	3,686	29,354	8,985	2,353	-	15,608	2,408
Minnesota	54,017	3,383	47,092	2,418	44,674	21,356	3,282	-	13,815	6,222
Mississippi	30,521	1,726	27,992	1,337	26,655	5,726	4,047	-	15,765	1,117
Missouri	44,606	2,017	41,710	2,336	39,374	13,347	11,911	126	11,656	2,332
Montana	94,109	27,122	65,656	1,096	64,561	15,035	3,370	36,835	5,156	4,165
Nebraska	49,507	739	48,137	1,252	46,885	19,239	2,066	22,669	777	2,135
Nevada	70,759	60,290	10,025	394	9,631	762	297	7,854	353	364
New Hampshire	5,938	747	4,952	563	4,389	142	98	-	3,932	217
New Jersey	4,984	159	4,549	1,588	2,961	650	159	-	1,766	386
New Mexico	77,819	27,394	50,196	866	49,330	1,892	212	39,792	4,600	2,835
New York	31,429	231	29,788	3,005	26,783	5,616	3,001	-	17,178	987
North Carolina	33,708	2,448	28,476	3,542	24,933	5,960	2,019	-	15,979	975
North Dakota	45,250	1,951	42,187	1,344	40,843	24,743	1,168	10,325	426	4,181
Ohio	26,451	375	25,654	3,558	22,096	11,929	2,269	-	6,624	1,275
Oklahoma	44,772	1,202	42,395	1,875	40,520	10,081	7,720	14,061	6,988	1,672
Oregon	62,127	32,291	29,155	1,125	28,030	3,776	1,900	9,375	11,839	1,142
Pennsylvania	28,997	682	27,813	3,432	24,381	5,596	2,326	-	15,316	1,143
Rhode Island	776	4	661	190	472	25	24	-	393	30
South Carolina	19,912	1,156	17,961	1,856	16,105	2,983	1,190	-	10,922	1,010
South Dakota	49,354	2,907	45,459	1,135	44,324	16,436	2,158	21,933	540	3,257
Tennessee	26,972	1,379	24,740	2,161	22,579	4,857	5,165	-	11,580	977
Texas	170,756	3,203	163,687	8,231	155,456	28,261	16,710	94,155	9,960	6,369
Utah	54,336	35,582	16,866	561	16,305	1,815	665	10,050	1,626	2,148
Vermont	6,153	368	5,521	324	5,197	635	349	-	4,138	75
Virginia	26,091	2,389	22,774	2,183	20,591	2,901	3,444	-	13,539	707
Washington	43,608	12,479	29,931	1,851	28,081	6,745	1,352	5,476	12,547	1,960
West Virginia	15,508	1,201	14,138	689	13,449	915	1,609	-	10,534	391
Wisconsin	35,938	1,829	32,747	2,357	30,390	10,813	2,954	-	13,410	3,212
Wyoming	62,598	30,020	32,012	541	31,471	2,272	901	26,015	975	1,309
Caribbean	2,334	90	2,211	407	1,804	367	712	145	521	59

- Represents zero. [1] Includes water area not shown separately. [2] Includes urban and built-up areas in units of 10 acres or greater, and rural transportation.

Source: U.S. Dept. of Agriculture, Soil Conservation Service, and Iowa State University, Statistical Laboratory; *Summary Report, 1992 National Resources Inventory.*

No. 366. Extreme and Mean Elevations States and Other Areas

[One foot=.305 meter]

STATE OR OTHER AREA	HIGHEST POINT Name	Elevation Feet	Meters	LOWEST POINT Name	Elevation Feet	Meters	APPROXIMATE MEAN ELEVATION Feet	Meters
U.S..	**Mt. McKinley (AK) . . . .**	**20,320**	**6,198**	**Death Valley (CA) . . .**	**-282**	**-86**	**2,500**	**763**
AL	Cheaha Mountain	2,405	733	Gulf of Mexico	(¹)	(¹)	500	153
AK	Mount McKinley.	20,320	6,198	Pacific Ocean	(¹)	(¹)	1,900	580
AZ	Humphreys Peak.	12,633	3,853	Colorado River.	70	21	4,100	1,251
AR	Magazine Mountain	2,753	840	Ouachita River.	55	17	650	198
CA	Mount Whitney	14,494	4,419	Death Valley	-282	-86	2,900	885
CO	Mt. Elbert	14,433	4,402	Arkansas River	3,350	1,022	6,800	2,074
CT	Mt. Frissell on South slope . . .	2,380	726	Long Island Sound . . .	(¹)	(¹)	500	153
DE	Ebright Road, [2]							
	New Castle County	448	137	Atlantic Ocean.	(¹)	(¹)	60	18
DC	Tenleytown at Reno Reservoir .	410	125	Potomac River.	1	(Z)	150	46
FL	Sec. 30, T6N, R20W, Walton							
	County.	345	105	Atlantic Ocean	(¹)	(¹)	100	31
GA	Brasstown Bald.	4,784	1,459	Atlantic Ocean	(¹)	(¹)	600	183
HI	Puu Wekiu	13,796	4,208	Pacific Ocean	(¹)	(¹)	3,030	924
ID	Borah Peak	12,662	3,862	Snake River	710	217	5,000	1,525
IL	Charles Mound	1,235	377	Mississippi River	279	85	600	183
IN	Franklin Twp., Wayne Co	1,257	383	Ohio River	320	98	700	214
IA	Sec. 29, T100N, R41W,							
	Osceola County [3]	1,670	509	Mississippi River	480	146	1,100	336
KS	Mount Sunflower	4,039	1,232	Verdigris River.	679	207	2,000	610
KY	Black Mountain	4,139	2,162	Mississippi River	257	78	750	229
LA	Driskill Mountain	535	163	New Orleans	-8	-2	100	31
ME	Mount Katahdin	5,267	1,606	Atlantic Ocean	(¹)	(¹)	600	183
MD	Backbone Mountain	3,360	1,025	Atlantic Ocean	(¹)	(¹)	350	107
MA	Mount Greylock.	3,487	1,064	Atlantic Ocean	(¹)	(¹)	500	153
MI	Mount Arvon.	1,979	604	Lake Erie	571	174	900	275
MN	Eagle Mountain, Cook Co	2,301	702	Lake Superior	600	183	1,200	366
MS	Woodall Mountain	806	246	Gulf of Mexico	(¹)	(¹)	300	92
MO	Taum Sauk Mountain	1,772	540	St. Francis River	230	70	800	244
MT	Granite Peak	12,799	3,904	Kootenai River.	1,800	549	3,400	1,037
NE	Johnson Twp., Kimball Co	5,424	1,654	Missouri River	840	256	2,600	793
NV	Boundary Peak	13,140	4,007	Colorado River.	479	146	5,500	1,678
NH	Mount Washington	6,288	1,918	Atlantic Ocean	(¹)	(¹)	1,000	305
NJ	High Point	1,803	550	Atlantic Ocean	(¹)	(¹)	250	76
NM	Wheeler Peak	13,161	4,014	Red Bluff Reservoir . .	2,842	867	5,700	1,739
NY	Mount Marcy.	5,344	1,630	Atlantic Ocean	(¹)	(¹)	1,000	305
NC	Mount Mitchell.	6,684	2,039	Atlantic Ocean	(¹)	(¹)	700	214
ND	White Butte, Slope Co	3,506	1,069	Red River	750	229	1,900	580
OH	Campbell Hill	1,549	472	Ohio River	455	139	850	259
OK	Black Mesa.	4,973	1,517	Little River	289	88	1,300	397
OR	Mount Hood	11,239	3,428	Pacific Ocean	(¹)	(¹)	3,300	1,007
PA	Mount Davis	3,213	980	Delaware River	(¹)	(¹)	1,100	336
RI	Jerimoth Hill	812	248	Atlantic Ocean	(¹)	(¹)	200	61
SC	Sassafras Mountain	3,560	1,086	Atlantic Ocean	(¹)	(¹)	350	107
SD	Harney Peak.	7,242	2,209	Big Stone Lake	966	295	2,200	671
TN	Clingmans Dome	6,643	2,026	Mississippi River	178	54	900	275
TX	Guadalupe Peak	8,749	2,668	Gulf of Mexico	(¹)	(¹)	1,700	519
UT	Kings Peak	13,528	4,126	Beaverdam Wash. . . .	2,000	610	6,100	1,861
VT	Mount Mansfield	4,393	1,340	Lake Champlain	95	29	1,000	305
VA	Mount Rogers	5,729	1,747	Atlantic Ocean	(¹)	(¹)	950	290
WA	Mount Rainier.	14,410	4,395	Pacific Ocean	(¹)	(¹)	1,700	519
WV	Spruce Knob.	4,861	1,483	Potomac River.	240	73	1,500	458
WI	Timms Hill	1,951	595	Lake Michigan	579	177	1,050	320
WY	Gannett Peak	13,804	4,210	Belle Fourche River . .	3,099	945	6,700	2,044
Other areas:								
Puerto Rico	Cerro de Punta	4,390	1,339	Atlantic Ocean	(¹)	(¹)	1,800	549
American Samoa. . .	Lata Mountain	3,160	964	Pacific Ocean	(¹)	(¹)	1,300	397
Guam	Mount Lamlam	1,332	406	Pacific Ocean	(¹)	(¹)	330	101
Virgin Is. . .	Crown Mountain	1,556	475	Atlantic Ocean	(¹)	(¹)	750	229

Z Less than 0.5 meter.　　[1] Sea level.　　[2] At DE-PA State line.　　[3] "Sec." denotes section; "T," township; "R," range; "N," north; and "W," west.

Source: U.S. Geological Survey, for highest and lowest points, *Elevations and Distances in the United States, 1990*; for mean elevations, 1983 edition.

No. 367. Water Areas for Selected Major Bodies of Water: 1990

[Includes only that portion of body of water under the jurisdiction of the United States, excluding Hawaii. One square mile=2.59 square kilometers]

BODY OF WATER AND STATE	AREA		BODY OF WATER AND STATE	AREA	
	Sq. mi.	Sq. km.		Sq. mi.	Sq. km.
Atlantic Coast water bodies:			Leech Lake (MN)	162	419
Chesapeake Bay (MD-VA)	2,747	7,115	Lake St Clair (MI) [1]	161	416
Pamlico Sound (NC)	1,622	4,200	Eufaula Lake (OK)	157	407
Long Island Sound (CT-NY)	914	2,368	Sam Rayburn Resevoir (TX)	150	389
Delaware Bay (DE-NJ)	614	1,591	Goose Lake (CA-OR)	147	381
Cape Cod Bay (MA)	598	1,548	Utah Lake (UT)	139	361
Albemarle Sound (NC)	492	1,274	Lake Marion (SC)	139	360
Biscayne Bay (FL)	218	565	Lake Francis Case (SD)	134	346
Buzzards Bay (MA)	215	558	Lake Pend Oreille (ID)	133	343
Tangier Sound (MD-VA)	172	445	Lake Texoma (OK-TX)	132	342
Currituck Sound (NC)	116	301	Yellowstone Lake (WY)	131	339
Pocomoke Sound (MD-VA)	111	286			
Chincoteague Bay (MD-VA)	105	272	Livingston Reservoir (TX)	127	330
Great South Bay (NY)	94	243	Franklin D Roosevelt Lake (WA)	124	322
Core Sound (NC)	88	229	Moosehead Lake (ME)	116	301
			Clark Hill Lake (GA-SC)	105	272
Gulf Coast water bodies:			Lake Maurepas (LA)	91	235
Mississippi Sound (AL-LA-MS)	813	2,105	Lake Moultrie (SC)	89	230
Laguna Madre (TX)	733	1,897	Lake Winnibigoshish (MN)	87	225
Lake Pontchartrain (LA)	631	1,635	Hartwell Lake (GA-SC)	86	224
Florida Bay (FL)	616	1,596	Upper Klamath Lake (OR)	85	221
Breton Sound (LA)	511	1,323	Harry S. Truman Reservoir (MO)	84	217
Mobile Bay (AL)	310	802	Oneida Lake (NY)	80	207
Lake Borgne (LA-MS)	271	702	Malheur Lake (OR)	75	195
Matagorda Bay (TX)	253	656			
Atchafalaya Bay (LA)	245	635	Alaska water bodies:		
Galveston Bay (TX)	236	611	Chatham Strait	1,559	4,039
Tampa Bay (FL)	212	549	Prince William Sound	1,382	3,579
Vermilion Bay (LA)	189	489	Clarence Strait	1,199	3,107
Corpus Christi Bay (TX)	151	392	Iliamna Lake	1,022	2,646
West Cote Blanche Bay (LA)	146	378	Frederick Sound	792	2,051
Trinity Bay (TX)	129	335	Sumner Strait	791	2,048
			Stephens Passage	702	1,819
Choctawhatchee Bay (FL)	122	315	Kvichak Bay	640	1,659
San Antonio Bay (TX)	118	306	Montague Strait	463	1,198
Timbalier Bay (LA)	112	291	Becharof Lake	447	1,158
Charlotte Harbor (FL)	112	291	Icy Strait	436	1,130
Aransas Bay (TX)	104	268	Hotham Inlet	433	1,120
Apalachicola Bay (FL)	101	262	Selawik Lake	403	1,044
Terrebonne Bay (LA)	99	256	Nushagak Bay	393	1,018
East Cote Blanche Bay (LA)	94	243	Baird Inlet	348	902
St George Sound (FL)	93	240			
Sabine Lake (LA-TX)	89	229	Yakutat Bay	345	894
White Lake (LA)	85	221	Teshekpuk Lake	324	839
Old Tampa Bay (FL)	83	214	Behm Canal	324	839
Bon Secour Bay (AL)	79	204	Turnagain Arm	322	834
Pine Island Sound (FL)	75	194	Kachemak Bay	310	803
			Glacier Bay	310	803
Pacific Coast water bodies:			Stefansson Sound	301	780
Puget Sound (WA)	808	2,092	Revillagigedo Channel	295	764
San Francisco Bay (CA)	264	684	Kasegaluk Lagoon	293	759
Willapa Bay (WA)	125	325	Cordova Bay	241	623
Hood Canal (WA)	117	303	Sitka Sound	229	593
			Naknek Lake	225	582
Interior water bodies:			Eschscholtz Bay	210	543
Lake Michigan (IL-IN-MI-WI)	22,342	57,866	Stepovak Bay	206	534
Lake Superior (MI-MN-WI) [1]	20,557	53,243	Keku Strait	206	534
Lake Huron (MI) [1]	8,800	22,792			
Lake Erie (MI-NY-OH-PA) [1]	5,033	13,036	Port Clarence	187	486
Lake Ontario (NY) [1]	3,446	8,926	Orca Bay	184	476
Great Salt Lake (UT)	1,836	4,756	Knik Arm	169	437
Green Bay (MI-WI)	1,396	3,617	Dall Lake	167	433
Lake Okeechobee (FL)	663	1,717	Knight Island Passage	167	432
Lake Sakakawea (ND)	563	1,459	Scammon Bay	163	423
Lake Oahe (ND-SD)	538	1,394	Port Moller	159	412
Lake of the Woods (MN) [1]	462	1,196	Ernest Sound	158	410
Lake Champlain (NY-VT) [1]	414	1,072	Spafarief Bay	157	405
Fort Peck Lake (MT)	379	981	Pavlov Bay	153	396
Salton Sea (CA)	364	944	Shishmaref Inlet	153	395
			Smith Bay	140	363
Toledo Bend Reservoir (LA-TX)	268	694	Seymour Canal	140	361
Lower Red Lake (MN)	257	666	Sitkalidak Strait	135	349
Lake Powell (AZ-UT)	250	649	Tlevak Strait	135	349
Kentucky Lake (KY-TN)	234	605			
Lake Mead (AZ-NV)	233	603	Lake Clark	130	336
Lake Winnebago (WI)	206	535	Lynn Canal	130	336
Mille Lacs Lake (MN)	200	518	Chignik Bay	119	309
Flathead Lake (MT)	191	495	Elson Lagoon	119	309
Lake Tahoe (CA-NV)	187	486	Bucareli Bay	119	307
Upper Red Lake (MN)	186	483	Hinchinbrook Entrance	118	306
Pyramid Lake (NV)	170	440			

[1] Area measurements for Lake Champlain, Lake Erie, Lake Huron, Lake Ontario, Lake St. Clair, Lake Superior, and Lake of the Woods include only those portions under the jurisdiction of the United States.

Source: U. S. Bureau of the Census, unpublished data from the Census TIGER [TM] data base.

No. 368. Flows of Largest U.S. Rivers—Length, Discharge, and Drainage Area

RIVER	Location of mouth	Source stream (name and location)	Length (miles) [1]	Average discharge at mouth (1,000 cubic ft. per second)	Drainage area (1,000 sq. mi.)
Missouri.	Missouri	Red Rock Creek, MT	2,540	76.2	[5]529
Mississippi.	Louisiana	Mississippi River, MN	[2]2,340	[3]593	[4][5]1,150
Yukon	Alaska	McNeil River, Canada	1,980	225	[5]328
St. Lawrence	Canada	North River, MN.	1,900	348	[5]396
Rio Grande	Mexico-Texas	Rio Grande, CO.	1,900	-	336
Arkansas	Arkansas	East Fork Arkansas River, CO	1,460	41	161
Colorado	Mexico	Colorado River, CO	1,450	-	246
Atchafalaya [6]	Louisiana	Tierra Blanca Creek, NM	1,420	58	95.1
Ohio.	Illinois-Kentucky	Allegheny River, PA	1,310	281	203
Red	Louisiana	Tierra Blanca Creek, NM	1,290	56	93.2
Brazos	Texas.	Blackwater Draw, NM	1,280	-	45.6
Columbia.	Oregon-Washington . .	Columbia River, Canada	1,240	265	[5]258
Snake.	Washington.	Snake River, WY	1,040	56.9	108
Platte	Nebraska	Grizzly Creek, CO	990	-	84.9
Pecos	Texas.	Pecos River, NM	926	-	44.3
Canadian.	Oklahoma	Canadian River, CO	906	-	46.9
Tennessee	Kentucky	Courthouse Creek, NC	886	68	40.9
Colorado (of Texas) . .	Texas.	Colorado River, TX.	862	-	42.3
North Canadian.	Oklahoma	Corrumpa Creek, NM	800	-	17.6
Mobile.	Alabama.	Tickanetley Creek, GA	774	67.2	44.6
Kansas	Kansas	Arikaree River, CO	743	-	59.5
Kuskokwim.	Alaska	South Fork Kuskokwim River, AK . .	724	67	48
Yellowstone	North Dakota.	North Folk Yellowstone River, WY . .	692	-	70
Tanana	Alaska	Nabesna River, AK.	659	41	44.5
Gila	Arizona.	Middle Fork Gila River, NM	649	-	58.2

- Represents zero.   [1] From source to mouth.   [2] The length from the source of the Missouri River to the Mississippi River and thence to the Gulf of Mexico is about 3,710 miles.   [3] Includes about 167,000 cubic ft. per second diverted from the Mississippi into the Atchafalaya River but excludes the flow of the Red River.   [4] Excludes the drainage areas of the Red and Atchafalaya Rivers.   [5] Drainage area includes both the United States and Canada.   [6] In east-central Louisiana, the Red River flows into the Atchafalaya River, a distributary of the Mississippi River. Data on average discharge, length, and drainage area include the Red River, but exclude all water diverted into the Atchafalaya from the Mississippi River.

Source: U.S. Geological Survey, *Largest Rivers in the United States*, Open File Report 87-242, May 1990.

No. 369. Water Withdrawals and Consumptive Use—States and Other Areas: 1990

[In millions of gallons per day, except as noted. Figures may not add due to rounding. Withdrawal signifies water physically withdrawn from a source. Includes fresh and saline water]

STATE OR OTHER AREA	WATER WITHDRAWN Total	Per capita (gal. per day) fresh	Source Ground water	Source Surface water	Consumptive use [1] fresh water	STATE OR OTHER AREA	WATER WITHDRAWN Total	Per capita (gal. per day) fresh	Source Ground water	Source Surface water	Consumptive use [1] fresh water
U.S. [2]	**407,900**	**1,340**	**80,640**	**327,260**	**93,980**	Montana	9,320	11,600	218	9,100	2,090
						Nebraska	8,940	5,660	4,800	4,150	4,230
Alabama.	8,090	2,000	403	7,680	454	Nevada	3,350	2,780	1,070	2,280	1,690
Alaska	641	517	112	529	26	New Hampshire .	1,310	378	64	1,250	26
Arizona.	6,570	1,790	2,740	3,830	4,350	New Jersey. . . .	12,800	287	566	12,200	211
Arkansas	7,840	3,330	4,710	3,130	4,140	New Mexico . . .	3,480	2,300	1,760	1,720	2,060
California	46,800	1,180	14,900	31,900	20,900	New York	19,000	583	840	18,100	562
Colorado.	12,700	3,850	2,800	9,910	5,250	North Carolina. . .	8,940	1,350	435	8,510	390
Connecticut. . . .	4,840	325	165	4,680	103	North Dakota. . .	2,680	4,190	141	2,540	228
Delaware	1,370	1,540	89	1,280	59	Ohio	11,700	1,080	904	10,800	901
District of						Oklahoma	1,670	452	905	760	659
Columbia	9	15	1	8	16	Oregon.	8,430	2,970	767	7,660	3,160
Florida	17,900	582	4,660	13,200	3,130	Pennsylvania. . . .	9,830	827	1,020	8,810	581
Georgia	5,350	816	996	4,360	822	Rhode Island. . .	526	132	25	501	18
Hawaii	2,740	1,070	590	2,150	627	South Carolina. .	6,000	1,720	282	5,720	293
Idaho	19,700	19,600	7,590	12,100	6,090	South Dakota. . .	592	851	251	341	345
Illinois	18,000	1,570	945	17,100	750	Tennessee	9,190	1,880	503	8,690	252
Indiana.	9,430	1,700	621	8,810	451	Texas.	25,200	1,180	7,880	17,300	9,020
Iowa	2,860	1,030	495	2,370	271	Utah	4,480	2,540	971	3,510	2,230
Kansas.	6,080	2,460	4,360	1,720	4,410	Vermont	632	1,120	45	587	29
Kentucky	4,320	1,170	247	4,070	309	Virginia.	6,860	762	443	6,420	224
Louisiana	9,350	2,200	1,340	8,010	1,590	Washington. . . .	7,940	1,630	1,450	6,490	2,830
Maine.	1,140	433	85	1,060	51	West Virginia. . .	4,580	2,560	728	3,860	509
Maryland	6,420	307	239	6,180	126	Wisconsin.	6,510	1,330	681	5,830	461
Massachusetts. . .	5,520	338	338	5,180	195	Wyoming	7,600	16,700	403	7,200	2,730
Michigan.	11,600	1,250	707	10,900	738						
Minnesota.	3,270	748	797	2,480	872	Puerto Rico. . . .	3,040	163	157	2,880	199
Mississippi	3,640	1,290	2,670	963	1,800	Virgin Islands. . .	164	91	3	160	2
Missouri.	6,930	1,150	728	6,200	529						

[1] Water that has been evaporated, transpired, or incorporated into products, plant, or animal tissue; and therefore, is not available for immediate reuse.   [2] Includes Puerto Rico and Virgin Islands.

Source: U.S. Geological Survey, *Estimated Use of Water in the United States in 1990*, circular 1081.

No. 370. U.S. Water Withdrawals and Consumptive Use Per Day, by End Use: 1940 to 1990

[Includes Puerto Rico. Withdrawal signifies water physically withdrawn from a source. Includes fresh and saline water; excludes water used for hydroelectric power. See also *Historical Statistics, Colonial Times to 1970*, series J 92-103]

YEAR	Total (bil. gal.)	Per capita [1] (gal.)	Irrigation (bil. gal.)	PUBLIC SUPPLY [2]		Rural [4] (bil. gal.)	Industrial and misc. [5] (bil. gal.)	Steam electric utilities (bil. gal.)
				Total (bil. gal.)	Per capita[3] (gal.)			
WITHDRAWALS								
1940	140	1,027	71	10	75	3.1	29	23
1950	180	1,185	89	14	145	3.6	37	40
1955	240	1,454	110	17	148	3.6	39	72
1960	270	1,500	110	21	151	3.6	38	100
1965	310	1,602	120	24	155	4.0	46	130
1970	370	1,815	130	27	166	4.5	47	170
1975	420	1,972	140	29	168	4.9	45	200
1980	440	1,953	150	34	183	5.6	45	210
1985	399	1,650	137	38	189	7.8	31	187
1990	408	1,620	137	41	195	7.9	30	195
CONSUMPTIVE USE								
1960	61	339	52	3.5	25	2.8	3.0	0.2
1965	77	403	66	5.2	34	3.2	3.4	0.4
1970	87	427	73	5.9	36	3.4	4.1	0.8
1975	96	451	80	6.7	38	3.4	4.2	1.9
1980	100	440	83	7.1	38	3.9	5.0	3.2
1985	92	380	74	(6)	(6)	9.2	6.1	6.2
1990	94	370	76	(6)	(6)	8.9	6.7	4.0

[1] Based on Bureau of the Census resident population as of July 1.   [2] Includes commercial water withdrawals.   [3] Based on population served.   [4] Rural farm and nonfarm household and garden use, and water for farm stock and dairies.   [5] For 1940 to 1960, includes manufacturing and mineral industries, rural commercial industries, air-conditioning, resorts, hotels, motels, military and other State and Federal agencies, and miscellaneous; thereafter, includes manufacturing, mining and mineral processing, ordnance, construction, and miscellaneous.   [6] Public supply consumptive use included in end-use categories.

Source: 1940-1960, U.S. Bureau of Domestic Business Development, based principally on committee prints, *Water Resources Activities in the United States*, for the Senate Committee on National Water Resources, U.S. Senate, thereafter, U.S. Geological Survey, *Estimated Use of Water in the United States in 1990*, circular 1081, and previous quinquennial issues.

No. 371. National Ambient Water Quality in Rivers and Streams—Violation Rate: 1980 to 1995

[In percent. Violation level based on U.S. Environmental Protection Agency water quality criteria. Violation rate represents the proportion of all measurements of a specific water quality pollutant which exceeds the "violation level" for that pollutant. "Violation" does not necessarily imply a legal violation. Data based on U.S. Geological Survey's National Stream Quality Accounting Network (NASQAN) data system; for details, see source. Years refer to water years. A water year begins in Oct. and ends in Sept. µg=micrograms; mg=milligrams. For metric conversion, see page ix]

POLLUTANT	VIOLATION LEVEL	1980	1985	1989	1990	1991	1992	1993	1994	1995
Fecal coliform bacteria. . . .	Above 200 cells per 100 ml. .	31	28	30	26	15	28	31	28	35
Dissolved oxygen	Below 5 mg per liter.	5	3	3	2	2	2	(Z)	2	1
Phosphorus, total, as phosporous	Above 1.0 mg per liter	4	3	2	3	2	2	2	2	4
Lead, dissolved	Above 50 µg per liter	(Z)	(Z)	(Z)	(Z)	(Z)	(Z)	(NA)	(NA)	(NA)
Cadmium, dissolved	Above 10 µg per liter	1	(Z)	(Z)	(Z)	(Z)	(Z)	(NA)	(NA)	(NA)

NA Not available.   Z Less than 1.

Source: U.S. Geological Survey, national-level data, unpublished; State-level data, *Water-Data Report*, annual series prepared in cooperation with the State governments.

No. 372. Oil Polluting Incidents Reported in and Around U.S. Waters: 1973 to 1993

YEAR	Incidents	Gallons	YEAR	Incidents	Gallons
1973	11,054	15,289,188	1986	5,818	4,427,544
1974	12,083	15,739,792	1987	5,693	3,759,983
1975	10,998	21,528,444	1988	6,733	10,650,138
1976	11,066	18,517,384	1989	8,562	25,531,292
1977	10,979	8,188,398	1990	10,186	13,907,783
1978	12,174	11,035,890	1991	10,405	2,156,063
1979	11,556	10,051,271	1992	9,131	1,572,341
1980	9,886	12,638,848			
1981	9,589	8,919,789	**1993**	**9,672**	**1,543,578**
1982	9,416	10,404,646	Tankships	185	14,138
1983	10,530	8,378,719	Tank barges	338	295,243
1984	10,089	19,007,332	Other vessels	5,220	412,430
1985	7,740	8,465,055	Non-vessels	3,929	821,767

Source: U.S. Coast Guard. Based on unpublished data from the *Marine Safety Information System*.

No. 373. National Ambient Air Pollutant Concentrations: 1985 to 1994

[Data represent annual composite averages of pollutant based on daily 24-hour averages of monitoring stations, except carbon monoxide is based on the second-highest, non-overlapping, 8-hour average; ozone, average of the second-highest daily maximum 1-hour value; and lead, quarterly average of ambient lead levels. Based on data from the Aerometric Information Retrieval System. μg/m³=micrograms of pollutant per cubic meter of air; ppm=parts per million]

POLLUTANT	Unit	Monitoring stations, number	Air quality standard [1]	1985	1988	1989	1990	1991	1992	1993	1994
Carbon monoxide	ppm	314	[2]9	6.96	6.4	6.35	5.86	5.55	5.16	4.86	5.01
Ozone	ppm	532	[3].12	0.124	0.136	0.117	0.114	0.116	0.107	0.110	0.109
Sulfur dioxide . .	ppm	474	.03	0.009	0.009	0.009	0.008	0.008	0.007	0.007	0.007
Particulates (PM-10) [4]	μg/m³	799	50	(X)	33.4	33.2	29.9	29.8	27.3	26.5	26.6
Nitrogen dioxide.	ppm	201	.053	0.022	0.022	0.022	0.020	0.020	0.020	0.019	0.020
Lead	μg/m³	204	[5]1.5	0.29	0.11	0.08	0.08	0.06	0.05	0.05	0.04

X Not applicable.   [1] Refers to the primary National Ambient Air Quality Standard that protects the public health.   [2] Based on 8-hour standard of 9 ppm.   [3] Based on 1-hour standard of .12 ppm.   [4] The particulates (PM-10) standard replaced the previous standard for total suspended particulates in 1987.   [5] Based on 3-month standard of 1.5 μg/m³.
Source: U.S. Environmental Protection Agency, *National Air Quality and Emissions Trends Report*, annual.

No. 374. National Air Pollutant Emissions: 1940 to 1994

[In thousands of tons, except lead in tons. PM-10=Particulate matter of less than ten microns. Methodologies to estimate data for 1900 to 1984 period and 1985 to present emissions differ. Beginning with 1985, the estimates are based on a modified National Acid Precipitation Assessment Program inventory]

YEAR	PM-10	PM-10, fugitive dust[1]	Sulfur dioxide	Nitrogen dioxides	Volatile organic compounds	Carbon monoxide	Lead
1940	15,956	(NA)	19,953	7,374	17,161	93,615	(NA)
1950	17,133	(NA)	22,358	10,093	20,936	102,609	(NA)
1960	15,558	(NA)	22,227	14,140	24,459	109,745	(NA)
1970	13,044	(NA)	31,161	20,625	30,646	128,079	219,471
1980	7,050	(NA)	25,905	23,281	25,893	115,625	74,956
1984	6,220	(NA)	23,470	23,172	25,572	114,262	42,217
1985	4,094	40,889	23,230	22,860	25,798	114,690	20,124
1986	3,890	46,582	22,442	22,348	24,991	109,199	7,296
1987	3,931	38,041	22,204	22,403	24,778	108,012	6,857
1988	4,750	55,851	22,647	23,618	25,719	115,849	6,513
1989	3,927	48,650	22,785	23,222	23,935	103,144	6,034
1990	3,882	39,451	22,433	23,038	23,599	100,650	5,666
1991	3,594	45,310	22,068	22,672	22,877	97,376	5,279
1992	3,485	40,233	21,836	22,847	22,420	94,043	4,899
1993	3,409	39,139	21,517	23,276	22,575	94,133	4,938
1994	3,705	41,726	21,118	23,615	23,174	98,017	4,956

NA Not available.   [1] Sources such as agricultural tilling, construction, mining and quarrying, paved roads, unpaved roads, and wind erosion.

No. 375. Air Pollutant Emissions, by Pollutant and Source: 1994

[In thousands of tons, except lead in tons. See headnote, table 374]

SOURCE	Particulates [1]	Sulfur dioxide	Nitrogen oxides	Volatile organic compounds	Carbon monoxide	Lead
Total	45,431	21,118	23,615	23,174	98,017	4,956
Fuel combustion, stationary sources.	1,033	18,497	11,728	886	4,884	493
Electric utilites	266	14,869	7,795	36	325	63
Industrial	237	3,029	3,206	135	671	15
Other fuel combustion	529	599	727	715	3,888	415
Residential	478	183	408	684	3,607	8
Industrial processes	621	1,986	798	2,695	5,355	2,021
Chemical and allied product manufacturing . . .	64	457	291	1,577	2,048	93
Metals processing	141	692	84	77	2,166	1,873
Petroleum and related industries	26	406	95	630	390	(NA)
Other	390	431	328	411	751	55
Solvent utilization	2	1	3	6,313	2	(NA)
Storage and transport	59	5	3	1,773	58	(NA)
Waste disposal and recycling	250	37	85	2,273	1,746	847
Highway vehicles	311	295	7,530	6,295	61,070	1,403
Light-duty gas vehicles and motorcycles	65	147	3,750	3,921	39,303	1,048
Light-duty trucks	31	61	1,432	1,664	15,139	336
Heavy-duty gas vehicles.	10	11	333	393	5,244	19
Diesels	206	76	2,015	317	1,383	(NA)
Off highway [2]	411	283	3,095	2,255	15,657	193
Miscellaneous [3]	42,743	14	374	685	9,245	(NA)

NA Not available.   [1] Represents both PM-10 and PM-10 fugitive dust; see table 374.   [2] Includes emissions from farm tractors and other farm machinery, construction equipment, industrial machinery, recreational marine vessels, and small general utility engines such as lawn mowers.   [3] Includes emissions such as from forest fires and other various agricultural activities, fugitive dust from paved and unpaved roads, and other construction and mining activities, and natural sources.
Source of tables 374 and 375: U.S. Environmental Protection Agency, *National Air Pollutant Emission Trends, 1900-1994*.

No. 376. Metropolitan Areas Failing to Meet National Ambient Air Quality Standards for Carbon Monoxide—Number of Days Exceeding Standards: 1993 and 1994

[Areas generally represent the officially defined metropolitan area, but may, in some cases, not have all the counties identified as part see *Federal Register,* 40 CFR, part 81, *Air Quality Designations: Revised,* July 1994. Nonattainment status was as of November 1995]

METROPOLITAN AREA	1993	1994	METROPOLITAN AREA	1993	1994	METROPOLITAN AREA	1993	1994
Albuquerque, NM	-	-	Klamath County, OR [1]	-	-	Philadelphia, PA-NJ-DE-		
Anchorage, AK	2	2	Lake Tahoe S. Shore,			MD CMSA	-	1
Baltimore, MD.	1	1	CA [1]	-	-	Phoenix, AZ	-	3
Boston, MA-NH CMSA. . . .	-	-	Las Vegas, NV	3	5	Portland, OR-WA CMSA. . .	-	1
Chico, CA	-	-	Longmont, CO[1]	-	-	Provo-Orem, UT	2	1
Colorado Springs, CO	-	-	Los Angeles, CA CMSA . . .	20	24	Raleigh-Durham, NC	-	-
Denver-Boulder, CO			Medford, OR	-	-	Reno, NV.	-	-
CMSA	2	1	Minneapolis-St. Paul,			Sacramento, CA	-	-
El Paso, TX	2	-	MN-WI.	-	-	San Diego, CA	-	-
Fairbanks, AK [1].	5	3	Missoula County, MT [1]	-	-	San Francisco, CA CMSA. .	-	-
Fort Collins, CO	-	-	Modesto, CA	-	-	Seattle-Tacoma, WA CMSA.	-	-
Fresno, CA	-	-	New York, NY-NJ-CT			Spokane, WA	1	-
Grant Pass, OR [1]	-	-	CMSA	-	2	Stockton, CA	-	-
Hartford, CT CMSA	-	-	Ogden, UT.	-	-	Washington, DC-MD-VA . . .	-	-

- Represents zero.   [1] Not a metropolitan area.

No. 377. Metropolitan Areas Failing to Meet National Ambient Air Quality Standards for Ozone—Average Number of Days Exceeding Standards: 1992 to 1994

[See headnote, table 376. Nonattainment status was as of November 1995]

METROPOLITAN AREA	1992-94, avg.	1994[1]	METROPOLITAN AREA	1992-94, avg.	1994[1]
Albany-Schenectady-Troy, NY	0.3	1.0	Manchester, NH	-	-
Allentown-Bethlehem-Easton, PA-NJ.	-	-	Manitowoc Co, WI.	2.0	2.0
Altoona, PA	-	-	Milwaukee-Racine, WI CMSA	1.7	3.0
Atlanta, GA	3.5	2.1	Monterey Bay, CA [6]	-	-
Atlantic City, NJ	0.3	-	Muskegon, MI.	1.0	1.0
Baltimore, MD.	3.8	5.0	Nashville, TN	1.0	1.0
Baton Rouge, LA	1.8	2.0	New York, NY-NJ-CT CMSA [7]	4.4	4.0
Beaumont-Port Arthur, TX.	1.1	1.1	Norfolk-Virginia Beach-Newport News, VA . .	1.7	-
Birmingham, AL	0.7	-	Philadelphia, PA-NJ-DE-MD CMSA.	4.0	4.0
Boston-Lawrence-Salem, MA-NH CMSA [2] . .	2.7	2.0	Phoenix, AZ	2.5	-
Buffalo-Niagara Falls, NY CMSA	-	-	Pittsburgh-Beaver Valley, PA CMSA	0.7	1.0
Canton, OH	-	-	Portland-Vancouver, OR-WA CMSA	0.3	-
Chicago-Gary-Lake County, IL-IN-WI			Portland, ME	2.0	1.2
CMSA	2.0	1.2	Portsmouth-Dover-Rochester, NH-ME.	0.7	1.0
Cincinnati-Hamilton, OH-KY-IN CMSA	0.3	2.0	Poughkeepsie, NY.	1.0	1.3
Cleveland-Akron-Lorain, OH CMSA	0.5	2.0	Providence, RI [8]	1.1	1.2
Columbus, OH	-	-	Reading, PA.	0.3	1.0
Dallas-Fort Worth, TX CMSA.	3.0	7.5	Reno, NV.	-	-
Door County, WI [3]	0.7	2.0	Richmond-Petersburg, VA.	1.4	-
El Paso, TX	3.4	5.7	Sacramento, CA	6.9	6.2
Erie, PA.	-	-	St. Louis, MO-IL	2.1	4.2
Essex County, NY [3]	-	-	Salt Lake City-Ogden, UT.	-	-
Evansville, IN-KY	-	-	San Diego, CA	10.5	9.0
Grand Rapids, MI	0.7	-	San Joaquin Valley, CA	20.9	32.1
Greater Connecticut, CT [4].	2.4	2.0	Santa Barbara-Santa Maria-Lompoc, CA . . .	1.7	3.1
Hancock and Waldo counties, ME [3]	-	-	Scranton-Wilkes-Barre, PA	-	-
Harrisburg-Lebanon-Carlisle, PA	-	-	Seattle-Tacoma, WA	0.7	2.0
Houston-Galveston-Brazoria, TX CMSA. . . .	6.5	15.2	Sheboygan, WI.	0.3	1.0
Jefferson County, NY [3]	-	-	Smyth County, VA [3]	(NA)	(NA)
Johnstown, PA	-	-	Southeast Desert Modified AQMD, CA [9] . . .	47.5	25.3
Kent County and Queen Anne's Co., MD [3]. .	0.7	-	Springfield, MA	2.4	3.1
Kewaunee County, WI [3]	1.0	1.0	Sunland Park, NM [3]	2.6	2.0
Knox and Lincoln counties, ME [3]	0.4	-	Sussex County, DE [3]	-	-
Lake Charles, LA	1.2	1.0	Tampa-St. Petersburg-Clearwater, FL	-	-
Lancaster, PA.	0.3	-	Ventura County, CA.	10.3	16.5
Lewiston-Auburn, ME.	-	-	Walworth County, WI	-	-
Lexington-Fayette, KY	-	-	Washington, DC-MD-VA	1.2	3.3
Louisville, KY-IN	2.0	3.0	York, PA	-	-
Los Angeles South Coast Air, CA [5]	103.3	88.0	Youngstown-Warren, OH [10].	-	-

- Represents zero.   NA Not available.   [1] May represent a different monitoring location than one used to calculate average.
[2] Includes also both the Worcester, MA, and New Bedford, MA MSA's.   [3] Not a metropolitan area.   [4] Primarily represents Hartford-New Haven area.   [5] Primarily represents Los Angeles and Orange counties.   [6] Primarily represents Monterey, Santa Cruz, and San Benito counties.   [7] Excludes the Connecticut portion.   [8] Covers entire State of Rhode Island.   [9] Represents primarily San Joaquin, Turlock, Merced, Madera, Fresno, Kings, Tulare, and Kern counties.   [10] Includes Sharon, PA.

Source of tables 376 and 377: U.S. Environmental Protection Agency, Published in *1994 Air Quality Update,* November 1995.

No. 378. Emissions of Greenhouse Gases, by Type and Source: 1988 to 1994

[Emission estimates were mandated by Congress through Section 1605(a) of the Energy Policy Act of 1992 (title XVI). Gases that contain carbon can be measured either in terms of the full molecular weight of the gas or just in terms of their carbon content]

TYPE AND SOURCE	Unit	1988	1989	1990	1991	1992	1993	1994
Carbon dioxide:								
Carbon content, total	Mil. metric tons . .	1,376.2	1,385.6	1,373.3	1,360.4	1,380.8	1,406.2	1,430.0
Energy sources	Mil. metric tons . .	1,344.0	1,355.8	1,344.2	1,324.6	1,346.3	1,372.5	1,396.2
Cement production	Mil. metric tons . .	8.7	8.7	8.8	8.5	8.6	9.1	9.5
Gas flaring	Mil. metric tons . .	1.7	1.7	1.8	2.1	2.1	1.4	1.5
Other industrial	Mil. metric tons . .	8.1	8.3	8.3	8.3	8.3	8.2	8.2
Other, adjustments	Mil. metric tons . .	13.7	11.2	10.2	16.9	15.5	14.9	14.6
Methane:								
Gas, total	Mil. metric tons . .	27.56	27.60	27.95	27.94	27.96	26.62	(NA)
Energy sources	Mil. metric tons . .	8.54	8.64	8.73	8.57	8.55	7.37	(NA)
Landfills	Mil. metric tons . .	10.64	10.65	10.81	10.72	10.60	10.43	(NA)
Agricultural sources	Mil. metric tons . .	8.26	8.19	8.28	8.54	8.69	8.69	9.00
Industrial sources	Mil. metric tons . .	0.12	0.12	0.12	0.11	0.12	0.12	0.12
Nitrous oxide, total	1,000 metric tons .	416	431	438	446	444	459	(NA)
Agriculture	1,000 metric tons .	154	159	164	167	168	176	186
Mobile sources	1,000 metric tons .	133	139	144	147	148	146	(NA)
Stationary combustion	1,000 metric tons .	38	38	37	37	37	38	39
Industrial sources	1,000 metric tons .	95	100	98	100	96	103	108
Nitrogen oxide, total	Mil. metric tons . .	21.05	21.08	21.02	20.83	20.84	21.22	(NA)
Energy related	Mil. metric tons . .	19.97	20.01	19.79	19.68	19.71	20.05	(NA)
Transportation	Mil. metric tons . .	9.59	9.55	9.37	9.22	9.36	9.45	(NA)
Industrial processes	Mil. metric tons . .	0.82	0.81	0.81	0.80	0.81	0.83	(NA)
Stationary source fuel combustion	Mil. metric tons . .	10.38	10.46	10.42	10.45	10.34	10.59	(NA)
Solid waste disposal	Mil. metric tons . .	0.08	0.08	0.07	0.07	0.08	0.08	(NA)
Other	Mil. metric tons . .	0.19	0.19	0.35	0.28	0.25	0.27	(NA)
Nonmethane volatile organic compounds								
(VOC's), total	Mil. metric tons . .	22.64	21.52	22.01	21.32	20.88	21.14	(NA)
Energy related	Mil. metric tons . .	10.13	9.11	8.80	8.48	8.09	8.11	(NA)
Industrial processes	Mil. metric tons . .	10.00	9.92	9.96	9.98	10.02	10.16	(NA)
Solid waste disposal	Mil. metric tons . .	2.10	2.08	2.05	2.01	2.06	2.06	(NA)
Other	Mil. metric tons . .	0.42	0.41	1.20	0.85	0.71	0.81	(NA)
Chloroflurocarbons (CFC's) gases [1]	1,000 metric tons .	278	272	231	210	187	166	133
Hydrochloroflurocarbons (HCFC's) gases[2] .	1,000 metric tons .	74	76	84	91	102	112	135

NA Not available.   [1] Covers principally CFC-11, CFC-12, and CFC-113.   [2] Covers principally HCFC-22.

Source: U.S. Energy Information Administration, *Emissions of Greenhouse Gases in the United States, 1987-1994.*

No. 379. Toxic Release Inventory, by Industry and Source: 1989 to 1993

[In millions of pounds. Based on reports from almost 23,000 manufacturing facilities which have 10 or more full-time employees and meet established thresholds for manufacturing, processing, or otherwise using the list of more than 300 chemicals covered. Only chemicals that were reportable in all years shown are compared so that data do not reflect any chemicals added or deleted from the list covered. The inventory was established under the Emergency Planning and Community Right-to-Know Act of 1986 (EPCRA)]

INDUSTRY	1987 SIC [1] code	1989	1990	1991	1992	1993 Total [2]	1993 Air [3], point	1993 Air [4], non-point	1993 Water
Total	(X)	4,405.2	3,719.7	3,393.5	3,190.4	2,791.4	1,175.1	480.2	271.1
Food and kindred products	20	37.2	39.2	39.8	38.7	38.0	15.7	11.5	1.4
Tobacco products	21	1.8	2.5	2.3	2.0	2.4	2.1	0.2	-
Textile mill products	22	32.2	27.2	25.2	21.9	20.4	15.3	4.8	0.3
Apparel and other textile prod . .	23	1.4	1.3	1.4	1.6	1.1	1.0	0.2	-
Lumber and wood products	24	38.0	35.8	32.6	31.0	29.5	24.6	4.7	0.1
Furniture and fixtures	25	65.5	62.6	56.6	56.7	58.1	50.8	7.0	-
Paper and allied products	26	262.8	254.5	246.4	234.1	216.1	171.9	21.1	18.1
Printing and publishing	27	58.7	56.0	47.2	41.1	36.5	17.2	19.3	-
Chemical and allied products . . .	28	2,093.3	1,629.5	1,546.9	1,543.0	1,308.4	320.9	148.1	234.1
Petroleum and coal products . . .	29	99.2	86.9	79.9	84.2	74.5	21.8	35.3	3.3
Rubber and misc. plastic prod. . .	30	184.6	178.7	151.5	135.6	125.1	86.9	37.5	0.4
Leather and leather products . . .	31	13.5	12.8	10.2	10.7	8.4	4.5	3.0	0.1
Stone, clay, glass products	32	37.2	31.2	29.8	26.1	26.7	15.4	2.6	0.2
Primary metal industries	33	522.9	476.7	424.7	348.6	328.6	106.0	30.6	6.8
Fabricated metals products	34	137.5	128.9	111.6	103.0	91.1	57.8	32.6	0.1
Industrial machinery and equip. .	35	58.4	49.4	39.3	34.1	27.5	17.0	10.1	0.2
Electronic, electric equipment . .	36	100.6	82.5	67.7	53.2	39.6	28.8	9.9	0.3
Transportation equipment	37	206.0	176.6	150.8	137.2	135.5	94.9	38.9	0.1
Instruments and related prod. . .	38	52.5	44.3	39.7	33.3	26.6	19.9	5.8	0.8
Misc. manufacturing industries . .	39	29.3	26.2	20.8	18.9	17.2	11.4	5.8	-
Multiple codes	20-39	362.0	303.0	242.1	220.3	159.6	84.1	46.2	4.5
No codes	20-39	10.8	13.8	27.1	15.1	20.4	7.0	4.7	0.3

- Represents zero.   X Not applicable.   [1] Standard Industrial Classification, see text, section 13.   [2] Includes other releases not shown separately.   [3] Stack.   [4] Fugitive.

Source: U.S. Environmental Protection Agency, *1993 Toxics Release Inventory,* March 1995.

No. 380. Municipal Solid Waste Generation, Recovery, and Disposal: 1960 to 1994

In millions of tons, except as indicated. Covers post-consumer residential and commercial solid wastes which comprise the major portion of typical municipal collections. Excludes mining, agricultural and industrial processing, demolition and construction wastes, sewage sludge, and junked autos and obsolete equipment wastes. Based on material-flows estimating procedure and wet weight as generated]

ITEM AND MATERIAL	1960	1970	1980	1985	1990	1991	1992	1993	1994
Waste generated	87.8	121.9	151.5	164.4	198.0	196.8	203.0	206.5	209.1
Per person per day (lb.)	2.7	3.3	3.7	3.8	4.3	4.3	4.4	4.4	4.4
Materials recovered	5.9	8.6	14.5	16.4	32.9	37.3	41.5	43.9	49.3
Per person per day (lb.)	0.18	0.23	0.35	0.38	0.7	0.8	0.9	0.9	1.0
Combustion for energy recovery	(NA)	0.4	2.7	7.6	29.7	31.1	30.5	31.3	31.2
Per person per day (lb.)	(NA)	0.02	0.06	0.17	0.7	0.7	0.7	0.7	0.7
Combustion without energy recovery	27.0	24.7	11.0	4.1	2.2	2.2	2.2	1.6	1.3
Per person per day (lb.)	0.82	0.66	0.27	0.10	0.05	0.05	0.05	0.03	0.03
Landfill, other disposal	54.9	88.2	123.3	136.4	133.2	126.2	128.8	129.7	127.3
Per person per day (lb.)	1.67	2.37	2.97	3.13	2.9	2.7	2.8	2.8	2.7
Percent distribution of generation:									
Paper and paperboard	34.1	36.3	36.1	37.4	36.7	36.1	36.6	37.5	38.9
Glass	7.6	10.4	9.9	8.0	6.7	6.5	6.5	6.6	6.3
Metals	12.0	11.6	9.6	8.6	8.3	8.5	8.3	8.2	7.6
Plastics	0.5	2.5	5.2	7.1	8.5	8.8	9.1	9.4	9.5
Rubber and leather	2.3	2.6	2.8	2.3	3.0	2.9	3.0	3.1	3.0
Textiles	1.9	1.6	1.7	1.7	3.3	3.1	3.2	2.9	3.1
Wood	3.4	3.3	4.4	5.0	6.2	6.4	6.3	6.6	7.0
Food wastes	13.9	10.5	8.7	8.0	6.7	6.8	6.6	6.7	6.7
Yard wastes	22.8	19.0	18.2	18.2	17.7	17.8	17.2	15.9	14.6
Other wastes	1.6	2.2	3.4	3.6	3.1	3.2	3.1	3.2	3.2

NA Not available.

Source: Franklin Associates, Ltd., Prairie Village, KS, *Characterization of Municipal Solid Waste in the United States: 1994.* Prepared for the U.S. Environmental Protection Agency.

No. 381. Generation and Recovery of Selected Materials in Municipal Solid Waste: 1960 to 1994

[In millions of tons, except as indicated. Covers post-consumer residential and commercial solid wastes which comprises the major portion of typical municipal collections. Excludes mining, agricultural and industrial processing, demolition and construction wastes, sewage sludge, and junked autos and obsolete equipment wastes. Based on material-flows estimating procedure and wet weight as generated]

ITEM AND MATERIAL	1960	1970	1980	1985	1990	1991	1992	1993	1994
Waste generated, total	**87.8**	**121.9**	**151.5**	**164.4**	**198.0**	**196.8**	**203.0**	**206.5**	**209.1**
Paper and paperboard	29.9	44.2	54.7	61.5	72.7	71.1	74.3	77.4	81.3
Ferrous metals	9.9	12.6	11.6	10.9	12.4	12.6	12.9	12.7	11.5
Aluminum	0.4	0.8	1.8	2.3	2.9	3.0	2.9	3.0	3.1
Other nonferrous metals	0.2	0.7	1.1	1.0	1.1	1.2	1.2	1.2	1.2
Glass	6.7	12.7	15.0	13.2	13.2	12.7	13.1	13.7	13.3
Plastics	0.4	3.1	7.9	11.6	16.8	17.2	18.5	19.5	19.8
Yard waste	20.0	23.2	27.5	30.0	35.0	35.0	35.0	32.8	30.6
Other wastes	20.3	24.6	31.9	33.9	43.9	44.0	45.1	46.2	48.3
Materials recovered, total	**5.9**	**8.6**	**14.5**	**16.4**	**32.9**	**37.3**	**41.5**	**43.9**	**49.3**
Paper and paperboard	5.4	7.4	11.9	13.1	20.3	22.5	24.5	25.5	28.7
Ferrous metals	0.1	0.1	0.4	0.4	1.7	2.3	2.8	3.4	3.7
Aluminum	-	-	0.3	0.6	1.0	1.0	1.1	1.0	1.2
Other nonferrous metals	-	0.3	0.5	0.5	0.7	0.7	0.7	0.7	0.8
Glass	0.1	0.2	0.8	1.0	2.6	2.6	2.9	3.0	3.1
Plastics	-	-	-	0.1	0.4	0.5	0.6	0.7	0.9
Yard waste	-	-	-	-	4.2	5.0	6.0	6.5	7.0
Other wastes	0.3	0.6	0.6	0.7	2.0	2.7	2.9	4.0	3.9
Percent of generation recovered, total	**6.7**	**7.1**	**9.6**	**10.0**	**16.6**	**19.0**	**20.4**	**21.2**	**23.6**
Paper and paperboard	18.1	16.7	21.8	21.3	27.9	31.7	32.9	32.9	35.3
Ferrous metals	1.0	0.8	3.4	3.7	13.7	18.5	21.6	27.0	32.3
Aluminum	-	-	16.7	26.1	35.3	34.9	38.1	34.7	37.6
Other nonferrous metals	-	42.9	45.5	50.0	66.4	64.3	62.1	59.8	66.1
Glass	1.5	1.6	5.3	7.6	20.0	20.1	22.0	21.9	23.4
Plastics	-	-	-	0.9	2.2	2.6	3.2	3.5	4.7
Yard waste	-	-	-	-	12.0	14.3	17.1	19.8	22.9
Other wastes	1.5	2.4	1.9	2.1	4.5	6.1	6.4	8.6	8.1

- Represents zero.

Source: Franklin Associates, Ltd., Prairie Village, KS, *Characterization of Municipal Solid Waste in the United States: 1994.* Prepared for the U.S. Environmental Protection Agency.

No. 382. Hazardous Waste Sites on the National Priority List, by State: 1995

[Includes both proposed and final sites listed on the National Priorities List for the Superfund program as authorized by the Comprehensive Environmental Response, Compensation, and Liability Act of 1980 and the Superfund Amendments and Reauthorization Act of 1986]

STATE	Total sites	Rank	Percent distribution	Federal	Non-Federal	STATE	Total sites	Rank	Percent distribution	Federal	Non-Federal
Total	1,283	(X)	(X)	159	1,124	Montana	9	41	0.71	-	9
						Nebraska	10	38	0.79	1	9
United States..	**1,270**	**(X)**	**100.00**	**157**	**1,113**	Nevada	1	50	0.08	-	1
						New Hampshire	17	23	1.34	1	16
Alabama	13	30	1.02	3	10	New Jersey	107	1	8.43	6	101
Alaska	8	42	0.63	6	2	New Mexico	11	36	0.87	2	9
Arizona	10	38	0.79	3	7	New York	80	4	6.30	4	76
Arkansas	12	32	0.94	-	12	North Carolina	23	17	1.81	2	21
California	96	3	7.56	23	73	North Dakota	2	49	0.16	-	2
Colorado	18	21	1.42	3	15	Ohio	38	9	2.99	5	33
Connecticut	15	27	1.18	1	14	Oklahoma	11	36	0.87	1	10
Delaware	19	20	1.50	1	18	Oregon	12	32	0.94	2	10
District of Columbia	-	(X)	0.00	-	-	Pennsylvania	103	2	8.11	6	97
Florida	55	6	4.33	5	50	Rhode Island	12	32	0.94	2	10
Georgia	14	28	1.10	2	12	South Carolina	25	15	1.97	2	23
Hawaii	4	45	0.31	3	1	South Dakota	4	45	0.31	1	3
Idaho	10	38	0.79	2	8	Tennessee	18	21	1.42	4	14
Illinois	38	9	2.99	4	34	Texas	27	14	2.13	4	23
Indiana	33	12	2.60	-	33	Utah	16	26	1.26	4	12
Iowa	17	23	1.34	1	16	Vermont	8	42	0.63	-	8
Kansas	13	30	1.02	2	11	Virginia	24	16	1.89	6	18
Kentucky	20	19	1.57	1	19	Washington	52	7	4.09	17	35
Louisiana	17	23	1.34	1	16	West Virginia	7	44	0.55	2	5
Maine	12	32	0.94	3	9	Wisconsin	41	8	3.23	-	41
Maryland	14	28	1.10	5	9	Wyoming	3	48	0.24	1	2
Massachusetts	30	13	2.36	8	22						
Michigan	78	5	6.14	1	77	Guam	2	(X)	(X)	1	1
Minnesota	37	11	2.91	3	34	Puerto Rico	9	(X)	(X)	1	8
Mississippi	4	45	0.31	-	4	Virgin Islands	2	(X)	(X)	-	2
Missouri	22	18	1.73	3	19						

- Represents zero.   X Not applicable.

Source: U.S. Environmental Protection Agency, *Supplementary Materials: National Priorities List, Proposed Rule,* November 1995.

No. 383. Environmental Industry—Revenues and Employment, by Industry Segment: 1980 to 1995

[Covers approximately 59,000 private and public companies engaged in environmental activities]

INDUSTRY SEGMENT	REVENUE (bil. dol.)					EMPLOYMENT (1,000)				
	1980	1990	1993	1994	1995	1980	1990	1993	1994	1995
Industry total	**52.0**	**146.4**	**163.1**	**172.5**	**179.9**	**462.5**	**1,174.3**	**1,222.5**	**1,278.0**	**1,314.0**
Analytical services [1]	0.4	1.5	1.6	1.6	1.5	6.0	20.2	20.0	20.0	17.7
Water treatment works	9.2	19.8	23.4	25.7	27.3	53.9	95.0	105.7	113.7	120.8
Solid waste management [2]	8.5	26.1	29.4	31.0	32.5	83.2	209.5	222.2	229.6	235.5
Hazardous waste management	0.6	6.3	6.5	6.4	6.2	6.8	56.9	55.2	53.3	52.5
Remediation/Industrial services	0.4	8.5	8.4	8.6	8.5	6.9	107.2	100.2	100.0	96.6
Consulting & engineering	1.5	12.5	14.6	15.3	15.4	20.5	144.2	158.0	162.8	160.4
Water equipment and chemicals	6.3	13.5	15.0	15.6	16.5	62.4	97.9	100.5	116.4	119.6
Instrument manufacturing	0.2	2.0	2.7	2.9	3.1	2.5	18.8	24.2	24.8	26.7
Air pollution control equipment	3.0	10.7	11.5	11.7	11.8	28.3	82.7	83.5	83.3	84.3
Waste management equipment	4.0	10.4	10.9	11.2	11.7	41.9	88.8	87.6	88.2	93.6
Process and prevention technology	0.1	0.4	0.7	0.8	0.8	2.1	8.9	14.0	15.2	19.0
Water utilities	11.9	19.8	23.1	24.2	25.3	76.9	104.7	115.0	118.0	123.4
Resource recovery	4.4	13.1	13.3	15.4	16.9	48.7	118.4	113.1	128.3	136.3
Environmental energy sources	1.5	1.8	2.1	2.2	2.3	22.4	21.1	23.3	24.4	27.1

[1] Covers environmental laboratory testing and services.   [2] Covers such activities as collection, transportation, transfer stations, disposal, landfill ownership and management for solid waste.

Source: Environmental Business International, Inc., San Diego, CA, *Environmental Business Journal,* monthly, (copyright).

No. 384. Pollution Abatement and Control Expenditures, in Current and Constant (1987) Dollars, 1973 to 1993, and by Media, 1993

[In millions of dollars]

YEAR	Total expenditures	POLLUTION ABATEMENT							Regulation and monitoring	Research and development
		Total	Personal consumption	Business	Government					
					Total	Federal	State and local	Govt. enterprise [1]		
CURRENT DOLLARS										
1973	19,404	18,011	1,867	12,261	3,883	203	1,433	2,246	490	903
1980	50,399	47,352	6,558	29,706	11,088	494	2,768	7,825	1,296	1,751
1981	54,241	51,153	8,122	32,370	10,660	506	3,144	7,011	1,378	1,711
1982	55,359	52,321	8,287	33,092	10,942	550	3,484	6,908	1,397	1,641
1983	58,873	55,893	9,742	34,804	11,346	795	3,842	6,709	1,385	1,595
1984	65,423	62,561	10,839	39,032	12,690	944	4,280	7,466	1,362	1,501
1985	71,169	68,268	11,991	42,058	14,220	1,225	4,858	8,137	1,279	1,621
1986	75,389	72,111	12,385	43,954	15,772	1,346	5,515	8,912	1,532	1,746
1987	77,649	74,349	11,075	45,432	17,842	1,237	6,266	10,339	1,519	1,781
1988	83,020	79,453	12,285	48,415	18,752	1,402	7,283	10,067	1,695	1,872
1989	87,622	83,774	10,950	52,429	20,395	1,379	8,705	10,312	1,803	2,044
1990 [2]	93,877	90,321	9,241	58,498	22,582	1,391	10,161	11,031	1,784	1,772
1991 [2]	95,893	92,012	7,425	60,594	23,634	1,417	11,417	10,800	1,868	2,013
1992 [2]	101,846	98,134	7,896	65,592	24,646	1,215	12,630	10,801	1,848	1,864
1993	109,044	105,386	8,458	69,983	26,945	1,068	14,583	11,295	1,924	1,734
Air	31,902	30,238	8,458	21,274	506	80	21	404	561	1,104
Water	39,015	37,984	-	25,932	12,052	567	595	10,890	789	243
Solid Waste	38,844	38,326	-	24,202	14,124	250	13,873	-	416	102
CONSTANT (1987) DOLLARS										
1973	49,683	46,166	4,543	31,997	9,626	539	3,723	5,364	1,190	2,327
1980	65,590	61,305	7,297	38,673	15,335	679	4,015	10,641	1,873	2,413
1981	63,613	59,681	8,472	37,731	13,477	627	4,070	8,780	1,810	2,123
1982	61,714	58,115	8,494	36,462	13,159	649	4,287	8,224	1,709	1,890
1983	63,836	60,465	9,990	37,454	13,021	911	4,527	7,583	1,608	1,763
1984	68,913	65,812	11,040	40,708	14,063	1,048	4,803	8,212	1,506	1,596
1985	72,813	69,773	11,935	42,833	15,005	1,300	5,200	8,505	1,361	1,678
1986	77,487	74,110	12,831	45,002	16,277	1,402	5,726	9,149	1,589	1,788
1987	77,649	74,349	11,075	45,432	17,842	1,237	6,266	10,339	1,519	1,781
1988	80,698	77,263	12,069	47,131	18,063	1,340	6,953	9,771	1,643	1,792
1989	81,802	78,266	10,445	48,901	18,920	1,271	7,982	9,667	1,657	1,879
1990 [2]	84,648	81,453	8,659	52,630	20,165	1,228	8,864	10,073	1,636	1,559
1991 [2]	84,152	80,806	6,783	53,667	20,356	1,220	9,661	9,475	1,654	1,692
1992 [2]	88,083	84,817	7,037	57,028	20,751	1,040	10,437	9,274	1,619	1,648
1993	91,826	88,731	7,356	59,299	22,077	902	11,691	9,484	1,656	1,438
Air	27,964	26,560	7,356	18,764	440	68	18	354	487	918
Water	33,503	32,612	-	22,463	10,150	480	541	9,129	690	201
Solid Waste	31,025	30,594	-	19,326	11,268	213	11,055	-	348	84

- Represents or rounds to zero.   [1] Fixed capital.   [2] Includes "other and unallocated" expenditures (such as for noise, radiation, and pesticide pollution and business expenditures not assigned to media) which may be either positive or negative; therefore, data may not add.

No. 385. Air and Water Pollution Abatement Expenditures in Constant (1987) Dollars: 1973 to 1993

[In millions of dollars. Excludes agricultural production of crops and livestock except feedlots]

YEAR	AIR							WATER				
	Total	Mobile sources [1]			Stationary sources			Total [5]	Industrial		Public sewer systems	
		Total	Cars [2]	Trucks [2]	Total [3]	Industrial			Facilities	Operations [4]	Facilities	Operations [4]
						Facilities	Operations [4]					
1973	18,272	6,832	5,586	1,247	11,440	6,348	4,673	19,732	3,709	2,756	5,136	3,510
1980	24,486	11,973	9,103	2,870	12,513	6,044	5,782	26,622	4,131	3,586	10,148	5,100
1981	25,688	13,818	11,092	2,726	11,870	5,851	5,360	23,892	3,306	4,011	8,270	5,297
1982	24,976	13,728	10,914	2,813	11,248	5,301	5,263	23,227	3,145	4,062	7,679	5,616
1983	25,906	15,943	12,756	3,186	9,963	3,879	5,353	23,328	2,564	4,231	7,063	5,959
1984	28,164	18,228	14,119	4,109	9,936	3,900	5,418	24,900	2,807	4,389	7,791	6,149
1985	29,050	19,373	14,896	4,477	9,677	3,409	5,730	26,017	2,771	4,590	8,124	6,550
1986	30,464	20,162	15,484	4,678	10,301	3,654	6,142	27,717	2,587	4,959	8,807	7,285
1987	27,421	17,614	13,166	4,448	9,807	3,482	5,843	29,420	2,566	5,257	10,035	7,792
1988	28,732	19,297	(NA)	(NA)	9,435	2,989	6,096	29,221	2,483	5,538	9,629	8,269
1989	25,817	16,412	(NA)	(NA)	9,405	3,008	5,963	30,127	2,976	5,649	9,412	8,803
1990	24,493	14,154	(NA)	(NA)	10,339	3,717	6,225	32,641	4,060	6,135	9,822	9,430
1991	23,031	12,076	(NA)	(NA)	10,955	4,885	5,689	32,225	4,191	5,719	9,253	10,171
1992	24,649	12,288	(NA)	(NA)	12,362	5,837	6,121	32,894	4,041	5,814	9,123	11,076
1993	26,560	13,134	(NA)	(NA)	13,426	6,798	6,052	32,612	3,426	6,133	9,088	11,088

NA Not available.   [1] Excludes expenditures to reduce emissions from sources other than cars and trucks.   [2] Includes expenditures for devices such as catalytic convertors, and expenditures for devices.   [3] Includes other expenditures not shown separately for fixed capital of government enterprises such as Tennessee Valley Authority.   [4] Operation of facilities.   [5] Includes expenditures for private connectors to sewer systems, by owners of animal feedlots, and by government enterprises.
Source of tables 384 and 385: U.S. Bureau of Economic Analysis, *Survey of Current Business*, May 1995.

No. 386. Pollution Abatement Capital Expenditures and Operating Costs of Manufacturing Establishments, 1990 to 1994, and by Selected Industry Group, 1994

[In millions of dollars. Based on probability sample of about 20,000 manufacturing establishments. Excludes apparel and other textile establishments and establishments with less than 20 employees]

YEAR AND INDUSTRY GROUP	POLLUTION ABATEMENT CAPITAL EXPENDITURES				POLLUTION ABATEMENT GROSS OPERATING COSTS [1]			
	Total	Air	Water	Solid contained waste	Total	Air	Water	Solid contained waste
1990	6,030.8	2,562.0	2,651.4	817.5	17,070.7	5,010.9	6,416.4	5,643.5
1991	7,390.1	3,706.3	2,814.6	869.1	17,386.8	5,033.5	6,345.0	6,008.2
1992	7,866.9	4,403.1	2,509.8	953.9	17,466.4	5,395.0	6,576.9	5,494.5
1993	7,177.9	4,122.0	2,294.9	760.9	17,555.0	5,574.6	6,631.8	5,348.6
All industries, 1994 [2].	7,578.0	4,310.6	2,428.9	838.5	18,722.0	6,139.1	7,031.5	5,601.4
Food and kindred products .	274.3	105.9	152.8	15.5	1,447.6	172.4	940.5	334.7
Paper and allied products. .	635.9	241.9	195.9	198.1	1,879.5	536.9	829.5	513.1
Chemical and allied products	1,931.0	676.9	1,005.6	248.4	4,566.9	1,138.7	1,996.7	1,431.5
Petroleum and coal products	2,572.0	1,982.3	466.9	122.9	2,914.9	1,742.0	755.7	417.2
Primary metal industries. . .	428.0	290.1	98.5	39.4	2,211.5	982.1	692.2	537.2
Machinery, exc. electrical . .	283.6	116.5	152.1	15.0	444.3	79.1	147.1	218.1
Electrical, electronic equipment	276.8	116.0	90.8	70.0	771.9	165.4	329.9	276.7
Transportation equipment. .	336.9	244.8	60.8	31.3	1,116.4	293.7	342.5	480.2

[1] Includes payments to governmental units.   [2] Includes industries not shown separately; excludes Major Group 23, Apparel and Other Textile Products.

Source: U.S. Bureau of the Census, *Current Industrial Reports*, series MA-200, annual.

No. 387. Threatened and Endangered Wildlife and Plant Species—Number: 1996

[As of **February 29.** Endangered species: One in danger of becoming extinct throughout all or a significant part of its natural range. Threatened species: One likely to become endangered in the foreseeable future]

ITEM	Mammals	Birds	Reptiles	Amphibians	Fishes	Snails	Clams	Crustaceans	Insects	Arachnids	Plants
Total listings	335	274	112	21	116	23	59	17	33	5	496
Endangered species, total	307	252	79	15	76	16	53	14	24	5	406
United States	55	74	14	7	65	15	51	14	20	5	405
Foreign	252	178	65	8	11	1	2	-	4	-	1
Threatened species, total.	28	22	33	6	40	7	6	3	9	-	90
United States	9	16	19	5	40	7	6	3	9	-	90
Foreign	19	6	14	1	-	-	-	-	-	-	-

- Represents zero.   [1] Species outside United States and outlying areas as determined by Fish and Wildlife Service.
Source: U.S. Fish and Wildlife Service, *Endangered Species Technical Bulletin*, quarterly.

No. 388. Tornadoes, Floods, and Tropical Storms: 1984 to 1994

[See also *Historical Statistics, Colonial Times to 1970*, series J 268-278]

ITEM	1984	1985	1986	1987	1988	1989	1990	1991	1992	1993	1994, prel.
Tornadoes, number [1]	907	684	764	656	702	856	1,133	1,132	1,303	1,173	1,082
Lives lost, total	122	94	15	59	32	50	53	39	39	33	69
Most in a single tornado	16	18	3	30	5	21	29	13	10	7	22
Property loss of $500,000 and over	125	69	75	38	48	60	91	64	108	72	83
Floods: Lives lost	126	304	80	82	29	81	147	63	87	101	72
Property loss (mil. dol.)	4,000	3,000	4,000	1,490	114	415	2,058	1,416	800	16,400	1,224
North Atlantic tropical storms and hurricanes: [2]											
Number reaching U.S. coast ...	12	11	6	7	12	11	14	8	7	8	7
Hurricanes only	1	6	2	1	1	3	-	1	1	1	-
Lives lost in U.S	4	30	9	-	6	56	10	17	26	9	38
Property loss (mil. (1990) dol.)[3].	77	4,457	18	8	9	7,840	57	1,500	25,000	57	973

- Represents zero. [1] A violent, rotating column of air descending from a cumulonimbus cloud in the form of a tubular- or funnel-shaped cloud, usually characterized by movements along a narrow path and wind speeds from 100 to over 300 miles per hour. Also known as a "twister" or "waterspout."   [2] Source: National Hurricane Center, Coral Gables, FL, unpublished data. Tropical storms have maximum winds of 39 to 73 miles per hour; hurricanes have maximum winds of 74 miles per hour or higher. [3] Source: Hebert, Jarrell, & Mayfield, "The Deadliest, Costliest, and Most Intense U.S. Hurricanes of this Century," NOAA Technical Memo, NHC-31, February 1993; and unpublished data.
Source: Except as noted, U.S. National Oceanic and Atmospheric Administration, *Storm Data*, monthly.

No. 389. Normal Daily Mean, Maximum, and Minimum Temperatures—Selected Cities

[In Fahrenheit degrees. Airport data except as noted. Based on standard 30-year period, 1961 through 1990. See *Historical Statistics, Colonial Times to 1970*, series J 110-136 and J 164-267, for related data]

STATE	STATION	DAILY MEAN TEMPERATURE Jan.	July	Annual average	DAILY MAXIMUM TEMPERATURE Jan.	July	Annual average	DAILY MINIMUM TEMPERATURE Jan.	July	Annual average
AL	Mobile	49.9	82.3	67.5	59.7	91.3	77.4	40.0	73.2	57.4
AK	Juneau	24.2	56.0	40.6	29.4	63.9	46.9	19.0	48.1	34.1
AZ	Phoenix	53.6	93.5	72.6	65.9	105.9	85.9	41.2	81.0	59.3
AR	Little Rock	39.1	81.9	61.8	49.0	92.4	72.5	29.1	71.5	51.0
CA	Los Angeles	56.8	69.1	63.0	65.7	75.3	70.4	47.8	62.8	55.5
	Sacramento	45.2	75.7	60.8	52.7	93.2	73.5	37.7	58.1	48.1
	San Diego	57.4	71.0	64.2	65.9	76.2	70.8	48.9	65.7	57.6
	San Francisco	48.7	62.7	57.1	55.6	71.6	65.2	41.8	53.9	49.0
CO	Denver	29.7	73.5	50.3	43.2	88.2	64.2	16.1	58.6	36.2
CT	Hartford	24.6	73.7	49.9	33.2	85.0	60.2	15.8	62.2	39.5
DE	Wilmington	30.6	76.4	54.2	38.7	85.6	63.6	22.4	67.1	44.8
DC	Washington	34.6	80.0	58.0	42.3	88.5	66.9	26.8	71.4	49.2
FL	Jacksonville	52.4	81.6	68.0	64.2	91.4	78.9	40.5	71.9	57.1
	Miami	67.2	82.6	75.9	75.2	89.0	82.8	59.2	76.2	69.0
GA	Atlanta	41.0	78.8	61.3	50.4	88.0	71.2	31.5	69.5	51.3
HI	Honolulu	72.9	80.5	77.2	80.1	87.5	84.4	65.6	73.5	70.0
ID	Boise	29.0	74.0	50.9	36.4	90.2	62.8	21.6	57.7	39.1
IL	Chicago	21.0	73.2	49.0	29.0	83.7	58.6	12.9	62.6	39.5
	Peoria	21.6	75.5	50.7	29.9	85.7	60.4	13.2	65.4	41.0
IN	Indianapolis	25.5	75.4	52.3	33.7	85.5	62.1	17.2	65.2	42.4
IA	Des Moines	19.4	76.6	49.9	28.1	86.7	59.8	10.7	66.5	40.0
KS	Wichita	29.5	81.4	56.2	39.8	92.8	67.4	19.2	69.9	45.0
KY	Louisville	31.7	77.2	56.1	40.3	87.0	66.0	23.2	67.3	46.0
LA	New Orleans	51.3	81.9	68.1	60.8	90.6	77.6	41.8	73.1	58.5
ME	Portland	20.8	68.6	45.4	30.3	78.8	54.9	11.4	58.3	35.8
MD	Baltimore	31.8	77.0	55.1	40.2	87.2	65.0	23.4	66.8	45.2
MA	Boston	28.6	73.5	51.3	35.7	81.8	59.0	21.6	65.1	43.6
MI	Detroit	22.9	72.3	48.6	30.3	83.3	58.1	15.6	61.3	39.0
	Sault Ste. Marie	12.9	63.8	39.7	21.1	76.3	49.6	4.6	51.3	29.8
MN	Duluth	7.0	66.1	38.5	16.2	77.1	47.9	-2.2	55.1	29.0
	Minneapolis-St. Paul	11.8	73.6	44.9	20.7	84.0	54.3	2.8	63.1	35.3
MS	Jackson	44.1	81.5	64.2	55.6	92.4	76.4	32.7	70.5	52.0
MO	Kansas City	25.7	78.5	53.6	34.7	88.7	63.6	16.7	68.2	43.7
	St. Louis	29.3	79.8	56.1	37.7	89.3	65.4	20.8	70.4	46.7
MT	Great Falls	21.2	68.2	44.8	30.6	83.3	56.4	11.6	53.2	33.1
NE	Omaha	21.1	76.9	50.6	31.3	87.9	61.5	10.9	65.9	39.5
NV	Reno	32.9	71.6	50.8	45.1	91.9	66.8	20.7	51.3	34.7
NH	Concord	18.6	69.5	45.1	29.8	82.4	57.0	7.4	56.5	33.1
NJ	Atlantic City	30.9	74.7	53.0	40.4	84.5	63.2	21.4	64.8	42.8
NM	Albuquerque	34.2	78.5	56.2	46.8	92.5	70.1	21.7	64.4	42.2
NY	Albany	20.6	71.8	47.4	30.2	84.0	58.1	11.0	59.6	36.6
	Buffalo	23.6	71.1	47.7	30.2	80.2	55.8	17.0	61.9	39.5
	New York [1]	31.5	76.8	54.7	37.6	85.2	62.3	25.3	68.4	47.1
NC	Charlotte	39.3	79.3	60.1	49.0	88.9	70.4	29.6	69.6	49.7
	Raleigh	38.9	78.1	59.3	48.9	88.0	70.1	28.8	68.1	48.4
ND	Bismarck	9.2	70.4	41.6	20.2	84.4	53.8	-1.7	56.4	29.4
OH	Cincinnati	28.1	75.1	53.2	36.6	85.5	63.2	19.5	64.8	43.2
	Cleveland	24.8	71.9	49.6	31.9	82.4	58.7	17.6	61.4	40.5
	Columbus	26.4	73.2	51.4	34.1	83.7	61.2	18.5	62.7	41.6
OK	Oklahoma City	35.9	82.0	60.0	46.7	93.4	71.1	25.2	70.6	48.8
OR	Portland	39.6	68.2	53.6	45.4	79.9	62.6	33.7	56.5	44.5
PA	Philadelphia	30.4	76.7	54.3	37.9	86.1	63.4	22.8	67.2	45.1
	Pittsburgh	26.1	72.1	50.3	33.7	82.6	59.9	18.5	61.6	40.7
RI	Providence	27.9	72.7	50.4	36.6	82.1	59.8	19.1	63.2	41.0
SC	Columbia	43.8	80.8	63.1	55.3	91.6	75.1	32.1	70.0	50.9
SD	Sioux Falls	13.8	74.3	45.5	24.3	86.3	56.8	3.3	62.3	34.2
TN	Memphis	39.7	82.6	62.3	48.5	92.3	72.1	30.9	72.9	52.4
	Nashville	36.2	79.3	59.1	45.9	89.5	69.8	26.5	68.9	48.4
TX	Dallas-Fort Worth	43.4	85.3	65.4	54.1	96.5	76.3	32.7	74.1	54.6
	El Paso	42.8	82.3	63.2	56.1	96.1	77.5	29.4	68.4	49.0
	Houston	50.4	82.6	67.9	61.0	92.7	78.6	39.7	72.4	57.3
UT	Salt Lake City	27.9	77.9	52.0	36.4	92.2	63.6	19.3	63.7	40.3
VT	Burlington	16.3	70.5	44.6	25.1	81.2	54.0	7.5	59.7	35.2
VA	Norfolk	39.1	78.2	59.2	47.3	86.4	67.8	30.9	70.0	50.6
	Richmond	35.7	78.0	57.7	45.7	88.4	68.8	25.7	67.5	46.6
WA	Seattle-Tacoma	40.1	65.2	52.0	45.0	75.2	59.4	35.2	55.2	44.6
	Spokane	27.1	68.8	47.3	33.2	83.1	57.5	20.8	54.4	36.9
WV	Charleston	32.1	75.1	55.0	41.2	85.7	65.8	23.0	64.4	44.2
WI	Milwaukee	18.9	70.9	46.1	26.1	79.9	54.3	11.6	62.0	37.9
WY	Cheyenne	26.5	68.4	45.6	37.7	82.2	58.0	15.2	54.6	33.2
PR	San Juan	77.0	82.6	80.2	83.2	88.5	86.4	70.8	76.8	74.0

[1] City office data.

Source: U.S. National Oceanic and Atmospheric Administration, *Climatography of the United States*, No. 81.

No. 390. Highest Temperature of Record—Selected Cities

[In **Fahrenheit degrees.** Airport data, except as noted. For period of record through 1994]

STATE	STATION	Length of record (yr.)	Jan.	Feb.	Mar.	Apr.	May	June	July	Aug.	Sept.	Oct.	Nov.	Dec.	Annual
AL	Mobile	53	84	82	90	94	100	102	104	102	99	93	87	81	104
AK	Juneau	50	57	57	59	71	82	86	90	83	72	61	56	54	90
AZ	Phoenix	57	88	92	100	105	113	122	118	116	118	107	93	88	122
AR	Little Rock	53	83	85	91	95	98	105	112	108	106	97	86	80	112
CA	Los Angeles	59	88	92	95	102	97	104	97	98	110	106	101	94	110
	Sacramento	44	70	76	88	93	105	115	114	109	108	101	87	72	115
	San Diego	54	88	88	93	98	96	101	95	98	111	107	97	88	111
	San Francisco	67	72	78	85	92	97	106	105	100	103	99	85	75	106
CO	Denver	60	73	76	84	90	96	104	104	101	97	89	79	75	104
CT	Hartford	40	65	73	87	96	97	100	102	101	99	91	81	74	102
DE	Wilmington	47	75	78	86	94	95	100	102	101	100	91	85	74	102
DC	Washington	53	79	82	89	95	99	101	104	103	101	94	86	75	104
FL	Jacksonville	53	85	88	91	95	100	103	105	102	100	96	88	84	105
	Miami	52	88	89	92	96	95	98	98	98	97	95	89	87	98
GA	Atlanta	46	79	80	86	93	95	101	105	102	98	95	84	79	105
HI	Honolulu	25	87	88	88	89	93	92	92	93	95	94	93	89	95
ID	Boise	55	63	71	81	92	98	109	111	110	102	94	74	65	111
IL	Chicago	36	65	71	88	91	93	104	102	101	99	91	78	71	104
	Peoria	55	70	72	86	92	93	105	103	103	100	90	81	71	105
IN	Indianapolis	55	71	74	85	89	93	102	104	102	100	90	81	74	104
IA	Des Moines	55	65	73	91	93	98	103	105	108	101	95	76	69	108
KS	Wichita	42	75	84	89	96	100	110	113	110	107	95	85	83	113
KY	Louisville	47	77	77	86	91	95	102	105	101	104	92	84	76	105
LA	New Orleans	48	83	85	89	92	96	100	101	102	101	92	87	84	102
ME	Portland	54	64	64	86	85	94	98	99	103	95	88	74	69	103
MD	Baltimore	44	75	79	87	94	98	101	104	105	100	92	83	77	105
MA	Boston	43	63	70	81	94	95	100	102	102	100	90	79	73	102
MI	Detroit	36	62	65	81	89	93	104	102	100	98	91	77	68	104
	Sault Ste. Marie	54	45	47	75	85	89	93	97	98	95	80	67	60	98
MN	Duluth	53	52	55	78	88	90	93	97	97	95	86	70	55	97
	Minneapolis-St. Paul	56	58	60	83	95	96	102	105	102	98	89	75	63	105
MS	Jackson	31	82	85	89	94	99	105	106	102	104	95	88	84	106
MO	Kansas City	22	69	76	86	93	92	105	107	109	102	92	82	70	109
	St. Louis	37	76	85	89	93	93	102	107	107	104	94	85	76	107
MT	Great Falls	57	67	70	78	89	93	101	105	106	98	91	76	69	106
NE	Omaha	58	69	78	89	97	99	105	114	110	104	96	80	72	114
NV	Reno	53	70	75	83	89	96	103	104	105	101	91	77	70	105
NH	Concord	53	68	66	85	95	97	98	102	101	98	90	80	68	102
NJ	Atlantic City	51	78	75	87	94	99	106	104	102	99	90	84	75	106
NM	Albuquerque	55	69	76	85	89	98	107	105	101	100	91	77	72	107
NY	Albany	48	62	67	86	92	94	99	100	99	100	89	82	71	100
	Buffalo	51	72	65	81	94	90	96	97	99	98	87	80	74	99
	New York[1]	126	72	75	86	96	99	101	106	104	102	94	84	72	106
NC	Charlotte	55	78	81	90	93	100	103	103	103	104	98	85	77	104
	Raleigh	50	79	84	92	95	97	104	105	105	104	98	88	79	105
ND	Bismarck	55	62	69	81	93	98	107	109	109	105	95	75	65	109
OH	Cincinnati	33	69	73	84	89	93	102	103	102	98	88	81	75	103
	Cleveland	53	73	69	83	88	92	104	103	102	101	90	82	77	104
	Columbus	55	74	73	85	89	94	102	100	101	100	90	80	76	102
OK	Oklahoma City	41	80	84	93	100	104	105	109	110	102	96	87	86	110
OR	Portland	54	63	71	80	87	100	100	107	107	105	92	73	65	107
PA	Philadelphia	53	74	74	87	94	97	100	104	101	100	96	81	72	104
	Pittsburgh	42	69	69	82	89	91	98	103	100	97	87	82	74	103
RI	Providence	41	66	72	80	98	94	97	102	104	100	86	78	70	104
SC	Columbia	47	84	84	91	94	101	107	107	107	101	101	90	83	107
SD	Sioux Falls	49	66	70	87	94	100	110	108	108	104	94	76	61	110
TN	Memphis	53	78	81	86	94	99	104	108	105	103	95	85	81	108
	Nashville	55	78	84	86	91	97	106	107	104	105	94	84	79	107
TX	Dallas-Fort Worth	41	88	88	96	95	103	113	110	108	106	102	89	88	113
	El Paso	55	80	83	89	98	104	114	112	108	104	96	87	80	114
	Houston	25	84	91	91	95	97	103	104	107	102	96	89	83	107
UT	Salt Lake City	66	62	69	78	86	93	104	107	106	100	89	75	67	107
VT	Burlington	51	63	62	84	91	93	97	99	101	94	85	75	65	101
VA	Norfolk	46	78	81	88	97	100	101	103	104	99	95	86	80	104
	Richmond	65	80	83	93	96	100	104	105	102	103	90	86	80	105
WA	Seattle-Tacoma	50	64	70	75	85	93	96	100	99	98	89	74	64	100
	Spokane	47	59	61	71	90	96	101	103	108	98	86	67	56	108
WV	Charleston	47	79	78	89	94	93	98	104	101	102	92	85	80	104
WI	Milwaukee	54	62	65	82	91	93	101	101	103	98	89	77	63	103
WY	Cheyenne	59	66	71	74	83	90	100	100	96	93	83	73	69	100
PR	San Juan	40	92	96	96	97	96	97	95	97	97	98	96	94	98

[1] City office data.

Source: U.S. National Oceanic and Atmospheric Administration, *Comparative Climatic Data*, annual.

No. 391. Lowest Temperature of Record—Selected Cities

[**In Fahrenheit degrees.** Airport data, except as noted. For period of record through 1994]

STATE	STATION	Length of record (yr.)	Jan.	Feb.	Mar.	Apr.	May	June	July	Aug.	Sept.	Oct.	Nov.	Dec.	Annual
AL	Mobile.........	53	3	11	21	32	43	49	60	59	42	30	22	8	3
AK	Juneau	50	-22	-22	-15	6	25	31	36	27	23	11	-5	-21	-22
AZ	Phoenix........	57	17	22	25	32	40	50	61	60	47	34	25	22	17
AR	Little Rock	53	-4	-5	11	28	40	46	54	52	37	29	17	-1	-5
CA	Los Angeles......	59	23	32	34	39	43	48	49	51	47	41	34	32	23
	Sacramento......	44	23	23	26	32	36	41	48	49	43	36	26	18	18
	San Diego.......	54	29	36	39	41	48	51	55	57	51	43	38	34	29
	San Francisco	67	24	25	30	31	36	41	43	42	38	34	25	20	20
CO	Denver	60	-25	-30	-11	-2	22	30	43	41	17	3	-8	-25	-30
CT	Hartford........	40	-26	-21	-6	9	28	37	44	36	30	17	1	-14	-26
DE	Wilmington.......	47	-14	-6	2	18	30	41	48	43	36	24	14	-7	-14
DC	Washington	53	-5	4	11	24	34	47	54	49	39	29	16	1	-5
FL	Jacksonville	53	7	19	23	34	45	47	61	63	48	36	21	11	7
	Miami	52	30	32	32	46	53	60	69	68	68	51	39	30	30
GA	Atlanta	46	-8	5	10	26	37	46	53	55	36	28	3	-	-8
HI	Honolulu	25	53	53	55	57	60	65	66	67	66	61	57	54	53
ID	Boise	55	-17	-15	6	19	22	31	35	34	23	11	-3	-25	-25
IL	Chicago.........	36	-27	-17	-8	7	24	36	40	41	28	17	1	-25	-27
	Peoria..........	55	-25	-18	-10	14	25	39	47	41	26	19	-2	-23	-25
IN	Indianapolis	55	-27	-21	-7	16	28	37	44	41	28	17	-2	-23	-27
IA	Des Moines	55	-24	-20	-22	9	30	38	47	40	26	14	-4	-22	-24
KS	Wichita	42	-12	-21	-2	15	31	43	51	48	31	18	1	-16	-21
KY	Louisville	47	-22	-19	-1	22	31	42	50	46	33	23	-1	-15	-22
LA	New Orleans	48	14	19	25	32	41	50	60	60	42	35	24	11	11
ME	Portland	54	-26	-39	-21	8	23	33	40	33	23	15	3	-21	-39
MD	Baltimore........	44	-7	-3	6	20	32	40	50	45	35	25	13	-	-7
MA	Boston	43	-12	-4	6	16	34	45	50	47	38	28	15	-7	-12
MI	Detroit..........	36	-21	-15	-4	10	25	36	41	38	29	17	9	-10	-21
	Sault Ste. Marie ...	54	-36	-35	-24	-2	18	26	36	29	25	16	-10	-31	-36
MN	Duluth	53	-39	-33	-29	-5	17	27	35	32	22	8	-23	-34	-39
	Minneapolis-St. Paul	56	-34	-28	-32	2	18	34	43	39	26	15	-17	-29	-34
MS	Jackson.........	31	2	11	15	27	38	47	51	55	35	26	17	4	2
MO	Kansas City	22	-17	-19	-10	12	30	42	52	43	33	17	1	-23	-23
	St. Louis........	37	-18	-10	-5	22	31	43	51	47	36	23	1	-16	-18
MT	Great Falls.......	57	-37	-35	-29	-6	15	31	40	30	21	-11	-25	-43	-43
NE	Omaha	58	-23	-21	-16	5	27	38	44	43	25	13	-9	-23	-23
NV	Reno	53	-16	-16	-2	13	18	25	33	24	20	8	1	-16	-16
NH	Concord	53	-33	-37	-16	8	21	30	35	29	21	10	-5	-22	-37
NJ	Atlantic City	51	-10	-11	5	12	25	37	42	40	32	20	10	-7	-11
NM	Albuquerque......	55	-17	-5	8	19	28	40	52	50	37	21	-7	-7	-17
NY	Albany	48	-28	-21	-21	10	26	36	40	34	24	16	5	-22	-28
	Buffalo	51	-16	-20	-7	12	26	35	43	38	32	20	9	-10	-20
	New York [1].......	126	-6	-15	3	12	32	44	52	50	39	28	5	-13	-15
NC	Charlotte........	55	-5	5	4	24	32	45	53	53	39	24	11	2	-5
	Raleigh	50	-9	5	11	23	31	38	48	46	37	19	11	4	-9
ND	Bismarck........	55	-44	-43	-31	-12	15	30	35	33	11	-10	-30	-43	-44
OH	Cincinnati........	33	-25	-11	-11	17	27	39	47	43	31	16	1	-20	-25
	Cleveland	53	-20	-15	-5	10	25	31	41	38	32	19	3	-15	-20
	Columbus	55	-22	-13	-6	14	25	35	43	39	31	20	5	-17	-22
OK	Oklahoma City	41	-4	-3	-3	20	37	47	53	51	36	16	11	-8	-8
OR	Portland	54	-2	-3	19	29	29	39	43	44	34	26	13	6	-3
PA	Philadelphia......	53	-7	-4	7	19	28	44	51	44	35	25	15	1	-7
	Pittsburgh	42	-22	-12	-1	14	26	34	42	39	31	16	-1	-12	-22
RI	Providence.......	41	-13	-7	1	14	29	41	48	40	33	20	6	-10	-13
SC	Columbia........	47	-1	5	4	26	34	44	54	53	40	23	12	4	-1
SD	Sioux Falls.......	49	-36	-31	-23	5	17	33	38	34	22	9	-17	-28	-36
TN	Memphis	53	-4	-11	12	29	38	48	52	48	36	25	9	-13	-13
	Nashville	55	-17	-13	2	23	34	42	51	47	36	26	-1	-10	-17
TX	Dallas-Fort Worth ..	41	4	7	15	29	41	51	59	56	43	29	20	-1	-1
	El Paso.........	55	-8	8	14	23	31	46	57	56	41	25	1	5	-8
	Houston	25	12	20	22	31	44	52	62	60	48	29	19	7	7
UT	Salt Lake City.....	66	-22	-30	2	14	25	35	40	37	27	16	-14	-21	-30
VT	Burlington	51	-30	-30	-20	2	24	33	39	35	25	15	-2	-26	-30
VA	Norfolk	46	-3	8	18	28	36	45	54	49	45	27	20	7	-3
	Richmond	65	-12	-10	11	23	31	40	51	46	35	21	10	-1	-12
WA	Seattle-Tacoma....	50	-	1	11	29	28	38	43	44	35	28	6	6	-
	Spokane	47	-22	-17	-7	17	24	33	37	35	24	10	-21	-25	-25
WV	Charleston.......	47	-16	-6	-	19	26	33	46	41	34	17	6	-12	-16
WI	Milwaukee	54	-26	-19	-10	12	21	33	40	44	28	18	-5	-20	-26
WY	Cheyenne	59	-29	-34	-21	-8	16	25	38	36	8	-1	-16	-28	-34
PR	San Juan........	40	61	62	60	64	66	69	69	70	69	67	66	63	60

- Represents zero.   [1] City office data.

Source: U.S. National Oceanic and Atmospheric Administration, *Comparative Climatic Data,* annual.

Geography and Environment

No. 392. Normal Monthly and Annual Precipitation—Selected Cities

[**In inches.** Airport data, except as noted. Based on standard 30-year period, 1961 through 1990. See *Historical Statistics, Colonial Times to 1970*, series J 164-267, for related data]

STATE	STATION	Jan.	Feb.	Mar.	Apr.	May	June	July	Aug.	Sept.	Oct.	Nov.	Dec.	Annual
AL	Mobile..........	4.76	5.46	6.41	4.48	5.74	5.04	6.85	6.96	5.91	2.94	4.10	5.31	63.96
AK	Juneau	4.54	3.75	3.28	2.77	3.42	3.15	4.16	5.32	6.73	7.84	4.91	4.44	54.31
AZ	Phoenix..........	0.67	0.68	0.88	0.22	0.12	0.13	0.83	0.96	0.86	0.65	0.66	1.00	7.66
AR	Little Rock	3.42	3.61	4.91	5.49	5.17	3.57	3.60	3.26	4.05	3.75	5.20	4.83	50.86
CA	Los Angeles	2.40	2.51	1.98	0.72	0.14	0.03	0.01	0.15	0.31	0.34	1.76	1.66	12.01
	Sacramento	3.73	2.87	2.57	1.16	0.27	0.12	0.05	0.07	0.37	1.08	2.72	2.51	17.52
	San Diego	1.80	1.53	1.77	0.79	0.19	0.07	0.02	0.10	0.24	0.37	1.45	1.57	9.90
	San Francisco	4.35	3.17	3.06	1.37	0.19	0.11	0.03	0.05	0.20	1.22	2.86	3.09	19.70
CO	Denver	0.50	0.57	1.28	1.71	2.40	1.79	1.91	1.51	1.24	0.98	0.87	0.64	15.40
CT	Hartford..........	3.41	3.23	3.63	3.85	4.12	3.75	3.19	3.65	3.79	3.57	4.04	3.91	44.14
DE	Wilmington.......	3.03	2.91	3.43	3.39	3.84	3.55	4.23	3.40	3.43	2.88	3.27	3.48	40.84
DC	Washington	2.72	2.71	3.17	2.71	3.66	3.38	3.80	3.91	3.31	3.02	3.12	3.12	38.63
FL	Jacksonville	3.31	3.93	3.68	2.77	3.55	5.69	5.60	7.93	7.05	2.90	2.19	2.72	51.32
	Miami	2.01	2.08	2.39	2.85	6.21	9.33	5.70	7.58	7.63	5.64	2.66	1.83	55.91
GA	Atlanta	4.75	4.81	5.77	4.26	4.29	3.56	5.01	3.66	3.42	3.05	3.86	4.33	50.77
HI	Honolulu	3.55	2.21	2.20	1.54	1.13	0.50	0.59	0.44	0.78	2.28	3.00	3.80	22.02
ID	Boise	1.45	1.07	1.29	1.24	1.08	0.81	0.35	0.43	0.80	0.75	1.48	1.36	12.11
IL	Chicago.........	1.53	1.36	2.69	3.64	3.32	3.78	3.66	4.22	3.82	2.41	2.92	2.47	35.82
	Peoria..........	1.51	1.42	2.91	3.77	3.70	3.99	4.20	3.10	3.87	2.65	2.69	2.44	36.25
IN	Indianapolis	2.32	2.46	3.79	3.70	4.00	3.49	4.47	3.64	2.87	2.63	3.23	3.34	39.94
IA	Des Moines	0.96	1.11	2.33	3.36	3.66	4.46	3.78	4.20	3.53	2.62	1.79	1.32	33.12
KS	Wichita	0.79	0.96	2.43	2.38	3.81	4.31	3.13	3.02	3.49	2.22	1.59	1.20	29.33
KY	Louisville	2.86	3.30	4.66	4.23	4.62	3.46	4.51	3.54	3.16	2.71	3.70	3.64	44.39
LA	New Orleans	5.05	6.01	4.90	4.50	4.56	5.84	6.12	6.17	5.51	3.05	4.42	5.75	61.88
ME	Portland	3.53	3.33	3.67	4.08	3.62	3.44	3.09	2.87	3.09	3.90	5.17	4.55	44.34
MD	Baltimore........	3.05	3.12	3.38	3.09	3.72	3.67	3.69	3.92	3.41	2.98	3.32	3.41	40.76
MA	Boston	3.59	3.62	3.69	3.60	3.25	3.09	2.84	3.24	3.06	3.30	4.22	4.01	41.51
MI	Detroit..........	1.76	1.74	2.55	2.95	2.92	3.61	3.18	3.43	2.89	2.10	2.67	2.82	32.62
	Sault Ste. Marie ...	2.42	1.74	2.30	2.35	2.71	3.14	2.71	3.61	3.69	3.23	3.45	2.88	34.23
MN	Duluth	1.22	0.80	1.91	2.25	3.03	3.82	3.61	3.99	3.84	2.49	1.80	1.24	30.00
	Minneapolis-St. Paul	0.95	0.88	1.94	2.42	3.39	4.05	3.53	3.62	2.72	2.19	1.55	1.08	28.32
MS	Jackson..........	5.24	4.70	5.82	5.57	5.05	3.18	4.51	3.77	3.55	3.26	4.81	5.91	55.37
MO	Kansas City	1.09	1.10	2.51	3.12	5.04	4.72	4.38	4.01	4.86	3.29	1.92	1.58	37.62
	St. Louis	1.81	2.12	3.58	3.50	3.97	3.72	3.85	2.85	3.12	2.68	3.28	3.03	37.51
MT	Great Falls.......	0.91	0.57	1.10	1.41	2.52	2.39	1.24	1.54	1.24	0.78	0.66	0.85	15.21
NE	Omaha	0.74	0.77	2.04	2.66	4.52	3.87	3.51	3.24	3.72	2.28	1.49	1.02	29.86
NV	Reno	1.07	0.99	0.71	0.38	0.69	0.46	0.28	0.32	0.39	0.38	0.87	0.99	7.53
NH	Concord	2.51	2.53	2.72	2.91	3.14	3.15	3.23	3.32	2.81	3.23	3.66	3.16	36.37
NJ	Atlantic City	3.46	3.06	3.62	3.56	3.33	2.64	3.83	4.14	2.93	2.82	3.58	3.32	40.29
NM	Albuquerque......	0.44	0.46	0.54	0.52	0.50	0.59	1.37	1.64	1.00	0.89	0.43	0.50	8.88
NY	Albany	2.36	2.27	2.93	2.99	3.41	3.62	3.18	3.47	2.95	2.83	3.23	2.93	36.17
	Buffalo	2.70	2.31	2.68	2.87	3.14	3.55	3.08	4.17	3.49	3.09	3.83	3.67	38.58
	New York [1]......	3.42	3.27	4.08	4.20	4.42	3.67	4.35	4.01	3.89	3.56	4.47	3.91	47.25
NC	Charlotte	3.71	3.84	4.43	2.68	3.82	3.39	3.92	3.73	3.50	3.36	3.23	3.48	43.09
	Raleigh	3.48	3.69	3.77	2.59	3.92	3.68	4.01	4.02	3.19	2.86	2.98	3.24	41.43
ND	Bismarck	0.45	0.43	0.77	1.67	2.18	2.72	2.14	1.72	1.49	0.90	0.49	0.51	15.47
OH	Cincinnati........	2.59	2.69	4.24	3.75	4.28	3.84	4.24	3.35	2.88	2.86	3.46	3.15	41.33
	Cleveland	2.04	2.19	2.91	3.14	3.49	3.70	3.52	3.40	3.44	2.54	3.17	3.09	36.63
	Columbus	2.18	2.24	3.27	3.21	3.93	4.04	4.31	3.72	2.96	2.15	3.22	2.86	38.09
OK	Oklahoma City	1.13	1.56	2.71	2.77	5.22	4.31	2.61	2.60	3.84	3.23	1.98	1.40	33.36
OR	Portland	5.35	3.85	3.56	2.39	2.06	1.48	0.63	1.09	1.75	2.67	5.34	6.13	36.30
PA	Philadelphia	3.21	2.79	3.46	3.62	3.75	3.74	4.28	3.80	3.42	2.62	3.34	3.38	41.41
	Pittsburgh	2.54	2.39	3.41	3.15	3.59	3.71	3.75	3.21	2.97	2.36	2.85	2.92	36.85
RI	Providence.......	3.88	3.61	4.05	4.11	3.76	3.33	3.18	3.63	3.48	3.69	4.43	4.38	45.53
SC	Columbia........	4.42	4.12	4.82	3.28	3.68	4.80	5.50	6.09	3.67	3.04	2.90	3.59	49.91
SD	Sioux Falls.......	0.51	0.64	1.64	2.52	3.03	3.40	2.68	2.85	3.02	1.78	1.09	0.70	23.86
TN	Memphis........	3.73	4.35	5.41	5.46	4.98	3.57	3.79	3.43	3.53	3.01	5.10	5.74	52.10
	Nashville	3.58	3.81	4.85	4.37	4.88	3.57	3.97	3.46	3.46	2.62	4.12	4.61	47.30
TX	Dallas-Fort Worth ..	1.83	2.18	2.77	3.50	4.88	2.98	2.31	2.21	3.39	3.52	2.29	1.84	33.70
	El Paso	0.40	0.41	0.29	0.20	0.25	0.67	1.54	1.58	1.70	0.76	0.44	0.57	8.81
	Houston	3.29	2.96	2.92	3.21	5.24	4.96	3.60	3.49	4.89	4.27	3.79	3.45	46.07
UT	Salt Lake City.....	1.11	1.23	1.91	2.12	1.80	0.93	0.81	0.86	1.28	1.44	1.29	1.40	16.18
VT	Burlington	1.82	1.63	2.23	2.76	3.12	3.47	3.65	4.06	3.30	2.88	3.13	2.42	34.47
VA	Norfolk	3.78	3.47	3.70	3.06	3.81	3.82	5.06	4.81	3.90	3.15	2.85	3.23	44.64
	Richmond	3.24	3.16	3.61	2.96	3.84	3.62	5.03	4.40	3.34	3.53	3.17	3.26	43.16
WA	Seattle-Tacoma....	5.38	3.99	3.54	2.33	1.70	1.50	0.76	1.14	1.88	3.23	5.83	5.91	37.19
	Spokane	1.98	1.49	1.49	1.18	1.41	1.26	0.67	0.72	0.73	0.99	2.15	2.42	16.49
WV	Charleston.......	2.91	3.04	3.63	3.31	3.94	3.59	4.99	4.01	3.24	2.89	3.59	3.39	42.53
WI	Milwaukee	1.60	1.45	2.67	3.50	2.84	3.24	3.47	3.53	3.38	2.41	2.51	2.33	32.93
WY	Cheyenne	0.40	0.39	1.03	1.37	2.39	2.08	2.09	1.69	1.27	0.74	0.53	0.42	14.40
PR	San Juan........	2.81	2.15	2.35	3.76	5.93	4.00	4.37	5.32	5.28	5.71	5.94	4.72	52.34

[1] City office data.

Source: U.S. National Oceanic and Atmospheric Administration, *Climatography of the United States*, No. 81.

No. 393. Average Number of Days With Precipitation of .01 Inch or More—Selected Cities

[Airport data, except as noted. For period of record through 1994, except as noted]

STATE	STATION	Length of record (yr.)	Jan.	Feb.	Mar.	Apr.	May	June	July	Aug.	Sept.	Oct.	Nov.	Dec.	Annual
AL	Mobile.	53	11	10	10	7	9	11	16	14	10	6	8	10	122
AK	Juneau [1]	50	19	17	18	17	17	16	17	17	21	24	20	21	222
AZ	Phoenix.	55	4	4	4	2	1	1	4	5	3	3	3	4	36
AR	Little Rock	52	10	9	10	10	10	8	8	7	7	7	8	9	105
CA	Los Angeles	59	6	6	6	3	1	(Z)	1	(Z)	1	2	3	5	35
	Sacramento	55	10	9	9	5	3	1	(Z)	(Z)	1	3	7	9	57
	San Diego	54	7	6	7	4	2	1	(Z)	1	1	2	5	6	42
	San Francisco	67	11	10	10	6	3	1	(Z)	(Z)	1	4	7	10	62
CO	Denver	60	6	6	9	9	11	9	9	9	6	5	6	5	89
CT	Hartford.	40	11	10	12	11	12	11	10	10	10	9	11	12	127
DE	Wilmington.	47	11	9	11	11	11	10	9	9	8	8	9	10	116
DC	Washington	53	10	9	11	10	11	9	10	9	8	7	8	9	113
FL	Jacksonville	53	8	8	8	6	8	12	15	15	13	9	7	8	116
	Miami	52	7	6	6	6	10	15	16	17	17	14	9	6	130
GA	Atlanta	60	11	10	11	9	9	10	12	10	8	7	8	10	115
HI	Honolulu	45	9	9	9	9	7	6	7	6	7	9	9	10	98
ID	Boise	55	12	10	10	8	8	6	2	3	4	6	10	11	90
IL	Chicago.	36	11	10	12	12	11	10	10	9	10	9	11	11	126
	Peoria	55	9	8	11	12	11	10	9	8	9	8	9	10	114
IN	Indianapolis	55	12	10	13	12	12	10	10	9	8	8	11	12	126
IA	Des Moines	55	8	7	10	11	11	11	9	9	9	8	7	8	108
KS	Wichita	41	5	5	8	8	11	9	7	8	8	6	5	6	86
KY	Louisville	47	11	11	13	12	12	10	11	8	8	8	10	11	124
LA	New Orleans	46	10	9	9	7	8	11	15	13	10	6	7	10	114
ME	Portland	54	11	10	11	12	13	11	10	9	9	9	12	12	129
MD	Baltimore.	44	11	9	11	11	11	9	9	10	8	7	9	9	113
MA	Boston	43	11	10	12	11	12	11	9	10	9	9	11	12	127
MI	Detroit.	36	13	11	13	13	11	10	10	9	10	10	12	14	136
	Sault Ste. Marie	53	19	14	13	11	11	11	10	11	13	14	17	19	165
MN	Duluth	53	12	9	11	11	12	13	11	11	12	10	11	12	134
	Minneapolis-St. Paul	56	9	7	10	10	11	12	10	10	10	8	9	9	115
MS	Jackson.	31	11	9	10	8	9	8	10	10	8	6	8	10	109
MO	Kansas City	22	7	7	10	11	11	10	9	9	8	8	8	8	106
	St. Louis	37	8	8	11	11	11	9	9	8	8	8	10	9	111
MT	Great Falls.	57	9	8	9	9	12	12	8	8	7	6	7	8	101
NE	Omaha	58	6	7	9	10	12	11	9	9	8	6	6	7	99
NV	Reno	52	6	6	6	4	4	3	2	2	2	3	5	6	50
NH	Concord	53	11	9	11	12	12	11	10	10	9	9	11	11	126
NJ	Atlantic City	51	11	10	11	11	10	9	9	9	8	7	9	10	112
NM	Albuquerque.	55	4	4	5	3	5	4	9	10	6	5	4	4	61
NY	Albany	48	12	11	12	12	13	11	10	10	10	9	12	12	135
	Buffalo	51	20	17	16	14	12	10	10	11	11	12	16	19	169
	New York [2]	125	11	10	11	11	11	10	11	10	8	8	9	10	121
NC	Charlotte	55	10	10	11	9	10	10	11	10	7	7	8	10	111
	Raleigh	50	10	10	10	9	10	9	11	10	8	7	8	9	112
ND	Bismarck	55	8	7	8	8	10	11	9	8	7	6	6	8	96
OH	Cincinnati.	47	12	11	13	13	12	10	10	9	8	8	11	12	130
	Cleveland	53	16	14	15	14	13	11	10	10	10	11	14	16	156
	Columbus	55	13	11	14	13	13	11	11	9	8	9	12	13	137
OK	Oklahoma City	55	6	6	7	8	10	9	6	7	7	7	5	6	83
OR	Portland	54	18	16	17	14	12	9	4	5	7	12	18	19	151
PA	Philadelphia	54	11	9	11	11	11	10	9	9	8	8	9	10	117
	Pittsburgh	42	16	14	16	14	13	11	11	10	10	10	13	16	153
RI	Providence.	41	11	10	12	11	11	11	9	9	8	9	11	12	124
SC	Columbia.	47	10	10	10	8	9	10	12	11	8	6	7	9	110
SD	Sioux Falls.	49	6	7	9	9	10	11	9	8	6	6	6	6	98
TN	Memphis	44	10	9	11	10	9	9	9	7	7	6	9	10	107
	Nashville	53	11	11	12	11	11	9	10	9	8	7	9	11	119
TX	Dallas-Fort Worth	41	7	7	7	8	9	6	5	5	7	6	6	7	79
	El Paso	55	4	3	2	2	2	3	8	8	5	4	3	4	49
	Houston	25	11	9	9	7	9	9	9	9	9	7	8	9	106
UT	Salt Lake City.	66	10	9	10	9	8	5	5	6	5	6	8	9	91
VT	Burlington	51	14	12	13	12	14	12	12	12	13	12	12	14	154
VA	Norfolk	46	11	10	11	10	10	9	11	10	8	8	8	9	115
	Richmond	57	10	9	11	9	11	9	11	10	8	7	8	9	113
WA	Seattle-Tacoma.	50	18	16	17	14	10	9	5	6	9	13	18	19	154
	Spokane	47	14	11	11	9	9	8	5	5	6	7	13	15	112
WV	Charleston	47	15	14	15	14	13	11	13	11	9	10	12	14	151
WI	Milwaukee	54	11	10	12	12	11	11	10	9	9	9	11	11	125
WY	Cheyenne	59	6	6	9	10	12	11	11	10	7	6	6	6	100
PR	San Juan	39	17	13	12	13	16	15	19	18	17	17	18	19	196

Z Less than 1/2 day. [1] For period of record through 1989. [2] City office data.

Source: U.S. National Oceanic and Atmospheric Administration, *Comparative Climatic Data*, annual.

No. 394. Snow and Ice Pellets—Selected Cities

[**In inches.** Airport data, except as noted. For period of record through 1994. T denotes trace]

STATE	STATION	Length of record (yr)	Jan.	Feb.	Mar.	Apr.	May	June	July	Aug.	Sept.	Oct.	Nov.	Dec.	Annual
AL	Mobile..........	53	0.1	0.1	0.1	T	T	-	T	-	-	-	T	0.1	0.4
AK	Juneau	50	26.7	19.2	15.1	3.4	-	T	-	-	T	1.1	13.1	22.7	101.3
AZ	Phoenix..........	57	T	-	T	T	T	-	-	-	-	T	-	-	T
AR	Little Rock	52	2.3	1.4	0.5	T	-	-	-	-	-	T	0.2	0.6	5.0
CA	Los Angeles	59	T	T	T	-	-	-	-	-	-	-	-	T	T
	Sacramento	46	T	-	T	-	T	-	-	-	-	-	-	T	T
	San Diego	54	T	-	T	-	-	-	-	-	-	T	T	T	T
	San Francisco	67	-	T	T	-	-	-	-	-	-	-	-	-	T
CO	Denver	60	8.2	7.4	12.5	8.9	1.6	-	T	T	1.6	3.7	9.1	7.3	60.3
CT	Hartford.........	40	12.4	11.8	10.1	1.5	-	T	-	-	-	0.1	2	10.1	48.0
DE	Wilmington.......	47	6.5	6.1	3.3	0.2	T	T	T	-	-	0.1	0.9	3.2	20.3
DC	Washington	51	5.3	5.2	2.1	-	T	-	T	T	-	-	0.8	3	16.4
FL	Jacksonville	53	T	-	-	-	-	-	T	-	-	-	-	-	T
	Miami	52	-	-	-	-	-	-	-	-	-	-	-	-	-
GA	Atlanta	60	0.9	0.5	0.4	T	-	-	-	-	-	T	-	0.2	2.0
HI	Honolulu	48	-	-	-	-	-	-	-	-	-	-	-	-	-
ID	Boise	55	6.7	3.6	1.7	0.6	0.1	T	T	T	-	0.1	2.4	5.8	21.0
IL	Chicago.........	36	10.8	8.6	6.8	1.7	0.1	T	T	T	T	0.4	1.8	8.3	38.5
	Peoria..........	51	6.6	5.6	4.1	0.8	-	-	T	-	T	0.1	2.0	5.8	25.0
IN	Indianapolis	63	6.2	5.8	3.4	0.5	-	T	T	-	T	0.2	1.8	4.9	22.8
IA	Des Moines	55	8.1	7.3	6.1	1.9	-	T	T	-	T	0.2	3.0	6.7	33.3
KS	Wichita	41	4.5	4.2	2.4	0.3	T	T	T	T	T	-	1.2	3.2	15.8
KY	Louisville	47	5.4	4.4	3.2	0.1	T	T	T	-	-	0.1	1	2.1	16.3
LA	New Orleans	48	-	0.1	T	T	T	-	-	-	-	-	T	0.1	0.2
ME	Portland	54	19.3	17.3	13.0	3.0	0.2	-	-	-	T	0.2	3	14.6	70.6
MD	Baltimore	44	5.8	6.5	3.8	0.1	T	-	T	-	-	-	1	3.4	20.6
MA	Boston	59	12.4	11.7	8.0	0.9	-	-	-	-	T	-	1.3	7.4	41.7
MI	Detroit..........	36	10.4	9.3	6.9	1.7	T	-	-	-	-	0.2	2.9	10.1	41.5
	Sault Ste. Marie ...	53	28.8	18.5	14.8	5.6	0.5	T	-	T	0.1	2.4	15.3	29.5	115.5
MN	Duluth	51	17.2	11.2	13.3	6.5	0.7	-	T	T	0.1	1.4	12.6	15.2	78.2
	Minneapolis-St. Paul	56	10.0	8.5	10.5	2.9	0.1	T	T	T	-	0.5	7.9	9.2	49.6
MS	Jackson.........	31	0.5	0.2	0.2	-	-	-	-	-	-	-	-	-	0.9
MO	Kansas City	60	5.7	4.6	3.5	0.8	T	T	T	-	T	-	1.1	4.3	20.0
	St. Louis	58	5.3	4.6	4.2	0.4	-	T	-	-	T	T	1.4	3.8	19.7
MT	Great Falls.......	57	9.8	8.4	10.3	7.3	1.7	0.3	T	0.1	1.5	3.4	7.6	8.6	59.0
NE	Omaha	59	7.4	6.6	6.3	1.0	0.1	T	-	-	T	0.3	2.6	5.6	29.9
NV	Reno	52	5.9	5.2	4.3	1.2	0.9	-	-	-	-	0.3	2.4	4.3	24.5
NH	Concord	53	18.1	14.6	11.1	2.3	0.1	T	-	-	T	0.1	3.8	13.4	63.5
NJ	Atlantic City	50	5.1	5.4	2.6	0.3	T	T	T	-	-	T	0.4	2.2	16.0
NM	Albuquerque......	55	2.5	2.1	1.8	0.6	-	T	T	T	T	0.1	1.2	2.6	10.9
NY	Albany	48	16.6	14.3	11.2	2.6	0.1	T	T	-	T	0.2	4.1	14.6	63.7
	Buffalo	51	23.5	18.3	11.7	3.2	0.3	T	T	T	T	0.3	11.3	22.4	91.0
	New York [1]	126	7.6	8.6	5.0	0.9	T	-	-	-	-	-	0.9	5.4	28.4
NC	Charlotte	55	2.0	1.7	1.2	-	T	-	-	-	-	T	0.1	0.5	5.5
	Raleigh	50	2.2	2.5	1.3	-	-	-	T	-	-	-	0.1	0.8	6.9
ND	Bismarck	55	7.3	6.8	8.2	3.9	0.9	T	T	T	0.2	1.7	6.5	6.9	42.4
OH	Cincinnati.	47	6.8	5.4	4.3	0.5	-	T	T	-	-	0.3	2.0	3.8	23.1
	Cleveland	53	12.9	12.3	10.6	2.3	0.1	T	T	-	T	0.6	4.9	11.7	55.4
	Columbus	47	8.4	6.2	4.5	0.9	-	T	T	-	T	0.1	2.2	5.4	27.7
OK	Oklahoma City	55	3	2.4	1.4	-	T	-	-	-	-	-	0.5	1.7	9.0
OR	Portland	54	3.3	1	0.4	T	-	T	-	T	-	T	0.4	1.4	6.5
PA	Philadelphia	52	6.3	6.5	3.8	0.3	T	T	T	-	-	-	0.6	3.3	20.8
	Pittsburgh	42	11.7	9.3	8.8	1.7	0.1	T	T	T	T	0.4	3.3	8.1	43.4
RI	Providence.	41	9.6	10	7.7	0.7	0.2	-	-	-	-	0.1	1.0	6.8	36.1
SC	Columbia........	47	0.4	0.8	0.2	T	-	-	-	T	-	-	T	0.3	1.7
SD	Sioux Falls.......	49	6.7	8.2	9.4	2.5	-	T	T	-	-	0.7	5.5	7.2	40.2
TN	Memphis	44	2.3	1.4	0.8	T	T	-	-	-	-	T	0.1	0.6	5.2
	Nashville	53	3.8	3	1.4	-	-	-	-	T	-	-	0.4	1.5	10.1
TX	Dallas-Fort Worth ..	41	1.2	0.9	0.2	T	T	-	-	-	-	T	0.1	0.2	2.6
	El Paso.........	55	1.4	0.8	0.4	0.3	T	T	T	-	T	-	0.9	1.7	5.5
	Houston	60	0.2	0.2	-	T	T	T	-	-	-	-	T	-	0.4
UT	Salt Lake City.....	66	13.4	9.5	9.3	4.9	0.6	T	T	T	0.1	1.3	7	12	58.1
VT	Burlington	51	19.2	16.8	12.7	3.9	0.2	-	T	T	-	0.2	6.6	17.9	77.5
VA	Norfolk	46	2.8	2.8	1.0	-	T	T	-	T	-	-	-	0.9	7.5
	Richmond	57	4.8	4.1	2.4	0.1	T	-	-	-	-	T	0.4	2.0	13.8
WA	Seattle-Tacoma....	50	4.9	1.7	1.4	0.1	T	-	-	-	T	-	1.2	2.5	11.8
	Spokane	47	15.9	7.7	4.0	0.6	0.1	T	-	-	T	0.4	6.4	14.9	50.0
WV	Charleston	47	10.6	8.7	5.0	0.9	-	T	T	-	T	0.2	2.2	5.0	32.6
WI	Milwaukee	54	13.1	10.2	8.6	1.8	0.1	T	T	T	T	0.2	3.0	10.4	47.4
WY	Cheyenne	59	6.5	6.1	12.0	9.0	3.3	0.2	-	-	0.8	3.7	7.3	6.2	55.1
PR	San Juan........	39	-	-	-	-	-	-	-	-	-	-	-	-	-

- Represents zero or rounds to zero.   [1] City office data.

Source: U.S. National Oceanic and Atmospheric Administration, *Comparative Climatic Data*, annual.

No. 395. Sunshine, Average Wind Speed, Heating and Cooling Degree Days, and Average Relative Humidity—Selected Cities

[Airport data, except as noted. For period of record through 1994, except as noted. M=morning. A=afternoon]

STATE	STATION	AVERAGE PERCENTAGE OF POSSIBLE SUNSHINE [1]		AVERAGE WIND SPEED (m.p.h.)				Heating degree days	Cooling degree days	AVERAGE RELATIVE HUMIDITY (percent)						
		Length of record (yr.)	Annual	Length of record (yr.)	Annual	Jan.	July			Length of record	Annual		Jan.		July	
											M	A	M	A	M	A
AL	Mobile	46	60	46	8.9	10.3	6.9	1,702	2,627	32	87	57	82	61	90	60
AK	Juneau	44	23	49	8.3	8.2	7.5	8,897	-	28	84	73	81	78	83	70
AZ	Phoenix	57	81	49	6.2	5.3	7.1	1,350	4,162	34	51	23	66	32	44	20
AR	Little Rock	35	60	52	7.8	8.4	6.7	3,155	2,005	34	84	58	80	62	88	56
CA	Los Angeles	59	72	46	7.5	6.7	7.9	1,458	727	35	79	64	70	59	86	68
	Sacramento	46	73	44	7.9	7.2	9.0	2,749	1,237	34	83	46	90	70	77	28
	San Diego	54	72	54	7.0	5.9	7.5	1,256	984	34	77	62	71	56	82	66
	San Francisco	67	72	67	10.6	7.2	13.6	3,016	145	35	84	62	86	66	86	59
CO	Denver	60	67	46	8.6	8.6	8.3	6,020	679	34	68	40	64	49	69	34
CT	Hartford	40	52	40	8.5	9.0	7.3	6,151	677	35	77	52	71	56	79	51
DE	Wilmington	47	55	46	9.0	9.8	7.8	4,937	1,046	47	78	55	75	60	79	54
DC	Washington	46	55	46	9.4	10.0	8.3	4,047	1,549	34	74	53	70	55	76	53
FL	Jacksonville	46	61	45	7.9	8.2	7.0	1,434	2,551	58	88	56	87	58	88	58
	Miami	45	68	45	9.3	9.6	8.0	200	4,198	30	84	61	84	59	84	63
GA	Atlanta	60	59	56	9.1	10.4	7.6	2,991	1,667	34	82	56	78	59	88	60
HI	Honolulu	45	74	45	11.3	9.5	13.1	-	4,474	25	72	55	81	61	67	51
ID	Boise	55	58	55	8.7	8.0	8.4	5,861	754	55	69	43	81	71	54	21
IL	Chicago	36	52	36	10.4	11.7	8.3	6,536	752	36	80	60	77	68	82	57
	Peoria	51	53	51	10.0	11.1	7.8	6,148	982	35	83	62	79	69	87	59
IN	Indianapolis	63	51	46	9.6	10.9	7.5	5,615	1,014	35	84	62	81	70	87	60
IA	Des Moines	45	55	45	10.7	11.5	8.9	6,497	1,036	33	80	60	76	67	82	58
KS	Wichita	39	62	41	12.3	12.1	11.4	4,791	1,628	41	80	56	79	63	79	49
KY	Louisville	47	53	47	8.3	9.5	6.8	4,514	1,288	34	81	58	77	64	85	58
LA	New Orleans	46	60	46	8.2	9.3	6.1	1,513	2,655	46	88	63	85	66	91	66
ME	Portland	54	55	54	8.8	9.1	7.6	7,378	268	54	79	59	76	60	80	59
MD	Baltimore	44	58	44	9.1	9.7	7.9	4,707	1,137	41	77	54	72	57	80	53
MA	Boston	59	55	37	12.5	13.8	10.9	5,641	678	30	72	58	67	57	74	56
MI	Detroit	36	50	36	10.4	12.0	8.6	6,569	626	36	81	60	80	69	82	54
	Sault Ste. Marie	53	43	53	9.2	9.7	7.8	9,316	131	53	85	67	81	74	89	62
MN	Duluth	46	49	45	11.0	11.6	9.4	9,818	180	33	81	63	77	70	85	59
	Minneapolis-St. Paul	56	54	56	10.5	10.5	9.4	7,981	682	35	79	60	74	67	81	54
MS	Jackson	30	59	31	7.3	8.4	5.8	2,467	2,215	31	91	58	87	65	94	60
MO	Kansas City	22	59	22	10.8	11.4	9.4	5,393	1,288	22	81	60	77	64	85	58
	St. Louis	46	55	45	9.7	10.6	8.0	4,758	1,534	34	83	59	81	66	84	56
MT	Great Falls	57	51	53	12.7	15.2	10.0	7,741	388	33	67	45	67	61	67	30
NE	Omaha	49	59	58	10.5	10.9	8.9	6,300	1,072	30	82	59	78	65	85	58
NV	Reno	52	69	52	6.6	5.6	7.1	5,674	508	31	70	31	79	50	62	18
NH	Concord	53	55	52	6.8	7.3	5.7	7,554	328	29	81	54	75	58	84	51
NJ	Atlantic City	36	56	36	9.9	10.9	8.4	5,169	826	30	82	56	78	58	83	57
NM	Albuquerque	55	76	55	8.9	8.0	9.0	4,425	1,244	34	60	29	70	40	60	27
NY	Albany	56	49	56	8.9	9.8	7.5	6,894	507	29	80	57	77	63	81	55
	Buffalo	51	43	55	11.9	14.2	10.3	6,747	477	34	80	62	79	72	78	55
	New York [2]	42	64	58	9.4	10.7	7.6	4,805	1,096	61	72	56	68	60	75	55
NC	Charlotte	46	58	45	7.4	7.8	6.6	3,341	1,582	34	82	53	78	55	86	56
	Raleigh	46	59	45	7.8	8.5	6.7	3,457	1,417	30	85	54	79	55	89	58
ND	Bismarck	55	55	55	10.2	10.0	9.2	8,968	488	35	80	57	75	69	84	47
OH	Cincinnati	43	49	47	9.0	10.6	7.2	5,248	996	32	82	60	79	68	85	57
	Cleveland	53	45	53	10.5	12.2	8.6	6,201	621	34	79	62	78	69	81	57
	Columbus	45	48	45	8.3	9.9	6.6	5,708	797	35	80	59	77	67	84	56
OK	Oklahoma City	44	64	46	12.3	12.6	10.9	3,659	1,859	29	80	55	78	59	80	50
OR	Portland	46	39	46	7.9	9.9	7.6	4,522	371	54	86	59	86	75	82	45
PA	Philadelphia	54	56	54	9.5	10.3	8.2	4,954	1,101	35	76	55	73	59	79	54
	Pittsburgh	42	44	42	9.1	10.6	7.3	5,968	654	34	79	58	76	66	83	54
RI	Providence	41	55	41	10.5	11.1	9.4	5,884	606	31	75	55	71	56	77	56
SC	Columbia	47	60	46	6.9	7.2	6.3	2,649	1,966	28	87	51	82	54	89	54
SD	Sioux Falls	49	57	46	11.1	11.0	9.8	7,809	744	31	82	60	77	68	83	54
TN	Memphis	42	59	46	8.9	10.0	7.5	3,082	2,118	55	81	57	78	63	84	57
	Nashville	53	57	53	8.0	9.1	6.5	3,729	1,616	29	84	57	80	63	89	57
TX	Dallas-Fort Worth	41	64	41	10.7	10.9	9.8	2,407	2,603	31	82	56	80	61	81	49
	El Paso	52	80	52	8.8	8.3	8.3	2,708	2,094	34	57	28	66	35	62	29
	Houston	25	56	25	7.9	8.2	7.0	1,599	2,700	25	90	60	86	64	93	57
UT	Salt Lake City	66	62	65	8.8	7.5	9.5	5,765	1,047	35	67	43	79	69	52	22
VT	Burlington	51	44	51	9.0	9.8	8.0	7,771	388	29	77	59	72	64	79	53
VA	Norfolk	46	58	46	10.6	11.5	8.9	3,495	1,422	46	78	57	75	59	81	59
	Richmond	49	56	46	7.7	8.1	6.9	3,963	1,348	60	83	53	80	57	85	56
WA	Seattle-Tacoma [2]	50	38	46	9.0	9.6	8.3	4,908	190	35	83	62	82	74	82	49
	Spokane	47	47	47	8.9	8.8	8.6	6,842	398	35	78	52	86	79	65	28
WV	Charleston	47	48	47	6.2	7.4	4.9	4,646	1,031	47	83	56	77	63	90	59
WI	Milwaukee	54	52	54	11.5	12.6	9.7	7,324	479	34	80	64	76	68	82	61
WY	Cheyenne	59	64	37	12.9	15.3	10.4	7,326	285	35	65	44	58	50	70	38
PR	San Juan	39	76	39	8.4	8.5	9.7	-	5,558	39	79	65	82	64	79	67

- Represents zero.   [1] Percent of days that are either clear or partly cloudy.   [2] Does not represent airport data.

Source: U.S. National Oceanic and Atmospheric Administration, *Comparative Climatic Data*, annual.

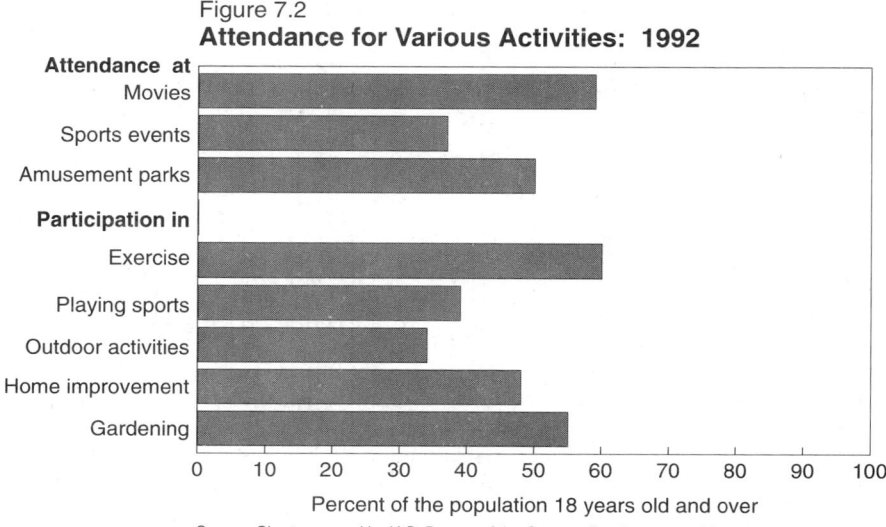

Figure 7.1
Participation in 10 Most Popular Sports Activities, by Sex: 1994

Male
Female

Exercise walking
Swimming
Bicycle riding
Exercising with equipment
Camping
Fishing (fresh water)
Bowling
Basketball
Hiking
Golf

0 5 10 15 20 25 30 35 40 45 50

Percent of the population 7 years old and over

Source: Chart prepared by U.S. Bureau of the Census. For data, see table 414.

Figure 7.2
Attendance for Various Activities: 1992

Attendance at
Movies
Sports events
Amusement parks

Participation in
Exercise
Playing sports
Outdoor activities
Home improvement
Gardening

0 10 20 30 40 50 60 70 80 90 100

Percent of the population 18 years old and over

Source: Chart prepared by U.S. Bureau of the Census. For data, see table 411.

Parks, Recreation, and Travel

This section presents data on national parks and forests, State parks, recreational activities, the arts and humanities, and domestic and foreign travel.

Parks and recreation—The Department of the Interior has responsibility for administering the national parks. As part of this function, it issues reports relating to the usage of public parks for recreation purposes. The National Park Service publishes information on visits to national park areas in its annual report, *National Park Statistical Abstract. The National Parks: Index (year)* is a biannual report which has appeared under a variety of *Index* titles prior to 1985. Beginning with the 1985 edition, the report has appeared under the current title. The *Index* contains brief descriptions, with acreages, of each area administered by the Service, plus certain "related" areas. A statistical summary of service-administered areas is also presented. The annual *Federal Recreation Fee Report* summarizes the prior year's recreation fee receipts and recreation visitation statistics for seven Federal land managing agencies.

Statistics for State parks are compiled by the National Association of State Park Directors which issues its annual *Information Exchange.* The Bureau of Land Management, in its *Public Land Statistics,* also issues data on recreational use of its lands. The Department of Agriculture's Forest Service, in its *Report of the Forest Service,* issues data on recreational uses of the national forests.

Visitation—Data on visitation to reporting areas are collected by several different agencies and groups. The methodology used to collect these results may vary accordingly, from visual counts and estimates to the use of electromagnetic traffic counters. In using and comparing these data, one should also be aware of several different definitions that follow: Recreation visit, which is the entry of any person into an area for recreation purposes; nonrecreation visits, which include visits going to and from inholdings, through traffic, tradespeople and personnel with business in the area; and visitor hour, which constitutes the presence of a person in a recreation

In Brief	
Persons who golf:	
1975	*13 million*
1994	*24 million*
Expenditures for sound recordings:	
1990	*$7.5 billion*
1993	*$10.0 billion*

area or site for recreational purposes for periods of time aggregating 60 minutes.

Recreation and leisure activities—Statistics on the participation in various recreation and leisure time activities are based on several sample surveys. Data on participation in fishing, hunting, and other forms of wildlife-associated recreation are published periodically by the U.S. Department of Interior, Fish and Wildlife Service. The most recent data are from the 1991 survey. Data on participation in various sports recreation activities are published by the National Sporting Goods Association.

Travel—Information on foreign travel and personal expenditures abroad, as well as expenditures by foreign citizens traveling in the United States, is compiled annually by the U.S. Bureau of Economic Analysis and published in selected issues of the monthly *Survey of Current Business.* Statistics on arrivals to the United States had been reported by the U.S. Travel and Tourism Administration (USTTA), in cooperation with the U.S. Immigration and Naturalization Service, and are published in *Summary and Analysis of International Travel to the United States.* Sources of statistics on departures from the United States included USTTA's in-flight survey, the Department of Transportation's *International Air Travel Statistics,* and other sources. Data on domestic travel, business receipts and employment of the travel industry, and travel expenditures are published by the U.S. Travel Data Center, the national nonprofit center for travel and tourism research which is located in Washington, DC. Other data on household transportation characteristics may be found in section 21.

No. 396. Visitation to Federal Recreation Areas: 1980 to 1994

[In **millions of visitor hours**. For years ending **September 30**. Covers persons entering and using a recreation area over a specified period of time. For definition of visitor hour, see text, section 7]

ADMINISTERING FEDERAL AGENCY	1980	1985	1987	1988	1989	1990	1991	1992	1994
All areas	6,367	6,403	7,332	7,419	7,475	7,567	7,829	7,995	(NA)
Fish and Wildlife Service	17	65	72	81	45	(NA)	(NA)	(NA)	(NA)
Forest Service	2,819	2,705	2,861	2,908	3,030	3,157	3,346	3,452	(NA)
U.S. Army Corps of Engineers [1]	1,926	1,721	2,176	2,290	2,296	2,280	2,306	2,306	(NA)
National Park Service	1,042	1,298	1,394	1,376	1,315	1,322	1,344	1,390	1,338
Bureau of Land Management [2]	68	246	515	461	493	518	540	563	(NA)
Bureau of Reclamation	407	289	306	294	286	280	280	269	(NA)
Tennessee Valley Authority [3]	87	79	8	9	10	10	13	14	(NA)

NA Not available. [1] Beginning 1987, not comparable with previous years. [2] Data not comparable for all years. [3] Beginning in 1989, the TVA discontinued reporting visitation to nonfee charging areas. Data for 1987 and 1988 have been adjusted to reflect this policy.

Source: 1980, U.S. Heritage Conservation and Recreation Service, *Federal Recreation Fee Report*, annual; thereafter, U.S. National Park Service.

No. 397. National Park System—Summary: 1985 to 1994

[**For fiscal years ending in year shown, except as noted;** see text, section 10. Includes data for five areas in Puerto Rico and Virgin Islands, one area in American Samoa, and one area in Guam. See also *Historical Statistics, Colonial Times to 1970*, series H 806-828]

ITEM	1985	1988	1989	1990	1991	1992	1993	1994
Finances (mil. dol.): [1]								
Expenditures reported	848.1	922.9	1,036.8	986.1	1,104.4	1,268.7	1,429.4	1,404.0
Salaries and wages	369.4	423.9	441.4	459.1	495.3	518.1	596.1	627.2
Improvements, maintenance	127.4	154.7	197.5	160.0	179.6	212.1	224.8	222.9
Construction	84.7	86.3	85.2	108.5	134.1	193.3	226.8	205.6
Other	266.6	258.0	312.7	258.5	295.4	345.2	379.7	348.3
Funds available	1,248.2	1,338.4	1,440.0	1,505.5	1,988.4	2,274.8	2,346.5	2,307.7
Appropriations.	821.6	874.6	996.7	1,052.5	1,284.7	1,392.8	1,334.0	1,388.8
Other [2]	426.6	463.8	443.3	453.0	703.7	882.0	1,012.5	918.9
Revenue from operations	50.6	77.2	86.3	78.6	78.1	88.3	89.5	97.0
Recreation visits (millions): [3]								
All areas . . . . [4]	263.4	282.5	269.4	258.7	267.8	274.7	273.1	267.6
National parks [4]	50.0	56.4	57.4	57.7	57.4	58.7	59.8	60.1
National monuments	15.9	23.2	23.7	23.9	25.8	26.6	26.5	26.5
National historical, commemorative, archaeological [5]	61.9	61.2	63.9	57.5	61.0	63.3	61.9	59.5
National parkways	40.0	42.0	31.2	29.1	28.8	30.7	30.4	29.3
National recreation areas [4]	49.4	54.5	49.6	47.2	49.8	50.3	50.8	52.3
National seashores and lakeshores. . .	25.3	23.2	21.9	23.3	24.4	23.9	24.1	24.0
National Capital Parks	8.3	9.0	8.9	7.5	7.5	8.1	9.1	5.4
Miscellaneous other areas.	12.6	12.9	12.8	12.5	13.1	13.1	10.5	10.5
Recreation overnight stays (millions) [3] . .	15.8	17.0	17.4	17.6	17.7	18.3	17.7	18.3
In commercial lodgings	3.5	3.8	3.9	3.9	4.0	4.1	4.0	3.9
In Park Service campgrounds	7.3	7.9	7.8	7.9	7.8	8.1	7.5	7.6
In tents.	3.6	3.9	3.9	4.1	4.2	4.4	4.1	4.2
In recreation vehicles	3.8	3.9	3.9	3.8	3.6	3.7	3.4	3.4
In backcountry	1.7	1.6	1.6	1.7	2.0	2.2	2.4	2.4
Other	3.2	3.7	4.1	4.2	3.9	3.9	3.8	4.4
Land (1,000 acres): [6]								
Total	75,749	76,176	76,331	76,362	76,607	76,492	75,515	74,905
Parks	45,739	45,955	46,081	46,089	46,135	46,208	45,521	48,111
Recreation areas.	3,335	3,339	3,342	3,344	3,346	3,347	3,349	3,351
Other	26,675	26,882	26,907	26,929	27,126	26,937	26,645	23,443
Acquisition, gross	34	38	73	21	66	23	39	26
By purchase	29	37	14	18	15	21	29	25
By gift	2	(Z)	58	2	43	1	10	(Z)
By transfer or exchange	3	1	1	3	8	1	1	(Z)
Exclusion	(Z)	(Z)	1	1	(Z)	(Z)	(Z)	(Z)
Acquisition, net.	34	38	71	21	66	23	39	26

Z Less than 500 acres. [1] Financial data are those associated with the National Park System. Certain other functions of the National Park Service (principally the activities absorbed from the former Heritage Conservation and Recreation Service in 1981) are excluded. [2] Includes funds carried over from prior years. [3] For calendar year. [4] Combined data for North Cascades National Park and two adjacent National Recreation Areas are included in National Parks total. [5] Includes military areas. [6] Federal land only, as of Dec. 31. Federal land acreages, in addition to National Park Service administered lands, also include lands within national park system area boundaries but under the administration of other agencies. Year-to-year changes in the federal lands figures include changes in the acreages of these other lands and hence often differ from "net acquisition."

Source: U.S. National Park Service, Visits, *National Park Statistical Abstract*, annual; and unpublished data. Other data are unpublished.

No. 398. National Forest Recreation Use, Summary: 1980 to 1993

[For year ending September 30. Estimated. Represents recreational use of National Forest land and water in States which have a Forest Service recreation program. See also *Historical Statistics, Colonial Times to 1970*, series H 829-835]

YEAR AND ACTIVITY	Recreation visitor-days [1] (1,000)	Per-cent	STATE	Recreation visitor-days [1], 1993 (1,000)	STATE OR OTHER AREA	Recreation visitor-days [1], 1993 (1,000)
1980	233,549	100.0	U.S.	295,473	NV	3,677
1981	235,709	100.0			NH	3,243
1982	233,438	100.0	AL	833	NM	8,775
1983	227,708	100.0	AK	5,515	NY	35
1984	227,554	100.0	AZ	30,973	NC	6,158
1985	225,407	100.0	AR	2,106	ND	135
1986	226,533	100.0	CA	69,981	OH	680
1987	238,458	100.0	CO	30,106	OK	358
1988	242,316	100.0	FL	3,124	OR	19,285
1989	252,495	100.0	GA	3,033	PA	2,950
1990	263,051	100.0	ID	13,455	SC	944
1991	278,849	100.0	IL	1,029	SD	3,352
1992	287,691	100.0	IN	501	TN	2,957
1993, total	**295,473**	**100.0**	KS	83	TX	2,303
Mechanized travel and viewing scenery	99,573	33.7	KY	2,106	UT	15,157
Camping, picnicking, and swimming	79,319	26.8	LA	533	VT	1,728
Hiking, horseback riding, and water travel	26,632	9.0	MA	114	VA	4,477
Winter sports	19,230	6.5	MI	5,011	WA	18,735
Hunting	17,279	5.8	MN	5,676	WV	1,354
Resorts, cabins, and organization camps	17,086	5.8	MS	1,318	WI	2,733
Fishing	16,299	5.5	MO	1,931	WY	7,454
Nature studies	2,711	0.9	MT	11,001		
Other [2]	17,343	6.0	NE	260	PR	296

[1] One recreation visitor-day is the recreation use of National Forest land or water that aggregates 12 visitor-hours. This may entail 1 person for 12 hours, 12 persons for 1 hour, or any equivalent combination of individual or group use, either continuous or intermittent.   [2] Includes team sports, gathering forest products, attending talks and programs, and other uses.

Source: U.S. Forest Service, unpublished data.

No. 399. Recreational Use of Public Lands Administered by Bureau of Land Management: 1982 to 1993

[In thousands. For year ending Sept. 30. Beginning 1987, increase due to an estimated longer length of stay per visit, especially in California. See text, section 7]

YEAR AND STATE	Number of visits	TYPE OF RECREATION USE (visitor hours)										
		Total	Off-highway vehicle travel	Other motor-ized travel	Non-motor-ized travel	Camp-ing	Hunting	Misc. site based	Fishing	Boating	Misc. water based	Snow- and ice-based recre-ational activity, winter sports
1982	58,135	316,959	19,471	32,646	11,237	63,928	108,996	44,587	19,287	10,101	1,043	5,663
1983	56,270	334,010	24,397	35,534	12,237	84,066	92,974	39,734	20,290	16,869	4,992	2,917
1984	59,228	271,373	21,348	25,433	9,579	73,032	73,898	37,650	14,263	11,184	2,092	2,894
1985	51,739	244,612	36,995	24,053	10,047	65,397	51,842	23,098	14,254	11,710	2,193	5,023
1986	54,253	284,142	49,688	25,866	14,397	95,196	35,570	19,331	18,227	15,891	3,951	6,025
1987	56,427	514,716	123,325	34,325	19,172	195,315	57,624	38,412	22,932	15,140	5,212	3,259
1988	57,460	492,756	122,014	35,748	19,761	178,703	55,285	38,340	21,617	13,294	4,979	3,015
1989	60,957	493,214	65,808	74,075	36,676	173,597	46,760	45,871	23,392	18,491	5,425	3,119
1990	71,820	523,753	63,016	83,445	41,316	165,366	47,053	57,958	28,664	20,806	8,313	7,816
1991	72,541	539,779	50,849	85,835	44,398	196,310	49,593	59,928	20,939	19,676	8,353	3,898
1992	69,418	519,429	46,411	93,477	43,845	181,536	44,557	59,857	19,768	18,735	3,657	3,657
1993, total	(NA)	428,825	40,197	61,113	27,780	162,663	47,246	42,500	19,466	17,127	7,009	3,724
AK	(NA)	5,924	152	466	87	3,719	567	201	432	173	5	122
AZ [1]	(NA)	59,022	749	619	2,473	36,351	2,334	8,748	756	4,927	2,061	4
CA	(NA)	132,143	24,989	10,159	7,177	66,608	7,727	9,213	2,745	1,584	1,688	253
CO	(NA)	27,795	1,418	6,122	946	5,692	9,204	1,535	791	1,710	54	323
Eastern States	(NA)	52	-	-	-	-	1	1	6	2	42	-
ID [2]	(NA)	18,199	1,032	1,326	692	5,168	2,568	1,588	2,288	1,433	570	1,534
MT [2]	(NA)	13,004	2,523	967	503	3,187	2,822	418	1,734	476	57	317
NV	(NA)	26,897	1,668	11,309	2,798	4,191	2,192	2,708	1,434	262	172	163
NM	(NA)	20,098	926	5,137	1,721	3,001	5,329	2,917	600	392	71	4
OR [3]	(NA)	60,564	1,828	8,291	5,625	15,759	6,627	9,718	7,232	3,026	1,902	556
UT	(NA)	56,000	4,618	15,988	5,481	17,341	4,868	3,985	465	2,812	336	114
WY	(NA)	9,119	294	729	277	1,646	3,007	1,468	983	330	51	334

- Represents zero.   NA Not available.   [1] Includes concession visitation data. These data relate to Bureau of Land Management concession leases along the Colorado River. The leases consist of boat docks and storage areas, trailer parks, restaurants, etc. The visitation by the recreating public to these areas and facilities is monitored and recorded.   [2] Includes North Dakota and South Dakota.   [3] Includes Washington.

Source: U.S. Bureau of Land Management, *Public Land Statistics*, annual.

No. 400. State Parks and Recreation Areas—States: 1992

[For year ending June 30. Data are shown as reported by State park directors. In some States, park agency has under its control forests, fish and wildlife areas, and/or other areas. In other States, agency is responsible for State parks only]

STATE	Acreage (1,000)	Visitors (1,000)[1]	REVENUE Total ($1,000)	Percent of operating expenditures	STATE	Acreage (1,000)	Visitors (1,000)[1]	REVENUE Total ($1,000)	Percent of operating expenditures
United States ...	11,831	724,805	488,984	45.0	Missouri	122	16,103	4,300	22.4
					Montana	41	4,491	1,330	48.6
Alabama	50	6,268	23,427	81.4	Nebraska	142	9,227	8,600	71.1
Alaska	3,169	6,321	1,063	19.9	Nevada	142	2,679	751	14.5
Arizona	33	1,750	3,734	35.9	New Hampshire ...	75	1,737	4,341	51.5
Arkansas	47	6,725	12,046	56.0	New Jersey	305	10,607	6,123	22.8
California	1,323	67,301	73,563	49.3	New Mexico	122	4,089	2,932	29.0
Colorado	340	9,522	13,373	109.0	New York	260	63,520	36,657	33.5
Connecticut	173	7,053	3,498	47.9	North Carolina	135	9,713	2,108	18.3
Delaware	13	3,619	4,176	43.0	North Dakota	19	990	809	49.1
Florida	444	12,232	18,061	38.9	Ohio	208	49,861	13,178	30.8
Georgia	57	16,284	15,029	42.5	Oklahoma	77	16,183	17,127	76.7
Hawaii	25	19,255	1,161	14.7	Oregon	91	42,334	9,171	38.5
Idaho	42	2,697	1,958	79.8	Pennsylvania	277	35,542	8,053	15.4
Illinois	403	38,555	3,528	11.6	Rhode Island	9	3,423	2,584	44.8
Indiana	57	10,570	9,111	73.7	South Carolina	80	7,876	10,955	60.7
Iowa	391	12,230	1,804	24.0	South Dakota	92	5,166	3,946	64.5
Kansas	324	4,425	2,523	45.5	Tennessee	133	27,360	20,270	59.0
Kentucky	43	27,831	36,529	63.3	Texas	501	24,423	16,366	49.8
Louisiana	39	1,226	2,142	25.0	Utah	97	5,577	3,923	31.9
Maine	75	2,005	1,478	34.9	Vermont	64	839	4,222	96.2
Maryland	241	8,891	6,176	26.0	Virginia	66	3,975	2,635	27.6
Massachusetts	274	11,549	9,256	64.9	Washington	241	47,289	7,360	36.1
Michigan	264	21,172	21,108	77.4	West Virginia	202	8,753	14,806	64.6
Minnesota	231	7,932	7,472	41.6	Wisconsin	125	11,646	8,338	70.0
Mississippi	23	4,033	5,607	48.0	Wyoming	120	1,949	275	10.2

[1] Includes overnight visitors.

Source: National Association of State Park Directors, Tallahassee, FL, *1993 Annual Information Exchange.*

No. 401. Personal Consumption Expenditures for Recreation in Real (1992) Dollars: 1970 to 1994

[In billions of dollars, except percent. Represents market value of purchases of goods and services by individuals and nonprofit institutions. For explanation of real dollars, see text, section 14]

TYPE OF PRODUCT OR SERVICE	1970	1980	1985	1990	1991	1992	1993	1994
Total recreation expenditures	93.8	159.7	215.8	291.8	295.0	310.8	337.2	369.9
Percent of total personal consumption[1]	4.3	5.3	6.1	7.1	7.2	7.4	7.8	8.3
Books and maps	12.8	12.5	13.9	17.6	17.3	17.7	18.4	19.1
Magazines, newspapers, and sheet music	16.7	23.3	21.7	23.8	22.8	21.6	21.8	22.5
Nondurable toys and sport supplies	10.8	20.1	25.7	32.6	33.3	34.2	36.2	39.3
Wheel goods, sports and photographic equipment[2]	11.7	21.4	25.2	31.2	30.0	29.9	32.5	38.2
Video and audio products, computer equipment, and musical instruments	6.2	12.7	24.7	47.9	53.6	61.2	73.4	89.0
Radio and television repair	3.2	4.1	4.0	4.6	4.2	4.2	4.4	4.4
Flowers, seeds, and potted plants	4.8	7.0	7.5	12.5	11.8	12.3	12.9	14.0
Admissions to specified spectator amusements	10.9	13.1	14.2	16.5	16.3	16.6	17.9	18.3
Motion picture theaters	5.5	5.1	4.7	5.6	5.5	5.0	5.1	5.2
Legitimate theaters and opera, and entertainments of nonprofit institutions[3]	1.7	3.5	4.7	6.1	6.2	6.8	7.8	8.2
Spectator sports[4]	3.7	4.5	4.8	4.8	4.6	4.8	5.0	4.9
Clubs and fraternal organizations except insurance[5]	4.5	4.8	7.5	9.5	9.9	10.3	11.0	11.5
Commercial participant amusements[6]	7.7	15.3	20.0	24.9	24.6	27.2	30.4	32.9
Pari-mutuel net receipts	3.8	4.8	4.1	3.7	3.5	3.3	3.1	3.0
Other[7]	14.2	32.2	52.7	68.3	68.0	72.4	75.5	79.3

[1] See table 695. [2] Includes boats and pleasure aircraft. [3] Except athletic. [4] Consists of admissions to professional and amateur athletic events and to racetracks, including horse, dog, and auto. [5] Consists of dues and fees excluding insurance premiums. [6] Consists of billiard parlors; bowling alleys; dancing, riding, shooting, skating, and swimming places; amusement devices and parks; golf courses; sightseeing buses and guides; private flying operations; casino gambling; and other commercial participant amusements. [7] Consists of net receipts of lotteries and expenditures for purchases of pets and pet care services, cable TV, film processing, photographic studios, sporting and recreation camps, video cassette rentals, and recreational services, not elsewhere classified.

Source: U.S. Bureau of Economic Analysis, *The National Income and Product Accounts of the United States,* forthcoming, and *Survey of Current Business,* January/February, 1996.

No. 402. Expenditures per Consumer Unit for Entertainment and Reading: 1985 to 1994

[Data are **annual averages. In dollars, except as indicated.** Based on Consumer Expenditure Survey; see text, section 14, for description of survey. See also headnote, table 704. For composition of regions, see table 27]

YEAR AND CHARACTERISTIC	ENTERTAINMENT AND READING		ENTERTAINMENT				Reading
	Total	Percent of total expenditures	Total	Fees and admissions	Television, radios, and sound equipment	Other equipment and services [1]	
1985.	1,311	5.6	1,170	320	371	479	141
1986.	1,289	5.4	1,149	308	371	470	140
1987.	1,335	5.5	1,193	323	379	491	142
1988.	1,479	5.7	1,329	353	416	560	150
1989.	1,581	5.7	1,424	377	429	618	157
1990.	1,575	5.6	1,422	371	454	597	153
1991.	1,635	5.5	1,472	378	468	627	163
1992.	1,662	5.6	1,500	379	492	629	162
1993.	1,792	5.8	1,626	414	590	621	166
1994, total	**1,732**	**5.5**	**1,567**	**439**	**533**	**595**	**165**
Age of reference person:							
Under 25 years old.	1,083	5.9	1,018	226	475	317	65
25 to 34 years old	1,655	5.4	1,519	364	563	592	136
35 to 44 years old	2,209	5.9	2,025	574	669	782	184
45 to 54 years old	2,308	5.6	2,104	560	635	908	204
55 to 64 years old	1,767	5.2	1,565	477	478	609	202
65 to 74 years old	1,224	4.9	1,055	373	392	290	169
75 years old and over.	789	4.1	656	253	240	164	133
Origin of reference person: Hispanic.	1,013	3.8	937	194	461	282	76
Non-Hispanic	1,790	5.6	1,618	459	539	620	172
Black	836	3.8	759	143	442	173	77
Other	1,908	5.7	1,724	498	551	675	184
Region of residence: Northeast	1,708	5.2	1,517	500	528	490	191
Midwest	1,712	5.6	1,551	404	531	615	161
South	1,553	5.2	1,417	383	510	525	136
West	2,066	5.8	1,875	514	578	783	191
Size of consumer unit: One person. .	1,072	5.5	945	273	351	322	127
Two or more persons	1,994	5.4	1,814	505	606	703	180
Two persons	1,814	5.5	1,623	469	522	632	191
Three persons	1,918	5.2	1,757	463	606	688	161
Four persons	2,314	5.6	2,128	588	721	818	186
Five persons or more	2,210	5.4	2,042	563	697	782	168

[1] Other equipment and services includes pets, toys, and playground equipment, and sports, exercise, and photographic equipment.

Source: U.S. Bureau of Labor Statistics, *Consumer Expenditure Survey*, annual.

No. 403. Motion Pictures and Amusement and Recreation Services—Annual Receipts: 1989 to 1994

[**In billions of dollars.** For taxable employer and nonemployer firms]

KIND OF BUSINESS	1987 SIC code [1]	1989	1990	1991	1992	1993	1994
Motion pictures.	78	36,173	39,982	42,838	45,662	50,185	54,238
Production, distribution, and allied services	781, 782	26,415	28,888	31,590	34,288	38,042	41,106
Theaters	783	5,408	6,088	6,213	5,879	6,121	6,512
Video tape rental.	784	4,350	5,006	5,035	5,495	6,022	[2]6,620
Amusement and recreation services	79	44,539	50,126	51,654	57,699	64,017	69,210
Dance studios, schools, and halls.	791	701	626	662	784	868	879
Theatrical producers (except motion picture), bands, orchestras, and entertainers	792	8,447	10,735	11,694	13,054	15,788	16,877
Bowling centers.	793	2,788	2,800	2,747	2,915	2,881	3,010
Commercial sports.	794	7,571	8,636	8,597	9,010	9,087	9,359
Professional sports clubs and promoters	7941	3,046	3,702	3,719	3,978	4,594	5,004
Racing, including track operation	7948	4,525	4,934	4,878	5,032	4,493	4,354
Miscellaneous amusement and recreation services [3].	799	25,032	27,329	27,954	31,936	35,393	39,085
Physical fitness facilities	7991	3,379	3,623	4,135	4,135	4,063	4,231
Public golf courses.	7992	1,790	2,254	2,386	2,609	2,913	3,245
Coin-operated amusement devices	7993	1,933	2,146	2,301	2,566	2,754	2,946
Amusement parks	7996	4,562	4,922	4,820	5,366	5,662	5,903
Membership sports and recreation clubs	7997	4,457	4,825	5,151	5,397	5,992	6,437

NA Not available.　[1] 1987 Standard Industrial Classification code; see text, section 13.　[2] Revised since published.
[3] Includes kinds of businesses, not shown separately.

Source: U.S. Bureau of the Census, *Current Business Reports, Service Annual Survey: 1994*, BS/94.

No. 404. Quantity of Books Sold and Value of U.S. Domestic Consumer Expenditures: 1982 to 1994

[Includes all titles released by publishers in the United States and imports which appear under the imprints of American publishers. Multi-volume sets, such as encyclopedias, are counted as one unit]

TYPE OF PUBLICATION AND MARKET AREA	UNITS SOLD (mil.)					CONSUMER EXPENDITURES (mil. dol.)				
	1982	1985	1990	1993	1994	1982	1985	1990	1993	1994
Total [1]	1,723	1,788	2,005	2,079	2,127	9,889	12,611	19,043	22,635	23,798
Hardbound, total	646	694	824	810	811	6,190	7,969	11,789	13,840	14,465
Softbound, total	1,077	1,094	1,181	1,269	1,316	3,699	4,642	7,254	8,795	9,333
Trade	459	553	705	762	806	2,484	3,660	6,498	8,353	9,162
Adult	315	360	403	463	489	2,028	2,871	4,777	6,393	7,155
Juvenile	144	193	301	299	317	456	789	1,721	1,960	2,006
Religious	144	134	130	139	142	706	926	1,362	1,651	1,690
Professional	106	110	131	137	142	1,630	2,043	2,957	3,646	3,867
Bookclubs	133	130	108	111	116	510	582	705	766	850
Elhi text	233	234	209	225	211	1,067	1,415	1,948	2,220	2,074
College text [1]	115	110	137	135	136	1,388	1,575	2,319	2,498	2,536
Mail order publications	134	121	138	102	96	581	650	752	601	576
Mass market paperbacks-rack sized	382	382	433	452	461	1,102	1,244	1,775	2,078	2,156
General retailers	756	829	1,010	1,074	1,122	3,743	5,103	8,465	10,597	11,456
College stores	224	225	255	264	269	1,910	2,309	3,403	3,916	4,061
Libraries and institutions [2]	80	80	88	94	96	888	1,090	1,592	1,911	2,012
Schools [2]	262	260	244	258	246	1,313	1,685	2,365	2,692	2,556
Direct to consumers	319	300	304	277	284	1,889	2,214	2,901	3,144	3,320
Other	82	94	104	106	110	146	210	316	375	394

[1] Types of publications include university press publications and subscription reference works, not shown separately.   [2] Elhi libraries included in schools.

Source: Book Industry Study Group, Inc., New York, NY, *Book Industry Trends, 1995*, annual, (copyright).

No. 405. Book Purchasing by Adults: 1991 and 1994

[In percent. Excludes books purchased for or by children under 13. Based on a survey of 16,000 households conducted over 12 months ending in December of year shown. For details, see source]

CHARACTERISTIC	TOTAL		MASS MARKET [1]		TRADE [2]		HARDCOVER	
	1991	1994	1991	1994	1991	1994	1991	1994
Total	100.0	100	100.0	100.0	100.0	100.0	100.0	100.0
Age of purchaser:								
Under 25 years old	3.9	4.2	3.4	3.7	4.7	4.8	3.7	4.1
25 to 34 years old	16.8	16.3	13.8	12.5	19.8	20.4	17.2	16.2
35 to 44 years old	28.6	27.3	26.6	25.0	31.7	30.4	27.7	26.4
45 to 54 years old	20.8	21.1	20.9	21.8	20.4	20.0	21.1	21.2
55 to 64 years old	14.2	14.8	15.6	16.1	12.1	13.2	14.7	15.3
65 years old and over	15.7	16.3	19.7	20.9	11.3	11.2	15.6	16.8
Household income:								
Under $30,000	31.2	31.4	36.3	37.9	27.2	26.7	28.9	28.7
$30,000 to 49,999	29.4	28.1	32.8	28.5	27.9	28.0	26.4	27.6
$50,000 to 59,999	8.6	9.3	7.2	9.9	9.4	9.0	9.5	8.9
$60,000 to 69,999	8.8	8.5	7.0	7.3	10.1	9.3	9.6	9.1
$70,000 and over	22.0	22.7	16.7	16.4	25.4	27.0	25.6	25.7
Household size:								
Singles	21.1	21.1	21.0	21.0	21.3	21.0	20.9	21.4
Families with no children	37.9	41.5	40.4	43.7	34.2	39.1	38.9	41.5
Families with children	41.0	37.4	38.6	35.3	44.5	39.9	40.2	37.1
Age of reader:								
Under 25 years old	8.5	8.3	5.9	6.0	11.4	10.8	8.5	8.1
25 to 34 years old	17.1	16.9	13.5	12.4	20.6	21.4	17.8	17.4
35 to 44 years old	26.3	25.5	25.3	24.0	28.0	27.3	25.7	25.1
45 to 54 years old	19.0	19.0	19.9	20.8	18.2	17.1	18.9	19.1
55 to 64 years old	13.5	13.7	15.6	15.5	10.9	11.8	13.8	13.7
65 years old and over	15.6	16.6	19.8	21.3	10.9	11.6	15.3	16.6
Category of book:								
Popular fiction	52.4	50.2	92.4	93.4	15.4	15.0	40.7	37.2
General nonfiction	10.5	9.9	3.6	3.3	15.3	13.5	14.4	13.8
Cooking/crafts	9.6	10.9	0.4	0.4	17.4	18.5	13.1	15.2
Other	27.5	29.0	3.6	2.9	51.9	53.0	31.8	33.8
Sales outlet:								
Independent	24.2	21.4	15.6	14.0	35.9	31.2	22.4	19.3
Chain book store	23.5	24.6	19.6	20.6	28.5	28.2	22.6	25.2
Book clubs	16.0	17.5	15.2	16.4	8.7	11.7	25.6	25.6
Other [3]	36.3	36.5	49.8	49.0	26.9	28.9	29.4	29.9

[1] "Pocket size" books sold primarily through magazine and news outlets, supermarkets, variety stores, etc.   [2] All paperbound books, except mass market.   [3] Includes mail order, price clubs, discount stores, food/drug stores, used book stores, and other outlets.

Source: Book Industry Study Group, Inc., New York, NY, *1995 Consumer Research Study on Book Purchasing*, (copyright).

No. 406. Profile of Consumer Expenditures for Sound Recordings: 1990 to 1993

[In percent, except total value. Based on monthly telephone surveys of the population 10 years old and over]

ITEM	1990	1992	1993	ITEM	1990	1992	1993
Total value (mil. dol.)	7,541.1	9,023.9	10,046.6	Other store	16.2	22.8	24.2
PERCENT DISTRIBUTION [1]				Music club	8.8	10.6	11.3
Age: 10 to 14 years	6.3	7.0	7.2	Mail order	3.5	4.0	4.4
15 to 19 years.	17.1	17.9	16.0	Music type: [2]			
20 to 24 years.	17.1	16.2	15.1	Rock	37.4	33.2	32.6
25 to 29 years.	15.0	14.3	13.6	Country	8.8	16.5	17.5
30 to 34 years.	13.5	12.8	12.4	Pop	13.6	11.4	11.7
35 to 39 years.	10.1	11.2	11.6	Urban contemporary.	(NA)	8.8	9.9
40 to 44 years.	8.3	7.3	8.7	Rap.	(NA)	7.9	7.8
45 years and over	11.8	12.3	14.6	Classical	4.1	4.4	4.0
Sex: Male	57.2	54.6	52.8	Jazz	5.2	4.0	3.3
Female	42.8	45.4	47.2	Gospel.	2.4	2.7	3.1
Sales outlet:				Soundtracks	1.0	0.9	0.8
Record store.	71.5	62.1	59.1	Children's.	0.4	0.5	0.3
				Other.	7.9	7.8	7.2

NA Not available.   [1] Percent distributions exclude nonresponses and responses of don't know.   [2] As classified by respondent.

Source: Recording Industry Association of America, Inc., Washington, DC, *Inside the Recording Industry: A Statistical Overview: 1993,* and earlier issues.

No. 407. Profile of Adults Living in Cable and Non-Cable TV Households: 1994-95

[Based on survey and subject to sampling error]

CHARACTERISTIC	ALL ADULTS	CABLE TV STATUS			
		No cable	Any cable		
			Total	Basic cable only	Pay cable
Total (mil.).	189.6	68.1	121.5	66.2	55.3
PERCENT DISTRIBUTION					
Age: 18 to 34 years old.	36	38	34	30	39
35 to 54 years old	36	32	39	36	44
55 years old and over	28	30	27	34	17
Household income:					
Under $20,000	25	36	20	23	14
$20,000 to 39,999.	29	32	28	30	26
$40,000 to 59,999.	21	16	23	22	25
$60,000 to 74,999.	10	7	11	11	13
$75,000 and over	15	9	18	14	22

Source: Media Dynamics, Inc. New York, NY, *TV Dimensions '96.* Based on data from Mediamark Research, Inc., (copyright).

No. 408. Household Participation in Lawn and Garden Activities: 1990 to 1994

[Based on national household sample survey conducted by the Gallup Organization. Subject to sampling variability; see source]

ACTIVITY	PERCENT HOUSEHOLDS ENGAGED IN—					RETAIL SALES (mil. dol.)				
	1990	1991	1992	1993	1994	1990	1991	1992	1993	1994
Total.	80	78	75	71	74	20,802	22,134	22,824	22,410	25,897
Lawn care.	66	62	54	54	56	6,412	6,890	7,460	6,446	8,417
Indoor houseplants	43	42	34	31	37	928	852	926	689	999
Flower gardening	48	41	39	39	44	2,275	2,302	2,167	2,396	3,147
Insect control.	39	35	27	24	28	1,370	1,260	1,593	1,080	1,127
Shrub care	38	32	27	28	30	1,099	1,030	1,437	1,274	1,133
Vegetable gardening.	37	31	31	26	31	1,384	1,652	1,440	1,063	1,476
Tree care	31	27	20	21	22	1,445	1,443	1,664	2,011	1,408
Landscaping	31	26	22	24	26	3,837	4,828	4,444	5,006	5,797
Flower bulbs	31	26	23	22	28	579	520	503	453	635
Fruit trees	19	15	13	13	14	502	371	350	759	389
Container gardening.	15	13	9	11	12	359	330	239	441	359
Raising transplants [1]	15	12	8	10	11	181	141	169	201	182
Herb gardening	9	9	7	8	10	84	161	135	175	112
Growing berries	9	7	6	6	6	79	90	62	126	85
Ornamental gardening.	7	7	5	6	5	268	264	235	290	264
Water gardening	(NA)	(NA)	(NA)	(NA)	5	(NA)	(NA)	(NA)	(NA)	367

NA Not available.   [1] Starting plants in advance of planting in ground.

Source: The National Gardening Association, Burlington, VT, *National Gardening Survey,* annual, (copyright).

No. 409. Sport Fishing and Hunting Licenses—Number and Cost: 1970 to 1994

[In millions, except as indicated. For fiscal years ending in year shown; see text, section 9.
See also *Historical Statistics, Colonial Times to 1970*, series H 875-876]

ITEM	1970	1975	1980	1985	1989	1990	1991	1992	1993	1994
Fishing licenses: Sales	31.1	34.7	35.2	35.7	36.6	37.0	37.0	37.4	37.9	37.9
Resident.	26.8	30.0	30.1	30.5	31.0	31.0	31.1	31.4	31.8	31.6
Nonresident	4.3	4.7	5.1	5.2	5.6	6.0	5.9	6.0	6.1	6.3
Paid license holders [1]	24.4	27.5	28.0	29.7	30.3	30.7	30.7	30.6	30.2	30.2
Cost to anglers (mil. dol.) . . .	91	142	196	282	341	363	375	398	412	425
Hunting licenses: Sales	22.2	25.9	27.0	27.7	29.3	30.0	30.7	31.3	31.6	31.6
Resident.	21.0	24.7	25.6	26.1	27.3	27.4	28.5	29.1	29.5	29.7
Nonresident	1.2	1.3	1.4	1.6	2.0	2.3	2.2	2.2	2.0	2.0
Paid license holders [1]	15.4	16.6	16.3	15.9	15.9	15.8	15.7	15.7	15.6	15.3
Cost to hunters (mil. dol.) . . .	102	155	222	301	400	422	439	481	492	502
Federal duck stamps sold (1,000)	2,072	2,222	2,090	1,914	1,395	1,401	1,420	1,330	1,401	1,449

[1] Resident and nonresident. Includes multiple counting of license holders who bought nonresident licenses as well as a home State license. "Licenses" includes licenses, tags, permits, and stamps.

Source: U.S. Fish and Wildlife Service, *Federal Aid in Fish and Wildlife Restoration*, annual.

No. 410. Anglers and Hunters: 1991

[**For persons 16 years old and over.** An angler or hunter is anyone who has fished or hunted in 1991. Based on the 1991 National Survey of Fishing, Hunting, and Wildlife-Associated Recreation conducted for the U.S. Fish and Wildlife Service by the U.S. Bureau of the Census]

TYPE OF FISHING	ANGLERS		Days of fishing [1] (mil.)	Expen- ditures [2] (mil. dol.)	TYPE OF HUNTING	HUNTERS		Days of hunt- ing [1] (mil.)	Expendi- tures [2] (mil. dol.)
	Number (1,000)	Percent of popu- lation				Number (1,000)	Percent of popu- lation		
All fishing.	[3]35,578	19	[3]511	23,990	All hunting. . . .	[3]14,063	7	[3]236	12,336
All freshwater fishing .	[3]31,041	16	[3]440	15,149	Big game.	10,745	6	128	5,090
Freshwater, except					Small game	7,642	4	77	1,550
Great Lakes.	30,186	16	431	13,812	Migratory birds	3,009	2	22	686
Great Lakes	2,552	1	25	1,337	Other animals.	1,411	1	19	255
Saltwater	8,885	5	75	4,992					

[1] Any part of a day constitutes a day. [2] Totals include expenditures for equipment, trips, magazines, membership dues, contributions, land leasing and ownership, licenses, stamps, tags, and other expenditures. Figures by type of fishing and hunting include only expenditures for trips and equipment. [3] Includes duplication for persons who participate in more than one category.

Source: U.S. Fish and Wildlife Service, *1991 National Survey of Fishing, Hunting, and Wildlife-Associated Recreation*.

No. 411. Participation in Various Leisure Activities: 1992

[In percent, except as indicated. Covers activities engaged in at least once in the prior 12 months. See headnote, table 419. See also table 420]

ITEM	Adult popu- lation (mil.)	ATTENDANCE AT—				PARTICIPATION IN—				
		Movies	Sports events	Amuse- ment park	Exercise program	Playing sports	Outdoor activ- ities [1]	Home improve- ment/ repair	Gar- dening
Total.	185.8	59	37	50	60	39	34	48	55
Sex: Male	89.0	60	44	51	61	50	39	53	46
Female	96.8	59	30	50	59	29	29	42	62
Race: White	158.8	60	38	51	61	40	37	50	57
Black	21.1	54	32	45	51	32	10	32	39
Other	5.9	62	20	46	51	38	28	31	42
Age: 18 to 24 years old	24.1	82	51	68	67	59	43	33	31
25 to 34 years old.	42.4	70	47	68	67	52	41	47	51
35 to 44 years old.	39.8	68	43	58	62	44	42	58	57
45 to 54 years old.	27.7	58	35	44	62	34	36	57	64
55 to 64 years old.	21.2	40	23	30	56	21	21	53	63
65 to 74 years old.	18.3	34	20	29	50	18	21	42	63
75 to 96 years old.	12.3	19	7	14	34	7	5	20	55
Education: Grade school	14.3	16	9	24	24	10	11	24	44
Some high school	18.6	35	19	35	39	18	21	34	50
High school graduate.	69.4	54	33	51	55	34	31	47	53
Some college.	39.2	21	45	59	71	49	42	53	55
College graduate	26.2	77	51	58	75	55	42	52	61
Graduate school	18.1	81	51	54	79	57	51	65	65

[1] Camping, hiking, and canoeing.

Source: U.S. National Endowment for the Arts, *Arts Participation in America: 1982 to 1992*.

No. 412. Selected Spectator Sports: 1985 to 1994

[See also *Historical Statistics, Colonial Times to 1970,* series H 865-870 and H 872]

SPORT	Unit	1985	1987	1989	1990	1991	1992	1993	1994
Baseball, major leagues: [1]									
Attendance	1,000	47,742	53,182	55,910	55,512	57,820	56,852	71,237	(NA)
Regular season	1,000	46,824	52,011	55,173	54,824	56,814	55,873	70,257	(NA)
National League	1,000	22,292	24,734	25,324	24,492	24,696	24,113	36,924	25,808
American League	1,000	24,532	27,277	29,849	30,332	32,118	31,760	33,333	(NA)
Playoffs	1,000	591	784	514	479	633	668	636	(X)
World Series	1,000	327	387	223	209	373	311	344	(X)
Players' salaries: [2]									
Average	$1,000	371	412	497	598	851	1,029	1,076	1,168
Basketball: [3][4]									
NCAA—Men's college:									
Teams	Number	753	760	772	767	796	813	831	858
Attendance	1,000	26,584	26,798	28,270	28,741	29,250	29,378	28,527	28,390
NCAA—Women's college:									
Teams	Number	746	756	765	782	806	815	826	859
Attendance	1,000	2,072	2,156	2,502	2,777	3,013	3,397	4,193	4,557
Pro: [5]									
Teams	Number	23	23	25	27	27	27	27	27
Attendance, total [6]	1,000	11,534	13,190	16,586	18,586	18,009	18,609	19,117	19,333
Regular season	1,000	10,506	12,065	15,465	17,369	16,876	17,367	17,778	17,984
Average per game	Number	11,141	12,795	15,088	15,690	15,245	15,689	16,060	16,246
Playoffs	1,000	985	1,091	1,077	1,203	1,109	1,228	1,338	1,349
Players' salaries:									
Average	$1,000	325	440	603	817	989	1,202	1,348	1,700
Football:									
NCAA College: [4]									
Teams	Number	509	507	524	533	548	552	560	568
Attendance	1,000	34,952	35,008	35,116	35,330	35,528	35,225	34,871	36,460
National Football League: [7]									
Teams	Number	28	28	28	28	28	28	28	(NA)
Attendance, total [8]	1,000	14,058	[9]15,180	17,400	17,666	17,752	17,784	14,772	(NA)
Regular season	1,000	13,345	[9]11,406	13,626	13,960	13,960	13,829	13,967	(NA)
Average per game	Number	59,567	[9]54,315	60,829	62,321	61,792	61,736	62,352	(NA)
Postseason games [10]	1,000	711	656	686	848	813	815	805	(NA)
Players' salaries: [11]									
Average	$1,000	194	203	295	352	415	645	683	636
Median base salary	$1,000	140	175	200	236	250	325	330	325
National Hockey league: [12]									
Regular season attendance	1,000	11,621	12,118	12,580	12,344	12,770	13,917	15,714	(NA)
Playoffs attendance	1,000	1,153	1,337	1,356	1,442	1,328	1,346	1,440	(NA)
Horseracing: [13][14]									
Racing days	Number	13,745	14,208	14,240	13,841	(NA)	13,644	13,237	13,082
Attendance	1,000	73,346	70,105	69,551	63,803	(NA)	49,275	45,688	42,065
Pari-mutuel turnover	Mil. dol.	12,222	13,122	13,867	7,162	14,094	14,078	13,718	14,143
Revenue to government	Mil. dol.	625	608	585	611	624	491.3	473	453
Greyhound: [13]									
Total performances	Number	9,590	11,156	13,393	14,915	(NA)	17,528	17,976	17,035
Attendance	1,000	23,853	26,215	33,818	28,660	(NA)	28,003	(NA)	(NA)
Pari-mutuel turnover	Mil. dol.	2,702	3,193	3,278	3,422	3,422	3,306	3,255	2,948
Revenue to government	Mil. dol.	201	221	239	235	(NA)	204.2	194.9	183.0
Jai alai: [13]									
Total performances	Number	2,736	2,906	3,835	3,620	3,619	3,288	3,200	3,146
Games played	Number	32,260	38,476	(NA)	(NA)	(NA)	45,067	43,056	42,607
Attendance	1,000	4,722	6,816	5,227	5,329	(NA)	4,634	4,194	3,684
Pari-mutuel turnover	Mil. dol.	664.0	707.5	553.0	545.5	(NA)	425.9	384.2	330.7
Revenue to government	Mil. dol.	50	51	39	39	39	30.1	26.6	21.5
Professional rodeo: [15]									
Rodeos	Number	617	637	741	754	798	791	791	782
Performances	Number	1,887	1,832	2,128	2,159	2,241	2,269	2,269	2,245
Members	Number	5,239	5,342	5,560	5,693	5,748	5,760	5,760	6,415
Permit-holders (rookies)	Number	2,534	2,746	3,584	3,290	3,006	2,888	2,888	3,346

NA Not available.   X Not applicable.   [1] Source: The National League of Professional Baseball Clubs, New York, NY, *National League Green Book;* and The American League of Professional Baseball Clubs, New York, NY, *American League Red Book.*   [2] Source: Major League Baseball Players Association, New York, NY.   [3] Season ending in year shown.   [4] Source: National Collegiate Athletic Assn., Overland Park, KS. For women's attendance total, excludes double-headers with men's teams.   [5] Source: National Basketball Assn., New York, NY.   [6] Includes All-Star game, not shown separately.   [7] Source: National Football League, New York, NY.   [8] 1988 through 1992 includes preseason attendance, not shown separately.   [9] Season was interrupted by a strike.   [10] Includes Pro Bowl, a nonchampionship game and Super Bowl.   [11] Source: National Football League Players Association, Washington, DC.   [12] For season beginning in year shown. Source: National Hockey League, Montreal, Quebec.   [13] Source: Association of Racing Commissioners International, Inc., Lexington, KY.   [14] Includes thoroughbred, harness, quarter horse, and fairs.   [15] Source: Professional Rodeo Cowboys Association, Colorado Springs, CO., *Official Professional Rodeo Media Guide,* annual, (copyright).

Source: Compiled from sources listed in footnotes.

No. 413. Selected Recreational Activities: 1975 to 1994

[See also *Historical Statistics, Colonial Times to 1970,* series H 862-864, H 871, H 874, and H 877]

ACTIVITY	Unit	1975	1980	1985	1990	1991	1992	1993	1994
Softball, amateur: [1]									
Total participants [2]	Million	26	30	41	41	41	41	42	42
Youth participants	1,000	450	650	712	1,100	1,205	1,207	1,208	1,208
Adult teams [3]	1,000	66	110	152	188	200	202	200	196
Youth teams [3]	1,000	9	18	31	46	51	57	62	68
Golfers (one round or more) [4][5]	1,000	13,036	15,112	17,520	27,800	24,800	24,800	24,600	24,300
Golf rounds played [5]	1,000	308,562	357,701	414,777	502,000	479,000	505,400	498,600	464,800
Golf facilities	Number	11,370	12,005	12,346	12,846	13,004	13,210	13,439	13,683
Classification:									
Private	Number	4,770	4,839	4,861	4,810	4,686	4,568	4,492	4,367
Daily fee	Number	5,014	5,372	5,573	6,024	6,272	6,552	6,803	7,126
Municipal	Number	1,586	1,794	1,912	2,012	2,046	2,090	2,144	2,190
Tennis: [6]									
Players	1,000	[7]34,000	(NA)	13,000	21,000	(NA)	22,630	21,500	18,700
Courts	1,000	130	(NA)	220	220	230	230	230	230
Indoor	1,000	8	(NA)	14	14	14	14	14	14
Tenpin bowling:									
Participants, total [8]	Million	62.5	72.0	67.0	71.0	82.0	82.0	79.0	(NA)
Male	Million	29.9	34.0	32.0	35.4	40.2	40.2	36.3	(NA)
Female	Million	32.6	38.0	35.0	35.6	41.8	41.8	42.6	(NA)
Establishments [9]	Number	8,577	8,591	8,275	7,544	7,395	7,250	7,183	(NA)
Lanes [9]	1,000	141	154	155	146	144	143	142	142
Membership, total [9][10]	1,000	8,751	9,595	8,064	6,357	5,881	5,601	5,202	4,925
American Bowling Congress	1,000	4,300	4,688	3,657	2,922	2,712	2,577	2,455	2,370
Women's Bowling Congress	1,000	3,692	4,118	3,714	2,742	2,523	2,403	2,191	2,036
Young American Bowling Alliance [11]	1,000	759	789	693	693	646	621	556	519
Motion picture theaters [12]	1,000	15	18	21	24	25	26	26	26
Four-wall	1,000	11	14	18	23	24	25	25	26
Drive-in	1,000	4	4	3	1	1	1	1	(Z)
Receipts, box office	Mil. dol.	2,115	2,749	3,749	5,022	4,803	4,871	5,154	5,396
Admission, average price	Dollars	2.05	2.69	3.55	4.23	4.21	4.15	4.14	4.18
Attendance	Million	1,033	1,022	1,056	1,187	1,141	1,173	1,244	1,292
Boating: [13]									
Recreational boats owned	Million	9.7	11.8	13.8	16.0	16.3	16.2	16.2	16.6
Outboard boats	Million	5.7	6.8	7.4	7.9	7.9	7.7	7.7	7.9
Inboard boats	Million	0.8	1.2	1.4	2.2	2.4	2.5	2.7	2.9
Sailboats	Million	0.8	1.0	1.2	1.3	1.3	1.3	1.3	1.3
Canoes	Million	2.4	1.3	1.8	2.3	2.4	2.4	2.4	2.4
Rowboats and other	Million	([14])	1.5	1.8	2.3	2.3	2.3	2.1	2.1
Expenditures, total [15]	Bil. dol.	4.8	7.4	13.3	13.7	10.6	10.3	11.3	14.1
Outboard motors in use	1,000	7,649	8,241	9,733	11,524	11,769	12,000	12,240	12,502
Motors sold	1,000	435	315	392	352	289	272	283	308
Value, retail	Mil. dol.	411	554	1,319	1,546	1,311	1,268	1,364	1,577
Outboard boats sold	1,000	328	290	305	227	195	192	205	220
Value, retail	Mil. dol.	263	408	759	978	871	839	914	1,122
Inboard/outdrive boats sold	1,000	70	56	115	97	73	75	75	90
Value, retail	Mil. dol.	420	616	1,663	1,794	1,293	1,239	1,244	1,669
Inboard cruisers sold	1,000	6.5	5.3	12.2	7.5	3.6	3.5	3.4	4.2
Value, retail	Mil. dol.	256	457	1,341	1,383	668	621	655	891

NA Not available.   Z Fewer than 500.   [1] Source: Amateur Softball Association, Oklahoma City, OK.   [2] Amateur Softball Association teams and other amateur softball teams.   [3] Amateur Softball Association teams only.   [4] Source: National Golf Foundation, Jupiter, FL.   [5] Prior to 1990, for persons 5 years of age and over; thereafter for persons 12 years of age and over. [6] Source: Tennis Industry Association, White Plains, NY. Players for persons 12 years old and over who played at least once. [7] 1974 data.   [8] For season ending in year shown. Persons 5 years old and over. Source: National Bowling Council, Arlington, VA.   [9] Source: American Bowling Congress, Greendale, WI. Season beginning in year shown.   [10] Membership totals are for U.S., Canada and for U.S. military personnel worldwide.   [11] Prior to 1985, represents American Jr. Bowling Congress and ABC/WIBC Collegiate Division.   [12] Source: Motion Picture Association of America, Inc., Encino, CA. Prior to 1975, figures represent theaters; thereafter, screens.   [13] Source: National Marine Manufacturers Association, Chicago, IL.   [14] Included in canoes.   [15] Represents estimated expenditures for new and used boats, motors, accessories, safety equipment, fuel, insurance, docking, maintenance, storage, repairs, and other expenses.

Source: Compiled from sources listed in footnotes.

No. 414. Participation in Selected Sports Activities: 1994

[In thousands, except rank. For persons 7 years of age or older. Except as indicated, a participant plays a sport more than once in the year. Based on a sampling of 10,000 households]

ACTIVITY	ALL PERSONS Number	ALL PERSONS Rank	SEX Male	SEX Female	AGE 7-11 years	AGE 12-17 years	AGE 18-24 years	AGE 25-34 years	AGE 35-44 years	AGE 45-54 years	AGE 55-64 years	AGE 65 years and over	HOUSEHOLD INCOME (dol.) Under 15,000	15,000-24,999	25,000-34,999	35,000-49,999	50,000-74,999	75,000 and over
Total	**232,986**	(X)	113,093	119,892	18,773	21,579	25,846	42,225	41,264	29,001	21,132	33,166	42,890	35,670	35,957	45,148	48,155	25,166
Number participated in:																		
Aerobic exercising [1]	23,200	11	4,435	18,765	464	1,083	4,566	6,945	4,994	2,236	1,280	1,633	3,161	2,898	3,281	4,799	5,404	3,657
Backpacking [2]	9,809	23	5,880	3,928	859	1,427	1,501	2,769	2,073	519	367	293	1,500	1,304	1,783	2,335	1,740	1,145
Badminton	5,424	26	2,413	3,011	1,073	1,099	733	1,104	778	447	165	24	1,010	928	992	854	1,167	473
Baseball	15,096	17	12,254	2,842	5,107	4,148	1,548	1,820	1,623	418	203	229	1,979	2,061	1,999	3,584	3,523	1,950
Basketball	28,191	8	20,492	7,699	5,554	7,951	5,165	4,768	3,462	797	287	208	3,537	4,394	4,428	5,580	6,603	3,649
Bicycle riding [1]	49,818	3	26,945	22,872	11,403	9,363	4,707	8,460	7,580	3,750	2,202	2,353	6,614	6,414	7,634	10,298	12,226	6,632
Bowling	37,356	7	19,544	17,812	4,501	4,833	6,476	9,215	6,185	2,846	1,346	1,954	5,217	5,708	5,892	8,154	7,995	4,389
Calisthenics [1]	8,536	24	3,634	4,902	1,259	1,178	1,414	1,654	1,239	682	371	738	924	1,159	1,189	1,851	2,170	1,243
Camping [3]	42,932	5	23,066	19,866	6,100	5,566	4,280	9,580	8,832	4,258	2,420	1,896	5,584	6,141	6,616	10,127	10,090	4,374
Exercise walking [1]	70,794	1	25,451	45,344	2,218	2,850	5,870	13,032	14,336	11,198	8,596	12,695	12,471	11,257	10,788	12,369	16,037	7,873
Exercise with equipment [1]	43,784	4	21,173	22,611	770	3,063	6,984	10,975	9,145	5,795	3,379	3,672	5,276	5,366	6,290	8,932	10,749	7,171
Fishing—fresh water	40,477	6	27,477	13,000	4,883	4,632	3,548	9,408	7,599	4,791	2,581	3,035	6,580	6,558	7,172	8,929	7,997	3,241
Fishing—salt water	11,515	21	7,941	3,574	855	1,037	1,026	2,532	2,668	1,353	784	1,260	1,374	1,399	1,941	2,572	2,786	1,444
Football	15,574	16	13,203	2,371	3,021	4,958	3,255	2,484	1,105	271	228	253	2,692	2,466	2,274	2,626	3,586	1,929
Golf	24,551	10	18,662	5,889	670	1,885	2,868	5,988	4,901	3,283	2,207	2,748	2,025	2,414	3,087	4,935	7,113	4,978
Hiking	25,301	9	13,976	11,326	2,710	2,811	3,125	5,690	5,440	2,808	1,432	1,285	3,350	3,826	3,248	5,058	6,339	3,480
Hunting with firearms	16,369	15	14,099	2,270	297	2,130	1,693	4,292	3,674	2,206	1,245	831	2,360	2,712	2,852	4,014	3,103	1,328
Racquetball	5,340	27	3,971	1,369	255	438	1,637	1,634	821	351	191	12	897	831	398	1,073	1,547	595
Running/jogging [1]	20,640	12	11,981	8,659	1,661	3,399	4,614	4,782	3,112	1,844	759	470	2,396	2,668	3,447	3,498	5,195	3,435
Skiing—alpine/downhill	10,620	22	6,356	4,264	646	1,966	2,493	2,683	1,620	931	173	107	741	883	1,167	2,011	2,881	2,936
Skiing—cross country	3,627	28	1,744	1,883	216	467	395	599	861	518	396	176	327	150	398	1,170	845	737
Soccer	12,508	18	8,223	4,284	5,494	3,536	1,394	1,023	778	157	59	67	1,262	1,614	1,507	2,640	3,414	2,070
Softball	18,143	13	10,162	7,982	3,292	3,567	3,070	4,340	2,667	893	246	68	1,941	2,783	3,019	3,666	4,551	2,183
Swimming	60,277	2	28,960	31,317	10,669	9,335	6,565	10,645	10,470	5,261	2,742	4,591	7,206	7,696	9,399	12,741	14,608	8,627
Table tennis	7,817	25	4,965	2,852	1,056	1,283	1,517	1,600	1,124	702	276	258	833	945	1,026	1,338	2,199	1,478
Target shooting	12,231	19	9,617	2,614	878	1,401	1,484	3,427	2,394	1,420	603	624	1,657	2,008	2,354	2,801	2,071	1,342
Tennis	11,590	20	6,535	5,055	941	2,083	2,155	2,655	1,725	1,172	480	378	1,254	1,491	1,058	1,972	3,450	2,364
Volleyball	17,383	14	8,492	8,891	1,739	4,222	3,374	4,538	2,551	591	314	55	2,455	2,744	2,627	3,689	3,984	1,882

X Not applicable. [1] Participant engaged in activity at least six times in the year. [2] Includes wilderness camping. [3] Vacation/overnight.

Source: National Sporting Goods Association, Mt. Prospect, IL, *Sports Participation in 1994: Series I* (copyright).

No. 415. Sporting Goods Sales, by Product Category: 1985 to 1995

[In millions of dollars, except percent. Based on a sample survey of consumer purchases of 80,000 households, except recreational transport, which was provided by industry associations. Excludes Alaska and Hawaii]

SELECTED PRODUCT CATEGORY	1985	1987	1988	1989	1990	1991	1992	1993	1994	1995, proj.
Sales, all products	29,608	34,875	42,080	45,638	44,886	43,659	43,682	45,412	48,732	50,557
Annual percent change [1] . . .	12.1	10.2	20.7	8.5	-1.6	-2.7	0.1	4.0	7.3	3.7
Percent of retail sales	2.2	2.3	2.5	2.6	2.4	2.4	2.2	2.2	2.2	2.2
Athletic and sport clothing [2]	3,796	4,645	9,555	10,286	10,130	10,731	8,990	8,596	8,442	8,744
Athletic and sport footwear [3]	4,025	4,457	4,940	7,488	8,290	8,342	8,303	7,853	7,837	8,095
Walking shoes	374	728	1,070	1,759	2,146	1,956	1,955	1,945	1,850	1,887
Gym shoes, sneakers	1,124	1,078	1,315	1,889	1,975	1,983	1,868	1,572	1,457	1,472
Jogging and running shoes. . . .	806	670	648	727	731	783	810	809	702	730
Tennis shoes	470	367	353	508	582	597	589	472	438	434
Aerobic shoes	178	401	327	425	389	381	376	318	226	208
Basketball shoes	277	253	338	436	638	670	680	604	600	624
Golf shoes.	109	130	128	129	157	173	182	192	167	170
Athletic and sport equipment [3] . . .	9,069	9,900	10,705	11,504	11,964	12,062	12,848	13,894	14,956	15,260
Firearms and hunting.	1,699	1,804	1,894	2,139	2,202	2,091	2,533	2,722	3,490	3,141
Exercise equipment.	1,216	1,191	1,452	1,748	1,824	2,106	2,050	2,602	2,449	2,571
Golf	730	946	1,111	1,167	1,219	1,149	1,338	1,248	1,342	1,436
Camping	724	858	945	996	1,072	1,006	903	906	1,017	1,098
Bicycles (10-12-15-18+ speed) .	975	930	819	906	1,092	(NA)	(NA)	(NA)	(NA)	(NA)
Fishing tackle.	681	830	766	769	776	711	678	716	717	731
Snow skiing	593	661	710	606	606	577	627	611	652	680
Tennis.	273	238	264	315	287	295	296	267	257	244
Archery.	212	224	235	261	265	270	334	285	312	308
Baseball and softball	176	173	174	206	217	214	245	323	305	317
Water skis	125	148	160	96	88	63	55	51	51	55
Bowling accessories	106	129	129	143	155	155	164	159	157	160
Recreational transport.	12,718	15,873	16,880	16,360	14,502	12,524	13,541	15,069	17,499	18,458
Pleasure boats	6,730	8,906	9,637	9,319	7,644	5,862	5,765	6,246	7,679	8,447
Recreational vehicles	3,717	4,507	4,839	4,481	4,113	3,615	4,412	4,775	5,690	5,871
Bicycles and supplies	2,109	2,272	2,131	2,259	2,423	2,686	2,973	3,534	3,470	3,435
Snowmobiles	162	188	273	301	322	362	391	515	659	705

NA Not available.   [1] Represents change from immediate prior year.   [2] Category expanded in 1988; not comparable with earlier years.   [3] Includes other products not shown separately.

Source: National Sporting Goods Association, Mt. Prospect, IL, *The Sporting Goods Market in 1995*; and prior issues (copyright).

No. 416. Consumer Purchases of Sporting Goods, by Consumer Characteristics: 1994

[In percent. Based on sample survey of consumer purchases of 80,000 households. Excludes Alaska and Hawaii]

CHARACTERISTIC	Total house-holds	FOOTWEAR				EQUIPMENT					
		Aerobic shoes	Gym shoes/ sneakers	Jogging/ running shoes	Walking shoes	Fishing tackle	Camping equipment	Exercise equipment	Hunting equipment guns	Team sports equipment	Golf equipment
Total.	100.0	100.0	100.0	100.0	100.0	100.0	100.0	100.0	100.0	100.0	100.0
Age of user:											
Under 14 years old	21	8.4	41.3	11.6	5.1	8	12	1	4	48	8
14 to 17 years old	5	3.8	9.6	10.6	2.8	3	8	2	4	20	8
18 to 24 years old	10	10.4	5.4	6.0	3.3	5	8	3	7	8	5
25 to 34 years old	16	29.8	12.4	19.1	11.9	18	22	21	27	11	18
35 to 44 years old	16	21.0	13.0	23.8	18.2	24	22	27	31	7	18
45 to 64 years old	19	21.6	13.3	24.8	34.9	28	19	34	22	3	33
65 years old and over	13	5.0	5.0	4.1	23.8	4	2	8	4	1	10
Multiple ages	-	-	-	-	-	9	7	4	1	1	-
Sex of user:											
Male	49	10.1	53.5	58.0	38.2	82	66	40	88	80	81
Female	51	89.9	46.5	42.0	61.8	12	28	55	11	20	18
Both sexes.	-	-	-	-	-	6	6	5	1	1	-
Education of household head:											
Less than high school	10	4.8	5.8	5.0	6.6	9	5	4	7	4	2
High school	26	20.8	26.6	14.7	24.8	26	19	18	25	18	13
Some college	34	36.9	34.4	31.6	34.8	39	36	37	40	32	32
College graduate.	30	37.5	33.2	48.7	33.8	27	39	40	27	44	53
Annual household income:											
Under $15,000	22	10.8	10.3	8.0	13.6	10	8	6	12	6	4
$15,000 to $24,999	17	14.4	13.6	11.0	15.8	16	13	8	16	10	7
$25,000 to $34,999	15	14.8	15.4	14.1	15.6	17	15	13	13	11	14
$35,000 to $49,999	18	18.6	23.5	19.6	19.5	21	22	21	24	21	15
$50,000 to $74,999	17	23.0	22.6	23.9	21.5	21	24	27	24	29	27
$75,000 and over	11	18.4	14.6	23.4	14.0	14	17	25	12	22	33

- Represents or rounds to zero.

Source: National Sporting Goods Association, Mt. Prospect, IL, *The Sporting Goods Market in 1995* (copyright).

No. 417. Gun Ownership: 1974 to 1993

[In percent. For the 50 States and DC, except prior to 1984 excludes Alaska and Hawaii. Represents respondents indicating there is a gun in the home or garage. Based on samples of noninstitutionalized English speaking persons 18 years old and older. For details, see source]

CHARACTERISTIC	1974	1976	1980	1984	1987	1990	1991	TYPE OF FIREARM, 1993			
								Total [1]	Pistol	Shotgun	Rifle
Total	46	47	48	45	46	43	40	42	24	27	23
Age:											
18 to 20 years old. . . .	34	38	48	44	43	40	22	48	21	34	21
21 to 29 years old. . . .	48	45	48	37	35	34	36	38	21	23	17
30 to 49 years old. . . .	49	52	50	48	51	46	40	44	27	27	24
50 years old and older.	44	44	46	49	47	42	42	42	22	28	25
Sex:											
Male.	51	52	56	53	51	53	50	53	28	38	31
Female	42	43	41	40	43	34	32	34	20	19	17
Race:											
White	48	58	50	48	49	45	42	45	25	29	26
Black/other	32	37	29	30	33	29	29	26	17	14	9
Education:											
Grade school	49	42	51	43	44	47	39	47	18	30	27
High school	48	50	51	48	50	47	46	46	25	32	27
College	42	44	41	42	43	37	34	38	24	22	20
Religion:											
Protestant	52	53	56	52	52	48	46	47	27	31	26
Catholic.	37	36	36	34	36	36	30	36	17	23	20
Jewish	7	26	6	22	25	6	10	9	-	4	4
None	40	43	39	36	39	34	31	37	24	17	20
Politics:											
Republican	49	50	53	56	51	48	42	51	29	34	28
Democrat	45	45	46	42	44	40	41	35	18	21	17
Independent.	47	48	47	40	44	42	37	42	26	28	25

- Represents or rounds to zero.   [1] Includes other types of firearms, not shown separately.

Source: U.S. Bureau of Justice Statistics, *Sourcebook of Criminal Justice Statistics,* annual.

No. 418. Arts and Humanities—Selected Federal Aid Programs: 1980 to 1994

[In millions of dollars, except as indicated. For fiscal years ending in year shown, see text, section 9]

TYPE OF FUND AND PROGRAM	1980	1985	1988	1989	1990	1991	1992	1993	1994
National Endowment for the Arts:									
Funds available [1]	188.1	171.7	171.1	166.7	170.8	166.5	163.0	159.7	158.1
Program appropriation	97.0	118.7	122.2	123.5	124.3	124.6	123.0	120.0	116.3
Matching funds [2]	42.9	29.5	32.9	23.6	32.4	32.4	30.3	27.4	29.4
Grants awarded (number).	5,505	4,801	4,628	4,604	4,475	4,239	4,229	4,096	3,843
Funds obligated [3]	166.4	149.4	156.3	148.3	157.6	158.0	154.6	148.4	145.2
Music.	13.6	15.3	15.3	15.3	16.5	14.1	14.9	12.4	10.9
State programs	22.1	24.4	24.9	25.5	26.1	37.7	37.0	42.0	40.7
Museums	11.2	11.9	12.6	12.7	12.1	11.3	11.1	9.9	9.4
Theater	8.4	10.6	10.7	10.7	10.6	9.4	9.4	8.3	8.8
Dance	8.0	9.0	9.2	9.5	9.6	8.5	8.2	7.9	7.6
Media arts	8.4	9.9	12.4	12.7	13.9	11.8	12.0	10.2	10.9
Challenge [4]	50.8	20.7	24.8	15.4	19.7	19.7	13.8	11.7	9.6
Visual arts.	7.3	6.2	6.0	6.1	5.9	5.3	5.6	5.1	4.8
Other.	36.6	41.3	40.4	40.2	43.1	40.2	42.7	40.9	42.5
National Endowment for the Humanities:									
Funds available [1]	186.2	125.6	125.2	137.1	140.6	152.1	156.5	158.5	157.9
Program appropriation	100.3	95.2	96.7	108.3	114.2	125.1	131.2	131.9	131.4
Matching funds [2]	38.4	30.4	28.5	28.7	26.3	27.0	25.2	26.5	26.5
Grants awarded (number).	2,917	2,241	2,113	2,285	2,195	2,171	2,199	2,197	1,881
Funds obligated [3]	185.5	125.7	125.2	137.1	141.0	149.8	159.1	160.3	159.0
Education programs	18.3	17.9	16.6	16.5	16.3	18.5	20.0	20.8	19.6
State programs	26.0	24.4	25.3	29.0	29.6	30.8	31.8	32.4	32.2
Research grants	32.0	24.4	21.9	22.1	22.5	24.0	25.3	23.7	23.4
Fellowship program	18.0	15.3	15.3	15.3	15.3	16.2	17.4	18.9	17.7
Challenge [4]	53.5	19.6	16.5	16.7	14.6	15.1	12.4	14.2	14.4
Public programs.	25.1	24.1	24.9	25.1	25.4	25.3	27.0	26.7	27.5
Preservation and access [5]	(X)	(X)	4.7	12.3	17.5	19.9	25.1	23.5	24.1
National Capital Arts and Cultural									
Affairs Program	(X)	(X)	(X)	(X)	(X)	(X)	(X)	(X)	(X)
Other.	12.6	(X)	(X)	(X)	(X)	(X)	(X)	(X)	(X)

X Not applicable.   [1] Includes other funds, shown separately. Excludes administrative funds. Gifts are included through 1980; excluded thereafter.   [2] Represents Federal funds obligated only upon receipt or certification by Endowment of matching non-Federal gifts.   [3] Includes obligations for new grants, supplemental awards on previous years' grants, and program contracts.   [4] Program designed to stimulate new sources and higher levels of giving to institutions for the purpose of guaranteeing long-term stability and financial independence. Program requires a match of at least 3 private dollars to each Federal dollar. Funds for challenge grants are not allocated by program area because they are awarded on a grant-by-grant basis.   [5] Program designed to support projects which preserve and guarantee access to print and nonprint media in danger of disintegration or deterioration.

Source: U.S. National Endowment for the Arts, *Annual Report;* and U.S. National Endowment for the Humanities, *Annual Report.*

Parks, Recreation, and Travel

No. 419. Attendance Rates for Various Arts Activities: 1992

[In percent. For persons 18 years old and over. Excludes elementary and high school performances. Based on 1992 household survey Public Participation in the Arts conducted January through December 1992. Data are subject to sampling error; see source. See also tables 411 and 420]

ITEM	ATTENDANCE AT LEAST ONCE IN THE PRIOR 12 MONTHS AT—								Reading litera-ture [1]
	Jazz perfor-mance	Classical music perfor-mance	Opera	Musical play	Non-musical play	Ballet	Art museum	Historic park	
Total	11	13	3	17	14	5	27	35	54
Sex: Male.	12	12	3	15	12	4	27	35	47
Female.	9	13	4	20	15	6	27	34	60
Race: White	10	13	3	18	14	5	28	37	56
Black	16	7	2	14	12	3	19	18	45
Other.	6	12	5	11	10	6	29	23	42
Age: 18 to 24 years old . .	11	10	3	16	13	5	29	33	53
25 to 34 years old	14	10	3	16	12	5	29	36	54
35 to 44 years old	13	12	3	19	14	5	30	40	59
45 to 54 years old	11	17	4	22	17	5	29	41	57
55 to 64 years old	8	15	4	19	15	5	25	33	53
65 to 74 years old	7	14	4	17	13	4	20	29	50
75 to 96 years old	2	8	2	9	7	2	10	12	40
Education: Grade school. .	1	2	1	3	2	1	4	8	17
Some high school.	2	3	1	5	4	1	7	15	32
High school graduate . .	6	7	1	12	8	2	16	26	49
Some college	14	14	3	21	16	6	35	43	65
College graduate	20	23	6	30	23	9	46	52	71
Graduate school.	25	36	12	37	35	12	59	64	79
Income: Under $5,000 . . .	6	5	2	8	8	2	12	17	37
$5,000 to $9,999	5	6	1	7	6	3	14	16	40
$10,000 to $14,999. . . .	5	6	2	8	7	2	13	20	43
$15,000 to $24,999. . . .	9	11	2	14	11	3	23	31	50
$25,000 to $49,999. . . .	11	13	3	18	14	5	29	40	58
$50,000 and over.	18	23	8	33	24	10	44	51	71
Not reported	11	13	4	18	15	5	28	33	50

[1] Includes novels, short stories, poetry, or plays.

Source: U.S. National Endowment for the Arts, *Arts Participation in America: 1982 to 1992.*

No. 420. Participation in Various Arts Activities: 1992

[In percent, except as indicated. Covers activities engaged in at least once in the prior 12 months. See headnote, table 419. See also table 411]

ITEM	Adult popu-lation (mil.)	IN THE PAST 12 MONTHS PERCENT ENGAGED AT LEAST ONCE IN—							
		Playing classical music	Modern danc-ing [1]	Pottery work [2]	Needle-work [3]	Photo-graphy [4]	Paint-ing [5]	Creative writing	Buying art work
Total.	185.8	4	8	8	25	12	10	7	22
Sex: Male	89.0	3	8	8	5	13	9	7	22
Female	96.8	5	8	9	43	10	10	8	22
Race: White	158.8	4	8	9	26	12	10	7	24
Black	21.1	3	8	8	15	11	5	6	12
Other	5.9	5	9	5	24	9	10	11	8
Age: 18 to 24 years old	24.1	6	11	9	18	11	19	14	13
25 to 34 years old	42.4	3	10	10	24	15	10	7	19
35 to 44 years old	39.8	4	7	10	25	13	10	8	27
45 to 54 years old	27.7	5	6	9	26	13	8	7	29
55 to 64 years old	21.2	5	6	6	27	10	6	5	26
65 to 74 years old	18.3	4	9	6	29	7	6	5	20
75 to 96 years old	12.3	3	5	3	26	2	4	2	17
Education: Grade school	14.3	1	4	2	22	3	1	(Z)	4
Some high school	18.6	1	4	7	25	5	5	3	11
High school graduate.	69.4	2	8	8	25	9	9	4	15
Some college	39.2	6	10	12	26	15	13	11	27
College graduate	26.2	8	8	9	26	16	12	12	32
Graduate school	18.1	9	10	8	21	22	13	16	49
Income: Under $5,000.	8.6	2	7	7	22	6	8	7	10
$5,000 to $9,999	15.2	2	7	4	27	7	8	7	10
$10,000 to $14,999	19.2	3	7	8	26	8	8	6	14
$15,000 to $24,999	32.9	4	9	8	26	9	10	7	17
$25,000 to $49,999	62.2	5	8	10	25	13	10	7	22
$50,000 and over	32.1	6	8	8	23	17	11	9	40
Not reported	15.6	4	8	8	24	12	11	9	24

Z Less than .05 percent. [1] Dancing other than ballet (e.g. folk and tap). [2] Includes ceramics, jewelry, leatherwork, and metalwork. [3] Includes weaving, crocheting, quilting, and sewing. [4] Includes making movies or video as an artistic activity. [5] Includes drawing, sculpture, and printmaking.

Source: U.S. National Endowment for the Arts, *Arts Participation in America: 1982 to 1992.*

No. 421. Performing Arts—Selected Data: 1980 to 1994

[Receipts and expenditures in millions of dollars. For season ending in year shown, except as indicated]

ITEM	1980	1985	1987	1988	1989	1990	1991	1992	1993	1994
Legitimate theater: [1]										
Broadway shows:										
New productions	67	31	40	31	29	35	28	36	(NA)	(NA)
Playing weeks [2] [3]	1,541	1,062	1,031	1,114	1,097	1,062	970	901	(NA)	(NA)
Number of tickets sold (1,000)	9,380	7,156	6,968	8,142	7,968	8,039	7,314	7,365	(NA)	(NA)
Gross box office receipts	143.4	208.0	207.2	253.4	262.0	283.3	267.2	292.4	(NA)	(NA)
Road shows:										
Playing weeks [3]	1,351	993	901	893	869	944	1,152	1,171	(NA)	(NA)
Gross box office receipts	181.2	225.9	224.2	222.9	255.5	367.1	450.2	502.7	(NA)	(NA)
Nonprofit professional theatres: [4]										
Companies reporting	147	217	188	189	192	185	184	182	177	231
Gross income	113.6	234.7	271.2	276.4	349.0	307.6	333.9	359.1	342.5	455.1
Earned income	67.3	146.1	165.2	167.0	224.6	188.4	202.6	222.5	209.7	277.4
Contributed income	46.3	88.6	106.0	109.4	124.4	119.2	131.3	136.6	132.8	177.7
Gross expenses	113.6	239.3	272.8	277.9	349.2	306.3	336.7	365.6	349.3	460.2
Productions	1,852	2,710	2,427	2,369	2,469	2,265	2,277	2,310	2,319	2,929
Performances	42,109	52,341	46,768	46,149	53,263	46,131	48,695	46,184	44,933	59,542
Total attendance (mil.)	14.2	14.2	14.6	13.9	18.7	15.2	16.9	16.0	16.5	20.7
OPERA America professional member companies: [5]										
Number of companies [6]	79	97	100	99	101	98	98	100	(NA)	(NA)
Expenses [6]	122.4	216.4	260.1	294.4	311.7	321.2	346.7	371.8	(NA)	(NA)
Performances [7]	1,372	1,909	2,254	2,378	2,429	2,336	2,283	2,424	(NA)	(NA)
Total attendance (mil.) [7] [8]	5.5	6.7	6.6	6.8	7.4	7.5	7.6	7.3	(NA)	(NA)
Main season attendance (mil.) [7] [9]	(NA)	3.3	3.8	3.9	4.0	4.1	4.3	4.3	(NA)	(NA)
Symphony orchestras: [10]										
Concerts	(NA)	19,573	19,319	21,306	20,630	18,931	18,074	19,778	18,599	17,795
Attendance (mil.)	(NA)	24.0	24.5	27.4	25.8	24.7	26.7	26.3	24.3	24.4
Gross revenue	(NA)	252.4	306.9	325.3	353.2	377.5	394.5	414.0	429.8	442.5
Concert income	(NA)	168.6	200.4	218.0	231.0	253.3	273.8	284.1	293.4	303.6
Endowment income	(NA)	(NA)	(NA)	42.6	46.8	52.1	52.5	55.3	59.8	60.4
Other earned income	(NA)	83.8	106.5	64.7	75.4	72.1	68.2	74.6	76.6	78.5
Operating expenses	(NA)	426.1	503.5	541.2	583.5	621.7	662.2	683.0	690.5	710
Artistic personnel	(NA)	231.9	270.0	288.0	310.2	327.3	355.8	398.9	378.9	389.9
Concert production	(NA)	69.2	79.5	85.8	89.0	104.3	110.3	117.2	114.3	129.3
Advertising and promotion	(NA)	32.5	40.4	42.0	47.5	51.3	57.3	58.3	63.3	67.3
General and administrative	(NA)	51.3	59.4	61.5	68.4	73.3	75.6	76.2	73.7	74.4
Other	(NA)	41.3	54.3	63.9	68.4	65.6	63.2	32.4	60.3	49.1
Support	(NA)	188.1	219.5	229.2	249.0	257.8	281.2	279.6	293.9	293.1
Tax supported grants	(NA)	42.2	49.3	52.1	54.5	55.6	58.3	49.1	48.2	46.4
Private sector support	(NA)	145.9	170.1	177.1	194.5	202.1	222.9	230.5	245.8	246.7

NA Not available. [1] Source: *Variety,* New York, NY, various June issues, (copyright). [2] All shows (new productions and holdovers from previous seasons). [3] Eight performances constitute one playing week. [4] Source: Theatre Communications Group, New York, NY. For years ending on or prior to Aug. 31. [5] Source: OPERA America, Washington, DC. [6] United States companies. [7] United States and Canadian companies. [8] Includes educational performances, outreach, etc. [9] For paid performances. [10] Source: American Symphony Orchestra League, Inc., Washington, DC. For years ending Aug. 31. Data represent all United States orchestras, excluding college/university and youth orchestras.

Source: Compiled from sources listed in footnotes.

No. 422. Boy Scouts and Girl Scouts—Membership and Units: 1970 to 1994

[In thousands. Boy Scouts as of Dec. 31; Girl Scouts as of Sept. 30. Includes Puerto Rico and outlying areas]

ITEM	1970	1975	1980	1985	1988	1989	1990	1991	1992	1993	1994
BOY SCOUTS OF AMERICA											
Membership	6,287	5,318	4,318	4,845	5,364	5,356	5,448	5,319	5,334	5,354	5,378
Boys	4,683	3,933	3,207	3,755	4,228	4,247	4,293	4,150	4,146	4,165	4,188
Adults	1,604	1,385	1,110	1,090	1,136	1,109	1,155	1,168	1,188	1,189	1,190
Total units (packs, troops, posts, groups)	157	150	129	134	131	130	130	128	128	128	129
GIRL SCOUTS OF THE U.S.A.											
Membership	3,922	3,234	2,784	2,802	3,052	3,166	3,269	3,383	3,510	3,438	3,363
Girls	3,248	2,723	2,250	2,172	2,345	2,415	2,480	2,561	2,647	2,612	2,561
Adults	674	511	534	630	707	751	788	822	863	826	802
Total units (troops, groups)	164	159	154	166	189	196	202	210	219	221	218

Source: Boy Scouts of America, National Council, Irving, TX, *Annual Report;* and Girl Scouts of the United States of America, New York, NY, *Annual Report.*

No. 423. Travel by U.S. Residents—Summary: 1985 to 1994

[In millions, except party size. See headnote table 424]

TYPE OF TRIP	1985	1987	1988	1989	1990	1991	1992	1993	1994
All travel: Total trips [1]	497.8	567.3	584.9	592.2	589.4	592.4	650.7	648.2	688.2
Person trips	808.3	893.5	924.5	945.2	956.0	980.1	1,063.0	1,057.5	1,127.4
Party size	1.5	1.6	1.6	1.6	1.6	1.7	1.6	1.6	1.6
Business travel: Total trips	156.6	185.0	182.8	199.3	182.8	176.9	210.8	210.4	220.8
Person trips	196.1	218.3	224.1	245.6	221.8	224.0	278.0	275.4	289.1
Party size	1.3	1.2	1.2	1.2	1.2	1.3	1.3	1.3	1.3
Pleasure travel: Total trips	301.2	348.6	356.7	358.3	361.1	364.3	411.7	413.4	434.3
Person trips	539.5	603.0	620.5	632.5	649.4	666.6	736.4	740.0	781.2
Party size	1.8	1.7	1.7	1.8	1.8	1.8	1.8	1.8	1.8
Vacation travel: Total trips	264.5	285.0	308.4	324.4	328.7	327.7	352.8	352.2	366.7
Person trips	487.8	518.9	556.2	587.9	591.6	605.3	637.1	633.2	671.3
Party size	1.8	1.8	1.8	1.8	1.8	1.9	1.8	1.8	1.8

[1] Includes other trips, not shown separately.

Source: U.S. Travel Data Center, Washington, DC, *National Travel Survey*, annual, (copyright).

No. 424. Characteristics of Business Trips and Pleasure Trips: 1985 to 1994

[Represents trips to places 100 miles or more from home by one or more household members traveling together. Based on a monthly telephone survey of 1,500 U.S. adults. For details, see source]

CHARACTERISTIC	Unit	BUSINESS TRIPS				PLEASURE TRIPS			
		1985	1990	1993	1994	1985	1990	1993	1994
Total trips	Million	156.6	182.8	210.4	220.8	301.2	361.1	413.4	434.3
Average household members on trip	Number	1.3	1.2	1.3	1.3	1.8	1.8	1.8	1.8
Average nights per trip [1]	Nights	3.6	3.7	3.5	3.0	5.6	4.4	4.0	3.7
Average miles per trip [2]	Miles	1,180	1,020	1,192	1,027	1,010	867	858	821
Traveled primarily by auto/truck/RV [3] rental car	Percent	51	58	55	56	73	77	79	78
Traveled primarily by air	Percent	44	37	43	43	21	18	18	17
Used a rental car while on trip	Percent	20	14	26	23	6	7	9	9
Stayed in a hotel while on trip	Percent	62	71	73	70	39	37	40	40
Used a travel agent	Percent	28	21	25	24	13	12	8	8
Also a vacation trip	Percent	13	17	14	12	80	82	76	75
Male travelers	Percent	67	71	72	74	48	49	55	52
Female travelers	Percent	33	29	28	26	52	51	45	48
Household income:									
Less than $40,000	Percent	58	42	30	21	73	63	47	49
$40,000 or more	Percent	42	56	70	79	27	38	53	51

[1] Includes no overnight stays.   [2] United States only.   [3] Recreational vehicle.

Source: U.S. Travel Data Center, Washington, DC, *National Travel Survey*, annual, (copyright).

No. 425. Arrangement of Passenger Transportation—Receipts and and Expenses, by Source: 1989 to 1994

[In millions of dollars. For taxable employer firms. Data are for SIC 472. Based on the 1987 Standard Industrial Classification code; see text, section 13]

ITEM	1989	1990	1991	1992	1993	1994
RECEIPTS						
Total	9,822	10,921	10,152	10,573	11,073	11,795
Air carriers	5,401	5,837	5,527	5,881	6,138	6,375
Water carriers	394	474	520	523	528	584
Hotels and motels	693	771	676	744	758	808
Motor coaches	343	403	385	379	388	397
Railroads	106	127	130	110	125	126
Rental cars	157	175	171	187	189	204
Packaged tours	1,978	2,250	1,931	1,989	2,158	2,425
Other	750	884	812	760	789	876
EXPENSES						
Total	8,799	9,912	9,469	9,705	10,136	10,889
Annual payroll	3,468	3,891	3,740	3,924	4,031	4,526
Employer contributions to Social Security and other supplemental benefits	464	519	516	526	558	628
Lease and rental payments	825	919	874	873	908	908
Advertising and promotion	588	722	636	653	713	746
Taxes and licenses	148	158	134	135	144	163
Utilities	295	352	341	371	386	388
Depreciation	371	409	379	326	339	361
Purchased office supplies	306	321	295	300	294	325
Purchased repair services	124	156	139	124	134	152
Other	2,210	2,465	2,415	2,473	2,629	2,692

Source: U.S. Bureau of the Census, *Current Business Reports, Service Annual Survey: 1994*, BS/94.

No. 426. Domestic Travel Expenditures, by State: 1993

[Represents U.S. spending on domestic overnight trips and day trips of 100 miles or more away from home. Excludes spending by foreign visitors and by U.S. residents in U.S. territories and abroad]

STATE	Total (mil. dol.)	Share of total (per-cent)	Rank	STATE	Total (mil. dol.)	Share of total (per-cent)	Rank	STATE	Total (mil. dol.)	Share of total (per-cent)	Rank
U.S., total .	323,272	100	(X)	KS	2,457	0.8	37	ND	828	0.3	50
				KY	3,567	1.1	29	OH	8,546	2.6	11
AL	3,682	1.1	28	LA	4,848	1.5	22	OK	2,698	0.8	35
AK	1,085	0.3	46	ME	1,483	0.5	40	OR	3,795	1.2	27
AZ	5,525	1.7	19	MD	4,922	1.5	21	PA	10,060	3.2	8
AR	2,745	0.8	33	MA	7,452	2.3	14	RI	708	0.2	51
CA	42,480	13.1	1	MI	7,498	2.3	13	SC	4,831	1.5	23
CO	6,122	1.9	17	MN	4,492	1.4	24	SD	834	0.3	49
CT	3,458	1.1	30	MS	2,236	0.7	38	TN	6,779	2.1	15
DE	836	0.3	48	MO	6,215	1.9	16	TX	20,215	6.3	3
DC	3,169	1	31	MT	1,434	0.4	42	UT	2,712	0.8	34
FL	28,629	8.9	2	NE	1,751	0.5	39	VT	1,030	0.3	47
GA	9,186	2.8	9	NV	12,539	3.9	6	VA	9,076	2.8	10
HI	5,866	1.8	18	NH	1,408	0.4	43	WA	5,318	1.6	20
ID	1,462	0.5	41	NJ	11,134	3.4	7	WV	1,371	0.4	44
IL	13,804	4.3	5	NM	2,695	0.8	36	WI	4,453	1.4	25
IN	4,220	1.3	26	NY	19,950	6.2	4	WY	1,142	0.4	45
IA	2,746	0.8	32	NC	7,884	2.4	12				

X Not applicable.
Source: U.S. Travel Data Center, Washington, DC, *Impact of Travel on State Economies, 1993* (copyright).

No. 427. International Travelers and Expenditures, With Projections: 1970 to 1995

[For coverage, see tables 428 and 429. Beginning 1985, receipts, payments, and fares not comparable with previous years. See source for details. Minus sign (-) indicates deficit. See also *Historical Statistics, Colonial Times to 1970,* series H 921, 928, 941, and 945]

YEAR	TRAVEL AND PASSENGER FARE (mil. dol.)				U.S. net travel and passenger payments (mil. dol.)	U.S. travelers to foreign countries (1,000)	Foreign visitors to the U.S. (1,000)
	Payments by U.S. travelers		Receipts from foreign visitors				
	Total [1]	Expenditures abroad	Total [1]	Travel receipts			
1970	5,195	3,980	2,708	2,331	-2,487	(NA)	12,362
1980	14,004	10,397	12,650	10,588	-1,354	[2]22,365	22,326
1985	31,042	24,558	22,173	17,762	-8,869	34,715	25,399
1987	36,593	29,310	30,566	23,563	-6,027	39,410	29,500
1988	39,843	32,114	38,409	29,434	-1,434	40,669	34,095
1989	41,666	33,418	46,863	36,250	5,197	41,138	36,564
1990	47,879	37,349	58,305	43,007	10,426	44,623	39,539
1991	45,334	35,322	64,237	48,384	18,904	41,566	42,986
1992	49,614	39,007	71,257	54,284	21,642	43,897	47,261
1993	51,980	40,564	74,171	57,621	22,191	44,385	45,779
1994, est. . .	55,618	43,059	77,653	60,001	22,035	46,426	45,504
1995, proj. .	57,900	44,825	76,485	58,370	18,585	47,419	42,983

NA Not available. [1] Includes passenger fares not shown separately. [2] Mexico visitation data are under-reported.
Source: Travelers and visitors: U.S. Travel and Tourism Administration (USTTA), and unpublished data. Fares and Payments: Through 1980, U.S. Bureau of Economic Analysis, (BEA) *Survey of Current Business;* beginning 1985, USTTA, based on data from BEA.

No. 428. U.S. Travel to Foreign Countries, With Projections: 1985 to 1995

[**Travelers in thousands; expenditures in millions of dollars.** Covers residents of the United States, its territories and possessions. See source for details. See also *Historical Statistics, Colonial Times to 1970,* series H 921-940]

ITEM AND AREA	1985	1989	1990	1991	1992	1993	1994, est.	1995, proj.
Total travelers	34,715	41,138	44,623	41,566	43,897	44,385	46,426	47,419
Canada	11,558	12,184	12,252	12,003	11,818	11,998	12,543	12,920
Mexico	10,461	14,163	16,381	15,042	16,114	15,285	15,759	15,759
Total overseas	12,696	14,791	15,990	14,521	15,965	17,102	18,124	18,740
Europe	6,780	7,233	8,043	6,316	7,136	7,491	(NA)	(NA)
Latin America [1]	3,592	4,392	4,749	5,155	5,285	5,729	(NA)	(NA)
Other	2,324	3,166	3,198	3,050	3,544	3,882	(NA)	(NA)
Expenditures abroad.	24,558	33,418	37,349	35,322	39,007	40,564	43,059	44,825
Canada	2,506	3,396	3,541	3,705	3,554	3,692	3,826	(NA)
Mexico	2,548	4,276	4,879	5,111	5,159	5,158	5,062	(NA)
Total overseas	19,504	25,746	28,929	26,506	30,293	31,714	34,172	(NA)
Europe	9,403	11,967	13,996	11,524	13,951	14,437	15,512	(NA)
Latin America [1]	3,995	5,123	5,395	3,072	6,351	6,987	7,570	(NA)
Other	6,106	8,656	9,538	11,910	9,991	10,290	11,090	(NA)
Fares to foreign carriers	6,444	8,248	10,530	10,012	10,608	11,416	12,558	(NA)

NA Not available. [1] Includes Central and South America and the Caribbean.
Source: Travelers: U.S. Travel and Tourism Administration (USTTA), unpublished data. Expenditures: USTTA, based on data from the Bureau of Economic Analysis.

No. 429. Foreign Travel to the United States, With Projections: 1985 to 1995

[Travelers in thousands; receipts in millions of dollars. Includes travelers for business and pleasure, foreigners in transit through the United States, and students; excludes travel by foreign government personnel and foreign businessmen employed in the United States. See source for details. See also *Historical Statistics, Colonial Times to 1970*, series H 946-951]

AREA OF ORIGIN	1985	1989	1990	1991	1992	1993	1994, est.	1995, proj.
International travelers	25,399	36,564	39,539	42,986	47,261	45,779	45,504	42,983
Canada	10,721	15,325	17,263	19,113	18,598	17,293	14,970	13,668
Mexico	7,141	7,240	7,217	7,718	10,872	9,824	11,325	9,610
Total overseas	7,537	13,999	15,059	16,155	17,791	18,662	19,209	19,705
Europe	2,905	6,251	6,659	7,360	8,262	8,630	8,509	8,803
Latin America [1]	1,795	2,627	2,877	3,080	3,255	3,678	3,672	3,751
Other	2,837	5,121	5,523	5,715	6,274	6,354	7,028	7,151
Total travel receipts	17,762	36,250	43,007	48,384	54,284	57,621	60,001	58,370
Canada	2,580	5,385	7,093	8,499	8,182	7,458	6,321	(NA)
Mexico	2,101	3,926	5,108	5,367	5,696	5,119	4,930	(NA)
Total overseas	13,081	26,939	30,806	34,518	40,407	45,044	48,749	(NA)
Europe	4,774	11,004	12,602	14,332	17,706	19,204	20,033	(NA)
Latin America [1]	3,122	4,418	5,126	5,927	6,883	8,300	8,816	(NA)
Other	5,185	11,517	13,078	14,259	15,818	17,540	19,900	(NA)
Fares to U.S. carriers	4,411	10,613	15,298	15,854	16,972	16,550	17,651	(NA)

NA Not available.   [1] Includes Central and South America and the Caribbean.

Source: Travelers: U.S. Travel and Tourism Administration (USTTA), unpublished data. Receipts: USTTA, based on data from the Bureau of Economic Analysis.

No. 430. Foreign Visitors for Pleasure Admitted, by Country of Last Residence: 1985 to 1994

[In thousands. For years ending September 30. See headnote, table 7, section 1]

COUNTRY	1985	1990	1993	1994	COUNTRY	1985	1990	1993	1994
Total [1]	6,609	13,418	16,918	17,155	Africa [2]	101	105	127	138
					Egypt	16	16	16	17
Europe [2]	2,048	5,383	7,349	6,944	Nigeria	25	11	11	10
Austria	34	87	146	132					
Belgium	39	95	147	153	Oceania [2]	282	562	535	478
Denmark	36	75	80	79	Australia	195	380	381	334
Finland	24	83	56	48	New Zealand	74	153	117	103
France	226	566	698	686	North America	1,664	2,463	2,712	2,763
Greece	34	43	44	47	Canada	79	119	160	144
Ireland	55	81	111	126	Mexico	773	1,061	1,259	1,324
Italy	155	308	491	457	Caribbean [2]	584	963	888	886
Netherlands	82	214	302	302	Bahamas, The	211	332	289	269
Norway	41	80	79	80	Barbados	17	34	41	38
Poland	40	55	32	33	Cayman Islands	18	31	31	33
Soviet Union	2	53	47	44	Dominican Republic . .	57	137	145	150
Spain	64	183	272	236	Haiti	56	57	31	27
Sweden	71	230	178	154	Jamaica	74	132	117	129
Switzerland	110	236	283	294	Netherlands Antilles . .	27	31	39	39
United Kingdom	598	1,899	2,566	2,461	Trinidad and Tobago . .	71	81	69	68
Germany [3]	373	969	1,667	1,450	Central America [2]	228	320	405	408
					El Salvador	38	46	64	63
Asia [2]	1,866	3,830	4,501	5,023	Guatemala	53	91	104	108
China (Mainland China					Panama	38	43	55	58
and Taiwan)	83	187	289	353					
Hong Kong	64	111	141	145	South America [2]	606	1,016	1,593	1,717
India	52	75	63	67	Argentina	66	136	312	338
Israel	80	128	142	150	Brazil	148	300	446	507
Japan	1,277	2,846	3,177	3,506	Chile	28	54	91	96
Korea	26	120	270	361	Colombia	123	122	162	174
Philippines	59	76	94	87	Ecuador	42	57	70	78
Saudi Arabia	31	33	45	47	Peru	44	97	102	99
Singapore	23	32	42	47	Venezuela	122	199	343	353

[1] Includes countries unknown or not reported.   [2] Includes countries not shown separately.   [3] Data prior to 1993 for former West Germany.

Source: U.S. Immigration and Naturalization Service, *Statistical Yearbook*, annual.

Elections

This section relates primarily to Presidential, congressional, and gubernatorial elections. Also presented are summary tables on congressional legislation; State legislatures; Black, Hispanic, and female officeholders; population of voting age; voter participation; and campaign finances.

Official statistics on Federal elections, collected by the Clerk of the House, are published biennially in *Statistics of the Presidential and Congressional Election* and *Statistics of the Congressional Election*. Federal and State elections data appear also in *America Votes*, a biennial volume of the Elections Research Center, Chevy Chase, MD. Federal elections data also appear in the U.S. Congress, *Congressional Directory*, and in official State documents. Data on reported registration and voting for social and economic groups are obtained by the U.S. Bureau of the Census as part of the Current Population Survey (CPS) and are published in *Current Population Reports*, P20 (see text, section 1).

Almost all Federal, State, and local governmental units in the United States conduct elections for political offices and other purposes. The conduct of elections is regulated by State laws or, in some cities and counties, by local charter. An exception is that the U.S. Constitution prescribes the basis of representation in Congress and the manner of electing the President, and grants to Congress the right to regulate the times, places, and manner of electing Federal officers. Amendments to the Constitution have prescribed national criteria for voting eligibility. The 15th Amendment, adopted in 1870, gave all citizens the right to vote regardless of race, color, or previous condition of servitude. The 19th Amendment, adopted in 1919, further extended the right to vote to all citizens regardless of sex. The payment of poll taxes as a prerequisite to voting in Federal elections was banned by the 24th Amendment in 1964. In 1971, as a result of the 26th Amendment, eligibility to vote in national elections was extended to all citizens, 18 years old and over.

In Brief

Percent of voting-age population voting for Representatives:

1990	33.1%
1994	36.0%

Members of Congress:

	1981	1995
Black	17	41
Asian, Pacific Islander	6	6
Hispanic	6	17
Female	21	55

Presidential election—The Constitution specifies how the President and Vice President are selected. Each State elects, by popular vote, a group of electors equal in number to its total of members of Congress. The 23d Amendment, adopted in 1961, grants the District of Columbia three presidential electors, a number equal to that of the least populous State. Subsequent to the election, the electors meet in their respective States to vote for President and Vice President. Usually, each elector votes for the candidate receiving the most popular votes in his or her State. A majority vote of all electors is necessary to elect the President and Vice President. If no candidate receives a majority, the House of Representatives, with each State having one vote, is empowered to elect the President and Vice President, again, with a majority of votes required.

The 22d Amendment to the Constitution, adopted in 1951, limits presidential tenure to two elective terms of 4 years each, or to one elective term for any person who, upon succession to the Presidency, has held the office or acted as President for more than 2 years.

Congressional election—The Constitution provides that Representatives be apportioned among the States according to their population; that a census of population be taken every 10 years as a basis for apportionment; and that each State have at least one Representative. At the time of each apportionment, Congress decides what the total number of

Representatives will be. Since 1912, the total has been 435, except during 1960 to 1962 when it increased to 437, adding one Representative each for Alaska and Hawaii. The total reverted to 435 after reapportionment following the 1960 census. Members are elected for 2-year terms, all terms covering the same period. The District of Columbia, American Samoa, Guam, and the Virgin Islands each elect one nonvoting Delegate and Puerto Rico elects a nonvoting Resident Commissioner.

The Senate is composed of 100 members, two from each State, who are elected to serve for a term of 6 years. One-third of the Senate is elected every 2 years. Senators were originally chosen by the State legislatures. The 17th Amendment to the Constitution, adopted in 1913, prescribed that Senators be elected by popular vote.

Voter eligibility and participation—The Census Bureau publishes estimates of the population of voting age and the percent casting votes in each State for Presidential and congressional election years. These voting-age estimates include a number of persons who meet the age requirement but are not eligible to vote, (e.g. aliens and some institutionalized persons). In addition, since 1964, voter participation and voter characteristics data have been collected during November of election years as part of the CPS. These survey data include noncitizens in the voting age population estimates, but exclude members of the Armed Forces and the institutional population.

Statistical reliability—For a discussion of statistical collection and estimation, sampling procedures, and measures of statistical reliability applicable to Census Bureau data, see Appendix III.

Historical statistics—Tabular head-notes provide cross-references, where applicable, to *Historical Statistics of the United States, Colonial Times to 1970.* See Appendix IV.

Figure 8.1
Popular Vote Cast for President, by Major Political Party: 1972 to 1992

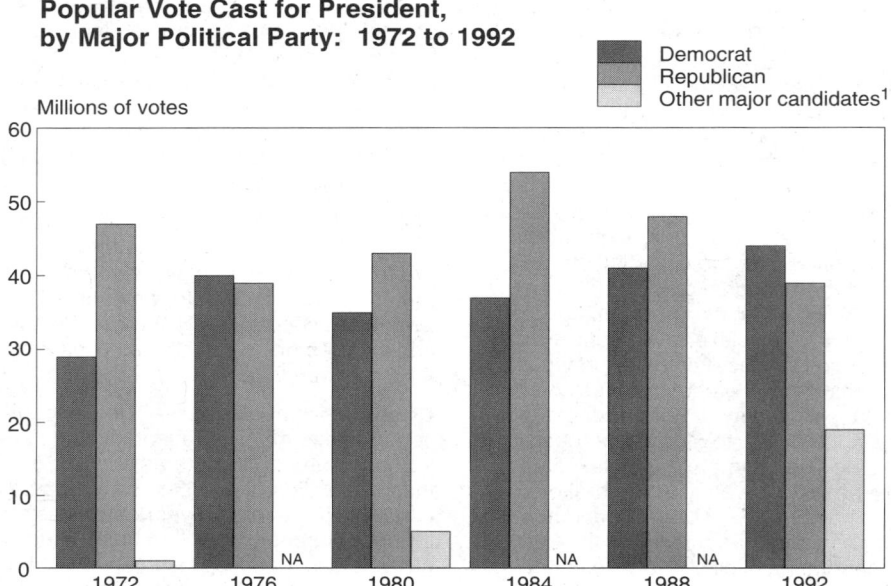

[1] 1972—American, John Schmitz; 1980—Independent, John Anderson; 1992—Independent, Ross Perot.
Source: Chart prepared by U.S. Bureau of the Census. For data, see table 431 and 432.

No. 431. Vote Cast for President, by Major Political Party: 1936 to 1992

[Prior to 1960, excludes Alaska and Hawaii; prior to 1964, excludes DC. Vote cast for major party candidates include the votes of minor parties cast for those candidates. See also *Historical Statistics, Colonial Times to 1970*, series Y 79-83 and Y 135]

YEAR	CANDIDATES FOR PRESIDENT		Total popular vote [1] (1,000)	VOTE CAST FOR PRESIDENT					
				Democratic			Republican		
	Democratic	Republican		Popular vote		Electoral vote	Popular vote		Electoral vote
				Number (1,000)	Percent		Number (1,000)	Percent	
1936	F. D. Roosevelt . .	Landon	45,655	27,757	60.8	523	16,684	36.5	8
1940	F. D. Roosevelt . .	Willkie	49,900	27,313	54.7	449	22,348	44.8	82
1944	F. D. Roosevelt . .	Dewey	47,977	25,613	53.4	432	22,018	45.9	99
1948	Truman	Dewey	48,794	24,179	49.6	303	21,991	45.1	189
1952	Stevenson	Eisenhower.	61,551	27,315	44.4	89	33,936	55.1	442
1956	Stevenson	Eisenhower.	62,027	26,023	42.0	73	35,590	57.4	457
1960	Kennedy	Nixon.	68,838	34,227	49.7	303	34,108	49.5	219
1964	Johnson.	Goldwater.	70,645	43,130	61.1	486	27,178	38.5	52
1968	Humphrey	Nixon.	73,212	31,275	42.7	191	31,785	43.4	301
1972	McGovern	Nixon.	77,719	29,170	37.5	17	47,170	60.7	520
1976	Carter	Ford	81,556	40,831	50.1	297	39,148	48.0	240
1980	Carter	Reagan	86,515	35,484	41.0	49	43,904	50.7	489
1984	Mondale.	Reagan	92,653	37,577	40.6	13	54,455	58.8	525
1988	Dukakis	Bush	91,595	41,809	45.6	111	48,886	53.4	426
1992	Clinton.	Bush	104,425	44,909	43.0	370	39,104	37.4	168

[1] Include votes for minor party candidates, independents, unpledged electors, and scattered write-in votes.

No. 432. Vote Cast for Leading Minority Party Candidates for President: 1936 to 1992

[See headnote, table 431]

YEAR	Candidate	Party	Popular vote (1,000)	Candidate	Party	Popular vote (1,000)
1936 . .	William Lemke	Union	892	Norman Thomas . . .	Socialist	188
1940 . .	Norman Thomas . . .	Socialist	116	Roger Babson	Prohibition.	59
1944 . .	Norman Thomas . . .	Socialist	79	Claude Watson	Prohibition.	75
1948 . .	Strom Thurmond . . .	States' Rights.	1,176	Henry Wallace	Progressive	1,157
1952 . .	Vincent Hallinan	Progressive	140	Stuart Hamblen	Prohibition.	73
1956 . .	T. Coleman Andrews .	States' Rights.	111	Eric Hass	Socialist Labor	44
1960 . .	Eric Hass	Socialist Labor	48	Rutherford Decker . .	Prohibition.	46
1964 . .	Eric Hass	Socialist Labor	45	Clifton DeBerry	Socialist Workers	33
1968 . .	George Wallace . . .	American Independent.	9,906	Henning Blomen . . .	Socialist Labor	53
1972 . .	John Schmitz.	American.	1,099	Benjamin Spock. . . .	People's	79
1976 . .	Eugene McCarthy . .	Independent	757	Roger McBride.	Libertarian.	173
1980 . .	John Anderson	Independent	5,720	Ed Clark	Libertarian.	921
1984 . .	David Bergland	Libertarian.	228	Lyndon H. LaRouche.	Independent	79
1988 . .	Ron Paul	Libertarian.	432	Lenora B. Fulani . . .	New Alliance	217
1992 . .	H. Ross Perot	Independent	19,742	Andre Marrou	Libertarian.	292

Source of tables 431 and 432: Elections Research Center, Chevy Chase, MD, *America at the Polls 2*, 1965, and *America Votes*, biennial (copyright).

No. 433. Democratic and Republican Percentages of Two-Party Presidential Vote, by Selected Characteristics of Voters: 1988 and 1992

[In percent. Covers citizens of voting age living in private housing units in the contiguous United States. Percentages for Democratic Presidential vote are computed by subtracting the percentage Republican vote from 100 percent; third-party or independent votes are not included as valid data. Data are from the National Election Studies and are based on a sample and subject to sampling variability; for details, see source]

CHARACTERISTIC	1988		1992		CHARACTERISTIC	1988		1992	
	Democratic	Republican	Democratic	Republican		Democratic	Republican	Democratic	Republican
Total [1] **. . . . . . .**	**47**	**53**	**58**	**42**	Race:				
Year of birth:					White.	41	59	53	47
1959 or later.	48	52	58	42	Black	92	8	94	6
1943 to 1958	47	53	58	42					
1927 to 1942	49	51	57	43	Education:				
1911 to 1926.	44	56	62	38	Grade school	61	39	70	30
1895 to 1910	47	53	55	45	High school.	51	49	63	37
					College	42	58	55	45
Sex:									
Male	44	56	55	45	Union household.	59	41	68	32
Female	50	50	61	39	Non-union household. .	44	56	56	44

[1] Includes other characteristics, not shown separately.

Source: Center for Political Studies, University of Michigan, Ann Arbor, MI, unpublished data, (copyright).

No. 434. Electoral Vote Cast for President, by Major Political Party—States: 1952 to 1992

[D=Democratic, R=Republican. For composition of regions, see table 27. See also *Historical Statistics, Colonial Times to 1970*, series Y 84-134]

REGION, DIVISION, AND STATE	1952	1956[1]	1960[2]	1964	1968[3]	1972[4]	1976[5]	1980	1984	1988[6]	1992
Democratic	89	73	303	486	191	17	297	49	13	111	370
Republican	442	457	219	52	301	520	240	489	525	426	168
Northeast: Democratic	-	-	121	126	102	14	86	4	-	53	106
Republican	133	133	12	-	24	108	36	118	113	60	-
Midwest: Democratic	-	13	71	149	31	-	58	10	10	29	100
Republican	153	140	82	-	118	145	87	135	127	108	29
South: Democratic	89	60	101	121	45	3	149	31	3	8	68
Republican	77	105	50	47	77	165	20	138	174	168	116
West: Democratic	-	-	10	90	13	-	4	4	-	21	96
Republican	79	79	75	5	82	102	97	98	111	90	23
New England: ME	R-5	R-5	R-5	D-4	D-4	R-4	R-4	R-4	R-4	R-4	D-4
NH	R-4	R-4	R-4	D-4	R-4	R-4	R-4	R-4	R-4	R-4	D-4
VT	R-3	R-3	R-3	D-3	R-3	R-3	R-3	R-3	R-3	R-3	D-3
MA	R-16	R-16	D-16	D-14	D-14	D-14	D-14	R-14	R-13	D-13	D-12
RI	R-4	R-4	D-4	D-4	D-4	R-4	D-4	D-4	R-4	D-4	D-4
CT	R-8	R-8	D-8	D-8	D-8	R-8	R-8	R-8	R-8	R-8	D-8
Middle Atlantic: NY	R-45	R-45	D-45	D-43	D-43	R-41	D-41	R-41	R-36	D-36	D-33
NJ	R-16	R-16	D-16	D-17	R-17	R-17	R-17	R-17	R-16	R-16	D-15
PA	R-32	R-32	D-32	D-29	D-29	R-27	D-27	R-27	R-25	R-25	D-23
East North Central: OH	R-25	R-25	R-25	D-26	R-26	R-25	D-25	R-25	R-23	R-23	D-21
IN	R-13	R-13	R-13	D-13	R-13	R-13	R-13	R-13	R-12	R-12	R-12
IL	R-27	R-27	D-27	D-26	R-26	R-26	R-26	R-26	R-24	R-24	D-22
MI	R-20	R-20	D-20	D-21	D-21	R-21	R-21	R-21	R-20	R-20	D-18
WI	R-12	R-12	R-12	D-12	R-12	R-11	D-11	R-11	R-11	D-11	D-11
West North Central: MN	R-11	R-11	D-11	D-10	D-10	R-10	D-10	D-10	D-10	D-10	D-10
IA	R-10	R-10	R-10	D-9	R-9	R-8	R-8	R-8	R-8	D-8	D-7
MO	R-13	D-13	D-13	D-12	R-12	R-12	D-12	R-12	R-11	R-11	D-11
ND	R-4	R-4	R-4	D-4	R-4	R-3	R-3	R-3	R-3	R-3	R-3
SD	R-4	R-4	R-4	D-4	R-4	R-4	R-4	R-4	R-3	R-3	R-3
NE	R-6	R-6	R-6	D-5	R-5	R-5	R-5	R-5	R-5	R-5	R-5
KS	R-8	R-8	R-8	D-7	R-7	R-7	R-7	R-7	R-7	R-7	R-6
South Atlantic: DE	R-3	R-3	D-3	D-3	R-3	R-3	D-3	R-3	R-3	R-3	D-3
MD	R-9	R-9	D-9	D-10	D-10	R-10	D-10	D-10	R-10	R-10	D-10
DC	(X)	(X)	(X)	D-3	D-3	D-3	D-3	D-3	D-3	D-3	D-3
VA	R-12	R-12	R-12	D-12	R-12	[4]R-11	R-12	R-12	R-12	R-12	R-13
WV	D-8	R-8	D-8	D-7	D-7	R-6	D-6	D-6	R-6	[6]D-5	D-5
NC	D-14	D-14	D-14	D-13	[3]R-12	R-13	D-13	R-13	R-13	R-13	D-14
SC	D-8	D-8	D-8	R-8	R-8	R-8	D-8	R-8	R-8	R-8	R-8
GA	D-12	D-12	D-12	R-12	([3])	R-12	D-12	D-12	R-12	R-12	D-13
FL	R-10	R-10	R-10	D-14	R-14	R-17	R-17	R-17	R-21	R-21	R-25
East South Central: KY	D-10	R-10	R-10	D-9	R-9	R-9	D-9	R-9	R-9	R-9	D-8
TN	R-11	R-11	R-11	D-11	R-11	R-10	R-10	D-10	R-11	R-11	D-11
AL	D-11	[1]D-10	[2]D-5	R-10	([3])	R-9	D-9	R-9	R-9	R-9	R-9
MS	D-8	D-8	([2])	R-7	([3])	R-7	D-7	R-7	R-7	R-7	R-7
West South Central: AR	D-8	D-8	D-8	D-6	([3])	R-6	D-6	R-6	R-6	R-6	D-6
LA	D-10	R-10	D-10	R-10	([3])	R-10	D-10	R-10	R-10	R-10	D-9
OK	R-8	R-8	[2]R-7	D-8	R-8	R-8	R-8	R-8	R-8	R-8	R-8
TX	R-24	R-24	D-24	D-25	D-25	R-26	D-26	R-26	R-29	R-29	R-32
Mountain: MT	R-4	R-4	R-4	D-4	R-4	R-4	R-4	R-4	R-4	R-4	D-3
ID	R-4	R-4	R-4	D-4	R-4	R-4	R-4	R-4	R-4	R-4	R-4
WY	R-3	R-3	R-3	D-3	R-3	R-3	R-3	R-3	R-3	R-3	R-3
CO	R-6	R-6	R-6	D-6	R-6	R-7	R-7	R-7	R-8	R-8	D-8
NM	R-4	R-4	D-4	D-4	R-4	R-4	R-4	R-4	R-5	R-5	D-5
AZ	R-4	R-4	R-4	R-5	R-5	R-6	R-6	R-6	R-7	R-7	R-8
UT	R-4	R-4	R-4	D-4	R-4	R-4	R-4	R-4	R-5	R-5	R-5
NV	R-3	R-3	D-3	D-3	R-3	R-3	R-3	R-3	R-4	R-4	D-4
Pacific: WA	R-9	R-9	R-9	D-9	D-9	R-9	[5]R-8	R-9	R-10	D-10	D-11
OR	R-6	R-6	R-6	D-6	R-6	R-6	R-6	R-6	R-7	D-7	D-7
CA	R-32	R-32	R-32	D-40	R-40	R-45	R-45	R-45	R-47	R-47	D-54
AK	(X)	(X)	R-3	D-3	R-3	R-3	R-3	R-3	R-3	R-3	R-3
HI	(X)	(X)	D-3	D-4	D-4	R-4	D-4	D-4	R-4	D-4	D-4

- Represents zero.   X Not applicable.   [1] Excludes one electoral vote cast for Walter B. Jones in Alabama.   [2] Excludes 15 electoral votes cast for Harry F. Byrd as follows: AL 6, MS 8, and OK 1.   [3] Excludes 46 electoral votes cast for American Independent George C. Wallace as follows: AL 10, AR 6, GA 12, LA 10, MS 7, and NC 1.   [4] Excludes one electoral vote cast for Libertarian John Hospers in Virginia.   [5] Excludes one electoral vote cast for Ronald Reagan in Washington.   [6] Excludes one electoral vote cast for Lloyd Bentsen for President in West Virginia.

Source: 1952-72, U.S. Congress, Clerk of the House, *Statistics of the Presidential and Congressional Election,* quadrennial; 1976-92, Elections Research Center, Chevy Chase, MD, *America Votes,* biennial (copyright).

No. 435. Popular Vote Cast for President, by Political Party—States: 1988 and 1992

[In thousands, except percent. See also Historical Statistics, Colonial Times to 1970, series Y 135-186]

REGION, DIVISION, AND STATE	1988 Total [1]	1988 Democratic Party	1988 Republican Party	1988 Percent for leading party [2]	1992 Total [1]	1992 Democratic Party	1992 Republican Party	1992 Perot (Independent)	1992 % Democratic Party	1992 % Republican Party	1992 % Perot (Independent)
United States..	91,595	41,809	48,886	R-53.4	104,425	44,909	39,104	19,742	43.0	37.4	18.9
Northeast.......	19,852	9,689	9,961	R-50.2	21,581	9,940	7,507	3,994	46.1	34.8	18.5
N.E	5,730	2,826	2,836	R-49.5	6,351	2,820	2,012	1,479	44.4	31.7	23.3
ME	555	244	307	R-55.3	679	263	207	207	38.8	30.4	30.4
NH	451	164	282	R-62.4	538	209	202	121	38.9	37.6	22.6
VT	243	116	124	R-51.1	290	134	88	66	46.1	30.4	22.8
MA	2,633	1,401	1,195	D-53.2	2,774	1,319	805	631	47.5	29.0	22.7
RI	405	225	178	D-55.6	453	213	132	105	47.0	29.0	23.2
CT	1,443	677	750	R-52.0	1,616	682	578	349	42.2	35.8	21.6
M.A	14,121	6,863	7,125	R-50.5	15,230	7,120	5,495	2,515	46.7	36.1	16.5
NY	6,486	3,348	3,082	D-51.6	6,927	3,444	2,347	1,091	49.7	33.9	15.7
NJ	3,100	1,320	1,743	R-56.2	3,344	1,436	1,357	522	43.0	40.6	15.6
PA	4,536	2,195	2,300	R-50.7	4,960	2,239	1,792	903	45.1	36.1	18.2
Midwest.........	24,663	11,556	12,915	R-52.4	27,735	11,692	10,234	5,668	42.2	36.9	20.4
E.N.C.........	16,982	7,819	9,038	R-53.2	19,102	8,199	7,104	3,702	42.9	37.2	19.4
OH	4,394	1,940	2,417	R-55.0	4,940	1,985	1,894	1,036	40.2	38.3	21.0
IN	2,169	861	1,298	R-59.8	2,306	848	989	456	36.8	42.9	19.8
IL	4,559	2,216	2,311	R-50.7	5,050	2,453	1,734	841	48.6	34.3	16.6
MI	3,669	1,676	1,965	R-53.6	4,275	1,871	1,555	825	43.8	36.4	19.3
WI	2,192	1,127	1,047	D-51.4	2,531	1,041	931	544	41.1	36.8	21.5
W.N.C.........	7,681	3,737	3,877	R-50.5	8,633	3,493	3,130	1,966	40.5	36.3	22.8
MN	2,097	1,109	962	D-52.9	2,348	1,021	748	563	43.5	31.9	24.0
IA	1,226	671	545	D-54.7	1,355	586	505	253	43.3	37.3	18.7
MO	2,094	1,002	1,085	R-51.8	2,392	1,054	811	519	44.1	33.9	21.7
ND	297	128	167	R-56.0	308	99	136	71	32.2	44.2	23.1
SD	313	146	165	R-52.8	336	125	137	73	37.1	40.7	21.8
NE	661	259	398	R-60.2	738	217	344	174	29.4	46.6	23.6
KS	993	423	554	R-55.8	1,157	390	450	312	33.7	38.9	27.0
South	28,558	12,004	16,327	R-57.2	33,625	14,118	14,014	5,325	42.0	41.7	15.8
S.A	14,234	5,927	8,207	R-57.7	17,195	7,352	7,103	2,667	42.8	41.3	15.5
DE	250	109	140	R-55.9	290	126	102	59	43.5	35.3	20.4
MD	1,714	826	876	R-51.1	1,985	989	707	281	49.8	35.6	14.2
DC	193	159	28	D-82.6	228	193	21	10	84.6	9.1	4.3
VA	2,192	860	1,309	R-59.7	2,559	1,039	1,151	349	40.6	45.0	13.6
WV	653	341	310	D-52.2	684	331	242	109	48.4	35.4	15.9
NC	2,134	890	1,237	R-58.0	2,612	1,114	1,135	358	42.7	43.4	13.7
SC	986	371	606	R-61.5	1,203	480	578	139	39.9	48.0	11.5
GA	1,810	715	1,081	R-59.8	2,321	1,009	995	310	43.5	42.9	13.3
FL	4,302	1,657	2,619	R-60.9	5,314	2,073	2,173	1,053	39.0	40.9	19.8
E.S.C.........	5,269	2,174	3,055	R-58.0	6,145	2,689	2,751	673	43.8	44.8	10.9
KY	1,323	580	734	R-55.5	1,493	665	617	204	44.6	41.3	13.7
TN	1,636	680	947	R-57.9	1,983	934	841	200	47.1	42.4	10.1
AL	1,378	550	816	R-59.2	1,688	690	804	183	40.9	47.6	10.8
MS	932	364	558	R-59.9	982	400	488	86	40.8	49.7	8.7
W.S.C.........	9,054	3,903	5,065	R-55.9	10,285	4,077	4,160	1,985	39.6	40.4	19.3
AR	828	349	467	R-56.4	951	506	337	99	53.2	35.5	10.4
LA	1,628	717	884	R-54.3	1,790	816	733	211	45.6	41.0	11.8
OK	1,171	483	678	R-57.9	1,390	473	593	320	34.0	42.6	23.0
TX	5,427	2,353	3,037	R-56.0	6,154	2,282	2,496	1,355	37.1	40.6	22.0
West	18,522	8,560	9,683	R-52.3	21,484	9,160	7,349	4,755	42.6	34.2	22.1
Mountain	5,014	2,043	2,887	R-57.6	5,970	2,167	2,272	1,437	36.3	38.1	24.1
MT	366	169	190	R-52.1	411	155	144	107	37.6	35.1	26.1
ID	409	147	254	R-62.1	482	137	203	130	28.4	42.0	27.0
WY	177	67	107	R-60.5	201	68	79	51	34.0	39.6	25.6
CO	1,372	621	728	R-53.1	1,569	630	563	366	40.1	35.9	23.3
NM	521	244	270	R-51.9	570	262	213	92	45.9	37.3	16.1
AZ	1,172	454	703	R-60.0	1,487	543	572	354	36.5	38.5	23.8
UT	647	207	428	R-66.2	744	183	323	203	24.7	43.4	27.3
NV	350	133	206	R-58.9	506	189	176	133	37.4	34.7	26.2
Pacific	13,509	6,517	6,797	R-50.3	15,514	6,993	5,076	3,318	45.1	32.7	21.4
WA	1,865	934	904	D-50.0	2,288	993	731	542	43.4	32.0	23.7
OR	1,202	616	560	D-51.3	1,463	621	476	354	42.5	32.5	24.2
CA	9,887	4,702	5,055	R-51.1	11,132	5,121	3,631	2,296	46.0	32.6	20.6
AK	200	73	119	R-59.6	259	78	102	73	30.3	39.5	28.4
HI	354	192	159	D-54.3	373	179	137	53	48.1	36.7	14.2

[1] Includes other parties. [2] D=Democratic, R=Republican. Leading party vote refers to the party vote representing either a majority or a plurality for the victorious party in the area shown.

Source: Elections Research Center, Chevy Chase, MD, America Votes, biennial, (copyright).

No. 436. Vote Cast for United States Senators, 1992 and 1994, and Incumbent Senators, 1996—States

[D=Democrat; R=Republican]

DIVISION AND STATE	1992 Total (1,000)	1992 Percent for leading party	1994 Total (1,000)	1994 Percent for leading party	INCUMBENT SENATORS AND YEAR TERM EXPIRES — Name, party, and year	Name, party, and year
N.E.:						
ME	(X)	(X)	511	R-60.3	William S. Cohen (R) 1997	Olympia Snowe (R) 2001
NH.	518	R-48.1	(X)	(X)	Judd Gregg (R) 1999	Robert C. Smith (R) 1997
VT.	286	D-54.2	212	R-50.3	Patrick J. Leahy (D) 1999	James M. Jeffords (R) 2001
MA	(X)	(X)	2,179	D-58.1	Edward M. Kennedy (D) 2001	John F. Kerry (D) 1997
RI	(X)	(X)	345	R-64.5	Claiborne Pell (D) 1997	John H. Chafee (R) 2001
CT.	1,501	D-58.8	1,080	D-67.0	Christopher J. Dodd (D) 1999	Joseph I. Lieberman (D) 2001
M.A.:						
NY.	6,459	R-49.0	4,790	D-55.2	Daniel P. Moynihan (D) 2001	Alfonse M. D'Amato (R) 1999
NJ	(X)	(X)	2,055	D-50.3	Bill Bradley (D) 1997	Frank R. Lautenberg (D) 2001
PA	4,802	R-49.1	3,513	R-49.4	Rick Santorum (R) 2001	Arlen Specter (R) 1999
E.N.C.:						
OH	4,794	D-51.0	3,437	R-53.4	John Glenn (D) 1999	Mike DeWine (R) 2001
IN	2,211	R-57.3	1,544	R-67.4	Dan Coats (R) 1999	Richard G. Lugar (R) 2001
IL	4,940	D-53.3	(X)	(X)	Carol Moseley Braun (D) 1999	Paul Simon (D) 1997
MI	(X)	(X)	3,043	R-51.9	Carl Levin (D) 1997	Spencer Abraham (R) 2001
WI	2,455	D-52.6	1,565	D-58.3	Herb Kohl (D) 2001	Russell Feingold (D) 1999
W.N.C.:						
MN	(X)	(X)	1,773	R-49.1	Paul David Wellstone (D) 1997	Rod Grams (R) 2001
IA	1,292	R-69.6	(X)	(X)	Tom Harkin (D) 1997	Charles E. Grassley (R) 1999
MO	2,355	R-51.9	1,775	R-59.7	Christopher S. Bond (R) 1999	John Ashcroft (R) 2001
ND.	304	D-59.0	237	D-58.0	Byron L. Dorgan (D) 1999	Kent Conrad (D) 2001
SD.	334	D-64.9	(X)	(X)	Thomas A. Daschle (D) 1999	Larry Pressler (R) 1997
NE.	(X)	(X)	579	D-54.8	J. James Exon (D) 1997	J. Robert Kerrey (D) 2001
KS.	1,126	R-62.7	(X)	(X)	Bob Dole (R) 1999	Nancy Kassebaum (R) 1997
S.A.:						
DE.	(X)	(X)	199	R-55.8	Joseph R. Biden Jr. (D) 1997	William V. Roth, Jr. (R) 2001
MD.	1,842	D-71.0	1,369	D-59.1	Barbara A. Mikulski (D) 1999	Paul S. Sarbanes (D) 2001
VA.	(X)	(X)	2,057	D-45.6	Charles S. Robb (D) 2001	John W. Warner (R) 1997
WV	(X)	(X)	421	D-69.0	Robert C. Byrd (D) 2001	John D. Rockefeller IV (D) 1997
NC.	2,578	R-50.3	(X)	(X)	Lauch Faircloth (R) 1999	Jesse Helms (R) 1997
SC.	1,180	D-50.1	(X)	(X)	Ernest F. Hollings (D) 1999	Strom Thurmond (R) 1997
GA	[1]1,254	[1]R-50.6	(X)	(X)	Paul Coverdell (R) 1999	Sam Nunn (D) 1997
FL	4,962	D-65.4	4,105	R-70.5	Bob Graham (D) 1999	Connie Mack (R) 2001
E.S.C.:						
KY.	1,331	D-62.9	(X)	(X)	Wendell H. Ford (D) 1999	Mitch McConnell (R) 1997
TN.	(X)	(X)	1,480	R-56.4	[2]Fred Thompson (R) 1997	Bill Frist (R) 2001
AL.	1,578	D-64.8	(X)	(X)	Howell Heflin (D) 1997	Richard C. Shelby (R) 1999
MS	(X)	(X)	608	R-68.8	Thad Cochran (R) 1997	Trent Lott (R) 2001
W.S.C.:						
AR.	920	D-60.2	(X)	(X)	Dale Bumpers (D) 1999	David Pryor (D) 1997
LA.	[3]843	[3]D-78.5	(X)	(X)	John B. Breaux (D) 1999	J. Bennett Johnston (D) 1997
OK	1,294	R-58.5	982	R-55.2	James Inhofe (R) 2001	Don Nickles (R) 1999
TX.	[4]1,765	[4]R-67.3	4,280	R-60.8	Kay Bailey Hutchison (R) 2001	Phil Gramm (R) 1997
Mountain:						
MT.	(X)	(X)	350	R-62.4	Max Baucus (D) 1997	Conrad Burns (R) 2001
ID	479	R-56.5	(X)	(X)	Larry E. Craig (R) 1997	Dirk Kempthorne (R) 1999
WY	(X)	(X)	202	R-58.9	Alan K. Simpson (R) 1997	Craig Thomas (R) 2001
CO	1,552	D-51.8	(X)	(X)	Ben N. Campbell (R) 1999	Hank Brown (R) 1997
NM	(X)	(X)	463	D-54.0	Jeff Bingaman (D) 2001	Pete V. Domenici (R) 1997
AZ	1,382	R-55.8	1,119	R-53.7	John McCain (R) 1999	Jon Kyl (R) 2001
UT.	758	R-55.4	519	R-68.8	Robert F. Bennett (R) 1999	Orrin G. Hatch (R) 2001
NV.	496	D-51.0	368	D-52.7	Harry Reid (D) 1999	Richard H. Bryan (D) 2001
Pacific:						
WA	2,219	D-54.0	1,700	R-55.7	Patty Murray (D) 1999	Slade Gorton (R) 2001
OR	1,376	R-52.1	[5]1,182	[5]D-48.4	Mark O. Hatfield (R) 1997	Ron Wyden (D) 1999
CA.	10,800	D-47.9	8,503	D-46.8	Barbara Boxer (D) 1999	Dianne Feinstein (D) 2001
AK.	240	R-53.0	(X)	(X)	Frank H. Murkowski (R) 1999	Ted Stevens (R) 1997
HI	364	D-57.3	357	D-71.8	Daniel K. Akaka (D) 2001	Daniel K. Inouye (D) 1999

X Not applicable.   [1] Results of run-off election. In the first election no candidate received more than 50 percent of the vote. First election: Total votes cast, 2,251,587; Democratic candidate, 1,108,416; Republican candidate, 1,073,282.   [2] In a special election in 1994 to fill an unexpired term, the Republican candidate received 60.4 percent of 1,465,835 total votes cast.   [3] Louisiana holds an open-primary election with candidates from all parties running on the same ballot. Any candidate who receives a majority is elected. In 1992 the indicated Senator received more than 50 percent of the vote in the October open-primary.   [4] Special election in June 1993 to fill the unexpired term of Senator Bentsen.   [5] Special election in January 1996 to fill the unexpired term of Senator Packwood.

Source: Elections Research Center, Chevy Chase, MD, *America Votes*, biennial, (copyright) and Congressional Quarterly, Inc., Washington, DC, *Congressional Quarterly Weekly Report*, vol. 53, No. 15, April 15, 1995, and unpublished data (copyright).

No. 437. Vote Cast for United States Representatives, by Major Political Party—States: 1990 to 1994

[In thousands, except percent. In each State, totals represent the sum of votes cast in each Congressional District or votes cast for Representative at Large in States where only one member is elected. In all years there are numerous districts within the State where either the Republican or Democratic party had no candidate. In some States the Republican and Democratic vote includes votes cast for the party candidate by endorsing parties. See also Historical Statistics, Colonial Times to 1970, series Y 211-214]

REGION, DIVISION, AND STATE	1990				1992				1994			
	Total[1]	Demo-cratic	Repub-lican	Percent for leading party	Total[1]	Demo-cratic	Repub-lican	Percent for leading party	Total[1]	Demo-cratic	Repub-lican	Percent for leading party
U.S. [2] . . .	61,513	32,565	27,648	D-52.9	96,239	48,964	43,833	D-50.9	69,770	31,698	36,590	R-52.4
Northeast . . .	12,792	6,483	5,868	D-50.7	19,417	9,567	8,871	D-49.3	14,398	7,016	6,927	D-48.7
N.E	4,453	2,523	1,742	D-56.7	5,910	3,007	2,334	D-50.9	4,410	2,431	1,754	D-55.1
ME	517	284	233	D-55.0	670	364	278	D-54.3	503	236	234	D-47.0
NH	291	141	149	R-51.2	511	266	227	D-52.0	309	117	180	R-58.2
VT	210	6	83	[3]I-56.0	282	22	87	[3]I-57.8	211	-	99	[3]I-49.9
MA	2,051	1,420	567	D-69.2	2,614	1,518	857	D-58.1	1,976	1,363	593	D-69.0
RI	347	182	165	D-52.5	399	193	186	D-48.3	342	209	132	D-61.3
CT	1,037	489	546	R-52.6	1,435	644	699	R-48.7	1,069	506	516	R-48.3
M.A.	8,339	3,959	4,126	R-47.1	13,507	6,560	6,537	D-48.6	9,987	4,585	5,173	R-51.8
NY [4]	3,662	1,830	1,662	D-50.0	5,925	3,051	2,687	D-51.5	4,611	2,213	2,251	R-48.8
NJ	1,827	837	911	R-49.9	2,992	1,355	1,503	R-50.2	2,005	880	1,091	R-54.4
PA	2,851	1,293	1,552	R-54.5	4,591	2,154	2,347	R-51.1	3,371	1,492	1,831	R-54.3
Midwest	17,484	9,370	7,970	D-53.6	26,232	13,260	12,238	D-50.5	18,769	8,414	10,147	R-54.1
E.N.C	11,699	6,202	5,363	D-53.0	17,899	9,149	8,315	D-51.1	12,348	5,421	6,803	R-55.1
OH	3,418	1,807	1,590	D-52.9	4,577	2,198	2,154	D-48.0	3,298	1,328	1,925	R-58.4
IN	1,514	831	683	D-54.9	2,219	1,206	998	D-54.3	1,546	667	875	R-56.6
IL	3,077	1,646	1,349	D-53.5	4,831	2,678	2,097	D-55.4	3,044	1,460	1,577	R-51.8
MI	2,434	1,321	1,089	D-54.3	3,884	1,913	1,855	D-49.3	3,001	1,418	1,532	R-51.0
WI	1,256	597	652	R-51.9	2,388	1,154	1,211	R-50.7	1,459	548	893	R-61.2
W.N.C	5,785	3,168	2,607	D-54.8	8,333	4,111	3,923	D-49.3	6,420	2,992	3,344	R-52.1
MN	1,781	1,042	736	D-58.5	2,275	1,178	931	D-51.8	1,748	884	847	D-50.6
IA	792	401	385	D-50.6	1,242	493	729	R-58.7	977	407	560	R-57.3
MO	1,353	728	625	D-53.8	2,349	1,269	1,036	D-54.1	1,766	894	834	D-50.6
ND	234	153	81	D-65.2	298	169	117	D-56.8	235	123	106	D-52.3
SD	257	174	83	D-67.6	333	230	89	D-69.1	306	183	112	D-59.8
NE	587	277	309	R-52.7	711	283	427	R-60.1	571	203	365	R-64.0
KS	781	394	387	D-50.4	1,125	488	592	R-52.6	817	298	519	R-63.5
South [2]	17,180	9,691	7,265	D-56.4	30,107	15,638	13,815	D-51.9	20,394	8,844	11,280	R-55.3
S.A. [2]	9,409	5,222	4,063	D-55.5	15,982	8,088	7,577	D-50.6	10,660	4,566	6,017	R-56.4
DE	177	116	58	D-65.5	276	117	153	R-55.4	195	52	138	R-70.7
MD	1,091	566	517	D-51.9	1,808	956	843	D-52.9	1,345	662	683	R-50.7
DC	160	98	42	D-61.7	197	167	20	D-84.8	(NA)	(NA)	(NA)	(NA)
VA	1,153	663	411	D-57.5	2,368	1,149	1,143	D-48.5	1,908	753	1,089	R-57.1
WV	375	251	123	D-67.1	562	439	123	D-78.1	407	269	138	D-66.1
NC	2,011	1,076	935	D-53.5	2,527	1,282	1,204	D-50.7	1,588	681	907	R-57.1
SC	670	383	275	D-57.2	1,115	506	581	R-52.1	867	313	552	R-63.6
GA [5]	1,394	855	539	D-61.3	2,214	1,215	999	D-54.9	1,498	681	816	R-54.5
FL [5]	2,378	1,213	1,163	D-51.0	4,915	2,257	2,511	R-51.1	2,852	1,156	1,694	R-59.4
E.S.C	2,866	1,712	1,070	D-59.7	5,655	3,170	2,292	D-56.1	3,936	1,839	2,041	R-51.9
KY	764	353	397	R-52.0	1,361	722	638	D-53.0	784	316	451	R-57.5
TN	717	369	289	D-51.5	1,726	883	738	D-51.2	1,416	615	776	R-54.8
AL	1,017	690	315	D-67.9	1,603	896	643	D-55.9	1,115	554	558	R-50.1
MS	369	299	69	D-81.2	965	670	273	D-69.4	620	354	256	D-57.1
W.S.C	4,906	2,758	2,132	D-56.2	8,470	4,380	3,946	D-51.7	5,798	2,438	3,222	R-55.6
AR [6]	665	369	296	D-55.5	889	525	357	D-59.1	709	336	373	R-52.6
LA [6]	106	106	-	D-100.0	684	285	399	R-58.3	(X)	(X)	(X)	(X)
OK	857	519	338	D-60.6	1,276	764	504	D-59.9	969	368	555	R-57.3
TX	3,278	1,763	1,498	D-53.8	5,622	2,806	2,686	D-49.9	4,120	1,734	2,294	R-55.7
West	14,057	7,022	6,545	D-50.0	20,483	10,499	8,910	D-51.5	16,209	7,424	8,237	R-50.8
Mountain . .	3,872	1,783	2,043	R-52.8	5,736	2,627	2,886	R-50.3	4,438	1,706	2,580	R-58.1
MT	317	157	160	R-50.5	404	204	190	D-50.5	352	171	149	D-48.7
ID	315	183	131	D-58.2	473	222	231	R-48.8	393	138	255	R-65.0
WY	158	71	87	R-55.1	197	77	114	R-57.8	196	81	104	R-53.2
CO	1,001	504	487	D-50.3	1,479	691	758	R-51.2	1,056	364	687	R-65.1
NM	359	146	214	R-59.5	556	273	278	R-50.0	462	188	263	R-57.1
AZ	966	345	621	R-64.3	1,409	582	740	R-52.5	1,099	410	653	R-59.4
UT	442	234	191	D-52.9	727	331	362	R-49.8	504	216	252	R-50.0
NV	313	144	151	R-48.2	492	245	214	D-49.9	376	138	216	R-57.4
Pacific. . . .	10,185	5,239	4,502	D-51.4	14,747	7,872	6,024	D-53.4	11,771	5,719	5,657	D-48.6
WA	1,313	696	596	D-53.0	2,223	1,237	912	D-55.6	1,687	827	854	R-50.6
OR	1,053	667	342	D-63.4	1,391	825	553	D-59.3	1,193	647	499	D-54.2
CA	7,287	3,568	3,347	D-49.0	10,535	5,447	4,365	D-51.7	8,328	3,958	4,066	R-48.8
AK	192	92	99	R-51.7	239	102	112	R-46.8	208	68	119	R-56.9
HI	341	216	118	D-63.3	358	261	82	D-72.8	354	219	120	D-61.9

- Represents zero.   NA Not available.   X Not applicable.   [1] Includes vote cast for minor parties.   [2] Includes vote cast for nonvoting Delegate at Large in District of Columbia, except for 1994.   [3] Leading party candidate was Independent.   [4] Includes votes cast by other endorsing parties for Democratic and Republican candidates.   [5] State law does not require tabulation of votes for unopposed candidates. In 1990 Districts 8, 10, 12, 13, and 16 were unopposed; in 1992 District 21 was unopposed; in 1994 Districts 4, 10, 13, 14, 18, and 23 were unopposed.   [6] 1990 data are for a general election runoff in one district. 1990 open primary totals-total, 1,186,253; Democratic, 706,004; Republican, 450,867. 1992 data are for general election runoffs in three districts. In 1994 all Representatives won their seats in the open primary.

Source: 1990 and 1992, Elections Research Center, Chevy Chase, MD, America Votes, biennial, (copyright); 1994, Congressional Quarterly Inc., Congressional Quarterly Weekly Report, vol. 53, No. 15, April 15, 1995, (copyright).

No. 438. Vote Cast for United States Representatives, by Major Political Party—Congressional Districts: 1994

[In some States the Democratic and Republican vote includes votes cast for the party candidate by endorsing parties]

STATE AND DISTRICT	Total vote cast (1,000)	DEMOCRATIC CANDIDATE Name	Percent of total	REPUBLICAN CANDIDATE Name	Percent of total	STATE AND DISTRICT	Total vote cast (1,000)	DEMOCRATIC CANDIDATE Name	Percent of total	REPUBLICAN CANDIDATE Name	Percent of total
AL	1,115	(X)	49.7	(X)	50.1	45th..	179	Williamson .	30.9	Rohrabacher	69.1
1st...	154	Womack ..	32.7	Callahan ...	67.3	46th..	88	Farber....	37.1	Dornan	57.1
2d...	169	Dowling...	26.4	Everett	73.6	47th..	213	Kingsbury .	24.9	Cox	71.7
3d...	148	Browder..	63.6	Hand	36.4	48th..	195	Leschick ..	22.3	Packard ...	73.4
4th...	121	Bevill.....	98.5	(¹)	(¹)	49th..	186	Schenk ...	46.0	Bilbray	48.5
5th...	176	Cramer ...	50.5	Parker	49.5	50th..	104	Filner	56.7	Acevedo ...	35.4
6th...	196	Fortenberry	20.9	Bachus....	79.0	51st..	207	Tamerius ..	27.7	Cunningham	66.9
7th...	151	Hilliard. ...	76.9	Middleton ..	23.0	52d ..	171	Gastil	31.1	Hunter	64.0
AK	208	Smith	32.7	Young.....	56.9	**CO**	1,056	(X)	34.5	(X).......	65.1
AZ	1,099	(X)	37.3	(X)	59.4	1st..	155	Schroeder .	60.0	Eggert	39.9
1st...	181	Blanchard .	39.0	Salmon....	56.0	2d ...	187	Skaggs ...	56.8	Miller	43.2
2d...	100	Pastor.....	62.3	MacDonald .	32.7	3d ...	209	Powers	30.4	McInnis....	69.6
3d...	207	Sprague ...	29.9	Stump	70.1	4th..	188	Kipp	27.7	Allard	72.3
4th...	194	Cure.....	36.0	Shadegg...	60.2	5th..	139	(¹)	(¹)	Hefley....	100.0
5th...	221	Auerbach..	28.7	Kolbe.....	67.7	6th..	178	Hallen....	28.0	Schaefer...	69.8
6th...	196	English ...	41.5	Hayworth..	54.6	**CT**	1,069	(X)	47.4	(X).......	48.3
AR	709	(X)	47.4	(X).......	52.6	1st..	189	Kennelly ..	73.4	Putman....	24.8
1st...	178	Lambert...	53.4	Dupwe	46.6	2d ...	186	Gejdenson .	42.6	Munster ...	42.5
2d...	170	Thornton ..	57.4	Powell	42.6	3d ...	175	DeLauro ...	63.4	Johnson ...	36.6
3d...	192	Seitz.....	32.3	Hutchinson .	67.7	4th..	147	Kantrowitz .	23.8	Shays.....	74.4
4th...	169	Bradford ..	48.2	Dickey	51.8	5th..	179	Maloney ...	45.5	Franks	52.2
CA	8,328	(X)	47.5	(X).......	48.8	6th..	193	Koskoff ...	31.5	Johnson ...	63.9
1st...	201	Hamburg ..	46.7	Riggs	53.3	**DE**	195	DeSantis ..	26.6	Castle.....	70.7
2d...	215	Jacobs	26.1	Herger	64.2	**FL**	2,852	(X)	40.5	(X).......	59.4
3d...	195	Fazio	49.8	Lefever....	46.1	1st..	183	Whibbs ...	38.4	Scarborough	61.6
4th...	236	Hirning ...	34.9	Doolittle ...	61.3	2d ...	191	Peterson ..	61.3	Griffin	38.7
5th...	183	Matsui.....	68.5	Dinsmore ..	29.0	3d ...	111	Brown.....	57.7	Little......	42.3
6th...	237	Woolsey ..	58.1	Nugent	37.6	4th..	(NA)	(¹)	(¹)	Fowler	(NA)
7th...	167	Miller.....	69.7	Hughes....	27.4	5th..	220	Thurman ...	57.2	Garlits....	42.8
8th...	168	Pelosi	81.8	Cheung....	18.2	6th..	150	(¹)	(¹)	Stearns....	99.1
9th...	179	Dellums ...	72.2	Wright.....	22.6	7th..	179	Goddard ..	26.6	Mica......	73.4
10th..	234	Schwartz ..	38.6	Baker	59.3	8th..	132	(¹)	(¹)	McCollum ..	99.7
11th..	160	Perry.....	34.9	Pombo	62.1	9th..	177	(¹)	(¹)	Bilirakis....	99.9
12th..	176	Lantos....	67.4	Wilder.....	32.6	10th..	(NA)	(¹)	(¹)	Young.....	(NA)
13th..	151	Stark.....	64.6	Molton	30.2	11th..	149	Gibbons ...	51.6	Sharpe	48.4
14th..	199	Eshoo....	60.6	Brink	39.4	12th..	163	Connors ..	35.0	Canady....	65.0
15th..	200	Mineta....	59.9	Wick.....	40.1	13th..	(NA)	(¹)	(¹)	Miller	(NA)
16th..	115	Lofgren ...	65.0	Smith	35.0	14th..	(NA)	(¹)	(¹)	Goss	(NA)
17th..	167	Farr	52.2	McCampbell.	44.5	15th..	218	Munsey....	46.2	Weldon....	53.7
18th..	139	Condit....	65.5	Carter.....	31.7	16th..	211	Comerford .	41.9	Foley	58.1
19th..	184	Lehman...	39.6	Radanovich.	56.8	17th..	76	Meek	100.0	(¹)	(¹)
20th..	101	Dooley ...	56.7	Young.....	43.3	18th..	(NA)	(¹)	(¹)	Ros-Lehtinen ..	(NA)
21st..	172	Evans	27.7	Thomas ...	68.1	19th..	223	Johnston ..	66.1	Tsakanikas .	33.9
22d ..	209	Capps....	48.5	Seastrand ..	49.3	20th..	187	Deutsch...	61.2	Kennedy ...	38.8
23d ..	172	Ready....	27.5	Gallegly ...	66.2	21st..	91	(¹)	(¹)	Diaz-Balart .	100.0
24th..	193	Beilenson .	49.4	Sybert	47.5	22d ..	189	Wiener ...	36.6	Shaw	63.4
25th..	170	Gilmartin ..	31.4	McKeon ...	64.9	23d ..	(NA)	Hastings ..	(NA)	(¹)	(¹)
26th..	88	Berman ...	62.6	Forsch	32.2	**GA**	1,498	(X)	45.5	(X).......	54.5
27th..	167	Kahn.....	42.1	Moorhead .	53.0	1st..	116	Beckworth .	23.4	Kingston ...	76.6
28th..	164	Randle	30.5	Dreier.....	67.1	2d ...	99	Bishop	66.2	Clayton....	33.8
29th..	190	Waxman ...	68.0	Stepanek ..	28.3	3d ...	145	Overby	34.5	Collins	65.5
30th..	66	Becerra ...	66.2	Ramirez ...	28.2	4th..	156	Yates	42.1	Linder.....	57.9
31st..	85	Martinez ...	59.1	Flores.....	40.9	5th..	123	Lewis	69.1	Dixon	30.9
32d ..	126	Dixon	77.6	Farhat	17.6	6th..	186	Jones	35.8	Gingrich ...	64.2
33d ..	42	Roybal-Allard ..	81.5	(¹)	(¹)	7th..	137	Darden ...	48.1	Barr	51.9
34th..	117	Torres	61.7	Nunez	34.1	8th..	143	Mathis.....	37.3	Chambliss ..	62.7
35th..	84	Waters ...	78.1	Truman....	21.9	9th..	137	Deal	57.9	Castello ...	42.1
36th..	196	Harman...	48.0	Brooks	47.6	10th..	147	Johnson ...	34.8	Norwood...	65.2
37th..	83	Tucker III..	77.4	(¹)	(¹)	11th..	109	McKinney..	65.6	Lovett.....	34.4
38th..	146	Mathews ..	36.8	Horn.....	58.5	**HI**	354	(X)	61.9	(X).......	33.8
39th..	170	Davis	29.0	Royce.....	66.4	1st..	177	Abercrombie ...	53.6	Swindle....	43.4
40th..	164	Rusk.....	29.3	Lewis	70.7	2d ...	177	Mink	70.1	Garner	24.2
41st..	132	Tessier ...	37.9	Kim	62.1	**ID**	393	(X)	35.0	(X).......	65.0
42d ..	115	Brown.....	51.1	Guzman ...	48.8	1st..	202	LaRocco ..	44.6	Chenoweth .	55.4
43d ..	154	Takano ...	38.4	Calvert....	54.7	2d ...	192	Fletcher...	25.0	Crapo.....	75.0
44th..	172	Clute.....	38.1	Bono	55.6						

See footnotes at end of table.

No. 438. Vote Cast for United States Representatives, by Major Political Party—Congressional Districts: 1994—Continued

[See headnote, p. 274]

STATE AND DISTRICT	Total vote cast (1,000)	DEMOCRATIC CANDIDATE Name	Percent of total	REPUBLICAN CANDIDATE Name	Percent of total
IL.....	3,044	(X)	48.0	(X)	51.8
1st...	149	Rush.....	75.7	Kelly.....	24.3
2d...	96	Reynolds..	98.1	[1]	[1]
3d...	171	Lipinski...	54.2	Nalepa....	45.8
4th...	62	Gutierrez..	75.2	Valtierra...	24.8
5th...	138	Rosten-kowski....	45.6	Flanagan...	54.4
6th...	157	Berry.....	23.6	Hyde.....	73.5
7th...	117	Collins....	79.6	Mobley....	20.4
8th...	136	Walberg...	35.1	Crane.....	64.9
9th...	143	Yates....	66.1	Larney....	33.9
10th..	153	Krupp....	24.9	Porter.....	75.1
11th..	160	Giglio....	39.4	Weller....	60.6
12th..	154	Costello...	65.9	Morris.....	34.1
13th..	170	Riley.....	26.9	Fawell....	73.1
14th..	144	Denari....	23.5	Hastert....	76.5
15th..	160	Alexander.	31.8	Ewing.....	68.2
16th..	166	Sullivan...	29.4	Manzullo...	70.6
17th..	175	Evans....	54.5	Anderson..	45.5
18th..	199	Stephens..	39.3	LaHood....	60.2
19th..	197	Poshard..	58.4	Winters....	41.6
20th..	197	Durbin....	54.8	Owens....	45.2
IN.....	1,546	(X)	43.2	(X)	56.6
1st...	122	Visclosky.	56.5	Larson....	43.5
2d...	172	Hogsett...	45.5	McIntosh..	54.5
3d...	131	Roemer...	55.2	Burkett....	44.8
4th...	160	Long.....	44.6	Souder....	55.4
5th...	160	Beaty....	28.3	Buyer....	69.5
6th...	178	Bruner....	23.0	Burton....	77.0
7th...	160	Harmless..	34.9	Myers.....	65.1
8th...	178	McCloskey.	47.6	Hostettler..	52.4
9th...	176	Hamilton..	52.0	Leising....	48.0
10th..	110	Jacobs....	53.5	Scott.....	46.5
IA.....	977	(X)	41.7	(X)	57.3
1st...	183	Winekauf..	37.9	Leach....	60.2
2d...	198	Nagle....	43.4	Nussle....	56.0
3d...	193	Baxter....	41.0	Lightfoot...	57.8
4th...	213	Smith....	46.4	Ganske....	52.5
5th...	189	McGuire..	39.0	Latham....	60.8
KS.....	817	(X)	36.5	(X)	63.5
1st...	219	Nichols...	22.6	Roberts....	77.4
2d...	207	Carlin....	34.4	Brownback.	65.6
3d...	181	Hancock...	43.4	Meyers....	56.6
4th...	211	Glickman..	47.1	Tiahrt.....	52.9
KY.....	784	(X)	40.3	(X)	57.5
1st...	127	Barlow....	49.0	Whitfield...	51.0
2d...	151	Adkisson..	40.2	Lewis.....	59.8
3d...	152	Ward.....	44.4	Stokes....	44.1
4th...	130	Skaggs...	25.9	Bunning...	74.1
5th...	104	Blevins...	20.6	Rogers....	79.4
6th...	119	Baesler...	58.8	Wills.....	41.2
LA[2]...	(X)	(X)	(X)	(X)	(X)
1st...	(X)	Jefferson[3]	(X)	Livingston[3]	(X)
2d...	(X)	(X)	(X)	(X)	(X)
3d...	(X)	Tauzin[3]	(X)	(X)	(X)
4th...	(X)	Fields[3]	(X)	(X)	(X)
5th...	(X)	(X)	(X)	McCrery[3]	(X)
6th...	(X)	(X)	(X)	Baker[3]	(X)
7th...	(X)	Hayes[3]	(X)	(X)	(X)
ME.....	503	(X)	47.0	(X)	46.6
1st...	263	Dutremble.	48.1	Longley....	51.9
2d...	240	Baldacci..	45.7	Bennett....	40.8
MD.....	1,345	(X)	49.2	(X)	50.7
1st...	179	Gies.....	32.3	Gilchrest...	67.7
2d...	199	Brewster..	37.2	Ehrlich....	62.8
3d...	165	Cardin....	71.0	Tousey....	29.0
4th...	124	Wynn....	75.0	Dyson.....	25.0
5th...	168	Hoyer....	58.8	Devine....	41.2
6th...	186	Muldowney.	34.1	Bartlett....	65.9
7th...	119	Mfume....	81.5	Kondner...	18.5
8th...	204	Van Grack.	29.7	Morella....	70.3
MA.....	1,976	(X)	69.0	(X)	30.0
1st...	151	Olver.....	99.4	[1]	[1]
2d...	200	Neal.....	58.6	Briare.....	36.4
3d...	212	O'Sullivan.	44.2	Blute.....	54.6
4th...	170	Frank.....	99.5	[1]	[1]
5th...	201	Meehan...	69.9	Coleman...	30.1

STATE AND DISTRICT	Total vote cast (1,000)	DEMOCRATIC CANDIDATE Name	Percent of total	REPUBLICAN CANDIDATE Name	Percent of total
6th...	239	Tierney...	47.4	Torkildsen..	50.5
7th...	227	Markey...	64.4	Bailey.....	35.6
8th...	114	Kennedy..	99.0	[1]	[1]
9th...	210	Moakley...	69.8	Murphy....	30.2
10th..	251	Studds...	68.8	Hemeon...	31.2
MI.....	3,001	(X)	47.3	(X)	51.0
1st...	213	Stupak...	56.9	Ziegler....	42.0
2d...	194	Hoover...	23.7	Hoekstra...	75.3
3d...	185	Flory.....	23.5	Ehlers.....	73.9
4th...	199	Frasier...	25.5	Camp.....	73.1
5th...	193	Barcia....	65.5	Anderson..	31.8
6th...	166	Taylor....	25.5	Upton.....	73.5
7th...	177	Mc-Caughtry..	32.3	Smith.....	65.1
8th...	212	Mitchell...	44.9	Chrysler...	51.6
9th...	189	Kildee....	51.2	O'Neill....	47.0
10th..	196	Bonior....	62.3	Lobsinger..	37.7
11th..	227	Breshgold.	30.5	Knollenberg.	68.2
12th..	198	Levin....	52.4	Pappa-george....	46.9
13th..	173	Rivers....	51.9	Schall.....	45.1
14th..	158	Conyers...	81.5	Fornier....	16.6
15th..	142	Collins....	84.1	Savage....	14.1
16th..	179	Dingell....	59.1	Larkin.....	39.8
MN.....	1,748	(X)	50.6	(X)	48.4
1st...	213	Hottinger..	44.7	Gutknecht..	55.2
2d...	220	Minge....	52.0	Revier.....	45.0
3d...	237	Olson....	26.3	Ramstad...	73.2
4th...	211	Vento....	54.9	Newinski...	41.9
5th...	196	Sabo.....	61.9	LeGrand...	37.3
6th...	228	Luther....	49.9	Jude......	49.7
7th...	211	Peterson..	51.2	Omann....	48.6
8th...	233	Oberstar...	65.7	Herwig....	34.2
MS.....	620	(X)	57.1	(X)	41.3
1st...	128	Wheeler...	36.9	Wicker....	63.1
2d...	127	Thompson.	53.7	Jordan....	38.9
3d...	123	Mont-gomery...	67.6	Dabbs....	32.4
4th...	121	Parker....	68.5	Wood.....	31.5
5th...	122	Taylor....	60.1	Barlos.....	39.9
MO.....	1,766	(X)	50.6	(X)	47.3
1st...	153	Clay.....	63.4	Counts....	32.9
2d...	230	Kelly.....	30.6	Talent....	67.3
3d...	204	Gephardt.	57.7	Gill......	39.7
4th...	203	Skelton...	67.8	Noland....	32.2
5th...	178	McCarthy..	56.6	Freeman...	43.4
6th...	212	Danner...	66.1	Tucker....	33.9
7th...	196	Fossard...	39.7	Hancock...	57.3
8th...	185	Thompson.	26.5	Emerson...	70.1
9th...	205	Volkmer...	50.5	Hulshof....	45.0
MT.....	352	Williams...	48.7	Jamison...	42.2
NE.....	571	(X)	35.6	(X)	64.0
1st...	189	Combs...	37.3	Bereuter...	62.6
2d...	185	Hoagland..	49.0	Christen-sen......	49.9
3d...	197	Chapin...	21.3	Barrett....	78.7
NV.....	376	(X)	36.6	(X)	57.4
1st...	152	Bilbray...	47.5	Ensign....	48.5
2d...	224	Greeson...	29.2	Vucanovich.	63.5
NH.....	309	(X)	37.7	(X)	58.2
1st...	148	Verge....	28.7	Zeliff.....	65.6
2d...	162	Swett....	46.0	Bass.....	51.4
NJ.....	2,005	(X)	43.9	(X)	54.4
1st...	150	Andrews..	72.3	Hogan....	27.7
2d...	159	Magazzu..	35.4	LoBiondo..	64.6
3d...	174	Smith....	31.2	Saxton....	66.4
4th...	162	Walsh....	30.6	Smith.....	67.9
5th...	189	Auer.....	21.9	Roukema..	74.2
6th...	147	Pallone...	60.4	Herson....	37.5
7th...	166	Carroll....	38.7	Franks....	59.6
8th...	141	Klein.....	48.6	Martini....	49.9
9th...	160	Torricelli...	62.5	Russo.....	36.1
10th..	98	Payne....	75.9	Ford.....	21.9
11th..	180	Herbert...	28.0	Freling-huysen....	71.2
12th..	184	Youssouf..	30.4	Zimmer....	68.3
13th..	95	Menendez..	70.9	Alonso....	25.2

See footnotes at end of table.

No. 438. Vote Cast for United States Representatives, by Major Political Party—Congressional Districts: 1994—Continued

[See headnote, p. 274]

STATE AND DIS-TRICT	Total vote cast (1,000)	DEMOCRATIC CANDIDATE Name	Percent of total	REPUBLICAN CANDIDATE Name	Percent of total	STATE AND DIS-TRICT	Total vote cast (1,000)	DEMOCRATIC CANDIDATE Name	Percent of total	REPUBLICAN CANDIDATE Name	Percent of total
NM....	462	(X)	40.6	(X)	57.1	12th..	172	Ruccia	33.3	Kasich	66.5
1st...	162	Zollinger	26.1	Schiff	73.9	13th..	190	Brown	49.1	White	45.5
2d...	142	Chavez	31.9	Skeen	63.3	14th..	185	Sawyer	51.9	Slaby	48.1
3d...	157	Richardson	63.6	Bemis	34.1	15th..	160	Buckel	29.1	Pryce	70.7
NY....	4,611	(X) Hoch-	48.0	(X)	48.8	16th..	183	Finn	25.0	Regula	75.0
1st...	172	brueckner	46.5	Forbes	52.5	17th..	192	Traficant	77.4	Meister	22.6
2d...	147	Manfre	28.0	Lazio	68.2	18th..	191	DiDonato	46.0	Ney	54.0
3d...	195	Grill	40.0	King	59.2	19th..	206	Fingerhut	43.5	LaTourette	48.5
4th...	175	Schiliro	37.3	Frisa	50.2	OK....	969	(X)	38.0	(X)	57.3
5th...	171	Ackerman	55.0	Lally	43.3	1st...	171	Price	37.3	Largent	62.7
6th...	85	Flake	80.4	Bhag-wandin	19.6	2d...	158	Cooper	47.9	Coburn	52.1
7th...	68	Manton	87.1	(¹)	(¹)	3d...	157	Brewster	73.8	Tallant	26.2
8th...	134	Nadler	82.0	Askren	15.8	4th...	155	Perryman	43.3	Watts	51.6
9th...	131	Schumer	72.6	McCall	27.4	5th...	175	(¹)	(¹)	Istook	78.1
10th..	87	Towns	89.0	Parker	9.2	6th...	152	Tollett	29.8	Lucas	70.2
11th..	70	Owens	88.9	Popkin	9.5	OR....	1,193	(X)	54.2	(X)	41.8
12th..	43	Velazquez	92.3	(¹)	(¹)	1st...	254	Furse	47.7	Witt	47.6
13th..	135	Butler	25.1	Molinari	71.4	2d...	234	Kupillas	38.7	Cooley	57.3
14th..	153	Maloney	64.2	Millard	35.4	3d...	223	Wyden	72.5	Hall	19.4
15th..	81	Rangel	96.5	(¹)	(¹)	4th...	238	DeFazio	66.8	Newkirk	33.2
16th..	61	Serrano	96.3	(¹)	(¹)	5th...	244	Webber	46.8	Bunn	49.8
17th..	94	Engel	77.6	Marshall	17.9	PA....	3,371	(X)	44.3	(X)	54.3
18th..	160	Lowey	57.3	Hartzell	40.9	1st...	122	Foglietta	81.5	Gordon	18.5
19th..	192	Fish	36.8	Kelly	52.1	2d...	140	Fattah	85.9	Watson	14.1
20th..	178	Julian	29.4	Gilman	67.5	3d...	148	Borski	62.7	Hasher	37.3
21st..	221	McNulty	67.0	Gomez	31.2	4th...	186	Klink	64.2	Peglow	35.8
22d..	215	Lawrence	26.6	Solomon	73.4	5th...	145	(¹)	(¹)	Clinger	99.9
23d..	176	Skeele	23.1	Boehlert	70.5	6th...	159	Holden	56.7	Levering	43.3
24th..	159	Francis	21.4	McHugh	78.6	7th...	197	Nichols	30.3	Weldon	69.7
25th..	198	Jezer	42.4	Walsh	57.6	8th...	167	Murray	26.7	Greenwood	66.1
26th..	195	Hinchey	49.1	Moppert	48.5	9th...	147	(¹)	(¹)	Shuster	99.7
27th..	205	Long	25.5	Paxon	74.5	10th..	163	Schreffler	31.1	McDade	65.7
28th..	196	Slaughter	56.6	Davison	40.1	11th..	153	Kanjorski	66.5	Podolak	33.5
29th..	187	LaFalce	55.2	Miller	43.0	12th..	171	Murtha	68.9	Choby	31.1
30th..	186	Franczyk	33.0	Quinn	67.0	13th..	195	Mezvinsky	45.2	Fox	49.4
31st..	143	(¹)	(¹)	Houghton	84.8	14th..	164	Coyne	64.1	Clark	32.4
NC....	1,588	(X)	42.9	(X)	57.1	15th..	151	McHale	47.8	Yeager	47.4
1st...	109	Clayton	61.1	Tyler	38.9	16th..	157	Chertok	30.3	Walker	69.7
2d...	141	Moore	44.0	Funderburk	56.0	17th..	134	(¹)	(¹)	Gekas	99.9
3d...	137	Lancaster	47.3	Jones	52.7	18th..	186	Doyle	54.8	McCarty	45.2
4th...	154	Price	49.6	Heineman	50.4	19th..	125	(¹)	(¹)	Goodling	99.5
5th...	148	Sands	42.7	Burr	57.3	20th..	179	Mascara	53.1	McCormick	46.9
6th...	98	(¹)	(¹)	Coble	100.0	21st..	181	Leavens	46.9	English	49.5
7th...	122	Rose	51.6	Anderson	48.4	RI....	342	(X)	61.3	(X)	38.7
8th...	120	Hefner	52.4	Morgan	47.6	1st...	166	Kennedy	54.1	Vigilante	45.9
9th...	127	Blake	35.0	Myrick	65.0	2d...	176	Reed	68.0	Elliot	32.0
10th..	151	Avery	28.5	Ballenger	71.5	SC....	867	(X)	36.1	(X)	63.6
11th..	193	Lauterer	39.9	Taylor	60.1	1st...	147	Barber	32.4	Sanford	66.3
12th..	88	Watt	65.8	Martino	34.2	2d...	134	(¹)	(¹)	Spence	99.8
ND....	235	Pomeroy	52.3	Porter	45.0	3d...	150	Bryan	39.9	Graham	60.1
OH....	3,298	(X)	40.3	(X)	58.4	4th...	149	Fowler	26.4	Inglis	73.5
1st...	166	Mann	43.9	Chabot	56.1	5th...	148	Spratt	52.1	Bigham	47.8
2d...	194	Mann	22.6	Portman	77.4	6th...	139	Clyburn	63.8	McLeod	36.2
3d...	178	Hall	59.3	Westbrock	40.7	SD....	306	Johnson	59.8	Berkhout	36.6
4th...	140	(¹)	(¹)	Oxley	100.0	TN....	1,416	(X)	43.4	(X)	54.8
5th...	185	Tudor	26.6	Gillmor	73.4	1st...	141	Christian	24.6	Quillen	72.9
6th...	179	Strickland	49.1	Cremeans	50.9	2d...	142	(¹)	(¹)	Duncan	90.5
7th...	140	(¹)	(¹)	Hobson	100.0	3d...	162	Button	45.6	Wamp	52.3
8th...	148	(¹)	(¹)	Boehner	99.9	4th...	144	Whorley	42.0	Hilleary	56.6
9th...	157	Kaptur	75.3	Whitman	24.7	5th...	159	Clement	60.2	Osborne	38.7
10th..	184	Gaul	38.6	Hoke	51.9	6th...	180	Gordon	50.6	Gill	49.4
11th..	148	Stokes	77.2	Sykora	22.8	7th...	170	Byrd	38.6	Bryant	60.2
						8th...	154	Tanner	63.8	Morris	36.2
						9th...	164	Ford	57.8	DeBerry	42.2

See footnotes at end of table.

No. 438. Vote Cast for United States Representatives, by Major Political Party— Congressional Districts: 1994—Continued

[See headnote, p. 274]

STATE AND DISTRICT	Total vote cast (1,000)	DEMOCRATIC CANDIDATE Name	Percent of total	REPUBLICAN CANDIDATE Name	Percent of total
TX	4,120	(X)	42.1	(X) Blanken-ship	55.7
1st...	156	Chapman	55.3	Blanken-ship	40.9
2d ...	154	Wilson	57.0	Peterson	43.0
3d ...	173	(¹)	(¹)	Johnson	91.0
4th...	169	Hall	58.8	Bridges	39.8
5th...	124	Bryant	50.1	Sessions	47.3
6th...	201	Jesmore	22.0	Barton	75.6
7th...	117	(¹)	(¹)	Archer	100.0
8th...	161	(¹)	(¹)	Fields	92.0
9th...	157	Brooks	45.7	Stockman	51.9
10th..	202	Doggett	56.3	Baylor	39.8
11th..	130	Edwards	59.2	Broyles	40.8
12th..	140	Geren	68.7	Anderson	31.3
13th..	143	Sarpalius	44.6	Thornberry	55.4
14th..	155	Laughlin	55.6	Deats	44.4
15th..	104	De La Garza	59.0	Haughey	39.4
16th..	87	Coleman	57.1	Ortiz	42.9
17th..	156	Stenholm	53.7	Boone	46.3
18th..	115	Lee	73.5	Burley	24.4
19th..	121	(¹)	(¹)	Combest	100.0
20th..	96	Gonzalez	62.5	Colyer	37.5
21st..	184	(¹)	(¹)	Smith	90.0
22d ..	163	Cunningham	23.8	DeLay	73.7
23d ..	118	Rios	37.4	Bonilla	62.6
24th..	123	Frost	52.8	Harrison	47.2
25th..	119	Bentsen	52.3	Fontenot	45.0
26th..	177	Bryant	22.4	Armey	76.4
27th..	110	Ortiz	59.4	Stone	40.6
28th..	104	Tejeda	70.9	Slatter	27.6
29th..	60	Green	73.4	Eide	26.6
30th..	101	Johnson	72.6	Cain	25.7
UT	504	(X)	42.8	(X)	50.0
1st...	163	Coray	35.5	Hansen	64.5
2d ...	187	Shepherd	35.9	Waldholtz	45.8
3d ...	155	Orton	59.0	Thompson	39.9
VT [4]	211	(¹)	(¹)	Carroll	46.6
VA	1,908	(X)	39.4	(X)	57.1
1st...	192	Sinclair	23.5	Bateman	74.3
2d ...	138	Pickett	59.1	Chapman	40.9
3d ...	137	Scott	79.4	Ward	20.6
4th...	187	Sisisky	61.6	Sweet	38.4
5th...	179	Payne	53.3	Landrith	46.7
6th...	127	(¹)	(¹)	Goodlatte	99.9
7th...	211	(¹)	(¹)	Bliley	84.0
8th...	203	Moran	59.4	McSlarrow	39.3
9th...	175	Boucher	58.8	Fast	41.2
10th..	176	(¹)	(¹)	Wolf	87.3
11th..	186	Byrne	45.3	Davis	52.9
WA	1,687	(X)	49.0	(X)	50.6
1st...	195	Cantwell	48.3	White	51.7
2d ...	197	Spanel	45.3	Metcalf	54.7
3d ...	193	Unsoeld	44.6	Smith	52.0
4th...	174	Inslee	46.7	Hastings	53.3
5th...	216	Foley	49.1	Nethercutt	50.9
6th...	181	Dicks	58.3	Gregg	41.7
7th...	197	McDermott	75.1	Harris	24.9
8th...	185	Wyrick	23.9	Dunn	76.1
9th...	150	Kreidler	48.2	Tate	51.8
WV	407	(X)	66.1	(X)	33.9
1st...	147	Mollohan	70.3	Riley	29.7
2d ...	142	Wise	63.7	Cravotta	36.3
3d ...	117	Rahall	63.9	Waldman	36.1
WI	1,459	(X)	37.6	(X)	61.2
1st...	170	Barca	48.8	Neumann	49.4
2d ...	193	Hecht	28.7	Klug	69.2
3d ...	160	Stower	41.0	Gunderson	55.7
4th...	175	Kleczka	53.7	Reynolds	44.8
5th...	141	Barrett	62.4	Hollings-head	36.4
6th...	120	(¹)	(¹)	Petri	99.5
7th...	179	Obey	54.3	West	45.7
8th...	179	Gruszynski	36.3	Roth	63.7
9th...	142	(¹)	(¹)	Sensen-brenner	99.8
WY	196	Schuster	41.3	Cubin	53.2

NA Not available.   X Not applicable.   ¹ No candidate.   ² Louisiana holds an open-primary election with candidates from all parties running on the same ballot. Any candidate who receives a majority is elected; if no candidate receives 50 percent, there is a run-off election in November between the top two finishers.   ³ Candidate listed won seat in open-primary.   ⁴ The winning candidate was Sanders, an Independent, who received 49.9 percent of the vote.

Source: Congressional Quarterly Inc., *Congressional Quarterly Weekly Report*, vol. 53, No. 15, April 15, 1995 (copyright).

No. 439. Composition of Congress, by Political Party: 1971 to 1996

[D=Democratic, R=Republican. Data for beginning of first session of each Congress (as of January 3), except as noted. Excludes vacancies at beginning of session. See also *Historical Statistics, Colonial Times to 1970*, series Y 204-210]

YEAR	Party and President	Congress	HOUSE Majority party	HOUSE Minority party	HOUSE Other	SENATE Majority party	SENATE Minority party	SENATE Other
1971 [1]	R (Nixon)	92d	D-254	R-180	-	D-54	R-44	2
1973 [1][2]	R (Nixon)	93d	D-239	R-192	1	D-56	R-42	2
1975 [3]	R (Ford)	94th	D-291	R-144	-	D-60	R-37	2
1977 [4]	D (Carter)	95th	D-292	R-143	-	D-61	R-38	1
1979 [4]	D (Carter)	96th	D-276	R-157	-	D-58	R-41	1
1981 [4]	R (Reagan)	97th	D-243	R-192	-	R-53	D-46	1
1983	R (Reagan)	98th	D-269	R-165	-	R-54	D-46	-
1985	R (Reagan)	99th	D-252	R-182	-	R-53	D-47	-
1987	R (Reagan)	100th	D-258	R-177	-	D-55	R-45	-
1989	R (Bush)	101st	D-259	R-174	-	D-55	R-45	-
1991 [5]	R (Bush)	102d	D-267	R-167	1	D-56	R-44	-
1993 [5]	D (Clinton)	103d	D-258	R-176	1	D-57	R-43	-
1995 [5]	D (Clinton)	104th	R-230	D-204	1	R-52	D-48	-
1996 [5][6]	D (Clinton)	104th	R-236	D-197	1	R-53	D-46	-

- Represents zero.   ¹ Senate had one Independent and one Conservative-Republican.   ² House had one Independent-Democrat.   ³ Senate had one Independent, one Conservative-Republican, and one undecided (New Hampshire).   ⁴ Senate had one Independent.   ⁵ House had one Independent-Socialist.   ⁶ As of beginning of second session.

Source: U.S. Congress, Joint Committee on Printing, *Congressional Directory*, annual; beginning 1977, biennial.

No. 440. Composition of Congress, by Political Party Affiliation—States: 1989 to 1996

[Figures are for the beginning of the first session (as of January 3), except as noted. Dem.=Democratic; Rep.=Republican]

REGION, DIVISION, AND STATE	REPRESENTATIVES								SENATORS							
	101st Cong.,[1] 1989		102d Cong.,[2] 1991		103rd Cong.,[2] 1993		104th Cong.,[2][3][4] 1996		101st Cong., 1989		102d Cong., 1991		103rd Cong., 1993		104th Cong.,[3][5] 1996	
	Dem.	Rep.	Dem.	Rep.	Dem.	Rep.	Dem.	Rep.	Dem.	Rep.	Dem.	Rep.	Dem.	Rep.	Dem.	Rep.
U.S.	259	174	267	167	258	176	197	236	55	45	56	44	57	43	46	53
Northeast.	55	40	56	38	50	37	47	40	10	8	10	8	11	7	9	9
N.E	14	10	16	7	14	8	14	8	7	5	7	5	7	5	6	6
ME	1	1	1	1	1	1	1	1	1	1	1	1	1	1	-	2
NH	-	2	1	1	1	1	-	2	-	2	-	2	-	2	-	2
VT	-	1	-	-	-	-	-	-	1	1	1	1	1	1	1	1
MA	10	1	10	1	8	2	8	2	2	-	2	-	2	-	2	-
RI	-	2	1	1	1	1	2	-	1	1	1	1	1	1	1	1
CT	3	3	3	3	3	3	3	3	2	-	2	-	2	-	2	-
M.A	41	30	40	31	36	29	33	32	3	3	3	3	4	2	3	3
NY	21	13	21	13	18	13	17	14	1	1	1	1	1	1	1	1
NJ	8	6	8	6	7	6	5	8	2	-	2	-	2	-	2	-
PA	12	11	11	12	11	10	11	10	-	2	-	2	1	1	-	2
Midwest.	64	48	68	45	61	44	46	59	13	11	14	10	15	9	13	11
E.N.C	47	32	49	31	43	31	32	42	7	3	7	3	8	2	6	4
OH	11	10	11	10	10	9	6	13	2	-	2	-	2	-	1	1
IN	6	3	8	2	7	3	4	6	-	2	-	2	-	2	-	2
IL	14	8	15	7	12	8	10	10	2	-	2	-	2	-	2	-
MI	11	7	11	7	10	6	9	7	2	-	2	-	2	-	1	1
WI	5	4	4	5	4	5	3	6	1	1	1	1	2	-	2	-
W.N.C	17	16	19	14	18	13	14	17	6	8	7	7	7	7	7	7
MN	5	3	6	2	6	2	6	2	-	2	1	1	1	1	1	1
IA	2	4	2	4	1	4	-	5	1	1	1	1	1	1	1	1
MO	5	4	6	3	6	3	6	3	-	2	-	2	-	2	-	2
ND	1	-	1	-	1	-	1	-	2	-	2	-	2	-	2	-
SD	1	-	1	-	1	-	1	-	1	1	1	1	1	1	1	1
NE	1	2	1	2	1	2	-	3	2	-	2	-	2	-	2	-
KS	2	3	2	3	2	2	-	4	-	2	-	2	-	2	-	2
South	95	46	95	47	92	57	66	83	22	10	22	10	20	12	15	17
S.A	47	22	45	24	42	33	30	45	11	5	11	5	9	7	9	7
DE	1	-	1	-	-	1	-	1	1	1	1	1	1	1	1	1
MD	6	2	5	3	4	4	4	4	2	-	2	-	2	-	2	-
VA	5	5	6	4	7	4	6	5	1	1	1	1	1	1	1	1
WV	4	-	4	-	3	-	3	-	2	-	2	-	2	-	2	-
NC	8	3	7	4	8	4	4	8	1	1	1	1	-	2	-	2
SC	4	2	4	2	3	3	2	4	1	1	1	1	1	1	1	1
GA	9	1	9	1	7	4	3	8	2	-	2	-	1	1	1	1
FL	10	9	9	10	10	13	8	15	1	1	1	1	1	1	1	1
E.S.C	18	9	20	8	19	8	13	14	5	3	5	3	5	3	2	6
KY	4	3	4	3	4	2	2	4	1	1	1	1	1	1	1	1
TN	6	3	6	3	6	3	4	5	2	-	2	-	2	-	-	2
AL	4	2	5	2	4	3	4	3	2	-	2	-	2	-	1	1
MS	4	1	5	-	5	-	3	2	-	2	-	2	-	2	-	2
W.S.C	30	15	30	15	31	16	23	24	6	2	6	2	6	2	4	4
AR	3	1	3	1	2	2	2	2	2	-	2	-	2	-	2	-
LA	4	4	4	4	4	3	2	5	2	-	2	-	2	-	-	2
OK	4	2	4	2	4	2	1	5	1	1	1	1	1	1	-	2
TX	19	8	19	8	21	9	18	12	1	1	1	1	1	1	1	1
West	45	40	48	37	55	38	38	54	10	16	10	16	11	15	9	16
Mountain . . .	9	15	11	13	11	13	6	18	6	10	6	10	6	10	4	12
MT	1	1	1	1	1	-	1	-	1	1	1	1	1	1	1	1
ID	1	1	2	-	1	1	-	2	-	2	-	2	-	2	-	2
WY	-	1	-	1	-	1	-	1	-	2	-	2	-	2	-	2
CO	3	3	3	3	2	4	2	4	1	1	1	1	1	1	1	1
NM	1	2	1	2	1	2	1	2	1	1	1	1	1	1	1	1
AZ	1	4	1	4	3	3	1	5	1	1	1	1	1	1	-	2
UT	1	2	2	1	2	1	1	2	-	2	-	2	-	2	-	2
NV	1	1	1	1	1	1	-	2	2	-	2	-	2	-	2	-
Pacific	36	25	37	24	44	25	32	36	4	6	4	6	5	5	5	4
WA	5	3	5	3	8	1	2	7	1	1	1	1	1	1	1	1
OR	3	2	4	1	4	1	3	2	-	2	-	2	-	2	1	1
CA	27	18	26	19	30	22	25	26	1	1	1	1	2	-	2	-
AK	-	1	-	1	-	1	-	1	-	2	-	2	-	2	-	2
HI	1	1	2	-	2	-	2	-	2	-	2	-	2	-	2	-

- Represents zero.   [1] Alabama and Indiana had one vacancy each.   [2] Vermont had one Independent-Socialist Representative.   [3] As of beginning of second session.   [4] California had one vacancy.   [5] Oregon had one vacancy.

Source: U.S. Congress, Joint Committee on Printing, *Congressional Directory*, biennial; and unpublished data.

No. 441. Members of Congress—Incumbents Re-elected: 1964 to 1994

YEAR	REPRESENTATIVES						SENATORS					
	Retirements[1]	Incumbent candidates					Retirements[1]	Incumbent candidates				
		Total	Re-elected		Defeated in—			Total	Re-elected		Defeated in—	
			Number	Percent of candidates	Primary	General election			Number	Percent of candidates	Primary	General election
PRESIDENTIAL-YEAR ELECTIONS												
1964	33	397	344	86.6	8	45	2	33	28	84.8	1	4
1968	23	409	396	96.8	4	9	6	28	20	71.4	4	4
1972	40	390	365	93.6	12	13	6	27	20	74.1	2	5
1976	47	384	368	95.8	3	13	8	25	16	64.0	-	9
1980	34	398	361	90.7	6	31	5	29	16	55.2	4	9
1984	22	411	392	95.4	3	16	4	29	26	89.7	-	3
1988	23	409	402	98.3	1	6	6	27	23	85.2	-	4
1992	65	368	325	88.3	[2]19	[3]24	7	28	23	82.1	1	4
MIDTERM ELECTIONS												
1966	22	411	362	88.1	8	41	3	32	28	87.5	3	1
1970	29	401	379	94.5	10	12	4	31	24	77.4	1	6
1974	43	391	343	87.7	8	40	7	27	23	85.2	2	2
1978	49	382	358	93.7	5	19	10	25	15	60.0	3	7
1982	40	393	354	90.1	[2]10	29	3	30	28	93.3	-	2
1986	40	394	385	97.7	3	6	6	28	21	75.0	-	7
1990	27	406	390	96.1	1	15	3	32	31	96.9	-	1
1994	[4]27	386	347	89.9	4	35	[4]8	26	24	92.3	-	2

- Represents zero. [1] Does not include persons who died or resigned before the election. [2] Number of incumbents defeated in primaries by other incumbents due to redistricting: six in 1982 and four in 1992. [3] Five incumbents defeated in general election by other incumbents due to redistricting. [4] As of September 9, 1994.

Source: Ornstein, Norman J., Thomas E. Mann, and Michael J. Malbin, *Vital Statistics on Congress, 1993-1994,* Congressional Quarterly, Inc., Washington, DC, 1994; Congressional Quarterly, Inc., Washington, DC, *Congressional Quarterly Weekly Report,* vol. 52, No. 44, Nov. 12, 1994, and selected prior issues; and *Congressional Monitor,* vol. 30, No. 161, Nov. 10, 1994 (copyright).

No. 442. Members of Congress—Selected Characteristics: 1981 to 1995

[As of beginning of first session of each Congress, (January 3). Figures for Representatives exclude vacancies]

MEMBERS OF CONGRESS AND YEAR	Male	Female	Black[1]	Asian, Pacific Islander[2]	Hispanic[3]	AGE[4] (in years)					SENIORITY[5]				
						Under 40	40 to 49	50 to 59	60 to 69	70 and over	Less than 2 yrs.	2 to 9 yrs.	10 to 19 yrs.	20 to 29 yrs.	30 yrs. or more
REPRESENTATIVES															
97th Cong., 1981	416	19	17	3	6	94	142	132	54	13	77	231	96	23	8
98th Cong., 1983	413	21	21	3	8	86	145	132	57	14	83	224	88	28	11
99th Cong., 1985	412	22	20	3	10	71	154	131	59	19	49	237	104	34	10
100th Cong., 1987	412	23	23	4	11	63	153	137	56	26	51	221	114	37	12
101st Cong., 1989	408	25	24	5	10	41	163	133	74	22	39	207	139	35	13
102d Cong., 1991	407	28	25	3	11	39	152	134	86	24	55	178	147	44	11
103d Cong., 1993[6]	388	47	38	4	17	47	151	128	89	15	118	141	132	32	12
104th Cong., 1995	388	47	40	4	17	53	155	135	79	13	92	188	110	36	9
SENATORS															
97th Cong., 1981	98	2	-	3	-	9	35	36	14	6	19	51	17	11	2
98th Cong., 1983	98	2	-	2	-	7	28	39	20	6	5	61	21	10	3
99th Cong., 1985	98	2	-	2	-	4	27	38	25	6	8	56	27	7	2
100th Cong., 1987	98	2	-	2	-	5	30	36	22	7	14	41	36	7	2
101st Cong., 1989	98	2	-	2	-	-	30	40	22	8	23	22	43	10	2
102d Cong., 1991	98	2	-	2	-	-	23	46	24	7	5	34	47	10	4
103d Cong., 1993[6]	93	7	1	2	-	1	16	48	22	12	15	30	39	11	5
104th Cong., 1995	92	8	1	2	-	1	14	41	27	17	12	38	30	15	5

- Represents zero. [1] Source: Joint Center for Political and Economic Studies, Washington, DC, *Black Elected Officials: A National Roster,* annual (copyright). [2] Source: Library of Congress, Congressional Research Service, "Asian Pacific Americans in the United States Congress", Report 94-767 GOV. [3] Source: National Association of Latino Elected and Appointed Officials, Washington, DC, *National Roster of Hispanic Elected Officials,* annual. [4] Some members do not provide date of birth. [5] Represents consecutive years of service. [6] Includes members elected to fill vacant seats through June 14, 1993.

Source: Except as noted, compiled by U.S. Bureau of the Census from data published in *Congressional Directory,* biennial.

No. 443. U.S. Congress—Measures Introduced and Enacted and Time in Session: 1977 to 1994

[Excludes simple and concurrent resolutions. See also *Historical Statistics, Colonial Times to 1970*, series Y 189-198]

ITEM	95th Cong., 1977-78	96th Cong., 1979-80	97th Cong., 1981-82	98th Cong., 1983-84	99th Cong., 1985-86	100th Cong., 1987-88	101st Cong., 1989-90	102d Cong., 1991-92	103d Cong., 1993-94
Measures introduced	19,387	12,583	11,490	11,156	9,885	9,588	6,664	6,775	8,544
Bills	18,045	11,722	10,582	10,134	8,697	8,515	5,977	6,212	7,883
Joint resolutions	1,342	861	908	1,022	1,188	1,073	687	563	661
Measures enacted	803	736	529	677	483	761	666	609	473
Public	633	613	473	623	466	713	650	589	465
Private.	170	123	56	54	17	48	16	20	8
HOUSE OF REPRESENTATIVES									
Number of days	323	326	303	266	281	298	281	280	265
Number of hours.	1,898	1,876	1,420	1,705	1,794	1,659	1,688	1,796	1,887
Number of hours per day	5.9	5.8	4.7	6.4	6.4	5.6	6.0	6.4	7.1
SENATE									
Number of days	337	333	312	281	313	307	274	287	291
Number of hours.	2,510	2,324	2,158	1,951	2,531	2,341	2,254	2,292	2,514
Number of hours per day	7.4	7.0	6.9	6.9	8.1	7.6	8.2	8.0	8.6

Source: U.S. Congress, *Congressional Record* and *Daily Calendar*, selected issues.

No. 444. Congressional Bills Vetoed: 1961 to 1994

[See also *Historical Statistics, Colonial Times to 1970*, series Y 199-203]

PERIOD	President	Total vetoes	Regular vetoes	Pocket vetoes	Vetoes sustained	Bills passed over veto
1961-63	Kennedy	21	12	9	21	-
1963-69	Johnson	30	16	14	30	-
1969-74	Nixon	43	26	17	36	7
1974-77	Ford	66	48	18	54	12
1977-81	Carter	31	13	18	29	2
1981-89	Reagan	78	39	39	69	9
1989-93	Bush.	44	29	15	43	1
1993-94	Clinton	-	-	-	-	-

- Represents zero.

Source: U.S. Congress, Senate Library, *Presidential Vetoes ... 1789-1968*; U.S. Congress, *Calendars of the U.S. House of Representatives and History of Legislation,* annual.

No. 445. Congressional Staff, by Location of Employment: 1970 to 1993

[Excludes those persons employed in Congressional support agencies such as the U.S. General Accounting Office, the Library of Congress, and the Congressional Budget Office]

YEAR	PERSONAL STAFF House	PERSONAL STAFF Senate	YEAR	STANDING COMMITTEE STAFF House	STANDING COMMITTEE STAFF Senate	LOCATION OF EMPLOYMENT	1981	1985	1990	1991	1993
1972 . .	5,280	2,426	1970. .	702	635	**Total**	17,422	18,136	17,625	17,821	(NA)
1980 . .	7,371	3,746	1980. .	1,917	1,191						
1981 . .	7,487	3,945	1981. .	1,843	1,022	House of Representatives. . . .	11,217	11,636	11,064	11,041	10,878
1982 . .	7,511	4,041	1982. .	1,839	1,047	Committee staff [2]	1,917	2,146	2,173	2,321	2,147
1983 . .	7,606	4,059	1983. .	1,970	1,075	Personal staff	7,487	7,528	7,496	7,278	7,400
1984 . .	7,385	3,949	1984. .	1,944	1,095	Leadership staff	127	144	156	149	137
1985 . .	7,528	4,097	1985. .	2,009	1,080	Officers of House, staff . . .	1,686	1,818	1,239	1,293	1,194
1986 . .	[1]7,920	[1]3,774	1986. .	1,954	1,075						
1987 . .	7,584	4,075	1987. .	2,024	1,074	Senate	6,079	6,369	6,425	6,635	6,397
			1988. .	1,976	970	Committee staff [2]	1,150	1,178	1,207	1,154	994
1989 . .	7,569	3,837	1989. .	1,986	1,013	Personal staff	3,945	4,097	4,162	4,294	4,138
1990 . .	7,496	4,162	1990. .	1,993	1,090	Leadership staff	106	118	94	95	100
1991 . .	7,278	4,294	1991. .	2,201	1,030	Officers of Senate, staff. . .	878	976	962	1,092	1,165
1992 . .	7,597	4,249	1992. .	2,178	1,008						
1993 . .	7,400	4,138	1993. .	2,118	897	Joint committee staff	126	131	136	145	(NA)

NA Not available. [1] House figure is average for year, and Senate figure only covers period following implementation of Gramm-Rudman budget reductions. [2] Covers standing, select, and special committees.

Source: Ornstein, Norman J., Thomas E. Mann, and Michael J. Malbin, *Vital Statistics on Congress, 1993-1994*, Congressional Quarterly, Inc., Washington, DC, 1994, and unpublished data (copyright).

No. 446. Number of Governors, by Political Party Affiliation: 1970 to 1996

[Reflects figures after inaugurations for each year]

YEAR	Demo-cratic	Re-pub-lican	Inde-pen-dent	YEAR	Demo-cratic	Re-pub-lican	Inde-pen-dent	YEAR	Demo-cratic	Re-pub-lican	Inde-pen-dent
1970	18	32	-	1987	26	24	-	1992	28	20	2
1975	36	13	1	1988	27	23	-	1993	30	18	2
1980	31	19	-	1989	28	22	-	1994	29	19	2
1985	34	16	-	1990	29	21	-	1995	19	30	1
1986	34	16	-	1991 [1]	29	19	2	1996	18	31	1

- Represents zero. [1] Reflects result of runoff election in Arizona in February 1991.
Source: National Governors' Association, Washington, DC, 1970-87 and 1991-96, *Directory of Governors of the American States, Commonwealths & Territories,* annual; and 1988-90, *Directory of Governors,* annual. (Copyright.)

No. 447. Vote Cast for and Governor Elected, by State: 1988 to 1994

[In thousands, except percent. D=Democratic, R=Republican, I=Independent]

DIVISION AND STATE	1988 Total vote [1]	1988 Percent leading party	1990 Total vote [1]	1990 Percent leading party	1992 Total vote [1]	1992 Percent leading party	1994 Total vote [1]	1994 Percent leading party	Candidate elected at most recent election
N.E.:									
ME	(X)	(X)	522	R-46.7	(X)	(X)	511	I-35.4	Angus King
NH	442	R-60.4	295	R-60.3	516	R-56.0	312	R-69.9	Steve Merrill
VT	243	D-55.4	211	R-51.8	286	D-74.7	212	D-68.7	Howard Dean
MA	(X)	(X)	2,343	R-50.2	(X)	(X)	2,164	R-70.9	William Weld
RI	401	R-50.8	357	D-74.1	425	D-61.5	361	R-47.4	Lincoln Almond
CT	(X)	(X)	1,141	I-40.4	(X)	(X)	1,147	R-36.2	John Rowland
M.A.:									
NY [2]	(X)	(X)	4,057	D-53.2	(X)	(X)	5,204	R-48.8	George Pataki
NJ [2]	(X)	(X)	2,254	D-61.2	2,506	R-49.3	(X)	(X)	Christine T. Whitman
PA	(X)	(X)	3,053	D-67.7	(X)	(X)	3,585	R-45.4	Thomas Ridge
E.N.C.:									
OH	(X)	(X)	3,478	R-55.7	(X)	(X)	3,346	R-71.8	George Voinovich
IN	2,141	D-53.2	(X)	(X)	2,229	D-62.0	(X)	(X)	Evan Bayh
IL	(X)	(X)	3,257	R-50.7	(X)	(X)	3,107	R-63.9	Jim Edgar
MI	(X)	(X)	2,565	R-49.8	(X)	(X)	3,088	R-61.5	John Engler
WI	(X)	(X)	1,380	R-58.2	(X)	(X)	1,563	R-67.3	Tommy Thompson
W.N.C.:									
MN	(X)	(X)	1,807	R-49.6	(X)	(X)	1,766	R-62.0	Arne Carlson
IA	(X)	(X)	976	R-60.6	(X)	(X)	997	R-56.8	Terry Branstad
MO	2,086	R-64.2	(X)	(X)	2,344	D-58.7	(X)	(X)	Mel Carnahan
ND	299	D-59.9	(X)	(X)	305	R-57.9	(X)	(X)	Edward T. Schafer
SD	(X)	(X)	257	R-58.9	(X)	(X)	312	R-55.4	William Janklow
NE	(X)	(X)	587	D-49.9	(X)	(X)	580	D-73.0	Ben Nelson
KS	(X)	(X)	783	D-48.6	(X)	(X)	821	R-64.1	Bill Graves
S.A.:									
DE	240	R-70.7	(X)	(X)	277	D-64.7	(X)	(X)	Thomas R. Carper
MD [2]	(X)	(X)	1,111	D-59.8	(X)	(X)	1,410	D-50.2	Parris Glendening
VA [2]	(X)	(X)	1,789	D-50.1	1,794	R-58.3	(X)	(X)	George F. Allen
WV	650	D-58.9	(X)	(X)	657	D-56.0	(X)	(X)	Gaston Caperton
NC	2,180	R-56.1	(X)	(X)	2,595	D-52.7	(X)	(X)	James B. Hunt
SC	(X)	(X)	761	R-69.5	(X)	(X)	934	R-50.4	David Beasley
GA	(X)	(X)	1,450	D-52.9	(X)	(X)	1,545	D-51.1	Zell Miller
FL	(X)	(X)	3,531	D-56.5	(X)	(X)	4,206	D-50.8	Lawton Chiles
E.S.C.:									
KY [3]	781	D-64.6	835	D-64.7	(X)	(X)	984	D-50.9	Paul Patton
TN	(X)	(X)	790	D-60.8	(X)	(X)	1,487	R-54.3	Don Sundquist
AL	(X)	(X)	1,216	R-52.1	(X)	(X)	1,202	R-50.3	Fob James, Jr.
MS [3]	722	D-53.4	711	R-50.8	(X)	(X)	819	R-55.6	Kirk Fordice
W.S.C.:									
AR	(X)	(X)	696	D-57.5	(X)	(X)	717	D-59.8	Jim Guy Tucker
LA	[4]1,559	[4]33.1	[5]1,728	[5]D-61.2	(X)	(X)	[6]1,550	[6]R-63.5	Mike Foster
OK	(X)	(X)	911	D-57.4	(X)	(X)	995	R-46.9	Frank Keating
TX	(X)	(X)	3,893	D-49.5	(X)	(X)	4,396	R-53.5	George W. Bush
Mountain:									
MT	367	R-51.9	(X)	(X)	408	R-51.3	(X)	(X)	Marc Racicot
ID	(X)	(X)	321	D-68.2	(X)	(X)	413	R-52.3	Phil Batt
WY	(X)	(X)	160	D-65.4	(X)	(X)	201	R-58.7	Jim Geringer
CO	(X)	(X)	1,011	D-61.9	(X)	(X)	1,116	D-55.5	Roy Romer
NM	(X)	(X)	411	D-54.6	(X)	(X)	468	R-49.8	Gary Johnson
AZ	(X)	(X)	[7]941	[7]R-52.4	(X)	(X)	1,129	R-52.5	Fife Symington
UT	649	R-40.1	(X)	(X)	763	R-42.2	(X)	(X)	Mike Leavitt
NV	(X)	(X)	321	D-64.8	(X)	(X)	371	D-53.9	Bob Miller
Pacific:									
WA	1,875	D-62.2	(X)	(X)	2,271	D-52.2	(X)	(X)	Mike Lowry
OR	(X)	(X)	1,113	D-45.7	(X)	(X)	1,221	D-50.9	John Kitzhaber
CA	(X)	(X)	7,699	R-49.2	(X)	(X)	8,659	R-55.2	Pete Wilson
AK	(X)	(X)	195	I-38.9	(X)	(X)	213	D-41.1	James Campbell
HI	(X)	(X)	340	D-59.8	(X)	(X)	369	D-36.6	Ben Cayetano

X Not applicable. [1] Includes minor party and scattered votes. [2] Voting years 1989 and 1993. [3] Voting years 1987, 1991, and 1995. [4] Primary election in Oct. 1987, held on a nonparty basis. Winner was Democratic. Runner-up withdrew from runoff. [5] Result of runoff election in 1991. [6] Result of runoff election in November 1995. [7] Result of runoff election in February 1991.
Source: Elections Research Center, Chevy Chase, MD, *America Votes,* biennial; and unpublished data, (copyright) and Congressional Quarterly, Inc., Washington, DC, *Congressional Quarterly Weekly Report,* vol. 53, No. 15, April 15, 1995, and unpublished data (copyright).

No. 448. Composition of State Legislatures, by Political Party Affiliation: 1988 to 1994

[Data reflect election results in year shown for most States; and except as noted, results in previous year for other States. Figures reflect immediate results of elections, including holdover members in State houses which do not have all of their members running for re-election. Dem.=Democrat, Rep.=Republican. In general, Lower House refers to body consisting of State Representatives; Upper House, of State Senators]

STATE	LOWER HOUSE								UPPER HOUSE							
	1988[1,2]		1990[3,4]		1992[5,6]		1994[7,8]		1988[1,9]		1990[3,10]		1992[5,11]		1994[7,12]	
	Dem.	Rep.	Dem.	Rep.	Dem.	Rep.	Dem.	Rep.	Dem.	Rep.	Dem.	Rep.	Dem.	Rep.	Dem.	Rep.
U.S.	3,277	2,176	3,242	2,202	3,186	2,223	2,817	2,603	1,192	751	1,186	757	1,132	799	1,021	905
AL[13]	85	17	82	23	82	23	74	31	28	6	28	7	27	8	23	12
AK[15]	23	17	23	17	20	18	17	22	8	12	10	10	10	10	8	12
AZ[14]	26	34	27	33	25	35	22	38	13	17	17	13	12	18	11	19
AR[14]	88	11	90	9	88	11	88	12	31	4	31	4	30	5	28	7
CA[14]	46	33	47	33	47	33	39	40	24	15	25	13	21	16	21	17
CO[14]	26	39	27	38	31	34	24	41	11	24	12	23	16	19	16	19
CT[15]	88	63	87	64	85	64	90	61	23	13	20	16	19	17	17	19
DE[14]	18	23	17	24	18	23	14	27	13	8	15	6	15	6	12	9
FL[14]	73	47	74	46	71	49	63	57	23	17	22	18	20	20	19	21
GA[15]	144	36	145	35	128	51	114	65	45	11	45	11	41	15	35	20
HI[14]	45	6	45	6	47	4	44	7	22	3	22	3	22	3	23	2
ID[15]	20	64	28	56	20	50	13	57	19	23	21	21	12	23	8	27
IL[14]	67	51	72	46	67	51	54	64	31	28	31	28	27	32	26	33
IN[14]	50	50	52	48	55	45	44	56	24	26	24	26	22	28	20	30
IA[14]	61	39	55	45	49	51	36	64	30	20	29	21	27	23	27	23
KS[14]	58	67	63	62	59	66	45	80	18	22	18	22	13	27	13	27
KY[14]	72	28	68	32	71	29	64	36	30	8	27	11	25	13	21	17
LA[13]	86	17	89	16	88	16	86	17	34	5	34	5	33	6	33	6
ME[15]	97	54	97	54	93	58	77	74	20	15	21	14	20	15	16	18
MD[13]	125	16	116	25	116	25	100	41	40	7	38	9	38	9	32	15
MA[15]	128	32	118	37	123	34	125	34	32	8	25	15	31	9	30	10
MI[14]	61	49	61	49	55	55	53	56	18	20	18	20	16	22	16	22
MN[14]	80	53	78	56	85	49	71	63	44	23	46	21	45	22	43	21
MS[13]	112	9	98	23	91	29	89	31	44	8	43	9	37	15	36	14
MO[14]	104	58	99	64	98	65	87	76	22	12	23	11	20	14	19	15
MT[14]	52	48	61	39	47	53	33	67	23	27	29	21	30	20	19	31
NE.	(16)	(16)	(16)	(16)	(16)	(16)	(16)	(16)	(16)	(16)	(16)	(16)	(16)	(16)	(16)	(16)
NV[14]	30	12	22	19	27	12	21	21	8	13	10	10	10	11	8	13
NH[14]	119	281	125	268	136	258	112	286	8	16	11	13	11	13	6	18
NJ[14]	44	36	22	58	27	53	28	52	22	17	13	27	16	24	16	24
NM[14]	45	25	49	21	53	17	46	24	26	16	26	16	27	15	27	15
NY[15]	92	58	95	55	100	50	94	56	27	34	26	35	26	35	25	36
NC[15]	74	46	81	39	78	42	52	68	37	13	36	14	39	11	26	24
ND[14]	45	61	48	58	33	65	23	75	32	21	27	26	25	24	20	29
OH[14]	59	40	61	38	53	46	43	56	14	19	12	21	13	20	13	20
OK[14]	68	32	68	33	70	31	65	36	33	15	37	11	37	11	35	13
OR[14]	32	28	28	32	28	32	26	34	19	11	20	10	16	14	11	19
PA[14]	104	99	107	94	105	98	101	102	23	27	24	26	24	25	21	29
RI[15]	83	17	89	11	85	15	84	16	41	9	45	5	39	11	40	10
SC[14]	87	37	79	43	71	52	58	62	35	11	33	13	30	16	29	17
SD[15]	24	46	25	45	28	42	24	46	15	20	17	18	20	15	16	19
TN[14]	59	40	57	42	63	36	59	40	22	11	20	13	19	14	18	15
TX[14]	93	57	93	57	91	58	89	61	23	8	22	9	18	13	17	14
UT[14]	28	47	31	44	26	49	20	55	7	22	10	19	11	18	10	19
VT[15]	74	76	73	75	87	57	86	61	16	14	15	15	14	16	12	18
VA[14]	59	39	58	41	52	47	52	47	30	10	22	18	22	18	22	18
WA[14]	63	35	58	40	65	33	38	60	24	25	24	25	28	21	25	24
WV[14]	81	19	74	26	79	21	69	30	29	5	33	1	32	2	26	8
WI[14]	56	43	58	41	51	47	48	51	20	13	19	14	16	17	16	17
WY[14]	23	41	22	42	19	41	13	47	11	19	10	20	10	20	10	20

[1] Status as of Jan. 1989, except for NJ and VA which are as of Jan. 1990. [2] Excludes one Independent for AR; two Independents for VA; one Independent Democrat for MS; one vacancy each for CA, MN, MO, and OK; two vacancies for LA; and three vacancies for AL. [3] Status as of May 1992; reflects results of elections held in LA, KY, MS, and NJ in 1991. [4] Excludes one Independent each for MA, MS, NH, SC, and VA; one Independent Democrat for NH; two Independents for VT; one vacancy each for AR, NV, and SC; two vacancies for PA; four vacancies for MA; and five vacancies for NH. [5] Status as of November 11, 1993. [6] Excludes one Independent each for AR, LA, NH, SC, and VA; two Independents each for AK and MS; four Independents for VT; members of political parties other than Democratic, Republican, or Independent (one in MA, two in VT, and four in NH); one vacancy each for GA, NH, TX, and WI; two vacancies each for CT and MA; and three vacancies for NV. [7] Status as of December 7, 1994. [8] Excludes one Independent each for AK, CA, LA, and VA; two Independents each for MS and VT; four Independents for SC; members of political parties other than Democratic, Republican, or Independent (one each in MA and VT and two in NH); one undecided in GA; and one vacancy each in LA, MI, and WV. [9] Excludes one Independent for CA and one vacancy each for AL and NJ. [10] Excludes two Independents for CA; and one vacancy for NV. [11] Excludes two Independents for CA; and one vacancy each for CA and PA. [12] Excludes one Independent in ME, two independents in CA, one vacancy in GA, two vacancies in MS, and three vacancies in MN. [13] Members of both houses serve 4-year terms. [14] Upper-House members serve 4-year terms and Lower House members serve 2-year terms. [15] Members of both houses serve 2-year terms. [16] Single chamber (unicameral body) of 49 members, elected without party designation.

Source: 1988 and 1990, The Council of State Governments, Lexington, KY, *State Elective Officials and the Legislatures*, biennial (copyright); 1992 and 1994, National Conference of State Legislatures, Denver, CO, unpublished data, (copyright).

No. 449. Political Party Control of State Legislatures, by Party: 1971 to 1995

[As of beginning of year. Until 1972 there were two nonpartisan legislatures in Minnesota and Nebraska. Since then only Nebraska has had a nonpartisan legislature]

YEAR	LEGISLATURES UNDER—			YEAR	LEGISLATURES UNDER—			YEAR	LEGISLATURES UNDER—		
	Democratic control	Split control or tie	Republican control		Democratic control	Split control or tie	Republican control		Democratic control	Split control or tie	Republican control
1971...	23	9	16	1981...	28	6	15	1990...	29	11	9
1973...	27	6	16	1983 [1] .	34	4	11	1992...	29	14	6
1975...	37	7	5	1985...	27	11	11	1993...	25	16	8
1977...	36	8	5	1987...	28	12	9	1994...	24	17	8
1979...	30	7	12	1989 [2] .	28	13	8	1995...	18	12	19

[1] Two 1984 midterm recall elections resulted in a change in control of the Michigan State Senate. At the time of the 1984 election, therefore, Democrats controlled 33 legislatures.   [2] A party change during the year by a Democratic representative broke the tie in the Indiana House of Representatives, giving the Republicans control of both chambers.

Source: National Conference of State Legislatures, Denver, CO, *State Legislatures*, periodic.

No. 450. Local Elected Officials, by Sex, Race, Hispanic Origin, and Type of Government: 1992

SEX, RACE, AND HISPANIC ORIGIN	Total	GENERAL PURPOSE			SPECIAL PURPOSE	
		County	Municipal	Town, township	School district	Special district
Total	**493,830**	**58,818**	**135,531**	**126,958**	**88,434**	**84,089**
Male	324,255	43,563	94,808	76,213	54,443	55,228
Female	100,531	12,525	26,825	27,702	24,730	8,749
Sex not reported	69,044	2,730	13,898	23,043	9,261	20,112
White	405,905	52,705	114,880	102,676	73,894	61,750
Black	11,542	1,715	4,566	369	4,222	670
American Indian, Eskimo, Aleut	1,800	147	776	86	564	227
Asian, Pacific Islander	514	80	97	16	184	137
Hispanic	5,859	906	1,701	216	2,466	570
Non-Hispanic	413,902	53,741	118,618	102,931	76,398	62,214
Race, Hispanic origin not reported	74,069	4,171	15,212	23,811	9,570	21,305

Source: U.S. Bureau of the Census, *1992 Census of Governments, Popularly Elected Officials*, (GC92(1)-2).

No. 451. Women Holding State Public Offices, by Office and State: 1995

[As of **January**. For data on women in U.S. Congress, see table 442]

STATE	Statewide elective executive office[1]	State legislature	STATE	Statewide elective executive office[1]	State legislature	STATE	Statewide elective executive office[1]	State legislature
United States	**84**	**1,535**	Kentucky	1	11	North Dakota	5	22
Alabama	3	5	Louisiana	2	14	Ohio	2	32
Alaska	1	14	Maine	-	50	Oklahoma	3	16
Arizona	3	27	Maryland	1	54	Oregon	1	24
Arkansas	2	17	Massachusetts	-	48	Pennsylvania	2	30
California	2	25	Michigan	2	33	Rhode Island	1	36
Colorado	3	31	Minnesota	3	50	South Carolina	1	21
Connecticut	2	50	Mississippi	-	20	South Dakota	3	19
Delaware	4	13	Missouri	[2]2	39	Tennessee	1	18
Florida	1	31	Montana	1	36	Texas	2	33
Georgia	1	43	Nebraska	1	12	Utah	2	15
Hawaii	1	16	Nevada	1	22	Vermont	1	53
Idaho	2	30	New Hampshire	-	128	Virginia	-	16
Illinois	2	42	New Jersey	1	16	Washington	4	58
Indiana	4	33	New Mexico	2	23	West Virginia	-	20
Iowa	1	27	New York	1	38	Wisconsin	-	32
Kansas	4	46	North Carolina	-	27	Wyoming	2	19

- Represents zero.   [1] Excludes women elected to the judiciary, women appointed to State cabinet-level positions, women elected to executive posts by the legislature, and elected members of university Board of Trustees or board of education.   [2] Includes one official who was appointed to an elective position.

Source: Center for the American Woman and Politics, Eagleton Institute of Politics, Rutgers University, New Brunswick, NJ, information releases, (copyright).

No. 452. Black Elected Officials, by Office, 1970 to 1993, and by Region and State, 1993

[As of **January 1993**, no Black elected officials had been identified in Hawaii, Idaho, Montana, North Dakota, or Utah]

REGION, DIVISION, AND STATE	Total	U.S. and State legislatures[1]	City and county offices[2]	Law enforcement[3]	Education[4]
1970 (Feb.)	1,469	179	715	213	362
1980 (July)	4,890	326	2,832	526	1,206
1985 (Jan.)	6,016	407	3,517	661	1,431
1990 (Jan.)	7,335	436	4,485	769	1,645
1991 (Jan.)	7,445	473	4,496	847	1,629
1992 (Jan.)	7,517	499	4,557	847	1,614
1993 (Jan.)	7,984	561	4,819	922	1,682
Northeast	777	96	291	126	264
N.E	109	35	60	4	10
ME	1	-	1	-	-
NH	2	2	-	-	-
VT	2	2	-	-	-
MA	30	8	18	2	2
RI	12	9	3	-	-
CT	62	14	38	2	8
M.A.	668	61	231	122	254
NY	299	30	63	70	136
NJ	211	13	113	-	85
PA	158	18	55	52	33
Midwest	1,361	106	757	171	327
E.N.C.	1,119	78	604	143	294
OH	219	16	124	30	49
IN	72	12	50	4	6
IL	465	25	282	37	121
MI	333	17	133	68	115
WI	30	8	15	4	3
W.N.C	242	28	153	28	33
MN	16	1	2	10	3
IA	11	1	6	1	3
MO	185	18	134	14	19
SD	3	1	2	-	-
NE	6	1	2	-	3
KS	21	6	7	3	5
South	5,492	328	3,675	518	971
S.A.	2,200	173	1,522	147	358
DE	23	3	14	-	6
MD	140	32	79	23	6
DC	198	[5]4	185	-	9
VA	155	14	126	15	-
WV	21	1	17	3	-
NC	468	28	328	31	81
SC	450	26	269	15	140
GA	545	43	371	32	99
FL	200	22	133	28	17
E.S.C.	1,681	85	1,175	175	246
KY	63	4	47	5	7
TN	168	16	104	24	24
AL	699	23	529	58	89
MS	751	42	495	88	126
W.S.C	1,611	70	978	196	367
AR	380	13	214	51	102
LA	636	33	346	104	153
OK	123	6	95	1	21
TX	472	18	323	40	91
West	354	31	96	107	120
Mountain	49	11	11	16	11
WY	1	-	-	-	1
CO	20	4	4	10	2
NM	3	-	-	2	1
AZ	15	4	3	3	5
NV	10	3	4	1	2
Pacific	305	20	85	91	109
WA	19	2	9	5	3
OR	10	4	2	4	-
CA	273	13	72	82	106
AK	3	1	2	-	-

- Represents zero. [1] Includes elected State administrators. [2] County commissioners and councilmen, mayors, vice mayors, aldermen, regional officials, and other. [3] Judges, magistrates, constables, marshals, sheriffs, justices of the peace, and other. [4] Members of State education agencies, college boards, school boards, and other. [5] Includes two shadow senators and one shadow representative.

Source: Joint Center for Political and Economic Studies, Washington, DC, *Black Elected Officials: A National Roster*, annual, (copyright).

No. 453. Hispanic Public Officials, by Office, 1985 to 1994, and by State, 1994

[As of **September**. For States not shown, no Hispanic public officials had been identified]

REGION, DIVISION, AND STATE	Total	State executives and legislators[1]	County and municipal officials[2]	Judicial and law enforcement	Education and school boards
1985	3,147	129	1,316	517	1,185
1990	4,004	144	1,819	583	1,458
1991	4,202	151	1,867	596	1,588
1992	4,994	150	1,908	628	2,308
1993	5,170	182	2,023	633	2,332
1994	5,459	199	2,197	651	2,412
Northeast	156	28	42	13	73
N.E	28	13	9	-	6
MA	1	-	-	-	1
RI	1	1	-	-	-
CT	26	12	9	-	5
M.A.	128	15	33	13	67
NY	83	12	13	11	47
NJ	37	2	17	1	17
PA	8	1	3	1	3
Midwest	917	15	43	8	851
E.N.C	903	8	39	7	849
OH	4	-	1	2	1
IN	8	1	5	1	1
IL	881	7	26	3	[2]845
MI	8	-	5	1	2
WI	2	-	2	-	-
W.N.C	14	7	4	1	2
MN	3	2	-	1	-
MO	1	-	1	-	-
NE	3	-	2	-	1
KS	7	5	1	-	1
South	2,298	61	1,059	410	768
S.A.	68	16	35	13	4
DE	1	-	1	-	-
MD	2	-	1	-	1
DC	1	-	-	1	-
FL	64	16	33	12	3
W.S.C	2,230	45	1,024	397	764
AR	2	1	-	-	1
LA	12	3	1	8	-
OK	1	-	1	-	-
TX	2,215	41	1,022	389	763
West	2,088	95	1,053	220	720
Mountain	1,270	74	697	167	332
MT	2	-	-	-	1
ID	3	1	2	-	-
WY	3	1	2	-	-
CO	201	9	140	10	42
NM	716	50	410	105	151
AZ	341	11	144	50	136
UT	1	1	-	-	-
NV	4	1	-	1	2
Pacific	818	21	356	53	388
WA	14	2	4	2	6
OR	5	-	3	1	1
CA	796	16	349	50	381
AK	1	1	-	-	-
HI	2	2	-	-	-

- Represents zero. [1] Includes U.S. Representatives. [2] Includes local school council members in the Chicago area.

Source: National Association of Latino Elected and Appointed Officials, Washington, DC, *National Roster of Hispanic Elected Officials*, annual.

No. 454. Public Confidence Levels in Selected Public and Private Institutions: 1994

[Based on a sample survey of 1,509 persons 18 years old and over conducted during the spring and subject to sampling variability; see source]

INSTITUTION	LEVEL OF CONFIDENCE				
	A great deal	Quite a lot	Some	Very little	Can't say/ no answer
Religious organizations	21.3	28.3	30.9	16.7	2.8
Private higher colleges or universities	14.4	33.9	30.9	12.4	8.4
Private elementary or secondary education	13.4	31.9	34.7	13.9	6.2
Federated charitable appeals	11.3	26.1	36.1	21.2	5.3
Health organizations	11.2	24.4	43.0	16.6	4.7
Environmental organizations	10.7	22.9	40.3	20.5	5.6
Human service organizations	10.3	22.9	45.0	15.4	6.5
Arts, culture, & humanities organizations	8.1	21.2	40.5	18.7	11.6
Private and community foundations	8.0	22.5	43.9	16.7	8.9
Public /society benefit organizations [1]	6.0	17.9	45.5	24.4	6.1
International/foreign organizations [2]	3.7	14.9	38.3	30.7	12.5
Small businesses	16.2	36.7	36.8	7.2	3.2
Military	15.8	32.8	34.0	14.1	3.2
Public higher colleges or universities	11.4	33.9	39.2	10.7	4.8
Public elementary or secondary education	11.3	30.7	40.6	14.7	2.7
Organized labor	6.7	15.9	43.9	29.1	4.4
Media (e.g. newspapers, TV, radio)	6.1	19.8	40.5	32.0	1.6
Major corporations	5.1	17.2	50.6	22.7	4.4
State government	4.4	16.4	46.0	31.2	1.9
Political organizations, parties	3.9	12.7	40.3	39.7	3.4
Local government	3.8	19.4	45.6	29.0	2.1
Federal government	3.5	15.5	44.2	34.8	1.9
Congress	3.2	12.0	40.9	41.3	2.6

[1] Civil rights, social justice, or community improvement organizations.   [2] Culture exchange or relief organizations.

Source: Hodgkinson, Virginia, Murray Weitzman, and the Gallup Organization, Inc., *Giving & Volunteering in the United States: 1994 Edition.* (Copyright and published by INDEPENDENT SECTOR, Washington, DC, 1994.)

No. 455. Political Party Identification of the Adult Population, by Degree of Attachment, 1972 to 1994, and by Selected Characteristics, 1994

[In percent. Covers citizens of voting-age living in private housing units in the contiguous United States. Data are from the National Election Studies and are based on a sample and subject to sampling variability; for details, see source]

YEAR AND SELECTED CHARACTERISTIC	Total	Strong Democrat	Weak Democrat	Independent Democrat	Independent	Independent Republican	Weak Republican	Strong Republican	Apolitical
1972	100	15	26	11	13	11	13	10	1
1980	100	18	23	11	13	10	14	9	2
1984	100	17	20	11	11	12	15	12	2
1986	100	18	22	10	12	11	15	11	2
1988	100	18	18	12	11	13	14	14	2
1990	100	20	19	12	11	12	15	10	2
1992	100	18	18	14	12	12	14	11	1
1994, total [1]	100	15	19	13	10	12	15	16	1
Age:									
17 to 24 years old	100	9	20	22	10	8	19	10	1
25 to 34 years old	100	11	19	14	12	11	16	16	1
35 to 44 years old	100	13	18	14	12	11	14	18	-
45 to 54 years old	100	15	16	15	7	16	12	17	1
55 to 64 years old	100	18	22	8	8	16	12	15	-
65 to 74 years old	100	28	17	6	8	13	14	15	-
75 to 99 years old	100	19	26	9	9	5	17	13	2
Sex:									
Male	100	13	17	12	11	14	14	18	1
Female	100	18	21	13	10	9	15	13	1
Race:									
White	100	12	19	12	10	13	16	17	1
Black	100	38	23	20	8	4	2	3	1
Education:									
Grade school	100	26	26	7	13	7	11	6	4
High school	100	15	22	14	13	10	13	11	1
College	100	14	16	13	7	13	16	21	-

- Represents zero.   [1] Includes other characteristics, not shown separately.

Source: Center for Political Studies, University of Michigan, Ann Arbor, MI, unpublished data. Data prior to 1988 published in Warren E. Miller and Santa A. Traugott, *American National Election Studies Data Sourcebook, 1952-1986,* Harvard University Press, Cambridge, MA, 1989 (copyright).

No. 456. Voting-Age Population, Percent Reporting Registered, and Voted: 1980 to 1994

[As of **November**. Covers civilian noninstitutional population 18 years old and over. Includes aliens. Figures are based on Current Population Survey (see text, section 1, and Appendix III) and differ from those in table 458 based on population estimates and official vote counts]

CHARACTERISTIC	VOTING-AGE POPULATION (mil.)								PERCENT REPORTING THEY REGISTERED								PERCENT REPORTING THEY VOTED							
									Presidential election years				Congressional election years				Presidential election years				Congressional election years			
	1980	1982	1984	1986	1988	1990	1992	1994	1980	1984	1988	1992	1982	1986	1990	1994	1980	1984	1988	1992	1982	1986	1990	1994
Total [1]	**157.1**	**165.5**	**170.0**	**173.9**	**178.1**	**182.1**	**185.7**	**190.3**	**66.9**	**68.3**	**66.6**	**68.2**	**64.1**	**64.3**	**62.2**	**62.0**	**59.2**	**59.9**	**57.4**	**61.3**	**48.5**	**46.0**	**45.0**	**44.6**
18 to 20 years old	12.3	12.1	11.2	10.7	10.7	10.8	9.7	10.3	44.7	47.0	44.9	48.3	35.0	35.4	35.4	37.2	35.7	36.7	33.2	38.5	19.8	18.6	18.4	16.5
21 to 24 years old	15.9	16.7	16.7	15.7	14.8	14.0	14.6	14.9	52.7	54.3	50.6	55.3	47.8	46.6	43.3	45.5	43.1	43.5	38.3	45.7	28.4	24.2	22.0	22.3
25 to 34 years old	35.7	38.8	40.3	41.9	42.7	42.7	41.6	41.1	62.0	63.3	57.8	60.6	57.1	55.8	52.0	51.5	54.6	54.5	48.0	53.2	40.4	35.1	33.8	32.2
35 to 44 years old	25.6	28.1	30.7	33.0	35.2	37.9	39.7	41.9	70.6	70.9	69.3	69.2	67.5	67.9	65.5	63.3	64.4	63.5	61.3	63.6	52.2	49.3	48.4	46.0
45 to 64 years old	43.6	44.2	44.3	44.8	45.9	46.9	49.1	50.9	75.8	76.6	75.5	75.3	75.6	74.8	71.4	71.0	69.3	69.8	67.9	70.0	62.2	58.7	55.8	56.0
65 years old and over	24.1	25.6	26.7	27.7	28.8	29.9	30.8	31.1	74.6	76.9	78.4	78.0	75.2	76.9	76.5	75.6	65.1	67.7	68.8	70.1	59.9	60.9	60.3	60.7
Male	74.1	78.0	80.3	82.4	84.5	86.6	88.6	91.0	66.6	67.3	65.2	66.9	63.7	63.4	61.2	60.8	59.1	59.0	56.4	60.2	48.7	45.8	44.6	44.4
Female	83.0	87.4	89.6	91.5	93.6	95.5	97.1	99.3	67.1	69.3	67.8	69.3	64.4	65.0	63.1	63.2	59.4	60.8	58.3	62.3	48.4	46.1	45.4	44.9
White	137.7	143.6	146.8	149.9	152.9	155.6	157.8	160.3	68.4	69.6	67.9	70.1	65.6	65.3	63.8	64.2	60.9	61.4	59.1	63.6	49.9	47.0	46.7	46.9
Black	16.4	17.6	18.4	19.0	19.7	20.4	21.0	21.8	60.0	66.3	64.5	63.9	59.1	64.0	58.8	58.3	50.5	55.8	51.5	54.0	43.0	43.2	39.2	37.0
Hispanic [2]	8.2	8.8	9.5	11.8	12.9	13.8	14.7	17.5	36.3	40.1	35.5	35.0	35.3	35.9	32.3	30.0	29.9	32.6	28.8	28.9	25.3	24.2	21.0	19.1
Region: [3]																								
Northeast	35.5	36.4	36.9	37.3	37.9	38.1	38.3	38.4	64.8	66.6	64.8	67.0	62.5	62.0	61.0	60.9	58.5	59.7	57.4	61.2	49.8	44.4	45.2	45.2
Midwest	41.5	41.9	42.1	42.8	43.3	43.9	44.4	44.5	73.8	74.6	72.5	74.6	71.1	70.7	68.2	68.7	65.8	65.7	62.9	67.2	54.7	49.5	48.6	48.8
South	50.6	55.4	57.6	59.2	60.7	62.4	63.7	66.4	64.8	66.9	65.6	67.2	61.7	63.0	61.3	60.7	55.6	56.8	54.5	59.0	41.8	43.0	42.4	40.5
West	29.5	31.9	33.4	34.6	36.2	37.7	39.3	41.0	63.3	64.7	63.0	63.6	60.6	60.8	57.7	58.1	57.2	58.5	55.6	58.5	50.7	48.4	45.0	46.4
School years completed:																								
8 years or less	22.7	22.4	20.6	19.6	19.1	17.7	15.4	14.7	53.0	53.4	47.5	43.9	52.3	50.5	44.0	40.1	42.6	42.9	36.7	35.1	35.7	32.7	27.7	23.2
High school: 1 to 3 years	22.5	22.3	22.1	21.4	21.1	21.0	[4]21.0	[4]20.7	54.6	54.9	52.8	[4]50.4	53.3	52.4	47.9	[4]44.7	45.6	44.4	41.3	[4]41.2	37.7	33.8	30.9	[4]27.0
4 years	61.2	65.2	67.8	68.6	70.0	71.5	[5]65.3	[5]64.9	66.4	67.3	64.6	[5]64.9	62.9	62.9	60.0	[5]58.9	58.9	58.7	54.7	[5]57.5	47.1	44.1	42.2	[5]40.5
College: 1 to 3 years	26.7	28.8	30.9	33.0	34.3	36.3	[6]46.7	[6]50.4	74.4	75.7	73.5	[6]75.4	70.0	70.0	68.7	[6]68.4	67.2	67.5	64.5	[6]68.7	53.3	49.9	50.0	[6]49.1
4 years or more	24.0	26.9	28.6	31.3	33.6	35.6	[7]37.4	[7]39.4	84.3	83.8	83.1	[7]84.8	79.4	77.8	77.3	[7]76.3	79.9	79.1	77.6	[7]81.0	66.5	62.5	62.5	[7]63.1
Employed	95.0	97.2	104.2	108.5	113.8	115.5	116.3	122.6	68.7	69.4	67.1	69.9	65.5	64.4	62.6	62.9	61.8	61.6	58.4	63.8	50.0	45.7	45.1	45.2
Unemployed	6.9	10.8	7.4	6.6	5.8	6.7	8.3	6.5	50.3	54.3	50.4	53.7	49.8	50.6	44.6	46.4	41.2	44.0	38.6	46.2	34.1	31.2	27.9	28.3
Not in labor force	55.2	57.5	58.4	58.8	58.5	59.9	61.1	61.2	65.8	68.1	67.2	66.8	64.3	65.4	63.4	61.9	57.0	58.9	57.3	58.7	48.7	48.2	46.7	45.3

[1] Includes other races not shown separately.   [2] Hispanic persons may be of any race.   [3] For composition of regions, see table 27.   [4] Represents those who completed 9th to 12th grade, but have no high school diploma.   [5] High school graduate.   [6] Some college or associate degree.   [7] Bachelor's or advanced degree.

Source: U.S. Bureau of the Census, *Current Population Reports*, P20-453 and P20-466; and unpublished data.

No. 457. Persons Reported Registered and Voted, by State: 1994

[See headnote, table 456]

STATE	Voting-age population (1,000)	PERCENT OF VOTING-AGE POPULATION		STATE	Voting-age population (1,000)	PERCENT OF VOTING-AGE POPULATION	
		Registered	Voted			Registered	Voted
U.S.....	190,267	62.0	44.6	DC	440	66.9	55.6
				VA.	4,760	60.0	45.7
Northeast....	38,386	60.9	45.2	WV	1,396	60.8	33.9
N.E.......	9,865	67.8	51.0	NC	5,211	60.8	35.7
ME	909	81.6	58.2	SC	2,681	60.8	45.2
NH	832	64.3	41.2	GA	5,105	54.9	35.4
VT.....	432	70.7	48.8	FL......	10,582	55.5	42.3
MA	4,532	65.6	51.6	E.S.C	11,662	66.7	41.9
RI	729	64.2	50.6	KY	2,807	62.5	34.5
CT	2,431	68.4	51.3	TN	3,856	63.7	43.0
M.A	28,521	58.5	43.1	AL.....	3,136	70.6	45.8
NY	13,599	56.8	44.6	MS	1,863	72.6	44.3
NJ.....	5,918	61.6	40.3	W.S.C.....	20,273	61.0	38.5
PA.....	9,004	58.9	42.7	AR	1,801	60.0	41.6
Midwest....	44,505	68.7	48.7	LA.....	3,013	70.6	34.2
E.N.C	31,463	66.4	46.1	OK	2,325	65.8	46.8
OH	8,152	64.6	46.6	TX.....	13,134	58.2	37.6
IN	4,191	55.6	38.7	West	41,009	58.1	46.4
IL.....	8,561	63.0	42.8	Mountain...	10,911	60.0	45.9
MI.....	6,921	73.7	52.2	MT	619	73.2	60.7
WI.....	3,638	77.2	49.6	ID	798	63.0	50.7
W.N.C....	13,042	74.3	55.2	WY	333	69.0	63.5
MN	3,296	80.9	58.4	CO	2,703	64.3	46.4
IA.....	2,059	71.7	52.5	NM	1,175	58.8	46.8
MO	3,797	72.3	54.5	AZ......	2,971	56.0	41.6
ND	441	93.3	61.1	UT	1,231	59.4	44.1
SD	495	75.4	63.9	NV	1,081	49.5	40.1
NE	1,156	72.6	54.3	Pacific	30,098	57.4	46.6
KS	1,798	65.3	50.5	WA	3,924	66.8	46.3
South.......	66,364	60.7	40.5	OR	2,309	72.7	60.9
S.A.......	34,429	58.4	41.2	CA	22,639	54.2	45.0
DE	528	58.7	41.2	AK	393	71.7	59.1
MD	3,726	62.6	46.2	HI	833	51.5	46.0

Source: U.S. Bureau of the Census, unpublished data.

No. 458. Participation in Elections for President and U.S. Representatives: 1932 to 1994

[As of **November**. Estimated resident population 21 years old and over, 1932-70, except as noted, and 18 years old and over thereafter; includes Armed Forces. Prior to 1960, excludes Alaska and Hawaii. District of Columbia is included in votes cast for President beginning 1964 and in votes cast for Representative from 1972 to 1992]

YEAR	Resident popula- tion (incl. aliens) of voting age [1] (1,000)	VOTES CAST				YEAR	Resident popula- tion (incl. aliens) of voting age [1] (1,000)	VOTES CAST			
		For Presi- dent [2] (1,000)	Per- cent of voting- age popu- lation	For U.S. Repre- senta- tives (1,000)	Per- cent of voting- age popu- lation			For Presi- dent [2] (1,000)	Per- cent of voting- age popu- lation	For U.S. Repre- senta- tives (1,000)	Per- cent of voting- age popu- lation
1932 ...	75,768	39,758	52.5	37,657	49.7	1964 ...	114,090	70,645	61.9	65,895	57.8
1934 ...	77,997	(X)	(X)	32,256	41.4	1966 ...	116,638	(X)	(X)	52,908	45.4
1936 ...	80,174	45,654	56.9	42,886	53.5	1968 ...	120,285	73,212	60.9	66,288	55.1
1938 ...	82,354	(X)	(X)	36,236	44.0	1970 ...	124,498	(X)	(X)	54,173	43.5
1940 ...	84,728	49,900	58.9	46,951	55.4	1972 ...	140,777	77,719	55.2	71,430	50.7
1942 ...	86,465	(X)	(X)	28,074	32.5	1974 ...	146,338	(X)	(X)	52,495	35.9
1944 ...	85,654	47,977	56.0	45,103	52.7	1976 ...	152,308	81,556	53.5	74,422	48.9
1946 ...	92,659	(X)	(X)	34,398	37.1	1978 ...	158,369	(X)	(X)	55,332	34.9
1948 ...	95,573	48,794	51.1	45,933	48.1	1980 ...	163,945	86,515	52.8	77,995	47.6
1950 ...	98,134	(X)	(X)	40,342	41.1	1982 ...	169,643	(X)	(X)	64,514	38.0
1952 ...	99,929	61,551	61.6	57,571	57.6	1984 ...	173,995	92,653	53.3	83,231	47.8
1954 ...	102,075	(X)	(X)	42,580	41.7	1986 ...	177,922	(X)	(X)	59,619	33.5
1956 ...	104,515	62,027	59.3	58,426	55.9	1988 ...	181,956	91,595	50.3	81,786	44.9
1958 ...	106,447	(X)	(X)	45,818	43.0	1990 ...	185,812	(X)	(X)	61,513	33.1
1960 ...	109,672	68,838	62.8	64,133	58.5	1992 ...	189,524	104,425	55.1	96,239	50.8
1962 ...	112,952	(X)	(X)	51,267	45.4	1994 ...	193,650	(X)	(X)	69,770	36.0

X Not applicable. [1] Population 18 and over in Georgia, 1944-70, and in Kentucky, 1956-70; 19 and over in Alaska and 20 and over in Hawaii, 1960-70. [2] Source: 1932-58, U.S. Congress, Clerk of the House, *Statistics of the Presidential and Congressional Election*, biennial.

Source: Except as noted, U.S. Bureau of the Census, *Current Population Reports*, P25-1085; Elections Research Center, Chevy Chase, MD, *America Votes*, biennial, (copyright); and 1994, Congressional Quarterly Inc., *Congressional Quarterly Weekly Report*, vol. 53, No. 15, April 15, 1995, (copyright).

No. 459. Resident Population of Voting Age and Percent Casting Votes—States: 1988 to 1996

[As of **November. Estimated population, 18 years old and over.** Includes Armed Forces stationed in each State, aliens, and institutional population]

REGION, DIVISION, AND STATE	VOTING-AGE POPULATION							PERCENT CASTING VOTES FOR—				
	1988 (1,000)	1990 (1,000)	1992 (1,000)	1994 (1,000)	1996, proj. (1,000)			Presidential electors		U.S. Representatives		
					Total	Black	His-panic [1]	1988	1992	1990	1992	1994
U.S.	181,956	185,812	189,524	193,650	196,509	22,857	18,609	50.3	55.1	33.1	50.8	36.0
Northeast	38,670	38,838	38,920	38,849	38,861	4,398	2,903	51.3	55.4	32.9	49.9	37.1
N.E.	10,069	10,137	10,091	10,017	10,081	473	459	56.9	62.9	43.9	58.6	44.0
ME.	902	924	932	931	939	4	6	61.5	72.9	56.0	71.8	54.0
NH.	817	835	838	843	860	5	9	55.2	64.2	34.8	61.0	36.7
VT	411	422	429	429	441	2	3	59.1	67.5	49.7	65.6	49.3
MA.	4,642	4,646	4,616	4,564	4,623	234	229	56.7	60.1	44.1	56.6	43.3
RI	772	776	768	764	750	29	39	52.5	59.0	44.7	51.9	44.8
CT	2,525	2,534	2,508	2,486	2,468	199	173	57.1	64.4	40.9	57.2	43.0
M.A.	28,601	28,701	28,829	28,832	28,780	3,925	2,444	49.4	52.8	29.1	46.9	34.6
NY	13,659	13,683	13,705	13,646	13,579	2,292	1,616	47.5	50.5	26.8	43.2	33.8
NJ	5,905	5,927	5,964	5,974	6,005	819	632	52.5	56.1	30.8	50.2	33.6
PA	9,037	9,091	9,161	9,212	9,196	814	196	50.2	54.1	31.4	50.1	36.6
Midwest	43,684	44,160	44,803	45,529	46,021	4,248	1,394	56.5	61.9	39.6	58.5	41.2
E.N.C.	30,775	31,133	31,636	32,083	32,382	3,594	1,156	55.2	60.4	37.6	56.6	38.5
OH.	7,986	8,066	8,207	8,313	8,358	866	112	55.0	60.2	42.4	55.8	39.7
IN	4,046	4,105	4,209	4,298	4,369	331	81	53.6	54.8	36.9	52.7	36.0
IL.	8,411	8,495	8,598	8,712	8,764	1,245	728	54.2	58.7	36.2	56.2	34.9
MI	6,774	6,851	6,947	6,983	7,067	972	159	54.2	61.5	35.5	55.9	43.0
WI	3,559	3,616	3,675	3,777	3,824	180	76	61.6	68.9	34.7	65.0	38.6
W.N.C	12,910	13,027	13,167	13,446	13,639	654	238	59.5	65.6	44.4	63.3	47.7
MN.	3,167	3,222	3,272	3,362	3,412	65	44	66.2	71.8	55.3	69.5	52.0
IA.	2,053	2,061	2,073	2,112	2,138	38	30	59.7	65.3	38.4	59.9	46.3
MO.	3,770	3,813	3,851	3,902	3,980	397	47	55.5	62.1	35.5	61.0	45.2
ND	470	462	462	467	473	3	3	63.2	66.7	50.6	64.5	50.4
SD	498	498	505	522	530	3	4	62.9	66.6	51.7	65.9	58.6
NE	1,145	1,152	1,164	1,192	1,208	41	35	57.7	63.4	50.9	61.1	47.9
KS	1,809	1,819	1,840	1,889	1,898	107	75	54.9	62.9	42.9	61.1	43.3
South	62,134	63,821	65,609	67,501	69,173	11,996	5,859	46.0	51.3	26.9	45.9	30.2
S.A	32,148	33,312	34,210	35,211	36,011	6,947	1,891	44.3	50.3	28.2	46.7	30.3
DE	490	507	521	534	547	92	15	51.0	55.6	35.0	53.0	36.5
MD.	3,536	3,640	3,705	3,750	3,811	982	110	48.5	53.6	30.0	48.8	35.9
DC	503	481	467	452	435	269	20	38.4	48.7	33.2	42.1	(NA)
VA	4,572	4,716	4,855	4,967	5,089	924	133	47.9	52.7	24.4	48.8	38.4
WV	1,358	1,349	1,376	1,389	1,414	40	7	48.1	49.7	27.8	40.9	29.3
NC	4,903	5,061	5,190	5,364	5,499	1,126	69	43.5	50.3	39.7	48.7	29.6
SC	2,505	2,587	2,669	2,740	2,777	771	27	39.4	45.1	25.9	41.8	31.7
GA	4,631	4,791	5,006	5,159	5,396	1,368	101	39.1	46.4	29.1	44.2	29.0
FL	9,651	10,180	10,422	10,856	11,043	1,375	1,409	44.6	51.0	[2]23.4	[2]47.2	[2]26.3
E.S.C.	11,085	11,252	11,547	11,813	12,124	2,166	76	47.5	53.2	25.5	49.0	33.3
KY	2,710	2,740	2,798	2,857	2,924	201	15	48.8	53.4	27.9	48.6	27.5
TN	3,609	3,685	3,796	3,913	4,021	589	29	45.3	52.2	19.5	45.5	36.2
AL	2,950	2,995	3,080	3,138	3,218	744	20	46.7	54.8	34.0	52.0	35.5
MS	1,816	1,832	1,873	1,905	1,961	632	12	51.3	52.4	20.1	51.5	32.6
W.S.C	18,901	19,257	19,852	20,477	21,038	2,883	3,892	47.9	51.8	25.5	42.7	28.3
AR	1,717	1,737	1,774	1,817	1,860	253	18	48.2	53.6	[3]38.3	[3]50.1	39.0
LA	3,006	2,988	3,045	3,100	3,137	902	75	54.2	58.8	[3]35.5	[3]22.4	[3](X)
OK.	2,300	2,310	2,352	2,394	2,419	164	69	50.9	59.1	37.1	54.2	40.5
TX	11,878	12,222	12,681	13,166	13,622	1,564	3,730	45.7	48.5	26.8	44.3	31.3
West	37,468	38,993	40,194	41,771	42,452	2,216	8,450	49.4	53.5	36.0	51.0	38.8
Mountain	9,524	9,856	10,370	10,906	11,494	311	1,750	52.6	57.6	39.3	55.3	40.7
MT	574	579	600	623	647	2	9	63.8	68.4	54.8	67.3	56.5
ID	683	707	750	803	845	4	49	59.9	64.3	44.5	63.0	49.0
WY.	321	319	329	343	352	3	20	55.1	61.0	49.5	59.9	57.2
CO.	2,397	2,447	2,579	2,713	2,843	113	351	57.2	60.8	40.9	57.4	38.9
NM.	1,047	1,075	1,121	1,167	1,210	22	505	49.8	50.8	33.4	49.6	39.6
AZ	2,610	2,696	2,812	2,923	3,094	85	602	44.9	52.9	35.8	50.1	37.6
UT	1,070	1,104	1,169	1,246	1,323	10	69	60.5	63.6	40.1	62.2	40.5
NV	824	929	1,011	1,088	1,180	72	145	42.5	50.1	33.7	48.7	34.6
Pacific	27,943	29,137	29,824	30,865	30,958	1,905	6,700	48.3	52.0	35.0	49.4	38.1
WA.	3,465	3,650	3,812	4,000	4,122	111	193	53.8	60.0	36.0	58.3	42.2
OR.	2,055	2,140	2,220	2,311	2,396	37	101	58.5	65.9	49.2	62.6	51.6
CA	21,250	22,124	22,521	23,225	23,133	1,716	6,323	46.5	49.4	32.9	46.8	35.9
AK	369	382	405	429	425	17	14	54.2	63.8	50.2	59.0	48.5
HI	804	841	866	900	882	24	18	44.0	43.1	40.5	41.4	39.3

NA Not available.   X Not applicable.   [1] Persons of Hispanic origin may be of any race.   [2] State law does not require tabulation of votes for unopposed candidates.   [3] See footnote 6, table 437.

Source: Compiled by U.S. Bureau of the Census. Population data from U.S. Bureau of the Census, *Current Population Reports*, P25-1117 and Statistical Brief (SB/96-2); votes cast from Elections Research Center, Chevy Chase, MD, *America Votes*, biennial, (copyright); and 1994, Congressional Quarterly Inc., *Congressional Quarterly Weekly Report*, vol. 53, No. 15, April 15, 1995, (copyright).

No. 460. Political Party Financial Activity, by Major Political Party: 1981 to 1994

[**In millions of dollars**. Covers financial activity during 2-year calendar period indicated. Some political party financial activities, such as building funds and State and local election spending, are not reported to the source. Also excludes contributions earmarked to Federal candidates through the party organizations, since some of those funds never passed through the committees' accounts]

YEAR AND TYPE OF COMMITTEE	DEMOCRATIC				REPUBLICAN			
	Receipts, net [1]	Dis-burse-ments, net [1]	Contri-butions to candi-dates	Monies spent on behalf of party's nomi-nees [2]	Receipts, net [1]	Dis-burse-ments, net [1]	Contri-butions to candi-dates	Monies spent on behalf of party's nomi-nees [2]
1981-82	39.3	40.1	1.7	3.3	215.0	214.0	5.6	14.3
1983-84	98.5	97.4	2.6	9.0	297.9	300.8	4.9	20.1
1985-86	64.8	65.9	1.7	9.0	255.2	258.9	3.4	14.3
1987-88	127.9	121.9	1.8	17.9	263.3	257.0	3.4	22.7
1989-90	85.8	90.9	1.5	8.7	206.3	213.5	2.9	10.7
1991-92, total	**177.7**	**171.9**	**1.9**	**28.1**	**267.3**	**256.1**	**3.0**	**33.9**
National committee	65.8	65.0	-	11.3	85.4	81.9	0.8	11.3
Senatorial committee.............	25.5	25.5	0.6	11.2	73.8	71.3	0.7	16.5
Congressional committee	12.8	12.7	0.8	4.1	35.3	34.3	0.7	5.2
Other national..................	9.8	8.6	-	-	-	-	-	-
State and local..................	63.9	60.2	0.5	1.4	72.8	68.6	0.8	0.9
1993-94, total	**143.3**	**141.8**	**2.2**	**21.2**	**254.4**	**243.7**	**3.0**	**20.6**
National committee	41.8	44.0	0.1	-0.3	87.4	85.3	0.5	4.7
Senatorial committee.............	26.4	26.4	0.5	12.3	65.3	65.4	0.6	10.9
Congressional committee	19.4	19.4	1.0	7.7	26.7	26.3	0.8	3.9
Other national..................	7.8	8.1	-	-	-	-	-	-
State and local..................	47.8	44.0	0.6	1.5	75.0	66.7	1.0	1.1

- Represents zero.   [1] Excludes monies transferred between affiliated committees.   [2] Monies spent in the general election. Minus sign (-) indicates refunds for expenditures.

Source: U.S. Federal Election Commission, *FEC Reports on Financial Activity, Final Report, Party and Non-Party Political Committees*, biennial.

No. 461. Independent Expenditures for Presidential and Congressional Campaigns: 1985 to 1994

[**In thousands of dollars**. Covers campaign finance activity during 2-year calendar period indicated. An "independent expenditure" is money spent to support or defeat a clearly identified candidate. According to Federal election law, such an expenditure must be made without cooperation or consultation with the candidate or his/her campaign. Independent expenditures are not limited, as are contributions]

TYPE OF OFFICE AND YEAR	ALL PARTIES			DEMOCRATS		REPUBLICANS		OTHERS	
	Total	For	Against	For	Against	For	Against	For	Against
TOTAL									
1985-86	10,205	8,832	1,373	3,450	888	5,376	485	6	-
1987-88	21,341	16,654	4,687	2,865	4,248	13,784	439	6	-
1989-90	5,774	4,177	1,597	1,530	735	2,645	862	2	-
1991-92	11,052	8,710	2,342	3,044	1,483	5,548	847	118	12
1993-94	4,980	3,256	1,724	672	1,119	2,571	590	13	15
PRESIDENTIAL									
1985-86	841	795	45	76	28	719	17	-	-
1987-88	14,127	10,628	3,499	568	3,352	10,054	146	6	-
1989-90	497	322	174	5	169	318	5	-	-
1991-92	4,431	3,695	736	583	561	3,052	163	60	12
1993-94	112	27	85	12	84	15	(Z)	-	1
SENATE									
1985-86	5,312	4,331	980	988	632	3,343	348	-	-
1987-88	4,401	3,641	761	831	617	2,810	143	(Z)	-
1989-90	3,506	2,362	1,144	756	428	1,604	716	2	-
1991-92	2,604	1,912	692	1,025	462	886	230	1	-
1993-94	2,627	1,612	1,015	261	476	1,351	539	(Z)	-
HOUSE OF REPRESENTATIVES									
1985-86	4,053	3,706	347	2,386	227	1,314	120	6	-
1987-88	2,813	2,385	427	1,466	279	920	149	(Z)	-
1989-90	1,772	1,493	279	770	138	723	141	-	-
1991-92	4,017	3,103	914	1,436	460	1,610	454	57	-
1993-94	2,241	1,617	624	399	559	1,205	51	13	14

- Represents zero.   Z Less than $500.

Source: U.S. Federal Election Commission, *FEC Index of Independent Expenditures, 1987-88*, May 1989; press release of May 19, 1989; and unpublished data.

No. 462. Political Action Committees—Number, by Committee Type: 1980 to 1995

[As of **December 31**]

COMMITTEE TYPE	1980	1985	1990	1991	1992	1993	1994	1995
Total	2,551	3,992	4,172	4,094	4,195	4,210	3,954	4,016
Corporate	1,206	1,710	1,795	1,738	1,735	1,789	1,660	1,674
Labor	297	388	346	338	347	337	333	334
Trade/membership/health	576	695	774	742	770	761	792	815
Nonconnected	374	1,003	1,062	1,083	1,145	1,121	980	1,020
Cooperative	42	54	59	57	56	56	53	44
Corporation without stock	56	142	136	136	142	146	136	129

Source: U.S. Federal Election Commission, press release of January 23, 1996.

No. 463. Political Action Committees—Financial Activity Summary, by Committee Type: 1989 to 1994

[**In millions of dollars.** Covers financial activity during 2-year calendar period indicated. Data have not been adjusted for transfers between affiliated committees]

COMMITTEE TYPE	RECEIPTS			DISBURSEMENTS [1]			CONTRIBUTIONS TO CANDIDATES		
	1989-90	1991-92	1993-94	1989-90	1991-92	1993-94	1989-90	1991-92	1993-94
Total	372.1	385.5	391.8	357.6	394.8	388.1	159.1	188.9	189.6
Corporate	106.5	112.5	115.0	101.1	112.4	116.8	58.1	68.4	69.6
Labor	88.9	89.9	90.3	84.6	94.6	88.4	34.7	41.4	41.9
Trade/membership/health	92.5	95.7	96.4	88.1	97.5	94.1	44.8	53.9	52.9
Nonconnected	71.6	73.8	76.9	71.4	76.2	75.1	15.1	18.3	18.2
Cooperative	5.0	4.8	4.4	4.8	4.9	4.5	2.9	3.0	3.0
Corporation without stock	7.6	8.7	8.9	7.7	9.2	9.2	3.4	4.0	4.1

[1] Comprises contributions to candidates, independent expenditures, and other disbursements.

Source: U.S. Federal Election Commission, *FEC Reports on Financial Activity, Final Report, Party and Non-Party Political Committees,* biennial.

No. 464. Presidential Campaign Finances—Federal Funds for General Election: 1980 to 1992

[**In millions of dollars.** Based on FEC certifications, audit reports, and Dept. of Treasury reports]

1980		1984		1988		1992	
Candidate	Amount	Candidate	Amount	Candidate	Amount	Candidate	Amount
Total	62.7	Total	80.3	Total	92.2	Total	110.4
Anderson [1]	4.2	Mondale	40.2	Bush	46.1	Bush	55.2
Carter	29.4	Reagan	40.1	Dukakis	46.1	Clinton	55.2
Reagan	29.2					Perot	-

- Represents zero.   [1] John Anderson, as the candidate of a new party, was permitted to raise funds privately. Total receipts for the Anderson campaign, including Federal funds, were $17.6 million, and total expenditures were $15.6 million.

Source: U.S. Federal Election Commission, periodic press releases.

No. 465. Presidential Campaign Finances—Primary Campaign Receipts and Disbursements: 1983 to 1992

[**In millions of dollars**. Covers campaign finance activity during 2-year calendar period indicated. Covers candidates who received Federal matching funds or who had significant financial activity]

ITEM	TOTAL			DEMOCRATIC			REPUBLICAN		
	1983-84 [1]	1987-88 [2]	1991-92 [3]	1983-84	1987-88	1991-92	1983-84	1987-88	1991-92
Receipts, total [4]	105.0	213.8	125.2	77.5	91.9	70.0	27.1	116.0	49.7
Individual contributions	62.8	141.1	82.4	46.2	59.4	44.7	16.4	76.8	34.4
Federal matching funds	34.9	65.7	41.5	24.6	30.1	24.4	10.1	34.7	15.0
Disbursements	103.6	210.7	118.7	77.4	90.2	64.4	25.9	114.6	48.8

[1] Includes Citizens Party candidate, not shown separately.   [2] Includes a minor party candidate who sought several party nominations and a Democratic candidate who did not receive Federal matching funds, but who had significant financial activity.   [3] Includes other parties, not shown separately.   [4] Includes other types of receipts, not shown separately.

Source: U.S. Federal Election Commission, *FEC Reports on Financial Activity, Final Report, Presidential Pre-Nomination Campaigns,* quadrennial.

No. 466. Congressional Campaign Finances—Receipts and Disbursements: 1989 to 1994

[Covers all campaign finance activity during 2-year calendar period indicated for primary, general, run-off, and special elections. for 1989-90 to 1,580 House of Representatives candidates and 179 Senate candidates; for 1991-92 to 2,585 House of Representatives candidates and 365 Senate candidates. for 1993-94 to 2,045 House of Representatives candidates and 331 Senate candidates; Data have been adjusted to eliminate transfers between all committees within a campaign. For further information on legal limits of contributions, see Federal Election Campaign Act of 1971, as amended]

ITEM	HOUSE OF REPRESENTATIVES						SENATE					
	Amount (mil. dol.)			Percent distribution			Amount (mil. dol.)			Percent distribution		
	1989-90	1991-92	1993-94	1989-90	1991-92	1993-94	1989-90	1991-92	1993-94	1989-90	1991-92	1993-94
Total receipts [1]	285.4	395.9	421.3	100	100	100	186.3	263.4	319.1	100	100	100
Individual contributions	129.9	192.4	216.1	46	49	51	119.6	162.8	186.4	64	62	58
Other committees	108.5	127.4	132.4	38	32	31	41.2	51.2	47.2	22	19	15
Candidate loans	20.9	43.0	43.9	7	11	10	10.0	28.7	43.5	5	11	14
Candidate contributions	4.8	11.4	10.3	2	3	2	2.4	6.5	24.9	1	2	8
Democrats	163.4	217.7	216.7	57	55	51	89.5	143.8	133.6	48	55	42
Republicans	120.9	174.3	201.8	42	44	48	96.8	118.3	183.6	52	45	58
Others	1.1	3.9	2.8	(Z)	1	1	(Z)	1.3	2.0	(Z)	(Z)	1
Incumbents	181.9	203.5	224.1	64	51	53	118.7	99.7	113.3	64	38	36
Challengers [2]	47.7	91.3	100.6	17	23	24	54.8	95.6	119.2	29	36	37
Open seats [2]	55.9	101.1	96.6	20	26	23	12.8	68.2	86.6	7	26	27
Total disbursements	265.8	407.6	407.2	100	100	100	180.4	272.1	318.8	100	100	100
Democrats	151.0	228.3	213.4	57	56	52	87.6	147.6	136.3	49	54	43
Republicans	113.7	176.0	191.0	43	43	47	92.9	123.2	180.6	52	45	57
Others	1.1	3.3	2.8	(Z)	1	1	(Z)	1.2	2.0	(Z)	(Z)	1
Incumbents	163.4	217.9	213.5	62	53	52	113.5	107.2	115.1	63	39	36
Challengers [2]	47.0	90.0	99.1	18	22	24	54.9	95.3	118.3	30	35	37
Open seats [2]	55.4	99.7	94.6	21	24	23	12.1	69.6	85.5	7	26	27

Z Less than $50,000 or 0.5 percent.   [1] Includes other types of receipts, not shown separately.   [2] Elections in which an incumbent did not seek re-election.

Source: U.S. Federal Election Commission, *FEC Reports on Financial Activity, Final Report, U.S. Senate and House Campaigns*, biennial.

No. 467. Contributions to Congressional Campaigns by Political Action Committees (PAC), by Type of Committee: 1981 to 1994

[In millions of dollars. Covers amounts given to candidates in primary, general, run-off, and special elections during the 2-year calendar period indicated. For number of political action committees, see table 462]

TYPE OF COMMITTEE	Total [1]	Democrats	Republicans	Incumbents	Challengers	Open seats [2]
HOUSE OF REPRESENTATIVES						
1981-82	61.1	34.2	26.8	40.8	10.9	9.4
1983-84	75.7	46.3	29.3	57.2	11.3	7.2
1985-86	87.4	54.7	32.6	65.9	9.1	12.4
1987-88	102.2	67.4	34.7	82.2	10.0	10.0
1989-90	108.5	72.2	36.2	87.5	7.3	13.6
1991-92	127.4	85.4	41.7	94.4	12.2	20.8
1993-94, total [3]	132.4	88.2	43.9	101.4	12.7	18.3
Corporate	43.5	23.6	19.9	36.3	2.9	4.3
Trade association [4]	38.8	22.1	16.6	30.0	3.3	5.5
Labor	33.4	31.9	1.4	23.6	4.1	5.6
Nonconnected [5]	11.8	7.4	4.4	7.4	2.0	2.4
SENATE						
1981-82	22.6	11.2	11.4	14.3	5.2	3.0
1983-84	29.7	14.0	15.6	17.9	6.3	5.4
1985-86	45.3	20.2	25.1	23.7	10.2	11.4
1987-88	45.7	24.2	21.5	28.7	8.0	9.0
1989-90	41.2	20.2	21.0	29.5	8.2	3.5
1991-92	51.2	29.0	22.2	31.9	9.4	10.0
1993-94, total [3]	47.2	24.0	23.2	26.3	5.7	15.1
Corporate	20.8	7.8	13.0	11.7	2.0	7.2
Trade association [4]	11.5	4.9	6.6	6.8	1.1	3.6
Labor	7.3	7.1	0.2	3.6	1.7	2.0
Nonconnected [5]	5.7	3.1	2.6	3.1	0.8	1.8

[1] Includes other parties, not shown separately.   [2] Elections in which an incumbent did not seek re-election.   [3] Includes other types of political action committees not shown separately.   [4] Includes membership organizations and health organizations.   [5] Represents "ideological" groups as well as other issue groups not necessarily ideological in nature.

Source: U.S. Federal Election Commission, *FEC Reports on Financial Activity, Party and Non-Party Political Committees, Final Report*, biennial.

Figure 9.1
State Government Tax Collections, by Type: 1970 and 1994

**Total collections
$48.0 billion**

1970

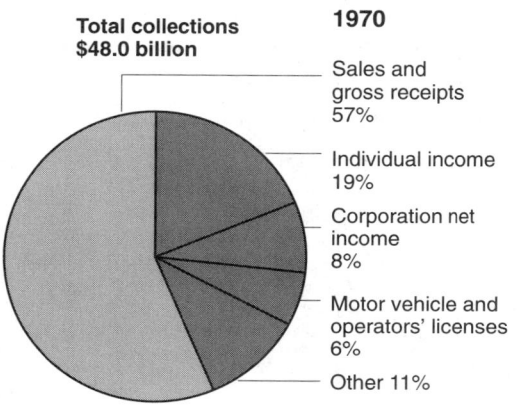

Sales and
gross receipts
57%

Individual income
19%

Corporation net
income
8%

Motor vehicle and
operators' licenses
6%

Other 11%

**Sales and gross receipts
$27.3 billion**

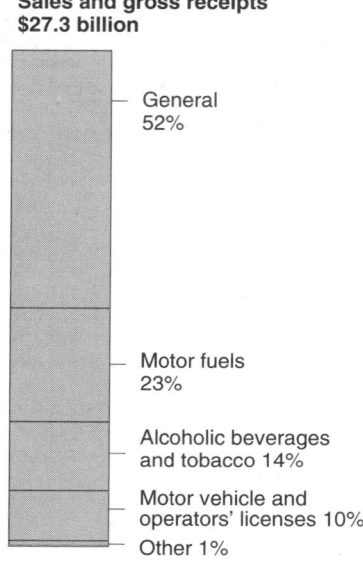

General
52%

Motor fuels
23%

Alcoholic beverages
and tobacco 14%

Motor vehicle and
operators' licenses 10%

Other 1%

**Total collections
$373.8 billion**

1994

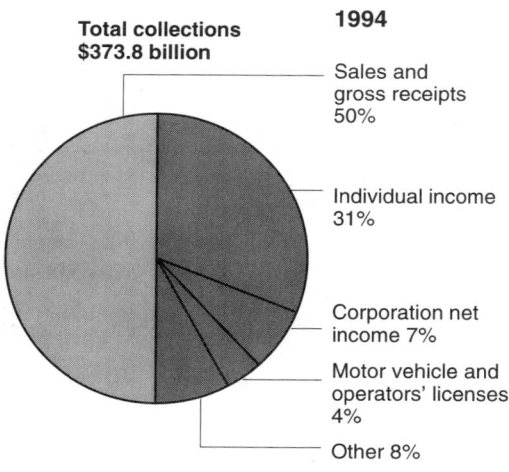

Sales and
gross receipts
50%

Individual income
31%

Corporation net
income 7%

Motor vehicle and
operators' licenses
4%

Other 8%

**Sales and gross receipts
$185.8 billion**

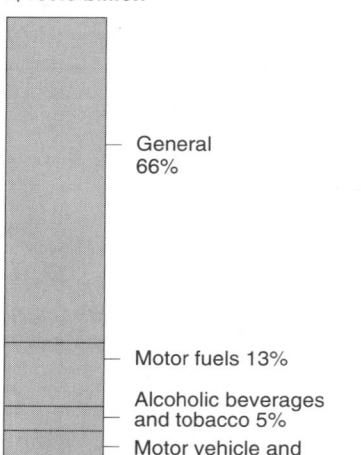

General
66%

Motor fuels 13%

Alcoholic beverages
and tobacco 5%

Motor vehicle and
operators' licenses 7%

Other 9%

Source: Chart prepared by U.S. Bureau of the Census. For data, see table 489.

State and Local Government Finances and Employment

This section presents data on revenues, expenditures, debt, and employment of State and local governments. Nationwide statistics relating to State and local governments, their numbers, finances, and employment, are compiled primarily by the Bureau of the Census through a program of censuses and surveys. Every fifth year (for years ending in "2" and "7") the Bureau conducts a census of governments involving collection of data for all governmental units in the United States. In addition, the Bureau conducts annual surveys which cover all the State governments and a sample of local governments.

Annually, the Bureau of the Census releases information on the Internet which present financial data for the Federal Government, nationwide totals for State and local governments, and State-local data by States. Also released annually is a series on State, city, county, and school finances, and on State and local public employment. There is also a series of quarterly data releases covering tax revenue and finances of major public employee retirement systems.

Basic information for Census Bureau statistics on governments is obtained by mail canvass from State and local officials; however, financial data for each of the State governments and for many of the large local governments are compiled from their official records and reports by Census Bureau personnel. In over two thirds of the States, all or part of local government financial data are obtained through central collection arrangements with State governments. Financial data on the Federal Government is primarily based on the *Budget* published by the Office of Management and Budget (see text, section 10).

Governmental units—The governmental structure of the United States includes, in addition to the Federal Government and the States, thousands of local governments—counties, municipalities, townships, school districts, and numerous kinds of "special districts." In

In Brief

State government revenue
(from own sources) in 1993:
$617,047 million

Taxes	57%
Insurance trust funds	23%
Charges	9%
Interest earnings	4%
Utility and liquor stores	1%

State government
direct expenditures in 1993:
$529,167 million

Public welfare	26%
Education	17%
Insurance trust funds	16%
Health and hospitals	8%

1992, 84,955 local governments were identified by the census of governments. As defined by the census, governmental units include all agencies or bodies having an organized existence, governmental character, and substantial autonomy. While most of these governments can impose taxes, many of the special districts—such as independent public housing authorities, and numerous local irrigation, power, and other types of districts—are financed from rentals, charges for services, benefit assessments, grants from other governments, and other non-tax sources. The count of governments excludes semi-autonomous agencies through which States, cities, and counties sometimes provide for certain functions—for example, "dependent" school systems, State institutions of higher education, and certain other "authorities" and special agencies which are under the administrative or fiscal control of an established governmental unit.

Finances—The financial statistics relate to government fiscal years ending June 30, or at some date within the 12 previous months. The following governments are exceptions and are included as though they were part of the June 30 group; ending September 30, the State governments of Alabama and Michigan, the District of

Columbia, and Alabama school districts; and ending August 31, the State government of Texas and Texas school districts. New York State ends its fiscal year on March 31. The Federal Government ended the fiscal year June 30 until 1976 when its fiscal year, by an act of Congress, was revised to extend from Oct. 1 to Sept. 30. A 3-month quarter (July 1 to Sept. 30, 1976) bridged the transition.

Nationwide government finance statistics have been classified and presented in terms of uniform concepts and categories, rather than according to the highly diverse terminology, organization, and fund structure utilized by individual governments. Accordingly, financial statistics which appear here for the Federal Government and for individual States or local governments have been standardized and may not agree directly with figures appearing in the original sources.

Statistics on governmental finances distinguish among general government, utilities, liquor stores, and insurance trusts. *General government* comprises all activities except utilities, liquor stores, and insurance trusts. Utilities include government water supply, electric light and power, gas supply, and transit systems. Liquor stores are operated by 17 States and by local governments in 6 States. Insurance trusts relate to employee retirement, unemployment compensation, and other social insurance systems administered by the Federal, State, and local governments.

Data for cities relate only to municipal corporations and their dependent agencies and do not include amounts for other local governments overlying city areas. Therefore, expenditure figures for "education" do not include spending by the separate school districts which administer public schools within most municipal areas. Variations in the assignment of governmental responsibility for public assistance, health, hospitals, public housing, and other functions to a lesser degree also have an important effect upon reported amounts of city expenditure, revenue, and debt. Therefore, any intercity comparisons based upon these figures should be made with caution and with due recognition of variations that exist among urban areas in the relative role of the municipal corporation.

Employment and payrolls—These data are based mainly on mail canvassing of State and local governments. Payroll includes all salaries, wages, and individual fee payments for the month specified, and employment relates to all persons on governmental payrolls during a pay period of the month covered—including paid officials, temporary help, and (unless otherwise specified) part-time as well as full-time personnel. Beginning 1986, statistics for full-time equivalent employment have been computed with a formula using hours worked by part-time employees. A payroll based formula was used prior to 1985. Full-time equivalent employment statistics were not computed for 1985. Figures shown for individual governments cover major dependent agencies such as institutions of higher education, as well as the basic central departments and agencies of the government.

Statistical reliability—For a discussion of statistical collection and estimation, sampling procedures, and measures of statistical reliability applicable to Census Bureau data, see Appendix III.

Historical statistics—Tabular headnotes provide cross-references, where applicable, to *Historical Statistics of the United States, Colonial Times to 1970.* See Appendix IV.

No. 468. Number of Governmental Units, by Type: 1942 to 1992

TYPE OF GOVERNMENT	1942	1952 [1]	1957 [1]	1962	1967	1972	1977	1982	1987	1992
Total	155,116	116,807	102,392	91,237	81,299	78,269	79,913	81,831	83,237	85,006
U.S. Government	1	1	1	1	1	1	1	1	1	1
State government	48	50	50	50	50	50	50	50	50	50
Local governments	155,067	116,756	102,341	91,186	81,248	78,218	79,862	81,780	83,186	84,955
County	3,050	3,052	3,050	3,043	3,049	3,044	3,042	3,041	3,042	3,043
Municipal	16,220	16,807	17,215	18,000	18,048	18,517	18,862	19,076	19,200	19,279
Township and town	18,919	17,202	17,198	17,142	17,105	16,991	16,822	16,734	16,691	16,656
School district	108,579	67,355	50,454	34,678	21,782	15,781	15,174	14,851	14,721	14,422
Special district	8,299	12,340	14,424	18,323	21,264	23,885	25,962	28,078	29,532	31,555

[1] Adjusted to include units in Alaska and Hawaii which adopted statehood in 1959.

No. 469. Number of Governments, by Type—States: 1992

[Governments in existence in January. Limited to governments actually in existence. Excludes, therefore, a few counties and numerous townships and "incorporated places" existing as areas for which statistics can be presented as to population and other subjects, but lacking any separate organized county, township, or municipal government]

STATE	All govern- mental units [1]	County	Muni- cipal	Town- ship [2]	School district	SPECIAL DISTRICT			
						Total [3]	Natural resources	Fire protection	Housing and com- munity develop- ment
U.S	85,006	3,043	19,279	16,656	14,422	31,555	6,228	5,260	3,470
Alabama	1,122	67	438	-	129	487	68	4	152
Alaska	175	12	148	-	-	14	-	-	13
Arizona	591	15	86	-	228	261	69	130	-
Arkansas	1,447	75	489	-	321	561	226	48	125
California	4,393	57	460	-	1,078	2,797	480	389	84
Colorado	1,761	62	266	-	180	1,252	167	239	91
Connecticut	564	-	29	149	17	368	1	59	94
Delaware	276	3	57	-	19	196	187	-	4
District of Columbia	2	-	1	-	-	1	-	-	-
Florida	1,014	66	390	-	95	462	135	53	105
Georgia	1,298	157	536	-	183	421	36	6	203
Hawaii	21	3	1	-	-	16	16	-	-
Idaho	1,087	44	199	-	115	728	165	129	12
Illinois	6,723	102	1,282	1,433	985	2,920	903	804	114
Indiana	2,899	91	566	1,008	294	939	132	-	61
Iowa	1,881	99	952	-	441	388	239	67	19
Kansas	3,892	105	627	1,353	324	1,482	258	-	203
Kentucky	1,321	119	435	-	176	590	128	92	22
Louisiana	459	61	301	-	66	30	2	-	-
Maine	797	16	22	468	91	199	13	-	26
Maryland	402	23	155	-	-	223	151	-	21
Massachusetts	844	12	39	312	84	396	14	15	253
Michigan	2,722	83	534	1,242	585	277	82	2	-
Minnesota	3,580	87	854	1,803	458	377	109	-	163
Mississippi	870	82	294	-	173	320	235	-	56
Missouri	3,310	114	933	324	552	1,386	168	204	142
Montana	1,276	54	128	-	537	556	125	145	17
Nebraska	2,924	93	534	452	797	1,047	93	418	133
Nevada	208	16	18	-	17	156	32	14	16
New Hampshire	528	10	13	221	167	116	10	15	22
New Jersey	1,513	21	320	247	550	374	17	169	2
New Mexico	342	33	98	-	94	116	71	-	5
New York	3,299	57	619	929	713	980	2	900	-
North Carolina	938	100	516	-	-	321	148	-	98
North Dakota	2,765	53	364	1,350	275	722	78	269	36
Ohio	3,524	88	942	1,314	666	513	98	40	59
Oklahoma	1,795	77	588	-	605	524	100	18	122
Oregon	1,451	36	239	-	340	835	188	263	22
Pennsylvania	5,159	66	1,022	1,548	516	2,006	8	1	88
Rhode Island	126	-	8	31	3	83	3	38	26
South Carolina	698	46	269	-	91	291	48	84	45
South Dakota	1,786	64	310	969	180	262	103	51	42
Tennessee	924	93	339	-	14	477	112	-	89
Texas	4,792	254	1,171	-	1,100	2,266	413	95	396
Utah	627	29	228	-	40	329	77	20	16
Vermont	682	14	50	237	276	104	14	21	9
Virginia	455	95	230	-	-	129	44	-	-
Washington	1,761	39	268	-	296	1,157	154	404	51
West Virginia	692	55	231	-	55	350	15	-	36
Wisconsin	2,739	72	583	1,266	440	377	168	-	177
Wyoming	550	23	97	-	56	373	123	54	-

- Represents zero.   [1] Includes the Federal Government and the 50 State governments not shown separately.   [2] Includes "town" governments in the six New England States and in Minnesota, New York, and Wisconsin.   [3] Includes other special districts not shown separately.

Source of tables 468 and 469: U.S. Bureau of the Census, *1992 Census of Governments, Government Organization.*

No. 470. County, Municipal, and Township Governments: 1992

[Number of governments as of **January 1992**. Population enumerated as of **April 1, 1990**. Consolidated city-county governments are classified as municipal rather than county governments. Township governments include "towns" in the six New England States, Minnesota, New York, and Wisconsin]

POPULATION-SIZE GROUP	COUNTY GOVERNMENTS			MUNICIPAL GOVERNMENTS			TOWNSHIP GOVERNMENTS		
	Number, 1992	Population, 1990		Number, 1992	Population, 1990		Number, 1992	Population, 1990	
		Number (1,000)	Percent		Number (1,000)	Percent		Number (1,000)	Percent
Total	3,043	224,924	100	19,279	153,819	100	16,656	53,051	100
200,000 or more	[1]174	[1]120,551	[1]54	76	47,809	31	6	2,140	4
100,000 to 199,999	[2]244	[2]37,336	[2]17	119	16,390	11	27	3,554	7
50,000 to 99,999	377	26,555	12	310	21,282	14	77	5,214	10
25,000 to 49,999	612	21,510	10	566	19,877	13	249	8,461	16
10,000 to 24,999	908	14,851	7	1,290	20,324	13	728	11,225	21
5,000 to 9,999	[3]728	[3]4,121	[3]2	1,566	11,135	7	1,019	7,112	13
2,500 to 4,999	(NA)	(NA)	(NA)	2,036	7,238	5	1,800	6,301	12
1,000 to 2,499	(NA)	(NA)	(NA)	3,670	5,894	4	3,626	5,796	11
Less than 1,000	(NA)	(NA)	(NA)	9,646	3,874	3	9,124	3,251	6

NA Not available. [1] For population-size group of 250,000 or more. [2] 100,000 to 249,999. [3] Less than 10,000.

Source: U.S. Bureau of the Census, *Census of Governments: 1992*, vol. 1, No. 1, *Government Organization*.

Figure 9.2
State Lottery Proceeds: 1980 to 1995

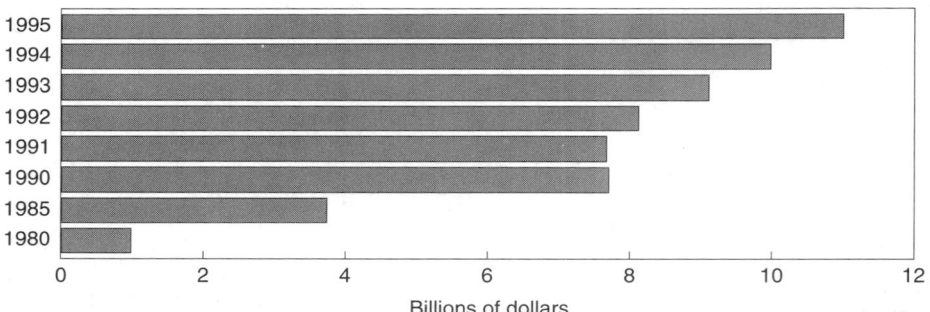

Billions of dollars

Percent distribution of 1964–1995
cumulative State lottery proceeds
($93 billion)

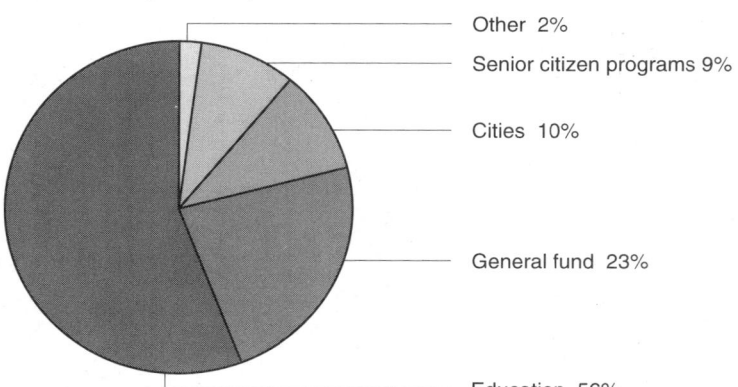

Other 2%

Senior citizen programs 9%

Cities 10%

General fund 23%

Education 56%

Source: Chart prepared by U.S. Bureau of the Census. For data, see table 493.

No. 471. All Governments—Revenue, Expenditure, and Debt: 1980 to 1993

[For fiscal year ending in year shown; see text, section 9. Local government amounts are estimates subject to sampling variation; see Appendix III and source. See also *Historical Statistics, Colonial Times to 1970*, series Y 505-637 and Y 652-848]

ITEM	All governments (bil. dol.)	FEDERAL [1] Total (bil. dol.)	FEDERAL [1] Percent of total	STATE AND LOCAL (bil. dol.) Total	STATE AND LOCAL (bil. dol.) State	STATE AND LOCAL (bil. dol.) Local	PER CAPITA [2] (dollars) Total	PER CAPITA [2] (dollars) Federal	PER CAPITA [2] (dollars) State and local
Revenue: [3] 1980	[4]932	565	60.7	[4]452	277	258	[4]4,115	2,496	1,993
1990	[4]2,047	1,155	56.4	[4]1,032	632	580	[4]8,230	4,642	4,150
1992	[4]2,262	1,259	55.7	[4]1,185	744	648	[4]8,869	4,938	4,647
1993	[4]2,374	1,308	55.0	[4]1,268	806	679	[4]9,209	5,066	4,918
Intergovernmental: 1980	(X)	2	(X)	[4]83	64	102	(X)	8	367
1990	(X)	3	(X)	[4]137	126	191	(X)	12	550
1992	(X)	3	(X)	[4]179	170	216	(X)	13	703
1993	(X)	3	(X)	[4]199	189	227	(X)	5	771
General, own sources:									
1980	717	417	58.2	299	169	130	3,163	1,842	1,321
1990	1,493	780	52.2	713	391	322	6,004	3,138	2,865
1992	1,645	851	51.8	793	436	357	6,449	3,338	3,111
1993	1,727	887	51.4	840	465	374	6,699	3,441	3,258
Taxes: [3] 1980	574	351	61.1	223	137	86	2,535	1,548	986
1990	1,134	632	55.7	502	301	201	4,559	2,542	2,017
1992	1,215	659	54.3	556	328	227	4,763	2,584	2,179
1993	1,306	713	54.6	593	354	239	5,066	2,765	2,300
Property: 1980	68	(X)	(X)	68	3	66	302	(X)	302
1990	156	(X)	(X)	156	6	150	626	(X)	626
1992	179	(X)	(X)	179	7	172	700	(X)	700
1993	189	(X)	(X)	189	8	181	733	(X)	731
Individual income:									
1980	286	244	85.3	42	37	5	1,263	1,077	186
1990	573	467	81.6	106	96	10	2,302	1,877	425
1992	592	476	80.5	115	105	11	2,320	1,868	452
1993	633	510	80.5	123	112	11	2,455	1,977	478
Corporate income:									
1980	78	65	82.9	13	13	-	344	285	59
1990	117	94	80.3	24	22	2	471	376	95
1992	124	100	81.0	24	22	2	486	393	93
1993	144	118	81.6	26	24	2	559	456	103
Sales or gross receipts:									
1980	112	[5]32	28.6	80	68	12	494	[5]141	353
1990	232	[5]54	23.3	178	147	31	932	[5]217	715
1992	260	[5]64	24.7	196	163	33	1,021	[5]252	769
1993	277	[5]67	24.3	210	175	35	1,074	[5]262	813
Current charges and miscellaneous: 1980	142	67	46.7	76	32	44	629	294	335
1990	359	148	41.3	211	91	120	1,445	596	849
1992	430	192	44.7	238	108	130	1,687	754	932
1993	421	174	41.4	247	111	135	1,633	676	958
Expenditures: [3] 1980	[4]959	617	64.4	[4]434	258	261	[4]4,232	2,724	1,916
1990	[4]2,219	1,393	62.8	[4]976	572	581	[4]8,921	5,601	3,924
1992	[4]2,488	1,527	61.4	[4]1,150	700	655	[4]9,755	5,989	4,510
1993	[4]2,572	1,570	61.0	[4]1,211	743	685	[4]9,977	6,088	4,697
Intergovernmental: 1980	(X)	91	(X)	[4]2	85	2	(X)	401	8
1990	(X)	147	(X)	[4]3	175	6	(X)	591	13
1992	(X)	186	(X)	[4]4	201	7	(X)	729	14
1993	(X)	205	(X)	[4]4	214	7	(X)	794	14
Direct: [3] 1980	959	526	54.9	432	173	259	4,232	2,323	1,908
1990	2,219	1,246	56.2	973	397	575	8,921	5,010	3,911
1992	2,488	1,341	53.9	1,147	499	648	9,755	5,259	4,496
1993	2,572	1,365	53.1	1,207	529	678	9,977	5,294	4,682
Current operation: 1980	517	209	40.5	308	108	200	2,282	923	1,359
1990	1,190	490	41.2	700	258	442	4,785	1,970	2,815
1992	1,324	500	37.7	823	322	501	5,191	1,962	3,229
1993	1,364	491	36.0	873	345	528	5,290	1,904	3,386
Capital outlay: 1980	99	36	36.7	63	23	40	439	161	278
1990	221	98	44.3	123	46	78	888	394	495
1992	228	93	40.9	135	50	84	892	365	527
1993	221	85	38.6	136	50	86	858	331	527
Debt outstanding: [6] 1980	1,250	914	73.2	336	122	214	5,517	4,036	1,486
1990	4,127	3,266	79.2	861	318	542	16,592	13,132	3,460
1992	5,054	4,083	80.8	970	372	598	19,816	16,009	3,804
1993	5,452	4,436	81.4	1,016	390	626	21,149	17,208	3,942

- Represents or rounds to zero.   X Not applicable.   [1] Data adjusted to system for reporting State and local data and therefore differ from figures in section 10 tables.   [2] 1990 based on enumerated resident population as of April 1; all other years based on estimated resident population as of July 1.   [3] Includes amounts not shown separately.   [4] Excludes duplicative transactions between levels of government; see source.   [5] Includes customs.   [6] End of fiscal year.

Source: U.S. Bureau of the Census, *Government Finances*, series GF, No. 5, annual; Internet site, http://www.census.gov/ftp/pub/govs/www/index.html (accessed 06/25/96) and unpublished data.

No. 472. All Governments—Detailed Finances: 1993

[For fiscal year ending in year shown, see text, section 9. Local government amounts are estimates subject to sampling variation; see Appendix III and source. See also *Historical Statistics, Colonial Times to 1970*, series Y 505-637 and Y 652-848]

ITEM	All governments (mil. dol.)	Federal (mil. dol.)	State/Local Total (mil. dol.)	State (mil. dol.)	Local (mil. dol.)	PER CAPITA[1] (dol.) Federal	PER CAPITA[1] (dol.) State and local
Revenue	2,374,185	1,308,349	1,485,036	805,607	679,429	5,067	5,760
Intergovernmental revenue	([2])	3,298	415,901	188,560	227,342	(X)	1,613
Revenue from own sources	2,374,185	1,305,051	1,069,134	617,047	452,087	5,055	4,147
General revenue from own sources	1,726,974	887,096	839,878	465,416	374,463	3,441	3,258
Taxes [3]	1,305,839	712,912	592,927	353,957	238,970	2,765	2,300
Property	188,535	(X)	188,535	7,796	180,738	(X)	731
Individual income	632,996	509,680	123,316	112,210	11,106	1,977	478
Corporation income	143,950	117,520	26,430	24,208	2,222	456	103
Sales and gross receipts	276,993	67,447	209,546	174,543	35,003	262	813
Customs duties	18,931	18,931	(X)	(X)	(X)	73	(X)
General	138,776	(X)	138,776	114,635	24,141	(X)	538
Selective [3]	127,121	56,351	70,770	59,908	10,862	219	275
Motor fuel	44,468	20,223	24,245	23,568	676	78	94
Alcoholic beverages	11,565	7,704	3,861	3,575	287	30	15
Tobacco products	12,121	5,700	6,421	6,232	189	22	25
Public utilities	22,196	7,835	14,361	8,265	6,097	30	56
Motor vehicle and operators' licenses	13,421	(X)	13,421	12,519	902	(X)	52
Death and gift	17,275	12,577	4,698	4,659	39	49	18
Charges and miscellaneous [3]	421,135	174,184	246,951	111,459	135,493	676	958
Current charges [3]	242,164	94,613	147,551	57,384	90,168	367	572
National defense and international relations	12,014	12,014	(X)	(X)	(X)	47	(X)
Postal service	46,502	46,502	(X)	(X)	(X)	180	(X)
Education [3]	42,025	-	42,025	31,270	10,756	-	163
School lunch sales	3,867	-	3,867	13	3,854	-	15
Higher education	34,940	-	34,940	30,861	4,079	-	136
Natural resources	15,176	13,149	2,027	1,532	495	51	8
Hospitals	41,209	143	41,066	13,953	27,112	1	159
Sewerage	7,231	(X)	7,231	318	6,913	(X)	28
Solid waste management	15,861	3	15,858	28	15,829	(Z)	62
Parks and recreation	4,169	109	4,060	867	3,193	(Z)	16
Housing and community development	6,231	3,061	3,170	254	2,916	12	12
Airports	6,632	23	6,609	726	5,884	(Z)	26
Water transport and terminals	3,133	1,427	1,706	409	1,297	6	7
Special assessments	2,660	(X)	2,660	152	2,508	(X)	10
Sale of property	4,440	3,602	838	200	638	14	3
Interest earnings	61,611	10,897	50,714	25,283	25,431	42	197
Utility and liquor store revenue	65,081	(X)	65,081	6,746	58,335	(X)	252
Insurance trust revenue	581,892	417,955	163,937	144,886	19,051	1,621	636
Expenditure	2,571,896	1,364,873	1,428,577	743,262	685,315	6,882	5,541
Intergovernmental expenditure	([2])	3,298	221,434	214,095	7,339	794	859
Direct expenditure	2,571,896	1,364,873	1,207,023	529,167	677,856	6,088	4,682
General expenditure [3]	1,902,481	878,625	1,023,856	432,813	591,043	4,202	3,972
Education [3]	368,473	25,878	342,595	90,368	252,228	100	1,329
Elementary and secondary education	240,588	(X)	240,588	2,530	238,058	(X)	933
Higher education	88,138	(X)	88,138	73,969	14,169	(X)	342
Public welfare	218,655	51,609	167,046	137,077	29,969	200	648
Hospitals	73,341	10,875	62,466	27,428	35,038	42	242
Health	45,628	13,443	32,185	17,173	15,012	52	125
Highways	68,753	619	68,134	42,056	26,078	2	264
Police protection	43,502	7,356	36,146	4,961	31,185	29	140
Fire protection	15,797	(X)	15,797	(X)	15,797	(X)	61
Corrections	32,036	2,422	29,614	19,091	10,523	9	115
Natural resources	62,311	49,143	13,168	10,514	2,653	191	51
Sewerage	22,692	(X)	22,692	1,097	21,595	11	88
Solid waste management	15,433	2,717	12,716	1,304	11,412	49	49
Housing and community development	31,121	12,582	18,539	1,797	16,742	49	72
Governmental administration	70,406	18,004	52,402	21,135	31,268	70	203
Parks and recreation	18,129	2,135	15,994	2,672	13,322	8	62
Interest on general debt	253,878	198,795	55,083	24,019	31,065	771	214
Utility and liquor store expenditure	84,361	(X)	84,361	9,376	74,985	(X)	327
Insurance trust expenditure	585,174	486,248	98,926	86,978	11,948	1,886	384
By character and object:							
Current operation	1,363,688	490,864	872,824	345,324	527,500	1,904	3,386
Capital outlay	221,304	85,328	135,976	50,152	85,824	331	527
Construction	109,892	9,661	100,231	39,604	60,627	37	389
Equip., land, and existing structures	111,412	75,667	35,745	10,548	25,197	294	139
Assistance and subsidies	138,274	103,638	34,636	21,884	12,752	402	134
Interest on debt (general and utility)	263,576	198,795	64,781	24,829	39,952	771	251
Insurance benefits and repayments	585,055	486,248	98,807	86,978	11,829	1,886	383
Expenditure for salaries and wages [4]	559,012	162,536	396,476	115,283	281,193	630	1,538

- Represents or rounds to zero.   X Not applicable.   Z Less than 50 cents.   [1] Based on estimated resident population as of July 1. See table 2.   [2] Aggregates exclude duplicative transactions between levels of government; see source.   [3] Includes amounts not shown separately.   [4] Included in items shown above.

Source: U.S. Bureau of the Census, Internet site, http://www.census.gov/ftp/pub/govs/www/index.html (accessed 06/25/96); and unpublished data.

No. 473. All Governments—Capital Outlays: 1970 to 1993

[In millions of dollars, except percent. For fiscal year ending in year shown; see text, section 9. Local government amounts are subject to sampling variation; see Appendix III and source. See also *Historical Statistics, Colonial Times to 1970*, series Y 523-524, Y 673-674, Y 740-741, and Y 787-788]

LEVEL AND FUNCTION	1970	1980	1985	1988	1989	1990	1991	1992	1993
Total	47,519	99,386	156,912	197,844	211,734	220,960	227,225	227,798	221,304
Federal Government:									
Total	17,869	36,492	77,014	93,531	99,790	97,891	95,575	93,095	85,328
Annual percent change [1]	-6	11	6	-3	7	-2	-2	-3	-7
Percent of direct expenditure . . .	10	7	8	8	9	8	6	7	6
By function:									
National defense [2]	14,027	28,161	64,154	74,790	78,891	75,624	72,775	69,061	61,754
Education	9	97	39	7	9	41	97	90	86
Highways	9	132	121	173	165	181	143	310	210
Health and hospitals	166	673	916	1,228	1,403	1,096	1,387	1,594	1,703
Natural resources	1,691	4,046	4,092	3,581	3,786	4,698	4,721	5,466	6,122
Housing [3]	853	317	1,935	5,180	5,032	4,343	4,147	4,017	3,942
Air transportation	234	151	785	407	658	664	778	879	916
Water transportation [4]	285	1,003	583	370	306	385	459	506	739
Other	595	1,912	4,389	7,792	9,540	10,859	10,068	11,172	10,856
State and local governments:									
Total	29,650	62,894	79,898	104,313	111,944	123,069	131,650	134,703	135,976
Annual percent change [1]	5	7	13	6	7	10	7	2	-
Percent of direct expenditure . . .	20	15	12	13	13	13	12	12	11
By function:									
Education [5]	7,621	10,737	13,477	18,529	21,854	25,997	27,251	30,845	31,551
Higher education	2,705	2,972	4,629	6,397	6,851	7,441	7,064	9,180	9,263
Elementary and secondary . . .	4,658	7,362	8,358	11,789	14,584	18,057	19,852	21,319	22,288
Highways	10,762	19,133	23,900	31,635	32,754	33,867	36,409	37,031	36,950
Health and hospitals	790	2,443	2,709	3,436	3,445	3,848	4,142	4,331	5,291
Natural resources	789	1,052	1,736	1,894	2,019	2,545	2,474	2,266	2,136
Housing [3]	1,319	2,248	3,217	3,619	3,765	3,997	4,389	4,182	4,890
Air transportation	691	1,391	1,875	2,896	2,965	3,434	3,941	4,605	5,413
Water transportation [4]	258	623	717	911	943	924	984	778	996
Sewerage	1,385	6,272	5,926	8,300	8,343	8,356	9,104	8,926	10,251
Parks and recreation.	684	2,023	2,196	3,142	3,350	3,877	4,702	3,934	3,839
Utilities	2,437	9,933	13,435	14,782	15,371	16,601	17,028	17,785	15,931
Water	1,201	3,335	4,160	6,052	6,372	6,873	7,499	7,567	6,490
Electric	820	4,572	5,247	4,473	4,291	3,976	3,579	3,950	3,760
Transit	366	1,921	3,830	3,998	4,430	5,443	5,636	5,836	5,253
Gas	50	105	198	259	279	310	314	432	428
Other	2,915	7,039	10,711	15,172	17,135	19,623	21,226	20,020	18,727

- Represents or rounds to zero.   [1] Change from prior year shown except 1970, change from 1969 and 1980, change from 1975.   [2] Includes international relations and U.S. service schools.   [3] Includes community development.   [4] Includes terminals.   [5] Includes other education.

Source: U.S. Bureau of the Census, *Historical Statistics on Governmental Finances and Employment*; and *Government Finances*, series GF, No. 5, annual; Internet site, http://www.census.gov/ftp/pub/govs/www/index.html (accessed 05/31/96); and unpublished data.

No. 474. All Governments—Expenditure for Public Works: 1980 to 1993

[In millions of dollars. Public works include expenditures on highways, airports, water transport and terminals, sewerage, solid waste management, water supply, and mass transit systems. Represents direct expenditures excluding intergovernmental grants]

ITEM	Total	Highways	Airport transportation	Water transport and terminals	Sewerage	Solid waste management	Water supply	Mass transit
1980: Total.	72,177	33,745	5,071	3,278	9,892	3,322	9,228	7,641
Federal	5,114	434	2,570	2,110	-	-	-	-
State	22,832	20,661	360	360	334	-	91	1,026
Local	44,231	12,650	2,141	808	9,558	3,322	9,137	6,615
Capital expenditures (percent) . . .	48	57	30	50	63	11	36	25
1990: Total.	146,762	61,913	10,983	4,524	18,309	10,144	22,101	18,788
Federal	7,911	856	4,499	2,556	-	-	-	-
State	43,787	36,464	635	504	636	891	136	4,521
Local	95,064	24,593	5,848	1,464	17,673	9,253	21,966	14,267
Capital expenditures (percent) . . .	42	55	37	29	46	18	31	29
1993: Total.	170,448	68,753	15,478	5,106	22,692	12,717	24,402	21,300
Federal	9,786	619	6,214	2,953	-	-	-	-
State	50,206	42,056	915	572	1,097	1,304	188	4,074
Local	110,456	26,078	8,349	1,581	21,595	11,413	24,214	17,226
Capital expenditures (percent) . . .	40	54	41	34	45	11	27	25

- Represents or rounds to zero.

Source: U.S. Bureau of the Census, *Government Finances*, series GF, No. 5, annual; Internet site, http://www.census.gov/ftp/pub/govs/www/index.html (accessed 06/03/96); and unpublished data.

No. 475. Federal Grants-in-Aid Summary: 1970 to 1996

[For fiscal year ending in year shown; see text, section 9. Minus sign (-) indicates decrease]

YEAR	CURRENT DOLLARS							CONSTANT (1987) DOLLARS	
	Total grants (bil. dol.)	Annual percent change [1]	Grants to individuals		Grants as percent of—			Total grants (bil. dol.)	Annual percent change [1]
			Total (bil. dol.)	Percent of total grants	State-local govt. outlays [2]	Federal outlays	Gross domestic product		
1970	24,065	19.3	8,727	36.3	19.0	12.3	2.4	73.6	11.9
1975	49,791	14.8	16,762	33.7	23.5	15.0	3.3	105.4	3.0
1980	91,451	9.7	32,652	35.7	26.3	15.5	3.5	127.5	-1.0
1985	105,852	8.5	49,352	46.6	21.3	11.2	2.7	112.9	4.2
1988	115,342	6.4	62,434	54.1	18.6	10.8	2.4	110.7	2.1
1989	121,928	5.7	67,353	55.2	18.6	10.7	2.4	112.2	1.4
1990	135,325	11.0	77,132	57.0	18.7	10.8	2.5	119.5	6.5
1991	154,519	14.2	92,497	59.9	19.5	11.7	2.7	130.9	9.5
1992	178,065	15.2	112,185	63.0	20.8	12.9	3.0	146.7	12.1
1993	193,612	8.7	124,289	64.2	21.2	13.7	3.1	155.5	6.0
1994	210,596	8.8	135,232	64.2	21.8	14.4	3.2	165.9	6.7
1995	224,992	6.8	145,793	64.8	22.2	14.8	3.2	172.7	4.1
1996 est.	236,730	5.2	150,583	63.6	(NA)	15.1	3.2	177.3	2.7

NA Not available. [1] Average annual percent change from prior year shown. For explanation, see Guide to Tabular Presentation. 1970, change from 1969. [2] Outlays as defined in the national income and product accounts.

Source: Office of Management and Budget, based on *Budget of the United States Government, FY 97.*

No. 476. Federal Aid to State and Local Governments: 1970 to 1996

[In millions of dollars. For fiscal year ending in year shown; see text, section 9. Includes trust funds. See *Historical Statistics, Colonial Times to 1970*, series Y 638-651, for related data]

PROGRAM	1970	1980	1990	1992	1993	1994	1995	1996,est.
Grant-in-aid shared revenue [1]	[2]24,065	91,451	135,325	178,065	193,612	210,596	224,992	236,730
National defense	37	93	241	318	152	169	68	25
Energy.	25	499	461	448	460	466	492	482
Natural resources and environment	411	5,363	3,745	3,929	3,796	3,765	4,148	4,009
Environmental Protection Agency.	194	4,603	2,874	3,038	2,852	2,700	2,912	2,828
Agriculture	604	569	1,285	1,142	1,117	937	780	676
Transportation [1]	4,599	13,087	19,174	20,556	22,292	23,633	25,787	26,617
Airports.	83	590	1,220	1,672	1,931	1,620	1,826	1,622
Highways	4,395	9,208	14,171	15,250	16,409	18,139	18,945	19,842
Urban mass transit	104	3,129	3,730	3,577	3,885	3,267	4,353	4,384
Community and regional development [1]	1,780	6,486	4,965	4,539	5,666	7,789	7,230	9,690
Appalachian development.	184	335	124	125	138	181	182	170
Community development block grants.	(X)	3,902	2,818	3,090	3,198	3,651	4,333	5,093
Education, employment, training, social services [1]	6,417	21,862	23,359	28,795	30,160	32,744	34,125	36,561
Compensatory education for the disadvantaged	1,470	3,370	4,437	6,129	6,582	6,819	6,785	7,098
School improvement programs	86	523	1,080	1,361	1,903	1,358	1,288	1,473
Bilingual and immigrant education	-	166	152	160	101	176	189	200
Federally affected areas impact aid	622	622	799	785	468	797	803	803
Vocational and adult education	285	854	1,287	1,020	1,133	1,292	1,449	1,481
Libraries	105	158	127	190	159	125	109	155
Payments to States for Family Support Activities	81	383	265	594	736	839	953	959
Social services-block grants to States.	574	2,763	2,749	2,708	2,785	2,728	2,797	3,183
Human development services	390	1,548	2,618	4,064	3,614	3,998	4,463	4,528
Training and employment assistance	954	6,191	3,042	3,388	3,245	3,310	3,620	3,618
Health [1]	3,849	15,758	43,890	71,416	79,665	86,265	93,587	99,173
Alcohol, drug abuse, and mental health [3] . .	146	679	1,241	1,778	1,994	2,132	2,444	2,105
Medicaid [4]	2,727	13,957	41,103	67,827	75,774	82,034	89,070	94,892
Income security [1]	5,795	18,495	35,189	43,486	46,991	51,532	55,123	54,909
Family support payments to States [3]	4,142	6,888	12,246	15,103	15,628	16,508	17,133	17,366
Food stamps-administration	559	412	2,130	2,607	2,611	2,688	2,740	3,061
Child nutrition and special milk programs [3] . .	380	3,388	4,871	5,993	6,589	6,938	7,387	8,111
Housing assistance [5]	436	3,435	9,516	12,262	14,100	15,791	18,416	16,825
Veterans benefits and services	18	90	134	164	189	199	253	254
Administration of justice.	42	529	574	987	987	992	1,222	2,142
General government [4]	479	8,616	2,309	2,274	2,131	2,098	2,172	2,178

- Represents or rounds to zero.   X Not applicable.   [1] Includes items not shown separately.   [2] Includes $5 million for international affairs subsequently provided to a private institution.   [3] Includes grants for payments to individuals.   [4] Includes general purpose fiscal assistance.

Source: U.S. Office of Management and Budget, *Historical Tables, Budget of the United States Government,* annual.

No. 477. Federal Aid to State and Local Governments—Selected Programs, by State: 1995

[In millions of dollars, except per capita. For fiscal year ending September 30]

STATE	FEDERAL AID [1] Total	Per capita [2] (dol.)	OE [3] compensatory education [4]	EPA [5] waste treatment facilities construction	HHS [6] Administration for Children and Families [7]	Medicaid	HUD [8] Lower income housing assistance [9]	Community development	ETA [10] employment/training	DOT [11] highway trust fund
United States [12]	228,936	863	6,817	2,451	33,156	89,070	15,943	4,339	6,897	19,091
Alabama	3,419	810	126	27	339	1,395	213	62	93	293
Alaska	1,125	1,856	15	13	135	169	90	9	41	258
Arizona	3,150	773	99	25	516	1,117	174	42	99	275
Arkansas	2,091	852	75	12	200	885	112	38	59	241
California	26,934	857	735	204	5,940	8,777	1,906	530	1,134	1,880
Colorado	2,391	654	66	13	316	832	174	42	76	249
Connecticut	3,195	976	53	27	472	1,280	327	47	112	392
Delaware	560	793	16	9	78	179	48	8	19	66
District of Columbia	2,238	3,926	21	8	225	384	100	43	36	104
Florida	9,078	651	280	62	1,205	3,516	604	173	286	876
Georgia	5,461	774	169	40	696	2,214	335	76	141	524
Hawaii	1,162	986	20	24	167	322	109	16	36	181
Idaho	849	749	22	5	101	253	40	13	32	141
Illinois	9,487	807	324	97	1,451	3,205	835	263	271	820
Indiana	3,546	616	110	49	501	1,305	253	93	96	369
Iowa	2,074	733	51	29	281	768	104	86	54	229
Kansas	1,649	646	53	22	253	594	71	30	42	167
Kentucky	3,437	898	126	26	414	1,503	198	56	88	248
Louisiana	5,291	1,226	191	19	444	3,071	198	86	110	246
Maine	1,315	1,060	26	12	163	578	105	22	42	116
Maryland	3,594	718	88	79	528	1,255	310	70	111	380
Massachusetts	6,829	1,130	122	277	870	2,447	722	120	182	964
Michigan	7,589	799	307	141	1,351	3,061	369	149	275	569
Minnesota	3,685	807	83	36	571	1,537	293	78	94	228
Mississippi	2,738	1,026	125	20	293	1,221	135	47	71	189
Missouri	4,159	788	113	32	532	1,699	265	134	122	399
Montana	933	1,090	26	6	116	259	62	11	28	146
Nebraska	1,440	887	28	10	172	641	81	28	26	140
Nevada	882	605	19	7	123	226	70	12	41	121
New Hampshire	866	762	17	9	103	387	63	10	29	78
New Jersey	6,639	840	143	69	800	2,632	767	123	226	545
New Mexico	1,866	1,128	60	10	253	597	78	22	42	227
New York	24,348	1,340	616	159	3,811	12,060	1,863	442	509	891
North Carolina	5,487	776	131	36	715	2,551	299	71	133	492
North Dakota	768	1,204	17	6	81	219	41	20	24	135
Ohio	9,115	821	304	183	1,391	3,796	702	193	207	688
Oklahoma	2,472	759	84	20	340	847	194	44	77	253
Oregon	2,763	895	67	19	366	943	170	39	92	189
Pennsylvania	10,354	859	306	64	1,558	4,255	761	259	337	883
Rhode Island	1,276	1,280	22	11	153	521	141	19	37	174
South Carolina	3,027	826	93	30	301	1,467	147	40	79	259
South Dakota	813	1,128	19	13	78	227	59	16	20	129
Tennessee	4,531	876	123	32	458	2,181	234	55	95	321
Texas	13,338	726	583	196	1,507	5,726	711	243	392	985
Utah	1,318	691	33	25	183	421	53	19	51	130
Vermont	625	1,078	15	9	102	219	39	7	20	85
Virginia	3,504	535	101	65	494	1,037	314	73	112	398
Washington	4,351	814	100	39	730	1,603	244	60	167	484
West Virginia	2,074	1,138	71	39	214	955	100	21	60	169
Wisconsin	3,729	734	124	58	644	1,494	217	76	99	296
Wyoming	748	1,571	16	5	55	116	19	4	20	133
Outlying areas	4,028	6,847	275	19	365	122	427	99	147	128

[1] Includes programs not shown separately. [2] Based on estimated resident population as of July 1, 1994. [3] Department of Education, Office of Elementary and Secondary Education. [4] For the disadvantaged. [5] Environmental Protection Agency. [6] Department of Health and Human Services. [7] Includes family support payments (Aid to Families with Dependent Children), social services block grants, children and family services, foster care and adoption assistance, low-income home energy assistance, community services block grants, refugee assistance, and assistance for legalized aliens. [8] Department of Housing and Urban Development. [9] Includes public housing, housing payments (section 8) to public agencies, and college housing. [10] Department of Labor, Employment and Training Administration, Insurance and Employment Service Operations, and Community Service. [11] Department of Transportation, Highway Trust Fund. [12] Includes undistributed amounts not shown separately.

Source: U.S. Bureau of the Census, *Federal Expenditures by State for Fiscal Year 1995*; Internet site, http://www.census.gov/ftp/pub/govs/ www/index.html (accessed 06/25/96).

No. 478. State and Local Governments—Summary of Finances: 1980 to 1993

[For fiscal year ending in year shown; see text, section 9. Local government amounts are estimates subject to sampling variation; see Appendix III and source. See also *Historical Statistics, Colonial Times to 1970,* series Y 652-709]

ITEM	TOTAL (mil. dol.)				PER CAPITA [1] (dol.)			
	1980	1990	1992	1993	1980	1990	1992	1993
Revenue [2]	**451,537**	**1,032,115**	**1,185,191**	**1,267,967**	**1,993**	**4,150**	**4,647**	**4,918**
From Federal Government	**83,029**	**136,802**	**179,184**	**198,833**	**367**	**550**	**703**	**771**
Public welfare	24,921	59,961	91,788	17,395	110	241	360	67
Highways	8,980	14,368	14,800	16,947	40	58	58	66
Education	14,435	23,233	27,821	30,380	64	93	109	118
Health and hospitals	2,513	5,904	7,293	8,635	11	24	29	33
Housing and community development	3,905	9,655	10,876	11,687	17	39	43	45
Other and unallocable	28,275	23,683	26,606	113,789	125	95	104	441
From State and local sources	**368,509**	**895,313**	**1,006,007**	**1,069,134**	**1,627**	**3,600**	**3,945**	**4,147**
General, net intergovernmental	299,293	712,700	793,399	839,878	1,321	2,865	3,111	3,258
Taxes	223,463	501,619	555,610	592,927	986	2,017	2,179	2,300
Property	68,499	155,613	178,536	188,535	302	626	700	731
Sales and gross receipts	79,927	177,885	196,112	209,546	353	715	769	813
Individual income	42,080	105,640	115,170	123,316	186	425	452	478
Corporation income	13,321	23,566	23,595	26,430	59	95	93	103
Other	19,636	38,915	42,197	45,101	87	156	165	175
Charges and miscellaneous	75,830	211,081	237,789	246,951	335	849	932	958
Utility and liquor stores	25,560	58,642	62,540	65,081	113	236	245	252
Water supply system	6,766	17,674	19,147	20,206	30	71	75	78
Electric power system	11,387	29,268	30,999	32,090	50	118	122	124
Transit system	2,397	5,216	5,742	5,828	11	21	23	23
Gas supply system	1,809	3,043	3,034	3,331	8	12	12	13
Liquor stores	3,201	3,441	3,618	3,626	14	14	14	14
Insurance trust revenue [3]	43,656	123,970	150,067	164,175	193	498	588	637
Employee retirement	25,441	94,268	108,310	113,054	112	379	425	439
Unemployment compensation	13,529	18,441	27,019	34,649	60	74	106	134
Direct expenditure	**432,328**	**972,662**	**1,146,610**	**1,207,142**	**1,908**	**3,911**	**4,496**	**4,682**
By function:								
Direct general expenditure [3]	367,340	834,786	971,973	1,023,856	1,622	3,356	3,811	3,972
Education [3]	133,211	288,148	326,769	342,595	588	1,159	1,281	1,329
Elementary and secondary	92,930	202,009	228,917	240,588	410	812	898	933
Higher education	33,919	73,418	84,329	88,138	150	295	331	342
Highways	33,311	61,057	66,477	68,134	147	245	261	264
Public welfare	45,552	110,518	154,235	167,046	201	444	605	648
Health	8,387	24,223	29,344	32,185	37	97	115	125
Hospitals	23,787	50,412	58,768	62,466	105	203	230	242
Police protection	13,494	30,577	34,545	36,146	60	123	135	140
Fire protection	5,718	13,186	14,358	15,797	25	53	56	61
Natural resources	5,509	12,330	13,049	13,168	24	50	51	51
Sanitation and sewerage	13,214	28,453	32,398	35,408	58	114	127	137
Housing and community development	6,062	15,479	17,067	18,539	27	62	67	72
Parks and recreation	6,520	14,326	15,728	15,994	29	58	62	62
Financial administration	6,719	16,217	18,090	19,300	30	65	71	75
Interest on general debt [4]	14,747	49,739	55,255	55,083	65	200	217	214
Utility and liquor stores [4]	36,191	77,801	84,361	84,361	160	313	331	327
Water supply system	9,228	22,101	24,378	24,401	41	89	96	95
Electric power system	15,016	30,997	31,983	32,338	66	125	125	125
Transit system	7,641	18,788	21,879	21,300	34	76	86	83
Gas supply system	1,715	2,989	3,058	3,274	8	12	12	13
Liquor stores	2,591	2,926	3,063	3,048	11	12	12	12
Insurance trust expenditure [3]	28,797	63,321	90,276	98,926	127	255	354	384
Employee retirement	14,008	38,355	46,419	51,662	62	154	182	200
Unemployment compensation	12,070	16,499	32,887	35,409	53	66	129	137
By character and object:								
Current operation	307,811	700,131	823,494	872,824	1,359	2,815	3,229	3,386
Capital outlay	62,894	123,069	134,521	135,976	278	495	527	527
Construction	51,492	89,114	100,533	100,231	227	358	394	389
Equipment, land, and existing structures	11,402	33,955	33,988	35,745	50	137	133	139
Assistance and subsidies	15,222	27,227	33,230	34,636	67	109	130	134
Interest on debt (general and utility)	17,604	58,914	64,789	64,781	78	237	254	251
Insurance benefits and repayments	28,797	63,321	90,276	98,926	127	255	354	384
Expenditure for salaries and wages	*163,896*	*341,158*	*378,804*	*396,476*	*723*	*1,372*	*1,485*	*1,538*
Debt outstanding, year end	**335,603**	**860,584**	**970,462**	**1,016,167**	**1,481**	**3,460**	**3,805**	**3,942**
Long-term	322,456	841,278	949,129	993,563	1,423	3,382	3,722	3,854
Short-term	13,147	19,306	21,333	22,605	58	78	84	88
Long-term debt:								
Issued	42,364	108,468	155,060	194,966	187	436	608	756
Retired	17,404	64,831	99,233	146,287	77	261	389	567

[1] 1980 and 1990 based on enumerated resident population as of April 1. Other years based on estimated resident population as of July 1; see table 2.   [2] Aggregates exclude duplicative transactions between State and local governments; see source.   [3] Includes amounts not shown separately.   [4] Interest on utility debt included in "utility expenditure." For total interest on debt, see "Interest on debt (general and utility)."

Source: U.S. Bureau of the Census, *Historical Statistics on Governmental Finances and Employment;* Internet site, http://www.census.gov/ftp/pub/govs/www/index.html (accessed 06/10/96), and unpublished data.

No. 479. State and Local Government Receipts and Current Expenditures in the National Income and Product Accounts: 1980 to 1995

[In billions of dollars. For explanation of national income, see text, section 14]

ITEM	1980	1985	1988	1989	1990	1991	1992	1993	1994	1995
Receipts	**361.4**	**528.7**	**631.4**	**681.0**	**728.9**	**784.2**	**844.3**	**897.1**	**946.4**	**996.1**
Personal tax and nontax receipts	56.2	94.0	117.6	131.4	139.1	147.8	159.7	166.2	170.0	179.4
Income taxes	42.6	72.1	89.9	101.4	106.3	110.4	118.1	123.4	125.7	133.5
Nontaxes	5.0	9.9	12.7	14.1	15.6	19.2	22.5	22.9	23.4	23.9
Other	8.6	11.9	15.0	15.9	17.3	18.2	19.1	19.9	20.9	22.0
Corporate profits tax accruals	14.5	20.2	26.0	24.2	22.5	23.6	24.4	26.3	30.9	34.4
Indirect business tax and nontax accruals [1]	172.3	271.4	324.6	353.0	377.6	398.4	423.7	451.8	479.9	504.3
Sales taxes	82.9	131.1	161.5	172.7	183.2	190.0	202.2	212.9	227.4	238.3
Property taxes	68.8	107.0	127.6	143.3	155.5	167.6	177.5	194.2	205.1	216.3
Contributions for social insurance	29.7	42.8	51.9	54.1	57.4	60.9	64.3	66.9	69.7	71.9
Federal grants-in-aid	88.7	100.3	111.2	118.2	132.4	153.4	172.2	185.7	195.9	206.1
Current expenditures	**307.0**	**437.8**	**545.5**	**585.9**	**648.8**	**708.4**	**758.0**	**802.2**	**846.6**	**901.1**
Consumption expenditures	261.3	382.6	471.3	507.2	550.1	579.4	603.6	627.9	651.7	682.6
Transfer payments to persons	65.7	101.9	131.0	144.5	166.5	199.0	227.2	246.8	267.4	291.6
Net interest paid	-19.3	-38.9	-44.6	-51.2	-51.7	-53.3	-54.7	-51.9	-49.8	-47.4
Interest received by government	38.7	81.0	99.0	108.8	112.1	116.8	119.4	116.3	114.0	111.4
Less: Dividends received	1.9	4.5	6.9	8.1	9.0	9.5	10.1	10.5	11.4	12.6
Subsidies	0.4	0.3	0.4	0.4	0.4	0.4	0.4	0.3	0.4	0.4
Less: Current surplus of govt. enterprises	-0.9	3.7	5.7	7.0	7.5	7.6	8.4	10.5	11.6	13.5
Current surplus or deficit	**54.4**	**91.0**	**85.9**	**95.1**	**80.1**	**75.8**	**86.3**	**94.9**	**99.7**	**95.0**
Social insurance funds	26.9	47.0	56.7	60.2	59.9	64.3	68.0	66.9	62.9	58.2
Other	27.5	44.0	29.2	34.9	20.2	11.5	18.3	28.0	36.9	36.8

[1] Includes other items not shown separately.

Source: U.S. Bureau of Economic Analysis, *National Income and Product Accounts of the United States,* to be published in late 1996, and *Survey of Current Business,* January/February 1996.

No. 480. State and Local Government Consumption Expenditures and Transfers in the National Income and Product Accounts: 1980 to 1994

[In billions of dollars. For explanation of national income, see text, section 14]

EXPENDITURE	1980	1985	1987	1988	1989	1990	1991	1992	1993	1994
Total	**324.4**	**464.9**	**537.2**	**574.7**	**617.9**	**672.6**	**703.4**	**735.8**	**767.8**	**798.4**
Consumption expenditures	261.3	382.6	441.1	471.3	507.2	550.1	579.4	603.6	627.9	651.7
Durable goods [1]	4.7	7.4	8.7	9.4	10.2	10.9	11.7	12.4	13.1	13.8
Nondurable goods	28.8	38.7	41.6	44.4	50.4	56.5	58.4	60.9	63.8	66.8
Services	227.8	336.5	390.7	417.5	446.6	482.8	509.4	530.3	551.0	571.2
Compensation of employees	193.1	285.4	329.5	353.7	380.2	413.9	437.9	460.0	480.9	500.0
Other services [2]	34.7	51.1	61.2	63.8	66.4	68.9	71.5	70.3	70.1	71.2
Structures	55.1	67.6	78.8	84.8	88.7	98.5	100.5	108.1	113.9	119.0
Transfers	65.7	101.9	120.7	131.0	144.5	166.5	199.0	227.2	246.8	267.4
Benefits from social insurance funds	17.8	30.4	37.5	41.1	44.7	49.6	55.1	61.0	65.7	73.1
State and local employee retirement	15.1	25.5	31.2	34.1	37.0	40.6	44.7	49.6	54.3	61.4
Temporary disability insurance	0.8	1.4	1.6	1.8	1.9	2.2	2.8	3.0	2.3	2.3
Workers' compensation	2.0	3.5	4.7	5.3	5.8	6.9	7.6	8.4	9.0	9.5
Public assistance	42.8	65.7	76.6	82.9	92.1	108.1	134.4	156.0	170.1	182.4
Medical care	24.6	41.8	50.7	55.9	63.8	76.7	100.2	119.7	132.5	143.5
Aid to Families with Dependent Children	12.4	15.4	16.7	17.3	18.0	19.8	22.0	23.3	23.9	24.2
Supplemental Security Income	2.0	2.3	2.9	3.1	3.4	3.8	3.8	4.1	3.9	3.8
General assistance	1.4	2.4	2.6	2.7	2.8	3.0	2.9	3.3	3.3	3.4
Energy assistance	1.3	2.1	1.7	1.8	1.4	1.6	1.6	1.6	1.6	1.9
Other [3]	1.0	1.6	1.9	2.3	2.7	3.2	3.8	4.0	4.8	5.7
Education	2.4	3.5	4.0	4.2	4.6	5.3	5.7	6.0	6.6	7.2
Employment and training	1.7	0.9	0.9	0.9	0.9	0.9	0.9	1.1	1.1	1.1
Other [4]	0.8	1.3	1.6	1.9	2.2	2.5	2.9	3.1	3.4	3.6

[1] Excludes expenditures classified as investment except goods transferred to foreign countries by the Federal Government. [2] Includes consumption of fixed capital or depreciation. [3] Consists of emergency assistance and medical insurance premium payments paid on behalf of indigents. [4] Consists largely of foster care, veterans benefits, Alaska dividends, and crime victim payments.

Source: U.S. Bureau of Economic Analysis, *National Income and Product Accounts of the United States,* to be published in late 1996, and *Survey of Current Business,* January/February 1996.

No. 481. New Issues of Long-Term State and Local Government Securities: 1980 to 1995

[In billions of dollars. Beginning 1985, includes outlying areas]

ITEM	1980	1985	1988	1989	1990	1991	1992	1993	1994	1995
All issues, new capital and refunding [1]	38.7	194.3	114.1	119.4	123.1	166.3	226.7	287.8	160.0	156.3
General obligations	11.2	37.1	30.5	36.8	39.7	55.9	78.8	90.9	55.3	60.4
Revenue	27.4	157.3	83.6	82.6	83.3	110.4	147.9	197.0	104.7	95.9
Type of issuer	38.7	194.3	114.1	119.4	123.1	166.3	[2]226.7	[2]287.8	[2]160.0	[2]156.3
City, town	6.4	34.6	20.6	23.2	22.5	30.7	44.1	51.0	26.5	28.0
College or university	0.1	2.7	1.9	2.0	1.6	3.7	4.0	5.1	2.8	2.5
County/parish	3.8	15.5	10.7	9.8	9.7	14.3	19.2	24.0	16.9	13.3
District	2.4	15.2	13.0	13.1	14.7	22.6	30.4	36.8	20.8	22.5
Local authority	7.9	49.8	21.7	23.1	20.8	27.7	41.0	57.4	26.3	27.8
State/territory	5.1	10.9	9.4	11.6	14.8	19.4	25.2	28.2	19.7	14.8
State authority	13.0	65.7	36.8	36.5	38.9	47.8	62.8	85.4	47.0	47.5
Issues for new capital	37.1	123.9	77.5	84.0	97.9	112.7	104.5	93.7	110.6	156.3
Use of proceeds:										
Airports	0.4	2.5	3.2	1.2	4.7	3.4	4.9	1.7	3.0	4.6
Economic development	0.1	1.8	1.3	1.6	1.5	2.2	1.9	2.2	3.0	2.5
Education	2.6	10.3	11.1	13.8	16.3	17.6	16.9	14.4	20.0	28.8
Electric & public power	3.6	8.4	1.2	2.1	1.3	3.3	2.8	3.2	2.4	4.9
General purpose/public improvement	9.6	21.4	24.7	28.2	32.2	40.8	34.2	31.3	39.1	44.5
Health care	1.7	15.9	5.6	8.0	8.2	11.1	8.1	8.5	7.5	11.4
Multi family housing	2.2	20.1	1.6	1.8	1.0	1.5	2.2	2.0	3.4	6.1
Pollution control	2.1	7.8	0.7	0.8	1.2	1.6	1.4	1.8	1.3	4.2
Single family housing	10.6	14.6	9.9	6.4	10.2	6.7	5.4	3.3	7.6	10.0
Solid waste/resource recovery	0.4	3.3	2.0	1.9	2.3	2.5	1.9	3.0	2.8	3.4
Student loans	0.2	2.7	2.9	1.3	0.9	1.4	2.6	3.0	2.3	4.1
Transportation	0.9	5.7	3.4	5.0	6.9	6.3	9.3	7.3	7.6	11.3
Water, sewer, and gas facilities	1.6	4.9	6.8	6.9	7.5	10.9	9.1	8.6	7.3	13.8

[1] Excludes short term issues, private placements, not-for-profit issuers. [2] Includes amounts not shown separately.

Source: Securities Data Company, Newark, NJ, Municipal New Issues Database (copyright).

No. 482. State and Local Governments—Indebtedness: 1980 to 1993

[In billions of dollars, except per capita. For fiscal year ending in year shown; see text, section 9. Local government amounts are estimates subject to sampling variation; see Appendix III and source. See *Historical Statistics, Colonial Times to 1970*, series Y 680, Y 747, and Y 794, for debt outstanding]

ITEM		DEBT OUTSTANDING					LONG TERM		
	Total	Per capita [1] (dol.)	Long-term			Short-term	Net long-term	Debt issued	Debt retired
			Local schools [2]	Utilities	All other				
1980: Total.........	335.6	1,481	32.3	55.2	235.0	13.1	262.9	42.4	17.4
State......	122.0	539	3.8	4.6	111.5	2.1	79.8	16.4	5.7
Local	213.6	943	28.5	50.6	123.5	11.0	183.1	25.9	11.7
1985: Total.........	568.6	2,390	43.8	90.8	414.5	19.6	430.5	101.2	43.5
State......	211.9	891	6.7	8.6	193.8	2.8	110.4	41.7	16.4
Local	356.7	1,499	37.1	82.2	220.6	16.8	320.1	59.5	27.2
1986: Total.........	658.9	2,744	43.0	104.8	492.8	18.3	458.9	162.0	74.4
State......	247.7	1,032	4.1	10.0	232.0	1.6	129.1	64.0	26.4
Local	411.2	1,712	38.9	94.9	260.6	16.7	329.8	98.1	48.0
1987: Total.........	727.1	3,001	49.2	120.5	541.5	15.9	518.3	134.4	83.0
State......	265.7	1,097	7.9	11.9	244.1	1.6	143.4	50.2	33.3
Local	461.5	1,905	41.3	108.6	297.3	14.3	375.0	84.1	49.8
1988: Total.........	755.0	3,088	47.5	124.9	566.9	15.7	425.4	89.7	63.8
State......	276.8	1,132	3.3	12.2	260.0	1.3	108.8	36.4	26.1
Local	478.2	1,956	44.2	112.7	306.9	14.4	316.5	53.3	37.6
1989: Total.........	798.4	3,235	52.7	127.5	600.2	18.0	445.5	102.2	63.8
State......	295.5	1,197	3.7	12.2	277.4	2.3	118.2	42.0	26.9
Local	502.9	2,037	49.0	115.3	322.8	15.7	327.2	60.2	36.8
1990: Total.........	860.6	3,451	60.4	134.8	646.1	19.3	477.0	108.5	64.8
State......	318.3	1,276	4.4	12.3	298.8	2.8	125.5	43.5	22.9
Local	542.3	2,175	56.0	122.4	347.4	16.5	351.5	65.0	42.0
1991: Total.........	915.8	3,632	71.0	141.2	681.8	21.7	509.9	118.1	65.7
State......	345.6	1,370	5.9	12.5	323.7	3.4	139.9	50.5	25.4
Local	570.2	2,261	65.1	128.7	358.1	18.3	369.9	67.6	40.3
1992: Total.........	970.5	3,805	78.4	150.4	720.4	21.3	561.6	155.1	99.2
State......	372.3	1,460	7.6	13.7	348.1	2.9	125.4	70.2	45.0
Local	598.1	2,345	70.9	136.7	373.1	18.4	409.1	85.0	54.3
1993: Total.........	1,016.2	3,942	89.2	157.5	746.9	22.6	617.1	195.0	146.3
State......	389.8	1,512	9.4	14.8	361.7	3.9	176.9	77.2	60.7
Local	626.4	2,430	79.8	142.7	385.2	18.7	440.2	117.8	85.6

[1] 1980 and 1990 based on enumerated resident population as of April 1; other years based on estimated resident population as of July 1; see table 2. [2] Includes debt for education activities other than higher education.

Source: U.S. Bureau of the Census, Internet site, http://www.census.gov/ftp/pub/govs/www/index.html (accessed 06/24/96); and unpublished data.

No. 483. Bond Ratings for State Governments, by State: 1995

[As of fourth quarter. Key to investment grade ratings are in declining order of quality. The ratings from AA to CCC may be modified by the addition of a plus or minus sign to show relative standing within the major rating categories. S&P:AAA,AA,A,BBB,BB,B,CCC,CC,C;Moody's:Aaa,Aa1,Aa,A1,A,Baa1,Baa,Ba1,Ba,B1,B; Fitch:AAA,AA,A,BBB,BB,B,CCC,CC,C]

STATE	Standard & Poor's	Moody's	Fitch	STATE	Standard & Poor's	Moody's	Fitch
Alabama	AA	Aa	AA	Montana	AA-	Aa	(1)
Alaska	AA	Aa	AA	Nebraska	(1)	(1)	(1)
Arizona	(1)	(1)	(1)	Nevada	AA	Aa	(1)
Arkansas	AA	Aa	(1)	New Hampshire	AA+	Aa	AA+
California	A	A1	A	New Jersey	AA+	Aa1	AA+
Colorado	(1)	(1)	(1)	New Mexico	AA1	Aa1	(1)
Connecticut	AA-	Aa	AA	New York	A-	A	A+
Delaware	AA+	Aa1	(1)	North Carolina	AAA	Aaa	AAA
Florida	AA	Aa	AA	North Dakota	AA-	Aa	(1)
Georgia	AA+	Aaa	AAA	Ohio	AA	Aa	(1)
Hawaii	AA	Aa	(1)	Oklahoma	AA	Aa	AA
Idaho	(1)	(1)	(1)	Oregon	AA-	Aa	AA
Illinois	AA-	A1	(2)	Pennsylvania	AA-	A1	AA-
Indiana	(1)	(1)	(1)	Rhode Island	AA-	A1	AA-
Iowa	(1)	(1)	(1)	South Carolina	AA+	Aaa	AAA
Kansas	(1)	(1)	(1)	South Dakota	(1)	(1)	(1)
Kentucky	AA	Aa	(1)	Tennessee	AA+	Aaa	AAA
Louisiana	A-	Baa1	(1)	Texas	AA	Aa+	AA+
Maine	AA+	Aa	(1)	Utah	AAA	Aaa	AAA
Maryland	AAA	Aaa	AAA	Vermont	AA-	Aa	AA
Massachusetts	A+	A1	A+	Virginia	AAA	Aaa	AAA
Michigan	AA	Aa	AA	Washington	AA	Aa	AA
Minnesota	AA+	Aa1	AAA	West Virginia	A+	A1	A+
Mississippi	AA-	Aa	(1)	Wisconsin	AA	Aa	(2)
Missouri	AAA	Aaa	AAA	Wyoming	(1)	(1)	(1)

[1] Not reviewed. [2] Under general review.

Source: Congressional Quarterly Inc., Washington, DC, *Governing Magazine* (copyright).

No. 484. Bond Ratings for City Governments, by Largest Cities: 1995

[As of fourth quarter. For key to ratings, see headnote in table above]

CITIES RANKED BY 1992 POPULATION	Standard & Poor's	Moody's	Fitch	CITIES RANKED BY 1992 POPULATION	Standard & Poor's	Moody's	Fitch
New York, NY	BBB+	Baa1	A-	Sacramento, CA	AA	Aa1	(1)
Los Angeles, CA	AA	Aa1	(1)	Fresno, CA	(1)	(1)	(1)
Chicago, IL	A	A	(1)	Tulsa, OK	AA	Aa	(1)
Houston, TX	AA-	Aa	AA	Oakland, CA	AA-	A1	(1)
Philadelphia, PA	BBB-	Ba	BBB-	Honolulu, HI	AA	Aa	(1)
San Diego, CA	AA+	Aaa	(1)	Miami, FL	A	A	(1)
Dallas, TX	AAA	Aa1	(1)	Pittsburgh, PA	(1)	Baa1	A-
Phoenix, AZ	AA+	Aa1	(1)	Cincinnati, OH	AA+	Aa	(1)
Detroit, MI	BBB	Ba1	(1)	Minneapolis, MN	AAA	Aaa	(1)
San Antonio, TX	AA	Aa	AA	Omaha, NE	AAA	Aaa	(1)
San Jose, CA	(1)	Aa	(1)	Toledo, OH	(1)	Baa1	(1)
Indianapolis, IN	(1)	Aaa	AAA	Buffalo, NY	BBB	Baa	(1)
San Francisco, CA	AA-	A1	AA	Wichita, KS	AA	Aa	(1)
Baltimore, MD	A	A1	AAA	Mesa, AZ	AA-	A1	(1)
Jacksonville, FL	AA	A1	AA	Colorado Springs, CO	AA-	Aa	(1)
Columbus, OH	AAA	Aaa	(1)	Santa Ana, CA	(1)	(1)	(1)
Milwaukee, WI	AA+	Aa	AA+	Tampa, FL	(1)	(1)	(1)
Memphis, TN	AA	Aa	(1)	Arlington, TX	AA	Aa	(1)
Washington, DC	B	Ba	BB	Anaheim, CA	AA	Aa1	(1)
Boston, MA	A	A	(1)	Louisville, KY	AA-	A1	(1)
El Paso, TX	AA	Aa	(1)	St. Paul, MN	AA+	Aa	(1)
Seattle, WA	AA+	Aa1	(1)	Newark, NJ	BBB+	Baa1	(1)
Cleveland, OH	A	A	A-	Corpus Christi, TX	AA-	A	(1)
Nashville-Davidson, TN	(1)	Aa	(1)	Birmingham, AL	AA	A1	(1)
Austin, TX	AA	Aa	AA	Norfolk, VA	AA	Aa	(1)
New Orleans, LA	A-	Baa	(1)	Anchorage, AK	(1)	A1	(1)
Denver, CO	BBB+	Aa	AA	Aurora, CO	AA-	A1	(1)
Fort Worth, TX	AA	Aa	AA	Riverside, CA	(1)	(1)	(1)
Oklahoma City, OK	AA	Aa	(1)	St Petersburg, FL	(1)	A1	(1)
Portland, OR	AA+	Aaa	(1)	Rochester, NY	AA	A1	(1)
Long Beach, CA	(1)	(1)	(1)	Lexington-Fayette, KY	AAA	(1)	(1)
Kansas City, MO	AA	Aa	(1)	Jersey City, NJ	BBB	Baa	(1)
Virginia Beach, VA	AA	Aa	(1)	Baton Rouge, LA	(1)	(1)	(1)
Charlotte, NC	AAA	Aaa	(1)	Akron, OH	AA-	A	(1)
Tucson, AZ	AA-	A1	(1)	Raleigh, NC	AAA	Aaa	(1)
Albuquerque, NM	AA	Aa	(1)	Stockton CA	(1)	(1)	(1)
Atlanta, GA	AA	Aa	(1)	Richmond, VA	AA	A1	(1)
St. Louis, MO	BBB+	Baa	BBB	Mobile, AL	(1)	A	(1)

[1] Not rated.

Source: Congressional Quarterly Inc., Washington, DC, *Governing Magazine* (copyright).

No. 485. State Governments—Revenue, by State: 1994

[**In millions of dollars, except as noted.** For fiscal year ending in year shown; see text, section 9]

STATE	Total revenue [1]	GENERAL REVENUE							
		Total		Per capita [2]		Intergovernmental revenue		Taxes	Charges and miscella- neous
		Amount	Rank	Total (dol.)	Rank	From Federal Govern- ment	From local govern- ments		
United States.	845,887	693,187	(X)	2,669	(X)	191,829	13,067	373,824	114,466
Alabama	11,599	10,014	24	2,374	40	3,024	53	4,767	2,170
Alaska.	6,203	5,279	36	8,712	1	914	6	1,240	3,119
Arizona	11,749	9,707	25	2,382	38	2,467	363	5,657	1,220
Arkansas	6,870	5,983	33	2,439	35	1,911	6	3,176	889
California	115,228	89,752	1	2,856	17	27,009	2,689	49,695	10,358
Colorado	10,425	8,035	28	2,198	46	2,164	20	4,154	1,696
Connecticut	11,993	11,287	21	3,446	7	2,623	5	6,788	1,870
Delaware	3,237	2,824	44	4,000	4	487	8	1,444	884
Florida.	34,805	29,484	5	2,113	49	7,084	322	17,808	4,269
Georgia	18,265	15,530	13	2,201	45	4,565	49	8,784	2,132
Hawaii.	5,698	5,057	37	4,289	2	1,093	4	2,993	967
Idaho	3,628	2,845	43	2,511	31	699	8	1,617	521
Illinois	31,897	26,595	8	2,263	43	6,857	318	15,472	3,948
Indiana	15,813	14,486	15	2,518	30	4,113	125	7,283	2,964
Iowa	8,961	7,619	29	2,693	23	1,958	81	4,130	1,450
Kansas	7,474	6,463	32	2,530	27	1,690	25	3,675	1,073
Kentucky	11,730	10,099	23	2,639	24	2,843	17	5,693	1,546
Louisiana	13,524	11,847	19	2,745	22	4,675	28	4,383	2,761
Maine	4,098	3,534	40	2,850	18	1,094	5	1,765	671
Maryland	15,581	12,870	18	2,571	25	2,856	110	7,583	2,322
Massachusetts	22,298	20,346	10	3,368	8	5,022	421	11,017	3,886
Michigan	31,814	27,050	7	2,849	19	6,866	273	15,419	4,491
Minnesota	17,182	14,212	17	3,112	11	3,199	274	8,651	2,089
Mississippi	7,697	6,607	31	2,476	33	2,394	100	3,325	787
Missouri.	13,359	11,345	20	2,135	47	3,684	34	5,910	1,717
Montana	3,166	2,518	46	2,942	14	824	16	1,161	518
Nebraska.	4,446	4,027	39	2,481	32	1,054	24	2,144	805
Nevada	4,767	3,460	41	2,375	39	675	45	2,381	360
New Hampshire	3,081	2,649	45	2,330	41	901	126	837	785
New Jersey	29,808	24,029	9	3,040	13	4,981	265	13,494	5,289
New Mexico	6,709	5,799	34	3,506	6	1,291	41	3,021	1,446
New York.	82,202	66,587	2	3,665	5	20,486	5,239	32,817	8,045
North Carolina	21,051	17,959	11	2,540	26	4,867	431	10,519	2,142
North Dakota	2,289	2,010	47	3,150	10	630	28	885	467
Ohio	40,836	27,052	6	2,437	36	7,932	286	14,188	4,646
Oklahoma	9,184	7,467	30	2,292	42	1,919	59	4,263	1,226
Oregon	10,886	8,511	27	2,758	21	2,568	58	4,039	1,846
Pennsylvania	38,252	30,462	4	2,528	28	8,293	71	17,142	4,956
Rhode Island	4,131	3,183	42	3,192	9	986	46	1,436	714
South Carolina	11,268	9,020	26	2,462	34	2,723	107	4,502	1,688
South Dakota	2,041	1,741	50	2,415	37	653	10	659	420
Tennessee	12,725	10,940	22	2,114	48	3,679	39	5,733	1,489
Texas	45,035	38,031	3	2,069	50	11,389	348	19,465	6,829
Utah	5,907	4,809	38	2,520	29	1,314	41	2,416	1,038
Vermont	2,026	1,782	49	3,072	12	617	2	833	330
Virginia	17,295	14,817	14	2,261	44	2,926	166	8,037	3,688
Washington	19,379	15,662	12	2,931	15	3,595	78	9,701	2,288
West Virginia	6,349	5,333	35	2,927	16	1,916	11	2,554	852
Wisconsin	19,617	14,467	16	2,847	20	3,525	174	8,428	2,340
Wyoming	2,308	2,004	48	4,211	3	792	13	739	460

X Not applicable.   [1] Includes items not shown separately.   [2] Based on estimated resident population as of July 1.

Source: U.S. Bureau of the Census, Internet site, http://www.census.gov/ftp/pub/govs/www/index.html (accessed 05/28/96), and unpublished data.

No. 486. State Governments—Expenditures and Debt, by State: 1994

[In millions of dollars, except as indicated. For fiscal year ending in year shown; see text, section 9]

STATE	Total expendi-ture [1]	GENERAL EXPENDITURE							DEBT OUTSTANDING	
		Total		Selected functions						
		Amount	Per capita [2] (dol.)	Educa-tion	Public welfare	High-ways	Health and hospi-tals	Correc-tions	Total	Per capita [2] (dol.)
United States	**779,459**	**686,300**	**2,642**	**230,791**	**185,186**	**53,849**	**56,577**	**23,135**	**410,998**	**1,582**
Alabama	10,815	9,922	2,352	3,969	2,168	884	1,310	217	3,854	913
Alaska	5,752	5,256	8,674	1,278	633	565	202	142	3,585	5,916
Arizona	10,522	9,530	2,339	3,307	2,319	1,054	557	384	3,170	778
Arkansas	6,078	5,642	2,300	2,217	1,387	599	523	132	1,812	739
California	105,831	91,377	2,907	28,115	28,568	4,658	7,603	3,499	48,121	1,531
Colorado	8,903	7,652	2,093	3,358	1,626	821	392	289	3,263	892
Connecticut	12,964	11,207	3,422	2,665	2,980	793	1,176	465	13,599	4,152
Delaware	2,617	2,389	3,383	828	352	250	179	84	3,397	4,812
Florida	32,284	29,991	2,149	10,231	6,725	2,711	2,329	1,247	14,565	1,044
Georgia	16,823	15,643	2,217	6,483	4,182	978	1,128	670	5,174	733
Hawaii	5,806	5,261	4,462	1,496	718	370	522	109	5,146	4,365
Idaho	2,989	2,650	2,339	1,112	454	313	113	70	1,281	1,130
Illinois	29,449	26,058	2,217	7,968	7,324	2,474	1,835	740	20,355	1,732
Indiana	15,048	14,337	2,492	5,449	3,911	1,347	877	330	5,572	969
Iowa	8,101	7,539	2,665	3,028	1,532	913	657	163	1,990	704
Kansas	6,654	6,092	2,385	2,734	1,095	764	513	181	1,103	432
Kentucky	10,541	9,559	2,498	3,846	2,518	867	576	207	6,744	1,762
Louisiana	12,936	11,786	2,731	3,968	2,860	861	1,432	327	8,782	2,035
Maine	3,902	3,450	2,782	1,041	1,173	281	187	56	2,993	2,414
Maryland	14,203	11,800	2,357	3,759	2,751	1,028	960	689	9,130	1,824
Massachusetts	22,454	20,428	3,381	3,716	5,865	1,485	1,874	633	26,681	4,417
Michigan	29,305	25,862	2,723	8,741	6,863	1,715	3,176	1,029	11,505	1,212
Minnesota	15,278	13,952	3,055	5,231	3,620	1,054	965	234	4,351	953
Mississippi	6,796	6,177	2,314	2,285	1,594	560	462	103	2,066	774
Missouri	11,549	10,590	1,992	3,943	2,666	1,111	859	222	6,512	1,225
Montana	2,778	2,393	2,796	896	438	302	139	41	2,108	2,462
Nebraska	3,991	3,887	2,395	1,354	873	517	411	79	1,468	905
Nevada	4,203	3,404	2,336	1,240	565	399	116	136	1,685	1,156
New Hampshire	3,179	2,797	2,460	535	1,082	214	144	53	5,651	4,970
New Jersey	29,606	24,432	3,091	7,614	5,892	1,780	1,524	702	22,894	2,897
New Mexico	5,995	5,570	3,367	2,158	909	719	518	143	1,735	1,049
New York	76,872	64,802	3,567	17,271	24,009	2,694	5,847	2,060	65,078	3,582
North Carolina	19,040	17,642	2,495	7,670	3,603	1,713	1,414	720	4,538	642
North Dakota	2,083	1,886	2,956	722	365	236	102	17	757	1,186
Ohio	33,422	26,869	2,420	8,867	7,952	2,296	2,208	885	12,117	1,091
Oklahoma	8,493	7,221	2,216	3,216	1,573	685	575	212	3,873	1,189
Oregon	9,104	7,817	2,533	2,617	1,645	785	736	218	5,645	1,829
Pennsylvania	37,818	32,579	2,703	9,170	11,786	2,342	2,503	800	13,671	1,134
Rhode Island	3,745	3,135	3,144	815	795	212	229	104	5,544	5,561
South Carolina	11,209	9,563	2,610	3,319	2,344	603	1,356	307	4,972	1,357
South Dakota	1,826	1,739	2,412	517	358	266	101	42	1,680	2,331
Tennessee	11,940	11,195	2,163	3,891	3,279	1,097	932	396	2,627	508
Texas	40,967	37,324	2,031	15,505	9,474	2,921	2,904	2,243	9,378	510
Utah	5,132	4,689	2,458	2,251	821	367	419	114	2,103	1,102
Vermont	1,913	1,770	3,052	569	454	195	65	30	1,570	2,707
Virginia	15,523	14,263	2,177	5,565	2,543	1,639	1,545	684	7,912	1,208
Washington	19,577	16,345	3,059	7,018	3,620	1,335	1,177	442	8,266	1,547
West Virginia	6,190	5,250	2,882	1,929	1,544	703	204	57	2,525	1,386
Wisconsin	15,281	13,823	2,720	4,660	3,154	1,098	896	394	7,748	1,525
Wyoming	1,975	1,752	3,681	655	225	275	108	31	702	1,476

[1] Includes items not shown separately.   [2] Based on estimated resident population as of July 1.

Source: U.S. Bureau of the Census, Internet site, http://www.census.gov/ftp/pub/govs/www/index.html (accessed 05/28/96); and unpublished data.

No. 487. State Governments—Summary of Finances: 1980 to 1994

[For fiscal year ending in year shown; see text section 9. See also *Historical Statistics, Colonial Times to 1970*, series Y 710-782]

ITEM	TOTAL (mil. dol.)				PER CAPITA [1] (dollars)			
	1980	1990	1993	1994	1980	1990	1993	1994
Borrowing and revenue	**293,356**	**672,994**	**882,014**	**925,473**	**1,295**	**2,706**	**3,421**	**3,555**
Borrowing	16,394	40,532	77,519	79,585	72	163	301	306
Revenue	276,962	632,462	804,495	845,887	1,223	2,543	3,121	3,249
General revenue	233,592	517,720	653,135	693,187	1,031	2,082	2,533	2,663
Taxes	137,075	300,779	353,328	373,827	605	1,209	1,371	1,436
Sales and gross receipts	67,855	147,404	174,218	185,853	300	593	676	714
General	43,168	99,929	114,909	123,298	191	402	446	474
Motor fuels	9,722	19,379	23,568	24,520	43	78	91	94
Alcoholic beverages	2,478	3,191	3,584	3,615	11	13	14	14
Tobacco products	3,738	5,541	6,229	6,605	17	22	24	25
Other	8,750	19,365	25,928	27,815	39	78	101	107
Licenses	8,690	18,849	23,319	24,203	38	76	90	93
Motor vehicles	4,936	9,850	11,502	11,946	22	40	45	46
Corporations in general	1,388	3,096	4,317	4,505	6	12	17	17
Other	2,366	5,903	7,500	7,752	10	24	29	30
Individual income	37,089	96,076	112,555	117,729	164	386	437	452
Corporation net income	13,321	21,751	24,208	25,500	59	87	94	98
Property	2,892	5,775	7,053	8,386	13	23	27	32
Other	7,227	10,922	11,975	12,158	32	44	46	47
Charges and miscellaneous	32,190	90,612	111,177	114,466	142	364	431	440
Intergovernmental revenue	64,326	126,329	188,630	204,897	284	508	732	787
From Federal Government	61,892	118,353	177,560	191,829	273	476	689	737
Public welfare	24,680	59,397	101,765	110,522	109	239	395	425
Education	12,765	21,271	28,164	30,186	56	86	109	116
Highways	8,860	13,931	16,475	17,767	39	56	64	68
Other	15,587	23,754	31,156	33,354	69	96	121	128
From local governments	2,434	7,976	11,070	13,067	11	32	43	50
Utility revenue	1,304	3,305	3,675	3,784	6	13	14	15
Liquor store revenue	2,765	2,907	3,070	3,052	12	12	12	12
Insurance trust revenue [2]	39,301	108,530	144,614	145,864	173	436	561	560
Employee retirement	21,146	78,898	94,347	98,550	93	317	366	379
Unemployment compensation	13,468	18,370	34,442	29,707	59	74	134	114
Expenditure and debt redemption	**263,494**	**592,213**	**805,076**	**824,804**	**1,163**	**2,381**	**3,123**	**3,168**
Expenditure	257,812	572,318	742,936	779,459	1,138	2,301	2,882	2,994
General expenditure	228,223	508,284	646,088	686,300	1,007	2,044	2,506	2,636
Education	87,939	184,935	221,342	230,791	388	744	859	886
Public welfare	44,219	104,971	168,421	185,186	195	422	653	711
Highways	25,044	44,249	51,268	53,849	111	178	199	207
Health and hospitals	17,855	42,666	53,202	56,577	79	172	206	217
Corrections	4,449	17,266	20,690	23,135	20	69	80	89
Natural resources	4,346	9,909	11,212	11,878	19	40	43	46
Police protection	2,263	5,166	5,600	6,000	10	21	22	23
Other and unallocable	42,108	99,122	114,352	118,882	186	399	444	457
Housing and community development	601	2,856	2,830	(3)	3	11	11	(3)
Other and unallocable	33,243	76,263	86,594	118,882	147	307	336	457
Utility expenditure	2,401	7,131	7,240	7,214	11	29	28	28
Liquor store expenditure	2,206	2,452	2,558	2,495	10	10	10	10
Insurance trust expenditure [2]	24,981	54,452	87,050	83,450	110	219	338	321
Employee retirement	10,256	29,552	40,117	40,045	45	119	156	154
Unemployment compensation	12,006	16,423	35,197	35,197	53	66	137	135
By character and object:								
Intergovernmental expenditure	84,504	175,028	213,937	225,166	373	704	830	865
Direct expenditure	173,307	397,291	528,999	554,293	765	1,597	2,052	2,129
Current operation	108,131	258,046	345,397	370,409	477	1,038	1,340	1,423
Capital outlay	23,325	45,524	49,776	52,929	103	183	193	203
Construction	19,736	34,803	39,220	39,604	87	140	152	152
Land and existing structure	1,345	3,471	3,129	5,020	6	14	12	19
Equipment	2,243	7,250	7,427	8,305	10	29	29	32
Assistance and subsidies	9,818	16,902	21,976	23,012	43	68	85	88
Interest on debt	7,052	22,367	24,800	24,494	31	90	96	94
Insurance benefits [4]	24,981	54,452	87,050	83,450	110	219	338	321
Debt outstanding, year end	**121,958**	**318,254**	**389,721**	**410,998**	**538**	**1,280**	**1,512**	**1,579**
Long-term	119,821	315,490	385,851	406,086	529	1,269	1,497	1,560
Full-faith and credit	49,364	74,972	103,517	112,475	218	301	402	432
Nonguaranteed	70,457	240,518	282,324	293,611	311	967	1,095	1,128
Short-term	2,137	2,764	3,870	4,912	9	11	15	19
Net long-term	79,810	125,524	180,944	200,785	352	505	702	771
Full-faith and credit only	39,357	63,481	93,077	103,007	174	255	361	396
Debt redemption	5,682	19,895	62,140	45,345	25	80	241	174

X Not applicable.   [1] 1980 and 1990 based on enumerated resident population as of April 1; other years based on estimated resident population as of July 1.   [2] Includes other items not shown separately.   [3] Included in Other and unallocable.   [4] Includes repayments.

Source: U.S. Bureau of the Census, *State Government Finances*, series GF, No. 3, annual; Internet site, http://www.census.gov/ftp/pub/govs/www/index.html (accessed 06/11/96); and unpublished data.

No. 488. State Resources, Expenditures, and Balances: 1994 and 1995

[For fiscal year ending in year shown; see text; section 9. **General funds** exclude special funds earmarked for particular purposes, such as highway trust funds and federal funds; they support most on-going broad-based State services and are available for appropriation to support any governmental activity. Minus sign (-) indicates deficit]

| STATE | EXPENDITURES BY FUND SOURCE | | | | | STATE GENERAL FUND | | | | | |
| | Total, 1994 (mil. dol.) | 1995 [1] | | | | Resources [3][4] | | Expenditures [4] | | Balance [5] | |
		Total [2] (mil. dol.)	General fund (per-cent)	Federal funds (per-cent)	Other State funds (per-cent)	1994 (mil. dol.)	1995 [1] (mil. dol.)	1994 (mil. dol.)	1995 [1] (mil. dol.)	1994 (mil. dol.)	1995 [1] (mil. dol.)
United States . . .	675,846	724,417	47	27	24	344,808	367,895	331,421	352,290	12,426	13,737
Alabama	10,693	11266	37	29	34	3,987	4,206	3,860	4,151	128	54
Alaska.	4,980	4,594	54	26	19	3,148	2,572	3,148	2,572	-	-
Arizona	9,059	10,026	44	32	23	4,164	4,695	3,935	4,425	229	270
Arkansas	6,609	7,073	34	26	40	2,270	2,453	2,270	2,453	-	-
California	85,493	86,431	48	36	14	39,162	42,644	39,130	41,961	[6]32	[6]683
Colorado	7,379	8,150	49	22	29	4,052	4,402	3,647	3,914	[6]405	[6]484
Connecticut	12,232	12,441	69	15	12	7,914	8,480	7,895	8,399	20	81
Delaware	3,021	3,331	46	15	34	1,659	1,915	1,345	1,541	[6]318	[6]374
Florida.	36,751	39,043	36	22	37	13,542	14,377	13,344	14,248	198	129
Georgia	16,477	18,080	54	27	15	9,005	9,745	8,741	9,500	120	224
Hawaii.	6,256	6,167	51	15	27	3,350	3,259	3,059	3,169	291	90
Idaho	2,388	2,745	46	29	25	1,146	1,271	1,108	1,268	38	3
Illinois	23,958	26,502	47	23	27	15,759	17,232	15,529	17,201	230	331
Indiana	12,523	12,038	52	28	19	6,730	7,367	6,640	6,332	90	679
Iowa	8,117	9,122	40	26	34	3,563	3,907	3,472	3,616	91	292
Kansas	6,782	7,447	45	20	34	3,565	3,677	3,111	3,310	454	367
Kentucky	10,779	11,413	44	25	31	4,869	5,411	4,646	5,006	98	261
Louisiana	14,502	14,970	31	35	33	4,449	4,794	4,389	4,729	213	146
Maine	3,576	3,825	44	28	26	1,650	1,712	1,596	1,687	4	4
Maryland	12,750	14,202	50	23	24	6,663	7,133	6,603	7,000	60	133
Massachusetts	17,933	18,850	68	25	3	15,166	15,923	14,977	15,705	125	[6]179
Michigan	22,370	26,573	31	27	43	8,317	8,040	7,719	8,041	-	[6]6.
Minnesota	13,113	14,341	62	21	15	9,040	9,662	8,136	8,605	[6]904	[6]1,057
Mississippi	5,877	6,725	39	36	26	2,481	2,790	2,149	2,675	332	[6]115
Missouri.	10,557	11,605	45	25	30	4,935	5,734	4,660	5,261	275	473
Montana	2,301	2,338	27	30	43	955	995	904	948	50	47
Nebraska.	3,854	4,092	41	25	34	1,764	1,858	1,612	1,683	152	176
Nevada.	3,659	3,747	29	18	51	1,094	1,500	1,043	1,103	129	102
New Hampshire	2,415	2,305	37	34	27	928	975	817	971	12	-
New Jersey	22,182	23,314	65	24	10	15,857	16,138	14,617	14,947	[6]1,240	[6]952
New Mexico	5,446	6,049	44	27	27	2,557	2,788	2,625	2,714	[6]156	-
New York.	57,907	61,899	51	31	14	32,296	33,557	31,897	33,399	399	[6]158
North Carolina	17,768	18,577	54	24	22	9,891	10,860	9,004	10,034	[6]888	[6]892
North Dakota	1,651	1,769	36	35	29	639	660	611	629	28	31
Ohio	28,618	29,451	51	14	33	15,019	16,011	14,433	14,979	300	70
Oklahoma	7,419	7,741	44	27	27	3,420	3,631	3,302	3,436	118	195
Oregon	9,851	10,693	31	19	49	3,512	3,829	3,073	3,333	439	496
Pennsylvania	28,874	31,708	50	30	19	15,270	16,215	14,935	15,732	302	429
Rhode Island	3,327	3,586	44	28	26	1,534	1,646	1,531	1,641	4	5
South Carolina	9,563	10,807	38	30	31	4,184	4,641	3,776	4,051	[6]407	[6]589
South Dakota	1,612	1,671	35	39	25	626	622	626	589	-	-
Tennessee	10,515	12,166	43	33	22	4,998	5,339	4,825	5,174	173	[6]138
Texas	35,766	39,398	52	28	16	21,129	22,492	19,200	20,640	1,929	1,852
Utah	4,402	4,808	49	23	27	2,183	2,402	2,119	2,341	64	61
Vermont	1,551	1,635	41	33	21	657	675	656	690	-	[6]-15
Virginia	15,382	16,825	43	17	38	7,076	7,507	6,742	7,490	[6]334	17
Washington	15,218	16,618	52	22	22	8,309	9,043	8,011	8,484	298	559
West Virginia	5,365	8,387	24	19	54	2,189	2,380	2,100	2,210	69	127
Wisconsin	15,242	16,074	48	22	29	7,603	8,228	7,353	7,827	[6]249	[6]401
Wyoming	1,783	1,799	31	25	44	532	502	500	476	31	26

- Represents zero.   [1] Estimated.   [2] Includes bonds not shown separately.   [3] Includes funds budgeted, adjustments, and balances from previous year.   [4] May or may not include budget stabilization fund transfers, depending on State accounting practices.   [5] Resources less expenditures.   [6] Ending balance is held in a budget stabilization fund.

Source: National Association of State Budget Officers, Washington, DC, *1995 State Expenditure Report,* and National Governors' Association and NASBO, *Fiscal Survey of the States,* semi-annual (copyright).

No. 489. State Government Tax Collections, by State: 1994

[In millions of dollars. **For fiscal year ending in year shown**; see text; section 9. Includes local shares of State-imposed taxes]

STATE	Total [1]	SALES AND GROSS RECEIPTS					Motor vehicle and operators' licenses	Individual income	Corporation net income	Death and gift	Severance
		Total [1]	General sales and gross receipts	Motor fuels	Alcoholic beverages and tobacco products	Public utilities					
United States [3] ..	373,827	185,853	123,298	24,520	10,220	8,506	13,000	117,726	25,498	5,042	4,298
Alabama.........	4,767	2,560	1,279	445	180	377	172	1,368	218	30	71
Alaska	1,240	100	(X)	41	29	3	27	(X)	176	2	828
Arizona.........	5,657	3,269	2,494	423	95	112	235	1,409	303	41	(X)
Arkansas	3,176	1,786	1,212	321	117	(X)	101	958	184	11	13
California	49,695	21,466	16,872	2,526	902	40	1,528	17,548	4,633	531	46
Colorado.........	4,154	1,776	1,125	406	85	6	117	1,925	146	34	15
Connecticut.......	6,788	3,262	2,184	406	167	147	210	2,237	702	223	(X)
Delaware	1,444	211	(X)	76	33	25	21	547	155	23	(X)
Florida	17,808	13,552	10,042	1,252	974	459	858	(X)	950	347	54
Georgia	8,784	4,151	3,267	491	195	(X)	242	3,581	521	88	(X)
Hawaii	2,993	1,852	1,332	76	72	92	58	962	68	28	(X)
Idaho...........	1,620	776	544	152	24	2	64	563	88	7	3
Illinois	15,472	7,870	4,661	1,096	364	799	753	5,050	1,229	155	(X)
Indiana..........	7,283	3,354	2,506	599	112	(X)	138	3,016	606	98	1
Iowa	4,130	1,965	1,389	354	109	(X)	256	1,509	174	88	(X)
Kansas..........	3,675	1,810	1,297	284	112	1	121	1,194	255	88	106
Kentucky	5,693	2,721	1,560	380	74	(X)	166	1,729	269	76	199
Louisiana	4,383	2,281	1,379	466	132	20	106	978	219	53	370
Maine...........	1,765	891	617	150	81	1	64	614	92	10	(X)
Maryland	7,583	3,274	1,815	588	164	138	205	3,225	320	82	(X)
Massachusetts.....	11,017	3,539	2,303	563	298	(X)	297	5,690	1,063	278	(X)
Michigan.........	15,419	6,081	4,538	795	518	(X)	609	5,553	2,175	57	33
Minnesota........	8,651	3,829	2,516	487	226	1	472	3,449	552	44	3
Mississippi	3,325	2,242	1,587	341	91	(X)	110	638	168	10	34
Missouri	5,910	2,986	2,196	472	122	(X)	233	2,142	252	54	-
Montana.........	1,161	242	(X)	158	29	13	46	346	69	11	91
Nebraska	2,144	1,149	747	256	62	2	70	716	113	12	2
Nevada	2,381	1,969	1,185	172	61	5	93	(X)	(X)	24	44
New Hampshire....	837	485	(X)	98	54	50	57	36	144	33	-
New Jersey.......	13,494	6,942	3,778	446	332	1,612	341	4,475	1,085	305	(X)
New Mexico	3,021	1,803	1,430	196	52	9	111	577	123	12	331
New York	32,817	11,596	6,365	490	923	1,750	705	16,034	3,120	799	(X)
North Carolina.....	10,519	4,598	2,589	909	196	279	360	4,288	737	120	2
North Dakota......	885	497	256	83	29	26	37	137	71	4	110
Ohio	14,188	7,151	4,480	1,242	367	663	557	5,110	653	86	9
Oklahoma........	4,263	1,774	1,091	378	131	15	452	1,315	162	59	372
Oregon..........	4,039	543	(X)	355	115	6	280	2,584	264	45	75
Pennsylvania......	17,142	8,119	5,134	751	454	650	512	4,736	1,486	594	(X)
Rhode Island......	1,436	722	413	120	50	69	55	528	79	9	(X)
South Carolina.....	4,502	2,322	1,673	304	141	39	102	1,531	219	27	(X)
South Dakota	659	512	339	87	24	1	28	(X)	37	24	7
Tennessee	5,733	4,502	3,081	684	146	6	213	99	422	44	1
Texas...........	19,465	15,868	9,926	2,171	974	263	814	(X)	(X)	152	919
Utah	2,416	1,257	984	187	45	(X)	58	925	125	8	19
Vermont	833	400	176	60	28	16	45	286	35	9	(X)
Virginia..........	8,037	3,253	1,781	671	122	114	290	3,812	307	83	2
Washington.......	9,701	7,238	5,798	632	344	202	243	(X)	(X)	35	84
West Virginia......	2,554	1,386	727	205	41	224	90	670	185	9	153
Wisconsin........	8,428	3,663	2,428	635	220	268	240	3,639	541	53	2
Wyoming	739	260	199	40	7	(X)	40	(X)	(X)	26	299

- Represents or rounds to zero. X Not applicable. [1] Includes amounts not shown separately.

No. 490. Estimated State and Local Taxes Paid by a Family of Four in Selected Cities: 1994

[Data based on average family of four (two wage earners and two school age children) owning their own home and living in a city where taxes apply. Comprises State and local sales, income, auto, and real estate taxes. For definition of median, see Guide to Tabular Presentation]

CITY	TOTAL TAXES PAID, BY GROSS FAMILY INCOME LEVEL (dollars)				TOTAL TAXES PAID AS PERCENT OF INCOME			
	$25,000	$50,000	$75,000	$100,000	$25,000	$50,000	$75,000	$100,000
Albuquerque, NM	1,671	3,789	6,548	9,196	6.7	7.6	8.7	9.2
Atlanta, GA	2,254	4,865	8,237	10,852	9.0	9.7	11.0	10.9
Baltimore, MD	2,724	5,626	8,874	11,724	10.9	11.3	11.8	11.7
Boston, MA	2,509	5,333	9,185	11,758	10.0	10.7	12.2	11.8
Charlotte, NC	2,061	4,576	7,611	10,064	8.2	9.2	10.1	10.1
Chicago, IL	2,690	5,333	8,355	10,852	10.8	10.7	11.1	10.9
Columbus, OH	2,163	4,641	7,624	10,516	8.7	9.3	10.2	10.5
Denver, CO	1,990	4,231	6,876	8,908	8.0	8.5	9.2	8.9
Detroit, MI	2,601	5,400	8,489	11,219	10.4	10.8	11.3	11.2
Honolulu, HI	1,977	4,542	7,696	10,456	7.9	9.1	10.3	10.5
Houston, TX	1,647	2,965	4,678	5,909	6.6	5.9	6.2	5.9
Indianapolis, IN	2,161	3,954	6,739	8,649	8.6	7.9	9.0	8.6
Jacksonville, FL	1,034	2,286	3,879	5,090	4.1	4.6	5.2	5.1
Kansas City, MO	1,915	4,035	6,680	8,598	7.7	8.1	9.0	8.6
Las Vegas, NV	1,412	2,355	3,862	4,698	5.6	4.7	5.1	4.7
Los Angeles, CA	1,666	4,001	8,002	11,216	6.7	8.0	10.7	11.2
Memphis, TN	1,894	3,197	5,022	6,348	7.6	6.4	6.7	6.3
Milwaukee, WI	2,719	6,034	9,689	12,815	10.9	12.1	12.9	12.8
Minneapolis, MN	1,811	4,462	7,830	10,468	7.2	8.9	10.4	10.5
New Orleans, LA	1,530	3,528	6,145	8,466	6.1	7.1	8.2	8.5
New York City, NY	2,641	6,726	11,380	15,608	10.6	13.5	15.2	15.6
Oklahoma City, OK	2,120	4,162	7,142	9,482	8.5	8.3	9.5	9.5
Omaha, NE	2,366	4,818	8,399	11,418	9.5	9.6	11.2	11.4
Philadelphia, PA	3,097	5,927	8,922	11,584	12.4	11.9	11.9	11.6
Phoenix, AZ	1,957	4,033	6,891	9,014	7.8	8.1	9.2	9.0
Portland, ME	2,947	6,369	11,058	14,609	11.8	12.7	14.7	14.6
Seattle, WA	1,800	3,060	5,056	6,179	7.2	6.1	6.7	6.2
Virginia Beach, VA	2,153	4,380	7,595	9,723	8.6	8.8	10.1	9.7
Washington, DC	2,071	4,531	7,808	10,777	8.6	9.1	10.4	10.8
Wichita, KS	1,922	3,814	6,829	9,162	7.7	7.6	9.1	9.2
Average	[1]2,111	4,417	7,437	9,823	8.4	8.8	9.9	9.8
Median	[1]1,990	4,380	7,420	9,723	8.0	8.8	9.9	9.7

[1] Based on the largest city in each state and District of Columbia. For complete list of cities, see table 491

Source: Government of the District of Columbia, Department of Finance and Revenue, *Tax Rates and Tax Burdens in the District of Columbia: A Nationwide Comparison,* annual.

No. 491. Residential Property Tax Rates in Selected Cities: 1994

[Effective tax rate is amount each jurisdiction considers based upon assessment level used. Assessment level is ratio of assessed value to assumed market value. Nominal rate is announced rates it levied at taxable value of house]

CITY	EFFECTIVE TAX RATE PER $100		Assessment level (percent)	Nominal rate per $100	CITY	EFFECTIVE TAX RATE PER $100		Assessment level (percent)	Nominal rate per $100
	Rank	Rate				Rank	Rate		
Milwaukee, WI	1	3.60	98.2	3.67	Phoenix, AZ	28	1.56	10.0	15.61
Bridgeport, CT	2	3.51	51.7	6.78	Chicago, IL	29	1.52	16.0	9.50
Newark, NJ	3	3.46	16.2	21.34	Boston, MA	30	1.40	100.0	1.40
Manchester, NH	4	3.20	112.0	2.86	Columbia, SC	31	1.40	4.0	34.90
Des Moines, IA	5	3.00	68.0	4.41	Louisville, KY	32	1.38	100.0	1.38
Providence, RI	6	2.82	100.0	2.82	Salt Lake City, UT	33	1.36	70.6	1.93
Detroit, MI	7	2.82	50.0	5.63	Minneapolis, MN	34	1.33	93.9	1.42
Houston, TX	8	2.73	100.0	2.73	Wichita, KS	35	1.30	11.5	11.34
Philadelphia, PA	9	2.64	32.0	8.26	Albuquerque, NM	36	1.27	33.3	3.82
Sioux Falls, SD	10	2.55	95.1	2.68	Little Rock, AR	37	1.27	18.9	6.72
Omaha, NE	11	2.53	90.0	2.81	Kansas City, MO	38	1.20	19.0	6.30
Portland, OR	12	2.47	100.0	2.47	Charlotte, NC	39	1.18	96.0	1.23
Baltimore, MD	13	2.42	40.0	6.06	Oklahoma City, OK	40	1.16	11.0	10.51
Jacksonville, FL	14	2.09	86.8	2.40	Virginia Beach, VA	41	1.14	100.0	1.14
Atlanta, GA	15	2.07	40.0	5.17	Las Vegas, NV	42	1.06	35.0	3.02
Fargo, ND	16	2.01	4.5	44.69	Denver, CO	43	1.04	12.9	8.07
Indianapolis, IN	17	1.97	15.0	13.15	Seattle, WA	44	0.96	91.1	1.05
Burlington, VT	18	1.90	100.0	1.90	Washington, DC	45	0.94	97.6	0.96
Boise City, ID	19	1.88	94.8	1.98	Charleston, WV	46	0.92	60.0	1.54
Portland, ME	20	1.80	100.0	1.80	New York City, NY	47	0.87	8.0	10.93
Columbus, OH	21	1.78	35.0	5.09	Cheyenne, WY	48	0.74	9.5	7.80
Anchorage, AK	22	1.75	100.0	1.75	Birmingham, AL	49	0.70	10.0	6.95
Wilmington, DE	23	1.68	83.0	2.02	Los Angeles, CA	50	0.67	61.2	1.09
New Orleans, LA	24	1.61	10.0	16.13	Honolulu, HI	51	O.33	93.4	0.35
Billings, MT	25	1.61	3.9	41.75					
Jackson, MS	26	1.60	10.0	15.95	Unweighted average	(X)	1.76	55.4	7.48
Memphis, TN	27	1.59	25.0	6.34	Median	(X)	1.60	(X)	(X)

X Not applicable.

Source: Government of the District of Columbia, Department of Finance and Revenue, *Tax Rates and Tax Burdens in the District of Columbia: A Nationwide Comparison,* annual.

No. 492. Gross Revenue From Parimutuel and Amusement Taxes and Lotteries, by State: 1994

[For fiscal years; see text, section 9]

STATE	Gross revenue (mil. dol.)	Parimutuel taxes (mil. dol.)	Amusement taxes [1] (mil. dol.)	LOTTERY REVENUE			
				Total [2] (mil. dol.)	Apportionment of funds (percent)		
					Prizes	Administration	Proceeds available from ticket sales
United States.	28,384	544	1,252	26,588	15,296	1,543	9,749
Alabama.	5	5	(Z)	(X)	(X)	(X)	(X)
Alaska	2	-	2	(X)	(X)	(X)	(X)
Arizona.	243	9	1	233	124	26	84
Arkansas	16	15	1	(X)	(X)	(X)	(X)
California	1,935	119	-	1,816	966	163	687
Colorado.	279	8	1	269	168	27	74
Connecticut.	615	41	51	524	309	23	191
Delaware	96	(Z)	-	96	53	7	35
Florida	2,137	93	(Z)	2,044	1,071	119	854
Georgia	1,010	-	-	1,010	550	89	370
Hawaii	(X)	(X)	(X)	(X)	(X)	(X)	(X)
Idaho	74	2	-	73	41	14	17
Illinois	1,627	47	207	1,374	795	53	526
Indiana.	527	-	-	527	312	29	186
Iowa	196	2	9	186	117	22	47
Kansas.	154	8	1	144	79	17	48
Kentucky	465	16	(Z)	449	291	35	123
Louisiana	332	6	2	325	175	24	126
Maine.	147	2	-	145	80	14	51
Maryland	940	3	5	932	507	39	386
Massachusetts.	2,328	13	8	2,306	1,659	69	578
Michigan.	1,267	17	-	1,250	684	52	514
Minnesota.	369	(Z)	58	312	192	59	60
Mississippi	127	-	127	(X)	(X)	(X)	(X)
Missouri	330	-	-	330	189	28	113
Montana	35	(Z)	-	35	18	8	9
Nebraska	65	1	11	53	27	12	14
Nevada	427	-	427	(X)	(X)	(X)	(X)
New Hampshire	113	6	2	104	61	6	38
New Jersey.	1,645	5	287	1,354	709	42	602
New Mexico	2	1	1	(X)	(X)	(X)	(X)
New York	2,244	67	1	2,176	1,107	64	1,005
North Carolina	(X)	(X)	(X)	(X)	(X)	(X)	(X)
North Dakota	11	-	11	(X)	(X)	(X)	(X)
Ohio	1,817	14	-	1,803	1,115	95	593
Oklahoma	16	4	12	(X)	(X)	(X)	(X)
Oregon.	706	3	(Z)	703	441	154	109
Pennsylvania.	1,478	16	(Z)	1,462	783	51	628
Rhode Island.	175	7	-	168	110	3	55
South Carolina.	18	-	18	(X)	(X)	(X)	(X)
South Dakota	92	(Z)	(Z)	92	18	7	68
Tennessee	(X)	(X)	(X)	(X)	(X)	(X)	(X)
Texas.	2,479	-	7	2,472	1,532	12	927
Utah	(X)	(X)	(X)	(X)	(X)	(X)	(X)
Vermont	50	(Z)	-	50	29	4	17
Virginia.	855	-	(Z)	855	466	85	305
Washington	319	4	(Z)	315	168	44	103
West Virginia	134	3	-	131	76	14	41
Wisconsin	479	8	1	470	274	31	165
Wyoming	(X)	(X)	(X)	(X)	(X)	(X)	(X)

- Represents or rounds to zero.   X Not applicable.   Z Less than $500,000.   [1] Represents nonlicense taxes.   [2] Excludes commissions.

Source: U.S. Bureau of the Census, Internet site, http://www.census.gov/ftp/pub/govs/www/index.html (accessed 06/27/96).

No. 493. Lottery Sales—Type of Game and Use of Proceeds: 1980 to 1995

[In millions of dollars. For fiscal years]

GAME	1980	1985	1990	1992	1994	1995	USE OF PROFITS	Cumulative [1]
Total ticket sales	2,393	9,035	20,017	22,069	28,514	31,931	Total	92,922
Passive [2]	206	88	(NA)	(NA)	(NA)	(NA)	Education.	52,061
Instant [3]	527	1,296	5,204	6,104	9,681	11,511	General fund.	21,133
Three-digit [4]	1,554	3,376	4,572	4,767	5,294	5,737	Cities.	9,013
Four-digit [4]	55	693	1,302	1,637	1,872	1,941	Senior citizen programs . .	8,708
Lotto [5]	52	3,583	8,563	8,506	10,024	10,594	Taxes	(NA)
Other [6]	(NA)	(NA)	409	1,055	1,642	2,148	Economic development. . .	1,385
							Infrastructure	(NA)
State proceeds (net income) [7] . .	978	3,735	7,703	8,118	9,977	11,100	Environment	485
							Other.	137

NA Not available.   [1] Cumulative profits tracks lottery revenue to government from March 12, 1964 - June 30, 1995   [2] Also known as draw game or ticket. Player must match his ticket to winning numbers drawn by lottery. Players cannot choose their numbers.   [3] Player scratches a latex section on ticket which reveals instantly whether ticket is a winner.   [4] Players choose and bet on three or four digits, depending on game, with various payoffs for different straight order or mixed combination bets.   [5] Players typically select six digits out of a large field of numbers. Varying prizes are offered for matching three through six numbers drawn by lottery.   [6] Includes breakopen tickets, spiel, keno, video lottery, etc.   [7] Sales minus prizes and expenses equal net government income.

Source: TLF Publications, Inc., Boyds, MD, 1996 World Lottery Almanac annual; LaFleur's Fiscal 1995 Lottery Special Report; and LaFleur's Lottery World Government Profits Report (copyright).

No. 494. State Government Intergovernmental Expenditures, by State: 1990 and 1994

[For fiscal year ending in year shown; see text, section 9]

STATE	TOTAL (mil. dol.)		PER CAPITA [1] (dol.)		RANK		PERCENT OF GENERAL EXPENDITURE	
	1990	1994	1990	1994	1990	1994	1990	1994
United States..................	175,028	225,166	704	865	(X)	(X)	34	33
Alabama......................	2,015	2,349	499	557	23	45	27	24
Alaska.......................	909	1,247	1,653	2,057	38	1	21	24
Arizona......................	2,433	3,578	664	878	19	12	32	38
Arkansas.....................	1,177	1,547	500	631	34	35	30	27
California....................	35,174	44,102	1,182	1,415	1	3	50	49
Colorado	1,816	2,554	551	698	28	26	32	33
Connecticut	1,858	2,257	565	689	27	27	21	20
Delaware.....................	359	420	538	594	46	41	18	18
Florida.......................	7,205	10,237	557	734	5	22	35	34
Georgia......................	3,667	4,474	566	634	15	34	32	29
Hawaii.......................	114	142	102	121	50	50	3	3
Idaho	585	859	581	758	41	20	32	32
Illinois......................	5,856	7,412	512	631	8	36	29	28
Indiana......................	3,385	4,595	611	799	17	16	34	32
Iowa........................	1,946	2,462	701	870	24	14	33	33
Kansas......................	1,312	2,114	529	828	33	15	30	35
Kentucky	1,913	2,581	519	675	25	30	27	27
Louisiana....................	2,331	2,844	552	659	21	33	27	24
Maine	664	739	540	596	40	40	24	21
Maryland.....................	2,288	2,805	477	560	20	44	25	24
Massachusetts	4,649	4,451	773	737	11	21	27	22
Michigan	6,314	8,864	679	933	7	10	32	34
Minnesota....................	4,277	5,379	978	1,178	13	5	41	39
Mississippi...................	1,691	2,071	657	776	29	18	38	34
Missouri.....................	2,561	3,250	501	616	18	37	33	31
Montana	420	676	525	789	44	17	25	28
Nebraska.....................	772	1,087	489	670	39	31	27	28
Nevada......................	949	1,277	790	877	37	13	40	38
New Hampshire	220	369	199	324	49	49	13	13
New Jersey	6,006	8,270	776	1,046	9	8	32	34
New Mexico	1,463	1,822	966	1,101	32	6	38	33
New York.....................	19,444	24,641	1,081	1,356	2	4	39	38
North Carolina	5,085	6,590	767	932	10	11	40	37
North Dakota	370	422	579	662	45	32	23	22
Ohio........................	7,386	8,532	681	768	3	19	36	32
Oklahoma	1,637	2,388	520	733	30	23	29	33
Oregon	1,479	2,261	520	733	31	24	27	29
Pennsylvania	6,921	8,683	583	721	6	25	33	27
Rhode Island	488	444	487	445	43	47	18	14
South Carolina	1,885	2,204	541	601	26	39	28	23
South Dakota	242	300	348	416	48	48	19	17
Tennessee....................	2,211	2,999	453	579	22	43	28	27
Texas	7,343	11,091	432	604	4	38	31	30
Utah........................	981	1,303	569	683	35	29	28	28
Vermont	265	302	472	520	47	46	18	17
Virginia	3,472	3,862	561	589	16	42	29	27
Washington	3,632	5,049	776	945	14	9	33	31
West Virginia	960	1,249	535	686	36	28	27	24
Wisconsin	4,316	5,328	882	1,048	12	7	41	39
Wyoming.....................	584	684	1,287	1,437	42	2	39	39

X Not applicable.   [1] 1990 based on enumerated resident population as of April 1, 1990. 1994 based on enumerated population as of July 1.

Source: U.S. Bureau of the Census, *State Government Finances,* series GF, No. 3 annual; Internet site, http://www.census.gov/ftp/pub/govs/www/index.html (accessed 05/31/96); and unpublished data.

No. 495. County Governments—Summary of Finances, by Population-Size Group: 1980 to 1992

[For fiscal year ending in year shown; see text, section 9. Represents all counties and their dependent agencies (including dependent school systems where applicable). Size classifications based on 1986 populations; counties distributed according to their 1990 enumerated population]

ITEM	ALL COUNTIES [1] (mil. dol.)			PER CAPITA (dollars), 1992								
				All counties		Counties with 1990 population (1,000) of—						
	1980	1990	1992	Total (3,043) [2]	Per-cent distri-bution	Less than 100 [1] (2,631)	100 to 149.9 (133)	150 to 199.9 (66)	200 to 299.9 (74)	300 to 499.9 (62)	500 to 999.9 (52)	1,000 or more (24)
General revenue	54,573	135,775	146,495	610	100	555	567	590	582	592	776	782
Intergovernmental revenue[3]	24,746	53,953	54,398	222	36	196	211	204	181	202	247	359
From State governments	18,969	49,225	48,936	198	32	177	192	184	159	184	217	326
From Federal government	4,948	2,780	3,070	14	2	12	13	13	14	10	16	17
Tax revenue [3]	18,813	48,750	54,926	232	38	195	196	247	225	241	348	256
Property	14,300	35,723	40,808	172	28	141	144	172	167	178	243	211
Charges and miscellaneous	11,014	33,072	37,172	157	26	164	159	140	175	148	181	167
General expenditure	54,291	127,626	148,268	619	100	557	579	607	590	605	786	790
Capital outlay	6,505	13,467	15,253	68	11	54	64	68	58	68	87	77
Current expenditure	47,786	114,159	133,015	551	89	503	515	540	532	537	699	713
Education	8,412	18,395	20,180	88	14	113	108	123	85	85	125	22
Public welfare	8,591	18,114	22,767	90	14	53	78	77	78	104	106	183
Hospitals	5,975	13,018	15,434	63	10	70	50	23	60	35	68	103
Health	2,806	8,791	10,289	42	7	34	45	43	46	43	50	60
Highways	5,227	9,415	10,198	46	7	69	43	43	38	39	34	29
Police protection	2,661	6,693	8,012	33	5	29	31	38	32	30	36	50
Correction	1,759	6,590	8,287	33	5	19	26	34	34	36	48	59
Natural resources	687	1,314	1,532	6	1	6	4	4	3	5	5	14
Parks and recreation	1,094	2,487	2,779	13	2	5	8	11	11	14	24	15
Financial administration	1,521	3,363	3,766	16	3	17	14	19	18	16	17	16
General control [4]	3,374	9,149	10,540	42	7	35	40	40	41	47	47	69
General public buildings	1,072	2,182	2,404	10	2	10	10	11	12	11	12	10
Interest on general debt	1,542	7,976	8,610	37	6	29	32	33	32	31	53	49
Other and unallocable	9,570	20,139	23,471	102	16	70	91	109	100	110	161	110
Debt outstanding, year end	32,993	118,608	129,760	541	100	384	487	513	502	546	808	747
Long-term	31,543	115,392	123,800	520	96	378	480	507	489	529	786	669
Short-term	1,450	3,216	5,961	21	4	6	7	6	14	17	22	78

[1] Data for counties under 100,000 population are estimates subject to sampling variation; see Appendix III and source.   [2] Figures in parentheses represent number of counties in each size group.   [3] Includes other revenues not shown separately.   [4] Includes judicial and legal as well as other administrative expenditures.

Source: U.S. Bureau of the Census, *County Government Finances,* series GF, No. 8, annual; Internet site,http://www.census.gov/ftp/pub/govs/www/index.html (accessed 06/03/96), and unpublished data.

No. 496. Gross Assessed Value of Property and Government Revenue From Property Taxes: 1975 to 1993

[In billions of dollars, except percent. Data are estimates subject to sampling variation; see Appendix III and source]

ITEM	1975	1979	1981	1984	1986	1989	1990	1991	1992	1993
Gross assessed value of property [1]	1,096	1,679	2,958	4,053	4,818	6,013	(NA)	6,924	(NA)	(NA)
State assessed	75	114	159	200	243	257	(NA)	286	(NA)	(NA)
Locally assessed	1,022	1,565	2,799	3,853	4,575	5,756	(NA)	6,638	(NA)	(NA)
Real property	882	1,359	2,515	3,447	4,105	5,220	(NA)	6,044	(NA)	(NA)
Percent of locally assessed	86	87	90	89	90	91	(NA)	91	(NA)	(NA)
Net assessed value of locally taxable property [2]	1,063	1,607	2,838	3,869	4,620	5,791	(NA)	6,682	(NA)	(NA)
Percent of gross assessed	97	96	96	96	96	96	(NA)	97	(NA)	(NA)
REVENUE FROM PROPERTY TAXES										
State and local governments	52	65	75	97	112	143	156	168	178	189
Percent of general revenue	23	19	18	18	17	18	18	19	18	18
Percent of tax revenue	36	32	31	30	30	30	31	32	32	32
State governments	2	3	3	4	4	5	6	6	7	8
Percent of general revenue	1	1	1	1	1	1	1	1	1	1
Percent of tax revenue	2	2	2	2	2	2	2	2	2	2
Local governments	50	63	72	93	107	137	150	162	172	181
Annual percent change from prior year	[3]7	6	7	8	8	8	9	9	6	5
Percent of general revenue	32	27	25	25	25	29	29	30	30	30
Percent of tax revenue	82	78	76	75	74	74	75	75	76	76

NA Not available.   [1] Gross assessed value amounts may include prior year components for those States unable to report data for indicated year at time of publication. See sources for definitions of terms and limitations of data.   [2] Value subject to local general property taxation, including State-assessed property, after deduction of partial exemptions.   [3] Change from 1971.

Source: U.S. Bureau of the Census, *1982* and *1987 Census of Governments,* vol. 2; *Property Values Subject to Local General Property Taxation in the United States: 1975* and *1979,* and *Government Finances,* series GF, No. 5, annual and unpublished data.

No. 497. City Governments—Summary of Finances: 1980 to 1993

[For fiscal year ending in year shown; see text, section 9. Represents all municipalities and their dependent agencies (including dependent school systems where applicable); excludes other local governments overlying city areas. Includes sample-based estimates for cities of less than 50,000; thus subject to sampling variation. See Appendix III and source]

ITEM	TOTAL (mil. dol.)				PER CAPITA [1] (dol.)			
	1980	1990	1992	1993	1980	1990	1992	1993
Revenue	94,862	202,393	220,048	228,067	672	1,316	1,430	1,483
General revenue	76,056	158,301	171,618	178,602	539	1,029	1,116	1,161
Intergovernmental revenue	28,270	45,306	48,152	50,592	200	295	313	329
From State governments only	15,939	34,243	36,222	37,666	113	223	235	245
Taxes	31,256	68,788	75,486	78,895	222	447	491	513
Property	16,859	35,024	39,706	41,525	119	228	258	270
Percent of total taxes	54	51	53	53	(X)	(X)	(X)	(X)
Sales and gross receipts	8,208	19,190	20,190	21,053	58	125	131	137
General	5,096	11,645	11,976	12,373	36	76	78	80
Selective	3,112	7,545	8,214	8,680	22	49	53	56
Income, licenses, and other	6,189	14,574	15,590	16,316	44	95	101	106
Charges and miscellaneous	16,530	44,207	47,980	49,115	117	287	312	319
Current charges only	9,875	25,265	29,449	31,423	70	164	191	204
Utility and liquor store revenue	15,719	33,266	35,460	36,446	111	216	231	237
Water system	4,989	11,578	12,724	13,266	35	75	83	86
Electric power system	8,007	17,312	18,232	18,464	57	113	119	120
Gas supply system	1,444	2,335	2,321	2,422	10	15	15	16
Transit system	1,032	1,766	1,892	2,019	7	11	13	13
Liquor stores	247	275	292	276	2	2	2	2
Insurance trust revenue	3,088	10,827	12,969	13,018	22	70	84	85
Expenditure	93,699	198,822	219,293	227,994	664	1,293	1,426	1,482
General expenditure	72,433	153,717	170,680	178,516	513	999	1,110	1,160
Police protection	8,200	18,183	20,420	21,511	58	118	133	140
Fire protection	4,535	9,487	10,412	10,777	32	62	68	70
Highways	5,977	12,106	12,961	12,814	42	79	84	83
Sewerage and sanitation	7,907	16,476	18,260	19,206	56	107	119	125
Public welfare	3,801	7,890	9,528	10,030	27	51	62	65
Education	9,284	17,368	19,382	20,395	66	113	126	133
Libraries	883	1,939	2,106	2,155	6	13	14	14
Health and hospitals	4,457	9,141	10,338	11,020	32	59	67	72
Parks and recreation	3,433	7,584	8,232	8,461	24	49	54	55
Housing and community development .	3,459	7,661	8,576	9,414	25	50	56	61
Airports	1,100	2,878	3,552	4,298	8	19	23	28
Financial administration	1,843	3,895	4,172	4,317	13	25	27	28
General control [2]	2,015	5,274	6,055	6,318	14	34	39	41
General public buildings	1,090	1,767	1,884	1,929	8	11	12	13
Interest on general debt	3,054	11,317	12,429	12,378	22	74	81	80
Other and unallocable	11,395	20,751	22,373	23,493	81	135	145	153
Utility and liquor store expenditure	18,274	38,436	40,740	40,637	130	250	265	265
Water system	5,933	13,579	14,661	14,849	42	88	95	97
Electric power system	8,596	17,490	18,023	17,996	61	114	117	117
Gas supply system	1,334	2,263	2,177	2,249	9	15	14	15
Transit system	2,189	4,855	5,613	5,288	16	32	36	34
Liquor stores	222	250	266	256	2	2	2	2
Insurance trust expenditure	2,993	6,669	7,873	8,841	21	43	51	57
By character and object:								
Direct expenditure	91,692	193,933	213,379	222,090	650	1,261	1,387	1,444
Current operation	66,687	138,818	153,501	160,771	473	902	998	1,045
Capital outlay	16,285	31,779	33,274	32,828	115	207	216	213
Construction	13,341	22,842	23,929	23,199	95	148	156	151
Land and existing structures [3] . . .	2,944	8,937	9,345	9,628	21	58	61	63
Assistance payments	1,546	2,212	2,788	3,011	11	14	18	20
Interest on debt	4,182	14,455	15,944	16,019	30	94	104	104
Insurance benefits, repayments	2,992	6,669	7,873	8,841	21	43	52	57
Intergovernmental expenditure	2,007	4,890	5,913	5,903	14	32	34	38
Expenditure for salaries and wages [4] . . .	34,709	66,973	74,192	75,694	246	435	482	492
Debt outstanding, year end	86,019	212,919	241,551	247,957	610	1,384	1,570	1,612
Long-term	82,346	207,487	236,144	243,013	584	1,349	1,535	1,580
Full faith and credit	39,570	68,510	81,748	87,812	280	445	531	571
Nonguaranteed	42,776	138,977	154,396	155,201	303	903	1,004	1,009
Short-term	3,673	5,432	5,407	4,944	26	35	34	32
Net long-term debt outstanding	72,528	139,109	167,329	177,790	514	904	1,088	1,156
Long-term debt issued	12,582	27,991	35,795	46,454	89	182	233	302
Long-term debt retired	5,541	17,980	22,227	35,664	39	117	144	232

X Not applicable.   [1] 1980 data based on April 1 enumerated urban population; all other years based on April 1, 1990 enumerated urban population.   [2] Includes judicial and legal as well as other governmental administration.   [3] Includes equipment.   [4] Included in items shown above.

Source: U.S. Bureau of the Census, *City Government Finances*, series; and unpublished data.

No. 498. City Governments—Total and Per Capita Finances for Largest Cities: 1992 and 1993

[For fiscal year ending in year shown; see text, section 9. Cities ranked by size of population enumerated as of April 1, 1990, except Honolulu and Baton Rouge ranked by county population. Data reflect inclusion of fiscal activity of dependent school systems where applicable. Intercity comparisons should be made with caution due to variations in responsibilities among urban areas; for details see text, section 9, and source]

CITIES RANKED BY 1990 POPULATION	GENERAL REVENUE		INTERGOV'T REVENUE		TAXES		GENERAL EXPENDITURE		DEBT OUTSTANDING	
	Total (mil. dol.)	Per capita [1] (dol.)	Total (mil. dol.)	Per capita [1] (dol.)	Total (mil. dol.)	Per capita [1] (dol.)	Total (mil. dol.)	Per capita [1] (dol.)	Total (mil. dol.)	Per capita [1] (dol.) 1993
1993 [2]										
New York City, NY [2]	37,870	5,172	14,856	2,029	17,703	2,418	39,431	5,385	37,814	5,164
Los Angeles, CA	3,890	1,116	541	155	1,896	544	3,534	1,014	8,035	2,305
Chicago, IL	3,342	1,200	796	286	1,677	602	3,552	1,276	6,371	2,289
Houston, TX [2]	1,413	866	79	48	762	467	1,530	939	3,751	2,300
Philadelphia, PA [2]	2,966	1,870	918	579	1,551	978	2,829	1,784	3,781	2,385
San Diego, CA	1,186	1,068	251	226	394	354	1,057	952	1,560	1,405
Detroit, MI	1,563	1,521	708	689	553	538	1,473	1,433	1,887	1,835
Dallas, TX	1,099	1,091	61	61	490	486	1,338	1,329	3,729	3,703
Phoenix, AZ	1,025	1,041	334	339	340	345	948	963	2,486	2,525
San Antonio, TX	575	602	141	148	243	255	739	775	4,328	4,537
Honolulu, HI [2]	968	1,158	138	165	514	615	995	1,190	1,356	1,621
San Jose, CA	687	878	97	125	345	441	717	917	1,211	1,548
Baltimore, MD [2]	1,745	2,371	836	1,135	684	929	1,491	2,026	1,258	1,709
Indianapolis, IN [2]	1,075	1,470	343	469	481	658	1,110	1,518	1,346	1,840
San Francisco, CA [2]	2,798	3,864	1,000	1,382	960	1,326	2,637	3,642	3,385	4,676
Jacksonville, FL [2]	844	1,354	199	313	302	476	797	1,254	4,646	7,314
Columbus, OH	601	949	102	161	303	478	640	1,011	1,316	2,079
Milwaukee, WI	614	978	324	516	166	264	615	979	587	934
Memphis, TN	910	1,491	600	983	175	287	909	1,490	833	1,365
Washington, DC [2]	4,683	7,716	1,662	2,739	2,539	4,184	4,791	7,894	4,083	6,727
Boston, MA [2]	1,679	2,925	708	1,233	695	1,210	1,605	2,794	1,087	1,894
Seattle, WA	748	1,449	104	202	383	743	747	1,448	1,151	2,230
El Paso, TX	281	545	30	58	142	275	269	523	472	915
Cleveland, OH	547	1,081	137	270	281	556	556	1,099	1,011	2,000
1992										
New Orleans, LA [2]	658	1,323	123	247	301	605	684	1,376	1,126	1,265
Nashville-Davidson, TN [2]	989	2,026	258	529	479	980	857	1,754	2,216	4,537
Denver, CO [2]	1,046	2,236	249	532	391	836	1,513	3,236	3,344	7,151
Austin, TX	560	1,203	34	74	176	378	611	1,313	3,190	6,850
Fort Worth, TX	381	851	42	94	196	437	436	974	935	2,067
Oklahoma City, OK	355	798	19	42	194	436	362	813	571	1,294
Portland, OR	402	920	66	150	203	464	495	1,131	759	1,735
Kansas City, MO	541	1,244	57	130	330	758	570	1,310	905	2,080
Long Beach, CA	604	1,407	115	267	183	425	598	1,393	791	1,841
Tucson, AZ	361	891	120	295	132	326	343	845	825	2,034
St. Louis, MO [2]	494	1,247	74	186	277	698	517	1,303	767	1,933
Charlotte, NC	428	1,080	111	279	165	416	500	1,263	999	2,523
Atlanta, GA	695	1,763	138	350	223	566	624	1,583	1,433	3,637
Virginia Beach, VA [2]	736	1,872	271	689	374	950	682	1,734	566	1,439
Albuquerque, NM	470	1,222	151	392	132	344	476	1,238	1,269	3,300
Oakland, CA	540	1,451	102	274	222	596	508	1,364	1,144	3,073
Pittsburgh, PA	373	1,009	91	245	237	640	379	1,024	661	1,787
Sacramento, CA	331	895	31	83	154	417	352	954	452	1,224
Minneapolis, MN	620	1,682	170	461	192	522	736	1,998	2,290	6,215
Tulsa, OK	416	1,133	29	79	167	454	444	1,210	1,585	4,315
Cincinnati, OH	523	1,437	96	263	238	653	525	1,443	260	713
Miami, FL	306	854	48	135	171	476	324	903	565	1,575
Fresno, CA	242	682	47	132	109	306	236	666	248	701
Omaha, NE	228	678	36	107	144	429	209	621	195	580
Toledo, OH	235	705	45	134	128	384	234	703	194	582
Buffalo, NY	690	2,101	467	1,425	143	436	757	2,308	500	1,524
Wichita, KS	247	812	76	250	80	262	260	857	539	1,772
Santa Ana, CA	180	613	39	134	103	349	204	694	304	1,035
Mesa, AZ	183	636	59	204	45	158	197	685	484	1,681
Colorado Springs, CO	286	1,016	27	96	85	302	306	1,087	730	2,597
Tampa, FL	306	1,094	50	178	126	449	327	1,169	683	2,438
Newark, NJ	453	1,646	265	963	97	353	450	1,634	207	750
St. Paul, MN	414	1,522	142	521	93	343	409	1,504	865	3,177
Louisville, KY	255	946	57	211	147	547	255	947	442	1,642
Anaheim, CA	267	1,003	39	145	112	421	333	1,252	766	2,874
Birmingham, AL	277	1,042	30	111	158	595	309	1,162	807	3,035
Arlington, TX	180	686	11	42	96	367	154	589	378	1,446
Norfolk, VA [2]	566	2,167	211	807	216	827	586	2,244	1,023	3,914
Las Vegas, NV	235	912	101	393	64	250	246	951	134	518
Corpus Christi, TX	164	637	15	59	71	276	154	596	429	1,668
St. Petersburg, FL	237	993	33	138	91	381	212	889	574	2,405
Rochester, NY	615	2,656	362	1,563	140	602	628	2,712	284	1,228
Riverside, CA	216	955	32	140	74	325	219	966	727	3,208
Anchorage, AK [2]	696	3,074	270	1,191	179	792	699	3,088	1,055	4,662
Lexington-Fayette, KY [2]	197	873	16	73	101	450	190	842	414	1,837
Akron, OH	200	898	41	182	95	426	200	895	152	683
Aurora, CO	173	777	16	74	100	452	157	706	429	1,932
Baton Rouge, LA [2]	414	1,089	56	147	203	533	395	1,040	754	1,984
Stockton, CA	146	693	21	102	68	322	382	145	687	1,342

[1] Based on enumerated population as of April 1, 1990. [2] Represents, in effect, city-county consolidated government.
Source: U.S. Bureau of the Census, *City Government Finances*, series GF, No. 4, 1991-92; Internet site, http://www.census.gov/ftp/pub/govs/www/index.html (accessed 06/06/96); and unpublished data.

No. 499. City Governments—Revenue and Debt for Largest Cities: 1992 and 1993

[**In millions of dollars.** For fiscal year ending in year shown; see text, section 9. See headnote, table 498]

CITIES RANKED BY 1990 POPULATION	REVENUE								Debt out-stand-ing
	Total [1]	General revenue						Utility and liquor store	
		Total [1]	Intergovernmental		Taxes				
			From State and local govts.	From Federal Government	Total [1]	Prop-erty	Sales and gross receipts 1993		
1993									
New York City, NY [2]	44,487	37,870	13,435	1,421	17,703	7,989	3,566	2,103	37,814
Los Angeles, CA	7,365	3,890	406	134	1,896	725	776	2,417	8,035
Chicago, IL	4,263	3,342	549	247	1,677	620	906	266	6,371
Houston, TX	1,828	1,413	21	58	762	399	345	234	3,751
Philadelphia, PA [2]	4,310	2,966	752	167	1,551	339	112	630	3,781
San Diego, CA	1,455	1,186	155	96	394	146	202	141	1,560
Detroit, MI	2,039	1,563	569	139	553	215	48	169	1,887
Dallas, TX	1,320	1,099	13	48	490	285	196	129	3,729
Phoenix, AZ	1,191	1,025	244	90	340	115	204	108	2,486
San Antonio, TX	1,488	575	118	23	243	132	104	880	4,328
Honolulu, HI [2]	1,060	968	68	69	514	418	59	92	1,356
San Jose, CA	854	687	87	10	345	127	151	10	1,211
Baltimore, MD [2]	1,979	1,745	781	55	684	476	46	55	1,258
Indianapolis, IN [2]	1,106	1,075	305	38	481	385	21	7	1,346
San Francisco, CA [2]	3,608	2,798	889	111	960	528	206	245	3,385
Jacksonville, FL [2]	1,690	844	136	62	302	199	93	740	4,646
Columbus, OH	697	601	65	37	303	24	7	96	1,316
Milwaukee, WI	776	614	274	50	166	154	5	49	587
Memphis, TN	1,916	910	583	17	175	134	30	851	833
Washington, DC [2]	4,929	4,683	74	1,588	2,539	1,012	664	52	4,083
Boston, MA [2]	1,888	1,679	674	34	695	651	25	76	1,087
Seattle, WA	1,155	748	83	21	383	130	163	343	1,151
El Paso, TX	372	281	10	19	142	73	64	44	472
Cleveland, OH	726	547	72	64	281	53	4	180	1,011
1992									
New Orleans, LA [2]	747	658	45	78	301	138	137	56	1,126
Nashville-Davidson, TN [2]	1,636	989	246	13	479	263	173	605	2,216
Denver, CO [2]	1,171	1,046	221	27	391	99	246	85	3,344
Austin, TX	1,130	560	26	8	176	98	74	500	3,190
Fort Worth, TX	501	381	23	19	196	130	61	65	935
Oklahoma City, OK	407	355	8	10	194	27	161	38	571
Portland, OR	455	402	54	12	203	138	31	52	759
Kansas City, MO	671	541	29	28	330	62	147	47	905
Long Beach, CA	725	604	73	42	183	72	91	120	791
Tucson, AZ	455	361	98	22	132	24	104	76	825
St. Louis, MO [2]	604	494	41	32	277	37	109	30	767
Charlotte, NC	473	428	89	22	165	140	12	34	999
Atlanta, GA	811	695	82	55	223	123	68	61	1,433
Virginia Beach, VA [2]	775	736	179	91	374	233	113	39	566
Albuquerque, NM	514	470	122	29	132	47	80	43	1,269
Oakland, CA	566	540	73	29	222	113	68	-	1,144
Pittsburgh, PA	407	373	70	21	237	122	29	-	661
Sacramento, CA	386	331	30	1	154	52	90	20	452
Minneapolis, MN	750	620	144	26	192	142	38	23	2,290
Tulsa, OK	473	416	14	15	167	19	144	44	1,585
Cincinnati, OH	675	523	69	27	238	43	4	64	260
Miami, FL	381	306	35	14	171	127	35	-	565
Fresno, CA	320	242	34	13	109	39	50	23	248
Omaha, NE	259	228	32	4	144	66	70	-	195
Toledo, OH	255	235	31	13	128	10	-	21	194
Buffalo, NY	709	690	422	45	143	122	15	20	500
Wichita, KS	313	247	66	10	80	52	25	25	539
Santa Ana, CA	197	180	22	17	103	48	47	17	304
Mesa, AZ	255	183	52	6	45	5	37	71	484
Colorado Springs, CO	546	286	15	12	85	18	66	260	730
Tampa, FL	383	306	38	12	126	58	59	30	683
Newark, NJ	491	453	203	62	97	62	8	37	207
St. Paul, MN	448	414	102	40	93	72	17	22	865
Louisville, KY	317	255	36	21	147	38	1	62	442
Anaheim, CA	510	267	17	21	112	38	65	243	766
Birmingham, AL	326	277	16	13	158	28	56	-	807
Arlington, TX	212	180	2	9	96	57	37	33	378
Norfolk, VA [2]	633	566	163	48	216	127	69	33	1,023
Las Vegas, NV	235	235	98	3	64	30	14	-	134
Corpus Christi, TX	214	164	5	10	71	36	34	50	429
St. Petersburg, FL	296	237	30	3	91	58	29	49	574
Rochester, NY	641	615	308	54	140	126	11	26	284
Riverside, CA	414	216	28	4	74	25	42	197	727
Anchorage, AK [2]	815	696	264	6	179	165	7	94	1,055
Lexington-Fayette, KY [2]	221	197	6	11	101	24	6	1	414
Akron, OH	226	200	18	22	95	18	-	25	152
Aurora, CO	205	173	14	2	100	16	80	25	429
Baton Rouge, LA [2]	455	414	32	24	203	54	137	3	754
Stockton, CA	152	146	17	5	68	18	40	6	283

- Represents or rounds to zero.   [1] Includes items not shown separately.   [2] Represents, in effect, city-county consolidated government.

Source: U.S. Bureau of the Census, *City Government Finances*, series GF, No. 4, 1991-92; Internet site, http://www.census.gov/ftp/pub/govs/www/index.html (accessed 06/06/96).

No. 500. City Governments—Expenditures for Largest Cities: 1992 and 1993

[In millions of dollars. For fiscal year ending in year shown; see text, section 9. See headnote, table 498]

CITIES RANKED BY 1990 POPULATION	Total expenditure [1]	GENERAL EXPENDITURE								Utility and liquor store
		Total [1]	Education	Housing and community development	Public welfare	Health and hospitals	Police protection	Fire protection	Highways	
1993										
New York City, NY [2]	47,224	39,431	8,750	3,098	7,093	4,084	1,985	747	797	4,256
Los Angeles, CA	6,707	3,534	14	278	-	11	652	251	149	2,519
Chicago, IL	4,226	3,552	33	123	106	104	680	244	305	207
Houston, TX	1,842	1,530	-	30	-	61	301	150	143	239
Philadelphia, PA [2]	3,792	2,829	16	121	239	364	333	121	77	646
San Diego, CA	1,285	1,057	-	94	-	1	164	71	66	182
Detroit, MI	2,002	1,473	7	57	-	94	283	90	95	280
Dallas, TX	1,601	1,338	-	16	-	21	200	76	66	164
Phoenix, AZ	1,120	948	1	57	-	1	149	82	60	146
San Antonio, TX	1,560	739	11	11	24	21	114	76	64	807
Honolulu, HI [2]	1,212	995	-	122	-	10	121	50	40	217
San Jose, CA	783	717	-	123	-	-	116	55	53	19
Baltimore, MD [2]	1,637	1,491	567	56	2	62	155	77	109	45
Indianapolis, IN [2]	1,169	1,110	1	155	91	187	84	38	47	24
San Francisco, CA [2]	3,370	2,637	59	83	353	607	177	107	45	471
Jacksonville, FL [2]	1,538	797	-	45	9	35	86	58	42	700
Columbus, OH	775	640	-	10	-	24	119	71	45	135
Milwaukee, WI	734	615	-	56	-	14	132	65	48	41
Memphis, TN	1,789	909	476	21	-	7	74	60	27	810
Washington, DC [2]	5,155	4,791	720	205	965	536	267	100	119	97
Boston, MA [2]	1,848	1,605	465	52	80	220	137	88	58	58
Seattle, WA	1,238	747	-	31	-	16	101	67	51	438
El Paso, TX	375	269	-	5	-	17	47	25	20	87
Cleveland, OH	798	556	-	45	-	13	126	65	46	242
1992										
New Orleans, LA [2]	773	684	-	82	6	14	77	37	39	54
Nashville-Davidson, TN [2]	1,525	857	271	5	11	80	64	39	35	629
Denver, CO [2]	1,649	1,513	-	11	133	134	92	53	65	113
Austin, TX	1,113	611	-	5	1	142	52	35	22	478
Fort Worth, TX	523	436	-	6	-	11	53	32	52	65
Oklahoma City, OK	417	362	-	6	-	1	68	48	41	49
Portland, OR	581	495	-	20	-	-	71	48	64	50
Kansas City, MO	662	570	24	8	(Z)	41	78	41	51	62
Long Beach, CA	737	598	-	70	-	25	95	56	26	137
Tucson, AZ	463	343	-	33	2	1	51	24	47	110
St. Louis, MO [2]	603	517	3	27	4	31	88	26	21	28
Charlotte, NC	566	500	-	12	1	3	43	33	53	61
Atlanta, GA	767	624	19	15	(Z)	-	74	39	25	82
Virginia Beach, VA [2]	716	682	334	5	15	17	41	19	56	34
Albuquerque, NM	546	476	-	17	5	7	55	29	38	70
Oakland, CA	554	508	4	46	1	-	75	40	17	-
Pittsburgh, PA	429	379	-	9	(Z)	7	58	43	22	16
Sacramento, CA	399	352	(Z)	-	-	2	73	40	49	28
Minneapolis, MN	795	736	-	131	-	10	56	29	49	29
Tulsa, OK	491	444	-	5	-	19	46	34	28	42
Cincinnati, OH	659	525	-	54	-	32	65	50	44	81
Miami, FL	359	324	-	17	1	(Z)	88	46	9	-
Fresno, CA	303	236	-	9	-	-	41	21	30	43
Omaha, NE	222	209	(Z)	10	-	1	33	25	30	-
Toledo, OH	258	234	-	10	-	5	46	31	28	24
Buffalo, NY	774	757	362	68	-	2	55	41	21	17
Wichita, KS	309	260	-	10	2	7	27	17	69	32
Santa Ana, CA	221	204	-	47	-	3	52	22	18	17
Mesa, AZ	265	197	-	4	(Z)	-	40	19	22	68
Colorado Springs, CO	590	306	-	4	-	109	34	19	54	284
Tampa, FL	408	327	-	5	-	4	54	22	26	54
Newark, NJ	491	450	(Z)	66	45	13	66	44	6	34
St. Paul, MN	451	409	-	59	-	8	34	25	55	27
Louisville, KY	291	255	-	23	11	7	33	22	18	37
Anaheim, CA	600	333	-	97	-	1	47	25	22	266
Birmingham, AL	329	309	3	1	-	3	36	28	25	-
Arlington, TX	189	154	-	13	-	1	24	16	21	34
Norfolk, VA [2]	646	586	196	66	32	30	34	21	20	44
Las Vegas, NV	246	246	-	4	(Z)	2	39	26	54	(Z)
Corpus Christi, TX	195	154	-	1	-	5	25	13	14	42
St. Petersburg, FL	285	212	-	3	-	5	40	16	33	58
Rochester, NY	645	628	320	54	-	-	38	27	18	17
Riverside, CA	398	219	-	18	-	1	37	17	28	180
Anchorage, AK [2]	868	699	284	2	6	27	40	22	43	162
Lexington-Fayette, KY [2]	203	190	-	21	5	13	22	19	8	5
Akron, OH	232	200	-	10	-	7	27	20	22	32
Aurora, CO	188	157	-	2	-	(Z)	30	17	22	29
Baton Rouge, LA [2]	423	395	-	11	1	31	39	20	41	6
Stockton, CA	152	145	-	4	-	1	35	21	9	7

- Represents or rounds to zero.   Z Less than $500,000.   [1] Includes items not shown separately.   [2] Represents, in effect, city-county consolidated government.

Source: U.S. Bureau of the Census, *City Government Finances*, series GF, No.4 1991-92; Internet site, http://www.census.gov/ftp/pub/govs/www/index.html (accessed 06/06/96).

No. 501. Governmental Employment and Payrolls: 1980 to 1993

[For **October**. Covers both full-time and part-time employees. Except for 1987, local government data are estimates subject to sampling variation; see Appendix III and source. See also *Historical Statistics, Colonial Times to 1970*, series Y 272-307]

TYPE OF GOVERNMENT	1980	1984	1985	1986	1987	1988	1989	1990	1991	1992	1993
EMPLOYEES (1,000)											
Total.............	**16,213**	**16,436**	**16,690**	**16,933**	**17,212**	**17,588**	**17,879**	**18,369**	**18,554**	**18,745**	**18,823**
Federal (civilian) [1]	2,898	2,942	3,021	3,019	3,091	3,112	3,114	3,105	3,103	3,047	2,999
State and local	13,315	13,494	13,669	13,913	14,121	14,476	14,765	15,263	15,452	15,698	15,824
Percent of total.........	82	82	82	82	82	82	83	83	83	84	84
State	3,753	3,898	3,984	4,068	4,116	4,236	4,365	4,503	4,521	4,595	4,673
Local	9,562	9,595	9,685	9,846	10,005	10,240	10,400	10,760	10,930	11,103	11,151
Counties	1,853	1,872	1,891	1,926	1,963	2,024	2,085	2,167	2,196	2,253	2,270
Municipalities	2,561	2,434	2,467	2,494	2,493	2,570	2,569	2,642	2,662	2,665	2,644
School districts	4,270	4,387	4,416	4,502	4,627	4,679	4,774	4,950	5,045	5,134	(NA)
Townships	394	386	392	400	393	415	405	418	415	424	(NA)
Special districts.	484	516	519	524	529	552	568	585	612	627	(NA)
OCTOBER PAYROLLS (mil. dol.)											
Total.............	**19,935**	**26,904**	**28,945**	**30,670**	**32,669**	**34,203**	**36,763**	**39,228**	**41,237**	**43,120**	**(NA)**
Federal (civilian) [1]	5,205	7,137	7,580	7,561	7,924	7,976	8,636	8,999	9,687	9,937	(NA)
State and local	14,730	19,767	21,365	23,109	24,745	26,227	28,127	30,229	31,551	33,183	34,540
Percent of total.........	74	74	74	75	76	77	77	77	77	77	(NA)
State	4,285	5,815	6,329	6,810	7,263	7,842	8,443	9,083	9,437	9,828	10,288
Local	10,445	13,952	15,036	16,298	17,482	18,385	19,684	21,146	22,113	23,355	24,252
Counties	1,936	2,596	2,819	3,009	3,270	3,532	3,855	4,192	4,404	4,698	4,839
Municipalities	2,951	3,872	4,191	4,407	4,770	4,979	5,274	5,564	5,784	6,207	6,328
School districts	4,683	6,283	6,746	7,517	7,961	8,298	8,852	9,551	9,975	10,394	(NA)
Townships	330	421	446	474	522	556	599	642	664	685	(NA)
Special districts........	546	780	834	892	959	1,020	1,104	1,197	1,287	1,370	(NA)

NA Not available.   [1] Includes employees outside the United States.

Source: U.S. Bureau of the Census, *Historical Statistics on Governmental Finances and Employment*, and *Public Employment*, series GE, No. 1, annual; Internet site, http://www.census.gov/ftp/pub/govs/www/index.html (accessed 06/14/96).

No. 502. All Governments—Employment and Payroll, by Function: 1993

[For **October**. Covers both full-time and part-time employees. Local government amounts are estimates subject to sampling variation; see Appendix III and source]

FUNCTION	EMPLOYEES (1,000)				OCTOBER PAYROLLS (mil. dol.)			
	Total	Federal (civil-ian) [1]	State and local		Total	Federal (civil-ian) [1]	State and local	
			Total	State	Local			Total	State	Local
Total	**18,823**	**2,999**	**15,824**	**4,673**	**11,151**	**(NA)**	**(NA)**	**34,540**	**10,288**	**24,252**
National defense [2]	926	926	(X)	(X)	(X)	(NA)	(NA)	(X)	(X)	(X)
Postal Service	796	796	(X)	(X)	(X)	(NA)	(NA)	(X)	(X)	(X)
Space research and technology	25	25	(X)	(X)	(X)	(NA)	(NA)	(X)	(X)	(X)
Education	8,372	13	8,359	2,112	6,247	(NA)	(NA)	17,370	3,999	13,371
Highways	560	4	556	262	294	(NA)	(NA)	1279	648	631
Health and hospitals	1,831	324	1,507	712	795	(NA)	(NA)	3,412	1,661	1,751
Public welfare	517	10	507	224	283	(NA)	(NA)	1055	496	559
Police protection	862	86	776	87	689	(NA)	(NA)	2142	256	1886
Fire protection	330	(X)	330	(X)	330	848	(X)	848	(X)	848
Sanitation and sewerage	240	(X)	240	3	237	556	(X)	556	8	548
Parks and recreation.......	362	27	335	46	289	(NA)	(NA)	456	77	379
Natural resources.	429	226	203	167	36	(NA)	(NA)	437	369	68
Financial administration	492	132	360	159	201	(NA)	(NA)	802	387	415
Other government administration	369	29	340	52	288	(NA)	(NA)	578	130	448
Judicial and legal	376	51	325	117	208	(NA)	(NA)	873	368	505
Other.................	2,336	350	1,986	732	1,254	(NA)	(NA)	4,732	1,889	2,843

NA Not available.   X Not applicable.   [1] Includes employees outside the United States.   [2] Includes international relations.

Source: U.S. Bureau of the Census, *Public Employment*, series GE, No. 1; Internet site, http://www.census.gov/ftp/pub/govs/www/index.html (accessed 06/14/96).

No. 503. State and Local Government—Full-Time Employment and Salary, by Sex and Race/Ethnic Group: 1973 to 1993

[As of June 30. Excludes school systems and educational institutions. Based on reports from State governments (44 in 1973, 48 in 1975, 1976, and 1979, 47 in 1977 and 1983, 45 in 1978, 42 in 1980, 49 in 1981 and 1984 through 1987, and 50 in 1989 through 1991) and a sample of county, municipal, township, and special district jurisdictions employing 15 or more nonelected, nonappointed full-time employees. Data for 1993 only for State and Local Governments with 100 or more employees. Data for 1974, 1982, 1988 and 1992 not available. For definition of median, see Guide to Tabular Presentation]

| YEAR AND OCCUPATION | EMPLOYMENT (1,000) | | | | | | | MEDIAN ANNUAL SALARY ($1,000) | | | | | |
| | Total | Male | Fe-male | White [1] | Minority | | | Male | Fe-male | White [1] | Minority | | |
					Total [2]	Black [1]	His-panic [3]				Total [2]	Black [1]	His-panic [3]
1973	3,809	2,486	1,322	3,115	693	523	125	9.6	7.0	8.8	7.5	7.4	7.4
1975	3,899	2,436	1,464	3,102	797	602	147	11.3	8.2	10.2	8.8	8.6	8.9
1976	4,369	2,724	1,645	3,490	880	664	165	11.8	8.6	10.7	9.2	9.1	9.4
1977	4,415	2,737	1,678	3,480	935	705	175	12.4	9.1	11.3	9.7	9.5	9.9
1978	4,447	2,711	1,736	3,481	966	723	181	13.3	9.7	12.0	10.4	10.1	10.7
1979	4,576	2,761	1,816	3,568	1,008	751	192	14.1	10.4	12.8	10.9	10.6	11.4
1980	3,987	2,350	1,637	3,146	842	619	163	15.2	11.4	13.8	11.8	11.5	12.3
1981	4,665	2,740	1,925	3,591	1,074	780	205	17.7	13.1	16.1	13.5	13.3	14.7
1983	4,492	2,674	1,818	3,423	1,069	768	219	20.1	15.3	18.5	15.9	15.6	17.3
1984	4,580	2,700	1,880	3,458	1,121	799	233	21.4	16.2	19.6	17.4	16.5	18.4
1985	4,742	2,789	1,952	3,563	1,179	835	248	22.3	17.3	20.6	18.4	17.5	19.2
1986	4,779	2,797	1,982	3,549	1,230	865	259	23.4	18.1	21.5	19.6	18.7	20.2
1987	4,849	2,818	2,031	3,600	1,249	872	268	24.2	18.9	22.4	20.9	19.3	21.1
1989	5,257	3,030	2,227	3,863	1,394	961	308	26.1	20.6	24.1	22.1	20.7	22.7
1990	5,374	3,071	2,302	3,918	1,456	994	327	27.3	21.8	25.2	23.3	22.0	23.8
1991	5,459	3,110	2,349	3,965	1,494	1,011	340	28.4	22.7	26.4	23.8	22.7	24.5
1993, total. .	**5,024**	**2,820**	**2,204**	**3,588**	**1,436**	**948**	**341**	**30.6**	**24.3**	**28.5**	**25.9**	**24.2**	**26.8**
Officials/admin-istrators	273	188	86	231	42	27	10	(NA)	40.9	(NA)	(NA)	(NA)	(NA)
Professionals. . .	1,206	587	619	923	283	168	59	37.8	32.5	35.3	32.8	31.8	34.1
Technicians. . . .	465	270	195	348	117	69	31	30.4	24.5	28.3	25.6	24.6	27.6
Protective service	846	725	120	632	214	145	58	31.4	27.2	30.9	30.3	28.8	34.3
Paraprofes-sionals	360	100	260	218	142	111	23	22.6	20.4	21.5	21.7	19.8	21.4
Admin. support .	897	116	781	610	287	183	75	22.7	21.1	21.0	21.9	21.2	21.8
Skilled craft. . . .	395	378	17	299	96	59	28	28.5	22.9	28.2	27.7	27.0	29.7
Service/mainte-nance.	582	455	127	327	255	186	57	23.1	17.8	22.2	22.6	21.0	23.0

NA Not available.   [1] Non-Hispanic.   [2] Includes other minority groups not shown separately.   [3] Persons of Hispanic origin may be of any race.

Source: U.S. Equal Employment Opportunity Commission, State and Local Government Information Report, biennially.

No. 504. State and Local Government—Employer Costs per Hour Worked: 1994

[As of March. Based on a sample; see source for details. For additional data, see table 669]

| ITEM | Total com-pensa-tion | Wages and salaries | BENEFITS | | | | | |
			Total	Paid leave	Supple-mental pay	Insur-ance	Retire-ment and savings	Legally required benefits	Other [1]
All State & local government	**$25.27**	**$17.57**	**$7.71**	**$1.94**	**$0.20**	**$2.15**	**$1.90**	**$1.49**	**$0.03**
Occupational group:									
White-collar occupations	28.60	20.38	8.22	2.05	0.12	2.31	2.11	1.60	0.03
Professional specialty and technical.	34.04	24.90	9.15	2.03	0.13	2.52	2.60	1.83	0.04
Teachers	37.22	27.77	9.45	1.78	0.04	2.72	2.97	1.90	0.04
Executive, admin., & managerial .	31.81	22.04	9.77	3.19	0.15	2.20	2.37	1.85	0.02
Admin. support including clerical .	16.10	10.53	5.58	1.50	0.09	1.94	1.01	1.02	(Z)
Blue-collar occupations.	19.42	12.49	6.93	1.78	0.36	1.94	1.34	1.49	0.02
Service occupations	17.71	11.25	6.45	1.66	0.39	1.73	1.53	1.12	0.02
Industry group:									
Services	26.94	19.25	7.69	1.80	0.14	2.24	1.97	1.50	0.03
Health services	20.03	13.37	6.65	2.05	0.52	1.60	1.08	1.39	0.02
Hospitals.	20.28	13.64	6.64	2.08	0.50	1.56	1.07	1.41	0.02
Educational services	28.60	20.67	7.93	1.75	0.07	2.37	2.17	1.54	0.03
Elementary and secondary education.	28.78	20.82	7.96	1.65	0.05	2.48	2.23	1.51	0.05
Higher education	28.94	20.91	8.03	2.03	0.13	2.15	2.07	1.65	(Z)
Public administration	22.11	14.47	7.64	2.19	0.29	1.90	1.86	1.37	0.02

Z Cost per hour is less than one cent.   [1] Includes severance pay and supplemental unemployment benefits.

Source: U.S. Bureau of Labor Statistics, News, Employer Costs for Employee Compensation, USDL 94-220.

No. 505. State and Local Government—Employee Benefits: 1994

[In percent. For January through July. Covers full-time employees in State and local governments. Covers only benefits for which the employer pays part or all of the premium or expenses involved, except unpaid maternity and paternity leave, and long-term care insurance. Based on sample. For data on employee benefits in businesses, see table 671]

BENEFIT	All employees	White collar employees[1]	Teachers[2]	Blue collar employees[3]	BENEFIT	All employees	White collar employees[1]	Teachers[2]	Blue collar employees[3]
Paid: Vacations	66	84	9	91	Life	87	87	85	87
Holidays	73	86	33	91	Noncontributory	86	85	85	88
Jury duty leave	94	94	94	93	Accident/sickness	21	24	11	26
Funeral leave	62	59	58	70	Noncontributory	76	72	86	79
Family leave	4	4	3	6	Long-term disability	30	31	37	23
Military leave	75	80	61	82	Noncontributory	77	77	77	79
Sick leave	94	93	96	94	Retirement and savings plans:				
Personal leave	38	30	58	31	Defined benefit pension	91	90	93	91
Unpaid:					Noncontributory	28	30	20	31
Family leave	93	93	96	90	Defined contribution	9	10	7	9
Insurance plans:					Money purchase pension[4]	7	7	5	7
Medical	87	89	84	86	Additional benefits:				
Dental	62	62	59	66	Child care	9	11	5	9
Extended care facility	81	83	81	78	Educational assistance:				
Home health care	84	84	86	84	Job related	64	69	51	66
Hospital/room & board	100	100	100	100	Not job related	20	22	15	20
In HMO's	30	34	24	28	Sabbatical leave	27	19	59	9
Inpatient surgery	100	100	100	100	Employee assistance program	68	73	55	74
Mental health care:					Flexible benefits plans	5	5	7	3
Inpatient	99	99	100	99	Financial counciling	6	7	6	4
Outpatient	97	98	97	97	Long-term care insurance	4	5	2	3
Vision	35	36	30	37	Nonproduction bonuses, cash	34	40	17	41
Alcohol abuse treatment:					Subsidized commuting	7	8	4	9
Inpatient detox	99	99	99	99	Recreation facilities	14	13	19	13
Inpatient rehab	77	76	78	76	Reimbursement accounts[5]	64	68	59	61
Outpatient	83	83	83	82	Severance pay	29	26	32	32
Drug abuse treatment:					Travel accident insurance	13	13	14	12
Inpatient detox	98	98	99	99	Wellness programs	34	38	29	32
Inpatient rehab	74	73	76	74					
Outpatient	80	79	82	80					

[1] Includes all professional, administrative, technical, and clerical employees except teachers. [2] Includes all personnel in primary and secondary schools, junior colleges, and universities whose primary duty is teaching or closely related activities. [3] Includes police, firefighters, and all production and service employees. [4] Fixed contributions are periodically placed in an employee's account and benefits are based on how much money has accumulated at retirement. [5] Account which is used throughout the year to pay for plan premiums or to reimburse the employee for benefit related expenses. Account may be financed by employer, employee, or both.

Source: U.S. Bureau of Labor Statistics, *Employee Benefits in State and Local Governments, 1994.*

No. 506. State and Local Government Major Collective Bargaining Agreements— Average Percent Changes in Wage and Compensation Rates Negotiated: 1987 to 1994

[In percent, except as indicated. Averages presented are means; for definition, see Guide to Tabular Presentation]

ITEM	1987	1988	1989	1990	1991	1992	1993	1994
Compensation rate changes,[1] all settlements:								
First year	4.9	5.4	5.1	5.1	1.8	0.6	0.9	2.8
Over life of contract[2]	4.8	5.3	4.9	5.1	2.9	1.9	1.8	3.1
State government: First year	4.3	5.3	4.9	4.4	1.9	0.2	1.2	2.8
Over life of contract[2]	4.3	4.9	4.6	3.9	2.8	2.0	2.1	2.9
Local government: First year	5.4	5.5	5.6	5.4	1.6	1.2	0.7	2.8
Over life of contract[2]	5.1	5.8	5.5	5.8	2.9	1.5	1.6	3.3
Wage rate changes,[3] all settlements:								
First year	4.9	5.1	5.1	4.9	2.3	1.1	1.1	2.7
Over life of contract[2]	5.1	5.3	5.1	5.0	2.8	2.1	2.1	3.0
State government: First year	4.1	5.3	5.0	4.7	2.0	0.5	1.3	3.0
Over life of contract[2]	4.2	5.0	4.7	4.2	3.0	2.0	2.4	3.2
Local government: First year	5.3	5.0	5.2	5.0	2.5	1.7	1.0	2.5
Over life of contract[2]	5.5	5.5	5.4	5.2	2.7	2.1	1.9	3.0
Number of workers affected (mil.)[4]	1.3	1.1	1.1	0.9	0.8	1.2	1.7	1.2
State government	0.5	0.4	0.5	0.2	0.4	0.6	0.6	0.4
Local government	0.8	0.7	0.6	0.7	0.4	0.6	1.1	0.8
Wage rate changes, all agreements[5]	4.9	4.7	5.1	4.6	2.6	1.9	2.8	3.3
Source: Current settlements	2.7	2.3	2.5	2.0	0.6	0.8	1.6	1.4
Prior settlements	2.2	2.4	2.6	2.6	1.8	1.1	1.1	1.9
Cost-of-living adjustments	(Z)	(Z)	(Z)	(Z)	0.1	(Z)	(Z)	(Z)
State government	4.3	4.1	4.0	4.7	2.5	1.6	3.4	1.1
Local government	5.3	5.1	5.9	4.6	2.6	2.1	2.2	1.7

Z Less than .05 percent. [1] Data relate to settlements of 5,000 workers or more in each calendar year, whether wages and benefits were changed or not. [2] Average annual rate of change. [3] Data relate to settlements covering 1,000 workers or more in each calendar year but exclude possible changes in wages under cost-of-living adjustment (COLA) clauses, except increases guaranteed by the contract. Includes all settlements, whether wages were changed or not. [4] Number of workers covered by settlements reached in each calendar year. [5] Data relate to all wage changes implemented in the year stemming from settlements reached in the year, deferred from prior-year agreements, and cost-of-living clauses.

Source: U.S. Bureau of Labor Statistics, *Current Wage Developments,* monthly.

No. 507. State and Local Government Full-Time Eqivalent Employment, by Selected Function and State: 1993

[**In thousands**, for **October.** Local government amounts are estimates subject to sampling variation; see Appendix III and source]

| STATE | EDUCATION | | | | HEALTH AND HOSPITALS | | HIGHWAYS | | POLICE AND FIRE PROTECTION | | PUBLIC WELFARE | |
| | Total | | Higher education | | | | | | | | | |
	State	Local	State	Local	State	Local	State	Local	State [1]	Local	State	Local
United States . . .	1,435.9	5,278.2	1,306.4	261.9	672.6	718.8	258.1	283.0	85.9	893.0	220.1	263.5
Alabama	35.5	83.5	31.5	-	19.5	20.9	4.3	6.2	1.0	13.9	4.6	1.4
Alaska.	6.9	12.0	3.4	-	0.9	0.7	2.9	0.7	0.4	1.8	1.7	0.2
Arizona	23.8	82.0	21.3	7.4	2.8	8.1	3.3	3.6	1.6	13.7	5.5	4.0
Arkansas	17.9	55.6	15.2	-	8.7	4.4	4.0	3.3	0.9	6.5	3.4	0.6
California	128.2	515.3	123.8	59.4	44.3	111.0	19.3	20.5	11.0	105.0	3.4	49.6
Colorado	30.0	67.8	28.9	1.4	5.9	10.1	3.1	4.4	1.0	11.6	1.3	4.2
Connecticut	17.7	61.1	14.8	-	14.6	1.3	3.8	3.6	1.5	11.9	4.6	1.9
Delaware	6.7	12.0	6.4	-	3.7	0.2	1.4	0.6	0.7	1.6	1.8	0.1
District of Columbia . . .	-	10.3	-	1.5	-	7.5	-	0.9	-	6.8	-	2.0
Florida.	41.6	258.4	38.4	20.7	29.1	32.7	11.3	13.5	3.7	59.2	10.2	5.5
Georgia.	40.6	156.6	35.4	0.7	28.5	44.6	6.1	6.7	2.1	24.7	8.2	0.8
Hawaii.	29.6	-	7.1	-	6.3	0.2	0.9	1.1	-	5.1	1.2	0.1
Idaho	7.7	24.9	7.0	0.9	2.0	4.3	1.8	1.4	0.4	3.0	1.8	0.1
Illinois	50.4	230.6	47.5	19.0	17.3	20.2	8.8	10.6	3.6	51.1	12.2	6.5
Indiana	43.7	116.2	38.9	-	12.9	22.9	4.8	5.7	2.0	16.8	5.2	2.5
Iowa	22.0	70.0	20.9	5.9	9.6	10.3	2.9	5.6	0.8	7.0	3.3	1.7
Kansas	20.8	72.0	20.1	5.6	7.8	8.9	3.6	5.2	1.0	8.4	1.7	0.6
Kentucky	28.8	83.7	24.7	-	7.6	7.6	5.6	3.2	1.7	8.3	4.7	0.5
Louisiana	30.8	95.9	27.0	-	25.9	13.0	5.6	4.8	1.1	14.8	5.8	0.6
Maine	6.8	29.1	5.6	-	2.8	1.3	2.8	1.4	0.5	3.5	1.9	0.2
Maryland	23.3	94.5	21.3	7.8	12.5	3.4	5.0	5.0	2.3	18.8	7.5	1.9
Massachusetts	23.5	114.2	22.8	0.2	15.8	8.7	4.6	5.7	1.9	28.4	6.4	2.0
Michigan	66.8	200.2	64.8	12.3	14.4	23.3	3.8	8.9	3.1	26.1	13.0	3.6
Minnesota	33.9	98.4	32.3	3.1	9.5	14.5	5.0	7.3	0.9	10.7	1.7	10.6
Mississippi	16.2	67.9	14.8	5.0	11.6	12.1	3.4	4.5	0.9	7.9	3.3	0.3
Missouri.	25.5	103.2	23.4	4.8	15.6	12.1	6.5	6.7	1.9	17.5	7.1	1.5
Montana	7.2	23.6	6.5	0.2	1.5	1.2	1.8	1.3	0.4	2.1	1.2	1.0
Nebraska.	10.6	39.3	9.9	2.5	5.1	3.7	2.4	3.2	0.7	4.5	2.8	1.0
Nevada	6.2	22.8	6.0	-	1.6	4.0	1.4	1.0	0.6	5.8	1.0	0.3
New Hampshire	5.5	21.6	5.2	-	1.9	0.1	2.0	1.4	0.4	3.8	1.3	2.5
New Jersey	35.1	166.0	27.3	8.9	20.5	10.8	8.2	11.0	3.6	33.3	5.8	10.8
New Mexico	18.1	39.5	17.3	2.0	7.8	2.6	2.7	1.5	0.6	5.3	1.4	0.4
New York.	49.4	406.5	43.9	21.0	69.7	82.7	15.1	31.5	5.5	84.1	8.1	57.8
North Carolina	42.0	163.4	38.9	13.4	17.2	31.1	13.0	3.2	3.3	21.5	1.2	12.4
North Dakota	7.0	14.3	6.7	0.0	2.7	0.2	1.1	1.1	0.2	1.4	0.2	1.0
Ohio	69.0	196.1	66.7	4.6	22.0	30.8	9.0	11.5	2.5	35.7	2.0	21.8
Oklahoma	25.1	75.7	22.5	-	11.4	8.0	4.2	5.5	1.6	11.3	6.8	0.3
Oregon	13.7	63.8	12.8	6.9	7.3	5.5	3.4	4.0	1.1	9.3	4.4	0.7
Pennsylvania	52.0	217.3	49.1	8.6	23.8	5.4	12.8	10.0	5.2	27.6	10.2	21.3
Rhode Island	6.7	17.3	5.8	-	2.7	0.1	1.0	0.9	0.3	4.8	1.6	0.2
South Carolina	27.8	75.1	24.9	-	17.9	13.4	5.2	2.1	1.8	9.8	4.8	0.4
South Dakota	5.0	17.3	4.5	-	2.1	0.7	1.3	1.6	0.3	1.6	1.1	0.2
Tennessee	32.3	88.6	30.1	-	13.8	22.4	4.8	6.5	1.5	17.6	4.5	3.7
Texas	83.9	477.2	79.3	28.0	51.6	52.8	13.7	22.4	3.1	66.9	22.9	3.1
Utah	21.8	36.1	20.9	-	6.1	1.4	1.8	1.5	0.7	4.6	2.7	0.5
Vermont	4.7	17.8	4.4	-	0.8	-	1.1	1.0	0.5	1.0	1.2	-
Virginia	46.2	140.0	43.1	-	26.2	8.6	11.3	3.7	2.4	20.1	2.4	8.0
Washington	36.6	82.4	34.9	-	15.6	11.5	6.4	6.2	1.9	15.9	7.2	1.1
West Virginia	13.0	39.2	11.4	-	2.9	4.2	5.7	0.9	0.8	3.2	2.5	-
Wisconsin	35.2	106.5	33.9	8.4	9.5	10.2	2.2	8.6	0.9	16.8	1.2	12.1
Wyoming	3.3	15.3	3.2	1.7	1.7	3.4	1.9	0.7	0.2	1.6	0.3	-

- Represents or rounds to zero.   [1] For State government, represents police protection only.

Source: U.S. Bureau of the Census, Internet site, http://www.census.gov/ftp/pub/govs/www/index.html (accessed 06/20/96).

No. 508. State and Local Government Employment and Average Earnings, by State: 1986 and 1993

[For **October**]

STATE	FULL-TIME EQUIVALENT EMPLOYMENT (1,000)				FULL-TIME EQUIVALENT EMPLOYMENT PER 10,000 POPULATION [2]				AVERAGE OCTOBER EARNINGS [3] (dol.)			
	State		Local [1]		State		Local [1]		State		Local [1]	
	1986	1993	1986	1993	1986	1993	1986	1993	1986	1993	1986	1993
United States	3,437	3,891	8,415	9,552	143	151	349	370	2,052	2,722	1,992	2,627
Alabama	70	83	131	157	174	198	324	374	1,884	2,307	1,532	1,908
Alaska	21	22	20	22	393	364	377	368	3,228	3,640	3,324	3,624
Arizona	43	57	119	149	128	144	358	378	2,126	2,424	2,185	2,694
Arkansas	39	47	71	84	163	192	299	348	1,724	2,261	1,388	1,754
California	279	344	965	1,085	104	110	358	348	2,751	3,644	2,535	3,390
Colorado	50	55	122	133	155	153	375	372	2,368	3,042	2,017	2,530
Connecticut	56	60	95	95	175	183	297	290	2,336	3,337	2,089	3,322
Delaware	17	20	16	18	272	292	252	251	1,795	2,469	1,991	2,714
District of Columbia	(X)	(X)	51	51	(X)	(X)	817	887	(X)	(X)	2,594	3,315
Florida	124	167	407	498	106	122	348	364	1,748	2,266	1,872	2,355
Georgia	91	119	239	293	149	171	391	423	1,811	2,309	1,589	2,054
Hawaii	41	52	12	14	389	442	113	122	1,844	2,627	2,010	2,900
Idaho	18	21	33	41	175	187	332	373	1,766	2,280	1,535	1,999
Illinois	130	132	385	431	113	113	333	368	2,165	2,839	2,166	2,799
Indiana	75	88	182	203	136	154	330	356	2,056	2,682	1,686	2,257
Iowa	57	51	101	113	199	181	355	400	2,049	2,971	1,735	2,214
Kansas	43	48	96	115	174	188	390	454	1,687	2,289	1,700	2,227
Kentucky	63	72	102	122	170	189	275	322	1,651	2,295	1,596	1,997
Louisiana	86	90	151	160	191	211	337	372	1,673	2,242	1,494	1,844
Maine	20	21	36	42	168	172	307	342	1,714	2,455	1,590	2,175
Maryland	80	84	143	161	178	169	321	324	2,046	2,742	2,233	2,977
Massachusetts	88	81	192	202	151	134	329	336	2,034	2,914	2,082	2,817
Michigan	128	136	315	326	140	143	344	344	2,541	3,231	2,329	3,064
Minnesota	61	67	137	177	145	148	326	391	2,428	3,127	2,318	2,810
Mississippi	42	48	95	107	161	181	364	404	1,430	2,177	1,324	1,634
Missouri	66	79	157	177	130	151	310	337	1,621	2,142	1,826	2,178
Montana	16	17	29	35	192	207	349	416	1,864	2,377	1,727	2,131
Nebraska	29	29	65	71	184	181	407	440	1,509	2,214	1,785	2,292
Nevada	15	19	33	46	154	137	343	332	1,990	2,795	2,140	2,909
New Hampshire	18	17	29	35	172	150	285	311	1,759	2,510	1,701	2,558
New Jersey	96	110	283	304	126	140	372	385	2,278	3,303	2,146	3,238
New Mexico	34	43	49	63	231	265	332	388	1,792	2,223	1,680	1,980
New York	272	267	810	855	153	147	456	470	2,355	3,335	2,266	3,323
North Carolina	93	111	216	279	147	159	341	401	1,935	2,416	1,662	2,172
North Dakota	15	16	22	23	222	247	318	356	1,805	2,318	2,017	2,366
Ohio	122	141	365	390	113	127	340	351	1,984	2,777	1,911	2,504
Oklahoma	64	68	109	122	195	211	329	376	1,733	1,897	1,595	1,949
Oregon	44	47	91	108	163	156	338	355	1,975	2,780	2,018	2,653
Pennsylvania	124	145	340	367	104	120	286	305	1,915	2,804	1,976	2,713
Rhode Island	19	20	24	28	195	198	245	277	2,041	2,949	2,215	2,961
South Carolina	69	78	109	125	204	214	322	342	1,705	2,091	1,558	2,037
South Dakota	13	14	23	26	177	194	330	366	1,684	2,238	1,441	1,926
Tennessee	71	77	157	182	147	151	327	356	1,746	2,238	1,554	2,059
Texas	193	247	633	768	115	137	379	426	1,927	2,426	1,748	2,140
Utah	33	42	47	56	197	226	283	300	1,654	2,206	1,900	2,253
Vermont	11	13	15	22	211	220	270	382	1,842	2,504	1,653	2,348
Virginia	102	118	195	234	177	182	336	360	1,895	2,355	1,787	2,381
Washington	79	96	143	171	177	183	320	326	2,231	2,987	2,134	3,140
West Virginia	34	33	61	57	180	184	317	314	1,574	2,015	1,625	2,127
Wisconsin	74	70	168	190	154	138	351	377	2,128	2,913	2,035	2,689
Wyoming	11	11	25	25	213	231	494	530	1,924	2,127	1,967	2,249

X Not applicable.   [1] Estimates subject to sampling variation; see Appendix III and source.   [2] Based on estimated resident population as of July 1.   [3] For full-time employees.

Source: U.S. Bureau of the Census, *Public Employment*, series GE, No.1, annual: Internet site, http://www.census.gov/www.census.gov/ftp/pub/govs/www/index.html (accessed 06/20/96), and unpublished data.

No. 509. City Government Employment and Payroll: 1980 to 1993

[For **October**. Includes only those school systems operated as part of the city government. 1982 and 1987 based on complete census of all cities; other years based on sample and subject to sampling variation]

YEAR	ALL EMPLOYEES, FULL TIME AND PART TIME (1,000)		OCTOBER PAYROLLS (mil. dol.)		ANNUAL PERCENT CHANGE		FULL-TIME EQUIVALENT EMPLOYMENT [1] (1,000)			AVERAGE EARNINGS IN OCTOBER, FULL-TIME EMPLOYEES (dollars)	
	Total	Excl. education	Total	Excl. education	All employees	October payroll	Total	Education	Other	Education	Other
1980	2,561	2,130	2,942	2,403	0.3	7.8	2,166	360	1,806	1,501	1,338
1981	2,469	2,056	3,222	2,640	-3.6	9.5	2,111	346	1,765	1,686	1,500
1982	2,396	2,015	3,428	2,861	-2.9	6.4	2,088	317	1,770	1,791	1,625
1983	2,423	2,051	3,640	3,059	1.1	6.2	2,060	300	1,760	1,962	1,739
1984	2,434	2,070	3,872	3,268	0.4	6.4	2,090	300	1,790	2,033	1,831
1985	2,467	2,102	4,191	3,536	1.4	8.2	(NA)	(NA)	(NA)	2,117	1,953
1986	2,494	2,126	4,407	3,724	1.1	5.1	2,181	320	1,860	2,186	2,044
1987	2,493	2,110	4,770	3,977	(Z)	8.2	2,223	337	1,885	2,406	2,163
1988	2,570	2,188	4,979	4,136	3.1	4.4	2,251	342	1,910	2,566	2,220
1989	2,569	2,190	5,274	4,405	(Z)	5.9	2,268	341	1,927	2,669	2,343
1990	2,642	2,237	5,564	4,675	2.8	5.5	2,295	338	1,957	2,683	2,449
1991	2,662	2,324	5,784	4,878	0.7	4.0	2,303	338	1,965	2,739	2,547
1992	2,665	2,312	6,207	5,146	0.1	7.3	2,340	371	1,969	2,931	2,683
1993	2,644	2,239	6,328	5,239	-0.8	1.9	2,307	352	1,955	3,176	2,755

NA Not available.   Z Less than .05 percent.   [1] Beginning 1986, data not comparable to previous years due to a change in how full-time equivalent is calculated; see text, section 9.   [2] Percent change from 1979.

Source: U.S. Bureau of the Census, *Compendium of Public Employment,* and *City Employment,* series GE, No. 2, annual. Internet site, http://www.census.gov/ftp/pub/govs/www/index.html (accessed 06/14/96); and unpublished data.

No. 510. City Government Employment and Payroll, by Function: 1980 to 1993

[For **October**]

ITEM	EMPLOYEES (1,000)					OCTOBER PAYROLLS (mil. dol.)				
	All cities [1]				Cities with 75,000 population or more, [2] 1992	All cities [1]				Cities with 75,000 population or more, [2] 1992
	1980	1990	1992	1993		1980	1990	1992	1993	
Total	2,561	2,642	2,665	2,644	1,568	2,942	5,564	6,207	6,328	4,281
Full-time	2,071	2,149	2,197	2,142	1,418	2,826	5,334	5,980	6,034	4,178
Part-time	489	493	468	502	150	116	229	227	294	103
Full-time equivalent [3]	2,166	2,295	2,340	2,307	1,480	(X)	(X)	(X)	(X)	(X)
Education [4]	360	338	371	352	301	539	889	1,061	1,089	880
Percent of total	17	15	16	15	20	18	16	17	17	21
Instructional staff	266	264	261	249	209	436	754	848	851	698
Others	94	74	110	103	92	102	134	212	238	182
Libraries	34	45	45	44	27	38	80	86	88	57
Public welfare	41	57	55	55	49	47	118	132	133	121
Hospitals	131	124	125	122	82	143	282	301	314	217
Health	35	42	43	41	35	47	93	104	107	89
Highways	121	133	130	134	56	141	274	301	315	152
Police protection	365	412	423	427	234	550	1,093	1,249	1,286	783
Fire protection	190	199	200	199	117	300	579	642	663	416
Correction	18	35	36	37	34	27	90	108	114	103
Parks and recreation.	103	121	123	126	71	116	211	232	242	141
Housing and community development	44	46	45	33	38	57	104	115	87	97
Sewerage	60	74	76	71	38	74	155	172	172	95
Solid waste management.	104	86	83	81	49	118	174	193	187	135
Financial administration.	69	74	74	74	35	85	164	179	184	96
Judicial, legal, other governmental administration	112	129	132	132	73	147	314	345	359	209
Local utilities [5]	209	226	226	219	144	306	594	615	598	439
Water supply	93	101	103	101	53	116	219	240	240	137
Electric power	44	51	51	50	28	67	142	159	160	101
Transit	66	66	64	61	60	115	217	198	180	191
Other	171	154	152	159	97	208	350	372	392	252

X Not applicable.   [1] Data are estimates subject to sampling variation; see Appendix III and source.   [2] Based on enumerated resident population as of April 1, 1990.   [3] 1980 data not directly comparable to later years due to a change in 1986 in how full-time equivalent was calculated; see text, section 9.   [4] City-operated schools and colleges only.   [5] Includes gas supply not shown separately.

Source: U.S. Bureau of the Census, *City Employment,* series GE, No. 2, annual; and unpublished data.

No. 511. City Government Employment and Payroll—Largest Cities: 1980 and 1993

[For October. See footnote 2, table 499, for those areas representing city-county consolidated governments]

| CITIES RANKED BY 1990 POPULATION | TOTAL EMPLOYMENT (1,000) | | FULL-TIME EQUIVALENT EMPLOYMENT [1] | | | | OCTOBER PAYROLL (mil. dol.) | | AVERAGE EARNINGS IN OCTOBER, FULL-TIME EMPLOYEES (dol.) | |
| | | | Total (1,000) | | Per 10,000 population [2] | | | | | |
	1980	1993	1980	1993	1980	1993	1980	1993	1980	1993
New York, NY [3][4]	364	422	319	381	451	520	504	1,279	1,587	3,416
Los Angeles, CA	42	47	41	48	138	138	73	183	1,806	3,896
Chicago, IL	47	40	45	40	150	144	71	131	1,569	3,315
Houston, TX	18	22	18	22	111	135	26	53	1,499	2,412
Philadelphia, PA	33	30	32	30	189	189	51	89	1,611	3,071
San Diego, CA	8	11	7	10	81	90	12	31	1,773	3,116
Detroit, MI	22	[5]19	22	[5]19	179	[5]185	40	[5]49	1,852	[5]2,700
Dallas, TX	14	14	14	14	153	139	20	35	1,465	2,647
Phoenix, AZ	9	11	9	11	114	112	14	43	1,517	3,211
San Antonio, TX	10	[6]14	10	[6]13	128	[6]139	13	[6]32	1,282	[6]2,472
San Jose, CA	[7]4	6	[7]4	6	[7]60	77	[7]7	24	[7]1,714	4,312
Baltimore, MD [3][6]	44	28	40	28	514	380	47	74	1,172	2,713
Indianapolis, IN	13	12	12	12	174	164	13	27	1,098	2,293
San Francisco, CA	21	24	21	24	310	332	37	93	1,761	3,892
Jacksonville, FL	[9]11	10	[9]11	10	[9]202	157	[9]11	28	[9]1,031	2,967
Columbus, OH	8	8	7	8	122	126	10	22	1,498	2,919
Milwaukee, WI	10	[6]8	9	[6]8	145	[6]127	15	[6]23	1,631	[6]2,782
Memphis, TN [3]	25	24	22	22	342	360	29	55	1,335	2,490
Washington, DC [3][4]	45	45	42	43	651	709	73	133	1,761	3,130
Boston, MA [3]	[7]28	21	[7]25	21	[7]444	366	[7]35	62	[7]1,398	3,034
Seattle, WA	10	11	9	10	188	194	77	37	1,830	3,691
El Paso, TX	5	6	4	6	104	116	3	12	942	2,225
Cleveland, OH	10	9	9	9	160	178	13	24	1,460	2,687
New Orleans, LA	[10]13	[11]10	[10]13	[11]10	[10]225	[11]201	[10]11	[11]16	[10]919	[11]1,623
Nashville-Davidson, TN [3]	[12]18	[6]18	[12]17	[6]17	[12]374	[6]348	[12]22	[6]40	[12]1,295	[6]2,430
Denver, CO	13	[6]14	12	[6]12	244	[6]257	18	[6]35	1,540	[6]2,859
Austin, TX	8	12	7	12	199	258	10	31	1,515	2,650
Fort Worth, TX	5	5	5	5	120	112	5	12	1,198	2,334
Oklahoma City, OK	5	[6]5	4	[6]5	104	[6]112	6	[6]12	1,323	[6]2,567
Portland, OR	5	5	4	5	115	114	8	17	1,916	3,679
Kansas City, MO	7	6	7	6	145	138	9	16	1,368	2,518
Long Beach, CA	[7]5	6	[7]4	5	[7]122	116	[7]7	19	[7]1,678	3,726
Tucson, AZ	4	5	4	5	124	123	6	13	1,474	2,714
St. Louis, MO	13	8	13	8	280	202	15	18	1,279	2,393
Charlotte, NC	4	5	4	5	125	126	5	12	1,290	2,578
Atlanta, GA	8	9	8	8	187	203	10	21	1,230	2,523
Virginia Beach, VA [3]	10	15	9	14	346	356	11	32	1,204	2,273
Albuquerque, NM	[9]4	7	[9]4	6	[9]119	156	[9]4	13	[9]1,135	2,148
Oakland, CA	4	5	4	5	[10]109	134	7	18	2,011	4,165
Pittsburgh, PA	[10]6	5	[10]6	5	[10]135	135	[10]6	15	[10]1,116	3,009
Sacramento, CA	3	[6]4	3	[6]4	119	[6]108	6	[6]13	1,762	[6]3,384
Minneapolis, MN	6	7	5	6	136	163	9	19	1,821	3,359
Tulsa, OK	[9]4	4	[9]4	4	[9]115	109	[9]5	11	[9]1,184	2,559
Honolulu, HI	9	10	9	10	117	120	12	29	1,401	2,966
Cincinnati, OH	7	8	7	7	174	192	10	20	1,527	2,973
Miami, FL	4	4	4	4	118	112	6	13	1,408	3,595
Fresno, CA	3	3	3	3	115	85	4	9	1,607	3,396
Omaha, NE	3	3	3	3	92	89	5	9	1,684	3,225
Toledo, OH [3]	4	3	3	3	96	90	6	10	1,758	3,054
Buffalo, NY [3]	14	14	13	13	348	396	18	35	1,475	2,862
Wichita, KS	3	[6]3	3	[6]3	111	[6]99	4	[6]7	1,327	[6]2,429
Santa Ana, CA	2	2	1	2	68	68	2	9	1,819	5,163
Mesa, AZ	1	2	1	2	89	69	2	8	1,592	3,091
Colorado Springs, CO	4	6	3	6	158	213	5	15	1,445	2,826
Tampa, FL [13][14]	5	4	5	4	165	143	5	12	1,178	3,128
Newark, NJ [13][14]	12	6	12	6	374	218	17	17	1,387	2,877
St. Paul, MN	4	3	3	3	125	110	6	11	1,734	3,629
Louisville, KY	6	4	6	4	186	149	7	7	1,358	1,936
Anaheim, CA	2	4	2	2	91	75	3	10	1,616	4,251
Birmingham, AL	4	4	4	4	128	150	5	9	1,333	2,320
Arlington, TX	[9]1	[5]2	[9]1	[5]2	[9]63	[5]76	[9]1	[5]5	[9]1,180	[5]2,721
Norfolk, VA [3]	11	12	10	10	380	383	12	25	1,222	2,523

[1] 1993 data not comparable with 1980 due to a change in 1986 in how full-time equivalent was calculated; see text, section 9. [2] 1980 based on enumerated resident population as of April 1, 1980. 1993 based on enumerated resident population as of April 1, 1990. [3] Includes city-operated elementary and secondary schools. [4] Includes city-operated university or college. [5] 1991 data. [6] 1992 data. [7] 1979 data. [8] Prior to 1990, includes data for city operated colleges. [9] 1978 data. [10] 1977 data. [11] 1989 data. [12] Noneducation data are for 1979. [13] Prior to 1983, city-operated elementary and secondary schools. [14] 1993 Employment increased when Housing Authority became city dependent.

Source: U.S. Bureau of the Census, City Employment, series GE, No. 2, annual; and unpublished data.

Figure 10.1
The Government of the United States
(As of July 1, 1993)

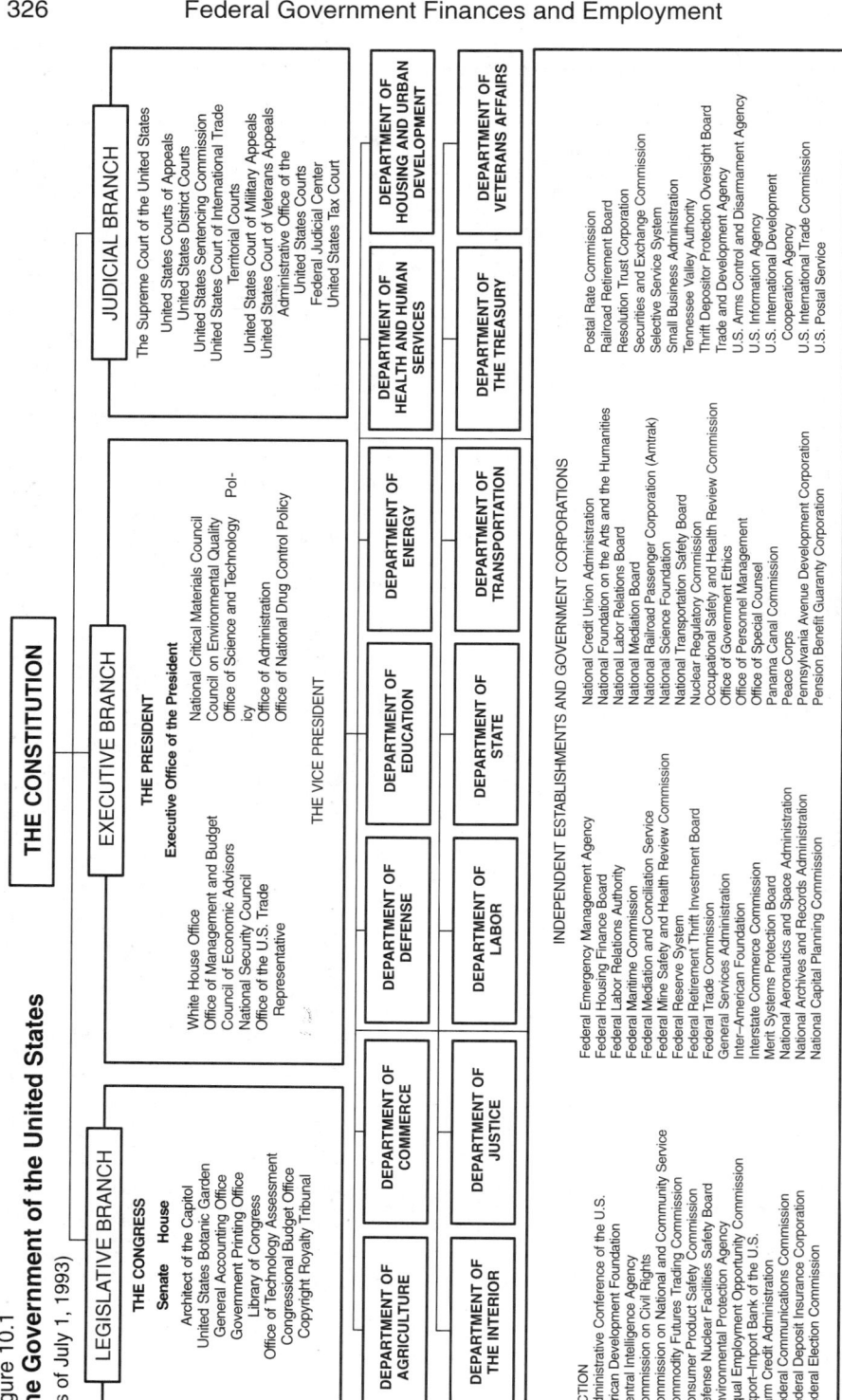

Source: Chart prepared by U.S. Bureau of the Census.

Federal Government Finances and Employment

This section presents statistics relating to the financial structure and the civilian employment of the Federal Government. The fiscal data cover taxes, other receipts, outlays, and debt. The principal sources of fiscal data are *The Budget of the United States Government* and related documents, published annually by the Office of Management and Budget (OMB), and the Department of the Treasury's *United States Government Annual Report* and its *Appendix*. Detailed data on tax returns and collections are published annually by the Internal Revenue Service. Personnel data relating to staffing and payrolls for the various public functions and agencies, to employee characteristics, and to civil service status; are published by the Office of Personnel Management and the Bureau of Labor Statistics. The primary source for data on public lands is *Public Land Statistics,* published annually by the Bureau of Land Management, Department of the Interior. Data on federally-owned land and real property are collected by the General Services Administration and presented in its annual *Inventory Report on Real Property Owned by the United States Throughout the World.*

Budget concept—Under the unified budget concept, all Federal monies are included in one comprehensive budget. These monies comprise both Federal funds and trust funds. Federal funds are derived mainly from taxes and borrowing and are not restricted by law to any specific government purpose. Trust funds, such as the Unemployment Trust Fund, collect certain taxes and other receipts for use in carrying out specific purposes or programs in accordance with the terms of the trust agreement or statute. Fund balances include both cash balances with Treasury and investments in U.S. securities. Part of the balance is obligated, part unobligated. Prior to 1985, the budget totals, under provisions of law, excluded some Federal activities—including the Federal Financing Bank, the Postal Service, the Synthetic Fuels Corporation, and the lending activities of

In Brief	
	1996
Gross Federal debt	*$5,207 bil.*
Interest on the public debt	*$345 bil.*
Net interest	*$241 bil.*

the Rural Electrification Administration. The Balanced Budget and Emergency Deficit Control Act of 1985 (P.L.99-177) repealed the off-budget status of these entities and placed social security (Federal old-age and survivors insurance and the Federal disability insurance trust funds) off-budget. Though social security is now off-budget and, by law, excluded from coverage of the congressional budget resolutions, it continues to be a Federal program.

Receipts arising from the Government's sovereign powers are reported as governmental receipts; all other receipts, i.e., from business-type or market-oriented activities, are offset against outlays. Outlays are reported on a checks-issued (net) basis (i.e., outlays are recorded at the time the checks to pay bills are issued).

Debt concept—For most of U.S. history, the total debt consisted of debt borrowed by the Treasury (i.e., public debt). The present debt series includes both public debt and agency debt. The *gross Federal debt* includes money borrowed by the Treasury and by various Federal agencies; it is the broadest generally used measure of the Federal debt. *Total public debt* is covered by a statutory debt limitation and includes only borrowing by the Treasury.

Treasury receipts and outlays—All receipts of the Government, with a few exceptions, are deposited to the credit of the U.S. Treasury regardless of ultimate disposition. Under the Constitution, no money may be withdrawn from the Treasury unless appropriated by the Congress.

The day-to-day cash operations of the Federal Government clearing through the accounts of the U.S. Treasury are reported in the *Daily Treasury Statement*. Extensive detail on the public debt is published in the *Monthly Statement of the Public Debt of the United States*.

Budget receipts such as taxes, customs duties, and outlays represented by checks issued and cash payments made by disbursing officers as well as government agencies are reported in the *Daily Treasury Statement of Receipts and Outlays of the United States Government* and in the Treasury's *United States Government Annual Report* and its *Appendix*. These deposits in and payments from accounts maintained by Government agencies are on the same basis as the unified budget.

The quarterly *Treasury Bulletin* contains data on fiscal operations and related Treasury activities, including financial statements of Government corporations and other business-type activities.

Income tax returns and tax collections—Tax data are compiled by the Internal Revenue Service of the Treasury Department. The *Annual Report of the Commissioner and Chief Counsel of the Internal Revenue Service Data Book* gives a detailed account of tax collections by kind of tax and by regions, districts, and States. The agency's annual *Statistics of Income* reports present detailed data from individual income tax returns and corporation income tax returns. The quarterly *Statistics of Income Bulletin* has, in general, replaced the supplemental *Statistics of Income* publications which presented data on such diverse subjects as tax-exempt organizations, unincorporated businesses, fiduciary income tax and estate tax returns, sales of capital assets by individuals, international income and taxes reported by corporations and individuals, and estate tax wealth.

Employment and payrolls—The Office of Personnel Management collects employment and payroll data from all departments and agencies of the Federal Government, except the Central Intelligence Agency, the National Security Agency, and the Defense Intelligence Agency. Employment figures represent the number of persons who occupied civilian positions at the end of the report month shown and who are paid for personal services rendered for the Federal Government, regardless of the nature of appointment or method of payment.

Federal payrolls include all payments for personal services rendered during the report month and payments for accumulated annual leave of employees who separate from the service. Since most Federal employees are paid on a biweekly basis, the calendar month earnings are partially estimated on the basis of the number of work days in each month where payroll periods overlap.

Federal employment and payroll figures are published by the Office of Personnel Management in its *Federal Civilian Workforce Statistics—Employment and Trends*. It also publishes biennial employment data for minority groups, data on occupations of white- and blue-collar workers, and data on employment by geographic area; reports on salary and wage distribution of Federal employees are published annually. General schedule is primarily white-collar; wage system primarily blue-collar. Data on Federal employment are also issued by the Bureau of Labor Statistics in its *Monthly Labor Review* and in *Employment and Earnings* and by the Bureau of the Census in its annual *Public Employment*.

Public lands—These data refer to transactions which involve the disposal, under public land laws, of Federal public lands to non-Federal owners. In general, original entries and selections are applications to secure title to public lands which have been accepted as properly filed (i.e., allowed). Some types of applications, however, are not reported until issuance of the final certificate, which passes equitable title to the land to the applicant. Applications are approved when full compliance with the requirements of the laws is shown and become final entries (perfected entries) upon issuance of a final certificate. Patents are Government deeds which pass legal title to the land to the applicant. Certifications are issued in lieu of patents in connection with certain State selections.

Historical statistics—Tabular headnotes provide cross-references, where applicable, to *Historical Statistics of the United States, Colonial Times to 1970*. See Appendix IV.

Figure 10.2
Federal Budget Summary: 1945 to 1996

Receipts, outlays, and surplus or deficit
Billions of dollars

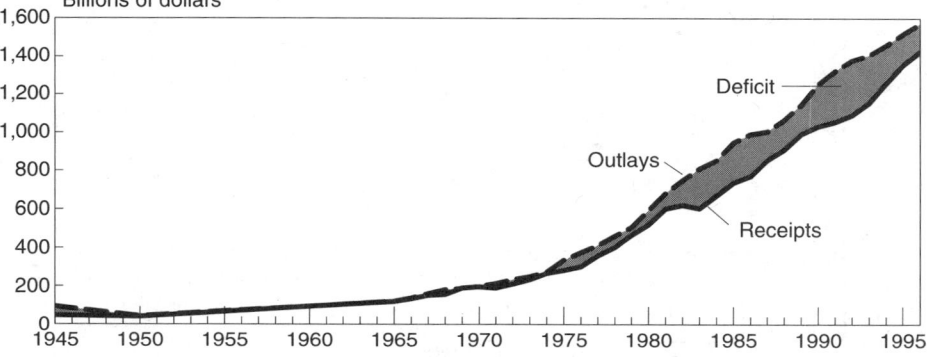

Outlays and debt as a percent of Gross Domestic Product
Percent

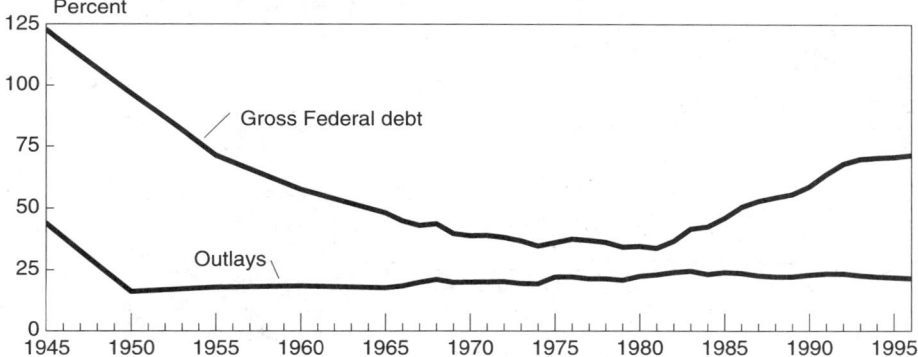

Gross Federal debt
Billions of dollars

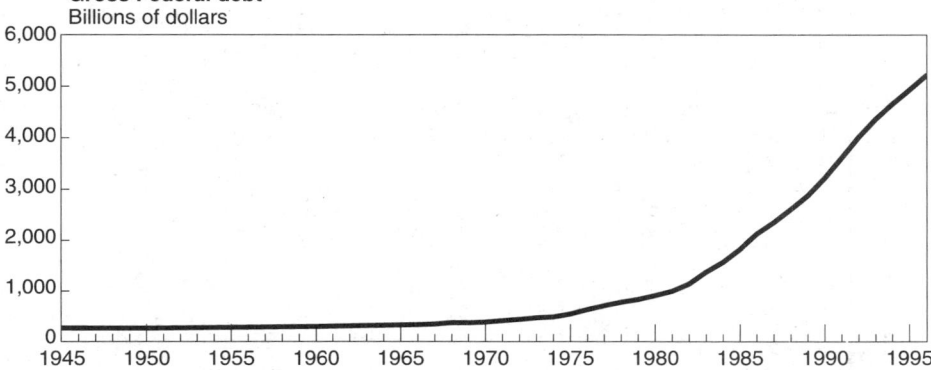

Source: Charts prepared by U.S. Bureau of the Census. For data, see table 512.

No. 512. Federal Budget—Summary: 1945 to 1996

[In millions of dollars, except percent. **For fiscal years ending in year shown;** see text, section 9. The Balanced Budget and Emergency Deficit Control Act of 1985 put all the previously off-budget Federal entities into the budget and moved Social Security off-budget. Minus sign (-) indicates deficit or decrease]

YEAR	OUTLAYS [1]						GROSS FEDERAL DEBT [3]					ANNUAL PERCENT CHANGE [4]			
	Receipts [1]	Total	Human resources	National defense	Percent of GDP [2]	Surplus or deficit (-)	Total	Federal Gov't Account	Held by— The public Total	Held by— The public Federal Reserve System	As percent of GDP [2]	Receipts	Outlays	Gross Federal debt [3]	Outlays, off-budget
1945	45,159	92,712	1,859	82,965	43.7	-47,553	260,123	24,941	235,182	21,792	122.7	3.2	1.5	27.5	143
1950	39,443	42,562	14,221	13,724	16.0	-3,119	256,853	37,830	219,023	18,331	96.6	0.1	9.6	1.7	524
1955	65,451	68,444	14,908	42,729	17.8	-2,993	274,366	47,751	226,616	23,607	71.3	-6.0	-3.4	1.3	3,983
1960	92,492	92,191	26,184	48,130	18.3	301	290,525	53,686	236,840	26,523	57.6	16.7	0.1	1.1	10,850
1965	116,817	118,228	36,576	50,620	17.6	-1,411	322,318	61,540	260,778	39,100	48.0	3.7	-0.3	2.0	16,529
1970	192,807	195,649	75,349	81,692	19.9	-2,842	380,921	97,723	283,198	57,714	38.7	3.2	6.5	4.1	27,607
1972	207,309	230,681	107,211	79,174	20.1	-23,373	435,936	113,559	322,377	71,426	38.0	10.8	9.8	6.8	36,857
1973	230,799	245,707	119,522	76,681	19.3	-14,908	466,291	125,381	340,910	75,181	36.6	11.3	6.5	7.0	45,589
1974	263,224	269,359	135,783	79,347	19.2	-6,135	483,893	140,194	343,699	80,648	34.5	14.0	9.6	3.8	52,089
1975	279,090	332,332	173,245	86,509	22.0	-53,242	541,925	147,225	394,700	84,993	35.9	6.0	23.4	12.0	60,440
1976	298,060	371,792	203,594	89,619	22.1	-73,732	628,970	151,566	477,404	94,714	37.3	6.8	11.9	16.1	69,609
1976 [5]	81,232	95,975	52,065	22,269	21.6	-14,744	643,561	148,052	495,509	96,702	36.2	(X)	(X)	(X)	19,421
1977	355,559	409,218	221,895	97,241	21.3	-53,659	706,398	157,295	549,103	105,004	36.8	19.3	10.1	12.3	80,716
1978	399,561	458,746	242,329	104,495	21.3	-59,186	776,602	169,477	607,125	115,480	36.0	12.4	12.1	9.9	89,657
1979	463,302	504,032	267,574	116,342	20.7	-40,729	829,470	189,162	640,308	115,594	34.1	16.0	9.8	6.8	99,978
1980	517,112	590,947	313,374	133,995	22.3	-73,835	909,050	199,212	709,838	120,846	34.4	11.6	17.2	9.6	114,329
1981	599,272	678,249	362,022	157,513	22.9	-78,976	994,845	209,507	785,338	124,466	33.6	15.9	14.8	9.4	135,196
1982	617,766	745,755	388,681	185,309	23.9	-127,989	1,137,345	217,560	919,785	134,497	36.4	3.1	10.0	14.3	151,404
1983	600,562	808,380	426,003	209,903	24.4	-207,818	1,371,710	240,114	1,131,596	155,527	41.4	-2.8	8.4	20.6	147,108
1984	666,457	851,846	432,042	227,413	23.1	-185,388	1,564,657	264,159	1,300,498	155,122	42.3	11.0	5.4	14.1	165,813
1985	734,057	946,391	471,822	252,748	23.9	-212,334	1,817,521	317,612	1,499,908	169,806	45.8	10.1	11.1	16.2	176,807
1986	769,091	990,336	481,594	273,375	23.5	-221,245	2,120,629	383,919	1,736,709	190,855	50.3	4.8	4.6	16.7	183,498
1987	854,143	1,003,911	502,196	281,999	22.1	-149,769	2,346,125	457,444	1,888,680	212,040	52.7	11.1	1.4	10.6	193,832
1988	908,954	1,064,140	533,404	290,361	22.1	-155,187	2,601,307	550,507	2,050,799	229,218	54.1	6.4	6.0	10.9	202,691
1989	990,691	1,143,172	568,668	303,559	22.1	-152,481	2,868,039	678,157	2,189,882	220,088	55.4	9.0	7.4	10.3	210,911
1990	1,031,321	1,252,515	619,329	299,331	22.8	-221,194	3,206,564	795,841	2,410,722	234,410	58.5	4.1	9.6	11.8	225,065
1991	1,054,272	1,323,631	689,666	273,292	23.3	-269,359	3,598,498	910,362	2,688,137	258,591	63.4	2.2	5.7	12.2	241,687
1992	1,090,453	1,380,856	772,440	298,350	23.3	-290,403	4,002,136	1,003,302	2,998,834	296,397	67.6	3.4	4.3	11.2	252,339
1993	1,153,535	1,408,675	827,535	291,086	22.5	-255,140	4,351,416	1,103,945	3,247,471	325,653	69.5	5.8	2.0	8.7	266,587
1994	1,257,737	1,460,841	869,414	281,642	22.0	-203,104	4,643,711	1,211,588	3,432,123	355,150	70.0	9.0	3.7	6.7	279,372
1995	1,355,213	1,519,133	923,769	272,066	21.7	-163,920	4,921,025	1,317,612	3,603,412	374,114	70.3	7.8	4.0	6.0	288,664
1996, est.	1,426,775	1,572,411	969,942	265,556	21.4	-145,636	5,207,298	1,438,614	3,768,684	(NA)	71.0	5.3	3.5	5.8	302,119

NA Not available.   X Not applicable.   [1] Includes off-budget receipts and outlays.   [2] Gross domestic product as of calendar year GDP; for calendar year GDP, see section 14.   [3] See text, section 10, for discussion of debt concept.   [4] Change from previous year. For explanation of average annual percent see section 14.   [5] Represents transition quarter, July-Sept.

Source: U.S. Office of Management and Budget, Historical Tables, annual.

No. 513. Federal Receipts, by Source: 1980 to 1996

[In millions of dollars. For fiscal years ending in year shown; see text, section 9. Receipts reflect collections. Covers both Federal funds and trust funds; see text, section 10. Excludes government-sponsored but privately-owned corporations, Federal Reserve System, District of Columbia government, and money held in suspense as deposit funds. See *Historical Statistics, Colonial Times to 1970*, series Y 343-351, and Y 472-487 for related data]

SOURCE	1980	1990	1992	1993	1994	1995	1996, est.
Total receipts [1]	517,112	1,031,321	1,090,453	1,153,535	1,257,737	1,355,213	1,426,775
Individual income taxes	244,069	466,884	475,964	509,680	543,055	590,244	630,873
Corporation income taxes	64,600	93,507	100,270	117,520	140,385	157,004	167,108
Social insurance	157,803	380,047	413,689	428,300	461,475	484,473	507,535
Employment taxes and contributions	138,748	353,891	385,491	396,939	428,810	451,045	473,186
Old-age and survivors insurance	96,581	255,031	273,137	281,735	302,607	284,091	311,713
Disability insurance	16,628	26,625	29,289	30,199	32,419	66,988	55,728
Hospital insurance	23,217	68,556	79,108	81,224	90,062	96,024	101,848
Railroad retirement/ pension fund	2,323	2,292	2,449	2,367	2,323	2,424	2,399
Railroad social security equivalent account	-	1,387	1,508	1,414	1,399	1,518	1,498
Unemployment insurance	15,336	21,635	23,410	26,556	28,004	28,878	29,810
Other retirement contributions	3,719	4,522	4,788	4,805	4,661	4,550	4,539
Excise taxes [1]	24,329	35,345	45,569	48,057	55,225	57,484	53,886
Federal funds	15,563	15,591	21,836	24,522	31,226	26,941	25,412
Alcohol	5,601	5,695	8,011	7,583	7,539	7,216	7,189
Tobacco	2,443	4,081	5,049	5,875	5,691	5,878	5,872
Ozone depletion	-	360	637	854	761	616	205
Trust funds [1]	8,766	19,754	23,733	23,535	23,999	30,543	28,474
Highways	6,620	13,867	16,733	18,039	16,668	22,611	24,554
Airport and airway	1,874	3,700	4,645	3,262	5,189	5,534	2,281
Black lung disability	272	665	626	634	567	608	620
Hazardous substance response	-	818	818	826	807	867	363
Aquatic resources	-	218	271	276	301	306	320
Leaking underground storage	-	122	157	153	152	165	54
Vaccine injury compensations	-	159	118	38	179	138	123
Oil spill liability	-	143	295	229	48	211	34
Estate and gift taxes	6,389	11,500	11,143	12,577	15,225	14,763	15,924
Customs duties	7,174	16,707	17,359	18,802	20,099	19,301	19,313
Federal Reserve deposits	11,767	24,319	22,920	14,908	18,023	23,378	23,752

- Represents or rounds to zero.   [1] Totals reflect interfund and intragovernmental transactions and/or other functions, not shown separately.

Source: U.S. Office of Management and Budget, *Historical Tables*, annual.

No. 514. Federal Trust Fund Receipts, Outlays, and Balances: 1993 to 1995

[In billions of dollars. For fiscal years ending in year shown; see text section 9. Receipts deposited. Outlays on a checks-issued basis less refunds collected. Balances: That which have not been spent. See text, section 10, for discussion of the budget concept and trust funds]

DESCRIPTION	INCOME			OUTLAYS			BALANCES [1]		
	1993	1994	1995, est.	1993	1994	1995, est.	1993	1994	1995, est.
Total [2]	702	749	783	602	653	684	1,080	1,181	1,281
Airport and airway trust fund	4	6	7	7	7	7	13	12	12
Federal employees retirement funds	63	65	67	35	37	38	319	346	375
Federal old-age, survivors and disability insurance trust funds	351	378	399	305	321	339	374	423	483
Foreign military sales trust fund	13	13	13	13	13	14	7	6	6
Health insurance trust fund	156	164	173	146	163	177	149	151	146
Medicare: Hospital insurance	(NA)	106	115	(NA)	103	112	(NA)	130	133
Supplemental medical insurance	(NA)	57	58	(NA)	60	66	(NA)	21	13
Transportation	(NA)	24	28	(NA)	29	29	(NA)	30	30
Surface transportation	(NA)	18	22	(NA)	22	22	(NA)	18	18
Federal employees health benefits	(NA)	16	16	(NA)	16	16	(NA)	8	8
Military retirement trust funds	35	35	34	26	27	27	98	120	127
Railroad retirement trust funds	11	11	12	11	11	11	12	12	13
Unemployment trust funds	41	34	32	40	31	26	37	40	47
Veterans life insurance trust funds	2	2	2	1	2	2	13	14	14
Other trust funds [3]	8	10	11	4	8	9	36	32	34

NA Not available.   [1] Balances available on a cash basis (rather than an authorization basis) at the end of the year. Balances are primarily invested in Federal debt securities.   [2] Includes funds not shown separately.   [3] Effective August 9, 1989, the permanent insurance fund of the FDIC was classified under law as a Federal fund.

Source: U.S. Office of Management and Budget, *Analytical Perspectives*, annual.

No. 515. Federal Budget Outlays—Defense, Human and Physical Resources, and Net Interest Payments: 1940 to 1996

[In millions of dollars. For fiscal year ending in year shown. Minus sign (-) indicates offsets]

YEAR	Outlays, total	National defense	HUMAN RESOURCES Total	Social Security	Income security	Medicare	Health	Education[1]	Veterans benefits	PHYSICAL RESOURCES Total[2]	Transportation	Commerce and housing	Net interest	Other	Undistributed offsets
1940	9,468	1,660	4,139	28	1,514	(NA)	55	1,972	570	2,312	392	550	899	775	-317
1945	92,712	82,965	1,859	267	1,137	(NA)	211	134	110	1,747	3,654	-2,630	3,112	4,418	-1,389
1950	42,562	13,724	14,221	781	4,097	(NA)	268	241	8,834	3,667	967	1,035	4,812	7,955	-1,817
1955	68,444	42,729	14,908	4,427	5,071	(NA)	291	445	4,675	2,732	1,246	92	4,850	6,718	-3,493
1960	92,191	48,130	26,184	11,602	7,378	(NA)	795	968	5,441	7,991	4,126	1,618	6,947	7,760	-4,820
1965	118,228	50,620	36,576	17,460	9,462	(NA)	1,791	2,140	5,723	11,264	5,763	1,157	8,591	17,086	-5,908
1966	134,532	58,111	43,257	20,694	9,671	64	2,543	4,363	5,923	13,410	5,730	3,245	9,386	16,911	-6,542
1967	157,464	71,417	51,272	21,725	10,253	2,748	3,351	6,453	6,743	14,674	5,936	3,979	10,268	17,126	-7,294
1968	178,134	81,926	59,375	23,854	11,806	4,649	4,390	7,634	7,042	16,002	6,316	4,280	11,090	17,786	-8,045
1969	183,640	82,497	66,410	27,298	13,066	5,695	5,162	7,548	7,642	11,869	6,526	-119	12,699	18,151	-7,986
1970	195,649	81,692	75,349	30,270	15,645	6,213	5,907	8,634	8,679	15,574	7,008	2,112	14,380	17,286	-8,632
1971	210,172	78,872	91,901	35,872	22,936	6,622	6,843	9,849	9,778	18,286	8,052	2,366	14,841	16,379	-10,107
1972	230,681	79,174	107,211	40,157	27,638	7,479	8,674	12,529	10,732	19,574	8,392	2,222	15,478	18,828	-9,583
1973	245,707	76,681	119,522	49,090	28,264	8,052	9,356	12,745	12,015	20,614	9,066	931	17,349	24,950	-13,409
1974	269,359	79,347	135,783	55,867	33,699	9,639	10,733	12,457	13,388	25,106	9,172	4,705	21,449	24,423	-16,749
1975	332,332	86,509	173,245	64,658	50,160	12,875	12,930	16,022	16,599	35,449	10,918	9,947	23,244	27,487	-13,602
1976	371,792	89,619	203,594	73,899	60,784	15,834	15,734	18,910	18,433	39,188	13,739	7,619	26,727	27,050	-14,386
1976³	95,975	22,269	52,065	19,763	14,981	4,264	3,924	5,169	3,963	9,512	3,358	931	6,949	9,388	-4,206
1977	409,218	97,241	221,895	85,061	61,044	19,345	17,302	21,104	18,038	40,746	14,829	3,093	29,901	34,315	-14,879
1978	458,746	104,495	242,329	93,861	61,488	22,768	18,524	26,710	18,978	52,591	15,521	6,254	35,458	39,594	-15,720
1979	504,032	116,342	267,574	104,073	66,359	26,495	20,494	30,223	19,951	54,555	17,532	4,686	42,636	40,396	-17,476
1980	590,947	133,995	313,374	118,547	86,540	32,090	23,169	31,843	21,185	65,985	21,329	9,390	52,538	44,996	-19,942
1981	678,249	157,513	362,022	139,584	99,723	39,149	26,866	33,709	22,991	61,752	23,379	8,206	68,774	47,095	-28,041
1982	745,755	185,309	388,681	155,964	107,717	46,567	27,445	27,029	23,958	57,600	20,625	6,256	85,044	51,069	-26,099
1983	808,380	209,903	426,003	170,724	122,598	52,588	28,641	26,606	24,846	57,938	21,334	6,681	89,828	59,023	-33,976
1984	851,846	227,413	432,042	178,223	112,668	57,540	30,417	27,579	25,614	58,614	23,669	6,917	111,123	55,287	-31,957
1985	946,391	252,748	471,822	188,623	128,200	65,822	33,542	29,342	26,292	54,932	25,838	4,229	129,504	68,227	-32,698
1986	990,336	273,375	481,594	198,757	119,796	70,164	35,936	30,585	26,356	68,283	28,117	4,890	136,047	73,713	-33,007
1987	1,003,911	281,999	502,196	207,353	123,250	75,120	39,967	29,724	26,782	81,069	27,272	6,182	138,652	62,588	-36,455
1988	1,064,140	290,361	533,404	219,341	129,332	78,878	44,487	31,938	29,428	80,822	27,608	18,815	151,838	57,222	-36,967
1989	1,143,172	303,559	568,668	232,542	136,031	84,964	48,390	36,674	30,066	80,549	29,485	29,211	169,266	57,822	-37,212
1990	1,252,515	299,331	619,329	248,623	147,022	98,102	57,716	38,755	29,112	125,356	31,099	66,952	184,221	60,893	-36,615
1991	1,323,631	273,292	689,666	269,015	170,276	104,489	71,183	43,354	31,349	134,407	33,333	75,502	194,541	71,081	-39,356
1992	1,380,856	298,350	772,440	287,585	196,948	119,024	89,497	45,248	34,138	74,789	34,407	10,093	199,421	75,136	-39,280
1993	1,408,675	291,086	827,535	304,585	207,250	130,552	99,415	50,012	35,720	45,896	35,004	-22,719	198,811	82,733	-37,386
1994	1,460,841	281,642	869,414	319,565	214,031	144,747	107,122	46,307	37,642	69,685	38,066	-5,118	202,957	74,914	-37,772
1995	1,519,133	272,066	923,769	335,846	220,449	159,855	115,418	54,131	37,938	62,921	39,350	-14,441	232,173	72,989	-44,455
1996, est.	1,572,411	265,756	969,942	350,924	228,342	177,586	121,211	54,131	37,748	66,670	39,769	-10,744	241,059	71,452	-42,268

NA Not available. [1] Also includes training, employment, and social services. [2] Includes outlays not shown separately. [3] Transition quarter, July to September.

Source: U. S. Office of Management and Budget, *Historical Tables*, annual.

No. 516. Federal Budget Outlays in Constant (1987) Dollars: 1980 to 1996

[Dollar amounts in billions of dollars. For fiscal years ending in year shown; see text, section 9. Given the inherent imprecision in deflating outlays, the data shown in constant dollars present a reasonable perspective—not precision. The deflators and the categories that are deflated are as comparable over time as feasible. See headnote, table 512. Minus sign (-) indicates offset]

OUTLAYS	1980	1985	1986	1987	1988	1989	1990	1991	1992	1993	1994	1995	1996, est.
Outlays, total	**832.0**	**1,001.3**	**1,017.3**	**1,003.9**	**1,027.1**	**1,057.2**	**1,110.2**	**1,123.3**	**1,133.4**	**1,125.8**	**1,140.1**	**1,159.3**	**1,170.5**
National defense	187.1	261.2	276.4	282.0	283.3	285.9	272.6	240.5	249.7	237.2	220.6	206.8	197.0
Nondefense outlays	645.0	740.0	740.8	721.9	743.8	771.3	837.5	882.9	883.7	888.6	919.5	952.5	973.5
Payments for individuals	394.9	458.6	467.5	471.3	480.0	490.4	509.6	541.3	587.3	614.9	634.8	660.2	674.2
Direct payments	-348.6	-405.6	-411.4	-413.5	-420.2	-428.8	-442.3	-464.2	-496.6	-517.1	-530.2	-549.9	-563.3
Grants to State and local gov'ts	-46.3	-53.0	-56.2	-57.8	-59.9	-61.6	-67.3	-77.1	-90.7	-97.8	-104.7	-110.3	-110.9
Other grants	81.1	59.8	59.5	50.5	50.7	50.3	51.9	53.6	55.7	57.4	61.0	62.3	66.2
Net interest	74.4	137.3	140.1	138.7	146.5	156.3	163.1	165.4	164.6	160.3	160.5	180.3	183.5
All other	123.0	118.8	107.7	98.0	102.4	108.7	145.4	155.8	108.0	85.1	91.4	81.5	79.2
Undistributed offsetting receipts	-28.5	-34.3	-34.0	-36.5	-35.8	-34.4	-32.4	-33.1	-32.0	-29.2	-28.2	-31.7	-29.5
PERCENT OF GDP													
Outlays, total	22.3	23.9	23.5	22.5	22.1	22.1	22.8	23.3	23.3	22.5	22.0	21.7	21.4
National defense	5.1	6.4	6.5	6.3	6.0	5.9	5.5	4.8	5.0	4.7	4.2	3.9	3.6
Nondefense outlays	17.3	17.5	17.0	16.2	16.1	16.2	17.4	18.5	18.3	17.9	17.8	17.8	17.8
Payments for individuals	10.5	10.8	10.7	10.6	10.4	10.4	10.7	11.5	12.3	12.5	12.4	12.5	12.5
Direct payments	-9.3	-9.5	-9.4	-9.3	-9.1	-9.1	-9.2	-9.8	-10.4	-10.5	-10.4	-10.4	-10.4
Grants to State and local gov'ts	-1.2	-1.2	-1.3	-1.3	-1.2	-1.3	-1.4	-1.6	-1.9	-2.0	-2.0	-2.1	-2.1
Other grants	2.2	1.4	1.4	1.1	1.1	1.1	1.1	1.1	1.1	1.1	1.1	1.1	1.2
Net interest	2.0	3.3	3.2	3.1	3.2	3.3	3.4	3.4	3.4	3.2	3.1	3.3	3.3
All other	3.3	2.9	2.5	2.2	2.2	2.3	3.0	3.2	2.2	1.7	1.8	1.5	1.4
Undistributed offsetting receipts	-0.8	-0.8	-0.8	-0.8	-0.8	-0.7	-0.7	-0.7	-0.7	-0.6	-0.6	-0.6	-0.6
PERCENT OF OUTLAYS													
Outlays, total	100.0	100.0	100.0	100.0	100.0	100.0	100.0	100.0	100.0	100.0	100.0	100.0	100.0
National defense	22.7	26.7	27.6	28.1	27.3	26.6	23.9	20.6	21.6	20.7	19.3	17.9	16.9
Nondefense outlays	77.3	73.3	72.4	71.9	72.7	73.4	76.1	79.4	78.4	79.3	80.7	82.1	83.1
Payments for individuals	47.1	45.2	45.6	46.9	47.0	46.9	46.6	49.1	52.7	55.6	56.3	57.6	58.3
Direct payments	-41.6	-39.9	-40.1	-41.2	-41.2	-41.0	-40.5	-42.1	-44.6	-46.7	-47.0	-48.0	-48.7
Grants to State and local gov'ts	-5.5	-5.2	-5.5	-5.8	-5.9	-5.9	-6.2	-7.0	-8.1	-8.8	-9.3	-9.6	-9.6
Other grants	9.9	6.0	5.8	5.0	5.0	4.8	4.6	4.7	4.7	4.9	5.1	5.2	5.5
Net interest	8.9	13.7	13.7	13.8	14.3	14.8	14.7	14.7	14.4	14.1	13.9	15.3	15.3
All other	14.8	12.0	10.6	9.8	9.9	10.3	13.1	13.8	9.4	7.4	8.0	7.0	6.7
Undistributed offsetting receipts	-3.4	-3.5	-3.3	-3.6	-3.5	-3.3	-2.9	-3.0	-2.8	-2.7	-2.6	-2.9	-2.7

Source: U.S. Office of Management and Budget, Historical Tables, annual.

Federal Government Finances and Employment

No. 517. Federal Outlays, by Branch and Detailed Function: 1990 to 1996

[In millions of dollars. For fiscal years ending in year shown; outlays stated in terms of checks issued or cash payments. See headnote, table 513]

BRANCH AND FUNCTION	1990	1992	1993	1994	1995	1996, est.
Total outlays	1,252,515	1,380,856	1,408,675	1,460,841	1,519,133	1,572,411
Legislative branch.	2,241	2,677	2,406	2,552	2,625	2,695
The Judiciary.	1,646	2,308	2,628	2,677	2,910	3,297
Funds appropriated to President [1]	10,087	11,113	11,526	10,511	11,161	10,445
Departments:						
Agriculture	46,012	56,437	63,144	60,753	56,665	54,840
Commerce	3,734	2,567	2,798	2,915	3,401	3,789
Defense-Military	289,755	286,632	278,574	268,646	259,556	254,325
Defense-Civil	24,975	28,270	29,266	30,407	31,669	32,255
Education	23,109	26,047	30,290	24,699	31,322	30,404
Energy	12,084	15,523	16,942	17,839	17,617	14,678
Health and Human Services	175,531	231,560	253,835	278,901	303,081	327,429
Housing and Urban Development.	20,167	24,470	25,181	25,845	29,044	26,432
Interior	5,790	6,539	6,784	6,900	7,405	6,939
Justice	6,507	9,802	10,170	10,005	10,788	12,964
Labor [2]	25,215	47,078	44,651	37,047	32,090	34,404
State.	3,979	5,007	5,384	5,718	5,344	5,500
Transportation.	28,650	32,491	34,457	37,228	38,777	38,994
Treasury	255,172	292,987	298,804	307,577	348,579	364,956
Veterans Affairs.	28,998	33,897	35,487	37,401	37,771	37,606
Independent agencies:						
Environmental Protection Agency	5,108	5,950	5,930	5,855	6,351	6,329
General Services Administration.	-123	469	743	334	707	469
NASA [3]	12,429	13,961	14,305	13,695	13,378	14,190
Office of Personnel Management	31,949	35,596	36,794	38,556	41,276	42,374
Small Business Administration	692	546	785	779	677	957
Other independent agencies	72,808	18,007	-11,428	10,281	4,199	9,503
Undistributed offsetting receipts.	-98,930	-117,111	-119,711	-123,469	-137,628	-139,866
Outlays, by function	1,252,515	1,380,856	1,408,675	1,460,841	1,519,133	1,572,411
National defense	299,331	298,350	291,086	281,642	272,066	265,556
Dept. of Defense—Military.	289,755	286,892	278,561	268,622	259,442	254,258
Military personnel.	75,622	81,171	75,904	73,137	70,809	67,449
Operation and maintenance	88,340	91,984	94,094	87,880	90,881	91,690
Procurement	80,972	74,881	69,936	61,769	54,982	48,131
R and D, test, and evaluation.	37,458	34,632	36,968	34,762	34,594	34,434
Military construction	5,080	4,262	4,831	4,979	6,823	6,524
Family housing	3,501	3,271	3,255	3,316	3,571	4,028
Other.	-1,218	-3,308	-6,428	2,779	-2,218	2,002
Atomic energy defense activities	8,988	10,619	11,017	11,892	11,777	10,245
Defense related activities	587	839	1,508	1,128	847	1,053
International affairs	13,764	16,107	17,248	17,083	16,434	14,830
International development and						
humanitarian assistance	5,498	6,133	5,827	7,049	7,599	6,895
Conduct of foreign affairs	3,050	3,894	4,325	4,557	4,192	4,138
Other	72,808	18,007	-11,428	10,281	4,199	9,503
Income security	147,022	196,948	207,250	214,031	220,449	228,342
General retirement and disability						
insurance	5,148	5,483	4,347	5,720	5,106	4,973
Federal employee retirement and						
disability.	51,983	57,572	60,047	62,487	65,834	67,936
Housing assistance	15,891	18,904	21,542	23,884	27,524	26,573
Food and nutrition assistance	23,964	32,622	35,148	36,773	37,594	39,034
Other income security	31,146	42,901	48,366	56,439	60,753	63,840
Unemployment compensation	18,889	39,466	37,802	28,729	23,638	25,986
Health.	57,716	89,497	99,415	107,122	115,418	121,211
Health care services	47,642	77,719	86,860	94,259	101,931	107,686
Health research	8,611	10,021	10,794	11,000	11,569	11,533
Consumer and occupational						
health and safety	1,462	1,757	1,762	1,863	1,918	1,992
Medicare.	98,102	119,024	130,552	144,747	159,855	177,586
Social Security	248,623	287,585	304,585	319,565	335,846	350,924
Veterans benefits and services	29,112	34,138	35,720	37,642	37,938	37,748
Income security for veterans	15,241	17,296	17,758	19,613	18,966	18,121
Educ., training, and rehab.	278	783	826	1,115	1,124	1,117
Hospital and medical care.	12,134	14,091	14,812	15,678	16,428	17,081
Housing for veterans	517	901	1,299	197	329	284
Other	943	1,067	1,025	1,039	1,091	1,145

See footnotes at end of table.

No. 517. Federal Outlays, by Branch and Detailed Function: 1990 to 1996—Continued

[In millions of dollars. See headnote, table 513]

FUNCTION	1990	1992	1993	1994	1995	1996, est.
Education, training, employment, and social services	38,755	45,248	50,012	46,307	54,263	54,131
Elementary, secondary, and vocational education.	9,918	12,402	13,481	14,258	14,694	16,002
Higher education	11,107	11,268	14,483	7,876	14,172	11,440
Research and general educ. aids	1,577	1,996	2,040	2,086	2,120	2,269
Training and employment	5,619	6,479	6,700	7,097	7,430	7,617
Other labor services.	810	884	948	958	965	962
Social services	9,723	12,219	12,360	14,031	14,882	15,841
Commerce and housing credit.	66,952	10,093	-22,719	-5,118	-14,441	-10,744
Mortgage credit.	3,845	4,320	1,554	-501	-1,038	-3,999
Postal Service.	2,116	1,169	1,602	1,233	-1,839	-189
Deposit insurance	57,891	2,518	-27,957	-7,570	-17,827	-13,465
Other commerce	3,100	2,085	2,083	1,719	6,263	6,909
Transportation	29,485	33,333	35,004	38,066	39,350	39,769
Ground transportation	18,954	20,347	21,251	23,940	25,297	26,124
Air transportation.	7,234	9,313	10,049	10,146	10,020	9,865
Water transportation.	3,151	3,430	3,423	3,648	3,732	3,471
Other transportation.	146	244	281	333	301	309
Natural resources and environment	17,080	20,025	20,239	21,064	22,105	21,550
Water resources	4,401	4,559	4,258	4,528	4,791	4,729
Conservation and land management. .	3,553	4,581	4,777	5,161	5,318	4,876
Recreational resources.	1,876	2,378	2,620	2,619	2,828	2,568
Pollution control and abatement	5,170	6,075	6,061	6,050	6,512	6,517
Other natural resources	2,080	2,432	2,522	2,706	2,656	2,860
Energy	3,341	4,500	4,319	5,219	4,936	3,217
Supply.	1,976	3,226	3,286	3,899	3,584	2,009
Conservation	365	468	521	582	671	681
Emergency preparedness	442	319	336	275	223	171
Information, policy, and regs	559	486	176	462	458	356
Community/regional develop.	8,498	6,838	9,052	10,454	10,641	12,878
Community development	3,530	3,643	3,681	4,133	4,744	5,519
Area and regional development	2,868	2,315	2,443	2,166	2,615	2,689
Disaster relief and insurance	2,100	881	2,928	4,156	3,282	4,670
Agriculture	11,958	15,205	20,490	15,046	9,773	7,718
Farm income stabilization	9,761	12,666	17,847	12,350	7,015	4,987
Research and services	2,197	2,539	2,643	2,695	2,758	2,731
Net interest	184,221	199,421	198,811	202,957	232,173	241,059
On-budget	200,212	223,059	225,599	232,160	265,478	277,499
Off-budget	-15,991	-23,637	-26,788	-29,203	-33,305	-36,440
Interest on the public debt.	264,724	292,323	292,502	296,278	332,414	344,628
Interest received by on-budget trust funds	-46,321	-54,193	-55,537	-56,494	-59,867	-61,158
Interest received by off-budget trust funds	-15,991	-23,637	-26,788	-29,203	-33,305	-36,440
Other interest	-18,191	-15,071	-11,367	-7,623	-7,069	-5,971
General science/space/technology	14,444	16,409	17,030	16,227	16,724	16,877
Gen. science and basic research	2,835	3,571	3,938	3,863	4,131	3,978
General government	10,734	12,990	13,009	11,303	13,835	13,590
Legislative functions.	1,763	2,124	2,124	2,042	1,995	2,066
Exec. direction and management	160	188	197	244	248	295
Central fiscal operations	6,004	6,612	6,976	7,417	7,936	7,576
General property and records management.	31	692	1,005	590	920	661
General purpose fiscal assistance . . .	2,161	1,865	1,935	1,899	2,057	2,096
Other general government	792	1,775	1,321	987	1,630	1,600
Deductions, offsetting receipts	-361	-480	-739	-2,087	-1,077	-854
Administration of justice	9,993	14,426	14,955	15,256	16,223	18,764
Federal law enforcement.	4,648	6,462	6,674	6,624	6,384	7,475
Federal litigative and judicial	3,577	5,054	5,336	5,470	6,123	6,368
Federal correctional activities.	1,291	2,114	2,124	2,315	2,749	3,013
Criminal justice assistance	477	795	822	847	967	1,908
Undistributed offsetting receipts.	-36,615	-39,280	-37,386	-37,772	-44,455	-42,268

[1] Represents international affairs funds mainly. [2] Includes Pension Benefit Guaranty Corporation. [3] National Aeronautics and Space Administration.

Source: U.S. Office of Management and Budget, Budget of the United States Government, annual.

No. 518. Tax Expenditures, by Function: 1994 to 1997

[**In millions of dollars.** For years ending, **Sept. 30, except as noted.** Tax expenditures are defined as *revenue losses* attributable to provisions of the Federal tax laws which allow a special exclusion, exemption, or deduction from gross income or which provide a special credit, a preferential rate of tax, or a deferral of liability. Represents tax expenditures of **$1 billion or more in 1997**]

DESCRIPTION	1994	1995	1996	1997
National defense:				
Excl. benefits/allowances to Armed Forces personnel	2,000	2,005	2,020	2,030
International affairs: [1]				
Exclusion of income of foreign sales corporations [2]	1,300	1,400	1,500	1,600
Deferral of income from controlled foreign corps. [2]	1,600	1,700	1,800	2,000
Inventory property sales source rules exception	1,200	1,300	1,400	1,500
General science, space, and technology: [1]				
Expensing of research and experimentation [2]	2,235	2,390	2,560	2,735
Energy:				
Excess of percent over cost depletion:				
Oil and gas	785	920	955	1,005
Commerce and housing credit: [1]				
Exclusion of interest on—				
Life insurance savings	9,410	10,365	11,160	12,000
Owner-occupied mortgage subsidy bonds	1,760	1,785	1,775	1,715
Capital gains (excl. agric., timber, iron ore and coal) [2]	5,745	6,135	6,205	6,335
Deferral of capital gains on home sales.	16,640	17,140	17,850	18,180
Exclusion of capital gains on home sales for persons age 55 and over. .	4,690	4,820	4,920	5,010
Deductibility of—				
Mortgage interest on owner-occupied homes	48,430	51,270	54,165	57,240
Property tax on owner-occupied homes . [2]	14,020	14,845	15,680	16,570
Accelerated depreciation on rental housing [2] . . . . [2]	1,145	1,290	1,425	1,580
Accelerated deprec. of bldgs. excl. rental housing [2].	5,145	4,920	4,385	3,580
Step-up basis of capital gains at death . . . . [2]. . . .	26,850	28,305	29,480	30,285
Accelerated depreciation of machinery and equipment [3].	17,620	19,400	20,850	21,885
Graduated corporation income tax rate [2]	3,775	3,960	4,120	4,240
Exception from passive loss rules for $25,000 rental loss	4,765	4,255	4,170	4,120
Transportation:				
Exclusion of reimbursed employee parking expenses	1,845	1,930	2,015	2,100
Community and regional development: [1]				
Credit for low income housing investments	1,925	2,260	2,600	2,945
Education, training, employment, and social services: [1]				
Deductibility of—				
Charitable contributions (education)	1,610	1,705	1,810	1,915
Charitable contributions other than education	2,085	2,210	2,340	2,490
Charitable contributions other than education and health	17,805	18,910	19,995	21,135
Credit for child and dependent care expenses	2,820	2,900	2,995	3,060
Health: [1]				
Excl. of employer contrib. for medical insurance				
premiums and medical care	56,000	60,670	66,620	72,300
Deductibility of medical expenses.	3,380	3,660	3,965	4,295
Excl. of interest on State and local debt for private				
nonprofit health facilities.	1,455	1,495	1,535	1,585
Deductibility of charitable contributions (health).	2,085	2,210	2,340	2,490
Social Security: [1]				
Exclusion of Social Security benefits:				
Disability insurance benefits.	1,815	1,895	2,100	2,300
OASI benefits for retired workers	18,295	16,875	17,395	18,110
Benefits for dependents and survivors	3,620	3,610	3,730	3,940
Income security: [1]				
Exclusion of workmen's compensation benefits	4,240	4,475	4,860	5,120
Net exclusion of pension contributions and earnings:				
Employer plans.	48,750	55,540	59,010	59,490
Individual Retirement Accounts	5,185	6,245	6,375	6,120
Keoghs	3,915	4,435	4,825	5,195
Exclusion of other employee benefits:				
Premiums on group term life insurance	2,750	2,880	3,020	3,170
Special ESOP rules (other than investment credit)	2,155	1,830	1,680	1,575
Additional deduction for the elderly [4]	1,470	1,490	1,510	1,520
Earned income credit.	4,020	5,110	5,740	6,440
Veterans benefits and services: [1]				
Exclusion of veterans disability compensation	1,910	1,985	1,930	1,975
Deferral of interest on savings bonds	1,250	1,360	1,470	1,600
General purpose fiscal assistance: [1]				
Excl. of interest on public State & local debt	11,970	12,350	12,690	13,085
Deductibility of nonbusiness State & local taxes other				
than on owner-occupied homes	25,745	27,250	28,795	30,425
Tax credit for corporations receiving income from doing				
business in United States possessions	2,890	2,630	2,680	2,735

[1] Total (after interactions). [2] Normal tax method. [3] Pre-1983 budget method. [4] Data on calendar year basis.

Source: U.S. Office of Management and Budget, *Budget of the United States Government*, annual.

No. 519. Summary of Federal Debt: 1985 to 1994

[In millions of dollars. As of end of fiscal year]

ITEM	1985	1990	1992	1993	1994
Debt outstanding, total	1,827,470	3,266,073	4,082,871	4,436,171	4,721,293
Public debt securities	1,823,103	3,233,313	4,064,621	4,411,489	4,692,750
Agency securities	4,366	32,758	18,250	24,682	28,543
Securities held by—					
Government accounts, total	317,612	795,907	1,016,453	1,116,713	1,213,115
Public debt securities	316,545	795,762	1,016,330	1,116,693	1,213,098
Agency securities	1,067	145	123	21	17
The public, total	1,509,857	2,470,166	3,066,418	3,319,458	3,508,178
Public debt securities	1,506,558	2,437,551	3,048,291	3,294,796	3,479,652
Agency securities	3,299	32,613	18,127	24,661	28,526
Interest-bearing public debt,	1,821,010	3,210,943	4,061,801	4,408,567	4,689,524
Marketable, total	1,360,179	2,092,759	2,677,476	2,904,910	3,091,602
Treasury bills	384,220	482,454	634,287	658,381	697,295
Treasury notes	776,449	1,218,081	1,566,349	1,734,161	1,867,507
Treasury bonds	199,510	377,224	461,840	497,367	511,800
Nonmarketable, total	460,831	1,118,184	1,384,325	1,503,657	1,597,922
U.S. savings bonds	77,011	122,152	148,266	167,024	176,413
Foreign series: Government	6,638	36,041	37,039	42,459	41,996
Government account series, total	313,928	779,412	1,011,020	1,114,289	1,211,689
Airport and airway trust fund	7,410	14,312	15,090	12,672	12,206
Bank insurance fund	16,130	8,438	4,664	4,325	13,972
Employees life insurance fund	6,312	9,561	12,411	13,575	14,929
Exchange stabilization fund	2,073	1,863	3,314	5,637	7,326
Federal disability insurance trust fund	5,443	11,254	12,774	10,162	6,025
Federal employees retirement funds	127,253	223,229	273,732	301,711	329,602
Federal hospital insurance trust fund	20,721	96,249	120,647	126,078	128,716
Federal Housing Administration	3,485	6,678	6,077	5,380	5,933
Fed. old-age & survivors insurance trust fund	30,968	203,717	306,524	355,510	413,425
Fed. S&L Corp., resolution fund	4,953	929	1,346	828	1,649
Fed. supplementary medical insur. trust fund	10,736	14,286	18,534	23,269	21,489
Government life insurance fund	269	184	134	125	114
Highway trust fund	9,422	9,530	11,167	11,475	7,751
National service life insurance fund	9,296	10,917	11,310	11,666	11,852
Postal Service fund	2,362	3,063	4,679	3,826	1,270
Railroad retirement account	4,232	8,356	10,081	10,457	10,596
Treasury deposit funds	681	304	212	147	130
Unemployment trust fund	16,454	50,186	34,898	36,563	39,745
Other	35,728	106,376	163,426	180,883	184,959
State and local government series	62,778	161,248	157,570	149,449	137,386
Domestic series	(X)	18,886	29,995	29,995	29,995
Other	477	447	435	442	445
MATURITY DISTRIBUTION					
Amount outstanding, privately held	1,185,675	1,841,903	2,363,802	2,562,336	2,719,861
Maturity class:					
Within 1 year	472,661	626,297	808,705	858,135	877,932
1-5 years	402,766	630,144	866,329	978,714	1,128,322
5-10 years	159,383	267,573	295,921	306,663	289,998
10-20 years	62,853	82,713	84,706	94,345	88,208
20 years and over	88,012	235,176	308,141	324,479	335,401

X Not applicable.

Source: U.S. Department of the Treasury, *Treasury Bulletin*, quarterly.

No. 520. U.S. Savings Bonds: 1980 to 1994

[In billions of dollars, except percent. As of end of fiscal year, see text, section 9. See *Historical Statistics, Colonial Times to 1970*, series Y 500, for similar but not exactly comparable data]

ITEM	1980	1985	1987	1988	1989	1990	1991	1992	1993	1994
Amounts outstanding, total [1]	73	77	97	107	114	123	134	149	167	177
Funds from sales	5	5	10	7	8	8	9	14	17	9
Accrued discounts	4	5	6	8	8	8	10	9	9	9
Redemptions [2]	17	6	5	6	7	8	8	7	8	9
Percent of total outstanding	23.0	7.4	5.1	5.6	6.3	6.1	5.6	5.0	4.7	5.1

[1] Interest-bearing debt only for amounts end of year.   [2] Matured and unmatured bonds.

Source: U.S. Dept. of the Treasury, *Treasury Bulletin*, quarterly.

No. 521. Federal Funds—Summary Distribution, by State: 1994

[In millions of dollars. For year ending Sept. 30. Data for grants, salaries and wages and direct payments to individuals are on an expenditures basis; procurement is on obligation basis]

REGION, DIVISION, AND STATE	FEDERAL FUNDS		Defense	Non-defense	Direct payments to individuals	Procurement	Grants to State and local governments	Salaries and wages
	Total [1]	Per capita [2] (dol.)						
U.S. [3]	1,320,132	4,996	227,525	1,092,607	691,666	197,959	214,239	168,951
Northeast	259,892	5,057	28,002	231,889	151,071	26,363	51,473	23,600
New England	71,193	5,365	12,402	58,790	37,284	11,478	13,160	6,631
Maine	6,708	5,409	1,502	5,206	3,518	1,023	1,269	773
New Hampshire	4,636	4,078	607	4,029	2,648	487	956	432
Vermont	2,411	4,157	155	2,256	1,435	109	546	268
Massachusetts	35,374	5,856	6,251	29,123	17,672	6,609	6,261	3,112
Rhode Island	5,473	5,489	845	4,628	3,109	499	1,100	641
Connecticut	16,591	5,066	3,042	13,548	8,902	2,751	3,028	1,405
Middle Atlantic	188,699	4,949	15,600	173,099	113,787	14,885	38,313	16,969
New York	90,346	4,973	5,533	84,813	51,909	6,142	22,445	7,428
New Jersey	37,328	4,723	4,719	32,609	22,685	4,218	6,163	3,739
Pennsylvania	61,025	5,064	5,348	55,677	39,193	4,525	9,705	5,802
Midwest	269,918	4,396	28,404	241,516	160,046	25,441	44,699	26,126
East North Central	178,708	4,138	14,645	164,064	112,810	13,432	30,992	16,253
Ohio	48,023	4,326	5,198	42,825	29,488	4,775	8,366	4,467
Indiana	22,104	3,843	2,470	19,634	13,804	1,674	3,553	2,101
Illinois	49,936	4,249	3,149	46,788	31,367	3,222	8,506	5,402
Michigan	38,975	4,104	2,601	36,374	25,535	2,479	7,117	2,887
Wisconsin	19,670	3,870	1,227	18,443	12,616	1,282	3,450	1,396
West North Central	91,210	5,009	13,759	77,452	47,236	12,009	13,707	9,873
Minnesota	18,797	4,116	1,585	17,212	10,113	1,798	3,515	1,617
Iowa	12,979	4,588	564	12,416	7,590	637	2,015	954
Missouri	31,766	6,019	7,797	23,968	14,889	7,455	3,971	3,332
North Dakota	3,909	6,127	473	3,436	1,704	210	702	566
South Dakota	3,814	5,289	331	3,483	1,848	197	1,114	541
Nebraska	7,439	4,584	936	6,504	4,178	561	1,666	971
Kansas	12,506	4,897	2,073	10,433	6,914	1,151		1,892
South	472,832	5,214	94,127	378,707	239,074	71,431	67,290	78,486
South Atlantic	265,846	5,730	59,141	206,706	128,265	42,355	32,311	52,763
Delaware	2,950	4,179	398	2,552	1,784	167	472	455
Maryland	36,576	7,306	7,588	28,988	13,600	8,228	3,637	7,414
District of Columbia	21,766	38,186	2,308	19,458	2,523	4,103	3,180	11,415
Virginia	45,890	7,004	19,023	26,867	17,168	11,689	2,222	12,147
West Virginia	9,550	5,242	416	9,134	6,003	445	2,166	788
North Carolina	28,858	4,082	5,313	23,546	16,481	1,897	4,862	4,833
South Carolina	17,097	4,666	3,494	13,603	8,839	2,721	2,726	2,503
Georgia	32,067	4,545	8,463	23,604	15,486	4,799	5,028	5,945
Florida	71,092	5,095	12,138	58,954	46,381	8,306	8,018	7,263
East South Central	78,924	4,966	12,039	66,873	42,833	11,459	12,752	9,941
Kentucky	17,504	4,574	2,618	14,886	10,068	1,322	3,096	2,608
Tennessee	25,056	4,842	2,272	22,784	13,461	4,478	3,940	2,669
Alabama	22,280	5,281	4,058	18,222	11,996	3,364	3,209	3,125
Mississippi	14,072	5,272	3,091	10,981	7,308	2,295	2,507	1,539
West South Central	128,074	4,509	22,947	105,128	67,976	17,617	22,227	15,782
Arkansas	11,376	4,638	1,072	10,305	7,298	596	1,966	1,020
Louisiana	21,672	5,022	3,541	18,131	10,656	3,037	5,233	2,136
Oklahoma	15,718	4,824	2,796	12,922	8,943	1,142	2,359	2,627
Texas	79,308	4,315	15,538	63,770	41,079	12,842	12,669	9,999
West	282,254	4,964	60,266	221,985	136,223	51,058	45,865	39,523
Mountain	74,919	4,924	13,634	61,284	35,279	14,151	11,216	11,222
Montana	4,638	5,418	330	4,307	2,250	204	906	611
Idaho	4,965	4,382	401	4,564	2,520	844	778	612
Wyoming	2,344	4,924	249	2,095	1,070	121	714	358
Colorado	18,989	5,194	4,897	14,092	7,987	4,472	2,102	3,540
New Mexico	11,274	6,816	1,764	9,510	4,041	3,596	1,714	1,590
Arizona	19,011	4,665	3,624	15,388	10,558	2,679	2,996	2,269
Utah	7,594	3,980	1,452	6,141	3,444	1,190	1,209	1,479
Nevada	6,104	4,189	917	5,187	3,409	1,045	797	763
Pacific	207,335	4,979	46,632	160,701	100,944	36,907	34,649	28,301
Washington	26,644	4,987	5,028	21,615	13,381	4,086	3,924	4,187
Oregon	13,057	4,231	643	12,415	8,275	493	2,355	1,419
California	155,391	4,944	36,198	119,192	75,466	30,416	26,219	18,830
Alaska	4,640	7,656	1,567	3,072	924	1,007	1,063	1,367
Hawaii	7,603	6,449	3,196	4,407	2,898	905	1,088	2,498
Undistributed	24,318	(X)	15,423	8,896	193	23,043	1,059	23

X Not applicable.   [1] Includes other programs not shown separately.   [2] Based on 1993 population estimates.   [3] Includes Outlying Areas, not shown separately.

Source: U.S. Bureau of the Census, *Federal Expenditures by State for Fiscal Year*, annual.

No. 522. Tax Returns Filed—Examination Coverage: 1988 to 1994

[In thousands, except as indicated. Return classification as Schedule C or C-EZ (nonfarm sole proprietorships) or Schedule F (farm proprietorships) for audit examination purposes was based on the largest source of income on the return and certain other characteristics. Therefore, some returns with business activity are reflected in the nonbusiness individual income tax return statistics in the table below (and vise versa), so that the statistics for the number of returns with Schedule C is not comparable to the number of nonfarm sole proprietorship returns in table 830. Series completely revised starting with fiscal year 1988; data not comparable to earlier years]

YEAR AND ITEM	Returns filed [1]	RETURNS EXAMINED					AVERAGE TAX AND PENALTY PER RETURN (dollars)		
		Total	Percent coverage	By—			Revenue agents [3]	Tax auditors	Service centers
				Revenue agents	Tax auditors	Service centers [2]			
INDIVIDUAL RETURNS									
1988	103,251	1,621	1.57	353	532	736	997,696	2,188	1,950
1989	107,029	1,385	1.29	243	543	599	246,371	1,827	1,649
1990	109,868	1,145	1.04	202	517	426	309,566	1,962	2,432
1991 [4]	112,305	1,313	1.17	200	500	613	664,440	2,398	2,738
1992 [4]	113,829	1,206	1.06	210	537	459	1,365,896	2,280	2,539
1993 [4]	114,719	1,059	0.92	251	506	303	103,250	2,625	2,974
1994 [4]									
Individual, total	113,754	1,226	1.08	364	456	406	246,785	3,113	1,963
1040A, TPI under $25,000 [5]	45,342	471	1.04	102	152	217	8,651	2,753	1,638
Non 1040, TPI under $25,000 [5]	14,719	129	0.88	31	57	41	184,674	1,952	1,813
TPI $25,000 under $50,000 [5]	26,963	143	0.53	30	77	36	45,432	2,028	2,018
TPI $50,000 under $100,000 [5]	15,230	110	0.72	23	54	33	70,110	2,810	1,982
TPI $100,000 and over [5]	3,746	110	2.94	38	28	44	350,155	5,658	3,329
Sch C—TGR under $25,000 [6]	2,418	106	4.39	57	37	13	3,234	2,844	2,165
Sch C—TGR $25,000 under $100,000	2,911	88	3.01	44	33	11	17,442	5,363	1,958
Sch C—TGR $100,000 and over [6]	1,620	58	3.57	35	14	8	80,485	9,442	3,505
Sch F—TGR under $100,000 [6]	536	6	1.16	2	3	1	51,699	1,618	1,172
Sch F—TGR $100,000 and over [6]	270	5	1.74	2	1	1	610,006	3,087	2,274
Corporation (except S Corporation)	2,516	58	2.31	54	(NA)	4	4,254,872	(NA)	2,937
Fiduciary	2,950	5	0.16	2	(NA)	3	122,962	(NA)	289
Estate	73	11	15.17	11	(NA)	0.2	115,187	(NA)	6,311
Gift	218	2	0.85	2	(NA)	(NA)	114,487	(NA)	(NA)
Employment	28,911	62	0.22	54	8	0.3	194,780	1,821	1,524
Excise	859	35	4.06	32	3	0.009	24,140	649	(NA)
Windfall Profit	(NA)	0.5	(NA)	0.02	(NA)	0.02	51,290	(NA)	2,408
Misc. Taxable	(NA)	0.5	(NA)	0.2	(NA)	0.04	140,249	(NA)	634
Partnerships	1,545	8	0.52	5	(NA)	3	(NA)	(NA)	(NA)
S Corporations (nontaxable)	1,906	19	1.02	18	(NA)	1	(NA)	(NA)	(NA)
Miscellaneous nontaxable [7]	(NA)	0.9	(NA)	0.04	(NA)	(NA)	(NA)	(NA)	(NA)

NA Not available. [1] Returns filed in previous calender year. [2] Includes taxpayer contacts by correspondence. [3] Mostly reflects coordinated examination of large corporations and related returns. [4] Includes activities to protect release of funds in Treasury in response to taxpayer efforts to recoup tax previously assessed and paid with penalty. [5] Total positive income, i.e., excludes losses. [6] Total gross receipts. [7] Includes Domestic International Sales Corporations, InterestCharge Domestic International Sales Corporations, Real Estate Investment Morgage Conduits, and other.

Source: U.S. Internal Revenue Service, *Annual Report of the Commissioner and Chief Counsel of the Internal Revenue Service.*

No. 523. Internal Revenue Gross Collections, by Source: 1980 to 1994

[For fiscal year ending in year shown; see text, section 9. See also *Historical Statistics, Colonial Times to 1970,* series Y 358-373]

SOURCE OF REVENUE	COLLECTIONS (bil. dol.)					PERCENT OF TOTAL				
	1980	1985	1990	1993	1994	1980	1985	1990	1993	1994
All taxes	519	743	1,056	1,177	1,276	100.0	100.0	100.0	100.0	100.0
Individual income taxes	288	397	540	586	620	54.9	53.4	51.1	49.8	48.9
Withheld by employers	224	299	388	431	460	43.1	40.2	36.8	36.6	36.1
Employment taxes [1]	128	225	367	412	444	24.7	30.2	34.8	35.0	34.8
Old-age and disability insurance	123	216	358	402	434	23.6	29.0	33.8	34.2	34.0
Unemployment insurance	3	6	6	6	6	0.6	0.8	0.5	0.5	0.5
Corporation income taxes	72	77	110	132	154	13.9	10.4	10.4	11.2	12.1
Estate and gift taxes	7	7	12	13	16	1.3	0.9	1.1	1.1	1.3
Excise taxes	25	37	27	35	43	4.7	5.0	2.6	3.0	3.4
Alcohol and tobacco	8	10	10	14	14	1.6	1.3	1.0	1.1	1.1
Manufactures	7	10	11	17	22	1.3	1.3	1.0	1.4	1.7
Windfall profits tax	3	5	(Z)	(Z)	(Z)	0.6	0.7	(Z)	(Z)	(Z)
Other	10	17	6	5	6	1.9	2.3	0.6	0.4	0.5

Z Less than $50 million or .05 percent. [1] Includes railroad retirement, not shown separately.

Source: U.S. Internal Revenue Service, *Annual Report,* and Bureau of Alcohol, Tobacco, and Firearms, *Alcohol and Tobacco Tax Collections.*

No. 524. Federal Individual Income Tax Returns With Adjusted Gross Income (AGI)—Summary: 1980 to 1993

[Includes Puerto Rico and Virgin Islands. Includes returns of resident aliens, based on a sample of unaudited returns as filed. Data are not comparable for all years because of tax changes and other changes, as indicated. See Statistics of Income, Individual Income Tax Returns publications for a detailed explanation. See Appendix III. See Historical Statistics, Colonial Times to 1970, series Y 393-411, for related data]

ITEM	NUMBER OF RETURNS (1,000)				ADJUSTED GROSS INCOME (mil. dol.)				AVERAGE AGI PER RETURN (dollars)			
	1980	1985	1990	1993	1980	1985	1990	1993	1980	1985	1990	1993
Total returns	93,902	101,660	113,717	114,602	1,613,731	2,305,951	3,405,427	3,723,340	17,185	22,683	29,947	32,489
Form 1040	57,123	67,006	69,270	66,358	1,310,088	1,938,263	2,772,625	2,973,799	22,935	28,927	40,026	44,814
Salaries and wages	83,802	87,198	96,730	98,003	1,349,843	1,928,201	2,599,401	2,892,120	16,108	22,113	26,873	29,511
Interest received	49,020	64,526	70,370	65,233	102,009	182,109	227,084	131,141	2,081	2,822	3,227	2,010
Dividends in AGI	10,739	15,528	22,904	24,691	38,761	55,046	80,169	79,729	3,609	3,545	3,500	3,229
Business or profession profit less loss	8,881	11,900	11,222	11,865	55,129	78,773	141,430	155,705	6,207	6,620	12,603	13,123
Sales of capital assets, net gain less loss, in AGI	9,971	11,126	14,288	18,408	30,029	67,694	114,231	144,172	3,012	6,084	7,995	7,832
Pensions and annuities in AGI	7,374	13,133	17,041	17,441	43,340	95,096	159,294	194,014	5,878	7,241	9,348	11,124
Rents and royalties, net income less loss	8,208	9,964	10,317	10,216	4,105	-10,946	-3,156	8,108	500	-1,099	-306	794
Partnerships and S Corporations [1], profit less loss	3,910	5,488	5,977	5,514	10,099	-2,527	67,022	92,868	2,583	-460	11,213	16,842
Farm profit less loss	2,608	2,621	2,321	2,272	-1,792	-12,005	-434	-3,667	-687	-4,580	-187	-1,614
Statutory adjustments, total	13,149	37,763	16,648	17,180	28,614	95,082	33,974	36,624	2,176	2,518	2,041	2,132
Individual Retirement Arrangements	2,564	16,206	5,224	4,385	3,431	38,212	9,858	8,527	1,338	2,358	1,887	1,945
Self-employed retirement (Keogh) plan	569	676	824	948	2,008	5,182	6,778	8,106	3,529	7,666	8,226	8,551
Married couples who both work	(NA)	24,835	(NA)	(NA)	(NA)	24,615	(NA)	(NA)	(NA)	991	(NA)	(NA)
Exemptions, total [2]	227,925	244,180	227,549	232,920	227,569	253,720	485,985	540,540	998	1,039	2,135	2,321
Age 65 or older	11,847	16,749	(NA)	(NA)	(NA)	(NA)	(NA)	(NA)	(NA)	(NA)	(NA)	(NA)
Blind	185	327	(NA)	(NA)	(NA)	(NA)	(NA)	(NA)	(NA)	(NA)	(NA)	(NA)
Standard and itemized deductions, total [3]	88,105	96,849	112,796	113,662	362,776	554,734	789,942	872,538	4,118	5,728	7,003	7,677
Itemized deductions, total [3]	28,950	39,848	32,175	32,821	218,028	405,024	458,485	490,404	7,531	10,164	14,250	14,942
Medical and dental expenses	19,458	10,777	5,091	5,490	14,972	22,926	21,457	26,510	769	2,127	4,215	4,829
Taxes paid	28,749	39,548	31,594	32,264	69,404	128,085	140,011	169,850	2,414	3,239	4,432	5,264
Interest paid	26,677	36,287	29,395	27,498	91,187	180,095	208,354	200,190	3,418	4,963	7,088	7,280
Contributions	26,621	36,162	29,230	29,799	25,810	47,963	57,243	68,354	970	1,326	1,958	2,294
Taxable income [4]	88,105	96,124	93,148	90,831	1,279,985	1,820,741	2,263,661	2,453,543	14,528	18,942	24,302	27,012
Income tax before credits	76,136	85,994	93,089	90,755	256,294	332,165	453,128	508,894	3,366	3,863	4,868	5,607
Tax credits, total [2] [5]	19,674	20,995	12,484	13,222	7,216	10,248	6,831	8,159	367	488	547	617
Child care	4,231	8,418	6,144	6,090	956	3,128	2,549	2,559	226	372	415	420
Elderly and disabled	562	463	339	223	135	109	61	49	240	235	180	220
Residential energy	4,670	2,979	(NA)	(NA)	562	812	(NA)	(NA)	120	273	(NA)	(NA)
Foreign tax	393	454	772	1,293	1,342	783	1,682	2,218	3,415	1,725	2,179	1,715
General business credit [6]	(NA)	4,614	263	255	(NA)	4,791	616	578	(NA)	1,038	2,342	2,267
Income tax, total [7]	73,906	82,846	89,862	86,436	250,341	325,710	447,127	502,788	3,387	3,932	4,976	5,817

NA Not available. [1] S Corporations are certain small corporations with up to 35 shareholders (25 for 1982; 15 for 1980-81; 10 for 1970-75), mostly individuals, electing to be taxed at the shareholder level. [2] Includes items not shown separately. Beginning 1991, total exemptions amount is after limitation. [3] For 1985, includes charitable deduction for nonitemizers. Starting 1989, includes additional standard deductions for age 65 or older or for blindness. Beginning 1991, total itemized deductions are after limitation. [4] For 1980 and 1985, includes amounts "taxed" at zero percent. [5] For 1981, includes tax reduction credit. [6] Investment credit was included in the more-inclusive general business tax credit starting with 1984. With exceptions, investment credit was repealed effective 1986. [7] Includes minimum tax or alternative minimum tax.

Source: U.S. Internal Revenue Service, Statistics of Income Bulletin, and Statistics of Income, Individual Income Tax Returns, annual.

No. 525. Individual Income Tax Returns—Number, Income Tax, and Average Tax, by Size of Adjusted Gross Income: 1992 and 1993

[Number in thousands; money amounts in billions of dollars, except as indicated]

SIZE OF ADJUSTED GROSS INCOME	NUMBER OF RETURNS		ADJUSTED GROSS INCOME (AGI)		TAXABLE INCOME		INCOME TAX TOTAL [1]		TAX AS PERCENT OF AGI [2]		AVERAGE TAX ($1,000) [2]	
	1992	1993, prel.	1992	1993, prel.	1992	1993, prel.	1992	1993, prel.	1992	1993, prel.	1992	1993, prel.
Total..........	113,605	114,602	3,629.1	3,723.3	2,395.7	2,453.5	476.2	502.8	13.7	13.5	5.5	5.8
Less than $1,000 [3]	3,515	3,550	-49.9	-50.7	0.1	0.1	0.1	0.1	3.2	-0.2	0.1	0.2
$1,000-$2,999	6,568	6,472	13.1	12.8	0.9	0.7	0.1	0.1	4.7	0.9	0.1	0.1
$3,000-$4,999	5,890	5,748	23.5	22.9	1.3	1.3	0.2	0.2	3.2	1.0	0.1	0.2
$5,000-$6,999	5,962	5,826	35.8	35.0	3.6	2.9	0.6	0.4	3.5	1.3	0.2	0.2
$7,000-$8,999	5,909	5,964	47.2	47.6	7.8	7.2	1.2	1.1	4.2	2.4	0.3	0.3
$9,000-$10,999 ...	5,694	5,701	56.8	56.9	12.9	12.5	1.9	1.8	5.9	3.3	0.6	0.6
$11,000-$12,999...	5,583	5,496	66.9	65.9	19.1	18.4	2.7	2.6	6.4	4.0	0.8	0.8
$13,000-$14,999 ..	4,968	5,210	69.5	72.7	24.7	24.4	3.3	3.2	6.9	4.4	1.0	0.9
$15,000-$16,999 ..	4,871	4,860	77.9	77.7	32.2	29.6	4.2	3.8	7.4	4.9	1.2	1.1
$17,000-$18,999 ..	4,506	4,306	81.0	77.5	36.8	34.3	4.9	4.4	7.1	5.7	1.3	1.3
$19,000-$21,999 ..	6,215	6,253	127.3	127.9	64.5	64.4	9.1	8.9	7.6	7.0	1.6	1.5
$22,000-$24,999 ..	5,451	5,427	128.0	127.4	70.9	70.4	10.5	10.4	8.3	8.1	2.0	2.0
$25,000-$29,999 ..	7,590	7,784	208.2	212.8	123.6	124.5	18.5	18.5	9.0	8.7	2.5	2.4
$30,000-$39,999 ..	12,325	12,358	428.5	429.4	274.0	272.8	43.7	43.3	10.3	10.1	3.6	3.5
$40,000-$49,999 ..	9,009	9,072	403.1	405.4	269.2	269.8	43.6	43.5	10.9	10.7	4.9	4.8
$50,000-$74,999 ..	11,796	12,248	712.3	741.5	495.9	516.9	88.5	91.1	12.4	12.3	7.5	7.5
$75,000-$99,999 ..	3,988	4,225	340.6	359.9	247.4	262.8	51.6	54.1	15.1	15.0	12.9	12.8
$100,000-$199,999.	2,811	3,108	368.4	408.0	280.7	313.4	67.4	75.3	18.3	18.5	24.0	24.3
$200,000-$499,999.	746	786	218.6	228.0	186.1	193.4	52.0	58.3	23.8	25.6	69.8	74.2
$500,000-$999,999.	141	141	95.4	94.4	84.3	82.9	24.8	28.3	26.0	30.0	175.7	201.5
$1,000,000 or more.	67	66	176.9	170.6	159.7	150.9	47.5	53.2	26.9	31.2	706.7	801.6

[1] Consists of income after credits, and alternative minimum tax.   [2] Computed using taxable returns only.   [3] In addition to low income taxpayers, this size class (and others) includes taxpayers with "tax preferences," not reflected in adjusted gross income or taxable income which are subject to the "alternative minimum tax" (included in total income tax).

Source: U.S. Internal Revenue Service, *Statistics of Income Bulletin*, quarterly and *Statistics of Income, Individual Income Tax Returns*, annual.

No. 526. Individual Income Tax Returns—Itemized Deductions and Statutory Adjustments, by Size of Adjusted Gross Income: 1993

[Preliminary]

ITEM	Unit	ADJUSTED GROSS INCOME CLASS							
		Total	Under $10,000	$10,000 to $19,999	$20,000 to $29,999	$30,000 to $39,999	$40,000 to $49,999	$50,000 to $99,999	$100,000 and over
Returns with itemized deductions:									
Number [1]	1,000 ..	32,821	782	2,305	3,562	4,539	4,952	12,820	3,863
Amount.................	Mil. dol .	490,404	8,406	22,416	33,757	46,551	55,387	186,694	137,193
Medical and dental expenses:									
Returns.................	1,000 ..	5,490	486	1,241	1,136	957	674	887	108
Amount	Mil. dol .	26,510	3,470	6,530	4,159	3,457	3,071	4,435	1,388
Taxes paid: Returns, total.....	1,000 ..	32,264	667	2,139	3,474	4,484	4,912	12,744	3,844
State, local income taxes..	1,000 ..	27,596	346	1,490	2,951	3,830	4,328	11,244	3,407
Real estate taxes.......	1,000 ..	29,083	550	1,780	2,973	3,913	4,395	11,834	3,637
Amount, total	Mil. dol .	169,850	1,234	3,995	7,844	12,446	16,367	63,283	64,682
State, local income taxes..	Mil. dol .	101,989	199	936	3,017	5,793	8,490	36,211	47,343
Real estate taxes.......	Mil. dol .	61,298	966	2,789	4,393	5,969	7,034	24,403	15,745
Interest paid: Returns	1,000 ..	27,498	453	1,504	2,804	3,768	4,262	11,384	3,323
Amount	Mil. dol .	200,190	3,029	8,038	13,283	20,874	24,692	81,636	48,638
Home mortgages interest:									
Returns.................	1,000 ..	27,173	446	1,487	2,779	3,734	4,235	11,303	3,188
Amount	Mil. dol .	188,594	2,952	7,878	13,030	20,407	24,117	79,295	40,914
Contributions: Returns.......	1,000 ..	29,799	517	1,862	3,033	4,057	4,500	12,104	3,726
Amount	Mil. dol .	68,354	580	2,614	3,810	5,591	6,892	23,360	25,508
Employee Business Expense:									
Returns.................	1,000 ..	9,263	64	431	907	1,389	1,551	3,952	969
Amount	Mil. dol .	28,213	197	1,373	2,278	3,350	3,804	11,632	5,579
Returns with statutory adjust-									
ments: [2] Returns	1,000 ..	17,180	2,939	3,021	2,689	2,170	1,732	3,164	1,463
Amount of adjustments	Mil. dol .	36,624	2,144	3,451	3,452	3,647	2,945	8,828	12,156
Payments to IRA's: [3] Returns....	1,000 ..	4,385	266	724	1,019	854	576	642	307
Amount...............	Mil. dol .	8,527	509	1,322	1,585	1,690	849	1,643	929
Payments to Keogh plans:									
Returns.................	1,000 ..	948	11	35	63	53	72	318	395
Amount	Mil. dol .	8,160	32	77	135	160	243	1,716	5,797
Alimony paid: Returns.........	1,000 ..	628	52	62	73	77	77	183	103
Amount	Mil. dol .	5,305	285	246	299	334	591	1,533	2,018

[1] After limitations.   [2] Includes disability income exclusion, employee business expenses, moving expenses, forfeited interest penalty, alimony paid, deduction for expense of living abroad, and other data not shown separately.   [3] Individual Retirement Account.

Source: U.S. Internal Revenue Service, *Statistics of Income, Individual Income Tax Returns*, annual.

No. 527. Federal Individual Income Tax Returns—Adjusted Gross Income (AGI), by Source of Income and Income Class for Taxable Returns: 1993

[In millions of dollars, except as indicated. Minus sign (-) indicates net loss was greater than net income. See headnote, table 524]

ITEM	Total [1]	Under $10,000	$10,000 to $19,999	$20,000 to $29,999	$30,000 to $39,999	$40,000 to $49,999	$50,000 to $99,999	$100,000 and over
Number of returns(1,000)	86,435	10,621	17,152	16,809	12,285	9,037	16,436	4,096
Source of income:								
Adjusted gross income (AGI)	3,563,976	60,862	258,789	414,731	426,792	403,802	1,099,056	899,943
Salaries and wages	2,723,086	49,348	187,910	339,167	360,875	337,999	915,569	532,218
Percent of AGI for taxable returns . .	76.4	81.1	72.6	81.8	84.6	83.7	83.3	59.1
Interest received	117,638	4,872	15,581	12,403	10,351	9,683	25,538	39,209
Dividends in AGI	74,749	1,757	5,185	5,491	5,502	5,434	17,448	33,933
Business; profession, net profit less loss	144,423	2,441	8,176	12,147	11,925	11,105	39,354	59,275
Pensions and annuities in AGI	181,212	4,295	31,351	31,611	23,502	21,934	49,322	19,196
Sales of property, [2] net gain less loss .	136,926	2,312	2,661	4,042	3,953	4,760	19,423	99,775
Rents and royalties, net income less loss	12,077	63	491	239	-348	-18	-429	12,080
Other sources, [3] net.	173,865	-4,226	7,434	9,631	11,032	12,905	32,831	104,257
Percent of all returns: [4]								
Number of returns.	75.4	12.3	19.8	19.5	14.2	10.5	19.0	4.7
Adjusted gross income.	95.7	1.7	7.3	11.6	12.0	11.3	30.8	25.3
Salaries and wages.	94.2	1.8	6.9	12.5	13.3	12.4	33.6	19.5
Interest received.	89.7	4.1	13.2	10.5	8.8	8.2	21.7	33.3
Dividends in AGI.	93.8	2.4	6.9	7.4	7.4	7.3	23.3	45.4
Business; profession, net profit less loss.	92.8	1.7	5.7	8.4	8.3	7.7	27.3	41.0
Pensions and annuities in AGI	93.4	2.4	17.3	17.4	13.0	12.1	27.2	10.6
Sales of property [2] net gain less loss . . .	91.8	1.7	1.9	3.0	2.9	3.5	14.2	72.9

[1] Includes a small number of taxable returns with no adjusted gross income. [2] Includes sales of capital assets and other property; net gain less loss. [3] Excludes rental passive losses disallowed in the computation of AGI; net income less loss. [4] Without regard to taxability.

Source: U.S. Internal Revenue Service, *Statistics of Income,*

No. 528. Federal Individual Income Tax Returns, by State, 1993

YEAR, DIVISION, STATE	Number of returns [1] (1,000)	Adjusted gross income (AGI) [2]	INCOME TAX Total [3] (mil. dol.)	INCOME TAX Per capita [4] (dol.)	YEAR, DIVISION, STATE	Number of returns [1] (1,000)	Adjusted gross income (AGI) [2]	INCOME TAX Total [3] (mil. dol.)	INCOME TAX Per capita [4] (dol.)
U.S.	**115,601**	**3,720,611**	**532,213**	**2,065**	VA	2,940	101,990	14,151	2,186
Northeast . .	**23,116**	**841,122**	**127,471**	**2,486**	WV	695	18,543	2,328	1,281
N.E	**6,134**	**225,028**	**34,153**	**2,608**	NC	3,166	92,645	11,992	1,725
ME	549	15,160	1,896	1,529	SC	1,581	43,494	5,327	1,467
NH. . . .	537	18,276	2,697	2,399	GA	3,023	94,470	12,947	1,876
VT	264	7,631	988	1,715	FL	6,282	193,995	29,539	2,152
MA . . .	2,784	101,965	15,514	2,578	**E.S.C . . .**	**6,620**	**183,687**	**24,485**	**1,559**
RI	447	14,341	1,975	1,975	KY	1,549	43,119	5,603	1,477
CT. . . .	1,553	67,655	11,443	3,491	TN	2,254	65,754	9,344	1,834
M.A.	**16,982**	**616,094**	**92,958**	**2,444**	AL	1,760	49,378	6,448	1,542
NY	7,844	293,197	45,165	2,488	MS	1,057	25,436	3,090	1,170
NJ	3,760	151,586	23,617	3,005	**W.S.C . . .**	**11,739**	**341,442**	**49,311**	**1,763**
PA	5,378	171,311	24,176	2,010	AR	995	25,665	3,250	1,340
Midwest . . .	**27,448**	**873,575**	**122,815**	**2,012**	LA	1,700	46,472	6,345	1,479
E.N.C . . .	**19,393**	**628,566**	**89,265**	**2,078**	OK	1,329	36,052	4,701	1,454
OH	5,101	153,217	20,993	1,898	TX	7,715	233,253	35,015	1,943
IN	2,549	78,734	10,883	1,907	**West. . . . . .**	**24,466**	**803,996**	**113,382**	**2,023**
IL	5,307	186,988	28,530	2,441	**Mountain . .**	**6,584**	**200,127**	**27,701**	**1,875**
MI	4,142	137,427	19,234	2,033	MT	376	9,594	1,243	1,478
WI	2,294	72,200	9,625	1,908	ID	468	13,272	1,719	1,563
W.N.C . . .	**8,055**	**245,009**	**33,550**	**1,855**	WY . . .	214	6,483	968	2,060
MN	2,061	69,040	9,577	2,117	CO	1,688	55,893	8,136	2,283
IA	1,256	35,719	4,648	1,648	NM . . .	699	18,364	2,314	1,432
MO	2,283	68,569	9,501	1,815	AZ	1,707	50,431	6,701	1,699
ND. . . .	284	7,600	1,030	1,617	UT	748	22,500	2,788	1,499
SD	321	8,546	1,231	1,580	NV	684	23,590	3,832	2,773
NE	741	21,073	2,814	1,745	**Pacific . . .**	**17,882**	**603,869**	**85,681**	**2,076**
KS	1,109	34,462	4,749	1,873	WA	2,401	82,320	12,132	2,307
South	**38,973**	**1,178,046**	**165,176**	**1,847**	OR	1,357	41,830	5,584	1,840
S.A.	**20,614**	**652,917**	**91,380**	**1,998**	CA	13,218	451,175	63,907	2,047
DE. . . .	331	11,424	1,572	2,252	AK	350	10,025	1,551	2,594
MD . . .	2,307	86,120	11,904	2,401	HI	556	18,519	2,507	2,150
DC. . . .	289	10,236	1,620	2,798	Other [5]. . .	1,057	23,872	3,370	(NA)

NA Not available. [1] Includes returns filed by nonresident aliens and certain self-employment tax returns. [2] Less deficit. [3] Includes additional tax for tax preferences, self-employment tax, tax from investment credit recapture, and other income-related taxes. Total is before earned income credit. [4] Based on resident population as of July 1. [5] Includes returns filed from Army Post Office and Fleet Post Office addresses by members of the armed forces stationed overseas; returns by other U.S. citizens abroad; and returns filed by residents of Puerto Rico with income from sources outside of Puerto Rico or with income earned as U.S. Government employees.

Source: U.S. Internal Revenue Service, *Statistics of Income Bulletin.* Quarterly.

No. 529. Federal Individual Income Tax—Tax Liability, Effective and Marginal Tax Rates, for Selected Income Groups: 1985 to 1994

[Refers to income after exclusions. Effective rate represents tax liability divided by stated income. The marginal tax rate is the percentage of the first additional dollar of income which would be paid in income tax. Computations assume the low income allowance, standard deduction, zero bracket amount, or itemized deductions equal to 10 percent of adjusted gross income, whichever is greatest. Excludes self employment tax. See *Historical Statistics, Colonial Times to 1970*, series Y 412-439, for similar data on net income]

ADJUSTED GROSS INCOME	1985	1988	1990	1991	1992	1993	1994
TAX LIABILITY							
Single person, no dependents:							
$5,000 [1]	177	8	-	-	-	-	-306
$10,000	888	758	705	668	615	593	563
$20,000	2,854	2,258	2,205	2,168	2,115	2,093	2,063
$25,000	4,125	3,294	2,988	2,918	2,865	2,843	2,813
$35,000	6,916	5,954	5,718	5,573	5,360	5,233	5,093
$50,000	12,067	9,734	9,498	9,353	9,168	9,069	8,957
$75,000	22,195	17,154	16,718	16,134	15,867	15,719	15,555
Married couple, two dependents: [2]							
$5,000 [3]	-550	-800	-700	-865	-920	-975	-1,500
$10,000 [3]	132	-858	-953	-1,235	-1,384	-1,511	2,528
$20,000 [4]	1,682	1,080	926	701	409	235	-359
$25,000	2,566	1,830	1,703	1,605	1,470	1,410	1,275
$35,000	4,916	3,330	3,203	3,105	2,970	2,910	2,828
$50,000	9,086	6,549	5,960	5,576	5,220	5,160	5,078
$75,000	17,649	12,849	12,386	12,072	11,670	11,471	11,216
EFFECTIVE RATE							
Single person, no dependents:							
$5,000 [1]	3.5	0.2	-	-	-	-	-6.1
$10,000	8.9	7.6	7.1	6.7	6.2	5.9	5.6
$20,000	14.3	11.3	11.0	10.8	10.6	10.5	10.3
$25,000	16.5	13.2	12.0	11.7	11.5	11.4	11.3
$35,000	19.8	17.0	16.3	15.9	15.3	15.0	14.6
$50,000	24.1	19.5	19.0	18.7	18.3	18.1	17.9
$75,000	29.6	22.9	22.3	21.5	21.2	21.0	20.7
Married couple, two dependents: [2]							
$5,000 [3]	-11.0	-14.0	-14.0	-17.3	-18.4	-19.5	-30.0
$10,000 [3]	1.3	-8.6	-9.5	-12.4	-13.8	-15.1	-25.3
$20,000 [4]	8.4	5.4	4.6	3.5	2.0	1.2	-1.8
$25,000	10.3	7.3	6.8	6.4	5.9	5.6	5.1
$35,000	14.0	9.5	9.2	8.9	8.5	8.3	8.1
$50,000	18.2	13.1	11.9	11.2	10.4	10.3	10.2
$75,000	23.5	17.1	16.5	16.1	15.6	15.3	15.0
MARGINAL TAX RATE							
Single person, no dependents:							
$5,000 [1]	12	15	-	-	-	-	7.7
$10,000	16	15	15	15	15	15	15
$20,000	26	15	15	15	15	15	15
$25,000	26	28	28	28	15	15	15
$35,000	34	28	28	28	28	28	28
$50,000	42	28	28	28	28	28	28
$75,000	48	33	33	31	31	31	31
Married couple, two dependents: [2]							
$5,000 [3]	-11.0	-14	-14	-17.3	-18.4	-19.5	-30
$10,000 [3]	24.2	10	-	-	-	-	-
$20,000 [4]	16	15	25	27.4	28.1	28.9	32.7
$25,000	18	15	15	15	15	15	32.7
$35,000	25	15	15	15	15	15	15
$50,000	33	28	28	28	15	15	15
$75,000	42	28	28	28	28	28	28

- Represents zero. [1] 1994, refundable earned income credit. [2] Only one spouse is assumed to work. [3] Refundable earned income credit. [4] Beginning 1990, refundable earned income credit.

Source: U.S. Dept. of the Treasury, Office of Tax Analysis, unpublished data.

No. 530. Federal Individual Income Tax—Current Income Equivalent to 1990 Constant Income for Selected Income Groups: 1985 to 1994

[Constant 1990 dollar incomes calculated by using the NIPA Personal Consumption Expenditure (PCE) deflator: 1970, 35.6; 1985, 93.1; 1988, 104.2; 1990, 114.9; 1991, 119.7; 1992, 123.5; 1993, 126.6; and 1994, 129.4 (estimated). See *Historical Statistics, Colonial Times to 1970*, series 412-439, for similar data on net income]

ADJUSTED GROSS INCOME	1985	1988	1990	1991	1992	1993	1994
REAL INCOME EQUIVALENT							
Single person, no dependents:							
$5,000	4,050	4,530	5,000	5,210	5,370	5,510	5,630
$10,000.	8,100	9,070	10,000	10,420	10,750	11,020	11,260
$20,000.	16,210	18,140	20,000	20,840	21,500	22,040	22,520
$25,000.	20,260	22,670	25,000	26,040	26,870	27,550	28,150
$35,000.	28,360	31,740	35,000	36,460	37,620	38,560	39,420
$50,000.	40,510	45,340	50,000	52,090	53,740	55,090	56,310
$75,000.	60,770	68,020	75,000	78,130	80,610	82,640	84,460
Married couple, two dependents: [1]							
$5,000	4,050	4,530	5,000	5,210	5,370	5,510	5,630
$10,000.	8,100	9,070	10,000	10,420	10,750	11,020	11,260
$20,000.	16,210	18,140	20,000	20,840	21,500	22,040	22,520
$25,000.	20,260	22,670	25,000	26,040	26,870	27,550	28,150
$35,000.	28,360	31,740	35,000	36,460	37,620	38,560	39,420
$50,000.	40,510	45,340	50,000	52,090	53,740	55,090	56,310
$75,000.	60,770	68,020	75,000	78,130	80,610	82,640	84,460
EFFECTIVE RATE (percent)							
Single person, no dependents:							
$5,000 [2]	1.7	-	-	-	-	-	-4.6
$10,000.	7.4	6.8	7.1	7.0	6.8	6.8	6.7
$20,000.	12.3	10.9	11.0	11.0	10.9	10.9	10.8
$25,000.	14.4	11.7	12.0	11.9	11.7	11.7	11.7
$35,000.	17.7	16.2	16.3	16.3	16.1	16.0	16.0
$50,000.	21.5	18.9	19.0	19.0	18.8	18.8	18.7
$75,000.	26.6	22.2	22.3	21.8	21.6	21.6	21.5
Married couple, two dependents: [1]							
$5,000 [3]	-11.0	-14.0	-14.0	-17.3	-18.4	-19.5	-30.0
$10,000 [3]	-3.8	-9.6	-9.5	-11.9	-12.9	-13.7	-22.0
$20,000 [4]	6.7	4.2	4.6	4.5	3.9	3.7	2.1
$25,000.	8.5	6.5	6.8	6.8	6.5	6.5	6.4
$35,000.	11.6	9.0	9.2	9.1	8.9	8.9	8.9
$50,000.	15.6	11.6	11.9	11.8	11.4	11.4	11.2
$75,000.	20.7	16.3	16.5	16.5	16.2	16.2	16.1
MARGINAL TAX RATE (percent)							
Single person, no dependents:							
$5,000 [2]	11	-	-	-	-	-	7.7
$10,000.	15	15	15	15	15	15	15
$20,000.	20	15	15	15	15	15	15
$25,000.	26	15	28	28	15	15	15
$35,000.	30	28	28	28	28	28	28
$50,000.	38	28	28	28	28	28	28
$75,000.	42	33	33	31	31	31	31
Married couple, two dependents: [1]							
$5,000 [3]	-11	-14	-14	-17.3	-18.4	-19.5	-30
$10,000 [3]	23.2	-	-	-	-	-	17.7
$20,000 [4]	14	25	25	27.4	28.1	28.9	32.7
$25,000.	16	15	15	15	15	15	15
$35,000.	22	15	15	15	15	15	15
$50,000.	28	28	28	28	28	28	28
$75,000.	38	28	28	28	28	28	28

- Represents zero.   [1] Only one spouse is assumed to work.   [2] 1994, refundable earned income credit.   [3] Refundable earned income credit.   [4] Beginning 1988, refundable earned income credit.

Source: U.S. Dept. of the Treasury, Office of Tax Analysis, unpublished data.

No. 531. Federal Civilian Employment, by Branch and Agency: 1990 to 1995

[As of September 30]

AGENCY	1990	1993	1994	1995	PERCENT CHANGE 1990-95	PERCENT CHANGE 1994-95
Total, all agencies	3,128,267	3,013,508	2,971,584	2,918,674	-6.7	-1.8
Legislative Branch, total [1]	37,495	38,258	35,357	33,367	-11.0	-5.6
Judicial Branch	23,605	28,120	28,035	28,993	22.8	3.4
Executive Branch, total	3,067,167	2,947,130	2,908,192	2,856,314	-6.9	-1.8
Executive Departments	2,065,542	1,972,569	1,907,895	[2]1,781,220	-13.8	-6.6
State.	25,288	26,077	25,596	24,859	-1.7	-2.9
Treasury	158,655	156,073	156,373	155,951	-1.7	-0.3
Defense	1,034,152	921,179	879,878	830,738	-19.7	-5.6
Justice	83,932	97,898	97,910	103,262	23.0	5.5
Interior	77,679	84,864	80,704	76,439	-1.6	-5.3
Agriculture	122,594	124,199	119,558	113,321	-7.6	-5.2
Commerce	69,920	38,680	37,642	36,803	-47.4	-2.2
Labor	17,727	17,407	16,732	16,204	-8.6	-3.2
Health & Human Services.	123,959	130,216	128,244	[4]59,788	-51.8	-53.4
Housing & Urban Development	13,596	13,459	13,218	11,822	-13.0	-10.6
Transportation	67,364	69,144	64,896	63,552	-5.7	-2.1
Energy	17,731	20,336	19,899	19,589	10.5	-1.6
Education	4,771	5,002	4,813	4,988	4.5	3.6
Veterans Affairs [3]	248,174	268,035	262,432	263,904	6.3	0.6
Independent agencies [1]	999,894	972,930	998,729	[2]1,073,521	7.4	7.5
American Battle Monuments Comm . . .	396	394	380	374	-5.6	-1.6
Armed Forces Retirement Home	966	875	1,056	960	-0.6	-9.1
Arms Control & Disarmament Agency . .	216	216	233	266	23.1	14.2
Board of Gov Fed Reserve System . . .	1,525	1,678	1,669	1,715	12.5	2.8
Commodity Futures Trading Comm. . . .	542	551	551	544	0.4	-1.3
Consumer Product Safety Comm	520	532	484	486	-6.5	0.4
Corp Natl & Community Service.	(X)	33	607	574	(X)	-5.4
Defense Nuclear Facilities Safety Bd . .	25	92	102	106	324.0	3.9
Environmental Protection Agency	17,123	18,415	18,092	17,910	4.6	-1.0
Equal Employment Opportunity Comm .	2,880	2,868	2,914	2,796	-2.9	-4.0
Export-Import Bank of US.	343	467	462	443	29.2	-4.1
Farm Credit Administration	515	436	412	380	-26.2	-7.8
Federal Communications Commission. .	1,778	1,807	2,015	2,116	19.0	5.0
Federal Deposit Insurance Corporation..	17,641	21,701	18,775	14,765	-16.3	-21.4
Federal Election Commission	250	272	316	327	30.8	3.5
Fed. Emergency Managmt Agency	3,137	5,099	5,221	5,256	67.5	0.7
Federal Housing Finance Board [4]	65	114	104	113	73.8	8.7
Federal Labor Relations Auth	251	250	229	221	-12.0	-3.5
Federal Maritime Commission	230	201	200	169	-26.5	-15.5
Federal Med & Council Svc.	316	308	309	297	-6.0	-3.9
Fed Ret Thrift Invest Board	93	102	105	110	18.3	4.8
Federal Trade Commission	988	971	969	996	0.8	2.8
General Services Administration	20,277	20,502	19,257	16,500	-18.6	-14.3
Holocaust Memorial Council	26	185	188	207	696.2	10.1
Int Boun & Wat Comm (US & Mex) . . .	260	258	248	236	-9.2	-4.8
International Trade Commission.	491	455	464	442	-10.0	-4.7
Interstate Commerce Comm	656	644	553	397	-39.5	-28.2
Merit Sys Protection Board	310	316	296	271	-12.6	-8.4
National Archives & Recds Admin.	3,120	3,082	3,073	2,833	-9.2	-7.8
National Aeronautics & Space Admin . .	24,872	24,826	23,338	21,635	-13.0	-7.3
Natl Credit Union Admin	900	962	921	912	1.3	-1.0
Natl Fnd Arts & Humanities	547	561	564	493	-9.9	-12.6
Natl Labor Relations Board	2,263	2,108	2,077	2,050	-9.4	-1.3
Natl Science Foundation	1,318	1,223	1,252	1,292	-2.0	3.2
Natl Trans Safety Board	366	365	358	368	0.5	2.8
Nuclear Regulatory Commission	3,353	3,476	3,336	3,212	-4.2	-3.7
Office of Personnel Management	6,636	6,776	5,340	4,354	-34.4	-18.5
Panama Canal Commission	8,240	8,568	8,562	9,060	10.0	5.8
Peace Corps	1,178	1,235	1,223	1,179	0.1	-3.6
Pension Benefit Guar Corp	574	727	697	716	24.7	2.7
Railroad Retirement Board	1,772	1,782	1,683	1,544	-12.9	-8.3
Securities & Exchange Comm	2,302	2,717	2,689	2,852	23.9	6.1
Selective Service System	288	267	230	218	-24.3	-5.2
Small Business Administration	5,128	5,526	6,824	5,085	-0.8	-25.5
Smithsonian Institution, Summary.	5,092	5,497	5,527	5,444	6.9	-1.5
Social Security Admin	(X)	(X)	(X)	[2]66,850	(X)	(X)
Tennessee Valley Authority	28,392	18,986	18,846	16,545	-41.7	-12.2
U.S. Information Agency.	8,555	8,283	7,888	7,480	-12.6	-5.2
U.S. International Development Cooperation Agency.	4,698	4,273	4,059	3,755	-20.1	-7.5
U.S. Postal Service	816,886	790,286	822,699	845,393	3.5	2.8

- Represents zero.   X Not applicable.   [1] Includes branches, or agencies, not shown separately.   [2] Sizable changes due to the Social Security Administration which was separated from the Department of Health and Human Services to become an independent agency effective April 1995.   [3] Formerly Veterans Administration.   [4] Formerly Federal Home Loan Bank Board.

Source: U.S. Office of Personnel Management, *Federal Civilian Workforce Statistics— Employment and Trends*, bimonthly.

No. 532. Federal Civilian Employment and Annual Payroll, by Branch: 1970 to 1995

[Average annual employment: For **fiscal year ending in year shown**; see text, section 9. Includes employees in U.S. territories and foreign countries. Data represent employees in active-duty status, including intermittent employees. Annual employment figures are averages of monthly figures. Excludes Central Intelligence Agency, National Security Agency, and, as of November 1984, the Defense Intelligence Agency. See also *Historical Statistics, Colonial Times to 1970*, series Y 308-317]

YEAR	EMPLOYMENT						PAYROLL (mil. dol.)				
	Total (1,000)	Percent of U.S. employed [1]	Executive		Legis-lative (1,000)	Judicial (1,000)	Total	Executive		Legis-lative	Judicial
			Total (1,000)	Defense				Total	Defense		
1970	[2]2,997	3.8	2,961	1,263	29	7	27,322	26,894	11,264	338	89
1971	2,899	3.7	2,861	1,162	31	7	29,475	29,007	11,579	369	98
1972	2,882	3.5	2,842	1,128	32	8	31,626	31,102	12,181	411	112
1973	2,822	3.3	2,780	1,076	33	9	33,240	32,671	12,414	447	121
1974	2,825	3.3	2,781	1,041	35	9	35,661	35,035	12,789	494	132
1975	2,877	3.4	2,830	1,044	37	10	39,126	38,423	13,418	549	154
1976	2,879	3.2	2,831	1,025	38	11	42,259	41,450	14,699	631	179
1977	2,855	3.1	2,803	997	39	12	45,895	44,975	15,696	700	219
1978	2,875	3.0	2,822	987	40	13	49,921	48,899	16,995	771	251
1979	2,897	2.9	2,844	974	40	13	53,590	52,513	18,065	817	260
1980	[3]2,987	3.0	2,933	971	40	14	58,012	56,841	18,795	883	288
1981	2,909	2.9	2,855	986	40	15	63,793	62,510	21,227	922	360
1982	2,871	2.9	2,816	1,019	39	16	65,503	64,125	22,226	980	398
1983	2,878	2.9	2,823	1,033	39	16	69,878	68,420	23,406	1,013	445
1984	2,935	2.8	2,879	1,052	40	17	74,616	73,084	25,253	1,081	451
1985	3,001	2.8	2,944	1,080	39	18	80,599	78,992	28,330	1,098	509
1986	3,047	2.8	2,991	1,089	38	19	82,598	80,941	29,272	1,112	545
1987	3,075	2.7	3,018	1,084	38	19	85,543	83,797	29,786	1,153	593
1988	3,113	2.7	3,054	1,073	38	21	88,841	86,960	29,609	1,226	656
1989	3,133	2.7	3,074	1,067	38	22	92,847	90,870	30,301	1,266	711
1990	[4]3,233	2.7	3,173	1,060	38	23	99,138	97,022	31,990	1,329	787
1991	3,101	2.7	3,038	1,015	38	25	104,273	101,965	32,956	1,434	874
1992	3,106	2.6	3,040	1,004	39	27	108,054	105,402	31,486	1,569	1,083
1993	3,043	2.5	2,976	952	39	28	114,323	111,523	32,755	1,609	1,191
1994	2,993	2.4	2,928	900	37	28	116,138	113,264	32,144	1,613	1,260
1995	2,943	2.4	2,880	852	34	28	118,290	115,314	31,743	1,598	1,379

[1] Civilian only. See table 616.   [2] Includes 33,000 temporary census workers.   [3] Includes 81,116 temporary census workers.   [4] Includes 111,020 temporary census workers.

Source: U.S. Office of Personnel Management, *Federal Civilian Workforce Statistics—Employment and Trends*, bimonthly; and unpublished data.

No. 533. Federal Executive Branch (Non-Postal) Employment, by Race and Hispanic Origin: 1990 to 1994

[As of **Sept. 30**. Covers total employment for only Executive branch agencies participating in OPM's Central Personnel Data File (CPDF)]

PAY SYSTEM	1990	1991	1992	1993	1994
All personnel	**2,150,359**	**2,183,403**	**2,175,715**	**2,110,510**	**2,043,449**
White, non-Hispanic.	1,562,846	1,581,388	1,570,812	1,515,700	1,462,185
General schedule and related.	1,218,188	1,239,964	1,228,634	1,190,705	1,146,990
Grades 1-4 ($11,903 - $21,307).	132,028	127,344	112,948	99,006	90,029
Grades 5-8 ($18,340 - $32,710).	337,453	344,483	338,182	320,410	303,999
Grades 9-12 ($27,789 - $52,385).	510,261	517,004	509,978	500,616	484,681
Grades 13-15 ($47,920 - $86,589).	238,446	251,133	267,526	270,673	268,281
Total Executives/Senior Pay Levels [1].	9,337	12,998	13,661	13,162	13,114
Wage pay system.	244,220	238,136	232,753	215,122	202,440
Other pay systems	91,101	90,290	95,764	96,711	99,641
Black.	356,867	363,864	360,725	351,879	340,512
General schedule and related.	272,657	281,559	277,264	272,393	265,926
Grades 1-4 ($11,903 - $21,307).	65,077	64,396	56,650	51,142	46,189
Grades 5-8 ($18,340 - $32,710).	114,993	119,566	120,259	118,438	115,966
Grades 9-12 ($27,789 - $52,385).	74,985	78,109	78,970	80,130	80,284
Grades 13-15 ($47,920 - $86,589).	17,602	19,488	21,385	22,683	23,487
Total Executives/Senior Pay Levels [1].	479	630	662	716	865
Wage pay system.	72,755	71,615	69,976	65,422	60,335
Other pay systems	10,976	10,060	12,823	13,348	13,386
Hispanic	115,170	118,769	120,296	117,935	116,863
General schedule and related.	83,218	88,051	87,947	87,200	86,816
Grades 1-4 ($11,903 - $21,307).	15,738	16,308	14,240	13,027	12,033
Grades 5-8 ($18,340 - $32,710).	28,727	30,852	31,708	30,985	30,749
Grades 9-12 ($27,789 - $52,385).	31,615	32,965	33,121	33,758	34,104
Grades 13-15 ($47,920 - $86,589).	7,138	7,926	8,878	9,430	9,930
Total Executives/Senior Pay Levels [1].	154	250	281	274	323
Wage pay system.	26,947	26,294	26,151	24,515	23,122
Other pay systems	4,851	4,174	5,917	5,946	6,602
American Indian, Alaska Natives, Asians, and Pacific	115,476	119,382	123,882	124,996	123,889

[1] General schedule pay rates as of January 1993. Senior Pay Levels effective as of October 1, 1991.

Source: Office of Personnel Management, Central Personnel Data File.

No. 534. Paid Civilian Employment in the Federal Government: 1994

[As of **December 31.** Excludes Central Intelligence Agency, Defense Intelligence Agency, seasonal and on-call employees, and National Security Agency]

DIVISION AND STATE	Total (1,000)	Percent defense	DIVISION AND STATE	Total (1,000)	Percent defense
United States	**2,903**	**27.6**	Virginia.	160	61.0
Northeast	**467**	**21.8**	West Virginia.	18	10.0
New England.	**123**	**20.8**	North Carolina	54	32.6
Maine	14	43.3	South Carolina	30	46.0
New Hampshire.	9	15.8	Georgia	92	37.9
Vermont	6	10.5	Florida	114	26.4
Massachusetts	60	16.1	**East South Central.**	**169**	**31.0**
Rhode Island.	11	36.7	Kentucky	36	34.2
Connecticut.	25	17.1	Tennessee	53	11.3
Middle Atlantic	**344**	**22.2**	Alabama.	55	43.4
New York	145	10.6	Mississippi	25	40.9
New Jersey.	72	29.8	**West South Central**	**273**	**31.2**
Pennsylvania.	127	31.1	Arkansas	20	20.2
North Central	**511**	**21.4**	Louisiana	35	25.0
East North Central	**330**	**22.8**	Oklahoma.	42	44.9
Ohio	92	34.2	Texas.	176	30.4
Indiana.	42	33.7	**West**	**629**	**32.1**
Illinois	106	15.9	**Mountain.**	**198**	**25.8**
Michigan	60	16.1	Montana.	13	9.5
Wisconsin.	30	10.9	Idaho.	11	11.3
West North Central	**180**	**18.7**	Wyoming	7	14.5
Minnesota.	34	7.9	Colorado	57	23.0
Iowa	21	6.8	New Mexico	27	31.6
Missouri	64	25.5	Arizona	40	22.4
North Dakota.	8	23.6	Utah	31	47.7
South Dakota	10	13.5	Nevada	12	17.8
Nebraska	16	22.7	**Pacific**	**430**	**34.9**
Kansas	26	23.3	Washington.	66	40.2
South.	**1,253**	**31.0**	Oregon	30	9.9
South Atlantic	**811**	**30.9**	California	295	33.3
Delaware	6	26.9	Alaska	15	32.1
Maryland	133	28.4	Hawaii	25	72.2
District of Columbia	204	7.6	Unspecified State	44	0.5

Source: U.S. Office of Personnel Management, *Biennial Report of Employment by Geographic Area.*

No. 535. Paid Full-Time Federal Civilian Employment, All Areas: 1990 to 1995

[**As of March 31.** Excludes employees of Congress and Federal courts, maritime seamen of Dept. of Commerce, and small number for whom rates were not reported. See text, section 10, for explanation of general schedule and wage system. See also *Historical Statistics, Colonial Times to 1970,* series Y 318-331]

COMPENSATION AUTHORITY	EMPLOYEES (1,000)				AVERAGE PAY			
	1990	1993	1994	1995	1990	1993	1994	1995
Total.	**2,697**	**2,709**	**2,681**	**(NA)**	**31,174**	**37,327**	**39,129**	**(NA)**
General Schedule	1,506	1,520	1,479	1,417	31,239	37,332	39,070	40,568
Wage System . . ;	369	315	290	269	26,565	30,136	31,299	32,084
Postal pay system [1]	661	692	729	(NA)	29,264	32,458	33,592	(NA)
Other	161	182	183	181	41,149	49,743	51,996	53,839

NA Not available.   [1] Source: Employees—U.S. Postal Service, *Annual Report of the Postmaster General.* Average pay—U.S. Postal Service, *Comprehensive Statement of Postal Operations,* annual.

Source: Except as noted, U.S. Office of Personnel Management, *Pay Structure of the Federal Civil Service,* annual.

No. 536. Federal General Schedule Employee Pay Increases: 1965 to 1994

[Percent change from prior year shown, except 1965, change from 1964. Represents legislated pay increases. For some years data based on range for details see source]

DATE	Pay increase	DATE	Pay increase	DATE	Pay increase
1965	3.6	1974	5.5	1985	3.5
1966	2.9	1975	5.0	1986	-
1967	4.5	1976	5.2	1987	3.0
1968	4.9	1977	7.0	1988	2.0
1969	9.1	1978	5.5	1989	4.1
1970	6.0	1979	7.0	1990	3.6
1971	6.0	1980	9.1	1991	4.1
1972	5.5	1981	4.8	1992	4.2
1972	5.1	1982	4.0	1993	3.7
1973	4.8	1984	4.0	1994	-

- Represents zero.

Source: U.S. Office of Personnel Management, *Pay Structure of the Federal Civil Service,* annual.

No. 537. Accessions to and Separations From Employment in the Federal Government: 1994 and 1995

[As of September 30]

AGENCY	ACCESSIONS				SEPARATIONS			
	Number		Rate		Number		Rate	
	1994	1995	1994	1995	1994	1995	1994	1995
Total, all agencies	529,026	556,602	18.0	19.2	565,035	638,761	19.2	22.1
Legislative Branch, total [1]	840	1,074	5.0	6.6	2,800	1,985	16.7	12.2
General Accounting Office	160	39	3.5	0.9	794	392	17.1	8.9
Government Printing Office.	84	77	1.9	1.8	593	318	13.4	7.6
Library of Congress.	360	540	7.8	11.6	860	642	18.6	13.8
Judicial Branch	3	-	(Z)	0.0	9	-	(Z)	0.0
Executive Branch, total	528,183	555,528	18.0	19.3	562,226	636,776	19.2	22.1
Executive Office of the President	311	384	19.6	24.3	367	373	23.1	23.6
Executive Departments	293,901	257,039	15.2	14.0	370,148	422,639	19.2	23.0
State.	3,502	3,338	13.5	13.3	3,893	3,919	15.1	15.6
Treasury	45,954	24,532	28.8	15.0	52,550	52,634	32.9	32.2
Defense	124,483	104,002	13.8	12.2	172,624	155,755	19.2	18.3
Justice	9,268	14,958	9.5	14.9	6,749	7,496	6.9	7.5
Interior	12,463	12,936	15.7	17.1	14,958	16,147	18.8	21.4
Agriculture	31,255	25,365	27.0	23.3	39,209	41,384	33.9	37.9
Commerce.	5,228	5,900	13.9	15.8	6,434	6,460	17.1	17.3
Labor	889	1,438	5.2	8.7	1,593	2,003	9.3	12.2
Health & Human Services.	13,042	8,774	10.1	9.3	14,362	78,780	11.1	83.7
Housing & Urban Development	675	489	5.1	4.0	1,124	1,952	8.6	15.8
Transportation	1,647	2,673	2.5	4.2	6,692	4,740	10.0	7.4
Energy	1,596	2,087	7.9	10.5	1,888	2,671	9.4	13.4
Education . . . . . [2]	628	683	12.8	13.8	613	354	12.5	7.2
Veterans Affairs [2]	43,271	49,864	16.4	19.0	47,459	48,344	18.0	18.5
Independent agencies [1]	233,971	298,105	23.5	28.6	191,711	213,764	19.3	20.5
Board of Governors, Fed RSRV System . . .	182	224	10.9	13.3	189	194	11.3	11.5
Environmental Protection Agency	1,451	2,232	8.0	12.3	1,732	2,078	9.5	11.5
Equal Employment Opportunity Comm	242	129	8.4	4.5	136	156	4.7	5.4
Federal Deposit Insurance Corporation. . . .	1,246	360	6.2	2.2	4,527	4,404	22.6	26.8
Fed. Emergency Management Agency	5,310	3,165	93.9	60.2	3,438	3,059	60.8	58.2
General Services Administration.	430	292	2.2	1.7	1,210	2,552	6.1	14.8
National Aeronautics & Space Admin	2,341	2,004	9.7	8.9	3,695	3,673	15.3	16.2
National Archives & Records Admin	585	583	18.8	20.0	200	307	6.4	10.5
Nuclear Regulatory Commission	127	98	3.7	3.0	240	263	7.0	8.0
Office of Personnel Management.	340	506	5.5	10.3	1,448	1,407	23.5	28.6
Panama Canal Comm	1,125	1,744	13.1	19.6	1,131	1,246	13.2	14.0
Railroad Retirement Board	50	46	2.9	2.9	151	185	8.8	11.6
Securities and Exchange Commission.	367	584	13.7	21.1	335	356	12.5	12.8
Small Business Administration	4,575	1,065	70.7	18.1	3,464	2,799.	53.5	47.6
Smithsonian Institution	793	707	14.5	13.1	853	980	15.6	18.2
Tennessee Valley Authority	674	674	3.6	4.1	716	2,873	3.8	17.3
U.S. Information Agency	338	356	4.2	4.7	830	836	10.2	11.0
U.S. International Dev. Coop. Agency	397	333	9.5	8.6	621	665	14.8	17.2
U.S. Postal Service	210,663	210,447	25.9	25.0	164,082	179,494	20.2	21.3

- Represents zero.   Z Less than .05.   [1] Includes other branches, or other agencies, not shown separately.   [2] Formerly Veterans Administration.

Source: U.S. Office of Personnel Management, *Federal Civilian Workforce Statistics—Employment and Trends,* bimonthly.

No. 538. Federal Land and Buildings Owned and Leased, and Predominant Land Usage: 1980 to 1991

[For fiscal years ending in years shown; see text, section 9. Covers Federal real property throughout the world, except as noted. Cost of land figures represent total cost of property owned in year shown. For further details see source. For data on Federal land by State, see table 364]

ITEM AND AGENCY	Unit	1980	1985	1986	1987	1988	1989	1990	1991
Federally owned: Land	Mil. acres. . . .	720	727	727	724	688	662	650	650
Buildings, number [1]	1,000	403	454	429	412	442	451	446	441
Cost of land, buildings, etc.[2] . . .	Bil. dol.	107	148	158	165	164	164	180	181
Federally leased: Land	Mil. acres. . . .	1.4	1.3	1.3	1.6	1.6	1.5	0.9	(NA)
Buildings, floor area [1]	Mil. sq/ft	214	237	246	246	248	254	234	242
Rental property, cost	Mil. dol	1,054	1,681	1,774	1,893	2,001	2,127	2,125	(NA)
Predominant usage (U.S. only) . . .	Mil. acres. . . .	720	727	727	724	688	662	650	650
Forest and wildlife.	Mil. acres. . . .	422	431	431	431	400	375	368	(NA)
Grazing.	Mil. acres. . . .	162	155	155	154	151	151	154	(NA)
Parks and historic sites	Mil. acres. . . .	93	94	96	96	99	98	96	(NA)
Other	Mil. acres. . . .	43	48	46	43	38	39	33	(NA)

NA Not available.   [1] Excludes data for Dept. of Defense military functions outside United States.   [2] Includes other uses not shown separately.

Source: U.S. General Services Administration, *Inventory Report on Real Property Owned by the United States Throughout the World,* annual.

National Defense and Veterans Affairs

This section presents data on national defense and its human and financial costs; active and reserve military personnel; ships, equipment and aircraft; and federally sponsored programs and benefits for veterans. The principal sources of these data are the annual *Selected Manpower Statistics* and the *Atlas/Data Abstract for the United States and Selected Areas* issued by the Office of the Secretary of Defense; *Annual Report of Secretary of Veterans Affairs, Department of Veterans Affairs,* and *The Budget of the United States Government,* Office of Management and Budget. For more data on expenditures, personnel, and ships, see section 31.

Department of Defense (DOD)—DOD is responsible for providing military forces of the United States. The President serves as Commander in Chief of the Armed Forces; from him, the authority flows to the Secretary of Defense and through the Joint Chiefs of Staff to the commanders of unified and specified commands (e.g., United States European Command).

Reserve components—Reserve personnel of the Armed Forces consist of the Army National Guard, Army Reserve, Naval Reserve, Marine Corps Reserve, Air National Guard, Air Force Reserve, and Coast Guard Reserve. They provide trained personnel available for active duty in the Armed Forces in time of war or national emergency and at such other times as authorized by law. The National Guard has dual Federal-State responsibilities and uses jointly provided equipment, facilities, and budget support. The President is empowered to mobilize the National Guard and to use such of the Armed Forces as he considers necessary to enforce Federal authority in any State.

The ready reserve includes selected reservists who are intended to assist active forces in a war and the individual ready reserve who, in a major war, would be used to fill out active and reserve units and later would be a source of combat replacements; a portion of the ready reserve serves in an active status. The

In Brief

	1996
U.S. military expenditures	$266 bil.
Defense outlays as percent of gross domestic product	3.6%

standby reserve cannot be called to active duty unless the Congress gives explicit approval. The retired reserve represents a low potential for mobilization.

Department of Veterans Affairs— The Department of Veterans Affairs administers laws authorizing benefits for eligible former and present members of the Armed Forces and for the beneficiaries of deceased members. Veterans benefits available under various acts of Congress include compensation for service-connected disability or death; pensions for nonservice-connected disability or death; vocational rehabilitation, education, and training; home loan insurance; life insurance; health care; special housing and automobiles or other conveyances for certain disabled veterans; burial and plot allowances; and educational assistance to families of deceased or totally disabled veterans, servicemen missing in action, or prisoners of war. Since these benefits are legislated by Congress, the dates they were enacted and the dates they apply to veterans may be different from the actual dates the conflicts occurred.

VA estimates of veterans cover all persons with active duty service during periods of war or armed conflict and until 1982 include those living outside the United States. Veteran population estimates for September 1982 are for the 50 States, the District of Columbia and Puerto Rico. Veterans whose active duty service was entirely during periods of peacetime are eligible for some veterans benefits and, where appropriate, are included in VA estimates.

Historical statistics—Tabular headnotes provide cross-references, where applicable, to *Historical Statistics of the United States, Colonial Times to 1970.* See Appendix IV.

Figure 11.1
Military and Civilian Personnel: 1985 to 1994

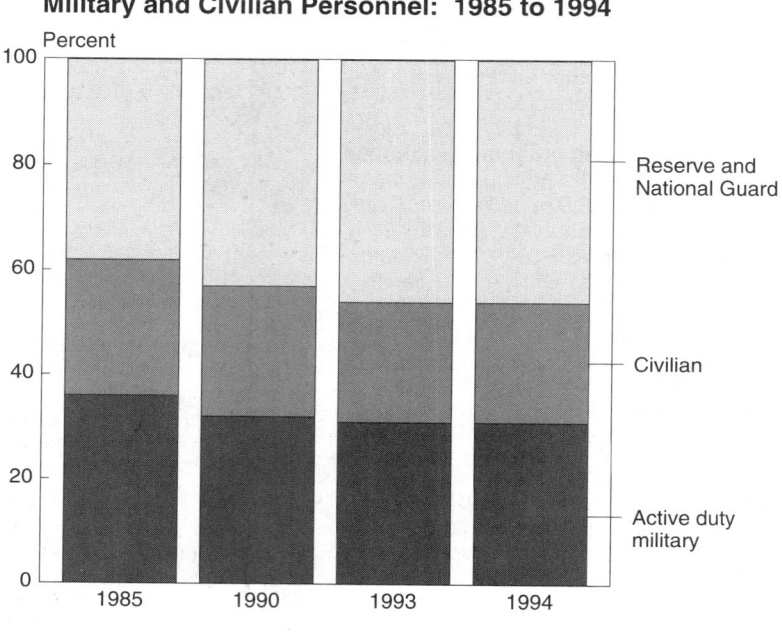

Source: Chart prepared by U.S. Bureau of the Census. For data, see table 543.

Figure 11.2
**Military and Civilian Expenditures,
by Major Location: 1994**

Source: Chart prepared by U.S. Bureau of the Census. For data, see table 543.

No. 539. National Defense Outlays and Veterans Benefits: 1960 to 1996

[For fiscal year ending in year shown; see text, section 9. Includes outlays of Department of Defense, Department of Veterans Affairs, and other agencies for activities primarily related to national defense and veterans programs. For explanation of average annual percent change, see Guide to Tabular Presentation. Minus sign (-) indicates decline. See Historical Statistics, Colonial Times to 1970, series Y 472, 473, and Y 476, for related data]

YEAR	NATIONAL DEFENSE AND VETERANS OUTLAYS				ANNUAL PERCENT CHANGE [1]			DEFENSE OUTLAYS, PERCENT OF—	
	Total outlays (bil. dol.)	Defense outlays		Veterans outlays (bil. dol.)	Total outlays	Defense outlays	Veterans outlays	Federal outlays	Gross domestic product [2]
		Current dollars	Constant (1987) dollars (bil. dol.)						
1960	53.5	48.1	220.1	5.4	2.5	2.4	3.1	52.2	9.5
1965	56.3	50.6	203.9	5.7	-6.8	-7.6	0.7	42.8	7.5
1966	64.0	58.1	225.9	5.9	13.7	14.8	3.5	43.2	7.9
1967	78.1	71.4	269.1	6.7	22.1	22.9	13.8	45.4	9.0
1968	88.9	81.9	295.5	7.0	13.8	14.7	4.4	46.0	9.7
1969	90.1	82.5	282.5	7.6	1.3	0.7	8.5	44.9	8.9
1970	90.4	81.7	262.9	8.7	0.3	-1.0	13.6	41.8	8.3
1971	88.7	78.9	236.9	9.8	-1.9	-3.5	12.7	37.5	7.5
1972	89.9	79.2	219.7	10.7	1.4	0.4	9.8	34.3	6.9
1973	88.7	76.7	197.2	12.0	1.3	-3.1	12.0	31.2	6.0
1974	92.7	79.3	185.3	13.4	4.6	3.5	11.4	29.5	5.7
1975	103.1	86.5	183.9	16.6	11.2	9.0	24.0	26.0	5.7
1976	108.1	89.6	177.8	18.4	4.8	3.6	11.0	24.1	5.3
1976, TQ [3]	26.2	22.3	42.4	4.0	(X)	(X)	(X)	23.2	5.0
1977	115.2	97.2	176.8	18.0	6.7	8.5	-2.1	23.8	5.1
1978	123.5	104.5	177.2	19.0	7.1	7.5	5.2	22.8	4.8
1979	136.2	116.3	180.4	19.9	10.4	11.3	5.0	23.1	4.8
1980	155.2	134.0	187.1	21.2	13.9	15.2	6.3	22.7	5.1
1981	180.5	157.5	198.2	23.0	16.3	17.6	8.5	23.2	5.3
1982	209.3	185.3	214.3	24.0	15.9	17.6	4.2	24.8	5.9
1983	234.7	209.9	230.4	24.8	12.1	13.3	3.3	26.0	6.3
1984	253.0	227.4	241.7	25.6	7.8	8.3	3.2	26.7	6.2
1985	279.0	252.7	261.2	26.3	10.3	11.1	2.7	26.7	6.4
1986	299.8	273.4	276.4	26.4	7.4	8.2	0.4	27.6	6.5
1987	308.8	282.0	282.0	26.8	3.0	3.1	1.5	28.1	6.3
1988	319.8	290.4	283.3	29.4	3.6	3.0	9.7	27.3	6.0
1989	333.7	303.6	285.9	30.1	4.3	4.5	2.4	26.6	5.9
1990	328.4	299.3	272.6	29.1	-1.6	-1.4	-3.3	23.9	5.5
1991	306.6	273.3	240.5	31.3	-7.2	-8.7	7.6	20.7	4.8
1992	332.5	298.4	249.7	34.1	12.0	12.4	8.0	21.6	5.0
1993	326.1	291.1	237.2	35.7	-1.9	-2.4	4.6	20.7	4.7
1994	319.2	281.6	220.6	37.6	-2.3	-3.3	5.3	19.3	4.2
1995	310.0	272.1	206.8	37.9	-2.9	-3.4	0.8	17.9	3.9
1996, est.	303.3	265.6	197.0	37.7	-2.2	-2.4	-0.5	16.9	3.6

X Not applicable.   [1] Change from prior year shown; for 1960, change from 1955.   [2] Represents fiscal year GDP; for definition, see text, section 14.   [3] Transition quarter, July–Sept.

Source: U.S. Office of Management and Budget, Historical Tables, annual.

No. 540. Federal Budget Outlays for National Defense Functions: 1970 to 1996

[In billions of dollars, except percent. For fiscal year ending in year shown; see text, section 9. Minus sign (-) indicates decline. See Historical Statistics, Colonial Times to 1970, series Y 473, for total]

DEFENSE FUNCTION	1970	1980	1985	1988	1989	1990	1991	1992	1993	1994	1995	1996, est.
Total.	81.7	134.0	252.7	290.4	303.6	299.3	273.3	298.4	291.1	281.6	272.1	265.6
Percent change [1]	10.1	15.2	11.1	3.0	4.5	-1.4	-8.7	9.2	-2.4	0.6	-3.4	-2.4
Defense Dept., military	80.1	130.9	245.2	281.9	294.9	289.8	262.4	286.9	278.6	268.6	259.4	254.3
Military personnel	29.0	40.9	67.8	76.3	80.7	75.6	83.4	81.2	75.9	73.1	70.8	67.4
Percent of military	36.2	31.2	27.7	27.1	27.0	26.1	31.8	28.3	27.2	27.2	27.3	26.5
Operation, maintenance.	21.6	44.8	72.4	84.5	87.0	88.3	101.8	92.0	94.1	87.9	90.9	91.7
Procurement	21.6	29.0	70.4	77.2	81.6	81.0	82.0	74.9	69.9	61.8	55.0	48.1
Research and development . .	7.2	13.1	27.1	34.8	37.0	37.5	34.6	34.6	37.0	34.8	34.6	34.4
Military construction	1.2	2.5	4.3	5.9	5.3	5.1	3.5	4.3	4.8	5.0	6.8	6.5
Family housing.	0.6	1.7	2.6	3.1	3.3	3.5	3.3	3.3	3.3	3.3	3.6	4.0
Other [2]	-1.1	-1.1	0.6	0.2	0.1	-1.2	-46.2	-3.3	-6.4	2.8	-2.2	2.0
Atomic energy activities [3]	1.4	2.9	7.1	7.9	8.1	9.0	10.0	10.6	11.0	11.9	11.8	10.2
Defense-related activities [4]	0.2	0.2	0.5	0.5	0.6	0.6	0.6	0.9	0.8	1.5	1.1	1.1

[1] Change from immediate prior year; for 1970, change from 1965.   [2] Revolving and management funds, trust funds, special foreign currency program, allowances, and offsetting receipts.   [3] Defense activities only.   [4] Includes civil defense activities.

Source: U.S. Office of Management and Budget, Historical Tables, annual.

No. 541. National Defense—Budget Authority and Outlays: 1980 to 1996

[In billions of dollars, except percent. For fiscal year ending in year shown, except as noted; see text, section 9. See *Historical Statistics, Colonial Times to 1970*, series Y 458-460 for outlays]

ITEM	1980	1985	1988	1989	1990	1991	1992	1993	1994	1995	1996, est.
Budget authority [1]	143.9	294.7	292.0	299.6	303.3	288.9	295.1	281.1	263.3	266.3	263.3
Department of Defense-Military [2]	140.6	286.8	283.8	290.8	293.0	276.2	282.1	267.2	251.4	255.7	251.8
Atomic energy [1] [3]	3.2	7.3	7.7	8.1	9.7	11.6	12.0	12.1	10.9	10.1	10.7
Outlays (Defense) [1]	134.0	252.7	290.4	303.6	299.3	273.3	298.4	291.1	281.6	272.1	265.6
Department of Defense-Military	130.9	245.2	281.9	294.9	289.8	262.4	286.9	278.6	268.6	259.4	254.3
Atomic energy [1] [3]	3.1	7.6	8.4	8.7	9.6	10.0	10.6	11.0	11.9	11.8	10.2

[1] Includes defense budget authority, balances, and outlays by other departments. [2] Excluding accruals. [3] Includes other defense related activities.

Source: U.S. Office of Management and Budget, *Historical Tables*, annual.

No. 542. Defense-Related Agencies: 1980 to 1993

[In thousands, except percent. Annual averages]

EMPLOYMENT	1980	1985	1987	1988	1989	1990	1991	1992	1993
Total U.S. employment [1]	100,907	108,856	114,177	116,677	119,030	119,550	118,440	119,164	120,791
Federal	4,386	4,608	4,709	4,690	4,662	4,577	4,541	4,549	4,403
Resident Armed Forces	1,604	1,706	1,737	1,709	1,688	1,637	1,564	1,566	1,485
Civilian personnel [2]	2,987	3,001	3,075	3,113	3,133	3,233	3,101	2,983	2,918
DOD-Civilian employment [3]	948	1,073	1,079	1,041	1,067	1,024	1,083	1,044	973
Percent of Federal civilian personnel	31.7	35.8	35.1	33.4	34.1	31.7	34.9	35.0	33.3
DOD-Military and civilian employment	2,552	2,779	2,816	2,750	2,755	2,661	2,647	2,610	2,458
Percent of total Federal	58.2	60.3	59.8	58.6	59.1	58.1	58.3	57.4	55.8
Percent of total U.S.	2.5	2.6	2.5	2.4	2.3	2.2	2.2	2.2	2.0

[1] Includes resident Armed Forces. [2] See table 532. [3] Source: Beginning 1980, U.S. Dept. of Defense, *Civilian Manpower Statistics*, annual (Sept. issues).

Source: Except as noted, U.S. Bureau of Labor Statistics, *Employment and Earnings*, monthly.

No. 543. Military and Civilian Personnel and Expenditures: 1985 to 1994

ITEM	1985	1990	1991	1992	1993	1994
Personnel, total [1] (1,000)	3,808	3,693	3,872	3,889	3,762	3,623
Active duty military	1,354	1,185	1,263	1,214	1,171	1,131
Civilian	976	931	911	899	847	810
Reserve and National Guard	1,478	1,577	1,697	1,777	1,744	1,682
Expenditures, total (mil. dol.)	216,045	209,904	221,089	211,534	214,655	210,138
Payroll outlays	75,949	88,650	96,970	99,250	100,510	99,822
Active duty military pay	29,818	33,705	39,118	39,447	38,782	37,694
Civilian pay	24,815	28,230	29,901	31,205	31,619	30,587
Retired military pay	17,029	21,159	22,584	23,936	25,658	26,386
Reserve and National Guard pay	4,287	5,556	5,366	4,661	4,451	5,154
Prime contract awards [2] (mil. dol.)	140,096	121,254	124,119	112,285	114,145	110,316
Supply contracts	92,375	66,895	66,981	54,880	54,856	48,642
Service contracts	24,224	28,540	31,222	30,503	32,163	33,040
R and D contracts	18,752	21,955	20,469	21,508	22,076	21,513
Construction contracts	3,245	2,088	3,469	2,894	2,829	4,786
Civil function contracts	1,500	1,775	1,979	2,500	2,222	2,335
Major area of work (mil. dol.):						
Aircraft, fixed wing	11,683	6,329	6,543	8,197	6,926	6,277
Research, devel'mt, testing and evaluation	(NA)	(NA)	(NA)	1,266	1,422	3,256
RDTE/Aircraft-Engineering development	(NA)	(NA)	(NA)	1,266	1,422	1,769
RDTE/Missile and space systems-op systems	(NA)	(NA)	(NA)	(NA)	(NA)	1,487
Gas turbines and jet engines	2,848	1,856	1,236	974	(NA)	(NA)
Guided missiles	(NA)	928	921	921	793	494
Guided missile handling and servicing equip	(NA)	446	921	921	757	(NA)
Major location of expenditures (mil. dol.):						
San Diego, CA	4,027	4,820	4,628	5,289	6,405	4,748
Pico Rivera, CA	(NA)	(NA)	2,600	4,284	2,428	3,272
St. Louis, MO	7,412	5,616	5,869	3,462	5,442	6,087
Norfolk, VA	2,200	2,741	2,928	3,257	3,265	3,228
Arlington, VA	(NA)	2,527	2,836	2,974	3,246	3,284
Fort Worth, TX	3,912	3,594	3,973	2,948	3,136	2,492
Washington, DC	(NA)	2,771	2,706	2,828	3,045	2,347
Marietta, GA	(NA)	(NA)	(NA)	2,573	2,734	2,828
Los Angeles, CA	7,125	2,459	(NA)	2,319	(NA)	(NA)
San Antonio, TX	(NA)	(NA)	(NA)	2,117	(NA)	(NA)

NA Not available. [1] Includes those based ashore and excludes those temporarily shore-based, in a transient status, or afloat. [2] Represents contract awards over $25,000.

Source: U.S. Dept. of Defense, *Atlas/Data Abstract for the United States and Selected Areas*, annual.

No. 544. Military Prime Contract Awards to All Businesses, by Program: 1980 to 1993

[In billions of dollars. Net values for **fiscal year ending in year shown;** see text, section 9. Includes all new prime contracts; debit or credit changes in contracts are also included. Actions cover official awards, amendments, or other changes in prime contracts to obtain military supplies, services, or construction. Excludes term contracts and contracts which do not obligate a firm total dollar amount or fixed quantity, but includes job orders, task orders, and delivery orders against such contracts]

DOD PROCUREMENT PROGRAM	1980	1985	1987	1988	1989	1990	1991	1992	1993
Total	83.7	163.7	156.5	151.4	139.3	144.7	150.9	136.3	138.3
Intragovernmental [1]	10.2	12.4	8.8	8.9	9.6	10.0	11.9	9.6	12.9
For work outside the U.S.	5.4	8.6	8.9	8.2	6.4	7.1	9.2	5.9	5.8
Educ. and nonprofit institutions	1.5	3.1	3.5	3.5	3.3	3.5	3.6	3.4	3.4
With business firms for work in the U.S. [2] . .	66.7	139.6	135.3	130.8	120.0	123.8	125.9	117.2	116.0
Major hard goods	41.0	98.1	93.0	85.9	79.9	79.1	74.1	67.1	64.5
Aircraft	12.5	34.6	27.7	25.0	24.2	24.0	23.6	24.1	23.0
Electronics and communication equip. .	9.6	22.0	22.6	17.8	18.1	18.5	15.2	14.2	14.2
Missiles and space systems	7.9	18.7	19.8	19.7	18.7	17.1	16.4	13.1	12.1
Ships	6.0	10.4	11.5	13.7	9.6	10.3	9.3	8.3	9.0
Tanks, ammo. and weapons	5.1	12.5	11.6	9.7	9.2	9.2	9.6	7.4	6.2
Services	5.9	9.1	11.0	12.0	11.7	14.6	16.9	17.3	17.5

[1] Covers only purchases from other Federal agencies and reimbursable purchases on behalf of foreign governments.
[2] Includes Department of Defense. Includes other business not shown separately. Contracts awarded for work in U.S. possessions, and other areas subject to complete sovereignty of United States; contracts in a classified location; and any intragovernmental contracts entered into overseas.

Source: U.S. Dept. of Defense, *Prime Contract Awards,* semiannual.

No. 545. Department of Defense Contract Awards, Payroll, and Civilian and Military Personnel—States: 1994

[For years ending **Sept. 30. Contracts** refer to awards made in year specified; expenditures relating to awards may extend over several years. **Civilian employees** include United States citizen and foreign national direct hire civilians subject to Office of Management and Budget (OMB) ceiling controls and civilian personnel involved in civil functions in the United States. Excludes indirect hire civilians and those direct hire civilian not subject to OMB ceiling controls. **Military personnel** include active duty personnel based ashore. Excludes personnel temporarily shore-based in a transient status, or afloat. **Payroll outlays** include the gross earnings of civilian and active duty military personnel for services rendered to the government and for cash allowances for benefits. Excludes employer's share of employee benefits, accrued military retirement benefits and most permanent change of station costs]

REGION, DIVISION, AND STATE	Contract awards [1] (mil. dol.)	Payroll (mil. dol.)	PERSONNEL (1,000) Civilian	PERSONNEL (1,000) Military	REGION, DIVISION, AND STATE	Contract awards [1] (mil. dol.)	Payroll (mil. dol.)	PERSONNEL (1,000) Civilian	PERSONNEL (1,000) Military
U.S..	110,316	99,822	810.2	1,130.7	DC	1,096	1,251	15.8	13.8
					VA	8,017	11,483	98.8	90.0
Northeast	18,752	9,116	103.8	56.1	WV	176	224	1.5	0.6
N.E.	9,329	3,053	26.1	18.0	NC	1,163	4,186	17.4	96.2
ME	925	584	6.0	2.2	SC	998	2,529	14.5	39.0
NH	369	236	1.4	0.3	GA	4,121	4,273	35.0	61.8
VT	57	94	0.6	0.2	FL	5,910	6,164	30.3	60.8
MA	5,106	1,081	9.9	6.1	E.S.C.	5,470	6,537	53.7	70.2
RI	422	436	4.0	3.6	KY	769	1,902	12.2	33.6
CT	2,450	621	4.2	5.6	TN	1,173	1,068	6.3	7.3
M.A.	9,424	6,064	77.6	38.1	AL	1,673	2,320	24.3	16.7
NY	3,629	1,894	15.5	23.7	MS	1,855	1,246	10.9	12.6
NJ	3,034	1,524	22.0	9.1	W.S.C.	11,426	11,272	86.7	157.0
PA	2,760	2,646	40.1	5.3	AR	374	701	4.2	5.9
Midwest	16,593	11,168	109.7	108.2	LA	2,148	1,355	8.6	20.3
E.N.C.	7,916	6,494	76.2	45.3	OK	759	2,015	19.6	28.3
OH	2,966	2,215	31.9	9.6	TX	8,145	7,201	54.3	102.5
IN	1,319	1,170	14.3	3.8	**West . . . .**	32,229	28,026	204.0	340.7
IL	1,256	1,810	16.8	27.3	Mountain . . .	6,234	7,307	52.4	99.5
MI	1,602	878	9.8	3.8	MT	63	258	1.1	4.6
WI	774	420	3.3	0.8	ID	66	315	1.5	4.3
W.N.C.	8,677	4,674	33.5	63.0	WY	56	189	1.0	3.9
MN	1,137	403	2.7	0.9	CO	2,620	2,298	13.3	34.2
IA	309	184	1.4	0.4	NM	658	1,056	8.6	16.2
MO	6,147	1,566	16.6	15.3	AZ	1,975	1,642	9.3	21.9
ND	120	340	1.7	9.8	UT	521	906	15.5	5.7
SD	75	251	1.3	5.0	NV	274	643	2.2	8.6
NE	310	612	3.6	9.7	Pacific	25,995	20,720	151.6	241.2
KS	580	1,266	6.2	21.9	WA	1,861	3,416	27.0	35.8
South.	42,741	51,511	392.8	625.8	OR	131	496	3.0	1.0
S.A.	25,844	33,702	252.4	398.6	CA	22,573	13,467	99.9	143.2
DE	108	285	1.6	4.6	AK	627	923	4.7	19.0
MD	4,256	3,308	37.5	31.8	HI	803	2,417	17.0	42.2

[1] Military awards for supplies, services, and construction. Net value of contracts of over $25,000 for work in each State and DC. Figures reflect impact of prime contracting on State distribution of defense work. Often the State in which a prime contractor is located is not the State where the subcontracted work is done. See also headnote, table 544. Undistributed civilians and military personnel, their payrolls, and prime contract awards for performance in classified locations are excluded.

Source: U.S. Dept. of Defense, *Atlas/Data Abstract for the United States and Selected Areas,* annual.

No. 546. Worldwide Military Expenditures: 1985 to 1993

[In billions of dollars. For military expenditures and Armed Forces by country, see section 30. GNP=Gross national product]

COUNTRY GROUP	1985	1986	1987	1988	1989	1990	1991	1992	1993
Current dollars, total [1]	**943**	**988**	**1,020**	**1,047**	**1,059**	**1,073**	**1,021**	**932**	**869**
United States	258	281	288	293	304	306	280	305	298
Percent of total	27.4	28.4	28.2	28.0	28.7	28.5	27.5	32.7	34.2
Developed countries [2]	756	797	833	860	867	849	787	689	648
Developing countries [2]	188	191	188	187	192	224	234	244	221
NATO countries [3]	405	432	448	456	475	486	467	489	480
Constant (1993) dollars, total [1].	**1,234**	**1,259**	**1,260**	**1,245**	**1,204**	**1,171**	**1,073**	**953**	**868**
United States	338	358	356	349	346	334	294	312	298
Percent of total	27.4	28.4	28.2	28.0	28.7	28.5	27.4	32.7	34.3
Developed countries [2]	989	1,016	1,028	1,023	986	926	827	704	648
Developing countries [2]	245	243	232	222	218	245	245	249	221
NATO countries [3]	530	550	553	542	541	530	490	500	480
Percent of GNP	**5.4**	**5.4**	**5.2**	**4.9**	**4.6**	**4.4**	**4.1**	**3.7**	**3.3**
United States	6.4	6.6	6.3	6.0	5.8	5.5	4.9	5.1	4.7
Developed countries [2]	5.4	5.4	5.4	5.1	4.8	4.5	4.0	3.7	3.4
Developing countries [2]	5.4	5.2	4.7	4.3	4.0	4.4	4.2	3.7	3.1
NATO countries [3]	4.8	4.9	4.8	4.5	4.3	4.2	3.8	3.8	3.6

[1] Includes countries not shown separately. [2] Twenty-eight developed countries; see table 547 for selected countries; for complete list, see source. [3] North Atlantic Treaty Organization.

No. 547. Arms Trade in Constant (1992) Dollars—Selected Countries: 1991 to 1993

[In millions of dollars, except percent. Because some countries exclude arms imports or exports from their trade statistics and their "total" imports and exports are therefore understated, and because arms transfers may be estimated independently of trade data, the ratio of arms to total imports or exports may be overstated and may even exceed 100 percent]

COUNTRY	1991	1992	1993 Total	1993 Arms imports as percent of total imports	COUNTRY	1991	1992	1993 Total	1993 Arms imports as percent of total imports
World total [1]	**31,790**	**24,710**	**21,960**	**0.6**	India	896	615	10	-
					Iran	2,215	369	1,000	6.2
Exporters: [1]					Iraq	-	-	-	-
Canada	517	1,025	200	0.1	Israel	554	795	850	3.8
China	1,582	897	950	1.0	Italy	200	82	50	(NA)
Czechoslovakia	243	144	(NA)	1.2	Japan	1,266	666	340	0.1
France	1,687	1,435	675	0.3	Jordan	53	21	20	0.6
Poland	116	21	10	0.1	Korea, North.	95	10	-	-
United Kingdom	4,957	4,511	4,300	2.4	Korea, South	633	349	875	1.0
United States	11,390	10,360	10,300	2.2	Kuwait.	380	769	650	9.9
Germany	2,531	1,128	1,100	0.3	Libya	432	82	-	-
					Morocco	32	51	20	0.3
Importers: [1]					Nicaragua	84	5	5	(NA)
Afghanistan	2,004	5	-	-	Oman	42	10	60	3.8
Algeria	137	-	10	0.1	Pakistan	211	379	430	4.5
Angola	53	10	100	(NA)	Peru	53	62	10	0.2
Argentina.	11	10	10	0.1	Poland	-	-	-	-
Australia	253	185	300	0.7	Romania	179	10	-	-
Canada	253	431	210	0.2	Saudi Arabia	6,538	7,382	5,100	(NA)
Cuba	554	103	100	5.9	Spain	190	215	190	0.2
Czechoslovakia.	53	-	(NA)	-	Syria	685	538	120	2.9
Egypt	712	897	1,100	13.4	Turkey.	1,055	846	975	3.3
El Salvador	63	31	30	1.6	United Kingdom	554	164	150	0.1
Ethiopia	84	-	-	-	United States	2,004	1,538	1,400	0.2
Germany	659	718	250	0.1	Venezuela	200	72	60	0.5
Greece	232	590	725	(NA)	Vietnam.	211	21	10	0.3
Hungary	-	-	875	0.1	Yemen (Sanaa).	32	5	20	1.3

- Represents or rounds to zero. NA Not available. [1] Includes countries not shown separately.

Source of tables 546 and 547: U.S. Arms Control and Disarmament Agency, *World Military Expenditures and Arms Transfers*, annual.

No. 548. Arms Transfers—Cumulative Value for Period 1991-93, by Major Supplier and Recipient Country

[In millions of dollars]

RECIPIENT	Total [1]	SUPPLIER				
		United States	France	United Kingdom	China	Germany
World, total	76,550	31,175	3,635	13,380	3,285	4,555
Africa [1]	2,015	195	95	230	295	15
Algeria	145	-	-	-	5	-
Angola	160	-	-	-	-	-
Ethiopia	80	-	-	-	-	-
Libya	480	-	-	-	50	10
Morocco	105	80	10	5	-	-
Mozambique	55	-	-	-	-10	-
Nigeria	295	5	50	190	-	-
Sudan	160	-	-	-	100	-
Zaire	30	-	-	-	10	-
Zimbabwe	155	-	-	30	80	-
Asia [1]	10,635	5,745	335	520	875	615
Afghanistan	1,905	-	-	-	-	-
Bahrain	190	190	-	-	-	-
Bangladesh	105	5	-	-	10	-
Burma	660	-	-	-	525	5
China	1,780	10	50	-	-	-
Taiwan	1,690	1,600	-	-	-	60
Cyprus	190	-	170	-	-	-
Egypt	2,695	2,400	20	10	-	5
Indonesia	210	70	100	-	-	40
India	1,430	70	-	-	-	150
Iran	3,575	-	-	-	875	40
Israel	2,200	2,000	-	-	-	200
Japan	2,230	2,200	-	-	-	30
Jordan	85	50	-	30	-	-
Korea, North	105	-	-	-	-	-
Korea, South	1,810	975	60	460	-	300
Kuwait	1,720	1,500	190	-	-	-
Laos	40	-	-	-	30	-
Malaysia	110	30	-	50	-	-
Oman	125	60	5	60	-	-
Pakistan	1,000	30	120	20	750	-
Philippines	240	180	-	-	-	-
Qatar	50	-	10	-	-	-
Saudi Arabia	18,570	5,200	1,000	10,200	280	525
Singapore	560	230	120	10	-	150
Sri Lanka	75	-	-	-	40	-
Syria	1,310	-	30	-	20	-
Thailand	925	450	-	-	320	30
United Arab Emir.	905	360	100	-	-	50
Vietnam	230	-	-	-	-	-
Europe [1]	14,240	7,485	1,030	475	-	2,255
Austria	90	20	10	-	-	-
Belgium	620	360	-	-	-	-
Czechoslovakia	50	-	-	-	-	-
Denmark	140	140	-	-	-	-
Finland	750	20	310	110	-	250
France	435	320	(NA)	10	-	-
Germany	1,560	1,100	50	100	-	(NA)
Greece	1,510	410	360	20	-	480
Hungary	865	-	-	-	-	40
Italy	330	270	-	50	-	-
Netherlands	770	675	20	5	-	-
Norway	670	130	-	50	-	280
Portugal	780	200	50	20	-	500
Romania	180	-	-	-	-	-
Slovakia	150	-	-	-	-	-
Spain	580	500	-	10	-	20
Sweden	275	140	100	-	-	5
Switzerland	660	80	80	100	-	400
Turkey	2,890	2,300	50	-	-	280
United Kingdom	840	800	-	(NA)	-	-
America:						
Canada	875	400	40	20	-	5
Chile	165	20	50	5	-	10
Colombia	320	60	-	-	-	160
El Salvador	120	120	-	-	-	-
Honduras	40	40	-	-	-	-
Nicaragua	80	-	-	-	-	-
Peru	120	10	-	-	20	-
United States	4,825	(X)	210	1,700	100	460
Venezuela	325	50	50	70	-	40
Oceania	980	640	-	20	-	-

- Nil or negligible ($2.5 million or less).   X Not applicable.   NA Not available.   [1] Includes countries not shown separately.

Source: U.S. Arms Control and Disarmament Agency, *World Military Expenditures and Arms Transfers,* annual.

No. 549. U.S. Military Sales and Assistance to to Foreign Governments: 1950 to 1994

[In millions of dollars, except as indicated. **For fiscal year ending in year shown;** see text, section 9. Department of Defense (DOD) sales deliveries cover deliveries against DOD sales orders sales orders authorized under Arms Export Control Act, as well as earlier and applicable legislation. For details regarding individual programs, see source]

ITEM	1950-85 [1]	1987	1988	1989	1990	1991	1992	1993	1994
Military sales agreements	165,691	6,074	11,171	10,009	11,831	20,367	14,557	32,173	12,812
Weapons and ammunition	65,038	1,739	4,521	4,117	4,510	6,008	7,395	17,013	5,161
Support equipment [2]	23,182	732	962	843	1,260	3,845	1,001	2,327	1,186
Spare parts and mods	33,746	1,547	2,845	2,280	2,583	4,375	2,657	6,703	3,145
Support services.	35,872	2,056	2,843	2,769	3,478	6,139	3,504	6,130	3,320
Military constr. sales agrmts	16,142	129	221	76	238	677	682	818	53
Military sales deliveries [3]	113,659	10,981	9,154	7,544	7,929	9,028	10,624	11,433	10,313
Military sales financing	49,371	4,053	4,049	4,273	4,758	4,693	4,274	4,124	3,917
Military assistance programs [4] . .	57,576	958	697	535	137	177	116	540	159
Military assist. program delivery [5] .	54,920	83	56	53	27	150	87	51	6
IMET program/deliveries [5]	2,001	53	45	46	43	46	42	43	22
Students trained (1,000).	538	6	6	5	5	5	4	4	3

[1] Includes transition quarter, July-September 1976.   [2] Includes aircraft, ships, support vehicles, communications equipment, and other supplies.   [3] Includes military construction sales deliveries.   [4] Also includes Military Assistance Service Funded (MASF) program data, section 506(a) drawdown authority, and MAP Merger Funds.   [5] Includes Military Assistance Service Funded (MASF) program data and section 506(a) drawdown authority.

Source: U.S. Defense Security Assistance Agency, *Foreign Military Sales, Foreign Military Construction Sales, and Military Assistance Facts,* annual; and unpublished data.

No. 550. U.S. Military Sales Deliveries to Foreign Governments, by Country: 1950 to 1994

[In millions of dollars. For **fiscal years ending in year shown;** see text, section 9. Represents Department of Defense military sales]

COUNTRY	1950-1986 [1]	1987	1988	1989	1990	1991	1992	1993	1994 Total	1994 Percent distribution
Total [2]	113,810	11,114	9,195	7,385	7,801	9,040	10,574	11,433	10,313	100.0
Australia	3,703	589	850	583	381	206	161	238	357	3.5
Belgium	1,889	27	185	136	156	163	37	51	95	0.9
Canada	2,022	127	212	144	103	164	107	122	156	1.5
China: Taiwan	3,239	366	484	353	460	556	823	727	768	7.4
Denmark.	1,066	62	149	93	38	47	44	55	31	0.3
Egypt.	4,112	962	498	322	441	573	1,093	1,311	1,072	10.4
El Salvador	348	76	93	92	87	58	65	43	28	0.3
France	649	99	37	36	109	32	35	41	78	0.8
Germany	8,228	315	382	632	359	480	503	346	158	1.5
Greece.	2,010	79	129	137	114	124	172	206	195	1.9
Indonesia	293	23	32	32	187	18	20	39	17	0.2
Israel	9,138	1,230	754	230	151	246	721	796	935	9.1
Italy	1,003	71	62	64	61	69	54	53	111	1.1
Japan	2,421	235	212	166	220	324	546	322	612	5.9
Jordan	1,474	50	55	60	42	23	20	25	33	0.3
Kuwait	884	58	41	46	52	112	858	882	229	2.2
Morocco.	721	42	74	32	41	20	39	19	21	0.2
Netherlands	2,973	417	327	391	381	371	306	122	218	2.1
Norway.	1,531	83	117	95	117	82	36	42	66	0.6
Pakistan	1,654	134	139	175	575	-	-	-	-	-
Philippines	252	32	69	72	62	97	96	44	47	0.5
Portugal	191	24	15	32	72	40	89	84	229	2.2
Saudi Arabia	32,245	3,324	1,327	986	1,152	3,041	2,674	3,659	2,266	22.0
Singapore	492	143	191	37	47	64	25	55	92	0.9
South Korea	3,089	344	326	316	328	230	310	306	380	3.7
Spain.	1,376	822	637	658	403	155	138	204	412	4.0
Sudan	245	26	24	30	-	-	-	-	-	-
Thailand	1,410	95	291	211	175	180	103	107	140	1.4
Tunisia	385	44	20	25	32	27	20	17	30	0.3
Turkey	2,108	277	699	619	720	601	703	750	896	8.7
United Kingdom	4,774	205	180	131	205	243	154	227	205	2.0
Venezuela.	686	50	27	13	20	23	16	21	17	0.2

- Represents or rounds to zero.   [1] Includes transactions for the transition quarter, July-September 1976.   [2] Includes countries not shown.

Source: U.S. Defense Security Assistance Agency, *Foreign Military Sales, Foreign Military Construction Sales,* and *Military Assistance Facts,* annual.

No. 551. Summary of Active and Reserve Military Personnel and Forces: 1989 to 1995

ITEM	1989	1994	1995, est.	ITEM	1989	1994	1995, est.
Military personnel (1,000):				Navy aircraft carrier..........	-	-	1
Active...................	2,130	1,611	1,523	Other navy ships	26	16	19
Guard and Reserve..........	1,171	1,025	965	Marine divisions and air wings...	1	1	1
Active Forces:				Air Force tactical wings	12	9	8
Army divisions............	18	12	12	Nuclear Deterrent:			
Navy aircraft carriers.........	16	12	11	Intercontinental Ballistic Missiles .	1,000	642	585
Navy air wings	13	11	10	Ballistic missile submarines.....	34	15	16
Navy combatants & attack subs..	287	196	197	Missiles.................	608	352	384
Marine divisions and air wings.. .	3	3	3	Bombers.................	268	152	140
Air Force tactical wings	25	13	13	Mobility Forces:			
Reserve Forces:				Strategic airlift aircraft	367	356	354
Army combat brigades........	56	48	48	Sealift ships [1]..............	163	174	149
Navy air wings	2	1	1				

- Represents or rounds to zero.   [1] Includes ships in the Ready Reserve Force funded.

Source: U.S. Office of Management and Budget, *Budget,* annual.

No. 552. Department of Defense Manpower: 1950 to 1993

[**In thousands. As of end of fiscal year;** see text, section 9. Includes National Guard, Reserve, and retired regular personnel on extended or continuous active duty. Excludes Coast Guard. Other officer candidates are included under enlisted personnel. See also *Historical Statistics, Colonial Times to 1970,* series Y 904-916]

YEAR	Total [1][2]	ARMY			NAVY [3]			MARINE CORPS			AIR FORCE		
		Total [2]	Officers	Enlisted	Total [2]	Officers	Enlisted	Total [2]	Officers	Enlisted	Total [2]	Officers	Enlisted
1950	1,459	593	73	519	381	45	333	74	7	67	411	57	354
1955	2,935	1,109	122	986	661	75	583	205	18	187	960	137	823
1960	2,475	873	101	770	617	70	545	171	16	154	815	130	683
1961	2,483	859	100	757	626	70	552	177	16	161	821	129	690
1962	2,806	1,066	116	949	664	75	585	191	17	174	884	135	746
1963	2,699	976	108	866	664	76	584	190	17	173	869	134	733
1964	2,686	973	111	861	666	76	585	190	17	173	857	133	721
1965	2,654	969	112	855	670	78	588	190	17	173	825	132	690
1966	3,092	1,200	118	1,080	743	80	659	262	21	241	887	131	753
1967	3,375	1,442	144	1,297	750	82	664	285	24	262	897	135	759
1968	3,546	1,570	166	1,402	764	85	674	307	25	283	905	140	762
1969	3,458	1,512	173	1,337	774	85	684	310	26	284	862	135	723
1970	3,065	1,323	167	1,153	691	81	606	260	25	235	791	130	657
1971	2,713	1,124	149	972	622	75	542	212	22	191	755	126	625
1972	2,322	811	121	687	587	73	511	198	20	178	726	122	600
1973	2,252	801	116	682	564	71	490	196	19	177	691	115	572
1974	2,162	783	106	674	546	67	475	189	19	170	644	110	529
1975	2,128	784	103	678	535	66	466	196	19	177	613	105	503
1976	2,082	779	99	678	525	64	458	192	19	174	585	100	481
1977	2,075	782	98	680	530	63	462	192	19	173	571	96	470
1978	2,062	772	98	670	530	63	463	191	18	172	570	95	470
1979	2,027	759	97	657	523	62	457	185	18	167	559	96	459
1980	2,051	777	99	674	527	63	460	188	18	170	558	98	456
1981	2,083	781	102	675	540	65	470	191	18	172	570	99	467
1982	2,109	780	103	673	553	67	481	192	19	173	583	102	476
1983	2,123	780	106	669	558	68	485	194	20	174	592	105	483
1984	2,138	780	108	668	565	69	491	196	20	176	597	106	486
1985	2,151	781	110	667	571	71	495	198	20	178	602	108	489
1986	2,169	781	110	667	581	72	504	199	20	179	608	109	495
1987	2,174	781	108	668	587	72	510	200	20	179	607	107	495
1988	2,138	772	107	660	593	72	516	197	20	177	576	105	467
1989	2,130	770	107	658	593	72	516	197	20	177	571	104	463
1990	2,044	732	104	624	579	72	503	197	20	177	535	100	431
1991	1,986	711	104	603	570	71	495	194	20	174	510	97	409
1992	1,807	610	95	511	542	69	468	185	19	165	470	90	376
1993	1,705	572	88	480	510	66	439	178	18	160	444	84	356

[1] Beginning 1980, excludes Navy Reserve personnel on active duty for Training and Administration of Reserves (TARS). From 1969, the full-time Guard and Reserve.   [2] Includes Cadets.   [3] Prior to 1980, includes Navy Reserve personnel on active duty for Training and Administration of Reserves (TARS).

Source: U.S. Dept. of Defense, *Selected Manpower Statistics,* annual.

No. 553. Military Installations in the United States: 1994

[Represents bases with active-duty populations of 300 or more. Excludes the Coast Guard]

STATE AND BRANCH	Active duty personnel	Family members	Civilians
United States	1,048,249	1,244,283	552,011
Alabama	24,679	29,615	29,495
Army	13,703	14,615	19,973
Navy	5,488	7,500	4,761
Air Force	5,488	7,500	4,761
Alaska	19,152	24,184	5,204
Army	7,700	9,635	2,640
Navy	1,405	-	86
Air Force	10,047	14,549	2,478
Arizona	22,444	38,249	9,909
Army	5,682	4,760	5,597
Marine Corps	6,553	6,789	1,113
Air Force	10,209	26,700	3,199
Arkansas	4,763	7,673	1,429
Army	350	247	622
Air Force	4,413	7,426	807
California	230,566	158,903	108,667
Army	9,842	7,302	4,465
Navy	133,630	44,293	46,022
Marine Corps	55,604	48,633	23,609
Air Force	31,490	58,675	34,571
Colorado	36,503	48,252	12,734
Army	17,918	37,572	4,703
Air Force	18,585	10,680	8,031
Connecticut	10,000	22,500	1,800
Navy	10,000	22,500	1,800
Delaware	4,388	6,446	1,616
Air Force	4,388	6,446	1,616
District of Columbia ..	9,617	90	10,945
Army	5,200	50	5,200
Navy	2,000	-	4,550
Marine Corps	1,168	40	-
Air Force	1,249	-	1,195
Florida	86,161	156,885	32,054
Navy	57,119	99,674	21,547
Air Force	29,042	57,211	10,507
Georgia	73,470	93,666	41,920
Army	56,544	62,789	20,986
Navy	7,400	18,350	4,250
Marine Corps	1,000	2,000	3,000
Air Force	8,526	10,527	13,684
Hawaii	56,720	50,952	21,947
Army	18,277	17,600	4,653
Navy	23,631	15,141	11,162
Marine Corps	10,007	10,604	2,118
Air Force	4,805	7,607	4,014
Idaho	4,004	3,700	467
Navy	500	300	-
Air Force	3,504	3,400	467
Illinois	22,753	28,166	14,137
Army	2,120	3,560	8,390
Navy	14,000	15,000	2,200
Air Force	6,633	9,606	3,547
Indiana	2,500	3,000	5,500
Army	2,500	3,000	5,500
Iowa	-	-	-
Kansas	21,008	28,341	4,986
Army	18,000	21,300	4,590
Air Force	3,008	7,041	396
Kentucky	34,600	41,194	8,304
Army	34,600	41,194	8,304
Louisiana	19,865	27,930	8,271
Army	10,396	18,438	4,952
Navy	3,669	1,295	2,119
Air Force	5,800	8,197	1,200
Maine	2,903	3,550	930
Navy	2,903	3,550	930
Air Force	-	-	-
Maryland	41,343	33,414	70,261
Army	21,538	15,026	52,903
Navy	9,796	8,400	14,158
Air Force	10,009	9,988	3,200
Massachusetts	6,163	6,143	4,585
Army	3,328	4,388	2,271
Navy	600	-	250
Air Force	2,235	1,755	2,064
Michigan	3,909	6,336	2,593
Air Force	3,909	6,336	2,593
Minnesota	-	-	-
Mississippi	13,763	22,438	8,760
Navy	7,400	6,900	2,994
Air Force	6,363	15,538	5,766
Missouri	8,716	12,297	5,120
Army	5,125	6,297	4,482
Air Force	3,591	6,000	638
Montana	4,611	7,158	527
Air Force	4,611	7,158	527
Nebraska	9,677	15,380	2,828
Air Force	9,677	15,380	2,828
Nevada	8,120	18,686	2,100
Navy	1,100	2,000	1,000
Air Force	7,020	16,686	1,100
New Hampshire	597	1,077	4,100
Navy	597	1,077	4,100
New Jersey	10,264	13,809	13,800
Army	2,910	5,489	8,867
Navy	3,014	1,200	3,283
Air Force	4,340	7,120	1,650
New Mexico	16,975	24,153	22,942
Army	1,061	1,626	7,505
Air Force	15,914	22,527	15,437
New York	25,695	35,383	9,584
Army	17,092	20,240	6,519
Navy	2,500	3,000	-
Air Force	6,103	12,143	3,065
North Carolina	104,793	101,619	18,061
Army	40,000	11,500	6,000
Marine Corps	55,076	77,737	10,576
Air Force	9,717	12,382	1,485
North Dakota	9,300	12,840	1,450
Air Force	9,300	12,840	1,450
Ohio	8,754	18,308	15,400
Air Force	8,754	18,308	15,400
Oklahoma	28,241	44,511	20,616
Army	16,806	38,911	5,930
Air Force	11,435	5,600	14,686
Oregon	-	-	-
Pennsylvania	6,001	7,045	7,396
Army	1,233	1,745	1,482
Navy	4,768	5,300	5,914
Rhode Island	3,652	3,000	3,976
Navy	3,652	3,000	3,976
South Carolina	36,718	75,586	13,478
Army	5,388	11,691	2,226
Navy	13,726	35,000	6,700
Marine Corps	7,151	9,286	1,646
Air Force	10,453	19,609	2,906
South Dakota	5,022	7,754	850
Air Force	5,022	7,754	850
Tennessee	9,839	4,050	3,269
Navy	9,839	4,050	3,269
Texas	133,847	183,152	61,899
Army	81,471	134,052	22,449
Navy	6,469	12,800	7,908
Air Force	45,907	36,300	31,542
Utah	5,000	-	11,000
Air Force	5,000	-	11,000
Vermont	-		-
Virginia	173,032	170,023	69,253
Army	22,989	23,511	19,993
Navy	139,493	141,512	46,469
Marine Corps	10,550	5,000	2,791
Air Force	8,811	10,573	2,613
Washington	48,550	72,872	35,895
Army	15,500	24,600	5,500
Navy	23,689	35,018	27,258
Air Force	9,361	13,254	3,137
West Virginia	-		-
Wisconsin	300	725	2,200
Army	300	725	2,200
Wyoming	3,500	5,000	650
Air Force	3,500	5,000	650

- Represents or rounds to zero.

Source: Army Times Publishing Co. Springfield, VA 22159, *Guide to Military Installations in the U. S.,* annual.

No. 554. Military Personnel on Active Duty, by Location: 1970 to 1994

[In thousands. 1970 as of Dec. 31; thereafter, as of end of fiscal year; see text, section 9]

ITEM	1970	1980	1985	1987	1988	1989	1990	1991	1992	1993	1994
Total	3,065	2,051	2,151	2,174	2,138	2,130	2,044	1,986	1,807	1,705	1,611
Shore-based [1]	2,798	1,840	1,920	1,928	1,891	1,884	1,794	1,743	1,589	1,505	1,431
Afloat [2]	268	211	231	246	248	246	252	243	218	200	180
United States [3]	2,033	1,562	1,636	1,650	1,598	1,620	1,437	1,539	1,463	1,397	1,324
Foreign countries	1,033	488	516	524	541	510	609	448	344	308	287

[1] Includes Navy personnel temporarily on shore.   [2] Includes Marine Corps.   [3] Includes outlying areas.

Source: U.S. Dept. of Defense, *Selected Manpower Statistics*, annual.

No. 555. Military Personnel on Active Duty in Foreign Countries: 1993

[As of end of fiscal year]

COUNTRY	1993	COUNTRY	1993	COUNTRY	1993
In foreign countries	308,020	Egypt	605	Norway	196
Ashore	263,194	El Salvador	42	Oman	26
Afloat	44,826	Ethopia	17	Pakistan	33
Antarctica	58	Finland	18	Panama	10,542
Antigua	71	France	74	Paraguay	11
Argentina	23	Germany	105,254	Peru	20
Australia	339	Greece	807	Philippines	53
Austria	34	Greenland	131	Poland	18
Bahamas, The	25	Guatemala	22	Portugal	1,320
Bahrain	379	Haiti	12	Rep. of Korea	34,830
Bangladesh	10	Honduras	696	Romania	12
Barbados	12	Hong Kong	34	Russia	70
Belgium	1,808	Hungary	18	Saudi Arabia	950
Bermuda	527	Iceland	2,878	Senegal	11
Bolivia	21	India	32	Singapore	162
Brazil	54	Indonesia	49	Somalia	6,345
Bulgaria	12	Israel	42	South Africa	24
Burma	10	Italy	10,333	Spain	3,820
Cameroon	10	Jamaica	16	Sri Lanka	11
Canada	547	Japan	46,131	Sudan	11
Chile	23	Jordan	21	Sweden	13
China	38	Kenya	33	Switzerland	30
Colombia	41	Korea, Republic of	34,830	Syria	10
Costa Rica	12	Kuwait	233	Thailand	106
Cote D'Ivoire	18	Liberia	10	Tonga	23
Croatia	10	Malaysia	20	Tunisia	19
Cuba (Guantanamo)	2,189	Mexico	30	Turkey	4,049
Cyprus	18	Morocco	22	United Arab Emirates	25
Czech Republic	17	Nepal	10	United Kingdom	16,100
Denmark	45	Netherlands	2,226	Uruguay	12
Diego Garcia	1,233	New Zealand	67	Venezuela	38
Dominican Republic	14	Nicaragua	15	Zambabwe	10
Ecuador	20	Nigeria	16		

[1] Includes areas not shown separately.

Source: U.S. Department of Defense, *Selected Manpower Statistics*, annual.

No. 556. Coast Guard Personnel on Active Duty: 1970 to 1994

[As of end of fiscal year]

YEAR	Total	Officers	Cadets	Enlisted	YEAR	Total	Officers	Cadets	Enlisted
1970	37,689	5,512	653	31,524	1991	38,377	7,192	900	30,285
1975	36,788	5,630	1,177	29,981	1992	39,388	7,507	919	30,962
1980	39,381	6,463	877	32,041	1993	39,234	7,628	907	30,699
1985	38,595	6,775	733	31,087	1994	37,802	7,656	881	29,265
1990	36,939	6,876	927	29,136					

Source: U.S. Dept. of Transportation, *Annual Report of the Secretary of Transportation*.

No. 557. Armed Forces Personnel—Summary of Major Conflicts

[For Revolutionary War, number of personnel serving not known, but estimates range from 184,000 to 250,000; for War of 1812, 286,730 served; for Mexican War, 78,718 served. Dates of the major conflicts may differ from those specified in various laws providing benefits for veterans. See table 548 for data on Vietnam conflict. See also *Historical Statistics, Colonial Times to 1970,* series Y 856-903]

ITEM	Unit	Civil War [1]	Spanish-American War	World War I	World War II	Korean conflict	Vietnam conflict
Personnel serving [2]	1,000 ...	2,213	307	4,735	[3]16,113	[4]5,720	[5]8,744
Average duration of service	Months ..	20	8	12	33	19	23
Service abroad: Personnel serving	Percent..	(NA)	[6]29	53	73	[7]56	(NA)
Average duration [8]	Months ..	(NA)	1.5	6	16	13	(NA)
Casualties: [9] Battle deaths [2]	1,000 ...	140	(Z)	53	292	34	[10]47
Wounds not mortal [2]	1,000 ...	282	2	204	671	103	[10]153
Draftees: Classified	1,000 ...	777	(X)	24,234	36,677	9,123	[5]75,717
Examined	1,000 ...	522	(X)	3,764	17,955	3,685	[5]8,611
Rejected	1,000 ...	160	(X)	803	6,420	1,189	[5]3,880
Inducted	1,000 ...	46	(X)	2,820	10,022	1,560	[5]1,759

NA Not available. X Not applicable. Z Fewer than 500. [1] Union forces only. Estimates of the number serving in Confederate forces range from 600,000 to 1.5 million. [2] Source: U.S. Department of Defense, *Selected Manpower Statistics,* annual. [3] Covers Dec. 1, 1941, to Dec. 31, 1946. [4] Covers June 25, 1950, to July 27, 1953. [5] Covers Aug. 4, 1964, to Jan. 27, 1973. [6] Army and Marines only. [7] Excludes Navy. Covers July 1950 through Jan. 1955. Far East area only. [8] During hostilities only. [9] For periods covered, see footnotes 3, 4, and 5. [10] Covers Jan. 1, 1961, to Jan. 27, 1973. Includes known military service personnel who have died from combat related wounds.

Source: Except as noted, the President's Commission on Veterans' Pensions, Veterans' *Benefits in the United States,* vol. I, 1956; and U.S. Dept. of Defense, unpublished data.

No. 558. Enlisted Military Personnel Accessions: 1990 to 1993

[In thousands. For years ending Sept. 30]

BRANCH OF SERVICE	1990	1991	1992	1993	BRANCH OF SERVICE	1990	1991	1992	1993
Total	461.0	433.1	427.5	406.0	First enlistments	62.0	49.8	42.7	51.1
First enlistments	216.0	184.9	186.0	187.4	Reenlistments	58.6	60.7	56.9	51.6
Reenlistments	237.0	218.9	221.5	200.7	Marine Corps	48.0	45.0	47.7	46.4
Reserves to active duty	15.6	29.3	19.9	17.9	First enlistments	33.0	29.7	32.1	34.0
Army	182.0	159.7	155.4	151.8	Reenlistments	14.4	14.1	14.9	11.9
First enlistments	85.0	75.1	75.8	70.5	Air Force	104.0	94.6	105.9	87.9
Reenlistments	96.5	79.9	79.4	81.2	First enlistments	37.0	30.3	35.4	31.9
Navy	135.0	133.8	118.8	119.9	Reenlistments	67.5	64.0	70.1	55.9

Source: U.S. Dept. of Defense, *Selected Manpower Statistics,* annual.

No. 559. Military Personnel on Active Duty and Monthly Basic Pay: 1990 to 1993

[Personnel as of Sept. 30; basic pay as of January, except as noted]

RANK/GRADE	PERSONNEL (1,000)				MONTHLY BASIC PAY (dollars)			
	1990	1991	1992	1993	1990	1991	1992	1993
Total [1]	2,043.7	1,985.6	1,807.2	1,705.1	(X)	(X)	(X)	(X)
Recruit—E-1	97.6	74.6	83.2	75.4	684	710	752	769
Private—E-2	140.3	125.8	110.9	114.1	803	838	873	909
Pvt. 1st class—E-3	280.1	275.6	233.5	214.6	871	900	937	976
Corporal—E-4	427.8	426.1	383.5	352.2	1,014	1,066	1,107	1,154
Sergeant—E-5	361.5	355.5	305.1	295.6	1,245	1,297	1,356	1,409
Staff Sgt.—E-6	239.1	238.9	227.4	214.6	1,480	1,563	1,634	1,711
Sgt. 1st class—E-7	134.1	134.2	130.5	124.7	1,784	1,866	1,946	2,028
Master Sgt.—E-8	38.0	36.1	33.2	31.6	2,117	2,210	2,302	2,406
Sgt. Major—E-9	15.3	14.8	13.5	12.8	2,583	2,682	2,794	2,933
Warrant Officer—W-1	3.2	2.8	2.2	2.4	1,686	1,747	1,809	1,849
Chief Warrant—W-4	3.0	3.0	2.7	2.4	2,943	3,085	3,214	3,383
2d Lt.—0-1	31.9	27.3	25.8	25.0	1,485	1,562	1,627	1,697
1st Lt.—0-2	37.9	37.6	33.5	29.7	2,056	2,135	2,220	2,311
Captain—0-3	106.6	106.1	100.2	93.0	2,618	2,727	2,829	2,924
Major—0-4	53.2	53.1	50.4	48.0	3,196	3,321	3,453	3,588
Lt. Colonel—0-5	32.3	32.2	30.9	29.5	3,894	4,041	4,197	4,359
Colonel—0-6	14.0	13.7	13.2	12.5	4,758	4,942	5,137	5,371
Brig. General—0-7	0.5	0.5	0.5	0.4	5,751	5,987	6,238	6,469
Major General—0-8	0.4	0.3	0.3	0.3	6,516	6,783	7,068	7,330
Lt. General—0-9	0.1	0.1	0.1	0.1	6,516	7,482	7,788	8,075
General—0-10	(Z)	(Z)	(Z)	(Z)	6,516	8,441	8,733	9,017

X Not applicable. Z Fewer than 50. [1] Includes cadets and midshipmen and warrant officers, W-2 and W-3.

Source: U.S. Dept. of Defense, *Selected Manpower Statistics,* annual, and Office of the Comptroller, unpublished data.

No. 560. Military Reserve Personnel: 1970 to 1994

[In thousands. As of end of fiscal year; see text, section 9. Excludes U.S. Coast Guard Reserve. The ready reserve includes selected reservists who are intended to assist active forces in a war and the individual ready reserve who, in a major war, would be used to fill out active and reserve units and later would be a source of combat replacements; a portion of the ready reserve serves in an active status. The standby reserve cannot be called to active duty unless the Congress gives its explicit approval. The retired reserve represents a low potential for mobilization]

RESERVE STATUS AND BRANCH OF SERVICE	1970	1975	1980	1985	1986	1987	1988	1989	1990	1991	1992	1993	1994
Total reserves	3,639	1,836	1,349	1,610	1,653	1,657	1,677	1,661	1,671	1,786	1,883	1,867	1,805
Ready reserve	2,574	1,471	1,263	1,566	1,612	1,620	1,642	1,631	1,641	1,758	1,858	1,841	1,779
Standby reserve	492	365	86	44	41	38	34	29	29	28	25	26	26
Retired reserve	573	(NA)	338	372	390	412	469	477	462	474	442	461	482
Army	2,221	1,168	804	1,045	1,067	1,064	1,070	1,062	1,050	1,124	1,156	1,132	1,077
Navy	808	273	207	214	228	238	244	248	252	271	297	302	317
Marine Corp	(NA)	124	94	92	93	88	87	82	83	96	107	112	109
Air Force.	610	271	243	259	266	268	275	270	286	295	323	321	302

NA Not available.

Source: U.S. Dept. of Defense, *Official Guard and Reserve Manpower Strengths and Statistics,* quarterly.

No. 561. Ready Reserve Personnel Profile—Race, and Sex: 1990 to 1994

ITEM	RACE					PERCENT DISTRIBUTION			
	Total	White	Black	Asian	American Indian	White	Black	Asian	American Indian
1990	1,558,867	1,269,278	271,470	14,608	3,511	81.4	17.4	0.9	0.2
1991	1,154,515	906,748	190,214	12,711	5,652	78.5	16.5	1.1	0.5
1992	1,114,905	725,963	172,770	11,479	4,842	65.1	15.5	1.0	0.4
1993	1,057,676	829,797	173,444	13,350	4,785	78.5	16.4	1.3	0.5
1994, total [1]	1,137,048	771,068	163,427	13,686	4,584	67.8	14.4	1.2	0.4
Male	998,330	681,062	124,683	11,897	3,800	68.2	12.5	1.2	0.4
Officers	153,809	117,107	7,630	1,620	292	76.1	5.0	1.1	0.2
Enlisted.	844,521	563,955	117,053	10,277	3,508	66.8	13.9	1.2	0.4
Female.	138,718	90,006	38,744	1,789	784	64.9	27.9	1.3	0.6
Officers	24,197	19,200	3,731	287	59	79.3	15.4	1.2	0.2
Enlisted.	114,521	70,806	35,013	1,502	725	61.8	30.6	1.3	0.6

[1] Includes unknown sex.

Source: U.S. Dept. of Defense, *Official Guard and Reserve Manpower Strengths and Statistics,* annual.

No. 562. Military Reserve Costs: 1980 to 1993

[In millions of dollars. As of end of fiscal year; see text, section 9. Army and Air Force data include National Guard]

TYPE OF COST	1980	1985	1987	1988	1989	1990	1991	1992	1993
Total	7,969	19,414	18,947	19,234	19,797	21,526	21,811	21,867	22,825
Operations and maintenance	3,526	5,734	6,168	6,670	6,694	6,687	7,398	7,714	8,095
Personnel	2,456	7,703	8,382	8,837	8,637	8,621	8,543	9,272	9,062
Procurement	1,459	5,009	3,316	2,533	3,520	4,914	4,480	3,533	4,398
Active-duty support	408	566	601	610	611	638	700	731	682
Construction	120	402	480	584	605	666	690	617	588

Source: U.S. Dept. of Defense, unpublished data.

No. 563. National Guard—Summary: 1980 to 1993

[As of end of fiscal year; see text, section 9. Includes Puerto Rico]

ITEM	Unit	1980	1985	1987	1988	1989	1990	1991	1992	1993
Army National Guard: Units .	Number . .	3,379	4,353	6,125	5,982	5,715	4,055	6,470	6,727	6,339
Personnel [1]	1,000	368	438	452	455	457	444	446	427	410
Funds obligated [2]	Bil. dol. . . .	1.8	4.4	5.0	5.3	5.4	5.2	5.4	5.4	4.8
Value of equipment	Bil. dol. . . .	7.6	18.8	22.3	27.4	30.1	29.0	29.0	29.0	31.0
Air National Guard: Units. . .	Number . .	1,054	1,184	1,281	1,272	1,339	1,339	1,450	1,425	1,330
Personnel [1]	1,000	96	109	115	115	116	118	115	119	117
Funds obligated [2]	Bil. dol. . . .	1.7	2.8	2.9	3.1	3.2	3.2	3.2	1.2	2.6
Value of equipment (est.) [3] .	Bil. dol. . . .	5.2	21.4	23.7	25.7	27.5	26.4	27.1	38.3	41.7

[1] Officers and enlisted personnel. [2] Federal funds; includes personnel, operations, maintenance, and military construction. [3] Beginning 1985, increase due to repricing of aircraft to current year dollars to reflect true replacement value. Beginning 1993 includes value of aircraft and support equipment.

Source: National Guard Bureau, *Annual Review of the Chief, National Guard Bureau;* and unpublished data.

No. 564. Wartime Veterans—States: 1994

[In thousands. **As of end of fiscal year**; see text, section 9. Data were estimated starting with veteran's place of residence as of April 1, 1980, based on 1980 Census of Population data, extended to later years on the basis of estimates of veteran interstate migration, separations from the Armed Forces, and mortality; not directly comparable with earlier estimates previously published by the VA. Excludes 423,000 veterans whose only active-duty military service occurred since September 8, 1980, and who failed to satisfy the minimum service requirement. Also excludes a small indeterminate number of National Guard personnel or reservists who incurred service-connected disabilities while on an initial tour of active duty for training only]

STATE	Total veterans [1]	War veterans [1]	World War I	World War II	Korean conflict	Vietnam era [2]	Persian Gulf War
United States . .	**26,365**	**20,327**	**18**	**7,770**	**4,563**	**8,246**	**1,230**
Northeast	5,126	3,980	4	1,672	887	1,405	195
New England.	1,418	1,088	1	441	246	412	48
Maine.	155	118	(Z)	42	26	50	8
New Hampshire	137	102	(Z)	35	23	46	5
Vermont	63	47	(Z)	16	10	20	3
Massachusetts	606	469	1	201	107	166	18
Rhode Island	111	87	(Z)	38	20	31	4
Connecticut	346	265	(Z)	109	60	99	10
Middle Atlantic	3,708	2,892	3	1,231	641	993	147
New York	1,569	1,215	1	507	269	416	67
New Jersey	756	590	1	255	137	201	23
Pennsylvania	1,383	1,087	1	469	235	376	57
North Central.	6,297	4,892	3	1,837	1,061	1,904	304
East North Central	4,370	3,382	3	1,281	720	1,304	210
Ohio.	1,204	936	1	362	197	357	59
Indiana	599	458	(Z)	168	100	181	29
Illinois.	1,092	854	1	332	186	321	49
Michigan	961	739	1	272	152	293	48
Wisconsin	514	395	(Z)	147	85	152	25
West North Central.	1,927	1,510	(Z)	556	341	600	94
Minnesota	468	360	(Z)	125	78	151	19
Iowa.	296	237	(Z)	90	53	87	16
Missouri	592	462	(Z)	175	106	183	29
North Dakota	60	48	(Z)	16	11	19	4
South Dakota	75	59	(Z)	21	15	22	5
Nebraska	170	134	(Z)	49	32	52	9
Kansas	266	210	(Z)	80	46	86	12
South.	9,293	7,156	3	2,705	1,627	3,013	504
South Atlantic	5,076	3,874	2	1,510	889	1,622	247
Delaware.	79	60	(Z)	23	13	24	4
Maryland.	536	394	(Z)	139	89	174	23
District of Columbia. . .	52	40	(Z)	16	11	15	3
Virginia	710	526	(Z)	175	125	261	33
West Virginia	202	163	(Z)	66	37	59	11
North Carolina	714	542	(Z)	195	121	232	38
South Carolina	381	289	(Z)	101	65	130	25
Georgia.	687	509	(Z)	157	111	247	41
Florida	1,715	1,351	2	638	317	480	69
East South Central	1,556	1,213	(Z)	447	277	490	100
Kentucky.	371	291	(Z)	108	63	117	21
Tennessee.	520	401	(Z)	144	89	170	28
Alabama	430	336	(Z)	123	81	135	31
Mississippi.	235	185	(Z)	72	44	68	20
West South Central . . .	2,661	2,069	1	748	461	901	157
Arkansas.	260	206	(Z)	82	46	79	18
Louisiana	384	304	(Z)	114	65	119	30
Oklahoma	355	282	(Z)	107	66	119	18
Texas	1,662	1,277	1	445	284	584	91
West	5,651	4,297	2	1,556	989	1,919	227
Mountain	1,608	1,242	(Z)	452	286	546	76
Montana	97	77	(Z)	28	17	31	6
Idaho	113	88	(Z)	33	19	36	7
Wyoming.	49	39	(Z)	13	8	17	3
Colorado	390	299	(Z)	94	67	148	19
New Mexico.	173	133	(Z)	48	30	60	9
Arizona.	460	355	(Z)	144	83	146	19
Utah.	140	112	(Z)	42	25	45	9
Nevada	186	139	(Z)	50	37	63	5
Pacific	4,043	3,055	2	1,104	703	1,373	151
Washington	636	480	(Z)	161	107	232	27
Oregon	374	291	(Z)	111	60	124	16
California.	2,852	2,152	2	796	507	945	101
Alaska	65	46	(Z)	8	8	30	2
Hawaii	116	86	(Z)	28	21	42	5

Z Less than 500.   [1] Veterans who served in more than one wartime period are counted only once. "All Veterans" includes Vietnam era (no prior wartime service), Korean conflict (no prior wartime service), World War II, post Vietnam era, Persian Gulf War era, and other.   [2] Excludes reservists.

Source: U.S. Dept. of Veterans Affairs, Management Sciences Service (008B2), *Annual Report of the Secretary of Veterans Affairs*.

No. 565. Veterans Living in the United States and Puerto Rico, by Age and by Service: 1994

[In thousands, except as indicated. As of July 1. Estimated. Excludes 500,000 veterans whose only active duty military service of less than 2 years occurred since Sept. 30, 1980. See headnote, table 564. See *Historical Statistics, Colonial Times to 1970,* series Y 943-956, for all veterans]

AGE	Total veterans	WARTIME VETERANS						Peace-time veterans
		Total [1]	Persian Gulf	Vietnam era	Korean con-flict	World War II	World War I	
1994	**26,497**	**20,425**	**1,236**	**8,281**	**4,597**	**7,795**	**19**	**6,072**
All ages	26,497	20,425	1,236	8,281	4,597	7,795	19	6,072
Under 30 years old . . .	1,236	675	675	(Z)	-	-	-	561
30-34 years old	1,328	215	203	12	-	-	-	1,113
35-39 years old	1,610	588	112	498	-	-	-	1,022
40-44 years old	2,194	1,951	126	1,920	-	-	-	244
45-49 years old	3,530	3,390	81	3,371	-	-	-	141
50-54 years old	2,545	1,548	28	1,538	-	-	-	997
55-59 years old	2,435	960	9	409	625	-	-	1,475
60-64 years old	3,037	2,653	2	260	2,524	110	-	384
65 years old and over .	8,581	8,446	(Z)	272	1,448	7,685	19	135

- Represents zero.   Z Less than 500.   [1] Veterans who served in more than one wartime period are counted only once.

Source: U.S. Dept. of Veterans Affairs, Office of Information Management and Statistics, *Veteran Population,* annual.

No. 566. Disabled Veterans Receiving Compensation: 1970 to 1994

[In thousands, except as indicated. As of end of fiscal year; see text, section 9. Represents veterans receiving compensation for service-connected disabilities. Totally disabled refers to veterans with any disability, mental or physical, deemed to be total and permanent which prevents the individual from maintaining a livelihood and are rated for disability at 100 percent]

MILITARY SERVICE	1970	1980	1985	1988	1989	1990	1991	1992	1993	1994
Disabled, all periods [1]	**2,092**	**2,274**	**2,240**	**2,199**	**2,192**	**2,184**	**2,179**	**2,181**	**2,198**	**2,218**
Peace-time	185	262	352	398	421	444	468	500	471	492
World War I [1]	85	30	12	6	5	3	3	2	1	1
World War II	1,416	1,193	1,049	947	912	876	841	805	769	731
Korea	239	236	223	215	212	209	205	202	198	195
Vietnam	167	553	604	633	643	652	662	671	682	694
Persian Gulf	(X)	(X)	(X)	(X)	(X)	(X)	(X)	(X)	76	106
Totally disabled, all periods [1].	**124**	**121**	**136**	**131**	**131**	**131**	**131**	**132**	**135**	**138**
Peace-time	16	20	26	26	26	27	27	28	28	29
World War I [1]	11	3	1	1	(Z)	(Z)	(Z)	(Z)	(Z)	(Z)
World War II	63	51	54	47	45	43	41	39	37	36
Korea	16	16	17	16	16	16	16	15	15	15
Vietnam	18	31	38	41	43	44	46	49	52	56
Persian Gulf	(X)	(X)	(X)	(X)	(X)	(X)	(X)	(X)	2	2
Compensation (mil. dol.) . . .	**2,393**	**6,104**	**8,270**	**8,722**	**8,937**	**9,284**	**9,612**	**10,031**	**10,545**	**10,977**

X Not applicable.   Z Less than 500.   [1] Includes Spanish-American War and Mexican Border service, not shown separately.

Source: U.S. Dept. of Veterans Affairs, *Annual Report of the Secretary of Veterans Affairs;* and unpublished data.

No. 567. Veterans Benefits—Expenditures, by Program: 1970 to 1992

[In millions of dollars. For fiscal years ending in year shown; see text, section 9. Beginning with fiscal year 1988, data are for outlays]

PROGRAM	1970	1980	1985	1987	1988	1989	1990	1991	1992
Total	**10,201**	**23,187**	**29,359**	**31,812**	**29,271**	**30,041**	**28,998**	**31,214**	**33,894**
Medical programs.	1,765	6,042	9,227	9,876	10,283	10,745	11,582	12,472	13,815
Construction	75	300	557	589	649	703	661	608	639
General operating expenses.	243	605	765	765	781	766	811	884	914
Compensation and pension	5,252	11,044	14,037	14,241	14,710	15,009	14,674	16,080	16,282
Vocational rehabilitation and education.	1,032	2,350	1,164	847	717	589	452	541	695
All other [1]	1,835	2,846	3,609	5,494	2,130	2,228	818	629	1,549

[1] Includes insurance and indemnities, and miscellaneous funds and expenditures. (Excludes expenditures from personal funds of patients.)

Source: U.S. Dept. of Veterans Affairs, *Trend Data, Fiscal Years 1968-1992.*

No. 568. Veterans Compensation and Pension Benefits—Number on Rolls and Average Payment, by Period of Service and Status: 1980 to 1993

[As of **Sept. 30.** Living refers to veterans receiving compensation for disability incurred or aggravated while on active duty and war veterans receiving pension and benefits for nonservice connected disabilities. Deceased refers to deceased veterans whose dependents were receiving pensions and compensation benefits. See also *Historical Statistics, Colonial Times to 1970,* series Y 998-999]

PERIOD OF SERVICE AND VETERAN STATUS	VETERANS ON ROLLS (1,000)					AVERAGE PAYMENT (annual basis) [1] (dol.)				
	1980	1990	1991	1992	1993	1980	1985	1990	1991	1992
Total	4,646	3,584	3,509	3,428	3,374	2,370	3,505	4,335	4,552	4,712
Living veterans	3,195	2,746	2,709	2,674	2,660	2,600	3,666	4,320	4,491	4,611
Service connected	2,273	2,184	2,179	2,181	2,198	2,669	3,692	4,250	4,406	4,593
Nonservice connected	922	562	530	493	462	2,428	3,581	4,591	4,837	4,689
Deceased veterans	1,451	838	800	754	714	1,863	3,066	4,382	4,761	5,071
Service connected	358	320	318	314	310	3,801	5,836	7,349	7,815	8,244
Nonservice connected	1,093	518	482	440	404	1,228	1,809	2,548	2,748	2,810
Prior to World War I	14	4	4	3	3	1,432	1,855	2,616	2,921	3,073
Living	(Z)	(Z)	(Z)	(Z)	(Z)	2,634	4,436	10,502	10,441	8,176
World War I	692	198	172	146	124	1,683	2,461	3,435	3,674	3,754
Living	198	18	13	9	6	2,669	4,439	6,922	7,239	6,476
World War II	2,520	1,723	1,638	1,543	1,453	2,307	3,317	4,052	4,238	4,334
Living	1,849	1,294	1,226	1,153	1,083	2,462	3,460	4,123	4,278	4,333
Korean conflict [2]	446	390	388	387	377	2,691	4,114	5,105	5,330	5,462
Living	317	305	304	300	296	2,977	4,260	5,103	5,288	5,390
Peacetime	312	495	518	550	518	3,080	3,973	4,132	4,216	4,292
Living	262	444	468	500	471	2,828	3,589	3,709	3,789	3,866
Vietnam era [3]	662	774	789	804	821	2,795	4,021	4,945	5,242	5,551
Living	569	685	698	711	727	2,709	3,849	4,671	4,936	5,234
Persian Gulf War [4]	(X)	(X)	(X)	(Z)	78	(X)	(X)	(X)	(X)	1,673
Living	(X)	(X)	(X)	(Z)	76	(X)	(X)	(X)	(X)	1,386

X Not applicable. Z Fewer than 500. [1] Averages calculated by multiplying average monthly payment by 12. [2] Service during period June 27, 1950, to Jan. 31, 1955. [3] Service from Aug. 5, 1964, to May 7, 1975. [4] Service from August 2, 1990, to the present.

Source: U.S. Dept. of Veterans Affairs, *Annual Report of the Secretary of Veterans Affairs;* and unpublished data.

No. 569. Veterans Administration Health Care Summary: 1980 to 1993

[For years ending **Sept. 30**]

ITEM	Unit	1980	1990	1993	ITEM	Unit	1980	1990	1993
Facilities operating:					Obligations [2]	Mil. dol .	6,215	11,827	15,079
Hospitals	Number .	172	172	171	Prescriptions dispensed. .	Millions .	36.7	58.6	59.1
Domiciliaries	Number .	16	32	37	Laboratory	Millions .	215	188	(NA)
Outpatient clinics	Number .	226	339	353	Inpatients treated [3].	1,000 . .	1,359	1,113	1,043
Nursing home units . . .	Number .	92	126	128	Average daily	1,000 . .	105	88	84
Employment [1]	1,000 . .	194	199	210	Outpatient visits	Millions .	18.0	22.6	24.2

NA Not available. [1] Net full-time equivalent. [2] 1980, cost basis; thereafter, obligation basis. [3] Based on the number of discharges and deaths during the fiscal year, plus the number on the rolls (bed occupants and patients on authorized leave of absence) at the end of the fiscal year. Excludes interhospital transfers.

Source: U.S. Dept. of Veterans Affairs, *Annual Report of the Secretary of Veterans Affairs; Directory of VA Facilities,* biennial; and unpublished data.

No. 570. Veterans Assistance—Education and Training: 1980 to 1994

[**In thousands, except where indicated. For fiscal years ending in year shown;** see text, section 9. Represents persons in training during year]

PROGRAM	1980	1985	1989	1990	1991	1992	1993	1994
Veteran Education Assistance [1]	1,107	402	164	102	143	195	246	284
Institutions of higher education	842	326	144	94	132	177	223	258
Resident schools other than college	149	54	13	6	9	14	18	19
Correspondence schools	42	7	3	1	1	3	3	4
On-the-job training	74	15	3	1	1	2	2	3
Children's Educational Assistance	82.6	55.3	38.7	37.5	37.3	37.2	36.4	35.7
Institutions of higher education	75.5	50.0	36.2	35.3	35.2	35.1	34.3	33.7
Schools other than college	6.5	5.2	2.4	2.1	2.1	2.1	2.0	1.9
Special restorative training	0.1	(Z)	(Z)	(Z)	(Z)	(Z)	(Z)	(Z)
On-the-job training	0.5	0.2	0.1	0.1	(Z)	(Z)	(Z)	(Z)
Spouses, Widows/Widowers Educational								
Assistance Program	13.0	6.6	4.6	4.5	4.4	4.5	4.4	4.6
Institutions of higher education	10.8	5.7	4.1	4.1	4.0	4.0	4.0	4.1
Schools other than college	2.2	1.0	0.5	0.4	0.4	0.4	0.4	0.4
Disabled Veterans Vocational Rehab.	25.5	26.9	27.0	27.8	35.9	36.8	40.7	44.2
Guaranteed and insured loans, (1,000) . . .	297.4	178.9	189.7	196.6	181.2	266.0	383.3	(NA)
Guaranteed and insured loans, (mil. dol.) . .	14,815	11,452	14,416	15,779	15,454	22,960	34,635	(NA)
Guaranty and insurance (mil. dol.)	6,370	4,363	5,211	5,561	5,299	7,819	11,601	(NA)

NA Not available. Z Fewer than 50. [1] Data for 1980-89 are for Post-Korean Conflict GI Bill (Title 38 USC Chapter 34). Data for 1990-94 are for the Active Duty Montgomery GI Bill (Title 38 USC Chapter 30).

Source: U.S. Dept. of Veterans Affairs, *Annual Report of the Secretary of Veterans Affairs;* and unpublished data.

Social Insurance and Human Services

This section presents data related to governmental expenditures for social welfare; governmental programs for old-age, survivors, disability, and health insurance (OASDHI); governmental employee retirement; private pension plans; government unemployment and temporary disability insurance; Federal supplemental security income payments and aid to the needy; child and other welfare services; and Federal food programs. Also included here are selected data on workers' compensation, vocational rehabilitation; child support; child care; charity contributions; and philanthropic trusts and foundations.

The principal sources for these data are the Social Security Administration's quarterly *Social Security Bulletin* and the *Annual Statistical Supplement to the Social Security Bulletin* which present current data on many of the programs. Current data on employment security are published annually in the Department of Labor's *Unemployment Insurance, Financial Data.* Statistics on aid to families with dependent children (AFDC) are presented in the U.S. Administration for Children and Families' annual publication, *Quarterly Public Assistance Statistics.*

Social insurance under the Social Security Act—Programs established by the Social Security Act provide protection against wage loss resulting from retirement, prolonged disability, death, or unemployment, and protection against the cost of medical care during old age and disability. The Federal OASDI program provides monthly benefits to retired or disabled insured workers and their dependents and to survivors of insured workers. To be eligible, a worker must have had a specified period of employment in which OASDI taxes were paid. A worker becomes eligible for full benefits at age 65, although reduced benefits may be obtained up to 3 years earlier; the worker's spouse is under the same limitations. Survivor benefits are payable to dependents of deceased insured

In Brief
In 1993, households below poverty level receiving:
Medicaid   49%
Food stamps   35%
Social Security beneficiaries, 1994:
Total   43 million
Retired workers   26 million

workers. Disability benefits are payable to an insured worker under age 65 with a prolonged disability and to the disabled worker's dependents on the same basis as dependents of retired workers. Disability benefits are provided at age 50 to the disabled widow or widower of a deceased worker who was fully insured at the time of death. Disabled children, aged 18 or older, of retired, disabled, or deceased workers are also eligible for benefits. A lump-sum benefit is generally payable on the death of an insured worker to a spouse or minor children. For information on the Medicare (HI) program, see section 3.

Retirement, survivors, disability, and hospital insurance benefits are funded by a payroll tax on annual earnings (up to a maximum of earnings set by law) of workers, employers, and the self-employed. The maximum taxable earnings are adjusted annually to reflect increasing wage levels (see table 580). Effective January 1994, there is no dollar limit on wages and self-employment income subject to hospital insurance tax. Tax receipts and benefit payments are administered through Federal trust funds. Special benefits for uninsured persons; hospital benefits for persons 65 and over with specified amounts of Social Security coverage less than that required for cash benefit eligibility; and that part of the cost of supplementary medical insurance not financed by contributions from participants are financed from Federal general revenues.

Unemployment insurance is presently administered by the U.S. Employment and Training Administration and each State's employment security agency. By agreement with the U.S. Secretary of Labor, State agencies also administer unemployment compensation for eligible ex-service members and Federal employees, unemployment assistance under the Disaster Relief Act of 1970, and workers assistance and relocation allowances under the Trade Act. Under State unemployment insurance laws, benefits related to the individual's past earnings are paid to unemployed eligible workers. State laws vary concerning the length of time benefits are paid and their amount. In most States, benefits are payable for 26 weeks and, during periods of high unemployment, extended benefits are payable under a Federal-State program to those who have exhausted their regular State benefits. The basic benefit can vary among States by over 100 percent. Some States also supplement the basic benefit with allowances for dependents.

Unemployment insurance is funded by a Federal unemployment tax levied on the taxable payrolls of most employers. Taxable payroll under the Federal Act and 12 State laws is the first $7,000 in wages paid each worker during a year. Forty-one States have taxable payrolls above $7,000. Employers are allowed a percentage credit of taxable payroll for contributions paid to States under State unemployment insurance laws. The remaining percent of the Federal tax finances administrative costs, the Federal share of extended benefits, and advances to States. About 93 percent of wage and salary workers are covered by unemployment insurance.

Retirement Programs for Government Employees—The Civil Service Retirement System (CSRS) and the Federal Employees' Retirement System (FERS) are the two major programs providing age and service, disability, and survivor annuities for Federal civilian employees. In general, employees hired after December 31, 1983, are covered under FERS and the social security program (OASDHI), and employees on staff prior to that date are members of CSRS and are covered under Medicare. CSRS employees were offered the option of

transferring to FERS during 1987. There are separate retirement systems for the uniformed services (supplementing OASDHI) and for certain special groups of Federal employees. State and local government employees are covered for the most part by State and local retirement systems similar to the Federal civil service retirement system. In many jurisdictions these benefits supplement OASDHI coverage.

Workers' compensation—All States provide protection against work-connected injuries and deaths, although some States exclude certain workers (e.g., domestic help). Federal laws cover Federal employees, private employees in the District of Columbia, and longshoremen and harbor workers. In addition, the Social Security Administration and the Department of Labor administer "Black Lung" benefits programs for coal miners disabled by pneumoconiosis and for specified dependents and survivors. Specified occupational diseases are compensable to some extent. In most States, benefits are related to the worker's salary. The benefits may or may not be augmented by dependents' allowances or automatically adjusted to prevailing wage levels.

Public aid—State-administered public assistance programs (Aid to Families with Dependent Children (AFDC), emergency assistance and general assistance) and the Federal Supplemental Security Income (SSI) program administered by the Social Security Administration provide benefits to persons who qualify. AFDC and emergency assistance are in part federally funded while the costs of general assistance are met entirely with State and local funds. The SSI program replaced Federal grants for aid to the aged, blind, and disabled in the 50 States and the District of Columbia in 1974. Residents of the Northern Mariana Islands became eligible in 1978. Federal grants continue for aid to the aged, blind, and disabled in Guam, Puerto Rico, and the Virgin Islands. The SSI program provides a minimum income for the aged, blind, and disabled and establishes uniform national basic eligibility requirements and payment standards. Most States supplement the basic SSI payment.

Federal Food Stamp program—Under the Food Stamp program, single persons and those living in households meeting nationwide standards for income and assets may receive coupons redeemable for food at most retail food stores. The monthly amount of coupons a unit receives is determined by household size and income. Households without income receive the determined monthly cost of a nutritionally adequate diet for their household size. This amount is updated to account for food price increases. Households with income receive the difference between the amount of a nutritionally adequate diet and 30 percent of their income, after certain allowable deductions.

To qualify for the program, a household must have less than $2,000 in disposable assets ($3,000 if one member is aged 60 or older), gross income below 130 percent of the official poverty guidelines, and net income below 100 percent of the poverty guidelines. Households with a person aged 60 or older or a disabled person receiving SSI, Social Security, or veterans' disability benefits may have gross income exceeding 130 percent of the poverty guidelines. All households must meet these requirements, even those receiving other Federal assistance payments. Households are certified for varying lengths of time, depending on their income sources and individual circumstances.

Health and welfare services—Programs providing health and welfare services are aided through Federal grants to States for child welfare services, vocational rehabilitation, activities for the aged, maternal and child health services, maternity and infant care projects, comprehensive health services, and a variety of public health activities. For information about the Medicaid program, see section 3.

Noncash benefits—The Bureau of the Census annually collects data on the characteristics of recipients of noncash (in-kind) benefits to supplement the collection of annual money income data in the Current Population Survey (see text, section 1, and section 15). Noncash benefits are those benefits received in a form other than money which serve to enhance or improve the economic well-being of the recipient. As for money income, the data for noncash benefits are for the calendar year prior to the date of the interview. The major categories of noncash benefits covered are public transfers (e.g. food stamps, school lunch, public housing, and Medicaid) and employer or union-provided benefits to employees.

Statistical reliability—For discussion of statistical collection, estimation, and sampling procedures and measures of statistical reliability applicable to HHS and Census Bureau data, see Appendix III.

Historical statistics—Tabular headnotes provide cross-references, where applicable, to *Historical Statistics of the United States, Colonial Times to 1970.* See Appendix IV.

No. 571. Social Welfare Expenditures Under Public Programs: 1970 to 1992

[In billions of dollars, except percent. See headnote, table 573]

YEAR	Total	Social insur- ance	Public aid	Health and medical programs [1]	Veterans pro- grams	Educa- tion	Housing	Other social welfare	All health and medical care [2]
Total:									
1970.	146	55	16	10	9	51	1	4	25
1980.	493	230	73	27	21	121	7	14	100
1985.	732	370	98	39	27	172	13	14	171
1989.	957	468	129	57	30	239	18	17	240
1990.	1,050	514	147	62	31	258	19	18	276
1991.	1,161	561	181	67	33	277	22	20	317
1992.	1,264	617	208	70	35	292	21	22	354
Federal:									
1970.	77	45	10	5	9	6	1	2	16
1980.	303	191	49	13	21	13	6	9	69
1985.	451	310	63	18	27	14	11	8	122
1989.	565	387	82	24	30	19	15	8	165
1990.	617	422	93	27	30	18	17	9	190
1991.	676	454	113	30	32	19	19	10	213
1992.	749	496	139	32	34	20	18	11	250
State and local:									
1970.	68	9	7	5	(Z)	45	(Z)	2	9
1980.	190	39	23	14	(Z)	108	1	5	31
1985.	281	59	35	21	(Z)	158	2	6	49
1989.	392	81	47	33	(Z)	220	3	8	75
1990.	433	92	54	35	(Z)	240	3	9	85
1991.	484	108	68	37	1	258	3	10	103
1992.	514	121	69	38	1	272	3	11	105
Percent Federal:									
1970.	53	83	59	48	99	12	83	55	65
1980.	62	83	68	47	99	11	91	65	69
1985.	62	84	64	46	99	8	88	56	71
1990.	59	82	64	44	98	7	85	50	69
1991.	58	81	62	44	98	7	87	50	68
1992.	59	80	67	46	98	7	87	50	71
Per capita (current dollars): [3]									
1970.	698	262	79	46	43	244	3	20	120
1980.	2,126	990	314	118	92	523	30	59	434
1985.	3,009	1,516	405	161	111	708	52	56	705
1990.	4,131	2,017	579	250	120	1,018	77	71	1,084
1991.	4,530	2,184	708	266	126	1,083	84	77	1,237
1992.	4,863	2,369	801	274	130	1,126	79	83	1,364
Per capita (constant (1992) dollars): [3] [4]									
1970.	2,421	908	275	160	150	847	12	69	418
1980.	3,678	1,712	544	204	159	905	51	102	750
1985.	3,993	2,011	537	215	147	940	69	74	940
1990.	4,440	2,168	622	269	129	1,094	83	76	1,171
1991.	4,531	2,185	705	271	126	1,083	87	77	1,234
1992.	4,863	2,369	801	274	130	1,126	79	83	1,364

Z Less than $500 million.   [1] Excludes program parts of social insurance, public aid, veterans, and other social welfare.
[2] Combines "Health and medical programs" with medical services included in social insurance, public aid, veterans, vocational rehabilitation, and antipoverty programs.   [3] Excludes payments within foreign countries for education, veterans, OASDHI, and civil service retirement.   [4] Constant dollar figures are based on implicit price deflators for personal consumption expenditures published by U.S. Bureau of Economic Analysis in *Survey of Current Business*, July 1994.

No. 572. Social Welfare Expenditures Under Public Programs as Percent of GDP and Total Government Outlays: 1970 to 1992

[See headnote, table 573]

YEAR	TOTAL EXPENDITURES				FEDERAL				STATE AND LOCAL GOVERNMENT			
	Total (bil. dol.)	Percent change [1]	Percent of—		Total (bil. dol.)	Percent change [1]	Percent of—		Total (bil. dol.)	Percent change [1]	Percent of—	
			Total GDP [2]	Total govt. outlays			Total GDP [2]	Total Federal outlays			Total GDP [2]	Total State and local outlays
1970. . . .	146	14.6	14.8	46.5	77	13.2	7.8	40.0	68	16.3	6.9	57.9
1980. . . .	493	14.7	18.6	57.2	303	15.2	11.4	54.4	190	13.8	7.2	62.9
1985. . . .	732	8.0	18.4	52.2	451	7.1	11.3	48.7	281	9.3	7.1	59.9
1989. . . .	957	7.9	18.5	55.2	565	7.2	10.9	49.5	392	8.8	7.6	68.0
1990. . . .	1,050	9.7	18.9	56.7	617	9.0	11.1	51.4	433	10.7	7.8	68.0
1991. . . .	1,161	10.6	20.3	58.6	676	9.7	11.8	52.8	484	12.0	8.5	70.4
1992. . . .	1,264	8.9	21.0	61.6	749	10.8	12.4	57.1	514	6.2	8.5	70.6

[1] Percent change from immediate prior year.   [2] Gross domestic product.
Source of tables 571 and 572: U.S. Social Security Administration, *Social Security Bulletin*, summer 1993; and unpublished data.

No. 573. Social Welfare Expenditures, by Source of Funds and Public Program: 1980 to 1992

[In millions of dollars. For fiscal years ending in year shown; see text, section 9. Represents outlays from trust funds (mostly social insurance funds built up by earmarked contributions from insured persons, their employers, or both) and budgetary outlays from general revenues. Includes administrative expenditures, capital outlay, and some expenditures and payments outside the United States. See *Historical Statistics, Colonial Times to 1970*, series H 1-47, for related but not comparable data]

PROGRAM	FEDERAL				STATE AND LOCAL			
	1980	1990	1991	1992	1980	1990	1991	1992
Total	**303,167**	**616,639**	**676,411**	**749,406**	**189,547**	**433,036**	**484,409**	**514,457**
Social insurance	**191,162**	**422,257**	**453,534**	**495,710**	**38,592**	**91,565**	**107,641**	**121,266**
Old-age, survivors, disability, health	152,110	355,264	382,290	416,564	(X)	(X)	(X)	(X)
Health insurance (Medicare).	34,992	109,709	116,651	132,246	(X)	(X)	(X)	(X)
Public employee retirement [1]	26,983	53,541	56,880	58,229	12,507	36,851	40,391	45,099
Railroad employee retirement	4,769	7,230	7,532	7,737	(X)	(X)	(X)	(X)
Unemployment insurance and employment services [2]	4,408	3,096	3,613	9,928	13,919	16,878	24,793	31,238
Other railroad employee insurance [3] . . .	224	105	94	95	(X)	(X)	(X)	(X)
State temporary disability insurance [4] . . .	(X)	(X)	(X)	(X)	1,377	3,224	3,879	4,009
Workers' compensation [5]	2,668	3,021	3,125	3,157	10,789	34,613	38,578	40,919
Hospital and medical benefits.	130	457	506	571	3,596	13,849	15,503	17,344
Public aid.	**49,394**	**92,858**	**113,235**	**138,704**	**23,309**	**53,953**	**68,104**	**69,241**
Public assistance [6]	23,542	54,747	69,315	86,747	21,522	50,347	64,354	65,264
Medical assistance payments [7]	14,550	40,690	53,393	69,766	13,020	35,485	48,521	47,848
Social services	1,757	2,065	2,117	2,031	586	688	706	677
Supplemental Security Income.	6,440	13,625	15,896	19,446	1,787	3,605	3,751	3,978
Food stamps	9,083	16,254	19,471	23,233	(X)	(X)	(X)	(X)
Other [8]	10,329	8,232	8,553	9,279	(X)	(X)	(X)	(X)
Health and medical programs.	**12,840**	**27,204**	**29,700**	**31,965**	**14,423**	**35,151**	**37,300**	**37,861**
Hospital and medical care.	6,636	14,816	17,128	17,781	5,667	11,479	11,836	11,407
Civilian programs	2,438	3,654	4,388	5,012	5,667	11,479	11,836	11,407
Defense Department [9]	4,198	11,162	12,740	12,769	(X)	(X)	(X)	(X)
Maternal and child health programs	351	492	522	580	519	1,374	1,461	1,532
Medical research.	4,428	9,172	9,445	10,641	496	1,679	1,854	1,931
Medical facilities construction.	210	413	-	-	1,450	1,922	2,056	2,388
Other	1,215	2,311	2,605	2,963	6,291	18,697	20,093	20,603
Veterans programs	**21,255**	**30,428**	**32,331**	**34,212**	**212**	**488**	**526**	**555**
Pensions and compensation	11,306	15,793	16,284	16,539	(X)	(X)	(X)	(X)
Health and medical programs	6,204	12,004	13,222	14,567	(X)	(X)	(X)	(X)
Hospital and medical care	5,750	11,321	12,190	13,452	(X)	(X)	(X)	(X)
Hospital construction	323	445	776	845	(X)	(X)	(X)	(X)
Medical and prosthetic research	131	238	256	270	(X)	(X)	(X)	(X)
Education	2,401	523	570	772	(X)	(X)	(X)	(X)
Life insurance [10]	665	1,038	1,039	1,114	(X)	(X)	(X)	(X)
Welfare and other	679	1,070	1,217	1,220	212	488	526	555
Education [11]	**13,452**	**18,374**	**19,084**	**20,188**	**107,597**	**240,011**	**258,063**	**272,011**
Elementary and secondary [12]	7,430	9,944	11,979	12,891	79,720	189,333	203,819	214,015
Construction [13]	41	23	39	43	6,483	10,613	12,324	14,638
Higher.	4,468	6,747	5,339	5,392	21,708	50,678	54,243	57,996
Construction . . . . [13]	42	-	31	30	1,486	3,953	3,950	4,839
Vocational and adult [13]	1,207	1,293	1,314	1,452	6,169	([12])	([12])	([12])
Housing.	**6,278**	**16,612**	**18,696**	**17,950**	**601**	**2,856**	**2,826**	**2,668**
Other social welfare	**8,786**	**8,905**	**9,831**	**10,677**	**4,813**	**9,012**	**9,949**	**10,855**
Vocational rehabilitation	1,006	1,661	1,751	1,912	245	466	485	534
Medical services and research	237	415	438	478	56	116	121	134
Institutional care [14]	74	143	142	144	408	486	523	541
Child nutrition [15]	4,209	5,470	6,098	6,722	643	1,696	1,869	2,054
Child welfare [16]	57	253	274	274	743	(NA)	(NA)	(NA)
Special CSA and ACTION programs [17] . .	2,303	169	192	194	(X)	(X)	(X)	(X)
Welfare, not elsewhere classified [18]	1,137	1,209	1,375	1,431	2,774	6,365	7,072	7,726

- Represents zero. NA Not available. X Not applicable. [1] Excludes refunds to those leaving service. Federal data include military retirement. [2] Includes compensation for Federal employees and ex-servicemen, trade adjustment and cash training allowance, and payments under extended, emergency, disaster, and special unemployment insurance programs. [3] Unemployment and temporary disability insurance. [4] Cash and medical benefits in five areas. Includes private plans where applicable. [5] Benefits paid by private insurance carriers, State funds, and self-insurers. Federal includes black lung benefit programs. [6] Includes payments under State general assistance programs and work incentive activities, not shown separately. [7] Medicaid payments and State and local general assistance medical payments. [8] Refugee assistance, surplus food for the needy, and work-experience training programs under the Comprehensive Employment and Training Act. Beginning 1990, includes low-income energy assistance program. [9] Includes medical care for military dependent families. [10] Excludes servicemen's group life insurance. [11] Federal expenditures include administrative costs (Department of Education) and research, not shown separately. [12] Beginning 1990, all State and local vocational education costs included with elementary-secondary. [13] Construction costs of vocational and adult education programs included under elementary-secondary expenditures. [14] Federal expenditures represent primarily surplus foods for nonprofit institutions. [15] Surplus food for schools and programs under National School Lunch and Child Nutrition Acts. [16] Represents primarily child welfare services under Title V of the Social Security Act. [17] Includes domestic volunteer programs under ACTION and community action and migrant workers programs under Community Services Administration. Beginning 1990, represents ACTION funds only. [18] Federal expenditures include administrative expenses of the Secretary of Health and Human Services; Indian welfare and guidance; and aging and juvenile delinquency activities. State and local include antipoverty and manpower programs, child care and adoption services, legal assistance, and other unspecified welfare services.

Source: U.S. Social Security Administration, *Social Security Bulletin*, summer 1993; and unpublished data.

No. 574. Private Expenditures for Social Welfare, by Type: 1980 to 1992

[In millions of dollars, except percent]

TYPE	1980	1985	1987	1988	1989	1990	1991	1992
Total expenditures	255,859	471,794	555,643	610,812	678,275	728,034	768,165	824,719
Percent of gross domestic product	9.4	11.7	12.2	12.5	12.9	13.1	13.4	13.7
Health.	145,800	259,400	298,600	336,100	370,700	410,000	432,900	462,900
Income maintenance . . . . [1][2] . . .	54,103	119,442	144,116	149,357	167,726	165,283	172,553	185,572
Private pension plan payments [1][2] . . .	37,560	98,450	120,442	124,546	140,911	137,739	144,237	156,888
Short-term sickness and disability [2] . .	9,214	11,261	12,579	13,613	14,457	14,566	14,720	15,526
Long-term disability [2]	1,282	1,937	2,293	2,295	2,892	2,926	3,172	3,143
Life insurance and death [3]	5,075	7,489	8,166	8,418	9,063	9,278	9,472	9,442
Supplemental unemployment [2].	972	305	636	485	403	774	952	573
Education	33,180	54,038	65,498	72,137	80,383	87,864	93,813	100,491
Welfare and other services	22,776	38,914	47,429	53,218	59,466	64,887	68,899	75,756

[1] Covers benefits paid for solely by employers and all benefits of employment-related pension plans to which employee contributions are made. Excludes individual savings plans such as IRA's and Keogh plans. Pension plan benefits include monthly benefits and lump-sum distributions to retired and disabled employees and their dependents and to survivors of deceased employees. Also includes preretirement lump-sum distributions. [2] Covers wage and salary workers in private industry. [3] Covers all wage and salary workers.

Source: U.S. Social Security Administration, *Annual Statistical Supplement* to the *Social Security Bulletin*, annual.

No. 575. Public Income-Maintenance Programs—Cash Benefit Payments: 1980 to 1994

[Includes payments outside the United States and benefits to dependents, where applicable]

PROGRAM	PAYMENTS (bil. dol.)									PERCENT		
	1980	1985	1988	1989	1990	1991	1992	1993	1994	1980	1990	1993
Total [1]	228.1	335.2	393.8	421.9	455.8	503.3	541.9	553.2	(NA)	100	100	100
Percent of personal income [2]	10.1	9.9	9.7	9.6	9.8	10.4	10.5	10.3	(NA)	(X)	(X)	(X)
OASDI [3]	120.3	186.1	216.4	229.6	245.6	265.6	284.3	301.2	315.9	53	54	54
Public employee retirement [4]. . .	40.6	63.0	78.0	83.8	90.4	97.3	103.7	111.4	(NA)	18	20	20
Railroad retirement	4.9	6.3	6.7	6.9	7.2	7.5	7.3	7.9	8.0	2	2	2
Veterans' pensions, compensation	11.4	14.1	14.7	15.3	15.8	16.3	16.5	16.9	18.7	5	3	3
Unemployment benefits [5]	18.9	14.4	13.2	16.4	20.0	31.3	37.3	21.5	21.6	8	4	4
Temporary disability benefits	1.4	1.8	2.8	2.9	3.2	3.9	4.0	3.3	(NA)	1	1	1
Workers' compensation [6]	9.7	22.3	30.3	33.8	37.6	41.7	44.1	43.4	(NA)	4	8	8
Public assistance	12.1	15.3	17.0	17.4	19.3	20.1	22.4	22.1	23.0	5	4	4
Supplemental Security Income. .	7.9	11.1	14.7	14.9	15.2	18.5	22.3	24.7	26.1	3	4	4

NA Not available.   X Not applicable.   [1] Includes lump sum death benefits, not shown separately. Lump sum death benefits for State and local government employee retirement systems are not available beginning 1987.   [2] For base data, see table 696.   [3] Old-age, survivors, and disability insurance under Federal Social Security Act; see text, section 12.   [4] Excludes refunds of contributions to employees who leave service.   [5] Beginning 1985, covers State unemployment insurance, Ex-Servicemen's Compensation Act and railroad unemployment insurance only.   [6] Includes black lung benefits.

Source: U.S. Social Security Administration, *Social Security Bulletin*, quarterly; and unpublished data.

No. 576. Number of Families Receiving Specified Sources of Income, by Characteristic of Householder and Family Income: 1994

[In thousands. Families as of March 1995. Based on Current Population Survey; see text, sections 1 and 14, and Appendix III]

SOURCE OF INCOME	Total families [1]	Under 65 years old	65 years old and over	White	Black	His-panic origin [2]	Under $15,000	$15,000 to $24,999	$25,000 to $34,000
Total	69,313	58,077	11,236	58,444	8,093	6,202	10,805	10,422	9,912
Earnings	58,628	54,009	4,619	49,708	6,500	5,279	6,022	7,658	8,439
Wages and salary	56,496	52,363	4,133	47,741	6,411	5,138	5,490	7,260	8,109
Social Security, railroad retirement . .	16,210	5,752	10,458	14,181	1,674	934	3,020	4,116	3,022
Supplemental Security Income (SSI) .	2,390	1,795	595	1,595	645	367	1,182	491	288
Public assistance	3,906	3,794	112	2,273	1,378	753	2,916	545	209
Veterans payments	1,822	1,073	749	1,595	177	53	192	356	312
Unemployment compensation	5,450	5,171	279	4,677	521	630	629	870	916
Workers compensation.	1,927	1,810	118	1,673	193	172	195	331	369
Retirement income	10,091	4,253	5,838	9,170	724	346	587	2,052	2,021
Private pensions	6,479	2,340	4,140	5,971	398	210	423	1,545	1,420
Military retirement	1,032	740	292	901	111	40	24	89	141
Federal employee pensions.	1,186	391	795	1,013	132	30	49	193	239
State or local employee pensions . .	1,814	804	1,010	1,666	119	62	78	273	371
Other income.	10,277	9,846	430	8,518	1,360	716	1,796	1,518	1,566
Alimony	212	199	13	195	12	10	25	34	51
Child support	4,247	4,196	51	3,506	627	309	1,032	761	720
Education assistance	4,770	4,631	139	3,964	606	308	610	627	657

[1] Includes other items not shown separately.   [2] Persons of Hispanic origin may be of any race.

Source: U.S. Bureau of the Census, 1994 Income and Poverty CD-ROM.

No. 577. Cash and Noncash Benefits for Persons With Limited Income: 1990 and 1994

[For years ending September 30, except as noted. Programs covered provide cash, goods, or services to persons who make no payment and render no service in return. In case of job and training programs and some educational benefits, recipients must work or study for wages, training allowances, stipends, grants, or loans. Most of the programs base eligibility on individual, household, or family income, but some use group or area income tests; and a few offer help on the basis of presumed need]

PROGRAM	AVERAGE MONTHLY RECIPIENTS (1,000)		EXPENDITURES (mil. dol.)					
			Total		Federal		State and local	
	1990	1994	1990	1994	1990	1994	1990	1994
Total [1]	(X)	(X)	210,817	344,861	151,478	246,240	59,339	98,621
Medical care [2]	(X)	(X)	86,785	161,139	50,190	93,892	36,595	67,247
Medicaid [3] [4]	25,253	34,047	72,492	143,593	41,103	82,147	31,389	61,446
Veterans [5] [6] [7]	585	1,537	6,624	8,162	6,624	8,162	-	-
General assistance [7]	(NA)	(NA)	4,853	5,370	-	-	4,853	5,370
Indian Health Services [3] [4]	1,100	1,333	1,176	1,943	1,176	1,943	-	-
Maternal and child health services	(NA)	11,600	907	1,118	554	687	353	431
Cash aid [2]	(X)	(X)	54,255	83,749	36,445	61,477	17,810	22,272
Supplemental Security Income [4] [8]	4,938	6,429	17,233	27,310	13,607	23,544	3,626	3,766
A.F.D.C. [4] [9]	11,465	14,229	21,200	25,920	11,507	14,141	9,693	11,779
Earned income tax credit (refunded portion) [10]	37,836	54,177	5,303	16,549	5,303	16,549	-	-
Foster care	168	246	2,741	5,159	1,473	2,748	1,268	2,411
General assistance [10]	1,205	1,113	2,924	3,250	-	-	2,924	3,250
Pensions for needy veterans [11] [12]	1,106	838	3,954	3,159	3,954	3,159	-	-
Food benefits [2] [13]	(X)	(X)	25,106	38,100	23,871	36,233	1,235	1,867
Food stamps [4] [13]	21,500	28,900	17,686	27,396	16,512	25,599	1,174	1,797
School lunch program [14] [15]	11,600	14,000	3,154	4,438	3,154	4,438	(NA)	(NA)
Women, infants and children [4] [16]	4,500	6,500	2,126	3,309	2,126	3,309	-	-
School breakfast [14]	3,600	5,200	548	936	548	936	-	-
Child and adult care food program [17]	842	1,116	447	774	447	774	-	-
Nutrition program for elderly [18]	3,540	(NA)	575	619	514	561	61	70
Housing benefits [2]	(X)	(X)	17,548	26,130	17,548	25,738	-	392
Low-income housing asst. (Sec. 8) [19]	2,500	2,926	10,577	14,576	10,577	14,576	-	-
Low-rent public housing [19] [20]	1,405	1,409	3,918	6,609	3,918	6,609	(NA)	(NA)
Rural housing loans [21] [22]	26	39	1,311	2,384	1,311	2,384	-	-
Interest reduction payments [19]	531	504	630	659	630	659	-	-
Home investment partnerships [4] [22] [23]	(NA)	68	3	595	3	219	-	376
Education aid [2]	(X)	(X)	14,390	15,707	13,761	14,804	629	903
Pell grants [24] [25]	3,214	3,819	4,484	6,459	4,484	6,459	-	-
Head Start [24]	541	740	1,940	4,156	1,552	3,325	388	831
Stafford loans [24]	4,496	3,854	5,648	2,757	5,648	2,757	-	-
Services [2]	(X)	(X)	6,460	11,982	3,781	6,737	2,679	5,245
Social services (Title 20) [26]	(NA)	(NA)	5,346	8,322	2,762	[27] 3,800	2,584	4,522
Child care for AFDC recipients and ex-recipients [28]	(NA)	519	211	1,199	116	700	95	499
Child care and development block grant	(X)	(NA)	(X)	893	(X)	893	(X)	-
Jobs and training [2]	(X)	(X)	4,242	5,531	3,975	4,870	267	661
Training for disadvantaged adults and youth [29]	630	759	1,745	1,597	1,745	1,597	-	-
JOBS (for AFDC recipients) [30]	444	579	452	1,417	265	850	187	567
Job Corps	61	100	803	1,040	803	1,040	-	-
Summer youth employment program [31]	585	569	709	877	709	877	-	-
Energy assistance [2]	(X)	(X)	1,728	1,871	1,604	1,837	124	34
Low-income energy assistance [4] [32] [33]	5,800	6,100	1,567	1,731	1,443	1,697	124	34

- Represents zero.   NA Not available.   X Not applicable.   [1] Includes State Legalization Impact Assistance Grants to offset State and local costs of welfare, health care, and education provided to legalized aliens.   [2] Includes other programs not shown separately.   [3] Recipient data represent unduplicated annual number.   [4] Expenditures include administrative expenses.   [5] Medical care for veterans with a nonservice-connected disability.   [6] Recipients are estimated number of inpatients.   [7] Estimated expenditures.   [8] Includes State-administered SSI supplements.   [9] Aid to Families with Dependent Children program. Excludes data for foster care program and child support operations (cost and collections).   [10] Estimated recipients.   [11] Estimated recipients as of September.   [12] Includes dependents and survivors.   [13] Includes Puerto Rico's nutritional assistance program.   [14] Free and reduced-price segments.   [15] Includes estimate of commodity assistance.   [16] Special supplemental food program for women, infants and children.   [17] Recipient data are numbers of children receiving free or reduced price meals and snacks in child care centers and estimates of children in family day care homes with incomes below 185 percent of poverty. Adult participants and funding are not included.   [18] No income test required but preference given to those with greatest need.   [19] Recipient data represent units eligible for payment at end of year.   [20] Includes operating subsidies and HUD-administered Indian housing.   [21] Recipient data represent total families or dwelling units during year.   [22] Expenditure data represent amounts obligated.   [23] Recipient data are housing units provided or rehabilitated.   [24] Recipient data are total numbers for the school year ending in year shown.   [25] Expenditure data are appropriations available for school year ending the fiscal year named.   [26] Non-Federal expenditure data are rough estimates.   [27] Includes one-time authorization of $1 billion for enterprise communities and empowerment zones.   [28] Recipient data are estimated number of children served.   [29] Recipient data are total number of participants.   [30] Job opportunities and basic skills training program (JOBS).   [31] Total participants (June-August).   [32] Households served during the year with heating and winter crisis aid.   [33] Federal funds include amounts transferred to other programs serving the needy.

Source: Library of Congress, Congressional Research Service, "Cash and Noncash Benefits for Persons With Limited Income: Eligibility Rules, Recipient, and Expenditure Data, FY's 1992-94," Report 96-159 EPW, and earlier reports.

No. 578. Households Receiving Means-Tested Noncash Benefits: 1980 to 1993

[In thousands, except percent. Households as of **March** of following year. Covers civilian noninstitutional population, including persons in the Armed Forces living off post or with their families on post. A means-tested benefit program requires that the household's income and/or assets fall below specified guidelines in order to qualify for benefits. The means-tested noncash benefits covered are food stamps, free or reduced-price school lunches, public or subsidized housing, and Medicaid. There are general trends toward underestimation of noncash beneficiaries. Households are classified according to poverty status of family or nonfamily householder; for explanation of poverty level, see text, section 14. Data for 1980-90 based on 1980 census population controls; beginning 1992, based on 1990 census population controls. Based on Current Population Survey; see text, section 1, and Appendix III]

TYPE OF BENEFIT RECEIVED	1980	1985	1990	1992	1993			
					Total	Below poverty level		Above poverty level
						Number	Percent distribution	
Total households	82,368	88,458	94,312	96,426	97,107	13,777	100	83,330
Receiving at least one noncash benefit . .	14,266	14,466	16,098	18,639	19,937	8,817	64	11,120
Not receiving cash public assistance . .	7,860	7,860	8,819	10,431	11,573	3,824	28	7,749
Receiving cash public assistance [1] . . .	6,407	6,607	7,279	8,208	8,365	4,993	36	3,372
Total households receiving—								
Food stamps.	6,769	6,779	7,163	8,669	9,167	4,827	35	4,340
School lunch.	5,532	5,752	6,252	7,264	8,109	3,929	29	4,180
Public housing.	2,777	3,799	4,339	4,550	5,183	2,909	21	2,274
Medicaid	8,287	8,178	10,321	12,476	13,134	6,746	49	6,388

[1] Households receiving money from Aid to Families with Dependent Children program, Supplemental Security Income program or other public assistance programs.

Source: U.S. Bureau of the Census, *Current Population Reports*, P60-155, and earlier reports; and unpublished data.

No. 579. Persons Participating in Selected Means-Tested Government Assistance Programs, by Selected Characteristics: 1991 and 1992

[**Average monthly participation**. Covers noninstitutionalized population. Persons are considered participants in Aid to Families with Dependent Children (AFDC), General Assistance, and the Food Stamp Program if they are the primary recipient or if they are covered under another persons's allotment. Persons receiving Supplemental Security Income (SSI) payments are considered to be participants in an assistance program as are persons covered by Medicaid or living in public or subsidized rental housing. Based on the Survey of Income and Program Participation; for details on sample survey, see source]

YEAR AND SELECTED CHARACTERISTIC	NUMBER OF PARTICIPANTS (1,000)					PERCENT OF POPULATION PARTICIPATING				
	Major means-tested assistance programs [1]	AFDC or General Assistance	Food stamps	Medicaid	Housing assistance	Major means-tested assistance programs [1]	AFDC or General Assistance	Food stamps	Medicaid	Housing assistance
1991	31,695	11,869	19,383	(NA)	(NA)	12.7	4.7	7.8	(NA)	(NA)
1992, total	33,954	11,862	20,700	23,924	10,878	13.4	4.7	8.2	9.4	4.3
Under 18 years old	15,222	7,292	10,780	11,918	4,344	22.5	10.8	15.9	17.6	6.4
18 to 64 years old	14,751	4,492	8,716	9,376	4,789	9.5	2.9	5.6	6.0	3.1
65 years old and over	3,982	78	1,204	2,630	1,745	13.0	0.3	3.9	8.6	5.7
White	21,690	6,379	12,583	14,921	6,178	10.3	3.0	6.0	7.1	2.9
Black	10,507	4,723	7,072	7,683	4,094	33.0	14.8	22.2	24.2	12.9
Hispanic origin [2]	6,410	2,439	4,222	4,635	1,687	26.9	10.2	17.7	19.4	7.1
Poverty status: [3]										
Below the poverty level.	20,031	9,288	15,926	15,320	6,050	56.5	26.2	44.9	43.2	17.1
At or above the poverty level .	13,923	2,574	4,774	8,604	4,828	6.4	1.2	2.2	3.9	2.2
Family status:										
In married-couple families . . .	12,895	3,012	7,313	8,298	2,964	7.5	1.7	4.2	4.8	1.7
With related children under 18 years	10,870	2,929	6,654	7,033	2,473	10.0	2.7	6.1	6.5	2.3
In families with female householder, no spouse present	15,068	8,287	10,968	12,012	5,146	40.7	22.4	29.7	32.5	13.9
With related children under 18 years old	13,630	8,116	10,377	10,958	4,765	49.0	29.2	37.3	39.4	17.1
Unrelated individuals	4,891	272	1,853	2,844	2,597	13.5	0.8	5.1	7.9	7.2

NA Not available. [1] Covers AFDC, General Assistance, SSI, food stamps, Medicaid, and housing assistance. [2] Persons of Hispanic origin may be of any race. [3] For explanation of poverty level, see text, section 14.

Source: U.S. Bureau of the Census, *Current Population Reports*, P70-46 and unpublished data.

No. 580. Social Security—Covered Employment, Earnings, and Contribution Rates: 1970 to 1994

[Includes Puerto Rico, Virgin Islands, American Samoa, and Guam. Represents all reported employment. Data are estimated. OASDHI=Old-age, survivors, disability, and health insurance; SMI=Supplementary medical insurance. See also *Historical Statistics, Colonial Times to 1970*, series H 172-185]

ITEM	Unit	1970	1980	1985	1988	1989	1990	1991	1992	1993	1994
Workers with insured status [1]	Million . . .	105.7	137.4	148.7	155.4	158.2	161.2	163.6	165.8	167.9	169.4
Male	Million . . .	61.9	75.4	79.7	82.6	83.7	85.1	86.1	87.2	88.1	88.6
Female	Million . . .	43.8	62.0	69.0	72.8	74.5	76.1	77.5	78.6	79.9	80.8
Under 25 years old	Million . . .	17.7	25.5	22.3	21.3	21.3	21.3	21.2	20.7	20.5	19.7
25 to 34 years old	Million . . .	22.3	34.9	39.9	41.0	41.4	41.5	41.5	41.2	40.8	40.3
35 to 44 years old	Million . . .	19.0	22.4	28.5	32.3	33.5	34.9	36.2	37.3	38.1	38.9
45 to 54 years old	Million . . .	19.0	18.6	19.0	20.5	21.4	22.1	22.8	24.1	25.5	26.8
55 to 59 years old	Million . . .	7.8	9.2	9.1	8.8	8.7	8.7	8.7	8.8	9.0	9.2
60 to 64 years old	Million . . .	6.3	7.9	8.7	8.7	8.6	8.7	8.7	8.7	8.5	8.5
65 to 69 years old	Million . . .	5.1	6.7	7.3	7.7	7.8	8.1	8.2	8.2	8.2	8.2
70 years old and over	Million . . .	8.5	12.1	13.9	15.0	15.5	15.8	16.3	16.8	17.3	17.7
Workers reported with—											
Taxable earnings [2]	Million . . .	93	113	120	130	132	134	133	134	136	139
Maximum earnings [2]	Million . . .	24	10	8	8	8	8	8	8	8	8
Earnings in covered employment [2]	Bil. dol . .	532	1,329	1,942	2,432	2,573	2,704	2,761	2,916	3,033	3,171
Reported taxable [2]	Bil. dol . .	416	1,178	1,725	2,092	2,238	2,358	2,422	2,533	2,644	2,784
Percent of total	Percent . .	78.2	88.6	88.8	86.0	87.0	87.2	87.7	86.9	87.2	87.8
Annual maximum taxable earnings [3]	Dollars . . .	7,800	25,900	39,600	45,000	48,000	51,300	53,400	55,500	57,600	60,600
Contribution rates for OASDHI: [4]											
Each employer and employee . .	Percent . .	4.80	6.13	7.05	7.51	7.51	7.65	7.65	7.65	7.65	7.65
Self-employed [5]	Percent . .	6.90	8.10	14.10	15.02	15.02	15.30	15.30	15.30	15.30	15.30
SMI, monthly premium [6]	Dollars . . .	5.30	9.60	15.50	24.80	31.90	28.60	29.90	31.80	36.60	41.10

[1] Fully insured for retirement and/or survivor benefits as of beginning of year. [2] Includes self-employment. [3] The maximum taxable earnings for HI was $125,000 in 1991; $130,200 in 1992, and 135,000 in 1993. Beginning 1994 upper limit on earnings subject to HI taxes was repealed. [4] As of January 1, 1995, and 1996, each employee and employer pays 7.65 percent and the self-employed pays 15.3 percent. [5] Self-employed pays 11.8 percent in 1985 and 13.02 percent in 1988 and 1989. The additional amount is supplied from general revenues. Beginning 1990, self-employed pays 15.3 percent, and half of the tax is deductible for income tax purposes and for computing self-employment income subject to social security tax. [6] 1970 and 1980, as of July 1; beginning 1985, as of January 1. As of January 1, 1996, the monthly premium is $42.50.

Source: U.S. Social Security Administration, *Annual Statistical Supplement* to the *Social Security Bulletin*; and unpublished data.

No. 581. Social Security Trust Funds: 1980 to 1994

[**In billions of dollars.** See also *Historical Statistics, Colonial Times to 1970*, series H 238-242]

TYPE OF TRUST FUND	1980	1985	1988	1989	1990	1991	1992	1993	1994
Old-age and survivors insurance (OASI):									
Net contribution income [1]	103.5	180.2	233.2	252.6	272.4	278.4	286.8	296.2	298.3
Interest received [2]	1.8	1.9	7.6	12.0	16.4	20.8	24.3	27.0	29.9
Benefit payments [3]	105.1	167.2	[4]195.5	208.0	223.0	240.5	[4]254.9	[4]267.8	279.1
Assets, end of year	22.8	[5]35.8	102.9	155.1	214.2	267.8	319.2	369.3	413.5
Disability insurance (DI):									
Net contribution income [1]	13.3	17.4	22.1	24.1	28.7	29.3	30.4	31.5	51.7
Interest received [2]	0.5	0.9	0.6	0.7	0.9	1.1	1.1	0.8	1.2
Benefit payments [3]	15.5	18.8	[4]21.7	22.9	24.8	27.7	[4]31.1	[4]34.6	37.7
Assets, end of year	3.6	[6]6.3	6.9	7.9	11.1	12.9	12.3	9.0	22.9
Hospital insurance (HI):									
Net contribution income [1] [7]	23.9	47.7	62.6	68.5	71.1	78.4	82.4	84.9	96.3
Interest received [2]	1.1	3.4	5.8	7.3	8.5	9.5	10.5	12.5	10.7
Benefit payments	25.1	47.5	52.5	60.0	66.2	71.5	83.9	93.5	103.3
Assets, end of year	13.7	[8]20.5	69.6	85.6	98.9	115.2	124.0	127.8	132.8
Supplementary medical insurance (SMI):									
Net premium income	3.0	5.6	8.8	10.8	11.3	11.9	14.1	14.2	17.4
Transfers from general revenue . . .	7.5	18.3	26.2	30.9	33.0	37.6	41.4	41.5	36.2
Interest received	0.4	1.2	0.9	1.1	1.6	1.7	1.8	2.0	2.0
Benefit payments	10.6	22.9	34.0	38.4	42.5	47.3	49.3	55.8	58.6
Assets, end of year	4.5	10.9	9.0	12.2	15.5	17.8	24.2	24.1	19.4

[1] Includes deposits by States and deductions for refund of estimated employee-tax overpayment. Beginning in 1985, includes government contributions on deemed wage credits for military service in 1957 and later. Beginning 1985 includes tax credits on net earnings from self-employment in 1985-89; and taxation of benefits (OASI and DI, only). [2] Beginning in 1985, includes interest on advance tax transfers and interest on reimbursement for unnegotiated checks. Data for 1985 reflect interest on interfund borrowing. [3] Includes payments for vocational rehabilitation services furnished to disabled persons receiving benefits because of their disabilities. Beginning in 1985, amounts reflect deductions for unnegotiated benefit checks. [4] Data adjusted to reflect 12 months of benefit payments. [5] Includes $13.2 billion borrowed from the DI and HI Trust Funds. [6] Excludes $2.5 billion lent to the OASI Trust Fund. [7] Includes premiums from aged ineligibles enrolled in HI. [8] Excludes $10.6 billion lent to the OASI Trust Fund.

Source: U.S. Social Security Administration, *Annual Report of Board of Trustees, OASI, DI, HI, and SMI Trust Funds*. Also published in *Social Security Bulletin*, quarterly.

No. 582. Social Security (OASDI)—Benefits, by Type of Beneficiary: 1970 to 1994

[A person eligible to receive more than one type of benefit is generally classified or counted only once as a retired-worker beneficiary. OASDI=Old-age, survivors, and disability insurance. See also headnote, table 580; Appendix III; and *Historical Statistics, Colonial Times to 1970*, series H 197-229]

TYPE OF BENEFICIARY	1970	1980	1985	1988	1989	1990	1991	1992	1993	1994
	BENEFITS IN CURRENT-PAYMENT STATUS [1] (end of year)									
Number of benefits (1,000)	26,229	35,585	37,058	38,627	39,151	39,832	40,592	41,507	42,246	42,883
Retired workers [2] (1,000)	13,349	19,562	22,432	23,858	24,327	24,838	25,289	25,758	26,104	26,408
Disabled workers [3] (1,000)	1,493	2,859	2,657	2,830	2,895	3,011	3,195	3,468	3,726	3,963
Wives and husbands [2][4] (1,000)	2,952	3,477	3,375	3,367	3,365	3,367	3,370	3,382	3,367	3,337
Children (1,000)	4,122	4,607	3,319	3,204	3,165	3,187	3,268	3,391	3,527	3,654
Under age 18	3,315	3,423	2,699	2,534	2,488	2,497	2,558	2,664	2,777	2,887
Disabled children [5]	271	450	526	574	586	600	616	637	656	673
Students [6]	537	733	94	96	91	89	95	90	94	94
Of retired workers	546	639	457	432	423	422	426	432	436	440
Of deceased workers	2,688	2,610	1,917	1,809	1,780	1,776	1,791	1,808	1,836	1,864
Of disabled workers	889	1,358	945	963	962	989	1,052	1,151	1,255	1,350
Widowed mothers [7] (1,000)	523	562	372	318	312	304	301	294	289	283
Widows and widowers [2][8] (1,000)	3,227	4,411	4,863	5,029	5,071	5,111	5,158	5,205	5,224	5,232
Parents [2] (1,000)	29	15	10	7	6	6	6	5	5	4
Special benefits [9] (1,000)	534	93	32	14	10	7	5	4	2	2
Average monthly benefit, current dollars										
Retired workers [2]	118	341	479	537	567	603	629	653	674	697
Retired worker and wife [2]	199	567	814	914	966	1,027	1,072	1,111	1,145	1,184
Disabled workers [3]	131	371	484	530	556	587	609	626	642	661
Wives and husbands [2][4]	59	164	236	265	281	298	311	322	332	343
Children of retired workers	45	140	198	228	242	259	273	285	297	309
Children of deceased workers	82	240	330	368	385	406	420	432	443	456
Children of disabled workers	39	110	142	151	157	164	168	170	173	178
Widowed mothers [7]	87	246	332	368	388	409	424	438	448	464
Widows and widowers, nondisabled [2]	102	311	433	493	522	557	584	608	630	655
Parents [2]	103	276	378	428	454	482	506	526	547	570
Special benefits [9]	45	105	138	151	158	167	173	178	183	187
Average monthly benefit, constant (1994) dollars [10]										
Retired workers [2]	444	592	656	667	673	675	683	689	692	697
Retired worker and wife [2]	749	984	1,115	1,135	1,147	1,149	1,164	1,172	1,176	1,184
Disabled workers [3]	493	644	663	658	660	657	661	660	659	661
Wives and husbands [2][4]	222	284	323	329	334	333	338	340	341	343
Children of deceased workers	308	416	453	457	457	454	456	456	455	456
Widowed mothers [7]	327	427	455	457	461	458	460	462	460	464
Widows and widowers, nondisabled [2]	384	539	593	612	620	622	633	641	647	655
	BENEFITS AWARDED DURING YEAR (1,000)									
Number of benefits	3,722	4,215	3,796	3,681	3,646	3,717	3,865	4,051	4,001	3,940
Retired workers [2]	1,338	1,620	1,690	1,654	1,657	1,665	1,695	1,708	1,661	1,625
Disabled workers [3]	350	389	377	409	426	468	536	637	635	632
Wives and husbands [2][4]	436	469	440	391	380	379	380	383	365	345
Children	1,091	1,174	714	706	675	695	727	795	816	824
Widowed mothers [7]	112	108	72	63	60	58	58	56	56	55
Widows and widowers [2][8]	363	452	502	458	449	452	469	472	466	459
Parents [2]	2	1	(Z)	(Z)	(Z)	(Z)	(Z)	(Z)	(Z)	(Z)
Special benefits [9]	30	1	1	(Z)	(Z)	(Z)	(Z)	(Z)	(Z)	(Z)
	BENEFIT PAYMENTS DURING YEAR (bil. dol.)									
Total amount [11]	31.9	120.5	186.2	217.2	230.9	247.8	268.1	286.0	302.4	316.8
Monthly benefits [12]	31.6	120.1	186.0	217.0	230.6	247.6	267.9	285.8	302.2	316.6
Retired workers [2]	18.4	70.4	116.8	137.0	146.0	156.8	169.1	179.4	188.4	196.4
Disabled workers [3]	2.4	12.8	16.5	19.2	20.3	22.1	24.7	27.9	30.9	33.7
Wives and husbands [2][4]	2.2	7.0	11.1	12.8	13.6	14.5	15.5	16.4	16.9	17.4
Children	3.5	10.5	10.7	11.3	11.5	12.0	12.8	13.6	14.6	15.4
Under age 18	2.7	7.4	8.5	8.7	8.7	9.0	9.5	10.1	10.8	11.4
Disabled children [5]	0.3	1.0	1.8	2.2	2.3	2.5	2.8	3.0	3.3	3.4
Students [6]	0.6	2.1	0.4	0.5	0.5	0.5	0.5	0.5	0.5	0.6
Of retired workers	0.3	1.1	1.1	1.2	1.2	1.3	1.4	1.5	1.6	1.6
Of deceased workers	2.8	7.4	7.8	8.1	8.3	8.6	9.0	9.4	9.9	10.3
Of disabled workers	0.5	2.0	1.8	2.0	2.0	2.2	2.4	2.7	3.1	3.4
Widowed mothers [7]	0.6	1.6	1.5	1.4	1.4	1.4	1.5	1.5	1.5	1.6
Widows and widowers [2][8]	4.1	17.6	29.3	35.2	37.7	40.7	44.1	47.1	49.7	52.1
Parents [2]	(Z)	0.1	0.1	(Z)	(Z)	(Z)	(Z)	(Z)	(Z)	(Z)
Special benefits [9]	0.3	0.1	0.1	0.2	0.2	0.2	0.2	0.2	0.2	(Z)
Lump sum	0.3	0.4	0.2	0.2	0.2	0.2	0.2	0.2	0.2	0.2

Z Fewer than 500 or less than $50 million. [1] Benefit payment actually being made at a specified time with no deductions or with deductions amounting to less than a month's benefits; i.e., the benefits actually being received. [2] 62 years and over. [3] Disabled workers under age 65. [4] Includes wife beneficiaries with entitled children in their care and entitled divorced wives. [5] 18 years old and over. Disability began before age 18 and, beginning 1973, before age 22. [6] Full-time students aged 18-21 through 1984 and aged 18 and 19 beginning 1985. [7] Includes surviving divorced mothers with entitled children in their care and, beginning 1980, widowed fathers with entitled children in their care. [8] Includes widows aged 60-61, surviving divorced wives aged 60 and over, disabled widows and widowers aged 50 and over; and beginning 1980, widowers aged 60-61. [9] Benefits for persons aged 72 and over not insured under regular or transitional provisions of Social Security Act. [10] Constant dollar figures are based on the consumer price index for December as published by the U.S. Bureau of Labor Statistics. [11] Represents total disbursements of benefit checks by the U.S. Dept. of the Treasury during the years specified. [12] Distribution by type estimated.

Source: U.S. Social Security Administration, *Annual Statistical Supplement* to the *Social Security Bulletin;* and unpublished data.

No. 583. Social Security—Beneficiaries, Annual Payments, and Average Monthly Benefit, 1980 to 1994, and by State and Other Areas, 1994

[Number of beneficiaries in current-payment status and average monthly benefit as of **December**. Data for number of beneficiaries based on 10-percent sample of administrative records. See also headnote, table 582, and Appendix III]

YEAR, DIVISION, STATE, AND OTHER AREA	NUMBER OF BENEFICIARIES (1,000)				ANNUAL PAYMENTS (mil. dol.)				AVERAGE MONTHLY BENEFIT (dol.)		
	Total	Retired workers and dependents [1]	Survivors	Disabled workers and dependents	Total	Retired workers and dependents [1]	Survivors [2]	Disabled workers and dependents	Retired workers [3]	Disabled workers	Widows and widowers [4]
1980.	35,585	23,309	7,598	4,678	120,472	78,025	27,010	15,437	341	371	311
1990.	39,832	28,369	7,197	4,266	247,796	172,042	50,951	24,803	603	587	557
1992.	41,497	29,296	7,297	4,903	285,980	196,688	58,203	31,089	653	626	608
1993.	42,238	29,633	7,341	5,264	302,402	206,365	61,440	34,598	674	642	630
1994, total [5]	42,878	29,913	7,371	5,592	316,835	214,895	64,223	37,717	697	661	655
United States	41,841	29,298	7,139	5,401	312,008	212,245	62,942	36,823	(NA)	(NA)	(NA)
New England	2,296	1,673	336	284	17,539	12,478	3,119	1,942	(NA)	(NA)	(NA)
Maine	232	162	36	34	1,593	1,078	304	211	642	600	613
New Hampshire.	180	132	26	22	1,363	972	240	151	700	666	675
Vermont.	97	67	15	14	703	478	132	93	686	641	649
Massachusetts	1,038	747	154	137	7,863	5,485	1,435	943	700	652	678
Rhode Island	188	139	26	22	1,419	1,032	237	150	696	634	668
Connecticut	561	426	79	55	4,598	3,433	771	394	765	672	716
Middle Atlantic	6,576	4,766	1,080	728	52,242	36,799	10,125	5,318	(NA)	(NA)	(NA)
New York	2,952	2,110	470	372	23,482	16,430	4,331	2,721	744	697	688
New Jersey	1,299	962	203	134	10,687	7,736	1,949	1,002	766	694	711
Pennsylvania	2,324	1,694	407	222	18,073	12,633	3,845	1,595	717	683	686
East North Central.	7,144	4,999	1,258	886	55,751	37,682	11,799	6,271	(NA)	(NA)	(NA)
Ohio	1,901	1,306	357	238	14,539	9,550	3,321	1,668	714	685	687
Indiana	957	668	164	125	7,442	5,045	1,537	861	726	674	691
Illinois	1,825	1,297	318	210	14,439	9,957	2,980	1,502	737	687	699
Michigan	1,584	1,090	281	212	12,614	8,396	2,669	1,549	745	719	700
Wisconsin	877	638	138	101	6,717	4,734	1,292	691	714	665	686
West North Central	3,164	2,270	537	357	23,267	16,089	4,808	2,373	(NA)	(NA)	(NA)
Minnesota	707	519	116	72	5,193	3,654	1,047	492	683	644	650
Iowa	537	392	90	55	4,009	2,809	834	367	697	650	657
Missouri.	960	664	165	131	7,018	4,704	1,438	876	683	651	643
North Dakota	115	82	22	11	799	537	191	71	656	618	604
South Dakota	135	95	25	15	919	625	204	91	645	600	598
Nebraska	280	205	47	28	2,059	1,447	430	182	687	631	651
Kansas	430	313	72	45	3,270	2,313	664	294	716	634	667
South Atlantic	7,903	5,522	1,322	1,060	57,060	38,806	11,093	7,161	(NA)	(NA)	(NA)
Delaware	118	86	19	14	915	647	170	98	725	687	688
Maryland	666	476	120	69	5,020	3,453	1,063	504	697	685	662
District of Columbia	78	54	16	9	509	340	110	60	594	593	497
Virginia	926	630	165	131	6,569	4,325	1,377	867	666	651	604
West Virginia	382	232	81	69	2,782	1,604	702	476	690	707	621
North Carolina.	1,203	805	205	193	8,389	5,518	1,607	1,264	659	630	568
South Carolina	611	398	108	105	4,226	2,711	819	696	657	643	560
Georgia	986	624	187	175	6,840	4,242	1,470	1,128	656	637	577
Florida.	2,933	2,217	421	295	21,810	15,966	3,775	2,068	695	671	665
East South Central	2,857	1,763	564	531	19,344	11,622	4,406	3,318	(NA)	(NA)	(NA)
Kentucky	700	417	139	144	4,763	2,736	1,112	915	647	663	577
Tennessee	907	581	170	156	6,285	3,924	1,364	998	657	627	586
Alabama	764	477	157	130	5,210	3,159	1,234	817	649	637	568
Mississippi	486	288	98	101	3,086	1,803	696	588	613	613	509
West South Central	4,191	2,749	846	597	29,230	18,530	6,932	3,769	(NA)	(NA)	(NA)
Arkansas	497	317	91	90	3,315	2,055	696	564	632	633	548
Louisiana	697	411	161	125	4,704	2,665	1,273	767	648	667	584
Oklahoma	568	391	104	73	4,025	2,670	881	474	665	642	619
Texas	2,429	1,630	490	309	17,186	11,140	4,082	1,964	676	650	624
Mountain	2,250	1,594	351	305	16,330	11,232	3,049	2,050	(NA)	(NA)	(NA)
Montana	150	104	25	21	1,078	719	214	145	678	668	647
Idaho	174	125	27	21	1,252	870	242	140	677	658	656
Wyoming	70	50	11	9	516	357	101	59	698	665	661
Colorado	484	334	78	72	3,485	2,314	687	485	678	657	653
New Mexico	252	167	46	39	1,686	1,094	354	237	655	642	613
Arizona	683	497	99	86	5,080	3,592	882	606	704	687	681
Utah	219	156	35	29	1,592	1,116	302	174	703	640	692
Nevada	218	161	30	28	1,641	1,170	267	204	705	695	674
Pacific	5,461	3,962	845	653	41,245	29,007	7,617	4,623	(NA)	(NA)	(NA)
Washington	778	570	115	92	6,002	4,264	1,083	655	724	672	693
Oregon	539	400	79	60	4,070	2,928	726	417	708	664	684
California	3,941	2,838	621	482	29,709	20,732	5,560	3,417	711	667	677
Alaska.	41	27	8	6	295	187	64	45	691	655	628
Hawaii	162	127	22	13	1,169	896	184	89	686	660	626
Puerto Rico	605	330	121	154	2,842	1,425	639	778	449	552	359
Guam	7	4	2	1	32	18	11	4	497	460	419
American Samoa	5	2	2	1	18	6	7	4	418	479	281
Virgin Islands.	12	8	2	2	68	44	14	10	584	627	486
Abroad.	365	258	91	16	1,866	1,157	610	98	466	568	463

NA Not available. [1] Includes special benefits; see footnote 9, table 582. [2] Includes lump-sum payments to survivors of deceased workers. [3] Excludes persons with special benefits. [4] Nondisabled only. [5] Number of beneficiaries includes those with State or area unknown.

Source: U.S. Social Security Administration, *Social Security Bulletin*, quarterly.

No. 584. Public Employee Retirement Systems—Participants and Finances: 1980 to 1993

[For fiscal year of retirement system, except data for the Thrift Savings Plan are for calendar year]

RETIREMENT PLAN	Unit	1980	1985	1987	1988	1989	1990	1991	1992	1993
TOTAL PARTICIPANTS [1]										
Federal retirement systems:										
Defined benefit:										
Civil Service Retirement System	1,000	4,629	4,919	4,295	4,261	4,332	4,167	4,086	4,014	3,808
Federal Employees Retirement System [2]	1,000	(X)	(X)	800	924	1,068	1,180	1,325	1,367	1,424
Military Service Retirement System [3]	1,000	3,380	3,672	3,765	3,762	3,790	3,763	3,732	3,579	3,511
Thrift Savings Plan [4]	1,000	(X)	(X)	1,022	1,317	1,446	1,625	1,700	1,900	2,000
State and local retirement systems [5][6]	1,000	(NA)	15,234	15,093	15,777	16,684	16,858	17,502	18,310	(NA)
ACTIVE PARTICIPANTS										
Federal retirement systems:										
Defined benefit:										
Civil Service Retirement System	1,000	2,700	2,800	2,080	2,011	1,918	1,826	1,726	1,654	1,525
Federal Employees Retirement System [2]	1,000	(X)	(X)	800	919	1,052	1,136	1,260	1,276	1,318
Military Service Retirement System [3]	1,000	2,050	2,192	2,229	2,196	2,188	2,130	2,064	1,868	1,763
Thrift Savings Plan [4]	1,000	(X)	(X)	960	1,099	1,269	1,419	1,200	1,300	1,500
State and local retirement systems [5][6]	1,000	(NA)	10,364	10,744	10,732	11,357	11,345	11,696	(NA)	(NA)
ASSETS										
Total	Bil. dol.	258	529	732	825	922	1,047	1,150	1,276	(NA)
Federal retirement systems	Bil. dol.	73	154	219	262	289	326	367	411	455
Defined benefit	Bil. dol.	73	154	218	260	284	318	355	394	434
Civil Service Retirement System	Bil. dol.	73	142	175	198	204	220	237	256	277
Federal Employees Retirement System [2]	Bil. dol.	(X)	(X)	4	8	12	18	24	32	41
Military Service Retirement System [3]	Bil. dol.	(7)	12	39	53	68	80	94	106	116
Thrift Savings Plan [4]	Bil. dol.	(X)	(X)	1	3	5	8	12	16	21
State and local retirement systems [5]	Bil. dol.	185	374	513	563	633	721	783	866	(NA)
CONTRIBUTIONS										
Total	Bil. dol.	83	106	98	103	104	103	111	107	(NA)
Federal retirement systems	Bil. dol.	19	54	56	59	60	61	65	68	68
Defined benefit	Bil. dol.	19	54	55	57	58	59	62	64	63
Civil Service Retirement System	Bil. dol.	19	27	24	25	26	28	29	30	31
Federal Employees Retirement System [2]	Bil. dol.	(X)	(X)	2	3	4	4	5	6	6
Military Service Retirement System [3]	Bil. dol.	(7)	27	29	29	28	27	28	28	26
Thrift Savings Plan [4]	Bil. dol.	(X)	(X)	1	2	2	2	3	4	5
State and local retirement systems [5]	Bil. dol.	64	52	42	44	44	42	46	39	(NA)
BENEFITS										
Total	Bil. dol.	39	62	71	77	83	89	96	101	(NA)
Federal retirement systems	Bil. dol.	27	40	44	47	50	53	57	58	62
Defined benefit	Bil. dol.	27	40	44	47	50	53	56	58	61
Civil Service Retirement System	Bil. dol.	15	23	26	28	30	31	33	33	35
Federal Employees Retirement System [2]	Bil. dol.	(X)	(X)	(Z)	(Z)	(Z)	(Z)	(Z)	(Z)	(Z)
Military Service Retirement System [3]	Bil. dol.	12	17	18	19	20	22	23	25	26
Thrift Savings Plan [4]	Bil. dol.	(X)	(X)	(Z)	(Z)	(Z)	(Z)	(Z)	(Z)	1
State and local retirement systems [5]	Bil. dol.	12	22	27	30	33	36	39	44	(NA)

NA Not available.   X Not applicable.   Z Less than $500 million.   [1] Includes active, separated vested, retired employees, and survivors.   [2] The Federal Employees Retirement system was established June 6, 1986.   [3] Includes nondisability and disability retirees, surviving families, and all active personnel with the exception of active reserves.   [4] The Thrift Savings Plan (a defined contribution plan) was established April 1, 1987.   [5] Excludes State and local plans that are fully supported by employee contributions.   [6] Not adjusted for double counting of individuals participating in more than one plan.   [7] The Military Retirement System was unfunded until October 1, 1984.

Source: Employee Benefit Research Institute, Washington, DC, *EBRI Databook on Employee Benefits, Fourth Edition* (copyright).

No. 585. Federal Civil Service Retirement: 1980 to 1995

[As of **Sept. 30** or for **year ending Sept. 30**. Covers both Civil Service Retirement System and Federal Employees Retirement System. See also *Historical Statistics, Colonial Times to 1970*, series H 262-270]

ITEM	Unit	1980	1985	1989	1990	1991	1992	1993	1994	1995
Employees covered [1]	1,000	2,720	2,750	2,880	2,945	2,885	2,933	2,843	2,778	2,668
Annuitants, total	1,000	**1,675**	**1,955**	**2,120**	**2,143**	**2,184**	**2,185**	**2,242**	**2,263**	**2,311**
Age and service	1,000	905	1,122	1,267	1,288	1,325	1,322	1,378	1,398	1,441
Disability	1,000	343	332	305	297	289	282	274	268	263
Survivors	1,000	427	501	548	558	570	581	589	597	607
Receipts, total [2]	Mil. dol.	**24,389**	**40,790**	**49,249**	**52,689**	**56,815**	**59,737**	**62,878**	**63,390**	**65,670**
Employee contributions	Mil. dol.	3,686	4,679	4,491	4,501	4,563	4,713	4,703	4,610	4,490
Federal government contributions	Mil. dol.	15,562	22,301	25,367	27,368	29,509	30,785	32,668	32,434	32,722
Disbursements, total [3]	Mil. dol.	**14,977**	**23,203**	**29,713**	**31,416**	**33,209**	**33,187**	**35,123**	**36,532**	**38,606**
Age and service annuitants [4]	Mil. dol.	12,639	19,414	25,095	26,495	27,997	27,684	29,288	30,440	32,150
Survivors	Mil. dol.	1,912	3,158	4,033	4,366	4,716	5,093	5,377	5,607	5,939
Average monthly benefit:										
Age and service	Dollars	992	1,189	1,310	1,369	1,439	1,493	1,537	1,587	1,643
Disability	Dollars	723	881	966	1,008	1,059	1,094	1,120	1,141	1,164
Survivors	Dollars	392	528	616	653	698	731	760	789	819
Cash and security holdings	Bil. dol.	73.7	142.3	216.7	238.0	261.6	289.6	317.4	344.3	371.3

[1] Excludes employees in Leave Without Pay status.   [2] Includes interest on investments.   [3] Includes refunds, death claims, and administration.   [4] Includes disability annuitants.

Source: U.S. Office of Personnel Management, *Civil Service Retirement and Disability Trust Fund Annual Report*.

No. 586. State and Local Government Retirement Systems— Beneficiaries and Finances: 1980 to 1994

[In billions of dollars, except as indicated. For fiscal years closed during the 12 months ending June 30]

YEAR AND LEVEL OF GOVERNMENT	Number of benefi-ciaries (1,000)	RECEIPTS					BENEFITS AND WITHDRAWALS			Cash and security holdings
		Total	Em-ployee contri-butions	Government contributions		Earn-ings on invest-ments	Total	Ben-efits	With-drawals	
				State	Local					
1980: All systems.	(NA)	37.3	6.5	7.6	10.0	13.3	14.0	12.2	1.8	185
State-administered . . .	(NA)	28.6	5.3	7.4	5.6	10.3	10.3	8.8	1.4	145
Locally administered . .	(NA)	8.7	1.2	0.2	4.3	3.0	3.8	3.4	0.4	41
1990: All systems.	4,026	111.3	13.9	14.0	18.6	64.9	38.4	36.0	2.4	721
State-administered . . .	3,232	89.2	11.6	14.0	11.5	52.0	29.6	27.6	2.0	575
Locally administered . .	794	22.2	2.2	(Z)	7.0	12.9	8.8	8.4	0.4	145
1993: All systems.	4,562	135.4	16.5	15.2	20.4	83.3	51.6	49.1	2.5	929
State-administered . . .	3,643	109.4	13.8	15.2	12.9	67.6	40.0	37.9	2.1	750
Locally administered . .	919	26.0	2.7	(Z)	7.5	15.8	11.6	11.2	0.4	180
1994: All systems.	4,889	138.7	17.3	15.5	21.2	84.6	56.4	53.4	3.0	1,025
State-administered . . .	3,979	113.2	14.7	15.5	13.6	69.4	43.8	41.2	2.6	826
Locally administered . .	910	25.5	2.6	(Z)	7.7	15.2	12.6	12.2	0.5	199

NA Not available.   Z Less than $50 million.
Source: U.S. Bureau of the Census, *Finances of Employee-Retirement Systems of State and Local Governments*, series GF, No. 2, annual.

No. 587. Private Pension Plans—Summary, by Type of Plan: 1980 to 1992

["Pension plan" is defined by the Employee Retirement Income Security Act (ERISA) as "any plan, fund, or program which was heretofore or is hereafter established or maintained by an employer or an employee organization, or by both, to the extent that such plan (a) provides retirement income to employees, or (b) results in a deferral of income by employees for periods extending to the termination of covered employment or beyond, regardless of the method of calculating the contributions made to the plan, the method of calculating the benefits under the plan, or the method of distributing benefits from the plan." A defined benefit plan provides a definite benefit formula for calculating benefit amounts - such as a flat amount per year of service or a percentage of salary times years of service. A defined contribution plan is a pension plan in which the contributions are made to an individual account for each employee. The retirement benefit is dependent upon the account balance at retirement. The balance depends upon amounts contributed, investment experience, and, in the case of profit sharing plans, amounts which may be allocated to the account due to forfeitures by terminating employees. Employee Stock Ownership Plans (ESOP) and 401(k) plans (see table 589) are included among defined contribution plans. Data are based on Form 5500 series reports filed with the Internal Revenue Service]

ITEM	Unit	TOTAL				DEFINED CONTRIBUTION PLAN				DEFINED BENEFIT PLAN			
		1980	1985	1990	1992	1980	1985	1990	1992	1980	1985	1990	1992
Number of plans [1]	1,000. . .	488.9	632.1	712.3	708.3	340.8	462.0	599.2	619.7	148.1	170.2	113.1	88.6
Total participants [2][3] . . .	Million . .	57.9	74.7	76.9	81.9	19.9	35.0	38.1	42.4	38.0	39.7	38.8	39.5
Active participants [2][4] .	Million . .	49.0	62.3	61.8	64.2	18.9	33.2	35.5	38.9	30.1	29.0	26.3	25.4
Contributions [5]	Bil. dol. .	66.2	95.1	98.8	128.8	23.5	53.1	75.8	93.6	42.6	42.0	23.0	35.2
Benefits [6]	Bil. dol. .	35.3	101.9	129.4	152.4	13.1	47.4	63.0	74.6	22.1	54.5	66.4	77.9

[1] Excludes all plans covering only one participant.   [2] Includes double counting of workers in more than one plan.   [3] Total participants include active participants, vested separated workers, and retirees.   [4] Any workers currently in employment covered by a plan and who are earning or retaining credited service under a plan. Includes any nonvested former employees who have not yet incurred breaks in service.   [5] Includes both employer and employee contributions.   [6] Benefits paid directly from trust and premium payments made from plan to insurance carriers. Excludes benefits paid directly by insurance carriers.
Source: U.S. Dept. of Labor, Pension and Welfare Benefits Administration, *Private Pension Plan Bulletin*, summer 1993; and unpublished data.

No. 588. Pension Plan Coverage of Workers, by Selected Characteristics: 1994

[Covers workers as of **March 1995** who had earnings in 1994. Based on Current Population Survey; see text, section 1, and Appendix III]

SEX AND AGE	NUMBER WITH COVERAGE (1,000)				PERCENT OF TOTAL WORKERS			
	Total [1]	White	Black	Hispanic [2]	Total [1]	White	Black	Hispanic [2]
Total	**57,424**	**49,144**	**6,190**	**3,215**	**41.3**	**41.6**	**41.0**	**26.1**
Male.	32,314	28,014	3,068	1,845	43.5	43.9	42.6	25.4
Under 65 years old	31,644	27,438	2,991	1,828	44.2	44.7	42.7	25.6
15 to 24 years old	1,524	1,292	174	150	12.2	12.1	12.9	9.6
25 to 44 years old	18,414	15,837	1,835	1,196	47.9	48.6	46.1	28.2
45 to 64 years old	11,706	10,310	982	482	56.8	56.8	58.5	36.0
65 years old and over	670	575	77	17	24.3	23.1	40.1	15.1
Female.	25,111	21,131	3,123	1,370	38.7	38.9	39.5	27.1
Under 65 years old	24,674	20,737	3,088	1,362	39.3	39.6	39.9	27.3
15 to 24 years old	1,240	1,029	176	82	10.9	10.9	12.4	7.8
25 to 44 years old	14,430	12,008	1,890	893	43.5	43.9	42.9	31.1
45 to 64 years old	9,004	7,700	1,022	388	49.5	49.4	53.3	35.9
65 years old and over	437	393	35	8	21.2	21.2	20.4	14.7

[1] Includes other races, not shown separately.   [2] Hispanic persons may be of any race.
Source: U.S. Bureau of the Census, unpublished data.

No. 589. 401(k) Plans—Summary: 1985 to 1992

[A 401(k) plan is a qualified retirement plan that allows participants to have a portion of their compensation (otherwise payable in cash) contributed pretax to a retirement account on their behalf]

ITEM	1985	1987	1988	1989	1990	1991	1992
Number of plans [1]	29,869	45,054	68,121	83,301	97,614	111,314	139,704
Active participants [2] (1,000)	10,339	13,131	15,203	17,337	19,548	19,126	22,404
Assets (mil. dol.)	143,939	215,477	276,995	357,015	384,854	440,259	552,959
Contributions (mil. dol.)	24,322	33,185	39,412	46,081	48,998	51,533	64,345
Benefits (mil. dol.)	16,399	22,215	25,235	30,875	32,028	32,734	43,166
Percentage of all private defined contribution plans:							
Assets	34	41	47	52	54	53	58
Contributions	46	53	61	63	65	64	69
Benefits	35	40	43	47	51	51	58

[1] Excludes single-participant plans.   [2] May include some employees who are eligible to participate in the plan but have not elected to join. 401(k) participants may participate in one or more additional plans.

Source: Employee Benefit Research Institute, Washington, DC, *EBRI Databook on Employee Benefits, Fourth Edition* (copyright).

No. 590. State Unemployment Insurance—Summary: 1980 to 1994

[Includes unemployment compensation for State and local government employees where covered by State law. See also *Historical Statistics, Colonial Times to 1970*, series H 305-317]

ITEM	Unit	1980	1985	1987	1988	1989	1990	1991	1992	1993	1994
Insured unemployment, avg. weekly	1,000	3,356	2,617	2,330	2,081	2,158	2,522	3,342	3,245	2,751	2,670
Percent of covered employment [1]	Percent	3.9	2.9	2.3	2.0	2.1	2.4	3.1	3.1	2.6	2.5
Percent of civilian unemployed	Percent	43.9	31.5	31.0	31.1	33.1	36.7	39.7	34.6	31.5	33.4
Unemployment benefits, avg. weekly	Dollars	100	128	141	145	152	162	170	174	180	182
Percent of weekly wage	Percent	36.6	35.3	35.5	34.9	35.4	36.0	36.4	35.4	36.0	35.7
Weeks compensated	Million	149.0	119.3	105.2	94.2	97.6	116.0	155.1	150.2	125.6	123.4
Beneficiaries, first payments	1,000	9,992	8,372	7,203	6,861	7,369	8,629	10,075	9,243	7,884	7,959
Average duration of benefits [2]	Weeks	14.9	14.2	14.6	13.7	13.2	13.4	15.4	16.2	15.9	15.5
Claimants exhausting benefits	1,000	3,072	2,575	2,408	1,979	1,940	2,323	3,472	3,838	3,204	2,977
Percent of first payment [3]	Percent	33.2	31.2	30.6	28.5	28.0	29.4	34.8	39.9	39.2	36.3
Contributions collected [4]	Bil. dol.	11.4	19.3	17.6	17.7	16.5	15.2	14.5	17.0	19.8	21.8
Benefits paid	Bil. dol.	13.8	14.1	13.6	12.8	13.6	17.3	24.6	24.0	20.7	20.4
Funds available for benefits [5]	Bil. dol.	11.6	16.2	25.2	31.9	37.5	38.4	31.5	27.1	28.2	31.3
Average employer contribution rate [6]	Percent	2.4	3.1	2.6	2.5	2.2	2.0	2.0	2.2	2.5	2.6

[1] Insured unemployment as percent of average covered employment in preceding year.   [2] Weeks compensated divided by first payment.   [3] Based on first payments for 12-month period ending June 30.   [4] Contributions from employers; also employees in States which tax workers.   [5] End of year. Sum of balances in State clearing accounts, benefit-payment accounts, and State accounts in Federal unemployment trust funds.   [6] As percent of taxable wages.

No. 591. State Unemployment Insurance, by State and Other Areas: 1994

[See headnote, table 590. For State data on insured unemployment, see table 650]

STATE OR OTHER AREA	Benefi-ciaries, first pay-ments (1,000)	Benefits paid (mil. dol.)	Avg. weekly unem-ploy-ment benefits (dol.)	STATE OR OTHER AREA	Benefi-ciaries, first pay-ments (1,000)	Benefits paid (mil. dol.)	Avg. weekly unem-ploy-ment benefits (dol.)	STATE OR OTHER AREA	Benefi-ciaries, first pay-ments (1,000)	Benefits paid (mil. dol.)	Avg. weekly unem-ploy-ment benefits (dol.)
Total	7,959	20,439	182	KY	164	215	159	OH	255	690	191
AL	137	174	131	LA	82	146	118	OK	48	106	168
AK	47	114	170	ME	51	102	161	OR	138	330	179
AZ	76	157	148	MD	119	325	180	PA	470	1,458	212
AR	81	146	161	MA	212	787	237	RI	57	175	220
CA	1,311	3,261	154	MI	324	829	213	SC	100	174	154
CO	73	180	195	MN	115	338	217	SD	8	12	138
CT	143	486	222	MS	58	90	129	TN	154	242	142
DE	23	59	183	MO	145	303	150	TX	375	975	185
DC	24	91	220	MT	27	53	156	UT	31	62	187
FL	285	684	168	NE	27	40	140	VT	23	50	164
GA	188	252	153	NV	52	127	185	VA	114	214	169
HI	41	172	266	NH	25	41	146	WA	242	822	206
ID	45	78	167	NJ	298	1,201	246	WV	57	125	167
IL	321	1,044	199	NM	28	62	140	WI	192	376	188
IN	106	222	158	NY	581	2,000	203	WY	12	25	173
IA	71	143	183	NC	190	262	175	PR	134	231	89
KS	60	143	192	ND	14	27	160	VI	4	18	191

Source of tables 590 and 591: U.S. Employment and Training Administration, *Unemployment Insurance Financial Handbook*, annual.

No. 592. Workers' Compensation Payments: 1980 to 1993

[**In billions of dollars**, except as indicated. See headnote, table 593. See also *Historical Statistics, Colonial Times to 1970*, series H 332-345]

ITEM	1980	1984	1985	1986	1987	1988	1989	1990	1991	1992	1993
Workers covered [1] (mil.)	79	82	84	86	88	91	94	95	94	95	96
Premium amounts paid . . .	22.3	25.1	29.2	34.0	38.1	43.3	48.0	53.1	55.2	55.5	57.3
Private carriers.	15.7	16.6	19.5	22.8	25.4	28.5	31.9	35.1	35.7	32.8	33.6
State funds	3.0	3.0	3.5	4.5	5.3	6.7	7.2	8.0	8.7	9.6	10.9
Federal programs [2]	1.1	1.6	1.7	1.8	1.8	1.9	2.0	2.2	2.1	2.2	2.3
Self-insurers	2.4	3.9	4.5	4.9	5.5	6.2	6.9	7.9	8.7	10.4	10.6
Annual benefits paid	13.6	19.7	22.2	24.6	27.3	30.7	34.3	38.2	42.2	44.7	42.9
By private carriers [3]	7.0	10.6	12.3	13.8	15.5	17.5	19.9	22.2	24.5	24.0	21.8
From State funds [4]	4.3	5.4	5.7	6.2	6.8	7.5	8.0	8.7	9.7	11.0	11.3
Employers' self-insurance [5]	2.3	3.7	4.1	4.5	5.1	5.7	6.4	7.4	7.9	9.6	9.9
Type of benefit:											
Medical/hospitalization	3.9	6.4	7.5	8.6	9.9	11.5	13.4	15.2	16.8	18.3	17.5
Compensation payments	9.7	13.3	14.7	16.0	17.4	19.2	20.9	23.1	25.3	26.4	25.4
Disability.	8.4	11.7	13.1	14.3	15.8	17.6	19.2	21.2	23.3	24.4	23.5
Survivor	1.3	1.6	1.7	1.6	1.6	1.6	1.7	1.8	2.0	2.0	2.0
Percent of covered payroll:											
Workers' compensation costs [6][7]	1.96	1.66	1.82	1.99	2.07	2.16	2.27	2.36	2.40	2.31	2.30
Benefits [7]	1.07	1.21	1.30	1.37	1.43	1.49	1.58	1.66	1.79	1.82	1.68

[1] Estimated per month.   [2] Includes Federal employer compensation program and that portion of Federal black lung benefits program financed from employer contributions.   [3] Net cash and medical benefits paid under standard workers' compensation policies.   [4] Net cash and medical benefits paid by competitive and exclusive State funds and by Federal workers' compensation programs, including black lung benefit program.   [5] Cash and medical benefits paid by self-insurers, plus value of medical benefits paid by employers carrying workers' compensation policies that exclude standard medical coverage.   [6] Premiums written by private carriers and State funds, and benefits paid by self-insurers increased by 5-10 percent to allow for administrative costs. Also includes benefits paid and administrative costs of Federal system for government employees.   [7] Excludes programs financed from general revenue—black lung benefits and supplemental pensions in some States.

Source: U.S. Social Security Administration, *Annual Statistical Supplement* to the *Social Security Bulletin.*

No. 593. Workers' Compensation Payments, by State: 1980 to 1993

[**In millions of dollars.** Calendar-year data, except fiscal-year data for Federal civilian and other programs and for a few States with State funds. Payments represent cash and medical benefits and include insurance losses paid by private insurance carriers (compiled from the *Spectator (Insurance by States . . . of Casualty Lines)*, from reports of State insurance commissions, and from A. M. Best Co.); net disbursements of State funds (from the *Spectator*, from *Argus Casualty and Surety Chart*, and from State reports), estimated for some States; and self-insurance payments, estimated from available State data. Includes benefit payments under Longshoremen's and Harbor Workers' Compensation Act and Defense Bases Compensation Act for States in which such payments are made]

STATE	1980	1990	1991	1992	1993	STATE	1980	1990	1991	1992	1993
Total	13,618	38,238	42,169	44,660	42,925	Nevada	69	339	392	529	553
						New Hampshire	48	169	203	206	194
Alabama.	112	444	472	481	461	New Jersey.	316	844	916	956	968
Alaska	60	113	124	127	122	New Mexico	54	228	232	216	182
Arizona.	120	371	368	399	402	New York	637	1,752	2,014	2,317	2,370
Arkansas	83	229	251	244	224	North Carolina	131	480	545	705	671
California	1,628	6,065	7,248	7,907	7,625	North Dakota.	17	60	73	71	60
Colorado.	114	595	657	722	683	Ohio	776	1,960	2,195	2,364	2,353
Connecticut.	147	694	773	783	798	Oklahoma	127	369	434	476	493
Delaware	21	75	80	89	84						
District of Columbia .	69	86	91	126	122	Oregon.	275	573	587	476	468
Florida	362	1,976	1,961	1,861	1,705	Pennsylvania.	572	2,019	2,329	2,531	2,551
Georgia	185	735	791	1,004	911	Rhode Island.	55	219	214	266	185
Hawaii	60	216	250	288	324	South Carolina.	79	277	292	350	344
Idaho	37	105	115	123	125	South Dakota.	13	56	64	69	72
Illinois	699	1,607	1,745	1,750	1,668	Tennessee	129	463	515	522	487
Indiana.	110	350	380	375	364	Texas	701	2,896	3,264	2,682	2,119
Iowa	99	231	241	259	240	Utah	39	187	183	219	248
Kansas.	84	266	295	297	307	Vermont	15	61	67	73	73
Kentucky	161	383	432	475	457	Virginia.	182	507	545	542	539
Louisiana	301	575	560	517	403	Washington	324	883	949	1,253	1,346
Maine.	81	380	419	429	341	West Virginia.	176	389	417	456	476
Maryland	187	505	523	565	548	Wisconsin	170	561	627	598	608
Massachusetts.	296	1,235	1,276	1,205	976	Wyoming	22	49	59	66	76
Michigan.	626	1,205	1,286	1,428	1,437						
Minnesota.	260	582	646	743	734	Federal programs:					
Mississippi	60	198	203	247	214	Civilian employ-					
Missouri	124	496	557	698	656	ees.	776	1,448	1,595	1,751	1,822
Montana.	41	150	168	260	210	Black lung					
Nebraska	42	137	146	157	160	benefits [1]	1,739	1,435	1,391	1,396	1,356
						Other [2]	8	11	11	11	11

[1] Includes payments by Social Security Administration and by Department of Labor.   [2] Primarily payments made to dependents of reservists who died while on active duty in the Armed Forces.

Source: U.S. Social Security Administration, *Social Security Bulletin,* summer 1995, and selected prior issues; and unpublished data.

No. 594. Persons With Work Disability, by Selected Characteristics: 1995

[In thousands, except percent. Covers civilian noninstitutional population and members of Armed Forces living off post or with their families on post. Persons are classified as having a work disability if they (1) have a health problem or disability which prevents them from working or which limits the kind or amount of work they can do; (2) have a service-connected disability or ever retired or left a job for health reasons; (3) did not work in survey reference week or previous year because of long-term illness or disability; or (4) are under age 65, and are covered by Medicare or receive Supplemental Security Income. Based on Current Population Survey; see text, section 1, and Appendix III]

AGE AND PARTICIPATION STATUS IN ASSISTANCE PROGRAMS	Total [1]	Male	Female	White	Black	Hispanic [2]
Persons with work disability	**16,846**	**8,444**	**8,402**	**12,993**	**3,191**	**1,650**
16 to 24 years old.	1,357	661	696	957	336	168
25 to 34 years old.	2,654	1,272	1,382	1,959	576	271
35 to 44 years old.	3,993	2,089	1,904	3,025	835	366
45 to 54 years old.	4,089	2,094	1,996	3,206	703	395
55 to 64 years old.	4,752	2,327	2,425	3,846	741	451
Percent work disabled of total population . . .	10.1	10.3	9.9	9.4	15.5	9.7
16 to 24 years old.	4.2	4.1	4.3	3.7	7.0	3.9
25 to 34 years old.	6.5	6.3	6.7	5.9	10.8	5.2
35 to 44 years old.	9.5	10.1	8.9	8.7	16.3	9.5
45 to 54 years old.	13.4	14.0	12.7	12.3	22.0	17.4
55 to 64 years old.	22.9	23.6	22.3	21.3	35.8	32.4
Percent of work disabled—						
Receiving Social Security income	28.1	30.6	25.6	28.4	28.9	26.1
Receiving food stamps	24.4	19.8	29.1	19.8	41.0	32.6
Covered by Medicaid.	31.7	27.2	36.2	26.9	48.9	42.7
Residing in public housing	5.6	4.4	6.8	3.2	15.0	8.0
Residing in subsidized housing	3.6	2.7	4.6	3.0	5.9	5.0

[1] Includes other races not shown separately.   [2] Hispanic persons may be of any race.
Source: U.S. Bureau of the Census, unpublished data.

No. 595. Vocational Rehabilitation—Summary: 1980 to 1994

[For fiscal years ending in year shown; see text, section 9. Includes Puerto Rico, Guam, Virgin Islands, American Samoa, Northern Mariana Islands, and the Republic of Palau. State agencies, using matching State and Federal funds, provide vocational rehabilitation services to eligible individuals with disabilities to enable them to prepare for and engage in gainful employment. Services may include counseling, guidance and work related placement services, physical and mental restoration, training and rehabilitation technology. See also *Historical Statistics, Colonial Times to 1970*, series H 392-397]

ITEM	Unit	1980	1985	1988	1989	1990	1991	1992	1993	1994
Federal and State expenditures [1]	Mil. dol . .	1,076	1,452	1,776	1,867	1,910	2,092	2,240	2,241	2,517
Federal expenditures	Mil. dol . .	817	1,100	1,373	1,446	1,525	1,622	1,731	1,691	1,891
Applicants processed for program eligibility .	1,000 . . .	717	594	606	623	625	619	713	713	675
Percent accepted into program	Percent .	58	60	58	58	57	57	57	61	47
Total persons rehabilitated [2]	1,000 . . .	277	228	218	220	216	203	192	194	203
Rehabilitation rate [3]	Percent .	64	64	63	63	62	60	58	56	49
Severely disabled persons rehabilitated [2] [4] .	1,000 . . .	143	135	141	147	146	140	134	139	149
Rehabilitation rate [3]	Percent .	61	62	62	62	62	59	57	55	49
Percent of total persons rehabilitated . . .	Percent .	51	59	65	67	68	69	70	72	74
Persons served, total [5]	1,000 . . .	1,095	932	919	929	938	942	949	1,049	1,194
Persons served, severely disabled [4] [5]	1,000 . . .	606	581	604	625	640	654	668	762	882
Percent of total persons served	Percent .	55	62	66	67	68	69	70	73	74

[1] Includes expenditures only under the basic support provisions of the Rehabilitation Act.   [2] Persons successfully placed into gainful employment.   [3] Persons rehabilitated as a percent of all active case closures (whether rehabilitated or not).   [4] An individual with a severe disability is an individual whose severe physical or mental impairment seriously limits one or more functional capacities in terms of an employment outcome, and whose vocational rehabilitation can be expected to require multiple vocational rehabilitation services over an extended period of time.   [5] Includes active cases accepted for rehabilitation services during year plus active cases on hand at beginning of year.
Source: U.S. Dept. of Education, Rehabilitation Services Administration, *Caseload Statistics of State Vocational Rehabilitation Agencies in Fiscal Years*, and *State Vocational Rehabilitation Agency Program Data in Fiscal Years*, both annual.

No. 596. Protection Against Short-Term Sickness Income Loss: 1980 to 1993

[In millions of dollars, except percent. "Short-term sickness" refers to short-term or temporary nonwork-connected disability (lasting not more than 6 months) and the first 6 months of long-term disability. See also *Historical Statistics, Colonial Times to 1970*, series H 115-124]

ITEM	1980	1985	1987	1988	1989	1990	1991	1992	1993
Short-term sickness: Income loss	33,933	48,745	55,839	60,115	63,788	67,661	69,522	73,565	77,843
Total protection provided [1]	**16,777**	**22,131**	**25,384**	**27,922**	**30,006**	**31,204**	**32,345**	**35,052**	**35,907**
Protection as percent of loss	49.4	45.4	45.5	46.4	47.0	46.1	46.5	47.6	46.1
Benefits provided by protection:									
Individual insurance.	1,280	1,796	2,062	2,057	2,451	2,701	2,588	3,497	3,560
Group benefits to workers in private employment	9,984	12,440	14,275	15,392	16,364	16,835	17,537	18,411	18,308
Private cash insurance [2]	3,271	2,601	2,692	2,903	2,732	2,711	2,645	2,739	2,608
Publicly operated cash sickness funds [3] . .	770	1,179	1,696	1,779	1,907	2,269	2,817	2,975	2,349
Sick leave	5,943	8,660	9,887	10,710	11,725	11,855	12,075	12,697	13,351
Sick leave for government employees.	5,338	7,700	8,827	10,266	10,967	11,393	11,910	12,748	13,644

[1] Provided by individual insurance, group benefits to workers in private employment, and sick leave for government employees. Includes benefits for the sixth month of disability payable under old-age, survivors, disability, and health insurance program, not shown separately.   [2] Group accident and sickness insurance and self-insurance privately written either on a voluntary basis or in compliance with State temporary disability insurance laws in CA, HI, NJ, and NY. Includes a small but undetermined amount of group disability insurance benefits paid to government workers and to self-employed persons through farm, trade, or professional associations.   [3] Includes State-operated plans in RI, CA, and NJ; State Insurance Fund and special fund for disabled unemployed in New York; and provisions of Railroad Unemployment Insurance Act.
Source: U.S. Social Security Administration, *Social Security Bulletin*, fall 1994 and unpublished data.

No. 597. Public Aid—Recipients and Average Monthly Cash Payments Under Supplemental Security Income (SSI) and Public Assistance: 1980 to 1994

[As of **December**, except as noted. Public assistance data for all years include Puerto Rico, Guam, and Virgin Islands; SSI data are for federally administered payments only. See text, section 12. Excludes payments made directly to suppliers of medical care. See also Appendix III and *Historical Statistics, Colonial Times to 1970*, series H 355-367]

PROGRAM	RECIPIENTS (1,000)					AVG. MONTHLY PAYMENTS (dol.)				
	1980	1990	1992	1993	1994	1980	1990	1992	1993	1994
SSI, total.	4,142	4,817	5,566	5,984	6,296	168	299	358	345	351
Aged.	1,808	1,454	1,471	1,475	1,466	128	213	227	237	243
Blind.	78	84	85	85	85	213	342	362	359	264
Disabled	2,256	3,279	4,010	4,424	4,745	198	337	407	381	384
Old-age assistance [1].	19	17	17	16	16	39	45	41	45	37
Aid to the blind [1].	(Z)	(Z)	(Z)	(Z)	(Z)	36	42	37	40	38
Aid to permanently, totally disabled [1] .	21	26	28	28	27	35	40	40	41	40
AFDC: [2] Families	3,843	4,218	4,936	5,050	4,981	288	392	381	377	378
Recipients [3]	11,101	12,159	14,035	14,257	13,974	100	136	133	133	135
Children.	7,599	8,208	9,471	9,598	9,469	(NA)	(NA)	(NA)	(NA)	(NA)
General assistance cases	796	1,060	979	971	909	161	(NA)	(NA)	(NA)	(NA)

NA Not available.   Z Fewer than 500.   [1] Average monthly recipients and payments for the year.   [2] Aid to Families with Dependent Children program.   [3] Includes the children and one or both parents, or one caretaker relative other than a parent, in families where the needs of such adults were considered in determining the amount of assistance.

No. 598. Public Aid Payments: 1980 to 1994

[**In millions of dollars.** See headnote, table 597. Supplemental Security Income data cover federally- and State-administered payments. See also Appendix III and *Historical Statistics, Colonial Times to 1970*, series H 346-354]

PROGRAM	1980	1985	1987	1988	1989	1990	1991	1992	1993	1994
Payments, total	[1]21,994	26,431	29,556	30,910	32,762	36,047	39,788	44,661	47,659	49,701
Supplemental Security Income [2] . .	7,941	11,060	12,951	13,786	14,980	16,599	18,524	22,233	24,557	25,877
Aged.	2,734	3,035	3,194	3,299	3,476	3,736	3,890	4,140	4,248	4,367
Blind.	190	264	291	302	316	334	347	371	375	372
Disabled	5,014	7,755	9,458	10,177	11,180	12,521	14,268	17,711	19,928	21,131
Public assistance	[1]14,048	15,371	16,605	17,124	17,782	19,448	21,264	22,428	23,102	23,824
Old-age assistance	9	8	7	7	7	7	11	8	9	8
Blind.	(Z)	(Z)	(Z)	(Z)	(Z)	(Z)	(Z)	(Z)	(Z)	(Z)
Permanently, totally disabled . . .	9	10	11	11	12	12	12	19	14	14
Families with dependent children.	12,475	15,196	16,373	16,827	17,466	19,078	20,931	22,106	22,688	22,867
Emergency assistance	113	157	214	279	297	349	303	301	391	937

Z Less than $500,000.   [1] Includes general assistance payments.   [2] Includes data not available by reason for eligibility.

Source of tables 597 and 598: U.S. Social Security Administration, *Social Security Bulletin*, quarterly and *Annual Statistical Supplement* to the *Social Security Bulletin*, and U.S. Administration for Children and Families, *Quarterly Public Assistance Statistics*, annual.

No. 599. Public Aid Recipients as Percent of Population, by State: 1990 and 1994

[Total recipients as of **June** of Aid to Families with Dependent Children and of Federal Supplemental Security Income as percent of resident population. Based on resident population as of April 1 for 1990 and as of July 1 for 1994]

DIVISION AND STATE	1990	1994	DIVISION AND STATE	1990	1994	DIVISION AND STATE	1990	1994	DIVISION AND STATE	1990	1994
U.S . . .	6.5	7.7	IL.	7.1	8.3	WV	8.9	9.6	**Mountain . .**	4.2	5.3
			MI	8.6	9.1	NC	5.6	7.2	MT	4.9	5.6
N.E	5.6	6.9	WI	6.6	6.5	SC	5.8	6.7	ID.	2.7	3.4
ME	6.6	7.4	**W.N.C.**	4.8	5.6	GA	7.1	8.2	WY	3.8	4.5
NH	2.2	3.5	MN	4.9	5.4	FL	4.6	6.8	CO	4.3	4.7
VT	5.7	7.0	IA	4.7	5.4	**E.S.C.**	7.9	8.8	NM	5.8	8.7
MA	6.4	7.5	MO	5.8	7.0	KY	7.9	9.3	AZ	4.7	6.5
RI	6.4	8.6	ND	3.6	3.9	TN	7.2	9.0	UT	3.3	3.6
CT	4.7	6.4	SD	4.2	4.4	AL	6.5	6.8	NV	2.9	3.8
M.A	6.7	8.3	NE	3.7	4.0	MS	11.4	10.9	**Pacific**	8.4	10.4
NY	7.7	10.0	KS	4.1	4.7				WA	6.0	7.1
NJ	5.3	6.0	**S.A**	5.4	6.9	**W.S.C.**	6.2	6.9	OR	4.3	5.1
PA	6.0	7.2	DE	4.4	5.2	AR	6.3	6.6	CA	9.4	11.7
E.N.C.	7.0	7.8	MD	5.1	5.9	LA	9.8	9.7	AK	4.6	7.4
OH	7.3	8.1	DC	10.9	16.7	OK	5.6	6.2	HI	5.2	6.9
IN.	3.9	5.2	VA	3.9	4.8	TX	5.4	6.3			

Source: Compiled by U.S. Bureau of the Census. Data from U.S. Social Security Administration, *Social Security Bulletin*, quarterly, and U.S. Administration for Children and Families, *Quarterly Public Assistance Statistics*, annual.

No. 600. Aid to Families With Dependent Children (AFDC) and Supplemental Security Income (SSI)—Recipients and Payments, by State and Other Areas: 1990 to 1994

[Recipients as of **December**. Data for SSI cover Federal SSI payments and/or federally-administered State supplementation except as noted. For explanation of methodology, see Appendix III]

DIVISION AND STATE OR OTHER AREA	AFDC								SSI			
	Recipients [1] (1,000)			Payments for year (mil. dol.)			Average monthly payment per family		Recipients (1,000)		Payments for year (mil. dol.)	
	1990	1993	1994	1990	1993	1994	1990	1994	1990	1994	1990	1994
Total	12,159	14,257	13,974	19,078	22,688	22,867	$392	$378	[2]4,817	[2]6,296	16,133	25,291
U.S.	11,958	14,061	13,790	18,995	22,598	22,777	396	382	4,817	6,295	16,133	25,289
New England	577	661	639	1,250	1,516	1,497	535	527	209	274	652	1,061
ME.	62	65	61	104	115	107	422	393	24	30	56	87
NH.	21	30	29	35	58	62	431	451	[3]7	[3]10	[3]19	[3]33
VT.	25	28	27	51	65	65	527	549	10	13	31	46
MA.	282	313	288	647	755	730	556	553	119	157	397	643
RI	52	63	63	104	136	136	499	499	17	23	53	89
CT.	135	163	171	309	388	397	571	553	[3]32	[3]43	[3]96	[3]162
Middle Atlantic	1,903	2,194	2,208	3,623	4,337	4,444	472	468	711	957	2,533	4,164
NY	1,031	1,240	1,273	2,337	2,887	2,993	556	543	415	564	1,557	2,542
NJ	323	340	324	459	531	524	352	358	105	140	340	562
PA	549	614	611	827	919	927	382	367	191	252	635	1,060
East North Central .	2,397	2,528	2,383	3,611	3,739	3,659	379	356	622	898	2,021	3,740
OH.	657	694	634	896	976	940	328	318	156	236	483	972
IN	164	220	203	174	209	229	263	263	[3]60	[3]86	[3]174	[3]324
IL	656	709	713	868	908	932	342	322	[3]177	[3]260	[3]593	[3]1,107
MI	684	676	619	1,232	1,208	1,136	464	430	143	207	483	870
WI	236	228	214	441	439	423	464	462	86	110	288	467
West North Central .	647	731	690	955	1,079	1,072	366	356	216	288	584	1,022
MN.	177	189	169	355	386	379	512	513	[3]40	[3]60	[3]110	[3]215
IA	96	109	105	154	165	169	371	356	33	41	86	139
MO	218	264	260	237	284	287	274	260	[3]85	[3]110	[3]237	[3]400
ND.	16	17	15	24	28	26	359	381	[3]7	[3]9	[3]18	[3]27
SD.	19	19	18	22	25	25	272	307	10	13	26	44
NE.	44	46	42	60	65	62	336	330	[3]16	[3]21	[3]42	[3]70
KS	77	87	82	103	126	124	332	347	25	36	65	127
South Atlantic	1,654	2,189	2,116	1,844	2,566	2,587	272	269	847	1,100	2,370	3,867
DE	22	28	26	30	40	40	292	293	8	10	22	36
MD.	198	215	227	304	306	313	370	324	60	[4]79	185	[4]308
DC.	54	74	75	87	118	127	380	389	16	20	54	79
VA.	158	195	190	181	233	253	265	282	[3]95	[3]125	[3]257	[3]431
WV.	109	116	109	112	122	126	249	260	[5]47	[5]64	[5]146	[5]255
NC.	255	334	322	257	358	356	237	227	[3]149	[3]182	[3]403	[3]592
SC.	118	142	133	97	118	115	203	186	[3]90	[3]108	[3]234	[3]360
GA.	320	394	390	333	434	430	265	254	159	194	415	646
FL	420	692	645	443	837	826	263	282	222	317	653	1,160
East South Central .	742	808	747	510	610	589	168	167	501	632	1,371	2,218
KY	204	211	195	185	208	199	224	210	[3]115	[3]156	[3]337	[3]578
TN	230	301	281	176	221	216	186	164	140	175	384	602
AL	132	135	124	63	95	92	115	155	[3]133	[3]162	[3]351	[3]558
MS.	176	161	147	86	86	82	120	123	114	140	300	480
West South Central .	1,154	1,258	1,248	811	942	937	180	176	564	735	1,478	2,521
AR.	73	70	66	57	59	58	190	188	76	94	187	310
LA	279	256	260	188	176	169	167	165	133	179	378	679
OK.	129	132	127	135	171	166	279	296	[3]60	[3]72	[3]158	[3]246
TX	673	799	794	431	536	544	165	159	[5]295	[5]390	[5]755	[5]1,286
Mountain	454	592	579	523	783	796	297	323	162	239	476	882
MT.	29	35	34	40	47	49	344	344	10	13	29	48
ID	17	23	24	20	30	30	266	285	[3]10	[3]16	[3]29	[3]57
WY.	16	17	15	20	25	21	313	310	[3]3	[3]6	[3]9	[3]19
CO.	109	126	115	138	163	158	320	321	[3]38	[3]55	[3]110	[3]203
NM.	67	101	105	66	124	144	273	352	[3]32	[3]43	[3]90	[3]152
AZ.	144	203	198	146	271	268	268	311	[3]45	[3]69	[3]139	[3]259
UT.	47	50	48	65	78	77	347	364	13	20	38	75
NV.	25	37	41	28	45	48	278	275	11	19	33	69
Pacific.	2,427	3,100	3,179	5,866	7,025	7,197	606	548	984	1,172	4,646	5,811
WA.	237	290	289	447	610	612	452	494	62	88	208	368
OR.	99	115	107	150	203	197	374	395	[3]32	[3]45	[3]95	[3]168
CA.	2,023	2,597	2,682	5,107	5,953	6,113	637	556	873	1,014	4,278	5,174
AK.	24	37	37	62	111	113	651	740	[3]5	[3]6	[3]14	[3]24
HI	44	60	65	100	148	163	581	652	14	18	51	76
PR	193	186	173	74	77	74	103	106	(X)	(X)	(X)	(X)
GU	4	6	7	6	10	12	418	509	(X)	(X)	(X)	(X)
VI	3	4	4	3	3	3	279	220	(X)	(X)	(X)	(X)
N. Mariana. . . .	(X)	(X)	(X)	(X)	(X)	(X)	(X)	(X)	[5]1	[5]1	[5]2	[5]2

X Not applicable.   [1] See footnote 3, table 597.   [2] Includes data for those recipients whose residence was "unknown."   [3] Data for persons with Federal SSI payments only; State has State-administered supplementation.   [4] Data for Federal SSI payments and federally-administered supplementation only; State also has State-administered supplementation.   [5] Data for persons with Federal SSI payments only; State supplementary payments not made.

Source: U.S. Social Security Administration, *Social Security Bulletin*, quarterly, and *Annual Statistical Supplement* to the *Social Security Bulletin*; and U.S. Administration for Children and Families, *Quarterly Public Assistance Statistics*, annual.

No. 601. Mothers Who Receive AFDC and/or Food Stamp Benefits— Socioeconomic Characteristics: 1993

[As of **summer**. Covers mothers 15 to 44 years old. AFDC=Aid to Families with Dependent Children program. Based on Survey of Income and Program Participation; see text, section 14]

CHARACTERISTIC	AFDC MOTHERS Number (1,000)	AFDC MOTHERS Percent distribution	FOOD STAMP MOTHERS Number (1,000)	FOOD STAMP MOTHERS Percent distribution	CHARACTERISTIC	AFDC MOTHERS Number (1,000)	AFDC MOTHERS Percent distribution	FOOD STAMP MOTHERS Number (1,000)	FOOD STAMP MOTHERS Percent distribution
Total	3,754	100	5,303	100	Married, husband absent [2]	648	17	906	17
Age:					Widowed or divorced . . .	851	23	1,244	23
15 to 19 years old	191	5	204	4	Never married	1,783	48	2,065	39
20 to 24 years old	866	23	1,162	22					
25 to 29 years old	865	23	1,150	22	Educational attainment:				
30 to 34 years old	921	25	1,335	25	Not a high school				
35 to 39 years old	604	16	922	17	graduate.	1,633	44	2,169	41
40 to 44 years old	307	8	530	10	High school, 4 years. . . .	1,422	38	2,141	40
Race:					College: 1 or more years.	698	19	992	19
White.	2,074	55	3,176	60					
Black.	1,471	39	1,903	36	Labor force status:				
Hispanic origin:					Worked all or some weeks	474	13	1,159	22
Hispanic [1].	784	21	1,060	20	No job last month.	3,280	87	4,144	78
Not Hispanic	2,970	79	4,242	80					
Marital status:					Monthly family income: [3]				
Married, husband					Less than $500	1,351	36	1,635	31
present.	472	13	1,087	20	$500 to $999	1,360	36	1,797	34
					$1,000 to $1,499	479	13	924	17
					$1,500 and over	552	15	861	16

[1] Persons of Hispanic origin may be of any race.   [2] Includes separated women.   [3] Excludes those who did not report income.

Source: U.S. Bureau of the Census, *Statistical Brief*, Nos. SB/95-2 and SB/95-22.

No. 602. Federal Food Programs: 1980 to 1995

[**For fiscal years ending in year shown**; see text, section 9. Program data include Puerto Rico, Virgin Islands, Guam, American Samoa, Northern Marianas, and the former Trust Territory when a Federal food program was operated in these areas. Participation data are average monthly figures except as noted. Participants are not reported for the nutrition program for the elderly and the commodity distribution programs. Cost data are direct Federal benefits to recipients; they exclude Federal administrative payments and applicable State and local contributions. Federal costs for commodities and cash-in-lieu of commodities are shown separately from direct cash benefits for those programs receiving both]

PROGRAM	Unit	1980	1985	1990	1991	1992	1993	1994	1995
Food Stamp:									
Participants	Million . .	21.1	19.9	20.1	22.6	25.4	27.0	27.5	26.6
Federal cost.	Mil. dol. .	8,721	10,744	14,187	17,339	20,906	22,006	22,749	22,768
Monthly average coupon value per recipient	Dollars . .	34.47	44.99	58.92	63.86	68.57	67.96	69.02	71.29
Nutrition assistance program for Puerto Rico: [1]									
Federal cost.	Mil. dol. .	(X)	825	937	963	1,002	1,040	1,079	1,131
National school lunch program (NSLP): [2]									
Free lunches served	Million . .	1,671	1,657	1,662	1,748	1,891	1,981	2,049	2,089
Reduced-price lunches served	Million . .	308	255	273	293	285	287	298	308
Children participating [3].	Million . .	26.6	23.6	24.1	24.2	24.6	24.9	25.3	25.6
Federal cost.	Mil. dol. .	2,279	2,578	3,214	3,525	3,856	4,081	4,291	4,464
School breakfast (SB):									
Children participating [3].	Million . .	3.6	3.4	4.1	4.4	4.9	5.4	5.8	6.3
Federal cost.	Mil. dol. .	288	379	596	685	787	869	959	1,048
Special supplemental food program (WIC): [4]									
Participants	Million . .	1.9	3.1	4.5	4.9	5.4	5.9	6.5	6.9
Federal cost.	Mil. dol. .	584	1,193	1,637	1,752	1,959	2,115	2,325	2,522
Child and adult care (CC): [5]									
Participants [6].	Million . .	0.7	1.0	1.5	1.6	1.8	2.0	2.2	2.3
Federal cost.	Mil. dol. .	207	390	720	834	966	1,082	1,196	1,295
Summer feeding (SF): [7]									
Children participating [8].	Million . .	1.9	1.5	1.7	1.8	1.9	2.1	2.2	2.1
Federal cost.	Mil. dol. .	104	103	145	160	182	195	205	211
Nutrition program for the elderly:									
Meals served	Million . .	166	225	246	245	245	244	247	251
Federal cost.	Mil. dol. .	75	134	142	140	151	153	153	147
Federal cost of commodities donated to— [9]									
Child nutrition (NSLP, CC, SF and SB)	Mil. dol. .	930	840	646	729	740	706	755	737
Emergency feeding [10]	Mil. dol. .	(X)	973	286	253	230	228	222	100

X Not applicable.   [1] Puerto Rico was included in the food stamp program until June 30, 1982.   [2] See headnote, table 603.
[3] Nine month (September through May) average daily meals (lunches or breakfasts) served divided by the ratio of average daily attendance to enrollment.   [4] WIC serves women, infants, and children.   [5] Program provides year-round subsidies to feed preschool children in child care centers and family day care homes. Certain care centers serving disabled or elderly adults also receive meal subsidies.   [6] Quarterly average daily attendance at participating institutions.   [7] Program provides free meals to children in poor areas during summer months.   [8] Peak month (July) average daily attendance at participating institutions.
[9] Includes the Federal cost of commodity entitlements, cash-in-lieu of commodities, and bonus foods.   [10] Provides free commodities to needy persons for home consumption through food banks, hunger centers, soup kitchens, and similar nonprofit agencies. Includes the Emergency Food Assistance Program, the commodity purchases for soup kitchens/food banks program, and commodity disaster relief.

Source: U.S. Dept. of Agriculture, Food and Nutrition Service. In "Annual Historical Review of FNS Programs" and unpublished data.

No. 603. Federal Food Stamp and National School Lunch Programs, by State: 1990 to 1995

[Cost data for years ending Sept. 30. Data on food stamp households and persons are average monthly number participating in year ending Sept. 30. Data on pupils participating in National School Lunch Program are for month in which the highest number of children participated nationwide. For National School Lunch Program, covers public and private elementary and secondary schools and residential child care institutions. Food Stamp costs are for benefits only and exclude administrative expenditures. National School Lunch Program costs include Federal cash reimbursements at rates set by law for each meal served but do not include the value of USDA donated commodities utilized in this program]

REGION, DIVISION, AND STATE	FOOD STAMP PROGRAM								NATIONAL SCHOOL LUNCH PROGRAM					
	Households participating (1,000)		Persons (1,000)			Cost (mil. dol.)			Persons (1,000)			Cost (mil. dol.)		
	1994	1995	1990	1994	1995	1990	1994	1995	1990	1994	1995	1990	1994	1995
Total [1]	11,094	10,883	20,067	27,468	26,615	14,187	22,749	22,768	24,589	25,742	26,235	3,214	4,291	4,464
U.S.	11,083	10,870	20,036	27,433	26,575	14,153	22,704	22,716	24,019	25,227	25,683	3,098	4,165	4,341
Northeast	2,203	2,207	3,589	4,927	4,876	2,462	4,191	4,347	4,033	4,144	4,257	489	673	711
N.E.	443	430	707	1,020	979	426	759	769	991	994	1,018	95	138	145
ME	61	60	94	136	132	63	111	112	108	107	105	11	15	16
NH	26	25	31	62	58	20	46	44	91	92	90	6	10	10
VT	29	27	38	65	59	22	44	46	47	50	50	4	6	7
MA	191	178	347	442	410	207	330	315	454	455	476	44	63	67
RI	40	40	64	93	93	42	76	82	60	60	61	7	11	12
CT	97	100	133	223	226	72	152	169	231	229	235	23	33	34
M.A.	1,760	1,777	2,882	3,907	3,897	2,036	3,432	3,578	3,042	3,151	3,239	393	535	566
NY	1,004	1,027	1,548	2,154	2,183	1,086	1,945	2,065	1,546	1,666	1,704	232	314	332
NJ	227	234	382	545	540	289	486	506	507	495	533	60	86	90
PA	530	515	952	1,208	1,173	661	1,001	1,006	990	990	1,002	102	136	143
Midwest	2,392	2,311	4,806	5,816	5,516	3,566	4,776	4,644	5,806	6,007	6,113	619	793	820
E.N.C.	1,783	1,713	3,616	4,312	4,067	2,765	3,615	3,482	3,687	3,840	3,876	421	536	555
OH	531	506	1,089	1,245	1,155	861	1,076	1,017	919	1,026	1,009	109	131	138
IN	196	183	311	518	470	226	415	382	635	602	605	54	69	70
IL	499	488	1,013	1,189	1,151	835	1,069	1,056	932	965	985	131	170	175
MI	434	418	917	1,031	971	663	834	806	733	758	770	82	108	112
WI	122	119	286	330	320	180	220	220	468	490	506	45	58	60
W.N.C	609	598	1,190	1,503	1,449	801	1,162	1,162	2,119	2,166	2,237	197	257	265
MN	133	131	263	314	308	165	234	240	489	525	535	42	56	58
IA	79	75	170	196	184	109	145	141	392	380	397	31	39	40
MO	240	237	431	593	576	312	482	488	547	543	581	58	76	79
ND	18	17	39	45	41	25	34	32	94	89	90	8	9	9
SD	19	19	50	53	50	35	41	40	102	107	109	12	14	14
NE	45	43	95	111	105	59	79	77	191	211	209	18	23	24
KS	76	75	142	192	184	96	146	144	302	312	316	29	39	40
South	4,379	4,242	8,040	11,185	10,701	5,928	9,351	9,201	9,890	10,351	10,485	1,334	1,768	1,835
S.A.	1,927	1,905	2,993	4,729	4,593	2,223	4,006	4,008	4,454	4,679	4,784	558	775	815
DE	22	21	33	59	57	25	48	47	59	65	68	6	9	9
MD	165	169	255	390	399	203	350	365	347	367	372	40	55	60
DC	41	43	62	91	94	43	86	93	47	47	50	10	13	14
VA	232	235	346	547	546	247	448	450	586	601	623	60	81	87
WV	126	123	262	321	309	192	261	253	198	204	241	29	31	33
NC	259	258	419	630	614	282	490	495	749	767	769	91	117	123
SC	146	140	299	385	364	240	303	297	451	461	463	60	80	82
GA	329	329	536	830	816	382	695	700	908	975	997	106	151	160
FL	607	588	781	1,474	1,395	609	1,324	1,307	1,110	1,192	1,200	158	239	248
E.S.C.	912	863	1,938	2,315	2,187	1,386	1,867	1,791	2,085	2,110	2,121	281	341	349
KY	196	187	458	522	520	334	416	413	498	518	519	61	76	79
TN	307	281	527	735	662	372	600	554	590	608	615	68	88	90
AL	215	209	454	548	525	328	453	441	570	567	568	77	92	93
MS	194	185	499	511	480	352	397	383	428	418	419	76	85	87
W.S.C.	1,540	1,474	3,109	4,141	3,922	2,319	3,479	3,402	3,351	3,561	3,580	495	652	671
AR	108	107	235	283	272	155	212	212	292	318	318	41	51	53
LA	278	267	727	756	711	549	642	629	694	687	689	104	125	126
OK	150	153	267	376	375	186	305	315	362	375	379	46	62	64
TX	1,003	948	1,880	2,726	2,564	1,429	2,320	2,246	2,003	2,182	2,194	304	414	428
West	2,109	2,110	3,601	5,504	5,482	2,197	4,385	4,524	4,289	4,725	4,827	657	930	974
Mountain	542	529	988	1,436	1,373	726	1,157	1,152	1,362	1,507	1,555	170	240	247
MT	28	28	57	71	71	41	56	57	84	91	88	10	12	13
ID	30	30	59	82	80	40	57	59	131	142	142	14	19	19
WY	13	13	28	34	34	21	27	28	57	59	58	5	7	7
CO	107	103	221	268	252	156	224	217	282	304	306	31	42	43
NM	86	87	157	244	239	117	194	196	179	187	192	30	39	40
AZ	187	178	317	512	480	239	418	414	331	381	422	47	73	76
UT	46	44	99	128	119	71	94	90	233	255	251	24	32	33
NV	44	46	50	97	99	41	88	91	67	87	97	8	15	16
Pacific	1,567	1,581	2,613	4,069	4,109	1,471	3,228	3,371	2,927	3,218	3,273	487	691	727
WA	196	204	340	468	476	229	386	417	361	411	434	43	65	69
OR	127	132	216	286	289	168	241	254	234	251	257	26	37	38
CA	1,179	1,176	1,955	3,155	3,175	968	2,395	2,472	2,147	2,350	2,392	396	558	587
AK	15	15	25	46	45	25	53	50	39	46	48	8	13	13
HI	50	55	77	115	125	81	153	177	145	160	142	14	18	20

[1] Includes Puerto Rico (for NSLP), other outlying areas and Dept. of Defense overseas.

Source: U.S. Dept. of Agriculture, Food and Nutrition Service. In "Annual Historical Review of FNS Programs" and unpublished data.

No. 604. Child Support—Award and Recipiency Status of Custodial Parent: 1991

[In thousands except as noted. Custodial parents 15 years and older with own children under 21 years of age present from absent parents as of spring 1992. Covers civilian noninstitutional population. Based on Current Population Survey; see text, section 1, and Appendix III. For definition of mean, see Guide to Tabular Presentation]

AWARD AND RECIPIENCY STATUS	ALL CUSTODIAL PARENTS				CUSTODIAL PARENTS BELOW THE POVERTY LEVEL			
	Total		Mothers	Fathers	Total		Mothers	Fathers
	Number	Percent distribu-tion			Number	Percent distribu-tion		
Total.......................	11,502	100	9,918	1,584	3,720	100	3,513	207
Payments awarded..................	6,190	54	5,542	648	1,438	39	1,368	71
Supposed to receive payments in 1991. .	5,326	46	4,883	443	1,257	34	1,200	57
Not supposed to receive payments	864	8	659	205	181	5	168	14
Payments not awarded	5,312	46	4,376	936	2,282	61	2,145	136
Supposed to receive payments	5,326	100	4,883	443	1,257	100	1,200	57
Actually received payments in 1991.	4,006	75	3,728	278	859	68	845	14
Received full amount.	2,742	51	2,552	189	499	40	497	2
Received partial amount.	1,265	24	1,176	89	360	29	348	12
Did not receive payments	1,320	25	1,156	164	398	32	355	43
MEAN INCOME AND CHILD SUPPORT								
Received child support payments in 1991:								
Mean total money income (dol.).	19,217	(X)	18,144	33,579	5,734	(X)	5,687	(B)
Mean child support received (dol.)	2,961	(X)	3,011	2,292	1,910	(X)	1,922	(B)
Received no payments in 1991:								
Mean total money income (dol.).	15,919	(X)	14,602	25,184	5,399	(X)	5,525	(B)
Without child support agreement or award:								
Mean total money income (dol.).	13,283	(X)	10,226	27,578	4,979	(X)	4,942	5,560

B Base too small to meet statistical standards for reliability.   X Not applicable.
Source: U.S. Bureau of the Census, *Current Population Reports*, P60-187.

No. 605. Child Support—Selected Characteristics of Custodial Parents: 1991

[See headnote, table 604. For definition of mean, see Guide to Tabular Presentation]

RECIPIENCY STATUS OF PARENT	Unit	Total [1]	AGE			RACE		His-panic [2]	CURRENT MARITAL STATUS			
			18 to 29 years	30 to 39 years	40 years and over	White	Black		Divor-ced	Mar-ried [3]	Never mar-ried	Sepa-rated
ALL CUSTODIAL PARENTS												
All parents, total	1,000 . .	11,502	3,197	5,058	3,154	8,319	2,886	1,160	3,599	3,428	2,685	1,705
Payments agreed to or awarded .	1,000 . .	6,190	1,321	2,997	1,862	5,035	1,009	410	2,477	2,208	712	755
Percent of total	Percent.	54	41	59	59	61	35	35	69	64	27	44
Supposed to receive child support in 1991.	1,000 . .	5,326	1,175	2,647	1,499	4,357	834	356	2,190	1,909	600	597
Percent received payment. .	Percent.	75	70	75	79	77	69	65	76	75	74	74
Mean child support	Dollars .	2,961	1,790	3,052	3,625	3,131	2,079	2,165	3,544	2,799	1,537	2,707
Percent of total income . .	Percent.	15	16	16	14	16	15	15	15	15	14	19
Parents with incomes below the poverty level in 1991	1,000 . .	3,720	1,529	1,555	575	2,134	1,478	591	935	410	1,487	874
Payments agreed to or awarded .	1,000 . .	1,438	545	664	224	962	438	152	514	221	362	333
Percent of total	Percent.	39	36	43	39	45	30	26	55	54	24	38
Supposed to receive child support in 1991.	1,000 . .	1,257	486	577	191	858	364	138	472	194	313	274
Percent received payment. .	Percent.	68	69	69	65	66	74	61	67	68	73	67
Mean child support	Dollars .	1,910	1,390	2,042	2,919	1,839	2,106	2,580	2,453	1,492	1,500	1,786
Percent of total income . .	Percent.	33	26	32	62	33	34	51	36	37	26	36
ALL CUSTODIAL MOTHERS												
All mothers, total	1,000 . .	9,918	3,022	4,379	2,429	6,966	2,698	1,043	3,052	2,707	2,565	1,514
Payments agreed to or awarded .	1,000 . .	5,542	1,269	2,691	1,571	4,459	958	368	2,221	1,888	693	702
Percent of total	Percent.	56	42	61	65	64	36	35	73	70	27	46
Supposed to receive child support in 1991.	1,000 . .	4,883	1,132	2,446	1,299	3,976	791	324	2,027	1,679	583	563
Percent received payment. .	Percent.	76	71	76	82	78	70	68	77	76	74	74
Mean child support	Dollars .	3,011	1,816	3,127	3,719	3,193	2,102	2,200	3,623	2,831	1,534	2,753
Percent of total income . .	Percent.	17	17	17	16	17	15	16	16	18	14	20
Mothers with incomes below the poverty level in 1991	1,000 . .	3,513	1,472	1,455	528	1,979	1,433	563	877	338	1,449	836
Payments agreed to or awarded .	1,000 . .	1,368	534	621	207	896	433	140	486	187	359	328
Percent of total	Percent.	39	36	43	39	45	30	25	55	55	25	39
Supposed to receive child support in 1991.	1,000 . .	1,200	474	539	184	804	361	126	448	169	311	268
Percent received payment. .	Percent.	70	70	72	67	68	74	67	69	73	72	68
Mean child support	Dollars .	1,922	1,399	2,058	2,939	1,869	2,083	2,580	2,474	1,477	1,515	1,786
Percent of total income . .	Percent.	34	26	33	62	34	33	51	36	40	26	36

[1] Includes other items, not shown separately.   [2] Hispanic persons may be of any race.   [3] Remarried parents whose previous marriage ended in divorce and persons in first marriage.
Source: U.S. Bureau of the Census, *Current Population Reports*, P60-187.

No. 606. Child Support Enforcement Program—Caseload and Collections: 1980 to 1994

[For years ending Sept. 30. Includes Puerto Rico, Guam, and the Virgin Islands. The Child Support Enforcement program locates absent parents, establishes paternity of children born out-of-wedlock, and establishes and enforces support orders. By law, these services are available to all families that need them. The program is operated at the State and local government level but 68 percent of administrative costs are paid by the Federal government. Child support collected for families not receiving Aid to Families with Dependent Children (AFDC) goes to the family to help it remain self-sufficient. Most of the child support collected on behalf of AFDC families goes to Federal and State governments to offset AFDC payments. Based on data reported by State agencies. Minus sign (-) indicates net outlay]

ITEM	Unit	1980	1985	1989	1990	1991	1992	1993	1994
Total cases	1,000 . . .	**5,432**	**8,401**	**11,876**	**12,796**	**13,423**	**15,159**	**17,115**	**18,608**
AFDC and AFDC arrears only caseload	1,000 . . .	(NA)	(NA)	7,610	7,953	8,034	8,705	9,620	10,415
AFDC cases.	1,000 . . .	4,583	6,242	5,709	5,872	6,166	6,753	7,473	7,984
AFDC arrears only cases [1]	1,000 . . .	(NA)	(NA)	1,901	2,082	1,868	1,952	2,148	2,430
Non-AFDC cases	1,000 . . .	849	2,159	4,266	4,843	5,389	6,454	7,495	8,193
Cases for which a collection was made:									
AFDC cases	1,000 . . .	503	684	658	701	755	831	874	926
AFDC arrears only cases [1]	1,000 . . .	(NA)	(NA)	202	224	278	255	289	308
Non-AFDC cases	1,000 . . .	243	654	1,247	1,363	1,555	1,749	1,956	2,169
Percentage of cases with collections:									
AFDC cases	Percent .	11.0	11.0	11.5	11.9	12.2	12.3	11.7	11.6
AFDC arrears only cases [1]	Percent .	(NA)	(NA)	10.6	10.8	14.9	13.1	13.5	12.7
Non-AFDC cases	Percent .	28.7	30.3	29.2	28.1	28.9	27.1	26.1	26.5
Absent parents located, total	1,000 . . .	643	878	1,628	2,062	2,577	3,706	4,499	4,104
Paternities established, total.	1,000 . . .	144	232	339	393	472	516	555	591
Support orders established, total [2]. . . .	1,000 . . .	374	669	938	1,022	821	893	1,025	1,023
FINANCES									
Collections, total	Mil. dol .	**1,478**	**2,694**	**5,241**	**6,010**	**6,886**	**7,965**	**8,907**	**9,869**
AFDC collections	Mil. dol .	603	1,090	1,593	1,750	1,984	2,259	2,416	2,558
State share	Mil. dol .	274	415	563	620	700	787	847	893
Incentive payments to States	Mil. dol .	72	145	266	264	278	299	339	407
Federal share	Mil. dol .	246	341	458	533	626	738	777	765
Payments to AFDC families [3]	Mil. dol .	10	189	307	334	381	435	453	493
Non-AFDC collections	Mil. dol .	874	1,604	3,648	4,260	4,902	5,706	6,491	7,311
Administrative expenditures, total	Mil. dol .	466	814	1,363	1,606	1,804	1,995	2,241	2,556
State share	Mil. dol .	117	243	426	545	593	652	724	816
Federal share.	Mil. dol .	349	571	938	1,061	1,212	1,343	1,517	1,741
Program savings, total.	Mil. dol .	127	86	-77	-190	-201	-171	-278	-492
State share	Mil. dol .	230	317	403	338	385	434	462	484
Federal share.	Mil. dol .	-103	-231	-480	-528	-586	-605	-740	-976
Total fees and costs recovered for non-AFDC cases	Mil. dol .	5	3	7	22	34	29	31	33
Percentage of AFDC payments recovered	Percent .	5.2	7.3	10.0	10.3	10.7	11.4	12.0	12.5

NA Not available.   [1] Reflects cases that are no longer receiving AFDC but still have outstanding child support due. [2] Through 1990 includes modifications to orders.   [3] Beginning 1985, States were required to pass along to the family the first $50 of any current child support collected each month. Beginning 1993 includes medical support payments.

Source: U.S. Department of Health and Human Services, Office of Child Support Enforcement, *Annual Report to Congress.*

No. 607. Regular Child Care Arrangements for Children Under 6 Years Old, by Type of Arrangement: 1995

[In percent, except as indicated. Estimates are based on children under 6 years old who have yet to enter kindergarten. Based on 14,064 interviews from a sample survey of the civilian, noninstitutional population in households with telephones; see source for details]

CHARACTERISTIC	CHILDREN		TYPE OF NONPARENTAL ARRANGEMENT				No nonpa-rental arrange-ment
	Number (1,000)	Percent distri-bution	Total [1]	In relative care	In nonrela-tive care	In center-based program [2]	
Total	**21,421**	**100**	**60**	**21**	**18**	**31**	**40**
Race-ethnicity:							
White, non-Hispanic.	13,996	65	62	18	21	33	38
Black, non-Hispanic.	3,344	16	66	31	12	33	34
Hispanic	2,838	13	46	23	12	17	54
Other	1,243	6	58	25	13	28	42
Mother's employment status: [3]							
35 or more hours per week.	7,101	34	88	33	32	39	12
Less than 35 hours per week	4,034	19	75	30	26	35	25
Looking for work	1,635	8	42	16	4	25	58
Not in labor force	8,354	40	32	7	6	22	68
Household income:							
Less than $10,001.	4,502	21	50	22	10	25	50
$10,001 to $20,000	2,909	14	54	27	12	24	46
$20,001 to $30,000	3,385	16	53	22	14	25	47
$30,001 to $40,000	3,047	14	60	23	20	27	40
$40,001 to $50,000	2,304	11	63	19	22	32	37
$50,001 to $75,000	3,063	14	74	20	26	40	26
$75,001 or more	2,211	10	77	14	30	49	23

[1] Columns do not add to total because some children participated in more than one type of nonparental arrangement. [2] Center-based programs include day care centers, head start programs, preschool, prekindergartens, and other early childhood programs.   [3] Children without mothers are not included.

Source: U.S. National Center for Education Statistics, *Statistics in Brief*, October 1995 (NCES 95-824).

No. 608. Percent of Adult Population Doing Volunteer Work: 1993

[Covers persons 18 years and over. Volunteers are persons who worked in some way to help others for no monetary pay during the previous year. Based on a sample survey conducted during the spring of the following year and subject to sampling variability; see source]

AGE, SEX, RACE, AND HISPANIC ORIGIN	Percent of population volunteering	Average hours volunteered per week	EDUCATIONAL ATTAINMENT AND HOUSEHOLD INCOME	Percent of population volunteering	Average hours volunteered per week	TYPE OF ACTIVITY	Percent of volunteers involved in activity
Total.	47.7	4.2	Elementary school	31.8	(B)	Arts, culture, humanities. .	4.4
			Some high school.	29.9	(B)	Education	15.7
18-24 years old	45.3	4.0	High school graduate	40.4	3.6	Environment	6.2
25-34 years old	46.1	3.1	Technical, trade, or			Health.	10.8
35-44 years old	54.5	4.8	business school	49.2	5.0	Human services	9.8
45-54 years old	53.8	5.2	Some college	56.9	4.3		
55-64 years old	46.6	4.1	College graduate	67.2	5.0	Informal	17.2
65-74 years old	42.9	4.8				International, foreign	1.3
75 years old and over.	36.4	(B)	Under $10,000.	34.0	(B)	Political organizations . . .	3.7
			$10,000-$19,999	37.0	3.7	Private, community	
Male	43.9	4.3	$20,000-$29,999	52.5	4.2	foundations	2.2
Female	51.2	4.2	$30,000-$39,999	56.3	4.9		
			$40,000-$49,999	55.1	3.6	Public and societal benefit	5.4
White.	51.1	4.2	$50,000-$59,999	56.9	4.1	Recreation - adults	5.4
Black.	29.1	3.7	$60,000-$74,999	66.6	6.1	Religion	24.1
			$75,000-$99,999	58.1	(B)	Work-related organizations	6.9
Hispanic [1]	32.4	(B)	$100,000 or more.	67.5	(B)	Youth development	11.7

B Base figure too small to meet statistical standards for reliability.   [1] Hispanic persons may be of any race.

No. 609. Charity Contributions—Average Dollar Amount and Percent of Household Income, 1987 to 1993, and by Age of Respondent and Household Income, 1993

[Estimates cover households' contribution activity for the year and are based on respondents' replies as to contribution and volunteer activity of household. See headnote, table 608]

YEAR AND AGE	ALL CONTRIBUTING HOUSEHOLDS Average amount (dol.)	ALL CONTRIBUTING HOUSEHOLDS Percent of household income	CONTRIBUTORS AND VOLUNTEERS Average amount (dol.)	CONTRIBUTORS AND VOLUNTEERS Percent of household income	HOUSEHOLD INCOME	ALL CONTRIBUTING HOUSEHOLDS Average amount (dol.)	ALL CONTRIBUTING HOUSEHOLDS Percent of household income	CONTRIBUTORS AND VOLUNTEERS Average amount (dol.)	CONTRIBUTORS AND VOLUNTEERS Percent of household income
1987	790	1.9	1,021	2.4	**1993—**				
1991	899	2.2	1,155	2.6	Under $10,000 . . .	207	2.7	(B)	(B)
1993, total.	880	2.1	1,193	2.6	$10,000-$19,999 . .	332	2.3	460	3.1
18-24 years	514	1.2	(B)	(B)	$20,000-$29,999 . .	668	2.7	862	3.4
25-34 years	520	1.4	666	1.6	$30,000-$39,999 . .	715	2.0	824	2.3
35-44 years	978	1.8	1,376	2.5	$40,000-$49,999 . .	572	1.3	713	1.6
45-54 years	1,241	2.5	1,766	3.3	$50,000-$59,999 . .	632	1.1	758	1.4
55-64 years	1,037	2.4	1,222	2.6	$60,000-$74,999 . .	1,572	2.3	2,006	3.0
65-74 years	1,135	3.9	1,832	4.8	$75,000-$99,999 . .	1,720	2.0	(B)	(B)
75 years and over. .	666	3.2	(B)	(B)	$100,000 and over.	3,213	3.2	(B)	(B)

B Base too small to meet statistical standards for reliability.

No. 610. Charity Contributions—Percent of Households Contributing, by Dollar Amount, 1987 to 1993, and Type of Charity, 1993

[In percent, except as noted. See headnote, tables 608 and 609]

ANNUAL AMOUNT OF HOUSEHOLD CONTRIBUTIONS	ALL HOUSEHOLDS 1987	ALL HOUSEHOLDS 1991	ALL HOUSEHOLDS 1993	GIVERS 1987	GIVERS 1991	GIVERS 1993	TYPE OF CHARITY	1993 Percentage of households	1993 Average contribution [1] (dol.)
None	28.9	27.8	26.6	(X)	(X)	(X)	Arts, culture, humanities .	8.1	139
Givers	71.0	72.2	73.4	100.0	100.0	100.0	Education	17.5	424
$1 to $100. . . .	20.8	14.9	20.9	32.7	24.9	32.3	Environment.	11.6	89
$101 to $200 . .	7.4	8.1	9.8	11.6	13.5	15.2	Health.	25.7	139
$201 to $300 . .	6.6	7.3	5.6	10.5	12.2	8.6	Human services	26.7	208
$301 to $400 . .	3.5	3.3	3.7	5.6	5.6	5.8	International	2.8	(B)
$401 to $500 . .	3.2	3.2	4.0	5.0	5.4	6.2	Private, community		
$501 to $600 . .	2.3	2.6	3.0	3.7	4.4	4.6	foundations	5.3	144
$601 to $700 . .	2.0	2.5	2.0	3.2	4.2	3.1	Public, societal benefit . .	11.2	160
$701 to $999 . .	3.7	3.4	2.9	5.8	5.7	4.6	Recreation - adults	4.6	193
$1,000 or more.	13.9	14.5	12.8	21.9	24.2	19.7	Religion.	49.2	817
Not reported . .	7.6	12.4	8.6	(X)	(X)	(X)	Youth development	17.9	106

B Base too small to meet statistical standards for reliability.   X Not applicable.   [1] Average contribution per contributing household.

Source of tables 608-610: Hodgkinson, Virginia, Murray Weitzman, and the Gallup Organization, Inc., *Giving and Volunteering in the United States: 1994 Edition.* (Copyright and published by INDEPENDENT SECTOR, Washington, DC, fall 1994.)

No. 611. Private Philanthropy Funds, by Source and Allocation: 1980 to 1994

[In billions of dollars. Estimates for sources of funds based on U.S. Internal Revenue Service reports of individual charitable deductions, household surveys of giving by Independent Sector, and, for years prior to 1986, an econometric model. For corporate giving, data are those prepared by the Council for Aid to Education. Data about foundation donations are based upon surveys of foundations and data provided by the Foundation Center. Estimates of the allocation of funds were derived from surveys of nonprofits conducted by source and other groups. See *Historical Statistics, Colonial Times to 1970*, series H 398-411, for similar but not comparable data]

SOURCE AND ALLOCATION	1980	1983	1984	1985	1986	1987	1988	1989	1990	1991	1992	1993	1994
Total funds	48.6	63.2	68.8	73.2	83.9	90.3	98.4	107.0	111.9	117.6	120.7	125.3	129.9
Individuals..............	40.7	52.1	56.5	58.7	67.6	72.3	80.1	87.8	91.2	96.1	98.0	101.2	105.1
Foundations..............	2.8	3.6	4.0	4.9	5.4	5.9	6.2	6.6	7.2	7.7	8.6	9.5	9.9
Corporations.............	2.2	3.7	4.3	4.8	5.1	5.5	5.6	5.8	5.9	6.0	5.9	6.1	6.1
Charitable bequests	2.9	3.9	4.0	4.8	5.7	6.6	6.6	7.0	7.6	7.8	8.2	8.5	8.8
Allocation:													
Religion................	22.2	31.8	35.6	38.2	41.7	43.5	45.2	47.8	49.8	53.9	54.9	56.3	58.9
Health.................	5.3	6.7	6.8	7.7	8.4	9.2	9.6	9.9	9.9	9.7	10.2	10.8	11.5
Education	5.0	6.7	7.3	8.2	9.4	9.8	10.2	11.0	12.4	13.5	14.3	15.4	16.7
Human service	4.9	7.2	7.9	8.5	9.1	9.8	10.5	11.4	11.8	11.1	11.6	12.5	11.7
Arts, culture and humanities ..	3.2	4.2	4.5	5.1	5.8	6.3	6.8	7.5	7.9	8.8	9.3	9.6	9.7
Public/societal benefit.......	1.5	1.9	1.9	2.2	2.5	2.9	3.2	3.8	4.9	4.9	5.1	5.4	6.1
Environment/wildlife	(1)	(1)	(1)	(1)	(1)	2.1	2.4	2.0	2.6	2.9	3.1	3.2	3.5
International	(1)	(1)	(1)	(1)	(1)	0.9	1.0	1.2	1.5	1.8	1.7	1.9	2.2
Unclassified	6.5	4.8	4.8	3.3	7.0	5.7	9.6	12.5	11.0	11.0	10.5	10.2	9.6

[1] Included in "Unclassified."

Source: AAFRC Trust for Philanthropy, New York, NY, *Giving USA*, annual, (copyright).

No. 612. Foundations—Number and Finances, by Asset Size

[Figures are for latest year reported by foundations, usually **1992** or **1993**. Covers nongovernmental nonprofit organizations with funds and programs managed by their own trustees or directors, whose goals were to maintain or aid social, educational, religious, or other activities deemed to serve the common good. Excludes organizations that make general appeals to the public for funds, act as trade associations for industrial or other special groups, or do not currently award grants]

ASSET SIZE	Number	Assets (mil. dol.)	Gifts received (mil. dol.)	Expenditures (mil. dol.)	Grants (mil. dol.)	PERCENT DISTRIBUTION				
						Number	Assets	Gifts received	Expenditures	Grants
Total	37,571	189,213	7,756	13,682	11,113	100.0	100.0	100.0	100.0	100.0
Under $50,000.	8,301	149	239	296	267	22.1	0.1	3.1	2.2	2.3
$50,000-$99,999	3,528	258	112	148	133	9.4	0.1	1.4	1.1	1.2
$100,000-$249,999.	6,227	1,022	239	302	259	16.6	0.5	3.1	2.2	2.3
$250,000-$499,999.	4,775	1,715	210	264	227	12.7	0.9	2.7	1.9	2.0
$500,000-$999,999.	4,407	3,146	300	396	327	11.7	1.7	3.9	2.9	2.9
$1,000,000-$4,999,999	6,781	15,075	1,323	1,549	1,280	18.0	8.0	17.1	11.3	11.5
$5,000,000-$9,999,999 ...	1,486	10,382	794	973	817	4.0	5.5	10.2	7.1	7.3
$10,000,000-$49,999,999 ...	1,575	32,706	2,084	2,675	2,140	4.2	17.3	26.9	19.6	19.3
$50,000,000-$99,999,999 ...	249	17,188	802	1,061	871	0.7	9.1	10.3	7.8	7.8
$100,000,000-$249,999,999 ..	143	21,757	730	1,497	1,048	0.4	11.5	9.4	10.9	9.4
$250,000,000 or more......	99	85,815	923	4,521	3,744	0.3	45.4	11.9	33.0	33.7

Source: The Foundation Center, New York, NY, *Guide to U.S. Foundations, Their Trustees, Officers, and Donors*, vol. 1, 1995.

No. 613. Foundations—Grants Reported, by Subject Field and Recipient Organization: 1994

[Covers grants of $10,000 or more in size. Based on reports of 1,029 foundations. Grant sample totaling $6.2 billion represented over half of all grant dollars awarded by private, corporate, and community foundations. For definition of foundations, see headnote, table 612]

SUBJECT FIELD	NUMBER OF GRANTS		DOLLAR VALUE		RECIPIENT ORGANIZATION [1]	NUMBER OF GRANTS		DOLLAR VALUE	
	Number	Percent distribution	Amount (mil. dol.)	Percent distribution		Number	Percent distribution	Amount (mil. dol.)	Percent distribution
Total	72,773	100.0	6,169	100.0	Community improvement				
Arts and culture	10,652	14.6	789	12.8	organizations	3,297	4.5	225	3.6
Education	15,883	21.8	1,804	29.2	Educational institutions.....	20,865	28.7	2,453	39.8
Environment & animals. ...	3,949	5.4	317	5.1	Colleges & universities ...	10,956	15.1	1,551	25.1
Health................	9,424	12.9	937	15.2	Educational support				
Human services	16,569	22.8	951	15.4	agencies............	4,314	5.9	350	5.7
International affairs,					Schools	3,718	5.1	360	5.8
development & peace....	2,128	2.9	211	3.4	Federated funds	2,400	3.3	218	3.5
Public/societal benefit	8,479	11.7	649	10.5	Hospitals/medical care				
Science and technology ...	2,497	3.4	250	4.0	facilities	3,431	4.7	330	5.3
Social sciences.........	1,401	1.9	151	2.5	Human service agencies....	13,233	18.2	704	11.4
Religion..............	1,705	2.3	104	1.7	Museums/historical societies .	2,904	4.0	267	4.3
Other	86	0.1	6	0.1	Performing arts groups.....	3,547	4.9	231	3.7

[1] Grants may be awarded to multiple types of recipient organizations and would thereby be double-counted.

Source: The Foundation Center, New York, NY, *The Foundation Grants Index, 1996*, 24th Edition, 1995.

Labor Force, Employment, and Earnings

This section presents statistics on the labor force; its distribution by occupation and industry affiliation; and the supply of, demand for, and conditions of labor. The chief source of these data is the Current Population Survey conducted by the U.S. Bureau of the Census. Comprehensive historical data are published by the Bureau of Labor Statistics (BLS) in *Labor Force Statistics Derived From the Current Population Survey, 1948-87, BLS Bulletin 2307.* These data are supplemented on a current basis by the BLS monthly publications *Employment and Earnings* and the *Monthly Labor Review.* Detailed data on the labor force are also available from the Census Bureau's decennial census of population.

Types of data—Most statistics in this section are obtained by two methods: household interviews or questionnaires, and reports of establishment payroll records. Each method provides data which the other cannot suitably supply. Population characteristics, for example, are readily obtainable only from the household survey, while detailed industrial classifications can be readily derived only from establishment records.

Household data are obtained from a monthly sample survey of the population. The Current Population Survey (CPS) is used to gather data for the calendar week including the 12th of the month and provides current comprehensive data on the labor force (see text, section 1). The CPS provides information on the work status of the population without duplication since each person is classified as employed, unemployed, or not in the labor force. Employed persons holding more than one job are counted only once, according to the job at which they worked the most hours during the survey week.

Monthly data from the CPS are published by the Bureau of Labor Statistics in *Employment and Earnings* and the related reports mentioned above. Data presented include national totals of the number of persons in the civilian labor force by sex, race, Hispanic origin, and age; the number employed; hours of work; industry and

---

In Brief

Labor force participation rate of married women with children under 6 years old:

1960	*18.6%*
1970	*30.3%*
1980	*45.1%*
1995	*63.5%*

Fastest growing occupations, 1994-2005:

Personal and home care aides	*+119%*
Home health aides	*+102%*
Systems analysts	*92%*
Computer engineers	*+91%*

---

occupational groups; and the number unemployed, reasons for, and duration of unemployment. Monthly data from the CPS also are presented for census regions and divisions. Annual data shown in this section are averages of monthly figures for each calendar year, unless otherwise specified.

The CPS also produces annual estimates of employment and unemployment for each State, 50 large metropolitan statistical areas, and selected cities. These estimates are published by BLS in its annual *Geographic Profile of Employment and Unemployment.* More detailed geographic data (e.g., for counties and cities) are provided by the decennial population censuses.

Data based on establishment records are compiled by BLS and cooperating State agencies as part of an ongoing Current Employment Statistics Program. Data, gathered from a sample of employers who voluntarily complete mail questionnaires monthly, are supplemented by data from other government agencies and adjusted at intervals to data from government social insurance program reports. The estimates exclude proprietors of unincorporated firms, self-employed persons, private household workers, unpaid family workers, agricultural workers, and the Armed Forces. In March 1995, reporting establishments employed 9 million manufacturing workers (50 percent of the total manufacturing employment at the time), 20 million workers in nonmanufacturing industries (26 percent of the total in nonmanufacturing), and 15 million Federal, State, and local government employees (78 percent of total government).

The establishment survey counts workers each time they appear on a payroll during the reference week (as with the CPS, the week including the 12th of the month). Thus, unlike the CPS, a person with two jobs is counted twice. The establishment survey is designed to provide detailed industry information for the Nation, States, and metropolitan areas on nonfarm wage and salary employment, average weekly hours, and average hourly and weekly earnings. Establishment survey data are published in *Employment and Earnings* and the *Monthly Labor Review*, cited above. Historical national data are published in *BLS Bulletin 2445, Employment, Hours, and Earnings, United States, 1909-94;* and *Employment, Hours, and Earnings, United States, 1988-96, Bulletin 2481.*

Labor force—According to the CPS definitions, the civilian labor force comprises all civilians in the noninstitutional population 16 years and over classified as "employed" or "unemployed" according to the following criteria: Employed civilians comprise (a) all civilians, who, during the reference week, did any work for pay or profit (minimum of an hour's work) or worked 15 hours or more as unpaid workers in a family enterprise, and (b) all civilians who were not working but who had jobs or businesses from which they were temporarily absent for noneconomic reasons (illness, weather conditions, vacation, labor-management dispute, etc.) whether they were paid for the time off or were seeking other jobs. Unemployed persons comprise all civilians who had no employment during the reference week, who made specific efforts to find a job within the previous 4 weeks (such as applying directly to an employer, or to a public employment service, or checking with friends), and who were available for work during that week, except for temporary illness. Persons on layoff from a job and expecting recall are also classified as unemployed. All other civilian persons,

16 years old and over, are "not in the labor force."

Beginning in 1982, changes in the estimation procedures and the introduction of 1980 census data caused substantial increases in the population and estimates of persons in all labor force categories. Rates on labor force characteristics, however, were essentially unchanged. In order to avoid major breaks in series, some 30,000 labor force series were adjusted back to 1970. The effect of the 1982 revisions on various data series and an explanation of the adjustment procedure used are described in "Revisions in the Current Population Survey in January 1982," in the February 1982 issue of *Employment and Earnings.* The revisions did not, however, smooth out the breaks in series occurring between 1972 and 1979, and data users should make allowances for them in making certain data comparisons.

Beginning in January 1985, and again in January 1986, the CPS estimation procedures were revised due to the implementation of a new sample design (for the 1985 revision) and to reflect an explicit estimate of the number of undocumented immigrants (for the 1986 revision). The greatest impact of these revisions was on estimates of persons of Hispanic origin. Where possible, these estimates were revised back to January 1980. A description of the changes and an indication of their effect on the national estimates of labor force characteristics appear in the February 1985 and February 1986 issues of *Employment and Earnings* respectively.

Beginning in January 1994, several changes were introduced into the CPS that effect all data comparisons with prior years. These changes include the results of a major redesign of the survey questionnaire and collection methodology, revisions to some of the labor force concepts and definitions, and the introduction of 1990 census population controls, adjusted for the estimated undercount. An explanation of the changes and their effects on the labor force data appears in "Revisions in the Current Population Survey Effective January 1994" in the February 1994 issue of *Employment and Earnings.*

Beginning in 1996, 1990 census population controls, adjusted for the estimated undercount were extended back to

January 1990. A discussion of the changes and their effects on the labor force data appears in "Revisions in Household Survey Data Effective February 1996" in the March 1996 issue of *Employment and Earnings.*

Hours and earnings—Average hourly earnings, based on establishment data, are gross earnings (i.e., earnings before payroll deductions) and include overtime premiums; they exclude irregular bonuses and value of payments in kind. Hours are those for which pay was received. Wages and salaries from the CPS consist of total monies received for work performed by an employee during the income year. It includes wages, salaries, commissions, tips, piece-rate payments, and cash bonuses earned before deductions were made for taxes, bonds, union dues, etc. Persons who worked 35 hours or more are classified as working full time.

Industrial and occupational groups— Establishments responding to the establishment survey are classified into industries on the basis of their principal product or activity (determined by annual sales volume) in accordance with the *Standard Industrial Classification (SIC) Manual,* Office of Management and Budget. The SIC is a classification structure for the entire national economy. The structure provides data on a division and industry code basis, according to the level of industrial detail. For example, manufacturing is a major industrial division; food and kindred products (code 20) is one of its major groups. One of the ways this group is further divided is into meat products (code 201) and meat packing plants (code 2011). Periodically, the SIC is revised to reflect changes in the industrial composition of the economy. The *1987 SIC Manual* has been issued; the previous was the *1972 SIC Manual.* Tables shown in this *Abstract* indicate which *SIC Manual* the data shown are based on.

Industry data derived from the CPS for 1983-91 utilize the 1980 census industrial classification developed from the 1972 SIC. CPS data from 1971 to 1982 were based on the 1970 census classification system which was developed from the 1967 SIC. Most of the industry categories were not affected by the change in classification.

The occupational classification system used in the 1980 census and in the CPS for 1983-91 evolved from the 1980 Standard Occupational Classification (SOC) system, first introduced in 1977. Occupational categories used in the 1980 census classification system are so radically different from the 1970 census system used in the CPS through 1982, that their implementation represented a break in historical data series. In cases where data have not yet been converted to the 1980 classifications and still reflect the 1970 classifications (e.g., table 668), comparisons between the two systems should not be made. To help users bridge the data gap, a limited set of estimates was developed for the 1972-82 period based on the new classifications. The estimates were developed by means of applying conversion factors created by double coding a 20-percent sample of CPS occupational records for 6 months during 1981-82. For further details, contact BLS.

Beginning in January 1992, the occupational and industrial classification system used in the 1990 census were introduced into the CPS. (These systems were largely based on the 1980 Standard Occupational Classification and the 1987 Standard Industrial Classification.) There were a few breaks in comparability between the 1980 and 1990 census-based systems, particularly within the "technical, sales, and administrative support" categories. The most notable changes in industry classification were the shift of several industries from "business services" to "professional services" and the splitting of some industries into smaller, more detailed categories. A number of industry titles were changed as well, with no change in content.

Productivity—BLS publishes data on productivity as measured by output per hour (labor productivity), output per combined unit of labor and capital input (multifactor productivity), and, for manufacturing industries, output per combined unit of capital, labor, energy, materials, and purchased service inputs. Labor productivity and related indexes are published for the business sector as a whole and its major subsectors: nonfarm business, manufacturing, nonfinancial corporations, 178 specific industries, and various functional areas of the Federal Government. Multifactor productivity and related measures are published for the private business sector and its major subsectors. Productivity indexes which take into account capital, labor, energy, materials, and service inputs are published for the 20 major 2-digit industry groups which comprise the manufacturing sector and for the following industries: cotton and synthetic broadwoven fabrics, household furniture, tire and inner tubes, footwear, steel, metal stampings, farm and garden machinery, refrigeration and heating equipment, motor vehicles, and railroad transportation industries. The major sector data are published in the BLS quarterly news release, *Productivity and Costs* and in the annual *Multifactor Productivity Measures* release. The specific industry productivity measures are published annually in the BLS Bulletin, *Productivity Measures for Selected Industries and Government Services,* and the *Handbook of Labor Statistics.* Detailed information on methods, limitations, and data sources appears in the *BLS Handbook of Methods,* BLS Bulletin 2414 (1992), chapters 10 and 11.

Unions—As defined here, unions include traditional labor unions and employee associations similar to labor unions. Data on union membership status provided by BLS are for employed wage and salary workers and relate to their principal job. Earnings by union membership status are usual weekly earnings of full-time wage and salary workers. The information is collected through the Current Population Survey. For a full description of the method of collection and comparability with earlier data, see "New Data on Union Members and Their Earnings" in the January 1985 issue of *Employment and Earnings,* and "Changing Employment Patterns of Organized Workers" in the February 1985 issue of the *Monthly Labor Review.* Collective bargaining settlements data are available for bargaining situations involving 1,000 or more workers in private industry and State and local government.

Work stoppages—Work stoppages include all strikes and lockouts known to BLS which last for at least 1 full day or shift and involve 1,000 or more workers. All stoppages, whether or not authorized by a union, legal or illegal, are counted. Excluded are work slowdowns and instances where employees report to work late, or leave early, to attend mass meetings or mass rallies.

Seasonal adjustment—Many economic statistics reflect a regularly recurring seasonal movement which can be estimated on the basis of past experience. By eliminating that part of the change which can be ascribed to usual seasonal variation (e.g., climate or school openings and closings), it is possible to observe the cyclical and other nonseasonal movements in the series. However, in evaluating deviations from the seasonal pattern—that is, changes in a seasonally adjusted series—it is important to note that seasonal adjustment is merely an approximation based on past experience. Seasonally adjusted estimates have a broader margin of possible error than the original data on which they are based, since they are subject not only to sampling and other errors, but also are affected by the uncertainties of the adjustment process itself.

Statistical reliability—For discussion of statistical collection, estimation, sampling procedures, and measures of statistical reliability applicable to Census Bureau and BLS data, see Appendix III.

Historical statistics—Tabular headnotes provide cross-references, where applicable, to *Historical Statistics of the United States, Colonial Times to 1970.* See Appendix IV.

No. 614. Employment Status of the Civilian Population: 1950 to 1995

[In thousands, except as indicated. Annual averages of monthly figures. For the civilian noninstitutional population 16 years old and over. Based on Current Population Survey; see text, section 1, and Appendix III. See also *Historical Statistics, Colonial Times to 1970*, series D 11-19 and D 85-86]

YEAR	Civilian noninsti-tutional population	CIVILIAN LABOR FORCE						NOT IN LABOR FORCE	
		Total	Percent of population	Employed	Employ-ment/population ratio [1]	Unemployed			
						Number	Percent of labor force	Number	Percent of population
1950	104,995	62,208	59.2	58,918	56.1	3,288	5.3	42,787	40.8
1960	117,245	69,628	59.4	65,778	56.1	3,852	5.5	47,617	40.6
1970	137,085	82,771	60.4	78,678	57.4	4,093	4.9	54,315	39.6
1980	167,745	106,940	63.8	99,303	59.2	7,637	7.1	60,806	36.2
1981	170,130	108,670	63.9	100,397	59.0	8,273	7.6	61,460	36.1
1982	172,271	110,204	64.0	99,526	57.8	10,678	9.7	62,067	36.0
1983	174,215	111,550	64.0	100,834	57.9	10,717	9.6	62,665	36.0
1984	176,383	113,544	64.4	105,005	59.5	8,539	7.5	62,839	35.6
1985	178,206	115,461	64.8	107,150	60.1	8,312	7.2	62,744	35.2
1986	180,587	117,834	65.3	109,597	60.7	8,237	7.0	62,752	34.7
1987	182,753	119,865	65.6	112,440	61.5	7,425	6.2	62,888	34.4
1988	184,613	121,669	65.9	114,968	62.3	6,701	5.5	62,944	34.1
1989 [2]	186,393	123,869	66.5	117,342	63.0	6,528	5.3	62,523	33.5
1990 [2]	189,164	125,840	66.5	118,793	62.8	7,047	5.6	63,324	33.5
1991	190,925	126,346	66.2	117,718	61.7	8,628	6.8	64,578	33.8
1992	192,805	128,105	66.4	118,492	61.5	9,613	7.5	64,700	33.6
1993 [2]	194,838	129,200	66.3	120,259	61.7	8,940	6.9	65,638	33.7
1994 [2]	196,814	131,056	66.6	123,060	62.5	7,996	6.1	65,758	33.4
1995	198,584	132,304	66.6	124,900	62.9	7,404	5.6	66,280	33.4

[1] Civilian employed as a percent of the civilian noninstitutional population. [2] Data beginning in 1990 and again in 1994, not strictly comparable with data for earlier years, See text, section 13, and February 1994 and March 1996 issues of *Employment and Earnings.*

Source: U.S. Bureau of Labor Statistics, Bulletin 2307; and *Employment and Earnings*, monthly.

No. 615. Civilian Labor Force and Participation Rates, With Projections: 1970 to 2005

[For civilian noninstitutional population 16 years old and over. Annual averages of monthly figures. Rates are based on annual average civilian noninstitutional population of each specified group and represent proportion of each specified group in the civilian labor force. Based on Current Population Survey; see text, section 1, and Appendix III. See also *Historical Statistics, Colonial Times to 1970*, series D 42-48]

RACE, SEX, AND AGE	CIVILIAN LABOR FORCE (millions)						PARTICIPATION RATE (percent)					
	1980	1990 [1]	1994 [1]	1995	2000, proj.	2005, proj.	1980	1990 [1]	1994 [1]	1995	2000, proj.	2005, proj.
Total [2]	106.9	125.8	131.1	132.3	140.0	147.1	63.8	66.5	66.6	66.6	67.1	67.1
White	93.6	107.4	111.1	112.0	117.7	122.9	64.1	66.9	67.1	67.1	67.8	68.1
Male	54.5	59.6	60.7	61.1	63.1	64.9	78.2	77.1	75.9	75.7	74.9	73.9
Female	39.1	47.8	50.4	50.8	54.6	58.0	51.2	57.4	58.9	59.0	61.6	62.6
Black	10.9	13.7	14.5	14.8	15.7	16.6	61.0	64.0	63.4	63.7	62.7	61.9
Male	5.6	6.8	7.1	7.2	7.5	7.9	70.3	71.0	69.1	69.0	67.4	65.8
Female	5.3	6.9	7.4	7.6	8.1	8.7	53.1	58.3	58.7	59.5	59.0	58.8
Hispanic [3]	6.1	10.7	12.0	12.3	14.3	16.3	64.0	67.4	66.1	65.8	65.4	64.7
Male	3.8	6.5	7.2	7.4	8.4	9.5	81.4	81.4	79.2	79.1	77.6	76.1
Female	2.3	4.2	4.8	4.9	5.8	6.8	47.4	53.1	52.9	52.6	53.3	53.6
Male	61.5	69.0	70.8	71.4	74.2	76.8	77.4	76.4	75.1	75.0	74.0	72.9
16 to 19 years	5.0	4.1	3.9	4.0	4.3	4.4	60.5	55.7	54.1	54.8	53.1	52.0
20 to 24 years	8.6	7.9	7.5	7.3	7.5	8.2	85.9	84.4	83.1	83.1	82.1	81.9
25 to 34 years	17.0	19.9	18.9	18.7	16.8	16.3	95.2	94.1	92.6	93.0	91.9	91.5
35 to 44 years	11.8	17.5	19.0	19.2	20.1	18.8	95.5	94.3	92.8	92.3	92.0	91.4
45 to 54 years	9.9	11.1	13.0	13.4	15.8	17.6	91.2	90.7	89.1	88.8	88.4	87.7
55 to 64 years	7.2	6.6	6.4	6.5	7.4	9.2	72.1	67.8	65.5	66.0	66.0	65.6
65 years and over. . . .	1.9	2.0	2.2	2.2	2.2	2.4	19.0	16.3	16.8	16.8	16.5	16.5
Female	45.5	56.8	60.2	60.9	65.8	70.3	51.5	57.5	58.8	58.9	60.6	61.7
16 to 19 years	4.4	3.7	3.6	3.7	4.0	4.2	52.9	51.6	51.3	52.2	51.2	50.7
20 to 24 years	7.3	6.8	6.6	6.3	6.5	7.1	68.9	71.3	71.0	70.3	70.5	70.7
25 to 34 years	12.3	16.1	15.5	15.5	14.3	14.2	65.5	73.5	74.0	74.9	75.3	76.4
35 to 44 years	8.6	14.7	16.3	16.6	17.8	17.1	65.5	76.4	77.1	77.2	78.7	80.0
45 to 54 years	7.0	9.1	11.4	11.8	14.8	17.1	59.9	71.2	74.6	74.4	78.2	80.7
55 to 64 years	4.7	4.9	5.3	5.4	6.6	8.6	41.3	45.2	48.9	49.2	53.4	56.6
65 years and over. . . .	1.2	1.5	1.7	1.6	1.8	2.0	8.1	8.6	9.2	8.8	9.5	10.2

[1] See footnote 2, table 614. [2] Includes other races, not shown separately. [3] Persons of Hispanic origin may be of any race.

Source: U.S. Bureau of Labor Statistics, Bulletin 2307; *Employment and Earnings*, monthly, January issues; *Monthly Labor Review*, November 1995; and unpublished data.

No. 616. Employment Status of the Civilian Population: 1960 to 1995

[In thousands, except as indicated. Annual averages of monthly figures. For the civilian noninstitutional population 16 years old and over. Based on Current Population Survey; see text, section 1, and Appendix III. See also *Historical Statistics, Colonial Times to 1970*, series D 11-19 and D 85-86]

YEAR, SEX, RACE, AND HISPANIC ORIGIN	Civilian noninsti-tutional popula-tion	CIVILIAN LABOR FORCE						NOT IN LABOR FORCE	
		Total	Percent of popula-tion	Employed	Employ-ment/ popula-tion ratio [1]	Unemployed			
						Number	Percent of labor force	Number	Percent of population
Total: [2]									
1960.	117,245	69,628	59.4	65,778	56.1	3,852	5.5	47,617	40.6
1970.	137,085	82,771	60.4	78,678	57.4	4,093	4.9	54,315	39.6
1980.	167,745	106,940	63.8	99,303	59.2	7,637	7.1	60,806	36.2
1985.	178,206	115,461	64.8	107,150	60.1	8,312	7.2	62,744	35.2
1990 [3].	189,164	125,840	66.5	118,793	62.8	7,047	5.6	63,324	33.5
1992.	192,805	128,105	66.4	118,492	61.5	9,613	7.5	64,700	33.6
1993.	194,838	129,200	66.3	120,259	61.7	8,940	6.9	65,638	33.7
1994 [3].	196,814	131,056	66.6	123,060	62.5	7,996	6.1	65,758	33.4
1995.	198,584	132,304	66.6	124,900	62.9	7,404	5.6	66,280	33.4
Male:									
1960.	55,662	46,388	83.3	43,904	78.9	2,486	5.4	9,274	16.7
1970.	64,304	51,228	79.7	48,990	76.2	2,238	4.4	13,076	20.3
1980.	79,398	61,453	77.4	57,186	72.0	4,267	6.9	17,945	22.6
1985.	84,469	64,411	76.3	59,891	70.9	4,521	7.0	20,058	23.7
1990 [3].	90,377	69,011	76.4	65,104	72.0	3,906	5.7	21,367	23.6
1992.	92,270	69,964	75.8	64,440	69.8	5,523	7.9	22,306	24.2
1993.	93,332	70,404	75.4	65,349	70.0	5,055	7.2	22,927	24.6
1994 [3].	94,355	70,817	75.1	66,450	70.4	4,367	6.2	23,538	24.9
1995.	95,178	71,360	75.0	67,377	70.8	3,983	5.6	23,818	25.0
Female:									
1960.	61,582	23,240	37.7	21,874	35.5	1,366	5.9	38,343	62.3
1970.	72,782	31,543	43.3	29,688	40.8	1,855	5.9	41,239	56.7
1980.	88,348	45,487	51.5	42,117	47.7	3,370	7.4	42,861	48.5
1985.	93,736	51,050	54.5	47,259	50.4	3,791	7.4	42,686	45.5
1990 [3].	98,787	56,829	57.5	53,689	54.3	3,140	5.5	41,957	42.5
1992.	100,535	58,141	57.8	54,052	53.8	4,090	7.0	42,394	42.2
1993.	101,506	58,795	57.9	54,910	54.1	3,885	6.6	42,711	42.1
1994 [3].	102,460	60,239	58.8	56,610	55.3	3,629	6.0	42,221	41.2
1995.	103,406	60,944	58.9	57,523	55.6	3,421	5.6	42,462	41.1
White:									
1960.	105,282	61,915	58.8	58,850	55.9	3,065	5.0	43,367	41.2
1970.	122,174	73,556	60.2	70,217	57.5	3,339	4.5	48,618	39.8
1980.	146,122	93,600	64.1	87,715	60.0	5,884	6.3	52,523	35.9
1985.	153,679	99,926	65.0	93,736	61.0	6,191	6.2	53,753	35.0
1990 [3].	160,625	107,447	66.9	102,261	63.7	5,186	4.8	53,178	33.1
1992.	162,972	108,837	66.8	101,669	62.4	7,169	6.6	54,135	33.2
1993.	164,289	109,700	66.8	103,045	62.7	6,655	6.1	54,589	33.2
1994 [3].	165,555	111,082	67.1	105,190	63.5	5,892	5.3	54,473	32.9
1995.	166,914	111,950	67.1	106,490	63.8	5,459	4.9	54,965	32.9
Black:									
1973.	14,917	8,976	60.2	8,128	54.5	846	9.4	5,941	39.8
1980.	17,824	10,865	61.0	9,313	52.2	1,553	14.3	6,959	39.0
1985.	19,664	12,364	62.9	10,501	53.4	1,864	15.1	7,299	37.1
1990 [3].	21,477	13,740	64.0	12,175	56.7	1,565	11.4	7,737	36.0
1992.	22,147	14,162	63.9	12,151	54.9	2,011	14.2	7,985	36.1
1993.	22,521	14,225	63.2	12,382	55.0	1,844	13.0	8,296	36.8
1994 [3].	22,879	14,502	63.4	12,835	56.1	1,666	11.5	8,377	36.6
1995.	23,246	14,817	63.7	13,279	57.1	1,538	10.4	8,429	36.3
Hispanic: [4]									
1980.	9,598	6,146	64.0	5,527	57.6	620	10.1	3,451	36.0
1985.	11,915	7,698	64.6	6,888	57.8	811	10.5	4,217	35.4
1990 [3].	15,904	10,720	67.4	9,845	61.9	876	8.2	5,184	32.6
1992.	16,961	11,338	66.8	10,027	59.1	1,311	11.6	5,623	33.2
1993.	17,532	11,610	66.2	10,361	59.1	1,248	10.8	5,922	33.8
1994 [3].	18,117	11,975	66.1	10,788	59.5	1,187	9.9	6,142	33.9
1995.	18,629	12,267	65.8	11,127	59.7	1,140	9.3	6,362	34.2
Mexican:									
1986.	7,377	4,941	67.0	4,387	59.5	555	11.2	2,436	33.0
1990 [3].	9,752	6,707	68.8	6,146	63.0	561	8.4	3,045	31.2
1993.	10,795	7,281	67.4	6,499	60.2	782	10.7	3,514	32.6
1994 [3].	11,174	7,567	67.7	6,800	60.9	766	10.1	3,608	32.3
1995.	11,609	7,765	66.9	7,016	60.4	750	9.7	3,844	33.1
Puerto Rican:									
1986.	1,494	804	53.8	691	46.3	113	14.0	690	46.2
1990 [3].	1,718	960	55.9	870	50.6	91	9.5	758	44.1
1993.	1,880	1,073	57.1	932	49.6	141	13.1	807	42.9
1994 [3].	1,854	1,026	55.4	907	48.9	119	11.6	828	44.6
1995.	1,896	1,098	57.9	974	51.4	123	11.2	798	42.1
Cuban:									
1986.	842	570	67.7	533	63.3	36	6.4	272	32.3
1990 [3].	918	603	65.7	559	60.9	44	7.2	315	34.3
1993.	1,004	604	60.1	556	55.4	47	7.9	400	39.8
1994 [3].	1,002	604	60.3	555	55.4	49	8.1	398	39.7
1995.	1,019	613	60.2	568	55.7	45	7.4	406	39.8

[1] Civilian employed as a percent of the civilian noninstitutional population.   [2] Includes other races, not shown separately. [3] See footnote 2, table 614.   [4] Persons of Hispanic origin may be of any race. Includes persons of other Hispanic origin, not shown separately.

Source: U.S. Bureau of Labor Statistics, Bulletin 2307; and *Employment and Earnings*, monthly, January issues.

No. 617. Civilian Labor Force and Participation Rates, by Educational Attainment, Sex, and Race: 1970 to 1991

[As of **March**. For civilian noninstitutional population 25 to 64 years of age. Beginning 1992, the method of computing attainment data was changed. See table 618 for later data. Based on Current Population Survey; see text, section 1, and Appendix III]

	CIVILIAN LABOR FORCE					PARTICIPATION RATE [1]				
		Percent distribution							College	
ITEM	Total (1,000)	Less than high school	High school graduate	College		Total	Less than high school	High school graduate	1-3 years	4 years or more
				1-3 years	4 years or more					
Total: [2] 1970	61,765	36.1	38.1	11.8	14.1	70.3	65.5	70.2	73.8	82.3
1980	78,010	20.6	39.8	17.6	22.0	73.9	60.7	74.2	79.5	86.1
1990	99,175	13.4	39.5	20.7	26.4	78.6	60.7	78.2	83.3	88.4
1991	100,480	13.0	39.4	21.1	26.5	78.6	60.7	78.1	83.2	88.4
Male: 1970	39,303	37.5	34.5	12.2	15.7	93.5	89.3	96.3	95.8	96.1
1980	45,417	22.2	35.7	17.7	24.3	89.4	78.8	91.9	92.4	95.3
1990	54,476	15.1	37.2	19.7	28.0	88.8	75.1	89.9	91.5	94.5
1991	55,165	14.7	37.5	20.2	27.6	88.6	75.1	89.3	92.0	94.2
Female: 1970	22,462	33.5	44.3	10.9	11.2	49.0	43.0	51.3	50.9	60.9
1980	32,593	18.4	45.4	17.4	18.7	59.5	43.7	61.2	66.4	73.4
1990	44,699	11.3	42.4	21.9	24.5	68.9	46.2	68.7	75.9	81.1
1991	45,315	10.9	41.6	22.2	25.2	69.1	46.2	68.6	75.2	81.8
White: 1970	55,044	33.7	39.3	12.2	14.8	70.1	65.2	69.7	73.3	81.9
1980	68,509	19.1	40.2	17.7	22.9	74.2	61.4	73.7	79.2	86.0
1990	85,238	12.6	39.6	20.6	27.1	79.2	62.5	78.4	83.3	88.3
1991	86,344	12.2	39.3	21.1	27.4	79.4	62.5	78.3	83.1	88.6
Black: 1970	6,721	55.5	28.2	8.0	8.3	72.0	67.1	76.8	81.0	87.4
1980	7,731	34.7	38.1	16.3	11.0	71.5	58.1	79.2	82.0	90.1
1990	10,537	19.9	42.5	22.1	15.5	74.6	54.5	78.2	84.2	92.0
1991	10,650	19.5	42.9	22.1	15.4	73.9	53.9	77.1	84.1	90.2

[1] Percent of the civilian population in each group in the civilian labor force.   [2] Includes other races, not shown separately. For 1970, White and Black races only.
Source: U.S. Bureau of Labor Statistics, Bulletin 2307; and unpublished data.

No. 618. Civilian Labor Force and Participation Rates, by Educational Attainment, Sex, Race, and Hispanic Origin: 1992 to 1995

[**As of March**. For the civilian noninstitutional population 25 to 64 years of age. See table 649 for unemployment data. Based on Current Population Survey; see text, section 1, and Appendix III]

	CIVILIAN LABOR FORCE (1,000)					PARTICIPATION RATE [1]				
		Percent distribution								
YEAR, SEX, AND RACE	Total	Less than high school diploma	High school graduate, no degree	Less than a bachelor's degree	College graduate	Total	Less than high school diploma	High school graduates, no degree	Less than a bachelor's degree	College graduate
Total: [2]										
1992	102,387	12.2	36.2	25.2	26.4	79.0	60.3	78.3	83.5	88.4
1993	103,504	11.5	35.2	26.3	27.0	78.9	59.6	77.7	82.9	88.3
1994 [3]	104,868	11.0	34.0	27.6	27.3	78.9	58.3	77.8	83.2	88.2
1995	106,519	10.8	33.1	27.8	28.3	79.3	59.8	77.3	83.2	88.7
Male:										
1992	55,917	13.9	34.7	23.8	27.5	88.6	75.1	89.0	91.8	93.7
1993	56,544	13.2	33.9	24.7	28.1	88.1	74.9	88.1	90.6	93.7
1994 [3]	56,633	12.7	32.9	25.8	28.6	87.0	71.5	86.8	90.3	93.2
1995	57,454	12.2	32.3	25.7	29.7	87.4	72.0	86.9	90.1	93.8
Female:										
1992	46,469	10.2	37.9	26.9	25.0	70.0	45.6	69.1	76.2	82.2
1993	46,961	9.3	36.7	28.2	25.8	70.0	44.2	68.8	76.1	82.2
1994 [3]	48,235	9.1	35.3	29.8	25.8	71.1	44.7	70.0	77.0	82.5
1995	49,065	9.1	34.1	30.2	26.6	71.5	47.2	68.9	77.3	82.8
White:										
1992	87,656	11.3	36.1	25.5	27.1	79.8	61.5	78.7	83.8	88.7
1993	88,457	10.7	35.0	26.4	27.9	79.7	61.1	78.2	83.1	88.8
1994 [3]	89,009	10.5	33.7	27.7	28.1	79.8	60.3	78.3	83.5	88.5
1995	90,192	10.0	32.8	27.8	29.3	80.1	61.6	77.9	83.4	88.8
Black:										
1992	10,936	19.2	40.3	24.9	15.6	74.4	55.4	76.9	83.4	89.1
1993	11,051	16.8	39.5	27.6	16.1	73.8	53.4	74.7	83.0	89.6
1994 [3]	11,368	14.5	39.3	29.2	17.0	73.5	49.4	75.2	82.5	89.5
1995	11,695	14.1	38.6	29.6	17.7	74.2	51.0	74.5	82.8	90.9
Hispanic: [4]										
1992	7,702	39.1	30.2	19.3	11.4	73.8	64.6	77.5	84.2	87.1
1993	8,010	38.7	29.4	21.0	10.9	73.9	64.9	76.8	84.0	87.3
1994 [3]	8,984	38.6	28.7	21.5	11.1	73.2	63.9	77.5	81.9	86.3
1995	9,298	38.9	28.2	21.3	11.6	73.2	64.7	75.9	81.9	87.9

[1] See footnote 1, table 617.   [2] Includes other races, not shown separately.   [3] See footnote 3, table 626.   [4] Persons of Hispanic origin may be of any race.
Source: U.S. Bureau of Labor Statistics, unpublished data.

No. 619. Civilian Labor Force—Percent Distribution, by Sex and Age: 1960 to 1995

[For civilian noninstitutional population 16 years old and over. Annual averages of monthly figures. Based on Current Population Survey; see text, section 1, and Appendix III. See *Historical Statistics, Colonial Times to 1970*, series D 29-41, for similar but not exactly comparable data]

YEAR AND SEX	Civilian labor force (1,000)	PERCENT DISTRIBUTION						
		16 to 19 years	20 to 24 years	25 to 34 years	35 to 44 years	45 to 54 years	55 to 64 years	65 yrs. and over
Total: 1960	69,628	7.0	9.6	20.7	23.4	21.3	13.5	4.6
1970	82,771	8.8	12.8	20.6	19.9	20.5	13.6	3.9
1980	106,940	8.8	14.9	27.3	19.1	15.8	11.2	2.9
1985	115,461	6.8	13.6	29.1	22.6	15.0	10.4	2.5
1990 [1]	125,840	6.2	11.7	28.6	25.5	16.1	9.2	2.7
1992	128,105	5.5	11.3	27.6	26.5	17.3	9.0	2.7
1993	129,200	5.5	11.1	26.9	26.8	18.0	9.0	2.7
1994 [1]	131,056	5.7	10.8	26.2	26.9	18.6	8.9	2.9
1995	132,304	5.9	10.3	25.8	27.0	19.1	9.0	2.9
Male: 1960	46,388	6.0	8.9	22.1	23.6	20.6	13.8	4.9
1970	51,228	7.8	11.2	22.1	20.4	20.3	13.9	4.2
1980	61,453	8.1	14.0	27.6	19.3	16.1	11.8	3.1
1985	64,411	6.4	12.9	29.2	22.5	15.3	11.0	2.7
1990 [1]	69,011	5.9	11.4	28.8	25.3	16.1	9.6	2.9
1992	69,964	5.4	11.1	27.9	26.2	17.2	9.4	2.9
1993	70,404	5.3	10.9	27.3	26.6	17.8	9.2	2.8
1994 [1]	70,817	5.5	10.6	26.6	26.8	18.3	9.1	3.1
1995	71,360	5.7	10.3	26.2	26.9	18.8	9.1	3.1
Female: 1960	23,240	8.8	11.1	17.8	22.8	22.7	12.8	3.9
1970	31,543	10.3	15.5	18.1	18.9	20.7	13.2	3.3
1980	45,487	9.6	16.1	26.9	19.0	15.4	10.4	2.6
1985	51,050	7.4	14.6	28.9	22.7	14.6	9.7	2.3
1990 [1]	56,829	6.5	12.0	28.3	25.8	16.1	8.7	2.6
1992	58,141	5.8	11.6	27.3	26.7	17.4	8.7	2.5
1993	58,795	5.8	11.4	26.5	27.0	18.3	8.7	2.5
1994 [1]	60,239	6.0	10.9	25.7	27.0	18.9	8.8	2.8
1995	60,944	6.1	10.4	25.5	27.2	19.4	8.8	2.7

[1] See footnote 2, table 614.

Source: U.S. Bureau of Labor Statistics, Bulletin 2307, and *Employment Earnings,* monthly, January issues.

No. 620. Civilian Labor Force, by Selected Metropolitan Area: 1995

[For the civilian noninstitutional population 16 years old and over. Annual averages of monthly figures. Except as noted, data are derived from the Local Area Unemployment Statistics Program. For composition of metropolitan areas, see Appendix II]

METROPOLITAN AREAS RANKED BY LABOR FORCE SIZE, 1995	Civilian labor force (1,000)	Unemploy-ment rate [1]	METROPOLITAN AREAS RANKED BY LABOR FORCE SIZE, 1995	Civilian labor force (1,000)	Unemploy-ment rate [1]
U.S. total	**132,304**	**5.6**	Fort Worth-Arlington, TX PMSA	816	4.9
Los Angeles-Long Beach, CA PMSA [2]	4,381	7.9	Cincinnati, OH-KY-IN PMSA	807	4.3
Chicago, IL PMSA	4,031	5.1	Columbus, OH MSA	782	3.1
New York, NY PMSA	3,792	7.6	Milwaukee-Waukesha, WI PMSA	782	3.5
Washington, DC-MD-VA-WV PMSA.	2,565	4.2	Orlando, FL MSA.	751	4.5
Philadelphia, PA-NJ PMSA	2,402	5.9	Norfolk-Virginia Beach-Newport News,		
Detroit, MI PMSA.	2,124	5.0	VA-NC MSA	729	4.9
Houston, TX PMSA	1,985	5.7	San Antonio, TX MSA.	720	4.4
Atlanta, GA MSA	1,880	4.3	Fort Lauderdale, FL PMSA	719	5.7
Boston, MA-NH PMSA	1,748	4.7	Sacramento, CA PMSA.	716	6.7
Dallas, TX PMSA.	1,709	4.6	Charlotte-Gastonia-Rock Hill, NC-SC MSA .	707	3.4
Minneapolis-St. Paul, MN-WI MSA	1,604	2.9	Bergen-Passaic, NJ PMSA	662	6.8
Nassau-Suffolk, NY PMSA.	1,356	5.0	Salt Lake City-Ogden, UT MSA	626	3.3
Phoenix-Mesa, AZ MSA	1,355	3.5	Greensboro-Winston-Salem-High Point,		
St. Louis, MO-IL MSA.	1,334	4.7	NC MSA.	612	3.3
Orange County, CA PMSA.	1,323	5.1	Austin-San Marcos, TX MSA	609	2.9
Riverside-San Bernardino, CA PMSA	1,284	8.7	Nashville, TN MSA.	607	3.4
Baltimore, MD PMSA	1,276	5.6	New Orleans, LA MSA	605	6.4
Seattle-Bellevue-Everett, WA PMSA	1,236	5.3	Middlesex-Somerset-Hunterdon, NJ PMSA.	600	4.8
San Diego, CA MSA.	1,226	6.4	Las Vegas, NV-AZ MSA	595	5.5
Pittsburgh, PA MSA	1,135	5.9	Hartford, CT MSA	592	6.0
Oakland, CA PMSA	1,133	5.8	Buffalo-Niagara Falls, NY MSA	569	5.4
Cleveland-Lorain-Elyria, OH PMSA	1,092	5.1	Rochester, NY MSA	564	4.6
Tampa-St. Petersburg-Clearwater,			Providence-Fall River-Warwick, RI-MA		
FL MSA	1,090	4.4	MSA	562	7.3
Denver, CO PMSA.	1,055	3.8	Raleigh-Durham-Chapel Hill, NC MSA. . . .	550	2.6
Miami, FL PMSA	1,033	7.3	Grand Rapids-Muskegon-Holland, MI MSA.	539	4.1
Newark, NJ PMSA	1,004	6.3	Louisville, KY-IN MSA.	530	4.4
Portland-Vancouver, OR-WA PMSA.	956	3.8	Memphis, TN-AR-MS MSA	525	4.9
Kansas City, MO-KS MSA.	924	4.3	Richmond-Petersburg, VA MSA	508	3.7
San Francisco, CA PMSA	892	5.1	Oklahoma City, OK MSA.	504	3.7
San Jose, CA PMSA	861	5.0	Jacksonville, FL MSA.	503	3.7
Indianapolis, IN MSA	824	3.9	Monmouth-Ocean, NJ PMSA	501	5.7

[1] Percent unemployed of the civilian labor force.   [2] Derived from the Current Population Survey.

Source: U.S. Bureau of Labor Statistics, *Employment and Earnings,* May 1996.

No. 621. Characteristics of the Civilian Labor Force, by State: 1995

[In thousands, except ratio and rate. Data are preliminary. For civilian noninstitutional population, 16 years old and over. Annual averages of monthly figures. Because of separate processing and weighting procedures, the totals for the United States may differ from results obtained by aggregating totals for States]

STATE	TOTAL		EMPLOYED		Employed/population ratio [1]	UNEMPLOYED					PARTICIPATION RATE [3]	
	Num-ber	Fe-male	Total	Fe-male		Total		Rate [2]			Male	Female
						Num-ber	Fe-male	Total	Male	Fe-male		
United States .	132,304	60,944	124,900	57,523	62.9	7,404	3,421	5.6	5.6	5.6	75.0	58.9
Alabama	2,062	957	1,933	898	59.3	129	58	6.3	6.4	6.1	72.4	55.3
Alaska	302	141	280	132	67.3	22	9	7.3	8.3	6.2	79.2	66.4
Arizona	2,120	968	2,012	914	64.4	108	54	5.1	4.7	5.6	76.7	59.6
Arkansas	1,223	579	1,163	545	61.7	59	34	4.9	4.0	5.9	58.4	58.4
California	15,415	6,792	14,206	6,258	60.3	1,210	534	7.8	7.8	7.9	74.8	56.5
Colorado	2,089	957	2,001	917	70.7	88	40	4.2	4.2	4.2	80.4	67.2
Connecticut	1,709	812	1,615	767	64.1	94	44	5.5	5.6	5.5	76.0	60.7
Delaware	381	180	365	173	66.7	17	7	4.3	4.6	4.1	77.2	62.9
District of Columbia .	283	145	258	133	59.6	25	13	8.9	9.0	8.8	70.4	61.4
Florida	6,830	3,160	6,455	2,982	58.6	375	177	5.5	5.4	5.6	70.4	54.5
Georgia	3,618	1,685	3,441	1,592	63.8	176	93	4.9	4.3	5.5	75.8	59.2
Hawaii	580	284	546	270	63.3	34	14	5.9	6.8	4.9	74.3	61.2
Idaho	598	263	565	252	66.3	32	11	5.4	6.3	4.3	78.0	62.1
Illinois	6,083	2,814	5,770	2,674	64.8	313	140	5.2	5.3	5.0	77.1	60.3
Indiana	3,134	1,473	2,988	1,398	67.8	146	75	4.7	4.3	5.1	78.8	64.2
Iowa	1,559	737	1,504	712	69.8	54	24	3.5	3.6	3.3	78.3	66.6
Kansas	1,330	622	1,270	591	67.2	59	31	4.4	4.0	5.0	77.8	63.4
Kentucky	1,861	864	1,761	820	59.6	100	44	5.4	5.6	5.1	70.7	56.0
Louisiana	1,956	905	1,821	844	57.0	135	61	6.9	7.0	6.8	69.8	53.6
Maine	642	305	605	290	63.0	37	15	5.7	6.4	5.0	72.3	61.6
Maryland	2,723	1,314	2,584	1,242	67.1	139	72	5.1	4.7	5.5	77.8	64.5
Massachusetts	3,168	1,498	2,998	1,425	63.9	170	73	5.4	5.8	4.8	75.0	60.8
Michigan	4,745	2,176	4,491	2,062	62.3	254	115	5.3	5.4	5.3	74.5	57.9
Minnesota	2,589	1,222	2,493	1,186	72.5	96	37	3.7	4.3	3.0	81.3	69.6
Mississippi	1,258	599	1,181	562	59.1	77	37	6.1	6.1	6.2	71.4	55.8
Missouri	2,832	1,361	2,697	1,293	67.3	135	67	4.8	4.6	4.9	76.8	65.0
Montana	436	202	410	192	62.4	26	10	5.9	6.6	5.1	73.5	59.6
Nebraska	897	431	873	419	72.0	24	12	2.6	2.5	2.8	79.9	68.4
Nevada	801	353	758	333	65.2	43	20	5.4	5.2	5.6	77.4	60.5
New Hampshire . . .	633	296	607	284	69.6	25	13	4.0	3.7	4.3	80.2	65.3
New Jersey	4,064	1,868	3,803	1,753	62.3	260	116	6.4	6.6	6.2	75.1	58.7
New Mexico	788	353	738	331	59.6	49	22	6.3	6.3	6.2	71.9	55.6
New York	8,493	3,931	7,955	3,700	57.0	538	231	6.3	6.7	5.9	70.1	52.8
North Carolina	3,636	1,737	3,479	1,647	63.9	158	90	4.3	3.6	5.2	74.7	59.8
North Dakota	334	159	323	154	68.5	11	5	3.3	3.5	3.1	77.1	64.9
Ohio	5,584	2,604	5,318	2,481	62.8	266	123	4.8	4.8	4.7	74.5	58.3
Oklahoma	1,547	719	1,474	687	60.3	73	33	4.7	4.8	4.5	71.9	55.7
Oregon	1,650	751	1,570	718	64.7	80	33	4.8	5.2	4.4	75.4	60.8
Pennsylvania	5,838	2,646	5,495	2,495	59.2	343	151	5.9	6.0	5.7	71.5	55.0
Rhode Island	485	235	451	219	60.1	34	16	7.0	7.2	6.7	71.7	58.4
South Carolina	1,859	878	1,765	822	63.3	94	56	5.1	3.9	6.3	74.1	59.9
South Dakota	382	176	371	171	69.9	11	5	2.9	3.0	2.9	78.2	65.8
Tennessee	2,712	1,284	2,571	1,218	63.5	141	66	5.2	5.3	5.1	74.4	60.3
Texas	9,568	4,215	8,991	3,939	65.3	576	276	6.0	5.6	6.6	79.3	60.0
Utah	971	415	936	400	69.2	35	15	3.6	3.6	3.6	82.5	61.2
Vermont	320	153	306	147	68.3	14	6	4.2	4.4	4.1	78.0	65.3
Virginia	3,496	1,657	3,338	1,573	66.9	158	83	4.5	4.0	5.0	78.0	63.0
Washington	2,805	1,261	2,626	1,181	64.0	179	80	6.4	6.4	6.4	76.5	60.6
West Virginia	790	356	728	331	50.1	62	25	7.9	8.6	7.0	63.4	46.3
Wisconsin	2,846	1,324	2,741	1,277	71.0	105	47	3.7	3.8	3.6	79.4	68.2
Wyoming	256	117	244	112	68.1	12	6	4.8	4.8	4.7	79.3	64.1

[1] Civilian employment as a percent of civilian noninstitutional population.   [2] Percent unemployed of the civilian labor force. [3] Percent of civilian noninstitutional population of each specified group in the civilian labor force.

Source: U.S. Bureau of Labor Statistics, *Geographic Profile of Employment and Unemployment, 1995.*

No. 622. Hispanic Persons—Civilian Labor Force Participation: 1994 and 1995

[For civilian noninstitutional population, 16 years old and over. Annual averages of monthly figures. Based on Current Population Survey; see text, section 1, and Appendix III]

ITEM	1994					1995				
	Total	Mexi-can	Puerto Rican	Cuban	Other His-panic origin [1]	Total	Mexi-can	Puerto Rican	Cuban	Other His-panic origin [1]
Total (1,000)	18,117	11,174	1,854	1,002	4,087	18,629	11,609	1,896	1,019	4,105
Percent in labor force:										
Male	79.2	81.5	67.6	70.3	79.7	79.1	80.9	70.6	69.9	79.5
Female	52.9	52.9	44.9	50.9	57.1	52.6	51.8	47.4	50.8	57.5
Employed (1,000)	10,788	6,800	907	555	2,526	11,127	7,016	974	568	2,569
Percent by occupation	100.0	100.0	100.0	100.0	100.0	100.0	100.0	100.0	100.0	100.0
Managerial and professional	14.1	11.6	19.5	25.5	16.3	13.9	11.7	19.6	22.0	16.0
Tech., sales, and admin. support .	24.5	22.4	31.0	36.5	24.9	24.4	21.7	29.8	37.5	26.9
Services	19.8	19.1	18.0	11.7	23.9	19.7	19.5	17.4	14.1	22.6
Precision production, craft, and repair.	13.0	13.9	10.1	10.6	12.3	12.9	13.5	10.8	10.4	12.5
Operators, fabricators and laborers	22.9	25.0	20.2	14.4	20.3	23.2	25.4	21.0	14.3	19.9
Farming, forestry, and fishing	5.7	8.0	1.3	1.3	2.3	5.9	8.3	1.4	1.8	2.1
Percent of labor force unemployed:										
Male	9.4	9.5	11.0	7.9	8.9	8.8	9.0	11.4	7.6	7.6
Female	10.7	11.1	12.4	8.4	9.4	10.0	10.8	11.0	7.0	8.3

[1] Includes Central or South American and other Hispanic origin.

Source: U.S. Bureau of Labor Statistics, *Employment and Earnings*, monthly, January issues.

No. 623. School Enrollment and Labor Force Status: 1980 and 1995

[In thousands, except percent. As of October. For the civilian noninstitutional population 16 to 24 years old. Based on Current Population Survey; see text, section 1, and Appendix III]

CHARACTERISTIC	POPULATION		CIVILIAN LABOR FORCE		EMPLOYED		UNEMPLOYED		
	1980	1995 [1]	1980	1995 [1]	1980	1995 [1]	1980, total	1995 [1]	
								Total	Rate [2]
Total, 16 to 24 years [3]	37,103	32,379	24,918	20,794	21,454	18,318	3,464	2,476	11.9
Enrolled in school [3]	15,713	16,842	7,454	8,301	6,433	7,346	1,021	954	11.5
16 to 19 years	11,126	11,272	4,836	4,931	4,029	4,169	807	762	15.5
20 to 24 years	4,587	5,570	2,618	3,370	2,404	3,178	214	192	5.7
Sex:									
Male	7,997	8,504	3,825	4,062	3,259	3,555	566	506	12.5
Female	7,716	8,337	3,629	4,239	3,174	3,791	455	448	10.6
College level	7,664	8,697	3,996	4,996	3,632	4,639	364	357	7.1
Full-time.	6,396	7,211	2,854	3,713	2,554	3,406	300	307	8.3
Race:									
White	13,242	13,379	6,687	7,030	5,889	6,322	798	708	10.1
Below college	6,566	6,251	3,095	2,793	2,579	2,357	516	435	15.6
College level	6,678	7,128	3,592	4,237	3,310	3,965	282	272	6.4
Black	2,028	2,431	595	862	406	667	189	195	22.6
Below college	1,282	1,418	294	376	174	248	120	128	34.0
College level	747	1,013	300	486	230	419	70	67	13.9
Not enrolled [3]	21,390	15,537	17,464	12,493	15,021	10,972	2,443	1,521	12.2
White	18,103	12,338	15,121	10,131	13,318	9,087	1,803	1,043	10.3
Black	2,864	2,408	2,055	1,745	1,451	1,349	604	396	22.7

[1] See footnote 3, table 626.　　[2] Percent of civilian labor force in each category.　　[3] Includes other races, not shown separately.

Source: U.S. Bureau of Labor Statistics, Bulletin 2307; *News*, USDL 96-152, April 25, 1996; and unpublished data.

No. 624. Labor Force Participation Rates, by Marital Status, Sex, and Age: 1960 to 1995

[Annual averages of monthly figures. See table 621 for definition of participation rate. Based on Current Population Survey; see text, section 1, and Appendix III]

MARITAL STATUS AND YEAR	MALE PARTICIPATION RATE							FEMALE PARTICIPATION RATE						
	Total	16-19 years	20-24 years	25-34 years	35-44 years	45-64 years	65 and over	Total	16-19 years	20-24 years	25-34 years	35-44 years	45-64 years	65 and over
Single:														
1960 ..	69.8	42.6	80.3	91.5	88.6	80.1	31.2	58.6	30.2	77.2	83.4	82.9	79.8	24.3
1970 ..	65.5	54.6	73.8	87.9	86.2	75.7	25.2	56.8	44.7	73.0	81.4	78.6	73.0	19.7
1975 ..	68.7	57.9	77.9	86.7	83.2	69.9	21.0	59.8	49.6	72.5	80.8	78.6	68.3	15.8
1980 ..	72.6	59.9	81.3	89.2	82.2	66.9	16.8	64.4	53.6	75.2	83.3	76.9	65.6	13.9
1985 ..	73.8	56.3	81.5	89.4	84.6	65.5	15.6	66.6	52.3	76.3	82.4	80.8	67.9	9.8
1990 [1]	74.8	55.1	81.6	89.9	84.5	67.3	15.7	66.7	51.7	74.5	80.9	80.8	66.2	12.1
1991 ..	74.1	52.6	80.6	89.6	84.6	67.1	13.9	66.2	50.1	73.2	80.0	80.9	68.4	12.7
1992 ..	74.6	52.9	80.8	89.7	84.7	67.7	16.3	66.2	49.1	73.4	80.2	80.4	68.2	11.2
1993 ..	74.2	52.6	80.5	89.2	84.3	68.4	15.0	66.2	49.6	73.8	78.9	78.9	68.8	12.4
1994 [1]	73.9	53.6	80.5	88.4	83.1	67.8	17.8	66.7	51.4	73.6	78.9	78.7	68.8	12.7
1995 ..	73.7	54.4	80.3	88.7	81.4	67.0	17.9	66.8	52.2	72.9	80.2	79.5	67.3	11.6
Married: [2]														
1960 ..	89.2	91.5	97.1	98.8	98.6	93.7	36.6	31.9	27.2	31.7	28.8	37.2	36.0	6.7
1970 ..	86.1	92.3	94.7	98.0	98.1	91.2	29.9	40.5	37.8	47.9	38.8	46.8	44.0	7.3
1975 ..	83.0	92.9	95.3	97.4	97.1	86.8	23.3	44.3	46.2	57.0	48.4	52.0	43.8	7.0
1980 ..	80.9	91.3	96.9	97.5	97.2	84.3	20.5	49.8	49.3	61.4	58.8	61.8	46.9	7.3
1985 ..	78.7	91.0	95.6	97.4	96.8	81.7	16.8	53.8	49.6	65.7	65.8	68.1	49.4	6.6
1990 [1]	78.6	92.1	95.6	96.9	96.7	82.6	17.5	58.4	49.5	66.1	69.6	74.0	56.5	8.5
1991 ..	78.1	92.9	95.4	96.5	96.5	82.4	16.7	58.5	48.2	64.6	69.9	74.2	57.0	8.3
1992 ..	78.0	90.2	94.7	96.5	96.1	82.7	17.1	59.3	48.8	65.8	70.8	74.7	58.6	7.8
1993 ..	77.6	91.3	95.0	96.5	96.0	82.5	16.5	59.4	49.8	65.1	70.6	74.7	59.9	7.6
1994 [1]	77.4	88.7	94.2	95.9	95.6	81.9	18.1	60.7	48.9	65.8	71.6	75.8	61.9	9.4
1995 ..	77.5	89.2	94.9	96.3	95.4	82.4	18.0	61.0	51.6	64.7	72.0	75.7	62.7	9.1
Other: [3]														
1960 ..	63.1	(B)	96.9	95.2	94.4	83.2	22.7	41.6	43.5	58.0	63.1	70.0	60.0	11.4
1970 ..	60.7	(B)	90.4	93.7	91.1	78.5	19.3	40.3	48.6	60.3	64.6	68.8	61.9	10.0
1975 ..	63.4	(B)	88.8	92.4	89.4	73.4	15.4	40.1	47.6	65.3	68.6	69.2	59.0	8.3
1980 ..	67.5	(B)	92.6	94.1	91.9	73.3	13.7	43.6	50.0	68.4	76.5	77.1	60.2	8.2
1985 ..	68.7	(B)	95.1	93.7	91.8	72.8	11.4	45.1	51.9	66.2	76.9	81.6	61.0	7.5
1990 [1]	68.9	(B)	93.1	93.0	90.7	74.9	12.0	47.2	53.9	65.4	77.0	82.1	65.0	8.4
1991 ..	68.2	(B)	94.1	92.0	90.4	73.8	12.2	46.8	45.5	62.9	74.6	81.9	65.2	8.3
1992 ..	68.6	(B)	92.0	93.5	90.2	75.0	12.1	47.1	47.3	66.7	75.5	81.4	66.4	8.3
1993 ..	67.9	(B)	91.9	91.9	89.5	74.5	12.0	47.2	53.0	64.8	75.0	81.4	66.9	8.2
1994 [1]	66.8	65.1	91.0	90.3	88.6	72.6	11.9	47.5	46.2	66.6	74.3	80.4	67.6	8.7
1995 ..	66.2	43.8	92.7	90.9	88.2	72.4	12.1	47.4	55.8	67.2	77.1	80.7	67.2	8.4

B For 1960, percentage not shown where base is less than 50,000; beginning 1970, 35,000.   [1] See footnote 2, table 614.   [2] Spouse present.   [3] Widowed, divorced, and married (spouse absent).

Source: U.S. Bureau of Labor Statistics, Bulletins 2217 and 2340; and unpublished data.

No. 625. Marital Status of Women in the Civilian Labor Force: 1960 to 1995

[Annual averages of monthly figures. For civilian noninstitutional population 16 years old and over. Based on Current Population Survey; see text, section 1, and Appendix III. See also *Historical Statistics, Colonial Times to 1970*, series D 49-62]

YEAR	FEMALE LABOR FORCE (1,000)				FEMALE PARTICIPATION RATE [3]			
	Total	Single	Married [1]	Other [2]	Total	Single	Married [1]	Other [2]
1960	23,240	5,410	12,893	4,937	37.7	58.6	31.9	41.6
1965	26,200	5,976	14,829	5,396	39.3	54.5	34.9	40.7
1970	31,543	7,265	18,475	5,804	43.3	56.8	40.5	40.3
1975	37,475	9,125	21,484	6,866	46.3	59.8	44.3	40.1
1980	45,487	11,865	24,980	8,643	51.5	64.4	49.9	43.6
1981	46,696	12,124	25,428	9,144	52.1	64.5	50.5	44.6
1982	47,755	12,460	25,971	9,324	52.6	65.1	51.1	44.8
1983	48,503	12,659	26,468	9,376	52.9	65.0	51.8	44.4
1984	49,709	12,867	27,199	9,644	53.6	65.6	52.8	44.7
1985	51,050	13,163	27,894	9,993	54.5	66.6	53.8	45.1
1986	52,413	13,512	28,623	10,277	55.3	67.2	54.9	45.6
1987	53,658	13,885	29,381	10,393	56.0	67.4	55.9	45.7
1988	54,742	14,194	29,921	10,627	56.6	67.7	56.7	46.2
1989	56,030	14,377	30,548	11,104	57.4	68.0	57.8	47.0
1990 [4]	56,829	14,612	30,901	11,315	57.5	66.7	58.4	47.2
1991	57,178	14,681	31,112	11,385	57.4	66.2	58.5	46.8
1992	58,141	14,872	31,700	11,570	57.8	66.2	59.3	47.1
1993	58,795	15,031	31,980	11,784	57.9	66.2	59.4	47.2
1994 [4]	60,239	15,333	32,888	12,018	58.8	66.7	60.7	47.5
1995	60,944	15,467	33,359	12,118	58.9	66.8	61.0	47.4

[1] Husband present.   [2] Widowed, divorced, or separated.   [3] See table 621 for definition of participation rate.   [4] See footnote 2, table 614.

Source: U.S. Bureau of Labor Statistics, Bulletin 2307; and unpublished data.

No. 626. Employment Status of Women, by Marital Status and Presence and Age of Children: 1960 to 1995

[As of **March**. For 1960, civilian noninstitutional persons 14 years and over, thereafter 16 years old and over. Based on Current Population Survey; see text, section 1, and Appendix III]

| ITEM | TOTAL | | | WITH ANY CHILDREN | | | | | | | | |
| | | | | Total | | | Children 6 to 17 only | | | Children under 6 | | |
	Single	Mar-ried[1]	Other[2]	Single	Mar-ried[1]	Other[2]	Single	Mar-ried[1]	Other[2]	Single	Mar-ried[1]	Other[2]
IN LABOR FORCE (mil.)												
1960	5.4	12.3	4.9	(NA)	6.6	1.5	(NA)	4.1	1.0	(NA)	2.5	0.4
1970	7.0	18.4	5.9	(NA)	10.2	1.9	(NA)	6.3	1.3	(NA)	3.9	0.6
1980	11.2	24.9	8.8	0.6	13.7	3.6	0.2	8.4	2.6	0.3	5.2	1.0
1985	12.9	27.7	10.3	1.1	14.9	4.0	0.4	8.5	2.9	0.7	6.4	1.1
1990	14.0	31.0	11.2	1.5	16.5	4.2	0.6	9.3	3.0	0.9	7.2	1.2
1992	14.1	31.7	11.5	1.7	16.8	4.2	0.7	9.5	3.0	1.0	7.3	1.2
1993	14.1	32.2	11.3	1.9	16.9	4.2	0.7	9.7	3.0	1.1	7.3	1.2
1994 [3]	14.9	32.9	11.9	2.2	17.6	4.4	0.8	9.9	3.2	1.4	7.7	1.2
1995	15.0	33.6	12.0	2.1	18.0	4.6	0.8	10.2	3.3	1.3	7.8	1.3
PARTICIPATION RATE [4]												
1960	44.1	30.5	40.0	(NA)	27.6	56.0	(NA)	39.0	65.9	(NA)	18.6	40.5
1970	53.0	40.8	39.1	(NA)	39.7	60.7	(NA)	49.2	66.9	(NA)	30.3	52.2
1980	61.5	50.1	44.0	52.0	54.1	69.4	67.6	61.7	74.6	44.1	45.1	60.3
1985	65.2	54.2	45.6	51.6	60.8	71.9	64.1	67.8	77.8	46.5	53.4	59.7
1990	66.4	58.2	46.8	55.2	66.3	74.2	69.7	73.6	79.7	48.7	58.9	63.6
1992	64.7	59.3	46.7	52.5	67.8	73.2	67.2	75.4	80.0	45.8	59.9	60.5
1993	64.5	59.4	45.9	54.4	67.5	72.1	70.2	74.9	78.3	47.4	59.6	60.0
1994 [3]	65.1	60.6	47.3	56.9	69.0	73.1	67.5	76.0	78.4	52.2	61.7	62.2
1995	65.5	61.1	47.3	57.5	70.2	75.3	67.0	76.2	79.5	53.0	63.5	66.3
EMPLOYMENT (mil.)												
1960	5.1	11.6	4.6	(NA)	6.2	1.3	(NA)	3.9	0.9	(NA)	2.3	0.4
1970	6.5	17.5	5.6	(NA)	9.6	1.8	(NA)	6.0	1.2	(NA)	3.6	0.6
1980	10.1	23.6	8.2	0.4	12.8	3.3	0.2	8.1	2.4	0.2	4.8	0.9
1985	11.6	26.1	9.4	0.9	13.9	3.5	0.3	8.1	2.6	0.5	5.9	0.9
1990	12.9	29.9	10.5	1.2	15.8	3.8	0.5	8.9	2.7	0.7	6.9	1.1
1992	12.8	30.1	10.6	1.4	15.9	3.7	0.6	9.1	2.7	0.8	6.8	1.0
1993	12.7	30.8	10.5	1.5	16.1	3.9	0.6	9.3	2.8	0.9	6.8	1.1
1994 [3]	13.4	31.4	11.0	1.7	16.8	4.0	0.7	9.5	2.9	1.1	7.3	1.0
1995	13.7	32.3	11.3	1.8	17.2	4.2	0.7	9.8	3.1	1.1	7.3	1.2
UNEMPLOY-MENT RATE [5]												
1960	6.0	5.4	6.2	(NA)	6.0	8.4	(NA)	4.9	6.8	(NA)	7.8	12.5
1970	7.1	4.8	4.8	(NA)	6.0	7.2	(NA)	4.8	5.9	(NA)	7.9	9.8
1980	10.3	5.3	6.4	23.2	5.9	9.2	15.6	4.4	7.9	29.2	8.3	12.8
1985	10.2	5.7	8.5	23.8	6.6	12.1	15.4	5.5	10.6	28.5	8.0	16.1
1990	8.2	3.5	5.7	18.4	4.2	8.5	14.5	3.8	7.7	20.8	4.8	10.2
1992	9.1	4.9	7.6	17.3	5.7	10.8	14.1	4.6	8.6	19.4	7.0	16.3
1993	9.8	4.4	6.9	19.2	4.8	8.5	13.7	3.8	7.0	22.8	6.2	12.5
1994 [3]	10.0	4.5	7.4	19.5	5.0	9.8	13.2	4.5	7.7	23.0	5.6	15.1
1995	8.7	3.9	5.8	16.6	4.3	8.1	11.8	3.6	7.1	19.5	5.3	10.8

NA Not available.   [1] Husband present.   [2] Widowed, divorced, or separated.   [3] Data beginning 1994 not strictly comparable with data for earlier years, See text, section 13, and February 1994 and March 1996 issues of *Employment and Earnings*. [4] Percent of women in each specific category in the labor force.   [5] Unemployed as a percent of civilian labor force in specified group.
Source: U.S. Bureau of Labor Statistics, Bulletin 2307; and unpublished data.

No. 627. Labor Force Participation Rates for Wives, Husband Present, by Age of Own Youngest Child: 1975 to 1995

[As of **March**. For civilian noninstitutional population, 16 years old and over. For definition of participation rate, see table 626. Based on Current Population Survey; see text, section 1, and Appendix III]

| PRESENCE AND AGE OF CHILD | TOTAL | | | WHITE | | | BLACK | | |
	1975	1985	1995 [1]	1975	1985	1995 [1]	1975	1985	1995 [1]
Wives, total	44.4	54.2	61.1	43.6	53.3	60.7	54.1	63.8	68.2
No children under 18	43.8	48.2	53.2	43.6	47.5	52.9	47.6	55.2	57.4
With children under 18	44.9	60.8	70.2	43.6	59.9	70.0	58.4	71.7	79.3
Under 6, total	36.7	53.4	63.5	34.7	52.1	63.0	54.9	69.6	77.3
Under 3	32.7	50.5	60.9	30.7	49.4	60.3	50.1	66.2	76.3
1 year or under	30.8	49.4	59.0	29.2	48.6	58.6	50.0	63.7	74.1
2 years	37.1	54.0	66.7	35.1	52.7	66.5	56.4	69.9	78.8
3 to 5 years	42.2	58.4	67.2	40.1	56.6	66.8	61.2	73.8	78.5
3 years	41.2	55.1	65.5	39.0	52.7	65.5	62.7	72.3	80.6
4 years	41.2	59.7	67.7	38.7	58.4	67.7	64.9	70.6	71.8
5 years	44.4	62.1	69.6	43.8	59.9	69.3	56.3	79.1	84.0
6 to 13 years	51.8	68.2	74.9	50.7	67.7	74.9	65.7	73.3	79.1
14 to 17 years	53.5	67.0	79.6	53.4	66.6	79.7	52.3	74.4	85.4

[1] See footnote 3, table 626.
Source: U.S. Bureau of Labor Statistics, Bulletin 2340; and unpublished data.

No. 628. Civilian Labor Force—Employment Status, by Sex, Race, and Age: 1995

[For civilian noninstitutional population 16 years old and over. Annual averages of monthly figures. Based on Current Population Survey; see text, section 1, and Appendix III]

| AGE AND RACE | TOTAL (1,000) | MALE (1,000) | | | FEMALE (1,000) | | | PERCENT OF LABOR FORCE | | | |
| | | | | | | | | Employed | | Unemployed | |
		Total	Em-ployed	Unem-ployed	Total	Em-ployed	Unem-ployed	Male	Fe-male	Male	Fe-male
All workers [1] ..	**132,304**	**71,360**	**67,377**	**3,983**	**60,944**	**57,523**	**3,421**	**94.4**	**94.4**	**5.6**	**5.6**
16 to 19 years	7,765	4,036	3,292	744	3,729	3,127	602	81.6	83.9	18.4	16.1
20 to 24 years	13,688	7,338	6,665	673	6,349	5,779	571	90.8	91.0	9.2	9.0
25 to 34 years	34,198	18,670	17,709	961	15,528	14,647	880	94.9	94.3	5.1	5.7
35 to 44 years	35,751	19,189	18,374	815	16,562	15,828	735	95.8	95.6	4.2	4.4
45 to 54 years	25,223	13,421	12,958	464	11,801	11,421	381	96.5	96.8	3.5	3.2
55 to 64 years	11,860	6,504	6,272	233	5,356	5,163	193	96.4	96.4	3.6	3.6
65 years and over ..	3,819	2,201	2,108	94	1,618	1,558	60	95.7	96.3	4.3	3.7
White	**111,950**	**61,146**	**58,146**	**2,999**	**50,804**	**48,344**	**2,460**	**95.1**	**95.2**	**4.9**	**4.8**
16 to 19 years	6,545	3,427	2,892	535	3,118	2,701	418	84.4	86.6	15.6	13.4
20 to 24 years	11,266	6,096	5,613	483	5,170	4,787	384	92.1	92.6	7.9	7.4
25 to 34 years	28,325	15,669	14,958	711	12,656	12,056	600	95.5	95.3	4.5	4.7
35 to 44 years	30,112	16,414	15,793	621	13,697	13,157	540	96.2	96.1	3.8	3.9
45 to 54 years	21,804	11,730	11,359	371	10,074	9,768	306	96.8	97.0	3.2	3.0
55 to 64 years	10,432	5,809	5,609	200	4,622	4,461	162	96.6	96.5	3.4	3.5
65 years and over ..	3,466	2,000	1,921	79	1,466	1,415	52	96.1	96.5	4.0	3.5
Black	**14,817**	**7,183**	**6,422**	**762**	**7,634**	**6,857**	**777**	**89.4**	**89.8**	**10.6**	**10.2**
16 to 19 years	911	453	285	168	458	301	157	62.9	65.7	37.1	34.3
20 to 24 years	1,754	866	714	153	887	729	158	82.4	82.2	17.6	17.8
25 to 34 years	4,267	2,089	1,895	195	2,177	1,949	228	90.7	89.5	9.3	10.5
35 to 44 years	4,165	1,987	1,836	150	2,178	2,025	153	92.4	93.0	7.6	7.0
45 to 54 years	2,404	1,148	1,085	63	1,256	1,202	53	94.5	95.7	5.5	4.2
55 to 64 years	1,046	490	468	21	556	536	20	95.7	96.4	4.3	3.6
65 years and over ..	271	150	138	11	121	114	7	92.0	94.2	7.6	5.8
Hispanic [2]	**12,267**	**7,376**	**6,725**	**651**	**4,891**	**4,403**	**488**	**91.2**	**90.0**	**8.8**	**10.0**
16 to 19 years	850	479	358	121	371	287	84	74.7	77.4	25.3	22.6
20 to 24 years	1,818	1,153	1,030	123	666	579	86	89.3	87.1	10.6	12.9
25 to 34 years	3,943	2,469	2,284	185	1,473	1,334	140	92.5	90.6	7.5	9.5
35 to 44 years	3,113	1,795	1,675	120	1,318	1,213	104	93.3	92.1	6.7	7.9
45 to 54 years	1,671	965	908	57	706	657	50	94.1	92.9	5.9	7.1
55 to 64 years	720	417	384	33	303	282	21	92.1	93.1	7.9	6.9
65 years and over ..	152	98	85	13	54	50	3	86.7	94.3	13.3	5.7

[1] Includes other races not shown separately. [2] Persons of Hispanic origin may be of any race.

Source: U.S. Bureau of Labor Statistics, *Employment and Earnings*, monthly, January 1996.

No. 629. Employed Civilians and Weekly Hours: 1970 to 1995

[**In thousands, except as indicated. For civilian noninstitutional population 16 years old and over.** Annual averages of monthly figures. Based on Current Population Survey; see text, section 1, and Appendix III]

ITEM	1970	1980	1985	1990 [1]	1992	1993	1994 [1]	1995
Total employed	**78,678**	**99,303**	**107,150**	**118,793**	**118,492**	**120,259**	**123,060**	**124,900**
Age:								
16 to 19 years old	6,144	7,710	6,434	6,581	5,669	5,805	6,161	6,419
20 to 24 years old	9,731	14,087	13,980	13,401	12,872	12,840	12,758	12,443
25 to 34 years old	16,318	27,204	31,208	33,935	32,667	32,385	32,286	32,356
35 to 44 years old	15,922	19,523	24,732	30,817	31,923	32,666	33,599	34,202
45 to 54 years old	16,473	16,234	16,509	19,525	21,022	22,175	23,348	24,378
55 to 64 years old	10,974	11,586	11,474	11,189	10,998	11,058	11,228	11,435
65 years old and over...........	3,118	2,960	2,813	3,346	3,341	3,331	3,681	3,666
Class of worker:								
Nonagriculture................	75,215	95,938	103,971	115,570	115,245	117,144	119,651	121,460
Wage and salary worker	69,491	88,525	95,871	106,598	106,437	107,966	110,517	112,448
Self-employed	5,221	7,000	7,811	8,719	8,575	8,959	9,003	8,902
Unpaid family workers..........	502	413	289	253	233	218	131	110
Agriculture	3,463	3,364	3,179	3,223	3,247	3,115	3,409	3,440
Wage and salary worker	1,154	1,425	1,535	1,740	1,750	1,689	1,715	1,814
Self-employed	1,810	1,642	1,458	1,378	1,385	1,320	1,645	1,580
Unpaid family workers..........	499	297	185	105	112	106	49	45
Weekly hours:								
Nonagriculture:								
Wage and salary workers........	38.3	38.1	38.7	39.2	38.7	39.2	39.1	39.2
Self-employed	45.0	41.2	41.1	40.8	40.1	40.6	39.5	39.4
Unpaid family workers..........	37.9	34.7	35.1	34.0	34.6	34.2	33.7	33.5
Agriculture:								
Wage and salary workers........	40.0	41.6	40.8	41.2	40.5	40.7	41.0	41.1
Self-employed	51.0	49.3	48.2	46.8	47.0	46.4	43.0	43.5
Unpaid family workers..........	40.0	38.6	38.5	38.5	40.4	36.9	39.0	42.0

[1] See footnote 2, table 614.

Source: U.S. Bureau of Labor Statistics, *Employment and Earnings,* monthly, January issues; and unpublished data.

No. 630. Persons At Work, by Hours Worked: 1995

[For civilian noninstitutional population 16 years old and over. Annual averages of monthly figures. Based on Current Population Survey; see text, section 1, and Appendix III]

HOURS OF WORK	PERSONS AT WORK (1,000)			PERCENT DISTRIBUTION		
	Total	Agriculture industries	Non-agriculture industries	Total	Agriculture industries	Non-agriculture industries
Total	119,318	3,247	116,071	100.0	100.0	100.0
1 to 34 hours	30,664	1,051	29,613	25.7	32.4	25.5
1 to 4 hours	1,297	83	1,214	1.1	2.6	1.0
5 to 14 hours	4,943	262	4,681	4.1	8.1	4.0
15 to 29 hours	15,120	476	14,644	12.7	14.7	12.6
30 to 34 hours	9,304	229	9,075	7.8	7.1	7.8
35 hours and over	88,654	2,196	86,458	74.3	67.6	74.5
35 to 39 hours	8,783	173	8,610	7.4	5.3	7.4
40 hours	42,228	635	41,592	35.4	19.6	35.8
41 hours and over	37,643	1,388	36,255	31.5	42.7	31.2
41 to 48 hours	13,958	250	13,708	11.7	7.7	11.8
49 to 58 hours	13,591	388	13,203	11.4	11.9	11.4
60 hours and over	10,094	750	9,344	8.5	23.1	8.1
Average weekly hours:						
Total at work	39.3	42.2	39.2	(X)	(X)	(X)
Persons usually working full time	43.4	49.7	43.2	(X)	(X)	(X)

X Not applicable.

Source: U.S. Bureau of Labor Statistics, *Employment and Earnings*, monthly, January, 1996.

No. 631. Self-Employed Workers, by Industry and Occupation: 1970 to 1995

[In thousands. For civilian noninstitutional population 16 years old and over. Annual averages of monthly figures. Data from 1992 forward are not fully comparable with data for prior years because of the introduction of the occupational and industrial classification used in the 1990 census. Based on the Current Population Survey; see text, section 1, and Appendix III]

ITEM	1970	1980	1985	1990 [1]	1992	1993	1994 [1]	1995
Total self-employed	7,031	8,642	9,269	10,097	9,960	10,280	10,648	10,482
Industry: Agriculture	1,810	1,642	1,458	1,378	1,385	1,320	1,645	1,580
Nonagriculture	5,221	7,000	7,811	8,719	8,575	8,960	9,003	8,902
Mining	14	28	20	24	22	17	13	16
Construction	687	1,173	1,301	1,457	1,460	1,549	1,506	1,460
Manufacturing	264	358	347	427	390	439	426	433
Transportation and public utilities	196	282	315	301	337	372	385	396
Trade	1,667	1,899	1,792	1,851	1,770	1,886	1,906	1,772
Finance, insurance, and real estate	254	458	558	630	622	655	625	660
Services	2,140	2,804	3,477	4,030	3,975	4,041	4,142	4,166
Occupation:								
Managerial and professional specialty	(NA)	(NA)	2,585	3,050	2,895	3,078	3,106	3,147
Technical, sales, and administrative support. .	(NA)	(NA)	2,059	2,240	2,176	2,319	2,380	2,341
Service occupations	(NA)	(NA)	980	1,207	1,079	1,044	1,178	1,190
Precision production, craft, and repair.	(NA)	(NA)	1,611	1,675	1,799	1,888	1,740	1,618
Operators, fabricators, and laborers	(NA)	(NA)	568	567	625	631	639	631
Farming, forestry, and fishing	(NA)	(NA)	1,465	1,358	1,377	1,320	1,605	1,556

NA Not available. [1] See footnote 2, table 614.

Source: U.S. Bureau of Labor Statistics, Bulletin 2307; *Employment and Earnings*, monthly, January issues; and unpublished data.

No. 632. Persons With a Job But Not at Work: 1970 to 1995

[In thousands, except percent. For civilian noninstitutional population 16 years old and over. Annual averages of monthly figures. Based on Current Population Survey; see text, section 1, and Appendix III. See *Historical Statistics, Colonial Times to 1970*, series D 116-126, for related but not comparable data]

REASON FOR NOT WORKING	1970	1975	1980	1985	1989	1990 [1]	1991	1992	1993	1994 [1]	1995
All industries, number	4,645	5,221	5,881	5,789	6,170	6,160	5,914	6,088	6,041	5,619	5,582
Percent of employed	5.9	6.1	5.9	5.4	5.3	5.2	5.0	5.1	5.0	4.6	4.5
Reason for not working:											
Vacation	2,341	2,815	3,320	3,338	3,437	3,529	3,291	3,409	3,328	2,877	2,982
Illness	1,324	1,343	1,426	1,308	1,405	1,341	1,305	1,259	1,295	1,184	1,084
Bad weather	128	139	155	141	133	90	119	128	153	165	122
Industrial dispute	156	95	105	42	63	24	17	19	24	15	21
All other	696	829	876	960	1,132	1,177	1,182	1,272	1,241	1,378	1,373

[1] See footnote 2, table 614.

Source: U.S. Bureau of Labor Statistics, *Employment and Earnings*, monthly, January issues; and unpublished data.

No. 633. Part-Time Workers, by Reason: 1995

[In thousands, except hours. For persons working 1 to 34 hours per week. For civilian noninstitutional population 16 years old and over. Annual average of monthly figures. Based on the Current Population Survey and subject to sampling error; see text, section 1, and Appendix III]

REASON	ALL INDUSTRIES			NONAGRICULTURAL INDUSTRIES		
	Total	Usually Work—		Total	Usually Work—	
		Full time	Part time		Full time	Part time
Total working fewer than 35 hours	**30,664**	**9,924**	**20,740**	**29,613**	**9,615**	**19,998**
Economic reasons	4,473	1,468	3,005	4,279	1,373	2,906
Slack work or business conditions	2,471	1,210	1,261	2,346	1,140	1,206
Could find only part-time work	1,702	-	1,702	1,663	-	1,663
Seasonal work	120	77	43	94	58	36
Job started or ended during the week	180	180	-	175	175	-
Noneconomic reasons	26,191	8,457	17,734	25,334	8,242	17,093
Child-care problems	774	71	703	765	70	695
Other family or personal obligations	5,585	719	4,866	5,393	700	4,693
Health or medical limitations	699	-	699	660	-	660
In school or training	5,986	79	5,907	5,831	77	5,755
Retired or Social Security limit on earnings	1,848	-	1,848	1,714	-	1,714
Vacation or personal day	3,303	3,303	-	3,250	3,250	-
Holiday, legal, or religious	1,005	1,005	-	998	998	-
Weather related curtailment	439	439	-	375	375	-
Other	6,551	2,841	3,711	6,348	2,772	3,575
Average hours per week:						
Economic reasons	22.9	24.1	22.3	23.0	24.2	22.4
Noneconomic reasons	21.4	25.6	19.4	21.5	25.7	19.5

- Represents or rounds to zero.

Source: U.S. Bureau of Labor Statistics, *Employment and Earnings*, monthly, January 1996 issue.

634. Multiple Jobholders: 1995

[Annual average of monthly figures. For the civilian noninstitutional population 16 years old and over. Multiple jobholders are employed persons who, either 1) had jobs as wage or salary workers with two employers or more; 2) were self-employed and also held a wage and salary job; or 3) were unpaid family workers on their primary jobs but also held wage and salary job. Based on the Current Population Survey; see text, section 1, and Appendix III]

CHARACTERISTIC	TOTAL		MALE		FEMALE	
	Number (1,000)	Percent of employed	Number (1,000)	Percent of employed	Number (1,000)	Percent of employed
Total [1]	**7,693**	**6.2**	**4,139**	**6.1**	**3,554**	**6.2**
Age:						
16 to 19 years old	350	5.4	153	4.7	196	6.3
20 to 24 years old	829	6.7	404	6.1	424	7.3
25 to 54 years old	5,874	6.5	3,217	6.6	2,657	6.3
55 to 64 years old	537	4.7	298	4.8	238	4.6
65 years old and over	104	2.8	66	3.1	38	2.5
Race and Hispanic origin:						
White	6,764	6.4	3,650	6.3	3,114	6.4
Black	688	5.2	362	5.6	326	4.8
Hispanic origin [2]	430	3.9	252	3.8	178	4.0
Marital status:						
Married, spouse present	4,398	5.9	2,683	6.4	1,715	5.3
Widowed, divorced, or separated	1,235	6.5	412	5.5	823	7.2
Single, never married	2,061	6.5	1,044	5.9	1,016	7.2
Full- or part-time status:						
Primary job full-time, secondary job part-time	4,446	(X)	2,664	(X)	1,781	(X)
Both jobs part-time	1,693	(X)	533	(X)	1,160	(X)
Both jobs full-time	257	(X)	185	(X)	72	(X)
Hours vary on primary or secondary job	1,262	(X)	740	(X)	521	(X)

X Not applicable.   [1] Includes a small number of persons who work part time on their primary job and full time on their secondary job(s), not shown separately. Includes other races, not shown separately.   [2] Persons of Hispanic origin may be of any race.

Source: U.S. Bureau of Labor Statistics, *Employment and Earnings*, monthly, January 1996 issue.

No. 635. Displaced Workers, by Selected Characteristics: 1992 and 1994

[In percent, except total. **As of January for 1992 and February for 1994.** For persons 20 years old and over with tenure of 3 years or more who lost or left a job between January 1987 and January 1992 for 1992 data or January 1991 and December 1993 for 1994 data because of plant closings or moves, slack work, or the abolishment of their positions. Based on Current Population Survey and subject to sampling error; see source and Appendix III]

SEX, AGE, RACE, AND HISPANIC ORIGIN	Total (1,000)	EMPLOYMENT STATUS			REASON FOR JOB LOSS		
		Employed	Unem-ployed	Not in the labor force	Plant or company closed down or moved	Slack work	Position or shift abolished
Total, 1992 [1]	**5,584**	**64.9**	**22.2**	**12.9**	**52.1**	**31.6**	**16.3**
Males	3,447	66.6	24.5	8.9	49.4	34.7	15.9
20 to 24 years old	127	55.6	32.5	11.8	45.0	49.4	5.6
25 to 54 years old	2,728	71.6	24.5	3.9	49.5	34.0	16.5
55 to 64 years old	488	52.3	24.2	23.5	49.0	34.6	16.4
65 years old and over	103	15.8	15.3	68.9	53.3	35.7	11.0
Females	2,137	62.2	18.6	19.2	56.6	26.4	17.0
20 to 24 years old	76	72.7	7.3	20.1	43.8	46.1	10.0
25 to 54 years old	1,688	65.8	19.9	14.3	54.4	26.7	18.9
55 to 64 years old	262	51.4	17.4	31.2	70.5	19.4	10.1
65 years old and over	111	26.5	8.7	64.8	66.3	25.1	8.6
White	4,828	65.7	21.2	13.0	52.5	30.6	16.9
Male	3,003	67.6	23.3	9.1	49.4	34.1	16.5
Female	1,825	62.7	17.8	19.5	57.6	24.8	17.6
Black	626	58.7	28.6	12.7	51.3	36.3	12.4
Male	356	58.9	33.4	7.7	52.3	36.6	11.1
Female	270	58.5	22.2	19.3	50.0	35.9	14.1
Hispanic origin [2]	511	60.4	27.4	12.3	57.0	34.5	8.5
Male	323	64.6	27.2	8.2	57.6	35.7	6.7
Female	188	53.0	27.7	19.3	56.0	32.5	11.6
Total, 1994 [1]	**4,473**	**68.0**	**19.1**	**12.9**	**42.3**	**29.9**	**27.7**
Males	2,614	71.6	19.9	8.4	40.9	33.0	26.1
20 to 24 years old	77	58.7	35.6	5.6	43.7	42.2	14.1
25 to 54 years old	2,097	76.2	19.1	4.7	40.7	32.8	26.4
55 to 64 years old	383	57.0	21.5	21.6	42.9	31.0	26.0
65 years old and over	57	(³)	(³)	(³)	(³)	(³)	(³)
Females	1,859	62.9	17.9	19.2	44.3	25.6	30.1
20 to 24 years old	76	68.6	13.1	18.3	47.4	30.3	22.4
25 to 54 years old	1,443	68.4	18.0	13.6	42.3	27.1	30.6
55 to 64 years old	228	47.4	23.0	29.6	54.4	16.2	29.4
65 years old and over	112	19.5	9.1	71.4	45.9	23.4	30.6
White	3,859	69.3	17.9	12.8	41.2	30.2	28.6
Male	2,291	73.4	18.4	8.2	40.2	33.1	26.6
Female	1,568	63.3	17.2	19.5	42.7	25.9	31.4
Black	427	61.5	26.1	12.4	51.4	25.3	23.3
Male	219	59.3	32.1	8.7	50.7	25.2	24.0
Female	209	63.7	19.8	16.4	52.1	25.3	22.6
Hispanic origin [2]	361	55.6	30.5	13.9	49.2	35.5	15.4
Male	243	57.8	34.0	8.1	44.9	42.0	13.1
Female	118	51.0	23.1	25.9	58.0	21.8	20.2

[1] Includes other races, not shown separately.　　[2] Persons of Hispanic origin may be of any race.　　[3] Data not shown where base is less than 75,000.

Source: U.S. Bureau of Labor Statistics, *News*, USDL 92-530 and 94-434.

No. 636. Persons Not in the Labor Force: 1995

[**In thousands. Annual average of monthly figures.** For the civilian noninstitutional population 16 years old and over. Based on the Current Population Survey; see text, section 1, and Appendix III]

STATUS AND REASON	Total	AGE			SEX	
		16 to 24 years old	25 to 54 years old	55 years old and over	Male	Female
Total not in the labor force	**66,280**	**10,922**	**18,854**	**36,503**	**23,818**	**42,462**
Do not want a job now [1]	60,610	8,807	16,246	35,557	21,536	39,074
Want a job now	5,670	2,115	2,608	947	2,282	3,388
In the previous year—						
Did not search for a job	3,286	1,153	1,436	697	1,231	2,054
Did search for a job [2]	2,384	963	1,172	250	1,050	1,334
Not available for work now	791	397	350	45	302	490
Available for work now, not looking for work	1,593	566	822	205	749	844
Reason for not currently looking:						
Discouraged over job prospects [3]	410	108	231	72	245	166
Family responsibilities	185	39	131	15	26	159
In school or training	245	199	44	2	131	114
Ill health or disability	131	19	84	28	60	71
Other [4]	621	201	331	89	287	334

[1] Includes some persons who are not asked if they want a job.　　[2] Persons who had a job in the prior 12 months must have searched since the end of that job.　　[3] Includes such things as believes no work available, could not find work, lacks necessary schooling or training, employer thinks too young or old, and other types of discrimination.　　[4] Includes such things as child care and transportation problems.

Source: U.S. Bureau of Labor Statistics, *Employment and Earnings*, monthly, January 1996 issue.

No. 637. Employed Civilians, by Occupation, Sex, Race, and Hispanic Origin: 1983 and 1995

[For civilian noninstitutional population 16 years old and over. Annual average of monthly figures. Based on Current Population Survey; see text, section 1, and Appendix III. Persons of Hispanic origin may be of any race. See headnote, table 631]

OCCUPATION	1983				1995 [1]			
	Total employed (1,000)	Percent of total			Total employed (1,000)	Percent of total		
		Female	Black	Hispanic		Female	Black	Hispanic
Total.............................	100,834	43.7	9.3	5.3	124,900	46.1	10.6	8.9
Managerial and professional specialty.............	**23,592**	**40.9**	**5.6**	**2.6**	**35,318**	**48.0**	**7.5**	**4.4**
Executive, administrative, and managerial [2]...........	10,772	32.4	4.7	2.8	17,186	42.7	7.2	4.8
Officials and administrators, public.............	417	38.5	8.3	3.8	618	49.8	13.6	4.7
Financial managers..........................	357	38.6	3.5	3.1	605	50.3	6.3	5.7
Personnel and labor relations managers...........	106	43.9	4.9	2.6	125	58.5	15.8	3.4
Purchasing managers.......................	82	23.6	5.1	1.4	135	41.5	6.6	3.1
Managers, marketing, advertising and public relations...	396	21.8	2.7	1.7	663	35.7	2.2	3.3
Administrators, education and related fields.........	415	41.4	11.3	2.4	701	58.7	11.2	4.7
Managers, medicine and health..............	91	57.0	5.0	2.0	653	79.9	9.0	5.1
Managers, properties and real estate............	305	42.8	5.5	5.2	522	49.8	6.8	7.1
Management-related occupations [2].............	2,966	40.3	5.8	3.5	4,325	53.8	9.2	5.0
Accountants and auditors..................	1,105	38.7	5.5	3.3	1,526	52.1	8.4	4.4
Professional specialty [2]......................	12,820	48.1	6.4	2.5	18,132	52.9	7.8	4.0
Architects..............................	103	12.7	1.6	1.5	163	19.8	2.5	5.8
Engineers [2]............................	1,572	5.8	2.7	2.2	1,934	8.4	4.7	3.3
Aerospace engineers...................	80	6.9	1.5	2.1	78	5.2	1.5	5.7
Chemical engineers....................	67	6.1	3.0	1.4	80	11.2	8.5	1.2
Civil engineers.......................	211	4.0	1.9	3.2	231	7.2	4.9	2.6
Electrical and electronic.................	450	6.1	3.4	3.1	611	8.7	5.8	3.7
Industrial engineers...................	210	11.0	3.3	2.4	250	14.9	6.0	4.0
Mechanical..........................	259	2.8	3.2	1.1	330	4.6	3.8	3.0
Mathematical and computer scientists [2]...........	463	29.6	5.4	2.6	1,195	32.0	7.2	2.8
Computer systems analysts, scientists.........	276	27.8	6.2	2.7	933	29.5	6.1	2.7
Operations and systems researchers and analysts...	142	31.3	4.9	2.2	217	39.1	10.0	3.4
Natural scientists [2].......................	357	20.5	2.6	2.1	519	27.3	3.9	2.6
Chemists, except biochemists..............	98	23.3	4.3	1.2	140	31.9	4.6	3.7
Geologists and geodesists................	65	18.0	1.1	2.6	60	15.0	0.5	0.6
Biological and life scientists..............	55	40.8	2.4	1.8	110	31.8	5.2	4.3
Medical scientists.....................	(3)	(3)	(3)	(3)	61	41.2	4.1	3.3
Health diagnosing occupations [2]..............	735	13.3	2.7	3.3	1,002	22.9	3.9	3.7
Physicians............................	519	15.8	3.2	4.5	693	24.4	4.9	4.3
Dentists..............................	126	6.7	2.4	1.0	155	13.4	1.9	2.6
Health assessment and treating occupations........	1,900	85.8	7.1	2.2	2,762	85.8	8.6	3.1
Registered nurses......................	1,372	95.8	6.7	1.8	1,977	93.1	8.4	2.6
Pharmacists..........................	158	26.7	3.8	2.6	170	36.2	4.3	1.8
Dietitians............................	71	90.8	21.0	3.7	94	93.2	18.4	7.5
Therapists [2].........................	247	76.3	7.6	2.7	466	75.1	9.2	4.6
Inhalation therapists..................	69	69.4	6.5	3.7	94	60.1	15.2	5.9
Physical therapists...................	55	77.0	9.7	1.5	130	70.2	2.7	4.4
Speech therapists....................	51	90.5	1.5	-	91	92.1	3.3	1.4
Physicians' assistants....................	51	36.3	7.7	4.4	55	53.2	7.6	5.7
Teachers, college and university...............	606	36.3	4.4	1.8	846	45.2	6.2	3.6
Teachers, except college and university [2].........	3,365	70.9	9.1	2.7	4,507	74.7	9.3	4.4
Prekindergarten and kindergarten............	299	98.2	11.8	3.4	498	98.2	13.9	6.9
Elementary school.....................	1,350	83.3	11.1	3.1	1,738	84.1	10.1	4.3
Secondary school......................	1,209	51.8	7.2	2.3	1,232	57.0	7.5	4.1
Special education......................	81	82.2	10.2	2.3	311	84.3	9.3	2.1
Counselors, educational and vocational...........	184	53.1	13.9	3.2	236	68.3	14.2	7.2
Librarians, archivists, and curators..............	213	84.4	7.8	1.6	211	83.2	7.5	2.3
Librarians............................	193	87.3	7.9	1.8	195	83.9	7.6	1.3
Social scientists and urban planners [2]............	261	46.8	7.1	2.1	453	54.3	8.6	4.6
Economists...........................	98	37.9	6.3	2.7	148	50.3	5.0	7.9
Psychologists.........................	135	57.1	8.6	1.1	260	59.2	10.2	3.4
Social, recreation, and religious workers [2]........	831	43.1	12.1	3.8	1,303	52.5	16.8	6.4
Social workers........................	407	64.3	18.2	6.3	727	67.9	23.7	7.8
Recreation workers.....................	65	71.9	15.7	2.0	110	74.7	7.6	4.9
Clergy...............................	293	5.6	4.9	1.4	356	11.1	9.2	3.6
Lawyers and judges.......................	651	15.8	2.7	1.0	926	26.2	3.6	3.1
Lawyers..............................	612	15.3	2.6	0.9	894	26.4	3.6	3.2
Writers, artists, entertainers, and athletes [2]........	1,544	42.7	4.8	2.9	2,054	49.4	6.2	4.8
Authors..............................	62	46.7	2.1	0.9	118	54.2	3.2	2.8
Technical writers......................	(3)	(3)	(3)	(3)	53	53.9	3.0	1.4
Designers............................	393	52.7	3.1	2.7	556	57.6	4.2	4.3
Musicians and composers.................	155	28.0	7.9	4.4	161	37.3	10.0	7.5
Actors and directors....................	60	30.8	6.6	3.4	114	38.9	9.8	3.0
Painters, sculptors, craft-artists, and artist printmakers.........................	186	47.4	2.1	2.3	233	50.1	4.2	3.3
Photographers.........................	113	20.7	4.0	3.4	136	27.1	6.5	4.8
Editors and reporters....................	204	48.4	2.9	2.1	273	53.2	4.7	3.5
Public relations specialists................	157	50.1	6.2	1.9	142	57.9	8.3	2.7
Announcers...........................	(3)	(3)	(3)	(3)	50	26.2	16.6	9.5
Athletes.............................	58	17.6	9.4	1.7	87	25.3	11.8	6.9

See footnotes at end of table.

No. 637. Employed Civilians, by Occupation, Sex, Race, and Hispanic Origin: 1983 and 1995—Continued

[See headnote, page 405]

OCCUPATION	1983 Total employed (1,000)	1983 Female	1983 Black	1983 Hispanic	1995[1] Total employed (1,000)	1995 Female	1995 Black	1995 Hispanic
Technical, sales, and administrative support	**31,265**	**64.6**	**7.6**	**4.3**	**37,417**	**64.4**	**10.2**	**7.3**
Technicians and related support	3,053	48.2	8.2	3.1	3,909	51.4	9.7	6.1
Health technologists and technicians [2]	1,111	84.3	12.7	3.1	1,648	79.7	12.9	6.6
Clinical laboratory technologists and technicians	255	76.2	10.5	2.9	374	71.7	13.6	8.5
Dental hygienists	66	98.6	1.6	-	95	99.4	1.0	5.1
Radiologic technicians	101	71.7	8.6	4.5	154	74.2	6.8	8.3
Licensed practical nurses	443	97.0	17.7	3.1	399	95.4	19.6	3.7
Engineering and related technologists and technicians [2]	822	18.4	6.1	3.5	880	17.8	8.0	6.2
Electrical and electronic technicians	260	12.5	8.2	4.6	334	11.1	10.6	5.8
Drafting occupations	273	17.5	5.5	2.3	229	18.4	5.1	6.6
Surveying and mapping technicians	(3)	(3)	(3)	(3)	62	13.2	8.7	3.1
Science technicians [2]	202	29.1	6.6	2.8	276	35.5	8.9	7.3
Biological technicians	52	37.7	2.9	2.0	96	50.0	6.6	6.7
Chemical technicians	82	26.9	9.5	3.5	84	21.5	10.5	6.3
Technicians, except health, engineering, and science [2]	917	35.3	5.0	2.7	1,106	39.9	6.3	5.2
Airplane pilots and navigators	69	2.1	-	1.6	114	3.4	1.2	3.9
Computer programmers	443	32.5	4.4	2.1	553	29.5	6.5	4.8
Legal assistants	128	74.0	4.3	3.6	285	80.0	6.8	6.9
Sales occupations	11,818	47.5	4.7	3.7	15,119	49.5	7.8	6.9
Supervisors and proprietors	2,958	28.4	3.6	3.4	4,480	38.9	5.6	5.6
Sales representatives, finance and business services [2]	1,853	37.2	2.7	2.2	2,399	42.1	5.5	5.1
Insurance sales	551	25.1	3.8	2.5	562	37.1	5.8	4.6
Real estate sales	570	48.9	1.3	1.5	718	50.7	3.4	4.5
Securities and financial services sales	212	23.6	3.1	1.1	397	31.3	5.7	5.0
Advertising and related sales	124	47.9	4.5	3.3	151	52.9	4.2	4.7
Sales representatives, commodities, except retail	1,442	15.1	2.1	2.2	1,529	21.2	2.7	4.9
Sales workers, retail and personal services	5,511	69.7	6.7	4.8	6,613	65.6	11.4	8.9
Cashiers	2,009	84.4	10.1	5.4	2,727	79.2	15.8	9.9
Sales-related occupations	54	58.7	2.8	1.3	99	75.6	4.5	7.8
Administrative support, including clerical	16,395	79.9	9.6	5.0	18,389	79.5	12.2	7.8
Supervisors	676	53.4	9.3	5.0	712	60.0	14.6	6.3
Computer equipment operators	605	63.9	12.5	6.0	491	60.4	15.5	8.9
Computer operators	597	63.7	12.1	6.0	485	60.5	15.7	8.9
Secretaries, stenographers, and typists [2]	4,861	98.2	7.3	4.5	4,106	97.8	10.0	6.6
Secretaries	3,891	99.0	5.8	4.0	3,361	98.5	8.7	6.4
Typists	906	95.6	13.8	6.4	656	94.3	17.7	8.1
Information clerks	1,174	88.9	8.5	5.5	1,872	88.0	10.0	8.0
Receptionists	602	96.8	7.5	6.6	939	96.5	8.8	8.4
Records processing occupations, except financial [2]	866	82.4	13.9	4.8	959	79.4	15.4	7.7
Order clerks	188	78.1	10.6	4.4	251	74.1	16.0	9.2
Personnel clerks, except payroll and time keeping	64	91.1	14.9	4.6	60	86.5	12.9	10.1
Library clerks	147	81.9	15.4	2.5	143	80.8	13.7	3.1
File clerks	287	83.5	16.7	6.1	317	80.2	17.0	8.6
Records clerks	157	82.8	11.6	5.6	172	80.2	14.1	6.7
Financial records processing [2]	2,457	89.4	4.6	3.7	2,255	92.4	6.1	5.3
Bookkeepers, accounting, and auditing clerks	1,970	91.0	4.3	3.3	1,776	92.8	4.9	4.9
Payroll and time keeping clerks	192	82.2	5.9	5.0	161	90.9	10.5	4.9
Billing clerks	146	88.4	6.2	3.9	176	90.4	11.8	8.3
Cost and rate clerks	96	75.6	5.9	5.3	52	89.5	6.0	6.2
Billing, posting, and calculating machine operators [3]	(3)	(3)	(3)	(3)	91	92.2	10.4	6.3
Duplicating, mail and other office machine operators	68	62.6	16.0	6.1	72	57.9	11.2	9.2
Communications equipment operators	256	89.1	17.0	4.4	185	87.4	25.6	7.4
Telephone operators	244	90.4	17.0	4.3	176	88.4	26.0	7.4
Mail and message distributing occupations	799	31.6	18.1	4.5	1,006	39.8	20.4	8.7
Postal clerks, except mail carriers	248	36.7	26.2	5.2	301	45.3	29.3	8.5
Mail carrier, postal service	259	17.1	12.5	2.7	362	31.9	13.8	7.4
Mail clerks, except postal service	170	50.0	15.8	5.9	187	54.5	26.2	8.9
Messengers	122	26.2	16.7	5.2	156	29.7	12.0	12.1
Material recording, scheduling, and distributing [2][4]	1,562	37.5	10.9	6.6	1,876	45.2	13.4	10.3
Dispatchers	157	45.7	11.4	4.3	247	54.1	10.2	5.6
Production coordinators	182	44.0	6.1	2.2	208	58.5	6.1	7.5
Traffic, shipping, and receiving clerks	421	22.6	9.1	11.1	639	32.5	16.2	14.0
Stock and inventory clerks	532	38.7	13.3	5.5	462	45.0	14.2	10.6
Weighers, measurers, and checkers	79	47.2	16.9	5.8	57	40.9	17.8	6.4
Expediters	112	57.5	8.4	4.3	194	67.2	9.9	7.5
Adjusters and investigators	675	69.9	11.1	5.1	1,414	74.9	13.2	7.0
Insurance adjusters, examiners, and investigators	199	65.0	11.5	3.3	365	73.9	10.1	4.5
Investigators and adjusters, except insurance	301	70.1	11.3	4.8	809	75.1	13.8	7.0
Eligibility clerks, social welfare	69	88.7	12.9	9.4	89	81.8	12.9	9.0
Bill and account collectors	106	66.4	8.5	6.5	151	72.2	17.6	12.0
Miscellaneous administrative support [2]	2,397	85.2	12.5	5.9	3,441	83.4	14.1	9.6
General office clerks	648	80.6	12.7	5.2	694	81.7	14.1	10.5
Bank tellers	480	91.0	7.5	4.3	443	90.1	11.0	7.6
Data entry keyers	311	93.6	18.6	5.6	652	82.9	17.5	8.3
Statistical clerks	96	75.7	7.5	3.4	94	84.3	24.8	8.5
Teachers' aides	348	93.7	17.8	12.6	634	90.9	14.9	15.1

See footnotes at end of table.

No. 637. Employed Civilians, by Occupation, Sex, Race, and Hispanic Origin: 1983 and 1995—Continued

[See headnote, page 405]

OCCUPATION	1983				1995 [1]			
	Total employed (1,000)	Percent of total			Total employed (1,000)	Percent of total		
		Female	Black	His-panic		Female	Black	His-panic
Service occupations	13,857	60.1	16.6	6.8	16,930	60.0	17.0	13.0
Private household [2]	980	96.1	27.8	8.5	821	95.5	16.7	24.8
Child care workers	408	96.9	7.9	3.6	312	96.8	9.6	19.3
Cleaners and servants	512	95.8	42.4	11.8	487	94.6	20.0	28.0
Protective service	1,672	12.8	13.6	4.6	2,237	15.9	18.2	7.4
Supervisors, protective service	127	4.7	7.7	3.1	193	10.9	13.4	5.5
Supervisors, police and detectives	58	4.2	9.3	1.2	102	12.9	7.8	7.1
Firefighting and fire prevention	189	1.0	6.7	4.1	249	2.7	15.1	5.1
Firefighting occupations	170	1.0	7.3	3.8	237	2.3	15.3	4.8
Police and detectives	645	9.4	13.1	4.0	949	13.5	16.9	7.4
Police and detectives, public service	412	5.7	9.5	4.4	519	10.4	11.2	8.7
Sheriffs, bailiffs, and other law enforcement officers	87	13.2	11.5	4.0	151	16.3	15.4	4.9
Correctional institution officers	146	17.8	24.0	2.8	278	17.8	28.2	6.4
Guards	711	20.6	17.0	5.6	846	23.7	21.6	8.6
Guards and police, except public service	602	13.0	18.9	6.2	709	16.4	23.4	9.1
Service except private household and protective	11,205	64.0	16.0	6.9	13,872	65.0	16.8	13.2
Food preparation and service occupations [2]	4,860	63.3	10.5	6.8	5,800	58.3	11.6	14.2
Bartenders	338	48.4	2.7	4.4	287	53.5	2.0	5.9
Waiters and waitresses	1,357	87.8	4.1	3.6	1,426	77.7	4.5	9.7
Cooks	1,452	50.0	15.8	6.5	2,001	44.5	17.6	18.1
Food counter, fountain, and related occupations	326	76.0	9.1	6.7	321	74.8	14.3	9.5
Kitchen workers, food preparation	138	77.0	13.7	8.1	280	70.7	10.7	10.4
Waiters' and waitresses' assistants	364	38.8	12.6	14.2	479	46.2	9.9	20.1
Health service occupations	1,739	89.2	23.5	4.8	2,315	88.2	27.6	8.4
Dental assistants	154	98.1	6.1	5.7	211	98.5	3.6	12.3
Health aides, except nursing	316	86.8	16.5	4.8	347	76.0	27.9	6.2
Nursing aides, orderlies, and attendants	1,269	88.7	27.3	4.7	1,757	89.4	30.4	8.4
Cleaning and building service occupations [2]	2,736	38.8	24.4	9.2	2,946	44.9	21.9	19.0
Maids and housemen	531	81.2	32.3	10.1	634	83.1	29.1	19.4
Janitors and cleaners	2,031	28.6	22.6	8.9	2,071	35.0	20.1	19.1
Personal service occupations [2]	1,870	79.2	11.1	6.0	2,810	80.7	13.5	8.8
Barbers	92	12.9	8.4	12.1	87	16.3	29.0	7.0
Hairdressers and cosmetologists	622	88.7	7.0	5.7	750	92.0	9.9	9.4
Attendants, amusement and recreation facilities	131	40.2	7.1	4.3	194	37.5	8.4	4.5
Public transportation attendants	63	74.3	11.3	5.9	94	81.7	16.9	3.1
Welfare service aides	77	92.5	24.2	10.5	93	85.1	29.4	11.8
Family child care providers	(NA)	(NA)	(NA)	(NA)	486	97.9	10.1	8.6
Early childhood teachers' assistants	(NA)	(NA)	(NA)	(NA)	396	95.8	16.5	10.8
Precision production, craft, and repair	12,328	8.1	6.8	6.2	13,524	8.9	7.9	10.6
Mechanics and repairers	4,158	3.0	6.8	5.3	4,423	3.9	8.3	8.3
Mechanics and repairers, except supervisors [2]	3,906	2.8	7.0	5.5	4,173	3.8	8.5	8.4
Vehicle and mobile equipment mechanics/repairers [2]	1,683	0.8	6.9	6.0	1,710	0.7	7.7	9.1
Automobile mechanics	800	0.5	7.8	6.0	819	0.6	7.8	11.2
Aircraft engine mechanics	95	2.5	4.0	7.6	121	1.7	10.4	6.7
Electrical and electronic equipment repairers [2]	674	7.4	7.3	4.5	642	9.4	9.3	6.7
Data processing equipment repairers	98	9.3	6.1	4.5	149	15.2	9.4	6.4
Telephone installers and repairers	247	9.9	7.8	3.7	163	16.0	6.2	6.0
Construction trades	4,289	1.8	6.6	6.0	5,098	2.3	7.1	11.4
Construction trades, except supervisors	3,784	1.9	7.1	6.1	4,372	2.3	7.6	12.2
Carpenters	1,160	1.4	5.0	5.0	1,255	0.8	5.7	9.4
Extractive occupations	196	2.3	3.3	6.0	136	3.6	2.6	7.8
Precision production occupations	3,685	21.5	7.3	7.4	3,867	23.3	8.8	12.3
Operators, fabricators, and laborers	16,091	26.6	14.0	8.3	18,068	24.3	15.0	14.3
Machine operators, assemblers, and inspectors [2]	7,744	42.1	14.0	9.4	7,907	37.3	15.4	15.8
Textile, apparel, and furnishings machine operators [2]	1,414	82.1	18.7	12.5	1,134	73.5	20.3	23.1
Textile sewing machine operators	806	94.0	15.5	14.5	607	85.7	17.0	26.9
Pressing machine operators	141	66.4	27.1	14.2	128	65.4	24.9	31.9
Fabricators, assemblers, and hand working occupations	1,715	33.7	11.3	8.7	2,059	29.9	13.1	13.6
Production inspectors, testers, samplers, and weighers	794	53.8	13.0	7.7	764	52.0	16.2	13.7
Transportation and material moving occupations	4,201	7.8	13.0	5.9	5,171	9.5	14.7	9.9
Motor vehicle operators	2,978	9.2	13.5	6.0	3,904	11.0	15.2	10.1
Trucks drivers	2,195	3.1	12.3	5.7	2,861	4.5	12.6	10.4
Transportation occupations, except motor vehicles	212	2.4	6.7	3.0	170	2.8	13.5	3.5
Material moving equipment operators	1,011	4.8	12.9	6.3	1,098	5.1	13.2	10.2
Industrial truck and tractor operators	369	5.6	19.6	8.2	500	7.1	19.5	13.3
Handlers, equipment cleaners, helpers, and laborers [2]	4,147	16.8	15.1	8.6	4,990	19.1	14.7	16.4
Freight, stock, and material handlers	1,488	15.4	15.3	7.1	1,925	22.1	14.7	13.1
Laborers, except construction	1,024	19.4	16.0	8.6	1,337	20.6	14.8	15.3
Farming, forestry, and fishing	3,700	16.0	7.5	8.2	3,642	19.9	4.2	18.1
Farm operators and managers	1,450	12.1	1.3	0.7	1,446	25.3	0.4	1.9
Other agricultural and related occupations	2,072	19.9	11.7	14.0	2,010	17.4	6.8	30.8
Farm workers	1,149	24.8	11.6	15.9	797	18.1	4.3	40.3
Forestry and logging occupations	126	1.4	12.8	2.1	129	3.6	8.6	3.7
Fishers, hunters, and trappers	53	4.5	1.8	2.5	58	7.3	1.3	9.5

- Represents or rounds to zero.   NA Not available.   [1] See footnote 2, table 614.   [2] Includes other occupations, not shown separately.   [3] Level of total employment below 50,000.   [4] Includes clerks.

Source: U.S. Bureau of Labor Statistics, *Employment and Earnings*, monthly, January issues.

No. 638. Civilian Employment in Occupations With the Largest Job Growth: 1994 to 2005

[Occupations are in descending order of absolute employment change 1994-2005 (moderate growth). Includes wage and salary jobs, self-employed, and unpaid family members. Estimates based on the Current Employment Statistics estimates and the Occupational Employment Statistics estimates. See source for methodological assumptions]

OCCUPATION	EMPLOYMENT (1,000)				PERCENT CHANGE 1994-2005		
	1994	2005 [1]			Low	Moderate	High
		Low	Moderate	High			
Total, all occupations [2]	**127,015**	**140,261**	**144,708**	**150,212**	**10.4**	**13.9**	**18.3**
Cashiers	3,005	3,493	3,567	3,645	16.2	18.7	21.3
Janitors and cleaners [3]	3,043	3,483	3,602	3,745	14.5	18.4	23.1
Salespersons, retail	3,842	4,244	4,374	4,508	10.5	13.8	17.3
Waiters and waitresses	1,847	2,361	2,326	2,291	27.8	25.9	24.0
Registered nurses	1,906	2,318	2,379	2,481	21.6	24.8	30.2
General managers and top executives	3,046	3,403	3,512	3,641	11.7	15.3	19.5
Systems analysts	483	893	928	972	84.9	92.1	101.3
Home health aides	420	832	848	863	98.3	102.0	105.7
Guards	867	1,248	1,282	1,322	44.0	47.9	52.5
Nursing aides, orderlies, and attendants	1,265	1,624	1,652	1,709	28.4	30.6	35.1
Teachers, secondary school	1,340	1,585	1,726	1,885	18.3	28.8	40.7
Marketing and sales worker supervisors	2,293	2,628	2,673	2,728	14.6	16.6	18.9
Teacher aides and educational assistants	932	1,211	1,296	1,393	29.9	39.0	49.5
Receptionists and information clerks	1,019	1,311	1,337	1,367	28.7	31.2	34.2
Truck drivers light and heavy	2,565	2,744	2,837	2,944	7.0	10.6	14.7
Secretaries, except legal and medical	2,842	2,983	3,109	3,258	5.0	9.4	14.6
Clerical supervisors and managers	1,340	1,550	1,600	1,658	15.7	19.5	23.8
Child care workers	757	1,009	1,005	1,006	33.2	32.8	33.0
Maintenance repairers, general utility	1,273	1,431	1,505	1,597	12.4	18.2	25.4
Teachers, elementary	1,419	1,509	1,639	1,787	6.3	15.5	25.9
Personal and home care aides	179	382	391	397	114.0	118.7	122.3
Teachers, special education	388	545	593	648	40.6	53.0	67.2
Licensed practical nurses	702	882	899	927	25.7	28.0	32.1
Food service and lodging managers	579	776	771	769	34.0	33.2	32.9
Food preparation workers	1,190	1,368	1,378	1,393	14.9	15.7	17.0
Social workers	557	712	744	778	27.9	33.5	39.8
Lawyers	656	824	839	856	25.6	27.9	30.6
Financial managers	768	919	950	988	19.7	23.6	28.5
Computer engineers	195	355	372	394	81.8	90.4	101.9
Hand packers and packagers	942	1,070	1,102	1,137	13.6	17.0	20.7
Correction officers	310	430	468	513	38.5	50.9	65.2
College and university faculty	823	893	972	1,062	8.6	18.2	29.1
Adjustment clerks	373	505	521	540	35.1	39.6	44.6
Teachers, preschool and kindergarten	462	588	602	620	27.2	30.3	34.2
Amusement and recreation attendants	267	398	406	414	49.2	52.0	55.2
Automotive mechanics	736	840	862	882	14.2	17.1	19.9
Residential counselors	165	284	290	295	72.7	76.5	79.5
General office clerks	2,946	2,959	3,071	3,204	0.5	4.3	8.8
Human services workers	168	284	293	303	68.8	74.5	80.0
Cooks, restaurant	704	839	827	815	19.3	17.5	15.8
Medical assistants	206	329	327	324	59.9	59.0	57.9
Accountants and auditors	962	1,056	1,083	1,119	9.7	12.6	16.3
Physicians	539	659	659	661	22.3	22.3	22.7
Marketing, advertising, and public relations managers	461	558	575	595	21.1	24.8	29.2
Police patrol officers	400	469	511	560	17.3	27.9	40.2
Counter and rental clerks	341	438	451	464	28.3	32.0	36.0
Cooks, short order and fast food	760	884	869	855	16.2	14.3	12.4
Instructors and coaches, sports and physical training	282	365	381	399	29.2	34.8	41.1
Engineering, mathematical, and natural science managers	337	415	432	453	23.3	28.1	34.5
Bill and account collectors	250	334	342	351	33.3	36.5	40.1
Securities and financial services sales workers	246	328	335	343	33.6	36.6	39.5
Instructors, adult (nonvocational) education	290	366	376	387	26.1	29.4	33.4
Hairdressers, hairstylists, and cosmetologists	595	675	677	680	13.4	13.8	14.3
Carpenters	992	1,044	1,074	1,122	5.2	8.3	13.2
Management analysts	231	308	312	319	33.4	35.4	38.2
Teachers and instructors, vocational ed. and training	299	356	381	409	19.0	27.2	36.6
Physical therapists	102	182	183	185	78.9	80.0	81.9
Dental assistants	190	271	269	266	43.1	41.9	40.0
Designers, except interior designers	238	308	314	322	29.3	31.9	35.1
Painters and paperhangers, construction and maintenance	439	497	509	529	13.3	16.0	20.6
Electrical and electronics engineers	349	402	417	439	15.3	19.7	25.9
Legal secretaries	281	341	350	358	21.3	24.3	27.3
Helpers, construction trades	513	549	581	630	6.9	13.2	22.8
Personnel, training, and labor relations specialists	307	360	374	391	17.2	21.9	27.4
Heat, air conditioning, and refrigeration mechanics [4]	233	286	299	319	22.9	28.5	36.8
Education administrators	393	431	459	491	9.8	16.9	25.0
Bus drivers, school	404	439	470	503	8.7	16.4	24.6
Computer programmers	537	577	601	631	7.4	12.0	17.6

[1] Based on low, moderate, or high trend assumptions.   [2] Includes other occupations, not shown separately.   [3] Includes maids and housekeepers.   [4] Includes installers.

Source: U.S. Bureau of Labor Statistics, *Monthly Labor Review*, November 1995.

No. 639. Civilian Employment in the Fastest Growing and Fastest Declining Occupations: 1994 to 2005

[Occupations are in order of employment percent change 1994-2005 (moderate growth). Includes wage and salary jobs, self-employed, and unpaid family members. Estimates based on the Current Employment Statistics estimates and the Occupational Employment Statistics estimates. See source for methodological assumptions. Minus sign (-) indicates decrease]

OCCUPATION	EMPLOYMENT (1,000)				PERCENT CHANGE 1994-2005		
	1994	2005 [1]			Low	Mod-erate	High
		Low	Mod-erate	High			
Total, all occupations [2]	127,015	140,261	144,708	150,212	10.4	13.9	18.3
FASTEST GROWING							
Personal and home care aides	179	382	391	397	114.0	118.7	122.3
Home health aides	420	832	848	863	98.3	102.0	105.7
Systems analysts	483	893	928	972	84.9	92.1	101.3
Computer engineers	195	355	372	394	81.8	90.4	101.9
Physical and corrective therapy assistants and aides	78	141	142	143	82.3	83.1	84.5
Electronic pagination systems workers	18	32	33	34	77.2	82.8	88.2
Occupational therapy assistants and aides	16	28	29	29	80.0	82.1	86.5
Physical therapists	102	182	183	185	78.9	80.0	81.9
Residential counselors	165	284	290	295	72.7	76.5	79.5
Human services workers	168	284	293	303	68.8	74.5	80.0
Occupational therapists	54	91	93	95	68.7	72.2	77.3
Manicurists	38	63	64	64	68.7	69.5	69.9
Medical assistants	206	329	327	324	59.9	59.0	57.9
Paralegals	110	170	175	179	54.3	58.3	62.4
Medical records technicians	81	125	126	130	53.5	55.8	59.8
Teachers, special education	388	545	593	648	40.6	53.0	67.2
Amusement and recreation attendants	267	398	406	414	49.2	52.0	55.2
Correction officers	310	430	468	513	38.5	50.9	65.2
Operations research analysts	44	65	67	69	45.5	50.0	55.8
Guards	867	1,248	1,282	1,322	44.0	47.9	52.5
Speech-language pathologists and audiologists	85	120	125	130	40.3	46.0	52.8
Detectives, except public	55	77	79	80	41.7	44.3	47.2
Surgical technologists	46	64	65	68	39.3	42.5	48.6
Dental hygienists	127	182	180	178	43.3	42.1	40.1
Dental assistants	190	271	269	266	43.1	41.9	40.0
Adjustment clerks	373	505	521	540	35.1	39.6	44.6
Teacher aides and educational assistants	932	1,211	1,296	1,393	29.9	39.0	49.5
Data processing equipment repairers	75	100	104	108	33.3	38.2	44.1
Nursery and greenhouse managers	19	26	26	26	38.3	37.5	37.3
Securities and financial services sales workers	246	328	335	343	33.6	36.6	39.5
Bill and account collectors	250	334	342	351	33.3	36.5	40.1
Respiratory therapists	73	96	99	104	32.3	36.4	43.8
Pest controllers and assistants	56	75	76	78	33.2	35.6	38.6
Emergency medical technicians	138	178	187	197	29.0	35.6	42.6
FASTEST DECLINING							
Letterpress operators	14	4	4	4	-72.2	-71.3	-70.5
Typesetting and composing machine operators [3]	20	6	6	6	-72.0	-71.1	-70.2
Directory assistance operators	33	10	10	10	-71.5	-70.4	-69.4
Station installers and repairers, telephone	37	10	11	11	-71.5	-70.4	-69.4
Central office operators	48	14	14	15	-71.4	-70.3	-69.2
Billing, posting, and calculating machine operators	96	32	32	33	-67.2	-66.7	-66.1
Data entry keyers, composing	19	6	6	7	-67.7	-66.6	-65.5
Shoe sewing machine operators and tenders	14	4	5	7	-70.9	-63.6	-53.8
Roustabouts	28	13	13	16	-54.2	-55.0	-43.5
Peripheral EDP equipment operators	30	13	13	14	-56.9	-54.8	-52.3
Cooks, private household	9	5	5	4	-48.1	-49.2	-50.5
Motion picture projectionists	8	4	4	4	-46.4	-47.3	-48.0
Rail yard engineers, dinkey operators, and hostlers	6	3	4	4	-44.3	-40.4	-36.5
Central office and PBX installers and repairers	84	50	51	53	-41.0	-39.1	-37.1
Computer operators, except peripheral equipment	259	157	162	168	-39.6	-37.7	-35.3
Statement clerks	25	15	16	16	-39.8	-37.7	-35.5
Housekeepers and butlers	20	13	12	12	-36.1	-37.5	-39.1
Drilling/boring machine tool setters and set-up operators [4]	45	28	30	32	-38.1	-34.9	-29.6
Fitters, structural metal, precision	14	9	9	10	-38.3	-34.6	-29.4
Mining, quarrying, and tunneling occupations	18	11	12	13	-39.5	-33.9	-27.8
Typists and word processors	646	418	434	452	-35.2	-32.8	-30.0
Photoengraving and lithographic machine operators [3]	5	3	3	3	-33.7	-32.1	-30.5
Boiler operators and tenders, low pressure	18	12	12	13	-34.5	-31.9	-29.1
Railroad brake, signal, and switch operators	19	12	13	14	-35.8	-30.8	-26.1
Lathe and turning machine tool setters and set-up operators [4]	71	47	50	54	-34.2	-30.6	-24.9
Cement and gluing machine operators and tenders	36	24	25	27	-34.0	-30.1	-25.3
EKG technicians	16	11	11	12	-31.5	-29.7	-26.6
Machine tool cutting operators and tenders, metal and plastic	119	80	85	92	-32.8	-28.9	-22.8
Paste-up workers	22	16	16	17	-30.1	-27.8	-25.7
Shoe and leather workers and repairers, precision	24	16	17	19	-33.8	-27.6	-19.4
Bank tellers	559	391	407	423	-30.1	-27.3	-24.4

[1] Based on low, moderate, or high trend assumptions. [2] Includes other occupations, not shown separately. [3] Includes tenders. [4] Includes metal and plastic.

Source: U.S. Bureau of Labor Statistics, *Monthly Labor Review*, November 1995.

No. 640. Occupations of the Employed, by Selected Characteristics: 1995

[In thousands. Annual averages of monthly figures. For civilian noninstitutional population 25 to 64 years old. Based on Current Population Survey; see text, section 1, and Appendix III]

SEX, RACE, AND EDUCATIONAL ATTAINMENT	Total employed	Managerial/ profes- sional	Tech./sales/ adminis- trative	Service [1]	Precision produc- tion [2]	Operators/ fabrica- tors [3]	Farming, forestry, fishing
Male, total [4]	55,312	16,860	10,650	4,511	10,805	10,473	2,012
Less than a high school diploma	6,205	308	437	735	1,677	2,416	632
High school graduates, no college	17,840	1,949	2,893	1,768	5,184	5,262	785
Less than a bachelor's degree.	14,641	3,493	3,805	1,460	3,220	2,282	380
College graduates	16,627	11,111	3,515	547	724	514	216
White.	47,720	15,154	9,323	3,381	9,610	8,439	1,812
Less than a high school diploma . .	5,035	259	356	522	1,430	1,950	517
High school graduates, no college .	15,228	1,773	2,510	1,269	4,675	4,281	720
Less than a bachelor's degree . . .	12,630	3,122	3,312	1,149	2,880	1,805	361
College graduates	14,828	9,999	3,146	440	626	404	213
Black.	5,285	1,045	878	840	829	1,590	104
Less than a high school diploma . .	713	30	45	125	155	310	48
High school graduates, no college .	2,061	133	295	401	376	811	45
Less than a bachelor's degree . . .	1,514	269	355	244	240	395	11
College graduates	997	612	184	70	57	73	1
Female, total [4]	47,059	15,464	18,962	7,354	1,057	3,653	568
Less than a high school diploma	3,930	221	760	1,602	186	1,035	126
High school graduates, no college	15,977	2,218	7,719	3,394	510	1,901	236
Less than a bachelor's degree.	14,249	3,921	7,453	1,887	273	586	131
College graduates	12,903	9,104	3,031	471	90	132	75
White.	39,442	13,504	16,236	5,570	845	2,754	533
Less than a high school diploma . .	2,983	176	638	1,141	140	781	107
High school graduates, no college .	13,459	1,969	6,829	2,581	408	1,447	225
Less than a bachelor's degree . . .	11,861	3,403	6,203	1,476	226	425	129
College graduates	11,139	7,956	2,566	372	71	101	73
Black.	5,712	1,396	2,076	1,430	139	659	12
Less than a high school diploma . .	656	30	90	358	21	152	5
High school graduates, no college .	2,012	193	711	670	70	363	6
Less than a bachelor's degree . . .	1,922	412	1,005	339	38	127	1
College graduates	1,121	761	270	62	11	16	-

- Represents or rounds to zero. [1] Includes private household workers. [2] Includes craft and repair. [3] Includes laborers. [4] Includes other races, not shown separately.

Source: U.S. Bureau of Labor Statistics, unpublished data.

No. 641. Employment, by Industry: 1970 to 1994

[In thousands, except percent. See headnote, table 622. Data from 1985 to 1990, and also beginning 1994, not strictly comparable with other years due to changes in industrial classification]

INDUSTRY	1970	1980	1990 [1]	1994 [1]	1995 Total	Percent Female	Percent Black	Percent Hispanic[2]
Total employed.	78,678	99,303	118,793	123,060	124,900	46.1	10.6	8.9
Agriculture	3,463	3,364	3,223	3,409	3,440	25.6	2.9	17.5
Mining	516	979	724	669	627	13.4	3.8	5.8
Construction	4,818	6,215	7,764	7,493	7,668	9.9	6.6	10.4
Manufacturing	20,746	21,942	21,346	20,157	20,493	31.6	10.4	10.2
Transportation, communication, and other public utilities.	5,320	6,525	8,168	8,692	8,709	28.9	14.5	7.7
Wholesale and retail trade.	15,008	20,191	24,622	25,699	26,071	47.2	8.6	9.8
Wholesale trade.	2,672	3,920	4,669	4,713	4,986	29.2	6.3	9.7
Retail trade	12,336	16,270	19,953	20,986	21,086	51.5	9.1	9.8
Finance, insurance, real estate.	3,945	5,993	8,051	8,141	7,983	58.3	9.3	6.7
Services [3]	20,385	28,752	39,267	42,986	43,953	61.9	12.0	7.9
Business and repair services [3]	1,403	3,848	7,485	7,304	7,526	36.5	11.3	10.2
Advertising.	147	191	277	272	267	52.3	3.8	7.0
Services to dwellings and buildings	(NA)	370	827	849	829	47.7	16.6	20.6
Personnel supply services	(NA)	235	710	804	853	59.4	19.6	9.0
Computer and data processing . . .	(NA)	221	805	1,017	1,136	34.8	8.2	3.9
Detective/protective services	(NA)	213	378	477	506	20.4	22.7	9.2
Automobile services	600	952	1,457	1,546	1,459	13.6	9.9	13.1
Personal services [3]	4,276	3,839	4,733	4,339	4,375	69.2	14.2	15.4
Private households	1,782	1,257	1,036	976	971	89.6	18.3	23.2
Hotels and lodging places.	979	1,149	1,818	1,464	1,495	55.7	15.6	15.9
Entertainment and recreation . . . . [3]	717	1,047	1,526	2,134	2,238	43.6	8.1	7.9
Professional and related services [3] . .	12,904	19,853	25,351	29,030	29,661	68.9	12.1	6.2
Hospitals.	2,843	4,036	4,700	5,009	4,961	76.1	16.2	6.0
Health services, except hospitals . .	1,628	3,345	4,673	5,579	5,967	79.1	13.5	6.8
Elementary, secondary schools . . .	6,126	5,550	5,994	6,447	6,653	74.6	11.7	7.3
Colleges and universities	(4)	2,108	2,637	2,743	2,768	52.9	10.3	5.2
Social services	828	1,590	2,239	3,046	2,979	80.8	17.5	7.7
Legal services	429	776	1,215	1,286	1,335	55.7	5.7	4.8
Public administration [5]	4,476	5,342	5,627	5,814	5,957	44.1	16.9	6.1

NA Not available. [1] See footnote 2, table 614. [2] Persons of Hispanic origin may be of any race. [3] Includes industries not shown separately. [4] Included with elementary/secondary schools. [5] Includes workers involved in uniquely governmental activities, e.g., judicial and legislative.

Source: U.S. Bureau of Labor Statistics, Employment and Earnings, monthly, January issues.

No. 642. Employment by Selected Industry, With Projections: 1983 to 2005

[Figures may differ from those in other tables since these data exclude establishments not elsewhere classified (SIC 99); in addition, agriculture services (SIC 074, 5, 8) are included in agriculture, not services. See source for details. Minus sign (-) indicates decrease]

INDUSTRY	1987 SIC [1] code	EMPLOYMENT (1,000)			ANNUAL GROWTH RATE	
		1983	1994	2005, proj. [2]	1983-1994	1994-2005, proj. [2]
Total	(X)	102,404	127,014	144,708	2.0	1.2
Nonfarm wage and salary	(X)	89,734	113,340	130,185	2.1	1.3
Goods-producing (excluding agriculture)	(X)	23,328	23,914	22,930	0.2	-0.4
Mining	10-14	952	601	439	-4.1	-2.8
Construction	15,16,17	3,946	5,010	5,500	2.2	0.9
Manufacturing	20-39	18,430	18,304	16,991	-0.1	-0.7
Durable manufacturing	24,25,32-39	10,707	10,431	9,290	-0.2	-1.0
Lumber and wood products	24	670	752	685	1.1	-0.9
Furniture and fixtures	25	448	502	515	1.0	0.2
Stone, clay and glass products	32	541	533	434	-0.1	-1.8
Primary metal industries	33	832	699	532	-1.6	-2.5
Blast furnaces/basic steel products	331	341	239	155	-3.2	-3.9
Fabricated metal products	34	1,368	1,387	1,181	0.1	-1.5
Industrial machinery and equipment	35	2,052	1,985	1,769	-0.3	-1.0
Computer equipment	357	474	351	263	-2.7	-2.6
Electronic and other electric equipment [3]	36	1,704	1,571	1,408	-0.7	-1.0
Communications equipment	366	279	244	210	-1.2	-1.3
Electronic components	367	563	544	553	-0.3	0.1
Transportation equipment	37	1,731	1,749	1,567	0.1	-1.0
Motor vehicles and equipment	371	754	899	775	1.6	-1.3
Instruments and related products [3]	38	990	863	798	-1.2	-0.7
Measuring/controlling devices	382	300	284	248	-0.5	-1.2
Medical instruments and supplies	384	198	265	306	2.7	1.3
Miscellaneous manufacturing industries	39	370	391	404	0.5	0.3
Nondurable manufacturing	20-23,26-31	7,723	7,873	7,700	0.2	-0.2
Food and kindred products	20	1,612	1,680	1,696	0.4	0.1
Tobacco manufactures	21	68	42	26	-4.2	-4.2
Textile mill products	22	742	673	568	-0.9	-1.5
Apparel and other textile products	23	1,163	969	772	-1.6	-2.1
Paper and allied products	26	654	691	708	0.5	0.2
Printing and publishing	27	1,298	1,542	1,627	1.6	0.5
Chemicals and allied products	28	1,043	1,061	1,067	0.2	0.1
Petroleum and coal products	29	196	149	140	-2.4	-0.5
Rubber/misc. plastics products	30	743	952	1,030	2.3	0.7
Leather and leather products	31	205	114	65	-5.2	-4.9
Service producing	(X)	66,407	89,425	107,256	2.7	1.7
Transportation, communications, utilities	40-42,44-49	4,958	6,006	6,431	1.8	0.6
Transportation	40-42,44-47	2,748	3,775	4,251	2.9	1.1
Communications	48	1,324	1,305	1,235	-0.1	-0.5
Electric, gas, and sanitary services	49	887	927	945	0.4	0.2
Wholesale trade	50,51	5,283	6,140	6,559	1.4	0.6
Retail trade	52-59	15,587	20,438	23,094	2.5	1.1
Eating and drinking places	58	5,038	7,069	8,089	3.1	1.2
Finance, insurance, and real estate	60-67	5,466	6,933	7,373	2.2	0.6
Services	70-87,89	19,242	30,792	42,810	4.4	3.0
Hotels and other lodging places	70	1,172	1,618	1,899	3.0	1.5
Personal services	72	869	1,139	1,374	2.5	1.7
Business services [3]	73	2,948	6,239	10,032	7.1	4.4
Advertising	731	171	224	250	2.5	1.0
Services to buildings	734	559	855	1,350	3.9	4.2
Personnel supply services	736	619	2,254	3,564	12.5	4.3
Computer and data processing services	737	416	950	1,611	7.8	4.9
Auto repair, services, and garages	75	619	971	1,345	4.2	3.0
Miscellaneous repair shops	76	287	334	400	1.4	1.7
Motion pictures	78	268	471	591	5.3	2.1
Video tape rental	784	54	138	165	8.9	1.7
Amusement and recreation services	79	853	1,344	1,844	4.2	2.9
Health services	80	5,986	9,001	12,075	3.8	2.7
Offices of health practitioners	801,2,3,4	1,503	2,546	3,525	4.9	3.0
Nursing and personal care facilities	805	1,106	1,649	2,400	3.7	3.5
Hospitals, private	806	3,037	3,774	4,250	2.0	1.1
Health services, n.e.c. [4]	807,8,9	341	1,032	1,900	10.6	5.7
Legal services	81	602	927	1,270	4.0	2.9
Educational services	82	1,225	1,822	2,400	3.7	2.5
Social services	83	1,188	2,181	3,639	5.7	4.8
Museums, botanical, zoological gardens	84	43	79	112	5.8	3.2
Membership organizations	86	1,510	2,059	2,336	2.9	1.2
Engineering, management, and services	87,89	1,673	2,607	3,494	4.1	2.7
Government	(X)	15,870	19,117	20,990	1.7	0.9
Federal government	(X)	2,774	2,870	2,635	0.3	-0.8
State and local government	(X)	13,096	16,247	18,355	2.0	1.1
Agriculture	01,02,07,08,09	3,508	3,623	3,399	0.3	-0.6
Private households	88	1,247	966	800	-2.3	-1.7
Nonagriculture self-employed and unpaid family	(X)	7,914	9,085	10,324	1.3	1.2

X Not applicable. [1] 1987 Standard Industrial Classification; see text, section 13. [2] Based on assumptions of moderate growth; see source. [3] Includes other industries, not shown separately. [4] N.e.c. means not elsewhere classified.

Source: U.S. Bureau of Labor Statistics, *Monthly Labor Review*, November 1995.

No. 643. High Technology Industries—Summary: 1994

[For workers on private industry payrolls and excludes the self-employed. Based on surveys of the Occupational Employment Statistics Program and subject to sampling error; for details see source]

INDUSTRY	1987 SIC [1] code	Establish-ments (1,000)	EMPLOYMENT		Average annual pay (dol.)
			Total (1,000)	Percent distribution	
All high technology industries [2]	(X)	**374.4**	**9,515**	**100.0**	**43,262**
Level I industries [3]	(X)	337.2	8,200	86.2	44,669
Crude petroleum and natural gas operations	131	9.2	162	1.7	58,425
Cigarettes	211	(Z)	30	0.3	55,698
Industrial inorganic chemicals	281	1.6	132	1.4	47,603
Plastics materials and synthetics	282	1.1	162	1.7	46,395
Drugs	283	1.9	263	2.8	50,500
Soap, cleaners, and toilet goods	284	2.6	152	1.6	41,857
Paints and allied products	285	1.6	58	0.6	38,639
Industrial organic chemicals	286	1.1	143	1.5	53,852
Agricultural chemicals	287	1.2	55	0.6	43,457
Miscellaneous chemical products	289	2.7	93	1.0	42,374
Petroleum refining	291	0.7	109	1.1	57,622
Miscellaneous petroleum and coal products	299	0.5	13	0.1	38,442
Nonferrous rolling and drawing	335	1.3	167	1.8	37,488
Computer and office equipment	357	2.9	353	3.7	50,534
Electrical industrial apparatus	362	2.0	156	1.6	32,390
Communications equipment	366	2.4	244	2.6	43,815
Electronic components and accessories	367	6.8	545	5.7	38,006
Motor vehicles and equipment	371	6.1	899	9.4	45,937
Aircraft and parts	372	2.8	480	5.0	46,696
Guided missiles, space vehicles, parts	376	0.3	108	1.1	52,389
Search and navigation equipment	381	0.9	182	1.9	49,110
Measuring and controlling devices	382	5.4	284	3.0	39,611
Medical instruments and supplies	384	4.6	265	2.8	36,929
Photographic equipment and supplies	386	0.9	88	0.9	47,981
Computer and data-processing services	737	72.5	955	10.0	47,384
Engineering and architectural services	871	67.4	774	8.1	42,687
Research and testing services	873	24.5	560	5.9	39,717
Management and public relations	874	102.7	728	7.7	44,000
Services, n.e.c. [4]	899	9.5	41	0.4	49,216
Level II industries [5]	(X)	37.2	1,315	13.8	34,483
Miscellaneous textile goods	229	1.0	53	0.6	28,825
Pulp mills	261	0.1	13	0.1	47,529
Miscellaneous converted paper products	267	3.2	246	2.6	33,650
Ordinance and accessories, n.e.c. [4]	348	0.5	53	0.6	36,828
Engines and turbines	351	0.5	90	0.9	45,401
General industry machinery	356	4.7	242	2.5	35,602
Industrial machines, n.e.c. [4]	359	23.0	321	3.4	30,927
Household audio and video equipment	365	1.2	89	0.9	37,093
Miscellaneous electrical equipment and supplies	369	1.9	158	1.7	35,221
Miscellaneous transportation equipment	379	1.2	50	0.5	29,597

X Not applicable.   Z Fewer than 50.   [1] 1987 Standard Industrial Classification; see text, section 13.   [2] Those industries whose proportion of R&D employment is at least equal to the average proportion of all industries surveyed.   [3] Industries whose proportion of R&D employment is at least 50 percent higher than the average of all industries surveyed.   [4] N.e.c. means not elsewhere classified.   [5] Industries whose proportion of R&D employment is at least equal to the average of all industries surveyed, but less than 50 percent higher than the average.

Source: U.S. Bureau of Labor Statistics, *Employment and Wages, Annual Averages 1994*, BLS Bulletin 2467.

No. 644. Unemployed Workers—Summary: 1980 to 1995

[**In thousands, except as indicated**. For civilian noninstitutional population 16 years old and over. Annual averages of monthly figures. For data on unemployment insurance, see table 590. See also *Historical Statistics, Colonial Times to 1970*, series D 87-101]

AGE, SEX, RACE, HISPANIC ORIGIN	1980	1985	1990 [1]	1991	1992	1993	1994 [1]	1995
UNEMPLOYED								
Total [2]	7,637	8,312	7,047	8,628	9,613	8,940	7,996	7,404
16 to 19 years old	1,669	1,468	1,212	1,359	1,427	1,365	1,320	1,346
20 to 24 years old	1,835	1,738	1,299	1,573	1,649	1,514	1,373	1,244
25 to 44 years old	2,964	3,681	3,323	4,166	4,678	4,291	3,694	3,390
45 to 64 years old	1,075	1,331	1,109	1,419	1,727	1,662	1,456	1,269
65 years and over	94	93	105	113	132	108	153	153
Male	4,267	4,521	3,906	4,946	5,523	5,055	4,367	3,983
16 to 19 years old	913	806	667	751	806	768	740	744
20 to 24 years old	1,076	944	715	911	951	865	768	673
25 to 44 years old	1,619	1,950	1,803	2,365	2,647	2,387	1,968	1,776
45 to 64 years old	600	766	662	855	1,053	972	803	697
65 years and over	58	55	59	64	67	64	88	94
Female	3,370	3,791	3,140	3,683	4,090	3,885	3,629	3,421
16 to 19 years old	755	661	544	608	621	597	580	602
20 to 24 years old	760	794	584	662	698	648	605	571
25 to 44 years old	1,345	1,732	1,519	1,799	2,031	1,905	1,726	1,615
45 to 64 years old	473	566	447	564	673	690	653	574
65 years and over	36	39	46	49	66	45	66	60
White [3]	5,884	6,191	5,186	6,560	7,169	6,655	5,892	5,459
16 to 19 years old	1,291	1,074	903	1,029	1,037	992	960	952
20 to 24 years old	1,364	1,235	899	1,132	1,156	1,057	952	866
Black [3]	1,553	1,864	1,565	1,723	2,011	1,844	1,666	1,538
16 to 19 years old	343	357	268	280	324	313	300	325
20 to 24 years old	426	455	349	378	421	387	351	311
Hispanic [3][4]	620	811	876	1,092	1,311	1,248	1,187	1,140
16 to 19 years old	145	141	161	179	219	201	198	205
20 to 24 years old	138	171	167	214	240	237	220	209
Full-time workers	6,269	6,793	5,677	7,088	7,923	7,305	6,513	5,909
Part-time workers	1,369	1,519	1,369	1,540	1,690	1,635	1,483	1,495
UNEMPLOYMENT RATE (percent) [5]								
Total [2]	7.1	7.2	5.6	6.8	7.5	6.9	6.1	5.6
16 to 19 years old	17.8	18.6	15.5	18.7	20.1	19.0	17.6	17.3
20 to 24 years old	11.5	11.1	8.8	10.8	11.4	10.5	9.7	9.1
25 to 44 years old	6.0	6.2	4.9	6.1	6.8	6.2	5.3	4.8
45 to 64 years old	3.7	4.5	3.5	4.4	5.1	4.8	4.0	3.4
65 years and over	3.1	3.2	3.0	3.3	3.8	3.2	4.0	4.0
Male	6.9	7.0	5.7	7.2	7.9	7.2	6.2	5.6
16 to 19 years old	18.3	19.5	16.3	19.8	21.5	20.4	19.0	18.4
20 to 24 years old	12.5	11.4	9.1	11.6	12.2	11.3	10.2	9.2
25 to 44 years old	5.6	5.9	4.8	6.3	7.0	6.3	5.2	4.7
45 to 64 years old	3.5	4.5	3.7	4.8	5.7	5.1	4.1	3.5
65 years and over	3.1	3.1	3.0	3.3	3.3	3.2	4.0	4.3
Female	7.4	7.4	5.5	6.4	7.0	6.6	6.0	5.6
16 to 19 years old	17.2	17.6	14.7	17.5	18.6	17.5	16.2	16.1
20 to 24 years old	10.4	10.7	8.5	9.8	10.3	9.7	9.2	9.0
25 to 44 years old	6.4	6.6	4.9	5.8	6.5	6.1	5.4	5.0
45 to 64 years old	4.0	4.6	3.2	3.9	4.4	4.4	3.9	3.3
65 years and over	3.1	3.3	3.1	3.3	4.5	3.1	4.0	3.7
White [3]	6.3	6.2	4.8	6.1	6.6	6.1	5.3	4.9
16 to 19 years old	15.5	15.7	13.5	16.5	17.2	16.2	15.1	14.5
20 to 24 years old	9.9	9.2	7.3	9.2	9.5	8.8	8.1	7.7
Black [3]	14.3	15.1	11.4	12.5	14.2	13.0	11.5	10.4
16 to 19 years old	38.5	40.2	30.9	36.1	39.7	38.8	35.2	35.7
20 to 24 years old	23.6	24.5	19.9	21.6	23.8	21.9	19.5	17.7
Hispanic [3][4]	10.1	10.5	8.2	10.0	11.6	10.8	9.9	9.3
16 to 19 years old	22.5	24.3	19.5	22.9	27.5	26.1	24.5	24.1
20 to 24 years old	12.1	12.6	9.1	11.6	13.2	13.1	11.8	11.5
Experienced workers [6]	6.9	6.8	5.3	6.6	7.2	6.6	5.9	5.4
Women maintaining families [2]	9.2	10.4	8.3	9.3	10.0	9.7	8.9	8.0
White	7.3	8.1	6.3	7.2	7.9	7.8	(NA)	(NA)
Black	14.0	16.4	13.2	13.9	14.8	13.9	(NA)	(NA)
Married men, wife present [2]	4.2	4.3	3.4	4.4	5.1	4.4	3.7	3.3
White	3.9	4.0	3.1	4.2	4.7	4.1	3.4	3.0
Black	7.4	8.0	6.2	6.6	8.3	7.2	6.0	5.0
Percent without work for—								
Fewer than 5 weeks	43.2	42.1	46.3	40.3	35.1	36.5	34.1	36.5
5 to 10 weeks	23.4	22.2	23.5	22.9	20.9	20.6	20.6	22.0
11 to 14 weeks	9.0	8.0	8.5	9.5	8.5	8.3	9.5	9.6
15 to 26 weeks	13.8	12.3	11.7	14.4	15.1	14.5	15.5	14.6
27 weeks and over	10.7	15.4	10.0	12.9	20.3	20.1	20.3	17.3
Unemployment duration, average (weeks)	11.9	15.6	12.0	13.7	17.7	18.0	18.8	16.6

NA Not available. [1] See footnote 2, table 614. [2] Includes other races, not shown separately. [3] Includes other ages, not shown separately. [4] Persons of Hispanic origin may be of any race. [5] Unemployed as percent of civilian labor force in specified group. [6] Wage and salary workers.

Source: U.S. Bureau of Labor Statistics, *Employment and Earnings*, monthly, January issues; and unpublished data.

No. 645. Unemployed Persons, by Sex and Reason: 1970 to 1995

[In thousands. For civilian noninstitutional population 16 years old and over. Annual averages of monthly figures. Based on Current Population Survey; see text, section 1, and Appendix III]

SEX AND REASON	1970	1980	1985	1986	1987	1988	1989	1990 [1]	1991	1992	1993	1994 [1]
Male, total	**2,238**	**4,267**	**4,521**	**4,101**	**3,655**	**3,525**	**3,906**	**4,946**	**5,523**	**5,055**	**4,367**	**3,983**
Job losers [2]	1,199	2,649	2,749	2,432	2,078	1,975	2,257	3,172	3,593	3,150	2,416	2,190
Job leavers	282	438	409	494	503	495	528	507	495	507	408	407
Reentrants	533	776	876	761	697	726	806	891	978	939	1,265	1,113
New entrants	224	405	487	413	376	328	315	375	457	459	278	273
Female, total	**1,855**	**3,370**	**3,791**	**3,324**	**3,046**	**3,003**	**3,140**	**3,683**	**4,090**	**3,885**	**3,629**	**3,421**
Job losers [2]	614	1,297	1,390	1,134	1,014	1,008	1,130	1,522	1,796	1,699	1,399	1,286
Job leavers	267	453	468	471	480	529	513	497	507	469	383	417
Reentrants	696	1,152	1,380	1,213	1,112	1,117	1,124	1,247	1,307	1,259	1,521	1,412
New entrants	279	468	552	506	440	349	373	416	480	459	326	306

[1] See footnote 2, table 614.   [2] Beginning 1994, persons who completed temporary jobs are identified separately and are included as job losers.

Source: U.S. Bureau of Labor Statistics, *Employment and Earnings,* monthly, January issues; Bulletin 2307; and unpublished data.

No. 646. Unemployment Rates, by Industry, 1975 to 1995, and by Sex, 1980 and 1995

[In percent. For civilian noninstitutional population 16 years old and over. Annual averages of monthly figures. Rate represents unemployment as a percent of labor force in each specified group. Data for 1985-90, and also beginning 1994, not strictly comparable with other years due to changes in industrial classification]

INDUSTRY	1975	1980	1985	1990 [1]	1994 [1]	1995	MALE		FEMALE	
							1980	1995	1980	1995
All unemployed [2]	**8.5**	**7.1**	**7.2**	**5.6**	**6.1**	**5.6**	**6.9**	**5.6**	**7.4**	**5.6**
Industry: [3]										
Agriculture	10.4	11.0	13.2	9.8	11.3	11.1	9.7	10.6	15.1	12.7
Mining	4.1	6.4	9.5	4.8	5.4	5.2	6.7	5.3	4.5	4.9
Construction	18.0	14.1	13.1	11.1	11.8	11.5	14.6	11.9	8.9	7.5
Manufacturing	10.9	8.5	7.7	5.8	5.6	4.9	7.4	4.2	10.8	6.5
Transportation and public utilities	5.6	4.9	5.1	3.9	4.8	4.5	5.1	4.4	4.4	4.5
Wholesale and retail trade	8.7	7.4	7.6	6.4	7.4	6.5	6.6	5.9	8.3	7.2
Finance, insurance, and real estate	4.9	3.4	3.5	3.0	3.6	3.3	3.2	3.0	3.5	3.4
Services	7.1	5.9	6.2	5.0	5.9	5.4	6.3	5.7	5.8	5.3
Government	4.1	4.1	3.9	2.7	3.4	2.9	3.9	2.9	4.3	3.0

[1] See footnote 2, table 614.   [2] Includes the self-employed, unpaid family workers, and persons with no previous work experience, not shown separately.   [3] Covers unemployed wage and salary workers.

Source: U.S. Bureau of Labor Statistics, *Employment and Earnings,* monthly, January issues.

No. 647. Unemployment by Occupation, 1990 to 1995, and by Sex, 1995

[For civilian noninstitutional population 16 years old and over. Annual averages of monthly data. Rate represents unemployment as a percent of the labor force for each specified group. Based on Current Population Survey; see text, section 1, and Appendix III. See also headnote, table 631]

OCCUPATION	NUMBER (1,000)			UNEMPLOYMENT RATE				
	1990 [1]	1994 [1]	1995	1990 [1]	1994 [1]	1995		
						Total	Male	Female
Total [2]	**7,047**	**7,996**	**7,404**	**5.6**	**6.1**	**5.6**	**5.6**	**5.6**
Managerial and professional specialty	666	907	880	2.1	2.6	2.4	2.3	2.6
Executive, administrative, and managerial	350	454	420	2.3	2.7	2.4	2.2	2.6
Professional specialty	316	453	460	2.0	2.5	2.5	2.4	2.6
Technical sales, and administrative support	1,641	1,962	1,744	4.3	5.0	4.5	3.8	4.8
Technicians and related support	116	127	113	2.9	3.2	2.8	2.7	2.9
Sales occupations	720	907	795	4.8	5.8	5.0	3.6	6.4
Administrative support, including clerical	804	928	836	4.1	4.7	4.3	4.8	4.2
Service occupations	1,139	1,471	1,378	6.6	8.0	7.5	7.5	7.6
Private household	47	91	99	5.6	10.0	10.7	17.4	10.4
Protective service	74	96	86	3.6	4.1	3.7	3.3	5.8
Service except private household and protective	1,018	1,285	1,193	7.1	8.5	7.9	8.9	7.4
Precision production, craft, and repair	861	910	860	5.9	6.3	6.0	6.0	5.6
Mechanics and repairers	175	201	182	3.8	4.3	4.0	4.0	4.0
Construction trades	483	518	501	8.5	9.4	9.0	8.9	9.9
Other precision production, craft, and repair	202	191	177	4.7	4.5	4.2	3.9	5.4
Operators, fabricators, and laborers	1,714	1,761	1,618	8.7	9.0	8.2	7.8	9.6
Machine operators, assemblers, inspectors	727	672	629	8.1	8.0	7.4	6.1	9.4
Transportation and material moving occupations	329	364	329	6.3	6.6	6.0	6.0	6.1
Handlers, equipment cleaners, helpers, laborers	657	725	660	11.6	12.7	11.7	11.7	11.8
Construction laborers	177	172	179	18.1	18.9	18.7	18.1	32.7
Farming, forestry, and fishing	237	333	311	6.4	8.4	7.9	7.5	9.4

[1] See footnote 2, table 614.   [2] Includes persons with no previous work experience and those whose last job was in the Armed Forces.

Source: U.S. Bureau of Labor Statistics, *Employment and Earnings,* monthly, January issues.

No. 648. Unemployment Rates, by Educational Attainment, Sex, and Race: 1970 to 1991

[In percent. As of March. For the civilian noninstitutional population 25 to 64 years of age. Due to a change in the method of reporting educational attainment, 1992 are not comparable with data for earlier years. See table 649 for data beginning 1992. Based on the Current Population Survey; see text, section 1, and Appendix III]

ITEM	1970	1975	1980	1984	1985	1986	1987	1988	1989	1990	1991
Total	**3.3**	**6.9**	**5.0**	**6.6**	**6.1**	**6.1**	**5.7**	**4.7**	**4.4**	**4.5**	**6.1**
Less than 4 years of high school [1] . .	4.6	10.7	8.4	12.1	11.4	11.6	11.1	9.4	8.9	9.6	12.3
4 years of high school, only	2.9	6.9	5.1	7.2	6.9	6.9	6.3	5.4	4.8	4.9	6.7
College: 1-3 years.	2.9	5.5	4.3	5.3	4.7	4.7	4.5	3.7	3.4	3.7	5.0
4 years or more.	1.3	2.5	1.9	2.7	2.4	2.3	2.3	1.7	2.2	1.9	2.9
Male: Total	2.9	6.7	4.9	6.9	6.1	6.2	6.0	5.1	4.7	4.8	6.8
Less than 4 years of high school [1] . .	4.0	10.5	8.2	12.3	11.2	11.7	11.2	10.0	9.4	9.6	13.4
4 years of high school, only	2.4	6.7	5.3	8.1	7.2	7.4	6.7	6.2	5.4	5.3	7.7
College: 1-3 years.	2.7	5.1	4.4	5.2	4.5	4.7	5.0	3.9	3.2	3.9	5.2
4 years or more.	1.1	2.2	1.7	2.7	2.4	2.3	2.5	1.6	2.3	2.1	3.2
Female: Total.	4.0	7.4	5.0	6.1	6.0	5.8	5.2	4.2	4.0	4.2	5.2
Less than 4 years of high school [1] . .	5.7	10.5	8.9	11.7	11.7	11.4	10.9	8.5	8.1	9.5	10.7
4 years of high school, only	3.6	7.1	5.0	6.3	6.5	6.3	5.8	4.6	4.2	4.6	5.5
College: 1-3 years.	3.1	6.3	4.1	5.3	4.8	4.8	4.0	3.4	3.7	3.5	4.8
4 years or more.	1.9	3.4	2.2	2.7	2.5	2.4	2.1	1.9	2.0	1.7	2.5
White: Total.	3.1	6.5	4.4	5.7	5.3	5.5	5.0	4.0	3.8	4.0	5.6
Less than 4 years of high school [1] . .	4.5	10.1	7.8	10.9	10.6	10.9	10.2	8.3	7.7	8.3	11.6
4 years of high school, only	2.7	6.5	4.6	6.4	6.1	6.2	5.5	4.6	4.2	4.4	6.2
College: 1-3 years.	2.8	5.1	3.9	4.6	3.9	4.2	4.1	3.2	3.0	3.3	4.6
4 years or more.	1.3	2.4	1.8	2.4	2.1	2.2	2.2	1.5	2.0	1.8	2.7
Black: Total [2]	4.7	10.9	9.6	13.3	12.0	10.7	10.6	10.0	9.2	8.6	10.1
Less than 4 years of high school [1] . .	5.2	13.5	11.7	17.4	15.3	15.3	14.8	14.6	14.6	15.9	15.9
4 years of high school, only	5.2	10.7	9.5	14.5	13.0	11.7	11.7	11.2	9.2	8.6	10.3
College: 1-3 years.	3.5	9.8	9.0	9.7	10.6	8.7	7.6	7.4	6.9	6.5	8.0
4 years or more.	0.9	3.9	4.0	6.2	5.4	3.2	4.2	3.3	4.7	1.9	5.2

[1] Includes persons reporting no school years completed.   [2] For 1970 and 1975, data refer to Black and other workers.
Source: U.S. Bureau of Labor Statistics, Bulletin 2307; and unpublished data.

No. 649. Unemployed and Unemployment Rates, by Educational Attainment, Sex, Race, and Hispanic Origin: 1992 to 1995

[As of March. For the civilian noninstitutional population 25 to 64 years old. See table 618 for civilian labor force and participation rate data. Based on Current Population Survey; see text, section 1, and Appendix III]

YEAR, SEX, AND RACE	UNEMPLOYED (1,000)					UNEMPLOYMENT RATE [1]				
	Total	Less than high school diploma	High school graduates, no degree	Less than a bachelor's degree	College graduate	Total	Less than high school diploma	High school graduate, no degree	Less than a bachelor's degree	College graduate
Total: [2]										
1992	6,846	1,693	2,851	1,521	782	6.7	13.5	7.7	5.9	2.9
1993	6,596	1,550	2,666	1,492	888	6.4	13.0	7.3	5.5	3.2
1994 [3]	6,126	1,463	2,388	1,453	823	5.8	12.6	6.7	5.0	2.9
1995	5,065	1,150	1,833	1,329	753	4.8	10.0	5.2	4.5	2.5
Male:										
1992 . . .	4,207	1,151	1,709	854	493	7.5	14.8	8.8	6.4	3.2
1993 . . .	4,152	1,059	1,667	882	543	7.3	14.1	8.7	6.3	3.4
1994 [3] . .	3,498	920	1,333	779	466	6.2	12.8	7.2	5.3	2.9
1995 . . .	2,925	765	1,064	656	440	5.1	10.9	5.7	4.4	2.6
Female:										
1992 . . .	2,639	542	1,142	666	289	5.7	11.4	6.5	5.3	2.5
1993 . . .	2,444	490	999	609	345	5.2	11.2	5.8	4.6	2.9
1994 [3] . .	2,628	543	1,055	674	357	5.4	12.4	6.2	4.7	2.9
1995 . . .	2,140	385	770	673	313	4.4	8.6	4.6	4.5	2.4
White:										
1992 . . .	5,247	1,285	2,146	1,176	641	6.0	12.9	6.8	5.3	2.7
1993 . . .	5,129	1,175	2,025	1,166	763	5.8	12.4	6.5	5.0	3.1
1994 [3] . .	4,598	1,092	1,738	1,109	659	5.2	11.7	5.8	4.5	2.6
1995 . . .	3,858	831	1,362	1,054	612	4.3	9.2	4.6	4.2	2.3
Black:										
1992 . . .	1,353	361	619	291	81	12.4	17.2	14.1	10.7	4.8
1993 . . .	1,201	321	542	266	72	10.9	17.3	12.4	8.7	4.1
1994 [3] . .	1,202	286	546	277	94	10.6	17.4	12.2	8.3	4.9
1995 . . .	905	225	377	218	86	7.7	13.7	8.4	6.3	4.1
Hispanic: [4]										
1992 . . .	757	408	224	88	36	9.8	13.6	9.6	5.9	4.2
1993 . . .	826	449	215	117	46	10.3	14.5	9.1	7.0	5.2
1994 [3] . .	871	465	215	139	52	9.7	13.4	8.3	7.2	5.2
1995 . . .	746	393	211	102	40	8.0	10.9	8.1	5.2	3.7

[1] Percent unemployed of the civilian labor force.   [2] Includes other races, not shown separately.   [3] See footnote 3, table 626.   [4] Persons of Hispanic origin may be of any race.
Source: U.S. Bureau of Labor Statistics, unpublished data.

No. 650. Total Unemployed and Insured Unemployed—States: 1980 to 1994

[For civilian noninstitutional population 16 years old and over. Annual averages of monthly figures. Total unemployment estimates based on the Current Population Survey (CPS); see text, section 1, and Appendix III. U.S. totals derived by independent population controls; therefore State data may not add to U.S. totals]

STATE	TOTAL UNEMPLOYED								INSURED UNEMPLOYED [3]			
	Number (1,000)				Percent [1]				Number (1,000)		Percent [4]	
	1980	1985	1990 [2]	1994 [2]	1980	1985	1990 [2]	1994 [2]	1993	1994	1993	1994
United States	7,637	8,312	7,047	7,996	7.1	7.2	5.6	6.1	[5]2,751	[5]2,670	[5]2.6	[5]2.5
Alabama.	147	160	130	122	8.8	8.9	6.9	6.0	33.4	31.0	2.1	1.9
Alaska	18	24	19	24	9.7	9.7	7.0	7.8	12.2	13.6	5.5	6.0
Arizona.	83	96	99	126	6.7	6.5	5.5	6.4	28.0	27.4	1.9	1.8
Arkansas	76	91	78	64	7.6	8.7	7.0	5.3	27.1	24.9	3.0	2.6
California	790	934	874	1,329	6.8	7.2	5.8	8.6	478.6	485.9	3.9	4.0
Colorado.	88	101	89	84	5.9	5.9	5.0	4.2	23.9	23.4	1.6	1.5
Connecticut.	94	83	95	97	5.9	4.9	5.2	5.6	49.5	47.8	3.3	3.2
Delaware	22	17	19	19	7.7	5.3	5.2	4.9	6.8	6.5	2.1	1.9
District of Columbia	24	27	22	24	7.3	8.4	6.6	8.2	9.8	8.9	2.3	2.1
Florida	251	320	390	446	5.9	6.0	6.0	6.6	122.5	99.5	2.3	1.8
Georgia	163	188	182	185	6.4	6.5	5.5	5.2	45.1	40.0	1.6	1.3
Hawaii	21	27	16	35	4.9	5.6	2.9	6.1	12.7	14.8	2.5	2.9
Idaho	34	37	29	33	7.9	7.9	5.9	5.6	13.4	13.2	3.3	3.1
Illinois	459	513	369	340	8.3	9.0	6.2	5.7	136.9	119.4	2.7	2.3
Indiana.	252	215	149	151	9.6	7.9	5.3	4.9	33.6	30.0	1.4	1.2
Iowa	82	112	62	57	5.8	8.0	4.3	3.7	22.4	18.6	1.9	1.5
Kansas.	53	62	57	70	4.5	5.0	4.5	5.3	20.1	18.6	1.9	1.7
Kentucky	133	161	104	98	8.0	9.5	5.9	5.4	29.1	31.6	2.1	2.2
Louisiana	121	229	117	156	6.7	11.5	6.3	8.0	32.1	29.4	2.1	1.9
Maine.	39	30	33	45	7.8	5.4	5.2	7.4	14.2	15.5	2.9	3.1
Maryland	140	104	122	138	6.5	4.6	4.7	5.1	47.2	45.8	2.5	2.4
Massachusetts.	162	120	195	190	5.6	3.9	6.0	6.0	78.7	80.1	2.9	2.9
Michigan.	534	433	350	281	12.4	9.9	7.6	5.9	108.4	92.0	2.9	2.4
Minnesota.	125	133	117	103	5.9	6.0	4.9	4.0	39.1	37.1	1.9	1.7
Mississippi	79	116	90	83	7.5	10.3	7.6	6.6	20.4	19.1	2.2	2.0
Missouri	167	158	151	132	7.2	6.4	5.8	4.9	51.5	47.5	2.3	2.1
Montana.	23	31	24	22	6.1	7.7	6.0	5.1	9.2	9.7	3.2	3.2
Nebraska	31	44	18	25	4.1	5.5	2.2	2.9	8.4	7.2	1.2	1.0
Nevada	27	41	33	48	6.2	8.0	4.9	6.2	17.8	16.0	2.9	2.4
New Hampshire	22	21	36	29	4.7	3.9	5.7	4.6	7.0	6.8	1.5	1.4
New Jersey.	260	217	206	273	7.2	5.7	5.1	6.8	109.9	106.8	3.3	3.2
New Mexico	42	57	46	49	7.5	8.8	6.5	6.3	11.8	11.5	2.2	2.0
New York	597	544	467	593	7.5	6.5	5.3	6.9	223.8	227.6	3.0	3.0
North Carolina	187	168	144	157	6.6	5.4	4.2	4.4	41.5	44.3	1.4	1.4
North Dakota.	15	20	13	13	5.0	5.9	4.0	3.9	4.1	3.9	1.7	1.5
Ohio	426	455	310	307	8.4	8.9	5.7	5.5	96.3	87.3	2.1	1.8
Oklahoma.	66	112	86	90	4.8	7.1	5.7	5.8	18.9	16.7	1.6	1.4
Oregon.	107	116	83	89	8.3	8.8	5.6	5.4	46.3	45.4	3.8	3.6
Pennsylvania.	425	443	315	360	7.8	8.0	5.4	6.2	164.0	169.4	3.4	3.5
Rhode Island.	34	25	35	35	7.2	4.9	6.8	7.1	16.4	18.9	4.0	4.6
South Carolina.	96	107	83	115	6.9	6.8	4.8	6.3	30.5	29.3	2.1	2.0
South Dakota	16	18	13	12	4.9	5.1	3.9	3.3	2.4	2.1	0.9	0.7
Tennessee	152	180	126	127	7.3	8.0	5.3	4.8	42.8	41.4	2.0	1.9
Texas.	352	565	544	605	5.2	7.0	6.3	6.4	137.5	128.7	2.0	1.8
Utah	40	43	35	36	6.3	5.9	4.3	3.7	9.5	8.4	1.4	1.1
Vermont	16	13	15	15	6.4	4.8	5.0	4.7	7.9	7.7	3.3	3.1
Virginia.	128	160	141	166	5.0	5.6	4.3	4.9	30.8	31.0	1.2	1.2
Washington.	156	170	125	174	7.9	8.1	4.9	6.4	83.9	94.4	3.9	4.3
West Virginia.	74	100	64	70	9.4	13.0	8.4	8.9	18.9	18.2	3.2	3.0
Wisconsin	167	171	114	132	7.2	7.2	4.4	4.7	53.9	49.8	2.4	2.2
Wyoming	9	18	13	13	4.0	7.1	5.5	5.3	3.6	3.7	1.9	1.9

[1] Total unemployment as percent of civilian labor force. [2] See footnote 2, table 614. [3] Source: U.S. Employment and Training Administration, *Unemployment Insurance, Financial Handbook,* annual updates. [4] Insured unemployment as percent of average covered employment in the previous year. [5] Includes 57,600 in Puerto Rico and the Virgin Islands in 1993 and 62,100 in 1994.

Source: Except as noted, U.S. Bureau of Labor Statistics, *Geographic Profile of Employment and Unemployment,* annual.

No. 651. Job Openings and Placements and Help-Wanted Advertising: 1970 to 1993

[Openings 1970 and 1980, for years ending Sept. 30; beginning 1985, for years ending June 30]

ITEM	1970	1980	1985	1989	1990	1991	1992	1993	1994
Job openings: [1] Received (1,000) . . .	6,130	8,122	7,529	6,998	5,651	5,635	5,752	6,343	6,619
Average per month	511	677	627	583	471	470	479	529	552
Nonagricultural placements [1] (1,000) .	4,604	5,610	3,270	4,284	3,714	3,507	3,396	3,375	3,360
Index of help-wanted advertising in newspapers [2] (1967=100)	93	128	138	151	129	93	92	101	128

[1] As reported by State employment agencies. Beginning 1985, all placements. Placements include duplication for individuals placed more than once. [2] Source: U.S. Bureau of Economic Analysis, *Survey of Current Business,* monthly (series published through January/February 1996 issue). Based on data from the Conference Board, New York, NY. Index based on the number of advertisements in classified sections of 51 newspapers, each in a major employment area.

Source: Except as noted, U.S. Employment and Training Administration, unpublished data.

No. 652. Nonfarm Establishments—Employees, Hours, and Earnings, by Industry: 1960 to 1995

[Based on data from establishment reports. Includes all full- and part-time employees who worked during, or received pay for, any part of the pay period reported. Excludes proprietors, the self-employed, farm workers, unpaid family workers, private household workers, and Armed Forces. Establishment data shown here conform to industry definitions in the 1987 Standard Industrial Classification and are adjusted to March 1994 employment benchmarks, and reflect historical corrections to previously published data. Based on the Current Employment Statistics Program; see Appendix III. See also *Historical Statistics, Colonial Times to 1970*, series D 127-141 and D 803, 878, 881, 884, and 890]

ITEM AND YEAR	Total	GOODS-PRODUCING				SERVICE-PRODUCING						
		Total	Mining	Construction	Manufacturing	Total	Transportation and public utilities	Wholesale trade	Retail trade	Finance, insurance, and real estate	Services	Government
EMPLOYEES (1,000)												
1960	54,189	20,434	712	2,926	16,796	33,755	4,004	3,153	8,238	2,628	7,378	8,353
1970	70,880	23,578	623	3,588	19,367	47,302	4,515	4,006	11,034	3,645	11,548	12,554
1975	76,945	22,600	752	3,525	18,323	54,345	4,542	4,430	12,630	4,165	13,892	14,686
1980	90,406	25,658	1,027	4,346	20,285	64,748	5,146	5,292	15,018	5,160	17,890	16,241
1985	97,387	24,842	927	4,668	19,248	72,544	5,233	5,727	17,315	5,948	21,927	16,394
1990	109,419	24,905	709	5,120	19,076	84,514	5,793	6,173	19,601	6,709	27,934	18,304
1991	108,256	23,745	689	4,650	18,406	84,511	5,762	6,081	19,284	6,646	28,336	18,402
1992	108,604	23,231	635	4,492	18,104	85,373	5,721	5,997	19,356	6,602	29,052	18,645
1993	110,730	23,352	610	4,668	18,075	87,378	5,829	5,981	19,773	6,757	30,197	18,841
1994	114,172	23,908	601	4,986	18,321	90,264	5,993	6,162	20,507	6,896	31,579	19,128
1995	117,203	24,206	580	5,158	18,468	92,997	6,165	6,412	21,173	6,830	33,107	19,311
PERCENT DISTRIBUTION												
1960	100.0	37.7	1.3	5.4	31.0	62.3	7.4	5.8	15.2	4.8	13.6	15.4
1970	100.0	33.3	0.9	5.1	27.3	66.7	6.4	5.7	15.6	5.1	16.3	17.7
1975	100.0	29.4	1.0	4.6	23.8	70.6	5.9	5.8	16.4	5.4	18.1	19.1
1980	100.0	28.4	1.1	4.8	22.4	71.6	5.7	5.9	16.6	5.7	19.8	18.0
1985	100.0	25.5	1.0	4.8	19.8	74.5	5.4	5.9	17.8	6.1	22.5	16.8
1990	100.0	22.8	0.6	4.7	17.4	77.2	5.3	5.6	17.9	6.1	25.5	16.7
1991	100.0	21.9	0.6	4.3	17.0	78.1	5.3	5.6	17.8	6.1	26.2	17.0
1992	100.0	21.4	0.6	4.1	16.7	78.6	5.3	5.5	17.8	6.1	26.8	17.2
1993	100.0	21.1	0.6	4.2	16.3	78.9	5.3	5.4	17.9	6.1	27.3	17.0
1994	100.0	20.9	0.5	4.4	16.0	79.1	5.2	5.4	18.0	6.0	27.7	16.8
1995	100.0	20.7	0.5	4.4	15.8	79.3	5.3	5.5	18.1	5.8	28.2	16.5
WEEKLY HOURS [1]												
1960	38.6	(NA)	40.4	36.7	39.7	(NA)	(NA)	40.5	38.0	37.2	(NA)	(NA)
1970	37.1	(NA)	42.7	37.3	39.8	(NA)	40.5	39.9	33.8	36.7	34.4	(NA)
1975	36.1	(NA)	41.9	36.4	39.5	(NA)	39.7	38.6	32.4	36.5	33.5	(NA)
1980	35.3	(NA)	43.3	37.0	39.7	(NA)	39.6	38.4	30.2	36.2	32.6	(NA)
1985	34.9	(NA)	43.4	37.7	40.5	(NA)	39.5	38.4	29.4	36.4	32.5	(NA)
1990	34.5	(NA)	44.1	38.2	40.8	(NA)	38.9	38.1	28.8	35.8	32.5	(NA)
1991	34.3	(NA)	44.4	38.1	40.7	(NA)	38.7	38.1	28.6	35.7	32.4	(NA)
1992	34.4	(NA)	43.9	38.0	41.0	(NA)	38.9	38.2	28.8	35.8	32.5	(NA)
1993	34.5	(NA)	44.3	38.5	41.4	(NA)	39.6	38.2	28.8	35.8	32.5	(NA)
1994	34.7	(NA)	44.8	38.9	42.0	(NA)	39.9	38.4	28.9	35.8	32.5	(NA)
1995	34.5	(NA)	44.7	38.8	41.6	(NA)	39.5	38.3	28.8	35.9	32.4	(NA)
HOURLY EARNINGS [1]												
1960	$2.09	(NA)	$2.60	$3.07	$2.26	(NA)	(NA)	$2.24	$1.52	$2.02	(NA)	(NA)
1970	3.23	(NA)	3.85	5.24	3.35	(NA)	3.85	3.43	2.44	3.07	2.81	(NA)
1975	4.53	(NA)	5.95	7.31	4.83	(NA)	5.88	4.72	3.36	4.06	4.02	(NA)
1980	6.66	(NA)	9.17	9.94	7.27	(NA)	8.87	6.95	4.88	5.79	5.85	(NA)
1985	8.57	(NA)	11.98	12.32	9.54	(NA)	11.40	9.15	5.94	7.94	7.90	(NA)
1990	10.01	(NA)	13.68	13.77	10.83	(NA)	12.97	10.79	6.75	9.97	9.83	(NA)
1991	10.32	(NA)	14.19	14.00	11.18	(NA)	13.22	11.15	6.94	10.39	10.23	(NA)
1992	10.57	(NA)	14.54	14.15	11.46	(NA)	13.45	11.39	7.12	10.82	10.54	(NA)
1993	10.83	(NA)	14.60	14.38	11.74	(NA)	13.62	11.74	7.29	11.35	10.78	(NA)
1994	11.12	(NA)	14.88	14.73	12.07	(NA)	13.86	12.06	7.49	11.83	11.04	(NA)
1995	11.44	(NA)	15.30	15.08	12.37	(NA)	14.23	12.43	7.69	12.33	11.39	(NA)
WEEKLY EARNINGS [1]												
1960	$81	(NA)	$105	$113	$90	(NA)	(NA)	$91	$58	$75	(NA)	(NA)
1970	120	(NA)	164	195	133	(NA)	156	137	82	113	97	(NA)
1975	164	(NA)	249	266	191	(NA)	233	182	109	148	135	(NA)
1980	235	(NA)	397	368	289	(NA)	351	267	147	210	191	(NA)
1985	299	(NA)	520	464	386	(NA)	450	351	175	289	257	(NA)
1990	345	(NA)	603	526	442	(NA)	505	411	194	357	319	(NA)
1991	354	(NA)	630	533	455	(NA)	512	425	198	371	331	(NA)
1992	364	(NA)	638	538	470	(NA)	523	435	205	387	343	(NA)
1993	374	(NA)	647	554	486	(NA)	539	448	210	406	350	(NA)
1994	386	(NA)	667	573	507	(NA)	553	463	216	424	359	(NA)
1995	395	(NA)	684	585	515	(NA)	562	476	221	443	369	(NA)

NA Not available. [1] Average hours and earnings. Private production and related workers in mining, manufacturing, and construction; nonsupervisory employees in other industries.

Source: U.S. Bureau of Labor Statistics, Bulletins 2445 and 2481, and *Employment and Earnings*, monthly, March and June issues.

No. 653. Employees in Nonfarm Establishments—States: 1980 to 1995

[**In thousands.** For coverage, see headnote, table 652. National totals differ from the sum of the State figures because of differing benchmarks among States and differing industrial and geographic stratification. Based on 1987 *Standard Industrial Classification Manual*, see text, section 13]

STATE	1980	1994	1995 Total [1]	1995 Con-struc-tion	1995 Manu-factur-ing	1995 Trans-porta-tion and public utilities	1995 Whole-sale and retail trade	1995 Finance, insur-ance, and real estate	1995 Serv-ices	1995 Govern-ment
United States	**90,406**	**114,172**	**117,203**	**5,158**	**18,468**	**6,165**	**27,585**	**6,830**	**33,107**	**19,311**
Alabama	1,356	1,759	1,803	87	391	89	411	77	395	343
Alaska	169	259	262	13	17	23	54	12	61	73
Arizona	1,014	1,692	1,783	117	193	86	449	107	520	299
Arkansas	742	1,034	1,069	44	259	64	242	42	237	177
California	9,849	12,160	12,434	488	1,790	630	2,927	737	3,730	2,102
Colorado	1,251	1,756	1,839	103	191	118	458	113	539	303
Connecticut	1,427	1,544	1,564	51	280	72	341	133	466	221
Delaware	259	356	366	19	62	16	83	41	96	50
District of Columbia	616	659	643	9	13	20	52	30	265	254
Florida	3,576	5,799	6,000	304	482	303	1,548	376	2,056	924
Georgia	2,159	3,266	3,417	152	588	215	865	174	838	575
Hawaii	405	536	533	[2]26	17	41	136	37	165	111
Idaho	330	461	477	30	71	23	121	24	109	96
Illinois	4,850	5,463	5,599	216	967	324	1,317	384	1,577	801
Indiana	2,130	2,713	2,781	130	684	140	669	131	632	389
Iowa	1,110	1,320	1,357	55	250	61	341	77	341	230
Kansas	945	1,166	1,201	52	192	68	296	58	290	238
Kentucky	1,210	1,597	1,643	73	314	91	396	65	392	287
Louisiana	1,579	1,722	1,775	105	188	108	417	80	473	357
Maine	418	532	542	22	92	22	139	26	148	93
Maryland	1,712	2,146	2,181	128	176	106	530	128	690	422
Massachusetts	2,652	2,904	2,974	90	445	128	688	204	1,024	394
Michigan	3,443	4,147	4,252	154	975	166	1,000	196	1,114	639
Minnesota	1,770	2,310	2,374	83	426	117	577	138	645	381
Mississippi	829	1,056	1,075	45	258	50	228	40	232	217
Missouri	1,970	2,471	2,521	111	421	159	603	146	685	390
Montana	280	340	351	16	23	21	96	16	96	77
Nebraska	628	796	815	34	112	49	205	52	210	151
Nevada	400	738	789	62	37	41	157	36	347	97
New Hampshire	385	523	539	19	102	20	141	29	152	76
New Jersey	3,060	3,553	3,606	124	500	252	851	228	1,081	569
New Mexico	465	657	690	46	45	31	164	30	193	165
New York	7,207	7,819	7,871	251	944	403	1,614	724	2,537	1,394
North Carolina	2,380	3,359	3,455	174	861	164	799	144	760	550
North Dakota	245	295	302	14	21	19	79	14	81	71
Ohio	4,367	5,076	5,232	207	1,101	229	1,276	270	1,387	749
Oklahoma	1,138	1,280	1,314	48	170	73	312	65	344	270
Oregon	1,045	1,363	1,417	68	228	71	359	87	364	239
Pennsylvania	4,753	5,192	5,248	201	939	272	1,197	303	1,596	720
Rhode Island	398	434	441	14	85	15	98	25	144	61
South Carolina	1,189	1,607	1,648	87	378	71	384	69	363	294
South Dakota	238	332	344	14	46	16	88	19	88	71
Tennessee	1,747	2,423	2,503	108	542	137	588	110	636	376
Texas	5,851	7,751	8,027	409	1,030	475	1,949	437	2,122	1,449
Utah	551	860	908	54	124	52	220	48	239	163
Vermont	200	264	270	12	45	12	64	12	79	45
Virginia	2,157	3,004	3,068	168	402	157	700	161	872	597
Washington	1,608	2,304	2,349	123	332	120	583	122	622	444
West Virginia	646	675	688	33	82	40	159	27	183	137
Wisconsin	1,938	2,491	2,555	100	601	119	587	136	631	378
Wyoming	210	217	220	14	10	14	52	8	48	58

[1] Includes mining, not shown separately. [2] Hawaii includes mining with construction.

Source: U.S. Bureau of Labor Statistics, *Employment and Earnings*, monthly, May issues. Compiled from data supplied by cooperating State agencies.

No. 654. Nonfarm Industries—Employees and Earnings: 1980 to 1995

[Annual averages of monthly figures. Covers all full- and part-time employees who worked during, or received pay for, any part of the pay period including the 12th of the month. For mining and manufacturing, data refer to production and related workers; for construction, to employees engaged in actual construction work; and for other industries, to nonsupervisory employees and working supervisors. See also headnote table 652. See *Historical Statistics, Colonial Times to 1970,* series D 127-151, D 802-810, and D 877-892, for related data]

INDUSTRY	1987 SIC [1] code	ALL EMPLOYEES TOTAL (1,000)			PRODUCTION WORKERS					
					Total (1,000)			Average hourly earnings (dollars)		
		1980	1990	1995	1980	1990	1995	1980	1990	1995
Total.	(X)	**90,406**	**109,419**	**117,203**	**(NA)**	**(NA)**	**(NA)**	**(NA)**	**(NA)**	**(NA)**
Private sector [2]	(X)	**74,166**	**91,115**	**97,892**	**60,331**	**73,800**	**80,123**	**6.66**	**10.01**	**11.44**
Mining	(B)	**1,027**	**709**	**580**	**762**	**509**	**424**	**9.17**	**13.68**	**15.30**
Metal mining	10	98	58	51	74	46	41	10.26	14.05	16.78
Coal mining	12	246	147	106	204	119	85	10.86	16.71	18.44
Oil and gas extraction	13	560	395	318	389	261	217	8.59	12.94	14.51
Nonmetallic minerals, except fuels	14	123	110	106	96	83	80	7.52	11.58	13.42
Construction	(C)	**4,346**	**5,120**	**5,158**	**3,421**	**3,974**	**3,992**	**9.94**	**13.77**	**15.08**
General building contractors	15	1,173	1,298	1,200	900	938	851	9.22	13.01	14.33
Heavy construction, except building	16	895	770	751	720	643	625	9.20	13.34	14.63
Special trade contractors	17	2,278	3,051	3,207	1,802	2,393	2,516	10.63	14.20	15.46
Manufacturing	(D)	**20,285**	**19,076**	**18,468**	**14,214**	**12,947**	**12,787**	**7.27**	**10.83**	**12.37**
Durable goods	(X)	**12,159**	**11,109**	**10,654**	**8,416**	**7,363**	**7,298**	**7.75**	**11.35**	**12.93**
Lumber and wood products [3]	24	704	733	764	587	603	628	6.57	9.08	10.12
Logging	241	88	85	82	71	70	66	8.64	11.22	11.66
Sawmills and planing mills	242	215	198	187	190	172	162	6.70	9.22	10.31
Millwork, plywood, and structural members	243	206	262	278	170	210	223	6.44	9.04	10.12
Wood containers	244	43	45	51	37	38	43	4.95	6.64	7.68
Mobile homes	2451	46	41	61	36	33	51	6.08	8.67	10.26
Furniture and fixtures [3]	25	466	506	509	376	400	402	5.49	8.52	9.82
Household furniture	251	301	289	281	253	241	235	5.12	7.87	9.29
Office furniture	252	51	68	63	40	51	46	5.91	9.64	10.53
Partitions and fixtures	254	63	78	86	47	57	63	6.68	9.77	10.92
Stone, clay, and glass products [3]	32	629	556	538	486	432	417	7.50	11.12	12.41
Flat glass	321	18	17	15	14	13	12	9.65	15.15	17.95
Glass and glassware, pressed and blown	322	124	83	73	105	72	62	7.97	12.40	14.11
Products of purchased glass	323	45	60	62	32	46	48	6.50	9.75	10.92
Cement, hydraulic	324	31	18	18	25	14	13	10.55	13.90	16.34
Structural clay products	325	46	36	34	34	28	26	6.14	9.55	10.95
Pottery and related products	326	47	39	41	39	31	33	6.25	9.62	10.70
Concrete, gypsum, and plaster	327	204	206	204	157	157	156	7.45	10.76	11.92
Primary metal industries [3]	33	1,142	756	710	878	574	552	9.77	12.92	14.62
Blast furnaces and basic steel products	331	512	276	241	396	212	184	11.39	14.82	17.35
Iron and steel foundries	332	209	132	130	167	105	107	8.20	11.55	13.42
Primary nonferrous metals	333	71	46	40	53	34	31	10.63	14.36	15.83
Nonferrous rolling and drawing	335	211	172	167	151	124	127	8.81	12.29	13.66
Nonferrous foundries (castings)	336	90	84	87	72	66	71	7.30	10.21	11.48
Fabricated metal products [3]	34	1,609	1,419	1,438	1,194	1,045	1,080	7.45	10.83	12.12
Metal cans and shipping containers	341	75	50	41	63	43	35	9.84	14.27	15.73
Cutlery, handtools, and hardware	342	164	131	128	125	96	97	7.02	10.78	12.17
Plumbing and heating, exc. electric	343	71	60	57	52	43	41	6.59	9.75	10.76
Fabricated structural metal products	344	506	427	428	351	303	312	7.27	10.16	11.35
Screw machine products	345	109	96	99	84	73	78	6.96	10.70	12.00
Metal forgings and stampings	346	260	225	252	205	178	202	8.56	12.70	14.23
Industrial machinery and equipment [3]	35	2,517	2,095	2,059	1,614	1,260	1,289	8.00	11.77	13.24
Engines and turbines	351	135	89	89	87	58	56	9.73	14.55	(NA)
Farm and garden machinery	352	169	106	100	116	78	74	8.78	10.99	12.80
Construction and related machinery	353	389	229	222	255	141	144	8.60	11.92	12.88
Metalworking machinery	354	398	330	340	290	236	242	8.13	12.27	13.99
Special industry machinery	355	194	159	172	125	94	99	7.53	11.90	13.64
General industrial machinery	356	300	247	196	196	158	162	7.95	11.32	12.95
Computer and office equipment	357	420	438	351	181	137	122	6.75	11.51	13.11
Refrigeration and service machinery	358	175	177	202	120	125	144	7.23	10.93	11.99
Electronic and other elec. equip. [3]	36	1,771	1,673	1,625	([4])	1,055	1,045	([4])	10.30	11.67
Electric distribution equipment	361	117	97	83	82	67	58	6.96	10.15	11.43
Electrical industrial apparatus	362	232	169	158	163	119	112	([4])	10.00	11.06
Household appliances	363	162	124	122	128	99	99	6.95	10.26	(NA)
Electric lighting and wiring equip.	364	211	189	178	157	136	128	6.43	10.12	11.56
Household audio and video equip.	365	109	85	84	79	59	57	6.42	9.68	10.91
Communications equipment	366	([4])	264	263	([4])	133	130	([4])	11.03	12.04
Electronic components and accessories	367	539	582	582	325	329	349	6.05	10.00	11.49
Transportation equipment [3]	37	1,881	1,989	1,785	1,220	1,224	1,196	9.35	14.08	16.75
Motor vehicles and equipment	371	789	812	968	575	617	759	9.85	14.56	17.36
Aircraft and parts	372	633	712	449	344	345	207	9.28	14.79	(NA)
Ship and boat building and repairing	373	221	188	159	176	141	123	8.22	10.94	12.65
Railroad equipment	374	71	33	37	53	25	28	9.93	13.41	15.07
Guided missiles, space vehicles, and parts	376	111	185	99	35	57	28	9.22	14.39	17.75

See footnotes at end of table.

No. 654. Nonfarm Industries—Employees and Earnings: 1980 to 1995—Continued

[See headnote, p. 419]

INDUSTRY	1987 SIC [1] code	ALL EMPLOYEES TOTAL (1,000)			PRODUCTION WORKERS					
					Total (1,000)			Average hourly earnings (dollars)		
		1980	1990	1995	1980	1990	1995	1980	1990	1995
Durable goods—Continued . . .	(X)									
Instruments and related products	38	1,022	1,006	837	[4]	499	414	[4]	11.29	12.71
Search and navigation equipment . . .	381	[4]	284	158	[4]	94	48	[4]	14.62	16.38
Measuring and controlling devices . . .	382	[4]	323	285	[4]	180	146	[4]	10.68	12.56
Medical instruments and supplies . . .	384	[4]	246	264	[4]	144	151	[4]	9.85	11.58
Ophthalmic goods	385	44	43	37	31	30	24	5.30	8.18	9.59
Photographic equipment and supplies	386	135	100	85	67	43	38	8.83	14.08	15.37
Watches, clocks, watchcases, and parts	387	22	11	8	17	8	6	5.24	7.70	8.90
Misc. manufacturing industries [3]	39	418	375	389	313	272	275	5.46	8.61	10.06
Jewelry, silverware, and plated ware.	391	56	52	50	40	37	35	5.76	9.23	10.22
Toys and sporting goods	394	117	104	118	88	76	84	5.01	7.94	9.48
Pens, pencils, office and art supplies	395	37	34	32	27	24	21	5.58	8.89	11.07
Costume jewelry and notions	396	[4]	34	26	[4]	25	18	[4]	7.40	8.65
Nondurable goods [3]	(X)	8,127	7,968	7,814	5,798	5,584	5,489	6.56	10.12	11.58
Food and kindred products [3]	20	1,708	1,661	1,680	1,175	1,194	1,238	6.85	9.62	10.94
Meat products	201	358	422	467	298	359	398	6.99	7.94	8.97
Dairy products	202	175	155	148	96	95	95	6.86	10.56	12.35
Preserved fruits and vegetables	203	246	247	242	202	206	202	5.94	8.95	10.49
Grain mill products	204	144	128	128	99	89	91	7.67	11.52	13.62
Bakery products.	205	230	213	209	139	133	140	7.14	10.85	11.87
Sugar and confectionery products . . .	206	108	99	101	81	78	78	6.56	10.26	11.83
Fats and oils	207	44	31	31	32	22	21	7.03	10.10	11.63
Beverages	208	234	184	175	105	78	82	8.12	13.51	15.48
Tobacco products	21	69	49	42	54	36	32	7.74	16.23	19.48
Cigarettes	211	46	35	29	35	26	22	9.23	19.57	24.46
Textile mill products [3]	22	848	691	667	737	593	563	5.07	8.02	9.41
Broadwoven fabric mills, cotton.	221	150	91	79	135	82	69	5.25	8.31	9.87
Broadwoven fabric mills, synthetics . .	222	116	77	70	104	68	59	5.30	8.63	10.37
Broadwoven fabric mills, wool.	223	19	17	16	16	14	13	5.21	8.61	9.84
Narrow fabric mills	224	23	24	23	20	20	19	4.63	7.39	8.74
Knitting mills	225	224	205	195	194	179	167	4.77	7.37	8.63
Textile finishing, except wool.	226	74	62	73	62	50	59	5.39	8.45	9.53
Carpets and rugs	227	54	61	63	44	50	51	5.20	8.25	9.38
Yarn and thread mills	228	125	103	95	113	92	84	4.76	7.68	9.18
Apparel and other textile products [3] . . .	23	1,264	1,036	930	1,079	869	772	4.56	6.57	7.64
Men's and boys' suits and coats	231	77	50	36	67	42	30	5.34	7.34	8.11
Men's and boys' furnishings	232	362	274	251	310	235	214	4.23	6.06	7.20
Women's and misses outerwear	233	417	328	277	360	274	228	4.61	6.26	7.27
Women's and children's undergarments.	234	90	62	48	76	51	40	4.15	6.18	7.24
Girls' and children's outerwear	236	64	56	43	55	47	36	4.20	5.95	6.85
Paper and allied products [3]	26	685	697	692	519	522	525	7.84	12.31	14.23
Papermills.	262	178	180	164	133	136	126	9.05	15.10	17.86
Paperboard mills	263	65	52	51	51	40	39	9.28	15.26	17.93
Paperboard containers and boxes . . .	265	205	209	220	157	162	172	6.94	10.39	12.02
Misc. converted paper products	267	220	241	244	163	174	177	6.89	10.79	12.39
Printing and publishing [3]	27	1,252	1,569	1,543	699	871	846	7.53	11.24	12.33
Newspapers	271	420	474	447	164	166	155	7.72	11.17	12.18
Periodicals	272	90	129	131	16	47	43	7.16	11.95	13.42
Books	273	101	121	123	52	66	65	6.76	10.10	11.57
Commercial printing	275	410	552	562	304	401	405	7.85	11.52	12.53
Blankbooks and bookbinding	278	62	72	70	51	56	54	5.78	8.83	9.68
Chemicals and allied products [3]	28	1,107	1,086	1,035	626	600	578	8.30	13.54	15.63
Industrial inorganic chemicals	281	161	138	119	88	70	54	9.07	14.66	17.32
Plastics materials and synthetics . . .	282	205	180	157	137	116	105	8.21	13.97	16.12
Drugs.	283	196	237	259	97	105	127	7.69	12.90	15.16
Soap, cleaners, and toilet goods	284	141	159	152	86	98	94	7.67	11.71	12.78
Paints and allied products	285	65	61	57	33	31	30	7.39	11.99	13.08
Industrial organic chemicals	286	174	155	147	88	86	83	9.67	15.97	19.11
Agricultural chemicals	287	72	56	53	45	34	31	8.12	13.73	15.72
Petroleum and coal products [3]	29	198	157	144	125	103	93	10.10	16.24	19.36
Petroleum refining	291	155	118	104	93	75	66	10.94	17.58	21.44
Asphalt paving and roofing materials.	295	31	27	27	24	21	20	7.69	12.87	14.48
Rubber and misc. plastics products [3] . .	30	764	888	976	588	687	760	6.58	9.76	10.91
Tires and inner tubes	301	115	84	80	81	62	58	9.74	15.42	17.58
Rubber and plastics footwear	302	22	11	8	20	9	6	4.43	6.66	8.43
Leather and leather products [3]	31	233	133	106	197	109	83	4.58	6.91	8.17
Leather tanning and finishing	311	19	15	14	16	12	11	6.10	9.04	11.07
Footwear, except rubber	314	144	74	53	123	63	43	4.42	6.61	7.67
Luggage.	316	16	11	11	12	8	8	4.90	6.91	8.13
Handbags and personal leather goods.	317	30	15	12	25	12	8	4.33	6.08	7.43

See footnotes at end of table.

No. 654. Nonfarm Industries—Employees and Earnings: 1980 to 1995—Continued

[See headnote, p. 419]

INDUSTRY	1987 SIC [1] code	ALL EMPLOYEES TOTAL (1,000)			PRODUCTION WORKERS					
					Total (1,000)			Average hourly earnings (dollars)		
		1980	1990	1995	1980	1990	1995	1980	1990	1995
Transp. and public utilities [3]	(E)	**5,146**	**5,793**	**6,165**	**4,293**	**4,807**	**5,164**	**8.87**	**12.97**	**14.23**
Railroad transportation	40	532	279	239	(4)	(4)	(4)	(4)	(4)	(4)
Class I railroads, plus Amtrak [5]	4011	482	241	212	(4)	(4)	(4)	[6]9.92	[6]16.08	[6]17.48
Local and interurban passenger transit	41	265	338	423	244	308	390	6.34	9.23	10.54
Trucking and warehousing	42	1,280	1,625	1,867	1,121	1,416	1,622	9.13	11.71	12.88
Water transportation	44	211	177	174	(4)	(4)	(4)	(4)	(4)	(4)
Transportation by air	45	453	745	788	(4)	(4)	(4)	(4)	(4)	(4)
Pipelines, except natural gas	46	21	19	15	15	14	12	10.50	17.04	20.28
Transportation services	47	198	345	413	159	278	330	6.94	10.43	12.46
Communication [3]	48	1,357	1,309	1,333	1,014	978	1,029	8.50	13.51	15.57
Telephone communication	481	1,072	913	915	779	658	684	8.72	14.13	16.22
Radio and television broadcasting	483	192	234	236	154	193	198	7.44	12.71	15.30
Cable and other pay television services	484	(4)	126	157	(4)	105	133	(4)	10.50	12.09
Electric, gas, and sanitary services [3]	49	829	957	914	678	759	722	8.90	15.23	17.66
Electric services	491	391	454	404	316	351	315	9.12	15.80	18.54
Gas production and distribution	492	168	165	154	138	129	120	8.27	14.25	17.30
Combination utility services	493	197	193	167	162	156	128	9.64	17.58	21.39
Sanitary services	495	50	115	157	44	99	135	7.16	11.55	12.90
Wholesale trade	(F)	**5,292**	**6,173**	**6,412**	**4,328**	**4,959**	**5,191**	**6.95**	**10.79**	**12.43**
Retail trade [3]	(G)	**15,018**	**19,601**	**21,173**	**13,484**	**17,358**	**18,624**	**4.88**	**6.75**	**7.69**
General merchandise stores	53	2,245	2,540	2,678	2,090	2,380	2,495	4.77	6.83	7.53
Food stores	54	2,384	3,215	3,364	2,202	2,953	3,059	6.24	7.31	8.15
Automotive dealers and service stations	55	1,689	2,063	2,190	1,430	1,718	1,825	5.66	8.92	10.40
Apparel and accessory stores	56	957	1,183	1,127	820	991	919	4.30	6.25	7.47
Furniture and home furnishings stores	57	606	820	942	502	670	762	5.53	8.53	10.15
Eating and drinking places	58	4,626	6,509	7,350	4,256	5,905	6,627	3.69	4.97	5.59
Finance, insurance, real estate	(H)	**5,160**	**6,709**	**6,830**	**3,907**	**4,860**	**4,978**	**5.79**	**9.97**	**12.33**
Depository institutions	60	(4)	2,251	2,026	(4)	1,632	1,458	(4)	8.43	9.62
Nondepository institutions	61	(4)	373	462	(4)	270	335	(4)	10.40	12.53
Security and commodity brokers	62	227	424	523	(4)	(4)	(4)	(4)	(4)	(4)
Insurance carriers	63	1,224	1,462	1,541	854	982	1,101	6.29	11.18	14.82
Insurance, agents, brokers, service	64	464	663	697	(4)	(4)	(4)	(4)	(4)	(4)
Real estate	65	989	1,315	1,354	(4)	(4)	(4)	(4)	(4)	(4)
Holding and other investment offices	67	115	221	227	(4)	(4)	(4)	(4)	(4)	(4)
Services [3]	(I)	**17,890**	**27,934**	**33,107**	**15,921**	**24,387**	**28,965**	**5.85**	**9.83**	**11.39**
Hotels and other lodging places	70	1,076	1,631	1,657	(4)	(4)	(4)	(4)	(4)	(4)
Hotels and motels	701	1,038	1,578	1,603	954	1,398	1,409	4.45	6.98	7.93
Personal services [3]	72	818	1,104	1,164	(4)	(4)	(4)	(4)	(4)	(4)
Laundry, cleaning, garment services	721	356	426	433	318	379	382	4.47	6.82	7.53
Beauty shops	723	284	372	390	264	333	350	4.26	7.10	8.56
Business services [3]	73	2,564	5,139	6,786	(4)	4,522	6,047	(4)	9.48	10.69
Advertising	731	153	235	236	116	169	172	8.07	13.51	15.91
Personnel supply services	736	543	1,535	2,475	(4)	(4)	(4)	(4)	(4)	(4)
Employment agencies	7361	(4)	246	286	(4)	(4)	(4)	(4)	(4)	(4)
Help supply services	7363	(4)	1,288	2,189	(4)	1,245	2,128	(4)	8.09	8.79
Computer and data processing services	737	304	772	1,080	254	603	871	7.16	15.11	17.76
Prepackaged software	7372	(4)	113	182	(4)	(4)	(4)	(4)	(4)	(4)
Data processing and preparation	7374	(4)	197	225	(4)	(4)	(4)	(4)	(4)	(4)
Auto repair, services, and parking	75	571	914	1,020	488	756	842	6.10	8.77	9.91
Automotive repair shops	753	350	524	566	297	429	458	6.52	9.67	11.07
Motion pictures	78	(4)	408	489	(4)	344	407	(4)	10.95	13.62
Motion picture theaters	783	124	112	118	(4)	(4)	(4)	(4)	(4)	(4)
Amusement and recreation services	79	(4)	1,076	1,436	(4)	944	1,259	(4)	8.11	8.76
Health services [3]	80	5,278	7,814	9,257	4,712	6,948	8,200	5.68	10.41	12.45
Offices and clinics of medical doctors	801	802	1,338	1,606	(4)	1,105	1,311	(4)	10.58	12.52
Nursing and personal care facilities	805	997	1,415	1,693	898	1,279	1,527	4.17	7.24	8.76
Hospitals	806	2,750	3,549	3,784	2,522	3,248	3,461	6.06	11.79	14.30
Home health care services	808	(4)	291	626	(4)	269	579	(4)	8.72	10.91
Legal services	81	498	908	923	427	748	737	7.35	14.16	16.07
Educational services	82	1,138	1,661	1,959	(4)	(4)	(4)	(4)	(4)	(4)
Social services	83	1,134	1,734	2,333	(4)	1,494	2,021	(4)	7.11	8.33
Membership organizations	86	1,539	1,946	2,132	(4)	(4)	(4)	(4)	(4)	(4)
Engineering and management services	87	(4)	2,478	2,747	(4)	1,886	2,110	(4)	13.56	15.78
Government	(J)	**16,241**	**18,304**	**19,310**	**(NA)**	**(NA)**	**(NA)**	**(NA)**	**(NA)**	**(NA)**
Federal government	(X)	2,866	3,085	2,822	(NA)	(NA)	(NA)	(NA)	(NA)	(NA)
State government	(X)	3,610	4,305	4,642	(NA)	(NA)	(NA)	(NA)	(NA)	(NA)
Local government	(X)	9,765	10,914	11,847	(NA)	(NA)	(NA)	(NA)	(NA)	(NA)

NA Not available.   X Not applicable.   [1] 1987 Standard Industrial Classification, see text, section 13.   [2] Excludes government.   [3] Includes industries not shown separately.   [4] Included in totals; not available separately.   [5] For changes in "Class I" classification, see text, section 21.   [6] Includes all employees except executives, officials, and staff assistants who received pay during the month.

Source: U.S. Bureau of Labor Statistics, Bulletins 2445 and 2481, and *Employment and Earnings*, March and June issues.

No. 655. Indexes of Output per Hour—Selected Industries: 1975 to 1994

[See text, section 13. Minus sign (-) indicates decrease. See also *Historical Statistics, Colonial Times to 1970,* series W 14, 17, and 19, W 30-54, and 62-65]

INDUSTRY	1987 SIC code [1]	INDEXES (1987=100)						AVERAGE ANNUAL PERCENT CHANGE [2], 1975-94
		1975	1980	1985	1990	1993	1994, prel.	
Mining:	(B)							
Coal mining	12	57.7	61.7	85.1	118.3	145.4	150.4	5.2
Crude petroleum and natural gas	1311	142.8	97.2	83.0	96.9	106.5	113.1	-1.2
Nonmetallic minerals, except fuels	14	81.0	86.9	95.1	101.4	100.2	103.9	1.3
Manufacturing:	(D)							
Red meat products	2011,13	71.3	89.7	102.2	96.3	104.5	100.9	1.8
Poultry dressing and processing	2015	67.6	81.6	100.5	108.6	119.8	119.9	3.1
Dairy products	202	66.5	76.7	92.8	105.4	110.3	112.1	2.8
Preserved fruits and vegetables	203	77.2	82.9	94.3	96.2	107.2	108.4	1.8
Grain mill products	204	57.3	70.9	92.5	106.0	109.4	110.5	3.5
Bakery products	2051,52	82.0	82.4	95.6	93.2	90.3	91.0	0.5
Bottled and canned soft drinks	2086	55.7	66.5	85.2	126.7	144.7	147.8	5.3
Cotton and synthetic broadwoven fabrics	2211,21	66.1	78.4	94.8	108.1	125.8	133.8	3.8
Hosiery	2251,52	81.4	91.7	100.9	109.2	117.3	126.1	2.3
Yarn spinning mills	2281	67.4	65.5	89.6	106.0	120.0	126.9	3.4
Sawmills and planing mills, general	2421	68.2	71.5	93.5	99.9	101.5	102.6	2.2
Millwork	2431	98.8	97.6	97.4	97.8	92.6	89.7	-0.5
Wood kitchen cabinets	2434	82.3	94.1	87.1	93.6	101.9	95.9	0.8
Household furniture	251	82.1	93.2	93.5	104.3	110.3	112.7	1.7
Pulp, paper, and paperboard mills	2611,21,31	63.5	77.1	87.6	102.6	104.5	111.4	3.0
Corrugated and solid fiber boxes	2653	78.6	90.5	99.6	100.9	105.5	110.6	1.8
Industrial inorganic chemicals	281	66.8	75.7	84.0	104.9	108.1	107.7	2.5
Synthetic fibers	2823,24	46.9	71.2	79.3	98.7	112.3	119.4	5.0
Cosmetics and other toiletries	2844	92.2	83.8	90.3	101.1	108.5	111.8	1.0
Industrial organic chemicals, n.e.c. [3]	2869	69.8	81.3	87.8	99.0	88.5	96.6	1.7
Petroleum refining	2911	80.0	81.7	84.7	109.2	120.1	123.8	2.3
Tires and inner tubes	3011	54.1	60.7	89.3	103.0	116.5	119.9	4.3
Miscellaneous plastics products, n.e.c. [3]	308	66.7	75.1	88.2	105.3	116.2	119.7	3.1
Concrete products	3271,72	91.5	89.2	99.5	103.8	109.3	107.9	0.9
Ready-mixed concrete	3273	93.3	90.0	93.6	100.2	96.9	93.1	(Z)
Steel	331	59.3	65.4	85.8	110.5	134.2	142.7	4.7
Gray and ductile iron foundries	3321	90.3	86.3	96.9	107.9	113.1	115.7	1.3
Fabricated structural metal	3441	82.0	86.0	99.0	101.2	108.1	109.6	1.5
Metal doors, sash, and trim	3442	88.3	90.5	104.8	103.1	105.4	103.2	0.8
Fabricated plate work	3443	(NA)	(NA)	87.5	94.1	98.3	108.4	[4]2.4
Metal stampings	3465,66,69	80.6	84.2	91.9	93.0	113.1	117.3	2.0
Valves and pipe fittings	3491,92,94	84.0	93.5	94.4	102.1	104.2	110.1	1.4
Farm and garden machinery	352	94.2	91.3	92.7	116.6	118.8	126.7	1.6
Construction machinery	3531	87.7	88.5	92.2	109.6	107.0	123.7	1.8
Pumps and compressors	3561,63,94	79.9	87.2	92.1	104.9	107.8	112.6	1.8
Refrigeration and heating equipment	3585	85.3	90.7	96.1	106.3	111.8	115.8	1.6
Motors and generators	3621	82.7	87.9	94.9	100.9	127.0	123.2	2.1
Major household appliances	3631,32,33,39	70.9	79.3	93.9	101.6	120.7	131.3	3.3
Lighting fixtures and equipment	3645,46,47,48	80.5	84.4	96.7	96.0	103.7	109.6	1.6
Motor vehicles and equipment	371	70.2	71.6	95.3	102.4	105.4	108.6	2.3
Aircraft	3721	80.9	97.9	94.2	112.9	142.4	131.7	2.6
Instruments to measure electricity	3825	67.2	76.2	95.4	106.2	122.4	145.0	4.1
Photographic equipment and supplies	3861	60.9	72.9	86.1	107.8	126.6	131.9	4.2
Service producing:	(E,G,H,I)							
Air transportation [5]	4512,13,22 (pts)	55.6	70.8	92.0	92.9	103.8	105.7	3.4
Telephone communications	481	49.3	67.6	88.9	113.3	134.5	135.7	5.5
Gas and electric utilities	491,2,3	107.0	107.2	98.0	106.2	116.7	120.7	0.6
Scrap and waste materials	5093	(NA)	79.2	93.4	98.6	109.4	106.6	[6]2.1
Hardware stores	5251	82.4	94.9	95.6	110.4	106.7	114.1	1.7
Department stores	5311	63.7	73.6	92.6	94.2	105.0	108.5	2.8
Variety stores	5331	151.6	128.6	129.2	151.3	170.4	155.2	0.1
Food stores	54	106.1	107.6	104.1	96.0	93.3	92.7	-0.7
New and used car dealers	5511	83.9	87.9	98.9	106.1	107.7	109.2	1.4
Auto and home supply stores	5531	70.3	82.8	94.5	102.8	98.9	101.4	1.9
Gasoline service stations	5541	58.5	72.1	93.5	102.6	112.4	115.0	3.6
Apparel and accessory stores	56	74.0	82.4	101.3	101.7	110.1	114.4	2.3
Home furniture, furnishings, & equipment stores	57	64.7	75.1	92.9	108.3	125.0	133.5	3.9
Eating and drinking places	581	107.9	106.8	96.2	104.0	103.1	103.8	-0.2
Drug stores and proprietary stores	5912	90.0	104.5	102.5	103.6	104.7	103.7	0.7
Liquor stores	5921	90.4	95.7	101.9	105.2	100.5	96.7	0.4
Miscellaneous shopping goods stores	594	(NA)	88.4	94.1	101.5	103.9	105.6	[6]1.3
Commercial banks	602	76.3	78.5	94.3	108.6	129.9	(NA)	[7]3.0
Hotels and motels	7011	99.9	103.9	101.2	96.0	106.5	110.0	0.5
Laundry, cleaning, and garment services	721	109.8	103.2	103.3	101.0	99.8	101.8	-0.4
Beauty and barber shops	7231,41	80.2	85.7	94.9	97.4	98.6	102.1	1.3
Automotive repair shops	753	106.6	100.4	99.4	107.0	103.7	111.6	0.2

NA Not available. Z Less than .05 percent. [1] 1987 Standard Industrial Classification; see text, section 13. [2] Average annual percent change based on compound rate formula. [3] N.e.c. means not elsewhere classified. [4] Change from 1985-94. [5] Refers to output per employee. [6] Change from 1980-94. [7] Change from 1975-93.

Source: U.S. Bureau of Labor Statistics, Bulletin 2480, *Productivity Measures for Selected Industries and Government Services,* June 1996.

No. 656. Productivity and Related Measures: 1970 to 1995

[See text, section 13. Minus sign (-) indicates decrease. See also *Historical Statistics, Colonial Times to 1970*, series D 689-704 and W 22-25]

ITEM	1970	1980	1985	1990	1991	1992	1993	1994	1995
INDEXES (1992=100)									
Output per hour, business sector	69.8	84.1	91.9	96.2	96.7	100.0	100.2	101.0	101.9
Nonfarm business	72.6	86.0	92.4	96.3	96.9	100.0	100.2	100.7	101.8
Manufacturing	55.0	71.2	83.7	94.2	96.5	100.0	102.1	106.3	110.3
Output, [1] business sector	51.8	72.9	85.9	98.7	96.9	100.0	102.6	106.9	109.6
Nonfarm business	52.2	73.5	85.8	98.8	97.1	100.0	102.9	106.9	109.8
Manufacturing	57.5	76.6	87.6	98.8	97.1	100.0	103.5	110.2	114.1
Hours, [2] business sector	74.3	86.8	93.4	102.6	100.3	100.0	102.4	105.9	107.6
Nonfarm business	71.8	85.4	92.8	102.7	100.2	100.0	102.7	106.2	107.9
Manufacturing	104.5	107.6	104.6	104.9	100.6	100.0	101.4	103.6	103.5
Compensation per hour, [3] business sector	23.4	54.4	73.1	90.8	95.1	100.0	102.6	104.8	108.5
Nonfarm business	23.8	54.8	73.5	90.6	95.1	100.0	102.3	104.5	108.2
Manufacturing	23.8	55.8	75.3	90.9	95.7	100.0	102.4	105.3	108.5
Real hourly compensation, [3] business sector	84.6	92.7	95.3	97.4	97.9	100.0	99.6	99.2	99.9
Nonfarm business	86.0	93.4	95.8	97.3	97.9	100.0	99.3	98.9	99.6
Manufacturing	86.1	94.9	98.1	97.6	98.6	100.0	99.4	99.7	99.9
Unit labor costs, [4] business sector	33.5	64.7	79.5	94.3	98.3	100.0	102.4	103.8	106.5
Nonfarm business	32.7	63.8	79.5	94.1	98.1	100.0	102.1	103.8	106.3
Manufacturing	43.3	78.3	89.9	96.5	99.1	100.0	100.3	99.0	98.4
ANNUAL PERCENT CHANGE [5]									
Output per hour, business sector	1.6	-0.3	1.9	0.8	0.5	3.4	0.2	0.7	0.9
Nonfarm business	1.4	-0.4	1.0	0.5	0.7	3.2	0.2	0.5	1.1
Manufacturing	3.0	0.7	3.7	1.8	2.5	3.6	2.1	4.2	3.7
Output, [1] business sector	-0.3	-1.1	4.1	0.9	-1.8	3.2	2.6	4.2	2.5
Nonfarm business	-0.2	-1.2	3.6	0.7	-1.8	3.0	2.9	4.0	2.7
Manufacturing	-3.0	-3.9	3.0	-0.4	-1.7	3.0	3.5	6.5	3.5
Hours, [2] business sector	-1.8	-0.9	2.1	0.1	-2.3	-0.3	2.4	3.4	1.6
Nonfarm business	-1.6	-0.8	2.5	0.2	-2.4	-0.2	2.7	3.4	1.6
Manufacturing	-5.9	-4.6	-0.7	-2.2	-4.1	-0.6	1.4	2.2	-0.2
Compensation per hour, [3] business sector	7.5	10.8	4.9	5.8	4.8	5.2	2.6	2.2	3.5
Nonfarm business	7.2	10.8	4.6	5.5	4.9	5.2	2.3	2.2	3.6
Manufacturing	7.1	12.0	5.4	4.8	5.2	4.5	2.4	2.8	3.1
Real hourly compensation, [3] business sector	1.7	-2.4	1.3	0.4	0.5	2.1	-0.4	-0.4	0.6
Nonfarm business	1.4	-2.4	1.0	0.1	0.7	2.1	-0.7	-0.4	0.7
Manufacturing	1.3	-1.4	1.8	-0.5	1.0	1.5	-0.6	0.3	0.2
Unit labor costs, [4] business sector	5.8	11.1	3.0	4.9	4.2	1.7	2.4	1.4	2.6
Nonfarm business	5.8	11.2	3.6	5.0	4.3	1.9	2.1	1.6	2.5
Manufacturing	4.0	11.2	1.6	3.0	2.7	0.9	0.3	-1.3	-0.6

NA Not available. [1] Refers to gross sectoral product, annual-weighted. [2] Hours at work of all persons engaged in the business and nonfarm business sectors (employees, proprietors, and unpaid family workers); employees' and proprietors' hours in manufacturing. [3] Wages and salaries of employees plus employers' contributions for social insurance and private benefit plans. Also includes an estimate of same for self-employed. Real compensation deflated by the consumer price index for all urban consumers, see text, section 15. [4] Hourly compensation divided by output per hour. [5] All changes are from the immediate prior year.

Source: U.S. Bureau of Labor Statistics, *News USDL 96-139, Productivity and Costs*.

No. 657. Workers Using Computers on the Job: 1993

[**In percent, except as indicated.** For workers 18 years old and over. Based on the Current Population Survey and subject to sampling error; see Appendix III and source]

CHARACTERISTIC	Number using computers [1] (1,000)	Per-cent of total	TYPE OF APPLICATION							
			Book-keeping/inventory	Word processing	Communications [2]	Analysis/spreadsheets	Data-bases	Desktop publishing	Sales and telemarketing
Total	51,106	45.8	36.1	45.0	38.7	34.5	22.3	16.2	44.4
Age:									
18 to 25 years old	4,965	34.4	25.0	45.3	27.1	27.1	15.9	19.9	34.7
25 to 29 years old	8,424	48.3	37.2	45.2	38.7	35.0	22.8	17.0	45.7
30 to 39 years old	14,969	50.7	38.8	45.4	40.4	36.0	25.0	16.4	45.0
40 to 49 years old	13,854	51.3	38.6	45.1	42.0	36.8	23.4	14.5	47.5
50 to 59 years old	6,881	43.9	34.5	44.3	38.8	33.3	20.4	15.0	43.9
60 years old and over	2,014	27.2	28.0	42.7	31.6	27.4	15.0	16.9	40.0
Sex: Male	24,414	40.3	41.1	45.2	39.4	35.2	25.3	18.1	40.7
Female	26,692	52.4	31.6	44.8	38.1	33.8	19.6	14.5	47.8
Race/ethnicity:									
White [3]	43,020	48.7	37.2	45.8	39.3	35.2	23.0	16.7	45.9
Black [3]	4,016	36.2	27.5	38.3	37.3	31.2	16.8	12.9	35.5
Hispanic	2,492	29.3	29.1	45.6	32.1	27.6	18.7	16.0	33.6
Other	1,578	43.9	39.7	39.4	37.2	33.5	22.6	10.2	44.5
Educational attainment:									
Not a high school graduate	1,190	10.0	19.1	54.4	20.4	22.2	9.9	20.6	16.0
High school graduate	13,307	34.2	23.7	52.5	29.4	25.8	13.3	17.6	30.8
Some college	11,548	50.4	33.5	49.5	38.5	33.9	20.6	18.0	40.9
Associate's degree	5,274	58.2	37.5	47.0	39.7	34.7	21.7	14.9	41.6
Bachelor's degree	13,162	68.8	46.9	40.0	45.1	41.5	28.8	17.0	54.8
Master's degree	4,628	71.2	47.9	29.3	48.5	41.9	35.3	10.4	63.8
Doctorate or professional degree	1,999	66.9	42.8	27.9	45.9	39.2	28.3	5.2	66.5

[1] Includes other applications, not shown separately. A person may be counted in more than one application. [2] Includes bulletin boards and electronic mail. [3] Non-Hispanic.

Source: U.S. National Center for Education Statistics, *Digest of Education Statistics*, 1994.

No. 658. Annual Total Compensation and Wages and Salaries Per Full-Time Equivalent Employee, by Industry: 1985 to 1994

[In dollars. Wage and salary payments include executives' compensation, bonuses, tips, and payments-in-kind; total compensation includes in addition to wages and salaries, employer contributions for social insurance, employer contributions to private and welfare funds, director's fees, jury and witness fees, etc. 1985 based on 1972 Standard Industrial Classification Code (SIC); beginning 1990, based on the 1987 SIC. See text, section 13]

INDUSTRY	ANNUAL TOTAL COMPENSATION				ANNUAL WAGES AND SALARIES			
	1985	1990	1993	1994	1985	1990	1993	1994
Domestic industries	25,871	32,093	36,123	36,821	21,285	26,396	29,351	29,909
Agriculture, forestry, and fisheries	13,224	18,638	20,320	21,325	11,864	16,014	17,365	18,294
Mining	38,858	46,053	54,015	55,496	32,202	38,081	43,598	44,166
Construction	27,270	33,701	36,338	36,726	22,836	27,832	29,417	29,568
Manufacturing	30,446	37,048	42,427	43,769	24,960	30,148	33,747	34,707
Transportation	31,880	36,636	40,394	39,946	25,333	29,019	31,675	31,418
Communication	39,509	46,481	54,535	53,010	32,012	38,930	45,123	43,729
Electric, gas, and sanitary services	39,894	48,057	56,324	58,594	32,443	39,538	45,346	47,010
Wholesale trade.	29,121	37,394	42,258	43,525	25,042	31,810	35,367	36,501
Retail trade	15,799	18,678	20,613	21,074	13,626	16,065	17,598	18,047
Finance, insurance, and real estate	28,300	37,905	46,360	47,245	24,132	32,071	38,776	39,539
Services	21,740	29,141	32,404	32,891	18,748	24,996	27,464	27,806
Government and government enterprises . .	29,955	37,142	42,150	43,190	22,479	28,195	31,850	32,704

Source: U.S. Bureau of Economic Analysis, *National Income and Product Accounts of the United States,* forthcoming; and *Survey of Current Business,* January/February 1996.

No. 659. Average Hourly and Weekly Earnings, by Private Industry Group: 1980 to 1995

[Average earnings include overtime. Data are for production and related workers in mining, manufacturing, and construction, and nonsupervisory employees in other industries. Excludes agriculture. See headnote, table 652. See also *Historical Statistics, Colonial Times to 1970,* series D 877-892]

PRIVATE INDUSTRY GROUP	CURRENT DOLLARS					CONSTANT (1982) DOLLARS [1]				
	1980	1985	1990	1994	1995	1980	1985	1990	1994	1995
TOTAL AVERAGE HOURLY EARNINGS										
Total	6.66	8.57	10.01	11.12	11.44	7.78	7.77	7.52	7.40	7.40
Mining	9.17	11.98	13.68	14.88	15.30	10.71	10.86	10.28	9.90	9.90
Construction	9.94	12.32	13.77	14.73	15.08	11.61	11.17	10.35	9.80	9.75
Manufacturing	7.27	9.54	10.83	12.07	12.37	8.49	8.65	8.14	8.03	8.00
Transportation, public utilities	8.87	11.40	12.97	13.86	14.23	10.36	10.34	9.74	9.22	9.20
Wholesale trade	6.95	9.15	10.79	12.06	12.43	8.12	8.30	8.11	8.02	8.04
Retail trade	4.88	5.94	6.75	7.49	7.69	5.70	5.39	5.07	4.98	4.97
Finance, insurance, real estate	5.79	7.94	9.97	11.83	12.33	6.76	7.20	7.49	7.87	7.98
Services	5.85	7.90	9.83	11.04	11.39	6.83	7.16	7.39	7.35	7.37
TOTAL AVERAGE WEEKLY EARNINGS										
Total	235	299	345	386	395	275	271	259	257	255
Mining	397	520	603	667	684	464	471	453	444	442
Construction	368	464	526	573	585	430	421	395	381	378
Manufacturing	289	386	442	507	515	337	350	332	337	333
Transportation, public utilities	351	450	505	553	562	410	408	379	368	364
Wholesale trade	267	351	411	463	476	312	319	309	308	308
Retail trade	147	175	194	217	221	172	158	146	144	143
Finance, insurance, real estate	210	289	357	424	443	245	262	268	282	286
Services	191	257	319	359	369	223	233	240	239	239

[1] Earnings in current dollars divided by the Consumer Price Index (CPI-W) on a 1982 base; see text, section 15.

Source: U.S. Bureau of Labor Statistics, Bulletins 2445 and 2481, and *Employment and Earnings,* monthly, March and June issues.

No. 660. Annual Percent Changes in Earnings and Compensation: 1980 to 1995

[Annual percent change from immediate prior year. Minus sign (-) indicates decrease]

ITEM	1980	1985	1989	1990	1991	1992	1993	1994	1995
Current dollars:									
Hourly earnings, total [1]	8.1	3.0	4.1	3.6	3.1	2.4	2.5	2.7	2.9
Hourly earnings, manufacturing	8.5	3.8	2.8	3.3	3.2	2.5	2.4	2.8	2.5
Compensation per employee-hour [1]	10.8	4.6	2.7	5.5	4.9	5.2	2.3	2.2	3.6
Constant (1982) dollars:									
Hourly earnings, total [1]	-4.8	-0.4	-0.7	-1.6	-0.9	-0.5	-0.3	0.1	-
Hourly earnings, manufacturing	-4.5	0.3	-1.9	-1.7	-0.9	-0.4	-0.4	0.2	-0.4
Compensation per employee-hour	-2.4	1.0	-2.1	0.1	0.7	2.1	-0.7	-0.4	0.7
Consumer Price Index (CPI-U) [2]	13.5	3.6	4.8	5.4	4.2	3.0	3.0	2.6	2.8

- Represents zero.   [1] Nonfarm business sector.   [2] See text, section 15.

Source: U.S. Bureau of Labor Statistics, *Monthly Labor Review;* and unpublished data.

No. 661. Average Annual Pay, by State: 1993 and 1994

[In dollars, except percent change. For workers covered by State unemployment insurance laws and for Federal civilian workers covered by unemployment compensation for Federal employees, approximately 96 percent of wage and salary civilian employment in 1994. Excludes most agricultural workers on small farms, all Armed Forces, elected officials in most States, railroad employees, most domestic workers, most student workers at school, employees of certain nonprofit organizations, and most self-employed individuals. Pay includes bonuses, cash value of meals and lodging, and tips and other gratuities]

STATE	AVERAGE ANNUAL PAY		Percent change, 1993-94 [1]	STATE	AVERAGE ANNUAL PAY		Percent change, 1993-94 [1]
	1993	1994			1993	1994	
United States.	26,361	26,939	2.2	Missouri	23,898	24,628	3.1
Alabama	22,786	23,616	3.6	Montana	19,932	20,218	1.4
Alaska	32,336	32,657	1.0	Nebraska	20,815	21,500	3.3
Arizona	23,501	24,276	3.3	Nevada	25,461	25,700	0.9
Arkansas	20,337	20,898	2.8	New Hampshire	24,962	25,555	2.4
California	29,470	29,878	1.4	New Jersey	32,722	33,439	2.2
Colorado	25,682	26,155	1.8	New Mexico	21,731	22,351	2.9
Connecticut	33,169	33,811	1.9	New York	32,919	33,439	1.6
Delaware	27,144	27,952	3.0	North Carolina	22,773	23,460	3.0
District of Columbia	39,199	40,919	4.4	North Dakota	19,382	19,893	2.6
Florida	23,571	23,918	1.5	Ohio	25,338	26,134	3.1
Georgia	24,865	25,313	1.8	Oklahoma	22,001	22,293	1.3
Hawaii	26,325	26,746	1.6	Oregon	24,093	24,780	2.9
Idaho	21,188	21,938	3.5	Pennsylvania	26,274	26,950	2.6
Illinois	28,425	29,107	2.4	Rhode Island	24,889	25,454	2.3
Indiana	24,109	24,908	3.3	South Carolina	21,933	22,477	2.5
Iowa	21,441	22,189	3.5	South Dakota	18,613	19,255	3.4
Kansas	22,430	22,907	2.1	Tennessee	23,368	24,106	3.2
Kentucky	22,170	22,747	2.6	Texas	25,523	25,959	1.7
Louisiana	22,633	23,178	2.4	Utah	22,250	22,811	2.5
Maine	22,026	22,389	1.6	Vermont	22,704	22,964	1.1
Maryland	27,686	28,416	2.6	Virginia	25,504	26,035	2.1
Massachusetts	30,229	31,024	2.6	Washington	25,760	26,362	2.3
Michigan	28,260	29,541	4.5	West Virginia	22,373	22,959	2.6
Minnesota	25,710	26,422	2.8	Wisconsin	23,610	24,324	3.0
Mississippi	19,693	20,382	3.5	Wyoming	21,745	22,054	1.4

Source: U.S. Bureau of Labor Statistics, *Employment and Wages, Annual Averages 1994*, Bulletin 2467.

No. 662. Average Annual Pay, by Selected Metropolitan Areas: 1993 and 1994

[In dollars. Metropolitan areas ranked by average pay 1994. Includes data for Metropolitan Statistical Areas and Primary Metropolitan Statistical Areas defined as of June 30, 1993. In the New England areas, the New England County Metropolitan Area (NECMA) definitions were used. See source for details. See also headnote table 661]

METROPOLITAN AREA	1993	1994	METROPOLITAN AREA	1993	1994
Metropolitan areas	**27,539**	**28,129**	Minneapolis-St. Paul, MN-WI	28,343	29,102
New York, NY	39,381	39,933	Saginaw-Bay City-Midland, MI	27,686	29,080
San Jose, CA	38,040	39,123	Denver, CO	28,607	28,965
Middlesex-Somerset-Hunterdon, NJ	35,597	36,690	Brazoria, TX	28,453	28,941
San Francisco, CA	35,278	36,510	Dutchess County, NY	29,730	28,860
Newark, NJ	35,132	35,910	Atlanta, GA	28,351	28,851
New Haven-Bridgeport-Stamford-Danbury-			Monmouth-Ocean, NJ	28,048	28,338
Waterbury, CT	35,058	35,535	Rochester, NY	27,645	28,299
Trenton, NJ	34,366	35,345	Rochester, MN	27,625	28,262
Bergen-Passaic, NJ	34,135	34,675	Sacramento, CA	27,476	28,125
Anchorage, AK	33,782	34,098	Lansing-East Lansing, MI	26,848	28,026
Washington, DC-MD-VA-WV	33,170	33,947	Springfield, IL	27,008	27,963
Kokomo, IN	29,672	33,231	Baltimore, MD	27,239	27,955
Flint, MI	30,512	33,220	Cleveland-Lorain-Elyria, OH	26,987	27,927
Detroit, MI	31,622	33,201	Yolo, CA	27,187	27,825
Hartford, CT	32,555	33,172	Bloomington-Normal, IL	26,282	27,769
Jersey City, NJ	32,815	33,012	Honolulu, HI	27,253	27,592
Oakland, CA	31,701	32,157	Indianapolis, IN	26,587	27,437
Los Angeles-Long Beach, CA	31,760	31,831	St. Louis, MO-IL	26,545	27,392
Boston-Worcester-Lawrence-Lowell-			San Diego, CA	26,531	27,261
Brockton MA-NH	30,642	31,403	Albany-Schenectady-Troy, NY	26,605	27,231
Chicago, IL	30,724	31,340	Pittsburgh, PA	26,478	27,121
Nassau-Suffolk, NY	30,226	30,765	Cincinnati, OH-KY-IN	26,462	27,106
Philadelphia, PA-NJ	29,839	30,519	Decatur, IL	26,037	27,071
Huntsville, AL	29,243	30,389	Portland-Vancouver, OR-WA	26,360	27,065
Houston, TX	30,069	30,349	Peoria-Pekin, IL	25,924	27,010
Orange County, CA	29,916	30,315	Milwaukee-Waukesha, WI	26,204	26,958
Seattle-Bellevue-Everett, WA	29,399	30,181	Boulder-Longmont, CO	26,215	26,948
Wilmington-Newark, DE-MD	29,232	30,175	Ventura, CA	26,567	26,905
Dallas, TX	29,489	30,105	Richland-Kennewick-Pasco, WA	25,673	26,835
New London-Norwich, CT	28,630	30,015	Dayton-Springfield, OH	25,900	26,721
Ann Arbor, MI	27,930	29,258	Reading, PA	25,610	26,705

Source: U.S. Bureau of Labor Statistics, *Employment and Wages, Annual Averages 1994*, Bulletin 2467.

No. 663. Full-Time Wage and Salary Workers—Number and Earnings: 1985 to 1995

[**In current dollars of usual weekly earnings**. Data represent annual averages of quarterly data. See text, section 13, and headnote table 631, for a discussion of occupational data. Based on Current Population Survey; see text, section 1, and Appendix III. For definition of median, see Guide to Tabular Presentation]

CHARACTERISTIC	NUMBER OF WORKERS (1,000)				MEDIAN WEEKLY EARNINGS (dol.)			
	1985	1990 [1]	1994 [1]	1995	1985	1990 [1]	1994 [1]	1995
All workers [2]	77,002	85,804	87,379	89,282	343	412	467	479
Male	45,589	49,564	49,992	51,222	406	481	522	538
16 to 24 years old	6,956	6,824	6,040	6,118	240	282	294	303
25 years old and over	38,632	42,740	43,952	45,104	442	512	576	588
Female	31,414	36,239	37,386	38,060	277	346	399	406
16 to 24 years old	5,621	5,227	4,403	4,366	210	254	276	275
25 years old and over	25,793	31,012	32,983	33,695	296	369	421	428
White	66,481	72,811	73,500	74,874	355	424	484	494
Male	40,030	42,797	42,816	43,747	417	494	547	566
Female	26,452	30,014	30,685	31,127	281	353	408	415
Black	8,393	9,820	10,199	10,596	277	329	371	383
Male	4,367	4,983	5,099	5,279	304	361	400	411
Female	4,026	4,837	5,100	5,317	252	308	346	355
Hispanic origin [3]	(NA)	7,812	8,274	8,719	(NA)	304	324	329
Male	(NA)	5,000	5,295	5,597	(NA)	318	343	350
Female	(NA)	2,812	2,979	3,122	(NA)	278	305	305
Family relationship:								
Husbands	30,260	(NA)	(NA)	(NA)	455	(NA)	(NA)	(NA)
Wives	16,270	(NA)	(NA)	(NA)	285	(NA)	(NA)	(NA)
Women who maintain families	4,333	(NA)	(NA)	(NA)	278	(NA)	(NA)	(NA)
Men who maintain families	1,313	(NA)	(NA)	(NA)	396	(NA)	(NA)	(NA)
Other persons in families:								
Men	6,173	(NA)	(NA)	(NA)	238	(NA)	(NA)	(NA)
Women	4,309	(NA)	(NA)	(NA)	213	(NA)	(NA)	(NA)
All other men [4]	7,841	(NA)	(NA)	(NA)	380	(NA)	(NA)	(NA)
All other women [4]	6,503	(NA)	(NA)	(NA)	305	(NA)	(NA)	(NA)
Occupation, male:								
Managerial and professional	11,078	12,255	13,021	13,684	583	729	803	829
Exec., admin., managerial	5,835	6,389	6,785	7,172	593	740	797	833
Professional specialty	5,243	5,866	6,236	6,512	571	719	809	827
Technical, sales, and administrative support	8,803	9,677	9,764	9,894	420	493	548	556
Tech. and related support	1,563	1,762	1,638	1,688	472	567	622	641
Sales	4,227	4,692	4,836	5,000	431	502	575	579
Admin. support, incl. clerical	3,013	3,224	3,289	3,206	391	436	482	489
Service	3,947	4,602	4,784	4,779	272	317	350	357
Private household	13	12	14	15	(B)	(B)	(B)	(B)
Protective	1,327	1,531	1,674	1,691	391	477	538	552
Other service	2,607	3,059	3,096	3,073	230	271	293	300
Precision production [5]	10,026	10,259	9,824	10,046	408	486	515	534
Mechanics and repairers	3,752	3,687	3,593	3,658	400	475	519	538
Construction trades	3,308	3,650	3,407	3,541	394	478	492	507
Other	2,966	2,922	2,824	2,847	433	508	553	574
Operators, fabricators and laborers	10,585	11,464	11,333	11,529	325	375	406	413
Machine operators, assemblers, and inspectors	4,403	4,594	4,469	4,576	341	387	415	421
Transportation and material moving	3,459	3,752	3,854	3,870	369	416	469	482
Handlers, equipment cleaners, helpers, and laborers	2,724	3,118	3,010	3,083	261	306	319	328
Farming, forestry, and fishing	1,150	1,306	1,266	1,290	216	261	290	294
Occupation, female:								
Managerial and professional	8,302	10,575	12,187	12,609	399	510	592	605
Exec., admin., managerial	3,492	4,758	5,548	5,803	383	484	541	570
Professional specialty	4,810	5,816	6,639	6,806	408	534	623	632
Technical, sales, and administrative support	14,622	16,290	15,954	16,004	269	331	376	383
Tech. and related support	1,200	1,476	1,536	1,506	331	417	466	480
Sales	2,929	3,554	3,633	3,862	226	290	324	330
Admin. support, incl. clerical	10,494	11,260	10,785	10,636	270	332	374	384
Service	3,963	4,577	4,702	4,838	185	230	257	264
Private household	330	305	311	324	130	171	177	193
Protective	156	217	277	266	278	405	430	438
Other service	3,477	4,055	4,115	4,249	188	230	256	264
Precision production [5]	906	900	970	957	268	316	370	371
Mechanics and repairers	144	139	160	150	392	458	520	550
Construction trades	53	50	52	66	265	393	408	400
Other	709	711	758	741	253	299	342	346
Operators, fabricators, and laborers	3,482	3,722	3,412	3,462	216	261	293	297
Machine operators, assemblers, and inspectors	2,778	2,878	2,563	2,559	216	259	292	296
Transportation and material moving	189	227	242	261	252	314	361	354
Handlers, equipment cleaners, helpers and laborers	514	616	608	642	209	249	279	284
Farming, forestry, and fishing	138	175	161	190	185	216	234	249

B Data not shown where base is less than 50,000.　NA Not available.　[1] See footnote 2, table 614.　[2] Includes other races, not shown separately.　[3] Persons of Hispanic origin may be of any race.　[4] The majority of these persons are living alone or with nonrelatives. Also included are persons in families where the husband, wife or other person maintaining the family is in the Armed Forces, and persons in unrelated subfamilies.　[5] Includes craft and repair.

Source: U.S. Bureau of Labor Statistics, Bulletin 2307, and *Employment and Earnings*, monthly, January issues; and unpublished data.

No. 664. Families With Earners—Number and Earnings: 1980 to 1993

[In current dollars of usual weekly earnings. Annual averages of quarterly figures based on Current Population Survey; see text, section 1, and Appendix III. For families with wage and salary earners]

CHARACTERISTIC	NUMBER OF FAMILIES (1,000)				MEDIAN WEEKLY EARNINGS (dollars)			
	1980	1985	1990	1993	1980	1985	1990	1993
TOTAL								
Total families with earners [1]	41,162	41,616	43,759	44,383	400	522	653	707
Married-couple families	33,825	33,459	34,219	34,257	433	582	732	804
One earner	14,797	13,347	12,166	12,185	303	385	455	481
Husband	12,127	10,346	8,994	8,643	336	440	520	565
Wife	2,059	2,243	2,407	2,773	159	217	267	314
Other family member	611	758	764	769	163	204	280	282
Two or more earners [2]	19,028	20,112	22,053	22,071	535	715	880	973
Husband and wife only	12,990	14,019	15,934	16,349	507	684	844	944
Husband and other family member(s) .	2,369	2,159	1,751	1,509	557	689	825	875
Wife and other family member(s)	426	514	527	574	350	454	557	613
Other family members only	139	176	176	150	356	468	554	605
Families maintained by women	5,690	6,470	7,323	7,792	222	297	363	393
One earner	4,022	4,397	4,983	5,452	184	234	288	307
Householder	3,104	3,432	3,937	4,402	188	243	296	315
Other family member	918	965	1,045	1,050	168	200	254	263
Two or more earners	1,668	2,073	2,340	2,340	370	487	607	655
Families maintained by men	1,647	1,688	2,218	2,334	360	450	514	523
One earner	1,016	1,031	1,352	1,523	283	346	396	429
Two or more earners	631	656	866	811	502	625	778	763
WHITE								
Total families with earners [1]	35,786	35,848	37,239	37,458	411	543	681	739
Married-couple families	30,316	29,899	30,361	30,288	438	589	745	816
One earner [2]	13,437	12,097	10,856	10,790	311	395	473	492
Husband	11,152	9,496	8,162	7,755	343	452	535	583
Wife	1,740	1,925	2,044	2,383	160	218	270	313
Two or more earners	16,878	17,802	19,505	19,497	542	723	892	984
Husband and wife only	11,448	12,394	14,148	14,546	511	691	855	954
Families maintained by women	4,140	4,616	5,127	5,355	233	311	382	415
Families maintained by men	1,331	1,333	1,751	1,816	374	475	539	547
BLACK								
Total families with earners [1]	4,503	4,668	5,082	5,268	299	378	459	490
Married-couple families	2,802	2,671	2,724	2,698	366	487	601	674
One earner [2]	1,103	902	893	909	210	257	304	344
Husband	769	580	527	539	244	292	345	381
Wife	279	257	290	287	151	206	243	321
Two or more earners	1,700	1,769	1,831	1,789	472	622	748	846
Husband and wife only	1,238	1,258	1,297	1,285	461	603	713	819
Families maintained by women	1,438	1,703	1,986	2,168	192	259	314	334
Families maintained by men	263	294	372	403	307	360	397	413
HISPANIC ORIGIN [3]								
Total families with earners [1]	(NA)	(NA)	3,624	3,879	(NA)	(NA)	496	505
Married-couple families	(NA)	(NA)	2,599	2,800	(NA)	(NA)	555	566
One earner [2]	(NA)	(NA)	1,050	1,177	(NA)	(NA)	322	334
Husband	(NA)	(NA)	814	912	(NA)	(NA)	356	365
Wife	(NA)	(NA)	164	183	(NA)	(NA)	236	262
Two or more earners	(NA)	(NA)	1,549	1,622	(NA)	(NA)	716	744
Husband and wife only	(NA)	(NA)	924	1,032	(NA)	(NA)	672	733
Families maintained by women	(NA)	(NA)	691	749	(NA)	(NA)	326	353
Families maintained by men	(NA)	(NA)	334	330	(NA)	(NA)	468	432

NA Not available.   [1] Excludes families in which there is no wage or salary earner or in which the husband, wife, or other person maintaining the family is either self-employed or in the Armed Forces.   [2] Includes other earners, not shown separately.   [3] Persons of Hispanic origin may be of any race.

Source: U.S. Bureau of Labor Statistics, Bulletin 2307; and *Employment and Earnings*, monthly, January issues.

No. 665. Workers With Earnings, by Occupation of Longest Held Job and Sex: 1994

[Covers persons 15 years old and over as of March 1995. Based on Current Population Survey; see text, section 1, and Appendix III. For definition of median, see Guide to Tabular Presentation]

MAJOR OCCUPATION OF LONGEST JOB HELD	ALL WORKERS				YEAR ROUND FULL-TIME			
	Women		Men		Women		Men	
	Number (1,000)	Median earn-ings	Number (1,000)	Median earn-ings	Number (1,000)	Median earn-ings	Number (1,000)	Median earn-ings
Total [1]	64,706	14,323	74,264	23,656	34,155	22,205	51,580	30,854
Executive, administrators, and managerial	7,570	25,980	9,906	41,410	5,657	30,299	8,368	45,944
Professional specialty	10,198	26,449	8,777	41,090	5,745	32,321	6,845	46,488
Technical and related support	2,340	22,524	1,977	30,642	1,430	27,202	1,551	35,235
Sales	8,626	9,070	8,364	25,790	3,565	18,986	6,037	32,850
Admin. support, incl. clerical	16,085	15,880	4,189	21,023	9,368	20,942	2,840	26,874
Precision production, craft and repair	1,362	15,815	13,333	24,681	825	21,637	9,540	29,527
Machine operators, assemblers, and inspectors	3,503	12,095	5,303	20,621	2,058	16,359	3,889	24,173
Transportation and material moving	589	11,686	5,061	21,546	234	23,249	3,364	26,036
Handlers, equipment cleaners, helpers, and laborers	1,156	7,893	4,944	10,905	481	14,800	2,251	18,239
Service workers	12,438	7,059	8,118	11,746	4,484	13,518	4,317	20,996
Private household	1,023	3,287	48	(B)	206	10,330	13	(B)
Service, except private household	11,415	7,453	8,070	11,823	4,279	13,719	4,304	21,037
Farming, forestry, and fishing	752	4,223	3,456	10,431	246	10,685	1,815	16,261

B Base less than 75,000.　　[1] Includes persons whose longest job was in the Armed Forces.

Source: U.S. Bureau of the Census, *Current Population Reports*, P60-189.

No. 666. Employment Cost Index (ECI), by Industry and Occupation: 1982 to 1995

[As of **December.** The ECI is a measure of the rate of change in employee compensation (wages, salaries, and employer costs for employee benefits). Data are not seasonally adjusted: 1982-1985 based on fixed employment counts from 1970 Census of Population; 1986-94 based on fixed employment counts from the 1980 Census of Population; 1995 based primarily on 1990 Occupational Employment Survey]

ITEM	INDEXES (June 1989=100)						PERCENT CHANGE FOR 12 MONTHS ENDING DEC.—				
	1982	1985	1990	1993	1994	1995	1985	1990	1993	1994	1995
Civilian workers [1]	74.8	86.8	107.6	120.2	123.8	127.4	4.3	4.9	3.5	3.0	2.9
Workers, by occupational group:											
White-collar occupations	72.9	85.8	108.3	120.6	124.4	128.2	4.9	5.2	3.4	3.2	3.1
Blue-collar occupations	78.2	88.4	106.5	119.4	122.7	125.9	3.3	4.4	3.6	2.8	2.6
Service occupations	74.3	87.2	108.0	120.5	124.3	127.5	3.9	5.1	3.3	3.2	2.6
Workers, by industry division:											
Manufacturing	76.9	87.8	107.2	121.3	125.1	128.4	3.3	5.1	4.1	3.1	2.6
Nonmanufacturing	73.9	86.4	107.8	119.8	123.4	127.0	4.7	4.9	3.3	3.0	2.9
Service industries [2]	70.5	84.1	110.2	122.9	126.4	129.7	4.7	6.3	3.1	2.8	2.6
Public administration [2]	71.9	85.4	108.7	120.0	124.2	128.5	4.9	5.3	3.2	3.5	3.5
Private industry workers [3]	75.8	87.3	107.0	119.8	123.5	126.9	3.9	4.6	3.6	3.1	2.8
Workers, by occupational group:											
White-collar occupations	73.7	86.4	107.4	120.2	124.1	127.9	4.9	4.9	3.7	3.2	3.1
Blue-collar occupations	78.4	88.5	106.4	119.3	122.6	125.7	3.1	4.4	3.7	2.8	2.5
Service occupations	76.3	88.4	107.3	119.5	122.9	125.3	3.0	4.7	3.1	2.8	2.0
Workers, by industry division:											
Manufacturing	76.9	87.8	107.2	121.3	125.1	128.4	3.3	5.1	4.1	3.1	2.6
Nonmanufacturing	75.1	87.0	106.9	119.0	122.6	126.2	4.3	4.5	3.4	3.0	2.9
Service industries	(NA)	84.1	109.3	123.1	126.6	129.7	(NA)	6.2	3.5	2.8	2.4
Business services	(NA)	(NA)	107.4	118.6	123.0	126.5	(NA)	6.0	2.3	3.7	2.8
Health services	(NA)	83.7	110.8	126.0	128.7	132.3	(NA)	6.8	3.4	2.1	2.8
Hospitals	(NA)	(NA)	110.7	125.6	128.6	131.4	(NA)	7.0	3.3	2.4	2.2
Workers by bargaining status:											
Union	79.6	90.1	106.2	120.9	124.2	127.9	2.6	4.3	4.3	2.7	3.0
Nonunion	74.3	86.3	107.3	119.5	123.2	126.7	4.6	4.8	3.5	3.1	2.8
State and local government	70.8	84.6	110.4	121.9	125.6	129.4	5.6	5.8	2.8	3.0	3.0
Workers, by occupational group:											
White-collar occupations	70.4	84.2	110.9	121.9	125.5	129.3	5.8	6.0	2.5	3.0	3.0
Blue-collar workers	73.9	86.7	108.7	121.4	124.7	128.1	5.3	4.8	3.1	2.7	2.7
Workers, by industry division:											
Service industries	70.0	84.0	111.3	122.6	126.1	129.8	5.9	6.3	2.5	2.9	2.9
Schools	69.0	83.6	111.6	122.9	126.3	129.9	6.2	6.0	2.5	2.8	2.9
Elementary and secondary	68.6	83.6	112.1	123.6	126.5	130.3	6.4	6.3	2.4	2.3	3.0
Colleges and universities [4]	(NA)	(NA)	110.2	120.7	125.5	129.0	(NA)	5.3	3.0	4.0	2.8
Services, excluding schools [4]	73.1	85.2	110.2	121.9	125.6	129.3	4.7	6.8	2.8	3.0	2.9
Public administration [2]	71.9	85.4	108.7	120.0	124.2	128.5	4.9	5.3	3.2	3.5	3.5

NA Not available.　　[1] Includes private industry and State and local government workers and excludes farm, household, and Federal government workers.　　[2] Consists of legislative, judicial, administrative, and regulatory activities.　　[3] Excludes farm and household workers.　　[4] Includes library, social, and health services. Formerly called hospitals and other services.

Source: U.S. Bureau of Labor Statistics, *News, Employment Cost Index*, quarterly; and Internet site http://stats.bls.gov/ecthome.htm

No. 667. Effective Federal Minimum Hourly Wage Rates: 1950 to 1996

[The Fair Labor Standards Act of 1938 and subsequent amendments provide for minimum wage coverage applicable to specified nonsupervisory employment categories. Exempt from coverage are executives and administrators or professionals]

IN EFFECT	MINIMUM RATES FOR NON-FARM			Minimum rates for farm work-ers [4]	IN EFFECT	MINIMUM RATES FOR NON-FARM			Minimum rates for farm work-ers [4]
	Laws prior to 1966 [1]	Percent, average earn-ings [2]	1966 and later [3]			Laws prior to 1966 [1]	Percent, average earn-ings [2]	1966 and later [3]	
Jan. 25, 1950. .	$0.75	54	(X)	(X)	Jan. 1, 1977 . .	([5])	42	2.30	2.20
Mar. 1, 1956 . .	1.00	52	(X)	(X)	Jan. 1, 1978 . .	2.65	44	2.65	2.65
Sept. 3, 1961. .	1.15	50	(X)	(X)	Jan. 1, 1979 . .	2.90	45	2.90	2.90
Sept. 3, 1963. .	1.25	51	(X)	(X)	Jan. 1, 1980 . .	3.10	44	3.10	3.10
Feb. 1, 1967 . .	1.40	50	$1.00	$1.00	Jan. 1, 1981 . .	3.35	43	3.35	3.35
Feb. 1, 1968 . .	1.60	54	1.15	1.15	Apr. 1, 1990. . .	3.80	35	3.80	3.80
Feb. 1, 1969 . .	([5])	51	1.30	1.30	Apr. 1, 1991. . .	4.25	38	4.25	4.25
Feb. 1, 1970 . .	([5])	49	1.45	([5])	Apr. 1, 1992. . .	([5])	37	([5])	([5])
Feb. 1, 1971 . .	([5])	46	1.60	([5])	Apr. 1, 1993. . .	([5])	36	([5])	([5])
May 1, 1974 . .	2.00	46	1.90	1.60	Apr. 1, 1994. . .	([5])	35	([5])	([5])
Jan. 1, 1975 . .	2.10	45	2.00	1.80	Apr. 1, 1995. . .	([5])	35	([5])	([5])
Jan. 1, 1976 . .	2.30	46	2.20	2.00	Apr. 1, 1996. . .	([5])	34	([5])	([5])

X Not applicable.   [1] Applies to workers covered prior to 1961 amendments and, after Sept. 1965, to workers covered by 1961 amendments. Rates set by 1961 amendments were: Sept. 1961, $1.00; Sept. 1964, $1.15; and Sept. 1965, $1.25. [2] Percent of gross average hourly earnings of production workers in manufacturing.   [3] Applies to workers newly covered by amendments of 1966, 1974, and 1977, and Title IX of Education amendments of 1972.   [4] Included in coverage as of 1966, 1974, and 1977 amendments.   [5] No change in rate.

Source: U.S. Department of Labor, Employment Standards Administration, *Minimum Wage and Maximum Hours Standards Under the Fair Labor Standards Act,* 1981, annual; and unpublished data.

No. 668. Workers Paid Hourly Rates, by Selected Characteristics: 1995

[Annual average of monthly figures; for employed wage and salary workers. Based on Current Population Survey; see text, section 1, and Appendix III]

CHARACTERISTIC	NUMBER OF WORKERS [1] (1,000)				PERCENT OF ALL WORKERS PAID HOURLY RATES			Median hourly earnings of workers paid hourly rates [2]
	Total paid hourly rates	At or below $4.25			At or below $4.25			
		Total	At $4.25	Below $4.25	Total	At $4.25	Below $4.25	
Total, 16 years and over [3]	68,354	3,655	1,956	1,699	5.3	2.9	2.5	$8.17
16 to 24 years	15,567	1,978	1,161	817	12.7	7.5	5.2	5.80
16 to 19 years	5,789	1,140	723	417	19.7	12.5	7.2	5.04
25 years and over	52,786	1,677	795	882	3.2	1.5	1.7	9.36
Male, 16 years and over	34,420	1,338	796	542	3.9	2.3	1.6	9.23
16 to 24 years	8,156	825	545	280	10.1	6.7	3.4	6.04
16 to 19 years	2,912	486	343	143	16.7	11.8	4.9	5.14
25 years and over	26,264	513	251	262	2.0	1.0	1.0	10.73
Women, 16 years and over. . . .	33,934	2,318	1,161	1,157	6.8	3.4	3.4	7.46
16 to 24 years	7,411	1,154	617	537	15.6	8.3	7.2	5.49
16 to 19 years	2,877	654	380	274	22.7	13.2	9.5	4.94
25 years and over	26,523	1,164	544	620	4.4	2.1	2.3	8.17
White	56,475	2,995	1,549	1,446	5.3	2.7	2.6	8.32
Black	8,957	498	314	184	5.6	3.5	2.1	7.66
Hispanic origin [4]	7,624	566	363	203	7.4	4.8	2.7	7.00
Full-time workers	51,347	1,347	657	690	2.6	1.3	1.3	9.14
Part-time workers [5]	16,898	2,301	1,294	1,007	13.6	7.7	6.0	5.86
Private sector industries	59,534	3,384	1,771	1,613	5.7	3.0	2.7	7.97
Goods-producing [6]	18,817	367	236	131	2.0	1.3	0.7	9.61
Service-producing [7]	40,717	3,017	1,535	1,482	7.4	3.8	3.6	7.23
Public sector	8,819	272	186	86	3.1	2.1	1.0	10.33

[1] Excludes the incorporated self-employed.   [2] For definition of median, see Guide to Tabular Presentation.   [3] Includes races not shown separately. Also includes a small number of multiple jobholders whose full- part- time status can not be determined for their principal job. [4] Persons of Hispanic origin may be of any race.   [5] Working fewer than 35 hours per week.   [6] Includes agriculture, mining, construction, and manufacturing.   [7] Includes transportation and public utilities; wholesale trade; finance, insurance, and real estate; private households; and other service industries, not shown separately.

Source: U.S. Bureau of Labor Statistics, unpublished data.

No. 669. Employer Costs for Employee Compensation per Hour Worked: 1995

[**In dollars.** As of **March,** for private industry workers. Based on a sample of establishments; see source for details]

COMPENSATION COMPONENT	Total	Goods produc- ing [1]	Service produc- ing [2]	Manufac- turing	Non- manufac- turing	Union mem- bers	Non- union mem- bers	Full- time workers	Part- time workers
Total compensation . . .	**17.10**	**20.75**	**15.88**	**20.47**	**16.29**	**22.40**	**16.26**	**19.44**	**8.98**
Wages and salaries	12.25	13.97	11.67	13.72	11.89	14.42	11.90	13.71	7.17
Total benefits	4.85	6.78	4.20	6.74	4.39	7.99	4.35	5.73	1.81
Paid leave	1.09	1.37	1.00	1.54	0.98	1.55	1.02	1.33	0.25
Vacation	0.54	0.73	0.47	0.80	0.47	0.84	0.49	(NA)	(NA)
Holiday	0.37	0.49	0.33	0.57	0.33	0.49	0.36	(NA)	(NA)
Sick	0.14	0.11	0.14	0.12	0.14	0.16	0.13	(NA)	(NA)
Other	0.05	0.04	0.05	0.05	0.04	0.06	0.04	(NA)	(NA)
Supplemental pay	0.47	0.78	0.37	0.80	0.39	0.73	0.43	0.57	0.14
Premium pay	0.19	0.40	0.12	0.40	0.14	0.49	0.14	(NA)	(NA)
Nonproduction bonuses .	0.23	0.31	0.20	0.30	0.21	0.12	0.24	(NA)	(NA)
Shift pay	0.05	0.07	0.05	0.09	0.05	0.12	0.04	(NA)	(NA)
Insurance	1.15	1.66	0.98	1.72	1.02	2.24	0.98	1.40	0.28
Health insurance	1.06	1.53	0.90	1.58	0.94	2.09	0.90	(NA)	(NA)
Retirement and savings . . .	0.52	0.82	0.41	0.75	0.46	1.15	0.42	0.63	0.10
Legally required [3]	1.59	2.08	1.43	1.86	1.53	2.24	1.49	1.76	1.02
Social Security	1.02	1.21	0.96	1.21	0.98	1.23	0.99	(NA)	(NA)
Federal unemployment . .	0.03	0.03	0.03	0.03	0.03	0.03	0.03	(NA)	(NA)
State unemployment . .	0.12	0.16	0.11	0.14	0.12	0.16	0.12	(NA)	(NA)
Workers compensation . .	0.39	0.67	0.30	0.48	0.37	0.72	0.34	(NA)	(NA)
Other benefits [4]	0.03	0.07	-	0.09	0.02	0.08	0.02	0.04	-

- Represents or rounds to zero.   NA Not available.   [1] Mining, construction, and manufacturing.   [2] Transportation, communications, public utilities, wholesale trade, retail trade, finance, insurance, real estate, and services.   [3] Includes railroad retirement, railroad unemployment, railroad supplemental unemployment, and other legally required benefits, not shown separately.   [4] Includes severance pay, and supplemental unemployment benefits.

Source: U.S. Bureau of Labor Statistics, *News, Employer Costs for Employee Compensation,* USDL, 95-225.

No. 670. Employees With Employer- or Union-Provided Pension Plans or Group Health Plans: 1994

[For wage and salary workers 15 years old and over as of **March 1995.** Based on Current Population Survey; see text, section 1, and Appendix III. Data based on 1990 population controls]

OCCUPATION	Total (1,000)	PERCENT— Included in pen- sion plan	PERCENT— With group health plan	CHARACTERISTIC	Total (1,000)	PERCENT— Included in pen- sion plan	PERCENT— With group health plan
Total	139,130	41.3	52.9	AGE			
Executive, admin., managerial . . .	17,484	54.7	68.9	Total	139,130	41.3	52.9
Professional specialty	18,980	59.5	67.1	15 to 24 years	23,891	11.6	23.5
				25 to 44 years old	71,621	45.9	57.6
Technical/related support	4,319	55.5	67.5	45 to 64 years	38,797	53.4	63.7
Sales workers	17,001	28.8	43.3	65 years and over	4,820	23.0	42.6
Admin. support, inc. clerical	20,318	47.4	57.1	WORK EXPERIENCE			
				Worked	139,130	41.3	52.9
Precision prod., craft/repair	14,704	42.2	56.6	Full time	108,218	49.5	62.6
				50 weeks or more	85,779	55.5	68.8
Mach. operators, assemblers [1] . . .	8,810	43.0	60.7	27 to 49 weeks	13,055	33.2	47.8
Transportation/material moving . . .	5,651	41.4	56.7	26 weeks or fewer	9,383	17.2	26.6
Handlers, equipment cleaners [2] . .	6,107	24.8	38.5	Part time	30,912	12.4	19.0
				50 weeks or more	13,012	17.6	24.8
Service workers	20,580	22.5	32.1	27 to 49 weeks	7,013	13.0	19.7
Private households	1,071	1.3	7.3	26 weeks or fewer	10,888	5.9	11.6
Other	19,510	23.6	33.5	EMPLOYER SIZE			
				Under 25 persons	41,912	12.7	27.5
Farming, forestry and fishing	4,251	10.0	21.4	25 to 99 persons	17,427	33.0	52.4
				100 to 999 persons	18,935	48.4	63.0
Armed Forces	924	78.4	23.9	500 to 999 persons	7,915	56.3	67.1
				Over 1,000 persons	52,941	61.9	67.6

[1] Includes inspectors.   [2] Includes helpers and laborers.

Source: U.S. Bureau of the Census, unpublished data.

No. 671. Employee Benefits in Private Establishments: 1993 and 1994

[Covers full-time employees in private industry. Medium and large establishments exclude establishments with fewer than 100 workers, and executive and traveling operating employees, and Alaska and Hawaii. Small establishments include those with fewer than 100 employees. Covers only benefits for which the employer pays part or all of the premium or expenses involved, except unpaid parental leave and long-term care insurance. Based on a sample survey of establishments; for details, see sources. For data on employee benefits in State and local governments, see table 505]

MEDIUM AND LARGE PRIVATE ESTABLISHMENTS, 1993	All employees	Professional, technical and related	Clerical and sales	Production and service	SMALL PRIVATE ESTABLISHMENTS, 1994	All employees	Professional, technical and related	Clerical and sales	Blue collar and service
Percent of employees participating in—					**Percent of employees participating in—**				
Paid: Vacations.	97	97	98	96	Paid time off: Holidays . . .	82	91	89	75
Holidays	91	89	93	92	Vacations	88	92	93	83
Jury duty leave	90	95	92	85	Personal leave.	13	21	17	7
Funeral leave	83	86	85	80	Funeral leave.	50	58	55	45
Rest time	68	54	66	76	Jury duty leave	58	74	66	48
Military leave	53	66	54	44	Military leave	17	23	19	13
Sick leave	65	85	80	45	Family leave	2	5	2	1
Personal leave	21	27	31	13	Unpaid family leave	47	53	50	43
Lunch time	9	5	5	13	Disability benefits:				
Maternity leave	3	4	3	1	Short-term disability . . .	61	75	69	50
Paternity leave	1	2	1	(Z)	Paid sick leave	50	69	61	36
Unpaid: Maternity leave . . .	60	63	60	59	Sickness and accident				
Paternity leave	53	55	51	52	insurance.	26	27	27	25
Insurance plans:					Long-term disability. . . .	20	36	27	10
Medical care.	82	84	79	82	Survivor benefits:				
Noncontributory	37	31	32	44	Life insurance	61	73	68	52
Hospital/room and board	82	84	79	82	Accidental death and				
Inpatient surgery	82	84	79	82	dismemberment	48	60	52	40
Mental health care:					Health care benefits:				
Inpatient care.	80	83	77	80	Medical care	66	80	70	57
Outpatient care. . . .	80	82	77	79	Dental care	28	40	31	22
Dental	62	68	63	58	Vision care	10	11	11	10
Extended care facility .	67	71	68	66	Outpatient prescription drug				
Home health care. . . .	71	74	70	68	coverage.	60	75	64	51
Hospice care	53	56	54	52	Retirement income benefits:				
Vision.	26	27	26	27	All retirement [1]	42	53	47	35
In HMO's	19	24	21	15	Defined benefit	15	16	16	15
Alcohol abuse treatment:					Defined contribution. . .	34	45	39	26
Inpatient detoxification	80	82	77	80	Savings and thrift. .	17	23	20	13
Inpatient rehabilitation	66	66	63	58	Deferred profit				
Outpatient	67	69	65	68	sharing.	13	16	17	10
Drug abuse treatment:					Employee stock				
Inpatient detoxification	80	82	77	80	ownership.	1	2	1	1
Inpatient rehabilitation	64	65	60	66	Money purchase				
Outpatient	66	68	64	65	pension	5	9	5	4
Life	91	95	92	89	Cash or deferred				
Noncontributory	87	84	87	89	arrangements:				
Accident/sickness	44	28	37	57	With employer				
Noncontributory	75	65	67	81	contributions . .	20	28	23	15
Long-term disability	41	64	50	23	No employer				
Noncontributory	73	69	71	80	contributions . .	3	5	3	2
Retirement and savings plans [1]	78	83	78	76	Income continuation plans:				
Defined benefit pension . . .	56	57	54	56	Severance pay.	15	24	22	8
Earnings-based					Supplemental unemploy-				
formula [2]	40	50	45	32	ment benefits	(Z)	(Z)	(Z)	(Z)
Defined contribution	49	60	54	40	Family benefits:				
Savings and thrift	29	38	34	21	Employer assistance for				
Employee stock owner-					child care	1	2	1	1
ship.	3	3	4	2	Employer provided funds	1	1	1	(Z)
Deferred profit sharing . .	13	12	16	12	On-site child care . . .	1	1	(Z)	1
Money purchase pension	8	13	7	6	Off-site child care . . .	(Z)	-	(Z)	(Z)
Additional benefits:					Eldercare	33	38	35	29
Parking [3]	88	86	85	92	Long-term care insurance	1	1	1	(Z)
Educational assistance . .	72	85	72	65	Health promotion programs:				
Travel accident insurance . .	44	59	52	32	Wellness programs	6	8	8	3
Severance pay	42	56	48	31	Employee assistance . .	15	19	18	11
Relocation allowance [3]	31	50	30	21	Miscellaneous benefits:. . .				
Recreation facilities [3]	26	34	25	23	Employer-subsidized				
Nonproduction bonuses, cash	38	37	38	38	recreation facilities . . .	5	7	5	4
Child care	7	12	6	4	Job-related travel accident				
Flexible benefits plans . . .	12	21	13	6	insurance	13	18	14	10
Reimbursement accounts [4] .	52	68	62	37	Nonproduction bonuses .	47	48	49	46
Eldercare	31	33	32	29	Financial counseling . . .	2	3	2	2
Long-term care insurance . .	6	8	8	3	Subsidized commuting. . .	1	2	(Z)	(Z)
Wellness programs	37	51	38	29	Sabbatical leave.	1	3	1	1
Employee assistance					Education assistance:				
programs.	62	74	64	53	Job-related.	37	49	46	27
					Not job-related	6	7	8	4
					Flexible benefit plans . . .	3	2	5	2
					Reimbursement accounts [4]	19	28	23	13

- Represents zero.   Z Less than .5 percent.   [1] Employees may participate in both defined benefit and contribution plans.
[2] Earnings-based formulas pay a percent of employee's annual earnings (usually earnings in the final years of employment) per year of service.   [3] 1991 data.   [4] Account which is used throughout the year to pay for plan premiums or to reimburse the employee for benefit related expenses. Account may be financed by employer, employee, or both.

Source: U.S. Bureau of Labor Statistics, *Employee Benefits in Medium and Large Private Establishments, 1993*, Bulletin 2456; and *Employee Benefits in Small Private Establishments, 1994*, Bulletin 2475.

No. 672. Major Collective Bargaining Agreements—Average Percent Wage Rate Changes Under All Agreements: 1970 to 1995

[In percent, except as indicated. Data represent all wage rate changes implemented under the terms of private nonfarm industry agreements affecting 1,000 workers or more. Series covers production and related workers in manufacturing and nonsupervisory workers in nonmanufacturing industries. Data measure all wage rate changes effective in the year stemming from settlements reached in the year, deferred from prior year settlements, and cost-of-living adjustment (COLA) clauses]

ITEM	1970	1975	1980	1985	1990	1991	1992	1993	1994	1995
Average wage rate change (prorated over all workers)	8.8	8.7	9.9	3.3	3.5	3.6	3.1	3.0	2.7	2.4
Source:										
Current settlements	5.1	2.8	3.6	0.7	1.3	1.1	0.8	0.9	0.6	0.7
Prior settlements	3.1	3.7	3.5	1.8	1.5	1.9	1.9	1.9	1.9	1.5
COLA provisions	0.6	2.2	2.8	0.7	0.7	0.5	0.4	0.2	0.2	0.2
Industry:										
Manufacturing	7.1	8.5	10.2	2.8	4.4	3.7	3.1	3.3	2.4	2.3
Nonmanufacturing	10.5	8.9	9.7	3.6	3.0	3.5	3.1	2.8	2.9	2.4
Construction	(NA)	8.1	9.9	3.0	3.4	3.4	3.4	2.7	2.7	2.8
Transportation and public utilities. . . .	(NA)	9.7	10.8	3.6	2.2	3.3	2.7	3.0	2.8	2.2
Wholesale and retail trade	(NA)	9.2	7.6	3.3	3.6	3.5	3.5	2.3	2.9	2.3
Services	(NA)	6.4	8.1	5.1	4.3	4.9	3.7	3.4	3.3	2.2
Nonmanufacturing, excluding construction.	(NA)	9.3	9.6	3.7	2.9	3.6	3.0	2.8	2.9	2.3
Average wage rate increase for workers receiving an increase	9.4	9.0	10.1	4.2	4.2	4.0	3.7	3.5	3.3	3.1
Source:										
Current settlements	11.9	10.2	9.4	4.1	4.1	4.2	3.6	3.2	3.2	3.2
Prior settlements	5.8	5.2	5.6	3.7	3.3	3.7	3.8	3.4	3.4	3.1
COLA provisions	3.7	4.8	7.7	2.2	2.7	2.0	2.0	1.3	1.7	1.7
Total number of workers receiving a wage rate increase (mil.)	10.2	9.7	8.9	5.5	4.9	5.1	4.7	4.8	4.6	4.2
Source (mil.):										
Current settlements	4.7	2.7	3.5	1.4	1.9	1.5	1.3	1.7	1.1	1.1
Prior settlements	5.7	7.3	5.6	3.4	2.7	3.0	2.8	3.0	3.0	2.6
COLA provisions	1.8	4.7	3.4	2.3	1.4	1.3	1.0	0.9	0.8	0.7
Number of workers not receiving a wage rate increase (mil.)	0.6	0.4	0.2	1.5	1.0	0.5	0.9	0.7	0.8	1.2

NA Not available.

Source: U.S. Bureau of Labor Statistics, *Compensation and Working Conditions*, monthly through 1995. Data series discontinued. Publication quarterly, beginning 1996.

No. 673. Major Collective Bargaining Settlements—Average Percent Changes in Wage and Compensation Rates Negotiated: 1970 to 1995

[In percent, except as indicated. Data represent private nonfarm industry settlements affecting production and related workers in manufacturing and nonsupervisory workers in nonmanufacturing industries. Wage data cover units with 1,000 workers or more. Compensation data relate to units of 5,000 workers or more. Data relate to contracts negotiated in each calendar year but exclude possible changes in wage rates under cost-of-living adjustment (COLA) clauses, except increases guaranteed by the contract. Includes all settlements, whether wage and benefit rates were changed or not. Minus sign (-) indicates decrease]

ITEM	1970	1975	1980	1985	1989	1990	1991	1992	1993	1994	1995
Compensation rates:											
First year.	13.1	11.4	10.4	2.6	4.5	4.6	4.1	3.0	3.0	2.3	2.6
Over life of contract [1].	9.1	8.1	7.1	2.7	3.4	3.2	3.4	3.1	2.4	2.4	2.5
Wage rates:											
All industries:											
First year	11.9	10.2	9.5	2.3	4.0	4.0	3.6	2.7	2.3	2.0	2.3
Contracts with COLA	(NA)	12.2	8.0	1.6	3.9	3.4	3.4	2.7	2.8	2.7	1.6
Contracts without COLA	(NA)	9.1	11.7	2.7	4.0	4.4	3.7	2.7	2.1	1.8	2.4
Over life of contract [1]	8.9	7.8	7.1	2.7	3.4	3.2	3.2	3.0	2.1	2.3	2.5
Contracts with COLA	(NA)	7.1	5.0	2.5	2.8	1.9	3.0	2.5	1.4	2.5	1.5
Contracts without COLA	(NA)	8.3	10.3	2.8	3.5	4.0	3.3	3.1	2.5	2.3	2.6
Manufacturing:											
First year	8.1	9.8	7.4	0.8	3.9	3.7	3.9	2.6	2.7	2.4	2.0
Over life of contract [1]	6.0	8.0	5.4	1.8	3.2	2.1	3.1	2.6	1.5	2.3	2.1
Nonmanufacturing:											
First year	15.2	10.4	10.9	3.3	4.0	4.3	3.4	2.7	2.1	1.8	2.4
Over life of contract [1]	11.5	7.8	8.3	3.3	3.4	4.0	3.3	3.0	2.5	2.3	2.6
Number of workers affected (mil.) . .	4.7	2.9	3.8	2.2	1.9	2.0	1.8	1.6	2.1	1.6	1.5
Manufacturing (mil.)	2.2	0.8	1.6	0.9	0.4	0.9	0.6	0.3	0.8	0.4	0.3
Nonmanufacturing (mil.)	2.5	2.1	2.2	1.3	1.5	1.1	1.2	1.3	1.3	1.1	1.2

NA Not available. [1] Average annual rate of change.

Source: U.S. Bureau of Labor Statistics, *Compensation and Working Conditions*, monthly through 1995. Data series discontinued. Publication quarterly, beginning 1996.

No. 674. Workers Killed or Disabled on the Job: 1960 to 1994

[Data for 1994 are preliminary estimates. Estimates based on data from the U.S. National Center for Health Statistics, State vital statistics departments, State industrial commissions and beginning 1992, Bureau of Labor Statisitcs, Census of Occupational Fatalities. Numbers of workers based on data from the U.S. Bureau of Labor Statistics]

YEAR	DEATHS						Dis-abling injur-ies [2] (mil.)	YEAR AND INDUSTRY GROUP	DEATHS		Dis-abling injur-ies [2] (1,000)
	Total		Manufacturing		Nonmanu-facturing				Number	Rate [1]	
	Number (1,000)	Rate [1]	Number (1,000)	Rate [1]	Number (1,000)	Rate [1]					
1960 . . .	13.8	21	1.7	10	12.1	25	2.0	**1994, total**	5,000	4	3,500
1965 . . .	14.1	20	1.8	10	12.3	24	2.1	Agriculture [3]	890	26	140
1970 . . .	13.8	18	1.7	9	12.1	21	2.2	Mining and quarrying [4] . .	160	27	20
1975 . . .	13.0	15	1.6	9	11.4	17	2.2	Construction	910	15	300
1980 . . .	13.2	13	1.7	8	11.5	15	2.2	Manufacturing	690	4	590
1985 . . .	11.5	11	1.2	6	10.3	12	2.0	Transportation and			
1986 . . .	11.1	10	1.0	5	10.1	11	1.8	utilities	740	12	260
1987 . . .	11.3	10	1.0	5	10.3	11	1.8	Trade [5]	450	2	800
1988 . . .	11.0	10	1.1	6	9.9	10	1.8	Services [6]	640	2	860
1989 . . .	10.9	9	1.1	6	9.8	10	1.7	Government	520	3	530
1990 . . .	10.1	9	1.0	5	9.1	9	3.9				
1991 . . .	9.8	8	0.8	4	9.0	9	3.5				
1992 . . .	5.0	4	0.7	4	4.3	4	3.3				
1993 . . .	5.0	4	0.7	4	4.3	4	3.2				
1994 . . .	5.0	4	0.7	4	4.3	4	3.5				

[1] Per 100,000 workers. [2] Disabling injury defined as one which results in death, some degree of physical impairment, or renders the person unable to perform regular activities for a full day beyond the day of the injury. Due to change in methodology, data beginning 1990 not comparable with prior years. [3] Includes forestry and fishing. [4] Includes oil and gas extraction. [5] Includes wholesale and retail trade. [6] Includes finance, insurance, and real estate.

Source: National Safety Council, Itasca, IL, *Accident Facts,* annual (copyright).

No. 675. Worker Deaths and Injuries and Production Time Lost: 1992 to 1994

ITEM	DEATHS (1,000)			DISABLING INJURIES [1] (mil.)			PRODUCTION TIME LOST (mil. days)					
							In the current year			In future years [2]		
	1992	1993	1994	1992	1993	1994	1992	1993	1994	1992	1993	1994
All accidents	36.7	38.3	41.1	8.6	8.4	9.1	200	195	215	420	430	410
On the job	5.0	5.0	5.0	3.6	3.2	3.5	80	75	75	120	120	60
Off the job	31.7	33.3	36.1	5.0	5.2	5.6	120	120	140	300	310	350
Motor vehicle	19.3	19.8	19.6	1.1	1.0	0.9	(NA)	(NA)	(NA)	(NA)	(NA)	(NA)
Public nonmotor vehicle . . .	6.2	7.0	7.6	2.0	2.3	2.4	(NA)	(NA)	(NA)	(NA)	(NA)	(NA)
Home	6.2	6.5	8.9	1.9	1.9	2.3	(NA)	(NA)	(NA)	(NA)	(NA)	(NA)

NA Not available. [1] See footnote 2, table 674 for a definition of disabling injuries. [2] Based on an average of 5,850 days lost in future years per fatality and 565 days lost in future years per permanent injury.

Source: National Safety Council, Itasca, IL, *Accident Facts,* annual (copyright).

No. 676. Industries with the Highest Total Case Incidence Rates for Nonfatal Injuries and Illnesses: 1993 and 1994

[**Rates per full-time employees.** Industries shown are those with highest rates in 1994. See headnote, table 677]

INDUSTRY	1987 SIC [1] code	1993	1994	INDUSTRY	1987 SIC [1] code	1993	1994
Private industry	(X)	8.5	8.4	Architectural metal work	3446	16.6	23.0
				Iron and steel forgings	3462	20.7	22.9
Meat packing plants	2011	39.0	36.4	Poultry slaughtering processing	2015	23.2	22.7
Motor vehicles and car bodies	3711	31.2	33.2	Truck and bus bodies	3713	22.7	22.2
Ship building and repairing	3731	34.3	31.8	Metal barrels, drums, and pails	3412	22.1	22.1
Gray and ductile iron foundries	3321	27.0	30.2	Travel trailers and campers	3792	19.0	21.9
Mobile homes	2451	27.5	29.3	Primary aluminum	3334	18.1	21.6
Metal sanitary ware	3431	29.0	28.3	Malleable iron foundries	3322	25.9	21.4
Truck trailers	3715	22.7	27.5	Flat glass	3211	20.9	21.3
Automotive stampings	3465	26.7	25.9	Prefabricated wood buildings	2452	22.8	20.8
Motorcycles, bicycles, and parts	3751	23.8	24.2	Knit underwear mills	2254	20.3	20.7
Aluminum die-castings	3363	22.8	23.3	Structural wood members, n.e.c. [2] . . .	2439	20.8	20.7
Steel foundries, n.e.c. [2]	3325	23.1	23.3	Sausages and other prepared meats .	2013	19.7	20.4
Household appliances, n.e.c. [2]	3639	27.5	23.2	Motor vehicle parts and accessories . .	3714	19.1	20.3
Public building and related furniture . .	2531	19.2	23.2	Metal doors, sash and trim	3442	16.6	19.4

(X) Not applicable. [1] 1987 Standard Industrial Classification; see text, section 13. [2] N.e.c. means not elsewhere classified.

Source: U.S. Bureau of Labor Statistics, *Occupational Injuries and Illnesses in the United States by Industry,* annual.

No. 677. Nonfatal Occupational Injury and Illness Incidence Rates: 1993 and 1994

[Rates per 100 full-time employees. For nonfarm employment data, see table 654. Rates refer to any occupational injury or illness resulting in (1) lost workday cases, or (2) nonfatal cases without lost workdays. Incidence rates were calculated as: Number of injuries and illnesses divided by total hours worked by all employees during year multiplied by 200,000 as base for 100 full-time equivalent workers (working 40 hours per week, 50 weeks a year)]

INDUSTRY	1987 SIC [1] code	1993	1994	INDUSTRY	1987 SIC [1] code	1993	1994
Private sector [2]	(X)	**8.5**	**8.4**	Local passenger transit	41	11.5	9.6
Agriculture, forestry, fishing [2]	A	**11.2**	**10.0**	Trucking and warehousing	42	13.8	14.8
Mining [3]	B	**6.8**	**6.3**	Water transportation	44	10.4	9.5
Metal mining [3]	10	5.9	5.6	Transportation by air	45	15.1	13.3
Coal mining [3]	12	10.3	9.9	Pipelines, except natural gas	46	3.8	2.4
Oil and gas extraction	13	6.1	5.4	Transportation services	47	4.0	4.2
Nonmetallic minerals, exc. fuels	14	6.3	5.9	Communications	48	3.9	3.3
Construction	C	**12.2**	**11.8**	Electric, gas, sanitary services	49	7.5	7.3
General building contractors	15	11.5	10.9	**Wholesale and retail trade**	F, G	**8.1**	**7.9**
Heavy construction, except				Wholesale trade	F	7.8	7.7
building	16	11.1	10.2	Retail trade	G	8.2	7.9
Special trade contractors	17	12.8	12.5	**Finance, insurance, real estate**	H	**2.9**	**2.7**
Manufacturing	D	**12.1**	**12.2**	Depository institutions	60	2.5	2.1
Durable goods	(X)	13.1	13.5	Nondepository institutions	61	1.3	1.5
Lumber and wood products	24	15.9	15.7	Security and commodity brokers	62	0.9	0.7
Furniture and fixtures	25	14.6	15.0	Insurance carriers	63	2.4	2.6
Stone, clay, and glass products	32	13.8	13.2	Insurance agents, brokers, and			
Primary metal industries	33	17.0	16.8	service	64	1.5	1.4
Fabricated metal products	34	16.2	16.4	Real estate	65	6.2	5.7
Industrial machinery and equip	35	11.1	11.6	Holding and other investment			
Electronic/other electric equip	36	8.3	8.3	offices	67	2.4	1.9
Transportation equipment	37	18.5	19.6	**Services [4]**	I	**6.7**	**6.5**
Instruments/related products	38	5.6	5.9	Hotels and other lodging places	70	10.7	10.1
Miscellaneous manufacturing				Personal services	72	4.3	4.1
industries	39	10.0	9.9	Business services	73	5.0	4.9
Nondurable goods	(X)	10.7	10.5	Auto repair, services, and			
Food and kindred products	20	17.6	17.1	parking	75	7.5	6.9
Tobacco products	21	5.8	5.3	Miscellaneous repair services	76	8.2	7.7
Textile mill products	22	9.7	8.7	Motion pictures	78	3.3	3.0
Apparel and other textile				Amusement and recreation			
products	23	9.0	8.9	services	79	10.3	9.0
Paper and allied products	26	9.9	9.6	Health services	80	9.6	9.4
Printing and publishing	27	6.9	6.7	Legal services	81	1.3	1.1
Chemicals and allied products	28	5.9	5.7	Educational services	82	4.6	4.2
Petroleum and coal products	29	5.2	4.7	Social services	83	7.3	7.5
Rubber and misc. plastics				Museums, botanical, zoological			
products	30	13.9	14.0	gardens	84	9.1	7.1
Leather and leather products	31	12.1	12.0	Engineering and management			
Transportation/public utilities [3]	E	**9.5**	**9.3**	services	87	2.6	2.6
Railroad transportation [3]	40	5.8	5.1	Services, n.e.c. [5]	89	2.4	(NA)

NA Not available.　X Not applicable.　[1] 1987 Standard Industrial Classification; see text, section 13.　[2] Excludes farms with fewer than 11 employees.　[3] Data conforming to OSHA definitions for employers in the railroad industry and for mining operators in coal, metal, and nonmetal mining. Independent mining contractors are excluded from the coal, metal, and nonmetal mining industries.　[4] Includes categories not shown separately.　[5] N.e.c means not elsewhere classified.

Source: U.S. Bureau of Labor Statistics, *Occupational Injuries and Illnesses in the United States by Industry*, annual.

No. 678. Fatal Work Injuries, by Cause: 1994

[For the 50 States and DC. Based on the 1994 Census of Fatal Occupational Injuries. Due to methodological differences, data differ from those in table 674. For details, see source]

CAUSE	Number of fatalities	Percent distribution	CAUSE	Number of fatalities	Percent distribution
Total	**6,588**	**100**	Contacts with objects and equipment [1]	1,015	15
			Struck by object [1]	589	9
Transportation accidents [1]	2,740	42	Struck by falling objects	371	6
Highway accidents [1]	1,336	20	Struck by flying object	67	1
Collision between vehicles, mobile			Caught in or compressed by—		
equipment	650	10	equipment or objects	280	4
Noncollision accidents	370	6	collapsing materials	132	2
Nonhighway accident (farm, industrial					
premises)	407	6	Falls	661	10
Aircraft accidents	424	6			
Workers struck by a vehicle	383	6	Exposure to harmful substances or		
Water vehicle accidents	92	1	environments [1]	638	10
Railway accidents	81	1	Contact with electric current	346	5
			Exposure to caustic, noxious		
Assaults and violent acts [1]	1,308	20	or allergenic substances	131	2
Homicides [1]	1,071	16	Oxygen deficiency	110	2
Shooting	925	14	Drowning, submersion	90	1
Stabbing	60	1	Fires and explosions	202	3
Self-inflicted injury	210	3	Other events and exposures	24	(Z)

(Z) Less than .5 percent.　[1] Includes other causes, not shown separately.

Source: U.S. Bureau of Labor Statistics, *USDL News*, Bulleitn 95-288, August 3, 1995.

No. 679. Fatal Occupational Injuries, by Industry and Event: 1994

[See headnote, table 678]

INDUSTRY	1987 SIC [1] code	Fatal-ities [2]	EVENT OR EXPOSURE—PERCENT DISTRIBUTION					Rate [5]
			Trans-portation incidents	Assaults/ violent acts	Contact with objects [3]	Falls	Expo-sure [4]	
Total.	(X)	6,588	42	20	15	10	10	5
Private industry	(X)	5,923	41	20	16	10	10	6
Agriculture, forestry, fishing	A	847	54	7	20	7	11	24
Mining [6].	B	180	31	-	34	6	15	27
Coal mining.	12	41	22	-	56	-	-	36
Oil and gas extraction	13	99	33	-	23	9	21	26
Construction	C	1,027	26	3	18	32	18	15
General building contractors	15	189	22	5	16	42	12	-
Heavy construction, except building.	16	247	41	-	21	8	24	-
Special trade contractors	17	591	20	3	17	39	17	-
Manufacturing [6].	D	787	31	7	39	7	10	4
Food and kindred products.	20	78	42	8	22	9	17	4
Lumber and wood products	24	199	19	-	68	2	7	27
Transportation and public utilities [6] . . .	E	944	67	14	9	3	6	13
Local passenger transit	41	114	18	80	-	-	-	22
Trucking and warehousing	42	502	79	4	11	2	3	22
Transportation by air	45	98	94	-	-	-	-	13
Electric, gas, sanitary services	49	88	48	5	10	8	26	8
Wholesale trade	F	269	51	10	20	8	7	6
Retail trade [6].	G	797	19	70	4	3	3	4
Food stores.	54	235	6	88	2	2	-	7
Automotive dealer and service stations	55	120	34	55	7	-	-	6
Eating and drinking places	58	181	12	77	-	4	3	3
Finance, insurance, real estate.	H	112	39	37	5	8	9	1
Services [6].	I	844	42	30	7	9	10	3
Business services.	73	253	40	31	5	13	10	5
Auto repair, services, and parking . .	75	89	28	28	22	4	8	6
Government.	J	665	51	21	7	7	6	3

- No data reported or data do not meet publication standards. X Not applicable. [1] 1987 Standard Industrial Classification code, see text section 13. [2] Includes 116 fatalities, not available by type of industry. Includes fatalities caused by other events and exposures, not shown separately. [3] Includes equipment. [4] Exposure to harmful substances or environments. [5] Rate per 100,000 employed civilians 16 years old and over. [6] Includes other industries, not shown separately.

Source: U.S. Bureau of Labor Statistics, USDL News, Bulleitn 95-288, August 3, 1995.

No. 680. Work Stoppages: 1960 to 1995

[Excludes work stoppages involving fewer than 1,000 workers and lasting less than 1 day. Information is based on reports of labor disputes appearing in daily newspapers, trade journals, and other public sources. The parties to the disputes are contacted by telephone, when necessary, to clarify details of the stoppages]

YEAR	Number of work stop-pages [1]	Workers involved [2] (1,000)	DAYS IDLE		YEAR	Number of work stop-pages [1]	Workers involved [2] (1,000)	DAYS IDLE	
			Number [3] (1,000)	Percent esti-mated working time [4]				Number [3] (1,000)	Percent esti-mated working time [4]
1960.	222	896	13,260	0.09	1982.	96	656	9,061	0.04
1965.	268	999	15,140	0.10	1983.	81	909	17,461	0.08
1969.	412	1,576	29,397	0.16	1984.	62	376	8,499	0.04
1970.	381	2,468	52,761	0.29	1985.	54	324	7,079	0.03
1971.	298	2,516	35,538	0.19					
					1986.	69	533	11,861	0.05
1972.	250	975	16,764	0.09	1987.	46	174	[5]4,481	0.02
1973.	317	1,400	16,260	0.08	1988.	40	118	[5]4,381	0.02
1974.	424	1,796	31,809	0.16	1989.	51	452	16,996	0.07
1975.	235	965	17,563	0.09	1990.	44	185	5,926	0.02
1976.	231	1,519	23,962	0.12					
					1991.	40	392	4,584	0.02
1977.	298	1,212	21,258	0.10	1992.	35	364	3,989	0.01
1978.	219	1,006	23,774	0.11	1993.	35	182	3,981	0.01
1979.	235	1,021	20,409	0.09	1994.	45	322	5,020	0.02
1980.	187	795	20,844	0.09	1995.	31	192	5,771	0.02
1981.	145	729	16,908	0.07					

[1] Beginning in year indicated. [2] Workers counted more than once if involved in more than one stoppage during the year. [3] Resulting from all stoppages in effect in a year, including those that began in an earlier year. [4] Agricultural and government employees are included in the total working time; private household and forestry and fishery employees are excluded. [5] Revised since originally published.

Source: U.S. Bureau of Labor Statistics, Compensation and Conditions, monthly through 1995, thereafter quarterly.

No. 681. Labor Union Membership, by Sector: 1983 to 1995

[See headnote, table 683]

SECTOR	1983	1985	1989	1990	1991	1992	1993	1994	1995
TOTAL (1,000)									
Wage and salary workers:									
Union members	17,717.4	16,996.1	16,960.5	16,739.8	16,568.4	16,390.3	16,598.1	16,740.3	16,359.6
Covered by unions	20,532.1	19,358.1	19,197.6	19,057.8	18,733.8	18,540.1	18,646.4	18,842.5	18,346.3
Public sector workers:									
Union members	5,737.2	5,743.1	6,424.2	6,485.0	6,632.0	6,653.1	7,017.8	7,091.0	6,927.4
Covered by unions	7,112.2	6,920.6	7,614.4	7,691.4	7,796.0	7,840.6	8,162.4	8,191.8	7,986.6
Private sector workers:									
Union members	11,980.2	11,253.0	10,536.2	10,254.8	9,936.5	9,737.2	9,580.3	9,649.4	9,432.1
Covered by unions	13,419.9	12,437.5	11,583.1	11,366.4	10,937.8	10,699.5	10,484.0	10,650.6	10,359.8
PERCENT									
Wage and salary workers:									
Union members	20.1	18.0	16.4	16.1	16.1	15.8	15.8	15.5	14.9
Covered by unions	23.3	20.5	18.6	18.3	18.2	17.9	17.7	17.4	16.7
Public sector workers:									
Union members	36.7	35.7	36.7	36.5	36.9	36.6	37.7	38.7	37.7
Covered by unions	45.5	43.1	43.5	43.3	43.3	43.2	43.8	44.7	43.5
Private sector workers:									
Union members	16.5	14.3	12.3	11.9	11.7	11.4	11.1	10.8	10.3
Covered by unions	18.5	15.9	13.5	13.2	12.9	12.5	12.1	11.9	11.3

Source: The Bureau of National Affairs, Inc., Washington, DC, *Union Membership and Earnings Data Book: Compilations from the Current Population Survey (1996 edition),* (copyright by BNA); authored by Barry Hirsch and David Macpherson of Florida State University. Internet site http://www.bna.com/bnaplus (operational fall 1996).

No. 682. U.S. Membership in AFL-CIO Affiliated Unions, by Selected Union: 1975 to 1995

[**In thousands.** Figures represent the labor organizations as constituted in 1995 and reflect past merger activity. Membership figures based on average per capita paid membership to the AFL-CIO for the 2-year period ending in June of the year shown and reflect only actively-employed members. Labor unions shown had a membership of 50,000 or more in 1995]

LABOR ORGANIZATION	1975	1985	1995	LABOR ORGANIZATION	1975	1985	1995
Total [1]	**11,199**	**13,287**	**13,014**	Machinists and Aerospace			
Actors and Artists	76	100	80	(IAM)	780	520	448
Automobile, Aerospace and				Mine Workers	(X)	(X)	75
Agriculture (UAW)	(X)	974	751	Office and Professional			
Bakery, Confectionery and				Employees	74	90	86
Tobacco	(X)	115	96	Oil, Chemical, Atomic			
Bricklayers	143	95	84	Workers (OCAW)	145	108	83
Carpenters	700	609	378	Painters	160	133	95
Clothing and Textile Workers				Paperworkers Int'l	275	232	233
(ACTWU)	(X)	228	129	Plumbing and Pipefitting	228	226	220
Communication Workers				Postal Workers	249	232	261
(CWA)	476	524	478	Retail, Wholesale Department			
Electrical Workers (IBEW)	856	791	679	Stores	118	106	76
Electronic, Electrical and				Rubber, Cork, Linoleum,			
Salaried [2]	(X)	(X)	135	Plastic	173	106	79
Operating Engineers	300	330	298	Seafarers	80	80	80
Fire Fighters	123	142	151	Service Employees			
Food and Commercial				(SEIU)	480	688	1,027
Workers (UFCW)	(X)	989	983	Sheet Metal Workers	120	108	106
Garment Workers (ILGWU)	363	210	123	Stage Employees, Moving			
Glass, Molders, Pottery, and				Picture Machine Operators	50	50	51
Plastics	(X)	72	69	State, County, Municipal			
Government, American				(AFSCME)	647	997	1,183
Federation (AFGE)	255	199	153	Steelworkers	1,062	572	403
Graphic Communications	(X)	141	94	Teachers (AFT)	396	470	613
Hotel Employees and				Teamsters [3]	(X)	(X)	1,285
Restaurant Employees	421	327	241	Transit Union	90	94	95
Iron Workers	160	140	82	Transport Workers	95	85	75
Laborers	475	383	352	Transportation-Communications	(X)	(X)	58
Letter Carriers (NALC)	151	186	210	Transportation Union, United	134	88	58
Longshoreman's Association	60	65	61				

X Not applicable. [1] Includes other AFL-CIO, not shown separately. [2] Includes Machine and Furniture Workers. [3] Includes Chauffeurs, Warehousemen and Helpers.

Source: American Federation of Labor and Congress of Industrial Organizations, Washington, DC, *Report of the AFL-CIO Executive Council,* biennial.

No. 683. Labor Union Membership, by State: 1983 and 1995

[Annual averages of monthly figures. For wage and salary workers in agriculture and non-agriculture. Data represent union members by place of residence. Based on the Current Population Survey and subject to sampling error. For methodological details, see source]

STATE	UNION MEMBERS (1,000)		WORKERS COVERED BY UNIONS (1,000)		PERCENT OF WORKERS—					
					Union members		Covered by unions		Private manufacturing sector union members	
	1983	1995	1983	1995	1983	1995	1983	1995	1983	1995
United States. .	17,717.4	16,359.6	20,532.1	18,346.3	20.1	14.9	23.3	16.7	27.8	17.6
Alabama [1].	228.2	235.5	268.2	256.5	16.9	13.6	19.8	14.9	25.9	19.5
Alaska	41.7	54.1	49.2	60.1	24.9	23.1	29.3	25.7	23.3	3.8
Arizona [1]	125.0	145.5	156.4	174.8	11.4	8.0	14.3	9.7	7.8	4.9
Arkansas [1]	82.2	79.4	103.2	98.7	11.0	7.8	13.8	9.7	18.7	14.0
California	2,118.9	2,176.4	2,505.2	2,462.9	21.9	17.7	25.9	20.0	21.0	12.1
Colorado.	177.9	170.0	209.6	207.7	13.6	9.9	16.0	12.0	13.1	9.2
Connecticut.	314.0	287.9	345.1	295.6	22.7	20.2	25.0	20.7	28.1	14.4
Delaware	49.2	42.9	54.1	48.2	20.1	13.0	22.1	14.6	27.3	18.7
District of Columbia .	52.4	37.2	69.4	44.2	19.5	15.1	25.9	18.0	17.6	10.8
Florida [1]	393.7	412.3	532.9	558.2	10.2	7.3	13.8	9.9	11.3	5.8
Georgia [1]	267.0	211.2	345.1	237.4	11.9	6.8	15.3	7.6	16.9	8.7
Hawaii	112.6	117.1	124.9	124.1	29.2	24.6	32.4	26.1	35.6	11.0
Idaho [1].	41.3	37.7	53.7	47.5	12.5	8.1	16.2	10.2	19.0	11.6
Illinois	1,063.8	1,041.7	1,205.1	1,094.9	24.2	20.2	27.4	21.2	32.4	23.5
Indiana.	503.3	443.1	544.5	482.5	24.9	16.5	27.0	17.9	48.7	29.9
Iowa [1]	185.9	152.1	231.3	191.9	17.2	12.1	21.5	15.2	40.3	20.1
Kansas [1]	125.2	110.6	170.4	138.5	13.7	10.2	18.7	12.7	25.5	17.7
Kentucky	223.7	195.3	259.8	223.0	17.9	12.6	20.8	14.4	37.4	22.0
Louisiana [1]	204.2	114.4	267.8	143.1	13.8	7.0	18.1	8.8	24.9	16.8
Maine.	88.0	78.1	100.4	89.4	21.0	15.6	24.0	17.8	24.8	21.9
Maryland	346.5	350.7	423.1	419.7	18.5	14.9	22.6	17.8	29.2	20.1
Massachusetts.	603.2	427.9	661.4	470.7	23.7	16.2	26.0	17.8	26.7	11.3
Michigan.	1,005.4	947.2	1,084.6	1,005.7	30.4	23.7	32.8	25.1	46.2	33.9
Minnesota.	393.9	430.6	439.4	457.9	23.2	20.3	25.9	21.6	22.3	16.8
Mississippi [1]	79.4	56.4	99.7	71.8	9.9	5.2	12.5	6.7	18.9	9.8
Missouri	374.4	342.2	416.7	387.0	20.8	14.6	23.2	16.5	36.6	23.9
Montana.	49.5	50.8	55.5	56.6	18.3	15.8	20.5	17.5	33.0	15.6
Nebraska [1]	80.6	65.4	94.8	88.5	13.6	9.1	16.0	12.4	19.1	14.4
Nevada [1]	90.0	137.0	106.7	160.6	22.4	20.2	26.6	23.6	10.8	8.5
New Hampshire	48.5	66.6	60.8	76.4	11.5	12.6	14.4	14.5	10.6	6.5
New Jersey.	822.1	739.3	918.2	801.9	26.9	21.9	30.0	23.8	31.4	20.5
New Mexico	52.6	57.7	70.6	71.9	11.8	9.4	15.8	11.7	11.9	9.6
New York	2,155.6	1,975.5	2,385.9	2,086.1	32.5	27.7	36.0	29.3	31.0	22.5
North Carolina [1]	178.7	132.2	238.1	169.0	7.6	4.2	10.2	5.4	6.9	2.9
North Dakota [1]	28.4	25.7	35.1	30.8	13.2	10.0	16.3	12.0	27.4	19.5
Ohio	1,011.0	885.2	1,125.0	979.0	25.1	18.5	27.9	20.5	40.9	28.9
Oklahoma.	131.5	116.9	168.2	134.9	11.5	9.3	14.7	10.7	25.2	14.0
Oregon.	222.9	266.8	261.9	288.3	22.3	20.1	26.2	21.7	28.7	15.1
Pennsylvania.	1,195.7	929.5	1,350.0	1,020.6	27.5	18.9	31.1	20.7	42.3	26.7
Rhode Island.	85.8	78.1	93.7	83.9	21.5	19.4	23.5	20.8	16.9	12.6
South Carolina [1] . . .	69.6	51.8	100.6	82.7	5.9	3.3	8.6	5.2	5.5	2.9
South Dakota [1]	26.8	22.3	34.8	27.2	11.5	7.7	14.9	9.4	19.0	9.1
Tennessee [1]	252.4	219.3	300.9	260.0	15.1	9.5	18.0	11.3	21.4	16.6
Texas [1].	583.7	511.9	712.8	633.7	9.7	6.5	11.9	8.0	16.1	8.9
Utah [1]	81.6	72.7	100.9	91.8	15.2	9.0	18.9	11.4	14.9	4.1
Vermont	25.9	23.9	31.5	29.4	12.6	9.3	15.3	11.5	13.5	7.2
Virginia [1]	268.3	200.5	346.1	266.6	11.7	6.7	15.1	8.9	21.2	8.3
Washington.	419.9	477.1	499.7	508.9	27.1	21.0	32.3	22.4	35.5	29.3
West Virginia.	142.7	104.5	160.6	114.1	25.3	16.3	28.5	17.8	41.3	30.5
Wisconsin	465.5	429.0	526.7	465.0	23.8	17.7	26.9	19.1	36.0	21.3
Wyoming [1]	27.1	22.2	31.8	26.1	13.9	11.2	16.2	13.1	14.6	21.9

[1] Right to work State.

Source: The Bureau of National Affairs, Inc., Washington, DC, *Union Membership and Earnings Data Book: Compilations from the Current Population Survey, (1996 edition)* (copyright by BNA); authored by Barry Hirsch and David Macpherson of Florida State University. Internet site http://www.bna.com/bnaplus (operational fall 1996).

No. 684. Union Members, by Selected Characteristics: 1983 and 1995

[Annual averages of monthly data. Covers employed wage and salary workers 16 years old and over. Excludes self-employed workers whose businesses are incorporated although they technically qualify as wage and salary workers. See headnote table 631 regarding data by occupation and industry. Based on Current Population Survey, see text, section 1, and Appendix III]

CHARACTERISTIC	EMPLOYED WAGE AND SALARY WORKERS						MEDIAN USUAL WEEKLY EARNINGS[4] (dol.)							
	Total (1,000)		Percent union members[2]		Percent represented by unions[3]		Total		Union members[2]		Represented by unions[3]		Not represented by unions	
	1983	1995[1]	1983	1995[1]	1983	1995[1]	1983	1995[1]	1983	1995[1]	1983	1995[1]	1983	1995[1]
Total[5]	88,290	110,038	20.1	14.9	23.3	16.7	313	479	388	602	383	598	288	447
16 to 24 years old	19,305	18,205	9.1	5.6	11.1	6.6	210	292	281	375	275	373	203	287
25 to 34 years old	25,978	29,761	19.6	12.1	23.1	13.7	321	451	382	542	376	534	304	433
35 to 44 years old	18,722	29,800	24.8	17.6	28.6	19.7	369	550	411	621	407	619	339	520
45 to 54 years old	13,150	20,623	27.0	21.7	30.5	24.1	366	582	404	665	402	663	335	536
55 to 64 years old	9,201	9,202	26.9	19.6	30.3	21.5	346	514	392	614	390	614	316	482
65 years and over	1,934	2,448	10.1	8.3	12.1	9.4	260	389	338	509	330	506	238	362
Men	47,856	57,669	24.7	17.2	27.7	18.8	378	538	416	640	414	638	349	507
Women	40,433	52,369	14.6	12.3	18.0	14.3	252	406	309	527	307	523	237	386
White	77,046	92,760	19.3	14.2	22.3	15.9	319	494	396	621	391	616	295	466
Men	42,168	49,162	24.0	16.6	26.9	18.2	387	566	423	661	421	658	362	526
Women	34,877	43,598	13.5	11.4	16.7	13.3	254	415	314	551	313	546	240	395
Black	8,979	12,644	27.2	19.9	31.7	22.3	261	383	331	503	324	500	222	348
Men	4,477	6,005	31.7	22.5	36.1	24.3	293	411	366	526	360	526	244	374
Women	4,502	6,639	22.7	17.6	27.4	20.5	231	355	292	473	287	468	209	325
Hispanic[6]	(NA)	10,401	(NA)	13.0	(NA)	14.8	(NA)	329	(NA)	499	(NA)	493	(NA)	311
Men	(NA)	6,223	(NA)	14.0	(NA)	15.6	(NA)	350	(NA)	528	(NA)	523	(NA)	321
Women	(NA)	4,178	(NA)	11.6	(NA)	13.5	(NA)	305	(NA)	423	(NA)	419	(NA)	291
Full-time workers	70,976	89,282	22.9	16.6	26.4	18.5	313	479	388	602	383	598	288	447
Part-time workers	17,314	20,550	8.4	7.5	10.3	8.7	(X)	(X)	(X)	(X)	(X)	(X)	(X)	(X)
Managerial and professional specialty	19,657	29,827	17.1	13.8	21.9	16.5	437	703	423	745	421	737	446	694
Technical, sales, and admin. support	28,024	33,842	12.1	9.9	15.0	11.5	281	426	350	522	341	516	270	414
Service occupations	12,875	15,648	15.3	13.5	17.9	15.1	205	299	305	484	299	477	182	275
Precision, production, craft, and repair	10,542	11,563	32.9	23.3	35.7	24.8	377	519	456	688	450	684	322	478
Operators, fabricators, and laborers	15,416	17,304	35.4	23.0	37.9	24.4	275	380	366	524	361	519	226	338
Farming, forestry, and fishing	1,775	1,855	5.5	4.9	6.9	5.6	196	287	292	404	287	404	189	280
Agricultural wage and salary workers	1,446	1,575	3.4	2.1	3.8	2.7	198	291	(B)	(B)	(B)	(B)	195	289
Private nonagri. wage and salary workers	71,225	90,121	16.8	10.4	18.8	11.4	307	462	389	573	385	567	286	443
Mining	869	609	20.7	13.8	23.1	14.4	481	667	470	684	470	682	488	663
Construction	4,109	5,135	27.5	17.7	29.4	18.8	348	487	518	741	510	730	296	442
Manufacturing	19,066	19,520	27.8	17.6	30.5	18.7	335	494	370	548	368	544	315	479
Transportation and public utilities	5,142	6,573	42.4	27.3	46.2	29.1	417	590	449	676	445	673	386	545
Wholesale and retail trade, total	18,081	23,028	8.7	6.1	9.8	6.7	252	370	353	466	348	454	242	363
Finance, insurance, and real estate	5,559	6,745	2.9	2.1	4.1	2.6	296	501	284	477	285	490	297	502
Services	18,400	28,511	7.7	5.7	9.6	6.9	272	444	303	489	303	491	268	440
Government	15,618	18,342	36.7	37.8	45.5	43.5	351	575	386	638	381	633	316	500

B Data not shown where base is less than 50,000. NA Not applicable. X Not applicable. [1] See footnote 2, table 614. [2] Members of a labor union or an employee association similar to a labor union. [3] Members of a labor union or an employee association similar to a union as well as workers who report no union affiliation but whose jobs are covered by a union or an employee association contract. [4] For full-time employed wage and salary workers; 1983 revised since originally published. [5] Includes races not shown separately. Beginning 1994, includes a small number of multiple jobholders whose full- part- time status can not be determined for their principal job. [6] Persons of Hispanic origin may be of any race.

Source: U.S. Bureau of Labor Statistics, Employment and Earnings, monthly, January issues.

Income, Expenditures, and Wealth

This section presents data on gross domestic product (GDP), gross national product (GNP), national and personal income, saving and investment, money income, poverty, and national and personal wealth. The data on income and expenditures measure two aspects of the U.S. economy. One aspect relates to the national income and product accounts (NIPA's), a summation reflecting the entire complex of the Nation's economic income and output and the interaction of its major components; the other relates to the distribution of money income to families and individuals, or consumer income.

The primary source for data on GDP, GNP, national and personal income, gross saving and investment, and fixed reproducible tangible wealth is the *Survey of Current Business,* published monthly by the Bureau of Economic Analysis (BEA). A comprehensive revision to the NIPA's was completed in January 1996. Discussions of the revision appeared in the July, September, and October 1995 and the January/February 1996 issues of the *Survey of Current Business.* Summary historical estimates appeared in the January/February 1996 issue of the *Survey of Current Business.* Detailed historical data will appear in the National Income and Product Accounts of the United States, volume 2, 1959-92 to be published in late 1996, and volume 1, 1929-58 to be published in early 1997.

Sources of income distribution data are the decennial censuses of population and the Current Population Survey (CPS), both products of the Bureau of the Census (see text, section 1). Annual data on income of families, individuals, and households are presented in *Current Population Reports- Consumer Income,* P60 series.

Data on individuals' saving and assets are published by the Board of Governors of the Federal Reserve System in the quarterly *Flow of Funds Accounts;* and detailed information on personal wealth is published periodically by the Internal Revenue Service (IRS) in *SOI Bulletin.*

In Brief

Gross domestic product, in chained (1992) dollars reached a record $6.7 trillion in 1995.

Gross state product reached $6 trillion in 1992.

Median household income in 1994: $32,264

Poverty status of persons in 1994:
*Number below poverty level:
38.1 million
Percent below poverty level: 14.5*

National income and product—

Gross domestic product is the total output of goods and services produced by labor and property located in the United States, valued at market prices. GDP can be viewed in terms of expenditure categories that comprise purchases of goods and services by consumers and government, gross private domestic investment, and net exports of goods and services. The goods and services included are largely those bought for final use (excluding illegal transactions) in the market economy. A number of inclusions, however, represent imputed values, the most important of which is rental value of owner-occupied housing. GDP, in this broad context, measures the output attributable to the factors of production located in the United States. *Gross State product* (GSP) is the gross market value of the goods and services attributable to labor and property located in a State. It is the State counterpart of the Nation's gross domestic product.

As part of the comprehensive revision released in January 1996, BEA replaced its fixed-weighted (1987 dollars) index as the featured measure of real GDP with an index based on chain-type annual weights. Changes in the new featured measures of real output and prices are calculated as the average of changes based on weights for the current and preceding years. (Components of real output are weighted by price and prices of components are weighted by output.) These annual changes are "chained" (multiplied) together to form a time series that allows for the effects of changes in relative prices and changes in the composition of output over time. Quarterly and monthly changes are also based on annual weights. The new output indexes are expressed in 1992 dollars and the new price indexes are based to 1992 = 100.

Gross national product measures the output attributable to all labor and property supplied by United States residents. GNP differs from "national income" mainly in that GNP includes allowances for depreciation and for indirect business taxes (sales and property taxes); see table 691.

In December 1991, the Bureau of Economic Analysis began featuring gross domestic product rather than gross national product as the primary measure of U.S. production. GDP is now the standard measure of growth because it is the appropriate measure for much of the short-term monitoring and analysis of the economy. In addition, the use of GDP facilitates comparisons of economic activity in the United States with that in other countries.

National income is the aggregate of labor and property earnings which arises in the current production of goods and services. It is the sum of employee compensation, proprietors' income, rental income of persons, corporate profits, and net interest. It measures the total factor costs of the goods and services produced by the economy. Income is measured before deduction of taxes.

Capital consumption adjustment for corporations, and for nonfarm sole proprietorships and partnerships is the difference between capital consumption based on income tax returns and capital consumption measured at straight-line depreciation, consistent service lives, and replacement cost. The tax return data are valued at historical costs and reflect changes over time in service lives and depreciation patterns as permitted by tax regulations. *Inventory valuation adjustment* represents the difference between the book value of inventories used up in production and the cost of replacing them.

Personal income is the current income received by persons from all sources minus their personal contributions for social insurance. Classified as "persons" are individuals (including owners of

unincorporated firms), nonprofit institutions that primarily serve individuals, private trust funds, and private noninsured welfare funds. Personal income includes transfers (payments not resulting from current production) from government and business such as Social Security benefits, public assistance, etc., but excludes transfers among persons. Also included are certain nonmonetary types of income—chiefly estimated net rental value to owner-occupants of their homes and the value of services furnished without payment by financial intermediaries.

Disposable personal income is personal income less personal tax and nontax payments. It is the income available to persons for spending or saving. Personal tax and nontax payments are tax payments (net of refunds) by persons (except personal contributions for social insurance) that are not chargeable to business expense, and certain personal payments to general government that are treated like taxes. Personal taxes include income, estate and gift, and personal property taxes and motor vehicle licenses. Nontax payments include passport fees, fines and forfeitures, and donations.

Consumer Expenditure Survey—The Consumer Expenditure Survey program was begun in late 1979. The principal objective of the survey is to collect current consumer expenditure data which provide a continuous flow of data on the buying habits of American consumers. The data are necessary for future revisions of the Consumer Price Index.

The survey conducted by the Bureau of the Census for the Bureau of Labor Statistics, consists of two components: (1) An interview panel survey in which the expenditures of consumer units are obtained in five interviews conducted every 3 months; and (2) a diary or recordkeeping survey completed by participating households for two consecutive 1-week periods.

Each component of the survey queries an independent sample of consumer units representative of the U.S. total population. Over 52 weeks of the year, 5,000 consumer units are sampled for the diary survey. Each consumer unit keeps a diary for two 1-week periods yielding approximately 10,000 diaries a year. The interview sample is selected on a rotating panel basis, targeted at 5,000 consumer units per quarter. Data are collected in 88 urban and 16 rural areas of the country that are representative of the U.S. total population. The survey includes students in student housing. Data from the two surveys are combined; integration is necessary to permit analysis of total family expenditures because neither the diary nor quarterly interview survey was designed to collect a complete account of consumer spending.

The Diary survey is designed to obtain expenditures on small, frequently purchased items which are normally difficult for respondents to recall. Detailed records of expenses are kept for food and beverages, both at home and in eating places, tobacco, housekeeping supplies, nonprescription drugs, and personal care products and services.

The Interview survey is designed to obtain data on the types of expenditures which respondents can be expected to recall for a period of 3 months or longer. In general, these include relatively large expenditures, such as those for property, automobiles, and major appliances, or expenditures which occur on a fairly regular basis, such as rent, utilities, or insurance premiums. Including "global estimates" for food, it is estimated that about 95 percent of expenditures are covered in the interview. Excluded are nonprescription drugs, household supplies, and personal care items. The interview survey also provides data on expenditures incurred while on trips. Both surveys exclude all business related expenditures for which the family is reimbursed.

Distribution of money income to families and individuals—Money income statistics are based on data collected in various field surveys of income conducted since 1936. Since 1947, the Bureau of the Census has collected the data on an annual basis and published them in *Current Population Reports,* P60 series. In each of the surveys, field representatives interview samples of the population with respect to income received during the previous year. Money income as defined by the Bureau of the Census differs from the BEA concept of "personal income."

Data on consumer income collected in the CPS by the Bureau of the Census cover money income received (exclusive of certain money receipts such as capital gains) before payments for personal income taxes, Social Security, union dues, Medicare deductions, etc. Therefore, money income does not reflect the fact that some families receive part of their income in the form of noncash benefits (see section 12) such as food stamps, health benefits, and subsidized housing; that some farm families receive noncash benefits in the form of rent-free housing and goods produced and consumed on the farm; or that noncash benefits are also received by some nonfarm residents which often take the form of the use of business transportation and facilities, full or partial payments by business for retirement programs, medical and educational expenses, etc. These elements should be considered when comparing income levels. For data on noncash benefits, see section 12. None of the aggregate income concepts (GDP, national income, or personal income) is exactly comparable with money income, although personal income is the closest.

Beginning in the March 1981 Current Population Survey, 1980 census population controls were used; for income years 1971 through 1979, 1970 census population controls had been used. This change had little impact on income summary measures (means and medians) and proportional measures (percent distributions and poverty rates); however, use of the controls may have significant impact on the absolute numbers.

Several changes were made in the collection and processing of the March 1994 CPS data. These changes included (1) a change in the data collection method from paper and pencil to computer-assisted interviewing, (2) revisions allowing for the coding of different income amounts on selected questionnaire items (limits either increased or decreased in the following categories: earnings increased to $999,999, Social Security increased to $49,999, Supplemental Security Income and Public Assistance increased to $24,999, Veterans' Benefits increased to $99,999, Child Support and Alimony decreased to $49,999), and (3) the introduction of 1990 census population controls. A detailed description of these changes and their effects on estimates can be found in *Current Population Reports*, Series P60–189.

In October 1983, the Census Bureau began to collect data under the new Survey of Income and Program Participation

(SIPP). The information supplied by this survey is expected to provide better measures of the status and changes in income distribution and poverty of households and persons in the United States. The data collected in SIPP will be used to study Federal and State aid programs (such as food stamps, welfare, Medicaid, and subsidized housing), to estimate program costs and coverage, and to assess the effects of proposed changes in program eligibility rules or benefit levels. The core questions are repeated at each interview and cover labor force activity, the types and amounts of income received, and participation status in various programs. The core also contains questions covering attendance in postsecondary schools and private health insurance coverage. Various supplements or topical modules covering areas such as educational attainment, assets and liabilities, and pension plan coverage are periodically included.

Poverty—Families and unrelated individuals are classified as being above or below the poverty level using the poverty index originated at the Social Security Administration in 1964 and revised by Federal Interagency Committees in 1969 and 1980. The poverty index is based solely on money income and does not reflect the fact that many low-income persons receive noncash benefits such as food stamps, Medicaid, and public housing. The index is based on the Department of Agriculture's 1961 Economy Food Plan and reflects the different consumption requirements of families based on their size and composition. The poverty thresholds are updated every year to reflect changes in the Consumer Price Index. The following technical changes to the thresholds were made in 1981: (1) distinctions based on sex of householder have been eliminated; (2) separate thresholds for farm families have been dropped; and (3) the matrix has been expanded to families of nine or more persons from the old cutoff of seven or more persons. These changes have been incorporated in the calculation of poverty data beginning with 1981.

In the recent past, the Bureau of the Census has published a number of technical papers that presented experimental poverty estimates based on income definitions that counted the value of selected government noncash benefits. The Census Bureau has also published annual reports on after-tax income. The *Current Population Reports,* series P60-186RD brings together the benefit and tax data that previously appeared in the separate reports. This report shows the distribution of income among households and the prevalence of poverty under the official definition of money income and under definitions that add or subtract income components.

The poverty statistics presented by the Bureau of the Census and Congressional Budget Office reflect alternative adjustments for inflation. The study used a variation of the Consumer Price Index to adjust poverty thresholds for the effects of changing prices since 1967. The alternative measure of inflation uses estimates of the cost of renting equivalent housing to assess homeownership costs; this methodology has been used in the official Consumer Price Index since 1983. See text, section 15, and source for more details.

Personal wealth—Personal wealth estimates, issued by the IRS, are based on a sample of Federal estate tax returns which must be filed for deceased persons. Estimates are weighted to adjust for age, sex, and "social class" (as determined by the IRS through insurance holdings). Gross estate is the gross value of all assets, including the full face value of life insurance (reduced by policy loans), before reduction by the amount of debts. The level of gross estate or gross assets required for filing estate tax returns was $600,000 in 1989. Net worth is one's level of worth after all debts have been removed.

Statistical reliability—For a discussion of statistical collection and estimation, sampling procedures, and measures of statistical reliability pertaining to Census Bureau data, see Appendix III.

Historical statistics—Tabular headnotes provide cross-references, where applicable, to *Historical Statistics of the United States, Colonial Times to 1970.* See Appendix IV.

No. 685. GDP in Current and Real (1992) Dollars: 1960 to 1995

[In billions of dollars. For explanation of gross domestic product and chained dollars, see text, section 14]

ITEM	1960	1970	1980	1981	1982	1983	1984	1985	1986
CURRENT DOLLARS									
Gross domestic product (GDP)	**526.6**	**1,035.6**	**2,784.2**	**3,115.9**	**3,242.1**	**3,514.5**	**3,902.4**	**4,180.7**	**4,422.2**
Personal consumption expenditures . .	332.2	648.1	1,760.4	1,941.3	2,076.8	2,283.4	2,492.3	2,704.8	2,892.7
Durable goods	43.3	85.0	213.5	230.5	239.3	279.8	325.1	361.1	398.7
Nondurable goods	152.9	272.0	695.5	758.2	786.8	830.3	883.6	927.6	957.2
Services	136.0	291.1	851.4	952.6	1,050.7	1,173.3	1,283.6	1,416.1	1,536.8
Gross private domestic investment. . .	78.8	150.2	465.9	556.2	501.1	547.1	715.6	715.1	722.5
Fixed investment	75.5	148.1	473.5	528.1	515.6	552.0	648.1	688.9	712.9
Nonresidential	49.2	106.7	350.3	405.4	409.9	399.4	468.3	502.0	494.8
Residential	26.3	41.4	123.2	122.6	105.7	152.5	179.8	186.9	218.1
Change in business inventories . . .	3.2	2.2	-7.6	28.2	-14.5	-4.9	67.5	26.2	9.6
Net exports of goods and services . . .	2.4	1.2	-14.9	-15.0	-20.5	-51.7	-102.0	-114.2	-131.5
Exports	25.3	57.0	278.9	302.8	282.6	277.0	303.1	303.0	320.7
Imports	22.8	55.8	293.8	317.8	303.2	328.6	405.1	417.2	452.2
Government consumption expenditures and gross investment.	113.2	236.1	572.8	633.4	684.8	735.7	796.6	875.0	938.5
Federal	65.6	115.9	248.4	284.1	313.2	344.5	372.6	410.1	435.2
National defense	54.9	90.6	174.2	202.0	230.9	255.0	282.7	312.4	332.4
State and local	47.6	120.2	324.4	349.2	371.6	391.2	424.0	464.9	503.3
CHAINED (1992) DOLLARS									
Gross domestic product (GDP)	**2,261.7**	**3,388.2**	**4,611.9**	**4,724.9**	**4,623.6**	**4,810.0**	**5,138.2**	**5,329.5**	**5,489.9**
Personal consumption expenditures . .	1,432.6	2,197.8	3,009.7	3,046.4	3,081.5	3,240.6	3,407.6	3,566.5	3,708.7
Durable goods	105.2	187.0	282.6	285.8	285.5	327.4	374.9	411.4	448.4
Nondurable goods	615.4	859.1	1,065.1	1,074.3	1,080.6	1,112.4	1,151.8	1,178.3	1,215.9
Services	717.4	1,155.4	1,670.7	1,696.1	1,728.2	1,809.0	1,883.0	1,977.3	2,041.4
Gross private domestic investment. . .	270.5	419.5	626.2	689.7	590.4	647.8	831.6	829.2	813.8
Fixed investment	269.2	432.1	648.4	660.6	610.4	654.2	762.4	799.3	805.0
Nonresidential	155.9	282.8	461.1	485.7	463.3	456.4	535.4	568.4	548.5
Residential	121.8	149.1	186.1	171.2	140.1	197.6	226.4	229.5	257.0
Change in business inventories . . .	10.6	5.7	-10.0	33.1	-15.6	-5.9	74.8	29.8	10.9
Net exports of goods and services . . .	-21.3	-65.0	10.1	5.6	-14.1	-63.3	-127.3	-147.9	-163.9
Exports	86.8	158.1	331.4	335.3	311.4	303.3	328.4	337.3	362.2
Imports	108.1	223.1	321.3	329.7	325.5	366.6	455.7	485.2	526.1
Government consumption expenditures and gross investment.	617.2	866.8	941.4	947.7	960.1	987.3	1,018.4	1,080.1	1,135.0
Federal	349.4	427.2	399.3	415.9	429.4	452.7	463.7	495.6	518.4
National defense	301.3	349.0	280.7	296.0	316.5	334.6	348.1	374.1	393.4
State and local	267.2	440.0	543.6	532.8	531.4	534.9	555.0	584.7	616.9

	1987	1988	1989	1990	1991	1992	1993	1994	1995
CURRENT DOLLARS									
Gross domestic product (GDP)	**4,692.3**	**5,049.6**	**5,438.7**	**5,743.8**	**5,916.7**	**6,244.4**	**6,550.2**	**6,931.4**	**7,245.8**
Personal consumption expenditures . .	3,094.5	3,349.7	3,594.8	3,839.3	3,975.1	4,219.8	4,454.1	4,698.7	4,924.3
Durable goods	416.7	451.0	472.8	476.5	455.2	488.5	530.7	580.9	606.4
Nondurable goods	1,014.0	1,081.1	1,163.8	1,245.3	1,277.6	1,321.8	1,368.9	1,429.7	1,486.1
Services	1,663.8	1,817.6	1,958.1	2,117.5	2,242.3	2,409.4	2,554.6	2,688.1	2,831.8
Gross private domestic investment. . .	747.2	773.9	829.2	799.7	736.2	790.4	871.1	1,014.4	1,065.3
Fixed investment	722.9	763.1	797.5	791.6	738.5	783.4	850.5	954.9	1,028.2
Nonresidential	495.4	530.6	566.2	575.9	547.3	557.9	598.8	667.2	738.5
Residential	227.6	232.5	231.3	215.7	191.2	225.6	251.7	287.7	289.8
Change in business inventories . . .	24.2	10.9	31.7	8.0	-2.3	7.0	20.6	59.5	37.0
Net exports of goods and services . . .	-142.1	-106.1	-80.4	-71.3	-20.5	-29.5	-64.9	-96.4	-102.3
Exports	365.7	447.2	509.3	557.3	601.8	639.4	660.0	722.0	804.5
Imports	507.9	553.2	589.7	628.6	622.3	669.0	724.9	818.4	906.7
Government consumption expenditures and gross investment.	992.8	1,032.0	1,095.1	1,176.1	1,225.9	1,263.8	1,289.9	1,314.7	1,358.5
Federal	455.7	457.3	477.2	503.6	522.6	528.0	522.1	516.3	516.7
National defense	350.4	354.0	360.6	373.1	383.5	375.8	362.2	352.0	345.7
State and local	537.2	574.7	617.9	672.6	703.4	735.8	767.8	798.4	841.7
CHAINED (1992) DOLLARS									
Gross domestic product (GDP)	**5,648.4**	**5,862.9**	**6,060.4**	**6,138.7**	**6,079.0**	**6,244.4**	**6,383.8**	**6,604.2**	**6,739.0**
Personal consumption expenditures . .	3,822.3	3,972.7	4,064.6	4,132.2	4,105.8	4,219.8	4,339.7	4,471.1	4,578.5
Durable goods	454.9	483.5	496.2	493.3	462.0	488.5	524.1	562.0	580.8
Nondurable goods	1,239.3	1,274.4	1,303.5	1,316.1	1,302.9	1,321.8	1,348.9	1,390.5	1,422.5
Services	2,126.9	2,212.4	2,262.3	2,321.3	2,341.0	2,409.4	2,466.8	2,519.4	2,576.1
Gross private domestic investment. . .	820.5	826.0	861.9	817.3	737.7	790.4	857.3	979.6	1,011.3
Fixed investment	799.4	818.3	832.0	805.8	741.3	783.4	836.4	921.1	976.9
Nonresidential	542.4	566.0	588.8	585.2	547.7	557.9	593.6	652.1	715.0
Residential	257.6	252.5	243.2	220.6	193.4	225.6	242.7	268.9	262.8
Change in business inventories . . .	26.2	11.6	33.3	10.4	-3.0	7.3	19.1	58.9	33.7
Net exports of goods and services . . .	-156.2	-114.4	-82.7	-61.9	-22.3	-29.5	-74.4	-108.1	-114.2
Exports	402.0	465.8	520.2	564.4	599.9	639.4	660.6	715.1	774.8
Imports	558.2	580.2	603.0	626.3	622.2	669.0	735.0	823.3	888.9
Government consumption expenditures and gross investment.	1,165.9	1,180.9	1,213.9	1,250.4	1,258.0	1,263.8	1,260.5	1,259.9	1,260.7
Federal	534.4	524.6	531.5	541.9	539.4	528.0	508.7	489.7	472.7
National defense	409.2	405.5	401.6	401.5	397.5	375.8	354.9	336.9	320.0
State and local	631.8	656.6	682.6	708.6	718.7	735.8	751.8	770.5	788.6

Source: U.S. Bureau of Economic Analysis, *National Income and Product Accounts of the United States* to be published in late 1996, and *Survey of Current Business*, January/February 1996.

No. 686. Gross Domestic Product, by Industry: 1980 to 1993

[In billions of dollars. **1980 data are based on the 1972 Standard Industrial Classification (SIC), and 1990-93 are based on the 1987 SIC.** Data include nonfactor charges (capital consumption allowances, indirect business taxes, etc.) as well as factor charges against gross product; corporate profits and capital consumption allowances have been shifted from a company to an establishment basis]

INDUSTRY	CURRENT DOLLARS				CONSTANT (1987) DOLLARS			
	1980	1990	1992	1993	1980	1990	1992	1993
Gross domestic product	2,708.0	5,546.2	6,020.3	6,343.4	3,776.3	4,897.3	4,979.3	5,134.5
Private industries	2,370.2	4,862.1	5,255.8	5,559.5	3,202.7	4,324.2	4,430.7	4,585.4
Agriculture, forestry, and fishing............	66.7	112.0	115.5	107.3	63.2	95.8	110.3	102.6
Farms	56.1	85.1	85.6	75.3	51.0	71.6	80.8	71.0
Agricultural services..................	10.6	26.9	29.9	32.0	12.2	24.2	29.5	31.7
Mining [1]	112.6	103.1	85.2	89.4	79.9	91.8	89.0	93.1
Construction	128.7	240.1	222.1	234.2	185.4	210.2	201.4	205.3
Manufacturing	588.3	1,024.7	1,063.0	1,118.3	725.4	928.5	924.6	970.7
Durable goods	348.9	563.7	568.0	603.5	424.3	537.0	533.6	573.3
Lumber and wood products	19.2	30.8	31.3	34.7	21.6	27.7	24.9	23.1
Furniture and fixtures	8.4	15.9	16.6	18.1	11.6	14.3	14.7	16.2
Stone, clay, and glass products.........	18.0	24.9	24.8	25.9	23.8	25.6	24.9	25.1
Primary metal industries	44.2	44.0	40.0	42.5	49.2	35.2	36.4	40.1
Fabricated metal products	45.4	66.5	70.1	71.3	54.6	59.7	59.7	63.7
Machinery, except electrical	76.7	(X)	(X)	(X)	81.2	(X)	(X)	(X)
Industrial machinery	(X)	109.1	102.7	107.7	(X)	102.4	107.6	125.4
Electric and electronic equipment	54.5	(X)	(X)	(X)	69.8	(X)	(X)	(X)
Electronic & other electric equipment......	(X)	85.7	85.5	93.3	(X)	90.9	93.1	103.0
Motor vehicles and equipment	26.8	46.3	56.7	67.5	39.8	49.4	51.3	55.8
Other transportation equipment..........	26.3	65.1	60.8	60.7	38.3	64.1	53.5	52.4
Instruments and related products	19.5	56.4	59.5	59.7	24.2	50.3	50.4	49.8
Misc. manufacturing industries	9.8	18.9	20.0	22.1	10.4	17.3	17.2	18.7
Nondurable goods	239.4	461.0	495.0	514.8	301.1	391.5	391.0	397.5
Food and kindred products	51.8	97.1	103.9	105.9	64.3	83.9	82.9	84.3
Tobacco manufactures	7.1	16.0	19.3	17.3	19.7	9.4	7.8	7.6
Textile mill products	14.8	21.9	24.3	24.8	17.3	21.0	22.5	23.3
Apparel and other textile products	17.3	25.3	27.1	28.2	20.4	24.1	24.6	25.3
Paper and allied products	22.8	46.2	46.2	47.3	30.9	41.9	43.7	46.1
Printing and publishing	32.7	72.1	76.6	80.3	52.7	61.9	57.5	57.1
Chemicals and allied products	47.6	103.6	110.8	117.0	57.5	87.6	87.8	87.7
Petroleum and coal products	24.3	40.1	43.4	47.7	15.0	25.8	25.2	24.7
Rubber and misc. plastic products.......	17.0	34.6	38.9	41.4	18.5	32.3	35.1	37.1
Leather and leather products	4.1	4.0	4.5	4.9	4.8	3.6	3.9	4.2
Transportation and public utilities.........	242.2	481.2	529.3	559.3	336.3	462.6	494.5	515.9
Transportation.......................	102.9	176.8	193.8	207.9	120.2	168.9	183.7	193.5
Railroad transportation	20.6	22.2	23.0	24.3	18.5	24.1	26.0	28.1
Local & interurban passenger transportation .	5.3	10.0	11.4	12.0	8.5	8.7	9.0	9.5
Trucking and warehousing	40.3	73.3	78.4	79.9	50.8	69.0	76.6	79.0
Water transportation	7.2	10.0	10.3	10.5	9.3	8.0	7.6	7.6
Transportation by air	18.1	39.8	46.0	54.2	19.2	39.7	44.5	47.8
Pipelines, except natural gas	5.2	4.2	4.7	5.1	5.3	4.5	4.8	5.4
Transportation services	6.3	17.3	20.1	21.8	8.7	15.0	15.1	16.1
Communications	68.9	146.7	162.1	169.8	94.4	140.8	153.8	158.9
Telephone and telegraph	61.7	122.5	134.6	142.6	80.9	120.8	131.2	137.4
Radio and television broadcasting.......	7.2	24.2	27.5	27.2	13.5	20.0	22.6	21.6
Electric, gas, and sanitary services.......	70.4	157.7	173.4	181.5	121.6	152.9	157.1	163.5
Wholesale trade	191.6	363.0	394.4	413.1	190.5	319.5	340.9	356.6
Retail trade	244.7	515.7	557.5	592.4	320.1	478.1	486.7	511.8
Finance, insurance, and real estate [2]	418.4	982.4	1,106.1	1,180.6	692.8	868.3	893.4	915.0
Depository institutions	(X)	158.7	193.9	198.5	(X)	135.1	125.3	123.3
Insurance carriers	36.9	69.9	84.8	104.1	61.1	60.1	73.0	67.7
Real estate........................	288.6	641.7	698.7	718.5	453.0	566.7	575.0	583.9
Nonfarm housing....................	207.9	458.7	512.0	533.4	325.4	398.3	409.4	419.5
Services [3]	377.0	1,040.0	1,182.7	1,264.8	609.0	869.4	889.9	914.2
Hotels and other lodging places	19.6	49.9	53.9	55.4	31.0	45.0	46.0	45.8
Personal services	17.5	36.3	39.0	41.4	27.6	31.0	30.4	30.6
Business services	69.3	198.2	220.5	241.6	103.9	172.6	173.7	184.2
Auto repair, services, and garages	19.1	46.2	48.8	53.5	31.7	38.9	37.1	38.1
Motion pictures	6.0	18.6	19.3	21.6	9.0	15.5	14.6	16.4
Amusement and recreation services	14.2	40.2	51.1	55.2	19.5	34.6	40.8	42.7
Health services.....................	111.5	304.4	364.4	389.4	196.1	241.4	252.0	255.3
Legal services......................	24.9	79.6	88.7	92.1	51.5	66.1	66.0	65.3
Social services & membership organizations. . .	26.1	60.6	70.2	75.0	37.8	55.0	59.6	61.9
Private households	6.1	9.4	10.1	10.8	7.2	8.9	8.8	9.0
Government	324.2	676.3	755.7	781.6	508.9	581.5	584.2	581.6
Federal............................	115.4	221.3	247.9	249.8	178.7	193.3	188.8	182.7
General government	96.3	180.1	199.5	203.6	139.2	156.2	151.9	146.0
Government enterprise	19.1	41.3	48.4	46.2	39.4	37.2	36.9	36.7
State and local......................	208.8	454.9	507.8	531.8	330.3	388.2	395.4	398.8
General government	193.5	412.7	461.7	483.0	301.1	353.3	360.1	363.6
Government enterprise	15.3	42.2	46.0	48.8	29.2	34.9	35.3	35.2

X Not applicable.   [1] For additional mining industries, see table 1139.   [2] For additional finance, real estate, and insurance industries, see table 766.   [3] For additional service industries, see table 1252.

Source: U.S. Bureau of Economic Analysis, *Survey of Current Business*, April 1995.

No. 687. Gross Domestic Product in Current and Real (1992) Dollars, by Type of Product and Sector: 1980 to 1995

[In billions of dollars]

ITEM	1980	1985	1988	1989	1990	1991	1992	1993	1994	1995
CURRENT DOLLARS										
Gross domestic product . . .	2,784.2	4,180.7	5,049.6	5,438.7	5,743.8	5,916.7	6,244.4	6,550.2	6,931.4	7,245.8
PRODUCT										
Goods.	1,191.1	1,669.8	1,942.9	2,124.0	2,203.8	2,234.0	2,321.0	2,421.5	2,593.8	2,697.4
Durable goods.	500.2	721.8	853.4	928.6	938.2	910.0	955.0	1,029.5	1,117.8	1,179.8
Nondurable goods	690.8	948.0	1,089.5	1,195.4	1,265.7	1,323.9	1,366.0	1,392.0	1,476.0	1,517.6
Services	1,274.1	1,871.8	2,398.1	2,600.0	2,795.3	3,201.3	3,411.1	3,581.7	3,742.3	3,920.8
Structures	319.1	423.6	489.3	506.7	519.4	481.4	512.3	547.0	595.3	627.6
SECTOR										
Business	2,346.3	3,520.2	4,233.4	4,563.7	4,796.9	4,908.5	5,184.4	5,448.9	5,794.0	6,070.2
Nonfarm.	2,290.2	3,453.1	4,169.6	4,487.5	4,717.3	4,835.6	5,103.8	5,376.7	5,711.7	5,991.6
Farm	56.1	67.1	63.8	76.2	79.6	72.9	80.6	72.1	82.3	78.6
Households and institutions.	87.1	140.9	195.1	214.6	237.9	257.4	279.1	294.9	310.3	323.0
Private households.	6.1	7.3	8.3	8.9	9.4	9.1	10.1	10.7	10.8	11.1
Nonprofit institutions.	81.0	133.6	186.8	205.7	228.5	248.3	269.0	284.2	299.5	311.8
General government	350.8	519.6	621.0	660.3	709.0	750.7	781.0	806.5	827.0	852.6
Federal	135.6	203.6	230.0	240.5	252.7	268.1	274.4	276.6	275.7	278.2
State and local	215.2	316.0	391.0	419.8	456.3	482.6	506.6	529.9	551.4	574.4
CHAINED (1992) DOLLARS										
Gross domestic product . . .	4,611.9	5,329.5	5,862.9	6,060.4	6,138.7	6,079.0	6,244.4	6,383.8	6,604.2	6,739.0
PRODUCT										
Goods.	1,687.4	1,971.7	2,178.9	2,300.2	2,307.1	2,262.3	2,321.0	2,389.6	2,524.3	2,590.8
Durable goods.	635.8	768.9	914.7	974.2	966.5	917.2	955.0	1,022.6	1,099.2	1,156.3
Nondurable goods	1,063.3	1,210.7	1,263.9	1,325.1	1,340.2	1,345.1	1,366.0	1,367.1	1,425.6	1,435.4
Services	2,441.4	2,797.8	3,128.6	3,208.5	3,295.4	3,332.3	3,411.1	3,464.9	3,521.7	3,578.5
Structures	475.9	550.3	550.8	546.0	533.3	484.5	512.3	529.4	559.8	571.7
SECTOR										
Business	3,777.0	4,431.3	4,880.0	5,047.8	5,099.4	5,025.9	5,184.4	5,313.0	5,525.8	5,659.1
Nonfarm.	3,740.8	4,357.5	4,826.8	4,984.8	5,026.5	4,954.9	5,103.8	5,242.0	5,442.2	5,582.4
Farm	46.2	71.9	56.6	64.8	72.9	71.2	80.6	71.0	83.9	76.4
Households and institutions.	178.7	203.4	240.6	253.4	264.1	272.1	279.1	287.9	296.2	302.5
Private households.	8.3	8.7	9.5	10.1	10.2	9.4	10.1	10.3	10.2	10.1
Nonprofit institutions.	169.8	194.6	231.0	243.3	253.8	262.6	269.0	277.5	286.0	292.4
General government	660.9	693.2	741.3	758.1	774.7	781.1	781.0	782.9	782.4	777.7
Federal	246.7	263.9	274.1	276.2	280.3	281.0	274.4	267.3	256.8	246.5
State and local	414.5	429.2	467.3	481.9	494.5	500.1	506.6	515.6	525.8	531.7

Source: U.S. Bureau of Economic Analysis, *National Income and Product Accounts of the United States* to be published in late 1996, and *Survey of Current Business,* January/February 1996.

No. 688. GDP Components—Annual Percent Change: 1980 to 1995

[Change from previous year; for 1980, change from 1979 and for 1987, change from 1986. Minus sign (-) indicates decrease]

ITEM	1980	1987	1988	1989	1990	1991	1992	1993	1994	1995
CURRENT DOLLARS										
Gross domestic product (GDP) . . .	8.9	6.1	7.6	7.7	5.6	3.0	5.5	4.9	5.8	4.5
Personal consumption expenditures.	10.5	7.0	8.2	7.3	6.8	3.5	6.2	5.6	5.5	4.8
Durable goods	-0.2	4.5	8.2	4.8	0.8	-4.5	7.3	8.6	9.5	4.4
Nondurable goods.	11.5	5.9	6.6	7.7	7.0	2.6	3.5	3.6	4.4	3.9
Services	12.7	8.3	9.2	7.7	8.1	5.9	7.5	6.0	5.2	5.3
Gross private domestic investment	-3.1	3.4	3.6	7.1	-3.6	-7.9	7.4	10.2	16.5	5.0
Fixed investment	2.1	1.4	5.5	4.5	-0.7	-6.7	6.1	8.6	12.3	7.7
Nonresidential.	8.5	0.1	7.1	6.7	1.7	-5.0	1.9	7.3	11.4	10.7
Residential	-12.6	4.3	2.2	-0.5	-6.7	-11.4	18.0	11.6	14.3	0.7
Exports	22.0	14.0	22.3	13.9	9.4	8.0	6.3	3.2	9.4	11.4
Imports	16.3	12.3	8.9	6.6	6.6	-1.0	7.5	8.4	12.9	10.8
Government consumption expenditures and gross investment	13.0	5.8	3.9	6.1	7.4	4.2	3.1	2.1	1.9	3.3
Federal	15.5	4.7	0.4	4.4	5.5	3.8	1.0	-1.1	-1.1	0.1
National defense	15.2	5.4	1.0	1.9	3.5	2.8	-2.0	-3.6	-2.8	-1.8
State and local	11.1	6.7	7.0	7.5	8.9	4.6	4.6	4.4	4.0	5.4
CHAINED (1992) DOLLARS										
Gross domestic product (GDP) . . .	-0.3	2.9	3.8	3.4	1.3	-1.0	2.7	2.2	3.5	2.0
Personal consumption expenditures.	-0.3	3.1	3.9	2.3	1.7	-0.6	2.8	2.8	3.0	2.4
Durable goods	-8.0	1.5	6.3	2.6	-0.6	-6.4	5.8	7.3	7.2	3.4
Nondurable goods.	-0.4	1.9	2.8	2.3	1.0	-1.0	1.5	2.0	3.1	2.3
Services	1.9	4.2	4.0	2.3	2.6	0.8	2.9	2.4	2.1	2.3
Gross private domestic investment	-11.1	0.8	0.7	4.3	-5.2	-9.7	7.1	8.5	14.3	3.2
Fixed investment	-6.8	-0.7	2.4	1.7	-3.1	-8.0	5.7	6.8	10.1	6.1
Nonresidential.	-0.5	-1.1	4.4	4.0	-0.6	-6.4	1.9	6.4	9.8	9.6
Residential	-21.1	0.2	-2.0	-3.7	-9.3	-12.3	16.6	7.6	10.8	-2.3
Exports	10.8	11.0	15.9	11.7	8.5	6.3	6.6	3.3	8.3	8.3
Imports	-6.7	6.1	3.9	3.9	3.9	-0.7	7.5	9.9	12.0	8.0
Government consumption expenditures and gross investment	1.8	2.7	1.3	2.8	3.0	0.6	0.5	-0.3	-	0.1
Federal	4.2	3.1	-1.8	1.3	2.0	-0.5	-2.1	-3.7	-3.7	-3.5
National defense	3.6	4.0	-0.9	-1.0	-	-1.0	-5.5	-5.6	-5.1	-5.0
State and local	-	2.4	3.9	4.0	3.8	1.4	2.4	2.2	2.5	2.4

- Represents or rounds to zero.
Source: U.S. Bureau of Economic Analysis, *National Income and Product Accounts of the United States* to be published in late 1996, and *Survey of Current Business,* January/February 1996.

No. 689. Gross State Product in Current and Constant (1987) Dollars: 1980 to 1992

[**In billions of dollars.** For definition of gross State product, see text, section 14]

DIVISION AND STATE	CURRENT DOLLARS					CONSTANT (1987) DOLLARS				
	1980	1985	1990	1991	1992	1980	1985	1990	1991	1992
United States	2,684.8	4,037.8	5,518.5	5,700.8	5,994.1	3,697.1	4,271.0	4,888.3	4,881.8	5,001.4
Northeast.	581.9	893.9	1,246.0	1,271.9	1,331.5	825.5	959.4	1,103.0	1,085.5	1,106.3
New England	141.2	230.0	327.1	331.0	343.9	199.9	247.0	290.3	283.6	287.0
Maine	10.1	15.6	23.0	23.2	24.1	14.2	16.8	20.5	19.9	20.1
New Hampshire.	9.1	16.7	23.6	24.3	25.5	12.8	17.8	21.0	21.0	21.6
Vermont.	4.8	7.5	11.2	11.2	11.8	6.7	8.0	10.1	9.7	10.0
Massachusetts	67.0	109.9	154.2	155.4	162.0	95.3	117.8	136.7	133.1	135.1
Rhode Island	9.5	14.7	20.7	20.8	21.6	13.4	15.8	18.3	17.7	17.8
Connecticut	40.6	65.7	94.3	96.1	98.9	57.6	70.7	83.8	82.2	82.5
Middle Atlantic	440.7	663.9	919.0	940.9	987.7	625.6	712.4	812.7	801.9	819.3
New York.	221.8	341.0	466.8	473.1	497.6	321.2	366.9	413.7	404.1	413.1
New Jersey	89.3	144.0	207.6	212.9	223.1	125.2	154.4	182.6	180.4	184.1
Pennsylvania	129.5	178.9	244.6	254.9	267.0	179.1	191.1	216.4	217.4	222.1
Midwest.	677.7	959.3	1,259.2	1,296.6	1,374.5	929.2	1,018.3	1,122.1	1,117.7	1,157.2
East North Central.	482.6	680.4	891.2	916.2	971.6	664.6	723.0	795.2	790.1	817.7
Ohio	122.8	170.3	223.1	228.8	241.6	167.6	180.4	198.7	197.2	203.2
Indiana	58.9	82.0	111.2	114.7	121.6	80.2	86.8	99.4	99.4	103.3
Illinois	144.7	202.3	270.3	278.9	294.4	199.3	215.2	240.1	239.4	246.8
Michigan	103.1	152.3	187.2	191.1	204.4	144.8	162.4	168.4	165.4	171.7
Wisconsin	53.2	73.4	99.5	102.7	109.5	72.7	78.1	88.6	88.8	92.8
West North Central	195.1	278.9	368.0	380.5	402.9	264.6	295.4	326.9	327.6	339.4
Minnesota	49.0	72.3	99.7	103.4	110.3	66.3	77.0	88.5	89.1	92.9
Iowa	33.8	41.5	54.8	56.0	59.5	45.2	43.9	48.6	48.3	50.5
Missouri	52.5	79.0	102.2	106.3	111.6	73.0	84.3	92.2	91.5	93.6
North Dakota	7.6	10.8	12.0	12.1	13.1	9.7	10.9	10.5	10.4	11.1
South Dakota	6.6	9.7	12.9	14.1	15.1	8.9	10.4	11.4	12.0	12.7
Nebraska	17.7	25.4	33.6	35.2	37.2	24.0	26.9	29.8	30.4	31.6
Kansas	27.8	40.2	51.7	53.3	56.2	37.5	41.9	45.9	45.8	47.1
South	856.3	1,308.3	1,761.6	1,838.1	1,940.6	740.4	886.8	1,055.7	1,064.0	1,096.6
South Atlantic.	385.0	626.8	920.0	960.0	1,016.4	550.7	674.1	812.9	816.1	838.4
Delaware	7.4	11.9	19.6	21.8	23.7	10.2	12.8	17.2	17.8	18.4
Maryland	45.1	73.8	109.2	112.1	116.2	65.1	79.7	96.2	94.8	95.4
District of Columbia	17.9	25.8	36.7	38.2	40.4	27.9	28.2	31.9	31.6	32.0
Virginia	58.0	94.7	140.3	145.3	153.8	85.3	102.2	123.3	122.5	125.1
West Virginia	18.8	23.1	28.2	29.1	30.7	24.3	23.7	25.8	26.0	26.8
North Carolina.	59.1	95.3	140.6	147.8	159.6	86.0	102.7	123.2	124.6	130.5
South Carolina	27.3	42.5	63.7	66.7	69.8	37.8	45.4	56.9	57.6	58.9
Georgia	55.6	96.2	137.0	143.7	153.5	77.4	102.9	122.1	123.7	128.6
Florida.	95.9	163.5	244.6	255.2	268.6	136.6	176.5	216.4	217.5	222.6
East South Central	139.0	200.9	272.3	287.5	306.9	189.7	212.7	242.7	247.9	258.2
Kentucky	36.6	50.1	67.0	70.1	75.6	50.0	52.9	60.1	60.6	63.7
Tennessee	45.1	67.9	95.2	101.3	108.9	62.1	72.5	84.7	87.0	91.3
Alabama	35.3	52.3	70.6	74.3	78.1	48.5	55.4	63.0	64.4	66.0
Mississippi	22.1	30.7	39.5	41.7	44.3	29.1	31.9	35.0	35.8	37.2
West South Central	332.3	480.6	569.3	590.7	617.3	418.2	479.4	499.1	506.1	518.0
Arkansas	19.9	28.9	38.4	40.7	44.0	26.9	30.4	34.2	35.3	37.3
Louisiana	64.7	84.9	91.8	95.6	96.2	77.0	80.4	79.1	80.9	79.9
Oklahoma	38.1	51.2	57.0	58.0	60.2	48.4	51.4	50.3	50.0	50.7
Texas	209.7	315.7	382.2	396.3	416.9	265.9	317.1	335.5	339.9	350.0
West	568.9	876.3	1,251.6	1,294.1	1,347.4	783.8	927.1	1,108.4	1,108.5	1,123.5
Mountain	140.3	208.5	274.3	291.4	310.1	188.0	218.2	244.6	253.0	262.7
Montana	9.3	11.0	13.4	14.5	15.2	12.0	11.4	12.0	12.6	13.0
Idaho	9.7	13.0	18.2	19.2	20.9	13.1	13.8	16.1	16.6	17.7
Wyoming	11.0	13.4	12.7	13.0	13.2	12.2	12.3	11.6	11.9	12.0
Colorado	37.4	57.1	72.6	77.0	82.5	51.4	60.4	64.5	66.2	69.0
New Mexico	16.4	23.1	27.1	30.3	31.9	20.4	23.0	24.0	26.6	27.3
Arizona	29.5	48.7	67.7	70.2	74.1	41.3	52.5	60.6	60.7	62.3
Utah	15.2	23.9	30.9	33.2	35.6	20.6	25.0	27.5	28.6	30.0
Nevada	11.7	18.3	31.7	34.0	36.8	16.8	19.8	28.4	29.7	31.4
Pacific	428.7	667.8	977.3	1,002.7	1,037.4	595.8	708.9	863.8	855.5	860.8
Washington	50.9	73.4	111.9	119.5	127.6	71.4	78.6	99.1	102.1	105.8
Oregon	30.0	39.6	56.3	58.9	62.7	41.7	42.5	49.9	50.7	52.5
California	319.8	511.1	752.8	767.2	787.9	447.3	545.6	665.3	653.2	652.3
Alaska.	15.6	25.8	27.3	26.0	26.0	17.5	22.6	23.8	23.3	23.0
Hawaii	12.4	18.0	29.1	31.1	33.2	17.9	19.5	25.7	26.3	27.2

Source: U.S. Bureau of Economic Analysis, *Survey of Current Business*, May 1995.

No. 690. Gross State Product in Constant (1987) Dollars, by Industry: 1992

[**In billions of dollars.** For definition of gross state product, see text, section 14. Industries based on 1987 Standard Industrial Classification]

DIVISION AND STATE	Total [1]	Farms, forestry, fisher-ies [2]	Con-struction	Manu-facturing	Trans-portation, public utilities	Whole-sale trade	Retail trade	Finance, insur-ance, real estate	Services	Govern-ment [3]
United States . .	5,001.4	110.3	201.4	924.6	494.5	340.9	486.7	893.4	889.9	570.8
Northeast	1,106.3	9.3	39.3	195.8	103.9	78.7	95.9	248.0	223.4	109.3
New England	287.0	2.9	9.6	59.4	22.5	19.7	27.0	61.0	58.4	26.2
Maine	20.1	0.5	0.9	3.8	1.8	1.2	2.5	3.5	3.4	2.6
New Hampshire . . .	21.6	0.2	0.8	5.2	1.8	1.2	2.3	4.4	3.8	1.9
Vermont	10.0	0.3	0.5	2.1	0.8	0.6	1.1	1.7	1.8	1.1
Massachusetts . . .	135.1	1.0	4.1	27.2	10.7	9.9	11.9	28.0	30.7	11.5
Rhode Island.	17.8	0.2	0.5	3.9	1.1	1.0	1.7	3.8	3.5	2.0
Connecticut.	82.5	0.7	2.8	17.3	6.3	5.9	7.5	19.7	15.3	7.1
Middle Atlantic	819.3	6.4	29.8	136.4	81.3	59.0	68.9	187.0	165.0	83.1
New York	413.1	2.5	13.6	58.9	38.8	27.9	32.2	109.1	86.3	43.3
New Jersey.	184.1	1.1	6.9	31.6	19.0	17.0	15.6	37.8	36.5	18.5
Pennsylvania.	222.1	2.8	9.3	45.9	23.5	14.1	21.0	40.1	42.2	21.3
Midwest	1,157.2	34.0	45.1	279.1	114.1	84.1	111.1	185.7	180.5	115.5
East North Central . .	817.7	14.6	32.2	212.6	78.2	58.1	77.7	132.1	129.0	78.3
Ohio	203.2	2.9	7.6	56.5	19.1	14.0	19.9	31.0	31.6	19.5
Indiana.	103.3	2.2	4.4	31.7	10.5	6.0	10.5	14.2	13.6	9.5
Illinois	246.8	4.2	10.3	48.1	28.0	20.7	22.3	45.1	43.8	22.6
Michigan	171.7	2.3	6.0	49.8	12.9	11.6	16.5	26.8	27.1	17.6
Wisconsin	92.8	3.0	3.9	26.6	7.8	5.8	8.5	15.0	12.9	9.2
West North Central .	339.4	19.4	12.9	66.5	35.9	26.0	33.4	53.6	51.5	37.2
Minnesota.	92.9	3.3	3.8	20.3	8.0	7.6	8.9	15.7	15.2	9.3
Iowa	50.5	4.1	1.8	11.9	4.5	3.6	4.8	7.7	6.6	5.4
Missouri	93.6	2.3	3.8	19.3	11.5	7.2	9.8	14.4	15.5	9.4
North Dakota.	11.1	1.5	0.4	0.8	1.1	0.9	1.1	1.6	1.5	1.5
South Dakota	12.7	1.8	0.4	1.2	1.1	0.8	1.4	2.5	1.7	1.5
Nebraska	31.6	3.6	1.0	4.2	3.9	2.5	2.8	5.0	4.4	4.2
Kansas	47.1	2.8	1.7	8.9	5.7	3.5	4.6	6.7	6.6	5.8
South.	1,614.5	36.2	66.4	289.4	175.2	105.6	164.0	250.6	266.0	209.8
South Atlantic	838.4	17.0	36.8	139.2	85.9	55.2	85.8	140.0	149.9	121.4
Delaware	18.4	0.2	0.7	3.9	1.1	0.7	1.2	6.6	2.3	1.5
Maryland	95.4	1.1	5.7	9.7	9.0	6.0	10.2	18.0	20.2	15.2
Dist. of Columbia . .	32.0	(Z)	0.4	1.0	2.2	0.6	1.3	4.1	10.5	12.1
Virginia.	125.1	1.7	5.7	19.5	12.5	7.2	12.1	20.1	22.0	23.1
West Virginia.	26.8	0.3	1.1	4.0	3.8	1.4	2.4	3.5	3.5	2.9
North Carolina. . . .	130.5	3.8	4.9	39.1	11.7	8.4	13.0	17.4	16.3	15.6
South Carolina . . .	58.9	0.9	2.9	16.7	5.5	2.8	6.6	7.5	7.4	8.6
Georgia	128.6	2.7	4.9	24.5	16.2	12.1	12.2	19.7	20.2	15.4
Florida.	222.6	6.2	10.4	20.9	23.9	16.1	26.9	43.1	47.6	26.9
East South Central. .	258.2	7.2	9.5	63.1	26.6	16.1	27.1	34.6	36.5	32.0
Kentucky	63.7	2.4	2.5	15.7	6.3	3.4	6.2	8.2	8.0	7.8
Tennessee	91.3	1.7	3.4	22.8	7.9	6.6	10.7	12.7	15.1	10.0
Alabama.	66.0	1.8	2.3	15.4	7.3	4.0	6.3	8.7	9.3	9.5
Mississippi	37.2	1.4	1.2	9.2	5.1	2.0	3.9	5.0	4.1	4.7
West South Central .	518.0	12.0	20.1	87.2	62.8	34.3	51.1	76.0	79.6	56.3
Arkansas	37.3	2.2	1.3	9.2	4.7	2.1	4.1	4.8	4.7	4.0
Louisiana	79.9	1.2	3.6	14.1	9.1	4.4	6.9	11.0	10.7	8.0
Oklahoma.	50.7	1.9	1.6	8.2	5.7	3.1	5.4	7.3	7.2	7.2
Texas.	350.0	6.8	13.7	55.7	43.3	24.8	34.7	52.8	56.9	37.1
West	1,123.5	30.8	50.5	160.3	101.3	72.4	115.7	209.1	220.0	136.2
Mountain.	262.7	7.3	12.5	31.8	28.1	14.7	27.6	41.3	50.6	34.3
Montana.	13.0	0.8	0.6	1.0	1.8	0.7	1.4	2.0	1.9	1.8
Idaho.	17.7	1.5	0.9	3.2	1.6	1.0	1.9	2.8	2.4	2.1
Wyoming	12.0	0.4	0.4	0.4	2.1	0.3	0.9	1.3	0.9	1.3
Colorado	69.0	1.6	3.4	9.0	7.9	4.5	7.4	11.4	13.4	9.2
New Mexico	27.3	0.8	1.1	3.8	2.9	1.2	2.7	3.7	4.3	4.4
Arizona	62.3	1.4	3.1	8.6	5.5	3.7	7.4	10.9	11.9	8.4
Utah	30.0	0.5	1.3	4.6	3.3	1.9	2.9	4.4	5.3	4.2
Nevada	31.4	0.3	1.7	1.1	2.9	1.3	3.0	4.9	10.6	3.0
Pacific	860.8	23.4	38.1	128.5	73.2	57.7	88.1	167.8	169.4	101.8
Washington.	105.8	3.9	5.6	17.8	8.9	7.9	11.5	17.3	18.5	14.1
Oregon	52.5	2.1	2.3	9.8	5.3	4.1	5.3	8.8	8.5	6.1
California	652.3	16.5	27.5	99.0	52.6	44.1	66.5	133.8	134.6	73.2
Alaska.	23.0	0.5	0.8	0.9	3.3	0.5	1.3	2.9	1.9	3.3
Hawaii	27.2	0.5	1.8	1.0	3.1	1.1	3.6	5.1	5.8	5.1

Z Less than $50 million.   [1] Includes mining not shown separately.   [2] Includes agricultural services.   [3] Includes Federal civilian and military and State and local government.

Source: U.S. Bureau of Economic Analysis, *Survey of Current Business*, May 1995.

No. 691. Relation of GDP, GNP, Net National Product, National Income, Personal Income, Disposable Personal Income, and Personal Saving: 1980 to 1995

[In billions of dollars. For definitions, see text, section 14]

ITEM	1980	1985	1989	1990	1991	1992	1993	1994	1995
Gross domestic product	2,784.2	4,180.7	5,438.7	5,743.8	5,916.7	6,244.4	6,550.2	6,931.4	7,245.8
Plus: Receipts of factor income from the rest of the world [1]	81.8	108.1	169.0	177.5	156.2	137.9	139.7	159.2	206.7
Less: Payments of factor income to the rest of the world [2]	46.5	87.7	154.8	156.4	140.5	126.8	129.9	168.1	215.0
Equals: Gross national product	2,819.5	4,201.0	5,452.8	5,764.9	5,932.4	6,255.5	6,560.0	6,922.4	7,237.5
Less: Consumption of fixed capital . .	368.0	519.5	662.2	693.1	723.1	754.2	773.8	818.8	825.9
Equals: Net national product [3]	2,451.5	3,681.5	4,790.6	5,071.9	5,209.3	5,501.3	5,786.2	6,103.7	6,411.6
Less: Indirect business tax and nontax liability	212.0	329.6	414.7	442.6	478.1	505.6	540.0	572.5	595.5
Plus: Subsidies [4]	15.2	21.9	24.2	25.3	23.6	27.1	31.7	25.1	18.2
Equals: National income [3]	2,216.1	3,351.5	4,362.1	4,611.9	4,719.7	4,950.8	5,194.4	5,495.1	5,799.2
Less: Corporate profits [5]	167.1	282.2	356.4	369.5	382.5	401.4	464.5	526.5	588.6
Net interest	191.9	337.2	456.6	467.3	448.0	413.3	398.1	392.8	401.0
Contributions for social insurance. . .	225.0	375.9	491.2	518.5	543.5	571.4	592.9	628.3	660.0
Wage accruals less disbursements. .	-	-0.2	-	0.1	-0.1	-15.8	4.6	14.8	-
Plus: Personal interest income	274.7	508.4	674.5	704.9	699.2	667.2	647.3	661.6	714.6
Personal dividend income.	57.5	88.3	130.9	142.9	153.6	159.4	186.8	199.6	214.8
Government transfer payments to persons	312.6	468.7	604.9	666.5	749.1	835.7	888.6	933.8	1,000.0
Business transfer payments to persons	8.8	17.8	21.1	21.3	20.8	22.5	22.1	22.6	22.6
Equals: Personal income.	2,285.7	3,439.6	4,489.3	4,791.6	4,968.5	5,264.2	5,479.2	5,750.2	6,101.7
Less: Personal tax and nontax payments	312.4	437.7	594.9	624.8	624.8	650.5	689.9	731.4	794.3
Equals: Disposable personal income	1,973.3	3,002.0	3,894.5	4,166.8	4,343.7	4,613.7	4,789.3	5,018.8	5,307.4
Less: Personal outlays	1,811.5	2,795.8	3,706.7	3,958.1	4,097.4	4,341.0	4,572.9	4,826.5	5,066.7
Equals: Personal saving	161.8	206.2	187.8	208.7	246.4	272.6	216.4	192.4	240.8

- Represents or rounds to zero.   [1] Consists largely of receipts by U.S. residents of interest and dividends and reinvested earnings of foreign affiliates of U.S. corporations.   [2] Consists largely of payments to foreign residents of interest and dividends and reinvested earnings of U.S. affiliates of foreign corporations.   [3] Includes items not shown separately.   [4] Less current surplus of government enterprises.   [5] With inventory valuation and capital consumption adjustments.

Source: U.S. Bureau of Economic Analysis, *National Income and Product Accounts of the United States* to be published in late 1996, and *Survey of Current Business,* January/February 1996.

No. 692. Selected Per Capita Income and Product Items: 1960 to 1995

[In dollars. Based on Bureau of the Census estimated population including Armed Forces abroad; based on quarterly averages]

YEAR	CURRENT DOLLARS					CHAINED (1992) DOLLARS			
	Gross domestic product	Gross national product	Personal income	Disposable personal income	Personal consumption expenditures	Gross domestic product	Gross national product	Disposable personal income	Personal consumption expenditures
1960	2,913	2,931	2,277	2,008	1,838	12,512	12,585	8,660	7,926
1961	2,965	2,985	2,335	2,062	1,865	12,571	12,651	8,794	7,954
1962	3,136	3,159	2,444	2,151	1,948	13,125	13,215	9,077	8,220
1963	3,261	3,285	2,531	2,225	2,023	13,492	13,587	9,274	8,434
1964	3,455	3,481	2,676	2,384	2,144	14,083	14,184	9,805	8,817
1965	3,700	3,728	2,860	2,541	2,286	14,792	14,897	10,292	9,257
1966	4,007	4,033	3,076	2,715	2,451	15,565	15,661	10,715	9,674
1967	4,194	4,222	3,269	2,877	2,563	15,800	15,896	11,061	9,854
1968	4,536	4,567	3,554	3,096	2,789	16,382	16,485	11,448	10,313
1969	4,845	4,875	3,839	3,297	2,982	16,712	16,809	11,708	10,593
1970	5,050	5,081	4,077	3,545	3,160	16,520	16,616	12,022	10,717
1971	5,419	5,456	4,328	3,805	3,383	16,853	16,959	12,345	10,975
1972	5,894	5,935	4,703	4,074	3,671	17,579	17,694	12,770	11,508
1973	6,524	6,584	5,217	4,553	4,018	18,412	18,572	13,539	11,950
1974	6,998	7,071	5,672	4,928	4,353	18,178	18,360	13,310	11,756
1975	7,550	7,611	6,091	5,367	4,765	17,896	18,032	13,404	11,899
1976	8,341	8,419	6,673	5,837	5,268	18,713	18,878	13,793	12,446
1977	9,201	9,295	7,315	6,362	5,797	19,426	19,611	14,095	12,846
1978	10,292	10,392	8,176	7,097	6,418	20,185	20,367	14,662	13,258
1979	11,361	11,507	9,105	7,861	7,079	20,541	20,794	14,899	13,417
1980	12,226	12,381	10,037	8,665	7,730	20,252	20,497	14,813	13,216
1981	13,547	13,698	11,132	9,566	8,440	20,542	20,756	15,009	13,245
1982	13,961	14,095	11,707	10,108	8,943	19,911	20,090	14,999	13,270
1983	14,998	15,135	12,340	10,764	9,744	20,527	20,702	15,277	13,829
1984	16,508	16,640	13,560	11,887	10,543	21,736	21,896	16,252	14,415
1985	17,529	17,614	14,421	12,587	11,341	22,345	22,443	16,597	14,954
1986	18,374	18,427	15,155	13,244	12,019	22,810	22,866	16,981	15,409
1987	19,323	19,389	15,966	13,849	12,743	23,260	23,296	17,106	15,740
1988	20,605	20,659	17,028	14,857	13,669	23,924	23,979	17,621	16,211
1989	21,984	22,042	18,147	15,742	14,531	24,497	24,553	17,801	16,430
1990	22,979	23,064	19,170	16,670	15,360	24,559	24,642	17,941	16,532
1991	23,416	23,478	19,663	17,191	15,732	24,058	24,119	17,756	16,249
1992	24,447	24,490	20,609	18,062	16,520	24,447	24,490	18,062	16,520
1993	25,373	25,411	21,224	18,552	17,253	24,728	24,767	18,075	16,810
1994	26,589	26,555	22,059	19,253	18,025	25,335	25,305	18,320	17,152
1995	27,541	27,510	23,193	20,174	18,717	25,615	25,588	18,757	17,403

Source: U.S. Bureau of Economic Analysis, *National Income and Product Accounts of the United States* to be published in late 1996, and *Survey of Current Business,* January/February 1996.

No. 693. National Income, by Type of Income: 1980 to 1995

[In billions of dollars]

INCOME	1980	1985	1989	1990	1991	1992	1993	1994	1995
National income	2,216.1	3,351.5	4,362.1	4,611.9	4,719.7	4,950.8	5,194.4	5,495.1	5,799.2
Compensation of employees	1,653.9	2,425.7	3,151.6	3,352.8	3,457.9	3,644.9	3,809.4	4,008.3	4,209.1
Wages and salaries	1,377.6	1,995.7	2,598.1	2,757.5	2,827.6	2,970.6	3,095.2	3,255.9	3,419.7
Government	261.2	373.5	479.4	517.2	546.0	567.8	584.2	602.5	621.7
Other	1,116.4	1,622.1	2,118.7	2,240.3	2,281.5	2,402.9	2,511.0	2,653.4	2,797.9
Supplements to wages and salaries . .	276.3	430.0	553.5	595.2	630.4	674.3	714.2	752.4	789.5
Employer contributions for social insurance	136.4	226.9	280.4	294.6	307.7	323	333.3	350.2	365.5
Other labor income	139.8	203.1	273.1	300.6	322.7	351.3	380.9	402.2	424
Proprietors' income [1] [2]	167.9	257.4	345	361	362.9	409.5	420	450.9	478.3
Farm	13.8	24.9	36.8	36.3	30.2	38	32	35	29
Nonfarm.	154.1	232.5	308.2	324.6	332.7	371.5	388.1	415.9	449.3
Rental income of persons [1]	35.3	49.1	52.4	61.4	68.4	80.6	102.5	116.6	122.2
Corporate profits [1] [2]	167.1	282.2	356.4	369.5	382.5	401.4	464.5	526.5	588.6
Corporate profits [2]	198.3	230.5	330.6	358.2	378.2	398.9	457.7	514.9	572.7
Profits before tax	241.4	229.9	348.1	371.7	374.2	406.4	464.3	528.2	600.8
Profits tax liability	84.8	96.5	141.3	140.5	133.4	143.0	163.8	195.3	218.7
Profits after tax	156.6	133.4	206.8	231.2	240.8	263.4	300.5	332.9	382.1
Dividends	59.3	92.8	138.9	151.9	163.1	169.5	197.3	211.0	227.4
Undistributed profits	97.3	40.6	67.9	79.4	77.7	93.9	103.3	121.9	154.7
Inventory valuation adjustment	-43.0	0.5	-17.5	-13.5	4.0	-7.5	-6.6	-13.3	-28.1
Capital consumption adjustment	-31.2	51.8	25.8	11.3	4.3	2.5	6.7	11.6	15.9
Net interest	191.9	337.2	456.6	467.3	448.0	414.3	398.1	392.8	401.0
Addenda:									
Corporate profits after tax	82.3	185.7	215.1	229.0	249.1	258.4	300.7	331.2	369.9
Net cash flow [1] [2]	219.1	374.7	435.5	455.0	479.3	491.9	520.3	561.2	596.5
Undistributed profits [1] [2]	23.0	92.9	76.2	77.2	86.0	88.9	103.4	120.2	142.5
Consumption of fixed capital	196.1	281.8	359.3	377.9	393.3	403.0	417.0	441.0	454.0
Less: Inventory valuation adjustment	-43.0	0.5	-17.5	-13.5	4.0	-7.5	-6.6	-13.3	-28.1
Equals: Net cash flow	262.2	374.2	453.0	468.5	475.3	499.4	526.9	574.5	624.6

[1] With capital consumption adjustment.   [2] With inventory valuation adjustment.

Source: U.S. Bureau of Economic Analysis, *National Income and Product Accounts of the United States* to be published in late 1996, and *Survey of Current Business,* January/February 1996.

No. 694. National Income, by Sector: 1980 to 1994

[In billions of dollars]

SECTOR	1980	1985	1989	1990	1991	1992	1993	1994
National income	2,216.1	3,351.5	4,362.1	4,611.9	4,719.7	4,950.8	5,194.4	5,495.1
Domestic business	1,798.1	2,745.9	3,567.8	3,744.8	3,802.3	3,989.8	4,198.0	4,486.1
Corporate business	1,313.0	1,979.5	2,557.2	2,677.2	2,716.6	2,839.3	3,012.6	3,231.6
Compensation of employees.	1,124.6	1,635.4	2,106.1	2,222.0	2,264.6	2,387.7	2,502.5	2,650.9
Corporate profits [1]	131.6	248.8	298.4	303.8	313.8	336.5	394.9	465.3
Net interest	56.7	95.3	152.7	151.4	138.2	115.1	115.2	115.5
Sole proprietorships and partnerships . .	304.6	469.4	623.5	647.3	646.2	694.1	716	758.9
Compensation of employees.	103.3	141.1	185.9	198.6	201.9	212.6	224.6	236.6
Proprietors' income [1]	165.8	254.9	342.4	358.3	360.1	406.4	416.8	447.5
Net interest	35.4	73.4	95.1	90.4	84.1	75.1	74.6	74.9
Other private business [2]	144.8	243.6	320.1	347.1	363	375.3	388	407.5
Compensation of employees.	7.6	10.7	12.6	13.1	13.3	13.7	14.4	15
Proprietors' income [1]	2.1	2.5	2.6	2.6	2.8	3	3.2	3.4
Rental income of persons [3]	35.3	49.1	52.4	61.4	68.4	80.6	102.5	116.6
Net interest	99.8	181.4	252.5	269.9	278.6	277.9	267.9	272.6
Government enterprises [4]	35.8	53.4	67.1	73.3	76.5	81	81.3	88.1
Households and institutions [5]	87.1	140.9	214.6	237.9	257.4	279.1	294.9	310.3
General government [4]	295.6	444.3	565.6	608.1	644.3	670.8	691.8	707.6
Rest of the world.	35.3	20.4	14.1	21.1	15.7	11.1	9.8	-8.9

[1] With inventory valuation and capital consumption adjustments.   [2] Consists of all business activities reported on the individual income tax return in Schedule E—Supplemental Income Schedule; tax-exempt cooperatives; and owner-occupied nonfarm housing and buildings and equipment owned and used by nonprofit institutions servicing individuals, which are considered to be business activities selling their current services to their owners.   [3] With capital consumption adjustment.   [4] Compensation of employees.   [5] Compensation of employees in private households; nonprofit social and athletic clubs; labor organizations; nonprofit schools and hospitals; religious, charitable, and welfare organizations; and all other nonprofit organizations serving individuals.

Source: U.S. Bureau of Economic Analysis, *National Income and Product Accounts of the United States* to be published in late 1996, and *Survey of Current Business,* January/February 1996.

No. 695. Personal Consumption Expenditures in Current and Real (1992) Dollars, by Type: 1980 to 1994

[In billions of dollars. For definition of "chained" dollars, see text, section 14]

EXPENDITURE	CURRENT DOLLARS				CHAINED (1992) DOLLARS			
	1980	1990	1993	1994	1980	1990	1993	1994
Total expenditures	1,760.4	3,839.3	4,454.1	4,698.7	3,009.7	4,132.2	4,339.7	4,471.1
Food and tobacco [1]	376.2	672.5	732.7	763.3	616	713.5	719.4	736.7
Food purchased for off-premise consumption	242.8	404.8	434.9	449.1	365.9	423.3	428.2	432.2
Purchased meals and beverages [2] . . .	105.9	218.0	242.9	258.4	181.9	231.6	238.2	249.0
Tobacco products	20.9	42.0	47.0	47.7	63.7	50.9	45.2	47.6
Clothing, accessories, and jewelry[1]	132.3	262.7	296.6	310.5	189.1	279.4	292.7	306.4
Shoes	17.4	31.9	34.4	35.5	23.6	34	34.1	35.3
Clothing	89.8	173.8	201.2	212.3	124.3	183.7	199.1	211.9
Jewelry and watches	15.0	31.2	35.6	36.7	22.6	34	34.7	34.8
Personal care	26.6	57.3	65.1	67.7	44.9	60.6	63.3	64.1
Housing [1]	255.2	586.3	673.2	706.6	486.6	627.2	655	668.2
Owner-occupied nonfarm dwellings-space rent	178.4	410.7	481.1	502.6	338.1	437.6	468.2	475.4
Tenant-occupied nonfarm dwellings-space rent	61.8	150.1	162.3	172.5	118.2	160	158.3	163.7
Household operation [1]	232.6	436.2	503.5	528.1	354.1	457	494	507.9
Furniture [3]	20.7	39.0	42.6	45.4	28.5	40.6	41.6	42.7
Semidurable house furnishings[4]	10.6	21.2	24.9	26.9	16.1	22	24.6	25.4
Cleaning and polishing preparations . .	21.9	41.9	48.5	50.6	35.1	43.7	48.3	50.1
Household utilities	81.1	138.3	160.2	162.2	133.4	146.7	155	154.8
Electricity	37.2	71.9	83.0	84.1	60.9	76.1	81.4	82.4
Gas	19.1	26.8	32.9	31.6	29.1	27.7	31	29.2
Water and other sanitary services . .	9.4	27.5	33.7	36.5	22.6	31.9	31.9	32.9
Fuel oil and coal	15.4	12.0	10.6	10.1	16.5	11.2	10.7	10.3
Telephone and telegraph	27.6	60.4	74.1	79.8	39.4	61.3	73.4	76.8
Medical care [1]	206.4	615.6	787.1	833.7	475.4	691.1	745.6	757.9
Drug preparations and sundries[5]	21.8	65.1	77.9	81.7	54.8	74.5	75.2	76.8
Physicians	42.8	140.8	172.9	179.8	101.3	158.5	163.8	163.1
Dentists	13.7	32.9	40.9	43.8	31.1	37.7	38.8	39.7
Hospitals and nursing homes [6]	97.5	265.7	344.4	363.8	222.6	299	329.7	337.6
Health insurance	12.8	37.4	51.7	57.0	34.9	41.3	41.9	40.8
Medical care [7]	7.6	31.3	41.9	44.5	26.1	35.3	37.1	37.4
Personal business [1]	101.2	290.1	354.0	361.9	234.5	331.3	347.6	347.6
Expense of handling life insurance[8] . .	23.9	56.4	68.2	71.0	48.8	61.2	65.5	66.4
Legal services	13.0	41.8	47.9	48.6	33.6	46.4	45.9	45.1
Funeral and burial expenses	4.6	9.0	10.8	11.1	11.3	10.1	10.3	10.1
Transportation [1]	238.4	463.3	503.8	536.6	334.1	491.3	490.3	510
User-operated transportation [1]	218.3	426.9	465.4	498.0	302.9	454.2	454	472.2
New autos	46.4	92.4	86.5	91.3	67.5	98.1	84.4	86.2
Net purchases of used autos	10.8	31.6	40.8	46.1	21.8	35	37.2	38.9
Tires, tubes, accessories, etc.	17.9	29.4	31.6	34.4	19.8	30	32.1	35
Repair, greasing, washing, parking, storage, rental, and leasing	32.2	84.1	94.4	102.0	62.5	94.7	94.4	98.3
Gasoline and oil	66.2	96.6	106.6	108.1	94	108.1	106.6	109.1
Purchased local transportation	4.8	7.8	8.3	8.6	9.8	8.6	8.1	8.2
Mass transit systems	2.9	5.2	5.5	5.6	6.5	5.7	5.4	5.4
Taxicab	1.9	2.6	2.8	2.9	3.2	2.9	2.7	2.8
Purchased intercity transportation[1] . . .	15.4	28.5	30.1	30.0	22	28.6	28.3	29.6
Railway (commutation)	0.3	0.8	0.8	0.7	0.7	0.8	0.8	0.7
Bus	1.4	1.0	0.9	0.8	2.8	1.1	0.9	0.8
Airline [1]	12.8	23.9	25.5	25.3	16.9	23.7	24	25.3
Recreation [1] [9]	116.3	281.6	339.0	374.8	159.7	291.8	337.2	369.9
Magazines, newspapers, and sheet music	12.0	21.5	22.6	24.0	23.3	23.8	21.8	22.5
Nondurable toys and sport supplies . .	14.6	31.6	36.5	40.1	20.1	32.6	36.2	39.3
Video and audio products, computing equipment, musical instruments	19.9	53.8	68.8	80.0	12.7	47.9	73.4	89
Education and research	33.3	80.7	99.3	105.4	66.4	89.3	95.1	97
Higher education	16.5	44.0	55.9	59.7	38.5	50.2	52.7	53.6
Religious and welfare activities	38.3	100.4	121.3	131.2	61	106.6	118.7	125.3
Foreign travel and other, net	3.5	-7.4	-21.4	-21.1	-3.2	-8.2	-19.1	-18.6
Foreign travel by U.S. residents	13.3	41.2	46.0	49.4	16.5	46.1	46.4	48.5
Less: Expenditures in the United States by nonresidents	11.6	51.6	68.8	71.9	22.7	57.7	66.9	68.4

[1] Includes other expenditures not shown separately. [2] Consists of purchases (including tips) of meals and beverages from retail, service, and amusement establishments; hotels; dining and buffet cars; schools; school fraternities; institutions; clubs; and industrial lunch rooms. Includes meals and beverages consumed both on and off-premise. [3] Includes mattresses and bedsprings. [4] Consists largely of textile house furnishings including piece goods allocated to house furnishing use. Also includes lamp shades, brooms, and brushes. [5] Excludes drug preparations and related products dispensed by physicians, hospitals, and other medical services. [6] Consists of (1) current expenditures (including consumption of fixed capital) of nonprofit hospitals and nursing homes and (2) payments by patients to proprietary and government hospitals and nursing homes. [7] Consists of (1) premiums, less benefits and dividends, for health, hospitalization, and accidental death and dismemberment insurance provided by commercial insurance carriers and (2) administrative expenses (including consumption of fixed capital) of Blue Cross and Blue Shield plans and of other independent prepaid and self-insured health plans. [8] Consists of (1) operating expenses of life insurance carriers and private noninsured pension plans and (2) premiums, less benefits and dividends of fraternal benefit societies. Excludes expenses allocated by commercial carriers to accident and health insurance. [9] For additional details, see table 401.

Source: U.S. Bureau of Economic Analysis, *National Income and Product Accounts of the United States* to be published in late 1996, and *Survey of Current Business*, January/February 1996.

No. 696. Personal Income and Its Disposition: 1980 to 1995

[In billions of dollars, except as indicated. For definition of personal income and chained dollars, see text, section 14]

ITEM	1980	1985	1990	1991	1992	1993	1994	1995
Personal income	**2,285.7**	**3,439.6**	**4,791.6**	**4,968.5**	**5,264.2**	**5,479.2**	**5,750.2**	**6,101.7**
Wage and salary disbursements	1,377.7	1,995.9	2,757.5	2,827.6	2,986.4	3,090.6	3,241.1	3,419.7
Commodity-producing industries [1] . .	472.5	620.7	754.2	746.3	765.7	781.3	825.0	858.7
Manufacturing.	356.4	468.9	561.2	562.5	583.5	593.1	621.3	642.8
Distributive industries [2]	336.7	476.5	634.1	646.6	680.3	698.4	739.3	787.9
Service industries [3]	307.2	525.0	852.1	888.6	972.6	1,026.6	1,074.3	1,151.3
Government	261.3	373.8	517.2	546.1	567.8	584.2	602.5	621.7
Other labor income.	139.8	203.1	300.6	322.7	351.3	380.9	402.2	424.0
Proprietors' income [4]	167.9	257.4	361.0	362.9	409.5	420.0	450.9	478.3
Rental income of persons [5]	35.3	49.1	61.4	68.4	80.6	102.5	116.6	122.2
Personal dividend income	57.5	88.3	142.9	153.6	159.4	186.8	199.6	214.8
Personal interest income	274.7	508.4	704.4	699.2	667.2	647.3	661.6	714.6
Transfer payments to persons	321.5	486.5	687.8	769.9	858.2	910.7	956.3	1,022.6
Old-age, survivors, disability, and health insurance benefits	154.2	253.4	352.0	382.3	414.0	444.4	472.9	507.4
Gov't unemployment insurance benefits	16.1	15.7	18.1	26.8	38.9	34.0	23.7	21.6
Veterans benefits	15.0	16.7	17.8	18.3	19.3	20.1	20.2	20.9
Gov't employees retirement benefits	43.0	66.6	94.5	102.2	109.0	116.4	125.8	135.5
Other transfer payments	93.2	134.2	205.3	240.2	277.1	295.7	313.7	337.2
Less: Personal contributions for social insurance	88.6	149.0	223.9	235.8	248.4	259.6	278.1	294.5
Less: Personal tax and nontax payments.	312.4	437.7	624.8	624.8	650.5	689.9	731.4	794.3
Equals: Disposable personal income. .	**1,973.3**	**3,002.0**	**4,166.8**	**4,343.7**	**4,613.7**	**4,789.3**	**5,018.8**	**5,307.4**
Less: Personal outlays	1,811.5	2,795.8	3,958.1	4,097.4	4,341.0	4,572.9	4,826.5	5,066.7
Personal consumption expenditures . .	1,760.4	2,704.8	3,839.3	3,975.1	4,219.8	4,454.1	4,698.7	4,924.3
Interest paid by persons	49.4	83.2	108.9	111.9	111.7	108.9	117.2	131.7
Personal transfer payments to the rest of the world (net).	1.6	7.8	9.9	10.4	9.6	9.9	10.6	10.6
Equals: Personal saving.	**161.8**	**206.2**	**208.7**	**246.4**	**272.6**	**216.4**	**192.4**	**240.8**
Addenda: Disposable personal income: Total, billions of chained (1992) dollars[1]	3,373.3	3,958.6	4,484.6	4,486.5	4,613.7	4,666.2	4,775.6	4,934.7
Per capita (dollars):								
Current dollars	8,665.0	12,587.0	16,670.0	17,191.0	18,062.0	18,552.0	19,253.0	20,174.0
Chained (1992) dollars	14,813.0	16,597.0	17,941.0	17,756.0	18,062.0	18,075.0	18,320.0	18,757.0
Personal saving as percentage of disposable personal income	8.2	6.9	5.0	5.7	5.9	4.5	3.8	4.5

[1] Comprises agriculture, forestry, fishing, mining, construction, and manufacturing. [2] Comprises transportation, communication, public utilities, and trade. [3] Comprises finance, insurance, real estate, services, and rest of world. [4] With capital consumption and inventory valuation adjustments. [5] With capital consumption adjustment.

Source: U.S. Bureau of Economic Analysis, *National Income and Product Accounts of the United States* to be published in late 1996, and *Survey of Current Business*, January/February 1996.

No. 697. Gross Saving and Investment: 1980 to 1995

[In billions of dollars]

ITEM	1980	1985	1989	1990	1991	1992	1993	1994	1995
Gross saving	**547.4**	**746.7**	**907.9**	**904.4**	**935.3**	**905.4**	**938.4**	**1,055.9**	**1,141.6**
Gross private saving	489.5	731.5	815.9	861.7	931.9	971.9	964.5	1,006.0	1,062.5
Personal saving.	161.8	206.2	187.8	208.7	246.4	272.6	216.4	192.4	240.8
Undistributed corporate profits [1]	23.0	92.9	76.2	77.2	86.0	88.9	103.4	120.2	142.5
Undistributed profits	97.3	40.6	67.9	79.4	77.7	93.9	103.3	121.9	154.7
Inventory valuation adjustment	-43.0	0.5	-17.5	-13.5	4.0	-7.5	-6.6	-13.3	-28.1
Capital consumption adjustment . . .	-31.2	51.8	25.8	11.3	4.3	2.5	6.7	11.6	15.9
Corporate consumption of fixed capital.	196.1	281.8	359.3	377.9	393.3	403.0	417.0	441.0	454.0
Noncorporate consumption of fixed capital	108.5	150.6	192.6	197.9	206.3	223.1	223.1	237.7	225.2
Wage accruals less disbursements . . .	-	-	-	-	-	-15.8	4.6	14.8	-
Gross government saving	56.8	15.2	92.0	42.7	3.3	-66.5	-26.0	49.9	79.1
Federal	-26.8	-116.9	-56.4	-94.0	-132.2	-215.0	-186.5	-119.3	-88.7
State and local	83.6	132.0	148.4	136.7	135.5	148.6	160.5	169.2	167.9
Capital grants received by the U.S. (net) .	1.2	-	-	-	-	-	-	-	-
Gross investment	**574.8**	**748.0**	**919.5**	**920.5**	**944.0**	**949.1**	**993.5**	**1,087.2**	**1,146.1**
Gross private domestic investment	465.9	715.1	829.2	799.7	736.2	790.4	871.1	1,014.4	1,065.3
Gross government investment	96.4	149.9	182.7	199.4	200.5	209.1	210.6	212.3	221.9
Net foreign investment	12.5	-116.9	-92.4	-78.6	7.3	-50.5	-88.2	-139.6	-141.1
Statistical discrepancy.	**27.4**	**1.3**	**11.6**	**16.1**	**8.8**	**43.7**	**55.1**	**31.3**	**4.5**

- Represents or rounds to zero. [1] With inventory valuation and capital consumption adjustments.

Source: U.S. Bureau of Economic Analysis, *National Income and Product Accounts of the United States* to be published in late 1996, and *Survey of Current Business*, January/February 1996.

No. 698. Personal Income, by State: 1980 to 1995

[In billions of dollars, except percent. 1995 preliminary. Represents a measure of income received from all sources during the calendar year by residents of each State. Data exclude Federal employees overseas and U.S. residents employed by private U.S. firms on temporary foreign assignment. Totals may differ from those in tables 691, 692, and 696. For definition of average annual percent change, see Guide to Tabular Presentation]

REGION, DIVISION, AND STATE	CURRENT DOLLARS				CONSTANT (1992) DOLLARS				Average annual percent change		Percent distribution	
	1980	1990	1994	1995	1980	1990	1994	1995	1980-1994	1994-1995	1980	1995
United States . .	2,259.0	4,655.4	5,649.0	5,987.5	3,861.5	5,010.7	5,375.4	5,567.2	2.4	3.5	100.0	100.0
Northeast	526.2	1,103.6	1,288.7	1,348.9	899.4	1,187.8	1,226.3	1,254.2	2.2	2.2	23.3	22.5
New England	130.9	290.0	334.5	352.9	223.7	312.1	318.3	328.1	2.5	3.0	5.8	5.9
Maine	9.3	21.0	24.2	25.5	15.8	22.6	23.0	23.7	2.7	3.0	0.4	0.4
New Hampshire . . .	9.1	22.5	26.9	28.9	15.5	24.2	25.6	26.9	3.7	4.8	0.4	0.5
Vermont	4.4	9.8	11.7	12.2	7.5	10.6	11.1	11.4	2.9	2.5	0.2	0.2
Massachusetts . . .	61.2	133.9	154.7	163.9	104.6	144.1	147.2	152.4	2.5	3.5	2.7	2.7
Rhode Island	9.1	19.1	21.9	23.1	15.5	20.6	20.8	21.5	2.1	3.0	0.4	0.4
Connecticut	37.9	83.6	95.1	99.2	64.7	90.0	90.5	92.3	2.4	1.9	1.7	1.7
Middle Atlantic	395.3	813.6	954.3	996.0	675.7	875.7	908.1	926.1	2.1	1.9	17.5	16.6
New York	191.6	401.8	467.5	485.7	327.5	432.5	444.9	451.6	2.2	1.5	8.5	8.1
New Jersey	85.9	187.2	219.3	229.3	146.9	201.4	208.6	213.2	2.5	2.1	3.8	3.8
Pennsylvania	117.8	224.6	267.5	281.0	201.4	241.8	254.5	261.3	1.7	2.6	5.2	4.7
Midwest	581.6	1,079.8	1,322.6	1,397.8	994.2	1,162.2	1,258.6	1,299.7	1.7	3.2	25.7	23.3
East North Central . .	420.3	769.9	942.5	998.7	718.4	828.7	896.9	928.6	1.6	3.5	18.6	16.7
Ohio	105.2	190.6	231.8	245.5	179.8	205.2	220.6	228.3	1.5	3.4	4.7	4.1
Indiana	50.6	93.4	116.5	123.5	86.5	100.5	110.9	114.8	1.8	3.5	2.2	2.1
Illinois	124.4	230.8	277.4	292.9	212.7	248.4	264.0	272.4	1.6	3.1	5.5	4.9
Michigan	94.0	169.8	210.6	224.9	160.6	182.8	200.4	209.1	1.6	4.3	4.2	3.8
Wisconsin	46.1	85.3	106.1	111.9	78.7	91.8	101.0	104.0	1.8	2.9	2.0	1.9
West North Central .	161.4	309.9	380.1	399.1	275.8	333.5	361.7	371.1	2.0	2.5	7.1	6.7
Minnesota	40.8	82.4	101.7	106.6	69.7	88.7	96.7	99.1	2.4	2.4	1.8	1.8
Iowa	27.3	46.4	57.1	59.7	46.6	49.9	54.3	55.5	1.1	2.2	1.2	1.0
Missouri	45.6	89.2	108.5	115.1	77.9	96.1	103.3	107.0	2.0	3.6	2.0	1.9
North Dakota	5.0	9.8	11.9	12.0	8.6	10.5	11.3	11.1	2.0	-1.6	0.2	0.2
South Dakota	5.3	10.9	14.2	14.2	9.1	11.7	13.5	13.2	2.8	-1.9	0.2	0.2
Nebraska	14.1	27.5	33.8	35.5	24.2	29.6	32.2	33.0	2.1	2.7	0.6	0.6
Kansas	23.3	43.8	53.0	56.0	39.8	47.1	50.5	52.1	1.7	3.1	1.0	0.9
South	678.4	1,448.4	1,807.9	1,924.6	1,159.7	1,558.9	1,720.3	1,789.5	2.9	4.0	30.0	32.1
South Atlantic	341.9	797.7	984.5	1,049.9	584.4	858.6	936.8	976.2	3.4	4.2	15.1	17.5
Delaware	6.2	13.2	16.3	17.3	10.5	14.2	15.5	16.1	2.8	3.9	0.3	0.3
Maryland	45.7	106.0	124.4	130.7	78.2	114.1	118.4	121.6	3.0	2.6	2.0	2.2
Dist. of Columbia . .	8.0	14.9	17.4	17.9	13.6	16.0	16.6	16.6	1.4	0.3	0.4	0.3
Virginia	52.9	121.4	147.4	156.2	90.5	130.7	140.3	145.2	3.2	3.5	2.3	2.6
West Virginia	15.6	25.0	31.1	32.8	26.6	26.9	29.6	30.5	0.8	2.7	0.7	0.5
North Carolina	47.2	108.3	138.4	148.3	80.7	116.6	131.7	137.8	3.6	4.6	2.1	2.5
South Carolina . . .	23.7	52.9	64.9	69.0	40.5	56.9	61.8	64.2	3.1	3.9	1.0	1.2
Georgia	45.8	111.4	142.5	153.2	78.3	119.9	135.6	142.5	4.0	5.0	2.0	2.6
Florida	96.8	244.6	302.1	324.6	165.4	263.3	287.5	301.8	4.0	5.0	4.3	5.4
East South Central . .	113.6	225.0	286.3	303.4	194.2	242.1	272.5	282.1	2.4	3.5	5.0	5.1
Kentucky	29.5	54.5	67.9	71.8	50.4	58.6	64.6	66.8	1.8	3.3	1.3	1.2
Tennessee	36.9	77.8	100.6	107.1	63.0	83.7	95.8	99.6	3.0	3.9	1.6	1.8
Alabama	29.9	60.3	75.6	79.9	51.1	64.9	72.0	74.3	2.5	3.2	1.3	1.3
Mississippi	17.4	32.4	42.2	44.6	29.7	34.9	40.1	41.5	2.2	3.3	0.8	0.7
West South Central .	223.0	425.8	537.0	571.3	381.1	458.2	511.0	531.2	2.1	3.9	9.9	9.5
Arkansas	16.9	32.5	41.2	43.3	28.9	34.9	39.2	40.3	2.2	2.5	0.7	0.7
Louisiana	36.7	60.2	76.0	81.8	62.7	64.8	72.3	76.0	1.0	5.0	1.6	1.4
Oklahoma	28.3	47.6	57.3	59.5	48.4	51.2	54.6	55.3	0.9	1.3	1.3	1.0
Texas	141.1	285.5	362.4	386.7	241.2	307.3	344.8	359.6	2.6	4.2	6.2	6.5
West	472.8	1,023.6	1,229.8	1,316.2	808.2	1,101.7	1,170.2	1,223.8	2.7	4.5	20.9	22.0
Mountain	108.3	227.5	301.1	327.0	185.1	244.9	286.5	304.0	3.2	6.1	4.8	5.5
Montana	6.9	11.8	15.3	16.1	11.8	12.7	14.5	15.0	1.5	3.0	0.3	0.3
Idaho	8.0	15.5	20.9	22.4	13.7	16.7	19.8	20.8	2.7	4.9	0.4	0.4
Wyoming	5.4	7.7	9.7	10.2	9.2	8.2	9.2	9.5	-	3.1	0.2	0.2
Colorado	30.9	62.2	81.6	87.9	52.8	66.9	77.6	81.7	2.8	5.2	1.4	1.5
New Mexico	10.7	21.6	28.2	30.4	18.2	23.3	26.8	28.3	2.8	5.6	0.5	0.5
Arizona	25.4	59.8	78.0	86.1	43.4	64.4	74.3	80.1	3.9	7.8	1.1	1.4
Utah	11.7	24.3	32.8	35.6	20.0	26.2	31.2	33.1	3.2	6.0	0.5	0.6
Nevada	9.4	24.7	34.7	38.3	16.0	26.6	33.0	35.6	5.3	7.7	0.4	0.6
Pacific	364.5	796.1	928.7	989.2	623.1	856.8	883.7	919.8	2.5	4.0	16.1	16.5
Washington	44.5	94.4	120.4	128.4	76.1	101.6	114.6	119.4	3.0	4.1	2.0	2.1
Oregon	26.1	49.2	63.2	68.3	44.5	52.9	60.1	63.5	2.2	5.5	1.2	1.1
California	278.0	617.7	702.6	748.6	475.2	664.8	668.5	696.1	2.5	4.1	12.3	12.5
Alaska	5.5	11.5	14.2	14.6	9.5	12.4	13.5	13.6	2.6	0.5	0.2	0.2
Hawaii	10.4	23.3	28.3	29.4	17.8	25.0	27.0	27.3	3.0	1.2	0.5	0.5

- Represents or rounds to zero.

Source: U.S. Bureau of Economic Analysis, *Survey of Current Business*, May 1996.

No. 699. Personal Income Per Capita in Current and Constant (1992) Dollars, by State: 1980 to 1995

[1995 data preliminary. See headnote, table 698]

REGION, DIVISION, AND STATE	CURRENT DOLLARS					CONSTANT (1992) DOLLARS					Income rank	
	1980	1990	1993	1994	1995	1980	1990	1993	1994	1995	1980	1995
United States ..	9,940	18,666	20,809	21,699	22,788	16,991	20,090	20,274	20,648	21,188	(X)	(X)
Northeast.	10,699	21,699	24,141	25,073	26,209	18,289	23,355	23,520	23,859	24,369	(X)	(X)
New England	10,582	21,934	24,148	25,203	26,506	18,089	23,608	23,527	23,982	24,645	(X)	(X)
Maine	8,218	17,039	18,687	19,481	20,527	14,048	18,339	18,206	18,537	19,086	38	34
New Hampshire. . . .	9,803	20,227	22,312	23,679	25,151	16,757	21,771	21,738	22,532	23,385	23	6
Vermont.	8,546	17,442	19,394	20,100	20,927	14,609	18,773	18,895	19,126	19,458	35	31
Massachusetts	10,659	22,247	24,410	25,608	26,994	18,221	23,945	23,782	24,368	25,099	12	3
Rhode Island	9,576	19,032	21,231	21,948	23,310	16,369	20,484	20,685	20,885	21,674	26	17
Connecticut	12,170	25,427	28,087	29,044	30,303	20,803	27,367	27,365	27,637	28,176	2	1
Middle Atlantic	10,738	21,617	24,139	25,028	26,106	18,356	23,267	23,518	23,816	24,273	(X)	(X)
New York.	10,906	22,321	24,844	25,726	26,782	18,643	24,024	24,205	24,480	24,902	7	4
New Jersey	11,648	24,182	26,834	27,741	28,858	19,911	26,027	26,144	26,397	26,832	4	2
Pennsylvania	9,923	18,883	21,314	22,195	23,279	16,962	20,324	20,766	21,120	21,645	17	18
Midwest.	9,872	18,067	20,328	21,542	22,617	16,875	19,446	19,805	20,499	21,029	(X)	(X)
East North Central. . .	10,077	18,297	20,627	21,825	22,982	17,226	19,693	20,096	20,768	21,369	(X)	(X)
Ohio	9,738	17,548	19,730	20,882	22,021	16,646	18,887	19,223	19,871	20,475	25	21
Indiana	9,215	16,816	19,219	20,261	21,273	15,752	18,099	18,725	19,280	19,780	31	29
Illinois	10,875	20,159	22,533	23,607	24,763	18,590	21,697	21,953	22,464	23,025	8	8
Michigan	10,154	18,237	20,599	22,172	23,551	17,357	19,629	20,069	21,098	21,898	15	15
Wisconsin	9,772	17,398	19,824	20,887	21,839	16,704	18,726	19,314	19,875	20,306	24	22
West North Central . .	9,374	17,520	19,619	20,870	21,753	16,024	18,857	19,114	19,859	20,226	(X)	(X)
Minnesota	9,982	18,779	20,911	22,257	23,118	17,063	20,212	20,373	21,179	21,495	16	19
Iowa	9,346	16,684	18,412	20,176	21,012	15,976	17,957	17,938	19,199	19,537	27	30
Missouri.	9,256	17,409	19,501	20,562	21,627	15,822	18,737	18,999	19,566	20,109	30	26
North Dakota	7,641	15,321	17,212	18,610	18,663	13,062	16,490	16,769	17,709	17,353	47	42
South Dakota	7,701	15,630	18,122	19,562	19,506	13,164	16,823	17,656	18,615	18,137	45	37
Nebraska	8,988	17,379	19,693	20,819	21,703	15,364	18,705	19,186	19,811	20,179	32	25
Kansas	9,829	17,642	19,880	20,762	21,825	16,802	18,988	19,369	19,756	20,293	22	23
South	8,958	16,895	19,085	19,936	20,945	15,313	18,184	18,594	18,970	19,475	(X)	(X)
South Atlantic	9,204	18,230	20,341	21,222	22,342	15,733	19,621	19,818	20,194	20,774	(X)	(X)
Delaware	10,356	19,719	22,015	22,919	24,124	17,703	21,224	21,449	21,809	22,430	14	11
Maryland	10,824	22,090	23,937	24,869	25,927	18,503	23,776	23,321	23,664	24,107	9	5
District of Columbia .	12,508	24,648	29,346	30,721	32,274	21,381	26,529	28,591	29,233	30,008	(X)	(X)
Virginia	9,857	19,537	21,650	22,503	23,597	16,850	21,028	21,093	21,413	21,940	19	14
West Virginia	7,972	13,967	16,230	17,089	17,915	13,627	15,033	15,813	16,261	16,657	43	48
North Carolina.	8,000	16,275	18,719	19,579	20,604	13,675	17,517	18,238	18,631	19,158	42	33
South Carolina	7,558	15,106	16,877	17,713	18,788	12,920	16,259	16,443	16,855	17,469	48	40
Georgia	8,353	17,123	19,244	20,198	21,278	14,279	18,430	18,749	19,220	19,784	37	28
Florida.	9,835	18,788	20,795	21,654	22,916	16,812	20,222	20,260	20,605	21,307	21	20
East South Central . .	7,730	14,792	17,089	18,020	18,884	13,214	15,921	16,649	17,147	17,558	(X)	(X)
Kentucky	8,051	14,747	16,887	17,752	18,612	13,762	15,872	16,453	16,892	17,305	40	43
Tennessee	8,010	15,905	18,458	19,446	20,376	13,692	17,119	17,983	18,504	18,946	41	36
Alabama	7,656	14,903	17,104	17,925	18,781	13,087	16,040	16,664	17,057	17,463	46	41
Mississippi	6,868	12,571	14,713	15,791	16,531	11,740	13,530	14,335	15,026	15,371	50	50
West South Central . .	9,329	15,908	18,151	18,906	19,816	15,947	17,122	17,684	17,990	18,425	(X)	(X)
Arkansas	7,371	13,784	15,980	16,818	17,429	12,600	14,836	15,569	16,003	16,205	49	49
Louisiana	8,672	14,281	16,555	17,615	18,827	14,824	15,371	16,129	16,762	17,505	34	39
Oklahoma	9,308	15,119	17,041	17,602	18,152	15,911	16,273	16,603	16,749	16,878	28	46
Texas	9,840	16,749	19,023	19,719	20,654	16,821	18,027	18,534	18,764	19,204	20	32
West	10,889	19,296	21,036	21,629	22,852	18,614	20,768	20,495	20,581	21,248	(X)	(X)
Mountain	9,455	16,589	18,975	19,789	20,900	16,162	17,855	18,487	18,831	19,433	(X)	(X)
Montana	8,728	14,741	17,624	17,824	18,482	14,920	15,866	17,171	16,961	17,185	33	44
Idaho	8,433	15,301	17,717	18,406	19,264	14,415	16,469	17,261	17,515	17,912	36	38
Wyoming	11,356	16,902	19,850	20,257	21,321	19,412	18,192	19,339	19,390	19,824	6	27
Colorado	10,616	18,814	21,560	22,320	23,449	18,147	20,250	21,005	21,239	21,803	13	16
New Mexico	8,147	14,213	16,295	17,025	18,055	13,926	15,298	15,876	16,200	16,788	39	47
Arizona	9,272	16,265	18,194	19,153	20,421	15,850	17,506	17,726	18,225	18,987	29	35
Utah	7,942	14,060	16,354	17,171	18,223	13,576	15,133	15,933	16,339	16,944	44	45
Nevada	11,559	20,254	22,727	23,817	25,013	19,759	21,800	22,142	22,663	23,257	5	7
Pacific	11,403	20,240	21,774	22,301	23,581	19,492	21,785	21,214	21,221	21,926	(X)	(X)
Washington	10,716	19,265	21,838	22,542	23,639	18,318	20,735	21,276	21,450	21,980	11	13
Oregon	9,863	17,199	19,534	20,467	21,736	16,860	18,511	19,032	19,476	20,210	18	24
California	11,681	20,654	21,893	22,353	23,699	19,968	22,230	21,330	21,270	22,035	3	12
Alaska.	13,692	20,881	22,887	23,431	24,182	23,405	22,474	22,298	22,296	22,484	1	10
Hawaii	10,774	20,906	23,566	24,043	24,738	18,417	22,501	22,960	22,878	23,001	10	9

X Not applicable.

Source: U.S. Bureau of Economic Analysis, *Survey of Current Business,* May 1996 issue.

No. 700. Disposable Personal Income Per Capita in Current and Constant (1992) Dollars, by State: 1980 to 1995

[1995 data preliminary]

REGION, DIVISION, AND STATE	CURRENT DOLLARS				Income rank			CONSTANT (1992) DOLLARS			
	1980	1990	1994	1995	1980	1990	1995	1980	1990	1994	1995
United States	8,569	16,173	18,852	19,729	(X)	(X)	(X)	14,648	17,407	17,939	18,344
Northeast	9,140	18,538	21,403	22,329	(X)	(X)	(X)	15,624	19,953	20,366	20,762
New England	9,055	18,827	21,488	22,502	(X)	(X)	(X)	15,479	20,264	20,447	20,922
Maine	7,283	15,062	17,425	18,282	38	27	32	12,450	16,211	16,581	16,999
New Hampshire	8,611	18,117	20,985	22,209	15	7	5	14,720	19,500	19,969	20,650
Vermont	7,485	15,223	17,713	18,389	35	25	30	12,795	16,385	16,855	17,098
Massachusetts	9,052	18,925	21,654	22,764	13	3	3	15,474	20,369	20,605	21,166
Rhode Island	8,306	16,568	19,141	20,263	26	14	16	14,198	17,832	18,214	18,841
Connecticut	10,321	21,605	24,278	25,130	2	1	1	17,643	23,254	23,102	23,366
Middle Atlantic	9,169	18,436	21,374	22,268	(X)	(X)	(X)	15,674	19,843	20,339	20,705
New York.	9,249	18,733	21,726	22,603	10	4	4	15,810	20,163	20,674	21,016
New Jersey	9,974	20,852	23,622	24,554	5	2	2	17,050	22,443	22,478	22,830
Pennsylvania	8,549	16,416	19,368	20,260	17	17	17	14,614	17,669	18,430	18,838
Midwest	8,494	15,676	18,710	19,568	(X)	(X)	(X)	14,520	16,872	17,804	18,194
East North Central	8,672	15,863	18,942	19,876	(X)	(X)	(X)	14,824	17,074	18,025	18,481
Ohio	8,405	15,248	18,197	19,123	24	24	22	14,368	16,412	17,316	17,781
Indiana	7,988	14,637	17,652	18,438	30	32	27	13,655	15,754	16,797	17,144
Illinois	9,276	17,412	20,448	21,371	9	11	9	15,856	18,741	19,458	19,871
Michigan	8,779	15,836	19,260	20,393	14	20	13	15,007	17,044	18,327	18,961
Wisconsin	8,401	15,046	17,954	18,725	25	28	26	14,361	16,194	17,087	17,411
West North Central	8,065	15,231	18,159	18,840	(X)	(X)	(X)	13,786	16,393	17,279	17,517
Minnesota	8,505	15,986	18,791	19,427	18	19	20	14,538	17,206	17,881	18,063
Iowa	7,987	14,517	17,578	18,270	31	33	33	13,653	15,625	16,727	16,987
Missouri	8,030	15,248	18,077	18,931	28	23	24	13,726	16,412	17,201	17,602
North Dakota	6,600	13,837	16,720	16,636	48	38	41	11,282	14,893	15,910	15,468
South Dakota	6,890	14,121	17,689	17,434	45	37	37	11,778	15,199	16,832	16,210
Nebraska.	7,769	15,340	18,546	19,250	32	21	21	13,280	16,511	17,648	17,899
Kansas	8,419	15,261	18,089	18,920	23	22	25	14,391	16,426	17,213	17,592
South	7,768	14,827	17,508	18,320	(X)	(X)	(X)	13,279	15,958	16,660	17,034
South Atlantic	7,956	15,859	18,452	19,347	(X)	(X)	(X)	13,600	17,069	17,558	17,989
Delaware.	8,502	16,544	19,426	20,333	19	15	14	14,533	17,806	18,485	18,906
Maryland	9,097	18,701	21,058	21,852	12	5	6	15,550	20,128	20,038	20,318
District of Columbia	10,542	20,316	25,787	27,012	(X)	(X)	(X)	18,021	21,866	24,538	25,116
Virginia	8,443	16,881	19,454	20,288	21	13	15	14,432	18,169	18,512	18,864
West Virginia	6,944	12,481	15,393	16,090	43	47	45	11,870	13,433	14,647	14,960
North Carolina	6,939	14,236	16,966	17,772	44	36	36	11,862	15,322	16,144	16,524
South Carolina	6,627	13,331	15,713	16,617	47	40	42	11,328	14,348	14,952	15,450
Georgia	7,309	14,893	17,546	18,404	37	29	28	12,494	16,029	16,696	17,112
Florida	8,595	16,538	19,030	20,074	16	16	18	14,692	17,800	18,108	18,665
East South Central	6,834	13,203	15,997	16,700	(X)	(X)	(X)	11,682	14,211	15,222	15,528
Kentucky	7,066	12,897	15,391	16,060	41	43	46	12,079	13,881	14,646	14,933
Tennessee.	7,117	14,317	17,343	18,105	40	35	34	12,166	15,410	16,503	16,834
Alabama	6,741	13,231	15,957	16,657	46	42	40	11,523	14,241	15,184	15,488
Mississippi	6,122	11,484	14,321	14,948	50	50	50	10,465	12,360	13,627	13,899
West South Central	8,050	14,063	16,810	17,548	(X)	(X)	(X)	13,761	15,136	15,996	16,316
Arkansas	6,502	12,240	14,897	15,349	49	48	49	11,115	13,174	14,175	14,272
Louisiana.	7,523	12,730	15,712	16,725	34	45	39	12,860	13,701	14,951	15,551
Oklahoma	8,017	13,293	15,445	15,827	29	41	47	13,704	14,307	14,697	14,716
Texas	8,459	14,787	17,564	18,332	20	30	31	14,460	15,915	16,713	17,045
West	9,422	16,642	18,845	19,825	(X)	(X)	(X)	16,106	17,912	17,932	18,433
Mountain	8,247	14,522	17,244	18,125	(X)	(X)	(X)	14,097	15,630	16,409	16,853
Montana	7,565	12,832	15,646	16,218	33	44	43	12,932	13,811	14,888	15,079
Idaho	7,452	13,834	16,378	17,122	36	39	38	12,738	14,890	15,585	15,920
Wyoming	9,705	15,111	18,213	19,021	6	26	23	16,590	16,264	17,331	17,686
Colorado	9,130	16,228	18,962	19,778	11	18	19	15,607	17,466	18,044	18,390
New Mexico	7,246	12,658	15,273	16,145	39	46	44	12,386	13,624	14,533	15,012
Arizona	8,147	14,340	16,814	17,850	27	34	35	13,926	15,434	16,000	16,597
Utah	6,987	12,154	14,890	15,692	42	49	48	11,944	13,081	14,169	14,590
Nevada	10,058	17,589	20,750	21,684	4	10	7	17,193	18,931	19,745	20,162
Pacific	9,843	17,381	19,430	20,459	(X)	(X)	(X)	16,826	18,707	18,489	19,023
Washington	9,317	16,888	19,922	20,808	7	12	11	15,926	18,177	18,957	19,347
Oregon	8,425	14,709	17,387	18,392	22	31	29	14,402	15,831	16,545	17,101
California	10,084	17,688	19,475	20,560	3	9	12	17,238	19,038	18,532	19,117
Alaska.	11,639	18,348	20,829	21,417	1	6	8	19,896	19,748	19,820	19,914
Hawaii.	9,286	17,693	20,641	21,157	8	8	10	15,874	19,043	19,641	19,672

X Not applicable.

Source: U.S. Bureau of Economic Analysis, *Survey of Current Business,* May 1996 issue.

No. 701. Personal Income, by Metropolitan Area: 1990 to 1994

[As defined **June 30, 1994.** CMSA=Consolidated Metropolitan Statistical Area; NECMA=New England County Metropolitan Area; MSA=Metropolitan Statistical Area. See Appendix II]

METROPOLITAN AREA RANKED BY 1990 POPULATION	PERSONAL INCOME				PER CAPITA PERSONAL INCOME			
	1990 (mil. dol.)	1993 (mil. dol.)	1994 (mil. dol.)	Annual percent change, 1993-94	1990 (dol.)	1993 (dol.)	1994 (dol.)	Percent of national average, 1994
United States [1]	4,655,420	5,365,006	5,648,263	5.3	18,666	20,812	21,696	100.0
New York-Northern New Jersey-Long Island, NY-NJ-CT-PA CMSA	491,234	552,201	571,868	3.6	25,230	28,105	29,021	133.8
Los Angeles-Riverside-Orange County, CA CMSA	301,614	324,298	329,646	1.6	20,659	21,321	21,542	99.3
Chicago-Gary-Kenosha, IL-IN-WI CMSA. .	178,641	205,074	215,361	5.0	21,635	24,223	25,257	116.4
Washington-Baltimore, DC-MD-VA-WV CMSA	159,226	181,186	189,819	4.8	23,594	25,957	26,919	124.1
San Francisco-Oakland-San Jose, CA CMSA	155,119	177,172	184,469	4.1	24,767	27,386	28,322	130.5
Philadelphia-Wilmington-Atlantic City, PA-NJ-DE-MD CMSA	126,512	143,257	149,311	4.2	21,444	24,108	25,055	115.5
Boston-Brockton-Nashua, MA-NH NECMA	128,494	141,685	149,517	5.5	22,589	24,858	26,093	120.3
Detroit-Ann Arbor-Flint, MI CMSA	104,758	118,481	128,545	8.5	20,174	22,585	24,458	112.7
Dallas-Fort Worth, TX CMSA	80,619	96,436	102,300	6.1	19,870	22,536	23,450	108.1
Houston-Galveston-Brazoria, TX CMSA . .	73,025	88,264	92,840	5.2	19,456	21,913	22,651	104.4
Miami-Fort Lauderdale, FL CMSA	62,388	70,760	74,698	5.6	19,464	21,098	21,918	101.0
Seattle-Tacoma-Bremerton, WA CMSA. . .	63,334	76,373	79,941	4.7	21,157	23,949	24,784	114.2
Atlanta, GA MSA	60,882	73,325	78,720	7.4	20,446	22,711	23,633	108.9
Cleveland-Akron, OH CMSA.	55,519	62,709	66,444	6.0	19,398	21,669	22,921	105.6
Minneapolis-St. Paul, MN-WI MSA	54,579	63,873	67,831	6.2	21,418	24,061	25,231	116.3
San Diego, CA MSA	49,587	55,046	56,923	3.4	19,729	21,075	21,627	99.7
St. Louis, MO-IL MSA	50,212	56,775	60,066	5.8	20,116	22,457	23,685	109.2
Pittsburgh, PA MSA	45,437	52,431	54,647	4.2	18,970	21,783	22,751	104.9
Phoenix-Mesa, AZ MSA.	40,237	47,638	51,938	9.0	17,919	19,914	20,999	96.8
Tampa-St. Petersburg-Clearwater, FL MSA.	37,291	43,231	46,059	6.5	17,966	20,232	21,358	98.4
Denver-Boulder-Greeley, CO CMSA	40,913	50,477	53,390	5.8	20,595	23,517	24,379	112.4
Cincinnati-Hamilton, OH-KY-IN CMSA . . .	33,873	39,188	41,447	5.8	18,588	20,830	21,883	100.9
Portland-Salem, OR-WA CMSA	33,612	41,086	43,949	7.0	18,610	21,131	22,172	102.2
Milwaukee-Racine, WI CMSA	31,851	36,884	38,849	5.3	19,784	22,569	23,728	109.4
Kansas City, MO-KS MSA	30,369	35,103	37,296	6.2	19,135	21,524	22,641	104.4
Sacramento-Yolo, CA CMSA	28,820	33,035	34,632	4.8	19,269	20,958	21,810	100.5
Norfolk-Virginia Beach-Newport News, VA-NC MSA	24,258	27,908	29,065	4.1	16,719	18,435	19,007	87.6
Indianapolis, IN MSA	26,638	31,817	33,865	6.4	19,227	22,048	23,169	106.8
Columbus, OH MSA	24,664	29,405	31,386	6.7	18,264	20,866	22,058	101.7
San Antonio, TX MSA	20,691	25,038	26,542	6.0	15,586	17,794	18,466	85.1
New Orleans, LA MSA	21,038	24,490	25,960	6.0	16,386	18,780	19,833	91.4
Orlando, FL MSA	21,645	25,802	27,391	6.2	17,468	19,344	20,119	92.7
Buffalo-Niagara Falls, NY MSA	21,277	23,952	25,067	4.7	17,877	20,086	21,079	97.2
Charlotte-Gastonia-Rock Hill, NC-SC MSA.	21,727	25,773	27,659	7.3	18,593	20,894	21,945	101.1
Hartford, CT NECMA	27,085	29,138	29,988	2.9	24,091	26,025	26,842	123.7
Salt Lake City-Ogden, UT MSA.	16,429	20,400	21,944	7.6	15,259	17,670	18,623	85.8
Rochester, NY MSA	21,245	23,784	24,640	3.6	19,954	21,834	22,593	104.1
Greensboro-Winston-Salem-High Point, NC MSA	19,457	22,720	24,121	6.2	18,467	20,806	21,789	100.4
Memphis, TN-AR-MS MSA.	18,001	21,243	22,774	7.2	17,824	20,382	21,564	99.4
Nashville, TN MSA	18,127	22,692	24,643	8.6	18,334	21,725	23,038	106.2
Oklahoma City, OK MSA	15,701	18,327	19,170	4.6	16,357	18,405	19,031	87.7
Dayton-Springfield, OH MSA	16,900	19,317	20,434	5.8	17,751	20,105	21,366	98.5
Louisville, KY-IN MSA	17,294	20,481	21,658	5.7	18,195	21,028	22,081	101.8
Grand Rapids-Muskegon-Holland, MI MSA.	16,308	19,556	21,338	9.1	17,317	20,073	21,663	99.8
Providence-Warwick, RI NECMA.	17,372	19,345	20,000	3.4	18,941	21,162	21,928	101.1
Jacksonville, FL MSA	16,443	19,284	20,348	5.5	18,015	20,038	20,938	96.5
West Palm Beach-Boca Raton, FL MSA. .	25,319	30,415	31,994	5.2	29,103	32,642	33,518	154.5
Richmond-Petersburg, VA MSA.	18,535	21,175	22,329	5.5	21,313	23,374	24,358	112.3

[1] Includes other areas not listed separately.

Source: U.S. Bureau of Economic Analysis, *Survey of Current Business,* June 1996 issue.

No. 702. Flow of Funds Accounts—Composition of Individuals' Savings: 1980 to 1994

[In billions of dollars. Combined statement for households, farm business, and nonfarm noncorporate business. Minus sign (-) indicates decrease. See *Historical Statistics, Colonial Times to 1970,* series F 566-594, for similar but not exactly comparable data]

COMPOSITION OF SAVINGS	1980	1985	1988	1989	1990	1991	1992	1993	1994
Increase in financial assets [1]	329.6	631.9	508.5	594.9	502.3	442.2	532.1	524.1	582.1
Checkable deposits and currency	9.3	29.0	27.2	-1.2	5.4	63.0	131.1	81.7	14.3
Time and savings deposits	121.6	117.2	136.2	79.6	38.5	-117.4	-112.1	-91.1	14.6
Money market fund shares	23.5	2.3	15.9	76.8	28.6	8.7	-41.8	-10.7	20.8
Securities	13.6	109.2	103.4	23.2	191.4	56.6	257.4	133.3	357.1
U.S. savings bonds	-7.3	5.3	8.5	8.2	8.5	11.9	19.1	14.7	8.0
Other U.S. Treasury securities	24.7	-3.2	60.9	12.5	106.8	-54.8	33.1	31.8	145.2
U.S. Government agency securities	7.7	13.1	63.4	46.3	12.7	7.9	49.2	-39.8	207.1
Tax-exempt securities	2.4	72.2	39.7	55.6	17.7	34.9	-34.8	-15.8	-29.6
Corporate and foreign bonds	-14.5	-0.8	-21.8	-17.2	38.0	10.3	-4.8	26.2	58.5
Open-market paper	2.9	58.4	31.3	-9.0	-8.3	-34.8	5.2	-37.7	-19.7
Mutual fund shares	2.1	75.5	14.1	36.0	37.7	115.1	146.5	187.0	76.6
Other corporate equities	-4.3	-111.2	-92.6	-109.1	-21.7	-33.8	43.8	-33.1	-89.0
Private life insurance reserves	9.7	10.4	24.9	26.8	25.3	25.6	27.7	35.7	20.4
Private insured pension reserves	22.3	63.4	85.0	77.8	84.4	81.1	75.2	102.0	80.7
Private noninsured pension reserves	59.0	136.2	-28.4	142.4	-10.9	192.5	75.0	96.9	-83.2
Government insurance and pension reserves	35.8	72.5	76.0	101.3	92.0	86.8	99.0	109.9	116.1
Gross investment in tangible assets	406.4	651.9	779.1	822.0	807.4	758.4	825.9	905.2	1,023.9
Owner-occupied homes	101.8	161.5	206.8	206.8	191.5	173.1	205.5	230.2	260.9
Other fixed assets [2]	98.4	130.8	145.2	152.8	144.5	129.4	122.2	140.7	163.0
Consumer durables	212.5	353.0	437.1	459.4	468.2	456.6	492.7	538.0	591.4
Inventories [2]	-6.3	6.7	-10.0	3.1	3.3	-0.7	5.5	-3.7	8.7
Capital consumption allowances	314.3	435.5	532.4	580.0	614.2	649.3	693.8	712.5	776.6
Net investment in tangible assets	92.0	216.4	246.7	242.0	193.2	109.2	132.1	192.7	247.4
Net increase in liabilities	200.2	444.3	363.1	360.0	252.2	159.7	191.8	309.4	396.5
Mortgage debt on nonfarm homes	94.1	171.7	234.3	223.8	185.0	163.3	179.0	183.3	191.3
Other mortgage debt [2]	50.9	98.1	44.1	43.8	18.3	-2.1	-27.6	-12.4	3.6
Consumer credit	4.8	82.3	50.1	45.8	16.0	-15.0	5.5	62.3	117.5
Other liabilities [2]	36.4	73.6	33.0	44.4	32.5	-7.5	30.9	47.9	80.2
Personal saving	221.5	404.0	392.1	476.9	443.3	391.7	472.4	407.4	433.0
Less: Government insurance and pension reserve	35.8	72.5	76.0	101.3	92.0	86.8	99.0	109.9	116.1
Net investment in consumer durables	26.3	95.8	112.6	109.0	90.0	52.2	62.6	88.9	100.2
Net saving by farm corporations	0.5	0.9	1.4	1.8	2.2	1.6	0.8	0.4	0.3
Equals: Personal saving, flow of funds basis	158.9	234.8	202.1	264.8	259.0	251.1	310.1	208.2	216.4

[1] Includes categories not shown separately. [2] Includes corporate farms.

Source: Board of Governors of the Federal Reserve System, *Flow of Funds Accounts,* quarterly.

No. 703. Annual Expenditure Per Child by Husband-Wife Families, by Family Income and Category: 1994

[In dollars. Expenditures based on data from the 1990 Consumer Expenditure Survey updated to 1994 dollars using the Consumer Price Index. For more on the methodology, see report cited below]

AGE OF CHILD	Total	EXPENDITURE TYPE						
		Housing	Food	Trans-portation	Clothing	Health care	Child care and educa-tion	Miscel-lan-eous [1]
INCOME: LESS THAN $32,800								
Less than 2 yrs. old	5,100	1,920	750	740	380	340	560	410
3 to 5 yrs. old	5,390	1,950	850	760	380	340	630	480
6 to 8 yrs. old	5,670	1,870	1,070	990	450	390	310	590
9 to 11 yrs. old	5,200	1,530	1,270	830	450	430	190	500
12 to 14 yrs. old	5,650	1,570	1,250	1,040	720	400	120	550
15 to 17 yrs. old	6,420	1,590	1,520	1,310	730	480	230	560
INCOME: $32,800-$55,500								
Less than 2 yrs. old	7,070	2,630	890	1,110	450	420	890	680
3 to 5 yrs. old	7,460	2,670	1,050	1,140	440	420	990	750
6 to 8 yrs. old	7,660	2,590	1,300	1,360	520	490	540	860
9 to 11 yrs. old	7,160	2,240	1,530	1,210	520	530	360	770
12 to 14 yrs. old	7,590	2,280	1,530	1,410	830	500	230	810
15 to 17 yrs. old	8,500	2,310	1,790	1,700	840	580	460	820
INCOME: MORE THAN $55,500								
Less than 2 yrs. old	10,510	4,150	1,230	1,370	600	500	1,390	1,270
3 to 5 yrs. old	10,940	4,190	1,400	1,400	600	500	1,510	1,340
6 to 8 yrs. old	11,020	4,110	1,650	1,620	690	580	920	1,450
9 to 11 yrs. old	10,500	3,770	1,920	1,470	690	630	660	1,360
12 to 14 yrs. old	10,940	3,800	1,930	1,680	1,090	590	450	1,400
15 to 17 yrs. old	12,110	3,830	2,190	1,970	1,110	690	910	1,410

[1] Expenses include personal care items, entertainment, and reading materials.

Source: Dept. of Agriculture, Center for Nutrition Policy and Promotion, *Expenditures on Children by Families, 1994 Annual Report.*

No. 704. Average Annual Expenditures of All Consumer Units, by Race and Age of Householder: 1994

[In dollars. Based on Consumer Expenditure Survey. Data are averages for the noninstitutional population. Expenditures reported here are out-of-pocket]

ITEM	All consumer units	White and other	Black	AGE					
				Under 25 yrs.	25 to 34 yrs.	35 to 44 yrs.	45 to 54 yrs.	55 to 64 yrs.	65 yrs. and over
Expenditures, total	**$31,751**	**$32,935**	**$22,418**	**$18,418**	**$30,466**	**$37,588**	**$41,444**	**$33,702**	**$22,557**
Food	4,411	4,542	3,390	2,793	4,159	5,367	5,614	4,549	3,251
Food at home	2,712	2,754	2,390	1,617	2,454	3,336	3,319	2,733	2,245
Cereals and bakery products	429	440	343	250	387	536	512	414	368
Cereals and cereal products	162	163	155	114	158	210	188	138	126
Bakery products	267	277	188	136	230	325	323	277	242
Meats, poultry, fish, and eggs	732	716	858	429	650	919	936	773	555
Beef	227	224	250	133	210	291	297	230	157
Pork	156	148	216	104	129	191	188	175	130
Other meats	94	95	88	51	80	119	119	90	80
Poultry	137	133	164	70	124	175	183	142	96
Fish and seafood	89	87	105	50	81	109	114	107	64
Eggs	30	29	34	22	27	34	35	29	28
Dairy products	289	301	193	180	261	360	338	272	253
Fresh milk and cream	127	131	94	83	123	157	145	112	111
Other dairy products	162	170	99	98	138	204	193	160	142
Fruits and vegetables	437	445	370	238	384	507	522	448	416
Fresh fruits	133	138	98	66	114	150	164	134	135
Fresh vegetables	135	138	108	69	119	160	163	145	122
Processed fruits	93	93	90	62	83	106	109	88	91
Processed vegetables	76	76	74	41	68	91	86	81	68
Other food at home	825	851	627	519	771	1,014	1,012	826	652
Nonalcoholic beverages	233	239	187	148	207	280	297	259	178
Food away from home	1,698	1,788	1,000	1,177	1,706	2,031	2,295	1,816	1,006
Alcoholic beverages	278	295	149	247	347	296	292	338	164
Housing	10,106	10,415	7,673	5,594	10,065	12,274	12,457	10,222	7,445
Shelter	5,686	5,866	4,261	3,481	5,972	7,173	7,024	5,253	3,733
Owned dwellings	3,492	3,719	1,695	473	2,709	4,963	5,069	3,691	2,307
Mortgage interest and charges	1,919	2,040	959	279	1,829	3,289	2,972	1,679	380
Property taxes	922	987	408	90	512	1,021	1,249	1,177	1,084
Maintenance, repair, insurance, other	651	692	329	105	369	654	848	835	844
Rented dwellings	1,799	1,718	2,443	2,840	3,074	1,841	1,318	1,007	1,013
Other lodging	395	429	124	168	188	368	636	555	412
Utilities, fuels, and public services	2,189	2,189	2,182	1,210	1,948	2,428	2,603	2,417	2,033
Natural gas	283	275	347	120	228	288	345	315	317
Electricity	861	866	830	422	752	990	1,019	983	784
Fuel oil and other fuels	98	106	31	24	48	98	110	118	150
Telephone	690	681	756	570	726	766	819	697	505
Water and other public services	257	262	217	74	195	285	310	304	278
Household operations	490	518	267	188	568	673	416	404	435
Personal services	230	235	192	145	450	412	102	53	58
Other household expenses	260	284	74	43	118	261	314	351	377
Housekeeping supplies	393	409	271	171	340	435	464	453	396
Household furnishings and equipment	1,348	1,432	692	544	1,237	1,565	1,950	1,696	847
Household textiles	100	106	52	20	76	102	161	129	84
Furniture	318	334	198	184	379	399	384	330	160
Floor coverings	120	128	53	10	58	100	264	265	48
Major appliances	149	156	94	74	140	160	189	165	129
Small appliances, misc. housewares	81	86	41	32	84	89	97	94	66
Miscellaneous household equipment	581	623	254	224	499	715	854	713	360
Apparel and services	1,644	1,651	1,592	1,107	1,748	2,054	2,262	1,586	873
Men and boys	395	398	366	269	399	517	573	358	193
Women and girls	652	657	612	349	626	810	937	728	364
Children under 2 years old	80	80	81	97	155	97	57	53	17
Footwear	254	250	278	181	291	320	348	210	131
Other apparel products and services	264	265	254	212	277	310	347	236	169
Transportation	6,044	6,268	4,271	4,409	6,523	6,796	7,893	6,504	3,572
Vehicle purchases (net outlay)	2,725	2,814	2,014	2,330	3,347	2,984	3,387	2,909	1,338
Cars and trucks, new	1,391	1,453	897	1,042	1,588	1,504	1,724	1,758	719
Cars and trucks, used	1,290	1,312	1,117	1,264	1,702	1,412	1,581	1,138	618
Gasoline and motor oil	986	1,020	713	670	982	1,193	1,295	1,005	614
Other vehicle expenses	1,953	2,037	1,283	1,201	1,931	2,248	2,720	2,113	1,202
Vehicle finance charges	235	243	173	170	306	299	343	191	59
Maintenance and repair	680	706	480	476	675	780	933	709	430
Vehicle insurance	690	718	468	417	633	771	935	759	509
Rent, lease, licenses, other	347	371	162	138	317	398	509	453	203
Public transportation	381	396	261	208	264	372	492	477	418
Health care [1]	1,755	1,860	923	505	1,086	1,616	1,855	2,144	2,678
Entertainment [2]	1,567	1,668	767	1,018	1,519	2,025	2,104	1,565	879
Personal care products and services	397	401	360	234	396	457	507	393	311
Reading	165	176	77	65	136	184	204	202	153
Education	460	485	259	812	368	483	882	351	114
Tobacco products and smoking supplies	259	266	202	217	270	319	327	302	117
Miscellaneous	749	789	428	255	620	908	1,071	814	573
Cash contributions	960	1,019	494	96	381	788	1,436	1,292	1,419
Personal insurance and pensions	2,957	3,099	1,833	1,067	2,847	4,022	4,539	3,440	1,007
Life and other personal insurance	398	407	321	62	232	439	590	554	382
Pensions and Social Security	2,559	2,692	1,512	1,005	2,616	3,583	3,949	2,886	624
Personal taxes	**3,083**	**3,234**	**1,806**	**956**	**2,873**	**4,090**	**4,972**	**3,399**	**1,294**

[1] For additional health care expenditures, see table 172. [2] For additional recreation expenditures, see table 402.
Source: U.S. Bureau of Labor Statistics, *Consumer Expenditures in 1994;* and unpublished data.

No. 705. Average Annual Expenditures of All Consumer Units, by Region and Size of Unit: 1994

[See headnote, page 457]

ITEM	REGION				SIZE OF CONSUMER UNIT				
	North-east	Mid-west	South	West	One person	Two per-sons	Three per-sons	Four per-sons	Five or more
Expenditures, total	**$32,565**	**$30,335**	**$30,086**	**$35,368**	**$19,345**	**$33,088**	**$36,750**	**$41,514**	**$40,732**
Food	4,706	4,201	4,251	4,639	2,464	4,324	5,135	6,063	6,614
Food at home	2,934	2,537	2,618	2,862	1,386	2,549	3,212	3,797	4,579
Cereals and bakery products	481	412	402	441	220	394	509	602	743
Cereals and cereal products	171	155	152	177	77	138	196	235	311
Bakery products	310	257	250	264	142	257	313	367	431
Meats, poultry, fish, and eggs	840	647	750	705	348	675	872	1,039	1,324
Beef	238	204	240	222	99	208	263	332	434
Pork	161	146	170	139	74	151	186	217	264
Other meats	111	95	87	87	42	88	115	133	169
Poultry	178	114	136	126	72	115	167	201	245
Fish and seafood	123	62	86	96	44	86	108	118	157
Eggs	29	25	31	36	17	28	33	40	55
Dairy products	319	269	271	313	151	267	339	407	495
Fresh milk and cream	132	122	122	137	66	107	153	179	245
Other dairy products	187	147	149	176	85	160	186	227	250
Fruits and vegetables	509	401	404	463	252	425	507	579	676
Fresh fruits	158	120	118	150	78	129	157	172	208
Fresh vegetables	168	113	124	147	76	131	155	191	200
Processed fruits	107	95	82	95	57	89	108	122	145
Processed vegetables	77	72	80	71	41	77	87	95	123
Other food at home	785	809	791	940	415	789	985	1,170	1,341
Nonalcoholic beverages	223	234	227	251	125	220	294	330	341
Food away from home	1,772	1,664	1,633	1,777	1,079	1,776	1,923	2,266	2,036
Alcoholic beverages	313	246	262	309	255	328	267	273	212
Housing	11,327	9,147	9,059	11,786	6,650	10,332	11,438	13,177	12,669
Shelter	6,724	4,922	4,723	7,171	4,089	5,729	6,193	7,241	7,037
Owned dwellings	4,088	3,153	2,919	4,252	1,691	3,636	3,997	5,224	4,848
Mortgage interest and charges	2,019	1,640	1,605	2,667	725	1,671	2,394	3,349	3,257
Property taxes	1,440	913	687	812	492	1,161	964	1,162	981
Maintenance, repair, insurance, other	629	600	628	774	475	804	639	712	610
Rented dwellings	2,119	1,389	1,498	2,475	2,179	1,532	1,804	1,603	1,831
Other lodging	517	380	305	443	219	561	392	415	358
Utilities, fuels, and public services	2,336	2,104	2,269	2,022	1,404	2,283	2,489	2,731	2,856
Natural gas	356	419	168	232	183	297	313	334	399
Electricity	806	724	1,080	729	497	909	1,009	1,130	1,127
Fuel oil and other fuels	254	86	56	31	79	107	100	111	102
Telephone	700	663	690	713	502	699	774	817	879
Water and other public services	220	212	274	317	144	272	294	339	349
Household operations	496	405	480	605	225	411	629	865	730
Personal services	247	210	214	262	30	80	407	598	457
Other household expenses	249	195	265	343	196	331	222	267	273
Housekeeping supplies	409	386	372	422	209	432	486	472	533
Household furnishings and equipment	1,362	1,330	1,217	1,567	722	1,477	1,641	1,869	1,513
Household textiles	112	99	101	86	54	109	112	133	128
Furniture	326	345	270	357	186	339	346	446	403
Floor coverings	151	119	74	165	48	109	281	138	79
Major appliances	130	142	151	172	78	157	180	205	196
Small appliances, misc. housewares	72	79	74	101	48	90	102	92	96
Miscellaneous household equipment	571	545	547	687	308	672	620	854	611
Apparel and services	1,913	1,622	1,459	1,710	876	1,519	2,124	2,338	2,436
Men and boys	439	417	331	427	173	369	496	558	701
Women and girls	786	649	579	642	378	600	817	946	899
Children under 2 years old	85	83	65	95	12	42	156	151	165
Footwear	316	241	225	255	143	209	346	365	397
Other apparel products and services	287	232	258	292	170	300	310	318	273
Transportation	5,111	6,201	6,141	6,592	3,374	6,361	7,452	7,961	7,660
Vehicle purchases (net outlay)	1,864	3,089	2,937	2,764	1,454	2,742	3,653	3,723	3,390
Cars and trucks, new	941	1,452	1,670	1,297	801	1,474	2,015	1,730	1,349
Cars and trucks, used	910	1,576	1,231	1,400	595	1,236	1,600	1,911	2,039
Gasoline and motor oil	832	977	1,035	1,064	526	1,029	1,159	1,347	1,360
Other vehicle expenses	1,866	1,815	1,889	2,306	1,119	2,090	2,301	2,531	2,506
Vehicle finance charges	148	265	269	229	98	244	304	352	320
Maintenance and repair	641	611	636	875	435	708	804	848	852
Vehicle insurance	707	627	693	744	399	756	838	889	789
Rent, lease, licenses, other	369	313	291	458	186	381	354	443	545
Public transportation	550	320	280	457	275	500	340	360	404
Health care [1]	1,679	1,698	1,854	1,737	1,178	2,171	1,801	1,865	1,859
Entertainment [2]	1,517	1,551	1,417	1,875	945	1,623	1,757	2,128	2,042
Personal care products and services	394	384	386	430	231	408	491	507	519
Reading	191	161	136	191	127	191	161	186	168
Education	504	451	404	517	284	385	572	698	671
Tobacco products and smoking supplies	255	291	271	202	159	263	325	312	346
Miscellaneous	669	767	681	910	558	787	757	959	852
Cash contributions	1,034	897	1,004	896	737	1,256	881	871	924
Personal insurance and pensions	2,950	2,717	2,760	3,573	1,507	3,139	3,587	4,177	3,760
Life and other personal insurance	412	395	432	332	159	485	470	528	501
Pensions and Social Security	2,538	2,322	2,328	3,241	1,348	2,654	3,117	3,648	3,259
Personal taxes	**2,841**	**2,734**	**2,712**	**4,215**	**2,038**	**3,437**	**3,430**	**3,853**	**3,381**

[1] For additional health care expenditures, see table 172.   [2] For additional recreation expenditures, see table 402.
Source: U.S. Bureau of Labor Statistics, *Consumer Expenditures in 1994;* and unpublished data.

No. 706. Average Annual Expenditures of All Consumer Units, by Type of Household Unit: 1994

[See headnote, page 457]

ITEM	Husband and wife only	HUSBAND AND WIFE WITH CHILDREN				One parent, at least one child under 18	Single person and other consumer units
		Total	Oldest child under 6	Oldest child 6 to 17	Oldest child 18 and over		
Expenditures, total	**36,198**	**44,088**	**38,560**	**44,145**	**48,489**	**21,671**	**21,861**
Food	4,650	6,276	4,880	6,558	6,921	3,599	2,986
Food at home	2,689	3,895	3,282	4,015	4,205	2,626	1,800
Cereals and bakery products	422	636	534	665	672	409	276
Cereals and cereal products	145	243	219	256	242	180	104
Bakery products	277	393	315	409	430	229	172
Meats, poultry, fish, and eggs	700	1,026	808	1,072	1,131	802	496
Beef	214	321	255	332	356	267	147
Pork	159	202	157	219	210	185	111
Other meats	93	139	101	151	151	91	60
Poultry	117	203	168	199	239	145	94
Fish and seafood	88	123	95	131	132	83	62
Eggs	29	39	32	39	43	31	22
Dairy products	280	423	346	446	448	268	192
Fresh milk and cream	110	190	162	199	197	123	86
Other dairy products	170	233	184	247	251	145	106
Fruits and vegetables	458	603	511	616	662	374	302
Fresh fruits	143	188	152	193	209	114	88
Fresh vegetables	137	186	146	186	221	111	96
Processed fruits	94	129	123	130	133	80	66
Processed vegetables	84	101	90	107	98	68	52
Other food at home	829	1,206	1,084	1,216	1,293	772	535
Nonalcoholic beverages	227	334	265	332	399	209	160
Food away from home	1,961	2,382	1,597	2,543	2,716	973	1,186
Alcoholic beverages	343	288	267	264	354	89	269
Housing	11,087	13,658	13,114	14,231	12,902	8,178	7,274
Shelter	6,048	7,531	7,315	7,951	6,815	4,675	4,323
Owned dwellings	4,250	5,605	4,818	6,047	5,283	1,763	1,843
Mortgage interest and charges	1,882	3,592	3,323	3,991	2,958	1,153	841
Property taxes	1,386	1,256	921	1,279	1,469	396	536
Maintenance, repair, insurance, other	982	757	573	777	856	214	466
Rented dwellings	1,091	1,453	2,300	1,444	810	2,810	2,256
Other lodging	707	474	198	459	722	102	224
Utilities, fuels, and public services	2,391	2,773	2,364	2,750	3,143	1,942	1,659
Natural gas	310	343	287	335	403	280	220
Electricity	967	1,146	926	1,169	1,268	766	603
Fuel oil and other fuels	124	119	90	111	160	45	78
Telephone	691	817	783	784	914	678	583
Water and other public services	300	349	278	351	399	174	175
Household operations	414	863	1,504	885	317	628	257
Personal services	17	571	1,309	543	53	510	65
Other household expenses	397	292	195	341	264	118	191
Housekeeping supplies	487	542	478	550	584	244	250
Household furnishings and equipment	1,746	1,948	1,453	2,096	2,044	689	786
Household textiles	124	140	104	153	142	48	63
Furniture	411	438	384	490	372	206	194
Floor coverings	144	227	106	221	345	27	43
Major appliances	178	203	157	217	212	112	90
Small appliances, misc. housewares	107	110	122	94	129	32	50
Miscellaneous household equipment	784	829	581	922	844	263	346
Apparel and services	1,639	2,427	2,071	2,485	2,597	1,624	1,042
Men and boys	409	611	418	670	662	401	220
Women and girls	647	964	669	980	1,168	654	423
Children under 2 years old	44	161	475	82	46	80	30
Footwear	208	366	251	390	422	320	175
Other apparel products and services	331	326	258	364	299	169	193
Transportation	6,929	8,770	8,382	7,765	11,188	3,246	4,005
Vehicle purchases (net outlay)	2,975	4,166	4,634	3,464	5,284	1,395	1,742
Cars and trucks, new	1,719	2,051	2,671	1,579	2,565	518	858
Cars and trucks, used	1,221	2,057	1,953	1,835	2,608	871	835
Gasoline and motor oil	1,105	1,419	1,176	1,342	1,773	619	654
Other vehicle expenses	2,264	2,779	2,313	2,555	3,605	1,048	1,318
Vehicle finance charges	257	377	346	366	424	146	133
Maintenance and repair	773	939	798	833	1,263	406	484
Vehicle insurance	795	940	742	823	1,343	392	489
Rent, lease, licenses, other	439	523	426	533	575	104	213
Public transportation	584	406	260	404	526	184	291
Health care [1]	2,555	2,049	1,775	2,008	2,347	884	1,233
Entertainment [2]	1,786	2,272	1,657	2,475	2,338	1,057	1,045
Personal care products and services	451	530	428	540	595	316	272
Reading	212	200	158	207	216	84	130
Education	392	787	203	715	1,407	299	307
Tobacco products and smoking supplies	232	316	266	287	415	219	225
Miscellaneous	785	916	689	951	1,014	535	629
Cash contributions	1,577	993	608	960	1,364	216	698
Personal insurance and pensions	3,561	4,605	4,061	4,699	4,832	1,326	1,747
Life and other personal insurance	599	584	440	582	702	189	185
Pensions and Social Security	2,962	4,021	3,621	4,117	4,130	1,137	1,562
Personal taxes	**3,860**	**4,222**	**3,821**	**4,267**	**4,468**	**948**	**2,219**

[1] For additional health care expenditures, see table 172. [2] For additional recreation expenditures, see table 402.
Source: U.S. Bureau of Labor Statistics, *Consumer Expenditures in 1994;* and unpublished data.

No. 707. Average Annual Expenditures of All Consumer Units, by Type of Expenditure: 1988 to 1994

[In dollars. See headnote, table 704]

TYPE	1988	1989	1990	1991	1992	1993	1994
Number of consumer units (1,000).	94,862	95,818	96,968	97,918	100,019	100,049	102,210
Total expenditures	**25,892**	**27,810**	**28,381**	**29,614**	**29,846**	**30,692**	**$31,751**
Food.	3,748	4,152	4,296	4,271	4,273	4,399	4,411
Food at home	2,136	2,390	2,485	2,651	2,643	2,735	2,712
Cereal and bakery products	312	359	368	404	411	434	429
Meats, poultry, fish, and eggs	551	611	668	709	687	734	732
Dairy products	274	304	295	294	302	295	289
Fruits and vegetables	373	408	408	429	428	444	437
Other food at home.	625	708	746	815	814	827	825
Food away from home	1,612	1,762	1,811	1,620	1,631	1,664	1,698
Alcoholic beverages.	269	284	293	297	301	268	278
Housing.	7,918	8,434	8,703	9,252	9,477	9,636	10,106
Shelter.	4,332	4,660	4,836	5,191	5,411	5,415	5,686
Fuels, utilities, public services	1,747	1,835	1,890	1,990	1,984	2,112	2,189
Household operations, furnishings. . . .	1,477	1,546	1,571	1,648	1,649	1,699	1,838
Housekeeping supplies	361	394	406	424	433	410	393
Apparel and services	1,489	1,582	1,618	1,735	1,710	1,676	1,644
Transportation	5,093	5,187	5,120	5,151	5,228	5,453	6,044
Vehicle purchase	2,361	2,291	2,129	2,111	2,189	2,319	2,725
Gasoline and motor oil	932	985	1,047	995	973	977	986
Other transportation	1,800	1,911	1,944	2,045	2,066	2,157	2,334
Health care	1,298	1,407	1,480	1,554	1,634	1,776	1,755
Tobacco products, smoking supplies.	242	261	274	276	275	268	259
Life and other personal insurance	314	346	345	356	353	399	398
Pensions and Social Security	1,935	2,125	2,248	2,431	2,397	2,509	2,559
Other expenditures	3,586	4,030	4,003	4,291	4,198	4,308	4,297

No. 708. Average Annual Expenditures of All Consumer Units, by Metropolitan Area: 1994

[In dollars. Metropolitan areas defined June 30, 1983, CMSA=Consolidated Metropolitan Statistical Area; MSA=Metropolitan Statistical Area; PMSA=Primary Metropolitan Statistical Area. See text, section 1, and Appendix II. See headnote, table 704]

METROPOLITAN AREA	Total expenditures [1]	Food	HOUSING		Apparel and services	TRANSPORTATION			Health care
			Total [1]	Shelter		Total [1]	Vehicle purchases	Gasoline and motor oil	
Anchorage, AK MSA	40,940	5,527	13,130	8,309	2,080	6,320	2,085	1,007	1,921
Atlanta, GA MSA	38,201	4,449	12,447	7,397	1,983	7,390	3,465	979	2,072
Baltimore, MD MSA	31,607	4,340	10,839	6,596	1,471	4,680	1,564	895	1,784
Boston-Lawrence-Salem, MA-NH CMSA	35,370	4,403	13,210	8,149	1,998	5,637	2,261	904	1,713
Buffalo-Niagara Falls, NY CMSA.	24,253	4,436	8,563	4,649	1,220	3,941	1,421	719	1,296
Chicago-Gary-Lake County, IL-IN-WI CMSA	36,854	5,156	12,159	7,337	2,340	6,816	3,429	975	1,946
Cincinnati-Hamilton, OH-KY-IN CMSA .	33,644	4,746	10,383	5,758	1,945	6,261	2,829	1,098	1,953
Cleveland-Akron-Lorain, OH CMSA . . .	27,480	4,194	8,499	4,621	1,416	5,433	2,499	815	1,536
Dallas-Fort Worth, TX CMSA	38,769	4,838	11,643	6,039	2,011	7,324	3,419	1,180	2,014
Detroit-Ann Arbor, MI CMSA.	34,418	4,577	11,164	6,585	2,136	7,541	3,699	1,004	1,293
Honolulu, HI MSA.	43,214	6,815	14,301	9,957	1,712	6,385	2,259	937	1,910
Houston-Galveston-Brazoria, TX CMSA	36,224	5,081	10,488	5,412	2,082	7,019	3,120	1,127	2,005
Kansas City, MO-Kansas City, KS CMSA	33,520	4,604	10,269	5,166	1,868	6,251	2,547	990	2,037
Los Angeles-Long Beach, CA PMSA . .	35,490	4,731	12,961	8,552	2,045	5,825	2,019	1,081	1,450
Miami-Fort Lauderdale, FL CMSA	32,403	4,982	10,920	6,387	1,635	6,000	2,340	967	1,537
Milwaukee, WI PMSA	33,600	4,074	10,494	6,381	1,943	6,930	3,714	1,049	1,535
Minneapolis-St. Paul, MN-WI MSA . . .	37,490	5,116	11,908	6,931	1,893	6,101	2,235	1,083	1,698
New York-Northern New Jersey-Long Island, NY-NJ-CT CMSA	36,111	5,378	13,388	8,452	2,367	4,942	1,274	799	1,727
Philadelphia-Wilmington-Trenton, PA-NJ-DE-MD CMSA	33,809	4,675	11,570	6,466	2,158	5,271	1,649	801	1,724
Pittsburgh-Beaver Valley, PA CMSA. . .	29,739	4,087	9,113	4,349	1,958	5,676	2,798	758	1,653
Portland-Vancouver, OR-WA CMSA. . .	33,579	4,292	11,375	6,982	1,696	6,314	3,003	981	1,540
San Diego, CA MSA	34,396	4,330	12,335	8,480	1,638	6,098	1,960	1,071	1,486
San Francisco-Oakland-San Jose, CA CMSA	41,440	5,349	14,457	9,434	1,741	6,779	2,621	1,091	1,663
Seattle-Tacoma, WA CMSA	35,216	4,446	11,514	7,039	1,619	6,316	2,573	1,034	1,537
St. Louis-East St. Louis-Alton, MO-IL CMSA.	28,734	3,976	8,732	4,568	1,298	5,958	3,073	945	1,582
Washington, DC-MD-VA MSA.	40,704	4,909	13,785	8,773	1,781	6,765	2,921	941	1,804

[1] Includes expenditures not shown separately.

Sources of tables 707 and 708: U.S. Bureau of Labor Statistics, *Consumer Expenditures in 1994.*

No. 709. Money Income of Households—Percent Distribution, by Income Level, Race, and Hispanic Origin, in Constant (1994) Dollars: 1970 to 1994

[Constant dollars based on CPI-U-X1 deflator. Households as of **March** of **following year.** Based on Current Population Survey; see text, sections 1 and 14, and Appendix III. For definition of median, see Guide to Tabular Presentation]

YEAR	Number of house-holds (1,000)	PERCENT DISTRIBUTION							Median income (dollars)
		Under $10,000	$10,000-$14,999	$15,000-$24,999	$25,000-$34,999	$35,000-$49,999	$50,000-$74,999	$75,000 and over	
ALL HOUSEHOLDS [1]									
1970	64,778	14.7	8.3	16.1	17.5	20.9	15.7	6.8	31,341
1975	72,867	14.0	9.3	17.0	16.2	19.7	16.2	7.5	31,117
1980	82,368	13.8	8.8	16.8	15.2	19.1	16.9	9.5	31,891
1985	88,458	13.9	8.4	16.6	14.9	17.9	16.9	11.5	32,530
1990	94,312	12.9	8.4	16.1	14.5	17.6	17.2	13.3	33,952
1992	96,426	13.8	9.1	16.1	14.8	16.8	16.7	12.6	32,361
1993	97,107	14.0	9.1	16.5	14.8	16.1	16.4	13.2	32,041
1994	98,990	13.6	9.1	16.7	14.2	16.3	16.5	13.6	32,264
WHITE									
1970	57,575	13.3	7.8	15.5	17.7	21.7	16.5	7.4	32,643
1975	64,392	12.5	8.9	16.7	16.4	20.3	17.1	8.1	32,541
1980	71,872	12.1	8.3	16.4	15.4	19.9	17.8	10.2	33,645
1985	76,576	12.2	7.9	16.2	15.1	18.5	17.7	12.4	34,306
1990	80,968	10.9	8.1	15.9	14.7	18.0	18.1	14.2	35,413
1992	81,795	11.8	8.7	15.9	15.1	17.3	17.7	13.5	34,023
1993	82,387	11.9	8.7	16.2	14.9	16.8	17.3	14.1	33,804
1994	83,737	11.7	8.7	16.4	14.4	16.7	17.3	14.7	34,028
BLACK									
1970	6,180	26.7	12.6	21.6	15.5	13.7	7.9	2.0	19,869
1975	7,489	26.9	13.8	19.6	15.4	13.7	8.4	2.2	19,535
1980	8,847	27.7	13.2	20.0	13.4	13.4	9.4	2.9	19,383
1985	9,797	27.7	11.6	19.6	13.4	13.4	10.2	4.0	20,411
1990	10,671	27.4	11.5	18.0	13.0	14.1	10.1	5.8	21,177
1992	11,269	29.0	12.1	17.9	13.5	13.0	9.6	4.8	19,811
1993	11,281	28.2	11.9	18.9	14.0	11.8	9.8	5.3	20,033
1994	11,655	26.3	11.5	18.9	12.8	13.3	10.8	6.3	21,027
HISPANIC [2]									
1975	2,948	17.9	12.4	22.6	18.1	17.1	9.0	2.8	23,377
1980	3,906	17.8	11.7	21.2	16.8	16.1	11.7	4.6	24,582
1985	5,213	19.8	12.1	20.2	15.7	15.4	11.3	5.5	24,055
1990	6,220	17.9	12.8	18.7	16.3	16.2	11.5	6.5	25,320
1992	7,153	19.7	11.9	20.5	16.1	14.9	11.3	5.7	23,869
1993	7,362	19.8	12.2	21.1	16.7	13.6	11.0	5.8	23,472
1994	7,735	20.5	12.2	20.4	14.9	14.4	10.9	6.7	23,421

[1] Includes other races not shown separately.   [2] Persons of Hispanic origin may be of any race. Income data for Hispanic origin households are not available prior to 1972.

No. 710. Money Income of Households—Median Income, by Race and Hispanic Origin, in Current and Constant (1994) Dollars: 1970 to 1994

[See headnote, table 709]

YEAR	MEDIAN INCOME IN CURRENT DOLLARS					MEDIAN INCOME IN CONSTANT (1993) DOLLARS				
	All house-holds [1]	White	Black	Asian, Pacific Islander	His-panic [2]	All house-holds [1]	White	Black	Asian, Pacific Islanders	His-panic [2]
1970	8,734	9,097	5,537	(NA)	(NA)	31,341	32,643	19,869	(NA)	(NA)
1975	11,800	12,340	7,408	(NA)	8,865	31,117	32,541	19,535	(NA)	23,377
1980	17,710	18,684	10,764	(NA)	13,651	31,891	33,645	19,383	(NA)	24,582
1981	19,074	20,153	11,309	(NA)	15,300	31,374	33,148	18,601	(NA)	25,166
1982	20,171	21,117	11,968	(NA)	15,178	31,269	32,736	18,553	(NA)	23,529
1983 [3]	20,885	21,902	12,429	(NA)	15,906	31,076	32,589	18,494	(NA)	23,667
1984	22,415	23,647	13,471	(NA)	16,992	31,972	33,729	19,215	(NA)	24,237
1985	23,618	24,908	14,819	(NA)	17,465	32,530	34,306	20,411	(NA)	24,055
1986	24,897	26,175	15,080	(NA)	18,352	33,665	35,394	20,391	(NA)	24,815
1987 [4]	26,061	27,458	15,672	(NA)	19,336	33,999	35,821	20,445	(NA)	25,225
1988	27,225	28,781	16,407	32,267	20,359	34,106	36,055	20,554	40,422	25,505
1989	28,906	30,406	18,083	36,102	21,921	34,547	36,340	21,612	43,148	26,199
1990	29,943	31,231	18,676	38,450	22,330	33,952	35,413	21,177	43,598	25,320
1991 [5]	30,126	31,569	18,807	36,449	22,691	32,780	34,350	20,464	39,660	24,690
1992 [5]	30,636	32,209	18,755	37,801	22,597	32,361	34,023	19,811	39,929	23,869
1993	31,241	32,960	19,533	38,347	22,886	32,041	33,804	20,033	39,329	23,472
1994	32,264	34,028	21,027	40,482	23,421	32,264	34,028	21,027	40,482	23,421

NA Not available.   [1] Includes other races not shown separately.   [2] Persons of Hispanic origin may be of any race. [3] Beginning 1983, data based on revised Hispanic population controls and not directly comparable with prior years.   [4] Beginning 1987, based on revised processing procedures and not directly comparable with prior years.   [5] Based on 1990 population controls.

Source of tables 709 and 710: U.S. Bureau of the Census, *Current Population Reports*, P60-189; and unpublished data.

Income, Expenditures, and Wealth

No. 711. Money Income of Households—Percent Distribution, by Income Level and Selected Characteristics: 1994

[See headnote, table 709. For composition of regions, see table 27]

CHARACTERISTIC	Number of house-holds (1,000)	PERCENT DISTRIBUTION							Median income (dollars)
		Under $10,000	$10,000-$14,999	$15,000-$24,999	$25,000-$34,999	$35,000-$49,999	$50,000-$74,999	$75,000 and over	
Total [1]	98,990	13.5	9.1	16.7	14.2	16.3	16.5	13.7	32,264
Age of householder:									
15 to 24 years	5,444	23.2	14.6	25.7	17.7	11.2	5.7	1.9	19,340
25 to 34 years	19,453	11.2	7.6	17.2	16.7	20.5	17.8	9.0	33,151
35 to 44 years	22,914	8.6	5.4	12.3	14.2	19.2	22.4	17.8	41,667
45 to 54 years	17,590	7.6	4.9	11.0	11.7	17.5	22.3	25.0	47,261
55 to 64 years	12,224	13.6	7.0	15.2	13.9	16.3	17.1	16.9	35,232
65 years and over. . . .	21,365	23.4	17.7	24.0	13.2	9.6	6.7	5.2	18,095
White	83,737	11.7	8.7	16.4	14.4	16.7	17.3	14.6	34,028
Black	11,655	26.3	11.5	18.9	12.8	13.3	10.8	6.3	21,027
Hispanic [2]	7,735	20.5	12.2	20.4	14.9	14.4	10.9	6.7	23,421
Northeast	19,593	13.9	8.4	14.8	12.9	15.8	17.1	17.0	34,926
Midwest	23,683	12.9	8.7	17.4	14.7	17.3	16.7	12.4	32,505
South	34,766	14.8	9.9	17.4	14.9	15.9	15.4	11.6	30,021
West	20,948	11.8	8.9	16.4	13.5	16.3	17.7	15.3	34,452
Size of household:									
One person	24,732	30.3	16.5	21.5	13.1	10.0	5.6	3.0	16,222
Two persons	31,834	8.1	8.4	18.7	16.2	17.8	17.1	13.6	33,955
Three persons	16,827	8.7	5.7	13.9	14.2	18.6	21.3	17.7	41,043
Four persons	15,321	7.1	4.5	10.3	12.3	19.4	24.7	21.7	46,757
Five persons	6,616	7.6	5.7	11.8	13.1	18.2	22.4	21.4	44,135
Six persons	2,279	7.2	6.0	12.7	12.9	19.7	20.0	21.5	42,683
Seven or more persons	1,382	9.9	8.2	15.8	14.3	16.7	17.9	17.1	36,622
Family households	69,305	8.1	6.7	14.9	14.5	18.2	20.2	17.4	39,390
Married-couple	53,858	3.9	5.1	13.4	14.2	19.2	23.2	21.1	45,041
Male householder, wife absent	3,226	10.7	8.9	19.9	17.0	19.0	15.8	8.6	30,472
Female householder, husband absent	12,220	26.0	13.3	20.3	15.0	13.7	8.1	3.6	19,872
Nonfamily households . . .	29,686	26.2	14.8	20.8	13.5	11.8	8.0	4.9	18,947
Male householder	13,190	17.7	11.8	21.3	15.8	15.1	11.1	7.2	24,593
Female householder . .	16,496	33.0	17.1	20.4	11.7	9.2	5.6	3.0	14,948
Educational attainment of householder: [3]									
Total	93,546	13.0	8.8	16.1	14.0	16.6	17.2	14.3	33,486
Less than 9th grade	8,242	34.0	18.3	22.6	11.3	7.8	4.2	1.9	14,275
9th to 12th grade (no diploma)	9,644	27.5	15.6	21.1	14.0	11.4	7.2	3.1	17,543
High school graduate . . .	29,647	13.3	10.0	18.4	16.4	18.5	15.6	8.0	30,071
Some college, no degree	16,786	9.1	7.2	16.8	15.4	19.8	19.8	11.8	35,879
Associate degree	6,403	6.9	5.7	14.4	14.6	20.0	22.6	15.8	40,258
Bachelor's degree or more	22,824	3.5	3.0	8.7	10.5	16.2	24.6	33.4	57,440
Bachelor's degree	14,380	3.9	3.5	9.9	12.1	17.1	25.4	28.2	52,370
Master's degree	5,506	2.6	2.2	7.2	9.1	17.1	25.3	36.6	61,045
Professional degree . .	1,710	2.6	2.1	6.7	6.6	11.1	18.8	52.2	18,002
Doctorate degree	1,227	2.9	2.4	5.3	4.6	9.9	21.5	53.5	78,157
Tenure:									
Owner occupied	64,045	8.2	7.2	14.2	13.6	17.8	20.6	18.5	40,299
Renter occupied	33,159	23.0	12.6	21.2	15.3	13.8	9.3	4.8	21,534
Occupier paid no cash rent	1,787	29.2	13.2	22.2	13.2	11.1	7.7	3.5	18,462

[1] Includes other races not shown separately.   [2] Persons of Hispanic origin may be of any race.   [3] 25 years old and over.

Source: U.S. Bureau of the Census, *Current Population Reports*, P60-189; and unpublished data.

No. 712. Money Income of Households—Aggregate and Average Income, by Race and Hispanic Origin: 1993

[See headnote, table 709]

CHARACTERISTIC	ALL RACES [1]		WHITE		BLACK		HISPANIC [2]	
	Aggre-gate income (bil. dol.)	Mean income (dollars)	Aggre-gate income (bil. dol.)	Mean income (dollars)	Aggre-gate income (bil. dol.)	Mean income (dollars)	Aggre-gate income (bil. dol.)	Mean income (dollars)
Total.	4,022.9	41,428	3,566.1	43,285	307.2	27,229	223	30,291
Age of householder:								
15 to 24 years old	121.3	23,041	102.7	24,298	12.4	16,009	12.7	21,423
25 to 34 years old	739.6	37,510	642.1	40,020	64.4	23,455	60.9	28,666
35 to 44 years old	1,102.9	49,473	966.7	52,205	89.5	31,666	64.1	34,520
45 to 54 years old	972.9	57,770	861.0	60,106	70.8	38,156	46.4	38,042
55 to 64 years old	546.2	44,814	493.2	46,650	38.7	29,450	22.5	29,316
65 years old and over.	540.2	25,965	500.5	26,761	31.4	17,782	16.3	20,459
Region:								
Northeast.	882.4	45,319	792.5	46,823	58.4	30,161	36.4	27,311
Midwest.	922.4	39,442	843.3	40,963	63.3	26,580	15.8	31,364
South	1,296.8	38,249	1,111.2	40,897	156.6	25,853	72.8	30,551
West	921.4	45,284	819.2	46,269	28.8	31,883	98.1	31,185
Size of household:								
One person	524.6	22,217	463.6	22,946	47.1	16,808	19.4	18,233
Two persons.	1,322.5	42,374	1,214.1	44,195	77.6	26,602	48.9	29,265
Three persons.	811.6	48,030	710.4	50,805	70.7	31,356	43.1	30,631
Four persons	836.8	55,516	735.4	58,306	63.4	36,018	48.0	34,042
Five persons.	354.1	52,473	305.7	55,456	26.8	30,862	34.1	35,474
Six persons	112.1	51,259	92.0	55,575	12.3	33,978	14.9	35,576
Seven or more persons.	61.2	44,401	45.1	47,388	9.2	29,373	14.7	33,937

[1] Includes other races not shown separately.   [2] Persons of Hispanic origin may be of any race.

Source: U.S. Bureau of the Census, *Current Population Reports*, P60-188; and unpublished data.

No. 713. Money Income of Households—Median Income and Income Level, by Household Type: 1994

[See headnote, table 709]

ITEM	All house-holds	FAMILY HOUSEHOLDS				NONFAMILY HOUSEHOLDS		
		Total	Married couple	Male house-holder, wife absent	Female house-holder, husband absent	Total [1]	Single-person household	
							Male house-holder	Female house-holder
MEDIAN INCOME (dollars)								
All households	**32,264**	**39,390**	**45,041**	**30,472**	**19,872**	**18,947**	**21,216**	**13,431**
White	34,028	41,334	45,555	32,227	22,605	19,783	22,153	13,912
Black	21,027	25,475	40,432	23,073	14,650	13,320	15,223	9,621
Hispanic [2]	23,421	25,210	29,915	25,596	13,200	15,789	17,474	8,382
NUMBER (1,000)								
All households	**98,990**	**69,305**	**53,858**	**3,226**	**12,220**	**29,686**	**10,140**	**14,592**
Under $5,000	4,044	1,947	648	102	1,197	2,097	665	1,327
$5,000 to $9,999.	9,368	3,687	1,458	244	1,984	5,682	1,489	4,006
$10,000 to $14,999	9,025	4,646	2,732	288	1,626	4,380	1,408	2,679
$15,000 to $19,999	8,346	5,036	3,362	342	1,333	3,310	1,208	1,693
$20,000 to $24,999	8,142	5,278	3,834	301	1,143	2,864	1,075	1,345
$25,000 to $34,999	14,032	10,016	7,630	548	1,838	4,016	1,617	1,619
$35,000 to $49,999	16,138	12,627	10,341	614	1,671	3,512	1,349	1,134
$50,000 to $74,999	16,373	13,989	12,487	508	993	2,384	831	550
$75,000 and over	13,521	12,081	11,368	277	435	1,443	498	239

[1] Includes other nonfamily households not shown separately.   [2] Persons of Hispanic origin may be of any race.

Source: U.S. Bureau of the Census, *Current Population Reports*, P60-189; and unpublished data.

No. 714. Money Income of Households—Percent Distribution, by Income Quintile and Top 5 Percent: 1993

[See headnote, table 709. For composition of regions, see table 27]

CHARACTERISTIC	Number (1,000)	PERCENT DISTRIBUTION						
		Total	Lowest fifth	Second fifth	Third fifth	Fourth fifth	Highest fifth	Top 5 percent
Total	97,107	100.0	20.0	20.0	20.0	20.0	20.0	5.0
Age of householder:								
15 to 24 years old	5,265	100.0	33.8	29.9	21.9	10.3	4.1	0.5
25 to 34 years old	19,717	100.0	16.8	20.7	24.0	23.1	15.3	2.8
35 to 44 years old	22,293	100.0	12.1	14.9	20.2	25.8	26.9	6.4
45 to 54 years old	16,837	100.0	11.4	12.9	17.2	23.7	34.8	9.9
55 to 64 years old	12,188	100.0	18.2	18.3	20.5	20.4	22.6	6.4
65 years old and over.	20,806	100.0	35.9	29.1	17.4	9.9	7.6	1.9
White	82,387	100.0	17.7	19.7	20.4	21.0	21.4	5.4
Black	11,281	100.0	36.8	22.6	18.0	13.3	9.3	1.7
Hispanic origin [1]	7,362	100.0	27.9	25.6	21.4	15.1	10.0	1.8
Northeast.	19,470	100.0	19.6	18.0	18.7	20.5	23.2	6.6
Midwest.	23,385	100.0	19.5	20.1	20.5	21.5	18.5	3.7
South.	33,904	100.0	22.2	21.6	20.4	18.5	17.4	4.1
West.	20,347	100.0	17.4	19.2	19.9	20.3	23.1	6.4
Family households.	68,490	100.0	13.1	17.9	20.7	23.2	25.1	6.4
Married-couple families	53,171	100.0	7.3	16.1	20.9	25.8	30.0	7.8
Male householder	2,913	100.0	16.7	24.1	24.7	20.5	14.0	3.1
Female householder.	12,406	100.0	37.4	24.4	19.0	12.6	6.6	0.9
Nonfamily households	28,617	100.0	36.5	25.0	18.3	12.4	7.8	1.8
Male householder	12,462	100.0	24.9	25.1	22.2	16.1	11.8	2.8
Living alone.	9,440	100.0	30.0	27.3	22.0	13.3	7.3	1.8
Female householder.	16,155	100.0	45.4	24.9	15.4	9.6	4.8	1.0
Living alone.	14,171	100.0	50.0	25.9	14.3	7.3	2.5	0.5
Worked	69,282	100.0	10.0	17.5	21.8	24.7	26.0	6.6
Worked at full-time jobs.	60,539	100.0	7.1	16.3	22.1	26.4	28.1	7.1
Worked at part-time jobs	8,744	100.0	30.2	25.9	19.3	13.1	11.4	2.8
Did not work.	27,825	100.0	44.8	26.3	15.6	8.2	5.1	1.1

[1] Persons of Hispanic origin may be of any race.

Source: U.S. Bureau of the Census, *Current Population Reports*, P60-188; unpublished data.

No. 715. Money Income of Households—Percent Distribution, by Income Level, Race, and Hispanic Origin: 1993

TYPE OF HOUSEHOLD	Number of house- holds (1,000)	PERCENT DISTRIBUTION							Median income (dollars)
		Under $10,000	$10,000- $14,999	$15,000- $24,999	$25,000- $34,999	$35,000- $49,999	$50,000- $74,999	$75,000 and over	
HOUSEHOLDS									
Total [1]	97,107	14.2	9.2	16.9	14.7	16.3	16.1	12.5	31,241
White.	82,387	12.2	8.9	16.6	14.9	17.0	17.0	13.4	32,960
Black	11,281	28.9	11.8	19.2	13.8	12.0	9.3	5.2	19,533
Asian, Pacific Islander	2,233	13.6	7.2	14.4	12.4	12.9	20.0	19.5	38,347
Hispanic [2].	7,362	20	12.4	21.5	16.5	13.4	10.8	5.4	22,886
FAMILIES									
Total [1]	68,490	9	7.1	15.3	15.0	18.2	19.6	15.8	37,484
White.	57,870	6.8	6.5	14.9	15.2	19.0	20.8	16.8	39,841
Black	7,989	24.7	11.2	18.5	14.1	13.3	11.3	6.8	22,221
Asian, Pacific Islander	1,737	9.9	6.4	12.3	11.6	13.9	22.7	23.1	45,251
Hispanic [2].	5,940	16.6	12.2	22.1	17.0	14.6	11.8	5.6	24,530
NONFAMILIES									
Total [1]	28,617	26.9	14.3	20.7	14.2	11.6	7.7	4.6	18,880
White.	24,518	25.2	14.5	20.7	14.3	12.1	8.1	5.1	19,639
Black	3,292	39	13.1	20.8	13.0	8.6	4.4	1.2	13,857
Asian, Pacific Islander	496	26	10.1	22.0	15.1	9.3	10.3	7.4	21,407
Hispanic [2].	1,423	34.4	13.4	19.0	14.3	8.1	6.8	4.1	15,799

[1] Includes other races not shown separately.   [2] Persons of Hispanic origin may be of any race.

Source: U.S. Bureau of the Census, *Current Population Reports*, P60-188; and unpublished data.

No. 716. Money Income of Households—Median Income, by State, in Constant (1994) Dollars: 1984 to 1994

[Constant dollars based on the CPI-U-X1 deflator. Data based on the Current Population Survey; see text, sections 1 and 14, and Appendix III. The CPS is designed to collect reliable data on income primarily at the national level and secondarily at the regional level. When the income data are tabulated by State, the estimates are considered less reliable and, therefore, particular caution should be used when trying to interpret the results]

STATE	1984	1987 [1]	1988	1989	1990	1991	1992 [2]	1993 [3]	1994
United States....	31,972	33,901	34,106	34,547	33,952	32,780	32,361	32,041	32,264
Alabama	24,690	25,745	24,990	25,438	26,484	26,491	27,261	25,724	27,196
Alaska	46,152	43,355	41,470	43,033	44,560	44,190	44,156	44,030	45,367
Arizona	30,560	34,896	33,116	34,124	33,137	33,445	31,011	31,291	31,293
Arkansas	22,357	24,561	25,270	25,616	25,837	25,500	25,227	23,629	25,565
California	36,069	39,328	37,942	39,451	37,747	36,630	36,868	34,945	35,331
Colorado	36,802	34,540	32,840	32,037	34,848	34,274	34,313	35,371	37,833
Connecticut	42,721	42,871	45,366	50,580	44,074	45,868	43,141	40,528	41,097
Delaware	36,827	38,151	38,215	38,326	34,928	35,456	37,687	36,987	35,873
District of Columbia	29,109	35,817	33,500	31,973	31,060	32,518	31,950	28,003	30,116
Florida	28,221	31,948	31,827	31,176	30,258	29,653	28,889	29,281	29,294
Georgia	28,505	34,850	33,280	32,917	31,251	29,610	30,419	32,474	31,467
Hawaii	41,189	45,689	41,371	41,872	44,132	40,528	44,484	43,754	42,255
Idaho	30,085	27,076	29,377	29,465	28,693	28,417	29,264	31,804	31,536
Illinois	33,879	35,333	36,986	37,409	36,899	34,693	33,328	33,698	35,081
Indiana	32,478	29,378	32,938	30,952	30,533	29,476	30,136	30,230	27,858
Iowa	28,332	28,949	30,448	31,391	30,942	31,069	30,361	29,397	33,079
Kansas	35,130	33,375	32,028	32,104	33,923	31,876	32,055	30,532	28,322
Kentucky	25,218	26,970	24,938	27,827	28,098	25,858	24,807	25,000	26,595
Louisiana	27,028	27,851	25,678	27,323	25,405	27,528	26,871	26,986	25,676
Maine	29,452	30,788	33,075	33,729	31,141	30,323	31,285	28,141	30,316
Maryland	42,375	45,621	45,790	43,045	44,060	40,208	39,298	40,962	39,198
Massachusetts	38,454	42,061	41,607	43,129	41,100	38,861	38,406	38,013	40,500
Michigan	32,757	36,139	36,921	36,781	33,945	34,947	34,084	33,498	35,284
Minnesota	34,855	36,635	36,439	36,076	35,678	32,076	32,725	34,544	33,644
Mississippi	22,009	24,152	22,757	23,804	22,880	21,191	21,728	22,759	25,400
Missouri	29,633	30,945	29,368	31,668	30,992	30,386	28,902	29,416	30,190
Montana	27,866	26,710	27,850	28,316	26,505	27,014	28,019	27,148	27,631
Nebraska	30,520	30,355	31,518	31,455	31,162	32,152	31,740	31,802	31,794
Nevada	36,766	35,064	35,056	35,066	36,311	36,311	33,705	36,731	35,871
New Hampshire	36,963	42,187	43,376	44,857	46,269	39,207	41,657	38,936	35,245
New Jersey	39,619	44,670	45,458	46,755	43,920	43,578	41,196	41,537	42,280
New Mexico	29,426	27,080	24,173	27,013	28,392	28,872	27,316	27,443	26,905
New York	31,419	34,420	36,223	37,643	35,821	34,595	32,799	32,509	31,899
North Carolina	29,339	29,692	30,586	31,559	29,854	29,219	29,335	29,558	30,114
North Dakota	29,627	29,452	30,181	30,153	28,647	28,173	28,477	28,838	28,278
Ohio	32,982	33,623	34,751	34,685	34,032	32,415	33,172	32,086	31,855
Oklahoma	30,165	28,298	29,649	28,286	27,649	27,705	26,708	26,932	26,991
Oregon	30,523	32,664	34,761	34,097	33,202	32,850	33,725	33,987	31,456
Pennsylvania	29,021	33,168	33,501	34,289	32,889	33,043	31,565	31,789	32,066
Rhode Island	30,827	36,909	37,384	36,003	36,248	33,553	32,146	34,367	31,928
South Carolina	28,968	32,678	31,986	28,442	32,582	29,883	29,131	26,720	29,846
South Dakota	27,684	27,593	27,929	28,813	27,861	26,810	27,738	28,447	29,733
Tennessee	23,937	27,630	26,127	27,024	25,617	26,607	25,687	25,745	28,639
Texas	32,841	32,250	31,272	30,938	32,008	30,176	29,527	29,463	30,755
Utah	32,888	34,609	32,964	36,712	34,178	30,484	36,180	36,702	35,716
Vermont	32,205	33,156	36,315	37,403	35,262	31,724	34,599	31,860	35,802
Virginia	37,835	39,132	40,900	40,777	39,769	39,321	40,349	37,366	37,647
Washington	35,684	35,640	40,498	38,199	36,412	36,963	35,809	36,568	33,533
West Virginia	24,024	22,448	24,244	25,908	25,908	25,101	21,412	22,995	23,564
Wisconsin	29,587	34,400	37,050	34,807	34,823	33,876	35,184	32,579	35,388
Wyoming	33,970	35,993	33,096	35,282	33,405	31,609	31,910	30,196	33,140

[1] Beginning 1987, data based on revised processing procedures and not directly comparable with prior years. [2] Implementation of 1990 census population controls. [3] Data collection method changed from paper and pencil to computer assisted interviewing. In addition, the March 1994 income supplement was revised to allow for the coding of different income amounts on selected questionnaire items.

Source: U.S. Bureau of the Census, *Current Population Reports*, P60-189.

No. 717. Money Income of Families—Percent Distribution, by Income Level, Race, and Hispanic Origin, in Constant (1994) Dollars: 1970 to 1994

[Constant dollars based on CPI-U-X1 deflator. Families as of **March** of following year. Beginning with 1980, based on householder concept and restricted to primary families. Based on Current Population Survey; see text, sections 1 and 14, and Appendix III. For definition of median, see Guide to Tabular Presentation. See also *Historical Statistics, Colonial Times to 1970*, series G 1-8, G 16-23, G 190-192, and G 197-199]

YEAR	Number of families (1,000)	PERCENT DISTRIBUTION							Median income (dollars)
		Under $10,000	$10,000-$14,999	$15,000-$24,999	$25,000-$34,999	$35,000-$49,999	$50,000-$74,999	$75,000 and over	
ALL FAMILIES [1]									
1970	52,227	7.9	7.0	15.8	18.8	24.1	18.3	8.0	35,407
1975	56,245	7.3	7.6	16.3	17.2	22.8	19.6	9.1	36,177
1980	60,309	7.7	6.8	15.4	15.7	21.9	20.7	11.8	37,857
1985	63,558	8.6	6.6	15.2	15.2	19.8	20.3	14.3	38,200
1990	66,322	7.9	6.4	14.4	14.4	19.4	20.6	16.9	40,087
1992	68,216	9.1	6.8	14.7	14.7	18.7	20.2	15.7	38,632
1993	68,506	9.4	7.0	15.1	14.8	17.7	19.6	16.4	37,905
1994	69,313	8.7	6.9	15.0	14.3	18.0	19.9	17.2	38,782
WHITE									
1970	46,535	6.7	6.5	15.0	18.9	25.0	19.3	8.6	36,731
1975	49,873	6.0	6.9	15.8	17.3	23.6	20.6	9.8	37,625
1980	52,710	6.2	6.0	14.8	15.9	22.7	21.8	12.7	39,443
1985	54,991	6.9	6.0	14.7	15.2	20.4	21.3	15.4	40,152
1990	56,803	6.0	5.7	13.9	14.6	20.0	21.8	17.9	41,858
1992	57,669	6.8	6.2	14.3	14.9	19.4	21.5	17.0	40,847
1993	57,881	7.1	6.4	14.7	15.0	18.5	20.8	17.6	40,306
1994	58,444	6.8	6.2	14.6	14.5	18.5	20.9	18.5	40,884
BLACK									
1970	4,928	19.5	12.7	23.3	17.2	15.8	9.4	2.2	22,531
1975	5,586	18.7	14.0	20.9	17.1	16.2	10.5	2.6	23,150
1980	6,317	20.0	13.5	20.8	14.6	15.4	12.0	3.7	22,822
1985	6,921	22.5	11.1	19.9	14.4	15.1	12.2	4.8	23,120
1990	7,471	22.0	11.5	18.3	13.0	15.8	12.1	7.4	24,291
1992	7,982	25.1	11.7	18.1	13.4	14.2	11.4	6.1	22,291
1993	7,993	25.2	11.4	18.4	14.0	12.7	11.4	7.0	22,094
1994	8,093	21.0	11.2	18.4	13.5	14.8	13.3	7.9	24,698
HISPANIC ORIGIN [2]									
1975	2,499	14.4	12.2	23.0	19.0	18.7	9.8	3.0	25,186
1980	3,235	14.2	11.4	21.4	17.8	17.5	12.8	4.9	26,500
1985	4,206	16.1	12.2	20.0	16.5	16.2	12.7	6.1	26,206
1990	4,981	15.3	12.6	19.5	16.2	16.9	12.4	7.1	26,568
1992	5,733	17.1	12.0	21.2	16.2	15.3	12.1	6.1	24,881
1993	5,946	17.5	12.2	21.8	16.9	14.1	11.5	5.9	24,260
1994	6,202	17.8	12.6	21.0	14.9	14.9	11.7	7.2	24,318

[1] Includes other races not shown separately.   [2] Persons of Hispanic origin may be of any race.

No. 718. Money Income of Families—Median Income, by Race and Hispanic Origin, in Current and Constant (1994) Dollars: 1970 to 1994

[See headnote, table 717]

YEAR	MEDIAN INCOME IN CURRENT DOLLARS					MEDIAN INCOME IN CONSTANT (1994) DOLLARS				
	All families [1]	White	Black	Asian, Pacific Islander	His-panic [2]	All families [1]	White	Black	Asian, Pacific Islander	His-panic [2]
1970	9,867	10,236	6,279	(NA)	(NA)	35,407	36,731	22,531	(NA)	(NA)
1975	13,719	14,268	8,779	(NA)	9,551	36,177	37,625	23,150	(NA)	25,186
1980	21,023	21,904	12,674	(NA)	14,716	37,857	39,443	22,822	(NA)	26,500
1981	22,388	23,517	13,266	(NA)	16,401	36,825	38,682	21,820	(NA)	26,977
1982	23,433	24,603	13,598	(NA)	16,227	36,326	38,140	21,080	(NA)	25,155
1983 [3]	24,580	25,757	14,506	(NA)	16,956	36,574	38,325	21,584	(NA)	25,230
1984	26,433	27,686	15,431	(NA)	18,832	37,703	39,491	22,010	(NA)	26,861
1985	27,735	29,152	16,786	(NA)	19,027	38,200	40,152	23,120	(NA)	26,206
1986	29,458	30,809	17,604	(NA)	19,995	39,833	41,660	23,804	(NA)	27,037
1987 [4]	30,970	32,385	18,406	(NA)	20,300	40,403	42,249	24,012	(NA)	26,483
1988	32,191	33,915	19,329	36,560	21,769	40,327	42,487	24,214	45,800	27,271
1989	34,213	35,975	20,209	40,351	23,446	40,890	42,996	24,153	48,226	28,022
1990	35,353	36,915	21,423	42,246	23,431	40,087	41,858	24,291	47,902	26,568
1991	35,939	37,783	21,548	40,974	23,895	39,105	41,112	23,447	44,584	26,000
1992 [5]	36,573	38,670	21,103	42,255	23,555	38,632	40,847	22,291	44,634	24,881
1993	36,959	39,300	21,542	44,456	23,654	37,905	40,306	22,094	45,594	24,260
1994	38,782	40,884	24,698	46,122	24,318	38,782	40,884	24,698	46,122	24,318

NA Not available.   [1] Includes other races not shown separately.   [2] Persons of Hispanic origin may be of any race.
[3] Beginning 1983, data based on revised Hispanic population controls and not directly comparable with prior years.   [4] Beginning 1987, data based on revised processing procedures and not directly comparable with prior years.   [5] Based on 1990 census population controls.

Source of tables 717 and 718: U.S. Bureau of the Census, *Current Population Reports*, P60-189; and unpublished data.

No. 719. Share of Aggregate Income Received by Each Fifth and Top 5 Percent of Families, by Race and Hispanic Origin of Householder: 1970 to 1994

[Families as of March of the following year. Income in constant 1994 CPI-U-X1 adjusted dollars]

YEAR	Number (1,000)	INCOME AT SELECTED POSITIONS (dollars)					PERCENT DISTRIBUTION OF AGGREGATE INCOME					
		Upper limit of each fifth				Top 5 percent	Low-est 5th	Sec-ond 5th	Third 5th	Fourth 5th	High-est 5th	Top 5 per-cent
		Lowest	Second	Third	Fourth							
1970	52,227	18,301	29,855	40,545	55,731	87,018	5.4	12.2	17.6	23.8	40.9	15.6
1980	60,309	18,728	31,531	44,658	62,665	99,040	5.1	11.6	17.5	24.3	41.6	15.3
1985	63,558	18,298	31,521	45,661	66,427	108,760	4.6	10.9	16.9	24.2	43.5	16.7
1990	66,322	19,102	32,933	47,669	69,723	116,063	4.6	10.8	16.6	23.8	44.3	17.4
1991	67,173	18,498	31,676	46,789	68,541	111,883	4.5	10.7	16.6	24.1	44.2	17.1
1992	68,216	17,654	31,345	46,478	67,657	111,981	4.3	10.5	16.5	24.0	44.7	17.6
1993	68,506	17,405	30,768	46,183	68,504	116,080	4.1	9.9	15.7	23.3	47.0	20.3
1994	69,313	17,940	31,300	47,000	69,998	120,043	4.2	10.0	15.7	23.3	46.9	20.1
White	58,444	19,946	33,406	49,228	72,200	124,090	4.6	10.3	15.8	23.0	46.3	20.0
Black	8,093	9,453	18,674	31,120	51,120	86,865	3.2	8.5	15.1	24.7	48.7	18.9
Hispanic origin . .	6,202	10,694	19,120	30,194	48,182	83,693	3.9	9.1	15.1	23.6	48.3	19.6

[1] Persons of Hispanic origin may be of any race.

Source: U.S. Bureau of the Census, Current Population Reports, series P60-189.

No. 720. Money Income of Families—Percent Distribution, by Income Quintile and Top 5 Percent: 1994

[See headnote, table 717]

CHARACTERISTIC	Number (1,000)	PERCENT DISTRIBUTION						
		Total	Lowest fifth	Second fifth	Third fifth	Fourth fifth	Highest fifth	Top 5 percent
All families	69,313	100.0	20.0	20.0	20.0	20.0	20.0	5.0
Age of householder:								
15 to 24 years old	3,079	100.0	50.0	27.3	14.7	5.9	2.1	0.2
25 to 34 years old	14,082	100.0	24.4	21.9	21.9	20.0	11.8	2.0
35 to 44 years old	18,274	100.0	16.0	15.7	20.9	24.1	23.3	5.8
45 to 54 years old	13,746	100.0	10.7	12.7	18.7	24.1	33.9	8.7
55 to 64 years old	8,895	100.0	15.6	18.8	20.3	21.4	23.8	7.1
65 years old and over	11,236	100.0	27.6	32.5	19.0	11.2	9.7	2.5
White	58,444	100.0	17.2	19.8	20.6	20.9	21.5	5.4
Black	8,093	100.0	38.5	21.7	16.2	14.1	9.5	1.7
Hispanic origin [1]	6,202	100.0	37.2	24.3	17.5	12.3	8.7	1.7
Type of family:								
Married-couple families	53,865	100.0	12.7	18.9	21.0	23.0	24.4	6.2
Male householder, wife absent	3,228	100.0	31.0	25.6	19.1	15.2	9.1	1.8
Female householder, husband absent .	12,220	100.0	49.3	23.5	15.8	8.0	3.3	0.4
Presence of related children under 18 years old:								
No related children	32,531	100.0	16.8	21.8	20.2	19.8	21.4	5.5
One or more related children	36,782	100.0	22.9	18.4	19.8	20.2	18.8	4.6
One child	15,084	100.0	22.4	19.5	19.6	19.8	18.7	4.2
Two children or more	21,698	100.0	23.2	17.6	19.9	20.5	18.9	4.9
Education attainment of householder: [2]								
Total	66,234	100.0	18.6	19.7	20.2	20.7	20.8	5.2
Less than 9th grade	5,223	100.0	46.2	29.3	14.4	6.8	3.3	0.6
9th to 12th grade (no diploma)	6,618	100.0	39.2	26.6	18.6	10.6	5.0	0.4
High school graduate (includes equiva-lency)	21,358	100.0	19.6	23.8	24.2	20.5	11.9	1.8
Some college, no degree	12,136	100.0	14.6	19.9	23.6	24.0	18.0	3.3
Associate degree	4,669	100.0	10.7	16.8	22.8	27.3	22.4	4.1
Bachelor's degree or more	16,230	100.0	5.2	8.9	14.4	25.0	46.4	15.0
Bachelor's degree	10,101	100.0	6.2	10.5	15.8	26.8	40.7	10.9
Master's degree	3,864	100.0	3.3	6.9	14.6	24.6	50.7	15.1
Professional degree	1,302	100.0	4.1	5.3	9.4	18.3	62.9	35.7
Doctorate degree	964	100.0	3.7	5.2	6.7	18.0	66.4	30.1

[1] Persons of Hispanic origin may be of any race.   [2] 25 years old and over.

Source: U.S. Bureau of the Census, Current Population Survey, unpublished data.

No. 721. Money Income of Families—Median Income, by Race and Hispanic Origin: 1993

[See headnote, table 717. For composition of regions, see table 27]

CHARACTERISTIC	NUMBER (1,000)				MEDIAN INCOME (dollars)			
	All families [1]	White	Black	His-panic [2]	All families [1]	White	Black	His-panic [2]
All families............	68,506	57,881	7,993	5,946	36,959	39,300	21,542	23,654
Region:								
Northeast................	13,456	11,690	1,298	1,001	40,987	42,526	25,002	19,580
Midwest.................	16,210	14,258	1,643	405	37,942	40,158	20,794	27,501
South	24,438	19,461	4,461	1,915	33,365	36,504	20,372	23,651
West....................	14,402	12,472	591	2,624	38,881	39,614	26,182	24,781
Type of family:								
Married-couple families.........	53,181	47,452	3,715	4,038	43,005	43,675	35,218	28,454
Wife in paid labor force......	32,194	28,539	2,417	2,121	51,204	51,630	44,805	35,973
Wife not in paid labor force ...	20,988	18,913	1,298	1,917	30,218	30,878	22,207	20,721
Male householder, wife absent...	2,914	2,298	450	410	26,467	28,269	19,476	21,717
Female householder, husband absent.................	12,411	8,131	3,828	1,498	17,443	20,000	11,909	12,047
With related children, under 18	36,456	29,234	5,525	4,153	36,200	39,837	18,671	22,117
Married couple	26,121	22,670	2,147	2,747	45,548	46,376	36,659	28,499
Male householder, wife absent...	1,577	1,202	295	239	22,348	24,272	18,857	17,835
Female householder, husband absent.................	8,758	5,361	3,084	1,167	13,472	16,020	10,375	10,497
Number of earners:								
No earners................	10,546	8,622	1,574	860	15,515	17,656	6,858	8,362
One earner	19,301	15,556	2,999	2,044	26,193	28,574	16,571	17,121
Two earners..............	30,137	26,336	2,620	2,248	47,424	48,332	37,124	32,172
Three earners.............	6,367	5,486	651	538	57,745	58,651	49,489	40,724
Four or more earners........	2,155	1,882	149	256	72,673	73,269	59,678	49,876

[1] Includes other races not shown separately.　　[2] Persons of Hispanic origin may be of any race.

No. 722. Money Income of Families—Percent Distribution, by Income Level and Selected Characteristics: 1993

[See headnote, table 717. See *Historical Statistics, Colonial Times to 1970,* series G 1-8 for U.S. data on total, White, Black, and other races. For composition of regions, see table 27]

ITEM	Number of fami-lies (1,000)	PERCENT DISTRIBUTION							Median income (dollars)
		Under $10,000	$10,000 to $14,999	$15,000 to $24,999	$25,000 to $34,999	$35,000 to $49,999	$50,000 to $74,999	$75,000 and over	
All families [1]........	68,506	9.6	7.2	15.5	14.8	17.9	19.4	15.5	36,959
White, total.............	57,881	7.3	6.6	15.1	15.1	18.8	20.6	16.6	39,300
Northeast.............	11,690	7.2	5.7	13.5	13.5	18.3	21.5	20.3	42,526
Midwest..............	14,258	6.4	5.8	14.9	15.6	20.7	21.8	14.8	40,158
South	19,461	7.8	7.6	16.4	16.0	18.4	19.0	14.9	36,504
West	12,472	7.5	6.7	14.9	14.5	17.7	20.8	17.8	39,614
Black, total.............	7,993	25.8	11.4	18.6	13.7	12.9	10.9	6.6	21,542
Northeast.............	1,298	25.1	9.6	15.3	14.1	14.0	13.4	8.5	25,002
Midwest..............	1,643	30.7	10.0	17.3	13.1	12.2	9.7	6.8	20,794
South	4,461	25.2	12.6	20.2	13.3	13.2	10.2	5.4	20,372
West	591	18.8	10.0	17.6	17.1	10.8	15.1	11.2	26,182
Hispanic, [2] total	5,946	17.9	12.5	22.2	16.6	14.0	11.4	5.4	23,654
Northeast.............	1,001	28.4	11.9	19.5	13.6	12.7	8.5	5.5	19,580
Midwest..............	405	15.1	10.6	20.2	17.5	18.0	13.6	5.2	27,501
South	1,915	17.0	13.3	23.1	16.9	12.4	11.1	6.2	23,651
West	2,624	15.0	12.3	22.9	17.3	14.9	12.4	4.9	24,781
Presence of related children under 18 years old:									
All families	68,506	9.6	7.2	15.5	14.8	17.9	19.4	15.5	36,959
No children	32,050	5.5	7.4	17.1	15.9	17.7	19.7	16.6	37,849
One or more children	36,456	13.2	7.1	14.2	13.9	18.1	19.1	14.5	36,200
Married-couple families.....	53,181	4.4	5.5	14.1	14.9	19.5	22.7	18.9	43,005
No children	27,060	4.7	6.7	16.2	15.6	17.6	20.8	18.5	40,293
One or more children	26,121	4.2	4.2	11.8	14.2	21.6	24.7	19.4	45,548
Female householder, no husband present	12,411	30.8	14.0	20.3	14.0	11.2	7.1	2.7	17,443
No children	3,653	10.9	11.8	22.5	18.0	18.0	13.1	5.6	27,184
One or more children	8,758	39.1	15.0	19.4	12.3	8.3	4.5	1.5	13,472

[1] Includes other races not shown separately.　　[2] Persons of Hispanic origin may be of any race.

Source of tables 721 and 722: U.S. Bureau of the Census, *Current Population Reports,* P60-188; and unpublished data.

No. 723. Money Income of Families—Distribution, by Type of Family and Income Level: 1994

[See headnote, table 717]

TYPE OF FAMILY	Number of families (1,000)	Under $10,000	$10,000-$14,999	$15,000-$19,999	$20,000-$24,999	$25,000-$34,999	$35,000-$49,999	$50,000-$74,999	$75,000 and over	Median income (dollars)
					DISTRIBUTION (1,000)					
All families	**69,313**	**6,012**	**4,794**	**5,098**	**5,323**	**9,912**	**12,471**	**13,819**	**11,883**	**38,782**
Married-couple families . .	53,865	2,118	2,741	3,382	3,845	7,619	10,360	12,481	11,320	44,959
Wife worked.	35,148	540	809	1,186	1,817	4,389	7,320	10,027	9,060	52,750
Wife did not work	18,717	1,581	1,932	2,196	2,028	3,230	3,039	2,453	2,258	29,783
Male householder [1]	3,228	422	353	356	520	558	474	223	27,751
Female householder [1] . . .	12,220	3,470	1,700	1,362	1,154	1,774	1,553	865	343	18,236
With related children [2] . . .	36,782	4,292	2,601	2,456	2,614	4,931	6,660	7,376	5,852	37,925
Married-couple	26,367	972	1,064	1,260	1,647	3,549	5,523	6,757	5,595	47,244
Female householder [1] .	8,665	3,048	1,307	986	780	1,116	857	413	160	14,902

[1] No spouse present.   [2] Children under 18 years old. Includes male householders not shown separately.

No. 724. Median Income of Families, by Type of Family in Current and Constant (1994) Dollars: 1970 to 1994

[See headnote, table 717. See also *Historical Statistics, Colonial Times to 1970*, series G 179-188]

YEAR	CURRENT DOLLARS						CONSTANT (1994) DOLLARS					
		Married-couple families			Male householder, no wife present	Female householder, no husband present		Married-couple families			Male householder, no wife present	Female householder, no husband present
	Total	Total	Wife in paid labor force	Wife not in paid labor force			Total	Total	Wife in paid labor force	Wife not in paid labor force		
1970	9,867	10,516	12,276	9,304	9,012	5,093	35,407	37,735	44,051	33,386	32,338	18,276
1980	21,023	23,141	26,879	18,972	17,519	10,408	37,857	41,671	48,402	34,163	31,547	18,742
1981	22,388	25,065	29,247	20,325	19,889	10,960	36,825	41,228	48,107	33,431	32,714	18,027
1982	23,433	26,019	30,342	21,299	20,140	11,484	36,326	40,335	47,036	33,018	31,221	17,803
1983	24,580	27,286	32,107	21,890	21,845	11,789	36,574	40,600	47,774	32,571	32,504	17,541
1984 [1]	26,433	29,612	34,668	23,582	23,325	12,803	37,703	42,238	49,449	33,637	33,270	18,262
1985	27,735	31,100	36,431	24,556	22,622	13,660	38,200	42,835	50,177	33,822	31,158	18,814
1986	29,458	32,805	38,346	25,803	24,962	13,647	39,833	44,359	51,851	34,891	33,753	18,453
1987 [2]	30,970	34,879	40,751	26,640	25,208	14,683	40,403	45,502	53,163	34,754	32,886	19,155
1988	32,191	36,389	42,709	27,220	26,827	15,346	40,327	45,586	53,504	34,100	33,607	19,225
1989	34,213	38,547	45,266	28,747	27,847	16,442	40,890	46,070	54,100	34,357	33,282	19,651
1990	35,353	39,895	46,777	30,265	29,046	16,932	40,087	45,237	53,040	34,317	32,935	19,199
1991	35,939	40,995	48,169	30,075	28,351	16,692	39,105	44,607	52,413	32,725	30,849	18,163
1992 [3]	36,573	41,890	49,775	30,174	27,576	17,025	38,632	44,249	52,578	31,873	29,129	17,984
1993	36,959	43,005	51,204	30,218	26,467	17,443	37,905	44,106	52,515	30,992	27,145	17,890
1994	38,782	44,959	53,309	31,176	27,751	18,236	38,782	44,959	53,309	31,176	27,751	18,236

[1] Beginning 1984, data based on revised Hispanic population controls and not directly comparable with prior years. [2] Beginning 1987, data based on revised processing procedures and not comparable with prior years.   [3] Based on 1990 census population controls.

No. 725. Median Income of Year-Round Full-Time Workers With Income: 1980 to 1994

[Age as of **March of following year.** Prior to 1990, earnings are for civilian workers only. For definition of median, see Guide to Tabular Presentation]

ITEM	FEMALE					MALE				
	1980	1990	1992	1993	1994	1980	1990	1992	1993	1994
Total with income . . .	**$11,591**	**$20,591**	**$22,093**	**$22,469**	**$23,265**	**$19,173**	**$28,979**	**$30,832**	**$31,077**	**$31,612**
15 to 19 years old	6,779	[1]13,944	[1]14,662	[1]15,227	[1]15,063	7,753	[1]15,462	[1]15,658	[1]15,948	[1]15,860
20 to 24 years old	9,407	(NA)	(NA)	(NA)	(NA)	12,109	(NA)	(NA)	(NA)	(NA)
25 to 34 years old	12,190	20,184	21,941	21,949	22,426	17,724	25,355	26,410	26,087	26,572
35 to 44 years old	12,239	22,505	24,125	25,282	25,744	21,777	32,607	34,714	35,233	35,586
45 to 54 years old	12,116	21,938	24,489	24,412	25,911	22,323	35,732	37,926	39,685	40,367
55 to 64 years old	11,931	20,755	22,581	22,587	22,875	21,053	33,169	35,537	35,736	37,799
65 years old and over. . . .	12,342	22,957	21,556	24,875	24,498	17,307	35,520	35,341	37,085	35,667
White.	11,703	20,839	22,349	22,979	23,894	19,720	30,081	31,565	31,832	32,440
Black.	10,915	18,544	20,258	20,315	20,628	13,875	21,481	22,991	23,566	24,405
Hispanic [2]	9,887	16,181	17,674	17,112	18,418	13,790	19,358	19,855	20,423	20,525

NA Not available. [1] 15 to 24 years old.   [2] Persons of Hispanic origin may be of any race.

Source of tables 723-725: U.S. Bureau of the Census, *Current Population Reports,* P60-189, and earlier reports; and unpublished data.

No. 726. Money Income of Persons—Percent Distribution, by Income Level, in Constant (1993) Dollars: 1970 to 1993

[Constant dollars based on CPI-U-X1 deflator. As of **March of following year.** For 1970, persons 14 years old and over; thereafter, 15 years old and over. For definition of median, see Guide to Tabular Presentation. See also *Historical Statistics, Colonial Times to 1970,* series G 257-268. For composition of regions, see table 27]

ITEM	All persons (mil.)	Total (mil.)	\$1 to \$2,499 or loss [1]	\$2,500 to \$4,999	\$5,000 to \$9,999	\$10,000 to \$14,999	\$15,000 to \$24,999	\$25,000 to \$49,999	\$50,000 to \$74,999	\$75,000 and over	Median income (dollars)
MALE											
1970	70.6	65.0	8.3	5.9	10.8	9.8	19.5	35.6	7.1	3.1	23,337
1980	82.9	78.7	7.2	5.1	11.9	11.1	20.0	32.9	8.1	3.6	22,000
1981	84.0	79.7	7.6	5.8	12.1	10.9	20.1	32.1	7.8	3.6	21,608
1982 [2]	85.0	79.7	8.2	5.6	12.2	10.6	21.1	30.6	7.6	4.0	21,086
1983 [2]	86.0	80.8	8.3	5.6	12.1	11.7	20.1	30.1	8.4	3.8	21,220
1984	87.3	82.2	7.6	5.5	12.6	11.1	19.0	31.3	8.7	4.1	21,696
1985	88.5	83.6	7.3	5.5	12.0	11.6	19.8	30.6	8.9	4.3	21,905
1986 [3]	89.4	84.5	7.0	5.1	11.8	11.1	19.3	31.3	9.6	4.8	22,564
1987 [3]	90.3	85.7	6.7	5.1	11.6	11.1	19.7	31.0	9.8	5.0	22,624
1988	91.0	86.6	6.7	4.9	11.7	11.0	20.1	31.1	9.5	5.0	23,096
1989	92.0	87.5	6.3	4.7	11.6	11.2	20.5	30.7	9.4	5.5	23,182
1990	92.8	88.2	6.4	4.7	12.3	11.5	20.9	30.4	9.0	5.0	22,436
1991	93.8	88.7	6.4	5.1	12.5	12.4	20.3	30.2	8.4	4.8	21,716
1992 [4]	94.9	89.6	6.9	5.1	12.9	12.3	20.6	29.0	8.4	4.8	21,067
1993	**96.8**	**90.2**	**7.0**	**4.9**	**12.1**	**12.4**	**20.8**	**28.8**	**8.7**	**5.2**	**21,102**
15 to 24 years old . .	18.2	13.8	27.7	15.0	21.0	14.9	15.2	5.6	0.5	0.2	6,429
25 to 34 years old . .	20.9	20.2	3.7	3.7	9.5	12.8	27.8	33.8	6.3	2.4	21,927
35 to 44 years old . .	20.5	19.9	3.7	2.2	6.9	8.1	18.9	39.3	13.3	7.6	30,342
45 to 54 years old . .	14.5	14.1	3.6	1.9	7.0	7.1	15.4	37.2	16.5	11.2	33,154
55 to 64 years old . .	9.9	9.6	3.8	3.1	11.0	11.7	20.1	31.6	10.7	7.9	25,139
65 yr. old and over . .	12.7	12.6	1.4	4.6	21.6	22.5	25.2	18.1	4.0	2.6	14,983
White	82.0	77.7	6.5	4.5	11.3	12.2	20.7	29.8	9.3	5.7	21,981
Black	10.6	8.9	11.1	7.5	18.0	14.1	21.8	22.2	4.1	1.2	14,605
Hispanic [5]	9.3	8.2	7.8	7.1	20.1	18.5	23.1	18.4	3.5	1.4	13,689
Northeast	19.3	17.9	6.4	4.8	11.3	11.8	19.9	29.5	10.0	6.3	22,283
Midwest	22.5	21.4	7.0	4.9	10.7	12.4	21.2	31.2	8.7	4.1	21,696
South	33.5	31.0	7.4	5.2	13.7	13.0	21.4	26.6	7.8	4.8	19,714
West	21.4	19.9	7.0	4.3	12.2	12.1	20.1	29.1	9.0	6.1	21,536
FEMALE											
1970	77.6	51.6	20.8	16.3	20.4	15.0	18.0	8.9	0.5	0.2	7,827
1980	91.1	80.8	20.3	12.8	22.3	14.4	18.3	10.8	0.8	0.3	8,638
1981	92.2	82.1	19.9	12.6	22.8	14.1	18.6	11.0	0.8	0.2	8,753
1982 [2]	93.1	82.5	19.8	12.2	22.4	13.6	18.9	11.7	1.0	0.4	8,898
1983 [2]	94.3	83.8	18.9	12.1	21.7	14.6	18.4	12.7	1.2	0.4	9,292
1984	95.3	85.6	18.1	11.9	22.0	14.1	18.2	13.9	1.4	0.5	9,552
1985	96.4	86.5	17.7	12.0	21.7	14.0	18.1	14.4	1.5	0.5	9,692
1986 [3]	97.3	87.8	17.1	11.6	21.6	13.7	18.4	15.2	1.7	0.6	10,033
1987 [3]	98.2	89.7	16.0	11.4	21.2	13.8	19.1	15.8	1.9	0.7	10,551
1988	99.0	90.6	15.9	11.1	21.3	14.0	18.9	16.1	2.1	0.7	10,852
1989	99.8	91.4	15.1	11.1	20.6	13.9	19.6	16.6	2.2	0.8	11,215
1990	100.7	92.2	14.9	11.2	20.9	14.4	19.1	16.4	2.3	0.8	11,133
1991	101.5	92.6	14.3	10.8	21.7	14.9	19.0	16.3	2.2	0.8	11,114
1992 [4]	102.4	93.2	14.6	10.9	21.3	14.7	18.7	16.7	2.2	0.8	11,035
1993	**104.0**	**94.4**	**14.1**	**10.9**	**21.4**	**14.4**	**19.1**	**16.5**	**2.6**	**0.9**	**11,046**
15 to 24 years old . .	18.1	13.5	30.5	17.4	23.5	13.2	12.2	3.0	0.1	0.1	5,351
25 to 34 years old . .	21.1	19.6	13.2	8.4	16.3	14.5	24.1	20.6	2.3	0.6	13,988
35 to 44 years old . .	21.0	19.7	13.0	7.1	14.6	13.3	21.5	25.0	4.0	1.7	15,844
45 to 54 years old . .	15.1	14.0	12.7	5.9	14.7	13.2	22.5	24.7	4.9	1.5	16,324
55 to 64 years old . .	10.8	10.0	15.8	11.2	20.3	14.1	18.4	16.1	3.0	1.1	10,829
65 yr. old and over . .	18.0	17.7	4.0	16.7	38.9	17.9	14.2	6.7	1.2	0.5	8,499
White	86.8	79.5	14.2	10.4	21.0	14.5	19.3	16.9	2.7	1.0	11,266
Black	12.9	11.3	11.8	14.7	25.3	14.7	17.7	13.8	1.5	0.5	9,508
Hispanic [5]	9.1	7.1	16.3	14.5	27.1	15.3	15.7	9.8	1.0	0.4	8,100
Northeast	21.3	19.5	13.3	10.6	21.8	13.1	18.4	17.8	3.5	1.4	11,375
Midwest	24.5	22.9	14.0	11.0	21.4	14.8	20.3	16.0	2.0	0.6	11,031
South	36.4	32.4	14.4	11.7	22.0	14.9	19.2	15.1	2.1	0.7	10,557
West	21.9	19.6	14.6	9.8	19.9	14.6	18.3	18.2	3.2	1.3	11,568

[1] Includes persons with income deficit.   [2] Beginning 1983, data based on revised Hispanic population controls not directly comparable with prior years.   [3] Beginning 1987, data based on revised processing procedures and not directly comparable with prior years.   [4] Based on 1990 populations controls.   [5] Persons of Hispanic origin may be of any race.

Source: U.S. Bureau of the Census, *Current Population Reports,* P60-188; and unpublished data.

No. 727. Median Income of Married-Couple Families, by Work Experience of Husbands and Wives: 1993

[As of **March 1994.** Based on Current Population Survey; see text, sections 1 and 14, and Appendix III]

WORK EXPERIENCE OF HUSBAND	NUMBER (1,000)				MEDIAN INCOME (dollars)			
	Total	Wife worked		Wife did not work	Total	Wife worked		Wife did not work
		Total	Worked year-round, full-time			Total	Worked year-round, full-time	
All families [1]	**53,181**	**34,411**	**18,657**	**18,770**	**43,005**	**50,798**	**56,078**	**28,779**
Husband worked.	42,072	31,419	17,170	10,653	49,450	52,494	57,891	37,482
Worked year-round, full-time	33,357	25,423	14,325	7,934	52,869	56,017	60,711	41,776
Husband did not work	11,109	2,992	1,487	8,117	23,128	30,131	34,661	20,987
White	47,452	30,574	16,231	16,878	43,675	51,205	56,519	29,571
Husband worked.	37,634	28,069	14,993	9,565	49,988	52,863	58,269	38,601
Worked year-round, full-time	29,808	22,690	12,470	7,118	53,356	56,341	61,062	42,456
Husband did not work	9,818	2,505	1,238	7,313	23,822	30,777	35,421	21,709
Black	3,715	2,562	1,617	1,153	35,218	44,446	51,192	20,953
Husband worked.	2,763	2,171	1,427	592	43,181	47,815	53,146	29,354
Worked year-round, full-time	2,214	1,759	1,210	455	47,002	51,442	55,517	30,966
Husband did not work	953	392	190	561	17,211	25,712	29,380	13,962
Hispanic [2]	4,038	2,236	1,166	1,802	28,454	35,919	43,856	19,989
Husband worked.	3,395	2,047	1,078	1,349	31,198	37,282	45,587	21,681
Worked year-round, full-time	2,483	1,543	885	939	35,357	42,191	48,607	25,254
Husband did not work	643	190	88	453	17,042	21,431	28,779	14,714

[1] Includes other races not shown separately.   [2] Persons of Hispanic origin may be of any race.

No. 728. Average Earnings of Year-Round, Full-Time Workers: 1994

[In dollars. For persons 25 years old and over as of March 1994]

AGE AND SEX	All workers	Less than 9th grade	HIGH SCHOOL			COLLEGE	
			9th to 12th grade (no diploma)	High school graduate (includes equivalency)	Some college, no degree	Associate degree	Bachelor's degree or more
Male, total.	**41,118**	**20,461**	**24,377**	**31,081**	**35,639**	**38,944**	**61,008**
25 to 34 years old	30,715	17,622	20,594	26,363	29,922	31,400	40,403
35 to 44 years old	43,058	17,576	24,089	31,452	36,298	40,198	65,358
45 to 54 years old	49,187	24,421	26,745	35,975	40,787	44,682	70,546
55 to 64 years old	47,044	23,855	30,380	35,373	41,595	47,127	73,318
65 years old and over. . . .	40,229	17,326	21,596	28,433	29,880	(B)	71,964
Female, total	**27,162**	**13,349**	**16,188**	**21,383**	**24,787**	**26,903**	**39,271**
25 to 34 years old	24,273	12,220	14,364	19,581	22,023	24,068	32,507
35 to 44 years old	29,189	14,153	15,416	21,321	25,976	28,855	43,954
45 to 54 years old	29,424	14,297	17,530	23,217	27,131	28,297	43,480
55 to 64 years old	24,816	12,541	18,351	21,770	24,327	27,726	37,134
65 years old and over. . . .	22,869	(B)	(B)	22,457	20,128	(B)	32,805

B Base figure too small to meet statistical standards for reliability of derived figure.

No. 729. Per Capita Money Income in Current and Constant (1994) Dollars, by Race and Hispanic Origin: 1970 to 1994

[In dollars. Constant dollars based on CPI-U-X1 deflator. **As of March of following year**]

YEAR	CURRENT DOLLARS				CONSTANT (1994) DOLLARS			
	All races [1]	White	Black	Hispanic [2]	All races [1]	White	Black	Hispanic [2]
1970	3,177	3,354	1,869	(NA)	11,400	12,035	6,707	(NA)
1980	7,787	8,233	4,804	4,865	14,022	14,825	8,651	8,761
1985 [3]	11,013	11,671	6,840	6,613	15,168	16,075	9,421	9,108
1986	11,670	12,352	7,207	7,000	15,780	16,702	9,745	9,465
1987 [4]	12,391	13,143	7,645	7,653	16,165	17,146	9,973	9,984
1988	13,123	13,896	8,271	7,956	16,440	17,408	10,361	9,967
1989	14,056	14,896	8,747	8,390	16,799	17,803	10,454	10,027
1990	14,387	15,265	9,017	8,424	16,313	17,309	10,224	9,552
1991	14,617	15,510	9,170	8,662	15,905	16,877	9,978	9,425
1992	15,033	15,981	9,296	8,874	(NA)	(NA)	(NA)	(NA)
1992 [5]	14,847	15,785	9,239	8,591	15,683	16,674	9,759	9,075
1993	15,777	16,800	9,863	8,830	16,181	17,230	10,116	9,056
1994	16,555	17,611	10,650	9,435	16,555	17,611	10,650	9,435

NA Not available.   [1] Includes other races not shown separately.   [2] Persons of Hispanic origin may be of any race.
[3] Beginning 1985, data based on revised Hispanic population controls   [4] Beginning 1987, data based on revised processing procedures and not directly comparable with prior years.   [5] Based on 1990 population controls.

Source of tables 727-729: U.S. Bureau of the Census, *Current Population Reports,* P60-189.

No. 730. Persons Below Poverty Level and Below 125 Percent of Poverty Level: 1960 to 1994

[Persons as of **March of the following year**. Based on Current Population Survey; see text, sections 1 and 14, and Appendix III]

YEAR	NUMBER BELOW POVERTY LEVEL (1,000)				PERCENT BELOW POVERTY LEVEL				BELOW 125 PERCENT OF POVERTY LEVEL		AVERAGE INCOME CUTOFFS FOR NONFARM FAMILY OF FOUR [3]	
	All races [1]	White	Black	His-panic [2]	All races [1]	White	Black	His-panic [2]	Number (1,000)	Per-cent of total popula-tion	At poverty level	At 125 percent of poverty level
1960	39,851	28,309	(NA)	(NA)	22.2	17.8	(NA)	(NA)	54,560	30.4	3,022	3,778
1966	28,510	19,290	8,867	(NA)	14.7	11.3	41.8	(NA)	41,267	21.3	3,317	4,146
1969	24,147	16,659	7,095	(NA)	12.1	9.5	32.2	(NA)	34,665	17.4	3,743	4,679
1970	25,420	17,484	7,548	(NA)	12.6	9.9	33.5	(NA)	35,624	17.6	3,968	4,960
1975	25,877	17,770	7,545	2,991	12.3	9.7	31.3	23.0	37,182	17.6	5,500	6,875
1976	24,975	16,713	7,595	2,783	11.8	9.1	31.1	26.9	35,509	16.7	5,815	7,269
1977	24,720	16,416	7,726	2,700	11.6	8.9	31.3	24.7	35,659	16.7	6,191	7,739
1978 [4]	24,497	16,259	7,625	2,607	11.4	8.7	30.6	22.4	34,155	15.8	6,662	8,328
1979 [4]	26,072	17,214	8,050	2,921	11.7	9.0	31.0	21.6	36,616	16.4	7,412	9,265
1980	29,272	19,699	8,579	3,491	13.0	10.2	32.5	21.8	40,658	18.1	8,414	10,518
1981	31,822	21,553	9,173	3,713	14.0	11.1	34.2	25.7	43,748	19.3	9,287	11,609
1982 [5]	34,398	23,517	9,697	4,301	15.0	12.0	35.6	26.5	46,520	20.3	9,862	12,328
1983 [5]	35,303	23,984	9,882	4,633	15.2	12.1	35.7	29.9	47,150	20.3	10,178	12,723
1984	33,700	22,955	9,490	4,806	14.4	11.5	33.8	28.0	45,288	19.4	10,609	13,261
1985	33,064	22,860	8,926	5,236	14.0	11.4	31.3	28.4	44,166	18.7	10,989	13,736
1986 [6]	32,370	22,183	8,983	5,117	13.6	11.0	31.1	29.0	43,486	18.2	11,203	14,004
1987 [6]	32,221	21,195	9,520	5,422	13.4	10.4	32.4	27.3	43,032	17.9	11,611	14,514
1988	31,745	20,715	9,356	5,357	13.0	10.1	31.3	28.0	42,551	17.5	12,092	15,115
1989	31,528	20,785	9,302	5,430	12.8	10.0	30.7	26.7	42,653	17.3	12,674	15,843
1990	33,585	22,326	9,837	6,006	13.5	10.7	31.9	26.2	44,837	18.0	13,359	16,699
1991 [7]	35,708	23,747	10,242	6,339	14.2	11.3	32.7	28.1	47,527	18.9	13,924	17,405
1992 [7]	38,014	25,259	10,827	7,592	14.8	11.9	33.4	29.6	50,592	19.7	14,335	17,919
1993	39,265	26,226	10,877	8,126	15.1	12.2	33.1	30.6	51,801	20.0	14,763	(NA)
1994	38,059	25,379	10,196	8,416	14.5	11.7	30.6	30.7	50,401	19.3	15,141	18,926

NA Not available. [1] Includes other races not shown separately. [2] Persons of Hispanic origin may be of any race. [3] Beginning 1981, income cutoffs for nonfarm families are applied to all families, both farm and nonfarm. [4] Population controls based on 1980 census; see text, sections 1 and 14. [5] Beginning 1983, data based on revised Hispanic population controls and not directly comparable with prior years. [6] Beginning 1987, data based on revised processing procedures and not directly comparable with prior years. [7] Beginning 1992, based on 1990 population controls.

Source: U.S. Bureau of the Census, *Current Population Reports*, P60-189.

No. 731. Children Below Poverty Level, by Race and Hispanic Origin: 1970 to 1994

[Persons as of **March of the following year**. Covers only related children in families under 18 years old. Based on Current Population Survey; see text, sections 1 and 14, and Appendix III]

YEAR	NUMBER BELOW POVERTY LEVEL (1,000)				PERCENT BELOW POVERTY LEVEL			
	All races [1]	White	Black	Hispanic [2]	All races [1]	White	Black	Hispanic [2]
1970	10,235	6,138	3,922	(NA)	14.9	10.5	41.5	(NA)
1975	10,882	6,748	3,884	1,619	16.8	12.5	41.4	33.1
1980	11,114	6,817	3,906	1,718	17.9	13.4	42.1	33.0
1981	12,068	7,429	4,170	1,874	19.5	14.7	44.9	35.4
1982	13,139	8,282	4,388	2,117	21.3	16.5	47.3	38.9
1983 [3]	13,427	8,534	4,273	2,251	21.8	17.0	46.2	37.7
1984	12,929	8,086	4,320	2,317	21.0	16.1	46.2	38.7
1985	12,483	7,838	4,057	2,512	20.1	15.6	43.1	39.6
1986 [4]	12,257	7,714	4,037	2,413	19.8	15.3	42.7	37.1
1987 [4]	12,275	7,398	4,234	2,606	19.7	14.7	44.4	38.9
1988	11,935	7,095	4,148	2,576	19.0	14.0	42.8	37.3
1989	12,001	7,164	4,257	2,496	19.0	14.1	43.2	35.5
1990	12,715	7,696	4,412	2,750	19.9	15.1	44.2	37.7
1991	13,658	8,316	4,637	2,977	21.1	16.1	45.6	39.8
1992 [5]	14,521	8,752	5,015	3,440	21.6	16.5	46.3	39.0
1993	14,961	9,123	5,030	3,666	22.0	17.0	45.9	39.9
1994	14,610	8,826	4,787	3,956	21.2	16.3	43.3	41.1

NA Not available. [1] Includes other races not shown separately. [2] Persons of Hispanic origin may be of any race. [3] Beginning 1983, data based on revised Hispanic population controls and not directly comparable with prior years. [4] Beginning 1987, data based on revised processing procedures and not directly comparable with prior years. [5] Beginning 1992, based on 1990 population controls.

Source: U.S. Bureau of the Census, *Current Population Reports*, P60-189.

No. 732. Weighted Average Poverty Thresholds: 1980 to 1994

[Official poverty thresholds; see text, section 14]

SIZE OF UNIT	1980[1]	1987	1988	1989	1990	1991	1992	1993	1994
One person (unrelated individual) . . .	$4,190	$5,778	$6,022	$6,310	$6,652	$6,932	$7,143	$7,363	$7,547
Under 65 years	4,290	5,909	6,155	6,451	6,800	7,086	7,299	$7,518	7,710
65 years and over	3,949	5,447	5,674	5,947	6,268	6,532	6,729	6,930	7,108
Two persons	5,363	7,397	7,704	8,076	8,509	8,865	9,137	9,414	9,661
Householder under 65 years	5,537	7,641	7,958	8,343	8,794	9,165	9,443	9,728	9,976
Householder 65 years and over . . .	4,983	6,872	7,157	7,501	7,905	8,241	8,487	8,740	8,967
Three persons	6,565	9,056	9,435	9,885	10,419	10,860	11,186	11,522	11,821
Four persons	8,414	11,611	12,092	12,674	13,359	13,924	14,335	14,763	15,141
Five persons	9,966	13,737	14,304	14,990	15,792	16,456	16,952	17,449	17,900
Six persons	11,269	15,509	16,146	16,921	17,839	18,587	19,137	19,718	20,235
Seven persons	12,761	17,649	18,232	19,162	20,241	21,058	21,594	22,383	22,923
Eight persons	14,199	19,515	20,253	21,328	22,582	23,605	24,053	24,838	25,427
Nine or more persons	16,896	23,105	24,129	25,480	26,848	27,942	28,745	29,529	30,300

[1] Poverty levels for nonfarm families.

Source: U.S. Bureau of the Census, *Current Population Reports*, P60-189; and earlier reports.

No. 733. Persons Below Poverty Level, by Selected Characteristics: 1994

[Persons as of **March 1995.** Based on Current Population Survey; see text, sections 1 and 14, and Appendix III. For composition of regions, see table 27]

AGE AND REGION	NUMBER BELOW POVERTY LEVEL (1,000)				PERCENT BELOW POVERTY LEVEL			
	All races [1]	White	Black	Hispanic [2]	All races [1]	White	Black	Hispanic [2]
Total	38,059	25,379	10,196	8,416	14.5	11.7	30.6	30.7
Under 18 years old	15,289	9,346	4,906	4,075	21.8	16.9	43.8	41.5
18 to 24 years old	4,538	3,157	1,068	1,042	18.0	15.7	29.0	30.2
25 to 34 years old	5,463	3,686	1,347	1,333	13.2	10.9	24.7	25.6
35 to 44 years old	4,467	3,022	1,135	889	10.6	8.6	21.9	23.0
45 to 54 years old	2,381	1,675	537	438	7.8	6.4	16.8	19.3
55 to 59 years old	1,129	827	239	170	10.4	8.9	21.2	23.2
60 to 64 years old	1,129	819	264	146	11.4	9.4	28.0	22.0
65 years old and over . . .	3,663	2,846	700	323	11.7	10.2	27.4	22.6
65 to 74 years old	1,842	1,370	401	214	10.1	8.5	26.0	22.3
75 years old and over .	1,821	1,476	299	109	13.9	12.5	29.4	23.2
Northeast	6,597	4,487	1,705	1,388	12.9	10.3	29.7	35.6
Midwest	7,965	5,438	2,221	423	13.0	10.1	35.2	24.1
South	14,729	8,614	5,575	2,719	16.1	12.2	30.1	30.2
West	8,768	6,840	694	3,886	15.3	14.1	25.0	30.4

[1] Includes other races not shown separately.   [2] Persons of Hispanic origin may be of any race.

Source: U.S. Bureau of the Census, *Current Population Reports*, P60-189; and unpublished data.

No. 734. Persons 65 Years Old and Over Below Poverty Level: 1970 to 1994

[Persons as of **March of following year**]

CHARACTERISTIC	NUMBER BELOW POVERTY LEVEL (1,000)					PERCENT BELOW POVERTY LEVEL				
	1970	1979 [1]	1990 [2]	1993	1994	1970	1979 [1]	1990 [2]	1993	1994
Total [3]	4,793	3,682	3,658	3,755	3,663	24.6	15.2	12.2	12.2	11.7
White	4,011	2,911	2,707	2,939	2,846	22.6	13.3	10.1	10.7	10.2
Black	683	740	860	702	700	48.0	36.2	33.8	28.0	27.4
Hispanic [4]	(NA)	154	245	297	323	(NA)	26.8	22.5	21.4	22.6
In families	2,013	1,380	1,172	1,343	1,254	14.8	8.4	5.8	6.5	6.0
Unrelated individuals	2,779	2,299	2,479	2,412	2,409	47.2	29.4	24.7	24.1	23.1

NA Not available.   [1] Population controls based on 1980 census; see text, section 14.   [2] Beginning 1987, data based on revised processing procedures and not directly comparable with prior years.   [3] Beginning 1979, includes members of unrelated subfamilies not shown separately. For earlier years, unrelated subfamily members are included in the "In families" category.   [4] Persons of Hispanic origin may be of any race.

Source: U.S. Bureau of the Census, *Current Population Reports*, P60-189; and earlier reports.

No. 735. Persons Below Poverty Level, by State: 1980 to 1994

[Based on the Current Population Survey; see text, sections 1 and 14, and Appendix III. The CPS is designed to collect reliable data on income primarily at the national level and secondarily at the regional level. When the income data are tabulated by State, the estimates are considered less reliable and, therefore, particular caution should be used when trying to interpret the results; for additional detail, see source]

STATE	NUMBER BELOW POVERTY LEVEL (1,000)					PERCENT BELOW POVERTY LEVEL				
	1980	1990 [1]	1992	1993	1994	1980	1990 [1]	1992	1993	1994
United States.	29,272	33,585	36,880	39,265	38,059	13.0	13.5	14.5	15.1	14.5
Alabama	810	779	715	725	704	21.2	19.2	17.1	17.4	16.4
Alaska.	36	57	53	52	61	9.6	11.4	10.0	9.1	10.2
Arizona	354	484	554	615	673	12.8	13.7	15.1	15.4	15.9
Arkansas	484	472	424	484	369	21.5	19.6	17.4	20.0	15.3
California.	2,619	4,128	4,925	5,803	5,658	11.0	13.9	15.8	18.2	17.9
Colorado	247	461	353	354	335	8.6	13.7	10.6	9.9	9.0
Connecticut	255	196	303	277	344	8.3	6.0	9.4	8.5	10.8
Delaware.	68	48	55	73	57	11.8	6.9	7.6	10.2	8.3
District of Columbia	131	120	108	158	129	20.9	21.1	20.3	26.4	21.2
Florida	1,692	1,896	2,097	2,507	2,128	16.7	14.4	15.3	17.8	14.9
Georgia	727	1,001	1,151	919	1,012	13.9	15.8	17.8	13.5	14.0
Hawaii.	81	121	129	91	97	8.5	11.0	11.0	8.0	8.7
Idaho	138	157	160	150	137	14.7	14.9	15.0	13.1	12.0
Illinois	1,386	1,606	1,836	1,600	1,464	12.3	13.7	15.3	13.6	12.4
Indiana	645	714	660	704	816	11.8	13.0	11.7	12.2	13.7
Iowa	311	289	327	290	302	10.8	10.4	11.3	10.3	10.7
Kansas	215	259	277	327	375	9.4	10.3	11.0	13.1	14.9
Kentucky	701	628	723	763	710	19.3	17.3	19.7	20.4	18.5
Louisiana.	868	952	1,020	1,119	1,117	20.3	23.6	24.2	26.4	25.7
Maine	158	162	170	196	113	14.6	13.1	13.4	15.4	9.4
Maryland	389	468	568	479	541	9.5	9.9	11.6	9.7	10.7
Massachusetts	542	626	580	641	585	9.5	10.7	10.0	10.7	9.7
Michigan	1,194	1,315	1,254	1,475	1,347	12.9	14.3	13.5	15.4	14.1
Minnesota	342	524	554	506	523	8.7	12.0	12.8	11.6	11.7
Mississippi	591	684	660	639	515	24.3	25.7	24.5	24.7	19.9
Missouri	625	700	797	832	797	13.0	13.4	15.6	16.1	15.6
Montana	102	134	113	127	97	13.2	16.3	13.7	14.9	11.5
Nebraska.	199	167	169	169	146	13.0	10.3	10.3	10.3	8.8
Nevada.	70	119	188	141	168	8.3	9.8	14.4	9.8	11.1
New Hampshire	63	68	99	112	87	7.0	6.3	8.6	9.9	7.7
New Jersey	659	711	771	866	730	9.0	9.2	10.0	10.9	9.2
New Mexico	268	319	327	282	356	20.6	20.9	21.0	17.4	21.1
New York.	2,391	2,571	2,699	2,981	3,097	13.8	14.3	15.3	16.4	17.0
North Carolina	877	829	1,047	966	980	15.0	13.0	15.7	14.4	14.2
North Dakota	99	87	73	70	65	15.5	13.7	11.9	11.2	10.4
Ohio	1,046	1,256	1,381	1,461	1,571	9.8	11.5	12.4	13.0	14.1
Oklahoma	406	481	600	662	540	13.9	15.6	18.4	19.9	16.7
Oregon	309	267	340	363	373	11.5	9.2	11.3	11.8	11.8
Pennsylvania	1,142	1,328	1,426	1,598	1,496	9.8	11.0	11.7	13.2	12.5
Rhode Island	97	71	116	108	99	10.7	7.5	12.0	11.2	10.3
South Carolina	534	548	687	678	501	16.8	16.2	18.9	18.7	13.8
South Dakota	127	93	105	102	107	18.8	13.3	14.8	14.2	14.5
Tennessee.	884	833	849	998	779	19.6	16.9	17.0	19.6	14.6
Texas	2,247	2,684	3,079	3,177	3,603	15.7	15.9	17.8	17.4	19.1
Utah	148	143	162	203	154	10.0	8.2	9.3	10.7	8.0
Vermont	62	61	63	59	45	12.0	10.9	10.4	10.0	7.6
Virginia	647	705	584	627	710	12.4	11.1	9.4	9.7	10.7
Washington	538	434	555	634	614	12.7	8.9	11.0	12.1	11.7
West Virginia	297	328	396	400	336	15.2	18.1	22.3	22.2	18.6
Wisconsin	403	448	551	636	453	8.5	9.3	10.8	12.6	9.0
Wyoming	49	51	49	64	45	10.4	11.0	10.3	13.3	9.3

[1] Beginning 1990, data based on revised processing procedures and not directly comparable with prior years.

Source: U.S. Bureau of the Census, Current Population Reports, P60-189.

No. 736. Persons Below Poverty Level, by Race and Family Status: 1979 to 1994

[Persons as of **March of following year.** Based on Current Population Survey; see text, sections 1 and 14, and Appendix III]

RACE AND FAMILY STATUS	NUMBER BELOW POVERTY LEVEL (mil.)					PERCENT BELOW POVERTY LEVEL				
	1979 [1]	1990 [2]	1992[3]	1993	1994	1979 [1]	1990 [2]	1992[3]	1993	1994
All persons [4]	**26.1**	**33.6**	**38.0**	**39.3**	**38.1**	**11.7**	**13.5**	**14.8**	**15.1**	**14.5**
In families	20.0	25.2	29.0	30.0	29.0	10.2	12.0	13.3	13.6	13.1
Householder.	5.5	7.1	8.1	8.4	8.1	9.2	10.7	11.9	12.3	11.6
Related children under 18 years .	10.0	12.7	14.5	15.0	14.6	16.0	19.9	21.6	22.0	21.2
Unrelated individuals	5.7	7.4	8.1	8.4	8.3	21.9	20.7	21.9	22.1	21.5
Male	2.0	2.9	3.2	3.3	3.3	16.9	16.9	18.2	18.1	17.8
Female	3.8	4.6	4.9	5.1	5.0	26.0	24.0	25.3	25.7	24.9
White [4]	**17.2**	**22.3**	**25.3**	**26.2**	**25.4**	**9.0**	**10.7**	**11.9**	**12.2**	**11.7**
In families	12.5	15.9	18.3	19.0	18.5	7.4	9.0	10.1	10.5	10.1
Householder.	3.6	4.6	5.3	5.5	5.3	6.9	8.1	9.1	9.4	9.1
Related children under 18 years .	5.9	7.7	8.8	9.1	8.8	11.4	15.1	16.5	17.0	16.3
Unrelated individuals	4.5	5.7	6.1	6.4	6.3	19.7	18.6	19.7	20.1	19.3
Black [4].	**8.1**	**9.8**	**10.8**	**10.9**	**10.2**	**31.0**	**31.9**	**33.4**	**33.1**	**30.6**
In families	6.8	8.2	9.1	9.2	8.4	30.0	31.0	32.9	32.9	29.6
Householder.	1.7	2.2	2.5	2.5	2.2	27.8	29.3	31.1	31.3	27.3
Related children under 18 years .	3.7	4.4	5.0	5.0	4.8	40.8	44.2	46.3	45.9	43.3
Unrelated individuals	1.2	1.5	1.6	1.5	1.6	37.3	35.1	35.6	33.4	34.8
In families with female										
householder, no spouse present. .	9.4	12.6	14.2	14.6	14.4	34.9	37.2	39.0	38.7	38.6
Householder.	2.6	3.8	4.3	4.4	4.2	30.4	33.4	35.4	35.6	34.6
Related children under 18 years .	5.6	7.4	8.4	8.5	8.4	48.6	53.4	54.6	53.7	52.9

[1] Population controls based on 1980 census; see text, section 14.   [2] Beginning 1987, data based on revised processing procedures and not directly comparable with prior years.   [3] Beginning 1992, based on 1990 population controls.   [4] Includes other races and members of unrelated subfamilies not shown separately.

Source: U.S. Bureau of the Census, *Current Population Reports,* P60-189; and unpublished data.

No. 737. Monthly Measures of Poverty Status, by Selected Characteristics: 1991-92 Period

[**In thousands, except percent.** Covers two-year calendar period. Based on Survey of Income and Program Participation, see text, section 14]

CHARACTERISTIC	PERSONS POOR IN AN AVERAGE MONTH OF 1991		PERSONS POOR 2 OR MORE MONTHS OF 1991		PERSONS POOR ALL 24 MONTHS OF 1991-92		Median duration of poverty spells (months)
	Number (1,000)	Percent	Number (1,000)	Percent	Number (1,000)	Percent	
Total [1]	**36,116**	**14.5**	**52,761**	**21.3**	**12,465**	**5.1**	**4.2**
Under 18 years old	14,668	22.2	20,427	30.6	5,842	8.7	4.8
18 to 64 years old	18,345	12.0	28,472	18.7	5,076	3.4	4.0
65 years old and over	3,103	10.2	3,862	13.6	1,547	5.8	5.9
White	24,671	11.8	37,351	18.1	6,960	3.4	4.0
Black	9,620	30.9	12,556	40.7	4,855	16.1	5.4
Hispanic origin [2]	6,476	29.8	9,361	40.9	2,723	12.2	5.6
Region: [3]							
Northeast.	6,953	13.6	10,144	20.0	2,587	5.1	4.0
Midwest.	7,428	11.7	10,850	17.1	2,185	3.4	3.9
South	14,074	17.3	20,287	25.2	5,672	7.2	4.9
West	7,662	14.3	11,480	21.8	2,022	4.0	4.0
Educational attainment: [4]							
Less than 4 years of high school	9,268	23.0	12,307	32.3	3,810	10.4	5.9
High school graduate, no college	7,280	10.6	11,495	16.6	1,969	2.9	4.0
One or more years of college	4,900	6.6	8,531	11.7	844	1.2	3.6
Disability status: [5]							
With a work disability	5,836	20.8	7,904	29.8	2,301	9.2	4.8
With no work disability	15,037	10.3	24,296	16.7	3,760	2.6	3.9

[1] Includes other characteristics not shown separately.   [2] Persons of Hispanic origin may be of any race.   [3] For compostion of regions, see table 27.   [4] Persons 18 years old and over.   [5] Persons 15 to 69 years old.

Source: U.S. Bureau of the Census, *Current Population Reports,* P70-45. Report revised after publication.

No. 738. Families Below Poverty Level and Below 125 Percent of Poverty Level: 1960 to 1994

[Families as of **March of the following year.** Based on Current Population Survey, see text, sections 1 and 14, and Appendix III]

YEAR	NUMBER BELOW POVERTY LEVEL (1,000)				PERCENT BELOW POVERTY LEVEL				BELOW 125 PERCENT OF POVERTY LEVEL	
	All races [1]	White	Black	His-panic [2]	All races [1]	White	Black	His-panic [2]	Number (1,000)	Percent
1960	8,243	6,115	(NA)	(NA)	18.1	14.9	(NA)	(NA)	11,525	25.4
1970	5,260	3,708	1,481	(NA)	10.1	8.0	29.5	(NA)	7,516	14.4
1971	5,303	3,751	1,484	(NA)	10.0	7.9	28.8	(NA)	(NA)	(NA)
1972	5,075	3,441	1,529	477	9.3	7.1	29.0	20.6	7,347	13.5
1973	4,828	3,219	1,527	468	8.8	6.6	28.1	19.8	7,044	12.8
1974	4,922	3,352	1,479	526	8.8	6.8	26.9	21.2	7,195	12.9
1975	5,450	3,838	1,513	627	9.7	7.7	27.1	25.1	7,974	14.2
1976	5,311	3,560	1,617	598	9.4	7.1	27.9	23.1	7,647	13.5
1977	5,311	3,540	1,637	591	9.3	7.0	28.2	21.4	7,713	13.5
1978	5,280	3,523	1,622	559	9.1	6.9	27.5	20.4	7,417	12.8
1979 [3]	5,461	3,581	1,722	614	9.2	6.9	27.8	20.3	7,784	13.1
1980	6,217	4,195	1,826	751	10.3	8.0	28.9	23.2	8,764	14.5
1981	6,851	4,670	1,972	792	11.2	8.8	30.8	24.0	9,568	15.7
1982	7,512	5,118	2,158	916	12.2	9.6	33.0	27.2	10,279	16.7
1983 [4]	7,647	5,220	2,161	981	12.3	9.7	32.3	25.9	10,358	16.7
1984	7,277	4,925	2,094	991	11.6	9.1	30.9	25.2	9,901	15.8
1985	7,223	4,983	1,983	1,074	11.4	9.1	28.7	25.5	9,753	15.3
1986	7,023	4,811	1,987	1,085	10.9	8.6	28.0	24.7	9,476	14.7
1987 [5]	7,005	4,567	2,117	1,168	10.7	8.1	29.4	25.5	9,338	14.3
1988	6,874	4,471	2,089	1,141	10.4	7.9	28.2	23.7	9,284	14.1
1989	6,784	4,409	2,077	1,133	10.3	7.8	27.8	23.4	9,267	14.0
1990	7,098	4,622	2,193	1,244	10.7	8.1	29.3	25.0	9,564	14.4
1991	7,712	5,022	2,343	1,372	11.5	8.8	30.4	26.5	10,244	15.3
1992 [6]	8,144	5,255	2,484	1,529	11.9	9.1	31.1	26.7	10,959	16.1
1993	8,393	5,452	2,499	1,625	12.3	9.4	31.3	27.3	11,203	16.4
1994	8,053	5,312	2,212	1,724	11.6	9.1	27.3	27.8	10,771	15.5

NA Not available.   [1] Includes other races not shown separately.   [2] Persons of Hispanic origin may be of any race.
[3] Population controls based on 1980 census; see text, section 14.   [4] Beginning 1983, data based on revised Hispanic population controls and not directly comparable with prior years.   [5] Beginning 1987, data based on revised processing procedures and not directly comparable with prior years.   [6] Beginning 1992, based on 1990 population controls.

Source: U.S. Bureau of the Census, *Current Population Reports*, P60-189.

No. 739. Families Below Poverty Level, by Selected Characteristics: 1994

[Families as of **March 1995.** Based on Current Population Survey; see text, sections 1 and 14, and Appendix III. For composition of regions, see table 27]

CHARACTERISTIC	NUMBER BELOW POVERTY LEVEL (1,000)				PERCENT BELOW POVERTY LEVEL			
	All races [1]	White	Black	His-panic [2]	All races [1]	White	Black	His-panic [2]
Total	8,053	5,312	2,212	1,724	11.6	9.1	27.3	27.8
Education of householder: [3]								
No high school diploma	2,936	1,901	770	1,042	24.8	20.6	40.1	38.0
High school diploma, no college	2,326	1,534	700	290	10.9	8.5	26.0	20.7
Some college, less than Bachelor's	1,305	888	351	132	7.8	6.2	17.7	12.8
Bachelor's degree or more	414	310	46	32	2.6	2.1	5.1	6.4
Work experience of householder:								
Total [4]	7,317	4,776	2,054	1,642	12.6	9.9	28.7	28.9
Worked during year	3,936	2,759	920	926	7.8	6.5	16.8	20.3
Year-round, full-time	1,367	997	262	390	3.6	3.0	6.6	12.2
Not year-round, full-time	2,569	1,762	658	535	21.7	18.0	43.2	39.1
Did not work	3,381	2,017	1,134	716	42.9	34.8	67.3	63.1

[1] Includes other races not shown separately.   [2] Hispanic persons may be of any race.   [3] Householder 25 years old and over.   [4] Persons 16 years old and over.

Source: U.S. Bureau of the Census, *Current Population Reports*, P60-189; and unpublished data.

No. 740. Persons Below Poverty Level, by Definition of Income: 1994

[Persons as of **March 1995**. For explanation of income definitions, see text, section 14]

Defi- nition num- ber	DEFINITION	NUMBER BELOW POVERTY LEVEL (1,000)				PERCENT BELOW POVERTY LEVEL			
		All races [1]	White	Black	His- panic [2]	All races [1]	White	Black	His- panic [2]
	All persons.....................	261,616	216,460	33,353	27,442	(X)	(X)	(X)	(X)
	INCOME BEFORE TAXES								
1	Money income excluding capital gains [3].....	34,443	22,751	9,461	7,674	13.2	10.5	28.4	28.0
2	Definition 1 less government money transfers.	56,416	40,950	12,506	9,533	21.6	18.9	37.5	34.7
3	Definition 2 plus capital gains...........	56,231	40,822	12,483	9,519	21.5	18.9	37.4	34.7
4	Definition 3 plus health insurance supplements to wage or salary income [4]...	54,462	39,515	12,136	9,071	20.8	18.3	36.4	33.1
	INCOME AFTER TAXES								
5	Definition 4 less Social Security payroll taxes.	56,574	41,223	12,387	9,631	21.6	19.0	37.1	35.1
6	Definition 5 less Federal income taxes (excluding EITC) [5]..............	56,892	41,440	12,451	9,727	21.7	19.1	37.3	35.4
7	Definition 6 plus EITC [5].............	53,969	39,315	11,877	8,926	20.6	18.2	35.6	32.5
8	Definition 7 less State income taxes.......	54,278	39,578	11,911	8,954	20.7	18.3	35.7	32.6
9	Definition 8 plus nonmeans-tested government cash transfers [6]..........	35,930	23,689	9,893	7,690	13.7	10.9	29.7	28.0
10	Definition 9 plus value of Medicare........	35,208	23,172	9,720	7,582	13.5	10.7	29.1	27.6
11	Definition 10 plus value of regular- price school lunches.................	35,195	23,161	9,718	7,582	13.5	10.7	29.1	27.6
12	Definition 11 plus means-tested government cash transfers [7]..........	31,799	20,982	8,791	6,950	12.2	9.7	26.4	25.3
13	Definition 12 plus value of Medicaid.......	29,765	19,623	8,240	6,330	11.4	9.1	24.7	23.1
14	Definition 13 plus means-tested government noncash transfers [8].................	25,577	17,227	6,680	5,490	9.8	8.0	20.0	20.0
15	Definition 14 plus net imputed return on equity in own home [9]...............	23,025	15,247	6,203	5,194	8.8	7.0	18.6	18.9

X Not applicable. [1] Includes other races not shown separately. [2] Persons of Hispanic origin may be of any race. [3] Official definition based on income before taxes and includes government cash transfers. [4] Employer contributions to the health insurance plans of employees. [5] Earned Income Tax Credit. [6] Includes Social Security and Railroad Retirement, veterans payments, unemployment and workers' compensation, Black Lung payments, Pell Grants, and other government educational assistance. [7] Includes AFDC and other public assistance or welfare payments, Supplemental Security Income, and veterans payments. Households must meet certain eligibility requirements in order to qualify for these benefits. [8] Includes Medicaid, food stamps, subsidies from free or reduced-price school lunches, and rent subsidies. [9] Estimated amount of income a household would receive if it chose to shift amount held as home equity into an interest bearing account.
Source: U.S. Bureau of the Census, *Current Population Reports*, P60-189.

No. 741. Nonfinancial Assets Held by Families, by Type of Asset: 1989 and 1992

[**Median value in thousands of constant 1992 dollars**. Constant dollar figures are based on consumer price index data published by U.S. Bureau of Labor Statistics. Families include one-person units; for definition of family, see text, section 1. Based on Survey of Consumer Finance; see Appendix III. For data on financial assets, see table 773. For definition of median, see Guide to Tabular Presentation]

AGE OF FAMILY HEAD AND FAMILY INCOME	Total	Vehicles	Primary residence	Investment real estate	Business	Other nonfinancial
PERCENT OF FAMILIES OWNING ASSET						
1989, total	89.1	83.6	63.8	20.0	13.2	11.9
1992, total	**91.3**	**86.4**	**63.8**	**20.0**	**14.9**	**8.5**
Under 35 years old.........	86.7	84.8	37.0	8.4	11.3	8.1
35 to 44 years old..........	93.0	89.3	64.1	17.1	20.1	9.3
45 to 54 years old..........	94.5	92.5	75.5	26.6	18.9	10.1
55 to 64 years old..........	93.1	87.2	77.9	35.8	19.2	6.7
65 to 74 years old..........	92.0	86.3	78.9	26.7	11.3	7.9
75 years old and over.......	90.7	72.4	76.7	16.6	4.1	8.4
Less than $10,000..........	67.8	55.8	38.8	5.9	3.6	5.0
$10,000 to $24,999..........	92.2	88.2	54.2	12.3	8.4	5.7
$25,000 to $49,999..........	97.5	93.9	68.8	20.3	14.1	8.2
$50,000 to $99,999..........	99.1	96.9	84.2	30.6	23.6	11.3
$100,000 and more.........	100.0	96.8	87.6	54.2	46.4	21.6
MEDIAN VALUE [1]						
1989, total	74.5	7.7	78.2	48.0	50.3	7.8
1992, total	**69.5**	**6.9**	**81.8**	**50.0**	**50.0**	**7.2**
Under 35 years old.........	16.6	5.9	69.0	40.0	19.3	3.5
35 to 44 years old..........	82.3	7.6	90.0	38.5	45.0	8.5
45 to 54 years old..........	101.5	8.6	95.0	70.0	100.3	11.3
55 to 64 years old..........	114.2	8.3	85.0	55.0	92.0	10.4
65 to 74 years old..........	79.0	5.6	70.0	60.0	80.0	11.0
75 years old and over.......	70.3	4.5	70.0	52.0	80.0	5.0
Less than $10,000..........	20.6	2.4	40.0	33.0	29.0	1.5
$10,000 to $24,999..........	34.3	4.3	50.0	21.0	20.0	5.0
$25,000 to $49,999..........	71.5	8.1	75.0	45.0	55.5	5.0
$50,000 to $99,999..........	140.3	11.0	115.0	65.0	25.0	12.0
$100,000 and more.........	442.3	14.9	225.0	160.0	260.0	20.0

[1] Median value of financial asset for families holding such assets.
Source: Board of Governors of the Federal Reserve System, *Federal Reserve Bulletin*, October 1994.

No. 742. Household and Nonprofit Organization Sector Balance Sheet: 1980 to 1993

[In billions of dollars. **As of December 31**. For details of financial assets and liabilities, see table 771]

ITEM	1980	1985	1986	1987	1988	1989	1990	1991	1992	1993
Assets	11,109	16,271	17,781	19,036	20,448	22,510	22,797	24,820	26,022	27,511
Tangible assets	4,703	6,603	7,100	7,656	8,103	8,709	8,775	9,286	9,557	9,973
Reproducible assets	3,339	4,392	4,758	5,157	5,409	5,774	6,107	6,358	6,662	7,067
Residential structures.	2,109	2,693	2,903	3,148	3,223	3,440	3,633	3,777	3,975	4,239
Owner-occupied housing.	2,062	2,634	2,841	3,082	3,157	3,370	3,560	3,704	3,902	4,164
Nonprofit institutions. . . .	47	58	62	66	67	70	73	73	73	75
Nonprofit plant & equipment	216	308	328	350	377	404	427	443	464	493
Consumer durable goods . .	1,014	1,391	1,527	1,660	1,808	1,930	2,047	2,139	2,222	2,336
Land	1,364	2,211	2,343	2,499	2,694	2,935	2,668	2,928	2,895	2,906
Owner-occupied [1]	1,227	2,016	2,138	2,287	2,463	2,688	2,456	2,780	2,807	2,836
Nonprofit institutions	137	195	205	211	231	247	212	148	88	70
Financial assets.	6,406	9,668	10,680	11,380	12,346	13,802	14,023	15,534	16,465	17,538
Liabilities	1,443	2,333	2,602	2,859	3,174	3,496	3,738	3,920	4,143	4,464
Home mortgages	905	1,379	1,574	1,795	2,023	2,253	2,455	2,614	2,788	2,970
Net worth	**9,666**	**13,938**	**15,178**	**16,177**	**17,274**	**19,014**	**19,059**	**20,900**	**21,879**	**23,047**
Memo:										
Owner-occupied real estate [2] . . .	3,289	4,650	4,978	5,369	5,620	6,059	6,016	6,484	6,709	7,000
Home mortgages as percent of owner-occupied real estate. .	28	30	32	33	36	37	41	40	42	42

[1] Includes vacant land.   [2] Owner-occupied housing plus owner-occupied land.

Source: Board of Governors of the Federal Reserve System, *Balance Sheets for the U.S. Economy.*

No. 743. Gross and Net Stock of Fixed Reproducible Tangible Wealth: 1970 to 1994

[In billions of dollars. **As of December 31**]

ITEM	1970	1980	1985	1987	1988	1989	1990	1991	1992	1993	1994
CURRENT DOLLARS											
Gross	**4,428**	**14,306**	**19,330**	**21,774**	**22,966**	**24,361**	**25,675**	**26,645**	**27,784**	**29,270**	**30,925**
Private	2,689	9,364	12,747	14,388	15,078	16,022	16,871	17,437	18,137	19,090	20,142
Nonresidential equipment.	679	2,389	3,374	3,775	4,010	4,257	4,506	4,636	4,783	4,974	5,238
Nonresidential structures.	790	2,683	3,783	4,156	4,478	4,755	4,979	5,109	5,269	5,516	5,772
Residential	1,219	4,292	5,590	6,457	6,590	7,010	7,387	7,692	8,085	8,600	9,131
Government	1,060	2,979	3,772	4,083	4,306	4,516	4,729	4,874	5,067	5,309	5,593
Equipment	274	488	695	764	814	873	952	1,017	1,085	1,132	1,200
Structures.	785	2,491	3,077	3,319	3,492	3,643	3,777	3,857	3,982	4,177	4,394
Federal	424	885	1,176	1,269	1,325	1,394	1,477	1,535	1,606	1,668	1,739
Military	276	493	678	738	776	818	881	922	977	1,015	1,060
State and local	636	2,094	2,596	2,814	2,981	3,122	3,252	3,339	3,461	3,640	3,855
Consumer durable goods . .	680	1,963	2,811	3,303	3,582	3,823	4,075	4,334	4,580	4,872	5,190
Net stock	**2,708**	**8,619**	**11,367**	**12,803**	**13,458**	**14,245**	**14,947**	**15,387**	**15,941**	**16,718**	**17,648**
Private	1,674	5,814	7,752	8,729	9,108	9,650	10,117	10,385	10,751	11,291	11,917
Government	662	1,790	2,224	2,414	2,542	2,665	2,784	2,864	2,967	3,091	3,240
Consumer durable goods . .	372	1,014	1,391	1,660	1,808	1,930	2,047	2,139	2,222	2,336	2,491
CONSTANT (1987) DOLLARS											
Gross	**12,476**	**17,469**	**20,091**	**21,400**	**22,062**	**22,717**	**23,344**	**23,883**	**24,437**	**25,096**	**25,839**
Private	8,131	11,585	13,322	14,112	14,504	14,886	15,245	15,525	15,803	16,162	16,599
Nonresidential equipment.	1,839	3,009	3,518	3,737	3,855	3,979	4,091	4,180	4,274	4,424	4,640
Nonresidential structures.	2,411	3,255	3,870	4,088	4,191	4,293	4,400	4,480	4,541	4,599	4,658
Residential	3,881	5,321	5,934	6,286	6,458	6,614	6,754	6,865	6,989	7,139	7,301
Government	3,001	3,544	3,849	4,026	4,115	4,204	4,309	4,412	4,514	4,613	4,701
Equipment	662	625	698	768	802	837	880	920	959	989	1,013
Structures.	2,339	2,918	3,152	3,259	3,313	3,429	3,492	3,492	3,556	3,623	3,688
Federal	1,141	1,122	1,204	1,266	1,293	1,319	1,352	1,382	1,411	1,432	1,444
Military	723	691	743	767	786	814	835	855	866	869	
State and local	1,860	2,421	2,645	2,760	2,822	2,885	2,957	3,029	3,104	3,181	3,257
Consumer durable goods . .	1,344	2,340	2,920	3,262	3,444	3,627	3,790	3,946	4,119	4,321	4,540
Net stock	**7,691**	**10,524**	**11,823**	**12,577**	**12,942**	**13,293**	**13,603**	**13,810**	**14,030**	**14,344**	**14,759**
Private	5,074	7,198	8,112	8,558	8,774	8,980	9,158	9,262	9,374	9,563	9,825
Government	1,884	2,123	2,269	2,380	2,430	2,482	2,539	2,595	2,646	2,690	2,726
Consumer durable goods . .	733	1,203	1,442	1,639	1,738	1,831	1,907	1,954	2,010	2,092	2,208

Source: U.S. Bureau of Economic Analysis, *Survey of Current Business,* June 1995.

Prices

This section presents indexes of producer and consumer prices, actual prices for selected commodities, and energy prices. The primary sources of these data are monthly publications of the Department of Labor, Bureau of Labor Statistics (BLS), which include *Monthly Labor Review, Consumer Price Index, Detailed Report; Producer Price Indexes;* and *U.S. Import and Export Price Indexes.* The Department of Commerce, Bureau of Economic Analysis, is the source for gross domestic product measures.

Producer price index (PPI)—This index, dating from 1890, is the oldest continuous statistical series published by BLS. It is designed to measure average changes in prices received by producers of all commodities, at all stages of processing, produced in the United States.

The index has undergone several revisions (see *Monthly Labor Review,* February 1962, April 1978, and August 1988). It is now based on approximately 3,200 commodity price series and 80,000 quotations per month. Indexes for the net output of manufacturing and mining industries have been added in recent years. Prices used in constructing the index are collected from sellers and generally apply to the first significant large volume commercial transaction for each commodity—i.e., the manufacturer's or other producer's selling price or the selling price on an organized exchange or at a central market.

The weights used in the index represent the total net selling value of commodities produced or processed in this country. Values are f.o.b. (free-on-board) production point and are exclusive of excise taxes. Effective with the release of data for January 1988, many important producer price indexes were changed to a new reference base year, 1982=100, from 1967=100. The reference year of the PPI shipment weights has been taken primarily from the 1987 Census of Manufactures. For further detail regarding the PPI, see the *BLS Handbook of Methods, Bulletin 2414,* Chapter 16.

Consumer price indexes (CPI)—The CPI is a measure of the average change in prices over time in a fixed "market

In Brief

Consumer price changes: 1994-95:

*All items index up 2.8 percent
Medical care index up 4.5 percent
Fuel oil index down -0.9 percent*

basket" of goods and services purchased either by urban wage earners and clerical workers or by all urban consumers.

In 1919, BLS began to publish complete indexes at semiannual intervals, using a weighting structure based on data collected in the expenditure survey of wage-earner and clerical-worker families in 1917-19 (BLS Bulletin 357, 1924). The first major revision of the CPI occurred in 1940, with subsequent revisions in 1953, 1964, 1978, and 1987.

Beginning with the release of data for January 1988 in February 1988, most Consumer Price Indexes shifted to a new reference base year. All indexes previously expressed on a base of 1967=100, or any other base through December 1981, have been rebased to 1982-84=100. Selection of the 1982-84 period was made to coincide with the updated expenditure weights, which are based upon data tabulated from the Consumer Expenditure Surveys for 1982, 1983, and 1984.

BLS publishes CPI's for two population groups: (1) a CPI for All Urban Consumers (CPI-U) which covers approximately 80 percent of the total population; and (2) a CPI for Urban Wage Earners and Clerical Workers (CPI-W) which covers 32 percent of the total population. The CPI-U includes, in addition to wage earners and clerical workers, groups which historically have been excluded from CPI coverage, such as professional, managerial, and technical workers, the self-employed, short-term workers, the unemployed, and retirees and others not in the labor force.

The current CPI is based on prices of food, clothing, shelter, fuels, transportation fares, charges for doctors' and dentists' services, drugs, etc., purchased for day-to-day living. Prices are collected in 85 areas across the country from over

57,000 housing units and 19,000 establishments. Area selection was based on the 1980 census. All taxes directly associated with the purchase and use of items are included in the index. Prices of food, fuels, and a few other items are obtained every month in all 85 locations. Prices of most other commodities and services are collected monthly in the five largest geographic areas and every other month in other areas.

In calculating the index, each item is assigned a weight to account for its relative importance in consumers' budgets. Price changes for the various items in each location are then averaged. Local data are then combined to obtain a U.S. city average. Separate indexes are also published for regions, area size-classes, cross-classifications of regions and size-classes, and for 29 local areas, usually consisting of the Metropolitan Statistical Area (MSA); see Appendix II. Area definitions are those established by the Office of Management and Budget in 1983. Definitions do not include revisions made since 1983. Area indexes do not measure differences in the level of prices among cities; they only measure the average change in prices for each area since the base period. For further detail regarding the CPI, see the BLS *Handbook of Methods,* Bulletin 2414, Chapter 19; the Consumer Price Index, and Report 736, the CPI: 1987 Revision. In January 1983, the method of measuring homeownership costs in the CPI-U was changed to a rental equivalence approach. This treatment calculates homeowner costs of shelter based on the implicit rent owners would pay to rent the homes they own. The rental equivalence approach was introduced into the CPI-W in 1985. The CPI-U was used to prepare the consumer prices tables in this section.

International price indexes—The BLS International Price Program produces export and import price indexes for non-military goods traded between the United States and the rest of the world. The export price index provides a measure of price change for all products sold by U.S. residents to foreign buyers. The import price index provides a measure of price change for goods purchased from other countries by U.S. residents. The reference period for the indexes is 1990=100, unless otherwise indicated.

The product universe for both the import and export indexes includes raw materials, agricultural products, semifinished manufactures, and finished manufactures, including both capital and consumer goods. Price data for these items are collected primarily by mail questionnaire. In nearly all cases, the data are collected directly from the exporter or importer, although in a few cases, prices are obtained from other sources.

To the extent possible, the data gathered refer to prices at the U.S. border for exports and at either the foreign border or the U.S. border for imports. For nearly all products, the prices refer to transactions completed during the first week of the month. Survey respondents are asked to indicate all discounts, allowances, and rebates applicable to the reported prices, so that the price used in the calculation of the indexes is the actual price for which the product was bought or sold.

In addition to general indexes for U.S. exports and imports, indexes are also published for detailed product categories of exports and imports. These categories are defined according to the five-digit level of detail for the Bureau of Economic Analysis End-Use Classification, the three-digit level of detail for the Standard International Trade Classification (SITC), and the four-digit level of detail for the Harmonized System. Aggregate import indexes by country or region of origin are also available.

Other price indexes—The *fixed-weighted price index* is a weighted average of the detailed price indexes used in the deflation of goods and services that make up the gross domestic product (GDP). These price indexes are combined using weights that reflect the composition of GDP in 1987. Because the same weights are used for each period, changes in this index measure changes in prices over any period.

Measures of inflation—Inflation is defined as a time of generally rising prices for goods and factors of production. The Bureau of Labor Statistics samples prices of items in a representative market basket and publishes the results as the CPI. The media invariably announce the inflation rate as the percent change in the CPI from month to month. A much more meaningful indicator of inflation is the percent change from the same month of the prior year.

The Producer Price Index (PPI) measures prices at the producer/manufacturing level only. The PPI shows the same general pattern of inflation as does the CPI, but is more volatile. The PPI can be roughly viewed as a leading indicator. It often tends to foreshadow trends that later occur in the CPI.

Other measures of inflation include the index of industrial materials prices; the Dow Jones Commodity Spot Price Index; Futures Price Index, the Employment Cost Index, the Hourly Compensation Index, or the Unit Labor Cost Index as a measure of

the change in cost of the labor factor of production, and changes in long-term interest rates that are often used to measure changes in the cost of the capital factor of production.

Statistical reliability—For a discussion of statistical collection and estimation, sampling procedures, and measures of statistical reliability pertaining to the producer price index and the CPI, see Appendix III.

Historical statistics—Tabular headnotes provide cross-references, where applicable, to *Historical Statistics of the United States, Colonial Times to 1970*. See Appendix IV.

No. 744. Purchasing Power of the Dollar: 1950 to 1995

[**Indexes: PPI, 1982=$1.00; CPI, 1982–84=$1.00.** Producer prices prior to 1961, and consumer prices prior to 1964, exclude Alaska and Hawaii. Producer prices based on finished goods index. Obtained by dividing the average price index for the 1982=100, PPI; 1982–84=100, CPI base periods (100.0) by the price index for a given period and expressing the result in dollars and cents. Annual figures are based on average of monthly data]

YEAR	ANNUAL AVERAGE AS MEASURED BY—		YEAR	ANNUAL AVERAGE AS MEASURED BY—		YEAR	ANNUAL AVERAGE AS MEASURED BY—	
	Producer prices	Consumer prices		Producer prices	Consumer prices		Producer prices	Consumer prices
1950	$3.546	$4.151	1966	2.841	3.080	1981	1.041	1.098
1951	3.247	3.846	1967	2.809	2.993	1982	1.000	1.035
1952	3.268	3.765	1968	2.732	2.873	1983	0.984	1.003
1953	3.300	3.735	1969	2.632	2.726	1984	0.964	0.961
1954	3.289	3.717	1970	2.545	2.574	1985	0.955	0.928
1955	3.279	3.732	1971	2.469	2.466	1986	0.969	0.913
1956	3.195	3.678	1972	2.392	2.391	1987	0.949	0.880
1957	3.077	3.549	1973	2.193	2.251	1988	0.926	0.846
1958	3.012	3.457	1974	1.901	2.029	1989	0.880	0.807
1959	3.021	3.427	1975	1.718	1.859	1990	0.839	0.766
1960	2.994	3.373	1976	1.645	1.757	1991	0.822	0.734
1961	2.994	3.340	1977	1.546	1.649	1992	0.812	0.713
1962	2.985	3.304	1978	1.433	1.532	1993	0.802	0.692
1963	2.994	3.265	1979	1.289	1.380	1994	0.797	0.675
1964	2.985	3.220	1980	1.136	1.215	1995	0.760	0.656
1965	2.933	3.166						

Source: U.S. Bureau of Labor Statistics. Monthly data in U.S. Bureau of Economic Analysis, *Survey of Current Business*.

Figure 15.1
**Annual Percent Change in Producer Price
Indexes by Stage of Processing: 1970 to 1995**

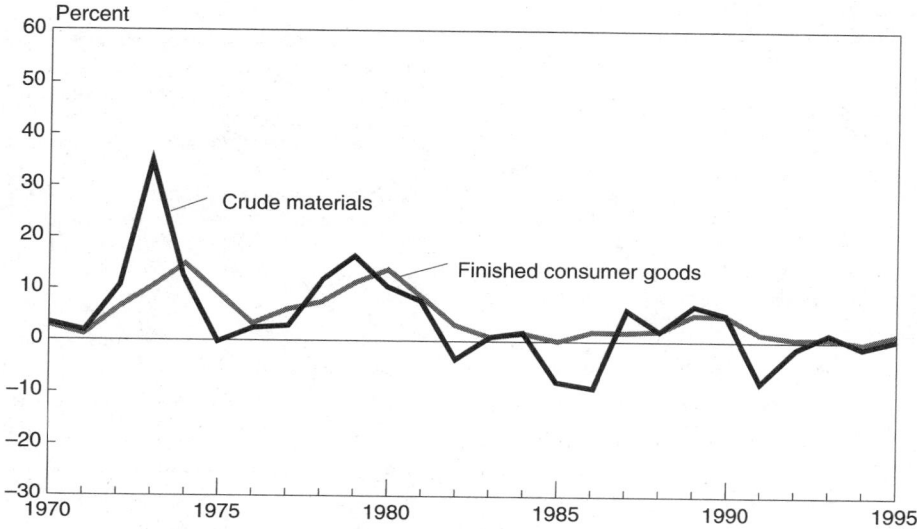

Source: Chart prepared by U.S. Bureau of the Census. For data, see table 751.

Figure 15.2
**Annual Percent Change in Consumer
Price Indexes: 1970 to 1995**

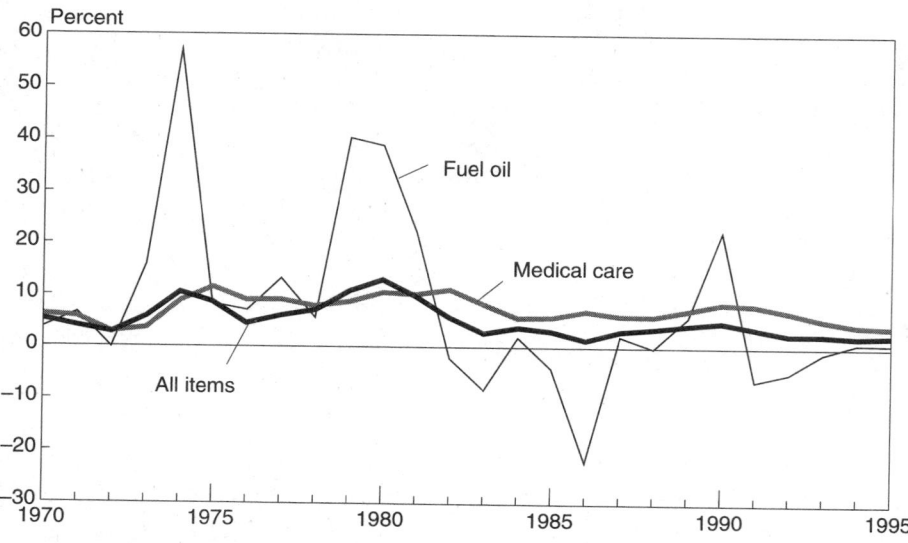

Source: Chart prepared by U.S. Bureau of the Census. For data, see table 746.

No. 745. Consumer Price Indexes (CPI-U), by Major Groups: 1939 to 1995

[1982-84=100. Represents annual averages of monthly figures. Reflects buying patterns of all urban consumers. Minus sign (-) indicates decrease. See text, section 15. See *Historical Statistics, Colonial Times to 1970*, series E 135-173 for similar data]

YEAR	All items	Com-modities	Energy	Food	Shelter	Apparel and upkeep	Trans-portation	Med-ical care	Fuel oil	Elec-tricity	Utility (piped) gas	Tele-phone serv-ices
1939	13.9	14.8	(NA)	11.8	(NA)	21.6	14.3	10.3	5.8	28.9	12.9	36.1
1940	14.0	14.9	(NA)	12.0	(NA)	21.8	14.2	10.4	6.1	28.6	12.8	36.1
1941	14.7	15.9	(NA)	13.1	(NA)	22.8	14.7	10.4	6.3	28.4	12.7	36.3
1942	16.3	18.2	(NA)	15.4	(NA)	26.7	16.0	10.7	7.2	28.3	12.6	38.3
1943	17.3	19.9	(NA)	17.1	(NA)	27.8	15.9	11.2	7.8	28.2	12.5	39.5
1944	17.6	20.1	(NA)	16.9	(NA)	29.8	15.9	11.6	7.9	28.2	12.4	40.7
1945	18.0	20.7	(NA)	17.3	(NA)	31.4	15.9	11.9	7.5	28.0	12.3	41.3
1946	19.5	22.9	(NA)	19.8	(NA)	34.4	16.7	12.5	7.6	26.9	12.1	41.3
1947	22.3	27.6	(NA)	24.1	(NA)	39.9	18.5	13.5	9.0	26.6	12.2	42.0
1948	24.1	29.6	(NA)	26.1	(NA)	42.5	20.6	14.4	11.5	26.8	12.6	44.1
1949	23.8	28.8	(NA)	25.0	(NA)	40.8	22.1	14.8	10.9	27.1	13.1	46.0
1950	24.1	29.0	(NA)	25.4	(NA)	40.3	22.7	15.1	11.0	27.2	13.2	49.5
1951	26.0	31.6	(NA)	28.2	(NA)	43.9	24.1	15.9	11.6	27.4	13.1	50.6
1952	26.5	32.0	(NA)	28.7	(NA)	43.5	25.7	16.7	11.9	27.6	13.4	52.5
1953	26.7	31.9	(NA)	28.3	22.0	43.1	26.5	17.3	12.5	28.0	13.8	54.3
1954	26.9	31.6	(NA)	28.2	22.5	43.1	26.1	17.8	12.6	28.1	14.1	53.4
1955	26.8	31.3	(NA)	27.8	22.7	42.9	25.8	18.2	13.0	28.5	14.6	52.9
1956	27.2	31.6	(NA)	28.0	23.1	43.7	26.2	18.9	13.6	28.6	14.9	53.5
1957	28.1	32.6	21.5	28.9	24.0	44.5	27.7	19.7	14.3	28.7	15.1	54.5
1958	28.9	33.3	21.5	30.2	24.5	44.6	28.6	20.6	13.5	29.1	16.0	56.1
1959	29.1	33.3	21.9	29.7	24.7	45.0	29.8	21.5	13.7	29.5	16.5	57.4
1960	29.6	33.6	22.4	30.0	25.2	45.7	29.8	22.3	13.5	29.9	17.6	58.3
1961	29.9	33.8	22.5	30.4	25.4	46.1	30.1	22.9	14.0	29.9	17.9	58.5
1962	30.2	34.1	22.6	30.6	25.8	46.3	30.8	23.5	14.0	29.9	17.9	58.5
1963	30.6	34.4	22.6	31.1	26.1	46.9	30.9	24.1	14.3	29.9	17.9	58.6
1964	31.0	34.8	22.5	31.5	26.5	47.3	31.4	24.6	14.0	29.8	17.9	58.6
1965	31.5	35.2	22.9	32.2	27.0	47.8	31.9	25.2	14.3	29.7	18.0	57.7
1966	32.4	36.1	23.3	33.8	27.8	49.0	32.3	26.3	14.7	29.7	18.1	56.5
1967	33.4	36.8	23.8	34.1	28.8	51.0	33.3	28.2	15.1	29.9	18.1	57.3
1968	34.8	38.1	24.2	35.3	30.1	53.7	34.3	29.9	15.6	30.2	18.2	57.3
1969	36.7	39.9	24.8	37.1	32.6	56.8	35.7	31.9	15.9	30.8	18.6	58.0
1970	38.8	41.7	25.5	39.2	35.5	59.2	37.5	34.0	16.5	31.8	19.6	58.7
1971	40.5	43.2	26.5	40.4	37.0	61.1	39.5	36.1	17.6	33.9	21.0	61.6
1972	41.8	44.5	27.2	42.1	38.7	62.3	39.9	37.3	17.6	35.6	22.1	65.0
1973	44.4	47.8	29.4	48.2	40.5	64.6	41.2	38.8	20.4	37.4	23.1	66.7
1974	49.3	53.5	38.1	55.1	44.4	69.4	45.8	42.4	32.2	44.1	26.0	69.5
1975	53.8	58.2	42.1	59.8	48.8	72.5	50.1	47.5	34.9	50.0	31.1	71.7
1976	56.9	60.7	45.1	61.6	51.5	75.2	55.1	52.0	37.4	53.1	36.3	74.3
1977	60.6	64.2	49.4	65.5	54.9	78.6	59.0	57.0	42.4	56.6	43.2	75.2
1978	65.2	68.8	52.5	72.0	60.5	81.4	61.7	61.8	44.9	60.9	47.5	76.0
1979	72.6	76.6	65.7	79.9	68.9	84.9	70.5	67.5	63.1	65.6	55.1	75.8
1980	82.4	86.0	86.0	86.8	81.0	90.9	83.1	74.9	87.7	75.8	65.7	77.7
1981	90.9	93.2	97.7	93.6	90.5	95.3	93.2	82.9	107.3	87.2	74.9	84.6
1982	96.5	97.0	99.2	97.4	96.9	97.8	97.0	92.5	105.0	95.8	89.8	93.2
1983	99.6	99.8	99.9	99.4	99.1	100.2	99.3	100.6	96.5	98.9	104.7	99.2
1984	103.9	103.2	100.9	103.2	104.0	102.1	103.7	106.8	98.5	105.3	105.5	107.5
1985	107.6	105.4	101.6	105.6	109.8	105.0	106.4	113.5	94.6	108.9	104.8	111.7
1986	109.6	104.4	88.2	109.0	115.8	105.9	102.3	122.0	74.1	110.4	99.7	117.2
1987	113.6	107.7	88.6	113.5	121.3	110.6	105.4	130.1	75.8	110.0	95.1	116.5
1988	118.3	111.5	89.3	118.2	127.1	115.4	108.7	138.6	75.8	111.5	94.5	116.0
1989	124.0	116.7	94.3	125.1	132.8	118.6	114.1	149.3	80.3	114.7	97.1	117.2
1990	130.7	122.8	102.1	132.4	140.0	124.1	120.5	162.8	98.6	117.4	97.3	117.7
1991	136.2	126.6	102.5	136.3	146.3	128.7	123.8	177.0	92.4	121.8	98.5	119.7
1992	140.3	129.1	103.0	137.9	151.2	131.9	126.5	190.1	88.0	124.2	100.3	120.4
1993	144.5	131.5	104.2	140.9	155.7	133.7	130.4	201.4	87.2	126.7	106.5	121.2
1994	148.2	133.8	104.6	144.3	160.5	133.4	134.3	211.0	85.6	126.7	108.5	123.1
1995	152.4	136.4	105.2	148.4	165.7	132.0	139.1	220.5	84.8	129.6	102.9	124.0

NA Not available.

Source: Bureau of Labor Statistics, *Monthly Labor Review and Handbook of Labor Statistics*, periodic.

No. 746. Consumer Price Indexes (CPI-U), Annual Percent Change by Major Groups: 1940 to 1995

[1982-84=100. Represents annual averages of monthly figures. Reflects buying patterns of all urban consumers. Minus sign (-) indicates decrease. Change from immediate prior year. See text, section 15. See *Historical Statistics, Colonial Times to 1970*, series E 135-173 for similar data]

YEAR	All items	Com-modities	Energy	Food	Shelter	Apparel and upkeep	Trans-portation	Med-ical care	Fuel oil	Elec-tricity	Utility (piped) gas	Tele-phone serv-ices
1940	0.7	0.7	(NA)	1.7	(NA)	0.9	-0.7	1.0	5.2	-1.0	-0.8	-
1941	5.0	6.7	(NA)	9.2	(NA)	4.6	3.5	-	3.3	-0.7	-0.8	0.6
1942	10.9	14.5	(NA)	17.6	(NA)	17.1	8.8	2.9	14.3	-0.4	-0.8	5.5
1943	6.1	9.3	(NA)	11.0	(NA)	4.1	-0.6	4.7	8.3	-0.4	-0.8	3.1
1944	1.7	1.0	(NA)	-1.2	(NA)	7.2	-	3.6	1.3	-	-0.8	3.0
1945	2.3	3.0	(NA)	2.4	(NA)	5.4	-	2.6	-5.1	-0.7	-0.8	1.5
1946	8.3	10.6	(NA)	14.5	(NA)	9.6	5.0	5.0	1.3	-3.9	-1.6	-
1947	14.4	20.5	(NA)	21.7	(NA)	16.0	10.8	8.0	18.4	-1.1	0.8	1.7
1948	8.1	7.2	(NA)	8.3	(NA)	6.5	11.4	6.7	27.8	0.8	3.3	5.0
1949	-1.2	-2.7	(NA)	-4.2	(NA)	-4.0	7.3	2.8	-5.2	1.1	4.0	4.3
1950	1.3	0.7	(NA)	1.6	(NA)	-1.2	2.7	2.0	0.9	0.4	0.8	7.6
1951	7.9	9.0	(NA)	11.0	(NA)	8.9	6.2	5.3	5.5	0.7	-0.8	2.2
1952	1.9	1.3	(NA)	1.8	(NA)	-0.9	6.6	5.0	2.6	0.7	2.3	3.8
1953	0.8	-0.3	(NA)	-1.4	(NA)	-0.9	3.1	3.6	5.0	1.4	3.0	3.4
1954	0.7	-0.9	(NA)	-0.4	2.3	-	-1.5	2.9	0.8	0.4	2.2	-1.7
1955	-0.4	-0.9	(NA)	-1.4	0.9	-0.5	-1.1	2.2	3.2	1.4	3.5	-0.9
1956	1.5	1.0	(NA)	0.7	1.8	1.9	1.6	3.8	4.6	0.4	2.1	1.1
1957	3.3	3.2	(NA)	3.2	3.9	1.8	5.7	4.2	5.1	0.3	1.3	1.9
1958	2.8	2.1	-	4.5	2.1	0.2	3.2	4.6	-5.6	1.4	6.0	2.9
1959	-	-	1.9	-1.7	0.8	0.9	4.2	4.4	1.5	1.4	3.1	2.3
1960	1.7	0.9	2.3	1.0	2.0	1.6	-	3.7	-1.5	1.4	6.7	1.6
1961	1.0	0.6	0.4	1.3	0.8	0.9	1.0	2.7	3.7	-	1.7	0.3
1962	1.0	0.9	0.4	0.7	1.6	0.4	2.3	2.6	-	-	-	-
1963	1.3	0.9	-	1.6	1.2	1.3	0.3	2.6	2.1	-	-	0.2
1964	1.3	1.2	-0.4	1.3	1.5	0.9	1.6	2.1	-2.1	-0.3	-	-
1965	1.6	1.1	1.8	2.2	1.9	1.1	1.6	2.4	2.1	-0.3	0.6	-1.5
1966	2.9	2.6	1.7	5.0	3.0	2.5	1.3	4.4	2.8	-	0.6	-2.1
1967	3.1	1.9	2.1	0.9	3.6	4.1	3.1	7.2	2.7	0.7	-	1.4
1968	4.2	3.5	1.7	3.5	4.5	5.3	3.0	6.0	3.3	1.0	0.6	-
1969	5.5	4.7	2.5	5.1	8.3	5.8	4.1	6.7	1.9	2.0	2.2	1.2
1970	5.7	4.5	2.8	5.7	8.9	4.2	5.0	6.6	3.8	3.2	5.4	1.2
1971	4.4	3.6	3.9	3.1	4.2	3.2	5.3	6.2	6.7	6.6	7.1	4.9
1972	3.2	3.0	2.6	4.2	4.6	2.0	1.0	3.3	-	5.0	5.2	5.5
1973	6.2	7.4	8.1	14.5	4.7	3.7	3.3	4.0	15.9	5.1	4.5	2.6
1974	11.0	11.9	29.6	14.3	9.6	7.4	11.2	9.3	57.8	17.9	12.6	4.2
1975	9.1	8.8	10.5	8.5	9.9	4.5	9.4	12.0	8.4	13.4	19.6	3.2
1976	5.8	4.3	7.1	3.0	5.5	3.7	10.0	9.5	7.2	6.2	16.7	3.6
1977	6.5	5.8	9.5	6.3	6.6	4.5	7.1	9.6	13.4	6.6	19.0	1.2
1978	7.6	7.2	6.3	9.9	10.2	3.6	4.6	8.4	5.9	7.6	10.0	1.1
1979	11.3	11.3	25.1	11.0	13.9	4.3	14.3	9.2	40.5	7.7	16.0	-0.3
1980	13.5	12.3	30.9	8.6	17.6	7.1	17.9	11.0	39.0	15.5	19.2	2.5
1981	10.3	8.4	13.6	7.8	11.7	4.8	12.2	10.7	22.3	15.0	14.0	8.9
1982	6.2	4.1	1.5	4.1	7.1	2.6	4.1	11.6	-2.1	9.9	19.9	10.2
1983	3.2	2.9	0.7	2.1	2.3	2.5	2.4	8.8	-8.1	3.2	16.6	6.4
1984	4.3	3.4	1.0	3.8	4.9	1.9	4.4	6.2	2.1	6.5	0.8	8.4
1985	3.6	2.1	0.7	2.3	5.6	2.8	2.6	6.3	-4.0	3.4	-0.7	3.9
1986	1.9	-0.9	-13.2	3.2	5.5	0.9	-3.9	7.5	-21.7	1.4	-4.9	4.9
1987	3.6	3.2	0.5	4.1	4.7	4.4	3.0	6.6	2.3	-0.4	-4.6	-0.6
1988	4.1	3.5	0.8	4.1	4.8	4.3	3.1	6.5	-	1.4	-0.6	-0.4
1989	4.8	4.7	5.6	5.8	4.5	2.8	5.0	7.7	5.9	2.9	2.8	1.0
1990	5.4	5.2	8.3	5.8	5.4	4.6	5.6	9.0	22.8	2.4	0.2	0.4
1991	4.2	3.1	0.4	2.9	4.5	3.7	2.7	8.7	-6.3	3.7	1.2	1.7
1992	3.0	2.0	0.5	1.2	3.3	2.5	2.2	7.4	-4.8	2.0	1.8	0.6
1993	3.0	1.9	1.2	2.2	3.0	1.4	3.1	5.9	-0.9	2.0	6.2	0.7
1994	2.6	1.7	0.4	2.4	3.1	-0.2	3.0	4.8	-	-	1.9	1.6
1995	2.8	1.9	0.6	2.8	3.2	-1.0	3.6	4.5	-0.9	2.3	-5.2	0.7

- Represents or rounds to zero.   NA Not available.

Source: Bureau of Labor Statistics, *Monthly Labor Review and Handbook of Labor Statistics*, periodic.

No. 747. Consumer Price Indexes for All Urban Consumers (CPI-U) for Selected Items and Groups: 1985 to 1995

[1982-84=100. Annual averages of monthly figures. See headnote, table 746]

ITEM	1985	1988	1989	1990	1991	1992	1993	1994	1995
All items	**107.6**	**118.3**	**124.0**	**130.7**	**136.2**	**140.3**	**144.5**	**148.2**	**152.4**
Food and beverages	105.6	118.2	124.9	132.1	136.8	138.7	141.6	144.9	148.9
Food	105.6	118.2	125.1	132.4	136.3	137.9	140.9	144.3	148.4
Food at home	104.3	116.6	124.2	132.3	135.8	136.8	140.1	144.1	148.8
Cereals and bakery products	107.9	122.1	132.4	140.0	145.8	151.5	156.6	163.0	167.5
Cereals and cereal products	107.2	122.5	133.8	141.1	147.5	153.3	157.9	164.8	167.1
Cereals	111.3	132.9	147.9	158.6	168.1	175.4	183.3	190.6	192.5
Rice, pasta, and cornmeal	102.1	114.4	120.0	122.0	126.5	128.3	129.7	139.7	140.2
Bakery products	108.2	121.8	131.5	139.2	144.7	150.4	155.7	161.9	167.4
White bread	105.8	118.6	129.4	136.4	139.3	146.2	152.2	159.0	165.5
Cookies, cakes, and cupcakes	110.2	125.0	134.5	142.7	151.1	155.6	159.3	165.1	169.1
Meats, poultry, fish and eggs	100.1	114.3	121.3	130.0	132.6	130.9	135.5	137.2	138.8
Meats	98.9	112.2	116.7	128.5	132.5	130.7	134.6	135.4	135.5
Beef and veal	98.2	112.1	119.3	128.8	132.4	132.3	137.1	136.0	134.9
Ground beef excl. canned	95.9	103.4	108.6	118.1	119.9	118.9	121.7	119.7	116.1
Chuck roast	95.6	108.1	116.8	130.3	135.8	137.1	141.9	140.3	138.7
Round steak	97.0	110.6	116.6	125.1	129.5	129.9	134.4	133.0	130.4
Sirloin steak	99.7	120.0	126.0	130.6	133.5	132.4	138.5	137.5	138.7
Pork	99.1	112.5	113.2	129.8	134.1	127.8	131.7	133.9	134.8
Bacon	101.3	100.9	95.8	113.4	119.8	104.6	110.8	118.1	120.0
Chops	98.7	118.8	122.7	140.2	141.7	138.9	144.6	144.2	144.2
Ham	99.8	116.5	117.3	132.4	139.9	135.6	137.9	139.3	139.6
Poultry	106.2	120.7	132.7	132.5	131.5	131.4	136.9	141.5	143.5
Fresh whole chicken	104.5	125.1	137.1	134.9	131.7	131.9	138.0	140.1	142.2
Fresh, frozen chicken parts	104.6	123.3	135.7	135.9	134.7	134.4	140.1	145.6	146.0
Fish and seafood	107.5	137.4	143.6	146.7	148.3	151.7	156.6	163.7	171.6
Canned fish and seafood	97.8	117.0	124.3	119.5	119.0	118.7	121.5	123.8	125.5
Fresh, frozen fish, seafood	112.9	144.2	155.2	161.4	163.8	168.7	174.5	183.6	194.1
Eggs	91.0	93.6	118.5	124.1	121.2	108.3	117.1	114.3	120.5
Dairy products	103.2	108.4	115.6	126.5	125.1	128.5	129.4	131.7	132.8
Fruits and vegetables	108.4	128.1	138.0	149.0	155.8	155.4	159.0	165.0	177.7
Fresh fruits and vegetables	(NA)	(NA)	(NA)	(NA)	(NA)	(NA)	(NA)	186.7	206.0
Fresh fruits	116.3	143.0	152.4	170.9	193.9	184.2	188.8	201.2	219.0
Apples	113.1	134.2	140.5	147.5	172.8	179.5	169.0	174.0	183.5
Bananas	99.9	119.2	131.3	138.2	145.0	139.9	135.5	143.6	153.8
Oranges, tangerines	119.7	144.6	147.0	160.6	249.4	176.2	190.1	189.9	224.5
Fresh vegetables	103.5	129.3	143.1	151.1	154.4	157.9	168.7	172.3	193.1
Potatoes	101.6	119.1	153.5	162.6	144.6	141.5	154.6	174.3	174.7
Lettuce	106.1	148.6	151.5	150.3	159.8	155.7	178.2	170.3	221.2
Tomatoes	103.6	123.1	136.2	160.8	153.1	171.8	168.0	173.5	188.3
Processed fruits and vegetables	(NA)	(NA)	(NA)	(NA)	(NA)	(NA)	(NA)	134.5	137.5
Processed fruits	109.5	122.0	125.9	136.9	131.8	137.7	132.3	133.1	137.2
Processed vegetables	104.4	112.2	124.2	127.5	128.5	128.8	130.8	136.6	138.3
Coffee	105.5	115.0	120.4	117.5	115.3	110.7	109.8	140.4	163.1
Food away from home	(NA)	(NA)	(NA)	(NA)	(NA)	(NA)	(NA)	145.7	149.0
Lunch	107.8	121.5	127.6	133.9	138.4	141.3	144.0	146.4	149.6
Dinner	108.8	121.6	126.9	132.3	136.3	138.9	141.3	143.8	147.1
Alcoholic beverages	106.4	118.6	123.5	129.3	142.8	147.3	149.6	151.5	153.9
Alcoholic beverages at home	105.2	114.2	117.9	123.0	137.8	141.6	142.2	142.5	143.1
Beer and ale	106.7	114.4	118.2	123.6	138.4	143.5	143.2	143.4	143.9
Distilled spirits	105.3	116.1	119.9	125.7	139.2	141.5	143.2	144.3	145.7
Wine	100.2	107.8	110.9	114.4	129.9	132.6	134.0	133.3	133.6
Alcoholic beverages away from home	111.1	130.6	137.4	144.4	156.9	162.5	167.4	171.6	176.5
Housing	107.7	118.5	123.0	128.5	133.6	137.5	141.2	144.8	148.5
Shelter	109.8	127.1	132.8	140.0	146.3	151.2	155.7	160.5	165.7
Renters' cost	115.4	133.6	138.9	146.7	155.6	160.9	165.0	169.4	174.3
Rent, residential	111.8	127.8	132.8	138.4	143.3	146.9	150.3	154.0	157.8
Tenants' insurance	109.4	124.9	128.3	130.6	133.2	136.5	140.8	145.8	150.9
Homeowners' costs	113.1	131.1	137.3	144.6	150.2	155.3	160.2	165.5	171.0
Owners' equivalent rent	113.2	131.1	137.4	144.8	150.4	155.5	160.5	165.8	171.3
Household insurance	112.4	129.0	132.6	135.3	138.4	142.2	146.9	152.3	157.4
Maintenance and repair	106.5	114.7	118.0	122.2	126.3	128.6	130.6	130.8	135.0
Fuels and other utilities	106.5	104.4	107.8	111.6	115.3	117.8	121.3	122.8	123.7
Fuels	104.5	98.0	100.9	104.5	106.7	108.1	111.2	111.7	111.5
Fuel oil and other	95.9	78.1	81.7	99.3	94.6	90.7	90.3	88.8	88.1
Fuel oil	94.6	75.8	80.3	98.6	92.4	88.0	87.2	85.6	84.8
Gas (piped) and electricity	107.1	104.6	107.5	109.3	112.6	114.8	118.5	119.2	119.2
Electricity	108.9	111.5	114.7	117.4	121.8	124.2	126.7	126.7	129.6
Utility (piped) gas	104.8	94.5	97.1	97.3	98.5	100.3	106.5	108.5	102.9
Telephone services	111.7	116.0	117.2	117.7	119.7	120.4	121.2	123.1	124.0
Local charges	120.4	141.3	146.5	149.3	153.9	155.7	156.4	156.9	160.4
Interstate toll charges	94.9	72.3	70.0	68.2	67.6	68.0	69.6	75.2	74.9
Intrastate toll charges	106.8	101.5	97.0	95.1	93.1	91.4	90.7	90.2	86.0
Water and sewerage maintenance	113.4	132.7	140.8	150.2	161.1	172.1	181.4	190.6	196.5
Cable television	110.6	132.9	144.0	158.4	175.7	186.2	198.9	197.4	200.7
Refuse collection	109.9	142.5	155.6	171.2	189.2	207.3	220.5	231.4	241.2

See footnotes at end of table.

No. 747. Consumer Price Indexes for All Urban Consumers (CPI-U) for Selected Items and Groups: 1985 to 1995—Continued

[1982-84=100. Annual averages of monthly figures. See headnote, table 745]

ITEM	1985	1988	1989	1990	1991	1992	1993	1994	1995
Household furnishings and operation	103.8	109.4	111.2	113.3	116.0	118.0	119.3	121.0	123.0
Housefurnishings.	101.7	105.1	105.5	106.7	107.5	109.0	109.5	111.0	111.2
Furniture and bedding.	104.9	113.2	113.9	115.7	116.6	120.6	123.5	128.2	130.9
Bedroom furniture.	107.4	117.7	117.6	118.5	120.1	126.8	132.5	135.1	136.4
Sofas	103.0	114.3	117.0	118.4	118.3	119.4	120.1	125.2	132.8
Living room chairs and tables	103.2	111.0	112.5	116.7	118.4	121.9	125.0	132.7	136.6
Appliances and electronic equipment . . .	95.2	90.2	89.1	87.8	86.0	84.6	83.4	82.3	80.0
Video and audio equipment	91.9	83.6	82.2	80.8	79.4	78.4	77.1	76.0	73.9
Television.	88.7	77.6	76.1	74.6	72.9	72.4	70.7	69.9	68.1
Video products other than TV	(NA)	(NA)	96.8	91.5	84.6	81.0	78.5	73.8	70.3
Audio products	94.4	92.7	92.8	93.2	94.6	94.4	93.9	93.8	92.1
Housekeeping supplies.	106.2	114.7	120.9	125.2	128.9	129.6	130.7	132.3	137.1
Housekeeping services.	106.1	114.3	117.3	120.1	127.5	132.1	135.8	138.5	143.7
Postage	108.8	121.4	125.1	125.1	143.6	145.3	145.3	145.3	160.3
Apparel and upkeep	105.0	115.4	118.6	124.1	128.7	131.9	133.7	133.4	132.0
Apparel commodities.	104.0	113.7	116.7	122.0	126.4	129.4	131.0	130.4	128.7
Apparel commodities less footwear.	104.3	114.4	117.1	122.8	127.4	130.2	131.9	131.2	129.3
Men's and boy's apparel	105.0	113.4	117.0	120.4	124.2	126.5	127.5	126.4	126.2
Women's and girl's apparel	104.9	114.9	116.4	122.6	127.6	130.4	132.6	130.9	126.9
Infants' and toddlers'.	107.2	116.4	119.1	125.8	128.9	129.3	127.1	128.1	127.2
Footwear.	102.3	109.9	114.4	117.4	120.9	125.0	125.9	126.0	125.4
Transportation	106.4	108.7	114.1	120.5	123.8	126.5	130.4	134.3	139.1
Private transportation.	106.2	107.6	112.9	118.8	121.9	124.6	127.5	131.4	136.3
New vehicles	106.1	116.5	119.2	121.4	126.0	129.2	132.7	137.6	141.0
New cars	106.1	116.9	119.2	121.0	125.3	128.4	131.5	136.0	139.0
New trucks	105.5	113.5	117.0	121.6	127.0	130.9	135.7	141.7	145.9
Used cars	113.7	118.0	120.4	117.6	118.1	123.2	133.9	141.7	156.5
Motor fuel	98.7	80.9	88.5	101.2	99.4	99.0	98.0	98.5	100.0
Automobile maintenance and repair	106.8	119.7	124.9	130.1	136.0	141.3	145.9	150.2	154.0
Automobile insurance.	119.2	156.6	166.6	177.9	191.5	205.5	216.7	224.8	234.3
Automobile finance charges.	94.5	91.3	100.5	99.6	98.0	86.1	78.6	83.8	99.0
Vehicle rental, registration, other	111.7	128.1	135.0	148.1	154.8	162.3	169.8	174.2	177.9
Public transportation	110.5	123.3	129.5	142.6	148.9	151.4	167.0	172.0	175.9
Airline fares	112.5	124.2	131.6	148.4	155.2	155.2	178.7	185.5	189.7
Other intercity transportation	114.7	132.6	138.5	143.3	149.0	152.5	150.9	152.8	153.3
Intracity transportation	107.7	121.7	125.2	133.5	138.9	146.9	150.7	152.7	157.5
Medical care	113.5	138.6	149.3	162.8	177.0	190.1	201.4	211.0	220.5
Medical care commodities	115.2	139.9	150.8	163.4	176.8	188.1	195.0	200.7	204.5
Prescription drugs	120.1	152.0	165.2	181.7	199.7	214.7	223.0	230.6	235.0
Nonprescription drugs, medical supplies . .	(NA)	108.1	114.6	120.6	126.3	131.2	135.5	138.1	140.5
Medical care services	113.2	138.3	148.9	162.7	177.1	190.5	202.9	213.4	224.2
Professional medical services	113.5	137.5	146.4	156.1	165.7	175.8	184.7	192.5	201.0
Physicians' services	113.3	139.8	150.1	160.8	170.5	181.2	191.3	199.8	208.8
Dental services	114.2	137.5	146.1	155.8	167.4	178.7	188.1	197.1	206.8
Eye care.	(NA)	108.7	112.4	117.3	121.9	127.0	130.4	133.0	137.0
Hospital and related services.	116.1	143.9	160.5	178.0	196.1	214.0	231.9	245.6	257.8
Hospital rooms	115.4	143.3	158.1	175.4	191.9	208.7	226.4	239.2	251.2
Entertainment	107.9	120.3	126.5	132.4	138.4	142.3	145.8	150.1	153.9
Entertainment commodities.	105.8	115.0	119.8	124.0	128.6	131.3	133.4	136.1	138.7
Reading materials	110.7	124.3	129.5	136.2	144.7	150.9	156.2	161.3	168.1
Newspapers	109.3	123.7	129.2	134.6	146.5	154.8	161.1	168.2	178.7
Magazines, periodicals, and books	112.1	125.0	130.0	137.9	143.3	147.4	151.8	155.1	158.4
Sporting goods, equipment	104.6	108.1	111.1	114.9	118.5	120.2	120.1	122.2	123.5
Sport vehicles, including bicycles	106.3	108.9	112.3	115.3	117.5	119.7	120.6	122.3	125.3
Toys, hobbies; other entertainment	103.3	113.2	118.5	121.5	123.9	124.7	126.0	127.4	127.8
Pet supplies and expenses	106.4	114.5	120.7	124.6	129.1	128.1	128.8	130.9	132.3
Entertainment services.	110.9	127.7	135.4	143.2	150.6	155.9	160.8	166.8	172.0
Club membership	(NA)	107.2	112.6	117.0	122.5	125.2	128.4	130.7	132.8
Admissions.	112.8	131.1	141.4	151.2	159.3	164.5	167.3	175.2	182.3
Tobacco and smoking products.	116.7	145.8	164.4	181.5	202.7	219.8	228.4	220.0	225.7
Personal care	108.3	119.4	125.0	130.4	134.9	138.3	141.5	144.6	147.1
Personal care services.	108.9	120.7	126.8	132.8	137.0	140.0	144.0	147.9	151.5
Beauty parlor services for women.	108.8	120.3	126.5	133.0	137.2	139.8	143.6	147.7	150.9
Haircuts, etc. for men.	109.0	121.7	127.3	131.5	135.9	140.3	144.6	147.9	153.4
Personal and educational expenses.	119.1	147.9	158.1	170.2	183.7	197.4	210.7	223.2	235.5
School books and supplies	118.2	148.1	158.0	171.3	180.3	190.3	197.6	205.5	214.4
Personal and educational services	119.2	148.0	158.3	170.4	184.2	198.1	211.9	224.8	237.3
Tuition and other school fees	119.7	151.0	162.7	175.7	191.4	208.5	225.3	239.8	253.8
College tuition.	119.9	150.0	161.9	175.0	192.8	213.5	233.5	249.8	264.8
Elementary and high school tuition	119.0	154.6	168.0	182.8	198.0	213.7	228.9	242.6	259.2
Day care and nursery school	(NA)	(NA)	(NA)	(NA)	103.2	108.3	113.6	119.6	124.5
All commodities	105.4	111.5	116.7	122.8	126.6	129.1	131.5	133.8	136.4
All commodities less food	105.2	107.7	112.0	117.4	121.3	124.2	126.3	127.9	129.8
Energy.	101.6	89.3	94.3	102.1	102.5	103.0	104.2	104.6	105.2

NA Not available.

Source: U.S. Bureau of Labor Statistics, *Monthly Labor Review* and *CPI Detailed Report*, January issues.

No. 748. Consumer Price Indexes (CPI-U)—Selected Areas: 1985 to 1995

[1982-84=100, except as indicated. Represents annual averages of monthly figures. Local area CPI indexes are byproducts of the national CPI program. Each local index has a smaller sample size than the national index and is therefore, subject to substantially more sampling and other measurement error. As a result, local area indexes show greater volatility than the national index, although their long- term trends are similar. Area definitions are those established by the Office of Management and Budget in 1983. For further detail see the U.S. Bureau of Labor Statistics Handbook of Methods, Bulletin 2285, Chapter 19, the Consumer Price Index, and Report 736, the CPI: 1987 Revision. See also text, section 15]

AREA	1985	1990	1991	1992	1993	1994	1995 All items	1995 Food and beverages	1995 Food	1995 Housing	1995 Apparel and upkeep	1995 Transportation	1995 Medical care	1995 Entertainment	1995 Fuel and other utilities
U.S. city average	107.6	130.7	136.2	140.3	144.5	148.2	152.4	148.9	148.4	148.5	132.0	139.1	220.5	153.9	123.7
Anchorage, AK MSA	105.8	118.6	124.0	128.2	132.2	135.0	138.5	139.1	138.2	125.0	130.7	140.7	206.3	179.1	145.3
Atlanta, GA MSA	108.9	131.7	135.9	138.5	143.4	146.7	148.7	145.0	147.1	144.2	149.3	125.9	234.3	169.5	129.1
Baltimore, MD MSA	108.2	130.8	136.4	140.1	143.1	146.9	149.7	153.7	154.6	139.7	127.5	139.5	225.4	164.1	111.8
Boston-Lawrence-Salem, MA-NH CMSA	109.4	138.9	145.0	148.6	152.9	154.9	157.4	152.1	151.9	150.0	150.7	140.1	259.9	169.9	121.0
Buffalo-Niagara Falls, NY CMSA	108.2	127.7	133.4	137.9	142.7	146.3	146.3	146.8	145.8	146.8	115.9	129.2	181.9	186.4	126.4
Chicago-Gary-Lake County, IL-IN-WI CMSA	107.7	131.7	137.0	141.1	145.4	148.6	148.4	151.6	150.4	141.4	125.1	133.5	227.0	160.1	112.8
Cincinnati-Hamilton, OH-KY-IN CMSA	106.6	126.5	131.4	134.1	137.8	142.4	143.4	138.8	137.6	134.8	135.7	137.3	220.5	143.7	115.3
Cleveland-Akron-Lorain, OH CMSA	107.8	129.0	134.2	136.8	140.3	144.4	140.2	148.4	148.7	133.3	125.2	129.8	199.2	148.4	120.6
Dallas-Fort Worth, TX CMSA	108.2	125.1	130.8	133.9	137.3	141.2	144.6	144.2	142.6	131.5	141.7	144.1	221.5	147.3	127.4
Denver-Boulder, CO CMSA	107.1	125.1	125.6	130.3	135.8	141.8	144.0	138.8	140.6	133.1	141.0	155.2	245.5	140.5	120.1
Detroit-Ann Arbor, MI CMSA	106.8	128.6	133.1	135.9	139.6	144.0	143.9	143.4	142.6	133.8	139.0	143.7	207.1	150.8	116.5
Honolulu, HI MSA	106.8	138.1	148.0	155.1	160.1	164.5	168.4	156.6	156.8	177.3	119.0	160.2	213.1	144.9	128.4
Houston-Galveston-Brazoria, TX CMSA	104.9	120.6	125.1	127.1	133.4	137.9	139.4	140.3	139.9	121.2	137.6	138.6	219.5	161.3	100.8
Kansas City, MO-KS CMSA	107.7	126.0	131.2	134.3	138.1	141.3	141.7	144.6	144.7	131.0	126.8	131.8	209.0	160.0	125.2
Los Angeles-Anaheim-Riverside, CA CMSA	108.4	135.9	141.4	146.5	150.3	152.3	149.4	153.5	151.3	146.4	126.8	138.4	218.8	142.1	148.7
Miami-Fort Lauderdale, FL CMSA	106.5	128.0	132.3	134.5	139.1	143.6	146.9	155.7	156.5	139.2	149.4	138.9	200.0	141.9	113.2
Milwaukee, WI PMSA	107.0	126.2	132.2	137.1	142.1	147.0	153.5	146.6	147.4	157.9	125.4	137.8	213.3	129.2	103.2
Minneapolis-St. Paul, MN-WI MSA	107.0	127.0	130.4	135.0	139.2	143.6	144.8	152.8	150.7	129.5	142.2	138.6	209.0	157.0	113.6
New Orleans, LA MSA [1]	(NA)	111.5	116.0	120.2	124.7	129.0	132.9	131.1	131.0	116.8	190.9	127.6	170.7	139.7	123.2
New York-Northern New Jersey-Long Island, NY-NJ-CT CMSA	108.7	138.5	144.8	150.0	154.5	158.2	158.3	155.3	155.3	158.0	121.8	146.0	227.6	158.1	111.2
Philadelphia-Wilmington-Trenton, PA-NJ-DE-MD CMSA	108.8	135.8	142.2	146.6	150.2	154.6	158.3	150.0	148.7	160.3	98.1	149.5	228.5	162.2	124.2
Pittsburgh-Beaver Valley, PA CMSA	106.9	126.2	131.3	136.0	139.9	144.6	142.9	143.4	141.8	138.5	128.9	128.5	208.6	154.6	136.7
Portland-Vancouver, OR-WA CMSA	106.7	127.4	133.9	139.8	144.7	148.9	149.9	136.4	136.0	149.4	124.3	143.0	197.0	166.7	128.1
San Diego, CA MSA	110.4	138.4	143.4	147.4	150.6	154.5	147.0	151.8	151.4	135.9	131.7	149.1	221.2	157.2	117.7
San Francisco-Oakland-San Jose, CA CMSA	108.4	132.1	137.9	142.5	146.3	148.7	149.3	151.8	152.4	151.1	120.0	132.1	206.8	154.8	145.1
Seattle-Tacoma, WA CMSA	105.6	126.8	134.1	139.0	142.9	147.8	149.3	151.0	151.2	144.5	120.4	143.1	209.1	142.4	115.2
St. Louis-East St. Louis, MO-IL CMSA	107.1	128.1	132.1	134.7	137.5	141.3	144.7	147.0	145.8	141.6	119.7	138.0	208.2	151.0	117.4
Tampa-St. Petersburg-Clearwater, FL MSA [1]	(NA)	111.7	116.4	119.2	124.0	126.5	128.0	124.8	124.5	123.5	123.3	124.6	182.6	114.9	115.6
Washington, DC-MD-VA MSA	109.0	135.6	141.2	144.7	149.3	152.2	152.7	147.4	147.6	150.4	140.7	144.0	212.0	156.7	125.5

NA Not available.   [1] 1987=100.

Source: U.S. Bureau of Labor Statistics, Monthly Labor Review and CPI Detailed Report, January issues.

No. 749. Cost of Living Index—Selected Metropolitan Areas: Third Quarter 1995

[Measures relative price levels for consumer goods and services in participating areas for a midmanagement standard of living. The nationwide average equals 100, and each index is read as a percent of the national average. The index does not measure inflation, but compares prices at a single point in time. Excludes taxes. Metropolitan areas as defined by the Office of Management and Budget. For definitions and components of MSA's, see source for details. Selection based on 1990 MSA population]

METROPOLITAN AREAS (MA)	Composite index (100%)	Grocery items (16%)	Housing (28%)	Utilities (8%)	Transportation (10%)	Health care (5%)	Misc. goods and services (33%)
Birmingham AL MSA	98.4	92.7	94.9	112.5	98.0	101.5	100.2
Decatur AL MSA: Decatur-Hartselle	92.3	95.2	80.4	99.4	99.8	83.9	98.7
Florence AL MSA	91.2	95.3	79.9	91.6	92.4	89.8	98.6
Gadsden AL MSA: Gadsden	92.5	95.6	77.1	109.7	99.0	95.3	97.5
Huntsville AL MSA: Huntsville	97.8	95.5	88.8	115.9	96.8	101.5	101.7
Mobile AL MSA: Mobile	91.5	94.7	74.8	111.3	105.6	86.5	96.3
Tuscaloosa AL MSA: Tuscaloosa	96.9	90.3	88.6	108.3	105.2	93.5	102.6
Anchorage AK MSA: Anchorage	124.8	122.1	130.9	99.9	110.4	171.3	122.4
Las Vegas NV-AZ MSA: Lake Havasu City AZ	99.1	105.9	89.0	109.6	98.6	112.6	99.4
Phoenix-Mesa AZ MSA:							
Phoenix	100.8	105.3	94.5	104.1	107.2	113.5	99.1
Scottsdale	102.7	103.7	108.9	104.0	110.1	116.9	91.9
Tucson AZ MSA: Tucson	99.8	107.9	98.6	103.2	96.8	106.2	95.6
Yuma AZ	93.3	101.6	80.2	113.9	107.7	100.1	90.1
Fayetteville-Springdale-Rogers AR MSA:							
Fayetteville	95.9	95.9	87.0	108.2	96.4	90.4	101.4
Fort Smith AR-OK MSA: Fort Smith AR	87.0	94.1	67.7	94.8	90.6	83.6	97.7
Little Rock-North Little Rock AR MSA:							
Little Rock-North Little Rock	87.3	93.2	72.0	125.3	92.7	75.3	88.8
Bakersfield CA MSA: Bakersfield	105.3	108.7	95.0	124.8	109.0	124.2	103.1
Fresno CA MSA: Fresno	108.7	112.3	105.8	104.5	108.9	124.9	107.3
Los Angeles-Long Beach CA PMSA	117.9	114.1	137.0	88.2	111.0	124.8	111.4
Riverside-San Bernardino CA PMSA:							
Palm Springs	115.5	114.6	116.1	132.4	110.1	137.9	108.8
Riverside City	108.7	107.6	110.1	98.6	111.7	125.6	106.7
San Diego CA MSA: San Diego	119.5	107.8	153.6	80.0	129.4	118.2	103.4
San Francisco CA PMSA:							
Marin County CA	155.3	111.8	259.6	98.5	114.8	148.7	113.8
San Francisco CA	174.2	128.1	307.6	96.2	122.2	177.7	115.8
San Mateo County CA	151.2	116.5	241.3	96.2	118.1	149.7	114.1
Santa Barbara-Santa Maria-Lompoc CA MSA:							
Lompoc CA	110.8	103.6	133.7	81.7	104.7	120.0	102.0
Santa Rosa CA PMSA: Santa Rosa	123.6	106.8	157.7	98.5	120.3	130.7	108.6
Visalia-Tulare-Porterville CA MSA:							
Visalia	107.3	104.9	106.1	115.6	107.1	104.2	108.2
Boulder-Longmont CO PMSA:							
Boulder	112.5	106.8	138.9	94.2	97.1	119.3	100.4
Longmont	102.4	103.9	110.0	77.0	111.9	122.5	95.1
Denver CO PMSA	104.3	101.3	115.4	93.6	104.2	122.9	95.6
Fort Collins-Loveland CO MSA: Fort Collins	109.4	104.4	130.7	90.8	101.0	114.3	99.7
Grand Junction CO MSA: Grand Junction	94.9	107.2	88.6	74.1	102.5	95.7	97.0
Provo-Orem UT MSA: Colorado Springs	99.6	100.6	108.2	75.9	94.9	117.3	95.7
Pueblo CO MSA: Pueblo	90.3	103.6	78.3	77.8	90.2	114.0	92.7
Dover DE MSA: Dover	102.8	107.5	93.1	112.6	99.1	107.7	106.6
Wilmington-Newark DE-MD PMSA: Wilmington DE	108.3	112.2	107.4	117.8	99.5	119.8	105.3
Washington DC-MD-VA-WV PMSA	124.6	117.8	154.0	106.8	132.4	120.4	105.9
Fort Walton Beach FL MSA: Fort Walton Beach	94.9	96.4	89.2	93.0	98.0	98.5	98.0
Gainesville FL MSA: Gainesville	97.0	98.0	93.3	101.1	95.8	94.5	99.4
Jacksonville FL MSA: Jacksonville	95.0	97.1	81.7	98.9	103.4	93.7	102.3
Miami FL PMSA:							
Miami/Dade County FL	110.2	101.7	111.0	100.5	105.8	124.1	114.7
Orlando FL MSA: Orlando	97.7	97.8	89.2	115.0	99.8	106.7	98.5
Panama City FL MSA	95.1	99.7	87.2	92.6	100.0	97.1	98.6
Pensacola FL MSA: Pensacola	93.8	95.8	78.3	95.5	100.6	109.0	100.9
Sarasota-Bradenton FL MSA: Sarasota	98.7	98.5	101.7	100.7	91.4	97.4	98.1
Tallahassee FL MSA: Tallahassee	100.7	99.4	101.3	105.4	102.2	100.4	99.4
Tampa-St. Petersburg-Clearwater FL MSA: Tampa	95.0	97.9	92.4	101.7	95.7	102.1	92.7
West Palm Beach-Boca Raton FL MSA:							
West Palm Beach	104.6	99.4	99.6	104.1	105.4	109.2	110.5
Albany GA MSA: Albany	91.0	94.2	75.7	100.8	98.1	89.3	98.5
Atlanta GA MSA: Atlanta	99.7	100.4	99.6	102.8	101.1	105.0	97.2
Macon GA MSA: Warner Robins	97.3	101.9	86.8	105.8	91.8	94.6	104.0
Honolulu HI MSA	182.8	164.4	309.1	139.9	145.2	136.9	113.6
Boise City ID MSA: Boise	101.7	97.7	107.5	79.0	96.6	113.8	103.4
Bloomington-Normal IL MSA: Bloomington-Normal	103.1	101.0	97.8	123.5	101.6	101.0	104.6
Champaign-Urbana IL MSA: Champaign-Urbana	102.0	100.2	96.7	111.7	104.9	110.5	102.7
Chicago IL PMSA: Joliet/Will County	107.2	103.2	111.6	112.8	118.4	104.9	101.5
Davenport-Moline-Rock Island IA-IL MSA:							
Quad Cities IL-IA	100.1	103.9	94.6	111.1	100.1	97.1	100.7
Decatur IL MSA: Decatur	92.5	104.9	79.6	108.6	97.7	90.0	96.2
Rockford IL MSA: Rockford	102.9	101.8	105.9	102.2	102.2	102.1	101.4
Springfield IL MSA: Springfield	96.3	111.4	87.3	88.8	92.9	109.0	97.1
Bloomington IN MSA: Bloomington	99.4	102.1	97.9	103.6	98.9	94.5	99.5
Elkhart-Goshen IN MSA: Elkhart-Goshen	96.8	94.8	92.1	111.0	96.2	99.6	98.0
Evansville-Henderson IN-KY MSA: Evansville IN	95.4	96.6	96.1	89.8	95.3	88.7	96.8
Fort Wayne IN MSA: Fort Wayne/Allen County	92.4	95.6	91.4	97.2	96.6	90.6	89.8

See footnote at end of table.

No. 749. Cost of Living Index—Selected Metropolitan Areas: Third Quarter 1995—Continued

[See headnote, page 488]

METROPOLITAN AREAS (MA)	Com-posite index (100%)	Gro-cery items (16%)	Hous-ing (28%)	Util-ities (8%)	Trans-por-tation (10%)	Health care (5%)	Misc. goods and services (33%)
Indianapolis IN MSA:							
Anderson	95.8	99.9	95.5	93.6	97.6	92.2	94.7
Indianapolis	95.5	99.9	90.9	93.0	97.5	95.9	97.4
Lafayette IN MSA: Lafayette	96.9	100.2	91.9	106.9	93.9	98.3	97.7
Muncie IN MSA: Muncie	99.0	101.9	106.1	91.5	101.4	88.7	94.7
South Bend IN MSA: South Bend	89.4	92.0	85.1	87.7	87.3	92.8	92.3
Terre Haute IN MSA: Terre Haute	97.3	94.9	102.5	95.7	95.9	92.9	95.5
Cedar Rapids IA MSA: Cedar Rapids	98.5	95.5	102.0	105.6	93.2	93.8	97.6
Des Moines IA MSA: Des Moines	93.0	93.5	84.7	105.3	94.6	99.0	95.4
Dubuque IA MSA: Dubuque	105.6	99.1	125.5	90.3	100.2	94.3	99.1
Waterloo-Cedar Falls IA MSA: Waterloo-Cedar Falls	98.4	92.9	107.5	80.5	94.1	88.0	100.6
Lawrence KS MSA: Lawrence	96.8	92.4	101.1	79.3	91.2	88.0	102.7
Cincinnati OH-KY-IN PMSA: Covington KY	92.2	92.8	89.3	99.6	89.9	98.3	92.1
Clarksville-Hopkinsville TN-KY MSA: Hopkinsville KY	93.6	102.5	83.6	85.6	91.5	87.6	101.3
Evansville-Henderson IN-KY MSA: Henderson KY	91.8	95.9	86.8	62.6	101.5	83.0	100.0
Lexington KY MSA	95.5	97.9	91.3	83.2	95.6	97.1	100.6
Louisville KY-IN MSA: Louisville KY	93.3	97.1	85.6	89.2	100.0	92.3	97.4
Baton Rouge LA MSA: Baton Rouge	98.2	100.8	89.5	111.5	104.7	95.9	99.6
Lafayette LA MSA: Lafayette	97.1	100.2	89.5	102.7	102.7	89.0	100.7
Lake Charles LA MSA: Lake Charles	93.7	90.0	84.9	104.4	96.7	86.8	100.9
Monroe LA MSA: Monroe	93.5	89.1	81.0	115.1	95.6	92.6	100.6
New Orleans LA MSA: New Orleans	94.4	97.4	83.1	122.6	100.8	86.1	95.4
Shreveport-Bossier City LA MSA: Shreveport-Bossier City	91.7	94.9	85.0	84.9	96.3	94.4	95.8
Baltimore MD PMSA: Baltimore	100.2	98.4	103.4	98.7	104.5	101.3	97.4
Cumberland MD-WV MSA: Cumberland MD	99.4	101.0	105.7	114.5	95.5	80.8	94.1
Hagerstown MD PMSA: Hagerstown	98.6	93.8	103.6	91.9	98.0	97.6	98.7
Boston MA-NH PMSA: Boston PMSA (MA Part)	139.2	121.1	188.6	159.9	119.3	136.7	106.9
Fitchburg-Leominster MA PMSA	102.3	109.6	90.5	119.9	101.5	110.9	103.2
Grand Rapids-Muskegon-Holland MI MSA:							
Grand Rapids MI	104.1	109.5	106.6	87.7	103.6	107.0	103.0
Holland MI	102.7	108.4	108.9	81.2	95.6	87.2	104.7
Lansing-East Lansing MI MSA: Lansing	104.5	109.2	113.9	86.4	96.9	109.6	99.7
Minneapolis-St Paul MN-WI MSA: Minneapolis MN	98.6	97.8	92.1	91.4	106.2	119.0	100.5
Rochester MN MSA: Rochester	97.6	97.7	87.1	100.1	109.4	99.3	102.4
St. Cloud MN MSA	96.8	104.0	85.9	87.0	109.3	96.6	101.5
Biloxi-Gulfport-Pascagoula MS MSA: Gulfport	93.5	93.8	84.0	97.2	95.0	101.7	98.7
Jackson MS MSA: Jackson	93.8	93.2	97.5	101.6	88.3	83.3	92.4
Columbia MO MSA: Columbia	92.5	96.7	82.6	77.9	98.6	101.8	99.0
Joplin MO MSA	88.5	91.5	82.7	81.0	83.6	97.4	93.4
Kansas City MO-KS MSA: Lee's Summit MO	96.1	98.1	89.3	100.4	95.0	106.8	98.3
St Joseph MO MSA	92.4	87.8	92.4	88.7	90.1	93.1	96.0
St Louis MO-IL MSA	97.8	102.5	94.1	110.0	91.7	108.9	95.5
Springfield MO MSA: Springfield	91.6	88.3	87.5	80.3	96.4	97.9	96.9
Billings MT MSA: Billings	102.7	103.9	107.4	74.6	113.1	101.0	102.3
Lincoln NE MSA: Lincoln	88.8	93.0	75.2	83.7	99.7	84.3	97.3
Omaha NE-IA MSA: Omaha NE	92.1	93.8	88.2	92.4	101.3	91.8	92.2
Las Vegas NV-AZ MSA: Las Vegas NV	106.4	102.2	105.9	98.3	119.5	117.5	105.2
Reno NV MSA: Reno-Sparks	111.6	101.8	125.1	96.0	108.7	119.3	108.1
Manchester NH PMSA: Manchester	109.4	99.6	119.7	134.6	103.4	108.6	101.2
Albuquerque NM MSA: Albuquerque	100.5	99.9	103.5	94.7	96.7	106.7	99.7
Las Cruces NM MSA	99.8	98.9	103.9	89.5	95.7	94.2	101.4
Santa Fe NM MSA:							
Los Alamos	116.1	111.9	147.2	81.1	114.2	118.4	100.3
Santa Fe	115.6	104.3	145.1	107.5	117.6	109.7	98.4
Albany-Schenectady-Troy NY MSA: Albany	107.5	106.2	110.7	114.8	106.5	112.5	103.1
Binghamton NY MSA: Binghamton/Broome County	104.6	107.6	97.4	127.7	105.6	93.0	105.4
Glens Falls NY MSA: Glens Falls	103.9	98.6	90.0	129.8	106.9	106.0	110.7
New York NY PMSA:							
New York (Manhattan)	221.1	142.5	424.3	144.9	126.8	195.1	135.8
Westchester County	140.7	130.5	178.1	161.4	125.1	120.3	116.9
Rochester NY MSA	107.8	116.2	107.0	128.8	111.6	88.5	101.8
Syracuse NY MSA: Syracuse	103.0	110.1	88.6	141.8	107.1	111.5	99.6
Utica-Rome NY MSA	102.9	102.6	94.8	142.0	110.6	93.2	100.1
Asheville NC MSA: Asheville	102.5	100.9	99.2	108.5	104.7	97.2	104.9
Charlotte-Gastonia-Rock Hill NC-SC MSA:							
Charlotte NC	97.5	97.6	94.6	100.1	96.4	99.1	99.3
Gastonia NC	94.0	96.6	86.4	99.5	96.9	88.7	97.9
Fayetteville NC MSA: Fayetteville	93.4	93.0	79.7	108.8	94.4	89.0	102.0
Goldsboro NC MSA: Goldsboro	100.8	100.8	93.9	107.8	92.3	104.3	106.5
Greensboro-Winston-Salem-High Point NC MSA:							
Burlington	92.9	96.1	88.7	99.1	86.6	88.8	95.9
Winston-Salem	99.4	96.0	97.0	98.9	102.3	90.5	103.9
Greenville NC MSA: Greenville	94.3	95.4	88.9	107.4	89.1	98.3	95.8
Hickory-Morganton-Lenoir NC MSA: Hickory	95.8	97.9	90.9	99.7	90.7	82.7	101.9
Raleigh-Durham-Chapel Hill NC MSA: Raleigh-Durham	97.4	93.8	98.1	109.3	92.4	101.5	96.3
Wilmington NC MSA: Wilmington	100.6	97.0	105.4	106.1	89.9	97.7	100.4
Bismarck ND MSA: Bismarck-Mandan	97.9	108.8	96.5	80.7	94.9	98.6	98.6
Fargo-Moorhead ND-MN MSA	99.5	103.6	97.1	98.2	91.4	103.4	101.4
Grand Forks ND-MN MSA: Grand Forks ND	95.6	101.9	90.4	76.8	104.6	93.3	99.6

See footnote at end of table.

No. 749. Cost of Living Index—Selected Metropolitan Areas: Third Quarter 1995—Continued

[See headnote, page 488]

METROPOLITAN AREAS (MA)	Com-posite index (100%)	Gro-cery items (16%)	Hous-ing (28%)	Util-ities (8%)	Trans-por-tation (10%)	Health care (5%)	Misc. goods and services (33%)
Akron OH PMSA: Akron	96.5	93.1	90.7	117.7	98.9	98.3	96.9
Cincinnati OH-KY-IN PMSA: Cincinnati	101.1	99.6	97.5	113.2	103.5	93.2	102.8
Cleveland-Lorain-Elyria OH PMSA: Cleveland	103.7	96.6	103.5	115.6	111.3	115.5	100.2
Columbus OH MSA: Columbus	102.5	100.5	92.9	125.3	106.2	97.7	106.0
Dayton-Springfield OH MSA: Dayton-Springfield	101.1	95.9	104.5	106.8	99.4	102.7	99.6
Mansfield OH MSA: Mansfield	96.9	94.2	93.7	119.9	95.9	88.3	97.2
Toledo OH MSA: Toledo	97.6	96.0	90.4	115.2	107.2	95.3	98.0
Youngstown-Warren OH MSA	94.5	98.0	105.1	110.3	88.0	89.8	82.7
Lawton OK MSA: Lawton	95.3	94.2	89.1	92.2	97.0	100.9	100.4
Oklahoma City OK MSA: Oklahoma City	91.9	91.1	77.2	106.3	90.3	94.9	101.1
Tulsa OK MSA: Tulsa	89.5	88.1	76.1	93.5	83.5	96.0	100.9
Eugene-Springfield OR MSA: Eugene	107.0	95.8	126.1	76.5	110.0	122.1	100.2
Portland-Vancouver OR-WA PMSA: Portland OR	109.1	99.9	124.8	74.0	108.3	125.2	105.9
Salem OR PMSA: Salem	104.0	93.7	107.1	93.0	103.2	114.2	107.3
Allentown-Bethlehem-Easton PA MSA:							
Allentown-Bethlehem-Easton	101.1	106.8	92.8	113.4	101.6	99.1	102.5
Altoona PA MSA: Altoona	98.1	100.6	99.6	107.4	93.5	89.5	96.3
Harrisburg-Lebanon-Carlisle PA MSA: Harrisburg	102.7	97.9	93.5	127.8	111.1	100.6	104.7
Lancaster PA MSA: Lancaster	104.6	99.9	98.0	124.1	113.3	92.8	107.4
Philadelphia PA-NJ PMSA: Philadelphia PA	128.6	117.2	149.2	185.5	117.9	104.8	110.2
Scranton-Wilkes Barre-Hazleton PA MSA:							
Wilkes Barre	95.5	100.0	92.2	87.5	94.2	93.1	98.9
York PA MSA:							
Hanover	97.9	94.3	103.5	85.8	99.0	82.1	100.5
York County	96.0	93.2	95.7	90.3	103.9	89.5	98.1
Charleston-North Charleston SC MSA	97.2	95.7	91.5	103.4	94.6	103.0	101.0
Charlotte-Gastonia-Rock Hill NC-SC MSA:							
Rock Hill SC	99.8	95.6	99.4	108.4	99.4	94.6	101.0
Columbia SC MSA: Columbia	93.7	95.4	87.3	98.5	89.9	91.4	98.6
Florence SC MSA: Florence	92.7	97.2	81.6	106.1	90.8	90.0	97.7
Greenville-Spartanburg-Anderson SC MSA:							
Greenville	99.6	103.2	98.3	100.2	92.2	92.5	102.0
Spartanburg	93.4	97.2	90.6	99.1	87.8	91.2	94.4
Myrtle Beach SC MSA: Myrtle Beach	98.6	95.3	98.9	95.2	95.2	96.3	102.1
Sumter SC MSA: Sumter	93.1	96.2	74.1	107.6	96.8	99.4	102.2
Rapid City SD MSA: Rapid City	101.7	101.3	105.4	105.6	100.2	94.4	99.4
Sioux Falls SD MSA: Sioux Falls	92.8	95.8	92.7	71.2	96.0	103.2	94.0
Chattanooga TN-GA MSA: Chattanooga	92.9	92.9	86.7	96.6	85.8	89.6	99.8
Clarksville-Hopkinsville TN-KY MSA: Clarksville TN	89.8	98.5	75.7	93.7	94.4	84.5	96.4
Jackson TN MSA: Jackson/Madison County TN	93.3	96.5	88.0	89.6	96.2	80.8	98.6
Johnson City-Kingsport-Bristol TN-VA MSA:							
Johnson City TN	93.9	96.0	93.4	85.7	95.7	89.9	95.5
Kingsport	91.1	94.5	82.6	80.2	104.2	87.4	96.4
Knoxville TN MSA: Knoxville	95.0	94.0	82.5	111.9	88.3	89.3	105.0
Memphis TN-AR-MS MSA: Memphis TN	93.6	100.8	85.5	95.0	102.4	96.2	93.8
Nashville TN MSA: Nashville-Franklin	91.5	97.4	80.1	90.0	95.9	93.9	96.9
Abilene TX MSA: Abilene	93.3	91.2	82.8	87.6	104.4	99.2	100.4
Amarillo TX MSA: Amarillo	89.9	93.5	85.3	76.3	99.9	90.3	92.7
Austin-San Marcos TX MSA:							
Austin TX	100.9	87.1	100.2	117.6	105.1	106.7	101.9
Georgetown TX	94.6	95.7	90.4	94.4	101.4	96.4	95.5
San Marcos TX	96.5	93.5	94.1	87.3	104.6	97.5	99.7
Beaumont-Port Arthur TX MSA: Beaumont	91.7	92.4	77.7	97.2	101.7	88.4	99.8
Brownsville-Harlingen-San Benito TX MSA: Harlingen	91.9	86.6	79.5	106.3	111.3	96.0	95.6
Bryan-College Station TX MSA:							
Bryan-College Station	89.7	88.3	84.4	92.7	90.8	89.6	93.8
Corpus Christi TX MSA	92.6	85.0	84.8	108.2	96.5	98.6	96.9
Dallas TX PMSA	100.4	96.5	90.7	125.3	106.8	107.3	101.5
Coppell TX	110.1	95.8	120.8	133.8	113.9	106.0	102.0
El Paso TX MSA: El Paso	92.0	95.2	80.1	86.4	109.0	91.5	97.5
Fort Worth-Arlington TX PMSA:							
Fort Worth	94.4	104.9	81.1	111.6	100.8	97.7	94.2
Weatherford	91.0	90.4	72.7	104.1	99.2	90.3	101.6
Houston TX PMSA	95.6	92.2	86.7	94.4	113.5	105.1	98.6
Killeen-Temple TX MSA: Killeen	93.4	93.7	85.3	110.0	93.3	96.6	95.7
Longview-Marshall TX MSA: Longview	94.2	93.4	89.9	93.8	98.6	93.8	97.1
Lubbock TX MSA: Lubbock	90.3	92.9	85.5	75.8	93.6	91.9	95.3
McAllen-Edinburg-Mission TX MSA: McAllen	93.9	90.9	83.8	109.8	97.4	88.8	99.9
Odessa-Midland TX MSA:							
Midland TX	91.1	92.1	74.0	111.1	98.1	97.3	97.2
Odessa TX	94.1	95.5	77.0	115.9	103.6	93.2	100.1
San Antonio TX MSA: San Antonio	92.1	93.4	87.5	82.9	103.5	87.0	95.3
Texarkana TX-AR MSA: Texarkana TX-AR	89.5	86.7	78.2	96.8	97.6	93.5	95.8
Tyler TX MSA: Tyler	92.9	90.3	78.5	117.4	95.9	96.4	99.0
Victoria TX MSA: Victoria	91.7	85.9	88.6	103.5	96.0	93.4	92.7
Waco TX MSA	91.3	88.6	78.0	123.2	103.9	81.7	94.4
Wichita Falls TX MSA: Wichita Falls	90.8	92.3	77.2	115.8	95.1	89.2	94.6

See footnote at end of table.

No. 749. Cost of Living Index—Selected Metropolitan Areas: Third Quarter 1995—Continued

[See headnote, page 488]

METROPOLITAN AREAS (MA)	Com-posite index (100%)	Gro-cery items (16%)	Hous-ing (28%)	Util-ities (8%)	Trans-por-tation (10%)	Health care (5%)	Misc. goods and services (33%)
Provo-Orem UT MSA: Provo-Orem	98.7	98.2	102.7	81.6	100.7	108.2	97.3
Salt Lake City-Ogden UT MSA: Salt Lake City.	95.6	94.4	92.1	94.3	98.5	103.8	97.2
Burlington VT MSA: Burlington	118.1	107.8	132.7	116.4	108.5	119.4	113.5
Johnson City-Kingsport-Bristol TN-VA MSA:							
Bristol VA	89.2	95.6	74.6	96.5	88.8	78.9	98.7
Lynchburg VA MSA: Lynchburg.	95.5	99.4	98.8	86.0	91.1	87.0	96.0
Norfolk-Virginia Beach-Newport News VA-NC MSA:							
Hampton Roads/SE Virginia	98.2	106.0	87.9	108.5	110.6	98.1	97.3
Virginia Peninsula VA	95.9	99.2	85.9	108.6	100.9	103.5	97.0
Richmond-Petersburg VA MSA: Richmond	105.0	102.6	104.7	110.8	106.3	109.3	104.0
Roanoke VA MSA: Roanoke.	91.7	98.9	88.3	87.0	91.7	89.9	92.5
Washington DC-MD-VA-WV PMSA: Prince William VA . .	110.1	102.5	122.2	117.2	108.4	112.2	102.0
Bellingham WA MSA: Bellingham	106.8	101.5	119.7	60.0	97.6	125.8	108.7
Richland-Kennewick-Pasco WA MSA:							
Richland-Kennewick-Pasco.	101.3	102.9	97.4	84.9	103.6	126.7	102.6
Spokane WA MSA	104.5	100.7	125.2	57.3	90.7	124.0	100.5
Tacoma WA PMSA: Tacoma.	101.4	101.4	100.7	68.4	106.5	137.5	101.9
Yakima WA MSA: Yakima	105.3	103.1	115.6	82.6	94.0	117.1	104.0
Charleston WV MSA.	94.3	97.5	88.5	103.0	104.3	92.6	93.0
Huntington-Ashland WV-KY-OH MSA:							
Huntington WV.	97.3	97.3	90.7	106.3	104.7	94.8	99.3
Washington DC-MD-VA-WV PMSA:							
Martinsburg/Berkeley County WV.	92.0	91.2	87.8	120.5	95.5	86.7	89.0
Appleton-Oshkosh-Neenah WI MSA:							
Appleton-Neenah-Menasha.	96.8	93.5	97.3	84.7	97.9	100.5	99.8
Oshkosh	99.0	103.3	103.2	74.5	91.5	95.3	101.9
Green Bay WI MSA: Green Bay	96.3	97.4	99.2	76.0	92.4	100.6	98.6
Janesville-Beloit WI MSA: Janesville	103.9	101.1	119.9	98.0	100.3	100.0	94.8
Milwaukee-Waukesha WI PMSA	104.3	105.5	117.8	93.3	102.6	103.6	95.5
Sheboygan WI MSA: Sheboygan	99.0	105.1	105.4	98.8	100.8	90.9	91.6
Wausau WI MSA: Wausau.	104.3	100.9	120.3	93.4	89.6	107.0	98.4
Casper WY MSA: Casper	102.2	105.6	103.6	81.5	95.2	103.5	106.0
Cheyenne WY MSA: Cheyenne	94.6	103.2	89.8	83.0	97.8	95.8	96.3

Source: ACCRA, 4232 King Street, Alexandria, VA 22302-1507, *ACCRA Cost of Living Index*, Third Quarter 1995 (copyright).

No. 750. Annual Percent Changes in Consumer Prices, United States and OECD Countries: 1975 to 1992

[Covers member countries of Organization for Economic Cooperation (OECD). For consumer price indexes for OECD countries, see section 30]

COUNTRY	1975	1980	1981	1982	1983	1984	1985	1986	1987	1988	1989	1990	1991	1992
United States	9.1	13.5	10.3	6.1	3.2	4.3	3.5	1.9	3.7	4.1	4.8	5.4	4.2	3.0
OECD	11.7	13.5	10.8	8.0	5.6	5.6	4.9	3.0	3.6	4.3	5.4	5.8	5.2	4.0
Australia	15.1	9.8	10.1	11.2	10.1	3.9	6.7	9.1	8.5	7.3	7.5	7.3	3.2	1.0
Canada	10.7	10.2	12.4	10.8	5.8	4.3	4.0	4.2	4.4	4.0	5.0	4.8	5.6	1.5
Japan	11.8	7.8	4.9	2.7	1.9	2.2	2.0	0.6	0.1	0.7	2.3	3.1	3.3	1.7
New Zealand.	14.7	17.2	15.4	16.2	7.3	6.2	15.4	13.2	15.8	6.4	5.7	6.1	2.6	1.0
Austria	8.4	6.3	6.8	5.4	3.3	5.7	3.2	1.7	1.4	1.9	2.6	3.3	3.3	4.0
Belgium	12.8	6.7	7.1	8.7	7.7	6.3	4.9	1.3	1.6	1.2	3.1	3.4	3.2	2.4
Denmark.	9.6	12.3	11.7	10.1	6.9	6.3	4.7	3.6	4.0	4.6	4.8	2.7	2.4	2.1
Finland.	17.9	11.6	12.0	9.6	8.3	7.1	5.9	2.9	4.1	5.1	6.6	6.1	4.3	2.9
France	11.8	13.6	13.4	11.8	9.6	7.4	5.8	2.7	3.1	2.7	3.6	3.4	3.2	2.4
Greece	13.6	24.7	24.5	21.0	20.2	18.5	19.3	23.0	16.4	13.5	13.7	20.4	19.5	15.9
Ireland	20.9	18.3	20.4	17.1	10.5	8.6	5.5	3.8	3.1	2.1	4.1	3.3	3.2	3.1
Italy [1]	17.2	21.1	18.7	16.3	15.0	10.6	8.6	6.1	4.6	5.0	6.6	6.1	6.5	5.3
Luxembourg	10.7	6.3	8.1	9.4	8.7	5.6	4.1	0.3	-0.1	1.4	3.4	3.7	3.1	3.2
Netherlands	10.2	6.5	6.7	5.9	2.7	3.3	2.3	0.1	-0.7	0.7	1.1	2.5	3.9	3.7
Norway.	11.7	10.9	13.7	11.3	8.4	6.3	5.7	7.2	8.7	6.7	4.6	4.1	3.4	2.3
Portugal [2]	20.4	16.6	20.0	22.4	25.5	28.8	19.6	11.8	9.4	9.7	12.6	13.4	11.4	8.9
Spain	17.0	15.6	14.5	14.4	12.2	11.3	8.8	8.8	5.2	4.8	6.8	6.7	5.9	5.9
Sweden	9.8	13.7	12.1	8.6	8.9	8.0	7.4	4.2	4.2	5.8	6.4	10.5	9.3	2.3
Switzerland	6.7	4.0	6.5	5.6	3.0	2.9	3.4	0.8	1.4	1.9	3.2	5.4	5.8	4.0
Turkey [2]	19.5	110.2	36.6	29.7	31.4	48.4	45.0	34.6	38.9	75.4	63.3	60.3	66.0	70.1
United Kingdom	24.2	18.0	11.9	8.6	4.6	5.0	6.1	3.4	4.1	4.9	7.8	9.5	5.9	3.7
Germany	5.9	5.5	6.3	5.3	3.3	2.4	2.2	-0.1	0.2	1.3	2.8	2.7	3.5	4.0

[1] Households of wage and salary earners. [2] Excludes rent.

Source: Organization for Economic Cooperation and Development, Paris, France, *Main Economic Indicators,* monthly.

No. 751. Producer Price Indexes, by Stage of Processing: 1960 to 1995

[1982=100. Minus sign (-) indicates decline. See text, section 15. See *Historical Statistics, Colonial Times to 1970*, series E 73-86 for similar data]

YEAR	CRUDE MATERIALS				Interme-diate materials, supplies, and compon-ents	FINISHED GOODS		CONSUMER FOODS		Finished con-sumer goods excl. food
	Total	Food-stuffs and feed-stuffs	Fuel	Crude nonfood materials except fuel		Con-sumer goods	Capital equip-ment	Crude	Proc-essed	
1960	30.4	38.4	10.5	26.9	30.8	33.6	32.8	39.8	35.2	33.5
1961	30.2	37.9	10.5	27.2	30.6	33.6	32.9	38.0	35.3	33.4
1962	30.5	38.6	10.4	27.1	30.6	33.7	33.0	38.4	35.6	33.4
1963	29.9	37.5	10.5	26.7	30.7	33.5	33.1	37.8	35.2	33.4
1964	29.6	36.6	10.5	27.2	30.8	33.6	33.4	38.9	35.2	33.3
1965	31.1	39.2	10.6	27.7	31.2	34.2	33.8	39.0	36.8	33.6
1966	33.1	42.7	10.9	28.3	32.0	35.4	34.6	41.5	39.2	34.1
1967	31.3	40.3	11.3	26.5	32.2	35.6	35.8	39.6	38.8	34.7
1968	31.8	40.9	11.5	27.1	33.0	36.5	37.0	42.5	40.0	35.5
1969	33.9	44.1	12.0	28.4	34.1	37.9	38.3	45.9	42.3	36.3
1970	35.2	45.2	13.8	29.1	35.4	39.1	40.1	46.0	43.9	37.4
1971	36.0	46.1	15.7	29.4	36.8	40.2	41.7	45.8	44.7	38.7
1972	39.9	51.5	16.8	32.3	38.2	41.5	42.8	48.0	47.2	39.4
1973	54.5	72.6	18.6	42.9	42.4	46.0	44.2	63.6	55.8	41.2
1974	61.4	76.4	24.8	54.5	52.5	53.1	50.5	71.6	63.9	48.2
1975	61.6	77.4	30.6	50.0	58.0	58.2	58.2	71.7	70.3	53.2
1976	63.4	76.8	34.5	54.9	60.9	60.4	62.1	76.7	69.0	56.5
1977	65.5	77.5	42.0	56.3	64.9	64.3	66.1	79.5	72.7	60.6
1978	73.4	87.3	48.2	61.9	69.5	69.4	71.3	85.8	79.4	64.9
1979	85.9	100.0	57.3	75.5	78.4	77.5	77.5	92.3	86.8	73.5
1980	95.3	104.6	69.4	91.8	90.3	88.6	85.8	93.9	92.3	87.1
1981	103.0	103.9	84.8	109.8	98.6	96.6	94.6	104.4	97.2	96.1
1982	100.0	100.0	100.0	100.0	100.0	100.0	100.0	100.0	100.0	100.0
1983	101.3	101.8	105.1	98.8	100.6	101.3	102.8	102.4	100.9	101.2
1984	103.5	104.7	105.1	101.0	103.1	103.3	105.2	111.4	104.9	102.2
1985	95.8	94.8	102.7	94.3	102.7	103.8	107.5	102.9	104.8	103.3
1986	87.7	93.2	92.2	76.0	99.1	101.4	109.7	105.6	107.4	98.5
1987	93.7	96.2	84.1	88.5	101.5	103.6	111.7	107.1	109.6	100.7
1988	96.0	106.1	82.1	85.9	107.1	106.2	114.3	109.8	112.7	103.1
1989	103.1	111.2	85.3	95.8	112.0	112.1	118.8	119.6	118.6	108.9
1990	108.9	113.1	84.8	107.3	114.5	118.2	122.9	123.0	124.4	115.3
1991	101.2	105.5	82.9	97.5	114.4	120.5	126.7	119.3	124.4	118.7
1992	100.4	105.1	84.0	94.2	114.7	121.7	129.1	107.6	124.4	120.8
1993	102.4	108.4	87.1	94.1	116.2	123.0	131.4	114.4	126.5	121.7
1994	101.8	106.5	82.4	97.0	118.5	123.3	134.1	111.3	127.9	121.6
1995	102.7	105.8	72.1	105.8	124.9	125.6	136.7	118.8	129.8	124.0
PERCENT CHANGE										
1960	-2.3	-1.0	1.0	3.7	-	0.9	0.3	6.7	1.4	0.6
1961	-0.7	-1.3	-	-4.3	-0.6	-	0.3	-4.5	0.3	-0.3
1962	1.0	1.8	-1.0	1.1	-	0.3	0.3	1.1	0.8	-
1963	-2.0	-2.8	1.0	-0.4	0.3	-0.6	0.3	-1.6	-1.1	-
1964	-1.0	-2.4	-	-1.5	0.3	0.3	0.9	2.9	-	-0.3
1965	5.1	7.1	1.0	1.9	1.3	1.8	1.2	0.3	4.5	0.9
1966	6.4	8.9	2.8	1.8	2.6	3.5	2.4	6.4	6.5	1.5
1967	-5.4	-5.6	3.7	2.2	0.6	0.6	3.5	-4.6	-1.0	1.8
1968	1.6	1.5	1.8	-6.4	2.5	2.5	3.4	7.3	3.1	2.3
1969	6.6	7.8	4.3	2.3	3.3	3.8	3.5	8.0	5.7	2.3
1970	3.8	2.5	15.0	4.8	3.8	3.2	4.7	0.2	3.8	3.0
1971	2.3	2.0	13.8	2.5	4.0	2.8	4.0	-0.4	1.8	3.5
1972	10.8	11.7	7.0	1.0	3.8	3.2	2.6	4.8	5.6	1.8
1973	36.6	41.0	10.7	9.9	11.0	10.8	3.3	32.5	18.2	4.6
1974	12.7	5.2	33.3	32.8	23.8	15.4	14.3	12.6	14.5	17.0
1975	0.3	1.3	23.4	27.0	10.5	9.6	15.2	0.1	10.0	10.4
1976	2.9	-0.8	12.7	-8.3	5.0	3.8	6.7	7.0	-1.8	6.2
1977	3.3	0.9	21.7	9.8	6.6	6.5	6.4	3.7	5.4	7.3
1978	12.1	12.6	14.8	2.6	7.1	7.9	7.9	7.9	9.2	7.1
1979	17.0	14.5	18.9	9.9	12.8	11.7	8.7	7.6	9.3	13.3
1980	10.9	4.6	21.1	22.0	15.2	14.3	10.7	1.7	6.3	18.5
1981	8.1	-0.7	22.2	21.6	9.2	9.0	10.3	11.2	5.3	10.3
1982	-2.9	-3.8	17.9	19.6	1.4	3.5	5.7	-4.2	2.9	4.1
1983	1.3	1.8	5.1	-8.9	0.6	1.3	2.8	2.4	0.9	1.2
1984	2.2	2.8	-	-1.2	2.5	2.0	2.3	8.8	4.0	1.0
1985	-7.4	-9.5	-2.3	2.2	-0.4	0.5	2.2	-7.6	-0.1	1.1
1986	-8.5	-1.7	-10.2	-6.6	-3.5	-2.3	2.0	2.6	2.5	-4.6
1987	6.8	3.2	-8.8	-19.4	2.4	2.2	1.8	1.4	2.0	2.2
1988	2.5	10.3	-2.4	16.4	5.5	2.5	2.3	2.5	2.8	2.4
1989	7.4	4.8	3.9	-2.9	4.6	5.6	3.9	8.9	5.2	5.6
1990	5.6	1.7	-0.6	11.5	2.2	5.4	3.5	2.8	4.9	5.9
1991	-7.1	-6.7	-2.2	12.0	-0.1	1.9	3.1	-3.0	-	2.9
1992	-0.8	-0.4	1.3	-9.1	0.3	1.0	1.9	-9.8	-	1.8
1993	2.0	3.1	3.7	-3.4	1.3	1.1	1.8	6.3	1.7	0.7
1994	-0.6	-1.8	-5.4	-0.1	2.0	0.2	2.1	-2.7	1.1	-0.1
1995	0.9	-0.7	-12.5	3.1	5.4	1.9	1.9	6.7	1.5	2.0

- Represents or rounds to zero.

Source: U.S. Bureau of Labor Statistics, *Producer Price Indexes*, monthly and annual.

No. 752. Producer Price Indexes for Selected Commodity Groupings: 1970 to 1995

[1982=100, except as indicated]

COMMODITY	1970	1980	1990	1991	1992	1993	1994	1995
All commodities.	36.9	89.8	116.3	116.5	117.2	118.9	120.4	124.7
Farm products	45.8	102.9	112.2	105.7	103.6	107.1	106.3	107.4
Fruits & melons, fresh/dry vegs. & nuts	44.0	94.1	117.5	114.7	96.9	106.9	104.6	108.5
Fresh fruits and melons.	42.3	100.3	118.1	129.9	84.0	84.5	82.7	85.8
Fresh and dry vegetables	47.5	88.9	118.1	103.8	115.0	135.2	129.0	144.4
Wheat	39.7	108.3	87.6	79.4	98.5	98.4	104.8	118.6
Barley	54.1	122.8	114.6	108.3	112.9	106.6	110.3	129.6
Corn	54.5	119.2	100.9	97.0	96.0	92.9	100.1	109.0
Slaughter livestock	45.3	98.0	115.6	107.9	104.7	107.0	96.4	92.8
Raw Cotton.	43.6	135.7	118.2	116.2	89.8	91.9	121.3	156.2
Wool	50.3	108.2	89.6	69.4	81.6	56.5	80.5	99.6
Fluid milk	40.8	96.0	100.8	89.5	96.1	94.1	95.7	93.6
Chicken eggs	71.0	95.7	117.6	110.7	94.1	105.9	97.8	104.1
Oilseeds.	45.8	116.1	112.1	106.4	107.5	115.9	117.4	112.6
Soybeans.	45.3	117.0	100.8	95.1	97.3	104.8	106.0	102.2
Leaf tobacco.	40.3	82.1	95.8	101.1	101.0	100.3	100.2	102.5
Farm products, processed foods and feeds.	44.9	98.3	118.6	116.4	115.9	118.4	119.1	120.5
Processed foods and feeds	44.6	95.9	121.9	121.9	122.1	124.0	125.5	127.0
Cereal and bakery products	42.4	93.0	134.2	137.9	144.2	147.6	151.1	154.7
Bakery products.	40.0	90.0	141.0	146.6	152.5	156.6	160.0	164.3
White pan bread	41.2	89.4	139.1	143.6	152.2	158.5	159.2	165.1
Flour and flour base mixes and doughs	50.9	98.3	107.9	103.8	111.5	112.0	113.8	120.8
Flour	55.3	102.3	103.6	96.8	109.5	108.9	110.4	123.0
Milled rice.	52.4	131.5	102.5	109.9	108.8	101.3	118.3	113.1
Meats, poultry, and fish	45.0	94.4	119.6	116.6	112.2	115.5	112.2	111.8
Meats	45.9	94.1	117.0	113.5	106.7	110.6	104.7	102.9
Beef and veal	46.7	106.2	116.0	112.2	109.5	112.9	103.6	100.9
Pork.	44.6	78.4	119.8	113.4	98.9	105.7	101.4	101.5
Processed poultry	63.4	108.2	113.6	109.9	109.0	111.7	114.7	114.2
Young chicken.	61.2	106.8	111.0	105.1	104.9	109.5	113.3	113.5
Turkeys	69.1	109.2	107.6	107.3	102.3	101.0	108.5	104.9
Fresh packaged fish and seafood	28.0	84.9	182.7	178.5	180.8	184.7	198.1	210.5
Frozen packaged fish and seafood	26.6	84.4	129.9	138.2	137.9	134.8	141.9	150.2
Canned and cured seafood	32.4	92.7	102.0	98.8	100.3	100.4	98.1	103.7
Dairy products.	44.7	92.7	117.2	114.6	117.9	118.1	119.4	119.7
Butter.	46.1	93.2	71.3	69.5	59.3	54.4	50.4	55.4
Ice cream and frozen desserts	45.3	90.1	123.1	123.1	124.9	127.2	127.4	128.2
Processed fruits and vegetables	40.3	83.3	124.7	119.6	120.8	118.2	121.1	122.4
Frozen fruits, juices and ades.	37.5	79.9	139.0	116.3	125.9	110.7	111.9	115.9
Frozen vegetables	41.0	79.4	118.4	117.6	116.4	120.9	125.9	124.2
Sugar and confectionery	42.9	119.6	123.1	128.4	127.7	127.9	132.5	134.0
Raw cane sugar.	39.9	148.3	119.2	113.7	112.1	113.2	115.2	119.7
Beverages and beverage materials	44.0	90.7	120.8	124.1	124.4	124.8	127.7	133.8
Alcoholic beverages	53.3	88.9	117.2	123.7	126.1	126.0	124.8	128.5
Malt beverages	54.8	91.5	116.2	122.3	124.8	123.4	121.1	125.2
Soft drinks	37.8	81.8	122.3	125.5	125.6	126.2	127.0	133.1
Coffee (whole bean, ground, & instant).	37.7	110.4	113.0	107.8	100.5	100.5	128.2	146.5
Fats and oils.	55.1	105.4	119.4	112.0	108.8	116.9	135.8	138.5
Textile products and apparel	52.4	89.7	115.0	116.3	117.8	118.0	118.3	120.8
Apparel	57.0	88.7	117.5	119.6	122.2	123.2	123.5	124.2
Textile housefurnishings	43.4	86.8	109.5	111.8	113.7	115.8	117.3	119.5
Footwear	46.2	95.2	125.6	128.6	132.0	134.4	135.5	139.2
Fuels and related products and power	15.3	82.8	82.3	81.2	80.4	80.0	77.8	78.0
Coal.	28.1	87.4	97.5	97.2	95.0	96.1	96.7	95.0
Natural gas (to pipelines).	7.9	63.3	80.4	79.1	80.6	84.7	78.8	66.6
Electric power	26.1	79.1	117.6	124.3	126.3	128.6	128.7	130.9
Petroleum products, refined	13.3	88.6	74.8	67.2	64.7	62.0	59.1	60.8
Gasoline.	14.4	93.3	78.7	69.9	68.1	63.9	61.7	63.7
Chemicals and allied products.	35.0	89.0	123.6	125.6	125.9	128.2	132.1	142.5
Industrial chemicals	28.6	91.9	113.2	111.8	109.3	110.4	114.3	128.4
Drugs and pharmaceuticals	48.2	83.0	170.8	182.6	192.2	200.9	206.0	210.9
Footwear	49.8	94.0	120.8	121.3	122.5	124.2	125.3	126.4
Lumber and wood products	39.9	101.5	129.7	132.1	146.6	174.0	180.0	178.1
Lumber	36.6	104.9	124.6	124.9	144.7	183.4	188.4	173.4
Wastepaper.	103.2	172.2	138.9	121.4	117.5	117.4	209.5	371.1
Paper.	38.8	89.7	128.8	126.9	123.2	123.8	126.0	159.0
Writing and printing papers	40.2	89.6	129.1	124.8	120.2	120.5	121.7	158.4
Newsprint	34.1	88.5	119.6	120.9	109.8	112.1	116.7	161.8
Paperboard.	39.7	92.0	135.7	130.2	134.3	130.0	140.5	183.1
Building paper & building board mill prods.	42.2	86.1	112.2	111.8	119.6	132.7	144.1	144.9
Hardboard, particleboard & fiberboard prods.	42.4	86.9	107.5	106.5	114.9	128.1	139.0	139.6
Metals and metal products.	38.7	95.0	122.9	120.2	119.2	119.2	124.8	134.5
Iron and steel	34.0	90.0	117.2	114.1	111.5	116.0	122.0	128.8
Iron ore	35.9	87.8	83.3	83.6	83.7	82.7	82.7	91.8
Iron and steel scrap	59.6	140.9	166.0	147.6	139.2	172.5	192.9	202.7

See footnote at end of table.

No. 752. Producer Price Indexes for Selected Commodity Groupings: 1970 to 1995—Continued

[1982=100, except as indicated]

COMMODITY	1970	1980	1990	1991	1992	1993	1994	1995
Blast and electric furnace products	36.3	97.1	120.1	116.9	115.5	115.7	117.0	126.0
Steel mill products	32.7	86.6	112.1	109.5	106.4	108.2	113.4	120.1
Plain wire, carbon steel	30.4	85.4	99.0	98.2	97.9	100.7	104.9	108.5
Mechanical tubing, welded, carbon	35.8	86.6	122.1	126.4	127.9	122.6	131.1	139.7
Nonferrous metals	47.3	115.7	133.8	123.4	120.9	114.4	126.6	149.6
Gold, refined (tr. oz.)	9.6	163.3	101.7	96.5	90.7	94.3	101.5	101.6
Copper base scrap	100.9	138.9	181.3	170.0	162.9	136.1	155.5	193.5
Aluminum base scrap	34.4	183.9	172.6	143.1	137.6	129.2	172.9	209.4
Nonferrous mill shapes	40.5	97.1	130.7	124.8	124.5	120.0	127.8	155.5
Aluminum mill shapes	36.7	89.3	127.9	123.2	121.9	120.4	127.7	160.4
Metal containers	34.3	90.9	114.0	115.5	113.9	109.7	108.1	117.2
Steel shipping barrels and drums	34.1	87.7	113.4	115.0	115.2	115.6	123.6	135.9
Hardware	39.8	85.8	125.9	130.2	132.7	135.2	137.5	141.1
Hand and edge tools	34.3	81.2	134.8	141.6	146.1	149.1	152.6	157.5
Plumbing fixtures and brass fittings	39.9	88.5	144.3	149.7	153.1	155.9	159.6	166.0
Heating equipment	46.6	87.0	131.6	134.1	137.3	140.4	142.5	147.5
Steam and hot water equipment	45.8	89.1	132.6	135.2	138.0	138.9	138.6	141.6
Gas heating boilers	44.7	86.9	127.1	130.8	132.9	134.2	137.0	140.4
Oil heating boilers	42.6	91.7	128.9	132.2	133.9	133.9	134.6	131.4
Warm air furnaces	46.5	84.2	129.6	131.5	134.8	137.3	138.0	141.2
Forced air, gas	45.0	83.0	131.6	133.4	136.4	138.2	138.2	141.1
Conversion burners and parts	48.0	84.9	134.4	138.5	142.3	147.1	150.1	154.8
Fabricated structural metal products	36.7	88.8	121.8	122.4	122.1	123.2	127.3	135.1
Lighting fixtures	41.7	81.8	127.5	129.8	131.0	131.2	132.2	135.9
Machinery and equipment	40.0	86.0	120.7	123.0	123.4	124.0	125.1	126.6
Agricultural machinery and equipment	36.4	83.3	121.7	125.7	129.5	133.6	137.0	142.9
Farm and garden tractors	36.0	81.8	123.2	128.1	133.4	135.3	138.3	141.5
Garden tractors	42.1	86.7	141.0	148.9	154.4	156.3	159.2	161.2
Agricultural equipment	44.0	86.5	119.2	121.3	124.0	129.9	132.1	140.5
Construction machinery and equipment	33.7	84.2	121.6	125.2	128.7	132.0	133.7	136.7
Metalworking machinery and equipment	35.6	85.5	123.0	127.6	130.9	133.5	136.5	139.8
Power driven hand tools	51.9	86.4	121.1	124.5	127.2	129.5	132.9	135.1
Welding machines and equipment	40.2	88.2	127.5	132.8	137.7	142.5	147.8	153.0
Cutting tools and accessories	41.9	86.0	118.5	121.5	123.9	125.8	128.1	131.9
Small cutting tools	41.5	86.0	113.2	115.9	117.8	119.7	121.4	125.0
Precision measuring tools	45.0	86.0	129.1	133.0	136.1	138.6	140.6	144.3
Metal cutting machine tools	30.8	85.1	129.8	134.6	138.9	141.1	143.1	148.0
Metal forming machine tools	28.6	85.7	128.7	133.5	135.9	138.4	141.9	145.7
Pumps, compressors, and equipment	33.0	82.8	119.2	124.6	129.1	132.8	135.2	139.4
Reciprocating pumps	21.6	76.5	109.9	118.9	121.5	124.9	126.4	130.5
Turbine pumps	37.0	76.7	124.3	127.4	130.4	135.7	136.9	137.7
Rotary pumps	34.9	80.5	135.3	140.9	145.7	151.2	155.7	160.2
Elevators, escalators, and other lifts	42.3	87.3	110.1	108.7	109.4	110.7	112.4	113.0
Industrial material handling equipment	39.8	88.4	115.0	117.4	118.4	120.2	122.4	125.3
Food products machinery	37.1	84.9	133.4	139.3	143.8	147.3	152.6	157.5
Dairy industry machinery	49.2	91.0	128.4	134.7	140.5	141.9	151.2	159.2
Commercial food production machinery	37.8	85.1	133.1	138.2	142.4	145.7	150.6	155.0
Textile machinery and equipment	45.4	87.2	128.8	135.0	138.9	143.7	144.9	146.7
Industrial sewing machines	43.0	81.7	118.0	122.8	124.4	123.8	125.8	129.4
Woodworking machinery and equipment	37.9	86.0	122.1	124.5	128.4	132.8	133.4	137.1
Printing trades machinery and equipment	42.5	89.7	124.9	126.5	126.8	129.5	130.9	133.6
Printing presses, offset	38.0	90.3	133.3	133.5	133.9	139.3	140.5	141.9
Bookbinding machinery and equipment	42.2	89.9	136.9	139.6	143.8	146.8	148.6	152.6
Electronic components and accessories	57.4	88.8	118.4	118.6	117.5	117.7	116.6	113.6
Power/transmitter/spec. purpose tubes	37.5	76.6	148.4	151.7	148.9	147.9	151.4	152.9
Capacitors	49.9	97.2	98.4	97.6	97.7	96.3	94.2	95.7
Resistors for electric applications	58.2	91.4	119.4	124.0	134.0	136.3	141.0	143.1
Relays	41.4	78.8	134.7	139.0	138.4	142.6	148.7	151.3
Connectors	47.8	95.0	128.0	134.5	137.0	142.1	143.1	143.3
Coaxial connectors (radio frequency)	43.6	91.6	163.7	177.4	190.5	206.5	211.4	210.1
Storage batteries	50.1	99.9	104.2	101.3	100.4	96.7	97.6	101.4
Mining machinery and equipment	30.9	85.2	121.0	125.2	127.4	129.5	131.1	135.6
Office and store machines and equipment	68.3	93.1	109.5	109.8	111.0	111.0	111.3	111.5
Internal combustion engines	34.5	81.7	120.2	126.0	128.4	130.2	132.9	135.6
Furniture and household durables	51.9	90.7	119.2	121.2	122.2	123.7	126.1	128.2
Household furniture	48.6	89.1	125.1	128.0	130.0	133.4	138.0	141.8
Commercial furniture	41.6	85.7	133.4	136.2	138.1	140.5	144.7	148.2
Household appliances	52.9	87.5	110.8	111.3	111.4	112.9	112.8	112.4
Home electronic equipment	106.0	103.8	82.7	83.2	82.0	80.2	80.3	78.9
Television receivers	106.4	103.4	78.9	78.9	77.1	74.5	74.3	72.2
Color console TV receiver	107.8	102.9	84.1	83.9	81.4	80.5	85.2	83.8
Lawn/garden equip. excl. garden tractors	46.8	87.5	123.0	124.7	125.3	126.2	128.4	130.4
Concrete products	37.7	92.0	113.5	116.6	117.2	120.2	124.6	129.4
Ceramic floor and wall tile	52.7	87.5	132.5	131.1	132.6	133.5	135.5	138.0
Gypsum products	38.9	100.1	105.2	99.3	99.9	108.3	136.1	154.5
Glass containers	33.9	82.3	120.4	125.4	125.1	125.8	127.5	130.5
Insulation materials	34.6	80.7	108.4	110.8	102.3	105.8	111.9	118.8
Transportation equipment	41.9	82.9	121.5	126.4	130.4	133.7	137.2	139.7
Motor vehicles and equipment	43.3	83.1	118.2	122.1	124.9	128.0	131.4	133.0
Motor vehicles	47.2	87.1	120.4	125.9	129.9	134.2	139.1	140.3
Passenger cars	50.0	88.9	118.3	124.1	126.9	129.8	133.9	134.1
Trucks, 10,000 lbs. GVW and under	42.0	83.3	130.0	135.5	142.4	150.3	157.1	159.0

Source: U.S. Bureau of Labor Statistics, *Producer Price Indexes*, monthly and annual.

No. 753. Producer Price Indexes for the Net Output of Selected Industries: 1985 to 1995

[Indexes are based on selling prices reported by establishments of all sizes by probability sampling. Industries selected by value added. N.e.c.= not elsewhere classified. See text, section 27]

ITEM	SIC code [1]	Index base	1985	1990	1992	1993	1994	1995
Meat packing plants	2011	12/80	90.9	119.8	108.9	113.6	108.0	105.9
Sausage and other prepared meats	2013	12/82	95.7	112.7	108.7	110.4	108.9	108.5
Fluid milk	2026	12/82	102.6	121.4	121.6	121.2	123.7	123.3
Canned fruits/vegetables/preserves/jams/jellies	2033	06/81	112.7	129.9	129.8	127.3	130.1	131.8
Frozen specialties	2038	12/82	110.8	127.3	131.0	130.7	132.2	133.2
Bread/other bakery prod., except cookies/crackers	2051	06/80	127.1	159.4	173.3	179.0	182.6	189.4
Cookies and crackers	2052	06/83	112.0	141.9	151.2	152.3	154.5	156.5
Malt beverages	2082	06/82	110.0	115.2	123.6	122.3	119.9	124.0
Bottled and canned soft drinks	2086	06/81	112.5	127.2	131.0	132.5	134.1	140.2
Coffee	2095	06/81	111.5	120.0	110.0	109.8	134.7	152.6
Cigarettes	2111	12/82	110.7	197.6	250.5	235.2	198.9	204.3
Women's, misses', and juniors' dresses	2335	12/80	108.0	125.6	129.7	130.1	127.0	124.9
Logging camps and logging contractors	2411	12/81	94.8	135.6	151.3	186.4	192.6	194.3
Sawmills and planing mills	2421	12/80	97.3	109.9	127.9	159.2	162.0	150.8
Millwork	2431	06/83	103.2	120.4	134.5	148.7	152.8	152.1
Wood household furniture, except upholstered	2511	12/79	133.3	158.9	166.9	173.3	180.3	186.3
Paper mills	2621	06/81	109.5	134.0	126.6	126.6	128.6	164.8
Paperboard mills	2631	12/82	112.0	146.0	142.6	138.3	152.6	203.2
Corrugated and solid fiber boxes	2653	03/80	119.7	139.6	137.3	135.8	146.2	186.5
Newspaper publishing	2711	12/79	164.0	220.4	248.7	259.5	269.5	286.7
Periodical publishing	2721	12/79	157.9	205.7	227.9	233.3	239.1	246.3
Book Publishing	2731	12/79	134.1	175.2	189.7	194.9	202.8	214.3
Commercial printing, lithographic	2752	06/82	111.0	127.9	130.8	135.0	136.5	145.0
Manifold business forms	2761	12/83	106.2	124.6	121.0	128.6	134.0	163.9
Industrial inorganic chemicals, n.e.c.	2819	12/82	100.4	117.9	118.9	117.3	115.7	125.2
Plastic materials and resins	2821	12/80	113.6	139.5	131.8	132.3	137.7	159.0
Noncellulosic manmade fibers	2824	06/81	97.6	102.7	101.6	101.7	103.0	107.9
Pharmaceutical preparations	2834	06/81	141.3	203.5	231.2	240.7	244.6	249.9
Soap and other detergents	2841	06/83	104.2	115.2	118.5	119.9	119.5	121.7
Specialty cleaning, polish, and sanitation preps	2842	06/83	103.9	118.6	123.1	124.7	126.4	129.2
Toilet preparations	2844	03/80	135.4	153.2	162.6	166.7	166.5	167.1
Paints and Allied Products	2851	06/83	104.9	125.0	132.3	133.5	136.0	143.1
Cyclic crudes/intermed., organic dyes/pigments	2865	12/82	96.9	114.1	113.3	116.2	117.5	125.0
Nitrogenous fertilizers	2873	12/79	122.4	119.9	121.7	122.9	136.6	157.5
Phosphatic fertilizers	2874	12/79	105.4	115.7	107.6	97.5	118.6	139.1
Fertilizers, mixing only	2875	12/79	117.1	124.9	124.4	122.8	131.0	140.6
Adhesives and sealants	2891	12/83	103.5	123.4	129.7	132.7	136.8	145.1
Explosives	2892	12/80	121.6	174.9	197.5	206.7	220.8	218.2
Printing ink	2893	06/84	101.1	120.3	127.6	128.8	129.4	135.7
Carbon black	2895	12/83	96.7	84.5	83.2	97.8	102.6	115.3
Petroleum Refining	2911	06/85	98.3	90.1	78.3	75.2	72.2	74.5
Tires and inner tubes	3011	06/81	96.8	103.0	106.0	106.2	106.4	108.5
Ready-mixed concrete	3273	06/81	108.6	114.3	117.4	121.0	125.8	131.3
Blast furnaces and steel mills	3312	06/82	104.9	110.8	105.8	107.4	112.4	118.5
Gray iron foundries	3321	12/80	115.6	123.4	127.0	128.3	131.7	137.7
Nonferrous wire drawing and insulating	3357	12/82	100.5	148.7	141.8	138.1	144.7	157.4
Metal cans	3411	06/81	110.4	116.6	117.0	113.3	110.8	118.7
Plumbing fixture fittings and brass goods	3432	06/83	105.2	143.2	153.6	157.8	162.1	169.0
Nonelectric heating equipment	3433	06/80	126.0	152.5	160.5	163.0	165.4	175.1
Fabricated structural metal	3441	06/82	103.0	118.6	116.6	118.1	121.7	126.2
Fabricated plate work (boiler shops)	3443	03/80	120.8	142.3	147.0	146.5	149.7	155.6
Sheet metal work	3444	12/82	107.2	129.4	126.6	127.1	129.9	137.6
Automotive stampings	3465	12/82	110.4	112.6	111.5	111.4	111.9	111.7
Internal combustion engines, n.e.c.	3519	12/82	103.4	115.7	123.3	125.5	128.0	131.2
Farm machinery and equipment	3523	12/82	105.3	116.8	124.1	126.7	129.6	133.2
Construction machinery	3531	12/80	119.5	137.6	146.9	151.2	153.8	157.2
Elevators and moving stairways	3534	06/81	109.4	122.4	121.9	122.8	124.8	126.0
Conveyors and conveying equipment	3535	06/84	101.2	116.0	119.0	120.2	123.4	125.8
Hoists, cranes and monorails	3536	12/82	101.9	111.0	116.5	120.0	124.5	129.3
Industrial trucks and tractors	3537	12/79	119.8	134.9	141.4	145.5	147.1	150.2
Special tools/dies/jigs/fixtures & indus. molds	3544	06/81	113.5	124.5	131.2	134.3	137.7	140.1
Electric motors and generators	3621	06/83	108.2	127.5	131.5	133.5	134.2	137.5
Telephone & telegraph apparatus	3661	12/85	(NA)	112.0	112.3	114.9	116.9	118.2
Semiconductors and related devices	3674	06/81	106.6	105.0	98.4	99.4	97.1	91.3
Electronic components, n.e.c.	3679	06/82	108.6	115.1	117.8	119.4	118.9	117.8
Motor vehicles and passenger car bodies	3711	06/82	107.2	119.9	129.1	133.2	138.0	139.1
Motor vehicle parts and accessories	3714	12/82	100.6	108.9	111.0	111.7	112.0	113.5
Aircraft	3721	12/85	(NA)	116.0	124.3	128.6	132.9	137.3
Photographic equipment and supplies	3861	12/83	101.5	112.2	112.1	112.1	111.7	113.8

NA Not available.   [1] Standard Industrial Classification code.

Source: U.S. Bureau of Labor Statistics, *Producer Price Indexes*, monthly.

Prices

No. 754. Chain-Type Price Indexes Personal Consumption Expenditures: 1960 to 1995

[1992=100. See text, section 14, for discussion of chain-type price index]

ITEM	1960	1965	1970	1975	1980	1985	1986	1987	1988	1989	1990	1991	1993	1994	1995
Personal consumption expenditures ..	23.2	24.7	29.5	40.0	58.5	75.8	78.0	81.0	84.3	88.4	92.9	96.8	102.6	105.1	107.6
Motor vehicles and parts.	34.6	35.6	38.9	48.4	68.3	83.2	85.6	89.3	90.5	93.1	93.8	97.1	103.4	107.5	112.0
Furniture and household equipment .	57.4	55.9	61.0	73.7	92.0	100.9	99.8	100.3	101.2	101.4	101.5	100.9	98.6	98.6	96.7
Food.	23.0	24.7	30.1	44.4	63.6	77.5	79.9	82.8	85.9	90.5	95.1	98.5	101.7	103.9	106.4
Clothing and shoes	38.9	40.4	50.4	61.2	72.5	81.6	81.6	84.9	88.5	90.6	94.5	97.9	101.0	100.3	98.9
Gasoline and oil	24.7	25.4	28.3	45.7	97.8	99.4	78.1	81.1	81.8	89.4	101.8	100.5	99.1	99.6	101.2
Fuel oil and coal	15.0	16.0	18.6	39.7	93.7	104.6	84.4	85.9	86.1	90.1	107.8	104.0	99.6	98.0	97.3
Services.	19.0	20.7	25.2	34.0	51.0	71.6	75.3	78.2	82.2	86.6	91.2	95.8	103.6	106.7	110.0
Housing.	23.4	24.9	28.5	35.8	52.4	73.9	78.2	81.7	85.4	89.1	93.5	97.1	102.8	105.7	109.1
Household operation	24.3	25.5	29.0	41.2	60.3	87.7	89.1	88.8	90.2	92.5	94.2	97.6	102.8	104.9	106.3
Electricity and gas	21.4	21.5	23.2	36.7	62.1	92.4	91.8	90.3	91.0	93.6	95.2	98.1	103.1	103.7	103.9
Other household operation	27.3	29.5	34.9	45.9	59.1	83.8	86.9	87.7	89.5	91.6	93.5	97.3	102.6	105.7	108.1
Transportation.	19.7	21.2	26.6	34.7	56.0	71.1	73.6	78.3	82.1	85.7	89.9	95.4	104.3	105.9	108.8
Medical care.	12.9	14.8	20.1	27.7	43.6	65.6	67.8	70.9	76.4	82.9	89.2	94.4	105.9	110.5	114.6
Other.	17.5	19.8	24.8	35.1	51.8	69.3	74.6	77.6	81.5	85.6	90.2	95.3	102.3	104.9	108.1
Addenda: Price indexes for personal consumption expenditures:															
Food.	23.0	24.7	30.1	44.4	63.6	77.5	79.9	82.8	85.9	90.5	95.1	98.5	101.7	103.9	106.4
Energy.	21.7	22.2	24.6	40.7	80.8	96.5	84.7	85.6	86.3	91.3	98.9	99.5	101.0	101.5	102.3
Personal consumption expenditures less food and energy	23.7	25.2	30.1	39.2	55.7	74.0	77.1	80.3	83.9	87.8	92.1	96.3	102.9	105.6	108.2

Source: U.S. Bureau of Economic Analysis, *The National Income and Product Accounts of the United States* (to be published in late 1996), and *Survey of Current Business*, January/February 1996.

No. 755. Chain-Type Price Indexes: 1980 to 1995

[1992=100. See text, section 14 for discussion of chain-type price index]

ITEM	1980	1985	1987	1988	1989	1990	1991	1993	1994	1995
Gross domestic product	60.4	78.6	83.1	86.1	89.7	93.6	97.3	102.6	105.0	107.6
Personal consumption expenditures.	58.5	75.8	81.0	84.3	88.4	92.9	96.8	102.6	105.1	107.6
Durable goods	75.6	87.8	91.6	93.3	95.3	96.6	98.5	101.3	103.4	104.8
Nondurable goods.	65.3	78.7	81.8	84.8	89.3	94.6	98.1	101.5	102.8	104.5
Services	51.0	71.6	78.2	82.2	86.6	91.2	95.8	103.6	106.7	110.0
Gross private domestic investment	74.5	87.0	91.0	93.5	96.1	98.4	99.7	101.7	103.6	105.6
Fixed investment.	73.0	86.2	90.4	93.2	95.9	98.2	99.6	101.7	103.7	105.5
Nonresidential	76.0	88.3	91.3	93.7	96.2	98.4	99.9	100.9	102.3	103.6
Structures.	68.7	84.9	87.9	92.1	95.6	98.8	100.1	103.3	106.7	110.2
Residential.	66.2	81.5	88.3	92.1	95.1	97.8	98.8	103.7	107.0	110.3
Exports of goods and services	84.2	89.8	91.0	96.0	97.9	98.7	100.3	99.9	101.0	104.3
Imports of goods and services	91.4	86.0	91.0	95.3	97.8	100.4	100.0	98.6	99.4	102.6
Government consumption expenditures and gross investment	60.9	81.0	85.2	87.4	90.2	94.1	97.4	102.3	104.3	107.8
Federal.	62.2	82.7	85.3	87.2	89.8	92.9	96.9	102.6	105.4	109.5
National defense.	62.0	83.5	85.6	87.3	89.8	92.9	96.5	102.1	104.5	108.3
Nondefense.	62.3	80.2	84.0	86.7	89.7	92.8	97.9	104.0	107.7	112.4
State and local.	59.7	79.5	85.0	87.5	90.5	94.9	97.9	102.1	103.6	106.7

Source: U.S. Bureau of Economic Analysis, *The National Income and Product Accounts of the United States to be published in late 1996,* and *Survey of Current Business,* January/February 1996.

No. 756. Chain-Type Price Indexes—Annual Percent Change: 1986 to 1995

[1992=100. See text, section 14 for discussion of chain-type price index]

ITEM	1986	1987	1988	1989	1990	1991	1992	1993	1994	1995
Gross domestic product	2.6	3.1	3.7	4.2	4.4	3.9	2.8	2.6	2.3	2.5
Personal consumption expend. . . .	2.8	3.8	4.2	4.9	5.1	4.2	3.3	2.6	2.4	2.4
Durable goods	1.3	3.0	1.8	2.2	1.4	2.0	1.5	1.3	2.1	1.4
Nondurable goods.	-	3.9	3.7	5.2	6.0	3.6	2.0	1.5	1.3	1.7
Services	5.1	3.9	5.0	5.4	5.4	5.0	4.4	3.6	3.0	3.1
Gross private domestic invest.:										
Fixed investment	2.7	2.1	3.1	2.8	2.5	1.4	0.4	1.7	1.9	1.8
Nonresidential	2.2	1.2	2.6	2.6	2.4	1.5	0.1	0.9	1.4	1.2
Structures.	1.9	1.6	4.8	3.8	3.3	1.3	-0.1	3.3	3.3	3.3
Producers' durable equip. .	2.3	1.1	1.5	2.0	1.8	1.6	0.2	-0.1	0.7	0.4
Residential	4.2	4.1	4.2	3.3	2.9	1.1	1.2	3.7	3.1	3.1
Exports of goods and services . . .	-1.4	2.8	5.5	2.0	0.8	1.6	-0.3	-0.1	1.1	3.3
Imports of goods and services . . .	0.0	5.9	4.8	2.6	2.6	-0.3	0.0	-1.4	0.8	3.3
Government purchases	2.1	3.0	2.6	3.2	4.3	3.6	2.6	2.3	2.0	3.4
Federal.	1.5	1.6	2.3	3.0	3.5	4.3	3.2	2.6	2.7	3.9
National defense	1.2	1.3	2.0	2.9	3.5	3.8	3.7	2.1	2.4	3.7
Nondefense	2.4	2.3	3.2	3.4	3.5	5.5	2.1	4.0	3.5	4.4
State and local.	2.6	4.2	2.9	3.4	4.9	3.1	2.2	2.1	1.5	3.0

- Represents zero.

Source: U.S. Bureau of Economic Analysis, *National Income and Product Accounts of the United States* to be published in late 1996, and *Survey of Current Business,* January/February 1996.

No. 757. Commodity Research Bureau Futures Price Index: 1975 to 1995

[1967=100. Index computed daily. Represents unweighted geometric average of commodity futures prices (through 9 months forward) of 21 major commodity futures markets. Represents end of year index]

ITEM	1975	1980	1985	1986	1987	1988	1989	1990	1991	1992	1993	1994	1995
All commodities	191.0	308.5	229.2	209.1	232.5	251.8	229.9	222.6	208.0	205.9	212.4	229.7	237.1
Imported	259.4	426.0	398.2	321.2	356.1	365.2	271.7	276.0	264.4	232.4	246.9	352.3	354.4
Industrial.	154.8	324.6	211.7	210.4	252.5	248.2	249.6	245.5	217.2	224.7	235.0	263.6	272.5
Grains	195.6	312.1	198.5	164.6	186.1	261.9	205.7	171.2	196.1	196.9	193.8	191.2	218.6
Oilseeds	181.6	314.6	245.4	189.8	223.6	309.6	254.2	223.6	195.4	218.8	239.8	259.9	277.5
Livestock and meats	180.8	217.4	206.9	200.2	189.9	199.1	206.5	226.2	174.0	179.8	201.4	192.3	192.4
Metals (precious)[1].	141.0	531.4	256.6	296.6	346.4	318.7	296.9	257.8	226.0	228.5	242.2	273.9	276.0

[1] Prior to 1980, index for metals only.

Source: Commodity Research Bureau, a Knight-Ridder Business Information Service, New York City, NY, *CRB Commodity Index Report,* weekly (copyright).

No. 758. Indexes of Spot Primary Market Prices: 1980 to 1995

[1967=100. Computed weekly for 1980; daily thereafter. Represents unweighted geometric average of price quotations of 23 commodities; much more sensitive to changes in market conditions than is a monthly producer price index]

ITEMS AND NUMBER OF COMMODITIES	1980 (6-24)	1985 (5-21)	1986 (5-20)	1987 (5-26)	1988 (5-27)	1989 (5-26)	1990 (5-25)	1991 (5-28)	1992 (5-26)	1993 (5-23)	1994 (5-24)	1995 (5-23)
All commodities (23)	265.1	251.4	218.0	250.0	270.3	281.3	279.2	235.3	242.3	237.7	261.5	290.6
Foodstuffs (10)	260.9	248.1	205.5	215.2	230.1	222.5	231.5	197.7	201.3	208.3	215.5	229.1
Raw industrials (13)	268.0	253.6	226.9	277.3	302.0	329.0	317.0	265.2	275.5	260.4	299.2	342.8
Livestock and products (5)	250.5	284.5	231.2	303.3	316.1	285.2	306.9	286.6	276.4	291.3	296.9	314.6
Metals (5)	257.9	220.2	191.2	239.5	276.7	347.1	313.9	348.8	262.7	236.2	262.1	306.7
Textiles and fibers (4)	234.7	220.8	216.9	247.1	247.3	253.5	259.4	201.8	218.6	205.3	252.6	286.0
Fats and oils (4)	229.5	273.1	168.5	201.2	230.4	208.1	193.3	185.0	180.7	190.1	209.6	228.3

Source: Commodity Research Bureau, a Knight-Ridder Business Information Service, New York, NY, *CRB Commodity Index Report*, weekly (copyright).

No. 759. Average Prices of Selected Fuels and Electricity: 1980 to 1994

[In dollars per unit, except electricity, in cents per kWh. Represents price to end-users, except as noted]

ITEM	Unit [1]	1980	1985	1986	1987	1988	1989	1990	1991	1992	1993	1994
Crude oil, composite [2]	Barrel	28.07	26.75	14.55	17.90	14.67	17.97	22.22	19.06	18.43	16.41	15.59
Motor gasoline: [3]												
Unleaded regular	Gallon	1.25	1.20	0.93	0.95	0.95	1.02	1.16	1.14	1.13	1.11	1.11
Unleaded premium	Gallon	(NA)	1.34	1.09	1.09	1.11	1.20	1.35	1.32	1.32	1.30	1.31
No. 2 heating oil	Gallon	0.79	0.85	0.56	0.58	0.54	0.59	0.73	0.67	0.63	0.60	0.57
No. 2 diesel fuel	Gallon	0.82	0.79	0.48	0.55	0.50	0.59	0.73	0.65	0.62	0.60	0.55
Residual fuel oil	Gallon	0.61	0.61	0.33	0.41	0.33	0.41	0.47	0.36	0.35	0.34	0.35
Natural gas, residential	1,000 cu/ft.	3.68	6.12	5.83	5.54	5.47	5.64	5.80	5.82	5.89	6.16	6.41
Electricity, residential	kWh	5.4	7.8	7.4	7.4	7.5	7.6	7.8	8.1	8.2	8.3	8.4

NA Not available. [1] See headnote. [2] Refiner acquisition cost. [3] Average, all service.

Source: U.S. Energy Information Administration, *Monthly Energy Review*.

No. 760. Weekly Food Cost: 1990 and 1995

[In dollars. Assumes that food for all meals and snacks is purchased at the store and prepared at home. See source for details on estimation procedures]

FAMILY TYPE	DECEMBER 1990				JANUARY 1995			
	Thrifty plan	Low-cost plan	Moderate-cost plan	Liberal plan	Thrifty plan	Low-cost plan	Moderate-cost plan	Liberal plan
FAMILIES								
Family of two:								
20-50 years	48.10	60.60	74.70	92.70	53.50	67.50	83.60	104.30
51 years and over	45.60	58.30	71.80	85.80	50.30	65.00	80.50	96.60
Family of four:								
Couple, 20-50 years and children—								
1-2 and 3-5 years	70.10	87.30	106.60	131.00	77.70	97.10	119.00	146.70
6-8 and 9-11 years	80.10	102.60	128.30	154.40	89.20	114.20	143.00	172.50
INDIVIDUALS [1]								
Child:								
1-2 years	12.70	15.40	18.00	21.80	14.00	17.10	20.00	24.30
3-5 years	13.70	16.80	20.70	24.90	15.10	18.60	23.00	27.60
6-8 years	16.60	22.20	27.90	32.50	18.50	24.70	30.90	36.00
9-11 years	19.80	25.30	32.50	37.60	22.10	28.10	36.10	41.70
Male:								
12-14 years	20.60	28.60	35.70	42.00	22.90	31.80	39.60	46.60
15-19 years	21.40	29.60	36.80	42.60	23.60	32.80	40.90	47.40
20-50 years	22.90	29.30	36.60	44.30	25.50	32.60	40.90	49.70
51 years and over	20.90	27.90	34.30	41.10	23.00	31.20	38.50	46.30
Female:								
12-19 years	20.80	24.80	30.10	36.30	22.90	27.50	33.40	40.40
20-54 years	20.80	25.80	31.30	40.00	23.10	28.80	35.10	45.10
55 years and over	20.60	25.10	31.00	36.90	22.70	27.90	34.70	41.50

[1] The costs given are for individuals in four-person families. For individuals in other size families, the following adjustments are suggested: one-person, add 20 percent; two-person, add 10 percent; three-person, add five percent; five- or six-person, subtract 5 percent; seven- (or more) person, subtract 10 percent.

Source: U.S. Dept. of Agriculture, *Agricultural Research Service*, monthly.

No. 761. Food—Retail Prices of Selected Items: 1989 to 1995

[In dollars per pound, except as indicated. As of December]

FOOD	1989	1990	1991	1992	1993	1994	1995
Cereals and bakery products:							
Flour, white, all purpose.	0.24	0.24	0.22	0.23	0.22	0.23	0.24
Rice, white, lg. grain, raw.	0.50	0.49	0.51	0.53	0.50	0.53	0.55
Spaghetti and macaroni.	0.87	0.85	0.86	0.86	0.84	0.87	0.88
Bread, white, pan	0.69	0.70	0.72	0.74	0.76	0.75	0.84
Meats, poultry, fish and eggs:							
Ground chuck, 100% beef	1.88	2.02	1.93	1.91	1.91	1.84	1.85
Rib roast, USDA Choice	4.21	4.54	4.59	4.69	4.73	4.88	4.81
Round steak, USDA Choice	3.17	3.42	3.38	3.34	3.32	3.24	3.20
Sirloin steak, bone-in	3.46	3.65	3.78	3.75	3.69	(NA)	(NA)
T-bone steak	5.04	5.45	5.21	5.39	5.77	5.86	5.92
Pork:							
Bacon, sliced.	1.96	2.28	1.99	1.86	2.02	1.89	2.17
Chops, center cut, bone-in	2.85	3.32	3.12	3.15	3.24	3.03	3.29
Shoulder picnic, bone-in, smoked	1.17	1.41	1.30	1.18	1.19	1.13	1.17
Sausage.	2.12	2.42	2.24	2.14	1.99	1.85	1.92
Poultry:							
Chicken, fresh, whole	0.88	0.86	0.86	0.88	0.91	0.90	0.94
Chicken breast, bone-in.	2.01	2.00	2.02	2.08	2.17	1.91	1.95
Chicken legs, bone-in	1.14	1.17	1.14	1.14	1.13	1.12	1.20
Turkey, frozen, whole	0.95	0.96	0.91	0.93	0.95	0.98	0.99
Eggs, Grade A, large, (dozen)	1.14	1.00	1.01	0.93	0.87	0.87	1.16
Dairy products:							
Milk, fresh, whole, fortified (1/2 gal.).	1.37	1.39	1.40	1.39	1.43	1.44	1.48
Butter, salted, grade AA, stick.	2.11	1.92	1.94	1.64	1.61	1.54	1.73
Ice cream, prepack., bulk,reg.(1/2 gal.). . . .	2.67	2.54	2.63	2.49	2.59	2.62	2.68
Fruits and vegetables:							
Fresh fruits and vegetables:							
Apples, red Delicious	0.57	0.77	0.86	0.76	0.78	0.72	0.83
Bananas.	0.42	0.43	0.42	0.40	0.41	0.46	0.45
Oranges, navel	0.53	0.56	0.65	0.52	0.56	0.55	0.64
Grapefruit	0.47	0.56	0.53	0.52	0.50	0.47	0.49
Lemons	0.96	0.97	1.21	0.90	1.05	1.04	1.12
Pears, Anjou	0.76	0.79	0.88	0.80	0.89	(NA)	(NA)
Potatoes, white	0.31	0.32	0.28	0.31	0.36	0.34	0.38
Lettuce, iceberg	0.52	0.58	0.69	0.66	0.53	0.91	0.61
Tomatoes, field grown	0.90	0.86	0.79	1.23	1.31	1.43	1.51
Cabbage	0.34	0.39	0.46	0.38	0.37	0.45	0.41
Carrots, short trimmed and topped	0.35	0.44	0.51	0.44	0.41	0.48	0.53
Celery	0.46	0.49	0.45	0.48	0.49	0.52	0.54
Cucumbers	0.64	0.56	0.55	0.51	0.93	0.69	0.53
Processed fruits and vegetables:							
Orange juice, frozen concentrate,							
12 oz. can, per 16 oz.	1.80	2.02	1.74	1.70	1.67	1.55	1.57
Potatoes, frozen, french fried	0.80	0.85	0.92	0.86	0.87	0.84	0.86

NA Not available.

Source: U.S. Bureau of Labor Statistics, *CPI Detailed Report, CPI Detailed Report,* January issues.

No. 762. Average Price of Energy in Selected Metropolitan Areas: 1995

[In dollars per unit shown. As of January. One therm contains approximately 100 cubic feet of natural gas. See Appendix II]

CITY/MSA	Utility (piped) gas (100 therms)	Electricity (500 kWh)	Fuel oil No. 2 (gallon)	GASOLINE		
				All types [1]	Unleaded regular	Unleaded premium
U.S. city average.	62.39	48.57	0.91	1.16	1.10	1.29
Baltimore, MD MSA	62.57	47.85	1.04	1.15	1.09	1.25
Boston-Lawrence-Salem, MA-NH CMSA.	96.05	62.02	0.92	1.18	1.13	1.33
Chicago-Gary-Lake County, IL-IN-WI CMSA	55.61	57.40	1.04	1.24	1.18	1.38
Cleveland-Akron-Lorain, OH CMSA	49.07	54.90	(NA)	1.10	1.06	1.25
Dallas-Fort Worth, TX CMSA	55.69	45.29	(NA)	1.09	1.02	1.22
Detroit-Ann Arbor, MI CMSA.	50.10	48.18	(NA)	1.09	1.05	1.25
Houston-Galveston-Brazoria, TX CMSA	43.78	40.00	(NA)	1.11	1.04	1.22
Los Angeles-Anaheim-Riverside, CA CMSA	67.69	64.95	(NA)	1.23	1.19	1.37
Miami-Fort Lauderdale, FL CMSA	97.07	44.05	(NA)	1.16	1.08	1.28
New York-N. NJ-Long Island, NY-NJ-CT CMSA	85.85	70.74	1.02	1.26	1.17	1.39
Philadelphia-Wilmington-Trenton, PA-NJ-DE-MD CMSA. .	71.03	62.09	0.87	1.12	1.07	1.26
Pittsburgh-Beaver Valley, PA CMSA.	50.59	51.59	(NA)	1.23	1.15	1.36
St. Louis-East St. Louis, MO-IL CMSA	52.06	37.28	(NA)	1.00	0.95	1.17
San Francisco-Oakland-San Jose, CA CMSA	68.87	62.98	(NA)	1.27	1.20	1.42
Washington, DC-MD-VA MSA.	71.23	40.43	(NA)	1.12	1.05	1.25

NA Not available.   [1] Includes types of gasoline not shown separately.

Source: U.S. Bureau of Labor Statistics, *CPI Detailed Report,* January issues.

No. 763. Import Price Indexes—Selected Commodities: 1985 to 1995

[1990=100. Indexes are weighted by the 1990 Tariff Schedule of the United States Annotated, a scheme for describing and reporting product composition and value of U.S. imports. Import prices are based on U.S. dollar prices paid by importer. F.o.b. = Free on board; c.i.f. = Cost, insurance, and freight; n.e.s.=Not elsewhere specified]

COMMODITY	1985	1989	1990 [1]	1991	1992	1993	1994	1995
All commodities....................	80.2	96.8	96.1	98.8	100.3	100.5	101.9	107.3
Food and live animals........................	87.2	98.2	98.6	102.4	97.9	101.1	109.0	116.3
Meat....................................	68.8	80.3	100.0	105.6	94.9	99.3	91.0	85.2
Meat of bovine animals..................	77.1	95.2	98.5	100.8	91.1	100.8	86.5	71.9
Fish......................................	75.5	94.1	96.7	107.6	107.9	107.9	121.2	126.1
Crustaceans; fresh, chilled, frozen, salted or dried. .	85.0	98.4	97.4	107.3	105.4	106.4	129.8	137.4
Cereals and cereal preparations	63.2	91.2	98.7	96.4	99.3	102.9	102.0	101.4
Sugar [2]...................................	87.4	95.5	99.7	96.7	95.3	95.1	98.2	103.9
Coffee, tea and cocoa	145.1	128.0	99.4	93.2	77.3	81.2	137.1	166.2
Beverages and tobacco.......................	77.1	91.1	99.2	110.8	113.4	112.6	113.2	114.9
Beverages..................................	75.9	92.6	99.3	110.3	112.5	112.9	112.8	114.8
Crude materials.............................	77.8	111.6	101.9	95.9	95.8	95.3	106.7	123.5
Crude rubber	98.3	100.6	101.2	98.4	100.8	102.9	106.3	156.8
Cork and wood............................	93.4	100.0	102.4	107.7	116.8	130.3	159.9	131.0
Pulp and waste paper	56.9	106.6	102.8	79.2	74.4	63.7	70.1	116.0
Crude fertilizers and minerals...............	102.8	106.9	99.6	100.9	89.0	82.5	82.3	100.7
Metalliferous ores and metal scrap...........	59.9	133.1	100.8	93.6	91.1	88.3	89.6	106.4
Crude animal and vegetable materials, n.e.s.	83.9	97.6	103.9	103.7	107.2	106.1	131.2	163.8
Mineral fuels and related products...............	114.5	84.2	73.1	83.2	86.7	79.9	76.3	82.7
Crude petroleum and petroleum products	112.1	83.8	72.0	82.8	86.7	79.2	75.7	82.7
Crude petroleum.......................	123.8	82.7	66.8	81.4	87.8	76.6	73.6	79.0
Natural gas	(NA)	88.5	89.4	88.1	83.7	90.3	83.7	80.3
Animal and vegetable oils, fats and waxes	115.5	123.3	100.6	102.2	134.9	117.8	135.1	159.3
Chemicals and related products	83.7	100.4	98.5	100.7	101.7	102.8	102.6	112.3
Intermediate manufactured products	73.1	100.3	99.5	99.2	99.4	99.3	101.0	111.8
Rubber manufactures	85.9	96.9	99.8	100.6	102.0	103.8	102.4	105.0
Cork and wood manufactures	69.0	97.2	100.4	98.6	108.1	120.6	126.5	119.3
Paper and paperboard products	82.7	100.0	100.4	101.0	94.1	96.7	95.6	125.1
Textiles..................................	77.6	95.8	98.7	103.0	106.0	108.1	108.9	114.8
Nonmetallic mineral manufactures	60.1	93.4	99.8	103.3	105.5	108.0	108.5	111.4
Iron and steel.............................	79.3	105.8	99.7	99.3	97.6	98.2	99.1	108.5
Nonferrous metals...........................	69.0	109.2	98.7	89.0	88.6	76.6	85.2	103.8
Silver, platinum and other platinum group metals...	71.2	89.6	93.6	90.2	75.5	69.1	74.8	78.0
Copper	57.6	98.5	98.6	88.7	88.5	75.9	89.3	110.5
Nickel	62.4	152.2	95.5	97.6	87.5	72.9	75.3	91.0
Aluminum..............................	(NA)	117.3	98.7	85.8	86.4	79.1	89.6	116.8
Zinc	56.7	108.9	113.4	77.2	89.3	67.7	65.8	72.4
Manufactures of metals, n.e.s.................	72.9	97.4	98.9	101.2	103.0	104.5	104.6	110.8
Machinery and transport equipment................	75.1	98.1	98.7	101.6	103.5	105.0	106.8	110.1
Machinery specialized for particular industries	59.1	89.3	97.3	101.7	105.4	107.5	109.7	117.0
Metalworking machinery.....................	64.8	92.0	98.7	100.6	103.9	107.7	110.1	124.4
General industrial machinery, parts, n.e.s.........	62.6	91.3	97.7	101.5	104.9	107.0	109.0	116.6
Computer equipment and office machines	85.0	103.0	99.8	97.3	95.7	91.9	87.1	84.1
Computer equipment	112.8	105.0	100.3	96.9	92.4	85.5	76.5	69.9
Telecommunications [3]	90.1	104.1	100.2	97.8	97.1	98.0	97.4	98.7
Electrical machinery and equipment	77.4	100.1	98.7	100.6	102.1	103.9	106.1	109.0
Electronic valves, diodes, transistors & integr. cir. . .	98.7	110.0	98.2	99.5	99.4	104.3	108.0	108.2
Road vehicles	75.1	98.5	98.4	103.5	105.6	108.4	112.7	116.7
Miscellaneous manufactured articles	74.3	94.9	98.9	100.6	103.7	105.2	105.4	107.8
Plumbing, heating & lighting fixtures............	68.9	91.9	98.4	98.0	101.5	102.0	99.6	103.7
Furniture and parts........................	74.0	94.0	99.1	101.2	103.4	104.1	103.9	106.5
Articles of apparel and clothing	81.7	98.1	100.5	98.8	101.8	102.1	102.2	103.1
Footwear.................................	70.6	92.0	99.0	100.9	102.6	101.2	100.2	101.9
Prof., scientific & contrlng instr & appratus, n.e.s.	64.4	91.4	97.5	102.1	104.4	104.1	113.0	117.2
Photographic apparatus [4]..................	73.5	95.1	98.0	100.1	102.9	106.9	109.1	115.3
Miscellaneous manufactured articles, n.e.s.........	71.1	93.8	97.9	101.8	106.0	108.3	108.5	110.7

NA Not available. [1] June 1990 may not equal 100 because indexes were reweighted to an "average" trade value in 1990. [2] Includes sugar preparations and honey. [3] Includes sound recording and reproducing equipment. [4] Includes photographic supplies, optical goods, watches, and clocks.

Source: U.S. Bureau of Labor Statistics, *News,* quarterly.

No. 764. Export Price Indexes—Selected Commodities: 1985 to 1995

[1990=100. Indexes are weighted by 1980 export values according to the Schedule B classification system of the U.S. Bureau of the Census. Prices used in these indexes were collected from a sample of U.S. manufacturers of exports and are factory transaction prices, except as noted. F.a.s. = free alongside ship. N.e.s. = not elsewhere specified. F.o.b. = free on board]

COMMODITY	1985	1989	1990 [1]	1991	1992	1993	1994	1995
All commodities.	**88.4**	**99.7**	**99.5**	**100.6**	**101.0**	**101.4**	**103.2**	**109.4**
Food and live animals	96.3	110.6	104.3	100.7	102.8	97.8	103.9	114.1
Meat	78.6	102.0	98.5	101.9	106.1	111.6	107.3	115.8
Fish	78.5	123.2	98.4	94.7	98.1	96.5	98.0	121.5
Cereals and cereal preparations	109.3	113.5	108.6	96.8	104.8	90.9	101.8	114.4
Wheat	115.5	134.4	112.1	91.2	108.4	94.1	91.2	127.2
Rice	110.9	104.5	101.7	112.1	106.7	92.5	113.6	101.2
Maize	107.8	105.2	108.6	97.8	102.2	87.7	105.6	109.1
Other cereals	105.0	103.6	104.7	97.6	104.6	88.7	112.0	111.3
Fruits and vegetables	88 6	100.6	102.0	121.5	100.0	103.0	109.6	117.4
Feeding stuff for animals	74.9	118.8	97.6	100.0	102.2	100.7	106.2	102.9
Miscellaneous food products	90.6	97.9	99.9	100.5	100.2	100.3	97.8	100.9
Beverages and tobacco	79.9	93.8	99.3	105.7	109.8	113.1	113.5	114.9
Tobacco and tobacco manufactures	79.6	93.8	99.4	105.7	109.6	112.8	113.1	114.8
Crude materials	74.4	104.7	100.5	95.4	93.4	99.6	108.1	130.3
Raw hides and skins	63.3	97.4	100.5	81.5	80.8	79.2	94.4	103.5
Oil seeds and oleaginous fruits	92.8	114.3	97.1	99.4	98.4	97.9	112.9	96.7
Crude rubber, f.a.s.	85.6	98.3	99.1	103.2	101.0	99.2	96.1	118.0
Cork and wood	56.2	97.2	102.1	97.9	110.1	161.4	149.4	156.8
Pulp and waste paper	57.6	111.2	100.2	86.6	82.6	70.2	94.6	172.7
Textile fibers	85.3	95.3	102.6	107.0	86.0	83.5	105.0	134.0
Cotton textile fibers	87.4	93.8	103.7	107.9	79.7	77.5	101.3	134.2
Crude fertilizers and minerals	100.8	99.6	100.1	101.1	99.7	95.0	95.6	97.7
Metalliferous ores and metal scrap	70.7	110.1	99.9	89.1	85.1	83.9	91.2	124.7
Ferrous waste and scrap	73.0	112.4	99.8	93.4	82.2	99.0	95.6	116.7
Nonferrous base metal waste and scrap	56.5	112.5	99.4	84.2	86.0	72.2	92.7	116.7
Mineral fuels and related materials	104.6	88.4	91.1	89.9	86.5	88.0	87.4	92.9
Coal, coke and briquettes	103.1	96.8	100.1	98.6	96.9	93.9	93.9	97.3
Crude petroleum and petroleum products	(NA)	81.4	83.9	80.1	77.2	80.7	80.3	87.0
Animal and vegetable oils, fats and waxes	123.5	95.1	103.0	93.8	94.9	98.4	110.0	114.8
Chemicals and related products	84.5	102.9	97.4	99.7	97.4	96.1	99.0	116.8
Organic chemicals	80.5	116.0	94.9	94.6	91.5	90.5	92.7	124.1
Hydrocarbons, n.e.s. and derivatives, f.a.s.	73.9	114.8	93.3	76.2	77.8	80.1	92.4	130.2
Alcohols, phenols, phenol-alcohols, & deriv., f.a.s.	78.6	147.1	96.3	101.8	93.1	93.2	89.3	131.7
Chemical materials and products, n.e.s.	86.7	95.0	98.7	103.4	102.9	105.7	108.7	115.0
Intermediate manufactured products	81.3	99.9	99.8	100.1	100.6	100.7	104.4	115.8
Rubber manufactures	86.6	97.6	98.9	105.0	105.6	108.5	109.2	116.3
Paper and paperboard products	76.7	102.1	99.5	99.5	98.4	93.9	96.2	126.8
Textiles	84.3	97.1	99.6	104.1	105.6	106.8	106.7	112.3
Nonmetallic mineral manufactures	(NA)	96.1	99.6	101.2	103.5	105.4	107.3	109.4
Nonferrous metals	77.1	110.2	100.2	88.1	87.9	81.3	92.5	113.0
Manufactures of metals, n.e.s.	84.9	97.1	99.8	102.7	103.6	105.1	107.3	113.5
Machinery and transport equipment [2]	90.7	97.2	99.8	102.9	104.4	104.5	104.1	104.8
Power generating machinery [3]	85.2	96.0	99.8	104.7	109.6	110.7	112.8	114.8
Rotating electric plant and parts thereof, n.e.s.	76.8	95.0	99.7	101.9	104.7	106.1	107.4	112.2
Machinery specialized for particular industries	87.7	95.4	99.3	103.3	105.5	108.0	108.9	112.8
Agricultural machinery and parts [4]	89.4	94.2	100.0	102.1	104.9	107.3	109.4	111.1
Civil engineering and contractors, plant and equip.	90.7	95.2	98.8	103.9	102.0	105.5	109.6	113.0
Metalworking machinery	82.1	96.5	99.6	106.5	109.1	111.0	110.7	112.0
General industrial machines, parts, n.e.s.	84.4	95.6	99.7	103.7	106.1	108.3	110.1	111.2
Computer equipment and office machines	105.9	100.6	100.3	98.4	94.7	87.7	81.0	76.6
Computer equipment	113.0	101.7	100.3	97.8	94.0	83.5	75.2	68.7
Telecommunications [5]	89.6	96.8	100.1	106.4	108.3	109.4	107.3	106.7
Electrical machinery and equipment	93.8	99.0	99.9	100.6	103.6	103.5	103.2	104.0
Electronic valves, diodes, transistors & integr. cir.	106.5	100.1	100.6	98.5	103.7	102.3	100.0	100.7
Road vehicles	89.8	96.8	99.6	102.4	104.0	105.2	106.3	107.9
Other transport equipment	81.7	94.4	99.8	112.4	113.0	117.4	120.1	123.4
Miscellaneous manufactured articles	85.4	96.1	99.1	104.2	106.2	106.9	107.1	108.0

NA Not available.   [1] June 1990 may not equal 100 because indexes were reweighted to an "average" trade value in 1990.   [2] Excludes military and commercial aircraft.   [3] Includes equipment.   [4] Excludes tractors.   [5] Includes sound recording and reproducing equipment.

Source: U.S. Bureau of Labor Statistics, *News,* quarterly.

No. 765. Refiner/Reseller Sales Price of Gasoline, by State: 1993 to 1995

[In cents per gallon. As of **March.** Represents all refinery and gas plant operators' sales through company-operated retail outlets. Gasoline prices exclude excise taxes]

STATE	Gasoline excise taxes 1994	AVERAGE, ALL GRADES 1993	1994	1995	LEADED REGULAR 1993	1994	1995	UNLEADED REGULAR 1993	1994	1995	PREMIUM 1993	1994	1995
United States	18	75.5	67.2	73.2	75.2	62.9	69.0	71.6	71.3	77.1	87.8	80.3	85.1
Northeast:													
New England:													
Maine	19	80.9	73.4	78.6	[1]	69.4	74.4	76.4	78.4	83.9	93.6	85.6	91.9
New Hampshire	19	80.3	72.2	78.9	[1]	67.2	74.0	75.2	77.3	84.8	94.6	85.9	93.2
Vermont	16	82.7	76.2	80.0	[1]	71.6	74.8	78.1	81.3	85.4	94.8	89.2	94.0
Massachusetts	21	79.0	69.2	78.2	[1]	62.6	72.5	73.3	74.4	83.2	92.6	83.3	92.4
Rhode Island	28	77.6	71.1	73.6	[1]	65.1	68.1	72.2	74.7	78.2	87.3	82.5	85.4
Connecticut	31	81.6	72.3	76.8	[1]	65.3	71.1	75.3	77.4	81.7	96.2	87.2	91.7
Middle Atlantic:													
New York	23	75.8	68.7	75.1	(D)	63.6	69.9	70.5	73.2	80.3	91.1	82.8	89.5
New Jersey	15	85.4	74.9	81.4	[1]	66.0	73.5	77.1	81.0	86.2	98.9	88.6	94.6
Pennsylvania	22	72.3	65.7	73.5	[1]	60.2	68.3	67.2	69.7	77.3	84.9	78.4	86.6
Midwest:													
East North Central:													
Ohio	22	71.4	66.3	69.6	71.0	62.3	65.4	68.1	70.6	74.8	80.2	77.6	78.5
Indiana	16	71.6	65.1	70.4	79.3	61.3	66.8	69.2	69.1	74.1	76.7	75.0	77.6
Illinois	19	74.1	64.0	72.0	80.9	60.9	68.9	71.0	68.1	73.6	83.6	75.7	79.3
Michigan	16	70.8	63.7	69.1	81.6	60.5	66.3	68.2	68.1	73.5	80.0	75.1	75.4
Wisconsin	26	73.5	64.4	70.5	77.5	61.9	68.1	71.4	70.1	75.2	84.1	76.0	79.3
West North Central:													
Minnesota	20	81.1	72.4	76.2	80.2	70.5	74.4	79.3	75.4	80.9	90.2	84.8	88.0
Iowa	20	72.9	62.2	67.5	75.2	61.1	66.4	71.9	67.2	71.0	81.3	71.8	76.7
Missouri	15	69.8	61.5	67.9	73.6	58.3	64.9	66.9	67.1	72.5	78.3	75.0	80.2
North Dakota	18	85.1	74.4	76.3	89.8	73.6	75.6	84.0	80.3	84.4	93.2	83.1	82.3
South Dakota	20	78.2	70.9	74.6	85.1	68.7	72.4	76.9	74.7	84.0	89.1	86.4	86.1
Nebraska	25	76.8	69.3	71.1	79.2	67.8	69.8	75.7	72.9	76.4	85.2	77.4	80.5
Kansas	18	73.1	62.5	68.4	75.5	60.8	66.5	71.3	68.2	74.1	84.8	73.2	80.3
South:													
South Atlantic:													
Delaware	22	74.8	65.2	75.5	[1]	59.1	70.2	69.7	70.5	80.5	88.3	79.1	89.9
Maryland	24	75.5	66.0	76.2	[1]	60.6	71.4	70.0	70.8	80.2	87.9	77.1	86.8
District of Columbia	23	(D)	(D)	(D)	[1]	(D)	(D)	(D)	(D)	(D)	(D)	(D)	(D)
Virginia	18	75.4	67.7	74.5	[1]	61.0	68.4	69.2	72.2	79.0	89.6	81.3	87.4
West Virginia	21	78.4	71.9	76.2	[1]	67.3	71.6	73.6	77.2	81.1	90.7	83.6	87.4
North Carolina	22	71.2	63.9	69.4	[1]	58.4	63.2	65.9	67.5	72.9	84.5	77.4	82.7
South Carolina	17	69.8	63.2	67.4	[1]	57.4	61.7	64.7	68.4	71.6	85.5	78.3	82.3
Georgia	8	72.6	63.5	68.7	73.1	57.2	62.8	77.1	67.6	73.0	86.9	77.0	82.5
Florida	12	77.2	68.2	73.2	[1]	61.5	67.1	70.6	73.4	78.2	91.2	82.0	86.4
East South Central:													
Kentucky	15	72.9	68.9	73.1	(D)	63.8	68.6	68.4	72.9	77.5	84.9	81.4	85.7
Tennessee	21	72.5	64.3	69.7	(D)	58.0	63.2	66.4	68.1	74.6	85.9	77.6	82.0
Alabama	18	74.5	68.3	73.3	(D)	62.8	68.0	69.7	71.3	76.9	87.6	80.6	85.6
Mississippi	18	74.5	66.1	74.1	(D)	61.0	68.9	69.9	70.1	78.5	86.7	78.6	87.5
West South Central:													
Arkansas	19	72.8	63.6	69.1	67.8	60.0	65.2	69.3	69.7	74.3	86.0	76.1	81.6
Louisiana	20	75.3	66.6	71.9	(D)	60.6	65.8	69.8	71.4	76.7	88.3	80.1	84.7
Oklahoma	17	71.5	59.9	66.0	75.7	57.3	63.3	69.1	64.4	70.1	82.3	70.3	76.8
Texas	20	74.8	65.0	74.5	79.4	60.1	69.8	70.0	70.0	79.1	87.7	78.0	87.8
West:													
Mountain:													
Montana	27	77.1	71.5	74.8	76.5	70.2	73.4	76.4	67.6	74.6	81.9	79.2	82.0
Idaho	22	72.6	64.5	72.0	72.4	63.2	70.1	71.7	65.5	76.1	82.4	74.0	81.5
Wyoming	9	80.2	72.8	79.7	79.7	70.8	77.3	78.9	76.0	83.0	88.4	82.7	89.7
Colorado	27	80.4	75.4	80.8	83.3	71.2	76.6	77.0	82.0	86.4	93.3	90.7	95.4
New Mexico	21	85.9	69.5	75.6	85.0	67.7	73.5	84.4	73.3	81.9	97.7	80.9	87.6
Arizona	18	84.6	80.9	79.8	79.7	78.1	76.7	83.2	87.5	87.1	99.3	96.3	94.2
Utah	20	74.8	63.1	73.1	75.7	59.6	68.9	72.0	65.5	76.6	82.3	73.0	83.3
Nevada	24	83.1	80.2	82.9	81.2	76.7	80.5	80.6	84.3	80.2	97.1	96.3	96.1
Pacific:													
Washington	23	69.6	70.8	78.3	64.0	68.0	75.3	68.0	70.8	82.0	84.9	85.8	93.5
Oregon	24	79.9	76.0	77.4	74.5	73.9	75.5	78.9	75.9	75.6	96.1	91.2	91.5
California	19	84.4	70.1	77.5	(D)	65.3	73.3	80.6	76.6	79.2	98.6	85.7	91.6
Alaska	8	107.7	107.7	112.4	104.7	107.0	113.8	(NA)	(NA)	102.9	109.1	107.9	114.5
Hawaii	16	108.5	110.1	105.0	[1]	105.2	99.8	103.0	107.1	106.2	119.2	123.5	117.7

D Withheld to avoid disclosure of individual company data.   NA Not available.   [1] No data reported.

Source: Except as noted, U.S. Energy Information Administration, *Petroleum Marketing Monthly.*

Banking, Finance, and Insurance

This section presents data on the Nation's finances, various types of financial institutions, money and credit, securities, and insurance. The primary sources of these data are publications of several departments of the Federal Government, especially the Treasury Department, and independent agencies such as the Federal Deposit Insurance Corporation, the Federal Reserve System, and the Securities and Exchange Commission. National data on insurance are available primarily from private organizations, such as the American Council of Life Insurance.

Flow of funds—The flow of funds accounts of the Federal Reserve System (see tables 768 to 771) bring together statistics on all of the major forms of financial transactions and financial claims to present an economy-wide view of asset and liability relationships. In flow form, the accounts relate borrowing and lending to one another and to the nonfinancial activities that generate income and production. Each claim outstanding is included simultaneously as an asset of the lender and as a liability of the debtor. The accounts also indicate the balance between asset totals and liability totals over the economy as a whole. Several publications of the Board of Governors of the Federal Reserve System contain information on the flow of funds accounts: Summary data on flows and outstandings, in the *Federal Reserve Bulletin, Flow of Funds Accounts* (quarterly), and *Annual Statistical Digest;* and concepts and organization of the accounts, in *Guide to the Flow of Funds Accounts* (1993).

Banking system—Banks in this country are organized under the laws of both the States and the Federal Government and are regulated by several bank supervisory agencies. National banks are supervised by the Comptroller of the Currency. *Reports of Condition* have been collected from national banks since 1863. Summaries of these reports are published in the Comptroller's *Annual Report,* which also presents data on the structure of the national banking system.

In Brief

Conventional new-home mortgage rates:

1980	*13.95%*
1990	*10.08%*
1995	*8.05%*

Dow-Jones industrial average:

1980	*964.0*
1990	*2,633.7*
1995	*5,117.1*

The Federal Reserve System was established in 1913 to exercise central banking functions, some of which are shared with the U.S. Treasury. It includes national banks and such State banks that voluntarily join the System. Statements of State bank members are consolidated by the Board of Governors of the Federal Reserve System with data for national banks collected by the Comptroller of the Currency into totals for all member banks of the System. Balance sheet data for member banks and other commercial banks are published quarterly in the *Federal Reserve Bulletin.* The Federal Deposit Insurance Corporation (FDIC), established in 1933, insures each depositor up to $100,000. Major item balance sheet and income data for all commercial banks are published in the *FDIC Quarterly Banking Profile.*

The FDIC is the primary federal regulator of State-chartered banks that are not members of the Federal Reserve System and of most savings banks insured by the Bank Insurance Fund (BIF). The agency also has certain back–up supervisory authority, for safety and soundness purposes, over State-chartered banks that are members of the Federal Reserve System, national banks, and savings associations.

Savings institutions—Savings institutions are primarily involved in credit extension in the form of mortgage loans. Statistics on savings institutions are collected by the U.S. Office of Thrift Supervision and the FDIC. The Financial Institutions Reform, Recovery, and Enforcement Act of 1989 (FIRREA) authorized the establishment of the Resolution Trust Corporation (RTC) which was responsible for the disposal of assets from failed savings institutions. FIRREA gave the FDIC the job of managing the federal deposit insurance fund for savings institutions (SAIF=Savings Association Insurance Fund). Major balance sheet and income data for all insured savings institutions are published in the *FDIC Quarterly Banking Profile*.

Credit Unions—Federally chartered credit unions are under the supervision of the National Credit Union Administration, established in 1970. State-chartered credit unions are supervised by the respective State supervisory authorities. The Administration publishes comprehensive program and statistical information on all Federal and federally insured State credit unions in the *Annual Report of the National Credit Union Administration*. Deposit insurance (up to $100,000 per account) is provided to members of all Federal and those State credit unions that are federally-insured by the National Credit Union Share Insurance Fund which was established in 1970. Deposit insurance for State chartered credit unions is also available in some States under private or State-administered insurance programs.

Other credit agencies—Insurance companies, finance companies dealing primarily in installment sales financing, and personal loan companies represent important sources of funds for the credit market. Statistics on loans, investments, cash, etc., of life insurance companies are published principally by the American Council of Life Insurance in its *Life Insurance Fact Book* and in the *Federal Reserve Bulletin*. Consumer credit data are published currently in the *Federal Reserve Bulletin*.

Government corporations and credit agencies make available credit of specified types or to specified groups of private borrowers, either by lending directly or by insuring or guaranteeing loans made by private lending institutions. Data on operations of Government credit agencies, along with other Government corporations, are available in reports of individual agencies; data on their debt outstanding are published in the *Federal Reserve Bulletin*.

Currency—Currency, including coin and paper money, represents about 31 percent of all media of exchange in the United States, with most payments made by check. All currency is now issued by the Federal Reserve Banks.

Securities—The Securities and Exchange Commission (SEC) was established in 1934 to protect the interests of the public and investors against malpractices in the securities and financial markets and to provide the fullest possible disclosure of information regarding securities to the investing public. Statistical data are published in the *SEC Annual Report*.

Insurance—Insuring companies, which are regulated by the various States or the District of Columbia, are classified as either life or property. Companies that underwrite accident and health insurance only and those that underwrite accident and health insurance in addition to one or more property lines are included with property insurance. Insuring companies, other than those classified as life, are permitted to underwrite one or more property lines provided they are so licensed and have the necessary capital or surplus.

There are a number of published sources for statistics on the various classes of insurance—life, health, fire, marine, and casualty. Individual States collect data on all insurers operating within their respective jurisdictions, and many of the States publish an annual insurance report giving individual company data and aggregates of certain items for the companies operating within the State. Organizations representing certain classes of insurers publish reports for these classes. Among them are the annual commercial publishers, such as The National Underwriter Company whose *Argus Health Chart* (annual) contains financial and operating data for individual health and accident insurance companies, including Blue Cross and Blue Shield Plans. The American Council of Life Insurance publishes statistics on life insurance purchases, ownership, benefit payments, and assets in its biennial *Life Insurance Fact Book*.

Historical statistics—Tabular headnotes provide cross-references, where applicable, to *Historical Statistics of the United States, Colonial Times to 1970*. See Appendix IV.

No. 766. Gross Domestic Product in Finance, Insurance, and Real Estate, in Current and Constant (1987) Dollars: 1990 to 1993

[In billions of dollars, except percent. For definition of gross domestic product, see text, section 14. Based on 1987 Standard Industrial Classification]

INDUSTRY	CURRENT DOLLARS				CONSTANT (1987) DOLLARS			
	1990	1991	1992	1993	1990	1991	1992	1993
Finance, insurance, real estate, total....	982.4	1,041.1	1,106.1	1,180.6	868.3	868.8	893.4	915.0
Percent of gross domestic product......	17.7	18.2	18.4	18.6	17.7	17.8	17.9	17.8
Depository institutions.................	158.7	181.3	193.9	198.5	135.1	129.4	125.3	123.3
Nondepository institutions	20.7	23.0	25.9	32.0	17.9	18.2	19.5	22.2
Security and commodity brokers...........	37.9	37.1	49.6	60.7	38.4	38.9	51.0	67.1
Insurance carriers....................	69.9	84.7	84.8	104.1	60.1	67.5	73.0	67.7
Insurance agents, brokers, and services......	37.7	38.5	40.4	42.3	32.1	31.2	31.3	31.1
Real estate........................	641.7	664.2	698.7	718.5	566.7	565.2	575.0	583.9
Nonfarm housing services	458.7	483.6	512.0	533.4	398.3	403.9	409.4	419.5
Other real estate....................	183.0	180.6	186.7	185.1	168.5	161.3	165.7	164.4
Holding and other investment offices	15.8	12.1	12.8	24.4	18.1	18.5	18.3	19.7

Source: U.S. Bureau of Economic Analysis, *Survey of Current Business*, April 1995 and previous issues.

No. 767. Finance, Insurance, and Real Estate—Establishments, Employees, and Payroll: 1990 and 1993

[Covers establishments with payroll. Employees are for the week including March 12. Most government employees are excluded. For statement on methodology, see Appendix III]

KIND OF BUSINESS	1987 SIC code [1]	ESTABLISHMENTS (1,000)		EMPLOYEES (1,000)		PAYROLL (bil. dol.)	
		1990	1993	1990	1993	1990	1993
Finance, insurance, real estate ..	(H)	544.7	608.6	6,957	6,905	197.4	232.3
Depository institutions [2][3].............	60	81.2	102.6	2,033	2,095	48.4	57.7
Central reserve depositories	601	0.1	0.1	31	26	0.9	1.0
Commercial banks	602	52.3	62.6	1,472	1,528	35.6	42.1
Savings institutions	603	21.7	19.3	417	319	8.8	8.3
Credit unions	606	3.6	15.3	51	147	1.0	3.0
Functions closely related to banking....	609	2.8	4.7	44	46	1.4	1.6
Nondepository institutions [2][3]..........	61	42.0	41.9	506	483	14.0	17.7
Federal and fed.-sponsored credit	611	0.6	1.4	14	22	0.4	1.0
Personal credit institutions	614	25.0	17.0	236	152	5.5	3.8
Business credit institutions	615	3.7	4.8	88	100	3.1	4.1
Mortgage bankers and brokers	616	10.9	18.5	153	208	4.6	8.8
Security and commodity brokers [2]......	62	25.2	34.3	411	450	26.6	39.5
Security brokers and dealers.........	621	15.9	19.6	308	310	20.8	28.9
Commodity contracts brokers, dealers ..	622	1.2	1.5	15	13	0.7	0.7
Security and commodity exchanges	623	0.2	0.1	9	7	0.5	0.4
Security and commodity services......	628	7.1	13.1	76	120	4.5	9.5
Insurance carriers [2]	63	43.3	43.8	1,407	1,570	41.5	52.7
Life insurance	631	14.1	12.7	572	618	16.3	19.7
Medical service and health insurance [2]..	632	2.1	2.9	188	256	5.1	8.1
Accident and health insurance	6321	1.1	1.1	48	54	1.3	1.5
Hospital and medical service plans ..	6324	1.0	1.8	139	202	3.8	6.6
Fire, marine, and casualty insurance ...	633	18.3	19.1	533	585	17.0	21.6
Surety insurance.................	635	0.6	0.6	15	12	0.5	0.5
Title insurance	636	3.2	2.3	57	40	1.6	1.4
Pension, health and welfare funds	637	3.8	6.0	25	54	0.6	1.2
Insurance agents, brokers, and service ...	64	110.8	122.3	712	656	20.3	20.3
Real estate [2]......................	65	217.0	235.0	1,374	1,335	28.5	29.7
Real estate operators and lessors	651	95.7	101.8	509	491	8.7	8.9
Real estate agents and managers	653	72.2	110.4	585	707	13.3	17.0
Title abstract offices..............	654	3.1	4.8	24	38	0.5	1.0
Subdividers and developers [2]	655	19.6	16.6	140	98	3.4	2.6
Subdividers and developers, n.e.c. [4]..	6552	10.8	9.4	88	57	2.3	1.7
Cemetery subdividers and developers .	6553	4.4	6.3	35	40	0.6	0.8
Holding and other investment offices [2]....	67	22.6	27.4	263	254	10.0	11.8
Holding offices	671	6.2	7.9	124	128	5.4	7.0
Investment offices................	672	1.0	0.8	16	12	1.0	0.7
Trusts.........................	673	7.8	10.4	65	65	1.4	1.7
Educational, religious, etc. trusts	6732	3.6	4.7	42	37	0.9	1.0
Miscellaneous investing	679	5.0	8.1	44	49	1.5	2.4
Patent owners and lessors	6794	0.9	1.6	15	18	0.4	0.8
Administrative and auxiliary	(X)	2.6	1.3	251	62	8.2	2.9

X Not applicable.   [1] Standard Industrial Classification; see text, section 13.   [2] Includes industries not shown separately.   [3] Includes government employees.   [4] N.e.c.=Not elsewhere classified.

Source: U.S. Bureau of the Census, *County Business Patterns*, annual.

No. 768. Flow of Funds Accounts—Financial Assets of Financial and Nonfinancial Institutions, by Holder Sector: 1980 to 1994

[In billions of dollars. As of Dec. 31. See also Historical Statistics, Colonial Times to 1970, series X 192, X 229, X 821, and X 835]

SECTOR	1980	1985	1987	1988	1989	1990	1991	1992	1993	1994
All sectors	13,527	22,319	27,282	29,724	33,098	34,188	37,338	39,679	42,776	44,435
Households [1]	6,406	9,668	11,380	12,346	13,802	14,023	15,534	16,465	17,538	17,997
Nonfinancial business	1,340	2,067	2,473	2,704	2,849	2,981	3,032	3,161	3,233	3,376
Farm	24	33	39	43	45	47	50	53	57	60
Nonfarm noncorporate	140	310	364	404	432	445	440	454	460	474
Nonfinancial corporations	1,176	1,723	2,070	2,257	2,373	2,489	2,542	2,654	2,716	2,842
State and local government	249	521	637	680	712	723	732	716	720	629
U.S. Government	229	372	371	361	369	441	499	474	474	432
U.S. Government-sponsored credit enterprises and mortgage pools	307	692	1,043	1,165	1,321	1,494	1,650	1,821	1,980	2,225
Monetary authorities	174	243	286	304	315	344	366	382	424	452
Commercial banking [2]	1,482	2,376	2,774	2,952	3,232	3,339	3,443	3,657	3,896	4,162
Domestic commercial banks	1,266	1,990	2,257	2,385	2,545	2,644	2,677	2,775	2,932	3,123
Foreign banking offices in U.S.	98	144	236	266	360	368	439	511	546	596
Nonbank finance	2,881	5,486	7,055	7,734	8,727	8,966	10,071	10,843	12,043	12,393
Funding corporations	14	46	71	99	117	153	178	235	291	345
Savings institutions	792	1,275	1,505	1,640	1,513	1,358	1,172	1,079	1,029	1,013
Credit unions	68	134	178	192	202	217	240	264	281	295
Life insurance	464	796	1,005	1,133	1,260	1,367	1,505	1,614	1,785	1,888
Other insurance	182	299	405	454	503	533	576	597	641	670
Private pension funds	504	1,093	1,367	1,422	1,706	1,629	2,056	2,214	2,450	2,356
State and local govt. retirement funds	197	399	524	609	767	820	941	1,059	1,151	1,223
Finance companies	205	365	484	535	571	611	634	637	654	742
Mortgage companies	16	25	24	29	49	49	60	60	60	34
Real estate investment trusts	3	8	10	14	15	13	14	14	17	18
Mutual funds	62	240	460	478	566	602	814	1,042	1,429	1,463
Closed-end funds	8	8	21	43	52	52	72	91	107	114
Money market funds	76	244	316	338	428	498	540	544	559	605
Security brokers, dealers	45	156	138	136	237	262	333	372	454	443
Asset-backed securities issuers	-	39	131	169	226	278	329	392	473	528
Bank personal trusts	245	358	414	444	515	522	608	630	661	656
Rest of the world	459	894	1,264	1,478	1,770	1,879	2,011	2,160	2,468	2,770

- Represents zero.   [1] Includes nonprofit organizations.   [2] Includes other sectors not shown separately.

No. 769. Flow of Funds Accounts—Credit Market Debt Outstanding: 1980 to 1994

[In billions of dollars. As of Dec. 31. N.e.c.=Not elsewhere classified]

ITEM	1980	1985	1987	1988	1989	1990	1991	1992	1993	1994
Credit market debt	4,700	8,462	10,697	11,704	12,725	13,597	14,232	15,036	16,018	17,051
U.S. government	735	1,590	1,950	2,105	2,251	2,498	2,776	3,080	3,336	3,492
Private domestic nonfinancial	3,189	5,382	6,612	7,208	7,819	8,215	8,405	8,640	9,027	9,490
Households [1]	1,391	2,243	2,771	3,074	3,380	3,614	3,785	4,002	4,292	4,641
Farm	161	173	144	134	134	135	135	136	138	141
Nonfarm noncorporate business . . .	440	860	1,034	1,097	1,137	1,147	1,116	1,074	1,049	1,069
Corporations	886	1,543	1,970	2,169	2,366	2,469	2,458	2,500	2,554	2,676
State and local government	310	563	693	735	803	849	911	928	993	964
Rest of the world	197	237	245	251	261	285	299	311	358	346
Financial sectors	579	1,254	1,890	2,140	2,393	2,599	2,752	3,005	3,297	3,722
Government-sponsored enterprises [2]	163	264	308	353	378	399	408	448	528	701
Federally-related mortgage pools . . .	114	369	670	745	870	1,020	1,156	1,272	1,353	1,448
Commercial banks	49	79	82	79	77	77	65	74	79	89
Bank holding companies	43	106	131	136	142	115	112	115	123	132
Funding corporations	13	39	80	118	130	146	139	162	170	201
Thrift institutions [3]	55	110	163	184	169	139	95	88	99	112
Life insurance companies	-	-	-	-	-	-	-	-	-	1
Finance companies	127	224	299	323	350	374	393	389	391	441
Mortgage companies	12	17	14	15	25	25	22	30	29	16
Real estate investment trusts	5	5	8	10	12	12	14	14	17	19
Security brokers, dealers	-	1	3	8	14	15	19	22	34	34
Asset-backed securities issuers	-	39	131	169	226	278	329	392	473	528
CORPORATE CREDIT MARKET DEBT OUTSTANDING, BY TYPE OF INSTRUMENT										
Total	886	1,543	1,970	2,169	2,366	2,469	2,458	2,500	2,554	2,676
Municipal debt [4]	46	127	116	116	115	115	114	114	114	112
Corporate bonds	366	578	784	887	961	1,008	1,087	1,154	1,230	1,252
Mortgages	114	96	191	186	204	192	193	166	153	152
Bank loans, n.e.c.	230	424	482	519	554	555	530	518	515	564
Commercial paper	28	72	74	86	107	117	98	107	118	139
Other loans	102	245	322	375	425	481	435	441	424	456
Savings institutions	1	15	20	25	24	17	10	6	5	5
Finance companies	71	127	171	196	216	235	234	237	236	269
U.S. government	8	14	11	10	10	9	8	8	8	9
Acceptance liabilities to banks	17	28	33	33	36	29	23	20	17	15
Rest of the world	5	60	86	111	138	187	153	160	141	140
Asset-backed securities issuers	-	-	-	-	2	5	7	9	17	19

- Represents zero.   [1] Includes nonprofit organizations.   [2] U.S. Government.   [3] Covers savings institutions and credit unions.   [4] Industrial revenue bonds. Issued by State and local governments to finance private investment and secured in interest and principal by the industrial user of the funds.

Source of tables 768 and 769: Board of Governors of the Federal Reserve System, Flow of Funds Accounts, March 1995 quarterly diskettes. Data are also published in the quarterly Z.1 release.

No. 770. Flow of Funds Accounts—Financial Assets and Liabilities of Financial and Nonfinancial Institutions, by Sector and Type of Instrument: 1995

[In billions of dollars. As of Dec. 31. Preliminary. A=Assets; L=Liabilities. SDR=Special drawing rights, IMF=International Monetary Fund. RP's=Repurchase Agreements. "N.e.c."=Not elsewhere classified]

TYPE OF INSTRUMENT	ALL SECTORS, TOTAL A	L	PRIVATE DOMESTIC NONFINANCIAL INSTITUTIONS — Total A	L	Households [1] A	L	Business A	L	State and local govts. A	L	U.S. GOVERNMENT A	L	FINANCIAL INSTITUTIONS — Total [2] A	L	Commercial banking A	L	Nonbank finance A	L	Federally sponsored credit agencies and mortgage pools A	L	FOREIGN SECTOR A	L
Total	52,265	40,725	27,061	13,757	21,036	5,199	5,283	7,464	742	1,093	418	4,152	21,683	20,923	4,497	4,333	14,247	13,670	2,468	2,452	3,103	1,894
Gold stock and SDR's	22	-	-	-	-	-	-	-	-	-	11	-	11	-	-	-	-	-	-	-	-	-
IMF position	15	15	-	-	-	-	-	-	-	-	15	-	21	21	-	-	-	-	-	-	-	15
Official foreign exchange	49	49	-	-	-	-	-	-	-	-	28	28	21	-	-	-	-	-	-	-	-	49
Treasury currency, SDR certificates	34	28	-	-	-	-	-	-	-	-	22	28	34	-	1	-	-	-	-	-	-	-
Checkable deposits, currency	1,192	1,230	1,076	-	701	-	342	-	33	-	1	-	67	1,230	-	711	65	128	1	-	27	-
Time and savings accounts	2,765	2,765	2,576	-	2,392	-	121	-	64	-	-	-	137	2,765	-	1,877	137	888	-	-	50	-
Fed. funds and security RP's	745	660	88	-	-	-	-	-	88	-	-	-	389	660	67	422	269	238	106	-	69	-
Money market fund shares	546	745	544	-	479	-	1	-	-	-	-	-	202	745	2	-	202	745	-	-	-	349
Life insurance reserves	546	546	546	-	546	-	-	-	-	-	-	11	20	535	-	-	20	535	-	-	-	-
Pension fund reserves	5,435	5,435	5,435	-	5,435	-	-	-	-	-	-	375	70	5,061	-	-	568	5,061	-	-	-	-
Interbank claims	296	287	-	-	-	-	45	-	-	-	-	-	570	287	67	217	3	-	-	-	-	-
Mutual fund shares [3]	1,865	1,865	1,295	-	1,250	-	64	-	-	-	-	-	570	1,865	5	-	568	1,865	-	-	-	-
Other corporate equities [4]	8,345	8,345	4,286	-	4,286	-	13	-	-	-	-	-	3,712	-	253	-	3,707	-	-	-	348	-
Credit market instruments [5]	18,551	18,551	2,903	10,241	2,019	-	362	4,172	522	1,063	184	3,637	13,937	4,244	3,518	253	7,715	1,609	2,323	2,382	1,527	429
U.S. Treasury securities [6]	3,609	3,609	481	-	753	-	75	-	160	-	-	3,609	1,794	-	280	-	1,080	-	56	-	827	-
Federal agency securities [7]	2,410	2,410	502	135	209	-	28	109	244	5	-	28	1,762	5	466	-	1,105	5	188	2,382	166	-
Municipal securities	1,301	1,301	396	1,301	435	-	63	-	-	1,057	57	-	799	-	93	-	701	-	5	-	-	-
Corporate and foreign bonds	2,760	2,760	400	1,328	396	-	97	1,328	114	-	-	-	1,995	1,150	111	162	1,862	988	22	-	368	282
Mortgages	4,724	4,724	83	3,572	189	-	83	1,128	-	-	57	-	4,267	24	1,090	-	1,351	24	1,826	-	-	-
Consumer credit	1,116	1,116	-	1,116	-	-	17	805	-	-	-	-	1,033	63	504	-	528	63	-	-	-	-
Bank loans, n.e.c.	946	946	-	848	-	-	-	157	-	-	-	-	946	488	946	53	573	435	-	-	-	45
Open-market paper	700	700	52	157	35	-	17	157	-	-	-	-	605	223	6	53	77	223	-	-	-	-
Security credit	300	300	123	77	123	98	-	-	-	-	26	95	176	10	100	-	104	10	-	-	43	34
Trade credit [8]	1,466	1,246	1,279	1,097	-	-	1,279	968	36	30	26	-	104	9	3	3	104	7	-	-	56	55
Taxes payable	51	89	36	80	-	-	-	80	36	-	15	9	-	-	-	-	-	-	-	-	-	-
Proprietors' equity	2,636	2,636	2,636	-	2,636	-	1,279	-	-	-	-	-	-	-	-	-	-	-	-	-	-	-
Investment in bank personal trusts	842	842	842	-	842	-	-	-	-	-	-	-	842	842	-	-	-	842	-	-	-	-
Miscellaneous claims	6,510	5,725	3,361	2,263	306	-	3,056	2,245	-	-	116	7	2,232	2,448	803	851	1,381	1,520	37	70	801	1,007

- Represents or rounds to zero. [1] Includes nonprofit organizations. [2] Includes monetary authority, not shown separately. [3] Nonbank finance liability is redemption value of shares of open-end investment companies for amounts outstanding. [4] Assets shown at market value. No specific liability attributed to issuers of stocks other than open-end investment companies. [5] Includes "Other loans", not shown separately. [6] Includes savings bonds and other nonmarketable debt held by public. [7] Issues by agencies in the budget and by Government-sponsored enterprises in financial sectors, issues backed by federally-related mortgage pools, and loan participation certificates. [8] Asset is corporate only; noncorporate credit deducted in liability total to conform to quarterly flow tables.

Source: Board of Governors of the Federal Reserve System, Flow of Funds Accounts, quarterly.

No. 771. Flow of Funds Accounts—Assets and Liabilities of Households: 1980 to 1994

[As of **December 31**. Includes nonprofit organizations. See table 770 for preliminary 1995 data. See also *Historical Statistics, Colonial Times to 1970*, series X 114-147]

TYPE OF INSTRUMENT	TOTAL (bil. dol.)							PERCENT DISTRIBUTION		
	1980	1985	1990	1991	1992	1993	1994	1980	1990	1994
Total financial assets	6,406	9,668	14,023	15,534	16,465	17,538	17,997	100.0	100.0	100.0
Deposits.	1,573	2,454	3,152	3,109	3,080	3,060	3,104	24.6	22.5	17.2
Checkable deposits and currency . .	264	348	449	511	635	713	722	4.1	3.2	4.0
Small time and savings deposits . . .	1,091	1,690	2,069	2,021	1,957	1,888	1,883	17.0	14.8	10.5
Large time deposits.	155	222	260	194	147	128	148	2.4	1.9	0.8
Money market fund shares	62	195	375	383	341	331	352	1.0	2.7	2.0
Credit market instruments	461	862	1,499	1,447	1,523	1,526	1,932	7.2	10.7	10.7
U.S. Government securities	212	350	648	600	699	702	1,084	3.3	4.6	6.0
Treasury issues.	181	306	449	406	462	503	677	2.8	3.2	3.8
Savings bonds.	73	80	126	138	157	172	180	1.1	0.9	1.0
Other Treasury	108	226	323	268	304	331	497	1.7	2.3	2.8
Agency issues	31	44	199	194	237	199	407	0.5	1.4	2.3
Municipal securities.	76	257	448	483	449	433	403	1.2	3.2	2.2
Corporate and foreign bonds.	31	31	95	105	107	142	198	0.5	0.7	1.1
Mortgages.	111	125	177	162	166	177	187	1.7	1.3	1.0
Open-market paper.	31	99	131	96	103	71	60	0.5	0.9	0.3
Mutual fund shares.	46	192	452	592	734	972	969	0.7	3.2	5.4
Corporate equities	934	1,210	1,717	2,469	2,810	3,088	2,913	14.6	12.2	16.2
Life insurance reserves.	216	257	380	406	433	468	488	3.4	2.7	2.7
Pension fund reserves [1]	949	2,032	3,484	4,138	4,516	4,975	5,061	14.8	24.8	28.1
Investment in bank personal trusts . . .	245	358	522	608	630	661	656	3.8	3.7	3.6
Equity in noncorporate business	1,892	2,134	2,529	2,444	2,412	2,422	2,485	29.5	18.0	13.8
Security credit	16	35	62	87	76	103	108	0.3	0.4	0.6
Miscellaneous assets	74	133	224	234	251	264	281	1.1	1.6	1.6
Total liabilities	1,443	2,333	3,738	3,920	4,143	4,464	4,821	100.0	100.0	100.0
Credit market instruments	1,391	2,243	3,614	3,785	4,002	4,292	4,641	96.4	96.7	96.3
Home mortgages	905	1,379	2,455	2,614	2,788	2,970	3,156	62.7	65.7	65.5
Consumer credit	355	602	812	797	803	867	984	24.6	21.7	20.4
Municipal debt	17	81	86	93	108	120	135	1.2	2.3	2.8
Commercial mortgages	31	63	139	152	164	181	190	2.2	3.7	3.9
Bank loans, not elsewhere classified	28	34	12	9	11	20	36	1.9	0.3	0.7
Other loans	55	84	110	120	128	134	141	3.8	2.9	2.9
Security credit	25	51	39	55	53	76	73	1.7	1.0	1.5
Trade credit.	14	24	69	64	72	80	89	1.0	1.8	1.8
Unpaid life insurance premiums [2]	13	15	16	16	16	17	18	0.9	0.4	0.4

[1] See also table 815.   [2] Includes deferred premiums.

Source: Board of Governors of the Federal Reserve System, *Flow of Funds Accounts*, March 1995 diskettes. Data are also published in the quarterly Z.1 release.

No. 772. Percent Distribution of Amount of Debt Held by Families, by Type and Purpose of Debt and Type of Lending Institution: 1989 and 1992

[Families include one-person units; for definition of family, see text, section 1. Based on Survey of Consumer Finance; see Appendix III]

TYPE OF DEBT	1989	1992	PURPOSE OF DEBT	1989	1992	TYPE OF LENDING INSTITUTION	1989	1992
Total.	100.0	100.0	Total	100.0	100.0	Total	100.0	100.0
Home mortgage and home equity lines of credit	56.7	63.3	Home purchase.	53.1	58.6	Commercial bank	29.7	31.8
			Home improvement . .	2.0	1.9	Savings and loan	23.5	18.9
Installment loans.	13.9	9.2	Investment, excluding real estate	2.6	1.4	Credit union	3.2	4.0
Credit card balances . .	2.3	2.8	Vehicles	8.6	5.7	Finance or loan company.	9.4	12.9
Other lines of credit. . .	1.0	0.8	Goods and services . .	4.8	4.9	Brokerage	3.0	3.9
Investment real estate mortgages	24.5	22.0	Investment real estate.	25.8	22.4	Real estate lender.	13.2	13.4
Other debt.	1.7	1.9	Education.	1.9	2.1	Individual lender	6.8	4.0
			Unclassifiable loans . .	1.2	2.9	Other nonfinancial.	1.9	2.5
						Government.	2.1	1.2
						Credit and store cards . .	2.3	2.9
						Unclassifiable loans . . .	4.9	4.5

Source: Board of Governors of the Federal Reserve System, *Federal Reserve Bulletin*, October 1994.

No. 773. Financial Assets Held by Families, by Type of Asset: 1989 and 1992

[**Median value in thousands of constant 1992 dollars**. Constant dollar figures are based on consumer price index data published by U.S. Bureau of Labor Statistics. Families include one-person units; for definition of family, see text, section 1. Based on Survey of Consumer Finance; see source. For definition of median, see Guide to Tabular Presentation]

AGE OF FAMILY HEAD AND FAMILY INCOME	Total [1]	Transaction accounts [2]	Certificates of deposit	Mutual funds [3]	Stocks [4]	Bonds [4]	Retirement accounts [5]	Savings bonds	Other managed [6]
PERCENT OF FAMILIES OWNING ASSET									
1989, total	88.4	85.1	19.4	7.1	16.2	5.3	35.4	23.8	3.5
1992, total	**90.7**	**87.5**	**16.6**	**11.2**	**17.8**	**4.7**	**39.3**	**22.7**	**4.3**
Under 35 years old	86.8	82.5	7.4	5.8	11.1	1.4	29.7	22.8	1.9
35 to 44 years old	90.9	86.9	9.0	10.8	20.7	3.1	47.3	29.4	3.3
45 to 54 years old	93.1	89.2	15.1	10.5	19.2	6.5	52.9	25.4	6.0
55 to 64 years old	92.9	90.7	21.2	16.6	23.0	5.0	53.4	21.4	6.0
65 to 74 years old	91.7	89.8	31.7	16.5	19.0	9.2	36.7	14.1	6.3
75 years old and over	92.6	91.7	36.6	13.4	18.2	8.3	6.3	14.5	5.6
Less than $10,000	70.2	63.7	11.1	3.3	4.2	1.0	7.0	6.6	0.9
$10,000 to $24,999	88.1	83.7	15.1	5.7	8.8	1.9	21.6	13.3	2.4
$25,000 to $49,999	98.2	95.4	17.1	11.8	18.2	3.7	45.2	27.9	4.7
$50,000 to $99,999	99.3	98.7	22.2	18.5	31.0	6.9	70.7	39.5	6.8
$100,000 and more	98.7	98.7	19.5	29.9	48.7	22.4	78.6	32.1	11.6
PERCENT DISTRIBUTION OF AMOUNT OF FINANCIAL ASSETS [7]									
1989	100.0	19.7	10.4	5.0	14.6	11.0	18.8	1.6	6.6
1992	100.0	16.4	7.9	7.2	21.0	7.7	22.7	1.1	6.4
MEDIAN VALUE [8]									
1989, total	12.0	2.3	12.6	11.2	7.3	27.9	11.2	0.6	22.3
1992, total	**13.1**	**2.4**	**13.5**	**18.0**	**10.0**	**25.0**	**15.0**	**0.7**	**25.0**
Under 35 years old	4.2	1.4	5.0	3.8	2.0	10.0	4.7	0.4	20.0
35 to 44 years old	10.8	2.2	5.0	18.0	5.0	19.3	9.8	0.6	20.0
45 to 54 years old	24.7	3.4	10.0	20.0	12.0	25.2	30.0	1.0	25.0
55 to 64 years old	40.1	4.0	20.0	20.4	20.0	40.0	35.7	1.0	30.0
65 to 74 years old	30.2	4.0	25.0	30.0	24.0	25.3	23.0	0.9	40.0
75 years old and over	20.2	4.0	24.0	22.3	28.0	52.0	28.0	1.1	55.0
Less than $10,000	1.5	0.7	7.0	15.0	10.0	15.7	9.0	0.5	12.0
$10,000 to $24,999	3.9	1.1	16.0	7.0	4.0	11.0	5.1	0.5	20.0
$25,000 to $49,999	14.1	2.3	13.0	15.0	5.0	25.0	10.0	0.5	20.0
$50,000 to $99,999	47.0	5.6	12.0	22.0	8.0	20.0	25.0	1.0	32.0
$100,000 and more	184.0	25.5	28.0	30.0	40.0	51.0	66.0	1.2	95.0

[1] Includes other types of financial assets, not shown separately.   [2] Checking, savings, and money market accounts.
[3] Excludes money market mutual funds, individual retirement accounts (IRA's), Keogh accounts, and any type of pension plan invested in mutual funds.   [4] Covers only those stocks and bonds that are directly held by families outside mutual funds, IRA's, Keogh or pension accounts.   [5] Covers IRA's, Keogh accounts, and employer-provided pension plans from which withdrawals can be made, such as 401(k) plans.   [6] Includes trusts, annuities, managed investment accounts, and other such assets.   [7] Of all families.   [8] Median value of financial asset for families holding such assets.

No. 774. Financial Debt Held by Families, by Type of Debt: 1989 and 1992

[See headnote, table 773]

AGE OF FAMILY HEAD AND FAMILY INCOME	Total	Mortgage and home equity	Installment	Credit cards	Other lines of credit	Investment real estate	Other debt [1]
PERCENT OF FAMILIES HOLDING DEBTS							
1989, total	73.0	40.0	50.1	40.4	3.2	7.3	6.7
1992, total	**73.3**	**38.7**	**45.8**	**43.4**	**2.5**	**8.3**	**8.7**
Under 35 years old	82.1	30.6	62.1	52.6	2.9	4.8	6.5
35 to 44 years old	86.5	55.5	58.2	50.3	3.3	9.3	12.6
45 to 54 years old	85.8	61.8	48.6	48.4	2.8	14.5	10.3
55 to 64 years old	69.2	40.0	38.0	36.7	2.3	13.8	10.8
65 to 74 years old	51.9	18.3	22.9	30.2	1.1	5.4	5.4
75 years old and over	30.2	6.7	8.0	19.5	(B)	0.7	4.5
Less than $10,000	47.5	9.6	29.8	23.7	(B)	0.6	5.2
$10,000 to $24,999	69.5	21.8	46.8	43.2	1.5	3.5	6.4
$25,000 to $49,999	82.5	47.4	54.6	54.8	2.9	7.3	10.7
$50,000 to $99,999	84.6	66.1	50.2	49.0	4.3	13.5	10.1
$100,000 and more	85.0	67.6	35.3	32.9	4.2	34.6	14.9
MEDIAN DEBT [2]							
1989, total	17.6	38.0	5.9	1.1	2.2	35.7	2.2
1992, total	**17.6**	**44.0**	**4.5**	**1.0**	**2.2**	**28.0**	**2.5**
Under 35 years old	10.2	52.0	4.6	0.9	1.6	18.0	1.2
35 to 44 years old	33.3	54.0	5.0	1.3	1.8	28.0	3.0
45 to 54 years old	30.9	42.0	5.0	1.7	5.0	49.5	3.0
55 to 64 years old	20.8	28.0	3.9	1.0	4.0	34.7	3.0
65 to 74 years old	5.6	17.0	4.2	0.7	4.0	17.0	2.0
75 years old and over	2.3	15.0	3.1	0.6	(B)	104.0	1.1
Less than $10,000	2.0	16.0	1.6	0.6	(B)	6.5	0.7
$10,000 to $24,999	5.6	17.4	2.7	0.8	3.0	6.1	1.0
$25,000 to $49,999	21.1	40.0	5.6	1.3	1.5	18.0	2.0
$50,000 to $99,999	57.2	58.0	7.8	1.5	2.0	41.0	3.0
$100,000 and more	131.0	103.0	10.8	3.9	18.0	75.0	6.0

B Base figure too small.   [1] Includes loans on insurance policies, loans against pension accounts, and other unclassified loans.   [2] Median amount of financial debt for families holding such debts.

Source of tables 773 and 774: Board of Governors of the Federal Reserve System, *Federal Reserve Bulletin*, October 1994.

No. 775. Selected Financial Institutions—Number and Assets, by Asset Size: 1995

[As of **December**. FDIC=Federal Deposit Insurance Corporation]

ASSET SIZE	NUMBER OF INSTITUTIONS			ASSETS (bil. dol.)		
	F.D.I.C.-insured		Credit unions [1]	F.D.I.C.-insured		Credit unions [1]
	Commercial banks	Savings institutions		Commercial banks [2]	Savings institutions	
Total	9,941	2,029	11,687	4,312.7	1,025.7	306.6
Less than $5.0 million	[3]	[3]	5,874	[3]	[3]	10.5
$5.0 million to $9.9 million	[3]	[3]	1,799	[3]	[3]	12.8
$10.0 million to $24.9 million	[3]1,756	[3]162	1,830	[3]28.8	[3]2.5	29.3
$25.0 million to $49.9 million	2,369	293	959	87.2	11.0	33.5
$50.0 million to $99.9 million	2,534	454	597	181.9	33.1	41.1
$100.0 million to $499.9 million. . .	2,593	822	568	511.3	184.6	114.1
$500.0 million to $999.9 million. . .	268	137	42	185.3	93.9	29.1
$1.0 billion to $2.9 billion	220	102	16	368.3	168.0	23.6
$3.0 billion or more.	201	59	2	2,949.8	532.6	12.7
	PERCENT DISTRIBUTION					
Total	100.0	100.0	100.0	100.0	100.0	100.0
Less than $5.0 million	[3]	[3]	50.3	[3]	[3]	3.4
$5.0 million to $9.9 million	[3]	[3]	15.4	[3]	[3]	4.2
$10.0 million to $24.9 million	[3]17.7	[3]8.0	15.7	[3]0.7	[3]0.2	9.6
$25.0 million to $49.9 million	23.8	14.4	8.2	2.0	1.1	10.9
$50.0 million to $99.9 million	25.5	22.4	5.1	4.2	3.2	13.4
$100.0 million to $499.9 million. . .	26.1	40.5	4.9	11.9	18.0	37.2
$500.0 million to $999.9 million. . .	2.7	6.8	0.4	4.3	9.2	9.5
$1.0 billion to $2.9 billion	2.2	5.0	0.1	8.5	16.4	7.7
$3.0 billion or more.	2.0	2.9	(Z)	68.4	51.9	4.1

Z Less than 0.05 percent.   [1] Source: National Credit Union Administration, *National Credit Union Administration Yearend Statistics 1995.* Excludes nonfederally insured State chartered credit unions and federally insured corporate credit unions.   [2] Includes foreign branches of U.S. banks.   [3] Data for institutions with assets less than $10 million included with those with assets of $10.0 million to $24.9 million.

Source: Except as noted, U.S. Federal Deposit Insurance Corporation, *Statistics on Banking, 1995.*

No. 776. Banking Offices, by Type of Bank: 1980 to 1995

[As of **December 31**. Includes Puerto Rico and outlying areas. Covers all FDIC-insured commercial banks and savings institutions. Data for 1980 include automatic teller machines which were reported by many banks as branches.

ITEM	1980	1985	1989	1990	1991	1992	1993	1994	1995
All banking offices	(NA)	85,083	84,632	84,672	84,098	82,002	81,745	82,673	81,893
Number of banks	(NA)	18,043	15,802	15,162	14,488	13,856	13,322	12,602	11,970
Number of branches	(NA)	67,040	68,830	69,510	69,610	68,146	68,423	70,071	69,923
Commercial banks	53,172	57,710	60,720	62,753	63,896	63,401	63,828	65,594	66,454
Number of banks.	14,434	14,417	12,715	12,347	11,927	11,466	10,960	10,450	9,941
Number of branches	38,738	43,293	48,005	50,406	51,969	51,935	52,868	55,144	56,513
Savings institutions	(NA)	27,373	23,912	21,919	20,202	18,601	17,917	17,079	15,439
Number of banks	(NA)	3,626	3,087	2,815	2,561	2,390	2,362	2,152	2,029
Number of branches	(NA)	23,747	20,825	19,104	17,641	16,211	15,555	14,927	13,410

NA Not available.

Source: U.S. Federal Deposit Insurance Corporation, *Historical Statistics on Banking, 1934-1994*, 1995 and *Statistics on Banking*, annual.

No. 777. Insured Commercial Banks—Selected Measures of Financial Condition, by Asset Size and Region: 1995

[**In percent, except as indicated**. Preliminary. See headnote, table 779]

ASSET SIZE AND REGION	Number of banks	Return on assets	Return on equity	Equity capital to assets	Noncurrent assets plus other real estate owned to total assets	Net charge-offs to loans and leases	Percentage of banks losing money
Total	9,941	1.17	14.68	8.11	0.85	0.49	3.4
Less than $100 million . .	6,659	1.18	11.37	10.43	0.78	0.24	4.0
$100 million to $1 billion .	2,861	1.25	13.48	9.39	0.80	0.36	2.1
$1 billion to $10 billion. . .	346	1.28	15.04	8.57	0.82	0.69	2.6
$10 billion or more	75	1.10	15.60	7.19	0.89	0.46	1.3
Northeast [1]	794	1.02	13.73	7.61	1.03	0.64	5.4
Southeast [2]	1,659	1.19	14.73	8.23	0.64	0.32	3.9
Central [3]	2,178	1.15	14.09	8.30	0.63	0.31	2.6
Midwest [4]	2,487	1.50	17.10	8.70	0.64	0.54	1.5
Southwest [5]	1,773	1.20	14.16	8.53	0.61	0.24	2.0
West [6]	1,050	1.41	16.58	8.54	1.09	0.62	9.5

[1] CT, DE, DC, ME, MD, MA, NH, NJ, NY, PA, PR, RI, and VT.   [2] AL, FL, GA, MS, NC, SC, TN, VA, and WV.   [3] IL, IN, KY, MI, OH, and WI.   [4] IA, KS, MN, MO, NE, ND, and SD.   [5] AR, LA, NM, OK, and TX.   [6] AK, AZ, CA, CO, HI, ID, MT, NV, OR, Pacific Islands, UT, WA, and WY.

Source: U.S. Federal Deposit Insurance Corporation, *The FDIC Quarterly Banking Profile*, Fourth Quarter 1995.

No. 778. Insured Commercial Banks—Assets and Liabilities: 1980 to 1995

[In billions of dollars, except as indicated. As of Dec. 31. Includes outlying areas. Except as noted, includes foreign branches of U.S. banks. See *Historical Statistics, Colonial Times to 1970*, series X 588-609, for related data]

ITEM	1980	1985	1989	1990	1991	1992	1993	1994	1995 [1]
Number of banks reporting	14,435	14,417	12,713	12,343	11,921	11,462	10,958	10,450	9,941
Assets, total.	**1,856**	**2,731**	**3,299**	**3,389**	**3,431**	**3,506**	**3,706**	**4,011**	**4,313**
Net loans and leases.	1,006	1,608	2,004	2,055	1,998	1,977	2,097	2,306	2,550
Real estate loans	269	438	762	830	851	868	923	998	1,080
Home equity lines of credit [2] . . .	(NA)	(NA)	51	61	70	73	73	76	79
Commercial and industrial loans. . .	391	578	618	615	559	536	539	589	662
Loans to individuals	187	309	401	404	392	385	419	487	535
Farm loans.	32	36	31	33	35	35	37	39	40
Other loans and leases.	158	288	261	242	227	216	239	251	292
Less: Reserve for losses.	10	23	54	56	55	54	53	52	53
Less: Unearned income	21	18	15	14	11	9	7	6	6
Investment securities	325	439	559	605	691	773	837	823	811
Other	524	684	736	730	742	755	773	882	952
Domestic office assets	1,533	2,326	2,897	2,999	3,033	3,110	3,258	3,484	3,727
Foreign office assets	323	406	402	390	398	396	448	527	585
Liabilities and capital, total	1,856	2,731	3,299	3,389	3,431	3,506	3,706	4,011	4,313
Noninterest-bearing deposits [3]	432	471	483	489	480	541	572	572	612
Interest-bearing deposits [4]	1,049	1,646	2,065	2,162	2,207	2,158	2,182	2,302	2,416
Subordinated debt.	7	15	19	24	25	34	37	41	44
Other liabilities	260	429	526	496	486	510	618	783	892
Equity capital	108	169	205	219	232	263	297	312	350
Domestic office deposits.	1,187	1,796	2,237	2,357	2,383	2,412	2,424	2,442	2,573
Foreign office deposits	294	322	312	293	305	287	330	432	454

NA Not available.   [1] Preliminary.   [2] For one- to four-family residential properties.   [3] Prior to 1985, demand deposits.   [4] Prior to 1985, time and savings deposits.

Source: U.S. Federal Deposit Insurance Corporation, *The FDIC Quarterly Banking Profile, Annual Report*, and *Statistics on Banking*, annual.

No. 779. Insured Commercial Banks—Income and Selected Measures of Financial Condition: 1980 to 1995

[In billions of dollars, except as indicated. Includes outlying areas. Includes foreign branches of U.S. banks. See *Historical Statistics, Colonial Times to 1970*, series X 588-609, for related data]

ITEM	1980	1985	1989	1990	1991	1992	1993	1994	1995 [1]
Interest income.	177.4	248.2	317.3	320.4	289.2	255.2	245.1	257.8	302.7
Interest expense.	120.1	157.3	205.1	204.9	167.3	121.8	105.7	111.3	148.4
Net interest income	57.3	90.9	112.2	115.5	121.9	133.4	139.3	146.6	154.2
Provisions for loan losses.	4.5	17.8	31.0	32.1	34.3	26.0	16.8	10.9	12.5
Noninterest income	13.3	31.1	50.9	54.9	59.7	65.6	75.0	76.3	82.4
Noninterest expense	46.7	82.4	108.1	115.7	124.8	130.9	139.7	144.2	149.7
Income taxes	5.0	5.6	9.5	7.7	8.3	14.5	19.8	22.4	26.2
Securities gain/loss, net	-0.5	1.6	0.8	0.5	3.0	4.0	3.1	-0.6	0.5
Extraordinary gains, net	-	0.2	0.3	0.6	0.7	0.4	2.1	-	-
Net income.	14.0	18.0	15.6	16.0	17.9	32.0	43.1	44.6	48.8
RATIOS OF CONDITION									
Return on assets [2] (percent)	0.80	0.70	0.49	0.48	0.53	0.93	1.20	1.15	1.17
Return on equity [3] (percent)	13.66	11.31	7.71	7.45	7.94	12.98	15.34	14.61	14.68
Equity capital to assets (percent)	5.80	6.20	6.21	6.45	6.75	7.51	8.00	7.78	8.11
Noncurrent assets plus other real estate owned to assets [4] (percent) . .	(NA)	1.87	2.30	2.94	3.02	2.54	1.61	1.01	0.85
Net charge-offs [5]	3.6	13.6	22.9	29.7	32.9	25.6	17.5	11.2	12.2
Net charge-offs to loans and leases (percent)	0.36	0.84	1.16	1.43	1.59	1.27	0.85	0.50	0.49
Net interest margin [6] (percent)	3.66	4.09	4.02	3.94	4.11	4.41	4.40	4.36	4.29
Percentage of banks losing money. . .	3.7	17.1	12.5	13.4	11.6	6.9	4.9	3.8	3.4

- Represents or rounds to zero.   NA Not available.   [1] Preliminary.   [2] Net income (including securities transactions and nonrecurring items) as a percentage of average total assets.   [3] Net income as a percentage of average total equity capital.   [4] The sum of loans, leases, debt securities and other assets that are 90 days or more past due, or in nonaccrual status plus foreclosed property.   [5] Total loans and leases charged off (removed from balance sheet because of uncollectibility), less amounts recovered on loans and leases previously charged off.   [6] Interest income less interest expense as a percentage of average earning assets (i.e. the profit margin a bank earns on its loans and investments).

Source: U.S. Federal Deposit Insurance Corporation, *Annual Report; Statistics on Banking*, annual; and *FDIC Quarterly Banking Profile*.

No. 780. Insured Commercial Banks, by State and Other Area: 1995

[In billions of dollars, except number of banks. As of December 31. Includes foreign branches of U.S. banks]

STATE	Number	Assets	Deposits	STATE	Number	Assets	Deposits
Total	**9,941**	**4,312.7**	**3,027.6**	North Carolina	61	180.5	110.8
United States	**9,920**	**4,282.8**	**3,005.9**	South Carolina	71	24.6	19.7
Northeast	**633**	**1,409.5**	**907.1**	Georgia	383	132.7	90.9
New England	**161**	**193.9**	**136.4**	Florida	333	150.8	125.0
Maine	20	9.0	6.7	**East South Central**	**812**	**199.6**	**154.7**
New Hampshire	23	10.1	7.6	Kentucky	276	49.6	37.9
Vermont	20	6.0	5.1	Tennessee	240	66.6	52.4
Massachusetts	51	117.9	82.3	Alabama	186	56.3	42.1
Rhode Island	8	17.0	10.6	Mississippi	110	27.1	22.3
Connecticut	39	34.0	24.0	**West South Central**	**1,705**	**311.7**	**246.4**
Middle Atlantic	**472**	**1,215.5**	**770.7**	Arkansas	243	29.2	25.3
New York	166	922.8	547.3	Louisiana	185	45.2	37.1
New Jersey	82	104.3	84.7	Oklahoma	342	34.5	28.8
Pennsylvania	224	188.4	138.7	Texas	935	202.7	155.3
Midwest	**4,389**	**933.1**	**686.9**	**West**	**1,114**	**654.2**	**489.7**
East North Central	**1,902**	**645.6**	**471.8**	**Mountain**	**578**	**179.2**	**124.0**
Ohio	260	157.8	109.2	Montana	104	8.2	7.0
Indiana	211	68.8	53.6	Idaho	18	12.9	9.4
Illinois	864	238.7	173.3	Wyoming	53	8.3	6.3
Michigan	180	118.9	87.9	Colorado	231	37.4	31.2
Wisconsin	387	61.4	47.8	New Mexico	68	14.8	11.5
West North Central	**2,487**	**287.5**	**215.1**	Arizona	34	51.4	34.1
Minnesota	525	70.2	49.5	Utah	45	19.9	13.8
Iowa	491	42.0	33.5	Nevada	25	26.3	10.6
Missouri	459	80.5	64.1	**Pacific**	**536**	**475.0**	**365.7**
North Dakota	127	8.0	6.9	Washington	87	49.2	37.9
South Dakota	116	28.6	11.9	Oregon	43	30.4	22.9
Nebraska	336	26.7	22.6	California	383	368.2	286.4
Kansas	433	31.4	26.6	Alaska	8	5.5	4.1
South	**3,784**	**1,286.0**	**922.2**	Hawaii	15	21.7	14.4
South Atlantic	**1,267**	**774.7**	**521.1**				
Delaware	40	108.4	39.6	American Samoa	1	0.1	(Z)
Maryland	91	68.9	53.8	Puerto Rico	15	29.0	20.8
District of Columbia	13	9.8	7.7	Guam	2	0.7	0.7
Virginia	157	77.8	56.4	Pacific Islands	1	0.1	(Z)
West Virginia	118	21.3	17.1	Virgin Islands	2	0.1	0.1

Z Less than $50 million.

Source: U.S. Federal Deposit Insurance Corporation, *Statistics on Banking*, annual.

No. 781. U.S. Banking Offices of Foreign Banks—Summary: 1980 to 1994

[In billions of dollars, except as indicated. As of December, except as indicated. Covers agencies, branches, subsidiary commercial banks, and New York State investment companies]

YEAR	Assets	LOANS		Deposits	COUNTRY	NUMBER OF—		Assets	Loans, commercial and industrial	Deposits
		Total	Business			Banks with U.S. offices	U.S. offices			
1980	200.6	121.4	59.6	80.4	**1994** [2]					
1985	440.8	247.4	108.8	236.7	Japan	52	142	392.6	101.1	223.7
1990	791.1	397.9	193.3	383.9	Canada	6	42	61.0	17.6	32.9
1991	860.7	412.3	206.4	444.5	Switzerland	6	15	44.6	14.0	19.7
1992	869.0	407.5	208.7	464.3	France	12	32	88.7	12.9	41.8
1993	855.6	383.3	196.5	468.7	Netherlands	3	22	48.8	12.4	28.9
1994	916.0	394.4	212.1	493.7	United Kingdom	9	32	61.9	10.1	38.2
Share: [1] 1980	11.9	13.4	18.2	6.6	Italy	12	24	35.6	5.1	15.3
1985	16.1	15.4	22.5	12.1	Hong Kong	10	33	22.9	4.5	15.7
1990	21.4	18.0	30.8	14.5	Germany	12	21	36.1	4.0	26.1
1994	21.3	16.2	33.6	17.3	Korea, South	8	30	12.1	3.8	2.3

[1] Percent of "domestically owned" commercial banks plus U.S. offices of foreign banks.   [2] As of June 30. Source: American Banker-Bond Buyer, New York, NY, *American Banker Ranking The Banks*, annual (copyright).

Source: Except as noted, Board of Governors of the Federal Reserve System, unpublished data.

No. 782. Foreign Lending by U.S. Banks, by Type of Borrower and Country: 1995

[In millions of dollars. As of December. Covers 137 U.S. banking organizations which do nearly all of the foreign lending in the country. Data represent claims on foreign residents and institutions held at all domestic and foreign offices of covered banks. Data cover only cross-border and nonlocal currency lending. These result from a U.S. bank's office in one country lending to residents of another country or lending in a currency other than that of the borrower's country. Excludes local currency loans and other claims and local currency liabilities held by banks' foreign offices on residents of the country in which the office was located (e.g. Deutsche mark loans to German residents booked at the German branch of the reporting U.S. bank). Criteria for country selection is $3 billion or more]

COUNTRY	Total	Bank	Public	Private non-bank	COUNTRY	Total	Bank	Public	Private non-bank
Total [1]	254,534	87,174	60,916	106,465	Italy	6,165	1,323	3,733	1,109
Argentina	11,311	1,506	2,770	7,035	Japan	18,495	9,313	2,374	6,809
Australia	3,479	834	529	2,117	Korea, South	8,120	4,877	218	3,025
Belgium-Luxembourg	7,563	3,660	1,244	2,659	Mexico	18,374	2,049	9,849	6,478
Brazil	14,802	2,996	5,803	6,004	Netherlands	6,061	1,822	1,869	2,371
Canada	7,466	1,701	1,240	4,527	Philippines	3,018	685	1,607	727
Cayman Islands	10,108	7,396	121	2,591	Singapore	6,426	3,117	117	3,192
Chile	4,307	693	1,343	2,270	Spain	4,993	1,237	2,958	798
Colombia	3,173	683	1,207	1,283	Switzerland	4,141	1,082	153	2,905
France	9,765	5,712	1,886	2,167	Thailand	4,312	1,460	52	2,801
Germany	8,060	2,477	4,261	1,323	United Kingdom	32,303	14,316	802	17,185
Hong Kong	7,433	2,904	60	4,469	Venezuela	3,121	59	2,007	1,056

[1] Includes other countries, not shown separately.

Source: Board of Governors of the Federal Reserve System, Federal Financial Institutions Examination Council, statistical release.

No. 783. Federal and State-Chartered Credit Unions—Summary: 1980 to 1995

[Except as noted, as of December 31. Federal data include District of Columbia, Puerto Rico, Canal Zone, Guam, and Virgin Islands. Excludes State-insured, privately-insured, and noninsured State-chartered credit unions and corporate central credit unions which have mainly other credit unions as members. See also Historical Statistics, Colonial Times to 1970, series X 864-878]

YEAR	OPERATING CREDIT UNIONS Federal	OPERATING CREDIT UNIONS State	Number of failed institutions [1]	MEMBERS (1,000) Federal	MEMBERS (1,000) State	ASSETS (mil. dol.) Federal	ASSETS (mil. dol.) State	LOANS OUTSTANDING (mil. dol.) Federal	LOANS OUTSTANDING (mil. dol.) State	SAVINGS (mil. dol.) Federal	SAVINGS (mil. dol.) State
1980 ...	12,440	4,910	239	24,519	12,338	40,092	20,870	26,350	14,582	36,263	18,469
1985 ...	10,125	4,920	94	29,579	15,689	78,188	41,525	48,241	26,168	71,616	37,917
1990 ...	8,511	4,349	164	36,241	19,454	130,073	68,133	83,029	44,102	117,892	62,082
1991 ...	8,229	4,731	130	37,081	21,619	143,940	83,133	84,150	49,268	130,164	75,626
1992 ...	7,908	4,686	114	38,124	23,238	162,066	96,312	87,350	52,192	145,637	87,371
1993 ...	7,696	4,621	37	39,756	23,997	172,854	104,316	94,640	57,695	153,506	93,482
1994 ...	7,498	4,493	33	40,837	24,295	182,529	106,937	110,090	65,769	160,226	94,797
1995 ...	7,329	4,358	26	42,163	24,927	193,781	112,860	120,514	71,606	170,300	99,838

[1] For year ending September 30, except 1995 reflects 15-month period from October 1994 through December 1995. A failed institution is defined as a credit union which has ceased operation because it was involuntarily liquidated or merged with assistance from the National Credit Union Share Insurance Fund. Assisted mergers were not identified until 1981.

Source: National Credit Union Administration, Annual Report of the National Credit Union Administration, and unpublished data.

No. 784. Insured Savings Institutions—Financial Summary: 1990 to 1995

[In billions of dollars, except number of institutions. As of December 31. Includes Puerto Rico, Guam, and Virgin Islands. Covers SAIF (Savings Association Insurance Fund)- and BIF (Bank Insurance Fund)-insured savings institutions. Minus sign (-) indicates debt or loss]

ITEM	INSURED SAVINGS INSTITUTIONS [1] 1990	1991	1992	1993	1994	1995 [2]	RTC CONSERVATORSHIPS [3] 1991	1992	1993	1994
Number of institutions	2,816	2,561	2,390	2,262	2,152	2,029	91	81	63	2
Assets, total	1,267	1,119	1,030	1,001	1,009	1,026	44	37	22	2
Loans and leases, net	816	727	648	626	635	648	24	17	10	1
Liabilities, total	1,200	1,051	956	923	929	940	48	42	27	2
Deposits	987	907	828	774	737	742	37	31	18	1
Equity capital	68	69	74	78	80	86	-4	-4	-5	(Z)
Interest and fee income	117	98	78	66	63	71	3	1	1	(Z)
Interest expense	91	70	46	35	33	43	3	1	1	(Z)
Net interest income	26	28	32	32	30	28	(Z)	(Z)	(Z)	(Z)
Net income	-5	1	7	7	6	8	-2	-3	-2	-2

Z Less than $500 million.   [1] Excludes institutions in RTC conservatorship and, beginning 1992, excludes one self-liquidating institution.   [2] Preliminary.   [3] RTC=Resolution Trust Corporation. These savings institutions are members of the Savings Association Insurance Fund. As of December 31, 1995 there were no institutions in RTC conservatorship.

Source: U.S. Federal Deposit Insurance Corporation, Statistics on Banking, annual and FDIC Quarterly Banking Profile.

No. 785. Volume of Long-Term Mortgage Loans Originated, by Type of Property, 1980 to 1994, and by Lender, 1994

[In billions of dollars. Covers credit extended in primary mortgage markets for financing real estate acquisitions]

TYPE OF PROPERTY	1980	1985	1989	1990	1991	1992	1993	1994, BY LENDER				
								Total [1]	Commercial banks	Mortgage companies	Savings and loan	Life insurance companies
Loans, total	197.2	430.0	642.3	710.5	793.3	1,124.0	1,241.7	1,019.2	391.3	408.1	133.3	27.5
1-4 unit family home . .	133.8	289.8	452.9	458.4	562.1	893.7	1,019.9	768.7	200.0	408.1	123.1	0.7
New units	49.1	59.0	90.4	110.7	120.0	132.4	117.3	114.6	43.2	54.5	14.1	0.2
Existing units	84.6	230.8	362.5	347.7	442.1	761.3	902.5	654.2	156.8	353.7	109.0	0.5
Multifamily residential .	12.5	31.9	31.1	32.6	25.5	25.7	31.7	32.7	20.9	-	5.8	1.3
New units	8.6	10.6	8.3	6.5	6.1	4.9	4.4	4.5	2.4	-	0.2	0.4
Existing units	3.9	21.3	22.8	26.0	19.4	20.9	27.3	28.2	18.6	-	5.6	0.8
Nonresidential	35.9	99.4	150.0	209.5	194.6	184.4	172.5	190.0	153.1	-	4.4	24.8
Farm properties	15.0	9.0	8.3	10.0	11.1	20.2	17.6	27.8	17.3	-	-	0.7

- Represents zero.　[1] Includes other lenders not shown separately.

Source: U.S. Dept. of Housing and Urban Development, monthly and quarterly press releases based on the Survey of Mortgage Lending Activity.

No. 786. Mortgage Debt Outstanding, by Type of Property and Holder: 1980 to 1995

[In billions of dollars. As of Dec. 31. Includes Puerto Rico and Guam. See also *Historical Statistics, Colonial Times to 1970*, series N 273 and N 276]

TYPE OF PROPERTY AND HOLDER	1980	1985	1987	1988	1989	1990	1991	1992	1993	1994	1995
Mortgage debt, total.	1,463	2,334	2,985	3,280	3,582	3,804	3,962	4,093	4,269	4,475	4,724
Residential nonfarm	1,110	1,741	2,237	2,495	2,748	2,966	3,134	3,312	3,498	3,707	3,929
One- to four-family homes.	969	1,536	1,976	2,217	2,459	2,676	2,850	3,037	3,228	3,432	3,640
Savings institutions.	487	554	602	672	669	600	538	490	470	477	488
Mortgage pools or trusts [1]	125	407	682	758	887	1,046	1,222	1,389	1,507	1,642	1,754
Government National Mortgage Assoc.	92	207	310	331	358	392	416	411	405	441	461
Federal Home Loan Mortgage Corp . .	13	100	206	220	266	308	352	402	441	483	515
Commercial banks	160	213	276	334	390	456	484	508	557	612	665
Individuals and others [2]	117	239	284	316	370	408	431	448	456	461	498
Federal and related agencies	61	110	120	126	131	153	163	192	229	232	226
Federal National Mortgage Assoc . . .	52	92	85	88	91	94	100	124	151	162	168
Life insurance companies	18	12	13	11	12	13	12	11	9	8	8
Five or more units	141	205	261	278	288	290	284	274	271	275	289
Commercial.	255	487	660	702	754	759	748	701	689	685	710
Farm	97	106	88	83	80	79	79	81	81	83	84
TYPE OF HOLDER											
Savings institutions	603	760	860	925	910	802	705	628	598	596	603
Commercial banks	263	429	592	674	767	845	876	895	940	1,004	1,080
Life insurance companies.	131	172	212	233	254	268	265	247	229	215	219
Individuals and others [2]	206	367	433	474	535	570	591	603	609	620	662
Mortgage pools or trusts [1]	146	439	699	783	918	1,081	1,258	1,434	1,563	1,716	1,850
Government National Mortgage Assoc. . . .	94	212	318	341	368	404	425	420	414	451	472
Federal Home Loan Mortgage Corp	17	100	213	226	273	316	359	408	446	486	518
Federal National Mortgage Association . . .	(X)	55	140	178	228	300	372	445	496	530	583
Farmers Home Administration [3]	32	48	(Z)	(Z)	(Z)	(Z)	(Z)	(Z)	(Z)	(Z)	(Z)
Federal and related agencies	115	167	189	192	198	239	266	286	329	323	310
Federal National Mortgage Association . . .	57	98	92	95	99	105	112	138	167	178	184
Farmers Home Administration [3]	3	1	43	42	41	41	42	42	41	42	42
Federal Land Banks.	38	47	34	32	30	29	29	29	28	29	28
Federal Home Loan Mortgage Corp	5	14	13	17	22	22	27	34	48	46	41
Federal Housing and Veterans Admin	4	4	5	5	7	7	9	11	11	10	9
Government National Mortgage Assoc. . . .	5	1	(Z)	(Z)	(Z)	(Z)	(Z)	(Z)	(Z)	(Z)	(Z)
Federal Deposit Insurance Corp.	(X)	(X)	(X)	(X)	(X)	(X)	(X)	(X)	(X)	14	4
Resolution Trust Corporation	(X)	(X)	(X)	(X)	(X)	(X)	33	46	32	17	2

X Not applicable.　Z Less than $500 million.　[1] Outstanding principal balances of mortgage pools backing securities insured or guaranteed by the agency indicated. Includes other pools not shown separately.　[2] Includes mortgage companies, real estate investment trusts, State and local retirement funds, noninsured pension funds, State and local credit agencies, credit unions, and finance companies.　[3] FmHA-guaranteed securities sold to the Federal Financing Bank were reallocated from FmHA mortgage pools to FmHA mortgage holdings in 1986 because of accounting changes by the Farmers Home Administration.

Source: Board of Governors of the Federal Reserve System, *Federal Reserve Bulletin*, monthly.

No. 787. Characteristics of Conventional First Mortgage Loans for Purchase of Single-Family Homes: 1990 to 1995

[In percent, except as indicated. Annual averages. Covers fully amortized conventional mortgage loans used to purchase single-family nonfarm homes. Excludes refinancing loans, nonamortized and balloon loans, loans insured by the Federal Housing Administration, and loans guaranteed by the Veterans Administration. Based on a sample of mortgage lenders, including savings and loans associations, savings banks, commercial banks, and mortgage companies]

LOAN CHARACTERISTICS	NEW HOMES						PREVIOUSLY OCCUPIED HOMES					
	1990	1991	1992	1993	1994	1995	1990	1991	1992	1993	1994	1995
Contract interest rate, [1]												
all loans	9.7	9.0	8.0	7.0	7.3	7.7	9.8	9.1	7.8	6.9	7.3	7.7
Fixed-rate loans	10.1	9.3	8.3	7.3	7.9	8.0	10.1	9.4	8.2	7.3	8.0	8.0
Adjustable-rate loans [2]	8.9	8.1	6.6	5.8	6.5	7.2	8.9	8.0	6.3	5.5	6.2	7.0
Initial fees, charges [3]	1.98	1.72	1.59	1.29	1.29	1.20	1.74	1.54	1.58	1.19	1.07	0.93
Effective interest rate, [4]												
all loans	10.1	9.3	8.2	7.2	7.5	7.9	10.1	9.3	8.1	7.1	7.5	7.8
Fixed-rate loans	10.4	9.6	8.5	7.5	8.1	8.2	10.4	9.7	8.5	7.5	8.2	8.2
Adjustable-rate loans [2]	9.2	8.4	6.9	5.9	6.6	7.4	9.2	8.2	6.5	5.7	6.4	7.1
Term to maturity (years)	27.3	26.8	25.6	26.1	27.5	27.7	27.0	26.5	25.4	25.4	27.1	27.4
Purchase price ($1,000)	154.1	155.2	158.1	163.7	170.7	175.4	140.3	145.8	144.1	139.6	136.4	137.3
Loan to price ratio	74.9	75.0	76.6	78.0	78.7	78.6	74.9	74.4	76.5	77.1	80.1	80.1
Percent of number of loans												
with adjustable rates	31	25	17	18	41	37	27	22	21	20	39	31

[1] Initial interest rate paid by the borrower as specified in the loan contract. [2] Loans with a contractual provision for periodic adjustments in the contract interest rate. [3] Includes all fees, commissions, discounts and "points" paid by the borrower, or seller, in order to obtain the loan. Excludes those charges for mortgage, credit, life or property insurance; for property transfer; and for title search and insurance. [4] Contract interest rate plus fees and charges amortized over a 10-year period.

Source: U.S. Federal Housing Finance Board, *Rates & Terms on Conventional Home Mortgages, Annual Summary.*

No. 788. Mortgage Delinquency and Foreclosure Rates: 1980 to 1995

[In percent, except as indicated. Covers one- to four-family residential nonfarm mortgage loans]

ITEM	1980	1985	1989	1990	1991	1992	1993	1994	1995
Number of mortgage loans outstanding (1,000)	30,033	34,004	39,578	40,638	41,586	42,562	45,336	48,667	50,880
Delinquency rates: [1]									
Total.	5.0	5.8	4.8	4.7	5.0	4.6	4.2	4.1	4.1
Conventional loans.	3.1	4.0	3.1	3.0	3.3	2.9	2.7	2.6	2.8
VA loans.	5.3	6.6	6.4	6.4	6.8	6.5	6.3	6.3	6.3
FHA loans	6.6	7.5	6.7	6.7	7.3	7.1	7.1	7.3	7.3
Foreclosure rates: [2]									
Total.	0.5	1.0	1.0	0.9	1.0	1.0	1.0	0.9	0.9
Conventional loans.	0.2	0.7	0.6	0.7	0.8	0.8	0.8	0.7	0.7
VA loans.	0.6	1.1	1.3	1.2	1.3	1.3	1.3	1.3	1.3
FHA loans	0.7	1.3	1.4	1.3	1.4	1.4	1.5	1.5	1.4

[1] Number of loans delinquent 30 days or more as percentage of mortgage loans serviced in survey. Annual average of quarterly figures. [2] Percentage of loans in the foreclosure process at yearend, not seasonally adjusted.

Source: Mortgage Bankers Association of America, Washington, DC, *National Delinquency Survey,* quarterly.

No. 789. Home Equity Lending—Percentage of Homeowners with Credit, Sources of Credit, and Uses for Funds Borrowed: 1988 and 1993-94

[In percent. A "traditional home equity loan" is a closed-end loan extended for a specific period that generally requires repayment of interest and principal in equal monthly installments. Such a loan typically has a fixed interest rate. A "home equity line of credit" is a revolving account that permits borrowing from time to time, at the homeowner's discretion, up to the amount of the credit line. It usually has a more flexible repayment schedule and a variable interest rate. Based on the Surveys of Consumers, a sample survey (2,527 households in 1993-94) conducted by the Survey Research Center of the University of Michigan]

ITEM	HOME EQUITY LINES OF CREDIT		TRADITIONAL HOME EQUITY LOANS		USES FOR FUNDS BORROWED	1993-94 [1]	
	1988	1993-94	1988	1993-94		Home equity lines of credit	Traditional home equity loans
Percentage of homeowners					Home improvement	64	38
with home equity credit . .	5.7	8.3	5.4	4.9	Repayment of other debts .	45	68
					Education.	21	4
SOURCE OF HOME EQUITY CREDIT					Real estate.	12	8
Total.	100	100	100	100	Auto or truck.	30	3
Commercial banks	54	60	33	29	Medical expenses	5	1
Savings institutions [2]	31	21	27	30	Business expenses	28	1
Credit unions	11	13	8	11	Vacation.	6	1
Other creditors [3]	4	7	32	29	Other [4]	1	3

[1] Percentages sum to more than 100 because respondents were allowed to cite multiple uses for a single loan or drawdown and more than one draw for one line of credit. [2] Includes savings banks and savings and loan associations. [3] Includes finance and loan companies, brokerage firms, mortgage companies, and individuals. [4] Includes purchase of furniture or appliance, purchase of boat or other recreational vehicle, payment of taxes, and personal financial investments.

Source: Board of Governors of the Federal Reserve System, *Federal Reserve Bulletin,* July 1994.

No. 790. Estimated Home Equity Debt Outstanding, by Type and Source of Credit: 1988 to 1994

[In billions of dollars. See headnote, table 789]

YEAR	Total	HOME EQUITY LINES OF CREDIT			TRADITIONAL HOME EQUITY LOANS		
		All lenders	Commercial banks	Other sources	All lenders	Commercial banks	Other sources
1988	210-265	75	40	35	135-190	(NA)	(NA)
1989	(NA)	90	51	39	(NA)	(NA)	(NA)
1990	258	105	61	44	153	54	99
1991	262	114	70	44	148	53	95
1992	258	114	73	41	144	50	94
1993	255	110	73	37	145	49	96
1994	(NA)	(NA)	76	(NA)	(NA)	54	(NA)

NA Not available.

Source: Board of Governors of the Federal Reserve System, *Federal Reserve Bulletin*, July 1994.

No. 791. Consumer Installment Credit Outstanding and Finance Rates: 1980 to 1995

[In billions of dollars, except percent. Estimated amounts of seasonally adjusted credit outstanding as of end of year; finance rates, annual averages. See also *Historical Statistics, Colonial Times to 1970*, series X 551-560]

TYPE OF CREDIT	1980	1985	1986	1987	1988	1989	1990	1991	1992	1993	1994	1995
Installment credit outstanding...	298.2	517.7	572.0	608.7	663.0	724.4	734.9	728.4	730.8	790.4	902.8	1,024.8
Automobile paper	112.0	210.2	247.8	266.3	285.5	292.5	283.1	259.6	257.4	280.6	317.2	353.3
Revolving [1]	55.1	121.8	135.8	153.1	174.3	198.5	223.5	245.3	258.1	286.6	334.5	395.2
Other	131.1	185.7	188.4	189.3	203.2	233.3	228.3	223.5	215.3	223.2	251.1	276.2
FINANCE RATES (percent)												
Commercial banks:												
New automobiles (48 months) [2] ...	14.30	12.91	11.33	10.46	10.85	12.07	11.78	11.13	9.28	8.08	8.13	9.57
Other consumer goods (24 months).	15.47	15.94	14.83	14.23	14.68	15.44	15.46	15.17	14.04	13.46	13.20	13.94
Credit-card plans	17.31	18.69	18.26	17.93	17.79	18.02	18.17	18.23	17.77	16.81	15.69	16.02
Finance companies:												
New automobiles	14.82	11.98	9.44	10.73	12.60	12.62	12.54	12.41	9.93	9.47	9.80	11.19
Used automobiles	19.10	17.59	15.95	14.61	15.11	16.18	15.99	15.59	13.80	12.78	13.51	14.47

[1] Consists mainly of outstanding balances on credit card accounts, but also includes borrowing under check credit and overdraft plans, and unsecured personal lines of credit. [2] For 1980, maturities were 36 months for new car loans.

Source: Board of Governors of the Federal Reserve System, *Federal Reserve Bulletin*, monthly; and *Annual Statistical Digest*.

No. 792. Usage of General Purpose Credit Cards by Families: 1989 and 1992

[General purpose credit cards include Mastercard, Visa, Optima, and Discover cards. All dollar figures are given in constant 1992 dollars based on consumer price index data as published by U.S. Bureau of Labor Statistics. Families include one-person units; for definition of family, see text, section 1. Based on Survey of Consumer Finance; see Appendix III. For definition of median, see Guide to Tabular Presentation]

AGE OF FAMILY HEAD AND FAMILY INCOME	Percent having a general purpose credit card	Median number of cards	Median new charges on last month's bills	Percent having a balance after last month's bills	Median balance [1]	PERCENT OF CARDHOLDING FAMILIES WHO—		
						Almost always pay off the balance	Some-times pay off the balance	Hardly ever pay off the balance
1989, total	56.4	2	$200	52.8	$1,100	52.0	21.8	26.1
1992, total	63.3	2	200	51.3	1,000	54.5	19.1	26.4
Under 35 years old	57.6	2	200	67.7	900	39.6	25.0	35.4
35 to 44 years old	64.2	2	200	61.6	1,500	45.5	22.0	32.5
45 to 54 years old	72.5	2	300	53.3	1,900	52.1	19.7	28.2
55 to 64 years old	68.0	2	200	40.0	1,000	64.8	16.3	18.9
65 to 74 years old	65.0	1	200	32.3	800	74.9	11.0	14.1
75 years old and over	52.1	1	100	19.1	800	78.9	10.6	10.5
Less than $10,000	25.9	1	100	45.5	800	57.4	12.2	30.4
$10,000 to $24,999	52.3	1	100	54.6	900	49.5	21.3	29.1
$25,000 to $49,999	73.1	2	200	61.1	1,200	47.0	21.2	31.7
$50,000 to $99,999	88.5	2	300	46.6	1,500	58.7	18.6	22.8
$100,000 and more	91.2	2	500	30.5	3,000	75.2	14.3	10.5

[1] Among families having a balance.

Source: Board of Governors of the Federal Reserve System, unpublished data.

No. 793. Credit Cards—Holders, Numbers, Spending, and Debt, 1990 and 1994, and Projections, 2000

TYPE OF CREDIT CARD	CARDHOLDERS (mil.)			NUMBER OF CARDS (mil.)			CREDIT CARD SPENDING (bil. dol.)			CREDIT CARD DEBT (bil. dol.)		
	1990	1994	2000, proj.	1990	1994	2000, proj.	1990	1994	2000, proj.	1990	1994	2000, proj.
Total [1]	113	124	141	1,026	1,131	1,344	466	731	1,443	236.4	366.4	660.9
Bank [2]	79	91	106	217	315	469	243	437	974	154.1	251.3	486.0
Oil company	85	84	82	123	114	105	27	26	31	3.3	3.5	4.1
Phone	97	106	132	141	161	203	14	17	24	1.7	2.1	3.0
Retail store	96	100	121	469	463	476	75	96	137	51.0	70.2	98.9
Travel and entertainment [3]	23	22	26	28	27	32	85	109	205	13.8	17.5	35.3
Other [4]	11	9	10	48	51	60	22	46	71	12.5	21.8	33.7

[1] Cardholders may hold more than one type of card.   [2] Visa and MasterCard credit cards. Excludes debit cards.   [3] Includes American Express and Diners Club.   [4] Includes Air Travel Card, automobile rental, Discover (except for cardholders), and miscellaneous cards.

Source: HSN Consultants Inc., Oxnard, CA, *The Nilson Report*, bimonthly. (Copyright used by permission.)

No. 794. Delinquency Rates on Bank Installment Loans, by Type of Loan: 1980 to 1995

[In percent, except as indicated. As of **end of year**; seasonally adjusted, except as noted. Number of loans having an installment past due for 30 days or more as a percentage of total installment loans outstanding]

TYPE OF CREDIT	1980	1985	1987	1988	1989	1990	1991	1992	1993	1994	1995
DELINQUENCY RATES											
Closed-end installment loans, total	2.82	2.32	2.47	2.49	2.64	2.57	2.58	2.43	1.77	1.72	2.12
Personal loans [1]	3.53	3.63	3.66	3.34	3.52	3.37	2.95	3.18	2.30	2.38	2.81
Automobile, direct loans [2]	1.81	1.64	1.59	1.92	2.03	2.22	2.14	2.08	1.58	1.46	1.87
Automobile, indirect loans [3]	2.29	2.02	2.20	2.46	2.61	2.59	2.66	2.33	1.65	1.65	2.17
Property improvement [4]	1.93	1.91	1.88	2.06	2.25	2.30	2.38	2.18	1.61	1.66	1.77
Home equity and second mortgage loans [5]	(NA)	2.06	2.01	1.86	1.85	1.45	2.06	1.89	1.66	1.38	1.41
Mobile home loans	3.14	2.39	2.57	3.12	2.51	3.03	2.86	4.02	3.70	3.68	4.02
Recreational vehicle loans	1.94	1.84	1.99	2.07	2.24	2.63	2.25	2.27	1.26	1.23	1.62
Marine financing [5]	(NA)	(NA)	(NA)	(NA)	(NA)	(NA)	(NA)	2.52	1.72	1.51	2.22
Bank card loans	2.72	2.95	2.33	2.19	2.24	2.86	3.29	2.93	2.49	2.93	3.34
Revolving credit loans	2.70	1.96	2.33	2.87	2.92	3.00	2.75	2.63	2.90	2.38	3.14
Home equity lines of credit loans (open-end) [5]	(NA)	(NA)	0.74	0.68	0.78	0.85	0.88	0.85	0.70	0.63	0.90
REPOSSESSIONS PER 1,000 LOANS OUTSTANDING											
Mobile home		1.57	1.21	1.58	1.77	1.63	1.19	1.62	1.30	1.21	1.18	0.86
Automobile, direct loans [2]	1.10	1.11	0.86	1.03	1.03	1.75	1.17	0.92	0.83	0.53	0.96
Automobile, indirect loans [3]	2.75	2.08	2.04	1.86	1.70	1.61	2.07	1.47	0.97	1.17	1.36
Marine financing [5]	(NA)	(NA)	(NA)	(NA)	(NA)	(NA)	(NA)	1.21	1.03	0.82	0.81

NA Not available.   [1] Beginning 1985, includes home appliance loans.   [2] Made directly by bank's lending function.   [3] Made by automobile dealerships; loans in bank's portfolio.   [4] Beginning 1985, own plan and FHA Title I loans.   [5] Not seasonally adjusted.

Source: American Bankers Association, Washington, DC, *Consumer Credit Delinquency Bulletin*, quarterly.

No. 795. Electronic Funds Transfer Volume: 1980 to 1995

[Electronic funds transfer cover automated teller machine (ATM) transactions and transactions at point-of-sale (POS) terminals. Point-of-sale terminals are electronic terminals in retail stores that allow a customer to pay for goods through a direct debit to a customer's account at the bank]

ITEM	Unit	1980	1985	1989	1990	1991	1992	1993	1994	1995
Total number of transactions	Million	(NA)	3,579	5,274	5,942	6,642	7,537	8,135	8,958	10,464
ATM transactions	Million	(NA)	3,565	5,116	5,751	6,418	7,206	7,705	8,334	9,689
POS transactions	Million	(NA)	14	157	191	223	289	430	624	775
ATM terminals, total [1]	1,000	18.5	60.0	75.6	80.2	83.5	87.3	94.8	109.1	122.7
Monthly transactions per terminal	Number	5,405	4,951	5,638	5,980	6,403	6,876	6,772	6,459	6,580
Shared terminals	1,000	(NA)	35.5	70.1	75.3	79.6	84.7	92.6	108.1	122.6
Proprietary terminals	1,000	(NA)	24.5	5.5	4.9	4.0	2.6	2.3	1.0	0.1
POS terminals, total [2]	1,000	(NA)	(NA)	(NA)	53.1	78.1	95.2	155.0	340.5	528.6
Grocery stores	1,000	(NA)	(NA)	(NA)	21.5	31.8	45.1	75.3	187.4	238.1
Gasoline service stations	1,000	(NA)	(NA)	(NA)	18.7	21.5	26.3	50.4	85.9	164.0
Specialty stores	1,000	(NA)	(NA)	(NA)	10.1	13.4	16.6	22.1	53.2	105.4
Convenience stores	1,000	(NA)	(NA)	(NA)	2.7	3.1	7.1	7.2	14.0	21.1

NA Not available.   [1] As of September.   [2] As of June.

Source: Faulkner & Gray, Chicago, IL, *Bank Network News*, November 24, 1995, (copyright).

No. 796. Money Stock and Liquid Assets: 1980 to 1995

[In billions of dollars. As of December. Seasonally adjusted averages of daily figures. See Historical Statistics, Colonial Times to 1970, series X 410-417 for similar data]

ITEM	1980	1981	1982	1983	1984	1985	1986	1987	1988	1989	1990	1991	1992	1993	1994	1995
M1, total	**409**	**437**	**474**	**521**	**552**	**620**	**724**	**750**	**787**	**794**	**826**	**897**	**1,024**	**1,129**	**1,149**	**1,125**
Currency[1]	115	123	133	146	156	168	181	197	212	223	247	267	293	322	355	373
Travelers checks[2]	4	4	4	5	6	6	6	7	7	7	8	8	8	8	8	9
Demand deposits[3]	261	231	234	238	244	267	302	287	287	279	277	290	339	384	382	390
Other checkable deposits[4]	28	78	104	132	147	180	236	260	281	285	294	332	384	414	403	353
M2, total	**1,601**	**1,756**	**1,911**	**2,128**	**2,312**	**2,498**	**2,735**	**2,834**	**2,998**	**3,164**	**3,282**	**3,384**	**3,439**	**3,494**	**3,509**	**3,660**
M1	409	437	474	521	552	620	724	750	787	794	826	897	1,024	1,129	1,149	1,125
Non-M1 components in M2	1,192	1,319	1,436	1,607	1,760	1,878	2,010	2,085	2,211	2,370	2,456	2,486	2,414	2,365	2,361	2,535
Money market funds, retail	63	152	185	138	167	177	210	224	246	322	358	374	356	359	388	465
Savings deposits (including MMDAs[5])	400	344	400	685	705	815	941	937	926	894	924	1,045	1,187	1,219	1,149	1,135
Commercial banks	186	159	190	363	389	457	534	535	542	541	582	665	754	785	752	775
Thrift institutions	215	185	210	322	315	359	407	403	384	353	342	380	433	434	397	360
Small time deposits[6]	729	823	851	784	889	886	859	923	1,039	1,154	1,175	1,068	871	788	824	936
Commercial banks	286	348	380	351	388	386	369	392	452	535	611	603	509	470	505	576
Thrift institutions	442	475	471	433	501	499	490	530	586	618	563	465	362	318	318	359
M3, total	**1,992**	**2,241**	**2,442**	**2,685**	**2,980**	**3,198**	**3,486**	**3,673**	**3,912**	**4,065**	**4,124**	**4,178**	**4,187**	**4,250**	**4,320**	**4,573**
M2	1,601	1,756	1,911	2,128	2,312	2,498	2,735	2,834	2,998	3,164	3,282	3,384	3,439	3,494	3,509	3,660
Non-M2 components in M3	391	485	531	557	667	700	752	839	915	902	842	795	749	756	810	912
Large time deposits[7]	260	304	325	316	403	422	420	467	518	541	481	417	354	334	363	417
Commercial banks[8]	215	250	261	220	256	271	270	304	344	380	360	333	287	272	299	342
Thrift institutions	45	54	64	97	147	152	150	163	175	161	121	83	67	62	65	75
Repurchase agreements[9]	57	65	67	95	105	120	143	173	189	158	139	119	128	158	181	177
Eurodollars[9]	58	77	90	105	97	94	104	108	117	95	89	79	67	66	82	91
Money market funds, institution only	16	39	49	41	62	64	84	91	90	107	134	180	200	198	184	226
L, total	**2,329**	**2,603**	**2,851**	**3,148**	**3,522**	**3,825**	**4,122**	**4,329**	**4,664**	**4,894**	**4,976**	**5,004**	**5,076**	**5,165**	**5,304**	**5,683**
M3	1,992	2,241	2,442	2,685	2,980	3,198	3,486	3,673	3,912	4,065	4,124	4,178	4,187	4,250	4,320	4,573
Savings bonds	72	68	68	71	74	79	92	101	109	118	126	138	157	172	180	185
Short-term Treasury securities[10]	134	149	183	213	262	298	276	249	267	324	334	329	346	343	387	477
Bankers acceptances[9]	32	40	44	45	45	42	37	45	40	41	36	24	21	15	14	12
Commercial paper[11]	99	105	114	133	161	207	231	261	335	346	355	335	365	386	402	437

[1] Currency outside U.S. Treasury, Federal Reserve Banks and the vaults of depository institutions. [2] Outstanding amount of nonbank issuers. [3] At commercial banks and foreign-related institutions. [4] Consists of negotiable order of withdrawal (NOW) and automatic transfer service (ATS) accounts at all depository institutions, credit union share draft balances, and demand deposits at thrift institutions. [5] Money market deposit accounts (MMDA). [6] Issued in amounts of less than $100,000. Includes retail repurchase agreements. Excludes individual retirement accounts (IRA's) and Keogh accounts. [7] Issued in amounts of $100,000 or more. Excludes those booked at international banking facilities. [8] Excludes those held by money market mutual funds, depository institutions, U.S. Government, foreign banks and official institutions. [9] Excludes those held by depository institutions and money market mutual funds. [10] U.S. Treasury bills and coupons with remaining maturities of less than 12 months held by other than depository institutions, Federal Reserve banks, money market mutual funds, and foreign entities. [11] Excludes commercial paper held by money market mutual funds.

Source: Board of Governors of the Federal Reserve System, Federal Reserve Bulletin, monthly, and Money Stock, Liquid Assets, and Debt Measures, Federal Reserve Statistical Release H.6, weekly.

No. 797. Bank Debits and Deposit Turnover: 1980 to 1995

[Debits in trillions of dollars; turnover as ratio of debits to deposits. Annual averages of monthly data]

ITEM	1980	1985	1986	1987	1988	1989	1990	1991	1992	1993	1994	1995
Debits to—												
Demand deposits, all banks [1]	63.1	156.3	188.8	214.9	219.2	256.2	277.6	277.8	313.1	334.8	369.0	397.6
Major New York City banks	25.3	70.7	91.6	110.4	115.5	129.7	131.9	137.3	165.4	171.2	191.2	201.2
Other banks	37.9	85.6	97.1	104.5	103.7	126.5	145.7	140.4	147.7	163.6	177.9	196.5
Other checkable deposits [2]	0.2	1.8	2.2	2.2	2.5	2.9	3.4	3.6	3.8	3.5	3.8	4.2
Money market deposit accounts	(NA)	1.2	1.6	1.9	2.3	2.7	2.9	[3]3.2	[3]3.3	[3]3.5	[3]3.8	[3]4.5
Savings deposits	(NA)	0.4	0.4	0.5	0.5	0.6	0.6	(3)	(3)	(3)	(3)	(3)
Deposit turnover:												
Demand deposits, all banks [1]	203	501	557	608	620	734	799	804	826	786	817	874
Major New York City banks	816	2,200	2,500	2,670	2,904	3,435	3,831	4,263	4,795	4,198	4,482	4,867
Other banks	135	306	322	335	331	406	466	448	429	425	435	475

NA Not available. [1] Represents accounts of individuals, partnerships, and corporations and of States and political subdivisions at insured commercial banks. [2] Accounts authorized for negotiable orders of withdrawal (NOW) and accounts authorized for automatic transfer to demand deposits (ATS). [3] Beginning 1991, savings deposits included in money market deposit accounts.

Source: Board of Governors of the Federal Reserve System, *Federal Reserve Bulletin*, monthly, and *Annual Statistical Digest*.

No. 798. Selected Time Deposits and Other Accounts at Insured Commercial Banks—Deposits and Interest Rates: 1990 to 1995

[As of **December**. Estimates based on data collected from a sample of about 500 banks]

TYPE OF DEPOSIT	AMOUNT OUTSTANDING (bil. dol.)						ANNUAL EFFECTIVE YIELD (percent)					
	1990	1991	1992	1993	1994	1995	1990	1991	1992	1993	1994	1995
NOW accounts [1]	209.9	245.1	287.1	305.2	304.9	252.4	4.89	3.77	2.33	1.86	1.96	1.92
Savings deposits	570.3	652.0	738.3	767.0	737.1	793.2	5.84	4.30	2.88	2.46	2.92	3.10
Interest-bearing time deposits: [2]												
7-91 day	50.2	47.1	38.5	29.4	32.3	32.8	6.94	4.18	2.90	2.65	3.79	4.11
92-182 day	168.0	158.6	127.8	109.0	96.7	96.9	7.19	4.41	3.16	2.91	4.44	4.69
183 day-1 year	221.0	209.7	163.1	145.4	163.1	187.8	7.33	4.59	3.37	3.13	5.12	5.03
1-2 1/2 years	150.2	171.7	153.0	139.8	164.4	211.4	7.42	4.95	3.88	3.55	5.74	5.18
2 1/2 years or more	139.4	157.1	169.7	180.5	192.7	203.2	7.53	5.52	4.77	4.28	6.30	5.41
All IRA and Keogh Plan deposits	131.0	147.3	147.4	144.0	144.1	152.4	(NA)	(NA)	(NA)	(NA)	(NA)	(NA)

NA Not available. [1] Estimates for all NOW accounts are based on reports of deposits. [2] All interest-bearing time deposits and open account time deposits with balances of less than $100,000, including those held in IRA's and Keogh Plan deposits.

Source: Board of Governors of the Federal Reserve System, *Money Stock, Liquid Assets, and Debt Measures, Federal Reserve Statistical Release H.6*, Special Supplementary Table, Monthly Survey of Selected Deposits, monthly.

No. 799. Commercial Paper Outstanding, by Type of Company: 1980 to 1995

[In billions of dollars. As of **December 31**. Seasonally adjusted. Commercial paper is an unsecured promissory note having a fixed maturity of no more than 270 days]

TYPE OF COMPANY	1980	1985	1987	1988	1989	1990	1991	1992	1993	1994	1995
All issuers	**124.4**	**298.8**	**359.0**	**458.5**	**525.8**	**562.7**	**528.8**	**545.6**	**555.1**	**595.4**	**671.6**
Financial companies [1]	87.7	213.8	277.1	354.7	394.6	414.7	395.5	398.1	399.3	430.7	482.1
Dealer-placed paper [2]	19.9	78.4	102.7	159.8	183.6	214.7	213.0	226.5	218.9	223.0	274.0
Directly-placed paper [3]	67.8	135.3	174.3	194.9	210.9	200.0	182.5	171.6	180.4	207.7	208.1
Nonfinancial companies [4]	36.7	85.0	81.9	103.8	131.3	147.9	133.4	147.6	155.7	164.6	189.5

[1] Institutions engaged primarily in activities such as, but not limited to, commercial, savings, and mortgage banking; sales, personal, and mortgage financing; factoring, finance leasing, and other business lending; insurance underwriting; and other investment activities. [2] Includes all financial company paper sold by dealers in the open market. [3] As reported by financial companies that place their paper directly with investors. [4] Includes public utilities and firms engaged primarily in such activities as communications, construction, manufacturing, mining, wholesale and retail trade, transportation, and services.

Source: Board of Governors of the Federal Reserve System, *Federal Reserve Bulletin*, monthly.

No. 800. Federal Reserve Bank of New York—Discount Rates: 1980 to 1996

[Percent per year. Rates for short-term adjustment credit. For rates applicable to other types of discount window credit, see source. See also *Historical Statistics, Colonial Times to 1970*, series X 454-455]

EFFECTIVE DATE	Rate	EFFECTIVE DATE	Rate	EFFECTIVE DATE	Rate	EFFECTIVE DATE	Rate
1980: [1] Nov. 17	12	Oct. 12	9 1/2	July 11	6	Nov. 6	4 1/2
Dec. 5	13	Nov. 22	9	Aug. 21	5 1/2	Dec. 20	3 1/2
1981: [1] May 5	14	Dec. 15	8 1/2	**1987:** Sept. 4	6	**1992:** July 2	3
Nov. 2	13	**1984:** April 9	9	**1988:** Aug. 9	6 1/2	**1994:** May 17	3 1/2
Dec. 4	12	Nov. 21	8 1/2	**1989:** Feb. 24	7	Aug. 16	4
1982: July 20	11 1/2	Dec. 24	8	**1990:** Dec. 19	6 1/2	Nov. 15	4 3/4
Aug. 2	11	**1985:** May 20	7 1/2	**1991:** Feb. 1	6	**1995:** Feb. 1	5 1/4
Aug. 16	10 1/2	**1986:** March 7	7	April 30	5 1/2	**1996:** Jan. 31	5
Aug. 27	10	April 21	6 1/2	Sept. 13	5	In effect, **Apr. 5, '96**	5

[1] The discount rates for 1980 and 1981 do not include the surcharge applied to frequent borrowings by large institutions. The surcharge reached 3 percent in 1980 and 4 percent in 1981. Surcharge was eliminated in Nov. 1981.

Source: Board of Governors of the Federal Reserve System, *Federal Reserve Bulletin*, monthly, and *Annual Statistical Digest*.

No. 801. Money Market Interest Rates and Mortgage Rates: 1980 to 1995

[Percent per year. Annual averages of monthly data, except as indicated. See also *Historical Statistics, Colonial Times to 1970*, series X 444-453]

TYPE	1980	1981	1982	1983	1984	1985	1986	1987	1988	1989	1990	1991	1992	1993	1994	1995
Federal funds, effective rate [1][2]	13.35	16.39	12.24	9.09	10.23	8.10	6.80	6.66	7.57	9.21	8.10	5.69	3.52	3.02	4.21	5.83
Commercial paper, 3-month [1][2]	12.61	15.34	11.90	8.88	10.12	7.95	6.49	6.82	7.66	8.99	8.06	5.87	3.75	3.22	4.66	5.93
Commercial paper, 6-month [1][2]	12.24	14.77	11.89	8.90	10.18	8.00	6.39	6.85	7.68	8.80	7.95	5.85	3.80	3.30	4.93	5.93
Prime rate charged by banks	15.26	18.87	14.85	10.79	12.04	9.93	8.33	8.21	9.32	10.87	10.01	8.46	6.25	6.00	7.15	8.83
Eurodollar deposits, 3-month	14.00	16.79	13.12	9.57	10.75	8.27	6.70	7.07	7.85	9.16	8.16	5.86	3.70	3.18	4.63	5.93
Finance paper, 3-month [3]	11.45	14.09	11.24	8.71	9.75	7.77	6.38	6.54	7.38	8.72	7.87	5.71	3.65	3.16	4.53	5.78
Finance paper, 6-month [2][3]	11.25	13.74	11.20	8.70	9.67	7.74	6.31	6.37	7.14	8.16	7.53	5.60	3.63	3.15	4.56	5.68
Bankers acceptances, 3-month [2][4]	12.67	15.34	11.89	8.91	10.17	7.91	6.38	6.75	7.56	8.87	7.93	5.70	3.62	3.13	4.56	5.81
Bankers acceptances, 6-month [2][4]	12.20	14.68	11.83	8.92	10.21	7.95	6.28	6.78	7.60	8.67	7.80	5.67	3.67	3.21	4.83	5.80
Large negotiable CD's, 3-month, secondary market [5]	13.07	15.91	12.27	9.07	10.37	8.05	6.52	6.86	7.73	9.09	8.15	5.83	3.68	3.17	4.63	5.92
Taxable money market funds [5]	12.68	16.82	12.23	8.58	10.04	7.71	6.26	6.12	7.11	8.87	7.82	5.71	3.37	2.70	3.75	5.48
Tax-exempt money market funds [5]	(NA)	(NA)	(NA)	(NA)	(NA)	(NA)	(NA)	(NA)	(NA)	(NA)	(NA)	(NA)	2.59	1.97	2.38	3.39
Certificates of deposit (CD's): [6]																
6-month	(NA)	(NA)	(NA)	(NA)	9.99	7.83	6.51	6.47	7.18	8.34	7.35	5.67	3.46	2.84	3.37	4.92
1-year	(NA)	(NA)	(NA)	(NA)	10.37	8.29	6.75	6.77	7.47	8.41	7.42	5.88	3.72	3.12	3.94	5.39
2 1/2-year	(NA)	(NA)	(NA)	10.06	10.82	9.00	7.13	7.16	7.77	8.33	7.52	6.29	4.47	3.73	4.49	5.69
5-year	(NA)	(NA)	(NA)	(NA)	11.25	9.66	7.60	7.66	8.11	8.30	7.71	6.83	5.62	4.88	5.30	6.00
U.S. Government securities: Secondary market: [7]																
3-month Treasury bill	11.39	14.04	10.60	8.62	9.54	7.47	5.97	5.78	6.67	8.11	7.50	5.38	3.43	3.00	4.25	5.49
6-month Treasury bill	11.32	13.81	11.06	8.74	9.78	7.65	6.02	6.03	6.91	8.03	7.46	5.44	3.54	3.12	4.64	5.56
1-year Treasury bill	10.85	13.16	11.07	8.80	9.94	7.81	6.07	6.33	7.13	7.92	7.35	5.52	3.71	3.29	5.02	5.60
Auction average: [8]																
3-month Treasury bill	11.51	14.03	10.69	8.63	9.35	7.47	5.98	5.82	6.68	8.12	7.51	5.42	3.45	3.02	4.29	5.51
6-month Treasury bill	11.37	13.78	11.08	8.75	9.77	7.64	6.03	6.05	6.92	8.04	7.47	5.49	3.57	3.14	4.66	5.59
1-year Treasury bill	10.75	13.16	11.10	8.86	9.91	7.76	6.07	6.33	7.17	7.91	7.36	5.54	3.75	3.33	4.98	5.69
Home mortgages: [9] HUD series:																
FHA insured, secondary market [10]	13.44	16.31	15.30	13.11	13.81	12.24	9.91	10.16	10.49	10.24	10.17	9.25	8.46	7.46	8.68	8.18
Conventional, new-home [11][12]	13.95	16.52	15.79	13.43	13.80	12.28	10.07	10.17	10.30	10.21	10.08	9.20	8.43	7.37	8.58	8.05
Conventional, existing-home [11]	13.95	16.55	15.82	13.44	13.81	12.29	10.09	10.17	10.31	10.22	10.08	9.20	8.43	7.37	8.59	8.05

NA Not available.   [1] Based on daily offering rates of dealers.   [2] Yields are quoted on a bank-discount basis, rather than an investment yield basis (which would give a higher figure).   [3] Placed directly; averages of daily offering rates quoted by finance companies.   [4] Based on representative closing yields. From Jan. 1, 1981, rates of top-rated banks only.   [5] 12 month return for period ending December 31. Source: IBC Financial Data, Inc., Ashland, MA, *IBC's Money Market Insight*, monthly (copyright).   [6] Annual averages. Source: Financial Rates, Inc., North Palm Beach, FL, *Bank Rate Monitor*, weekly (copyright).   [7] Averages based on daily closing bid yields in secondary market; bank discount basis.   [8] Averages computed on an issue-date basis; bank discount basis.   [9] HUD=Housing and Urban Development.   [10] Averages based on quotations for 1 day each month as compiled by FHA.   [11] Primary market.   [12] Average contract rates on new commitments.

Source: Except as noted, Board of Governors of the Federal Reserve System, *Federal Reserve Bulletin*, monthly, and *Annual Statistical Digest*.

No. 802. Security Prices: 1980 to 1995

[Annual averages of daily figures, except as noted. See also Historical Statistics, Colonial Times to 1970, series X 492-498]

CLASS OR ITEM	1980	1981	1982	1983	1984	1985	1986	1987	1988	1989	1990	1991	1992	1993	1994	1995
BOND PRICES (dollars per $100 bond)																
Dow Jones and Co., Inc.: [1][2]																
Yearly high	76.6	65.8	71.5	77.8	72.9	83.7	93.7	95.5	91.3	94.2	93.0	98.9	103.9	109.8	105.6	105.3
Yearly low	61.0	55.0	55.7	69.4	64.8	72.3	83.7	81.3	86.9	87.4	88.4	91.3	98.4	103.5	93.6	93.6
STOCK PRICES																
Standard & Poor's common index (500 stocks) (1941-43=10) [3]	118.7	128.0	119.7	160.4	160.5	186.8	236.3	268.8	265.9	323.1	335.0	376.2	415.7	451.6	460.4	541.7
Industrial	134.5	144.2	133.6	180.5	181.3	207.8	262.2	330.5	306.5	392.9	391.4	445.8	489.8	517.4	540.6	641.3
N.Y. Stock Exchange common stock index (Dec. 31, 1965=50):																
Composite	68.1	74.0	68.9	92.6	92.5	108.1	136.0	161.8	150.0	180.1	183.7	206.4	229.0	249.7	254.2	291.2
Yearly high [4]	81.0	79.1	82.4	99.6	98.1	121.9	145.8	188.0	159.4	199.3	201.1	229.4	242.1	260.7	267.7	331.2
Yearly low [4]	55.3	65.0	58.8	79.8	85.1	94.6	117.8	125.9	136.7	155.0	162.2	171.0	217.9	236.2	243.1	250.7
Industrial	78.6	85.4	78.2	107.5	108.0	123.8	155.9	195.3	180.8	228.0	226.1	258.2	284.3	300.1	315.3	367.4
Transportation	60.5	72.6	60.4	89.4	85.6	104.1	119.9	140.5	134.1	174.9	158.8	174.0	201.0	242.7	247.2	270.1
Utility	37.3	38.9	39.8	47.0	46.4	56.8	71.4	74.3	72.2	94.3	90.7	92.6	99.5	114.6	105.0	114.6
Finance	64.3	73.5	72.0	95.3	89.3	114.2	147.2	146.5	127.4	162.0	133.2	150.8	179.3	216.6	209.8	238.5
American Stock Exchange Market Value Index (Aug. 31, 1973=50) [5]	150.6	171.8	141.3	216.5	208.0	229.1	264.4	316.4	295.1	356.7	338.3	360.3	391.3	438.8	449.5	498.1
NASDAQ composite index [5]	202.3	195.9	232.4	278.6	247.4	324.9	348.8	330.5	381.4	454.8	373.9	586.3	677.0	776.8	752.0	1,052.1
Industrial	261.4	229.3	273.6	323.7	260.7	330.2	349.3	338.9	379.0	448.0	406.1	669.0	724.9	805.8	753.8	964.7
Insurance	166.8	194.3	226.4	257.6	283.1	382.1	404.1	351.1	429.1	546.0	451.8	601.1	803.9	920.6	925.9	1,292.6
Banks	118.4	143.1	156.4	203.8	229.8	349.4	412.5	390.7	435.3	391.0	254.9	350.6	532.9	689.4	697.1	1,009.4
Dow Jones and Co., Inc.: [1][6]																
Composite (65 stocks)	373.4	347.8	409.2	502.9	489.9	616.5	736.8	714.3	825.9	1,035.1	920.6	1,156.8	1,204.6	1,381.0	1,274.4	1,693.2
Industrial (30 stocks)	964.0	875.0	1,046.5	1,258.6	1,211.6	1,546.7	1,896.0	1,938.8	2,168.6	2,753.2	2,633.7	3,168.8	3,301.1	3,754.1	3,834.4	5,117.1
Transportation (20 stocks)	398.1	380.3	448.4	589.6	558.1	708.2	807.2	748.9	969.8	1,177.8	910.2	1,358.0	1,449.2	1,762.3	1,455.0	1,981.0
Utility (15 stocks)	114.4	109.0	119.5	131.8	149.5	174.8	206.0	175.1	186.3	235.0	209.7	226.2	221.0	229.3	181.5	225.4
Wilshire 5000 equity index (Dec. 31, 1980=1404.596) [7]	1,220.7	1,343.7	1,233.7	1,691.5	1,644.6	1,923.8	2,418.8	2,843.7	2,636.9	3,172.6	3,187.3	3,604.6	4,041.1	4,468.0	4,571.3	5,337.1

[1] Source: Dow Jones and Co., Inc., New York, NY. Reprinted by permission of Dow Jones & Company, Inc., 1996. All rights reserved worldwide. [2] A 20-bond average consisting of 10 utility bonds and 10 industrial bonds. [3] The index includes 400 industrial stocks, 20 transportation, 40 public utility, and 40 financial stocks. [4] Source: New York Stock Exchange, Inc., New York, NY, Fact Book, annual (copyright). [5] Source: National Association of Securities Dealers, Washington, DC, Fact Book, annual. December monthly closing values. [6] Based on stocks listed on the New York Stock Exchange and NASDAQ/NMS. Averages are as of end-of-year. [7] Represents return on the market value of all common equity securities for which daily pricing is available. Source: Wilshire Associates, Santa Monica, CA, releases.

Source: Except as noted, Board of Governors of the Federal Reserve System, Federal Reserve Bulletin, monthly; Annual Statistical Digest; and unpublished data.

No. 803. Dow-Jones U.S. Equity Market Index, by Industry: 1990 to 1995

[As of end of year]

INDUSTRY	1990	1991	1992	1993	1994	1995
U.S. Equity Market Index, total	305.59	391.90	413.29	442.19	433.07	581.43
Basic materials.	299.67	372.44	401.09	443.38	456.55	540.47
Consumer, cyclical	325.98	446.65	527.62	596.43	532.55	635.01
Consumer, noncyclical.	543.87	784.85	734.03	684.89	740.25	1,052.90
Conglomerates.	354.20	471.90	530.30	655.57	638.07	891.54
Energy	262.85	265.79	264.73	290.55	286.70	358.74
Financial services.	233.04	338.52	410.85	436.98	408.25	611.76
Industrial.	288.12	364.55	390.48	432.52	399.79	499.93
Technology	242.10	302.07	320.10	361.45	406.48	570.55
Utilities	248.91	278.77	286.74	316.02	272.82	362.66

Source: Dow Jones & Company, Inc., New York, NY, *Wall Street Journal*, selected issues, (copyright).

No. 804. Bond and Stock Dividend Yields: 1980 to 1995

[**Percent per year**. Annual averages of daily figures, except as indicated. See also *Historical Statistics, Colonial Times to 1970*, series X 474-491]

TYPE	1980	1985	1987	1988	1989	1990	1991	1992	1993	1994	1995
U.S. Treasury, constant maturities: [1] [2]											
3-year.	11.51	9.64	7.68	8.26	8.55	8.26	6.82	5.30	4.44	6.27	6.25
5-year.	11.45	10.12	7.94	8.47	8.50	8.37	7.37	6.19	5.14	6.69	6.38
7-year.	11.40	10.50	8.23	8.71	8.52	8.52	7.68	6.63	5.54	6.91	6.50
10-year	11.43	10.62	8.39	8.85	8.49	8.55	7.86	7.01	5.87	7.69	6.57
20-year	(NA)	(NA)	(NA)	(NA)	(NA)	(NA)	(NA)	(NA)	6.29	7.47	6.95
30-year	11.27	10.79	8.59	8.96	8.45	8.61	8.14	7.67	6.59	7.37	6.88
U.S. Govt., long-term bonds [2] [3]. . . .	10.81	10.75	8.64	8.98	8.58	8.74	8.16	7.52	6.45	7.41	6.93
State and local govt. bonds, Aaa [4] . . .	7.86	8.60	7.12	7.36	7.00	6.96	6.56	6.09	5.38	5.78	5.79
State and local govt. bonds, Baa [4] . . .	9.02	9.58	8.17	7.84	7.40	7.29	6.99	6.48	5.82	6.18	6.04
Municipal (Bond Buyer, 20 bonds) . . .	8.59	9.11	7.63	7.68	7.23	7.27	6.92	6.44	5.60	6.18	5.95
Corporate Aaa seasoned [4]	11.94	11.37	9.38	9.71	9.26	9.32	8.77	8.14	7.22	7.97	7.59
Corporate Baa seasoned [4]	13.67	12.72	10.58	10.83	10.18	10.36	9.80	8.98	7.93	8.63	8.20
Corporate (Moody's) [4] [5].	12.75	12.05	9.91	10.18	9.66	9.77	9.23	8.55	7.54	8.26	7.83
Industrials (49 bonds) [6]	12.35	11.80	9.83	9.91	9.66	9.77	9.25	8.52	7.51	8.21	7.76
Public utilities (51 bonds) [7]	13.15	12.29	9.98	10.45	9.66	9.76	9.21	8.57	7.56	8.30	7.90
Stocks (Standard & Poor's):											
Common: Composite (500 stocks) .	5.26	4.25	3.08	3.64	3.45	3.61	3.24	2.99	2.78	2.82	2.56

NA Not available.   [1] Yields on the more actively traded issues adjusted to constant maturities by the U.S. Treasury.   [2] Yields are based on closing bid prices quoted by at least five dealers.   [3] Averages (to maturity or call) for all outstanding bonds neither due nor callable in less than 10 years, including several very low yielding "flower" bonds.   [4] Source: Moody's Investors Service, New York, NY.   [5] For 1980-88 includes railroad bonds which were discontinued as part of composite in 1989.   [6] Covers 40 bonds for 1980, 38 bonds for 1985, and 37 bonds for 1987 and 1988.   [7] Covers 40 bonds for period 1980-88.

Source: Except as noted, Board of Governors of the Federal Reserve System, *Federal Reserve Bulletin*, monthly.

No. 805. New Security Issues of Corporations, by Type of Offering and Industry Group: 1990 to 1994

[**In billions of dollars**. Represents gross proceeds of issues maturing in more than one year. Figures are the principal amount or the number of units multiplied by the offering price. Excludes secondary offerings, employee stock plans, investment companies other than closed-end, intracorporate transactions, equities sold abroad, and Yankee bonds. Stock data include ownership securities issued by limited partnerships]

TYPE OF OFFERING AND INDUSTRY GROUP	1990	1991	1992	1993	1994	TYPE OF OFFERING AND INDUSTRY GROUP	1990	1991	1992	1993	1994
Total.	339.1	465.2	559.8	769.1	583.2	Stocks, total	40.2	75.4	88.3	122.5	85.2
Bonds, total	298.9	389.8	471.5	646.6	498.0	Preferred	4.0	17.1	21.3	18.9	12.5
Public, domestic. .	188.8	286.9	378.1	487.0	365.2	Common.	19.4	48.2	57.1	82.7	47.8
Private placement, domestic.	87.0	74.9	65.9	121.2	76.1	Private place- ment	16.7	10.1	9.9	20.9	24.8
Sold abroad	23.1	28.0	27.6	38.4	56.8						
Manufacturing . . .	51.8	86.6	82.1	88.2	43.4	Manufacturing . . .	5.6	24.1	22.7	22.3	17.8
Commercial and miscellaneous . .	40.7	36.7	43.1	58.6	40.7	Commercial and miscellaneous . .	10.2	19.4	20.2	25.8	15.7
Transportation . . .	12.8	13.6	10.0	10.8	6.9	Transportation . . .	0.4	2.4	2.6	2.2	2.2
Public utility.	17.6	23.9	48.1	56.3	13.3	Public utility.	0.4	3.5	6.5	7.1	2.2
Communication . .	6.7	9.4	15.4	31.9	13.3	Communication . .	3.8	0.5	2.4	3.4	0.5
Real estate and financial	169.3	219.6	272.9	400.8	380.4	Real estate and financial	19.7	25.5	33.9	61.0	46.7

Source: Board of Governors of the Federal Reserve System, *Federal Reserve Bulletin*, monthly, and *Annual Statistical Digest*.

No. 806. Equities, Corporate Bonds, and Tax-Exempt Securities—Holdings and Net Purchases, by Type of Investor: 1980 to 1994

[In billions of dollars. Holdings as of Dec. 31. Minus sign (-) indicates net sales]

TYPE OF INVESTOR	HOLDINGS					NET PURCHASES				
	1980	1990	1992	1993	1994	1980	1990	1992	1993	1994
EQUITIES [1]										
Total [2]	1,535	3,530	5,463	6,186	6,049	14.5	-45.6	84.1	120.1	31.6
Household sector [3]	934	1,717	2,810	3,088	2,913	-4.3	-21.7	43.8	-33.1	-89.0
Rest of the world [4]	65	222	300	340	341	4.2	-16.0	-5.8	20.5	0.9
Life insurance companies	46	98	122	146	159	0.4	-5.7	2.7	7.8	8.2
Other insurance companies	32	80	97	103	105	3.1	-7.0	-0.4	0.8	5.3
Private pension funds	223	658	962	1,079	1,047	16.4	-14.4	-2.6	-13.6	-26.7
State and local retirement funds	44	296	449	507	520	5.3	12.3	16.7	48.0	30.9
Mutual funds	42	233	452	669	738	-1.8	14.4	67.2	128.9	122.7
Bank personal trusts	135	190	217	181	156	-7.2	0.5	-37.0	-55.2	-20.4
CORPORATE & FOREIGN BONDS										
Total [2]	508	1,696	2,023	2,277	2,417	36.2	114.7	160.4	252.9	142.4
Household sector [3]	31	95	107	142	198	-14.5	38.0	-4.8	26.2	58.5
Rest of the world [4]	37	217	252	273	311	9.2	5.3	18.1	30.0	38.2
Commercial banking	11	89	95	98	104	1.1	4.6	-1.6	3.5	6.0
Life insurance companies	179	567	654	719	766	8.7	55.8	58.9	65.5	46.7
Other insurance companies	24	89	98	103	105	-	9.9	0.7	5.3	1.6
Private pension funds	78	235	292	309	295	14.0	9.3	16.4	17.4	-14.9
State and local retirement funds	92	169	223	238	258	9.2	2.8	27.8	14.8	19.9
Mutual funds	8	88	120	176	173	1.3	13.6	19.8	56.1	-2.9
MUNICIPAL SECURITIES [5]										
Total [2]	365	1,040	1,140	1,218	1,203	23.9	48.7	31.1	78.1	-15.1
Household sector [3]	76	448	449	433	403	2.4	17.7	-34.8	-15.8	-29.6
Commercial banking	149	117	98	99	98	13.2	-16.4	-5.7	1.7	-1.5
Other insurance companies	81	137	134	146	153	7.7	2.2	7.5	11.8	7.3
Mutual funds	4	109	173	218	213	0.4	15.6	36.3	44.6	-5.4
Money market mutual funds	2	84	95	103	111	1.6	14.3	5.0	8.3	7.5
Bank personal trusts	26	81	96	109	120	-1.6	7.7	6.1	12.9	11.3

- Represents or rounds to zero.   [1] Excludes mutual fund shares.   [2] Includes other types not shown separately.   [3] Includes nonprofit organizations.   [4] Holdings of U.S. issues by foreign residents.   [5] Includes small amounts of taxable securities.

Source: Board of Governors of the Federal Reserve System, *Flow of Funds Accounts*, March 1995 quarterly diskettes. Data are also published in the quarterly Z.1 release.

No. 807. United States Purchases and Sales of Foreign Stocks and Bonds, 1980 to 1995, and by Selected Country, 1995

[In billions of dollars. See headnote, table 808. Minus sign (-) indicates net sales by U.S. investors or a net inflow of capital into the United States]

YEAR AND COUNTRY	NET PURCHASES			TOTAL TRANSACTIONS [1]			PURCHASES		SALES	
	Total	Bonds	Stocks	Total	Bonds	Stocks	Bonds	Stocks	Bonds	Stocks
1980	3.1	1.0	2.1	53.1	35.2	17.9	18.1	10.0	17.1	7.9
1990	31.2	21.9	9.2	906.7	652.2	254.5	337.1	131.9	315.1	122.6
1991	46.8	14.8	32.0	948.6	675.5	273.2	345.1	152.6	330.3	120.6
1992	47.9	15.6	32.3	1,375.1	1,042.8	332.4	529.2	182.3	513.6	150.1
1993	143.1	80.4	62.7	2,126.0	1,572.3	553.7	895.2	313.9	834.5	246.1
1994	57.3	9.2	48.1	2,526.2	1,706.0	820.3	924.9	431.1	904.6	384.0
1995, total [2]	98.1	46.8	51.3	2,573.6	1,832.0	741.6	939.4	396.4	892.6	345.2
United Kingdom	29.0	19.0	10.0	1,135.4	861.1	274.3	440.0	142.1	421.1	132.1
Canada	7.8	8.0	-0.2	414.6	370.7	43.9	189.4	21.8	181.3	22.0
Japan	25.1	5.3	19.8	246.8	123.2	123.6	64.3	71.7	59.0	51.9
France	0.5	-1.0	1.4	60.0	38.4	21.6	18.7	11.5	19.7	10.1
Hong Kong	1.6	-0.6	2.2	58.5	19.4	39.1	9.4	20.6	10.0	18.5
Germany	1.0	0.5	0.5	33.8	12.1	21.6	6.3	11.1	5.8	10.6
Mexico	0.6	0.5	0.2	26.5	11.0	15.5	5.7	7.8	5.3	7.7

[1] Total purchases plus total sales.   [2] Includes other countries, not shown separately.

Source: U.S. Dept. of Treasury, *Treasury Bulletin*, quarterly.

No. 808. Foreign Purchases and Sales of U.S. Securities, by Type of Security, 1980 to 1995, and by Selected Country, 1995

[In billions of dollars. Covers transactions in all types of long-term domestic securities by foreigners as reported by banks, brokers, and other entities in the United States (except nonmarketable U.S. Treasury notes, foreign series; and nonmarketable U.S. Treasury bonds and notes, foreign currency series). Data cover new issues of securities, transactions in outstanding issues, and redemptions of securities. Includes transactions executed in the United States for the account of foreigners, and transactions executed abroad for the account of reporting institutions and their domestic customers. Data by country show the country of domicile of the foreign buyers and sellers of the securities; in the case of outstanding issues, this may differ from the country of the original issuer. The term "foreigner" covers all institutions and individuals domiciled outside the United States, including U.S. citizens domiciled abroad, and the foreign branches, subsidiaries and other affiliates abroad of U.S. banks and businesses; the central governments, central banks, and other official institutions of foreign countries; and international and regional organizations. "Foreigner" also includes persons in the United States to the extent that they are known by reporting institutions to be acting on behalf of foreigners. Minus sign (-) indicates net sales by foreigners or a net outflow of capital from the United States]

YEAR AND COUNTRY	NET PURCHASES					TOTAL TRANSACTIONS [4]				
	Total	Treasury bonds and notes [1]	U.S. Govt. corporations [2] bonds	Corporate bonds [3]	Corporate rate stocks	Total	Treasury bonds and notes [1]	U.S. Govt. corporations [2] bonds	Corporate bonds [3]	Corporate rate stocks
1980	15.8	4.9	2.6	2.9	5.4	198	97	17	9	75
1985	78.3	29.2	4.3	39.8	4.9	1,256	968	46	84	159
1990	25.0	17.9	6.3	9.7	-15.1	4,204	3,620	104	117	362
1991	58.1	19.9	10.2	16.9	11.1	4,706	4,016	124	155	411
1992	73.2	39.3	18.3	20.8	-5.1	5,282	4,444	204	187	448
1993	111.1	23.6	35.4	30.6	21.6	6,314	5,195	263	239	618
1994	140.6	78.8	21.7	38.2	1.9	6,562	5,343	297	222	699
1995, total [5]	230.1	134.0	28.7	56.3	11.2	7,242	5,828	222	277	915
United Kingdom	98.9	34.8	17.1	39.0	8.0	2,729	2,278	59	146	245
Japan	16.4	16.9	1.1	1.2	-2.7	1,001	912	32	13	45
Canada	1.3	0.3	1.0	1.6	-1.5	548	435	3	13	96
British West Indies	19.4	17.4	-0.4	1.3	1.1	333	212	42	11	69
Netherlands Antilles	27.3	23.5	(Z)	-0.2	4.0	298	206	3	10	79
Bermuda	-2.4	-6.0	1.1	1.9	0.6	283	171	20	13	78

Z Less than $50 million. [1] Marketable bonds and notes. [2] Includes federally-sponsored agencies. [3] Includes transactions in directly placed issues abroad by U.S. corporations and issues of States and municipalities. [4] Total purchases plus total sales. [5] Includes other countries, not shown separately.

Source: U.S. Dept. of Treasury, *Treasury Bulletin*, quarterly.

No. 809. Sales of Stocks and Options on Registered Exchanges: 1980 to 1994

[Excludes over-the-counter trading. See also *Historical Statistics, Colonial Times to 1970*, series X 517-530]

EXCHANGE	Unit	1980	1985	1987	1988	1989	1990	1991	1992	1993	1994
Market value of all sales, all exchanges [1] [2]	Bil. dol	522	1,260	2,492	1,702	2,010	1,752	1,903	2,149	2,734	2,966
New York	Bil. dol	398	1,024	1,987	1,380	1,581	1,394	1,534	1,759	2,278	2,483
American	Bil. dol	47	38	102	59	80	65	67	69	83	83
Chicago [3]	Bil. dol	21	79	122	87	101	74	77	87	107	98
CBOE [4]	Bil. dol	28	38	124	64	88	81	74	63	65	87
Pacific	Bil. dol	13	40	71	49	64	53	63	65	70	70
Philadelphia	Bil. dol	11	23	48	34	50	41	39	49	55	51
STOCKS [5]											
Shares sold, all exchanges [2] . . .	Million.	15,488	37,046	63,771	52,533	54,239	53,338	58,025	65,463	82,808	90,482
New York	Million.	12,390	30,222	53,038	44,018	44,140	43,829	47,674	53,344	68,732	76,665
American	Million.	1,659	2,115	3,496	2,576	3,248	3,125	3,103	3,631	4,470	4,300
Chicago [3]	Million.	598	2,274	3,329	2,771	2,960	2,511	2,715	3,035	3,792	3,526
Pacific	Million.	435	1,352	2,034	1,576	1,791	1,682	2,068	2,087	2,330	2,147
Market value, all exchanges [2] . .	Bil. dol	476	1,200	2,284	1,587	1,845	1,612	1,776	2,032	2,610	2,817
New York	Bil. dol	398	1,023	1,983	1,378	1,577	1,390	1,532	1,758	2,276	2,482
American	Bil. dol	35	26	53	31	43	36	40	42	54	56
Chicago [3]	Bil. dol	21	79	122	87	101	74	77	87	107	98
Pacific	Bil. dol	11	37	57	41	52	45	63	58	62	59
OPTIONS [6]											
Contracts traded, all exchanges [2].	Million.	97	233	305	196	227	210	199	202	233	281
CBOE [4]	Million.	53	149	182	112	127	130	122	122	141	184
American	Million.	29	49	71	45	50	41	39	42	48	46
Market value of contracts traded, all exchanges [2]	Bil. dol	45.8	59.1	118.9	62.6	76.8	79.0	76.1	72.2	75.2	94.5
CBOE [4]	Bil. dol	27.9	38.4	76.9	39.7	47.3	55.4	50.7	44.5	45.5	67.2
American	Bil. dol	12.5	11.6	25.7	12.4	15.1	12.8	14.0	14.1	14.9	13.2
Options exercised:											
Number of contracts	Million.	4.9	10.5	17.0	11.4	15.6	12.1	10.8	9.9	11.5	13.0
Value	Bil. dol	20.4	49.2	85.9	51.5	85.2	55.8	49.2	43.9	48.4	53.8

[1] Includes market value of stocks, rights, warrants, and options trading beginning 1987. [2] Includes other registered exchanges, not shown separately. [3] The Chicago Stock Exchange, Inc. was formerly the Midwest Stock Exchange. [4] Chicago Board Options Exchange, Inc. [5] Includes voting trust certificates, American Depository Receipts, and certificate of deposit for stocks. [6] Data for 1980 exclude nonequity options.

Source: U.S. Securities and Exchange Commission, *SEC Monthly Statistical Review* (discontinued Feb. 1989); and unpublished data.

No. 810. Volume of Trading on New York Stock Exchange: 1980 to 1995

[**Round lot**: A unit of trading or a multiple thereof. On the NYSE the unit of trading is generally 100 shares in stocks. For some inactive stocks, the unit of trading is 10 shares. **Odd lot**: An amount of stock less than the established 100-share unit or 10-share unit of trading]

ITEM	Unit	1980	1985	1988	1989	1990	1991	1992	1993	1994	1995
Shares traded.........	Million .	11,562	27,774	41,118	42,022	39,946	45,599	51,826	67,461	74,003	87,873
Round lots...............	Million..	11,352	27,511	40,850	41,699	39,665	45,266	51,376	66,923	73,420	87,218
Average daily shares	Million..	44.9	109.2	161.5	165.5	156.8	178.9	202.3	264.5	291.4	346.1
High day	Million..	84.3	181.0	343.9	416.4	292.4	317.4	389.0	379.5	482.8	652.8
Low day................	Million..	16.1	62.1	72.1	68.9	56.9	69.6	95.1	89.9	113.8	117.7
Odd lots	Million..	209	263	268	324	282	333	450	538	583	656
Value of shares traded ..	Bil. dol .	382	981	1,366	1,556	1,336	1,534	1,765	2,305	2,477	3,110
Round lots...............	Bil. dol..	375	970	1,356	1,543	1,325	1,520	1,745	2,283	2,454	3,083
Odd lots	Bil. dol..	8	10	10	13	11	[1]13	19	22	22	27
Bond volume [2]........	Mil. dol .	5,190	9,047	7,702	8,836	10,893	12,698	11,629	9,743	7,197	6,979
Daily average	Mil. dol .	20.5	35.9	30.4	35.1	43.1	50.2	45.8	38.5	28.6	27.7

[1] Excludes odd lot statistics for February which were not available.   [2] Par value.

Source: New York Stock Exchange, Inc., New York, NY, *Fact Book*, annual (copyright).

No. 811. Securities Listed on New York Stock Exchange: 1980 to 1995

[As of **December 31**, except **cash dividends** are for **calendar year**]

ITEM	Unit	1980	1985	1987	1988	1989	1990	1991	1992	1993	1994	1995
BONDS												
Number of issuers	Number .	1,045	1,010	885	846	794	743	705	636	574	583	564
Number of issues......	Number .	3,057	3,856	3,346	3,106	2,961	2,912	2,727	2,727	2,103	2,141	2,097
Face value	Bil. dol .	602	1,327	1,651	1,610	1,435	1,689	2,219	2,009	2,342	2,526	2,773
Market value.........	Bil. dol..	508	1,339	1,621	1,561	1,412	1,610	2,227	2,044	2,528	2,367	2,748
Average price	Percent .	84.41	100.90	98.20	96.94	98.42	95.31	100.34	101.77	107.96	93.73	99.09
STOCKS												
Companies	Number .	1,570	1,541	1,647	1,681	1,720	1,774	1,885	2,088	2,361	2,570	2,675
Number of issues......	Number .	2,228	2,298	2,244	2,234	2,246	2,284	2,426	2,658	2,904	3,060	3,126
Shares listed.........	Billion..	33.7	52.4	71.8	76.2	83.0	90.7	99.6	115.8	131.1	142.3	154.7
Market value.........	Bil. dol .	1,243	1,950	2,216	2,457	3,030	2,820	3,713	4,035	4,541	4,448	6,013
Average price	Dollars ..	36.87	37.20	30.87	32.26	36.51	31.08	37.27	34.83	34.65	31.26	38.86
Cash dividends on common stock	Bil. dol ..	53.1	74.2	84.4	102.2	101.8	103.2	123.4	109.7	120.2	130.0	147.0

Source: New York Stock Exchange, Inc., New York, NY, *Fact Book*, annual (copyright).

No. 812. NASDAQ—Securities Listed and Volume of Trading: 1980 to 1995

ITEM	Unit	1980	1985	1988	1989	1990	1991	1992	1993	1994	1995
Member firms..........	Number...	2,932	6,307	6,432	6,141	5,827	5,386	5,254	5,296	5,426	5,451
Branch offices..........	Number...	7,555	15,375	22,714	29,998	24,457	29,158	33,484	44,181	57,105	58,119
Companies listed........	Number...	2,894	4,136	4,451	4,293	4,132	4,094	4,113	4,611	4,902	5,112
Issues................	Number...	3,050	4,784	5,144	4,963	4,706	4,684	4,768	5,393	5,761	5,955
Shares traded.........	Million....	6,692	20,699	31,070	33,530	33,380	41,311	48,455	66,541	74,353	101,158
Average daily volume ...	Million....	26.5	82.1	122.8	133.1	131.9	163.3	190.8	263.0	295.1	401.4
Value of shares traded	Bil. dol. ...	69	234	347	431	452	694	891	1,350	1,449	2,398

Source: National Association of Securities Dealers, Washington, DC, *Fact Book*, annual.

No. 813. Commodity Futures Trading on U.S. Exchanges—Volume of Trading: 1980 to 1994

[In millions. For year ending Sept. 30]

COMMODITY	1980	1985	1986	1987	1988	1989	1990	1991	1992	1993	1994
Number of contracts traded ..	82.7	152.6	183.1	213.5	241.8	267.7	272.2	261.4	289.5	325.5	411.1
Grain.....................	18.3	10.7	10.3	10.9	15.9	15.9	17.0	16.6	17.6	16.0	20.0
Oilseeds/products.............	15.7	14.9	13.8	14.2	22.5	21.1	20.4	19.8	18.6	20.7	21.0
Livestock/products............	11.8	7.9	8.6	8.8	9.6	8.2	8.0	6.9	6.4	5.8	6.1
Other agriculturals	7.8	5.1	6.7	5.7	9.8	10.7	11.0	9.5	9.4	10.8	12.3
Energy products.............	1.1	7.0	11.5	20.3	26.3	31.3	35.2	31.8	38.4	42.8	50.5
Metals	14.1	18.4	16.2	19.4	18.9	17.9	17.8	13.9	12.2	15.2	18.2
Financial instruments	10.2	72.1	96.9	114.3	117.6	136.7	135.7	134.1	148.2	185.4	252.6
Currencies	3.7	16.4	19.1	19.9	21.2	25.7	27.2	28.8	38.7	28.8	30.4

Source: U.S. Commodity Futures Trading Commission, *Annual Report*.

No. 814. Securities Industry—Revenues and Expenses: 1980 to 1995

[In millions of dollars]

TYPE	ALL SECURITIES FIRMS								MEMBERS OF NY STOCK EXCHANGE [1]	
	1980	1985	1989	1990	1991	1992	1993	1994	1994	1995, proj.
Revenues, total	**19,829**	**49,844**	**76,864**	**71,356**	**84,890**	**90,584**	**108,843**	**112,815**	**71,355**	**96,303**
Commissions	6,777	10,955	13,452	12,032	14,210	16,249	19,905	19,896	13,504	15,998
Trading/investment gains	5,091	14,549	16,247	15,746	22,641	21,838	25,427	20,217	13,338	18,902
Underwriting profits	1,571	4,987	4,537	3,728	6,593	8,300	11,249	6,848	5,856	7,799
Margin interest	2,151	2,746	3,860	3,179	2,771	2,690	3,235	4,674	4,525	6,239
Mutual fund sales	278	2,754	3,038	3,242	4,176	5,950	8,115	6,909	3,192	3,406
Other	3,960	13,854	35,731	33,428	34,498	35,557	40,913	54,272	30,939	43,960
Expenses, total	**16,668**	**43,342**	**74,041**	**70,566**	**76,234**	**81,467**	**95,805**	**109,287**	**70,227**	**88,899**
Interest expense	3,876	11,470	29,822	28,093	27,512	24,576	26,616	40,255	23,731	38,175
Compensation	7,619	18,112	23,740	22,931	26,916	32,071	39,125	37,604	27,340	30,309
Commissions/clearance paid	1,055	2,314	3,057	2,959	3,200	3,722	5,338	5,363	2,620	2,728
Other	4,119	11,446	17,422	16,583	18,605	21,098	24,726	26,065	16,536	17,686
Net income, pretax	**3,160**	**6,502**	**2,823**	**790**	**8,656**	**9,117**	**13,039**	**3,528**	**1,128**	**7,405**

[1] Covers all members of New York Stock Exchange doing public business. Source: Securities Industry Association, New York, NY, *Securities Industry Association Fact Book*, annual.

Source: Except as noted, U.S. Securities and Exchange Commission, *Annual Report*.

No. 815. Assets of Private and Public Pension Funds, by Type of Fund: 1980 to 1994

[In billions of dollars. As of end of year. Except for corporate equities, represents book value. Excludes Social Security trust funds and U.S. Government pension funds; see tables 581 and 585]

TYPE OF PENSION FUND	1980	1985	1988	1989	1990	1991	1992	1993	1994
Total, all types	**873**	**1,883**	**2,653**	**3,172**	**3,234**	**3,862**	**4,213**	**4,644**	**4,702**
Private funds	676	1,485	2,044	2,405	2,413	2,921	3,154	3,492	3,480
Insured	172	392	622	700	784	865	940	1,042	1,123
Noninsured [1][2]	504	1,093	1,422	1,706	1,629	2,056	2,214	2,450	2,356
Small time and savings deposits	28	74	120	144	134	174	183	186	162
Mutual fund shares	7	11	31	42	45	64	86	137	151
Corporate equities	223	464	609	735	658	889	962	1,079	1,047
Credit market instruments [2]	151	378	509	590	607	693	730	771	728
U.S. government securities	51	190	250	311	322	363	384	401	378
Treasury	32	115	164	209	221	254	271	286	276
Agency	18	74	86	102	101	109	112	115	103
Corporate and foreign bonds	78	155	204	226	235	276	292	309	295
State and local pension funds [2]	197	399	609	767	820	941	1,059	1,151	1,223
Corporate equities	44	120	220	300	296	387	449	507	520
Credit market instruments [2]	147	257	353	399	434	480	514	543	586
U.S. government securities	40	124	182	198	225	235	238	251	273
Treasury	21	83	124	125	142	151	155	171	187
Agency	19	41	58	73	82	84	83	79	86
Corporate and foreign bonds	92	107	135	167	169	195	223	238	258

[1] Covers all pension funds of corporations, nonprofit organizations, unions, and multi-employer groups. Also includes deferred profit-sharing plans and Federal Employees Retirement System (FERS) Thrift Savings Fund. Excludes health, welfare, and bonus plans. [2] Includes other types of assets not shown separately.

Source: Board of Governors of the Federal Reserve System, *Flow of Funds Accounts*, March 1995 quarterly diskettes. Data are also published in the quarterly Z.1 release.

No. 816. Individual Retirement Accounts (IRA) Plans—Value, by Type of Holder: 1985 to 1995

[As of **December 31**. Estimated]

TYPE OF HOLDER	AMOUNT (bil. dol.)									PERCENT DISTRIBUTION		
	1985	1988	1989	1990	1991	1992	1993	1994	1995	1985	1990	1995
Total	200	390	455	529	657	746	868	941	1,169	100	100	100
Savings institutions	56	90	98	95	91	85	76	72	71	28	18	6
Commercial banks	52	88	99	119	134	137	134	136	145	26	22	12
Mutual funds	32	86	112	127	169	211	284	305	411	16	24	35
Self directed.	29	68	82	117	181	225	271	318	415	15	22	36
Life insurance companies. . . .	17	33	38	42	50	56	70	79	94	9	8	8
Credit unions	14	25	26	29	32	32	32	32	33	7	6	3

Source: Investment Company Institute, Washington, DC, *Mutual Fund Fact Book*, annual (copyright).

No. 817. 401(k) Plan Assets—Summary, 1985 to 1995, and Projections, 2000

YEAR	Total assets (bil. dol.)	TYPE OF ASSET	Percent of compa- nies offering invest- ment option, 1995	ASSETS, 1995		FINANCIAL INSTITUTION MANAGING ASSETS	ASSETS, 1995	
				Amount (bil. dol.)	Percent distri- bution		Amount (bil. dol.)	Percent distri- bution
1985	105	Total	(X)	675	100	All defined contribution plans [2]	1,225	100
1987	190	Guaranteed investment account [1]	62	150	22	Insurance companies. . .	395	32
1988	230					Banks	355	29
1989	270	Equity	91	140	21	Mutual fund groups	305	25
1990	300	Money market.	50	40	6	Other	170	14
1991	350	Balanced account . . .	48	95	14			
1992	410							
1993	475	Bond fund	59	55	8	401(k) plans	675	100
1994	525	Company stock	24	155	23	Insurance companies. . .	195	29
1995	675	Other.	18	40	6	Banks	160	24
						Mutual fund groups	225	33
2000, proj. .	1,300					Other	95	14

X Not applicable.   [1] Covers bank certificate of deposits, guaranteed investment contracts (GIC's), GIC alternatives, and insurance company participating contracts.   [2] Includes 401(k) plans.

Source: Access Research, Inc., Windsor, CT, *1995 Marketplace Update*, 1995, (copyright).

No. 818. Mutual Funds—Summary: 1980 to 1995

[Number of funds, accounts, and assets as of **December 31**. A mutual fund is an open-end investment company that continuously issues and redeems shares that represent an interest in a pool of financial assets. See also *Historical Statistics, Colonial Times to 1970*, series X 536-539]

TYPE OF FUND	Unit	1980	1985	1989	1990	1991	1992	1993	1994	1995
Number of funds, total	Number. .	564	1,528	2,917	3,105	3,427	3,850	4,558	5,357	5,761
Equity funds.	Number . .	267	579	1,080	1,127	1,217	1,356	1,615	1,944	2,211
Income and bond funds [1]	Number . .	191	492	1,173	1,235	1,389	1,629	2,023	2,450	2,553
Money market funds, tax-exempt [2] . .	Number . .	10	111	201	235	267	279	292	319	325
Money market funds, taxable [3]	Number . .	96	346	463	508	554	586	628	644	672
Shareholder accounts, total. . . .	Millions. .	12.1	34.7	58.2	62.6	68.6	80.3	95.5	114.8	131.8
Equity funds.	Millions . .	5.8	11.5	21.5	23.0	26.1	33.2	42.1	59.0	70.7
Income and bond funds [1]	Millions . .	1.5	8.3	15.4	16.6	18.9	23.4	29.7	30.5	30.9
Money market funds, tax-exempt [2] . .	Millions . .	(NA)	0.5	1.1	1.4	1.7	1.9	2.0	2.0	2.3
Money market funds, taxable [3]	Millions . .	4.8	14.4	20.2	21.6	21.9	21.8	21.6	23.3	27.9
Assets, total	Bil. dol . .	135	496	982	1,067	1,396	1,646	2,075	2,161	2,820
Equity funds.	Bil. dol . .	44	117	249	246	412	523	749	866	1,269
Income and bond funds [1]	Bil. dol . .	14	135	305	323	441	577	761	684	798
Money market funds, tax-exempt [2] . .	Bil. dol . .	2	36	69	84	90	95	103	111	123
Money market funds, taxable [3]	Bil. dol . .	74	208	359	415	453	451	462	500	630
Sales, total	Bil. dol . .	248	954	1,445	1,565	2,037	2,751	3,189	3,077	3,602
Equity funds.	Bil. dol . .	6	30	55	71	99	145	229	271	307
Income and bond funds [1]	Bil. dol . .	4	84	71	79	138	220	282	203	170
Money market funds, tax-exempt [2] . .	Bil. dol . .	5	109	185	197	231	286	342	369	397
Money market funds, taxable [3]	Bil. dol . .	232	730	1,135	1,219	1,570	2,100	2,336	2,234	2,728
Redemptions, total	Bil. dol . .	217	865	1,327	1,471	1,879	2,548	2,905	2,929	3,315
Equity funds.	Bil. dol . .	6	18	38	45	54	62	93	142	172
Income and bond funds [1]	Bil. dol . .	3	15	53	53	62	103	139	188	141
Money market funds, tax-exempt [2] . .	Bil. dol . .	4	99	181	190	227	282	337	370	386
Money market funds, taxable [3]	Bil. dol . .	204	732	1,055	1,183	1,536	2,101	2,337	2,229	2,616

NA Not available.   [1] Includes municipal bond funds.   [2] Funds invest in municipal securities with relatively short maturities.   [3] Funds invest in short-term, high-grade securities sold in the money market.

Source: Investment Company Institute, Washington, DC, *Mutual Fund Fact Book*, annual (copyright).

No. 819. Mutual Fund Shares—Holdings and Net Purchases, by Type of Investor: 1980 to 1994

[In billions of dollars. Holdings as of Dec. 31. Minus sign (-) indicates net sales]

TYPE OF INVESTOR	HOLDINGS					NET PURCHASES				
	1980	1990	1992	1993	1994	1980	1990	1992	1993	1994
Total	61.8	602.1	1,042.1	1,429.3	1,463.0	3.5	65.3	211.9	317.0	128.3
Households, nonprofit organizations	45.6	451.9	733.9	972.5	968.5	2.1	37.7	146.5	187.0	76.6
Nonfinancial corporate business. . .	1.5	8.2	15.6	22.4	20.3	0.3	-1.3	4.7	6.8	-1.3
Commercial banking	-	1.9	3.4	3.9	2.0	-	-0.3	-0.4	0.5	-1.9
Credit unions	-	1.4	4.1	4.2	-	-	0.2	1.5	0.1	-4.2
Life insurance companies	1.1	30.7	70.7	105.6	128.0	0.1	12.6	18.7	34.8	26.1
Private pension funds	7.2	45.4	86.4	137.3	150.5	1.4	6.7	15.2	42.8	17.9
Bank personal trusts	6.4	62.7	128.1	183.5	193.7	-0.3	9.7	25.8	44.9	15.1

- Represents or rounds to zero.

Source: Board of Governors of the Federal Reserve System, *Flow of Funds Accounts*, March 1995 quarterly diskettes. Data are also published in the quarterly Z.1 release.

No. 820. Households Owning Mutual Funds, by Age of Head of Household and Income: 1989 and 1992

[In percent. Income in thousands of constant 1992 dollars. Constant dollar figures are based on consumer price index data published by U.S. Bureau of Labor Statistics. Families include one-person units; for definition of family, see text, section 1. Based on Survey of Consumer Finance; see source]

AGE AND ANNUAL INCOME	PERCENT OF HOUSEHOLDS OWNING LONG-TERM MUTUTAL FUNDS [1]		PERCENT OF HOUSEHOLDS' TOTAL FINANCIAL ASSETS HELD IN—			
			Long-term mutual funds [1]		Short-term mutual funds and bank deposits	
	1989	1992	1989	1992	1989	1992
Total.	11.8	15.5	9.8	13.2	36.7	30.7
Less than 35 years old	6.1	8.4	3.6	5.2	37.5	41.3
35 to 44 years old.	14.3	18.7	9.6	12.4	33.5	33.6
45 to 54 years old.	14.6	18.0	10.8	14.0	33.0	23.0
55 to 64 years old.	14.9	22.2	10.9	17.2	41.0	22.1
65 years old and over	12.3	14.6	9.7	11.9	36.8	36.0
Less than $30,000	4.9	5.7	4.1	7.7	60.5	51.4
$30,000 to $49,999	12.5	19.9	8.6	17.0	42.9	35.5
$50,000 to $99,999.	26.2	28.4	11.0	13.1	36.9	30.2
$100,000 to $199,999	42.6	41.8	12.2	14.2	33.2	23.0
$200,00 or more.	51.7	55.5	11.8	14.4	19.2	18.7

[1] Excludes all money market mutual funds except those in retirement accounts.

Source: Board of Governors of the Federal Reserve System, *Federal Reserve Bulletin*, November 1993.

No. 821. Health Insurance—Premium Income and Benefit Payments of Insurance Companies: 1980 to 1993

[In billions of dollars. Includes Puerto Rico and other U.S. outlying areas. Represents premium income of and benefits paid by insurance companies only. Excludes Blue Cross-Blue Shield plans, medical-society sponsored plans, and all other independent plans]

ITEM	1980	1983	1984	1985	1986	1987	1988	1989	1990	1991	1992	1993
Premiums [1]	43.7	63.2	70.4	75.2	75.5	84.1	98.2	108.0	112.9	116.4	125.0	124.7
Group policies [2]	36.8	54.9	60.8	64.4	65.9	74.0	87.6	96.1	100.2	103.0	110.4	110.2
Individual and family policies. .	6.9	8.3	9.6	10.8	9.6	10.1	10.6	11.8	12.7	13.3	14.6	14.5
Benefit payments	37.0	51.7	56.0	60.0	64.3	72.5	83.0	89.4	92.5	97.6	104.8	103.4
Group policies [2]	33.0	46.9	50.3	53.7	58.9	66.5	76.4	82.2	84.4	88.8	95.2	94.1
Individual and family policies. .	4.0	4.8	5.7	6.3	5.4	5.9	6.6	7.2	8.2	8.8	9.6	9.3
Type of coverage:												
Loss of income	5.3	4.9	5.2	5.6	5.6	6.4	6.4	7.2	7.4	7.5	8.3	8.1
Medical expense	27.9	41.5	44.1	47.2	50.9	57.4	66.4	72.0	73.8	77.9	82.9	81.4
Dental	2.8	4.4	4.9	5.3	5.3	5.9	6.3	6.5	6.4	6.4	7.1	7.0
Medicare supplement	1.0	1.0	1.8	1.9	2.5	2.8	3.8	3.7	5.0	5.8	6.4	6.9

[1] Earned premiums. [2] Insurance company group premiums and benefit payments include administrative service agreements and minimum premium plans.

Source: Health Insurance Association of America, Washington, DC, *Source Book of Health Insurance Data*, annual.

No. 822. Property and Casualty Insurance—Summary: 1987 to 1994

[In billions of dollars. Minus sign (-) indicates loss]

ITEM	1987	1988	1989	1990	1991	1992	1993	1994
Premiums, net written	193.2	202.0	208.4	217.8	223.0	227.8	241.7	250.7
Automobile, private [1]	64.3	69.5	73.6	78.4	82.8	88.4	93.4	96.8
Automobile, commercial [1]	16.9	16.9	17.3	17.0	16.6	16.1	16.3	16.7
Liability other than auto.	24.9	23.1	22.7	22.1	20.9	21.1	22.1	23.6
Fire and allied lines	7.7	6.9	7.0	7.1	7.2	7.1	7.9	8.7
Homeowners' multiple peril	16.7	17.1	17.7	18.6	19.3	20.5	21.5	22.6
Commercial multiple peril	17.2	17.7	17.5	17.7	17.0	16.4	17.3	17.8
Workers' compensation.	23.4	26.1	28.5	31.0	31.3	29.7	30.3	28.9
Marine, inland and ocean	5.5	5.5	5.6	5.7	5.5	5.5	6.1	6.7
Accident and health	3.8	4.7	4.6	5.0	5.1	5.4	6.8	7.2
Other lines	12.8	14.5	14.2	15.2	17.4	17.6	20.0	21.7
Losses and expenses	196.4	208.6	223.6	234.7	239.3	259.6	250.7	263.4
Underwriting gain/loss	-9.6	-11.2	-19.2	-20.9	-19.4	-33.3	-15.1	-19.0
Net investment income.	24.0	27.7	31.2	32.9	34.2	33.7	32.6	33.7
Operating earnings after taxes.	11.0	12.9	9.0	9.0	10.4	5.8	19.3	10.9
Assets.	426.7	476.9	527.0	556.3	601.4	637.3	671.5	704.6
Policyholders' surplus.	104.0	118.2	134.0	138.4	158.7	163.1	182.3	193.3

[1] Includes premiums for automobile liability and physical damage.

Source: Insurance Information Institute, New York, NY, The Fact Book, Property/Casualty Insurance Facts, annual (copyright).

No. 823. Automobile Insurance—Average Expenditures Per Insured Vehicle, by State: 1991 to 1993

[In dollars. The average expenditures for automobile insurance in a State are affected by a number of factors, including the underlying rate structure, the coverages purchased, the deductibles and limits selected, the types of vehicles insured, and the distribution of driver characteristics]

STATE	1991	1992	1993	STATE	1991	1992	1993	STATE	1991	1992	1993
U.S.	597	616	638	KS	368	392	422	ND	329	319	349
				KY	435	473	506	OH	494	503	493
AL	475	498	513	LA	679	724	752	OK	422	448	470
AK	643	685	712	ME	484	468	477	OR	529	535	564
AZ	647	667	700	MD	689	702	707	PA	610	642	645
AR	398	424	445	MA	814	860	909	RI	823	837	871
CA	783	766	803	MI	606	662	677	SC	502	534	569
CO	588	653	698	MN	530	566	595	SD	309	333	364
CT	841	878	925	MS	482	519	541	TN	466	478	488
DE	718	745	738	MO	469	493	517	TX	612	646	666
DC	863	880	879	MT	370	393	432	UT	436	463	515
FL	669	684	698	NE	346	352	403	VT	474	484	501
GA	546	514	536	NV	640	673	726	VA	506	503	508
HI	874	974	953	NH	646	638	649	WA	549	588	641
ID	386	402	429	NJ	879	957	961	WV	519	557	581
IL	552	534	572	NM	517	543	589	WI	463	492	503
IN	474	497	494	NY	754	799	832	WY	330	366	401
IA	359	379	397	NC	432	448	440				

Source: National Association of Insurance Commissioners, Kansas City, MO, State Average Expenditures and Premiums for Personal Automobile Insurance, annual (copyright).

No. 824. Life Insurance in Force in the United States—Summary: 1980 to 1994

[As of December 31 or calendar year, as applicable. Covers life insurance with life insurance companies only. Represents all life insurance in force on lives of U.S. residents whether issued by U.S. or foreign companies. For definition of household, see text, section 1. See also Historical Statistics, Colonial Times to 1970, series X 879-889]

YEAR	LIFE INSURANCE IN FORCE						AVERAGE SIZE POLICY IN FORCE (dollars)				AVERAGE AMOUNT ($1,000)		Dispos- able per- sonal income per house- hold ($1,000)
	Number of poli- cies, total (mil.)	Value (bil. dol.)					Ordi- nary	Group	Indus- trial	Cred- it [1]	Per house- hold	Per in- sured house- hold	
		Total	Ordi- nary	Group	Indus- trial	Cred- it [1]							
1980	402	3,541	1,761	1,579	36	165	11,920	13,410	620	2,110	41.9	51.1	24.2
1985	386	6,053	3,247	2,562	28	216	22,780	19,720	640	3,100	66.6	82.2	33.9
1988	391	8,020	4,512	3,232	25	251	31,390	23,410	660	3,570	84.5	105.6	38.8
1989	394	8,694	4,940	3,470	24	260	34,410	24,510	670	3,600	89.9	112.4	40.8
1990	389	9,393	5,367	3,754	24	248	37,910	26,630	670	3,500	98.4	124.5	44.1
1991	375	9,986	5,678	4,058	22	228	41,450	28,760	680	3,580	102.7	130.0	44.9
1992	366	10,406	5,942	4,241	21	202	42,960	29,930	700	3,610	106.6	136.6	47.1
1993	363	11,105	6,428	4,456	21	200	45,770	31,430	700	3,850	111.6	143.1	48.6
1994	371	11,674	6,835	4,609	20	210	48,950	32,690	700	3,530	118.7	152.2	51.7

[1] Insures borrower to cover consumer loan in case of death.

Source: American Council of Life Insurance, Washington, DC, Life Insurance Fact Book, biennial.

No. 825. Life Insurance Purchases in the United States—Number and Amount: 1980 to 1994

[Excludes revivals, increases, dividend additions, and reinsurance acquired. Includes long-term credit insurance (life insurance on loans of more than 10 years' duration). See also headnote, table 824]

YEAR	NUMBER OF POLICIES PURCHASED (1,000)						AMOUNT PURCHASED (bil. dol.)					
		Ordinary						Ordinary				
	Total	Total	Percent—		Group	Indus-trial	Total	Total	Percent—		Group	Indus-trial
			Whole life [1]	Term [2]					Whole life [1]	Term [2]		
1980	29,007	14,750	78	22	11,379	2,878	573	386	43	57	183	4
1985	33,880	17,104	78	22	16,243	533	[3]1,231	911	57	43	[3]320	1
1988	31,589	15,579	81	19	15,793	217	1,407	996	56	44	411	(Z)
1989	29,960	14,694	80	20	15,110	156	1,442	1,021	53	47	421	(Z)
1990	28,791	14,066	79	21	14,592	133	1,529	1,070	52	48	459	(Z)
1991	29,813	13,471	78	22	16,230	112	[4]1,616	1,042	50	50	[4]574	(Z)
1992	28,382	13,350	76	24	14,930	102	1,489	1,048	49	51	441	(Z)
1993	31,238	13,574	75	25	17,574	90	1,678	1,101	56	44	577	(Z)
1994	31,955	13,780	(NA)	(NA)	18,061	114	1,657	1,107	(NA)	(NA)	550	(Z)

NA Not available.　Z Less than $500 million.　[1] Life insurance payable to a beneficiary at the death of the insured whenever that occurs. Premiums may be payable for a specified number of years or for life. Includes a small number of endowment and retirement income policies.　[2] Life insurance payable to a beneficiary only when an insured dies within a specified period.　[3] Includes Federal Employees' Group Life Insurance: $10.8 billion in 1985.　[4] Includes Servicemen's Group Life Insurance: $167 billion in 1991.

Source: American Council of Life Insurance, Washington, DC, Life Insurance Fact Book, biennial.

No. 826. U.S. Life Insurance Companies—Summary: 1980 to 1994

[As of **December 31** or **calendar year**, as applicable. Covers domestic and foreign business of U.S. companies. See also Historical Statistics, Colonial Times to 1970, series X 879 and X 890-917]

ITEM	Unit	1980	1985	1987	1988	1989	1990	1991	1992	1993	1994
U.S. companies	Number .	1,958	2,261	2,337	2,343	2,270	2,195	2,064	1,944	1,844	1,715
Sales...................	Bil. dol..	655	[1]1,530	1,656	1,716	1,788	2,024	[2]2,014	1,881	2,130	2,086
Ordinary	Bil. dol ..	461	1,187	1,267	1,287	1,343	1,368	1,403	1,395	1,520	1,463
Group	Bil. dol ..	190	[1]342	388	428	444	655	[1]611	485	610	623
Industrial	Bil. dol ..	4	1	(Z)	(Z)	(Z)	(Z)	(Z)	1	(Z)	(Z)
Income.................	Bil. dol..	130.9	234.0	314.3	338.1	367.3	402.2	411.0	426.9	466.4	480.8
Life insurance premiums.....	Bil. dol ..	40.8	60.1	76.7	73.5	73.3	76.7	79.3	83.9	94.5	96.3
Percent of total	Percent .	31.2	25.7	24.4	21.7	20.0	19.1	19.3	19.6	20.3	20.0
Annuity considerations	Bil. dol ..	22.4	53.9	88.7	103.3	115.0	129.1	123.6	132.6	156.4	153.8
Health insurance premiums...	Bil. dol ..	29.4	41.8	47.6	52.3	56.1	58.2	60.9	65.5	68.7	76.2
Investment and other.......	Bil. dol ..	38.3	78.2	101.3	109.0	122.9	138.2	147.2	144.9	146.8	154.5
Disbursements	Bil. dol..	88.2	151.8	202.3	221.4	246.8	277.1	299.2	305.0	318.9	346.3
Payments to policyholders [2][3] .	Bil. dol ..	59.0	95.7	144.4	156.8	178.3	200.9	218.6	222.1	231.9	252.9
Percent of total........	Percent .	66.9	63.0	71.4	70.8	72.2	72.5	73.1	72.8	72.7	73.1
Death payments	Bil. dol ..	12.9	18.5	20.7	22.4	23.5	25.5	26.4	28.0	29.8	31.6
Matured endowments	Bil. dol ..	0.8	0.8	0.8	0.8	0.8	0.8	0.7	0.7	0.6	0.7
Annuity payments	Bil. dol ..	7.4	19.7	20.3	21.9	26.0	28.6	31.8	32.4	36.4	40.2
Policy dividends.	Bil. dol ..	8.1	12.4	13.0	13.8	14.9	15.7	15.8	15.3	15.8	16.2
Surrender values [3]	Bil. dol ..	6.4	15.9	53.7	58.1	73.4	90.2	101.2	100.5	103.1	110.4
Disability benefits	Bil. dol ..	0.5	0.5	0.5	0.4	0.5	0.5	0.6	0.6	0.5	0.6
Commissions, expenses, etc. [3]	Bil. dol ..	27.8	53.1	54.7	61.3	63.5	70.2	75.1	77.8	80.1	87.4
Dividends to stockholders	Bil. dol ..	1.4	3.0	3.3	3.4	5.0	6.0	5.5	5.1	6.9	5.9
BALANCE SHEET											
Assets.................	Bil. dol..	479	826	1,044	1,167	1,300	1,408	1,551	1,665	1,839	1,942
Government securities	Bil. dol ..	33	125	151	160	178	211	269	320	384	396
Corporate securities........	Bil. dol ..	227	374	502	585	664	711	789	863	982	1,072
Percent of total assets...	Percent .	47.4	45.3	48.1	50.1	51.1	50.5	50.8	51.8	53.4	55.2
Bonds	Bil. dol ..	180	297	406	480	538	583	624	670	730	791
Stocks	Bil. dol ..	47	77	97	104	126	128	165	193	252	282
Mortgages	Bil. dol ..	131	172	213	233	254	270	265	247	229	215
Real estate	Bil. dol ..	15	29	34	37	40	43	47	51	54	54
Policy loans	Bil. dol ..	41	54	54	54	57	63	66	72	78	85
Other	Bil. dol ..	32	72	90	98	106	110	115	112	112	120
Interest earned on assets [4].....	Percent .	8.02	9.63	9.10	9.03	9.10	8.89	8.63	8.08	7.52	7.14
Liabilities [2][5]	Bil. dol ..	445	769	977	1,092	1,216	1,317	1,445	1,549	1,711	1,806
Policy reserves [2]	Bil. dol..	390	665	862	969	1,084	1,197	1,305	1,407	1,550	1,644
Annuities	Bil. dol ..	181	410	562	642	730	815	895	960	1,062	1,118
Group...	Bil. dol ..	140	303	393	434	474	516	548	560	602	613
Individual [6]	Bil. dol ..	41	107	169	208	256	299	347	400	460	505
Life insurance	Bil. dol ..	198	236	276	300	324	349	372	402	436	468
Health insurance	Bil. dol ..	11	19	24	27	30	33	38	45	52	58
Asset valuation reserve [7]	Bil. dol ..	6	11	16	18	19	15	19	21	25	25
Capital and surplus [2]........	Bil. dol ..	34	57	67	75	84	91	106	115	128	137

Z Less than $500 million.　[1] Data for 1985 include Federal Employees' Group Life Insurance: $11 billion; data for 1991 include Servicemen's Group Life Insurance: $167 billion.　[2] Includes operations of accident and health departments of life insurance companies.　[3] Beginning in 1987, data not comparable to prior years due to change in accounting method.　[4] Net rate.　[5] Includes other obligations not shown separately.　[6] Includes reserves for supplementary contracts with and without life contingencies.　[7] The asset valuation reserve is carried as a liability in financial statements but functions as surplus.

Source: American Council of Life Insurance, Washington, DC, Life Insurance Fact Book, biennial; and unpublished data.

Business Enterprise

This section relates to the place and behavior of the business firm and to business initiative in the American economy. It includes data on the number, type, and size of businesses; financial data of domestic and multinational U.S. corporations; business investment, expenditures, and profits; sales and inventories; and business failures. Additional business data may be found in other sections, particularly 27 and 28.

In Brief

Patents issued in 1994: 113,600
  Percent issued to foreign country
  residents: 43%
Bankruptcies filed in 1994: 845,257
  Business: 7%
  Nonbusiness: 93%
  Change from 1993   –8%

The principal sources of these data are the *Survey of Current Business,* published by the Bureau of Economic Analysis (BEA), the *Federal Reserve Bulletin,* issued by the Board of Governors of the Federal Reserve System, the annual *Statistics of Income* reports of the Internal Revenue Service (IRS), *The Business Failure Record* issued by The Dun & Bradstreet Corporation, Milton, CT, and *Fortune* and *The Fortune Directory,* issued by Time, Inc., New York.

Business firms—A **firm** is generally defined as a business organization under a single management and may include one or more establishments (i.e., a single physical location at which business is conducted). The terms **firm, business, company,** and **enterprise** are used interchangeably throughout this section. Examples of series where the industrial distribution is based on data collected from establishments are those on capital stock, those on gross domestic product by industry, and those on employment and earnings (section 13). Examples of company-based series are those on business expenditures for new plant and equipment, those from IRS *Statistics of Income*, and those on corporation profits by industry. A firm doing business in more than one industry is classified by industry according to the major activity of the firm as a whole. The industrial classification is based on the *Standard Industrial Classification (SIC) Manual* (see text, section 13). The IRS concept of a business firm relates primarily to the legal entity used for tax reporting purposes. The IRS *Statistics of Income* reports present data, based on a sample of tax returns before audit, separately for sole proprietorships, partnerships, and corporations. Data presented are for active

enterprises only. A **sole proprietorship** is an unincorporated business owned by one person including large enterprises with many employees and hired managers and part-time operations in which the owner is the only person involved. A **partnership** is an unincorporated business owned by two or more persons, each of whom has a financial interest in the business. The "persons" could be individuals, estates, trusts, other partnerships, or corporations. A **corporation** is a business that is legally incorporated under State laws. The IRS recognizes many types of businesses as corporations, including joint-stock companies, insurance companies, and unincorporated associations such as business trusts, etc. While many corporations file consolidated tax returns, most corporate tax returns represent individual corporations, some of which are affiliated through common ownership or control with other corporations filing separate returns.

Assets and liabilities—In its annual report, *Statistics of Income, Corporation Income Tax Returns,* the IRS presents balance sheet and income estimates for all active U.S. corporations. The Bureau of the Census issues the *Quarterly Financial Report for Manufacturing, Mining, and Trade Corporations* (QFR), which presents quarterly income account and balance sheet data for manufacturing, mining, and trade industries. This report was prepared by the Federal Trade Commission until responsibilities for QFR were transferred to Census beginning with the fourth quarter 1982 report.

One of the most comprehensive measures of the investment position of the business sector (and the only measure adjusted to current replacement cost) is the BEA capital stock series. See

Survey of Current Business, January 1992, September 1993, and August 1994.

Income, profits, dividends, and taxes—Several agencies, among them IRS and BEA, compile corporate income account data. These data, however, are not comparable because of differing definitions and methods of compilation. A reconciliation of the two can be found in table 8.22 of *Survey of Current Business,* published by BEA. The IRS publishes financial data for all business enterprises. These data appear in *Statistics of Income, Corporation Income Tax Returns,* and the *Statistics of Income Bulletin* (partnerships and sole proprietorships). Data on international income and taxes reported by U.S. corporations are also included in the *Statistics of Income Bulletin* and in the periodic *Compendium of Studies of International Income and Taxes.*

Corporate data issued by BEA are a part of its national income and product accounts (see text, section 14). The primary sources for BEA estimates of profits, taxes, dividends, and undistributed profits are the original corporate tax returns submitted to IRS. Various adjustments of IRS data are required by the national income treatment—particularly with respect to profits which would be disclosed if all tax returns were audited: depletion, capital gain or loss, treatment of bad debts, measurement of income received from abroad, and intercorporate dividends—to make the figures comparable with other entries in the national income accounts. For a discussion of two types of adjustments (inventory valuation and capital consumption), see text, section 14. The BEA's corporate profits data also include net earnings of Federal Reserve banks, credit unions, private noninsured pension funds, and several quasi-government credit agencies not included in IRS data.

Sources and uses of corporate funds—These data show capital requirements of corporations and the manner in which they are financed. Sources of funds should be equal to their uses. Certain discrepancies, however, interfere with this equality due to omission of (1) money accruing to corporations from an excess of sales over purchases of used plant and equipment, (2) transactions in securities held as permanent investments except public offerings, and (3) net purchases of land. Also, the balance sheet data upon which many of the financial flow estimates are based are not fully comparable with the tax-return based estimates of internal sources or the establishment series underlying the figures on inventory change.

Fortune 500—Sales include service and rental revenues but exclude dividends, interest, and other nonoperating revenues. All companies must have derived more than 50 percent of their sales from manufacturing and/or mining. Sales of subsidiaries are included when they are consolidated. **Assets** are those shown at the company's yearend. **Net income** is shown after taxes and after extraordinary credits or charges when any are shown on the income statement. **Stockholder's equity** is the sum of capital stock, surplus, and retained earnings at the company's yearend. Redeemable preferred stock is excluded when its redemption is either mandatory or outside the control of the company, except in the case of cooperatives. **Total returns to investors** include both price appreciation and dividend yield. Returns are adjusted for stock splits, stock dividends, recapitalizations, and corporate reorganizations as they occur. For further discussion, see Time, Inc., New York, NY, *The Fortune Directories.*

Economic censuses—The economic censuses constitute comprehensive and periodic canvasses of the Nation's industrial and business activities. The first economic census of the United States was conducted as part of the 1810 decennial census, when inquiries on manufacturing were included with the census of population. Minerals data were collected in 1840. The first censuses of construction and business were taken for 1929. An integrated economic census program was begun for 1954. In that year, the censuses covered the retail and wholesale trades, selected service industries, manufactures, and mineral industries. The economic censuses are taken at 5-year intervals covering years ending in "2" and "7." Special surveys are conducted every 5 years as part of the economic censuses to determine the extent of business ownership by specific minority groups and women.

No. 827. Number of Returns and Business Receipts, by Size of Receipts and Type of Business: 1970 to 1993

[Covers active enterprises only. Figures are estimates based on sample of unaudited tax returns; see Appendix III. The industrial distribution is based on data collected from companies; see text, section 17. See also *Historical Statistics, Colonial Times to 1970,* series V 1-12]

SIZE-CLASS OF RECEIPTS	RETURNS (1,000)					BUSINESS RECEIPTS [1] (bil. dol.)				
	1970	1980	1990	1992	1993	1970	1980	1990	1992	1993
Corporations	**1,665**	**2,711**	**3,717**	**3,869**	**3,965**	**1,706**	**6,172**	**10,914**	**11,272**	**11,814**
Under $25,000 [2]	452	557	879	936	968	3	4	5	5	3
$25,000 to $49,999	171	208	252	256	256	6	8	9	9	10
$50,000 to $99,999	220	323	359	376	397	16	22	26	28	29
$100,000 to $499,999	517	926	1,162	1,216	1,218	123	224	291	305	306
$500,000 to $999,999	141	280	416	423	439	99	197	294	300	313
$1,000,000 or more	165	418	649	662	687	1,459	5,717	10,289	10,625	11,153
Partnerships	**936**	**1,380**	**1,554**	**1,485**	**1,467**	**92**	**286**	**541**	**571**	**627**
Under $25,000 [2]	502	638	963	921	887	4	5	4	4	3
$25,000 to $49,999	125	182	126	113	121	5	7	5	4	4
$50,000 to $99,999	120	184	133	126	129	9	13	10	9	9
$100,000 to $499,999	162	290	222	220	222	33	64	51	50	50
$500,000 to $999,999	17	48	52	50	49	12	33	36	35	35
$1,000,000 or more	10	37	57	56	59	30	164	435	470	524
Nonfarm proprietorships [3]	**6,494**	**9,730**	**14,783**	**15,495**	**15,848**	**199**	**411**	**731**	**737**	**757**
Under $25,000 [2]	4,738	6,916	10,196	10,392	10,615	30	44	69	71	73
$25,000 to $49,999	746	1,079	1,660	1,817	1,838	27	39	58	64	65
$50,000 to $99,999	562	836	1,282	1,269	1,330	40	59	91	92	93
$100,000 to $499,999	420	796	1,444	1,454	1,454	76	159	296	297	294
$500,000 to $999,999	21	74	143	133	139	14	50	97	90	94
$1,000,000 or more	7	29	57	58	66	12	60	119	123	125

[1] Excludes investment income except for partnerships and corporations in finance, insurance, and real estate. Starting 1983, investment income no longer included for S corporations. S corporations are certain small companies with 35 shareholders (15 in 1980 and 10 in 1970), mostly individuals, electing to be taxed through shareholders.   [2] Includes firms with no receipts.   [3] Number of businesses for 1970 and 1980. Number of nonfarm sole proprietorship returns is not available by size prior to 1981. However, the number of returns and the number of businesses are very closely related. The ratio of number of returns to the number of businesses is approximately 1 to 1.3.

Source: U.S. Internal Revenue Service, *Statistics of Income; Statistics of Income Bulletin;* and unpublished data.

No. 828. Number of Returns, Receipts, and Net Income, by Type of Business and Industry: 1980 to 1993

[See headnote, table 827. Minus sign (-) indicates net loss]

ITEM	NUMBER OF RETURNS (1,000)			BUSINESS RECEIPTS [2] (bil. dol.)			NET INCOME (less loss) [3] (bil. dol.)		
	Non-farm propri-etor-ships [1]	Partner-ships	Corpo-rations	Non-farm propri-etor-ships [1]	Partner-ships	Corpo-rations	Non-farm propri-etor-ships [1]	Partner-ships	Corpora-tions
1980	8,932	1,380	2,711	411	286	6,172	55	8	239
1985	11,929	1,714	3,277	540	349	8,050	79	-9	240
1988	13,679	1,654	3,563	672	516	9,804	126	15	413
1989	14,298	1,635	3,628	693	524	10,440	133	14	389
1990	14,783	1,554	3,717	731	541	10,914	141	17	371
1991 [4]	15,181	1,515	3,803	713	539	10,963	142	21	345
1992	15,495	1,485	3,869	737	571	11,272	154	43	402
1993 [4]	15,848	1,468	3,965	757	627	11,814	156	67	498
Agriculture, forestry, fishing [5]	497	120	141	20	10	92	3	2	2
Mining	124	32	35	6	17	102	1	2	3
Construction	1,927	62	417	107	27	529	18	2	8
Manufacturing	472	25	307	27	90	3,652	3	4	173
Transportation, public utilities	711	21	176	36	59	981	5	4	53
Wholesale and retail trade [6]	2,860	157	1,073	245	111	3,623	15	3	50
Wholesale	416	19	338	39	37	1,717	5	1	21
Retail	2,444	138	729	206	74	1,898	10	2	28
Finance, insurance, real estate	1,273	793	641	53	128	1,940	19	15	185
Services	7,718	256	1,157	260	184	893	92	34	25

[1] In 1980, represents individually owned businesses, including farms; thereafter, represents only nonfarm proprietors, i.e., business owners.   [2] Excludes investment income except for partnerships and corporations in finance, insurance, and real estate. Starting 1985, investment income no longer included for S corporations.   [3] Net income (less loss) is defined differently by form of organization, basically as follows: (a) Proprietorships: Total taxable receipts less total business deductions, including cost of sales and operations, depletion, and certain capital expensing, excluding charitable contributions and owners' salaries; (b) Partnerships: Total taxable receipts (including investment income except capital gains) less deductions, including cost of sales and operations and certain payments to partners, excluding charitable contributions, oil and gas depletion, and certain capital expensing; (c) Corporations: Total taxable receipts (including investment income, capital gains, and income from foreign subsidiaries deemed received for tax purposes, except for S corporations beginning 1983) less business deductions, including cost of sales and operations, depletion, certain capital expensing, and officers' compensation excluding S corporation charitable contributions and investment expenses starting 1983; net income is before income tax.   [4] Includes businesses not allocable to individual industries.   [5] Represents agricultural services only.   [6] Includes trade business not identified as wholesale or retail.

Source: U.S. Internal Revenue Service, *Statistics of Income;* and various publications.

No. 829. Number of Returns and Business Receipts, by Industry, Type of Business, and Size of Business Receipts: 1991

[Number of returns in thousands; receipts and net income in billions of dollars. Covers active enterprises only. Figures are estimates based on a sample of unaudited tax returns; see Appendix III. The industrial distribution is based on data collected from establishments; see text, section 17. See also *Historical Statistics, Colonial Times to 1970,* series V 42-53, for number of active corporations. Minus sign (-) indicates net loss]

INDUSTRY	Non-farm pro-prietor-ships	Partner-ships	CORPORATIONS				
			Under $1 mil. [1]	$1 mil.-$4.9 mil.	$5 mil.-$9.9 mil.	$10 mil.-$49.9 mil.	$50 mil. or more
Total: [2] Number	15,181	1,515	3,156	483	82	66	15
Business receipts [3]	713	539	633	1,029	571	1,330	7,399
Net income (less loss)	142	21	-13	9	9	36	304
Agriculture, forestry, fishing: Number	432	127	117	11	1	1	(Z)
Business receipts [3]	17	8	18	23	8	13	19
Mining: Number	150	39	34	4	1	1	(Z)
Business receipts [3]	7	18	4	8	4	12	62
Construction: Number	1,735	57	335	66	9	6	1
Business receipts [3]	93	27	85	134	66	107	110
Manufacturing: Number	427	24	199	67	15	14	5
Business receipts [3]	23	66	54	150	104	294	2,807
Transportation, public utilities: Number	660	26	132	25	4	3	1
Business receipts [3]	33	38	26	56	30	50	734
Wholesale and retail trade: Number	2,678	171	774	198	36	31	5
Business receipts [3]	246	100	214	427	251	614	1,786
Finance, insurance, real estate: Number	1,291	804	571	31	6	7	3
Business receipts [3]	44	113	61	67	43	137	1,615
Services: Number.	7,642	260	965	81	10	5	1
Business receipts [3]	247	171	168	161	66	102	265

Z Less than 500 returns. [1] Includes businesses without receipts. [2] Includes businesses not allocable to individual industries. [3] Excludes investment income except for partnerships and corporations (other than S corporations) in finance, insurance, and real estate.

Source: U.S. Internal Revenue Service, *Statistics of Income,* various publications; and unpublished data.

No. 830. Sole Proprietorships—Selected Income and Deduction Items: 1970 to 1993

[In millions of dollars, except as indicated. Covers nonfarm sole proprietorships. All figures are estimates based on sample. Tax law changes have affected the comparability of the data over time; see *Statistics of Income* reports for a description. See also *Historical Statistics, Colonial Times to 1970,* series V 4-6]

ITEM	1970	1980	1985	1988	1989	1990	1991	1992	1993
Number of returns (1,000)	5,770	8,932	11,929	13,679	14,298	14,783	15,181	15,495	15,848
Businesses with net income (1,000).	(NA)	(NA)	8,641	10,492	11,018	11,222	11,551	11,720	11,872
Inventory, end of year	11,061	21,996	24,970	27,313	30,060	30,422	29,783	29,898	31,795
Business receipts	198,582	411,206	540,045	671,970	692,811	730,606	712,568	737,082	757,215
Income from sales and operations .	(NA)	407,169	528,675	658,687	678,616	719,008	700,681	725,666	746,306
Business deductions [1]	168,045	356,258	461,273	545,735	560,175	589,250	571,154	583,147	600,765
Cost of goods sold/operations [1] . .	109,149	209,890	232,294	277,880	283,709	291,010	272,627	274,220	289,578
Purchases	88,586	168,302	(NA)	197,220	204,681	210,225	200,861	204,317	210,260
Labor costs...............	7,704	10,922	14,504	21,143	22,540	22,680	21,918	18,838	20,685
Materials and supplies	6,216	12,909	(NA)	27,800	29,870	30,195	28,072	28,825	32,701
Commissions	1,274	3,333	(NA)	6,540	6,843	8,816	7,628	10,457	8,707
Salaries and wages (net)	15,107	26,561	38,266	43,007	45,469	46,998	48,890	52,316	52,046
Car and truck expenses	(NA)	13,378	17,044	19,640	20,789	21,766	22,594	23,920	26,714
Rent paid	4,637	9,636	15,259	19,470	20,952	23,392	23,643	25,148	25,008
Repairs	2,445	5,032	(NA)	8,104	8,149	8,941	9,159	9,706	9,847
Taxes paid	3,776	7,672	(NA)	9,495	9,948	10,342	10,629	12,618	13,062
Utilities	(NA)	4,790	(NA)	14,618	13,601	13,539	13,260	14,547	16,069
Insurance.................	2,310	6,003	(NA)	12,528	12,879	13,358	13,065	13,260	13,173
Interest paid	1,784	7,190	11,914	12,071	13,280	13,312	12,077	10,406	9,431
Depreciation...............	5,452	13,953	26,291	26,078	24,479	23,735	23,076	23,274	24,964
Pension and profit sharing plans ..	73	141	311	450	539	586	519	528	636
Net income (less loss)	30,537	54,947	78,773	126,323	132,738	141,430	141,516	153,960	156,459
Businesses with net income	33,736	68,010	98,776	145,518	152,416	161,657	162,427	173,473	176,983

NA Not available. [1] Includes other amounts not shown separately.

Source: U.S. Internal Revenue Service, *Statistics of Income Bulletin.*

No. 831. Partnerships—Selected Items, by Industry: 1980 to 1992

[In millions of dollars, except number of partners and partnerships in thousands. Covers active partnerships only. Includes partnerships not allocable by industry. Figures are estimates based on samples. See Appendix III]

YEAR	NUMBER OF PARTNERSHIPS			Number of part-ners	Total assets [1]	Business re-ceipts [2][3]	Total deduc-tions [3]	Net income less loss [3]	Net in-come [3]	Net loss [3]
	Total	With net income	With net loss							
All industries:										
1980	1,380	774	605	8,420	597,504	285,967	283,749	8,249	45,062	36,813
1985	1,714	876	838	13,245	1,269,434	349,169	376,001	-8,884	77,045	85,928
1989	1,635	898	737	18,432	1,791,027	523,774	475,434	14,099	113,886	99,787
1990	1,554	854	700	17,095	1,735,285	540,647	549,603	16,610	116,318	99,708
1991	1,515	856	660	15,801	1,816,567	539,027	541,230	21,406	113,408	92,002
1992	1,485	856	629	15,735	1,907,345	571,427	553,770	42,916	121,834	78,918
Agriculture, forestry, fishing:										
1980	126	72	54	381	24,595	21,611	22,859	472	2,539	2,067
1985	136	76	60	585	27,027	6,529	10,495	-1,049	2,797	3,846
1989	131	83	48	591	25,219	7,708	10,133	1,380	3,679	2,299
1990	125	77	48	503	27,580	9,497	11,805	1,667	3,905	2,238
1991	127	78	49	552	32,391	8,422	10,892	1,740	3,992	2,252
1992	125	81	44	504	32,884	8,932	10,547	2,227	3,951	1,724
Mining:										
1980	35	15	20	722	24,742	13,201	18,248	-4,208	3,920	8,128
1985	62	33	30	2,207	66,930	19,922	21,920	1,482	7,884	6,402
1989	46	26	20	3,771	62,073	19,701	20,751	1,965	7,027	5,062
1990	41	29	14	2,149	58,246	19,967	20,869	2,183	7,009	4,825
1991	39	26	13	1,415	53,725	18,147	19,966	780	5,285	4,505
1992	36	23	13	1,389	53,697	16,706	18,230	1,009	5,271	4,263
Construction:										
1980	67	51	16	160	9,811	18,407	17,202	1,560	2,119	559
1985	57	41	16	134	15,008	21,476	20,080	2,207	2,743	536
1989	62	46	16	165	21,150	30,052	28,397	2,647	3,313	666
1990	59	45	15	162	17,989	30,716	29,672	1,908	3,020	1,112
1991	57	42	15	152	16,730	26,625	25,766	1,494	2,563	1,069
1992	59	42	17	158	15,663	25,946	24,501	1,906	2,648	743
Transportation, public utilities:										
1980	20	11	10	73	9,291	5,868	5,821	248	1,092	844
1985	25	15	10	186	26,468	11,253	14,814	-3,066	1,360	4,426
1989	22	10	12	435	54,171	26,727	30,319	-1,977	3,695	5,671
1990	25	14	11	503	63,334	32,800	35,989	-117	5,887	6,004
1991	26	14	12	519	72,512	37,611	40,873	-1,431	4,710	6,142
1992	24	12	12	527	81,070	42,081	43,127	1,054	6,585	5,531
Manufacturing:										
1980	30	20	10	92	11,252	15,327	16,142	-472	1,199	1,671
1985	30	12	18	105	24,838	22,588	24,225	-1,085	1,228	2,314
1989	26	14	12	185	56,601	55,336	55,816	1,398	4,154	2,756
1990	28	15	13	246	59,789	65,354	65,833	1,166	4,791	3,626
1991	24	13	11	175	65,140	65,818	66,385	904	4,909	4,005
1992	24	14	11	225	74,240	78,028	78,996	1,870	5,779	3,909
Wholesale and retail trade:										
1980	200	123	77	487	17,727	65,793	63,988	2,475	3,374	900
1985	201	113	88	493	20,568	69,079	68,119	1,977	3,467	1,490
1989	173	98	75	496	27,294	90,306	89,418	2,529	4,550	2,021
1990	176	100	77	481	28,423	98,120	97,131	2,610	4,717	2,107
1991	171	97	74	448	29,786	99,749	98,940	2,628	4,718	2,090
1992	162	86	76	425	32,777	107,870	106,639	2,553	4,758	2,205
Finance, insurance, and real estate:										
1980	637	313	325	5,566	454,531	87,133	91,382	-4,249	15,169	19,418
1985	844	369	475	7,755	979,787	92,309	118,237	-25,929	30,383	56,311
1989	853	419	434	11,327	1,394,319	71,243	91,965	-20,824	47,753	68,576
1990	822	401	422	10,846	1,329,452	64,313	87,011	-19,213	47,577	66,790
1991	804	410	394	10,317	1,386,914	57,398	126,042	-12,786	47,595	60,381
1992	797	427	370	10,328	1,438,303	87,773	72,853	-752	50,044	50,796
Services:										
1980	263	169	94	938	45,510	58,627	48,106	12,424	15,649	3,224
1985	341	207	134	1,713	106,597	104,197	96,202	16,541	26,942	10,400
1989	299	189	110	2,370	148,688	162,325	147,280	26,652	39,296	12,643
1990	267	173	96	2,153	150,063	161,702	145,789	26,453	39,383	12,930
1991	260	170	91	2,207	159,117	169,073	152,011	28,036	39,588	11,552
1992	253	169	84	2,167	178,577	181,603	158,260	33,004	42,748	9,744

[1] Total assets are understated because not all partnerships file complete balance sheets. [2] Includes investment income for partnerships in finance, insurance, and real estate. [3] Beginning 1985, only net (not gross) income from farming, rents, and royalties are included.

Source: U.S. Internal Revenue Service, *Statistics of Income Bulletin,* various publications.

No. 832. Partnerships—Selected Income and Balance Sheet Items: 1980 to 1993

[In billions of dollars, except as indicated. Covers active partnerships only. All figures are estimates based on samples. See Appendix III and *Historical Statistics, Colonial Times to 1970*, series V 7-9]

ITEM	1980	1985	1987	1988	1989	1990	1991	1992	1993
Number of returns (1,000)	1,380	1,714	1,648	1,654	1,635	1,554	1,515	1,485	1,468
Number with net income (1,000). . .	774	876	865	901	898	854	856	856	870
Number with balance sheets (1,000)	1,194	1,227	1,129	1,155	1,149	1,081	1,048	975	977
Number of partners (1,000).	8,420	13,245	16,963	17,291	18,432	17,095	15,801	15,735	15,627
Assets [1] [2]	598	1,269	1,381	1,580	1,791	1,735	1,817	1,907	2,118
Depreciable assets (net)	239	696	567	621	670	681	696	701	698
Inventories, end of year	33	27	45	51	59	57	57	62	71
Land	70	152	178	200	214	215	213	213	207
Liabilities [1] [2]	489	1,069	1,386	1,580	1,791	1,415	1,460	1,508	1,620
Accounts payable	34	41	41	49	52	67	63	79	80
Short-term debt [3].	48	103	82	87	87	88	117	115	131
Long-term debt [4].	178	382	430	474	512	498	491	486	489
Nonrecourse loans.	119	328	388	437	461	470	474	476	478
Partners' capital accounts [2]	109	200	247	267	356	320	357	399	499
Receipts [1].	292	367	443	541	551	566	563	597	656
Business receipts [5]	271	303	428	516	524	483	483	515	561
Interest received [6]	11	21	18	19	21	21	20	16	16
Deductions [1]	284	376	423	465	475	550	541	554	589
Cost of goods sold/operations	114	146	237	253	233	243	237	249	273
Salaries and wages	22	34	41	47	54	56	58	62	65
Taxes paid	10	8	7	8	9	9	10	10	11
Interest paid	28	29	20	23	33	30	28	25	27
Depreciation	22	54	19	20	20	60	58	60	60
Net income (less loss)	8	-9	-5	14	14	17	21	43	67
Net income.	45	77	88	111	114	116	113	122	137

[1] Includes items not shown separately. [2] Assets, liabilities, and partners' capital accounts are understated because not all partnerships file complete balance sheets. [3] Mortgages, notes, and bonds payable in less than 1 year. [4] Mortgages, notes, and bonds payable in 1 year or more. [5] Includes investment income for partnerships in finance, insurance, and real estate. [6] 1985 also includes dividends.

Source: U.S. Internal Revenue Service, *Statistics of Income Bulletin*, various publications.

No. 833. Corporate Funds—Sources and Uses: 1980 to 1995

[In billions of dollars, except percent. Covers nonfarm nonfinancial corporate business. See text, section 17]

ITEM	1980	1985	1988	1989	1990	1991	1992	1993	1994	1995
Sources	**336.1**	**493.8**	**634.2**	**567.9**	**535.5**	**471.7**	**600.0**	**619.4**	**785.7**	**885.3**
Internal	199.7	351.9	404.3	399.6	411.6	426.0	438.6	480.1	521.6	538.1
U.S. undistributed profits.	69.2	21.7	73.6	32.2	20.5	4.7	33.7	48.2	81.4	82.4
IVA and CCA [1]	-61.4	54.4	15.7	19.8	21.8	35.2	-9.1	-7.5	-8.7	-18.4
Capital consumption allowances. .	173.2	256.0	295.1	314.8	326.6	338.6	372.6	386.0	408.2	421.1
Foreign earnings [2]	18.7	19.8	19.9	32.8	42.8	47.6	41.5	53.4	40.7	53.0
External [3]	136.4	142.0	229.9	168.2	123.9	45.7	161.3	139.3	264.1	347.1
Credit market funds	78.4	84.7	95.0	68.0	48.3	8.7	61.1	73.3	84.4	135.1
Securities and mortgages	35.9	13.2	-4.7	-37.6	-20.1	96.1	67.1	85.7	-28.1	4.8
Equity issues	10.4	-84.5	-129.5	-124.2	-63.0	18.3	27.0	21.3	-44.9	-76.0
Bonds and mortgages [4]	25.5	97.7	124.8	86.6	42.9	77.8	40.1	64.4	16.8	80.8
Loans and short-term paper. . .	42.4	71.5	99.8	105.6	68.3	-87.4	-5.9	-12.4	112.5	130.4
Other	21.7	31.8	100.7	96.2	95.1	-9.3	100.2	66.0	179.7	212.0
Profit taxes payable	2.9	-3.2	1.7	-3.1	-5.0	-8.2	7.2	2.0	2.4	-0.8
Trade debt	38.0	34.0	59.2	30.5	29.3	12.3	33.4	21.1	92.6	79.5
Foreign direct investment in U.S.	13.2	17.8	69.4	61.8	55.9	12.0	59.5	42.9	84.7	133.3
Uses	**334.5**	**467.2**	**575.8**	**509.4**	**488.7**	**435.3**	**554.4**	**612.0**	**768.7**	**838.2**
Capital expenditures	252.4	370.2	391.0	401.1	402.8	379.8	386.9	430.6	485.0	551.5
Increase in financial assets.	82.1	97.0	184.8	108.3	85.9	55.6	167.5	181.4	283.7	286.7
Discrepancy (sources less uses) . . .	1.6	26.7	58.4	58.4	46.7	36.4	45.6	7.4	17.0	47.0

[1] Inventory valuation and capital consumption adjustment. [2] Foreign earnings of subsidiaries retained abroad. [3] Net increases in liability. [4] Includes industrial pollution control revenue bonds issued by State and local governments.

Source: Board of Governors of the Federal Reserve System. Data derived from *Flow of Funds Accounts*, annual.

No. 834. Nonfinancial Corporate Business-Sector Balance Sheet: 1980 to 1994

[In billions of dollars. Represents yearend outstandings]

ITEM	1980	1984	1985	1986	1987	1988	1989	1990	1991	1992	1993	1994
Assets.	4,455	5,829	6,122	6,445	6,821	7,313	7,707	7,815	7,585	7,473	7,681	8,097
Tangible assets (current cost)	3,278	4,215	4,399	4,546	4,751	5,057	5,334	5,326	5,043	4,819	4,965	5,230
Reproducible	2,771	3,514	3,658	3,771	3,937	4,182	4,394	4,573	4,620	4,709	4,875	5,136
Land	508	702	741	775	814	875	940	753	422	110	90	93
Financial assets	1,176	1,613	1,723	1,899	2,070	2,257	2,373	2,489	2,542	2,654	2,716	2,868
Liquid assets [1]	197	459	508	595	643	674	741	783	801	811	813	857
Checkable deposits and currency . .	57	105	132	154	172	171	185	193	201	191	194	195
Time deposits	38	74	80	88	92	106	103	99	104	97	101	102
Consumer credit	29	38	43	47	54	61	64	67	63	65	80	90
Mutual fund shares	2	7	11	16	13	11	10	8	11	16	22	20
Trade credit	478	585	624	649	694	766	810	825	822	854	867	942
Miscellaneous assets	471	524	538	593	666	745	749	806	845	908	933	957
Liabilities.	1,416	2,084	2,313	2,606	2,910	3,246	3,537	3,705	3,724	3,825	3,914	4,152
Credit market debt	886	1,369	1,543	1,774	1,970	2,169	2,366	2,469	2,458	2,500	2,561	2,681
Profit taxes payable	44	42	39	43	48	50	47	42	33	41	43	45
Trade debt.	348	452	486	500	540	599	629	659	671	701	727	800
Miscellaneous liabilities	138	221	245	290	352	428	496	536	562	583	584	627
Net worth.	3,039	3,745	3,809	3,838	3,911	4,068	4,170	4,109	3,861	3,648	3,767	3,945

[1] Includes other assets not shown separately.
Source: Board of Governors of the Federal Reserve System, *Balance Sheets for the U.S. Economy.*

No. 835. Corporations—Selected Financial Items: 1980 to 1993

[In billions of dollars, except as noted. Covers active corporations only. All corporations are required to file returns except those specifically exempt. See source for changes in law affecting comparability of historical data. Based on samples; see Appendix III. See also *Historical Statistics, Colonial Times to 1970*, series Y 381-392]

ITEM	1980	1985	1987	1988	1989	1990	1991	1992	1993
Number of returns (1,000)	2,711	3,277	3,612	3,563	3,628	3,717	3,803	3,869	3,965
Number with net income (1,000)	1,597	1,820	1,995	1,909	1,922	1,911	1,942	2,064	2,145
S Corporation returns [1] (1,000)	545	725	1,128	1,257	1,423	1,575	1,698	1,785	1,902
Assets [2]	7,617	12,773	15,311	16,568	17,647	18,190	19,030	20,002	21,816
Cash	529	683	754	785	824	771	787	806	812
Notes and accounts receivable	1,985	3,318	3,763	4,099	4,196	4,198	4,191	4,169	4,532
Inventories.	535	715	829	846	879	894	884	915	947
Investments in Govt. obligations	266	917	1,092	1,095	1,262	921	1,069	1,248	1,290
Mortgage and real estate	894	1,259	1,455	1,605	1,610	1,538	1,529	1,567	1,627
Other investments.	1,214	2,414	3,227	3,614	3,971	4,137	4,750	4,971	5,701
Depreciable assets	2,107	3,174	3,603	3,821	4,070	4,318	4,549	4,755	4,969
Depletable assets	72	112	123	124	134	129	142	131	137
Land.	93	141	159	177	191	210	215	221	230
Liabilities [2]	7,617	12,773	15,311	16,568	17,647	18,190	19,030	20,002	21,816
Accounts payable	542	892	998	1,023	1,090	1,094	1,681	1,605	1,466
Short-term debt [3]	505	1,001	1,247	1,431	1,602	1,803	1,500	1,560	1,569
Long-term debt [4]	987	1,699	2,141	2,352	2,490	2,665	2,698	2,742	2,871
Capital stock	417	920	1,292	1,429	1,477	1,585	1,741	1,881	2,042
Paid-in or capital surplus	532	1,421	1,988	2,154	2,595	2,814	3,257	3,656	4,223
Retained earnings [5].	1,070	1,366	1,417	1,493	1,522	1,410	1,441	1,431	1,662
Net worth	1,944	3,304	3,947	4,207	4,603	4,739	5,277	5,700	(NA)
Receipts [3][6].	6,361	8,398	9,582	10,265	10,935	11,410	11,436	11,742	12,270
Business receipts [6][7]	5,732	7,370	8,415	8,950	9,427	9,860	9,966	10,360	10,866
Interest [8]	367	635	706	805	967	977	920	829	808
Rents and royalties	54	105	113	116	129	133	137	140	130
Deductions [3][6]	6,125	8,158	9,244	9,853	10,545	11,033	11,087	11,330	11,765
Cost of sales and operations [7]	4,205	4,894	5,596	5,945	6,317	6,611	6,654	6,772	7,052
Compensation of officers	109	171	200	203	198	205	201	221	226
Rent paid on business property	72	135	154	161	173	185	193	196	201
Taxes paid.	163	201	211	222	236	251	258	274	290
Interest paid.	345	569	590	672	832	825	733	597	546
Depreciation	157	304	317	328	337	333	334	346	364
Advertising	52	92	107	114	124	126	129	134	140
Net income (less loss) [6][9]	239	240	328	413	389	371	345	402	498
Net income	297	364	465	556	556	553	536	570	659
Deficit	58	124	137	143	167	182	191	168	161
Income subject to tax	247	266	312	383	371	366	350	378	437
Income tax before credits [10].	104	109	115	127	123	119	116	126	149
Tax credits [3]	42	48	31	35	32	32	29	30	35
Foreign tax credit	25	24	21	27	24	25	21	22	23
Income tax after credits [11]	62	61	84	92	96	96	93	102	(NA)

NA Not available. [1] Represents certain small corporations with up to 35 shareholders (15 in 1980), mostly individuals, electing to be taxed at the shareholder level. [2] Includes items not shown separately. [3] Payable in less than 1 year. [4] Payable in 1 year or more. [5] Appropriated and unappropriated. [6] Except for 1980, receipts, deductions and net income of S corporations are limited to those from trade or business. Those from investments are excluded. [7] Beginning 1987, includes gross sales and cost of sales of securities, commodities, and real estate by exchanges, brokers, or dealers selling on their own accounts. Previously, net gain included in total receipts only. Excludes investment income. [8] Includes tax-exempt interest in State and local government obligations. [9] Excludes regulated investment companies. [10] Consists of regular (and alternative tax) only. [11] Includes minimum tax, alternative minimum tax, adjustments for prior year credits, and other income-related taxes.
Source: U.S. Internal Revenue Service, *Statistics of Income, Corporation Income Tax Returns*, annual.

No. 836. Corporations—Selected Financial Items, by Industry: 1980 to 1993

[**In billions of dollars, except as indicated.** Covers active corporations only. Industrial distribution based on d collected from companies; see text, section 17. Excludes corporations not allocable by industry]

INDUSTRY	1980	1985	1988	1989	1990	1991	1992	1993
Agriculture, forestry, and fishing:								
Returns (1,000)	81	103	120	123	126	130	138	141
Assets	40.7	52.7	60.5	63.4	68.3	67.8	71.8	74.6
Liabilities [1]	29.3	37.2	40.2	42.3	45.0	45.0	46.7	46.9
Receipts [2]	52.1	70.5	86.3	86.6	88.1	85.9	95.6	98.3
Deductions [2]	51.4	70.6	84.6	85.1	86.9	85.3	94.0	96.7
Net income (less loss) [2]	0.7	-0.1	1.6	1.6	1.2	0.6	1.6	1.6
Mining:								
Returns (1,000)	26	41	41	42	40	39	37	35
Assets	126.9	240.8	225.6	236.3	219.2	213.0	218.2	224.0
Liabilities [1]	72.9	136.0	113.8	109.9	108.9	106.4	112.1	112.6
Receipts [2]	176.7	142.0	100.4	102.4	111.4	103.3	112.8	112.1
Deductions [2]	169.1	145.4	96.8	99.5	106.5	99.5	110.3	109.6
Net income (less loss) [2]	7.8	-2.5	4.1	3.1	5.3	4.0	2.7	2.6
Construction:								
Returns (1,000)	272	318	381	393	407	417	408	417
Assets	132.9	215.3	241.4	249.7	243.8	243.0	231.1	240.4
Liabilities [1]	100.1	160.6	178.9	183.0	180.0	172.4	159.5	164.6
Receipts [2]	267.2	387.2	499.7	517.5	534.7	515.1	499.4	538.3
Deductions [2]	262.1	382.8	488.4	508.8	527.8	509.2	493.9	530.7
Net income (less loss) [2]	5.3	4.4	11.3	8.7	6.8	6.1	5.5	7.5
Manufacturing:								
Returns (1,000)	243	277	300	301	302	300	300	307
Assets	1,709.5	2,644.4	3,390.4	3,721.2	3,921.3	4,028.4	4,113.1	4,225.1
Liabilities [1]	960.3	1,544.7	2,137.2	2,347.7	2,529.1	2,547.2	2,701.2	2,784.4
Receipts [2]	2,404.3	2,831.1	3,349.0	3,531.2	3,688.7	3,658.5	3,760.3	3,890.7
Deductions [2]	2,290.6	2,733.1	3,170.0	3,377.1	3,545.1	3,548.7	3,633.8	3,741.6
Net income (less loss) [2]	125.7	113.8	205.1	180.5	171.4	132.3	143.6	173.2
Transportation and public utilities:								
Returns (1,000)	111	138	149	156	160	165	178	176
Assets	758.4	1,246.4	1,411.2	1,474.4	1,522.0	1,573.8	1,642.0	1,770.7
Liabilities [1]	467.7	755.9	891.8	963.1	1,013.4	1,044.9	1,106.3	1,190.9
Receipts [2]	523.8	772.4	838.8	906.5	936.3	954.9	997.6	1,037.2
Deductions [2]	504.0	747.8	792.5	867.6	901.0	917.8	956.5	984.9
Net income (less loss) [2]	20.0	25.1	46.9	39.1	35.4	37.7	41.8	52.9
Wholesale and retail trade:								
Returns (1,000)	800	917	985	1,013	1,023	1,044	1,053	1,073
Assets	646.9	1,010.0	1,295.8	1,390.6	1,447.3	1,483.4	1,581.9	1,702.8
Liabilities [1]	424.6	723.7	963.9	1,047.8	1,092.5	1,108.6	1,177.7	1,254.2
Receipts [2]	1,955.5	2,473.9	2,978.0	3,184.9	3,309.0	3,380.6	3,503.9	3,709.5
Deductions [2]	1,919.5	2,440.4	2,935.5	3,148.8	3,279.1	3,350.9	3,463.4	3,659.8
Net income (less loss) [2]	38.3	33.1	42.8	36.2	30.1	30.0	41.3	49.7
Finance, insurance, and real estate:								
Returns (1,000)	493	518	572	593	609	618	635	641
Assets	4,022.2	7,029.5	9,411.5	9,957.5	10,193.3	10,780.7	11,480.5	12,831.7
Liabilities [2][3]	3,491.7	5,867.5	7,632.1	7,929.3	8,051.3	8,267.1	8,531.3	9,288.5
Receipts [2]	697.5	1,182.0	1,714.4	1,868.0	1,954.7	1,924.3	1,900.4	1,940.3
Deductions [2]	652.6	1,104.6	1,596.0	1,730.5	1,809.9	1,771.2	1,724.3	1,723.3
Net income (less loss) [2]	33.1	60.7	91.9	108.9	109.9	124.5	147.0	185.2
Services:								
Returns (1,000)	671	939	995	990	1,029	1,062	1,100	1,158
Assets	178.2	331.0	530.3	552.1	572.8	636.8	661.6	744.8
Liabilities [1]	125.3	241.1	402.2	419.8	429.7	459.1	465.0	508.6
Receipts [2]	279.9	534.6	695.3	735.5	779.3	809.7	869.5	941.6
Deductions [2]	271.8	528.7	686.3	724.9	769.0	800.2	851.1	916.5
Net income (less loss) [2]	8.2	5.9	9.3	11.0	10.6	9.8	18.5	25.4
ANNUAL PERCENT CHANGE RECEIPTS [4]								
Agriculture, forestry, and fishing	-2.4	5.9	11.9	0.3	1.7	-2.5	11.3	2.8
Mining	33.3	15.0	3.7	2.0	8.8	-7.3	9.2	-0.6
Construction	5.7	14.4	9.9	3.6	3.3	-3.7	-3.0	7.8
Manufacturing	11.7	2.3	6.6	5.4	4.5	-0.8	2.8	3.5
Transportation and public utilities	17.5	6.4	6.7	8.1	3.3	2.0	4.5	4.0
Wholesale and retail trade	11.6	7.2	7.6	6.9	3.9	2.2	3.6	5.9
Finance, insurance, and real estate	24.3	14.4	7.9	9.0	4.6	-1.6	-1.2	2.1
Services	14.2	9.0	4.9	5.8	6.0	3.9	7.4	8.3

[1] Liabilities does not include net worth.　[2] Beginning 1988, receipts, deductions, and net income of S corporations are limited to those from trade or business; those from investments are generally excluded. S corporations are certain small corporations with up to 35 shareholders (15 in 1980), mostly individuals, electing to be taxed at the shareholder level.　[3] Beginning 1988, includes gross sales (previously net sales) of securities, commodities, and real estate by exchanges, brokers, or dealers selling on their own account.　[4] Change from preceding year.

Source: U.S. Internal Revenue Service, *Statistics of Income, Corporation Income Tax Returns*, annual.

No. 837. Corporations, by Asset-Size Class and Industry: 1991

[In millions of dollars, except number of returns and percent distribution. Covers active corporations only. Excludes corporations not allocable by industry. The industrial distribution is based on data collected from companies; see text, section 17. Detail may not add to total because of rounding. See also *Historical Statistics, Colonial Times to 1990*, series V 167-183 and V 193-196]

INDUSTRY	Total	ASSET-SIZE CLASS					
		Under $10 mil. [1]	$10-$24.9 mil.	$25-$49.9 mil.	$50-$99.9 mil.	$100-$249.9 mil.	$250 mil. and over
Agriculture, forestry, and fishing:							
Returns	129,886	129,373	316	110	52	24	12
Assets	67,757	46,567	4,861	3,895	3,765	3,925	4,744
Receipts	85,946	60,551	5,260	5,317	4,837	4,952	5,028
Deductions	85,332	60,195	5,263	5,242	4,897	4,885	4,849
Net income (less loss)	626	341	(Z)	74	-62	67	206
Mining:							
Returns	39,199	38,272	450	186	113	80	97
Assets	212,963	16,971	6,919	6,751	8,110	13,687	160,525
Receipts	103,286	20,208	5,862	4,222	4,954	8,148	59,893
Deductions	99,538	19,956	5,859	4,282	4,931	7,963	56,546
Net income (less loss)	4,001	244	-6	-63	22	186	3,618
Construction:							
Returns	416,987	414,894	1,476	348	155	71	43
Assets	243,036	134,116	22,168	12,032	12,506	11,354	50,860
Receipts	515,129	366,281	44,501	21,493	19,089	17,157	46,607
Deductions	509,248	363,033	43,847	21,139	18,910	16,944	45,373
Net income (less loss)	6,104	3,207	635	348	166	227	1,520
Manufacturing:							
Returns	300,122	288,768	5,728	2,292	1,292	952	1,091
Assets	4,028,360	194,210	89,369	79,953	91,337	172,063	3,401,427
Receipts	3,658,501	460,024	160,241	123,824	128,380	205,641	2,580,391
Deductions	3,548,747	456,013	156,315	120,039	124,944	199,369	2,492,066
Net income (less loss)	132,269	3,981	3,908	3,769	3,463	6,802	110,346
Transportation and public utilities:							
Returns	164,980	162,537	1,207	421	247	201	367
Assets	1,573,824	57,739	18,493	15,056	17,364	31,602	1,433,570
Receipts	954,945	148,430	22,889	17,799	16,185	26,925	722,716
Deductions	917,838	148,218	22,902	17,650	16,398	26,389	686,280
Net income (less loss)	37,743	197	-24	148	-217	608	37,031
Wholesale and retail trade:							
Returns	1,043,534	1,034,263	5,902	1,670	765	496	439
Assets	1,483,428	419,387	88,349	57,811	53,106	79,406	785,368
Receipts	3,380,512	1,500,494	252,213	158,692	139,379	192,858	1,136,963
Deductions	3,350,909	1,496,314	250,041	157,188	137,781	191,740	1,117,845
Net income (less loss)	29,951	4,112	2,156	1,512	1,602	1,132	19,437
Finance, insurance, and real estate:							
Returns	617,557	593,275	7,277	5,073	4,446	3,844	3,642
Assets [2]	10,780,681	246,705	118,301	181,633	315,463	601,295	9,317,284
Receipts [2]	1,924,318	196,406	28,096	27,643	45,987	89,921	1,536,266
Deductions	1,771,169	194,879	28,043	25,820	41,605	78,102	1,402,720
Net income (less loss)	124,546	1,043	-209	1,290	3,218	8,918	110,285
Services:							
Returns	1,061,657	1,057,496	2,252	906	446	314	242
Assets	636,752	183,809	34,864	31,714	31,481	49,476	305,408
Receipts	809,724	468,297	44,147	34,727	34,877	45,927	181,750
Deductions	800,164	462,686	43,911	34,609	34,822	45,344	178,792
Net income (less loss)	9,770	5,589	226	98	39	571	3,247
PERCENT DISTRIBUTION RECEIPTS							
Agriculture, forestry, and fishing	100	70	6	6	6	6	6
Mining	100	20	6	4	5	8	58
Construction	100	71	9	4	4	3	9
Manufacturing	100	13	4	3	4	6	71
Transportation and public utilities	100	16	2	2	2	3	76
Wholesale and retail trade	100	44	7	5	4	6	34
Finance, insurance, and real estate [2]	100	10	1	1	2	5	80
Services	100	58	5	4	4	6	22

Z less than $500,000.   [1] Includes returns with zero assets.   [2] Includes investment income.

Source: U.S. Internal Revenue Service, *Statistics of Income, Corporation Income Tax Returns*, annual.

No. 838. Employees and Payroll, by Employment-Size Class: 1980 to 1993

[Excludes government employees, railroad employees, self-employed persons, etc. See "General Explanation" in source for definitions and statement on reliability of data. An **establishment** is a single physical location where business is conducted or where services or industrial operations are performed]

EMPLOYMENT-SIZE CLASS	Unit	1980	1985	1987	1988	1989	1990	1991	1992	1993
Employees, total [1]	1,000 .	74,844	81,111	85,484	87,882	91,631	93,476	92,302	92,801	94,789
Under 20 employees	1,000 .	19,423	21,810	23,069	23,583	23,992	24,373	24,482	25,000	25,233
20 to 99 employees	1,000 .	21,168	23,539	25,221	25,930	26,829	27,414	26,906	27,030	27,443
100 to 499 employees	1,000 .	17,840	19,410	20,615	21,307	22,387	22,926	22,369	22,227	23,195
500 to 999 employees	1,000 .	5,689	5,716	5,922	6,078	6,442	6,551	6,325	6,270	6,449
1,000 or more employees	1,000 .	10,716	10,645	10,657	10,984	11,981	12,212	12,220	12,275	12,470
Annual payroll, total [1]	Bil. dol	1,035	1,514	1,724	1,860	1,990	2,104	2,145	2,272	2,363
Under 20 employees	Bil. dol.	231	352	414	440	461	485	502	536	554
20 to 99 employees	Bil. dol.	261	388	449	485	514	547	555	586	611
100 to 499 employees	Bil. dol.	249	362	417	452	488	518	523	550	582
500 to 999 employees	Bil. dol.	91	126	140	152	163	174	175	186	191
1,000 or more employees	Bil. dol.	208	286	305	331	364	381	390	413	424

[1] Prior to 1987, totals for employees and annual payroll have been revised. Detail may not add to totals because revisions for size class are not available.

Source: U.S. Bureau of the Census, *County Business Patterns,* annual.

No. 839. Establishments, Employees, and Payroll, by Industry: 1980 to 1993

[Beginning 1990, data are based on the 1987 Standard Industrial Classification (SIC). Prior to 1990, data are based on the 1972 SIC]

INDUSTRY	ESTABLISHMENTS (1,000)				EMPLOYEES (1,000)				PAYROLL (bil. dol.)			
	1980	1985	1990	1993	1980	1985	1990	1993	1980	1985	1990	1993
All industries [1] . . .	4,543	5,701	6,176	6,403	74,844	81,111	93,476	94,789	1,035	1,513	2,104	2,363
Agricultural services [2] . . .	46	64	85	100	290	380	531	588	3	5	9	10
Mining	30	37	30	29	994	943	723	608	22	28	27	25
Construction	418	476	578	598	4,473	4,480	5,239	4,524	75	98	132	125
Manufacturing [3]	319	358	378	387	21,165	19,429	19,173	18,183	355	458	544	576
Transportation [3]	168	203	235	267	4,623	4,809	5,592	5,622	88	123	166	182
Wholesale trade	385	438	476	509	5,211	5,624	6,328	6,258	89	130	181	201
Retail trade	1,223	1,407	1,530	1,552	15,047	16,851	19,815	19,777	124	178	242	265
Finance and insurance [4]	421	488	545	609	5,295	6,005	6,956	6,905	77	132	197	232
Services	1,278	1,712	2,059	2,289	17,186	21,549	28,800	32,259	197	346	599	746

[1] Includes nonclassifiable establishments not shown separately. [2] Includes forestry and fisheries. [3] Includes public utilities. [4] Includes real estate.

Source: U.S. Bureau of the Census, *County Business Patterns,* annual.

No. 840. Establishments, Employees, and Payroll, by Employment-Size Class and Industry: 1993

[See headnote, table 838. Data are based on the 1987 Standard Industrial Classification]

EMPLOYMENT SIZE-CLASS	Unit	All industries [1]	Agricultural services [2]	Mining	Construction	Manufacturing	Transportation [3]	Wholesale trade	Retail trade	Finance and insurance [4]	Services
Establishments, total . . .	1,000 . .	6,403	100	29	598	387	267	509	1,552	609	2,289
Under 20 employees	1,000 . .	5,577	95	23	554	262	219	440	1,317	552	2,051
20 to 99 employees	1,000 . .	688	5	5	41	88	38	62	210	48	191
100 to 499 employees	1,000 . .	123	(Z)	1	4	32	8	7	24	7	41
500 to 999 employees	1,000 . .	9	(Z)	(Z)	(Z)	3	1	(Z)	1	1	3
1,000 or more employees	1,000 . .	6	(Z)	(Z)	(Z)	2	(Z)	(Z)	(Z)	(Z)	3
Employees, total	1,000 . .	94,789	588	608	4,524	18,183	5,622	6,258	19,777	6,905	32,259
Under 20 employees	1,000 . .	25,233	344	109	2,099	1,516	1,011	2,268	6,954	2,239	8,636
20 to 99 employees	1,000 . .	27,443	(D)	175	1,506	3,891	1,580	2,363	8,252	1,855	7,652
100 to 499 employees	1,000 . .	23,195	(D)	(D)	666	6,476	1,479	1,202	3,939	1,451	7,717
500 to 999 employees	1,000 . .	6,449	12	(D)	105	2,357	437	211	387	511	2,365
1,000 or more employees	1,000 . .	12,470	(D)	(D)	148	3,944	1,115	214	244	849	5,890
Annual payroll, total . . .	Bil. dol . .	2,363	10.3	24.6	125.5	575.9	182.1	200.7	265.3	232.3	745.7
Under 20 employees	Bil. dol .	554	6.0	3.5	50.8	25.3	66.6	88.9	64.1	210.3
20 to 99 employees	Bil. dol .	611	(D)	6.2	44.3	106.1	46.1	73.6	103.0	61.7	167.4
100 to 499 employees	Bil. dol .	582	(D)	(D)	22.4	188.7	50.1	42.4	58.6	52.6	157.1
500 to 999 employees	Bil. dol .	191	0.3	(D)	3.0	77.6	17.0	8.6	8.1	18.7	54.7
1,000 or more employees	Bil. dol .	424	(D)	(D)	4.5	165.5	43.7	9.6	6.6	35.2	156.1

D Withheld to avoid disclosing data for individual companies; data are included in higher-level totals. Z Less than 500 establishments. [1] Includes nonclassifiable establishments not shown separately. [2] Includes forestry and fisheries. [3] Includes public utilities. [4] Includes real estate.

Source: U.S. Bureau of the Census, *County Business Patterns,* annual.

No. 841. Black-Owned Firms by Major Industry Group: 1992

[Includes individual proprietorships, partnerships and subchapter S corporations. Detail may not add to total due to rounding. N.e.c. not elsewhere classified]

MAJOR INDUSTRY GROUP	SIC code	ALL FIRMS		FIRMS WITH PAID EMPLOYEES			
		Firms (number)	Sales and receipts ($1,000)	Firms (number)	Sales and receipts ($1,000)	Employees (number)	Annual payroll ($1,000)
All industries.................	(X)	**620,912**	**32,197,361**	**64,478**	**22,589,676**	**345,193**	**4,806,624**
Agricultural services, forestry, & fishing...	9,820	265,089	1,491	159,119	(NA)	45,547	
Agricultural services.............	7	8,771	244,356	1,426	155,105	(NA)	44,668
Forestry.........................	8	371	8,550	47	2,555	(NA)	581
Fishing, hunting, and trapping.........	9	678	12,183	18	1,459	(NA)	298
Mining............................	(X)	490	65,621	51	46,000	(NA)	6,454
Metal mining......................	10	21	620	2	(D)	(NA)	(D)
Coal mining.......................	12	14	10,778	5	10,730	(NA)	2,272
Oil and gas extraction..............	13	424	49,224	37	32,716	187	3,497
Nonmetallic minerals, except fuels.......	14	31	4,999	7	(D)	(D)	(D)
Construction	(X)	43,381	2,651,356	8,798	1,962,727	28,545	447,362
General building contractors..........	15	6,023	840,456	1,715	697,311	6,077	104,932
Heavy construction, except building.....	16	730	156,055	241	146,986	1,234	28,068
Special trade contractors............	17	36,057	1,465,642	6,759	987,598	20,117	293,863
Subdividers and developers, nec........	6552	571	189,203	82	130,832	1,117	20,498
Manufacturing	(X)	10,469	1,319,193	1,958	1,155,011	12,977	251,322
Food and kindred products	20	364	203,986	67	200,378	1,272	23,629
Tobacco products.................	21	-	-	-	-	-	-
Textile mill products................	22	102	28,331	42	27,924	310	5,385
Apparel and other textile products......	23	1,054	82,592	92	74,018	1,267	18,387
Lumber and wood products...........	24	3,793	248,306	842	177,569	2,249	26,453
Furniture and fixtures	25	300	35,130	55	31,196	699	8,409
Paper and allied products	26	147	23,272	13	22,032	345	5,618
Printing and publishing	27	2,365	180,062	380	145,474	1,855	42,409
Chemicals and allied products	28	26	64,281	13	63,894	459	14,341
Petroleum and coal products	29	15	3,346	1	(D)	(D)	(D)
Rubber and misc. plastics products	30	36	81,418	20	81,213	808	18,165
Leather and leather products	31	79	8,126	20	7,450	119	1,727
Stone, clay, and glass products........	32	279	32,421	47	30,453	279	6,716
Primary metal industries	33	73	6,661	9	(D)	(D)	(D)
Fabricated metal products	34	432	91,041	96	84,158	974	21,390
Industrial machinery and equipment.....	35	372	69,820	110	62,736	570	19,605
Electronic & other electric equipment....	36	194	66,713	28	64,856	645	16,478
Transportation equipment	37	37	32,201	13	27,745	218	4,880
Instruments and related products	38	26	20,547	20	20,486	447	8,934
Transportation & public utilities	(X)	49,095	2,498,102	4,072	1,305,091	20,308	308,376
Local and interurban passenger transit...	41	15,974	462,237	637	195,242	6,067	66,246
Trucking and warehousing	42	25,756	1,346,941	2,778	538,453	7,336	116,437
Water transportation	44	97	10,265	10	8,545	151	4,324
Transportation by air................	45	145	7,288	13	5,466	131	1,524
Pipelines, except natural gas	46	-	-	-	-	-	-
Transportation services	47	4,882	160,875	335	74,011	1,335	25,327
Communications	48	1,517	400,528	198	383,885	4,906	88,883
Electric, gas, and sanitary services	49	724	109,968	101	99,490	381	5,634
Wholesale trade	(X)	7,550	2,944,321	1,510	2,745,412	8,649	203,544
Wholesale trade-durable goods........	50	4,088	1,107,372	927	1,016,558	4,744	105,620
Wholesale trade-nondurable goods	51	3,461	1,836,949	583	1,728,854	3,904	97,923
Retail trade	(X)	86,840	6,967,644	12,096	5,591,522	82,931	760,051
Building materials and garden supplies....	52	855	139,679	208	116,176	961	16,387
General merchandise stores...........	53	1,198	46,636	95	23,882	275	2,804
Food stores......................	54	8,466	979,773	1,915	635,336	6,741	61,312
Automotive dealers and service stations...	55	4,040	2,384,443	1,127	2,250,442	8,222	146,850
Apparel and accessory stores.........	56	6,391	203,985	796	125,457	1,836	18,020
Furniture and home furnishings stores	57	2,677	180,560	514	128,120	1,320	16,404
Eating and drinking places	58	13,832	1,785,569	4,571	1,590,634	54,393	404,464
Finance, insurance, and real estate	(X)	40,924	3,777,171	3,194	2,771,537	17,606	380,056
Depository institutions	60	53	(D)	51	(D)	(D)	(D)
Nondepository institutions	61	501	63,478	93	40,989	321	10,793
Security and commodity brokers	62	1,161	(D)	114	(D)	(D)	(D)
Insurance carriers.................	63	10	2,627	9	(D)	(D)	(D)
Insurance agents, brokers, and service ...	64	12,199	308,003	1,414	158,469	2,534	35,944
Real estate ²	65pt	24,187	1,552,796	1,400	792,740	7,614	127,428
Holding and other investment offices	67	2,814	(D)	114	(D)	(D)	(D)
Services	(X)	332,981	11,057,136	30,081	6,773,932	169,248	2,393,563
Hotels and other lodging places	70	1,657	207,731	431	168,897	5,057	45,161
Personal services	72	76,988	1,468,760	5,240	583,994	20,004	184,961
Business services..................	73	80,330	2,371,433	6,774	1,576,771	72,130	705,681
Auto repair, services, and parking	75	14,814	551,800	2,244	313,519	5,370	72,871
Miscellaneous repair services	76	5,691	169,785	605	95,795	2,203	32,520
Motion pictures	78	1,916	85,727	170	60,315	690	14,413
Amusement and recreation services	79	23,786	664,978	996	300,042	3,670	93,076
Health services	80	43,860	2,858,582	6,164	2,010,937	29,578	601,966
Legal services....................	81	7,016	551,363	1,732	391,175	4,500	110,680
Educational services................	82	7,309	70,718	297	30,926	1,294	15,287
Social services...................	83	35,391	582,275	3,356	304,435	12,009	111,769
Museums, botanical, zoos, gardens......	84	-	-	-	-	-	-
Engineering and management services	87	29,916	1,352,798	1,940	916,084	12,399	399,943
Services, n.e.c....................	89	4,307	121,187	130	21,043	344	5,237
Industries not classified	(X)	39,363	651,727	1,226	79,325	731	10,350

- Represents zero.   D Withheld to avoid disclosing data for individual companies; data are included in higher-level totals.
NA Not available.   X Not applicable.   ¹ Standard Industrial Classification; see section 13.   ² Excludes 6552 which is included in construction industries.
Source: U.S. Bureau of the Census, *Black-Owned Businesses, 1992* WB92-1.

No. 842. Women-Owned Firms by Major Industry Group: 1992

[Based on the 1987 SIC system. Includes individual proprietorships, partnerships and subchapter S corporations. Detail may not add to total due to rounding. N.e.c. not elsewhere classified]

MAJOR INDUSTRY GROUP	SIC code [1]	ALL FIRMS		FIRMS WITH PAID EMPLOYEES			
		Firms (number)	Sales and receipts ($1,000)	Firms (number)	Sales and receipts ($1,000)	Employees (number)	Annual payroll ($1,000)
All industries	(X)	**5,888,883**	**642,484,352**	**817,773**	**550,425,116**	**6,252,029**	**104,786,488**
Agricultural services, forestry, & fishing .	(X)	82,526	4,987,572	15,254	3,787,251	69,542	1,002,688
Agricultural services	7	72,595	4,525,599	14,431	3,486,805	66,811	952,898
Forestry	8	2,102	197,768	322	162,728	1,697	27,069
Fishing, hunting, and trapping	9	7,829	264,205	501	137,718	1,034	22,721
Mining	(X)	37,205	6,905,374	2,731	5,940,020	30,563	841,127
Metal mining	10	329	992,742	49	984,357	6,603	174,849
Coal mining	12	269	815,858	184	806,709	4,495	153,234
Oil and gas extraction	13	35,782	4,489,037	2,112	3,557,951	14,507	375,722
Nonmetallic minerals, except fuels	14	824	607,737	386	591,004	4,958	137,322
Construction [2]	(X)	183,695	45,978,168	64,746	41,579,094	371,788	8,827,641
General building contractors	15	37,019	17,280,614	18,098	15,639,397	84,674	1,974,815
Heavy construction, except building	16	4,915	4,978,394	2,985	4,914,118	36,888	1,179,061
Special trade contractors	17	131,697	19,422,242	41,942	17,745,585	221,322	5,170,625
Manufacturing	(X)	152,346	90,634,753	41,038	88,751,252	803,428	18,574,330
Food and kindred products	20	5,964	9,313,985	2,161	9,235,119	54,558	1,140,681
Tobacco products	21	5	(D)	3	(D)	(D)	(D)
Textile mill products	22	2,702	10,134,708	641	10,107,936	72,142	1,646,085
Apparel and other textile products	23	27,387	6,931,681	4,695	6,676,915	94,757	1,500,348
Lumber and wood products	24	14,719	4,934,635	3,532	4,679,332	45,605	881,754
Furniture and fixtures	25	4,536	2,005,893	1,140	1,952,537	22,953	476,424
Paper and allied products	26	1,396	2,668,991	393	2,656,294	19,316	501,351
Printing and publishing	27	33,762	9,347,365	10,927	8,902,714	110,034	2,584,322
Chemicals and allied products	28	911	5,953,234	589	5,935,309	31,014	826,518
Petroleum and coal products	29	192	989,996	114	984,590	2,584	89,446
Rubber and misc. plastics products	30	1,658	3,739,465	1,148	3,720,652	36,304	826,412
Leather and leather products	31	1,532	(D)	236	(D)	(D)	(D)
Stone, clay, and glass products	32	12,346	2,864,999	1,739	2,748,111	23,779	624,495
Primary metal industries	33	872	4,575,183	501	4,566,460	22,232	649,275
Fabricated metal products	34	7,527	6,866,234	2,879	6,751,520	64,282	1,657,898
Industrial machinery and equipment	35	7,169	5,883,316	4,123	5,801,935	58,037	1,663,434
Electronic & other electric equipment	36	4,382	3,562,432	1,304	3,507,481	38,020	904,508
Transportation equipment	37	1,386	4,981,568	997	4,951,185	48,093	1,246,814
Instruments and related products	38	1,214	2,148,366	921	2,137,522	20,259	544,185
Transportation & public utilities	(X)	141,623	25,822,193	31,049	23,026,912	290,081	5,841,177
Local and interurban passenger transit . . .	41	15,230	1,403,896	2,464	1,172,639	32,495	427,963
Trucking and warehousing	42	61,541	10,022,377	13,771	8,600,975	99,318	2,147,697
Water transportation	44	2,293	981,307	1,058	918,650	8,671	186,475
Transportation by air	45	2,717	(D)	678	(D)	(D)	(D)
Pipelines, except natural gas	46	13	(D)	1	(D)	(D)	(D)
Transportation services	47	42,809	4,805,220	10,282	4,048,530	71,111	1,359,742
Communications	48	13,592	5,884,932	2,003	5,681,750	59,091	1,288,344
Electric, gas, and sanitary services	49	3,429	2,231,373	791	2,169,096	13,523	318,341
Wholesale trade	(X)	154,542	12,487,093	45,591	120,625,000	385,814	9,846,339
Wholesale trade-durable goods	50	91,440	58,900,129	27,217	56,443,187	213,675	5,603,049
Wholesale trade-nondurable goods	51	63,101	65,946,965	18,374	64,181,813	172,139	4,243,290
Retail trade [3]	(X)	1,093,342	155,852,751	244,488	139,694,945	1,850,074	19,926,963
Building materials and garden supplies . . .	52	17,446	6,582,726	7,834	6,253,807	48,593	879,104
General merchandise stores	53	13,785	2,511,601	2,327	2,196,644	23,526	260,709
Food stores	54	61,238	23,136,159	27,443	21,212,922	212,271	2,232,248
Automotive dealers and service station . . .	55	31,527	43,268,554	15,080	41,956,683	159,390	3,216,977
Apparel and accessory stores	56	61,890	8,034,197	20,615	6,966,468	96,994	1,059,712
Furniture and home furnishings stores . . .	57	41,540	8,529,458	14,484	7,647,724	70,519	1,116,531
Eating and drinking places	58	128,441	27,668,320	81,725	26,356,092	922,918	7,347,321
Finance, insurance, and real estate . . .	(X)	602,802	51,748,279	56,040	33,084,796	295,871	6,347,967
Depository institutions	60	663	273,113	582	266,810	4,076	72,156
Nondepository institutions	61	6,366	1,099,701	1,963	972,388	9,339	258,294
Security and commodity brokers	62	12,569	2,373,407	2,285	1,982,138	12,253	710,255
Insurance carriers	63	264	1,215,458	202	1,211,998	5,654	176,762
Insurance agents, brokers, and services . .	64	83,005	4,637,170	14,128	3,321,440	44,325	1,055,598
Real estate [2]	65pt	457,705	39,106,288	35,113	23,380,255	201,316	3,578,079
Holding and other investment offices	67	42,231	3,043,142	1,767	1,949,767	18,908	496,823
Services	(X)	3,158,444	130,745,314	307,443	92,823,096	2,145,482	33,415,073
Hotels and other lodging places.	70	28,478	8,080,838	10,127	7,572,262	194,569	2,098,978
Personal services	72	654,769	15,698,876	65,472	8,722,382	296,619	3,063,956
Business services	73	800,034	32,476,240	60,502	23,068,120	614,305	9,192,298
Auto repair, services, and parking	75	39,240	6,126,347	15,819	5,503,642	85,986	1,439,956
Motion pictures	78	22,951	3,432,550	6,458	3,078,055	48,111	732,953
Amusement and recreation services	79	169,254	6,688,081	14,366	4,775,079	107,656	1,836,104
Health services	80	325,255	24,924,940	43,540	18,714,738	382,362	7,127,848
Legal services	81	62,535	5,031,519	14,152	3,892,616	41,334	1,230,707
Educational services	82	130,739	1,938,562	4,870	1,070,137	27,650	394,470
Social services	83	426,857	6,538,673	26,087	3,285,633	147,555	1,394,435
Museums, botanical, zoos, gardens	84	50	9,334	49	9,334	128	1,856
Engineering and management services . . .	87	397,500	14,403,312	35,205	9,763,942	151,985	3,817,235
Services, n.e.c.	89	67,368	2,932,151	2,806	1,297,271	15,761	481,327
Industries not classified	(X)	282,358	4,962,855	9,394	1,112,750	9,386	163,185

D Figure withheld to avoid disclosure.   X Not applicable.   [1] Standard Industrial Classification; see text, section 13. [2] Includes SIC 6552 formerly included in Real estate.   [3] Includes items not shown separately.
Source: U.S. Bureau of the Census, *Women-Owned Businesses* WB92-1.

No. 843. New Business Incorporations and Business Failures: 1970 to 1994

[1970 excludes Hawaii; 1970 and 1975 exclude Alaska. Total concerns and failure data prior to 1984 exclude agriculture, forestry, and fishing; finance, insurance, and real estate; and services; therefore, are not directly comparable with data for 1984 and later. See also *Historical Statistics, Colonial Times to 1970*, series V 20-30]

YEAR	Total concerns in business [1] (1,000)	Index of net business formations [2] (1967 =100)	New incorporations (1,000)	FAILURES [3] Number	FAILURES [3] Rate per 10,000 concerns	FAILURES [3] Current liabilities [4] (mil. dol.)	YEAR	Total concerns in business [1] (1,000)	Index of net business formations [2] (1967 =100)	New incorporations (1,000)	FAILURES [3] Number	FAILURES [3] Rate per 10,000 concerns	FAILURES [3] Current liabilities [4] (mil. dol.)
1970....	2,442	108.8	264	10,748	44	1,888	1987....	6,004	121.2	686	61,111	102	34,724
1975....	2,679	109.9	326	11,432	43	4,380	1988....	5,804	124.1	685	57,098	98	39,573
1980....	2,780	129.9	534	11,742	42	4,635	1989....	7,694	124.8	677	50,361	65	42,329
1981....	2,745	124.8	581	16,794	61	6,955	1990....	8,038	120.7	647	60,747	74	56,130
1982....	2,806	116.4	567	24,908	88	15,611	1991....	8,218	115.2	629	88,140	107	96,825
1983....	2,851	117.5	600	31,334	110	16,073	1992....	8,805	116.3	667	97,069	110	94,318
1984....	4,885	121.3	635	52,078	107	29,269	1993....	8,966	121.1	707	86,133	96	47,755
1985....	4,990	120.9	664	57,078	115	36,937	1994, prel.	(NA)	125.5	(NA)	71,520	79	29,357
1986....	5,119	120.4	703	61,616	120	44,724							

NA Not available.   [1] Data through 1983 represent number of names listed in July issue of *Dun & Bradstreet Reference Book*. Data for 1984-93 represent the number of establishments listed in the Dun's Census of American Business. The base has been changed due to expanded business failure coverage.   [2] Source: U.S. Bureau of Economic Analysis, *Survey of Current Business*.   [3] Includes concerns discontinued following assignment, voluntary or involuntary petition in bankruptcy, attachment, execution, foreclosure, etc.; voluntary withdrawals from business with known loss to creditors; also enterprises involved in court action, such as receivership and reorganization or arrangement which may or may not lead to discontinuance; and businesses making voluntary compromise with creditors out of court.   [4] Liabilities exclude long-term publicly held obligations; offsetting assets are not taken into account.

Source: Except as noted, Dun & Bradstreet Corporation, Wilton, CT 06897, *New Business Incorporations*, monthly; and *Monthly Failure Report*.

No. 844. New Business Incorporations and Business Failures, by State: 1992 to 1994

[**1993** preliminary]

DIVISION AND STATE	NEW BUSINESS INCORPORATIONS 1992	NEW BUSINESS INCORPORATIONS 1993	NUMBER OF FAILURES 1993	NUMBER OF FAILURES 1994	DIVISION AND STATE	NEW BUSINESS INCORPORATIONS 1992	NEW BUSINESS INCORPORATIONS 1993	NUMBER OF FAILURES 1993	NUMBER OF FAILURES 1994
United States . . .	**666,800**	**706,537**	**86,133**	**71,520**	Virginia	16,936	17,212	1,741	1,455
Northeast	143,119	146,557	18,242	14,215	West Virginia	2,236	2,406	316	297
New England	**28,686**	**30,233**	**5,339**	**3,757**	North Carolina	12,580	13,424	1,194	1,051
Maine	2,431	2,664	383	334	South Carolina	6,189	6,483	397	499
New Hampshire	2,577	2,884	621	410	Georgia	21,046	23,084	2,355	1,958
Vermont.	1,589	1,617	174	131	Florida.	86,037	88,048	5,091	3,605
Massachusetts	12,197	12,850	2,712	2,097	**East South Central . . .**	**26,514**	**28,184**	**3,217**	**2,585**
Rhode Island	2,553	2,696	346	212	Kentucky	7,155	7,758	845	706
Connecticut	7,339	7,522	1,103	573	Tennessee	8,514	8,859	1,210	957
Middle Atlantic	**114,433**	**116,324**	**12,903**	**10,458**	Alabama	7,087	7,179	839	669
New York.	67,503	69,835	6,924	5,533	Mississippi	3,758	4,388	323	253
New Jersey	29,983	29,603	2,848	2,182	**West South Central . . .**	**58,135**	**58,805**	**9,389**	**8,026**
Pennsylvania	16,947	16,886	3,131	2,743	Arkansas	6,078	5,410	186	365
Midwest	127,541	138,387	13,540	11,470	Louisiana	10,839	10,656	668	657
East North Central. . . .	**92,792**	**101,052**	**9,097**	**7,768**	Oklahoma	7,207	7,832	1,443	116
Ohio	18,730	20,082	2,131	1,988	Texas	34,011	34,907	7,092	5,838
Indiana	11,119	11,542	1,098	904	West	113,428	125,490	28,767	24,490
Illinois	30,928	32,756	2,092	1,749	**Mountain . . . .**	**49,841**	**56,871**	**5,606**	**4,293**
Michigan	24,726	28,790	2,554	1,956	Montana	1,948	2,261	174	179
Wisconsin	7,289	7,882	1,222	1,171	Idaho	2,127	2,511	351	277
West North Central . . .	**34,749**	**37,335**	**4,443**	**3,702**	Wyoming	1,707	1,747	90	84
Minnesota	10,002	10,845	918	723	Colorado	14,876	15,452	1,548	1,311
Iowa	4,918	4,804	508	473	New Mexico	2,843	3,232	449	328
Missouri.	10,020	11,544	1,231	1,064	Arizona	9,148	11,170	2,069	1,405
North Dakota	984	932	145	89	Utah	4,582	5,270	356	261
South Dakota	1,218	1,337	174	168	Nevada	12,610	15,228	569	448
Nebraska.	3,302	3,458	398	315	**Pacific . . . .**	**63,587**	**68,619**	**23,161**	**20,197**
Kansas	4,305	4,415	1,069	870	Washington	12,500	13,444	2,032	2,000
South	282,712	296,103	25,584	21,345	Oregon	8,861	9,874	969	1,025
South Atlantic.	**198,063**	**209,114**	**12,978**	**10,734**	California	36,973	40,072	19,746	16,803
Delaware	33,582	39,111	138	88	Alaska.	1,461	1,437	108	111
Maryland	17,201	17,090	1,549	1,614	Hawaii.	3,792	3,792	306	258
District of Columbia . .	2,256	2,256	197	167					

Source: Dun & Bradstreet Corporation, Wilton, CT 06897, *New Business Incorporations*, monthly; and *Business Failure Record*, annual, (copyright).

No. 845. Business Failures, by Industry: 1990 to 1994

INDUSTRY	NUMBER					RATE PER 10,000 FIRMS				
	1990	1991	1992	1993	1994	1990	1991	1992	1993	1994
Total	60,747	88,140	97,069	86,133	71,520	74	107	109	90	74
Agriculture, forestry, fishing	1,733	2,256	2,871	2,289	1,872	50	65	80	64	62
Mining.	388	411	430	310	241	88	95	99	73	62
Construction.	8,162	11,963	12,452	10,552	8,301	91	128	129	109	91
Manufacturing.	4,740	6,595	7,120	6,163	4,643	92	127	131	114	90
Food and kindred products	232	305	350	299	204	91	122	133	116	82
Textile mill products	102	143	171	149	99	97	135	158	139	98
Apparel, other textile products . .	318	505	566	567	410	114	177	191	191	146
Lumber and wood products	420	576	554	440	327	97	129	122	98	86
Furniture and fixtures	258	383	398	305	233	151	223	226	174	139
Paper and allied products	68	86	88	86	70	105	129	128	124	102
Printing and publishing	734	1,062	1,245	1,059	823	74	105	118	100	78
Chemicals and allied products . .	139	207	219	169	141	86	128	129	101	89
Petroleum refining	21	33	35	17	15	83	137	161	78	73
Rubber and misc. products	158	209	185	197	150	101	134	113	119	92
Leather and leather products . . .	40	40	35	43	42	113	114	95	120	127
Stone, clay, and glass products .	161	220	215	168	132	80	111	107	85	74
Primary metal products.	115	145	141	95	81	123	157	152	104	91
Fabricated metal products	397	593	662	584	400	90	135	145	128	90
Machinery, exc. electric.	656	823	951	860	618	84	105	117	107	79
Electric and electronic										
equipment.	287	380	421	327	271	114	149	157	124	108
Transportation equipment	242	318	263	229	170	147	198	158	140	114
Instruments and related										
equipment.	120	192	175	157	148	68	106	92	83	81
Miscellaneous	272	375	446	412	309	74	98	106	97	73
Transportation, public utilities	2,630	3,891	3,922	3,102	2,448	94	134	126	99	77
Wholesale trade	4,423	6,170	6,744	6,014	4,635	77	109	113	73	55
Retail trade	12,972	17,242	19,084	15,661	12,575	65	90	76	78	66
Finance, insurance, real estate . . .	3,819	5,962	6,260	4,989	3,907	60	90	87	68	52
Services	16,119	22,852	26,871	24,371	20,595	49	87	93	65	50
Public administration	10	20	30	24	20	(NA)	(NA)	(NA)	(NA)	(NA)
Nonclassifiable establishments . . .	5,751	10,778	11,285	12,658	12,283	(NA)	(NA)	(NA)	(NA)	(NA)

NA Not available.

Source: The Dun and Bradstreet Corporation, Wilton, CT 06897, *Business Failure Record*, annual, (copyright).

No. 846. Bankruptcy Cases, by State: 1991 to 1994

[In thousands. For years ending June 30. Includes outlying areas, not shown separately. Covers only bankruptcy cases filed under the Bankruptcy Reform Act of 1978. **Bankruptcy:** legal recognition that a company or individual is insolvent and must restructure or liquidate. Petitions "filed" means the commencement of a proceeding through the presentation of a petition to the clerk of the court]

STATE	1991	1992	1993	1994	STATE	1991	1992	1993	1994
United States. . .	880.4	972.5	918.7	845.3	Missouri	17.3	19.2	16.6	14.4
Alabama	27.8	27.8	25.7	23.7	Montana	2.1	2.1	1.9	1.9
Alaska	1.1	1.1	1.0	0.9	Nebraska	4.5	4.4	3.9	3.6
Arizona	19.3	20.4	18.5	17.0	Nevada	6.9	7.7	7.9	7.7
Arkansas	7.7	8.6	7.5	6.7	New Hampshire . . .	3.4	4.0	3.7	3.3
California.	124.2	152.8	159.7	150.9	New Jersey	19.4	24.0	24.9	23.7
Colorado	17.0	16.6	14.9	13.2	New Mexico.	4.5	4.5	4.3	3.5
Connecticut	6.9	8.9	9.4	8.7	New York	40.3	49.6	51.3	47.8
Delaware.	1.3	1.4	1.6	1.3	North Carolina	15.5	16.3	13.8	13.0
District of Columbia .	1.2	1.4	1.4	1.3	North Dakota	1.2	1.2	1.1	1.1
Florida	43.4	52.4	46.6	41.9	Ohio	42.8	44.0	37.9	32.5
Georgia	49.0	48.7	42.9	40.5	Oklahoma	16.2	15.3	13.9	13.0
Hawaii	1.0	1.3	1.5	1.5	Oregon	13.5	14.3	13.3	12.7
Idaho	4.2	4.1	3.9	3.4	Pennsylvania	20.8	24.3	23.0	20.2
Illinois	40.5	43.4	41.4	38.4	Rhode Island	3.1	3.6	3.5	3.1
Indiana	26.8	28.2	24.8	22.0	South Carolina	6.9	7.4	6.8	6.4
Iowa.	5.8	6.4	5.9	5.3	South Dakota	1.6	1.4	1.4	1.3
Kansas	9.6	9.6	8.3	7.9	Tennessee.	40.6	41.6	38.2	35.6
Kentucky	15.6	15.5	12.8	11.6	Texas	46.6	49.5	47.3	41.8
Louisiana	13.3	14.2	13.2	12.3	Utah	8.0	8.3	7.5	6.6
Maine.	2.2	2.3	2.0	1.8	Vermont	0.8	1.0	0.9	0.8
Maryland.	12.8	16.0	16.2	15.4	Virginia	25.3	29.1	26.8	24.4
Massachusetts	12.9	15.9	16.4	14.8	Washington	17.2	18.7	17.9	17.5
Michigan	23.3	26.7	25.1	22.9	West Virginia	4.0	4.5	4.0	3.6
Minnesota	16.7	17.8	15.5	13.9	Wisconsin	12.1	12.4	11.3	10.2
Mississippi	12.3	12.7	11.1	9.8	Wyoming.	1.5	1.4	1.3	1.2

Source: Administrative Office of the U.S. Courts, unpublished data.

No. 847. Bankruptcy Petitions Filed and Pending, by Type and Chapter: 1985 to 1994

[For years ending June 30. Covers only bankruptcy cases filed under the Bankruptcy Reform Act of 1978. **Bankruptcy:** legal recognition that a company or individual is insolvent and must restructure or liquidate. Petitions "filed" means the commencement of a proceeding through the presentation of a petition to the clerk of the court; "pending" is a proceeding in which the administration has not been completed]

ITEM	1985	1987	1988	1989	1990	1991	1992	1993	1994
Total, filed	**364,536**	**561,278**	**594,567**	**642,993**	**725,484**	**880,399**	**972,490**	**918,734**	**845,257**
Business [1]	66,651	88,278	68,501	62,534	64,688	67,714	72,650	66,428	56,748
Nonbusiness [2]	297,885	473,000	526,066	580,459	660,796	812,685	899,840	852,306	788,509
Voluntary	362,939	559,658	593,158	641,528	723,886	878,626	971,047	917,350	844,087
Involuntary	1,597	1,620	1,409	1,465	1,598	1,773	1,443	1,384	1,170
Chapter 7 [3]	244,650	397,551	423,796	457,240	505,337	612,330	679,662	638,916	578,903
Chapter 9 [4]	3	10	3	7	7	20	15	9	17
Chapter 11 [5]	21,425	22,566	18,891	17,465	19,591	22,495	24,029	20,579	17,098
Chapter 12 [6]	(X)	4,824	3,099	1,717	1,351	1,358	1,634	1,434	976
Chapter 13 [7]	98,452	136,300	148,771	166,539	199,186	244,192	267,121	257,777	248,246
Section 304 [8]	6	27	7	25	12	4	29	19	17
Total, pending . . .	**608,945**	**808,504**	**814,195**	**869,340**	**961,919**	**1,123,433**	**1,237,357**	**1,183,009**	**1,134,036**

X Not applicable. [1] Business bankruptcies include those filed under chapters 7, 9, 11, or 12. [2] Bankruptcies include those filed under chapters 7, 11, or 13. [3] Chapter 7, liquidation of nonexempt assets of businesses or individuals. [4] Chapter 9, adjustment of debts of a municipality. [5] Chapter 11, individual or business reorganization. [6] Chapter 12, adjustment of debts of a family farmer with regular income, effective November 26, 1986. [7] Chapter 13, adjustment of debts of an individual with regular income. [8] Chapter 11 U.S.C., Section 304, cases ancillary to foreign proceedings.

Source: Administrative Office of the U.S. Courts, *Annual Report of the Director.*

No. 848. Small Business Administration Loans to Small Businesses: 1980 to 1994

[For fiscal year ending in year shown; see text, section 9. A small business must be independently owned and operated, must not be dominant in its particular industry, and must meet standards set by the Small Business Administration as to its annual receipts or number of employees. Loans include both direct and guaranteed loans to small business establishments. Does not include Disaster Assistance Loans]

LOANS APPROVED	Unit	1980	1985	1986	1987	1988	1989	1990	1991	1992	1993	1994
Loans, all businesses	1,000. . .	31.7	19.3	16.8	17.1	17.1	17.0	18.8	19.4	25.1	28.0	38.8
Loans, minority-owned businesses. .	1,000. . .	6.0	2.8	2.0	2.1	2.2	2.4	2.4	2.9	3.6	4.3	6.9
Percent of all business loans	Percent .	19	15	12	12	13	14	13	15	14	15	18
Value of total loans [1]	Mil. dol. .	3,858	3,217	3,013	3,232	3,434	3,490	4,354	4,625	6,339	7,412	8,426
Value of loans to minority-operated businesses [2]	Mil. dol. .	470	324	265	299	343	385	473	601	808	928	1,328

[1] Includes both SBA and bank portions of loans. [2] SBA direct loans and guaranteed portion of bank loans only.

Source: U.S. Small Business Administration, unpublished data.

No. 849. Venture Capital Commitments, by Source: 1980 to 1994

[1993 data preliminary. **Venture capital commitment:** investment in venture capital partnerships]

SOURCE	1980	1985	1987	1988	1989	1990	1991	1992	1993	1994
Capital commitments (mil. dol.). .	**661**	**2,327**	**4,184**	**2,947**	**2,399**	**1,847**	**1,271**	**2,548**	**2,545**	**3,764**
PERCENT DISTRIBUTION										
Individuals/families	16	13	12	8	6	11	12	11	7	12
Endowments/foundations	14	8	10	12	12	13	24	18	11	21
Insurance companies/banks	13	11	15	9	13	9	5	15	11	9
Foreign investors	8	23	13	14	13	7	12	11	4	2
Corporations	19	12	11	11	20	7	5	3	8	9
Pension funds	30	33	39	46	36	53	42	42	59	46

Source: Venture Economics Investor Services, Boston, MA, *Venture Capital Journal*, monthly.

No. 850. Mergers and Acquisitions—Summary: 1985 to 1993

[Covers transactions valued at $5 million or more. Values based on transactions for which price data revealed. **All activity** includes mergers, acquisitions, acquisitions of partial interest that involve a 40% stake in the target or an investment of at least $100 million, divestitures, and leveraged transactions that result in a change in ownership. **Divestiture:** sale of a business, division, or subsidiary by corporate owner to another party. **Leveraged buyout:** acquisition of a business in which buyers use mostly borrowed money to finance purchase price and incorporate debt into capital structure of business after change in ownership]

ITEM	Unit	1985	1986	1987	1988	1989	1990	1991	1992	1993
All activity: Number	Number . .	1,719	2,497	2,479	2,970	3,752	4,239	3,446	3,502	(NA)
Value	Bil. dol. . .	149.6	223.1	198.8	281.8	316.8	205.6	141.5	125.3	(NA)
Divestitures: Number.	Number . .	780	1,090	1,004	1,274	1,615	1,907	1,759	1,598	1,993
Value	Bil. dol. . .	51	84.7	77.8	115.8	94.9	90.8	61.4	57.2	213.4
Leveraged buyouts: Number.	Number . .	154	233	208	291	293	177	171	199	621
Value	Bil. dol. . .	16.3	46.5	40.5	55.2	75.5	17.6	7.3	7.2	16.4
Foreign acquisitions of U.S. companies:										
Number	Number . .	259	345	365	536	693	773	504	361	(NA)
Value	Bil. dol. . .	27.9	31.4	55.3	66	69.2	56.4	29.1	17.6	(NA)
U.S. acquisitions overseas:										
Number	Number . .	91	111	162	223	347	392	402	455	(NA)
Value	Bil. dol. . .	3.7	3.4	6.9	11.1	27.1	20.5	14.8	13.7	(NA)

NA Not available.

Source: Securities Data Company, Newark, NJ, Merger & Corporate Transactions Database (copyright).

No. 851. Mergers and Acquisitions, by Industry: 1994

[See headnote table 850]

INDUSTRY	TOTAL		U.S. COMPANY ACQUIRING U.S. COMPANY		FOREIGN COMPANY ACQUIRING U.S. COMPANY		U.S. COMPANY ACQUIRING FOREIGN COMPANY	
	Number	Value (mil. dol.)	Number	Value (mil. dol.)	Number	Value (mil. dol.)	Number	Value (mil. dol.)
Total activity [1]	3,129	358,718	1,497	186,181	173	38,169	149	17,612
Construction firms.	46	2,926	17	760	3	524	2	248
Food and kindred products.	107	19,451	23	8,730	5	3,954	8	632
Textile and apparel products	56	5,387	23	1,775	2	37	1	5
Wood products, furniture, and fixtures.	29	1,415	9.00	223	(NA)	(NA)	1	299
Paper and allied products.	44	5,684	7	604	4	2,295	3	178
Chemicals and allied products.	71	7,262	21	2,126	3	86	5	328
Drugs	41	26,419	17	14,715	8	8,889	6	214
Soaps, cleaners, & personal-care products . . .	16	4,494	7.00	1,250	1	1,550	(NA)	(NA)
Rubber & misc. plastic products	41	1,441	16	714	3	40	1	55
Stone, clay, glass and concrete products. . . .	53	4,085	10	900	7	206	3	177
Metal and metal products	95	6,610	27	1,071	10	838	9	509
Machinery	83	5,274	36	2,647	6	229	9	452
Computer and office equipment	31	2,030	20	1,720	5	87	1	15
Prepackaged software	51	4,727	34	3,856	5	483	5	208
Electronic and electrical equipment	80	7,210	31.00	4,223	10	897	8	912
Communications equipment	35	3,005	16	1,576	4	56	3	203
Transportation equipment.	39	2,943	13	995	2	59	4	429
Aerospace and aircraft.	13	9,166	9	7,995	2	536	(NA)	(NA)
Measuring, medical, photo equip; clocks	71	5,859	38	4,102	9	1,032	3	165
Miscellaneous manufacturing	19	1,089	13	838	(NA)	(NA)	1	78
Air transportation and shipping	19	1,713	3	344	(NA)	(NA)	1	17
Transportation and shipping (except air)	107	4,648	27.00	1,750	5	276	3	84
Telecommunications	52	14,129	39	5,844	(NA)	(NA)	3	5,623
Radio & television broadcasting stations	85	15,064	62	12,641	2	823	4	301
Printing, publishing, and allied services.	59	6,627	24.00	3,115	1	8	4	820
Electric, gas, water distribution	41	5,315	19	2,809	(NA)	(NA)	2	705
Sanitary services	17	1,227	10	704	2	291	1	46
Services: Hotels and casinos	99	6,478	40	3,338	5	301	4	594
Amusement and recreation services.	30	2,240	19.00	1,965	2	21	(NA)	(NA)
Motion picture production and distribution	20	9,150	12	8,928	1	119	(NA)	(NA)
Business services.	183	16,702	114	10,504	10	3,367	10	421
Advertising services	15	1,047	8	604	(NA)	(NA)	(NA)	(NA)
Health services.	84	14,760	64	14,139	4	243	1	86
Wholesale trade-durable goods	101	3,716	44	1,629	6	267	8	800
Wholesale trade-nondurable goods	66	7,642	35	4,334	5	1,922	2	76
Retail trade-general merchandise and apparel .	26	3,063	11	915	(NA)	(NA)	2	307
Retail trade-food stores	29	2,890	11	1,880	3	483	(NA)	(NA)
Miscellaneous retail trade	54	5,393	21	1,684	3	708	3	181
Commercial banks, bank holding companies . .	212	23,629	145.00	10,609	4	822	1	72
Savings and loans, mutual savings banks	78	6,664	77	6,656	1	8	(NA)	(NA)
Credit institutions	14	3,399	8.00	3,120	(NA)	(NA)	(NA)	(NA)
Real estate, mortgage bankers and brokers. . .	210	12,088	110	4,905	1	79	(NA)	(NA)
Investment & commodity firms, dealers, exc . .	107	13,996	33.00	5,686	4	1,715	5	146
Insurance	90	18,175	44	7,234	1	7	5	606
Mining	55	9,689	7	718	5	2,011	4	392
Oil and gas; petroleum refining	140	14,545	77.00	6,807	9	493	11	1,114

NA Not available.   [1] Includes other items not shown separately.

Source: Securities Data Company, Newark, NJ, Merger & Corporate Transactions Database, (copyright).

No. 852. Patents and Trademarks: 1980 to 1994

[In thousands. Calendar year data. Covers patents issued to citizens of the United States and residents of foreign countries. For data on foreign countries, see table 1353. See also *Historical Statistics, Colonial Times to 1970*, series W 96-108]

ITEM	1980	1985	1988	1989	1990	1991	1992	1993	1994
Patent applications filed.	113.0	127.1	151.9	166.3	176.7	178.4	187.2	189.4	206.9
Inventions	104.3	117.0	139.8	152.8	164.6	164.3	173.1	174.7	189.9
Designs	7.8	9.6	11.3	12.6	11.3	13.1	13.1	13.6	15.8
Botanical plants	0.2	0.2	0.4	0.4	0.4	0.4	0.4	0.4	0.5
Reissues	0.6	0.3	0.4	0.5	0.5	0.6	0.6	0.6	0.7
Patents issued	66.2	77.3	84.4	102.7	99.2	106.8	107.4	109.7	113.6
Inventions	61.8	71.7	77.9	95.5	90.4	96.5	97.4	98.3	101.7
Individuals	13.8	12.9	14.3	18.0	17.3	18.1	17.3	16.5	17.3
Corporations: United States	27.7	31.2	31.5	38.7	36.1	39.2	40.3	41.8	44.0
Foreign [1]	19.1	26.4	31.4	38.0	36.0	38.1	38.7	38.8	38.8
U.S. Government	1.2	1.1	0.7	0.9	1.0	1.2	1.2	1.2	1.3
Designs	3.9	5.1	5.7	6.1	8.0	9.6	9.3	10.6	11.1
Botanical plants	0.1	0.2	0.4	0.6	0.3	0.4	0.3	0.4	0.5
Reissues	0.3	0.3	0.2	0.3	0.4	0.3	0.4	0.3	0.3
U.S. residents [2]	40.8	43.3	44.6	54.6	52.8	57.7	58.7	61.1	64.2
Foreign country residents [2]	25.4	33.9	39.7	47.9	46.2	49.0	48.7	48.7	49.3
Percent of total . . . . . , ...	38.4	43.9	47.1	46.7	46.7	46.0	45.3	44.3	43.4
Other published documents [3]	(Z)	(Z)	0.2	0.2	0.1	0.1	0.1	0.1	0.1
Trademarks:									
Applications filed	46.8	65.1	78.3	94.4	127.3	123.3	127.8	150.4	161.1
Issued	24.7	71.7	54.3	63.1	60.8	52.4	85.8	86.9	70.1
Trademarks	18.9	65.8	47.4	55.3	53.6	46.6	80.2	80.6	63.9
Trademark renewals	5.9	5.9	6.9	7.8	7.2	5.8	5.6	6.3	6.2

Z Less than 50.   [1] Includes patents to foreign governments.   [2] Includes patents for inventions, designs, botanical plants, and reissues.   [3] Includes Defensive Publications, a practice which began in November 1968 and ended in July 1986; and Statutory Invention Registrations, the current practice, which began May 1985. These documents are patent applications, which are published to provide the defensive properties of a patent, but do not have the enforceable rights of a patent.

Source: U.S. Patent and Trademark Office. Fiscal-year figures are published in the *Commissioner of Patents and Trademarks Annual Report*.

No. 853. Patents, by State: 1994

[Includes only U.S. patents granted to residents of the United States and territories]

STATE	Total	Inventions	Designs	Botanical plants	Reissues	STATE	Total	Inventions	Designs	Botanical plants	Reissues
United States [1] . .	64,241	56,066	7,698	283	194	Dist. of Columbia .	47	43	4	-	-
						Virginia	968	858	104	1	5
Northeast.	17,292	15,472	1,763	14	43	West Virginia	163	142	21	-	-
New England	5,519	4,825	675	3	16	North Carolina . . .	1,189	1,015	169	4	1
Maine	140	118	22	-	-	South Carolina . . .	510	436	71	2	1
New Hampshire . .	455	407	47	-	1	Georgia.	963	801	160	-	2
Vermont	172	140	32	-	-	Florida	2,295	1,888	375	27	5
Massachusetts . . .	2,645	2,335	299	3	8	East South Central .	1,524	1,252	266	4	2
Rhode Island	274	217	56	-	1	Kentucky	339	285	53	-	1
Connecticut	1,833	1,608	219	-	6	Tennessee	685	591	93	1	-
Middle Atlantic	11,773	10,647	1,088	11	27	Alabama	338	259	76	3	-
New York	5,442	4,905	512	6	19	Mississippi	162	117	44	-	1
New Jersey	3,248	2,926	314	4	4	West South Central.	5,474	4,946	502	3	23
Pennsylvania	3,083	2,816	262	1	4	Arkansas	159	120	39	-	-
Midwest.	15,981	13,838	2,062	23	58	Louisiana	442	403	33	-	6
East North Central .	12,181	10,559	1,553	21	48	Oklahoma	621	545	70	-	6
Ohio	3,091	2,593	476	12	10	Texas	4,252	3,878	360	3	11
Indiana	1,165	1,038	123	1	3	West	16,178	13,849	2,079	201	49
Illinois	3,318	2,834	477	2	5	Mountain	3,704	3,257	432	3	12
Michigan	3,217	2,930	261	3	23	Montana	98	84	14	-	-
Wisconsin	1,390	1,164	216	3	7	Idaho	367	331	33	-	3
West North Central .	3,800	3,279	509	2	10	Wyoming	53	42	11	-	-
Minnesota	1,963	1,720	235	2	6	Colorado	1,180	1,045	130	-	5
Iowa	460	394	65	-	1	New Mexico	260	232	27	1	-
Missouri	759	633	126	-	-	Arizona	1,054	930	121	2	-
North Dakota	60	51	9	-	-	Utah	481	422	57	-	2
South Dakota	47	44	3	-	-	Nevada	211	171	39	-	1
Nebraska	185	166	18	-	1	Pacific	12,474	10,592	1,647	198	37
Kansas	326	271	53	-	2	Washington	1,149	960	173	11	5
South	14,756	12,879	1,789	44	44	Oregon	780	556	206	17	1
South Atlantic	7,758	6,681	1,021	37	19	California	10,392	8,956	1,237	168	31
Delaware	451	440	11	-	-	Alaska	54	47	7	-	-
Maryland	1,172	1,058	106	3	5	Hawaii	99	73	24	2	-

- Represents zero.   [1] Includes U.S. territories not shown separately.

Source: U.S. Patent and Trademark Office, Technology Assessment and Forecast Data Base.

No. 854. Patents, by Industry: 1980 to 1994

[Based on the 1972 Standard Industrial Classification (SIC). Includes all patents for inventions granted to residents of the United States, its territories, and foreign citizens. Individual industries may not add to total since a patent may be recorded in more than one industry category. Except for total, data for all years have been revised to reflect the U.S. Patent Classification System as of 1993]

INDUSTRY	SIC code	1980	1985	1990	1992	1993	1994
Total	(X)	**61,819**	**71,661**	**90,366**	**97,443**	**98,344**	**101,675**
Durable goods:							
Stone, clay, and glass products	32	1,280	1,345	1,678	1,857	1,857	1,811
Primary metals	33, 3462-3	673	750	894	922	1,028	926
Fabricated metal products [1]	34	5,154	5,589	6,864	6,531	6,169	6,458
Machinery, except electrical	35	14,387	16,693	18,880	20,455	20,865	20,995
Electronic and other electric equipment	36, 3825	10,645	13,962	19,369	21,614	21,921	23,950
Transportation equipment	37, 348	2,942	3,668	4,560	4,699	4,472	4,331
Instruments and related products [2]	38	7,402	8,846	12,203	13,057	13,532	14,938
Nondurable goods:							
Food and kindred products	20	483	547	727	668	635	579
Textile mill products	22	421	503	507	558	600	579
Chemicals and allied products	28	9,825	10,242	12,417	14,161	14,679	13,240
Oil and gas extraction, petroleum products . .	13, 29	731	965	843	777	788	1,010
Rubber and miscellaneous plastics products .	30	2,615	3,075	3,846	4,271	4,314	4,287
Other industries	(X)	5,261	5,477	7,576	7,875	7,484	8,571

X Not applicable. [1] Excludes SIC groups 3462, 3463, and 348. [2] Excludes SIC group 3825.

Source: U.S. Patent and Trademark Office, *Patenting Trends in the United States, State Country Report, 1964-1994.*

No. 855. New Product Introductions of Consumer Packaged Goods: 1980 to 1994

[**Consumer packaged goods:** consumable products packaged by the manufacturer for retail sale primarily through grocery and drug stores. **New product:** a product not previously offered for sale by a particular manufacturer including new varieties, formats, sizes, and packaging for existing products]

ITEM	Food	Beverages	Health and beauty	Household products	Pet products	Miscellaneous products
Domestic and imports:						
1980	1,192	256	834	331	86	197
1981	1,356	262	868	315	74	237
1982	1,762	332	919	390	103	113
1983	3,013	587	1,355	473	138	105
1984	2,678	569	1,094	303	108	227
1985	2,327	585	1,222	463	139	294
1986	2,764	657	1,327	365	107	194
1987	2,895	634	1,526	362	152	292
1988	2,781	597	1,496	310	151	222
1989	2,866	524	1,492	313	204	206
1990	3,453	630	1,531	432	164	154
1991	3,130	589	1,614	422	175	113
1992	2,987	587	1,869	417	213	127
1993	3,107	767	2,068	376	173	161
1994, total	**3,883**	**807**	**2,655**	**378**	**161**	**97**
Percent:						
New brands [1]	21.1	32.6	19.3	17.2	31.7	39.2
Brand extensions [2]	1.4	1.1	1.0	2.9	0.6	4.1
Line extensions [3]	77.5	66.3	79.7	79.9	67.7	56.7
Types of new product innovation (percent): [4]						
Formulation [5]	56.5	50.8	47.8	51.9	50.0	51.8
New market [6]	0.9	-	3.4	-	11.1	3.4
Packaging [7]	13.3	17.5	8.6	11.1	-	3.4
Positioning [8]	29.3	31.7	39.1	37.0	33.3	34.5
Technology [9]	-	-	1.1	-	5.6	6.9
CUMULATIVE						
Domestic, except imports, 1980-94	36,289	7,127	20,636	5,409	2,078	2,563
Imports, 1980-94 [10]	3,905	1,256	1,234	241	70	176
International, 1985-94 [11]	13,938	4,000	12,194	2,523	567	832

- Represents or rounds to zero. [1] Product introduced under completely or partly new brand name. [2] Product introduced in a category with an existing brand name which has not been used in the category before. [3] Introduction of a new variety, format, size, or package of an existing product/brand name. [4] Product which offers consumers something significantly different from existing products. [5] Added or new ingredient which offers a benefit not previously provided by existing products in its category. [6] Special category for new products which do not compete with any existing category of products. [7] New product packaged in a way that makes it easier to store, handle, prepare, or dispense than others in its category. [8] New product presented for new users or uses compared to existing products in its category. [9] New product with added consumer benefits resulting from use of a new technology. [10] New products introduced in the United States by foreign companies. [11] New products introduced by U.S. and foreign companies outside the United States.

Source: Marketing Intelligence Service Ltd., Naples, NY, *Product Alert Weekly.* Publication contains extract from data base, Productscan.

No. 856. Gross Stock of Fixed Private Capital, by Industry: 1991 to 1994

[**In billions of dollars.** Estimates as of **Dec. 31.** Based on the 1987 Standard Industrial Classification]

INDUSTRY	CURRENT DOLLARS				CONSTANT (1987) DOLLARS			
	1991	1992	1993	1994	1991	1992	1993	1994
Fixed private capital	17,437	18,137	19,090	20,142	15,525	15,803	16,162	16,599
Nonresidential	9,745	10,052	10,490	11,010	8,660	8,814	9,023	9,298
Agriculture, forestry, and fishing	416	416	423	434	363	356	352	351
Farms.	364	360	362	366	318	308	300	295
Agr. services, forestry, fishing	51	56	61	68	45	49	52	57
Mining.	527	492	477	463	434	414	396	377
Metal mining	40	40	40	40	36	35	34	33
Coal mining	48	48	49	51	43	42	42	42
Oil and gas extraction	409	374	358	341	330	312	295	277
Nonmetallic minerals, exc. fuels.	29	30	30	32	26	25	25	26
Construction	115	117	120	125	101	100	100	101
Manufacturing	2,177	2,250	2,347	2,471	1,917	1,952	2,000	2,065
Durable goods	1,161	1,188	1,234	1,291	1,030	1,040	1,062	1,093
Lumber and wood products	41	41	42	44	36	35	36	36
Furniture and fixtures	20	20	21	22	17	18	18	19
Stone, clay, glass products	64	64	65	67	57	56	57	58
Primary metal industries	207	209	212	217	179	177	176	176
Fabricated metal products	129	130	134	138	112	112	112	112
Industrial machinery and equipment	202	208	216	228	184	188	194	203
Electronic and electric equipment	174	181	190	200	157	161	167	173
Motor vehicles and equipment	123	125	132	142	107	107	111	117
Other transportation equipment	100	104	110	118	89	91	94	98
Instruments, related products.	82	86	91	94	75	78	80	82
Misc. manufacturing industries	20	20	21	22	17	17	18	18
Nondurable goods.	1,016	1,062	1,113	1,180	887	912	938	972
Food and kindred products	201	213	225	242	175	182	188	198
Tobacco products	15	15	15	15	13	13	13	12
Textile mill products	52	53	54	56	45	45	45	45
Apparel, other textile products	18	18	19	19	16	16	16	15
Paper and allied products	151	156	161	170	130	132	135	138
Printing and publishing	85	89	94	100	77	80	83	88
Chemicals, allied products.	286	305	324	347	250	261	272	285
Petroleum and coal products	132	136	140	144	116	117	118	118
Rubber, misc. plastic products	71	74	78	84	62	64	65	68
Leather and leather products	4	4	4	4	4	4	3	3
Transportation, communication,								
and public utilities.	2,442	2,511	2,600	2,688	2,155	2,173	2,193	2,221
Transportation	613	620	636	642	541	534	528	523
Railroad transportation	246	248	259	260	221	217	213	211
Local, interurban passenger transit	12	12	12	11	11	11	10	10
Trucking and warehousing.	104	102	101	101	91	87	83	82
Water transportation.	55	55	55	55	48	47	46	45
Transportation by air	110	116	120	122	95	98	100	101
Pipelines, exc. natural gas.	42	43	44	46	36	36	36	36
Transportation services.	44	45	46	46	40	40	39	39
Communications	622	639	663	684	569	575	580	590
Telephone and telegraph.	535	545	561	574	488	488	488	493
Radio and television.	88	94	102	110	81	86	92	98
Electric, gas, and sanitary services.	1,206	1,252	1,300	1,362	1,046	1,065	1,085	1,108
Electric services	930	958	991	1,031	802	811	822	835
Gas services.	214	224	233	247	185	189	193	197
Sanitary services	63	70	77	85	59	65	70	77
Wholesale trade	415	435	458	484	388	404	422	444
Retail trade	636	673	726	796	574	600	636	685
Finance, insurance, real estate.	2,136	2,238	2,372	2,526	1,930	1,995	2,075	2,163
Depository institutions	439	467	497	531	401	423	447	471
Nondepository institutions.	114	123	135	149	103	111	121	133
Security and commodity brokers	13	13	14	14	13	13	13	14
Insurance carriers	133	145	159	174	134	148	163	179
Insurance agents, brokers, and service	6	6	6	7	6	6	6	7
Real estate	1,404	1,456	1,533	1,622	1,247	1,268	1,297	1,331
Holding, other investment offices	27	28	29	30	27	27	28	29
Services	882	920	966	1,023	799	821	851	891
Hotels, other lodging places	131	132	135	137	117	115	114	113
Personal services	33	36	39	43	31	33	36	39
Business services	234	246	259	279	208	215	225	240
Auto repair, services, parking	157	165	172	182	144	150	155	163
Misc. repair services	15	16	17	19	14	14	15	17
Motion pictures.	22	23	25	28	20	22	23	26
Amusement, recreation services	42	43	45	47	38	38	39	40
Other services	248	260	274	289	228	236	245	255
Health services	136	144	153	161	122	126	131	135
Legal services.	27	28	29	31	26	27	28	29
Educational services	6	6	7	7	5	6	6	6
Other [1]	80	83	86	91	75	77	80	84
Residential	7,692	8,085	8,600	9,131	6,865	6,989	7,139	7,301
Farms	163	166	171	176	145	143	141	140
Real estate	7,530	7,919	8,429	8,955	6,720	6,846	6,998	7,161

[1] Consists of social services, membership organizations, and miscellaneous professional services.

Source: U.S. Bureau of Economic Analysis, *Survey of Current Business*, January 1992, August 1992, September 1993, and August 1994.

No. 857. Fixed Nonresidential Private Capital: 1980 to 1994

[In billions of dollars. Stocks as of Dec. 31; depreciation over entire calendar year. Data refer to privately owned based on the fixed capital formation components of the gross domestic product. Excludes residential capital and government enterprises; includes nonprofit institutions. Gross stocks allow for retirement; net stocks allow for retirement and depreciation. Net stock and depreciation estimates are based on the straight-line depreciation formula. For manufacturing industry, see table 1215]

ITEM	CURRENT DOLLARS						CONSTANT (1987) DOLLARS					
	1980	1990	1991	1992	1993	1994	1980	1990	1991	1992	1993	1994
Gross stocks . . .	5,072	9,485	9,745	10,052	10,490	11,010	6,264	8,491	8,660	8,814	9,023	9,298
Equipment . . .	2,389	4,506	4,636	4,783	4,974	5,238	3,009	4,091	4,180	4,274	4,424	4,640
Structures . . .	2,683	4,979	5,109	5,270	5,516	5,773	3,255	4,400	4,480	4,541	4,599	4,658
Net stocks.	2,974	5,321	5,420	5,550	5,770	6,061	3,677	4,773	4,829	4,877	4,980	5,145
Equipment . . .	1,360	2,417	2,463	2,525	2,631	2,800	1,709	2,202	2,231	2,268	2,360	2,512
Structures . . .	1,615	2,904	2,957	3,025	3,139	3,261	1,968	2,571	2,598	2,609	2,620	2,633
Depreciation . . .	240	471	489	506	519	545	308	436	447	461	472	493
Equipment . . .	161	321	335	347	357	376	211	303	313	324	335	354
Structures . . .	78	150	154	158	162	169	97	132	134	137	137	138

Source: U.S. Bureau of Economic Analysis, *Survey of Current Business*, August 1992, September 1993, and August 1994 issues, unpublished data.

No. 858. Business Investment and Plans—Capital Expenditures: 1993 to 1996

[In millions of dollars. Based on 1987 Standard Industrial Classification (SIC)]

INDUSTRY	SIC code [1]	1993	1994	1995	1996, plans
Expenditures, total	(X)	489,682	549,912	594,465	603,395
By industry	(X)	488,249	547,762	591,680	600,701
Mining and construction	10-17	31,227	36,061	35,985	33,565
Manufacturing	(X)	134,066	153,338	172,308	184,786
Durable goods	24-25,32-3	66,361	78,898	91,381	100,151
Nondurable goods	20-23,26-3	67,705	74,440	80,927	84,634
Transportation	40-42,44-4	30,610	33,344	37,021	35,171
Communications	48	37,050	41,547	46,040	46,319
Utilities	(X)	41,257	42,173	42,816	40,599
Electric	491	21,029	23,513	21,410	18,932
Gas transmission, distribution, and other utilities	492-497	20,228	18,660	21,405	21,667
Wholesale and retail trade	(X)	60,316	68,853	75,093	71,855
Wholesale trade	50-51	18,963	23,269	21,851	19,654
Retail trade	52-59	41,353	45,584	53,242	52,202
Finance, insurance, and real estate	(X)	40,242	46,787	57,260	57,655
Finance	60-62,67	26,024	29,823	30,971	34,581
Insurance and real estate	63-65	14,218	16,964	26,289	23,074
Services	(X)	111,760	123,487	123,696	129,429
Personal and business services, incl. agricultural . . .	07-09,70-7	57,376	66,220	68,406	67,429
Health services	80	30,857	31,177	31,291	34,758
Social, educational and other professional services .	81-87,89	23,527	26,089	23,999	27,243
Expenditures serving multiple industries	(X)	1,722	2,172	1,462	1,321
Not distributed by industry	(X)	1,433	2,150	2,785	2,694

X Not applicable.

Source: U.S. Bureau of the Census. *Annual Capital Expenditures Survey.*

No. 859. Gross Private Domestic Investment: 1960 to 1994

[In billions of dollars]

ITEM	1960	1970	1980	1985	1986	1987	1988	1989	1990	1991	1992	1993	1994
Gross private domestic investment.	78.8	150.2	465.9	715.1	722.5	747.2	773.9	829.2	799.7	736.2	790.4	871.1	1,014.4
Less: Consumption of fixed capital.	46.1	86.1	304.6	432.4	459.4	483.2	516.0	551.9	575.8	599.6	626.1	640.0	678.7
Equals: Net private domestic investment.	32.6	64.1	161.3	282.7	263.1	264.0	258.0	277.3	223.9	136.6	164.3	231.1	335.8
Fixed investment.	75.5	148.1	473.5	688.9	712.9	722.9	763.1	797.5	791.6	738.5	783.4	850.5	954.9
Less: Consumption of fixed capital.	46.1	86.1	304.6	432.4	459.4	483.2	516.0	551.9	575.8	599.6	626.1	640.0	678.7
Equals: Net fixed investment	29.4	62.0	168.9	256.5	253.5	239.8	247.1	245.6	215.8	138.9	157.3	210.5	276.2
Nonresidential	49.2	106.7	350.3	502.0	494.8	495.4	530.6	566.2	575.9	547.3	557.9	598.8	667.2
Less: Consumption of fixed capital.	38.4	71.3	253.7	361.4	385.1	403.8	431.0	458.0	481.0	500.3	513.3	531.1	561.0
Equals: Net nonresidential . .	10.9	35.4	96.5	140.5	109.7	91.6	99.6	108.2	94.9	47.0	44.6	67.7	106.2
Structures	19.6	40.3	133.9	193.3	175.8	172.1	181.3	192.3	200.8	181.7	169.2	171.8	180.2
Producers' durable equipment	29.7	66.4	216.4	308.7	319.0	323.3	349.3	373.9	375.1	365.6	388.7	427.0	487.0
Residential	26.3	41.4	123.2	186.9	218.1	227.6	232.5	231.3	215.7	191.2	225.6	251.7	287.7
Change in business inventories	3.2	2.2	-7.6	26.2	9.6	24.2	10.9	31.7	8.0	-2.3	7.0	20.6	59.5
Gross government investment	28.2	44.0	96.4	149.9	163.5	173.5	172.9	182.7	199.4	200.5	209.1	210.6	212.3
Structures	16.6	29.2	65.3	81.1	89.0	95.5	99.0	102.0	112.6	114.3	123.6	129.9	134.4
Equipment.	11.6	14.8	31.0	68.7	74.5	78.0	73.9	80.7	86.8	86.2	85.5	80.7	78.0

Source: U.S. Bureau of Economic Analysis, *National Income and Product Accounts of the United States* to be published in late 1996, and *Survey of Current Business,* Jan./Feb. 1996.

No. 860. Composite Indexes of Economic Cyclical Indicators: 1980 to 1995

[See source for discussion of composite indexes. Minus sign (-) indicates decrease. **Leading indicators** are economic time series that tend to reach their cyclical high and low points earlier than the corresponding peaks and troughs in the overall economy. **Coincident indicators** are economic time series that tend to reach their cyclical high and low points about the same time as the corresponding peaks and troughs in the overall economy. **Lagging indicators** are economic time series that tend to reach their cyclical high and low points later than the corresponding peaks and troughs in the overall economy]

ITEM	Unit	1980	1985	1988	1989	1990	1991	1992	1993	1994	1995
LEADING INDICATORS											
Composite index.	1987=100 ...	88.6	95.3	100.1	99.7	98.5	97.2	98.2	98.9	101.8	101.3
Building permits [1]	1987=100 ...	78.6	112.4	94.2	87.6	72.9	61.4	71.2	78.3	86.4	84.2
Common stock prices, index [2] . .	1941-43=10 ..	118.8	186.8	265.8	322.8	334.6	376.2	415.7	451.4	460.3	541.6
Initial claims, unemployment insurance . .	1,000	480	383	305	327	383	444	411	364	337	355
Change in sensitive materials prices [3][4] . .	Percent	4.3	-8.2	5.0	0.6	-3.0	-7.3	3.2	-3.1	22.1	2.86
Vendor performance, slower deliveries . .	Percent	40.6	48.0	57.7	47.6	47.9	47.3	50.2	51.6	60.1	52.8
Average workweek, manufacturing [5] . .	Hours	39.7	40.5	41.1	41.0	40.8	40.7	41.0	41.4	42.0	41.6
Plant and equipment contracts and orders (1987 dol.)	Bil. dol.	359	350	422	438	421	381	401	447	535	623
Manufacturers new orders for consumer goods and materials (1987 dol.) . . .	Bil. dol.	1,016	1,144	1,264	1,264	1,250	1,227	1,186	1,231	1,305	1,431	1,455
Money supply (M2) [6] (1987 dol.)	Bil. dol.	2,163	2,631	2,908	2,885	2,883	2,855	2,829	2,784	2,688	2,670
Consumer expectations index [7]	1966=100 . . .	56.8	86.5	85.2	85.3	70.2	70.3	70.3	72.8	83.8	83.2
Change in manufacturers' unfilled orders, durable goods (1987 dol.) [4]	Bil. dol.	-13	3	18	22	13	-15	-37	-35	-9	-
COINCIDENT INDICATORS											
Composite index.	1987=100 ...	85.6	95.0	103.5	105.8	106.7	105.3	106.9	109.7	114.2	117.7
Industrial production index	1987=100 ...	84.1	94.4	104.4	106.0	106.0	104.2	107.7	111.5	118.1	122.0
Employees, nonagricultural payrolls . . .	Million	90.4	97.4	105.2	107.9	109.4	108.3	108.6	110.7	114.0	116.6
Personal income less transfer payments (1987 dol.)	Bil. dol.	2,722	3,110	3,357	3,436	3,469	3,416	3,477	3,523	4,562	4,722
Sales, mfg. and trade (1987 dol.)	Bil. dol.	4,522	5,109	5,735	5,822	5,834	5,749	5,922	6,255	6,688	6,963
LAGGING INDICATORS											
Composite index.	1987=100 ...	99.0	98.9	102.1	104.6	104.8	102.1	97.2	96.4	97.4	101.7
Change in labor cost per unit of output, manufacturing [4].	Percent	10.1	1.8	4.6	2.6	3.0	2.8	0.1	-0.2	-2.3	-0.5
Ratio, consumer installment credit to personal income	Percent	13.2	14.3	15.7	16.0	15.7	15.0	14.2	14.1	14.73	15.91
Average prime rate charged by banks. . .	Percent	15.3	9.9	9.3	10.9	10.0	8.5	6.2	6.0	7.1	8.83
Average duration of unemployment.	Weeks.	11.9	15.6	13.5	11.9	12.1	13.8	17.9	18.1	18.8	16.6
Ratio, mfg. and trade inventories to sales (1987 dol.)	Ratio.	1.61	1.59	1.54	1.59	1.62	1.64	1.59	1.53	1.47	1.47
Commercial and industrial loans outstanding (1987 dol.) [8]	Bil. dol.	231	338	375	400	413	398	373	371	384	513
Change in CPI for services [4][9].	Percent	15.2	5.0	4.7	5.0	5.9	4.6	3.8	3.9	3.1	3.5

- Represents or rounds to zero. [1] New private housing units authorized. [2] Standard and Poor's 500 stocks. [3] Producer prices of selected crude and intermediate materials and spot market prices of selected raw industrial materials. [4] Smoothed by an autoregressive-moving-average filter developed by Statistics Canada. [5] Production workers. [6] See table 815. [7] Copyrighted by the University of Michigan's Survey Research Center. [8] Includes commercial paper issued by nonfinancial companies. [9] Consumer Price Index.

Source: U.S. Bureau of Economic Analysis, *Survey of Current Business,* monthly.

No. 861. Business Cycle Expansions and Contractions—Months of Duration: 1919 to 1994

[A trough is the low point of a business cycle; a peak is the high point. Contraction, or recession, is the period from peak to subsequent trough; expansion is the period from trough to subsequent peak. Business cycle reference dates are determined by the National Bureau of Economic Research, Inc.]

BUSINESS CYCLE REFERENCE DATE		Contraction (trough from previous peak)	Expansion (trough to peak)	LENGTH OF CYCLE	
Trough	Peak			Trough from previous trough	Peak from previous peak
March 1919.	January 1920.	[1]7	10	[2]51	[1]17
July 1921.	May 1923	18	22	28	40
July 1924	October 1926.	14	27	36	41
November 1927.	August 1929.	13	21	40	34
March 1933.	May 1937	43	50	64	93
June 1938	February 1945	13	80	63	93
October 1945	November 1948	8	37	88	45
October 1949	July 1953.	11	45	48	56
May 1954.	August 1957.	10	39	55	49
April 1958.	April 1960	8	24	47	32
February 1961.	December 1969	10	106	34	116
November 1970.	November 1973	11	36	117	47
March 1975.	January 1980	16	58	52	74
July 1980	July 1981.	6	12	64	18
November 1982.	July 1990.	16	92	28	108
March 1991.	(X)	8	(X)	100	(X)
Average, all cycles:					
1919 to 1945 (six cycles)	. . . .	18	35	53	53
1945 to 1991 (nine cycles)	. . . .	11	50	61	61

X Not applicable.   [1] Previous peak: August 1918.   [2] Previous trough: December 1914.

Source: U.S. Bureau of Economic Analysis, *Survey of Current Business,* October 1994.

No. 862. Manufacturing and Trade—Sales and Inventories: 1980 to 1994

[In billions of dollars, except ratios]

ITEM	1980	1985	1988	1989	1990	1991	1992	1993	1994
CURRENT DOLLARS									
Sales, average monthly	393	507	595	628	651	646	674	712	768
Manufacturing	185	233	268	279	287	283	293	310	337
Retail trade	96	138	166	176	184	186	195	207	224
Merchant wholesalers	112	136	161	173	179	178	185	194	207
Inventories [1]	(NA)	664	765	811	834	830	839	861	917
Manufacturing	(NA)	335	367	387	399	386	379	377	392
Retail trade	(NA)	182	219	237	240	243	252	268	290
Merchant wholesalers	(NA)	147	179	187	196	200	208	216	235
Inventory-sales ratios [2]	(NA)	1.31	1.29	1.29	1.28	1.28	1.24	1.21	1.19
Manufacturing	(NA)	1.44	1.37	1.39	1.39	1.36	1.29	1.22	1.16
Retail trade	(NA)	1.32	1.32	1.35	1.30	1.31	1.29	1.29	1.29
Merchant wholesalers	(NA)	1.08	1.11	1.08	1.09	1.12	1.12	1.11	1.14

NA Not available.   [1] Seasonally adjusted end-of-year data. See text, section 17.   [2] End-of-year seasonally adjusted inventories to seasonally adjusted sales.

Source: U.S. Bureau of the Census, Current Business Reports, *"Manufacturing and Trade Inventories and Sales"* February 1994, and unpublished data.

No. 863. Manufacturing Corporations—Number, Assets, and Profits, by Asset Size: 1980 to 1995

[Corporations and assets as of **end of 4th quarter;** profits for **entire year.** Based on complete canvass. The asset value for complete canvass was $25 million in 1980 and raised in 1988 to $50 million. Asset sizes less than these values are sampled, except as noted. For details regarding methodology, see source for first quarter, 1988]

YEAR	Unit	Total	ASSET-SIZE CLASS						
			Under [1] $10 mil.	$10-$25 mil.	$25-$50 mil.	$50-$100 mil.	$100-$250 mil.	$250 mil.-$1 bil.	$1 bil. and over
Corporations:									
1980.	Number .	(NA)	(NA)	(NA)	1,777	941	590	491	369	244
1985.	Number .	(NA)	(NA)	(NA)	896	744	608	428	281
1988.	Number .	(NA)	(NA)	(NA)	(NA)	783	729	550	334
1989.	Number .	(NA)	(NA)	(NA)	(NA)	781	750	579	347
1990.	Number .	(NA)	(NA)	(NA)	(NA)	834	774	597	367
1991.	Number .	(NA)	(NA)	(NA)	(NA)	868	799	608	373
1992.	Number .	(NA)	(NA)	(NA)	(NA)	881	829	621	387
1993.	Number .	(NA)	(NA)	(NA)	(NA)	956	843	648	407
1994.	Number .	(NA)	(NA)	(NA)	(NA)	983	903	712	417
Assets:									
1980.	Mil. dol. .	1,384,474	126,639	43,569	34,930	41,963	75,284	179,959	882,129
1985.	Mil. dol. .	1,932,766	153,883	64,324	52,669	58,019	96,748	208,403	1,298,720
1988.	Mil. dol. .	2,339,690	149,276	77,068	53,461	62,190	110,411	261,880	1,625,404
1989.	Mil. dol. .	2,501,097	144,814	73,487	56,548	68,149	117,014	282,056	1,759,029
1990.	Mil. dol. .	2,629,458	142,498	74,477	55,914	72,554	123,967	287,512	1,872,536
1991.	Mil. dol. .	2,688,422	140,056	70,567	58,549	72,694	127,748	295,743	1,923,066
1992.	Mil. dol. .	2,798,625	143,766	70,446	65,718	75,967	132,742	302,287	2,007,698
1993.	Mil. dol. .	2,904,869	149,763	72,854	61,243	81,389	134,388	317,774	2,087,457
1994.	Mil. dol. .	3,080,231	148,751	81,505	66,405	82,116	138,950	358,100	2,204,404
1995.	Mil. dol. .	3,313,287	156,403	87,254	68,344	87,744	159,814	371,110	2,382,618
Net profit: [2]									
1980.	Mil. dol. .	92,443	7,770	2,235	1,904	2,479	4,532	11,485	62,041
1985.	Mil. dol. .	87,647	8,601	2,551	2,305	2,819	3,628	7,312	60,431
1988.	Mil. dol. .	154,583	11,364	4,488	3,199	3,978	5,473	13,994	112,086
1989.	Mil. dol. .	136,490	10,381	5,173	2,921	3,105	4,434	11,824	98,651
1990.	Mil. dol. .	111,561	8,527	5,160	2,769	2,676	3,531	7,245	81,652
1991.	Mil. dol. .	67,516	6,820	4,271	2,564	1,714	1,730	5,119	45,299
1992.	Mil. dol. .	23,212	9,567	4,748	3,245	3,050	4,585	5,976	-7,956
1993.	Mil. dol. .	83,922	11,195	5,415	3,439	3,225	3,624	4,662	52,362
1994.	Mil. dol. .	176,639	14,131	7,057	4,072	4,999	6,787	14,875	124,719
1995.	Mil. dol. .	201,310	13,251	5,679	3,769	5,756	7,067	17,028	148,758

NA Not available.   [1] Beginning 1986, excludes estimates for corporations with less than $250,000 in assets at time of sample selection. Prior periods include estimates for corporations in this size category.   [2] After taxes.

Source: U.S. Bureau of the Census, *Quarterly Financial Report for Manufacturing, Mining and Trade Corporations.*

No. 864. U.S. Largest Public Companies—Profitability and Growth: 1994

[In percent, except ranks. **For fiscal years ending in the 12 month period ending September 30.** Included in the Forbes Universe of 1,305 companies is every firm with revenue of over $400 million in **1993,** electric and banking firms $800 million. Represents industry medians; calculated by listing companies in rank order and selecting the midpoint. Where there is an even number of companies, an arithmetic average of the two middle companies is substituted. Minus sign (-) indicates decrease]

INDUSTRY	PROFITABILITY					GROWTH					
	Return on equity [1]			Return on capital, [2] latest 12 months	Debt/ capital	Sales [3]			Earnings per share		
	5-year rank	5-year average	Latest 12 months			5-year rank	5-year average	Latest 12 months	5-year rank	5-year average	Latest 12 months
All industries, median	(X)	11.4	12.6	9.4	32.8	(X)	5.5	6.3	(X)	-18.8	11.8
Health.	1	17.3	17.9	13.4	24.2	1	12.7	8.1	1	9.5	16.5
Food, drink and tobacco.	3	15.9	14.1	10.6	38.1	7	6.4	4.3	6	-8.7	1.7
Consumer nondurables	2	16.9	16.1	11.5	26.5	4	8.0	5.2	7	-11.5	3.0
Retailing	6	12.8	11.8	9.3	32.6	2	12.1	8.5	8	-13.5	9.4
Chemicals	10	12.1	15.5	11.3	29.3	19	3.4	6.1	13	-29.6	14.8
Insurance	5	14.2	12.1	10.9	19.8	8	6.2	3.9	2	7.7	5.1
Food distribution	9	12.1	8.6	8.1	41.5	12	4.5	3.2	5	-4.1	10.7
Financial services	4	14.5	16.0	12.3	33.1	16	3.8	4.4	3	6.8	12.0
Bus. services/supplies	11	11.9	14.0	11.2	30.2	6	6.8	9.9	9	-15.5	15.8
Computers/communication	15	10.2	13.7	10.7	19.6	3	12.0	15.2	15	(NS)	31.1
Electric utilities	12	11.5	11.7	6.2	37.3	18	3.5	3.3	4	-4.0	-0.8
Entertainment and information . .	8	12.2	14.8	13.2	28.0	9	5.3	7.0	15	(NS)	15.2
Aerospace and defense	7	12.7	11.3	10.2	37.3	21	-3.0	-0.8	11	-20.8	10.3
Capital goods	13	10.8	13.0	10.2	29.8	11	5.2	8.4	15	(NS)	17.6
Forest prod./packaging.	19	7.1	5.6	4.7	41.6	15	3.8	5.2	15	(NS)	13.2
Transport	16	10.1	12.8	8.2	36.2	10	5.3	9.4	10	-15.5	27.6
Energy	17	9.1	8.9	6.6	39.6	13	4.5	1.1	12	-23.4	0.9
Consumer durables	18	8.4	15.2	11.6	31.7	14	3.9	11.3	15	(NS)	30.4
Metals.	21	4.6	6.7	7.3	34.0	20	-2.4	7.8	15	(NS)	27.4
Construction.	20	5.9	8.4	6.2	39.1	17	3.7	10.4	14	-31.8	24.1
Travel	14	10.7	8.3	6.5	53.8	5	7.6	7.8	15	(NS)	18.8

NS Not significant.   X Not applicable.   [1] Represents primary earnings per share before extraordinary item divided by common shareholders' equity per share. Common shareholders' equity is total shareholders' equity including the stated value of all preferred stock at the beginning of each year minus the involuntary liquidating value of nonconvertible preferred shares.   [2] After-tax profits, the amount remaining if the interest paid on long-term debt was taxed, and minority interest divided by a firm's total capitalization. Total capitalization is long-term debt, common and preferred equity, deferred taxes, investment tax credits, and minority interest in consolidated subsidiaries.   [3] Net sales plus other operating revenue.

Source: Forbes, Inc., New York, NY, *Forbes Annual Report on American Industry* (copyright).

No. 865. 500 Largest Industrial Corporations—Sales, Assets, and Profits by Sales Rank: 1990 to 1993

[In billions of dollars. Excludes large privately owned companies that do not publish sales. Includes service and rental revenues, but companies must derive more than 50 percent of revenues from manufacturing or mining for years ending not later than Dec. 31 of year stated; sales exclude excise taxes collected by manufacturer and include discontinued operations. Minus sign (-) indicates decrease]

SALES RANK	SALES				ASSETS [1]				PROFITS [2]			
	1990	1991	1992	1993	1990	1991	1992	1993	1990	1991	1992	1993
Total	2,303	2,264	2,365	2,370	2,443	2,466	2,565	2,676	93	[3]55	[3](-Z)	62.6
Top 100	(NA)	1,619	1,681	1,676	(NA)	1,844	1,902	2,015	(NA)	38	-8	49.0
101-200	(NA)	323	341	343	(NA)	328	351	337	(NA)	9	3	12.0
201-300	(NA)	160	171	175	(NA)	151	160	163	(NA)	4	3	2.0
301-400	(NA)	96	104	107	(NA)	77	91	102	(NA)	3	2	-1.0
401-500	(NA)	65	69	70	(NA)	57	60	59	(NA)	1	(Z)	1.0

NA Not available.   Z Less than $500 million.   [1] Total assets employed in business at end of fiscal year, less depreciation and depletion.   [2] After taxes, special charges, and credits.   [3] Total profits of $55 billion in 1991 and $200 million in 1992 include charge-offs for accounting rule change on retiree health benefits. Profits before charge-offs were $60 billion and $71 billion in 1991 and 1992 respectively.

Source: Time Warner, New York, NY, *The Fortune Directories* (copyright).

No. 866. 500 Largest Industrial Corporations—Selected Financial Items: 1980 to 1995

ITEM	Unit	1980	1985	1989	1990	1991	1992	1993	1994	1995
Sales per employee	$1,000 . . .	78.1	106.0	146.0	153.9	159.2	169.3	174.5	(NA)	(NA)
Changes in profits.	Percent . . .	3.6	-19.1	-8.1	-11.6	[1]-41.0	[1]-100.4	[1]1.8	13.8	15.0
Sales per dollar of stockholder's equity . .	Dollar	3.00	2.80	2.96	2.97	2.81	2.91	3.02	(NA)	(NA)
Return on stockholder's equity	Percent . . .	14.4	11.6	15.0	12.7	[2]10.2	[2]9.0	[2]10.3	13.7	14.0
Return on sales	Percent . . .	4.8	3.9	4.7	4.1	3.1	2.4	2.9	(NA)	(NA)
Total return to investors [3]	Percent . . .	21.1	26.3	17.5	-10.2	29.5	9.1	11.1	-1.0	32.8

NA Not available.   [1] Changes in profits of -41% in 1991 and -100.4% in 1992 include charge-offs for accounting rule change on retiree health benefits. Changes before charge-offs were -35.8%, 18.3%, and 15.1% in 1991, 1992, and 1993 respectively.   [2] For 1991-92 data, the return is on common stockholders' equity. For prior years and again with 1993 data, the return is on total equity.   [3] Includes both price appreciation and dividend yield, i.e., to an investor in the company's stock.

No. 867. 500 Largest Industrial Corporations—Selected Financial Items, by Industry: 1994 and 1995

[Data are medians and are ranked based on sales per employee for latest year shown. See headnote, table 865. Minus sign (-) indicates decrease. For definition of median, see Guide to Tabular Presentation]

INDUSTRY	REVENUES PER EMPLOYEE ($1,000)		CHANGES IN PROFITS FROM PREVIOUS YEAR [1] (percent)		RETURN ON EQUITY (percent)		TOTAL RETURN TO INVESTORS (percent)	
	1994	1995	1994	1995	1994	1995	1994	1995
Total	**213.6**	**248.4**	**13.8**	**15.0**	**11.9**	**14.0**	**-1.0**	**32.8**
Petroleum refining	623.8	741.2	-1.7	-4.3	11.6	8.6	3.2	17.6
Mining, crude-oil production	(NA)	(NA)	(NA)	(NA)	(NA)	(NA)	(NA)	(NA)
Tobacco	(NA)	(NA)	(NA)	(NA)	(NA)	(NA)	(NA)	(NA)
Soaps, cosmetics	186.8	224.1	48.2	19.6	28.5	25.0	9.8	33.4
Food	200.9	226.5	4.4	15.6	19.1	21.4	5.8	31.0
Beverages	241.6	247.5	32.0	17.9	21.0	17.9	12.9	41.7
Chemicals.	263.8	284.6	299.1	29.5	18.5	19.8	3.7	27.1
Metals	227.2	249.6	63.9	116.9	9.6	17.4	7.8	3.7
Forest and paper products	197.6	249.3	17.6	75.1	9.6	17.6	7.4	12.5
Pharmaceuticals.	207.0	228.9	25.6	11.3	31.2	30.7	13.9	57.0
Toys, sporting goods	(NA)	(NA)	(NA)	(NA)	(NA)	(NA)	(NA)	(NA)
Computers, office equipment	263.5	374.2	20.1	61.8	15.7	16.9	10.2	52.5
Publishing, printing	143.3	159.6	18.8	11.2	14.0	(NA)	-3.3	22.7
Building materials, glass	136.8	163.7	126.4	45.3	20.8	12.9	-25.7	42.6
Industrial and farm equipment. . . .	161.4	168.1	44.6	28.0	17.0	18.3	-6.5	33.0
Aerospace	158.3	168.5	14.2	21.7	15.6	15.7	4.5	55.8
Motor vehicles and parts	170.8	153.2	92.5	24.9	18.5	20.2	-12.2	20.7
Metal products.	177.5	195.9	41.7	-14.5	12.1	8.0	-7.2	38.8
Rubber and plastic products.	(NA)	(NA)	(NA)	(NA)	(NA)	(NA)	(NA)	(NA)
Scientific, photo, control equip . . .	174.7	190.3	-4.4	9.8	15.2	16.9	0.1	48.7
Electronics, electrical equip	155.9	183.4	12.1	26.3	16.5	17.4	-1.0	35.0
Transportation equipment [2]	(NA)	(NA)	(NA)	(NA)	(NA)	(NA)	(NA)	(NA)
Furniture.	(NA)	(NA)	(NA)	(NA)	(NA)	(NA)	(NA)	(NA)
Textiles.	(NA)	(NA)	(NA)	(NA)	(NA)	(NA)	(NA)	(NA)
Apparel	(NA)	(NA)	(NA)	(NA)	(NA)	(NA)	(NA)	(NA)

NA Not available.   [1] Changes in profits of -41% in 1991 and -100.4% in 1992 include charge-offs for accounting rule change on retiree health benefits. Changes before charge-offs were -35.8%, 18.3, and 15.1% in 1991, 1992, and 1993 respectively.   [2] Excludes motor vehicles and aircraft.

Source of tables 866 and 867: Time Warner, New York, NY, The Fortune Directories (copyright).

No. 868. Corporate Profits, Taxes, and Dividends: 1980 to 1995

[In billions of dollars. Covers corporations organized for profit and other entities treated as corporations. Represents profits to U.S. residents, without deduction of depletion charges and exclusive of capital gains and losses; intercorporate dividends from profits of domestic corporations are eliminated; net receipts of dividends, reinvested earnings of incorporated foreign affiliates, and earnings of unincorporated foreign affiliates are added]

ITEM	1980	1985	1986	1987	1988	1989	1990	1991	1992	1993	1994	1995
Profits before tax	241	230	223	294	354	348	372	374	406	464	528	601
Profits tax liability	85	97	107	127	137	141	141	133	143	164	195	219
Profits after tax	157	133	116	167	217	207	231	241	263	301	333	382
Dividends	59	93	110	107	117	139	152	163	170	197	211	227
Undistributed profits	97	41	6	60	101	68	79	78	94	103	122	155
Inventory valuation adjustment (IVA)	-43	1	11	-21	-29	-18	-14	4	-8	-7	-13	-28
Capital consumption adjustment	-31	52	37	37	32	26	11	4	3	7	12	16
Net interest	192	337	363	372	399	457	467	448	414	398	393	401
Addenda:												
Corporate profits after tax with IVA/CCA	82	186	165	183	220	215	229	249	258	301	331	370
Net cash flow with inventory IVA/CCA [1]	219	375	355	392	442	436	455	479	492	520	561	597
Undistributed profits with IVA/CCA [1]	23	93	54	76	103	76	77	86	89	103	120	143
Consumption of fixed capital	196	282	301	316	338	359	378	393	403	417	441	454
Less: Inventory valuation adjustment (IVA)	-43	1	11	-21	-29	-18	-14	4	-8	-7	-13	-28
Equals: Net cash flow	262	374	344	413	471	453	469	475	499	527	575	625

[1] Inventory valuation adjustment/capital consumptiom adjustment.

No. 869. Corporate Profits, by Industry: 1990 to 1994

[In millions of dollars. Profits are without inventory valuation and capital consumption adjustments. Minus sign (-) indicates loss. See headnote, table 868]

INDUSTRY	BEFORE TAXES				AFTER TAXES			
	1990	1992	1993	1994	1990	1992	1993	1994
Corporate profits	371,685	406,415	464,312	528,208	231,221	263,391	300,535	332,907
Domestic industries	305,945	341,518	394,712	466,933	165,481	198,494	230,935	271,632
Agriculture, forestry, and fishing	1,619	1,947	2,055	2,322	993	1,345	1,317	1,487
Mining	2,459	2,382	2,326	3,064	876	1,260	1,499	2,224
Construction	10,999	8,075	10,631	12,943	8,781	6,427	8,695	9,964
Manufacturing	115,543	98,168	110,236	149,085	67,503	57,044	63,599	85,459
Transportation	934	2,251	7,169	10,855	-1,993	-605	3,655	6,825
Communications	20,014	27,801	33,050	36,734	11,831	19,090	22,553	25,089
Wholesale trade	19,839	24,085	28,134	37,240	13,695	17,523	20,775	27,208
Retail trade	24,382	35,130	41,604	44,857	15,426	25,296	30,307	32,664
Finance, insurance, and real estate	65,354	82,260	92,788	95,899	17,873	27,856	29,486	25,822
Services	20,241	31,086	36,853	40,784	14,901	24,695	29,530	33,008
Rest of the world [1]	65,740	64,897	69,600	61,275	65,740	64,897	69,600	61,275

[1] Consists of receipts by all U.S. residents, including both corporations and persons, of earnings of unincorporated foreign affiliates, dividends from their incorporated foreign affiliates, and their share of their incorporated foreign affiliates, net of corresponding outflows.

No. 870. Corporate Profits With Inventory Valuation and Capital Consumption Adjustments—Financial and Nonfinancial Industries: 1980 to 1995

[In billions of dollars. Minus sign (-) indicates loss. See headnote, table 868]

ITEM	1980	1985	1988	1989	1990	1991	1992	1993	1994	1995
Corporate profits with IVA/CCA [1]	167.1	282.2	357.2	356.4	369.5	382.5	401.4	464.5	526.5	588.6
Domestic industries	131.6	248.8	306.4	298.4	303.8	313.8	336.5	394.9	465.3	510.0
Rest of the world	35.5	33.4	50.7	58.0	65.7	68.7	64.9	69.6	61.3	78.6
Corporate profits with IVA [1]	198.3	230.5	325.0	330.6	358.2	378.2	398.9	457.7	514.9	572.7
Domestic industries	162.9	197.1	274.3	272.6	292.5	309.5	334.0	388.1	453.7	494.1
Financial	24.3	29.0	43.0	53.1	68.6	87.4	83.7	91.0	94.4	119.1
Nonfinancial	138.5	168.1	231.2	219.6	223.8	222.1	250.3	297.2	359.3	375.0
Manufacturing	75.8	81.6	115.1	109.3	112.3	92.7	96.3	109.7	142.7	145.7
Transportation and public utilities	18.3	34.3	48.7	42.6	43.2	53.9	57.8	70.6	81.3	94.8
Wholesale trade	16.7	20.6	19.3	20.4	17.2	20.6	23.0	25.5	34.5	29.6
Retail trade	6.1	22.5	19.6	20.7	20.6	26.1	32.2	39.2	42.2	38.7
Other	21.6	9.1	28.5	26.6	30.6	28.9	41.0	52.1	58.6	66.2

[1] Inventory valuation adjustment and capital consumption adjustment.

Source of tables 868-870: U.S. Bureau of Economic Analysis, *National Income and Product Accounts of the United States* to be published in late 1996, and *Survey of Current Business*, January/February 1996.

No. 871. Manufacturing, Mining, and Trade Corporations—Profits and Stockholders' Equity Ratios: 1990 to 1995

[Averages of quarterly figures at annual rates. Beginning 1990, manufacturing data exclude estimates for corporations with less than $250,000 in assets at time of sample selection. Data are not necessarily comparable from year to year due to changes in accounting procedures, industry classifications, sampling procedures, etc.; for detail, see source. Based on sample; see source for discussion of methodology. Minus sign (-) indicates loss]

INDUSTRY	RATIO OF PROFITS TO STOCKHOLDERS' EQUITY (percent)				PROFITS PER DOLLAR OF SALES (cents)				RATIO OF STOCKHOLDERS' EQUITY TO DEBT			
	1990	1993	1994	1995	1990	1993	1994	1995	1990	1993	1994	1995
Manufacturing corporations	10.7	8.1	15.7	16.3	4.0	2.8	5.4	5.7	1.3	1.3	1.4	1.4
Durable goods	8.0	5.7	16.3	15.7	3.0	1.9	5.2	5.4	1.6	1.5	1.7	1.8
Lumber and wood products	(NA)	18.6	21.8	12.9	(NA)	4.7	5.7	3.6	(NA)	1.6	1.8	1.8
Furniture and fixtures	(NA)	13.5	14.7	13.7	(NA)	3.4	3.5	3.5	(NA)	1.7	1.6	1.7
Stone, clay, and glass products	5.4	5.8	9.1	12.9	1.8	2.1	3.4	4.7	0.8	0.8	1.1	1.1
Primary metal industries	9.5	-2.5	13.6	19.0	2.6	-0.7	3.6	5.4	1.1	1.0	1.1	1.4
Iron and steel	6.6	-2.0	16.4	14.5	1.0	-0.4	3.8	3.8	0.6	0.8	1.1	1.4
Nonferrous metals	10.4	-2.8	11.6	22.3	4.0	-0.9	3.4	6.7	1.6	1.1	1.1	1.3
Fabricated metal products	11.7	7.1	13.4	12.6	3.4	2.1	3.7	3.5	1.3	1.3	1.3	1.2
Machinery, exc. electrical.	8.1	-6.0	12.4	12.4	4.4	-2.3	4.4	4.5	2.2	1.5	1.7	1.9
Electrical and electronic equipment . . .	7.5	21.6	16.0	18.8	3.0	5.0	6.7	8.2	1.6	2.0	2.2	2.3
Transportation equipment	3.8	9.8	24.3	17.4	1.3	1.9	5.1	4.5	1.9	1.3	1.8	2.1
Motor vehicles and equipment	-1.0	6.9	32.1	21.1	-0.5	1.1	5.4	4.7	2.2	1.3	2.0	2.6
Aircraft, guided missiles and parts . .	11.5	13.1	14.8	11.1	3.4	3.6	4.7	3.8	1.6	1.4	1.6	1.8
Instruments and related products	12.9	21.6	17.0	15.1	6.6	5.1	9.2	8.6	1.6	1.9	2.1	2.3
Miscellaneous manufacturing	(NA)	14.6	17.8	12.8	(NA)	4.1	4.9	4.1	(NA)	1.6	1.7	1.5
Nondurable goods	13.3	10.1	15.2	16.8	4.9	3.7	5.5	6.1	1.2	1.1	1.2	1.2
Food and kindred products [1]	16.1	13.5	18.0	18.5	4.1	3.7	5.0	5.5	0.8	0.9	0.9	1.0
Tobacco products.	(¹)	(¹)	(¹)	(¹)	(¹)	(¹)	(¹)	(¹)	(¹)	(¹)	(¹)	(¹)
Textile mill products	3.4	7.7	9.7	4.9	0.8	2.3	2.8	1.3	0.7	1.2	1.0	1.0
Apparel (includes leather)	(NA)	16.8	11.7	12.1	(NA)	3.3	2.6	2.8	(NA)	1.1	1.3	1.2
Paper and allied products	10.6	-0.4	11.0	21.5	4.2	-0.2	3.7	7.0	1.1	0.8	0.8	0.9
Printing and publishing	8.3	9.1	12.6	15.1	3.6	3.6	5.1	6.1	1.2	1.0	1.2	1.3
Chemicals and allied products	17.3	10.2	19.1	21.7	8.2	4.7	8.5	9.2	1.4	1.3	1.3	1.2
Industrial.	13.8	6.7	13.5	17.4	7.0	3.3	6.0	7.1	1.4	1.1	1.1	1.0
Drugs.	27.1	22.0	25.4	26.9	15.7	12.4	14.3	15.1	2.2	2.0	1.8	1.4
Residual of chemicals	(NA)	2.6	19.6	21.0	(NA)	0.9	6.9	7.2	(NA)	1.3	1.2	1.0
Petroleum and coal products	12.8	10.3	11.5	10.6	5.7	4.9	5.6	4.9	1.7	1.5	1.6	1.7
Rubber and misc. plastics products . . .	6.9	11.9	17.1	15.6	1.8	3.0	4.3	4.1	1.0	1.0	1.2	1.3
Mining corporations [2]	8.1	4.1	2.2	2.9	5.7	3.7	1.9	2.6	1.3	1.5	1.4	1.4
Retail trade corporations [2]	8.4	9.7	13.5	10.2	1.1	1.5	2.1	1.7	0.6	0.8	0.9	1.0
Wholesale trade corporations [2] . .	5.0	6.6	5.2	9.1	0.6	0.9	0.7	1.2	1.0	0.8	0.8	0.8

NA Not available.　[1] After 1980, tobacco included in food and kindred products.　[2] Asset cut-off raised to $50 million from $25 million in 1985.

No. 872. Manufacturing Corporations—Selected Finances: 1980 to 1995

[**In billions of dollars.** Data are not necessarily comparable from year to year due to changes in accounting procedures, industry classifications, sampling procedures, etc.; for detail, see source. See also *Historical Statistics, Colonial Times to 1970*, series P 93-106]

YEAR	ALL MANUFACTURING CORPS.				DURABLE GOODS INDUSTRIES				NONDURABLE GOODS INDUSTRIES			
	Sales	Profits		Stock-holders' equity [1]	Debt [1]	Sales	Profits		Stock-holders' equity [1]	Debt [1]	Sales	Profits		Stock-holders' equity [1]	Debt [1]
		Before taxes	After taxes				Before taxes	After taxes				Before taxes	After taxes		
1980 . .	1,897	145	92	665	292	883	57	36	316	143	1,014	88	57	349	149
1982 . .	2,039	108	71	770	371	913	35	22	356	177	1,126	74	49	415	193
1983 . .	2,114	133	86	813	368	973	49	30	372	168	1,141	84	56	440	200
1984 . .	2,335	166	108	864	405	1,108	76	49	396	166	1,228	90	59	469	239
1985 [2] . .	2,331	137	88	866	454	1,143	61	39	421	187	1,189	76	49	445	267
1986 [2] . .	2,221	129	83	875	501	1,126	52	33	436	203	1,096	77	51	438	298
1987 . .	2,378	173	116	901	553	1,178	78	53	444	229	1,200	95	63	457	324
1988 . .	2,596	216	155	958	622	1,285	92	67	469	265	1,312	124	88	489	357
1989 . .	2,745	189	136	999	733	1,357	75	56	501	308	1,388	114	81	498	425
1990 . .	2,812	160	112	1,044	782	1,357	58	41	515	328	1,454	102	71	529	453
1991 . .	2,761	100	68	1,064	814	1,304	14	7	507	338	1,457	86	60	557	476
1992 . .	2,890	33	23	1,035	819	1,390	-34	-24	474	335	1,500	66	47	561	485
1993 . .	3,014	119	84	1,040	819	1,490	39	28	483	327	1,524	79	56	557	492
1994 . .	3,261	244	175	1,114	815	1,660	121	87	533	316	1,601	123	89	581	500
1995 . .	3,519	279	201	1,239	863	1,799	183	97	616	333	1,720	145	105	623	529

[1] Annual data are average equity or debt for the year using four end-of-quarter figures.　[2] Beginning 1986, data exclude estimates for corporations with less than $250,000 in assets at time of sample selection.

Source of tables 871 and 872: Through 1981, U.S. Federal Trade Commission; thereafter, U.S. Bureau of Census, *Quarterly Financial Report for Manufacturing, Mining, and Trade Corporations.* In U.S. Council of Economic Advisers, *Economic Report of the President,* annual.

No. 873. U.S. Multinational Companies—Gross Product: 1982 and 1989

[In millions of dollars. Gross product measures valued added by a firm. Consists of nonbank U.S. parent companies and their nonbank foreign affiliates. A U.S. parent comprises the domestic operations of a multinational and is a U.S. person that owns or controls 10 percent or more of the voting securities, or the equivalent, of a foreign business enterprise. A U.S. person can be an incorporated business enterprise. A majority-owned foreign affiliate is a foreign business enterprise in which a U.S. parent company owns or controls 50 percent or more of the voting securities]

INDUSTRY	U.S. MULTINATIONALS		U.S. PARENTS		MAJORITY-OWNED FOREIGN AFFILIATES	
	1982	1989	1982	1989	1982	1989
All industries.	1,019,734	1,364,878	796,017	1,044,884	223,717	319,994
Petroleum.	211,937	165,680	134,096	93,128	77,841	72,552
Manufacturing.	542,689	793,771	421,050	586,568	121,639	207,203
Food and kindred products	46,069	79,472	35,804	60,310	10,265	19,162
Chemical and allied products	93,054	141,006	66,234	97,119	26,820	43,887
Primary and fabricated metals.	43,592	45,775	37,215	37,556	6,377	8,219
Machinery, except electrical	84,046	116,146	60,597	70,887	23,449	45,259
Electric and electronic equipment.	69,259	68,515	59,323	56,139	9,936	12,376
Transportation equipment.	91,170	160,292	71,256	121,141	19,914	39,151
Other	115,499	182,567	90,621	143,417	24,878	39,150
Wholesale trade.	17,427	28,766	13,604	22,587	3,823	6,179
Finance, insurance, real estate.	31,823	62,715	22,801	50,535	9,022	12,180
Finance, except banking	4,991	16,948	4,730	15,103	261	1,845
Insurance	23,539	41,233	17,954	34,948	5,585	6,285
Real estate	135	668	120	558	15	110
Holding companies	3,005	2,808	-2	-75	3,007	2,883
Services.	29,362	66,999	25,997	57,090	3,365	9,909
Hotels and other lodging places.	2,838	6,676	2,693	5,780	145	896
Business services.	10,026	24,067	8,501	18,756	1,525	5,311
Advertising	2,627	3,960	1,947	2,349	680	1,611
Equipment rental (exc. auto, computers) . .	652	193	646	175	6	18
Computer and data processing	2,313	6,361	2,135	5,353	178	1,008
Other	4,434	13,551	3,773	10,878	661	2,673
Automotive rental and leasing	(¹)	4,998	(¹)	4,212	(¹)	786
Motion pictures, television tape and film	941	3,465	825	2,663	116	802
Health services.	5,420	8,965	5,234	8,559	186	406
Engineering, architectural, surveying	3,350	3,498	2,422	2,998	928	500
Management and public relations.	(¹)	1,702	(¹)	1,180	(¹)	522
Other	6,787	13,629	6,322	12,943	465	686
Other industries	186,496	246,946	178,469	234,975	8,027	11,971

¹ Included in "other" services.

Source: U.S. Bureau of Economic Analysis, *Survey of Current Business*, February 1994.

No. 874. U.S. Multinational Companies—Selected Characteristics: 1992

[Preliminary. In billions of dollars, except as indicated. Consists of nonbank U.S. parent companies and their nonbank foreign affiliates. U.S. parent is a U.S. person that owns or controls directly or indirectly, 10 percent or more of the voting securities of an incorporated foreign business enterprise, or an equivalent interest in an unincorporated foreign business enterprise. A U.S. person can be an incorporated business enterprise. A foreign affiliate is a foreign business enterprise owned or controlled by a U.S. parent company]

INDUSTRY ¹	U.S. PARENTS				FOREIGN AFFILIATES				U.S. exports shipped to foreign affiliates	U.S. imports shipped from foreign affiliates
	Total assets	Sales	Employment (1,000)	Employee compensation	Total assets	Sales	Employment (1,000)	Employee compensation		
All industries.	5,570.5	3,353.0	17,617.2	722.8	1,746.8	1,578.7	6,727.5	201.4	120.3	109.2
Petroleum.	523.2	383.8	553.9	31.9	228.7	306.4	230.2	11.1	2.5	12.5
Manufacturing	2,071.5	1,638.9	9,307.4	417.4	591.6	757.6	4,006.5	121.7	82.2	85.9
Food and kindred products .	200.1	223.8	1,167.2	33.3	69.1	89.2	495.1	11.1	2.4	1.4
Chemical and allied products	341.6	267.3	1,194.9	61.5	131.4	143.0	587.1	21.2	9.7	4.9
Primary and fabricated metals.	87.1	86.2	557.2	24.5	26.7	27.9	198.9	5.6	2.0	1.8
Machinery (except electrical).	379.3	223.8	1,306.8	67.3	91.9	124.9	507.2	20.7	13.3	15.3
Electric and electronic equipment	103.5	95.4	685.1	28.7	47.8	56.8	557.0	10.7	9.6	12.9
Transportation equipment . .	476.1	367.2	1,808.8	97.5	102.6	183.9	738.7	25.7	33.5	39.6
Other	483.8	375.1	2,587.4	104.6	122.0	131.9	922.4	26.7	11.7	9.9
Wholesale trade.	100.9	184.0	406.7	14.4	142.6	263.2	550.8	24.2	32.7	9.1
Finance (except banking), insurance, real estate	1,936.6	416.2	1,033.4	53.8	594.0	79.0	150.3	7.4	0.0	0.0
Services.	154.8	125.3	1,610.7	47.4	73.6	61.1	569.1	17.5	0.8	0.1
Other.	783.6	604.9	4,705.1	157.8	116.3	111.4	1,220.8	19.4	2.0	1.7

¹ Represents industry of U.S. parent or industry of foreign affiliate.

Source: U.S. Bureau of Economic Analysis, *Survey of Current Business*, May 1994.

Figure 18.1
Media Usage by Consumers: 1989 to 1999

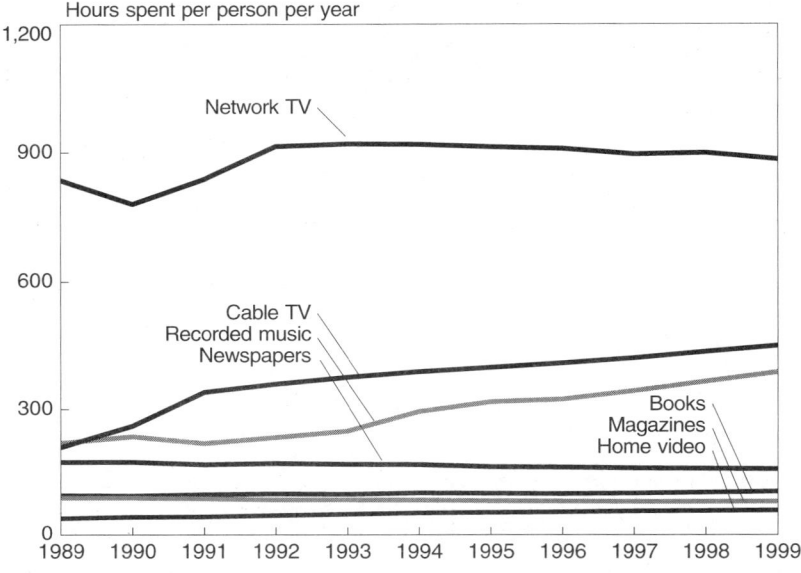

Hours spent per person per year

Network TV

Cable TV
Recorded music
Newspapers

Books
Magazines
Home video

Note: Data for 1995 to 1999 are projected.
Source: Chart prepared by U.S. Bureau of the Census. For data, see table 878.

Figure 18.2
Microcomputer Software Sales: 1994 and 1995

1994
1995

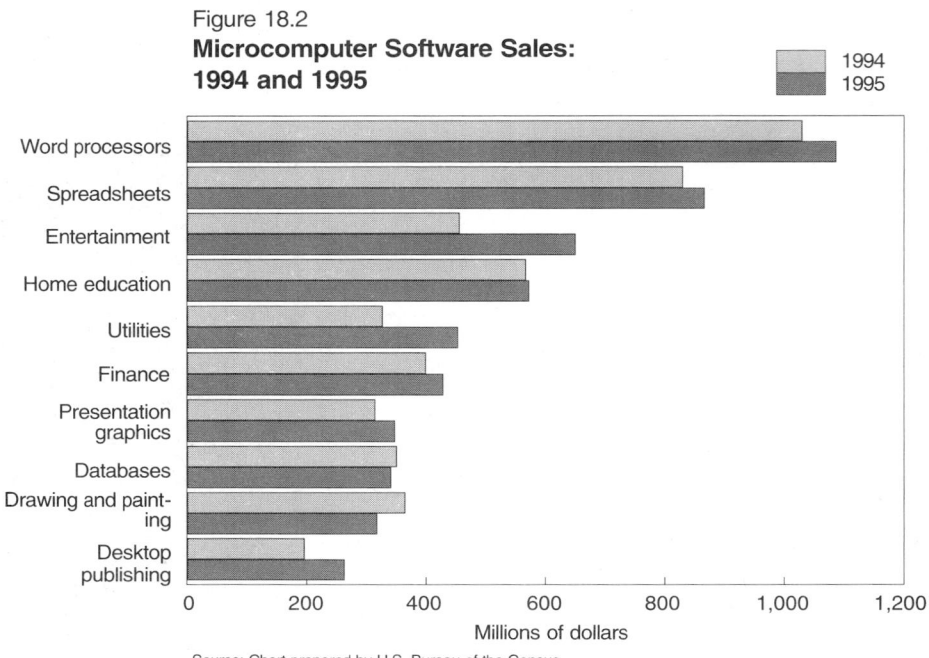

- Word processors
- Spreadsheets
- Entertainment
- Home education
- Utilities
- Finance
- Presentation graphics
- Databases
- Drawing and paint-ing
- Desktop publishing

Millions of dollars

Source: Chart prepared by U.S. Bureau of the Census.
For data, see table 893.

Communications and Information Technology

This section presents statistics on the various communications media: telephone, telegraph, radio, television, newspapers and periodicals, and the usage, finances, and operations of the Postal Service. Expenditure data for advertising in the media are also included.

Communication media—The Bureau of the Census *Annual Survey of Communication Services* (ASCS) covers all employer firms with one or more establishments that are primarily engaged in providing point-to-point communication services, whether by wire or radio, and whether intended to be received aurally or visually. This includes telephone communications, including cellular and other radiotelephone services; telegraph and other message communications, such as electronic mail services, facsimile transmission services, telex services, and so on; radio and television broadcasting stations and networks; cable and other pay television services; and other communication services, such as radar station operations, satellite earth stations, satellite or missile tracking stations, and so on. The report presents statistics that are summarized by kind-of-business classification based on the 1987 edition of the *Standard Industrial Classification Manual.*

The Federal Communications Commission (FCC), established in 1934, regulates wire and radio communications. Only the largest carriers and holding companies file annual or monthly financial reports. The FCC has jurisdiction over interstate and foreign communication services, but not over intrastate or local services. The gross operating revenues of the telephone carriers reporting annually to the FCC, however, are estimated to cover about 90 percent of the revenues of all U.S. telephone companies. Data are not comparable with Bureau of the Census *Annual Survey of Communication Services* because of coverage (*ASCS* includes all domestic long-distance telephone companies, all local exchange carriers, and all cellular telephone companies) and different

---

In Brief

Consumer spending per person in 1994:

Basic cable	$110
Books	$79
Home video	$73
Recorded music	$56
Daily newspapers	$49
Magazines	$36
On-line/Internet access services	$7

---

accounting practices for those telephone companies which report to the FCC.

Reports filed by the broadcasting industry cover substantially all radio and television stations operating in the United States. The private radio services represent the largest and most diverse group of licensees regulated by the FCC. These services provide voice, data communications, point-to-point and point-to-multipoint radio communications for fixed and mobile communicators. Major users of these services are small businesses, the aviation industry, the maritime trades, the land transportation industry, manufacturing industries, State and local public safety and governmental authorities, emergency medical service providers, amateur radio operators, and personal radio operations (CB and the General Mobile Radio Service). The FCC also licenses entities as private and common carriers. Private and common carriers provide fixed and land mobile communications service on a for-profit basis. Principal sources of wire, radio, and television data are the FCC's *Annual Report* and its annual *Statistics of Communications Common Carriers.*

Statistics on the printed media are available from the U.S. Bureau of the Census, as well as from various private agencies. The censuses of manufactures (conducted by the Census Bureau every 5 years, for the years ending in "2" and "7") provide statistics on the number and circulation of newspapers and periodicals and on sales of books and pamphlets.

Editor & Publisher Co., New York, NY, presents annual data on the number and circulation of daily and Sunday newspapers in its *International Year Book.* Monthly data on new books and new editions appear in *Publishers Weekly,* issued by R. R. Bowker Company, New York. (See table 900 for annual data.)

Advertising—Data on advertising expenditures are compiled primarily by McCann-Erickson, Inc., (see table 907). Monthly index figures of advertising in certain media are also published periodically by McCann-Erickson in *Advertising Age.*

The Broadcast Advertisers Reports distinguishes between spot and local advertising primarily on the basis of the type of advertiser to whom the time is sold, rather than how and by whom it is sold. In general, time purchased on behalf of retail or service establishments in the market is considered local, even though the establishments may be part of a national or regional chain. That is, spot advertising promotes a product, while local advertising promotes a given establishment. Network advertising, mutually exclusive of spot and local, is broadcast through the network system.

Postal Service—The Postal Service provides mail processing and delivery services within the United States. The Postal Reorganization Act of 1970 created the Postal Service, effective July 1971, as an independent establishment of the Federal Executive Branch.

Revenue and cost analysis describes the Postal Service's system of attributing revenues and costs to classes of mail and service. This system draws primarily upon probability sampling techniques to develop estimates of revenues, volumes, and weights, as well as costs by class of mail and special service. The costs attributed to classes of mail and special services are primarily incremental costs which vary in response to changes in volume; they account for roughly 60 percent of the total costs of the Postal Service. The balance represents "institutional costs." Statistics on revenues, volume of mail, and distribution of expenditures are presented in the Postal Service's annual report, *Cost and Revenue Analysis,* and its *Annual Report of the Postmaster General* and its *Annual Comprehensive Statement on Postal Operations.*

Statistical reliability—For a discussion of statistical collection and estimation, sampling procedures, and measures of statistical reliability applicable to Census Bureau data, see Appendix III.

Historical statistics—Tabular headnotes provide cross-references, where applicable, to *Historical Statistics of the United States, Colonial Times to 1970.* See Appendix IV.

No. 875. Communications Industry—Summary: 1992

[For establishments with payroll]

INDUSTRY	1987 SIC[1] code	Establishments	Revenue ($1,000)	Payroll ($1,000)	Paid employees[2]
Communications	48	39,244	230,667,167	47,057,941	1,294,236
Total, except broadcasting and cable ..	**481, 2, 9**	**26,227**	**174,926,125**	**36,522,874**	**943,518**
Telephone	481	24,730	171,580,095	35,900,576	928,245
Radiotelephone	4812	3,063	12,269,735	2,091,368	61,077
Other telephone	4813	21,667	159,310,360	33,809,208	867,168
Telegraph communications	482	489	988,142	217,800	5,536
Communication services, n.e.c.[3]	489	1,008	2,357,888	404,498	9,737
Broadcasting and cable	483, 4	13,017	55,741,042	10,535,067	350,718
Radio and television broadcasting	483	8,549	28,228,942	6,976,376	221,755
Radio	4832	6,956	6,865,419	2,547,700	112,385
Television	4833	1,593	21,363,523	4,428,676	109,370
Cable and other pay television	484	4,468	27,512,100	3,558,691	128,963

[1] 1987 Standard Industrial Classification code; see text, section 13.   [2] For the pay period including March 12.
[3] N.e.c. means not elsewhere classified.
Source: U.S. Bureau of the Census, *Census of Transportation, Communications, and Utilities,* UC92-A-1.

No. 876. Utilization of Selected Media: 1970 to 1994

ITEM	Unit	1970	1980	1985	1988	1989	1990	1991	1992	1993	1994
Households with—											
Telephone service [1]	Percent .	(NA)	93.0	91.8	92.9	93.0	93.3	93.6	93.9	94.2	93.9
Radio [2]	Millions .	71.4	78.6	87.1	91.1	92.8	94.4	95.5	96.6	97.3	98.0
Percent of total households . .	Percent .	98.6	99.0	99.0	99.0	99.0	99.0	99.0	99.0	99.0	99.0
Average number of sets	Number .	5.6	5.5	5.5	5.6	5.6	5.6	5.6	5.6	5.6	5.6
Television [3]	Millions .	69	76	85	89	90	92	93	92	93	94
Percent of total households . .	Percent .	97.1	97.9	98.1	98.1	98.2	98.2	98.2	98.3	98.3	98.3
Television sets in homes. . . .	Millions .	105	128	155	168	176	193	193	192	201	211
Average number of sets per home	Number .	1.5	1.7	1.8	1.9	1.9	2.1	2.1	2.1	2.2	2.2
Color sets	Millions .	47	63	78	85	87	90	91	91	92	93
Cable television [4]	Millions .	9	15	36	44	48	52	55	55	57	59
Percent of TV households . . .	Percent .	12.6	19.9	42.8	49.4	52.8	56.4	58.9	60.2	61.4	62.4
VCR's [4]	Millions .	(NA)	1	18	51	58	63	67	69	72	74
Percent of TV households . . .	Percent .	(NA)	1.1	20.8	58.0	64.6	68.6	71.9	75.0	77.1	79.0
Commercial radio stations: [2]											
AM.	Number .	4,463	4,589	[5]4,718	4,932	4,975	4,987	4,985	4,961	4,994	4,913
FM.	Number .	2,767	3,282	[5]3,875	4,155	4,269	4,392	4,570	4,785	4,971	5,109
Television stations: [6] Total	Number .	953	1,011	1,182	1,362	1,403	1,442	1,459	1,481	1,506	1,512
Commercial [3]	Number .	706	734	883	1,028	1,061	1,092	1,099	1,118	1,137	1,145
VHF	Number .	514	516	520	539	545	547	547	551	552	561
UHF	Number .	192	218	363	489	516	545	552	567	585	584
Cable television:											
Systems [6]	Number .	3,506	4,225	6,844	8,500	9,050	9,575	10,704	11,075	11,217	11,230
Subscribers served [7]	Millions .	9.8	17.7	39.9	48.6	52.6	54.9	55.8	56.4	57.2	60.5
Daily newspaper circulation [8]	Millions .	61	62	63	63	63	62	61	60	60	60

NA Not available. [1] For occupied housing units. 1970 and 1980 as of April 1; all other years as of March. Source: U.S. Bureau of the Census, 1970 and 1980 Census of Housing, vol. 1; and unpublished data. [2] As of December 31, except as noted. Source: Radio Advertising Bureau, New York, NY, through 1992, Radio Facts, annual, (copyright); beginning 1993, Radio Marketing Guide and Fact Book for Advertisers, annual, (copyright). Number of stations on the air compiled from Federal Communications Commission reports. [3] 1970, as of September of prior year; all other years as of January of year shown. Excludes Alaska and Hawaii. Source: Television Bureau of Advertising, Inc., Trends in Television, annual, (copyright). [4] As of February. Excludes Alaska and Hawaii. Source: See footnote 3. [5] As of February 1986. [6] As of January 1. Source: Warren Publishing, Washington DC, Television and Cable Factbook. [7] Source: Nielsen Media Research, Nielsen Station Index, November diary estimates (copyright). [8] As of September 30. Source: Editor & Publisher, Co., New York, NY, Editor & Publisher International Year Book, annual (copyright).

Source: Compiled from sources mentioned in footnotes.

No. 877. Multimedia Audiences—Summary: 1996

[In percent, except total. As of spring. For persons 18 years old and over. Represents the percent of persons participating during a specified time period. Based on sample and subject to sampling error; see source for details]

ITEM	Total population (1,000)	Television viewing	Television prime time viewing	Cable viewing	Radio listening	Newspaper reading	Accessed Internet [1]
Total	191,663	90.9	75.4	64.1	83.4	81.6	9.4
18 to 24 years old.	24,848	89.1	69.2	61.8	91.6	75.8	12.2
25 to 34 years old.	42,530	89.4	73.3	63.9	91.0	79.7	12.7
35 to 44 years old.	41,652	89.8	75.1	65.9	89.4	82.5	13.0
45 to 54 years old.	29,737	90.6	75.6	68.1	86.7	85.9	10.2
55 to 64 years old.	21,537	92.3	76.6	67.8	77.8	84.4	3.8
65 years old and over	31,359	95.3	82.4	57.4	59.1	81.6	1.0
Male.	91,780	90.9	74.2	65.3	86.0	81.9	11.5
Female.	99,882	91.0	76.5	63.0	81.0	81.3	7.4
White	162,526	90.6	74.8	66.2	83.4	83.1	10.0
Black	21,957	92.8	79.5	54.7	84.3	77.1	5.7
Other	7,179	91.6	75.8	45.9	80.1	62.0	6.7
Spanish speaking	14,144	92.2	75.8	50.4	85.3	68.4	7.3
Not high school graduate	36,567	92.0	77.1	48.1	72.9	65.9	1.4
High school graduate	64,414	92.5	78.3	65.6	82.5	80.8	3.4
Attended college.	51,083	90.3	73.6	69.6	88.4	86.6	11.9
College graduate	39,600	88.1	71.3	69.4	88.0	90.9	23.4
Employed:							
Full time	104,602	89.0	73.1	67.6	90.6	83.7	13.6
Part time	18,438	89.3	71.7	64.5	87.3	84.9	9.6
Not employed.	68,622	94.2	79.9	58.7	71.3	77.5	2.9
Household income:							
Less than $10,000.	18,491	90.8	76.0	41.8	71.8	65.8	1.9
$10,000 to $19,999	28,635	94.6	79.9	54.6	75.7	73.8	2.3
$20,000 to $29,999	29,109	92.3	78.6	57.8	79.6	78.7	3.4
$30,000 to $34,999	14,010	90.7	75.3	65.3	84.8	79.7	5.5
$35,000 to $39,999	12,263	92.2	77.9	65.8	86.9	83.3	8.5
$40,000 to $49,999	21,774	90.2	76.0	70.1	85.8	84.4	8.4
$50,000 or more	67,380	88.8	71.2	74.5	89.7	89.7	18.4

[1] In the past 30 days.

Source: Mediamark Research Inc., New York, NY, Multimedia Audiences, spring 1996 (copyright).

No. 878. Media Usage and Consumer Spending: 1989 to 1999

[Estimates of time spent were derived using rating data for television and radio, survey research and consumer purchase data for recorded music, newspapers, magazines, books, home video, admissions for movies, and consumer on-line/Internet access services. Adults 18 and older except for recorded music where estimates include persons 12 and older]

| YEAR | Total [1] | TELEVISION | | | | | Re-corded music | Daily news-papers | Con-sumer maga-zines | Con-sumer books | Home video [4] | Con-sumer on-line/Internet access services |
		Net-work sta-tions [2]	Inde-pen-dent sta-tions [2]	Basic cable [3]	Pay cable						
HOURS PER PERSON PER YEAR											
1989	3,278	835	345	210	95	220	175	90	96	39	(Z)
1990	3,267	780	340	260	90	235	175	90	95	42	1
1991	3,257	838	227	340	90	219	169	88	98	43	1
1992	3,329	914	159	359	78	233	172	85	100	46	2
1993	3,302	920	162	375	78	248	170	85	99	49	2
1994	3,402	919	172	388	81	294	169	84	102	52	3
1995 proj.	3,434	913	185	398	84	317	164	82	101	53	5
1996 proj.	3,457	909	205	408	78	323	163	81	100	54	8
1997 proj.	3,489	896	221	420	78	343	161	80	101	56	11
1998 proj.	3,528	899	224	435	77	365	160	80	103	57	13
1999 proj.	3,560	884	231	449	81	387	159	80	105	58	14
CONSUMER SPENDING PER PERSON PER YEAR (dollars)											
1989	331.65	-	-	77.86	(5)	32.25	45.71	31.49	61.24	50.71	2.22
1990	365.43	-	-	87.90	(5)	36.64	47.55	33.14	63.90	56.35	2.93
1991	378.77	-	-	94.44	(5)	37.73	46.56	33.45	68.18	58.69	3.61
1992	403.15	-	-	101.28	(5)	43.05	48.54	34.26	71.37	63.23	4.39
1993	428.19	-	-	108.54	(5)	47.42	48.25	35.27	74.90	68.42	5.35
1994	456.26	-	-	110.00	(5)	56.35	49.28	36.36	79.22	72.97	7.44
1995 proj.	492.35	-	-	117.84	(5)	62.36	52.67	38.79	84.20	78.19	11.23
1996 proj.	525.74	-	-	128.65	(5)	65.07	55.78	40.53	88.89	81.47	16.34
1997 proj.	563.32	-	-	137.16	(5)	70.76	58.08	42.12	93.91	86.47	21.82
1998 proj.	601.55	-	-	145.75	(5)	77.29	60.61	43.75	100.03	89.85	27.03
1999 proj.	639.17	-	-	154.30	(5)	83.92	62.76	45.53	107.19	93.56	29.95

- Represents zero.   Z less than 1 hour.   [1] Includes other media, not shown separately.   [2] Affiliates of the Fox network are counted as network affiliates for part of 1991 and all latter years, but as independent stations in earlier years.   [3] Includes TBS beginning in 1992.   [4] Playback of prerecorded tapes only.   [5] Included with basic cable.

Source: Veronis, Suhler & Associates Inc., New York, NY, *Communications Industry Report*, annual (copyright).

No. 879. Communications Industry—Finances: 1990 to 1994

[**In millions of dollars.** Covers 420 publicly reporting companies with revenues of over $1 million in 11 communication industry segments]

| INDUSTRY | REVENUE | | | | OPERATING INCOME | | | |
	1990	1992	1993	1994	1990	1992	1993	1994
Total	117,072	131,852	138,410	152,528	15,658	17,769	19,368	22,026
Television & radio broadcasting [1] . . .	19,325	19,960	20,840	23,193	2,763	2,505	3,354	4,459
Television network companies	12,011	12,510	12,893	14,185	1,644	1,268	1,873	2,444
TV & radio station broadcasters.	7,314	7,450	7,948	9,009	1,119	1,238	1,481	2,015
Subscription video services	15,946	19,129	20,552	22,729	2,220	3,737	3,982	3,718
Subscription video services operators.	11,267	13,494	14,447	14,962	1,668	2,759	2,918	2,735
Cable and pay-per-view networks	4,679	5,635	6,105	7,767	553	977	1,064	982
Filmed entertainment	10,524	13,878	14,896	16,476	1,139	1,343	1,285	1,475
Recorded music.	6,104	7,064	7,393	8,471	613	766	797	1,004
Newspaper publishing.	19,875	18,956	19,381	20,878	3,147	2,677	2,752	3,322
Book publishing.	7,282	9,549	10,253	11,180	997	1,270	1,304	1,368
Magazine publishing.	8,537	9,461	9,615	9,771	916	928	1,008	1,083
Consumer magazine	6,631	7,616	7,802	7,965	667	738	825	861
Business and professional	1,905	1,846	1,813	1,806	249	190	182	221
Business information services.	16,740	19,189	19,958	22,519	2,472	2,904	3,058	3,604
Advertising agencies [2]	6,807	7,782	7,666	8,206	630	711	716	824
Interactive digital media [3].	745	1,192	1,651	2,364	79	166	167	200
Miscellaneous communications.	5,188	5,693	6,205	6,742	682	763	944	970

[1] Excludes agency commissions.   [2] Net revenue including only commissions, fees, and other income, not gross billings.   [3] Software for consumer data and transactions, consumer reference, education, games, home shopping, and infomercials.

Source: Veronis, Suhler & Associates Inc., New York, NY, *Communications Industry Report*, annual (copyright).

No. 880. Telephone and Telegraph Systems: 1980 to 1994

[Covers principal carriers filing annual reports with Federal Communications Commission. Minus sign (-) indicates loss. See *Historical Statistics, Colonial Times to 1970,* series R 46-70 and R 75-88, for data on telegraph systems]

ITEM	Unit	1980	1985	1988	1989	1990	1991	1992	1993	1994
DOMESTIC TELEPHONE [1]										
Carriers [2]	Number .	59	39	54	53	53	54	56	55	54
Access lines	Million . .	(NA)	103	122	126	130	137	140	149	157
Miles of wire	Million . .	1,131	1,313	1,483	1,502	1,528	(NA)	(NA)	(NA)	(NA)
Gross book cost of plant	Bil. dol. .	147	195	250	260	265	270	279	289	299
Depreciation reserves [3]	Bil. dol. .	27	50	85	94	98	102	108	117	127
Ratio to book cost	Percent .	18	26	34	36	37	38	39	41	42
Capital stock and premium	Bil. dol. .	31	48	45	46	46	47	48	42	42
Operating revenues	Bil. dol. .	56	89	100	102	104	106	109	113	117
Operating expenses [4]	Bil. dol. .	37	61	74	77	78	80	81	85	88
Net operating income [5]	Bil. dol. .	10	12	17	16	16	16	17	17	17
Net income	Bil. dol. .	7	10	13	12	13	12	12	8	12
Return on investment (domestic and overseas) [6]	Percent .	9	9	10	10	10	9	10	10	10
Employees	1,000. .	938	(NA)	688	663	648	616	608	592	553
Compensation of employees	Bil. dol. .	20	(NA)	25	24	26	25	26	27	26
OVERSEAS TELEPHONE										
Number of overseas calls	Million . .	200	412	706	1,008	1,201	2,279	2,750	3,136	3,713
Revenue from overseas calls [7]	Mil. dol. .	1,535	1,799	2,573	3,513	4,362	5,835	6,974	7,800	8,140
Ocean cable systems	Number .	24	26	26	23	24	26	(NA)	(NA)	(NA)
Communications satellites [8]	Number .	5	6	14	15	16	16	(NA)	(NA)	(NA)
TELEGRAPH [9]										
Carriers	Number .	8	7	6	6	3	3	2	2	2
Revenue messages transmitted	Million . .	75	42	(NA)	(NA)	(NA)	(NA)	(NA)	(NA)	(NA)
Message revenues [10]	Mil. dol. .	676	708	483	521	259	219	(NA)	(NA)	(NA)
Total operating revenues	Mil. dol. .	1,232	1,367	882	1,019	408	383	317	367	471
Operating revenue deductions	Mil. dol. .	1,008	1,292	942	995	447	421	343	416	579
Operating income [11]	Mil. dol. .	147	102	-56	24	-28	-28	-77	-76	-107
Return on investment [6]	Percent .	16	7	-6	4	1	-12	(NA)	(NA)	(NA)

NA Not available.   [1] Includes Virgin Islands, and prior to 1991, Puerto Rico. Excludes intercompany duplications. Gross operating revenues of carriers reporting estimated at 90 percent of all carriers. Beginning 1988, based on new accounting rules; prior years not directly comparable.   [2] Beginning 1985, number of carriers changed due to change in dollar requirement of reporting carriers from $1 million to $100 million.   [3] Includes amortization reserves.   [4] Excludes taxes.   [5] After tax deductions.   [6] Ratio of net operating income (after taxes) to average net book cost of communications plant.   [7] Beginning 1991, includes calls to and from Alaska, Hawaii, Puerto Rico, Canada, and Mexico.   [8] Excludes contingency and retired satellites.   [9] Domestic and overseas except for South American and most Caribbean operations of All America Cables and Radio, Inc.   [10] Includes telex service; for domestic telegraph, excludes TWX.   [11] After Federal income taxes.

Source: U.S. Federal Communications Commission, *Statistics of Communications Common Carriers,* annual; and unpublished data.

No. 881. Telephone Communications—Operating Revenue and Expenses: 1990 to 1994

[Based on a sample of employer firms with one or more establishments that are primarily engaged in providing telephone, voice, and data communication services. For SIC 481. Based on the 1987 Standard Industrial Classification code; see text, section 13]

ITEM	TOTAL (mil. dol.)					PERCENT DISTRIBUTION		
	1990	1991	1992	1993	1994	1990	1993	1994
OPERATING REVENUE								
Total	160,482	164,738	171,578	181,700	195,333	100.0	100.0	100.0
Local service	40,180	41,354	43,341	45,313	46,994	25.0	24.9	24.1
Long-distance service	67,698	69,006	69,446	72,306	77,711	42.2	39.8	39.8
Network access	30,044	29,947	30,998	31,884	33,485	18.7	17.5	17.1
Cellular and other radiotelephone	6,002	6,870	9,181	12,050	15,930	3.7	6.6	8.2
Directory advertising	8,373	8,680	8,923	9,126	9,467	5.2	5.0	4.8
Other	8,185	8,881	9,689	11,021	11,746	5.1	6.1	6.0
OPERATING EXPENSES								
Total	131,493	137,593	143,033	156,573	156,730	100.0	100.0	100.0
Annual payroll	34,903	35,320	35,900	36,801	37,476	26.5	23.5	23.9
Employer contributions to Social Security and other supplemental benefits	8,121	8,924	9,584	9,326	9,245	6.2	6.0	5.9
Access charges	23,214	24,039	24,539	25,510	26,849	17.7	16.3	17.1
Depreciation	22,927	23,600	23,623	24,614	26,535	17.4	15.7	16.9
Lease and rental	3,543	3,867	4,247	4,102	4,917	2.7	2.6	3.1
Purchased repairs	2,977	2,954	2,915	3,125	3,636	2.3	2.0	2.3
Insurance	193	218	222	217	242	0.1	0.1	0.2
Telephone and other purchased communication services	504	544	707	838	1,051	0.4	0.5	0.7
Purchased utilities	1,106	1,150	1,178	1,197	1,312	0.8	0.8	0.8
Purchased advertising	2,328	2,546	2,637	3,277	4,306	1.8	2.1	2.7
Taxes	5,086	5,233	5,194	5,365	5,546	3.9	3.4	3.5
Other	26,591	29,198	32,287	42,201	35,615	20.2	27.0	22.7

Source: U.S. Bureau of the Census, *Annual Survey of Communication Services: 1994* (BC/94).

No. 882. Telephone Companies—Summary: 1988 to 1993

[**As of Dec. 31** or **calendar year,** as applicable. January 1, 1988, marked the beginning of significant rules changes in the way local exchange carriers account for assets, liabilities, revenue, expenses, and income. Any comparisons with earlier data would not be meaningful. See also *Historical Statistics, Colonial Times to 1970,* series R 1-12 and 31-45]

ITEM	Unit	INDEPENDENT COMPANIES [1]				ALL TELEPHONE COMPANIES			
		1988	1990	1992	1993	1988	1990	1992	1993
All companies	Number .	1,349	1,310	1,308	1,305	1,371	1,332	1,327	1,324
Access lines	Millions .	29	32	34	35.4	130	138	145	150.2
Total telephone plant.	Bil. dol. .	59	65	71	74.1	238	256	272	281.7
Operating revenues	Bil. dol. .	21	22	26	26.7	90	90	95	98
Avg. daily conversations [2] . .	Millions .	(NA)	(NA)	(NA)	(NA)	1,700	9,515	9,885	10,665
Reporting companies [3]	Number .	585	594	622	573	607	616	641	592
Access lines	Millions .	29	30	32	33.8	130	136	143	148.7
Telephone plant in service . .	Bil. dol. .	57	63	68	70.7	233	251	265	274.8
Depreciation reserves [4]	Bil. dol. .	20	24	27	29	80	95	106	113.8
Operating revenues	Bil. dol. .	21	22	24	24.2	86	89	92	95.5
Operating expenses [5]	Bil. dol. .	14	16	16	17.3	61	65	67	70
Net income	Bil. dol. .	3	3	4	2	12	12	10	7
Stockholders' equity	Bil. dol. .	20	22	24	24.2	76	80	83	79.6
Net income to stockholders									
equity.	Percent .	16	15	15	8.3	16	14	12	8.8
Employees	1,000. . .	170	161	152	140	639	606	560	536

NA Not available. [1] Companies independent of the Bell System, prior to divestiture of January 1984. [2] Average business day conversations in 1988. Average business day minutes of use beginning in 1990. [3] Comprises only companies submitting operating information to source cited below. [4] Total accumulated depreciation and amortization. [5] Excludes Federal income tax.

Source: United States Telephone Association, Washington, DC, *Statistics of the Local Exchange Carriers,* annual (copyright).

No. 883. Percent of Households with Telephone Service: 1984 and 1994

[**Annual averages of quarterly data.** Based on Current Population Survey; see text, section 1, and Appendix III]

CHARACTERISTIC	1984				1994			
	All races	White	Black	Hispanic [1]	All races	White	Black	Hispanic [1]
Total	92	93	80	81	94	95	86	86
Age of householder:								
15 to 24 years old [2]	77	80	58	61	84	86	74	72
25 to 54 years old	92	93	80	83	93	95	85	86
55 to 59 years old	95	96	87	87	96	96	91	89
60 to 64 years old	95	96	87	87	96	97	90	92
65 to 69 years old	96	97	88	90	97	97	92	93
70 years old and over.	95	96	88	84	97	97	92	92
Household size:								
1 person	88	90	75	73	92	93	82	82
2 to 3 persons.	93	95	82	82	95	96	88	87
4 to 5 persons.	93	94	82	84	94	96	87	88
6 or more persons	87	90	76	79	89	91	82	83
Household level:								
Under $5,000	71	75	63	55	76	80	69	66
$5,000 to $7,499	83	86	75	70	83	85	77	73
$7,500 to $9,999	87	88	77	75	87	89	81	81
$10,000 to $12,499	90	91	81	80	90	91	82	83
$12,500 to $14,999	92	93	85	87	92	93	86	85
$15,000 to $19,999	(NA)	(NA)	(NA)	(NA)	94	94	87	88
$15,000 to $17,499.	94	94	89	88	(NA)	(NA)	(NA)	(NA)
$17,500 to $19,999.	95	96	92	91	(NA)	(NA)	(NA)	(NA)
$20,000 to $24,999	97	97	93	93	95	96	90	91
$25,000 to $29,999	98	98	95	96	97	97	94	92
$30,000 to $34,999	99	99	97	99	97	98	94	92
$35,000 to $39,999	99	99	98	98	98	98	94	95
$40,000 to $49,999	99	99	97	99	99	99	97	96
$50,000 to $74,999	99	100	98	100	(NA)	(NA)	(NA)	(NA)
$50,000 to $59,999.	(NA)	(NA)	(NA)	(NA)	99	99	96	100
$60,000 to $74,999.	(NA)	(NA)	(NA)	(NA)	99	99	100	98
$75,000 and over.	99	99	97	98	99	99	99	99
Labor force status of persons, 15 years old and over: [3]								
Total civilian noninstitutional population.	93	94	83	83	95	96	88	87
Employed	94	95	86	86	96	96	90	89
Unemployed	82	84	75	74	88	90	81	84
Not in labor force	92	94	81	80	93	95	85	86

NA Not available. [1] Persons of Hispanic origin may be of any race. [2] 16 to 24 years old in 1984. [3] 16 years old and over in 1984.

Source: Federal Communications Commission, *Telephone Subscribership in the U.S.,* April 1995.

No. 884. Cellular Telephone Industry: 1988 to 1995

[Calendar year data, except as noted. Based on a survey mailed to all cellular systems. For 1994 data, the universe was 1,581 systems and the response rate was 85 percent]

ITEM	UNIT	1988	1989	1990	1991	1992	1993	1994	1995
Systems.............	Number .	517	584	751	1,252	1,506	1,529	1,581	1,627
Subscribers.........	1,000 ..	2,069	3,509	5,283	7,557	11,033	16,009	24,134	33,786
Cell sites [1]	Number .	3,209	4,169	5,616	7,847	10,307	12,805	17,920	22,663
Employees..........	Number .	11,400	15,927	21,382	26,327	34,348	39,775	53,902	68,165
Service revenue......	Mil. dol. .	1,959	3,340	4,548	5,708	7,822	10,891	14,229	19,081
Roamer revenue [2].....	Mil. dol. .	89	294	456	704	974	1,360	1,830	2,542
Capital investment	Mil. dol. .	3,274	4,480	6,282	8,672	11,262	13,946	18,939	24,080
Average monthly bill [3].....	Dollars..	98.02	89.30	80.90	72.74	68.68	61.48	56.21	51.00
Average length of call [3]....	Minutes .	2.26	2.48	2.20	2.38	2.58	2.41	2.24	2.15

NA Not available.   [1] The basic geographic unit of a cellular system. A city or county is divided into smaller "cells," each of which is equipped with a lowpowered radio transmitter/receiver. The cells can vary in size depending upon terrain, capacity demands, etc. By controlling the transmission power, the radio frequencies assigned to one cell can be limited to the boundaries of that cell. When a cellular phone moves from one cell toward another, a computer at the Switching Office monitors the movement and at the proper time, transfers or hands off the phone call to the new cell and another radio frequency.   [2] Service revenue generated by subscribers' calls outside of their system areas.   [3] For 6 months ending December 31.

Source: Cellular Telecommunications Industry Association, Washington, DC, State of the Cellular Industry, annual, (copyright).

No. 885. Private Radio Stations Authorized, by Class: 1990 to 1994

[In thousands. As of September 30. Includes Puerto Rico and Virgin Islands. See also Historical Statistics, Colonial Times to 1970, series R 140-148]

CLASS	1990	1992	1993	1994	CLASS	1990	1992	1993	1994
Private radio services [1] .	2,880	2,956	3,007	2,995	Railroad	16	18	18	18
Personal	528	611	655	682	Taxicab............	6	6	5	5
General mobile	32	28	27	31	Interurban property....	6	6	6	7
Amateur and disaster ..	496	583	628	652	Other.............	12	12	11	10
Aviation	251	210	191	192	Marine.............	623	634	664	686
Aircraft	210	193	182	173	Ship..............	607	619	648	668
Aeronautical and fixed..	12	12	13	13	Alaskan	2	2	2	2
Civil air patrol	24	(Z)	(Z)	(Z)	Coastal and other.....	13	13	14	15
Other.............	5	5	5	5	Public safety.........	235	245	251	252
Industrial	865	840	828	795	Police.............	51	53	54	55
Power	46	48	49	50	Fire..............	44	46	47	48
Business...........	628	27	591	563	Forestry conservation ...	11	12	12	17
Petroleum..........	27	603	26	25	Highway maintenance ..	15	16	16	12
Forest products	12	12	12	11	Special emergency....	41	41	40	38
Special industrial	114	110	108	103	Other.............	73	78	81	83
Other.............	39	41	43	43	Operational fixed				
Land transportation	40	41	41	40	services [2]..........	33	36	37	38

Z Fewer than 500.   [1] Includes items not shown separately. Each license, construction permit, or combination construction permit and license is counted one as station; therefore, a station might include a transmitter and many mobile units.   [2] Includes microwave operations.

Source: U.S. Federal Communications Commission, Annual Report; and unpublished data.

No. 886. Radio and Television Broadcasting Services—Finances: 1990 to 1994

[In millions of dollars. Based on a sample of taxable employer firms with one or more establishments primarily engaged in broadcasting to the public, except cable and other pay television services. Based on the 1987 Standard Industrial Classification Code; see text, section 13]

ITEM	TOTAL (SIC 483)			RADIO (SIC 4832)			TELEVISION (SIC 4833)		
	1990	1993	1994	1990	1993	1994	1990	1993	1994
Operating revenue	28,017	28,281	31,064	6,954	7,231	7,980	21,063	21,050	23,084
Station time sales..............	19,019	19,227	21,352	6,397	6,693	7,397	12,622	12,534	13,955
Network compensation.........	549	444	455	105	87	95	444	357	360
National/regional advertising	7,226	6,922	7,794	1,522	1,433	1,646	5,704	5,489	6,148
Local advertising	11,244	11,861	13,103	4,770	5,173	5,656	6,474	6,688	7,447
Network time sales	7,905	8,053	8,702	305	285	338	7,600	7,768	8,364
Other	1,093	1,001	1,010	252	253	245	841	748	765
Operating expenses	24,145	23,448	25,038	6,317	6,257	6,769	17,828	17,191	18,269
Annual payroll	6,333	6,641	7,178	2,428	2,535	2,709	3,905	4,106	4,469
Employer contributions to Social Security and other supplemental benefits..................	998	1,118	1,197	326	356	362	672	762	835
Broadcast rights..............	7,642	7,172	7,396	264	235	236	7,378	6,937	7,160
Music license fees	373	339	347	159	161	181	214	178	166
Depreciation	1,345	1,187	1,192	477	431	441	868	756	751
Lease and rental..............	469	469	487	197	207	228	272	262	259
Purchased repairs.............	232	233	257	79	79	83	153	154	174
Insurance	143	156	168	64	67	73	79	89	95
Telephone and other purchased communication services	240	234	251	115	115	122	125	119	129
Purchased utilities............	246	253	269	99	98	106	147	155	163
Purchased advertising	947	808	942	368	310	367	579	498	575
Taxes	176	184	200	60	69	72	116	115	128
Other......................	5,001	4,654	5,154	1,681	1,594	1,789	3,320	3,060	3,365

Source: U.S. Bureau of the Census, Annual Survey of Communication Services: 1994 (BC/94).

No. 887. Copyright Registration, by Subject Matter: 1990 to 1995

[In thousands. For years ending September 30. Comprises claims to copyrights registered for both U.S. and foreign works. See also *Historical Statistics Colonial Times to 1970*, series W 82-95]

SUBJECT MATTER	1990	1993	1994	1995	SUBJECT MATTER	1990	1993	1994	1995
Total	643.5	564.9	530.4	609.2	Sound recordings	37.5	32.4	35.9	34.0
Monographs [1]	179.7	185.8	163.0	196.0	Renewals.	51.8	37.7	33.3	30.6
Semiconductor chip products. .	1.0	1.0	1.0	0.8	Musical works [2]	185.3	152.3	136.1	163.6
Serials.	111.5	82.6	75.0	88.7	Works of the visual arts [3]	76.7	73.5	86.1	95.5

[1] Includes computer software and machine readable works.   [2] Includes dramatic works, accompanying music, choreography, pantomimes motion pictures, and filmstrips.   [3] Two-dimensional works of fine and graphic art, including prints and art reproductions; sculptural works; technical drawings and models; photographs; commercial prints and labels; works of applied arts, cartographic works, and multimedia works.

Source: The Library of Congress, Copyright Office, *Annual Report*.

No. 888. Public Television Programming: 1980 to 1992

[For October through September seasons. General programming is directed at the general community. Instructional programming is directed at students in the classroom or otherwise in the general context of formal education]

ITEM	1980	1982	1984	1986	1988	1990	1992
Stations broadcasting	281	291	303	305	322	341	349
Number of broadcasters [1]	160	164	169	178	186	193	198
Average annual hours per broadcaster.	5,128	5,421	5,542	5,650	6,135	6,392	6,303
BROADCAST HOURS, PERCENT DISTRIBUTION							
Program content	100	100	100	100	100	100	100
General.	87	87	88	86	85	86	90
News and public affairs [2]	12	12	14	16	16	18	17
Information and skills	23	25	26	30	32	32	29
Cultural	22	23	20	21	18	19	18
General children's and youth's.	9	8	8	7	6	6	15
Sesame Street	16	15	15	11	12	11	11
Other	6	5	6	2	1	1	1
Instructional [3].	15	14	13	15	16	14	12
Children and youth	14	13	12	(NA)	(NA)	(NA)	9
Adult	1	1	1	(NA)	(NA)	(NA)	3
Producer	100	100	100	100	100	100	100
Local	7	7	6	5	5	5	5
Any public TV source.	46	46	44	38	27	32	35
Consortium	3	3	3	3	10	10	1
Children's TV Workshop.	17	16	16	[4]29	16	15	14
Independent producer	8	11	9	([4])	19	19	25
Foreign producer, international coproduction	13	10	13	15	14	12	11
Commercial producer.	3	4	3	6	4	4	5
Other	4	4	5	4	4	4	3
Distributor	100	100	100	100	100	100	100
Local distribution only	7	6	6	5	6	6	5
Public broadcasting service.	70	67	65	64	62	59	63
Regional public television network	8	11	13	14	18	24	23
Other	16	16	16	17	14	11	9

NA Not available.   [1] Beginning 1990, only broadcasters in the 50 U.S. States were surveyed. In prior years, the stations in the outlying areas were also included.   [2] Beginning 1988, this category includes "Business or Consumer."   [3] Some general audience programs with instructional applications were double counted if aired during school hours when school was in session. "The Electric Company" was one such program.   [4] Independent producer included with Children's TV Workshop for 1986.

Source: Corporation for Public Broadcasting, Washington, DC, *PTV Programming Survey*, biennial.

No. 889. Public Broadcasting Systems—Income, by Source: 1980 to 1994

[In millions of dollars, except number of stations and percents. Stations as of Dec. 31; fiscal year data for income. Includes nonbroadcast income]

NUMBER OF STATIONS AND INCOME SOURCE	1980	1985	1990	1991	1992	1993	1994	PERCENT DISTRIBUTION		
								1980	1990	1994
CPB-qualified public radio stations [1] . .	217	288	318	373	391	400	(NA)	(X)	(X)	(X)
Public television stations	290	317	341	349	349	352	(NA)	(X)	(X)	(X)
Total income.	705	1,096	1,581	1,721	1,790	1,790	1,795	100	100	100
Federal government	193	179	267	333	374	370	330	27	17	18
State and local government [2]	272	358	474	503	485	475	510	39	30	28
Subscribers and auction/marathon.	102	248	364	384	404	412	420	15	23	23
Business and industry.	72	171	262	290	300	285	301	10	17	17
Foundation	24	43	71	70	80	100	97	3	5	5
Other	43	97	143	139	148	149	137	6	9	8

NA Not available.   X Not applicable.   [1] Includes CPB-supported developmental grantees/stations, and excludes repeater stations.   [2] Includes income received from State and other public colleges and universities.

Source: Corporation for Public Broadcasting (CPB), Washington, DC, *Public Broadcasting Income, Fiscal Year, 1994*; and unpublished data.

No. 890. Cable Television—Systems and Subscribers: 1970 to 1995

[Subscribers in thousands, except percent. Estimated]

YEAR (As of Jan. 1)	Sys-tems	Sub-scribers	YEAR (As of Jan. 1)	Sys-tems	Sub-scribers	SUBSCRIBER SIZE-GROUP	NUMBER OF [1]— Sys-tems	NUMBER OF [1]— Sub-scribers	PERCENT OF [1]— Sys-tems	PERCENT OF [1]— Sub-scribers
1970	2,490	4,500	1985	6,600	32,000	1995, total [2]	10,495	59,289	100	100
1975	3,506	9,800	1986	7,600	37,500	50,000 and over	256	26,631	2	45
1976	3,681	10,800	1987	7,900	41,100	20,000 to 49,999	437	13,461	4	23
1977	3,832	11,900	1988	8,500	44,000	10,000 to 19,999	512	7,208	5	12
1978	3,875	13,000	1989	9,050	47,500	5,000 to 9,999	658	4,522	6	8
1979	4,150	14,100	1990	9,575	50,000	3,500 to 4,999	421	1,736	4	3
1980	4,225	16,000	1991	10,704	51,000	1,000 to 3,499	1,968	3,743	19	6
1981	4,375	18,300	1992	11,075	53,000	500 to 999	1,458	1,043	14	2
1982	4,825	21,000	1993	11,100	55,000	250 to 499	1,513	542	14	1
1983	5,600	25,000	1994	11,200	57,000	Less than 250	3,272	403	31	1
1984	6,200	30,000	1995	11,126	58,000					

[1] As of October 1.   [2] Excludes 631 systems not available by subscriber size-group.
Source: Warren Publishing, Inc., Washington, DC, Television & Cable Factbook, annual, (copyright).

No. 891. Cable and Pay TV—Summary: 1970 to 1994

[Cable TV for calendar year. Pay TV as of Dec. 31 of year shown]

YEAR	CABLE TV Avg. basic sub-scribers (1,000)	CABLE TV Avg. monthly basic rate (dol.)	CABLE TV Revenue [1] (mil. dol.) Total	CABLE TV Revenue [1] (mil. dol.) Basic	PAY TV Units [2] (1,000) Total [3]	PAY TV Units [2] (1,000) Pay cable	PAY TV Monthly rate (dol.) Total pay [3]	PAY TV Monthly rate (dol.) Pay cable	PAY TV Percent of homes passed by cable with pay TV	PAY TV Percent of homes with cable TV with pay TV
1970	5,100	5.50	345	337	(X)	(X)	(X)	(X)	(X)	(X)
1980	17,500	7.69	2,549	1,615	10,389	9,144	9.09	8.80	28	51
1985	35,500	9.73	8,938	4,145	31,063	30,596	10.46	10.42	47	84
1988	44,200	13.86	13,595	7,351	39,127	38,819	10.25	10.18	50	85
1989	47,500	15.21	15,678	8,670	41,234	41,095	10.26	10.21	50	83
1990	50,520	16.78	17,855	10,169	41,656	41,505	10.43	10.38	48	80
1991	52,600	18.10	19,463	11,414	43,314	39,900	10.35	10.27	45	75
1992	54,300	19.08	21,045	12,433	44,714	40,700	10.18	10.06	45	74
1993	56,200	[4]19.39	22,782	13,528	46,397	41,500	9.27	9.11	46	73
1994	58,500	21.62	22,786	15,164	51,000	45,000	[5]8.62	8.37	49	75

X Not applicable.   [1] Includes installation revenue, subscriber revenue, and nonsubscriber revenue.   [2] Individual program services sold to subscribers.   [3] Includes multipoint distribution service (MDS) and satellite TV (STV).   [4] Weighted average representing 8 months of unregulated basic rate and 4 months of FCC rolled-back rate.   [5] Direct broadcast satellite average rate not included.
Source: Paul Kagan Associates Inc., Carmel, CA, The Cable TV Financial Databook, annual, (copyright); The Kagan Census of Cable and Pay TV, 1991, and The Cable TV Investor, June 1995.

No. 892. Cable and Pay TV—Revenue and Expenses: 1990 to 1994

[Based on a sample of taxable employer firms with one or more establishments that are primarily engaged in the dissemination of visual and textual television programs on a subscription or fee basis. For SIC 4841. Based on the 1987 Standard Industrial Classification code; see text, section 13]

ITEM	TOTAL (mil. dol.) 1990	TOTAL (mil. dol.) 1991	TOTAL (mil. dol.) 1992	TOTAL (mil. dol.) 1993	TOTAL (mil. dol.) 1994	PERCENT DISTRIBUTION 1990	PERCENT DISTRIBUTION 1993	PERCENT DISTRIBUTION 1994
Revenue	22,165	23,895	26,653	29,333	30,563	100.0	100.0	100.0
Advertising	1,882	2,100	2,491	2,873	3,353	8.5	9.8	11.0
Program revenue	3,816	4,112	4,423	4,868	5,626	17.2	16.6	18.4
Basic service	10,933	11,985	13,532	14,851	14,477	49.3	50.6	47.3
Pay-per-view and other premium service	4,351	4,465	4,708	5,190	5,346	19.6	17.7	17.5
Installation fees	302	324	390	436	469	1.4	1.5	1.6
Other cable and pay TV revenue	881	909	1,109	1,115	1,292	4.0	3.8	4.2
Operating expenses	19,354	20,154	21,232	22,852	23,915	100.0	100.0	100.0
Annual payroll	2,816	2,973	3,533	3,861	4,011	14.5	16.9	16.8
Employer contributions to Social Security and other supplemental benefits	588	667	801	886	957	3.0	3.9	4.0
Program and production costs [1]	5,926	6,317	6,763	7,447	7,926	30.6	32.6	33.1
Depreciation	3,611	3,634	3,704	3,917	4,087	18.7	17.1	17.1
Lease and rental payments	513	516	589	633	652	2.7	2.8	2.7
Purchased repairs	343	341	373	406	399	1.8	1.8	1.7
Insurance	110	115	145	166	167	0.6	0.7	0.7
Telephone, other purchased communications	133	139	158	180	200	0.7	0.8	0.8
Purchased utilities	188	201	220	241	255	1.0	1.1	1.1
Purchased advertising	467	472	537	588	683	2.4	2.6	2.9
Taxes	310	332	408	437	454	1.6	1.9	1.9
Other operating expenses	4,349	4,447	4,001	4,090	4,124	22.5	17.9	17.2

[1] Includes costs from basic cable, pay-per-view, premium services, in-house programs, and other program and production costs.
Source: U.S. Bureau of the Census, Annual Survey of Communication Services: 1994, (BC/94).

No. 893. Microcomputer Software Sales: 1994 and 1995

[**In millions of dollars**. Estimated North American retail sales. Figures may not add to totals because individual applications and totals are derived independently]

APPLICATION	1994					1995				
	Total	PC/ MS-DOS	Win- dows	Macin- tosh	Other	Total	PC/ MS-DOS	Win- dows	Macin- tosh	Other
Total	6,717.8	1,132.5	4,441.2	1,225.1	103.8	7,525.3	717.4	5,654.3	1,054.7	98.9
Entertainment	454.8	182.1	190.6	82.0	(B)	649.1	288.0	274.2	86.9	(B)
Home education.	566.2	171.7	324.4	116.3	8.4	571.6	36.3	423.6	108.9	2.9
Finance	398.5	116.2	233.6	46.5	(B)	427.7	82.3	294.8	50.7	(B)
Word processors	1,029.3	95.3	826.9	94.0	13.1	1,085.7	25.5	987.3	63.5	9.3
Spreadsheets	829.2	62.2	689.3	69.0	8.7	865.2	12.3	803.4	46.8	2.8
Databases	350.1	29.6	279.5	41.1	1.3	340.4	9.2	305.3	25.1	(B)
Integrated	130.2	6.8	75.1	48.4	(B)	132.1	2.1	84.7	45.3	(B)
Utilities	326.6	104.1	154.7	50.5	15.3	452.4	76.2	297.9	51.6	26.7
Presentation graphic	314.2	9.5	258.7	45.0	1.0	347.1	1.5	315.0	29.9	(B)
Drawing and painting . . .	364.3	(B)	119.6	209.9	10.6	317.0	(B)	150.5	159.0	7.5
Desktop publishing	195.5	(B)	123.2	72.2	(B)	262.0	(B)	179.4	82.6	(B)
Other graphics	313.2	38.0	211.3	67.6	1.3	364.1	17.2	278.3	68.2	(B)
Project management	172.1	18.6	135.4	14.0	(B)	188.7	7.6	164.2	16.8	(B)
Personal info. manager . .	163.9	4.4	135.9	23.4	(B)	232.6	1.0	204.0	27.3	(B)
Languages and tools . . .	176.9	17.1	143.4	13.7	2.9	249.3	8.6	231.6	8.0	1.2
Other productivity	816.9	160.7	458.1	174.3	36.0	1,040.3	149.5	660.1	184.1	46.5

B Base figure too small to meet statistical standards for reliability of a derived figure.

Source: Software Publishers Association, Washington, DC, *SPA Software Sales Report,* News Release, April 19, 1996.

No. 894. Recording Media—Manufacturers' Shipments and Value: 1975 to 1994

[Domestic shipments based on reports of manufacturers representing more than 85 percent of the market. Domestic value data based on list prices of records and other media]

YEAR	UNIT SHIPMENTS [1] (mil.)					MANUFACTURES' VALUE (mil. dol.)				
	Vinyl singles	Albums- LP's/EP's	CD's	Cassettes	Cassette singles	Vinyl singles	Albums- LP's/EP's	CD's	Cassettes	Cassette singles
1975 . . .	164.0	257.0	(X)	16.2	(X)	211.5	1,485.0	(X)	98.8	(X)
1980 . . .	164.3	322.8	(X)	110.2	(X)	269.3	2,290.3	(X)	776.4	(X)
1984 . . .	131.5	204.6	5.8	332.0	(X)	298.7	1,548.8	103.3	2,383.9	(X)
1985 . . .	120.7	167.0	22.6	339.1	(X)	281.0	1,280.5	389.5	2,411.5	(X)
1986 . . .	93.9	125.2	53.0	344.5	(X)	228.1	983.0	930.1	2,499.5	(X)
1987 . . .	82.0	107.0	102.1	410.0	[2]5.1	203.3	793.1	1,593.6	2,959.7	[2]14.3
1988 . . .	65.6	72.4	149.7	450.1	22.5	180.4	532.2	2,089.9	3,385.1	57.3
1989 . . .	36.6	34.6	207.2	446.2	76.2	116.4	220.3	2,587.7	3,345.8	194.6
1990 . . .	27.6	11.7	286.5	442.2	87.4	94.4	86.5	3,451.6	3,472.4	257.9
1991 . . .	22.0	4.8	333.3	360.1	69.0	63.9	29.4	4,337.7	3,019.6	230.4
1992 . . .	19.8	2.3	407.5	336.4	84.6	66.4	13.5	5,326.5	3,116.3	298.8
1993 . . .	15.1	1.2	495.4	339.5	85.6	51.2	10.6	6,511.4	2,915.8	298.5
1994 . . .	11.7	1.9	662.1	345.4	81.1	47.2	17.8	8,464.5	2,976.4	274.9

X Not applicable.   [1] Net units, after returns.   [2] Represents 6 months of sales.

Source: Recording Industry Association of America, Washington, DC, *Inside the Recording Industry: A Statistical Overview- 1994 Update.*

No. 895. Publishing Industry—Summary: 1987 to 1994

[**In millions of dollars,** except as noted. Number in parentheses represents Standard Industrial Classification code; see text, section 13]

ITEM	NEWSPAPERS (SIC 2711)			PERIODICALS (SIC 2721)			BOOKS (SIC 2731)		
	1987	1992	1994	1987	1992	1994	1987	1992	1994
Establishments	9,091	8,679	(NA)	4,020	4,699	(NA)	2,298	2,644	(NA)
With 20 or more employees	2,617	2,629	(NA)	876	991	(NA)	424	500	(NA)
Employees [1] (1,000)	435	417	410	110	116	116	70	80	87
Payroll	9,025	10,506	10,585	2,983	4,075	4,274	1,860	2,676	2,936
Value of receipts	31,849	34,124	35,837	17,329	22,034	21,723	12,620	16,731	19,419
Cost of materials	7,533	6,874	7,018	5,873	6,201	5,903	3,663	5,338	5,827
Value added [2]	24,311	27,247	28,818	11,452	15,833	15,821	9,111	11,494	13,681
New capital expends.	1,523	1,667	1,330	246	234	307	240	327	283
Fixed assets, gross assets	14,028	20,042	(NA)	2,528	2,769	(NA)	1,680	2,402	(NA)
Inventories, Dec. 31	857	767	759	902	1,067	1,095	2,091	2,944	3,027

NA Not available.   [1] Represents the average number of production workers plus the number of other employees in mid-March.   [2] By manufacture, derived by subtracting the cost of materials, supplies, containers, fuel, purchased electricity, and contract work from the value of shipments. This result is then adjusted by the addition of value added by merchandising operations, plus the net change in finished goods and work-in-process inventories between the beginning and the end of the year.

Source: U.S. Bureau of the Census, *1992 Census of Manufactures,* Industry Reports, series MC92-I-27A (P) and *Annual Survey of Manufactures.*

No. 896. Newspapers and Periodicals—Number, by Type: 1980 to 1995

[Data refer to year of compilation of the Directory cited as the source, i.e., generally to year preceding year shown. See also *Historical Statistics, Colonial Times to 1970*, series R 232-243]

TYPE	1980	1985	1987	1988	1989	1990	1991	1992	1993	1994	1995
Newspapers [1] . .	9,620	9,134	9,031	10,088	10,457	11,471	11,689	11,339	12,597	12,513	12,246
Semiweekly.	537	517	510	555	567	579	574	562	639	661	705
Weekly.	7,159	6,811	6,750	7,438	7,622	8,420	8,546	8,293	9,177	9,067	9,011
Daily	1,744	1,701	1,646	1,745	1,773	1,788	1,781	1,755	1,850	1,831	1,710
Periodicals [1] . . .	10,236	11,090	11,593	11,229	11,556	11,092	11,239	11,143	11,863	12,136	11,179
Weekly. . . . , ...	1,716	1,367	1,400	880	828	553	511	466	485	487	513
Semimonthly [2].	645	801	858	619	622	435	412	371	199	209	216
Monthly	3,985	4,088	4,031	4,192	4,445	4,239	4,340	4,326	4,545	4,494	4,067
Bimonthly	1,114	1,361	1,402	1,558	1,880	2,087	2,116	2,143	2,359	2,475	2,568
Quarterly	1,444	1,759	1,984	2,245	2,513	2,758	2,861	3,024	3,199	3,370	3,621

[1] Includes other items not shown separately.   [2] Includes fortnightly (every 2 weeks).

Source: Gale Research Inc., *1995 Gale Directory of Publications and Broadcast Media*, 127th edition; and earlier editions (copyright).

No. 897. Daily and Sunday Newspapers—Number and Circulation: 1970 to 1995

[Number of newspapers as of **February 1** the following year. Circulation figures as of **September 30** of year shown. For English language newspapers only. See also *Historical Statistics, Colonial Times to 1970*, series R 224-231]

TYPE	1970	1975	1980	1985	1987	1988	1989	1990	1991	1992	1993	1994	1995
NUMBER													
Daily: Total [1]	1,748	1,756	1,745	1,676	1,645	1,642	1,626	1,611	1,586	1,570	1,556	1,548	1,533
Morning	334	339	387	482	511	529	530	559	571	596	623	635	656
Evening	1,429	1,436	1,388	1,220	1,166	1,141	1,125	1,084	1,042	996	954	935	891
Sunday	586	639	736	798	820	840	847	863	875	891	884	886	888
CIRCULATION (mil.)													
Daily: Total [1]	62.1	60.7	62.2	62.8	62.8	62.7	62.6	62.3	60.7	60.1	59.8	59.3	58.2
Morning	25.9	25.5	29.4	36.4	39.1	40.5	40.7	41.3	41.5	42.4	43.1	43.4	44.3
Evening	36.2	35.2	32.8	26.4	23.7	22.2	21.9	21.0	19.2	17.8	16.7	15.9	13.9
Sunday	49.2	51.1	54.7	58.8	60.1	61.5	62.0	62.6	62.1	62.2	62.6	62.3	61.2
PER CAPITA CIRCULATION [2]													
Daily: Total [1]	0.30	0.28	0.27	0.26	0.26	0.26	0.25	0.25	0.24	0.24	0.23	0.23	0.22
Morning	0.13	0.12	0.13	0.15	0.16	0.17	0.16	0.17	0.16	0.17	0.17	0.17	0.17
Evening	0.18	0.16	0.14	0.11	0.10	0.09	0.09	0.08	0.08	0.07	0.06	0.06	0.05
Sunday	0.24	0.24	0.24	0.25	0.25	0.25	0.25	0.25	0.25	0.24	0.24	0.24	0.23

[1] All-day newspapers are counted in both morning and evening columns but only once in total. Circulation is divided equally between morning and evening.   [2] Based on U.S. Bureau of the Census estimated resident population as of July 1.

Source: Editor & Publisher Co., New York, NY, *Editor & Publisher International Year Book*, annual (copyright).

No. 898. Daily Newspapers—Number and Circulation, by Size of City: 1980 to 1995

[Number of newspapers as of **February 1** the following year. Circulation as of **September 30** of year shown. For English language newspapers only. See table 45 for number of cities by population size. All-day newspapers are counted in both morning and evening columns; circulation is divided equally between morning and evening]

TYPE OF DAILY AND POPULATION-SIZE CLASS	NUMBER					NET PAID CIRCULATION (1,000)				
	1980	1985	1990	1994	1995	1980	1985	1990	1994	1995
Morning dailies, total . .	**387**	**482**	**559**	**635**	**654**	**29,413**	**36,361**	**41,311**	**43,382**	**44,310**
In cities of—										
1,000,001 or more	20	22	18	27	25	8,795	9,367	6,508	10,144	10,173
500,001 to 1,000,000.	27	24	22	23	22	5,705	6,897	4,804	5,174	5,587
100,001 to 500,000.	99	121	138	153	153	8,996	12,197	20,051	17,210	17,214
50,001 to 100,000.	75	87	100	134	138	2,973	3,653	4,373	5,520	5,602
25,001 to 50,000	64	83	102	106	115	1,701	2,145	3,209	2,935	3,150
Less than 25,000	102	145	179	192	201	1,243	2,099	2,365	2,399	2,584
Evening dailies, total . .	**1,388**	**1,220**	**1,084**	**935**	**893**	**32,788**	**26,407**	**21,017**	**15,924**	**13,883**
In cities of—										
1,000,001 or more	11	8	7	8	3	2,984	2,169	1,423	791	390
500,001 to 1,000,000.	23	14	12	10	7	4,101	1,626	1,350	1,479	1,017
100,001 to 500,000.	123	102	71	48	45	8,178	6,987	4,687	2,929	2,529
50,001 to 100,000.	156	127	94	81	72	4,896	3,942	2,941	2,273	2,029
25,001 to 50,000	246	229	204	166	158	5,106	4,606	4,278	2,979	2,819
Less than 25,000	829	740	696	622	608	7,523	7,075	6,338	5,473	5,099

Source: Editor & Publisher Co., New York, NY, *Editor & Publisher International Year Book*, annual (copyright).

No. 899. Daily and Sunday Newspapers—Number and Circulation, by State: 1995

[Number of newspapers as of February 1 the following year. Circulation as of September 30 of the year shown. For English language newspapers only. New York, Massachusetts, and Virginia Sunday newspapers include national circulation]

STATE	DAILY Num-ber	DAILY Circulation [1] Net paid (1,000)	DAILY Circulation [1] Per capita [2]	SUNDAY Num-ber	SUNDAY Net paid circulation [1] (1,000)	STATE	DAILY Num-ber	DAILY Circulation [1] Net paid (1,000)	DAILY Circulation [1] Per capita [2]	SUNDAY Num-ber	SUNDAY Net paid circulation [1] (1,000)
U.S. ...	1,533	58,193	0.22	888	61,229	MO	44	1,008	0.19	23	1,330
AL	26	743	0.17	18	754	MT	11	196	0.23	7	202
AK	7	113	0.18	4	129	NE	17	470	0.29	6	443
AZ	22	781	0.18	16	917	NV	9	286	0.20	4	317
AR	31	478	0.19	16	530	NH	12	237	0.19	6	200
CA	98	6,094	0.18	62	6,416	NJ	20	1,481	0.18	16	1,776
CO	30	1,057	0.28	11	1,254	NM	18	300	0.17	13	300
CT	18	794	0.23	11	831	NY	69	6,576	0.35	44	5,440
DE	3	150	0.21	2	184	NC	50	1,395	0.19	38	1,518
DC	2	895	1.47	2	1,193	ND	10	181	0.28	7	185
FL	40	3,123	0.21	35	3,972	OH	84	2,621	0.24	37	2,878
GA	35	1,069	0.15	19	1,294	OK	46	696	0.21	39	858
HI	6	239	0.19	5	261	OR	19	683	0.22	10	716
ID	12	225	0.20	8	241	PA	87	2,978	0.24	40	3,331
IL	68	2,487	0.21	31	2,665	RI	6	262	0.25	3	295
IN	71	1,452	0.25	21	1,344	SC	15	639	0.17	14	758
IA	38	677	0.25	12	711	SD	11	167	0.24	4	139
KS	47	491	0.19	15	449	TN	27	906	0.17	16	1,107
KY	23	643	0.17	12	679	TX	89	2,986	0.16	85	4,040
LA	26	750	0.17	21	849	UT	6	317	0.17	6	361
ME	7	258	0.20	4	223	VT	8	129	0.21	3	106
MD	14	647	0.12	7	682	VA	28	2,603	0.39	15	1,010
MA	36	1,825	0.29	14	1,450	WA	24	1,204	0.23	16	1,286
MI	50	2,066	0.21	27	2,366	WV	22	396	0.22	11	402
MN	25	922	0.20	14	1,185	WI	35	1,006	0.20	18	1,190
MS	22	403	0.15	16	396	WY	9	89	0.19	4	66

[1] Circulation figures based on the principal community served by a newspaper which is not necessarily the same location as the publisher's office.   [2] Per capita based on estimated resident population as of July 1.

Source: Editor & Publisher Co., New York, NY, *Editor & Publisher International Year Book*, annual (copyright).

No. 900. New Books and Editions Published and Imports, by Subject: 1980 to 1992

[Covers listings in Bowker's Weekly Record in year shown, plus titles issued in that year which were listed in following 6 months. Comprises new books (published for first time) and new editions (with changes in text or format). Excludes government publications; books sold only by subscription; dissertations; periodicals and quarterlies; and pamphlets under 49 pages. See also *Historical Statistics, Colonial Times to 1970*, series R 191-216]

SUBJECT	NEW BOOKS AND NEW EDITIONS 1980	1985	1989	1990	1991	1992	IMPORTS 1980	1985	1989	1990	1991	1992
Total [1]	42,377	50,070	53,446	46,738	48,146	49,276	5,390	7,304	7,315	6,414	5,867	6,506
Agriculture	461	536	562	514	523	565	104	118	104	86	81	93
Art	1,691	1,545	1,569	1,262	1,283	1,392	157	166	128	94	101	156
Biography	1,891	1,953	2,193	1,957	2,120	2,007	126	216	144	115	124	124
Business	1,185	1,518	1,569	1,191	1,421	1,367	74	196	152	134	140	126
Education	1,011	1,085	1,054	1,039	1,129	1,184	133	211	233	234	176	232
Fiction	2,835	5,105	5,941	5,764	5,424	5,690	71	171	119	166	250	246
General works	1,643	2,905	2,332	1,760	1,886	2,153	132	329	322	266	252	313
History	2,220	2,327	2,563	2,243	2,331	2,322	296	395	376	329	314	348
Home economics	879	1,228	949	758	789	826	40	41	31	19	23	25
Juvenile	2,859	3,801	5,413	5,172	5,111	5,144	58	92	101	103	69	50
Language	529	632	586	649	566	617	134	216	182	202	171	164
Law	1,102	1,349	1,096	896	1,177	1,063	112	170	156	138	171	197
Literature	1,686	1,964	2,298	2,049	2,087	2,227	183	267	275	242	196	274
Medicine	3,292	3,579	3,447	3,014	3,027	3,234	671	598	712	588	447	514
Music	357	364	375	289	300	346	35	70	78	52	71	69
Philosophy, psychology	1,429	1,559	2,058	1,683	1,766	1,806	218	267	348	284	256	291
Poetry and drama	1,179	1,166	1,128	874	890	899	120	220	147	119	115	136
Religion	2,055	2,564	2,586	2,285	2,389	2,540	94	173	173	176	129	165
Science	3,109	3,304	3,288	2,742	2,710	2,729	1,069	1,242	1,187	1,030	795	840
Sociology, economics	7,152	7,441	7,971	7,042	7,241	7,432	1,050	1,559	1,575	1,368	1,278	1,521
Sports, recreation	971	1,154	1,077	973	1,063	1,113	85	107	94	75	93	112
Technology	2,337	2,526	2,690	2,092	2,421	2,152	373	419	638	546	558	458
Travel	504	465	701	495	492	468	55	61	39	48	57	52

[1] Increase in new books and editions after 1980 is due largely to a major improvement in the recording of paperbound books.

Source: R. R. Bowker Co., New York, NY, *Publishers Weekly*. (Copyright by Reed Publishing USA.)

No. 901. Books—Average Retail Prices: 1980 to 1993

[In dollars. Covers listings in Bowker's Weekly Record in year shown, plus titles issued in that year which were listed in following 6 months. Comprises new books (published for first time) and new editions (with changes in text or format). See also *Historical Statistics, Colonial Times to 1970*, series R 191-216. For definition of mean see Guide to Tabular Presentation]

SUBJECT	1980	1985	1987	1988	1989	1990	1991	1992	1993, prel.
Hardcover [1]	24.64	31.46	36.29	39.00	40.61	42.12	44.17	45.05	43.26
Agriculture	27.55	36.77	46.25	49.36	51.17	54.24	57.73	53.76	57.15
Art	27.70	35.15	37.72	39.96	50.30	42.18	44.99	44.59	46.29
Biography	19.77	22.20	25.05	25.99	27.34	29.58	27.52	30.41	30.38
Business	22.45	28.84	33.31	37.51	37.94	45.48	43.38	43.91	42.34
Education	17.01	27.28	31.59	33.55	37.62	38.72	41.26	48.77	42.02
Fiction	12.46	15.29	18.20	17.63	18.69	19.83	21.30	20.39	20.35
General works	29.84	37.91	43.82	50.35	49.73	54.77	51.74	56.29	53.58
History	22.78	27.02	31.74	33.44	37.95	36.43	39.87	39.19	40.69
Home economics	13.31	17.50	20.14	21.38	22.17	23.80	24.23	24.88	20.70
Juvenile	8.16	9.95	11.48	11.79	13.01	13.01	16.64	14.46	14.30
Language	22.16	28.68	37.80	40.42	47.35	42.98	51.71	49.68	60.87
Law	33.25	41.70	49.65	50.85	58.62	60.78	64.89	76.21	70.70
Literature	18.70	24.53	28.70	30.85	32.74	35.80	36.76	39.23	38.58
Medicine	34.28	44.36	57.68	66.59	69.87	72.24	71.44	75.22	75.17
Music	21.79	28.79	35.83	36.95	41.73	41.86	41.04	47.37	41.65
Philosophy, psychology	21.70	28.11	33.33	34.75	36.55	40.58	42.74	46.85	44.91
Poetry and drama	17.85	22.14	28.59	28.02	31.12	32.19	33.29	36.76	38.11
Religion	17.61	19.13	24.52	26.73	28.12	31.31	32.33	35.31	32.22
Science	37.45	51.19	62.16	66.91	68.90	74.39	80.14	81.95	79.39
Sociology, economics	31.76	33.33	34.39	37.25	41.26	42.10	48.43	45.53	46.46
Sports, recreation	15.92	23.43	23.96	27.33	29.42	30.52	30.68	34.62	33.42
Technology	33.64	50.37	60.24	65.26	71.04	76.80	76.40	82.18	78.40
Travel	16.80	24.66	28.08	26.22	31.37	30.41	32.43	33.28	28.51
Paperbacks:									
Mass market [2]	(NA)	3.63	4.00	4.54	4.32	4.57	5.08	5.22	5.70
Trade	8.60	13.98	14.56	15.01	17.16	17.45	18.40	18.81	19.24

NA Not available.   [1] Excludes publications of the United States and other governmental units, books sold only by subscription, and dissertations.   [2] "Pocket-sized" books sold primarily through magazine and news outlets, supermarkets, variety stores, etc.

Source: R. R. Bowker Co., New York, NY, *Publishers Weekly*, March 1994 and *Bowker Annual: Library and Book Trade Almanac*. (Copyright by Reed Publishing USA.)

No. 902. Periodicals—Average Retail Prices: 1991 to 1995

[In dollars]

SUBJECT	1991	1992	1993	1994	1995
Agriculture	221.06	233.13	270.85	284.78	316.45
Anthropology	109.01	118.80	127.57	139.65	156.45
Art and architecture	85.89	91.91	98.61	99.54	104.93
Astronomy	542.66	600.12	740.86	686.52	771.32
Biology	462.61	487.11	561.74	579.79	646.96
Botany	346.43	364.98	438.66	444.69	503.20
Business and economics	159.76	174.88	198.60	213.44	247.35
Chemistry	678.57	806.66	916.54	923.42	1,020.00
Education	97.53	104.42	121.99	127.35	138.91
Engineering and technology	384.37	440.82	492.86	534.42	585.37
Food science	297.32	320.19	375.80	387.76	424.35
General science	234.29	264.80	318.35	341.36	382.69
General works	57.66	61.32	65.80	65.71	69.98
Geography	194.15	221.62	242.65	265.00	290.46
Geology	321.57	356.17	407.51	420.31	467.71
Health sciences	281.40	307.53	345.57	361.87	401.28
History	62.41	68.72	73.04	78.04	85.49
Language and literature	59.00	62.52	67.39	68.89	77.00
Law	71.15	79.68	88.49	90.38	97.33
Library and information science	117.35	132.33	142.50	150.53	167.69
Math and computer science	433.92	473.07	527.78	582.64	637.36
Military and naval science	78.5	90.75	103.63	117.13	136.75
Music	45.66	49.77	54.22	54.24	58.87
Philosophy and religion	72.16	75.47	86.18	87.33	97.54
Physics	744.92	846.84	987.04	1,009.56	1,126.50
Political science	96.85	104.12	118.91	124.93	141.20
Psychology	125.00	140.30	154.36	169.84	189.99
Recreation	59.54	70.05	74.47	80.07	82.62
Sociology	120.58	133.34	146.81	156.13	173.09
Technology	355.94	385.94	436.48	479.57	536.64
Zoology	342.36	367.65	419.29	441.85	498.36

Source: Library Journal, New York, NY, *Library Journal*, April 15, 1995, and earlier issues. (Copyright by Reed Publishing USA.)

No. 903. U.S. Postal Service—Summary: 1980 to 1995

[**Employees in thousands; revenue and expenditures in millions of dollars,** except as indicated. **For fiscal years;** see text, section 9. Includes Puerto Rico and all outlying areas. See text, section 18. See also *Historical Statistics, Colonial Times to 1970,* series R 163-171]

ITEM	1980	1985	1989	1990	1991	1992	1993	1994	1995
Number of post offices	30,326	29,557	29,083	28,959	28,912	28,837	28,728	28,657	28,392
Pieces of mail handled (bil.)	106.3	140.1	161.6	166.3	165.9	166.4	171.2	178.0	180.7
First-class, number (bil.) [1]	60.3	72.4	85.9	89.3	90.3	90.8	92.2	95.3	96.4
Percent	56.7	51.7	53.2	53.7	54.4	54.5	53.8	53.3	53.3
Second class (bil.)	8.4	10.4	10.5	10.7	10.4	10.3	10.3	10.2	10.2
Employees, total	**667**	**744**	**817**	**819**	**808**	**819**	**818**	**852**	**875**
Regular	536	586	764	757	746	725	692	729	753
Postmasters.	29	28	27	27	27	26	25	27	27
Office supervisors and tech. personnel . .	36	46	55	53	54	54	42	46	46
Office clerks and mail handlers [2]	229	249	345	333	324	318	308	320	331
City carriers and vehicle drivers.	160	179	243	240	235	232	221	238	249
Rural carriers	33	35	41	42	43	43	44	45	46
Other	49	48	54	62	64	52	52	53	55
Substitute (part-time).	130	159	53	62	62	84	84	86	90
Transitional	(X)	(X)	(X)	(X)	(X)	10	42	38	32
Compensation and employee benefits (mil. dol.)	16,541	24,349	32,368	34,214	36,076	37,122	38,447	39,609	41,931
Avg. salary per employee (dol.) [3]	24,799	29,621	35,045	37,570	39,597	41,509	42,711	44,342	45,001
Pieces of mail per employee, avg	159	188	198	203	205	203	209	209	207
Total revenue [4]	**19,106**	**28,956**	**38,920**	**40,074**	**44,202**	**47,105**	**47,986**	**49,576**	**54,509**
Operating postal revenue.	17,143	27,736	37,979	39,201	43,323	46,151	47,418	49,252	54,176
Stamps, postal cards, etc	4,287	6,520	8,381	8,638	9,148	10,071	10,357	10,851	11,846
Second-class postage paid in money (pound rates) [5]	881	1,339	1,519	1,509	1,668	1,751	1,740	1,757	1,971
Other postage paid under permit and meter	10,828	17,747	24,534	25,311	28,019	29,777	30,621	32,079	35,023
Box rents	160	230	362	394	413	457	481	489	532
Miscellaneous	892	1,774	2,959	3,124	3,877	3,941	4,053	4,246	4,635
Money-order revenues.	95	126	148	154	148	154	166	154	169
Government appropriations	1,610	970	436	453	562	545	164	131	117
Percent of total revenue.	8.4	3.3	1.1	1.1	1.3	1.2	0.3	0.3	0.2
Investment income, net	353	250	504	420	317	409	404	193	216
Mail and service:									
First-class mail [1]	10,146	16,740	23,234	24,023	26,649	28,296	28,828	29,377	31,955
Priority mail [6]	612	960	1,416	1,555	1,765	2,070	2,300	2,653	3,075
Second-class publishers' mail [7]	864	1,093	1,519	1,509	1,668	1,751	1,740	1,757	1,972
Third-class mail [8]	2,412	4,887	7,924	8,082	8,956	9,490	9,817	10,514	11,791
Bulk rate	2,168	4,697	7,668	7,844	8,699	9,209	9,553	10,242	11,550
Single piece rate and fees.	244	190	256	238	257	281	264	272	241
Fourth-class mail [9]	805	763	908	920	1,001	1,186	1,183	1,353	1,525
Zone rate mail (parcels, catalogs, etc.)	500	524	612	655	721	873	882	1,019	1,115
Special fourth-class rate	272	199	235	215	234	266	257	292	360
Library rate and fees	33	40	61	50	46	48	44	42	50
Government mail [10]	745	934	(NA)	(NA)	(NA)	(NA)	(NA)	(NA)	(NA)
International mail [11]	596	882	1,081	1,163	1,206	1,276	1,407	1,412	1,459
Special services	518	918	1,314	1,310	1,403	1,434	1,509	1,513	1,687
Express mail	184	544	572	631	668	639	627	671	711
Mailgrams	15	15	10	8	7	8	7	2	2
Other [12]	2,205	1,220	938	873	879	955	568	323	332
Expenditures [13]	**19,412**	**29,207**	**38,370**	**40,490**	**43,291**	**45,653**	**46,322**	**48,455**	**50,730**

NA Not available.　X Not applicable.　[1] Items mailed at 1st-class rates and weighing 12 ounces or less.　[2] Includes mobile unit employees.　[3] Beginning 1985, for career bargaining unit employees. Includes fringe benefits.　[4] Net revenues after refunds of postage. Includes operating reimbursements, embossed envelope purchases, indemnity claims, and miscellaneous revenue and expenditure offsets. Shown in year which gave rise to the earnings.　[5] Includes controlled circulation publications.　[6] Items otherwise qualified as 1st-class or airmail that exceeds 12 ounces and 8 ounces, respectively.　[7] Includes mail paid at other than bulk rates. Publishers' mail includes printed publications periodically issued and mailed at a known post office to paid subscribers, such as regular rate newspapers and magazines, and classroom and nonprofit rate publications. See source for further detail.　[8] Items less than 16 ounces in weight not mailed at either 1st- or 2d-class rates.　[9] Items not mailed at 1st-, 2d-, or 3d-class rates, except government and international mail. May include parcel post, catalogs weighing 16 ounces or more, books, films, and records.　[10] Penalty and franked. Beginning in 1988 penalty and franked mail are included in their appropriate classes of mail.　[11] Mail from United States to foreign countries paid at international mail rates.　[12] Consists of unassignable revenues.　[13] Shown in year in which obligation was incurred.

Source: U.S. Postal Service, *Annual Report of the Postmaster General* and *Comprehensive Statement on Postal Operations,* annual; and unpublished data.

No. 904. U.S. Postal Service—Volume of Mail, by Class: 1980 to 1995

[In millions, except per capita. For fiscal years; see text section 9. Includes Puerto Rico and all outlying. For definition of classes of mail, see footnotes, table 903. See also *Historical Statistics, Colonial Times to 1970*, series R 172-186]

CLASS OF MAIL	PIECES OF MAIL					WEIGHT OF MAIL (lbs.)				
	1980	1990	1993	1994	1995	1980	1990	1993	1994	1995
Total	106,311	166,301	171,220	178,039	180,734	12,958	18,826	19,598	21,027	21,926
Domestic.	105,348	165,503	170,313	177,177	179,933	12,742	18,577	19,353	20,787	21,677
1st class and express [1]	60,332	89,343	92,229	95,394	96,357	2,213	3,452	3,733	3,846	3,928
Priority mail.	248	518	664	770	869	591	1,007	1,175	1,333	1,484
2d class	10,221	10,680	10,306	10,228	10,194	3,478	4,233	4,041	4,088	4,211
3d class	30,381	63,725	65,773	69,416	71,112	3,240	7,648	8,007	8,798	9,234
4th class	633	663	744	872	936	2,661	2,109	2,284	2,621	2,709
Penalty.	2,992	(NA)	(NA)	(NA)	(NA)	503	(NA)	(NA)	(NA)	(NA)
US Postal Service and free for blind	540	574	596	499	464	56	127	114	100	112
International.	963	798	907	862	801	216	249	245	240	249
Per capita: [2]										
Total, all domestic mail [3] . .	463	662	656	675	683	56	74	74	79	82
1st class and express. . .	265	354	355	363	366	10	14	14	15	15
2d class	45	43	40	39	39	15	17	16	16	16
3d class.	133	255	253	264	270	14	31	31	33	35
4th class	3	3	3	3	4	12	8	9	10	10

NA Not available.   [1] Includes mailgrams.   [2] 1980 and 1990 based on April 1 population, including Armed Forces abroad; other years based on estimated total population as of July 1, including Armed Forces abroad.   [3] Includes types of mail not shown separately.

Source: U.S. Postal Service, *Annual Report of the Postmaster General;* and unpublished data.

No. 905. U.S. Postal Service Rates for Letters and Post Cards: 1958 to 1995

[Domestic airmail letters, as a separate class of service, discontinued in 1973 at 13 cents per ounce. See also *Historical Statistics Colonial Times to 1970*, series R 188-191]

DATE OF RATE CHANGE	Letters			Postal and post cards	Ex-press mail [1]	DATE OF RATE CHANGE	Letters			Postal and post cards	Ex-press mail [1]
	Each oz.	First oz.	Each added oz.				Each oz.	First oz.	Each added oz.		
1958 (Aug. 1) . .	$0.04	(X)	(X)	$0.03	(X)	1978 (May 29). .	(X)	$0.15	$0.13	$0.10	(X)
1963 (Jan. 7). .	$0.05	(X)	(X)	$0.04	(X)	1981 (Mar. 22). .	(X)	$0.18	$0.17	$0.12	(X)
1968 (Jan. 7). .	$0.06	(X)	(X)	$0.05	(X)	1981 (Nov. 1) . .	(X)	$0.20	$0.17	$0.13	$9.35
1971 (May 16). .	$0.08	(X)	(X)	$0.06	(X)	1985 (Feb.17) . .	(X)	$0.22	$0.17	$0.14	$10.75
1974 (Mar. 2). .	$0.10	(X)	(X)	$0.08	(X)	1988 (Apr. 3). . .	(X)	$0.25	$0.20	$0.15	[3]$12.00
1975 (Sept. 14).	(X)	$0.10	$0.09	$0.07	(X)	1991 (Feb. 3) . .	(X)	$0.29	$0.23	$0.19	[3]$13.95
1975 (Dec. 31) [2].	(X)	$0.13	$0.11	$0.09	(X)	1995 (Jan. 1). . .	(X)	$0.32	$0.23	$0.20	[3]$15.00

X Not applicable.   [1] Post Office to addressee rates. Rates shown are for weights up to 2 pounds, all zones. Beginning Feb. 17, 1985, for weights between 2 and 5 lbs, $12.85 is charged. Prior to Nov. 1, 1981, rate varied by weight and distances. Beginning 1995, price varies by weight, not distance.   [2] As of October 11, 1975, surface mail service upgraded to level of airmail. [3] Over 8 ounces and up to 2 pounds. For 1995, up to 8 oz. is $10.75.

No. 906. International Air Mail Rates From the United States: 1961 to 1995

[Excludes Canada and Mexico. Zones discontinued as of February 1991]

DATE OF RATE CHANGE	ZONE 1 [1]		ZONE 1 [2]		ZONE 1 [3]		Postal and post cards	Aero-grammes
	Each 1/2 oz. up to 2 ozs.	Each added 1/2 oz.	Each 1/2 oz. up to 2 ozs.	Each added 1/2 oz.	Each 1/2 oz. up to 2 ozs.	Each added 1/2 oz.		
1961 (July 1).	$0.13	$0.13	$0.15	$0.15	$0.25	$0.25	$0.11	$0.11
1967 (May 1).	$0.15	$0.15	$0.20	$0.20	$0.25	$0.25	$0.13	$0.13
1971 (July 1).	$0.17	$0.17	$0.21	$0.21	$0.21	$0.21	$0.13	$0.13
1974 (March 2)	$0.21	$0.21	$0.26	$0.21	$0.26	$0.21	$0.18	$0.18
1976 (January 3)	$0.25	$0.21	$0.31	$0.26	$0.31	$0.26	$0.21	$0.22
1981 (January 1)	$0.35	[4]$0.30	$0.40	[5]$0.35	$0.40	[5]$0.35	$0.28	$0.30
1985 (February 17).	$0.39	[6]$0.33	$0.44	[7]$0.39	$0.44	[7]$0.39	$0.33	$0.36
1988 (April 17) [8]	$0.45	$0.42	$0.45	$0.42	$0.45	$0.42	$0.36	$0.39
1991 (February 3) [8] [9]	(X)	(X)	(X)	(X)	(X)	(X)	$0.40	$0.45
1995 (July 9) [10]	(X)	(X)	(X)	(X)	(X)	(X)	$0.50	$0.50

X Not applicable.   [1] Caribbean, Central and South America. The airmail letter rate to South America, 1961 to 1967, was the same as that to Europe. Beginning January 3, 1976, the airmail letter rate to all South American countries except Colombia and Venezuela is the same as Europe; Columbia and Venezuela are included in the first zone.   [2] Europe and Mediterranean Africa. [3] Rest of world.   [4] Up to 32 oz.; 30 cents per additional ounce over 32.   [5] Up to 32 oz.; 35 cents per additional ounce over 32. [6] Up to 32 oz.; 33 cents per additional ounce over 32.   [7] Up to 32 oz.; 39 cents per additional ounce over 32.   [8] Air letters collapsed to a single schedule.   [9] First 1/2 ounce= 50 cents; second 1/2 ounce= 45 cents, 39 cents for each additional 1/2 ounce up to the limit of 64 oz.   [10] First 1/2 ounce= 60 cents; 40 cents for each additional 1/2 ounce up to limit of 64 ounces.

Sources of tables 905 and 906: U.S. Postal Service, *"United States Domestic Postage Rate: Recent History;"* and unpublished data.

No. 907. Advertising—Indexes of National Advertising Expenditures, by Medium: 1980 to 1994

[1982-84=100. Based on the average monthly expenditure for those major media which give national coverage. See also *Historical Statistics, Colonial Times to 1970*, series T 472-484]

MEDIUM	1980	1984	1985	1986	1987	1988	1989	1990	1991	1992	1993	1994
General index	71	115	121	126	132	141	149	157	151	160	165	182
Network television [1]	72	119	119	124	130	142	150	160	160	172	178	194
Spot television	67	112	123	134	140	146	150	159	145	154	159	184
Magazines	73	115	120	124	131	142	156	159	152	163	171	184
Newspapers	71	112	122	123	127	130	135	140	134	131	131	142

[1] Includes the 3 networks, Fox, cable, and syndication.

Source: McCann-Erickson, Inc., New York, NY. Compiled for Crain Communications, Inc. in *Advertising Age* (copyright).

No. 908. Advertising—Estimated Expenditures, by Medium: 1980 to 1995

[In millions of dollars. See text, section 18, for definitions of types of advertising. See also *Historical Statistics, Colonial Times to 1970*, series R 106-109, R 123-126, and T 444-471]

MEDIUM	1980	1985	1988	1989	1990	1991	1992	1993	1994	1995 [1]
Total	53,550	94,750	118,050	123,930	128,640	126,400	131,290	138,080	150,030	161,860
National	29,815	53,355	65,610	68,990	72,780	72,635	76,020	80,010	87,325	94,620
Local	23,735	41,395	52,440	54,940	55,860	53,765	55,270	58,070	62,705	67,240
Newspapers	14,794	25,170	31,197	32,368	32,281	30,409	30,737	32,025	34,356	36,760
National	1,963	3,352	3,586	3,720	3,867	3,685	3,602	3,620	3,906	4,180
Local	12,831	21,818	27,611	28,648	28,414	26,724	27,135	28,405	30,450	32,580
Magazines	3,149	5,155	6,072	6,716	6,803	6,524	7,000	7,357	7,916	8,550
Weeklies	1,418	2,297	2,646	2,813	2,864	2,670	2,739	2,850	3,140	3,420
Women's	782	1,294	1,504	1,710	1,713	1,671	1,853	2,009	2,106	2,270
Monthlies	949	1,564	1,922	2,193	2,226	2,183	2,408	2,498	2,670	2,860
Farm publications	130	186	196	212	215	215	231	243	262	285
Television.	11,469	21,022	25,686	26,891	28,405	27,402	29,409	30,584	34,167	36,680
TV networks [2]	5,130	8,060	9,172	9,110	9,863	9,533	10,249	10,229	10,942	11,490
Cable networks . . .	45	594	942	1,197	1,393	1,521	1,685	1,970	2,321	2,645
Syndication (nat'l) [2] .	50	520	901	1,288	1,109	1,253	1,370	1,576	1,734	1,940
Spot (national).	3,269	6,004	7,147	7,354	7,788	7,110	7,551	7,800	8,993	9,575
Spot (local).	2,967	5,714	7,270	7,612	7,856	7,565	8,079	8,435	9,464	10,175
Cable (non-network).	8	130	254	330	396	420	475	594	713	855
Radio	3,702	6,490	7,798	8,323	8,726	8,476	8,654	9,457	10,529	11,500
Network	183	365	425	476	482	490	424	458	463	510
Spot	779	1,335	1,418	1,547	1,635	1,575	1,505	1,657	1,902	2,090
Local	2,740	4,790	5,955	6,300	6,609	6,411	6,725	7,342	8,164	8,900
Yellow Pages	2,900	5,800	7,781	8,330	8,926	9,182	9,320	9,517	9,825	10,340
National	330	695	944	1,011	1,132	1,162	1,188	1,230	1,314	1,405
Local	2,570	5,105	6,837	7,319	7,794	8,020	8,132	8,287	8,511	8,935
Direct mail	7,596	15,500	21,115	21,945	23,370	24,460	25,391	27,266	29,638	32,600
Business papers	1,674	2,375	2,610	2,763	2,875	2,882	3,090	3,260	3,358	3,560
Outdoor.	578	945	1,064	1,111	1,084	1,077	1,031	1,090	1,167	1,260
Miscellaneous.	7,558	12,107	14,531	15,271	15,955	15,773	16,427	17,281	18,812	20,325

[1] Projected from 4 months of data.   [2] Beginning 1990, Fox included in TV networks, rather than syndication; therefore, data not comparable with previous years.

Source: McCann-Erickson, Inc., New York, NY. Compiled for Crain Communications, Inc. in *Advertising Age* (copyright).

No. 909. Magazine Advertising—Expenditures, by Product: 1980 to 1994

[In millions of dollars. Space cost based on one-time rate; special rates used where applicable. Year-to-year data not strictly comparable, as a few minor publications are added or deleted]

PRODUCT	1980	1985	1988	1989	1990	1991	1992	1993	1994
Total	2,846	4,961	5,943	6,611	6,753	6,608	7,186	7,667	8,505
Apparel, footwear, accessories	112	251	363	396	428	419	496	513	540
Automotive, accessories, equipment . .	230	549	801	881	900	941	1,035	1,064	1,210
Beer, wine, and liquor	239	240	213	255	277	279	247	204	198
Computers, office equipment	79	250	252	284	283	291	354	364	414
Business and consumer services	190	463	466	522	516	453	513	625	657
Drugs and remedies	79	135	145	135	163	167	299	368	434
Food and food products	199	342	377	435	444	437	459	470	511
Household equipment and supplies . . .	65	100	102	104	118	115	161	141	145
Household furnishings	73	87	116	126	116	123	117	146	166
Jewelry, cameras, optical goods	79	101	142	156	157	157	158	168	179
Mail orders/direct response	(NA)	328	467	513	531	574	617	725	832
Publishing and media	146	188	192	191	212	197	202	214	258
Retail	(NA)	121	176	211	255	201	190	219	215
Smoking materials	290	383	352	393	305	265	224	210	285
Toiletries and toilet goods	206	385	554	651	679	640	734	811	853
Travel, hotels, and resorts	123	245	311	374	380	346	350	378	445
Other	736	793	914	984	989	1,005	1,030	1,047	1,163

NA Not available.

Source: Publishers Information Bureau, Inc., New York, NY, as compiled by Competitive Media Reporting.

No. 910. Television—Expenditures for Network Advertising: 1992 to 1994

[In millions of dollars. See text, section 18, for a definition of network advertising]

PRODUCT	1992	1993 [1]	1994 [1]	PRODUCT	1992	1993 [1]	1994 [1]
Total	9,973	10,893	11,893	Home electronics equipment	121	105	150
Apparel, footwear, accessories	305	332	320	Horticulture	26	32	40
Automotive	1,541	1,589	1,696	Household equipment, supplies,			
Beer and wine	313	330	341	and furnishings	307	286	315
Building material, equipment,				Insurance	142	147	141
fixtures	77	64	65	Jewelry, cameras, optical goods	118	116	121
Computers, office equipment,				Laundry soaps, cleansers,			
and stationery	124	150	187	polishes	285	348	280
Confectionery, soft drinks	531	941	679	Movies	236	373	446
Consumer services	501	783	916	Pet products	67	73	75
Department, discount stores	318	308	383	Proprietary medicines	882	957	988
Financial planning services	95	99	97	Publishing and media	56	51	50
Food and food products	1,375	1,306	1,429	Restaurants and drive-ins	601	743	839
Freight, industrial development	91	77	61	Toiletries and toilet goods	937	1,064	1,095
Gas, lubricants, etc.	67	57	77	Toys and sporting goods	157	271	305
Home centers and hardware				Travel, hotels, and resorts	122	97	181
stores	51	58	68	Other	527	136	548

[1] Includes the Fox network.

Source: Television Bureau of Advertising, Inc., New York, NY. Data compiled by Competitive Media Reporting, New York, NY.

No. 911. Television—Estimated Time Charges for Spot Advertising: 1992 to 1994

[In millions of dollars. Data represent activity in the top 75 markets monitored by Competitive Media Reporting, currently covering approximately 382 stations. Beginning 1990, data exclude National Syndicated Activity and therefore are not directly comparable to prior years. See text, section 18, for definitions of types of advertising]

PRODUCT	1992	1993	1994	PRODUCT	1992	1993	1994
Total	5,469	5,619	6,580	Horticulture	40	34	42
				Household equipment,			
Agriculture and farming	12	11	13	supplies, and furnishings	111	139	166
Apparel, footwear, accessories	85	88	84	Insurance	115	135	199
Automotive	1,635	1,820	2,312	Jewelry, cameras, optical			
Beer and wine	201	196	179	goods	25	32	31
Building material, equipment,				Laundry soaps, cleaners,			
fixtures	56	58	60	polishes	110	94	84
Computers, office equipment				Pet products	28	20	29
and stationery	14	16	26	Political, unions, religious	76	46	55
Confectionery, soft drinks	316	308	315	Proprietary medicines	238	177	172
Consumer services	442	498	666	Publishing and media	108	100	95
Food and food products	856	867	963	Toiletries and toilet goods	248	249	276
Freight, industrial development	48	39	34	Toys and sporting goods	245	293	277
Gasoline, lubricants, etc.	134	136	140	Travel, hotels, and resorts	185	140	189
Home electronics equipment	108	83	129	Other	32	40	44

Source: Television Bureau of Advertising, Inc., New York, NY. Data compiled by Competitive Media Reporting, New York, NY, in the top 75 markets.

No. 912. Television—Expenditures for Retail/Local Advertising: 1992 to 1994

[In millions of dollars. See headnote, table 911]

PRODUCT	1992	1993	1994	PRODUCT	1992	1993	1994
Total	5,271	5,566	6,313	Hotels, resorts, U.S.	69	84	86
Amusements, entertainment	144	151	160	Insurance agencies	20	26	31
Appliance stores	203	231	269	Jewelry stores	21	26	27
Auto repair, service stations	83	84	93	Legal services	113	126	129
Auto supply, accessory stores	40	41	62	Leisure time stores and services	147	173	201
Auto, truck dealers	283	338	405	Loan, mortgage companies	38	55	75
Banks, S&L associations	183	187	157	Medical, dental services	141	146	158
Builders, home improvement	24	32	35	Movies	242	296	314
Carpet, floor covering stores	52	58	61	Newspapers	30	29	29
Clothing stores	133	143	163	Office equipment/supply stores	16	18	35
Department stores	213	185	198	Optical services, supplies	56	54	57
Discount department stores	119	119	149	Political	170	69	352
Drug stores	118	101	97	Radio, cable TV	186	192	208
Education services	102	99	105	Realtors, real estate developers	21	25	29
Financial planning services	28	28	25	Rental services (nonauto)	30	28	27
Food stores, supermarkets	316	300	289	Restaurants, drive-ins	892	991	1,075
Furniture stores	268	302	359	Shoe stores	31	33	32
Gas, electric, water companies	41	40	42	Shopping centers	24	28	29
Health clubs, reducing salons	128	140	99	Sport, hobby, toy stores	44	58	64
Home centers and hardware	131	138	172	Other	371	392	415

Source: Television Bureau of Advertising, Inc., New York, NY. Data compiled by Competitive Media Reporting, New York, NY, in the top 75 markets.

Figure 19.1
Energy Supply and Disposition: 1970 to 1994

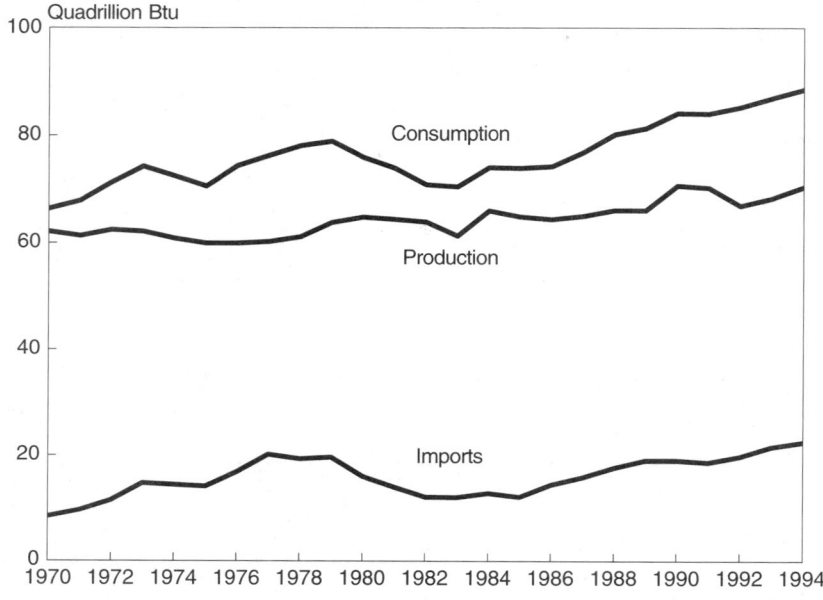

Quadrillion Btu

Source: Chart prepared by U.S. Bureau of the Census. For data, see table 913.

Figure 19.2
**Commercial Nuclear Power Generation—
Top 10 Countries: 1993**

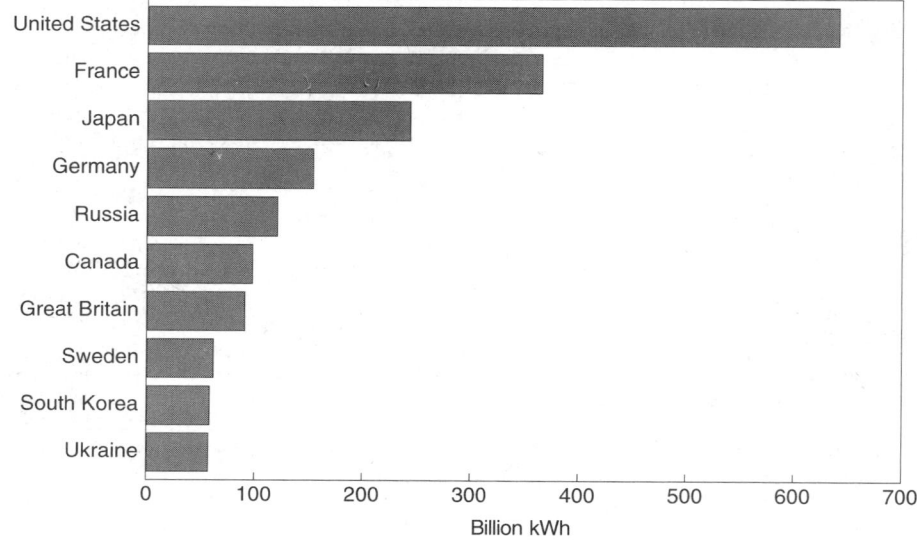

Billion kWh

Source: Chart prepared by U.S. Bureau of the Census. For data, see table 945.

This section presents statistics on fuel resources, energy production and consumption, electric energy, hydroelectric power, nuclear power, solar energy, wood energy and the electric and gas utility industries. The principal sources are the U.S. Department of Energy's Energy Information Administration (EIA), the Edison Electric Institute, Washington, DC, and the American Gas Association, Arlington, VA. For additional data on transportation, see section 21; on fuels, see section 24; and on energy-related housing characteristics, see section 25.

The EIA, in its *Annual Energy Review,* provides statistics and trend data on energy supply, demand, and prices. Information is included on petroleum and natural gas, coal, electricity, hydroelectric power, nuclear power, solar, wood, and geothermal energy. Among its annual reports are *Annual Energy Review, Electric Power Annual, Natural Gas Annual, Petroleum Supply Annual, State Energy Data Report, State Energy Price and Expenditure Report, Financial Statistics of Selected Electric Utilities, Performance Profiles of Major Energy Producers, Annual Energy Outlook,* and *International Energy Annual.* These various publications contain State, national, and international data on production of electricity, net summer capability of generating plants, fuels used in energy production, energy sales and consumption, and hydroelectric power. The EIA also issues the *Monthly Energy Review,* which presents current supply, disposition, and price data, and monthly publications on petroleum, coal, natural gas, and electric power. Data on residential energy consumption, expenditures, and conservation activities are available from EIA's Residential Energy Consumption Survey and are published triennially in *Residential Energy Consumption Survey: Consumption and Expenditures,* and *Residential Energy Consumption Survey: Housing Characteristics,* and several other reports.

The Edison Electric Institute's monthly bulletin and annual *Statistical Year Book of the Electric Utility Industry for the Year* contain data on the distribution of electric energy by public utilities; information on the

In Brief

Renewable energy sources provided 6.3 quadrillion Btu's in 1994, which represented 7.1 percent of U.S. consumption.

Crude oil imports surpassed domestic production for the second year in a row in 1995 with 7.2 million barrels per day compared to 6.5 for production.

Net generation of electric energy by utilities reached a record 3.0 trillion kWh in 1995.

electric power supply, expansion of electric generating facilities, and the manufacture of heavy electric power equipment is presented in the annual *Year End Summary of the Electric Power Situation in the United States.* The American Gas Association, in its monthly and quarterly bulletins and its yearbook, *Gas Facts,* presents data on gas utilities, including sales, revenues, customers, prices, and other financial and operating statistics.

Btu conversion factors.—Various energy sources are converted from original units (e.g., short tons, cubic feet, barrels, kilowatt-hours) to the thermal equivalent using British thermal units (Btu). A Btu is the amount of energy required to raise the temperature of 1 pound of water 1 degree Fahrenheit (F) at or near 39.2 degrees F. Factors are calculated annually from the latest final annual data available; some are revised as a result. The following list provides conversion factors used in 1995 for production and consumption, in that order, for various fuels: Petroleum, 5.800 and 5.358 mil. Btu per barrel; total coal, 21.278 and 20.852 mil. Btu per short ton; and natural gas (dry), 1,028 Btu per cubic foot for both. The factors for the production of nuclear power and geothermal power were 10,676 and 20,914 Btu per kilowatt-hour, respectively. The fossil fuel steam-electric power plant generation factor of 10,272 Btu per kilowatt-hour was used for hydroelectric power generation and for wood and waste, wind, photovoltaic, and solar thermal energy consumed at electric utilities.

No. 913. Energy Supply and Disposition, by Type of Fuel: 1970 to 1994

[In quadrillion British thermal units (Btu). For Btu conversion factors, see text, section 19]

TYPE OF FUEL	1970	1973	1975	1980	1985	1988	1989	1990	1991	1992	1993	1994
Production [2]	62.1	62.1	59.9	64.8	64.9	66.1	66.1	[1]70.7	70.3	69.9	68.3	70.4
Crude oil [2]	20.4	19.5	17.7	18.3	19.0	17.3	16.1	15.6	15.7	15.2	14.5	14.0
Natural gas liquids	2.5	2.6	2.4	2.3	2.2	2.3	2.2	2.2	2.3	2.4	2.4	2.4
Natural gas	21.7	22.2	19.6	19.9	17.0	17.6	17.9	18.4	18.2	18.4	18.7	19.4
Coal	14.6	14.0	15.0	18.6	19.3	20.7	21.4	22.5	21.6	21.6	20.2	22.0
Nuclear electric power	0.2	0.9	1.9	2.7	4.2	5.7	5.7	6.2	6.6	6.6	6.5	6.8
Renewable energy	2.6	2.9	3.2	3.0	3.2	2.6	3.0	[1]6.0	6.0	5.8	6.0	5.9
Hydroelectric power	2.6	2.9	3.2	2.9	3.0	2.3	2.8	[3]3.0	3.0	2.6	2.9	2.7
Geothermal	(Z)	(Z)	0.1	0.1	0.2	0.2	0.2	[1]0.3	0.3	0.3	0.3	0.3
Biofuels [4]	(Z)	(Z)	(Z)	(Z)	(Z)	(Z)	(Z)	[1]2.6	2.6	2.8	2.7	2.8
Net trade [5]	-5.7	-12.7	-11.8	-12.3	-7.9	-13.1	-14.2	-14.1	-13.4	-14.4	-17.2	-18.3
Exports	2.7	2.1	2.4	3.7	4.2	4.4	4.8	4.9	5.2	5.0	4.4	4.1
Coal	1.9	1.4	1.8	2.4	2.4	2.5	2.6	2.8	2.9	2.7	2.0	1.9
Natural gas	0.1	0.1	0.1	0.1	0.1	0.1	0.1	0.1	0.1	0.2	0.1	0.2
Petroleum	0.6	0.5	0.4	1.2	1.7	1.7	1.8	1.9	2.1	2.0	2.1	2.0
Imports	8.4	14.7	14.1	16.0	12.1	17.6	19.0	19.0	18.6	19.7	21.5	22.4
Coal	(Z)	(Z)	(Z)	(Z)	0.1	0.1	0.1	0.1	0.1	0.1	0.2	0.2
Natural gas	0.9	1.1	1.0	1.0	1.0	1.3	1.4	1.6	1.8	2.2	2.4	2.6
Petroleum [6]	7.5	13.5	13.0	14.7	10.6	15.8	17.2	17.1	16.3	17.0	18.5	19.0
Consumption [7]	66.4	74.3	70.6	76.0	74.0	80.2	81.3	84.1	84.0	85.2	86.9	88.5
Petroleum [8]	29.5	34.8	32.7	34.2	30.9	34.2	34.2	33.6	32.9	33.5	33.8	34.7
Natural gas [8]	21.8	22.5	20.0	20.4	17.8	18.6	19.4	19.3	19.6	20.1	20.8	21.2
Coal	12.3	13.0	12.7	15.4	17.5	18.8	18.9	19.1	18.8	18.9	19.4	19.5
Nuclear electric power	0.2	0.9	1.9	2.7	4.2	5.7	5.7	6.2	6.6	6.6	6.5	6.8
Renewable energy [9]	2.7	3.1	3.3	3.2	3.6	2.9	3.1	[1]6.0	6.2	6.0	6.3	6.3
Hydroelectric power [9]	2.7	3.0	3.2	3.1	3.4	2.7	2.9	[3]3.0	3.2	2.9	3.2	3.1
Geothermal	(Z)	(Z)	0.1	0.1	0.2	0.2	0.2	[1]0.3	0.2	0.3	0.3	0.3
Biofuels [4]	(Z)	(Z)	(Z)	(Z)	(Z)	(Z)	(Z)	[1]2.6	2.6	2.8	2.7	2.8

Z Less than 50 trillion.   [1] There is a discontinuity in this time series between 1989 and 1990 due to the expanded coverage of non-electric utility use of renewable energy beginning in 1990.   [2] Includes lease condensate.   [3] There is a discontinuity in this time series between 1989 and 1990; beginning in 1990, pumped storage is removed and expanded coverage of industrial use of hydroelectric power is included.   [4] Includes wood, wood waste, peat, wood liquors, railroad ties, pitch, wood sludge, municipal solid waste, agricultural waste, straw, tires, landfill gases, fish oils, and/or other waste.   [5] Exports minus imports.   [6] Includes imports of crude oil for the Strategic Petroleum Reserve, which began in 1977. Includes imports of unfinished oils and natural gas plant liquids.   [7] Petroleum products supplied, including natural gas plant liquids and crude oil burned as fuel.   [8] Includes supplemental gaseous fuels.   [9] Includes net imports of electricity.

Source: U.S. Energy Information Administration, *Annual Energy Review*.

No. 914. Energy Supply and Disposition, by Type of Fuel—Estimates, 1993 to 1995, and Projections, 2000 to 2015

[Quadrillion Btu per year, except percent change. Projections are "reference" or mid-level forecasts. See report for methodology and assumptions used in generating projections]

TYPE OF FUEL	1993	1994	1995	2000	2005	2010	2015
Production, total	69.64	72.08	71.79	71.87	74.50	77.79	81.08
Crude oil and lease condensate	14.50	14.10	13.84	11.96	11.10	11.51	12.30
Natural gas plant liquids	2.49	2.47	2.43	2.54	2.74	2.97	3.20
Natural gas	18.97	19.41	19.47	20.24	21.89	23.52	25.72
Coal	20.23	22.01	21.89	22.59	23.95	24.94	26.14
Nuclear power	6.52	6.84	7.02	7.09	6.93	6.52	4.63
Renewable energy and other [1] [2]	6.94	7.25	7.13	7.45	7.88	8.33	9.09
Imports, total	21.38	22.53	23.25	27.70	30.43	31.65	32.25
Crude oil [3]	14.76	15.33	16.33	19.67	21.13	21.05	20.87
Petroleum products [4]	3.73	3.92	3.53	4.03	5.23	6.16	6.40
Natural gas [5]	2.39	2.60	2.78	3.30	3.48	3.84	4.42
Other imports [5]	0.50	0.67	0.62	0.69	0.59	0.61	0.56
Exports, total	4.23	4.04	4.33	4.56	4.56	4.74	5.38
Petroleum [6]	2.12	2.00	2.28	2.12	1.88	1.77	1.91
Natural gas	0.15	0.16	0.17	0.27	0.31	0.32	0.33
Coal	1.96	1.88	1.88	2.16	2.37	2.66	3.14
Consumption, total [7]	87.38	89.14	90.60	95.07	100.38	104.69	108.02
Petroleum products [7]	33.83	34.56	34.88	36.88	39.12	40.68	41.69
Natural gas	20.80	21.36	21.95	23.00	24.79	26.76	29.52
Coal	19.55	19.65	19.66	20.67	21.83	22.55	23.27
Nuclear power	6.52	6.84	7.02	7.09	6.93	6.52	4.63
Renewable energy/other [1] [8]	6.69	6.73	7.08	7.43	7.71	8.18	8.92

[1] Includes utility and nonutility electricity from hydroelectric, wood and wood waste, municipal solid and wood waste, municipal solid waste, other biomass, wind, photovoltaic and solar thermal sources; nonelectric energy from renewable sources, such as active and passive solar systems, and wood; and both the ethanol and gasoline components of E85, but not the ethanol components of blends less than 85 percent. Excludes nonmarketed blends less than 85 percent. Excludes nonmarketed renewable energy.   [2] Includes liquid hydrogen, methanol, supplemental natural gas, and some domestic inputs to refineries.   [3] Includes imports of crude oil for the Strategic Petroleum Reserve.   [4] Includes imports of finished petroleum products, imports of unfinished oils, alcohols, ethers, and blending components.   [5] Includes coal, coal coke (net), and electricity (net).   [6] Includes crude oil and petroleum products.   [7] Includes natural gas plant liquids, crude oil consumed as a fuel, and nonpetroleum based liquids for blending, such as ethanol.   [8] Includes net electricity imports, methanol, and liquid hydrogen.

Source: U.S. Energy Information Administration, *Annual Energy Outlook 1996*.

No. 915. Selected Energy Indicators—Summary: 1970 to 1995

[Btu=British thermal unit. For Btu conversion factors, see text, section 19. Minus sign (-) indicates decrease]

ITEM	1970	1973	1975	1980	1985	1988	1989	1990	1991	1992	1993	1994	1995
AVERAGE ANNUAL PERCENT CHANGE [1]													
Gross domestic product [2] ...	3.3	1.9	-0.3	-0.1	0.7	1.2	3.3	1.3	-1.0	2.7	2.2	3.4	2.0
Energy production, total [3][4] ..	4.6	-0.2	-1.8	0.3	-0.3	0.6	-	2.6	-0.5	-0.9	-2.6	3.3	0.6
Crude oil [5]	4.2	-0.9	-4.7	0.2	0.2	-0.8	-6.9	-3.4	0.8	-3.1	-4.9	-2.7	-2.0
Natural gas	6.4	-	-6.1	-0.2	-1.2	0.9	1.4	2.8	-0.7	0.8	1.1	3.6	-0.2
Coal.	2.2	-0.2	3.4	1.2	-0.4	1.0	2.9	5.1	-3.9	(Z)	-6.5	8.8	-0.7
Energy consumption, total [3][4] .	4.6	1.4	-2.6	-0.8	-	1.4	1.4	-0.1	-0.2	1.3	2.1	2.1	1.8
Petroleum products	4.8	1.9	-3.1	-1.6	-0.1	1.3	-	-1.9	-2.1	2.1	0.9	2.6	-0.3
Natural gas (dry).	6.5	-0.3	-6.0	-0.3	-0.7	1.5	4.4	-0.5	1.6	2.6	3.4	2.4	4.0
Coal.	1.1	2.4	-1.2	0.5	0.5	1.5	0.4	0.9	-1.7	0.5	2.9	0.6	0.4
PER CAPITA [6] (mil. Btu)													
Energy production	304	294	278	285	273	270	268	272	268	262	253	259	258
Energy consumption	327	351	327	334	311	328	329	326	322	322	325	329	332
Energy consumption per dollar of GDP [2] (1,000 Btu) .	19.6	19.0	18.3	16.5	13.9	13.7	13.4	13.2	13.3	13.2	13.1	13.0	12.9

- Represents zero.   Z Less than .05 percent.   [1] Represents percent change from immediate prior year; for example, 1970, change from 1965. Percent change derived from Btu values.   [2] Gross domestic product in chained (1992) dollars. For definition of chained, see text, section 14.   [3] Includes types of fuel or power, not shown separately.   [4] Due to a lack of consistant historical data, some renewable energy sources are not included.   [5] Includes lease condensate.   [6] Based on resident population estimated as of July 1.

Source: U.S. Energy Information Administration, *Annual Energy Review,* and *Monthly Energy Review.*

No. 916. Energy Consumption, by End-Use Sector: 1970 to 1994

[There exits a discontinuity in the series between 1989 and 1990 due to the expanded coverage of non-lectric utility use of renewable energy beginning 1990. Btu=British thermal units. For Btu conversion factors, see text, section 19]

YEAR	Total consumption (quad. Btu)	Residential and commercial (quad. Btu)	Industrial and miscellaneous (quad. Btu)	Transportation (quad. Btu)	PERCENT OF TOTAL		
					Residential and commercial	Industrial and miscellaneous	Transportation
1970	66.4	21.7	28.6	16.1	32.7	43.1	24.2
1973	74.3	24.1	31.5	18.6	32.5	42.4	25.0
1975	70.6	23.9	28.4	18.3	33.9	40.3	25.9
1976	74.4	25.0	30.2	19.1	33.6	40.7	25.7
1977	76.3	25.4	31.1	19.8	33.3	40.7	26.0
1978	78.1	26.1	31.4	20.6	33.4	40.2	26.4
1979	78.9	25.8	32.6	20.5	32.7	41.3	25.9
1980	76.0	25.7	30.6	19.7	33.8	40.3	25.9
1981	74.0	25.2	29.2	19.5	34.1	39.5	26.4
1982	70.9	25.6	26.1	19.1	36.2	36.9	26.9
1983	70.5	25.6	25.8	19.1	36.3	36.5	27.1
1984	74.1	26.5	27.9	19.8	35.7	37.6	26.7
1985	74.0	26.7	27.2	20.1	36.1	36.8	27.1
1986	74.3	26.9	26.6	20.8	36.1	35.8	28.0
1987	76.9	27.6	27.8	21.5	35.9	36.2	27.9
1988	80.2	28.9	29.0	22.3	36.1	36.1	27.8
1989	81.3	29.4	29.4	22.6	36.1	36.1	27.7
1990	84.1	29.4	32.0	22.6	35.0	38.1	26.9
1991	84.0	30.1	31.7	22.2	35.9	37.7	26.4
1992	85.2	29.8	32.8	22.5	35.0	38.5	26.5
1993	86.9	30.8	33.1	23.0	35.5	38.1	26.4
1994	88.5	31.3	33.7	23.5	35.4	38.1	26.5

Source: U.S. Energy Information Administration, *Annual Energy Review.*

No. 917. Energy Consumption—End-Use Sector and Selected Source, by State: 1993

[In trillions of Btu, except as indicated. For Btu conversion factors, see text, section 19]

REGION, DIVISION, AND STATE	Total[1]	Per capita[2] (mil. Btu)	END-USE SECTOR				SOURCE				
			Residential	Commercial	Industrial	Transportation	Petroleum	Natural gas (dry)	Coal	Hydroelectric power	Nuclear electric power
United States ..	83,958	322.0	17,095	13,230	[3]30,748	22,885	33,842	20,868	19,483	3,050	6,519
Northeast..........	12,972	253.0	3,326	2,764	3,436	3,445	5,818	2,805	1,947	514	1,660
New England......	3,182	240.4	927	676	691	889	1,706	546	168	154	473
Maine	380	299.6	83	55	136	106	236	5	11	48	61
New Hampshire...	246	218.9	73	40	57	76	147	17	38	23	97
Vermont........	142	244.9	43	26	25	48	81	7	-	37	36
Massachusetts ...	1,408	228.5	420	333	262	393	743	324	99	20	46
Rhode Island.....	245	246.6	66	46	75	57	99	78	-	11	-
Connecticut......	762	232.3	242	176	136	208	402	115	21	15	233
Middle Atlantic	9,790	257.3	2,400	2,088	2,745	2,557	4,112	2,260	1,779	361	1,187
New York.......	3,702	199.7	1,013	1,050	742	897	1,592	971	307	350	287
New Jersey......	2,422	307.0	510	488	650	774	1,198	572	63	[4]-1	266
Pennsylvania.....	3,666	299.9	876	550	1,353	886	1,322	717	1,410	12	634
Midwest...........	20,385	334.0	4,712	3,319	7,302	5,052	7,005	5,171	6,710	234	1,781
East North Central..	14,250	331.7	3,318	2,321	5,273	3,338	4,627	3,727	4,677	52	1,371
Ohio	3,791	338.7	866	595	1,499	832	1,162	866	1,432	2	107
Indiana.........	2,514	425.6	461	284	1,182	587	839	525	1,319	5	-
Illinois	3,582	300.3	901	672	1,201	809	1,154	1,053	812	1	837
Michigan	2,899	295.1	724	526	899	750	967	932	708	20	305
Wisconsin.......	1,465	281.2	367	245	493	360	506	352	406	25	123
West North Central .	6,135	339.3	1,395	998	2,029	1,714	2,378	1,444	2,033	182	409
Minnesota.......	1,432	306.4	326	195	507	405	561	332	325	76	128
Iowa	966	330.6	221	150	360	235	330	249	340	8	35
Missouri........	1,597	288.8	417	306	363	512	674	281	466	32	90
North Dakota.....	331	516.1	53	39	165	74	116	42	400	29	-
South Dakota	219	289.4	54	34	57	74	109	31	34	27	-
Nebraska	533	315.9	129	106	145	153	206	123	166	10	73
Kansas	1,057	403.0	194	168	432	263	383	387	302	-	84
South.............	35,102	392.6	6,226	4,527	15,237	9,112	14,514	9,029	8,445	478	2,429
South Atlantic.....	13,166	287.9	3,147	2,400	3,697	3,922	5,499	1,692	3,761	166	1,688
Delaware	257	343.7	51	38	100	68	142	43	64	-	-
Maryland	1,246	244.8	346	191	364	345	526	186	262	17	131
Dist. of Columbia..	179	297.4	36	83	32	28	37	33	1	-	-
Virginia.........	1,911	289.8	462	412	458	580	756	228	348	5	242
West Virginia.....	826	439.0	138	90	431	167	302	150	804	11	-
North Carolina....	2,104	299.7	504	362	672	565	789	192	643	54	254
South Carolina ...	1,279	339.8	262	174	528	315	420	146	330	28	493
Georgia	2,237	309.3	496	347	645	749	892	360	659	49	291
Florida	3,128	227.4	853	701	468	1,106	1,636	355	652	2	277
East South Central..	6,042	384.6	1,166	573	2,642	1,660	2,137	1,013	2,516	212	310
Kentucky	1,577	408.2	292	184	689	413	544	213	922	32	-
Tennessee	1,832	356.7	393	128	821	490	624	263	686	86	35
Alabama........	1,669	399.5	304	161	783	422	541	301	808	93	190
Mississippi	963	370.0	177	101	350	335	428	235	99	-	84
West South Central .	15,894	568.2	1,913	1,554	8,898	3,529	6,877	6,324	2,168	101	431
Arkansas	853	332.5	177	111	323	243	298	234	200	46	144
Louisiana	3,605	831.4	299	211	2,353	741	1,506	1,644	223	-	154
Oklahoma.......	1,355	406.2	254	182	553	367	464	594	332	44	-
Texas..........	10,081	560.7	1,183	1,050	5,670	2,179	4,610	3,852	1,413	10	133
West	15,482	276.2	2,831	2,620	4,756	5,276	6,505	3,863	2,381	1,823	649
Mountain..........	4,765	322.4	898	880	1,502	1,484	1,802	1,090	2,173	324	236
Montana........	358	414.3	63	53	150	93	160	54	158	99	-
Idaho..........	399	362.6	85	70	142	102	132	58	10	94	-
Wyoming	406	908.1	37	42	240	87	127	111	467	8	-
Colorado	1,023	276.8	228	241	247	307	374	287	339	19	-
New Mexico	595	369.3	78	98	194	226	239	225	270	3	-
Arizona	958	246.5	209	208	185	356	377	118	390	72	236
Utah	579	307.4	109	92	213	166	211	149	368	8	-
Nevada	446	308.0	92	76	132	147	182	88	172	21	-
Pacific	10,717	259.7	1,932	1,740	3,254	3,791	4,703	2,773	207	1,499	413
Washington......	1,944	387.2	397	296	662	589	776	206	98	657	76
Oregon	957	317.1	216	166	285	290	357	141	37	399	-
California	6,988	229.6	1,256	1,196	1,900	2,638	3,151	2,048	57	429	337
Alaska	599	1, 040.0	44	59	348	148	196	376	14	13	-
Hawaii	229	227.6	20	23	60	127	224	3	2	1	-

- Represents zero. [1] Sources of energy includes geothermal, wood and waste, and net interstate sales of electricity, including losses, not shown separately. [2] Based on estimated resident population as of July 1. [3] Includes 17.3 trillion Btu of net imports of coal coke not allocated by State. [4] A negative number occurs when more electricity is expended than is created to provide electricity during peak demand periods.

Source: U.S. Energy Information Administration, *State Energy Data Report, 1993.*

No. 918. Energy Expenditures—End-Use Sector and Selected Source, by State: 1993

[In millions of dollars, except as indicated. End-use sector and electric utilities exclude expenditures on energy sources such as hydropower, solar, wind, and geothermal. Also excludes expenditures for reported amounts of energy consumed by the energy industry for production, transportation, and processing operations]

REGION, DIVISION, AND STATE	Total[1]	Per capita[2] (dol.)	END-USE SECTOR				SOURCE				
			Resi-dential	Com-mercial	Indus-trial	Trans-porta-tion	Petroleum products		Natural gas	Coal	Elec-tricity sales
							Total	Gaso-line			
U.S.	493,337	1,914	124,430	86,736	[3]103,853	178,318	225,842	130,021	75,982	27,857	103,853
Northeast.	95,546	1,863	29,436	21,780	15,638	28,692	40,356	21,961	15,572	2,999	15,638
N.E	25,787	1,948	8,231	5,430	3,932	8,193	12,394	6,813	3,400	294	3,932
ME	2,669	2,152	740	404	576	949	1,542	725	31	27	576
NH	2,091	1,861	682	341	372	696	1,052	618	110	62	372
VT	1,167	2,026	368	202	159	439	679	348	36	1	159
MA	11,327	1,882	3,631	2,575	1,591	3,529	5,216	2,865	1,964	169	1,591
RI	1,926	1,926	585	380	418	543	784	458	463	-	418
CT	6,607	2,015	2,225	1,528	815	2,038	3,121	1,799	797	36	815
M.A	69,759	1,834	21,205	16,350	11,706	20,500	27,963	15,149	12,172	2,705	11,706
NY	30,368	1,673	9,933	8,724	3,704	8,008	11,336	6,431	5,790	479	3,704
NJ	16,408	2,088	4,435	3,792	2,870	5,312	7,155	3,364	2,842	110	2,870
PA	22,984	1,911	6,837	3,834	5,133	7,180	9,472	5,354	3,540	2,116	5,133
Midwest.	118,874	1,948	30,872	19,841	27,372	40,789	51,036	30,443	22,732	9,123	27,372
E.N.C	83,625	1,947	22,139	14,405	19,899	27,182	33,829	20,500	17,166	6,831	19,899
OH	22,495	2,034	5,911	3,769	5,723	7,092	8,832	5,469	4,222	2,051	5,723
IN	12,318	2,159	2,825	1,511	3,627	4,354	5,369	2,878	2,281	1,805	3,627
IL	22,605	1,934	6,498	4,408	4,943	6,757	8,280	5,080	5,101	1,360	4,943
MI	17,538	1,854	4,496	3,378	3,818	5,848	7,339	4,640	3,882	1,101	3,818
WI	8,669	1,719	2,409	1,339	1,789	3,132	4,010	2,434	1,681	514	1,789
W.N.C.	35,249	1,949	8,733	5,436	7,473	13,607	17,207	9,943	5,566	2,292	7,473
MN	8,286	1,831	2,013	1,021	1,879	3,373	4,165	2,566	1,355	392	1,879
IA	5,561	1,971	1,464	824	1,331	1,942	2,505	1,490	1,084	364	1,331
MO	9,806	1,873	2,649	1,714	1,581	3,862	4,750	2,840	1,323	582	1,581
ND	1,634	2,564	304	201	510	619	827	428	125	471	510
SD	1,391	1,943	341	185	253	611	823	454	132	41	253
NE	3,175	1,968	725	549	567	1,334	1,619	884	512	131	567
KS	5,397	2,129	1,238	942	1,351	1,866	2,518	1,282	1,036	310	1,351
South	184,520	2,064	43,756	27,165	45,972	67,626	88,309	48,442	24,994	12,862	45,972
S.A	82,908	1,813	23,334	14,661	14,158	30,755	37,812	24,048	7,470	6,156	14,158
DE	1,494	2,141	409	243	306	536	755	403	171	106	306
MD	8,583	1,731	2,631	1,218	1,704	3,031	3,951	2,446	996	413	1,704
DC	1,222	2,109	265	525	180	253	293	212	232	3	180
VA	11,816	1,825	3,311	2,278	1,548	4,679	5,572	3,546	1,116	533	1,548
WV	3,927	2,160	832	488	1,234	1,373	2,010	1,017	501	1,145	1,234
NC	13,621	1,959	3,877	2,194	2,781	4,769	6,011	3,821	891	1,096	2,781
SC	7,095	1,955	1,814	1,003	1,831	2,447	2,925	1,940	599	528	1,831
GA	13,833	2,004	3,564	2,352	2,645	5,272	6,039	3,817	1,789	1,175	2,645
FL	21,316	1,553	6,632	4,360	1,929	8,395	10,256	6,846	1,178	1,158	1,929
E.S.C	31,505	2,006	6,944	3,282	8,610	12,669	14,938	8,914	3,519	3,587	8,610
KY	7,757	2,044	1,588	878	2,106	3,185	3,885	2,108	799	1,129	2,106
TN	9,892	1,942	2,168	734	3,015	3,976	4,580	2,904	1,068	880	3,015
AL	8,746	2,092	2,017	1,015	2,395	3,319	3,889	2,421	1,063	1,415	2,395
MS	5,111	1,936	1,172	655	1,094	2,190	2,584	1,480	590	163	1,094
W.S.C	70,108	2,506	13,479	9,221	23,205	24,202	35,559	15,480	14,004	3,119	23,205
AR	5,095	2,100	1,279	662	1,178	1,976	2,329	1,411	762	343	1,178
LA	13,095	3,052	2,117	1,402	5,320	4,256	6,601	2,273	2,965	354	5,320
OK	6,427	1,988	1,564	992	1,254	2,616	3,053	1,815	1,430	415	1,254
TX	45,490	2,524	8,518	6,166	15,452	15,354	23,576	9,982	8,848	2,008	15,452
West	94,341	1,683	20,365	17,951	14,814	41,210	46,141	29,175	12,685	2,873	14,814
Mt	27,711	1,875	5,810	5,000	4,808	12,095	13,948	8,532	3,344	2,511	4,808
MT	1,851	2,201	333	250	430	839	1,090	568	198	115	430
ID	2,081	1,892	417	299	456	909	1,111	649	205	18	456
WY	1,667	3,546	191	189	624	664	848	345	281	386	624
CO	5,872	1,648	1,293	1,225	722	2,633	2,955	1,964	928	375	722
NM	3,192	1,975	560	620	533	1,480	1,809	1,085	388	370	533
AZ	7,380	1,871	1,849	1,555	928	3,047	3,284	2,222	487	536	928
UT	2,922	1,571	603	444	553	1,323	1,463	892	513	459	553
NV	2,746	1,987	564	418	563	1,201	1,389	807	346	253	563
Pac	66,629	1,614	14,556	12,952	10,006	29,116	32,193	20,643	9,341	362	10,006
WA	8,628	1,641	1,812	1,234	1,386	4,196	4,612	2,838	771	142	1,386
OR	5,366	1,768	1,093	781	963	2,529	2,865	1,803	560	44	963
CA	48,816	1,564	11,008	10,265	7,095	20,448	22,256	15,140	7,759	108	7,095
AK	1,845	3,085	324	351	175	995	1,197	321	214	65	175
HI	1,975	1,693	318	321	387	949	1,262	540	37	3	387

- Represents zero. [1] Includes sources not shown separately. Total expenditures are the sum of purchases for each source (including electricity sales) less electric utility purchases of fuel. [2] Based on estimated resident population as of July 1. [3] Includes net imports of coal coke not shown separately by State.

Source: U.S. Energy Information Administration, *State Energy Price and Expenditure Report*, annual.

No. 919. Energy Expenditures and Average Fuel Prices, by Source and Sector: 1970 to 1993

[For definition of Btu, see text, section 19. End-use sector and electric utilities exclude expenditures and prices on energy sources such as hydropower, solar, wind, and geothermal. Also excludes expenditures for reported amounts of energy consumed by the energy industry for production, transportation, and processing operations]

SOURCE AND SECTOR	1970	1973	1975	1980	1985	1988	1989	1990	1991	1992	1993
EXPENDITURES (mil. dol.)											
Total[1][2]	82,579	111,638	171,782	373,900	435,444	407,597	434,354	469,785	467,408	472,699	493,337
Natural gas	10,891	13,933	20,061	51,061	72,938	61,089	65,383	64,102	64,697	68,401	75,982
Petroleum products[2]	48,088	65,305	103,858	238,408	223,196	189,261	206,277	234,826	222,298	221,701	225,842
Motor gasoline	31,596	39,667	59,446	124,408	118,044	103,211	112,585	126,472	123,051	125,158	130,021
Coal	4,594	6,251	13,047	22,648	29,719	28,371	28,106	28,381	27,866	27,417	27,857
Electricity sales	23,351	33,780	50,680	98,098	149,242	162,070	169,340	176,742	184,822	186,956	196,585
Residential sector	20,083	27,078	36,844	68,825	98,307	102,773	108,423	109,266	114,738	115,148	124,430
Commercial sector	10,668	15,107	22,835	46,881	70,263	71,579	75,467	78,922	81,482	82,408	86,736
Industrial sector	16,458	23,549	41,169	94,520	105,723	91,315	93,827	101,057	99,767	102,259	103,853
Transportation sector[2]	35,370	45,904	70,934	163,674	161,150	141,930	156,637	180,540	171,421	172,884	178,318
Motor gasoline	30,525	38,598	57,992	121,809	115,201	100,988	110,168	123,775	120,557	122,700	128,116
Electric utilities	4,316	7,817	16,396	37,435	42,558	37,435	38,895	38,443	36,501	35,764	36,653
AVERAGE FUEL PRICES (dol. per mil. Btu)											
All sectors	1.65	2.02	3.33	6.91	8.42	7.30	7.69	8.38	8.33	8.26	8.42
Residential sector	2.12	2.73	3.83	7.55	11.14	10.90	11.26	12.14	12.34	12.27	12.52
Commercial sector	1.97	2.56	4.09	7.88	11.71	10.91	11.40	12.03	12.21	12.33	12.65
Industrial sector	0.83	1.09	2.20	4.71	6.09	5.03	5.11	5.40	5.35	5.3	5.30
Transportation sector	2.31	2.57	4.02	8.61	8.26	6.56	7.16	8.27	7.98	7.92	8.03
Electric utilities	0.32	0.46	0.96	1.75	1.85	1.45	1.48	1.46	1.37	1.34	1.35

[1] Includes electricity sales; excludes electricity generation.   [2] Includes sources or fuel types not shown separately.

Source: U.S. Energy Information Administration, *State Energy Price and Expenditure Report*, annual.

No. 920. Residential Energy Consumption, Expenditures, and Average Price, 1980 to 1993, and by Region, 1993

[For period April to March for 1980-1985; January to December for 1987 to 1993. Excludes Alaska and Hawaii in 1980. Covers occupied units only. Excludes household usage of gasoline for transportation and the use of wood or coal. Based on Residential Energy Consumption Survey; see Appendix III. For composition of regions, see table 27. Btu=British thermal unit; see text, section 19]

TYPE OF FUEL	Unit	1980	1983	1985	1987	1990	1993 Total	1993 North-east	1993 Mid-west	1993 South	1993 West
CONSUMPTION											
Total	Quad. Btu	9.74	8.62	9.04	9.13	9.22	10.01	2.38	3.13	2.95	1.55
Avg. per household	Mil. Btu	126	103	105	101	98	103.6	122.4	134.3	87.9	76.0
Natural gas	Quad. Btu	5.31	4.77	4.98	4.83	4.86	5.27	1.11	2.07	1.18	0.91
Electricity	Quad. Btu	2.42	2.42	2.48	2.76	3.03	3.28	0.47	0.74	1.51	0.56
Fuel oil, kerosene	Quad. Btu	1.71	1.14	1.26	1.22	1.04	1.07	0.78	0.13	0.13	0.03
Liquid petroleum gas	Quad. Btu	0.31	0.29	0.31	0.32	0.28	0.38	0.03	0.19	0.13	0.04
EXPENDITURES											
Total	Bil. dol.	63.2	87.8	97.0	97.7	110.2	123.91	29.72	31.12	43.67	19.41
Avg. per household	Dollars	815	1,048	1,123	1,080	1,172	1,282	1,526	1,336	1,304	953
Natural gas	Bil. dol.	17.8	27.1	29.8	26.1	27.3	32.04	8.60	11.13	7.24	5.07
Electricity	Bil. dol.	32.6	48.4	54.5	61.6	71.5	81.08	15.76	17.55	34.08	13.69
Fuel oil, kerosene	Bil. dol.	10.7	9.6	9.6	7.2	8.3	6.98	5.00	0.84	0.9	0.24
Liquid petroleum gas	Bil. dol.	2.1	2.7	3.1	2.8	3.1	3.81	0.35	1.59	1.46	0.41
AVERAGE PRICE											
Total	Dol./mil. Btu	6.49	10.18	10.73	10.71	12.0	12.38	12.47	9.94	14.82	12.54
Natural gas	Dol./mil. Btu	3.36	5.67	5.97	5.41	5.6	6.07	7.73	5.38	6.13	5.55
Electricity	Dol./mil. Btu	13.46	19.98	21.94	22.34	23.6	24.69	33.55	23.67	22.61	24.23
Fuel oil, kerosene	Dol./mil. Btu	6.29	8.42	7.64	5.89	7.9	6.5	6.4	6.5	6.9	8.0
Liquid petroleum gas	Dol./mil. Btu	6.71	9.42	9.91	8.91	11.2	10.04	13.90	8.55	11.13	10.99

Source: U.S. Energy Information Administration, *Household Energy Consumption and Expenditures, 1993*, and prior reports. Survey not conducted in 1984, 1986, 1988, and 1989.

No. 921. Residential Energy Consumption and Expenditures, by Type of Fuel and Selected Household Characteristic: 1993

[For period January through December. Quad.=quadrillion. See headnote, table 920]

CHARACTERISTIC	CONSUMPTION (Btu's)					EXPENDITURES				
	Total [1] (quad.)	Avg. per house-hold[1] (mil.)	Natural gas (quad.)	Elec-tricity (quad.)	Fuel oil[2] (quad.)	Total[1] (bil. dol.)	Avg. per house-hold[1] (dol.)	Natural gas (bil. dol.)	Elec-tricity (bil. dol.)	Fuel oil[2] (bil. dol.)
Total households	10.01	104	5.27	3.28	1.02	123.9	1,282	32.04	81.08	6.61
Single family detached.	7.21	121	3.77	2.34	0.78	87.0	1,462	22.23	56.44	5.20
Single family attached	0.70	96	0.41	0.24	0.05	9.3	1,266	2.65	6.22	0.34
Two-to-four unit building	0.80	100	0.54	0.17	0.09	8.9	1,112	3.56	4.72	0.58
Five-or-more unit building	0.83	52	0.43	0.32	0.08	12.0	740	2.84	8.76	0.37
Mobile home	0.46	82	0.14	0.21	0.02	6.7	1,203	0.76	4.93	0.12
Year house built:										
1939 or earlier	2.63	129	1.55	0.51	0.43	27.0	1,325	9.60	13.34	2.75
1940 to 1949	0.77	112	0.44	0.20	0.10	8.6	1,240	2.70	4.91	0.64
1950 to 1959	1.49	114	0.85	0.42	0.19	18.1	1,387	5.28	11.22	1.28
1960 to 1969	1.55	103	0.90	0.49	0.11	18.9	1,257	5.35	12.26	0.69
1970 to 1979	1.59	88	0.69	0.71	0.12	22.2	1,222	3.92	16.74	0.78
1980 to 1984	0.68	80	0.29	0.35	0.02	10.6	1,247	1.73	8.48	0.13
1985 to 1987	0.47	85	0.20	0.23	0.02	7.1	1,284	1.22	5.47	0.11
1988 to 1990	0.43	90	0.18	0.21	0.02	6.2	1,322	1.05	4.81	0.13
1991 to 1993	0.40	89	0.20	0.16	0.01	5.4	1,200	1.19	3.85	0.09
1993 family income:										
Less than $5,000	0.32	80	0.18	0.1	0.03	4.0	991	1.14	2.52	0.18
$5,000 to $9,999.	0.86	81	0.48	0.26	0.08	10.3	977	2.94	6.42	0.47
$10,000 to $14,999	1.00	90	0.58	0.29	0.09	11.7	1,051	3.51	7.17	0.58
$15,000 to $19,999	0.95	99	0.52	0.30	0.09	11.2	1,163	3.08	7.08	0.55
$20,000 to $24,999	0.84	97	0.43	0.28	0.08	10.3	1,182	2.62	6.75	0.51
$25,000 to $34,999	1.45	104	0.70	0.51	0.16	18.3	1,302	4.20	12.24	1.05
$35,000 to $49,999	1.90	109	0.96	0.65	0.21	24.1	1,379	5.87	16.18	1.36
$50,000 to $74,999	1.51	119	0.78	0.52	0.17	18.9	1,493	4.66	12.66	1.11
$75,000 or more	1.17	140	0.64	0.38	0.12	15.1	1,809	4.02	10.06	0.81

[1] Includes liquid petroleum gas not shown separately. [2] Includes kerosene.
Source: U.S. Energy Information Administration, *Household Energy Consumption and Expenditures, 1993.*

No. 922. Manufacturing Primary Energy Consumption for all Purposes, by Type of Fuel and Major Industry Group: 1991

[In trillions of Btu. Estimates represented in this table are for the primary consumption of energy for heat and power and as feedstocks or raw material inputs. Primary consumption is defined as the consumption of the energy that was originally produced offsite or was produced onsite from input materials not classified as energy. Examples of the latter are hydrogen produced from the electrolysis of brine; the output of captive (onsite) mines or wells; woodchips, bark, and woodwaste from wood purchased as a raw material input; and waste materials such as wastepaper and packing materials. Primary consumption excludes quantities of energy that are produced from other energy inputs and, therefore, avoids double counting. Based on the 1991 Manufacturing Energy Consumption Survey and subject to sampling variability]

INDUSTRY	SIC[1] code	Total	Net elec-tricity[2]	Residual fuel oil	Distil-late fuel oil[3]	Natural gas[4]	LPG	Coal	Coke and breeze	Other[5]
All industries	(X)	20,257	2,370	454	146	6,095	1,574	2,006	308	7,304
Food and kindred products.	20	956	169	27	17	(D)	5	154	(D)	(D)
Tobacco products	21	24	3	1	(Z)	4	(Z)	15	-	(Z)
Textile mill products.	22	274	101	12	6	108	2	31	-	13
Apparel and other textile products .	23	44	19	(S)	1	19	1	2	-	1
Lumber and wood products	24	451	61	2	16	41	4	2	-	325
Furniture and fixtures	25	68	17	1	1	19	1	4	-	26
Paper and allied products.	26	2,506	201	156	9	(D)	5	296	(D)	(D)
Printing and publishing	27	108	53	(Z)	2	48	1	-	-	4
Chemicals and allied products. . . .	28	5,051	440	(D)	14	2,227	(D)	(D)	10	526
Petroleum and coal products	29	5,967	105	65	21	838	(D)	(D)	(D)	4,864
Rubber and misc. plastic products .	30	238	116	8	3	96	3	7	-	6
Leather and leather products	31	12	3	1	1	5	(Z)	(S)	-	1
Stone, clay, and glass products . . .	32	880	105	9	20	381	(D)	293	(D)	(D)
Primary metal industries.	33	2,467	499	(D)	11	708	(D)	853	278	72
Fabricated metal products	34	307	102	3	6	175	4	5	(D)	(D)
Industrial machinery & equipment .	35	237	101	3	4	109	2	11	1	5
Electric and electronic equipment .	36	212	102	4	2	79	1	(D)	(D)	(D)
Transportation equipment.	37	323	118	12	7	133	2	(D)	(D)	17
Instruments and related products. .	38	98	42	3	(D)	26	(S)	(D)	-	(D)
Misc. manufacturing industries . . .	39	92	32	12	1	(D)	15	(Z)	-	(S)

- Represents or rounds to zero. D Withheld to avoid disclosing data for individual establishments. S Withheld because Relative Standard Error is greater than 50 percent. X Not applicable. Z Less than 0.5 trillion Btu. [1] Standard Industrial Classification Code; see text, section 13. [2] Net electricity is obtained by aggregating purchases, transfers in, and generation from noncombustible renewable resources minus quantities sold and transferred out. Excludes electricity inputs from onsite cogeneration or generation from combustible fuels because that energy has already been included as generating fuel (for example, coal). [3] Includes Nos.1, 2, and 4 fuel oils and Nos. 1, 2, and 4 diesel fuels. [4] Includes natural gas obtained from utilities, transmission pipelines, and any other supplier such as brokers and producers. [5] Includes net steam, and other energy that respondents indicated was used to produce heat and power or as feedstock/raw material inputs.
Source: U.S. Energy Information Administration, *Manufacturing Energy Consumption 1991.*

No. 923. Commercial Buildings—Energy Consumption and Expenditures, by Major Fuel Type Used: 1992

[Covers buildings using one or more major fuel. Excludes industrial buildings predominantly residential buildings, and buildings of less than 1,000 sq.ft. Based on a sample survey of building representatives and energy suppliers; therefore, subject to sampling variability. For characteristics of commercial buildings, see tables in section 25. Tril. = trillion]

TYPE OF FUEL	MAJOR FUEL CONSUMPTION				MAJOR FUEL EXPENDITURES			
	Total (tril. Btu)	Per building (mil. Btu)	Per square ft. (1,000 Btu)	Per worker (mil. Btu)	Total (mil. dol.)	Per building (1,000 dol.)	Per square ft. (dollars)	Per mil. Btu (dollars)
All buildings.	5,490	1,142	80.9	77.1	71,821	14.9	1.06	13.08
Energy sources (more than one may apply):								
Electricity	5,490	1,190	82.5	77.1	71,817	15.6	1.08	13.08
Natural gas.	4,264	1,605	94.8	83.3	51,785	19.5	1.15	12.15
Fuel oil.	1,440	2,574	109.0	79.7	17,748	31.7	1.34	12.32
District heat	839	8,872	160.0	117.5	9,106	96.3	1.74	10.85
District chilled water	292	10,369	152.6	107.8	3,167	112.5	1.65	10.85
Propane.	220	653	64.9	76.3	3,561	10.6	1.05	16.18
Other.	67	411	43.3	50.9	992	6.1	0.64	14.78

Source: Energy Information Administration, *Commercial Buildings Energy Consumption and Expenditures, 1992.*

No. 924. Commercial Buildings—Energy Consumption and Expenditures: 1992

[Covers buildings using one or more major fuel. Excludes industrial buildings, predominantly residential buildings, and buildings of less than 1,000 sq. ft. Based on a sample survey of building representatives and energy suppliers; therefore, subject to sampling variability. For characteristics of commercial buildings, see tables in section 25. For composition of regions, see table 27]

BUILDING CHARACTERISTIC	ALL BUILDINGS USING ANY MAJOR FUEL		CONSUMPTION (tril. Btu)			EXPENDITURES (mil. dol.)		
	Number (1,000)	Square feet (mil.)	Major fuel, total [1]	Elec- tricity	Natural gas	Major fuel, total [1]	Elec- tricity	Natural gas
All buildings	4,615	66,538	5,490	2,609	2,174	71,821	57,619	9,901
Region:								
Northeast	755	13,235	1,090	419	354	16,226	12,250	2,014
Midwest	1,141	16,909	1,578	622	747	16,957	12,745	3,011
South	1,874	23,979	1,825	1,002	697	22,843	19,097	2,998
West.	845	12,415	998	566	376	15,795	13,527	1,878
Year constructed:								
1899 or before	169	1,721	118	38	62	1,447	1,029	281
1900 to 1919	244	3,401	213	67	102	2,516	1,711	516
1920 to 1945	681	8,385	666	217	310	7,534	5,263	1,442
1946 to 1959	839	10,135	800	332	355	9,797	7,477	1,665
1960 to 1969	757	12,473	1,125	528	426	14,532	11,617	1,903
1970 to 1979	945	13,781	1,261	629	528	16,459	13,659	2,187
1980 to 1989	855	14,153	1,133	689	345	16,834	14,510	1,668
1990 to 1992	127	2,489	173	109	48	2,702	2,354	239
Principal activity within building:								
Assembly [2]	704	9,123	510	233	202	6,460	4,939	995
Education	301	8,470	637	235	291	7,389	5,526	1,271
Food sales/services.	390	2,248	444	251	181	6,669	5,609	952
Health care	63	1,763	403	138	189	3,733	2,640	662
Lodging.	154	2,891	463	189	193	5,459	4,030	929
Mercantile/services	1,270	12,399	892	444	381	12,907	10,583	1,899
Office	749	12,319	1,247	704	388	18,102	15,511	1,618
Public order and safety	24	1,652	52	B	9	811	743	43
Warehouse	685	11,179	527	253	196	6,750	5,386	939
Other	65	1,124	184	78	84	1,954	1,479	302
Vacant	210	3,371	131	47	61	1,585	1,172	290
Square footage:								
1,001 to 5,000	2,539	6,995	703	334	321	10,559	8,536	1,716
5,001 to 10,000	954	7,057	555	251	251	7,995	6,336	1,342
10,001 to 25,000	628	10,097	1,865	335	438	10,126	7,758	1,882
25,001 to 50,000	275	9,856	794	347	324	9,864	7,619	1,559
50,001 to 100,000.	114	7,926	642	308	255	8,483	6,806	1,184
100,001 to 200,000	70	9,658	640	347	206	8,413	6,935	893
200,001 to 500,000	25	7,678	711	361	215	8,457	6,847	742
500,001 and over	9	7,271	581	325	165	7,924	6,783	582

B Base figure too small to meet statistical standards for reliability of a derived figure.   [1] Includes fuel oil, propane, and purchased steam not shown separately.   [2] Includes public assembly, public order and safety, and religious worship.

Source: U.S. Energy Information Administration, *Commercial Buildings Energy Consumption and Expenditures, 1992.*

No. 925. Fossil Fuel Prices in Current and Constant (1987) Dollars: 1970 to 1994

[In cents per million British thermal units (Btu), except as indicated. All fuel prices taken as close to the point of production as possible. See text, section 19, for explanation of Btu conversions from mineral fuels]

FUEL	1970	1973	1975	1980	1985	1987	1988	1989	1990	1991	1992	1993	1994
CURRENT DOLLARS													
Composite [1]	31.7	39.8	82.1	204.2	251.2	170.0	153.3	167.1	184.3	167.0	165.8	166.8	152.3
Crude oil	54.8	67.1	132.2	372.2	415.3	265.5	216.9	273.4	345.3	285.2	275.7	245.7	227.4
Natural gas	15.4	20.1	40.2	144.8	225.7	150.2	152.4	152.7	154.6	148.0	156.8	183.5	165.5
Bituminous coal [2]	26.2	36.5	83.9	109.4	114.8	104.9	100.8	100.0	99.5	98.9	96.9	92.6	91.0
Anthracite coal	48.8	61.7	149.5	185.9	204.2	188.9	189.8	183.6	174.5	161.0	151.7	145.7	143.1
CONSTANT (1987) DOLLARS													
Composite [1]	90.1	96.4	166.9	284.8	266.1	170.0	147.5	154.0	162.7	142.0	137.1	135.1	120.8
Crude oil	155.7	162.5	268.7	519.1	439.9	265.5	208.8	252.0	304.8	242.5	228.0	198.9	180.3
Natural gas	43.8	48.7	81.7	202.0	239.1	150.2	146.7	140.7	136.5	125.9	129.7	148.6	131.2
Bituminous coal [2]	74.4	88.4	170.5	152.6	121.6	104.9	97.0	92.2	87.8	84.1	80.1	75.0	72.2
Anthracite coal	138.6	149.4	303.9	259.3	216.3	188.9	182.7	169.2	154.0	136.9	125.5	118.0	113.5
GDP implicit price deflator[3] (1987=100)	35.2	41.3	49.2	71.7	94.4	100.0	103.9	108.5	113.2	117.8	120.9	123.5	126.1

[1] Weighted by relative importance of individual fuels in total fuels production.   [2] Includes subbituminous and lignite.
[3] GDP=Gross domestic product; see text, section 15.
Source: U.S. Energy Information Administration, *Annual Energy Review.*

No. 926. World Energy Consumption, by Region and Energy Source: 1970 to 1994

[In tons of coal equivalent. Metric ton=1.1023 short tons. Kilogram=2.205 pounds. See text, section 30, for general comments about the data]

REGION AND ENERGY SOURCE	CONSUMPTION (mil. metric tons)				PER CAPITA (kilograms)				PERCENT DISTRIBUTION			
	1970	1980	1990	1994	1970	1980	1990	1994	1970	1980	1990	1994
World, total	6,412	8,783	10,826	11,258	1,208	1,626	2,004	1,993	100.0	100.0	100.0	100.0
North America [1]	2,486	2,825	3,196	3,550	5,949	6,667	7,543	7,906	38.8	32.2	29.5	31.5
United States	2,205	2,391	2,687	2,969	8,910	9,566	10,749	11,391	34.4	27.2	24.8	26.4
South America	142	247	313	372	490	841	1,064	1,184	2.2	2.8	2.9	3.3
Europe	1,709	2,230	2,346	3,413	2,963	3,854	4,056	4,699	26.7	25.4	21.7	30.3
Soviet Union	999	1,592	1,919	(2)	3,476	5,502	6,592	(2)	15.6	18.1	17.7	(2)
Asia	904	1,592	2,624	3,455	292	506	834	1,009	14.1	18.1	24.2	30.7
Oceania	72	107	149	159	2,753	3,993	5,597	5,657	1.1	1.2	1.4	1.4
Africa	101	191	279	309	(NA)	(NA)	434	436	1.6	2.2	2.6	2.7
Energy source:												
Solid fuels	2,143	2,650	3,238	3,356	586	595	612	594	33.5	30.8	29.9	29.8
Liquid fuels	2,802	3,806	4,000	4,054	770	855	756	718	44.0	44.2	36.9	36.0
Natural gas	1,289	1,838	2,539	2,671	351	413	480	473	20.1	21.5	23.5	23.7
Electricity	178	489	1,049	1,177	48	110	198	208	2.4	3.5	9.7	10.5

[1] Includes Central America.   [2] Beginning 1992, Soviet Union included with Europe.
Source: Statistical Office of the United Nations, New York, NY, *Energy Statistics Yearbook,* annual (copyright).

No. 927. World Primary Energy Production, by Region and Type: 1980 to 1993

[In quadrillion Btu. Btu=British thermal units. For Btu conversion factors, see source]

REGION AND TYPE	1980	1985	1986	1987	1988	1989	1990	1991	1992	1993
World total	286.38	304.89	315.05	322.94	335.12	341.96	347.74	345.19	343.64	345.76
North America	80.85	84.55	83.31	84.73	86.83	86.85	88.80	89.31	89.12	88.52
United States	64.76	64.87	64.35	64.95	66.11	66.13	67.85	67.48	66.85	65.31
Central and South America	12.11	13.59	14.47	14.44	15.29	15.86	16.81	17.64	17.73	18.32
Western Europe	30.66	37.62	38.49	38.90	39.10	39.02	38.74	39.23	38.91	39.28
Eastern Europe and former USSR	66.72	75.85	78.68	80.80	83.17	81.89	80.36	74.38	69.01	65.32
Middle East	42.17	25.77	30.75	32.21	36.12	39.72	41.03	40.35	43.56	46.34
Africa	18.05	19.29	19.07	19.45	20.54	21.39	22.43	23.43	22.74	22.91
Far East and Oceania	35.82	48.22	50.27	52.41	54.08	57.23	59.57	60.84	62.59	65.07
Crude oil	128.12	115.40	120.24	121.16	125.93	127.98	129.50	128.77	129.12	129.72
Natural gas	52.65	61.38	62.60	65.61	68.78	71.20	72.91	73.99	73.80	75.34
Natural gas liquids	5.10	5.82	6.12	6.32	6.63	6.68	6.85	7.16	7.34	7.63
Coal	74.48	85.77	88.06	90.27	91.92	93.93	94.97	90.43	88.62	86.67
Hydroelectric power	18.05	20.56	20.96	21.03	21.81	21.62	22.46	22.80	22.67	23.51
Nuclear electric power	7.58	15.37	16.34	17.80	19.30	19.82	20.30	21.27	21.30	22.10
Geothermal, solar and wind	0.40	0.60	0.73	0.75	0.75	0.75	0.75	0.77	0.79	0.79

Source: U.S. Energy Information Administration, *International Energy Annual.*

No. 928. Energy Imports and Exports, by Type of Fuel: 1970 to 1994

[In quadrillion of Btu. For definition of Btu, see text, section 19]

TYPE OF FUEL	1970	1973	1975	1980	1985	1988	1989	1990	1991	1992	1993	1994
Net imports:[1]												
Coal.	-1.93	-1.42	-1.74	-2.39	-2.39	-2.45	-2.57	-2.70	-2.77	-2.59	-1.78	-1.69
Natural Gas (dry)	0.77	0.98	0.90	0.96	0.90	1.22	1.28	1.46	1.67	1.94	2.25	2.43
Petroleum	6.92	12.98	12.51	13.50	8.95	14.01	15.33	15.29	14.22	14.96	16.40	17.12
Other [2]	-0.04	0.14	0.08	0.18	0.41	0.37	0.14	0.03	0.24	0.32	0.31	0.46
Imports:												
Coal.	(Z)	(Z)	0.02	0.03	0.05	0.05	0.07	0.07	0.08	0.10	0.18	0.19
Natural Gas (dry)	0.85	1.06	0.98	1.01	0.95	1.30	1.39	1.55	1.80	2.16	2.40	2.58
Petroleum	7.47	13.47	12.95	14.66	10.61	15.75	17.16	17.12	16.35	16.97	18.51	19.11
Other [2]	0.07	0.20	0.16	0.28	0.49	0.47	0.33	0.25	0.35	0.43	0.44	0.53
Exports:												
Coal.	1.94	1.43	1.76	2.42	2.44	2.50	2.64	2.77	2.85	2.68	1.96	1.88
Natural Gas (dry)	0.07	0.08	0.07	0.05	0.06	0.07	0.11	0.09	0.13	0.22	0.14	0.15
Petroleum	0.55	0.49	0.44	1.16	1.66	1.74	1.84	1.82	2.13	2.01	2.12	1.99
Other [2]	0.11	0.06	0.08	0.09	0.08	0.10	0.18	0.23	0.11	0.11	0.13	0.07

Z Less than .005 quadrillion Btu.   [1] Net imports equals imports minus exports.   Minus sign (-) denotes an excess of exports over imports.   [2] Coal coke and small amounts of electricity transmitted across U.S. borders with Canada and Mexico.
Source: U.S. Energy Information Administration, *Annual Energy Review.*

No. 929. U.S. Foreign Trade in Selected Mineral Fuels: 1970 to 1995

[Minus sign (-) indicates an excess of imports over exports. See also *Historical Statistics, Colonial Times to 1970,* series M 100, 101, 127, 128, 140, 141, 178, and 181]

MINERAL FUEL	Unit	1970	1973	1975	1980	1985	1990	1992	1993	1994	1995
NATURAL GAS											
Imports	Bil. cu. ft.. . . .	821	1,033	953	985	950	1,532	2,138	2,350	2,624	2,735
Exports	Bil. cu. ft.. . . .	70	77	73	49	55	86	216	140	162	161
Net trade	Bil. cu. ft.. . . .	-751	-956	-880	-936	-894	-1,446	-1,922	-2,210	-2,462	-2,574
CRUDE OIL											
Imports [1]	Mil. bbl..	483	1,184	1,498	1,926	1,168	2,151	2,220	2,477	2,578	2,608
Exports	Mil. bbl..	5	1	2	105	75	40	32	36	36	32
Net trade	Mil. bbl..	-478	-1,183	-1,496	-1,821	-1,093	-2,112	-2,188	-2,441	-2,542	-2,576
PETROLEUM PRODUCTS											
Imports	Mil. bbl..	765	1,099	712	603	681	775	659	669	706	581
Exports	Mil. bbl..	89	84	74	94	211	273	314	330	308	312
Net trade	Mil. bbl..	-676	-1,015	-638	-509	-470	-502	-345	-339	-398	-269
COAL											
Imports	1,000 sh. tons	36	127	940	1,194	1,952	2,699	3,803	7,309	7,584	7,201
Exports	1,000 sh. tons	71,733	53,587	66,309	91,742	92,680	105,804	102,516	74,519	71,359	88,547
Net trade	1,000 sh. tons	71,697	53,460	65,369	90,548	90,728	103,105	98,713	67,210	63,775	81,346

[1] Beginning 1980, includes strategic petroleum reserve imports.
Source: U.S. Energy Information Administration, *Natural Gas Monthly, Petroleum Supply Monthly,* and *Monthly Energy Review.*

No. 930. Daily International Flow of Crude Oil, by Area: 1991

[In thousands of barrels per day]

EXPORTING AREA	Total [1]	IMPORTING AREA							
		North America		Central and South America	Western Europe	Eastern Europe	Middle East and Africa	Japan	Other Far East and Oceania
		U.S.	Canada						
World total.	28,406	5,782	551	1,641	10,245	834	1,143	4,180	4,030
United States	116	(X)	5	[2]111	-	-	-	-	-
North America, except U.S. . . .	2,121	1,502	15	58	346	-	32	157	11
Central and South America	1,842	927	35	615	208	-	-	9	48
Western Europe.	2,939	183	348	11	2,374	-	23	-	-
Eastern Europe and U.S.S.R.	1,205	1	-	5	637	493	16	2	51
Middle East.	12,947	1,770	89	682	3,567	246	731	3,034	2,828
Africa.	4,969	1,160	59	147	3,101	95	323	11	73
Far East and Oceania	2,267	239	-	12	12	-	18	967	1,019

- Represents zero.   X Not applicable.   [1] Includes stocks at sea, exchanges, transshipments, and other statistical discrepancies not shown separately.   [2] Includes shipments to Puerto Rico and Virgin Islands.
Source: U.S. Energy Information Administration, *International Energy Annual.*

No. 931. Crude Oil Imports Into U.S., by Country of Origin: 1970 to 1995

[In millions of barrels. Barrels contain 42 gallons]

COUNTRY OF ORIGIN	1970	1973	1975	1980	1985	1988	1989	1990	1991	1992	1993	1994	1995
Total imports . .	483	1,184	1,498	1,921	1,168	1,864	2,133	2,151	2,110	2,220	2,477	2,578	2,643
Total OPEC [1]	222	765	1,172	1,410	479	984	1,232	1,283	1,233	1,243	1,317	1,307	1,303
Persian Gulf [2], total. . . .	62	293	409	550	89	495	633	657	636	597	598	589	539
Iran.	12	79	101	3	10	(Z)	-	-	12	-	-	-	-
Iraq. . . ., ...	-	1	1	10	17	125	161	188	-	-	-	-	-
Kuwait [3].	12	15	1	10	1	29	57	29	2	14	126	112	78
Qatar . . . ., ...	-	3	7	8	-	-	1	1	-	-	-	-	-
Saudi Arabia [3]	15	169	256	456	48	333	407	436	622	585	468	473	460
United Arab Emirates .	23	26	43	63	13	8	8	3	1	-	4	4	1
Other OPEC [2], total . . .	160	472	763	860	390	489	599	625	596	646	720	717	764
Algeria. . ., ...	2	44	96	166	31	21	22	23	16	9	9	8	10
Ecuador [4]	-	17	21	6	20	12	29	14	19	23	44	4	-
Gabon.	-	-	10	9	19	5	18	23	31	45	55	71	84
Indonesia.	26	73	138	115	107	68	58	36	37	26	24	34	23
Libya.	17	49	81	200	-	-	-	-	-	-	-	-	-
Nigeria	17	164	272	307	102	222	292	286	249	243	264	228	226
Venezuela	98	126	144	57	112	160	181	243	244	302	369	377	421
Non-OPEC [5], total .	245	419	326	511	689	880	900	869	878	977	1,160	1,271	1,340
Canada.	245	365	219	73	171	249	230	235	271	292	329	359	380
Ecuador [4]	(4)	(4)	(4)	(4)	(4)	(4)	(4)	(4)	(4)	(4)	28	33	36
Malaysia.	(NA)	(NA)	(NA)	(NA)	(NA)	(NA)	(NA)	(NA)	(NA)	(NA)	4	2	2
Mexico	-	-	(Z)	26	185	261	246	261	251	277	288	315	343	375
Norway.	-	-	-	4	53	11	23	46	35	27	43	50	69	95
Trinidad and Tobago . . .	(Z)	22	42	42	.36	26	27	28	26	26	20	23	23
United Kingdom	-	-	(Z)	63	101	93	58	57	39	73	114	145	125

- Represents zero.   NA Not available.   Z Less than 500,000 barrels.   [1] OPEC (Organization of Petroleum Exporting Countries)includes the Persian Gulf nations shown below, except Bahrain, which is not a member of OPEC, and also includes nations shown under "Other OPEC".   [2] Excludes petroleum imported into the United States indirectly from members of the OPEC countries.   [3] Imports from the Neutral Zone between Kuwait and Saudi Arabia are included in Saudi Arabia.   [4] Ecuador withdrew from OPEC on Dec. 31, 1992; therefore, it is included under OPEC for the period 1973 to 1992.   [5] Includes petroleum imported into the United States indirectly from member of OPEC, primarily from Caribbean and West European areas, as petroleum products that were refined from crude oil produced by OPEC.

Source: 1970, U.S. Bureau of Mines, *Minerals Yearbooks, vol. I;* thereafter, U.S. Energy Information Administration, *Petroleum Supply Annual,* vol. I.

No. 932. Crude Oil and Refined Products—Summary: 1973 to 1995

[Barrels of 42 gallons. Data are averages]

YEAR	CRUDE OIL (1,000 bbl. per day)				REFINED OIL PRODUCTS (1,000 bbl. per day)			Total oil imports[2] (1,000 bbl. per day)	CRUDE OIL STOCKS [3] (mil. bbl.)	
	Input to refin-eries	Domestic produc-tion	Imports		Exports	Domestic demand	Imports	Exports		Total	Stra-tegic reserve
			Total [1]	Stra-tegic reserve							
1973	12,431	9,208	3,244	(X)	2	17,308	3,012	229	6,256	242	(X)
1974	12,133	8,774	3,477	(X)	3	16,653	2,635	218	6,112	265	(X)
1975	12,442	8,375	4,105	(X)	6	16,322	1,951	204	6,056	271	(X)
1976	13,416	8,132	5,287	(X)	8	17,461	2,026	215	7,313	285	(X)
1977	14,602	8,245	6,615	21	50	18,431	2,193	193	8,807	348	7
1978	14,739	8,707	6,356	161	158	18,847	2,008	204	8,363	376	67
1979	14,648	8,552	6,519	67	235	18,513	1,937	236	8,456	430	91
1980	13,481	8,597	5,263	44	287	17,056	1,646	258	6,909	466	108
1981	12,470	8,572	4,396	256	228	16,058	1,599	367	5,996	594	230
1982	11,774	8,649	3,488	165	236	15,296	1,625	579	5,113	644	294
1983	11,685	8,688	3,329	234	164	15,231	1,722	575	5,051	723	379
1984	12,044	8,879	3,426	197	181	15,726	2,011	541	5,437	796	451
1985	12,002	8,971	3,201	118	204	15,726	1,866	577	5,067	814	493
1986	12,716	8,680	4,178	48	154	16,281	2,045	631	6,224	843	512
1987	12,854	8,349	4,674	73	151	16,665	2,004	613	6,678	890	541
1988	13,246	8,140	5,107	51	155	17,283	2,295	661	7,402	890	560
1989	13,401	7,613	5,843	56	142	17,325	2,217	717	8,061	921	580
1990	13,409	7,355	5,894	27	109	16,988	2,123	748	8,018	908	586
1991	13,301	7,417	5,782	-	116	16,714	1,844	885	7,627	893	569
1992	13,411	7,171	6,083	10	89	17,033	1,805	861	7,888	893	575
1993	13,613	6,847	6,787	15	98	17,237	1,833	904	8,620	922	587
1994	13,866	6,662	7,063	12	99	17,718	1,933	843	8,996	929	592
1995	13,977	6,524	7,249	-	91	17,712	1,585	834	8,834	894	592

- Represents zero.   X Not applicable.   [1] Includes Strategic Petroleum Reserve.   [2] Crude oil (including Strategic Petroleum Reserve) imports) plus refined products.   [3] End of year.

Source: U.S. Energy Information Administration, *Monthly Energy Review,* February 1996.

No. 933. Strategic Petroleum Reserve: 1977 to 1994

[**Million barrels, except as noted.** The Strategic Petroleum Reserve is a stock of petroleum maintained by the Federal Government for use during periods of major supply interruption]

YEAR	Crude oil imports	Domestic crude oil deliveries	Domestic crude oil sales	STOCKS AT YEAR-END			Days of net petroleum imports [3]
				Quantity [1]	Percent of crude oil stocks [2]	Percent of total petroleum stocks	
1977	7.54	[4]0.37	-	7.46	2.1	0.6	1
1980	16.07	1.30	-	107.80	23.1	7.7	17
1985	43.12	0.17	-	493.32	60.6	32.5	115
1987	26.52	2.69	-	540.65	60.8	33.6	91
1988	18.76	0.01	-	559.52	62.9	35.0	85
1989	20.35	-	-	579.86	62.9	36.7	81
1990	9.77	-	3.91	585.69	64.5	36.1	82
1991	-	-	17.22	568.51	63.7	35.2	86
1992	3.59	2.60	-	574.72	64.4	36.1	83
1993	5.37	6.96	-	587.08	63.6	35.6	78
1994	4.49	0.11	-	591.67	63.7	35.8	74

- Represents zero. [1] Stocks do not include imported quantities in transit to Strategic Petroleum Reserve terminals, pipeline fill, and above ground storage. [2] Including lease condensate stocks. [3] Derived by dividing end-of-year strategic petroleum reserve stocks by annual average daily net imports of all petroleum. Calculated prior to rounding. [4] The quantity of domestic fuel oil which was in storage prior to injection of foreign crude oil.
Source: U.S. Energy Information Administration, *Annual Energy Review.*

No. 934. World Petroleum Consumption, by Major Consuming Country: 1983 to 1993

[**Million barrels per day**]

REGION AND COUNTRY	1983	1985	1986	1987	1988	1989	1990	1991	1992	1993
World, total	**58.74**	**60.10**	**61.76**	**63.01**	**64.83**	**66.03**	**66.16**	**66.71**	**66.57**	**66.72**
North America, total	18.03	18.70	19.28	19.74	20.53	20.73	20.41	20.14	20.51	20.75
Canada	1.45	1.50	1.51	1.55	1.69	1.73	1.69	1.62	1.64	1.66
Mexico	1.35	1.47	1.49	1.52	1.55	1.66	1.73	1.80	1.83	1.84
United States	15.23	15.73	16.28	16.67	17.28	17.33	16.99	16.71	17.03	17.24
Central & South America, total	3.19	3.19	3.41	3.52	3.57	3.58	3.60	3.65	3.74	3.89
Brazil	0.98	1.08	1.24	1.26	1.30	1.32	1.34	1.35	1.37	1.41
Western Europe, total	12.38	12.39	12.79	12.93	13.08	13.16	13.25	13.66	13.81	13.80
France	1.84	1.78	1.77	1.79	1.80	1.86	1.82	1.94	1.93	1.91
Germany	2.66	2.70	2.86	2.77	2.74	2.58	2.66	2.83	2.84	2.90
Italy	1.75	1.72	1.74	1.86	1.84	1.93	1.87	1.86	1.94	1.88
United Kingdom	1.53	1.63	1.65	1.60	1.70	1.74	1.75	1.80	1.80	1.80
Eastern Europe and former U.S.S.R.	10.47	10.46	10.46	10.51	10.38	10.19	9.73	9.43	7.85	6.81
Middle East, total	2.61	2.85	2.98	3.06	3.15	3.36	3.47	3.40	3.40	3.49
Africa, total	1.70	1.83	1.83	1.84	1.91	1.99	2.10	2.15	2.18	2.17
Far East & Oceania, total	10.36	10.69	11.03	11.42	12.21	13.03	13.61	14.28	15.09	15.82
China	1.73	1.89	2.00	2.12	2.28	2.38	2.30	2.50	2.66	3.11
India	0.77	0.90	0.95	0.99	1.08	1.15	1.17	1.19	1.28	1.29
Japan	4.40	4.38	4.44	4.48	4.75	4.98	5.14	5.28	5.45	5.38

Source: U.S. Energy Information Administration, *Annual Energy Review* and *Monthly Energy Review*, monthly

No. 935. Energy Producing Companies—Selected Financial and Investment Indicators: 1985 to 1994

[Based on data from major publicly-owned domestic crude oil producing companies which either had at least 1 percent of domestic production or reserves of oil, natural gas, coal, or uranium, or at least 1 percent of refining capacity or petroleum product sales. There were 25 companies in 1993 and 1994; 22 during 1985 through 1987; and 23 in 1988 to 1992]

ITEM	1985	1986	1987	1988	1989	1990	1991	1992	1993	1994
INCOME STATEMENT (bil. dol.)										
Operating revenues	492.5	378.5	417.4	419.8	433.6	510.4	469.3	472.8	448.1	446.6
Operating expenses	444.2	354.4	383.7	381.6	397.7	470.1	443.3	449.5	423.0	416.5
Operating income	48.3	24.0	33.7	38.2	35.9	40.2	26.0	23.3	25.1	30.1
Pretax income	43.6	20.6	25.0	34.3	32.3	37.5	25.1	22.5	24.8	29.6
Net income	17.4	9.2	11.3	22.3	19.8	21.6	14.7	1.8	15.5	16.5
Funds from operations [1]	63.5	53.1	51.6	57.8	48.3	54.9	47.8	44.8	50.2	48.3
BALANCE SHEET (bil. dol.)										
Net property, plant, and equipment	297.7	291.1	297.6	293.6	293.2	302.5	305.5	309.7	307.9	308.7
Net investment in place [2]	315.4	310.0	316.4	309.6	309.9	319.7	325.6	331.6	331.5	334.6
Total assets	438.4	427.0	443.6	437.8	434.5	457.2	447.1	453.6	451.3	457.4
RATIOS (percent)										
Net income to operating revenues	3.5	2.4	2.7	5.3	4.6	4.2	3.1	[3]0.4	3.5	3.7
Net income to total assets	4.0	2.2	2.5	5.1	4.6	4.7	3.3	0.4	3.4	3.6
Net income to stockholders' equity	10.5	5.6	6.8	13.5	12.3	12.9	8.8	1.1	9.6	10.0
Long-term debt to stockholders' equity [4]	54.3	56.0	57.6	56.6	56.4	53.0	54.3	59.4	55.3	53.1
Long-term debt to total assets [4]	20.5	21.6	21.5	21.3	20.9	19.4	20.3	20.6	19.8	19.3

[1] The sum of net income, depreciation, depletion and amortization, deferred taxes, dry hole expenses, etc. [2] Composed of net property, plant and equipment plus investment, and advances to unconsolidated subsidiaries. [3] The implementation of the new "Financial Accounting Standard No. 106" greatly reduced the reported profitability of large publicly traded corporations. Net income without these accounting changes would have been $12.5 billion. [4] Long-term debt includes amounts applicable to capitalized leases.
Source: U.S. Energy Information Administration, *Performance Profiles of Major Energy Producers*, annual.

No. 936. Petroleum and Coal Products Corporations—Sales, Net Profit, and Profit Per Dollar of Sales: 1980 to 1995

[Represents SIC group 29. Profit rates are averages of quarterly figures at annual rates. Beginning 1986, excludes estimates for corporations with less than $250,000 in assets]

ITEM	Unit	1980	1985	1986	1987	1988	1989	1990	1991	1992	1993	1994	1995
Sales	Bil. dol . .	333.2	320.9	226.5	248.3	252.2	265.3	318.5	282.2	278.0	266.1	268.2	290.3
Net profit:													
Before income taxes	Bil. dol . .	39.1	17.7	9.8	14.2	27.3	23.7	23.3	12.2	2.0	15.0	17.3	16.7
After income taxes	Bil. dol . .	25.5	12.7	8.8	10.9	21.2	19.5	18.0	10.9	3.2	13.1	15.0	14.2
Depreciation[1].	Bil. dol . .	11.6	22.1	21.9	20.3	20.0	18.5	18.7	18.0	18.3	17.4	17.1	17.1
Profits per dollar of sales:													
Before income taxes	Cents . .	11.7	5.5	4.1	5.8	10.8	9.0	7.4	4.3	0.4	5.6	6.4	5.7
After income taxes	Cents . .	7.7	4.0	3.8	4.5	8.5	7.4	5.7	3.9	0.9	4.9	5.5	4.9
Profits on stockholders' equity:													
Before income taxes	Percent .	30.7	11.7	6.8	10.1	19.2	17.8	16.6	8.6	1.5	11.9	13.3	12.4
After income taxes	Percent .	20.0	8.5	6.1	7.7	14.9	14.6	12.8	7.7	2.4	10.3	11.5	10.6

[1] Includes depletion and accelerated amortization of emergency facilities.
Source: 1980, U.S. Federal Trade Commission; thereafter, U.S. Bureau of the Census, *Quarterly Financial Report for Manufacturing, Mining and Trade Corporations.*

No. 937. Major Petroleum Companies—Financial Data Summary: 1973 to 1994

[Data represent a composite of approximately 42 major worldwide petroleum companies aggregated on a consolidated, total company basis]

ITEM	1973	1975	1980	1985	1988	1989	1990	1991	1992	1993	1994
FINANCIAL DATA (bil. dol.)											
Net income	11.8	11.6	32.9	19.4	24.6	24.7	26.8	18.7	12.1	18.8	20.2
Depreciation, depletion, etc	10.5	11.3	32.5	53.0	34.3	33.7	38.7	36.5	43.3	39.0	37.7
Cash flow[1]	22.3	22.8	65.4	72.4	58.9	58.4	65.5	55.2	55.4	57.0	57.9
Dividends paid	4.0	4.7	9.3	12.0	14.0	16.0	15.9	16.3	16.5	15.5	16.1
Net internal funds available for investment											
or debt repayment [2].	18.3	18.1	56.1	60.4	44.9	42.4	49.6	38.9	38.9	41.5	41.8
Capital and exploratory expenditures . . .	16.3	26.9	62.1	58.3	62.4	55.1	59.6	61.5	53.6	51.8	51.5
Long-term capitalization	102.9	121.1	211.4	272.1	287.8	290.0	300.0	307.4	290.7	291.7	301.1
Long-term debt	22.5	28.9	49.8	93.5	88.5	91.4	90.4	95.9	94.0	91.6	91.0
Preferred stock	0.4	0.4	2.0	3.3	4.5	6.4	5.2	4.1	5.3	5.8	5.5
Common stock and retained earnings [3].	80.0	91.9	159.6	175.3	194.8	192.2	204.4	207.4	191.4	194.3	204.6
Excess of expenditures over cash											
income [4]	-2.0	8.9	6.0	-2.1	17.5	12.7	10.0	22.6	14.7	10.3	9.7
RATIOS [5] (percent)											
Long-term debt to long-term											
capitalization	22.0	23.8	23.6	34.4	30.8	31.5	30.1	31.2	32.3	31.4	30.2
Net income to total average capital	12.0	10.0	17.0	7.0	8.6	8.3	9.1	6.2	4.1	6.5	6.8
Net income to average common equity . .	15.6	13.1	22.5	10.8	12.8	12.4	13.5	9.1	6.1	9.8	10.1

[1] Generally represents internally-generated funds from operations. Sum of net income and noncash charges such as depreciation, depletion, and amortization.   [2] Cash flow minus dividends paid.   [3] Includes common stock, capital surplus, and earned surplus accounts after adjustments.   [4] Capital and exploratory expenditures plus dividends paid minus cash flow.
[5] Represents approximate year-to-year comparisons because of changes in the makeup of the group due to mergers and other corporate changes.
Source: Carl H. Pforzheimer & Co., New York, NY, *Comparative Oil Company Statements, 1994-1993,* and earlier reports.

No. 938. Electric Utility Sales and Average Prices, by End-Use Sector: 1970 to 1994

[Prior to 1980, covers Class A and B privately-owned electric utilities; thereafter, Class A utilities whose electric operating revenues were $100 million or more during the previous year]

YEAR	SALES (bil. kWh)				AVERAGE PRICE OF ELECTRICITY SOLD (cents per kWh)							
					Current dollars				Constant (1987) dollars [2]			
	Total [1]	Resi-dential	Com-mer-cial	Indus-trial	Total [1]	Resi-dential	Com-mer-cial	Indus-trial	Total [1]	Resi-dential	Com-mer-cial	Indus-trial
1970	1,392	466	307	571	1.7	2.2	2.1	1.0	4.8	6.3	6.0	2.8
1973	1,713	579	388	686	2.0	2.5	2.4	1.3	4.8	6.1	5.8	3.1
1975	1,747	588	403	688	2.9	3.5	3.5	2.1	5.9	7.1	7.1	4.3
1980	2,094	717	488	815	4.7	5.4	5.5	3.7	6.6	7.5	7.7	5.2
1981	2,147	722	514	826	5.5	6.2	6.3	4.3	7.0	7.9	8.0	5.4
1982	2,086	730	526	745	6.1	6.9	6.9	5.0	7.3	8.2	8.2	6.0
1983	2,151	751	544	776	6.3	7.2	7.0	5.0	7.2	8.3	8.0	5.7
1984	2,286	780	583	838	6.3	7.2	7.1	4.8	6.9	7.9	7.8	5.3
1985	2,324	794	606	837	6.4	7.4	7.3	5.0	6.8	7.8	7.7	5.3
1986	2,369	819	631	831	6.4	7.4	7.2	4.9	6.6	7.6	7.4	5.1
1987	2,457	850	660	858	6.4	7.4	7.1	4.8	6.4	7.4	7.1	4.8
1988	2,578	893	699	896	6.4	7.5	7.0	4.7	6.2	7.2	6.7	4.5
1989	2,647	906	726	926	6.5	7.6	7.2	4.7	6.0	7.0	6.6	4.3
1990	2,713	924	751	946	6.6	7.8	7.3	4.7	5.8	6.5	6.5	4.2
1991	2,762	955	766	947	6.8	8.0	7.5	4.8	5.7	6.4	6.4	4.1
1992	2,763	936	761	973	6.8	8.2	7.7	4.8	5.6	6.3	6.3	4.0
1993	2,861	995	795	977	6.9	8.3	7.7	4.9	5.6	6.3	6.3	3.9
1994	2,924	1,008	820	1,008	6.9	8.4	7.7	4.8	5.5	6.1	6.1	3.8

[1] Includes other sectors not shown separately.   [2] Based on the GDP implicit price deflator.
Source: U.S. Energy Information Administration, *Annual Energy Review.*

No. 939. Electric Utility Industry—Net Generation, Net Summer Capability, Generating Units, and Consumption of Fuels: 1980 to 1995

[Net Generation for **calendar years**; other data as of **December 31.** See also *Historical Statistics, Colonial Times to 1970,* series S 32-52, S 78-82, and S 86-107]

ITEM	Unit	1980	1985	1988	1989	1990	1991	1992	1993	1994	1995, prel.
RETAIL SALES											
Retail sales, total	**Bil. kWh.** . .	2,094	2,324	2,578	2,647	2,713	2,762	2,763	2,861	2,935	3,005
Net generation by electric utilities. . .	Bil. kWh. . .	2,286	2,470	2,704	2,784	2,808	2,825	2,797	2,883	2,911	2,995
Purchases by utilities from nonutility purchasers.	Bil. kWh. . .	1	26	68	90	116	139	166	189	209	(NA)
Imports	Bil. kWh. . .	25	46	39	26	23	31	37	39	52	45
Exports	Bil. kWh. . .	4	5	7	15	21	9	9	11	8	8
Losses and unaccounted for	Bil. kWh. . .	214	212	226	238	214	225	229	238	230	(NA)
NET GENERATION											
Total	**Bil. kWh** . .	2,286	2,470	2,704	2,784	2,808	2,825	2,797	2,883	2,911	2,995
Average annual change [1]	Percent . . .	3.5	1.5	3.0	2.9	0.9	0.6	-1.0	3.0	1.0	2.8
Net generation, kWh per kW of net summer capability [2]	Rate	3,951	3,770	3,990	4,064	4,067	4,076	4,024	4,119	4,146	4,246
Source of energy:											
Coal [3]	Percent . . .	50.8	56.8	57.4	56.2	55.6	54.9	56.3	56.9	56.2	55.2
Nuclear	Percent . . .	11.0	15.5	19.5	19.0	20.5	21.7	22.1	21.2	22.0	22.5
Oil	Percent . . .	10.8	4.0	5.5	5.7	4.2	3.9	3.2	3.5	3.1	2.0
Gas	Percent . . .	15.1	11.8	9.3	9.6	9.4	9.3	9.4	9.0	10.0	10.3
Hydro	Percent . . .	12.1	11.4	8.2	9.5	10.1	9.9	8.7	9.3	8.5	9.9
Type of prime mover: [4]											
Hydro	Bil. kWh. . .	276	281	223	265	280	276	240	265	244	294
Steam conventional [5]	Bil. kWh. . .	1,726	1,778	1,921	1,950	1,919	1,905	1,908	1,964	1,982	1,977
Gas turbine and internal combustion	Bil. kWh. . .	28	16	22	29	14	22	21	25	36	44
Steam nuclear	Bil. kWh. . .	251	384	527	529	577	613	619	610	640	673
Other	Bil. kWh. . .	6	11	12	11	11	10	10	10	9	6
NET SUMMER CAPABILITY											
Total [6]	**Mil. kW** . . .	579	655	678	685	691	693	695	700	702	705
Average annual change [1] . . .	Percent . . .	3.3	2.5	1.1	1.1	0.8	0.4	0.3	0.7	0.3	0.4
Hydro	Mil. kW . . .	82	89	90	91	91	92	93	96	96	97
Steam conventional [7]	Mil. kW . . .	397	437	442	444	448	447	447	447	446	446
Gas turbine	Mil. kW . . .	43	44	44	45	46	48	50	52	55	57
Steam nuclear	Mil. kW . . .	52	79	95	98	100	100	99	99	99	99
Internal combustion	Mil. kW . . .	5	5	5	5	5	5	5	5	5	5
Geothermal and other	Mil. kW . . .	1	2	2	2	2	2	2	2	2	2
NUMBER OF GENERATING UNITS											
Total [8]	**Number** . .	11,084	(NA)	10,305	10,325	10,296	10,260	10,221	10,471	10,427	(NA)
Hydro	Number . . .	3,275	(NA)	3,496	3,479	3,479	3,476	3,497	3,388	3,362	(NA)
Steam conventional	Number . . .	2,862	(NA)	2,383	2,363	2,354	2,284	2,307	2,221	2,170	(NA)
Gas turbine	Number . . .	1,447	(NA)	1,397	1,438	1,460	1,485	1,501	1,411	1,446	(NA)
Steam nuclear	Number . . .	74	(NA)	108	110	111	111	109	109	109	(NA)
Internal combustion	Number . . .	3,410	(NA)	2,872	2,889	2,847	2,803	2,807	2,976	2,953	(NA)
CONSUMPTION OF FOSSIL FUELS											
Net generation by fuel [9]	**Quad. Btu** . . .	18.56	18.79	20.12	20.54	20.32	20.07	19.99	20.58	20.92	20.92
Coal	Quad. Btu . .	12.12	14.54	15.85	15.99	16.19	16.03	16.21	16.79	16.90	17.00
Percent of total	Percent . . .	65.30	77.38	78.78	77.85	79.68	79.87	81.09	81.58	80.78	81.26
Petroleum	Quad. Btu .	2.63	1.09	1.56	1.69	1.25	1.18	0.95	1.05	0.97	0.66
Gas	Quad. Btu .	3.81	3.16	2.71	2.87	2.88	2.86	2.83	2.74	3.05	3.26
Fuel consumed:											
Coal	Mil. sh. tons	569	694	758	767	774	772	780	814	817	829
Petroleum	Mil. bbl. . . .	421	175	250	270	200	189	152	169	155	106
Gas	Bil cu. ft. . .	3,682	3,044	2,636	2,787	2,787	2,789	2,766	2,682	2,987	3,195

NA Not available. [1] Change from immediate prior year except for 1980, change from 1975. For explanation of average annual percent change, see Guide to Tabular Presentation. [2] Net summer capability is the steady hourly output that generating equipment is expected to supply to system load, exclusive of auxiliary power as demonstrated by test at the time of summer peak demand. [3] Includes small percentage (.5 percent) from wood and waste, geothermal, and petroleum coke. [4] A prime mover is the engine, turbine, water wheel, or similar machine which drives an electric generator. [5] Fossil fuels only. [6] Includes wind, solar thermal, and photovoltaic, not shown separately. [7] Includes fossil steam, wood, and waste. [8] Each prime mover type in combination plants counted separately. Includes geothermal, wind, and solar, not shown separately. [9] Includes small amounts of wood, waste, wind, geothermal, solar thermal, and photovoltaic.

Source: U.S. Energy Information Administration, 1980, *Power Production, Fuel Consumption, and Installed Capacity Data-Annual,* and unpublished data; thereafter, *Electric Power Annual, Annual Energy Review,* and unpublished data.

No. 940. Electric Utility Industry—Capability, Peak Load, and Capacity Margin: 1980 to 1994

[Excludes Alaska and Hawaii. Capability represents the maximum kilowatt output with all power sources available and with hydraulic equipment under actual water conditions, allowing for maintenance, emergency outages, and system operating requirements. Capacity margin is the difference between capability and peak load]

| YEAR | CAPABILITY AT THE TIME OF— | | | | NON-COINCIDENT PEAK LOAD | | CAPACITY MARGIN | | | |
| | Summer peak load (1,000 kW) | | Winter peak load (1,000 kW) | | | | Summer | | Winter | |
	Amount	Change from prior year	Amount	Change from prior year	Summer	Winter	Amount (1,000 kW)	Percent of capability	Amount (1,000 kW)	Percent of capability
1980	558,237	13,731	572,195	17,670	427,058	384,567	131,179	23.5	187,628	32.8
1981	572,219	13,982	586,569	14,374	429,349	397,800	142,870	25.0	188,769	32.2
1982	586,142	13,923	598,066	11,497	415,618	373,985	170,524	29.1	224,081	37.5
1983	596,449	10,307	612,453	14,387	447,526	410,779	148,923	25.0	201,674	32.9
1984	604,240	7,791	622,125	9,672	451,150	436,374	153,090	25.3	185,751	29.9
1985	621,597	17,357	636,475	14,350	460,503	423,660	161,094	25.9	212,815	33.4
1986	633,291	11,694	646,721	10,246	476,320	422,857	156,971	24.8	223,864	34.6
1987	648,118	14,827	662,977	16,256	496,185	448,277	151,933	23.4	214,700	32.4
1988	661,580	13,462	676,940	13,963	529,460	466,533	132,120	20.0	210,407	31.1
1989	673,316	11,736	685,249	8,309	523,432	496,378	149,884	22.3	188,871	27.6
1990	685,091	11,775	696,757	11,508	545,537	484,014	139,554	20.4	212,743	30.5
1991	690,915	5,824	703,212	6,455	551,320	485,435	139,595	20.2	217,777	31.0
1992	695,436	4,521	707,752	4,540	548,707	492,983	146,729	21.1	214,769	30.3
1993	694,250	1,186	711,957	4,205	575,356	521,733	118,894	17.1	190,224	26.7
1994	702,985	8,735	715,090	3,133	585,320	518,253	117,665	16.7	196,837	27.5

Source: Edison Electric Institute, Washington, DC, *Statistical Yearbook of the Electric Utility Industry,* annual.

No. 941. Electric Energy Sales, by Class of Service, 1970 to 1994, and by State, 1994

[In billions of kilowatt-hours]

REGION, DIVISION, AND STATE	Total[1]	Residential	Commercial	Industrial	REGION, DIVISION, AND STATE	Total[1]	Residential	Commercial	Industrial
1970	1,392.3	466.3	306.7	570.9	Kansas	29.6	10.1	10.1	9.0
1973	1,712.9	579.2	388.3	686.1	**South**	**1,253.7**	**467.1**	**310.6**	**435.2**
1975	1,747.1	588.1	403.0	687.7	**South Atlantic**	**592.4**	**237.8**	**177.0**	**158.9**
1980	2,094.4	717.5	488.2	815.1	Delaware	9.3	3.1	2.7	3.4
1985	2,309.5	791.0	609.0	824.5	Maryland	54.8	21.7	13.3	19.0
1988	2,578.1	892.9	699.1	896.5	Dist. of Columbia	10.3	1.6	8.1	0.3
1989	2,646.8	905.5	725.9	925.7	Virginia	82.2	32.3	22.9	18.2
1990	2,712.6	924.0	751.0	945.5	West Virginia	24.8	8.7	5.5	10.5
1991	2,762.0	955.4	765.7	946.6	North Carolina	99.8	37.2	27.5	33.3
1992	2,763.3	935.9	761.3	972.7	South Carolina	61.9	19.9	13.4	27.8
1993	2,861.5	994.8	794.6	977.2	Georgia	89.9	32.7	26.2	29.9
1994, total [2]	**2,934.5**	**1,008.4**	**820.3**	**1,008.0**	Florida	159.5	80.6	57.4	16.5
Northeast	**426.8**	**143.0**	**152.0**	**115.4**	**East South Central**	**259.2**	**89.1**	**34.2**	**130.8**
New England	**106.3**	**38.5**	**40.4**	**25.6**	Kentucky	72.5	19.5	10.1	40.0
Maine	11.6	3.7	2.8	5.0	Tennessee	82.5	32.8	5.2	43.6
New Hampshire	9.0	3.4	3.2	2.2	Alabama	67.6	23.2	11.8	31.9
Vermont	5.1	2.0	1.6	1.4	Mississippi	36.6	13.6	7.1	15.3
Massachusetts	46.1	16.0	19.4	9.7	**West South Central**	**402.1**	**140.2**	**99.5**	**145.5**
Rhode Island	6.6	2.5	2.6	1.4	Arkansas	32.6	11.6	6.9	13.5
Connecticut	28.0	10.9	10.8	5.9	Louisiana	70.1	22.6	15.0	29.9
Middle Atlantic	**320.5**	**104.5**	**111.6**	**89.8**	Oklahoma	41.1	16.1	11.1	11.7
New York	131.2	40.1	48.8	29.5	Texas	258.2	89.8	66.5	90.3
New Jersey	66.3	22.2	29.4	14.3	**West**	**539.6**	**176.0**	**168.9**	**174.6**
Pennsylvania	123.0	42.2	33.4	46.1	**Mountain**	**180.3**	**56.7**	**54.8**	**61.2**
Midwest	**714.4**	**222.4**	**188.8**	**282.9**	Montana	13.2	3.6	3.1	6.0
East North Central	**506.2**	**147.4**	**132.0**	**212.0**	Idaho	19.9	6.2	5.6	7.6
Ohio	154.4	41.8	34.1	74.0	Wyoming	11.7	1.9	2.4	7.3
Indiana	83.8	25.0	17.5	40.8	Colorado	34.5	10.9	13.0	9.6
Illinois	121.5	35.7	35.7	41.8	New Mexico	15.9	4.1	5.0	5.2
Michigan	91.2	27.2	30.4	32.7	Arizona	47.3	18.2	15.6	11.3
Wisconsin	55.4	17.7	14.4	22.7	Utah	17.8	5.0	5.5	6.5
West North Central	**208.2**	**75.0**	**56.8**	**70.9**	Nevada	20.0	6.8	4.6	7.8
Minnesota	51.2	16.0	9.0	25.5	**Pacific**	**359.3**	**119.2**	**114.0**	**113.3**
Iowa	33.0	11.1	7.5	13.2	Washington	87.1	29.7	19.8	34.1
Missouri	59.7	24.1	20.6	14.1	Oregon	45.0	16.5	12.7	15.1
North Dakota	7.7	3.2	1.9	2.0	California	213.7	68.9	76.9	59.9
South Dakota	7.2	3.1	1.9	1.8	Alaska	4.5	1.7	2.2	0.5
Nebraska	19.8	7.3	5.8	5.3	Hawaii	8.9	2.6	2.5	3.8

[1] Includes other service not shown separately.   [2] Preliminary.

Source: U.S. Energy Information Administration, *Electric Power Annual.*

No. 942. Electric Energy—Net Generation and Net Summer Capability, by State: 1990 to 1994

[Capacity as of **Dec. 31.** Covers utilities for public use]

DIVISION AND STATE	NET GENERATION (bil. kWh)				NET SUMMER CAPA- BILITY (mil. kW)		DIVISION AND STATE	NET GENERATION (bil. kWh)				NET SUMMER CAPA- BILITY (mil. kW)	
			1994							1994			
	1990	1993	Total	Per- cent from coal	1990	1994		1990	1993	Total	Per- cent from coal	1990	1994
U.S. . . .	2,808.2	2,882.5	2,910.7	56.2	690.5	702.7	VA	47.2	52.2	52.7	42.6	13.7	14.0
							WV. . . .	77.4	71.1	77.7	99.2	14.4	14.5
N.E	94.1	83.9	80.9	19.1	23.4	22.2	NC	79.8	88.8	91.5	58.2	20.2	20.0
ME. . . .	9.1	8.1	9.0	-	2.4	2.4	SC	69.3	75.6	74.2	36.4	14.9	16.7
NH	10.8	14.6	11.9	26.8	2.6	2.5	GA	97.6	95.7	98.8	65.5	20.7	22.0
VT	5.0	4.3	5.3	-	1.1	1.1	FL	123.6	140.1	141.8	42.9	32.7	35.5
MA	36.5	28.2	27.5	37.2	9.9	9.3	E.S.C	246.9	274.0	280.3	72.7	59.5	59.1
RI. . . .	0.6	0.1	0.1	-	0.3	0.1	KY	73.8	85.0	84.1	95.0	15.5	15.5
CT	32.2	28.7	27.2	7.7	7.1	6.7	TN	73.9	71.6	74.9	69.6	17.0	16.6
M.A.	330.8	306.8	304.7	39.2	78.4	79.9	AL	76.2	94.1	95.2	66.0	20.0	19.9
NY	128.7	106.3	103.8	20.1	31.2	32.8	MS	22.9	23.2	26.2	33.9	7.0	7.1
NJ	36.5	34.3	31.9	14.6	13.7	13.5	W.S.C. . . .	374.3	394.4	400.2	47.5	101.2	103.5
PA	165.7	166.2	169.0	55.6	33.4	33.5	AR	37.1	38.0	39.5	50.0	9.6	9.7
E.N.C. . . .	485.8	513.8	503.4	76.2	113.1	114.5	LA	58.2	59.4	60.2	33.4	16.8	16.9
OH	126.5	133.7	129.0	91.0	27.0	27.2	OK	45.1	48.8	45.4	60.5	12.8	12.9
IN. . . .	97.7	100.0	103.5	98.6	20.6	20.7	TX	234.0	248.2	255.1	48.1	62.0	64.1
IL. . . .	127.0	140.1	137.7	44.4	32.6	33.0	Mountain .	247.4	255.0	263.9	76.6	49.3	50.4
MI	89.1	92.3	83.7	80.7	22.3	22.4	MT	25.7	23.4	24.7	66.7	4.9	4.9
WI	45.6	47.8	49.4	71.4	10.6	11.3	ID.	8.6	9.0	7.3	-	2.3	2.5
W.N.C. . . .	218.4	218.4	230.6	74.5	54.2	55.3	WY	39.4	40.2	42.3	97.7	5.8	5.9
MN	41.6	41.3	40.9	64.5	8.8	9.0	CO	31.3	32.7	33.3	94.2	6.6	6.7
IA. . . .	29.0	31.0	32.0	82.9	8.0	8.2	NM	28.5	28.4	30.0	89.1	5.0	5.1
MO. . . .	59.0	53.2	61.5	79.0	15.2	15.5	AZ	62.3	68.0	71.2	53.5	14.9	15.1
ND	26.8	28.5	29.0	93.4	4.5	4.5	UT	32.3	33.5	34.5	95.1	4.8	4.8
SD	6.4	5.3	8.0	35.5	2.7	3.0	NV	19.3	19.8	20.5	74.7	4.9	5.5
NE	21.6	22.7	21.9	63.8	5.5	5.5	Pacific . . .	276.7	261.0	257.4	5.4	82.1	81.1
KS	33.9	36.4	37.3	71.0	9.6	9.7	WA	100.5	83.8	82.3	11.9	24.2	24.3
S.A	533.8	575.4	589.2	56.9	129.2	136.6	OR	49.2	40.7	37.5	10.2	11.2	10.2
DE	7.1	8.3	8.5	55.9	2.0	2.3	CA	114.5	125.8	126.7	-	43.7	43.3
MD	31.5	43.5	43.8	58.0	9.8	10.8	AK	4.5	4.6	4.8	6.2	1.5	1.7
DC	0.4	0.2	0.3	-	0.8	0.8	HI. . . .	8.0	6.1	6.1	-	1.5	1.6

- Represents zero.
Source: U.S. Energy Information Administration, 1980, *Power Production, Fuel Consumption, and Installed Capacity Data,* annual; thereafter, *Electric Power Annual, Electric Power Monthly,* December issues, and *Inventory of Power Plants in the United States,* annual.

No. 943. Nuclear Power Plants—Number of Units, Net Generation, and Net Summer Capability, by State: 1994

REGION, DIVISION, AND STATE	Number of units	NET GENERATION		NET SUMMER CAPABILITY		REGION, DIVISION, AND STATE	Number of units	NET GENERATION		NET SUMMER CAPABILITY	
		Total (mil. kWh)	Percent of total[1]	Total (mil. kW)	Percent of total[1]			Total (mil. kWh)	Percent of total[1]	Total (mil. kW)	Percent of total[1]
U.S.	109	640,440	22.0	99,148	14.1	South	43	266,561	21.0	40,366	13.5
Northeast . .	27	159,738	41.4	23,856	23.4	S.A	27	169,086	28.7	23,689	17.3
N.E	8	41,170	50.9	6,375	28.7	MD. . . .	2	11,235	25.7	1,675	15.5
ME. . . .	1	6,632	73.6	870	35.8	VA	4	25,429	48.2	3,349	24.0
NH	1	6,204	52.2	1,150	46.0	NC	5	32,346	35.4	4,639	23.2
VT	1	4,316	81.5	496	45.4	SC	7	44,466	59.9	6,364	38.1
MA	1	3,859	14.1	665	7.2	GA	4	28,927	29.3	3,840	17.4
CT	4	20,160	74.1	3,194	47.4	FL	5	26,682	18.8	3,822	10.8
M.A	19	118,568	38.9	17,481	21.9	E.S.C. . . .	8	42,027	15.0	8,195	13.9
NY	6	29,231	28.2	4,831	14.7	TN	2	11,932	15.9	2,217	13.3
NJ	4	22,129	69.3	3,862	28.6	AL	5	20,480	21.5	4,835	24.3
PA	9	67,207	39.8	8,788	26.2	MS. . . .	1	9,615	36.7	1,143	16.1
Midwest . .	31	150,479	20.5	25,720	15.1	W.S.C . . .	8	55,448	13.9	8,482	8.2
E.N.C. . . .	23	109,267	21.7	20,112	17.6	AR	2	13,924	35.2	1,694	17.5
OH	2	10,952	8.5	2,037	7.5	LA	2	12,779	21.2	2,006	11.9
IL. . . .	13	72,654	52.7	12,609	38.3	TX	4	28,745	11.3	4,782	7.5
MI	5	14,144	16.9	3,967	17.7	West.	8	63,663	12.2	9,206	7.0
WI	3	11,516	23.3	1,499	13.3	Mt	3	23,171	8.8	3,810	7.6
W.N.C . . .	8	41,212	17.9	5,608	10.1	AZ	3	23,171	32.5	3,810	25.3
MN	3	12,224	29.9	1,564	17.5	Pac	5	40,492	15.7	5,396	6.7
IA. . . .	1	4,107	12.8	515	6.3	WA. . . .	1	6,740	8.2	1,086	4.5
MO. . . .	1	10,006	16.3	1,115	7.2	CA	4	33,752	26.6	4,310	10.0
NE	2	6,345	28.9	1,254	22.7						
KS	1	8,529	22.9	1,160	11.9						

[1] For total capability and generation, see table 942.
Source: U.S. Energy Information Administration, *Electric Power Annual* and *Electric Power Monthly,* December issues.

No. 944. Nuclear Power Plants—Number, Capacity, and Generation: 1970 to 1995

ITEM	1970	1975	1980	1985	1988	1989	1990	1991	1992	1993	1994	1995
Operable generating units[1]	18	54	70	95	108	110	111	111	109	109	109	109
Net summer capability[1][2] (mil. kW). .	7.0	37.3	51.8	79.4	94.7	98.2	99.6	99.6	99.0	99.0	99.1	99.1
Net generation (bil. kWh)	21.8	172.5	251.1	383.7	527.0	529.4	576.9	612.6	618.8	610.3	640.4	673.4
Percent of total electric utility generation	1.4	9.0	11.0	15.5	19.5	19.0	20.5	21.7	22.1	21.2	22.0	22.5
Capacity factor [3]	(NA)	55.9	56.3	58.0	63.5	62.2	66.0	70.2	70.9	70.5	73.8	77.5

NA Not available. [1] As of yearend. [2] Net summer capability is the peak steady hourly output that generating equipment is expected to supply to system load, exclusive of auxiliary and other powerplant, as demonstrated by test at the time of summer peak demand. [3] Weighted average of monthly capacity factors. Monthly factors are derived by dividing actual monthly generation by the maximum possible generation for the month (hours in month times net maximum dependable capacity).
Source: U.S. Energy Information Administration, *Annual Energy Review* and *Monthly Energy Review*, March 1996.

No. 945. Commercial Nuclear Power Generation, by Country: 1970 to 1993

[Generation for **calendar years**; other data as of **December**]

COUNTRY	REACTORS				GROSS ELECTRICITY GENERATED (bil. kWh)				GROSS CAPACITY (1,000 kW)			
	1970	1980	1990	1993	1970	1980	1990	1993	1970	1980	1990	1993
Total.	64	208	368	421	73.9	617.8	1,743.9	2,134.6	15,186	128,847	301,745	349,171
United States . .	15	74	112	110	23.2	265.2	606.4	641.2	5,211	56,529	105,998	105,276
Argentina	-	1	2	2	-	2.3	7.0	7.7	-	357	1,005	1,005
Belgium	1	3	7	7	0.3	12.5	42.7	41.9	11	1,744	5,740	5,843
Brazil	-	-	1	1	-	-	2.0	4.4	-	-	657	657
Bulgaria	(NA)	(NA)	(NA)	6	(NA)	(NA)	(NA)	14.0	(NA)	(NA)	(NA)	3,760
Canada	1	9	19	22	0.9	40.4	74.0	97.5	220	5,588	13,855	16,709
China: Taiwan . .	-	2	6	6	-	8.2	32.9	34.3	-	1,272	5,146	5,146
Czech Republic .	(NA)	(NA)	(NA)	4	(NA)	(NA)	(NA)	3.6	(NA)	(NA)	(NA)	1,782
Finland	-	4	4	4	-	7.0	18.9	19.6	-	2,296	2,400	2,400
France	4	22	58	56	5.7	61.2	314.1	365.8	1,606	15,412	58,862	59,751
Germany	4	11	22	22	5.3	43.7	147.2	153.5	907	8,996	23,973	24,143
Great Britain . . .	27	33	42	37	26.5	37.2	68.8	90.5	4,783	9,012	15,274	14,832
Hungary	-	-	4	4	-	-	13.6	13.8	-	-	1,760	1,840
India	2	4	6	9	2.2	2.9	6.0	6.2	400	860	1,330	2,020
Italy	3	4	2	-	3.3	2.2	-	-	631	1,490	1,132	-
Japan	3	22	40	46	3.3	81.0	191.9	243.5	828	15,117	31,645	37,351
Mexico	-	-	1	1	-	-	2.1	4.9	-	-	675	675
Netherlands . . .	1	2	2	2	0.4	4.2	3.4	3.9	55	529	540	540
Pakistan	-	1	1	1	-	0.1	0.4	0.4	-	137	137	137
Russia	(NA)	(NA)	(NA)	29	(NA)	(NA)	(NA)	120.4	(NA)	(NA)	(NA)	21,316
Slovenia [1]	-	-	1	1	-	-	4.6	4.0	-	-	664	664
South Africa . . .	-	-	2	2	-	-	8.9	7.7	-	-	1,930	1,930
South Korea . . .	-	1	9	9	-	3.5	52.8	58.1	-	587	7,616	7,616
Spain	1	3	10	9	0.9	5.2	54.3	56.0	160	1,117	7,984	7,405
Sweden	1	8	12	12	(Z)	26.7	68.2	61.4	12	5,770	10,344	10,394
Switzerland	1	4	5	5	1.9	14.3	23.6	23.3	364	2,034	3,079	3,099
Ukraine	(NA)	(NA)	(NA)	14	(NA)	(NA)	(NA)	57.0	(NA)	(NA)	(NA)	12,880

- Represents zero. NA Not available. Z Less than 50 million kWh. [1] Formerly Yugoslavia.
Source: McGraw-Hill, Inc., New York, NY, *Nucleonics Week,* March issues (copyright).

No. 946. Uranium Supply and Discharged Commercial Reactor Fuel: 1980 to 1994

[Years ending **Dec. 31**, except as noted. For additional data on uranium, see section 25 on mining]

ITEM	Unit	1980	1985	1988	1989	1990	1991	1992	1993	1994
URANIUM CONCENTRATE										
Production	Mil. lb	43.70	11.31	13.13	13.84	8.89	7.95	5.65	3.06	3.35
Exports	Mil. lb	5.80	5.30	3.30	2.10	2.00	3.50	2.80	3.00	3.50
Imports	Mil. lb	3.60	11.70	15.80	13.10	23.70	16.30	23.30	21.00	22.70
Utility purchases from domestic suppliers	Mil. lb	(NA)	21.7	17.6	18.4	20.5	26.8	23.4	15.5	15.4
Loaded into U.S. Nuclear reactors [1] .	Mil. lb	(NA)	(NA)	(NA)	(NA)	(NA)	34.6	42.9	45.1	(NA)
Inventories, total	Mil. lb	(NA)	176.9	144.8	138.1	129.1	118.7	117.3	104.4	(NA)
At domestic suppliers	Mil. lb	(NA)	23.7	19.3	22.2	26.4	20.7	25.2	23.7	(NA)
At electric utilities	Mil. lb	(NA)	153.1	125.5	115.8	102.7	98.0	92.1	80.7	(NA)
Average prices:										
Purchased imports	Dol. per lb .	(NA)	20.08	19.03	16.75	12.55	15.55	11.34	10.53	(NA)
Domestic purchases	Dol. per lb .	(NA)	31.43	26.15	19.56	15.70	13.66	13.45	13.14	(NA)
DISCHARGED COMMERCIAL REACTOR FUEL [2]										
Annual discharge	Metric tons .	1,193	1,330	1,672	1,914	2,028	1,794	2,255	2,082	1,812
Inventory, year-end [3]	Metric tons .	6,434	12,481	17,178	19,092	21,120	22,914	25,169	27,251	29,257

NA Not available. [1] Does not include any fuel rods removed from reactors and later reloaded into the reactor. [2] Uranium content. Source: Nuclear Assurance Corporation, Atlanta, GA. [3] Reprocessed fuel not included as inventory.
Source: Except as noted, U.S. Energy Information Administration, *Annual Energy Review, Uranium Industry Annual* and unpublished data.

No. 947. Electric Utilities—Generation, Sales, Revenue, and Customers: 1980 to 1994

[Sales and revenue are to and from ultimate customers]

CLASS	Unit	1980	1985	1988	1989	1990	1991	1992	1993	1994, prel.
Generation [1]	Bil. kWh . .	2,286	2,470	2,704	2,784	2,808	2,825	2,797	2,883	2,911
Sales [2]	Bil. kWh .	2,126	2,306	2,554	2,621	2,684	2,737	2,735	2,850	2,930
Residential or domestic	Bil. kWh . .	734	793	886	899	916	949	929	994	1,008
Percent of total	Percent . .	34.5	34.4	34.7	34.3	34.1	34.7	34.0	34.9	34.4
Commercial [3]	Bil. kWh . .	524	606	698	716	739	753	756	803	834
Industrial [4]	Bil. kWh . .	794	820	882	913	932	935	949	957	990
Revenue [2]	Bil. dol . .	95.5	149.2	162.4	169.6	176.5	185.1	187.3	197.9	202.5
Residential or domestic	Bil. dol. . .	37.6	58.6	66.4	68.8	71.7	76.4	76.4	82.4	84.5
Percent of total	Percent . .	39.4	39.3	40.9	40.5	40.7	41.2	40.8	41.7	41.7
Commercial [3]	Bil. dol. . .	27.4	44.1	49.1	51.6	54.2	56.8	58.0	62.0	64.4
Industrial [4]	Bil. dol. . .	27.3	41.4	41.6	43.7	44.9	45.9	46.8	46.6	46.8
Ultimate customers, Dec. 31 [2]	Million. . .	92.7	101.6	106.4	108.5	110.1	111.4	113.1	115.2	116.9
Residential or domestic	Million . . .	82.2	89.8	93.9	95.6	97.0	98.2	99.6	101.3	102.7
Commercial [3]	Million . . .	9.7	10.9	11.6	12.0	12.1	12.3	12.5	12.5	12.8
Industrial [4]	Million . . .	0.5	0.5	0.5	0.5	0.5	0.5	0.5	0.5	0.6
Avg. kWh used per customer	1,000. . . .	23.2	22.9	24.2	24.4	24.6	24.7	24.4	24.9	25.2
Residential.	1,000. . . .	9.0	8.9	9.5	9.5	9.5	9.7	9.4	9.9	9.9
Commercial [3]	1,000. . . .	54.5	56.1	60.4	60.6	61.3	61.6	61.0	64.4	65.7
Avg. annual bill per customer. .	Dollar . . .	1,040	1,482	1,536	1,576	1,614	1,670	1,667	1,727	1,741
Residential.	Dollar . . .	462	658	712	725	744	782	772	818	827
Commercial [3]	Dollar . . .	2,848	4,080	4,256	4,363	4,494	4,646	4,681	4,977	5,076
Avg. revenue per kWh sold . . .	Cents . . .	4.49	6.47	6.36	6.47	6.57	6.76	6.85	6.94	6.91
Residential.	Cents . . .	5.12	7.39	7.49	7.65	7.83	8.05	8.22	8.29	8.38
Commercial [3]	Cents . . .	5.22	7.27	7.04	7.20	7.33	7.55	7.67	7.73	7.73
Industrial [4]	Cents . . .	3.44	5.04	4.71	4.79	4.81	4.91	4.93	4.87	4.73

[1] Source: U.S. Energy Information Administration, *Monthly Energy Review*, monthly.   [2] Includes other types not shown separately.   [3] Small light and power.   [4] Large light and power.
Source: Except as noted, Edison Electric Institute, Washington, DC, *Statistical Yearbook of the Electric Utility Industry*, annual.

No. 948. Major Investor-Owned Electric Utilities—Balance Sheet and Income Account of Privately Owned Companies: 1984 to 1994

[In billions of dollars. As of Dec. 31. As of 1990, covers approximately 180 investor-owned electric utilities that during each of the last 3 years met any one or more of the following conditions — 1 mil. megawatthours of total sales; 100 megawatthours of sales for resale, 500 megawatthours of gross interchange out, and 500 megawatthours of wheeling for other. See also *Historical Statistics, Colonial Times to 1970*, series S 133-146 and V 197-212]

ITEM	1984	1985	1987	1988	1989	1990	1991	1992	1993	1994
COMPOSITE BALANCE SHEET										
Total assets and other debits	375.6	404.7	446.3	454.3	465.7	477.9	487.5	506.4	566.6	574.5
Total electric utility plant.	364.7	396.9	434.6	449.4	462.4	480.6	497.9	518.8	537.3	553.1
Electric depreciation and amortization	77.1	85.1	103.2	113.5	125.0	135.7	148.3	160.5	173.4	186.1
Net electric utility plant	287.5	311.8	331.4	335.9	337.5	344.9	349.6	358.3	363.8	366.9
Total other utility plant	17.6	19.9	23.1	24.6	26.3	28.5	31.0	33.4	36.4	38.6
Other utility depreciation and amortization. .	6.1	6.5	7.8	8.5	9.2	10.0	10.8	11.7	12.4	13.4
Net other utility plant.	12.1	13.4	15.2	16.1	17.1	18.6	20.2	21.7	24.0	25.2
Total all utility plant	395.3	431.1	475.7	493.0	507.9	528.7	548.4	571.9	593.6	610.7
All utility plant depreciation and amortization.	88.0	97.4	118.7	131.3	144.6	157.4	171.7	185.1	199.8	212.9
Net all utility plant.	307.3	333.8	357.0	361.6	363.2	371.3	376.8	386.9	393.8	397.8
Other property and investments	10.8	12.1	15.6	15.2	16.1	17.7	17.4	18.0	20.1	23.5
Current and accrued assets	37.9	39.4	40.9	39.1	41.5	41.5	43.4	43.4	42.4	41.3
Deferred debits	19.3	19.4	32.9	38.3	44.8	47.3	50.0	58.0	110.3	112.0
Liabilities and other credits.	375.3	404.7	446.3	454.3	465.7	477.9	487.5	506.4	566.6	574.5
Capital stock [1]	79.0	82.8	79.9	80.7	82.9	83.2	83.6	86.1	87.1	87.2
Other paid-in capital [2]	34.0	36.3	40.3	40.4	39.1	40.5	42.9	44.7	47.2	48.9
Retained earnings	37.1	41.1	48.0	47.1	47.7	48.1	49.0	49.7	49.9	51.8
Subsidiary earnings	1.9	2.2	2.6	2.5	2.8	2.9	3.0	2.7	2.9	3.2
Long-term debt	140.6	152.7	158.4	160.7	162.9	167.9	171.9	174.1	174.9	175.4
Current and accrued liabilities.	32.0	32.0	39.3	38.4	42.0	44.3	43.4	45.6	48.9	48.0
Deferred credits and operating reserves [3] . .	19.0	20.9	25.6	28.1	28.5	28.8	29.2	31.1	40.9	41.2
Deferred income taxes as deferred credits .	28.1	32.7	45.9	50.2	53.3	56.5	59.2	65.0	105.0	107.1
COMPOSITE INCOME ACCOUNTS										
Electric operating revenues	128.3	135.3	138.5	143.9	150.9	157.3	166.8	169.5	176.4	179.3
Electric operating expenses	105.5	111.1	111.6	115.3	121.6	127.9	135.9	139.0	146.1	148.7
Net electric utility operating income	22.8	24.1	27.0	28.6	29.4	29.4	30.9	30.5	30.2	30.6
Other than electric utility operating income .	1.1	1.2	1.1	1.2	1.2	1.1	1.2	1.3	1.5	1.3
Net utility operating income	24.0	25.3	28.1	29.8	30.6	30.5	32.1	31.8	31.7	32.1
Total other income	6.8	7.4	6.6	5.0	5.2	4.1	3.9	2.9	2.8	2.8
Total income [4]	30.8	32.7	34.6	34.8	35.8	34.6	36.0	34.7	34.6	34.9
Income deductions [5]	11.1	14.0	15.6	18.8	18.5	17.7	19.1	16.3	16.7	15.0
Net income	19.7	18.7	19.0	16.0	17.3	16.9	16.9	18.4	17.9	19.9

[1] Composed of Common Stock Issued and Preferred Stock Issued.   [2] Composed of Capital Stock Subscribed, Liability and Premium and Other Paid-in Capital.   [3] Composed of Total Deferred Credits less Accumulated Deferred Income Taxes as Deferred Credits.   [4] Composed of Net Utility Operating Income plus Total Other Income.   [5] Composed of the difference between Total Income less Net Income.
Source: U.S. Energy Information Administration, 1984, *Financial Statistics of Selected Electric Utilities*, annual; thereafter, *Financial Statistics of Major U.S. Investor-Owned Electric Utilities*, annual.

No. 949. Nonutility Electric Power Producers—Summary, by Type of Fuel: 1989 to 1994

MAJOR SELECTED TYPES OF FUEL	INSTALLED CAPACITY OF 5 MEGAWATT OR MORE						INSTALLED CAPACITY OF 1 MEGAWATT OR MORE	
	1989	1990	1991	1992	1993	1994	1993	1994
Installed capacity (megawatts)	36,645	42,869	48,171	56,814	59,055	66,633	60,778	68,461
Coal [1]	6,229	6,712	7,291	8,503	9,712	10,322	9,772	10,372
Petroleum [2]	917	811	1,207	1,730	1,869	2,061	2,043	2,262
Natural gas [3]	13,999	16,682	20,259	21,542	23,009	26,454	23,463	26,925
Other gas [4]	(NA)	(NA)	(NA)	(NA)	(NA)	1,122	(NA)	1,130
Petroleum/natural gas (combined)	4,439	6,167	5,049	8,478	8,377	9,667	8,505	9,820
Hydroelectric.	1,386	1,477	1,587	2,684	2,173	2,783	2,741	3,364
Geothermal.	944	1,031	1,048	1,254	1,307	1,324	1,318	1,335
Solar	200	360	360	360	360	354	360	354
Wind [5]	1,339	1,405	1,652	1,822	1,775	1,700	1,813	1,737
Wood [5]	5,254	5,786	6,580	6,805	6,983	7,354	7,046	7,416
Waste [6]	1,742	2,230	2,627	3,006	2,910	2,900	3,131	3,150
Gross generation (mil. kWh)	187,356	217,241	248,448	296,001	318,843	348,189	325,226	354,925
Coal [1]	31,511	32,131	40,587	47,363	53,166	58,839	53,367	59,035
Petroleum [2]	5,742	7,330	7,814	10,963	13,089	14,751	13,364	15,069
Natural gas [3]	98,875	116,706	131,340	158,798	171,765	177,058	174,282	179,735
Other gases [4]	(NA)	(NA)	(NA)	(NA)	(NA)	12,441	(NA)	12,480
Hydroelectric.	5,931	6,235	6,243	9,446	9,583	11,293	11,511	13,227
Geothermal.	5,046	6,872	7,651	8,578	9,704	10,080	9,749	10,122
Solar	489	663	779	746	897	824	897	824
Wind [5]	1,833	2,251	2,606	2,916	2,999	3,424	3,052	3,482
Wood [5]	27,835	30,812	33,785	36,255	37,206	38,395	37,421	38,595
Waste [6]	8,296	11,415	13,956	17,352	17,187	17,532	18,325	18,797

NA Not available.   [1] Includes coal, anthracite, culm and coal waste.   [2] Includes petroleum, petroleum coke, diesel, kerosene, and petroleum sludge and tar.   [3] Includes natural gas, butane, ethane, propane, waste heat and waste gases.   [4] Includes butane, ethane, propane, and other gases.   [5] Includes wood, wood waste, peat, wood liquors, railroad ties, pitch and wood sludge.   [6] Includes municipal solid waste, agricultural waste, straw, tires, landfill gases and other waste.
Source: Energy Information Administration, *Electric Power Annual.*

No. 950. Water Power—Developed and Undeveloped Capacity, by Division: 1960 to 1995

[In millions of kilowatts. As of **Dec. 31.** Excludes all capacity of reversible equipment at pumped storage projects. Also excludes capacity precluded from development due to wild and scenic river legislation. For composition of divisions, see table 27. See also *Historical Statistics, Colonial Times to 1970,* series S 160-175]

DIVISION	DEVELOPED INSTALLED CAPACITY							ESTIMATED UNDEVELOPED CAPACITY						
	1960	1970	1980	1990	1993	1994	1995	1960	1970	1980	1990	1993	1994	1995
United States	33.2	52.0	64.4	73.0	74.0	74.1	74.2	114.2	128.0	129.9	73.9	73.6	73.5	71.0
New England	1.5	1.5	1.5	1.9	1.9	1.9	1.9	2.9	3.3	4.7	4.4	4.4	4.4	4.4
Middle Atlantic	2.5	4.3	4.3	4.9	4.9	4.9	4.9	7.6	4.5	5.1	5.1	4.9	4.9	4.9
East North Central	0.9	0.9	0.9	1.1	1.2	1.2	1.2	3.0	1.6	2.0	1.7	1.7	1.7	1.7
West North Central	1.6	2.7	2.8	3.1	3.1	3.1	3.1	6.4	4.4	3.4	3.1	3.1	3.1	3.1
South Atlantic	3.8	5.3	5.9	6.7	6.7	6.7	6.7	8.4	9.6	9.6	7.0	7.2	7.2	7.2
East South Central	3.8	5.2	5.6	5.9	5.9	5.9	5.9	4.6	3.8	3.3	2.4	2.4	2.4	2.3
West South Central	0.9	1.9	2.3	2.7	2.7	2.7	2.7	3.9	3.3	4.7	4.6	4.6	4.6	4.6
Mountain	4.6	6.2	7.4	9.2	9.5	9.5	9.5	23.6	26.7	34.2	19.4	19.1	19.1	18.8
Pacific	13.6	23.9	33.7	37.5	38.1	38.2	38.3	53.8	70.9	62.9	26.2	26.2	26.1	24.0

Source: U.S. Federal Energy Regulatory Commission (formerly U.S. Federal Power Commission), *Hydroelectric Power Resources of the United States, Developed and Undeveloped,* January 1, 1988; and unpublished data.

No. 951. Solar Collector Shipments, by Type, End Use, and Market Sector: 1984 to 1994

[In thousands of square feet, except number of manufacturers. Solar collector is a device for intercepting sunlight, converting the light to heat, and carrying the heat to where it will be either used or stored. 1985 data are not available]

YEAR	Number of manufac- turers	Total ship- ments [1]	COLLECTOR TYPE		END USE			MARKET SECTOR		
			Low tem- perature	Medium tempera- ture, spe- cial, other	Pool heating	Hot water	Space heating	Resi- dential	Com- mercial	Indus- trial
1984 [2]	225	17,191	4,479	11,939	4,427	8,930	2,370	13,980	2,091	289
1986 [2]	98	9,360	3,751	1,111	3,494	1,181	127	4,131	703	13
1987 [2]	59	7,269	3,157	957	3,111	964	23	3,775	305	11
1988 [2]	51	8,174	3,326	732	3,304	726	7	3,796	255	7
1989 [2]	44	11,482	4,283	1,989	4,688	1,374	205	5,804	424	42
1990	51	11,409	3,645	2,527	5,016	1,091	2	5,835	294	22
1991	48	6,574	5,585	989	5,535	989	24	6,322	225	13
1992	45	7,086	6,187	897	6,210	801	35	6,832	204	27
1993	41	6,968	6,025	931	6,040	880	15	6,694	215	31
1994	41	7,627	6,823	803	6,813	790	19	7,026	583	16

[1] Includes high temperature collectors, end uses such process heating, and utility and other market sectors not shown separately.   [2] Declines between 1984 and 1989 are primarily due to the expiration of the Federal energy tax credit and industry consolidation.
Source: U.S. Energy Information Administration, *Solar Collector Manufacturing Activity,* annual.

No. 952. Renewable Energy Consumption Estimates, by Type: 1990 to 1994

[**In quadrillion Btu**. Renewable energy is obtained from sources that are essentially inexhaustible unlike fossil fuels of which there is a finite supply]

SOURCE AND SECTOR	1990	1991	1992	1993	1994
SOURCES					
Total	6.16	6.27	6.11	6.40	6.35
Consumption for electricity.	3.94	4.10	3.83	4.15	4.05
Electric utilities	3.23	3.30	2.97	3.22	3.07
Hydroelectric power.	2.93	2.90	2.51	2.77	2.54
Geothermal energy	0.18	0.17	0.17	0.16	0.15
Biofuels [1]	0.02	0.02	0.02	0.02	0.02
Wind energy [2].	(Z)	(Z)	(Z)	(Z)	(Z)
Nonutility power generators.	0.70	0.79	0.87	0.93	0.99
Hydroelectric power	0.08	0.08	0.10	0.12	0.14
Geothermal, solar, and wind energy	0.18	0.20	0.22	0.24	0.26
Biofuels [1]	0.44	0.51	0.55	0.57	0.59
Net imported electricity.	0.10	0.21	0.26	0.27	0.36
Consumption for other uses [3]	2.22	2.17	2.28	2.25	2.30
Biofuels [1]	2.63	2.64	2.79	2.78	2.85
Solar and photovoltaic energy	0.07	0.07	0.07	0.07	0.07
SECTORS					
Total	6.16	6.27	6.11	6.40	6.35
Residential and commercial	0.64	0.67	0.71	0.65	0.64
Industrial.	2.21	2.22	2.36	2.45	2.54
Transportation	0.08	0.07	0.08	0.09	0.10
Electric utilities.	3.23	3.30	2.97	3.22	3.07

Z Less than 0.005 quadrillion Btu. [1] Biofuels are fuelwood, wood byproducts, waste wood, municipal solid waste, manufacturing process waste, and alcohol fuels. [2] Also includes photovoltaic and solar thermal energy. [3] Included are nonutility thermal energy uses, such as space heating and industrial process heat production. Excluded are estimates for mechanical energy, such as shaft power from dams, wind machines, and solar-powered motors and activators.
Source: U.S. Energy Information Administration, *Annual Energy Review.*

No. 953. Privately Owned Gas Utility Industry—Balance Sheet and Income Account: 1980 to 1994

[**In millions of dollars.** The gas utility industry consists of pipeline and distribution companies. Excludes operations of companies distributing gas in bottles or tanks. See also *Historical Statistics, Colonial Times to 1970,* series S 205-218]

ITEM	1980	1985	1988	1989	1990	1991	1992	1993	1994
COMPOSITE BALANCE SHEET									
Assets, total [1]	75,851	104,478	121,667	123,820	121,686	124,120	129,400	135,813	138,086
Total utility plant.	67,071	88,121	99,933	106,017	112,863	119,772	129,272	135,859	139,187
Depreciation and amortization. . . .	26,162	36,377	44,423	47,054	49,483	52,400	53,005	60,152	61,355
Utility plant (net).	40,909	51,744	55,510	58,963	63,380	67,372	76,267	75,707	77,832
Investment and fund accounts [1] . .	15,530	23,871	31,552	28,111	23,872	22,883	21,883	23,342	23,108
Current and accrued assets	17,243	24,771	23,402	24,836	23,268	23,023	23,783	21,451	20,799
Deferred debits [2]	2,169	4,092	9,658	10,364	9,576	9,277	9,776	13,369	14,257
Liabilities, total [1]	75,851	104,478	121,667	123,820	121,686	124,120	129,400	135,813	138,086
Capitalization, total [1].	51,382	65,799	69,875	74,753	74,958	75,463	81,183	82,755	85,823
Capital stock [1]	29,315	39,517	39,898	43,889	43,810	43,435	46,318	49,051	50,570
Long-term debts	22,067	26,282	29,977	30,864	31,148	32,028	34,865	33,693	35,215
Current and accrued liabilities. . . .	18,119	26,125	33,735	31,005	29,550	28,128	26,438	27,321	25,536
Deferred income taxes [3]	4,149	7,769	10,685	11,292	11,360	10,527	10,952	13,070	13,760
Other liabilities and credits	2,201	4,785	7,372	6,770	5,818	10,002	10,827	12,667	12,967
COMPOSITE INCOME ACCOUNT									
Operating revenues, total . .	85,918	103,945	69,754	70,363	66,027	63,922	66,405	69,966	63,831
Operating expenses [4]	81,789	98,320	64,696	64,262	60,137	59,165	60,042	62,977	56,896
Operation and maintenance . . .	74,508	88,572	57,032	55,990	51,627	50,867	48,054	50,468	44,014
Federal, State, and local taxes .	4,847	6,590	4,241	4,843	4,957	4,446	6,031	6,185	6,515
Operating income.	4,129	5,625	5,058	6,101	5,890	4,756	6,363	6,988	6,934
Utility operating income	4,471	6,030	5,202	6,274	6,077	4,962	6,572	7,177	7,126
Income before interest charges [1] . .	6,929	7,636	7,472	8,764	8,081	5,530	7,223	8,754	8,500
Net income [1]	4,194	3,785	3,352	4,641	4,410	1,894	3,750	5,589	5,325
Dividends	2,564	4,060	3,151	3,113	3,191	4,341	3,889	3,149	3,930

[1] Beginning 1980, not comparable with earlier years due to Federal Power Commission ruling requiring adoption of the equity method in reporting earnings of subsidiaries. [2] Includes capital stock discount and expense and reacquired securities. [3] Includes reserves for deferred income taxes. [4] Includes expenses not shown separately.
Source: American Gas Association, Arlington, VA, *Gas Facts,* annual, (copyright).

No. 954. Gas Utility Industry—Summary: 1980 to 1994

[Covers natural, manufactured, mixed, and liquid petroleum gas. Based on questionnaire mailed to all privately and municipally owned gas utilities in United States, except those with annual revenues less than $25,000. See also *Historical Statistics, Colonial Times to 1970,* series S 190-204]

ITEM	Unit	1980	1985	1988	1989	1990	1991	1992	1993	1994
End users [1]	1,000	47,223	49,971	52,422	53,356	54,261	55,174	56,132	57,028	57,960
Residential	1,000 ...	43,489	45,929	48,133	48,980	49,802	50,634	51,525	52,358	53,243
Commercial	1,000 ...	3,498	3,816	4,069	4,161	4,246	4,322	4,397	4,428	4,474
Industrial and other	1,000 ...	187	179	168	168	166	168	165	181	181
Sales [2]	Tril. Btu ..	15,413	12,616	10,705	10,551	9,842	9,605	9,906	10,021	9,480
Residential	Tril. Btu ...	4,826	4,513	4,695	4,798	4,468	4,550	4,694	5,054	4,972
Percent of total	Percent ...	31.3	35.8	43.9	45.5	45.4	47.4	47.4	50.4	52.4
Commercial	Tril. Btu ...	2,453	2,338	2,306	2,322	2,192	2,198	2,209	2,397	2,351
Industrial	Tril. Btu ...	7,957	5,635	3,544	3,243	3,010	2,631	2,772	2,404	2,009
Other	Tril. Btu ...	177	130	160	188	171	226	231	167	148
Revenues [2]	Mil. dol ...	48,303	63,293	46,162	47,493	45,153	44,647	46,178	49,847	49,864
Residential	Mil. dol ...	17,432	26,864	24,828	26,172	25,000	25,729	26,702	29,787	30,563
Percent of total	Percent ...	36.1	42.4	53.8	55.1	55.4	57.6	57.8	59.8	61.3
Commercial	Mil. dol ...	8,183	12,722	10,681	11,074	10,604	10,669	10,865	12,076	12,254
Industrial	Mil. dol ...	22,215	23,086	10,113	9,666	8,996	7,576	7,913	7,351	6,475
Other	Mil. dol ...	473	621	538	581	553	674	698	632	572
Prices per mil. Btu [3]	Dollars ...	3.13	5.02	4.31	4.50	4.59	4.65	4.66	4.94	5.23
Residential	Dollars ...	3.61	5.95	5.29	5.45	5.60	5.66	5.69	5.89	6.14
Commercial	Dollars ...	3.34	5.44	4.63	4.77	4.84	4.85	4.92	5.04	5.21
Industrial	Dollars ...	2.79	4.10	2.85	2.98	2.99	2.88	2.85	3.02	3.17
Gas mains mileage	1,000	1,052	1,119	1,169	1,185	1,207	1,225	1,254	1,251	1,267
Field and gathering	1,000 ...	84	94	92	91	90	86	86	73	72
Transmission	1,000 ...	266	271	276	276	280	282	285	270	276
Distribution	1,000 ...	702	754	801	818	837	857	883	908	919
Construction expenditures [4]	Mil. dol ...	5,350	5,671	6,166	7,341	7,899	9,036	11,068	9,140	9,282
Transmission	Mil. dol ...	1,583	1,562	1,568	2,081	2,886	3,656	5,739	3,288	3,065
Distribution	Mil. dol ...	1,869	2,577	3,389	3,980	3,714	3,842	3,867	4,286	4,550
Production and storage	Mil. dol ...	1,150	790	268	276	309	430	349	253	230

[1] Annual average.   [2] Excludes sales for resale.   [3] For definition, see text, section 19.   [4] Includes general.

Source: American Gas Association, Arlington, VA, *Gas Facts,* annual (copyright).

No. 955. Gas Utility Industry—Customers, Sales, and Revenues, by State: 1994

[See headnote, table 954. For definition of Btu, see text, section 19]

REGION, DIVISION, AND STATE	CUSTOMERS[1] (1,000) Total[2]	Resi-dential	SALES[3] (tril. Btu) Total[2]	Resi-dential	REVENUES[3] (mil. dol.) Total[2]	Resi-dential	REGION, DIVISION, AND STATE	CUSTOMERS[1] (1,000) Total[2]	Resi-dential	SALES[3] (tril. Btu) Total[2]	Resi-dential	REVENUES[3] (mil. dol.) Total[2]	Resi-dential
U.S. . .	57,960	53,243	9,480	4,972	49,864	30,563	DC ..	147	132	32	13	231	110
							VA. . .	785	707	134	62	831	469
Northeast .	11,342	10,383	1,962	1,070	13,286	8,520	WV ..	398	363	101	40	452	264
N.E. . . .	2,112	1,905	406	186	2,938	1,672	NC ..	721	632	150	49	781	346
ME ..	20	14	5	1	32	7	SC ..	436	387	121	24	548	180
NH ..	84	71	19	7	124	54	GA ..	1,560	1,441	329	165	1,334	796
VT ..	30	26	8	3	42	19	FL ..	599	546	85	18	458	154
MA ..	1,281	1,166	226	112	1,658	990	E.S.C .	2,815	2,536	494	209	2,450	1,235
RI ..	220	198	35	19	277	166	KY ..	742	669	128	66	610	351
CT ..	478	429	113	45	805	436	TN ..	838	738	165	61	814	351
M.A . . .	9,230	8,478	1,556	884	10,348	6,848	AL ..	796	734	117	54	652	381
NY ..	4,331	4,005	615	395	4,713	3,344	MS ..	440	395	85	28	375	152
NJ . . .	2,309	2,081	493	213	2,767	1,521	W.S.C .	6,192	5,672	1,330	386	5,029	2,168
PA...	2,590	2,392	448	276	2,868	1,983	AR ..	585	520	86	42	415	236
Midwest . .	17,798	16,269	3,025	1,941	15,262	10,397	LA ..	1,024	959	360	56	1,080	339
E.N.C . .	12,730	11,714	2,182	1,469	11,287	7,929	OK ..	941	850	176	77	676	378
OH ..	3,153	2,908	531	358	2,894	2,028	TX . .	3,643	3,344	709	212	2,858	1,215
IN ..	1,593	1,452	280	166	1,580	1,016	West . . .	14,172	13,260	1,547	911	8,211	5,347
IL . . .	3,689	3,394	605	448	3,131	2,377	Mt	3,711	3,385	497	285	2,365	1,489
MI...	2,937	2,720	519	368	2,361	1,702	MT ..	221	195	35	21	162	99
WI...	1,357	1,241	246	129	1,320	806	ID . . .	183	160	22	12	115	69
W.N.C . .	5,068	4,555	843	472	3,975	2,468	WY ..	134	119	24	12	104	59
MN ..	1,177	1,069	247	122	1,103	632	CO ..	1,209	1,092	178	106	788	493
IA . . .	837	749	136	78	657	413	NM ..	448	407	58	33	270	182
MO ..	1,405	1,272	196	127	1,028	698	AZ..	609	569	60	26	353	198
ND ..	107	94	21	11	96	54	UT ..	543	503	81	52	340	242
SD ..	135	120	25	12	116	63	NV ..	365	340	39	22	233	145
NE ..	504	441	87	45	384	222	Pac . . .	10,461	9,875	1,050	626	5,846	3,858
KS ..	903	811	129	76	591	386	WA ..	671	599	143	54	621	292
South. . . .	14,648	13,332	2,946	1,049	13,105	6,299	OR ..	446	392	74	30	397	202
S.A. . .	5,641	5,124	1,122	454	5,626	2,896	CA ..	9,218	8,774	799	526	4,683	3,300
DE ..	109	100	27	9	138	64	AK ..	90	78	32	15	102	54
MD ..	886	816	144	74	853	513	HI . . .	36	33	3	1	44	10

[1] Averages for the year.   [2] Includes other service, not shown separately.   [3] Excludes sales for resale.

Source: American Gas Association, Arlington, VA, *Gas Facts,* annual (copyright).

Figure 20.1
Research and Development Expenditures: 1960 to 1995

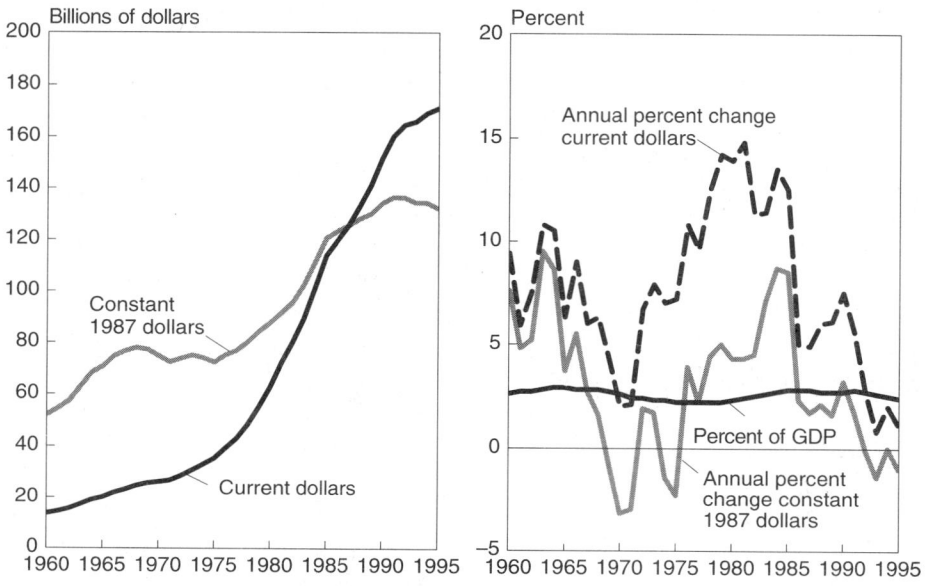

Source: Chart prepared by U.S. Bureau of the Census. For data, see table 957.

Figure 20.2
**Research and Development Scientists and Engineers
in Private Industry: 1975 to 1993**

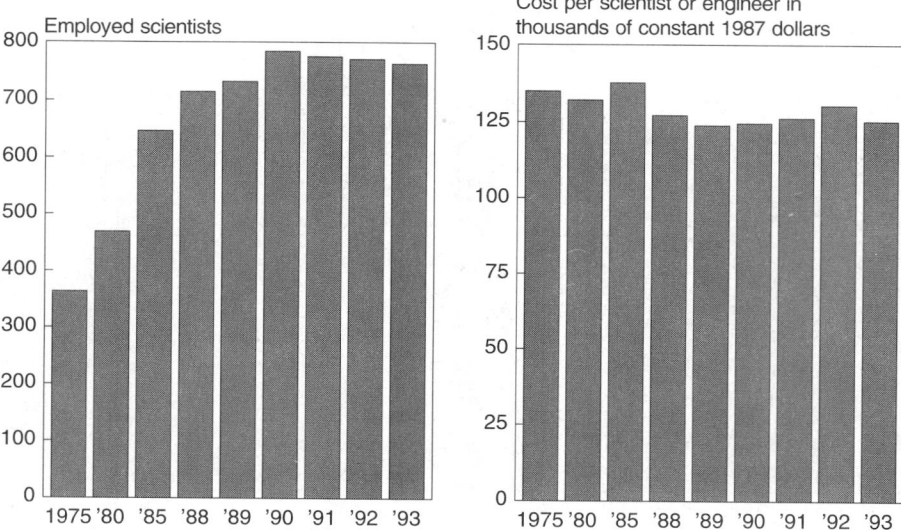

Source: Chart prepared by U.S. Bureau of the Census. For data, see table 969.

Science and Technology

This section presents statistics on scientific, engineering, and technological resources, with emphasis on patterns of research and development (R&D) funding and on scientific, engineering, and technical personnel, education, and employment. Also included are statistics on space program outlays and accomplishments. Principal sources of these data are the National Science Foundation (NSF) and the National Aeronautics and Space Administration (NASA).

NSF gathers data chiefly through recurring surveys. Current NSF publications containing data on funds for research and development and on scientific and engineering personnel include the *Science Resources Studies Highlights* summaries series; Detailed Statistical Tables; and annual, biennial, triennial, and special reports. Titles or the areas of coverage of these reports include the following: *Science and Engineering Indicators; National Patterns of R&D Resources; Science and Engineering Personnel—A National Overview; Women and Minorities in Science and Engineering;* science and technology data presented in chart and tabular form in a pocket-size publication; *International Science and Technology Data Update;* profiles on human resources and funding in individual fields of science and engineering; *Federal Funds for Research and Development; Federal R&D Funding by Budget Function; Federal Support to Universities, Colleges, and Selected Nonprofit Institutions; Scientific and Engineering Facilities at Universities and Colleges; Geographic Distribution of Industrial R&D Expenditures; Research and Development in Industry;* R&D funds and graduate enrollment and support in academic science and engineering; characteristics of doctoral scientists and engineers and of recent graduates in the United States; *U.S. Scientists and Engineers;* and scientists, engineers, and technicians in manufacturing, nonmanufacturing, and trade and regulated industries. Statistical surveys in these areas pose problems of concept and definition and the data should, therefore, be regarded as broad estimates

In Brief
R&D expenditures in constant (1987) dollars:

1970	74.6 bil.
1980	87.6 bil.
1995	132.1 bil.

Federal outlays for space and technologies in constant 1987 dollars:

1970	11.0 bil.
1980	6.3 bil.
1990	10.3 bil.
1996	9.5 bil.

rather than precise quantitative statements. See sources for details.

The National Science Board's biennial *Science and Engineering Indicators* contains data and analyses of international and domestic science and technology, including measures of inputs and outputs. *The Budget of the United States Government,* published by the U.S. Office of Management and Budget, contains summary financial data on Federal R&D programs.

Research and development outlays—NSF defines research as a "systematic and intensive study directed toward a fuller knowledge of the subject studied" and development as "the systematic use of scientific knowledge directed toward the production of useful materials, devices, systems, methods, or processes." National coverage of R&D expenditures is developed primarily from periodic surveys in four principal economic sectors: (1) *Government,* made up primarily of Federal executive agencies; (2) *industry,* consisting of manufacturing and nonmanufacturing firms and the federally funded research and development centers (FFRDC's) they administer; (3) *universities and colleges,* composed of universities, colleges, and their affiliated institutions, agricultural experiment stations, and associated schools of agriculture, and FFRDC's administered by educational institutions; and (4) *other nonprofit institutions,* consisting of such organizations as private philanthropic foundations, nonprofit research institutes, voluntary health agencies, and FFRDC's administered by nonprofit organizations. The R&D funds reported consist of current operating costs, including planning and administration costs, except as otherwise noted. They exclude funds for routine testing, mapping and surveying, collection of general-purpose data, dissemination of scientific information, and training of scientific personnel.

Scientists, engineers, and technicians—Scientists and engineers are defined as persons engaged in scientific and engineering work at a level requiring a knowledge of sciences equivalent at least to that acquired through completion of a 4-year college course. Technicians are defined as persons engaged in technical work at a level requiring knowledge acquired through a technical institute, junior college, or other type of training less extensive than 4-year college training. Craftsmen and skilled workers are excluded.

Historical statistics—Tabular headnotes provide cross-references, where applicable, to *Historical Statistics of the United States, Colonial Times to 1970.* See Appendix IV.

Figure 20.3
Top 15 Universities—Federal Research and Development Obligations: 1993

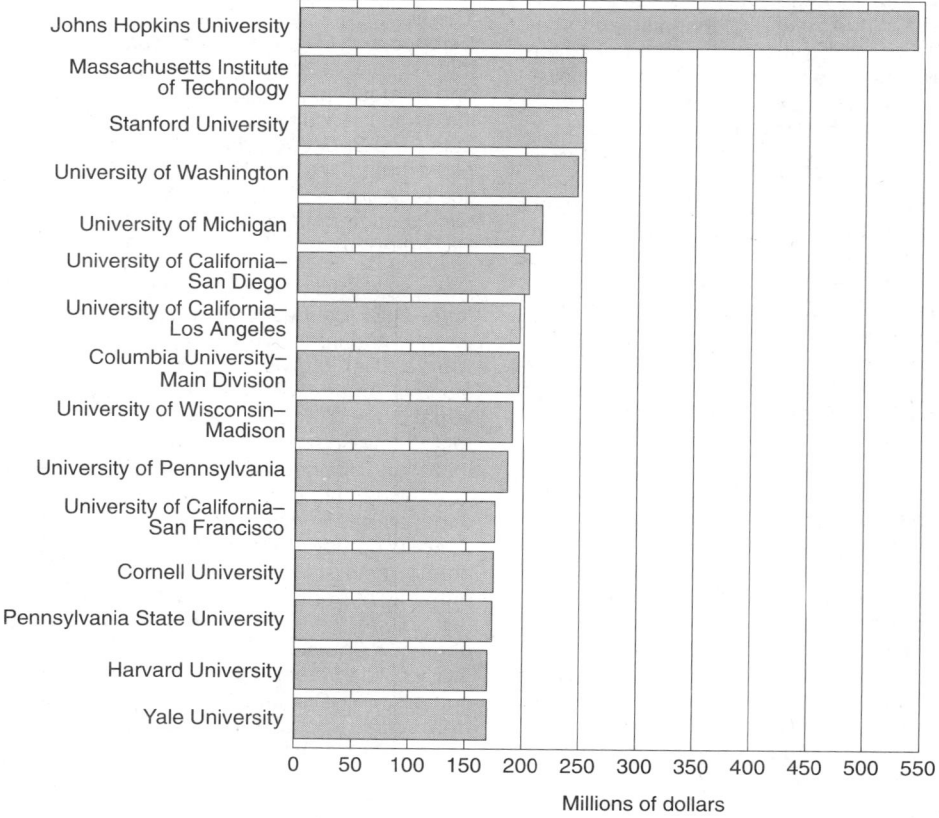

Millions of dollars

Source: Chart prepared by U.S. Bureau of the Census. For data, see table 965.

No. 956. R&D Expenditures: 1960 to 1995

[Includes basic research, applied research, and development. Defense-related outlays comprise all research and development spending by Dept. of Defense, including space activities, and a portion of Department of Energy funds. Space-related outlays are those of the National Aeronautics and Space Administration; they exclude space activities of other Federal agencies, estimated at less than 5 percent of all space research and development spending. Minus sign (-) indicates decrease]

YEAR	CURRENT DOLLARS (bil. dol.)			CONSTANT (1987) DOLLARS [1]		ANNUAL PERCENT CHANGE [3]		PERCENT OF TOTAL R&D OUTLAYS				
	Total	Defense space related	Other	Total (bil. dol.)	Percent of GDP [2]	Current dollars	Constant dollars	Federally funded defense/space-related			Other outlays	
								Total	Defense	Space	Non-Federal	Federal
1960	13.5	7.5	6.0	52.0	2.6	9.4	7.6	55	52	3	35	9
1965	20.0	10.8	9.3	70.6	2.9	6.3	3.7	54	33	21	35	11
1970	26.1	11.4	14.7	74.6	2.6	2.0	-3.2	44	33	10	43	13
1973	30.7	11.9	18.9	74.9	2.3	7.9	1.7	39	32	7	47	15
1974	32.9	11.8	21.1	73.9	2.3	7.0	-1.4	36	29	7	49	15
1975	35.2	12.3	23.0	72.2	2.2	7.2	-2.3	35	27	7	49	17
1976	39.0	13.4	25.6	75.0	2.2	10.8	3.9	34	27	8	49	17
1977	42.8	14.3	28.5	76.7	2.2	9.6	2.2	33	27	7	50	17
1978	48.1	15.3	32.8	80.1	2.2	12.5	4.4	32	26	6	50	18
1979	54.9	16.6	38.4	84.1	2.2	14.2	5.0	30	25	6	51	19
1980	62.6	18.4	44.2	87.6	2.3	13.9	4.3	29	24	5	53	18
1981	71.9	21.2	50.6	91.4	2.4	14.8	4.3	30	24	5	54	17
1982	80.0	24.6	55.4	95.5	2.5	11.3	4.5	31	26	5	54	15
1983	89.1	28.3	60.9	102.3	2.6	11.4	7.1	32	27	4	54	14
1984	101.2	31.8	69.3	111.2	2.7	13.5	8.7	31	28	3	55	14
1985	113.8	37.5	76.3	120.6	2.8	12.5	8.5	33	30	3	54	13
1986	119.6	40.5	79.1	123.3	2.8	5.0	2.3	34	31	3	55	12
1987	125.4	43.2	82.2	125.4	2.8	4.9	1.7	34	31	3	54	12
1988	132.9	43.7	89.2	128.0	2.7	6.0	2.1	33	30	3	55	12
1989	141.0	43.4	97.6	130.0	2.7	6.1	1.6	31	27	4	58	12
1990	151.5	44.4	107.1	134.1	2.7	7.5	3.2	29	25	4	59	11
1991	160.1	42.9	117.2	136.4	2.8	5.6	1.7	27	22	4	62	11
1992	164.5	41.1	123.4	136.3	2.7	2.7	-0.1	25	21	4	63	12
1993	165.8	40.6	125.2	134.4	2.6	0.8	-1.4	25	21	4	64	12
1994, prel . .	169.1	41.3	127.8	134.3	2.5	2.0	-0.0	24	20	4	64	12
1995, est. . .	171.0	41.0	130.0	132.1	2.4	1.1	-1.6	24	20	4	65	11

[1] Based on GDP implicit price deflator.   [2] GDP = Gross Domestic Product.   [3] Change from immediate prior year.

Source: U.S. National Science Foundation, *National Patterns of R&D Resources,* annual.

No. 957. R&D Source of Funds and Performance Sector: 1970 to 1995

[**In millions of dollars.** See headnote, table 958]

YEAR	Total	SOURCE OF FUNDS				PERFORMANCE SECTOR				
		Federal Govt.	Industry	Univ., colleges	Other [1]	Federal Govt.	Industry	Univ., colleges	Associated FFRDC's [2]	Other [1]
Current dollars:										
1970	26,134	14,891	10,444	462	337	4,079	18,067	2,335	737	916
1975	35,213	18,109	15,820	749	535	5,354	24,187	3,409	987	1,276
1980	62,596	29,455	30,912	1,326	903	7,632	44,505	6,063	2,246	2,150
1985	113,818	52,127	57,978	2,369	1,344	12,945	84,239	9,686	3,523	3,425
1987	125,376	57,913	62,643	3,192	1,628	13,413	92,155	12,152	4,206	3,450
1988	132,889	59,546	68,044	3,463	1,836	14,281	97,015	13,462	4,531	3,600
1989	140,981	59,893	75,046	3,921	2,121	15,121	102,055	14,975	4,730	4,100
1990	151,544	61,493	83,380	4,329	2,342	16,002	109,727	16,283	4,832	4,700
1991	160,096	60,219	92,485	4,835	2,557	15,238	116,952	17,577	5,079	5,250
1993	165,849	60,224	97,645	5,111	2,869	16,556	118,334	19,911	5,298	5,750
1994, prel.	169,100	61,050	99,650	5,350	3,050	17,200	119,700	20,950	5,250	6,000
1995, est.	171,000	60,700	101,650	5,500	3,150	16,700	121,400	21,600	5,300	6,000
Constant (1987) dollars: [3]										
1970	74,597	42,622	29,673	1,335	966	11,789	51,327	6,749	2,130	2,602
1975	72,237	37,396	32,162	1,574	1,105	11,248	49,161	7,162	2,074	2,593
1980	87,649	41,385	43,118	1,878	1,268	10,810	62,071	8,588	3,181	2,999
1985	120,599	55,245	61,418	2,512	1,425	13,727	89,236	10,271	3,736	3,628
1987	125,376	57,913	62,643	3,192	1,628	13,413	92,155	12,152	4,206	3,450
1988	127,991	57,386	65,492	3,343	1,770	13,785	93,373	12,994	4,374	3,465
1989	130,025	55,275	69,169	3,624	1,958	13,975	94,060	13,840	4,372	3,779
1990	134,135	54,587	73,604	3,865	2,079	14,288	96,846	14,538	4,314	4,148
1991	136,385	51,407	78,652	4,143	2,183	13,057	99,449	15,062	4,352	4,464
1993	134,428	48,876	79,069	4,155	2,328	13,460	95,817	16,188	4,307	4,656
1994, prel.	134,292	48,569	79,031	4,266	2,426	13,716	94,925	16,707	4,187	4,758
1995, est.	132,078	46,989	78,381	4,270	2,437	12,966	93,601	16,770	4,115	4,626

[1] Nonprofit institutions.   [2] University associated federally-funded R&D centers.   [3] Based on gross domestic product implicit price deflator.

Source: U.S. National Science Foundation, *National Patterns of R&D Resources,* annual.

No. 958. R&D Funds, by Performance Sector: 1980 to 1995

[In millions of dollars, except percent. Data primarily on calendar year basis—calendar year data for industry and other nonprofit institutions combined with Federal and university fiscal year data. Data refer, in general, to natural sciences including engineering, and to social sciences in all but industry sector. Excludes capital expenditures data. Expenditures at associated federally funded research and development centers administered by industry and other nonprofit institutions included in totals of respective sectors. See also *Historical Statistics, Colonial Times to 1970*, series W 109-125]

PERFORMANCE SECTOR	1980	1985	1990	1991	1992	1993	1994, prel.	1995, est.
Total R&D [1]	**62,596**	**113,818**	**151,544**	**160,096**	**164,493**	**165,849**	**169,100**	**171,000**
In 1987 dollars [2]	87,649	120,599	134,135	136,385	136,276	134,428	134,292	132,078
Percent Federal as source	47.1	45.8	40.6	37.6	36.7	36.3	36.1	35.5
Percent of gross domestic product	2.3	2.8	2.7	2.8	2.7	2.6	2.5	2.4
Federal Government	7,632	12,945	16,002	15,238	15,690	16,556	17,200	16,700
Industry	44,505	84,239	109,727	116,952	119,110	118,334	119,700	121,400
Federal funds	14,029	27,196	28,125	26,372	24,722	22,813	22,300	22,100
Industry funds	30,476	57,043	81,602	90,580	94,388	95,521	97,400	99,300
Universities and colleges	6,063	9,686	16,283	17,577	18,794	19,911	20,950	21,600
Federal funds	4,098	6,063	9,634	10,230	11,090	11,957	12,600	13,000
Industry funds	236	560	1,128	1,205	1,291	1,374	1,450	1,500
University and college funds [3]	1,326	2,369	4,329	4,835	5,018	5,111	5,350	5,500
Other nonprofit institutions funds [3]	403	694	1,192	1,307	1,395	1,469	1,550	1,600
Universities and colleges, associated federally funded R&D centers	2,246	3,523	4,832	5,079	5,249	5,298	5,250	5,300
Other nonprofit institutions	2,150	3,425	4,700	5,250	5,650	5,750	6,000	6,000
Federal funds	1,450	2,400	2,900	3,300	3,550	3,600	3,700	3,600
Industry funds	200	375	650	700	750	750	800	850
Other [4]	500	650	1,150	1,250	1,350	1,400	1,500	1,550
Total research, basic and applied	**22,045**	**39,537**	**57,144**	**65,030**	**65,133**	**66,263**	**68,260**	**69,310**
In 1987 dollars [2]	30,981	41,901	50,682	55,469	54,026	53,751	54,268	53,608
Percent Federal as source	54.8	50.8	47.9	44.8	44.7	45.7	45.6	45.4
Federal Government	3,666	5,056	5,953	6,539	6,616	7,360	7,600	7,600
Industry	9,775	21,117	29,913	35,283	33,680	32,803	33,500	33,800
Federal funds	2,190	5,836	7,721	7,733	6,468	5,892	5,900	5,800
Industry funds	7,585	15,281	22,192	27,550	27,212	26,911	27,600	28,000
Universities and colleges	5,566	8,973	14,986	16,079	17,218	18,277	19,290	19,950
Federal funds	3,739	5,604	8,802	9,245	10,053	10,880	11,520	11,960
Industry funds	219	521	1,049	1,121	1,201	1,278	1,350	1,390
University and college funds [3]	1,233	2,203	4,026	4,497	4,667	4,753	4,980	5,110
Other nonprofit institutions funds [3]	375	645	1,109	1,216	1,297	1,366	1,440	1,490
Universities and colleges, associated federally funded R&D centers	1,553	2,351	3,052	3,519	3,779	3,903	3,840	3,850
Other nonprofit institutions	1,485	2,040	3,240	3,610	3,840	3,920	4,030	4,110
Federal funds	930	1,250	1,850	2,100	2,200	2,250	2,250	2,250
Industry funds	160	300	520	560	610	610	640	680
Other [4]	395	490	870	950	1,030	1,060	1,140	1,180
Total basic research	**8,435**	**14,210**	**22,322**	**26,399**	**26,860**	**28,902**	**29,110**	**29,560**
In 1987 dollars [2]	11,902	15,064	19,860	22,557	22,314	23,464	23,220	22,900
Percent of total R&D	13.5	12.5	14.7	16.5	16.3	17.4	17.3	17.3
Percent Federal as source	70.1	64.7	61.9	56.7	57.0	56.0	57.6	57.7
Federal Government	1,182	1,923	2,366	2,446	2,397	2,605	2,700	2,700
Industry	1,325	2,862	5,128	7,837	7,075	7,926	7,200	7,150
Federal funds	290	489	1,368	1,712	1,210	1,000	1,000	950
Industry funds	1,035	2,373	3,760	6,125	5,865	6,926	6,200	6,200
Universities and colleges	4,036	6,555	10,640	11,601	12,504	13,270	14,100	14,500
Federal funds	2,861	4,342	6,645	7,123	7,713	8,379	8,900	9,200
Industry funds	141	342	678	734	803	845	900	900
University and college funds [3]	793	1,447	2,601	2,947	3,120	3,143	3,350	3,400
Other nonprofit institutions funds [3]	241	424	716	797	868	903	950	1,000
Universities and colleges, associated federally funded R&D centers	1,132	1,765	2,428	2,595	2,844	2,941	3,000	3,000
Other nonprofit institutions	760	1,105	1,760	1,920	2,040	2,160	2,170	2,210
Federal funds	450	675	1,000	1,100	1,150	1,250	1,200	1,200
Industry funds	95	170	300	320	350	350	370	390
Other [4]	215	260	460	500	540	560	600	620
Total development	**40,551**	**74,281**	**94,400**	**95,066**	**99,360**	**99,586**	**100,840**	**101,690**
In 1987 dollars [2]	56,669	78,698	83,453	80,916	82,250	80,677	80,024	78,470
Percent of total R&D	64.8	65.3	62.3	59.4	60.4	60.0	59.6	59.5
Percent Federal as source	42.9	43.1	36.1	32.7	31.4	30.1	29.7	28.8

[1] Basic research, applied research, and development.   [2] Based on gross domestic product implicit price deflator.   [3] Includes State and local government funds received by these institutions and used for research and development.   [4] Includes estimates for independent nonprofit hospitals and voluntary health agencies.

Source: U.S. National Science Foundation, *National Patterns of R&D Resources*, annual.

No. 959. Funds for R&D—Performance Sector, by State: 1991

[In millions of dollars. See headnote, table 958. Data shown here are unrevised]

STATE	Total	Federal government[1]	Industry	Universities and colleges[2]	Other nonprofit[3]	STATE	Total	Federal government[1]	Industry	Universities and colleges[2]	Other nonprofit[3]
U.S.	145,385	15,238	102,246	22,701	5,200	MO	(NA)	71	(7)	306	22
						MT	(NA)	26	(6)	38	1
AL	1,503	701	521	245	36	NE	211	22	59	124	6
AK	146	59	18	67	2	NV	261	109	83	67	3
AZ	1,399	132	944	311	11	NH	(NA)	88	(9)	79	-
AR	198	35	106	55	2	NJ	8,768	513	7,810	433	12
CA	28,337	1,885	21,279	4,700	473	NM	2,582	393	1,064	1,111	15
CO	(NA)	275	(4)	340	106	NY	10,363	174	8,268	1,751	170
CT	1,913	47	1,535	317	15	NC	1,965	151	1,285	502	27
DE	(NA)	9	(5)	45	3	ND	(NA)	24	(7)	31	1
DC	1,737	1,433	40	118	145	OH	5,975	689	4,726	504	57
FL	3,700	658	2,599	438	5	OK	604	41	392	153	18
GA	1,479	121	868	484	6	OR	600	47	349	179	24
HI	145	45	11	78	11	PA	7,621	315	6,262	906	138
ID	(NA)	37	(6)	42	1	RI	485	226	152	88	18
IL	6,417	68	5,027	1,275	47	SC	595	14	419	151	10
IN	2,347	92	1,988	262	4	SD	32	9	5	16	2
IA	777	27	461	286	3	TN	1,139	124	737	251	28
KS	(NA)	12	(7)	124	5	TX	6,635	405	4,755	1,218	257
KY	317	62	154	98	2	UT	665	103	356	202	4
LA	457	43	172	240	2	VT	(NA)	5	(8)	47	5
ME	(NA)	14	(8)	27	16	VA	2,771	1,107	1,115	366	182
MD	5,864	3,432	1,203	1,078	151	WA	3,890	133	3,215	350	193
MA	8,561	278	6,335	1,338	610	WV	(NA)	76	(10)	73	5
MI	8,851	92	8,116	601	42	WI	1,573	32	1,140	388	13
MN	2,228	41	1,810	332	46	WY	41	9	2	23	7
MS	299	157	41	97	4	Other[11]	3,835	577	675	349	2,234

- Represents or rounds to zero.   NA Not available.   [1] Total funds used by Federal government from Federal sources.
[2] Distribution by States includes R&D performed in only doctoral degree granting institutions; U.S. total includes R&D performed in all institutions.   [3] For other sector, funds distributed by State include only Federal obligations to organizations in the nonprofit sector. Nonprofit R&D performance using non-Federal funds are undistributed.   [4] Between $1,751 and $2,593 million. [5] Between $863 and $995 million.   [6] Under $95 million.   [7] Under $1,963 million.   [8] Under $284 million.   [9] Between $102 and $120 million.   [10] Between $69 and $201 million.   [11] Includes unknown.

Source: U.S. National Science Foundation, Science and Engineering Indicators, 1993.

No. 960. Federal Obligations for R&D, by Agency: 1975 to 1995

[In millions of dollars. For fiscal years ending in year shown; see text, section 9. Includes those agencies with obligations of $1 billion or more in 1995. See Historical Statistics, Colonial Times to 1970, series W 142, for total R&D expenditures]

AGENCY	1975	1980	1985	1990	1991	1992	1993	1994	1995, est.
CURRENT DOLLARS									
Obligations, total[1]	19,039	29,830	48,360	63,668	61,295	65,593	67,314	69,594	69,366
Dept. of Defense	9,013	13,981	29,792	37,268	32,135	36,130	35,849	35,650	34,927
Dept. of Health and Human Services	2,281	3,780	5,451	8,406	9,756	8,988	10,349	11,031	11,481
National Aeronautics and Space Administration.	3,064	3,234	3,327	6,533	7,280	7,658	8,020	8,766	8,585
Dept. of Energy	2,047	4,754	4,966	5,631	5,983	6,172	6,262	6,530	6,370
National Science Foundation.	595	882	1,346	1,690	1,785	1,868	1,882	2,031	2,219
Dept. of Agriculture	420	688	943	1,108	1,237	1,327	1,328	1,388	1,397
CONSTANT (1987) DOLLARS[2]									
Obligations, total[1]	39,998	42,253	51,283	56,846	52,524	54,615	54,727	55,498	53,856
Dept. of Defense	18,935	19,803	31,592	33,275	27,536	30,083	29,146	28,429	27,117
Dept. of Health and Human Services	4,792	5,354	5,780	7,505	8,360	7,484	8,414	8,797	8,914
National Aeronautics and Space Administration.	6,437	4,581	3,528	5,833	6,238	6,376	6,520	6,990	6,665
Dept. of Energy	4,300	6,733	5,266	5,028	5,127	5,139	5,691	5,207	4,946
National Science Foundation.	1,250	1,249	1,427	1,509	1,530	1,555	1,530	1,620	1,723
Dept. of Agriculture	882	974	1,000	989	1,060	1,105	1,080	1,107	1,085

[1] Includes other agencies, not shown separately.   [2] Based on gross domestic product implicit price deflator.

Source: U.S. National Science Foundation, Federal Funds for Research and Development, annual.

No. 961. Federal Funding for R&D, by Selected Budget Functions: 1970 to 1996

[In millions of dollars. For fiscal years ending in year shown; see text, section 9. Excludes R&D plant. Represents budget authority. Functions shown are those for which $1 billion or more was authorized for 1996. See *Historical Statistics, Colonial Times to 1970*, series W 126, for total obligations]

FUNCTION	1970	1980	1985	1990	1992	1993	1994	1995	1996, est.
CURRENT DOLLARS									
Total [1]	15,339	29,739	49,887	63,781	68,398	69,884	68,331	70,309	70,503
Eight functions, percent of total	96.6	96.5	98.3	98.0	98.0	98.1	97.9	97.5	97.4
National defense	7,981	14,946	33,698	39,925	40,083	41,249	37,764	39	37,571
Health	1,084	3,694	5,418	8,308	10,055	10,280	10,993	11,356	11,785
Space research and technology	3,606	2,738	2,725	5,765	6,744	6,988	7,414	7,874	7,863
Energy	574	3,603	2,389	2,715	3,099	2,677	2,873	2,856	3,069
General science	452	1,233	1,862	2,410	2,659	2,691	2,712	2,843	3,011
Natural resources and environment	340	999	1,059	1,386	1,688	1,802	2,062	2,067	2,208
Transportation	535	887	1,030	1,045	1,523	1,703	1,888	1,865	1,984
Agriculture	238	585	836	950	1,155	1,152	1,193	1,179	1,187
CONSTANT (1987) DOLLARS [2]									
Total [1]	44,332	42,123	52,902	56,947	56,951	56,816	54,490	54,588	53,170
National defense	23,066	21,170	35,735	35,647	33,375	33,536	30,115	29,905	28,334
Health	3,133	5,232	5,745	7,418	8,372	8,358	8,766	8,817	8,888
Space research and technology	10,422	3,878	2,890	5,147	5,615	5,681	5,912	6,113	5,930
Energy	1,659	5,103	2,533	2,424	2,580	2,176	2,291	2,217	2,314
General science	1,306	1,746	1,975	2,152	2,214	2,188	2,163	2,207	2,271
Natural resources and environment	983	1,415	1,123	1,238	1,405	1,465	1,644	1,605	1,665
Transportation	1,546	1,256	1,092	933	1,268	1,385	1,506	1,448	1,496
Agriculture	688	829	887	848	962	937	951	915	895

[1] Includes other functions, not shown separately. [2] Based on gross domestic product implicit price deflator.

Source: U.S. National Science Foundation, *Federal R&D Funding by Budget Function*, annual.

No. 962. National R&D Expenditures as a Percent of Gross Domestic Product, by Country: 1975 to 1993

YEAR	TOTAL R&D						NONDEFENSE R&D [1]					
	United States	Japan	Unified Germany	France	United Kingdom	Italy	United States	Japan	Unified Germany	France	United Kingdom	Italy
1975	2.22	1.91	2.24	1.79	2.05	0.84	1.61	1.90	2.10	1.44	1.42	0.83
1980	2.31	2.01	2.45	1.82	(NA)	0.75	1.76	2.00	2.33	1.41	(NA)	0.74
1985	2.82	2.58	2.72	2.25	2.27	1.13	1.98	2.56	2.58	1.78	1.68	1.06
1990	2.73	2.89	2.75	2.42	2.19	1.30	2.01	2.87	2.61	1.85	1.81	1.25
1991	2.80	2.87	2.65	2.42	2.13	1.32	2.11	2.84	2.53	1.92	1.73	1.26
1992	2.77	2.80	2.53	2.36	2.12	1.38	2.10	2.77	2.42	1.92	1.71	1.33
1993	2.67	(NA)	(NA)	(NA)	(NA)	1.40	2.02	(NA)	(NA)	(NA)	(NA)	1.35

NA Not available. [1] Estimated.

Source: National Science Foundation, *National Patterns of R&D Resources*, annual; and Organization for Economic Co-operation and Development.

No. 963. R&D Expenditures in Science and Engineering at Universities and Colleges: 1981 to 1994

[In millions of dollars]

CHARACTERISTIC	1981	1990	1994	CHARACTERISTIC	1981	1990	1994
CURRENT DOLLARS				**CONSTANT (1987) DOLLARS [1]**			
Total	6,846	16,334	21,081	Total	8,799	14,493	16,811
Basic research	4,593	10,680	14,095	Basic research	5,904	9,476	11,240
Applied R&D	2,253	5,654	6,986	Applied R&D	2,896	5,017	5,571
Source of funds:				Source of funds:			
All governments	5,115	10,976	14,223	All governments	6,575	9,739	11,342
Institutions' own funds	1,004	3,033	3,838	Institutions' own funds	1,290	2,691	3,061
Industry	292	1,130	1,430	Industry	375	1,003	1,140
Other	435	1,195	1,590	Other	559	1,060	1,268
Fields:				Fields:			
Physical sciences	765	1,809	2,171	Physical sciences	983	1,605	1,731
Environmental sciences	550	1,080	1,426	Environmental sciences	707	958	1,137
Mathematical sciences	87	221	279	Mathematical sciences	112	196	222
Computer sciences	144	514	660	Computer sciences	185	456	526
Life sciences	3,695	8,748	11,521	Life sciences	4,749	7,762	9,187
Psychology	127	258	359	Psychology	163	229	286
Social sciences	366	706	951	Social sciences	470	626	758
Other sciences	145	335	392	Other sciences	186	297	313
Engineering	967	2,663	3,324	Engineering	1,243	2,363	2,651

[1] Based on gross domestic product implicit price deflator.

Source: U.S. National Science Foundation, *Survey of Scientific and Engineering Expenditures at Universities and Colleges*, annual.

No. 964. Federal Obligations to Universities and Colleges: 1970 to 1993

[In millions of dollars, except percent. For fiscal years ending in year shown; see text, section 9.
Minus sign (-) indicates decrease]

ITEM	1970	1980	1985	1989	1990	1991	1992	1993
CURRENT DOLLARS								
Federal obligations, total	3,237	8,299	10,972	15,504	15,198	17,554	19,056	(NA)
Annual percent change [1]	-6.5	9.1	9.3	10.2	-2.0	15.5	8.6	(NA)
Academic science/engineering obligations	2,188	4,791	7,258	10,075	10,443	11,831	12,739	12,725
Percent of total	67.6	57.7	66.2	65.0	68.7	67.4	66.9	(NA)
Research and development	1,447	4,161	6,246	8,523	9,006	10,027	10,859	10,940
Research and development plant.	45	38	114	237	125	152	205	259
Other science/engineering activities	696	593	898	1,315	1,312	1,652	1,676	1,525
Nonscience/engineering activities	1,049	3,508	3,714	5,429	4,755	5,722	6,317	(NA)
CONSTANT (1987) DOLLARS [2]								
Federal obligations, total	9,355	11,755	11,635	14,329	13,570	15,042	15,867	(NA)
Annual percent change [1]	-11.4	-	5.4	5.5	-5.9	10.8	5.5	(NA)
Academic science/engineering obligations	6,324	6,786	7,697	9,311	9,324	10,138	10,607	10,345
Percent of total	67.6	57.7	66.2	65.0	68.7	67.4	66.9	(NA)
Research and development	4,182	5,894	6,624	7,877	8,041	8,592	9,042	8,894
Research and development plant.	130	54	121	219	111	130	170	211
Other science/engineering activities	2,012	840	952	1,215	1,172	1,416	1,395	1,240
Nonscience/engineering activities	3,032	4,969	3,938	5,018	4,245	4,903	5,260	(NA)

- Represents or rounds to zero. NA Not available. [1] Percent change from immediate prior year. [2] Based on gross domestic product implicit price deflator.

Source: U.S. National Science Foundation, *Survey of Federal Support to Universities, Colleges, and Nonprofit Institutions,* annual.

No. 965. Federal R&D Obligations to Selected Universities and Colleges: 1981 to 1993

[For fiscal years ending in year shown; see text, section 9. For the top 45 institutions receiving Federal R&D funds in 1993. Awards to the administrative offices of university systems are excluded from totals for individual institutions because that allocation of funds is unknown, but those awards are included in "total all institutions"]

MAJOR INSTITUTION RANKED BY TOTAL 1993 FEDERAL R&D OBLIGATIONS	OBLIGATIONS ($1,000)			RANK		
	1981	1985	1993	1981	1985	1993
Total, all institutions [1]	4,410,931	6,246,181	10,940,124	(X)	(X)	(X)
45 institutions, percent of total	62.6	61.3	58.6	(X)	(X)	(X)
Johns Hopkins University.	363,429	297,374	543,873	1	1	1
Massachusetts Institute of Technology	146,035	189,558	251,845	2	2	2
Stanford University	106,073	174,961	249,575	3	3	3
University of Washington	99,965	146,179	246,013	4	4	4
University of Michigan	73,999	108,035	214,612	11	11	5
University of California—San Diego	91,403	103,633	204,063	6	13	6
University of California—Los Angeles.	94,945	128,211	195,788	5	5	7
Columbia University—Main Division	83,659	127,331	194,910	9	6	8
University of Wisconsin—Madison	86,918	124,604	190,469	8	7	9
University of Pennsylvania	76,136	103,119	186,002	10	15	10
University of California—San Francisco	64,814	98,536	175,388	15	16	11
Cornell University.	72,671	119,966	174,226	13	8	12
Pennsylvania State University.	47,099	76,726	173,070	21	19	13
Harvard University	87,830	109,414	169,173	7	9	14
Yale University.	73,526	109,227	169,151	12	10	15
University of Minnesota	72,001	103,272	168,675	14	14	16
University of Colorado	46,146	71,424	145,497	22	23	17
Duke University	44,287	69,169	138,839	23	26	18
University of Pittsburgh	38,512	58,620	136,780	29	28	19
University of California—Berkeley	64,065	106,710	133,232	16	12	20
Washington University.	54,170	71,978	133,210	17	22	21
University of North Carolina at Chapel Hill	38,447	63,105	129,071	30	27	22
University Southern California	49,221	89,706	125,297	20	17	23
University of Texas at Austin.	43,756	72,379	117,225	24	21	24
University of Illinois—Urbana Champaign	53,583	83,122	116,116	19	18	25
University of Arizona	36,308	49,740	107,819	33	37	26
Boston University	27,019	46,152	102,642	51	43	27
University of Chicago	53,992	71,194	99,378	18	24	28
University of Rochester	42,983	70,379	98,935	25	25	29
University of Alabama—Birmingham	29,970	44,093	90,737	44	46	30
Case Western Reserve University	33,744	47,994	89,608	38	40	31
Baylor Col of Medicine	35,062	45,837	88,276	35	45	32
University of Iowa.	35,300	55,117	87,875	34	31	33
California Inst of Tech	32,959	55,083	87,702	40	32	34
University of California—Davis	31,757	43,156	84,495	42	47	35
Ohio State University	42,899	56,065	84,121	26	30	36
Northwestern University.	32,446	48,260	82,636	47	39	37
Vanderbilt University	27,426	39,909	82,091	49	48	38
Indiana University.	29,276	39,118	81,374	45	49	39
University of Virginia	24,333	37,415	79,221	52	52	40
New York University	40,636	74,577	77,694	28	20	41
University of Utah.	38,163	50,938	77,407	31	36	42
University of Florida	30,845	47,716	77,341	43	41	43
University of Maryland— College Park	27,313	51,073	76,300	50	35	44
Purdue University.	36,549	51,544	74,920	32	34	45

X Not applicable. [1] Includes other institutions, not shown separately.

Source: U.S. National Science Foundation, *Federal Support to Universities and Colleges and Nonprofit Institutions,* annual.

No. 966. Funds for Performance of Industrial R&D, by Source of Funds and Selected Industries: 1980 to 1993

[In millions of dollars. For calendar years. Covers basic research, applied research, and development. See also *Historical Statistics, Colonial Times to 1970*, series W 144-160]

INDUSTRY	1987 SIC [1] code	1980	1985	1990	1991	1992	1993
CURRENT DOLLARS							
Total funds	(X)	44,505	84,239	109,727	116,952	119,110	118,334
Chemicals and allied products	28	4,636	8,540	13,291	14,648	15,381	(D)
Petroleum refining and extraction	13,29	1,552	(D)	2,306	2,498	2,277	2,117
Machinery.	35	5,901	12,216	14,446	14,775	14,938	8,270
Electrical equipment	36	9,175	14,432	13,400	13,415	13,360	12,686
Motor vehicles and motor vehicles equipment	371	4,955	6,984	(D)	(D)	(D)	(D)
Aircraft and missiles	372,376	9,198	22,231	20,635	16,629	17,158	15,615
Professional and scientific instruments	38	3,029	5,013	7,055	8,705	9,542	10,288
All other [2]	(X)	6,059	(D)	(D)	(D)	(D)	(D)
Company funds.	(X)	30,476	57,043	81,602	90,580	94,388	95,521
Chemicals and allied products	28	4,264	8,310	13,168	14,439	15,091	16,747
Petroleum refining and extraction	13,29	1,401	2,194	2,289	2,487	2,268	2,103
Machinery.	35	5,254	10,721	13,575	13,720	13,903	8,182
Electrical equipment	36	5,431	9,271	9,267	8,865	9,516	11,285
Motor vehicles and motor vehicles equipment	371	4,300	6,164	8,594	9,063	9,132	10,652
Aircraft and missiles	372,376	2,570	5,649	5,387	5,533	6,871	6,246
Professional and scientific instruments	38	2,456	4,622	6,318	6,840	7,321	7,521
All other [2]	(X)	4,800	10,132	23,004	29,633	30,286	32,785
CONSTANT (1987) DOLLARS [3]							
Total funds	(X)	62,071	89,236	96,846	99,449	98,519	95,817
Chemicals and allied products	28	6,466	9,047	11,730	12,455	12,722	(D)
Petroleum refining and extraction	13,29	2,165	(D)	2,035	2,124	1,883	1,714
Machinery.	35	8,230	12,941	12,750	12,563	12,355	6,696
Electrical equipment	36	12,796	15,288	11,827	11,407	11,050	10,272
Motor vehicles and motor vehicles equipment	371	6,911	7,398	(D)	(D)	(D)	(D)
Aircraft and missiles	372,376	12,828	23,550	18,212	14,140	14,191	12,643
Professional and scientific instruments	38	4,225	5,310	6,226	7,402	7,892	8,330
All other [2]	(X)	8,450	(D)	(D)	(D)	(D)	(D)
Company funds.	(X)	42,505	60,427	72,022	77,023	78,071	77,344
Chemicals and allied products	28	5,947	8,803	11,622	12,278	12,482	13,560
Petroleum refining and extraction	13,29	1,954	2,324	2,020	2,114	1,875	1,702
Machinery.	35	7,328	11,357	11,981	11,666	11,499	6,625
Electrical equipment	36	7,575	9,821	8,179	7,538	7,871	9,137
Motor vehicles and motor vehicles equipment	371	5,997	6,530	7,585	7,706	7,553	8,625
Aircraft and missiles	372,376	3,584	5,984	4,754	4,704	5,683	5,057
Professional and scientific instruments	38	3,425	4,896	5,576	5,816	6,055	6,089
All other [2]	(X)	6,695	10,733	20,303	25,198	25,050	26,546

D Figure withheld to avoid disclosure of information pertaining to a specific organization or individual.   X Not applicable.
[1] Prior to 1992, 1972 Standard Industrial Classification; beginning 1992, 1987 Standard Industrial Classification; see text, section 13.   [2] All other manufacturing and nonmanufacturing.   [3] Based on gross domestic product implicit price deflator.

Source: U.S. National Science Foundation, *Research and Development in Industry,* annual.

No. 967. R&D Funds in R&D-Performing Manufacturing Companies, by Industry: 1980 to 1993

INDUSTRY	1987 SIC [1] code	TOTAL R&D FUNDS AS A PERCENT OF NET SALES					COMPANY R&D FUNDS AS A PERCENT OF NET SALES				
		1980	1985	1990	1992	1993	1980	1985	1990	1992	1993
Total [2]	(X)	3.0	4.4	4.2	4.2	3.8	2.1	3.0	3.1	3.3	3.1
Food and kindred products [3]	20	0.4	(D)	(D)	0.5	0.4	(D)	0.6	0.5	0.5	0.4
Paper and allied products	26	1.0	(D)	1.0	(D)	(D)	1.0	0.8	1.0	1.0	1.1
Chemicals and allied products . . .	28	3.6	5.0	5.3	5.5	(D)	3.3	4.9	5.3	5.4	5.8
Petroleum refining and extraction .	13,29	0.6	(D)	0.9	0.9	0.9	0.5	0.9	0.9	0.9	0.8
Rubber products	30	2.2	(D)	(D)	(D)	0.9	0.9	0.9	0.9	0.9	0.4
Stone, clay, and glass products. . .	32	1.4	(D)	(D)	(D)	(D)	(D)	1.8	2.1	2.3	2.1
Primary metals.	33	0.7	(D)	0.8	0.6	0.7	1.3	2.3	1.7	1.6	1.5
Fabricated metal products	34	1.4	1.5	1.4	1.5	(D)	0.5	0.9	0.8	0.6	0.7
Machinery.	35	5.0	7.6	7.7	7.8	4.5	1.2	1.4	1.1	1.1	1.1
Electrical equipment	36	6.6	7.6	6.5	5.6	5.8	4.5	6.7	7.2	7.3	4.5
Motor vehicles and motor vehicle equipment.	371	4.9	3.8	(D)	(D)	(D)	3.9	4.8	4.5	4.0	5.1
Aircraft and missiles	372,376	13.7	14.9	11.8	11.8	13.2	4.2	3.1	3.7	4.0	3.6
Professional and scientific instruments	38	7.5	8.9	8.0	9.4	9.6	3.8	3.9	3.1	4.7	5.2
							6.1	8.3	7.1	7.2	7.0

D Figure withheld to avoid disclosure of information pertaining to a specific organization or individual.   X Not applicable.
[1] Prior to 1992, 1972 Standard Industrial Classification; beginning 1992, 1987 Standard Industrial Classification; see text, section 13.   [2] Includes all manufacturing industries.   [3] Includes tobacco products (SIC 21) beginning 1985.

Source: U.S. National Science Foundation, *Research and Development in Industry*, annual.

No. 968. Federal Obligations for Research, by Field of Science: 1980 to 1995

[In millions of dollars. For fiscal years ending in year shown; see text, section 9. Excludes R&D plant]

FIELD	1980	1985	1988	1990	1991	1992	1993	1994	1995, est.
CURRENT DOLLARS									
Research, total	**11,597**	**16,133**	**20,766**	**21,731**	**23,968**	**24,491**	**26,890**	**28,034**	**28,161**
Basic	4,674	7,819	10,602	11,286	12,171	12,490	13,399	14,043	14,201
Applied	6,923	8,315	10,164	10,446	11,798	12,001	13,491	13,990	13,960
Life sciences	4,192	6,363	8,495	8,830	9,622	9,910	10,772	11,350	11,609
Psychology	199	327	422	449	482	298	551	569	574
Physical sciences	2,001	3,046	3,705	3,809	4,235	4,439	4,427	4,449	4,379
Environmental sciences	1,261	1,404	1,773	2,174	2,150	2,208	2,608	2,832	2,690
Mathematics and computer sciences . . .	241	575	735	841	904	1,160	1,225	1,410	1,526
Engineering	2,830	3,618	4,442	4,335	4,945	4,977	5,499	5,701	5,629
Social sciences	524	460	551	630	727	690	675	708	699
Other sciences, n.e.c. [1]	350	342	642	664	903	808	1,133	1,014	1,055
CONSTANT (1987) DOLLARS [2]									
Research, total	**16,427**	**17,109**	**19,192**	**19,403**	**20,538**	**20,392**	**21,862**	**22,356**	**21,864**
Basic	6,621	8,291	9,799	10,077	10,429	10,400	10,893	11,199	11,026
Applied	9,806	8,817	9,394	9,327	10,110	9,993	10,968	11,156	10,839
Life sciences	5,938	6,747	7,851	7,884	8,245	8,251	8,758	9,051	9,013
Psychology	282	347	390	401	413	248	448	454	446
Physical sciences	2,834	3,230	3,424	3,401	3,629	3,696	3,599	3,548	3,400
Environmental sciences	1,786	1,489	1,639	1,941	1,842	1,838	2,120	2,258	2,089
Mathematics and computer sciences . . .	341	610	679	751	775	966	996	1,124	1,185
Engineering	4,009	3,836	4,105	3,871	4,237	4,144	4,471	4,546	4,370
Social sciences	742	488	509	563	623	575	549	565	543
Other sciences, n.e.c. [1]	495	362	593	593	774	673	921	809	819

[1] N.e.c. = Not elsewhere classified.   [2] Based on gross domestic product implicit price deflator.

Source: U.S. National Science Foundation, *Federal Funds for Research and Development,* annual.

No. 969. R&D Scientists and Engineers— Employment and Cost, by Industry: 1975 to 1993

[Data are estimates; on average full-time-equivalent (FTE) basis. See *Historical Statistics, Colonial Times to 1970,* series W 167, for total cost per scientist or engineer]

INDUSTRY	1987 SIC [1] code	1975	1980	1985	1988	1989	1990	1991	1992	1993
EMPLOYED SCIENTISTS										
Average FTE of scientists and engineers (1,000) [2] [3]	(X)	363.9	469.2	646.8	715.6	733.1	758.5	776.4	772.0	764.5
Chemicals [4]	28	44.8	53.1	73.5	77.1	79.4	81.0	83.6	86.1	90.7
Machinery . . . . [5]	35	54.3	65.7	85.7	99.4	106.9	111.5	104.5	98.4	83.3
Electrical equipment [5]	36	81.5	100.7	115.6	127.5	113.9	100.6	93.9	90.6	90.8
Motor vehicles	371	25.7	36.7	31.3	46.6	47.6	47.4	44.9	44.8	48.1
Aircraft and missiles	372,376	67.2	90.6	137.5	135.6	125.1	107.8	96.6	95.4	85.2
CONSTANT (1987) DOLLARS [6]										
Cost per scientist or engineer ($1,000) [3] [7]	(X)	135.2	132.3	138.0	127.3	124.0	124.7	126.4	130.6	125.4
Chemicals [4]	28	123.8	121.9	123.2	134.2	137.3	140.3	142.5	151.8	162.4
Machinery . . . . [5]	35	119.7	125.4	151.0	(D)	119.8	122.2	125.7	126.4	80.4
Electrical equipment [5]	36	127.5	127.0	132.4	119.4	122.0	126.0	125.1	124.2	113.1
Motor vehicles	371	185.2	188.5	236.4	(D)	(D)	(D)	(D)	184.4	197.2
Aircraft and missiles	372,376	173.0	141.7	171.3	186.0	191.1	188.6	150.5	149.3	148.5

D Withheld to avoid disclosure.   X Not applicable.   [1] Prior to 1992, 1972 Standard Industrial Classification; beginning 1992, 1987 Standard Industrial Classification; see text, section 13.   [2] The mean number of FTE R&D scientists and engineers employed in January of the year shown and the following January.   [3] Includes industries not shown separately.   [4] Includes allied products.   [5] Includes communication.   [6] Based on gross domestic product implicit price deflator.   [7] Represents the arithmetic mean of the numbers of R&D scientists and engineers reported in each industry for January in 2 consecutive years divided into total R&D expenditures in each industry.

Source: U.S. National Science Foundation, *Research and Development in Industry,* annual.

No. 970. Scientists and Engineers Employed in R&D: 1970 to 1993

[For full-time equivalent employees. Data are estimates. Yearly averages for industry sector only. Excludes those employed by State and local government agencies]

SECTOR	1970	1980	1983	1984	1985	1987	1989	1991	1993
Total [1] (1,000)............	543.8	651.1	751.6	797.6	801.9	877.8	924.2	960.4	962.7
PERCENT DISTRIBUTION									
Industry (excl. social scientists)	69.1	72.1	74.8	75.6	80.9	80.0	79.3	80.8	79.4
Federal Government	12.4	9.0	8.2	7.8	6.5	6.2	6.4	6.1	6.2
Other [2]	18.5	18.9	17.0	16.6	12.6	13.8	14.3	13.1	14.3

[1] Due to change in methodology, data beginning 1985 are not comparable with data for previous years.   [2] Includes professional R&D personnel employed at universities and colleges, other nonprofit institutions, and federally funded R&D centers administered by organizations in these sectors and graduate students engaged in R&D at universities and colleges.

Source: U.S. National Science Foundation, *National Patterns of R&D Resources*, annual.

No. 971. Civilian Employment of Scientists, Engineers, and Technicians, by Occupation and Industry: 1994

[In thousands. Based on sample and subject to sampling error. For details, see source]

OCCUPATION	Total [1]	WAGE AND SALARY WORKERS								Self em-ployed
		Min-ing [2]	Con-struc-tion	Manu-fac-turing	Trans-por-tation [3]	Trade	FIRE [4]	Serv-ices	Govern-ment	
Scientists and engineers .	2,822.7	36.6	31.5	866.0	116.7	96.5	109.7	891.1	480.6	185.0
Scientists	1,495.3	16.3	2.4	261.1	46.9	60.3	98.7	554.8	300.0	146.0
Physical scientists	209.2	10.4	0.3	58.1	3.0	2.3	0.7	76.0	46.3	12.0
Life scientists............	185.9	0.2	0.1	28.1	1.3	1.3	0.6	61.4	75.2	10.0
Mathematical scientists	14.0	(NA)	(NA)	1.5	0.4	(NA)	3.0	4.1	5.0	-
Social scientists	258.7	1.5	(NA)	(NA)	0.8	(NA)	7.6	105.0	68.9	75.0
Computer systems analysts, engineers and scientists....	827.5	4.1	2.0	173.4	41.3	56.7	86.9	308.3	104.7	49.0
Engineers [5]	1,327.4	20.3	29.1	604.9	69.9	36.2	11.0	336.3	180.6	39.0
Civil engineers	184.4	0.6	10.4	7.7	5.5	0.4	0.5	79.5	70.8	9.0
Electrical/electronics	348.6	0.6	8.5	156.7	35.2	12.4	1.3	86.4	37.5	10.0
Mechanical engineers	230.5	1.7	4.8	134.5	4.4	6.7	1.1	56.2	13.1	8.0
Engineering and science technicians...........	1,219.6	16.8	27.2	441.8	67.8	84.8	4.4	385.2	161.9	25.0
Electrical/electronics technicians	314.0	1.0	7.1	122.9	21.4	64.0	1.5	62.4	26.6	7.0
Engineering technicians	371.1	5.3	4.0	128.9	25.8	10.6	0.3	96.3	92.8	7.0
Drafters	303.6	2.1	15.7	102.2	17.1	6.6	1.3	137.2	12.0	9.0
Science technicians	230.9	8.4	0.4	87.7	3.5	3.5	1.3	89.3	32.3	2.0
Surveyors	95.5	2.5	2.5	(NA)	3.0	(NA)	0.8	57.5	22.2	7.0
Computer programmers	536.7	2.7	1.5	77.8	22.1	38.3	78.6	254.8	35.1	26.0

- Represents or rounds to zero.   NA Not available.   [1] Includes agriculture, forestry, and fishing not shown separately.   [2] Includes oil and gas extraction.   [3] Includes communications and public utilities.   [4] Finance, insurance, and real estate.   [5] Includes kinds of engineers and technicians not shown separately.

Source: U.S. Bureau of Labor Statistics, unpublished data.

No. 972. Graduate Science/Engineering Students in Doctorate-Granting Colleges: 1985 to 1992

[As of fall. Includes outlying areas]

FIELD OF SCIENCE OR ENGINEERING	TOTAL (1,000)			PERCENT—							
				Female			Foreign		Part-time		
	1985	1990	1992	1985	1990	1992	1990	1992	1985	1990	1992
Total, all surveyed fields	353.8	394.8	427.8	34.5	37.5	38.6	25.6	25.1	32.2	30.7	29.9
Science/engineering	314.8	347.4	374.8	29.4	32.2	33.2	27.9	27.5	30.4	28.5	27.7
Engineering, total	89.7	99.1	108.3	11.5	13.6	14.4	36.7	36.3	39.5	35.6	33.7
Sciences, total	225.1	248.2	266.5	36.6	39.6	40.8	24.3	23.9	26.8	25.6	25.3
Physical sciences	29.4	32.4	33.6	20.5	23.4	24.5	37.1	36.8	11.7	11.2	10.7
Environmental.........	14.3	13.0	14.0	25.4	29.2	31.0	20.1	21.0	23.9	23.6	24.3
Mathematical sciences ..	15.2	17.2	17.9	29.1	30.4	31.2	36.1	33.9	26.9	23.4	22.4
Computer sciences	23.4	27.4	29.0	24.9	22.8	21.8	33.2	35.0	42.8	46.6	46.4
Agricultural sciences	10.7	10.4	10.9	25.6	29.2	31.5	29.1	27.8	18.2	17.7	18.2
Biological sciences.....	42.1	46.2	50.2	42.4	45.5	46.3	24.2	24.9	16.0	14.6	14.8
Psychology..........	30.4	34.7	37.7	59.7	65.5	67.3	4.6	4.7	30.1	28.1	27.9
Social sciences	59.6	66.8	73.2	39.7	42.9	44.1	21.9	20.4	34.1	32.4	31.3
Health fields, total.	39.0	47.4	53.0	75.5	76.6	76.4	8.6	8.1	46.2	47.1	45.7

Source: U.S. National Science Foundation, *Survey of Graduate Science Engineering Students and Postdocturates*, annual.

No. 973. Science and Engineering Degree Recipients in 1991 and 1992: 1993

[Based on survey and subject to sampling error; see source for details]

DEGREE AND FIELD	Graduates 1991 and 1992 (1,000)	1993 [1]—PERCENT DISTRIBUTION				Median salary [4] ($1,000)
		In school [2]	Employed		Not employed or FT students	
			In S&E [3]	In other		
Bachelor's recipients	**639.4**	**22**	**22**	**50**	**6**	**24.0**
All science fields	521.1	24	13	57	6	22.1
Computer and mathematical sciences	77.6	11	32	51	5	28.5
Life and related sciences	99.7	38	14	43	6	21.0
Physical and related sciences	33.8	39	28	29	4	26.0
Social and related sciences	310.0	21	6	66	6	21.0
All engineering fields	118.4	15	60	20	5	33.8
Aerospace and related engineering	7.3	23	35	37	6	29.0
Chemical engineering	6.7	16	70	10	4	40.0
Civil and architectural engineering	15.6	12	69	15	4	31.0
Electrical, electronics, computer and communications engineering	41.8	16	59	18	7	35.0
Industrial engineering	7.7	7	59	30	3	33.0
Mechanical engineering	25.1	13	65	19	3	35.0
Other engineering	14.1	17	53	25	5	33.0
Master's recipients	**115.6**	**23**	**48**	**24**	**5**	**38.1**
All science fields	74.6	26	37	31	5	33.8
Computer and mathematical sciences	24.1	16	48	31	5	40.0
Life and related sciences	13.2	28	35	31	6	29.0
Physical and related sciences	10.6	38	46	13	4	34.0
Social and related sciences	26.7	31	24	39	6	28.0
All engineering fields	41.0	17	68	11	4	42.9
Aerospace and related engineering	1.9	26	56	16	3	40.0
Chemical engineering	1.7	33	56	7	4	44.0
Civil and architectural engineering	4.9	15	74	7	5	38.8
Electrical, electronics, computer and communications engineering	15.7	15	71	10	4	44.0
Industrial engineering	2.6	13	63	20	4	42.5
Mechanical engineering	6.4	17	72	6	4	42.0
Other engineering	7.9	18	61	18	3	43.0

[1] As of April.   [2] Full-time graduate students.   [3] In science and engineering.   [4] Excludes students and the self-employed.
Source: National Science Foundation/SRS, *National Survey of Recent College Graduates: 1993.*

No. 974. Doctorates Conferred, by Recipients' Characteristics: 1980 and 1994

[In percent, except as indicated]

CHARACTERISTIC	1980, total	1994									
		All fields [1]	Engineering	Physical sciences [2]	Earth sciences	Mathematics	Computer sciences	Biological sciences [3]	Agricultural	Social sciences [4]	Psychology
Total conferred (number)	31,020	41,011	5,826	3,975	824	1,118	904	5,197	1,078	3,900	3,389
Male	69.7	61.5	89.1	79.2	77.8	78.9	84.8	59.5	76.9	63.0	37.8
Female	30.3	38.5	10.9	20.8	22.2	21.1	15.2	40.5	23.1	37.0	62.2
Median age [5]	32.2	34.1	31.7	31	33.7	31.2	32.1	31.5	34.5	35.2	33.1
CITIZENSHIP [6]											
Total conferred (number)	30,156	4,239	5,706	3,893	808	1,084	887	5,139	1,069	3,799	3,296
U.S. citizen	83.6	67.4	38.7	56.4	62.6	45.8	48.0	66.5	48.6	61.1	92.8
Foreign citizen	16.4	32.6	61.3	43.6	37.4	54.2	52.0	33.5	51.4	38.9	7.2
RACE/ETHNICITY [7]											
Total conferred (number)	26,512	3,846	3,050	2,785	612	647	543	4,083	616	2,690	3,145
White [8]	84.7	79.6	66.1	72.6	82.2	72.8	73.8	76.1	79.1	79.3	87.1
Black [8]	4.2	4.1	1.8	1.7	1.0	1.7	1.8	1.8	3.6	5.5	3.9
Asian/Pacific [8]	4.2	11.5	28.5	21.5	14.5	21.8	21.5	17.6	11.7	10.1	3.5
Indian/Alaskan [8]	0.3	0.5	0.2	0.2	0.2	0.3	0.2	0.4	0.2	0.7	0.4
Hispanic	1.8	3.3	2.2	3.2	1.3	2.0	1.3	3.2	4.1	2.8	4.2
Other/unknown	4.9	1.0	1.2	0.8	0.8	1.4	1.4	0.9	1.3	1.6	0.9

[1] Includes other fields, not shown separately.   [2] Astronomy, physics, and chemistry.   [3] Biochemistry, botany, microbiology, physiology, zoology, and related fields.   [4] Anthropology, sociology, political science, economics, international relations and related fields.   [5] For definition of median, see Guide to Tabular Presentation.   [6] For those with known citizenship. Includes those with temporary visas.   [7] Excludes those with temporary visas.   [8] Non-Hispanic.

Source: U.S. National Science Foundation, Division of Science Resources Studies, Survey of Earned Doctorates, *Selected Data on Science and Engineering Doctorate Awards,* annual.

No. 975. Space Vehicle Systems—Net Sales and Backlog Orders: 1965 to 1994

[In millions of dollars. Backlog orders as of Dec. 31. Based on data from major companies engaged in manufacture of aerospace products. Includes parts but excludes engines and propulsion units]

YEAR	NET SALES			BACKLOG ORDERS			YEAR	NET SALES			BACKLOG ORDERS		
	Total	Military	Non-military	Total	Military	Non-military		Total	Military	Non-military	Total	Military	Non-military
1965 .	2,449	602	1,847	2,203	503	1,700	1986 .	6,304	4,579	[1]1,725	8,063	6,028	[1]2,035
1970 .	1,956	1,025	931	1,184	786	398	1987 .	8,051	5,248	[1]2,803	12,393	9,460	[1]2,933
1975 .	2,119	1,096	1,023	1,304	1,019	285	1988 .	8,622	6,190	[1]2,432	10,838	7,880	[1]2,958
1980 .	3,483	1,461	2,022	1,814	951	863	1989 .	9,758	6,457	[1]3,301	13,356	9,192	[1]4,164
1981 .	3,856	1,736	2,120	3,174	2,164	1,010	1990 .	9,691	6,556	[1]3,135	12,462	8,130	[1]4,332
1982 .	4,749	2,606	2,143	4,337	2,403	1,934	1991 .	10,515	6,770	[1]3,745	11,664	6,221	[1]5,443
1983 .	4,940	2,420	2,520	4,865	2,733	2,132	1992 .	9,266	5,887	[1]3,379	12,809	7,622	[1]5,187
1984 .	5,225	3,019	2,206	4,624	3,099	1,525	1993 .	8,309	4,175	[1]4,133	15,203	8,332	[1]6,871
1985 .	6,300	4,241	2,059	6,707	4,941	1,766	1994 .	10,284	5,360	[1]4,924	13,139	7,079	6,059

[1] Includes data for nonmilitary missile systems and parts.

Source: U.S. Bureau of the Census, *Current Industrial Reports*, MA-37D, *Aerospace Industry (Orders, Sales, and Backlog)*.

No. 976. Federal Outlays for General Science, Space, and Other Technology: 1970 to 1996

[In billions of dollars. For fiscal years ending in year shown; see text, section 9]

YEAR	CURRENT DOLLARS			CONSTANT (1987) DOLLARS		
	Total	General science/basic research	Space and other technologies	Total	General science/basic research	Space and other technologies
1970	4.5	0.9	3.6	13.9	2.9	11.0
1975	4.0	1.0	3.0	8.2	2.1	6.0
1980	5.8	1.4	4.4	8.2	1.9	6.3
1982	7.2	1.6	5.6	8.5	1.9	6.6
1983	7.9	1.6	6.3	8.9	1.8	7.1
1984	8.3	1.8	6.5	9.0	2.0	7.0
1985	8.6	2.0	6.6	9.1	2.1	6.9
1986	9.0	2.2	6.8	9.2	2.3	6.9
1987	9.2	2.2	7.0	9.2	2.2	7.0
1988	10.8	2.4	8.4	10.5	2.3	8.2
1989	12.8	2.6	10.2	11.9	2.4	9.5
1990	14.4	2.8	11.6	12.8	2.5	10.3
1991	16.1	3.1	13.0	13.7	2.7	11.0
1992	16.4	3.5	12.8	13.7	3.0	10.7
1993	17.0	3.9	13.1	13.9	3.2	10.7
1994	16.2	3.8	12.4	12.7	3.0	9.7
1995, est.	16.9	4.1	12.8	13.0	3.2	9.8
1996, est.	16.8	4.0	12.8	12.5	3.0	9.5

Source: U.S. Office of Management and Budget, *Budget of the United States,* annual.

No. 977. NASA Financial Summary: 1970 to 1994

[In millions of dollars. For fiscal year ending in year shown; see text, section 9]

YEAR	TOTAL		R&D		COMMUNICA-TIONS [1]		FACILITIES CONSTRUCTION		RESEARCH AND PROGRAM DEVELOPMENT	
	Appro-priations	Outlays	Appro-priations	Outlays	Appro-priations	Outlays	Appro-priations	Outlays	Appro-priations	Outlays
1970	3,749	3,753	3,006	2,992	-	-	53	54	690	707
1975	3,231	3,267	2,331	2,420	-	-	140	85	760	761
1980	5,243	4,852	4,091	3,701	-	-	156	140	996	1,010
1985	7,552	7,318	2,468	2,118	3,602	3,707	150	170	1,332	1,323
1986	7,764	7,404	2,638	2,615	3,689	3,267	133	189	1,303	1,332
1987	10,621	7,592	3,166	2,436	5,561	3,597	469	149	1,425	1,409
1988	9,002	9,092	3,414	2,916	3,908	4,362	178	166	1,501	1,648
1989 [2]	10,898	11,051	4,267	3,922	4,464	5,030	305	190	1,862	1,908
1990 [2]	12,296	12,428	5,221	5,094	4,555	5,117	588	218	1,923	1,991
1991 [2]	15,078	13,877	6,024	5,766	6,334	5,590	498	326	2,212	2,185
1992 [2]	14,302	13,818	6,396	6,261	5,124	5,311	525	448	2,242	1,784
1993, est. [2] .	14330	(NA)	7089	(NA)	5,086	(NA)	525	(NA)	1,615	(NA)
1994, est. [2] .	14,551	(NA)	7,529	(NA)	4,854	(NA)	518	(NA)	1,636	(NA)

- Represents zero.   NA Not available.   [1] Space flight, control, and data communications.   [2] Include appropriations and outlays for the Inspector General, not shown separately.

Source: U.S. National Aeronautics and Space Administration, *1995 Budget Summary*.

No. 978. National Aeronautics and Space Administration—Budget Summary: 1995 to 1997

[**In millions of dollars.** Data represent budget authority for fiscal years]

ITEM	1995	1996	1997
Total	[1]14,463.7	13,820.7	13,804.2
Human space flight.	5,514.9	5,456.6	5,362.9
Space station.	1,889.6	1,863.6	1,802.0
Russian cooperation	150.1	129.2	138.2
Space shuttle.	3,155.1	3,148.8	3,150.9
Payload and utilization operations	320.1	315.0	271.8
Science, aeronautics and technology	5,943.6	5,845.9	5,862.1
Space science	2,012.6	2,032.6	1,857.3
Life and microgravity sciences and applications	483.1	488.5	498.5
Mission to planet earth.	1,340.1	1,289.4	1,402.1
Space access and technology.	642.4	641.3	725.0
Aeronautical research and technology	882.0	845.9	857.8
Mission communication services	481.2	441.3	420.6
Academic programs.	102.2	106.9	100.8
Mission support	2,589.2	2,502.2	2,562.2
Safety, reliability and quality assurance	38.7	37.6	36.7
Space communication services	226.5	269.4	291.4
Research and program management	2,189.0	2,052.8	2,078.8
Construction of facilities	135.0	142.4	155.3
Inspector General.	16.0	16.0	17.0

[1] Includes $400 million for national aeronautical facilities.

Source: U.S. National Aeronautics and Space Administration, *Budget Summary, 1996* and *1997*.

No. 979. U.S. Commercial Space Revenues: 1990 to 1995

[**In millions of dollars.** For calendar years]

INDUSTRY	1990	1991	1992	1993	1994	1995 [1]
Total	3,385	4,370	4,860	5,295	6,640	7,850
Commercial satellites delivered	1,000	1,300	1,300	1,100	1,400	1,550
Satellite services	800	1,200	1,500	1,850	2,330	2,740
Fixed	735	1,115	1,275	1,600	1,980	2,340
Mobile.	65	85	225	250	350	400
Satellite ground equipment.	860	1,300	1,400	1,600	1,970	2,570
Mobile-equipment	145	280	350	420	480	510
Commercial launches	570	380	450	465	580	600
Remote sensing data and services	155	190	210	250	300	330
Commercial R&D infrastructure	-	-	-	30	60	60

- Represents zero.   [1] Forecast.

Source: U.S. Department of Commerce, International Trade Administration, *U.S. Industrial Outlook, 1994*; and unpublished data.

No. 980. NASA Space Shuttle Operations Expenditures: 1993 to 1995

[**In millions of dollars.** Data are funding requirements fiscal years shown]

OPERATION	1993	1994	1995
Total.	2,857.2	2,570.6	2,420.1
Orbiter.	477.0	364.1	292.8
System integration	200.6	211.2	190.5
External tank.	300.2	305.3	379.6
Space shuttle main engine.	239.9	191.8	144.4
Redesigned solid rocket	409.4	368.9	373.1
Solid rocket booster	172.0	156.4	144.9
Launch and landing operations.	697.1	650.1	596.4
Mission and crew operations	361.0	322.8	298.4

Source: U.S. National Aeronautics and Space Administration, *1995 Budget Summary*.

No. 981. Space Shuttle Flights—Summary: 1981 to March 1996

FLIGHT NUMBER	Date	Mission/Orbiter name	Crew size	Days duration	FLIGHT NUMBER	Date	Mission/Orbiter name	Crew size	Days duration
1	4/12/81	Columbia	2	2	39	4/28/91	Discovery	7	8
4	6/27/81	Columbia	2	7	37	4/5/91	Atlantis	5	6
2	11/12/81	Columbia	2	2	40	6/5/91	Columbia	7	9
3	3/22/82	Columbia	2	8	43	8/2/91	Atlantis	5	9
5	11/11/82	Columbia	4	5	44	11/24/91	Atlantis	6	7
6	4/4/83	Challenger	4	5	42	1/22/92	Discovery	7	8
7	6/18/83	Challenger	5	6	45	3/24/92	Atlantis	7	8
8	8/30/83	Challenger	5	6	49	5/7/92	Endeavour	7	8
9	11/28/83	Columbia	6	10	50	6/25/92	Columbia	7	13
10	2/3/84	Challenger	5	8	46	7/31/92	Atlantis	7	7
11	4/6/84	Challenger	5	7	47	9/12/92	Endeavour	7	7
12	8/30/84	Discovery	6	6	52	10/22/92	Columbia	6	9
13	10/5/84	Challenger	7	8	53	12/2/92	Discovery	5	7
14	11/8/84	Discovery	5	8	54	1/13/93	Endeavour	5	6
15	1/24/85	Discovery	5	3	56	4/8/93	Discovery	5	9
16	4/12/85	Discovery	7	7	55	4/26/93	Columbia	7	10
17	4/29/85	Challenger	7	7	57	6/21/93	Endeavour	6	10
18	6/17/85	Discovery	7	7	51	9/12/93	Discovery	5	10
19	7/29/85	Challenger	7	8	58	10/18/93	Columbia	7	14
20	8/27/85	Discovery	5	7	61	12/2/93	Endeavour	7	11
21	10/3/85	Atlantis	5	4	60	2/3/94	Discovery	6	8
22	10/30/85	Challenger	8	7	62	3/4/94	Columbia	5	14
23	11/26/85	Atlantis	7	7	59	4/9/94	Endeavour	6	11
24	1/12/86	Columbia	7	6	65	7/8/94	Columbia	7	14
25	1/28/86	Challenger	7	-	64	9/9/94	Discovery	6	10
26	9/29/88	Discovery	5	4	68	9/30/94	Endeavour	6	11
27	12/2/88	Atlantis	4	4	66	11/3/94	Atlantis	6	10
29	3/13/89	Discovery	5	5	63	2/3/95	Discovery	6	8
30	5/4/89	Atlantis	5	4	67	3/2/95	Endeavour	7	16
28	8/8/89	Columbia	5	5	71	6/27/95	Atlantis	10	9
34	10/18/89	Atlantis	5	5	70	7/13/95	Discovery	5	8
33	11/22/89	Discovery	5	5	69	9/7/95	Endeavour	5	10
32	1/9/90	Columbia	5	10	73	10/20/95	Columbia	7	15
36	2/28/90	Atlantis	5	5	74	11/12/95	Atlantis	9	8
31	4/24/90	Discovery	5	6	72	1/11/96	Endeavour	6	8
41	10/6/90	Discovery	5	4	75	2/22/96	Columbia	7	15
38	11/15/90	Atlantis	5	4	76	3/22/96	Atlantis	6	9
35	12/2/90	Columbia	7	9					

- Represents zero.
Source: Rockwell, Media Relations, Downey, CA, *Reporter's Space Flight Note Pad*, May, 1996.

No. 982. World-Wide Successful Space Launches: 1957 to 1995

[Criterion of success is attainment of Earth orbit or Earth escape]

COUNTRY	Total	1957-1964	1965-1969	1970-1974	1975-1979	1980-1984	1985-1989	1990	1991	1992	1993	1994	1995
Total	3,733	289	586	555	607	605	550	116	88	94	79	89	75
Soviet Union/CIS [1]	2,495	82	302	405	461	483	447	75	59	54	47	48	32
United States	1,054	207	279	139	126	93	61	27	18	28	23	26	27
Japan	49	-	-	5	10	12	11	3	2	1	1	2	2
ESA [2]	74	-	-	-	1	8	21	5	8	7	7	6	11
China	40	-	-	2	6	6	9	5	1	3	1	5	2
France	10	-	4	3	3	-	-	-	-	-	-	-	-
India	6	-	-	-	-	3	-	-	-	1	-	2	-
Israel	3	-	-	-	-	-	1	1	-	-	-	-	1
Australia	1	-	1	-	-	-	-	-	-	-	-	-	-
United Kingdom	1	-	-	1	-	-	-	-	-	-	-	-	-

- Represents zero.   [1] Commonwealth of Independent States.   [2] European Space Agency.
Source: Library of Congress, Congressional Research Service, Science Policy Research Division, *Space Activities of the United States, CIS, and Other Launching Countries/Organizations 1957-1994*, July 31, 1995; and forthcoming report.

No. 983. Nobel Prize Laureates in Chemistry, Physics, and Physiology/Medicine—Selected Countries: 1901 to 1994

[Presented by location of award-winning research and by date of award]

COUNTRY	1901-1994				1901-1930	1931-1945	1946-1960	1961-1975	1976-1990	1991-1994
	Total	Physics	Chemistry	Physiology/Medicine						
Total	425	146	120	159	93	49	74	92	98	19
United States	174	60	39	75	6	14	38	41	63	12
United Kingdom	69	21	24	24	15	11	14	20	9	-
Germany [1]	59	17	28	14	27	11	4	8	7	2
France	24	10	7	7	13	2	-	5	2	2
Soviet Union	10	7	1	2	2	-	4	3	1	-
Japan	4	3	1	-	-	-	1	2	1	-
Other countries	85	28	20	37	30	11	13	13	15	3

- Represents zero.   [1] Between 1946 and 1991, data are for the former West Germany only.
Source: U.S. National Science Foundation, unpublished data.

Transportation—Land

This section presents statistics on revenues, passenger and freight traffic volume, and employment in various revenue-producing modes of the transportation industry, including motor vehicles, trains, and pipelines. Data are also presented on commuting travel, highway mileage and finances, motor vehicle travel, accidents, sales, and registrations, automobile operating costs, and characteristics of public transit, railroads, and pipelines.

In Brief

Transportation outlays reached $1,064 billion in 1993

State gasoline tax rates for 1995—
Lowest rate, 7.5 cents/gallon in Georgia
Highest rate, 34 cents/gallon in Connecticut

The principal compiler of data on public roads and on operation of motor vehicles is the U.S. Department of Transportation's (DOT) Federal Highway Administration (FHWA). These data appear in FHWA's annual *Highway Statistics* and other publications. The U.S. Interstate Commerce Commission (ICC) presents data on interstate land transport in its publications, the *Annual Report to Congress* and the *Transport Statistics in the United States,* which contain data on railroads and motor carriers subject to ICC regulations.

The U.S. National Highway Traffic Safety Administration issues data on traffic accident deaths and death rates in two annual reports: the *Fact Book* and the *Fatal Accident Reporting System Annual Report.* DOT's Federal Railroad Administration presents data on accidents involving railroads in its annual *Accident/Incident Bulletin,* and the *Rail-Highway Crossing Accident/Incident and Inventory Bulletin.*

Various censuses and surveys conducted by the U.S. Bureau of the Census also provide data. Results of the censuses of transportation are presented in the *Truck Inventory and Use Survey.* The *Annual Survey of Manufactures* and reports of the censuses of manufactures, wholesale and retail trade, and service industries contain statistics on the motor vehicle and equipment industry and on retail, wholesale, and services aspects of this industry. Data on persons commuting to work were collected as part of the 1980 census and are in various census reports.

Data are also presented in many nongovernment publications. Among them are the weekly and annual *Cars of Revenue Freight Loaded* and the annual *Yearbook of Railroad Facts,* both published by the Association of American Railroads, Washington, DC; and the *Transit Fact Book,* containing electric railway and motorbus statistics, published annually by the American Public Transit Association, Washington, DC. Useful annual handbooks in the field of transportation are *Motor Vehicle Facts and Figures* and *World Motor Vehicle Data,* issued by the American Automobile Manufacturers Association (AAMA), Detroit, MI; *Accident Facts,* issued by the National Safety Council, Chicago, IL; and *Transportation in America,* issued by the ENO Foundation for Transportation, Westport, Connecticut.

Urban and rural highway mileage—
Beginning in 1980, mileage is classified in urban and rural categories, rather than municipal and rural. Urban denotes the Federal-aid legislation definition of an area. Such areas include, as a minimum, a census place with a population of 5,000 to 49,999 or a designated urbanized area with a population of 50,000 or more. These Federal-aid urban areas may extend beyond corporate and census boundaries, and thus are not necessarily coextensive with municipal boundaries. Rural in 1980 refers to non-Federal-aid urban area mileage. Prior to 1980, municipal referred to roads within incorporated places, densely populated New England towns, and certain of the

more populous unincorporated areas and rural to non-municipal roads.

Federal-aid Highway Systems—The Intermodal Surface Transportation Efficiency Act (ISTEA of 1991 eliminated the historical Federal-aid Systems and created the National Highway System (NHS) and other Federal-aid highway categories. The final NHS was approved by Congress in December of 1995 under the National Highway System Designation Act.

Functional Systems—Roads and streets are assigned to groups according to the character of service they are intended to provide. The functional systems are (1) arterial highways that generally handle the long trips, (2) collector facilities that collect and disperse traffiC between the arterials and the lower systems, and (3) local roads and streets that primarily serve direct access to residential areas.

Regulatory bodies—The ICC, created by the U.S. Congress to regulate transportation in interstate commerce, has jurisdiction over railroads, trucking companies, bus lines, freight forwarders, water carriers, coal slurry pipelines, and transportation brokers. The Federal Energy Regulatory Commission is responsible for setting rates and charges for transportation and sale of natural gas and for establishing rates or charges for transportation.

Motor carriers—For 1960-73, class I for-hire motor carriers of freight were classified by the ICC as those with $1 million or more of gross annual operating revenue; 1974-79, the class I minimum was $3 million. Effective January 1, 1980, class I carriers are those with $5 million or more in revenue. For 1960-68, class I motor carriers of passengers were classified by the ICC as those with $200,000 or more of gross annual operating revenue; for 1969-76, as those with revenues of $1 million or more; and since 1977, as those with $3 million or more. Effective January 1, 1988, class I motor carriers of passengers are those with $5 million or more in operating revenues; class II less than $5 million in operating revenues.

Railroads—Railroad companies reporting to the ICC are divided into specific groups as follows: (1) Regular line-haul (interstate) railroads (and their non-operating subsidiaries); (2) switching and terminal railroads; (3) private railroads prior to 1964 (identified by ICC as "circular" because they reported on brief circulars); and (4) unofficial railroads, so designated when their reports are received too late for tabulation. For the most part, the last three groups are not included in the statistics shown here.

For years prior to 1978, class I railroads were those with annual revenues of $1 million or more for 1950-55; $3 million or more for 1956-64; $5 million or more for 1965-75; and $10 million or more for 1976-77. In 1978, the classification became class I, those having more than $50 million gross annual operating revenue; class II, from $10 million to $50 million; and class III, less than $10 million. Effective January 1, 1982, the ICC adopted a procedure to adjust the threshold for inflation by restating current revenues in constant 1978 dollars. In 1990, the criteria for class I and class II railroads were $94.4 million and $18.9 million, respectively. Also effective January 1, 1982, the ICC adopted a *Carrier Classification Index Survey Form* for carriers not filing annual report form R-1 with the commission. Effective January 1, 1992, the ICC adopted new revenue classification levels as follows: Class I–$250 million or more; Class II–less than $250 million but in excess of $20 million; Class III–$20 million or less. The inflation adjustment index still applies. Class II and class III railroads are currently exempted from filing any financial report with the Commission. The form is used for reclassifying carriers.

Statistical reliability—For a discussion of statistical collection and estimation, sampling procedures, and measures of statistical reliability, see Appendix III.

Historical statistics—Tabular headnotes provide cross-references, where applicable, to *Historical Statistics of the United States, Colonial Times to 1970.* See Appendix IV.

No. 984. Passenger and Freight Transportation Outlays, by Type of Transport: 1975 to 1993

[In billions of dollars. Freight data include outlays for mail and express. ICC=Interstate Commerce Commission]

TYPE OF TRANSPORT	1975	1980	1981	1982	1983	1984	1985	1986	1987	1988	1989	1990	1991	1992	1993
Total outlays [1]	298	543	593	591	643	716	753	761	808	869	916	965	952	997	1,064
Passenger, total	187	338	374	379	411	460	492	493	528	572	604	630	613	638	683
Private transportation	161	285	317	321	348	387	418	415	445	481	508	528	509	532	571
Automobiles [2]	157	277	307	313	340	379	410	407	436	472	498	517	499	522	560
New and used cars	46	73	83	86	105	126	139	157	151	164	164	166	153	164	173
Tires, tubes, accessories	12	22	25	25	26	27	30	29	21	23	24	25	26	26	28
Gasoline and oil	54	100	111	105	106	106	107	82	94	97	107	121	114	115	115
Insurance less claims	5	12	11	11	12	12	12	14	17	19	20	20	25	27	29
Interest on debt	7	18	21	22	20	25	27	27	29	34	37	36	32	26	30
Registration and operator's permit fees	2	3	4	4	4	5	5	6	6	6	7	7	7	8	9
Repair, greasing, washing, parking, tolls [3]	22	39	42	45	47	52	60	60	75	84	90	94	94	102	112
Air	5	8	9	8	7	8	8	8	9	10	10	10	10	10	11
For-hire transportation	26	53	57	59	63	72	74	77	84	91	96	103	104	106	112
Local [4]	11	20	22	23	24	27	27	30	31	32	33	34	36	36	37
Bus and transit [5]	5	9	10	11	12	13	14	15	15	16	16	17	18	18	18
School bus	5	4	5	5	5	6	6	6	6	7	7	8	8	8	8
Taxi	3	5	5	6	5	6	6	6	6	7	7	8	8	7	8
Intercity	13	28	30	30	33	39	40	40	44	48	51	53	53	53	58
Air	11	25	27	27	30	34	36	36	40	44	47	50	49	49	54
Rail [6]	1	2	2	2	2	2	2	2	2	2	2	2	2	2	2
Bus	1	2	2	2	2	2	2	2	2	2	2	2	2	2	2
International	3	5	5	5	6	7	7	7	9	11	12	15	16	17	18
Freight, total [4]	116	214	228	222	243	268	274	281	294	313	329	352	356	376	397
Highway	85	155	165	163	182	200	206	213	225	239	254	271	274	293	311
Truck, intercity	47	95	97	100	111	121	123	158	135	143	151	162	165	177	190
Truck, local	37	61	68	63	71	79	82	85	90	96	103	108	110	116	122
Rail	17	28	31	27	27	31	29	28	29	30	30	30	30	31	31
Water	8	16	17	16	16	18	18	19	19	20	20	21	20	20	21
Oil pipeline	2	8	8	8	9	9	9	9	9	8	8	8	8	9	9
Air carrier	2	4	4	4	5	6	7	8	9	10	12	14	14	15	16
Percent change, total:															
Passenger, total	5.4	10.3	9.1	-0.2	8.8	11.3	5.2	1.0	6.1	7.6	5.4	5.4	-1.4	4.7	6.7
Private transportation	9.4	9.9	10.6	1.4	8.3	11.9	7.1	0.1	7.2	8.3	5.6	4.4	-2.7	4.1	7.0
Automobiles [2]	9.2	7.9	11.2	1.3	8.4	11.4	8.0	-0.7	7.0	8.2	5.6	4.0	-3.5	4.5	7.3
Air	9.3	7.7	11.1	1.7	8.8	11.4	8.3	-0.8	7.1	8.1	5.6	3.9	-3.5	4.5	7.3
For-hire transportation	6.8	14.1	16.0	-12.8	-9.8	10.8	-3.7	3.8	3.7	11.8	-	9.5	-2.9	1.0	7.8
Air	11.0	23.3	7.3	2.1	8.0	8.0	2.4	4.6	8.2	8.7	5.8	6.7	1.3	2.5	5.7
Freight	-0.4	10.8	6.9	-2.8	9.5	10.2	2.1	2.7	4.7	6.4	5.1	6.9	1.0	5.6	5.6

[1] Total outlays less than sum of passenger and freight totals, as estimated freight costs included in costs of new cars, gasoline, oil, tires, and tubes have been excluded to prevent duplication. [2] Includes business-owned vehicles. [3] Includes storage and rental. [4] Includes items not shown separately. [5] Includes Federal, State, and local government operating subsidies and capital grants. [6] Includes Federal operating subsidies and capital grants for Amtrak.

Source: Eno Transportation Foundation, Inc.., Lansdowne, VA, Transportation in America, annual (copyright).

No. 985. Employment and Earnings in Transportation, by Industry: 1980 to 1995

[Annual averages of monthly figures. Based on Current Employment Statistics program; see Appendix III. See also *Historical Statistics, Colonial Times to 1970*, series Q36-42]

INDUSTRY	SIC [1] code	1980	1985	1989	1990	1991	1992	1993	1994	1995
NUMBER (1,000)										
Total transportation.	(X)	**2,960**	**2,997**	**3,415**	**3,527**	**3,502**	**3,498**	**3,587**	**3,769**	**3,918**
Railroads.	40	532	359	293	279	262	254	250	241	239
Class I railroads	4011	482	323	252	241	231	222	218	214	212
Local and interurban passengers . .	41	265	277	326	338	354	361	374	404	423
Trucking and warehousing	42	1,280	1,361	1,595	1,625	1,606	1,611	1,685	1,794	1,867
Water transportation	44	211	185	172	177	184	173	167	172	174
Air transportation.	45	453	522	683	745	733	730	737	753	788
Pipelines, exc. natural gas	46	21	19	19	19	19	19	18	17	15
Transportation services	47	198	275	329	345	344	348	356	389	413
AVERAGE WEEKLY EARNINGS (dol.)										
Class I railroads	4011	427	595	693	727	707	736	782	786	811
Local and interurban passengers . .	41	217	261	305	310	323	334	339	354	356
Trucking and warehousing	42	358	405	437	451	455	468	479	495	501
Pipelines, exc. natural gas	46	441	629	671	711	733	772	817	872	888

X Not applicable.   [1] 1987 Standard Industrial Classification, see text, section 13.

Source: U.S. Bureau of Labor Statistics, Bulletin 2445 and, and Earnings, March and June issues.

No. 986. Volume of Domestic Intercity Freight and Passenger Traffic, by Type of Transport: 1970 to 1993

[**Freight traffic in bil. ton-miles; passenger traffic in bil. passenger-miles.** A ton-mile is the movement of 1 ton (2,000 pounds) of freight for the distance of 1 mile. A passenger-mile is the movement of one passenger for the distance of 1 mile. Comprises public and private traffic, both revenue and nonrevenue. See also *Historical Statistics, Colonial Times to 1970*, series Q1-22]

TYPE OF TRANSPORT	TRAFFIC VOLUME						PERCENT DISTRIBUTION					
	1970	1980	1985	1990	1992	1993	1970	1980	1985	1990	1992	1993
Freight traffic, total	**1,936**	**2,487**	**2,458**	**2,895**	**3,009**	**3,105**	**100.0**	**100.0**	**100.0**	**100.0**	**100.0**	**100.0**
Railroads.	771	932	895	1,091	1,138	1,183	39.8	37.5	36.4	37.7	37.8	38.1
Truck:												
ICC truck	167	242	250	311	342	365	8.6	9.7	10.2	10.7	11.4	11.8
Non-ICC truck.	245	313	360	424	473	506	12.7	12.6	14.6	14.6	15.7	16.3
Water:												
Rivers/canals	205	311	306	390	397	393	10.6	12.5	12.4	13.5	13.2	12.7
Great Lakes	114	96	76	85	77	74	5.9	3.9	3.1	2.9	2.6	2.4
Oil pipelines.	431	588	564	584	571	572	22.3	23.6	23.0	20.2	19.0	18.4
Domestic airways [1] . . .	3	5	7	10	11	12	0.2	0.2	0.3	0.4	0.4	0.4
Passenger traffic, total. . . .	**1,181**	**1,467**	**1,635**	**1,993**	**2,079**	**2,126**	**100.0**	**100.0**	**100.0**	**100.0**	**100.0**	**100.0**
Private automobiles. . .	1,026	1,210	1,310	1,598	1,675	1,718	86.9	82.5	80.1	80.2	80.6	80.8
Domestic airways [2] . . .	119	219	290	359	367	370	10.1	14.9	17.7	18.1	17.6	17.4
Bus [3]	25	27	24	23	24	23	2.1	1.8	1.5	1.2	1.1	1.1
Railroads [4]	11	11	11	13	14	14	0.9	0.8	0.7	0.7	0.7	0.7

[1] Revenue service only for scheduled and nonscheduled carriers, with small section 418 all-cargo carriers included from 1980. Includes express mail and excess baggage.   [2] Includes general aviation (mostly private business) flying.   [3] Excludes school and urban transit buses.   [4] Includes intercity (Amtrak) and rail commuter service.

Source: Eno Transportation Foundation, Inc., Lansdowne VA, *Transportation in America*, annual (copyright).

No. 987. Highway Mileage—Urban and Rural, by Type and Control, and Federal-Aid Highway System: 1980 to 1994

[**In thousands, except percent. As of Dec. 31.** Data for urban and rural mileage are not comparable to years prior to 1980 because of classification changes; see text, section 21. See also *Historical Statistics, Colonial Times to 1970*, series Q 50, 51, and 55]

TYPE AND CONTROL	1980	1985	1988	1989	1990	1991	1992	1993	1994
Total mileage [1]	[2]**3,955**	**3,862**	**3,871**	**3,877**	**3,880**	**3,889**	**3,902**	**3,905**	**3,906**
Urban mileage.	624	691	739	754	757	750	785	803	814
Under State control	79	111	96	97	96	96	104	106	110
Under local control	543	578	642	656	661	653	680	696	702
Rural mileage	[2]**3,331**	3,171	3,132	3,123	3,123	3,139	3,117	3,102	3,093
Percent surfaced [3]	77.5	88.1	88.1	88.4	88.6	89.7	88.9	88.7	91.3
Under State control	702	773	704	706	703	703	697	675	690
Under local control	2,270	2,173	2,244	2,238	2,242	2,255	2,239	2,247	2,229
Under Federal control	262	225	183	178	178	182	181	180	174

[1] Beginning 1985, includes only public road mileage as defined 23 USC 402.   [2] Includes 98,000 miles of nonpublic road mileage previously contained in other rural categories.   [3] Covers soil-surfaced roads and roads with slag, gravel, stone, bituminous, or concrete surfaces.

Source: U.S. Federal Highway Administration, *Highway Statistics*, annual.

No. 988. Commodity Flow Survey (CFS) Shipment Characteristics: 1993

MODE OF TRANSPORTATION	VALUE		TONS		TON-MILES		
	Amount (mil. dol.)	Percent	Total (1,000)	Percent	Total (mil.)	Percent	Avg. miles per shipment [1]
All modes, total.............	**6,037,200**	**100.0**	**9,865,526**	**100.0**	**2,517,089**	**100.0**	**403**
Single modes:							
Parcel, U.S. postal service or courier	563,603	9.3	18,682	0.2	12,901	0.5	715
Private truck	1,789,798	29.6	3,556,030	36.0	237,617	9.4	51
For-hire truck.................	2,775,836	46.0	2,921,436	29.6	634,599	25.2	470
Air.........................	41,520	0.7	492	(Z)	613	(Z)	1,390
Rail	250,534	4.1	1,570,087	15.9	958,658	38.1	803
Inland water	41,645	0.7	366,207	3.7	164,514	6.5	356
Great Lakes	624	(Z)	34,337	0.3	12,293	0.5	266
Deep sea water..............	(S)	(S)	(S)	(S)	(S)	(S)	(S)
Pipeline [2]	84,053	1.4	466,578	4.7	(S)	(S)	(S)
Multiple modes:							
Private truck and for-hire truck.........	22,567	0.4	32,418	0.3	4,654	0.2	209
Truck and air.................	107,736	1.8	2,296	(Z)	2,822	0.1	1,315
Truck and rail.................	82,895	1.4	38,014	0.4	43,127	1.7	1,482
Truck and water..............	8,232	0.1	72,051	0.7	48,256	1.9	1,269
Truck and pipeline [2]	649	(Z)	3,386	(Z)	(S)	(S)	(S)
Rail and water................	3,260	0.1	66,740	0.7	55,719	2.2	917
Inland water & Great Lakes	(S)	(S)	(S)	(S)	(S)	(S)	(S)
Inland water & deep sea	16,514	0.3	80,042	0.8	126,386	5.0	(S)
Other and unknown modes	246,056	4.1	624,846	6.3	131,635	5.2	216

S Data do not meet publication standards due to high sampling variability or other reasons.   Z Insignifcant.   [1] Excludes shipments of STCC 27, printed matter.   [2] Excludes most shipments of crude oil.

Source: U.S. Bureau of Transportation Statistics, *National Transportation Statistics, 1996*. Data from U.S. Bureau of the Census, *1993 Commodity Flow Survey, U.S. Preliminary Report, TC92-CF-52(P)*, July 1995.

No. 989. Transportation Accidents, Deaths, and Injuries: 1985 to 1994

[For related data, see also table 1013]

YEAR AND CASUALTY	Motor vehi-cle [1] (1,000)	Rail-road [2]	TYPE OF TRANSPORT										
			Air carriers				General avia-tion	Recre-ational boat-ing [6]	Gas pipe-lines [7]	Liquid pipe-lines [8]	Water-borne [9]	Rail Rapid Trans-it [10]	Haz-ardous mate-rials [11]
			Total	Air-lines [3]	Com-muter air car-riers [4]	On demand air car-riers [5]							
Accidents:													
1980....	6,216	8,451	228	19	38	171	3,590	5,513	1,524	246	4,624	6,789	15,737
1985....	6,081	3,275	195	22	21	152	2,738	6,237	331	183	3,439	1,014	6,019
1990....	6,471	2,879	147	24	15	108	2,216	6,411	199	180	3,613	12,178	8,882
1991....	6,117	2,658	136	26	22	88	2,177	6,573	234	216	2,222	14,102	9,110
1992....	6,000	2,359	117	18	23	76	2,075	6,048	176	212	3,297	15,512	9,355
1993....	6,105	2,611	110	23	16	71	2,042	6,335	217	230	2,654	15,082	12,832
1994....	6,492	2,504	116	22	10	84	1,989	6,906	222	244	2,833	15,258	16,084
Deaths:													
1980....	51.1	584	143	1	37	105	1,239	1,360	15	4	206	83	19
1985....	43.8	454	639	526	37	76	955	1,116	26	5	131	17	8
1990....	44.6	599	94	39	6	49	766	865	6	3	85	117	8
1991....	41.5	586	200	50	77	73	785	924	14	-	30	103	10
1992....	39.3	591	120	33	21	70	860	816	10	5	105	91	15
1993....	40.2	653	67	1	24	42	737	800	17	-	95	83	15
1994....	40.7	611	328	239	25	64	706	784	21	-	52	76	11
Injuries:													
1980....	2,848	58,356	74	17	14	43	675	2,650	177	15	176	6,801	626
1985....	3,363	31,617	89	30	16	43	517	2,577	106	18	172	1,039	253
1990....	3,231	22,736	86	39	11	36	391	3,822	69	7	175	10,036	423
1991....	3,097	21,374	83	26	30	27	420	3,967	89	9	110	9,285	439
1992....	3,070	19,408	37	13	5	19	418	3,683	80	38	172	10,446	604
1993....	3,125	17,284	42	16	2	24	386	3,559	102	10	133	10,532	626
1994....	3,215	14,850	73	35	6	32	452	4,084	112	1,858	146	11,170	576

- Represents or rounds to zero.   NA Not available.   [1] Data on deaths are from U.S. National Highway Traffic Safety Administration and are based on 30 day definition.   [2] Accidents which result in damages to railroad property. Grade crossing accidents are also included when classified as a train accident. Deaths exclude fatalities in railroad-highway grade crossing accidents.   [3] Includes scheduled and nonscheduled (charter) air carriers. Represents serious injuries.   [4] All scheduled service. Represents serious injuries.   [5] All nonscheduled service. Represents serious injuries.   [6] Accidents resulting in death; injury or requiring medical treatment beyond first aid; damages exceeding $200; or a person's disappearance.   [7] Beginning 1985, pipeline accidents/incidents are credited to year of occurrence; prior data are credited to the year filed.   [8] Pipelines carrying hazardous materials, petroleum, and liquid petroleum products.   [9] Covers accidents involving commercial vessels which must be reported to U.S. Coast Guard if there is property damage exceeding $1,500; material damage affecting the seaworthiness or efficiency of a vessel; stranding or grounding; loss of life; or injury causing a person's incapacity for more than 3 days.   [10] Reporting criteria and source of data changed between 1989 and 1990; these data from 1990 to present are not comparable to earlier years.   [11] Accidents, deaths, and injuries involving hazardous materials cover all types of transport.

Source: U.S. Bureau of Transportation Statistics, *National Transportation Statistics*, annual.

No. 990. Highway Mileage—Functional Systems and Urban/Rural: 1994

[As of Dec. 31. For definition of urban, rural, see text, section 21]

STATE	FUNCTIONAL SYSTEMS					Urban	Rural
	Total	Inter-state	Other arterial	Collector	Local		
U.S	**3,906,544**	**45,583**	**385,103**	**799,234**	**2,676,624**	**813,591**	**3,092,953**
AL	93,032	904	8673	19,366	62,272	20,069	72,963
AK	14,325	1,086	1509	1,648	8,759	1,782	12,543
AZ	54,380	1,169	4768	15,123	40,787	16,212	38,168
AR	77,216	543	6799	7,691	49,626	7,677	69,539
CA	169,047	2,427	28138	79,986	106,090	81,117	87,930
CO	84,195	954	8335	12,777	53,195	13,324	70,871
CT	20,384	346	2967	11,496	13,900	11,555	8,829
DE	5,592	41	619	1,855	3,945	1,907	3,685
DC	1,104	12	279	1,104	656	1,104	-
FL	113,478	1,472	12088	48,637	85,349	48,394	65,084
GA	111,252	1,242	13148	26,147	73,443	26,396	84,856
HI	4,106	43	793	1,799	2,647	1,813	2,293
ID	59,897	611	3580	3,314	44,990	3,462	56,435
IL	137,149	2,054	13983	32,266	99,727	35,312	101,837
IN	92,476	1,138	8061	19,109	60,572	19,315	73,161
IA	112,793	785	9410	9,096	71,016	9,319	103,474
KS	133,280	872	9297	9,508	90,097	9,596	123,684
KY	72,981	762	5458	10,008	48,840	10,311	62,670
LA	60,021	878	5337	12,319	40,873	13,949	46,072
ME	22,561	366	2324	2,479	13,872	2,605	19,956
MD	29,474	482	3775	13,574	20,073	13,758	15,716
MA	30,599	565	5825	21,017	18,725	19,745	10,854
MI	117,671	1,238	12307	28,012	78,136	28,147	89,524
MN	130,198	914	12704	14,523	87,316	15,016	115,182
MS	72,910	685	7032	7,888	49,623	7,913	64,997
MO	122,311	1,178	9561	15,398	85,996	16,499	105,812
MT	69,346	1,190	6008	2,348	46,105	2,385	66,961
NE	92,730	482	7895	5,030	63,596	5,083	87,647
NV	46,152	560	2754	4,513	37,550	4,590	41,562
NH	15,022	224	1584	2,440	10,416	2,899	12,123
NJ	35,432	420	5511	22,503	24,496	24,188	11,244
NM	61,221	1,000	4522	5,828	48,532	6,081	55,140
NY	112,004	1,498	14497	39,063	75,355	39,907	72,097
NC	96,479	970	9099	21,451	68,028	21,899	74,580
ND	86,731	571	5869	1,825	61,500	1,819	84,912
OH	114,464	1,572	10949	31,568	78,865	33,085	81,379
OK	112,467	929	7995	12,281	78,186	12,794	99,673
OR	84,029	727	6885	9,494	70,104	10,148	73,881
PA	118,445	1,589	13754	30,823	82,096	33,233	85,212
RI	5,973	70	841	4,597	4,194	4,613	1,360
SC	64,253	810	6874	10,517	43,078	10,518	53,735
SD	83,317	678	6285	1,858	57,061	1,907	81,410
TN	85,527	1,062	8681	16,314	57,583	16,826	68,701
TX	294,491	3,234	28968	76,143	200,284	80,903	213,588
UT	40,842	940	3342	6,084	28,545	6,201	34,641
VT	14,180	320	1319	1,314	9,415	1,333	12,847
VA	68,943	1,106	8298	15,581	45,420	18,196	50,747
WA	79,799	763	7593	17,025	54,313	17,501	62,298
WV	34,822	549	3211	3,090	22,473	3,151	31,671
WI	110,923	638	11934	14,841	76,957	15,725	95,198
WY	36,520	914	3665	2,489	22,457	2,309	34,211

- Represents zero.

Source: U.S. Federal Highway Administration, *Highway Statistics,* annual.

No. 991. Highway Pavement Condition, by Type of Road System: 1993

CONDITION	URBAN AREAS						RURAL AREAS				
			Other						Other		
	Total	Inter-state	Free-ways and express-ways	Prin-cipal arter-ial	Minor arter-ial	Collec-tor	Total	Inter-state	prin-cipal arter-ial	Minor arter-ial	Major collec-tor
Percent of road mileage rated—											
Poor	9	12	4	11	7	10	6	6	2	3	7
Mediocre	15	28	10	13	12	16	12	26	8	10	13
Fair	38	24	47	41	38	40	43	24	55	55	37
Good	20	26	22	20	21	17	21	33	27	25	18
Very Good	18	9	16	16	22	16	18	11	8	7	25

Source: U.S. Federal Highway Administration, *Highway Statistics*, annual.

No. 992. Funding for Highways, by Level of Government: 1980 to 1994

[**In millions of dollars.** Data compiled from reports of State and local authorities. For Federal highway trust fund receipts, disbursements, and balances, see table 514. State data include District of Columbia]

TYPE	1980	1985	1990	1992	1993	1994		
						Total [1]	Federal	State
Total receipts	39,715	61,506	75,294	86,703	88,380	88,296	16,337	48,469
Current income	37,604	54,957	69,730	77,404	80,610	80,514	16,337	44,282
Imposts on highway users [2]	22,559	35,599	44,264	50,889	54,401	54,476	14,235	38,534
Other taxes and fees	11,808	15,127	19,827	19,933	19,375	19,872	1,348	3,756
Investment income, other receipts	3,237	4,231	5,639	6,582	6,834	6,166	754	1,992
Bond issue proceeds [3]	2,111	6,549	5,564	9,299	7,770	7,782	-	4,187
Intergovernmental payments [4]	(X)	(X)	(X)	(X)	(X)	(X)	-18,714	9,751
Funds from (+) or to (-) reserves [4]	2,080	-4,058	114	-3,155	-1,955	962	3,598	-2,651
Total funds available	41,795	57,448	75,408	83,548	86,425	89,258	1,221	55,569
Total disbursements	41,795	57,448	75,408	83,548	86,425	89,258	1,221	55,569
Current disbursements	40,084	54,725	72,457	78,959	81,233	85,109	1,221	53,388
Capital outlay	20,337	27,138	35,151	38,309	39,528	41,780	344	32,059
Maintenance and traffic services	11,445	16,032	20,365	22,223	22,894	23,607	71	10,136
Administration and research	3,022	4,033	6,501	7,718	7,921	8,398	806	4,847
Law enforcement and safety	3,824	5,334	7,235	7,088	7,157	7,518	-	4,209
Interest on debt	1,456	2,188	3,205	3,621	3,733	3,806	-	2,137
Debt retirement [3]	1,711	2,723	2,951	4,589	5,192	4,149	-	2,181

- Represents zero. X Not applicable. [1] Includes other levels of government not shown separately. [2] Excludes amounts later allocated for nonhighway purposes. [3] Excludes issue and redemption of short-term notes or refunding bonds. [4] Plus sign (+) indicates net receipt of funds from other levels of government; minus sign (-) indicates net disbursement of funds to other levels.

No. 993. Disbursements of State Highway Funds, by State: 1990 to to 1994

[**In millions of dollars.** Comprises disbursements from current revenues or loans for construction, maintenance, interest and principal payments on highway bonds, transfers to local units, and miscellaneous. Includes transactions by State toll authorities. Excludes amounts allocated for collection expenses and nonhighway purposes, and bonds redeemed by refunding. See also *Historical Statistics, Colonial Times to 1970*, series Q 90-94]

STATE	1990	1993	1994	STATE	1990	1993	1994	STATE	1990	1993	1994
U.S.	53,580	62,192	64,113	KS	697	780	919	ND	189	230	264
				KY	1,008	1,127	1,303	OH	2,271	2,523	2,604
AL	866	942	834	LA	923	980	1,106	OK	827	738	760
AK	336	436	436	ME	332	339	349	OR	765	825	907
AZ	1,525	1,188	1,255	MD	1,464	1,171	1,263	PA	2,885	3,065	3,214
AR	456	645	658	MA	1,055	2,034	2,108	RI	214	316	348
CA	4,294	5,186	5,073	MI	1,526	1,734	1,804	SC	585	668	632
CO	714	914	979	MN	1,228	1,320	1,202	SD	232	287	297
CT	1,204	1,050	1,101	MS	529	685	645	TN	1,174	1,117	1,144
DE	315	360	420	MO	937	1,111	1,265	TX	3,001	3,380	3,553
DC	273	289	205	MT	302	328	339	UT	355	410	397
FL	1,677	2,882	2,892	NE	449	537	618	VT	165	210	187
GA	1,278	1,294	1,236	NV	309	355	445	VA	1,874	1,578	2,019
HI	297	400	400	NH	299	368	354	WA	1,251	1,602	1,655
ID	300	312	348	NJ	1,831	2,457	2,312	WV	650	765	776
IL	2,645	2,802	2,602	NM	409	519	534	WI	979	1,214	1,262
IN	1,218	1,303	1,297	NY	2,874	4,529	4,728	WY	297	261	288
IA	869	1,000	999	NC	1,428	1,626	1,778				

Source of tables 992-993: U.S. Federal Highway Administration, *Highway Statistics*, annual.

No. 994. Federal Grants to State and Local Governments for Highway Trust Fund and Federal Transit Administration (FTA), by State: 1995

[Year ending Sept. 30]

STATE	HIGHWAY TRUST FUND Total (mil. dol.)	Per capita [1]	FTA [2] Total (mil. dol.)	Per capita [1]	STATE	HIGHWAY TRUST FUND Total (mil. dol.)	Per capita [1]	FTA [2] Total (mil. dol.)	Per capita [1]	STATE	HIGHWAY TRUST FUND Total (mil. dol.)	Per capita [1]	FTA [2] Total (mil. dol.)	Per capita [1]
U.S.	19,091	72.3	4,818	18.2	KS...	167	65.4	8	3.0	ND...	135	211.8	3	4.0
					KY...	248	64.8	17	4.5	OH...	688	61.9	92	8.3
AL...	293	69.4	17	4.0	LA...	246	57.1	46	10.7	OK...	253	77.6	11	3.3
AK...	258	425.9	6	9.4	ME...	116	93.9	5	4.2	OR...	189	61.2	194	62.9
AZ...	275	67.5	44	10.9	MD...	380	76.0	113	22.5	PA...	883	73.3	276	22.9
AR...	241	98.4	6	2.5	MA...	964	159.5	277	45.8	RI...	174	174.7	16	16.0
CA...	1,880	59.8	762	24.2	MI...	569	59.9	64	6.8	SC...	259	70.6	8	2.2
CO...	249	68.1	28	7.6	MN...	228	50.0	39	8.5	SD...	129	178.6	3	4.3
CT...	392	119.7	84	25.5	MS...	189	70.8	8	2.8	TN...	321	62.1	25	4.9
DE...	66	93.9	3	3.8	MO...	399	75.5	50	9.4	TX...	985	53.6	181	9.8
DC...	104	182.6	322	564.6	MT...	146	171.1	4	5.1	UT...	130	68.3	10	5.3
FL...	876	62.8	163	11.7	NE...	140	86.0	9	5.8	VT...	85	146.7	6	10.4
GA...	524	74.3	104	14.8	NV...	121	83.0	12	8.2	VA...	398	60.7	47	7.2
HI...	181	153.9	45	38.6	NH...	78	68.2	4	3.7	WA...	484	90.6	54	10.2
ID...	141	124.4	7	6.6	NJ...	545	68.9	272	34.4	WV...	169	92.6	11	6.1
IL...	820	69.8	403	34.3	NM...	227	137.4	7	4.2	WI...	296	58.3	37	7.3
IN...	369	64.1	35	6.1	NY...	891	49.0	806	44.3	WY...	133	279.2	2	4.8
IA...	229	80.8	18	6.5	NC...	492	69.5	27	3.9					

[1] Based on Bureau of the Census resident population as of July 1, 1994; excluding population of the territories.   [2] Federal Transit Administration.

Source: U.S. Bureau of the Census, *Federal Expenditures by State for Fiscal Year,* annual.

No. 995. State Gasoline Tax Rates, 1994 and 1995, and Motor Fuel Tax Receipts, 1994

[See also *Historical Statistics, Colonial Times to 1970,* series Q 233-234]

STATE	RATE [1] (cents/gal.) 1994	1995	Receipts, [2] 1994 (mil. dol.)	STATE	RATE [1] (cents/gal.) 1994	1995	Receipts, [2] 1994 (mil. dol.)	STATE	RATE [1] (cents/gal.) 1994	1995	Receipts, [2] 1994 (mil. dol.)
Federal .	18.4	18.4	(NA)	KS...	18	18	283	ND...	18	18	82
State..	(NA)	(NA)	(NA)	KY [3]..	16.4	16.4	363	OH....	22	22	1,255
AL...	18	18	518	LA...	20	20	473	OK [4]..	17	17	353
AK...	8	8	22	ME..	19	19	139	OR...	24	24	347
AZ...	18	18	423	MD..	23.5	23.5	593	PA...	22.35	22.35	1,363
AR...	18.7	18.7	319	MA..	21	21	556	RI...	28	29	116
CA...	18	18	2,440	MI..	15	15	716	SC...	16	16	378
CO..	22	22	414	MN..	20	20	478	SD [5]..	18	18	88
CT..	31	34	431	MS..	18.4	18.4	318	TN [5]..	20	20	633
DE...	22	23	89	MO..	15.05	15	498	TX...	20	20	2,169
DC...	20	20	36	MT..	27	27	150	UT...	19	19	191
FL...	12.1	12.3	1,189	NE...	25.4	25.4	236	VT [3]..	16	16	64
GA...	7.5	7.5	374	NV...	24	24	207	VA [3]..	17.5	17.5	682
HI...	16	16	66	NH..	18.7	18.7	104	WA...	23	23	639
ID...	21	21	143	NJ...	10.5	10.5	441	WV...	25.35	25.35	276
IL...	19	19	1,074	NM...	21	18	224	WI...	23.1	23.4	630
IN...	15	15	609	NY...	22.56	21.92	1,365	WY..	9	9	50
IA...	20	20	347	NC...	21.3	21.6	888				

NA Not available.   [1] In effect Dec. 31.   [2] Represents net gallonage receipts.   [3] Trucks or combinations with more than two axles pay tax of 2 cents per gallon more in Kentucky and 3.5 cents per gallon more in Virginia.   [4] .08 cents per gallon is for inspection fee.   [5] Includes 1 cent per gallon inspection fee.

No. 996. Public Highway Debt—State and Local Governments: 1970 to 1994

[In millions of dollars. Long-term obligations. Data are for varying calendar and fiscal years. Excludes duplicated and interunit obligations. See also *Historical Statistics, Colonial Times to 1970,* series Q 136-147]

ITEM	1970	1980	1985	1988	1989	1990	1991	1992	1993	1994 [1]
Total debt issued	1,892	2,357	8,194	4,594	5,900	5,838	9,516	12,988	14,178	9,334
State	1,306	1,135	5,397	2,702	3,775	3,277	6,252	9,460	10,035	5,739
Local	586	1,222	2,797	1,892	2,125	2,561	3,264	3,528	4,143	3,595
Total debt redeemed ..	1,270	1,982	4,606	2,774	3,729	5,158	6,138	7,665	10,823	5,590
State	800	1,109	3,835	1,547	2,813	2,041	4,352	5,388	8,082	3,622
Local	470	873	771	1,227	916	3,117	1,786	2,277	2,741	1,968
Total debt outstanding .	19,124	27,519	33,379	41,663	43,834	44,514	47,892	53,539	58,373	64,158
Local	5,104	7,427	12,100	15,927	17,136	16,580	18,058	19,353	22,965	26,709

[1] Estimated.

Source of tables 995 and 996: U.S. Federal Highway Administration, *Highway Statistics,* annual.

No. 997. Price Trends for Federal-Aid Highway Construction: 1980 to 1994

YEAR	Common exca-vation (cu.yd.)	SURFACING				STRUCTURES				Com-posite index
		Portland cement concrete (sq. yd.)	Bitumi-nous concrete (ton)	Index		Rein forcing steel (lb.)	Struc-tural steel (lb.)	Struc-tural concrete (cu. yd.)	Index	
Average contract price:										
1980............	1.83	14.92	25.29	(X)		0.48	0.94	226.68	(X)	(X)
1985............	2.24	14.31	28.52	(X)		0.44	0.80	243.60	(X)	(X)
1986............	2.28	15.63	26.48	(X)		0.44	0.85	236.37	(X)	(X)
1987............	2.42	14.80	24.65	(X)		0.44	0.89	240.81	(X)	(X)
1988............	2.72	14.33	24.91	(X)		0.49	0.92	274.12	(X)	(X)
1989............	2.40	15.17	24.08	(X)		0.56	1.02	283.40	(X)	(X)
1990............	2.38	15.91	24.52	(X)		0.53	1.01	286.18	(X)	(X)
1991............	2.32	16.58	25.52	(X)		0.51	1.03	264.98	(X)	(X)
1992............	2.20	17.80	24.66	(X)		0.52	0.92	259.61	(X)	(X)
1993............	2.50	18.81	26.26	(X)		0.47	0.86	261.89	(X)	(X)
1994 (3d qtr.).......	3.12	21.09	30.29	(X)		0.49	0.86	285.08	(X)	(X)
Index (1987=100):										
1980............	75.5	101.3	102.6	102.2		109.6	106.3	94.1	100.0	97.2
1985............	92.4	97.1	115.7	109.6		100.7	89.9	101.2	98.1	102.0
1986............	94.0	106.1	107.4	107.0		100.3	96.0	98.2	98.0	101.1
1987............	100.0	100.0	100.0	100.0		100.0	100.0	100.0	100.0	100.0
1988............	112.2	97.3	100.1	99.8		112.1	104.4	113.8	111.0	106.6
1989............	99.0	103.0	97.7	99.4		126.2	115.0	117.7	118.4	107.7
1990............	98.1	108.0	99.5	102.3		120.0	114.1	118.8	117.8	108.5
1991............	95.5	112.5	103.6	106.5		114.6	116.4	110.0	112.5	107.5
1992............	90.8	120.8	100.1	106.9		117.9	103.5	107.8	108.4	105.1
1993............	103.2	127.7	106.6	113.5		106.0	97.3	108.7	105.3	108.3
1994 (3d qtr.).......	128.6	143.2	122.9	129.5		111.1	96.9	118.4	111.5	121.4

X Not applicable.
Source: U.S. Federal Highway Administration, *Price Trends for Federal-Aid Highway Construction, Third Quarter 1994.*

No. 998. New Plant and Equipment Expenditures and Capacity Utilization: 1980 to 1995

[In percent]

YEAR	NEW PLANT AND EQUIPMENT EXPENDITURES					CAPACITY UTILIZATION			
	Total United States	Total manufac-turing	Motor vehicle and parts mfg.			All manufacturing		Motor vehicle and parts mfg.	
			Total	Percent of—		Total	Percent change	Total	Percent change
				Total mfg.	Total U.S.				
1980	286.40	112.60	8.54	7.6	3.0	80.2	-6.1	57.8	-27.0
1985	410.12	152.88	13.39	8.8	3.3	79.5	-1.1	83.4	6.1
1986	399.36	137.95	12.79	9.3	3.2	79.0	-0.6	79.5	-4.7
1987	410.52	141.06	10.88	7.7	2.7	81.4	3.0	78.1	-1.8
1988	455.49	163.45	9.75	6.0	2.1	83.9	3.1	80.5	3.1
1989	507.40	183.80	11.49	6.3	2.3	83.9	0.0	79.2	-1.6
1990	532.61	192.61	11.28	5.9	2.1	81.1	-3.3	72.6	-8.3
1991	528.39	182.81	10.20	5.6	1.9	77.8	-4.1	67.5	-7.0
1992	546.60	174.02	8.67	5.0	1.6	78.6	1.0	71.9	6.5
1993	585.64	179.18	12.23	6.8	2.1	80.6	1.4	78.7	9.6
1994	634.02	191.60	15.69	8.2	2.5	83.3	3.3	85.1	8.1
1995	(NA)	(NA)	(NA)	(NA)	(NA)	83.1	-0.3	81.2	-4.6

NA Not available.
Source: American Automobile Manufacturers Association, Washington, DC, *Facts and Figures*, annual.

No. 999. Alternative Fueled Vehicles in Use, by Fuel Type: 1994 to 1996

FUEL	ALTERNATIVE FUELED VEHICLES			FUEL CONSUMPTION (1,000 gasoline-equivalent gallons)		
	1994	1995	1996	1994	1995	1996
Fuels	**324,401**	**362,190**	**421,294**	**281,210**	**312,919**	**322,970**
Liquified petroleum gases (LPG)	264,000	272,000	279,000	248,550	259,940	263,130
Compressed natural gas (CNG)	41,227	65,849	84,319	24,160	43,631	48,230
Liquified natural gas (LNG).	399	482	563	2,320	3,110	3,150
M85 (Mixture: 85% methanol + 15% gasoline) . . .	15,484	20,170	22,284	2,340	2,372	3,540
Neat methanol (M100)...................	415	413	411	3,190	3,050	3,160
E85 (Mixture: 85% ethanol+15% gasoline)	605	894	32,224	80	105	1,030
E95 (Mixture: 95% ethanol + 5% gasoline)	33	32	33	140	140	140
Electricity	2,238	2,350	2,460	430	571	590

[1] Values represents lower bound estimates.   [2] Consumption includes gasoline portion of the mixture.   [3] Primarily tertiary amyl menthyl ether (TAME) and ethyl tertiary butyl ether (ETBE).   [4] Gasoline consumption includes ethanol in gasohol and MTBE.
Source: Energy Information Administration, *Alternatives to Traditional Transportation Fuels 1993.*

No. 1000. Motor Vehicle Registrations, 1990 to 1994, Vehicle Miles of Travel, 1994, and Drivers Licenses, 1994, by State

[**In thousands, except as indicated.** Motor vehicle registrations cover publicly, privately, and commercially owned vehicles. For uniformity, data have been adjusted to a calendar-year basis as registration years in States differ; figures represent net numbers where possible, excluding re-registrations and nonresident registrations]

STATE	AUTOMOBILES, TRUCKS, AND BUSES [1]					1994				
				1994		Motor-cycle [1] regis-tration (incl. official)	Public road and street mileage (1,000 mi.)	Vehicle miles of travel		Drivers licenses
	1990	1992	1993	Total	Auto-mobiles (incl. taxis)			Total (bil. mi.)	Per mile of road (1,000)	
U.S	188,798	190,362	194,063	198,045	133,930	3,718	3,907	2,360	604	175,403
AL.	3,744	3,304	3,390	3,177	1,948	39	93	49.0	526	2,861
AK.	477	486	489	533	300	13	14	4.2	290	436
AZ.	2,825	2,801	2,892	2,813	1,850	68	54	38.8	713	2,849
AR.	1,448	1,501	1,528	1,567	775	14	77	24.9	323	1,768
CA.	21,926	22,202	22,824	22,339	14,743	542	169	271.9	1,609	20,156
CO	3,155	2,915	3,032	2,750	1,652	96	84	33.7	400	2,733
CT.	2,623	2,569	2,594	2,599	2,046	48	20	27.1	1,331	2,319
DE.	526	545	555	578	404	9	6	7.0	1,256	513
DC	262	256	264	249	211	1	1	3.4	3,123	362
FL.	10,950	10,232	10,170	10,252	7,519	177	113	122.0	1,075	11,005
GA	5,489	5,899	5,632	5,990	4,168	57	111	82.8	744	4,817
HI	771	774	763	779	509	12	4	7.9	1,933	745
ID	1,054	1,034	1,023	1,035	545	33	60	11.7	195	801
IL	7,873	7,982	8,070	8,698	6,226	188	137	92.3	673	7,502
IN	4,366	4,516	4,670	4,889	3,231	97	92	62.1	672	3,860
IA	2,632	2,706	2,738	2,766	1,806	115	113	25.7	228	1,897
KS	2,012	1,921	1,922	2,083	1,094	45	133	24.7	185	1,772
KY.	2,909	2,983	2,629	2,666	1,732	34	73	39.8	546	2,516
LA.	2,995	3,094	3,166	3,426	1,978	35	60	37.4	624	2,595
ME	977	978	1,028	946	611	26	23	12.5	553	914
MD	3,607	3,689	3,560	3,640	2,732	39	29	44.2	1,498	3,308
MA	3,726	3,663	3,837	4,027	3,068	66	31	47.0	1,536	4,472
MI	7,209	7,311	7,399	7,574	5,277	113	118	85.2	724	6,602
MN	3,508	3,484	3,716	4,057	2,677	130	130	43.3	333	2,706
MS	1,875	1,954	2,000	2,063	1,341	29	73	28.5	392	1,672
MO	3,905	4,004	4,066	4,208	2,741	57	122	57.3	468	3,382
MT	783	907	939	950	512	21	69	9.1	131	526
NE.	1,384	1,355	1,439	1,458	841	21	93	15.5	167	1,146
NV.	853	921	937	985	538	20	46	13.0	282	1,007
NH	946	894	959	992	644	33	15	10.5	699	877
NJ.	5,652	5,591	5,641	5,839	4,602	86	35	60.5	1,707	5,433
NM	1,301	1,352	1,421	1,422	735	31	61	20.5	335	1,167
NY.	10,196	9,780	10,163	10,196	7,907	175	112	113.0	1,009	10,377
NC	5,162	5,307	5,365	5,443	3,525	64	96	71.9	746	4,840
ND	630	655	662	685	373	18	87	6.3	73	439
OH	8,410	9,030	9,279	9,664	7,177	224	114	98.2	858	7,142
OK	2,649	2,737	2,771	2,806	1,559	56	112	37.0	329	2,344
OR	2,445	2,583	2,624	2,753	1,530	61	84	29.5	351	2,543
PA.	7,971	8,179	8,282	8,482	6,026	169	118	92.3	780	8,115
RI	672	622	695	699	545	17	6	7.1	1,188	688
SC.	2,521	2,601	2,684	2,743	1,817	34	64	37.2	580	2,492
SD.	704	720	808	769	469	26	83	7.6	92	508
TN.	4,444	4,645	4,964	5,059	3,712	57	86	54.5	638	3,826
TX.	12,800	12,767	13,118	13,626	8,699	143	294	178.3	606	12,110
UT.	1,206	1,252	1,335	1,415	808	23	41	18.1	443	1,245
VT.	462	465	483	489	315	18	14	6.2	434	446
VA.	4,938	5,239	5,408	5,507	3,921	58	69	67.6	981	4,601
WA	4,257	4,466	4,413	4,465	2,882	97	80	47.4	594	3,775
WV	1,225	1,273	1,345	1,462	879	16	35	17.1	491	1,298
WI	3,815	3,735	3,815	3,926	2,461	150	111	50.3	453	3,554
WY	528	483	558	508	269	17	37	6.7	183	342

[1] Excludes vehicles owned by military services.

Source: U.S. Federal Highway Administration, *Highway Statistics,* annual; and *Selected Highway Statistics and Charts,* annual.

No. 1001. Motor Vehicle Production and Trade: 1980 to 1994

ITEM	Unit	1980	1985	1989	1990	1991	1992	1993	1994
United States	1,000. . .	8,010	11,653	10,876	9,784	8,811	9,729	10,898	12,263
Passenger car production	1,000. . .	6,376	8,185	6,825	6,078	5,439	5,664	5,981	6,614
Truck and bus production	1,000. . .	1,634	3,468	4,051	3,706	3,372	4,065	4,917	5,649
Imports:									
Passenger cars (new) [1] [2]	1,000. . .	3,116	4,398	4,043	3,945	3,736	3,615	3,808	4,097
Canada	1,000. . .	595	1,145	1,151	1,220	1,196	1,200	1,468	1,591
Germany, Federal Republic of . . .	1,000. . .	339	473	217	245	172	206	184	188
Japan	1,000. . .	1,992	2,527	2,052	1,868	1,789	1,678	1,597	1,593
Trucks and buses (new) [2]	1,000. . .	747	1,253	953	766	716	777	722	708
Japan	1,000. . .	483	800	420	302	283	197	154	170
All-terrain vehicles	1,000. . .	(NA)	683	121	100	100	(NA)	(NA)	(NA)
Motorcycles, total [3]	1,000. . .	1,120	733	253	169	(NA)	(NA)	(NA)	(NA)
Import value:									
Passenger cars (new) [1]	Mil. dol. .	16,675	36,474	44,417	45,716	45,564	46,729	52,208	61,367
Trucks and buses, (new) [1]	Mil. dol. .	1,985	7,734	8,591	8,155	8,221	10,000	10,104	10,909
Motorcycles [3] [4]	Mil. dol. .	1,142	783	542	361	(NA)	(NA)	(NA)	(NA)
Exports, number:									
Passenger cars (new) [1]	1,000. . .	617	704	778	794	755	851	864	1,019
Trucks and buses (new) exports . . .	1,000. . .	186	183	189	159	208	161	181	274
Export value [1] [5]	Mil. dol. .	16,015	22,820	31,574	38,086	(NA)	(NA)	(NA)	(NA)
Passenger cars (new) [5]	Mil. dol. .	3,932	6,027	8,895	9,708	9,886	11,893	12,476	14,591
Trucks and buses (new) [5]	Mil. dol. .	2,977	2,789	3,471	2,845	3,388	3,073	3,399	5,238
Parts and accessories [6]	Mil. dol. .	9,106	14,004	19,208	24,996	(NA)	(NA)	(NA)	(NA)
Factory sales:									
Passenger cars	1,000. . .	6,400	8,002	6,807	6,050	5,407	5,685	5,962	6,549
Trucks and buses	1,000. . .	1,667	3,357	4,062	3,725	3,387	4,062	4,895	5,640
Retail sales:									
Passenger cars (new) [1]	1,000. . .	8,979	11,042	9,772	9,300	8,175	8,213	8,518	8,991
Domestics [7]	1,000. . .	6,581	8,205	7,073	6,897	6,137	6,277	6,742	7,255
Imports [8]	1,000. . .	2,398	2,838	2,699	2,403	2,038	1,937	1,776	1,735
Trucks and buses [9]	1,000. . .	2,232	3,984	4,483	4,261	3,842	4,513	5,318	6,091
Light duty (up to 14,000 GVW) [10]	1,000. . .	1,964	3,700	4,171	3,984	3,621	4,264	5,015	5,703
Med. duty (14,001-26,000 GVW) [10]	1,000. . .	92	53	73	71	50	57	64	80
Heavy duty (over 26,000 GVW) [10]	1,000. . .	176	231	239	207	171	192	239	308
Under 6,000 pounds	1,000. . .	985	2,408	2,854	2,866	2,724	3,217	3,756	4,031
Utility	1,000. . .	51	429	447	490	549	666	721	1,258
Van	1,000. . .	79	115	43	31	17	21	18	12
Minivan (cargo)	1,000. . .	(X)	103	97	83	66	63	70	73
Station wagon (truck chassis) . .	1,000. . .	(X)	86	138	112	110	201	321	-
Mini-passenger carrier	1,000. . .	(X)	301	688	750	706	840	1,002	1,113
6,000 to 10,000 pounds [11]	1,000. . .	975	1,280	1,297	1,097	876	1,021	1,232	1,631
Utility	1,000. . .	108	108	93	68	37	51	60	144
Van	1,000. . .	172	261	289	254	203	241	279	274
Pickup, conventional	1,000. . .	546	628	663	568	476	524	647	967
Station wagon (truck chassis) . .	1,000. . .	39	95	100	85	55	80	60	109
10,001 pounds and over	1,000. . .	271	295	331	298	242	275	330	428

- Represents zero.   NA Not available.   X Not applicable.   [1] Based on data from U.S. Dept. of Commerce.   [2] Includes other countries, not shown separately.   [3] Source: Motorcycle Industry Council, Inc., Irvine, CA. Data from U.S. Dept. of Commerce. Excludes mopeds/motorized bicycles and all-terrain vehicles. Excludes moped imports (motorcycle imports less than 51 cc's) from all countries (except Japan).   [4] Represents c.i.f. value.   [5] Covers assembled and unassembled vehicles.   [6] Includes rubber tires and tubes and used vehicles.   [7] Includes domestic models produced in Canada and Mexico.   [8] Excludes domestic models produced in Canada.   [9] Excludes motorcoaches and light-duty imports from foreign manufactures. Includes imports sold by franchised dealers of U.S. manufacturers. Starting in 1987, includes sales of trucks over 10,000 lbs. GVW by foreign manufacturers.   [10] Gross vehicle weight (fully loaded vehicle).   [11] Includes vehicles, not shown separately.

Source: Except as noted, American Automobile Manufacturers Association Inc., Detroit, MI, *Motor Vehicle Facts and Figures*, annual (copyright); and *World Motor Vehicle Data*, annual (copyright).

No. 1002. Motor Vehicles in Use: 1980 to 1994

ITEM	Unit	1980	1985	1989	1990	1991	1992	1993	1994
Cars in use, total	Million. .	**104.6**	**114.7**	**122.8**	**123.3**	**123.3**	**120.3**	**121.1**	**122.0**
Under 5 years	Million . .	52.3	48.7	57.6	56.5	54.6	50.4	47.0	45.4
6-8 years	Million . .	25.2	27.8	20.7	22.6	25.5	27.5	28.7	27.7
9-11 years	Million . .	14.6	17.2	21.1	19.1	16.7	16.0	22.5	25.1
12 years and over	Million . .	12.5	21.0	23.4	25.1	26.6	26.4	31.1	31.4
Average age	Years. . .	6.6	7.6	7.6	7.8	7.9	8.1	8.3	8.4
Cars retired from use [1]	1,000. . .	8,405	7,729	8,981	8,897	8,565	11,194	7,366	7,824
Trucks in use, total	Million. .	**35.2**	**42.4**	**53.2**	**56.0**	**58.2**	**61.2**	**82.5**	**71.4**
Under 3 years	Million . .	8.8	9.0	12.5	12.8	12.0	11.3	12.1	13.7
3-5 years	Million . .	8.1	6.3	12.6	13.2	14.0	14.0	12.9	12.7
6-8 years	Million . .	7.4	10.2	6.3	8.0	9.9	11.9	14.0	13.6
9-11 years	Million . .	4.4	6.2	7.9	6.6	5.3	5.6	11.7	11.3
12 years and over	Million . .	6.5	10.7	14.0	15.5	17.0	18.3	23.2	20.1
Average age	Years. . .	7.1	8.1	7.9	8.0	8.1	8.4	8.6	8.4
Trucks retired from use [1]	1,000. . .	1,732	2,100	2,189	2,177	2,284	1,587	1,048	4,545

[1] For years ending June 30. Represents vehicles failing to re-register.

Source: Except as noted, American Automobile Manufacturers Association Inc., Detroit, MI, *Motor Vehicle Facts and Figures*, annual (copyright); and *World Motor Vehicle Data*, annual (copyright).

No. 1003. Motor Vehicle Registrations: 1980 to 1994

[**In thousands.** Beginning 1994, personal passenger vans, passenger minivans, and utility type vehicles are no longer included in atuomobiles. These vehicles are now included in light trucks]

ITEM	1980	1985	1989	1990	1991	1992	1993	1994
Total [1]	155,796	171,654	187,261	188,798	188,136	190,362	194,063	198,045
Automobiles	121,601	131,864	143,081	143,550	142,569	144,213	146,314	133,930
Buses	529	593	625	627	631	645	654	670
Private and commercial:								
Commercial	107	109	113	114	114	114	115	118
School and other	147	157	162	161	161	161	161	165
Publicly owned:								
Federal	4	4	4	5	5	5	5	5
School	271	323	346	347	352	365	374	383
Private and commercial trailers, total . .	14,372	15,008	16,115	16,098	16,269	16,715	17,498	18,195
Motorcycles	5,694	5,444	4,434	4,259	4,177	4,065	3,978	3,718
Truck tractors	1,402	1,150	1,237	1,240	1,236	1,279	1,289	1,315
Light trucks [2]	(NA)	32,146	36,530	37,380	37,728	38,257	39,786	55,603

NA Not available.   [1] Components may not add to total because of double counting.   [2] Excludes farm trucks.
Source: U.S. Federal Highway Administration, *Highway Statistics*, annual.

No. 1004. Motor Vehicle Tires and Batteries: 1980 to 1993

[**In millions**]

ITEM	1980	1985	1988	1989	1990	1991	1992	1993
Tires, passenger car, total [1]	145.9	200.9	218.8	214.8	213.6	214.5	228.6	235.0
Radials	83.5	164.7	200.2	200.4	202.1	205.7	221.4	227.4
Replacement	106.9	141.5	155.3	151.2	152.3	155.4	165.8	165.1
Tires, truck and bus, total [1]	31.1	41.1	46.0	46.9	46.9	42.4	45.0	48.4
Radials	3.8	19.7	29.4	30.6	32.5	32.4	36.1	40.3
Replacement	24.4	32.1	33.9	35.2	36.6	32.9	33.7	35.7
Batteries, total [2]	61.7	74.4	80.1	80.3	79.7	79.8	(NA)	(NA)
Replacement automobile batteries . .	50.1	58.7	63.5	64.4	65.2	66.6	(NA)	(NA)

NA Not available.   [1] Includes original equipment. Also includes exports, not shown separately.   [2] Source: Battery Council International, Chicago, IL, and U.S. Bureau of the Census.
Source: Except as noted, The Rubber Manufacturers Association, Inc., Washington, DC, *RMA Monthly Tire Report*.

No. 1005. Automobile Output and Trade in National Income Accounts: 1980 to 1995

[**In billions of dollars**. Vehicle output equals final dollar sales value of new vehicles, plus net dollar value of used vehicle sales adjusted for changes in inventories and net balance of vehicle exports and imports]

ITEM	CURRENT DOLLARS					CHAINED (1992) DOLLARS				
	1980	1990	1993	1994	1995	1980	1990	1993	1994	1995
Auto output, total	59.7	118	131	143.6	134.8	84.8	125.2	125.7	133.2	120.3
Final sales	60.6	121	129.2	141.8	133.8	87	129.8	125	132	120.1
Personal consumption expenditures . .	57.2	124	127.3	137.4	137.3	88.8	133.3	121.6	125.1	117.9
Producers' durable equipment	14.3	30.8	37.7	46.9	42.2	19.7	33	38.2	46.6	43.3
Net exports	-12.3	-36.1	-37.7	-44.7	-48	-22.8	-38.7	-36.6	-41.2	-43
Government purchases	1.4	2.3	1.9	2.1	2.4	2.3	2.4	1.9	2	2.2
Change in business inventories	-0.9	-3.1	1.8	1.8	1	-2.4	-4.6	0.6	1.1	0.2
New	-0.1	-2.1	1.8	1.7	-	-1.1	-3.6	0.6	1.1	-0.5
Used	-0.8	-1	-	0.1	1	-1.4	-1	-	-	0.6

- Represents or rounds to zero.
Source: U.S. Bureau of Economic Analysis, *The National Income and Product Accounts of the United States* to be published in late 1996, and *Survey of Current Business*, January/February 1996.

No. 1006. Recreational Vehicles—Number and Retail Value of Shipments: 1970 to 1993

ITEM	1970	1975	1980	1985	1986	1987	1988	1989	1990	1991	1992	1993
NUMBER (1,000)												
Total	380.3	339.6	181.4	351.7	371.7	393.6	420.0	388.3	347.3	293.7	382.7	420.2
Motorized homes	30.3	96.6	99.9	233.5	249.6	255.7	277.1	261.6	226.5	172.6	226.3	(NA)
Travel trailers	138.0	150.6	52.0	75.4	78.2	86.2	89.6	82.9	80.4	77.6	102.5	113.6
Folding camping trailers	116.1	48.1	24.5	35.9	36.5	41.6	42.3	33.9	30.7	33.9	43.3	(NA)
Truck campers	95.9	44.3	5.0	6.9	7.4	10.1	11.0	9.9	9.7	9.6	10.6	(NA)
RETAIL VALUE (mil. dol.)												
Total	1,122	2,320	1,952	6,904	7,434	8,288	9,061	9,019	8,101	6,623	8,774	9,518
Motorized homes	318	1,251	1,381	5,724	6,155	6,826	7,543	7,420	6,660	5,284	6,963	(NA)
Travel trailers	445	856	485	997	1,083	1,219	1,254	1,252	1,220	1,107	1,523	1,644
Folding camping trailers	175	101	69	137	144	167	175	147	134	146	189	(NA)
Truck campers	183	112	17	46	53	76	88	81	86	87	99	(NA)

NA Not available.
Source: Recreation Vehicle Industry Association, Reston, VA, *RV's ... A Year-End Report/1989*. Data also in American Automobile Manufacturers Association of the United States, Inc., Detroit, MI, *Motor Vehicle Facts and Figures*, annual.

No. 1007. Transportation to Work: 1990

[In thousands, except as indicated. Based on workers 16 years old or older]

REGION, DIVISION, AND STATE	MEANS OF TRANSPORTATION TO WORK			Worked at home	Average travel time to work [1] (minutes)	HOUSEHOLDS WITH VEHICLES AVAILABLE		
	Car, truck, van		Percent using public transport-ation			None	One vehicle	Two or more vehicles
	Drove alone	Carpooled						
United States	84,215	15,378	5.3	3,406	22.4	10,602	31,039	50,306
Northeast	15,902	2,771	12.8	630	24.5	3,603	6,408	8,862
New England	4,892	749	5.1	191	21.5	568	1,699	2,676
Maine	424	80	0.9	24	19.0	40	159	266
New Hampshire.	443	70	0.7	20	21.9	26	132	254
Vermont.	200	36	0.7	17	18.0	17	72	122
Massachusetts	2,148	318	8.3	75	22.7	321	819	1,107
Rhode Island	376	58	2.5	10	19.2	40	132	206
Connecticut	1,301	187	3.9	45	21.1	124	386	721
Middle Atlantic	11,010	2,023	15.7	438	25.7	3,035	4,709	6,186
New York.	4,461	861	24.8	213	28.6	1,994	2,153	2,492
New Jersey	2,731	472	8.8	80	25.3	360	966	1,468
Pennsylvania	3,818	690	6.4	145	21.6	681	1,589	2,226
Midwest	21,091	3,207	3.5	987	20.7	2,238	7,365	12,714
East North Central	14,749	2,206	4.3	551	21.7	1,693	5,230	8,674
Ohio	3,889	521	2.5	119	20.7	416	1,351	2,320
Indiana	2,040	332	1.3	73	20.4	175	670	1,221
Illinois	3,742	653	10.1	144	25.1	588	1,476	2,138
Michigan	3,328	429	1.6	100	21.2	344	1,133	1,943
Wisconsin	1,751	270	2.5	114	18.3	170	600	1,052
West North Central	6,342	1,002	1.9	436	18.4	545	2,135	4,040
Minnesota	1,593	247	3.6	116	19.1	142	517	988
Iowa	971	157	1.2	89	16.2	75	332	657
Missouri.	1,816	312	2.0	84	21.6	191	652	1,118
North Dakota	210	31	0.6	24	13.0	16	73	152
South Dakota	233	33	0.3	31	13.8	17	76	166
Nebraska	590	87	1.2	44	15.8	43	182	377
Kansas	929	136	0.6	49	17.2	60	302	583
South.	29,495	5,886	2.6	936	22.0	3,208	10,987	17,627
South Atlantic.	15,481	3,156	3.4	501	22.5	1,725	5,725	9,053
Delaware	258	43	2.4	8	20.0	20	80	147
Maryland	1,733	376	8.1	65	27.0	216	554	979
District of Columbia	107	37	36.6	9	27.1	93	103	53
Virginia	2,281	500	4.0	103	24.0	205	717	1,370
West Virginia	493	107	1.1	16	21.0	94	247	347
North Carolina.	2,528	530	1.0	71	19.8	242	786	1,489
South Carolina	1,235	277	1.1	31	20.5	137	402	720
Georgia	2,379	468	2.8	65	22.7	244	730	1,393
Florida.	4,468	819	2.0	132	21.8	474	2,106	2,555
East South Central	5,110	1,005	1.2	149	21.1	607	1,814	3,231
Kentucky	1,195	229	1.6	47	20.7	159	447	773
Tennessee	1,763	324	1.3	52	21.5	181	593	1,079
Alabama	1,374	267	0.8	31	21.2	156	466	885
Mississippi	777	184	0.8	19	20.6	111	307	494
West South Central	8,904	1,725	2.0	286	21.6	876	3,448	5,343
Arkansas	765	153	0.5	28	19.0	88	303	501
Louisiana	1,239	247	3.0	31	22.3	209	542	749
Oklahoma	1,079	191	0.6	41	19.3	91	414	701
Texas	5,821	1,134	2.2	185	22.2	489	2,190	3,392
West	17,727	3,513	4.1	854	22.7	1,553	6,279	11,103
Mountain.	4,586	873	2.1	229	19.7	343	1,697	2,993
Montana	250	41	0.6	22	14.8	20	91	194
Idaho	330	53	1.9	21	17.3	17	101	243
Wyoming	154	28	1.4	9	15.4	8	48	113
Colorado	1,217	210	2.9	67	20.7	89	412	781
New Mexico	472	96	1.0	24	19.1	38	185	320
Arizona	1,178	239	2.1	48	21.6	107	532	730
Utah	541	111	2.3	26	18.9	29	153	355
Nevada	444	94	2.7	12	19.8	36	174	256
Pacific	13,141	2,640	4.8	625	23.8	1,210	4,582	8,111
Washington	1,701	282	4.5	86	22.0	141	582	1,149
Oregon	949	165	3.4	56	19.6	88	355	660
California	9,982	2,036	4.9	453	24.6	923	3,452	6,006
Alaska	165	40	2.4	11	16.7	23	64	102
Hawaii	344	116	7.4	19	23.8	35	129	193

[1] Excludes persons who worked at home.

Source: U.S. Bureau of the Census, *Census of Population and Housing, 1990*.

No. 1008. National Personal Transportation Survey (NPTS)— Summary of Travel Trends: 1969 to 1990

[Data obtained by collecting information on all trips taken by the respondent on a specific day (known as travel day), combined with longer trips taken over a 2-week period (known as travel period). Contains data from previous NPTS surveys. For compatibility with previous survey data, all data are based only on trips taken during travel day. Be aware that terminology changes from survey to survey. See source for details]

CHARACTERISTICS	Unit	1969	1977	1983	1990	Percent change, 1969-90	Annual percent change, 1969-90
Households, total.	1,000. . .	62,504	75,412	85,371	93,347	49.0	1.9
1 person	1,000. . .	10,980	16,214	19,354	22,999	109.0	3.6
2 persons	1,000. . .	18,448	22,925	27,169	30,114	63.0	2.4
3 persons	1,000. . .	10,746	13,046	14,756	16,128	50.0	2.0
4 persons or more	1,000. . .	22,330	23,227	24,092	24,106	8.0	0.4
Persons, total	1,000. . .	197,213	213,141	229,453	[1]239,416	21.0	0.9
Under 16 yrs. old	1,000. . .	60,100	54,958	53,682	54,303	-10.0	-0.5
16-19 yrs. old	1,000. . .	14,598	16,552	15,268	13,851	-5.0	-0.2
20-34 yrs. old	1,000. . .	40,060	52,252	60,788	59,517	49.0	1.9
35-64 yrs. old	1,000. . .	62,982	66,988	75,353	82,480	31.0	1.3
65 yrs. old and over	1,000. . .	19,473	22,391	24,362	26,955	38.0	1.6
5 yrs. old and over	1,000. . .	(NA)	198,434	212,932	222,101	12.0	0.9
Males, total	1,000. . .	94,465	102,521	111,514	114,441	21.0	0.8
16 yrs. old and over.	1,000. . .	66,652	74,542	83,645	86,432	30.0	1.1
Females	1,000. . .	102,748	110,620	117,939	124,975	22.0	0.8
16 yrs. old and over.	1,000. . .	73,526	83,721	92,080	96,371	31.0	1.1
Licensed drivers	1,000. . .	102,986	127,552	147,015	163,025	58.0	2.2
Male.	1,000. . .	57,981	66,199	75,639	80,289	38.0	1.6
Female	1,000. . .	45,005	61,353	71,376	82,707	84.0	2.9
Workers.	1,000. . .	75,758	93,019	103,244	118,343	56.0	2.1
Male.	1,000. . .	48,487	55,625	58,849	63,996	32.0	1.3
Female	1,000. . .	27,271	37,394	44,395	54,334	99.0	3.3
Households with—							
No vehicle	1,000. . .	12,876	11,538	11,548	8,573	-33.0	-1.9
One vehicle	1,000. . .	30,252	26,092	28,780	30,654	1.0	0.1
Two vehicles.	1,000. . .	16,501	25,942	28,632	35,872	117.0	3.8
Three or more Vehicles	1,000. . .	2,875	11,840	16,411	18,248	535.0	9.2
All vehicles available	1,000. . .	72,500	120,098	143,714	165,221	128.0	4.0
Vehicle trips.	Millions .	87,284	108,826	126,874	158,927	82.0	2.9
Vehicle miles of travel (VMT)	Millions .	775,940	907,603	1,002,139	1,409,600	82.0	2.9
Person trips.	Millions .	145,146	211,778	224,385	249,562	72.0	2.6
Person miles of travel	Millions .	1,404,137	1,879,215	1,946,662	2,315,300	65.0	2.4
Ratios:							
Persons per household.	Number .	[2]3.16	2.83	2.69	2.56	(NA)	(NA)
Vehicles per household.	Number .	[2]1.16	1.59	1.68	1.77	(NA)	(NA)
Licensed drivers per household	Number .	[2]1.65	1.69	1.72	1.75	(NA)	(NA)
Vehicles per licensed driver	Number .	[2]0.70	0.94	0.98	1.01	(NA)	(NA)
Workers per household.	Number .	[2]1.21	1.23	1.21	1.27	(NA)	(NA)
Vehicles per worker	Number .	[2]0.96	1.29	1.39	1.40	(NA)	(NA)
Daily vehicle trips per household	Number .	[2]3.83	3.95	4.07	4.66	(NA)	(NA)
Daily VMT per household	Number .	[2]34.01	32.97	32.16	41.37	(NA)	(NA)
Average vehicle trip length (miles)	Number .	[2]8.89	8.34	7.90	8.87	(NA)	(NA)
Average annual VMT.	Miles . . .	12,423	12,036	11,739	15,100	22.0	(NA)
Home to work	Miles . . .	4,183	3,815	3,538	4,853	16.0	(NA)
Shopping	Miles . . .	929	1,336	1,567	1,743	88.0	(NA)
Other family or personal business.	Miles . . .	1,270	1,444	1,816	3,014	137.0	(NA)
Social and recreational	Miles . . .	4,094	3,286	3,534	4,060	-1.0	(NA)
Average annual vehicle trips	Number .	1,396	1,442	1,486	1,702	22.0	(NA)
Home to work	Number .	445	423	414	448	0.7	(NA)
Shopping	Number .	213	268	297	345	62.0	(NA)
Other family or personal business.	Number .	195	215	272	411	111.0	(NA)
Social and recreational.	Number .	312	320	335	349	12.0	(NA)
Average vehicle trip length	Miles . . .	8.9	8.4	7.9	9.0	1.0	(NA)
Home to work	Miles . . .	9.4	9.1	8.5	11.0	17.0	(NA)
Shopping	Miles . . .	4.4	5.0	5.3	5.1	16.0	(NA)
Other family or personal business.	Miles . . .	6.5	6.8	6.7	7.4	14.0	(NA)
Social and recreational	Miles . . .	13.1	10.3	10.5	11.8	-10.0	(NA)
Average vehicle occupancy [3]	Persons .	(NA)	1.9	1.7	1.6	[4]-1.3	(NA)
Home to work	Persons .	(NA)	1.3	1.3	1.1	[4]-1.3	(NA)
Shopping	Persons .	(NA)	2.1	1.8	1.7	[4]-1.6	(NA)
Other family or personal business.	Persons .	(NA)	2.0	1.8	1.8	[4]-0.8	(NA)
Social and recreational	Persons .	(NA)	2.4	2.1	2.1	[4]-1.0	(NA)
Journey-to-work trip mode	Percent .	100.0	100.0	100.0	100.0	(NS)	(NS)
Auto	Percent .	82.7	80.5	77.6	91.4	(NS)	(NS)
Truck [5]	Percent .	8.1	12.5	14.8	(NA)	(NS)	(NS)
Public transit.	Percent .	8.4	4.7	5.8	5.5	(NS)	(NS)
Other	Percent .	0.8	2.3	1.8	3.1	(NS)	(NS)

NA Not available. NS Percent change irrelevant. [1] Includes "don't know" and "refusals". [2] Excludes pickups and other light-trucks as household vehicles. [3] Includes other purposes not shown separately. [4] Change from 1977. [5] Household based trucks, primarily pickups.

Source: Federal Highway Administration, *National Personal Transportation Survey, Summary of Travel Trends, 1969, 1977, 1983,* and *1990.*

No. 1009. Roadway Congestion: 1991

[Various Federal, State, and local information sources were used to develop the data base with the primary source being the Federal Highway Administration's Highway Performance Monitoring System]

URBANIZED AREAS	FREEWAY DAILY VEHICLE MILES OF TRAVEL		DAILY VEHICLE HOURS OF DELAY		CONGESTION COST		Delay and fuel cost (mil. dol.)
	Total miles (1,000)	Per lane-mile of freeway	Total hours	Per 1,000 persons	Per reg. vehicle (dol.)	Per capita (dol.)	
Total, average	25,740	1,840	207,170	80	480	340	880
Northeastern cities	41,260	3,070	432,060	90	720	380	1,840
Baltimore, MD	25,820	2,010	130,470	60	530	270	550
Boston, MA	34,900	2,450	356,220	120	920	510	1,520
Hartford, CT.	10,050	930	30,260	50	250	210	130
New York, NY.	133,650	9,530	1,544,140	90	1,090	390	6,620
Philadelphia, PA	29,620	2,440	272,760	60	410	270	1,140
Pittsburgh, PA	13,280	1,630	115,340	60	390	260	480
Washington, DC	41,470	2,460	575,280	180	1,440	740	2,430
Midwestern cities	23,580	1,920	120,860	40	300	190	510
Chicago, IL	62,760	3,920	555,790	70	580	310	2,360
Cincinnati, OH	18,680	1,470	44,440	40	210	160	190
Cleveland, OH	22,490	1,840	49,780	30	140	120	220
Columbus, OH	13,690	1,300	41,570	50	240	200	180
Detroit, MI	38,160	2,870	383,690	100	560	400	1,610
Indianapolis, IN	13,120	1,230	17,130	20	130	80	70
Kansas City, MO.	20,150	2,190	28,390	20	160	100	120
Louisville, KY	10,060	950	21,470	30	190	110	90
Milwaukee, WI	12,570	970	47,960	40	380	170	200
Minneapolis-St. Paul, MN	29,320	2,410	105,880	50	270	220	450
Oklahoma City, OK	11,310	1,170	22,070	30	190	130	90
St. Louis, MO.	30,670	2,730	132,170	70	540	280	550
Southern cities.	11,530	930	87,620	80	400	330	370
Atlanta, GA	40,200	2,770	239,490	130	640	530	1,010
Charlotte, NC.	4,010	480	36,550	80	410	340	150
Ft. Lauderdale, FL	11,480	970	71,040	60	290	230	300
Jacksonville, FL	8,810	720	55,100	70	390	310	230
Memphis, TN	7,080	630	21,600	20	150	110	90
Miami, FL	14,140	990	228,860	120	670	510	950
Nashville, TN	8,390	810	40,090	70	330	290	170
New Orleans, LA	8,110	590	69,730	60	330	270	290
Norfolk, VA	8,960	760	78,150	80	400	350	330
Orlando, FL	9,730	970	74,330	80	420	360	310
Tampa, FL.	5,880	490	48,840	70	320	290	210
Southwestern cities.	16,560	1,300	116,140	70	390	300	500
Albuquerque, NM	3,990	350	19,840	40	200	150	80
Austin, TX	8,860	730	49,020	90	410	400	210
Corpus Christi, TX.	2,580	300	3,470	10	70	50	10
Dallas, TX	38,480	2,760	274,030	130	780	570	1,180
Denver, CO	18,390	1,440	146,110	90	450	390	620
El Paso, TX	5,460	570	9,670	20	120	80	40
Fort Worth, TX	19,800	1,660	105,680	90	450	380	450
Houston, TX.	47,500	3,240	409,970	140	780	600	1,750
Phoenix, AZ	13,140	1,030	179,060	90	600	390	750
Salt Lake City, UT.	8,830	830	17,850	20	110	90	80
San Antonio, TX	15,090	1,340	62,910	50	310	230	270
Western cities	45,140	2,560	404,710	130	770	550	1,730
Honolulu, HI.	7,570	550	57,640	90	500	380	250
Los Angeles, CA.	177,550	8,410	1,834,240	160	1,000	660	7,790
Portland, OR	12,110	900	87,280	80	550	360	380
Sacramento, CA	15,920	1,220	82,020	70	280	300	350
San Bernardino-River, CA.	24,100	1,460	249,720	200	1,340	870	1,070
San Diego, CA.	44,600	2,780	159,710	70	490	300	690
San Francisco-Oakland, CA . . .	67,620	3,850	658,550	180	930	760	2,830
San Jose, CA.	26,600	1,890	236,310	160	990	670	1,010
Seattle-Everett, WA.	30,590	1,960	276,930	150	890	660	1,190

Source: Texas Transportation Institute, College Station, Texas; *Roadway Congestion in Major Urban Areas*, annual (copyright).

No. 1010. Motor Vehicle Accidents—Number and Deaths: 1972 to 1994

[See also *Historical Statistics, Colonial Times to 1970,* series Q 208 and Q 224-232]

ITEM	Unit	1972 [1]	1980	1985	1989	1990	1991	1992	1993	1994
Motor vehicle accidents [2]	Million .	17.0	17.9	19.3	12.8	11.5	11.3	(NA)	11.9	11.2
Cars	Million .	24.5	22.8	25.6	15.3	14.3	13.7	(NA)	14.1	13.5
Trucks	Million .	3.5	5.5	6.1	6.5	4.4	4.7	(NA)	5.9	5.2
Motorcycles	1,000 .	343	560	480	211	180	239	(NA)	187	178
Motor vehicle deaths within 1 yr. [3]	1,000 .	56.3	53.2	45.9	47.6	46.8	43.5	41.0	42.2	43.0
Noncollision accidents	1,000 .	15.8	14.7	12.6	4.9	4.9	4.7	4.1	4.2	4.3
Collision accidents:										
With other motor vehicles	1,000 .	23.9	23.0	19.9	20.3	19.9	18.2	17.6	18.3	19.3
With pedestrians	1,000 .	10.3	9.7	8.5	7.8	7.3	6.6	6.3	6.1	5.6
With fixed objects	1,000 .	3.9	3.7	3.2	12.9	13.1	12.6	11.7	12.1	12.4
Deaths within 30 days [4]	1,000 .	54.6	51.1	43.8	45.6	44.6	41.5	39.3	40.1	40.7
Vehicle occupants	1,000 .	41.4	36.8	31.5	34.9	33.9	31.9	30.5	31.1	32.0
Pedestrians	1,000 .	9.2	8.1	6.8	6.6	6.5	5.8	5.5	5.6	5.5
Motorcyclists [5]	1,000 .	3.0	5.1	4.6	3.1	3.2	2.8	2.4	2.4	2.3
Bicyclists [4] [6]	1,000 .	1.0	1.0	0.9	0.8	0.9	0.8	0.7	0.8	0.8
Traffic death rates:										
Per 100,000 resident population	Rate . .	26.2	22.5	18.4	18.4	17.9	16.5	15.4	15.6	15.6
Per 100,000 registered vehicles	Rate . .	44.5	34.8	24.8	23.6	23.1	21.6	21.2	21.3	21.2
Per 100 million vehicle miles	Rate . .	4.3	3.3	2.5	2.2	2.1	1.9	1.8	1.8	1.7
Per 100,000 licensed drivers	Rate . .	46.1	35.2	27.9	27.6	26.7	24.6	22.7	22.8	23.2
Motor vehicle accidents [7]	Million .	24.9	24.1	32.5	34.4	33.4	31.3	31.8	32.8	33.9
Injuries [7]	1,000 .	5,190	5,230	5,044	5,560	5,560	5,285	5,445	5,675	5,885
Economic loss [7] [8]	Bil. dol.	28.7	57.1	76.0	93.9	95.9	93.8	98.1	104.1	110.5

NA Not available.   [1] Represents peak year for deaths from motor vehicle accidents.   [2] Covers only accidents occurring on the road.   [3] Deaths that occur within 1 year of accident. Includes collision categories not shown separately.   [4] Within 30 days of accident.   Source: U.S. National Highway Traffic Safety Administration, unpublished data from Fatal Accident Reporting System.   [5] Includes motor scooters and motorized bicycles (mopeds).   [6] Based on 30-day definition of traffic deaths.   [7] Source: Insurance Information Institute, New York, NY, *Insurance Facts.* Estimates based on official reports from a representative cross-section of States. Includes all motor vehicle accidents on and off the road and all injuries regardless of length of disability.   [8] Wage loss; legal, medical, hospital, and funeral expenses; insurance administrative costs; and property damage.

Source: Except as noted, National Safety Council, Itasca, IL, *Accident Facts,* annual (copyright).

No. 1011. Motor Vehicle Deaths, by State: 1985 to 1994

[Includes both traffic and nontraffic motor vehicle deaths. See source for definitions]

REGION DIVISION STATE	1985	1990	1993	1994	MILEAGE RATE [1] 1985	MILEAGE RATE [1] 1994	REGION DIVISION STATE	1985	1990	1993	1994	MILEAGE RATE [1] 1985	MILEAGE RATE [1] 1994
U.S. . .	45,901	47,151	42,200	43,000	2.6	1.8	DC . .	96	91	(NA)	(NA)	3.0	(NA)
							VA. . .	1,021	1,091	875	925	2.1	1.4
Northeast .	6,797	6,610	5,391	5,030	(NA)	(NA)	WV . .	461	502	435	356	3.6	2.1
N.E. . .	1,873	1,617	1,310	1,193	(NA)	(NA)	NC . .	1,553	1,489	1,384	1,428	3.1	2.0
ME . .	224	215	186	185	2.4	1.5	SC . .	943	987	845	832	3.5	2.3
NH . .	198	154	122	119	2.6	1.1	GA . .	1,462	1,659	1,407	1,438	2.7	1.8
VT . .	117	94	112	77	2.5	1.3	FL . .	2,968	3,049	2,693	2,735	3.4	2.2
MA . .	761	655	474	439	1.9	0.9	E.S.C . .	3,664	4,259	3,879	3,873	(NA)	(NA)
RI . .	124	104	74	63	2.1	0.9	KY . .	749	850	875	791	2.5	2.0
CT . .	449	395	342	310	2.0	1.1	TN . .	1,219	1,312	1,175	1,208	2.4	2.3
M.A . . .	4,924	4,993	4,081	3,837	(NA)	(NA)	AL . . .	1,005	1,234	1,016	1,082	2.0	2.2
NY . .	2,121	2,318	1,764	1,636	2.3	1.4	MS . .	691	863	813	792	2.9	2.9
NJ. . .	986	908	787	761	1.9	1.2	W.S.C . .	6,197	5,713	5,175	5,271	(NA)	(NA)
PA. . .	1,817	1,767	1,530	1,440	2.4	1.6	AR . .	580	625	583	611	2.9	2.5
Midwest . .	9,760	10,248	8,719	9,189	(NA)	(NA)	LA . . .	1,011	1,023	883	823	2.7	2.2
E.N.C . .	6,602	6,913	5,884	6,026	(NA)	(NA)	OK . .	781	684	672	695	2.1	1.9
OH . .	1,581	1,708	1,484	1,368	2.1	1.4	TX. . .	3,825	3,381	3,037	3,142	2.1	1.8
IN . .	1,045	1,097	891	979	2.6	1.6	West	10,352	10,561	8,245	8,728	(NA)	(NA)
IL . . .	1,594	1,650	1,392	1,554	2.3	1.7	Mt	3,409	3,379	2,908	3,178	(NA)	(NA)
MI . . .	1,605	1,633	1,414	1,419	2.4	1.6	MT . .	233	225	194	202	2.7	2.3
WI . .	777	825	703	706	2.1	1.4	ID . .	268	259	233	249	2.6	2.1
W.N.C . .	3,158	3,335	2,835	3,163	(NA)	(NA)	WY . .	145	130	120	144	2.2	2.1
MN . .	657	644	538	644	2.0	1.5	CO . .	628	583	561	584	2.1	1.7
IA . .	478	481	437	475	2.4	1.9	NM . .	561	534	433	447	3.3	2.3
MO . .	1,005	1,174	949	1,089	2.6	1.9	AZ . .	942	947	801	915	2.7	2.3
ND . .	117	128	89	88	2.2	1.4	UT . .	335	296	303	343	4.0	2.0
SD . .	142	166	140	154	2.3	2.0	NV . .	297	405	263	294	3.9	2.5
NE . .	259	289	254	271	2.1	1.8	Pac . . .	6,943	7,182	5,337	5,550	(NA)	(NA)
KS . .	500	453	428	442	2.6	1.8	WA . .	786	875	661	641	2.3	1.4
South. . . .	19,250	19,732	17,478	17,626	(NA)	(NA)	OR . .	605	608	522	491	2.8	1.7
S.A. . . .	9,389	9,760	8,424	8,482	(NA)	(NA)	CA . .	5,294	5,411	3,903	4,212	2.6	1.5
DE . .	119	151	113	112	2.2	1.6	AK . .	124	102	117	84	3.2	2.1
MD . .	766	741	672	656	2.3	1.5	HI . . .	134	186	134	122	2.0	1.5

NA Not available.   [1] Deaths per 100 million vehicle miles.

Source: 1985: National Center for Health Statistics; thereafter, National Safety Council, Itasca, IL, *Accident Facts,* annual (copyright).

No. 1012. Fatal Motor Vehicle Accidents—National Summary: 1980 to 1994

[Based on data from the Fatal Accident Reporting System (FARS). FARS gathers data on accidents that result in loss of human life. FARS is operated and maintained by National Highway Traffic Safety Administration's (NHTSA) National Center for Statistics and Analysis (NCSA). FARS data are gathered on motor vehicle accidents that occurred on a roadway customarily open to the public, resulting in the death of a person within 30 days of the accident. Collection of these data depend on the use of police, hospital, medical examiner/coroner, and Emergency Medical Services reports; State vehicle registration, driver licensing, and highway department files; and vital statistics documents and death certificates. See source for further detail]

ITEM	1980	1985	1989	1990	1991	1992	1993	1994
Fatal accidents, total	**45,284**	**39,196**	**40,741**	**39,836**	**36,937**	**34,942**	**35,780**	**36,223**
One vehicle involved.	28,306	22,875	23,742	23,445	21,910	20,388	20,569	20,505
Two or more vehicles involved	16,978	16,321	16,999	16,391	15,027	14,554	15,211	15,718
Persons killed in fatal accidents	**51,091**	**43,825**	**45,582**	**44,599**	**41,508**	**39,250**	**40,150**	**40,676**
Occupants [1]	41,927	36,043	38,087	37,134	34,740	32,880	33,574	34,293
Drivers	28,816	25,337	26,389	25,750	23,930	22,584	23,142	23,695
Passengers	12,972	10,619	11,624	11,276	10,688	10,211	10,361	10,502
Nonmotorists [1]	9,164	7,782	7,495	7,465	6,768	6,370	6,576	6,383
Pedestrians	8,070	6,808	6,556	6,482	5,801	5,549	5,649	5,472
Pedalcyclists	965	890	832	859	843	723	816	802
Occupant fatalities by type								
of vehicle, total	**41,927**	**36,043**	**38,087**	**37,134**	**34,740**	**32,880**	**33,574**	**34,293**
Passenger cars [1]	27,449	23,212	25,063	24,092	22,385	21,387	21,566	21,903
Mini-compact	3,141	3,571	3,812	3,556	3,039	2,714	2,635	2,294
Subcompact	4,158	4,422	4,928	4,753	4,655	4,314	4,333	4,642
Compact	927	2,635	5,099	5,310	5,338	5,354	5,707	6,245
Intermediate	3,878	4,391	5,055	4,849	4,681	4,418	4,483	4,334
Full size	4,831	2,974	2,641	2,386	2,073	2,120	2,067	2,064
Largest size	6,746	3,612	2,610	2,249	1,967	1,676	1,608	1,463
Motorcycles	4,961	4,417	3,036	3,129	2,703	2,291	2,336	2,176
Other motorized cycles	183	147	105	115	103	104	113	128
Multipurpose vehicles	895	855	1,135	1,214	1,476	1,335	1,521	1,751
Light trucks	6,591	5,834	7,416	7,387	6,915	6,763	6,990	7,126
Pickup	5,483	4,640	5,870	5,979	5,671	5,385	5,538	5,562
Van	1,000	791	1,214	1,154	1,154	1,292	1,365	1,497
Medium trucks	285	157	128	134	115	99	90	110
Heavy trucks	977	820	730	571	546	486	515	553
Buses	46	57	50	32	31	28	18	21
Persons involved in fatal accidents.	**113,289**	**104,045**	**109,866**	**107,777**	**99,369**	**95,691**	**97,589**	**98,858**
Occupants [1]	103,049	95,482	101,401	99,297	91,707	88,367	90,150	91,573
Drivers	62,957	57,883	6,435	58,893	54,391	51,901	53,401	54,514
Passengers	39,892	37,477	40,816	40,229	37,108	36,330	36,599	36,885
Nonoccupants	10,240	8,563	8,465	8,480	7,662	7,324	7,439	7,285
Vehicle miles traveled (VMT) (100 million). .	15,273	17,742	21,070	21,444	21,721	22,471	22,967	23,600
Licensed drivers (1,000)	145,295	156,868	165,555	167,015	168,995	173,125	173,149	175,403
Registered vehicles (1,000)	161,490	177,098	191,694	192,915	192,314	194,427	198,041	201,763
Fatalities by road type [1]	(NA)	(NA)	45,582	44,599	41,508	39,250	(NA)	(NA)
Interstate	4,427	4,148	4,971	4,993	4,574	4,350	(NA)	(NA)
Federal-aid primary	(NA)	14,526	14,732	14,203	13,158	12,052	(NA)	(NA)
Federal-aid secondary	(NA)	6,429	6,769	6,892	6,249	5,849	(NA)	(NA)
Federal-aid urban	(NA)	8,116	8,398	8,432	7,511	6,582	(NA)	(NA)
Non-Federal-aid	(NA)	10,408	10,579	10,039	9,924	8,826	(NA)	(NA)
Fatal accidents by the highest blood alcohol concentration (BAC) in accident:								
0.00 percent	(NA)	48.5	51.1	50.6	52.1	54.5	56.5	59.1
0.01 to 0.09 percent	(NA)	10.3	9.8	9.7	9.4	9.1	8.5	8.4
0.10 percent and over	(NA)	41.2	39.1	39.7	38.5	36.4	35.0	32.5
Rates:								
Fatality rate by age group:								
Under 5 years old.	6.9	5.2	5.4	4.9	4.6	4.5	4.5	4.8
5 years to 15 years old	8.7	7.4	7.0	6.4	6.1	5.9	5.8	5.9
16 years to 24 years old	46.0	37.1	36.7	35.2	33.0	29.5	30.2	30.8
25 years to 44 years old	24.6	19.6	20.0	19.7	17.7	16.6	16.9	16.3
45 years to 64 years old	17.2	14.5	15.0	14.9	13.5	13.1	13.0	13.3
65 years to 79 years old	19.6	18.0	19.1	18.8	18.0	17.9	17.9	18.6
80 years old and over	25.3	25.1	28.8	26.8	26.9	26.0	28.0	28.2
Fatalities per 100 million VMT.	3.3	2.5	2.2	2.1	1.9	1.8	1.7	1.7
Fatalities per 100,000 licensed drivers	35.2	27.9	27.5	26.7	24.6	22.7	23.2	23.2
Licensed driver per person.	0.6	0.7	0.7	0.7	0.7	0.7	0.7	0.7
VMT per registered vehicle	9,458	10,018	10,936	11,107	11,294	11,558	12,189	12,281
Fatalities per 100,000 registered vehicles . .	31.6	24.8	23.8	23.1	21.6	20.2	21.3	21.2
Fatal crashes per 100 million VMT	2.9	2.2	1.9	1.9	1.7	1.6	1.6	1.5
Involved vehicles per fatal crash	1.4	1.5	1.5	1.5	1.5	1.5	1.5	1.5
Fatalities per fatal crash	1.2	1.1	1.1	1.1	1.1	1.1	1.1	1.1
Average occupants per fatal crash.	2.3	2.4	2.5	2.5	2.5	2.5	2.5	2.5
Fatalities per 100,000 population.	22.5	18.4	18.4	17.9	16.5	15.4	15.6	15.6

NA Not available.   [1] Includes items not shown separately.

Source: National Highway Traffic Safety Administration, *Fatal Accident Reporting System,* annual.

No. 1013. Highway Mileage, Vehicle Miles of Travel, Accidents, and Fatalities, 1980 to 1994, and by Type of Highway System, 1994

YEAR AND TYPE OF SYSTEM	Highway mileage (1,000)	Vehicle miles of travel (bil.)	Daily vehicle miles per mile	FATAL ACCIDENTS		NONFATAL INJURY ACCIDENTS		FATALITIES [2]	
				Number	Rate [1]	Number (1,000)	Rate [1]	Number	Rate [1]
1980	3,857	1,527	1,082	45,284	2.96	2,008	131	51,091	3.35
1985	3,862	1,774	1,259	39,168	2.21	2,219	125	43,825	2.47
1986	3,880	1,835	1,298	41,062	2.23	2,254	123	46,087	2.51
1987	3,874	1,921	1,361	41,434	2.15	2,294	119	46,390	2.41
1988	3,871	2,026	1,430	42,119	2.08	2,302	114	47,087	2.32
1989	3,877	2,096	1,489	40,718	1.93	2,384	113	45,582	2.16
1990	3,880	2,148	1,516	39,779	1.85	2,501	116	44,529	2.07
1991	3,889	2,172	1,530	36,895	1.70	2,210	102	41,462	(NA)
1992	3,902	2,240	1,568	34,928	1.56	2,216	99	39,235	1.75
1993	3,905	2,297	1,611	35,750	1.56	(NA)	(NA)	40,115	1.75
1994, total	3,907	2,360	1,655	36,223	1.53	(NA)	(NA)	40,676	1.72
Urban	814	1,451	4,884	15,627	1.08	(NA)	(NA)	16,983	1.17
Rural	3,092	909	805	20,596	2.26	(NA)	(NA)	23,693	2.61
Interstate	45	547	33,303	4,047	0.74	(NA)	(NA)	4,641	0.85
Urban	14	331	64,775	1,907	0.58	(NA)	(NA)	2,107	0.64
Rural	32	216	18,493	2,140	0.99	(NA)	(NA)	2,534	1.17
Noninterstate	3,860	1,813	1,287	32,176	1.80	(NA)	(NA)	36,035	1.99
Urban	800	1,120	3,836	13,720	1.72	(NA)	(NA)	14,876	1.33
Rural	3,060	693	620	18,456	2.66	(NA)	(NA)	21,159	3.05

NA Not available. [1] Rate per 100 million vehicle miles of travel. [2] Represents fatalities occurring within 30 days of accident. Excludes nontraffic accidents which, for example, occur outside the rights-of-way or other boundaries of roads that are open for public use.

Source: U.S. Federal Highway Administration, *Fatal and Injury Accident Rates on Public Roads in the United States,* annual.

No. 1014. Motor Vehicle Safety Defect Recalls, by Domestic and Foreign Manufacturers: 1980 to 1995

[Covers manufacturers reporting to U.S. National Highway Traffic Administration under section 151 of National Traffic and Motor Vehicle Safety Act of 1966, as amended]

MANUFACTURER	Unit	1980	1985	1988	1989	1990	1991	1992	1993	1994	1995
Motor vehicles:											
Total recall campaigns [1]	Number	167	173	197	237	208	220	187	221	244	264
Domestic	Number	129	137	152	182	159	168	142	178	178	189
Foreign	Number	38	36	45	55	49	52	45	43	66	75
Total vehicles recalled	1,000	4,868	5,629	4,486	7,137	5,985	8,279	10,122	10,922	6,063	18,295
Domestic	1,000	3,943	4,995	3,171	6,173	4,070	6,646	6,545	7,655	4,280	9,041
Foreign	1,000	925	634	1,315	964	1,915	1,633	3,577	3,267	1,784	9,254
Motor vehicle tires:											
Recall campaigns [1]	Number	24	19	12	11	13	12	7	5	5	3
Tires recalled	1,000	7,070	28	215	115	172	153	8	6	93	10

[1] A recall campaign is the notification to the Secretary of the U.S. Dept. of Transportation and to owners, purchasers, and dealers of motor vehicles and motor vehicle equipment.

Source: U.S. National Highway Traffic Safety Administration, *Motor Vehicles Recall Campaigns,* annual.

No. 1015. Cost of Owning and Operating an Automobile: 1980 to 1993

ITEM	Unit	1980	1985	1988	1989	1990	1991	1992	1993
Cost per mile [1]	Cents	27.95	27.20	33.40	38.20	40.96	43.64	45.77	45.14
Cost per 10,000 miles [1]	Dollars	2,795	2,720	3,341	3,820	4,096	4,364	4,577	4,514
Variable cost	Cents/mile	7.62	8.04	7.60	7.90	8.40	9.80	9.10	9.30
Gas and oil	Cents/mile	5.86	6.16	5.20	5.20	5.40	6.70	6.00	6.00
Maintenance	Cents/mile	1.12	1.23	1.60	1.90	2.10	2.20	2.20	2.40
Tires	Cents/mile	0.64	0.65	0.80	0.80	0.90	0.90	0.90	0.90
Fixed cost	Dollars	2,033	2,441	3,061	3,534	3,877	4,217	4,538	4,486
Insurance	Dollars	490	503	573	663	675	726	747	724
License and registration	Dollars	82	115	139	151	165	169	179	183
Depreciation	Dollars	1,038	1,253	1,784	2,094	2,357	2,543	2,780	2,883
Finance charge	Dollars	423	570	565	626	680	779	832	696

[1] Beginning 1985, not comparable to previous data.

Source: American Automobile Manufacturers Association Inc., Detroit, MI, *Motor Vehicle Facts and Figures,* annual (copyright).

No. 1016. State Legislation—Alcohol and Road Safety Laws: Various Years

REGION, DIVISION, AND STATE	ALCOHOL LEGISLATION			MANDATORY BELT USE LAW			Child safety seat law date[5]	Motor-cycle helmet law[6]	65 SPEED LIMIT	
	21 year drinking age since[1]	Open container law[2]	BAC limit[3]	Effective date	Enforcement[4]	Seating positions			Effective date[7]	Applicable vehicles
Northeast:										
N.E:										
ME	1985	no	0.08	none	(X)	(X)	9/83	[8][9]15	6/87	all
NH	1985	yes	0.08	none	(X)	(X)	7/89	18	4/87	all
VT	1986	no	0.08	1/94	2	all	7/84	yes	4/87	all
MA	1985	yes	0.10	2/94	2	all	1/82	yes	12/91	all
RI	1984	no	[10]0.10	7/91	2	all	7/87	([11])	none	(X)
CT	1985	no	0.10	1/86	1	front	1982	18	none	(X)
M.A:										
NY	1985	no	0.10	12/84	1	front	4/82	yes	none	(X)
NJ	1982	yes	[10]0.10	3/85	2	front	4/83	yes	none	(X)
PA	1935	no	0.10	11/87	2	front	11/83	yes	none	(X)
Midwest:										
E.N.C:										
OH	1987	yes	[10]0.10	5/86	2	front	6/83	[9]18	7/87	some
IN	1935	yes	[10]0.10	7/87	2	front	1/84	18	6/87	some
IL	1980	yes	0.10	7/85	2	front	7/83	no	4/87	some
MI	1978	yes	[10]0.10	7/85	2	all	3/82	yes	12/87	some
WI	1986	yes	[10]0.10	12/87	2	front	4/84	[8]18	6/87	all
W.N.C:										
MN	1986	yes	[10]0.10	8/86	2	front	8/83	[8]18	6/87	all
IA	1986	yes	0.10	7/86	1	front	1/85	no	5/87	all
MO	1945	no	0.10	9/85	2	front	1/84	yes	4/87	some
ND	1936	yes	0.10	12/94	2	front	1/84	18	4/87	all
SD	1987	yes	0.10	11/94	2	front	7/84	18	4/87	all
NE	1985	no	0.10	1/93	2	front	8/83	yes	4/87	all
KS	1985	yes	0.08	7/86	2	front	7/81	18	5/87	some
South:										
S.A:										
DE	1983	yes	0.10	1992	2	front	6/82	[8][12]19	none	(X)
MD	1982	no	0.10	7/86	2	[13]front	1/84	yes	none	(X)
DC	1986	no	[10]0.10	12/85	2	[13]front	7/83	yes	none	(X)
VA	1986	no	0.08	1/88	2	front	1/83	yes	7/88	all
WV	1986	no	0.10	9/93	2	front	7/81	yes	5/87	all
NC	1986	yes	0.08	10/85	1	front	7/85	yes	4/87	all
SC	1986	yes	0.10	7/89	2	front	1/89	21	7/87	all
GA	1986	yes	[10]0.10	9/88	2	front	7/84	yes	2/88	all
FL	1985	yes	0.08	7/86	2	front	7/83	yes	4/87	all
E.S.C:										
KY	1938	no	0.10	7/94	2	all	7/82	yes	6/87	all
TN	1984	no	0.10	4/86	2	front	1/78	yes	5/87	all
AL	1985	no	0.10	7/92	2	front	1982	yes	1987	all
MS	1986	no	0.10	3/90	2	front	7/83	yes	4/87	all
W.S.C:										
AR	1967	no	[10]0.10	7/91	2	front	8/83	yes	4/87	all
LA	1987	no	[10]0.10	7/86	2	front	1/85	yes	4/87	all
OK	1983	yes	[10]0.10	2/87	2	front	11/83	18	4/87	all
TX	1985	no	[10]0.10	9/85	1	front	1/85	yes	5/87	some
West:										
Mountain:										
MT	1987	no	0.10	10/87	2	all	10/83	18	4/87	all
ID	1987	[14]yes	0.10	7/86	2	front	1/85	18	5/87	all
WY	1988	no	0.10	6/89	2	front	4/85	18	5/87	all
CO	1987	no	0.10	7/87	2	front	1/84	no	4/87	all
NM	1934	yes	[10]0.08	1/86	1	front	5/83	18	4/87	all
AZ	1984	no	0.10	1/91	2	front	1984	18	5/87	all
UT	1935	yes	0.08	4/86	2	front	4/83	18	5/87	all
NV	1933	yes	0.10	7/87	2	all	7/83	yes	4/87	all
Pacific:										
WA	1934	yes	[10]0.10	6/86	2	all	1/84	yes	4/87	some
OR	1935	yes	[10]0.08	12/90	1	all	1/84	yes	10/87	some
CA	1933	yes	[10]0.08	1/86	1	all	1/83	yes	5/87	some
AK	1983	yes	0.10	9/90	2	all	6/85	18	8/92	all
HI	1986	yes	0.10	12/85	2	front	1983	18	none	(X)

X Not applicable.   [1] Year in which original law became effective, not when grandfather clauses expired.   [2] Law prohibiting open liquor containers in motor vehicles.   [3] Percent blood alcohol concentration (BAC) which constitutes the threshold of legal intoxication.   [4] "1" indicates primary enforcement (law can be enforced on its own), "2" indicates secondary enforcement. (Law enforced only if vehicle stopped for a separate offense.)   [5] Effective data of original law, not of subsequent revisions.   [6] Presence of law or age below which riders are required to wear helmet.   [7] Includes administrative action as well as legislation.   [8] Plus instruction permit holders.   [9] Plus novice license holders.   [10] Different legal limit for minors; repeat offenders (WI only).   [11] Operators under 21 for first year; passengers.   [12] Possession of helmet required by all.   [13] Excluding front center seat.   [14] Does not include beer.

Source: National Safety Council, Itasca, IL, *Accident Facts*, annual (copyright).

No. 1017. Estimated Arrests for Driving Under the Influence, by Age: 1980 and 1989

[Total drivers and arrests in thousands. Represents licensed drivers and arrests for those 16 years old and over]

AGE	1980			1989			Percent change in rate, 1980-89
	Drivers	Arrests	Arrests per 100,000 drivers	Drivers	Arrests	Arrests per 100,000 drivers	
Total	145,207	1,425	981	165,518	1,735	1,048	6.9
Percent distribution.	100.0	100.0	(X)	100.0	100.0	(X)	(X)
16 to 17 years old. . . .	3.2	2.2	668	2.3	1.1	503	-24.7
18 to 24 years old. . . .	7.2	12.9	1,757	5.4	8.3	1,607	-8.5
25 to 29 years old. . . .	13.0	17.9	1,347	12.4	22.2	1,869	38.8
30 to 34 years old. . . .	12.0	13.1	1,076	12.4	17.6	1,486	38.1
35 to 39 years old. . . .	9.4	9.6	996	11.2	12.0	1,123	12.8
40 to 44 years old. . . .	7.7	7.4	944	9.7	8.1	872	-7.6
45 to 49 years old. . . .	6.9	5.9	837	7.6	5.3	725	-13.4
50 to 54 years old. . . .	6.9	4.9	686	6.2	3.3	558	-18.7
55 to 59 years old. . . .	6.7	3.5	509	5.7	2.2	400	-21.4
60 to 64 years old. . . .	5.7	1.9	335	5.6	1.4	262	-21.8
65 years old and over .	10.7	1.5	140	13.0	1.2	100	-28.6

X Not applicable.
Source: U.S. Bureau of Justice Statistics, *Drunk Driving, Special Report.*

No. 1018. Police-Reported Traffic Accidents, by Age Group: 1994

[Based on probability sample of police-reported accidents. See source for details]

ITEM	Total	15 yrs. and under	16 to 20 yrs.	21 to 24 yrs.	25 to 34 yrs.	35 to 44 yrs.	45 to 54 yrs.	55 to 64 yrs.	65 yrs. and older
Crash-involved	11,430,000	74,000	1,831,000	1,304,000	2,881,000	2,450,000	1,378,000	719,000	823,000
Percent male	61	64	60	59	62	61	62	64	61
Percent female	39	36	40	41	38	39	38	36	39
Percent alcohol-involved . .	4	5	2	4	5	4	3	2	1
Passengers injured or killed .	3,090,000	324,000	521,000	356,000	684,000	506,000	293,000	179,000	227,000
Percent male	48	46	50	50	50	47	44	47	43
Percent female	52	54	50	50	50	53	56	53	57
Pedestrians injured or killed .	95,000	32,000	11,000	6,000	12,000	13,000	8,000	5,000	8,000
Percent during day	61	69	45	50	50	62	62	60	75
Percent at night	39	31	55	50	50	38	38	40	25
Pedalcyclists injured or killed.	60,000	26,000	8,000	5,000	11,000	5,000	3,000	1,000	1,000

Source: U.S. National Highway Traffic Safety Administration, *General Estimates System,* annual; and unpublished data.

No. 1019. Domestic Motor Fuel Consumption, by Type of Vehicle: 1970 to 1994

[Comprises all fuel types used for propulsion of vehicles under State motor fuels laws. Excludes Federal purchases for military use. Minus sign (-) indicates decrease. See also *Historical Statistics, Colonial Times to 1970,* series Q 156-162]

YEAR	FUEL CONSUMPTION					AVG. FUEL CONSUMPTION PER VEHICLE (gal.)			AVG. MILES PER GALLON		
	All vehicles (bil. gal.)	Avg. annual percent change [1]	Cars [2] (bil. gal.)	Buses [3] (bil. gal.)	Trucks [4] (bil. gal.)	Cars [2]	Buses [3]	Trucks [4]	Cars [2]	Buses [3]	Trucks [4]
1970 . .	92.3	5.4	67.8	0.8	23.6	760	2,172	1,257	13.5	5.5	7.9
1975 . .	109.0	2.5	76.4	1.1	31.4	716	2,279	1,217	13.5	5.8	9.0
1980 . .	115.0	-5.9	71.9	1.0	41.9	591	1,926	1,243	15.5	6.0	9.5
1981 . .	114.5	-0.4	71.0	1.1	42.2	576	1,938	1,219	15.9	5.9	9.6
1982 . .	113.4	-0.9	70.1	1.0	42.1	566	1,756	1,191	16.7	5.9	9.8
1983 . .	116.1	2.4	69.9	0.9	45.1	553	1,507	1,229	17.1	5.9	9.8
1984 . .	118.7	2.3	68.7	0.8	49.0	536	1,359	1,308	17.8	5.9	9.8
1985 . .	121.3	2.2	69.3	0.8	51.0	525	1,407	1,302	18.2	5.8	9.8
1986 . .	125.2	3.2	71.4	0.9	52.9	526	1,463	1,320	18.3	5.8	9.8
1987 . .	127.5	1.8	70.6	0.9	55.8	514	1,500	1,357	19.2	5.9	9.9
1988 . .	130.1	2.0	71.9	0.9	57.2	509	1,496	1,345	20.0	5.9	10.2
1989 . .	131.8	1.3	72.7	0.9	57.9	509	1,518	1,328	20.4	6.0	10.4
1990 . .	130.8	-0.8	72.0	0.9	57.7	502	1,428	1,290	21.0	6.4	10.7
1991 . .	128.6	-1.7	70.7	0.9	56.8	496	1,369	1,264	21.7	6.7	11.0
1992 . .	132.9	3.2	73.9	0.9	58.0	512	1,360	1,275	21.7	6.6	10.9
1993 . .	[3]137.2	3.1	73.6	0.9	26.0	559	1,447	4,249	21.0	6.5	6.2
1994 . .	[3]140.1	2.1	73.8	1.0	27.6	551	1,454	4,375	21.5	6.6	6.2

[1] From prior year, except 1970, change from 1965. [2] Includes taxicabs. The format used to report some vehicle types was changed. In previous years, some other 2-axle 4-tire vehicles were included in the passenger car category. Other 2-axle 4-tire vehicles are now separate from the truck category. [3] Includes school buses. [4] Includes combinations.
Source: U.S. Federal Highway Administration, *Highway Statistics Summary to 1985,* and *Highway Statistics,* annual.

No. 1020. U.S. Vehicle, by Model Year and Vehicle Fuel Efficiency: 1991

[For composition of regions, see table 27]

1990 HOUSEHOLD CHARACTERISTICS	U.S. VEHICLES (mil.)					U.S. VEHICLE FUEL EFFICIENCY (mpg)				
	All model years	Model year				All model years	Model year			
		1991 to 1992	1990	1989	1986 to 1988		1991 to 1992	1990	1989	1986 to 1988
Total	151.2	5.5	10.5	12.5	39.0	19.3	21.8	21.5	21.8	22.0
Urban	114.3	4.5	8.5	10.2	30.8	19.8	21.8	21.9	22.1	22.2
Rural	36.9	1.0	2.0	2.4	8.2	18.0	21.6	19.6	20.6	21.5
Household size:										
1 person	22.1	0.7	1.4	1.5	4.9	19.1	(S)	21.0	21.7	23.4
2 persons	49.9	1.9	3.7	4.0	13.1	19.3	20.9	21.1	22.1	21.3
3 persons	30.3	1.1	2.0	2.8	8.5	20.1	22.5	22.3	21.8	22.9
4 persons	29.3	1.3	2.0	2.9	7.7	19.4	21.7	21.7	21.6	22.2
5 persons	13.6	0.4	0.9	0.9	3.5	18.9	(S)	21.4	21.8	21.4
6 persons or more	6.0	(S)	(S)	(S)	1.2	17.6	(S)	(S)	(S)	19.3
Households with children	65.1	2.5	4.5	5.5	16.8	19.4	21.9	21.8	22.0	22.0
Households without children	86.2	3.0	6.0	7.0	22.2	19.3	21.7	21.2	21.7	22.0
One adult	22.1	0.7	1.4	1.5	4.9	19.1	(S)	21.0	21.7	23.4
Two or more adults	64.0	2.3	4.5	5.5	17.2	19.4	21.3	21.2	21.7	21.7
White	135.3	5.1	9.4	11.1	35.8	19.3	21.8	21.4	21.6	21.9
Black	12.8	(S)	0.7	1.1	2.5	19.4	(S)	(S)	24.3	23.5
Other	3.1	(S)	(S)	(S)	0.6	19.3	(S)	(S)	(S)	(S)
Hispanic descent:										
Yes	9.4	(S)	(S)	(S)	2.3	18.3	(S)	(S)	(S)	20.1
No	141.8	5.3	10.0	12.0	36.6	19.4	21.8	21.4	21.8	22.1

S Figure does not meet publications standards.

Source: U.S. Energy Information Administration, *Household Vehicles Energy Consumption, 1991.*

No. 1021. Household Vehicles—Annual Mileage, Fuel Consumption, and Fuel Expenditures: 1991

1990 HOUSEHOLD CHARACTERISTICS	VEHICLES		VEHICLE MILES TRAVELED		CONSUMPTION			EXPENDITURES	
	Total (mil.)	Percent	Total (bil.)	Percent	Total (bil. gal.)	Gallon (per-cent	Btu. (quadril-lion)	Total (bil. dol.)	Percent
Total	151.2	100.0	1,602	100.0	82.8	100.0	10.3	98.2	100.0
Households with children	65.1	43.0	753	47.0	38.9	46.9	4.8	46.1	46.9
Households without children	86.2	57.0	849	53.0	44.0	53.1	5.5	52.2	53.1
One adult	22.1	14.6	198	12.4	10.4	12.5	1.3	12.3	12.5
Two or more adults	64.0	42.3	651	40.6	33.6	40.6	4.2	39.9	40.6
White	135.3	89.5	1,429	89.2	73.9	89.2	9.1	87.5	89.1
Black	12.8	8.4	143	8.9	7.4	8.9	0.9	8.9	9.0
Other	3.1	2.1	30	1.9	1.6	1.9	0.2	1.8	1.9
Hispanic descent:									
Yes	9.4	6.2	95	5.9	5.2	6.3	0.6	6.1	6.3
No	141.8	93.8	1,507	94.1	77.6	93.7	9.6	92.1	93.7
Eligible for Federal assistance	29.8	19.7	279	17.4	15.6	18.8	1.9	18.3	18.6
Number of drivers (fall 1990):									
1	34.6	22.9	321	20.0	16.8	20.3	2.1	20.0	20.3
2	86.7	57.3	934	58.3	48.5	58.6	6.0	57.5	58.6
3	22.0	14.5	258	16.1	13.0	15.7	1.6	15.5	15.8
4 or more	7.2	4.7	84	5.2	4.2	5.1	0.5	4.9	5.0
Average number of vehicles per household during the year:									
Part-year vehicle	2.1	1.4	21	1.3	1.1	1.3	0.1	1.3	1.4
Only 1	27.5	18.2	269	16.8	13.4	16.2	1.7	16.0	16.3
Between 1 and 2	14.1	9.3	152	9.5	7.9	9.5	1.0	9.4	9.5
Only 2	49.4	32.6	534	33.3	27.1	32.7	3.4	32.3	32.9
Between 2 and 3	19.3	12.8	219	13.7	11.6	14.1	1.4	13.7	14.0
Only 3	17.6	11.6	187	11.7	9.8	11.8	1.2	11.6	11.8
Between 3 and 4	10.6	7.0	112	7.0	6.0	7.2	0.7	7.0	7.1
4 or more	10.8	7.2	108	6.8	5.9	7.1	0.7	7.0	7.1

Source: U.S. Energy Information Administration, *Household Vehicles Energy Consumption, 1991.*

No. 1022. Motor Vehicle Travel, by Type of Vehicle and by Speed: 1970 to 1994

[Travel in billions of vehicle-miles, except as indicated. Travel estimates based on automatic traffic recorder data. Speed trend data for 1970 were collected by several State highway agencies, normally during summer months; beginning Oct. 1975 all States have monitored speeds at locations on several highway systems Monitoring Program. See also *Historical Statistics, Colonial Times to 1970*, series Q 199-207]

YEAR	VEHICLE-MILES OF TRAVEL (bil.)				AVG. MILES PER VEHICLE (1,000)			MOTOR VEHICLE SPEED ON RURAL INTERSTATE				
	Total	Cars [1]	Buses	Trucks	Passenger vehicles		Trucks	Citations recorded (1,000) [2]	Avg. speed (miles per hour)	Percent of vehicles exceeding—		
					Cars [1]	Buses				55 mph	60 mph	65 mph
1970	1,110	917	4.5	186	10.3	12.0	9.9	200	63.8	87	69	44
1980	1,527	1,111	6.1	399	9.1	11.5	11.9	667	57.5	66	25	7
1985	1,774	1,261	4.9	500	9.6	8.2	12.7	8,449	59.5	75	44	17
1986	1,835	1,301	5.1	519	9.6	8.5	13.0	8,549	59.7	76	46	18
1987	1,921	1,355	5.3	551	9.9	8.8	13.4	7,992	59.7	74	46	19
1988	2,026	1,430	5.5	581	10.1	8.9	13.7	7,566	59.5	74	46	19
1989	2,096	1,478	5.7	603	10.3	9.0	13.8	7,488	60.1	77	49	22
1990	2,144	1,513	5.7	616	10.5	9.1	13.8	7,511	60.4	78	50	23
1991	2,172	1,543	5.7	624	10.8	9.1	13.9	7,594	59.9	76	48	21
1992	2,247	1,601	5.8	631	11.1	8.9	13.9	7,004	61.2	81	56	28
1993	2,297	1,547	6.1	160	11.8	9.4	26.1	6,433	60.8	78	51	24
1994	2,360	1,586	6.4	170	11.8	9.6	27.0	(NA)	(NA)	(NA)	(NA)	(NA)

NA Not available.   [1] Includes motorcycles.   [2] Citations issued for 55 mph violations.

Source: U.S. Federal Highway Administration, *Highway Statistics Summary, annual.*

No. 1023. Passenger Transit Industry—Summary: 1985 to 1994

[Includes Puerto Rico. Includes aggregate information for all transit systems in the United States. Excludes nontransit services such as taxicab, school bus, unregulated jitney, sightseeing bus, intercity bus, and special application mass transportation systems (e.g., amusement parks, airports, island, and urban park ferries) Includes active vehicles only]

ITEM	Unit	1985	1989	1990	1991	1992	1993	1994, prel.
Operating systems	Number. . .	4,972	5,046	5,078	5,084	5,086	5,088	5,973
Motor bus systems.	Number. . .	2,631	2,665	2,688	2,689	2,693	2,693	2,250
Passenger vehicles owned [1] . . .	Number. . .	94,368	92,293	92,961	96,399	102,251	107,316	118,589
Motor bus.	Number. . .	64,258	58,919	58,714	60,377	63,080	64,850	67,492
Trolley bus	Number. . .	676	725	832	752	907	851	877
Heavy rail.	Number. . .	9,326	10,506	10,419	10,331	10,245	10,261	10,138
Light rail.	Number. . .	717	755	913	1,095	1,058	1,025	1,054
Commuter rail	Number. . .	4,035	4,472	4,415	4,370	4,413	4,494	4,517
Demand response	Number. . .	14,490	15,856	16,471	17,879	20,695	23,527	31,872
Operating funding, total	Mil. dol . . .	12,195	14,985	16,053	16,533	16,915	17,276	18,134
Passenger funding	Mil. dol . . .	4,575	5,420	5,891	6,037	6,152	6,351	6,841
Other operating funding [2] . . .	Mil. dol . . .	702	837	895	767	646	764	802
Operating assistance	Mil. dol . . .	6,918	8,728	9,267	9,729	10,117	10,161	10,491
Federal.	Mil. dol . . .	940	937	970	956	969	966	929
Local	Mil. dol . . .	[3]5,979	4,995	5,327	5,573	5,268	5,491	5,683
State	Mil. dol . . .	([3])	2,796	2,970	3,200	3,898	3,704	3,879
Total expense.	Mil. dol . . .	14,077	17,169	17,979	19,332	20,034	20,679	22,695
Operating expense.	Mil. dol . . .	12,381	14,972	15,742	16,541	16,781	17,350	18,782
Vehicle operations	Mil. dol . . .	5,655	6,275	6,654	6,727	7,660	7,941	9,654
Maintenance	Mil. dol . . .	3,672	4,493	4,631	4,597	4,831	4,894	5,270
General administration. . . .	Mil. dol . . .	2,505	3,251	3,450	3,585	2,674	2,715	2,919
Purchased transportation . .	Mil. dol . . .	549	953	1,008	1,633	1,616	1,800	1,939
Reconciling expense	Mil. dol . . .	1,696	2,196	2,237	2,791	3,253	3,329	3,913
Capital expenditure, Federal . . .	Mil. dol . . .	2,510	2,590	2,380	2,396	2,613	3,465	3,577
Vehicle-miles operated [1]	Mil. dol . . .	2,791	3,203	3,242	3,306	3,355	3,435	3,556
Motor bus.	Million	1,863	2,109	2,130	2,167	2,178	2,210	2,163
Trolley bus	Million	16	15	14	14	14	14	14
Heavy rail.	Million	451	532	537	527	525	522	532
Light rail.	Million	17	21	24	28	29	28	34
Commuter rail	Million	183	210	213	215	219	224	231
Demand response	Million	247	300	306	335	364	406	553
Passengers carried [1]	Million	8,636	8,931	8,799	8,575	8,501	8,217	8,435
Motor bus.	Million	5,675	5,620	5,677	5,624	5,517	5,381	5,402
Trolley bus	Million	142	130	126	125	126	121	118
Heavy rail.	Million	2,290	2,542	2,346	2,172	2,207	2,046	2,206
Light rail.	Million	132	162	175	184	188	188	203
Commuter rail	Million	275	330	328	318	314	322	338
Demand response	Million	59	70	68	71	72	81	87
Avg. funding per passenger. . . .	Cents	53.0	60.7	66.9	70.4	72.4	77.3	81.1
Employees, number (avg.) [4] . . .	1,000	270	272	273	276	279	299	312
Payroll, employee	Mil. dol . . .	5,843	6,898	7,226	7,395	7,671	7,932	8,648
Fringe benefits, employee.	Mil. dol . . .	2,868	3,737	3,986	3,998	4,319	4,400	4,769

[1] Includes other not shown separately.   [2] Includes other operating revenue, nonoperating revenue, and auxiliary income.   [3] For 1985, State and local combined.   [4] Thru 1992, represents employee equivalents of 2,080 hours = one employee; beginning 1993, equals actual employees.

Source: American Public Transit Association, Washington, DC, *Transit Fact Book, annual.*

No. 1024. Transportation Industry Summary: 1992

[Includes only establishments with payroll]

KIND OF BUSINESS	SIC code	Establish- ments (number)	Revenue ($1,000)	Annual payroll ($1,000)	First- quarter payroll	Paid employees for pay period including March 12 (number)
Total transportation, except U.S. Post Office		(NA)	327,623	92,211	(NA)	3,356,872
Railroad transportation [1]	40	(NA)	28,349	8,753	(NA)	197,421
Passenger transportation.	41	17,805	12,649	5,191	1,246	354,913
Local and suburban passenger transportation	411	8,275	5,968	2,624	613	153,278
Local and suburban transit	4111	1,135	1,364	838	199	37,653
Other local passenger transportation.	4119	7,140	4,604	1,786	414	115,625
Sightseeing bus.	4119 pt	277	342	104	22	5,565
Limousine service	4119 pt	2,430	964	278	64	20,739
Ambulance or rescue service, except by air	4119 pt	3,070	2,507	1,104	256	66,885
Other local passenger transportation, n.e.c	4119 pt	1,363	791	300	72	22,436
Taxicabs	412	3,337	992	306	75	26,338
Other bus transportation and terminal service.	413, 4, 5, 7	6,193	5,689	2,261	558	175,297
Intercity and rural bus service	413	607	1,092	483	116	20,404
Charter bus service	414	1,307	1,269	394	86	24,604
Local charter bus	4141	429	375	125	29	7,699
Charter bus, except local.	4142	878	894	269	58	16,905
School buses	415	4,260	3,315	1,380	355	130,093
Bus terminal and service facilities.	417	19	12	4	1	196
Motor freight transportation and warehousing	42	110,908	143,794	39,896	9,196	1,580,095
Trucking and courier services, except air.	421	101,169	135,437	37,760	8,691	1,484,655
Local trucking without storage	4212	49,870	33,554	8,043	1,799	354,742
Household goods moving	4212 pt	2,566	661	196	43	13,237
General freight.	4212 pt	12,186	8,404	2,250	522	97,594
Garbage and trash collection	4212 pt	7,405	10,985	2,473	577	94,054
Dump trucking.	4212 pt	13,383	6,807	1,418	277	66,956
Other local trucking without storage.	4212 pt	14,330	6,698	1,707	380	82,901
Hazardous materials	4212 pt	1,279	885	238	57	9,270
Agricultural products	4212 pt	6,203	2,188	478	106	26,897
Other local trucking without storage, n.e.c	4212 pt	6,848	3,625	990	218	46,734
Trucking, except local.	4213	40,821	78,358	20,974	4,808	758,435
Household goods moving	4213 pt	3,248	7,433	1,354	302	61,592
General freight trucking	4213 pt	25,014	55,257	15,880	3,650	553,202
Other trucking, except local	4213 pt	12,559	15,668	3,741	856	143,641
Hazardous products	4213 pt	1,666	2,759	720	170	25,617
Agricultural products	4213 pt	4,483	3,304	665	146	30,518
Other trucking, except storage, n.e.c	4213 pt	6,410	9,605	2,356	540	87,506
Local trucking with storage	4214	4,512	4,191	1,346	303	64,417
Household goods moving	4214 pt	2,641	2,175	703	155	36,483
Other local trucking with storage	4214 pt	1,871	2,016	643	149	27,934
Courier services, except by air.	4215	5,966	19,334	7,396	1,780	307,061
Public warehousing and storage	422	9,718	8,330	2,127	504	95,145
Farm products warehousing and storage	4221	584	656	130	31	6,497
Refrigerated warehousing and storage	4222	929	1,745	464	111	18,963
General warehousing and storage	4225	6,753	3,919	983	233	49,091
General goods warehousing.	4225 pt	2,251	2,641	832	196	37,814
Self-service or miniwarehousing	4225 pt	4,502	1,279	151	37	11,277
Special warehousing and storage, n.e.c	4226	1,452	2,009	551	129	20,594
Trucking terminal facilities.	423	21	27	8	2	295
Pipelines, except natural gas	46	844	7,063	821	203	16,779
Refined petroleum pipelines	4613	358	2,010	252	61	5,578
Other pipelines	4612, 9	486	5,053	569	142	11,201
Crude petroleum pipelines	4612	405	4,409	531	132	10,355
Pipelines, n.e.c	4619	81	644	38	10	846
Transportation services	47	46,593	23,890	7,850	1,854	329,202
Arrangement of passenger transportation	472	31,793	10,573	3,921	931	192,981
Travel agencies.	4724	27,688	6,964	2,836	673	149,140
Other arrangement of passenger transportation. . . .	4725,9	4,105	3,608	1,086	258	43,841
Tour operators	4725	3,008	1,865	690	155	30,519
Arrangement of passenger transportation, n.e.c . .	4729	1,097	1,744	396	102	13,322
Freight shipping services	473	12,553	9,159	3,233	761	106,979
Freight forwarding	4731 pt	5,308	4,156	1,437	335	48,903
Arrangement of freight and cargo, n.e.c	4731 pt	7,245	5,002	1,796	426	58,076
Other transportation services	474, 8	2,247	4,158	696	162	29,242
Rental of railroad cars	474	125	1,881	85	23	1,926
Miscellaneous services incidental to transportation. .	478	2,122	2,277	612	140	27,316
Packing and crating	4783	835	522	155	33	8,123
Fixed facilities, inspection and weighing services .	4785	263	221	65	15	2,810
Transportation services, n.e.c	4789	1,024	1,534	392	91	16,383

NA Not available. [1] Includes Class I Freight railroads only. Source, Association of American Railroads, Washington DC, *Railroad Facts*, annual. Source: U.S. Bureau of the Census, *Census of Transportation, Communications and Utilities: 1992*

No. 1025. Class I Intercity Motor Carriers of Passengers: 1980 to 1992

[Carriers subject to ICC regulations. See text, section 21. Minus sign (-) indicates deficit. See also *Historical Statistics, Colonial Times to 1970, series Q 69-75*]

ITEM	Unit	1980	1983	1984	1985	1986	1987	1988	1989	1990	1991	1992
Carriers reporting [1]	Number.	48	45	43	43	29	32	21	20	21	21	21
Number of employees, average....	1,000 ..	31	25	25	24	20	(NA)	(NA)	(NA)	(NA)	(NA)	(NA)
Compensation of employees......	Mil. dol .	599	570	551	518	443	(NA)	(NA)	(NA)	(NA)	(NA)	(NA)
Operating revenue	Mil. dol .	1,397	1,276	1,255	1,233	1,117	1,079	1,122	1,205	943	980	938
Passenger revenue [2].........	Mil. dol .	947	876	861	836	765	751	825	890	738	793	755
Special bus revenue and other ..	Mil. dol .	215	180	180	184	155	165	155	165	90	187	183
Operating expenses	Mil. dol .	1,318	1,283	1,254	1,168	1,082	1,081	1,059	1,133	1,015	967	874
Net operating revenue.........	Mil. dol .	79	-7	1	65	35	-2	63	72	-72	13	64
Ordinary income:												
Before income taxes	Mil. dol .	107	16	53	65	50	-11	(NA)	(NA)	(NA)	(NA)	(NA)
After income taxes..........	Mil. dol .	90	26	43	53	36	-21	(NA)	12	-180	162	21
Passenger vehicles in service [2]....	1,000 ..	8.6	7.3	7.0	8.4	8.3	(NA)	(NA)	(NA)	(NA)	(NA)	(NA)
Vehicle-miles, passenger	Million..	781	591	585	567	495	(NA)	(NA)	(NA)	(NA)	(NA)	(NA)
Revenue passengers carried	Million..	134	94	89	88	74	82	55	54	43	42	41
Expense per vehicle-mile.......	Dollar..	1.69	2.17	2.14	2.06	2.18	(NA)	(NA)	(NA)	(NA)	(NA)	(NA)

NA Not available. [1] Excludes carriers preponderantly in local or suburban service and carriers engaged in transportation of both property and passengers. [2] Regular route, intercity, and local.

Source: U.S. Interstate Commerce Commission, *Transport Statistics in the United States*, part 2, annual.

No. 1026. Passenger Transportation Arrangement: 1992 to 1994

[In millions of dollars, except percent. Represents SIC 4722]

SOURCE OF RECEIPTS	1992	1993	1994	OPERATING EXPENSES	1992	1993	1994
Receipts, total [1] ...	10,573	11,073	11,795	Expenses, total [1]	9,705	10,136	10,889
Air carriers	5,881	6,138	6,375	Payroll, annual	3,924	4,031	4,526
Water carriers	523	528	584	Employer contributions [2].	526	558	628
Hotels and motels	744	758	808	Lease and rental payments	873	908	908
Motor coaches........	379	388	397	Advertising and promotion	653	713	746
Railroads	110	125	126	Taxes and licenses	135	144	163
Rental cars	187	189	204	Utilities	371	386	388
Package tours	1,989	2,158	2,425	Depreciation	326	339	361
Other..............	760	789	876	Office Supplies	300	294	325
				Repair Services	124	134	152
				Other	2,473	2,629	2,692

[1] Receipts for firms primarily engaged in arranging passenger transportation. These estimates exclude receipts of transportation companies (airlines, railroads, etc.). [2] Includes contributions to Social Security and other supplemental benefits.

Source: U.S. Bureau of the Census, *Service Annual Survey.*

No. 1027. Motor Freight Transportation and Warehousing Services—Revenues, Expenses, and Payroll: 1993 and 1994

[In millions of dollars. Estimates for 1993 reflect a benchmarking to the results of the 1992 Census of Transportation, Communications, and Utilities]

KIND OF BUSINESS	SIC [1] code	OPERATING REVENUE		OPERATING EXPENSES		ANNUAL PAYROLL	
		1993	1994	1993	1994	1993	1994
Motor frgt. transport. and warehousing services [2]	42	152,694	167,865	142,803	156,227	42,266	46,137
Trucking and courier services, except by air [3]....	421	143,601	157,910	135,144	147,911	39,889	43,580
Local trucking without storage	4212	35,953	39,400	33,383	36,444	8,434	9,193
Trucking, except local..................	4213	82,558	91,971	78,716	87,078	22,277	24,658
Local trucking with storage	4214	4,259	4,282	4,052	4,131	1,351	1,362
Courier services, except by air	4215	20,831	22,257	18,993	20,258	7,827	8,367
Public warehousing and storage	422	9,056	9,911	7,622	8,271	2,364	2,540
Farm product warehousing and storage	4221	718	773	615	652	144	152
Refrigerated warehousing and storage.......	4222	1,805	1,970	1,541	1,667	488	522
General warehousing and storage.	4225	4,352	4,652	3,597	3,803	1,120	1,170
Special warehousing and storage [4]	4226	2,181	2,516	1,869	2,149	612	696

[1] Standard Industrial Classification. [2] Includes terminal and joint terminal maintenance facilities for motor carrier transportation (SIC 4231) not shown separately. [3] Excludes private motor carriers that operate as auxiliary establishments to nontransportation companies and independent owner-operators with no paid employees. [4] Includes household goods warehousing.

Source: U.S. Bureau of the Census, *Current Business Reports, 1994 Motor Freight Transportation and Warehousing Survey.*

No. 1028. Bus Profile: 1980 to 1994

ITEM	Unit	1980	1990	1992	1993	1994
FINANCIAL						
Expenditures, school bus	Mil. dol. .	3,833	7,605	8,060	8,074	8,316
Operating revenues, intercity buc, Class I	Mil. dol. .	1,397	943	938	928	(NA)
Operating expenses, intercity bus, Class I	Mil. dol. .	1,318	1,026	874	880	(NA)
INVENTORY						
Operating companies, intercity bus, Class I	Number .	61	31	31	30	(NA)
Vehicles:						
Commercial & Federal bus	Number .	110,576	118,726	118,894	119,560	122,705
School & other bus	Number .	418,225	508,261	525,838	534,872	547,718
PERFORMANCE						
Vehicle-miles, all buses:						
Rural & urban highway	Millions .	6,059	5,719	5,759	6,126	6,416
School bus	Millions .	3,000	3,800	4,400	4,300	4,400
Revenue:—						
Passenger miles, intercity bus	Millions .	27,400	23,000	22,600	24,600	25,300
Passengers, intercity bus	1,000. . .	370,000	334,000	339,000	339,900	343,200
Avg. miles traveled per vehicle, all buses	Miles . . .	11,458	9,121	8,932	9,361	9,570
Avg. annual fuel consumption, all buses	Gallon . .	1,926	1,428	1,360	1,447	1,454
Avg. miles per gallon, all buses	Mpg . . .	6.0	6.4	6.6	6.5	6.6
Average revenue per passenger mile	Cents . .	7.3	11.6	11.8	12.0	11.6
SAFETY						
Fatalities:						
School bus related	Number .	150	115	124	141	105
School bus occupants	Number .	9	11	10	13	3
Other vehicle occupants	Number .	88	64	83	86	64
Non-occupants	Number .	53	40	31	42	38
Fatalities in vehicular accidents, all buses	Number .	390	340	300	286	282
Occupant fatality rate:						
Per 100 million vehicle-miles, all buses	Rate . . .	0.8	0.6	0.5	0.3	(NA)
Per 10,000 registered vehicles, all buses	Rate . . .	0.9	0.5	0.4	0.3	(NA)

NA Not available.

Source: U.S. Bureau of Transportation Statistics, *National Transportation Statistics, 1996*.

No. 1029. Truck Profile: 1980 to 1994

ITEM	Unit	1980	1990	1992	1993	1994
FINANCIAL						
Revenues:						
Local	Mil. dol . .	60,545	108,350	116,000	122,050	125,712
Intercity	Mil. dol . .	94,551	162,300	176,800	189,700	204,876
Class I intercity motor carriers of property:						
Operating revenue, total	Mil. dol . .	1,290	46,710	51,072	55,303	(NA)
Operating expenses, total	Mil. dol . .	29,012	44,827	48,259	52,695	(NA)
INVENTORY						
Truck registrations, total	1,000 . . .	33,637	44,479	45,504	61,828	63,445
PERFORMANCE						
Vehicle miles, total	Millions . .	399,426	615,902	630,996	733,302	757,699
Average miles traveled per vehicle:						
All trucks, total	Avg. miles	11,864	13,773	13,867	11,860	11,943
Ton-miles, intercity	Millions . .	555,000	735,000	815,000	861,000	908,000
Average fuel consumption per vehicle	Gallons . .	1,243	1,290	1,275	1,010	1,026
Highway-user taxes, total	Mil. dol . .	9,888	19,356	19,759	(NA)	(NA)
SAFETY						
Occupant fatalities	Number . .	8,748	9,306	8,681	9,116	9,539
Vehicle involvement, total (per 100 million vehicle-miles)	Rate. . . .	4.5	2.9	2.3	2.4	(NA)

NA Not available.

Source: U.S. Bureau of Transportation Statistics, *National Transportation Statistics, 1996*.

No. 1030. Trucking and Courier Services—Operating Revenue, Operating Expenses, and Equipment, by Type of Carrier: 1992 to 1994

[In millions of dollars, except as indicated. Data cover SIC group 421. Excludes private motor carriers that operate as auxiliary establishments to nontransportation companies and independent owner-operators with no paid employees. Estimates for years 1992 and 1993 reflect a benchmarking to the results of the 1992 Census of Transportation, Communications, and Utilities]

ITEM	ALL CARRIERS			SPECIALTY CARRIERS			GENERAL CARRIERS		
	1992	1993	1994	1992	1993	1994	1992	1993	1994
Operating revenues:									
Total [1]	135,437	143,601	157,910	36,729	38,335	41,205	98,708	105,266	116,705
Motor carrier	127,049	135,383	149,160	32,690	34,279	37,015	94,359	101,104	112,145
Local trucking	31,120	34,086	38,157	16,366	17,442	19,231	14,754	16,644	18,926
Long-distance trucking	95,929	101,297	111,003	16,324	16,837	17,784	79,605	84,460	93,219
Operating expenses:									
Total [1]	127,687	135,144	147,911	34,101	35,902	38,403	93,586	99,242	109,508
Annual payroll	37,761	39,889	43,580	8,362	8,735	9,349	29,399	31,154	34,231
Employer contrib. to Soc. Sec. and other benefits	10,125	10,745	11,502	1,973	2,042	2,283	8,152	8,703	9,219
Purchased fuels	11,345	12,119	13,287	2,111	2,314	2,498	9,234	9,805	10,789
Purchased transportation	24,760	26,678	29,329	6,805	7,586	7,906	17,955	19,092	21,423
Lease and rental	2,521	2,545	2,732	711	719	765	1,810	1,826	1,967
Insurance	4,801	5,097	5,489	1,383	1,473	1,577	3,418	3,624	3,912
Maintenance and repair	7,985	8,542	9,442	2,298	2,367	2,645	5,687	6,175	6,797
Depreciation	6,998	7,450	8,218	1,886	1,950	2,016	5,112	5,500	6,202
Taxes and licenses	3,212	3,351	3,676	667	688	746	2,545	2,663	2,930
Drug and alcohol testing and rehabilitation programs	53	64	82	15	18	23	38	46	59
Other operating expenses	18,126	18,664	20,574	7,890	8,010	8,595	10,236	10,654	11,979
Equipment (1,000 units): [2]									
Trucks	246	260	287	112	131	147	134	129	140
Truck-tractors	575	622	681	110	129	133	465	493	548
Trailers (full and semi)	1,276	1,337	1,456	202	200	212	1,074	1,137	1,244

[1] Includes other revenue not shown separately.   [2] Represents revenue generating equipment as of December 31, 1994. Includes owned and leased equipment.
Source: U.S. Bureau of the Census, *Current Business Reports, 1994 Motor Freight Transportation and Warehousing Survey.*

No. 1031. Class I Intercity Motor Carriers of Property, by Carrier: 1975 to 1992

[See headnote, table 1025. Common carriers are carriers offering regular scheduled service. Contract carriers provide service at request of user. Minus sign (-) indicates loss]

ITEM	Unit	1975	1980	1985	1987	1988	1989	1990	1991	1992
Common carriers, gen. freight										
reporting	Number	368	298	237	200	209	192	191	201	208
Number of employees, average	1,000	379	413	376	405	430	461	465	474	490
Compensation of employees	Mil. dol	5,726	9,803	10,217	11,208	12,074	12,854	13,556	14,032	14,967
Operating revenues	Mil. dol	11,116	19,725	22,314	23,087	25,234	27,405	29,682	31,619	34,594
Operating expenses	Mil. dol	10,571	18,870	21,037	22,326	24,000	26,242	28,340	30,269	32,977
Ordinary income before taxes	Mil. dol	432	701	1,198	647	1,135	988	1,146	1,180	1,453
Net income	Mil. dol	225	-72	658	406	804	659	746	749	878
Intercity vehicle-miles	Million	6,246	6,547	5,760	5,524	5,913	6,557	6,804	7,615	8,674
Intercity revenue freight carried	Mil. ton	191	178	136	129	124	145	157	169	196
Common carriers, other reporting [1]	Number	330	441	397	339	360	337	322	295	330
Number of employees, average	1,000	94	101	76	83	82	84	87	74	78
Compensation of employees	Mil. dol	1,046	1,931	1,783	1,961	2,010	2,105	2,236	1,920	2,358
Operating revenues	Mil. dol	3,907	8,792	7,962	8,047	8,344	8,321	9,042	7,761	9,367
Operating expenses	Mil. dol	3,758	8,426	7,752	7,835	8,018	8,081	8,702	7,509	8,942
Ordinary income before taxes	Mil. dol	109	230	123	129	248	117	198	122	309
Net income	Mil. dol	65	14	94	97	194	88	153	85	221
Intercity vehicle-miles	Million	4,776	6,889	5,714	5,761	6,263	6,320	6,566	5,372	6,696
Intercity revenue freight carried	Mil. ton	264	324	303	295	299	278	302	253	298
Contract carrier, other reporting [1]	Number	50	69	64	64	74	77	87	83	113
Number of employees, average	1,000	10	14	22	20	30	29	34	34	42
Compensation of employees	Mil. dol	175	336	630	561	925	893	1,082	989	1,325
Operating revenues	Mil. dol	453	1,272	1,942	1,922	3,026	2,946	3,486	3,644	4,501
Operating expenses	Mil. dol	432	1,207	1,807	1,833	2,923	2,888	3,422	3,547	4,333
Ordinary income before taxes	Mil. dol	17	48	103	59	55	15	3	53	127
Net income	Mil. dol	9	28	69	38	38	3	-13	20	80
Intercity vehicle-miles	Million	454	934	1,227	1,304	1,882	1,826	2,044	2,339	2,933
Intercity revenue freight carried	Mil. ton	21	37	41	41	69	80	80	76	110
Carriers of household goods										
reporting	Number	32	28	40	37	36	36	36	36	32
Number of employees, average	1,000	4	10	11	11	11	12	13	12	12
Compensation of employees	Mil. dol	70	157	240	247	254	276	290	298	291
Operating revenues	Mil. dol	866	1,824	2,684	2,931	3,038	3,114	3,152	3,026	3,180
Operating expenses	Mil. dol	849	1,781	2,635	2,862	2,971	3,059	3,129	2,973	3,159
Ordinary income before taxes	Mil. dol	32	74	79	74	33	41	12	27	-1
Net income	Mil. dol	18	42	54	57	25	28	8	17	8
Intercity vehicle-miles	Million	688	969	1,171	1,234	1,289	1,229	1,366	1,086	1,136
Intercity revenue freight carried	Mil. ton	3	5	7	8	8	7	8	7	9

[1] Other than general freight.
Source: U.S. Interstate Commerce Commission, *Transport Statistics in the United States,* part 2, annual.

No. 1032. Railroads, Class I—Summary: 1980 to 1994

[As of **Dec. 31**, or **calendar year** data, except as noted. Compiled from annual reports of class I railroads only except where noted. Beginning 1985, financial data are not comparable with earlier years due to change in method of accounting for track and related structures. Minus sign (-) indicates deficit. See also *Historical Statistics, Colonial Times to 1970*, series Q 284-312, Q 319, Q 330, Q 356-378, and Q 400-401]

ITEM	Unit	1980	1985	1988	1989	1990	1991	1992	1993	1994
Class I line-hauling companies [1] . . .	Number.	40	23	17	15	14	14	13	13	13
Employees [2]	1,000 . .	458	302	236	228	216	206	197	193	190
Compensation	Mil. dol .	11,318	10,563	9,301	9,043	8,654	8,695	8,753	8,732	8,874
Average per hour	Dollars .	10.2	14.3	15.6	15.8	15.8	16.8	17.8	17.9	18.5
Average per year	Dollars .	24,695	34,991	39,431	39,742	39,987	42,131	44,336	45,354	46,714
Mileage:										
Railroad line owned [3]	1,000 . .	178	162	150	149	146	143	139	137	132
Railroad track owned [4]	1,000 . .	292	269	251	250	244	241	234	231	222
Equipment:										
Locomotives in service	Number.	28,094	22,548	19,364	19,015	18,835	18,344	18,004	18,161	18,505
Average horsepower	1,000 lb	2,302	2,469	2,579	2,624	2,665	2,714	2,750	2,777	2,832
Cars in service:										
Passenger train	Number.	4,347	2,502	2,332	(NA)	(NA)	(NA)	(NA)	(NA)	(NA)
Freight train [5]	1,000 . .	1,711	1,422	1,239	1,224	1,212	1,190	1,173	1,173	1,192
Freight cars [6]	1,000 . .	1,168	867	725	682	659	633	605	587	591
Income and expenses:										
Operating revenues	Mil. dol .	28,258	27,586	27,934	27,956	28,370	27,845	28,349	28,825	30,809
Operating expenses	Mil. dol .	26,355	25,225	24,811	25,038	24,652	28,061	25,325	24,517	25,511
Net revenue from operations . . .	*Mil. dol* .	*1,902*	*2,361*	*3,123*	*2,918*	*3,718*	*-216*	*3,024*	*4,308*	*5,298*
Income before 'xed charges . . .	Mil. dol .	2,897	3,393	4,460	4,162	4,627	928	4,127	4,990	6,184
Provision for taxes [7]	Mil. dol .	592	660	1,162	1,040	1,088	-156	1,092	1,810	1,935
Ordinary income.	Mil. dol .	1,129	1,788	2,286	2,009	1,961	-91	2,055	2,258	3,315
Net income	Mil. dol .	1,129	1,882	2,382	2,203	1,977	-281	1,800	2,240	3,298
Net railway operating income . . .	Mil. dol .	1,339	1,746	1,980	1,894	2,648	-37	1,955	2,517	3,392
Total taxes [8]	Mil. dol .	2,585	3,169	3,871	3,742	3,780	2,649	3,732	4,343	4,512
Indus. return on net investment. .	Percent.	4.2	4.6	6.7	6.3	8.1	1.3	6.3	7.1	9.4
Gross capital expenditures.	Mil. dol .	3,238	4,485	3,546	3,865	3,591	3,439	3,680	4,504	5,035
Balance sheet:										
Total property investment.	Mil. dol .	43,923	64,241	68,550	67,661	70,348	71,622	72,677	75,217	78,384
Accrued depreciation and										
amortization	Mil. dol .	10,706	19,756	21,497	21,481	22,222	23,057	23,378	23,892	24,200
Net investment.	Mil. dol .	33,419	46,237	47,053	47,370	48,126	48,565	49,299	51,325	54,184
Shareholder's equity	Mil. dol .	19,860	27,605	26,467	25,753	23,662	22,603	22,055	24,658	27,389
Net working capital	Mil. dol .	922	1,084	-190	-2119	-3505	-3,988	-4,372	-3,295	-3,059
Cash dividends	Mil. dol .	610	1,444	1,814	1,910	2,074	915	830	1,054	1,398
AMTRAK passenger traffic:										
Passenger revenue.	Mil. dol .	(NA)	604.9	784.2	893.0	941.9	962.3	933.2	924.4	(NA)
Revenue passengers carried . . .	1,000 . .	21,303	20,945	21,490	21,394	22,382	21,693	21,672	21,841	(NA)
Revenue passenger miles	Million. .	4,645	4,977	5,686	5,912	6,125	6,249	6,181	6,064	(NA)
Averages:										
Revenue per passenger	Dollars .	(NA)	28.9	36.5	41.8	42.1	44.4	43.0	42.3	(NA)
Revenue per passenger mile. .	Cents . .	(NA)	12.2	13.8	15.1	15.4	15.4	15.1	15.2	(NA)
Trip per passenger	Miles . .	218.1	237.6	264.6	276.3	273.7	288.0	285.1	277.7	(NA)
Freight service:										
Freight revenue	Mil. dol .	26,200	26,688	27,092	27,059	24,471	26,949	27,508	27,991	29,931
Per ton-mile	Cents . .	2.8	3.0	2.7	2.7	2.7	2.6	2.6	2.5	2.5
Per ton originated.	Dollar . .	17.7	20.2	19.0	19.3	19.3	19.5	19.7	20.0	20.4
Revenue-tons originated	Million. .	1,492	1,320	1,430	1,402	1,425	1,383	1,399	1,397	1,470
Revenue-tons carried	Million. .	2,434	1,985	2,045	1,988	2,024	1,987	2,022	2,047	2,185
Tons carried one mile	Billion . .	919	877	996	1,014	1,034	1,039	1,067	1,109	1,201
Average miles of road operated .	1,000 . .	179	161	141	138	133	130	126	124	123
Revenue ton-miles per mile of										
road	1,000 . .	5,133	5,446	7,052	7,373	7,763	8,001	8,451	8,965	9,735
Revenue per ton-mile	Cents . .	3	3	3	3	3	3	3	3	2
Train miles	Million. .	428	347	379	383	380	375	390	405	441
Net ton-miles per train-mile [9] . . .	Number.	2,175	2,574	2,662	2,683	2,755	2,796	2,759	2,759	2,746
Net ton-miles per loaded										
car-mile [9]	Number.	63.5	62.7	65.5	67.0	69.1	71.6	70.9	71.6	72.2
Train-miles per train-hour.	Miles . .	18.2	21.9	21.5	23.0	23.7	23.7	23.7	23.1	22.4
Haul per ton, U.S. as a system . .	Miles . .	616	664	697	723	726	751	763	794	817
Accident: [10]										
All railroads	Number.	63,663	35,340	28,253	28,039	26,440	24,662	22,553	20,400	19,455
Persons killed.	Number.	1,417	1,036	1,199	1,324	1,297	1,194	1,170	1,279	1,226
Persons injured	Number.	62,246	34,304	27,054	26,715	25,143	23,468	21,383	19,121	18,229
Class I railroads	Number.	57,755	29,388	22,093	21,809	20,450	18,728	17,055	15,058	12,428
Persons killed.	Number.	1,344	955	1,076	1,195	1,166	1,069	1,047	1,124	1,080
Persons injured	Number.	56,411	28,433	21,017	20,614	19,284	17,659	16,008	13,934	11,348

NA Not available. [1] See text, section 21, for definition of Class I. [2] Average midmonth count. [3] Represents the aggregate length of roadway of all line-haul railroads. Excludes yard tracks, sidings, and parallel lines. (Includes estimate for class II and III railroads). [4] Includes multiple main tracks, yard tracks, and sidings owned by both line-haul and switching and terminal. (Includes estimate for class II and III railroads). [5] Includes cars owned by all railroads, private car companies, and shippers. [6] Class I railroads only. [7] Includes State income taxes. [8] Includes payroll, income, and other taxes. [9] Revenue and nonrevenue freight. [10] Source: Federal Railroad Admin., *Accident Bulletin*, annual. Includes highway grade crossing casualties.

Source: Except as noted, Association of American Railroads, Washington, DC, *Railroad Facts, Statistics of Railroads of Class I*, annual, and *Analysis of Class I Railroads*, annual.

No. 1033. Railroads, Class I-Cars of Revenue Freight Loaded, 1970 to 1995, and by Commodity Group, 1994 and 1995

[In thousands. Figures are 52-week totals. N.e.c.= Not elsewhere classified]

YEAR	CARLOADS		COMMODITY GROUP	CARLOADS		COMMODITY GROUP	CARLOADS	
	Total	Piggy-back		1994	1995		1994	1995
1970 . .	27,160	1,450	Coal	6,477	6,600	Metals and products	566	571
1975 . .	23,217	1,308	Metallic ores	436	463	Stone, clay, and glass products . .	491	499
1980 . .	22,598	1,661	Chemicals, allied products. . . .	1,547	1,585	Crushed stone, gravel, sand	661	674
1985 . .	19,574	2,863	Grain.	1,312	1,496	Nonmetalic minerals, n.e.c	464	481
1990 . .	16,177	(NA)	Motor vehicles and equipment .	1,095	1,099	Waste and scrap materials	503	519
1992 . .	15,798	(NA)	Pulp, paper, allied products . . .	520	543	Lumber, wood products, n.e.c. [1] . .	296	265
1993 . .	15,911	(NA)	Primary forest products.	397	392	Coke.	293	287
1994 . .	16,763	(NA)	Food and kindred prod., n.e.c. .	482	475	Petroleum product	267	273
1995 . .	17,181	(NA)	Grain mill products.	534	541	All other carloads	423	418

NA Not available. [1] Excludes furniture.

Source: Association of American Railroads, Washington, DC, *Weekly Railroad Traffic*, annual.

No. 1034. Railroads, Class I Line-Haul-Revenue Freight Originated, by Commodity Group: 1980 to 1994

[See *Historical Statistics, Colonial Times to 1970*, series Q 332, for total carloads originated]

COMMODITY GROUP	1980	1985	1988	1989	1990	1991	1992	1993	1994
Carloads (1,000) [1]	**22,223**	**19,501**	**21,600**	**21,226**	**21,401**	**20,868**	**21,205**	**21,683**	**23,179**
Coal.	5,789	5,684	5,621	5,672	5,912	5,683	5,572	5,310	5,681
Farm products	1,866	1,494	1,977	1,781	1,689	1,605	1,646	1,636	1,459
Chemicals, allied products	1,322	1,296	1,497	1,486	1,531	1,556	1,568	1,606	1,695
Food and kindred products	1,767	1,224	1,318	1,284	1,307	1,316	1,352	1,380	1,381
Nonmetallic minerals [2]	1,474	1,196	1,290	1,254	1,202	1,075	1,029	1,044	1,138
Transportation equipment	1,004	1,202	1,160	1,141	1,091	1,068	1,181	1,355	1,448
Lumber and wood products [3]	1,384	948	910	843	780	716	726	710	771
Pulp, paper, allied products	954	703	646	615	611	616	618	620	651
Petroleum and coal products	596	491	568	561	573	533	583	584	602
Stone, clay, and glass products. . .	776	551	577	565	539	479	483	487	512
Metallic ores	1,258	511	582	523	508	499	489	443	440
Primary metal products	756	449	479	452	477	469	481	528	579
Waste and scrap materials	632	429	471	444	439	433	487	558	604
Machinery, exc. electrical.	77	35	40	38	39	39	39	37	40
Fabricated metal products [4]	72	31	26	27	31	34	32	37	37
Tons (mil.) [1].	**1,492**	**1,320**	**1,429**	**1,403**	**1,425**	**1,383**	**1,399**	**1,397**	**1,470**
Coal.	522	538	543	551	579	560	554	534	574
Farm products	156	127	170	154	147	144	149	147	131
Chemicals, allied products	108	106	123	123	126	127	130	134	142
Nonmetallic minerals [2]	125	108	115	111	109	99	94	96	106
Food and kindred products	92	74	81	79	81	83	86	88	88
Lumber and wood products [3]	86	63	62	57	53	48	50	49	54
Metallic ores	105	47	52	47	47	45	45	41	40
Stone, clay, and glass products. . .	54	44	46	47	44	39	40	40	42
Petroleum and coal products	38	33	39	39	40	37	41	41	43
Primary metal products	53	34	38	36	38	37	39	43	47
Pulp, paper, allied products	42	36	35	34	33	33	34	34	37
Waste and scrap materials.	34	26	30	28	28	27	30	35	37
Transportation equipment	24	27	25	24	23	22	25	29	30
Machinery, exc. electrical.	2	1	1	1	1	1	1	1	1
Fabricated metal products [4]	2	1	1	1	1	1	1	1	1
Gross revenue (mil. dol.) [1].	**26,938**	**28,225**	**29,529**	**29,328**	**29,775**	**29,319**	**29,777**	**30,376**	**32,424**
Coal.	4,956	6,556	6,430	6,581	6,954	6,903	6,717	6,481	7,021
Chemicals, allied products	2,946	3,342	3,795	3,788	3,933	4,043	4,123	4,277	4,520
Transportation equipment	1,917	3,110	3,218	3,269	3,100	2,633	2,753	3,021	3,257
Farm products	2,801	1,977	2,534	2,444	2,422	2,332	2,454	2,528	2,407
Food and kindred products	2,837	2,256	2,198	2,128	2,188	2,254	2,308	2,336	2,427
Pulp, paper, allied products [3]	1,652	1,641	1,540	1,514	1,486	1,502	1,508	1,511	1,510
Lumber and wood products [3]	1,543	1,525	1,626	1,500	1,390	1,282	1,342	1,324	1,421
Primary metal products	1,332	872	1,013	972	979	977	970	1,021	1,114
Stone, clay, and glass products. . .	1,025	960	965	960	931	878	911	944	1,009
Petroleum and coal products	865	861	903	917	918	888	943	929	967
Nonmetallic minerals [2]	948	949	890	868	885	824	812	818	862
Waste and scrap materials.	513	446	526	492	504	515	558	613	655
Metallic ores	597	403	415	397	408	400	409	385	378
Machinery, exc. electrical.	176	72	63	66	67	62	61	59	65
Fabricated metal products [4]	110	48	38	38	42	48	45	50	50

[1] Includes commodity groups and small packaged freight shipments, not shown separately. [2] Except fuels. [3] Except furniture. [4] Except ordnance, machinery, and transport.

Source: Association of American Railroads, Washington, DC, *Freight Commodity Statistics*, annual.

No. 1035. Railroad Freight—Producer Price Indexes: 1980 to 1994

[**Dec. 1984=100.** Reflects prices for shipping a fixed set of commodities under specified and unchanging conditions]

COMMODITY	1980	1985	1987	1988	1989	1990	1991	1992	1993	1994
Total railroad freight	**75.9**	**99.9**	**100.1**	**104.8**	**106.4**	**107.5**	**109.3**	**109.9**	**110.9**	**111.8**
Coal	75.8	100.0	100.1	104.3	105.3	104.2	105.2	105.9	106.6	107.5
Farm products	75.6	99.0	99.3	105.5	108.5	110.4	111.4	111.1	113.7	114.5
Food products	75.2	100.0	98.6	103.1	103.9	105.4	108.1	108.7	109.0	111.0
Metallic ores	74.5	100.2	99.0	103.9	105.8	106.5	106.7	106.6	106.7	104.6
Chemicals or allied products	75.6	100.1	100.8	106.9	110.0	111.7	113.5	115.6	116.2	117.6
Nonmetallic minerals	72.2	100.1	101.1	106.1	108.3	111.7	115.9	117.6	119.3	119.7
Wood or lumber products	72.7	100.0	100.4	105.3	105.9	107.5	108.6	108.8	109.7	110.0
Transportation equipment	81.7	100.0	99.3	103.4	106.4	107.5	109.7	110.8	113.1	115.3
Pulp, paper, or allied products	76.7	100.0	100.6	104.0	105.1	108.0	111.5	111.8	112.6	111.1
Primary metal products	77.8	99.7	99.7	108.8	112.3	113.1	116.1	117.5	116.3	115.6
Clay, concrete, glass, or stone products	74.2	100.0	102.2	107.5	110.5	114.1	117.1	116.5	117.9	120.1

Source: U.S. Bureau of Labor Statistics, *Producer Price Indexes*, monthly and annual.

No. 1036. Petroleum Pipeline Companies—Characteristics: 1980 to 1994

[Covers pipeline companies operating in interstate commerce and subject to jurisdiction of Federal Energy Regulatory Commission]

ITEM	Unit	1980	1985	1988	1989	1990	1991	1992	1993	1994
Miles of pipeline, total	1,000	173	171	171	169	168	172	164	164	159
Gathering lines	1,000	36	35	34	33	32	31	29	29	30
Trunk lines	1,000	136	136	136	135	136	141	136	135	128
Total deliveries	Mil. bbl	10,600	10,745	11,484	11,281	11,378	11,496	11,447	12,219	12,159
Crude oil	Mil. bbl	6,405	6,239	6,509	6,435	6,563	6,685	6,541	6,708	6,785
Products	Mil. bbl	4,195	4,506	4,974	4,847	4,816	4,811	4,906	5,511	5,373
Total trunk line traffic	Bil. bbl-miles	3,405	3,342	3,619	3,505	3,500	3,470	3,428	3,051	3,560
Crude oil	Bil. bbl-miles	1,948	1,842	1,970	1,918	1,891	1,899	1,853	1,382	1,845
Products	Bil. bbl-miles	1,458	1,500	1,649	1,587	1,609	1,571	1,575	1,669	1,715
Carrier property value	Mil. dol	19,752	21,605	24,332	24,638	25,828	26,943	27,106	31,625	26,363
Operating revenues	Mil. dol	6,356	7,461	6,861	6,512	7,149	6,798	7,154	6,931	7,281
Net income	Mil. dol	1,912	2,431	2,505	2,227	2,340	1,788	2,061	1,763	2,148

Source: PennWell Publishing Co., Tulsa, OK, *Oil & Gas Journal*, annual (copyright).

No. 1037. Major Interstate Natural Gas Pipeline Companies—Summary: 1985 to 1991

[The classification of A and B interstate natural gas pipeline companies changed to major companies and nonmajor companies. Major natural gas pipeline companies are those whose combined sales for resale and natural gas transported or stored for a fee exceed 50 billion cubic feet. They account for more than 85 percent of all interstate natural gas]

ITEM	Unit	1985	1986	1987	1988	1989	1990	1991
Sales	Tril. cu. ft	11.3	7.8	6.5	6.4	5.6	4.5	3.9
Residential	Tril. cu. ft	0.3	0.2	0.2	0.3	0.1	0.2	0.2
Commercial, industrial	Tril. cu. ft	1.1	0.5	0.4	0.5	0.5	0.4	0.3
For resale	Tril. cu. ft	9.9	7.1	5.8	5.6	4.9	3.9	3.3
Operating revenues	Mil. dol	49,106	33,859	27,565	27,501	25,695	22,574	21,420
From sales [1]	Mil. dol	44,996	29,508	22,942	22,512	19,786	15,981	14,135
From transportation of gas of others	Mil. dol	2,272	3,027	3,622	4,059	4,959	5,505	6,117
Other	Mil. dol	1,838	1,325	1,002	929	950	1,088	1,167
Operation, maintenance expenses	Mil. dol	42,528	27,460	21,794	22,742	20,829	17,446	17,335
Production	Mil. dol	36,739	22,208	16,955	17,625	15,257	12,124	11,663
Storage	Mil. dol	418	420	409	436	458	417	460
Transmission	Mil. dol	3,409	2,984	2,598	2,589	2,589	2,720	2,880
Distribution	Mil. dol	132	80	80	127	94	112	133
Administrative, general, and other	Mil. dol	1,830	1,768	1,752	1,966	2,430	2,074	2,048
Pipeline mileage	1,000	230.2	217.3	249.5	246.9	253.2	230.2	249.5
Transmission lines	1,000	189.7	184.6	181.2	191.6	194.1	195.5	146.8
Field lines	1,000	69.6	64.5	62.9	55.5	55.1	54.0	50.7
Storage	1,000	4.8	4.6	4.3	4.8	4.8	5.0	4.7

[1] Includes other ultimate customers not shown separately.

Source: U.S. Energy Information Administration, *Statistics of Interstate Natural Gas Pipeline Companies*, annual.

Figure 22.1
**Revenue Passengers Enplaned—
Top 10 Airports: 1994**

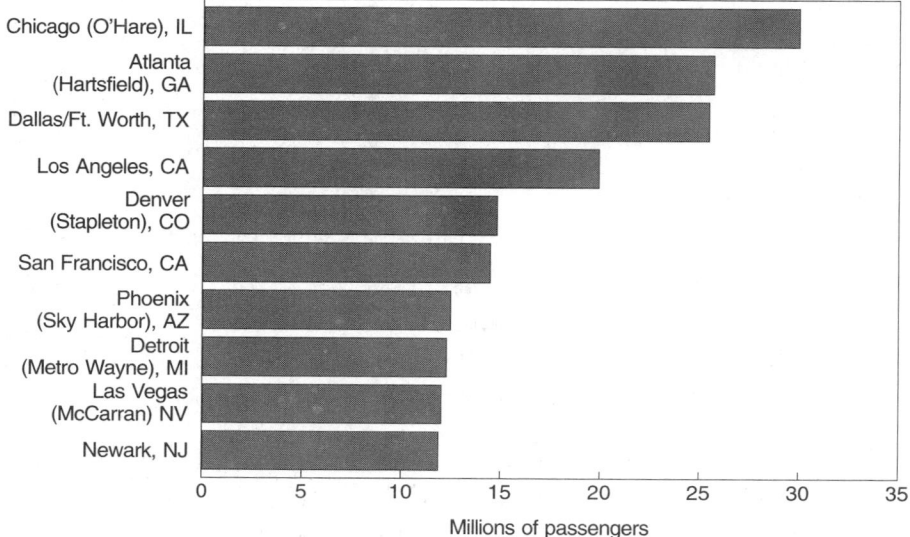

Source: Chart prepared by U.S. Bureau of the Census. For data, see table 1041.

Figure 22.2
**Consumer Complaints Against
U.S. Airlines: 1988 to 1995**

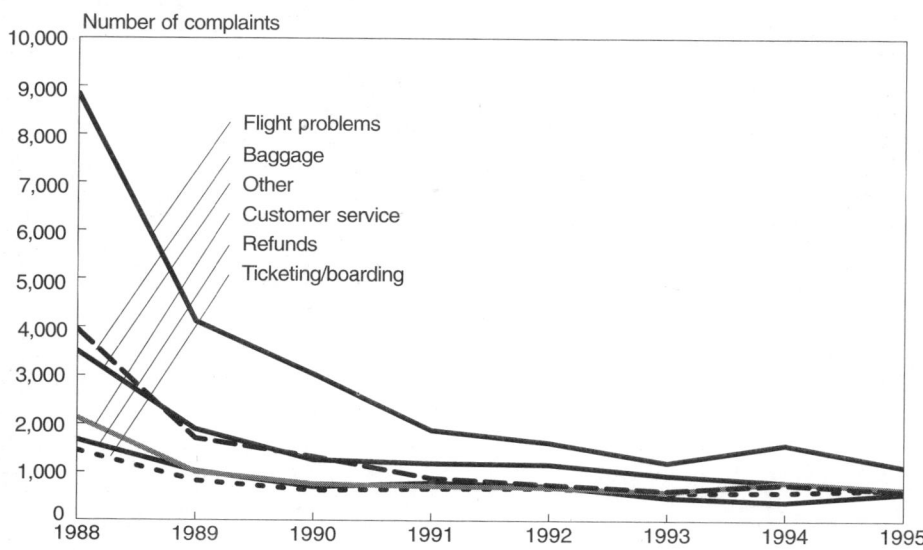

Source: Chart prepared by U.S. Bureau of the Census. For data, see table 1047.

Transportation— Air and Water

This section presents data on civil air transportation, both passenger and cargo, and on water transportation, including inland waterways, oceanborne commerce, the merchant marine, cargo and vessel tonnages, and shipbuilding. Comparative data on various types of transportation carriers are presented in section 21.

Principal sources of these data are the annual *FAA Statistical Handbook of Aviation* issued by the Federal Aviation Administration (FAA); the annual *Waterborne Commerce of the United States* issued by the Corps of Engineers of the Department of the Army; the monthly and annual issues of *U.S. Waterborne Exports and General Imports,* and the annual *Vessel Entrances and Clearances,* and the monthly *Highlights of U.S. Export and Import Trade,* issued by the Bureau of the Census. In addition, the Bureau of the Census in its commodity transportation survey (part of the census of transportation, taken every 5 years, for years ending in "2" and "7") provides data on the type, weight, and value of commodities shipped by manufacturing establishments in the United States, by means of transportation, origin, and destination.

Air transportation data are also presented annually by the Air Transport Association of America, Washington, DC, in *Air Transport Facts and Figures.* Additional sources of data on water transportation include *Merchant Fleets of the World* issued periodically by the U.S. Maritime Administration; *The Bulletin,* issued monthly by the American Bureau of Shipping, New York, NY; and *World Fleet Statistics* and the *Register Book,* published by Lloyd's Register of Shipping, London, England.

Civil aviation—Federal promotion and regulation of civil aviation have been carried out by the FAA and the Civil Aeronautics Board (CAB). The CAB promoted and regulated the civil air transportation industry within the United States and between the United States and foreign

In Brief
SCHEDULED AIR CARRIERS
Revenue passengers enplaned:

1985	382 million
1994	528 million

Net profit:

1985	+$863 million
1994	-$279 million

countries. The Board granted licenses to provide air transportation service, approved or disapproved proposed rates and fares, and approved or disapproved proposed agreements and corporate relationships involving air carriers. In December 1984, the CAB ceased to exist as an agency. Some of its functions were transferred to the Department of Transportation (DOT), as outlined below. The responsibility for investigation of aviation accidents resides with the National Transportation Safety Board.

The Office of the Secretary, DOT aviation activities include the following: negotiation of international air transportation rights, selection of U.S. air carriers to serve capacity controlled international markets, oversight of international rates and fares, maintenance of essential air service to small communities, and consumer affairs. DOT's Bureau of Transportation Statistics (BTS) handles aviation information functions formerly assigned to CAB. Prior to BTS, the Research and Special Programs Administration handled these functions.

The principal activities of the FAA include the promotion of air safety, controlling the use of navigable airspace, prescribing regulations dealing with the competency of airmen, airworthiness of aircraft, and air traffic control, operation of air route traffic control centers, airport traffic control towers, and flight service stations, the design, construction, maintenance, and inspection of navigation, traffic control, and communications equipment, and the development of general aviation.

The CAB published monthly and quarterly financial and traffic statistical data for the certificated route air carriers. BTS continues these publications, including both certificated and noncertificated (commuter) air carriers. The FAA publishes data annually on the use of airway facilities; data related to the location of airmen, aircraft, and airports; the volume of activity in the field of nonair carrier (general aviation) flying; and aircraft production and registration.

General aviation comprises all civil flying (including such commercial operations as small demand air taxis, agriculture application, powerline patrol, etc.) but excludes certificated route air carriers, supplemental operators, large-aircraft commercial operators and commuter airlines.

Air carriers and service—The CAB previously issued "certificates of public convenience and necessity" under Section 401 of the Federal Aviation Act of 1958 for scheduled and nonscheduled (charter) passenger services and cargo services. It also issued certificates under Section 418 of the Act to cargo air carriers for domestic all-cargo service only. The DOT Office of the Secretary now issues the certificates under a "fit, willing, and able" test of air carrier operations. Carriers operating only 60 seat or less aircraft are given exemption authority to carry passengers, cargo, and mail in scheduled and nonscheduled service under Part 298 of the DOT (formerly CAB) regulations. Exemption authority carriers who offer scheduled passenger service to an essential air service point must meet the "fit, willing, and able" test.

Vessel shipments, entrances, and clearances—Shipments by dry cargo vessels comprise shipments on all types of watercraft, except tanker vessels; shipments by tanker vessels comprise all types of cargo, liquid and dry, carried by tanker vessels.

A vessel is reported as entered only at the first port which it enters in the United States, whether or not cargo is unloaded at that port. A vessel is reported as cleared only at the last port at which clearance is made to a foreign port, whether or not it takes on cargo. Army and Navy vessels entering or clearing without commercial cargo are not included in the figures.

Units of measurement—Cargo (or freight) tonnage and shipping weight both represent the gross weight of the cargo including the weight of containers, wrappings, crates, etc. However, shipping weight excludes lift and cargo vans and similar substantial outer containers. Other tonnage figures generally refer to stowing capacity of vessels, 100 cubic feet being called 1 ton. Gross tonnage comprises the space within the frames and the ceiling of the hull, together with those closed-in spaces above deck available for cargo, stores, passengers, or crew, with certain minor exceptions. Net or registered tonnage is the gross tonnage less the spaces occupied by the propelling machinery, fuel, crew quarters, master's cabin, and navigation spaces. Substantially, it represents space available for cargo and passengers. The net tonnage capacity of a ship may bear little relation to weight of cargo. Deadweight tonnage is the weight in long tons required to depress a vessel from light water line (that is, with only the machinery and equipment on board) to load line. It is, therefore, the weight of the cargo, fuel, etc., which a vessel is designed to carry with safety.

Historical statistics—Tabular headnotes provide cross-references, where applicable, to *Historical Statistics of the United States, Colonial Times to 1970.* See Appendix IV.

No. 1038. Air and Water Transportation Industries—Summary: 1992

[For establishments with payroll]

INDUSTRY	1987 SIC [1] Code	Establish-ments	Revenue (mil. dol.)	Annual payroll (mil. dol.)	Paid employees [2] (1,000)
Air transportation [3].............................	45	(NA)	82,670	24,530	707
Air transportation, including air courier services [3].......................	451,2	(NA)	76,503	22,734	627
Scheduled and air courier services [3]...........	451	(NA)	73,070	22,026	604
Scheduled [3]...................	4512	(NA)	62,057	19,090	505
Air courier services..................	4513	2,639	11,013	2,935	99
Nonscheduled......................	452	1,791	3,433	708	23
Airport terminal services.....................	458	3,252	6,168	1,796	80
Water transportation........................	44	8,147	29,207	5,170	171
Water transportation of freight................	441,2,3,4	836	14,704	1,523	37
Deep sea foreign and domestic freight	441, 2	615	11,948	1,148	27
Deep sea foreign freight	4412	334	8,490	629	13
Deep sea domestic freight	4424	281	3,458	519	13
Other water transportation of freight..........	443,4	221	2,756	375	10
Great Lakes-St. Lawrence Seaway freight	4432	26	559	81	1
Water transportation of freight, n.e.c. [4].......	4449	195	2,197	293	9
Water transportation of passengers	448	1,033	4,133	508	23
Ferries...............................	4482	118	155	51	2
Water transportation of passengers, except by ferry	4481,9	915	3,978	457	22
Deep sea transportation, except by ferry ...	4481	72	3,268	275	13
Water transportation of passengers, n.e.c. [4] ...	4489	843	710	182	9
Services incidental to water transportation........	449	6,278	10,370	3,140	111
Marinas.................................	4493	3,348	1,651	346	18
Other services incidental to water transportation ..	4491,2,9	2,930	8,719	2,794	93
Marine cargo handling...................	4491	871	5,066	1,841	59
Towing and tugboat services	4492	941	2,682	689	25
Water transportation services, n.e.c. [4]	4499	1,118	971	263	9

NA Not available.   [1] 1987 Standard Industrial Classification code; see text, section 13.   [2] For the pay period including March 12.   [3] Revenue for scheduled air transportation includes revenues for large certificated passenger carriers that was reported to the Office of Airline Statistics, U.S. Dept. of Transportation, as published in *Air Carrier Financial Statistics Quarterly*.   [4] N.e.c. means not elsewhere classified.
Source: U.S. Bureau of the Census, *Census of Transportation, Communications, and Utilities: 1992*, UC92-A-1.

No. 1039. U. S. Scheduled Airline Industry—Summary: 1985 to 1994

[**For calendar years or Dec. 31.** For domestic and international operations. Covers carriers certificated under Section 401 of the Federal Aviation Act. Minus sign (-) indicates loss]

ITEM	Unit	1985	1988	1989	1990	1991	1992	1993	1994
SCHEDULED SERVICE									
Revenue passengers enplaned .	Mil.	382.0	454.6	453.7	465.6	452.3	475.1	488.5	528.4
Revenue passenger miles......	Bil.....	336.4	423.3	432.7	457.9	448.0	478.6	489.7	519.2
Available seat miles.........	Bil.....	547.8	676.8	684.4	733.4	715.2	752.8	771.6	783.8
Revenue passenger load factor .	Percent .	61.4	62.5	63.2	62.4	62.6	63.6	63.5	66.2
Mean passenger trip length [1]...	Miles ...	881	931	954	984	990	1,007	1,002	983
Freight and express ton miles ..	Mil.	6,030.5	9,632.2	10,275.0	10,546.3	10,225.2	11,129.7	11,943.6	11,720.6
Aircraft departures............	1,000 . .	5,835.5	6,699.6	6,622.1	6,923.6	6,782.8	7,050.6	7,245.4	7,510.5
FINANCES									
Total operating revenue [2] ...	Mil. dol.	46,664	63,749	69,316	76,142	75,159	78,140	84,559	87,568
Passenger revenue.........	Mil. dol.	39,236	50,296	53,802	58,453	57,092	59,829	63,945	64,850
Freight and express revenue...	Mil. dol.	2,681	7,478	6,893	5,432	5,509	5,916	6,662	7,114
Mail revenue	Mil. dol.	890	972	955	970	957	1,184	1,212	1,189
Charter revenue	Mil. dol.	1,280	1,698	2,052	2,877	3,717	2,801	3,082	3,471
Total operating expense	Mil. dol.	45,238	60,312	67,505	78,054	76,943	80,585	83,121	84,801
Operating profit............	Mil. dol.	1,426	3,437	1,811	-1,912	-1,785	-2,445	1,438	2,766
Interest expense...........	Mil. dol.	1,588	1,846	1,944	1,978	1,177	1,743	2,027	2,335
Net profit.................	Mil. dol.	863	1,686	128	-3,921	-1,940	-4,791	-2,136	-279
Revenue per passenger mile...	Cents...	11.7	11.9	12.4	12.8	12.7	12.5	13.1	12.5
Rate of return on investment...	Percent .	9.6	10.8	6.3	-6.0	-0.5	-9.3	-0.4	5.3
Operating profit margin.......	Percent .	3.1	5.4	2.6	-2.5	-2.3	-3.1	1.7	3.2
Net profit margin...........	Percent .	1.8	2.6	0.2	-5.1	-2.6	-6.1	-2.5	-0.3
EMPLOYEES									
Total	1,000 . . .	355	481	507	546	534	540	537	543
Pilots, copilots, and other flight personnel	1,000 . . .	40	52	52	56	56	59	60	61
Flight attendants	1,000 . . .	63	76	78	83	82	86	85	87
Mechanics	1,000 . . .	43	55	57	61	59	59	58	56
Aircraft and traffic servicing personnel	1,000 . . .	101	212	225	252	237	243	243	249
Other	1,000 . . .	108	86	95	94	98	93	92	90

[1] For definition of mean, see Guide to Tabular Presentation.   [2] Includes other types of revenues, not shown separately.
Source: Air Transport Association of America, Washington, DC, *Air Transport*, annual, and *Air Transport, Facts and Figures*, annual.

No. 1040. Airline Cost Indexes: 1980 to 1994

[Covers U.S. major and national service carriers. Major carriers have operating revenues of $1 billion or more; nationals have operating revenues from $75 million to $1 billion. Minus sign (-) indicates decrease]

ITEM	INDEX (1982=100)								PERCENT DISTRIBUTION OF CASH OPERATING EXPENSES [1]			
	1980	1985	1989	1990	1991	1992	1993	1994	1980	1985	1990	1994
INDEX												
Composite	86.3	103.1	102.4	109.0	117.0	124.0	123.3	100.0	100.0	100.0	100.0	100.0
Labor	84.8	111.1	115.0	118.4	121.1	140.7	147.7	35.1	34.9	32.6	34.8	36.0
Interest [2]	88.7	105.5	99.6	111.5	107.3	89.1	94.3	2.9	3.5	2.5	2.6	3.0
Fuel	91.6	81.4	54.2	61.2	78.7	60.8	55.6	29.7	22.3	17.6	12.7	11.7
Passenger food	94.3	102.0	111.9	122.8	132.6	131.6	123.7	2.9	3.2	3.6	3.6	3.5
Advertising and promotion	69.5	99.8	96.9	105.0	107.6	80.3	77.6	1.7	2.3	2.1	1.7	1.6
Landing fees	90.0	101.2	129.1	137.1	148.1	183.1	185.4	1.7	1.7	1.9	2.1	2.2
Passenger traffic commissions	77.3	117.6	148.3	163.4	176.8	200.9	170.3	4.8	7.4	9.8	11.3	10.0
All other	85.6	112.7	123.9	129.4	134.7	147.5	150.5	21.3	24.6	29.9	31.2	32.0
PERCENT CHANGE [3]												
Composite	23.3	0.3	4.1	6.4	7.3	1.6	-0.6	(X)	(X)	(X)	(X)	(X)
Labor	10.0	2.9	4.4	3.0	2.3	4.7	5.0	(X)	(X)	(X)	(X)	(X)
Interest [2]	16.9	-3.2	2.2	11.9	-3.8	5.1	5.8	(X)	(X)	(X)	(X)	(X)
Fuel	55.8	-5.7	-4.6	12.9	28.6	-5.1	-8.6	(X)	(X)	(X)	(X)	(X)
Passenger food	11.9	-4.2	6.0	9.7	8.0	-8.7	-6.0	(X)	(X)	(X)	(X)	(X)
Advertising and promotion	24.3	-0.2	6.6	8.4	2.5	-10.6	-3.4	(X)	(X)	(X)	(X)	(X)
Landing fees	9.6	-0.2	6.3	6.2	8.0	2.0	1.3	(X)	(X)	(X)	(X)	(X)
Passenger traffic commissions	40.0	0.8	15.1	10.2	8.2	4.5	-15.2	(X)	(X)	(X)	(X)	(X)
All other	9.3	3.7	3.9	4.4	4.1	2.2	2.1	(X)	(X)	(X)	(X)	(X)

X Not applicable.   [1] Total operating expenses plus interest on long term debt, less depreciation and amortization. [2] Interest on debt.   [3] Change from immediate prior year.

Source: Air Transport Association of America, Washington, DC, *Air Transport*, annual; and unpublished data.

No. 1041. Top 10 Airports—Traffic Summary: 1994

[In thousands, except percent change. For calendar year. Airports ranked by revenue passengers enplaned. For scheduled carriers only; excludes charter-only carriers]

AIRPORT	Rank	AIRCRAFT DEPARTURES		REVENUE PASSENGERS ENPLANED		ENPLANED REVENUE TONS		
		Total [1]	Completed scheduled	Total	Percent change, 1980-1994	Total	Freight	U.S. mail
All airports [2]	(X)	7,513	7,206	508,458	82.3	8,718	6,802	1,916
Atlanta, Hartsfield International . . .	2	317	315	25,670	28.4	315	198	117
Chicago, O'Hare	1	387	374	29,970	55.9	472	335	137
Dallas/Ft. Worth International	3	371	366	25,435	143.8	275	178	97
Denver International	5	168	166	14,789	53.8	147	91	56
Detroit, Metro Wayne	8	156	152	12,256	143.9	142	92	50
Los Angeles International.	4	203	198	19,885	40.5	493	409	84
Newark International . .	10	146	139	11,864	182.1	341	287	54
Phoenix, Sky Harbor International .	7	157	152	12,452	268.4	95	59	36
San Francisco International	6	134	133	14,452	53.7	280	207	73
Las Vegas McCarran	9	109	108	11,998	159.2	32	16	16

X Not applicable.   [1] Includes completed scheduled and unscheduled.   [2] Includes other airports, not shown separately.

Source: U.S. Federal Aviation Administration and Research and Special Programs Administration, *Airport Activity Statistics*, annual.

No. 1042. Domestic Airline Markets: 1994

[For calendar year. Data are for the 30 top markets and include all commercial airports in each metro area. Data do not include connecting passengers]

MARKET	Passengers	MARKET	Passengers
New York to—from Chicago	2,968,730	Chicago to—from Detroit	1,450,170
New York to—from Los Angeles	2,951,850	New York to—from West Palm Beach. . . .	1,436,150
New York to—from Miami.	2,676,200	Los Angeles to—from Phoenix	1,382,970
New York to—from Boston	2,618,180	Los Angeles to—from Honolulu	1,282,460
Honolulu to—from Kahului, Maui	2,481,440	Los Angeles to—from Oakland	1,254,230
Dallas/Ft. Worth to—from Houston.	2,270,580	Chicago to—from Los Angeles	1,205,220
New York to—from Washington	2,227,950	Honolulu to—from Hilo, Hawaii	1,203,280
Los Angeles to—from San Francisco	2,136,880	Honolulu to—from Kona, Hawaii	1,200,110
New York to—from Orlando	2,072,000	New York to—from Tampa	1,122,790
New York to—from San Francisco	2,023,430	Chicago to—from Denver.	1,100,400
New York to—from Atlanta	1,838,410	Boston to—from Washington.	1,064,620
New York to—from Ft. Lauderdale	1,807,750	Chicago to—from St. Louis.	1,055,640
Los Angeles to—from Las Vegas	1,780,460	San Francisco to—from San Diego	1,049,790
New York to—from San Juan	1,632,980	Chicago to—from Atlanta	1,023,890
Honolulu to—from Lihue, Kauai	1,463,690	Chicago to—from Cleveland	998,120

Source: Air Transport Association of America, Washington, DC, *Air Transport 1995*.

No. 1043. Worldwide Airline Fatalities: 1970 to 1995

[For scheduled air transport operations]

YEAR	Fatal accidents	Passenger deaths	Death rate [1]	Death rate [2]	YEAR	Fatal accidents	Passenger deaths	Death rate [1]	Death rate [2]
1970	29	700	0.29	0.18	1988 [3] ...	28	729	0.07	0.04
1975	20	467	0.13	0.08	1989 [3] ...	27	817	0.07	0.05
1980	22	814	0.14	0.09	1990 [3] ...	25	495	0.04	0.03
1983	20	809	0.13	0.08	1991 [3] ...	30	653	0.06	0.04
1984	16	223	0.03	0.02	1992 [3] ...	29	1,097	0.09	0.06
1985	22	1,066	0.15	0.09	1993 [3] ...	34	936	0.08	0.05
1986 [3] ...	22	546	0.06	0.04	1994 [3][4] ..	28	941	0.07	0.05
1987 [3] ...	26	901	0.09	0.06	1995 [3][4] ..	26	710	0.04	0.03

[1] Rate per 100 million passenger miles flown.   [2] Rate per 100 million passenger kilometers flown.   [3] Includes former USSR which began reporting in 1986.   [4] Preliminary.

Source: International Civil Aviation Organization, Montreal, Canada, *Civil Aviation Statistics of the World,* annual.

No. 1044. Airline Passenger Screening Results: 1980 to 1994

[Calendar year data]

YEAR	Passengers screened (mil.)	WEAPONS DETECTED				PERSONS ARRESTED	
		Firearms		Other [1]	Explosive/ incendiary devices	Carrying firearms/ explosives	Giving false information
		Handguns	Long guns				
1980	585	1,878	36	108	8	1,031	32
1982	630	2,559	57	60	1	1,314	27
1983	709	2,634	67	83	4	1,282	34
1984	776	2,766	98	91	6	1,285	27
1985	993	2,823	90	74	12	1,310	42
1986	1,055	2,981	146	114	11	1,415	89
1987	1,096	3,012	99	141	14	1,581	81
1988	1,055	2,591	74	108	11	1,493	222
1989	1,113	2,397	92	390	26	1,436	83
1990	1,145	2,490	59	304	15	1,336	18
1991	1,015	1,597	47	275	94	893	28
1992	1,111	2,503	105	(NA)	(NA)	1,282	13
1993	1,150	2,707	91	(NA)	(NA)	1,354	31
1994	1,261	2,860	134	(NA)	(NA)	1,433	35

NA Not available.   [1] Though 1991, includes other firearms; beginning 1992, includes stunning guns, chemical agents, martial arts equipment, knives, bludgeons, and other designated items.

Source: U.S. Federal Aviation Administration, *Annual Report to Congress on Civil Aviation Security.*

No. 1045. Aircraft Accidents and Hijackings: 1975 to 1994

[For years ending December 31]

ITEM	Unit	1975	1980	1985	1990	1992	1993	1994
Aircraft accidents: [1] General aviation [2]	Number...	3,995	3,590	2,738	2,214	2,076	2,042	1,989
Fatal	Number...	633	618	498	442	448	399	392
Rate per 100,000 aircraft hours flown	Rate	2.20	1.69	1.75	1.55	1.88	1.78	1.87
Fatalities	Number...	1,252	1,239	955	766	860	737	706
Air carrier, all services [3]	Number...	(NA)	19	22	24	18	23	22
Fatal	Number...	(NA)	1	7	6	4	1	4
Rate per 1,000,000 aircraft miles flown	Rate	(NA)	(Z)	0.002	0.001	0.001	(Z)	0.001
Fatalities	Number...	(NA)	1	526	39	33	1	239
Air carrier, scheduled services	Number...	29	15	17	22	16	22	20
Fatal	Number...	2	-	4	6	4	1	4
Rate per 1,000,000 aircraft miles flown ...	Rate	0.001	-	0.001	0.001	0.001	(Z)	0.001
Fatalities	Number...	122	-	197	39	33	1	239
Commuter air carriers [4]	Number...	48	38	21	15	23	18	10
Fatal	Number...	12	8	7	3	7	4	3
Rate per 1,000,000 aircraft miles flown	Rate	0.07	0.04	0.02	0.01	0.02	0.01	0.01
Fatalities	Number...	28	37	37	6	21	24	25
Air taxis [5]	Number...	152	171	154	106	76	69	84
Fatal	Number...	24	46	35	28	24	19	27
Rate per 100,000 aircraft hours flown	Rate	0.95	1.27	1.36	1.24	1.19	0.80	1.35
Fatalities	Number...	69	105	76	50	70	42	34
Hijacking incidents, worldwide.	Number...	19	39	26	40	12	31	23
U.S. registered aircraft.	Number...	6	21	4	1	-	-	-
Successful [6]	Number...	4	13	2	(NA)	-	-	-
Foreign-registered aircraft.	Number...	13	18	22	39	12	31	23
Successful [6]	Number...	3	9	18	(NA)	(NA)	(NA)	(NA)
Bomb threats:								
U.S. airports.	Number...	449	268	256	448	188	304	250
Explosions	Number...	4	1	-	-	-	-	-
U.S. worldwide and foreign aircraft in U.S.......	Number...	1,853	1,179	372	338	215	248	218
Explosions	Number...	2	1	1	-	-	-	-

- Represents zero.   NA Not available.   Z Rounds to zero.   [1] Data from National Transportation Safety Board.   [2] See text, section 22.   [3] U.S. air carriers operating under 14 CFR 121.   [4] All scheduled service of U.S. air carriers operating under 14 CFR 135.   [5] All nonscheduled service of U.S. air carriers operating under 14 CFR 135.   [6] Hijacker controls flight and reaches destination or objective.

Source: U.S. Federal Aviation Administration, *FAA Statistical Handbook of Aviation,* annual; and unpublished data. Includes data from U.S. Department of Transportation, Research and Special Programs Administration.

No. 1046. On-Time Flight Arrivals and Departures at Major U.S. Airports: 1995

[In percent. Quarterly, based on gate arrival and departure times for domestic scheduled operations in the 48 contiguous States of major U.S. airlines, per DOT reporting rule effective September 1987. All U.S. airlines with 1 percent or more of total U.S. domestic scheduled airline passenger revenues are required to report on-time data. A flight is considered on time if it operated less than 15 minutes after the scheduled time shown in the carrier's computerized reservation system. Cancelled and diverted flights are considered late. Excludes flight operations delayed/cancelled due to aircraft mechanical problems reported on FAA maintenance records (4-5 percent of the reporting airlines' scheduled operations). See source for data on individual airlines]

AIRPORT	ON-TIME ARRIVALS				ON-TIME DEPARTURES			
	1st. qtr.	2d. qtr.	3d. qtr.	4th. qtr.	1st. qtr.	2d. qtr.	3d. qtr.	4th. qtr.
Total, all airports	77.3	79.3	81.8	75.9	81.5	84.4	85.3	79.7
Total 27 major airports.	76.7	78.7	81.5	75.3	79.8	82.9	83.6	77.8
Atlanta, Hartsfield International	78.2	77.4	75.3	67.5	82.2	80.0	79.9	68.6
Boston, Logan International	73.6	76.2	78.2	69.3	81.3	85.7	84.8	76.2
Charlotte, Douglas	78.8	84.4	84.6	79.3	79.6	83.1	83.6	77.9
Chicago, O'Hare	81.4	78.9	80.1	75.5	78.7	80.1	79.2	74.5
Cincinnati International	83.6	84.3	84.1	77.6	84.2	85.5	84.5	78.6
Dallas/Ft. Worth International	74.9	80.8	86.4	80.6	74.8	82.2	85.9	80.6
Denver, Stapleton International	79.2	80.9	84.6	80.2	78.0	83.7	84.8	81.3
Detroit, Metro Wayne	80.4	82.0	82.3	81.2	79.2	80.9	78.1	77.1
Houston Intercontinental	78.5	78.3	85.4	82.3	83.4	83.6	88.2	87.6
Las Vegas, McCarran International	76.3	79.4	83.9	77.2	78.3	82.4	84.8	78.8
Los Angeles International.	68.1	70.1	78.6	65.8	74.6	80.0	82.5	72.2
Miami International.	75.7	77.3	76.3	75.2	82.8	85.5	81.1	82.9
Minneapolis/St. Paul International	82.7	83.7	81.4	79.0	83.3	85.6	83.1	81.1
Newark International.	73.0	73.2	80.4	74.5	80.1	81.3	85.3	79.6
New York, Kennedy International.	72.9	74.6	73.5	71.2	83.7	84.6	80.4	76.3
New York, LaGuardia	79.2	81.4	82.3	79.3	83.0	86.4	87.1	82.2
Orlando International	78.0	78.3	79.6	73.4	85.3	87.5	87.6	84.5
Philadelphia International.	77.6	81.3	81.7	78.7	83.2	85.8	85.5	80.1
Phoenix, Sky Harbor International	75.7	78.4	84.3	78.2	78.2	81.9	84.8	79.7
Pittsburgh, Greater International	78.6	83.1	84.8	77.4	80.2	83.7	83.8	77.7
St. Louis, Lambert	72.2	74.1	82.3	74.9	75.8	78.4	82.7	75.7
Salt Lake City International	80.0	79.4	81.7	71.5	80.2	83.2	82.4	74.8
San Diego International, Lindbergh	74.2	77.5	83.0	76.0	80.6	85.4	88.4	79.8
San Francisco International	65.8	73.7	79.8	65.0	74.3	83.1	84.2	70.5
Seattle-Tacoma International	75.9	78.1	77.9	68.1	84.2	86.6	84.8	79.1
Tampa International	77.4	76.7	77.5	71.6	85.3	85.9	87.2	82.5
Washington National.	78.7	81.1	81.4	78.1	85.3	88.2	88.2	84.2

Source: U.S. Department of Transportation, Office of Consumer Affairs, *Air Travel Consumer Report*, monthly.

No. 1047. Consumer Complaints Against U.S. Airlines: 1987 to 1995

[Calendar year data. See source for data on individual airlines]

COMPLAINT CATEGORY	1987	1988	1989	1990	1991	1992	1993	1994	1995
Total	40,985	21,493	10,553	7,703	6,106	5,639	4,438	5,179	4,629
Flight problems [1]	18,019	8,831	4,111	3,034	1,877	1,624	1,211	1,586	1,133
Customer service [2]	3,888	2,120	1,002	758	714	695	599	805	667
Ticketing/boarding [3]	2,458	1,445	821	624	659	680	577	598	666
Baggage.	7,438	3,938	1,702	1,329	883	752	627	761	628
Refunds	3,313	1,667	1,023	701	783	721	482	393	576
Oversales [4]	2,122	1,353	607	399	301	265	257	301	263
Fares [5]	937	455	341	312	388	573	398	267	185
Advertising	344	141	89	96	96	54	51	94	66
Tours	90	37	22	29	23	12	16	127	18
Smoking.	888	546	232	74	30	25	30	20	15
Credit.	101	35	19	5	10	10	4	2	4
Other.	1,387	925	584	342	342	228	186	225	408

[1] Cancellations, delays, etc. from schedule.　　[2] Unhelpful employees, inadequate meals or cabin service, treatment of delayed passengers.　　[3] Errors in reservations and ticketing; problems in making reservations and obtaining tickets.　　[4] All bumping problems, whether or not airline complied with DOT regulations.　　[5] Incorrect or incomplete information about fares, discount fare conditions, and availability, etc.

Source: U.S. Dept. of Transportation, Office of Consumer Affairs, *Air Travel Consumer Report*, monthly.

No. 1048. Commuter/Regional Airline Operations—Summary: 1980 to 1994

[**Calendar year data.** Commuter/regional airlines operate primarily aircraft of predominately 75 passengers or less and 18,000 pounds of payload capacity serving short haul and small community markets. Represents operations within all North America by U.S. Regional Carriers. Averages are means. For definition of mean, see Guide to Tabular Presentation]

ITEM	Unit	1980	1985	1989	1990	1991	1992	1993	1994
Passenger carriers operating	Number.	214	179	151	150	144	127	130	125
Passengers enplaned	Millions .	14.8	[1]26.0	37.4	42.1	42.0	48.9	52.7	57.1
Average passengers enplaned per carrier. .	1,000 . .	69.2	152.4	247.4	277.5	291.4	385.0	405.2	456.9
Revenue passenger miles (RPM)	Billions .	1.92	[1]4.41	6.77	7.61	7.80	9.46	10.61	12.02
Average RPM's per carrier.	Millions .	8.97	[1]24.64	44.84	50.75	54.18	74.50	81.59	96.15
Airports served	Number.	732	854	817	811	811	802	829	805
Average trip length	Miles. . .	129	173	181	183	186	194	201	210
Passenger aircraft operated	Number.	1,339	1,745	1,907	1,917	1,992	2,103	2,208	2,172
Average seating capacity (seats).	Number.	13.9	19.2	21.8	22.1	22.8	23.4	23.0	23.7
Fleet flying hours	1,000 . .	1,740	2,854	3,266	3,447	3,671	4,259	4,490	4,565
Average annual utilization aircraft	Hours . .	1,299	1,635	1,712	1,798	1,843	2,025	2,033	2,102

[1] Adjusted to exclude a merger in 1986.
Source: Regional Airline Association, Washington, DC, Annual Report of the Regional Airline Industry (copyright).

No. 1049. Civil Flying—Summary: 1970 to 1994

[As of **Dec. 31** or for years ending **Dec. 31**, except as noted. See also *Historical Statistics, Colonial Times to 1970,* series Q 604-623]

ITEM	Unit	1970	1980	1985	1990	1992	1993	1994
Airports in operation [1]	Number. . .	11,261	15,161	16,318	17,490	17,846	18,317	18,343
Heliports	Number. . .	790	2,336	3,120	4,085	4,323	4,569	4,617
Public	Number. . .	4,260	4,814	5,861	5,078	5,116	5,157	5,137
Private	Number. . .	7,001	10,347	10,457	12,412	12,730	13,160	13,206
Airports with runway lights	Number. . .	3,554	4,738	4,941	4,822	4,831	4,842	4,830
Airports with paved runways.	Number. . .	3,805	5,833	6,721	7,694	7,936	8,186	8,230
Airport Improvement Program [2].	Mil. dol. . . .	50.5	639.0	842.1	1,244.7	1,765.0	1,830.0	1,628.0
Total civil aircraft.	1,000 . . .	154.5	259.4	274.9	275.9	277.0	279.0	281.0
Active aircraft [3].	1,000 . . .	134.5	214.8	215.4	218.9	191.7	183.3	178.0
Air carriers, total [4]	1,000 . . .	2.8	3.8	4.7	6.7	7.3	7.3	7.4
General aviation aircraft [5]	1,000 . . .	131.7	211.0	210.7	212.2	184.4	176.0	170.6
Fixed-wing aircraft: Multi-engine . . .	1,000 . . .	18.4	31.7	33.6	32.7	27.3	24.6	23.8
Single-engine.	1,000 . . .	109.5	168.4	164.4	165.1	143.5	130.7	123.3
Rotorcraft [6].	1,000 . . .	2.2	6.0	6.4	7.4	5.8	4.5	4.4
Balloons, blimps, gliders, etc	1,000 . . .	1.6	5.0	6.3	7.0	7.8	5.2	6.2
Airman certificates held	1,000 . . .	1,002	1,195	1,105	1,195	1,224	1,225	1,225
Pilot [7]	1,000 . . .	733	827	710	703	683	665	654
Held by women	Percent . . .	4.0	6.4	6.1	5.8	5.9	5.9	5.9
Airline transport	1,000 . . .	34	70	83	108	116	117	117
Commercial	1,000 . . .	187	183	152	149	146	143	139
Private	1,000 . . .	304	357	311	299	288	284	284
Student	1,000 . . .	196	200	147	128	115	104	96
Nonpilot [8]	1,000 . . .	269	368	395	492	541	560	571
Ground technicians [9]	1,000 . . .	241	321	341	421	478	485	498
FAA employees: Total	Number. . .	53,125	55,340	47,245	51,269	53,871	52,680	48,932
Air traffic control specialists [10].	Number. . .	(NA)	27,190	23,580	24,339	24,983	24,630	23,628
Full performance [11]	Number. . .	(NA)	16,317	11,672	12,985	14,377	14,931	14,997
Developmental [11]	Number. . .	(NA)	4,387	4,304	5,042	3,759	3,040	2,548
Assistants [11].	Number. . .	(X)	(X)	1,465	1,153	792	632	507
Traffic management coordinators [12] . .	Number. . .	(X)	(X)	(X)	370	471	482	544
Electronic technicians/ATSS [13]	Number. . .	(NA)	8,871	6,856	6,458	6,572	6,262	6,531
Aviation safety inspectors	Number. . .	(NA)	2,038	1,897	2,984	3,017	2,920	2,813
Engineers	Number. . .	(NA)	2,436	2,457	2,745	3,208	3,198	2,891
Other	Number. . .	(NA)	14,805	12,445	14,743	16,091	15,670	13,069
General aviation: [5]								
Hours flown	Million	26.0	41.0	34.1	34.8	26.5	24.3	23.9
Fuel consumed: [14]								
Gasoline.	Mil. gal. . . .	362	520	420	353	314	268	264
Jet fuel [15].	Mil. gal. . . .	415	766	691	663	494	454	471

NA Not available. X Not applicable. [1] Existing airports, heliports, seaplane bases, etc. recorded with FAA. Includes military airports with joint civil and military use. Includes U.S. outlying areas. Airport-type definitions: Public—publicly owned and under control of a public agency; private—owned by a private individual or corporation. May or may not be open for public use. [2] Fiscal year data. Does not include System Planning Grants. Includes U.S. outlying areas. 1970-1980 data is obligated Federal funds for the Airport Development Aid Program. Thereafter, data are appropriated Federal funds under the Airport and Airway Improvement Act of 1982. [3] Registered aircraft that flew 1 or more hours during the year. [4] Includes helicopters. [5] See text, section 22. Beginning 1993, excludes commuters and includes experimental aircraft, not shown separately. Prior to 1993, experimental aircraft were included in the appropriate type. [6] Includes autogyros; excludes air carrier helicopters. [7] Includes all active pilots. An active pilot is one with a pilot certificate and a valid medical certificate. Also includes pilots who hold only a helicopter, glider, or lighter than air certificate, not shown separately. [8] Includes dispatchers, flight navigators and engineers, and ground technicians—mechanics, parachute riggers, and ground instructors. [9] No medical examinations are required, therefore, data represent all certificates on record and include retired or otherwise inactive technicians. [10] Includes all air traffic control specialists (staff positions, managers, supervisors, and for 1970-1985 traffic management coordinators, not shown separately) and air traffic assistants. [11] Serving in-flight service stations, towers, and centers. [12] Prior to 1990, included in total air traffic control specialists. [13] Airway Transportation Systems Specialists [14] Source: 1970, U.S. Bureau of Mines; thereafter, FAA General Aviation Activity and Avionics Survey. [15] Includes kerosene-type and naphtha-type jet fuels.

Source: Except as noted, U.S. Federal Aviation Administration, *FAA Statistical Handbook of Aviation,* annual; and unpublished data. Includes data from U.S. Department of Transportation, Research and Special Programs Administration.

No. 1050. Net Orders for U.S. Civil Jet Transport Aircraft: 1985 to 1995

[Value in millions of dollars. 1985-1992 are net new firm orders; beginning 1993, net announced orders. Minus sign (-) indicates net cancellations]

TYPE OF AIRCRAFT AND CUSTOMER	1985	1990	1991	1992	1993	1994	1995
Total number [1]	468	670	280	231	31	79	421
U.S. customers	242	259	36	82	44	12	138
Foreign customers	226	411	244	149	-13	67	283
Boeing 737, total	253	189	75	91	-34	49	189
U.S. customers	146	38	-8	43	-29	9	85
Foreign customers	107	151	83	48	-5	40	104
Boeing 747, total	37	153	48	41	-25	-5	35
U.S. customers	13	24	-5	-	-25	-1	2
Foreign customers	24	129	53	41	-	-4	33
Boeing 757, total	51	66	80	7	20	5	-7
U.S. customers	39	33	42	29	46	-1	-6
Foreign customers	12	33	38	-22	-26	6	-1
Boeing 767, total	10	60	58	20	43	27	26
U.S. customers	4	23	28	10	41	11	4
Foreign customers	6	37	30	10	2	16	22
Boeing 777, total	-	34	52	36	29	-	83
U.S. customers	-	34	-	-	5	-	-
Foreign customers	-	-	52	36	24	-	83
McDonnell Douglas MD-11, total	-	52	-31	1	-1	2	-6
U.S. customers	-	16	-26	4	-	2	3
Foreign customers	-	36	-5	-3	-1	-	-9
McDonnell Douglas MD-80/90, total	114	116	-2	35	-1	1	51
U.S. customers	37	91	5	-4	6	-8	-
Foreign customers	77	25	-7	39	-7	9	51
McDonnell Douglas MD-95, total	-	-	-	-	-	-	50
U.S. customers	-	-	-	-	-	-	50
Foreign customers	-	-	-	-	-	-	-
Total value	14,811	45,485	23,351	16,640	(NA)	(NA)	(NA)
U.S. customers	7,869	14,828	2,144	3,200	(NA)	(NA)	(NA)
Foreign customers	6,942	30,657	21,207	13,440	(NA)	(NA)	(NA)

- Represents zero.   NA Not available.   [1] Includes types of aircraft not shown separately.
Source: Aerospace Industries Association of America, Washington, DC, Research Center, Statistical Series 23.

No. 1051. U.S. Aircraft Shipments With Projections: 1970 to 1994

[Value in millions of dollars]

YEAR	TOTAL		CIVIL						MILITARY	
	Units	Value	Large transports		General Aviation [1]		Helicopters		Units	Value
			Units	Value	Units	Value	Units	Value		
1970	11,632	7,511	311	3,158	7,292	337	495	49	3,534	3,967
1975	16,958	9,355	285	4,006	14,056	1,033	838	266	1,779	4,050
1980	14,660	18,845	383	9,793	11,877	2,486	1,353	674	1,047	5,892
1985	3,597	29,312	273	9,375	2,029	1,431	376	505	919	18,001
1989	3,675	34,228	398	15,074	1,535	1,803	515	251	1,227	17,100
1990	3,486	39,206	521	22,215	1,144	2,007	603	254	1,218	14,730
1991	2,934	40,776	589	26,856	1,021	1,968	571	211	753	11,741
1992 [2]	2,507	41,832	610	30,268	941	1,840	324	142	632	9,582
1993 [2]	2,282	37,108	408	26,456	964	2,144	260	122	650	8,386
1994 [3]	2,146	30,589	306	20,437	960	2,150	260	82	620	7,920

[1] Excludes off-the-shelf military aircraft.   [2] Estimated.   [3] Forecast.
Source: U.S. Department of Commerce, International Trade Administration, U.S. Industrial Outlook, 1994; and unpublished data.

No. 1052. Employment and Earnings in Aircraft Industries: 1985 to 1995

[Annual averages of monthly figures. See headnote, table 652]

ITEM	1987 SIC [1] code	Unit	1985	1990	1993	1994	1995
Employment: Total	(X)	1,000 . . .	794	898	665	589	549
Aircraft	3721	1,000 . . .	326	381	301	271	244
Aircraft engines and engine parts.	3724	1,000 . . .	148	152	109	95	93
Aircraft equipment, n.e.c. [2]	3728	1,000 . . .	143	180	131	115	113
Guided missiles, space vehicles, and parts . .	376	1,000 . . .	177	185	124	108	99
Average weekly earnings: [3]							
Aircraft	3721	Dollars . .	(NA)	(NA)	(NA)	(NA)	(NA)
Aircraft engines and parts.	3724	Dollars . .	542	637	715	753	(NA)
Guided missiles, space vehicles, and parts . .	376	Dollars . .	515	612	696	738	765
Average hourly earnings: [3]							
Aircraft [4]	3721	Dollars . .	13.18	15.66	18.43	19.50	19.97
Aircraft engines and parts.	3724	Dollars . .	12.85	14.84	16.70	17.31	(NA)
Guided missiles, space vehicles, and parts . .	376	Dollars . .	12.14	14.39	16.80	17.48	17.75

NA Not available.   X Not applicable.   [1] 1987 Standard Industrial Classification; see text, section 13.   [2] N.e.c. means not elsewhere classified.   [3] For production workers.   [4] Excludes lump-sum payments. Earnings which include proration of lump-sum payments were: $13.40 in 1985; $16.32 in 1990; $19.00 in 1993; $19.57 in 1994; and $20.02 in 1995.
Source: U.S. Bureau of Labor Statistics, Bulletins 2445 and 2481; and Employment and Earnings, monthly, March and June issues.

No. 1053. Aerospace—Sales, New Orders, and Backlog: 1980 to 1994

[In billions of dollars, except as indicated. Reported by establishments in which the principal business is the development and/or production of aerospace products]

ITEM	1980	1985	1987	1988	1989 [1]	1990 [1]	1991 [1]	1992 [1]	1993 [1]	1994 [1]
Net sales.	58.4	100.5	110.3	113.5	122.1	136.6	123.9	118.7	108.1	100.3
Percent U.S. Government	45.6	63.2	62.2	60.0	58.0	54.0	48.9	50.0	48.8	54.8
Complete aircraft and parts [2]	22.6	34.2	37.0	35.7	38.4	49.9	52.9	54.0	46.1	40.2
Aircraft engines and parts	6.9	9.7	12.0	15.0	15.4	16.4	15.6	13.7	12.2	10.8
Missiles and space vehicles, parts . . .	8.4	16.7	20.7	21.5	22.6	22.0	23.3	21.3	19.1	18.2
Other products, services	20.5	39.8	40.5	41.3	45.7	48.3	32.0	29.7	30.7	31.1
Net, new orders	70.4	111.0	121.2	147.1	173.6	146.0	122.5	100.3	76.5	87.0
Backlog, Dec. 31	90.5	143.0	158.7	191.5	252.4	250.1	245.2	236.1	207.1	183.5

[1] Data beginning 1989 are not comparable with earlier years. Data are being reported which were previously not available. The extent of this noncomparability is not known.   [2] Except engines sold separately.

Source: U.S. Bureau of the Census, *Current Industrial Reports*, series MA-37D.

No. 1054. Aerospace Industry Sales, by Product Group and Customer: 1985 to 1996

[In billions of dollars. Due to reporting practices and tabulating methods, figures may differ from those in table 1053]

ITEM	CURRENT DOLLARS					CONSTANT (1987) DOLLARS [3]				
	1985	1990	1994	1995 [1]	1996 [2]	1985	1990	1994	1995 [1]	1996 [2]
Total sales.	**96.6**	**134.4**	**111.2**	**107.1**	**110.6**	**97.8**	**121.6**	**90.9**	**85.4**	**85.7**
PRODUCT GROUP										
Aircraft, total	50.5	71.4	58.1	54.5	58.8	51.1	64.6	47.5	43.5	45.5
Civil [4]	13.7	31.3	26.0	23.6	29.2	13.9	28.3	21.2	18.8	22.6
Military	36.8	40.1	32.1	30.9	29.6	37.2	36.3	26.3	24.7	22.9
Missiles	11.4	14.2	7.9	7.3	5.7	11.6	12.8	6.5	5.9	4.4
Space	18.6	26.4	26.7	27.1	28.1	18.8	23.9	21.8	21.6	21.7
Related products and services [5] . .	16.1	22.4	18.6	18.2	18.1	16.3	20.3	15.2	14.5	14.0
CUSTOMER GROUP										
Aerospace, total	80.5	112.0	92.7	88.9	92.5	81.5	101.3	75.8	70.9	71.7
DOD [6]	53.2	60.5	44.0	42.0	39.0	53.9	54.8	36.0	33.5	30.2
NASA [7] and other agencies . . .	6.3	11.1	11.9	11.0	10.8	6.3	10.0	9.8	8.8	8.4
Other customers [8]	21.0	40.4	36.7	35.9	42.6	21.3	36.5	30.0	28.6	33.0
Related products and services [5] . .	16.1	22.4	18.6	18.2	18.1	16.3	20.3	15.2	14.5	14.0

[1] Preliminary.   [2] Estimate.   [3] Based on AIA's aerospace composite price deflator.   [4] All civil sales of aircraft (domestic and export sales of jet transports, commuters, business, and personal aircraft and helicopters).   [5] Electronics, software, and ground support equipment, plus sales of non-aerospace products which are produced by aerospace-manufacturing use technology, processes, and materials derived from aerospace products.   [6] Department of Defense.   [7] National Aeronautics and Space Administration.   [8] Includes civil aircraft sales (see footnote 4), commercial space sales, all exports of military aircraft and missiles and related propulsion and parts.

Source: Aerospace Industries Association of America, Inc., Washington, DC, *1995 Year-end Review and Forecast.*

No. 1055. Aerospace Industry—Net Profits After Taxes: 1980 to 1995

[For calendar year. Minus sign (-) indicates loss]

YEAR	AEROSPACE INDUSTRY PROFITS				ALL MANUFACTURING CORPORATIONS PROFITS AS A PERCENT OF—		
	Total (mil. dol.)	As percent of—			Sales	Assets	Equity
		Sales	Assets	Equity			
1980	2,588	4.3	5.2	16.0	4.8	6.9	13.9
1982	2,193	3.3	3.7	12.0	3.5	4.5	9.2
1983	2,829	3.5	4.1	12.1	4.1	5.1	10.5
1984	3,639	4.1	4.7	14.1	4.6	6.0	12.5
1985	3,274	3.1	3.6	11.1	3.8	4.6	10.1
1986	3,093	2.8	3.1	9.4	3.7	4.2	9.5
1987	4,582	4.1	4.4	14.6	4.9	5.6	12.8
1988	4,883	4.3	4.4	14.9	6.0	6.9	16.2
1989	3,866	3.3	3.3	10.7	5.0	5.6	13.7
1990	4,487	3.4	3.4	11.5	4.0	4.3	10.7
1991	[1]2,484	1.8	1.9	6.1	2.5	2.6	6.4
1992	[1]-1,836	-1.4	-1.2	-5.2	1.0	1.0	2.6
1993	4,621	3.6	3.5	13.2	2.8	2.9	8.1
1994	5,655	4.7	4.3	14.8	5.4	5.8	15.6
1995, prel.	4,635	3.8	3.5	11.1	5.7	6.2	16.3

[1] Reflects unusually large nonoperating expenses totalling $3.4 billion in 1991 and $8.7 billion in 1992 due to the initial implementation of a change in accounting for future retirement benefit costs and defense-downsizing restructuring charges. Many large aerospace corporations chose to write off against first quarter earnings amounts required to comply with FASB 106.

Source: Aerospace Industries Association of America, Washington, DC, *1995 Year-end Review and Forecast.*

No. 1056. U.S. Exports of Aerospace Vehicles and Equipment: 1990 to 1993

ITEM	NUMBER OF UNITS				VALUE (mil. dol.)			
	1990	1991	1992	1993 [1]	1990	1991	1992	1993 [1]
Aerospace vehicles and equipment .	(NA)	(NA)	(NA)	(NA)	39,083	43,796	45,030	39,426
Civilian aircraft	3,779	3,329	2,086	1,758	18,148	22,388	24,337	19,845
Under 4,536 kg. unladen weight, new .	1,134	911	586	555	324	311	297	234
4,536-15,000 kg. unladen weight, new .	79	69	60	58	245	279	295	324
Over 15,000 kg. unladen weight, new .	306	385	387	276	16,691	20,881	22,379	18,146
Rotocraft, new.	349	318	212	175	161	168	118	120
Nonpowered aircraft, new	(NA)	(NA)	(NA)	(NA)	15	15	7	9
Used or rebuilt.	1,911	1,646	841	694	712	734	1,241	1,012
Military aircraft, new and used	445	490	428	632	1,481	1,784	2,083	1,460
Aircraft engines and parts	(NA)	(NA)	(NA)	(NA)	6,883	7,049	6,699	6,278
Piston engines and parts.	(NA)	(NA)	(NA)	(NA)	421	417	315	294
Complete engines, new and used . .	6,411	7,812	7,278	7,613	110	111	104	123
Engine parts	(NA)	(NA)	(NA)	(NA)	311	306	211	172
Turbine engines and parts	(NA)	(NA)	(NA)	(NA)	6,462	6,632	6,384	5,984
Complete engines, new and used . .	24,687	17,565	18,540	17,088	1,856	2,229	2,484	2,409
Engine parts	(NA)	(NA)	(NA)	(NA)	4,606	4,403	3,900	3,575
Propellers, rotors, and parts	(NA)	(NA)	(NA)	(NA)	343	317	289	308
Landing gear and parts	(NA)	(NA)	(NA)	(NA)	276	333	362	338
Aircraft parts and accessories, n.e.c. [2] . .	(NA)	(NA)	(NA)	(NA)	8,982	9,386	8,496	8,574
Guided missiles and parts.	(NA)	(NA)	(NA)	(NA)	1,306	1,204	1,428	1,231
Flight simulators	(NA)	(NA)	(NA)	(NA)	255	245	205	197
Space vehicles and parts	(NA)	(NA)	(NA)	(NA)	660	308	336	548
Avionics.	(NA)	(NA)	(NA)	(NA)	747	780	795	646

NA Not available.   [1] Estimated.   [2] N.e.c.=Not elsewhere classified.
Source: U.S. Dept. of Commerce, International Trade Administration, *U.S. Industrial Outlook, 1994;* and unpublished data.

No. 1057. International Transportation Transactions of the United States, by Type: 1980 to 1995

[In millions of dollars. Data are international transportation transactions recorded for balance of payment purposes (see table 1283). Receipts include freight on exports carried by U.S.-operated carriers and foreign carrier expenditures in U.S. ports. Payments include freight on imports carried by foreign carriers and U.S. carrier port expenditures abroad. Freight on exports carried by foreign carriers is excluded since such payments are directly or indirectly for foreign account. Similarly, freight on U.S. imports carried by U.S. carriers is a domestic rather than an international transaction. Minus sign (-) indicates excess of payments over receipts. See *Historical Statistics, Colonial Times to 1970,* series U 3 and U 10, for totals]

ITEM	1980	1985	1989	1990	1991	1992	1993	1994	1995 [1]
Total receipts	**14,209**	**19,085**	**31,764**	**38,043**	**39,185**	**40,309**	**40,594**	**43,555**	**46,767**
Ocean passenger fares	(Z)	60	132	154	156	176	237	192	192
Other ocean transportation	7,757	8,846	11,704	12,141	12,252	12,403	12,437	13,452	15,046
Freight	3,229	3,440	3,896	4,104	4,011	3,980	3,998	4,537	5,300
Port expenditures	4,435	5,274	7,609	7,815	8,041	8,267	8,335	8,859	9,678
Charter hire	93	132	199	222	200	156	104	56	68
Air passenger fares [2]	2,591	4,351	10,526	15,144	15,698	16,442	16,374	17,285	18,021
Other air transportation	3,355	5,347	7,890	8,878	9,256	9,206	9,420	10,314	11,140
Freight	742	706	1,719	2,432	2,722	2,589	2,856	3,241	3,658
Port expenditures	2,613	4,641	5,591	5,742	5,834	5,785	5,753	6,209	6,574
Aircraft leasing	(NA)	(NA)	580	704	700	832	811	864	908
Miscellaneous receipts.	506	481	1,512	1,726	1,823	2,082	2,126	2,312	2,368
Total payments.	**15,397**	**22,087**	**30,509**	**35,699**	**35,216**	**36,015**	**37,871**	**41,069**	**42,891**
Ocean passenger fares	268	154	193	248	279	301	341	341	341
Other ocean transportation	8,179	10,698	12,227	13,078	12,276	11,861	12,700	13,943	14,339
Import freight	5,809	8,114	9,391	10,290	9,593	9,269	10,028	10,965	11,206
Port expenditures	1,905	2,048	2,228	2,174	2,093	2,029	2,143	2,465	2,635
Charter hire	465	536	608	614	590	563	529	513	498
Air passenger fares [2]	3,339	6,290	8,056	10,283	9,733	10,255	10,972	12,355	13,044
Other air transportation	3,366	4,719	8,168	10,083	10,742	11,290	11,438	11,675	12,279
Import freight	562	1,666	2,197	2,207	2,257	2,376	2,580	2,914	3,210
Port expenditures	2,804	3,053	5,883	7,674	8,256	8,657	8,597	8,468	8,765
Aircraft leasing	(NA)	(NA)	88	202	229	257	261	293	304
Miscellaneous payments	245	226	1,865	2,007	2,186	2,308	2,420	2,755	2,888
Balance.	**-1,188**	**-3,002**	**1,255**	**2,345**	**3,969**	**4,294**	**2,722**	**2,486**	**3,876**

NA Not available.   Z Less than $500,000.   [1] Preliminary.   [2] Beginning 1990, includes interairline settlements.
Source: U.S. Bureau of Economic Analysis, *Survey of Current Business,* June issues; and unpublished data.

No. 1058. Exports and Imports, by Method of Transport: 1980 to 1994

[Exports are free alongside ship (f.a.s.) value (see text, section 28) for all years; imports are f.a.s. value for 1980 and customs value for other years. Export data include both domestic and foreign; import data for general imports only. For details, see source]

ITEM	Unit	EXPORTS					IMPORTS				
		1980	1985	1990	1993	1994	1980	1985	1990	1993	1994
All methods [1]	Bil. dol.	220.7	213.1	393.0	464.9	512.4	240.8	345.3	495.3	580.5	663.4
Vessel	Bil. dol.	120.9	91.7	150.8	166.6	177.6	165.1	208.4	283.4	310.4	339.4
Air	Bil. dol.	46.1	52.3	110.5	135.1	150.3	28.0	51.3	90.9	119.7	143.0
Shipping weight: Vessel . . .	Bil. kg .	363.7	317.7	372.4	349.5	334.5	443.1	361.5	496.3	531.0	586.9
Air	Bil. kg .	1.0	0.8	1.5	1.7	2	0.6	1.3	1.7	1.9	2.2

[1] Includes types other than vessel and air and revisions that are not distributed by method of transport.
Source: U.S. Bureau of the Census, *Highlights of U.S. Export and Import Trade,* through 1985, FT 990, monthly; thereafter, *U.S. Merchandise Trade: Selected Highlights,* FT-920, monthly.

No. 1059. Federal Expenditures for Civil Functions of the Corps of Engineers, United States Army: 1965 to 1993

[In millions of dollars. For fiscal years ending in year shown, see text, section 9. These expenditures represent the work of the Corps of Engineers to plan, design, construct, operate, and maintain civil works projects and activities, particularly in the management and improvement of rivers, harbors, and waterways for navigation, flood control, and multiple purposes. The amounts listed below do not include the expenditure of funds contributed, advanced, or reimbursed by other government agencies or local interests. Includes Puerto Rico and outlying areas]

FISCAL YEAR	Total program [1]	Navigation	Flood control	Multiple purpose	FISCAL YEAR	Total program [1]	Navigation	Flood control	Multiple purpose
1965	1,169	426	447	283	1986	3,163	1,345	1,300	402
1970	1,128	398	379	331	1987	2,937	1,135	1,272	411
1975	2,070	694	904	439	1988	3,086	1,271	1,271	423
1980	3,061	1,225	1,228	551	1989	3,252	1,395	1,253	462
1982	2,940	1,331	1,083	453	1990	3,297	1,391	1,397	375
1983	2,959	1,290	1,088	482	1991	3,511	1,473	1,447	443
1984	3,085	1,383	1,154	445	1992	3,675	1,562	1,469	469
1985	2,956	1,234	1,187	419	1993	3,335	1,461	1,243	464

[1] Includes expenditures which are not associated with a specific purpose (e.g., headquarters staff supervision, management, and administration activities, and some research and development activities).

Source: U.S. Army Corps of Engineers, *Report of Civil Works Expenditures by State and Fiscal Year,* annual.

No. 1060. Freight Carried on Inland Waterways, by System: 1960 to 1989

[In billions of ton-miles. Excludes Alaska and Hawaii, except as noted. Includes waterways, canals, and connecting channels]

ITEM	1960	1970	1980	1982	1983	1984	1985	1986	1987	1988	1989
Total	220.3	318.6	406.9	351.2	359.0	399.0	381.7	392.6	410.7	438.2	448.7
Atlantic coast waterways	28.6	28.6	30.4	25.4	22.5	24.7	24.8	25.7	25.9	28.1	28.2
Gulf coast waterways	16.9	28.6	36.6	31.8	32.4	36.7	36.5	39.0	37.9	44.6	42.5
Pacific coast waterways [1]	6.0	8.4	14.9	12.8	13.2	20.5	19.9	20.8	22.8	24.5	24.0
Mississippi River system [2]	69.3	138.5	228.9	218.0	223.0	234.6	224.7	239.3	251.6	257.8	268.1
Great Lakes System [3]	99.5	114.5	96.0	63.2	67.9	82.5	75.8	67.9	72.5	83.1	85.8

[1] Includes Alaskan waterways.   [2] Comprises main channels and all tributaries of the Mississippi, Illinois, Missouri, and Ohio Rivers.   [3] Does not include traffic between foreign ports.

Source: U.S. Army Corps of Engineers, *Waterborne Commerce of the United States,* annual.

No. 1061. Waterborne Commerce, by Type of Commodity: 1980 to 1993

[In millions of short tons. Domestic trade includes all commercial movements between United States ports and on inland rivers, Great Lakes, canals, and connecting channels of the United States, Puerto Rico, and Virgin Islands]

COMMODITY	1980		1985		1990		1993	
	Total	Domestic	Total	Domestic	Total	Domestic	Total	Domestic
Net total	1,998.9	1,077.5	1,788.4	1,014.1	2,163.9	1,122.3	2,128.2	1,068.2
Petroleum products [1] ...	423.2	339.2	368.8	259.0	437.5	281.4	428.3	273.4
Gasoline	87.3	81.0	94.0	78.0	116.8	96.4	112.3	95.1
Distillate fuel oil	74.6	72.1	70.0	55.0	77.3	58.3	83.2	58.5
Residual fuel oil	188.0	141.3	130.0	83.7	145.1	90.4	123.1	81.3
Crude petroleum	480.2	174.2	357.7	194.7	485.7	176.2	505.6	147.4
Coal and lignite	256.4	164.1	273.9	179.9	333.7	222.5	292.3	209.5
Nonmetallic minerals [1][2]	157.1	111.6	150.7	108.5	167.5	119.0	167.3	116.7
Sand and gravel [3]	65.1	60.8	66.4	62.0	62.8	57.4	65.4	56.1
Limestone	34.2	23.9	24.5	21.9	43.0	38.1	45.9	38.9
Phosphate rock	23.7	9.5	19.4	8.4	14.5	6.7	9.9	5.4
Iron and concentrates ...	98.4	64.9	72.7	50.0	86.1	62.8	82.2	60.7
Farm products [1]	216.8	63.4	172.8	60.0	215.5	78.7	208.1	75.3
Corn.............	98.6	30.8	76.3	29.0	96.1	39.6	78.8	35.3
Wheat............	53.4	14.3	38.0	10.6	44.4	13.3	52.5	13.2
Soybeans	39.6	16.1	32.9	14.9	32.2	15.9	37.7	17.7
Chemicals and allied products	91.9	49.4	108.5	53.3	123.7	67.3	136.1	71.4
Food and kindred products	54.8	20.4	52.5	17.6	56.7	17.3	62.6	22.3
Lumber and wood products [4]	52.0	22.7	47.2	18.8	57.9	22.4	49.9	20.3
Primary metal products ..	28.9	9.0	33.4	8.5	28.3	8.1	32.1	9.2
Waste and scrap	31.1	18.8	37.4	23.9	60.6	31.9	53.9	26.9
Other.............	108.1	39.8	112.8	40.0	110.7	35.7	109.8	35.1

[1] Includes categories not shown separately.   [2] Excludes fuels.   [3] Includes crushed rock.   [4] Excludes furniture.

Source: U.S. Army Corps of Engineers, *Waterborne Commerce of the United States,* annual.

No. 1062. Waterborne Imports and Exports, by Coastal District: 1980 to 1993

[Exports are free alongside ship (f.a.s.) value for all years; imports are f.a.s. value for 1980 and customs value for other years, see text, section 28. Includes commodities classified for security reasons as "Special Category" (exports only) and exports by Dept. of Defense (grant-aid shipments), and merchandise shipped in transit through the United States. See source]

DISTRICT	CARGO TONNAGE (mil. sh. tons)						VALUE (bil. dol.)					
	1980	1985	1990	1991	1992	1993	1980	1985	1990	1991	1992	1993
Imports:												
Atlantic	183	190	207	176	185	197	71.5	94.4	110.8	101.1	108.2	117.7
Gulf	243	141	225	217	232	267	56.4	32.8	41.0	36.4	36.3	38.7
Pacific.	56	51	55	49	55	58	45.0	90.4	143.3	143.7	156.6	168.8
Great Lakes	16	17	16	13	14	16	1.9	2.8	7.6	8.4	9.2	10.3
Exports:												
Atlantic	117	93	101	107	102	83	51.0	35.2	62.4	70.1	78.2	75.4
Gulf	163	144	148	167	165	155	41.5	31.8	41.2	44.2	45.0	39.9
Pacific.	78	81	100	102	101	96	25.2	25.8	53.7	56.6	60.4	59.9
Great Lakes	45	34	26	18	24	21	4.6	2.4	1.7	1.2	1.6	1.5

Source: U.S. Bureau of the Census, *U.S. Waterborne Exports and General Imports,* through 1985, FT 985, annual; thereafter TM 985, monthly.

No. 1063. Vessels Entered and Cleared in Foreign Trade, Net Registered Tonnage: 1966 to 1993

[In millions of net registered tons, except as indicated. Includes Puerto Rico and Virgin Islands. Seaports comprise all ports except Great Lakes ports. See also *Historical Statistics, Colonial Times to 1970,* series Q 507-517]

YEARLY AVERAGE OR YEAR	Number of vessels	ALL PORTS			SEAPORTS					
		Tonnage, all vessels			Tonnage, all vessels			Tonnage, with cargo		
		Total	U.S.	Foreign	Total	U.S.	Foreign	Total	U.S.	Foreign
Entered:										
1966-70	53,459	232	29	203	206	27	180	157	18	139
1971-75	53,760	319	30	290	292	28	264	220	24	196
1976-80	53,700	458	40	418	425	38	387	316	30	286
1981-85	50,124	452	57	395	424	55	369	277	36	241
1986-90	61,978	548	46	502	521	45	476	346	30	315
1970.	53,293	254	26	226	227	24	202	171	19	152
1975.	51,443	355	32	323	326	30	297	240	26	215
1980.	53,645	492	52	440	460	50	410	310	34	276
1985.	53,531	451	53	398	426	52	374	283	34	249
1989.	64,946	587	44	543	558	42	516	367	31	335
1990.	66,424	589	41	548	564	40	524	367	30	337
1991.	57,254	516	39	476	494	38	455	311	28	283
1992.	55,056	515	37	478	493	36	457	312	28	284
1993.	54,834	515	35	480	493	33	460	329	26	303
Cleared:										
1966-70	52,415	232	30	202	206	27	179	122	23	99
1971-75	53,039	324	31	293	296	29	267	149	21	127
1976-80	52,931	453	41	412	420	38	382	203	26	177
1981-85	50,291	460	57	403	432	55	377	251	34	217
1986-90	60,249	551	47	504	524	46	478	284	31	253
1970.	52,195	253	27	226	226	25	201	132	20	112
1975.	51,017	363	34	329	334	31	303	168	23	144
1980.	52,928	487	54	433	456	51	405	246	33	213
1985.	53,095	461	55	406	435	53	382	253	36	217
1989.	63,042	590	45	545	561	44	517	304	30	274
1990.	63,648	592	43	550	566	41	525	304	29	275
1991.	55,100	521	40	480	498	39	459	282	28	253
1992.	54,127	519	38	481	496	37	460	276	28	248
1993.	53,637	519	36	483	497	35	462	262	28	234

Source: U.S. Bureau of the Census, *Vessel Entrances and Clearances,* through 1989, FT 975, annual; thereafter TA 987, annual.

No. 1064. Domestic Merchant Vessels Completed by U.S. Shipyards: 1970 to 1994

[Vessels of 1,000 gross tons and over. See also *Historical Statistics, Colonial Times to 1970,* series Q 438-48]

TYPE	Unit	1970	1975	1980	1985	1986	1987	1988	1992	1993	1994
Merchant vessels	Number. . .	13	15	10	8	5	4	4	3	-	1
Gross tons.	1,000	342	452	375	172	215	153	153	44	-	17
Cargo.	Number. . .	6	3	6	4	2	3	3	1	-	-
Gross tons.	1,000	120	65	105	113	66	58	58	32	-	-
Deadweight tons.	1,000	134	71	114	97	53	63	63	29	-	-
Tankers	Number. . .	7	12	4	4	3	1	1	2	-	1
Gross tons.	1,000	222	387	270	59	149	95	95	12	-	17
Deadweight tons.	1,000	427	742	354	92	271	209	209	16	-	22

- Represents zero.

Source: U.S. Maritime Administration, *New Ship Construction,* annual.

No. 1065. United States Flag Merchant Vessels: 1995

[As of January. Covers ocean-going vessels of 1,000 gross tons and over engaged in foreign and domestic trade, and inactive vessels. Excludes vessels operating exclusively on Great Lakes, inland waterways, and those owned by the United States Army and Navy, and special types such as cable ships, tugs, etc. See also *Historical Statistics, Colonial Times to 1970*, series Q 487-502]

VESSEL TYPE	NUMBER						DEADWEIGHT TONS (1,000)					
	Total	Passenger [1]	Cargo [2]	Inter-coastal	Bulk carrier [3]	Tanker [4]	Total	Passenger [1]	Cargo [2]	Inter-coastal	Bulk carrier [3]	Tanker [4]
Total	543	13	133	175	22	200	19,968	115	1,948	4,918	1,042	11,945
Active vessels.	343	7	29	131	20	156	15,279	56	470	3,890	966	9,897
Privately owned.	331	2	25	129	20	155	15,151	14	420	3,871	966	9,880
U.S. foreign trade	128	-	16	69	14	29	4,633	-	241	2,294	757	1,341
Foreign-to-foreign	26	-	1	9	-	16	1,972	-	12	379	-	1,581
Domestic trade.	129	2	1	26	5	95	7,318	14	15	574	173	6,542
Coastal	66	-	1	3	4	58	2,476	-	15	88	143	2,230
Noncontiguous	63	2	-	23	1	37	4,842	14	-	486	30	4,312
Military Sea Lift Command .	48	-	7	25	1	15	1,228	-	152	624	36	416
Government owned	12	5	4	2	-	1	128	42	50	19	-	17
Ready reserve force	2	1	1	-	-	-	24	9	15	-	-	-
Other Custody	1	-	-	1	-	-	16	-	-	16	-	-
Other Reserve	9	4	3	1	-	1	88	33	35	3	-	17
Inactive vessels	200	6	104	44	2	44	4,689	59	1,478	1,028	76	2,048
Privately owned.	23	-	3	1	2	17	1,326	-	52	19	76	1,179
Temporarily inactive	2	-	-	-	-	2	117	-	-	-	-	117
Lay-up	19	-	3	1	2	13	1,141	-	52	19	76	994
Lay-up (MARAD Custody) [5]	2	-	-	-	-	2	68	-	-	-	-	68
Government owned (MARAD Custody):[5]												
National defense reserve fleet	177	6	101	43	-	27	3,363	59	1,426	1,009	-	869
Ready reserve fleet	87	-	42	38	-	7	1,838	-	608	940	-	290
Other reserve	44	-	27	5	-	12	871	-	446	69	-	356
Nonretention [6]	46	6	32	-	-	8	654	59	372	-	-	223

- Represents zero.   [1] Includes combination passenger and cargo vessels.   [2] General cargo.   [3] Includes tug barges.   [4] Includes tanker barges and liquified natural gas vessels.   [5] In the custody of the Maritime Administration.   [6] Vessels not actively maintained.

Source: U.S. Maritime Administration, *Employment Report of the United States Flag Merchant Fleet Ocean-Going Vessels 1,000 Gross Tons and Over*, annual.

No. 1066. Private Shipyards—Summary: 1980 to 1993

[For calendar year, unless noted. See also *Historical Statistics, Colonial Times to 1970*, series Q 449-458 and series Q 467-472]

ITEM	Unit	1980	1985	1987	1988	1989	1990	1991	1992	1993
Employment [1]	1,000. . .	177.3	130.3	120.4	121.0	123.4	121.8	127.2	123.5	111.0
Production workers	1,000. . .	141.8	99.0	90.8	90.9	88.6	86.4	95.5	93.3	84.3
Value of work done. . . . . . .`.	Mil. dol. .	9,269	9,358	8,531	(NA)	(NA)	(NA)	(NA)	(NA)	(NA)
On ships only	Mil. dol. .	8,889	9,483	8,377	(NA)	(NA)	(NA)	(NA)	(NA)	(NA)
Value added	Mil. dol. .	5,338	5,740	5,227	(NA)	(NA)	(NA)	(NA)	(NA)	(NA)
Building activity:										
Merchant vessels: [2]										
Under construction [3] . . .	Number .	69	10	6	-	-	-	3	3	1
Ordered	Number .	7	-	-	-	-	3	-	1	-
Delivered	Number .	23	3	4	-	-	-	-	3	-
Cancelled.	Number .	4	-	-	-	-	-	-	-	-
Under contract [4]	Number .	49	7	-	-	-	3	3	1	1
Naval vessels: [2]										
Under construction [3] . . .	Number .	99	100	79	83	105	98	91	90	82
Ordered	Number .	11	11	20	32	16	8	13	10	12
Delivered	Number .	19	26	16	10	23	15	14	18	19
Under contract [4] [5]	Number .	91	85	83	105	98	91	90	82	73
Repairs/conversions:										
Commercial ships	Mil. dol. .	1,335	852	806	202	279	373	380	226	292
Naval ships	Mil. dol. .	1,134	2,311	1,930	1,238	1,091	1,119	993	526	573
Unfinished work: [3]										
Commercial ships	Mil. dol. .	2,070	450	53	-	-	-	-	99	42
Naval ships	Mil. dol. .	7,107	12,091	8,265	10,500	16,010	15,450	14,151	12,286	(NA)

- Represents zero.   NA Not available.   [1] Annual average of monthly data.   [2] Vessels of 1,000 tons or larger.   [3] As of Jan. 1.   [4] As of Dec. 31.   [5] Two ships were cancelled in August 1993.

Source: Shipbuilders Council of America, Arlington, VA., *Annual Report*, for 1980; thereafter, unpublished data.

No. 1067. Employees in Government and Private Shipyards: 1960 to 1995

[**In thousands.** Annual average employment in establishments primarily engaged in building and repairing all types of ships, barges, canal boats, and lighters of 5 gross tons and over, whether propelled by sail or motor power or towed by other craft. Includes all full- and part-time employees]

YEAR	Total	Private yards	Navy yards	YEAR	Total	Private yards	Navy yards	YEAR	Total	Private yards	Navy yards
1960	208	112	96	1986	206	131	75	1991	193	131	62
1970	216	134	83	1987	200	124	75	1992	183	124	59
1975	217	154	65	1988	197	124	73	1993	163	113	50
1980	250	178	72	1989	196	126	71	1994	148	107	41
1985	219	138	80	1990	198	130	68	1995	139	105	34

Source: U.S. Bureau of Labor Statistics, Bulletins 2445 and 2481; *Employment and Earnings*, monthly, March and June issues; and unpublished data.

No. 1068. Employment on U.S. Flag Merchant Vessels, and Basic Monthly Wage Scale for Able-Bodied Seamen: 1975 to 1995

[**Employment in thousands.** See also *Historical Statistics, Colonial Times to 1970*, series Q 414-416]

YEAR	Employment [1]	YEAR	Employment [1]	YEAR	East coast wage rate [2]	West coast wage rate [2]	YEAR	East coast wage rate [2]	West coast wage rate [2]
1975	20.5	1990	11.1	1975	612	900	1991	$1,581	$2,329
1980	19.6	1991	11.7	1980	967	1,414	1992	1,655	2,438
1985	13.1	1992	9.2	1985	1,419	2,029	1993	1,721	2,438
1987	10.4	1993	9.3	1988	1,419	2,175	1994	1,790	2,536
1988	10.7	1994	9.1	1989	1,448	2,218	1995	1,918	2,637
1989	9.9	1995	7.9	1990	1,505	2,218			

[1] As of June 30, except beginning 1980, as of Sept. 30. Estimates of personnel employed on merchant ships, 1,000 gross tons and over. Excludes vessels on inland waterways, Great Lakes, and those owned by, or operated for, U.S. Army and Navy, and special types such as cable ships, tugs, etc. [2] As of January. Basic monthly wage, over and above subsistence (board and room); excludes overtime and fringe pay benefits. West coast incorporates extra pay for Saturdays and Sundays at sea into base wages but east coast does not.

Source: U.S. Maritime Administration, *U.S. Merchant Marine Data Sheet*, monthly; and unpublished data.

No. 1069. Worldwide Tanker Casualties: 1975 to 1994

[Data for **1975** and **1980** covers tankers, ore/oil carriers and bulk/oil vessels of 6,000 deadweight tons and over; beginning **1985**, 10,000 deadweight tons and over; excludes liquid gas carriers. Incident is counted in the year it is reported. Based on data from "Lloyd's List" published by Lloyd's of London. "Casualties" include weather damage, strandings, collisions and other contact, fires and explosions, machinery damage, and other mishaps]

ITEM	Unit	1975	1980	1985	1988	1989	1990	1991	1992	1993	1994
Casualties	Number	906	(NA)	340	456	528	541	507	396	314	270
Total losses [1]	Number	22	15	12	3	8	10	11	11	9	11
Deaths	Number	90	132	53	63	74	119	205	86	26	88
Oil spills	Number	45	32	9	13	31	31	26	17	24	29
Amount	1,000 tons	188	136	80	178	188	61	439	152	120	110
Amount	Mil. gallons	58	42	25	55	58	19	136	47	37	33

NA Not available. [1] Excludes losses due to hostilities.

Source: Tanker Advisory Center, Inc., New York, NY, "Worldwide Tanker Casualty Returns," quarterly.

No. 1070. Merchant Vessels—World and United States: 1960 to 1993

[**Through 1992, as of mid-year; thereafter for year-end.** For propelled sea-going merchant ships of not less than 100 gross tonnage. See also *Historical Statistics, Colonial Times to 1970*, series Q 473-480]

YEAR	WORLD: COMPLETED Number	WORLD: COMPLETED Gross tonnage (1,000)	WORLD: OWNED Number	WORLD: OWNED Gross tonnage (1,000)	U.S.: COMPLETED Number	U.S.: COMPLETED Gross tonnage (1,000)	U.S.: REGISTERED Number	U.S.: REGISTERED Gross tonnage (1,000)
1960	2,005	8,382	36,311	129,770	49	379	4,059	24,837
1970	2,814	20,980	52,444	227,490	156	375	2,983	18,463
1980	2,412	13,101	73,832	419,911	205	555	5,579	18,464
1985	1,964	18,157	76,395	416,269	66	180	6,447	19,518
1989	1,593	13,236	76,100	410,481	10	4	6,375	20,588
1990	1,672	15,885	78,336	423,627	16	15	6,348	21,328
1991	1,574	16,095	80,030	436,027	17	9	6,222	20,291
1992	1,506	18,633	79,845	444,305	27	54	5,737	18,228
1993	1,505	20,025	80,655	457,915	30	14	5,646	14,087

Source: Through 1992, Lloyd's Register of Shipping, London, England, *Statistical Tables*, annual; and *Annual Summary of Merchant Ships Completed in the World*; thereafter, *World Fleet Statistics*, annual.

No. 1065. United States Flag Merchant Vessels: 1995

[**As of January.** Covers ocean-going vessels of 1,000 gross tons and over engaged in foreign and domestic trade, and inactive vessels. Excludes vessels operating exclusively on Great Lakes, inland waterways, and those owned by the United States Army and Navy, and special types such as cable ships, tugs, etc. See also *Historical Statistics, Colonial Times to 1970*, series Q 487-502]

VESSEL TYPE	NUMBER						DEADWEIGHT TONS (1,000)					
	Total	Pas-sen-ger [1]	Car-go [2]	Inter-coastal	Bulk car-rier [3]	Tank-er [4]	Total	Pas-sen-ger [1]	Car-go [2]	Inter-coastal	Bulk car-rier [3]	Tank-er [4]
Total	543	13	133	175	22	200	19,968	115	1,948	4,918	1,042	11,945
Active vessels.	343	7	29	131	20	156	15,279	56	470	3,890	966	9,897
Privately owned.	331	2	25	129	20	155	15,151	14	420	3,871	966	9,880
U.S. foreign trade	128	-	16	69	14	29	4,633	-	241	2,294	757	1,341
Foreign-to-foreign	26	-	1	9	-	16	1,972	-	12	379	-	1,581
Domestic trade.	129	2	1	26	5	95	7,318	14	15	574	173	6,542
Coastal	66	-	1	3	4	58	2,476	-	15	88	143	2,230
Noncontiguous	63	2	-	23	1	37	4,842	14	-	486	30	4,312
Military Sea Lift Command .	48	-	7	25	1	15	1,228	-	152	624	36	416
Government owned	12	5	4	2	-	1	128	42	50	19	-	17
Ready reserve force	2	1	1	-	-	-	24	9	15	-	-	-
Other Custody	1	-	-	1	-	-	16	-	-	16	-	-
Other Reserve	9	4	3	1	-	1	88	33	35	3	-	17
Inactive vessels	200	6	104	44	2	44	4,689	59	1,478	1,028	76	2,048
Privately owned	23	-	3	1	2	17	1,326	-	52	19	76	1,179
Temporarily inactive	2	-	-	-	-	2	117	-	-	-	-	117
Lay-up	19	-	3	1	2	13	1,141	-	52	19	76	994
Lay-up (MARAD Custody) [5]	2	-	-	-	-	2	68	-	-	-	-	68
Government owned (MARAD Custody):[5]												
National defense reserve fleet	177	6	101	43	-	27	3,363	59	1,426	1,009	-	869
Ready reserve fleet	87	-	42	38	-	7	1,838	-	608	940	-	290
Other reserve	44	-	27	5	-	12	871	-	446	69	-	356
Nonretention [6]	46	6	32	-	-	8	654	59	372	-	-	223

- Represents zero.   [1] Includes combination passenger and cargo vessels.   [2] General cargo.   [3] Includes tug barges.   [4] Includes tanker barges and liquified natural gas vessels.   [5] In the custody of the Maritime Administration.   [6] Vessels not actively maintained.

Source: U.S. Maritime Administration, *Employment Report of the United States Flag Merchant Fleet Ocean-Going Vessels 1,000 Gross Tons and Over*, annual.

No. 1066. Private Shipyards—Summary: 1980 to 1993

[**For calendar year, unless noted.** See also *Historical Statistics, Colonial Times to 1970*, series Q 449-458 and series Q 467-472]

ITEM	Unit	1980	1985	1987	1988	1989	1990	1991	1992	1993
Employment [1]	1,000. . .	177.3	130.3	120.4	121.0	123.4	121.8	127.2	123.5	111.0
Production workers	1,000. . .	141.8	99.0	90.8	90.9	88.6	86.4	95.5	93.3	84.3
Value of work done.	Mil. dol. .	9,269	9,358	8,531	(NA)	(NA)	(NA)	(NA)	(NA)	(NA)
On ships only	Mil. dol. .	8,889	9,483	8,377	(NA)	(NA)	(NA)	(NA)	(NA)	(NA)
Value added	Mil. dol. .	5,338	5,740	5,227	(NA)	(NA)	(NA)	(NA)	(NA)	(NA)
Building activity:										
Merchant vessels: [2]										
Under construction [3] . . .	Number .	69	10	6	-	-	-	3	3	1
Ordered	Number .	7	-	-	-	-	3	-	1	-
Delivered	Number .	23	3	4	-	-	-	-	3	-
Cancelled.	Number .	4	-	-	-	-	-	-	-	-
Under contract [4]	Number .	49	7	-	-	-	-	3	3	1
Naval vessels: [2]										
Under construction [3] . . .	Number .	99	100	79	83	105	98	91	90	82
Ordered	Number .	11	11	20	32	16	8	13	10	12
Delivered	Number .	19	26	16	10	23	15	14	18	19
Under contract [4][5]	Number .	91	85	83	105	98	91	90	82	73
Repairs/conversions:										
Commercial ships	Mil. dol. .	1,335	852	806	202	279	373	380	226	292
Naval ships	Mil. dol. .	1,134	2,311	1,930	1,238	1,091	1,119	993	526	573
Unfinished work: [3]										
Commercial ships	Mil. dol. .	2,070	450	53	-	-	-	-	99	42
Naval ships	Mil. dol. .	7,107	12,091	8,265	10,500	16,010	15,450	14,151	12,286	(NA)

- Represents zero.   NA Not available.   [1] Annual average of monthly data.   [2] Vessels of 1,000 tons or larger.   [3] As of Jan. 1.   [4] As of Dec. 31.   [5] Two ships were cancelled in August 1993.

Source: Shipbuilders Council of America, Arlington, VA., *Annual Report,* for 1980; thereafter, unpublished data.

No. 1067. Employees in Government and Private Shipyards: 1960 to 1995

[In thousands. Annual average employment in establishments primarily engaged in building and repairing all types of ships, barges, canal boats, and lighters of 5 gross tons and over, whether propelled by sail or motor power or towed by other craft. Includes all full- and part-time employees]

YEAR	Total	Private yards	Navy yards	YEAR	Total	Private yards	Navy yards	YEAR	Total	Private yards	Navy yards
1960	208	112	96	1986	206	131	75	1991	193	131	62
1970	216	134	83	1987	200	124	75	1992	183	124	59
1975	217	154	65	1988	197	124	73	1993	163	113	50
1980	250	178	72	1989	196	126	71	1994	148	107	41
1985	219	138	80	1990	198	130	68	1995	139	105	34

Source: U.S. Bureau of Labor Statistics, Bulletins 2445 and 2481; Employment and Earnings, monthly, March and June issues; and unpublished data.

No. 1068. Employment on U.S. Flag Merchant Vessels, and Basic Monthly Wage Scale for Able-Bodied Seamen: 1975 to 1995

[Employment in thousands. See also Historical Statistics, Colonial Times to 1970, series Q 414-416]

YEAR	Employment [1]	YEAR	Employment [1]	YEAR	East coast wage rate [2]	West coast wage rate [2]	YEAR	East coast wage rate [2]	West coast wage rate [2]
1975.	20.5	1990	11.1	1975	612	900	1991	$1,581	$2,329
1980.	19.6	1991	11.7	1980	967	1,414	1992	1,655	2,438
1985.	13.1	1992	9.2	1985	1,419	2,029	1993	1,721	2,438
1987.	10.4	1993	9.3	1988	1,419	2,175	1994	1,790	2,536
1988.	10.7	1994	9.1	1989	1,448	2,218	1995	1,918	2,637
1989.	9.9	1995	7.9	1990	1,505	2,218			

[1] As of June 30, except beginning 1980, as of Sept. 30. Estimates of personnel employed on merchant ships, 1,000 gross tons and over. Excludes vessels on inland waterways, Great Lakes, and those owned by, or operated for, U.S. Army and Navy, and special types such as cable ships, tugs, etc. [2] As of January. Basic monthly wage, over and above subsistence (board and room); excludes overtime and fringe pay benefits. West coast incorporates extra pay for Saturdays and Sundays at sea into base wages but east coast does not.

Source: U.S. Maritime Administration, U.S. Merchant Marine Data Sheet, monthly; and unpublished data.

No. 1069. Worldwide Tanker Casualties: 1975 to 1994

[Data for 1975 and 1980 covers tankers, ore/oil carriers and bulk/oil vessels of 6,000 deadweight tons and over; beginning 1985, 10,000 deadweight tons and over; excludes liquid gas carriers. Incident is counted in the year it is reported. Based on data from "Lloyd's List" published by Lloyd's of London. "Casualties" include weather damage, strandings, collisions and other contact, fires and explosions, machinery damage, and other mishaps]

ITEM	Unit	1975	1980	1985	1988	1989	1990	1991	1992	1993	1994
Casualties.	Number	906	(NA)	340	456	528	541	507	396	314	270
Total losses [1]	Number	22	15	12	3	8	10	10	11	9	11
Deaths	Number	90	132	53	63	74	119	205	86	26	88
Oil spills	Number	45	32	9	13	31	31	26	17	24	29
Amount	1,000 tons . .	188	136	80	178	188	61	439	152	120	110
Amount	Mil. gallons . .	58	42	25	55	58	19	136	47	37	33

NA Not available. [1] Excludes losses due to hostilities.

Source: Tanker Advisory Center, Inc., New York, NY, "Worldwide Tanker Casualty Returns," quarterly.

No. 1070. Merchant Vessels—World and United States: 1960 to 1993

[Through 1992, as of mid-year; thereafter for year-end. For propelled sea-going merchant ships of not less than 100 gross tonnage. See also Historical Statistics, Colonial Times to 1970, series Q 473-480]

YEAR	WORLD: COMPLETED		WORLD: OWNED		U.S.: COMPLETED		U.S.: REGISTERED	
	Number	Gross tonnage (1,000)	Number	Gross tonnage (1,000)	Number	Gross tonnage (1,000)	Number	Gross tonnage (1,000)
1960	2,005	8,382	36,311	129,770	49	379	4,059	24,837
1970	2,814	20,980	52,444	227,490	156	375	2,983	18,463
1980	2,412	13,101	73,832	419,911	205	555	5,579	18,464
1985	1,964	18,157	76,395	416,269	66	180	6,447	19,518
1989	1,593	13,236	76,100	410,481	10	4	6,375	20,588
1990	1,672	15,885	78,336	423,627	16	15	6,348	21,328
1991	1,574	16,095	80,030	436,027	17	9	6,222	20,291
1992	1,506	18,633	79,845	444,305	27	54	5,737	18,228
1993	1,505	20,025	80,655	457,915	30	14	5,646	14,087

Source: Through 1992, Lloyd's Register of Shipping, London, England, Statistical Tables, annual; and Annual Summary of Merchant Ships Completed in the World; thereafter, World Fleet Statistics, annual.

Agriculture

This section presents statistics on farms and farm operators; land use and irrigation; farm income, expenditures, and debt; farm output, productivity, and marketings; foreign trade in agricultural products; specific crops; and livestock, poultry, and their products.

The principal sources are the reports issued by the U.S. Bureau of the Census and by the National Agricultural Statistics Service (NASS) and the Economic Research Service (ERS) of the U.S. Department of Agriculture. The 1992 Census of Agriculture is the 24th taken by the Bureau of the Census. The information is available in printed form in the volume 1, Geographic Area Series, and in electronic format on CD-ROM. The Department of Agriculture publishes annually *Agricultural Statistics*, a general reference book on agricultural production, supplies, consumption, facilities, costs, and returns. The Economic Research Service publishes data on farm assets, debt, and income in the annual *Farm Business Economic Report*. Sources of current data on agricultural exports and imports include *Foreign Agricultural Trade of the United States*, published by the ERS, and the reports of the Bureau of the Census, particularly *U.S. Imports for Consumption and General Imports— HTSUSA Commodity by Country of Origin* (FT247), *U.S. Exports, Harmonized Schedule B, Commodity by Country* (FT447) and *U.S. Merchandise Trade: Exports, General Imports, and Imports for Consumption* (FT925).

The 45 field offices of the NASS collect data on crops, livestock and products, agricultural prices, farm employment, and other related subjects mainly through sample surveys. Information is obtained on some 75 crops and 50 livestock items as well as scores of items pertaining to agricultural production and marketing. State estimates and supporting information are sent to the Agricultural Statistics Board of NASS which reviews the estimates and issues reports containing State and national data. Among these reports are annual summaries such as *Crop Production, Crop*

In Brief

Number of farms, 1995: 2.1 million
 Leading States—

Texas	*202,000*
Missouri	*106,000*
Iowa	*100,000*

Farm marketings cash receipts, 1994: $180 billion
 Leading commodities—

Cattle, calves	*$36 billion*
Dairy products	*$20 billion*
Corn	*$15 billion*

Values, Agricultural Prices, and *Livestock Production, Disposition and Income*. For more information about concepts and methods underlying USDA's statistical series, see *Major Statistical Series of the U.S. Department of Agriculture* (Agricultural Handbook No. 671), a 12-volume set of publications.

Farms and farmland—The Bureau of the Census has used varying definitions of a farm. Since 1850, when minimum criteria defining a farm for census purposes first were established, the farm definition has been changed nine times. The current definition, first used for the 1974 census, is any place from which $1,000 or more of agricultural products were produced and sold, or normally would have been sold, during the census year.

Acreage designated as "land in farms" consists primarily of agricultural land used for crops, pasture, or grazing. It also includes woodland and wasteland not actually under cultivation or used for pasture or grazing, provided it was part of the farm operator's total operation. Land in farms includes acres set aside under annual commodity acreage programs as well as acres in the Conservation Reserve and Wetlands Reserve Programs for places meeting the farm definition. Land in farms is an operating unit concept and includes land owned and operated as well as land rented from others. All grazing land, except land used under government permits on a per-head basis, was included as "land in farms" provided it was part of a farm or ranch.

Coverage estimates for 1987 and 1992 indicate about 7.2 and 11.1 percent of all farms, respectively, were not included in census totals. Farms undercounted in these censuses were usually small and accounted for approximately 1 percent of the total value of agricultural products sold and approximately 2 percent of the land in farms. For more explanation about mail list compilation and census coverage, see appendixes A and C, *1992 Census of Agriculture*, volume 1 reports and *Coverage Evaluation*, volume 2, part 2.

Farm income—Gross farm income comprises cash receipts from farm marketings of crops and livestock, Federal government payments made directly to farmers for farm-related activities, rental value of farm homes, value of farm products consumed in farm homes, and other farm-related income such as machine hire and custom work. Farm marketings represent quantities of agricultural products sold by farmers multiplied by prices received per unit of production at the local market. Information on prices received for farm products is generally obtained by the NASS Agricultural Statistics Board from surveys of firms (such as grain elevators, packers, and processors) purchasing agricultural commodities directly from producers. In some cases, the price information is obtained directly from the producers.

Crops—Estimates of crop acreage and production by the NASS are based on current sample survey data obtained from individual producers and objective yield counts, reports of carlot shipments, market records, personal field observations by field statisticians, and reports from other sources. Prices received by farmers are marketing year averages.

These averages are based on U.S. monthly prices weighted by monthly marketings during specific periods. U.S. monthly prices are State average prices weighted by marketings during the month. Marketing year average prices do not include allowances for outstanding loans, government purchases, deficiency payments or disaster payments.

All State prices are based on individual State marketing years, while U.S. marketing year averages are based on standard marketing years for each crop. For a listing of the crop marketing years and the participating States in the monthly program, see *Crop Values*, January 1992. Value of production is computed by multiplying State prices by each State's production. The U.S. value of production is the sum of State values for all States. Value of production figures shown in tables 1105, 1107-1109, 1111, and 1112 should not be confused with cash receipts from farm marketings which relate to sales during a calendar year, irrespective of the year of production.

Livestock—Annual inventory numbers of livestock and estimates of livestock, dairy, and poultry production prepared by the Department of Agriculture are based on information from farmers and ranchers obtained by probability survey sampling methods.

Statistical reliability—For a discussion of statistical collection and estimation, sampling procedures, and measures of statistical reliability pertaining to Census Bureau and Department of Agriculture data, see Appendix III.

Historical statistics—Tabular headnotes provide cross-references, where applicable, to *Historical Statistics of the United States, Colonial Times to 1970*. See Appendix IV.

No. 1073. Farms—Number and Acreage, by Size of Farm: 1982 to 1992

[See also *Historical Statistics, Colonial Times to 1970*, series K 162-173]

SIZE OF FARM	NUMBER OF FARMS (1,000)			LAND IN FARMS (mil. acres)			CROPLAND HARVESTED (mil. acres)			PERCENT DISTRIBUTION, 1992		
	1982	1987	1992	1982	1987	1992	1982	1987	1992	Number of farms	All land in farms	Cropland harvested
Total	2,241	2,088	1,925	986.8	964.5	945.5	326.3	282.2	295.9	100.0	100.0	100.0
Under 10 acres.	188	183	166	0.7	0.7	0.7	0.3	0.2	0.2	8.6	0.1	0.1
10 to 49 acres	449	412	388	12.1	11.1	10.3	4.5	3.9	3.5	20.1	1.1	1.2
50 to 99 acres	344	311	283	24.8	22.5	20.4	9.5	7.9	7.2	14.7	2.2	2.4
100 to 179 acres.	368	334	301	49.9	45.3	40.7	21.2	17.1	15.4	15.6	4.3	5.2
180 to 259 acres.	211	192	172	45.7	41.5	37.2	21.7	17.2	15.5	8.9	3.9	5.2
260 to 499 acres.	315	286	255	113.0	103.0	91.7	60.5	47.3	43.6	13.3	9.7	14.7
500 to 999 acres.	204	200	186	140.5	138.5	129.3	77.6	67.4	68.6	9.7	13.7	23.2
1,000 to 1,999 acres . .	97	102	102	132.4	138.8	139.0	64.5	61.1	69.3	5.3	14.7	23.4
2,000 acres and over. .	65	67	71	467.5	463.2	476.3	66.6	60.2	72.5	3.7	50.4	24.5

No. 1074. Farms—Number and Acreage, by Tenure of Operator: 1978 to 1992

[*Full owners* own all the land they operate. *Part owners* own a part and rent from others the rest of the land they operate. See also *Historical Statistics, Colonial Times to 1970*, series K 109-113 and 142-146]

ITEM AND YEAR	Unit	Total	Full owner	Part owner	Tenant	PERCENT DISTRIBUTION			
						Total	Full owner	Part owner	Tenant
NUMBER OF FARMS									
1978.	1,000. . . .	2,258	1,298	681	279	100.0	57.5	30.1	12.4
1982.	1,000. . . .	2,241	1,326	656	259	100.0	59.2	29.3	11.5
1987.	1,000. . . .	2,088	1,239	609	240	100.0	59.3	29.2	11.5
1992.	1,000. . . .	1,925	1,112	597	217	100.0	57.7	31.0	11.3
Under 50 acres	1,000. . . .	554	444	58	52	100.0	80.1	10.5	9.4
50 to 179 acres	1,000. . . .	584	395	130	59	100.0	67.6	22.3	10.1
180 to 499 acres	1,000. . . .	428	190	183	55	100.0	44.4	42.8	12.8
500 to 999 acres	1,000. . . .	186	48	111	27	100.0	25.8	59.7	14.5
1,000 acres or more.	1,000. . . .	173	35	114	24	100.0	20.2	65.9	13.9
LAND IN FARMS									
1978.	Mil. acres .	1,015	332	561	122	100.0	32.7	55.3	12.0
1982.	Mil. acres .	987	342	531	114	100.0	34.7	53.8	11.6
1987.	Mil. acres .	964	318	520	127	100.0	32.9	53.9	13.2
1992.	Mil. acres .	946	296	527	123	100.0	31.3	55.7	13.0

No. 1075. Farm Operators—Tenure and Characteristics: 1987 and 1992

[**In thousands, except as indicated**. See also *Historical Statistics, Colonial Times to 1970*, series K 82-113]

CHARACTERISTIC	ALL FARMS		FARMS WITH SALES OF $10,000 AND OVER		CHARACTERISTIC	ALL FARMS		FARMS WITH SALES OF $10,000 AND OVER	
	1987	1992	1987	1992		1987	1992	1987	1992
Total operators	2,088	1,925	1,060	1,019	Tenant.	240	217	161	148
White	2,043	1,882	1,046	1,003					
Black.	23	19	4	5	Principal occupation:				
American Indian, Eskimo,					Farming	1,138	1,053	811	754
andAleut	7	8	2	3	Other.	950	872	248	265
Asian or Pacific Islander	8	8	5	5					
Other	7	8	2	3	Place of residence: [2]				
					On farm operated.	1,488	1,379	776	736
Operators of Hispanic origin [1].	17	21	6	8	Not on farm operated	443	409	215	215
Female	132	145	42	50	Years on present farm: [2]				
					2 years or less.	114	95	49	41
Under 25 years old	36	28	21	17	3 to 4 years	135	133	56	58
25 to 34 years old	243	179	147	112	5 to 9 years	304	259	138	121
35 to 44 years old	411	382	212	217	10 years or more	1,163	1,113	653	648
45 to 54 years old	455	429	228	223					
55 to 64 years old	496	430	263	229	Days worked off farm: [2]				
65 years old and over	447	478	188	220	None	844	802	561	536
Average age (years)	52.0	53.3	50.6	51.9	Less than 100 days	200	165	124	104
					100 to 199 days.	178	162	80	76
Full owner	1,239	1,112	445	422	200 days or more.	737	666	219	226
Part owner	609	597	454	448					

[1] Operators of Hispanic origin may be of any race. [2] Excludes not reported.

Source of tables 1073-1075: U.S. Bureau of the Census, *Census of Agriculture: 1987*, vol. 1; and *1992*, vol. 1.

No. 1076. Farms—Number, Acreage, and Value, by Type of Organization: 1987 and 1992

ITEM	Unit	Total [1]	Indi-vidual or family	Partner-ship	Corpo-ration	PERCENT DISTRIBUTION			
						Total [1]	Indi-vidual or family	Partner-ship	Corpo-ration
ALL FARMS									
Number of farms: 1987	1,000 ...	2,088	1,809	200	67	100.0	86.7	9.6	3.2
1992	1,000 ...	1,925	1,653	187	73	100.0	85.9	9.7	3.8
Land in farms: 1987	Mil. acres.	964	628	153	119	100.0	65.1	15.9	12.4
1992	Mil. acres.	946	604	153	123	100.0	63.9	16.2	13.0
Value of land and buildings: [2] 1987	Bil. dol. ...	604	424	95	69	100.0	70.1	15.7	11.4
1992	Bil. dol. ...	687	474	109	85	100.0	69.0	15.8	12.4
Value of farm products sold: 1987	Bil. dol. ...	136	77	23	35	100.0	56.3	17.1	25.6
1992	Bil. dol. ...	163	88	29	44	100.0	54.1	18.0	27.2
FARMS WITH SALES OF $10,000 AND OVER									
Number of farms: 1987	1,000 ...	1,060	861	136	56	100.0	81.3	12.8	5.3
1992	1,000 ...	1,019	820	131	61	100.0	80.5	12.8	6.0
Land in farms: 1987	Mil. acres.	829	525	143	116	100.0	63.3	17.3	14.0
1992	Mil. acres.	822	512	143	119	100.0	62.2	17.4	14.4

[1] Includes other types, not shown separately. [2] Based on a sample of farms.

No. 1077. Corporate Farms—Characteristics, by Type: 1992

ITEM	Unit	All corpora-tions	FAMILY HELD CORPORATIONS			OTHER CORPORATIONS		
			Total	1-10 stock-holders	11 or more stock-holders	Total	1-10 stock-holders	11 or more stock-holders
Farms	Number...	72,567	64,528	62,755	1,773	8,039	6,914	1,125
Percent distribution	Percent...	100.0	88.9	86.5	2.4	11.1	9.5	1.6
Land in farms	Mil. acres..	122.8	110.8	100.9	9.9	11.9	8.0	4.0
Average per farm	Acres	1,692	1,718	1,608	5,597	1,484	1,152	3,524
Value of—								
Land and buildings [1]	Bil. dol. ...	85.1	72.5	66.5	6.0	12.5	8.1	4.4
Average per farm	$1,000 ...	1,172	1,131	1,068	3,385	1,484	1,105	3,950
Farm products sold	Bil. dol. ...	44.2	34.4	29.7	4.7	9.8	6.5	3.3
Average per farm	$1,000 ...	609	533	474	2,626	1,218	941	2,915

[1] Based on a sample of farms.

No. 1078. Farms—Number, Acreage, and Value of Sales, by Size of Sales: 1992

VALUE OF PRODUCTS SOLD	Farms (1,000)	ACREAGE		VALUE OF SALES		PERCENT DISTRIBUTION		
		Total (mil.)	Average per farm	Total (mil. dol.)	Average per farm (dol.)	Farms	Acreage	Value of sales
Total	**1,925**	**945.5**	**491**	**162,608**	**84,459**	**100.0**	**100.0**	**100.0**
Less than $10,000	907	123.5	136	3,043	3,357	47.1	13.1	1.9
Less than $2,500	423	55.7	132	411	972	22.0	5.9	0.3
$2,500-$4,999	232	26.9	116	836	3,605	12.1	2.8	0.5
$5,000-$9,999	252	40.9	162	1,797	7,132	13.1	4.3	1.1
$10,000 or more	1,019	822.0	807	159,565	156,623	52.9	86.9	98.1
$10,000-$24,999	302	81.8	271	4,841	16,039	15.7	8.7	3.0
$25,000-$49,999	195	91.4	477	6,967	35,662	10.1	9.7	4.3
$50,000-$99,999	188	133.9	713	13,517	71,990	9.8	14.2	8.3
$100,000-$249,999	208	228.0	1,094	32,711	156,958	10.8	24.1	20.1
$250,000-$499,999	79	130.9	1,666	26,914	342,653	4.1	13.8	16.6
$500,000-$999,999	31	80.6	2,598	20,953	675,368	1.6	8.5	12.9
$1,000,000 or more	16	75.5	4,751	53,663	3,377,175	0.8	8.0	33.0

Source of tables 1076-1078: U.S. Bureau of the Census, *1992 Census of Agriculture*, vol. 1.

No. 1079. Farms—Number, Acreage, and Value, by State: 1987 and 1992

[See also *Historical Statistics, Colonial Times to 1970*, series K 17-18]

REGION, DIVISION, AND STATE	ALL FARMS								FARMS WITH SALES OF $10,000 OR MORE, 1992			
	Number of farms (1,000)		Land in farms (mil. acres)		Average size of farm (acres)		Total value [1] (mil. dol.)		Number of farms (1,000)	Land in farms (mil. acres)	Average size of farm (acres)	Total value [1] (mil. dol.)
	1987	1992	1987	1992	1987	1992	1987	1992				
U.S.....	2,088	1,925	964.5	945.5	462	491	604,168	687,432	1,019	822.0	807	555,056
Northeast...	123	109	21.4	19.4	174	177	32,045	38,305	56	14.7	261	27,504
N.E......	25	23	4.2	3.9	169	168	7,866	8,834	10	2.7	257	5,449
ME	6	6	1.3	1.3	214	218	1,321	1,396	3	0.9	340	842
NH	2	2	0.4	0.4	169	158	900	836	1	0.2	257	418
VT....	6	5	1.4	1.3	240	235	1,521	1,730	3	1.0	328	1,219
MA	6	5	0.6	0.5	99	100	2,154	2,421	2	0.3	145	1,478
RI.....	1	1	0.1	0.1	84	76	295	313	(Z)	(Z)	118	194
CT	4	3	0.4	0.4	111	105	1,674	2,138	1	0.2	173	1,299
M.A	98	86	17.2	15.5	175	180	24,179	29,472	46	12.0	261	22,055
NY	38	32	8.4	7.5	223	231	8,263	9,130	18	6.0	332	7,012
NJ....	9	9	0.9	0.8	99	93	3,579	5,590	4	0.6	179	3,734
PA....	51	45	7.9	7.2	153	160	12,337	14,752	24	5.4	221	11,309
Midwest....	862	777	350.5	343.6	407	442	228,073	263,320	514	310.8	605	235,102
E.N.C	365	326	86.6	82.7	237	254	96,291	110,003	200	73.7	368	96,755
OH	79	71	15.0	14.2	189	201	18,023	20,626	38	11.9	314	16,799
IN	70	63	16.2	15.6	229	249	18,716	21,732	37	14.1	384	19,151
IL	89	78	28.5	27.3	321	351	35,779	41,844	56	26.0	464	39,607
MI....	51	47	10.3	10.1	202	217	10,034	11,517	24	8.3	352	8,999
WI....	75	68	16.6	15.5	221	228	13,740	14,285	46	13.4	290	12,199
W.N.C	497	451	263.8	260.9	531	578	131,782	153,317	313	237.2	757	138,347
MN	85	75	26.6	25.7	312	342	18,616	23,319	53	23.2	438	21,005
IA	105	97	31.6	31.3	301	325	29,830	38,063	77	29.9	388	36,345
MO	106	98	29.2	28.5	275	291	18,634	22,070	47	22.5	477	16,771
ND	35	31	40.3	39.4	1,143	1,267	12,934	13,163	25	36.8	1,449	12,194
SD	36	34	44.2	44.8	1,214	1,316	11,871	12,264	27	39.0	1,452	10,955
NE	60	53	45.3	44.4	749	839	20,828	22,713	42	42.6	1,007	21,640
KS	69	63	46.6	46.7	680	738	19,068	21,725	41	43.2	1,041	19,438
South......	824	775	281.2	277.0	341	357	207,777	222,294	315	222.2	706	158,473
S.A......	240	223	51.2	48.6	214	218	64,886	76,544	93	36.5	393	54,951
DE	3	3	0.6	0.6	205	224	1,096	1,351	2	0.5	309	1,184
MD	15	13	2.4	2.2	162	171	5,419	6,570	7	1.8	282	4,862
VA	45	42	8.7	8.3	194	197	10,409	13,534	17	6.0	355	9,100
WV	17	17	3.4	3.3	196	192	2,255	2,810	4	1.5	394	1,229
NC	59	52	9.4	8.9	159	172	11,845	13,950	25	7.0	281	10,118
SC	20	20	4.8	4.5	232	221	4,127	5,093	7	3.0	452	2,986
GA	44	41	10.7	10.0	247	246	9,852	11,437	17	7.5	431	7,547
FL....	37	35	11.2	10.8	306	306	19,884	21,801	15	9.2	614	17,924
E.S.C	250	235	45.6	43.5	183	185	38,811	45,055	90	30.4	337	29,328
KY	92	90	14.0	13.7	152	151	12,545	14,775	41	10.0	248	10,603
TN	80	75	11.7	11.2	147	149	11,648	13,977	24	7.3	298	8,007
AL....	43	38	9.1	8.5	211	223	7,284	8,350	14	5.7	410	5,152
MS	34	32	10.7	10.2	315	318	7,333	7,952	12	7.5	640	5,566
W.S.C	335	317	184.4	185.0	551	583	104,079	100,695	131	155.2	1,181	74,195
AR	48	44	14.4	14.1	298	322	10,884	12,407	21	11.3	536	9,668
LA	27	26	8.0	7.8	293	306	7,348	7,474	11	6.4	604	5,645
OK	70	67	31.5	32.1	449	480	15,102	15,754	30	26.3	889	11,851
TX....	189	181	130.5	130.9	691	725	70,746	65,060	70	111.2	1,586	47,031
West	278	264	311.3	305.6	1,118	1,158	136,274	163,513	134	274.3	2,046	133,977
Mountain..	124	118	244.1	240.7	1,965	2,035	62,906	69,720	65	217.3	3,362	58,517
MT	25	23	60.2	59.6	2,451	2,613	12,418	13,578	15	53.6	3,612	11,658
ID	24	22	13.9	13.5	577	609	8,126	9,077	13	11.6	909	7,829
WY	9	9	33.6	32.9	3,650	3,772	4,909	5,242	6	29.7	5,376	4,516
CO	27	27	34.0	34.0	1,248	1,252	12,519	14,568	15	30.7	2,029	11,932
NM	14	14	46.0	46.8	3,230	3,281	8,291	9,220	6	42.4	7,273	7,298
AZ....	8	7	36.3	35.0	4,732	5,173	10,111	10,984	3	32.7	10,260	9,837
UT	14	14	10.0	9.6	710	712	4,259	4,704	6	8.2	1,372	3,546
NV	3	3	10.0	9.3	3,300	3,205	2,272	2,347	1	8.3	6,081	1,902
Pacific ...	154	146	67.3	64.8	466	445	73,367	93,793	69	57.0	821	75,461
WA	34	30	16.1	15.7	480	520	11,948	14,178	15	13.5	915	11,060
OR	32	32	17.8	17.6	556	552	9,597	11,824	12	15.6	1,289	8,534
CA	83	78	30.6	29.0	368	373	48,567	63,689	40	25.8	639	52,685
AK	1	1	1.0	0.9	1,789	1,803	317	249	(Z)	0.6	3,788	138
HI	5	5	1.7	1.6	353	298	2,938	3,854	2	1.5	729	3,044

Z Less than 500 farms or 50,000 acres. [1] Value of land and buildings. Based on reports for a sample of farms.

Source: U.S. Bureau of the Census, *1992 Census of Agriculture*, vol. 1.

No. 1080. Irrigated Farms and Acreage, by State: 1987 and 1992

[See also *Historical Statistics, Colonial Times to 1970*, series J 85-91]

STATE	IRRIGATED FARMS				LAND IN IRRIGATED FARMS				IRRIGATED LAND			
	Number (1,000)		Percent of all farms		Acreage (1,000)		Percent of all land in farms		Acreage (1,000)		Percent of all land in farms	
	1987	1992	1987	1992	1987	1992	1987	1992	1987	1992	1987	1992
U.S. [1]	291.6	279.4	13.9	14.5	241,069	231,853	24.9	24.5	46,386	49,404	4.8	5.2
California	58.9	56.5	70.7	72.8	17,567	16,444	57.4	54.9	7,596	7,571	24.8	26.1
Colorado.	14.9	15.2	54.6	56.0	16,729	16,648	49.1	49.0	3,014	3,170	8.9	9.3
Florida	12.0	13.5	32.7	38.3	4,670	4,937	41.7	45.9	1,623	1,783	14.5	16.6
Idaho	16.6	15.5	68.8	70.0	9,053	8,579	64.9	63.7	3,219	3,260	23.1	24.2
Kansas.	7.4	6.5	10.7	10.3	10,654	10,519	22.8	22.5	2,463	2,680	5.3	5.7
Montana	9.5	8.9	38.7	38.9	23,259	22,024	38.6	36.9	1,997	1,978	3.3	3.3
Nebraska	22.6	19.3	37.3	36.5	22,499	22,027	49.6	49.6	5,682	6,312	12.5	14.2
Oregon.	14.4	15.0	45.0	47.0	11,340	10,419	63.6	59.2	1,648	1,622	9.3	9.2
Texas.	19.8	18.8	10.4	10.4	20,270	19,353	15.5	14.8	4,271	4,912	3.3	3.8
Washington	15.4	14.1	45.9	46.5	5,468	5,101	33.9	32.4	1,519	1,641	9.4	10.4
Wyoming	5.2	5.1	56.7	58.2	18,207	17,955	54.1	54.6	1,518	1,465	4.5	4.5

[1] Includes other States not shown separately.

Source: U.S. Bureau of the Census, *1992 Census of Agriculture*, vol. 1.

No. 1081. Farms—Number and Acreage: 1980 to 1995

[As of **June 1**. Based on 1974 census definition; for definition of farms and farmland, see text, section 23. Data for census years (indicated by italics) have been adjusted for underenumeration and are used as reference points along with data from acreage and livestock surveys in estimating data for other years. Minus sign (-) indicates decrease. See also *Historical Statistics, Colonial Times to 1970*, series K 4-7]

YEAR	FARMS		LAND IN FARMS		YEAR	FARMS		LAND IN FARMS	
	Number (1,000)	Annual change [1] (1,000)	Total (mil. acres)	Average per farm (acres)		Number (1,000)	Annual change [1] (1,000)	Total (mil. acres)	Average per farm (acres)
1980	2,440	3	1,039	426	1990	2,146	-29	987	460
1985	2,293	-41	1,012	441	1991	2,117	-29	982	464
1986	2,250	-43	1,005	447	*1992*	*2,108*	*-9*	*979*	*464*
1987	*2,213*	*-37*	*999*	*451*	1993	2,083	-25	976	469
1988	2,201	-12	994	452	1994	2,065	-18	973	471
1989	2,175	-26	991	456	1995	2,073	8	972	469

[1] Annual change from immediate preceding year.

No. 1082. Farms—Number and Acreage, by State: 1990 and 1995

[See headnote, table 1081]

STATE	FARMS (1,000)		ACREAGE (mil.)		ACREAGE PER FARM		STATE	FARMS (1,000)		ACREAGE (mil.)		ACREAGE PER FARM	
	1990	1995	1990	1995	1990	1995		1990	1995	1990	1995	1990	1995
U.S.	2,146	2,073	987	972	460	469	Missouri	108	106	30	30	281	283
							Montana	25	22	61	60	2,449	2,714
Alabama	47	47	10	10	215	217	Nebraska	57	56	47	47	826	841
Alaska	1	1	1	1	1,707	1,769	Nevada.	3	3	9	9	3,560	3,520
Arizona	8	7	36	35	4,641	4,784	New Hampshire	3	2	(Z)	(Z)	163	191
Arkansas.	47	44	16	15	330	341	New Jersey . . .	8	9	1	1	107	94
California.	85	80	31	30	362	375	New Mexico. . .	14	14	45	44	3,296	3,259
Colorado.	27	25	33	33	1,249	1,308	New York	39	36	8	8	218	214
Connecticut . . .	4	4	(Z)	(Z)	108	100	North Carolina .	62	58	10	9	156	159
Delaware.	3	3	1	1	207	228	North Dakota . .	34	32	41	40	1,209	1,259
Florida	41	39	11	10	266	264	Ohio.	83	74	16	15	188	205
Georgia	48	45	13	12	260	267	Oklahoma	70	71	33	34	471	479
Hawaii	5	5	2	2	357	331	Oregon	37	39	18	18	488	455
Idaho	22	22	14	14	628	628	Pennsylvania . .	53	50	8	8	153	154
Illinois.	83	77	28	28	342	365	Rhode Island . .	1	1	(Z)	(Z)	95	90
Indiana	68	63	16	16	240	252	South Carolina .	25	22	5	5	208	230
Iowa.	104	100	34	33	322	332	South Dakota . .	35	33	44	44	1,266	1,333
Kansas.	69	66	48	48	694	724	Tennessee. . . .	87	82	12	12	139	146
Kentucky.	93	89	14	14	152	157	Texas	196	202	132	129	673	639
Louisiana	32	27	9	9	278	315	Utah.	13	13	11	11	856	828
Maine	7	8	1	1	201	178	Vermont	7	6	1	1	222	228
Maryland.	15	14	2	2	148	154	Virginia	46	47	9	9	193	183
Massachusetts .	6	6	1	1	100	98	Washington . . .	37	36	16	16	432	439
Michigan	54	54	11	11	200	198	West Virginia . .	21	20	4	4	180	185
Minnesota	89	87	30	30	337	343	Wisconsin	80	80	18	17	220	211
Mississippi. . . .	40	40	13	13	325	323	Wyoming.	9	9	35	35	3,899	3,761

Z Less than 500,000 acres.

Source of tables 1081 and 1082: U.S. Dept. of Agriculture, National Agricultural Statistics Service, *Farm Numbers, 1975-80; Farms and Land in Farms, Final Estimates by States, 1979-1987; Farms and Land in Farms, Final Estimates, 1988-1992;* and *Farms and Land In Farms,* July releases.

No. 1083. Farm Real Estate—Summary: 1980 to 1995

[**1980** and **1987-89**, value data as of **Feb. 1; 1985**, as of **April 1; 1990-95**, as of **January 1**. Excludes Alaska and Hawaii. Total value of land and buildings is estimated by multiplying the number of acres of farmland by the average value per acre of land and buildings. Per acre values are based on data from the census of agriculture. For intercensal years, estimates are based on surveys conducted by the U.S. Dept. of Agriculture]

ITEM	Unit	1980	1985	1987	1988	1989	1990	1991	1992	1993	1994	1995
Total value.	Bil. dol	763.3	719.4	597.1	626.9	660.6	672.3	688.9	696.3	717.1	759.2	807.0
Average value per acre.	Dollars.	737	713	599	632	668	683	703	713	736	782	832
Average value, operating unit. . .	$1,000	313.5	314.5	270.5	286.0	305.1	314.8	328.1	333.4	345.1	368.7	390.2

No. 1084. Farm Real Estate—Value of Land and Buildings, by State: 1990 to 1995

[See headnote, table 1083. See also *Historical Statistics, Colonial Times to 1970*, series K 16]

STATE	VALUE OF LAND AND BUILDINGS (mil. dol.)			AVERAGE VALUE OF LAND AND BUILDINGS, PER ACRE			STATE	VALUE OF LAND AND BUILDINGS (mil. dol.)			AVERAGE VALUE OF LAND AND BUILDINGS, PER ACRE		
	1990	1994	1995	1990	1994	1995		1990	1994	1995	1990	1994	1995
U.S. .	672,273	759,217	807,017	$683	$782	$832	MT	13,431	15,165	16,529	222	254	277
							NE	24,680	26,485	28,074	524	562	596
AL	8,989	11,393	12,875	890	1,117	1,262	NV	1,842	2,355	2,543	207	268	289
AZ	9,612	11,522	12,282	267	325	347	NH	1,112	1,082	1,094	2,269	2,459	2,486
AR	12,338	13,992	14,747	796	927	983	NJ	4,780	6,370	6,844	5,494	7,407	8,052
CA	58,027	66,169	66,456	1,884	2,213	2,215	NM	8,233	9,184	9,883	185	208	225
CO	12,379	15,658	17,020	374	479	520	NY	8,518	10,925	10,628	1,014	1,383	1,380
CT	2,114	2,533	2,495	5,033	6,495	6,567	NC	13,144	14,965	16,092	1,355	1,609	1,749
DE	1,262	1,431	1,533	2,214	2,511	2,689	ND	13,001	14,278	15,041	321	353	373
FL	22,563	22,303	22,860	2,070	2,165	2,219	OH	19,986	24,212	27,359	1,273	1,593	1,800
GA	13,488	13,959	15,076	1,079	1,154	1,256	OK	16,203	17,572	18,609	491	517	547
ID.	9,015	10,450	11,286	658	774	836	OR	10,199	13,076	14,776	573	747	844
IL.	40,043	47,588	52,346	1,405	1,694	1,863	PA	15,625	17,528	18,013	1,929	2,247	2,339
IN.	20,440	24,061	26,302	1,254	1,504	1,654	RI.	389	433	438	5,564	6,871	6,947
IA.	36,515	42,532	44,786	1,090	1,281	1,349	SC	5,257	6,141	6,749	1,011	1,204	1,337
KS	21,555	24,035	25,573	450	503	535	SD	12,891	12,658	13,306	291	286	302
KY	13,790	16,021	17,498	978	1,136	1,250	TN	13,231	15,000	16,035	1,067	1,250	1,336
LA	8,233	8,402	9,199	925	1,000	1,082	TX	66,924	67,396	70,968	507	522	550
ME	1,556	1,675	1,681	1,073	1,232	1,245	UT	4,497	5,957	6,731	398	537	606
MD. . . .	5,767	7,282	8,155	2,563	3,310	3,707	VT	1,906	2,048	2,026	1,262	1,463	1,479
MA	2,874	3,203	3,077	4,227	5,339	5,398	VA	14,819	14,534	15,232	1,665	1,690	1,771
MI	10,854	12,985	14,219	1,005	1,214	1,329	WA	13,136	16,194	16,825	821	1,025	1,065
MN	24,300	27,135	27,907	810	914	936	WV	2,457	3,217	3,368	664	869	910
MS	9,568	10,701	11,432	736	836	886	WI	14,098	16,367	18,004	801	968	1,065
MO. . . .	21,310	24,835	26,411	701	825	880	WY	5,324	6,211	6,633	153	180	192

Source of tables 1083 and 1084: U.S. Dept. of Agriculture, Economic Research Service, 1980, *Farm Real Estate Market Developments*, annual; 1985-88, *Agricultural Resources, Agricultural Land Values and Markets, Situation and Outlook Report*, annual; 1989-95, *AREI Updates, Number 17: Agricultural Land Values*, annual.

No. 1085. Balance Sheet of the Farming Sector: 1980 to 1994

[**In billions of dollars, except as indicated**. As of **December 31**. See *Historical Statistics, Colonial Times to 1970*, series K 204-219, for data before revisions]

ITEM	1980	1985	1986	1987	1988	1989	1990	1991	1992	1993	1994
Assets	983.2	772.7	724.4	757.4	789.6	815.3	838.8	843.7	868.4	902.9	933.5
Real estate.	782.8	586.2	542.3	563.5	583.7	600.9	618.4	624.4	640.6	670.9	703.3
Nonreal estate.	173.7	153.3	147.6	158.8	170.5	177.6	182.1	178.8	184.7	185.4	182.4
Livestock and poultry	60.6	46.3	47.8	58.0	62.2	66.2	70.9	68.1	71.0	72.8	68.3
Machinery, motor vehicles . . .	80.3	82.9	81.5	80.0	81.2	85.1	85.4	85.8	85.6	85.2	85.7
Crops stored	32.7	22.9	16.3	17.7	23.6	23.7	23.0	22.2	24.2	23.3	23.4
Purchased inputs	(NA)	1.2	2.1	3.2	3.5	2.6	2.8	2.7	3.9	4.2	5.0
Financial assets.	26.7	33.3	34.5	35.1	35.4	36.8	38.3	40.6	43.1	46.6	47.7
Investment in cooperatives. . .	19.3	24.3	24.4	25.3	25.1	26.3	27.5	28.7	29.4	31.3	32.3
Other financial assets	7.4	9.0	10.0	9.9	10.3	10.5	10.9	11.8	13.6	15.3	15.5
Claims	983.2	772.7	724.4	757.4	789.6	815.3	838.8	843.7	868.4	902.9	933.5
Debt	166.8	177.6	157.0	144.4	139.6	137.9	138.0	139.2	139.1	142.0	146.8
Real estate debt.	89.7	100.1	90.4	82.4	77.8	76.0	74.7	74.9	75.4	76.0	77.6
Nonreal estate debt	77.1	77.5	66.6	62.0	61.7	61.9	63.2	64.3	63.6	65.9	69.1
Equity	816.4	595.1	567.5	613.0	650.0	677.4	700.8	704.5	729.4	761.0	786.7
Farm debt/asset ratio (percent).	17.0	23.0	21.7	19.1	17.7	16.9	16.4	16.5	16.0	15.7	15.7

NA Not available.

Source: U.S. Dept. of Agriculture, Economic Research Service, *Farm Business Economic Report, 1994* (ECI-1995).

No. 1086. Gross Farm Product—Summary: 1980 to 1994

[In billions of dollars. For definition of gross product, see text, section 14. Minus sign (-) indicates decrease]

ITEM	1980	1985	1986	1987	1988	1989	1990	1991	1992	1993	1994
CURRENT DOLLARS											
Farm output, total	142.9	152.7	144.0	152.0	158.5	177.2	185.6	180.3	187.7	186.0	201.6
Cash receipts from farm marketings	140.3	136.3	135.3	147.8	159.6	166.7	172.3	170.4	172.2	181.3	179.2
Farm housing	5.1	5.0	4.9	4.9	4.8	5.0	5.1	5.2	5.3	5.5	5.7
Farm products consumed on farms	1.2	0.9	0.9	0.7	0.7	0.7	0.7	0.6	0.6	0.5	0.5
Other farm income	2.4	4.6	4.4	5.0	5.2	4.9	4.8	5.1	4.6	4.8	4.7
Change in farm inventories	-6.1	5.8	-1.5	-6.4	-11.9	-	2.6	-1.1	5.0	-6.2	11.5
Less: Intermediate goods and services purchased[1]	86.8	85.6	81.1	86.9	94.7	101.0	106.0	107.3	107.1	113.9	119.3
Equals: **Gross farm product**	56.1	67.1	63.0	65.1	63.8	76.2	79.6	72.9	80.6	72.1	82.3
Less: Consumption of fixed capital	16.9	19.2	19.3	19.4	19.7	20.6	20.8	21.4	22.3	22.4	23.1
Indirect business tax[2]	3.0	3.3	3.3	3.6	3.7	3.9	4.4	4.4	4.5	4.6	5.0
Plus: Subsidies to operators	1.0	6.3	9.5	13.5	11.7	9.3	7.5	6.8	7.7	11.3	6.6
Equals: **Farm national income**	37.3	50.9	49.9	55.6	52.2	61.0	62.0	54.0	61.5	56.4	60.8
CHAINED (1992) DOLLARS [3]											
Farm output, total	143.9	169.2	161.8	164.9	158.3	168.4	179.2	178.2	187.7	182.2	198.0
Cash receipts from farm marketings	146.9	149.5	152.5	164.3	161.5	159.8	164.0	168.9	172.2	177.6	176.7
Farm housing	7.4	6.2	6.0	5.8	5.8	5.6	5.6	5.5	5.3	5.1	4.9
Farm products consumed on farms	1.4	1.1	1.1	0.8	0.8	0.7	0.6	0.6	0.6	0.5	0.5
Other farm income	2.4	4.7	4.9	5.3	5.0	4.5	4.7	5.0	4.6	4.8	4.3
Change in farm inventories	-6.9	6.5	-1.8	-9.0	-12.7	-	2.5	-1.7	5.4	-7.2	12.3
Less: Intermediate goods and services purchased[1]	102.0	96.6	96.3	101.7	103.0	104.1	106.2	107.1	107.1	111.2	114.3
Equals: **Gross farm product**	46.2	71.9	65.5	63.7	56.6	64.8	72.9	71.2	80.6	71.0	83.9

- Represents zero.   [1] Includes rent paid to nonoperator landlords.   [2] Includes nontax liability.   [3] See text, section 14.

Source: U.S. Bureau of Economic Analysis, *National Income and Product Accounts of the United States* to be published in late 1996, and *Survey of Current Business*, January/February 1996.

No. 1087. Value Added to Economy by Agricultural Sector: 1980 to 1994

[In billions of dollars. Data are consistent with the net farm income accounts and include income and expenses related to the farm operator dwellings. The concept presented is consistent with that employed by the Organization for Economic Co-operation and Development]

ITEM	1980	1985	1986	1987	1988	1989	1990	1991	1992	1993	1994
Final agricultural sector output	148.0	153.5	144.3	151.5	162.9	181.0	189.2	183.6	191.3	189.6	205.6
Final crop output (sales)[1]	64.4	74.1	63.3	64.5	69.2	81.5	83.4	80.9	89.0	81.6	98.9
Final animal output (sales)[1]	70.3	68.7	70.7	75.7	78.6	83.8	90.2	87.3	87.0	91.6	89.9
Services and forestry	13.3	10.7	10.3	11.3	15.0	15.8	15.6	15.4	15.3	16.4	16.8
Machine hire and customwork	0.7	1.5	1.2	1.5	1.5	1.7	1.8	1.7	1.5	2.0	2.3
Forest products sold	1.0	1.4	1.5	1.7	1.8	2.0	1.9	1.9	2.2	2.5	2.7
Other farm income	0.6	3.2	3.0	3.2	4.5	4.9	4.5	4.7	4.4	4.6	4.1
Gross imputed rental value of farm dwellings	11.0	4.7	4.6	4.9	7.1	7.2	7.3	7.1	7.2	7.3	7.6
Less: Intermediate consumption outlays	77.0	73.5	71.4	76.2	84.4	89.0	93.2	94.7	93.7	100.8	105.1
Farm origin	34.9	29.3	30.4	32.6	37.4	38.2	39.8	38.9	38.9	41.6	41.6
Manufactured inputs	20.9	18.3	16.5	15.9	16.6	18.0	19.4	20.6	20.1	20.5	21.7
Other intermediate expenses	21.2	26.0	24.5	27.7	30.3	32.8	34.0	35.3	34.6	38.8	41.8
Repair and maintenance of capital items	7.1	6.4	6.4	6.8	7.7	8.4	8.6	8.6	8.5	9.2	9.2
Machine hire and customwork	1.8	2.4	2.1	2.5	3.1	3.4	3.6	3.5	3.8	4.4	4.8
Marketing, storage, and transportation expenses	3.1	4.1	3.7	4.1	3.5	4.2	4.2	4.7	4.5	5.6	6.7
Contract labor	1.0	1.5	1.0	1.3	1.1	1.3	1.6	1.6	1.7	1.8	1.8
Miscellaneous expenses	8.2	11.6	11.3	13.1	14.9	15.5	16.1	16.8	16.1	17.8	19.3
Plus: Net government transactions[2]	-2.8	2.9	7.0	11.6	9.2	5.4	3.2	2.1	2.8	6.8	1.0
Direct Government payments	1.3	7.7	11.8	16.7	14.5	10.9	9.3	8.2	9.2	13.4	7.9
Motor vehicle registration and licensing fees	0.2	0.3	0.2	0.3	0.3	0.3	0.4	0.3	0.4	0.4	0.3
Property taxes	3.9	4.5	4.6	4.9	5.0	5.2	5.7	5.8	6.0	6.3	6.6
Equals: **Gross value added**	68.2	82.9	79.9	87.0	87.7	97.4	99.3	90.9	100.4	95.5	101.5
Less: Capital consumption	21.5	19.3	17.8	17.1	17.6	18.2	18.3	18.2	18.3	18.4	18.5
Equals: Net value added	46.7	63.6	62.1	69.9	70.1	79.2	81.0	72.7	82.1	77.2	83.0
Less: Employee compensation	8.3	8.5	8.4	8.7	9.8	10.7	12.5	12.3	12.3	13.2	13.5
Equals: Net operating surplus	38.5	55.1	53.6	61.2	60.3	68.5	68.5	60.3	69.8	63.9	69.5
Less: Net rent received by nonoperator landlords	6.1	7.7	6.1	8.2	8.5	9.6	10.3	9.9	10.7	11.0	11.1
Less: Real estate and nonreal estate interest	16.3	18.6	16.5	15.0	14.3	13.9	13.4	12.1	11.2	10.8	11.7
Equals: **Net farm income**	16.1	28.8	31.1	38.0	37.5	45.0	44.8	38.4	47.9	42.1	46.7

[1] Includes home consumption and value of inventory adjustment.   [2] Direct Government payments minus motor vehicle registration and licensing fees and property taxes.

Source: U.S. Dept. of Agriculture, Economic Research Service, *Farm Business Economic Report, 1994* (ECI-1995).

No. 1088. Farm Income and Expenses: 1980 to 1994

[In billions of dollars. See also *Historical Statistics, Colonial Times to 1970,* series K 192, K 259-260, K 264-285, and K 326]

ITEM	1980	1985	1986	1987	1988	1989	1990	1991	1992	1993	1994
Gross farm income	**149.3**	**161.2**	**156.1**	**168.3**	**177.3**	**191.9**	**198.5**	**191.8**	**200.5**	**203.0**	**213.5**
Cash income	143.3	157.9	152.9	165.0	173.6	180.3	187.0	184.3	188.6	199.6	196.7
Farm marketings	139.7	144.1	135.4	141.8	151.2	160.8	169.4	167.8	171.3	177.1	179.7
Crops	71.7	74.3	63.8	65.8	71.6	76.9	80.3	82.0	85.7	87.1	91.6
Livestock and products	68.0	69.8	71.6	76.0	79.6	83.9	89.2	85.8	85.6	90.0	88.1
Government payments	1.3	7.7	11.8	16.7	14.5	10.9	9.3	8.2	9.2	13.4	7.9
Other farm income [1]	2.3	6.0	5.7	6.4	7.9	8.6	8.2	8.3	8.2	9.1	9.2
Value of home consumption	1.2	0.9	0.9	0.7	0.7	0.7	0.7	0.6	0.6	0.5	0.5
Rental value of dwellings [2]	11.0	4.7	4.6	4.9	7.1	7.2	7.3	7.1	7.2	7.3	7.6
Value of inventory adjustment [3]	-6.3	-2.3	-2.2	-2.3	-4.1	3.8	3.5	-0.2	4.2	-4.5	8.7
Expenses of farm production	**133.1**	**132.4**	**125.1**	**130.2**	**139.8**	**146.9**	**153.7**	**153.4**	**152.6**	**160.9**	**166.7**
Intermediate products	76.1	72.3	70.6	75.2	83.6	88.0	91.9	93.5	92.3	99.4	103.6
Farm origin	34.9	29.3	30.4	32.6	37.4	38.2	39.8	38.9	38.9	41.6	41.6
Feed purchased	21.0	16.9	17.5	17.5	20.2	20.7	20.4	19.3	20.1	21.4	22.6
Livestock, poultry purchased	10.7	9.2	9.8	11.8	13.1	13.1	14.9	14.4	13.9	15.0	13.6
Seed purchased [4]	3.2	3.1	3.2	3.3	4.1	4.4	4.5	5.1	4.9	5.2	5.4
Manufactured inputs	20.9	18.3	16.5	15.9	16.6	18.0	19.4	20.6	20.1	20.5	21.7
Fertilizer and lime	9.5	7.5	6.8	6.5	7.7	8.2	8.2	8.7	8.3	8.4	9.2
Pesticides	3.5	4.3	4.3	4.5	4.1	5.0	5.4	6.3	6.5	6.7	7.2
Fuel and oil	7.9	6.4	5.3	5.0	4.8	4.8	5.8	5.6	5.3	5.3	5.3
Repairs and maintenance [5]	7.1	6.4	6.4	6.8	7.7	8.4	8.6	8.6	8.5	9.2	9.2
Other [6]	13.3	18.4	17.3	19.9	21.8	23.4	24.2	25.4	24.8	28.2	31.1
Interest	16.3	18.6	16.5	15.0	14.3	13.9	13.4	12.1	11.2	10.8	11.7
Real estate	7.5	9.9	9.1	8.2	7.6	7.2	6.7	6.0	5.8	5.5	5.7
Nonreal estate	8.7	8.7	7.4	6.8	6.7	6.7	6.7	6.1	5.4	5.3	6.0
Contract, hired labor expenses [7]	9.3	10.0	9.5	10.0	10.9	12.0	14.1	13.9	14.0	15.0	15.3
Net rent to nonoperator landlords [8]	6.1	7.7	6.1	8.2	8.5	9.6	10.3	9.9	10.7	11.0	11.1
Capital consumption [9]	21.5	19.3	17.8	17.1	17.6	18.2	18.3	18.2	18.3	18.4	18.5
Property taxes	3.9	4.5	4.6	4.9	5.0	5.2	5.7	5.8	6.0	6.3	6.6
Net farm income	**16.1**	**28.8**	**31.1**	**38.0**	**37.5**	**45.0**	**44.8**	**38.4**	**47.9**	**42.1**	**46.7**

[1] Includes forest product sales.   [2] Data for 1980 are not comparable with later data.   [3] Minus sign (-) indicates decrease in inventories.   [4] Includes bulbs, plants, and trees.   [5] Expenditures for repairs and maintenance of farm buildings, motor vehicles, and machinery.   [6] Includes machine hire and customwork expenses; marketing, storage, and transportation expenses and miscellaneous expenses. Significant differences in the items included exist between 1987 and prior years.   [7] Includes Social Security payments and perquisites.   [8] Data for 1980 are based on different sources from those for 1985 and later, creating potential inconsistencies in estimates among these periods. Forest product sales by nonoperators are included beginning in 1987. Includes landlord capital consumption.   [9] Capital replacement and accidental damage.

No. 1089. Farm Income—Cash Receipts From Farm Marketings: 1990 to 1994

[In millions of dollars. Represents gross receipts from commercial market sales as well as net Commodity Credit Corporation loans. See also *Historical Statistics, Colonial Times to 1970,* series K 286-302]

COMMODITY	1990	1992	1993	1994	COMMODITY	1990	1992	1993	1994
Total	**169,449**	**171,258**	**177,137**	**179,669**	Avocados	245	205	140	262
All crops [1]	80,256	85,662	87,102	91,562	Cherries	156	233	225	247
Barley	823	815	655	678	Grapefruit	355	373	322	310
Corn	13,348	14,665	14,607	15,031	Grapes	1,677	1,846	2,002	1,854
Cotton lint, seed	5,488	5,192	5,249	5,730	Lemons	306	239	283	264
Hay	3,271	3,084	3,521	3,579	Oranges	1,721	1,474	1,514	1,580
Oats	221	176	143	134	Peaches	374	380	399	313
Peanuts	1,258	1,286	1,032	1,231	Pears	261	275	247	227
Rice	1,052	1,256	699	1,654	Plums and				
Sorghum	1,002	1,314	1,225	1,142	prunes	295	254	262	250
Soybean	10,756	11,619	11,781	13,404	Strawberries	590	698	671	824
Sunflower/safflower	217	304	298	446	Almonds	598	691	911	894
Tobacco	2,733	2,962	2,949	2,646	Pecans	248	241	214	200
Wheat	6,412	7,194	7,464	7,794	Walnuts	236	286	361	317
Vegetables [2]	11,424	11,824	13,144	13,033	Sugar beets	1,178	1,205	1,021	1,242
Dry beans	692	489	519	568	Sugarcane	820	877	868	882
Snap beans	198	253	271	285	Mushrooms	667	668	701	721
Broccoli	268	284	278	336	Greenhouse,				
Carrots	281	353	296	310	nursery	8,677	9,304	9,663	10,044
Celery	215	259	319	226					
Sweet corn	476	480	532	631	All livestock and				
Cucumbers	231	295	304	286	products [1]	89,193	85,596	90,036	88,107
Lettuce	844	1,172	1,469	1,111	Cattle and calves	39,302	37,272	39,362	36,445
Onions	486	533	918	633	Dairy products	20,153	19,742	19,244	19,934
Green peppers	150	386	437	468	Hogs	11,525	10,017	10,911	9,859
Potatoes	2,448	1,977	2,326	2,529	Broilers	8,365	9,177	10,416	11,370
Tomatoes	1,627	1,906	1,708	1,683	Eggs	4,010	3,385	3,779	3,777
Cantaloups	195	251	297	308	Turkeys	2,393	2,396	2,509	2,672
					Sheep and lambs	414	460	545	507
Fruits, tree nuts [2]	9,418	10,175	10,260	10,146	Horses and mules	490	433	441	489
Apples	1,080	1,589	1,366	1,321	Aquaculture	541	572	630	657

[1] Includes other commodities not shown separately.   [2] Melons included with vegetables.

Source of tables 1088 and 1089: U.S. Dept. of Agriculture, Economic Research Service, *Farm Business Economic Report, 1994* (ECI-1995).

No. 1090. Indexes of Prices Received and Paid by Farmers: 1990 to 1995

[1990-92=100, except as noted. See also *Historical Statistics, Colonial Times to 1970*, series K 344-353]

ITEM	1990	1993	1994	1995, prel.	ITEM	1990	1993	1994	1995, prel.
Prices received, all products	**104**	**101**	**100**	**102**	Prices paid, total [3]	99	103	106	109
					Production	99	103	106	108
					Feed	103	99	105	103
Crops [1]	103	102	105	112	Livestock & poultry	102	104	95	84
Food grains	100	105	119	134	Seed	102	105	109	110
Feed grains and hay	105	99	106	112	Fertilizer	97	97	106	117
Cotton	107	89	109	128	Agricultural chemicals	95	107	112	115
Tobacco	97	101	101	103	Fuels	100	92	84	88
Oil-bearing crops	105	108	110	104	Supplies & repairs	96	107	110	112
Fruits	97	91	89	98	Autos and trucks	101	109	115	121
Commercial vegetables [2]	102	116	109	119	Farm machinery	96	106	110	116
Potatoes & dry beans	133	107	110	106	Building materials	99	105	109	114
					Farm services	97	108	113	117
Livestock and products	105	100	95	92	Interest	107	88	92	102
Meat animals	105	100	90	85	Taxes	95	107	112	117
Dairy products	105	98	99	98	Wage rates	96	108	111	113
Poultry and eggs	105	105	106	107	Parity ratio (1910-14=100) [4]	51	47	46	46

[1] Includes other items not shown separately.   [2] Excludes potatoes and dry beans.   [3] Includes production items, interest, taxes, wage rates, and a family living component. The family living component is the Consumer Price Index for all urban consumers from the Bureau of Labor Statistics. See text, section 15, and table 745.   [4] Ratio of prices received by farmers to prices paid.

Source: U.S. Dept. of Agriculture, National Agricultural Statistics Service, *Agricultural Prices: Annual Summary*.

No. 1091. Commodity Credit Corporation—Net Outlays, by Commodity and Function: 1990 to 1995

[In millions of dollars. For fiscal year ending in year shown; see text, section 9. Excludes value of commodity certificates which may also be issued to farmers in lieu of cash under certain programs. Minus sign (-) indicates a net receipt (excess of repayments or other receipts over gross outlays of funds)]

COMMODITY	1990	1993	1994	1995	FUNCTION	1990	1993	1994	1995
Total	**6,471**	**16,047**	**10,336**	**6,030**	**Total**	**6,471**	**16,047**	**10,336**	**6,030**
Feed grains	2,693	5,765	972	2,392	Price support loans [4]	-399	2,065	527	-119
Wheat	796	2,185	1,729	803	Direct payments [5]	4,370	9,143	5,057	4,125
Cotton, upland	-79	2,239	1,539	99	Deficiency payments	4,178	8,607	4,391	4,008
Dairy	505	253	158	4	Loan deficiency payments	3	387	495	29
Rice	667	887	836	814					
Wool	104	179	211	108	1988/93 crop disaster	[3]5	872	2,461	584
Honey	47	22	-	-9	Emergency livestock/forage				
Peanuts	1	-13	37	120	assistance	156	72	105	76
Sugar	15	-35	-24	-3	Purchases [6]	-48	525	293	-51
Tobacco	-307	235	693	-298	Producer storage payments	185	9	12	23
Soybeans	5	109	-183	77	Processing, storage and				
Operating expense [1]	618	6	6	6	transportation	278	136	112	72
Interest expenditure	632	129	-17	-1	Operating expense [1]	618	6	6	6
Export programs [2]	-34	2,193	1,950	1,361	Interest expenditure	632	129	-17	-1
1988/93 disaster/livestock					Export programs [2]	-34	2,193	1,950	1,361
assistance	[3]161	944	2,566	660	Other	708	897	-170	-46
Other	647	949	-137	-103					

- Represents zero.   [1] Excludes CCC transfers to the general sales manager.   [2] Covers the direct export credit sales program, the export guarantee program, transfers to the general sales manager, market promotion program (beginning 1991), and beginning 1992, the export guarantee program-credit reform, export enhancement program, dairy export incentive program, and technical assistance to emerging democracies.   [3] Approximately $1.5 billion in benefits to farmers under the Disaster Assistance Act of 1989 were paid in generic certificates and were not recorded directly as disaster assistance outlays.   [4] Price support loans made less loans repaid.   [5] Cash payments only. Excludes generic certificates.   [6] Purchases less sales proceeds.

Source: U.S. Agricultural Stabilization and Conservation Service, *Commodity Credit Corporation Report of Financial Condition and Operations*, annual, and *Agricultural Outlook*, monthly.

No. 1092. Average Income to Farm Operator Households: 1991 to 1995

[In dollars per operator household. Data are expanded to represent the total number of farms and ranches in the contiguous United States]

ITEM	1991	1992	1993	1994	1995 [1]
Farm income to household [2]	5,810	7,180	4,815	5,200	4,898
Self-employment farm income	4,458	5,172	3,623	3,983	(NA)
Other farm income to household	1,352	2,008	1,192	1,217	(NA)
Plus: Total off-farm income	31,638	35,731	35,408	38,939	38,512
Income from wages, salaries, and nonfarm businesses	23,551	27,022	25,215	29,355	(NA)
Income from interest, dividends, transfer payments, etc.	8,086	8,709	10,194	9,584	(NA)
Equals: Farm operator household income	37,447	42,911	40,223	44,140	43,410

NA Not available.   [1] Preliminary.   [2] Farm income to the household equals self-employment income plus amounts that operators pay themselves and family members to work on the farm, income from renting out acreage (1991 and 1992), and net income from a farm business other than the one being surveyed. In 1993 and 1994, income from renting out acreage is included in income from interest, dividends, transfer payments, etc.

Source: U.S. Dept. of Agriculture, Economic Research Service, *Agricultural Income and Finance Situation and Outlook*, December 1995.

No. 1093. Farm Assets, Debt, and Income, by State: 1993 and 1994

[Assets and debt, as of December 31. Farm income data are after inventory adjustment and include income and expenses related to the farm operator's dwelling]

DIVISION AND STATE	ASSETS (mil. dol.)		DEBT (mil. dol.)		DEBT/ASSET RATIO (percent)		GROSS FARM INCOME (mil. dol.)		NET FARM INCOME (mil. dol.)	
	1993	1994	1993	1994	1993	1994	1993	1994	1993	1994
United States.	902,924	933,458	141,953	146,762	15.7	15.7	202,969	213,471	42,061	46,730
New England:										
Maine.	2,006	2,019	303	323	15.1	16.0	550	556	129	98
New Hampshire	1,048	1,060	73	74	6.9	7.0	190	194	48	46
Vermont	2,478	2,457	336	342	13.6	13.9	520	539	116	114
Massachusetts	3,144	3,048	290	287	9.2	9.4	552	530	186	140
Rhode Island	403	412	38	39	9.5	9.4	89	90	44	42
Connecticut	2,413	2,380	188	197	7.8	8.3	519	523	178	167
Middle Atlantic:										
New York	13,551	13,064	2,095	2,142	15.5	16.4	3,124	3,095	533	337
New Jersey	6,287	6,638	451	414	7.2	6.2	811	900	202	249
Pennsylvania	19,956	20,038	2,428	2,487	12.2	12.4	4,096	4,160	833	673
East North Central:										
Ohio.	27,238	29,370	3,095	3,316	11.4	11.3	5,087	5,416	868	1,170
Indiana	27,995	29,331	4,510	4,648	16.1	15.9	5,824	5,712	918	857
Illinois	55,129	58,708	7,431	7,660	13.5	13.1	9,026	9,715	1,233	1,919
Michigan	15,936	16,612	2,548	2,591	16.0	15.6	3,921	3,835	460	193
Wisconsin	23,061	23,497	4,770	4,892	20.7	20.8	6,009	6,483	507	626
West North Central:										
Minnesota	35,199	35,546	6,927	7,252	19.7	20.4	7,043	8,928	35	1,407
Iowa	53,784	55,587	10,473	10,817	19.5	19.5	10,618	13,116	630	2,793
Missouri	30,282	30,852	4,634	4,770	15.3	15.5	4,951	5,379	639	964
North Dakota	20,540	21,177	3,340	3,569	16.3	16.9	3,488	3,968	521	859
South Dakota	18,471	18,696	3,552	3,725	19.2	19.9	3,811	4,276	982	1,354
Nebraska	35,389	36,185	7,222	7,544	20.4	20.9	9,787	9,973	1,912	2,264
Kansas	30,831	31,919	5,778	5,929	18.7	18.6	8,583	9,053	1,512	1,678
South Atlantic:										
Delaware	1,519	1,595	309	308	20.4	19.3	670	734	114	127
Maryland	7,536	8,153	974	989	12.9	12.1	1,512	1,573	280	276
Virginia	15,991	16,679	1,900	1,908	11.9	11.4	2,333	2,523	455	608
West Virginia	3,405	3,436	400	411	11.8	12.0	475	503	88	90
North Carolina	16,952	18,030	2,661	2,907	15.7	16.1	7,036	7,678	2,538	2,873
South Carolina	7,084	7,441	832	845	11.7	11.4	1,429	1,620	304	461
Georgia	16,365	17,097	2,749	2,854	16.8	16.7	4,912	5,650	1,488	2,055
Florida	25,057	25,425	3,893	4,074	15.5	16.0	6,438	6,278	2,471	2,251
East South Central:										
Kentucky	18,835	20,037	2,674	2,761	14.2	13.8	3,860	3,879	1,126	1,209
Tennessee	17,071	17,153	2,169	1,993	12.7	11.6	2,585	2,713	513	647
Alabama	12,576	13,424	1,481	1,517	11.8	11.3	3,444	3,631	1,034	1,123
Mississippi	12,238	12,831	2,434	2,444	19.9	19.1	3,234	3,679	345	670
West South Central:										
Arkansas	16,839	17,318	3,233	3,313	19.2	19.1	5,451	6,010	1,018	1,419
Louisiana	8,149	8,661	1,636	1,602	20.1	18.5	2,301	2,485	377	520
Oklahoma	21,802	22,484	3,717	3,890	17.1	17.3	4,605	4,827	1,192	1,133
Texas	79,750	82,071	9,628	9,872	12.1	12.0	15,653	15,334	3,952	3,744
Mountain:										
Montana	18,751	19,525	2,461	2,584	13.1	13.2	2,558	2,412	826	454
Idaho	12,821	13,201	2,561	2,685	20.0	20.3	3,337	3,394	1,042	665
Wyoming	7,623	7,744	811	884	10.6	11.4	1,037	894	294	122
Colorado	18,844	19,647	2,937	3,055	15.6	15.6	4,775	4,581	1,006	608
New Mexico	10,588	11,244	1,111	1,131	10.5	10.1	1,704	1,775	455	378
Arizona	12,200	12,847	1,217	1,256	10.0	9.8	2,149	2,048	702	482
Utah	6,406	6,955	652	675	10.2	9.7	968	1,000	309	241
Nevada	2,607	2,704	231	239	8.9	8.9	330	340	106	67
Pacific:										
Washington	16,388	17,912	2,899	3,018	17.7	16.9	5,677	5,462	1,307	922
Oregon	14,382	15,445	2,172	2,187	15.1	14.2	3,551	3,593	661	523
California	71,306	70,968	13,452	14,066	18.9	19.8	21,777	21,838	5,518	5,077
Alaska	561	577	16	16	2.8	2.8	35	37	9	9
Hawaii	4,136	4,254	260	261	6.3	6.1	538	538	48	27

Source: U.S. Dept. of Agriculture, Economic Research Service, *Farm Business Economic Report, 1994* (ECI-1995).

No. 1094. Farm Income—Farm Marketings, 1993 and 1994, Government Payments, 1994, and Principal Commodities, 1994, by State

[In millions of dollars. Cattle include calves; sheep include lambs; and greenhouse includes nursery]

DIVISION AND STATE	1993 Farm marketings Total	Crops	Live-stock and prod-ucts	1994 Farm marketings Total	Crops	Live-stock and prod-ucts	Gov-ern-ment pay-ments	State rank for total farm marketings and four principal commodities in order of marketing receipts
U.S..	177,137	87,102	90,036	179,669	91,562	88,107	7,881	Cattle, dairy products, corn, soybeans
N.E.....	2,140	1,009	1,131	2,127	1,017	1,110	27	(X)
ME ...	453	185	269	483	207	276	14	42-Potatoes, eggs, dairy products, aquaculture
NH ...	152	86	66	152	88	64	1	48-Dairy products, greenhouse, Christmas trees, apples
VT ...	489	87	402	481	91	390	4	43-Dairy products, cattle, greenhouse, hay
MA ...	491	370	121	459	341	117	5	45-Greenhouse, cranberries, dairy products, eggs
RI....	80	67	14	81	68	12	(Z)	49-Dairy products, dairy products, eggs, sweet corn
CT ...	475	214	260	473	222	251	2	44-Greenhouse, eggs, dairy products, aquaculture
M.A	7,366	2,667	4,699	7,381	2,700	4,682	83	(X)
NY ...	2,860	978	1,882	2,858	971	1,887	42	27-Dairy products, greenhouse, cattle, apples
NJ....	700	502	197	768	586	183	8	39-Greenhouse, dairy products, green peppers, tomatoes
PA....	3,807	1,187	2,620	3,755	1,143	2,612	33	19-Dairy products, cattle, greenhouse, mushrooms
E.N.C...	26,705	15,433	11,272	26,339	15,577	10,762	896	(X)
OH ...	4,491	2,835	1,656	4,475	2,898	1,577	117	16-Soybeans, corn, dairy products, greenhouse
IN	5,341	3,428	1,913	4,838	3,072	1,765	137	12-Corn, soybeans, hogs, cattle
IL	8,151	5,916	2,234	8,223	6,158	2,065	303	5-Corn, soybeans, hogs, cattle
MI....	3,328	1,959	1,368	3,419	2,009	1,410	102	20-Dairy products, greenhouse, soybeans, corn
WI....	5,395	1,294	4,101	5,384	1,439	3,945	236	10-Dairy products, cattle, corn, hogs
W.N.C...	43,191	18,110	25,082	43,657	20,154	23,503	3,185	(X)
MN ...	6,334	2,580	3,755	6,522	3,075	3,447	622	7-Dairy products, soybeans, corn, cattle
IA ...	10,390	4,606	5,784	10,084	4,964	5,120	733	3-Corn, hogs, soybeans, cattle
MO ...	4,112	1,836	2,276	4,524	2,072	2,452	267	15-Cattle, soybeans, hogs, corn
ND ...	2,949	2,348	600	2,935	2,307	627	457	24-Wheat, cattle, barley, sunflower
SD ...	3,200	1,236	1,964	3,343	1,699	1,644	289	21-Cattle, corn, soybeans, wheat
NE ...	8,871	3,025	5,846	8,561	3,158	5,403	348	4-Cattle, corn, hogs, soybeans
KS ...	7,335	2,478	4,857	7,687	2,879	4,809	468	6-Cattle, wheat, corn, soybeans
S.A.....	22,026	11,467	10,559	22,991	12,170	10,822	397	(X)
DE ...	611	144	467	660	155	505	6	40-Broilers, soybeans, greenhouse, corn
MD ...	1,345	525	821	1,345	551	793	16	36-Broilers, greenhouse, dairy products, soybeans
VA...	2,095	697	1,398	2,159	773	1,386	34	29-Broilers, cattle, dairy products, turkeys
WV...	405	81	323	403	74	329	6	46-Broilers, cattle, turkeys, dairy products
NC ...	6,019	2,829	3,190	6,369	3,037	3,333	78	8-Broilers, hogs, tobacco, greenhouse
SC ...	1,249	649	600	1,362	747	615	60	35-Broilers, tobacco, greenhouse, cattle
GA ...	4,232	1,684	2,549	4,716	2,047	2,669	140	14-Broilers, peanuts, cotton, eggs
FL....	6,069	4,858	1,211	5,978	4,786	1,192	59	9-Oranges, greenhouse, sugar, tomatoes
E.S.C ...	10,929	4,546	6,383	11,203	4,710	6,493	465	(X)
KY ...	3,414	1,690	1,725	3,230	1,585	1,645	55	22-Tobacco, cattle, horses/mules, corn
TN ...	2,026	1,064	962	2,152	1,170	982	96	30-Cattle, dairy products, cotton, tobacco
AL...	2,857	728	2,129	2,904	745	2,159	89	26-Broilers, cattle, chickens, cotton
MS ...	2,632	1,064	1,568	2,916	1,210	1,706	225	25-Broilers, cotton, soybeans, aquaculture
W.S.C ...	22,761	8,177	14,584	23,705	8,959	14,746	1,555	(X)
AR ...	4,354	1,454	2,901	5,276	2,162	3,114	303	11-Broilers, rice, soybeans, cotton
LA...	1,795	1,090	705	2,013	1,309	704	182	31-Cotton, broilers, rice, sugar
OK ...	3,949	1,141	2,808	3,864	1,165	2,700	207	18-Cattle, wheat, broilers, greenhouse
TX ...	12,662	4,492	8,170	12,552	4,324	8,228	863	2-Cattle, cotton, dairy products, greenhouse
Moun-tain....	14,340	5,724	8,617	14,130	5,954	8,175	769	(X)
MT ...	1,802	854	948	1,857	990	867	256	33-Cattle, wheat, barley, hay
ID ...	2,890	1,723	1,167	2,955	1,756	1,199	127	23-Cattle, potatoes, dairy products, wheat
WY ...	841	181	660	778	157	621	38	38-Cattle, sugar beets, hay, sheep
CO ...	4,197	1,205	2,992	4,029	1,250	2,779	177	17-Cattle, wheat, corn, dairy products
NM ...	1,537	413	1,123	1,524	425	1,099	61	34-Cattle, dairy products, hay, chili peppers
AZ ...	1,946	1,028	918	1,869	1,045	824	72	32-Cattle, cotton, dairy products, lettuce
UT ...	831	218	614	819	221	598	32	37-Cattle, dairy products, hay, turkeys
NV ...	296	103	193	299	110	189	5	47-Cattle, hay, dairy products, potatoes
Pacific ..	27,678	19,970	7,709	28,136	20,321	7,815	504	(X)
WA ...	4,633	3,075	1,558	4,720	3,112	1,609	153	13-Cattle, dairy products, apples, wheat
OR ...	2,557	1,809	748	2,652	1,926	726	74	28-Greenhouse, cattle, hay, dairy products
CA ...	19,954	14,643	5,311	20,238	14,841	5,398	273	1-Dairy products, greenhouse, grapes, cattle
AK ...	27	21	6	28	22	6	1	50-Greenhouse, dairy products, hay, potatoes
HI....	507	422	85	498	422	77	3	41-Sugar, pineapples, greenhouse, nuts

X Not applicable.   Z Less than $500,000.

Source: U.S. Dept. of Agriculture, Economic Research Service, *Farm Business Economic Report, 1994* (ECI-1995).

No. 1095. Civilian Consumer Expenditures for Farm Foods—Farm Value and Marketing Bill: 1980 to 1994

[In billions of dollars, except percent. Excludes imported and nonfarm foods, such as coffee and seafood, as well as food consumed by the military, or exported. See *Historical Statistics, Colonial Times to 1970*, series K 358-360 for data before revisions]

ITEM	1980	1985	1986	1987	1988	1989	1990	1991	1992	1993	1994
Consumer expenditures, total	264.4	345.4	359.6	375.5	398.8	419.4	449.8	465.1	474.5	489.2	510.6
Farm value, total	81.7	86.4	88.8	90.4	96.8	103.8	106.2	101.6	105.1	109.6	109.6
Marketing bill, total [1]	182.7	259.0	270.8	285.1	301.9	315.6	343.6	363.5	369.4	379.6	401.0
Percent of total consumer expenditures	69.1	75.0	75.3	75.9	75.7	75.3	76.4	78.2	77.9	77.6	78.5
At-home expenditures [2]	180.1	220.8	226.0	230.2	242.1	255.5	276.2	286.1	289.6	294.9	304.6
Farm value.	65.9	66.6	67.6	67.5	72.5	77.9	80.2	76.7	76.9	76.4	75.4
Marketing bill [1]	114.2	154.2	158.4	162.7	169.6	177.6	196.0	209.4	212.7	218.5	229.2
Percent of at-home expenditures	63.4	69.8	70.1	70.7	70.1	69.5	71.0	73.2	73.4	74.1	75.2
Away-from-home expenditures	84.3	124.6	133.6	145.3	156.7	163.9	173.6	179.0	184.9	194.3	206.0
Farm value.	15.8	19.8	21.2	22.9	24.3	25.9	26.0	24.9	28.2	33.2	34.2
Marketing bill [1]	68.5	104.8	112.4	122.4	132.4	138.0	147.6	154.1	156.7	161.1	171.8
Percent of away-from-home expenditures	81.3	84.1	84.1	84.2	84.5	84.2	85.0	86.1	84.7	82.9	83.4
Marketing bill cost components:											
Labor cost [3]	81.5	115.6	122.9	130.0	137.9	145.1	154.0	160.9	168.4	178.0	188.7
Packaging materials.	21.0	26.9	27.7	29.9	32.6	35.2	36.5	38.1	39.2	39.4	42.1
Rail and truck transport [4]	13.0	16.5	16.8	17.2	17.8	18.6	19.8	20.4	20.6	21.2	21.8
Corporate profits before taxes	9.9	10.4	10.3	11.1	12.0	12.9	13.2	15.2	14.9	14.2	16.0
Fuels and electricity.	9.0	13.1	13.2	13.6	14.1	14.8	15.2	16.3	16.7	17.2	17.9
Advertising.	7.3	12.5	13.5	13.8	14.1	15.7	17.1	17.5	17.9	18.3	18.9
Depreciation.	7.8	15.4	15.8	15.8	16.2	16.4	16.3	15.8	16.2	16.8	17.4
Net interest	3.4	6.1	6.7	8.1	9.7	12.3	13.5	12.2	12.4	13.1	13.5
Net rent.	6.8	9.3	9.7	10.9	11.7	12.7	13.9	15.9	16.4	17.0	17.8
Repairs	3.6	4.8	5.0	5.1	5.2	5.7	6.2	6.4	6.5	6.8	7.1
Taxes	8.3	11.7	12.2	12.6	13.7	14.6	15.7	16.5	16.9	17.6	18.3
Other	11.0	16.7	17.0	17.1	16.8	11.5	22.2	28.3	23.2	20.1	21.3

[1] The difference between expenditures for domestic farm-originated food products and the farm value or payment farmers received for the equivalent farm products.   [2] Food primarily purchased from retail food stores for use at home.   [3] Covers employee wages and salaries, and their health and welfare benefits. Also includes imputed earnings of proprietors, partners, and family workers not receiving stated remuneration.   [4] Excludes local hauling.

Source: U.S. Dept. of Agriculture, Economic Research Service, *Food Cost Review*, annual; *FoodReview*, periodic; and *Agricultural Statistics*, annual.

No. 1096. Selected Indexes of Farm Inputs: 1970 to 1993

[1982=100. Inputs based on physical quantities of resources used in production. See *Historical Statistics, Colonial Times to 1970*, series K 486-495 for data before revisions]

INPUT	1970	1980	1985	1986	1987	1988	1989	1990	1991	1992	1993
Total	95	105	94	91	89	86	86	89	90	90	90
Farm labor	133	102	90	85	84	86	85	85	87	82	81
Farm real estate.	95	102	97	95	91	90	92	92	91	91	89
Durable equipment.	78	102	86	80	74	70	67	65	64	62	60
Energy.	92	110	90	84	93	93	92	92	92	92	92
Agricultural chemicals [1]	76	133	100	110	101	92	96	98	103	103	106
Feed, seed, and livestock purchases [2]	83	102	93	94	91	89	86	94	91	96	96
Other purchased inputs [3]	89	116	103	93	97	86	91	103	110	114	126

[1] Includes fertilizer, lime, and pesticides.   [2] Includes nonfarm portion of feed, seed, and livestock purchases.   [3] Includes purchased services and miscellaneous inputs.

Source: U.S. Dept. of Agriculture, Economic Research Service, *Agricultural Outlook*, monthly. Also published in the U.S. Council of Economic Advisers, *Economic Report of the President*, annual.

No. 1097. Farm Machinery and Equipment: 1980 to 1994

[See also *Historical Statistics, Colonial Times to 1970*, series K 184-191]

ITEM	Unit	1980	1984	1985	1986	1987	1988	1989	1990	1991	1992	1993	1994
Value of farm implements and machinery [1]	Bil. dol. .	80.3	85.0	82.9	81.5	80.0	81.2	85.1	85.4	85.8	85.6	85.2	85.7
Farmers' expenditures:													
Motor vehicles [2]	Mil. dol. .	5,813	4,583	3,699	3,227	4,275	4,912	5,484	5,750	4,993	5,126	5,189	5,453
Tractors	Mil. dol. .	3,683	2,539	1,937	1,513	2,104	2,540	2,903	3,119	2,593	2,826	2,689	2,893
Machinery, equipment	Mil. dol. .	6,956	4,682	3,232	3,094	4,297	4,222	5,087	5,589	5,410	5,132	5,488	5,182
Repair and maintenance	Mil. dol. .	5,205	4,908	4,834	4,825	5,017	5,869	6,607	6,311	6,414	5,966	6,474	6,370
Tractors, machinery and equipment	Mil. dol. .	3,746	3,592	3,442	3,428	3,540	4,050	4,571	4,437	4,547	4,210	4,508	4,437
Autos and trucks	Mil. dol. .	1,459	1,316	1,392	1,397	1,477	1,821	2,039	1,876	1,870	1,758	1,969	1,937
Retail sales: [3]													
Tractors, total [4]	1,000. . .	119.3	66.7	58.5	47.1	48.3	52.0	59.7	66.3	58.1	52.8	57.8	63.2
Two-wheel drive	1,000. . .	108.4	62.7	55.5	45.1	46.6	49.3	55.5	61.2	54.0	50.1	54.5	59.5
Four-wheel drive	1,000. . .	10.9	4.0	3.0	2.0	1.7	2.7	4.2	5.1	4.1	2.7	3.3	3.7
Combines	1,000. . .	25.7	11.4	8.4	7.7	7.2	6.0	9.1	10.4	9.7	7.7	7.9	8.5

[1] Farm inventory valuations as of December 31. [2] For farm business use. [3] Source: Equipment Manufacturers Institute, Chicago, IL, unpublished data. [4] Covers tractors over 40 hp. only.

Source: Except as noted, U.S. Dept. of Agriculture, Economic Research Service, *Farm Business Economic Report, 1994* (ECI-1995). Also in *Agricultural Statistics*, annual.

No. 1098. Farm Output Indexes: 1970 to 1993

[1982=100. See also *Historical Statistics, Colonial Times to 1970*, series K 414-429]

ITEM	1970	1980	1984	1985	1986	1987	1988	1989	1990	1991	1992	1993
Farm output [1]	73	92	99	103	100	101	95	103	108	108	116	108
Per unit of total input	77	87	103	110	110	115	111	120	122	121	129	119
Gross production:												
Livestock and products [2]	90	100	101	104	104	107	109	109	111	114	116	117
Meat animals	100	104	100	99	99	100	102	102	102	105	106	106
Dairy products	87	95	99	105	106	105	107	106	109	109	112	111
Poultry and eggs	76	96	103	108	112	122	125	130	138	144	151	157
Crops [3]	63	86	97	102	96	98	86	99	106	104	115	101
Feed crops	64	81	97	107	102	90	67	91	94	92	107	82
Food grains	50	87	94	88	77	77	70	77	99	76	93	88
Oil crops	52	81	87	96	88	88	72	87	87	93	99	85
Cotton and cottonseed	92	95	112	114	83	128	134	104	133	152	152	140
Tobacco	98	90	89	77	58	61	69	71	83	86	88	83
Vegetables and melons	76	93	102	109	110	119	108	114	124	130	134	126
Fruits and nuts	71	102	99	98	95	108	116	111	110	108	114	120
Other crops	59	93	111	113	122	136	144	149	154	154	159	154

[1] Annual production available for eventual human use. [2] Includes livestock products not shown separately. [3] Includes crops not shown separately.

Source: U.S. Dept. of Agriculture, Economic Research Service, *Agricultural Outlook*, monthly. Also published in the U.S. Council of Economic Advisors, *Economic Report of the President*, annual.

No. 1099. Agricultural Exports and Imports—Volume, by Principal Commodities: 1980 to 1994

[In thousands of metric tons]

EXPORTS	1980	1990	1993	1994	IMPORTS	1980	1990	1993	1994
Animal products [1]	2,575	2,737	3,824	4,529	Fruits, nuts, vegetables	2,325	4,573	5,113	5,379
Wheat and products [2]	37,130	28,282	36,691	31,680	Bananas	2,352	3,094	3,513	3,694
Feed grains and products	72,970	61,397	48,282	43,579	Green coffee	1,089	1,174	1,081	995
Rice	3,075	2,509	2,775	2,983	Cocoa and products	325	765	801	672
Feeds and fodders	6,888	10,979	11,724	11,638	Meat and products [5]	931	1,165	1,153	1,150
Protein meal	7,427	5,138	6,352	5,372					
Oilseeds and products [3]	23,631	15,778	20,020	18,834	Vegetable oils	704	1,183	1,419	1,588
Vegetable oils	1,837	1,204	1,708	1,891	Rubber, crude natural	931	840	1,000	992
Fruits, nuts, vegetables [4]	4,147	5,552	6,172	6,839	Sugar	3,744	1,856	1,617	1,545
Cotton and linters	1,880	1,733	1,184	1,829	Spices	86	129	144	164
Tobacco, unmanufactured	272	223	208	197	Tobacco, unmanufactured	392	187	461	244

[1] Includes meat and products, poultry meats, dairy products, and fats, oils and greases. Excludes live animals, hides, skins, and eggs. [2] Includes flour and bulgur. [3] Includes soybeans, sunflowerseeds, peanuts, cottonseed, safflowerseed, flaxseed, and nondefatted soybean flour. [4] Excludes fruit juices. [5] Excludes poultry.

Source: U.S. Dept. of Agriculture, Economic Research Service, *Foreign Agricultural Trade of the United States*, Jan./Feb. 1995, and calendar year supplements.

No. 1100. Agricultural Exports and Imports—Value: 1980 to 1994

[In billions of dollars, except percent. Includes Puerto Rico. Excludes forest products and distilled liquors; includes crude rubber and similar gums (now mainly plantation products). Includes shipments under foreign aid programs. See also *Historical Statistics, Colonial Times to 1970*, series K 251-255]

YEAR	Trade bal- ance	Ex- ports, domes- tic prod- ucts	Per- cent of all ex- ports	Imports for con- sump- tion	Per- cent of all im- ports	YEAR	Trade bal- ance	Ex- ports, domes- tic prod- ucts	Per- cent of all ex- ports	Imports for con- sump- tion	Per- cent of all im- ports
1980	23.9	41.2	18	17.4	7	1989	18.2	39.9	11	21.7	5
1984	18.5	37.8	17	19.3	6	1990	16.6	39.4	10	22.8	5
1985	9.1	29.0	13	20.0	6	1991	16.5	39.2	10	22.7	5
1986	4.8	26.2	13	21.5	6	1992	18.3	42.9	10	24.6	5
1987	8.3	28.7	12	20.4	5	1993	17.6	42.6	10	25.0	4
1988	16.1	37.1	12	21.0	5	1994	18.9	45.7	9	26.8	4

Source: U.S. Dept. of Agriculture, Economic Research Service, *Foreign Agricultural Trade of the United States*, Jan.-Feb. issues, and calendar year supplements. Also in *Agricultural Statistics*, annual.

No. 1101. Agricultural Exports—Value, by Principal Commodities and Selected Countries of Destination: 1980 to 1994

[See headnote, table 1100. Data by country of destination for 1980 are not adjusted for transshipments]

COMMODITY AND COUNTRY	VALUE (mil. dol.)								PERCENT		
	1980	1985	1989	1990	1991	1992	1993	1994	1980	1990	1994
Total agricultural exports [1]	41,234	29,041	39,909	39,363	39,204	42,930	42,608	45,704	100.0	100.0	100.0
Grains and feeds [2]	19,126	11,882	17,155	14,378	12,746	14,174	13,979	13,515	46.4	36.5	29.6
Feed grains and products	9,852	6,112	7,870	7,151	5,869	5,881	5,174	4,912	23.9	18.2	10.7
Corn	8,492	5,206	6,580	6,027	4,922	4,708	4,220	3,936	20.6	15.3	8.6
Wheat and products	6,660	3,898	6,136	4,033	3,516	4,675	4,909	4,316	16.2	10.2	9.4
Rice	1,289	665	971	800	751	725	770	1,008	3.2	2.0	2.2
Oilseeds and products [2]	9,394	5,794	6,345	5,710	6,397	7,197	7,270	7,207	22.8	14.5	15.8
Soybeans	5,880	3,732	3,942	3,551	3,957	4,387	4,599	4,330	14.3	9.0	9.5
Soybean oilcake and meal	1,666	870	1,181	992	1,157	1,242	1,074	907	4.1	2.5	2.0
Vegetable oils and waxes	1,216	870	872	808	768	1,018	1,056	1,376	3.0	2.1	3.0
Animals and animal products [2]	3,768	4,150	6,378	6,712	7,007	7,925	7,931	9,149	9.2	17.1	20.0
Hides and skins, incl. furskins	1,046	1,295	1,747	1,747	1,371	1,346	1,285	1,523	2.6	4.4	3.3
Cattle hides	637	1,007	1,383	1,428	1,136	1,132	1,079	1,239	1.6	3.6	2.7
Meats and meat products	890	905	2,348	2,558	2,853	3,339	3,325	3,704	2.2	6.5	8.1
Beef and veal	249	467	1,420	1,579	1,757	2,043	1,995	2,304	0.6	4.0	5.0
Fats, oils, and greases	769	619	512	424	442	525	504	594	1.9	1.1	1.3
Poultry and poultry products	603	384	713	954	1,094	1,211	1,376	1,880	1.5	2.4	4.1
Cotton, excluding linters	2,864	1,633	2,250	2,783	2,480	1,999	1,528	2,653	7.0	7.1	5.8
Tobacco, unmanufactured	1,334	1,521	1,301	1,441	1,428	1,651	1,306	1,303	3.3	3.7	2.9
Fruits and preparations	1,335	1,186	1,835	2,359	2,498	2,732	2,764	3,091	3.3	6.0	6.8
Fresh fruits	739	743	1,143	1,486	1,561	1,683	1,707	1,954	1.8	3.8	4.3
Vegetables and preparations	1,188	930	1,601	2,302	2,615	2,872	3,277	3,876	2.9	5.8	8.5
Nuts and preparations	757	683	846	976	1,020	1,139	1,182	1,285	1.9	2.5	2.8
Other	1,468	1,262	2,198	2,702	3,013	3,241	3,371	3,625	3.6	6.9	7.9
Asia [1]	15,046	11,191	18,828	17,640	16,450	17,924	18,074	20,430	36.5	44.8	44.7
Japan	6,133	5,409	8,162	8,104	7,729	8,437	8,739	9,268	14.9	20.6	20.3
Korea, South	1,797	1,413	2,593	2,644	2,104	2,222	1,932	2,330	4.4	6.7	5.1
Taiwan [3]	1,095	1,231	1,754	1,661	1,899	1,900	2,043	2,145	2.7	4.2	4.7
China [3]	2,277	157	1,435	814	722	545	376	1,080	5.6	2.1	2.4
Hong Kong	437	389	611	701	771	862	875	1,233	1.1	1.8	2.7
Western Europe [1,4]	12,917	7,002	7,070	7,353	7,467	7,805	7,324	7,365	31.4	18.7	16.1
European Union [5]	12,177	6,542	6,578	6,851	6,916	7,291	6,839	6,775	29.6	17.4	14.8
Netherlands	3,476	1,869	1,722	1,581	1,698	1,853	1,702	1,708	8.5	4.0	3.7
Germany	2,373	1,009	1,075	1,158	1,076	1,163	1,071	1,052	5.8	2.9	2.3
Spain [6]	1,488	837	820	937	928	936	782	862	3.6	2.4	1.9
United Kingdom	996	604	703	829	831	910	945	946	2.5	2.1	2.1
Italy	1,203	669	637	710	674	670	600	549	3.0	1.8	1.2
France	765	403	458	528	581	595	593	450	1.9	1.3	1.0
Latin America [1]	6,154	4,224	5,337	5,092	5,684	6,668	6,793	8,035	15.0	13.0	17.6
Mexico	2,469	1,439	2,724	2,553	2,999	3,791	3,603	4,513	6.0	6.5	9.9
Canada	1,908	1,622	2,221	4,197	4,554	4,902	5,271	5,504	4.7	10.7	12.0
Soviet Union (former)	1,138	1,923	3,597	2,271	2,508	2,346	1,758	999	2.8	5.8	2.2
Eastern Europe	1,644	414	327	537	234	317	432	335	4.0	1.4	0.7
Africa [1]	2,237	2,488	2,260	1,935	1,908	2,570	2,485	2,494	5.5	4.9	5.5
Algeria	195	227	504	513	483	437	516	595	0.5	1.3	1.3
Egypt	774	891	989	693	687	766	661	872	1.9	1.8	1.9

[1] Includes areas not shown separately. [2] Includes commodities not shown separately. [3] See text, section 30. [4] Includes Canary Islands and Madeira Islands for all years. [5] Includes Belgium, Luxembourg, Denmark, Greece, Ireland, and Portugal, not shown separately. As of Jan. 1, 1981, Greece became a member of the European Union. As of Jan. 1, 1986, Spain and Portugal became members of the European Union. For consistency, data for all years are shown on same basis. [6] As of Jan. 1, 1984, includes Canary Islands and Spanish Africa, not elsewhere classified.

Source: U.S. Dept. of Agriculture, Economic Research Service, *Foreign Agricultural Trade of the United States*, Jan./Feb. 1995, and calendar year supplements. Also in *Agricultural Statistics*, annual.

No. 1102. Agricultural Imports—Value, by Selected Commodity, 1980 to 1994, and by Leading Countries of Origin, 1994

[In millions of dollars]

COMMODITY	1980	1985	1990	1991	1992	1993	1994	Leading countries of origin, 1994
Total	17,366	19,968	22,770	22,719	24,624	24,981	26,818	Canada, Mexico, Brazil
Competitive products	10,374	13,067	17,202	17,139	18,946	19,362	20,087	Canada, Mexico, Australia
Cattle, live	237	307	978	952	1,245	1,341	1,152	Canada, Mexico, Japan
Beef and veal	1,780	1,276	1,872	1,964	1,891	1,938	1,798	Australia, New Zealand, Canada
Pork	486	861	938	795	620	694	706	Canada, Denmark, Poland
Dairy products	488	765	867	772	857	873	963	New Zealand, Italy, Ireland
Fruits and preparations . .	564	1,738	2,219	2,131	2,216	2,037	2,154	Mexico, Chile, Brazil
Vegetables and preparations	864	1,385	2,266	2,211	2,184	2,450	2,731	Mexico, Canada, Spain
Wine	692	998	917	915	1,087	976	1,035	France, Italy, Spain
Malt beverages	367	633	923	825	864	941	1,050	Netherlands, Canada, Mexico
Grains and feeds	371	623	1,189	1,321	1,586	1,813	2,339	Canada, Italy, Thailand
Sugar and related products	2,205	1,190	1,172	1,065	1,139	1,065	1,129	Canada, Dominican Republic, Brazil
Oilseeds and products . .	599	756	949	974	1,219	1,193	1,563	Canada, Italy, Philippines
Noncompetitive products . .	6,992	6,902	5,568	5,580	5,678	5,618	6,731	Indonesia, Colombia, Brazil
Coffee and products	4,186	3,322	1,915	1,859	1,706	1,522	2,485	Brazil, Colombia, Mexico
Rubber, crude natural . . .	817	654	707	663	770	852	965	Indonesia, Thailand, Malaysia
Cocoa and products	920	1,351	1,094	1,092	1,080	1,062	1,034	Canada, Cote d'Ivoire, Indonesia
Bananas and plantains . .	430	763	939	1,006	1,097	1,071	1,072	Costa Rica, Colombia, Ecuador

Source: U.S. Dept. of Agriculture, Economic Research Service, *Foreign Agricultural Trade of the United States*, calendar year supplement.

No. 1103. Selected Farm Products—United States and World Production and Exports: 1993 to 1995

[In metric tons, except as indicated. Metric ton=1.102 short tons or .984 long tons]

ITEM	Unit	AMOUNT						UNITED STATES AS PERCENT OF WORLD		
		United States			World			1993	1994	1995
		1993	1994	1995	1993	1994	1995			
PRODUCTION [1]										
Wheat	Million	65	63	59	559	522	530	11.7	12.1	11.2
Corn for grain	Million	161	257	192	471	556	506	34.2	46.2	37.8
Soybeans	Million	51	68	60	117	136	125	43.4	50.2	47.6
Rice, milled	Million	5.2	6.5	5.8	347	354	351	1.5	1.8	1.7
Tobacco, unmanufactured [2]	1,000	732	674	(NA)	8,345	7,775	(NA)	8.8	8.7	(NA)
Cotton [3]	Million bales [4] . .	16.2	16.1	19.7	82.8	77.0	85.6	19.6	20.9	23.0
EXPORTS [5]										
Wheat [6]	Million	33.1	32.2	32.5	100.1	97.2	95.4	33.1	33.1	34.1
Corn	Million	33.1	58.0	51.0	56.5	69.9	63.1	58.7	82.9	80.8
Soybeans	Million	16.0	23.0	21.8	28.0	32.1	31.6	57.2	71.7	68.9
Rice, milled basis	Million	2.8	3.1	2.9	16.0	19.4	16.1	17.4	16.0	18.0
Tobacco, unmanufactured [7]	1,000	208	200	(NA)	1,814	1,712	(NA)	11.5	11.7	(NA)
Cotton [3]	Million bales [4] . .	5.2	6.9	9.4	25.6	27.3	29.0	20.3	25.2	32.4

NA Not available.   [1] Production years vary by commodity. In most cases, includes harvests from July 1 of the year shown through June 30 of the following year.   [2] Farm sales weight basis.   [3] For production and trade years ending in year shown. [4] Bales of 480 lb. net weight.   [5] Trade years may vary by commodity.   [6] Includes wheat flour on a grain equivalent.   [7] Dried weight basis.

Source: U.S. Department of Agriculture, Foreign Agricultural Service, *Foreign Agricultural Commodity Circular Series*, periodic.

No. 1104. Cropland Used for Crops and Acreages of Crops Harvested: 1980 to 1995

[In millions of acres, except as indicated. See also *Historical Statistics, Colonial Times to 1970*, series K 496-501]

ITEM	1980	1985	1988	1989	1990	1991	1992	1993	1994	1995, prel.
Cropland used for crops	382	372	327	341	341	337	337	330	339	332
Index (1977=100)	101	98	87	90	90	89	89	87	90	88
Cropland harvested [1]	342	334	287	306	310	306	305	297	310	302
Crop failure	10	7	10	8	6	7	8	11	7	8
Cultivated summer fallow	30	31	30	27	25	24	24	22	22	22
Acres of crops harvested [2] . . .	352	342	298	318	322	318	317	308	321	314

[1] Land supporting one or more harvested crops.   [2] Area in principal crops harvested as reported by Crop Reporting Board plus acreages in fruits, vegetables for sale, tree nuts, and farm gardens.

Source: U.S. Dept. of Agriculture, Economic Research Service, *Economic Indicators of the Farm Sector: Production and Efficiency Statistics*, annual. Also in *Agricultural Statistics*, annual. Beginning 1991 *Agricultural Resources and Environmental Indicators*, periodical, and *AREI Updates: Cropland Use*, No. 12, annual.

No. 1105. Principal Crops—Production, Supply, and Disappearance: 1990 to 1995

[Marketing year beginning May 1 for hay, June 1 for wheat, August 1 for cotton and rice, September 1 for soybeans, corn, and sorghum. Acreage, production, and yield of all crops periodically revised on basis of census data. See also *Historical Statistics, Colonial Times to 1970*, series K 506-563]

CROP AND YEAR	ACREAGE (mil.)— Set aside[1]	Plant- ed	Har- vested	Yield per acre	Pro- duction	Farm price[2]	Farm value (mil. dol.)	Total sup- ply[3]	DISAPPEAR- ANCE Total[4]	Ex- ports	Ending stocks
Corn for grain:				Bu.	Mil. bu.	$/bu.			Mil. bu.		
1990.	10.7	74.2	67.0	118.5	7,934	2.28	18,192	9,282	7,761	1,725	1,521
1992.	5.3	79.3	72.1	131.5	9,477	2.07	19,723	10,584	8,471	1,663	2,113
1993.	10.9	73.2	62.9	100.7	6,336	2.50	16,032	8,470	7,620	1,328	850
1994.	2.4	79.2	72.9	138.6	10,103	2.26	22,992	10,962	9,405	2,177	1,558
1995.	7.7	71.2	65.0	113.5	7,374	3.15	23,145	8,947	8,535	2,250	412
Soybeans:				Bu.	Mil. bu.	$/bu.			Mil. bu.		
1990.	-	57.8	56.5	34.1	1,926	5.74	11,042	2,169	1,840	557	329
1992.	-	59.2	58.2	37.6	2,190	5.56	12,168	2,471	2,179	770	292
1993.	-	60.1	57.3	32.6	1,871	6.40	11,950	2,170	1,961	589	209
1994.	-	61.7	60.9	41.4	2,517	5.48	13,756	2,731	2,396	838	335
1995.	-	62.6	61.6	34.9	2,152	6.80	14,564	2,492	2,292	810	200
Hay:				Sh. tons	Mil. sh. tons	$/ton			Mil. sh. tons		
1990.	-	(NA)	61.0	2.40	147	[5][6]80.60	10,462	173	146	(NA)	27
1992.	-	(NA)	58.9	2.49	147	[5][6]74.30	10,436	175	154	(NA)	21
1993.	-	(NA)	59.7	2.46	147	[5][6]84.70	10,957	168	146	(NA)	22
1994.	-	(NA)	58.7	2.56	150	[5][6]86.70	11,114	172	151	(NA)	21
1995.	-	(NA)	60.2	2.61	157	[5][6]85.00	10,977	178	(NA)	(NA)	(NA)
Wheat:				Bu.	Mil. bu.	$/bu.			Mil. bu.		
1990.	7.5	77.0	69.1	39.5	2,730	2.61	7,184	3,303	2,435	1,069	868
1992.	7.3	72.2	62.8	39.3	2,467	3.24	8,010	3,012	2,481	1,354	531
1993.	5.7	72.2	62.7	38.2	2,396	3.26	7,648	3,036	2,467	1,228	568
1994.	5.2	70.3	61.8	37.6	2,321	3.45	7,968	2,981	2,475	1,188	507
1995.	6.1	69.2	61.0	35.8	2,186	4.45	9,744	2,762	2,416	1,275	346
Cotton:				Lb.	Mil. bales[7]	cents/lb.			Mil. bales[7]		
1990.	2.0	12.3	11.7	634	[8]15.5	68.2	5,076	18.5	16.5	7.8	[9]2.3
1992.	1.7	13.2	11.1	700	[8]16.2	54.9	4,274	19.9	15.5	5.2	[9]4.7
1993.	1.4	13.4	12.8	606	[8]16.1	58.4	4,521	20.8	17.3	6.9	[9]3.5
1994.	1.7	13.7	13.3	708	[8]19.7	72.0	6,797	23.2	20.6	9.4	[9]2.7
1995.	0.2	16.9	16.0	540	[8]18.0	75.9	6,551	20.8	17.9	7.4	[9]2.9
Potatoes:				Cwt.	Mil. cwt.	$/cwt.			Mil. cwt.		
1990.	(NA)	1.4	1.4	293	402	6.08	2,431	582	[10]319	[11]14	(NA)
1992.	(NA)	1.3	1.3	323	425	5.52	2,336	640	[10]338	[11]18	(NA)
1993.	(NA)	1.4	1.3	326	429	6.17	2,637	642	[10]353	[11]19	(NA)
1994.	(NA)	1.4	1.4	338	468	5.58	2,596	692	[10]367	[11]24	(NA)
1995.	(NA)	1.4	1.4	323	442	6.35	2,799	687	[10]369	[11]30	(NA)
Tobacco: [12]				Lb.	Mil. lb.	$/lb.			Mil. lb.		
1990.	(NA)	(NA)	0.7	2,218	1,626	[6]1.74	2,827	4,026	1,794	631	[13]2,232
1992.	(NA)	(NA)	0.8	2,195	1,722	[6]1.78	3,059	4,002	1,590	630	[13]2,412
1993.	(NA)	(NA)	0.7	2,159	1,614	[6]1.75	2,831	4,026	1,438	538	[13]2,588
1994.	(NA)	(NA)	0.7	2,358	1,583	[6]1.77	2,840	4,170	1,630	529	[13]2,541
1995.	(NA)	(NA)	0.7	1,962	1,323	[6]1.81	2,394	3,864	(NA)	(NA)	(NA)
Rice, rough:				Lb.	Mil. cwt.	$/cwt.			Mil. cwt.		
1990.	1.0	2.9	2.8	5,529	156	6.68	1,047	187	163	71	25
1992.	0.4	3.2	3.1	5,736	180	5.89	1,057	213	174	77	39
1993.	0.7	2.9	2.8	5,510	156	7.98	1,247	203	177	75	26
1994.	0.3	3.4	3.3	5,964	198	6.78	1,337	231	199	101	31
1995.	0.5	3.1	3.1	5,621	174	8.65	1,514	213	188	84	25
Sorghum for grain:				Bu.	Mil. bu.	$/bu.			Mil. bu.		
1990.	3.3	10.5	9.1	63.1	573	2.12	1,221	793	651	232	143
1992.	2.0	13.2	12.1	72.6	875	1.89	1,667	928	753	277	175
1993.	2.3	9.9	8.9	59.9	534	2.31	1,235	709	662	202	48
1994.	1.6	9.8	8.9	72.8	649	2.13	1,324	697	625	223	72
1995.	1.7	9.5	8.3	55.6	460	3.15	1,408	532	492	185	40

- Represents zero. NA Not available. [1] Acreage set aside under diversion, PIK (payment-in-kind) and acreage reduction programs. [2] Except as noted, marketing year average price. U.S. prices are computed by weighting U.S. monthly prices by estimated monthly marketings and do not include an allowance for outstanding loans and government purchases and payments. [3] Comprises production, imports, and beginning stocks. [4] Includes feed, residual, and other domestic uses not shown separately. [5] Prices are for hay sold baled. [6] Season average prices received by farmers. U.S. prices are computed by weighting State prices by estimated sales and include an allowance for outstanding loans and government purchases, if any, for crops under government programs. [7] Bales of 480 pounds, net weight. [8] State production figures, which conform with U.S. totals. [9] Stock estimates based on Census Bureau data which results in an unaccounted difference between supply and use estimates and changes in ending stocks. [10] Covers potatoes used for table use, frozen and canned products, chips, and dehydration. [11] Covers fresh potatoes, chips, frozen and dehydrated products. [12] Flue-cured and cigar wrapper, crop year July-June; all other types October-September. Farm-sales-weight basis. [13] Includes tobacco carried over on farms.

Source: Production—U.S. Dept. of Agriculture, National Agricultural Statistics Service. In *Crop Production*, annual; and *Crop Values*, annual. Supply and disappearance—U.S. Dept. of Agriculture, Economic Research Service, *Feed Situation*, quarterly; *Fats and Oils Situation*, quarterly; *Wheat Situation*, quarterly; *Tobacco Situation*, quarterly; *Cotton and Wool Outlook Statistics*, periodic; and *Agricultural Supply and Demand Estimates*, periodic. All data are also in *Agricultural Statistics*, annual; and *Agricultural Outlook*, monthly.

No. 1106. Crops—Acreage and Value, by State: 1993 to 1995

STATE	ACREAGE PLANTED (1,000)			ACREAGE HARVESTED (1,000)			FARM VALUE (mil. dol.)		1995	
	1993	1994	1995	1993	1994	1995	1993	1994	Value	Rank
U.S.[1]	319,553	323,968	318,458	295,529	308,138	301,186	84,147	96,511	99,174	(X)
AL	2,256	2,258	2,204	2,116	2,141	2,093	561	691	539	34
AZ	710	750	795	695	744	787	969	985	1,330	28
AR	8,575	8,360	8,435	8,305	8,160	8,188	1,782	2,185	2,205	15
CA	4,791	5,132	5,351	4,402	4,682	4,791	12,734	12,898	12,585	1
CO	6,052	6,093	6,104	5,661	5,622	5,748	1,421	1,349	1,560	22
CT	117	130	112	111	123	107	84	95	97	45
DE	512	510	507	499	494	499	122	139	144	43
FL	1,133	1,089	1,079	1,077	1,047	1,036	3,536	3,386	3,216	10
GA	4,068	4,269	4,237	3,551	3,876	3,862	1,426	1,987	2,087	20
HI	70	69	69	70	69	50	326	332	315	38
ID	4,506	4,402	4,483	4,322	4,244	4,306	1,870	1,980	2,185	16
IL	23,533	23,695	23,221	22,241	23,288	22,526	6,535	7,021	6,985	3
IN	12,038	12,137	11,942	11,768	11,970	11,785	3,585	3,539	3,715	7
IA	23,662	24,207	23,502	22,001	23,967	22,872	4,226	7,184	7,447	2
KS	21,899	22,590	22,428	20,485	21,764	21,363	2,930	3,453	3,477	9
KY	5,600	5,558	5,716	5,375	5,354	5,461	1,915	1,955	1,867	21
LA	3,947	3,895	3,857	3,811	3,809	3,786	1,119	1,380	1,399	24
ME	379	349	364	364	337	355	191	167	171	42
MD	1,627	1,569	1,548	1,569	1,506	1,463	359	401	409	36
MA	138	139	134	133	134	131	163	174	72	46
MI	6,726	7,008	6,790	6,554	6,811	6,647	2,096	2,073	2,456	13
MN	19,277	20,050	19,577	16,940	19,510	18,972	2,757	4,775	5,162	4
MS	4,841	4,790	4,850	4,709	4,722	4,739	1,035	1,471	1,346	27
MO	12,749	12,719	12,055	11,483	12,483	11,687	2,069	2,566	2,441	14
MT	9,378	9,355	9,697	8,816	8,986	9,245	1,264	1,137	1,549	23
NE	18,532	19,103	18,280	17,718	18,570	17,769	3,435	4,443	4,478	6
NV	530	497	516	527	491	512	165	160	181	41
NH	109	98	85	107	96	83	30	34	31	48
NJ	456	458	452	413	410	413	278	315	268	40
NM	1,276	1,243	1,282	986	985	869	383	400	433	35
NY	3,187	3,118	3,045	3,101	3,070	2,981	959	1,037	952	31
NC	4,482	4,729	4,644	4,168	4,488	4,341	1,894	2,304	2,128	18
ND	21,982	21,714	20,706	19,832	20,720	20,114	2,386	2,686	2,903	12
OH	10,231	10,406	10,025	10,009	10,275	9,884	2,622	2,840	3,046	11
OK	10,690	10,741	10,631	8,780	8,804	8,628	1,025	1,098	1,056	30
OR	2,317	2,321	2,436	2,240	2,242	2,292	1,170	1,239	1,375	25
PA	4,111	4,153	4,146	4,035	4,062	4,050	1,305	1,367	1,366	26
RI	13	12	11	13	12	11	7	8	7	49
SC	1,837	2,038	1,973	1,602	1,923	1,871	498	716	701	33
SD	15,231	16,371	14,334	14,073	15,679	13,947	1,651	2,191	2,168	17
TN	4,690	4,655	4,897	4,458	4,394	4,535	1,039	1,253	1,222	29
TX	22,012	21,822	22,600	18,108	17,536	17,870	4,186	4,473	4,695	5
UT	1,083	1,114	1,099	1,032	1,049	1,042	255	289	277	39
VT	413	418	387	404	409	379	71	73	64	47
VA	2,854	2,906	2,910	2,682	2,749	2,749	727	859	863	32
WA	4,378	4,057	4,130	4,227	3,922	3,997	2,937	2,881	3,641	8
WV	630	646	650	621	636	642	132	114	120	44
WI	8,020	8,432	8,195	7,511	8,069	7,793	1,606	2,126	2,091	19
WY	1,890	1,716	1,898	1,806	1,638	1,835	311	285	349	37

X Not applicable.　　[1] Excludes Alaska. Acreage data include sunflower and sugarbeet acreage unallocated by State.

Source: U.S. Dept. of Agriculture, National Agricultural Statistics Service, *Crop Production*, annual; and *Crop Values*, annual.

No. 1107. Corn—Acreage, Production, and Value, by Leading States: 1992 to 1994

[One bushel of corn=56 pounds. See also *Historical Statistics, Colonial Times to 1970*, series K 502-508]

STATE	ACREAGE HARVESTED (1,000 acres)			YIELD PER ACRE (bu.)			PRODUCTION (mil. bu.)			PRICE ($/bu.)			FARM VALUE (mil. dol.)		
	1992	1993	1994	1992	1993	1994	1992	1993	1994	1992	1993	1994	1992	1993	1994
U.S.[1]	72,077	62,921	72,917	132	101	139	9,477	6,336	10,103	2.07	2.50	2.20	19,723	16,032	22,158
IA	12,950	11,000	12,700	147	80	152	1,904	880	1,930	2.00	2.44	2.15	3,807	2,147	4,150
IL	11,050	10,000	11,450	149	130	156	1,646	1,300	1,786	2.11	2.57	2.20	3,474	3,341	3,930
NE	7,900	7,550	8,300	135	104	139	1,067	785	1,154	2.09	2.52	2.25	2,229	1,979	2,596
MN	6,500	4,600	6,450	114	70	142	741	322	916	1.91	2.26	2.10	1,415	728	1,923
IN	5,970	5,400	5,960	147	132	144	878	713	858	2.09	2.51	2.15	1,834	1,789	1,845
OH	3,550	3,280	3,500	143	110	139	508	361	487	2.06	2.57	2.10	1,046	927	1,022
WI	2,950	2,350	3,100	104	92	141	307	216	437	2.12	2.46	2.15	650	532	940
SD	3,300	2,550	3,400	84	63	108	277	161	367	1.84	2.27	1.90	510	365	698
KS	1,730	1,800	2,130	150	120	143	260	216	305	2.15	2.61	2.35	558	564	716
MO	2,400	1,850	2,300	135	90	119	324	167	274	2.11	2.58	2.25	684	430	616
MI	2,300	2,050	2,230	105	110	117	242	226	261	1.95	2.46	2.15	471	555	561
TX	1,620	1,850	2,040	125	115	117	203	213	239	2.41	2.61	2.55	488	555	609
KY	1,300	1,220	1,220	132	104	128	172	127	156	2.23	2.58	2.25	383	327	351

[1] Includes other States, not shown separately.

Source: U.S. Dept. of Agriculture, National Agricultural Statistics Service, *Crop Production*, annual; and *Crop Values*, annual.

No. 1108. Soybeans—Acreage, Production, and Value, by Leading States: 1992 to 1994

[One bushel of soybeans=60 pounds. See also *Historical Statistics, Colonial Times to 1970*, series K 520-522]

STATE	ACREAGE HARVESTED (1,000 acres) 1992	1993	1994	YIELD PER ACRE (bu.) 1992	1993	1994	PRODUCTION (mil. bu.) 1992	1993	1994	PRICE ($/bu.) 1992	1993	1994	FARM VALUE (mil. dol.) 1992	1993	1994
U.S.[1]	58,233	57,347	61,129	38	33	42	2,190	1,871	2,558	5.56	6.40	5.35	12,168	11,950	13,785
IA	8,170	8,300	8,770	44	31	51	359	257	447	5.54	6.34	5.35	1,992	1,631	2,393
IL	9,430	9,000	9,530	43	43	46	405	387	438	5.69	6.49	5.50	2,307	2,512	2,411
MN	5,400	5,000	5,600	32	23	41	173	115	230	5.52	6.18	5.35	954	711	1,228
IN	4,520	4,850	4,680	43	46	47	194	223	220	5.61	6.31	5.40	1,090	1,408	1,188
OH	3,680	4,110	3,990	40	38	44	147	156	176	5.65	6.42	5.35	832	1,003	939
MO	4,250	3,600	4,560	38	33	38	162	119	173	5.45	6.36	5.30	880	756	918
NE	2,460	2,500	2,860	42	36	48	103	90	137	5.37	6.20	5.15	555	558	707
AR	3,160	3,550	3,400	33	26	34	104	92	116	5.64	6.65	5.75	588	614	665
SD	2,250	1,750	2,420	28	22	39	63	39	94	5.18	6.03	5.00	326	232	472
KS	1,850	1,900	2,100	37	28	36	68	53	76	5.42	6.41	5.30	371	341	401
MS	1,750	1,950	1,920	34	22	31	60	43	60	5.69	6.53	5.55	339	280	330
MI	1,440	1,440	1,540	33	38	38	48	55	59	5.53	6.32	5.45	263	346	319

[1] Includes other States, not shown separately.

Source: U.S. Dept. of Agriculture, National Agricultural Statistics Service, *Crop Production*, annual; and *Crop Values*, annual.

No. 1109. Wheat—Acreage, Production, and Value, by Leading States: 1992 to 1994

[One bushel of wheat= 60 pounds. See also *Historical Statistics, Colonial Times to 1970*, series K 506-508]

STATE	ACREAGE HARVESTED (1,000 acres) 1992	1993	1994	YIELD PER ACRE (bu.) 1992	1993	1994	PRODUCTION (mil. bu.) 1992	1993	1994	PRICE ($/bu.) 1992	1993	1994	FARM VALUE (mil. dol.) 1992	1993	1994
U.S.[1]	62,761	62,712	61,771	39.3	38.2	37.6	2,467	2,396	2,321	3.24	3.26	3.50	8,010	7,645	8,233
KS	10,700	11,100	11,400	34.0	35.0	38.0	364	389	433	3.13	3.00	3.40	1,139	1,166	1,473
ND	11,500	10,850	11,238	41.1	31.0	31.7	473	337	356	3.14	4.04	4.00	1,490	1,329	1,400
MT	4,947	5,264	5,378	30.1	39.2	31.7	149	206	171	3.42	3.50	3.80	509	715	646
OK	5,900	5,400	5,300	28.5	29.0	27.0	168	157	143	3.19	2.94	3.45	536	460	494
WA	2,420	2,790	2,545	49.4	63.6	52.7	120	178	134	3.80	3.24	4.10	453	574	551
ID	1,440	1,390	1,410	69.5	79.4	71.1	100	110	100	3.48	2.88	3.80	348	319	380
SD	3,733	3,488	3,353	32.0	32.0	28.4	120	112	95	3.21	3.35	3.65	385	377	347
CO	2,397	2,583	2,592	30.9	37.5	30.8	74	97	80	3.15	3.21	3.50	233	310	279
TX	3,800	3,700	2,900	34.0	32.0	26.0	129	118	75	3.18	2.86	3.20	411	339	241
MN	2,805	2,298	2,572	49.9	31.0	28.0	140	71	72	3.17	3.31	3.60	443	235	259
NE	1,850	2,100	2,100	30.0	35.0	34.0	56	74	71	3.16	3.04	3.50	175	223	250

[1] Includes other States, not shown separately.

Source: U.S. Dept. of Agriculture, National Agricultural Statistics Service, *Crop Production*, annual; and *Crop Values*, annual.

No. 1110. Greenhouse and Nursery Crops—Summary, by Type of Product: 1990 to 1995

[In millions of dollars, except per capita. Based on a survey of 36 commercial floriculture States and estimates by source]

ITEM	Total	Cut flowers	Potted flowering plants	Foliage plants	Bedding plants	Cut cultivated greens	Other[1]
Domestic production:[2]							
1990	8,677	529	701	693	1,032	121	5,601
1992	9,304	519	823	623	1,391	126	5,821
1993	9,617	480	871	609	1,456	131	6,071
1994	10,078	501	844	714	1,593	135	6,291
1995	10,229	462	865	724	1,649	128	6,401
Imports:							
1990	526	326	18	25	(NA)	14	143
1992	586	352	27	30	(NA)	15	162
1993	638	382	27	37	(NA)	20	171
1994	697	420	28	43	(NA)	20	186
1995	855	512	30	53	(NA)	42	218
RETAIL CONSUMER EXPENDITURES[3]							
Total:							
1990	29,273	4,826	2,707	2,510	1,548	679	17,003
1992	30,880	4,932	3,203	2,299	2,087	707	17,652
1993	31,924	4,893	3,383	2,292	2,184	773	18,399
1994	33,574	5,264	3,288	2,712	2,390	769	19,151
1995	34,768	5,669	3,376	2,790	2,473	811	19,649
Per capita (dol.):[4]							
1990	117	19	11	10	6	3	68
1995	132	21	13	11	9	3	75

NA Not available. [1] Includes turfgrass (sod), bulbs, nursery stock, groundcovers, and other greenhouse and nursery products except the following: seeds, cut Christmas trees, and food crops grown under cover. [2] Equivalent wholesale values. [3] Excludes services such as landscaping, installation, and maintenance. [4] Based on U.S. Bureau of the Census estimated resident population as of July 1.

Source: U.S. Dept. of Agriculture, Economic Research Service, unpublished data.

No. 1111. Commercial Vegetable and Other Specified Crops—Area, Production, and Value, 1992 to 1994, and Leading Producing States, 1994

[Except as noted, relates to commercial production for fresh market and processing combined. Includes market garden areas but excludes minor producing acreage in minor producing States. Excludes production for home use in farm and nonfarm gardens. Value is for season or crop year and should not be confused with calendar-year income]

CROP	AREA [1] (1,000 acres)			PRODUCTION [2] (1,000 short tons)			VALUE [3] (mil. dol.)			Leading States in order of production, 1994
	1992	1993	1994	1992	1993	1994	1992	1993	1994	
Beans, snap	278	281	302	843	857	1,011	251	270	285	WI, OR, MI [4]
Beans, dry edible. .	1,530	1,622	1,845	1,131	1,096	1,459	457	540	628	ND, MI, NE
Broccoli	111	107	111	622	540	569	284	278	336	CA, AZ, OR
Cabbage	87	85	81	1,329	1,403	1,467	213	290	244	NY,TX,CA [5]
Cantaloups.	109	108	103	906	954	947	251	297	308	CA, AZ, TX
Carrots	107	103	106	1,640	1,584	1,525	353	296	310	CA, WA, MI
Corn, sweet	708	682	741	4,175	3,663	4,787	480	532	630	(NA)
Fresh market. . . .	221	210	225	924	942	1,056	271	335	374	FL, CA, NY
Processed.	486	472	516	3,252	2,721	3,731	210	197	256	WI, MN, WA
Cucumbers.	151	167	173	1,016	1,059	1,085	292	296	282	MI, NC, TX [4]
Lettuce, head	215	208	196	3,541	3,391	3,143	882	1,087	819	CA, AZ, FL
Mushrooms [6]	142	(NA)	(NA)	373	388	377	670	686	721	(NA)
Onions.	142	151	160	2,737	2,853	3,152	629	813	602	CA, OR, WA
Peppers, green . . .	67	65	64	721	725	793	386	437	468	FL, CA, NJ
Potatoes	1,315	1,317	1,377	21,268	21,435	22,967	2,336	2,641	2,449	ID, WA, CO
Strawberries	49	51	49	657	724	813	684	671	824	CA, FL, OR
Tomatoes	406	442	469	10,729	11,452	13,321	1,906	1,708	1,683	(NA)
Fresh market. . .	132	135	129	1,952	1,775	1,779	1,397	1,126	966	FL, CA, VA
Processed. . . .	274	307	340	8,777	9,677	11,542	509	582	717	CA, OH, IN
Watermelons.	230	205	208	1,889	1,889	1,999	223	262	256	FL, TX, CA

NA Not available.　[1] Area of crops for harvest for fresh market, including any partially harvested or not harvested because of low prices or other factors, plus area harvested for processing.　[2] Excludes some quantities not marketed.　[3] Fresh market vegetables valued at f.o.b. shipping point. Processing vegetables are equivalent returns at packinghouse door.　[4] Processing only.　[5] Fresh market only.　[6] Area is shown in million square feet. All data are for marketing year ending June 30.

Source: U.S. Dept. of Agriculture, National Agricultural Statistics Service, *Vegetables*, annual summary. Also in *Agricultural Statistics*, annual.

No. 1112. Fruits and Nuts—Utilized Production and Value, 1992 to 1994, and Leading Producing States, 1994

FRUIT OR NUT	Unit	UTILIZED PRODUCTION [1]			FARM VALUE (mil. dol.)			Leading States in order of production, 1994
		1992	1993	1994	1992	1993	1994	
Apples (36 States) [2]	Mil. lb	10,474	10,605	10,733	1,431	1,370	1,323	WA, NY, MI
Apricots	1,000 tons . .	106	97	145	38	39	51	CA, WA, UT
Avocados	1,000 tons . .	185	292	144	196	118	255	CA, FL, HI
Bananas	Mil. lb	12	12	13	5	4	5	HI
Cherries, sweet	1,000 tons . .	192	161	193	176	191	200	WA, OR, CA
Cherries, tart	Mil. lb	313	257	280	55	30	(NA)	MI, UT, NY
Cranberries	1,000 bbl. [3]	4,160	3,919	4,529	215	197	(NA)	MA, WI, NJ
Dates (CA)	1,000 tons . .	21	25	25	22	25	30	CA
Figs (fresh) (CA).	1,000 tons . .	47	61	49	19	24	21	CA
Grapefruit (4 States)	Mil. boxes [4]	55	68	65	428	311	327	FL, CA, AZ
Grapes (13 States)	1,000 tons . .	6,032	6,018	5,923	1,848	2,010	1,801	CA, WA, NY
Kiwifruit (CA)	1,000 tons . .	48	45	38	14	17	(NA)	CA
Lemons (2 States)	Mil. boxes [5]	20	25	26	257	240	238	CA, AZ
Limes (FL).	Mil. boxes [6]	2	1	(Z)	23	7	4	FL
Nectarines (CA)	1,000 tons . .	236	205	242	74	102	68	CA
Olives (CA)	1,000 tons . .	165	122	84	91	57	40	CA
Oranges and tangerines (4 States) .	Mil. boxes [7]	216	262	247	1,649	1,573	1,676	FL, CA, AZ
Papayas	Mil. lb	71	64	58	14	14	13	HI
Peaches (31 States)	Mil. lb	2,480	2,487	2,352	379	398	313	CA, GA, SC
Pears	1,000 tons . .	924	948	1,036	273	232	220	CA, WA, OR
Pineapples	1,000 tons . .	550	370	365	102	80	79	HI
Plums and prunes (fresh)	1,000 tons [8]	828	522	812	261	239	(NA)	CA, WA, MI
Tangelos (FL).	Mil. boxes [8]	3	3	3	24	16	18	FL
Temples (FL)	Mil. boxes [8]	2	3	2	20	12	12	FL
Almonds (shelled basis) (CA)	Mil. lb	548	490	660	691	911	776	CA
Hazelnuts (in the shell)	1,000 tons . .	28	41	20	15	26	17	OR, WA
Macadamia nuts	Mil. lb	48	49	50	33	33	35	HI
Pecans (in the shell) (11 States) . . .	Mil. lb	166	365	175	240	214	184	GA, TX, NM
Pistachios	Mil. lb	147	152	128	151	163	118	CA
Walnuts, English (in the shell)	1,000 tons . .	203	260	228	286	361	(NA)	CA

NA Not available.　Z Less than 500,000 boxes.　[1] Excludes quantities not harvested or not marketed.　[2] Production in commercial orchards with 100 or more bearing age trees.　[3] Barrels of 100 pounds.　[4] Approximate average, net weight, is 65 lb. in AZ and CA through 1993 and 67 starting in 1994; 85 in FL; and 80 in TX.　[5] About 76 lb. net.　[6] Approximate net weight is 88 lb.　[7] Net contents of box varies. In CA and AZ approximate average for oranges and tangerines is 75 lb.; FL oranges, 90 lb.; TX oranges, 85 lb.; and FL tangerines, 95 lb.　[8] Approximate net weight is 90 lb.

Source: U.S. Dept. of Agriculture, National Agricultural Statistics Service, *Noncitrus Fruits and Nuts*, annual; and *Citrus Fruits*, annual.

No. 1113. Red Meats—Slaughter, Supply, and Use: 1980 to 1995

[Quantities in millions of pounds (carcass weight equivalent), except as noted. Carcass weight equivalent is the weight of the animal minus entrails, head, hide, and internal organs; includes fat, and bone. Covers Federal and State inspected, and farm slaughter. See also Historical Statistics, Colonial Times to 1970, series K 583-594]

YEAR AND TYPE OF MEAT	Animals slaughtered (mil. head)	Produc- tion	Imports	Supply, [1] total	Consump- tion [2]	Exports	Ending stocks
All red meats:							
1980.	139.7	38,978	2,668	42,481	41,170	429	882
1990.	126.3	38,787	3,295	42,742	40,784	1,250	707
1992.	135.3	40,977	3,135	44,932	42,435	1,739	758
1993.	133.5	40,759	3,194	44,711	42,093	1,718	900
1994.	136.6	42,683	3,161	46,744	43,589	2,151	1,004
1995.	138.4	43,604	2,831	47,439	43,912	2,598	930
Beef:							
1980.	34.1	21,643	2,064	24,166	23,560	173	432
1990.	33.4	22,743	2,356	25,434	24,031	1,006	397
1992.	33.1	23,086	2,440	25,945	24,261	1,324	360
1993.	33.5	23,049	2,401	25,810	24,006	1,275	529
1994.	34.4	24,386	2,369	27,284	25,125	1,611	548
1995.	35.8	25,149	2,103	27,800	25,460	1,821	519
Pork:							
1980.	97.2	16,617	550	17,521	16,838	252	431
1990.	85.4	15,354	898	16,565	16,031	238	296
1992.	95.2	17,233	645	18,266	17,474	407	385
1993.	93.3	17,088	740	18,213	17,419	435	359
1994.	95.9	17,696	743	18,798	17,829	531	438
1995.	96.5	17,850	664	18,952	17,785	771	396
Veal:							
1980.	2.7	400	21	432	420	2	9
1990.	1.8	327	(NA)	331	325	(NA)	6
1992.	1.4	310	(NA)	317	312	(NA)	5
1993.	1.2	285	(NA)	290	286	(NA)	4
1994.	1.3	293	(NA)	297	290	(NA)	7
1995.	1.5	318	(NA)	325	318	(NA)	7
Lamb and mutton:							
1980.	5.7	318	33	362	351	1	9
1990.	5.7	363	41	412	397	6	8
1992.	5.6	348	50	404	388	8	8
1993.	5.3	337	53	398	381	8	8
1994.	5.0	308	49	365	345	9	11
1995.	4.6	287	64	362	348	6	8

NA Not available. [1] Total supply equals production plus imports plus ending stocks of previous year. [2] Includes shipments to territories.

Source: U.S. Dept. of Agriculture, Economic Research Service, Livestock and Meat Statistics, quarterly. Also published in Agricultural Outlook, monthly.

No. 1114. Livestock Inventory and Production: 1980 to 1995

[Production in live weight; includes animals for slaughter market, younger animals shipped to other States for feeding or breeding purposes, farm slaughter and custom slaughter consumed on farms where produced, minus livestock shipped into States for feeding or breeding with an adjustment for changes in inventory. See also Historical Statistics, Colonial Times to 1970, series K 564-569 and 575-582]

TYPE OF LIVESTOCK	Unit	1980	1985	1987	1988	1989	1990	1991	1992	1993	1994	1995
ALL CATTLE [1]												
Inventory: [2] Number on farms	Mil	111.2	109.6	102.1	99.6	96.7	95.8	96.4	97.6	99.2	101.0	103.3
Total value.	Bil. dol. .	55.8	44.0	41.6	52.1	56.2	59.0	63.1	61.5	64.4	66.5	63.6
Value per head.	Dol	502	402	407	523	581	616	655	630	649	659	616
Production: Quantity	Bil. lb . .	40.3	40.1	40.5	39.7	38.9	39.2	39.8	40.3	40.9	42.7	(NA)
Beef, price per 100 lb . .	Dol	62.40	53.70	61.10	66.60	69.50	74.60	72.70	71.30	72.60	66.70	(NA)
Calves, price per 100 lb.	Dol	76.80	62.10	78.50	89.20	90.80	95.60	98.00	89.00	91.20	87.20	(NA)
Value of production	Bil. dol. .	25.5	21.2	24.8	26.6	27.1	29.3	29.4	28.6	30.3	28.7	(NA)
HOGS AND PIGS												
Inventory: [3] Number on farms	Mil	67.3	54.1	51.0	54.4	55.5	53.8	54.4	57.6	58.2	57.9	59.6
Total value.	Bil. dol. .	3.8	4.1	4.7	4.1	3.7	4.3	4.6	4.0	4.2	4.3	3.2
Value per head.	Dol	56.00	75.00	91.90	76.00	66.30	79.10	85.40	68.80	71.20	74.90	53.20
Production: Quantity	Bil. lb . .	23.4	20.2	20.4	21.7	21.9	21.3	22.7	23.9	23.7	24.5	(NA)
Price per 100 lb	Dol	38.00	44.00	51.20	42.30	42.50	53.70	49.10	41.60	45.20	39.90	(NA)
Value of production	Bil. dol. .	8.9	8.9	10.4	9.2	9.3	11.3	11.1	9.9	10.6	9.7	(NA)
SHEEP AND LAMBS												
Inventory: [2] Number on farms	Mil	12.7	10.7	10.6	10.9	10.9	11.4	11.2	10.8	10.2	9.7	8.9
Total value.	Mil. dol .	993	654	799	985	894	901	732	661	714	681	664
Value per head.	Dol	78.20	61.10	75.70	90.00	82.40	79.30	65.60	61.20	70.00	69.90	74.70
Production: Quantity	Mil. lb . .	746	704	733	731	811	781	796	746	689	626	(NA)
Sheep, price per 100 lb .	Dol	21.30	23.90	29.50	25.60	24.40	23.20	19.70	25.80	28.60	30.90	(NA)
Lambs, price per 100 lb .	Dol	63.60	67.70	77.60	69.10	66.10	55.50	52.20	59.50	64.40	65.60	(NA)
Value of production	Mil. dol	403	434	503	434	468	374	357	394	394	373	(NA)

NA Not available. [1] Includes milk cows. [2] As of Jan. 1. [3] As of Dec. 1 of preceding year.

Source: U.S. Dept. of Agriculture, National Agricultural Statistics Service, Meat Animals—Production, Disposition, und Income, annual; and annual livestock summaries. Also in Agricultural Statistics, annual.

No. 1115. Cattle and Calves; and Hogs and Pigs—Number, Production, and Value, by State: 1991 to 1994

[See headnote, table 1114]

STATE	NUMBER ON FARMS [1] (1,000)			QUANTITY PRODUCED (mil. lb.)			VALUE OF PRODUCTION (mil. dol.)			COMMERCIAL SLAUGHTER [2] (mil. lb.)		
	1992	1993	1994	1992	1993	1994	1992	1993	1994	1991	1992	1993
CATTLE AND CALVES [3]												
U.S. [4]	97,556	99,176	100,988	40,253	40,875	42,721	28,633	30,330	28,702	38,029	38,417	38,686
CA.	4,550	4,600	4,550	1,909	1,838	1,997	1,143	1,215	1,162	1,338	1,116	1,050
CO.	2,900	2,950	3,000	1,895	1,938	1,924	1,411	1,498	1,336	2,634	2,938	2,915
ID.	1,720	1,680	1,700	836	795	865	542	546	536	(5)	(5)	(5)
IA.	4,300	4,200	4,100	2,108	2,052	1,961	1,467	1,468	1,284	1,952	1,952	1,953
KS.	5,650	5,900	6,000	3,245	3,173	3,652	2,429	2,438	2,549	6,937	7,027	7,191
MN.	2,700	2,750	2,700	1,190	1,187	1,205	795	798	720	1,344	1,262	1,319
MO.	4,450	4,550	4,750	1,232	1,278	1,179	952	1,034	863	299	263	218
MT.	2,550	2,500	2,550	1,020	1,048	1,061	705	809	774	21	22	23
NE.	5,800	5,900	6,150	3,776	3,788	3,905	2,783	2,847	2,694	7,424	7,808	7,811
OK.	5,300	5,200	5,100	1,824	1,895	2,092	1,349	1,533	1,559	44	46	42
SD.	3,550	3,750	3,750	1,445	1,425	1,475	1,088	1,120	1,041	625	482	292
TX.	13,400	14,100	14,800	6,391	6,768	7,271	4,722	5,131	4,972	6,158	6,264	6,591
WI.	4,000	3,950	3,850	1,158	1,037	1,095	752	687	651	1,347	1,584	1,716
HOGS AND PIGS												
U.S. [4]	57,649	58,202	57,904	23,947	23,693	24,459	9,854	10,628	9,691	22,200	23,952	23,611
IL.	5,900	5,900	5,450	2,484	2,435	2,385	1,024	1,072	924	2,221	2,239	2,041
IN.	4,600	4,550	4,300	1,801	1,728	1,719	711	757	657	924	1,148	1,012
IA.	15,000	14,900	15,000	6,303	6,000	6,100	2,656	2,716	2,427	7,121	7,636	7,488
MN.	4,900	4,700	4,750	1,941	1,955	1,976	827	909	810	1,827	2,093	2,029
NE.	4,500	4,600	4,300	1,833	1,784	1,782	763	816	728	1,355	1,443	1,398
NC.	3,650	4,500	5,400	1,823	2,074	2,592	756	954	1,053	(5)	(5)	(5)

[1] Cattle and calves, as of January 1; hogs and pigs as of December 1 of preceding year. [2] Data for cattle and calves cover cattle only. Includes slaughter in federally inspected and other slaughter plants; excludes animals slaughtered on farms. [3] Includes milk cows. [4] Includes other States not shown separately. [5] Included in U.S. total. Not printed to avoid disclosing individual operation.

Source: U.S. Dept. of Agriculture, National Agricultural Statistics Service, *Meat Animals-Production, Disposition and Income,* annual.

No. 1116. Milk Production and Commercial Use: 1980 to 1995

[In billions of pounds milkfat basis]

YEAR	Produc-tion	Farm use	COMMERCIAL		Imports	Commer-cial supply, total	CCC net remov-als [1]	COMMERCIAL		Milk price per 100 lb. [2] (dol.)
			Farm market-ings	Begin-ning stock				Ending stock	Disap-pear-ance	
1980	128.4	2.3	126.1	5.3	2.1	133.5	8.8	5.6	119.0	13.1
1990	147.7	2.0	145.7	4.1	2.7	152.5	8.5	5.1	138.8	13.7
1992	150.8	1.9	149.0	4.5	2.5	155.9	9.9	4.7	141.3	13.2
1993	150.6	1.9	148.7	4.7	2.8	156.2	6.6	4.5	145.0	12.8
1994	153.6	1.9	151.7	4.6	3.0	159.1	4.8	4.3	150.1	13.1
1995	155.6	1.7	153.9	4.3	2.9	161.1	2.1	4.1	154.9	12.8

[1] Removals from commercial supply by Commodity Credit Corporation. [2] Wholesale price received by farmers for all milk delivered to plants and dealers.

Source: U.S. Dept. of Agriculture, Economic Research Service, *Agricultural Outlook,* monthly.

No. 1117. Milk Cows—Number, Production, and Value, by State: 1992 to 1994

STATE	NUMBER ON FARMS [1] (1,000)			MILK PRODUCED ON FARMS (mil. lb.)			VALUE OF PRODUCTION [2] (mil. dol.)		
	1992	1993	1994	1992	1993	1994	1992	1993	1994
United States [3]	9,688	9,589	9,525	150,885	150,582	153,622	19,994	19,484	20,167
California	1,180	1,210	1,235	22,092	22,927	25,019	2,615	2,667	2,951
Iowa	268	264	265	4,006	4,054	3,962	521	519	511
Michigan.	333	330	328	5,435	5,435	5,545	726	715	746
Minnesota.	653	635	609	9,858	9,693	9,342	1,267	1,241	1,208
New York	735	727	718	11,557	11,415	11,420	1,553	1,488	1,523
Ohio	313	305	294	4,695	4,620	4,520	629	601	601
Pennsylvania.	646	640	639	10,368	10,181	10,230	1,500	1,424	1,460
Texas.	386	394	402	5,590	5,910	6,225	770	786	834
Washington.	249	257	261	4,836	4,980	5,203	648	639	681
Wisconsin.	1,618	1,543	1,494	23,844	22,844	22,412	3,140	2,945	2,912

[1] Average number during year. Represents cows and heifers that have calved, kept for milk; excluding heifers not yet fresh. [2] Valued at average returns per 100 pounds of milk in combined marketings of milk and cream. Includes value of milk fed to calves. [3] Includes other States not shown separately.

Source: U.S. Dept. of Agriculture, National Agricultural Statistics Service, *Dairy Products,* annual; and *Milk: Production, Disposition, and Income,* annual.

No. 1118. Milk Production and Manufactured Dairy Products: 1980 to 1994

[See also *Historical Statistics, Colonial Times to 1970*, series K 595-601]

ITEM	Unit	1980	1985	1988	1989	1990	1991	1992	1993	1994
Number of farms with milk cows	1,000	334	269	216	203	193	181	171	159	150
Cows and heifers that have calved, kept for milk.	Mil. head . .	10.8	11.0	10.2	10.0	10.0	9.8	9.7	9.6	9.5
Milk produced on farms.	Bil. lb	128	143	145	144	148	148	151	151	154
Production per cow	1,000 lb. . . .	11.9	13.0	14.2	14.3	14.8	15.0	15.6	15.7	16.1
Whole milk sold from farms [1]	Bil. lb	126	141	143	142	146	146	149	149	152
Sales to plants and dealers.	Bil. lb	125	139	142	141	145	145	148	148	151
Value of milk produced	Bil. dol. . . .	16.9	18.4	17.9	19.6	20.4	18.3	20.0	19.5	20.2
Gross farm income, dairy products.	Bil. dol. . . .	16.7	18.1	17.7	19.4	20.2	18.1	19.8	19.3	20.0
Cash receipts from marketing of milk and cream [1]	Bil. dol. . . .	16.6	18.1	17.6	19.4	20.1	18.0	19.7	19.2	19.9
Sales to plants and dealers	Bil. dol. . . .	16.3	17.8	17.4	19.1	19.9	17.8	19.5	19.0	19.6
Number of dairy manufacturing plants	Number . . .	2,257	2,061	1,846	1,754	1,723	1,680	1,603	1,534	1,531
Manufactured dairy products:										
Butter (incl. whey butter)	Mil. lb	1,145	1,248	1,208	1,295	1,302	1,336	1,365	1,315	1,296
Cheese, total [2]	Mil. lb	3,984	5,081	5,572	5,615	6,059	6,055	6,488	6,528	6,730
American (excl. full-skim American). . .	Mil. lb	2,376	2,855	2,757	2,674	2,894	2,769	2,937	2,957	2,977
Cream and Neufchatel	Mil. lb	229	294	376	401	431	447	517	540	573
All Italian varieties	Mil. lb	983	1,491	1,937	2,043	2,207	2,329	2,509	2,495	2,622
Cottage cheese: Creamed [3]	Mil. lb	825	716	647	572	531	498	457	431	410
Curd, pot, and bakers.	Mil. lb	667	599	557	527	493	491	502	471	463
Condensed bulk milk	Mil. lb	952	1,232	1,364	1,417	1,426	1,530	1,624	1,605	1,504
Evaporated and condensed canned milk .	Mil. lb	740	656	612	545	615	543	853	557	565
Nonfat dry milk [4]	Mil. lb	1,168	1,398	998	893	902	885	872	964	1,227
Dry whey [5]	Mil. lb	690	987	1,137	1,069	1,143	1,167	1,237	1,196	1,164
Ice cream of all kinds.	Mil. gal . . .	830	901	882	831	824	863	875	866	876
Ice milk.	Mil. gal . . .	293	301	355	377	352	345	329	325	360

[1] Comprises sales to plants and dealers, and retail sales by farmers direct to consumers. [2] Includes varieties not shown separately. [3] Includes partially creamed (low fat). [4] Includes dry skim milk for animal feed. [5] Includes animal but excludes modified whey production.

Source: U.S. Dept. of Agriculture, National Agricultural Statistics Service, *Dairy Products*, annual; and *Milk: Production, Disposition, and Income*, annual.

No. 1119. Broiler, Turkey, and Egg Production: 1980 to 1994

[For year ending November 30. See also *Historical Statistics, Colonial Times to 1970*, series K 614-623]

ITEM	Unit	1980	1985	1986	1987	1988	1989	1990	1991	1992	1993	1994
Broilers:[1]												
Number.	Million . .	3,963	4,470	4,649	5,004	5,238	5,517	5,864	6,137	6,402	6,694	7,018
Weight	Bil. lb. . .	15.5	18.9	19.7	21.5	22.5	24.0	25.6	27.2	28.8	30.6	32.5
Price per lb	Cents . .	27.7	30.1	34.5	28.7	33.1	36.6	32.6	30.8	31.8	34.0	35.0
Production value.	Mil. dol. .	4,303	5,668	6,784	6,177	7,435	8,778	8,366	8,383	9,174	10,417	11,374
Turkeys:												
Number.	Million . .	165	185	207	240	242	261	282	285	289	288	289
Weight	Bil. lb. . .	3.1	3.7	4.1	4.9	5.1	5.5	6.0	6.1	6.3	6.4	6.6
Price per lb	Cents . .	41.3	49.1	47.1	34.8	38.6	40.9	39.4	38.0	37.7	39.0	40.4
Production value.	Mil. dol. .	1,272	1,820	1,951	1,703	1,951	2,235	2,393	2,353	2,396	2,509	2,672
Eggs:												
Number.	Billion . .	69.7	68.4	69.1	70.4	69.7	67.2	67.9	69.0	70.5	71.9	73.9
Price per dozen	Cents . .	56.3	57.2	61.5	54.7	52.8	68.9	70.9	67.8	57.6	63.4	61.4
Production value.	Mil. dol. .	3,268	3,262	3,543	3,209	3,073	3,877	4,021	3,915	3,397	3,800	3,777

[1] Young chickens of the heavy breeds and other meat-type birds, to be marketed at 2-5 lbs. live weight and from which no pullets are kept for egg production.

Source: U.S. Dept. of Agriculture, National Agricultural Statistics Service, *Poultry—Production and Value*, annual; *Turkeys*, annual; and *Layers and Egg Production*, annual.

No. 1120. Broiler and Turkey Production, by State: 1992 to 1994

[In millions of pounds, liveweight production. See *Historical Statistics, Colonial Times to 1970*, series K 614 and 621 for U.S. totals]

STATE	BROILERS			TURKEYS			STATE	BROILERS			TURKEYS		
	1992	1993	1994	1992	1993	1994		1992	1993	1994	1992	1993	1994
U.S. [1] . .	28,829	30,618	32,529	6,334	6,433	6,610	MS.	2,145	2,430	2,712	(NA)	(NA)	(NA)
AL.	3,855	3,970	4,184	(NA)	(NA)	(NA)	MO	542	580	658	431	447	478
AR.	4,499	4,615	4,854	518	513	510	NC.	2,852	3,138	3,218	1,321	1,366	1,362
CA.	1,188	1,102	1,131	509	486	449	OH.	117	137	166	145	158	176
DE	1,256	1,295	1,369	(NA)	(NA)	(NA)	OK.	600	666	799	(NA)	(NA)	(NA)
FL	541	552	571	(NA)	(NA)	(NA)	PA	572	547	597	178	169	202
GA	4,026	4,416	4,724	61	44	42	SC.	447	514	589	196	195	173
IN	(NA)	(NA)	(NA)	350	334	336	TN.	509	552	599	(NA)	(NA)	(NA)
IA	92	90	83	232	231	250	TX	1,582	1,623	1,670	(NA)	(NA)	(NA)
KY	173	174	237	(NA)	(NA)	(NA)	VA	1,048	1,124	1,188	363	393	409
MD.	1,262	1,332	1,311	3	4	3	WA	169	180	200	(NA)	(NA)	(NA)
MN.	231	238	249	800	815	847	WV	177	303	384	77	80	104

NA Not available. [1] Includes other States not shown separately.

Source: U.S. Dept. of Agriculture, National Agricultural Statistics Service, *Poultry—Production and Value*, annual; and *Turkeys*, annual.

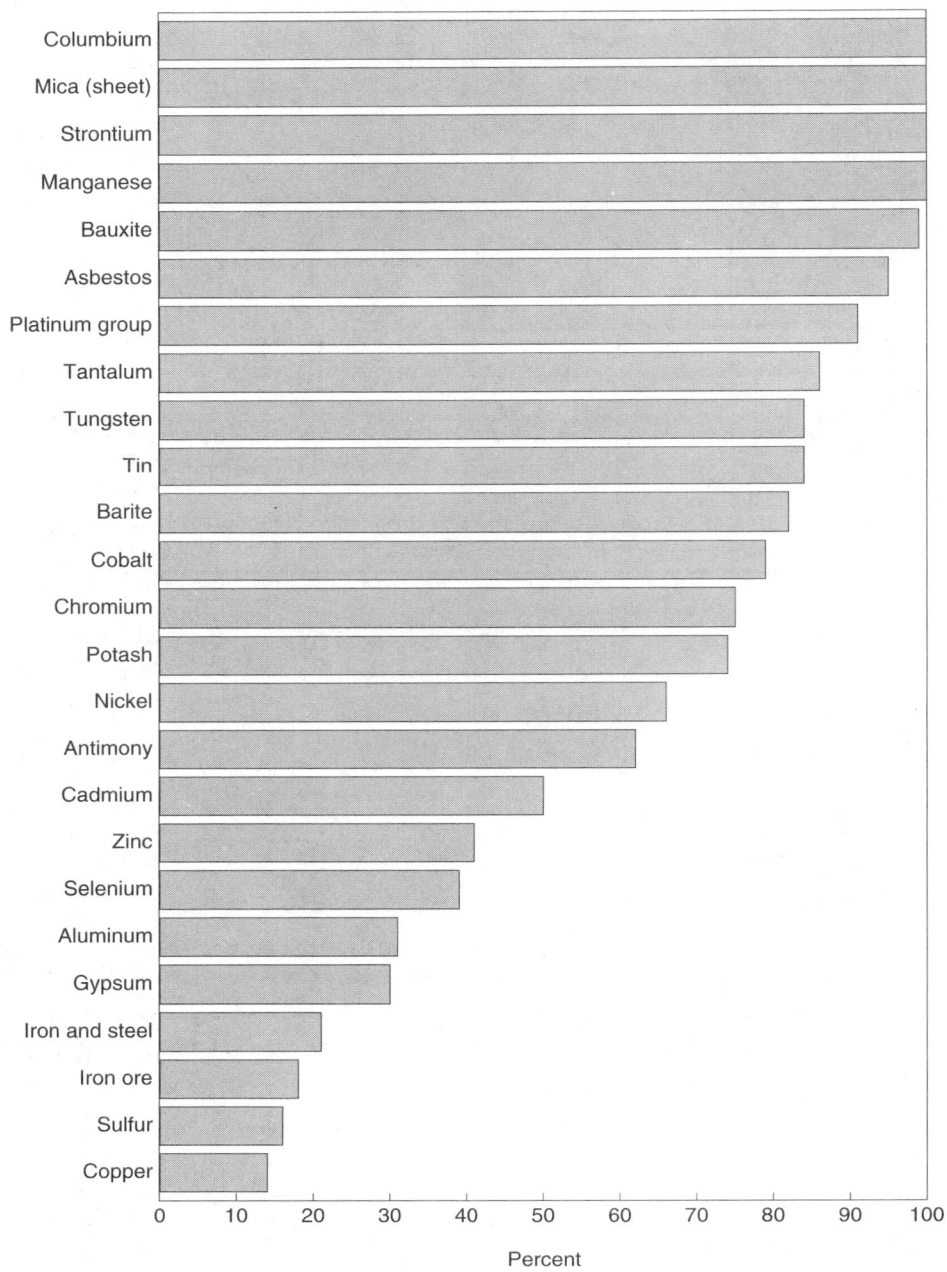

Figure 24.1
Net U.S. Imports of Selected Minerals and Metals as a Percent of Apparent Consumption: 1994

Percent

Source: Chart prepared by U.S. Bureau of the Census. For data, see table 1154.

Natural Resources

This section presents data on the area, ownership, production, trade, reserves, and disposition of natural resources. Natural resources is defined here as including forestry, fisheries, and mining and mineral products.

Forestry—Presents data on the area, ownership, and timber resource of commercial timberland; forestry statistics covering the National Forests and Forest Service cooperative programs; product data for lumber, pulpwood, woodpulp, paper and paperboard, and similar data.

The principal sources of data relating to forests and forest products are *An Analysis of the Timber Situation in the United States, 1989-2040, 1990; Forest Resources of the United States, 1992, 1993; U.S. Timber Production, Trade, Consumption, and Price Statistics; Land Areas of the National Forest System*, issued annually by the Forest Service of the Department of Agriculture; *Agricultural Statistics* issued by the Department of Agriculture; and reports of the census of manufactures (taken every 5 years) and the annual Current Industrial Reports, issued by the Bureau of the Census. Additional information is published in the monthly *Survey of Current Business* of the Bureau of Economic Analysis; and the annual *Wood Pulp and Fiber Statistics* and *The Statistics of Paper, Paperboard, and Wood Pulp* of the American Forest and Paper Association, Washington, DC.

The completeness and reliability of statistics on forests and forest products vary considerably. The data for forest land area and stand volumes are much more reliable for areas which have been recently surveyed than for those for which only estimates are available. In general, more data are available for lumber and other manufactured products such as particle board and softwood panels, etc., than for the primary forest products such as poles and piling and fuelwood.

Fisheries—The principal source of data relating to fisheries is *Fisheries of the United States*, issued annually by the National Marine Fisheries Service

In Brief

Petroleum balance, 1994:

	Barrels
Products supplied	6.5 billion
Net imports	2.5 billion
Stocks	1.7 billion

(NMFS), National Oceanic and Atmospheric Administration (NOAA).

The NMFS collects and disseminates data on commercial landings of fish and shellfish. Annual reports include quantity and value of commercial landings of fish and shellfish disposition of landings, number of fishermen, and number and kinds of fishing vessels and fishing gear. Reports for the fish-processing industry include annual output for the wholesaling and fish processing establishments, annual and seasonal employment. The Magnuson Fishery Conservation and Management Act of 1976 (Magnuson Act), Public Law 94-265 as amended, provides for the conservation and management of all fishery resources within the U.S. Exclusive Economic Zone (EEZ), and gives the Federal Government exclusive authority over domestic and foreign fisheries within 200 nautical miles of U.S. shores and over certain living marine resources beyond the EEZ. Within the EEZ, the total allowable level of foreign fishing, if any, is that portion of the "optimum yield" not harvested by U.S. vessels. Adjustments in the "optimum yield" level may occur periodically. For details, see Fisheries of the United States, 1993. The NMFS collects and disseminates data on catches by foreign fishing vessels in the EEZ.

Mining and mineral products—Presents data relating to mineral industries and their products, general summary measures of production and employment, and more detailed data on production, prices, imports and exports, consumption, and distribution for specific industries and products. Data on mining and mineral products may also be found in sections 26 and 30 of this *Abstract*; data on mining employment may be found in section 13.

Mining comprises the extraction of minerals occurring naturally (coal, ores, crude petroleum, natural gas) and quarrying, well operation, milling, refining and processing and other preparation customarily done at the mine or well site or as a part of extraction activity. (Mineral preparation plants are usually operated together with mines or quarries.) Exploration for minerals is included as is the development of mineral properties.

The principal governmental sources of these data are the *Minerals Yearbook*, published by the U.S. Geological Survey, Department of the Interior, and various monthly and annual publications of the Energy Information Administration, Department of Energy. See text, section 19, for list of Department of Energy publications. In addition, the Bureau of the Census conducts a census of mineral industries every 5 years. Nongovernment sources include the *Annual Statistical Report* of the American Iron and Steel Institute, Washington, DC; *Metals Week* and the monthly *Engineering and Mining Journal*, issued by the McGraw-Hill Publishing Co., New York, NY; *The Iron Age*, issued weekly by the Chilton Co., Philadelphia, PA; and the *Joint Association Survey* of the U.S. Oil and Gas Industry, conducted jointly by the American Petroleum Institute, Independent Petroleum Association of America, and Mid-Continent Oil and Gas Association.

Mineral statistics, with principal emphasis on commodity detail, have been collected by the U.S. Geological Survey since 1880. Current data in U.S. Geological Survey publications include quantity and value of nonfuel minerals produced, sold or used by producers, or shipped; quantity of minerals stocked; crude materials treated and prepared minerals recovered; and consumption of mineral raw materials. The U.S. Mine Safety and Health Administration also collects and publishes data on workhours, employment, accidents, and injuries in the mineral industries, except petroleum and natural gas. In October 1977, mineral fuel data collection activities of the U.S. Geological Survey were transferred to the Energy Information Administration.

Censuses of mineral industries have been conducted by the Bureau of the Census at various intervals since 1840. Beginning with the 1967 census, legislation provides for a census to be conducted every 5 years for years ending in "2" and "7." The censuses provide, for the various types of mineral establishments, information on operating costs, capital expenditures, labor, equipment, and energy requirements in relation to their value of shipments and other receipts. Commodity statistics on many manufactured mineral products are also collected by the Bureau at monthly, quarterly, or annual intervals and issued in its *Current Industrial Reports* series.

In general, figures shown in the individual commodity tables include data for outlying areas and may therefore not agree with summary tables. Except for crude petroleum and refined products, the export and import figures include foreign trade passing through the customs districts of United States and Puerto Rico, but exclude shipments between U.S. territories and the customs districts.

Historical statistics—Tabular headnotes provide cross-references, where applicable, to *Historical Statistics of the United States, Colonial Times to 1970*. See Appendix IV.

No. 1121. National Forest System—Summary: 1970 to 1993

[For fiscal years ending in year shown; see text, section 9. Includes Alaska and Puerto Rico, except as noted. See *Historical Statistics, Colonial Times to 1970*, series J 33-34, for similar grazing data, and L 15-31]

ITEM	Unit	1970	1980	1985	1988	1989	1990	1991	1992	1993
Timber cut, total value	Mil. dol	309	737	725	1,243	1,313	1,191	1,012	938	918
Commercial and cost sales: [1]										
Volume.	Mil. bd.	11,527	9,178	10,941	12,649	11,951	10,500	8,475	7,290	5,917
Value	Mil. dol	308	730	721	1,240	1,310	1,188	1,009	935	914.6
Free use:										
Volume.	Mil. bd.	179	2,070	399	223	214	151	121	80	80
Value [2].	Mil. dol	0.3	5.7	2.2	1.2	1.2	1.0	1.0	0.8	0.8
Misc. forest products:										
Value	Mil. dol	0.7	1.1	1.7	2.0	2.2	2.6	2.7	2.7	2.8
Livestock grazing: [3]										
Cattle and horses [4]	1,000 .	1,607	1,521	1,565	1,313	1,526	1,236	1,265	1,216	(NA)
Sheep and goats	1,000 .	2,105	1,328	1,183	1,067	972	958	1,029	1,017	(NA)
Roads and trails:										
Road construction [5]	Miles. .	942	925	1,903	1,352	866	857	910	853	816
Trail construction [5][6].	Miles. .	278	2,419	987	1,834	1,944	1,635	1,921	1,976	1976
Receipts, total	Mil. dol	300	703	636	980	1,051	971	772	614	503
Timber use	Mil. dol	284	625	515	888	910	849	667	520	425
Grazing use	Mil. dol	4	16	9	9	11	10	11	11	11
Special land use, etc	Mil. dol	11	62	112	83	130	112	93	84	67
Payments to local govt. [7]	Mil. dol	73	240	229	325	368	368	335	322	323
25-percent fund [8].	Mil. dol	72	234	212	317	354	358	327	(NA)	(NA)
Other [9]	Mil. dol	1	7	17	8	15	10	8	(NA)	(NA)
Allotments to Forest Service [10] . . .	Mil. dol	30	73	60	104	111	106	88	(NA)	(NA)
Roads and trails	Mil. dol	29	65	55	92	96	91	73	(NA)	(NA)
Other.	Mil. dol	1	8	5	12	15	14	14	(NA)	(NA)

NA Not available. [1] Includes land exchanges. [2] Includes some free use timber not reducible to board feet. [3] For 1970, data for livestock permitted to graze; thereafter, for number actually grazed. Calendar-year data, prior to 1980. Excludes Puerto Rico. [4] Excludes animals under 6 months of age. 1970 includes swine. Beginning 1980, includes burros. [5] Includes reconstruction. [6] Beginning 1980, includes work accomplished by Human Resource Programs and volunteers. [7] Payments made in following year. [8] Includes Tongass Alaska suspense account. [9] Includes Arizona and New Mexico School Fund (through 1980), State of Minnesota, and receipts paid to counties under Bankhead-Jones Farm Tenant Act. [10] For use in following year.

Source: U.S. Forest Service. In *Agricultural Statistics*, annual; and unpublished data.

No. 1122. Forest and Timberland Area, Sawtimber and Stock: 1970 to 1992

[As of **Jan. 1**]

YEAR AND REGION	Total forest land (mil. acres)	TIMBERLAND, OWNERSHIP [1]				SAWTIMBER, NET VOLUME [3]		GROWING STOCK, NET VOLUME [4]	
		All ownerships (mil. acres)	Federally owned or managed [2] (mil. acres)	State, county, and municipal (mil. acres)	Private (mil. acres)	Total (bil. bd. ft.)	Softwood (bil. bd. ft.)	Total (bil. cu. ft.)	Softwood (bil. cu. ft.)
United States, 1970 .	754	504	116	29	360	2,587	2,035	694	458
North	(NA)	154	11	18	126	295	81	146	39
South.	(NA)	203	15	3	185	569	302	191	87
Rocky Mountains	(NA)	65	42	2	20	398	384	101	95
Pacific Coast.	(NA)	82	47	5	29	1,325	1,268	257	238
United States, 1987 .	731	485	97	34	354	2,853	2,040	766	453
North	165	154	11	19	124	459	126	190	48
South.	203	197	16	4	177	781	388	245	106
Rocky Mountains	142	61	39	3	20	411	394	108	100
Pacific Coast.	220	72	31	8	32	1,202	1,132	223	199
United States, 1992 .	737	490	97	35	358	2,992	2,047	786	450
North	168	158	11	19	127	540	137	207	51
South.	212	199	16	4	179	842	389	251	103
Rocky Mountains	140	63	40	3	20	415	397	110	101
Pacific Coast.	217	70	30	8	32	1,196	1,124	218	195

NA Not available. [1] Timberland is forest land that is producing or is capable of crops of industrial wood and not withdrawn from timber utilization by statute or administrative regulation. Areas qualifying as timberland have the capability of producing in excess of 20 cubic feet per acre per year of industrial wood in natural stands. Currently inaccessible and inoperable areas are included. [2] Includes Indian lands. [3] Sawtimber is timber suitable for sawing into lumber. Live trees of commercial species containing at least one 12-foot sawlog or two noncontiguous 8-foot logs, and meeting regional specifications for freedom from defect. Softwood trees must be at least 9.0-inches diameter, and hardwood trees must be at least 11.0-inches diameter at 4 1/2 feet above ground. International 1/4-inch rule. [4] Live trees of commercial species meeting specified standards of quality or vigor. Cull trees are excluded. Includes only trees 5.0-inches diameter or larger at 4 1/2 feet above ground.

Source: U.S. Forest Service, *Forest Resources of the United States, 1992.*

No. 1123. National Forest System Land—States and Other Areas: 1990 and 1992

[In thousands of acres. As of Sept. 30. See also *Historical Statistics, Colonial Times to 1970*, series L 10-11]

STATE	GROSS AREA WITHIN UNIT BOUNDARIES [1]		NATIONAL FOREST SYSTEM LAND [2]		OTHER LANDS WITHIN UNIT BOUNDARIES	
	1990	1992	1990	1992	1990	1992
United States.	231,443	231,502	191,324	191,453	40,119	40,049
Alabama.	1,280	1,288	658	659	622	629
Alaska	24,345	24,345	22,220	22,193	2,126	2,152
Arizona.	11,880	11,887	11,239	11,247	642	641
Arkansas	3,490	3,490	2,509	2,529	981	961
California	24,401	24,401	20,619	20,616	3,782	3,785
Colorado.	16,039	16,037	14,462	14,467	1,577	1,570
Connecticut.	-	(Z)	-	(Z)	-	-
Delaware	-	-	-	-	-	-
Florida	1,246	1,254	1,128	1,135	118	119
Georgia	1,846	1,846	859	860	987	986
Hawaii	-	(Z)	-	(Z)	-	-
Idaho.	21,674	21,674	20,438	20,441	1,236	1,233
Illinois	840	840	266	268	573	572
Indiana.	644	644	188	189	456	455
Iowa	-	-	-	-	-	-
Kansas.	116	116	108	108	8	8
Kentucky	2,102	2,102	670	673	1,431	1,428
Louisiana	1,022	1,022	601	601	422	421
Maine.	93	93	53	53	40	40
Maryland	-	-	-	-	-	-
Massachusetts.	-	-	-	-	-	-
Michigan.	4,885	4,895	2,816	2,849	2,069	2,046
Minnesota.	5,467	5,467	2,810	2,815	2,657	2,652
Mississippi	2,310	2,310	1,150	1,153	1,160	1,157
Missouri	3,082	3,082	1,475	1,478	1,606	1,603
Montana.	19,101	19,102	16,806	16,806	2,295	2,296
Nebraska	442	442	352	352	90	90
Nevada	6,275	6,275	5,797	5,801	478	474
New Hampshire	825	825	720	721	105	104
New Jersey.	-	-	-	-	-	-
New Mexico	10,367	10,367	9,321	9,321	1,046	1,045
New York	13	13	13	13	-	-
North Carolina	3,165	3,165	1,232	1,234	1,934	1,932
North Dakota.	1,106	1,106	1,106	1,106	-	(Z)
Ohio	833	833	203	212	630	622
Oklahoma.	461	465	297	301	165	164
Oregon.	17,502	17,504	15,651	15,655	1,851	1,849
Pennsylvania.	744	744	513	513	231	231
Rhode Island.	-	-	-	-	-	-
South Carolina.	1,376	1,376	607	609	768	767
South Dakota	2,344	2,352	1,996	2,013	349	339
Tennessee	1,212	1,212	628	628	585	585
Texas.	1,994	1,994	753	755	1,241	1,240
Utah	9,186	9,186	8,099	8,099	1,087	1,087
Vermont.	815	816	340	345	475	471
Virginia.	3,223	3,223	1,645	1,648	1,578	1,575
Washington.	10,050	10,061	9,151	9,160	899	901
West Virginia.	1,863	1,863	1,025	1,025	838	838
Wisconsin	2,023	2,023	1,517	1,518	506	505
Wyoming	9,704	9,704	9,255	9,255	449	449

- Represents zero. Z Less than half the unit of measure. [1] Comprises all publicly and privately owned land within authorized boundaries of national forests, purchase units, national grasslands, Land utilization projects, research and experimental areas, and other areas. [2] Federally owned land within the "gross area within unit boundaries."

Source: U.S. Forest Service, *Land Areas of the National Forest System*, annual.

No. 1124. Public Lands—Disposal: 1980 to 1993

[For fiscal year ending in year shown: see text, section 9. Period figures are totals, not annual averages. See also *Historical Statistics, Colonial Times to 1970*, series J 10-15 and J 28-32]

ITEM	Unit	1980	1985	1987	1988	1989	1990	1991	1992	1993
Applications, entries, and selections allowed [1]	1,000 acres	1,167	1,404	1	1	1	7	1	1	-
Applications, entries, and selections approved [1]	1,000 acres	175	6,491	1,812	1,387	579	238	436	1,219	819
Patents and certificates [1]	1,000 acres	2,495	4,217	3,000	5,419	780	1,052	476	1,585	1,460
Mineral class, total	Number	106,125	119,419	89,789	82,585	83,762	81,355	83,358	72,337	59,631
Leases	Number	105,963	119,101	89,546	82,450	83,656	81,248	83,259	72,192	59,523
Permits [2]	Number	132	316	231	121	96	96	88	121	84
Licenses	Number	30	2	12	14	10	11	11	24	24
Grazing Leases [3]	Number	7,700	7,387	7,164	7,197	7,263	7,105	7,185	7,036	6,994
Permits [4]	Number	14,741	12,493	12,368	12,537	12,362	12,153	12,312	12,128	12,069

- Represents or rounds to zero. [1] Excludes Indian fee and reissue trust and corrective patents. [2] Excludes free-use permits for disposition of mineral materials. [3] Beginning 1985, as of September 30. [4] Licenses and permits within grazing districts.

Source: U. S. Bureau of Land Management, *Public Land Statistics*, annual.

No. 1125. Timber-Based Industries—Summary of Manufactures: 1991 and 1992

[Data based on *1987 Standard Industrial Classification Manual*, published by the Office of Management and Budget, see text, section 26. N.e.c. = Not elsewhere classified]

INDUSTRY	SIC [1] code	1991 All employees Number (1,000)	1991 All employees Payroll (mil. dol.)	1991 Value of shipments (bil. dol.)	1992 All employees Number (1,000)	1992 All employees Payroll (mil. dol.)	1992 Value of shipments (bil. dol.)
Logging and sawmills	241/242	207.6	4,307	28.9	221.7	4,739	31.3
Millwork and veneer [2]	243	209.9	4,487	21.4	224.6	5,027	24.9
Wood containers	244	39.8	634	2.9	40.0	639	2.9
Wood buildings, mobile homes	245	54.1	1,106	6.0	56.2	1,230	6.6
Miscellaneous wood products	249	90.9	1,706	9.5	84.9	1,740	10.3
Pulp mills	261	16.8	697	5.3	15.9	688	5.5
Paper mills	262	130.3	5,224	33.3	130.7	5,425	32.8
Paperboard mills	263	50.6	2,027	15.0	51.5	2,135	16.1
Paperboard containers and boxes	265	198.6	5,392	30.6	199.0	5,710	32.6
Converted paper and paperboard products [3]	267	224.3	6,043	44.6	229.2	6,521	46.0

[1] Standard Industrial Classification code; see text, section 13. [2] Includes plywood and structural members. [3] Except containers and boxes.

Source: U.S. Bureau of the Census, *Census of Manufactures, 1992 Final Industry Series*, MC87-I-24A-D and MC87-I-26A-C, and *Annual Survey of Manufactures*.

No. 1126. Timber Products—Production, Foreign Trade, and Consumption, by Type of Product: 1970 to 1988

[In millions of cubic feet, roundwood equivalent. See also *Historical Statistics, Colonial Times to 1970*, series L 72-97]

ITEM	Unit	1970	1975	1980	1983	1984	1985	1986	1987	1988, prel.
Industrial roundwood:										
Domestic production	Mil. cu. ft.	11,105	10,575	12,120	12,065	12,725	12,515	13,845	14,670	14,985
Imports	Mil. cu. ft.	2,430	2,215	3,250	3,710	4,165	4,340	4,375	4,575	4,445
Exports	Mil. cu. ft.	1,540	1,685	2,350	2,110	2,060	2,070	2,300	2,650	3,200
Consumption	Mil. cu. ft.	11,995	11,105	13,020	13,665	14,830	14,785	15,920	16,595	16,230
Lumber:										
Domestic production	Mil. cu. ft.	5,215	4,890	5,300	5,370	5,770	5,665	6,545	6,990	6,920
Plywood and veneer:										
Domestic production	Mil. cu. ft.	1,020	1,165	1,175	1,365	1,400	1,420	1,505	1,650	1,630
Pulp products:										
Domestic production	Mil. cu. ft.	3,835	3,485	4,390	4,165	4,355	4,165	4,545	4,670	4,885
Logs:										
Imports	Mil. cu. ft.	25	15	25	30	30	20	15	15	15
Pulpwood chips, exports	Mil. cu. ft.	145	195	275	155	145	145	150	160	215
Fuelwood consumption	Mil. cu. ft.	540	570	3,105	3,235	3,620	3,450	3,115	3,150	3,360
Timber products, per capita	Cu. ft	61.1	54.0	70.8	72.0	77.9	76.2	78.8	81.0	79.5
Industrial roundwood	Cu. ft	58.5	51.4	57.2	58.2	62.6	61.8	65.9	68.0	65.9
Fuelwood	Cu. ft	2.6	2.6	13.6	13.8	15.3	14.4	12.9	12.9	13.6
Lumber	Bd. ft	193.0	171.0	188.0	190.0	205.0	207.0	224.0	233.0	221.0
Plywood and veneer	Bd. ft	34.0	32.0	30.0	34.0	34.0	35.0	37.0	39.0	37.0
Pulp products	Cords (128 cu. ft.).	0.3	0.2	0.3	0.3	0.3	0.3	0.3	0.3	0.3

Source: U.S. Forest Service, *U.S. Timber Production, Trade, Consumption, and Price Statistics, 1960-88*, annual.

No. 1127. Selected Species—Stumpage Prices In Current and Constant (1982) Dollars: 1980 to 1993

[In dollars per 1,000 board feet. Stumpage prices are based on sales of sawtimber from National Forests. See also *Historical Statistics, Colonial Times to 1970*, series L 199-205]

SPECIES	1980	1983	1984	1985	1986	1987	1988	1989	1990	1991	1992	1993
CURRENT DOLLARS												
Softwoods:												
Douglas fir [1]	432	162	133	126	161	190	256	390	466	395	477	318
Southern pine [2]	155	141	139	91	104	136	142	131	127	166	198	217
Sugar pine [3]	667	138	84	110	170	288	260	289	285	241	492	598
Ponderosa pine [3][4]	206	104	123	101	157	209	182	292	252	238	292	535
Western hemlock [5]	213	62	62	51	75	105	163	223	203	164	165	364
Hardwoods:												
All eastern hardwoods [6]	52	60	90	65	70	88	151	136	146	160	167	264
Oak, white, red, and black [6]	66	88	145	95	108	147	146	179	188	164	211	195
Maple, sugar [7]	70	55	81	70	66	81	108	129	135	121	145	220
CONSTANT (1982) DOLLARS [8]												
Softwoods:												
Douglas fir [1]	481	160	128	122	160	185	240	347	401	339	407	270
Southern pine [2]	173	139	134	88	103	132	133	117	109	143	169	184
Sugar pine [3]	742	136	81	106	169	280	244	258	245	207	419	508
Ponderosa pine [3][4]	230	103	118	98	156	204	170	260	217	204	249	455
Western hemlock [5]	237	61	60	49	75	103	152	199	175	141	140	309
Hardwoods:												
All eastern hardwoods [6]	58	59	87	63	70	86	142	121	126	137	142	224
Oak, white, red, and black [6]	73	87	140	92	108	143	137	159	162	140	180	166
Maple, sugar [7]	78	54	78	68	66	78	101	115	116	104	123	187

[1] Western Washington and western Oregon.   [2] Southern region.   [3] Pacific Southwest region (formerly California region). [4] Includes Jeffrey pine.   [5] Pacific Northwest region.   [6] Eastern and Southern regions.   [7] Eastern region.   [8] Deflated by the producer price index, all commodities.

Source: U.S. Forest Service, *U.S. Timber Production, Trade, Consumption, and Price Statistics*, annual.

No. 1128. Lumber Consumption, by Species Group and End Use: 1970 to 1992

[In million board feet, except per capita in board feet. Per capita consumption based on estimated resident population as of July 1]

ITEM	1970	1986	1991	1992	END-USE	1970	1976	1986	1991
Total	39.9	57.0	54.8	56.0	New housing	13.3	17.0	19.3	15.0
					Residential upkeep and				
Per capita	194	237	217	219	improvements	4.7	5.7	10.1	11.6
					New nonresidential				
Species group:					construction [1]	4.7	4.5	5.3	5.4
Softwoods	32.0	48.0	44.0	45.7	Manufacturing	4.7	4.9	4.8	5.6
Hardwoods	7.9	9.0	10.8	10.3	Shipping	5.7	5.9	6.8	8.2
					Other [2]	6.8	6.7	10.9	8.8

[1] In addition to new construction, includes railroad ties laid as replacements in existing track and lumber used by railroads for railcar repair.   [2] Includes upkeep and improvement of nonresidential buildings and structures; made-at-home projects, such as furniture, boats, and picnic tables; made-on-the-job items such as advertising and display structures; and miscellaneous products and uses.

Source: U.S. Forest Service. *The 1993 RPA Timber Assessment Update*, forthcoming.

No. 1129. Selected Timber Products—Producer Price Indexes: 1980 to 1994

[See also *Historical Statistics, Colonial Times to 1970*, series L 206-210]

PRODUCT	Unit	1980	1985	1990	1992	1993	1994
Lumber and wood products, except furniture	Dec. 1984=100	(NA)	100.3	117.0	129.7	148.3	154.4
Logging camps and logging contractors	Dec. 1981=100	(NA)	94.8	135.6	151.3	186.4	192.6
Sawmills and planing mills	Dec. 1984=100	(NA)	99.7	113.7	131.3	161.8	165.2
Millwork, veneer, and plywood [1]	Dec. 1984=100	(NA)	99.9	115.4	128.4	142.8	148.7
Softwood plywood	Dec. 1980=100	91.4	90.0	102.5	124.2	145.4	153.1
Wood containers	June 1985=100	(NA)	(NA)	113.9	123.5	141.7	147.4
Wood buildings and mobile homes	Dec. 1984=100	(NA)	100.6	115.5	121.5	129.5	139.8
Particleboard	Dec. 1982=100	92.1	110.0	117.1	120.7	138.6	156.2
Paper and allied products	Dec. 1984=100	(NA)	98.8	121.9	121.2	120.2	123.6
Pulp mills	Dec. 1982=100	105.5	100.9	153.8	118.5	105.8	117.2
Paper mill products; except building paper	June 1981=100	93.5	109.5	134.0	126.6	126.6	128.4
Paperboard mills	Dec. 1982=100	97.3	112.0	146.0	142.6	138.3	152.2
Converted paper and paperboard products [2]	June 1993=100	(NA)	(NA)	(NA)	(NA)	(NA)	100.6
Paperboard containers and boxes	Dec. 1984=100	(NA)	98.4	117.7	118.5	118.0	123.7

NA Not available.   [1] Includes structural wood members.   [2] Excludes containers and boxes.

Source: U.S. Bureau of Labor Statistics, *Producer Price Indexes*, monthly.

No. 1130. Paper and Paperboard—Production, New Supply, and Ratio of New Supply to Real GDP: 1990 to 1993

[In thousands of short tons. See also *Historical Statistics, Colonial Times to 1970*, series L 172, L 174, and L 178-191]

ITEM	PRODUCTION				NEW SUPPLY				RATIO OF NEW SUPPLY TO REAL GDP [1]			
	1990	1991	1992	1993	1990	1991	1992	1993	1990	1991	1992	1993
Total paper	39,361	39,084	40,973	41,745	49,494	47,379	49,424	51,244	10.106	9.734	9.926	9.980
Total paperboard	39,423	40,416	41,985	43,213	36,406	36,826	38,543	40,045	7.434	7.566	7.741	7.799
Unbleached Kraft	20,357	20,950	21,658	21,447	17,780	17,794	18,515	18,456	3.631	3.656	3.718	3.595
Semichemical	5,640	5,552	5,762	5,672	5,609	5,482	5,730	5,774	1.145	1.126	1.151	1.125
Bleached Kraft	4,399	4,572	4,503	4,583	3,638	3,781	3,690	3,788	0.743	0.777	0.741	0.738
Recycled	9,026	9,332	10,063	11,510	9,378	9,768	10,608	12,026	1.915	2.007	2.130	2.342

[1] GDP = Gross domestic product.

Source: American Forest and Paper Association, Washington, DC, *Monthly Statistical Summary of Paper, Paperboard and Woodpulp*.

No. 1131. Newsprint—Production, Stocks, Consumption, and Price Index: 1970 to 1992

[In thousands of metric tons, except price index. See also *Historical Statistics, Colonial Times to 1970*, series L 192-198]

COUNTRY AND ITEM	1970	1980	1985	1987	1988	1989	1990	1991	1992
Canada: Production	7,808	8,625	8,890	9,630	9,840	9,640	9,068	8,977	8,931
Shipments from mills	7,795	8,622	8,899	9,718	9,740	9,606	9,074	8,728	9,143
Stocks at mills, end of year	236	165	288	189	288	321	315	564	351
United States:									
Consumption, estimate	6,468	10,088	11,507	12,303	12,245	12,241	12,125	11,381	11,634
Production	3,142	4,239	4,924	5,300	5,427	5,523	5,997	6,206	6,424
Shipments from mills	3,136	4,234	4,927	5,310	5,415	5,515	6,007	6,152	6,464
Stocks, end of year: At mills	33	21	57	36	48	56	46	98	59
At and in transit to publishers	749	732	910	900	932	749	801	932	938
Producer price index (1982=100)	34.1	[1]88.5	105.3	112.3	127.6	122.5	119.5	120.9	109.9

[1] Average for 11 months.

Source: U.S. Bureau of Economic Analysis, *Survey of Current Business*, monthly. Data from American Forest and Paper Association, Washington, DC, and Canadian Pulp & Paper Association.

No. 1132. Selected Timber Products—Imports and Exports: 1970 to 1993

ITEM	Unit	1970	1980	1985	1988	1989	1990	1991	1992	1993, prel.
IMPORTS [1]										
Lumber, total [2]	Mil. bd. ft	6,114	9,866	14,996	14,226	15,277	12,159	11,756	13,474	15,625
From Canada	Percent	96.0	97.5	97.6	97.5	91.3	98.5	98.3	98.3	97.6
Softwoods	Mil. bd. ft	5,778	9,573	14,632	13,841	14,928	11,927	11,545	13,214	15,260
Hardwoods	Mil. bd. ft	337	293	364	386	349	232	210	260	335
Logs, total	Mil. bd. ft.[3]	144	128	99	68	42	28	15	46	94
From Canada	Percent	79.6	97.4	81.8	91.9	61.5	67.5	74.5	88.9	77.7
Softwoods	Mil. bd. ft.[3]	107	114	71	56	24	18	9	40	86
Hardwoods	Mil. bd. ft.[3]	38	13	28	12	18	10	6	7	8
Paper and board [4]	1,000 tons	7,115	8,780	11,522	13,110	13,100	13,148	12,167	12,543	13,971
Woodpulp	1,000 tons	3,518	4,051	4,466	4,938	5,105	4,893	4,997	5,029	5,413
Plywood	Mil. sq. ft.[5]	2,049	1,235	1,817	1,698	1,955	1,687	1,457	1,776	1,798
EXPORTS										
Lumber, total [2]	Mil. bd. ft	1,243	2,494	1,945	4,527	4,243	3,802	3,997	3,603	3,385
To: Canada	Percent	21.7	25.3	23.7	17.6	15.6	18.1	15.1	17.3	17.4
Japan	Percent	30.8	26.0	32.1	34.5	38.1	33.5	30.5	30.9	36.3
Europe	Percent	24.1	23.8	15.1	20.5	16.6	19.1	19.6	21.2	15.9
Softwoods	Mil. bd. ft	1,115	2,007	1,518	3,266	3,379	2,941	3,055	2,613	2,376
Hardwoods	Mil. bd. ft	128	487	427	1,261	863	861	942	990	1,008
Logs, total	Mil. bd. ft.[3]	2,741	3,261	3,843	4,798	4,745	4,262	3,816	3,316	2,877
To: Canada	Percent	10.6	9.7	11.6	7.9	5.8	9.3	11.2	12.6	13.6
Japan	Percent	86.3	78.0	49.4	50.3	63.5	62.5	56.7	62.1	65.4
China: Mainland	Percent	(NA)	2.7	27.8	23.4	9.6	8.5	9.7	7.1	4.6
Softwoods	Mil. bd. ft.[3]	2,672	3,109	3,732	4,594	4,532	4,044	3,532	3,092	2,640
Hardwoods	Mil. bd. ft.[3]	69	152	111	204	214	218	283	224	237
Paper and board [4]	1,000 tons	2,817	5,214	4,071	5,691	6,300	6,796	8,331	8,971	9,126
Woodpulp	1,000 tons	3,095	3,806	3,796	5,528	6,231	5,906	6,337	7,222	6,499
Plywood	Mil. sq. ft.[5]	172	413	358	1,093	1,562	1,767	1,552	1,759	1,648

NA Not available. [1] Customs value of imports; see text, section 28. [2] Includes railroad ties. [3] Log scale. [4] Includes paper and board products. Excludes hardboard. [5] 3/8 inch basis.

Source: U.S. Foreign Agricultural Service, unpublished data. Trade, Consumption, and Price Statistics: 1960-89, forthcoming.

No. 1133. Fishery Products—Domestic Catch and Imports, Summary: 1970 to 1993

[Live weight, in millions of pounds, except percent. 1979-1993 preliminary. For data on commercial catch for selected countries, see table 1361, section 30. See *Historical Statistics, Colonial Times to 1970*, series L 224-226, for domestic catch]

ITEM	1970	1980	1984	1985	1986	1987	1988	1989	1990	1991	1992	1993
Total	11,474	11,357	12,552	15,150	14,368	15,744	14,628	15,485	16,349	16,364	16,106	20,334
For human food.	6,213	8,006	8,498	9,337	9,620	10,561	10,505	12,268	12,662	13,020	13,242	13,821
For industrial use	5,261	3,351	4,054	5,813	4,748	5,183	4,123	3,217	3,687	3,344	2,864	6,513
Domestic catch	4,917	6,482	6,438	6,258	6,031	6,896	7,192	8,463	9,404	9,484	9,637	10,467
For human food	2,537	3,654	3,320	3,294	3,393	3,946	4,588	6,204	7,041	7,031	7,618	8,214
For industrial use	2,380	2,828	3,118	2,964	2,638	2,950	2,604	2,259	2,363	2,453	2,019	2,253
Imports [2]	6,557	4,875	6,114	8,892	8,337	8,848	7,436	7,022	6,945	6,879	6,469	9,867
For human food	3,676	4,352	5,178	6,043	6,227	6,615	5,917	6,064	5,621	5,989	5,624	5,607
For industrial use [3] . . .	2,881	523	936	2,849	2,110	2,233	1,519	958	1,324	890	845	4,260
Disposition	4,917	6,482	6,438	6,258	6,031	6,896	7,192	8,463	9,404	9,484	9,637	10,467
Fresh and frozen	1,595	2,621	2,336	2,242	2,487	3,157	3,813	5,585	6,501	6,541	7,288	7,744
Canned	1,150	1,161	1,128	1,232	1,134	1,009	1,017	798	751	674	543	649
Cured.	71	96	82	70	60	89	86	128	126	119	100	115
Reduced to meal, oil, etc.	2,101	2,604	2,892	2,714	2,350	2,641	2,276	1,952	2,026	2,150	1,696	1,959

[1] For univalve and bivalve mollusks (conchs, clams, oysters, scallops, etc.), the weight of meats, excluding the shell, is reported. [2] Excludes imports of edible fishery products consumed in Puerto Rico; includes landings of tuna caught by foreign vessels in American Samoa. [3] Fish meal and sea herring.

No. 1134. Fisheries—Quantity and Value of Domestic Catch: 1970 to 1993

[1979-1993 preliminary. See also *Historical Statistics, Colonial Times to 1970*, series L 224-226, L 229, and L 310]

YEAR	QUANTITY (mil. lb. [1]) Total	For human food	For indus-trial prod-ucts [2]	Value (mil. dol.)	Average price per lb. (cents)	YEAR	QUANTITY (mil. lb. [1]) Total	For human food	For indus-trial prod-ucts [2]	Value (mil. dol.)	Average price per lb. (cents)
1970	4,917	2,537	2,380	613	12.5	1986	6,031	3,393	2,638	2,763	45.8
1975	4,877	2,465	2,412	977	20.0	1987	6,896	3,946	2,950	3,115	45.2
1980	6,482	3,654	2,828	2,237	34.5	1988	7,192	4,588	2,604	3,520	48.9
1981	5,977	3,547	2,430	2,388	40.0	1989	8,463	6,204	2,259	3,238	38.30
1982	6,367	3,285	3,082	2,390	37.5	1990	9,404	7,041	2,363	3,522	37.50
1983	6,439	3,238	3,201	2,355	36.6	1991	9,484	7,031	2,453	3,308	34.90
1984	6,438	3,320	3,118	2,350	36.5	1992	9,637	7,618	2,019	3,678	38.19
1985	6,258	3,294	2,964	2,326	37.2	1993	10,467	8,214	2,253	3,471	33.2

[1] Live weight. [2] Meal, oil, fish solubles, homogenized condensed fish, shell products, bait, and animal food.

No. 1135. Domestic Fish and Shellfish Catch and Value, by Species: 1985 to 1993

SPECIES	QUANTITY (1,000 lb.) 1988-92 5-year average	1985	1990	1993	VALUE ($1,000) 1985	1990	1993
Total	(X)	6,257,642	9,403,571	10,466,895	2,326,237	3,521,995	3,471,460
Fish, total [1]	(X)	5,214,363	8,091,068	8,999,142	1,193,427	1,900,097	1,884,121
Cod: Atlantic	80,859	82,823	95,881	50,503	35,140	61,329	44,956
Pacific.	453,996	120,275	526,396	482,799	18,556	91,384	116,172
Flounder	347,282	195,718	254,519	599,180	129,121	112,921	135,598
Herring, sea; Atlantic. . . .	104,642	57,133	113,095	109,645	2,968	5,746	6,511
Herring, sea; Pacific	128,219	142,074	108,120	106,572	47,025	32,178	18,711
Menhaden	1,931,671	2,739,401	1,962,160	1,983,319	100,680	93,896	103,258
Pollock, Alaska	2,506,943	92,833	3,108,031	3,257,990	5,409	268,344	358,378
Salmon.	724,855	726,946	733,146	888,134	439,795	612,367	423,530
Shellfish, total [1]	(X)	1,043,279	1,312,503	1,467,753	1,132,810	1,621,898	1,587,339
Clams	137,159	150,551	139,198	147,752	128,349	130,194	138,030
Crabs.	537,548	337,632	499,416	604,437	203,044	483,837	510,494
Lobsters: American.	56,353	46,152	61,017	56,513	114,895	154,677	151,746
Oysters	31,805	44,173	29,193	(NA)	70,053	93,718	86,698
Scallops: Calico	19,583	12,513	(NA)	(NA)	1,281	(NA)	(NA)
Sea	35,412	15,829	39,917	44,494	18,116	153,696	105,603
Shrimp	337,347	333,691	346,494	292,887	472,850	491,433	412,896
Squid: Atlantic	65,250	7,157	59,809	90,809	7,256	21,178	38,323
Pacific	55,219	22,276	36,082	71,550	4,047	2,636	8,079

NA Not available.   X Not applicable.   [1] Includes other types of fish and shellfish, not shown separately.
Source of tables 1133-1135: U.S. National Oceanic and Atmospheric Administration, National Marine Fisheries Service, *Fisheries of the United States*, annual.

No. 1136. U.S. Private Aquaculture—Trout and Catfish Production and Value: 1988 to 1994

[Periods are from Sept. 1 of the previous year to Aug. 31 of stated year. Data are for foodsize fish, those over 12 inches long]

ITEM	Unit	1988	1989	1990	1991	1992	1993	1994
TROUT								
Number sold	Mil	70.5	67.4	67.8	67.7	64.5	60.9	58.3
Total weight	Mil. lb	56.0	55.5	56.8	58.9	55.2	54.6	52.1
Total value of sales	Mil. dol . . .	57.9	60.0	64.6	58.3	51.0	54.3	52.7
Average price received	$/lb	1.03	1.08	1.14	0.99	0.92	0.99	1.01
Average weight	Lb	0.8	0.8	0.8	0.9	0.9	0.9	0.9
CATFISH								
Fish sold to processors	Mil. lb	295.1	341.9	360.4	390.9	457.4	459.0	(NA)
Avg. price paid by processors	Cents/lb. . .	76.4	71.7	75.8	63.1	59.8	71.0	(NA)
Value	Mil. dol . . .	225.5	245.1	273.2	246.7	273.5	325.9	(NA)
Processor sales.	Mil. lb	149.6	176.3	183.1	199.8	231.3	233.5	(NA)
Avg. price received by processors.	Cents/lb. . .	220.8	211.2	224.0	208.6	200.3	218.7	(NA)
Value.	Mil. dol . . .	330.3	372.3	410.1	416.8	463.3	510.7	(NA)
Inventory (Jan. 1).	Mil. lb	5.3	8.8	8.1	9.4	9.6	11.6	9.5

NA Not available.

Source: U.S. Dept. of Agriculture, National Agricultural Statistics Service, USDA.

No. 1137. Supply of Selected Fishery Items: 1980 to 1993

[**In millions of pounds.** Totals available for U.S. consumption are supply minus exports plus imports. Round weight is the complete or full weight as caught. Data are preliminary]

ITEM	Unit	1980	1984	1985	1987	1988	1989	1990	1991	1992	1993
Tuna, canned	Canned weight. . .	666	777	759	866	843	1,028	856	933	922	835
Shrimp	Heads-off weight. .	425	584	633	773	767	743	734	744	820	840
Clams	Meat weight.	102	144	164	151	145	150	152	144	155	156
Salmon, canned.	Canned weight. . .	126	150	113	76	59	159	148	131	73	114
American lobster	Round weight. . . .	69	100	108	116	121	85	95	107	95	92
Spiny lobster	Round weight. . . .	127	153	154	151	139	89	89	85	81	76
Scallops	Meat weight.	51	87	72	79	74	79	74	62	69	66
Sardines, canned	Canned weight. . .	69	58	76	77	63	61	61	52	41	41
Oysters	Meat weight.	71	84	90	92	78	66	56	47	50	48
Crab meat, canned.	Canned weight. . .	9	7	8	8	8	8	8	9	11	9
Snow crab	Round weight. . . .	54	23	45	29	30	58	37	60	88	66
King crab	Round weight. . . .	133	13	11	14	10	18	19	20	15	8

Source: U.S. National Oceanic and Atmospheric Administration, National Marine Fisheries Service, *Fisheries of the United States,* annual.

No. 1138. Canned, Fresh, and Frozen Fishery Products: 1980 to 1993

[Fresh fishery products exclude Alaska and Hawaii. Canned fishery products data are for natural pack only. See also *Historical Statistics, Colonial Times to 1970,* series L 338-357 (production data in cases) and L 358]

PRODUCT	PRODUCTION (mil. lb.)						VALUE (mil. dol.)					
	1980	1985	1990	1991	1992	1993	1980	1985	1990	1991	1992	1993
Canned, [1]	1,516	1,161	1,178	1,386	1,343	1,615	1,928	1,360	1,562	1,644	1,577	1,626
Tuna	602	545	581	593	609	619	1,144	821	902	877	888	904
Salmon.	200	159	196	196	152	199	376	228	366	413	293	307
Clam products	77	117	110	129	126	116	66	109	76	84	88	90
Mackerel [2]	38	15	23	9	5	(NA)	12	7	11	3	2	(NA)
Sardines, Maine.	20	20	13	14	17	14	32	38	17	19	25	25
Shrimp	16	4	1	1	1	1	80	19	3	4	4	4
Crabs.	5	1	1	(Z)	(Z)	(Z)	19	2	4	(Z)	1	1
Oysters [3]	(Z)	2	1	1	(NA)	(Z)	(Z)	2	1	2	(NA)	(Z)
Fish fillets and steaks [4] . .	202	246	441	473	449	409	261	440	843	1,021	912	829
Cod	31	57	65	71	65	54	43	89	132	180	158	131
Flounder.	49	69	54	48	46	35	87	157	154	147	120	100
Haddock.	17	8	7	8	5	4	29	19	24	30	19	17
Ocean perch, Atlantic	7	2	1	1	1	1	9	3	1	1	3	2
Rockfish	14	18	33	22	19	18	13	25	53	36	30	28
Pollock, Atlantic	9	15	12	8	9	8	9	17	21	18	19	18
Pollock, Alaska	(NA)	11	164	152	165	154	(NA)	24	174	206	205	179
Other	74	66	105	163	139	135	71	106	284	403	358	354

NA Not available. Z Less than 500,000 pounds or $500,000. [1] Includes other products, not shown separately. [2] Includes Jack and a small amount of Pacific mackerel. [3] Includes oyster specialties. [4] Fresh and frozen.

Source: U.S. National Oceanic and Atmospheric Administration, National Marine Fisheries Service, *Fisheries of the United States,* annual.

No. 1139. Gross Domestic Product (GDP) in Mining: 1980 to 1993

[In millions of dollars, except percent. For definition of gross domestic product, see text, section 14. For 1977-87, based on 1972 Standard Industrial Classification (SIC); For 1987, estimates are shown first based on the 1972 SIC and then on the 1987 SIC. Estimates thereafter based on 1987 SIC]

MINING INDUSTRY	1980	1985	1987	1988	1989	1990	1991	1992	1993
Current dollars, total	**112.6**	**130.6**	**83.0**	**87.9**	**84.2**	**103.1**	**92.0**	**85.2**	**89.4**
Metal mining	4.4	2.5	2.6	4.8	5.2	6.2	6.3	6.3	6.8
Coal mining	13.6	13.8	12.5	12.5	12.9	12.7	12.4	13.1	12.3
Oil and gas extraction	89.1	108.4	60.8	63.2	58.8	76.9	66.1	58.5	62.7
Nonmetallic minerals, except fuels	5.5	5.9	7.2	7.3	7.4	7.2	7.1	7.3	7.6
Constant (1987) dollars, total	**79.9**	**83.3**	**83.0**	**94.2**	**83.3**	**91.8**	**92.3**	**89.0**	**93.1**
Metal mining	1.6	2.5	2.6	4.3	5.0	6.6	7.7	8.0	8.6
Coal mining	10.1	11.3	12.5	13.8	14.8	15.3	15.5	16.7	16.2
Oil and gas extraction	61.8	63.2	60.8	69.0	56.2	62.9	62.2	57.2	61.1
Nonmetallic minerals, except fuels	6.4	6.3	7.2	7.1	7.3	7.0	6.9	7.1	7.2

Source: U.S. Bureau of Economic Analysis, *Survey of Current Business*, October 1994.

No. 1140. Mining and Primary Metal Production Indexes: 1970 to 1994

[1987=100. See also *Historical Statistics, Colonial Times to 1970*, series M 68-71]

INDUSTRY GROUP	1970	1980	1985	1986	1988	1989	1990	1991	1992	1993	1994
Mining	**100.4**	**110.0**	**109.0**	**101.0**	**101.3**	**100.0**	**102.0**	**100.2**	**98.9**	**98.2**	**99.8**
Coal	67.2	90.2	96.3	97.1	103.1	107.0	112.2	108.2	108.2	102.9	112.0
Anthracite	274.1	169.6	132.8	120.8	115.6	96.3	103.2	72.7	66.1	(NA)	(NA)
Bituminous	66.0	89.7	96.1	96.9	105.0	105.8	113.3	109.4	105.8	(NA)	(NA)
Oil and gas extraction	104.8	112.1	111.9	102.0	99.7	96.0	96.8	95.9	93.2	93.0	92.9
Metal mining	129.5	108.8	91.3	95.2	120.3	140.5	153.1	153.7	163.8	162.4	159.4
Iron ore	194.4	149.4	104.9	84.4	119.4	122.5	117.9	118.3	116.3	115.7	122.5
Nonferrous ores	111.5	95.0	86.4	99.1	120.5	144.1	160.2	160.8	173.3	171.7	166.4
Copper ore	123.2	93.1	86.9	91.2	113.7	120.0	126.8	131.1	141.9	143.3	145.4
Primary metals, manufacturing	**115.2**	**110.8**	**101.8**	**93.7**	**108.7**	**107.2**	**106.5**	**98.7**	**101.9**	**106.9**	**114.5**
Nonferrous metals	77.1	92.5	98.5	97.3	103.1	101.7	99.5	96.1	97.6	101.0	109.3
Copper	135.2	94.7	99.8	99.1	100.1	98.9	102.2	110.0	124.8	135.3	137.5
Aluminum	107.8	138.7	104.7	90.9	117.6	120.5	121.0	123.2	120.5	110.5	98.6
Iron and steel	148.2	126.0	104.5	90.8	112.7	111.2	111.5	100.5	105.1	111.4	118.3

NA Not available.

Source: Board of Governors of the Federal Reserve System, *Federal Reserve Bulletin*, monthly.

No. 1141. Summary of Mineral Operations: 1963 to 1992

[Represents mineral operations only. Beginning 1967, excludes single unit establishments without paid employees. See also *Historical Statistics, Colonial Times to 1970*, series M 1-11]

ITEM	Unit	1963	1967	1972	1977	1982	1987	1992
Establishments	Number	38,651	28,579	25,269	31,359	42,241	33,617	30,828
With 20 or more employees	Number	5,499	5,682	5,312	6,632	(NA)	6,299	5,581
Including all operations in manufactures	Number	40,532	29,688	29,688	31,967	42,585	34,041	(NA)
Excluding oil and gas extraction	Number	19,290	13,330	11,680	13,520	12,267	10,707	9,951
Employees, total	1,000	616	567	595	799	1,114	698	637
Production workers [1]	1,000	482	433	443	593	762	451	414
All other	1,000	134	134	152	206	352	247	223
Worker-hours, production workers [1]	Million	973	892	909	1,183	1,578	942	873
Worker-hours per production workers	1,000	2.0	2.1	2.1	2.1	2.0	2.1	2.1
Payroll, total	Mil. dol.	3,743	4,187	6,226	13,167	28,637	21,739	24,303
Wages, production workers [1]	Mil. dol.	2,680	2,888	4,250	9,082	18,030	12,443	13,874
Salaries, all other employees	Mil. dol.	1,063	1,299	1,976	4,085	10,607	9,296	10,429
Cost of supplies, etc. [2]	Mil. dol.	8,974	10,576	14,884	46,079	109,697	62,423	64,602
Value added in mining	Mil. dol.	15,910	19,330	26,471	68,013	188,056	110,959	113,780
Metal mining	Mil. dol.	1,418	1,557	2,382	3,504	3,215	4,610	7,180
Coal mining	Mil. dol.	1,727	2,091	3,754	11,266	18,631	17,068	17,283
Oil and gas extraction	Mil. dol.	11,020	13,394	17,612	48,587	159,937	80,049	79,700
Nonmetallic minerals mining	Mil. dol.	1,745	2,288	2,723	4,656	6,273	9,233	9,619
Value of shipments and receipts [3]	Mil. dol.	18,804	22,784	36,319	96,375	250,000	157,964	162,339
Capital expenditures	Mil. dol.	3,264	4,058	5,036	17,718	47,753	15,418	16,043

NA Not available.   [1] See footnote 3, table 1142.   [2] Includes purchased machinery installed.   [3] See footnote 5, table 1142.

Source: U.S. Bureau of the Census, *Census of Mineral Industries, 1972, 1977, 1982, 1987*, and *1992*.

No. 1142. Mineral Industries—Summary: 1987 and 1992

["N.e.c." means not elsewhere classified. See also Historical Statistics, Colonial Times to 1970, series M1-12]

MINERAL INDUSTRY	1987							1992									
	Establishments, total	All employees: Number[1] (1,000)	All employees: Payroll[2] (mil. dol.)	Production workers[3]: Number[1] (1,000)	Production workers[3]: Wages (mil. dol.)	Value added in mining[4] (mil. dol.)	Value of shipments and receipts[5] (mil. dol.)	Establishments: Total	Establishments: With 20 or more employees	All employees: Number[1] (1,000)	All employees: Payroll[2] (mil. dol.)	Production workers[3]: Number[1] (1,000)	Production workers[3]: Hours[6] (mil.)	Production workers[3]: Wages (mil. dol.)	Value added in mining[4] (mil. dol.)	Value of shipments and receipts[5] (mil. dol.)	Capital expenditures (mil. dol.)
All industries	33,617	698	21,739	451	12,443	110,959	157,964	30,828	5,581	637	24,303	414	873	13,874	113,780	162,339	16,043
Metal mining	1,027	44	1,354	34	952	4,610	6,852	1,063	273	53	2,113	42	89	1,542	7,180	10,327	1,574
Iron ores	51	7	224	6	166	768	1,360	40	18	9	348	7	15	274	985	1,715	53
Copper ores	61	14	405	11	283	1,301	2,150	62	35	15	550	12	25	405	1,730	2,935	516
Lead and zinc ores	39	2	58	1	40	176	268	44	24	3	113	2	5	86	287	472	22
Gold and silver ores	372	13	423	10	305	1,814	2,261	428	116	19	827	16	33	601	3,641	4,453	(D)
Ferroalloy ores, except vanadium	58	1	46	1	24	61	110	(NA)	(NA)	(NA)	(NA)	(NA)	(NA)	(NA)	(NA)	(NA)	(NA)
Metal mining services	268	3	81	2	60	176	251	303	38	3	120	3	6	92	263	357	(D)
Miscellaneous metal ores	236	5	162	4	99	374	559	186	42	4	155	3	5	84	274	396	58
Coal mining	3,905	163	5,567	129	4,251	17,068	25,955	3,086	1,239	134	5,438	108	227	4,197	17,283	26,984	1,899
Bituminous coal and lignite mining	3,507	158	5,410	124	4,125	16,679	25,347	2,642	1,155	128	5,247	103	216	4,051	16,792	26,269	1,869
Anthracite mining	107	2	41	2	32	109	206	76	19	1	47	1	2	30	97	161	4
Coal mining services	291	4	116	3	94	280	402	368	65	5	145	4	9	116	394	554	26
Oil and gas extraction	22,910	378	11,961	206	5,283	80,049	112,363	20,877	2,686	344	13,526	187	391	5,992	79,700	111,518	11,423
Crude petroleum and natural gas	10,203	199	7,510	69	2,154	67,955	76,518	9,388	1,017	174	8,409	64	131	2,601	66,297	72,298	9,850
Natural gas liquids	714	13	433	10	320	4,025	24,750	591	197	13	532	9	18	360	4,246	27,206	619
Oil and gas field services	11,993	167	4,018	127	2,809	8,069	11,095	10,898	1,472	157	4,585	114	242	3,031	9,156	12,014	955
Drilling oil and gas wells	2,591	55	1,318	46	1,012	2,550	3,626	2,129	450	48	1,371	38	81	982	2,516	3,584	289
Oil, gas exploration services	1,917	17	452	13	311	771	1,096	1,489	85	14	462	9	19	238	742	980	182
Oil, gas field services, n.e.c.	7,485	95	2,248	69	1,486	4,748	6,373	7,280	937	96	2,753	67	143	1,811	5,899	7,451	484
Nonmetallic mining	5,775	113	2,858	83	1,956	9,233	12,795	5,802	1,383	106	3,226	77	166	2,144	9,619	13,510	1,147
Dimension stone[7]	149	1	25	1	18	65	86	171	17	2	31	2	2	22	79	101	5
Crushed and broken stone[8]	2,002	44	1,082	33	754	3,465	4,768	2,142	664	42	1,222	31	68	840	3,670	5,071	430
Sand and gravel	2,750	33	772	24	551	2,320	3,139	2,678	440	30	889	21	47	594	2,321	3,160	262
Clay and related minerals[8]	197	10	272	7	165	827	1,249	200	100	10	320	8	17	211	935	1,400	87
Chemical and fertilizer minerals	148	16	501	12	336	1,999	2,772	156	76	15	564	10	22	347	2,071	3,017	308
Nonmetallic minerals, services	177	2	45	1	32	119	165	175	14	2	47	1	3	35	128	170	14
Miscellaneous[8]	352	7	162	5	101	438	616	280	72	5	154	4	8	96	415	590	42

D Withheld to avoid disclosure. NA Not available. [1] Excludes proprietors and firm members of unincorporated concerns. [2] Gross earnings paid to all employees on payroll. [3] Represents employees up through the working foreman level engaged in manual work. Includes development and exploration workers. [4] Computed by subtracting cost of supplies, minerals received for preparation, purchased fuel and electric energy, contract work, and purchased machinery from the value of shipments and capital expenditures. [5] Represents value of shipments of primary and secondary products of the industry and amount received for other establishments on a contract, fee, or other basis. [6] Excludes paid vacations, holidays, and sick leave; includes actual overtime hours (not straight-time equivalent). [7] Excludes data for dimension stone quarries operated in conjunction with dressing plants. [8] Excludes data for mining included in establishments classified in manufacturing industries.

Source: U.S. Bureau of the Census, Census of Mineral Industries: 1987, and 1992, final industry series reports.

No. 1143. Mineral Industries—Gross Assets and Capital Expenditures: 1977 to 1992

[In millions of dollars]

INDUSTRY AND YEAR	END OF YEAR GROSS VALUE OF DEPRECIABLE ASSETS					CAPITAL EXPENDITURES					
	Total [1]	Buildings and other structures	Machinery and equipment	Mineral exploration and development [1]	Mineral land and rights [1]	Total [1]	New buildings and other structures	New machinery and equipment	Used buildings and other structures	Used machinery and equipment	Mineral exploration and development [1]
Mineral industries: [2]											
1977.........	44,664	6,099	33,068	2,625	2,871	6,802	785	5,068	30	399	520
1982.........	94,613	10,228	73,419	5,036	5,930	13,472	1,229	10,551	78	937	677
1987.........	84,286	9,314	64,143	5,034	5,795	4,869	349	3,234	88	797	401
1992.........	(NA)	(NA)	(NA)	(NA)	(NA)	6,193	(NA)	(NA)	(NA)	(NA)	(NA)
Crude oil, nat. gas:											
1977.........	94,414	(NA)	(NA)	(NA)	(NA)	10,916	571	2,269	14	93	7,969
1982.........	233,052	(NA)	(NA)	(NA)	(NA)	34,281	1,967	5,550	20	215	26,529
1987.........	(NA)	(NA)	(NA)	(NA)	(NA)	10,549	590	3,176	18	218	6,548
1992.........	(NA)	(NA)	(NA)	(NA)	(NA)	9,850	(NA)	(NA)	(NA)	(NA)	(NA)

NA Not available. [1] Excludes data for mineral exploration and development, and mineral land and rights portions for mining service industries and natural gas liquids industry. [2] Excludes crude petroleum and natural gas. [3] Not collected separately. Data for mineral exploration and development are combined with mineral land and rights. Data for used buildings and other structures are combined with used machinery and equipment.

Source: U.S. Bureau of the Census, Census of Mineral Industries, 1987 and preliminary summary for 1992.

No. 1144. Mineral Industries—Employment, Hours, and Earnings: 1992 to 1994

ITEM	Unit	1992	1993	1994	ITEM	Unit	1992	1993	1994
All mining:						Avg. weekly hours	No ...	43.8	43.8	44.1
All employees.........	1,000 .	635	611	605	Avg. weekly earnings ..	Dol...	614	619	622
Production workers	1,000 .	448	432	431	Metal mining:				
Avg. weekly hours	No ...	43.9	44.3	44.7	All employees.........	1,000 .	53	50	51
Avg. weekly earnings ..	Dol...	638	647	666	Production workers	1,000 .	42	40	41
Coal mining:					Avg. weekly hours	No ...	42.9	43.1	43.6
All employees.........	1,000 .	127	109	114	Avg. weekly earnings ..	Dol...	655	659	703
Production workers	1,000 .	103	87	92	Nonmetallic minerals,				
Avg. weekly hours	No ...	44.0	44.4	45.2	except fuels:				
Avg. weekly earnings ..	Dol...	755	766	802	All employees.........	1,000 .	102	101	101
Oil and gas extraction:					Production workers	1,000 .	76	76	76
All employees.........	1,000 .	353	351	339	Avg. weekly hours	No ...	44.9	46.1	46.5
Production workers	1,000 .	228	229	222	Avg. weekly earnings ..	Dol...	551	585	608

Source: U.S. Bureau of Labor Statistics, Bulletin 2370 and Employment and Earnings, March and June issues.

No. 1145. Selected Mineral Products—Average Prices: 1970 to 1995

[Excludes Alaska and Hawaii, except as noted. See Historical Statistics, Colonial Times to 1970, series M 96, M 139, M 209, M 248, and M 262, for bituminous coal, crude petroleum, iron ore, lead, and aluminum, respectively]

YEAR	Tantalum (dol. per lb.) [1]	Copper, electrolytic [2] (cents per lb.)	Platinum [3] (dol./ troy oz.)	Gold (dol./ fine oz.)	Silver (dol./ fine oz.)	Lead [4] (cents per lb.)	Tin (New York) [5] (cents per lb.)	Zinc [6] (cents per lb.)	Sulfur, crude [7] (dol./ metric ton)	Bituminous coal [8] (dol./ short ton)	Crude petroleum [8] (dol./ bbl.)	Natural gas [8] (dol./ 1,000 cu. ft.)
1970	9.15	58	133	36	1.77	16	174	15	[9]22.41	6.26	3.18	0.17
1975	18.32	64	164	161	4.42	22	340	39	[9]44.20	19.23	7.67	0.44
1980	126.37	101	677	613	20.63	43	846	37	89.06	24.52	21.59	1.59
1982	49.95	73	327	376	7.95	26	654	39	108.27	27.14	28.52	2.46
1983	30.60	77	424	424	11.44	22	655	41	87.24	25.85	26.19	2.59
1984	37.44	67	357	361	8.14	26	624	49	94.31	25.51	25.88	2.66
1985	33.68	67	291	318	6.14	19	596	40	106.46	25.10	24.09	2.51
1986	23.74	66	461	368	5.47	22	383	38	105.22	23.70	12.51	1.94
1987	27.08	83	553	478	7.01	36	419	42	89.78	23.00	15.40	1.67
1988	47.37	121	523	438	6.53	37	441	60	85.95	22.00	12.58	1.69
1989	44.93	131	507	383	5.50	39	520	82	86.62	21.76	15.86	1.69
1990	38.06	123	467	385	4.82	46	386	75	80.14	21.71	20.03	1.71
1991	36.70	109	371	363	4.04	34	363	53	71.45	21.45	16.54	1.64
1992	34.42	107	356	345	3.94	35	402	58	48.14	20.98	15.99	1.74
1993	(NA)	92	370	361	4.30	32	350	46	31.86	19.79	14.25	2.03
1994	(NA)	111	406	385	5.29	37	369	49	28.60	19.43	13.19	1.83
1995, prel..	(NA)	137	430	385	5.30	42	420	53	35.00	(NA)	14.62	(NA)

NA Not available. [1] Dollars per pound of tantalum content. [2] Domestic market prices for wirebar, 1970, 1975-77; prices for cathode thereafter. [3] Average annual dealer prices. [4] 1970, New York prices; beginning 1975, nationwide delivered basis. [5] Straits tin through 1975; thereafter, composite price. [6] Prime western. Beginning 1975, delivered price. [7] F.o.b. works. [8] Average value at the point of production. Source: U.S. Energy Information Administration, Annual Energy Review.

Source: Except as noted, U.S. Bureau of Mines, Mineral Facts and Problems, 1980 edition; and Mineral Commodity Summaries, annual.

No. 1146. Mineral Production: 1990 to 1995

[Data represent production as measured by mine shipments, mine sales or marketable production]

MINERAL	Unit	1990	1993	1994	1995
FUEL MINERALS					
Coal, total	Mil. sh. tons	1,029.1	945.4	1,033.5	(NA)
Bituminous	Mil. sh. tons	693.2	576.7	640.3	(NA)
Subbituminous	Mil. sh. tons	244.3	274.9	300.5	(NA)
Lignite	Mil. sh. tons	88.1	89.5	88.1	(NA)
Anthracite	Mil. sh. tons	3.5	4.3	4.6	(NA)
Natural gas (marketed production)	Tril. cu. ft.	18.59	18.98	19.64	19.62
Petroleum (crude)	Mil. bbl. [1]	2,686	2,500	2,420	(NA)
Uranium (recoverable content)	Mil. lb.	8.9	3.1	3.4	(NA)
NONFUEL MINERALS					
Abrasive stone [2]	Metric tons	3,709	(Z)	(Z)	(Z)
Asbestos (sales)	1,000 metric tons	(D)	13.0	10.0	10.0
Asphalt and related bitumens (native) [3]	Mil. metric tons	25	27	(3)	(3)
Barite, primary, sold/used by producers	1,000 metric tons	430	315	583	525
Boron minerals, sold or used by producers	1,000 metric tons	1,094	574	550	546
Bromine, sold or used by producers	1,000 metric tons	177	177	(D)	211
Calcium chloride (natural)	1,000 sh. tons	(D)	-	-	-
Carbon dioxide, natural (estimate)	Mil. cu. ft.	-	-	-	-
Cement:					
Portland	Mil. sh. tons	75.6	71.6	74.3	72.1
Masonry	Mil. sh. tons	3.3	3.0	4.0	4.0
Clays	1,000 metric tons	42,904	40,700	42,200	46,600
Diatomite	1,000 metric tons	631	599	613	672
Feldspar [4]	1,000 metric tons	630	770	765	770
Fluorspar, finished shipments	1,000 metric tons	64	60	50	(D)
Garnet (abrasive)	1,000 metric tons	47.0	(D)	51	(D)
Gypsum, crude	Mil. metric tons	16.4	15.8	17.2	17.2
Helium [5]	Mil. cu. meters	87	96	100	102
Lime, sold or used by producers	Mil. sh. tons	17.5	16.8	17.4	18.4
Mica, scrap & flake, sold/used by producers	1,000 metric tons	109	88	110	104
Peat, sales by producers	1,000 sh. tons	795	612	552	577
Perlite, processed, sold or used	1,000 metric tons	576	569	644	719
Phosphate rock (marketable)	Mil. metric tons	46.3	35.0	41.0	46
Potash (K₂O equivalent) sales	1,000 metric tons	1,713	1,470	1,470	1,470
Pumice & pumicite, producer sales	1,000 metric tons	443	469	490	544
Pyrites	1,000 metric tons	(D)	(D)	(D)	(NA)
Salt, common, sold/used by producers	Mil. metric tons	36.9	38.7	39.2	39.2
Sand & gravel, sold/used by producer	Mil. metric tons	852	895	918	907
Construction	Mil. metric tons	829	869	891	879
Industrial	Mil. metric tons	26	26	27	28
Sodium carbonate (natural) (soda ash)	1,000 metric tons	9,156	8,959	9,320	9,800
Sodium sulfate (natural)	1,000 metric tons	349	(D)	298	325
Stone [6]	Mil. metric tons	1,110	1,117	1,230	1,280
Crushed and broken	Mil. metric tons	1,109	1,116	1,230	1,280
Dimension	1,000 metric tons	1,118	1,235	(D)	(D)
Sulfur: Frasch mines (shipments)	1,000 metric tons	3,676	1,904	3,010	(D)
Talc, and pyrophyllite, crude	1,000 metric tons	1,267	(D)	(D)	1,110
Tripoli	1,000 metric tons	94	94	82	(D)
Vermiculite concentrate	1,000 metric tons	209	187	177	170
METALS					
Antimony ore and concentrate	Metric tons	(D)	(D)	(D)	(D)
Bauxite (dried)	1,000 metric tons	(D)	(D)	(D)	(D)
Copper (recoverable content)	1,000 metric tons	1,590	1,800	1,810	1,890
Gold (recoverable content)	Metric tons	294	331	326	320
Iron ore (gross weight) [7]	Mil. metric tons	57.0	56.3	57.6	62
Lead (recoverable content)	1,000 metric tons	497	355	363	374
Magnesium metal	1,000 metric tons	139	132	128	140
Manganiferous ore (gross weight) [8]	1,000 metric ton	(D)	(D)	(D)	(D)
Mercury [9]	Metric tons	562	(D)	(D)	(D)
Molybdenum (concentrate)	1,000 metric tons	62	39	46	(D)
Nickel	1,000 metric tons	0.3	2.5	(NA)	1.7
Palladium metal	Kilograms	5,930	6,500	6,440	6400
Platinum metal	Kilograms	1,810	1,800	1,960	2000
Silver (recoverable content)	Metric tons	2,121	1,645	1,480	1500
Titanium concentrate: Ilmenite (gross weight)	1,000 metric tons	(D)	(D)	(D)	(D)
Tungsten ore and concentrate [10]	Metric tons	(D)	(D)	(D)	(D)
Zinc (recoverable content)	1,000 metric tons	515	488	570	600

- Represents zero.   D Withheld to avoid disclosing individual company data.   NA Not available.   Z Less than half the unit of measure.   [1] 42 gal. bbl.   [2] Includes grindstones, oilstones, whetstones, and deburring media. Excludes grinding pebbles, and tubemill liners.   [3] Contains bituminous limestone and sandstone, and gilsonite. Includes road oil, 1990-93. Discontinued.   [4] Includes aplite, 1992-93.   [5] Refined only.   [6] Excludes abrasive stone, bituminous limestone and sandstone, and ground soapstone, all included elsewhere in table; 1993 excludes dimension stone. Includes calcareous marl and slate.   [7] Represents shipments; includes byproduct ores.   [8] 5 to 35 percent manganiferous ore.   [9] Mercury produced as a byproduct of gold ores only.   [10] Content of ore and concentrate.

Source: U.S. Bureau of Mines, *Minerals Yearbook* thru 1991; thereafter, *Annual Reports and Mineral Commodities Summaries*, annual. U.S. Energy Information Administration, *Annual Energy Review.*

No. 1147. Mineral Production Value: 1990 to 1994

[**In millions of dollars**. See *Historical Statistics, Colonial Times to 1970*, series M 13-37 for selected values]

MINERAL	1990	1992	1993	1994
Mineral production, total	**150,530**	**135,797**	**113,395**	**97,025**
Mineral fuels, total	**117,066**	**103,764**	**101,519**	**97,025**
Coal, total.	31,336	29,287	27,020	28,926
Bituminous [1]	22,266	20,856	18,624	19,953
Anthracite	138	120	142	120
Natural gas.	31,789	32,555	38,834	36,179
Petroleum (crude)	53,801	41,846	35,625	31,920
Uranium u_3o_8	140	76	40	(NA)
Industrial minerals, total	**21,022**	**20,496**	**(NA)**	**(NA)**
Abrasive stone [2]	(Z)	(Z)	(Z)	(NA)
Asbestos (sales)	(⁴)	6	6	5
Asphalt, related bitumens (native) [3]	3,480	2,794	(NA)	(NA)
Barite, primary, sold/used by producers	16	20	19	13
Boron minerals, sold/used by producers.	436	339	373	370
Bromine, sold/used by producers	173	170	123	157
Calcium chloride (natural)	(⁴)	(⁴)	(X)	(X)
Carbon dioxide, natural (estimate).	-	-	(X)	(X)
Cement:				
Portland	3,683	3,500	3,916	4,155
Masonry.	225	195	229	264
Clays.	1,620	1,482	1,488	1,597
Diatomite [5]	138	141	150	162
Feldspar [5]	28	29	31	30
Fluorspar, finished shipments	(⁴)	(⁴)	(⁴)	(⁴)
Garnet (abrasive)	7	5	4	5
Gemstones (estimate).	53	66	58	52
Gypsum, crude	100	101	107	118
Helium [6]	113	187	189	191
Lime, sold/used by producers	902	950	977	996
Mica, scrap and flake, sold/used by producers	6	5	4	5
Peat (sales by producers)	19	17	17	18
Perlite, processed, sold/used by producers	17	16	17	19
Phosphate rock (marketable)	1,075	1,058	759	902
Potash (K_2O equivalent)	303	334	286	274
Pumice and pumicite (sales by producers)	11	15	12	14
Pyrites	(⁴)	(⁴)	(⁴)	(⁴)
Salt (common), sold/used by producers	827	803	894	906
Sand and gravel, sold/used by producers.	3,686	3,766	3,988	4,293
Construction	3,249	3,341	3,534	3,835
Industrial.	436	425	454	458
Sodium carbonate (natural) (soda ash)	836	836	734	650
Sodium sulfate (natural)	34	26	(D)	25
Stone [7]	5,822	5,775	5,987	6,731
Crushed and broken	5,591	5,594	5,770	6,731
Dimension.	231	181	217	(NA)
Sulfur: Frasch mines (shipments)	335	159	101	135
Talc and pyrophyllite, crude [8]	31	31	(D)	32
Tripoli	3	3	4	(NA)
Vermiculite concentrate.	19	15	15	(D)
Industrial minerals, undistributed.	504	478	212	136
Metals, total	**12,442**	**11,537**	**11,876**	**(NA)**
Antimony ore and concentrate [9]	(¹⁰)	(¹⁰)	(¹⁰)	(¹⁰)
Bauxite (dried equivalent)	(¹⁰)	(¹⁰)	(¹⁰)	(¹⁰)
Copper (recoverable content).	4,311	4,179	3,636	4,382
Gold (recoverable content)	3,650	3,662	3,841	3,843
Iron ore (gross weight) [11]	1,741	1,732	1,643	1,700
Lead (recoverable content)	491	308	249	286
Magnesium metal [12]	433	360	377	(D)
Manganiferous ore (gross weight) [13]	(¹⁰)	(¹⁰)	(¹⁰)	(¹⁰)
Mercury [14]	(¹⁰)	0.4	(D)	(D)
Molybdenum (concentrate)	348	209	165	215
Palladium metal.	22	18	25	25
Platinum metal	27	21	21	21
Silver (recoverable content)	329	229	227	192
Titanium concentrate: Ilmenite (gross weight)	(¹⁰)	(¹⁰)	(¹⁰)	(¹⁰)
Tungsten ore and concentrate	(¹⁰)	(¹⁰)	(¹⁰)	(¹⁰)
Vanadium (recoverable content)	(¹⁰)	(¹⁰)	(¹⁰)	(¹⁰)
Zinc mine production (recoverable content).	847	674	497	549
Metals, undistributed	242	156	306	113

- Represents or rounds to zero. D Withheld to avoid disclosing individual company data. NA Not available. X Not applicable. Z Less than $500,000. [1] Includes subbituminous and lignite. [2] Includes grindstones, oilstones, whetstones, and deburring media. [3] 1990-92, excluded from industrial minerals. [4] Included in "Industrial minerals, undistributed." [5] 1992-93, includes aplite. [6] Refined only. [7] Excludes abrasive stone, bituminous limestone and sandstone, and ground soapstone; 1993 excludes dimension stone. State ranks based on publishable data. Includes calcareous marl and slate. [8] 1990-92, talc only. [9] Antimony content. [10] Included with "Metals, undistributed." [11] Represents shipments; includes byproduct ores. [12] Canvass for magnesium chloride for magnesium metal discontinued in 1986. [13] 5 to 35 percent manganiferous ore. [14] Mercury produced as a byproduct of gold ores only.

Source: U.S. Bureau of Mines, Minerals Yearbook thru 1991; Annual Reports and Mineral Commodities Summaries, annual. U.S. Energy Information Administration, Annual Energy Review.

No. 1148. Nonfuel Mineral Commodities—Summary: 1994

[Preliminary estimates. Average price in dollars per metric tons except as noted]

MINERAL	Unit	MINERAL DISPOSITION				Average price per unit (dollars)	Employ-ment (number)
		Production	Exports	Net import reliance[1] (percent)	Consumption, apparent		
Aluminum	1,000 metric tons	4,950	1,700	25	6,500	[2]0.85	21,500
Antimony (contained)	Metric tons	[3]43,000	2,600	60	50,200	[2]2.40	100
Arsenic	Metric tons	-	100	100	24,000	[2]0.72	100
Asbestos	1,000 metric tons	9	13	46	24	[4](D)	30
Barite	1,000 metric tons	600	20	65	1,710	[4]41.00	400
Bauxite and alumina	1,000 metric tons	(D)	130	99	4,000	[4]15-18	20
Beryllium (contained)	Metric tons	225	55	[5]	200	[2][6]275.00	425
Bismuth (contained)	Metric tons	(D)	120	(D)	[1]1,500	[2]3.75	30
Boron (B_2O_3 content)	1,000 metric tons	602	230	[5]	287	[4][8]294.00	900
Bromine (contained)	1,000 metric tons	211	25	[5]	206	[9]88.00	1,700
Cadmium (contained)	Metric tons	[3]1,300	1,050	21	1,600	[2][10]1.84	125
Cement	1,000 metric tons	77,000	600	17	92,000	62.00	18,000
Chromium	1,000 metric tons	[11]117	13	78	537	[4][12]230.00	(NA)
Clays	1,000 metric tons	46,600	4,510	[5]	42,100	(NA)	13,900
Cobalt (contained)	Metric tons	[11]1,500	1,400	82	8,400	[2]28.70	(NA)
Columbium (contained)	Metric tons	-	400	100	3,900	[2][13]2.90	(NA)
Copper (Mine, contained)	1,000 metric tons	1,890	850	6	2,570	[2]137.00	13
Diamond (industrial)	Million carats ...	141.1	120	36	222	[14]0.46	(NA)
Diatomite	1,000 metric tons	670	145	[5]	525	[4]259.00	1,000
Feldspar	1,000 metric tons	770	17	[5]	761	[4]41.56	400
Fluorspar	1,000 metric tons	150	52	92	603	(NA)	180
Gallium (contained)	Kilograms	-	(NA)	(NA)	(NA)	425.00	20
Garnet (industrial)	Metric tons	53,300	7,260	[5]	44,900	85-1500	180
Gemstones	Million dollars ...	99.9	2,510	98	4,110	(NA)	850
Germanium (contained)	Kilograms	[3]10,000	(NA)	(NA)	[1]25,000	[15]1375.00	110
Gold (contained)	Metric tons	320	365	[5]	(NA)	[16]385.00	13,900
Graphite (crude)	1,000 metric tons	-	30	100	30	[4][17]635.00	-
Gypsum (crude)	1,000 metric tons	17,300	110	30	25,900	[4]6.80	[18]6,700
Indium	Metric tons	-	(NA)	(NA)	[1]43	[19]375.00	(NA)
Iodine	Metric tons	1,800	1,300	62	4,800	[20]9.32	35
Iron ore (usable)	Million metric tons	62	5	18	75.3	[21]72.5-74.0	7,000
Iron and steel scrap (metal)	Million metric tons	83	10.4	[5]	74	[4][22]130.00	37,000
Iron and steel slag (metal)	1,000 metric tons	21,000	4	1	[1]21,000	[4]7.33	2,500
Lead (contained)	1,000 metric tons	390	10	15	1,450	[23]42.00	1,900
Lime	1,000 metric tons	18,500	75	1	18,700	[4]62.70	5,500
Magnesium compounds	1,000 metric tons	300	50	50	600	(NA)	600
Magnesium metal	1,000 metric tons	200	37	[5]	167	[24]2.10	1,400
Manganese (gross weight)	1,000 metric tons		22	100	[25]710	[26]2.40	(NA)
Mercury	Metric tons	[27]450	220	(D)	[1]480	[28]250.00	-
Mica, scrap and flake	1,000 metric tons	104	7	10	100	[4]65.00	360
Molybdenum (contained)	Metric tons	59,000	40,000	[5]	29,000	[29]5.00	700
Nickel (contained)	Metric tons	9,850	9,900	61	159,000	[30]8,245	15
Nitrogen (fixed)-ammonia	1,000 metric tons	13,200	200	20	16,600	[4][31]230.00	2,500
Nonrenewable organics	Million metric tons	(NA)	(NA)	(NA)	(NA)	(NA)	(NA)
Peat	1,000 metric tons	580	20	55	1,290	[4]27.00	650
Perlite	1,000 metric tons	719	25	8	779	[4]29.40	125
Phosphate rock	1,000 metric tons	45,500	3,000	[5]	43,600	[4]20.50	5,000
Platinum-group metals	Kilograms	8,000	47,000	(NA)	(NA)	[32]430.00	400
Potash (K_2O equivalent)	1,000 metric tons	1,460	450	74	5,670	[4][33]135.00	1,740
Pumice and pumicite	1,000 metric tons	544	18	29	763	[4]23.15	55
Salt	1,000 metric tons	43,300	825	15	49,500	[4][34]115.00	4,150
Silicon (contained)	1,000 metric tons	390	60	33	580	[35]54.50	(NA)
Silver (contained)	Metric tons	1,500	1,500	(NA)	(NA)	[16]5.30	1,000
Sodium carbonate (soda ash)	1,000 metric tons	9,800	3,600	[5]	6,280	[4][36]105.00	2,800
Sodium sulfate	1,000 metric tons	325	70	15	675	[37]114.00	240
Stone (crushed)	Million metric tons	1,280	6	-	1,280	[4]5.48	77,500
Sulfur (all forms)	1,000 metric tons	11,800	1,000	18	13,900	[4][38]35.00	3,100
Talc	1,000 metric tons	1,050	190	[5]	970	[4]7-560	750
Thallium (contained)	Kilograms	-	(NA)	100	[1]700	300.00	-
Tin (contained)	Metric tons	[11]11,900	2,000	84	47,000	[2]290.00	-
Titanium dioxide	1,000 metric tons	1,280	381	[5]	1,090	[2][39].96	4,600
Tungsten (contained)	Metric tons	(D)	-	87	[7]15,900	[40]60.00	20
Vermiculite	1,000 metric tons	170	5	15	130	(D)	230
Zinc (contained)	1,000 metric tons	600	400	41	[41]1,210	[23]53.00	2,700
Zirconium (Z,02) content	Metric tons	(D)	23,600	(D)	(D)	[42](NA)	(NA)

- Represents zero or rounds to zero. D Withheld to avoid disclosure. NA Not available. [1] Calculated as a percent of apparent consumption. [2] Price per pound. [3] Refinery production. [4] Price per metric ton. [5] Net exporter. [6] Metal, vacuum-cast ingot. [7] Estimated consumption. [8] Granulated pentahydrate borax in bulk, f.o.b mine. [9] Cents per kilogram, bulk, purified bromine. [10] 1- to 5-short ton lots. [11] Secondary production. [12] Turkish, chromite price. [13] Columbite price. [14] Value of imports per carat. [15] Zone refined, first reduction quality. [16] Price per troy ounce. [17] Price of flake imports. [18] Includes employment at calcining plants. [19] 99.97% indium, per kilogram. [20] O.i.f. value, crude, per kilogram. [21] Lake Superior pellets. Cents per long ton unit of iron. [22] Delivered, No. 1 Heavy Melting composite price. [23] Cents per pound. [24] Year-end price, per pound. [25] Estimated manganese content. [26] 46%-48% Mn metallurgical ore, per unit contained Mn, c.i.f. U.S. ports. [27] Secondary industrial production. [28] Price per 76-pound flask. [29] Price per kilogram. [30] London Metal Exchange cash price. [31] F.o.b. gulf coast. [32] Dealer price of platinum. Per troy ounce. [33] Price of K20, muriate. [34] Vacuum and open pan, bulk, pellets and packaged, f.o.b. mine and plant. [35] Ferrosilicon, 50% Si. [36] Quoted year-end price, dense, bulk, f.o.b. Green River, WY. [37] Quoted price, bulk, f.o.b. works, East, per short ton. [38] Elemental sulfur, f.o.b. mine and/or plant. [39] Rutile, list, year-end. [40] Price per unit W03 (7.93 kilograms of contained tungsten per unit). [41] All forms. [42] Price for imported zircon, f.o.b. U.S. east coast.

Source: U.S. Bureau of Mines, *Mineral Commodity Summaries*, annual.

No. 1149. Value of Domestic Nonfuel Mineral Production: 1980 to 1995

[In millions of dollars]

AREA	1980	1985	1989	1990	1991	1992	1993	1994	1995
U.S. [1]	25,140	23,303	32,220	33,452	30,579	32,012	31,912	35,000	37,600
Northeast.....	1,581	1,964	2,450	2,479	2,095	2,308	2,451	2,620	2,670
N.E	268	325	455	446	347	423	424	444	467
ME	37	41	65	55	41	56	60	61	59
NH	25	33	33	36	30	42	37	44	39
VT	43	50	89	87	60	60	53	53	53
MA	91	117	144	128	112	147	160	178	206
RI	6	12	11	18	13	21	23	26	30
CT	66	72	113	122	91	98	91	82	81
M.A	1,313	1,639	1,995	2,033	1,748	1,885	2,027	2,180	2,210
NY	496	657	745	773	699	766	852	893	863
NJ	149	178	249	229	205	240	262	289	289
PA	668	804	1,001	1,031	844	881	913	997	1,050
Midwest......	6,610	6,034	6,980	7,163	6,755	7,261	7,357	7,880	8,080
E.N.C......	2,930	2,869	3,551	3,483	3,479	3,762	3,875	4,000	4,030
OH	562	594	699	733	684	742	851	880	871
IN	288	303	434	428	403	477	472	555	581
IL	443	460	633	667	673	734	734	823	820
MI	1,485	1,387	1,599	1,440	1,503	1,587	1,510	1,460	1,460
WI	152	125	185	215	216	244	256	284	295
W.N.C......	3,680	3,165	3,429	3,680	3,276	3,499	3,482	3,870	4,050
MN	1,782	1,548	1,376	1,482	1,289	1,364	1,300	1,340	1,490
IA	252	228	283	310	344	391	398	451	484
MO	1,054	735	1,050	1,105	880	897	855	1,090	1,110
ND	22	24	14	25 [2]	17	26	25	25	25
SD	228	208	284	319	290	301	337	323	315
NE	80	100	104	90	89	115	126	146	142
KS	262	322	318	349	367	405	442	497	492
South	7,320	8,029	8,966	9,291	8,285	8,560	8,578	9,520	10,000
S.A	3,454	3,998	4,985	5,132	4,497	4,651	4,689	5,090	5,290
DE [2]	2	4	6	10	5	9	10	9	9
MD	186	258	342	368	348	339	314	340	341
VA	305	381	509	507	428	462	465	502	517
WV	106	105	125	133	117	112	149	181	193
NC	380	466	582	586	557	596	617	710	743
SC	195	276	425	450	340	347	391	433	426
GA	771	946	1,387	1,504	1,306	1,346	1,432	1,550	1,670
FL	1,509	1,562	1,608	1,574	1,396	1,440	1,311	1,370	1,390
E.S.C......	1,030	1,251	1,537	1,692	1,533	1,640	1,564	1,790	1,860
KY	204	268	331	359	343	401	388	428	401
TN	394	473	638	663	548	576	510	602	660
AL	328	407	461	559	540	543	562	626	678
MS	104	103	108	111	102	121	100	135	125
W.S.C......	2,836	2,780	2,443	2,467	2,255	2,269	2,325	2,630	2,850
AR	293	270	382	381	361	404	347	405	479
LA	584	521	380	368	352	309	232	350	362
OK	224	252	219	259	276	253	298	356	388
TX	1,735	1,737	1,462	1,459	1,266	1,303	1,430	1,520	1,620
West........	9,629	7,276	13,809	14,512	13,435	13,858	13,424	15,000	16,600
Mountain....	7,223	4,669	9,985	10,380	9,581	10,154	9,736	11,000	12,400
MT	280	200	566	573	534	539	484	543	581
ID	522	359	365	375	298	306	274	346	399
WY	761	551	827	911	929	949	844	880	976
CO	1,265	408	458	377	338	385	399	410	448
NM	766	657	1,122	1,103	986	871	804	930	1,080
AZ	2,471	1,550	3,046	3,085	2,877	3,160	2,780	3,280	4,150
UT	764	313	1,290	1,335	1,190	1,348	1,314	1,520	1,810
NV	394	631	2,310	2,621	2,429	2,588	2,820	3,070	2,920
Pacific	2,406	2,607	3,824	4,132	3,854	3,704	3,688	4,030	4,250
WA	207	222	481	483	483	469	505	570	613
OR	152	130	183	205	198	214	226	243	261
CA	1,872	2,112	2,854	2,771	2,538	2,370	2,440	2,580	2,680
AK	115	90	213	577	494	526	378	519	594
HI	60	53	92	106	141	149	139	[2]116	[2]106

[1] Includes undistributed not shown separately. [2] Partial data only.

Source: U.S. Bureau of Mines, *Annual Reports, and Mineral Commodities Summary,* annual.

No. 1150. Principal Fuels, Nonmetals, and Metals—U.S. Production, as Percent of World Production: 1980 to 1994

MINERAL	Unit	WORLD PRODUCTION				PERCENT U.S. OF WORLD			
		1980	1985	1990	1994	1980	1985	1990	1994
Fuels: [1]									
Coal	Bil. sh. ton	4.2	4.8	5.2	(NA)	20	18	20	(NA)
Petroleum (crude)	Bil. bbl	21.7	19.6	22	(NA)	14	17	12	(NA)
Natural gas (dry, marketable).	Tril. cu. ft	53.1	62	74.3	(NA)	37	26	24	(NA)
Natural gas plant liquids	Bil. bbl	1.4	1.5	1.8	(NA)	43	38	32	(NA)
Nonmetals:									
Asbestos	1,000 metric tons	4,699	4,249	4,003	2,410	2	1	(D)	(Z)
Barite	1,000 metric tons	7,495	6,067	5,633	4,470	27	11	8	17
Feldspar	1,000 metric tons	3,202	4,039	5,456	6,250	20	16	12	12
Fluorspar	1,000 metric tons	5,006	4,979	5,131	3,850	2	1	1	1
Gypsum.	Mil. metric tons .	78	87	100	101	14	15	15	17
Mica (incl. scrap).	1,000 metric tons	228	255	215	214	46	49	51	51
Nitrogen, (fixed) - ammonia . .	Mil. metric tons .	74	91	97	92	20	14	13	15
Phosphate rock, gross wt. . . .	Mil. metric tons .	144	149	162	124	38	34	29	33
Potash (k₂O equivalent)	Mil. metric tons .	28	29	28	23	8	4	6	6
Sulfur, elemental	Mil. metric tons .	55	54	58	51	22	22	20	23
Metals, mine basis:									
Bauxite	Mil. metric tons .	89	84	109	107	2	1	(D)	(NA)
Columbian concentrates									
(Nb content)	1,000 metric tons	15	15	15	37	(NA)	-	(NA)	-
Copper	1,000 metric tons	7,405	7,988	9,017	9,260	16	14	18	20
Gold	Metric tons	1,219	1,532	2,133	2,290	2	5	14	14
Iron ore	Mil. metric tons .	891	861	982	995	8	6	6	6
Lead [2]	1,000 metric tons	3,470	3,431	3,353	2,800	17	12	15	13
Mercury.	Metric tons	6,806	6,136	4,523	1,760	16	9	12	(NA)
Molybdenum.	1,000 metric tons	111	98	128	104	62	50	48	45
Nickel [2]	1,000 metric tons	779	813	965	(NA)	2	1	(Z)	(NA)
Silver	1,000 metric tons	11	13	16	14	9	9	13	11
Tantalum concentrates									
(ta content)	Metric tons	544	315	400	(NA)	(NA)	(NA)	(NA)	(NA)
Titanium concentrates:									
Ilmenite	1,000 metric tons	3,726	3,457	4,072	(NA)	14	(D)	[1] (D)	(NA)
Rutile	1,000 metric tons	436	373	481	(NA)	(D)	(D)	(D)	(NA)
Tungsten [2]	1,000 metric tons	52	47	43	26	5	2	14	(NA)
Vanadium [2]	1,000 metric tons	37	30	31	34	12	(D)	(D)	8
Zinc [2]	1,000 metric tons	5,954	6,758	7,184	6,810	6	4	8	9
Metals, smelter basis:									
Aluminum.	1,000 metric tons	15,383	15,398	19,292	19,100	30	23	21	17
Cadmium.	1,000 metric tons	18	19	20	18	9	8	8	6
Copper	1,000 metric tons	7,649	8,630	9,472	11,200	14	14	15	20
Iron, pig.	Mil. metric tons .	514	499	532	512	12	9	9	10
Lead [3]	1,000 metric tons	5,430	5,641	5,763	5,380	23	20	23	24
Magnesium [4]	1,000 metric tons	316	325	354	267	49	42	39	48
Raw Steel	Mil. metric tons .	717	718	771	726	14	11	12	13
Tin [5]	1,000 metric tons	251	193	223	199	1	2	-	(NA)
Zinc	1,000 metric tons	6,049	6,786	7,060	7,360	6	5	5	5

- Represents or rounds to zero.   D Withheld to avoid disclosing company data.   NA Not available.   Z Less than half the unit of measure.   [1] Source: Energy Information Administration, *International Energy Annual.*   [2] Content of ore and concentrate.   [3] Refinery production.   [4] Primary production; no smelter processing necessary.   [5] Production from primary sources only.

Source: Except as noted, U.S. Bureau of Mines, *Annual Reports,* and *Mineral Commodity Summaries,* annual.

No. 1151. Federal Strategic and Critical Materials Inventory: 1980 to 1994

[As of **Dec. 31.** Covers strategic and critical materials essential to military and industrial requirements in time of national emergency]

MINERAL	Unit	QUANTITY [1]				VALUE (mil. dol.) [2]			
		1980	1985	1990	1994	1980	1985	1990	1994
Tin.	1,000 metric ton.	200	185	169	145	3,158	2,324	962	684
Silver	1,000 troy oz. . .	139,500	136,006	92,151	59,507	2,288	801	374	158
Cobalt	Mil. lb.	41	53	53	52	1,020	590	443	561
Bauxite [3]	1,000 lg. ton . . .	14,333	17,957	18,033	16,549	583	871	888	191
Manganese [4]	1,000 sh. ton . .	5,130	4,470	4,017	2,792	599	520	962	468
Tungsten [5]	Mil. lb.	97	87	82	82	817	369	253	178
Zinc	1,000 sh. ton . .	380	378	379	360	317	268	483	307
Titanium	1,000 sh. ton . .	43	48	37	37	432	405	402	221
Platinum	1,000 troy oz. . .	466	466	453	453	215	154	186	131
Chromium [6]	1,000 sh. ton . .	804	854	1,074	1,149	773	836	917	837
Diamonds: Stones . .	Carat 1,000. . . .	19,224	12,549	7,777	6,457	349	336	267	533
Industrial, bort . . .	Carat 1,000. . . .	23,693	22,001	17,353	4,012	73	39	16	3

[1] Consists of stockpile and nonstockpile grades and reflects uncommitted balances.   [2] Market values are estimated trade values of similar materials and not necessarily amounts that would be realized at time of sale.   [3] Consists of abrasive grade, metallic grade Jamaica, metallic grade Suriname, and refractory.   [4] Consists of chemical grade, dioxide battery natural, dioxide battery synthetic, electrolytic, ferro-high carbon, ferro-med. carbon, ferro-silicon, and metal.   [5] Consists of carbide powder, ferro, metal powder, and ores and concentrates.   [6] Consists of ferro-high carbon, ferro-low carbon, ferro-silicon, and metal.

Source: U.S. Defense Logistics Agency, *Statistical Supplement, Stockpile Report to the Congress* (AP-3).

No. 1152. Selected Mineral and Metal Products—Quantity and Value of Imports and Exports: 1990 to 1993

[Imports represent imports for consumption. Exports include shipments under foreign aid programs. Import and export data are not necessarily comparable to prior data due to change in tariff schedule to Harmonized System]

PRODUCT	Unit	QUANTITY				VALUE (mil. dol.)			
		1990	1991	1992	1993	1990	1991	1992	1993
IMPORTS									
Petroleum (crude) [1]	Mil. bbls.	2,222	2,124	2,295	2,543	43,833	37,123	38,553	38,469
Gem stones: Diamonds	Mil. carats	7.5	8.5	9.4	11.5	3,955	3,992	4,144	5,096
Ores and concentrates:									
Chromium (Cr_2O_3 content) .	1,000 metric tons	134	94	99	123	22	15	15	17
Copper	1,000 metric tons	91.5	60.8	102.1	37	131	69	125	46
Iron	Mil. metric tons .	18.1	13.3	12.5	14	560	437	396	421
Tungsten	1,000 metric tons	6.4	7.8	2.5	1.7	31	43	16	8
Metals:									
Aluminum	1,000 metric tons	960	1,025	1,156	1,836	1,597	1,428	1,501	2,147
Cobalt [2]	1,000 metric tons	6.0	6.4	5.3	5.4	107	158	246	166
Copper refined ingots, etc .	1,000 metric tons	262	289	289	343	675	685	660	669
Gold (refined bullion)	Metric tons	65	147	141	130	795	1,722	1,568	1,495
Iron and steel products									
(major)	Mil. metric tons .	17.8	16.2	17.4	20.0	11,612	11,962	10,977	(NA)
Platinum group [3]	Metric tons	125	126	132	153	1,906	1,743	1,484	1,311
Silver (refined bullion)	Metric tons	2,698	2,525	2,662	2,183	437	339	341	297
Zinc: Blocks, pigs, slabs. . .	1,000 metric tons	632	549	644	724	992	620	784	699
EXPORTS									
Fuels: [1]									
Bituminous coal	Mil. sh. tons . . .	95.3	98.4	(NA)	(NA)	4,464	4,588	4,427	3,197
Petroleum (crude)	Mil. bbls.	8.0	2.7	(NA)	(NA)	198.6	54.1	32.4	20.0
Nonmetallic minerals:									
Gem stones: Diamonds . . .	Mil. carats	1.2	1.8	1.9	1.6	1,433	1,383	1,362	1,499
Nitrogen compounds (maj.).	Mil. metric tons .	11.9	13.9	12.8	11.5	(NA)	(NA)	(NA)	(NA)
Phosphatic fertilizers [4]	Mil. metric tons .	9.2	11.5	10.3	9.2	1,515	1,974	(NA)	(NA)
Metals:									
Aluminum: Ingots, slabs,									
crude	1,000 metric tons	684	793	604	400	1,169	1,274	843	541
Plates, sheets, bars, etc .	1,000 metric tons	419	489	534	571	1,278	1,384	1,416	1,346
Gold (refined bullion)	Metric tons	141	174	257	658	1,719	2,039	2,877	7,611
Iron and steel products									
(major)	Mil. metric tons .	4.7	6.6	4.7	4.5	4,665	5,753	5,374	4,848
Magnesium [5]	1,000 metric tons	51.8	55.2	52	39	164	150	132	103
Molybdenum [6]	Metric tons	180	88	74	52	2	1	1	1
Silver (refined bullion)	Metric tons	736	787	911	705	120	115	126	100
Scrap exports:									
Aluminum	1,000 metric tons	537	461	295	212	719	542	300	211
Iron and steel.	Mil. metric tons .	11.7	9.5	9.4	10	1,653	1,253	1,113	1,341

NA Not available. [1] Source: U.S. Bureau of the Census, *U.S. Imports for Consumption* and *General Imports, TSUSA Commodity and Country*, FT 246, annual; and *U.S. Exports, Schedule B Commodity and Country*, FT 446, annual; 1989 and 1990, *U.S. Exports of Merchandise* and *U.S. Imports of Merchandise* compact discs, December issues. [2] Includes unwrought metal, waste and scrap. [3] Unwrought and semimanufactured. [4] Superphosphates and ammonium phosphates. [5] Metal and alloys, scrap, semimanufactured forms. [6] Metals and alloys, crude and scrap.

Source: Except as noted, U.S. Bureau of Mines, *Minerals Yearbook*, and *Annual Reports*.

No. 1153. Mineral Industries—Lost Workday Injuries and Fatalities: 1994

[Excludes office workers. Lost workday injuries are nonfatal occurrences that result in days away from work, days of restricted work activity or a permanent disability. Data for all years includes injuries to independent contractors at mine sites. Rates for the noncoal industries are based only on employment and hours worked by mine employees. See also *Historical Statistics, Colonial Times to 1970*, series M 271-286]

ITEM	Coal mining	Quarrying; related indus- tries [1]	Metal/ nonmetal mining [3]	Sand and gravel mining
Injuries, total [1]	11,353	5,369	4,498	1,863
Fatal	44	22	13	5
Rate per million work-hours: [2]				
Fatal.	0.04	0.03	0.02	0.02
Nonfatal	7.24	4.70	3.35	4.05
Fatalities per 1,000 employed.	0.33	0.26	0.18	0.15

[1] Includes contractor data. [2] Average number of persons at work each day mines were active.

Source: U.S. Mine Safety and Health Administration, Denver, CO, unpublished data.

No. 1154. Net U.S. Imports of Selected Minerals and Metals as Percent of Apparent Consumption, 1980 to 1994

[**Percent,** based on net imports which equal the difference between imports and exports plus or minus Government stockpile and industry stock changes]

MINERAL	1980	1985	1988	1989	1990	1991	1992	1993	1994
Columbium	100	100	100	100	100	100	100	100	100
Manganese. . . .	98	100	100	100	100	100	100	100	100
Mica (sheet) . . .	100	100	100	100	100	100	100	100	100
Strontium	100	100	100	100	100	100	100	100	100
Bauxite [1]	94	96	97	96	98	100	100	100	99
Asbestos	78	65	75	90	90	95	95	95	95
Platinum group .	87	92	91	90	88	90	87	89	91
Tantalum	90	89	86	86	86	86	85	85	86
Cobalt	93	94	87	83	84	80	75	79	79
Chromium.	91	75	78	78	71	72	76	74	75
Tungsten	53	68	86	84	81	91	86	82	84
Nickel.	76	71	74	71	64	61	59	63	66
Tin.	79	72	78	77	71	74	80	84	84
Barite.	44	74	76	77	71	66	52	70	82
Potash	65	76	71	65	68	69	68	72	74
Antimony	47	63	65	56	51	53	60	62	62
Cadmium	55	57	64	48	46	50	52	61	50
Selenium	59	(D)	52	55	46	50	48	39	39
Zinc[2]	60	70	69	61	41	24	30	45	41
Gypsum	35	38	36	35	36	31	31	31	30
Iron ore	25	21	18	22	21	11	12	14	18
Iron and steel . .	13	22	19	13	13	12	13	15	21
Sulfur.	14	3	16	1	15	19	20	12	16
Copper.	16	28	13	7	3	(NA)	2	7	14
Aluminum	(3)	16	7	(NA)	(3)	(NA)	1	19	31
Silver.	7	(NA)	(NA)	(NA)	(NA)	(NA)	(NA)	(NA)	(NA)
Mercury	27	(NA)	(NA)	(NA)	(D)	(3)	(D)	(NA)	(D)
Titanium	32	(D)	(D)	(D)	(D)	(D)	(D)	(D)	(3)
Vanadium	35	(D)	(D)	(D)	(D)	(D)	(D)	(D)	(D)

D Withheld to avoid disclosure. NA Not available. [1] Includes alumina. [2] Beginning 1990, effect of sharp rise in exports of concentrates. If calculated on a refined zinc-only basis, reliance would be about the same as pre-1990 level. [3] Net exports.

Source: U.S. Bureau of Mines, *Mineral Commodity Summaries;* import and export data from U.S. Bureau of the Census.

No. 1155. Federal Offshore Leasing, Exploration, Production, and Revenue: 1980 to 1994

[See source for explanation of terms and for reliability statement]

ITEM	Unit	1980	1985	1988	1989	1990	1991	1992	1993	1994
Tracts offered	Number. .	483	15,754	28,382	11,013	10,459	16,600	9,618	10,164	10,861
Tracts leased.	Number. .	218	681	1,621	1,049	825	676	204	336	560
Acres offered	1,000 . .	2,563	87,029	158,016	60,098	56,789	90,288	52,380	55,070	58,895
Acres leased	1,000 . . .	1,134	3,574	8,839	5,581	4,263	3,414	1,021	1,714	2,775
Bonus paid for leased tracts	Bil. dol. . .	4.2	1.6	1.3	0.6	0.6	0.3	0.1	0.1	0.3
New wells being drilled:										
Active	Number. .	191	195	116	123	120	64	104	129	120
Suspended	Number. .	739	348	289	361	266	249	180	193	222
Wells completed.	Number. .	9,638	12,285	12,827	12,938	13,167	13,184	13,209	13,181	13,342
Wells plugged and abandoned.	Number. .	8,057	10,487	13,164	13,846	14,677	15,430	16,348	16,709	17,427
Revenue, total [1]	Bil. dol. . .	6.4	5.3	3.4	2.9	3.4	2.8	2.6	2.9	2.6
Bonuses	Bil. dol. . .	4.2	1.6	1.3	0.6	0.6	0.3	0.1	0.1	0.3
Oil and gas royalties [1]	Bil. dol. . .	2.1	3.6	2.1	2.1	2.6	2.3	2.3	2.5	2.3
Rentals	Bil. dol. . .	(Z)	0.1	0.1	0.1	0.1	0.1	0.1	(Z)	(Z)
Sales value [2]	Bil. dol. . .	13.1	22.2	12.9	13.4	17.0	14.9	15.1	16.4	15.0
Crude oil	Bil. dol. . .	4.8	9.6	4.2	4.4	5.9	5.2	5.3	4.9	4.4
Condensate	Bil. dol. . .	0.4	1.0	0.7	0.8	1.1	1.1	1.0	0.9	0.7
Natural gas	Bil. dol. . .	7.9	11.4	7.9	7.8	9.5	7.9	8.2	9.9	9.8
Sales volume:										
Crude oil	Mil. bbls. .	259	351	279	260	274	263	302	307	319
Condensate	Mil. bbls. .	19	38	41	45	51	52	52	55	51
Natural gas	Bil. cu. ft .	4,641	4,001	4,310	4,200	5,093	4,516	4,686	4,533	4,700

Z Less than $50 million. [1] Includes condensate royalties. [2] Production value is value at time of production, not current value.

Source: U.S. Dept. of the Interior, Minerals Management Service, *Federal Offshore Statistics,* annual.

No. 1156. Petroleum Industry—Summary: 1980 to 1994

[Includes all costs incurred for drilling and equipping wells to point of completion as productive wells or abandonment after drilling becomes unproductive. Based on sample of operators of different size drilling establishments]

ITEM	Unit	1980	1985	1988	1989	1990	1991	1992	1993	1994
Crude oil producing wells (Dec. 31).	1,000...	548	647	612	603	602	614	594	584	582
Daily output per well.........	Bbl.....	15.9	13.9	13.5	12.6	12.2	12.1	12.1	11.7	11.4
Completed wells drilled, total.....	1,000...	56.93	57.88	25.58	22.82	26.22	24.75	19.78	20.32	16.01
Crude oil..............	1,000...	30.50	33.14	12.53	9.76	11.53	11.36	8.26	7.65	5.69
Gas................	1,000...	15.13	12.97	7.58	8.57	9.85	8.77	7.59	8.36	7.22
Dry................	1,000...	11.30	11.76	5.48	4.49	4.83	4.61	3.94	4.32	3.10
Average depth per well [1]........	Feet...	4,188	4,225	4,570	4,558	4,662	4,805	5,194	5,422	5,644
Average cost per well [1].........	$1,000..	368	349	355	362	384	422	383	427	(NA)
Offshore..............	$1,000..	3,024	4,073	3,112	3,197	3,112	3,550	3,223	3,250	(NA)
Average cost per foot [1]........	Dollars..	77.02	75.35	70.23	73.55	76.07	82.64	70.27	75.30	(NA)
Crude oil production, total.......	Mil. bbl..	3,138	3,274	2,971	2,779	2,685	2,707	2,617	2,499	2,419
Value at wells...........	Bil. dol..	67.9	78.9	37.5	44.1	54.8	44.7	42.0	35.6	(NA)
Average price per barrel......	Dollars..	21.59	24.09	12.58	15.86	20.03	16.54	15.99	14.24	(NA)
Refinery input of crude oil.......	Mil. bbl..	4,934	4,381	4,848	4,891	4,895	4,855	4,909	4,969	(NA)
Imports: Crude oil...........	Mil. bbl..	1,926	1,168	1,869	2,133	2,151	2,111	2,223	2,472	(NA)
Refined petroleum products....	Mil. bbl..	603	681	840	809	775	500	471	(NA)	(NA)
Import value...............	Bil. dol..	78.7	53.5	42.6	51.9	63.8	53.5	54.8	55.0	55.0
Export value..............	Bil. dol..	7.9	9.9	7.1	7.5	9.2	9.7	9.1	7.7	6.6
Operable refineries...........	Number.	319	223	213	204	205	202	199	187	179
Capacity (Jan. 1)..........	Mil. bbl..	6,566	5,716	5,811	5,712	5,683	5,723	5,731	5,519	5,486
Output...............	Mil. bbl..	5,352	5,019	5,498	5,539	5,570	5,933	6,050	(NA)	(NA)
Utilization rate............	Percent.	75.4	77.6	84.7	86.6	87.1	86.0	87.9	91.5	92.6
Proved reserves............	Bil. bbl..	29.8	28.4	26.8	26.5	26.3	24.7	23.7	23.0	22.5

NA Not available.   [1] Source: American Petroleum Institute, *Joint Association Survey on Drilling Costs,* annual.

Source: Except as noted, U.S. Energy Information Administration, *Annual Energy Review, Petroleum Supply Annual; U.S. Crude Oil, Natural Gas,* and *Natural Gas Liquids Reserves.*

No. 1157. Natural Gas—Financial Performance Measure: 1985 to 1994

[LT = Long term. S&P = Standard & Poor's]

ITEM	1985	1987	1988	1989	1990	1991	1992	1993	1994
Producer segment, majors:									
Average adjusted stock price........	28.24	37.01	41.64	51.79	49.20	50.01	48.50	57.50	(NA)
S&P bond rating.................	AA-	A	AA-	AA	AA	AA	AA	BBB-	BB+
LT debt as a percent of invested capital.	32.06	28.33	30.54	30.35	27.76	29.19	30.10	42.15	40.40
Times interest earned ratio........	5.09	3.76	4.42	4.32	5.07	4.04	3.93	2.25	2.55
Rate of return on common equity (%)...	14.30	10.64	17.67	18.56	17.78	12.54	9.05	7.30	6.72
Price/earnings ratio..............	7.35	11.69	9.11	10.65	9.98	15.15	15.14	23.53	33.63
Market/book value ratio............	1.18	1.69	1.65	1.99	1.92	2.01	2.07	2.61	2.51
Producer segment, independents:									
Average adjusted stock price........	14.66	12.33	12.84	17.34	15.14	12.01	11.93	14.53	(NA)
S&P bond rating.................	A-	BBB	BBB-	BBB-	BBB-	BBB-	BB+	BB+	BB+
LT debt as a percent of invested capital.	47.39	61.13	73.47	68.00	63.00	55.87	53.93	45.01	45.64
Times interest earned ratio.........	0.36	0.52	0.91	1.46	1.46	1.21	1.46	1.83	1.04
Rate of return on common equity (%)...	-10.39	-7.85	-1.69	6.51	1.93	-1.17	1.99	5.14	0.61
Price/earnings ratio..............	6.78	15.70	17.96	16.45	23.75	31.28	21.50	26.46	35.71
Market/book value ratio............	1.23	1.96	1.84	2.32	2.63	2.05	1.85	2.30	2.35
Pipeline segment, w/Columbia:									
Average adjusted stock price........	19.68	17.96	20.52	27.84	23.76	20.10	23.49	26.26	(NA)
S&P bond rating.................	BBB-	BBB-	BBB	BBB	BBB	BBB-	BB+	BBB-	BBB
LT debt as a percent of invested capital.	53.35	52.92	52.29	52.99	53.24	55.91	54.61	50.24	47.30
Times interest earned ratio.........	1.89	1.75	1.44	1.79	1.65	1.00	1.74	2.33	2.72
Rate of return on common equity (%)...	6.32	7.97	6.18	8.63	7.47	1.01	6.23	10.88	12.25
Price/earnings ratio..............	10.94	12.04	13.42	14.66	16.00	17.36	13.18	16.68	14.42
Market/book value ratio............	1.11	1.31	1.28	1.51	1.55	1.52	1.53	1.86	1.77
Average adjusted stock price..........	17.69	18.84	18.66	23.29	21.21	20.53	22.78	26.06	(NA)
S&P bond rating.................	BBB+	A	A	A	A	A	A	A	A
LT debt as a percent of invested capital...	44.21	44.27	47.30	46.31	47.28	48.62	48.83	46.62	47.93
Times interest earned ratio...........	2.81	3.01	2.51	2.49	2.04	1.95	2.42	2.88	2.92
Rate of return on common equity (%).....	8.55	12.19	10.35	12.35	9.17	7.17	4.09	10.95	11.45
Price/earnings ratio...............	8.42	11.96	10.16	12.01	12.69	15.15	14.38	14.83	13.02
Market/book value ratio..............	1.29	1.48	1.36	1.49	1.51	1.47	1.56	1.77	1.56

NA Not available.

Source: U.S. Energy Information Administration, *Natural Gas 1995: Issues and Trends.*

No. 1158. World Crude Oil Production: 1980 to 1995

[In thousands of barrels]

COUNTRY	1980	1985	1990	1991	1992	1993	1994	1995
Total [1]	59,599	53,981	60,566	60,210	60,213	60,640	60,916	62,227
Algeria	1,106	1,037	1,175	1,230	1,214	1,190	1,170	1,197
Kuwait	1,656	1,023	1,175	190	1,058	1,872	2,034	2,061
Libya	1,787	1,059	1,375	1,483	1,433	1,377	1,378	1,390
Saudi Arabia	9,900	3,388	6,410	8,115	8,332	8,198	8,147	8,231
United Arab Emirates	1,709	1,193	2,117	2,386	2,266	2,191	2,263	2,277
Indonesia	1,577	1,325	1,462	1,592	1,504	1,528	1,514	1,523
Iran	1,662	2,250	3,088	3,312	3,429	3,650	3,635	3,643
Nigeria	2,055	1,495	1,810	1,892	1,943	2,050	2,037	2,026
Venezuela	2,168	1,677	2,137	2,375	2,371	2,450	2,514	2,750
Canada	1,435	1,471	1,553	1,548	1,598	1,680	1,743	1,814
Mexico	1,936	2,745	2,553	2,680	2,668	2,671	2,689	2,618
United Kingdom	1,622	2,530	1,820	1,797	1,825	1,915	2,375	2,489
United States	8,597	8,971	7,355	7,417	7,171	6,847	6,662	6,530
China	2,114	2,505	2,774	2,835	2,838	2,911	2,939	3,015
U.S.S.R (former)	11,706	11,585	10,975	9,992	8,931	7,717	6,611	6,550

[1] Includes countries not shown separately.

Source: U. S. Energy Information Administration, *Monthly Energy Review.*

No. 1159. World Natural Gas Production: 1985 to 1993

[In quadrillion Btu's]

REGION AND COUNTRY	1985	1986	1987	1988	1989	1990	1991	1992 [1]	1993 [1]
World total	61.42	62.24	65.46	68.62	71.59	72.48	73.99	73.84	75.15
North America	20.98	20.33	21.11	22.12	22.59	23.23	23.31	23.86	24.66
Canada	3.08	2.90	3.15	3.63	3.85	3.96	4.18	4.60	5.04
United States	16.98	16.54	17.14	17.60	17.85	18.36	18.23	18.38	18.74
Central and South America	1.84	1.86	1.82	1.94	2.21	2.22	2.22	2.07	2.24
Western Europe	6.83	6.74	6.99	6.63	6.88	6.99	7.58	7.64	8.08
Eastern Europe	23.11	24.54	25.61	27.29	27.96	28.32	28.03	26.68	26.04
Middle East	2.50	2.76	3.18	3.47	3.87	3.89	4.02	4.33	4.75
Africa	1.97	1.99	2.23	2.37	2.53	2.60	2.85	2.93	2.99
Far East and Oceania	4.16	4.38	4.67	4.96	5.16	5.66	5.98	6.29	6.59

NA Not available. [1] Preliminary.
Source: U. S. Energy Information Administration, *International Energy Annual.*

No. 1160. Domestic Motor Gasoline Supply: 1980 to 1996

[In 1,000 barrels per day, except as noted]

ITEM	1980	1985	1988	1989	1990	1991	1992	1993	1994	1995	1996
Supply [1]	6,579	6,831	7,336	7,328	7,235	7,188	7,268	7,476	7,601	7,785	7,416
Production	6,506	6,419	6,956	6,963	6,959	6,975	7,058	7,360	7,312	7,586	7,375
Net imports	140	381	405	369	342	297	294	247	356	264	407
Stocks (mil. bbl.) [2]	261	223	228	213	220	219	216	226	215	202	214

NA Not available. [1] Production plus net imports less net increase in primary stocks. [2] End of year, includes motor gasoline blending components.

Source: U.S. Energy Information Administration, *Monthly Energy Review.*

No. 1161. Natural Gas Plant Liquids—Production and Value: 1970 to 1994

[Barrels of 42 gallons. See also *Historical Statistics, Colonial Times to 1970,* series M 143-146]

ITEM	Unit	1970	1980	1985	1988	1989	1990	1991	1992	1993	1994
Field production [1]	Mil. bbl	606	576	587	595	564	566	606	621	634	630
Pentanes plus	Mil. bbl	197	126	103	111	113	112	118	121	122	119
Liquefied petroleum gases	Mil. bbl	400	441	479	483	451	454	488	500	512	511
Natural gas processed	Tril. cu. ft.	19	15	13	13	13	15	16	16	16	(NA)

NA Not available. [1] Includes other finished petroleum products, not shown separately.

Source: Through 1975, U.S. Bureau of Mines, *Minerals Yearbook;* thereafter, U.S. Energy Information Administration, *Energy Data Reports, Petroleum Statement Annual, Petroleum Supply Annual,* and *Natural Gas Annual.*

No. 1162. U.S. Petroleum Balance: 1980 to 1994

[In millions of barrels]

ITEM	1980	1985	1989	1990	1991	1992	1993	1994
Petroleum products supplied	**6,242**	**5,740**	**6,324**	**6,201**	**6,101**	**6,234**	**6,291**	**6,467**
Production of products	5,765	5,363	5,874	5,934	5,933	6,050	6,182	6,244
Crude input to refineries	4,934	4,381	4,891	4,894	4,855	4,909	4,969	5,061
Oil, field production	3,138	3,274	2,779	2,685	2,707	2,617	2,499	2,431
Alaska	592	666	684	647	656	627	577	569
Lower 48 States	2,555	2,608	2,095	2,037	2,050	1,997	1,922	1,863
Net imports	1,821	1,094	2,081	2,112	2,068	2,194	2,441	2,542
Imports (gross excluding SPR) [1] . . .	1,910	1,125	2,112	2,142	2,111	2,223	2,472	2,574
SPR [1] imports	16	43	20	10	-	4	5	4
Exports	-105	75	52	40	42	32	36	36
Other sources	33	12	32	98	80	90	28	88
Natural gas plant liquids (NGPL), supply .	577	604	563	574	613	628	664	694
Other liquids	253	378	420	465	466	513	550	489
Net imports of refined products	484	313	396	326	177	156	134	217
Imports	578	523	656	598	500	471	461	518
Exports	94	210	260	272	323	315	327	302
New supply of products	6,249	5,676	6,270	6,259	6,110	6,206	6,316	6,461
Stock withdrawal, refined products	-7	64	53	-59	-10	28	-24	6
Ending stocks, all oils	1,392	1,519	1,581	1,621	1,617	1,592	1,647	1,653
Crude oil and lease condensate	358	321	341	323	325	318	335	337
Strategic Petroleum Reserve (SPR) [1]	108	493	580	586	569	575	587	592
Unfinished oils	124	107	(NA)	(NA)	(NA)	(NA)	(NA)	(NA)
Gasoline blending components	17	33	(NA)	(NA)	(NA)	(NA)	(NA)	(NA)
Pentanes plus	(NA)	8	(NA)	(NA)	(NA)	(NA)	(NA)	(NA)
Finished refined products	785	557	580	712	724	(NA)	(NA)	(NA)
PRODUCT TYPE SUPPLIED								
Total products	**6,242**	**5,740**	**6,324**	**6,201**	**6,101**	**6,234**	**6,291**	**6,467**
Finished motor gasoline	2,407	2,493	2,675	2,641	2,623	2,660	2,729	2,774
Distillate fuel oil	1,049	1,047	1,152	1,103	1,066	1,090	1,110	1,154
Residual fuel oil	918	439	500	449	423	401	394	373
Liquified petroleum gases [2]	414	584	609	568	616	642	633	686
Pentanes plus, other liquids, etc	1,454	1,155	1,378	1,431	1,365	(NA)	(NA)	(NA)
Crude oil	(NA)	22	10	9	7	5	4	3

- Represents zero. NA Not available. [1] SPR=Strategic petroleum reserve. See table 933. [2] Includes ethane.

Source: U.S. Energy Information Administration, *Petroleum Supply Annual.*

No. 1163. Crude Petroleum and Natural Gas—Production, by State: 1985 to 1994

[See also *Historical Statistics, Colonial Times to 1970,* series M 138, M 142, and M 147-161]

STATE	CRUDE PETROLEUM						NATURAL GAS MARKETED PRODUCTION [1]					
	Quantity (mil. bbl.)			Value (mil. dol.)			Quantity (bil. cu. ft.)			Value (mil. dol.)		
	1985	1990	1994	1985	1990	1994	1985	1990	1994	1985	1990	1994
Total [2] . . .	3,274	2,685	2,431	78,884	32,071	32,071	17,270	18,594	19,635	43,343	31,658	36,850
AL	22	18	18	579	275	275	107	135	515	398	373	1,119
AK	666	658	569	10,655	5,559	5,559	321	403	453	236	554	578
AR	19	10	10	443	131	131	155	175	188	393	360	497
CA	424	322	286	8,386	3,467	3,467	491	363	309	1,653	857	940
CO	30	31	29	758	442	442	178	243	453	517	377	629
FL	11	6	6	(NA)	(NA)	(NA)	11	6	7	26	15	10
IL	30	20	17	795	270	270	1	1	(Z)	4	1	1
IN	5	3	2	134	39	39	(Z)	(Z)	(Z)	1	1	(Z)
KS	75	59	47	1,939	687	687	528	574	713	671	893	1,139
KY	8	5	4	201	62	62	73	75	73	174	169	164
LA	508	148	126	5,387	1,973	1,973	5,014	5,242	5,170	13,355	9,587	10,728
MI	27	20	12	726	188	188	132	140	223	475	420	436
MS	31	30	20	796	271	271	144	95	63	456	167	95
MT	30	20	17	734	222	222	52	50	50	125	90	73
NE	7	5	4	163	57	57	2	1	3	6	2	5
NM	79	66	66	2,028	1,009	1,009	905	965	1,558	2,370	1,629	2,463
NY	1	(Z)	(Z)	25	-	-	32	25	20	106	55	48
ND	51	39	28	1,307	388	388	73	52	58	138	93	(NA)
OH	15	8	9	361	140	140	182	155	132	560	393	321
OK	163	117	91	4,256	1,395	1,395	1,936	2,258	1,935	4,930	3,548	3,290
PA	5	2	3	114	41	41	150	178	150	474	417	414
TX	889	674	591	23	8,849	8,849	6,053	6,343	6,354	14,097	9,939	11,985
UT	41	23	21	773	338	338	83	146	271	293	249	417
WV	4	2	2	86	30	30	145	178	182	558	568	480
WY	129	103	80	3,061	1,087	1,087	417	736	516	1,252	856	1,429

NA Not available. Z Less than 500 million cubic feet or less than $500,000. [1] Excludes nonhydrocarbon gases.
[2] Includes other States not shown separately. State production does not include State offshore production.

Source: U.S. Energy Information Administration, *Energy Data Reports, Petroleum Supply Annual, Natural Gas Annual,* and *Natural Gas Monthly.*

No. 1164. Natural Gas—Supply, Consumption, Reserves, and Marketed Production: 1970 to 1994

[See also *Historical Statistics, Colonial Times to 1970*, series M 147-161]

ITEM	Unit	1970	1975	1980	1985	1988	1989	1990	1991	1992	1993	1994
Producing wells (year-end)	1,000	117	130	182	243	257	262	270	277	276	286	288
Production value at wells .	Bil. dol	3.7	8.9	32.1	43.4	30.3	30.6	31.8	30.4	32.6	38.8	36.2
Avg. per 1,000 cu. ft . .	Dollars	0.17	0.44	1.59	2.51	1.69	1.69	1.71	1.64	1.74	2.03	1.83
Proved reserves [1]	Tril. cu. ft . .	291	228	199	193	168	167	169	167	165	162	164
Marketed production [2] . . .	Tril. cu. ft . .	21.9	20.1	20.2	17.3	17.9	18.1	18.6	18.5	18.7	19.1	19.8
Drawn from storage	Tril. cu. ft . .	1.5	1.8	1.9	2.4	2.2	2.8	1.9	2.7	2.7	2.7	2.5
Imports [3]	Tril. cu. ft . .	0.8	1.0	1.0	1.0	1.3	1.4	1.5	1.8	2.1	2.4	2.6
Consumption, total	Tril. cu. ft . .	21.1	19.5	19.9	17.3	18.0	18.8	18.7	19.0	19.5	20.3	20.8
Residential.	Tril. cu. ft . .	4.8	4.9	4.8	4.4	4.6	4.8	4.4	4.6	4.7	5.0	4.8
Commercial [4]	Tril. cu. ft . .	2.4	2.5	2.6	2.4	2.7	2.7	2.6	2.7	2.8	2.9	2.9
Industrial	Tril. cu. ft . .	9.3	7.0	8.2	6.9	7.5	7.9	8.2	8.3	8.7	9.2	9.4
Lease and plant fuel	Tril. cu. ft . .	1.4	1.4	1.0	1.0	1.1	1.1	1.2	1.1	1.2	1.2	1.2
Other industrial	Tril. cu. ft . .	7.9	7.0	7.2	5.9	6.4	6.8	7.0	7.2	7.5	8.0	8.2
Electric utilities .	Tril. cu. ft . .	3.9	3.2	3.7	3.0	2.6	2.8	2.8	2.8	2.8	2.7	3.0
Transportation [5]	Tril. cu. ft . .	0.7	0.6	0.6	0.5	0.6	0.6	0.7	0.6	0.6	0.6	0.7
Extraction losses [6]	Tril. cu. ft . .	0.9	0.9	0.8	0.8	0.8	0.8	0.8	0.8	0.9	0.9	0.9
Exports	Tril. cu. ft . .	0.1	0.1	0.1	0.1	0.1	0.1	0.1	0.1	0.2	0.1	0.2
Additions to storage [7] . . .	Tril. cu. ft . .	1.9	2.1	1.9	2.1	2.2	2.5	2.4	2.6	2.6	2.8	2.8
World production (dry) . . .	Tril. cu. ft . .	(NA)	44.1	53.1	62.0	69.8	71.9	74.3	74.8	(NA)	(NA)	(NA)
U.S. production (dry) . .	Tril. cu. ft . .	21.0	19.2	19.4	16.5	17.1	17.3	17.8	17.7	17.8	18.1	18.7
Percent U.S. of world	Percent . . .	56.0	43.6	36.5	26.4	24.4	24.0	24.0	23.7	(NA)	(NA)	(NA)

NA Not available.   [1] Estimated, end of year. Source: 1970-1976; American Gas Association, Arlington, VA, (copyright); thereafter, U.S. Energy Information Administration, *U.S. Crude Oil, Natural Gas*, and *Natural Gas Liquids Reserves, annual*.   [2] Marketed production includes gross withdrawals from reservoirs less quantities used for reservoir repressuring and quantities vented or flared. For 1980 and thereafter, it excludes the nonhydrocarbon gases subsequently removed.   [3] Includes imports of liquefied natural gas.   [4] Includes deliveries to municipalities and public authorities for institutional heating and other purposes.   [5] Pipeline fuel and vehicle fuel.   [6] Volumetric reduction in natural gas resulting from the extraction of natural gas constituents at natural gas processing plants.   [7] Beginning with 1980, includes liquefied natural gas (LNG) storage in above ground tanks.

Source: Except as noted, U.S. Energy Information Administration, *Annual Energy Review, International Energy Annual, Natural Gas Annual*, Volume I and II and *Monthly Energy Review*.

No. 1165. Liquefied Petroleum Gases—Summary: 1980 to 1994

[In millions of 42-gallon barrels. Includes ethane]

ITEM	1980	1990	1993	1994	ITEM	1980	1990	1993	1994
Production	561	638	850	734	**Consumption**	538	568	633	(NA)
At natural gas plants	441	456	634	511	Ethane [1]	164	186	217	(NA)
At refineries	121	182	216	223	Propane [1] [2]	298	335	367	(NA)
Imports	79	68	70	67	Butane (incl. isobutane) [2] .	76	47	49	(NA)
Refinery input	85	107	179	108	Stocks, Dec. 31.	116	98	117	99
Exports	9	14	16	14					

NA Not available.   [1] Reported consumption of ethane-propane mixtures have been allocated 70 percent ethane and 30 percent propane.   [2] Reported consumption of butane-propane mixtures have been allocated 60 percent butane and 40 percent propane.

Source: U.S. Energy Information Administration, *Petroleum Supply Annual*.

No. 1166. World Coal Trade: 1980 to 1991

[In millions of short tons]

COUNTRIES	1980	1982	1983	1984	1985	1986	1987	1988	1989	1990	1991
Exporting countries, total [1]	277.2	292.0	284.5	332.9	370.2	376.3	383.0	415.0	423.5	440.2	434.6
United States	88.7	106.5	78.2	82.0	93.2	85.5	79.6	94.9	100.8	105.8	109
Australia	46.6	48.8	62.3	82.2	96.6	101.3	111.9	109.8	108.5	116.9	132.5
South Africa	30.7	30.5	32.7	40.9	49.8	50.1	46.9	47.4	51.6	54.5	52.7
Soviet Union	26.2	23.0	22.8	22.8	26.5	36.9	39.1	46.0	43.9	42.7	31
Germany [2]	13.8	11.2	11.5	12.4	10.5	7.9	6.9	5.5	5.9	6.0	3.9
Canada	16.1	16.6	18.6	26.8	30.3	28.6	29.5	35.0	36.1	34.2	37.6
Poland	34.6	30.6	38.7	47.2	39.7	37.9	34.2	35.5	31.8	61.8	19.8
China: Mainland	4.2	5.1	6.8	7.7	8.6	10.9	14.4	16.2	16.9	19.1	20.7
Importing countries, total [1]	277.2	292.0	284.5	332.9	370.2	376.3	383.0	415.0	423.5	440.2	434.6
Western Europe/Mediterranean	126.9	126.5	112.9	132.4	152.3	149.0	145.6	146.2	154.7	172.1	180.6
Japan	75.6	86.5	82.8	96.2	103.0	99.6	100.2	111.6	111.7	113.9	123.5
Eastern Europe	34.8	37.0	39.7	39.9	39.1	45.4	44.9	45.1	39.6	30.6	21.9
Canada	17.4	17.3	16.7	20.3	16.1	14.7	15.8	19.3	15.1	15.7	13.7

[1] Includes areas not shown separately.   [2] Beginning 1990, represents United Germany.

Source: U.S. Energy Information Administration, 1975-84, *Outlook for U.S. Coal Imports;* thereafter, *Annual Prospects for World Coal Trade*.

No. 1167. Coal and Coke—Summary: 1970 to 1994

[Includes coal consumed at mines. Demonstrated coal reserve base for United States on Jan. 1, 1992, was an estimated 476 billion tons. Recoverability varies between 40 and 90 percent for individual deposits; 50 percent or more of overall U.S. coal reserve base is believed to be recoverable. See also *Historical Statistics, Colonial Times to 1970*, series M 93-126]

ITEM	Unit	1970	1980	1985	1990	1991	1992	1993	1994
Coal production, total [1]	Mil. sh. tons ..	613	830	884	1,029	996	998	945	1,034
Value.	Mil. dol.	3,882	20,453	22,277	(NA)	(NA)	(NA)	(NA)	(NA)
Anthracite production	Mil. sh. tons . . .	9.7	6.1	4.7	3.5	3.4	3.1	4.3	4.7
Bituminous coal and lignite: [2]									
Number of mines	Number.	5,601	5,598	4,547	3,243	2,846	2,134	2,326	2,209
Production.	Mil. sh. tons . .	603	824	879	1,026	993	992	941	1,029
Value, total	Mil. dol.	3,774	20,196	22,061	22,274	21,598	(NA)	(NA)	(NA)
Average per ton	Dollars	6.26	24.52	25.10	21.71	21.45	20.98	19.79	19.43
Exports	Mil. sh. tons . .	72	92	93	106	109	103	75	71
Value.	Mil. dol.	961	4,627	4,465	4,510	4,619	(NA)	(NA)	(NA)
Imports	1,000 sh. tons .	36	1,194	1,952	2,699	3,390	3,803	7,309	7,583
Method of mining:									
Underground	Mil. sh. tons . . .	339	337	350	425	407	407	351	399
Surface	Mil. sh. tons . . .	264	487	529	605	589	590	594	634
Percent of total prod . .	Percent	43.8	59.1	60.2	58.7	59.1	59.1	62.0	61.0
Value	Mil. dol.	(Z)	30	70	(NA)	(NA)	(NA)	(NA)	(NA)
Consumption [3]	Mil. sh. tons . . .	523	703	818	896	888	892	926	930
Electric power utilities. . .	Mil. sh. tons . . .	320	569	694	774	772	780	814	817
Industrial	Mil. sh. tons . . .	184	126	116	76	75	74	75	75
Productivity average: [4]									
Daily employment	1,000	140	225	169	131	121	110	101	97.5
Days worked	Number.	228	210	204	271	274	280	280	285
Tons per worker:									
Per day	Sh. tons	18.84	16.32	23.13	32.90	35.18	37.71	(NA)	(NA)
Per year	Sh. tons	4,296	3,427	4,719	7,106	7,880	(NA)	(NA)	(NA)
Production, by State:									
Alabama	Mil. sh. tons . . .	21	26	28	29	27	26	25	24
Illinois.	Mil. sh. tons . . .	65	63	59	60	60	60	41	53
Indiana.	Mil. sh. tons . . .	22	31	33	36	32	31	29	31
Kentucky.	Mil. sh. tons . . .	125	150	152	173	159	161	156	162
Montana	Mil. sh. tons . . .	3	30	33	38	38	39	36	42
Ohio.	Mil. sh. tons . . .	55	39	36	35	31	30	29	30
Pennsylvania	Mil. sh. tons . . .	90	93	71	71	65	69	60	62
Virginia	Mil. sh. tons . . .	35	41	41	47	42	43	39	37
West Virginia	Mil. sh. tons . . .	144	122	128	169	167	162	131	162
Wyoming.	Mil. sh. tons . . .	7	95	141	184	194	190	210	237
Other States	Mil. sh. tons . . .	44	140	161	187	181	189	(NA)	(NA)
World production	Mil. sh. tons . . .	3,295	4,103	4,779	5,214	4,952	4,996	4,885	(NA)
Coke production [5]	Mil. sh. tons ..	66.5	46.1	28.4	27.6	24.1	23.4	23.1	22.2
Oven coke [6]	Mil. sh. tons . . .	65.7	46.1	28.7	27.6	24.0	23.0	(NA)	(NA)
Value of product at plant	Mil. dol.	2,193	6,029	(NA)	(NA)	(NA)	(NA)	(NA)	(NA)
Coke and breeze	Mil. dol.	1,899	4,784	(NA)	(NA)	(NA)	(NA)	(NA)	(NA)
Avg. market value per ton . . .	Dollars	28	103	103	(NA)	(NA)	(NA)	(NA)	(NA)
Coal carbonized.	Mil. sh. tons . . .	96.5	66.7	41.1	38.9	33.9	32.4	31.3	31.7
Average value per ton	Dollars	12.47	56.26	54.30	47.73	48.88	47.9	47.4	46.5
Yield of coke from coal	Percent	69.1	69.2	69.8	71.0	71.0	(NA)	(NA)	(NA)

NA Not available.   Z Less than $500,000.   [1] Includes bituminous coal, lignite, and anthracite.   [2] All domestic production data for 1970 are for mines producing 1,000 short tons or more per year; thereafter, data are for all mines.   [3] Includes some categories not shown separately.   [4] Data for 1970 are for mines producing 1,000 short tons or more per year; thereafter, for mines producing 10,000 short tons more. Beginning 1985, includes anthracite.   [5] Includes beehive coke.   [6] Prior to 1980, excludes screenings or breeze; thereafter, includes beehive and other nonrecoverable coke-oven operations.

Source: 1970, U.S. Bureau of Mines, *Minerals Yearbook;* thereafter, U.S. Energy Information Administration, *Coal Industry,* annual; *Annual Energy Review,* and *Quarterly Coal Report,* and unpublished data.

No. 1168. Uranium Concentrate (U_3O_8) Industry—Summary: 1980 to 1993

[Middle demand case. See table 969. See also *Historical Statistics, Colonial Times to 1970*, series M 266-267]

ITEM	Unit	1980	1985	1986	1987	1988	1989	1990	1991	1992	1993
Production	1,000 sh. tons .	21.9	5.6	6.8	6.5	6.5	6.9	4.4	4.0	2.8	3.1
Net imports (U_3O_8)	1,000 sh. tons .	-1.1	3.2	6.4	7.5	6.4	5.6	12.1	9.8	12.3	(NA)
Utility and Suppliers inventories											
(U_3O_8 equivalent)	1,000 sh. tons .	54.4	[1]68.3	[1]66.2	[1]64.5	[1]59.1	[1]54.9	45.6	36.70	(NA)	(NA)
Price (1988 dol./lb. U_3O_8):											
Long-term contract price	Dollars	41.4	24.7	19.3	18.5	(NA)	(NA)	(NA)	(NA)	(NA)	(NA)
Spot market price.	Dollars	45.0	17.0	18.1	17.3	14.5	14.2	(NA)	(NA)	(NA)	(NA)
Delivered price	Dollars	39.9	[2]33.6	[2]31.9	[2]19.6	[2]25.7	[2]27.8	(NA)	(NA)	(NA)	(NA)
Capital expenditures											
(1988 dollars)	Mil. dol.	1,107	37	29	63	36	35	(NA)	(NA)	(NA)	(NA)
Employment.	1,000	19.9	2.4	2.1	2.0	2.10	1.6	1.3	1.0	0.7	0.4

NA Not available.   [1] Includes natural U_3O_8 (uranium oxide), natural UF_6 (uranium hexafluoride), natural UF_6 under usage agreement, UF_6 at enrichment suppliers, enriched UF_6 and fabricated fuel.   [2] Average U.S. contract prices and market price settlements.

Source: U.S. Department of Energy, *Domestic Uranium Mining and Milling Industry,* annual, and *Uranium Industry,* annual.

Construction and Housing

This section presents data on the construction industry and on various indicators of its activity and costs; on housing units and their characteristics and occupants; and on the characteristics and vacancy rates for commercial buildings. There are new data on industrial buildings and the construction value series changed its base year to 1992 dollars for its constant dollar series.

The principal source of these data is the U.S. Bureau of the Census, which issues a variety of current publications. Construction statistics compiled by the Bureau appear in its monthly *Current Construction Reports* series with various quarterly or annual supplements; *Housing Starts* and *Housing Completions* present data by type of structure and by four major census regions; *New One-Family Houses Sold and For Sale* also provides statistics annually on physical and financial characteristics for all new housing by the four major census regions; *Price Index of New One-Family Houses Sold* presents quarterly figures and annual regional data; and *Housing Units Authorized by Building Permits* covers approximately 19,000 permit-issuing jurisdictions in the United States (prior to 1995, 17,000 places). Statistics on expenditures by owners of residential properties are issued quarterly and annually in *Expenditures for Residential Upkeep and Improvements. Value of New Construction Put in Place* presents data on all types of construction and includes monthly composite cost indexes. Reports of the censuses of construction industries (see below) are also issued on various topics.

Other Census Bureau publications include the *Current Housing Reports* series, which comprises the quarterly *Housing Vacancies,* the quarterly *Market Absorption of Apartments,* the American Housing Survey (formerly Annual Housing Survey) and reports of the censuses of housing and of construction industries. *Construction Review,* published quarterly by the International Trade Administration, U.S. Department of Commerce, contains many of the census series and other construction statistics series from the Federal Government and private agencies.

In Brief

Value of new construction in constant (1992) dollars reached $470 billion in 1995, its highest level since 1986.

Sales of existing one-family homes declined 3.6% between 1994 and 1995 to just over 3.8 million units.

The Nation's office vacancy rate declined to 14.3% at yearend 1995, the lowest rate since 1984.

Other sources include the monthly *Dodge Construction Potentials* of F. W. Dodge Division, McGraw-Hill Information Systems Company, New York, NY, which presents national and State data on construction contracts; the National Association of Home Builders with–State-level data on housing starts; the NATIONAL ASSOCIATION OF REALTORS, which presents data on existing home sales; the Society of Industrial and Office Realtors and Oncor International on commercial 2nd industrial office space; the Bureau of Economic Analysis, which presents data on residential capital and gross housing product; and the U.S. Energy Information Administration, which provides data on commercial buildings through its periodic sample surveys.

Censuses and surveys—Censuses of the construction industry were first conducted by the Bureau of the Census for 1929, 1935, and 1939; beginning in 1967, a census has been taken every five years (for years ending in "2" and "7"). The latest reports are for 1992.

The 1992 Census of Construction Industries, in accordance with the 1987 *Standard Industrial Classification Manual* (see text, section 13), covers all employer establishments primarily engaged in (1) building construction by general contractors or operative builders; (2) heavy (nonbuilding) construction by general contractors; and (3) construction by special trade contractors.

From 1850 through 1930, the Bureau of the Census collected some housing data as part of its censuses of population and agriculture. Beginning in 1940, separate censuses of housing have been taken at 10-year intervals. For the 1970 and 1980 censuses, data on year-round housing units were collected and issued on occupancy and structural characteristics, plumbing facilities, value, and rent; for 1990 such characteristics were presented for all housing units.

The American Housing Survey (*Current Housing Reports* series H-150 and H-170), which began in 1973, provided an annual and ongoing series of data on selected housing and demographic characteristics until 1983. In 1984 the name of the survey was changed from the Annual Housing Survey. It is currently based on a biennial national sample and on 11 annual MSA samples. All samples represent a cross section of the housing stock in their respective areas. Estimates are subject to both sampling and non-sampling errors; caution should therefore, be used in making comparisons with 1970 and 1980 census data.

Data on residential mortgages were collected continuously from 1890 to 1970,

except 1930, as part of the decennial census by the Bureau of the Census. Since 1973, mortgage status data, limited to single family homes on less than ten acres with no business on the property, have been presented in the American Housing Survey. Data on mortgage activity are covered in section 16.

Housing units—In general, a housing unit is a group of rooms or a single room occupied or intended for occupancy as separate living quarters; that is, the occupants do not live and eat with any other persons in the structure and there is direct access from the outside or through a common hall. Transient accommodations, barracks for workers, and institutional-type quarters are not counted as housing units.

Statistical reliability—For a discussion of statistical collection and estimation, sampling procedures, and measures of statistical reliability applicable to Census Bureau data, see Appendix III.

Historical statistics—Tabular headnotes provide cross-references, where applicable, to *Historical Statistics of the United States, Colonial Times to 1970*. See Appendix IV.

No. 1169. Construction Industries—Summary, by Industry: 1992

[Based on a probability sample of about 160,000 construction establishments with payroll in 1987; see Appendix III. N.e.c.= Not elsewhere classified]

INDUSTRY	SIC [1] code	Estab-lish-ments with payroll (1,000)	EMPLOYEES (1,000)		PAYROLL (mil. dol.)		VALUE OF CONSTRUC-TION WORK (mil. dol.)		Value added [3] (mil. dol.)
			Total	Con-struction workers	Total	Con-struction workers	Total	Net [2]	
All industries, total	(X)	**572.9**	**4,668**	**3,596**	**117,730**	**83,048**	**528,106**	**391,190**	**234,618**
General building contractors	15	168.4	1,097	759	27,078	16,125	215,629	114,722	63,117
Single-family houses.	1521	107.5	404	296	7,278	4,869	48,633	33,660	17,183
Other residential buildings	1522	6.5	49	35	1,161	718	7,835	4,338	2,454
Operative builders	1531	17.0	114	50	3,359	1,045	44,588	26,843	15,289
Industrial buildings and warehouses	1541	7.7	123	92	3,476	2,310	20,586	10,967	6,438
Nonresidential buildings, n.e.c	1542	29.7	407	286	11,804	7,183	93,987	38,913	21,754
Heavy construction contractors	16	37.2	799	647	23,728	17,622	95,571	77,526	49,165
Highway and street construction	1611	10.1	257	211	7,358	5,457	35,332	27,863	15,711
Bridge, tunnel, and elevated highway . . .	1622	1.0	44	36	1,485	1,125	7,198	5,316	3,078
Water, sewer, and utility lines	1623	10.2	194	160	5,624	4,252	20,205	17,587	11,734
Heavy construction, n.e.c	1629	15.8	304	240	9,261	6,788	32,837	26,760	18,642
Special trade contractors	17	367.3	2,772	2,190	66,924	49,302	216,905	198,942	122,336
Plumbing, heating, air-conditioning	1711	75.4	613	455	16,613	11,781	56,902	50,756	29,432
Painting and paperhanging	1721	32.0	163	136	3,164	2,470	8,690	8,095	5,855
Electrical work	1731	54.0	487	379	13,624	10,039	40,259	38,541	23,548
Masonry and other stonework	1741	22.6	148	130	2,883	2,366	8,458	7,956	5,146
Plastering, drywall, insulation	1742	18.6	207	173	4,910	3,826	14,056	12,824	8,143
Terrazzo, tile, marble, and mosaic work . .	1743	6.5	34	27	775	568	2,439	2,323	1,358
Carpentry	1751	38.2	178	145	3,489	2,683	12,852	11,334	6,760
Floorlaying and other floor work	1752	10.2	49	36	1,065	724	4,428	4,032	2,166
Roofing, siding, and sheet metal work . . .	1761	27.6	216	169	4,623	3,230	16,788	15,590	8,906
Concrete work	1771	26.1	193	161	4,038	3,093	14,423	13,179	7,703
Water well drilling	1781	3.6	19	15	444	323	1,727	1,676	995
Structural steel erection	1791	3.8	58	47	1,629	1,227	4,952	4,487	3,021
Glass and glazing work	1793	4.6	32	21	796	495	2,724	2,634	1,424
Excavation work	1794	13.9	77	62	1,817	1,401	6,870	6,129	4,340
Wrecking and demolition work	1795	1.0	13	10	296	215	1,059	928	775
Installing building equipment, n.e.c	1796	3.9	83	64	2,324	1,742	6,611	6,132	4,494
Special trade contractors, n.e.c	1799	25.3	204	157	4,435	3,120	13,667	12,325	8,270

X Not applicable.   [1] Standard Industrial Classification; see, text, section 13.   [2] Value of construction work less payments for construction work subcontracted to others, not shown separately.   [3] Dollar value of business done less (a) payments for materials, components, and supplies, and (b) payments for construction work subcontracted to others, not shown separately.
Source: U.S. Bureau of the Census, *Census of Construction Industries, 1992,* series CC92-I-1(P) through CC92-I-27(P).

No. 1170. Construction Materials—Producer Price Indexes: 1980 to 1995

[1982=100, except as noted. For discussion of producer price index, see text, section 15. This index, more formally known as the special commodity grouping index for construction materials, covers materials incorporated as integral part of a building or normally installed during construction and not readily removable. Excludes consumer durables such as kitchen ranges, refrigerators, etc. This index is not the same as the stage-of-processing index of intermediate materials and components for construction. See *Historical Statistics, Colonial Times to 1970,* series N 140-155 for similar data]

COMMODITY	1980	1985	1988	1989	1990	1991	1992	1993	1994	1995
Construction materials	**92.5**	**107.6**	**115.7**	**119.5**	**119.6**	**120.4**	**122.5**	**128.6**	**133.8**	**(NA)**
Interior solvent based paint	91.3	107.3	120.3	128.8	133.0	140.2	141.7	142.9	148.1	164.5
Plastic construction products	103.9	108.6	121.1	120.1	117.2	115.1	112.7	116.6	122.7	133.8
Douglas fir, dressed	132.6	126.5	135.7	151.6	138.4	139.6	169.5	237.6	236.4	198.8
Southern pine, dressed	104.0	105.2	112.4	108.0	111.2	111.0	130.6	168.8	182.5	166.9
Millwork	93.2	111.7	121.9	127.3	130.4	135.5	143.3	156.6	162.4	163.8
Softwood plywood	109.5	107.4	109.1	124.2	119.6	120.8	147.2	169.7	176.8	188.1
Hardwood plywood and related products	97.5	89.9	94.2	99.8	102.7	102.8	106.9	115.4	122.3	122.2
Softwood plywood veneer, ex. reinforced/backed.	126.0	100.1	117.3	142.1	142.3	138.5	168.3	216.0	207.8	203.5
Building paper and building board mill products .	86.1	107.4	113.3	115.6	112.2	111.8	119.6	132.9	144.1	144.9
Tube, drawn, 6000 alloy series	85.6	109.7	128.9	131.0	127.1	124.1	123.4	(NA)	(NA)	(NA)
Builders hardware	84.9	113.5	122.5	127.8	133.0	138.1	141.4	144.9	147.9	153.2
Plumbing fixtures and brass fittings	88.5	111.9	128.7	137.7	144.3	149.7	153.1	155.9	159.7	166.0
Heating equipment	87.0	109.5	119.2	125.1	131.6	134.1	137.3	140.4	142.5	147.5
Metal doors, sash, and trim	87.8	107.3	122.4	130.0	131.4	134.6	135.0	136.6	142.0	156.5
Incandescent outdoor lighting fixtures	82.7	109.2	122.4	128.0	137.3	136.5	139.1	138.5	141.0	151.8
Bright nails	90.9	100.2	104.7	110.4	(NA)	(NA)	115.1	115.9	118.0	119.8
Welded steel wire fabric for concrete reinforcing.	98.9	101.3	109.2	108.6	109.7	100.0	101.3	104.5	108.7	109.0
Elevators, escalators, and other lifts.	87.3	97.7	103.6	107.1	110.1	108.7	109.4	110.7	112.4	113.0
Stamped metal outlet box	82.7	119.7	168.7	171.7	179.4	179.7	187.2	195.7	(NA)	(NA)
Concrete ingredients and related products	88.4	108.5	112.0	113.2	115.3	118.4	119.4	123.4	128.7	134.7
Concrete products	92.0	107.5	110.0	111.2	113.5	116.6	117.2	120.2	124.6	129.4
Clay construction products exc. refractories. . . .	88.8	113.5	124.9	127.0	129.9	130.2	132.0	135.1	138.3	141.3
Prep. asphalt and tar roofing and siding products.	105.5	100.5	94.4	95.6	95.8	96.2	94.3	94.9	92.9	97.8
Gypsum products	100.1	132.3	112.9	110.0	105.2	99.3	99.9	108.3	136.1	154.5
Insulation materials.	80.7	105.2	105.8	106.7	108.4	110.8	102.3	105.8	111.9	118.8
Paving mixtures and blocks	83.7	111.6	102.7	101.0	101.2	103.2	100.2	102.0	103.2	105.8

NA Not available.
Source: U.S. Bureau of Labor Statistics, *Producer Price Indexes,* monthly and annual.

No. 1171. Price and Cost Indexes for Construction: 1980 to 1995

[1992=100. Excludes Alaska and Hawaii. Indexes of certain sources are published on bases different from those shown here. See *Historical Statistics, Colonial Times to 1970*, series N 118-137, for construction cost indexes on a 1947-49 base]

NAME OF INDEX	1980	1985	1989	1990	1991	1992	1993	1994	1995
Bureau of the Census:									
Composite fixed-weighted [1]	68.8	83.0	95.9	98.5	99.3	100.0	103.7	107.9	112.1
Implicit price deflator [2]	69.7	83.4	96.0	98.6	99.3	100.0	103.7	108.1	112.0
Bureau of the Census houses under construction: [3]									
Fixed-weighted	67.6	81.4	95.8	98.6	98.9	100.0	104.9	109.4	113.7
Price deflator	69.4	82.2	95.9	98.5	99.0	100.0	104.8	109.5	113.4
Federal Highway Administration, composite [4]	92.5	97.1	102.5	103.2	102.3	100.0	103.0	109.5	116.5
Bureau of Reclamation composite [5]	70	84	92	96	99	100	103	106	110
Turner Construction Co.: Building construction [6]	61	83	95	98	100	100	102	105	109
E. H. Boeckh, building cost index: [7]									
Residences	(NA)	82.4	91.1	94.2	96.8	100.0	104.5	107.4	(NA)
Apartments, hotels, and office buildings	(NA)	83.8	92.4	94.9	97.5	100.0	102.8	105.6	(NA)
Commercial and factory buildings	(NA)	82.3	91.3	94.4	97.3	100.0	102.6	105.7	(NA)
Engineering News-Record: [8]									
Buildings	68.5	85.7	93.0	95.4	97.1	100.0	105.7	109.8	109.8
Construction	64.9	84.2	92.6	94.9	97.0	100.0	104.5	108.5	109.8
Handy-Whitman public utility: [9]									
Buildings	78	90	100	101	98	100	105	112	114
Electric [10]	68	83	94	97	99	100	103	107	110
Gas	67	85	94	96	98	100	103	108	111
Water [11]	73	88	97	98	98	100	104	109	111
C. A. Turner Telephone Plant [12]	90	89	97	99	100	100	102	103	109

NA Not available. [1] Weighted average of the various indexes used to deflate the Construction Put in Place series. In calculating the index, the weights (i.e., the composition of current dollar estimates in 1987 by category) are held constant. [2] Derived ratio of total current to constant dollar Construction Put in Place (multiplied by 100). [3] Excludes value of site. [4] Based on average contract unit bid prices for composite mile (involving specific average amounts of excavation, paving, reinforcing steel, structural steel, and structural concrete). [5] Derived from the four quarterly indexes which are weighted averages of costs of labor, materials, and equipment for the construction of dams and reclamation projects. [6] Based on firm's cost experience with respect to labor rates, materials prices, competitive conditions, efficiency of plant and management, and productivity. [7] Average of 20 cities for types shown. Weights based on surveys of building costs. [8] Building index computed on the basis of a hypothetical unit of construction requiring 6 bbl. of portland cement, 1,088 M bd. ft. of 2" x 4" lumber, 2,500 lb. of structural steel, and 68.38 hours of skilled labor. Construction index based on same materials components combined with 200 hours of common labor. [9] Based on data covering public utility construction costs in six geographic regions. Covers skilled and common labor. [10] As derived by U.S. Bureau of the Census. Covers steam generation plants only. [11] As derived by U.S. Bureau of the Census. Reflects costs for structures and improvements at water pumping and treatment plants. [12] Computed by the Census Bureau by averaging the weighted component indexes published for six geographic regions.
Source: U.S. Bureau of the Census. In U.S. Department of Commerce, International Trade Administration, *Construction Review*, bimonthly.

No. 1172. Value of New Construction Put in Place in Current and Constant (1992) Dollars: 1964 to 1995

[In millions of dollars. Represents value of construction put in place during year; differs from building permit and construction contract data in timing and coverage. Includes installed cost of normal building service equipment and selected types of industrial production equipment (largely site fabricated). Excludes cost of shipbuilding, land, and most types of machinery and equipment. For methodology, see Appendix III. See also *Historical Statistics, Colonial Times to 1970*, series N 1-29 and N 66-69]

YEAR	CURRENT DOLLARS					CURRENT (1992) DOLLARS				
	Total	Private			Public	Total	Private			Public
		Total	Residential buildings	Nonresidential buildings			Total	Residential buildings	Nonresidential buildings	
1964	72,124	51,921	30,526	14,412	20,203	330,986	239,924	141,223	68,831	91,062
1970	100,727	72,819	35,863	23,008	27,908	347,988	255,546	129,217	81,126	92,443
1971	117,311	87,612	48,514	24,204	29,699	379,941	288,737	164,820	78,602	91,203
1972	133,318	103,288	60,693	26,568	30,030	406,561	319,510	192,738	80,731	87,051
1973	146,826	114,477	65,085	30,683	32,348	411,534	324,531	188,309	86,162	87,004
1974	147,476	109,344	55,967	32,195	38,132	365,614	275,357	147,346	79,099	90,257
1975	145,623	102,330	51,581	28,397	43,293	329,751	237,442	124,429	66,628	92,309
1976	165,441	121,462	68,273	27,936	43,979	356,947	267,307	154,776	62,824	89,641
1977	193,126	150,044	92,004	30,871	43,083	385,186	302,002	187,573	64,453	83,184
1978	230,178	180,032	109,838	39,135	50,146	412,385	324,036	197,295	73,721	88,349
1979	259,839	203,194	116,444	51,732	56,646	415,092	327,150	186,242	87,239	87,943
1980	259,746	196,100	100,381	58,290	63,646	372,868	285,544	144,867	88,847	87,325
1981	271,950	207,259	99,241	68,450	64,691	360,614	278,633	132,364	95,497	81,981
1982	260,594	197,531	84,676	73,953	63,064	332,485	254,418	108,738	98,006	78,067
1983	294,945	231,494	125,521	70,438	63,450	371,969	293,573	159,839	90,741	78,396
1984	348,838	278,600	153,849	87,493	70,238	428,833	343,795	190,762	108,429	85,038
1985	377,358	299,543	158,474	103,455	77,815	452,317	361,534	192,633	124,868	90,783
1986	407,682	323,100	187,148	98,674	84,582	472,889	377,346	218,648	115,183	95,543
1987	419,386	328,738	194,656	100,933	90,648	470,180	369,847	218,391	113,413	100,332
1988	432,251	337,516	198,101	106,994	94,735	467,175	365,750	214,021	115,973	101,426
1989	443,651	345,477	196,551	113,988	98,174	462,185	360,501	204,789	119,238	101,684
1990	442,161	334,683	182,856	117,971	107,478	448,478	339,888	185,592	119,775	108,591
1991	403,404	293,295	157,835	97,841	110,109	406,351	296,245	159,527	98,808	110,107
1992	435,021	315,696	187,869	87,241	119,326	435,198	315,826	187,915	87,266	119,372
1993	464,501	339,160	210,455	90,065	125,341	447,798	325,401	200,729	86,912	122,396
1994	506,904	376,566	238,883	97,704	130,338	469,005	346,099	217,886	90,465	122,906
1995	526,598	383,886	236,111	109,721	142,711	470,202	341,020	208,081	98,441	129,182

Source: U.S. Bureau of the Census, *Current Construction Reports*, series C30.

No. 1173. Value of New Construction Put in Place in Current and Constant (1992) Dollars: 1990 to 1995

[In millions of dollars. Represents value of construction put in place during year; differs from building permit and construction contract data in timing and coverage. Includes installed cost of normal building service equipment and selected types of industrial production equipment (largely site fabricated). Excludes cost of shipbuilding, land, and most types of machinery and equipment. For details on derivation of constant values and description of revised series, see source. For description of nature of revisions and deflators used, see *Construction Reports*, series C30-9005. For methodology, see Appendix III. See also *Historical Statistics, Colonial Times to 1970*, series N 1-29 and N 66-69]

TYPE OF CONSTRUCTION	CURRENT DOLLARS					CONSTANT (1992) DOLLARS				
	1990	1992	1993	1994	1995	1990	1992	1993	1994	1995
Total new construction .	442,161	435,021	464,501	506,904	526,598	448,478	435,198	447,798	469,005	470,202
Private construction	334,683	315,696	339,160	376,566	[1]383,886	339,888	315,826	325,401	346,099	341,020
Residential buildings	182,856	187,869	210,455	238,883	236,111	185,592	187,915	200,729	217,886	208,081
New housing units	127,987	129,600	144,071	167,928	162,412	129,912	129,640	137,397	153,177	143,131
1 unit	108,737	116,505	133,282	153,838	143,992	110,371	116,529	127,102	140,339	126,897
2 or more units	19,250	13,094	10,788	14,090	18,420	19,540	13,112	10,295	12,838	16,234
Improvements	54,869	58,269	66,384	70,955	(NA)	55,681	58,275	63,332	64,708	(NA)
Nonresidential buildings . . .	117,971	87,241	90,065	97,704	109,721	119,775	87,266	86,912	90,465	98,441
Industrial	23,848	20,719	19,531	21,122	24,154	24,212	20,728	18,855	19,552	21,673
Office	28,722	17,241	15,414	17,074	19,422	29,168	17,255	14,882	15,810	17,430
Hotels, motels	9,673	3,507	4,286	4,121	6,424	9,824	3,506	4,136	3,821	5,760
Other commercial	34,140	24,283	27,211	31,478	35,735	34,660	24,280	26,246	29,131	32,054
Religious	3,390	3,382	3,636	3,648	3,877	3,440	3,381	3,509	3,377	3,478
Educational	4,219	4,254	4,229	4,418	5,003	4,282	4,257	4,080	4,095	4,489
Hospital and institutional .	9,450	10,110	11,001	10,332	9,775	9,592	10,111	10,620	9,571	8,774
Miscellaneous [2]	4,528	3,746	4,756	5,511	5,332	4,598	3,746	4,586	5,108	4,782
Farm nonresidential	2,670	2,391	3,191	3,287	(NA)	2,710	2,391	3,078	3,044	(NA)
Public utilities	28,228	34,626	32,169	33,801	(NA)	28,813	34,685	31,452	31,942	(NA)
Telecommunications	9,803	8,993	9,619	10,771	10,775	9,891	9,005	9,468	10,471	9828
Other public utilities	18,425	25,633	22,550	23,030	(NA)	18,922	25,680	21,985	21,471	(NA)
Railroads	2,600	2,928	3,108	3,905	(NA)	2,633	2,926	3,056	3,731	(NA)
Electric light and power.	10,594	14,955	12,811	12,256	(NA)	10,848	15,010	12,428	11,411	(NA)
Gas	4,820	6,901	5,645	5,871	(NA)	5,013	6,895	5,536	5,410	(NA)
Petroleum pipelines . . .	411	849	986	998	(NA)	428	849	965	919	(NA)
All other private [3]	2,957	3,570	3,281	2,890	2,829	2,997	3,569	3,229	2,763	2,585
Public construction	107,478	119,326	125,341	130,338	142,711	108,591	119,372	122,396	122,906	129,182
Buildings	43,615	50,281	51,457	52,308	58,009	44,269	50,303	49,610	48,370	51,967
Housing and development	3,808	3,825	4,036	4,616	5,182	3,864	3,828	3,851	4,211	4,568
Industrial	1,433	1,876	1,718	1,465	1,506	1,455	1,875	1,658	1,357	1,352
Educational	16,055	20,736	22,065	23,194	25,913	16,292	20,742	21,288	21,477	23,244
Hospital	2,860	3,271	3,684	3,856	4,262	2,905	3,272	3,556	3,573	3,825
Other [4]	19,458	20,574	19,954	19,176	21,146	19,752	20,584	19,258	17,752	18,978
Highways and streets	32,104	34,899	37,432	39,883	42,219	31,777	34,933	37,284	38,602	38,640
Military facilities	2,665	2,502	2,453	2,318	2,904	2,674	2,502	2,406	2,195	2,635
Conservation and development	4,686	6,021	5,977	6,228	6,317	4,870	6,015	5,811	5,869	5,743
Sewer systems	10,276	10,180	10,433	11,334	12,161	10,670	10,171	10,145	10,678	11,046
Water supply facilities	4,909	5,171	6,022	6,164	7,110	4,987	5,179	5,765	5,630	6,380
Miscellaneous public [5] . . .	9,223	10,272	11,568	12,104	13,992	9,344	10,270	11,375	11,563	12,770

NA Not available. [1] Includes estimates for types of construction indicated as (NA). [2] Includes amusement and recreational buildings, bus and airline terminals, animal hospitals and shelters, etc. [3] Includes privately owned streets and bridges, parking areas, sewer and water facilities, parks and playgrounds, golf courses, airfields, etc. [4] Includes federal administrative buildings, prisons, police and fire stations, courthouses, civic centers, passenger terminals, space facilities, postal facilities, etc. [5] Includes open amusement and recreational facilities, power generating facilities, transit systems, airfields, open parking facilities, etc.

Source: U.S. Bureau of the Census, *Current Construction Reports*, series C30, monthly.

No. 1174. Value of Privately Owned Nonresidential Building Projects, by Construction Status, 1987 to 1995, and by Type of Project, 1995

[In billions of dollars]

CONSTRUCTION STATUS	1987	1988	1989	1990	1991	1992	1993	1994	1995				
									Total	Industrial	Office building	Other commercial	Other[1]
Value of projects—													
Started	95.7	107.7	109.9	89.5	72.9	81.3	81.3	98.7	113.2	19.5	19.8	40.0	33.9
Completed	91.4	101.6	107.7	114.0	109.5	100.1	94.8	104.7	102.5	23.4	18.1	32.7	28.4

[1] Privately owned hotels and motels, religious, educational, hospital and institutional, and miscellaneous nonresidential building projects.

Source: U.S. Bureau of the Census, *Current Construction Reports*, series C30.

No. 1175. Construction Contracts—Value of Construction and Floor Space of Buildings, by Class of Construction: 1980 to 1995

[Includes new structures and additions, and major alterations to existing structures which affect only valuation, since no additional floor area is created by "alteration". See also *Historical Statistics, Colonial Times to 1970*, series N 78-100]

YEAR	Total	Resi-dential build-ings	NONRESIDENTIAL BUILDINGS									Non-build-ing con-struc-tion
			Total	Com-mer-cial [1]	Manu-fac-turing	Educa-tional [2]	Hos-pital	Public build-ings	Reli-gious	Social and recrea-tional	Mis-cella-neous	
VALUE (bil. dol.)												
1980	151.8	60.4	56.9	27.7	9.2	7.4	5.4	1.6	1.2	2.7	1.7	34.5
1981	157.3	56.3	65.5	35.2	9.3	6.6	6.4	1.4	1.2	3.4	2.0	35.4
1982	157.1	55.0	64.6	32.3	9.6	6.8	8.0	1.9	1.2	2.8	2.0	37.5
1983	194.1	88.4	67.9	38.3	5.4	7.1	8.5	2.1	1.5	2.9	2.1	37.8
1984	214.3	95.3	82.1	48.2	7.9	8.5	7.4	2.7	1.7	3.3	2.4	36.9
1985	235.6	102.1	92.1	54.6	8.1	10.0	7.8	3.1	2.0	4.0	2.5	41.4
1986	249.3	115.6	91.6	52.4	7.3	11.7	7.9	3.2	2.1	4.2	2.8	42.1
1987	259.0	114.1	98.8	53.7	8.6	13.2	9.0	4.7	2.1	4.3	3.2	46.1
1988	262.2	116.2	97.9	51.6	9.5	14.1	8.2	4.4	2.2	4.7	3.2	48.1
1989	271.3	116.2	106.1	53.6	12.7	15.9	8.8	5.2	2.0	5.0	2.9	49.0
1990	246.0	100.9	95.4	44.8	8.4	16.6	9.2	5.7	2.2	5.3	3.1	49.7
1991	230.8	94.4	86.2	32.7	8.3	19.0	9.6	6.2	2.4	5.1	3.0	50.2
1992	252.2	110.6	87.0	32.8	8.9	17.6	10.9	5.8	2.5	5.5	3.1	54.6
1993	271.5	123.9	88.8	34.2	9.0	19.3	10.5	3.9	2.4	6.8	2.6	58.9
1994	296.2	133.6	101.0	40.9	10.7	21.0	10.5	6.1	2.5	6.5	3.0	61.6
1995	303.8	127.9	112.4	46.5	12.4	22.9	10.7	6.1	2.9	7.1	3.8	63.5
FLOOR SPACE (mil. sq. ft.)												
1980	3,102	1,839	1,263	738	220	103	55	18	28	49	52	(X)
1981	2,805	1,562	1,243	787	188	83	60	14	25	46	41	(X)
1982	2,455	1,440	1,015	631	119	82	71	19	25	38	30	(X)
1983	3,387	2,276	1,111	716	112	84	84	20	29	36	31	(X)
1984	3,661	2,311	1,350	901	157	100	70	23	29	37	34	(X)
1985	3,853	2,324	1,529	1,039	165	111	73	28	32	44	38	(X)
1986	3,935	2,481	1,454	960	148	129	73	30	32	44	39	(X)
1987	3,756	2,288	1,469	933	160	139	78	42	32	46	38	(X)
1988	3,594	2,181	1,413	883	162	142	71	38	32	49	37	(X)
1989	3,516	2,115	1,400	867	158	151	72	41	27	48	35	(X)
1990	3,020	1,817	1,203	694	128	152	69	47	29	51	32	(X)
1991	2,634	1,653	981	476	100	177	72	50	29	45	33	(X)
1992	2,799	1,864	936	462	95	156	77	41	30	42	32	(X)
1993	3,062	2,091	971	481	110	165	75	30	30	51	29	(X)
1994	3,410	2,266	1,144	601	142	172	72	45	30	51	31	(X)
1995	3,448	2,172	1,276	700	160	185	69	39	33	56	33	(X)

X Not applicable. [1] Includes nonindustrial warehouses. [2] Includes science.

No. 1176. Construction Contracts—Value, by State: 1990 to 1995

[In millions of dollars. See headnote, table 1175. Represents value of construction in States in which work was actually done]

STATE	1990	1993	1994	1995 Total (incl. non-bldg.)	1995 Resi-den-tial	1995 Non-resi-den-tial	STATE	1990	1993	1994	1995 Total (incl. non-bldg.)	1995 Resi-den-tial	1995 Non-resi-den-tial
U.S .	246,022	271,529	296,212	303,790	127,890	112,395	MO ...	3,833	5,151	5,554	6,429	2,381	2,747
AL ...	2,939	3,831	4,278	4,140	1,841	1,381	MT ...	332	765	760	842	350	204
AK ...	1,919	927	882	1,659	339	438	NE ...	1,318	1,593	1,831	1,679	582	591
AZ ...	4,553	6,491	8,004	8,764	5,262	2,413	NV ...	3,334	3,828	4,784	5,545	2,714	1,891
AR ...	1,438	2,171	2,757	2,897	1,193	915	NH ...	1,021	923	1,110	1,027	443	390
CA ...	37,318	28,215	30,572	28,677	10,916	9,993	NJ ...	6,141	6,277	6,539	6,448	2,260	2,754
CO ...	3,235	6,081	6,494	6,461	3,626	1,958	NM ...	1,124	1,666	1,966	2,103	755	690
CT ...	3,058	3,236	2,941	3,124	1,057	1,605	NY ...	14,137	12,778	13,527	13,271	3,257	5,893
DE ...	787	709	726	863	321	330	NC ...	6,614	8,959	10,097	10,541	5,409	3,654
DC ...	795	1,132	789	664	50	553	ND ...	506	641	850	791	229	314
FL ...	16,975	19,117	22,140	21,570	10,868	6,938	OH ...	9,885	11,185	12,067	12,364	4,828	5,391
GA ...	7,120	9,458	10,682	12,170	6,304	4,340	OK ...	2,164	2,427	2,981	2,975	1,248	1,035
HI ...	2,831	2,243	2,234	2,273	868	1,010	OR ...	3,101	3,581	4,197	4,944	2,280	1,839
ID ...	986	1,746	1,790	1,681	931	507	PA ...	10,117	10,367	9,678	9,292	3,214	4,407
IL ...	10,796	11,337	12,009	11,682	4,625	4,435	RI ...	594	1,289	661	464	244	133
IN ...	6,350	7,152	7,666	7,908	3,825	2,762	SC ...	3,664	4,157	4,171	4,570	2,167	1,747
IA ...	2,034	2,364	2,744	2,874	892	1,159	SD ...	468	758	846	701	226	232
KS ...	2,193	2,685	3,144	3,274	1,212	1,221	TN ...	4,388	5,604	6,392	7,161	3,453	2,450
KY ...	3,174	4,319	4,247	4,452	1,913	1,538	TX ...	13,197	19,155	20,900	22,583	9,538	8,040
LA ...	3,191	3,701	4,085	4,287	1,256	1,881	UT ...	1,884	3,149	3,436	3,701	1,812	1,382
ME ...	897	959	1,055	1,077	401	373	VT ...	515	512	558	482	216	181
MD ...	6,056	5,271	6,369	6,276	2,738	1,989	VA ...	7,180	7,575	8,471	8,800	3,821	3,276
MA ...	5,135	6,330	6,446	7,391	2,270	2,843	WA ...	6,185	6,998	7,850	7,275	3,340	2,896
MI ...	7,646	7,994	9,656	9,933	4,400	3,807	WV ...	1,253	1,167	1,199	1,213	227	405
MN ...	4,953	5,329	5,504	5,593	2,371	2,113	WI ...	4,654	5,169	5,453	5,653	2,398	2,042
MS ...	1,569	2,379	2,555	2,714	867	1,154	WY ...	462	679	561	532	152	153

Source of tables 1175 and 1176: F. W. Dodge, McGraw-Hill, Inc., New York, NY. Figures reported currently in *Dodge Construction Potentials* (copyright).

No. 1177. New Privately-Owned Housing Units Authorized, by State: 1994 and 1995

[Based on about 19,000 places in United States having building permit systems]

STATE	HOUSING UNITS (1,000) 1994	1995 Total	1995 1 unit	VALUATION (mil. dol.) 1994	1995 Total	1995 1 unit	STATE	HOUSING UNITS (1,000) 1994	1995 Total	1995 1 unit	VALUATION (mil. dol.) 1994	1995 Total	1995 1 unit
U.S.	1,371.6	1,332.5	997.3	123,278	120,811	104,739	MO ...	26.4	24.3	19.0	2,149	2,033	1,818
							MT ...	3.0	3.1	1.7	233	224	160
AL ...	19.1	20.1	13.4	1,357	1,429	1,142	NE ...	7.9	8.2	5.2	574	570	471
AK ...	2.1	2.2	1.7	230	257	213	NV ...	31.1	32.8	22.5	2,185	2,738	2,246
AZ ...	51.8	52.7	39.9	5,075	5,133	4,431	NH ...	4.7	4.4	4.1	454	464	446
AR ...	12.4	11.7	7.3	795	766	614	NJ ...	25.4	21.5	18.3	2,318	1,947	1,815
CA ...	97.0	83.9	68.1	11,937	10,836	9,687	NM ...	11.5	11.0	8.6	969	899	800
CO ...	37.2	38.6	28.4	3,906	3,859	3,302	NY ...	31.1	28.1	19.9	2,787	2,616	2,189
CT ...	9.5	8.6	7.6	1,030	956	909	NC ...	62.9	60.9	47.7	5,277	5,275	4,774
DE ...	5.0	4.6	4.3	337	332	321	ND ...	3.4	3.2	1.5	211	201	141
DC ...	0.2	(Z)	(Z)	18	5	5	OH ...	47.2	44.8	32.6	4,799	4,375	3,901
FL ...	128.6	122.9	84.1	11,076	10,827	8,403	OK ...	9.5	10.1	7.8	903	878	794
GA ...	64.9	72.2	55.0	5,095	5,581	4,904	OR ...	24.1	26.2	15.4	2,276	2,492	1,945
HI ...	7.3	6.6	3.9	801	752	498	PA ...	40.2	36.3	32.0	3,728	3,318	3,124
ID ...	12.6	10.7	8.4	1,043	944	840	RI ...	2.5	2.3	2.1	233	214	203
IL ...	49.3	47.5	35.4	5,012	4,844	4,220	SC ...	24.6	24.0	19.3	2,019	1,984	1,784
IN ...	34.4	35.7	27.9	3,324	3,378	3,056	SD ...	4.6	3.8	2.2	288	258	189
IA ...	12.5	11.3	7.3	998	976	799	TN ...	31.9	35.1	27.7	2,539	2,838	2,581
KS ...	13.0	12.7	8.7	1,177	1,175	1,008	TX ...	102.6	105.1	70.4	8,098	8,324	7,066
KY ...	18.6	17.6	12.8	1,370	1,276	1,121	UT ...	18.6	20.9	15.2	1,717	1,870	1,564
LA ...	14.8	14.7	12.5	1,141	1,141	1,056	VT ...	2.4	2.3	2.0	205	205	190
ME ...	4.6	4.4	4.2	377	391	376	VA ...	46.8	43.1	34.7	3,965	3,658	3,354
MD ...	29.0	26.6	23.2	2,395	2,293	2,142	WA ...	44.0	38.2	26.8	4,018	3,578	2,918
MA ...	18.1	16.4	14.4	2,046	1,895	1,752	WV ...	3.9	3.7	2.9	283	261	232
MI ...	46.5	47.2	39.3	4,149	4,411	4,065	WI ...	34.6	32.4	20.7	2,917	2,727	2,177
MN ...	25.6	25.5	20.7	2,558	2,590	2,304	WY ...	2.0	1.7	1.4	210	168	155
MS ...	10.9	10.8	7.3	660	651	538							

Z Less than 50 units.

Source: U.S. Bureau of the Census, *Construction Reports,* series C40, annual.

No. 1178. New Privately-Owned Housing Units Started—Selected Characteristics: 1970 to 1995

[**In thousands.** For composition of regions, see table 27. See also *Historical Statistics, Colonial Times to 1970,* series N 156-163 and 170]

YEAR	Total units	STRUCTURES WITH— One unit	2 to 4 units	5 or more units	REGION North-east	Mid-west	South	West	CONDOMINIUM UNITS [1] Total	Single-family	Multi-family
1970	1,434	813	85	536	218	294	612	311	(NA)	(NA)	(NA)
1971	2,052	1,151	120	781	264	434	869	486	(NA)	(NA)	(NA)
1972	2,357	1,309	141	906	330	443	1,057	527	(NA)	(NA)	(NA)
1973	2,045	1,132	118	795	277	440	899	429	241	69	172
1974	1,338	888	68	382	183	317	553	285	175	46	130
1975	1,160	892	64	204	149	294	442	275	65	20	45
1976	1,538	1,162	86	289	169	400	569	400	95	30	64
1977	1,987	1,451	122	414	202	465	783	538	118	41	77
1978	2,020	1,433	125	462	200	451	824	545	156	42	114
1979	1,745	1,194	122	429	178	349	748	470	198	43	156
1980	1,292	852	110	331	125	218	643	306	186	35	150
1981	1,084	705	91	288	117	165	562	240	181	36	145
1982	1,062	663	80	320	117	149	591	205	170	40	130
1983	1,703	1,068	113	522	168	218	935	382	276	77	199
1984	1,750	1,084	121	544	204	243	866	436	291	96	194
1985	1,742	1,072	93	576	252	240	782	468	225	79	146
1986	1,805	1,179	84	542	294	296	733	483	214	80	134
1987	1,620	1,146	65	409	269	298	634	420	196	73	123
1988	1,488	1,081	59	348	235	274	575	404	148	53	95
1989	1,376	1,003	55	318	179	266	536	396	118	37	82
1990	1,193	895	37	260	131	253	479	329	75	22	53
1991	1,014	840	36	138	113	233	414	254	60	21	39
1992	1,200	1,030	31	139	127	288	497	288	74	35	40
1993	1,288	1,126	29	133	126	298	562	302	86	45	41
1994	1,457	1,198	35	224	138	329	639	351	96	48	48
1995	1,354	1,076	38	244	118	290	615	331	93	47	47

NA Not available. [1] Type of ownership under which the owners of the individual housing units are also joint owners of the common areas of the building or community. Includes a small number of cooperatively-owned units.

Source: U.S. Bureau of the Census, *Current Construction Reports,* series C20, monthly.

Construction and Housing

No. 1179. New Privately-Owned Housing Units Started, by State: 1992 to 1995

[In thousands of units]

REGION, DIVISION, AND STATE	1992	1993	1994	1995 Total units	1995 Single-family units	REGION, DIVISION, AND STATE	1992	1993	1994	1995 Total units	1995 Single-family units
U.S. ...	1,201.0	1,288.0	1,457.0	1,348.0	1,068.0	DC ...	0.2	0.3	0.2	0.2	0.1
Northeast..	126.7	125.0	137.4	129.0	107.3	VA ...	40.9	46.9	49.4	40.2	32.8
N.E.	39.5	38.9	42.1	42.3	36.8	WV ...	4.0	4.4	5.6	5.2	4.7
ME ...	5.0	4.4	4.8	4.7	4.4	NC ...	53.5	60.8	69.6	62.3	52.5
NH ...	4.2	4.2	4.6	5.1	4.2	SC ...	22.0	23.4	26.8	27.2	22.3
VT ...	2.5	2.5	2.5	2.7	2.2	GA ...	49.9	57.3	65.5	63.0	48.0
MA ...	16.2	16.7	18.1	17.5	15.6	FL ...	106.1	115.1	131.8	129.7	94.4
RI ...	2.6	2.5	2.5	2.6	2.3	E.S.C. ...	74.2	87.2	97.5	93.7	76.7
CT ...	8.8	8.5	9.5	9.7	8.1	KY ...	18.1	20.7	22.5	20.7	17.0
M.A.	87.2	86.1	95.3	86.7	70.5	TN ...	29.0	33.6	37.2	36.8	31.6
NY ...	29.1	24.9	29.9	25.7	18.5	AL ...	18.5	21.9	24.4	23.5	18.3
NJ ...	19.3	22.5	25.1	24.6	20.2	MS ...	8.6	11.1	13.4	12.7	9.8
PA ...	38.9	38.7	40.2	36.4	31.8	W.S.C. ...	108.6	130.1	155.4	144.0	111.1
Midwest...	290.6	297.9	328.2	289.2	228.2	AR ...	10.6	13.0	15.6	14.3	10.3
E.N.C.	202.2	205.2	228.9	205.2	165.0	LA ...	12.1	14.3	16.3	15.0	12.7
OH ...	47.8	48.8	52.4	46.6	37.5	OK ...	11.0	12.9	13.1	11.0	9.9
IN ...	35.5	35.7	40.2	36.0	31.4	TX	74.9	89.9	110.4	103.7	78.2
IL	42.3	45.9	51.4	42.9	33.2	West	288.2	301.8	352.6	334.5	264.3
MI	43.1	41.6	49.4	47.3	40.0	Mountain	114.9	140.7	173.8	166.1	130.4
WI ...	33.6	33.1	35.4	32.4	22.9	MT ...	3.3	3.7	4.0	3.1	2.5
W.N.C. ...	88.4	92.7	99.3	84.0	63.2	ID	11.8	13.1	14.0	10.0	8.4
MN ...	26.9	26.6	25.8	22.5	18.7	WY ...	1.6	2.1	2.2	2.0	1.9
IA ...	12.3	12.2	13.8	10.6	7.3	CO ...	25.6	32.4	39.4	39.0	29.5
MO ...	22.7	24.9	28.3	24.2	19.3	NM ...	6.3	7.8	10.1	10.5	8.9
ND ...	2.9	3.3	3.8	3.7	1.7	AZ ...	32.9	38.7	52.8	49.4	40.4
SD ...	3.8	4.3	4.8	4.1	2.5	UT ...	15.2	19.3	20.5	20.1	15.9
NE ...	8.3	8.8	9.0	8.6	5.2	NV ...	17.7	23.6	30.1	31.9	22.9
KS ...	11.6	12.5	13.7	10.3	8.5	Pacific ..	173.3	161.1	178.7	168.4	133.9
South	495.6	562.8	639.2	594.8	468.1	WA ...	40.4	41.1	44.4	43.4	32.0
S.A. ...	312.7	345.5	386.2	357.1	280.3	OR ...	19.7	21.6	24.6	24.7	18.3
DE ...	5.5	5.8	6.0	6.0	5.4	CA ...	105.1	90.3	100.9	91.7	77.5
MD ...	30.5	31.3	31.3	23.3	20.1	AK ...	1.6	2.1	2.2	2.0	1.7
						HI	6.6	6.0	6.7	6.6	4.4

Source: National Association of Home Builders, Economics, Mortgage Finance, and Housing Policy Division, *Forecast of Housing Activity.*

No. 1180. Characteristics of New Privately Owned One-Family Houses Completed: 1970 to 1995

[Percent distribution, except as indicated. Data beginning 1980 show percent distribution characteristics for all houses completed (includes new houses completed, houses built for sale completed, contractor-built and owner-built houses completed, and houses completed for rent). Data for 1970 cover contractor-built, owner-built, and houses for rent for year construction started and houses sold for year of sale. Percents exclude houses for which characteristics specified were not reported]

CHARACTERISTIC	1970	1980	1990	1994	1995	CHARACTERISTIC	1970	1980	1990	1994	1995
Total houses (1,000)....	793	957	966	1,160	1,066	Bedrooms...........	100	100	100	100	100
						2 or less.............	13	17	15	12	13
Financing	100	100	100	100	100	3.................	63	63	57	58	57
Mortgage	84	82	82	89	88	4 or more..........	24	20	29	30	30
FHA-insured	30	16	14	8	8	Bathrooms	100	100	100	100	100
VA-guaranteed	7	8	4	5	5	1 1/2 or less	52	27	13	11	11
Conventional	47	55	62	74	74	2.................	32	48	42	40	41
Farmers Home Administration	(1)	3	2	1	1	2 1/2 or more	16	25	45	49	48
Cash or equivalent....	16	18	18	11	12	Heating fuel	100	100	100	100	100
Floor area..........	100	100	100	100	100	Electricity	28	50	33	29	28
Under 1,200 sq. ft	36	21	11	9	10	Gas..............	62	41	59	67	67
1,200 to 1,599 sq. ft...	28	29	22	21	22	Oil...............	8	5	5	3	3
1,600 to 1,999 sq. ft...	16	22	22	24	23	Other.............	1	5	3	1	1
2,000 to 2,399 sq. ft...	21	13	17	18	17	Heating system	100	100	100	100	100
2,400 sq. ft. and over ..	(2)	15	29	29	28	Warm air furnace.....	71	57	65	67	67
Average (sq. ft.)......	1,500	1,740	2,080	2,100	2,095	Electric heat pump....	(NA)	18	23	24	25
Median (sq. ft.)	1,385	1,595	1,905	1,940	1,920	Other.............	29	19	12	9	9
Number of stories	100	100	100	100	100	Central air-conditioning .	100	100	100	100	100
1.................	74	60	46	49	49	With	34	63	76	79	80
2 or more	17	31	49	47	48	Without	66	37	24	21	20
Split level	10	8	4	3	3	Fireplaces...........	100	100	100	100	100
Foundation	100	100	100	100	100	No fireplace	65	43	34	36	37
Full or partial basement.	37	36	38	39	39	1 or more	35	56	66	64	63
Slab	36	45	40	41	42	Parking facilities	100	100	100	100	100
Crawl space	27	19	21	20	19	Garage	58	69	82	86	84
						Carport	17	7	2	2	2
						No garage or carport ..	25	24	16	13	14

NA Not available.   [1] Included with "Conventional" financing.   [2] Included with floor area of 2,000 to 2,399 square feet.

Source: U.S. Bureau of the Census and U.S. Dept. of Housing and Urban Development, *Current Construction Reports,* series C25, *Characteristics of New Housing,* annual.

No. 1181. Characteristics of New One-Family Houses Sold, by Metropolitan Area: 1992 to 1994

METROPOLITAN AREA	MEDIAN SALES PRICE (dollars)			AVERAGE SALES PRICE (dollars)			FINISHED FLOOR AREA — Average square footage (square feet)			FINISHED FLOOR AREA — Median square footage (square feet)			NUMBER OF HOUSES SOLD (1,000)			Detached housing		
	1992	1993	1994	1992	1993	1994	1992	1993	1994	1992	1993	1994	1992	1993	1994	1992	1993	1994
Atlanta, GA MSA [1]	101,600	118,200	123,900	129,100	140,700	146,300	2,180	2,260	2,250	1,940	2,120	2,115	23.8	27.8	27.9	23.4	27.5	27.5
Charlotte, Gastonia-Rock Hill, NC-SC MSA	98,600	115,100	117,100	116,400	132,900	135,500	1,960	2,150	2,065	1,740	1,945	2,000	6.7	7.8	7.5	6.7	7.7	7.2
Chicago-Gary-Kenosha, IL-IN-WI CMSA	200,700	159,500	171,900	216,900	183,400	203,200	2,445	2,155	2,170	2,425	2,020	2,025	14.1	18.9	20.0	11.6	14.4	16.6
Colorado Springs, CO MSA	129,700	138,600	139,300	143,500	147,500	149,900	2,605	2,390	2,210	2,210	2,210	2,085	2.6	3.0	2.7	2.5	2.7	2.5
Dallas-Fort Worth, TX CMSA [1]	121,300	123,000	121,400	137,000	137,000	145,300	2,500	2,425	2,440	2,380	2,325	2,265	18.9	19.2	19.7	18.8	19.2	19.6
Denver-Boulder-Greeley, CO CMSA [1]	148,900	174,600	186,500	168,800	187,800	208,200	2,270	2,250	2,290	2,110	2,225	2,165	9.8	11.9	11.7	9.6	11.3	11.0
Houston-Galveston-Brazoria, TX CMSA [1]	111,600	114,200	116,600	125,700	133,800	145,200	2,705	2,800	2,675	2,560	2,680	2,535	9.7	10.2	10.9	9.7	10.1	10.8
Jacksonville, FL MSA [1]	89,800	95,000	92,100	106,500	111,700	116,500	1,885	2,025	1,955	1,840	1,995	1,850	4.6	5.0	4.6	4.6	5.0	4.5
Kansas City, MO-KS MSA [1]	87,500	99,300	111,900	103,400	118,400	126,900	1,825	1,965	1,910	1,585	1,720	1,815	7.1	6.5	7.3	6.8	6.4	7.2
Las Vegas, NV-AZ MSA [1]	118,100	121,700	128,300	129,200	133,400	138,100	1,945	1,930	2,015	1,745	1,770	1,915	11.3	18.5	17.4	10.7	16.8	15.8
Los Angeles-Riverside-Orange County, CA CMSA	135,100	139,800	146,400	187,500	196,100	211,200	2,025	2,050	2,060	1,760	1,820	1,875	25.2	23.4	24.3	24.0	22.5	22.6
Miami-Fort Lauderdale, FL CMSA [1]	122,000	131,500	127,600	138,800	142,300	143,000	2,455	2,475	2,195	2,260	2,185	2,085	10.8	11.2	9.6	9.5	10.4	7.7
Minneapolis-St. Paul, MN-WI MSA [1]	133,500	155,600	152,600	155,100	173,800	173,900	1,945	2,000	1,920	1,880	2,030	1,820	11.9	10.6	9.6	10.4	8.8	8.7
New Orleans, LA MSA [1]	92,000	99,200	131,200	92,600	123,600	149,900	2,020	2,215	2,330	1,865	2,045	2,210	1.3	1.6	1.7	1.3	1.5	1.6
New York-Northern NJ-Long Island, NY-NJ-CT-PA, CMSA [1]	194,200	191,400	192,300	247,400	226,700	252,300	2,245	2,290	2,450	2,060	2,140	2,165	17.1	17.9	18.1	9.3	9.5	11.3
Norfolk-Virginia Beach- Newport News, VA-NC MSA [1]	113,800	120,200	127,200	128,800	129,600	140,900	2,220	2,195	2,275	2,165	2,245	2,260	6.7	6.0	5.2	5.7	4.9	4.3
Orlando, FL MSA [1]	105,800	107,500	108,000	129,300	122,800	127,100	2,165	1,925	1,965	1,935	1,725	1,795	8.2	10.5	10.2	8.0	10.5	9.7
Phoenix-Mesa, AZ MSA [1]	114,800	113,900	125,500	128,700	136,700	149,200	2,445	2,260	2,190	2,275	2,180	2,015	17.8	21.9	23.8	17.5	21.7	22.7
Sacramento-Yolo, CA CMSA	152,100	144,000	143,300	167,400	158,100	160,200	1,685	1,640	1,650	1,610	1,540	1,560	5.9	6.5	6.8	5.4	6.2	6.5
St. Louis, MO-IL MSA	129,100	144,500	144,400	155,500	153,900	166,500	2,195	2,080	2,175	1,995	1,995	2,090	4.5	6.9	6.0	4.5	6.7	5.6
Salt Lake City-Ogden, UT MSA [1]	83,800	100,300	100,000	114,300	119,500	119,800	1,740	1,765	1,695	1,400	1,545	1,545	5.2	3.0	5.0	5.2	6.5	5.0
San Antonio, TX MSA [1]	96,300	117,900	119,800	109,200	119,900	131,200	2,225	2,345	2,320	2,145	2,375	2,300	2.0	3.8	3.8	2.0	2.9	3.7
San Diego, CA MSA	234,400	225,000	212,800	239,700	246,000	237,600	2,335	2,410	2,320	2,200	2,375	2,245	4.1	3.8	5.1	4.1	3.5	4.8
Seattle-Tacoma-Bremerton, WA CMSA [1]	167,800	159,700	165,300	182,200	181,700	191,300	2,150	2,050	2,055	2,060	1,885	1,960	8.7	10.8	10.3	8.2	10.1	9.3
Tampa-St. Petersburg-Clearwater, FL MSA	109,600	113,700	126,300	120,100	126,100	132,700	2,250	2,325	2,400	2,135	2,240	2,260	7.2	8.4	8.2	6.2	7.6	7.2
Tucson, AZ MSA	106,800	106,600	131,900	125,200	123,400	152,800	1,990	1,900	2,000	1,875	1,810	1,870	3.3	3.8	4.2	3.0	3.5	3.9
Washington-Baltimore, DC-MD-VA CMSA [2]	(NA)	184,400	182,600	(NA)	205,500	207,800	(NA)	2,470	2,435	(NA)	2,305	2,270	26.0	31.1	28.3	15.9	19.3	16.7
Baltimore, MD PMSA	152,500	161,400	157,400	169,200	202,200	207,400	2,305	2,440	2,435	2,115	2,080	2,060	7.3	9.5	8.4	4.4	5.7	4.9
Washington, DC-MD-VA-WV PMSA [1]	185,100	196,500	197,500	211,300	207,000	207,900	2,425	2,480	2,435	2,285	2,395	2,365	18.7	21.2	19.5	11.5	13.4	11.6
West Palm Beach-Boca Raton, FL MSA	144,900	158,400	137,000	(S)	178,300	165,200	2,500	2,305	2,205	2,210	2,150	2,050	4.4	5.6	3.5	3.8	4.6	3.3

NA Not available.   S Withheld because estimate did not meet publication standards.   [1] Beginning 1993, data reflect the new metropolitan area definition.   [2] This is a newly created CMSA. Data prior to 1993 are not available.

Source: U.S. Bureau of the Census, *Current Construction Reports*, series C21.

No. 1182. New Privately Owned One-Family Houses Sold, by Region and Type of Financing, 1980 to 1995, and by Sales-Price Group, 1995

[In thousands. Based on a national probability sample of monthly interviews with builders or owners of one-family houses for which building permits have been issued or, for nonpermit areas, on which construction has started. For details, see source. For composition of regions, see table 27]

YEAR AND SALES-PRICE GROUP	Total sales	REGION				FINANCING TYPE			
		North-east	Midwest	South	West	Conven-tional	FHA and VA	Farmers Home Admin.	Cash
1980	545	50	81	267	145	302	196	14	32
1981	436	46	60	219	112	244	142	14	36
1982	412	47	48	219	99	193	173	11	34
1983	623	76	71	323	152	350	217	8	49
1984	639	94	76	309	160	423	149	9	58
1985	688	112	82	323	170	403	208	11	64
1986	750	136	96	322	196	411	268	12	59
1987	671	117	97	271	186	408	190	8	64
1988	676	101	97	276	202	437	171	6	62
1989	650	86	102	260	202	416	162	14	58
1990	534	71	89	225	149	337	138	10	50
1991	509	57	93	215	144	329	128	9	43
1992	610	65	116	259	170	428	134	7	41
1993	666	60	123	295	188	476	147	6	37
1994	670	61	123	295	191	490	130	9	41
1995	667	55	125	300	187	490	128	9	39
Under $80,000	58	2	6	42	8	24	25	6	3
$80,000 to $119,999	200	8	41	98	53	114	69	2	14
$120,000 to $149,999	144	9	27	63	44	111	24	(B)	8
$150,000 to $199,999	127	13	25	49	40	110	9	(B)	8
$200,000 and over	138	23	26	47	42	131	(B)	(B)	6

B Withheld because estimate did not meet publication standards on the basis of sample size.
Source: U.S. Bureau of the Census and U.S. Dept. of Housing and Urban Development, *Current Construction Reports*, series C25, *Characteristics of New Housing*, annual; and *New One-Family Houses Sold*, monthly.

No. 1183. Median Sales Price of New Privately Owned One-Family Houses Sold, by Region: 1980 to 1995

[In dollars. For definition of median, see Guide to Tabular Presentation. For composition of regions, see table 27]

YEAR	U.S.	North-east	Midwest	South	West	YEAR	U.S.	North-east	Midwest	South	West
1980	64,600	69,500	63,400	59,600	72,300	1988	112,500	149,000	101,600	92,000	126,500
1981	68,900	76,000	65,900	64,400	77,800	1989	120,000	159,600	108,800	96,400	139,000
1982	69,300	78,200	68,900	66,100	75,000	1990	122,900	159,000	107,900	99,000	147,500
1983	75,300	82,200	79,500	70,900	80,100	1991	120,000	155,900	110,000	100,000	141,100
1984	79,900	88,600	85,400	72,000	87,300	1992	121,500	169,000	115,600	105,500	130,400
1985	84,300	103,300	80,300	75,000	92,600	1993	126,500	162,600	125,000	115,000	135,000
1986	92,000	125,000	88,300	80,200	95,700	1994	130,000	169,000	132,900	116,900	140,400
1987	104,500	140,000	95,000	88,000	111,000	1995	133,900	180,000	134,000	124,500	141,400

Source: U.S. Bureau of the Census and U.S. Dept. of Housing and Urban Development, *Current Construction Reports*, series C25, *Characteristics of New Housing*, annual; and *New One-Family Houses Sold*, monthly.

No. 1184. New Mobile Homes Placed for Residential Use and Average Sales Price, by Region: 1980 to 1995

[A mobile home is a moveable dwelling, 10 feet or more wide and 35 feet or more long, designed to be towed on its own chassis and without need of a permanent foundation. Excluded are travel trailers, motor homes, and modular housing. Data are based on a probability sample and subject to sampling variability; see source. For composition of regions, see table 27]

YEAR	UNITS PLACED (1,000)					AVERAGE SALES PRICE (dol.)				
	Total	North-east	Mid-west	South	West	U.S.	North-east	Mid-west	South	West
1980	233.7	12.3	32.3	140.3	48.7	19,800	18,500	18,600	18,200	25,400
1981	229.2	12.0	30.1	143.5	43.6	19,900	19,000	18,900	18,400	25,600
1982	234.1	12.4	25.6	161.1	35.0	19,700	19,800	18,500	18,500	24,700
1983	278.1	16.3	34.3	186.0	41.4	21,000	21,400	20,400	19,700	27,000
1984	287.9	19.8	35.2	193.4	39.4	21,500	22,200	21,100	20,200	27,400
1985	283.4	20.2	38.6	187.6	36.9	21,800	22,700	21,500	20,400	28,700
1986	256.1	21.2	37.2	162.3	35.4	22,400	24,400	21,800	20,700	29,900
1987	239.2	23.6	40.0	145.5	30.1	23,700	25,600	23,700	21,900	31,000
1988	224.3	22.7	39.1	130.7	31.8	25,100	27,000	24,600	22,700	33,900
1989	202.8	20.2	39.1	112.8	30.6	27,200	30,200	26,700	24,100	37,800
1990	195.4	18.8	37.7	108.4	30.6	27,800	30,000	27,000	24,500	39,300
1991	174.3	14.3	35.4	97.6	27.0	27,700	30,400	27,600	24,500	38,600
1992	212.0	15.0	42.2	124.4	30.4	28,400	30,900	28,800	25,400	39,000
1993	242.5	15.4	44.5	146.7	35.9	30,500	32,000	31,400	27,700	40,500
1994	286.1	16.2	53.0	174.4	42.5	33,500	33,900	34,600	30,500	44,600
1995	306.1	14.4	55.5	195.2	41.0	36,300	37,500	36,700	33,900	46,900

Source: U.S. Bureau of the Census, *Current Construction Reports*, series C20.

No. 1185. Existing One-Family Houses Sold and Price, by Region: 1970 to 1995

[Based on data (adjusted and aggregated to regional and national totals) reported by participating real estate multiple listing service. For definition of median, see Guide to Tabular Presentation. For composition of regions, see table 27]

YEAR	HOUSES SOLD (1,000)					MEDIAN SALES PRICE (dol.)				
	Total	North-east	Mid-west	South	West	Total	North-east	Mid-west	South	West
1970	1,612	251	501	568	292	23,000	25,200	20,100	22,200	24,300
1971	2,018	311	583	735	389	24,800	27,100	22,100	24,300	26,500
1972	2,252	361	630	788	473	26,700	29,800	23,900	26,400	28,400
1973	2,334	367	674	847	446	28,900	32,800	25,300	29,000	31,000
1974	2,272	354	645	839	434	32,000	35,800	27,700	32,300	34,800
1975	2,476	370	701	862	543	35,300	39,300	30,100	34,800	39,600
1976	3,064	439	881	1,033	712	38,100	41,800	32,900	36,500	46,100
1977	3,650	515	1,101	1,231	803	42,900	44,400	36,700	39,800	57,300
1978	3,986	516	1,144	1,416	911	48,700	47,900	42,200	45,100	66,700
1979	3,827	526	1,061	1,353	887	55,700	53,600	47,800	51,300	77,400
1980	2,973	403	806	1,092	672	62,200	60,800	51,900	58,300	89,300
1981	2,419	353	632	917	516	66,400	63,700	54,300	64,400	96,200
1982	1,990	354	490	780	366	67,800	63,500	55,100	67,100	98,900
1983	2,697	477	692	1,004	524	70,300	72,200	56,600	69,200	94,900
1984	2,829	478	720	1,006	624	72,400	78,700	57,100	71,300	95,800
1985	3,134	561	806	1,063	704	75,500	88,900	58,900	75,200	95,400
1986	3,474	635	922	1,145	773	80,300	104,800	63,500	78,200	100,900
1987	3,436	618	892	1,163	763	85,600	133,300	66,000	80,400	113,200
1988	3,513	606	865	1,224	817	89,300	143,000	68,400	82,200	124,900
1989	3,346	531	855	1,185	775	93,100	145,200	71,300	84,500	139,900
1990	3,211	469	831	1,202	709	95,500	141,200	74,000	85,900	139,600
1991	3,220	479	840	1,199	702	100,300	141,900	77,800	88,900	147,200
1992	3,520	534	939	1,292	755	103,700	140,000	81,700	92,100	143,800
1993	3,802	571	1,007	1,416	808	106,800	139,500	85,200	95,000	142,600
1994	3,946	592	1,027	1,464	863	109,800	139,100	87,900	96,000	146,700
1995	3,802	575	992	1,429	806	112,900	136,900	93,600	97,700	147,200

Source: National Association of REALTORS, Washington, DC, *Real Estate Outlook: Market Trends & Insights* (copyright).

No. 1186. Median Sales Price of Existing One-Family Homes, by Selected Metropolitan Area: 1990 to 1995

[**In thousands of dollars.** Areas are metropolitan statistical areas (MSA's) except as indicated; for definitions and components, see Appendix II]

METROPOLITAN AREA	1990	1993	1994	1995	METROPOLITAN AREA	1990	1993	1994	1995
U.S., all areas.	95.5	106.8	109.8	112.9	Memphis, TN-AR-MS.	78.1	87.0	86.3	86.5
Albany-Schenectady-Troy, NY. . .	106.9	112.3	112.0	105.9	Miami-Hialeah, FL PMSA	89.3	98.8	103.2	107.1
Anaheim-Santa Ana, CA MSA. . .	242.4	217.2	211.0	208.8	Milwaukee, WI PMSA	84.4	104.1	109.0	114.7
Atlanta, GA	(NA)	91.8	93.6	97.5	Minneapolis-St. Paul, MN-WI . . .	88.7	98.2	101.5	106.8
Baltimore, MD	105.9	115.7	115.4	111.3	Nashville, TN.	81.8	90.4	96.5	107.3
Birmingham, AL	80.8	96.5	100.2	103.6	New Orleans, LA	67.8	76.8	76.9	78.0
Boston, MA PMSA	174.1	173.2	179.3	179.0	New York-Northern New Jersey-				
Buffalo-Niagara Falls, NY CMSA .	77.2	83.5	82.3	81.3	Long Island, NY-NJ-CT CMSA. .	174.9	173.2	173.2	169.7
Charlotte-Gastonia-Rock Hill,					Oklahoma City, OK	53.2	64.9	66.7	70.4
NC-SC	93.1	106.1	106.5	107.8	Orlando, FL.	82.8	90.1	90.7	89.2
Chicago, IL PMSA	116.8	142.0	144.1	147.9	Philadelphia, PA-NJ PMSA	108.7	118.0	119.5	118.7
Cincinnati, OH-KY-IN PMSA	79.8	91.4	96.5	100.4	Phoenix, AZ.	84.0	89.1	91.4	96.8
Cleveland, OH PMSA	80.6	95.0	98.5	104.7	Pittsburgh, PA PMSA.	70.1	82.2	80.7	82.1
Columbus, OH	81.6	91.8	94.8	99.1	Portland, OR PMSA	79.5	106.0	116.9	128.4
Dallas, TX PMSA	89.5	94.5	95.0	96.4	Richmond-Petersburg VA	87.5	94.1	95.4	103.1
Denver, CO PMSA	86.4	104.7	116.8	127.3	Riverside/San Bernardino, CA				
Detroit, MI PMSA	76.7	86.0	87.0	98.2	PMSA.	132.1	134.4	129.1	120.9
Ft. Lauderdale-Hollywood-					Rochester, NY	79.8	84.8	85.6	85.0
Pompano Beach, FL PMSA . . .	92.6	103.1	103.1	105.9	St. Louis, MO-IL	76.7	84.8	85.0	87.7
Ft. Worth-Arlington TX PMSA . . .	76.7	82.9	82.5	83.7	Sacramento, CA.	137.5	129.2	124.5	120.2
Hartford, CT PMSA.	157.3	135.3	133.4	133.4	Salt Lake City-Ogden, UT.	69.4	84.9	98.0	113.7
Honolulu, HI.	352.0	358.5	360.0	349.0	San Antonio, TX	63.6	77.0	78.2	80.8
Houston, TX PMSA	70.7	80.9	80.5	79.2	San Diego, CA.	183.2	176.9	176.0	171.6
Indianapolis, IN	74.8	86.6	90.7	94.6	San Francisco, CA PMSA.	259.3	254.4	255.6	254.4
Jacksonville, FL	72.4	77.1	81.9	83.1	Seattle-Tacoma, WA CMSA	142.0	150.2	155.9	159.0
Kansas City, MO-KS	74.1	83.6	87.1	91.7	Tampa-St. Petersburg-				
Las Vegas, NV.	93.0	108.2	110.5	113.5	Clearwater, FL	71.4	75.0	76.2	78.3
Los Angeles-Long Beach, CA					Washington, DC-MD-VA.	150.5	158.3	157.9	156.5
PMSA.	212.1	195.4	189.1	179.9	West Palm Beach-Boca Raton-				
Louisville, KY-IN	60.8	74.5	80.5	86.4	Delray Beach, FL	108.0	114.6	117.6	121.3

NA Not available.
Source: National Association of REALTORS, Washington, DC, *Real Estate Outlook: Market Trends & Insights* (copyright).

No. 1187. Existing Home Sales, by State: 1990 to 1995

[In thousands]

STATE	1990	1992	1993	1994	1995	STATE	1990	1992	1993	1994	1995
United States [1]...	**3,211**	**3,520**	**4,203**	**4,383**	**4,230**	Missouri	84.1	98.8	106.4	110.2	108.3
Alabama	61.1	72.5	77.9	77.4	74.6	Montana	12.7	16.6	16.2	15.6	14.8
Alaska	(NA)	(NA)	(NA)	(NA)	(NA)	Nebraska	19.3	22.4	23.2	23.3	21.0
Arizona	86.3	89.8	107.9	123.8	122.0	Nevada	26.2	25.6	30.5	32.9	31.9
Arkansas	44.8	47.8	52.8	52.3	55.3	New Hampshire	7.9	12.0	13.6	16.2	0.0
California [2]	452.1	427.3	435.0	482.6	425.4	New Jersey	114.8	132.1	139.0	145.4	138.3
Colorado	54.2	71.4	82.1	80.6	76.9	New Mexico	23.6	29.2	31.0	30.4	28.9
Connecticut	34.3	40.0	45.9	49.8	51.4	New York	125.5	136.3	143.0	156.3	150.4
Delaware	9.7	10.0	9.4	10.4	10.3	North Carolina	135.9	160.2	185.0	204.1	200.1
District of Columbia	13.1	12.4	12.3	12.3	11.7	North Dakota	10.4	11.9	11.8	10.9	10.6
Florida	183.3	179.2	208.9	229.7	220.8	Ohio	151.6	167.4	179.1	186.4	181.4
Georgia	73.2	(NA)	(NA)	(NA)	(NA)	Oklahoma	53.4	57.6	61.5	59.7	58.1
Hawaii	19.2	11.6	12.5	13.1	10.0	Oregon	56.6	52.5	58.8	58.1	57.7
Idaho	18.1	21.6	23.4	23.1	22.8	Pennsylvania	182.7	204.4	216.1	216.4	217.2
Illinois	160.9	186.2	193.9	188.4	181.2	Rhode Island	7.8	10.0	11.0	11.6	11.9
Indiana	80.1	84.8	100.8	103.3	100.3	South Carolina	57.8	58.9	62.2	67.3	69.1
Iowa	51.9	53.1	53.5	54.3	51.3	South Dakota	11.6	12.7	13.7	13.2	13.2
Kansas	38.8	46.2	53.7	55.7	54.2	Tennessee	92.7	102.2	120.5	129.8	133.2
Kentucky	66.4	78.7	83.3	81.1	78.2	Texas	240.0	242.7	258.8	266.9	260.2
Louisiana	41.6	47.0	49.3	51.4	50.1	Utah	22.1	31.5	31.2	32.4	33.8
Maine	(NA)	10.3	11.6	13.0	0.0	Vermont	6.1	9.5	11.0	10.9	9.0
Maryland	67.1	69.0	73.4	69.5	59.2	Virginia	96.9	101.3	104.2	99.5	94.0
Massachusetts	44.0	57.6	66.0	68.7	68.1	Washington	87.7	91.3	97.0	101.2	95.5
Michigan	145.0	157.3	170.6	184.2	176.3	West Virginia	42.0	46.8	45.7	45.8	44.5
Minnesota	64.8	75.7	81.8	82.1	78.5	Wisconsin	71.7	91.5	94.6	94.3	93.2
Mississippi	34.7	39.2	43.6	43.5	43.8	Wyoming	7.4	9.9	10.9	11.0	10.5

NA Not available.   [1] U.S. totals are derived independently and therefore are not equal to the sum of the States.   [2] Provided by the California Association of Realtors.

Source: National Association of REALTORS, Washington, DC, *Real Estate Outlook: Market Trends & Insights* (copyright).

No. 1188. New Apartments Completed and Rented in 3 Months, by Region: 1980 to 1994

[Structures with five or more units, privately financed, nonsubsidized, unfurnished apartments. Based on sample and subject to sampling variability. For composition of regions, see table 27]

YEAR AND RENT	NUMBER (1,000)					PERCENT RENTED IN 3 MONTHS				
	U.S.	North-east	Mid-west	South	West	U.S.	North-east	Mid-west	South	West
1980	196.1	14.2	43.8	91.5	46.6	75	77	77	74	75
1981	135.3	4.9	36.9	68.4	25.1	80	85	86	78	75
1982	117.0	4.6	21.9	66.8	23.7	72	74	79	70	72
1983	191.5	3.5	41.1	115.1	31.8	69	73	86	63	69
1984	313.2	3.8	41.2	194.4	73.9	67	64	79	63	70
1985	365.2	8.1	54.0	166.1	137.0	65	69	72	59	68
1986	407.6	16.9	64.5	171.7	154.5	66	70	70	62	67
1987	345.6	11.3	66.0	124.5	143.9	63	73	65	59	64
1988	284.5	8.7	60.4	91.7	123.8	66	52	73	58	69
1989	247.8	13.4	45.8	86.3	102.3	70	74	74	68	69
1990	214.3	12.7	44.3	77.2	80.0	67	66	75	64	65
1991	165.3	6.8	37.9	63.6	57.0	70	83	78	65	68
1992	110.2	10.9	34.0	37.4	28.0	74	75	80	72	70
1993	77.2	3.7	25.3	27.7	20.5	75	37	81	76	73
1994	**104.0**	**3.7**	**32.2**	**44.5**	**23.6**	**80**	**96**	**78**	**78**	**85**
Less than $350	6.7	0.1	2.0	3.6	1.0	81	95	90	74	89
$350-$549	39.5	0.7	14.5	16.2	8.1	79	95	75	78	86
$350-$449	14.5	0.7	3.8	6.1	3.9	83	99	78	83	87
$450-$549	25.1	(Z)	10.7	10.1	4.2	76	(Z)	74	75	85
$550-$749	37.1	2.6	14.2	12.5	7.8	83	97	80	82	87
$550-$649	21.9	1.6	8.9	7.6	3.7	83	100	80	81	84
$650-$749	15.2	1.0	5.3	4.8	4.1	84	93	80	82	90
$750 or more	20.7	0.2	1.5	12.3	6.7	79	90	70	78	82
Median asking rent	$576	$614	$546	$582	$621	(X)	(X)	(X)	(X)	(X)

X Not applicable.   Z Less than 50 units.

Source: U.S. Bureau of the Census, *Current Housing Reports*, series H130 and H131, and unpublished data.

No. 1189. Housing Units—Historical Trends for Selected Characteristics: 1950 to 1993

[As of **April 1**, except **1993**, as of **fall**. Based on the Census of Population and Housing and American Housing Survey; see Appendix III]

CHARACTERISTIC	NUMBER OF UNITS						PERCENT DISTRIBUTION					
	1950	1960	1970	1980	1990	1993	1950	1960	1970	1980	1990	1993
UNITS IN STRUCTURE												
All housing units [1]	45,983	58,315	67,699	86,759	102,264	106,611	100.0	100.0	100.0	100.0	100.0	100.0
1 detached	29,116	40,103	44,801	53,596	60,383	64,283	63.3	68.8	66.2	61.8	59.0	60.3
1 attached	[2]2,799	3,655	1,990	3,587	5,378	6,079	[2]6.1	6.3	2.9	4.1	5.3	5.7
2	5,302	4,464	5,444	5,309	4,948	[3]	11.5	7.7	8.0	6.1	4.8	[3]
3 or 4	3,374	3,088	3,563	4,373	4,928	[3] 10,732	7.3	5.3	5.3	5.0	4.8	[3]10.1
5 or more	5,078	6,238	9,829	15,478	18,105	18,444	11.0	10.7	14.5	17.8	17.7	17.3
Mobile home or trailer	315	767	2,073	4,416	7,400	7,072	0.7	1.3	3.1	5.1	7.2	6.6
Other	(NA)	(NA)	(NA)	(NA)	1,121	(NA)	(NA)	(NA)	(NA)	(NA)	1.1	(NA)
PLUMBING FACILITIES												
All housing units [1]	44,502	58,315	67,657	86,693	102,264	106,611	100.0	100.0	100.0	100.0	100.0	100.0
Complete plumbing facilities .	28,729	48,537	62,984	84,359	101,162	104,302	64.6	83.2	93.1	97.3	98.9	97.8
Lacking complete plumbing facilities	15,773	9,778	4,672	2,334	1,102	1,854	35.4	16.8	6.9	2.7	1.1	1.7
Not reported	1,481	(NA)	(NA)	(NA)	(NA)	(NA)	(X)	(NA)	(NA)	(NA)	(NA)	(NA)
TELEPHONE IN HOUSING UNIT [4]												
Occupied housing units .	41,829	53,024	63,450	80,390	91,947	94,724	(NA)	100.0	100.0	100.0	100.0	100.0
With telephone	(NA)	41,618	55,177	74,720	87,130	88,442	(NA)	78.5	87.0	92.9	94.8	93.4
No telephone	(NA)	11,406	8,273	5,670	4,817	6,282	(NA)	21.5	13.0	7.1	5.2	6.6

NA Not available.   X Not applicable.   [1] Data for 1970 and 1980 are "Year-round housing units," which exclude seasonal and migratory vacant units.   [2] Includes 1,588,902 units classified as "1 and 2 dwelling unit."   [3] Structures with "2 units" included with units of "3 or 4."   [4] Beginning 1980, data are not completely comparable with earlier years due to change in question asked.
Source: U.S. Bureau of the Census, *1990 Census of Housing*, series CH-1, and earlier census reports; and *Current Housing Reports*, series H150/93, American Housing Survey in the United States.

No. 1190. Occupied Housing Units—Tenure, by Race of Householder: 1920 to 1993

[In thousands, except as indicated. As of **April 1**, except **1991**, as of **fall**. Prior to 1960, excludes Alaska and Hawaii. Statistics on the number of occupied units are essentially comparable although identified by various terms. See also *Historical Statistics, Colonial Times to 1970*, series N 238-245]

RACE AND TENURE	1920	1930	1940	1950	1960	1970	1980	1990	1993
ALL RACES									
Occupied units, total	24,352	29,905	34,855	42,826	53,024	63,445	80,390	91,947	94,724
Owner occupied	11,114	14,280	15,196	23,560	32,797	39,886	51,795	59,025	61,252
Percent of occupied	45.6	47.8	43.6	55.0	61.9	62.9	64.4	64.2	64.7
Renter occupied	13,238	15,624	19,659	19,266	20,227	23,560	28,595	32,923	33,472
WHITE									
Occupied units, total	21,826	26,983	31,561	39,044	47,880	56,606	68,810	76,880	80,029
Owner occupied	10,511	13,544	14,418	22,241	30,823	37,005	46,671	52,433	54,878
Percent of occupied	48.2	50.2	45.7	57.0	64.4	65.4	67.8	68.2	68.6
Renter occupied	11,315	13,439	17,143	16,803	17,057	19,601	22,139	24,447	25,151
BLACK AND OTHER									
Occupied units, total	2,526	2,922	3,293	3,783	5,144	6,839	11,580	15,067	14,695
Owner occupied	603	737	778	1,319	1,974	2,881	5,124	6,592	6,374
Percent of occupied	23.9	25.2	23.6	34.9	38.4	42.1	44.2	43.8	43.4
Renter occupied	1,923	2,185	2,516	2,464	3,170	3,959	6,456	8,475	8,321

Source: U.S. Bureau of the Census, *Census of Housing: 1960*, vol. 1; *1970*, vol. 1; *1980 Census of Housing*, vol. 1, chapter A (HC80-1-A); and *1990 Census of Housing, General Housing Characteristics*, series CH-90-1; 1993 data, *Current Housing Reports*, series H150/93, American Housing Survey in the United States.

No. 1191. Occupied Housing Units—Tenure, by Race and Hispanic Origin of Householder: 1980 and 1990

[As of **April 1**. Based on the Census of Population and Housing; see Appendix III]

RACE AND HISPANIC ORIGIN OF HOUSEHOLDER	ALL HOUSEHOLDS			OWNER OCCUPIED		PERCENT OWNER OCCUPIED		RENTER OCCUPIED	
	1980	1990	Percent change, 1980-1990	1980	1990	1980	1990	1980	1990
Total units	80,389,673	91,947,410	14.4	51,794,545	59,024,811	64.4	64.2	28,595,128	32,922,599
White	68,810,123	76,880,105	11.7	46,670,775	52,432,648	67.8	68.2	22,139,348	24,447,457
Black	8,381,668	9,976,161	19.0	3,724,251	4,327,265	44.4	43.4	4,657,417	5,648,896
American Indian, Eskimo, or Aleut	397,252	591,372	48.9	212,209	318,001	53.4	53.8	185,043	273,371
Asian or Pacific Islander .	993,182	2,013,735	102.7	521,230	1,050,182	52.5	52.2	472,228	963,553
Other race	1,807,172	2,486,037	37.6	666,080	896,715	36.9	36.1	1,141,092	1,589,322
Hispanic origin [1]	4,007,896	6,001,718	49.7	1,738,920	2,545,584	43.4	42.4	2,268,976	3,456,134

[1] Persons of Hispanic origin may be of any race.
U.S. Bureau of the Census, *1980 Census of Housing*, vol. 1, chapter A (HC80-1-A); and *1990 Census of Housing, General Housing Characteristics*, series CH-90-1.

No. 1192. Homeownership Rates, by Age of Householder: 1985 to 1995

[**In percent**. Represents the proportion of households that are owners or the number of owner occupied households divided by the total number of households]

AGE	1985	1986	1987	1988	1989	1990	1991	1992	1993[1]	1994	1995
United States	63.9	63.8	64.0	63.8	63.9	63.9	64.1	64.1	64.0	64.0	64.7
Less than 25 yrs. old	17.2	17.2	16.0	15.8	16.6	15.7	15.3	14.9	14.8	14.9	15.9
25 to 29 yrs. old	37.7	36.7	36.4	35.9	35.3	35.2	33.8	33.6	33.6	34.1	34.4
30 to 34 yrs. old	54.0	53.6	53.5	53.2	53.2	51.8	51.2	50.5	50.8	50.6	53.1
35 to 39 yrs. old	65.4	64.8	64.1	63.6	63.4	63.0	62.2	61.4	61.8	61.2	62.1
40 to 44 yrs. old	71.4	70.5	70.8	70.7	70.2	69.8	69.5	69.1	68.6	68.2	68.6
45 to 49 yrs. old	74.3	74.1	74.6	74.4	74.1	73.9	73.7	74.2	73.7	73.8	73.7
50 to 54 yrs. old	77.5	78.1	77.8	77.1	77.2	76.8	76.1	76.2	77.2	76.8	77.0
55 to 59 yrs. old	79.2	80.0	80.0	79.3	79.1	78.8	79.5	79.3	78.9	78.4	78.8
60 to 64 yrs. old	79.9	79.8	80.4	79.8	80.1	79.8	80.5	81.2	80.9	80.1	80.3
65 to 69 yrs. old	79.5	79.4	79.5	80.0	80.0	80.0	81.4	80.8	80.7	80.6	81.0
70 to 74 yrs. old	76.8	77.2	77.7	77.7	77.8	78.4	78.8	79.0	79.9	80.1	80.9
75 yrs. old and over	69.8	70.0	70.8	70.8	71.2	72.3	73.1	73.3	73.4	73.5	74.6

[1] Based on 1990 census controls.

Source: Bureau of the Census, *Current Housing Reports*, series H111/95.

No. 1193. Homeownership Rates, by State: 1984 to 1995

[**In percent**. See headnote, table 1192]

STATE	1984	1990	1993	1994	1995	STATE	1984	1990	1993	1994	1995
United States	64.5	64.1	64.0	64.0	64.7	Missouri	69.5	64.2	66.4	68.4	69.4
Alabama	73.7	69.9	70.2	68.5	70.1	Montana	66.4	69.6	69.7	68.8	68.7
Alaska	57.6	57.1	55.4	58.8	60.9	Nebraska	69.3	67.5	67.7	68.0	67.1
Arizona	65.2	66.3	69.1	67.7	62.9	Nevada	58.9	55.8	55.8	55.8	58.6
Arkansas	65.9	68.6	70.5	68.1	67.2	New Hampshire	67.1	66.8	65.4	65.1	66.0
California	53.7	54.5	56.0	55.5	55.4	New Jersey	63.4	64.8	64.5	64.1	64.9
Colorado	64.7	59.8	61.8	62.9	64.6	New Mexico	68.0	69.5	69.1	66.8	67.0
Connecticut	67.8	65.5	64.5	63.8	68.2	New York	51.1	52.6	52.8	52.5	52.7
Delaware	70.4	70.2	74.1	70.5	71.7	North Carolina	68.8	69.3	68.8	68.7	70.1
Dist. of Columbia	37.3	35.1	35.7	37.8	38.2	North Dakota	70.1	65.4	62.7	63.3	67.3
Florida	66.5	66.1	65.5	65.7	66.6	Ohio	67.7	68.7	68.5	67.4	67.9
Georgia	63.6	65.7	66.5	63.4	66.6	Oklahoma	71.0	69.2	70.3	68.5	69.8
Hawaii	50.7	55.2	52.8	52.3	50.2	Oregon	61.9	65.2	63.8	63.9	63.2
Idaho	69.7	68.4	72.1	70.7	72.0	Pennsylvania	71.1	74.0	72.0	71.8	71.5
Illinois	62.4	63.0	61.8	64.2	66.4	Rhode Island	60.9	58.2	57.6	56.5	57.9
Indiana	69.9	66.1	68.7	68.4	71.0	South Carolina	69.1	73.1	71.1	72.0	71.3
Iowa	71.3	68.4	68.2	70.1	71.4	South Dakota	69.6	66.1	65.6	66.4	67.5
Kansas	72.7	69.7	68.9	69.0	67.5	Tennessee	67.6	68.0	64.1	65.2	67.0
Kentucky	70.2	67.2	68.8	70.6	71.2	Texas	62.5	59.0	58.7	59.7	61.4
Louisiana	70.1	68.9	65.4	65.8	65.3	Utah	69.9	70.7	68.9	69.3	71.5
Maine	74.1	72.0	71.9	72.6	76.7	Vermont	66.9	70.8	68.5	69.4	70.4
Maryland	67.8	63.8	65.5	64.1	65.8	Virginia	68.3	68.9	68.5	69.3	68.1
Massachusetts	61.7	60.2	60.7	60.6	60.2	Washington	65.7	61.8	63.1	62.4	61.6
Michigan	72.7	70.6	72.3	72.0	72.2	West Virginia	72.0	72.4	73.3	73.7	73.1
Minnesota	72.6	68.9	65.8	68.9	73.3	Wisconsin	65.2	68.9	65.7	64.2	67.5
Mississippi	72.3	71.8	69.7	69.2	71.1	Wyoming	68.8	68.7	67.1	65.8	69.0

Source: U.S. Bureau of the Census, *Current Housing Reports*, series H111/95-A.

No. 1194. Housing Units—Summary of Characteristics and Equipment, by Tenure and Region: 1993

[**In thousands of units, except as indicated.** Based on the American Housing Survey; see Appendix III. For composition of regions, see table 27]

ITEM	Total housing units	Sea-sonal	YEAR-ROUND UNITS							Vacant
			Occupied							
			Total	Owner	Renter	North-east	Mid-west	South	West	
Total units.	**106,611**	**3,088**	**94,724**	**61,252**	**33,472**	**18,906**	**23,031**	**32,936**	**19,850**	**8,799**
Percent distribution.	100.0	2.9	88.9	57.5	31.4	17.7	21.6	30.9	18.6	8.3
Units in structure:										
Single family detached.	64,283	1,808	58,918	50,490	8,428	9,749	15,411	21,668	12,091	3,557
Single family attached	6,079	114	5,375	2,824	2,550	1,535	970	1,779	1,091	591
2 to 4 units	10,732	127	9,279	1,774	7,505	3,099	2,353	2,073	1,754	1,327
5 to 9 units	5,521	76	4,724	409	4,315	923	1,054	1,605	1,142	721
10 to 19 units.	5,025	102	4,190	359	3,831	735	846	1,597	1,011	733
20 to 49 units.	3,826	107	3,154	335	2,819	886	611	755	902	566
50 or more units.	4,072	93	3,429	579	2,850	1,432	676	692	628	551
Mobile home or trailer	7,072	663	5,655	4,482	1,173	547	1,110	2,766	1,232	754
Stories in structure: [1]										
One story	2,807	32	2,424	266	2,158	82	387	1,156	799	350
2 stories	10,742	173	9,101	976	8,125	1,009	1,328	3,627	3,137	1,469
3 stories	8,373	166	7,137	1,204	5,934	2,432	2,564	1,204	937	1,070
4 to 6 stories	4,543	61	3,829	595	3,234	2,125	895	407	402	652
7 or more stories	2,721	72	2,294	420	1,873	1,429	366	330	169	356
Foundation: [2]										
Full or partial basement	31,516	344	29,910	26,280	3,630	9,662	12,478	4,902	2,869	1,262
Crawlspace	18,774	761	16,564	13,026	3,538	625	2,218	8,946	4,775	1,449
Concrete slab.	18,453	498	16,697	13,196	3,501	894	1,492	8,982	5,329	1,257
Other	1,619	319	1,121	811	310	102	193	618	208	179
Year structure built: [3]										
1939 and earlier.	22,676	502	19,886	11,290	8,596	7,357	6,406	3,766	2,358	2,290
1940 to 1949.	8,529	252	7,539	4,696	2,843	1,635	1,791	2,554	1,559	737
1950 to 1959.	13,633	406	12,360	8,855	3,505	2,521	3,212	3,959	2,667	867
1960 to 1969.	16,070	538	14,405	9,482	4,923	2,421	3,389	5,266	3,329	1,127
1970 to 1979.	23,474	859	20,818	13,290	7,528	2,629	4,622	8,475	5,092	1,797
1980 or later.	22,228	532	19,716	13,637	6,079	2,342	3,612	8,916	4,846	1,979
Median year.	1965	1967	1965	1966	1964	1952	1960	1971	1970	1964
Main heating equipment:										
Warm-air furnace	55,763	818	51,248	36,603	14,645	6,525	17,074	16,918	10,730	3,697
Electric heat pump	9,697	348	8,422	6,078	2,344	422	593	6,190	1,218	927
Steam or hot water system.	14,896	75	13,657	7,338	6,320	9,548	2,549	830	729	1,164
Floor, wall, or pipeless furnace	5,625	214	4,746	2,070	2,676	184	435	1,533	2,594	665
Built-in electric units	8,084	460	6,722	2,891	3,831	1,325	1,327	1,934	2,136	903
Room heaters with flue	2,163	168	1,766	984	782	249	219	965	333	229
Room heaters without flue	1,893	53	1,597	919	677	42	52	1,422	81	244
Stoves	3,477	354	2,831	2,091	740	412	425	1,298	697	292
Fireplaces	1,076	138	884	740	143	36	97	419	332	54
None	1,644	361	911	366	545	38	46	355	472	372
Portable elec. heaters	833	61	682	330	352	4	14	431	233	90
Other	1,459	38	1,257	840	417	121	200	641	295	163
Air conditioning:										
Central	46,277	762	42,183	30,560	11,622	3,397	10,430	21,764	6,592	3,332
Percent of total units	43.4	24.7	44.5	49.9	34.7	18.0	45.3	66.1	33.2	37.9
One or more room units.	27,968	434	26,090	15,620	10,470	8,251	6,540	8,543	2,756	1,444
Source of water:										
Public system or private company	90,327	1,659	81,028	50,064	30,963	15,990	19,110	28,007	17,921	7,640
Percent of total units	84.7	53.7	85.5	81.7	92.5	84.6	83.0	85.0	90.3	86.8
Well serving 1 to 5 units.	13,880	936	11,967	10,140	1,826	2,698	3,674	4,396	1,198	978
Other	2,404	494	1,730	1,047	683	218	247	534	732	181
Means of sewage disposal:										
Public sewer	80,830	1,226	72,797	42,722	30,075	14,684	18,088	23,175	16,849	6,807
Percent of total units	75.8	39.7	76.9	69.7	89.9	77.7	78.5	70.4	84.9	77.4
Septic tank, cesspool, chemical toilet.	25,221	1,550	21,807	18,444	3,362	4,214	4,927	9,672	2,994	1,864
Other	559	312	121	85	35	8	16	90	7	127

[1] Limited to multiunit structures.   [2] Limited to single-family units.   [3] For mobile home, oldest category is 1939 or earlier.

Source: U.S. Bureau of the Census, *Current Housing Reports*, series H-150/93, American Housing Survey in the United States.

No. 1195. Occupied Housing Units—Housing Value and Gross Rent, by Region: 1993

[Based on the American Housing Survey; see Appendix III. For composition of regions, see table 27]

CATEGORY	NUMBER (1,000)					PERCENT DISTRIBUTION				
	Total units	North-east	Midwest	South	West	Total units	North-east	Midwest	South	West
VALUE										
Owner occupied units.	**61,252**	**11,751**	**15,617**	**21,841**	**12,043**	**100.0**	**100.0**	**100.0**	**100.0**	**100.0**
Less than $10,000.	1,856	192	445	969	251	3.0	1.6	2.8	4.4	2.1
$10,000 to $19,999	2,391	282	704	1,102	303	3.9	2.4	4.5	5.0	2.5
$20,000 to $29,999	2,685	348	810	1,236	292	4.4	3.0	5.2	5.7	2.4
$30,000 to $39,999	3,353	355	1,173	1,613	212	5.5	3.0	7.5	7.4	1.8
$40,000 to $49,999	4,148	394	1,517	1,895	342	6.8	3.4	9.7	8.7	2.8
$50,000 to $59,999	4,101	471	1,331	1,915	384	6.7	4.0	8.5	8.8	3.2
$60,000 to $69,999	4,802	590	1,564	2,117	532	7.8	5.0	10.0	9.7	4.4
$70,000 to $79,999	4,666	730	1,393	1,971	572	7.6	6.2	8.9	9.0	4.7
$80,000 to $99,999	8,034	1,582	2,256	2,840	1,356	13.1	13.5	14.4	13.0	11.3
$100,000 to $119,999	5,171	1,158	1,316	1,622	1,075	8.4	9.9	8.4	7.4	8.9
$120,000 to $149,999	5,922	1,586	1,253	1,619	1,463	9.7	13.5	8.0	7.4	12.1
$150,000 to $199,999	6,284	1,943	939	1,440	1,963	10.3	16.5	6.0	6.6	16.3
$200,000 to $249,999	2,999	899	405	551	1,144	4.9	7.7	2.6	2.5	9.5
$250,000 to $299,999	1,734	474	195	365	700	2.8	4.0	1.2	1.7	5.8
$300,000 or more	3,104	748	315	586	1,455	5.1	6.4	2.0	2.7	12.1
Median value (dol.)	86,529	116,102	71,898	70,376	134,430	(X)	(X)	(X)	(X)	(X)
GROSS RENT										
Renter occupied units.	**33,472**	**7,155**	**7,415**	**11,096**	**7,808**	**100.0**	**100.0**	**100.0**	**100.0**	**100.0**
Less than $100.	551	82	165	242	63	1.6	1.1	2.2	2.2	0.8
$100 to $199	2,079	465	552	764	298	6.2	6.5	7.4	6.9	3.8
$200 to $249	1,424	258	426	530	210	4.3	3.6	5.7	4.8	2.7
$250 to $299	1,728	293	527	685	223	5.2	4.1	7.1	6.2	2.9
$300 to $349	2,071	335	616	758	363	6.2	4.7	8.3	6.8	4.6
$350 to $399	2,741	420	769	1,102	451	8.2	5.9	10.4	9.9	5.8
$400 to $449	2,850	453	833	1,048	516	8.5	6.3	11.2	9.4	6.6
$450 to $499	2,851	513	694	1,026	618	8.5	7.2	9.4	9.2	7.9
$500 to $599	4,817	1,084	1,040	1,499	1,194	14.4	15.2	14.0	13.5	15.3
$600 to $699	3,683	1,036	668	947	1,032	11.0	14.5	9.0	8.5	13.2
$700 to $799	2,382	678	287	607	810	7.1	9.5	3.9	5.5	10.4
$800 to $999	2,257	692	208	514	843	6.7	9.7	2.8	4.6	10.8
$1,000 to $1,249.	971	251	72	201	447	2.9	3.5	1.0	1.8	5.7
$1,250 to $1,499.	379	91	32	65	191	1.1	1.3	0.4	0.6	2.4
$1,500 or more.	275	95	14	46	120	0.8	1.3	0.2	0.4	1.5
No cash rent	2,414	408	514	1,062	430	7.2	5.7	6.9	9.6	5.5
Median gross rent (dol.) . . .	487	551	424	445	579	(X)	(X)	(X)	(X)	(X)

X Not applicable.
Source: U.S. Bureau of the Census, *Current Housing Reports*, series H-150/93, American Housing Survey in the United States.

No. 1196. Heating Equipment and Fuels for Occupied Units: 1950 to 1993

[As of **April 1, except 1993**, as of **fall**. Based on the Census of Population and Housing and American Housing Survey; see Appendix III]

ITEM	NUMBER (1,000)					PERCENT DISTRIBUTION				
	1950	1960	1970	1980	1993	1950	1960	1970	1980	1993
Occupied units, total	**42,826**	**53,024**	**63,445**	**80,390**	**94,724**	**100.0**	**100.0**	**100.0**	**100.0**	**100.0**
Heating equipment:										
Warm air furnace	[1]11,508	17,378	27,515	39,279	51,248	[1]26.9	32.8	43.4	48.9	54.1
Heat pumps.	(NA)	(NA)	(NA)	2,835	8,422	(NA)	(NA)	(NA)	3.5	8.9
Steam or hot water	10,071	11,990	13,211	13,859	13,657	23.5	22.6	20.8	17.2	14.4
Floor, wall, or pipeless furnace . .	([1])	6,088	5,552	4,693	4,746	([1])	11.5	8.8	5.8	5.0
Built-in electric units	-	664	3,236	6,370	6,722	-	1.3	5.1	7.9	7.1
Room heaters with flue	[2]15,399	[2]11,183	7,209	6,098	1,766	[2]36.0	[2]21.1	11.4	7.6	1.9
Room heaters without flue	5,268	5,218	3,558	2,736	1,597	12.3	9.8	5.6	3.4	1.7
Fireplaces, stoves, portable heaters or other	([2])	([2])	2,766	3,977	5,654	([2])	([2])	4.4	4.9	6.0
None	581	503	398	541	911	1.4	0.9	0.6	0.7	1.0
House heating fuel:										
Utility gas	11,387	22,851	35,014	42,658	47,669	26.6	43.1	55.2	53.1	50.3
Fuel oil, kerosene, etc	9,686	17,158	16,473	14,655	12,189	22.6	32.4	26.0	18.2	12.9
Electricity.	283	933	4,876	14,768	25,107	0.7	1.8	7.7	18.3	26.5
Bottled, tank, or LP gas	787	2,686	3,807	4,535	3,922	1.8	5.1	6.0	5.6	4.1
Wood and other fuel	4,855	2,460	1,060	2,729	4,630	11.3	4.6	1.7	3.4	4.9
Coal or coke	14,828	6,456	1,821	504	297	34.6	12.2	2.9	0.6	0.3
None	999	478	395	541	910	2.3	0.9	0.6	0.7	1.0
Cooking fuel:										
Electricity.	6,403	16,351	25,768	41,906	55,887	15.0	30.8	40.6	52.1	59.0
Gas [3]	25,501	33,787	36,558	37,944	37,996	59.6	63.7	57.6	47.2	40.1
Other fuel	10,796	2,603	908	398	479	25.2	4.9	1.4	0.5	0.5
None	124	280	213	142	362	0.3	0.5	0.3	0.2	0.4

- Represents zero.   NA Not available.   [1] "Floor, wall, or pipeless furnace" included in "Warm air furnace."   [2] "Fireplaces, stoves, or portable heaters" included in "Room heaters with flue."   [3] Includes utility, bottled, tank, and LP gas.
Source: U.S. Bureau of the Census, *Census of Housing, 1960*, vol. 1; *1970 and 1980*, vol. 1; and *1990 Census of Housing, Detailed Housing Characteristics*, series CH-2, and *Current Housing Reports*, series H-150/93, American Housing Survey in the United States.

No. 1197. Appliances Used by Households, by Region and Family Income: 1993

[In millions, except percent. As of **November**. Represents appliances possessed and generally used by the household. Based on the Residential Energy Consumption Survey; see Appendix III. For composition of regions, see table 27]

TYPE OF APPLIANCE	HOUSEHOLDS USING APPLIANCE		REGION				FAMILY INCOME IN 1993			
	Number	Percent of total	North-east	Midwest	South	West	Under $25,000	$25,000 -$34,999	$35,000 -$49,999	$50,000 and over
Total households ..	96.6	100.0	19.5	23.3	33.5	20.4	35.4	22.8	10.8	27.6
Air conditioners	66.1	68.4	11.3	17.1	29.9	7.8	21.7	15.7	7.9	20.8
Room	25.7	26.6	7.6	6.6	9.0	2.6	11.4	5.8	3.0	5.5
Central system [1]	42.1	43.5	3.9	10.8	21.8	5.5	10.6	10.5	5.1	15.9
Clothes washer	74.5	77.1	14.4	18.4	27.0	14.7	21.9	18.4	9.3	24.9
Clothes dryer.	68.8	71.2	12.5	18.0	24.6	13.6	18.2	17.5	8.9	24.2
Dehumidifier	9.1	9.4	2.5	5.1	1.2	0.2	1.7	1.8	1.4	4.1
Dishwasher.	43.7	45.2	8.1	9.4	15.7	10.5	7.7	10.2	6.5	19.4
Freezer . . . . [2]	33.4	34.5	5.0	10.2	12.5	5.7	9.9	8.2	4.2	11.0
Microwave oven [2]	81.3	84.1	15.1	20.8	27.8	17.5	25.6	20.3	9.8	25.5
Office equipment	23.3	24.2	4.8	5.5	7.2	5.8	3.2	4.7	3.8	11.7
Facsimile machine . . .	2.9	3.0	0.6	0.4	1.0	0.8	(B)	0.5	0.5	1.6
Laser printer	5.3	5.5	0.9	1.0	1.8	1.6	0.5	0.9	0.7	3.0
Personal computer . . .	22.6	23.3	4.7	5.3	6.9	5.7	3.2	4.4	3.6	11.4
Outdoor gas grill	27.5	28.5	7.0	7.4	8.5	4.7	4.0	6.9	4.3	12.4
Oven: Electric	59.4	61.5	9.2	13.5	23.8	12.9	19.0	14.5	7.2	18.9
Gas	30.7	31.8	8.6	8.4	6.9	6.7	13.0	6.6	3.2	7.9
Range: Electric	59.3	61.4	9.3	13.6	23.9	12.6	19.1	14.5	7.2	18.6
Gas	32.2	33.3	9.0	8.7	7.2	7.2	13.7	6.8	3.3	8.4
Refrigerator: Frost-free . .	81.8	84.6	16.1	19.3	29.4	17.0	26.4	19.9	9.8	25.6
Nonfrost-free [3]	14.7	15.2	3.4	4.0	4.0	3.4	8.9	2.8	1.0	2.0
Television set: Color	94.4	97.7	19.1	22.8	32.7	19.9	33.7	22.6	10.7	27.4
Black and white	19.0	19.6	3.9	5.5	6.5	3.1	6.7	4.3	2.0	6.0
Toaster oven	27.5	28.5	7.2	4.5	10.1	5.7	9.2	5.8	3.5	9.0
Water heater: [4] Gas	51.2	53.0	10.1	15.3	12.6	13.2	18.4	11.0	5.8	16.0
Electric	37.1	38.4	4.5	6.9	19.2	6.5	14.1	9.8	4.1	9.3
Ceiling fan	51.8	53.6	8.6	13.2	22.1	8.0	15.2	12.6	7.0	17.1

B Base figure too small to meet statistical standards for reliability. [1] Includes the .9 million households with both central air conditioning and window or wall air conditioning units. [2] Microwave is first or second most used oven. [3] Includes refrigerators without freezer compartments. [4] Excludes water heaters that serve more than one household.
Source: U.S. Energy Information Administration, *Housing Characteristics: 1993*.

No. 1198. Expenditures by Residential Property Owners for Improvements and Maintenance and Repairs, by Type of Property and Activity: 1980 to 1994

[In millions of dollars]

YEAR AND TYPE OF EXPENDITURE	Total	1-unit proper-ties with owner occupant	Other proper-ties	ADDITIONS AND ALTERATIONS				To prop-erty out-side of struc-tures	Major replace-ments	Mainte-nance and repairs
				Total	To structures					
					Addi-tions	Alter-ations				
1980	46,338	31,481	14,857	21,336	4,183	11,193	5,960	9,816	15,187
1981	46,351	30,201	16,150	20,414	3,164	11,947	5,303	9,915	16,022
1982	45,291	29,779	15,512	18,774	2,641	10,711	5,423	9,707	16,810
1983	49,295	32,524	16,771	20,271	4,739	11,673	3,859	10,895	18,128
1984	69,784	43,781	26,003	27,822	6,007	14,486	7,329	13,067	28,894
1985	80,267	47,742	32,525	28,775	3,966	17,599	7,211	16,134	35,358
1986	91,274	54,298	36,976	38,608	7,377	21,192	10,040	16,695	35,971
1987	94,082	54,791	39,291	39,978	9,557	21,641	8,779	15,875	38,229
1988	101,117	60,822	40,295	43,339	11,333	22,703	9,303	16,893	40,885
1989	100,891	59,858	41,033	39,786	6,828	23,129	9,828	18,415	42,690
1990	106,773	59,683	47,090	37,253	8,561	21,920	6,771	18,215	51,305
1991	97,528	58,083	39,445	30,944	7,914	16,076	6,954	16,744	49,840
1992, total [1]	103,734	67,316	36,418	40,186	6,783	22,700	10,704	18,393	45,154
Heating and air conditioning [2]	6,952	5,302	1,650	1,103	(NA)	1,103	(NA)	3,546	2,303
Plumbing	9,549	5,653	3,896	1,540	(NA)	1,540	(NA)	3,104	4,905
Roofing	10,714	5,327	5,387	(NA)	(NA)	(NA)	(NA)	6,257	4,457
Painting	11,147	5,867	5,280	(NA)	(NA)	(NA)	(NA)	(NA)	11,147
1993, total [1]	108,305	70,746	37,559	45,797	12,757	24,781	8,259	20,809	41,699
Heating and air conditioning [2]	7,918	5,814	2,103	1,259	(NA)	1,259	(NA)	4,040	2,618
Plumbing	8,700	4,488	4,212	1,597	(NA)	1,597	(NA)	2,990	4,114
Roofing	8,943	5,559	3,385	(NA)	(NA)	(NA)	(NA)	4,821	4,122
Painting	12,566	6,567	5,998	(NA)	(NA)	(NA)	(NA)	(NA)	12,566
1994, total [1]	115,030	77,270	37,760	48,828	9,647	28,672	10,509	23,248	42,953
Heating and air conditioning [2]	8,581	5,712	2,869	2,060	(NA)	2,060	(NA)	3,904	2,617
Plumbing	8,941	5,222	3,719	1,677	(NA)	1,677	(NA)	2,836	4,428
Roofing	11,406	6,371	5,034	(NA)	(NA)	(NA)	(NA)	7,008	4,398
Painting	11,446	6,439	5,007	(NA)	(NA)	(NA)	(NA)	(NA)	11,446

NA Not available. [1] Includes types of expenditures not separately specified. [2] Central air-conditioning.
Source: U.S. Bureau of the Census, *Current Construction Reports*, series C50.

No. 1199. Gross Housing Product in Real (1992) Dollars: 1990 to 1994

[**In billions of dollars.** For definition of chained dollars, see text, section 14]

ITEM	CURRENT DOLLARS					CHAINED (1992) DOLLARS				
	1990	1991	1992	1993	1994	1990	1991	1992	1993	1994
Housing output [1]	565.9	595.2	623.7	649.0	680.7	603.1	612.6	623.7	631.5	644.0
Less: Intermediate goods and services consumed	78.5	81.0	76.2	86.8	83.1	82.5	81.3	76.2	84.8	78.8
Equals: **Gross housing product** .	487.4	514.1	547.5	562.2	597.6	520.4	531.2	547.5	546.8	565.1
Less: Indirect business tax and nontax liability plus business transfer payments	91.0	98.2	104.2	114.0	120.6	(NA)	(NA)	(NA)	(NA)	(NA)
Plus: Subsidies less current surplus of government enterprises	15.0	16.0	17.0	18.8	20.6	(NA)	(NA)	(NA)	(NA)	(NA)
Equals: Housing national income. .	320.7	337.1	352.1	362.9	385.2	(NA)	(NA)	(NA)	(NA)	(NA)

NA Not available. [1] Equals personal consumption expenditures (see text, section 14) for housing, less expenditures for transient hotels, motels, clubs, schools, and other group housing.

Source: U.S. Bureau of Economic Analysis, *National Income and Product Accounts of the United States* to be published in late 1996, and *Survey of Current Business,* January/February 1996.

No. 1200. Residential Capital—Year-End Stocks and Average Age: 1970 to 1994

[As of **Dec. 31.** Data based on fixed residential capital formation components of the gross national product. For definition of current and constant dollars, see Guide to Tabular Presentation]

ITEM	CURRENT DOLLARS (bil. dol.)				CONSTANT (1987) DOLLARS (bil. dol.)				AVERAGE AGE [1] (years)			
	1970	1980	1990	1994	1970	1980	1990	1994	1970	1980	1990	1994
Gross stocks [2]	1,244	4,391	7,563	9,339	3,961	5,443	6,916	7,477	24.8	23.2	23.6	24.0
Private nonfarm:												
1 to 4 units.	1,001	3,502	6,074	7,636	3,208	4,356	5,556	6,066	25.3	23.9	24.2	24.4
5 or more units	131	522	933	1,059	421	647	853	887	17.7	17.8	19.8	21.8
Farm (1 to 4 units) . . .	55	136	163	176	176	170	150	140	43.9	42.8	43.2	43.2
Other nonfarm structures [3]	10	24	32	35	32	29	29	27	14.6	19.3	23.7	22.5
Mobile homes.	15	79	124	152	31	88	112	112	5.1	7.7	10.7	11.0
Public: Federal, State and local	25	99	176	208	80	122	162	177	14.9	17.2	19.5	20.5
Net stocks [2][4]	813	2,910	4,913	5,992	2,590	3,607	4,491	4,795	16.2	15.8	16.8	17.4
Private nonfarm:												
1 to 4 units.	656	2,334	3,991	4,979	2,102	2,902	3,649	3,953	16.8	16.3	17.2	17.6
5 or more units	93	371	629	676	301	459	575	566	11.0	12.8	15.2	17.4
Farm (1 to 4 units) . . .	24	58	68	73	76	73	62	58	28.7	26.4	26.6	26.7
Other nonfarm structures [3]	6	12	14	14	21	15	12	11	9.0	16.0	18.4	19.1
Mobile homes.	11	48	62	75	23	54	55	55	3.8	6.0	7.5	7.3
Public: Federal, State and local	18	70	117	135	60	87	107	115	12.7	13.5	14.6	14.9

[1] Constant-dollar stocks. [2] Includes equipment, not shown separately. [3] Consists of dormitories, fraternity and sorority houses, nurses' homes, etc. [4] Based on straight-line depreciation.

Source: U.S. Bureau of Economic Analysis, *Fixed Reproducible Tangible Wealth in the United States, 1925-89,* and *Survey of Current Business,* and August 1994; and unpublished data.

No. 1201. Vacancy Rates for Housing Units—Characteristics: 1990 to 1995

[**In percent.** Annual averages. Based on Current Population Survey and Quarterly Household Survey. Rate is relationship between vacant housing for rent or for sale and the total rental and homowner supply, which comprises occupied units, units rented or sold and awaiting occupancy, and vacant units available for rent or sale. For composition of regions, see table 27. See also *Historical Statistics, Colonial Times to 1970,* series N 249-2]

CHARACTERISTIC	RENTAL UNITS					HOMEOWNER UNITS				
	1990	1992	1993 [1]	1994	1995	1990	1992	1993 [1]	1994	1995
Total units. . . .	**7.2**	**7.4**	**7.3**	**7.4**	**7.6**	**1.7**	**1.5**	**1.4**	**1.5**	**1.5**
Inside MSA's.	7.1	7.4	7.5	7.3	7.6	1.7	1.6	1.4	1.5	1.5
Outside MSA's.	7.6	7.0	6.5	7.7	7.9	1.8	1.5	1.5	1.5	1.5
Northeast	6.1	6.9	7.0	7.1	7.2	1.6	1.3	1.3	1.5	1.6
Midwest	6.4	6.7	6.6	6.8	7.2	1.3	1.2	1.1	1.5	1.5
South	8.8	8.2	7.9	8.0	8.3	2.1	1.7	1.7	1.1	1.3
West	6.6	7.1	7.4	7.1	7.5	1.8	1.9	1.4	1.6	1.7
Units in structure:										
1 unit	4.0	3.8	3.7	4.5	5.4	1.4	1.3	1.2	1.3	1.4
2 units or more. . . .	9.0	9.4	9.4	9.0	9.0	7.1	5.8	5.3	5.1	4.8
5 units or more. . .	9.6	10.0	10.2	9.7	9.5	8.4	7.4	6.8	5.3	5.1
Units with—										
3 rooms or less . .	10.3	11.4	10.7	11.1	11.4	10.2	8.6	6.9	9.7	9.2
4 rooms	8.0	7.9	8.1	7.9	8.2	3.2	2.6	2.5	3.0	2.8
5 rooms	5.7	5.3	5.7	5.7	5.8	2.0	1.9	1.7	1.8	1.8
6 rooms or more. .	3.0	3.1	3.2	3.4	3.8	1.1	1.1	1.0	0.9	1.1

[1] Beginning 1993, based on 1990 population census controls.

Source: U.S. Bureau of the Census, *Current Housing Reports,* series H111/95 and prior reports.

No. 1202. Recent Home Buyers—General Characteristics: 1976 to 1995

[As of **October.** Based on a sample survey; subject to sampling variability]

ITEM	Unit	1976	1980	1985	1990	1991	1992	1993	1994	1995
Median purchase price . .	Dollars . .	43,340	68,714	90,400	131,200	134,300	141,000	141,900	145,400	147,700
First-time buyers	Dollars . .	37,670	61,450	75,100	106,000	118,700	122,400	121,100	125,000	128,300
Repeat buyers [1]	Dollars . .	50,090	75,750	106,200	149,400	152,500	158,000	159,600	163,500	164,300
Average monthly mortgage										
payment	Dollars . .	329	599	896	1,127	1,144	1,064	1,015	1,028	1,062
Percent of income. . . .	Percent. .	24.0	32.4	30.0	33.8	34.0	33.2	31.5	31.4	32.6
Percent buying—										
New houses.	Percent. .	15.1	22.4	23.8	21.2	19.7	20.5	22.3	22.0	21.5
Existing houses	Percent. .	84.9	77.6	76.2	78.8	80.3	79.5	77.7	78.0	78.5
Single-family houses . .	Percent. .	88.8	82.4	87.0	83.8	85.3	85.0	84.2	83.9	83.1
Condominiums [2]	Percent. .	11.2	17.6	10.6	13.1	11.5	13.1	12.8	12.1	14.0
For the first time	Percent. .	44.8	32.9	36.6	41.9	45.1	47.7	46.0	47.1	46.2
Average age:										
First-time buyers	Years . . .	28.1	28.3	28.4	30.5	30.7	31.0	31.6	31.6	32.1
Repeat buyers [1]	Years . . .	35.9	36.4	38.4	39.1	39.8	40.8	41.0	41.7	40.7
Downpayment/sales price	Percent. .	25.2	28.0	24.8	23.3	22.6	21.4	20.2	20.2	20.4
First-time buyers	Percent. .	18.0	20.5	11.4	15.7	14.7	14.3	14.0	13.7	13.3
Repeat buyers [1]	Percent. .	30.8	32.7	32.7	28.9	29.1	28.0	25.4	26.1	26.8

[1] Buyers who previously owned a home.   [2] Includes multiple-family houses.
Source: Chicago Title Insurance Company, Chicago, IL, *The Guarantor*, quarterly (copyright).

No. 1203. Low-Income Public Housing Units, by Progress Stage: 1970 to 1993

[**In thousands.** As of **Dec. 31.** Housing for the elderly intended for persons 62 disabled, or handicapped. Includes Puerto Rico and Virgin Islands. Covers units subsidized by HUD under annual contributions contracts. See also *Historical Statistics, Colonial Times to 1970,*

YEAR	Total[1]	Occupied units [2]	Under construction	YEAR	Total[1]	Occupied units [2]	Under construction
1970	1,155.3	893.5	126.8	1990	1,305.3	1,028.1	7.6
Elderly.	249.4	143.4	65.7	Elderly.	(NA)	342.2	(NA)
1980	1,321.1	1,195.6	20.9	1992	1,323.3	1,199.4	7.2
Elderly.	358.3	317.7	11.5	Elderly.	(NA)	513.5	(NA)
1985	1,378.0	1,344.6	9.6	1993	1,324.7	1,207.6	(NA)
Elderly.	373.5	361.1	2.1	Elderly. . . .	(NA)	507.5	(NA)

NA Not available.   [1] Includes units to be constructed or to go directly "under management" because no rehabilitation need
[2] Under management or available for occupancy.
Source: U.S. Dept. of Housing and Urban Development, unpublished data based on the Field Office Report Monitoring System.

No. 1204. Office Buildings—Vacancy Rates for Major Cities, 1980 to 1995, and Status of Supply, 1995

[**As of December.** Excludes government owned and occupied, owner-occupied, and medical office buildings]

CITY	VACANCY RATE FOR EXISTING SPACE (percent)									SUPPLY STATUS, December 1995 (mil. sq. ft.)		
	1980	1985	1989	1990	1991	1992	1993	1994	1995	Existing space Total	Available for lease	Space under construction
Total [1]	4.6	16.9	19.5	20.0	20.2	20.5	19.4	16.2	14.3	2,834.1	441.2	12.2
Atlanta, GA	10.0	21.0	19.9	19.1	19.5	19.4	16.8	13.0	10.4	88.8	9.2	2.1
Baltimore, MD	7.2	11.5	16.4	20.0	21.0	20.6	17.3	15.5	17.0	41.0	7.0	0.2
Boston, MA	3.8	13.1	15.3	19.6	19.1	17.5	17.7	13.3	10.4	136.3	14.2	0.1
Charlotte, NC.	(NA)	16.7	14.3	16.5	19.4	(NA)	(NA)	10.0	8.9	21.2	1.9	0.7
Chicago, IL	7.0	16.5	17.0	18.6	20.0	22.1	21.4	18.7	15.5	188.8	29.3	0.0
Dallas, TX	8.6	23.0	26.9	25.8	26.0	31.3	29.5	21.7	18.7	116.4	21.8	0.2
Denver, CO	6.6	24.7	26.1	24.8	23.0	21.5	15.9	12.8	12.1	68.5	8.3	0.4
Detroit, MI	(NA)	(NA)	(NA)	(NA)	(NA)	(NA)	21.4	19.7	16.9	67.2	11.4	0.0
Houston, TX	4.0	27.6	27.5	24.9	27.3	27.0	25.1	24.7	21.9	157.6	34.5	0.0
Indianapolis, IN	(NA)	(NA)	20.0	21.2	21.4	22.4	18.8	18.4	14.3	26.0	3.7	0.2
Kansas City, MO. . . .	4.2	16.2	15.8	14.1	16.9	15.2	13.9	11.5	9.1	30.7	2.8	0.1
Los Angeles, CA. . .	0.9	15.3	19.7	16.8	20.2	21.2	21.0	19.6	23.2	220.5	51.2	0.5
Miami, FL	2.4	20.9	22.0	23.4	22.6	18.5	19.0	15.4	13.8	40.6	5.6	0.7
Milwaukee, WI	(NA)	(NA)	20.4	22.9	19.5	18.4	21.0	17.6	16.3	24.0	3.9	0.3
New Orleans, LA . . .	(NA)	21.8	25.7	29.0	25.0	(NA)	(NA)	(NA)	(NA)	(NA)	(NA)	(NA)
New York, NY [2] . . .	3.1	7.9	15.1	16.0	18.8	18.3	17.9	16.3	17.0	319.2	54.2	0.0
Philadelphia, PA . . .	6.3	14.5	16.3	18.2	17.3	19.0	17.8	16.3	16.2	70.9	11.5	0.1
Pittsburgh, PA	1.2	(NA)	16.3	16.3	14.2	(NA)	17.0	15.8	14.5	36.6	5.3	0.1
San Diego, CA	(NA)	24.7	17.6	19.5	23.7	23.8	22.1	18.8	17.4	37.5	6.5	0.3
San Francisco, CA . .	0.4	13.7	15.7	14.7	13.3	12.5	13.7	11.7	10.2	53.4	5.4	0.0
Seattle, WA	(NA)	(NA)	12.4	12.3	12.8	15.9	17.6	14.7	7.1	24.8	1.8	0.0
St. Louis, MO.	(NA)	(NA)	22.6	21.0	20.5	21.8	19.1	18.1	12.7	32.3	4.1	0.1
Washington, DC . . .	2.5	9.0	14.4	19.0	17.6	15.4	14.1	13.4	10.8	220.8	23.9	1.7

NA Not available.   [1] Includes other cities not shown separately. In 1993, 51 cities were covered.   [2] Refers to Manhattan.
Source: ONCOR International, Houston, TX, 1980-1985, *National Office Market Report*, semi-annual; 1986-1990, *International Office Market Report*, semi-annual; thereafter, *Market Data Book* (copyright).

No. 1205. Commercial Office Space—Inventory and Vacancy Rates for the Largest Metropolitan Areas: 1995

[As of **December 31, except population as July 1.** Data based on responses from individuals knowledgeable in the local markets. Represents primarily the metropolitan areas as indicated, but in many cases may exclude outlying countries beyond the central portion]

METROPOLITAN AREAS	Resident population, 1992 (1,000)	Inventory (1,000 sq. ft.)	Vacant space (1,000 sq. ft.)	Vacancy rate (percent)	Construction (1,000 sq. ft.)	Absorption (1,000 sq. ft.)
Albany-Schenectady-Troy, NY MSA	872	13,524	1,386	10.2	122	427
Atlanta, GA MSA	3,143	89,136	10,286	11.5	2,150	3,096
Austin-San Marcos, TX MSA	901	19,808	2,099	10.6	-	185
Baltimore, MD PMSA	2,433	43,200	7,225	16.7	-	-
Birmingham, AL MSA	859	16,000	1,143	7.1	-	1,075
Boston, MA-NH PMSA	3,211	92,155	10,602	11.5	66	1,433
Buffalo-Niagara Falls, NY MSA	1,194	7,543	1,060	14.1	217	13
Charlotte, NC MSA	1,212	20,534	1,737	8.5	1,114	560
Chicago, IL PMSA	7,561	145,769	21,873	15.0	221	1,688
Cincinnati, OH PMSA	1,560	30,092	4,655	15.5	216	-
Cleveland-Lorain-Elyria, OH PMSA	2,221	35,720	5,463	15.3	-	1,386
Columbus, OH MSA	1,394	26,280	1,116	4.2	1,634	695
Dallas, TX PMSA	4,215	116,250	24,289	20.9	-	2,093
Dayton, OH MSA	962	11,632	1,504	12.9	20	278
Denver, CO PMSA	1,715	54,369	5,131	9.4	1,081	639
Detroit, MI PMSA	4,308	56,299	8,266	14.7	99	1,849
Fort Lauderdale, FL PMSA	1,301	14,905	1,855	12.4	118	710
Fort Worth, TX PMSA	1,419	17,530	3,021	17.2	-	552
Grand Rapids-Muskegon-Holland, MI MSA	964	8,348	1,570	18.8	-	571
Greensboro-Winston Salem-High Point, NC MSA	1,078	12,622	1,089	8.6	-	984
Greenville-Spartanburg-Anderson, SC MSA	853	4,064	657	16.2	-	69
Hartford, CT MSA	1,156	20,800	3,400	16.3	-	100
Honolulu, HI MSA	863	14,642	2,139	14.6	637	10
Houston TX PMSA	3,530	127,626	22,627	17.7	-	629
Indianapolis, IN MSA	1,424	18,733	2,690	14.4	260	911
Jacksonville, FL MSA	953	19,352	1,706	8.8	476	847
Kansas City, MO-KS MSA	1,617	34,317	3,237	9.4	-	1,336
Las Vegas, NV MSA	971	7,734	584	7.6	626	1,155
Los-Angeles, CA PMSA [1]	9,054	98,847	20,050	20.3	-	689
Louisville, KY MSA	968	13,786	2,110	15.3	48	480
Memphis, TN MSA	1,034	18,484	1,400	7.6	1,480	442
Miami, FL PMSA	2,008	27,504	4,289	15.6	256	228
Minneapolis-St. Paul, MN-WI MSA	2,618	45,875	5,071	11.1	-	292
Nashville, TN MSA	1,023	13,129	992	7.6	161	586
Nassau-Suffolk, NY PMSA [2]	2,640	37,390	6,617	17.7	100	1,560
New Jersey-Central/Northern [2]	1,846	151,357	24,179	16.0	507	2,002
New Orleans, LA MSA	1,303	18,079	3,895	21.5	-	169
New York, NY PMSA [3]	8,552	428,722	62,696	14.6	-	1,844
Norfolk-Virginia Beach-Newport News, VA MSA	1,497	16,302	1,826	11.2	308	377
Oakland, CA PMSA [4]	2,148	14,306	1,809	12.6	-	336
Oklahoma City, OK MSA	984	14,070	3,136	22.3	-	475
Orange County, CA PMSA	2,485	54,310	8,378	15.4	-	1,203
Orlando, FL MSA	1,305	21,098	2,012	9.5	69	1,025
Philadelphia, PA PMSA	4,944	82,697	13,498	16.3	175	461
Phoenix, AZ MSA	2,330	22,907	2,347	10.2	-	679
Pittsburgh, PA MSA	2,406	33,236	4,341	13.1	-	581
Portland-Vancouver, OR PMSA	1,897	16,589	1,302	7.8	130	411
Providence, RI MSA	1,131	8,741	1,795	20.5	-	1
Raleigh-Durham-Chapel Hill, NC MSA	909	21,140	1,902	9.0	920	1,778
Richmond-Petersburg, VA MSA [5]	896	13,838	757	5.5	160	217
Sacramento-Yolo, CA MSA	1,563	26,352	2,845	10.8	579	485
St. Louis, MO MSA	2,519	38,842	4,517	11.6	-	12
Salt Lake City-Ogden, UT MSA	1,128	10,807	500	4.6	407	228
San Antonio, TX MSA [6]	1,379	15,767	2,399	15.2	42	186
San Diego, CA MSA	2,601	58,474	9,061	15.5	19	399
San Francisco, CA PMSA	1,626	74,019	6,664	9.0	60	1,478
San Jose, CA PMSA	1,528	36,500	3,687	10.1	-	6,000
Seattle, WA PMSA [7]	2,124	44,711	3,880	8.7	-	1,284
Tampa-St. Petersburg-Clearwater, FL MSA [8]	2,107	19,469	2,684	13.8	23	338
Washington, DC-MD-VA-WV PMSA [9]	4,630	167,826	22,306	13.3	2,267	2,593
West Palm Beach-Boca Raton, FL MSA	901	6,782	1,039	15.3	-	80

- Represents zero. [1] Excludes the San Gabriel Valley and western portions of the metropolitan area. [2] Data are for area identified by source as New Jersey-Central/Northern with a market area of Bergen, Essex, Hudson, Morris, and Passaic, Hunterdon, Mercer, Middlesex, Monmouth, Somerset, and Union counties. [3] Represents primarily Brooklyn, Manhattan, Queens, Rockland, and Westchester counties. [4] Excludes Contra Costa county. [5] Covers only outside the central business district. [6] Represents only Bexar County. [7] Represents only the central business district portion of Seattle. [8] Represents only Pinnellas and Hillsborough counties. [9] Excludes the Maryland portion of the metropolitan area and some outlying counties in Virginia.

Source: Resident population, U.S. Bureau of the Census. Office data, Society of Industrial and Office REALTORS, Washington, DC, *Comparative Statistics of Industrial and Office Real Estate Markets*, (copyright).

No. 1206. Commercial Buildings—Selected Characteristics, by Square Footage of Floorspace: 1992

[Excludes buildings 1,000 square feet or smaller. Building type based on predominant activity in which the occupants were engaged. Based on a sample survey of building representatives conducted between August and December 1992; therefore, subject to sampling variability. For composition of regions, see table 27]

CHARACTERISTIC	Number of buildings (1,000)	FLOORSPACE (mil. sq. ft.)							Mean sq. ft. per building (1,000)	Median sq. ft. per building (1,000)
		Total	Within all buildings having square footage of—							
			5,000 or less	5,001 to 10,000	10,001 to 25,000	25,001 to 50,000	50,001 to 100,000	100,001 and over		
All buildings	**4,806**	**67,876**	**7,327**	**7,199**	**10,375**	**10,069**	**8,062**	**24,845**	**14.1**	**4.5**
Region:										
Northeast	771	13,400	1,074	1,337	1,663	1,976	1,752	5,597	17.4	5.2
Midwest	1,202	17,280	1,889	1,763	2,689	2,353	2,097	6,488	14.4	4.5
South	1,963	24,577	3,155	2,723	3,782	3,696	2,842	8,379	12.5	4.0
West	870	12,619	1,208	1,376	2,241	2,043	1,371	4,380	14.5	5.0
Year constructed:										
1899 or before	169	1,721	251	397	297	431	(S)	(S)	10.2	5.5
1900 to 1919	255	3,608	336	523	503	522	319	(S)	14.1	5.0
1920 to 1945	724	8,712	1,150	1,106	1,507	1,267	927	1,934	12.0	4.2
1946 to 1959	880	10,421	1,352	1,255	1,775	1,792	1,236	2,531	11.8	4.2
1960 to 1969	783	12,612	1,167	986	1,892	1,856	1,625	5,085	16.1	4.5
1970 to 1979	982	14,014	1,536	1,505	1,902	2,216	1,776	5,079	14.3	4.5
1980 to 1989	884	14,287	1,339	1,251	2,189	1,658	1,717	6,132	16.2	4.8
1990 to 1992	128	2,502	197	176	309	327	268	1,224	19.6	4.8
Principal activity within building:										
Public assembly [1]	644	8,303	1,002	1,056	1,742	1,278	378	418	12.9	(NA)
Education	301	8,470	292	307	997	1,551	2,045	3,262	28.2	9.0
Food sales	130	757	286	(S)	(S)	(S)	(S)	(S)	5.8	2.6
Food service	260	1,491	485	343	325	(S)	(S)	(S)	5.7	3.4
Health care	63	1,763	108	(S)	(S)	(S)	(S)	1,286	27.9	4.3
Lodging	154	2,891	159	294	412	711	420	758	18.8	8.0
Mercantile/services	1,272	12,402	2,203	1,987	2,003	1,369	1,268	3,570	9.7	4.0
Office	749	12,319	1,018	1,248	1,656	1,823	1,355	5,218	16.4	5.0
Parking garage	24	1,652	(S)	(S)	(S)	(S)	(S)	694	69.9	6.0
Public order and safety	60	820	91	(S)	(S)	(S)	(S)	(S)	13.7	5.0
Warehouse	761	11,484	1,089	1,106	2,066	1,631	1,250	4,343	15.1	5.0
Other	69	1,130	99	(S)	110	(S)	(S)	(S)	16.4	4.0
Vacant	319	4,396	473	459	635	768	503	821	13.8	4.2
Government owned	599	15,124	689	848	1,735	1,953	2,241	7,659	25.2	6.7
Nongovernment owned	4,206	52,752	6,638	6,351	8,640	8,116	5,821	17,186	12.5	4.3
Fuels used alone or in combination:										
Electricity	4,616	66,549	6,996	7,057	10,097	9,856	7,936	24,607	14.4	4.7
Natural gas	2,665	45,097	3,761	4,266	6,865	6,510	5,735	17,959	16.9	5.1
Fuel oil	559	13,218	829	925	978	1,377	1,539	7,570	23.7	5.0
Propane	337	3,393	573	466	456	501	411	500	10.1	3.5
District heat	95	5,339	56	73	450	545	653	3,562	56.0	17.0
District chilled water	28	2,066	(S)	(S)	115	311	(S)	1,504	72.6	26.5
Any other	163	1,551	250	311	(S)	(S)	(S)	(S)	9.5	3.6
Workers:										
Fewer than 5	2,718	17,944	5,095	3,329	3,053	2,107	910	(S)	6.6	3.0
5 to 9	895	7,524	1,554	1,612	1,801	1,348	595	(S)	8.4	4.8
10 to 19	561	8,077	537	1,446	2,323	1,538	643	(S)	14.4	8.0
20 to 49	405	10,556	120	757	2,608	3,049	1,899	(S)	26.1	16.3
50 to 99	130	7,763	(S)	(S)	450	1,445	2,151	(S)	59.7	38.5
100 to 249	64	7,378	(S)	(S)	(S)	517	1,303	5,433	114.6	79.0
250 or more	31	8,633	(S)	(S)	(S)	(S)	561	7,992	274.4	150.0
Weekly operating hours:										
39 or less	1,039	8,246	1,797	1,341	1,592	1,309	1,007	(S)	7.9	3.5
40 to 48	1,278	14,998	1,904	2,186	2,994	2,553	1,698	3,662	11.7	4.9
49 to 60	1,004	14,046	1,430	1,610	2,549	2,536	1,440	4,482	14.0	5.0
61 to 84	645	12,062	926	1,098	1,408	1,443	1,769	5,418	18.7	5.0
85 to 167	478	8,467	772	492	1,022	1,151	1,132	3,897	17.7	4.0
168 (open continuously)	362	10,057	498	472	810	1,077	1,015	6,185	27.8	5.0

NA Not available.   S Figure does not meet publication standards.   [1] Includes religious worship.

Source: U.S. Energy Information Administration, *Commercial Buildings Characteristics, 1992.*

No. 1207. Commercial Buildings—Number and Square Footage of Floorspace, by Type of Building and Characteristic: 1992

[For composition of regions, see table 27]

BUILDING CHARACTERISTICS	All build-ings [1]	Public as-sembly[2]	Educa-tion	Food sales	Food service	Health care	Lodg-ing	Mer-cantile/serv-ices	Offices	Public order and safety	Ware-house
NUMBER (1,000)											
All buildings	**4,806**	**644**	**301**	**130**	**260**	**63**	**154**	**1,272**	**749**	**60**	**761**
Region:											
Northeast	771	70	38	(S)	54	12	31	246	126	16	109
Midwest	1,202	162	46	29	73	14	26	329	170	(S)	233
South	1,963	314	112	57	83	15	56	510	299	24	316
West.	870	99	104	32	50	23	41	187	154	(S)	103
Year constructed:											
1899 or before	169	(S)	(S)	(S)	(S)	(S)	(S)	34	31	(NA)	(S)
1900 to 1919	255	48	12	(S)	(S)	(S)	(S)	59	38	(S)	27
1920 to 1945	724	98	28	(S)	43	7	14	210	108	(S)	112
1946 to 1959	880	131	76	(S)	51	10	24	235	136	(S)	117
1960 to 1969	783	111	72	(S)	33	15	38	208	102	(S)	107
1970 to 1979	982	107	46	28	73	14	27	247	163	16	185
1980 to 1986	671	69	37	(S)	23	9	22	200	113	(S)	125
1987 to 1989	212	(S)	12	(S)	(S)	(S)	(S)	47	42	(S)	50
1990 to 1992	128	(S)	17	(S)	(S)	(S)	4	32	15	(S)	21
Government owned	599	65	201	(NA)	10	13	15	63	69	49	59
Nongovernment owned . .	4,206	578	99	130	250	51	139	1,210	680	(S)	702
FLOORSPACE (mil. sq. ft.)											
All buildings	**67,876**	**8,303**	**8,470**	**757**	**1,491**	**1,763**	**2,891**	**12,402**	**12,319**	**820**	**11,484**
Region:											
Northeast	13,400	1,229	1,968	(S)	445	386	616	2,798	2,525	269	1,763
Midwest	17,280	1,998	2,386	182	432	487	577	3,156	2,804	(S)	3,108
South	24,577	3,635	2,620	245	407	597	1,043	4,233	4,152	238	4,964
West.	12,619	1,441	1,496	209	208	292	654	2,214	2,838	(S)	1,649
Year constructed:											
1899 or before	1,721	(S)	(S)	(S)	(S)	(S)	(S)	239	435	(NA)	(S)
1900 to 1919	3,608	575	441	(S)	(S)	(S)	(S)	422	716	(S)	269
1920 to 1945	8,712	850	1,077	(S)	246	227	410	1,381	1,389	(S)	1,853
1946 to 1959	10,421	1,434	1,903	(S)	283	152	328	1,883	1,400	(S)	1,805
1960 to 1969	12,612	1,180	2,405	(S)	187	492	482	2,680	2,187	(S)	1,815
1970 to 1979	14,014	1,601	1,728	155	365	544	579	2,607	2,283	168	2,397
1980 to 1986	10,149	819	480	(S)	103	240	550	2,109	2,419	(S)	2,233
1987 to 1989	4,138	(S)	173	(S)	(S)	(S)	(S)	535	899	(S)	610
1990 to 1992	2,502	(S)	253	(S)	(S)	(S)	97	545	590	(S)	377
Government owned	15,124	(S)	6,961	(NA)	157	521	370	1,082	1,654	767	599
Nongovernment owned . .	52,752	6,945	1,508	757	1,334	1,242	2,520	11,319	10,665	(S)	10,885

NA Not available. S Figure does not meet publication standards. [1] Includes parking garages, vacant, and other commercial buildings, not shown separately. [2] Includes religious worship.

Source: U.S. Energy Information Administration, *Commercial Building Characteristics, 1992.*

No. 1208. Industrial Buildings—Floorspace and Vacancy Rates for Major Cities: 1995

CITY	FLOORSPACE (sq. ft.)			VACANCY RATES (percent)		
	Total	General warehouse	Office warehouse [1]	Total	General warehouse	Office warehouse [1]
Atlanta, GA	(NA)	138,327,298	111,040,435	(NA)	4.5	5.6
Baltimore, MD	(NA)	96,071,812	24,442,980	(NA)	11.3	14.6
Boston, MA	46,907,777	(NA)	(NA)	21.2	(NA)	(NA)
Charlotte, NC	(NA)	15,629,816	5,047,755	(NA)	14.2	8.5
Dallas, TX.	(NA)	284,922,831	65,379,388	(NA)	7.5	8.3
Denver, CO.	(NA)	108,102,500	14,986,800	(NA)	4.0	13.0
Detroit, MI.	263,643,540	(NA)	(NA)	8.6	(NA)	(NA)
Houston, TX	(NA)	127,126,065	20,665,401	(NA)	14.0	19.0
Indianapolis, IN	(NA)	43,500,000	25,100,000	(NA)	2.5	10.0
Kansas City, MO	(NA)	123,212,825	(NA)	(NA)	13.4	(NA)
Los Angeles, CA	775,000,000	(NA)	(NA)	12.0	(NA)	(NA)
Miami, FL	(NA)	130,000,000	10,000,000	(NA)	7.5	9.5
Milwaukee , WI	(NA)	(NA)	191,244,500	(NA)	(NA)	4.2
New Orleans, LA	(NA)	(NA)	(NA)	(NA)	(NA)	(NA)
New York, NY	(NA)	(NA)	(NA)	(NA)	(NA)	(NA)
Philadelphia, PA.	(NA)	99,000,000	37,000,000	(NA)	18.0	6.0
Pittsburgh, PA	(NA)	12,600,000	6,700,000	(NA)	18.7	11.1
San Diego, CA.	(NA)	17,776,729	(NA)	(NA)	11.0	(NA)
San Francisco. CA	(NA)	(NA)	(NA)	(NA)	(NA)	(NA)
Seattle, WA.	(NA)	62,350,096	9,453,841	(NA)	4.3	2.8
St. Louis, MO	198,918,000	(NA)	(NA)	4.0	(NA)	(NA)
Washington, DC.	70,242,369	(NA)	(NA)	13.4	(NA)	(NA)

NA Not available. [1] Space is between 10 - 50 percent used for office.

Source: ONCOR International, Houston, TX, *Market Data Book,* 1995 (copyright).

Manufactures

This section presents summary data for manufacturing as a whole and more detailed information for major industry groups and selected products. The types of measures shown at the different levels include data for establishments; employment and wages; raw materials, fuels, and electricity consumed; plant and equipment expenditures; value and quantity of production and shipments; value added by manufacture; inventories; and various indicators of financial status.

The principal sources of these data are Bureau of the Census reports of the censuses of manufactures conducted every 5 years; the *Annual Survey of Manufactures;* and the *Current Industrial Reports* series, which presents monthly, quarterly, or annual data on production, shipments, and stocks for particular commodities. Indexes of industrial production are presented monthly in the Federal Reserve Board's *Federal Reserve Bulletin.* Reports on current activities of industries, or current movements of individual commodities, are compiled by such government agencies as the Bureau of Labor Statistics; the Economic Research Service of the Department of Agriculture; the International Trade Administration; and by private research or trade associations such as The Conference Board, Inc., New York, NY, and the American Iron and Steel Institute, Washington, DC.

Data on financial aspects of manufacturing industries are collected by the Bureau of Economic Analysis (BEA) and the Bureau of the Census. Industry aggregates in the form of balance sheets, profit and loss statements, analyses of sales and expenses, lists of subsidiaries, and types and amounts of security issues are published for leading manufacturing corporations registered with the Securities and Exchange Commission. The BEA issues data on capital in manufacturing industries and capacity utilization rates in manufacturing. See also section 17, Business Enterprise.

Censuses and annual surveys—The first census of manufactures covered the year 1809. Between 1809 and 1963, a census was conducted at periodic intervals. Since 1967 it has been taken every

In Brief

Personal computer shipments topped 14.8 million units in 1993.

1-megabit DRAM chips:

	1993
Revenue (millions)	*$2,031*
Shipments (mil. units)	*601*

5 years (for years ending in "2" and "7"). Census data, either direct reports or estimates from administrative records, are obtained for every manufacturing plant with one paid employee or more.

The *Annual Survey of Manufactures (ASM),* conducted for the first time in 1949, collects data for the years between censuses for the more general measures of manufacturing activity covered in detail by the censuses. The annual survey data are estimates derived from a scientifically selected sample of establishments. The 1991 annual survey is based on a sample of about 55,000 establishments of an approximate total of 200,000. These establishments represent all manufacturing establishments of multiunit companies and all single-establishment manufacturing companies mailed schedules in the 1987 Census of Manufactures. The 1989 through 1993 ASM sample is similar to the previous sample. For the current panel, all establishments of companies with 1987 shipments in manufacturing in excess of $500 million were included in the survey with certainty. For the remaining portion of the mail survey, the establishment was defined as the sampling unit. For this portion, all establishments with 250 employees or more and establishments with a very large value of shipments also were included. Therefore, of the 55,000 establishments included in the ASM panel, approximately 28,000 are selected with certainty. These establishments account for approximately 80 percent of total value of shipments in the 1987 census. Smaller establishments in the remaining portion of the mail survey were selected by sample.

The basic statistical measures of manufacturing activity, such as employment, payrolls, value added, etc., are defined in essentially the same way for both the annual surveys and the census of manufactures. However, the bases for computing average employment vary for different years. For example, beginning with 1949, average employment was calculated from the figures reported for the pay periods ending nearest the 15th of March, May, August, and November; whereas, for 1947 such averages were based on 12 monthly employment figures. In 1967, the average employment calculation was revised to the pay periods which include the 12th of March, May, August, and November to provide data more comparable with other statistical series.

Establishments and classification— The censuses of manufactures for 1947 through 1992 cover operating manufacturing establishments as defined in the *Standard Industrial Classification Manual (SIC)*, issued by the U.S. Office of Management and Budget (see text, section 13). The *Manual* is also used for classifying establishments in the annual surveys. The comparability of manufactures data over time is affected by changes in the official definitions of industries as presented in the *Manual*. It is important to note, therefore, that the 1987 edition of the *Manual* was used for the 1987 and 1992 censuses; and the 1972 edition of the *Manual* and the *1977 Supplement* were used for the 1972 through 1982 censuses. For the censuses from 1947 to 1963, reports were required from all establishments employing one or more persons at any time during the census year. Beginning with the 1967 census, an effort was made to relieve the very small establishments from the necessity of filing a census report. Approximately 150,000 small single-unit manufacturing firms identified as having less than 20 employees (cutoff varied by industry) benefited from this procedure. Data for these single-unit companies were estimated on the basis of government administrative records and industry averages. Each of the establishments tabulated was classified in 1 of the approximately 459

manufacturing industries as defined by the *SIC Manual* in 1987. The *Manual* defines an industry as a number of establishments producing a single product or a closely related group of products. In the main, an establishment is classified in a particular industry if its production of a product or product group exceeds in value added its production of any other product group. While some establishments produce only the products of the industry in which they are classified, few within an industry specialize to that extent. The statistics on employment, payrolls, value added, inventories, and expenditures, therefore, reflect both the primary and secondary activities of the establishments in that industry. For this reason, care should be exercised in relating such statistics to the total shipments figures of products primary to the industry.

The censuses for 1947 through 1992 were conducted on an establishment basis. The term "establishment" signifies a single physical plant site or factory. It is not necessarily identical to the business unit or company, which may consist of one or more establishments. A company operating establishments at more than one location is required to submit a separate report for each location. An establishment engaged in distinctly different lines of activity and maintaining separate payroll and inventory records is also required to submit separate reports.

Durable goods—Items with a normal life expectancy of 3 years or more. Automobiles, furniture, household appliances, and mobile homes are common examples.

Nondurable goods—Items which generally last for only a short time (3 years or less). Food, beverages, clothing, shoes, and gasoline are common examples.

Statistical reliability—For a discussion of statistical collection and estimation, sampling procedures and measures of statistical reliability applicable to Census Bureau data, see Appendix III.

Historical statistics—Tabular headnotes provide cross-references, where applicable, to *Historical Statistics of the United States, Colonial Times to 1970*. See Appendix IV.

No. 1209. Gross Domestic Product in Manufacturing: 1980 to 1993

[In billions of dollars. **1980** and **1985** data are shown on the basis of the 1972 Standard Industrial Classification (SIC). Beginning 1988, data are based on the 1987 SIC. Data include nonfactor charges (capital consumption allowances, indirect business taxes, etc.) as well as factor charges against gross product; corporate profits and capital consumption allowances have been shifted from a company to an establishment basis]

ITEM	1972 SIC BASIS		1987 SIC BASIS					
	1980	1985	1988	1989	1990	1991	1992	1993
CURRENT DOLLARS								
Gross domestic product	2,708	4,039	4,900	5,251	5,546	5,725	6,020	6,343
Manufacturing	588	798	961	1,005	1,025	1,033	1,063	1,118
Durable goods	349	472	541	563	564	554	568	603
Lumber and wood products	19	24	32	33	31	29	31	35
Furniture and fixtures	8	14	16	16	16	16	17	18
Stone, clay, and glass products	18	24	24	25	25	23	25	26
Primary metal industries	44	36	43	46	44	42	40	42
Fabricated metal products	45	57	63	67	67	65	70	71
Machinery, exc. electrical	77	87	(X)	(X)	(X)	(X)	(X)	(X)
Industrial machinery and equipment	(X)	(X)	100	106	109	101	103	108
Electric and electronic equipment	55	84	(X)	(X)	(X)	(X)	(X)	(X)
Electronic and other electric equipment	(X)	(X)	81	87	86	88	86	93
Motor vehicles and equipment	27	58	59	53	46	45	57	68
Other transportation equipment	26	48	56	60	65	66	61	61
Instruments and related products	20	27	50	52	56	59	60	60
Misc. manufacturing industries	10	14	17	18	19	19	20	22
Nondurable goods	239	327	420	442	461	478	495	515
Food and kindred products	52	72	83	88	97	102	104	106
Tobacco manufactures	7	11	14	14	16	17	19	17
Textile mill products	15	17	20	21	22	22	24	25
Apparel and other textile products	17	21	24	25	25	26	27	28
Paper and allied products	23	33	44	47	46	46	46	47
Printing and publishing	33	52	65	71	72	73	77	80
Chemicals and allied products	48	67	94	100	104	107	111	117
Petroleum and coal products	24	24	41	38	40	44	43	48
Rubber and misc. plastics products	17	26	31	34	35	36	39	41
Leather and leather products	4	4	4	4	4	4	5	5
CONSTANT (1987) DOLLARS								
Gross domestic product	3,776	4,280	4,719	4,838	4,897	4,868	4,979	5,135
Manufacturing	725	811	924	932	929	911	925	971
Durable goods	424	468	536	543	537	526	534	573
Lumber and wood products	22	25	30	29	28	26	25	23
Furniture and fixtures	12	14	15	15	14	14	15	16
Stone, clay, and glass products	24	25	25	26	26	23	25	25
Primary metal industries	49	35	34	33	35	38	36	40
Fabricated metal products	55	58	62	61	60	57	60	64
Machinery, exc. electrical	81	78	(X)	(X)	(X)	(X)	(X)	(X)
Industrial machinery and equipment	(X)	(X)	97	102	102	101	108	125
Electric and electronic equipment	70	83	(X)	(X)	(X)	(X)	(X)	(X)
Electronic and other electric equipment	(X)	(X)	85	91	91	94	93	103
Motor vehicles and equipment	40	63	63	57	49	44	51	56
Other transportation equipment	38	47	58	61	64	61	54	52
Instruments and related products	24	27	50	50	50	51	50	50
Misc. manufacturing industries	10	14	17	17	17	17	17	19
Nondurable goods	301	342	387	389	392	385	391	398
Food and kindred products	64	75	82	79	84	83	83	84
Tobacco manufactures	20	14	12	10	9	9	8	8
Textile mill products	17	18	20	21	21	21	23	23
Apparel and other textile products	20	21	24	25	24	24	25	25
Paper and allied products	31	36	40	39	42	42	44	46
Printing and publishing	53	59	63	64	62	59	58	57
Chemicals and allied products	58	67	83	84	88	86	88	88
Petroleum and coal products	15	23	30	31	26	25	25	25
Rubber and misc. plastic products	19	26	30	32	32	33	35	37
Leather and leather products	5	4	4	4	4	4	4	4

X Not applicable.

Source: U.S. Bureau of Economic Analysis, *Survey of Current Business*, May and November 1993.

No. 1210. Manufactures—Summary: 1972 to 1994

[For establishment coverage, see text, section 27. For compostion of regions, see table 26. See also, *Historical Statistics, Colonial Times to 1970*, series P 1-12]

ITEM	Unit	1972	1977	1982	1987	1992	1993 [1]	1994 [1]
ALL ESTABLISHMENTS								
Number of establishments [2]	1,000	321	360	358	369	382	(NA)	(NA)
With 20 or more employees	1,000	114	119	123	126	125	(NA)	(NA)
Employee size-class:								
Establishments [3]	1,000	313	351	348	359	371	(NA)	(NA)
Under 20	1,000	203	237	230	238	252	(NA)	(NA)
20 to 99	1,000	76	78	84	86	85	(NA)	(NA)
100 to 249	1,000	21	22	21	22	22	(NA)	(NA)
250 to 999	1,000	11	12	11	11	11	(NA)	(NA)
1,000 and over	1,000	3	2	2	2	2	(NA)	(NA)
Form of organization:								
Corporate	1,000	233.2	284.2	283.2	287.4	304.0	(NA)	(NA)
Noncorporate [4]	1,000	87.5	75.7	74.0	81.5	77.7	(NA)	(NA)
Individual proprietorship	1,000	42.5	52.3	45.6	35.4	40.9	(NA)	(NA)
Partnership	1,000	17.7	18.3	15.0	13.2	10.3	(NA)	(NA)
All employees: [5]								
Annual average [6]	Million	19.0	19.6	19.1	18.9	18.2	18.2	18.3
Payroll	Bil. dol.	174	264	380	476	559	573	594
Payroll per employee	$1,000	9.2	13.5	19.9	25.2	30.7	31.5	32.4
Production workers:								
Annual average	Million	13.5	13.7	12.4	12.2	11.6	11.7	11.9
Percent of all employees	Percent	71.1	69.9	64.9	64.6	63.8	64.3	65.1
Hours	Billion	26.7	26.7	23.5	24.3	23.6	23.8	24.5
Hours per worker	1,000	2.0	1.9	1.9	2.0	2.0	2.0	2.1
Wages	Bil. dol.	106	157	205	251	282	290	304
Percent of payroll for all employees	Percent	60.9	59.5	53.9	52.8	50.4	50.6	51.2
Wages per worker	$1,000	7.9	11.5	16.5	20.6	24.2	24.8	25.5
Wages per worker hour	Dollar	3.97	5.89	8.72	10.35	11.95	12.17	12.40
Value added by manufacture [7]	Bil. dol.	354	585	824	1,166	1,425	1,483	1,598
Per production worker	$1,000	26.2	42.7	66.5	95.5	122.6	126.5	133.9
Per production worker hour	Dollar	13.26	21.91	35.06	47.97	60.56	62.20	65.14
Per dollar of workers' wages	Dollar	3.34	3.73	4.02	4.64	5.07	5.11	5.25
Value added, percent distribution:								
Northeast	Percent	26.3	23.7	23.7	23.7	19.9	(NA)	(NA)
North Central	Percent	34.9	34.4	29.8	29.8	30.2	(NA)	(NA)
South	Percent	25.5	27.4	29.5	29.5	32.1	(NA)	(NA)
West	Percent	13.4	14.5	17.0	17.0	17.8	(NA)	(NA)
Cost of materials	Bil. dol.	407	782	1,130	1,320	1,571	1,647	1,752
Value of shipments [8]	Bil. dol.	757	1,359	1,960	2,476	3,006	3,128	3,340
Per production worker	$1,000	56.1	99.2	158.1	203.0	258.0	266.7	279.7
End-of-year inventories	Bil. dol.	108	188	307	333	374	383	397
New capital expenditures [9]	Bil. dol.	24.1	47.5	75.0	78.6	104.0	103.0	112.0
Gross book value of depreciable assets	Bil. dol.	301	439	692	868	1,128	(NA)	(NA)
Machinery and equipment	Bil. dol.	218	328	527	671	896	(NA)	(NA)
Assets per employee	$1,000	16.4	22.4	36.2	48.6	66.6	(NA)	(NA)
Operation ratios:								
Value added to shipments	Ratio	46.7	42.9	42.0	47.1	47.9	47.4	47.9
Inventories to shipments	Ratio	14.2	13.8	15.7	13.1	12.5	12.2	11.9
Payroll to value added	Ratio	49.1	45.2	46.1	40.8	34.7	38.7	37.2
MULTIUNIT COMPANIES								
Establishments	1,000	70.2	81.2	81.7	80.9	81.0	(NA)	(NA)
Employees	Million	14.3	15.0	14.3	13.8	13.1	(NA)	(NA)
Production workers	Million	9.8	10.1	8.8	8.5	8.0	(NA)	(NA)
Payroll	Bil. dol.	138.8	214.2	307.5	377.3	436.0	(NA)	(NA)
Wages, production workers	Bil. dol.	81.9	124.9	159.1	191.8	211.2	(NA)	(NA)
Value added by manufacture	Bil. dol.	286.1	485.0	678.4	953.6	1,160	(NA)	(NA)
New capital expenditures	Bil. dol.	20.0	41.0	65.2	66.5	87.8	(NA)	(NA)
SINGLE UNIT COMPANIES [10]								
Establishments	1,000	250.5	278.7	276.3	288.0	300.7	(NA)	(NA)
Employees	Million	4.8	4.6	4.8	5.1	5.1	(NA)	(NA)
Payroll	Bil. dol.	35.4	49.8	72.1	98.3	123.1	(NA)	(NA)
Value added by manufacture	Bil. dol.	67.9	100.1	145.7	212.1	265.0	(NA)	(NA)

NA Not available. [1] Estimated data based on *Annual Survey of Manufactures;* see text, section 26. [2] Includes administrative and auxiliary units. [3] Excludes administrative offices and auxiliary units. [4] Includes forms of organization not shown separately. [5] Includes data for employees of manufacturing establishments engaged in distribution and construction work. [6] Data are based on pay periods ending nearest 15th of March, May, August, and November. [7] Adjusted value added; takes into account (a) value added by merchandising operations (that is, difference between the sales value and cost of merchandise sold without further manufacture, processing, or assembly), plus (b) net change in finished goods and work-in-process inventories between beginning and end of year. [8] Includes extensive and unmeasurable duplication from shipments between establishments in the same industry classification. [9] Includes plants under construction and not yet in operation. [10] Beginning 1972, includes data obtained from Federal administrative records.

Source: Except as noted, U.S. Bureau of the Census, *Census of Manufactures, 1972, 1977, 1982, 1987* and *1992* and *Annual Survey of Manufactures.*

No. 1211. Manufactures—Summary, by Industry: 1987 to 1994

[Data based on various editions of the Standard Industrial Classification (SIC) Manual, published by the Office of Management and Budget; see text, section 26. N.e.c.=Not elsewhere classified. See also Historical Statistics, Colonial Times to 1970, series P 58-67]

INDUSTRY	SIC code	Establish-ments	1987 All employees Number (1,000)	1987 All employees Payroll (mil. dol.)	1987 Value added by manufacture (mil. dol.)	1992 All employees Number (1,000)	1992 All employees Payroll (mil. dol.)	1992 Production workers (1,000)	1992 Value added by manufacture (mil. dol.)	1994 All employees Number (1,000)	1994 All employees Payroll (mil. dol.)	1994 Production workers (1,000)	1994 Value added by manufacture (mil. dol.)	1994 Value of shipments (mil. dol.)
All manufacturing establishments	(X)	358,952	**17,718**	**428,480**	**1,165,741**	**16,949**	**494,109**	**11,641**	**1,424,700**	**18,344**	**594,104**	**11,941**	**1,598,464**	**3,340,223**
Food and kindred products	20	20,624	**1,449**	**30,268**	**122,073**	**1,503**	**36,772**	**1,100**	**157,260**	**1,512**	**38,492**	**1,112**	**171,988**	**430,994**
Meat products	201	3,267	341	5,701	13,740	400	7,564	343	19,141	420	8,262	362	22,510	98,116
Dairy products	202	2,366	142	3,217	11,909	135	3,720	85	15,258	132	3,802	82	15,385	53,761
Preserved fruits and vegetables	203	1,912	209	3,784	17,272	216	4,825	179	23,644	213	4,997	178	24,609	50,239
Grain mill products	204	2,610	102	2,704	15,271	107	3,375	74	21,000	105	3,410	72	23,964	54,273
Bakery products	205	2,850	217	4,761	15,252	215	5,599	133	17,905	222	5,944	138	19,939	31,471
Sugar and confectionery products	206	1,094	90	1,991	8,927	91	2,402	71	10,950	90	2,546	70	11,252	23,913
Fats and oils	207	595	30	702	3,246	28	778	19	3,770	26	787	18	4,301	20,775
Beverages	208	2,214	161	4,521	22,694	144	4,786	74	29,260	139	4,873	71	31,409	61,347
Miscellaneous foods and kindred products	209	3,716	158	2,887	13,762	166	3,723	121	16,333	165	3,872	120	18,619	37,099
Tobacco products	21	138	45	1,486	14,261	38	1,524	27	27,207	34	1,441	24	22,131	30,021
Cigarettes	211	11	32	1,486	12,967	25	1,205	19	24,802	23	1,152	16	19,759	24,879
Cigars	212	20	3	36	106	3	53	2	190	3	55	2	193	291
Chewing and smoking tobacco	213	29	3	77	792	3	92	2	1,213	3	98	2	1,500	1,871
Tobacco stemming and redrying	214	78	7	139	395	7	174	5	1,002	6	137	4	678	2,980
Textile mill products	22	6,412	672	11,410	26,014	616	12,398	529	30,060	624	13,587	534	32,905	78,267
Broadwoven fabric mills, cotton	221	301	72	1,260	2,609	56	1,147	50	2,504	56	1,250	51	3,549	6,262
Broadwoven fabric mills, manmade	222	441	88	1,596	3,648	87	1,850	77	4,008	81	1,869	71	4,172	9,424
Broadwoven fabric mills, wool	223	119	14	236	494	14	279	12	691	15	337	13	729	1,810
Narrow fabric mills	224	277	19	296	612	17	323	14	706	18	358	14	834	1,470
Knitting mills	225	2,130	203	2,988	6,409	195	3,400	170	8,052	194	3,578	170	9,238	19,128
Textile finishing, except wool	226	971	56	1,036	2,364	51	1,143	41	2,786	55	1,359	45	3,216	7,855
Carpets and rugs	227	477	53	1,039	3,190	49	1,088	39	3,480	55	1,314	43	3,959	10,961
Yarn and thread mills	228	610	114	1,850	3,821	92	1,744	84	4,059	90	1,857	81	4,040	12,125
Miscellaneous textile goods	229	1,086	53	1,109	2,867	55	1,423	42	3,775	62	1,665	47	4,166	9,231
Apparel and other textile products	23	22,872	1,081	13,904	33,311	985	15,325	824	36,423	953	15,593	798	38,700	76,898
Men's and boys' suits and coats	231	347	55	779	1,964	44	723	37	1,375	34	604	29	1,431	2,362
Men's and boys' furnishings	232	2,195	280	3,246	8,675	261	3,649	228	9,864	243	3,561	213	9,764	18,224
Women's and misses' outerwear	233	10,290	349	4,297	10,000	306	4,597	256	10,836	309	4,740	259	11,141	22,734
Women's and children's undergarments	234	557	68	839	2,071	54	798	46	2,193	47	747	39	2,122	4,245

See footnotes at end of table.

No. 1211. Manufactures—Summary, by Industry: 1987 to 1994—Continued

[See headnote, page 733]

SIC code	INDUSTRY	Establish-ments	1987 All employees Number (1,000)	1987 All employees Payroll (mil. dol.)	1987 Value added by manufacture (mil. dol.)	1992 All employees Number (1,000)	1992 All employees Payroll (mil. dol.)	1992 Production workers (1,000)	1992 Value added by manufacture (mil. dol.)	1994 All employees Number (1,000)	1994 All employees Payroll (mil. dol.)	1994 Production workers (1,000)	1994 Value added by manufacture (mil. dol.)	1994 Value of shipments (mil. dol.)
	Apparel, other textile products—Con.													
235	Hats, caps, and millinery	461	17	204	361	19	280	16	572	18	296	14	573	990
236	Girls' and children's outerwear	834	72	826	1,967	53	775	44	1,667	48	791	39	2,190	3,926
237	Fur goods	380	2	48	137	1	21	1	68	1	16	1	55	137
238	Miscellaneous apparel and accessories	986	41	518	1,169	37	566	30	1,260	33	545	27	1,426	2,637
239	Miscellaneous fabricated textile products	6,822	198	3,143	6,969	211	3,918	169	8,586	221	4,295	178	9,998	21,645
24	Lumber and wood products	33,982	698	12,707	28,591	656	13,882	540	33,154	719	15,901	595	40,689	103,642
241	Logging	11,952	86	1,518	4,164	83	1,689	69	5,017	87	1,820	72	5,948	16,818
242	Sawmills and planing mills	6,696	180	3,297	7,635	168	3,585	144	8,848	178	4,063	153	10,924	29,714
243	Millwork, plywood, and structural members	7,930	240	4,658	9,806	224	5,005	181	10,844	246	5,691	200	12,813	30,689
244	Wood containers	2,216	37	483	874	40	645	33	1,321	46	768	38	1,708	3,708
245	Wood buildings and mobile homes	1,077	65	1,215	2,453	56	1,234	44	2,531	70	1,654	56	3,618	9,787
249	Miscellaneous Wood Products	4,104	90	1,536	(NA)	84	1,725	69	4,593	92	1,905	76	5,679	12,927
25	Furniture and fixtures	11,613	511	9,082	20,239	471	10,227	372	22,840	496	11,284	399	25,185	50,039
251	Household furniture	5,606	284	4,452	9,481	253	4,804	213	10,942	267	5,327	229	11,735	23,663
252	Office Furniture	986	81	1,790	(NA)	68	1,868	51	4,626	70	2,022	53	5,041	8,663
253	Public building and related furniture	484	22	397	844	30	732	23	1,736	34	840	26	1,905	5,641
254	Partitions and fixtures	2,455	74	1,552	3,094	75	1,818	55	3,633	76	1,930	56	3,912	7,238
259	Miscellaneous furniture and fixtures	2,084	50	892	2,062	45	1,005	31	2,353	49	1,166	35	2,593	4,834
26	Paper and allied products	6,342	611	16,860	49,726	626	20,492	479	60,174	621	21,547	479	63,347	143,762
261	Pulp mills	39	14	535	2,247	16	689	12	2,554	12	570	9	1,926	4,424
262	Paper mills	281	129	4,597	13,694	131	5,421	100	14,848	123	5,519	95	15,012	35,071
263	Paperboard mills	199	52	1,859	7,002	52	2,136	39	8,195	55	2,392	41	8,894	18,749
265	Paperboard containers and boxes	2,796	194	4,618	9,815	199	5,722	151	12,406	202	6,212	156	13,706	36,124
267	Miscellaneous converted paper products	3,027	222	5,251	16,969	229	6,524	176	22,171	229	6,853	177	23,809	49,393
27	Printing and publishing	61,774	1,494	33,440	89,208	1,492	41,136	785	112,446	1,502	42,989	784	120,534	176,382
271	Newspapers	9,079	434	9,022	24,300	414	10,437	134	26,920	410	10,585	134	28,818	35,837
272	Periodicals	4,017	110	2,983	11,802	115	4,077	20	15,880	116	4,274	18	15,821	21,723
273	Books	2,856	114	2,821	10,316	130	4,037	57	14,325	134	4,287	54	16,521	24,117
274	Miscellaneous publishing	2,376	70	1,513	5,514	65	1,720	24	8,473	71	1,982	25	9,523	12,332
275	Commercial printing	36,103	553	12,301	25,025	567	15,337	408	31,898	579	16,431	418	34,709	60,527
276	Manifold business forms	853	53	1,281	3,883	48	1,341	34	3,922	45	1,249	30	3,706	6,982
277	Greeting cards	162	22	471	2,197	23	584	12	3,389	23	628	13	3,660	4,507
278	Blankbooks and bookbinding	1,545	69	1,265	2,918	66	1,461	51	3,640	65	1,496	51	3,846	5,362
279	Printing trade services	4,783	69	1,784	3,253	65	2,142	46	3,999	58	2,058	42	3,929	4,994

See footnotes at end of table.

No. 1211. Manufactures—Summary, by Industry: 1987 to 1994—Continued

[See headnote, page 733]

SIC code	INDUSTRY	1987 Establishments	1987 All employees Number (1,000)	1987 All employees Payroll (mil. dol.)	1987 Value added by manufacture (mil. dol.)	1992 All employees Number (1,000)	1992 All employees Payroll (mil. dol.)	1992 Production workers (1,000)	1992 Value added by manufacture (mil. dol.)	1994 All employees Number (1,000)	1994 All employees Payroll (mil. dol.)	1994 Production workers (1,000)	1994 Value added by manufacture (mil. dol.)	1994 Value of shipments (mil. dol.)
28	**Chemicals and allied products**	12,109	814	25,016	121,242	849	32,502	479	164,346	824	33,811	471	181,189	333,259
281	Industrial inorganic chemicals	1,405	94	3,099	11,154	103	4,214	55	16,724	87	3,669	47	15,058	24,940
282	Plastics materials and synthetics	680	123	4,013	17,882	129	5,137	86	20,979	128	5,302	85	24,497	55,314
283	Drugs	1,356	172	5,304	28,176	194	7,840	93	48,602	206	8,935	102	55,528	76,238
284	Soap, cleaners, and toilet goods	2,399	119	3,099	21,620	123	3,927	75	26,182	118	3,960	71	27,767	46,314
285	Paints and allied products	1,431	55	1,492	6,238	51	1,710	26	7,154	50	1,911	27	8,501	17,544
286	Industrial organic chemicals	961	126	4,541	21,542	125	5,495	72	26,132	115	5,595	68	28,942	69,596
287	Agricultural chemicals	973	40	1,171	6,379	40	1,451	25	8,659	40	1,550	26	10,302	20,899
289	Miscellaneous chemical products	2,904	85	2,298	8,249	84	2,727	48	9,915	80	2,890	47	10,595	22,413
29	**Petroleum and coal products**	2,254	116	3,996	18,399	114	4,967	74	23,408	112	5,224	73	28,594	143,150
291	Petroleum refining	331	75	2,845	14,128	75	3,640	48	18,607	72	3,796	46	23,232	128,236
295	Asphalt paving and roofing materials	1,367	28	786	2,883	26	846	18	3,006	27	935	20	3,245	8,668
299	Miscellaneous petroleum and coal products	556	13	365	1,388	14	481	7	1,796	14	493	7	2,118	6,246
30	**Rubber and misc. plastics products**	14,515	831	17,581	44,293	907	23,156	698	58,652	972	25,851	762	69,613	134,553
301	Tires and inner tubes	164	65	2,070	5,561	65	2,499	53	6,504	64	2,589	53	7,202	12,883
302	Rubber and plastics footwear	66	11	153	325	14	216	11	464	11	198	9	476	961
305	Hose and belting and plastics and packing	693	52	1,159	2,756	52	1,411	38	3,290	57	1,650	42	4,072	7,222
306	Fabricated rubber products, n.e.c	1,573	104	2,245	4,680	105	2,617	79	6,024	112	2,799	87	7,132	12,949
308	Miscellaneous plastics products, n.e.c.	12,019	599	11,955	30,971	671	16,413	516	42,370	728	18,616	571	50,731	100,538
31	**Leather and leather products**	2,193	129	1,831	4,275	101	1,806	83	4,527	92	1,712	78	4,623	9,545
311	Leather tanning and finishing	344	15	292	745	17	420	13	891	16	416	13	985	3,038
313	Footwear cut stock	128	5	70	142	4	63	3	149	3	62	3	143	319
314	Footwear, except rubber	479	71	913	2,106	49	762	41	2,060	47	759	40	2,191	3,923
315	Leather gloves and mittens	77	3	34	75	3	35	2	69	3	35	2	63	143
316	Luggage	241	11	196	467	10	191	8	509	9	174	7	549	991
317	Handbags and personal leather goods	529	17	232	519	11	202	9	470	8	142	7	416	697
319	Leather goods, n.e.c.	395	7	95	221	8	133	6	304	7	123	6	276	434

See footnotes at end of table.

No. 1211. Manufactures—Summary, by Industry: 1987 to 1994—Continued

[See headnote, page 733]

INDUSTRY	SIC code	1987 Establishments	1987 All employees Number[1] (1,000)	1987 All employees Payroll (mil. dol.)	1987 Value added by manufacture (mil. dol.)	1992 All employees Number[1] (1,000)	1992 All employees Payroll (mil. dol.)	1992 Production workers (1,000)	1992 Value added by manufacture (mil. dol.)	1994 All employees Number[1] (1,000)	1994 All employees Payroll (mil. dol.)	1994 Production workers (1,000)	1994 Value added by manufacture (mil. dol.)	1994 Value of shipments (mil. dol.)
Stone, clay, and glass products	**32**	**16,166**	**524**	**12,349**	**33,076**	**469**	**13,113**	**357**	**34,641**	**485**	**14,145**	**374**	**39,557**	**71,227**
Flat glass	321	81	15	507	1,618	12	451	10	1,311	11	503	9	1,651	2,600
Glass and glassware, pressed or blown	322	522	77	1,959	4,944	66	2,075	56	5,900	63	2,051	54	6,198	9,628
Products of purchased glass	323	1,432	51	1,060	2,847	55	1,369	42	3,757	58	1,535	46	4,254	7,935
Cement, hydraulic	324	215	19	599	2,284	17	595	13	2,149	17	629	12	2,800	4,808
Structural clay products	325	598	35	689	1,733	31	734	24	1,695	31	778	24	1,944	3,247
Pottery and related products	326	1,006	38	762	1,638	37	863	29	1,995	41	974	33	2,322	3,301
Concrete, gypsum, and plaster products	327	9,814	203	4,632	11,762	174	4,741	126	11,008	184	5,194	136	12,783	26,853
Cut stone and stone products	328	745	13	243	449	12	282	9	604	13	311	10	662	1,112
Miscellaneous nonmetallic mineral products	329	1,753	73	1,898	5,803	66	2,004	49	6,222	68	2,172	50	6,944	11,744
Primary metal industries[2]	**33**	**6,771**	**701**	**19,777**	**46,471**	**662**	**22,202**	**508**	**52,027**	**664**	**23,974**	**516**	**61,554**	**160,771**
Blast furnace and basic steel products	331	1,241	253	8,166	21,081	239	9,179	182	22,173	226	9,643	175	27,665	69,729
Iron and steel foundries	332	1,231	130	3,426	6,187	122	3,739	99	6,873	123	4,176	101	8,242	14,032
Primary nonferrous metals	333	169	32	996	2,975	35	1,334	27	3,391	34	1,275	26	4,198	14,546
Secondary nonferrous metals	334	397	13	312	947	13	407	9	1,233	14	466	11	1,955	7,152
Nonferrous rolling and drawing	335	1,066	163	4,298	10,140	147	4,635	109	12,335	153	5,076	116	14,762	41,854
Nonferrous foundries (castings)	336	1,687	80	1,805	3,382	75	1,942	59	3,927	82	2,251	67	4,899	8,672
Fabricated metal products	**34**	**36,105**	**1,458**	**35,000**	**75,503**	**1,362**	**38,962**	**994**	**83,761**	**1,407**	**42,020**	**1,054**	**96,698**	**190,172**
Metal cans and shipping containers	341	538	48	1,527	4,224	40	1,465	33	3,736	39	1,493	32	3,770	13,025
Cutlery, handtools, and hardware	342	2,327	145	3,389	8,055	134	3,648	99	9,044	139	3,955	106	10,560	18,277
Plumbing and heating, except electric	343	828	46	1,005	2,780	29	1,152	29	3,105	44	1,288	31	3,972	6,806
Fabricated structural metal products	344	12,579	407	9,042	18,798	389	10,362	275	21,256	401	11,069	289	24,314	51,452
Screw machine products, bolts, etc.	345	2,569	95	2,270	4,762	91	2,624	68	5,269	95	2,875	74	6,250	10,463
Metal forgings and stampings	346	4,062	255	7,235	13,223	234	7,749	185	14,913	247	8,882	200	17,897	36,747
Metal services, n.e.c.	347	5,251	113	2,167	4,730	108	2,652	83	5,679	119	3,026	92	6,966	12,314
Ordnance and accessories, n.e.c.	348	374	88	2,458	5,343	62	2,124	35	4,536	45	1,539	28	3,994	5,555
Miscellaneous fabricated metal products	349	7,577	262	5,906	13,589	263	7,185	186	16,224	278	7,893	203	18,975	35,532
Industrial machinery and equipment	**35**	**52,135**	**1,844**	**50,553**	**119,018**	**1,739**	**57,231**	**1,086**	**132,923**	**1,827**	**62,947**	**1,176**	**161,200**	**314,423**
Engines and turbines	351	356	87	2,906	7,018	83	3,135	52	7,738	81	3,382	55	10,239	21,754
Farm and garden machinery	352	1,804	82	1,917	5,638	86	2,354	63	7,318	95	2,794	71	9,634	20,037
Construction and related machinery	353	3,467	188	5,272	11,331	176	5,664	108	12,489	185	6,264	118	15,303	33,989
Metalworking machinery	354	11,470	268	7,301	13,766	255	8,571	178	16,542	264	9,318	188	19,788	31,313
Special industry machinery	355	4,550	169	4,588	9,699	162	5,515	91	11,667	171	6,383	98	15,075	26,786
General industrial machinery	356	3,929	240	6,203	13,757	244	7,742	154	17,817	247	8,293	161	20,339	36,036
Computer and office equipment	357	2,134	328	10,668	33,167	251	10,143	89	29,229	250	10,403	88	34,181	79,573
Refrigeration and service machinery	358	2,129	190	4,752	11,622	179	5,264	125	13,597	190	5,895	138	15,878	33,537
Industrial machinery, n.e.c.	359	22,296	292	6,946	13,218	304	8,843	227	16,527	344	10,215	260	20,764	31,398

See footnotes at end of table.

No. 1211. Manufactures—Summary, by Industry: 1987 to 1994—Continued

[See headnote, page 733]

INDUSTRY	SIC code	1987 Establishments	1987 All employees Number (1,000)	1987 All employees Payroll (mil. dol.)	1987 Value added by manufacture (mil. dol.)	1992 All employees Number (1,000)	1992 All employees Payroll (mil. dol.)	1992 Production workers (1,000)	1992 Value added by manufacture (mil. dol.)	1994 All employees Number (1,000)	1994 All employees Payroll (mil. dol.)	1994 Production workers (1,000)	1994 Value added by manufacture (mil. dol.)	1994 Value of shipments (mil. dol.)
Electronics; other electric equip.	**36**	15,962	1,565	38,738	95,958	1,439	44,197	911	121,158	1,470	47,617	949	145,671	257,800
Electric distribution equipment	361	766	77	1,791	4,577	68	1,946	48	5,437	70	2,126	49	5,996	10,813
Electrical industrial apparatus	362	2,213	166	3,882	9,020	157	4,387	106	10,850	165	4,850	114	12,440	22,784
Household appliances	363	480	117	2,642	7,444	103	2,571	83	7,964	110	2,992	90	10,305	22,794
Electric lighting and wiring equipment	364	1,986	167	3,732	10,314	148	3,974	107	11,307	154	4,336	113	12,487	22,204
Household audio and video equipment	365	854	44	850	3,004	47	1,123	35	3,486	47	1,241	37	4,279	12,628
Communications equipment	366	1,437	260	7,537	19,804	239	9,111	114	26,522	230	9,159	108	29,031	48,052
Electronic components and accessories	367	5,911	546	13,623	30,635	530	16,752	317	44,305	546	18,297	336	58,357	93,635
Misc. electrical equipment and supplies	369	2,315	188	4,682	11,160	147	4,332	100	11,287	146	4,617	102	12,775	24,891
Transportation equipment	**37**	10,500	1,817	58,790	135,783	1,647	62,734	1,080	158,326	1,554	64,061	1,062	173,940	452,363
Motor vehicles and equipment	371	4,422	751	23,910	65,778	703	26,213	565	80,935	776	31,935	636	102,049	314,440
Aircraft and parts	372	1,618	596	20,590	40,189	548	22,647	281	47,661	424	19,446	205	43,610	84,287
Ship and boat building and repairing	373	2,766	177	4,266	7,657	163	4,634	122	8,560	150	4,408	114	8,049	15,289
Railroad equipment	374	173	22	631	1,285	28	900	21	2,015	30	1,076	22	2,535	6,569
Motorcycles, bicycles, and parts	375	246	7	158	368	13	343	10	891	16	483	12	1,149	2,632
Guided missiles, space vehicles, parts	376	156	214	8,114	18,152	146	6,780	50	15,246	111	5,453	38	13,351	20,715
Miscellaneous transportation equipment	379	1,119	49	1,122	2,354	46	1,218	33	3,018	48	1,261	35	3,197	8,430
Instruments and related products	**38**	10,326	982	28,778	71,487	907	33,067	460	89,394	830	31,941	430	92,880	138,798
Search and navigation equipment	381	1,137	369	12,368	24,648	253	10,962	103	24,299	199	9,396	80	21,900	30,103
Measuring and controlling devices	382	4,240	285	7,807	17,326	276	9,632	138	21,775	264	9,782	138	24,427	38,800
Medical instruments and supplies	384	3,443	204	5,027	14,865	264	8,522	154	26,082	266	9,143	154	27,945	42,776
Ophthalmic goods	385	494	24	475	1,094	29	714	20	1,938	28	719	19	2,096	2,929
Photographic equipment and supplies	386	791	88	2,878	13,059	77	3,061	39	14,862	65	2,717	35	16,057	23,368
Watches, clocks, watchcases and parts	387	221	12	223	496	8	177	6	438	7	185	5	456	823
Misc. manufacturing industries	**39**	16,544	374	6,884	17,432	366	8,417	255	21,975	383	9,070	272	24,466	44,156
Jewelry, silverware, and plated ware	391	2,978	50	941	2,487	46	1,068	32	2,501	44	1,070	29	2,723	6,095
Musical instruments	393	425	12	218	518	12	273	9	589	12	281	10	638	1,062
Toys and sporting goods	394	2,711	89	1,512	4,868	98	2,133	71	6,816	103	2,345	77	7,372	13,489
Pens, pencils, office, and art supplies	395	1,013	29	540	1,431	30	684	21	2,030	32	749	23	2,282	3,985
Costume jewelry and notions	396	1,020	32	498	1,155	27	557	19	1,366	27	569	20	1,502	2,526
Miscellaneous manufactures	399	8,397	163	3,174	6,972	153	3,702	103	8,674	165	4,055	114	9,951	16,999
Administrative and auxiliary [3]	(X)	9,480	1,234	47,202	-					1,265	70,898			-

- Represents zero. NA Not available. X Not applicable. [1] Represents the average of production workers plus all other employees for the payroll period ended nearest the 15th of March. [2] Includes other industries not shown separately. [3] Manufacturing concerns often reported separately for central offices or auxiliaries which serve the manufacturing establishment of a company, rather than the general public. Separate reports were obtained from such units if at a different location or if they serviced more than one establishment.

Source: U.S. Bureau of the Census, *1992 Census of Manufactures and Annual Survey of Manufactures.*

No. 1212. Manufactures—Summary, by Industry: Selected Based on Value Added: 1987 to 1994

[Data based on various editions of the *Standard Industrial Classification (SIC) Manual*, published by the Office of Management and Budget; see text, section 26. N.e.c.=Not elsewhere classified. See also *Historical Statistics, Colonial Times to 1970*, series P 58-67]

INDUSTRY	SIC code	1987 Establishments	1987 All employees Number (1,000)	1987 All employees Payroll (mil. dol.)	1987 Value of shipments (mil. dol.)	1992 All employees Number (1,000)	1992 All employees Payroll (mil. dol.)	1992 Value of shipments (mil. dol.)	1994 All employees Number (1,000)	1994 All employees Payroll (mil. dol.)	1994 Production workers (1,000)	1994 Value added by manufacture (mil. dol.)	1994 Value of shipments (mil. dol.)
Meat packing plants	2011	1,434	113.2	2,141	44,991	121.2	2,441	50,167	119.5	2,597	102.2	8,350	50,444
Sausages and other prepared meats	2013	1,344	79.1	1,619	16,623	85.4	2,023	19,940	84.8	2,059	67.0	5,836	20,257
Poultry slaughtering and processing	2015	463	147.7	1,919	14,912	193.8	3,100	23,965	216.0	3,605	193.2	8,324	27,415
Fluid milk	2026	946	72.4	1,681	20,591	63.4	1,840	21,926	61.6	1,850	30.9	6,088	22,474
Canned fruits and vegetables	2033	647	65.6	1,163	11,890	63.6	1,465	15,071	60.1	1,438	50.6	6,424	14,481
Frozen specialties, n.e.c.	2038	288	37.5	669.1	5,625	46.7	972	7,886	46.1	991	38.4	4,540	8,864
Cereal breakfast foods	2043	53	16.0	599	6,566	16.1	745	9,737	17.1	765	14.1	8,177	11,507
Bread, cake, and related products	2051	2,357	161.6	3,556	16,202	154.9	4,059	18,130	159.0	4,263	88.6	12,177	19,329
Cookies and crackers	2052	380	45.4	1,010	6,309	47.0	1,247	8,668	48.7	1,335	37.7	6,630	10,094
Candy and other confectionery products	2064	685	45.8	900	6,980	51.5	1,261	10,202	51.2	1,347	40.7	6,504	10,911
Malt beverages	2082	134	31.9	1,355	13,619	34.5	1,567	17,340	33.5	1,566	23.6	9,847	16,795
Bottled and canned soft drinks	2086	1,190	95.6	2,277	22,006	77.1	2,163	25,423	73.4	2,213	29.0	11,647	28,334
Flavoring extracts and syrups, n.e.c.	2087	280	9.1	258	4,665	10.3	342	6,923	11.0	372	6.4	5,517	7,440
Food preparations, n.e.c.	2099	1,658	57.9	1,110	9,787	61.4	1,413	12,165	64.3	1,547	45.7	6,530	13,315
Cigarettes	2111	12	32.0	1,234	17,372	25.4	1,205	29,746	23.0	1,152	16.4	19,759	24,879
Logging	2411	11,936	85.7	1,516	10,880	83.2	1,689	13,592	87.2	1,820	71.7	5,948	16,818
Sawmills and planing mills, general	2421	5,742	148.2	2,817	17,357	137.6	3,040	21,061	142.2	3,413	121.8	9,476	26,761
Wood household furniture	2511	2,948	135.8	2,017	7,980	121.1	2,174	8,730	125.4	2,363	110.6	5,248	9,919
Paper mills	2621	282	129.1	4,597	28,916	130.6	5,421	32,786	122.8	5,519	94.9	15,012	35,071
Paperboard mills	2631	205	52.3	1,859	13,730	51.5	2,136	16,140	54.9	2,392	41.4	8,894	18,749
Corrugated and solid fiber boxes	2653	1,601	105.8	2,610	16,107	112.3	3,276	19,834	119.1	3,713	89.1	7,766	22,802
Sanitary paper products	2676	133	38.4	1,155	11,698	40.6	1,454	15,647	39.7	1,470	32.6	8,859	16,200
Newspapers	2711	9,091	434.6	9,025	31,849	413.9	10,437	33,782	410.1	10,585	133.7	28,818	35,837
Periodicals	2721	4,020	110.0	2,983	17,329	115.1	4,077	22,104	116.4	4,274	18.3	15,821	21,723
Book publishing	2731	2,298	70.1	1,860	12,620	79.0	2,676	16,698	87.1	2,936	25.3	13,681	19,419
Miscellaneous publishing	2741	2,369	69.4	1,513	7,810	65.1	1,720	10,908	71.2	1,982	18.7	9,523	12,332
Commercial printing, lithographic	2752	24,980	403.0	9,132	32,698	438.2	12,016	43,352	439.8	12,618	319.3	26,474	45,847
Commercial printing, n.e.c.	2759	10,796	126.2	2,490	8,973	107.4	2,588	9,265	117.1	2,752	79.8	6,454	10,973
Manifold business forms	2761	853	53.2	1,276	7,359	47.9	1,341	7,429	45.1	1,249	29.6	3,706	6,982
Industrial inorganic chemicals, n.e.c.	2819	662	72.2	2,425	13,212	78.9	3,266	18,129	64.6	3,150	32.7	9,766	16,033
Plastics materials and resins	2821	480	56.3	2,006	26,246	61.2	2,698	31,601	69.2	3,150	40.6	15,117	36,965
Organic fibers, noncellulosic	2824	72	45.7	1,347	10,112	44.4	1,545	11,113	40.7	1,417	31.6	6,437	12,213
Pharmaceutical preparations	2834	732	131.6	4,168	32,094	122.9	4,958	50,415	134.2	5,754	68.6	42,615	56,961
Soap and other detergents	2841	764	31.7	956	11,559	32.8	1,171	14,729	31.3	1,167	18.5	7,377	14,528
Polishes and sanitation goods	2842	726	20.6	500	5,594	21.2	662	6,659	21.2	649	12.9	5,468	8,372
Toilet preparations	2844	694	58.5	1,353	14,593	59.8	1,774	18,629	57.6	1,797	35.3	13,327	19,736
Paints and allied products	2851	1,426	55.2	1,491	12,701	51.1	1,710	14,973	50.1	1,911	27.0	8,501	17,544
Industrial organic chemicals, n.e.c.	2869	699	100.3	3,696	42,189	99.8	4,494	54,103	89.3	4,501	52.6	24,329	57,671
Agricultural chemicals, n.e.c.	2879	277	16.1	518	6,300	16.8	669	9,142	15.3	700	8.8	5,898	9,636
Chemical preparations, n.e.c.	2899	1,529	37.9	1,021	8,024	37.1	1,233	9,927	36.5	1,365	20.1	5,724	11,370

See footnotes at end of table.

INDUSTRY	SIC code	1987				1992			1994				
		Establish-ments	All employees Number¹ (1,000)	Payroll (mil. dol.)	Value of shipments (mil. dol.)	All employees Number¹ (1,000)	Payroll (mil. dol.)	Value of shipments (mil. dol.)	All employees Number¹ (1,000)	Payroll (mil. dol.)	Production workers (1,000)	Value added by manufacture (mil. dol.)	Value of shipments (mil. dol.)
Petroleum refining	2911	309	74.6	2,846	118,216	74.9	3,640	136,551	71.7	3,796	46.3	23,232	105,723
Tires and inner tubes	3011	163	65.4	2,070	10,427	64.6	2,499	11,814	63.7	2,589	52.7	7,202	12,883
Unsupported plastics film and sheet	3081	594	48.4	1,256	8,140	54.7	1,680	10,619	56.3	1,822	41.7	6,103	12,562
Plastics products, n.e.c.	3089	8,571	384.7	7,286	33,774	427.8	9,998	45,376	470.7	11,443	372.8	29,248	54,297
Ready-mixed concrete	3273	5,321	96.9	2,289	12,975	82.4	2,293	12,015	87.2	2,551	67.6	6,168	13,831
Blast furnaces and steel mills	3312	342	188.9	6,451	38,663	170.1	7,022	42,154	156.1	7,272	121.7	20,693	50,634
Nonferrous wiredrawing and insulating	3357	487	64.9	1,504	10,827	60.6	1,724	13,044	64.3	1,952	48.2	6,019	15,347
Hardware, n.e.c.	3429	1,240	85.6	2,056	8,175	75.4	2,063	8,806	79.1	2,259	60.2	5,585	10,518
Fabricated structural metal	3441	2,454	80.9	1,881	8,667	72.0	1,964	8,919	71.3	2,009	51.5	4,242	9,832
Fabricated plate work (boiler shops)	3443	1,740	74.6	1,842	9,700	78.4	2,312	8,975	80.4	2,426	57.8	5,263	10,079
Sheet metal work	3444	4,297	100.3	2,237	15,252	103.9	2,834	11,299	108.0	3,049	79.9	6,760	13,163
Automotive stampings	3465	713	119.8	3,977	8,331	105.1	4,094	15,803	114.0	4,882	95.4	9,075	19,653
Metal stampings, n.e.c.	3469	2,815	95.5	2,132	11,123	91.8	2,470	9,559	97.7	2,765	76.9	6,020	11,362
Internal combustion engines, n.e.c.	3519	278	64.0	2,043	6,880	55.5	2,029	11,707	54.2	2,145	39.9	6,292	14,953
Farm machinery and equipment	3523	1,634	57.0	1,416	12,773	61.5	1,786	9,620	67.1	2,111	48.1	6,855	13,218
Construction machinery	3531	955	81.2	2,429	7,550	74.6	2,458	13,139	77.9	2,706	52.9	7,674	17,697
Special dies, tools, jigs, and fixtures	3544	7,317	114.4	3,164	8,275	110.8	3,883	9,265	119.5	4,353	92.4	8,090	11,195
Special industry machinery, n.e.c.	3559	2,531	83.3	2,286	33,627	83.3	2,947	11,479	87.7	3,473	49.1	8,748	15,192
Electronic computers	3571	974	151.9	4,953	13,692	110.6	4,849	38,202	109.4	5,074	30.4	21,066	48,547
Refrigeration and heating equipment	3585	892	133.3	3,355	6,753	120.7	3,594	19,739	130.6	4,103	99.1	11,286	24,397
Industrial machinery, n.e.c.	3599	21,545	228.4	5,119	6,101	248.9	7,040	19,117	288.8	8,286	221.2	16,488	23,955
Motors and generators	3621	462	74.6	1,664	17,583	67.9	1,762	8,168	74.0	1,914	58.1	4,777	9,429
Relays and industrial controls	3625	1,168	66.6	1,631	14,229	62.5	1,864	7,741	64.8	2,122	37.6	5,560	9,473
Telephone and telegraph apparatus	3661	469	112.3	3,776	19,795	91.1	3,739	20,510	86.1	3,577	41.2	12,354	20,877
Radio and TV communications equip.	3663	655	126.0	5,495	15,439	124.9	4,721	19,521	120.2	4,837	55.0	14,436	20,877
Semiconductors and related devices	3674	853	184.6	5,495	19,795	172.0	6,884	32,191	173.6	7,464	89.1	32,084	42,252
Electronic components, n.e.c.	3679	2,900	162.6	3,891	15,439	180.2	5,119	23,670	196.5	5,965	118.9	14,922	31,610
Motor vehicles and car bodies	3711	413	284.4	10,376	133,346	227.8	10,434	151,682	234.0	12,438	202.5	52,918	197,554
Motor vehicle parts and accessories	3714	2,807	389.1	11,947	62,000	400.0	13,955	75,058	454.1	17,229	364.1	43,598	100,983
Aircraft	3721	155	268.2	9,680	39,093	264.6	11,493	62,940	217.9	10,312	92.8	23,606	50,944
Aircraft engines and engine parts	3724	453	139.6	4,814	20,262	120.4	4,966	22,408	86.9	3,786	46.4	7,957	16,664
Aircraft parts and equipment, n.e.c.	3728	1,013	187.7	6,088	17,923	163.1	6,187	19,511	119.5	5,348	65.4	12,047	16,679
Ship building and repairing	3731	590	120.2	3,218	8,504	118.2	3,631	10,601	101.5	3,311	75.6	5,760	9,864
Guided missiles and space vehicles	3761	40	166.7	6,415	21,566	97.7	4,637	19,423	76.8	3,806	25.0	10,121	15,397
Search and navigation equipment	3812	1,084	369.4	12,373	36,267	253.0	10,962	35,039	199.4	9,396	79.7	21,900	30,103
Instruments to measure electricity	3825	930	85.2	2,477	7,780	68.5	2,544	8,826	62.6	2,547	31.8	6,661	10,098
Surgical and medical instruments	3841	1,136	73.1	1,786	7,780	98.2	3,099	13,396	100.5	3,404	60.0	10,272	14,812
Surgical appliances and supplies	3842	1,500	78.5	1,786	8,533	96.4	2,846	13,801	96.1	3,000	59.4	9,366	14,573
Photographic equipment and supplies	3861	787	88.0	2,878	19,241	77.3	3,061	22,119	64.8	2,717	34.8	16,057	23,368

¹ Represents the average of production workers plus all other employees for the payroll period ended nearest the 15th of the month.

Source: U.S. Bureau of the Census, 1992 Census of Manufactures and Annual Survey of Manufactures.

No. 1213. Manufactures Summary: 1992

[Sum of State totals may not add to U.S. total because U.S. and State figures were independently derived]

REGION, DIVISION, AND STATE	Establish-ments [1]	ALL EMPLOYEES [2]			PRODUCTION WORKERS [2]		Value added by manu-facture [3] (mil. dol.)	Value of ship-ments [4] (mil. dol.)
		Number (1,000)	Payroll (mil. dol.)	Payroll per employee (dol.)	Total (1,000)	Wages (mil. dol.)		
U.S.	381,870	18,253	560,485	30,706	11,654	281,737	1,428,707	3,006,275
Northeast	82,967	3,699	122,862	33,215	2,162	53,564	283,865	525,662
N.E.	24,967	1,124	37,791	33,622	660	16,765	81,692	145,315
ME	2,200	91	2,447	26,890	67	1,589	5,458	11,611
NH	2,332	94	2,820	30,000	60	1,470	6,493	11,260
VT	1,343	45	1,289	28,644	30	659	3,379	6,386
MA	10,145	480	16,421	34,210	273	7,085	36,519	65,702
RI	2,664	88	2,403	27,307	59	1,229	5,166	9,578
CT	6,283	326	12,411	38,071	171	4,733	24,677	40,778
M.A.	58,000	2,575	85,071	33,037	1,502	36,799	202,173	380,347
NY	26,617	1,049	35,225	33,580	592	14,354	86,349	154,211
NJ	13,281	574	20,616	35,916	301	7,676	46,091	86,885
PA	18,102	952	29,230	30,704	609	14,769	69,733	139,251
Midwest	73,020	5,470	175,883	32,154	3,525	94,148	432,051	942,160
E.N.C.	72,979	4,098	135,913	33,166	2,646	73,551	323,581	697,113
OH	18,292	1,046	34,904	33,369	681	19,317	86,161	184,637
IN	9,285	619	19,114	30,879	435	11,662	49,662	104,871
IL	18,784	970	31,605	32,582	588	14,977	74,860	158,129
MI	16,531	917	34,207	37,303	574	18,452	71,724	161,409
WI	10,087	546	16,083	29,456	368	9,143	41,174	88,067
W.N.C.	26,740	1,372	39,970	29,133	879	20,597	108,470	245,047
MN	7,934	394	12,664	32,142	225	5,391	27,175	57,324
IA	3,913	227	6,484	28,564	158	3,852	20,502	46,432
MO	7,846	408	11,868	29,088	260	6,049	33,995	73,746
ND	666	19	438	23,053	13	257	1,423	3,678
SD	889	35	739	21,114	25	448	2,267	5,956
NE	2,028	100	2,516	25,160	72	1,555	7,952	21,816
KS	3,464	189	5,261	27,836	126	3,045	15,156	36,095
South	112,543	5,908	158,853	26,888	4,095	88,503	458,531	1,019,572
S.A.	56,717	2,989	80,393	26,896	2,052	43,314	228,773	461,046
DE	736	67	2,770	41,343	31	850	4,881	13,000
MD	4,337	195	6,291	32,261	114	3,005	15,588	31,047
DC	458	13	553	42,538	4	116	1,570	2,008
VA	6,521	408	11,265	27,610	283	6,400	35,933	65,860
WV	1,786	78	2,337	29,962	56	1,457	6,511	13,217
NC	11,877	831	20,456	24,616	609	11,842	65,446	128,599
SC	4,839	367	9,425	25,681	272	5,689	24,725	51,996
GA	9,767	556	14,278	25,680	394	8,159	41,038	90,999
FL	16,396	474	13,018	27,464	289	5,796	33,081	64,320
E.S.C.	22,123	1,399	34,389	24,581	1,045	21,746	98,705	221,601
KY	4,310	277	7,524	27,162	203	4,691	25,265	60,029
TN	7,610	504	12,618	25,036	370	7,755	35,799	76,209
AL	6,436	380	9,217	24,255	284	5,934	23,653	52,708
MS	3,767	238	5,030	21,134	188	3,366	13,988	32,655
W.S.C.	33,703	1,520	44,071	28,994	998	23,443	131,053	336,925
AR	3,913	227	4,878	21,489	179	3,353	14,204	34,050
LA	4,048	179	5,460	30,503	126	3,308	20,509	60,940
OK	4,064	157	4,282	27,274	109	2,611	13,808	30,287
TX	21,678	957	29,451	30,774	584	14,171	82,532	211,648
West	86,641	3,183	102,889	32,325	1,873	45,520	254,261	518,884
Mountain	19,211	631	18,453	29,244	387	8,975	50,939	100,596
MT	1,375	22	544	24,727	16	364	1,421	4,137
ID	1,838	66	1,769	26,803	46	1,022	4,465	10,557
WY	577	9	225	25,000	6	146	856	2,385
CO	5,295	184	5,926	32,207	107	2,773	15,300	29,220
NM	1,594	39	965	24,744	27	564	4,946	9,492
AZ	4,758	177	5,420	30,621	99	2,244	14,960	25,767
UT	2,525	106	2,860	26,981	68	1,477	7,271	15,750
NV	1,249	28	744	26,571	18	385	1,720	3,288
Pacific	67,430	2,552	84,436	33,086	1,486	36,545	203,322	418,288
WA	8,521	342	11,612	33,953	200	5,531	27,765	72,800
OR	6,865	213	6,076	28,526	144	3,453	14,444	32,215
CA	50,513	1,960	65,766	33,554	1,117	26,955	158,240	305,805
AK	513	16	426	26,625	12	313	1,347	3,678
HI	1,018	21	556	26,476	13	293	1,526	3,790

[1] Includes central administrative offices and auxiliary units. [2] Includes employment and payroll at administrative offices and auxiliary units. All employees represents the average of production workers plus all other employees for the payroll period ended nearest the 12th of March. Production workers represents the average of the employment for the payroll periods ended nearest the 12th of March, May, August, and November. [3] Adjusted value added; takes into account (a) value added by merchandising operations (that is, difference between the sales value and cost of merchandise sold without further manufacture, processing, or assembly), plus (b) net change in finished goods and work-inprocess inventories between beginning and end of year. [4] Includes extensive and unmeasurable duplication from shipments between establishments in the same industry classification.

Source: U.S. Bureau of the Census, *1992 Census of Manufactures.*

No. 1214. Average Hourly Earnings of Production Workers in Manufacturing Industries, by State: 1980 to 1995

[In dollars]

DIVISION AND STATE	1980	1985	1989	1990	1991	1992	1993	1994	1995
United States.	7.27	9.54	10.48	10.83	11.18	11.46	11.74	12.06	12.35
New England:									
Maine.	6.00	8.40	9.92	10.59	11.08	11.40	11.63	11.91	12.39
New Hampshire	5.87	8.39	10.37	10.83	10.84	11.22	11.62	11.74	11.93
Vermont	6.14	8.41	9.99	10.52	11.00	11.52	11.82	11.96	12.21
Massachusetts.	6.51	9.00	10.87	11.39	11.81	12.15	12.36	12.59	12.79
Rhode Island	5.59	7.59	9.06	9.45	9.73	9.92	10.20	10.35	10.62
Connecticut	7.08	9.57	11.21	11.53	11.99	12.46	13.01	13.53	13.72
Middle Atlantic:									
New York	7.18	9.67	10.67	11.11	11.43	11.72	11.97	12.19	12.50
New Jersey	7.31	9.86	11.17	11.76	12.17	12.57	12.98	13.36	13.56
Pennsylvania	7.59	9.57	10.66	11.04	11.46	11.78	12.11	12.49	12.81
East North Central:									
Ohio.	8.57	11.38	12.26	12.64	13.12	13.49	14.05	14.40	14.42
Indiana	8.49	(NA)	11.70	12.03	12.43	12.79	13.17	13.55	13.92
Illinois	8.02	10.37	11.21	11.44	11.68	11.84	12.04	12.25	12.63
Michigan	9.52	12.64	13.51	13.86	14.52	14.81	15.36	16.13	16.31
Wisconsin	8.03	10.26	10.77	11.11	11.47	11.85	12.17	12.41	12.76
West North Central:									
Minnesota	7.61	10.05	10.95	11.23	11.52	11.92	12.23	12.58	12.80
Iowa	8.67	10.32	10.82	11.27	11.62	11.92	12.22	12.45	12.73
Missouri	7.26	9.57	10.49	10.74	10.86	11.24	11.55	11.77	12.18
North Dakota	6.56	8.05	8.80	9.27	9.25	9.60	9.86	10.19	10.75
South Dakota	6.50	7.43	8.30	8.48	8.79	8.84	8.89	9.19	9.56
Nebraska	7.38	9.02	9.53	9.66	9.84	10.22	10.46	10.94	11.20
Kansas	7.37	9.45	10.68	10.94	11.24	11.60	11.99	12.15	12.40
South Atlantic:									
Delaware.	7.58	9.86	12.36	12.39	12.20	12.35	13.29	13.92	14.17
Maryland	7.61	9.73	11.19	11.57	11.92	12.50	12.83	13.15	13.50
District of Columbia	8.46	10.48	11.79	12.51	13.05	13.17	13.18	13.46	(NA)
Virginia	6.22	8.51	9.69	10.07	10.43	10.62	10.85	11.24	11.73
West Virginia	8.08	10.24	11.17	11.53	11.77	12.11	12.27	12.60	12.64
North Carolina	5.37	7.29	8.42	8.79	9.19	9.49	9.81	10.19	10.57
South Carolina	5.59	7.61	8.54	8.84	9.17	9.48	9.80	10.00	10.15
Georgia.	5.77	8.10	8.87	9.17	9.56	9.86	10.09	10.34	10.71
Florida	5.98	7.86	8.67	8.98	9.30	9.59	9.76	9.97	10.19
East South Central:									
Kentucky	7.34	9.53	10.37	10.70	11.00	11.28	11.47	11.81	12.22
Tennessee	6.08	8.29	9.22	9.55	9.92	10.13	10.33	10.50	10.77
Alabama	6.49	8.48	9.10	9.39	9.72	9.99	10.35	10.75	11.14
Mississippi	5.44	7.22	8.03	8.37	8.67	8.91	9.16	9.41	9.74
West South Central:									
Arkansas.	5.71	7.57	8.26	8.51	8.81	9.05	9.36	9.65	10.05
Louisiana	7.74	10.43	11.13	11.61	11.86	12.19	12.66	13.11	13.43
Oklahoma	7.36	9.86	10.48	10.73	11.09	11.38	11.41	11.42	11.51
Texas	7.15	9.41	10.25	10.47	10.84	10.92	11.02	11.13	11.47
Mountain:									
Montana	8.78	10.95	11.15	11.51	11.57	12.18	12.40	12.49	12.92
Idaho	7.55	9.41	10.21	10.60	11.11	11.42	11.88	11.88	11.46
Wyoming.	7.01	9.64	10.58	10.83	10.98	11.10	11.53	11.79	11.97
Colorado.	7.63	9.52	10.44	10.94	11.33	11.32	12.01	12.26	12.52
New Mexico.	5.79	8.41	8.74	9.04	9.40	9.68	9.74	10.13	10.70
Arizona	7.29	9.48	9.92	10.21	10.70	10.96	11.06	11.17	11.19
Utah.	7.02	9.64	10.14	10.32	10.77	11.09	11.10	11.28	11.63
Nevada	7.72	9.15	10.33	11.05	11.04	11.55	11.65	11.83	12.62
Pacific:									
Washington	(NA)	11.63	12.12	12.61	13.13	13.59	14.01	14.86	13.68
Oregon.	8.65	10.50	10.81	11.15	11.53	11.97	12.18	12.31	12.76
California.	7.70	10.12	11.16	11.48	11.87	12.19	12.38	12.44	12.54
Alaska	10.22	12.19	12.01	12.46	11.40	10.75	11.14	10.96	11.00
Hawaii	6.83	8.65	10.37	10.99	11.39	11.61	11.98	12.22	12.82

NA Not available.

Source: U.S. Bureau of Labor Statistics, *Employment and Earnings,* monthly.

No. 1215. Capital in Manufacturing Establishments: 1980 to 1994

[**In billions of dollars, except percent.** Data refer to privately owned manufacturing establishments and are based on the capital expenditures data from the Census of Manufactures, the *Annual Survey of Manufactures,* and the inventory investment component of GNP. For details, see source]

ITEM	CURRENT DOLLARS						CONSTANT (1987) DOLLARS					
	1980	1985	1990	1992	1993	1994	1980	1985	1990	1992	1993	1994
Purchases of equipment and structures	80	98	128	121	135	157	103	102	118	111	126	147
Percent equipment	71	65	66	69	73	75	69	65	67	70	76	78
Depreciation (straight line) [1].	54	78	101	109	113	119	72	83	93	98	102	107
Percent equipment	76	74	73	73	73	73	76	74	74	74	74	75
Net investment [2]	26	20	27	12	22	38	31	19	25	12	25	40
Net stock, end of year [1] . . .	976	1,238	1,576	1,615	1,665	1,756	1,222	1,285	1,403	1,421	1,447	1,494
Equipment and structures	666	898	1,153	1,219	1,270	1,343	860	950	1,026	1,061	1,087	1,130
Percent equipment . . .	62	58	57	56	56	56	61	58	57	56	57	58
Inventories	310	340	424	397	395	413	361	336	377	360	360	364

[1] Depreciation and net stock estimates for equipment and structures are derived using the perpetual inventory method and the straight-line depreciation formula. [2] Represents the difference between purchases and depreciation.

Source: U.S. Bureau of Economic Analysis, *The National Income and Product Accounts of the United States, to be published in late 1996,* and *Survey of Current Business,* January/February 1996; and *Fixed Reproducible Tangible Wealth in the United States, 1925-89.*

No. 1216. Manufacturers' Shipments, Inventories, and Orders: 1950 to 1995

[**In billions of dollars, except ratio.** See also *Historical Statistics, Colonial Times to 1970,* series P 74-92]

YEAR	Shipments	Inventories (Dec. 31) [1]	Ratio of inventories to shipments [2]	New orders	Unfilled orders (Dec. 31)	YEAR	Shipments	Inventories (Dec. 31) [1]	Ratio of inventories to shipments [2]	New orders	Unfilled orders (Dec. 31)
1950	224	32	1.41	242	41	1973	875	124	1.63	913	158
1951	261	39	1.78	287	67	1974	1,018	158	1.86	1,047	187
1952	270	42	1.71	279	76	1975	1,039	160	1.77	1,023	171
1953	298	44	1.90	283	60	1976	1,186	175	1.66	1,194	180
1954	280	42	1.71	268	48	1977	1,358	188	1.58	1,381	202
1955	318	45	1.63	330	60	1978	1,523	209	1.55	1,580	259
1956	333	51	1.74	340	68	1979	1,727	239	1.61	1,771	303
1957	345	52	1.90	331	53	1980	1,853	262	1.61	1,876	326
1958	327	50	1.75	324	47	1981	2,018	280	1.74	2,015	323
1959	363	53	1.68	369	52	1982	1,960	307	1.91	1,947	309
1960	371	54	1.79	363	45	1983	2,071	308	1.80	2,105	343
1961	371	55	1.67	373	47	1984	2,288	334	1.78	2,315	370
1962	400	58	1.76	401	48	1985	2,334	330	1.72	2,348	384
1963	421	60	1.66	426	53	1986	2,336	318	1.66	2,342	390
1964	448	63	1.62	460	65	1987	2,476	333	1.64	2,513	427
1965	492	68	1.58	505	79	1988	2,682	361	1.64	2,724	469
1966	538	78	1.70	557	97	1989	2,793	380	1.66	2,831	507
1967	558	84	1.71	565	104	1990	2,874	392	1.66	2,888	522
1968	603	90	1.76	608	110	1991	2,826	380	1.64	2,812	508
1969	642	98	1.81	647	115	1992	2,934	373	1.55	2,899	472
1970	634	101	1.91	625	106	1993	3,102	370	1.46	3,068	438
1971	671	102	1.76	672	107	1994	3,370	384	1.40	3,383	452
1972	756	108	1.58	770	120	1995	3,599	409	1.40	3,609	461

[1] Beginning in 1982, inventories are stated at current cost and are not comparable to the book value estimates for prior years. [2] Ratio based on December seasonally adjusted data.

Source: U.S. Bureau of the Census, *Current Industrial Reports, Manufacturers' Shipments, Inventories, and Orders: 1982-1992,* series M3; and monthly press releases.

No. 1217. Value of Manufactures Shipments and Inventories, by Industry: 1985 to 1995

[In billions of dollars. Based on 1987 Standard Industrial Classification (SIC). See also *Historical Statistics, Colonial Times to 1970*, series P 74-79]

INDUSTRY	SIC code	1985	1990	1991	1992	1993	1994	1995
Shipments	(X)	**2,334.5**	**2,912.2**	**2,878.2**	**3,004.7**	**3,127.6**	**3,343.8**	**3,566.9**
Durable goods [1]	(X)	1,215.4	1,485.3	1,452.0	1,541.9	1,630.6	1,787.0	1,910.6
Stone, clay, and glass prods.	32	55.8	63.7	60.0	62.5	65.6	71.2	75.5
Primary metals	33	112.3	148.8	136.4	138.3	142.7	160.8	184.5
Fabricated metal products	34	143.3	165.1	159.8	166.5	175.1	190.2	198.7
Industrial machinery and equip	35	218.4	259.4	247.5	258.7	278.1	314.4	353.6
Engines and turbines	351	15.1	17.0	17.2	17.6	18.8	21.8	21.2
Construction, mining [2]	353	27.6	30.8	27.9	27.2	30.6	34.0	39.9
Computer and office equipment ...	357	60.4	65.3	60.4	66.7	69.2	79.6	93.4
Electronic and other	36	164.0	195.9	199.3	216.8	233.6	261.4	300.6
Elec. transmission/distrib	361-2	23.8	27.7	26.7	29.1	31.4	33.6	36.9
Household appliances	363	16.1	17.7	17.2	18.6	20.4	22.8	23.3
Household audio and video equip. .	365	11.5	9.3	9.8	10.6	11.1	12.6	14.1
Communications equipment	366	35.4	38.6	38.1	43.0	45.5	51.7	63.2
Electronic components	367	42.2	62.6	67.5	73.6	81.0	93.6	116.3
Transportation equipment [1]	37	307.4	370.3	367.2	399.3	414.7	452.4	451.3
Motor vehicles and parts........	371	193.4	217.3	209.2	238.4	267.4	314.4	314.0
Aircraft, missiles, and parts	372, 6	91.3	125.8	132.2	131.4	116.3	105.0	102.3
Instruments and related prod. [1]	38	96.2	128.0	132.8	134.9	137.4	138.8	145.1
Measuring/controlling devices	382	25.9	32.2	33.3	34.7	35.4	38.8	44.3
Nondurable goods [1]	(X)	1,119.1	1,426.9	1,426.2	1,462.9	1,497.0	1,556.8	1,656.3
Food and kindred products [1]	20	308.6	391.7	397.9	407.0	422.2	431.0	440.9
Beverages	208	43.7	53.4	56.3	58.0	58.6	61.3	63.6
Tobacco products	21	18.6	29.9	31.9	35.2	28.4	30.0	31.9
Textile mill products............	22	54.6	65.5	65.4	70.8	74.0	78.3	78.8
Paper and allied products [1]	26	94.7	132.4	130.1	133.2	133.3	143.8	171.8
Paper/pulp/paperboard mill prod. .	261-3,6	39.1	57.6	53.7	54.4	52.6	58.2	75.8
Paperboard containers and boxes .	265	23.2	30.6	30.7	32.7	33.5	36.1	43.6
Chemicals and allied prods. [1]	28	204.8	292.8	298.5	305.4	314.9	333.3	358.5
Industrial chemicals	281,2,6,8,9	114.7	158.4	155.4	157.6	158.8	168.9	186.7
Drugs, soaps, toiletries........	283-4	61.3	98.4	107.1	110.7	117.9	122.6	126.9
Petroleum and coal products	29	176.6	173.4	159.1	150.2	144.8	143.1	154.1
Rubber and plastics products	30	75.6	105.3	105.8	113.6	122.8	134.6	143.3
Inventories (Dec. 31)	(X)	**329.6**	**397.9**	**383.5**	**374.9**	**382.5**	**397.4**	**422.6**
Durable goods [1]	(X)	214.0	257.4	244.1	232.3	237.4	248.4	263.5
Stone, clay, and glass products.....	32	6.9	8.1	7.8	7.8	7.6	7.7	8.2
Primary metals	33	19.8	22.6	20.7	20.0	20.0	22.5	23.6
Fabricated metal products	34	22.5	24.6	23.5	23.4	23.5	25.1	25.7
Industrial machinery and equip	35	45.6	48.4	46.5	45.7	47.3	51.3	56.5
Engines and turbines	351	2.7	3.3	3.2	3.0	3.2	3.7	3.7
Construction, mining [2]	353	7.8	6.9	6.4	6.1	6.3	6.6	6.9
Computer and office equip	357	11.5	10.7	10.7	10.4	10.6	10.6	12.7
Electronic and other	36	29.8	31.9	30.0	29.7	31.6	34.1	39.5
Elec. transmission and distrib.....	361-2	4.7	4.7	4.5	4.5	4.5	4.9	5.0
Household appliances	363	2.5	2.8	2.3	2.1	2.3	2.5	2.5
Household audio and video equip..	365	1.3	1.1	1.1	1.0	1.0	1.1	1.4
Communications equipment	366	8.0	7.0	6.5	6.7	7.3	8.2	10.2
Electronic components	367	7.5	9.8	9.8	9.8	10.6	11.2	13.7
Transportation equipment [1]	37	51.5	75.7	71.1	61.5	61.2	61.5	61.6
Motor vehicles and parts........	371	11.8	13.4	13.0	12.9	13.5	15.3	15.0
Aircraft, missiles, and parts	372, 6	36.2	57.9	53.5	44.2	43.2	41.7	41.8
Instruments and related products [1] ...	38	21.0	25.7	25.0	23.9	23.3	22.2	23.2
Measuring and controlling devices .	382	6.2	7.2	7.0	6.8	6.6	6.7	7.4
Nondurable goods [1]	(X)	115.6	140.5	139.4	142.6	145.1	149.0	159.1
Food and kindred products [1]	20	24.4	30.2	30.5	31.4	32.2	32.7	33.3
Beverages	208	4.7	5.3	5.4	5.7	5.8	5.9	6.1
Tobacco products	21	6.3	6.1	6.5	6.8	6.5	6.1	5.9
Textile mill products............	22	7.2	8.3	8.1	8.3	8.8	9.3	9.9
Paper and allied products [1]	26	10.1	13.5	13.7	13.8	14.0	14.2	17.4
Paper, pulp, paperboard mill prod..	261-3,6	3.8	5.2	5.5	5.7	5.7	5.4	7.1
Paperboard containers and boxes .	265	2.5	3.3	3.4	3.5	3.4	3.7	4.6
Chemicals and allied products [1]	28	26.0	33.8	34.3	35.5	36.1	36.8	38.3
Industrial chemicals	281,2,6,8,9	14.0	17.8	17.4	17.5	17.6	17.7	19.0
Drugs, soaps, toiletries.........	283-4	7.8	11.4	12.5	13.5	13.9	14.5	14.6
Petroleum and coal products	29	13.7	13.1	11.3	11.0	9.9	10.8	11.3
Rubber and plastics products	30	9.1	12.3	12.1	12.5	13.1	14.2	15.1

X Not applicable.   [1] Includes industries not shown separately.   [2] Also includes material handling industries.

Source: U.S. Bureau of the Census, Current Industrial Reports, *Manufactures' Shipments, Inventories, and Orders: 1982-1995*, and monthly press releases.

No. 1218. Industrial Production Indexes, by Industry: 1970 to 1995

[1987=100. Beginning 1990, data based on 1987 Standard Industrial Classification (SIC), earlier years based on 1977 SIC; see text, section 26. See also *Historical Statistics, Colonial Times to 1970,* series P 13 and P 18-39]

INDUSTRY	SIC code	1970	1975	1980	1985	1990	1991	1992	1993	1994	1995
Total index	(X)	61.4	66.3	84.1	94.4	106.0	104.2	107.7	111.5	118.1	121.9
Manufacturing	(X)	56.4	61.1	78.8	91.6	106.1	103.8	108.2	112.3	119.7	123.9
Durable goods.	(X)	53.3	56.7	75.7	91.8	107.4	104.1	109.3	115.6	125.8	132.5
Lumber and products	24	66.7	66.5	76.9	88.0	97.1	90.2	95.2	97.1	104.0	104.5
Furniture and fixtures	25	55.6	59.4	78.5	88.1	100.1	94.1	99.2	104.8	111.1	111.6
Stone, clay, and glass products. .	32	71.1	77.8	92.0	93.6	100.3	92.8	95.3	97.7	102.3	104.1
Primary metals.	33	115.2	107.2	110.8	101.8	106.5	98.6	101.9	107.7	116.4	119.2
Fabricated metal products	34	75.9	76.7	92.5	94.5	99.5	94.5	99.0	103.1	110.5	113.9
Industrial, commercial machinery [1]	35	32.8	38.1	60.6	86.8	117.6	114.7	124.0	138.1	157.7	177.8
Electrical machinery	36	40.5	45.1	73.3	93.1	111.4	113.9	123.5	134.1	154.3	174.9
Transportation equipment.	37	55.5	59.7	72.3	91.8	107.0	101.1	104.8	109.2	115.3	113.3
Instruments	38	38.8	52.4	78.8	95.7	104.9	106.2	106.3	106.8	109.1	110.7
Nondurable goods	(X)	61.1	67.7	83.1	91.5	104.4	103.4	106.7	108.6	113.0	114.3
Foods.	20	64.0	71.4	84.6	94.9	103.7	105.3	106.9	109.5	113.2	115.3
Tobacco products	21	90.6	97.8	103.6	97.3	100.8	94.7	95.8	81.8	88.1	90.0
Textile mill products.	22	74.4	77.7	92.1	89.7	97.1	96.5	104.0	109.9	113.5	112.6
Paper and products.	26	62.9	65.9	83.1	92.2	105.6	106.5	110.0	114.9	119.2	119.8
Printing and publishing	27	52.7	53.7	70.3	87.6	100.8	97.0	98.1	98.8	100.1	99.4
Chemicals and products.	28	55.9	69.1	87.8	91.4	111.8	110.5	114.4	115.4	121.3	125.0
Petroleum products.	29	83.9	91.5	99.0	92.6	103.3	101.7	102.6	105.7	106.7	108.3
Rubber and plastics products . . .	30	37.6	47.4	61.7	85.8	107.2	105.5	116.2	123.9	135.9	139.4
Leather and products	31	208.0	182.5	161.7	112.5	96.0	87.5	89.0	89.9	87.5	81.3
Mining.	(X)	100.4	98.0	110.0	109.0	102.0	100.2	98.9	98.0	100.3	99.9
Utilities	(X)	72.9	84.3	95.9	99.5	109.9	112.3	111.9	116.3	117.9	122.0

X Not applicable.   [1] Includes computer equipment.
Source: Board of Governors of the Federal Reserve System, *Federal Reserve Bulletin,* monthly.

No. 1219. Index of Manufacturing Capacity: 1950 to 1995

[1987 output=100. Annual figures are averages of quarterly data. Capacity represents estimated quantity of output relative to output in 1967 which the *current* stock of plant and equipment in manufacturing industries was capable of producing. Primary processing industries comprise textiles, lumber, paper and pulp, petroleum, rubber, stone, clay, glass, primary metals, fabricated metals, and a portion of chemicals. Advanced processing industries comprise chemical products, food, beverages, tobacco, apparel, furniture, printing and publishing, leather, machinery, transportation equipment, instruments, ordnance, and miscellaneous industry groups]

YEAR	Index of capacity	RELATION OF OUTPUT TO CAPACITY (percent)			YEAR	Index of capacity	RELATION OF OUTPUT TO CAPACITY (percent)		
		All manu-facturing	Primary pro-cessing	Advanced pro-cessing			All manu-facturing	Primary pro-cessing	Advanced pro-cessing
1950	29	83	88	80	1986	119	79	81	78
1955	36	87	92	84	1987	123	82	85	80
1960	44	80	80	80	1988	125	84	87	82
1965	54	90	91	89	1989	128	83	86	82
1970	71	80	80	79	1990	131	81	84	80
1975	84	73	73	74	1991	133	78	80	77
1980	98	80	78	81	1992	136	80	82	78
1982	105	73	69	75	1993	140	81	84	81
1983	108	75	75	75	1994	144	83	88	81
1984	111	80	80	80	1995	150	83	87	81
1985	115	80	80	79					

Source: Board of Governors of the Federal Reserve System, *Capacity Utilization In Manufacturing, Mining, Utilities, and Industrial Materials,* G.3., monthly. (Based on data from Federal Reserve Board, U.S. Department of Commerce, U.S. Bureau of Labor Statistics, and McGraw-Hill Information Systems Company, New York, NY, and other sources.)

No. 1220. Finances of Manufacturing Corporations: 1970 to 1995

[In billions of dollars. Beginning 1986, data exclude estimates for corporations with less than $250,000 in assets at time of sample selection. Prior years include estimates for corporations in this size category. See table 871 for individual industry data]

ITEM	1970	1980	1985	1986	1987	1988	1989	1990	1991	1992	1993	1994	1995
Net sales.	709	1,897	2,331	2,221	2,378	2,596	2,745	2,811	2,761	2,890	3,015	3,261	3,519
Net operating profit	50	129	138	125	159	190	182	173	133	151	180	241	270
Net profit:													
Before taxes	48	145	137	129	173	216	189	160	100	33	119	244	279
After taxes	29	92	88	83	116	155	136	112	68	23	84	175	201
Cash dividends.	15	36	46	46	50	57	65	62	60	63	67	70	81
Net income retained in business.	14	58	42	37	66	98	71	49	7	-40	17	105	120

Source: 1970 and 1980, U.S. Federal Trade Commission; thereafter, U.S. Bureau of the Census, *Quarterly Financial Report for Manufacturing, Mining, and Trade Corporations.*

No. 1221. Manufacturing Technology—Percent of Establishments Using and Planning to Use: 1993

[Based on the Survey of Manufacturing Technology, which surveyed companies in SIC groups 34 to 38 and establishments of 20 or more employees]

ESTABLISHMENT CHARACTERISTIC	ESTABLISHMENTS USING SELECTED TECHNOLOGIES							PLANNING TO USE WITHIN 2 YEARS						
	Computer aided design (CAD) or computer aided engineering	Numerically controlled machines	Automated storage and retrieval	Automated sensor based inspection or testing	Programmable controllers	Computer control on factory floor	Inter-company computer network	Computer aided design (CAD) or computer aided engineering	Numerically controlled machines	Automated storage and retrieval	Automated sensor based inspection or testing	Programmable controllers	Computer control on factory floor	Inter-company computer network
Major SIC [1] group:														
34, Fabricated metal products	46.5	40.4	1.2	9.6	30.2	20.2	16.7	5.1	2.5	0.9	4.1	3.2	9.2	8.0
35, Industrial mach. and equip.	64.1	61.9	2.3	10.6	29.0	28.1	15.4	4.1	2.1	0.9	4.0	4.3	9.1	7.5
36, Electronic and other	64.2	34.5	3.8	17.5	30.7	33.2	21.9	4.2	2.4	1.7	5.1	3.5	9.9	9.8
37, Transportation equip.	53.9	44.1	3.8	16.2	30.7	26.8	23.4	5.3	2.9	0.8	4.4	3.2	8.2	7.0
38, Instruments, related prod.	65.5	35.1	4.8	14.7	29.8	29.0	15.3	3.3	2.3	1.6	4.4	4.4	8.7	10.2
Employment size:														
20 to 99	49.5	41.4	0.6	7.9	20.5	18.8	12.0	4.7	2.4	0.4	3.8	3.6	9.0	6.7
100 to 499	76.4	56.5	4.1	20.0	49.1	41.8	28.4	4.5	2.1	2.5	5.7	4.5	10.1	12.4
500 and over	87.2	67.1	23.6	38.8	69.8	62.8	47.1	1.0	2.3	3.1	4.5	2.4	5.6	11.1
Age of plant (years):														
Less than 5	63.5	38.4	2.5	11.0	25.6	27.5	15.0	5.7	3.8	1.5	6.7	4.6	13.1	9.7
5 to 15	62.0	47.9	2.5	13.3	30.4	28.2	18.0	5.2	2.5	1.0	4.6	4.1	10.7	8.9
16 to 30	64.4	53.7	2.5	13.3	33.1	29.4	20.5	4.8	2.9	1.0	4.5	3.6	8.9	9.4
Over 30	63.1	57.3	4.0	15.6	39.1	30.7	22.0	4.1	6.5	1.3	3.7	4.3	8.2	8.3
Manufacturing process:														
Fabrication/machining	51.5	57.1	2.1	13.1	29.5	26.6	16.3	4.5	3.4	0.6	5.2	3.4	10.0	7.7
Assembly	67.3	14.6	1.8	15.7	25.1	28.5	20.7	4.4	1.9	1.8	4.3	3.8	9.4	9.9
Both	69.0	62.7	2.8	13.5	36.0	30.8	20.5	5.3	2.7	1.0	4.9	4.6	10.6	9.5
Neither	29.3	12.8	1.1	10.5	29.8	20.9	12.3	3.4	0.7	1.4	2.2	1.3	4.9	6.2
Market for most products:														
Consumer	48.2	33.9	2.7	12.6	35.3	25.2	20.6	4.8	2.6	1.4	4.6	3.6	10.8	9.8
Commercial	66.3	44.4	3.0	11.6	30.2	32.2	18.7	2.8	1.9	1.8	4.2	5.2	10.4	10.8
Industrial	64.3	55.6	2.4	12.2	32.2	27.4	18.2	5.4	2.8	0.9	3.8	4.0	9.5	9.0
Transportation	64.3	54.9	3.5	21.1	44.3	34.2	32.2	6.2	2.4	0.7	7.8	3.6	11.4	6.8
Government	74.1	62.9	6.3	18.4	29.3	33.6	15.7	1.4	1.5	1.0	5.7	4.2	9.4	7.8
Other	63.7	42.2	2.4	12.7	24.1	26.9	13.6	5.8	3.2	1.3	5.8	3.3	8.2	8.6
Market price for most products:														
Less than $5	46.3	39.4	2.1	18.1	45.1	30.4	26.1	7.4	3.4	1.4	7.5	3.5	10.9	11.3
$5 to $100	53.6	51.1	1.9	13.3	36.1	29.8	22.3	5.4	2.9	1.5	4.9	4.6	10.9	10.2
$101 to $1,000	63.6	54.6	3.0	13.8	30.6	28.1	16.4	4.1	2.0	0.7	4.7	4.0	10.3	8.4
$1,001 to $2,000	68.3	43.7	3.9	13.6	23.5	26.3	16.2	3.7	3.2	1.6	3.5	3.8	8.7	6.2
$2,001 to $10,000	73.5	54.9	2.5	9.7	24.5	27.3	14.9	5.8	1.5	1.1	4.3	4.5	10.0	6.9
Over $10,000	83.3	54.2	4.8	12.7	30.0	30.1	18.5	2.9	2.6	1.2	3.2	4.0	8.8	8.8

[1] Standard Industrial Classification; see text, section 13.

Source: U.S. Bureau of the Census, Current Industrial Reports, Manufacturing Technology, series SMT(93)-3.

No. 1222. Employment Related to Manufactured Exports, by Industry: 1985 to 1991

[Total employment related to manufactured exports is the sum of employment directly calculated for the plants shipping the exported product, the supplying industries and service organizations, and the central offices and auxiliaries. For manufacturing industries, employment is limited to paid employees in manufacturing plants, while for nonmanufacturing it includes an estimate for working proprietors and partners]

| INDUSTRY | EMPLOYMENT RELATED TO MANUFACTURED EXPORTS | | | | | | CIVILIAN EMPLOYMENT (1,000) | | |
| | Employees (1,000) | | | Percent of civilian employment | | | | | |
	1985	1990	1991	1985	1990	1991	1985	1990	1991
Total	4,413	5,729	6,092	4.0	4.8	5.1	100,260	119,943	120,040
Manufacturing	2,295	3,212	3,363	12.2	17.1	18.6	20,647	18,840	18,062
Nonmanufacturing	2,118	2,516	2,730	2.3	2.5	2.7	79,613	101,103	101,978
Trade	949	1,211	1,427	4.3	5.1	6.0	19,737	23,718	23,780
Business services	227	256	268	1.1	1.0	1.0	17,245	25,611	26,206
Transportation [1]	282	401	397	4.6	6.2	6.0	6,369	6,500	6,641
Agriculture	127	139	139	3.7	4.1	4.0	3,225	3,382	3,470
Mining	50	68	78	4.9	9.2	10.2	947	738	767
Other	483	442	421	1.3	1.1	1.0	32,090	41,154	41,114

[1] Includes communications and utilities.

No. 1223. Manufacturing Establishments—Export-Related Shipments and Employment, 1977 to 1990, and by Industry, 1991

[The export-related employment data do not include the jobs involved in the export of nonmanufactured goods and various services sold to foreign buyers. Thus, jobs in the manufacturing sector that relate to the export of nonmanufactured goods are excluded from the estimates. In addition, all of the indirect exports being reported are domestically produced; that is, they exclude imports. See source for further details on methodology]

| INDUSTRY | SIC code[1] | MANUFACTURER'S SHIPMENT VALUE | | | | MANUFACTURING EMPLOYMENT | | | |
| | | Total [2] (bil. dol.) | Export related | | Export related as per-cent of ship-ments | Total (1,000) | Export related | | Export related as per-cent of total employ-ment |
			Total (bil. dol.)	Direct exports [3] (bil. dol.)			Total (1,000)	Direct exports [4] (1,000)	
1977	(X)	1,358.4	142.4	85.8	10.4	19,590	1,990	1,106	10.2
1980	(X)	1,852.7	249.8	151.2	13.5	20,647	2,639	1,486	12.8
1981	(X)	2,017.5	271.7	164.3	13.4	20,264	2,604	1,486	12.9
1983	(X)	2,055.3	246.4	141.6	12.0	18,737	2,173	1,118	11.6
1984	(X)	2,253.8	268.3	151.0	11.9	19,141	2,179	1,083	11.4
1985	(X)	2,278.9	286.7	156.9	12.6	18,788	2,295	1,083	12.2
1986	(X)	2,260.3	294.3	159.4	13.0	18,371	2,318	1,061	12.6
1987	(X)	2,475.9	378.8	193.6	15.3	18,900	2,771	1,185	14.7
1988	(X)	2,684.7	395.3	242.9	14.7	19,147	2,638	1,412	13.8
1989	(X)	2,793.0	460.5	287.4	16.5	19,042	2,948	1,610	15.5
1990	(X)	2,873.5	515.0	293.7	17.9	18,840	3,214	1,614	17.1
1991, total.	(X)	2,826.2	546.9	314.1	19.4	18,062	3,363	1,697	18.6
Food and kindred products	20	387.6	26.5	17.6	6.8	1,475	91	63	6.2
Tobacco products	21	32.0	6.5	4.7	20.2	40	9	7	23.1
Textile mill products.	22	65.7	10.0	4.2	15.2	598	85	32	14.3
Apparel, other textile products. . .	23	65.3	4.8	3.6	7.4	960	61	45	6.3
Lumber and wood products	24	70.6	14.1	6.2	20.0	631	105	41	16.6
Furniture and fixtures.	25	40.0	2.1	1.4	5.3	466	24	16	5.2
Paper and allied products.	26	128.4	19.8	8.0	15.4	621	87	31	14.0
Printing and publishing.	27	156.7	13.0	3.1	8.3	1,488	123	23	8.3
Chemical and allied products . . .	28	292.3	76.2	38.6	26.1	846	221	117	26.2
Petroleum and coal products . . .	29	158.1	15.7	5.7	9.9	113	11	5	10.1
Rubber, misc. plastics products . .	30	100.7	19.4	6.8	19.3	840	160	53	19.0
Leather, leather products	31	9.1	1.9	1.5	20.9	106	15	11	13.7
Stone, clay, glass products	32	59.6	6.8	3.0	11.5	476	51	22	10.7
Primary metal industries.	33	132.8	39.5	10.5	29.8	677	198	43	29.3
Fabricated metal products	34	157.1	28.5	9.9	18.2	1,359	256	83	18.8
Machinery, except electric	35	243.5	79.2	53.9	32.5	1,774	512	323	28.8
Electric, electronic equipment . . .	36	197.9	61.2	39.5	30.9	1,427	484	321	33.9
Transportation equipment.	37	364.0	89.7	72.2	24.6	1,634	377	293	23.1
Instruments and related products .	38	127.2	26.3	19.7	20.7	901	183	137	20.3
Misc. manufacturing	39	37.1	5.6	3.9	15.0	363	49	33	13.6
Administrative and auxiliary	(X)	(X)	(X)	(X)	(X)	1,269	261	(X)	20.5

X Not applicable.   [1] Standard Industrial Classification; see text, section 13.   [2] Includes total domestic and export shipments for all manufacturing establishments.   [3] Includes only the value of manufactured products exported by the producing plants.   [4] Employment is limited to paid employees in manufacturing plants producing the export product. The number of employees related to export shipments was calculated for each establishment, aggregated by industry and by States, and inflated to a level comparable to the plant value of exports reported in the official foreign trade statistics at port value.

Source of tables 1222 and 1223: U.S. Bureau of the Census, *Annual Survey of Manufactures, 1987* and *1992 Census of Manufactures*; and *Exports from Manufacturing Establishments*, series AR91-1.

No. 1224. Export-Related Shipments and Employment of Manufacturing Establishments, by State: 1991

[Export-related figures exclude jobs in the manufacturing sector that are involved in the export of nonmanufactured goods and various services sold to foreign buyers. In addition, all of the indirect exports being reported are domestically produced, that is they exclude imports. Includes central administration and auxiliary office employees]

REGION, DIVISION, AND STATE	MANUFACTURES SHIPMENT VALUE					MANUFACTURING EMPLOYMENT				
	Total (bil. dol.)	Export related			Export related shipments, percent of total	Total (1,000)	Export related			Export related employment, percent of total
		Total exports (bil. dol.)	Direct exports (bil. dol.)	Supporting exports (bil. dol.)			Total (1,000)	Direct exports (1,000)	Supporting exports (1,000)	
United States........	2,826.2	546.9	314.1	232.8	19.4	18,061.7	3,362.5	1,697.2	1,665.3	18.6
Northeast............	506.8	95.7	54.5	41.2	18.9	3,757.2	715.4	352.9	362.5	18.8
New England	138.6	32.5	20.6	11.9	23.4	1,150.3	254.1	141.5	112.6	22.1
Maine	11.6	2.4	1.3	1.2	20.9	98.8	17.9	9.7	8.2	18.1
New Hampshire.......	9.8	2.2	1.3	0.9	22.1	85.8	18.2	9.0	9.2	21.2
Vermont............	5.8	1.2	0.5	0.7	20.6	42.8	7.9	3.7	4.2	18.5
Massachusetts	61.9	14.4	9.5	4.9	23.4	489.7	111.0	63.9	47.1	22.7
Rhode Island	9.6	1.9	1.0	0.9	19.4	94.6	17.0	8.2	8.8	18.0
Connecticut	40.0	10.4	7.0	3.3	25.9	338.6	82.1	47.0	35.1	24.2
Middle Atlantic	368.1	63.2	33.9	29.3	17.1	2,606.9	461.3	211.4	249.9	17.7
New York...........	148.4	27.6	16.5	11.1	18.6	1,054.0	189.5	98.8	90.7	18.0
New Jersey	85.7	13.0	6.4	6.5	15.2	590.9	102.0	39.0	63.0	17.3
Pennsylvania	134.0	22.6	10.9	11.7	16.8	962.0	169.8	73.6	96.2	17.7
Midwest............	877.2	155.4	86.2	69.4	17.7	5,351.7	979.3	450.5	528.8	18.3
East North Central.....	647.2	121.1	67.1	53.9	18.7	4,006.8	764.8	348.7	416.1	19.1
Ohio	174.9	35.9	20.4	15.5	20.5	1,045.4	209.5	96.4	113.1	20.0
Indiana	97.3	17.6	8.9	8.7	18.1	594.1	105.9	47.9	58.0	17.8
Illinois	151.9	27.4	14.4	12.9	18.0	976.1	181.9	80.9	101.0	18.6
Michigan	143.1	27.3	16.5	10.8	19.1	858.2	175.4	81.9	93.5	20.4
Wisconsin	80.0	12.9	6.9	6.0	16.2	533.0	92.1	41.6	50.5	17.3
West North Central	230.0	34.3	19.1	15.5	14.9	1,344.9	214.5	101.8	112.7	16.1
Minnesota	53.3	8.8	4.9	3.9	16.4	384.5	69.4	32.9	36.5	18.0
Iowa	45.0	6.6	3.6	3.0	14.6	224.0	33.3	16.6	16.7	14.9
Missouri...........	66.4	10.0	5.5	4.6	15.1	401.4	61.6	27.5	34.1	15.3
North Dakota	3.1	0.4	0.3	0.2	14.4	17.2	2.1	1.1	1.0	12.2
South Dakota	4.5	0.6	0.3	0.3	13.7	30.3	5.0	2.6	2.4	16.5
Nebraska..........	21.0	2.7	1.6	1.2	13.1	100.5	13.8	6.6	7.2	13.7
Kansas	36.7	5.2	2.9	2.3	14.3	187.0	29.3	14.5	14.8	15.7
South	955.1	177.1	92.6	84.4	18.5	5,788.2	988.7	492.5	496.2	17.1
South Atlantic........	425.5	76.8	41.9	34.8	18.0	2,935.5	469.2	218.8	250.4	16.0
Delaware	11.9	2.0	1.2	0.9	17.1	62.4	12.4	3.3	9.1	19.9
Maryland	29.6	4.9	2.8	2.1	16.7	200.6	31.3	14.4	16.9	15.6
District of Columbia	2.1	0.2	0.1	0.1	10.4	13.3	1.2	0.2	1.0	9.0
Virginia	61.6	10.6	6.1	4.5	17.2	408.4	57.2	26.3	30.9	14.0
West Virginia	12.5	3.3	1.4	1.9	26.2	78.1	15.8	5.5	10.3	20.2
North Carolina.......	118.2	20.7	10.6	10.1	17.5	801.9	122.2	54.9	67.3	15.2
South Carolina	47.5	10.2	5.2	4.9	21.4	352.6	63.4	27.8	35.6	18.0
Georgia	82.8	13.0	6.8	6.2	15.7	545.1	80.9	37.7	43.2	14.8
Florida............	59.3	11.9	7.7	4.1	20.0	473.1	84.8	48.7	36.1	17.9
East South Central	202.7	35.8	18.0	17.7	17.7	1,366.4	209.7	98.6	111.1	15.4
Kentucky	53.5	9.3	5.0	4.3	17.4	272.9	45.2	22.0	23.2	16.6
Tennessee	69.5	12.0	6.1	5.8	17.2	493.0	77.5	37.2	40.3	15.7
Alabama	48.5	9.3	4.1	5.2	19.1	363.3	56.5	24.1	32.4	15.6
Mississippi	31.2	5.2	2.8	2.4	16.6	237.2	30.5	15.3	15.2	12.9
West South Central	326.9	64.5	32.7	31.9	19.7	1,486.3	309.8	175.1	134.7	20.8
Arkansas	31.1	5.0	2.4	2.6	16.0	220.2	32.3	15.2	17.1	14.7
Louisiana	63.4	12.2	5.5	6.6	19.2	174.8	29.8	13.7	16.1	17.0
Oklahoma	28.4	4.2	2.0	2.3	14.9	168.6	26.9	12.3	14.6	16.0
Texas	204.0	43.1	22.8	20.4	21.1	922.7	220.8	133.9	86.9	23.9
West	487.1	118.9	80.7	38.0	24.4	3,165.1	679.2	401.4	277.8	21.5
Mountain	91.4	18.2	10.0	8.0	19.9	607.4	113.4	57.4	56.0	18.7
Montana	3.8	0.6	0.1	0.4	15.1	19.8	2.8	0.6	2.2	14.1
Idaho	9.8	2.8	2.0	0.8	28.8	60.5	13.3	7.7	5.6	22.0
Wyoming	2.7	0.4	0.1	0.3	13.3	9.8	1.4	0.4	1.0	14.3
Colorado	26.8	4.5	2.6	1.9	16.9	176.3	32.0	17.3	14.7	18.2
New Mexico	8.0	1.7	0.6	1.0	20.7	40.7	5.9	2.5	3.4	14.5
Arizona	23.0	5.3	3.1	2.2	23.0	173.5	36.1	17.7	18.4	20.8
Utah	14.5	2.5	1.3	1.2	17.2	101.8	18.0	9.4	8.6	17.7
Nevada	2.8	0.4	0.2	0.2	15.6	25.6	3.9	1.8	2.1	15.2
Pacific	395.7	100.7	70.7	30.0	25.4	2,557.7	565.8	344.0	221.8	22.1
Washington	68.0	29.6	25.3	4.3	43.6	353.8	110.4	81.2	29.2	31.2
Oregon	30.7	7.1	4.1	3.0	23.1	208.4	43.6	24.0	19.6	20.9
California	289.6	61.6	39.3	22.3	21.3	1,961.8	402.0	230.7	171.3	20.5
Alaska............	3.6	1.8	1.6	0.2	49.7	14.4	7.1	6.3	0.8	49.3
Hawaii............	3.8	0.6	0.4	0.2	16.3	19.3	2.7	1.8	0.9	14.0

Source: U.S. Bureau of the Census, *Exports from Manufacturing Establishments* AR91-1.

No. 1225. U.S. Exports of Manufactures, Origin of World Exports of Manufacture: 1975 to 1994

[In millions of dollars, except percents]

ITEM	1975-79	1980-84	1985-89	1990	1991	1992	1993	1994
Manufactures export value	88	143	185	281	305	327	339	381
Machinery & transport equipment	56	91	120	174	190	203	211	233
Chemicals	12	21	28	39	40	44	45	52
Other.	20	31	38	68	75	80	83	97
Origin of world exports of manu. (percent):								
United States[1]	12.4	12.8	10.7	11.3	12.0	11.8	12.7	(NA)
Machinery & transport equip.	16.9	17.3	14.2	14.4	15.1	14.9	(NA)	(NA)
Chemicals.	13.8	15.2	13.0	13.1	13.3	13.1	(NA)	(NA)
Other	6.9	6.9	5.6	7.0	7.6	7.4	(NA)	(NA)
Germany [2]	15.4	13.7	14.4	14.6	14.2	14.0	12.5	(NA)
Japan	10.9	12.8	13.0	11.2	11.9	11.8	13.0	(NA)
Other G-7 countries [3]	23.5	22.1	21.3	22.0	21.6	21.0	20.8	(NA)
East Asian NICs [4]	4.1	6.0	7.7	7.6	8.2	8.1	9.3	(NA)

NA Not available.   [1] U.S. exports are domestic exports only.   [2] Prior to 1991, data for are for former West Germany only.
[3] Other Group of Seven (G-7) Countries: Canada, France, Italy, United Kingdom.   [4] East Asian newly industrialized countries (NICs): Hong Kong, S. Korea, Singapore, Taiwan.

Source: U.S. Dept. of Commerce, International Trade Administration, Office of Trade and Economic Analysis. Based on United Nations Commodity Trade Statistics, *Statistical Yearbook of the Republic of China*, and unpublished data.

No. 1226. Foreign Direct Investment Position in the United States—Manufacturing: 1993 and 1994

[In millions of dollars. Book value at year end. Covers U.S. firms in which foreign interest or ownership was 10% or more. Minus sign (-) indicates a negative position]

AREA OR COUNTRY	TOTAL [1]		FOOD AND KINDRED PRODUCTS		CHEMICALS AND ALLIED PRODUCTS		PRIMARY AND FABRICATED METALS		MACHINERY	
	1993	1994	1993	1994	1993	1994	1993	1994	1993	1994
All countries [2]	166,397	184,484	22,997	20,880	58,316	67,303	12,034	14,325	29,677	31,856
Canada	15,306	16,911	(D)	5,431	(D)	1,018	2,032	2,420	2,617	2,365
Europe.	124,454	135,804	16,058	13,423	52,376	59,668	8,025	9,583	20,726	21,948
Latin America	4,273	6,466	288	647	1,138	2,327	198	229	-73	-45
Asia and Pacific	21,694	23,433	(D)	1,376	(D)	3,992	1,791	2,084	6,038	7,173

D Data withheld to avoid disclosure of individual companies.   [1] Includes other manufacturing industries not shown separately.   [2] Includes other countries not shown separately.

Source: U.S. Bureau of Economic Analysis, *Survey of Current Business*, August 1995.

No. 1227. Alcoholic Beverages—Summary: 1980 to 1994

[For 1980-1985, stocks on hand for years ending June 30; later data for years ending September 30. All other items for fiscal years ending in year shown; see text, section 9. Includes Puerto Rico. Excludes imports. See *Historical Statistics, Colonial Times to 1970*, series P 235 for beer and P 236a for distilled spirits]

ITEM	Unit	1980	1985	1989	1990	1991	1992	1993	1994
Beer: Breweries operated . . .	Number	86	103	245	286	333	392	480	619
Production [1]	Mil. bbl. [2]	193	194	198	202	204	202	202	203
Value of shipments [3]	Mil. dol.	9,362	12,216	14,321	15,186	15,925	17,302	16,629	16,714
Tax-paid withdrawals	Mil. bbl. [2]	172	175	179	182	183	182	180	180
Stocks on hand.	Mil. bbl. [2]	15	14	14	14	14	13.4	13.7	13.4
Distilled spirits:									
Production facilities operated. . .	Number	143	117	140	143	145	143	132	150
Production [1][4]	Mil. tax gal. [5] . .	236	117	135	122	129	110	111	99
Tax-paid withdrawals [6]	Mil. tax gal. [5] . .	330	306	251	251	242	246	240	229
Stocks on hand [4]	Mil. tax gal. [5] . .	696	588	456	451	459	365	420	410
Whiskey: Production [1]	Mil. tax gal. [5] . .	87	65	75	77	75	62	59	59
Stocks on hand	Mil. tax gal. [5] . .	566	467	361	365	368	309	361	354
Still wines: Production [1]	Mil. wine gal. [7] . .	982	622	611	577	478	484	417	438
Tax-paid withdrawals [8]	Mil. wine gal. [7] . .	340	414	464	468	387	387	354	356
Stocks on hand [9]	Mil. wine gal. [7] . .	486	602	558	562	539	525	520	477
Effervescent wines [10]: Prod. [1] .	Mil. wine gal. [7] . .	26.8	32.0	30.9	26.9	22.8	24.7	27.7	23.7
Tax-paid withdrawals	Mil. wine gal. [7] . .	24.1	30.9	27.0	26.2	24.6	24.1	24.4	23.7
Stocks on hand.	Mil. wine gal. [7] . .	11.9	21.3	19.4	22.1	20.4	18.8	19.5	16.5

NA Not available.   [1] Production represents total amount removed from fermenters, including distilling material, and includes increase after fermentation (by amelioration, sweetening, and addition of wine spirits).   [2] Barrels of 31 wine gallons.   [3] Source: U.S. Bureau of the Census, *Census of Manufactures*, and *Annual Survey of Manufactures*.   [4] Excludes alcohol produced for industrial use. Also excludes vodka and gin production.   [5] For spirits of 100 proof or over, a tax gallon is equivalent to the proof gallon; for spirits of less than 100 proof, the tax gallon is equivalent to the wine gallon. A proof gallon is the alcoholic equivalent of a U.S. gallon at 60 degrees F, containing 50 percent of ethyl alcohol by volume.   [6] Includes ethyl alcohol.   [7] A wine gallon is the U.S. gallon equivalent to the volume of 231 cubic inches.   [8] Includes special natural wines.   [9] Excludes distilling materials.   [10] Includes champagne, other effervescent wines, and artificially carbonated wines.

Source: Except as noted, through 1982, U.S. Bureau of Alcohol, Tobacco, and Firearms, *Alcohol and Tobacco Summary Statistics*, annual; thereafter, *Statistical Release*, No. 76.

No. 1228. Tobacco Products—Production, Consumption, and Expenditures: 1970 to 1994

[Production data are for calendar years. Excludes cigars produced in customs bonded manufacturing warehouses. See also *Historical Statistics, Colonial Times to 1970*, series P 239-241]

ITEM	Unit	1970	1980	1985	1986	1987	1988	1989	1990	1991	1992	1993	1994
PRODUCTION													
Cigarettes.............	Billions .	583	714	669	665	658	689	695	677	710	695	719	661
Cigars	Billions .	8	4	4	3	3	2	2	2	2	2	2	2
Tobacco [1].............	Mil. lb. .	165	163	163	158	147	143	142	141	142	142	141	133
Consumption per person[2]..	Lb. [3]...	10	8	7	7	7	6	6	6	6	5	5	5
Cigarettes.............	1,000 ..	4	4	3	3	3	3	3	3	3	3	3	3
Cigars [4].............	Number.	60	24	20	18	17	15	14	14	13	12	12	11
Consumer expenditures ...	Bil. dol .	11.5	21.0	30.7	32.2	33.7	35.4	37.8	40.9	43.8	47.4	48.4	49.0
Cigarettes.............	Bil. dol .	10.4	19.4	28.8	30.3	31.8	33.6	35.9	38.3	41.6	45.2	45.8	46.2
Cigars	Bil. dol .	0.7	0.7	0.7	0.7	0.7	0.6	0.6	0.7	0.7	0.7	0.6	0.7
Other................	Bil. dol .	0.4	0.9	1.2	1.2	1.2	1.3	1.4	1.4	1.5	1.8	2.0	2.1

[1] Smoking and chewing tobaccos and snuff output. [2] Based on estimated population 18 years old and over, as of July 1, including Armed Forces abroad. [3] Unstemmed processing weight equivalent. [4] Weighing over 3 pounds per 1,000.

Source: U.S. Dept. of Agriculture, Economic Research Service, *Tobacco Situation and Outlook*, quarterly.

No. 1229. Cotton, Wool, and Manmade Fibers—Consumption, by End-Use: 1990 to 1993

[Represents products manufactured by U.S. mills. Excludes glass fiber]

YEAR	Total (mil. lb.)	COTTON		WOOL		MAN-MADE FIBERS					
		Total (mil. lb.)	Percent of end-use	Total (mil. lb.)	Percent of end-use	Total (mil. lb.)	Percent of end-use	Cellulosic [1]		Noncellulosic [2]	
								Total (mil. lb.)	Percent of end-use	Total (mil. lb.)	Percent of end-use
Total:											
1990..........	14,011	4,699	33.5	185	1.3	9,127	65.2	599	4.3	8,528	60.9
1993..........	16,177	5,656	34.9	236	1.5	10,285	63.6	594	3.7	9,691	59.9
Apparel:											
1990..........	5,204	2,897	55.7	118	2.3	2,189	42.0	287	5.5	1,902	36.5
1993..........	6,193	3,489	56.4	151	2.4	2,553	41.2	287	4.6	2,266	36.6
Home furnishings:											
1990..........	2,235	1,325	59.3	14	0.6	896	40.1	104	4.7	792	35.4
1993..........	2,606	1,632	62.6	16	0.6	958	36.8	104	4.0	854	32.8
Floor coverings:											
1990..........	3,075	18	0.6	21	0.7	3,036	98.7	-	-	3,036	98.7
1993..........	3,508	24	0.6	30	0.9	3,454	98.5	-	-	3,454	98.5
Exports of domestic products:											
1990..........	532	146	27.4	22	4.1	364	68.5	29	5.5	335	63.0
1993..........	657	174	26.5	24	3.7	459	69.8	37	5.6	422	64.2
Industrial: [3]											
1990..........	2,965	313	10.6	10	0.3	2,642	88.1	179	6.0	2,463	83.1
1993..........	3,213	337	10.4	15	0.5	2,861	89.1	166	5.2	2,695	83.9

- Represents or rounds to zero. [1] Rayon and acetate. [2] Nylon, polyester, acrylic, and olefin. [3] Includes consumer-type products.

Source: Fiber Economics Bureau, Inc., Roseland, NJ, *Textile Organon*, monthly, (copyright).

No. 1230. Textiles and Apparel Products—U.S. Exports and Imports: 1992 to 1994

[**In millions of dollars.** Excludes glass fibers, rubber and leather apparel, and clothing donated for charity. Minus sign (-) indicates deficit]

PRODUCT	EXPORTS			GENERAL IMPORTS			MERCHANDISE TRADE BALANCE		
	1992	1993	1994	1992	1993	1994	1992	1993	1994
Total...................	10,120	10,977	12,208	39,070	42,225	45,952	-28,950	-31,248	-33,744
Textile yarn fabrics..............	5,911	6,025	6,592	7,844	8,438	9,208	-1,933	-2,413	-2,616
Textile yarn..................	1,179	1,045	1,213	955	1,146	1,335	224	-101	-122
Cotton fabric, woven	591	641	725	1,493	1,552	1,498	-902	-911	-773
Woven fabric of manmade textiles ..	825	883	925	1,206	1,261	1,291	-381	-378	-366
Woven fabric of textile material	185	210	236	666	662	695	-481	-452	-459
Special yarns.................	1,335	1,418	1,588	797	878	977	538	540	611
Other......................	1,796	1,828	1,905	2,727	3,412	3,412	-931	-1,111	-1,507
Apparel	4,209	4,952	5,616	31,226	33,787	36,744	-27,017	-28,835	-31,128

Source: U.S. Bureau of the Census, *U.S. Merchandise Trade: Exports, General Imports, and Imports for Consumption*, Report FT925, monthly.

No. 1231. Iron and Steel Industry—Summary: 1980 to 1995

[For financial data, the universe in 1992 consists of the companies that produced 68 percent of the total reported raw steel production. The financial data represent the operations of the steel segment of the companies. Minus sign (-) indicates net loss]

ITEM	Unit	1980	1985	1988	1989	1990	1991	1992	1993	1994	1995
Steel mill products, apparent supply . . .	Mil. tons [1] . .	95.2	96.4	102.7	96.8	97.8	88.3	95.0	104.6	121.3	114.8
Net shipments.	Mil. tons [1] . .	83.9	73.0	83.8	84.1	85.0	78.8	82.2	89.0	95.1	97.5
Exports	Mil. tons [1] . .	4.1	1.0	2.1	4.6	4.3	6.3	4.3	4.0	3.8	7.1
Imports	Mil. tons [1] . .	15.5	24.3	20.9	17.3	17.2	15.8	17.1	19.5	30.1	24.4
Scrap consumed.	Mil. tons [1] . .	66.6	53.2	56.3	51.7	50.1	50.5	51.9	58.5	60.0	(NA)
Scrap inventory.	Mil. tons [1] . .	6.9	4.0	3.5	3.5	3.6	3.7	3.3	3.6	4.0	(NA)
Iron and steel products: Exports.	Mil. tons [1] . .	5.1	1.6	2.8	5.4	5.3	7.4	5.3	4.7	4.9	8.2
Imports	Mil. tons [1] . .	17.9	27.6	25.7	22.1	21.9	20.2	21.9	21.8	32.7	27.3
Capacity by steelmaking process	Mil. net tons	153.7	133.6	112.0	115.9	116.7	117.6	113.1	109.9	108.2	112.5
Revenue	Bil. dol.	37.7	28.4	32.7	31.8	30.9	27.1	26.9	29.5	33.5	(NA)
Net income	Bil. dol.	0.7	-1.8	-0.6	1.6	0.1	-2.0	-4.1	1.9	1.3	(NA)
Stockholders' equity.	Bil. dol.	14.5	6.9	2.2	2.1	4.3	2.8	-0.6	3.7	7.1	(NA)
Total assets	Bil. dol.	30.8	24.0	24.2	24.6	28.3	27.4	28.8	30.6	32.0	(NA)
Capital expenditures [2]	Bil. dol.	2.7	1.6	1.8	2.3	2.6	2.3	1.8	1.5	2.2	(NA)
Working capital ratio [2]	Ratio	1.6	1.3	1.7	1.6	1.6	1.4	1.4	1.3	1.6	(NA)
Inventories.	Bil. dol.	4.7	3.5	3.8	4.0	4.7	4.4	4.5	4.6	4.9	(NA)
Average employment	1,000	399	208	169	169	164	146	140	127	126	123
Hours worked. . . . . [3]	Million	758	419	363	360	350	304	293	274	273	269
Producer price indexes: [3]											
Iron and steel, total	1982=100 . .	90.0	104.8	115.7	119.1	117.2	114.1	116.0	121.9	(NA)	(NA)
Steel mill products	1982=100 . .	86.6	104.7	110.7	114.5	112.1	109.5	108.2	113.4	(NA)	(NA)
Blast and electric furnace products . .	1982=100 . .	97.1	95.6	119.6	129.4	120.1	116.9	115.7	116.6	(NA)	(NA)
Iron ore	1982=100 . .	87.8	97.5	82.8	82.8	83.3	83.6	82.7	82.8	(NA)	(NA)
Scrap, iron and steel	1982=100 . .	140.9	112.6	177.1	173.7	166.0	147.6	172.5	192.5	(NA)	(NA)
Foundry and forge shop products . . .	1982=100 . .	89.7	105.2	109.6	114.6	117.2	119.0	121.3	123.8	(NA)	(NA)

NA Not available.　　[1] In millions of short tons.　　[2] Current assets to current liabilities.　　[3] Source: U.S. Bureau of Labor Statistics, *Producer Price Indexes*, monthly and annual.

No. 1232. Raw Steel, Pig Iron, and Ferroalloys Production: 1970 to 1995

[**In millions, except percent.** See also *Historical Statistics, Colonial Times to 1970*, series P 265-269]

ITEM	1970	1980	1985	1988	1989	1990	1991	1992	1993	1994	1995
Raw steel (net tons):											
World production.	654.2	790.4	792.9	859.2	865.3	848.8	811.1	810.2	814.6	800.1	(NA)
U.S. production	131.5	111.8	88.3	99.9	97.9	98.9	87.9	92.9	97.9	100.6	104.9
Percent of world	20	14	11	12	11	12	11	12	12	13	(NA)
Basic oxygen process . .	63.3	67.6	51.9	58.0	58.3	58.5	52.7	57.6	59.3	61.0	62.5
Electric	20.2	31.2	29.9	36.8	35.2	36.9	33.8	35.3	38.5	39.6	42.4
Open hearth	48.0	13.0	6.4	5.1	4.4	3.5	1.4	-	-	-	-
Carbon	117.4	94.7	76.7	86.8	86.2	86.6	77.9	82.5	86.9	89.5	92.7
Alloy and stainless.	14.1	17.1	11.6	13.1	11.7	12.3	10.0	10.4	11.0	11.1	12.3
Pig iron and ferroalloys, production (sh. tons) [1]	93.5	68.7	50.4	55.7	55.9	54.8	48.6	52.2	53.1	54.4	56.1

- Represents or rounds to zero.　　NA Not available.　　[1] For 1970, excludes blast furnace ferroalloys.

No. 1233. Steel Products—Net Shipments, by Market Classes: 1970 to 1994

[**In thousands of short tons.** Comprises carbon, alloy, and stainless steel]

MARKET CLASS	1970	1980	1985	1989	1990	1991	1992	1993	1994
Total [1]	**90,798**	**83,853**	**73,043**	**84,100**	**84,981**	**78,846**	**82,241**	**89,022**	**95,084**
Automotive.	14,475	12,124	12,950	11,763	11,100	10,015	11,092	12,719	14,753
Steel service centers, distributors.	16,025	16,172	18,439	20,769	21,111	19,464	21,328	23,714	24,153
Construction, incl. maintenance	8,913	8,742	7,900	8,318	9,245	9,161	9,536	13,429	10,935
Containers, packaging, shipping.	7,775	5,551	4,089	4,459	4,474	4,278	3,974	4,355	4,495
Machinery, industrial equipment, tools . .	5,169	4,543	2,271	2,409	2,388	1,982	1,951	2,191	2,427
Steel for converting and processing . . .	3,443	4,117	5,484	8,235	9,441	8,265	9,226	9,451	10,502
Rail transportation	3,098	3,155	1,061	1,229	1,080	999	1,052	1,223	1,248
Contractors' products	4,440	3,148	3,330	3,182	2,870	2,306	2,694	2,913	3,348
Oil and gas industries	3,550	5,371	2,044	1,203	1,892	1,425	1,454	1,526	1,703
Electrical equipment.	2,694	2,441	1,869	2,449	2,453	2,102	2,136	2,213	2,299
Appliances, utensils, and cutlery	2,160	1,725	1,466	1,721	1,540	1,388	1,503	1,592	1,736

[1] Includes nonclassified shipments and other classes not shown separately.

Source of tables 1231-1233: American Iron and Steel Institute, Washington, DC, *Annual Statistical Report* (copyright).

No. 1234. Computer Shipments and Revenues: 1991 to 1993

[Revenue is in if-sold, end-user dollars]

ITEM	FACTORY REVENUE (mil. dol.)			SHIPMENTS (units)		
	1991	1992	1993	1991	1992	1993
United States:						
Supercomputer	876	938	701	558	571	405
Mainframe	9,713	7,453	4,643	3,227	2,421	1,929
Midrange	7,967	8,534	6,705	151,574	124,745	107,034
Workstation	3,458	3,719	4,375	210,541	237,730	262,869
Personal computer	24,589	25,858	29,695	10,903,000	12,544,374	14,775,000
Canada:						
Supercomputer	22	37	38	17	26	29
Mainframe	671	623	243	204	156	123
Midrange	485	618	509	10,117	9,094	6,794
Workstation	188	185	181	8,017	11,806	10,687
Personal computer	2,077	2,405	2,730	926,000	1,175,000	1,415,000
Western Europe:						
Supercomputer	529	479	448	241	269	213
Mainframe	9,629	7,490	5,782	4,088	2,455	1,963
Midrange	9,699	6,727	7,157	198,780	155,142	145,353
Workstation	2,540	2,604	2,828	154,581	175,762	171,744
Personal computer	17,517	18,872	17,999	8,406,937	9,495,441	10,323,974
Japan:						
Supercomputer	494	450	558	140	108	122
Mainframe	6,252	5,367	5,569	5,631	3,630	4,191
Midrange	5,673	4,916	4,808	286,626	233,967	194,385
Workstation	1,885	1,883	2,143	124,712	124,073	133,750
Personal computer	4,586	4,750	5,885	2,354,300	2,223,810	2,464,093
Asia/Pacific:						
Supercomputer	54	83	82	44	63	58
Mainframe	544	642	784	568	238	265
Midrange	263	522	784	3,978	8,757	12,883
Workstation	256	327	351	15,871	23,842	20,374
Personal computer	4,574	5,219	7,053	2,235,000	3,031,398	3,935,135
Rest of world:						
Supercomputer	16	67	31	13	50	18
Mainframe	382	584	473	158	200	246
Midrange	476	506	625	15,063	13,209	18,862
Workstation	373	340	408	15,808	24,038	24,006
Personal computer	4,237	6,991	10,256	2,140,763	3,940,777	5,929,798

No. 1235. Microcontrollers and Chip Shipments: 1990 to 1993

ITEM	REVENUE (mil. dol.)				SHIPMENTS (millions of units)			
	1990	1991	1992	1993	1990	1991	1992	1993
Microcontrollers, worldwide	3,667	4,519	4,613	5,813	1,365	1,562	1,895	2,155
8-bit	2,079	2,618	(NA)	3,612	567	729	844	1,096
4-bit	1,394	1,598	(NA)	1,705	781	801	1,003	999
16-bit	194	303	(NA)	496	17	32	48	60
32-bit processors	1,402	2,456	4,363	8,427	26	44	61	77
RISC [1]	175	270	305	642	1	1	3	7
CISC [2]	1,227	2,186	4,057	7,785	25	42	27	70
256K DRAM [3] chips	1,322	622	270	162	620	299	193	105
1-Megabit DRAM chips	4,229	3,776	2,644	2,031	665	835	821	601

NA Not available.   [1] RISC=Reduced Instruction Set Computer.   [2] CISC=Complex Instruction Set Computer.
[3] DRAM=Dynamic Random Access Memory.

Source of tables 1234 and 1235: Dataquest, Inc., San Jose, CA, Consolidate Data Base, January 1994, and unpublished data.

No. 1236. Computers and Industrial Electronics—Shipments: 1985 to 1994

[In millions of dollars]

ITEM	1985	1987	1988	1989	1990	1991	1992	1993	1994
Total	43,993	48,275	49,797	51,339	50,793	50,121	51,932	54,821	63,478
Computer and peripheral equipment:									
Computers	21,107	24,410	24,354	25,610	25,973	26,691	29,036	30,002	38,423
Peripheral equipment	22,887	23,865	25,443	25,729	24,820	23,430	22,896	24,819	25,005
Total	20,121	21,325	22,100	24,799	26,183	26,126	27,250	27,225	29,757
Industrial electronics:									
Controlling, processing equipment	8,719	9,193	9,861	11,992	12,728	12,633	12,881	13,961	15,077
Testing, measuring equipment	6,008	6,009	5,807	5,953	6,859	7,492	7,484	7,332	8,121
Nuclear electronic equipment	519	601	616	606	567	571	533	519	521
Robots, accessories, and components	345	284	229	256	275	294	(NA)	(NA)	(NA)
Other electronic equipment	4,530	5,238	5,588	5,992	5,754	5,137	5,880	5,438	6,038

NA Not available.

Source: Electronic Industries Association, Washington, DC, *Electronic Market Data Book,* annual (copyright).

No. 1237. Factory Sales of Consumer Electronics (including imports), and Electronic Components in the United States: 1985 to 1995

[In millions of dollars]

CATEGORY	1985	1988	1989	1990	1991	1992	1993	1994	1995
Total	22,940	32,236	33,373	43,033	42,668	46,165	51,215	56,292	61,693
Television sets:									
Direct-view color TV.	5,514	6,247	6,490	6,197	5,979	6,591	7,316	7,225	6,798
LCD color TV	7	30	40	50	66	60	60	60	60
Projection TV	488	529	478	626	683	714	841	1,117	1,417
TV/VCR combinations	(NA)	(NA)	(NA)	178	266	376	699	710	723
Monochrome TV	308	196	116	99	61	47	40	38	34
LCD Monochrome TV.	(NA)	40	40	33	31	32	33	32	31
Other video:									
VCR decks.	4,173	2,848	2,625	2,439	2,454	2,947	2,851	2,869	2,767
Camcorders	793	1,972	2,007	2,260	2,013	1,841	1,958	1,985	2,135
Laserdisc players	23	34	50	72	81	93	123	122	108
Home satellite earth stations	(NA)	331	365	421	370	379	408	900	1,265
Videocassette players	(NA)	57	63	65	71	49	61	64	69
Audio:									
Audio systems	1,372	1,225	1,217	1,270	1,264	1,370	1,464	1,703	1,623
Separate audio components	1,132	1,854	1,871	1,935	1,805	1,586	1,635	1,686	1,911
Home radios.	379	377	379	360	310	324	307	306	284
Portable audio equipment	1,140	1,547	1,595	1,645	1,780	2,096	2,187	2,495	2,506
Aftermarket autosound equipment .	961	1,187	1,125	1,192	1,232	1,467	1,604	1,898	1,931
Factory installed autosound.	1,800	2,750	3,000	3,100	2,875	2,990	3,199	3,225	3,585
Pagers	(NA)	(NA)	(NA)	118	139	168	198	230	300
Vehicle security.	(NA)	(NA)	(NA)	190	210	240	294	401	485
Home information:									
Cordless telephones	280	681	830	842	1,125	1,091	1,046	1,106	1,377
Corded telephones	630	441	532	638	605	575	617	610	557
Telephone answering devices	325	755	838	827	1,000	934	1,026	1,153	1,077
Cellular telephones	115	430	653	1,133	962	1,146	1,257	1,275	1,431
Home computers.	2,175	3,340	3,711	4,187	4,287	5,573	6,921	8,070	10,920
Computer peripherals.	(NA)	(NA)	(NA)	1,980	2,060	2,220	2,450	3,100	3,850
Computer software (inc.CDROM) . .	(NA)	(NA)	(NA)	971	1,045	1,250	1,600	2,050	2,500
Personal Wordprocessors	(NA)	650	688	666	600	555	558	504	451
Home fax machines.	(NA)	(NA)	(NA)	920	869	826	888	964	919
Home security systems.	(NA)	900	1,000	1,440	1,030	830	940	1,110	1,130
Electronic Gaming Hardware	(NA)	(NA)	(NA)	975	1,275	1,575	1,650	1,575	1,500
Electronic Gaming Software	(NA)	(NA)	(NA)	2,400	2,325	2,400	2,625	2,925	3,000
Blank media:									
Blank audio cassettes	270	354	367	376	373	376	362	353	334
Blank videocassettes	1,055	936	923	948	980	872	779	730	708
Blank floppy diskettes.	(NA)	258	297	314	308	320	345	353	373
Accessories:									
Electronic accessories	(NA)	847	829	793	721	715	759	936	944
Total primary batteries	(NA)	1,420	1,244	1,383	1,424	1,538	2,215	2,412	2,600
U.S. electronic component ship. .	44,064	55,287	59,120	61,303	61,698	65,295	71,480	83,593	(NA)
Electron tubes	2,068	2,299	2,586	2,646	2,586	2,655	3,038	3,457	(NA)
Solid State products	14,651	19,790	22,246	23,543	26,238	27,292	31,534	39,500	(NA)
Passive and other components	27,345	33,197	34,288	35,114	32,874	35,349	36,909	40,635	(NA)

NA Not available.
Source: Electronic Industries Association, Washington, DC, *Electronic Market Data Book,* annual (copyright).

No. 1238. Machine Tools—New Orders and Shipments: 1970 to 1994

[In millions of dollars. Data represents total industry volume based on reports from over 200 manufacturers]

YEAR	METAL CUTTING TOOLS					METAL FORMING TOOLS				
	New orders (net)		Shipments		Order backlog, end of period	New orders (net)		Shipments		Order backlog, end of period
	Total	Domestic	Total	Domestic		Total	Domestic	Total	Domestic	
1970	651	507	993	827	471	261	227	450	412	235
1975	916	781	1,879	1,548	1,062	361	284	573	485	388
1980	3,885	3,496	3,681	3,206	4,750	870	744	1,011	879	701
1984	1,916	1,700	1,607	1,484	1,132	1,000	932	679	609	542
1985	1,853	1,652	1,742	1,549	1,243	675	610	803	743	414
1986	1,544	1,377	1,890	1,685	897	581	507	688	621	307
1987	1,451	1,294	1,677	1,499	672	667	536	647	538	327
1988	2,708	2,316	1,575	1,400	1,806	883	749	825	702	386
1989	1,977	1,723	2,359	2,059	1,423	832	719	837	704	380
1990	2,070	1,772	2,330	2,004	1,164	894	761	970	851	304
1991	1,894	1,549	1,872	1,595	1,186	748	546	802	625	251
1992	1,756	1,532	1,918	1,605	1,025	726	609	678	547	299
1993	2,322	2,177	2,160	1,955	1,187	971	825	1,044	881	225
1994	2,914	2,775	2,515	2,333	1,587	1,527	1,382	1,184	1,038	568

Source: The Association For Manufacturing Technology, McLean, VA, *The Economic Handbook of The Machine Tool Industry,* annual, (copyright); and Bureau of Economic Analysis, *Survey of Current Business,* monthly.

No. 1239. Semiconductors and Related Devices: 1980 to 1993

[In millions of dollars, except percent. Semiconductors and related devices represent SIC 3674]

ITEM	1980	1985	1988	1989	1990	1991	1992	1993
Consumption, North American market [1]	6,053	9,420	15,844	17,070	16,540	16,990	20,426	27,998
Revenues (North American companies)	8,062	11,051	18,586	19,515	21,047	22,940	27,105	37,453
Capital expenditures (North America) [2]	1,438	2,629	3,434	3,642	3,855	4,077	4,296	5,809
Percent of sales	17.8	23.8	18.5	18.7	18.3	17.8	15.9	15.5
Japan capital expend. as a percent of revenues	11.0	11.4	14.9	15.5	20.5	20.4	22.2	16.2
R&D (North America)	423	1,159	3,873	4,269	5,172	5,652	6,122	5,587
Imports, total [3]	2,223	4,870	9,502	10,758	(NA)	(NA)	(NA)	(NA)
Shipments [4]	9,455	15,253	20,332	23,488	23,978	26,302	25,964	30,425
Integrated microcircuits	6,768	10,872	14,857	16,682	16,372	19,151	20,065	24,084
Semiconductor devices, n.e.c. [5]	1,398	2,569	3,337	4,875	5,584	5,761	5,899	6,341
Assets, beginning of year	4,014	12,200	(NA)	(NA)	(NA)	(NA)	(NA)	(NA)

NA Not available.   [1] Source: Dataquest Inc., San Jose, CA, unpublished data. Revenue from shipments by all companies into Canada and the United States.   [2] Capital expenditures by all companies in Canada and the United States.   [3] Imports for consumption. Includes imports not shown separately.   [4] Includes items not shown separately.   [5] N.e.c.=Not elsewhere classified.

Source: Except as noted, U.S. Bureau of the Census, *Current Industrial Reports*, series MA-36Q; *U.S. Imports, FT 210, 1980-1988; Import CD-ROM Disc 1989; and Annual Survey of Manufactures*.

No. 1240. Fiber, Rugs, Carpeting, and Sheets—Shipments: 1989 to 1995

PRODUCT	Unit	1989	1990	1991	1992	1993	1994	1995
All fibers [1]	Mil. lbs.	743	812	837	926	1,008	1,036	953
Raw wool [2] [3]	Mil. lbs.	135	133	152	151	157	153	142
Noils, and fiber [4]	Mil. lbs.	24	20	21	21	23	19	20
Other fibers	Mil. lbs.	584	659	664	754	829	864	792
Knit fabric production	Mil. lbs.	1,935	1,901	1,963	2,179	2,188	2,230	(NA)
Rugs, carpet and carpeting	Mil. dol.	8,431	8,527	7,980	8,749	9,283	9,895	(NA)
Sheets	1,000 doz	15,663	15,408	14,001	15,198	16,331	16,190	15,210
Pillow cases	1,000 doz	13,089	12,665	11,301	12,523	14,464	14,622	14,199
Terry towels	1,000 doz	62,741	42,376	43,158	48,789	47,161	48,348	47,933

NA Not available.   [1] Includes man-made fiber top converted from tow without combing. A number of companies were added for 1990 based on information in the 1987 Census of Manufactures. Data were received from these companies for 1990; therefore, the information shown for years prior to 1990 may not be directly comparable. These changes represent approximately 20 percent of the total fibers consumed on the woolen system and worsted combing.   [2] Data are shown on a scoured basis for greasy wool.   [3] Shorn and pulled wool of sheep excludes raw wool consumed in cotton system spinning to avoid disclosing figures for individual companies.   [4] Includes reprocessed and reused wool, mohair, alpaca, vicuna, and other specialty fibers as well as tops and noils consumed in woolen spinning and mohair consumed in worsted combing. Does not include wool tops consumed in cotton system spinning.

Source: U.S. Bureau of the Census, *Current Industrial Reports*, MA22K, MA22Q, and MQ23X, annual.

No. 1241. Glass Containers, Clay Construction Products, and Refractories—Shipments: 1989 to 1995

[In millions of dollars]

PRODUCT	1989	1990	1991	1992	1993	1994	1995
Glass container shipments	286	285	279	283	290	285	269
Brick shipments [1]	1,088	1,014	883	920	1,006	1,103	1,040
Clay tile shipments [2]	698	687	639	646	701	723	680
Clay pipe and fittings shipments	63	60	51	38	32	33	38
Refractory shipments	2,011	2,003	1,947	1,956	1,930	1,997	(NA)
Clay	823	771	784	786	773	851	(NA)
Nonclay	1,188	1,232	1,163	1,170	1,157	1,146	(NA)

NA Not available.   [1] Building or common and face bricks.   [2] Floor and wall tile including quarry tile.

Source: U.S. Bureau of the Census, *Current Industrial Reports*, M32G, MQ32D, and MA32C, annual.

No. 1242. Mining and Mineral Processing Equipment—Shipments: 1993 and 1994

PRODUCT	Product code	Number of companies 1993	QUANTITY (units)		VALUE (mil. dol.)	
			1993	1994	1993	1994
Portable crushing, screening, washing, and combination plants	3531K	16	574	605	75	83
Underground mining machinery [1]	35325	33	3,312	(NA)	338	356
Mineral processing and beneficiation equip. [1]	35326	(NA)	(NA)	(NA)	(NA)	(NA)
Crushing/pulverizing/screening machinery [2]	35327	47	3,297	4,010	229	278

NA Not available.   [1] Excludes parts.   [2] Excludes portables and parts.

Source: U.S. Bureau of the Census, *Current Industrial Reports*, MA35F, annual.

Manufactures

No. 1243. Inorganic Materials and Pharmaceutical Preparations: 1990 to 1994

PRODUCT	Product code	Unit	1990	1992	1993	1994
INORGANIC FERTILIZERS						
Ammonia, synthetic anhydrous:	28731 31					
Total production.		1,000 sh. tons	17,003	17,924	17,195	17,256
Shipments		1,000 sh. tons	10,382	10,642	10,436	10,411
Shipments value		Mil. dol..	1,072	1,095	1,174	1,509
Ammonium nitrate, original solution:	28731 50					
Total production.		1,000 sh. tons	7,714	7,981	8,281	8,517
Ammonium sulfate:	28731 57					
Total production.		1,000 sh. tons	2,519	2,391	2,432	2,588
Shipments		1,000 sh. tons	2,529	2,239	2,417	2,489
Shipments value		Mil. dol..	130	140	150	165
Urea (100%):	28732					
Total production.		1,000 sh. tons	8,217	8,766	8,330	7,952
Shipments		1,000 sh. tons	5,362	5,343	5,255	5,099
Shipments value		Mil. dol.. . . .	640	696	630	657
Nitric acid (100%):	28731 11					
Total production.		1,000 sh. tons	7,931	8,136	8,254	8,611
Shipments		1,000 sh. tons	647	672	678	964
Shipments value		Mil. dol..	81	85	89	118
Phosphoric acid (100% P2O5):	28741 81					
Total production.	28741 85	1,000 sh. tons	12,035	12,826	11,515	12,792
Shipments		1,000 sh. tons	4,170	4,375	3,688	4,228
Shipments value		Mil. dol.. . . .	1,226	1,182	969	1,085
Sulfuric acid, gross (100%):	28193					
Total production.		1,000 sh. tons	44,337	44,524	39,839	44,813
Shipments		1,000 sh. tons	11,879	10,950	11,362	11,916
Shipments value		Mil. dol..	589	529	516	488
Superphosphates and other fertilizer materials (100% P2O5):	28742					
Total production.		1,000 sh. tons	8,982	9,696	8,801	10,024
Shipments		1,000 sh. tons	9,016	9,666	8,814	9,973
Shipments value		Mil. dol..	2,711	2,530	2,057	2,830
INORGANIC CHEMICAL SHIPMENTS						
Alkalies and chlorine.	2812	Mil. dol..	3,187	2,761	2,278	2,281
Chlorine (100% Cl).	28121	Mil. dol..	478	194	546	840
Sodium hydroxide (caustic soda)	28123	Mil. dol..	2,341	2,206	1,370	1,053
Other alkalies	28125	Mil. dol..	361	353	355	381
Alkalies and chlorine n.s.k.	28120 00	Mil. dol..	7	7	7	7
Inorganic color pigments	2816	Mil. dol..	2,261	2,428	2,391	2,471
Titanium dioxide (composite and pure) (commodity weight)	28161 00	Mil. dol..	2,131	2,316	2,253	2,318
Inorganic chemicals n.e.c.	2819	Mil. dol..	13,612	12,838	11,860	12,442
Sulfuric acid, gross (new and fortified)	28193	Mil. dol..	589	529	516	487
Inorganic acids, except nitric, phosphoric and sulfuric	28194	Mil. dol.. . . .	603	505	506	578
Aluminum oxide, except natural alumina	28195	Mil. dol.. . . .	1,499	947	920	813
Aluminum compounds	28196	Mil. dol.. . . .	665	595	574	598
Potassium and sodium compounds (except bleaches, alkalies, and alums)	28197	Mil. dol.. . . .	1,956	1,932	1,884	1,866
Chemical catalytic preparations	28198	Mil. dol.. . . .	1,221	1,350	1,380	1,422
Other inorganic chemicals n.e.c.	28199	Mil. dol.. . . .	6,846	6,533	5,883	6,467
Industrial inorganic chemicals n.s.k.	28190 00	Mil. dol.. . . .	232	220	197	211
Household bleaching compounds	28422 00	Mil. dol..	724	920	915	950
PHARMACEUTICAL PREP. SHIPMENTS						
Affecting neoplasms, endocrine systems, and metabolic disease	28341	Mil. dol..	2,743	3,318	3,820	4,132
Acting on the central nervous system and sense organs	28342	Mil. dol..	7,219	8,319	8,927	9,065
Acting on the cardiovascular system	28343	Mil. dol..	4,815	4,909	5,234	5,547
Acting on the respiratory system.	28344	Mil. dol..	3,724	5,277	5,510	5,675
Acting on the digestive system	28345	Mil. dol..	4,840	7,111	7,996	8,827
Acting on the skin	28346	Mil. dol..	1,558	1,760	1,980	2,219
Vitamin, nutrient, and hematinic preps.	28347	Mil. dol..	2,588	2,924	3,560	4,408
Affecting parasitic and infective disease	28348	Mil. dol..	5,411	7,018	7,234	8,189
Pharmaceutical preps. for veterinary use	28349	Mil. dol..	1,057	1,327	1,353	1,315

Source: U.S. Bureau of the Census, *Current Industrial Reports*, MA28A, MA28B, and MA28G, annual.

No. 1244. Engines, Refrigeration and Heating Equipment, and Pumps and Compressors—Shipments: 1992 to 1994

PRODUCT	Product code	Unit	1992	1993	1994
Internal combustion engines produced	**(X)**	**1,000**	**18,868**	**21,342**	**24,178**
Gasoline (except outboard, aircraft, and auto).	35191	1,000	18,217	20,561	23,287
Nonautomotive diesel (except aircraft).	35193	1,000	178	197	220
Automotive diesel	35194	1,000	469	608	661
Natural gas and LPG	35196	1,000	4	6	9
Air-conditioning, heating equipment shipments:					
Heat transfer equipment	35851	Mil. dol. . . .	4,118	4,951	5,509
Unitary air-conditioners.	35852	Mil. dol. . . .	3,913	3,937	4,339
Commercial refrigeration equipment	35853 pt	Mil. dol. . . .	(D)	183	220
Compressors and compressor units	35854	Mil. dol. . . .	2,931	3,101	3,717
Condensing units, refrigeration (complete)	35855	Mil. dol. . . .	203	240	277
Room air-conditioners and dehumidifiers	35856	Mil. dol. . . .	774	824	1,106
Nonelectric warm air furnaces and humidifiers	3585C pt	Mil. dol. . . .	1,216	1,334	1,426
Pumps and compressors[1]	**(X)**	**Mil. dol. . .**	**5,916**	**6,216**	**6,563**
Industrial pumps	35611	Mil. dol. . . .	2,465	2,571	2,638
Hydraulic fluid power pumps and motors	35617,8	Mil. dol. . . .	(NA)	(NA)	(NA)
Domestic water systems.	35613	Mil. dol. . . .	331	330	339
Oil well, oilfield, and other pumps (including laboratory pumps)	35615	Mil. dol. . . .	805	916	907
Compressors and vacuum pumps	35631	Mil. dol. . . .	2,315	2,400	2,680

D Data withheld to avoid disclosure of company data. NA Not available. X Not applicable. [1] Excludes hand pumps, automotive circulating pumps, compressors for icemaking and refrigeration equipment, air conditioning units, and replacements and repair parts for pumps and compressors.

Source: U.S. Bureau of the Census, *Current Industrial Reports*, MA35L, MA35M, and MA35P, annual.

No. 1245. Computers and Office and Accounting Machines—Shipments: 1993 and 1994

PRODUCT	Product code	Number of companies, 1994	QUANTITY (number)		VALUE (mil. dol.)	
			1993	1994	1993	1994
Electronic computers (automatic data processors).	3571	207	(X)	(X)	29,659	38,132
Large-scale processing equipment [1]	35713	27	31	(NA)	4,104	4,459
Medium- and small-scale processing equipment [2] .	35714	45	190	(NA)	2,442	3,089
Personal computers and workstations	35715	90	13,383	(NA)	18,889	24,494
Portable computers	35716	31	2,694	(NA)	2,576	4,560
Computer storage devices and equipment	35721	103	12,537	(NA)	5,731	5,512
Parts for computer storage devices and subassemblies	35722	23	(X)	(X)	1,496	1,955
Computer terminals	35751	68	4,360	(NA)	1,531	1,240
Parts for computer terminals	35752	14	(X)	(X)	276	(3)
Computer peripheral equipment, n.e.c.[3]	35771	277	(X)	(X)	9,810	10,412
Calculating and accounting machines	35784	46	(X)	(X)	1,454	1,464
Automatic typing and word processing machines. .	35792	5	1,717	(NA)	343	290
Mailing, letter handling, addressing machines	35795	32	1,258	(NA)	1,268	967
Other office machines, n.e.c.[3]	35799	44	(X)	(X)	(D)	570
Magnetic and optical recording media	36950	64	(X)	(X)	4,483	4,782

D Data withheld to avoid disclosure of company data. NA Not available. X Not applicable. [1] 64 megabytes in MINIMUM main memory configuration. [2] Up to 64 megabytes in MINIMUM main memory configuration. [3] N.e.c. = Not elsewhere classified.

Source: U.S. Bureau of the Census, *Current Industrial Report*, MA35R, annual.

No. 1246. Metalworking Machinery—Shipments: 1988 to 1994

[In millions of dollars]

PRODUCT	Product code	1988	1989	1990	1991	1992	1993	1994
Metalworking machinery	(X)	2,858	3,514	3,426	3,172	3,074	3,222	3,780
Metal cutting type	(X)	1,735	2,429	2,371	2,139	2,000	2,085	2,463
Machining centers [1]	3541A	334	442	437	362	378	485	552
Station type machines	3541B	225	563	502	450	435	375	455
Other metal cutting machine tools [2] . . .	3541C	165	174	142	196	167	166	200
Metal forming type.	(X)	1,123	1,086	1,065	1,033	1,074	1,140	1,277

X Not applicable. [1] Multi-function numerically controlled machines. [2] Excludes those designed primarily for home workshops, labs, etc.

Source: U.S. Bureau of the Census, *Current Industrial Reports*, MQ35W, annual.

No. 1247. Switchgear, Switchboard Apparatus, Relays, and Industrial Controls—Shipments: 1990 to 1994

[In millions of dollars]

PRODUCT	Product code	Companies, 1994 (number)	1990	1991	1992	1993	1994
Power circuit breakers	36132	26	388	368	481	516	531
Low volt panelboards & dist. boards [1]	36133	130	1,722	1,643	1,531	1,681	1,744
Fuses and fuse equipment [2]	36134	21	419	409	413	320	332
Molded case circuit breakers, 1,000 volts and under	36135	32	959	917	955	1,010	1,107
Duct [3]	36136	25	194	184	189	200	228
Switchgear, except ducts	36139	128	1,324	1,398	1,615	1,581	1,636
General purpose and other relays	36251	116	805	772	782	751	676
Specific purpose industrial controls	36252	244	2,020	1,993	1,916	2,322	2,732
General purpose industrial controls	36253	272	2,912	2,879	2,778	3,326	3,699
Motor controller accessories [4]	36254	123	452	434	448	476	502

[1] Includes other switching and interruption devices, 1,000 volts and below. [2] Under 2,300 volts, except power distribution cutouts. [3] Includes plug-in units and accessories, 1,000 volts and under, consisting of enclosed sectionalized prefabricated bus bars rated 20 amperes or more, associated structures and fittings. [4] Includes parts for industrial controls.

Source: U.S. Bureau of the Census, *Current Industrial Reports*, MA36A, annual.

No. 1248. Selected Industrial Air Pollution Control Equipment—Shipments: 1994

[Quantity in number of units, value in thousands of dollars]

PRODUCT	Product code	Number of companies	NEW ORDERS Quantity	NEW ORDERS Value	SHIPMENTS Quantity	SHIPMENTS Value	BACKLOG (Dec. 31) Quantity	BACKLOG (Dec. 31) Value
Selected indus. air pollution control equip.	35646	110	69,532	630,689	67,927	711,390	7,738	408,655
Particulate emissions collectors	(X)	90	56,392	477,873	54,744	453,261	6,987	226,340
Electrostatic precipitators	35646 51	19	530	161,817	552	136,763	100	104,802
Fabric filters	35646 54	59	48,551	207,221	47,213	211,340	5,772	50,085
Mechanical collectors	35646 55	39	5,999	63,511	5,692	68,028	844	22,907
Wet scrubbers	35646 58	31	1,312	45,324	1,287	37,130	271	48,546
Gaseous emissions control devices	(X)	38	1,198	103,822	1,169	206,546	356	153,402
Catalytic oxidation systems	35646 70	10	145	30,363	(S)	28,267	(S)	15,501
Thermal and direct oxidation systems	35646 72	14	300	34,419	272	30,878	48	12,084
Scrubbers (gas absorber)	35646 73	11	687	14,441	658	13,997	181	4,163
Dry flue gas desulfurization systems	35646 75	9	(D)	(D)	(S)	117,354	(S)	(S)
Gas absorbers	35646 76	9	51	7,968	(D)	(D)	27	4,562
Other	35646 79	19	11,942	48,994	12,014	51,583	395	28,913

D Data withheld to avoid disclosure of company data.   S Figure does not meet publication standards.   X Not applicable.

Source: U.S. Bureau of the Census, *Current Industrial Reports*, MA35J, annual.

No. 1249. Fluid Power Products—Shipments: 1989 to 1994

[In millions of dollars. Includes aerospace]

PRODUCT	Product code	1989	1990	1991	1992	1993	1994
Fluid power products, incl. aerospace	(X)	6,915	7,207	6,475	6,330	6,742	7,738
Hydraulic valves, nonaerospace type	34921	629	663	606	583	64	765
Pneumatic valves, nonaerospace type	34922	463	458	434	458	418	525
Aerospace type hydraulic & pneumatic valves	34923	451	498	527	443	356	284
Fittings for metal and plastic tubing [1]	34924	505	500	471	516	518	604
Hydraulic and pneumatic fittings and couplings for hose (nonaerospace)	34925	625	620	552	630	489	652
Hydraulic and pneumatic hose or tube end fitting and assemblies (aerospace)	34926	(X)	336	394	386	354	304
Parts for hydraulic & pneumatic valves	34927	206	209	161	151	151	188
Filters for hydraulic and pneumatic fluid power systems	35692	352	385	409	395	381	391
Hydraulic and pneumatic cylinders etc.: Nonaerospace	35931	909	941	800	864	1,075	1,254
Aerospace	35932	646	636	510	479	464	388
Parts for hydraulic and pneumatic cylinders [2]	35933	281	264	269	171	197	202
Hydraulic fluid power pumps and motors	35941	1,180	1,240	997	974	1,014	(NA)
Parts for pumps and motors	35942	333	399	354	312	321	347

NA Not available.   X Not applicable.   [1] Used in fluid and power transfer systems (nonaerospace).   [2] Includes parts for actuators, accumulators, cushions, and nonvehicular shock absorbers.

Source: U.S. Bureau of the Census, *Current Industrial Reports*, MA35N, annual.

No. 1250. Selected Instruments and Related Products—Shipments: 1988 to 1994

[In millions of dollars]

PRODUCT	Product code	1988	1989	1990	1991	1992	1993	1994
Automatic regulating and control valves	34918	1,262	1,331	1,418	1,537	1,579	1,648	1,802
Solenoid-operated valves (except nuclear and fluid power transfer)	34919	338	374	346	360	405	406	419
Aeronautical, nautical, and navigational instruments	38121	2,365	2,521	2,518	2,672	2,517	2,121	1,998
Search & detection, navigation & guidance systems and equipment	38122	31,145	30,840	32,420	31,774	31,311	28,604	25,762
Laboratory apparatus and laboratory furniture [1]	38210	1,565	1,698	1,675	1,612	1,715	1,598	1,655
Controls for monitoring residential and commercial environments and appliance	38220	2,207	2,224	1,982	1,982	2,197	2,310	2,462
Process control instruments	38230	4,348	4,743	5,224	5,230	5,731	5,935	6,165
Integrating and totalizing meters for gas and liquids	38242	610	647	725	698	727	777	854
Counting devices	38243	193	206	210	226	273	285	340
Motor vehicle instruments [2]	38244	682	637	1,457	1,330	1,576	1,768	2,188
Integrating instruments, electrical	38251	388	401	396	390	439	461	486
Test equipment for testing electrical, radio and communication circuits, and motors	38252	6,248	6,134	6,156	6,525	6,493	6,572	7,228
Instruments to measure electricity	38253	663	620	586	584	558	526	551
Analytical, scientific instruments (except optical)	38260	3,442	4,042	4,412	4,519	4,886	4,766	4,923
Sighting, tracking, and fire-control equipment, optical type	38271	609	595	581	547	771	769	652
Optical instruments and lenses [3]	38274	1,270	1,274	1,252	1,292	1,322	1,456	1,559
Aircraft engine instruments (except flight)	38291	505	508	579	682	590	552	491
Physical properties and kinematic testing equip.	38292	894	946	1,012	1,024	1,149	1,175	1,237
Nuclear radiation detection and monitoring instruments	38294	654	606	567	570	533	519	522
Commercial, geophysical, meteorological, and general purpose instruments	38295	1,072	1,035	1,140	1,335	1,361	1,271	1,276
Surveying and drafting instruments	38296	270	270	274	235	281	255	318

[1] Beginning 1987, includes laboratory furniture. Prior to 1987, laboratory furniture was included in product class 38296. [2] Beginning 1990, includes some data previously classified in product class 37149, "Other motor vehicle parts and accessories, new, n.e.c." [3] Beginning 1992, product classes 38272, "Binoculars and astonomical instruments," and 38273, "Other optical instruments and lenses" were combined into product class 38274; prior years have been restated to reflect revision.

Source: U.S. Bureau of the Census, *Current Industrial Reports*, MA38B, annual.

No. 1251. Robots—Shipments: 1987 to 1989

[Based on a survey of all known manufacturers of robots, robot accessories, and components. Shipment value represents the net sales price, f.o.b. plant, to the customer or branch to which the products are shipped, net of discounts, allowances, freight charges and returns. A robot is a reprogrammable multifunctional manipulator designed to move materials, parts, tools, or specialized devices through variable programmed motions for the performance of a variety of tasks]

ROBOTS, ACCESSORIES, AND COMPONENTS	QUANTITY (number)			VALUE (mil. dol.)		
	1987	1988	1989	1987	1988	1989
Robots, robot accessories, and components	(X)	(X)	(X)	284	238	256
Robots, complete	6,037	4,603	2,217	220	164	151
Servo-controlled robots	2,677	2,072	1,840	203	138	136
Point-to-point type:						
Welding, etc	675	304	273	65	32	29
Foundry, forging, and/or heat treating [1]	28	31	34	3	3	9
Assembly for nonelectronic/elec. prods.	535	296	238	20	8	8
Material handling and/or parts transfer	726	247	162	48	27	26
Continuous-path type:						
Welding, etc.	110	79	31	9	4	2
Spraying, painting, gluing, and/or sealing	297	292	254	41	30	35
Fettling/grinding/polishing, and/or deburring [2]	306	823	848	17	33	26
Nonservo-controlled robots	215	336	377	8	17	15
Other robots	3,145	2,195	(3)	9	9	(3)
Robot accessories, subassemblies, etc	(X)	(X)	(X)	65	74	105
Miscellaneous receipts	(X)	(X)	(X)	8	6	3

X Not applicable. [1] Includes all point-to-point robots, except assembly, material handling, and/or parts transfer. [2] Includes other continuous-path type, not elsewhere classified. [3] Beginning 1989, data no longer available for other robots which included education hobby, experimental, and nonindustrial robots.

Source: U.S. Bureau of the Census, *Current Industrial Reports*, MA35X(89-1).

Figure 27.1
**Percent Change in Sales and Annual
Payroll: 1987 to 1992**

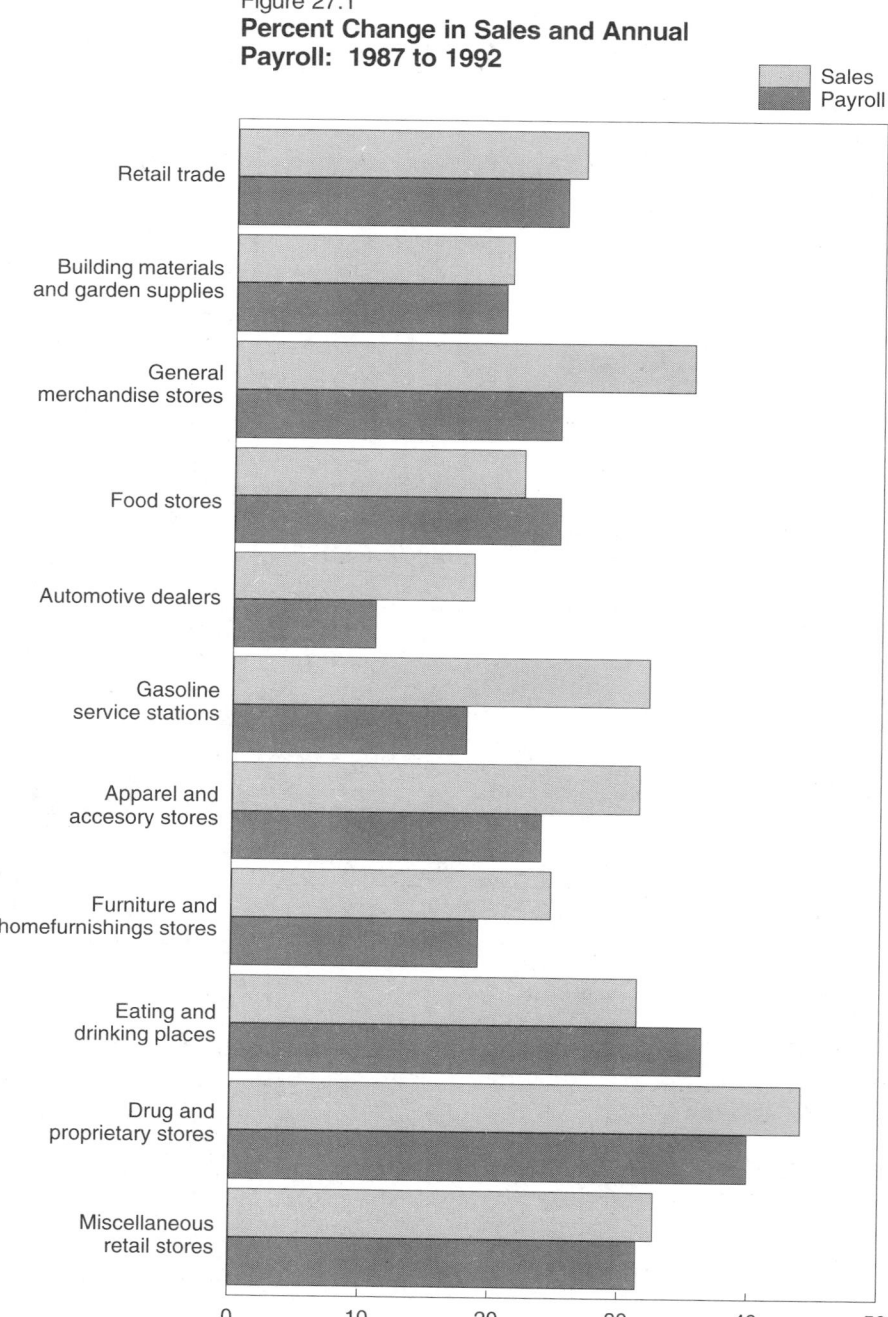

Source: Chart prepared by U.S. Bureau of the Census. For data, see table 1255.

Domestic Trade and Services

This section presents statistics relating to the distributive trades and service industries. Data shown for the trades, classified by kind of business, and for the various categories of services (e.g., personal, business, repair, hotel) cover sales or receipts, establishments, employees, payrolls, and other items. The principal sources of these data are census reports and survey reports of the Bureau of the Census. Data on gross product in trade and service industries usually appear in the *Survey of Current Business*, issued by the U.S. Bureau of Economic Analysis. Financial data for firms engaged in retail, wholesale, or service activities appear in the annual *Statistics of Income,* published by the Internal Revenue Service.

Censuses—Censuses of retail trade and wholesale trade have been taken at various intervals since 1929. Limited coverage of the service industries started in 1933. Beginning with the 1967 census, legislation provides for a census of each area to be conducted every 5 years (for years ending in "2" and "7"). The industries covered in the censuses and surveys of business are those classified in three divisions defined in the *Standard Industrial Classification Manual* (see text, section 13). *Retail trade* refers to places of business primarily engaged in selling merchandise for personal or household consumption; *wholesale trade,* to establishments primarily engaged in selling goods to dealers and distributors for resale or to purchasers who buy for business and farm uses; and *services,* to establishments primarily engaged in providing a wide range of services for individuals and for businesses.

Beginning with the 1954 Censuses of Retail Trade and Service Industries, data for nonemployer establishments are included and published separately. The census of wholesale trade excludes establishments with no paid employees. Beginning in 1977, sales taxes and finance charges are excluded from sales (or receipt) figures of the three censuses. In 1982 and prior censuses, the count of establishments represented the number

In Brief		
Retail sales, 1995:		
Total		$2.3 trillion
Automotive dealers		$.6 trillion
Food stores		$.4 trillion

Annual receipts of taxable service firms ($ billions):

	1990	1994
Business services	281	379
Health services	271	357

in business at the end of the year. Beginning 1987, the count of establishments represents those in business at any time during the year.

For the 1987 and 1992 Censuses of Service Industries, hospitals operated by governmental organizations are included. Government-operated facilities in other service kind-of-business classifications are excluded from the census. In 1987 and 1992, data were not collected for elementary and secondary schools, colleges and universities, labor unions and similar organizations, and political organizations.

The census of retail trade beginning in 1977, excludes nonemployer direct sellers. Beginning 1982, the census treated each leased department in a store as a separate establishment and classified it according to the kind of business it conducted. In prior years, data for leased departments were consolidated with the data for stores in which they were located.

Current surveys—Current sample surveys conducted by the Bureau of the Census cover various aspects of the retail and wholesale trade and selected service industries. Its *Monthly Retail Trade Report* contains monthly estimates of sales, inventories, inventory/sales ratios, and sales of organizations operating 11 or more retail stores, for the United States, by kind of business. In addition, monthly retail sales data for census regions and divisions, large States, metropolitan areas, and cities are included.

Annual figures on sales, year-end inventories, and sales/inventory ratios, by kind of business, appear in the *Combined Annual and Revised Monthly Retail Trade Report.*

Statistics from the Bureau's monthly wholesale trade survey include national estimates of merchant wholesalers' sales, inventories, and stock-sales ratios by major summary groups—durable and nondurable—and selected kinds of business. Merchant wholesalers are those wholesalers who take title to the goods they sell (e.g., jobbers, exporters, importers, major distributors). These data, based on reports submitted by a sample of firms, appear in the *Monthly Wholesale Trade Report.* Annual figures on sales, sales-inventory ratios, and year-end inventories appear in the *Combined Annual and Revised Monthly Wholesale Trade Report.* The *Service Annual Survey* provides annual estimates of receipts for selected service kinds of business for the United States as a whole.

For the current sample survey programs, retail trade coverage is the same as for the census; wholesale trade coverage is limited to merchant wholesalers; and selected services coverage is less inclusive than the census.

Estimates obtained from annual and monthly surveys are based on sample data and are not expected to agree exactly with results that would be obtained from a complete census of all establishments. Data include estimates for sampling units not reporting.

Statistical reliability—For a discussion of statistical collection and estimation, sampling procedures, and measures of statistical reliability applicable to Census Bureau data, see Appendix III.

Historical statistics—Tabular headnotes provide cross-references, where applicable, to *Historical Statistics of the United States, Colonial Times to 1970.* See Appendix IV.

Figure 27.2
U.S. Mail Order Sales, by Kind of Business: 1993

1993 Mail Order Sales: $186.7 Billion

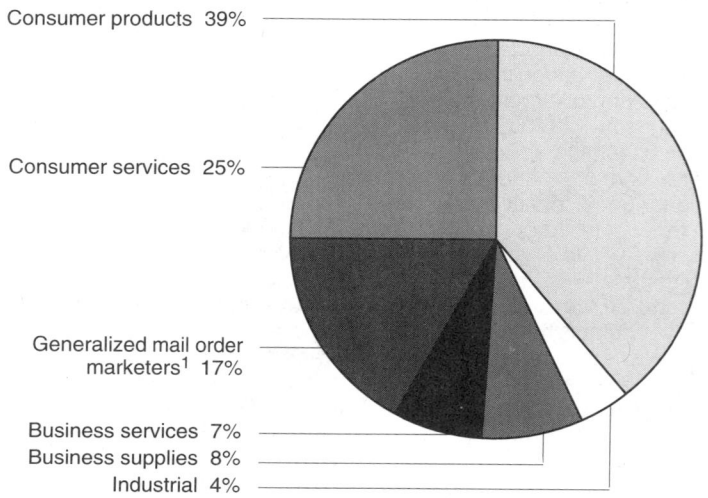

Consumer products 39%

Consumer services 25%

Generalized mail order marketers[1] 17%

Business services 7%
Business supplies 8%
Industrial 4%

[1]Mail order as part of the overall selling channel mix of multichannel industrial marketers not specializing in mail order selling.

Source: Chart prepared by U.S. Bureau of the Census. For data, see table 1266.

No. 1252. Gross Domestic Product in Domestic Trade and Service Industries in Current and Constant (1987) Dollars: 1990 to 1993

[In billions of dollars, except percent. For definition of gross domestic product, see text, section 14. Based on 1987 Standard Industrial Classification]

INDUSTRY	CURRENT DOLLARS				CONSTANT (1987) DOLLARS			
	1990	1991	1992	1993	1990	1991	1992	1993
Wholesale and retail trade	**878.8**	**905.3**	**951.9**	**1,005.5**	**797.6**	**797.7**	**827.6**	**868.4**
Percent of gross domestic product	15.8	15.8	15.8	15.9	16.3	16.4	16.6	16.9
Wholesale trade.	363.0	373.4	394.4	413.1	319.5	324.5	340.9	356.6
Retail trade	515.7	531.9	557.5	592.4	478.1	473.2	486.7	511.8
Services	**1,040.0**	**1,093.3**	**1,182.7**	**1,264.8**	**869.4**	**871.4**	**889.9**	**914.2**
Percent of gross domestic product	18.8	19.1	19.6	19.9	17.8	17.9	17.9	17.8
Hotels and other lodging places	49.9	52.4	53.9	55.4	45.0	45.5	46.0	45.8
Personal services	36.3	36.8	39.0	41.4	31.0	29.9	30.4	30.6
Business services	198.2	199.2	220.5	241.6	172.6	167.9	173.7	184.2
Auto repair, services, and garages	46.2	48.1	48.8	53.5	38.9	38.9	37.1	38.1
Miscellaneous repair services	17.1	16.2	16.9	18.0	15.9	14.6	13.9	13.6
Motion pictures	18.6	18.3	19.3	21.6	15.5	14.6	14.6	16.4
Amusement and recreation services	40.2	44.8	51.1	55.2	34.6	36.8	40.8	42.7
Health services	304.4	335.2	364.4	389.4	241.4	248.0	252.0	255.3
Legal services	79.6	82.3	88.7	92.1	66.1	64.7	66.0	65.3
Educational services	38.1	43.4	45.6	47.8	32.1	34.8	35.1	35.5
Social services, membership organizations	60.6	65.0	70.2	75.0	55.0	57.5	59.6	61.9
Other services	141.3	142.4	154.1	163.2	112.3	110.0	112.2	115.7
Private households	9.4	9.2	10.1	10.8	8.9	8.2	8.8	9.0

Source: U.S. Bureau of Economic Analysis, *Survey of Current Business,* April 1995 and previous issues.

No. 1253. Retail Trade—Summary: 1963 to 1992

[1972 through 1982 based on 1972 Standard Industrial Classification (SIC) code; beginning 1987 based on 1987 SIC code. Prior years based on earlier editions of SIC. Comparability of data over time is affected by changes in the SIC code. See also *Historical Statistics, Colonial Times to 1970,* series T 43-47 and T 79-91]

ITEM	Unit	1963	1967	1972	1977	1982	1987	1992
Firms, total [1]	1,000	1,532	1,577	1,665	1,567	1,573	1,992	2,212
Multiunit establishments [1][2]	1,000	240	234	301	343	415	498	528
Establishments, total [1]	1,000	1,708	1,763	1,780	1,855	1,923	2,420	2,672
With payroll	1,000	1,206	1,192	1,265	1,304	1,324	1,504	1,526
With sales of $1,000,000 or more	1,000	(NA)	(NA)	74	119	193	259	326
Consumer Price Index: [3]								
All items	1982-84=100 . .	30.6	33.4	41.8	60.6	96.5	113.6	140.3
All commodities	1982-84=100 . .	34.4	36.8	44.5	64.2	97.0	107.7	129.1
Sales	Bil. dol.	244	310	457	723	1,066	1,540	1,949
By establishments with payroll	Bil. dol.	233	295	440	700	1,039	1,493	1,895
By multiunit establishments [2]	Bil. dol.	90	124	202	341	567	844	1,137
Percent of total sales	Percent	36.6	39.8	44.0	47.1	53.2	56.5	60.0
Percent of multiunit sales by 100-or-more establishment multiunits [2][4]	Percent	43.1	46.7	55.8	53.8	54.5	54.6	57.0
In 1987 dollars [5]	Bil. dol.	712	843	1,042	1,170	1,175	1,540	1,669
Percent of sales by corporations	Percent	61.9	67.4	76.4	79.8	84.6	88.9	89.9
Per capita sales: [6]								
Current dollars	Dollars	1,296	1,571	2,186	3,291	4,601	6,357	7,643
Constant (1987) dollars [5]	Dollars	3,777	4,269	4,978	5,325	5,073	6,357	6,544
Sales as percent of personal income	Percent	51.3	48.0	46.6	45.2	39.6	40.5	37.9
Payroll, entire year [7]	Bil. dol.	27.6	36.2	55.4	85.9	123.6	177.5	222.9
Percent of sales [7]	Percent	11.9	12.3	12.6	12.3	11.9	11.9	11.8
Paid employees, March 12 pay period [8]	1,000	8,410	9,381	11,211	13,040	14,468	17,780	18,407

NA Not available. [1] Through 1982, represents the number of establishments and firms in business at the end of year. Beginning 1987, represents the number of establishments and firms in business at any time during year. [2] Establishments of firms that operate at two or more locations. [3] Source: U.S. Bureau of Labor Statistics, *Monthly Labor Review.* Beginning 1982, CPI-U annual averages, see text, section 14. [4] Prior to 1982, data provided for percent of multiunit sales by 101-or-more establishment units. [5] Based on implicit price deflators for retail sales supplied by U.S. Bureau of Economic Analysis. [6] Based on estimated resident population as of July 1. [7] Covers only establishments with payroll. [8] For 1963 week including November 15.

Source: Except as noted, U.S. Bureau of the Census, *U.S. Census of Business: 1963,* vol. I; *1967,* vol. I; and *Census of Retail Trade, 1972,* RC72-S-1; *1977,* RC77-52; *1982,* RC82-A-52 and RC82-I-1; *1987,* RC87-A-52, RC87-N-1, and RC87-S-1; and *1992,* RC92-A-52, RC92-N-1, and RC92-S-1.

No. 1254. Retail Trade—Establishments, Employees, and Payroll: 1990 and 1993

[Covers establishments with payroll. Employees are for the week including March 12. Most government employees are excluded. For statement on methodology, see Appendix III]

KIND OF BUSINESS	1987 SIC code [1]	ESTABLISHMENTS (1,000)		EMPLOYEES (1,000)		PAYROLL (bil. dol.)	
		1990	1993	1990	1993	1990	1993
Retail trade, total	(G)	1,529.7	1,551.5	19,815	19,777	241.7	265.3
Building materials and garden supplies [2]	52	71.9	70.0	703	696	11.9	13.0
Lumber and other building materials	521	27.5	25.9	403	411	7.5	8.4
Paint, glass, and wallpaper stores	523	10.2	10.2	54	49	0.9	0.9
Hardware stores	525	19.0	18.6	143	138	1.9	1.9
Retail nurseries and garden stores	526	10.1	11.1	76	73	1.0	1.1
Mobile home dealers	527	4.2	4.1	23	25	0.4	0.6
General merchandise stores [2]	53	36.6	35.6	2,135	2,142	22.9	25.7
Department stores	531	10.1	10.6	1,710	1,739	18.3	20.6
Variety stores	533	10.0	12.9	109	119	1.0	1.1
Misc. general merchandise stores	539	15.0	12.1	310	284	3.6	3.9
Food stores [2]	54	186.1	181.9	3,124	3,028	35.8	38.3
Grocery stores	541	132.5	133.0	2,757	2,729	32.4	35.2
Meat and fish markets	542	9.3	8.8	54	46	0.6	0.6
Fruit and vegetable markets	543	2.9	3.1	19	17	0.2	0.2
Candy, nut, confectionery stores	544	5.4	5.1	29	26	0.2	0.2
Retail bakeries	546	19.9	20.7	176	161	1.5	1.6
Automotive dealers and service stations [2]	55	207.3	198.9	2,104	1,993	40.0	43.5
New and used car dealers	551	26.1	24.6	917	899	23.9	27.6
Used car dealers	552	14.3	19.3	56	67	1.0	1.3
Auto and home supply stores	553	43.4	41.1	305	276	5.1	5.0
Gasoline service stations	554	104.8	101.4	701	672	7.5	7.9
Boat dealers	555	4.6	4.8	34	28	0.6	0.6
Recreational vehicle dealers	556	2.7	2.8	24	23	0.5	0.6
Motorcycle dealers	557	3.4	3.6	22	23	0.4	0.5
Apparel and accessory stores [2]	56	150.2	143.5	1,193	1,194	12.2	12.8
Men's and boys' clothing stores	561	14.7	14.7	108	109	1.5	1.4
Women's clothing stores	562	50.2	50.2	439	449	4.0	4.2
Women's accessory and specialty stores	563	7.7	8.6	46	43	0.5	0.5
Children's and infants' wear stores	564	5.6	5.4	36	37	0.3	0.3
Family clothing stores	565	17.8	19.4	283	325	3.0	3.6
Shoe stores	566	37.4	35.2	206	186	2.2	2.2
Misc. apparel and accessory stores	569	9.1	9.2	47	43	0.5	0.5
Furniture and homefurnishings stores [2]	57	108.1	112.3	749	754	12.3	13.2
Furniture and homefurnishings stores [2]	571	61.1	66.4	430	437	7.2	7.8
Furniture stores	5712	30.8	32.9	245	245	4.3	4.7
Floor covering stores	5713	13.2	13.9	77	72	1.5	1.5
Drapery and upholstery stores	5714	3.4	2.8	16	11	0.2	0.2
Misc. homefurnishings stores	5719	13.3	16.5	92	108	1.1	1.4
Household appliance stores	572	10.0	9.8	63	67	1.1	1.2
Radio, television, and computer stores [2]	573	34.2	36.0	245	250	3.9	4.2
Radio, TV, and electronic stores	5731	16.5	16.9	120	126	2.1	2.3
Computer and software stores	5734	5.1	6.5	33	38	0.8	0.8
Record and prerecorded tape stores	5735	7.1	8.2	60	63	0.6	0.6
Eating and drinking places [2]	58	402.6	441.5	6,461	6,728	49.6	57.4
Eating places	5812	286.8	360.2	5,700	6,346	43.8	53.9
Drinking places	5813	43.8	52.8	267	314	2.0	2.4
Miscellaneous retail [2]	59	349.0	352.1	2,487	2,423	33.2	35.4
Drug stores and proprietary stores	591	50.0	47.1	593	590	8.3	9.4
Liquor stores [3]	592	30.8	30.2	141	130	1.6	1.6
Used merchandise stores	593	15.0	20.8	79	105	0.9	1.3
Sporting goods and bicycle shops	5941	21.4	24.0	139	149	1.6	1.9
Book stores	5942	11.7	13.5	86	99	0.8	1.0
Stationery stores	5943	4.8	4.4	34	25	0.4	0.3
Jewelry stores	5944	26.6	27.6	161	148	2.3	2.3
Hobby, toy, and game shops	5945	9.4	10.7	83	93	0.8	1.0
Camera, photo supply stores	5946	3.6	3.0	22	18	0.4	0.3
Gift, novelty, and souvenir shops	5947	29.5	34.1	164	174	1.4	1.6
Sewing, needlework, and piece goods	5949	8.2	8.0	68	64	0.5	0.5
Catalog and mail-order houses	5961	7.2	7.4	141	150	2.6	3.0
Merchandising machine operators	5962	5.1	5.9	76	67	1.3	1.2
Direct selling establishments	5963	8.8	13.3	107	121	1.7	2.1
Fuel dealers	598	12.0	11.0	100	86	2.2	2.1
Florists	5992	25.8	27.2	131	122	1.2	1.2
Optical goods stores	5995	13.2	13.8	66	67	1.1	1.2
Administrative and auxiliary	(X)	18.0	15.7	860	819	23.7	26.0

X Not applicable. [1] Based on 1987 Standard Industrial Classification; see text, section 13. [2] Includes kinds of business not shown separately. [3] Includes government employees.

Source: U.S. Bureau of the Census, *County Business Patterns,* annual.

No. 1255. Retail Trade Establishments—Number, Sales, Payroll, and Employees, by Kind of Business: 1987 and 1992

[Each kind-of-business classification includes leased departments classified in that kind of business as if they were separate establishments. See *Historical Statistics, Colonial Times to 1970*, series T 79-196 for similar but not comparable data]

KIND OF BUSINESS	1987 SIC code [1]	ALL ESTABLISHMENTS				ESTABLISHMENTS WITH PAYROLL		
		Number [2] (1,000)		Sales (mil. dol.)		Annual payroll, 1992 (mil. dol.)	Paid employees [3] (1,000)	
		1987	1992	1987	1992		1987	1992
Retail trade, total [4]		**2,420**	**2,672**	**1,540,263**	**1,949,193**	**222,868**	**17,780**	**18,407**
Building materials & garden supplies	52	107	105	83,454	100,837	11,790	668	666
Building materials, supply stores	521, 3	51	51	61,302	75,358	8,423	432	435
Lumber and other building materials	521	36	36	55,868	68,930	7,519	380	386
Paint, glass, and wallpaper stores	523	15	15	5,434	6,428	903	52	49
Hardware stores	525	27	25	11,036	12,729	1,871	138	136
Retail nurseries and garden stores	526	21	22	5,809	6,773	1,018	71	71
Mobile home dealers	527	8	7	5,307	5,978	478	27	23
General merchandise stores	53	57	63	181,971	246,420	24,503	2,003	2,079
Department stores (incl. leased depts.) [5]	531	10	11	153,679	190,785	(NA)	(NA)	(NA)
Department stores (excl. leased depts.) [5]	531	10	11	144,017	186,423	20,136	1,651	1,719
Variety stores	533	21	23	7,134	9,516	1,088	121	116
Misc. general merchandise stores	539	26	29	30,819	50,481	3,279	231	243
Food stores [6]	54	290	278	309,460	377,098	37,228	2,855	2,969
Grocery stores	541	197	186	290,979	358,148	34,425	2,502	2,682
Meat and fish markets	542	[7]11	[7]9	[7]5,616	[7]5,041	556	59	45
Retail bakeries	546	31	31	5,194	5,732	1,407	185	157
Automotive dealers [6]	55 ex. 554	194	207	342,896	406,936	31,807	1,373	1,268
New and used car dealers	551	28	24	280,529	333,801	24,421	940	860
Used car dealers	552	75	92	18,295	25,511	1,132	55	63
Auto and home supply stores	553	67	63	26,622	29,817	4,683	286	269
Boat dealers	555	[7]5	[7]5	[7]6,824	[7]5,537	558	35	27
Recreational vehicle dealers	556	[7]3	[7]3	[7]5,538	[7]6,314	514	25	22
Motorcycle dealers	557	[7]4	[7]4	[7]3,475	[7]4,163	427	27	22
Gasoline service stations	554	137	120	104,769	136,950	7,569	702	675
Apparel and accessory stores [6]	56	197	221	79,322	104,211	12,039	1,121	1,145
Men's and boys' clothing stores	561	19	19	9,017	10,197	1,440	115	105
Women's clothing, specialty stores	562, 3	77	87	29,208	35,749	4,170	455	467
Women's clothing stores	562	64	65	26,366	31,828	3,690	419	423
Family clothing stores	565	27	33	21,472	33,222	3,469	268	310
Shoe stores	566	43	42	14,594	18,122	2,185	205	184
Furniture and homefurnishings stores	57	180	189	78,072	96,947	11,869	703	702
Furniture stores	5712	46	48	26,740	31,216	4,355	247	233
Homefurnishings stores	5713, 4, 9	63	64	17,737	21,132	2,835	176	181
Floor covering stores	5713	[7]14	[7]14	[7]9,226	[7]9,616	1,382	75	69
Household appliance stores	572	17	16	8,642	8,407	965	65	54
Radio, television, computer stores [6]	573	54	61	24,953	36,192	3,714	215	235
Radio, TV, and electronic stores	5731	31	28	15,679	20,275	2,112	123	121
Computer and software stores	5734	8	15	2,799	7,120	607	22	30
Record and prerecorded tape stores	5735	[7]6	[7]8	[7]3,930	[7]5,860	593	44	60
Eating and drinking places	58	490	558	153,462	200,163	52,570	6,100	6,548
Eating places [6]	5812	402	474	142,627	187,758	50,307	5,787	6,244
Restaurants and lunchrooms	5812 pt.	[7]155	[7]170	[7]66,364	[7]85,178	25,369	2,822	2,989
Refreshment places	5812 pt.	[7]138	[7]164	[7]56,870	[7]77,686	18,808	2,352	2,652
Cafeterias	5812 pt.	[7]7	[7]6	[7]3,778	[7]3,619	1,037	138	109
Drinking places	5813	88	84	10,834	12,406	2,263	313	304
Drug stores and proprietary stores	591	56	51	54,142	77,788	9,060	574	588
Miscellaneous retail stores [4] [6]	59 ex. 591	710	881	152,716	201,842	24,434	1,682	1,769
Liquor stores	592	45	40	19,826	21,698	1,523	157	133
Used merchandise stores	593	89	124	5,217	8,219	1,124	69	93
Misc. shopping goods stores [6]	594	263	311	53,777	71,650	8,563	706	750
Sporting goods, bicycle shops	5941	50	55	11,256	15,617	1,733	121	137
Book stores	5942	19	23	5,338	8,329	928	72	92
Jewelry stores	5944	50	55	12,925	15,259	2,224	163	148
Hobby, toy, and game shops	5945	28	38	7,451	11,298	992	76	95
Gift, novelty, souvenir shops	5947	79	104	8,446	12,036	1,467	151	164
Nonstore retailers [4]	596	66	116	34,878	52,790	6,280	318	339
Catalog and mail-order houses	5961	31	66	20,765	35,538	3,079	123	150
Merchandising machine operators	5962	24	36	6,258	7,082	1,232	74	70
Direct selling establishments [4]	5963	11	14	7,855	10,170	1,969	121	119
Fuel dealers	598	17	15	14,503	14,202	1,928	99	82
Florists	5992	50	55	5,441	6,433	1,207	125	122
Optical goods stores	5995	15	16	3,480	4,917	1,114	54	65

NA Not available. [1] Based on 1987 Standard Industrial Classification; see text, section 13. [2] Represents the number of establishments in business at any time during year. [3] For pay period including March 12. [4] Excludes nonemployer direct sellers, SIC 5963. [5] Includes sales from catalog order desks. [6] Includes other kinds of businesses, not shown separately. [7] Covers only establishments with payroll.

Source: U.S. Bureau of the Census, *1987* and *1992 Census of Retail Trade*, RC87-N-1, RC92-A-52, and RC92-N-1.

No. 1256. Retail Trade—Sales, by Broad Merchandise Lines: 1987 and 1992

[For establishments with payroll]

MERCHANDISE LINES	1987			1992		
		Sales of specified merchandise lines			Sales of specified merchandise lines	
	Estab-lish-ments (1,000)	Total (mil. dol.)	Percent distri-bution	Estab-lish-ments (1,000)	Total (mil. dol.)	Percent distri-bution	Percent of total sales of estab-lishments handling line
Retail trade, total [1]...............	[2]1,504	1,493,309	100.0	[2]1,526	1,894,880	100.0	(X)
Groceries and other food................	369	247,410	16.6	371	308,488	16.3	41.4
Meals and snacks	478	137,954	9.2	548	183,957	9.7	34.4
Alcoholic drinks	170	18,721	1.3	187	22,318	1.2	24.5
Packaged alcoholic beverages	179	29,651	2.0	179	35,589	1.9	9.3
Cigars, cigarettes, and tobacco..........	275	23,231	1.6	284	31,328	1.7	4.5
Drugs, health and beauty aids	219	69,040	4.6	224	107,336	5.7	14.9
Soaps, detergents, and household cleaners	116	9,902	0.7	140	14,979	0.8	3.1
Paper and related products	119	9,232	0.6	152	14,159	0.8	2.8
Men's wear...........................	(NA)	(NA)	(NA)	116	48,519	2.6	13.4
Women's, junior's and misses' wear...........	(NA)	(NA)	(NA)	162	91,972	4.9	24.2
Children's wear	(NA)	(NA)	(NA)	75	21,862	1.2	7.4
Footwear	(NA)	(NA)	(NA)	110	29,198	1.5	9.3
Sewing, knitting, and needlework goods	37	4,155	0.3	35	5,127	0.3	3.5
Curtains, draperies, and dry goods	68	13,037	0.9	66	15,763	0.8	5.1
Major household appliances................	66	17,571	1.2	56	17,866	0.9	7.2
Small electric appliances................	80	6,245	0.4	76	6,404	0.3	2.1
TV's, video equipment, videotapes	66	13,380	0.9	66	18,567	1.0	6.8
Audio equipment, musical instruments and supplies .	86	16,944	1.1	86	21,710	1.2	8.2
Furniture and sleep equipment	79	29,843	2.0	73	34,359	1.8	12.0
Floor coverings	59	11,385	0.8	47	11,902	0.6	5.6
Computer hardware, software, and supplies	30	5,828	0.4	25	11,437	0.6	8.9
Kitchenware and home furnishings	167	21,512	1.4	162	24,885	1.3	5.1
Jewelry.............................	118	20,691	1.4	131	25,872	1.4	6.6
Books	(NA)	(NA)	(NA)	69	10,475	0.6	5.3
Photographic equipment and supplies	64	5,381	0.4	55	5,524	0.3	2.1
Toys, hobby goods, and games	106	12,917	0.9	105	18,059	1.0	5.1
Optical goods	29	3,717	0.2	35	5,300	0.3	4.3
Sporting goods	73	21,190	1.4	81	25,361	1.3	9.0
Recreational vehicles, parts, and accessories	9	6,092	0.4	7	6,449	0.3	13.6
Hardware, tools, plumbing, and electrical supplies ..	107	20,784	1.4	106	28,581	1.5	7.8
Lawn and garden equipment	119	16,847	1.1	111	20,952	1.1	4.9
Lumber, millwork, building materials........	65	45,491	3.0	57	50,103	2.6	28.8
Paint and related preservatives and supplies......	57	7,103	0.5	53	10,399	0.6	5.0
Mobile homes	5	4,866	0.3	4	5,607	0.3	89.0
Cars, vans, trucks, and other powered vehicles	51	251,243	16.8	50	299,852	15.8	83.9
Automotive fuels	151	87,432	5.9	141	114,754	6.1	57.6
Automotive lubricants	154	3,021	0.2	146	3,503	0.2	0.8
Automobile tires, batteries, accessories	158	37,734	2.5	131	45,158	2.4	7.0
Household fuels.......................	26	12,450	0.8	24	12,121	0.6	27.4
Pets, pet food, and supplies................	82	5,009	0.3	87	8,197	0.4	2.5
All other merchandise	261	37,211	2.5	301	48,118	2.5	7.2
Unclassified merchandise	161	6,708	0.4	133	9,930	0.5	3.4
Nonmerchandise receipts.................	342	52,381	3.5	316	62,841	3.3	7.5

NA Not available.   X Not applicable.   [1] Includes other merchandise lines not shown separately.   [2] Detail will not add to total because establishments may carry more than one merchandise line.

Source: U.S. Bureau of the Census, *Census of Retail Trade 1987*, and *1992, Merchandise Line Sales*, RC87-S-3 and RC92-S-3RV.

No. 1257. Retail Trade Sales—Summary: 1980 to 1995

[Sales and inventories for leased departments and concessions are tabulated in the kind-of-business category of the leased department or concession. Based on Current Business Survey, see Appendix III. Minus sign (-) indicates decrease. See also *Historical Statistics, Colonial Times to 1970*, series T 245, 246, and 255]

YEAR	CURRENT DOLLARS							CONSTANT (1987) DOLLARS [4]		
	Total sales (bil. dol.)	Annual percent change [1]	Per capita [2] (dol.)	Index of sales (1982= 100)	Durable goods (bil. dol.)	Nondurable goods (bil. dol.)		Total sales (bil. dol.)	Annual percent change [1]	Per capita [2] (dol.)
						Total	Dept. stores [3]			
1980	957	6.7	4,213	89.5	299	658	86	1,193	-3.8	5,252
1985	1,375	6.8	5,779	128.6	498	877	126	1,420	4.4	5,969
1986	1,450	5.4	6,037	135.6	541	909	134	1,498	5.5	6,240
1987	1,541	6.3	6,361	144.2	576	965	144	1,539	2.7	6,351
1988	1,656	7.5	6,774	154.9	629	1,027	152	1,598	3.8	6,536
1989	1,759	6.2	7,127	164.5	657	1,102	161	1,639	2.6	6,640
1990	1,845	4.9	7,396	172.5	669	1,176	166	1,650	0.7	6,616
1991	1,856	0.6	7,361	173.6	650	1,206	173	1,613	-2.2	6,397
1992	1,952	5.2	7,652	182.5	704	1,248	186	1,664	3.2	6,524
1993	2,075	6.3	8,049	194.0	778	1,298	200	1,752	5.3	6,796
1994	2,231	7.5	8,570	208.6	877	1,355	219	1,864	6.4	7,160
1995	2,341	4.9	8,909	218.9	936	1,405	231	(NA)	(NA)	(NA)

NA Not available. [1] Change from immediate prior year. [2] Based on Bureau of the Census estimates of resident population as of July 1. [3] Excludes leased departments. [4] Source: U.S. Bureau of Economic Analysis, *Survey of Current Business*, monthly; and unpublished data.

No. 1258. Retail Trade—Sales, by Kind of Business: 1980 to 1995

[In billions of dollars. See headnote, table 1257. Based on Current Business Survey, see Appendix III. See also *Historical Statistics, Colonial Times to 1970*, series T 245-271]

KIND OF BUSINESS	1987 SIC code [1]	1980	1985	1990	1991	1992	1993	1994	1995
Retail trade, total		957.4	1,375.0	1,844.6	1,855.9	1,951.6	2,075.1	2,231.2	2,340.8
Durable goods stores, total [2]		299.2	498.1	668.8	650.0	703.6	777.5	876.5	936.2
Building materials and garden supplies [2] . .	52	50.8	71.2	94.6	91.5	100.8	109.6	122.7	124.6
Building materials, supply stores	521,3	35.0	50.8	70.3	68.2	75.4	82.4	93.0	95.6
Hardware stores	525	8.3	10.5	12.5	12.1	12.7	13.2	14.2	13.7
Automotive dealers	55 exc. 554	164.1	303.2	387.6	372.6	406.9	456.9	519.7	560.6
Motor vehicle, misc. automotive dealers .	551,2,5,6,7,9	146.2	278.0	356.8	343.0	377.1	426.1	486.7	525.9
Motor vehicle dealers	551,2	137.7	263.1	338.7	325.2	359.3	405.7	463.7	498.2
Motor vehicle dealers, franchised . .	551	130.5	251.6	316.0	301.3	333.8	377.2	430.3	459.0
Auto and home supply stores	553	18.0	25.2	30.8	29.6	29.8	30.8	33.0	34.7
Furniture and homefurnishings stores [2] . . .	57	44.2	68.3	91.5	91.7	97.0	105.7	119.4	129.9
Furniture, homefurnishings stores [2]	571	26.3	38.3	50.5	49.5	52.3	55.7	61.1	64.7
Furniture stores	5712	(NA)	23.9	30.8	30.2	31.2	33.4	36.1	38.1
Floor covering stores	5713	(NA)	7.9	10.7	10.1	10.4	10.6	11.4	11.0
Household appliance, radio, TV, and computer stores	5722,31,34	14.0	25.1	33.0	33.6	35.8	40.7	48.1	54.7
Household appliance stores	5722	(NA)	8.4	8.8	8.3	8.4	9.0	8.8	8.8
Radio, TV, and computer stores	5731,34	(NA)	16.7	24.3	25.3	27.4	31.7	39.4	45.9
Sporting goods and bicycle shops	5941	(NA)	8.7	15.0	15.1	15.6	17.1	19.3	21.0
Book stores	5942	(NA)	4.5	7.4	7.7	8.3	9.0	10.0	10.3
Jewelry stores	5944	(NA)	11.2	15.2	14.7	15.3	16.5	17.8	19.4
Nondurable goods stores, total [2] . . .		658.1	876.9	1,175.8	1,206.0	1,248.0	1,297.5	1,354.7	1,404.6
General merchandise stores	53	109.0	158.6	215.5	226.7	246.4	264.6	283.2	296.9
Department stores [3]	531	85.5	126.4	165.8	172.9	186.4	200.5	218.6	230.9
Variety stores	533	7.8	8.5	8.3	8.3	9.5	9.0	8.1	7.7
Misc. general merchandise stores	539	15.7	23.8	41.4	45.5	50.5	55.1	56.5	58.4
Food stores	54	220.2	285.1	368.3	374.5	377.1	385.4	399.3	410.5
Grocery stores	541	205.6	269.5	348.2	354.3	358.1	365.4	378.6	389.1
Gasoline service stations	554	94.1	113.3	138.5	137.3	137.0	138.3	142.4	148.2
Apparel and accessory stores [2]	56	49.3	70.2	95.8	97.4	104.2	107.2	109.9	110.0
Men's and boys' clothing stores	561	7.7	8.5	10.5	10.4	10.2	10.3	10.7	10.1
Women's clothing specialty stores	562,3	17.6	26.1	32.8	32.9	35.8	36.8	35.9	34.6
Women's clothing stores	562	15.9	23.6	29.8	29.9	31.8	33.0	32.0	30.7
Family clothing stores	565	10.8	17.8	28.4	30.5	33.2	34.9	37.2	38.9
Shoe stores	566	10.5	13.1	18.0	17.5	18.1	18.2	18.7	18.8
Eating and drinking places	58	90.1	127.9	190.1	194.4	200.2	213.7	223.4	233.6
Eating places [2]	5812	80.4	117.6	178.7	182.6	187.8	201.4	211.4	222.3
Restaurants, lunchrooms, cafeterias . .	5812 pt	(NA)	68.2	99.9	102.4	103.6	110.1	117.3	126.9
Refreshment places	5812 pt	(NA)	48.1	75.7	77.2	81.5	88.4	91.0	92.4
Drinking places	5813	(NA)	10.3	11.5	11.8	12.4	12.3	11.9	11.3
Drug stores and proprietary stores	591	31.0	47.0	70.6	75.5	77.8	79.6	81.4	84.2
Liquor stores	592	16.9	19.5	21.7	22.5	21.7	21.6	22.1	22.5
Nonstore retailers	596	22.8	28.3	45.6	49.1	55.2	58.4	64.0	69.8
Catalog and mail-order houses	5961	(NA)	15.8	26.6	30.0	35.5	39.2	43.5	46.0
Fuel dealers	598	(NA)	16.8	15.6	14.6	14.2	14.0	13.8	13.7

NA Not available. [1] Based on 1987 Standard Industrial Classification code; see text, section 13. [2] Includes kinds of business, not shown separately. [3] Excludes leased departments.

Source of tables 1257 and 1258: Except as noted, U.S. Bureau of the Census, *Current Business Reports, Combined Annual and Revised Monthly Retail Trade, January 1986 Through December 1995*, (BR/95-RV) and prior issues.

No. 1259. Retail Trade—Sales of Multiunit Organizations, by Kind of Business: 1980 to 1995

[Data based on sales of companies which had 11 or more retail establishments according to the most recent update of multiestablishment files selected with certainty (i.e., their sales size exceeded specified dollar volume cutoffs which varied by kind of business). For details, see source. See also *Historical Statistics, Colonial Times to 1970*, series T 197-219]

KIND OF BUSINESS	1987 SIC code [1]	SALES (bil. dol.) 1980	1990	1992	1993	1994	1995	PERCENT OF TOTAL RETAIL SALES 1980	1990	1995
Total		361.3	733.4	804.8	847.2	901.1	945.4	37.3	39.8	40.4
Durable goods stores		35.2	96.5	109.5	120.5	138.4	152.0	11.4	14.4	16.2
Auto and home supply stores	553	4.7	9.6	10.3	11.0	12.0	12.9	26.2	31.1	37.0
Nondurable goods stores [2]		326.0	636.9	695.3	726.7	762.7	793.4	49.1	54.2	56.5
General merchandise stores	53	101.6	205.1	233.5	252.1	271.7	285.9	90.6	95.2	96.3
Department stores	531	83.2	162.8	183.7	198.0	216.3	228.8	96.1	98.2	99.0
Variety stores	533	6.3	5.5	6.5	6.2	5.5	5.3	80.9	66.6	66.3
Misc. general merchandise stores	539	12.1	36.8	43.4	47.9	50.0	51.7	58.1	88.9	89.1
Food stores	54	119.8	217.2	226.4	230.5	238.6	248.9	54.4	59.0	60.6
Grocery stores . . . . ; .	541	118.1	214.1	223.3	227.5	235.5	245.6	57.4	61.5	63.1
Apparel and accessory stores [2]	56	21.1	58.0	65.5	68.8	72.2	73.1	42.7	60.5	66.5
Women's clothing specialty stores	562,3	8.3	19.5	22.0	22.9	22.3	21.6	47.1	59.5	61.7
Family clothing	565	(NA)	21.0	25.2	26.9	29.5	31.0	(NA)	74.0	79.5
Shoe stores	566	5.3	11.8	12.2	12.6	13.0	12.9	50.8	65.6	67.9
Eating places	5812	22.6	45.7	47.3	50.0	50.9	51.8	28.1	25.6	23.3
Drug stores and proprietary stores	591	16.8	42.6	48.1	49.4	51.6	54.5	54.3	60.4	64.9

NA Not available.   [1] Based on 1987 Standard Industrial Classification code; see text, section 13.   [2] Includes kinds of business not shown separately.

No. 1260. Retail Trade—Merchandise Inventories and Inventory/Sales Ratios, by Kind of Business: 1990 to 1995

[As of **Dec. 31**. Includes warehouses. Adjusted for seasonal variations. Sales data also adjusted for holiday, and trading-day differences. See headnote, table 1257]

KIND OF BUSINESS	1987 SIC code [1]	INVENTORIES AT COST [2] (bil. dol.) 1990	1993	1994	1995	INVENTORY/SALES RATIOS 1990	1993	1994	1995
Total		239.8	267.9	290.6	302.9	1.57	1.49	1.52	1.52
Excluding automotive group		*176.7*	*198.4*	*211.3*	*216.8*	*1.45*	*1.44*	*1.45*	*1.44*
Durable goods stores [3]		121.1	133.9	150.4	160.4	2.27	1.92	1.98	1.98
Building materials and garden supplies. . . .	52	17.0	18.5	20.4	21.0	2.28	1.86	1.97	1.98
Automotive dealers.	55 exc. 554	63.1	69.5	79.3	86.1	2.05	1.67	1.74	1.77
Furniture and homefurnishings stores.	57	17.4	20.2	22.6	24.4	2.36	2.17	2.11	2.14
Nondurable goods stores [3]		118.7	134.0	140.2	142.5	1.19	1.22	1.22	1.21
General merchandise stores.	53	42.4	52.4	55.1	57.6	2.34	2.32	2.29	2.33
Department stores	531	33.4	41.2	43.5	46.1	2.40	2.38	2.33	2.38
Food stores	54	25.0	26.1	26.8	27.7	0.81	0.80	0.79	0.80
Apparel and accessory stores.	56	19.7	22.8	24.1	23.2	2.50	2.54	2.62	2.53

[1] Based on 1987 Standard Industrial Classification code; see text, section 13.   [2] Excludes supplies and equipment used in store and warehouse operations that are not for resale.   [3] Includes kinds of business not shown separately.

Source of tables 1259 and 1260: U.S. Bureau of the Census, *Current Business Reports, Combined Annual and Revised Monthly Retail Trade, January 1986 Through December 1995* (BR/95-RV).

No. 1261. Motor Vehicle Factory Sales and Retail Sales: 1980 to 1995

[**In thousands**. See also *Historical Statistics, Colonial Times to 1970*, series Q 148 and 150]

YEAR	1980	1985	1987	1988	1989	1990	1991	1992	1993	1994	1995
Factory sales, total	**8,067**	**11,359**	**10,907**	**11,225**	**10,869**	**9,769**	**8,783**	**9,747**	**10,857**	**12,189**	**12,023**
Passenger cars	6,400	8,002	7,085	7,105	6,807	6,050	5,407	5,685	5,962	6,549	6,310
Trucks and buses	1,667	3,357	3,821	4,121	4,062	3,719	3,375	4,062	4,895	5,640	5,713
Retail sales, total	**11,466**	**15,724**	**15,189**	**15,679**	**14,713**	**14,146**	**12,539**	**13,116**	**14,199**	**15,411**	**15,116**
Passenger cars (new), total	8,979	11,042	10,277	10,530	9,772	9,300	8,175	8,213	8,518	8,991	8,635
Domestic	6,581	8,205	7,081	7,526	7,073	6,897	6,137	6,277	6,742	7,255	7,129
Imports	2,398	2,838	3,196	3,004	2,699	2,403	2,038	1,937	1,776	1,735	1,506
Trucks (new), total	2,487	4,682	4,912	5,149	4,941	4,846	4,365	4,903	5,681	6,421	6,481
Domestic	2,001	3,902	4,055	4,508	4,403	4,215	3,813	4,481	5,287	5,995	6,064
Imports	486	780	857	641	538	631	551	422	394	426	417

Source: American Automobile Manufacturers Association, Detroit, MI, *AAMA Motor Vehicle Facts and Figures*, annual (copyright).

No. 1262. Franchised New Car Dealerships—Summary: 1980 to 1995

ITEM	Unit	1980	1985	1988	1989	1990	1991	1992	1993	1994	1995
Dealerships [1]	Number .	27,900	24,725	25,025	25,000	24,825	24,200	23,500	22,950	22,850	22,800
Sales	Bil. dol . .	130.5	251.6	303.3	311.6	316.0	301.3	333.8	377.2	434.1	464.1
New cars	1,000. . .	8,979	10,983	10,544	9,770	9,296	8,176	8,211	8,519	8,991	8,635
Used vehicles	1,000. . .	9,717	13,300	14,570	14,610	14,180	14,270	15,140	16,300	17,760	18,480
Employment	1,000. . .	745.2	856.9	960.1	956.4	926.4	886.4	876.0	907.4	964.4	1,010.0
Annual payroll	Bil. dol . .	11.0	20.1	24.7	24.4	24.1	23.5	25.1	26.7	29.8	32.0
Advertising expenses	Bil. dol . .	1.2	2.8	4.1	3.9	3.7	3.5	3.8	4.1	4.3	4.7
Dealer pretax profits as a percentage of sales	Percent .	0.6	2.2	1.7	1.0	1.0	1.0	1.4	1.6	1.8	1.4
Inventory: [2] Domestic: [3]											
Total	1,000. . .	1,506	1,510	1,549	1,677	1,436	1,296	1,260	1,347	1,397	1,668
Days' supply	Days . . .	71	58	65	72	66	66	63	62	60	72
Imported: [3]											
Total	1,000. . .	458	271	647	648	597	584	504	450	381	354
Days' supply	Days . . .	55	30	65	70	74	86	81	78	69	72

[1] At beginning of year. [2] Annual average. [3] Classification based on where automobiles are produced (i.e., automobiles manufactured by foreign companies but produced in the United States are classified as domestic).
Source: National Automobile Dealers Association, McLean, VA, *NADA Data*, annual.

No. 1263. Retail Foodstores—Number and Sales, by Type: 1990 to 1994

TYPE OF FOODSTORE	NUMBER [1] (1,000)					SALES [2] (bil. dol.)					PERCENT DISTRIBUTION			
											Number		Sales	
	1990	1991	1992	1993	1994	1990	1991	1992	1993	1994	1990	1994	1990	1994
Total	253.3	252.1	250.8	249.6	248.4	368.3	374.5	377.1	385.4	399.3	100.0	100.0	100.0	100.0
Grocery stores	170.2	168.0	165.9	163.8	161.7	348.2	354.3	358.1	365.7	378.6	67.2	65.1	94.5	94.8
Supermarkets [3]	25.0	24.9	24.6	24.5	24.6	260.1	268.9	275.9	281.0	289.0	9.9	9.9	70.6	72.4
Conventional	13.7	12.8	12.5	12.2	12.0	90.7	81.8	84.7	78.6	81.5	5.4	4.8	24.6	20.4
Superstore [4]	5.8	5.9	6.0	6.3	6.5	87.6	91.1	93.3	100.6	107.6	2.3	2.6	23.8	26.9
Warehouse [5]	3.4	3.5	3.4	3.1	2.9	33.1	35.3	33.1	31.9	27.7	1.3	1.2	9.0	6.9
Combination food and drug [6]	1.6	2.1	2.1	2.2	2.4	34.8	46.0	42.3	45.8	51.7	0.6	1.0	9.4	12.9
Superwarehouse [7]	0.3	0.5	0.5	0.5	0.5	12.6	13.8	13.9	15.3	16.2	0.1	0.2	3.4	4.1
Hypermarket [8]	0.1	0.1	0.1	0.2	0.2	1.3	0.9	7.0	8.8	4.3	0.0	0.1	0.4	1.1
Convenience stores [9]	51.5	52.4	53.8	54.2	54.2	37.0	37.9	39.1	39.8	40.3	20.3	21.8	10.0	10.1
Superette [10]	93.7	90.7	87.5	85.9	82.9	51.1	47.5	43.1	44.9	49.2	37.0	33.4	13.9	12.3
Specialized food stores [11]	83.2	84.0	84.9	85.8	86.7	20.1	20.2	19.0	19.7	20.7	32.8	34.9	5.5	5.2

[1] Estimated. [2] Includes nonfood items. [3] A grocery store, primarily self-service in operation, providing a full range of departments, and having at least $2.5 million in annual sales in 1985 dollars. [4] Contains greater variety of products than conventional supermarkets, including specialty and service departments, and considerable nonfood (general merchandise) products. [5] Contains limited product variety and fewer services provided, incorporating case lot stocking and shelving practices. [6] Contains a pharmacy, a nonprescription drug department, and a greater variety of health and beauty aids than that carried by conventional supermarkets. [7] A larger warehouse store that offers expanded product variety and often service meat, deli, or seafood departments. [8] A very large store offering a greater variety of general merchandise—like clothes, hardware, and seasonal goods—and personal care products than other grocery stores. [9] A small grocery store selling a limited variety of food and nonfood products, typically open extended hours. [10] A grocery store, primarily self-service in operation, selling a wide variety of food and nonfood products with annual sales below $2.5 million (1985 dollars). [11] Primarily engaged in the retail sale of a single food category such as meat and seafood stores and retail bakeries.
Source: U.S. Dept. of Agriculture, Economic Research Service, *Food Marketing Review*, annual.

No. 1264. Percent of Supermarkets Offering Selected Services and Product Lines: 1990 and 1993

[In percent. Based on a sample survey of chain and independent supermarkets and subject to sampling variability; for details, see source]

SERVICE OR PRODUCT LINE OFFERED	TOTAL		CHAINS		INDEPENDENTS	
	1990	1993	1990	1993	1990	1993
Service delicatessen	73	79	76	81	69	77
Service bakery	60	62	66	66	53	55
Hot takeout food	55	55	59	57	49	52
Chilled prepared food	50	46	55	47	42	40
Service meat	42	47	45	47	37	46
Self-service delicatessen	38	50	38	52	39	46
Service fish	33	37	43	47	20	21
Separate cheese department	33	34	43	44	19	20
Salad bar	18	19	22	23	13	13
Plastic grocery bags	88	94	94	97	79	89
Reusable grocery bags	58	61	68	65	44	54
Carryout services	82	82	81	79	84	86
Scanning checkouts	71	85	79	91	61	75
Automated teller machines (ATM's)	20	38	28	46	10	25
Accept credit cards	19	51	23	55	13	44
Accept debit cards	(NA)	31	(NA)	36	(NA)	23
Pharmacy	15	20	22	28	6	8
Home delivery	(NA)	16	(NA)	10	(NA)	25

NA Not available.
Source: Maclean Hunter Media Inc., Stamford, CT, *Progressive Grocer, 61st Annual Report of the Grocery Industry* (copyright).

No. 1265. Commercial and Institutional Groups—Food and Drink Sales: 1980 to 1996

[Excludes military. Data refer to sales to consumers of food and alcoholic beverages. Sales are estimated. For details, see source]

TYPE OF GROUP	Number, 1993	SALES (mil. dol.)							
		1980	1990	1991	1992	1993	1994 [1]	1995 [1]	1996 [1]
Total	771,857	119,004	237,700	245,417	257,561	268,828	275,647	297,012	311,772
Commercial foodservice [2][3]	595,203	101,529	211,083	217,983	229,704	240,419	246,114	267,482	281,424
Eating places [2]	367,531	72,276	154,227	159,272	168,675	177,469	182,488	198,589	209,529
Full-service restaurants	173,416	39,307	76,072	78,355	83,561	87,011	85,290	95,702	100,008
Limited-service restaurants [4]	169,601	28,699	69,458	71,889	76,975	82,061	87,082	93,864	100,153
Bars and taverns [5]	36,435	7,785	9,212	9,442	10,203	10,162	9,106	10,864	11,201
Food contractors [2]	19,117	6,818	14,149	14,829	15,400	15,951	16,358	17,656	18,491
Manufacturing and industrial plants .	(NA)	2,121	3,856	3,918	4,040	4,153	4,275	4,513	4,716
Colleges and universities	(NA)	1,140	2,788	3,072	3,238	3,455	3,505	3,893	4,157
Lodging places [2]	27,251	6,768	14,272	14,601	15,053	15,565	16,219	17,095	17,847
Hotel restaurants	17,369	4,964	12,907	13,281	13,733	14,253	14,917	15,714	16,437
Motel restaurants	8,281	1,151	820	790	788	783	775	818	833
Retail hosts [2][6]	123,937	3,264	9,888	10,380	10,689	11,220	11,779	12,407	13,015
Department store restaurants	4,721	857	950	980	906	941	(NA)	(NA)	(NA)
Grocery store restaurants [6]	54,369	830	5,733	6,013	5,808	6,017	(NA)	(NA)	(NA)
Gasoline service stations	38,695	492	1,681	1,824	2,055	2,199	(NA)	(NA)	(NA)
Recreation and sports	14,627	1,452	2,916	2,949	3,085	3,185	3,291	3,453	3,617
Institutional foodservice [2]	176,654	17,475	26,617	27,435	27,857	28,409	29,533	29,529	30,348
Employee foodservice	7,370	1,635	1,985	1,913	1,835	1,728	1,753	1,731	1,730
Industrial, commercial organizations .	2,776	1,377	1,603	1,535	1,457	1,344	(NA)	(NA)	(NA)
Educational foodservice	97,106	4,610	7,671	8,223	8,548	8,697	9,077	9,139	9,391
Elementary and secondary schools . .	94,254	2,312	3,700	3,878	4,012	4,183	4,239	4,528	4,739
Hospitals	6,439	6,668	8,968	9,018	8,988	9,208	9,582	9,557	9,702
Miscellaneous [2]	31,568	1,521	2,845	2,993	3,053	3,231	3,376	3,645	3,883
Clubs	10,310	1,056	1,993	2,039	2,010	2,090	2,339	(NA)	(NA)

NA Not available.   [1] Projection.   [2] Includes other types of groups, not shown separately.   [3] Data for establishments with payroll.   [4] Fast-food restaurants.   [5] For establishments serving food.   [6] Beginning 1990, a portion of delicatessen sales in grocery stores are considered foodservice.

Source: National Restaurant Association, Washington, DC, *Foodservice Numbers: A Statistical Digest for the Foodservice Industry*, 1992; *Foodservice Industry in Review*, annual; and *National Restaurant Association Foodservice Industry Forecast*, December 1995, (copyright).

No. 1266. U.S. Mail Order Sales, by Kind of Business: 1985 to 1993

[**In millions of dollars**. Mail order sales represent orders placed by mail, phone, or electronically without the person ordering coming to the point of sale to place the order, or the seller coming to the office or home of the orderer to take the order or using an agent to collect the order. Excludes orders placed at catalog desks or elsewhere in stores even in response to a catalog but does include products or services delivered in the store as long as the order was placed by mail, phone, or electronically. Statistics are generated independently each year and are not adjusted for any discontinuities of available data]

KIND OF BUSINESS	1985	1986	1987	1988	1989	1990	1991	1992	1993
Total mail order sales	93,780	99,540	111,240	122,720	137,390	151,640	162,050	168,050	186,700
Consumer, total	58,690	61,900	69,670	77,160	87,000	98,190	107,970	110,740	118,970
Products	38,470	39,750	43,380	48,380	54,490	57,500	64,940	65,210	71,960
Specialty [1]	26,770	28,720	34,370	38,370	41,990	44,520	50,010	50,560	57,720
Apparel	2,360	2,540	2,980	3,760	3,640	4,250	4,410	4,820	5,230
Books	2,080	2,150	2,230	2,500	2,520	2,760	2,770	3,120	3,100
Collectibles	1,410	1,240	1,460	1,580	1,510	1,690	1,810	2,000	2,360
Computer software & hardware	(NA)	740	760	840	920	1,000	1,330	2,160	3,350
Health products	1,090	1,180	1,860	2,510	2,530	2,480	2,770	2,940	4,010
Magazines	4,310	4,660	4,900	5,320	6,360	6,020	6,580	6,340	6,280
Multi-products	2,610	3,020	4,700	5,400	7,020	7,410	8,440	6,860	10,190
Newspapers	2,600	2,600	3,020	3,020	3,020	3,020	3,020	3,020	3,020
Sporting goods	1,310	1,670	2,010	2,380	2,750	3,460	3,910	3,650	4,030
General merchandise	11,700	11,030	9,010	10,010	12,500	12,980	14,930	14,650	14,240
Services	20,220	22,150	26,290	28,780	32,510	40,690	43,030	45,530	47,010
Non-financial	10,710	12,030	13,690	16,180	19,390	21,660	25,740	26,620	26,980
Financial	9,510	10,120	12,600	12,600	13,120	19,030	17,290	18,910	20,030
Business products and services	35,090	37,640	41,570	45,560	50,390	53,450	54,080	57,310	67,730
Business supplies [1]	3,660	4,760	4,520	5,820	6,800	7,160	9,180	10,060	14,080
Data processing-oriented supplies	750	950	1,020	1,300	1,520	1,520	2,060	2,320	1,840
Computer hardware	(NA)	730	540	590	650	700	1,800	2,400	6,000
Business services [1]	4,890	5,210	7,420	7,200	7,690	8,900	8,940	10,410	13,300
Communications	1,850	2,150	3,700	3,420	3,450	4,240	4,140	5,580	8,050
Information	1,600	1,900	1,970	2,200	2,460	2,500	2,500	2,500	2,850
Industrial	1,340	1,440	1,580	2,160	3,640	5,390	5,560	6,440	8,150
Generalized mail order marketers [2].	25,200	26,460	28,050	30,290	32,260	32,000	30,400	30,400	32,200

NA Not available.   [1] Includes other kinds of business not shown separately.   [2] Mail order as part of the overall selling channel mix of multichannel industrial marketers not specializing in mail order selling.

Source: Fishman, Arnold L., data are extracted from *Annual Guides to Mail Order Sales, 1981-1994*, Marketing Logistics, Inc., Highland Park, IL, 60035 (copyright). For 1989-92, *Portable Mail Order Industry Statistics, 1993 Edition*, Richard D. Irwin, Inc., Burr Ridge, IL, 1994 (copyright).

No. 1267. Retail Trade—Summary of Establishments, by State: 1993

[Covers establishments with payroll. Employees are for the week including March 12. Most government employees are excluded. Kind-of-business classification based on 1987 Standard Industrial Classification code; see text, section 13. For statement on methodology, see Appendix III]

DIVISION AND STATE	Estab-lish-ments (1,000)	Paid employ-ees (1,000)	Annual payroll (mil. dol.)	DIVISION AND STATE	Estab-lish-ments (1,000)	Paid employ-ees (1,000)	Annual payroll (mil. dol.)	DIVISION AND STATE	Estab-lish-ments (1,000)	Paid employ-ees (1,000)	Annual payroll (mil. dol.)
U.S ..	1,551.5	19,777	265,268	IA	20.0	240	2,670	MS	15.5	164	1,868
				MO	32.8	418	5,318	W.S.C. . . .	159.5	2,071	26,349
N.E	89.8	1,079	15,766	ND	4.9	54	562	AR	15.3	172	2,105
ME	9.5	98	1,328	SD	5.7	61	663	LA	23.3	305	3,512
NH	8.7	101	1,404	NE	11.5	140	1,487	OK	19.9	227	2,669
VT	5.3	49	630	KS	16.8	205	2,445	TX	101.0	1,368	18,063
MA	38.7	503	7,384	S.A	286.5	3,711	48,647	Mountain .	91.5	1,198	15,482
RI	6.6	72	963	DE	4.8	62	823	MT	7.1	69	794
CT	21.2	256	4,056	MD	28.2	381	5,606	ID	7.3	84	1,040
M.A	232.6	2,608	38,276	DC	3.7	49	766	WY	3.9	39	461
NY	111.2	1,133	17,264	VA	38.1	511	6,748	CO	23.9	313	4,180
NJ	49.5	566	9,321	WV	10.7	115	1,337	NM	9.7	122	1,485
PA	71.9	909	11,692	NC	45.1	557	6,958	AZ	22.2	318	4,168
E.N.C. . . .	251.1	3,458	43,936	SC	23.4	281	3,355	UT	9.6	146	1,741
OH	64.1	900	11,369	GA	42.4	562	7,171	NV	7.8	107	1,613
IN	34.1	473	5,542	FL	90.1	1,194	15,882	Pacfic . . .	226.4	2,979	44,575
IL	65.8	907	12,428					WA	32.4	416	6,055
MI	54.9	752	9,650	E.S.C	94.1	1,145	13,890	OR	20.0	250	3,476
WI	32.2	427	4,945	KY	22.5	285	3,312	CA	162.2	2,162	32,604
W.N.C. . . .	120.0	1,528	18,348	TN	31.3	402	5,216	AK	3.8	40	733
MN	28.2	409	5,203	AL	24.7	295	3,495	HI	7.9	111	1,707

Source: U.S. Bureau of the Census, *County Business Patterns*, annual.

No. 1268. Retail Trade—Sales, by Metropolitan Area: 1992

[Covers only establishments with payroll. Areas as defined by U.S. Office of Management and Budget, June 30, 1993. CMSA=consolidated metropolitan statistical area. MSA=metropolitan statistical area. For definition, see Appendix II]

METROPOLITAN AREAS RANKED BY VOLUME OF SALES	Total sales (mil. dol.)	Sales per capita (dol.)	METROPOLITAN AREAS RANKED BY VOLUME OF SALES	Total sales (mil. dol.)	Sales per capita (dol.)
New York-Northern New Jersey-Long Island, NY-NJ-CT-PA CMSA	140,681	7,159	Atlanta, GA MSA	26,525	8,461
Los Angeles-Riverside-Orange County, CA CMSA	107,567	7,141	Seattle-Tacoma-Bremerton, WA CMSA. . . .	26,436	8,440
			Minneapolis-St. Paul, MN-WI MSA	22,603	8,637
Chicago-Gary-Kenosha, IL-IN-WI CMSA. . .	64,858	7,721	Cleveland-Akron, OH CMSA.	20,840	7,218
Washington-Baltimore, DC-MD-VA-WV CMSA	54,251	7,849	San Diego, CA MSA	19,216	7,386
San Francisco-Oakland-San Jose, CA			St. Louis, MO-IL MSA	19,145	7,609
CMSA	52,731	8,226	Phoenix-Mesa, AZ MSA.	18,724	8,027
Philadelphia-Wilmington-Atlantic City,			Tampa-St. Petersburg-Clearwater, FL MSA .	18,487	8,734
PA-NJ-DE-MD CMSA	46,633	7,867	Denver-Boulder-Greeley, CO CMSA	17,743	8,499
Boston-Worcester-Lawrence, MA-NH-			Pittsburgh, PA MSA	17,575	7,309
ME-CT CMSA	44,532	8,181	Portland-Salem, OR-WA CMSA	15,542	8,183
Detroit-Ann Arbor-Flint, MI CMSA	41,636	7,952	Cincinnati-Hamilton, OH-KY-IN CMSA	13,739	7,379
Dallas-Fort Worth, TX CMSA	35,359	8,406	Milwaukee-Racine, WI CMSA.	12,747	7,825
Miami-Fort Lauderdale, FL CMSA	32,182	9,702	Kansas City, MO-KS MSA	12,655	7,840
Houston-Galveston-Brazoria, TX CMSA . . .	30,576	7,740	Indianapolis, IN MSA	12,352	8,671
			Orlando, FL MSA	12,343	9,470
			Columbus, OH MSA	12,224	8,787

Source: U.S. Bureau of the Census, *1992 Census of Retail Trade*, RC92-A-52.

No. 1269. Retail Sales, by Type of Store and State: 1993 and 1994

[In millions of dollars, except as indicated. Kind-of-business classification based on 1987 Standard Industrial Classification code; see text, section 13. Data are estimates]

REGION, DIVISION, AND STATE	ALL STORES [1] 1993, total	ALL STORES [1] 1994 Total	1994 Sales per household [2] Amount (dol.)	1994 Sales per household [2] Per-cent change, 1993-94	FOOD STORES Total 1993	FOOD STORES Total 1994	FOOD STORES Supermarkets 1993	FOOD STORES Supermarkets 1994	GENERAL MERCHANDISE STORES Total 1993	GENERAL MERCHANDISE STORES Total 1994	GENERAL MERCHANDISE STORES Department stores 1993	GENERAL MERCHANDISE STORES Department stores 1994
U.S....	2,079,201	2,241,319	23,209	7.0	392,206	406,018	367,100	385,202	266,511	285,351	212,802	219,239
Northeast..	405,976	429,674	22,565	6.1	80,469	82,731	73,131	76,536	42,894	45,382	35,400	34,995
N.E.....	114,720	121,796	24,493	6.1	24,270	25,356	22,152	23,678	12,687	13,133	10,069	9,391
ME ...	11,992	11,681	24,748	-2.6	2,844	2,689	2,681	2,575	1,170	1,225	822	747
NH ...	12,566	12,761	30,112	0.2	2,775	2,818	2,633	2,702	1,554	1,754	1,111	1,163
VT....	5,090	5,125	23,380	-	1,206	1,241	1,130	1,199	392	357	275	261
MA ...	48,498	52,466	23,254	8.1	9,906	10,564	8,857	9,695	5,498	5,483	4,379	3,904
RI	7,593	7,538	20,177	1.0	1,595	1,610	1,387	1,467	947	813	749	591
CT	28,980	32,224	26,247	11.1	5,945	6,433	5,465	6,040	3,125	3,501	2,732	2,726
M.A	291,257	307,878	21,884	6.1	56,199	57,375	50,979	52,859	30,207	32,248	25,331	25,604
NY ...	127,516	134,422	20,252	6.2	24,728	25,391	22,002	22,943	12,843	13,467	10,476	10,432
NJ...	67,277	72,315	25,378	7.4	12,950	13,654	11,889	12,713	6,500	7,412	5,594	5,807
PA....	96,464	101,141	22,075	5.1	18,520	18,329	17,088	17,203	10,864	11,370	9,261	9,365
Midwest..	510,728	549,225	23,836	7.3	87,222	89,528	81,674	84,812	68,330	73,708	56,557	60,748
E.N.C. ...	355,228	381,998	23,766	7.4	58,816	59,780	54,729	56,318	47,589	51,577	40,092	42,670
OH ...	92,428	98,330	23,430	6.7	16,739	16,808	15,676	15,921	12,836	13,086	10,610	10,684
IN	45,787	49,462	22,916	7.4	7,348	7,624	6,991	7,260	5,874	6,720	4,682	5,435
IL	95,828	99,964	23,217	4.2	15,276	15,534	14,160	14,569	11,767	11,963	10,040	9,819
MI	79,236	87,884	25,052	10.7	12,392	12,396	11,307	11,538	11,741	13,997	10,449	12,193
WI	41,949	46,358	24,338	9.9	7,061	7,419	6,596	7,030	5,370	5,811	4,311	4,538
W.N.C.	155,500	167,227	23,999	7.1	28,406	29,748	26,945	28,494	20,741	22,131	16,465	18,079
MN ...	39,583	42,137	24,362	5.8	6,630	6,995	6,256	6,588	5,466	5,140	3,936	4,184
IA	24,293	25,538	23,434	5.0	4,919	5,036	4,709	4,796	3,111	3,300	2,467	2,712
MO ...	44,823	48,783	23,984	8.3	8,061	8,636	7,706	8,347	6,175	6,875	5,255	5,876
ND ...	5,921	6,182	25,336	4.3	1,011	1,001	968	967	787	924	623	753
SD ...	6,276	6,853	25,391	8.8	1,171	1,178	1,121	1,144	661	849	509	663
NE ...	13,266	15,227	24,481	14.3	2,477	2,760	2,199	2,627	1,695	1,899	1,382	1,485
KS ...	21,338	22,506	22,993	5.2	4,137	4,141	3,986	4,024	2,846	3,144	2,293	2,406
South...	714,817	780,018	22,927	7.7	136,330	141,266	129,601	135,791	96,761	104,057	76,481	80,429
S.A.....	388,230	418,512	23,609	6.5	71,631	75,662	67,867	72,458	48,478	51,349	38,622	39,081
DE ...	6,860	6,578	24,890	-5.2	1,148	1,109	1,061	1,036	1,060	1,000	932	773
MD ...	40,364	44,184	24,037	8.8	7,175	8,518	6,713	8,063	5,216	5,249	4,192	3,952
DC ...	3,740	3,762	16,188	2.2	589	641	527	565	376	224	330	193
VA...	58,251	62,293	25,471	5.7	11,267	12,105	10,832	11,642	7,148	7,616	5,581	5,543
WV ...	11,586	13,056	18,547	12.5	2,576	2,809	2,411	2,754	1,841	1,903	1,248	1,488
NC ...	55,206	60,196	22,117	7.3	10,331	11,199	9,946	10,773	6,206	7,182	4,657	5,703
SC ...	27,914	29,754	22,217	6.0	5,603	5,871	5,393	5,732	3,227	3,613	2,497	2,917
GA ...	54,313	60,877	23,389	10.1	9,770	10,710	9,384	10,277	7,286	8,125	5,923	6,466
FL....	129,996	137,812	24,702	4.5	23,172	22,700	21,600	21,617	16,118	16,437	13,262	12,047
E.S.C ...	114,507	128,070	21,452	10.5	23,304	23,392	22,123	22,657	17,245	18,917	13,491	15,000
KY ...	27,507	30,968	21,505	11.6	5,877	5,800	5,588	5,651	4,180	4,531	3,246	3,771
TN ...	41,884	45,897	23,071	7.8	7,863	7,705	7,446	7,520	6,336	6,565	5,057	5,156
AL....	29,779	33,586	21,161	11.9	6,015	6,200	5,705	5,976	4,237	4,881	3,447	3,838
MS ...	15,336	17,619	18,478	13.3	3,549	3,687	3,384	3,510	2,492	2,939	1,740	2,234
W.S.C ...	212,081	233,436	22,610	8.5	41,396	42,211	39,610	40,676	31,038	33,792	24,368	26,348
AR ...	16,998	19,091	20,371	11.4	3,182	3,275	3,061	3,199	2,742	3,127	2,288	2,511
LA ...	31,410	35,422	23,044	12.7	7,011	7,117	6,669	6,852	4,918	5,382	3,718	4,168
OK ...	20,818	25,620	20,511	22.5	4,082	4,457	3,885	4,279	2,972	3,780	2,420	3,018
TX....	142,855	153,303	23,225	5.2	27,121	27,363	25,995	26,346	20,406	21,503	15,942	16,652
West	447,679	482,403	23,568	6.5	88,185	92,493	82,694	88,062	58,527	62,204	44,364	43,066
Mountain..	124,102	137,910	24,120	7.7	26,776	27,964	25,719	27,150	15,397	17,169	11,785	12,998
MT ...	7,220	7,592	22,832	2.1	1,680	1,535	1,617	1,489	757	866	591	613
ID ...	8,147	10,489	25,306	24.9	1,871	2,211	1,808	2,161	865	1,178	661	869
WY ...	3,531	4,385	24,389	21.4	743	830	724	816	402	556	305	400
CO ...	33,261	35,670	24,543	4.7	6,742	6,894	6,482	6,682	4,350	4,394	3,473	3,358
NM ...	12,337	14,092	23,494	11.4	2,547	2,741	2,419	2,653	1,571	1,804	1,138	1,432
AZ ...	33,825	36,517	23,516	4.8	7,634	7,604	7,357	7,375	4,166	4,665	2,941	3,456
UT ...	13,390	14,268	23,818	3.6	2,982	3,110	2,849	3,030	1,754	1,834	1,369	1,379
NV ...	12,390	14,898	25,426	12.3	2,575	3,039	2,461	2,942	1,531	1,872	1,307	1,493
Pacific ..	323,577	344,492	23,353	6.0	61,409	64,529	56,976	60,913	43,130	45,036	32,579	30,068
WA ...	43,370	48,468	23,520	10.3	9,143	9,065	8,716	8,733	5,724	6,345	4,304	4,525
OR ...	27,767	29,609	24,522	5.1	5,056	4,978	4,735	4,795	4,422	4,738	3,449	3,289
CA ...	233,725	247,689	22,752	5.8	43,358	46,882	39,931	43,976	29,940	30,960	22,752	20,786
AK ...	5,471	6,041	28,714	10.1	1,378	1,333	1,331	1,295	842	850	617	606
HI	13,244	12,685	32,845	-4.7	2,474	2,272	2,263	2,114	2,203	2,142	1,764	862

See footnotes at end of table.

No. 1269. Retail Sales, by Type of Store and State: 1993 and 1994—Continued

[See headnote, page 770]

REGION, DIVISION, AND STATE	AUTOMOTIVE DEALERS		EATING AND DRINKING PLACES		GASOLINE SERVICE STATIONS		BUILDING MATERIALS DEALERS [3]		APPAREL AND ACCESSORIES STORES		FURNITURE AND APPLIANCE STORES [4]	
	1993	1994	1993	1994	1993	1994	1993	1994	1993	1994	1993	1994
U.S .	453,308	521,583	208,023	229,542	135,802	142,342	112,997	116,109	105,961	107,916	114,345	125,302
Northeast. .	77,677	88,514	39,817	42,320	22,606	23,130	21,090	20,597	26,956	27,184	20,553	21,725
N.E.	19,393	21,381	12,467	13,244	6,763	7,033	7,010	6,395	6,984	6,934	4,889	5,369
ME . . .	2,009	1,982	1,124	1,069	747	673	872	759	509	586	374	368
NH . . .	2,361	2,349	1,130	1,105	616	616	967	794	600	621	585	585
VT. . . .	873	950	534	514	334	329	446	390	241	219	188	170
MA . . .	8,060	9,160	5,923	6,476	2,672	2,933	2,516	2,425	3,261	3,333	2,097	2,419
RI	1,156	1,193	905	945	503	511	427	325	466	363	265	309
CT . . .	4,934	5,747	2,852	3,135	1,891	1,972	1,782	1,702	1,907	1,811	1,380	1,518
M.A	58,284	67,134	27,349	29,076	15,843	16,097	14,081	14,203	19,971	20,250	15,664	16,356
NY . . .	22,929	25,411	12,880	13,856	6,015	6,515	6,050	6,274	9,674	10,166	7,235	7,585
NJ. . . .	14,731	17,432	5,823	6,140	3,851	3,903	3,105	3,090	4,943	5,137	4,017	4,325
PA. . . .	20,624	24,290	8,646	9,080	5,977	5,679	4,926	4,839	5,355	4,947	4,412	4,445
Midwest . . .	120,040	136,512	53,217	57,306	35,103	36,298	27,176	30,066	22,230	21,920	26,656	29,979
E.N.C. . .	82,326	94,116	38,661	41,077	22,563	23,576	18,450	20,385	16,163	15,869	19,446	22,506
OH . . .	21,688	23,645	10,254	11,039	6,086	6,235	4,561	5,006	3,588	3,641	4,795	5,440
IN	11,100	11,962	4,782	5,294	3,101	3,453	2,650	2,790	1,796	1,670	2,226	2,609
IL	21,025	24,157	10,548	11,111	5,454	5,517	4,546	4,690	5,367	5,139	5,522	6,616
MI . . .	19,310	23,010	8,250	8,852	4,964	5,282	4,274	4,858	3,867	3,874	4,536	5,157
WI . . .	9,202	11,343	4,827	4,781	2,958	3,089	2,418	3,042	1,545	1,545	2,367	2,685
W.N.C. . .	37,714	42,396	14,556	16,229	12,540	12,722	8,726	9,680	6,067	6,050	7,211	7,473
MN . . .	8,868	10,121	3,638	3,941	2,914	3,073	2,462	2,801	1,621	1,631	2,024	1,975
IA	6,013	6,525	2,168	2,347	2,081	2,053	1,319	1,627	941	838	1,027	1,067
MO . . .	11,334	12,697	4,351	5,030	3,671	3,819	2,408	2,577	1,715	1,779	1,931	2,062
ND . . .	1,523	1,695	530	559	532	499	361	395	241	200	219	219
SD . . .	1,577	1,831	564	647	594	595	361	401	240	238	256	276
NE . . .	3,082	3,633	1,318	1,533	1,103	1,123	664	750	531	575	725	823
KS . . .	5,316	5,895	1,988	2,172	1,645	1,560	1,151	1,129	778	788	1,029	1,051
South.	163,441	192,032	68,262	78,886	49,247	52,644	39,360	40,172	35,043	36,079	39,758	41,954
S.A.	88,008	100,456	38,573	43,329	24,816	25,257	23,455	22,399	19,882	20,515	22,893	25,994
DE . . .	1,469	1,363	607	641	365	362	445	379	319	278	407	454
MD . . .	9,197	9,698	3,828	4,623	2,503	2,596	2,016	2,087	2,355	2,408	2,468	2,870
DC . . .	176	146	899	1,080	131	185	77	52	373	348	233	294
VA. . . .	13,252	13,584	5,355	6,017	3,944	3,926	3,291	3,160	2,938	3,209	3,540	4,277
WV . . .	2,413	2,997	942	1,116	845	976	786	865	449	432	491	571
NC . . .	12,432	14,030	5,391	6,448	3,602	3,792	4,239	4,169	2,813	2,647	3,453	3,636
SC . . .	5,915	6,795	2,696	3,158	2,048	2,118	2,041	1,982	1,584	1,486	1,574	1,647
GA . . .	12,021	14,460	5,376	6,433	3,794	4,065	3,489	3,350	2,682	2,873	3,042	3,600
FL. . . .	31,135	37,383	13,479	13,812	7,584	7,237	7,072	6,355	6,371	6,834	7,684	8,645
E.S.C . . .	24,015	30,267	10,207	12,341	8,925	10,649	6,751	7,560	4,643	4,944	6,197	5,624
KY . . .	5,081	6,538	2,611	3,152	2,318	2,885	1,667	1,948	949	1,039	1,437	1,304
TN . . .	9,193	11,587	3,856	4,689	3,358	3,681	2,439	2,623	1,712	1,821	2,484	2,135
AL. . . .	6,684	8,102	2,543	3,033	2,176	2,757	1,770	1,992	1,415	1,469	1,569	1,502
MS . . .	3,057	4,041	1,198	1,467	1,073	1,326	875	997	568	615	708	682
W.S.C . .	51,418	61,308	19,482	23,215	15,506	16,739	9,154	10,213	10,518	10,620	10,668	10,336
AR . . .	4,276	5,193	1,224	1,537	1,375	1,671	1,077	1,118	671	640	732	675
LA. . . .	6,472	8,462	2,799	3,501	2,257	2,655	1,403	1,715	1,441	1,503	1,517	1,444
OK . . .	5,300	7,237	1,944	2,577	1,535	1,950	908	1,078	1,051	1,020	1,005	1,022
TX. . . .	35,370	40,416	13,516	15,600	10,339	10,463	5,766	6,303	7,354	7,458	7,415	7,195
West	92,150	104,525	46,728	51,030	28,847	30,270	25,372	25,274	21,732	22,734	27,378	31,644
Mountain.	25,000	29,780	13,903	17,376	7,910	8,511	7,674	7,265	4,556	5,073	7,397	8,405
MT . . .	1,403	1,680	851	1,027	547	501	504	525	249	236	369	427
ID . . .	1,761	2,644	814	1,129	596	697	582	749	282	336	449	624
WY . . .	689	925	409	559	348	495	212	189	131	141	145	176
CO . . .	6,473	7,568	4,042	4,672	1,974	1,936	1,879	1,854	1,254	1,296	2,090	2,434
NM . . .	2,556	2,915	1,428	1,871	832	1,057	855	725	462	514	637	773
AZ. . . .	6,990	7,934	3,673	4,629	1,983	2,140	1,981	1,662	1,137	1,371	2,123	2,095
UT . . .	2,679	3,173	1,294	1,590	916	906	812	776	563	575	917	1,001
NV . . .	2,449	2,941	1,391	1,899	713	780	849	785	477	604	667	876
Pacific . .	67,150	74,745	32,825	33,654	20,937	21,758	17,697	18,009	17,176	17,661	19,982	23,239
WA . . .	8,465	10,822	4,203	4,461	3,000	3,091	2,689	3,089	2,103	2,169	2,414	3,008
OR . . .	6,216	7,232	2,537	2,589	1,881	1,842	1,497	1,822	1,241	1,233	1,448	1,699
CA . . .	49,765	53,675	23,487	24,113	14,982	15,841	12,786	12,346	12,572	12,957	15,411	17,638
AK . . .	756	1,082	632	674	281	355	299	366	288	278	188	252
HI	1,947	1,934	1,966	1,817	792	629	426	387	971	1,023	521	642

- Represents or rounds to zero.   [1] Includes other types of stores, not shown separately.   [2] Based on number of households as of July 1 as estimated by source. Minus sign (-) indicates decrease.   [3] Includes hardware dealers.   [4] Includes homefurnishings stores.

Source: Market Statistics, New York, NY, *The Survey of Buying Power Data Service,* annual (copyright).

No. 1270. Shopping Centers—Number, Gross Leasable Area, and Retail Sales, by Gross Leasable Area: 1990 to 1994

[As of **December 31**. A shopping center is a group of architecturally unified commercial establishments built on a site that is planned, developed, owned, and managed as an operating unit related in its location, size, and type of shops to the trade area that the unit serves. The unit provides on-site parking in definite relationship to the types and total size of the stores. The data base attempts to include all centers with three or more stores. Estimates are based on a sample of data available on shopping center properties; for details, contact source]

YEAR	Total	GROSS LEASABLE AREA (sq. ft.)					
		Less than 100,001	100,001- 200,000	200,001- 400,000	400,001- 800,000	800,001- 1,000,000	More than 1 million
NUMBER							
1990	36,515	23,231	8,756	2,781	1,102	288	357
1992	38,966	24,578	9,467	3,086	1,170	294	371
1993	39,633	24,993	9,611	3,166	1,194	295	374
1994	40,368	25,450	9,784	3,251	1,210	297	376
Percent distribution	100.0	63.0	24.2	8.1	3.0	0.7	0.9
Percent change, 1993-94	1.9	1.8	1.8	2.7	1.3	0.7	0.5
GROSS LEASABLE AREA							
1990 (mil. sq. ft.)	4,390	1,125	1,197	734	618	259	457
1992 (mil. sq. ft.)	4,679	1,190	1,289	807	653	264	475
1993 (mil. sq. ft.)	4,771	1,214	1,312	834	666	265	479
1994 (mil. sq. ft.)	4,861	1,239	1,339	859	675	267	482
Percent distribution	100.0	25.5	27.5	17.7	13.9	5.5	9.9
Percent change, 1993-94	1.9	2.0	2.0	3.0	1.4	0.8	0.6
RETAIL SALES							
1990 (bil. dol.)	706.4	205.1	179.5	108.0	91.7	45.1	77.0
1992 (bil. dol.)	768.2	223.3	195.3	117.2	99.6	49.0	83.8
1993 (bil. dol.)	806.6	234.4	205.0	123.1	104.6	51.5	88.1
1994 (bil. dol.)	851.3	247.3	216.3	129.9	110.3	54.3	93.1
Percent distribution	100.0	29.1	25.4	15.3	13.0	6.4	10.9
Percent change, 1993-94	5.5	5.5	5.5	5.6	5.5	5.5	5.6

No. 1271. Shopping Centers—Number, Gross Leasable Area, and Retail Sales, by State: 1994

[See headnote, table 1270]

DIVISION AND STATE	Num- ber	Gross leas- able area (mil. sq. ft.)	Retail sales (bil. dol.)	PERCENT CHANGE, 1993-94			DIVISION AND STATE	Num- ber	Gross leas- able area (mil. sq. ft.)	Retail sales (bil. dol.)	PERCENT CHANGE, 1993-94		
				Num- ber	Gross leas- able area	Retail sales per sq. ft.					Num- ber	Gross leas- able area	Retail sales per sq. ft.
U.S . .	40,368	4,861	851.3	1.9	1.9	3.6	VA	1,162	151	25.8	2.1	2.7	3.1
							WV	155	21	3.2	-	-	4.2
N.E	2,347	253	44.5	2.2	2.4	4.0	NC	1,412	147	24.1	1.9	1.1	4.2
ME	196	17	3.2	3.7	5.9	1.1	SC	760	73	13.1	1.5	0.8	4.2
NH	206	22	3.3	2.0	2.4	5.6	GA	1,418	150	26.3	1.5	2.4	2.7
VT	106	7	1.3	2.9	2.0	4.6	FL	3,086	390	75.1	1.4	1.3	4.9
MA	925	104	18.9	2.0	2.7	3.3	**E.S.C . . . .**	2,749	297	51.0	1.3	1.3	3.6
RI	187	17	3.1	1.6	2.0	3.5	KY	593	64	11.7	1.4	0.9	4.0
CT	727	86	14.7	2.3	1.4	5.2	TN	1,137	125	19.1	1.4	1.3	4.0
M.A	4,170	580	92.8	2.5	2.1	3.5	AL	601	70	13.2	1.3	1.4	3.2
NY	1,598	219	37.0	2.2	2.3	3.0	MS	418	39	7.2	1.0	1.8	2.1
NJ	1,051	144	22.7	3.9	2.9	3.3	**W.S.C. . . .**	4,395	501	106.1	1.3	1.4	3.6
PA	1,521	216	33.1	1.9	1.4	4.1	AR	339	32	6.4	1.8	1.7	2.7
							LA	676	79	15.6	1.5	2.3	2.8
E.N.C	5,923	766	119.8	1.6	1.6	3.7	OK	556	58	11.4	1.3	1.9	2.2
OH	1,559	221	34.8	1.3	1.3	3.8	TX	2,824	331	72.7	1.2	1.1	4.1
IN	848	112	18.0	1.6	1.3	3.7							
IL	1,961	235	34.1	2.3	2.2	3.6	**Mountain .**	2,681	320	60.5	1.9	1.5	4.1
MI	967	127	21.0	0.9	1.5	3.8	MT	91	9	1.7	-	-	5.5
WI	588	72	12.0	1.0	1.4	4.2	ID	140	16	2.8	2.2	0.6	4.0
W.N.C. . . .	2,385	301	54.0	1.8	1.3	3.9	WY	53	6	1.2	-	-	4.8
MN	436	62	11.5	1.9	0.3	5.2	CO	674	87	18.5	0.9	0.8	5.3
IA	277	37	6.3	1.8	1.8	3.3	NM	288	27	5.4	2.1	1.2	3.7
MO	834	103	18.9	1.6	1.6	3.6	AZ	933	110	20.1	1.6	1.7	4.0
ND	84	9	1.8	5.0	3.1	2.3	UT	210	29	5.5	1.4	0.9	3.7
SD	51	7	1.1	-	-	5.1	NV	292	34	5.4	5.8	4.5	1.5
NE	245	32	4.8	2.1	1.2	3.9							
KS	458	51	9.7	1.6	1.6	3.5	**Pacific . . .**	6,691	769	129.5	2.5	3.3	2.2
							WA	672	87	14.5	3.2	3.2	2.5
S.A	9,027	1,074	193.1	1.6	1.5	4.2	OR	441	50	7.6	1.6	1.8	4.1
DE	126	19	3.4	1.6	1.3	5.3	CA	5,350	607	102.8	2.5	3.4	2.0
MD	837	114	20.6	1.3	0.8	4.7	AK	63	8	1.6	5.0	0.6	6.3
DC	71	9	1.4	7.6	3.8	1.6	HI	165	17	3.1	3.1	5.8	2.3

- Represents zero.

Source of tables 1270 and 1271: National Research Bureau, Chicago, IL. Data for 1990 published by Monitor Publishing, Clearwater, FL, in *Monitor Magazine*, November/December 1991, (copyright). Data for 1992 published by Communication Channels, Inc., Atlanta, GA, in *Shopping Center World*, March 1993, (copyright). Data for 1993 and 1994 published by International Council of Shopping Centers in *Shopping Centers Today*, April 1994 and 1995, (copyright—Blackburn Marketing Services (U.S.), Inc.).

No. 1272. Merchant Wholesalers—Summary: 1990 to 1995

[Inventories and stock/sales ratios, as of December, seasonally adjusted. Data reflect latest revision. Based on Current Business Survey; see Appendix III. See *Historical Statistics, Colonial Times to 1970*, series T 280-371, for related sales data]

KIND OF BUSINESS	1987 SIC code [1]	1990	1991	1992	1993	1994	1995
SALES (bil. dol.)							
Merchant wholesalers		1,793.8	1,779.6	1,843.7	1,940.6	2,077.4	2,253.2
Durable goods	50	881.2	859.9	906.0	987.1	1,082.3	1,172.9
Motor vehicles, parts, and supplies	501	173.9	166.4	170.3	179.5	197.2	199.0
Furniture and homefurnishings	502	33.9	32.3	33.1	34.9	36.7	39.3
Lumber and construction materials	503	63.6	58.2	63.7	71.7	78.2	75.4
Professional and commercial equipment.	504	114.3	124.0	139.2	159.1	165.8	191.3
Metals and minerals, except petroleum.	505	77.8	76.0	76.6	80.3	92.6	100.1
Electrical goods	506	116.5	113.3	115.0	131.7	150.2	173.1
Hardware, plumbing and heating equipment . . .	507	52.7	49.9	52.9	55.4	63.7	69.2
Machinery, equipment and supplies	508	157.0	146.5	148.8	160.7	170.0	180.5
Miscellaneous durable goods	509	91.4	93.2	106.3	113.7	127.9	144.9
Nondurable goods.	51	912.6	919.7	937.7	953.5	995.1	1,080.3
Paper and paper products	511	51.6	52.1	54.6	59.2	67.8	82.0
Drugs, proprietaries, and sundries	512	51.5	59.6	66.8	72.2	83.5	93.6
Apparel, piece goods, and notions	513	64.9	64.6	67.7	70.2	72.6	72.0
Groceries and related products	514	272.5	277.2	278.3	285.7	288.8	301.3
Farm-product raw materials	515	107.6	104.7	105.9	96.0	95.7	111.7
Chemicals and allied products	516	35.7	37.1	39.0	39.2	41.9	46.6
Petroleum and petroleum products	517	148.5	140.0	142.1	139.5	143.4	154.6
Beer, wine, and distilled beverages	518	49.3	51.6	50.2	51.1	53.0	53.7
Miscellaneous nondurable goods	519	131.0	133.0	133.1	140.4	148.5	164.8
INVENTORIES (bil. dol.)							
Merchant wholesalers		195.6	200.1	207.7	215.9	234.9	254.6
Durable goods	50	126.2	127.1	131.1	135.6	149.0	162.0
Motor vehicles, parts, and supplies	501	23.5	24.1	24.1	24.4	25.5	27.1
Furniture and homefurnishings	502	4.6	4.6	4.8	4.8	4.9	5.0
Lumber and construction materials	503	6.0	5.8	6.3	6.7	7.4	7.6
Professional and commercial equipment.	504	15.8	16.8	17.0	17.9	20.5	23.3
Metals and minerals, except petroleum.	505	10.7	10.0	10.0	11.1	12.8	12.9
Electrical goods	506	15.9	16.1	17.2	17.5	20.2	23.4
Hardware, plumbing and heating equipment . . .	507	8.5	8.4	8.8	9.3	10.8	11.1
Machinery, equipment and supplies	508	31.5	29.7	30.0	29.2	31.6	35.1
Miscellaneous durable goods	509	9.8	11.4	12.8	14.6	15.2	16.5
Nondurable goods.	51	69.4	73.0	76.6	80.2	85.9	92.7
Paper and paper products	511	4.9	5.2	5.6	6.3	7.0	8.6
Drugs, proprietaries, and sundries	512	6.5	7.7	9.0	10.4	11.6	12.8
Apparel, piece goods, and notions	513	9.8	9.5	10.6	11.4	12.2	12.0
Groceries and related products	514	14.7	15.6	16.0	15.7	16.1	16.2
Farm-product raw materials	515	8.8	9.1	9.0	10.0	10.4	12.0
Chemicals and allied products	516	3.1	3.1	3.2	3.7	4.1	4.7
Petroleum and petroleum products	517	4.4	4.5	4.4	4.0	4.9	4.9
Beer, wine, and distilled beverages	518	4.4	4.7	4.3	4.5	4.6	4.6
Miscellaneous nondurable goods	519	12.7	13.6	14.4	14.2	14.9	16.9
STOCK/SALES RATIO							
Merchant wholesalers		1.31	1.34	1.33	1.33	1.29	1.31
Durable goods	50	1.75	1.77	1.67	1.61	1.56	1.59
Motor vehicles, parts, and supplies	501	1.66	1.75	1.64	1.63	1.51	1.55
Furniture and homefurnishings	502	1.71	1.78	1.62	1.69	1.48	1.50
Lumber and construction materials	503	1.33	1.22	1.12	1.01	1.06	1.20
Professional and commercial equipment.	504	1.58	1.54	1.39	1.35	1.38	1.35
Metals and minerals, except petroleum.	505	1.60	1.58	1.55	1.62	1.53	1.56
Electrical goods	506	1.71	1.72	1.72	1.50	1.50	1.54
Hardware, plumbing and heating equipment . . .	507	1.90	2.01	2.01	1.94	1.90	1.87
Machinery, equipment and supplies	508	2.49	2.47	2.34	2.16	2.11	2.19
Miscellaneous durable goods	509	1.27	1.45	1.37	1.52	1.36	1.35
Nondurable goods.	51	0.90	0.94	0.98	1.03	0.99	1.00
Paper and paper products	511	1.16	1.17	1.20	1.21	1.11	1.24
Drugs, proprietaries, and sundries	512	1.49	1.43	1.51	1.65	1.61	1.57
Apparel, piece goods, and notions	513	1.77	1.83	1.80	2.12	2.08	2.00
Groceries and related products	514	0.66	0.67	0.68	0.67	0.64	0.62
Farm-product raw materials	515	1.04	1.08	1.01	1.20	1.20	1.25
Chemicals and allied products	516	0.97	0.98	0.97	1.14	1.10	1.16
Petroleum and petroleum products	517	0.33	0.38	0.39	0.39	0.40	0.37
Beer, wine, and distilled beverages	518	0.95	1.04	1.06	1.06	1.03	1.00
Miscellaneous nondurable goods	519	1.17	1.21	1.41	1.22	1.15	1.19

[1] Based on 1987 Standard Industrial Classification code; see text, section 13.

Source: U.S. Bureau of the Census, *Current Business Reports, Combined Annual and Revised Monthly Wholesale Trade, January 1986 Through January 1996*, (BW/95-RV).

No. 1273. Wholesale Trade—Summary: 1963 to 1992

[Data prior to 1972 based on earlier editions of Standard Industrial Classification (SIC) code. Comparability of data over time is affected by changes in the SIC code; for details, see source. See also *Historical Statistics, Colonial Times to 1970*, series T 43-47, and T 274-279]

ITEM	Unit	1963	1967	1972 [1]	1977 [1]	1982 [1]	1987 [1]	1987 [2]	1992 [2]
Firms, total [3]	1,000	232	233	276	289	335	(NA)	364	387
Establishments, total [3]	1,000	308	311	370	383	435	467	470	495
With sales of $1,000,000 or more	1,000	62	75	103	152	(NA)	(NA)	222	285
Sales, all establishments	Bil. dol	358	459	695	1,258	1,998	2,524	[4]2,508	[4]3,239
Merchant wholesalers	Bil. dol	157	206	354	678	1,159	1,477	[4]1,462	[4]1,847
Inventories, end of year	Bil. dol	20.1	28.1	45.7	82.3	130.7	(NA)	165.1	213.4
Payroll, entire year	Bil. dol	18.1	23.9	36.9	58.3	95.2	133.2	133.4	173.3
Paid employees, Mar. 12 workweek [5]	1,000	3,089	3,519	4,026	4,397	4,985	5,581	5,596	5,791

NA Not available.   [1] Based on 1972 SIC code.   [2] Based on 1987 SIC code.   [3] Through 1977 number of firms and establishments in business at end of year; beginning 1982 number of firms and establishments in business at any time during year.   [4] Revised since publication of report.   [5] 1963 data for workweek including Nov. 15.

No. 1274. Wholesale Trade, by Type of Operation and Kind of Business: 1987 and 1992

[Based on 1987 Standard Industrial Classification (SIC) code; see text, section 13. See *Historical Statistics, Colonial Times to 1970*, series T 274-287 and T 352-369 for similar but not comparable data]

TYPE OF OPERATION AND KIND OF BUSINESS	ESTABLISH-MENTS [1] (1,000)		SALES (mil. dol.)		ANNUAL PAYROLL (mil. dol.)		PAID EMPLOYEES [2] (1,000)	
	1987	1992	1987	1992	1987	1992	1987	1992
Wholesale trade	469.5	495.5	2,508,258	3,238,520	133,357	173,272	5,596	5,791
Merchant wholesalers	391.0	414.8	1,461,700	1,847,274	100,413	127,987	4,476	4,588
Other operating types	78.6	80.6	1,046,557	1,391,247	32,944	45,285	1,120	1,203
Durable goods	297.3	313.5	1,262,302	1,593,874	82,767	105,155	3,332	3,349
Motor vehicles, parts, and supplies	45.8	47.3	326,625	394,104	9,872	12,065	483	489
Furniture and home furnishings	14.5	16.5	48,123	58,927	3,652	4,612	153	161
Lumber and construction materials	19.1	19.5	79,946	89,764	5,476	6,060	231	211
Professional & commercial equipment	44.2	46.8	175,149	262,974	19,728	26,380	698	685
Metals and minerals, except petroleum	11.1	11.2	114,528	118,322	4,038	4,684	143	138
Electrical goods	35.3	39.3	179,727	227,784	12,104	15,070	441	436
Hardware, plumbing, heating equipment	23.1	24.7	57,126	76,088	5,610	7,106	235	241
Machinery, equipment, supplies	71.7	73.9	178,892	230,004	16,731	21,267	682	690
Miscellaneous durable goods	32.3	34.3	102,185	135,906	5,556	7,912	266	299
Nondurable goods	172.2	182.0	1,245,956	1,644,647	50,589	68,117	2,264	2,442
Paper and paper products	16.8	19.7	83,173	106,580	5,202	6,939	228	269
Drugs, proprietaries, and sundries	4.9	6.1	64,280	129,306	2,968	5,368	120	158
Apparel, piece goods, and notions	16.9	19.6	81,476	109,203	4,661	6,522	181	196
Groceries and related products	42.1	42.9	380,945	504,567	16,729	21,723	763	812
Farm-product raw materials	12.6	11.6	117,606	136,869	1,847	2,100	117	109
Chemicals and allied products	12.7	14.2	94,620	132,471	3,847	5,596	131	147
Petroleum and petroleum products	16.7	16.1	234,874	281,585	3,658	4,447	175	169
Beer, wine, and distilled beverages	5.8	5.3	49,433	59,487	3,849	4,670	146	142
Miscellaneous nondurable goods	43.7	46.8	139,550	184,577	7,828	10,754	404	441

[1] Number of establishments in business at any time during the year.   [2] Revised since publication of report.   [3] For pay period including March 12.

Source of tables 1273 and 1274: U.S. Bureau of the Census, *U.S. Census of Business: 1963*, vol. IV; *1967*, vol. III; and *Census of Wholesale Trade: 1972*, vol. I; *1977*, WC77-A-52; *1982*, WC82-A-52; *1987*, WC87-A-52 and *1992*, WC92-A-52.

No. 1275. Exported Services, by Selected Kinds of Business: 1992

[For establishments with payroll]

KIND OF BUSINESS	1987 SIC code [1]	Estab-lishments	Receipts (mil. dol.)	ESTABLISHMENTS WITH RECEIPTS FROM EXPORTED SERVICES		Receipts from exported services (mil. dol.)
				Number	Receipts (mil. dol.)	
Business services	73	306,551	274,892	12,326	38,254	6,961
Advertising	731	19,023	19,456	1,408	1,640	91
Credit reporting and collection	732	7,472	6,151	106	105	6
Mailing, reproduction, stenographic	733	32,086	18,339	939	1,041	107
Services to dwellings and other buildings	734	57,649	19,003	198	95	6
Miscellaneous equipment rental and leasing	735	24,816	21,778	329	1,265	192
Personnel supply services	736	31,166	38,163	588	721	205
Computer and data processing services	737	59,052	101,073	6,770	30,024	5,802
Miscellaneous business services	738	75,287	50,929	1,988	3,363	551
Legal services	81	151,737	101,114	5,365	20,524	1,482
Engineering and architectural services	871	68,127	78,770	3,832	18,729	2,739
Accounting, auditing, and bookkeeping	872 873 ex.	79,097	34,038	1,131	3,575	91
Research and testing services	8733	13,531	22,690	1,771	5,012	1,006
Management and public relations	874	72,130	57,321	5,655	7,212	2,002

[1] Based on 1987 Standard Industrial Classification; see text, section 13.
Source: U.S. Bureau of the Census, *1992 Census of Service Industries*, Subject Series, SC92-S-5.

No. 1276. Selected Service Industries—Summary: 1987 and 1992

[For establishments with payroll]

KIND OF BUSINESS	1987 SIC code [1]	ESTABLISH-MENTS [2] (1,000)		RECEIPTS OR EXPENSES [3] (mil. dol.)		PAID EMPLOYEES [4] (1,000)	
		1987	1992	1987	1992	1987	1992
Firms subject to Federal income tax [5]	(X)	1,626	1,825	772,194	1,202,613	16,055	19,290
Hotels and other lodging places [6]	70 ex. 704	47	49	51,865	69,204	1,411	1,489
Personal services	72	185	197	31,491	43,280	1,105	1,218
Business services	73	252	307	166,322	274,892	4,414	5,542
Automotive repair, services, and parking	75	151	172	51,423	70,033	785	864
Miscellaneous repair services	76	66	72	20,838	30,732	346	428
Amusement and recreation services and museums [7]	78, 79, 84	99	115	57,638	92,915	1,094	1,382
Health services	80	407	442	182,289	299,067	3,592	4,453
Legal services	81	138	152	66,998	101,114	808	924
Social services	83 87 ex.	43	59	7,330	13,349	357	505
Engineering and management services [8]	8733	205	233	127,344	192,819	1,969	2,271
Firms exempt from Federal income tax [5]	(X) 8011 pt.;	176	209	253,284	423,900	6,737	8,109
Selected health services	8021 pt 805, 6, 8, 9	19	24	184,920	312,050	4,648	5,565
Social services	83	63	82	26,884	47,170	1,110	1,407
Selected membership organizations	861, 2, 4, 9 873, 4 ex.	68	72	22,028	33,795	539	603
Research, testing, and consulting services [9]	8744	4	6	8,837	14,314	121	147

X Not applicable.   [1] Based on 1987 Standard Industrial Classification; see text, section 13.   [2] Number of establishments in business at any time during the year.   [3] Receipts refer to establishments subject to Federal income tax. Expenses refer to establishments exempt from Federal income tax.   [4] For pay period including March 12.   [5] Includes other kinds of business, not shown separately.   [6] Excludes membership lodging.   [7] Includes motion pictures.   [8] Except noncommercial research organizations.   [9] Excludes facilities support management services.

Source: U.S. Bureau of the Census, *1992 Census of Service Industries*, Geographic Area Series, SC92-A-52.

No. 1277. Selected Service Industries—Revenue and Expenses for Tax-Exempt Firms: 1990 to 1994

[**In billions of dollars**. Estimated from a sample of employer firms only]

KIND OF BUSINESS	1987 SIC code [1]	REVENUE			EXPENSES		
		1990	1993	1994	1990	1993	1994
Selected amusement and recreation services [2]	792, 7991, 7997, 7999	7.9	9.8	10.5	7.6	9.7	10.6
Offices and clinics of doctors of medicine	801	12.9	19.1	20.7	12.5	18.6	20.1
Nursing and personal care facilities	805	12.1	16.6	18.0	12.0	16.3	17.7
Hospitals	806	233.6	293.3	304.8	225.6	285.1	301.4
Home health care services	808	3.9	6.8	7.9	3.6	6.5	7.6
Health and allied services, n.e.c.	809	5.3	8.0	9.0	5.2	7.8	8.7
Social services	83	45.3	58.7	62.8	39.4	51.8	55.4
Individual and family social services	8322	13.0	17.5	19.4	12.6	16.9	18.8
Job training and related services	8331	4.9	6.2	6.7	4.5	6.1	6.5
Child day care services	8351	2.9	4.1	4.5	3.0	3.9	4.4
Residential care	8361	8.8	12.0	12.8	8.6	11.4	12.2
Selected membership organizations [3]	86 (pt)	31.5	38.2	39.4	28.6	36.0	36.4
Research and testing services	873	11.0	13.2	14.0	10.0	13.0	13.4

[1] Standard Industrial Classification; see text, section 13.   [2] Covers theatrical producers, bands, orchestras, and entertainers (SIC 792); physical fitness facilities (SIC 7991); membership sports and recreation clubs (SIC 7997); and amusement and recreation services, not elsewhere classified (SIC 7999).   [3] Includes business associations (SIC 861); professional membership organizations (SIC 862); civic, social, and fraternal organizations (SIC 864); and other membership organizations, except labor unions and political and religious organizations (SIC 869).

Source: U.S. Bureau of the Census, *Current Business Reports, Service Annual Survey: 1994* (BS/94).

No. 1278. National Nonprofit Associations—Number, by Type: 1980 to 1994

[Data compiled during last few months of year previous to year shown and the beginning months of year shown]

TYPE	1980	1985	1990	1994	TYPE	1980	1985	1990	1994
Total	**14,726**	**19,121**	**22,289**	**22,512**	Fraternal, foreign interest, nationality, ethnic	435	492	573	548
Trade, business, commercial	3,118	3,719	3,918	3,768	Religious	797	953	1,172	1,227
Agriculture	677	882	940	1,119	Veteran, hereditary, patriotic	208	281	462	577
Legal, governmental, public admin., military	529	658	792	781	Hobby, avocational	910	1,311	1,475	1,555
Scientific, engineering, tech	1,039	1,270	1,417	1,347	Athletic sports	504	737	840	838
Educational	[1]2,376	[1]2,822	1,291	1,289	Labor unions	235	252	253	245
Cultural	([1])	([1])	1,886	1,904	Chambers of Commerce [2]	105	142	168	169
Social welfare	994	1,450	1,705	1,852	Greek and non-Greek letter societies	318	331	340	335
Health, medical	1,413	1,886	2,227	2,331	Fan clubs	(NA)	(NA)	581	458
Public affairs	1,068	1,935	2,249	2,169					

NA Not available.   [1] Data for cultural associations included with educational associations.   [2] National and binational.

Source: Gale Research Inc., Detroit, MI. Compiled from *Encyclopedia of Associations*, annual (copyright).

No. 1279. Service Industries—Summary of Establishments, by Tax Status: 1992

[See *Historical Statistics, Colonial Times to 1970*, series T 391-443, for similar but not comparable data]

KIND OF BUSINESS	1987 SIC code [1]	ALL ESTABLISHMENTS		ESTABLISHMENTS WITH PAYROLL			
		Establish-ments [2] (1,000)	Receipts or reve-nues [3] (mil. dol.)	Establish-ments [2] (1,000)	Receipts or reve-nues [3] (mil. dol.)	Annual payroll (mil. dol.)	Paid employ-ees [4] (1,000)
Firms subject to Federal income tax [5] ...	(X)	8,593.5	1,345,146	1,825.4	1,202,613	452,697	19,290
Hotels and other lodging places [5][6]	70 ex. 704	92.9	71,038	48.6	69,204	19,633	1,489
Hotels and motels....................	701	69.1	68,508	41.7	67,193	19,187	1,456
Personal services [5]	72	1,320.9	59,598	197.1	43,280	14,379	1,218
Laundry, cleaning, and garment services	721	124.4	18,805	55.8	17,140	5,588	426
Beauty and barber shops...............	723, 4	471.6	15,951	87.7	10,347	4,428	402
Funeral service and crematories	726	25.2	7,588	15.6	7,145	1,856	88
Business services [5]	73	2,056.2	309,439	306.6	274,892	109,299	5,542
Advertising [5]	731	91.6	22,673	19.0	19,456	7,223	196
Advertising agencies	7311	(NA)	(NA)	13.9	13,608	5,649	132
Credit reporting and collection.	732	14.6	6,377	7.5	6,151	2,163	98
Mailing, reproduction, stenographic [5]	733	154.5	20,990	32.1	18,339	5,522	235
Direct mail advertising services	7331	(NA)	(NA)	3.9	6,434	1,777	79
Services to dwellings and other buildings	734	460.5	23,586	57.6	19,003	9,164	818
Miscellaneous equipment rental and leasing ..	735	52.4	22,782	24.8	21,778	4,905	200
Personnel supply services [5]	736	54.1	38,709	31.2	38,163	26,436	1,975
Help supply services	7363	(NA)	(NA)	19.0	33,587	24,075	1,842
Computer and data processing services [5] ...	737	223.6	104,650	59.1	101,073	35,598	886
Computer programming services	7371	(NA)	(NA)	23.3	23,548	10,890	243
Prepackaged software	7372	(NA)	(NA)	7.1	20,802	6,614	131
Computer integrated systems design	7373	(NA)	(NA)	5.0	14,805	4,151	98
Data processing and preparation	7374	(NA)	(NA)	7.3	20,200	6,796	230
Computer maintenance and repair	7378	(NA)	(NA)	5.0	7,353	2,300	63
Detective and armored car services	7381	(NA)	(NA)	11.6	9,193	5,794	482
Auto repair, services, and parking [5].......	75	454.3	78,512	172.0	70,033	15,550	864
Automotive rentals, no drivers [5]	751	22.2	20,906	10.6	20,574	2,757	132
Truck rental and leasing, no drivers	7513	(NA)	(NA)	4.3	7,445	1,029	42
Passenger car rental	7514	(NA)	(NA)	4.9	10,280	1,475	81
Automotive repair shops [5]	753	334.5	46,200	128.7	39,746	10,337	520
Top and body repair and paint shops	7532	(NA)	(NA)	35.0	12,262	3,445	166
General automotive repair shops	7538	(NA)	(NA)	64.8	17,773	4,406	230
Automotive services, except repair........	754	85.8	7,661	22.5	6,047	1,776	160
Miscellaneous repair services [5]	76	269.8	35,237	71.6	30,732	9,695	428
Electrical repair shops	762	71.6	11,875	21.2	10,667	3,707	162
Amusement and recreation services [5][7]	78, 79, 84	691.7	103,556	114.8	92,915	25,357	1,382
Motion picture prod., distribution, services....	781, 2	54.1	34,289	13.0	33,062	8,084	249
Producers, orchestras, entertainers [8]	792	288.6	13,054	10.1	8,625	2,895	69
Commercial sports	794	71.6	9,010	3.8	7,594	4,022	90
Health services [5]	80	1,005.5	321,650	441.7	299,067	129,093	4,453
Offices and clinics of doctors of medicine	801	328.9	151,824	197.7	141,429	68,732	1,357
Offices and clinics of dentists	802	138.5	36,939	108.8	35,523	13,039	555
Offices, clinics of other health practitioners ...	804	243.0	23,892	74.7	18,926	6,150	283
Nursing and personal care facilities	805	51.8	34,742	15.0	33,990	15,954	1,135
Hospitals [5]	806	(NA)	(NA)	1.4	31,083	10,556	428
General medical and surgical hospitals	8062	(NA)	(NA)	0.7	24,162	8,013	323
Medical and dental laboratories [5]	807	29.4	15,172	16.0	14,460	4,804	178
Medical laboratories..................	8071	(NA)	(NA)	8.4	12,511	3,980	139
Home health care services	808	(NA)	(NA)	8.0	10,414	4,853	342
Legal services........................	81	326.9	108,443	151.7	101,114	39,328	924
Selected educational services	823, 4, 9	240.7	9,158	14.7	7,242	2,457	133
Social services	83	617.4	18,201	59.1	13,349	5,466	505
Engineering and architectural services [5]......	871	225.4	83,033	68.1	78,770	32,745	825
Engineering services..................	8711	131.3	67,716	41.8	65,245	27,247	658
Architectural services	8712	71.6	12,682	17.9	11,244	4,408	122
Accounting, auditing, and bookkeeping	872	325.5	37,191	79.1	34,038	14,001	521
Research and testing services [9]	873 ex. 8733	30.4	22,910	13.5	22,690	9,227	282
Management and public relations [5]	874	735.8	72,490	72.1	57,321	23,371	644
Management services	8741	111.0	23,774	19.7	21,728	8,516	278
Management consulting services..........	8742	(NA)	(NA)	33.8	22,629	9,620	212
Firms exempt from Federal income tax [5] .	(X)	(NA)	(NA)	208.9	446,256	186,672	8,109
Nursing and personal care facilities	805	(NA)	(NA)	5.9	15,220	7,591	498
Hospitals	806	(NA)	(NA)	5.7	279,735	126,202	4,566
Hospitals, excluding government	806	(NA)	(NA)	3.6	203,360	87,062	3,252
Social services [5]	83	(NA)	(NA)	81.7	53,672	19,331	1,407
Individual and family social services........	832	(NA)	(NA)	28.9	16,046	6,381	434
Residential care	836	(NA)	(NA)	15.0	10,615	4,830	319
Business associations	861	(NA)	(NA)	14.3	11,068	3,157	102
Civic, social, and fraternal associations	864	(NA)	(NA)	41.8	13,176	3,657	355
Research and testing services	873	(NA)	(NA)	3.8	12,535	4,511	126

NA Not available. [1] Based on 1987 Standard Industrial Classification; see text, section 13. [2] Represents the number of establishments in business at any time during year. [3] Receipts refer to establishments subject to Federal income tax. Revenues refer to establishments exempt from Federal income tax. [4] For pay period including March 12. [5] Includes other kinds of business, not shown separately. [6] Excludes membership lodging. [7] Includes motion pictures and museums. [8] Excludes motion picture producers. [9] Excludes noncommercial research organizations.

Source: U.S. Bureau of the Census, *1992 Census of Service Industries*, SC92-A-52 and SC92-N-1.

No. 1280. Services—Establishments, Employees, and Payroll: 1990 and 1993

[Covers establishments with payroll. Employees are for the week including March 12. Most government employees are excluded. For statement on methodology, see Appendix III]

KIND OF BUSINESS	1987 SIC code [1]	ESTABLISHMENTS (1,000)		EMPLOYEES (1,000)		PAYROLL (bil. dol.)	
		1990	1993	1990	1993	1990	1993
Services, total [2]	(I)	**2,059.3**	**2,289.3**	**28,800**	**32,259**	**599.4**	**745.7**
Hotels and other lodging places	70	50.6	52.9	1,529	1,527	19.1	21.5
Hotels and motels	701	39.2	42.6	1,463	1,477	18.3	20.7
Personal services [2]	72	186.1	200.5	1,196	1,253	13.5	15.2
Laundry, cleaning, and garment services	721	50.4	56.6	418	442	5.2	5.9
Drycleaning plants, except rug	7216	17.6	22.6	148	167	1.6	1.9
Beauty shops	723	76.1	83.2	371	397	3.9	4.4
Barber shops	724	5.1	4.8	16	15	0.2	0.2
Funeral service and crematories	726	14.9	15.3	85	90	1.7	1.9
Business services [2]	73	292.3	322.7	5,119	5,832	98.1	123.0
Advertising	731	19.1	19.7	204	211	7.3	7.7
Advertising agencies	7311	11.1	13.6	137	133	5.4	5.8
Credit reporting and collection	732	6.6	7.4	94	106	2.0	2.4
Mailing, reproduction, stenographic [2]	733	26.2	32.6	233	251	5.1	5.9
Direct mail advertising services	7331	3.5	4.0	84	84	1.7	1.9
Commercial art and graphic design	7336	9.0	12.3	52	52	1.5	1.6
Services to buildings	734	48.5	60.2	802	863	8.3	9.9
Misc. equipment rental and leasing	735	22.6	24.9	209	209	4.9	5.4
Personnel supply services [2]	736	27.0	32.1	1,518	1,992	20.6	30.2
Employment agencies	7361	12.8	12.4	247	175	4.3	3.3
Help supply services	7363	13.3	19.6	1,210	1,817	15.6	26.9
Computer and data processing services [2]	737	40.5	62.6	773	966	28.5	40.5
Computer programming services	7371	12.4	23.2	217	262	8.9	12.1
Prepackaged software	7372	3.8	7.0	76	142	3.5	7.4
Computer integrated systems design	7373	3.3	5.2	82	115	3.5	5.1
Data processing and preparation	7374	6.8	7.1	229	236	6.4	7.6
Computer maintenance and repair	7378	3.3	4.9	53	62	1.9	2.4
Miscellaneous business services	738	62.7	80.0	1,093	1,230	17.2	20.7
Detective and armored car services	7381	9.4	11.7	467	490	5.2	6.2
Automotive repair, services, and parking [2]	75	156.6	174.6	877	904	15.2	17.0
Automotive rentals, no drivers [2]	751	10.5	10.3	147	139	2.9	3.1
Truck rental and leasing, no drivers	7513	4.0	4.1	51	47	1.2	1.2
Passenger car rental	7514	4.5	4.8	78	83	1.3	1.6
Automotive repair shops [2]	753	112.7	131.6	507	537	9.6	11.2
Top and body repair and paint shops	7532	30.5	35.1	164	171	3.2	3.7
General automotive repair shops	7538	54.8	67.3	214	240	3.8	4.8
Automotive services, except repair	754	18.1	23.3	145	171	1.5	2.0
Miscellaneous repair services	76	67.4	72.8	403	439	8.7	10.4
Electrical repair shops	762	17.2	21.1	115	161	2.6	3.9
Motion pictures [2]	78	35.4	42.5	430	501	8.6	10.2
Motion picture production and services	781	9.2	12.0	189	228	5.9	7.3
Motion picture distribution and services	782	1.0	1.6	24	33	0.9	1.1
Motion picture theaters	783	7.0	6.8	107	104	0.8	0.8
Video tape rental	784	16.4	22.0	103	134	0.8	1.0
Amusement and recreation services [2]	79	75.2	88.1	1,032	1,201	16.1	21.1
Producers, orchestras, entertainers	792	9.7	13.9	126	162	3.3	4.3
Commercial sports	794	3.3	4.0	79	93	3.0	4.6
Amusement parks	7996	0.7	0.9	69	85	1.1	1.4
Membership sports and recreation clubs	7997	13.1	14.7	242	265	3.4	4.1
Health services [2]	80	436.7	471.9	8,811	10,403	213.8	283.0
Offices and clinics of medical doctors	801	193.6	200.6	1,387	1,577	63.0	76.3
Offices and clinics of dentists	802	104.7	109.8	533	581	11.6	14.2
Offices of other health practitioners	804	62.5	77.7	250	312	5.0	6.9
Offices and clinics of chiropractors	8041	22.9	28.3	73	89	1.3	1.7
Nursing and personal care facilities	805	19.1	21.4	1,461	1,689	18.6	24.7
Hospitals [3]	806	6.3	7.4	4,325	5,093	99.2	136.7
Medical and dental laboratories	807	14.4	16.0	158	187	3.8	5.1
Medical laboratories	8071	7.1	8.4	118	147	3.0	4.2
Home health care services	808	7.7	11.6	351	594	4.8	9.6
Legal services	81	142.4	158.3	932	962	36.0	40.7
Elementary and secondary schools	821	14.3	16.7	451	539	6.6	8.7
Colleges and universities	822	3.0	3.5	1,082	1,219	19.2	24.5
Social services [2]	83	115.6	146.0	1,750	2,029	20.9	26.9
Child day care services	835	39.0	52.5	405	503	3.4	4.8
Residential care	836	21.0	27.9	417	491	5.4	6.9
Museums, botanical, zoological gardens	84	3.2	3.6	64	74	1.1	1.3
Business associations	861	12.7	14.5	99	106	2.7	3.4
Civic and social associations	864	40.0	41.9	366	369	3.7	3.9
Engineering and management services [2]	87	201.1	249.8	2,473	2,590	79.8	91.2
Engineering services	8711	33.1	41.5	652	656	24.9	27.4
Architectural services	8712	15.7	17.8	140	122	4.8	4.5
Accounting, auditing, and bookkeeping	872	67.9	81.4	524	543	13.8	15.2
Research and testing services	873	14.9	18.2	393	429	12.3	14.8
Management services	8741	15.3	21.9	286	358	7.7	10.8
Management consulting services	8742	24.5	35.8	226	253	8.6	11.1
Facilities support services	8744	0.7	1.0	70	76	2.2	2.3

[1] Based on 1987 Standard Industrial Classification; see text, section 13.   [2] Includes kinds of business not shown separately.   [3] Includes government employees.

Source: U.S. Bureau of the Census, *County Business Patterns*, annual.

No. 1281. Service Industries—Annual Receipts of Taxable Firms: 1985 to 1994

[In billions of dollars. Covers employer and nonemployer firms except as noted. Estimated]

KIND OF BUSINESS	1987 SIC code [1]	1985	1989	1990	1991	1992	1993	1994
Hotels and other lodging places [2]	70 ex. 704	45.4	61.2	64.2	65.3	71.0	74.5	80.3
Hotels and motels	701	43.5	59.1	62.0	63.1	68.5	71.8	77.2
Personal services [3]	72	36.7	51.8	54.7	54.6	59.6	61.5	63.7
Laundry, cleaning, and garment services	721	12.8	16.6	17.3	17.6	18.8	19.1	19.8
Drycleaning plants, except rug cleaning	7216	3.8	4.8	4.4	4.5	5.5	5.5	5.7
Beauty shops	723	9.0	12.5	12.8	13.1	14.4	14.6	15.2
Barber shops	7241	1.2	1.4	1.4	1.5	1.5	1.5	1.6
Funeral service and crematories	726	5.2	6.4	6.8	7.1	7.6	8.2	8.5
Business services [3]	73	155.9	251.6	280.7	287.2	309.4	338.5	379.1
Advertising	731	14.9	20.3	22.0	21.3	22.7	23.9	25.2
Advertising agencies	7311	11.1	14.8	16.1	15.2	16.0	16.9	17.7
Credit reporting and collection	732	3.7	5.4	5.8	6.0	6.4	7.0	7.2
Mailing, reproduction, stenographic [3]	733	14.5	19.7	20.8	20.4	21.0	22.8	24.1
Direct mail advertising services	7331	3.8	6.0	7.0	6.5	6.8	7.7	8.1
Commercial art and graphic design	7336	(NA)	(NA)	6.1	6.1	6.2	6.3	6.9
Services to dwellings and other buildings	734	13.3	20.3	22.3	22.4	23.6	24.0	26.8
Miscellaneous equipment rental and leasing	735	(NA)	21.0	23.1	22.6	22.8	24.6	26.6
Personnel supply services	736	14.7	28.6	32.5	33.4	38.7	43.0	49.8
Employment agencies	7361	3.7	5.4	6.2	5.2	5.0	5.5	6.3
Help supply services	7363	(NA)	23.2	26.4	28.3	33.7	37.4	43.4
Computer and data processing services [3]	737	45.1	78.7	88.3	94.4	104.7	117.0	133.6
Computer programming services	7371	(NA)	(NA)	21.3	23.4	25.0	28.0	32.6
Prepackaged software	7372	(NA)	(NA)	16.5	18.3	21.2	24.7	27.7
Computer integrated systems design	7373	(NA)	(NA)	12.9	13.8	15.2	17.1	19.0
Data processing and preparation	7374	(NA)	(NA)	17.8	18.8	20.4	22.6	26.7
Computer maintenance and repair	7378	(NA)	(NA)	7.0	6.9	7.7	7.5	7.7
Miscellaneous business services	738	(NA)	57.7	65.8	66.6	69.7	76.2	85.9
Detective and armored car services	7381	(NA)	(NA)	9.0	9.6	9.7	10.2	10.6
Automotive repair, services, and parking [3]	75	51.7	71.0	73.7	71.5	78.5	84.3	91.7
Automotive rentals, no drivers [3]	751	14.6	19.6	20.8	20.3	20.9	22.2	23.3
Truck rental and leasing, without drivers	7513	5.5	7.9	8.5	7.9	7.6	7.7	8.1
Passenger car rental	7514	(NA)	9.0	9.0	9.5	10.4	11.4	12.1
Automotive repair shops [3]	753	30.5	42.0	43.5	41.2	46.2	49.6	54.5
Top & body repair & paint shops	7532	(NA)	13.1	13.5	12.8	13.9	14.8	16.0
General automotive repair shops	7538	(NA)	(NA)	19.6	17.7	21.3	23.0	25.8
Automotive services, except repair	754	(NA)	6.2	6.5	6.7	7.7	8.4	9.6
Miscellaneous repair services	76	20.7	30.1	32.8	32.4	35.2	36.2	39.5
Electrical repair shops	762	(NA)	9.6	11.3	11.3	11.9	12.3	13.0
Motion pictures	78	21.5	36.2	40.0	42.8	45.7	50.2	54.2
Motion picture produc., distribution, allied services	781,2	15.0	26.4	28.9	31.6	34.3	38.0	41.1
Motion picture theaters	783	3.8	5.4	6.1	6.2	5.9	6.1	6.5
Video tape rental	784	(NA)	4.4	5.0	5.0	5.5	6.0	6.7
Amusement and recreation services [3]	79	31.2	44.5	50.1	51.7	57.7	64.0	69.2
Producers, orchestras, entertainers	792	6.4	8.4	10.7	11.7	13.1	15.8	16.9
Commercial sports	794	5.0	7.6	8.6	8.6	9.0	9.1	9.4
Amusement parks	7996	2.6	4.6	4.9	4.8	5.4	5.7	5.9
Membership sports and recreation clubs	7997	3.5	4.5	4.8	5.2	5.4	6.0	6.4
Health services [3][4]	80	147.4	241.6	271.2	293.9	321.7	337.9	356.5
Offices and clinics of doctors of medicine	801	72.1	117.2	128.9	138.6	151.8	155.2	161.6
Offices and clinics of dentists	802	20.6	29.3	31.5	33.3	36.9	39.2	42.1
Offices of other health practitioners	804	7.9	17.1	20.1	21.4	23.9	25.6	26.3
Offices and clinics of chiropractors	8041	2.7	5.0	5.5	5.6	6.6	7.1	7.2
Nursing and personal care facilities	805	17.5	25.8	30.1	32.9	34.7	37.4	39.6
Hospitals	806	15.7	23.5	26.5	28.8	31.1	32.9	34.1
Medical and dental laboratories	807	5.4	10.3	12.0	13.6	15.2	16.3	18.1
Medical laboratories	8071	3.9	8.5	10.0	11.5	12.9	14.0	15.6
Home health care services	808	(NA)	5.6	7.6	9.1	11.2	13.0	14.9
Legal services [4]	81	52.8	89.1	97.6	100.0	108.4	111.7	113.7
Social services [4]	83	(NA)	(NA)	15.5	16.4	18.2	19.9	22.0
Child day care services	8351	2.6	6.0	7.1	7.4	8.7	9.6	10.6
Residential care	8361	(NA)	4.1	4.6	4.9	4.9	5.3	5.7
Museums, botanical, zoological gardens [4]	84	(NA)	(NA)	0.1	0.2	0.2	0.2	0.2
Engineering and management services [3]	87	(NA)	183.5	198.4	202.7	215.6	225.1	239.7
Engineering services	8711	(NA)	(NA)	64.8	65.8	67.7	67.8	69.6
Architectural services	8712	(NA)	(NA)	13.0	12.3	12.7	13.5	14.6
Accounting, auditing, & bookkeeping	8721	21.2	32.3	32.6	33.7	37.2	40.1	43.3
Research and testing services [5]	873, ex. 8733	(NA)	18.1	20.4	20.9	22.9	25.1	26.6
Management services	8741	(NA)	(NA)	20.6	21.8	23.8	24.7	27.1
Management consulting services	8742	(NA)	(NA)	28.9	29.8	31.9	33.8	37.0
Facilities support services	8744	(NA)	4.8	5.3	5.6	5.6	5.4	6.3
Arrangement of passenger transportation [4]	472	6.3	11.0	12.3	11.4	11.9	12.5	13.4
Real estate agents and managers [4]	653	31.3	62.3	63.0	63.2	73.1	80.9	84.6

NA Not available.   [1] Standard Industrial Classification; see text, section 13.   [2] Excludes those on membership basis. [3] Includes other kinds of businesses, not shown separately.   [4] Covers employer firms only.   [5] Excludes noncommercial research organizations.

Source: U.S. Bureau of the Census, *Current Business Reports, Service Annual Survey: 1994* (BS/94); and unpublished data.

No. 1282. Service Industries—Summary of Establishments, by State: 1992

[Based on 1987 Standard Industrial Classification code; see text, section 13]

DIVISION AND STATE	FIRMS SUBJECT TO FEDERAL INCOME TAX						TAX-EXEMPT FIRMS			
	All establishments		Establishments with payroll				Establishments with payroll			
	Establishments [1] (1,000)	Receipts (mil. dol.)	Establishments [1] (1,000)	Receipts (mil. dol.)	Payroll (mil. dol.)	Paid employees [2] (1,000)	Establishments [1] (1,000)	Revenues (mil. dol.)	Payroll (mil. dol.)	Paid employees [2] (1,000)
U.S ..	8,593.5	1,345,146	1,825.4	1,202,613	452,697	19,290	208.9	446,256	186,672	8,109
N.E	524.0	81,419	104.9	71,871	27,908	1,070	15.9	31,225	14,154	573
ME....	46.7	4,246	9.0	3,597	1,367	68	1.7	2,068	956	45
NH....	46.7	5,413	9.2	4,612	1,840	83	1.4	1,933	767	36
VT	27.7	2,325	5.0	1,946	633	37	1.1	1,021	449	22
MA....	246.2	43,676	46.6	38,949	15,103	545	7.2	16,940	7,698	302
RI.....	33.3	4,196	7.6	3,664	1,413	64	1.1	2,217	1,003	43
CT	123.4	21,562	27.4	19,102	7,551	273	3.4	7,046	3,280	125
M.A	1,227.9	227,191	277.4	202,649	75,238	2,812	33.6	89,401	40,752	1,631
NY	617.1	115,939	133.7	103,025	38,012	1,344	16.3	49,030	22,980	871
NJ	265.2	55,842	65.9	50,242	18,485	671	4.8	13,855	6,282	245
PA	345.6	55,409	77.8	49,383	18,741	797	12.4	26,516	11,490	514
E.N.C....	1,273.3	185,044	277.5	167,019	65,455	2,946	35.7	77,872	32,219	1,482
OH....	321.5	45,210	69.9	40,844	16,137	758	9.3	20,111	8,361	394
IN.....	164.6	19,610	34.5	17,548	6,742	355	5.2	9,009	3,649	180
IL.....	370.7	63,955	79.8	57,927	22,077	902	9.0	23,341	9,521	417
MI	278.3	39,049	61.3	35,124	14,203	614	7.5	16,757	7,154	306
WI	138.1	17,220	32.0	15,577	6,295	317	4.8	8,654	3,534	185
W.N.C....	636.2	72,240	122.4	64,468	24,808	1,235	20.9	32,693	14,274	738
MN....	176.5	21,146	31.0	18,764	7,544	349	5.6	9,718	4,346	208
IA.....	95.3	8,755	17.8	7,711	2,899	163	3.7	4,656	2,065	121
MO....	166.6	22,388	36.4	20,339	7,699	374	4.4	9,484	3,996	195
ND	22.2	1,795	4.2	1,576	616	33	1.1	1,312	585	37
SD	25.2	2,076	4.8	1,790	592	34	1.1	1,258	552	33
NE	59.3	6,492	11.3	5,828	2,290	120	1.9	2,572	1,118	59
KS	91.0	9,589	16.9	8,460	3,168	162	3.0	3,693	1,611	86
S.A	1,460.4	239,872	335.5	217,306	82,773	3,637	32.6	75,442	29,708	1,261
DE	21.2	3,142	5.3	2,823	1,170	54	0.6	1,324	588	26
MD....	179.1	29,822	36.8	26,937	10,765	419	3.9	9,853	3,925	163
DC	26.0	11,752	7.4	11,238	4,299	121	2.6	9,782	3,118	96
VA	200.8	36,436	45.9	33,606	13,138	526	4.7	10,782	4,191	176
WV....	44.0	4,951	9.5	4,466	1,575	84	1.6	2,718	1,138	57
NC....	196.1	24,631	42.2	22,155	8,410	425	4.8	9,777	4,152	185
SC	90.0	12,169	21.5	10,930	4,349	233	2.1	4,200	1,694	76
GA	207.7	34,081	46.9	30,802	11,409	502	3.8	9,122	3,706	163
FL.....	495.6	82,890	120.0	74,347	27,658	1,274	8.4	17,885	7,195	318
E.S.C....	406.6	55,607	88.7	49,925	18,598	930	10.2	20,583	8,317	398
KY	103.8	11,685	21.0	10,378	3,864	211	2.6	4,753	1,922	99
TN	148.3	22,712	32.0	20,410	7,581	362	3.5	7,549	3,028	139
AL	98.7	14,933	23.0	13,649	5,162	248	2.4	5,319	2,148	99
MS	55.9	6,277	12.8	5,487	1,991	108	1.6	2,961	1,219	61
W.S.C....	894.1	130,736	185.9	116,445	44,205	2,057	17.9	34,160	13,778	655
AR	67.8	6,902	14.0	6,007	2,250	133	1.9	2,946	1,206	64
LA	117.1	17,943	27.1	16,067	5,912	296	2.6	5,587	2,338	110
OK	112.1	11,169	21.2	9,607	3,641	196	2.5	3,935	1,620	83
TX	597.2	94,721	123.6	84,763	32,402	1,430	10.9	21,692	8,614	398
Mountain .	558.2	80,847	113.0	72,714	26,295	1,258	12.1	19,276	7,667	360
MT	34.3	2,629	6.9	2,197	722	44	1.4	1,243	524	29
ID.....	38.3	3,918	7.3	3,440	1,305	64	0.9	1,089	447	22
WY....	19.2	1,612	4.1	1,384	436	26	0.7	561	257	15
CO....	168.2	21,229	32.9	18,810	7,183	319	3.3	6,301	2,401	104
NM....	53.2	6,880	10.7	6,191	2,332	111	1.5	1,899	849	43
AZ	132.4	18,648	28.7	16,616	6,220	299	2.6	5,386	2,075	94
UT	65.4	8,389	11.7	7,491	2,667	139	1.0	1,784	732	35
NV	47.2	17,541	10.8	16,585	5,431	256	0.7	1,013	382	16
Pacfic ...	1,612.8	272,189	320.2	240,217	87,418	3,346	30.1	65,604	25,804	1,011
WA	185.1	24,125	39.5	21,448	8,091	355	5.0	8,837	3,778	162
OR	118.9	12,382	23.3	10,663	3,963	195	3.1	4,479	1,857	87
CA	1,243.0	224,885	244.5	198,432	71,824	2,646	20.1	49,179	18,799	707
AK	24.2	2,770	4.5	2,382	884	32	0.9	1,028	445	17
HI.....	41.6	8,027	8.5	7,291	2,654	118	1.0	2,081	924	37

[1] Number of establishments in business at any time during year. [2] For the pay period including March 12.

Source: U.S. Bureau of the Census, *1992 Census of Service Industries*, Geographic Area Series, SC92-A-1 to 52 and Nonemployer Statistics Series, SC92-N-1.

Figure 28.1
U.S. International Transaction Balances: 1960 to 1995

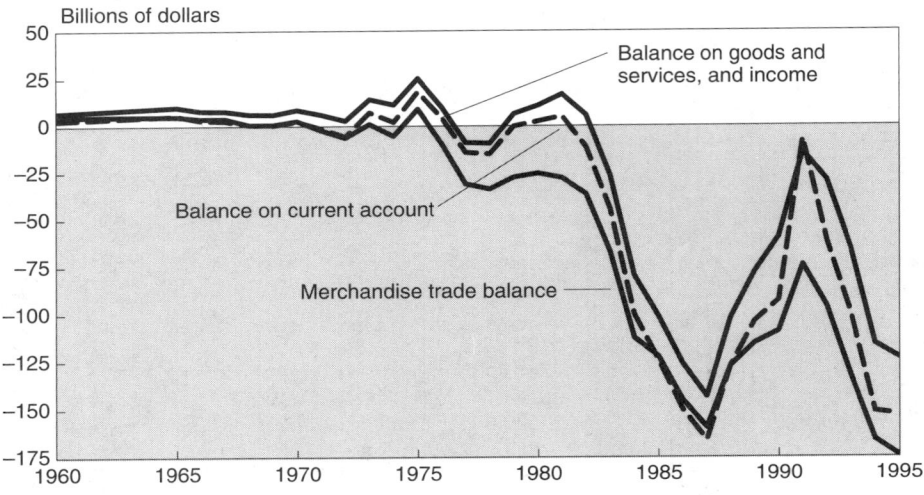

Source: Chart prepared by U.S. Bureau of the Census. For data, see table 1283.

Figure 28.2
**Top Purchasers of U.S. Exports and Suppliers
of U.S. General Imports: 1995**

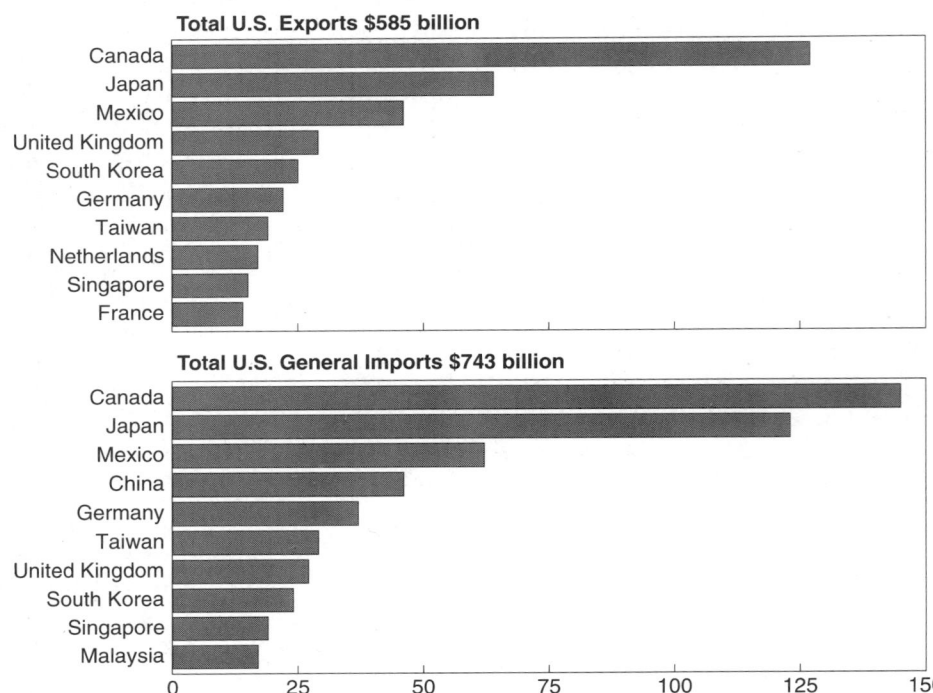

Source: Chart prepared by U.S. Bureau of the Census. For data, see table 1305.

Foreign Commerce and Aid

This section presents data on the flow of goods, services, and capital between the United States and other countries; changes in official reserve assets of the United States; international investments; foreign assistance programs; and import duties.

The Bureau of Economic Analysis publishes current figures on U.S. international transactions and the U.S. international investment position in its monthly *Survey of Current Business.* Statistics for the foreign aid programs are presented by the Agency for International Development (AID) in its annual *U.S. Overseas Loans and Grants and Assistance from International Organizations;* and by the Department of Agriculture in its *Foreign Agricultural Trade of the United States.*

The principal source of merchandise import and export data is the Bureau of the Census. Current data are presented monthly in *U.S. Merchandise Trade,* (beginning 1994, retitled *U.S. International Trade in Goods and Services*) report series FT900, and *U.S. Merchandise Trade: Exports, General Imports, and Imports for Consumption*, report series FT925. The *Bureau of the Census Catalog* and the *Guide to Foreign Trade Statistics* lists the Bureau's monthly and annual reports in this field. In addition, the International Trade Administration and the Bureau of Economic Analysis present summary as well as selected commodity and country data for U.S. foreign trade in the *Overseas Business Reports* and the *Survey of Current Business,* respectively. The merchandise trade data in the latter source include balance of payments adjustments to the Census data. The Treasury Department's *Monthly Treasury Statement of Receipts and Outlays of the United States Government* contains information on import duties.

International accounts—The international transactions tables (Nos. 1283 to 1285) show, for given time periods, the transfer of goods, services, grants, and financial assets and liabilities between the United States and the rest of the world. The international investment

In Brief

The U.S. international trade in goods and services saw the deficit increase slightly from $104.4 billion in 1994 to $105.1 billion in 1995.

Foreign direct investors increased their outlays in the U.S. for the third year in a row to $47.2 billion in 1994. The rise in outlays occurred mostly in manufacturing and by European investors.

position table (No. 1286) presents, for specific dates, the value of U.S. investments abroad and of foreign investments in the United States. The movement of foreign and U.S. capital as presented in the balance of payments is not the only factor affecting the total value of foreign investments. Among the other factors are changes in the valuation of assets or liabilities, including changes in prices of securities, defaults, expropriations, and write-offs.

Direct investment abroad means the ownership or control, directly or indirectly, by one person of 10 percent or more of the voting securities of an incorporated business enterprise or an equivalent interest in an unincorporated business enterprise. Direct investment position is the value of U.S. parents' claims on the equity of, and receivables due from, foreign affiliates, less foreign affiliates' receivables due from their U.S. parents. Income consists of parents' shares in the earnings of their affiliates plus net interest received by parents on intercompany accounts, less withholding taxes on dividends and interest.

Foreign aid—Foreign assistance is divided into three major categories—grants (military supplies and services and other grants), credits, and other assistance (through net accumulation of foreign currency claims from the sale of agricultural commodities). *Grants* are transfers for which no payment is expected (other than a limited percentage of the foreign currency "counterpart" funds generated by the grant), or which at most involve an obligation on the part of the receiver to extend aid to the United States or other countries to achieve a common objective. *Credits* are loan disbursements or transfers under other agreements which give rise to specific obligations to repay, over a period of years, usually with interest. All known returns to the U.S. Government stemming from grants and credits (reverse grants, returns of grants, and payments of principal) are taken into account in net grants and net credits, but no allowance is made for interest or commissions. *Other assistance* represents the transfer of U.S. farm products in exchange for foreign currencies (plus, since enactment of Public Law 87-128, currency claims from principal and interest collected on credits extended under the farm products program), *less* the Government's disbursements of the currencies as grants, credits, or for purchases. The net acquisition of currencies represents net transfers of resources to foreign countries under the agricultural programs, in addition to those classified as grants or credits.

The basic instrument for extending military aid to friendly nations has been the Mutual Defense Assistance Program authorized by the Congress in 1949. Prior to 1952, economic and technical aid was authorized in the Foreign Assistance Act of 1948, the 1950 Act for International Development, and other legislation which set up programs for specific countries. In 1952, these economic, technical, and military aid programs were combined under the Mutual Security Act, which in turn was followed by the Foreign Assistance Act passed in 1961. Appropriations to provide military assistance were also made in the Department of Defense Appropriation Act (rather than the Foreign Assistance Appropriation Act) beginning in 1966 for certain countries in Southeast Asia and in other legislation concerning program for specific countries (such as Israel). Figures on activity under the Foreign Assistance Act as reported in the *Foreign Grants and Credits* series differ from data published by AID or its immediate predecessors, due largely to differences in reporting, timing, and treatment of particular items.

Exports—The Bureau of the Census compiles export data primarily from Shipper's Export Declarations required to be filed with customs officials for shipments leaving the United States. They include U.S. exports under mutual security programs and exclude shipments to U.S. Armed Forces for their own use.

The value reported in the export statistics is generally equivalent to a free alongside ship (f.a.s.) value at the U.S. port of export, based on the transaction price, including inland freight, insurance, and other charges incurred in placing the merchandise alongside the carrier at the U.S. port of exportation. This value, as defined, excludes the cost of loading merchandise aboard the exporting carrier and also excludes freight, insurance, and any other charges or transportation and other costs beyond the U.S. port of exportation. The country of destination is defined as the country of ultimate destination or country where the merchandise is to be consumed, further processed, or manufactured, as known to the shipper at the time of exportation. When ultimate destination is not known, the shipment is statistically credited to the last country to which the shipper knows the merchandise will be shipped in the same form as exported.

For certain "low-valued" shipments, the export statistics include estimates based upon selected samples of such shipments. The dollar value of the "low-valued" shipments has varied. For instance, effective January 1987 through September 1989, data are estimated for shipments valued under $1,501; from October 1989 through December 1989, data are estimated for shipments valued under $2,501 to all countries.

Effective January 1990, the United States began substituting Canadian import statistics for U.S. exports to Canada. As a result of the data exchange between the United States and Canada, the United States has adopted the Canadian import exemption level for its export statistics based on shipments to Canada.

Data are estimated for shipments valued under $2,501 to all countries, except Canada, using factors based on the ratios of low-valued shipments to individual country totals. These shipments represent slightly less than 2.5 percent of the monthly value of U.S. exports to those countries. Data are estimated for shipments reported on Canadian import documents which total less than $900 (Canadian). Such shipments represent 2 percent of the monthly value of U.S. exports to Canada.

Prior to 1989, exports were based on Schedule B, Statistical Classification of Domestic and Foreign Commodities Exported from the United States. These statistics were retabulated and published using Schedule E, Standard International Trade Classification, Revision 2. Beginning in 1989, Schedule B classifications were based on the Harmonized System and made to coincide with the Standard International Trade Classification, Revision 3. This revision will affect the comparability of most export series beginning with the 1989 data for commodities.

Imports—The Bureau of the Census compiles import data from various customs forms required to be filed with customs officials. Data on import values are presented on two bases in this section: the c.i.f. (cost, insurance, and freight) and the customs import value (as appraised by the U.S. Customs Service in accordance with legal requirements of the Tariff Act of 1930, as amended). This latter valuation, primarily used for collection of import duties, frequently does not reflect the actual transaction value. Country of origin is defined as country where the merchandise was grown, mined, or manufactured. If country of origin is unknown, country of shipment is reported.

Imports are classified either as "General imports" or "Imports for consumption." *General imports* are a combination of entries for immediate consumption, entries into customs bonded warehouses, and entries into U.S. Foreign Trade Zones, thus generally reflecting total arrivals of merchandise. *Imports for consumption* are a combination of entries for immediate consumption, withdrawals from warehouses for consumption, and entries of merchandise into U.S. customs territory from U.S. Foreign Trade Zones, thus generally reflecting the total of the commodities entered into U.S. consumption channels.

Since July 1953, the import statistics include estimates, not classified by commodity, for certain low-valued shipments. For instance, from January 1985 through September 1989, import statistics include estimates for shipments valued under $1,001. Effective October 1989, import statistics are fully compiled on shipments valued over $1,250 or, under certain textile programs, for any article which must be reported on a formal entry. Value data for shipments valued under $1,251 and not required to be reported on formal entries are estimated for individual countries using factors based on the ratios of low-valued shipments to individual country totals for past periods. The estimated low-valued shipments generally amount to slightly less than 4 percent of the import total.

Prior to 1989, imports were based on the Tariff Schedule of the United States Annotated. The statistics were retabulated and published using Schedule A, Standard International Trade Classification, Revision 2. Beginning in 1989, the statistics are based on the Harmonized Tariff Schedule of the United States, which coincides with the Standard International Trade Classification, Revision 3. This revision will affect the comparability of most import commodity series beginning with the 1989 data.

Area coverage—Except as noted, the geographic area covered by the export and import trade statistics is the United States Customs area (includes the 50 States, the District of Columbia and Puerto Rico), the U.S. Virgin Islands (effective January 1981), and U.S. Foreign Trade Zones (effective July 1982). Data for selected tables and total values for 1980, have been revised to reflect the U.S. Virgin Islands' trade with foreign countries, where possible.

No. 1283. U.S. International Transactions, by Type of Transaction: 1980 to 1995

[In millions of dollars. Minus sign (-) indicates debits. See also Historical Statistics, Colonial Times to 1970, series U 1-25]

TYPE OF TRANSACTION	1980	1985	1987	1988	1989	1990	1991	1992	1993	1994	1995
Exports of goods and services [1]	344,440	382,747	449,514	560,426	642,025	697,426	718,194	737,394	763,826	838,820	965,008
Merchandise, excl. military [2][3]	224,250	215,915	250,208	320,230	362,120	389,307	416,913	440,352	456,823	502,485	574,879
Foods, feeds, and beverages	36,278	24,566	25,229	33,770	37,475	35,172	35,829	40,336	40,692	42,017	50,543
Industrial supplies and materials	72,088	61,159	70,052	90,019	99,826	105,503	109,826	109,592	111,871	121,552	146,221
Capital goods, except automotive	76,283	79,322	92,707	119,103	138,908	152,543	166,453	176,070	182,216	205,390	233,315
Automotive vehicles and parts [4]	17,443	24,945	27,583	33,397	34,888	36,465	40,008	47,027	52,405	57,614	60,506
Consumer goods (nonfood) [5]	17,751	14,593	20,307	26,981	37,317	43,719	46,858	51,424	54,655	59,981	64,456
Services	47,584	73,155	98,539	111,126	127,387	147,819	164,278	178,617	187,755	198,716	208,828
Transfers under U.S. military agency sales contracts	9,029	8,718	11,106	9,284	8,564	9,932	11,135	11,693	12,650	12,418	12,674
Travel	10,588	17,762	23,563	29,434	36,205	43,007	48,385	54,742	57,875	60,406	60,278
Passenger fares	2,591	4,411	7,003	8,976	10,657	15,298	15,854	16,618	16,611	17,477	18,213
Other transportation	11,618	14,674	17,471	19,811	21,106	22,745	23,331	23,691	23,983	26,078	28,553
Royalties and license fees	7,085	6,678	10,183	12,146	13,818	16,634	18,114	20,015	20,637	22,436	25,852
Other private services	6,276	20,035	28,688	30,812	36,450	39,535	46,770	50,997	55,101	59,022	62,488
U.S. Government misc. services	398	878	526	664	587	668	690	861	899	880	771
Income on U.S. assets abroad	72,606	93,677	100,767	129,070	152,070	160,300	137,003	118,425	119,248	137,619	181,301
Direct investment	37,146	30,547	39,608	52,092	55,368	58,740	52,198	51,912	61,579	67,702	91,195
Other private receipts	32,898	57,631	55,848	70,275	91,049	91,048	76,781	59,399	52,561	65,835	85,511
U.S. Government receipts	2,562	5,499	5,311	6,703	5,653	10,512	8,023	7,114	5,108	4,082	4,595
Imports of goods, services and income	-333,774	-484,037	-592,745	-662,487	-719,758	-756,694	-732,486	-766,796	-829,668	-954,304	-1,087,827
Merchandise, excl. military [2][3]	-249,750	-338,088	-409,765	-447,189	-477,365	-498,337	-490,981	-536,458	-589,441	-668,584	-749,348
Foods, feeds, and beverages	-18,564	-21,850	-24,809	-24,928	-24,898	-26,407	-26,205	-27,610	-27,866	-30,958	-33,179
Industrial supplies and materials	-132,472	-114,008	-113,746	-122,684	-135,363	-145,168	-132,963	-140,591	-152,437	-164,863	-183,900
Capital goods, except automotive	-31,576	-61,287	-85,128	-102,202	-112,156	-116,061	-120,802	-134,252	-152,366	-184,425	-221,604
Automotive vehicles and parts [4]	-28,257	-64,905	-85,174	-87,947	-87,356	-88,480	-85,696	-91,787	-102,419	-118,269	-124,485
Consumer goods (nonfood) [5]	-34,268	-66,336	-88,824	-96,425	-103,053	-105,053	-107,777	-122,656	-134,015	-146,299	-160,004
Services	-41,491	-72,862	-91,678	-99,491	-103,535	-118,783	-119,614	-121,991	-129,979	-138,829	-145,777
Direct defense expenditures	-10,851	-13,108	-14,950	-15,604	-15,313	-17,531	-16,409	-13,835	-13,202	-10,270	-9,864
Travel	-10,397	-24,558	-29,310	-32,114	-33,416	-37,349	-35,322	-38,552	-40,713	-43,562	-45,496
Passenger Fares	-3,607	-6,444	-7,283	-7,729	-8,249	-10,531	-10,012	-10,556	-11,313	-12,696	-13,385
Other transportation	-11,790	-15,643	-19,057	-20,969	-22,260	-25,168	-25,204	-25,459	-26,558	-28,373	-29,505
Royalties and license fees	-724	-1,170	-1,857	-2,601	-2,528	-3,135	-4,035	-5,074	-4,863	-5,666	-6,561
Other private services	-2,900	-10,203	-17,328	-18,554	-19,898	-23,150	-26,516	-26,214	-31,999	-35,605	-38,147
U.S. Government miscellaneous services	-1,214	-1,735	-1,893	-1,921	-1,871	-1,919	-2,116	-2,301	-2,331	-2,657	-2,818
Income on foreign assets in the United States	-42,532	-73,087	-91,302	-115,806	-138,858	-139,574	-121,892	-108,346	-110,248	-146,891	-192,703
Direct investment	-8,635	-7,213	-7,425	-11,693	-6,507	-2,871	3,433	-317	-5,250	-22,621	-32,062
Other private payments	-21,214	-42,745	-57,659	-72,398	-93,987	-95,661	-83,796	-67,549	-63,437	-77,251	-99,362
U.S. Government payments	-12,684	-23,129	-26,218	-31,715	-38,364	-41,042	-41,529	-40,480	-41,561	-47,019	-61,279
Unilateral transfers (excl. military grants, net	-8,349	-22,954	-23,107	-25,023	-26,106	-33,393	6,869	-32,148	-34,084	-35,761	-30,095
U.S. Government grants	-5,486	-11,268	-10,227	-10,513	-10,892	-17,417	24,194	-15,083	-16,311	-15,814	-11,027
U.S. Government pensions	-1,818	-2,138	-2,221	-2,501	-2,516	-2,934	-3,461	-3,735	-3,785	-4,247	-3,114
Private remittances and other transfers	-1,044	-9,549	-10,599	-12,009	-12,698	-13,042	-13,864	-13,330	-13,988	-15,700	-15,954

TYPE OF TRANSACTION	1980	1985	1987	1988	1989	1990	1991	1992	1993	1994	1995
U.S. assets abroad, net (increase/capital outflow (-))...	**-86,967**	**-39,889**	**-72,617**	**-100,087**	**-168,744**	**-74,011**	**-57,881**	**-65,875**	**-184,589**	**-125,851**	**-280,096**
U.S. official reserve assets, net	-8,155	-3,858	9,149	-3,912	-25,293	-2,158	5,763	3,901	-1,379	5,346	-9,742
Special drawing rights	-16	-897	-509	127	-535	-192	-177	2,316	-537	-441	-808
Reserve position in the International Monetary Fund	-1,667	908	2,070	1,025	471	731	-367	-2,692	-44	494	-2,466
Foreign currencies	-6,472	-3,869	7,588	-5,064	-25,229	-2,697	6,307	4,277	-797	5,293	-6,468
U.S. Govt. assets, other than official reserve assets, net	-5,162	-2,821	1,006	2,967	1,259	2,307	2,911	-1,661	-330	-322	-326
U.S. credits and other long-term assets	-9,860	-7,657	-6,506	-7,680	-5,590	-8,430	-12,874	-7,403	-6,299	-5,182	-4,744
Repayments on U.S. credits and other long-term assets [7]	4,456	4,719	7,625	10,370	6,723	10,867	16,776	5,809	6,270	5,044	4,352
U.S. foreign currency holdings and U.S. short-term assets, net	242	117	-113	277	125	-130	-992	-66	-301	-184	66
U.S. private assets, net	-73,651	-33,211	-82,771	-99,141	-144,710	-74,160	-66,555	-68,115	-182,880	-130,875	-270,028
Direct investments abroad	-19,222	-14,065	-28,355	-16,175	-36,834	-29,950	-31,369	-42,640	-72,601	-49,370	-96,897
Foreign securities	-3,568	-7,481	-5,251	-7,846	-22,070	-28,765	-45,673	-46,415	-141,807	-49,799	-93,769
U.S. claims on unaffiliated foreigners reported by U.S. nonbanking concerns	-4,023	-10,342	-7,046	-21,193	-27,646	-27,824	11,097	45	1,531	-32,621	-20,358
U.S. claims reported by U.S. banks, n.i.e. [8]	-46,838	-1,323	-42,119	-53,927	-58,160	12,379	-610	20,895	29,947	915	-59,004
Foreign assets in the U.S., net (increase/capital inflow (+))..	**58,112**	**141,183**	**242,983**	**240,265**	**218,490**	**122,192**	**94,241**	**153,823**	**248,529**	**291,365**	**426,325**
Foreign official assets in the U.S., net	15,497	-1,119	45,387	39,758	8,503	33,910	17,389	40,466	72,146	39,409	110,483
U.S. Government securities	11,895	-1,139	44,802	43,050	1,532	30,243	16,147	22,403	53,014	36,748	72,507
U.S. Treasury securities	9,708	-838	43,238	41,741	149	29,576	14,846	18,454	48,952	30,723	68,773
Other	2,187	-301	1,564	1,309	1,383	667	1,301	3,949	4,062	6,025	3,734
Other U.S. Government liabilities [8]	615	844	-2,326	-467	160	1,868	1,367	2,180	1,706	2,211	1,814
Other U.S. liabilities reported by U.S. banks, n.i.e. [8]	-159	645	3,918	-319	4,976	3,385	-1,484	16,571	14,841	2,923	32,896
Other foreign official assets	3,145	-1,469	-1,007	-2,506	1,835	-1,586	1,359	-688	2,585	-2,473	3,266
Other foreign assets in the United States, net	42,615	142,301	197,596	200,507	209,987	88,282	76,853	113,358	176,383	251,956	315,842
Direct investments in the United States	16,918	20,010	58,219	57,278	67,736	47,915	22,004	17,600	41,108	49,448	74,701
U.S. Treasury securities	2,645	20,433	-7,643	20,239	29,618	-2,534	18,826	36,857	24,063	33,811	99,081
U.S. securities other than U.S. Treasury securities	5,457	50,962	42,120	26,353	38,767	1,592	35,144	29,867	79,864	58,625	94,576
U.S. liabilities to unaffiliated foreigners reported by U.S. nonbanking concerns	6,852	9,851	18,363	32,893	22,086	45,133	-3,115	13,573	10,489	-4,324	27,578
U.S. liabilities reported by U.S. banks, n.i.e. [8]	10,743	41,045	86,537	63,744	51,780	-3,824	3,994	15,461	20,859	114,396	19,906
Allocations of special drawing rights.	**1,152**	(X)	(X)	(X)	(X)	(X)	(X)	(X)	(X)	(X)	(X)
Statistical discrepancy	25,386	22,950	-4,028	-13,095	54,094	44,480	-28,936	-26,399	35,985	-14,269	6,684
Balance on merchandise trade	-25,500	-122,173	-159,557	-126,959	-115,245	-109,030	-74,068	-96,106	-132,618	-166,099	-174,469
Balance on services	6,093	294	6,861	11,635	23,853	29,037	44,664	56,626	57,777	59,887	63,052
Balance on investment income	30,073	20,590	9,465	13,264	13,659	20,725	1,511	10,079	9,000	-9,272	-11,402
Balance on goods, services, and income	10,666	-101,290	-143,231	-102,060	-77,733	-59,268	-14,293	-29,402	-65,841	-115,484	-122,819
Unilateral transfers, net	-8,349	-22,954	-23,107	-25,023	-26,106	-33,393	6,869	-32,148	-34,084	-35,761	-30,095
Balance on current account	2,317	-124,243	-166,338	-127,083	-103,839	-92,661	-7,424	-61,549	-99,925	-151,245	-152,914

- Represents zero. X Not applicable. [1] Excludes transfers of goods and services under U.S. military grant programs. [2] Excludes exports of goods under U.S. military agency sales contracts identified in Bureau of the Census export documents, excludes imports of goods under direct defense expenditures identified in Census import documents, and reflects various other adjustments (for valuation, coverage, and timing) of Census statistics to a balance of payments basis. [3] Includes other end-use items, not shown separately. [4] Includes engines. [5] Excludes engines. [6] Break in series due to inclusion of new data. [7] Includes sales of foreign obligations to foreigners. [8] Not included elsewhere. Major revisions to these data appear in the July 1996 issue of the Survey of Current Business.

See Technical Note in Survey of Current Business, June 1979.

Source: U.S. Bureau of Economic Analysis, Survey of Current Business, June 1995 and April 1996 issues.

No. 1284. U.S. Balances on International Transactions, by Area and Selected Country: 1993 to 1995

[In millions of dollars. Minus sign (-) indicates debits]

AREA OR COUNTRY	1993, BALANCE ON—			1994, BALANCE ON—			1995, BALANCE ON—		
	Merchandise trade [1]	Goods, services, and income	Current account	Merchandise trade [1]	Goods, services, and income	Current account	Merchandise trade [1]	Goods, services, and income	Current account
All areas	-132,618	-65,841	-99,925	-166,099	-115,484	-151,245	-174,469	-122,820	-152,915
Western Europe	-9,692	-8,724	-8,163	-17,563	-27,616	-26,785	-15,581	-25,468	-24,133
European Economic	-7,248	-8,863	-6,923	-11,957	-22,748	-21,205	-13,005	-23,100	-21,225
United Kingdom	4,164	-6,762	-5,287	1,111	-16,956	-15,676	1,278	-26,246	-24,968
Other Western Europe	-12,481	-5,251	-4,297	-13,843	-9,339	-8,518	-11,814	-871	190
Eastern Europe	2,658	2,829	359	-482	-545	-4,033	-1,276	-1,019	-3,844
Canada	-12,155	677	362	-16,246	-5,358	-5,724	-20,281	-7,068	-7,450
Latin America, other Western Hemisphere	3,023	16,919	8,066	3,505	16,765	8,451	-8,748	603	-7,779
Australia	4,813	9,725	9,656	6,384	11,939	11,854	7,100	12,578	12,481
Japan [2]	-60,544	-54,263	-54,441	-67,318	-64,992	-65,144	-60,600	-59,362	-59,499
Other Asia and Africa	-60,945	-43,762	-57,976	-74,468	-57,592	-71,763	-75,083	-55,465	-65,419
International and unallocated	224	10,758	2,212	89	11,916	1,900	-	12,381	2,728

- Represets or rounds to zero. [1] Adjusted to balance of payments basis; excludes exports under U.S. military sales contracts and imports under direct defense expenditures. [2] Includes Ryukyu Islands.
Source: U.S. Bureau of Economic Analysis, *Survey of Current Business,* June 1995 and April 1996. Major revisions to these data appear in the July 1996 issue of the *Survey of Current Business.*

No. 1285. Private Services Transaction, by Type of Service and Country: 1990 to 1994

[In millions of dollars]

TYPE OF SERVICE AND COUNTRY	EXPORTS				IMPORTS			
	1990	1992	1993	1994	1990	1992	1993	1994
Total private services	137,219	166,062	174,207	185,419	99,333	105,855	115,446	125,902
Travel	43,007	54,742	57,875	60,406	37,349	38,552	40,713	43,562
Overseas	30,806	40,864	45,298	49,225	28,929	29,838	31,859	34,585
Canada	7,093	8,182	7,458	6,251	3,541	3,554	3,692	3,912
Mexico	5,108	5,696	5,119	4,930	4,879	5,160	5,162	5,065
Passenger fares	15,298	16,618	16,611	17,477	10,531	10,556	11,313	12,696
Other transportation	22,745	23,691	23,983	26,078	25,168	25,459	26,558	28,373
Freight	8,063	8,450	8,755	9,836	14,353	13,784	14,846	16,444
Port services	13,662	14,164	14,222	15,213	9,920	10,762	10,817	11,011
Other	1,020	1,077	1,005	1,029	895	914	895	919
Royalties and license fees	16,634	20,015	20,637	22,436	3,135	5,074	4,863	5,666
Other private services	39,535	50,997	55,101	59,022	23,150	26,214	31,999	35,605
Affiliated services	13,622	16,295	16,191	17,215	9,118	9,690	10,606	11,602
Unaffilated services	25,913	34,701	38,910	41,807	14,003	16,524	21,395	24,003
Education	5,126	6,186	6,732	7,140	658	719	753	791
Financial services	4,417	5,484	6,606	6,962	2,475	3,520	5,558	6,835
Insurance, net	572	1,222	1,380	1,640	1,910	1,324	3,107	3,405
Telecommunications	2,735	2,885	2,784	2,757	5,583	6,052	6,193	6,828
Business, professional, and technical services	6,951	11,994	13,294	14,813	1,891	3,295	4,046	4,227
Advertising	130	315	338	399	243	450	644	736
Computer and data processing services	1,031	1,902	2,306	2,546	44	141	304	386
Data base and other information services	283	641	694	823	54	72	88	94
Research, development, and testing services	384	611	443	537	210	225	247	281
Management, consulting, and public relations services	354	728	849	986	135	243	280	283
Legal services	451	1,358	1,446	1,558	111	311	317	428
Construction, engineering, architectural, and mining services	867	1,935	2,358	2,704	170	261	336	296
Other services	947	1,549	1,586	1,631	135	830	849	881
Canada	16,145	18,205	17,777	17,258	9,282	9,936	10,617	11,669
Europe	48,644	61,561	63,676	66,739	39,849	41,951	47,363	51,662
Belgium-Luxembourg	1,795	2,300	2,222	2,453	1,023	933	975	1,113
France	5,565	7,145	6,931	6,728	4,168	4,681	4,965	5,535
Germany [2]	7,478	10,924	11,350	11,559	6,824	6,560	7,112	7,549
Italy	3,319	4,506	4,136	4,344	3,474	3,560	3,549	3,809
Netherlands	3,278	3,710	4,169	5,012	1,937	2,428	2,109	2,436
United Kingdom	13,027	16,167	17,495	17,480	11,567	11,987	15,744	16,929
Other	(NA)	8,348	8,905	10,221	(NA)	6,515	7,229	8,208
Other Western Europe	(NA)	(NA)	(NA)	(NA)	(NA)	(NA)	(NA)	(NA)
Eastern Europe	1,003	1,244	1,703	2,023	799	1,412	1,511	1,891
Latin America and other Western Hemisphere	21,226	25,547	27,993	30,314	19,401	21,144	21,924	23,847
Mexico	7,387	8,676	8,555	8,909	7,386	8,062	8,319	8,380
Venezuela	1,284	1,992	2,512	2,189	669	638	730	760
Other	(NA)	6,563	7,117	7,599	(NA)	4,099	3,932	4,423
Other countries	45,883	56,059	59,979	66,499	28,095	30,515	33,853	37,027
Int'l organizations and unallocated	5,325	4,690	4,782	4,609	2,708	2,310	1,690	1,700

NA Not available.
Source: U.S. Bureau of Economic Analysis, Survey of Current Business, September 1995. Major revisions to these data appear in the October 1996 issue of the *Survey of Current Business.*

No. 1286. International Investment Position: 1980 to 1994

[**In millions of dollars.** Estimates for end of year; subject to considerable error due to nature of basic data. See *Historical Statistics, Colonial Times to 1970*, series U 26-39, for similar data]

TYPE OF INVESTMENT	1980	1985	1989	1990	1991	1992	1993	1994
U.S. net international investment position:								
Current cost	392,547	132,845	-250,341	-251,112	-355,070	-515,734	-545,312	-680,824
Market value	(NA)	135,767	-77,107	-211,670	-349,035	-570,571	-453,861	-583,990
U.S. assets abroad:								
Current cost	936,275	1,303,965	1,979,348	2,066,383	2,131,715	2,142,172	2,393,577	2,477,749
Market value	(NA)	1,295,557	2,251,399	2,178,114	2,314,945	2,282,948	2,708,685	2,765,170
U.S. official reserve assets	171,412	117,930	168,714	174,664	159,223	147,435	164,945	163,394
Gold	155,816	85,834	105,164	102,406	92,561	87,168	102,556	100,110
Special drawing rights	2,610	7,293	9,951	10,989	11,240	8,503	9,039	10,039
Reserve position in IMF	2,852	11,947	9,048	9,076	9,488	11,759	11,818	12,030
Foreign currencies	10,134	12,856	44,551	52,193	45,934	40,005	41,532	41,215
U.S. Government assets, other . .	63,865	87,752	84,489	81,993	79,063	80,723	81,001	81,306
U.S. loans and other long-term assets	62,023	85,814	83,903	81,365	77,417	79,010	79,021	79,161
U.S. foreign currency holdings and short-term assets	1,842	1,938	586	628	1,646	1,713	1,980	2,145
U.S. private assets:								
Current cost	700,998	1,098,283	1,726,145	1,809,726	1,893,429	1,914,014	2,147,631	2,233,049
Market value	(NA)	1,089,875	1,998,196	1,921,457	2,076,659	2,054,790	2,462,739	2,520,470
Direct investments abroad:								
Current cost	396,249	394,760	560,409	620,031	644,307	657,854	706,636	760,980
Market value	(NA)	386,352	832,460	731,762	827,537	798,630	1,021,744	1,048,401
Foreign securities	62,454	114,288	217,612	228,693	302,425	333,834	542,867	538,605
U.S. claims on unaffiliated foreigners [1]	38,429	141,872	234,307	265,315	256,295	254,303	250,434	286,772
U.S. claims reported by U.S. banks [2]	203,866	447,363	713,817	695,687	690,402	668,023	647,694	646,692
Foreign assets in the U.S.								
Current cost	543,728	1,171,120	2,229,689	2,317,495	2,486,785	2,657,906	2,938,889	3,158,573
Market value	(NA)	1,159,790	2,328,506	2,389,784	2,663,980	2,853,519	3,162,546	3,349,160
Foreign official assets in the U.S.	176,062	202,482	341,829	375,339	401,678	442,742	516,695	545,260
U.S. Government securities . . .	118,189	145,063	263,725	295,005	315,932	335,695	388,312	414,930
Other U.S. Government liabilities	13,367	15,803	15,374	17,243	18,610	20,790	22,496	24,707
U.S. liabilities reported by U.S. banks [2]	30,381	26,734	36,495	39,880	38,396	54,967	69,808	72,731
Other foreign official assets	14,125	14,882	26,265	23,211	28,740	31,290	36,079	32,892
Other foreign assets in the U.S:								
Current cost	367,666	968,638	1,887,830	1,942,156	2,085,107	2,215,164	2,422,194	2,613,313
Market value	(NA)	957,308	1,986,647	2,014,445	2,262,302	2,410,777	2,645,851	2,803,900
Direct investments:								
Current cost	125,944	231,326	435,917	467,312	491,942	498,599	535,805	580,503
Market value	(NA)	219,996	534,734	539,601	669,137	694,212	759,462	771,090
U.S. securities other than U.S. Treasury securities	74,114	207,868	482,864	467,437	559,180	620,033	732,157	755,728
U.S. liabilities to unaffiliated foreigners [1]	30,426	86,993	167,093	213,406	208,908	220,666	229,038	225,149
U.S. liabilities reported by U.S. banks [2]	121,069	354,497	635,467	631,597	635,571	651,031	671,890	786,286
U.S. Treasury securities	16,113	87,954	166,489	162,404	189,506	224,835	253,304	265,647

NA Not available.   [1] Reported by U.S. nonbanking concerns.   [2] Not included elsewhere.

Source: U.S. Bureau of Economic Analysis, *Survey of Current Business*, June 1995. Major revisions to these data appear in the July 1996 issue of the *Survey of Current Business*.

No. 1287. U.S. Reserve Assets: 1980 to 1995

[**In billions of dollars.** As of **end of year**, except as indicated]

TYPE	1980	1985	1987	1988	1989	1990	1991	1992	1993	1994	1995
Total	26.8	43.2	45.8	47.8	74.6	83.3	77.7	71.3	73.4	74.3	85.8
Gold stock [1]	11.2	11.1	11.1	11.1	11.1	11.1	11.1	11.1	11.1	11.1	11.1
Special drawing rights	2.6	7.3	10.3	9.6	10.0	11.0	11.2	8.5	9.0	10.0	11.0
Foreign currencies	10.1	12.9	13.1	17.4	44.6	52.2	45.9	40.0	41.5	41.2	49.1
Reserve position in IMF [2]	2.9	11.9	11.3	9.7	9.0	9.1	9.5	11.8	11.8	12.0	14.6

[1] Includes gold in Exchange Stabilization Fund; excludes gold held under earmark at Federal Reserve banks for foreign and international accounts. Beginning 1975, gold assets were valued at $42.22 pursuant to the amending of Section 2 of the Par Value Modification Act, PL-93-110, approved September 21, 1973.   [2] International Monetary Fund.

Source: Board of Governors of the Federal Reserve System, *Federal Reserve Bulletin*, monthly; and Department of the Treasury, *Treasury Bulletin*, monthly.

No. 1288. Foreign Direct Investment Position in the U.S. on a Historical Cost Basis— Value, by Area and Industry: 1980 to 1994

[In millions of dollars. Book value at year end. Covers U.S. firms, including real estate investments in which foreign interest or ownership was 10 percent or more. Minus sign (-) indicates a negative position. See also *Historical Statistics, Colonial Times to 1970*, series U 47-74]

AREA AND INDUSTRY	1980	1985	1987	1988	1989	1990	1991	1992	1993	1994, prel.
All areas [1]	83,046	184,615	263,394	314,754	368,924	394,911	419,108	427,566	464,110	504,401
Petroleum	12,200	28,270	37,815	36,006	40,345	42,882	40,051	37,555	31,740	34,048
Manufacturing	32,993	59,584	93,865	122,582	150,949	152,805	157,115	158,873	166,397	184,484
Finance and insurance	12,027	27,429	39,455	44,010	59,597	35,482	44,748	48,780	74,733	76,048
Trade, wholesale and retail . .	15,210	35,873	45,399	53,590	54,005	60,152	65,334	67,888	72,808	79,542
Canada	12,162	17,131	24,684	26,566	30,370	29,544	36,834	37,843	40,143	43,223
Petroleum	1,817	1,589	1,088	1,181	1,141	1,373	2,468	2,443	2,455	2,585
Manufacturing	5,227	4,607	8,085	9,730	9,766	9,201	15,716	15,598	15,306	16,911
Finance and insurance. . . .	1,612	4,008	5,797	5,769	7,356	6,033	7,354	7,235	8,168	8,496
Europe	54,688	121,413	181,006	208,942	239,190	247,320	256,053	255,570	287,084	312,876
Petroleum	10,137	25,636	35,700	33,499	32,649	34,284	31,436	29,167	24,396	25,818
Manufacturing	21,953	45,841	74,300	95,641	118,129	115,831	114,248	115,215	124,454	136,804
Finance and insurance. . . .	8,673	17,022	26,336	27,121	33,157	21,310	27,715	28,550	46,895	45,194
United Kingdom	14,105	43,555	75,519	95,698	103,458	98,676	100,085	90,931	102,351	113,504
Petroleum	-257	12,155	17,950	19,522	16,666	15,900	14,068	11,080	9,963	10,906
Manufacturing.	6,159	11,687	30,372	41,708	50,166	42,365	41,924	40,818	42,783	48,190
Finance and insurance . .	3,350	6,483	9,801	11,256	12,790	11,609	13,391	12,436	19,927	16,343
Netherlands	19,140	37,056	46,636	48,128	56,734	64,671	63,113	69,191	72,172	70,645
Petroleum	9,265	11,481	(D)	9,045	10,061	13,267	12,444	11,590	12,067	12,770
Manufacturing	4,777	13,351	15,615	17,843	23,090	24,734	19,540	22,793	23,286	19,881
Switzerland	5,070	10,568	13,772	14,372	18,746	17,674	18,482	19,048	22,161	25,330
Manufacturing.	3,116	6,881	6,921	7,613	11,798	10,651	10,222	10,280	11,337	13,111
Finance and insurance . .	1,033	5,425	3,211	3,506	4,492	4,833	4,806	4,460	5,497	6,923
Germany [2].	7,596	14,816	21,905	25,250	28,386	28,232	29,335	29,768	34,849	39,550
Manufacturing.	3,875	6,015	10,298	13,980	15,560	15,718	15,659	15,765	17,903	21,321
Finance and insurance . .	1,248	(D)	3,442	2,683	3,139	1,652	1,413	2,073	4,893	5,508
Other Europe [3].	8,777	15,417	23,174	25,494	31,866	38,067	45,038	46,632	55,551	63,847
Petroleum	991	(D)	(D)	4,580	4,786	4,835	4,653	5,768	1,959	1,604
Manufacturing	4,026	7,907	11,094	14,497	17,515	22,363	26,903	25,559	29,145	34,301
Finance and insurance . .	1,193	(D)	2,189	406	2,519	-1,817	-589	-298	5,433	5,398
Japan	4,723	19,313	34,421	51,126	67,268	83,091	95,142	99,628	99,208	103,120
Other areas	11,472	26,758	23,283	28,120	32,096	34,956	31,079	34,525	37,675	45,182

[2] D Withheld to avoid disclosure of data of individual companies.   [1] Area totals include industries not shown separately.
[2] For 1980 to 1989, includes only the Federal Republic of Germany. For 1990 to 1994, also includes the former German Democratic Republic (GDR). This change has no effect on the data because, prior to 1990, there were no U.S. affiliates of the former GDR.
[3] Direct investments in 1994 (in millions of dollars): Belgium and Luxembourg, 5,673; France, 33,496; Italy, 2,437; and Sweden, 8,077. France, 33,496; Italy, 2,437; and Sweden, 9,112.
Source: U.S. Bureau of Economic Analysis, *Survey of Current Business*, August 1995, and earlier issues.

No. 1289. U.S. Affiliates of Foreign Companies—Assets, Sales, Employment, Land, Exports, and Imports: 1993

[A U.S. affiliate is a U.S. business enterprise in which one foreign owner (individual, branch, partnership, association, trust, corporation, or government) has a direct or indirect voting interest of 10 percent or more. Universe estimates based on a sample survey of nonbank affiliates with assets, sales, or net income of $10 million or more]

INDUSTRY	Total assets (mil. dol.)	Sales (mil. dol.) [1]	Employment (1,000) [2]	Employee compensation (mil. dol.)	GROSS BOOK VALUE (mil. dol.) Plant and equipment [3]	GROSS BOOK VALUE (mil. dol.) Land	Land owned (1,000 acres)	Merchandise exports[4] (mil. dol.)	Merchandise imports[4] (mil. dol.)
Total.	2,049,263	1,302,131	4,722.3	190,304	638,907	65,065	13,844	105,088	198,469
Petroleum	98,243	115,426	109.2	6,223	101,902	2,726	467	3,349	17,433
Manufacturing.	508,827	457,532	2,235.5	101,551	268,505	17,293	5,619	42,305	58,250
Chemicals and allied products	171,879	129,931	508.3	27,182	105,245	9,910	976	12,958	12,775
Wholesale trade [5]	195,215	382,826	445.0	20,044	57,384	2,878	417	55,477	118,071
Motor vehicles and auto parts and supplies	65,427	105,621	74.2	4,069	28,559	829	27	8,032	38,328
Farm-product raw materials.	8,115	36,473	20.0	648	2,491	91	37	14,513	1,645
Retail trade	46,322	89,077	769.9	13,838	23,688	2,606	77	1,254	3,164
Finance, except banking. . .	455,486	29,630	46.9	5,490	6,380	782	64	(D)	1
Insurance	422,080	84,646	153.2	7,946	21,128	1,324	86	-	-
Real estate	106,901	15,768	38.6	1,184	69,386	23,718	2,230	(D)	3
Services	123,019	55,408	536.5	17,115	44,667	7,735	207	717	388
Other	93,170	71,818	387.5	16,915	45,867	6,002	4,678	1,949	1,159

- Represents zero.   [1] Excludes returns, discounts, allowances, and sales and excise taxes. [2] Average number of full-time and part-time employees.   [3] Includes mineral rights and minor amounts of property other than land.   [4] F.a.s. value at port of exportation.   [5] includes industries not shown separately.
Source: U.S. Bureau of Economic Analysis, *Survey of Current Business*, May 1995; and *Foreign Direct Investment in the United States, Operations of U.S. Affiliates of Foreign Companies*, Preliminary 1993 Estimates and Revised 1992 Estimates.

No. 1290. Foreign Direct Investment in the United States—Gross Book Value and Employment of U.S. Affiliates of Foreign Companies, by State: 1981 to 1993

[A U.S. affiliate is a U.S. business enterprise in which one foreign owner (individual, branch, partnership, association, trust corporation, or government) has a direct or indirect voting interest of 10 percent or more. Universe estimates based on a sample survey of nonbank affiliates with assets, sales, or net income of $10 million or more]

DIVISION, STATE, AND OTHER AREA	GROSS BOOK VALUE OF PROPERTY, PLANT, AND EQUIPMENT (mil. dol.)				TOTAL EMPLOYMENT			1993	
	1981	1990	1992	1993	1981 (1,000)	1990 (1,000)	1992 (1,000)	Total (1,000)	Percent of all businesses
Total	187,956	578,355	660,826	703,972	2,416.6	4,734.5	4,715.4	4,722.3	(X)
United States	178,003	552,902	631,956	672,604	2,402.3	4,704.4	4,680.9	4,681.7	4.9
New England	5,686	19,524	23,465	25,212	143.9	280.6	269.2	270.7	(NA)
Maine	1,637	2,080	2,398	2,504	17.7	26.6	24.1	24.4	5.6
New Hampshire	409	1,446	1,852	2,042	13.9	25.9	27.9	31.2	7.1
Vermont	315	631	833	891	6.0	7.7	7.5	7.1	3.2
Massachusetts	1,712	8,890	9,815	10,759	55.6	131.2	114.3	116.7	4.6
Rhode Island	359	1,120	1,820	2,021	9.9	13.3	12.9	13.9	3.6
Connecticut	1,254	5,357	6,747	6,995	40.8	75.9	82.5	77.4	5.7
Middle Atlantic	20,216	71,619	85,982	93,388	480.2	796.1	773.0	798.9	(NA)
New York	7,892	36,424	44,312	47,839	210.3	347.5	340.8	350.0	5.3
New Jersey	6,552	18,608	21,890	23,624	134.9	227.0	216.3	213.0	7.1
Pennsylvania	5,772	16,587	19,780	21,925	135.0	221.6	215.9	235.9	5.2
East North Central	19,215	74,495	89,000	94,471	388.6	812.8	811.8	788.9	(NA)
Ohio	5,178	20,549	24,702	25,279	99.9	219.1	211.4	205.6	4.8
Indiana	1,883	13,426	14,905	15,848	47.0	126.9	127.2	122.6	5.3
Illinois	5,646	23,420	27,958	30,106	113.6	245.8	247.2	235.8	5.0
Michigan	4,188	12,012	15,115	16,404	65.9	139.6	143.8	148.6	4.3
Wisconsin	2,320	5,088	6,320	6,834	62.2	81.4	82.2	76.3	3.6
West North Central	8,400	28,155	23,902	24,304	112.2	248.4	256.1	244.3	(NA)
Minnesota	2,902	11,972	8,310	8,180	33.0	89.8	92.3	84.9	4.4
Iowa	1,032	2,712	3,422	3,813	21.6	32.8	33.3	30.9	2.8
Missouri	1,894	5,757	6,666	6,678	32.6	73.7	77.6	74.7	3.6
North Dakota	1,155	1,251	1,229	1,231	3.5	3.1	4.6	4.6	2.0
South Dakota	299	553	635	647	1.3	4.5	4.8	4.8	1.9
Nebraska	241	776	926	1,023	5.6	14.9	16.3	16.0	2.5
Kansas	877	5,134	2,714	2,732	14.6	29.6	27.2	28.4	3.0
South Atlantic	33,271	94,766	111,517	118,766	476.0	934.7	931.4	956.0	(NA)
Delaware	1,869	5,818	6,210	6,457	36.0	43.1	35.8	32.9	10.7
Maryland	2,103	5,713	6,165	6,481	45.1	79.6	73.5	74.4	4.3
District of Columbia	547	3,869	4,651	4,662	3.2	11.4	9.9	9.9	2.4
Virginia	3,046	10,702	12,987	14,251	49.8	113.3	122.1	124.9	5.2
West Virginia	3,992	7,975	8,733	8,966	35.4	34.9	34.6	34.8	6.7
North Carolina	5,543	15,234	19,047	21,335	89.0	181.0	191.4	209.0	7.5
South Carolina	5,318	10,067	12,028	13,122	65.1	104.7	111.7	105.1	8.1
Georgia	4,558	16,729	19,649	20,154	78.5	161.0	156.4	163.5	6.2
Florida	6,295	18,659	22,247	23,338	73.9	205.7	196.0	201.5	4.1
East South Central	9,802	29,798	37,784	41,726	121.7	261.9	280.5	282.1	(NA)
Kentucky	1,848	9,229	12,018	13,749	26.0	65.7	71.2	74.4	5.7
Tennessee	3,747	10,280	13,235	14,816	57.4	116.9	124.2	123.6	6.1
Alabama	2,776	7,300	9,191	9,557	27.0	55.7	61.7	60.3	4.3
Mississippi	1,431	2,989	3,340	3,604	11.3	23.6	23.4	23.8	2.9
West South Central	34,651	82,904	89,000	95,663	268.5	433.7	451.1	437.0	(NA)
Arkansas	636	2,344	2,794	3,065	17.5	29.2	30.8	29.9	3.5
Louisiana	7,872	17,432	21,033	22,013	47.0	61.4	62.1	59.3	4.4
Oklahoma	2,760	6,049	5,781	5,906	25.0	43.6	42.9	38.9	3.9
Texas	23,383	57,079	59,432	64,679	179.0	299.5	315.3	308.9	4.9
Mountain	12,353	33,197	34,529	36,921	97.9	197.1	198.3	194.0	(NA)
Montana	1,235	2,181	2,150	2,536	3.0	5.1	5.1	5.2	2.0
Idaho	312	776	810	834	3.8	11.7	13.7	11.2	3.1
Wyoming	2,144	2,782	3,014	3,118	4.2	5.8	5.6	6.1	3.9
Colorado	2,369	6,544	6,916	7,272	24.7	56.3	61.5	59.8	4.2
New Mexico	997	4,312	4,169	4,882	7.9	17.4	13.6	16.1	3.3
Arizona	2,949	7,234	6,456	6,684	30.6	57.1	52.7	51.2	3.8
Utah	1,791	3,918	4,362	4,637	16.8	21.0	22.9	23.1	3.4
Nevada	556	5,450	6,652	6,958	6.9	22.7	23.2	21.3	3.5
Pacific	34,409	118,445	136,738	142,151	313.3	738.7	708.4	709.5	(NA)
Washington	2,430	7,985	10,155	10,321	26.0	77.5	80.2	76.4	4.0
Oregon	845	3,427	4,741	4,633	13.1	39.1	41.9	42.1	3.8
California	20,404	75,768	85,661	86,462	248.4	555.9	522.7	529.1	5.0
Alaska	(D)	19,435	20,727	24,696	8.8	13.2	9.8	9.3	5.1
Hawaii	(D)	11,830	15,454	16,039	17.0	53.0	53.8	52.6	11.8
Puerto Rico	413	1,499	2,047	2,249	9.5	16.1	19.8	27.2	(X)
Other territories and offshore	7,496	18,484	17,502	17,404	3.1	9.0	10.0	10.5	(X)
Foreign	2,044	5,470	9,321	11,715	1.6	5.0	5.2	2.9	(X)

D Withheld to avoid disclosure of data of individual companies.   NA Not available.   X Not applicable.

Source: U.S. Bureau of Economic Analysis, *Survey of Current Business*, May 1995, and *Foreign Direct Investment in the United States, Operations of U.S. Affiliates of Foreign Companies*, annual; and *Foreign Direct Investment in the United States, 1992 Benchmark Survey.*

No. 1291. U.S. Businesses Acquired or Established by Foreign Direct Investors— Investment Outlays, by Industry of U.S. Business Enterprise and Country of Ultimate Beneficial Owner: 1988 to 1994

[In millions of dollars. Foreign direct investment is the ownership or control, directly or indirectly, by one foreign individual branch, partnership, association, trust, corporation, or government of 10 percent or more of the voting securities of a U.S. business enterprise or an equivalent interest in an unincorporated one. Data represent number and full cost of acquisitions of existing U.S. business enterprises, including business segments or operating units of existing U.S. business enterprises and establishments of new enterprises. Investments may be made by the foreign direct investor itself, or indirectly by an existing U.S. affiliate of the foreign direct investor. Covers investments in U.S. business enterprises with assets of over $1 million, or ownership of 200 acres of U.S. land]

INDUSTRY AND COUNTRY	1988	1989	1990	1991	1992	1993	1994, prel.
Total	72,692	71,163	65,932	25,538	15,333	26,229	47,244
INDUSTRY							
Petroleum	4,740	1,189	1,141	702	463	882	452
Manufacturing	36,136	35,958	23,898	11,461	6,014	11,090	23,889
Wholesale trade	2,454	2,634	1,676	623	698	837	2,109
Retail trade	8,022	1,861	1,250	1,605	256	1,495	1,732
Banking [1]	1,800	349	897	482	529	958	2,313
Finance, except banking [1]	972	4,186	2,121	2,199	797	1,599	635
Insurance	5,855	1,901	2,093	2,102	291	1,105	277
Real estate	3,518	6,438	7,771	3,823	2,161	1,883	1,963
Services	5,597	10,058	19,369	2,256	2,023	4,162	7,995
Other [2]	3,597	6,587	5,716	284	2,101	2,218	5,879
COUNTRY							
Canada	11,360	4,403	3,430	3,454	1,351	3,797	3,640
Europe	37,173	40,724	36,011	13,994	8,344	16,845	34,475
France	4,199	3,469	10,217	4,976	406	1,249	1,335
Germany [3]	2,090	2,435	2,363	1,922	1,964	2,841	3,578
Netherlands	2,214	3,629	2,247	1,661	1,331	2,074	1,346
Switzerland	2,063	4,923	3,905	1,327	1,259	804	5,669
United Kingdom	22,559	23,047	13,096	2,169	2,255	8,238	18,987
Other Europe	4,048	3,221	4,183	1,939	1,129	1,639	3,560
Latin America and other Western Hemisphere	(D)	1,084	796	375	1,438	874	1,507
South and Central America	(D)	650	399	108	1,152	527	1,142
Other Western Hemisphere	187	434	397	267	286	347	365
Africa	296	(D)	(D)	(D)	(D)	(D)	(D)
Middle East	1,613	243	472	1,006	238	1,308	(D)
Asia and Pacific	21,819	24,530	23,170	6,560	3,716	3,004	4,448
Australia	4,556	4,574	1,412	251	164	129	1,308
Japan	16,188	17,410	19,933	5,357	2,921	2,065	2,044
Other Asia and Pacific	1,075	2,546	1,825	952	631	810	1,096

D Suppressed to avoid disclosure of data of individual companies.   [1] Prior to 1992, "banking" excludes, and "finance, except banking" includes, savings institutions and credit unions. Beginning with 1992, savings institutions and credit unions have been reclassified from "finance, except banking" to "banking".   [2] For investments in which more than one investor participated, each investor and each investor's outlays are classified by country of each ultimate beneficial owner.   [3] Prior to 1990, this line includes data only for the Federal Republic of Germany. Beginning in 1990, this line also includes the former German Democratic Republic (GDR). This change has no effect on the data because, prior to 1991, there were no U.S. affiliates of the former GDR.

Source: U.S. Bureau of Economic Analysis, Survey of Current Business, May 1995.

No. 1292. U.S. Businesses Acquired by Foreign Direct Investors—Assets, Sales, and Employment, by Industry of U.S. Business Enterprise: 1993 and 1994

[See headnote, table 1291. Minus sign (-) indicates loss]

INDUSTRY	1993					1994, prel.				
	Total assets (mil. dol.)	Sales (mil. dol.)	Net income (mil. dol.)	Employment (1,000)	Acres of land owned (1,000)	Total assets (mil. dol.)	Sales (mil. dol.)	Net income (mil. dol.)	Employment (1,000)	Acres of land owned (1,000)
Total	104,367	52,882	-1,934	289	300	75,937	59,889	1,241	310	1,229
Petroleum	1,896	(D)	(D)	(D)	(D)	1,253	(D)	4	(D)	1
Manufacturing	15,194	14,066	(D)	81	27	25,605	23,885	391	113	(D)
Wholesale trade	1,050	(D)	31	6	1	2,520	3,867	(D)	7	(D)
Retail trade	(D)	(D)	29	(D)	(D)	3,188	8,207	(D)	(D)	1
Banking	10,295	811	-43	(D)	(D)	14,286	(D)	(D)	(D)	(D)
Finance, except banking .	19,674	1,073	(D)	3	(D)	1,926	234	2	(D)	-
Insurance	11,220	(D)	(D)	(D)	(D)	1,303	(D)	5	(D)	(D)
Real estate	(D)	225	14	(Z)	12	3,420	(D)	20	(D)	14
Services	(D)	13,292	17	71	4	5,907	3,351	-49	31	6
Other [1]	10,171	9,123	(D)	62	(D)	16,527	(D)	608	69	122

- Represents or rounds to zero.   D Withheld to avoid disclosure of data of individual companies.   Z Less than 500.
[1] Includes agriculture, forestry, and fishing; mining; construction; transportation; and communication and public utilities.

Source: U.S. Bureau of Economic Analysis, Survey of Current Business, May 1995; and unpublished data.

No. 1293. U.S. Direct Investment Position Abroad, by Country: 1980 to 1994

[In millions of dollars. Direct investments represent private enterprises in one country owned or controlled by investors in another country or in the management of which foreign investors have an important role. Negative position occurs when U.S. parent company's liabilities to the foreign affiliate are greater than its equity in, and loans to the foreign affiliate. See Historical Statistics, Colonial Times to 1970, series U 41-46]

COUNTRY	1980	1990	1991	1992	1993	1994 Total [1]	1994 Manu-facturing	1994 Petro-leum	1994 Finance [2]
All countries	215,375	430,521	467,844	502,063	559,733	612,109	220,328	65,711	175,045
Canada	45,119	69,508	70,711	68,690	69,612	72,808	35,037	8,553	12,159
Europe [3]	96,287	214,739	235,163	248,744	280,506	300,177	108,655	25,344	94,004
Austria	524	1,113	1,268	1,371	1,333	1,611	834	192	(D)
Belgium	6,259	9,464	10,611	11,381	11,488	13,966	7,108	318	3,175
Denmark	1,266	1,726	1,940	1,676	1,740	1,993	298	(D)	380
Finland	188	544	386	343	419	602	217	(D)	(D)
France	9,347	19,164	21,569	25,157	24,281	27,894	14,521	1,177	4,724
Germany [4]	15,415	27,609	32,411	33,003	36,879	39,886	22,131	2,020	6,716
Greece	347	282	306	372	410	446	124	(D)	32
Ireland	2,319	5,894	6,471	7,607	9,224	10,337	5,766	(D)	3,729
Italy	5,397	14,063	15,085	13,015	12,750	14,998	8,582	422	2,263
Luxembourg	652	1,697	1,734	2,031	5,376	5,730	1,374	24	3,956
Netherlands	8,039	19,120	20,293	20,700	20,945	24,150	8,908	1,484	7,959
Norway	1,679	4,209	4,318	3,825	3,768	4,286	592	3,089	174
Portugal	257	897	1,034	1,290	1,260	1,458	438	(D)	126
Spain	2,678	7,868	8,088	8,757	6,734	8,048	4,512	135	665
Sweden	1,474	1,787	2,323	1,881	2,428	2,719	1,279	48	778
Switzerland	11,280	25,099	25,682	28,698	32,782	34,485	2,858	726	15,996
Turkey	207	522	545	732	997	1,084	693	(D)	(Z)
United Kingdom	28,460	72,707	79,819	85,176	104,313	102,244	27,247	14,320	42,494
Latin America	39,581	71,413	77,677	91,308	101,602	114,986	31,933	6,264	53,615
South America [3]	16,342	22,933	24,607	28,760	31,457	37,972	19,331	4,146	5,057
Argentina	2,540	2,531	2,831	3,327	4,331	5,666	2,467	773	756
Brazil	7,704	14,384	14,997	16,313	16,822	18,977	13,681	768	2,258
Chile	536	1,896	2,069	2,544	2,847	4,457	376	(D)	1,590
Colombia	1,012	1,677	1,876	3,053	3,075	3,442	994	1,318	(D)
Ecuador	322	280	321	295	549	728	129	546	-
Peru	1,665	599	492	620	628	836	49	(D)	-
Venezuela	1,908	1,087	1,427	1,972	2,419	2,978	1,536	212	85
Central America [3]	11,013	20,415	23,939	25,579	28,317	31,321	11,513	1,154	13,934
Costa Rica	303	251	417	274	315	584	355	(D)	(Z)
Guatemala	229	130	107	115	137	133	88	37	8
Honduras	288	262	255	239	213	198	174	(D)	24
Mexico	5,986	10,313	12,501	13,730	15,229	16,375	10,697	(D)	1,982
Panama	3,170	9,289	10,484	11,038	12,190	13,775	168	806	11,915
Other W. Hemisphere [3]	12,226	28,065	29,131	36,969	41,828	45,693	1,089	964	34,624
Bahamas, The	2,712	4,004	3,864	4,167	3,564	3,260	7	56	1,214
Barbados	40	252	291	340	466	488	7	98	(D)
Bermuda	11,045	20,169	22,262	26,736	28,696	29,232	5	-161	28,014
Dominican Republic	316	529	661	779	1,047	1,196	206	(D)	3
Jamaica	407	625	763	892	1,053	1,272	161	(D)	5
Netherlands Antilles	-4,336	-4,501	-5,072	-1,989	32	2,007	(D)	(D)	2,048
Trinidad and Tobago	951	485	510	565	693	817	(D)	511	11
U.K. Islands, Caribbean . .	979	5,929	5,397	5,401	5,638	6,667	421	76	2,845
Other Africa [3]	6,128	3,650	4,427	4,469	5,473	5,472	1,274	2,185	647
Egypt	1,038	1,231	1,246	1,334	1,463	1,360	85	1,017	(D)
Nigeria	18	-401	529	301	544	402	81	(D)	(D)
South Africa	2,350	775	868	879	903	1,044	623	(D)	(D)
Middle East [3]	2,163	3,959	4,963	5,759	6,573	6,727	1,853	2,390	1,143
Israel	379	746	826	1,335	1,604	1,350	930	(D)	(D)
Saudi Arabia	1,037	1,899	2,303	2,351	2,618	2,717	920	157	(D)
United Arab Emirates	384	409	416	429	524	589	3	(D)	-28
Other Asia and Pacific [3]	22,963	64,716	72,218	79,963	92,561	108,403	41,577	18,917	12,956
Australia	7,654	15,110	16,072	16,928	19,054	20,504	8,002	2,942	2,056
China	-6	354	426	563	933	1,699	765	675	(D)
Hong Kong	2,078	6,055	6,656	8,693	10,177	11,986	1,902	552	3,013
India	398	372	415	484	611	818	308	(D)	(D)
Indonesia	1,314	3,207	3,826	4,384	4,770	5,015	181	4,341	(D)
Japan	6,225	22,599	25,403	26,591	31,184	37,027	15,844	6,124	6,400
Korea, Republic of	575	2,695	2,900	2,912	3,124	3,612	1,391	88	204
Malaysia	632	1,466	1,774	1,596	1,988	2,382	1,582	396	153
New Zealand	579	3,156	2,949	3,314	3,090	3,577	1,274	282	209
Philippines	1,259	1,355	1,395	1,666	1,945	2,374	1,167	(D)	(D)
Singapore	1,204	3,975	5,363	6,715	8,867	10,972	5,316	2,127	690
Taiwan	498	2,226	2,666	2,827	3,128	3,882	2,459	(D)	168
Thailand	361	1,790	2,025	2,594	2,947	3,762	1,341	1,185	63
International . . . . [5]	3,955	2,535	2,684	3,131	3,407	3,537	-	1,346	-
Addendum: OPEC [5]	6,090	7,145	9,729	10,692	11,762	12,586	2,724	6,022	1,085

- Represents zero.   D Suppressed to avoid disclosure of data of individual companies.   Z Less than $500,000.   [1] Includes industries not shown separately.   [2] Includes insurance.   [3] Includes countries not shown separately.   [4] Prior to 1990, West Germany only.   [5] OPEC=Organization of Petroleum Exporting Countries. Includes Algeria, Ecuador, Gabon, Indonesia, Iran, Iraq, Kuwait, Libya, Nigeria, Qatar, Ecuador was also a member and was included in this line.

Source: U.S. Bureau of Economic Analysis, Survey of Current Business, August 1995.

No. 1294. U.S. Government Foreign Grants and Credits, by Type and Country: 1946 to 1994

[In millions of dollars. See text, section 28. Negative figures (-) occur when the total of grant returns, principal repayments, and/or foreign currencies disbursed by the U.S. Government exceeds new grants and new credits utilized and/or acquisitions of foreign currencies through new sales of farm products. See also *Historical Statistics, Colonial Times to 1970*, series U 75-186]

TYPE AND COUNTRY	1946-1955, total	1956-1965, total	1966-1975, total	1976-1985, total	1990	1991	1992	1993	1994, prel.
Total, net	51,509	49,723	70,355	104,153	14,280	-32,018	17,042	16,638	15,965
Investment in financial institutions . . .	635	655	2,719	10,432	1,301	1,498	1,419	1,132	1,417
Under assistance programs	50,875	49,067	67,636	93,720	12,979	-33,517	15,623	15,506	14,548
Western Europe.	33,067	6,752	1,004	1,612	-69	-5,985	324	124	166
Austria.	1,001	193	-19	34	-10	-19	-1	-1	-1
Belgium and Luxembourg	1,570	305	17	-46	-9	-3	-	-	-
Bosnia and Hercegovina	-	-	-	-	-	-	40	30	50
Croatia	-	-	-	-	-	-	62	37	50
Denmark	596	276	64	-58	-	-	-	-	-
Finland	86	-26	-19	21	-8	-5	-5	-26	-1
France.	8,661	-171	-93	-222	-15	-8	-2	-2	-1
Germany	3,881	10	-117	-117	-338	-6,117	-	-1	-
Iceland	34	33	-8	-12	(Z)	-	-	-	-
Ireland.	146	-16	-51	7	2	-6	-6	-8	25
Italy	3,851	1,435	85	133	-30	-14	-	(Z)	-
Macedonia	-	-	-	-	-	-	67	1	3
Netherlands	1,716	322	116	-180	-	-	-	-	-
Norway	697	362	379	-257	-	-1	-15	-	-
Portugal.	248	241	34	1,003	56	44	159	53	115
Slovenia	-	-	-	-	-	-	118	-6	-18
Spain	258	1,203	607	965	-122	-76	-104	-114	-55
Sweden	107	-20	17	-1	-	-	-	-	-
United Kingdom.	7,458	105	-546	-964	-111	-113	-115	-118	-120
Yugoslavia	1,356	1,151	84	174	-39	-58	-308	1	-1
Other [1] and unspecified	1,399	1,351	454	1,132	555	391	435	279	120
Eastern Europe	823	501	226	1,029	965	779	707	2,888	2,711
Albania	9	-	-	-	-	9	59	29	10
Armenia.	-	-	-	-	-	-	19	62	78
Belarus	-	-	-	-	-	-	27	74	36
Bulgaria	-	-	-	-	-	17	1	20	5
Czechoslovakia	136	-	-	-5	(Z)	1	1	15	1
Czech Republic.	-	-	-	-	-	-	-	2	2
Estonia	-	-	-	-	-	-	21	1	(Z)
Georgia	-	-	-	-	-	-	5	72	53
Hungary.	18	5	-5	6	1	3	2	3	4
Kazakhstan	-	-	-	-	-	-	17	9	12
Kyrgyzstan	-	-	-	-	-	-	1	59	22
Latvia	-	-	-	-	-	-	21	1	2
Lithuania	-	-	-	-	-	-	21	24	15
Moldova.	-	-	-	-	-	-	9	25	22
Poland.	350	555	-75	1,017	919	646	57	21	5
Romania	-	-	92	55	64	39	10	14	9
Russia.	-	-	-	-	-	-	145	1,902	1,134
Soviet Union.	292	-59	214	-44	-30	3	-	5	-
Tajikistan	-	-	-	-	-	-	10	17	19
Turkmenistan	-	-	-	-	-	-	7	24	13
Ukraine	-	-	-	-	-	-	8	66	103
Other [2] and unspecified	17	(Z)	-	-	11	60	266	444	1,166
Near East and South Asia.	4,944	16,828	17,195	50,777	6,602	-24,672	7,493	7,631	7,060
Afghanistan	31	227	185	56	57	59	70	49	8
Bangladesh	-	-	701	1,670	175	168	154	109	176
Cyprus.	-	19	20	138	16	18	10	14	16
Egypt	41	1,009	271	13,600	4,976	2,508	2,537	2,760	2,236
Greece	2,026	1,281	905	362	282	-179	402	205	332
India	370	4,890	3,810	1,021	-8	100	78	54	32
Iran.	314	1,061	914	-847	-	-23	(Z)	-	-
Iraq 3/.	13	81	-5	5	-7	365	119	115	135
Israel.	390	483	3,760	25,417	4,379	2,002	4,691	3,276	3,132
Jordan.	26	495	618	1,320	139	67	121	127	94
Kuwait	-	-	-	-	-2,506	-13,550	-2	-	-
Lebanon	15	78	90	233	8	5	11	7	5
Nepal	3	86	105	177	20	16	19	20	20
Oman	-	-	(Z)	79	4	3	13	24	1
Pakistan	189	3,092	2,048	1,971	526	346	123	-39	-162
Saudi Arabia.	12	35	23	-20	-1,614	-13,913	-1,328	-	-
Sri Lanka	(Z)	89	153	512	72	109	53	77	34
Syria	1	57	15	262	(Z)	-	-	2	-
Turkey	1,295	3,020	2,703	3,760	367	798	300	629	226
United Arab Emirates	-	-	-	-	-361	-3,709	-	-	-
Yemen (Sanaa)	-	40	24	216	14	-	-	-	-
Yemen.	-	-	-	-	28	19	14	21	1
UNRWA [4].	131	274	296	596	7	76	69	140	7
Other and unspecified	85	510	559	248	27	43	41	43	765

See footnotes at end of table.

No. 1294. U.S. Government Foreign Grants and Credits, by Type and Country: 1946 to 1994—Continued

[In millions of dollars. See headnote, p. 792]

COUNTRY	1946-1955, total	1956-1965, total	1966-1975, total	1976-1985, total	1990	1991	1992	1993	1994, prel.
Africa.........................	147	2,272	3,610	11,066	1,841	1,483	1,624	1,773	1,861
Algeria......................	1	135	263	345	59	-42	-14	-11	28
Angola.......................	-	-	6	115	-15	-4	-20	8	37
Benin........................	-	7	12	44	5	10	17	12	16
Botswana....................	-	(Z)	35	169	17	11	8	15	14
Burkina	-	5	40	287	15	32	17	20	13
Burundi	-	4	5	62	18	6	16	19	36
Cameroon	-	16	50	150	42	57	42	23	14
Cape Verde	-	-	1	68	6	7	9	5	5
Chad.........................	(Z)	5	20	145	24	26	26	22	9
Eritrea	-	-	-	-	-	-	-	4	19
Ethiopia	13	200	297	310	54	123	88	137	126
Ghana.......................	(Z)	64	203	152	14	32	36	48	55
Guinea.......................	-	58	68	74	15	22	21	34	33
Ivory Coast..................	-	14	57	57	25	58	46	21	38
Kenya	(Z)	34	76	549	110	87	90	79	40
Lesotho	-	(Z)	27	197	15	11	16	7	6
Liberia	24	139	86	459	31	64	40	29	42
Madagascar	(Z)	7	13	86	33	31	20	26	22
Malawi.......................	-	5	30	56	34	48	47	41	33
Mali.........................	-	12	58	199	31	44	31	37	30
Mauritania	-	1	20	161	11	6	3	7	2
Morocco.....................	7	464	413	948	95	100	26	21	26
Mozambique	-	-	1	175	80	89	72	75	68
Niger........................	-	5	64	223	33	44	34	29	15
Nigeria......................	(Z)	87	284	267	156	34	31	18	52
Rwanda	-	2	13	91	13	27	10	32	271
Senegal......................	-	18	48	361	60	39	47	54	31
Sierra Leone.................	(Z)	22	36	85	2	10	16	8	7
Somalia......................	(Z)	42	47	582	77	11	337	506	24
South Africa	20	-101	-11	2	20	28	44	66	71
Sudan	-	86	52	1,358	145	113	32	35	44
Swaziland....................	-	(Z)	8	58	14	13	13	14	10
Tanzania	2	34	123	259	40	42	28	28	24
Togo	-	9	18	60	10	19	12	8	7
Tunisia.......................	2	407	376	563	38	5	16	-4	1
Uganda......................	-	12	33	40	43	39	26	58	51
Zaire	(Z)	258	342	938	241	48	33	9	(Z)
Zambia	-	1	35	331	63	50	76	52	21
Zimbabwe....................	-	(Z)	(Z)	271	10	27	67	28	34
Other and unspecified............	76	219	361	769	156	113	165	154	484
Far East and Pacific..............	9,678	16,199	34,767	9,622	35	-8,991	777	-1	722
Australia.....................	-9	(Z)	276	-12	-34	-26	-18	-2	-1
Burma	25	134	43	31	1	-3	(Z)	-2	-2
Cambodia....................	28	327	1,760	87	5	6	14	29	16
China........................	-	-	-	49	71	55	31	14	6
Hong Kong...................	3	35	41	11	-8	-	-	1	1
Indonesia....................	246	501	1,390	1,661	46	23	82	-64	23
Japan and Ryukyu Islands.........	3,267	1,318	-345	-210	-635	-9,377	-30	-2	-1
South Korea	1,420	4,744	5,426	3,518	-192	-331	-133	-431	-55
Laos	37	647	1,868	8	(Z)	(Z)	1	(Z)	(Z)
Malaysia.....................	1	30	86	39	-1	-2	(Z)	(Z)	1
Mongolia	-	-	-	-	-	17	2	36	17
New Zealand.................	3	2	95	-68	-2	-2	-1	-	-
Pacific Islands, Trust Territory of the [5] .	28	89	488	1,260	221	178	204	152	317
Philippines	1,028	554	729	1,466	556	391	534	129	-53
Singapore....................	-	(Z)	78	110	(Z)	(Z)	(Z)	(Z)	(Z)
Taiwan.......................	1,267	2,681	1,523	648	-7	-8	-7	-9	-8
Thailand.....................	192	727	996	733	-19	49	44	84	245
Vietnam.....................	244	3,566	19,720	18	2	1	2	2	-7
Other and unspecified............	1,898	844	595	273	33	38	54	60	224
Western Hemisphere	1,248	5,181	6,816	9,847	2,003	2,014	2,465	673	798
Argentina....................	86	342	34	21	64	87	90	80	26
Bolivia.......................	77	288	270	413	112	197	185	129	111
Brazil........................	509	1,400	1,518	399	260	-22	410	-188	-60
Canada	-1	4	272	317	-41	-50	-38	-41	-120
Chile	100	740	724	-565	-32	-40	-55	-39	-36
Colombia	43	446	846	298	-30	7	-78	-235	-8
Costa Rica	15	83	103	687	108	63	24	15	-7
Dominican Republic	2	184	360	550	27	25	3	163	9
Ecuador.....................	32	131	144	153	61	26	30	17	19
El Salvador..................	3	56	93	1,681	303	308	278	212	87
Guatemala...................	23	146	160	270	96	82	109	74	51
Guyana......................	(Z)	7	71	36	42	11	9	6	8
Haiti	27	75	42	370	53	69	54	59	162
Honduras....................	6	53	113	801	223	193	130	92	49
Jamaica......................	16	3	120	643	108	109	84	34	99

See footnotes at end of table.

No. 1294. U.S. Government Foreign Grants and Credits, by Type and Country: 1946 to 1994—Continued

[In millions of dollars. See headnote, p. 792]

COUNTRY	1946-1955, total	1956-1965, total	1966-1975, total	1976-1985, total	1990	1991	1992	1993	1994, prel.
Western Hemisphere— Continued:									
Mexico	225	178	305	1,162	140	38	-110	-160	-231
Nicaragua..................	8	67	150	197	100	396	207	37	41
Panama....................	10	103	210	205	102	153	193	49	6
Paraguay	4	67	86	22	(Z)	1	(Z)	1	2
Peru	55	304	274	757	87	139	671	113	41
Trinidad and Tobago.........	-	35	21	151	5	5	-10	-11	-9
Uruguay...................	8	90	116	-9	-4	-5	2	-1	2
Venezuela	6	156	115	-35	-18	-14	-2	1	(Z)
Other [6] and unspecified	-6	224	671	1,325	237	236	280	266	557
Other international organizations and unspecified areas..............	969	1,335	4,018	9,768	1,603	1,855	2,234	2,419	1,230

Z Less than $500,000.   [1] Includes European Atomic Energy Community, European Coal and Steel Community, European Payments Union, European Productivity Agency, North Atlantic Treaty Organization, and Organization for European Economic Cooperation.   [2] Foreign assistance in 1989-94 to the countries of Eastern Europe and to the Newly Independent States of the former Soviet Union was reported primarily on a regional basis.   [3] Foreign assistance to Iraq in 1991-94 was direct humanitarian assistance to ethnic minorities of Northern Iraq after the conflict in the Persian Gulf.   [4] United Nations Relief and Works Agency for Palestine refugees.   [5] Excludes transactions with Commonwealth of the Northern Mariana Islands after October 1986; includes transactions with Federated States of Micronesia, Republic of the Marshall Islands, and Republic of Palau.   [6] Includes Andean Development Corporation, Caribbean Development Bank, Central American Bank for Economic Integration, Eastern Caribbean Central Bank, Inter-American Institute of Agricultural Science, Organizations of American States, and Pan American Health Organization.

Source: U.S. Bureau of Economic Analysis, press releases, and unpublished data.

No. 1295. U.S. Foreign Economic and Military Aid Programs: 1946 to 1993

[In millions of dollars. For years ending June 30 except, beginning 1977, ending Sept. 30. Economic aid shown here represents U.S. economic aid—not just aid under the Foreign Assistance Act. Major components in recent years include AID, Food for Peace, Peace Corps, and paid-in subscriptions to international financial institutions, such as IBRD, and IDB. Cumulative totals for 1946-1993 are true totals net of deobligation; annual figures however, are gross unadjusted program figures. Military aid includes Military Assistance Program (MAP) grants, foreign military credit sales, service-funded programs, and excess defense articles]

PERIOD OR YEAR AND REGION	Total economic and military aid	ECONOMIC AID			MILITARY AID		
		Total	Loans	Grants	Total	Loans	Grants
1946-1993, total	439,565	287,850	63,253	224,598	151,715	39,877	111,837
1946 to 1952	41,661	31,116	8,518	22,598	10,545	-	10,545
1953 to 1961	43,358	24,053	5,850	18,203	19,305	161	19,144
1962 to 1969	50,254	33,392	15,421	17,972	16,862	1,620	15,242
1970 to 1979	87,986	49,171	17,659	31,515	38,812	14,180	24,631
1980 to 1989	140,130	92,082	13,740	78,342	48,048	21,884	26,164
1970......................	6,568	3,676	1,389	2,288	2,892	70	2,822
1975......................	6,916	4,908	1,679	3,229	2,009	750	1,259
1976......................	6,412	3,878	1,759	2,119	2,535	1,442	1,093
1976, TQ [1].................	2,603	1,931	840	1,091	672	494	178
1977......................	7,784	5,594	2,083	3,511	2,190	1,411	779
1978......................	9,014	6,661	2,530	4,131	2,353	1,601	752
1979......................	13,845	7,120	1,900	5,220	6,725	5,173	1,552
1980......................	9,695	7,573	1,993	5,580	2,122	1,450	672
1981......................	10,550	7,305	1,460	5,845	3,245	2,546	699
1982......................	12,324	8,129	1,454	6,675	4,195	3,084	1,111
1983......................	14,202	8,603	1,619	6,984	5,599	3,932	1,667
1984......................	15,524	9,038	1,621	7,417	6,486	4,401	2,085
1985......................	18,128	12,327	1,579	10,748	5,801	2,365	3,436
1986......................	16,739	10,900	1,330	9,570	5,839	1,980	3,859
1987......................	14,488	9,386	1,138	8,248	5,102	953	4,149
1988......................	13,792	8,961	852	8,109	4,831	763	4,068
1989......................	14,688	9,860	694	9,166	4,828	410	4,418
1990......................	15,727	10,834	756	10,078	4,893	404	4,489
1991......................	16,663	11,904	354	11,550	4,760	428	4,332
1992......................	15,589	11,242	494	10,748	4,347	345	4,002
1993	28,196	24,054	462	23,592	4,143	855	3,288
Near East and South Asia........	5,373	2,215	61	2,154	3,158	-	3,158
East Asia..................	842	821	70	751	22	-	22
Europe	1,534	671	72	599	863	855	8
New Independent States [2]	1,007	1,005	148	857	1	-	1
Latin America...............	1,392	1,318	96	1,223	74	-	74
Africa	1,553	1,529	15	1,514	24	-	24
Oceania and other............	32	32	-	32			
Nonregional.................	16,462	16,462	-	16,462	1	-	1

- Represents zero.   [1] Transition quarter, July-Sept.   [2] Former republics of the Soviet Union.

Source: U.S. Agency for International Development, *U.S. Overseas Loans and Grants and Assistance from International Organizations,* annual.

No. 1296. U.S. Foreign Military Aid, by Region and Selected Countries: 1985 to 1993

[In millions of dollars. For years ending **Sept. 30.** Military aid data include Military Assistance Program (MAP) grants, foreign military credit sales, International Military Education and Training, and excess defense articles]

REGION AND COUNTRY	1985	1990	1991	1992	1993	REGION AND COUNTRY	1985	1990	1991	1992	1993
Total	**5,801**	**4,894**	**4,760**	**4,348**	**4,143**	Philippines	42	143	203	28	18
						South Korea. . . .	232	1	1	1	-
Europe.	**1,736**	**939**	**1,007**	**960**	**863**	Thailand	102	5	1	-	2
Greece	501	349	351	350	315	**Africa [1] . . . .**	**279**	**39**	**38**	**17**	**24**
Portugal.	128	87	101	102	91	Kenya	22	11	1	1	1
Spain	403	2	2	1	-	Liberia.	13	-	-	-	-
Turkey.	704	501	554	504	453	Somalia.	34	1	-	-	-
South Asia	**2,833**	**3,236**	**3,182**	**3,158**	**3,158**	Sudan.	46	1	-	-	-
Egypt	1,177	1,296	1,302	1,302	1,302	**Latin America [1] . . .**	**269**	**234**	**237**	**124**	**74**
Israel	1,400	1,792	1,800	1,800	1,800	Colombia.	1	73	50	49	29
Jordan.	92	70	21	21	10	Costa Rica.	11	-	-	-	-
Morocco	50	44	44	23	41	El Salvador	136	81	67	23	11
Oman	40	-	3	1	1	Honduras.	67	21	34	6	3
Tunisia	67	31	12	11	3	Panama.	11	-	-	-	-
East Asia	**416**	**383**	**233**	**32**	**22**	Peru	9	2	25	-	-
Indonesia.	34	2	27	2	-	**Nonregional . . . . .**	**58**	**63**	**61**	**56**	**1**
Pakistan	326	230	-	-	-						

- Represents zero.   Z Less than $500,000.   [1] Includes countries not shown separately.
Source: U.S. Agency for International Development, *U.S. Overseas Loans and Grants and Assistance from International Organizations,* annual.

No. 1297. U.S. Foreign Aid—Commitments for Economic Assistance, by Region and Selected Countries: 1985 to 1993

[In millions of dollars. For years ending Sept. 30. Falls under economic portion of the Foreign Assistance Act. Data cover commitments for economic and technical assistance by AID. See text, section 28]

REGION AND COUNTRY	1985	1990	1991	1992	1993	REGION AND COUNTRY	1985	1990	1991	1992	1993
Total	**8,132**	**6,964**	**7,668**	**6,819**	**7,059**	Guinea	4	15	31	27	24
						Kenya.	40	36	25	20	16
Europe [1]	**284**	**160**	**606**	**514**	**469**	Liberia.	60	-	-	1	-
Portugal	80	39	43	40	-	Madagascar.	5	17	11	42	44
Turkey	175	14	250	1	200	Malawi	25	23	57	28	55
East European						Mali	32	21	37	36	34
Regional	(X)	97	294	411	249	Mozambique	13	50	60	69	54
New Independent						Niger	28	20	28	29	17
States [2]	(X)	(X)	(X)	130	487	Rwanda	19	12	40	21	6
						Senegal	44	37	25	34	22
Near East [1]	**3,270**	**2,199**	**2,754**	**2,205**	**2,124**	Somalia.	51	1	1	11	28
Egypt	1,065	901	783	893	748	South Africa.	-	33	50	80	80
Israel	1,950	1,195	1,850	1,200	1,200	Sudan.	149	8	2	3	-
Jordan	100	4	31	-	65	Tanzania	(Z)	9	39	17	23
Lebanon	20	8	9	9	10	Uganda.	9	43	45	42	39
Morocco	38	31	50	41	33	Zaire.	36	31	22	-	-
Oman	20	13	16	30	-	Zambia	42	17	35	40	26
Tunisia	23	14	4	4	5	Zimbabwe	41	28	43	41	49
West Bank/Gaza.	-	-	-	6	30	Regional	96	73	92	98	97
Yemen Arab Republic .	28	23	3	3	4						
Regional	23	12	8	17	28	**Latin America [1] . . . .**	**1,506**	**1,486**	**1,075**	**855**	**780**
						Belize	23	6	7	5	5
Asia [1]	**781**	**873**	**749**	**511**	**375**	Bolivia	18	58	100	127	86
Bangladesh	76	56	49	57	35	Costa Rica.	196	78	42	24	9
India.	89	23	30	48	25	Dominican Rep.	126	18	14	16	20
Indonesia	72	48	60	43	48	Ecuador	33	17	16	22	13
Kampuchea	-	-	-	-	57	El Salvador	376	200	180	234	172
Nepal	18	17	24	17	21	Guatemala.	76	86	60	34	33
Pakistan	250	276	96	-	6	Haiti	31	42	51	31	47
Philippines	183	314	328	201	83	Honduras	205	167	99	65	33
Sri Lanka	35	21	28	20	17	Jamaica	115	28	27	38	43
Thailand	36	14	3	2	8	Nicaragua	-	220	215	43	128
Regional	7	106	118	105	42	Panama	74	396	40	15	6
						Peru	38	22	69	24	41
Sub-Saharan Africa [1]. . .	**839**	**621**	**865**	**891**	**783**	ROCAP [3]	107	30	21	12	17
Burundi	4	20	15	15	17	Regional	30	88	96	134	59
Cameroon	24	22	20	22	10						
Gambia, The	6	5	15	46	38	**South Pacific Regional .**	**6**	**18**	**20**	**21**	**23**
Ghana	2	15	29	31	40	**Nonregional . . . .**	**1,453**	**1,607**	**1,598**	**1,693**	**2,018**

- Represents zero.   Z Less than $500,000.   [1] Includes countries not shown separately.   [2] Former republics of the Soviet Union.   [3] Regional programs covering Costa Rica, El Salvador, Guatemala, Honduras, Nicaragua, and Panama.

Source of tables 1296 and 1297: U.S. Agency for International Development, *U.S. Overseas Loans and Grants and Assistance from International Organizations,* annual; and unpublished data.

No. 1298. U.S. International Trade in Goods and Services: 1993 to 1995

[In millions of dollars. Data presented on a balance of payments basis and will not agree with the following merchandise trade tables 1297 to 1308]

CATEGORY	EXPORTS			IMPORTS			TRADE BALANCE		
	1993	1994	1995	1993	1994	1995	1993	1994	1995
Total	642,953	698,301	786,529	714,990	802,682	891,593	-72,037	-104,381	-105,064
Goods	456,834	502,462	575,939	589,441	668,585	749,363	-132,607	-166,123	-173,424
Services	186,119	195,839	210,590	125,549	134,097	142,230	60,570	61,742	68,360
Travel	57,875	58,417	61,137	40,713	43,782	45,855	17,162	14,635	15,282
Passenger fares	16,611	17,083	18,534	11,313	12,885	14,313	5,298	4,198	4,221
Other transportation	23,894	25,861	28,063	26,328	27,983	29,205	-2,434	-2,122	-1,142
Royalties and license fees	20,323	22,272	26,953	4,765	5,518	6,312	15,558	16,754	20,641
Other private services	53,436	59,071	61,724	27,897	30,980	33,970	25,539	28,091	27,754
Direct defense expenditures	13,082	12,255	13,405	12,202	10,292	9,820	880	1,963	3,585
U.S. Government miscellaneous services	899	880	775	2,331	2,657	2,755	-1,432	-1,777	-1,980

Source: U.S. Bureau of the Census, *U.S. International Trade in Goods and Services*, series FT-900(95).

No. 1299. U.S. Exports and Imports of Merchandise: 1970 to 1995

[In billions of dollars, except percent. Includes silver ore and bullion; beginning 1974, includes shipments of nonmonetary gold. Data may differ from those shown in other tables due to revisions and inclusion of the Virgin Islands since 1974. For basis of dollar values, see text, section 28. See also *Historical Statistics, Colonial Times to 1970*, series U 190-195 and U 207-21

YEAR	Mer-chandise trade balance	EXPORTS [1]					GENERAL IMPORTS [4]				AVERAGE ANNUAL PERCENT CHANGE [5]	
		Total [2]	Domestic				Total [3]	Petro-leum	Machin-ery	Trans-port equip-ment	Domes-tic exports	General imports
			Total [3]	Agri-cultural	Machin-ery	Trans-port equip-ment						
1970	2.7	42.7	42.0	7.2	11.4	6.5	40.0	2.8	5.3	5.9	14.1	10.8
1971	-2.0	43.5	42.9	7.7	11.6	7.9	45.6	3.3	6.0	7.9	1.9	14.0
1972	-6.4	49.2	48.4	9.4	13.2	8.3	55.6	4.3	7.8	9.6	13.1	21.9
1973	1.3	70.8	69.7	17.7	17.1	10.7	69.5	7.6	10.0	11.1	43.9	25.0
1974	-4.5	98.1	96.5	22.0	23.7	14.5	102.6	24.3	11.6	12.5	38.6	47.6
1975	9.1	107.7	106.1	21.9	28.5	17.2	98.5	24.8	12.0	12.2	9.8	-4.0
1976	-8.3	115.2	113.5	23.0	31.3	18.2	123.5	31.8	15.2	14.6	7.0	25.4
1977	-29.2	121.2	118.9	23.7	32.5	18.5	150.4	41.5	17.7	17.8	5.2	21.8
1978	-31.1	143.7	141.0	29.4	37.0	22.3	174.8	39.1	24.4	23.2	18.6	16.2
1979	-27.6	181.9	178.6	34.8	44.7	25.8	209.5	56.0	28.0	25.6	26.6	19.9
1980	-24.2	220.6	216.5	41.3	55.8	28.8	244.9	77.6	31.9	28.6	21.3	16.9
1981	-27.3	233.7	228.9	43.3	62.9	32.8	261.0	75.6	38.2	31.4	5.9	6.6
1982	-31.8	212.3	207.1	36.6	60.3	23.6	244.0	59.4	39.7	33.6	-9.2	-6.5
1983	-57.5	200.5	196.0	36.1	54.3	28.3	258.0	52.3	47.0	39.2	-5.6	5.7
1984	-107.9	217.9	212.1	37.8	60.3	29.7	325.7	55.9	68.4	50.8	8.7	26.2
1985	-132.1	213.1	206.9	29.2	59.5	34.8	345.3	49.6	75.3	62.0	-2.2	6.0
1986	-152.7	217.3	206.4	26.1	60.4	34.9	370.0	34.1	87.5	74.0	2.0	7.2
1987	-152.1	254.1	243.9	28.6	69.6	39.0	406.2	41.5	99.4	78.4	16.9	9.8
1988	-118.6	322.4	310.0	37.0	88.4	46.7	441.0	38.8	117.3	79.8	26.9	8.6
1989	-109.6	363.8	349.4	40.0	98.3	50.5	473.4	49.1	126.8	79.0	12.8	7.3
1990	-101.7	393.6	375.1	38.7	122.4	32.1	495.3	60.5	134.8	72.4	8.2	4.6
1991	-65.4	421.7	401.1	38.5	139.7	34.9	487.1	50.1	131.8	70.6	7.1	-1.7
1992	-84.5	448.2	425.7	42.2	126.6	36.9	532.7	50.4	148.3	75.5	6.3	9.4
1993	-115.6	465.1	439.3	41.9	136.4	36.6	580.7	49.7	168.7	83.3	3.8	9.0
1994	-151.1	512.7	472.3	45.0	156.7	44.9	663.8	49.6	204.6	95.1	10.2	14.3
1995	-159.6	583.9	548.1	54.9	182.7	27.7	743.4	52.8	241.7	75.1	13.9	12.0

[1] Includes "Special Category" items and beginning 1974, includes trade of Virgin Islands with foreign countries. F.a.s. value basis.　[2] Domestic and foreign exports excluding M.A.P. Grant-Aid shipments, through 1985; 1986 through 1988 include Grant-Aid shipments.　[3] Includes commodity groups not shown separately.　[4] 1970-73, 1982-91, customs value basis; 1974-81, f.a.s. value basis. Beginning 1974, includes trade of Virgin Islands with foreign countries.　[5] 1970, change from 1965; thereafter, from previous year. For explanation of average annual percent change, see Guide to Tabular Presentation.

Source: U.S. Bureau of the Census, 1970-88, *Highlights of U.S. Export and Import Trade*, FT 990, monthly; beginning 1989, *U.S. Merchandise Trade: Export, General Imports, and Imports for Consumption*, series FT 925, monthly.

No. 1300. U.S. Exports and Imports for Consumption of Merchandise, by Major Customs District: 1980 to 1995

[In billions of dollars. Exports are f.a.s. (free alongside ship) value all years; imports are on customs value basis. See also *Historical Statistics, Colonial Times to 1970*, series U 264-273]

CUSTOMS DISTRICT	EXPORTS						IMPORTS FOR CONSUMPTION					
	1980	1990	1992	1993	1994	1995	1980	1990	1992	1993	1994	1995
Total [1]	220.8	393.0	448.2	465.1	512.6	584.7	244.0	490.6	525.3	575.1	657.3	739.6
Anchorage, AK	1.0	3.7	5.1	4.8	5.3	5.9	0.2	0.7	1.3	2.0	3.6	5.7
Baltimore, MD	9.0	6.7	7.7	7.6	8.2	9.0	6.0	11.2	10.8	11.7	13.4	14.4
Boston,	0.8	5.6	4.4	4.4	4.7	4.6	5.0	12.2	12.0	11.7	12.6	13.4
Buffalo, NY	6.3	15.8	18.1	19.5	21.3	30.5	7.4	19.2	21.2	24.2	27.0	29.3
Charleston, SC [2]	3.1	6.7	7.3	7.3	7.9	10.1	1.8	6.8	6.6	7.5	8.6	10.4
Chicago, IL	4.2	10.2	11.9	13.1	15.2	18.4	4.1	18.3	22.4	25.1	28.5	31.3
Cleveland, OH	1.8	4.0	4.1	4.3	5.3	7.8	1.5	11.3	13.8	15.5	18.2	21.7
Dallas/Fort Worth, TX	0.5	3.4	3.9	4.2	4.1	4.4	1.2	4.8	5.3	6.3	7.7	8.8
Detroit, MI	14.6	35.6	37.8	44.7	54.4	56.8	12.7	37.8	41.9	47.6	58.1	65.4
Duluth, MN	1.5	0.8	0.9	0.9	1.1	1.4	3.0	3.9	3.6	4.1	4.7	6.0
El Paso, TX	1.8	3.9	6.0	6.5	7.4	7.9	1.4	5.0	6.5	8.1	11.2	12.9
Great Falls, MT	1.8	2.4	3.2	3.5	3.2	3.0	3.2	4.7	4.9	5.9	7.1	6.9
Honolulu, HI	0.2	0.5	0.6	1.1	1.0	1.1	1.8	2.1	2.1	2.2	2.5	2.7
Houston/Galveston, TX	15.7	17.6	20.2	19.9	21.2	27.4	20.1	21.6	18.7	19.7	21.9	23.4
Laredo, TX	8.3	15.2	21.7	22.7	28.3	24.3	2.7	10.0	11.8	13.7	17.5	24.7
Los Angeles, CA	14.8	42.1	49.4	48.3	55.8	67.0	20.0	64.1	72.1	79.4	89.4	96.3
Miami, FL	6.9	11.2	16.0	17.1	19.5	22.7	2.6	7.1	8.4	9.4	10.3	11.9
Milwaukee, WI	0.4	0.1	0.1	0.1	0.1	0.1	0.4	1.1	1.2	1.2	1.4	1.5
Minneapolis, MN	0.1	0.9	1.1	1.1	1.3	1.3	0.3	2.0	2.7	2.5	2.6	2.8
Mobile, AL [2]	2.6	1.9	2.2	2.1	2.7	3.4	3.0	3.4	3.2	3.1	3.8	3.9
New Orleans, LA	19.5	18.0	20.2	19.8	20.7	28.4	22.5	24.1	23.3	24.7	29.1	34.4
New York, NY	38.9	50.9	53.3	58.7	56.4	61.4	43.4	68.0	72.8	75.6	81.8	87.6
Nogales, AZ	0.8	2.1	2.8	3.0	4.1	4.0	1.2	4.2	4.6	5.7	7.5	7.7
Norfolk, VA [2]	8.0	11.7	11.9	11.0	12.4	14.4	4.7	7.4	7.5	7.3	7.9	8.6
Ogdensburg, NY	3.8	7.9	7.9	8.0	8.9	9.2	4.6	9.8	10.0	11.4	12.3	14.4
Pembina, ND	2.3	3.4	4.3	4.8	5.9	5.5	3.0	4.1	4.5	5.3	6.1	7.2
Philadelphia, PA	3.2	4.0	4.4	4.4	5.1	6.7	15.6	18.3	16.4	16.1	16.8	18.3
Port Arthur, TX	2.0	0.9	0.8	0.9	0.9	1.3	9.4	3.2	3.1	3.8	4.0	4.8
Portland, ME	4.3	1.7	1.9	2.3	2.0	2.1	1.6	4.3	4.0	4.0	4.3	4.4
Portland, OR	3.8	5.8	7.2	7.3	8.1	10.2	2.6	5.6	5.1	5.7	7.0	7.9
Providence, RI	2.7	(Z)	(Z)	0.1	0.1	0.1	1.5	1.3	1.1	1.1	0.9	0.9
San Diego, CA	1.4	3.4	4.6	4.5	5.6	6.1	1.0	4.3	5.5	6.2	7.4	8.9
San Francisco, CA	10.6	23.1	27.2	29.4	34.2	43.7	8.3	28.0	33.1	38.8	46.2	58.8
San Juan, PR	0.9	2.5	2.5	2.7	2.6	2.6	3.7	5.4	5.1	4.9	5.7	6.8
Savannah, GA	2.4	7.4	8.9	8.7	9.3	10.9	2.2	9.8	11.3	12.9	13.3	14.7
Seattle, WA	12.0	32.6	35.4	35.0	33.1	31.4	9.2	20.9	20.4	21.8	23.6	24.1
St. Albans, VT	0.7	4.0	4.0	3.8	4.1	4.4	1.6	5.2	5.2	5.5	6.2	7.4
St. Louis, MO	0.2	0.3	0.7	0.3	0.3	0.3	0.9	3.0	3.4	3.9	4.3	4.4
Tampa, FL	2.8	4.3	5.2	4.7	5.7	6.7	3.7	7.0	7.0	7.3	9.1	9.2
Virgin Islands of the U.S.	0.1	0.2	0.1	0.2	0.2	0.2	4.1	2.1	1.8	1.6	2.1	2.1
Washington, DC	0.3	1.1	1.6	1.9	2.0	2.3	0.4	0.8	0.8	0.8	0.9	1.2
Wilmington, NC	1.3	3.0	3.9	3.0	3.9	4.4	1.1	3.3	4.5	5.6	6.0	7.4

Z Less than $50 million.   [1] Totals shown for exports reflect the value of estimated parcel post and Special Category shipments, and beginning 1990, adjustments for undocumented exports to Canada which are not distributed by customs district. Beginning 1990, the value of bituminous coal exported through Norfolk, VA; Charleston, SC; and Mobile, AL is reflected in the total but not distributed by district.   [2] Beginning 1990, excludes exports of bituminous coal.

Source: U.S. Bureau of the Census, 1980, *Highlights of U.S. Export and Import Trade*, FT 990; beginning 1990, *U.S. Merchandise Trade: Selected Highlights*, series FT 920, monthly; and *U.S. Export History, Historical Summary 1991-1995* and *U.S. Import History, Historical Summary 1991-1995* on compact disc.

No. 1301. Export and Import Unit Value Indexes—Selected Countries: 1991 to 1995

[Indexes in U.S. dollars, 1990=100. A unit value is an implicit price derived from value and quantity data]

COUNTRY	EXPORT UNIT VALUE					IMPORT UNIT VALUE				
	1991	1992	1993	1994	1995	1991	1992	1993	1994	1995
United States	100.9	101.0	101.4	103.6	108.8	100.0	100.8	100.1	101.8	106.4
Australia	91.2	87.7	82.3	86.0	93.6	100.8	99.3	99.4	104.3	109.6
Austria	94.2	98.0	88.6	(NA)	(NA)	97.6	102.2	93.4	(NA)	(NA)
Belgium-Luxembourg	96.0	100.5	(NA)	(NA)	(NA)	96.5	99.2	(NA)	(NA)	(NA)
Canada	98.2	95.3	94.4	94.6	101.2	100.4	99.2	98.6	99.1	102.6
Denmark	96.9	101.6	91.4	95.1	(NA)	97.3	99.7	89.2	92.8	(NA)
France	96.2	99.6	90.1	98.3	111.1	95.5	97.9	87.0	92.4	104.5
Germany	96.8	102.1	92.0	92.9	107.6	99.0	102.0	91.1	94.6	110.0
Italy	99.4	100.8	87.9	88.9	96.2	95.8	95.9	83.9	85.2	(NA)
Japan	107.2	114.0	124.5	134.1	144.5	97.4	96.3	97.0	97.2	105.1
Netherlands	95.8	98.4	90.1	92.4	106.7	97.0	101.0	89.7	91.6	104.4
Norway	92.4	88.7	77.7	75.4	86.6	95.0	97.2	85.8	86.4	97.2
Sweden	98.7	98.9	81.2	78.1	(NA)	97.3	98.4	80.9	75.8	(NA)
United Kingdom	100.4	101.8	97.6	101.5	113.4	100.5	100.9	94.3	99.4	113.7

NA Not available.

Source: International Monetary Fund, Washington, DC, *International Financial Statistics*, monthly.

No. 1302. U.S. Exports, by State of Origin: 1990 to 1995

[**In millions of dollars.** Exports are on a f.a.s. value basis]

STATE AND OTHER AREAS	1990	1994	1995 Total	1995 Rank	STATE AND OTHER AREAS	1990	1994	1995 Total	1995 Rank
Total......	394,045	512,670	583,865	(X)	MT.......	229	328	358	49
					NE.......	693	1,573	1,759	38
U.S.........	315,065	429,808	487,761	(X)	NV.......	394	621	665	44
AL.......	2,834	3,895	4,764	26	NH.......	973	1,000	1,253	42
AK.......	2,850	2,456	2,772	32	NJ.......	7,633	10,519	11,071	14
AZ.......	3,729	6,467	7,327	21	NM.......	249	526	432	46
AR.......	920	1,672	1,994	36	NY.......	22,072	25,912	28,095	3
CA.......	44,520	66,292	77,529	1	NC.......	8,010	11,863	14,313	10
CO.......	2,274	3,802	4,460	27	ND.......	360	458	526	45
CT.......	4,356	5,664	5,666	23	OH.......	13,378	19,007	20,967	7
DE.......	1,344	1,498	1,402	40	OK.......	1,646	2,110	2,079	34
DC.......	320	546	231	(X)	OR.......	4,065	6,103	7,667	20
FL.......	11,634	16,287	18,909	9	PA.......	8,491	11,650	13,031	11
GA.......	5,763	8,237	10,291	16	RI.......	595	923	897	43
HI.......	179	297	241	50	SC.......	3,116	5,236	6,423	22
ID.......	898	1,466	1,804	37	SD.......	205	295	388	48
IL.......	12,965	19,097	22,163	5	TN.......	3,746	6,749	7,778	18
IN.......	5,273	8,256	10,383	15	TX.......	32,931	51,818	59,116	2
IA.......	2,189	3,214	3,842	29	UT.......	1,596	2,355	3,282	31
KS.......	2,113	3,028	3,433	30	VT.......	1,154	1,371	1,620	39
KY.......	3,175	4,803	5,253	24	VA.......	9,333	9,573	11,512	13
LA.......	14,199	14,549	19,793	8	WA.......	24,432	23,629	21,879	6
ME.......	870	1,090	1,357	41	WV.......	1,550	1,586	2,040	35
MD.......	2,592	4,874	5,223	25	WI.......	5,158	7,722	8,931	17
MA.......	9,501	11,199	12,946	12	WY.......	264	360	411	47
MI.......	18,474	25,830	25,275	4					
MN.......	5,091	6,621	7,747	19	PR.........	3,600	4,473	4,501	(X)
MS.......	1,605	1,846	2,592	33	VI	51	139	216	(X)
MO.......	3,130	3,541	3,876	28	Other [1]......	75,328	78,250	91,387	(X)

X Not applicable.   [1] Includes unreported, not specified, special category, estimated shipments, foreign trade zone, re-exports, and any timing adjustments.

Source: U.S. Bureau of the Census, *U.S. Merchandise Trade*, series FT 900, December issues.

No. 1303. U.S. Trade in Advanced Technology Products: 1990 to 1995

[**In billions of dollars.** Exports are f.a.s. value basis and imports are on customs value basis]

PRODUCT CATEGORY	EXPORTS					GENERAL IMPORTS				
	1990	1992	1993	1994	1995	1990	1992	1993	1994	1995
Total...................	93.4	105.1	108.4	120.8	138.4	59.3	71.8	81.2	98.4	124.8
Advanced materials [1].........	6.4	0.6	0.7	0.9	(NA)	1.0	0.4	0.5	0.6	(NA)
Aerospace...'..2............	37.0	42.5	37.4	35.0	(NA)	10.7	12.8	11.6	11.4	(NA)
Biotechnology [2].............	0.6	0.7	0.8	1.0	(NA)	(Z)	(Z)	0.1	0.1	(NA)
Electronics.................	7.5	16.5	19.6	25.8	(NA)	11.0	15.4	19.4	25.9	(NA)
Flexible manufacturing [3].......	3.1	3.4	4.0	5.2	(NA)	1.7	1.7	2.2	2.9	(NA)
Information and communications ..	31.4	32.5	36.7	42.9	(NA)	30.2	33.9	40.1	49.9	(NA)
Life science................	4.9	5.8	6.1	6.8	(NA)	3.4	4.8	4.7	4.8	(NA)
Nuclear technology	1.3	1.5	1.4	1.6	(NA)	(Z)	(Z)	(Z)	(Z)	(NA)
Opto-electronics [4]...........	0.5	0.6	0.7	0.9	(NA)	1.1	2.6	2.5	2.5	(NA)
Weapons...................	0.7	0.8	0.7	0.7	(NA)	0.1	(Z)	0.2	0.1	(NA)

NA Not available.   Z Less than $50 million.   [1] Encompasses recent advances in the development of materials that allow for further development and application of other advanced technologies. Examples are semiconductor materials, optical fiber cable and video discs.   [2] Biotechnology is the medical and industrial application of advanced scientific discoveries in genetics to the creation of new drugs, hormones and other therapeutic items for both agricultural and human use.   [3] Encompasses advances in robotics, numerically—controlled machine tools, and similar products involving industrial automation that allow for greater flexibility to the manufacturing process and reduce the amount of human intervention. Includes robots, numerically controlled machine tools and semiconductor production and assembly machines.   [4] Encompasses electronic products and components that involve the emitting and/or detection of light. Examples of products included are optical scanners, optical disc players, solar cells, photo-sensitive semiconductors and laser printers.

Source: U. S. Bureau of the Census, *U. S. Merchandise Trade*, series FT 900, December issues.

No. 1304. U.S. Exports and General Imports of Major SITC Commodity Groups— Value, by Area: 1995

[In millions of dollars. SITC=Standard International Trade Classification. Includes nonmonetary gold. Exports are f.a.s. (free alongside ship) transaction value basis; imports are customs value basis]

COMMODITY GROUPS	Total [1]	WESTERN HEMISPHERE		WESTERN EUROPE				ASIA	
		Canada	Mexico	United King-dom	Ger-many	France	Italy	Japan	China
Exports, total [1]	**583,031**	**126,024**	**46,311**	**28,827**	**22,376**	**14,241**	**8,862**	**64,298**	**11,748**
Meat and meat preparations	6,478	634	380	14	10	30	3	2,920	39
Fish (except marine mammal) crustaceans, etc., preparations	3,298	521	38	104	24	83	30	1,927	75
Cereals and cereal preparations	16,054	642	981	58	31	34	131	2,816	1,147
Vegetables and fruit	7,697	2,468	170	300	360	138	90	1,604	6
Feeding stuff for animals not including unmilled cereal	3,798	506	204	163	97	89	89	645	15
Miscellaneous edible products and preparations	2,018	480	121	35	28	7	8	185	7
Tobacco and tobacco manufactures	6,668	23	23	48	303	15	36	1,803	6
Hides, skins, and furskins, raw	1,777	98	64	4	7	13	62	268	100
Oil seeds and oleaginous fruits	5,921	116	531	103	296	105	149	1,028	52
Cork and wood	5,666	926	135	92	156	36	172	3,025	21
Pulp and waste paper	6,279	639	601	324	307	275	472	927	184
Textile fibers & their wastes (excluding wool tops, etc)	5,403	282	284	113	76	12	92	505	1,041
Crude fertilizers & crude minerals [2]	1,577	312	74	50	83	14	51	285	10
Metalliferous ores and metal scrap	5,595	1,489	210	315	101	18	32	690	247
Crude animal and vegetable materials, n.e.s.	1,325	259	135	52	77	31	28	143	14
Coal, coke and briquettes	3,714	459	51	193	68	160	400	462	-
Petroleum, petroleum products, and related materials	5,946	822	924	78	42	64	185	382	27
Organic chemicals	16,395	1,583	1,136	557	342	324	327	1,455	261
Inorganic chemicals	4,581	641	329	134	153	76	35	1,084	38
Dyeing, tanning and coloring materials	2,621	816	216	115	54	35	17	140	31
Medicinal and pharmaceutical products	6,554	1,028	155	458	471	400	316	948	36
Essential oils, etc; toilet, polishing, preparations	3,943	1,016	223	203	100	108	67	423	16
Fertilizers [3]	3,226	256	69	7	13	10	8	204	1,204
Plastics in primary forms	10,756	2,266	999	295	259	96	84	552	283
Plastics in nonprimary forms	4,337	1,164	658	203	160	123	47	248	34
Chemical materials and products, n.e.s.	9,288	1,883	482	444	565	406	169	1,075	111
Rubber manufactures, n.e.s.	3,554	1,627	439	103	116	46	26	311	7
Cork and wood manufactures other than furniture	1,718	411	121	148	193	13	37	220	8
Paper, paperboard and articles	9,675	2,521	1,237	305	210	94	147	924	141
Textile yarn, fabrics, made-up articles, n.e.s.	7,372	2,111	951	336	248	100	94	289	55
Nonmetallic mineral manufactures, n.e.s.	6,708	1,509	376	228	174	120	50	499	62
Iron and steel	5,803	2,157	732	127	95	42	150	217	159
Nonferrous metals	7,514	2,181	695	684	162	138	71	964	132
Manufactures of metals, n.e.s.	10,282	3,647	1,922	442	421	152	95	526	96
Power generating machinery and equipment	22,430	6,450	1,752	1,375	849	1,470	346	1,537	395
Machinery specialized for particular industries	24,286	4,324	1,197	1,168	998	845	320	1,507	680
Metalworking machinery	4,865	911	289	243	304	152	134	377	231
General industrial machinery, equipment, parts	25,048	7,371	1,895	1,096	888	609	292	1,093	717
Office machines and automatic data processing machines	41,947	6,844	1,765	3,951	3,364	2,024	513	4,693	315
Telecommunications, sound recording, reproduction apparatus and equipment	20,332	3,137	1,671	1,210	595	331	305	2,054	724
Electrical machinery, apparatus, and appliances, n.e.s.	65,638	12,768	8,640	3,964	2,369	1,284	713	5,688	429
Road vehicles (incl. air-cushion vehicles)	49,222	25,795	4,482	665	1,721	259	206	4,134	147
Transport equipment, n.e.s.	27,720	2,117	192	1,956	1,103	829	845	2,949	1,189
Furniture, bedding, mattresses, etc.	3,306	1,602	559	95	50	30	13	220	15
Articles of apparel and clothing accessories	6,651	566	1,378	90	99	61	40	961	10
Professional scientific and control instruments and apparatus	19,372	3,064	1,088	1,310	1,394	892	489	2,764	335
Photo apparatus, equipment and optical goods n.e.s.; watch and clocks	5,200	888	285	450	357	209	102	747	52
Miscellaneous manufactured articles	28,515	5,944	2,066	2,018	1,281	765	376	3,125	185
Special transactions and commodities not classified by kind	4,695	1,882	161	230	184	37	24	259	66
Gold, nonmonetary (excluding ores and concentrates)	5,098	404	49	926	198	442	9	221	4
Shipments under $10,000 and under $1,500 documented exports	13,005	2,051	1,728	879	591	410	210	778	83

See footnotes at end of table.

No. 1304. U.S. Exports and General Imports of Major SITC Commodity Groups— Value, by Area: 1995—Continued

[In millions of dollars. See headnote, page 799]

COMMODITY GROUPS	Total [1]	WESTERN HEMISPHERE		WESTERN EUROPE				ASIA	
		Canada	Mexico	United Kingdom	Germany	France	Italy	Japan	China
Imports, total [1]	**743,505**	**145,119**	**61,705**	**26,891**	**36,847**	**17,177**	**16,498**	**123,577**	**45,555**
Meat and meat preparations	2,322	837	8	1	1	4	10	2	1
Fish (except marine mammal) crustaceans, etc., preps	6,741	1,120	446	24	5	31	2	127	306
Vegetables and fruit.	6,581	467	1,952	8	108	29	40	44	162
Coffee, tea, cocoa, spices manufactures thereof	4,856	319	639	37	129	42	41	5	61
Beverages	4,567	633	395	649	199	1,052	398	29	9
Cork and wood	6,153	5,390	154	2	3	2	7	-	2
Pulp and waste paper	3,827	3,226	5	12	5	-	-	-	-
Metalliferous ores and metal scrap	4,000	1,187	486	78	38	21	10	23	30
Petroleum, petroleum products, and related materials	52,569	8,007	5,714	2,764	97	78	64	32	326
Gas, natural and manufactured	5,079	4,636	74	18	5	19	14	3	-
Organic chemicals.	13,325	1,474	360	1,443	1,510	666	500	1,813	229
Inorganic chemicals.	4,655	1,343	240	200	417	250	39	340	201
Medicinal and pharmaceutical products . .	5,544	366	33	914	785	321	404	520	173
Chemical materials and products, n.e.s. . .	3,921	547	84	318	554	254	61	774	120
Rubber manufactures, n.e.s.	5,149	1,473	183	112	255	183	107	1,382	117
Cork and wood manufactures other than furniture	3,798	1,685	150	15	43	73	61	8	223
Paper, paperboard and articles	12,472	8,883	350	262	428	193	84	295	240
Textile yarn, fabrics, made-up articles, n.e.s.	9,985	1,067	722	328	379	249	630	556	1,152
Nonmetallic mineral manufactures, n.e.s..	14,363	1,190	699	533	563	398	734	927	827
Iron and steel.	14,211	2,637	923	523	963	687	366	1,677	244
Nonferrous metals.	14,524	6,101	828	345	538	194	80	383	175
Manufactures of metals, n.e.s.	13,729	2,307	1,109	390	879	382	325	2,140	1,229
Power generating machinery and equipment	20,486	3,319	2,781	1,779	2,044	1,612	300	6,275	281
Machinery specialized for particular industries	18,990	2,184	302	1,299	3,858	905	1,247	5,094	102
Metalworking machinery	5,925	458	17	215	937	65	297	2,402	64
General industrial machinery, equipment, parts	24,113	4,010	1,970	1,223	3,234	651	1,070	5,667	813
Office machines and automatic data processing machines	62,824	4,227	2,186	1,981	892	484	619	18,273	2,903
Telecommunications, sound recording, reproduction apparatus and equipment .	34,384	2,004	6,357	455	216	121	39	8,759	4,308
Electrical machinery, apparatus and appliances, n.e.s.	75,169	4,375	9,226	1,690	3,018	1,466	729	19,168	3,099
Road vehicles (incl air-cushion vehicles) .	100,254	40,239	10,286	1,977	7,648	838	518	31,336	414
Transport equipment, n.e.s.	8,336	2,978	59	908	406	1,780	287	605	31
Furniture, bedding, mattresses, etc.	8,339	2,435	1,194	131	147	68	632	152	883
Travel goods, handbags and similar containers	3,411	25	87	6	20	133	307	6	1,612
Articles of apparel and clothing accessories	39,526	889	2,877	184	122	212	1,188	90	5,854
Footwear.	12,106	97	237	120	72	56	1,022	4	5,824
Professional scientific and control instruments and apparatus	11,572	961	1,737	943	1,409	317	135	2,816	394
Photo apparatus, equipment and optical goods,n.e.s.; watch and clocks.	10,164	378	171	374	478	176	418	3,875	921
Miscellaneous manufactured articles. . . .	36,467	2,754	1,762	1,895	1,215	1,076	2,056	3,849	10,332
Special transactions and commodities not classified by kind	18,024	5,963	2,072	1,285	970	618	321	1,059	172
Estimate of low valued import transactions	5,157	1,426	425	284	446	142	132	828	202

- Represents zero or rounds to zero.   Z Less than $500,000.   [1] Includes countries and commodities not shown separately.
[2] Other than fertilizers covered in SITC division 56 (Fertilizers).   [3] Other than crude fertilizers covered in SITC division 272.

Source: U.S. Bureau of the Census, *U.S. Merchandise Trade: Exports, General Imports, and Imports for Consumption*, series FT 927.

No. 1305. U.S. Exports, Imports, and Merchandise Trade Balance, by Country: 1991 to 1995

[In millions of dollars. Includes silver ore and bullion. Country totals include exports of special category commodities, if any. Data include nonmonetary gold and includes trade of Virgin Islands with foreign countries; see footnote 2 for exception. Minus sign (-) denotes an excess of imports over exports. See *Historical Statistics, Colonial Times to 1970*, series U 317-352, for selected countries]

COUNTRY	EXPORTS, DOMESTIC, AND FOREIGN					GENERAL IMPORTS [1]					MERCHANDISE TRADE BALANCE				
	1991	1992	1993	1994	1995	1991	1992	1993	1994	1995	1991	1992	1993	1994	1995
Total [2]	421,730	448,164	464,767	512,670	584,742	487,129	532,665	580,511	663,768	743,445	-65,399	-84,501	-115,744	-151,098	-158,703
Afghanistan	3	4	10	5	4	5	2	3	6	5	-2	2	7	-1	-1
Albania	18	36	34	16	14	3	5	7	6	10	15	31	27	10	4
Algeria	727	688	938	1,191	774	2,103	1,586	1,583	1,525	1,674	-1,376	-898	-645	-334	-900
Andorra	17	16	15	5	16	(Z)	(Z)	(Z)	(Z)	(Z)	17	16	15	5	16
Angola	186	158	174	197	260	1,775	2,303	2,092	2,061	2,212	-1,589	-2,145	-1,918	-1,864	-1,953
Anguilla	11	11	14	13	15	1	(Z)	(Z)	(Z)	(Z)	10	11	14	13	15
Antigua	74	68	73	65	97	4	5	15	6	3	70	63	58	59	94
Argentina	2,045	3,223	3,776	4,466	4,189	1,287	1,256	1,206	1,725	1,761	758	1,967	2,570	2,741	2,428
Armenia	(X)	25	78	74	70	(X)	2	1	1	16	(X)	23	77	73	54
Aruba	235	288	266	274	247	100	212	457	462	420	135	76	-191	-188	-173
Australia	8,404	8,876	8,277	9,781	10,789	3,988	3,688	3,298	3,200	3,323	4,416	5,188	4,979	6,581	7,466
Austria	1,056	1,256	1,326	1,373	2,017	1,264	1,306	1,411	1,750	1,963	-208	-50	-85	-377	54
Azerbaijan	(X)	(Z)	37	27	36	(X)	(Z)	(Z)	(Z)	1	(X)	(Z)	37	27	35
Bahamas, The	721	712	704	685	661	469	605	328	203	156	252	107	376	482	505
Bahrain	500	489	636	443	255	87	61	97	155	134	413	428	539	288	121
Bangladesh	179	188	255	234	325	524	831	887	1,080	1,257	-345	-643	-632	-846	-932
Barbados	166	128	146	161	186	31	31	35	34	38	135	97	111	127	148
Byelarus	(X)	25	92	47	48	(X)	25	34	54	45	(X)	(Z)	58	-7	3
Belgium	10,572	9,775	8,878	10,944	12,466	3,929	4,476	5,149	6,342	6,054	6,643	5,299	3,729	4,602	6,412
Belize	114	117	136	115	100	45	59	54	51	52	69	58	82	64	48
Benin	26	27	22	26	34	22	10	6	10	10	4	17	16	16	24
Bermuda	233	242	265	300	299	8	7	15	9	11	225	236	250	291	288
Bolivia	192	222	218	186	214	209	162	191	260	263	-17	60	27	-74	-49
Bosnia-Hercegovina [3]	(X)	5	25	39	28	(X)	9	7	4	3	(X)	-4	18	35	25
Botswana	31	47	25	23	36	13	13	8	14	21	18	34	17	9	15
Brazil	6,148	5,751	6,058	8,118	11,439	6,717	7,609	7,479	8,708	8,830	-569	-1,858	-1,421	-590	2,610
British Virgin Islands	45	44	46	47	49	2	3	14	15	11	43	41	32	32	38
Brunei	162	453	473	376	190	26	29	31	46	38	136	424	442	330	152
Bulgaria	142	85	115	110	132	56	78	159	212	189	86	7	-44	-102	-57
Burkina	24	13	18	7	15	1	(Z)	(Z)	(Z)	(Z)	23	13	18	7	15
Cameroon	45	57	49	54	46	127	84	102	56	48	-82	-27	-53	-2	-2
Canada	85,150	90,594	100,444	114,441	127,226	91,064	98,630	111,216	128,948	145,349	-5,914	-8,036	-10,772	-14,506	-18,123
Cayman Islands	117	282	164	202	180	18	10	34	52	18	99	272	130	150	162
Chad	14	5	8	8	11	(Z)	(Z)	(Z)	2	3	14	5	8	6	8
Chile	1,839	2,466	2,599	2,776	3,615	1,302	1,388	1,462	1,822	1,931	537	1,078	1,137	954	1,684
China	6,278	7,418	8,763	9,287	11,754	18,969	25,728	31,540	38,781	45,543	-12,691	-18,309	-22,777	-29,494	-33,790
Colombia	1,952	3,286	3,235	4,070	4,624	2,736	3,751	3,032	3,171	3,751	-784	-465	203	899	873
Congo (Brazzaville)	43	59	27	38	55	410	510	500	403	207	-367	-451	-473	-365	-152
Costa Rica	1,034	1,357	1,542	1,867	1,737	1,154	1,411	1,541	1,647	1,844	-120	-54	1	220	-107
Croatia [3]	(X)	91	103	147	140	(X)	43	106	115	94	(X)	48	-3	32	46
Cyprus	119	166	138	209	258	12	11	16	18	13	107	155	122	191	245
Czechoslovakia	123	413	(X)	(X)	(X)	145	242	(X)	(X)	(X)	-22	171	(X)	(X)	(X)
Czech Republic	(X)	(X)	267	297	363	(X)	(X)	277	316	364	(X)	(X)	-10	-18	-1
Denmark	1,574	1,473	1,092	1,215	1,518	1,661	1,667	1,664	2,122	1,945	-87	-194	-572	-907	-427

See footnotes at end of table.

No. 1305. U.S. Exports, Imports, and Merchandise Trade Balance, by Country: 1991 to 1995—Continued

[See headnote, page 801]

COUNTRY	EXPORTS, DOMESTIC AND FOREIGN					GENERAL IMPORTS [1]					MERCHANDISE TRADE BALANCE				
	1991	1992	1993	1994	1995	1991	1992	1993	1994	1995	1991	1992	1993	1994	1995
Djibouti	10	11	13	7	9	(Z)	(Z)	(Z)	-	(Z)	10	11	13	7	9
Dominica	42	34	27	26	27	5	6	6	7	7	37	29	22	19	20
Dominican Republic	1,743	2,100	2,350	2,800	3,015	2,008	2,372	2,672	3,094	3,399	-265	-273	-322	-294	-384
Ecuador	948	999	1,100	1,196	1,538	1,327	1,343	1,399	1,727	1,929	-379	-344	-299	-531	-391
Egypt	2,720	3,088	2,768	2,844	2,985	206	435	613	548	606	2,514	2,654	2,155	2,295	2,379
El Salvador	534	742	873	932	1,111	303	384	488	609	812	231	358	385	323	298
Equatorial Guinea	13	11	3	2	5	(Z)	(Z)	(Z)	(Z)	31	13	11	3	2	-26
Estonia	(X)	59	54	33	139	(X)	13	20	29	62	(X)	46	34	4	77
Ethiopia	210	250	139	143	148	15	9	22	34	33	196	241	117	109	115
Federated States of Micronesia	46	32	25	25	23	6	13	14	13	13	41	19	11	11	10
Fiji	18	59	27	118	32	43	67	69	97	78	-25	-8	-42	21	-46
Finland	952	785	848	1,069	1,250	1,085	1,185	1,608	1,803	2,270	-133	-400	-761	-734	-1,020
France	15,346	14,593	13,267	13,622	14,245	13,333	14,797	15,279	16,775	17,200	2,013	-205	-2,013	-3,152	-2,964
French Guiana	150	82	323	196	442	1	3	3	3	5	150	78	321	193	436
French Polynesia	80	82	102	72	82	12	11	8	14	14	68	71	94	58	68
Gabon	85	55	48	40	54	712	921	961	1,155	1,449	-627	-866	-913	-1,114	-1,395
Gambia	11	10	10	4	6	2	(Z)	9	2	2	9	10	1	2	4
Georgia	(X)	16	48	79	95	(X)	7	21	2	10	(X)	9	27	77	85
Germany	21,302	21,249	18,932	19,237	22,394	26,137	28,820	28,562	31,749	36,844	-4,835	-7,572	-9,630	-12,512	-14,450
Ghana	142	124	215	125	167	152	96	216	199	196	-10	27	-1	-74	-29
Gibraltar	10	11	8	23	18	1	2	4	4	5	9	9	5	19	13
Greece	1,039	901	880	830	1,519	429	370	348	455	397	610	531	533	375	1,122
Greenland	4	3	3	3	2	4	11	13	9	7	-	-8	-10	-6	-5
Grenada	31	24	24	24	27	8	8	8	8	5	23	16	16	16	22
Guadeloupe	83	60	49	51	69	2	1	5	2	1	81	59	44	49	68
Guatemala	945	1,205	1,312	1,355	1,647	899	1,081	1,194	1,283	1,527	46	124	118	72	120
Guinea	88	61	59	50	67	138	103	117	92	99	-50	-42	-58	-42	-32
Guyana	86	118	122	110	141	83	102	91	98	107	3	17	32	12	34
Haiti	395	209	229	211	550	284	107	154	59	130	111	102	74	152	420
Honduras	625	811	899	1,012	1,279	557	783	914	1,097	1,441	68	28	-15	-86	-162
Hong Kong	8,137	9,077	9,874	11,445	14,231	9,279	9,793	9,554	9,698	10,291	-1,142	-716	319	1,748	3,940
Hungary	256	295	435	309	295	367	347	401	470	547	-111	-52	34	-161	-252
Iceland	156	119	147	112	171	209	165	233	249	233	-53	-46	-86	-137	-62
India	1,999	1,917	2,778	2,296	3,296	3,193	3,780	4,554	5,302	5,726	-1,194	-1,863	-1,776	-3,005	-2,430
Indonesia	1,892	2,780	2,770	2,811	3,360	3,241	4,530	5,435	6,523	7,435	-1,349	-1,750	-2,665	-3,712	-4,076
Iran	528	748	616	329	277	231	1	(Z)	1	(Z)	297	747	616	328	277
Iraq	(Z)	1	4	(Z)	(Z)	(Z)	(Z)	(Z)	(Z)	(Z)	(Z)	1	4	(Z)	(Z)
Ireland	2,681	2,862	2,728	3,416	4,109	1,948	2,262	2,519	2,890	4,079	733	600	209	525	30
Israel	3,911	4,077	4,429	5,006	5,621	3,484	3,816	4,420	5,223	5,709	427	261	9	-217	-88
Italy	8,570	8,721	6,464	7,193	8,862	11,764	12,314	13,216	14,711	16,348	-3,194	-3,593	-6,752	-7,518	-7,487
Ivory Coast	81	87	89	111	173	223	188	178	185	214	-142	-100	-90	-74	-41
Jamaica	961	939	1,116	1,066	1,420	576	599	720	747	847	385	340	397	319	573
Japan	48,125	47,813	47,892	53,481	64,343	91,511	97,414	107,246	119,149	123,479	-43,386	-49,601	-59,355	-65,669	-59,137
Jordan	219	258	361	288	335	6	18	19	29	29	213	240	342	259	307
Kazakhstan	(X)	15	68	131	81	(X)	21	41	60	123	(X)	-6	27	71	-42
Kenya	91	124	131	170	114	69	73	92	109	102	22	51	39	61	13
Kiribati	27	35	31	23	2	1	(Z)	2	(Z)	1	26	35	29	23	1

See footnotes at end of table.

COUNTRY	EXPORTS, DOMESTIC AND FOREIGN					GENERAL IMPORTS[1]					MERCHANDISE TRADE BALANCE				
	1991	1992	1993	1994	1995	1991	1992	1993	1994	1995	1991	1992	1993	1994	1995
Kuwait	1,228	1,337	999	1,175	1,437	36	281	1,819	1,445	1,336	1,192	1,055	-819	-270	102
Kyrgyzstan	(X)	2	18	6	25	(X)	1	2	8	8	(X)	1	16	-2	16
Latvia	(X)	55	90	101	90	(X)	11	22	51	82	(X)	44	67	51	8
Lebanon	165	311	377	443	592	27	28	27	25	35	138	283	351	418	557
Lesotho	4	3	7	3	2	28	53	53	63	62	-24	-50	-48	-60	-60
Liberia	50	31	39	46	42	9	13	3	4	10	41	18	36	43	32
Liechtenstein	10	12	11	14	15	21	36	100	96	126	-11	-23	-89	-82	-111
Lithuania	(X)	44	57	41	52	(X)	5	16	16	26	(X)	39	41	26	26
Luxembourg	217	272	560	228	374	188	227	253	288	234	29	45	307	-59	140
Macao	10	19	28	21	30	581	721	669	791	895	-571	-702	-641	-770	-865
Macedonia[3]	(X)	4	11	14	21	(X)	46	111	82	89	(X)	-42	-100	-68	-68
Madagascar	14	6	11	14	10	47	53	43	23	57	-33	-47	-32	-9	-47
Malawi	55	14	26	48	18	73	60	58	57	41	-18	-46	-32	-38	-23
Malaysia	3,900	4,363	6,064	6,965	8,816	6,102	8,294	10,563	13,977	17,453	-2,202	-3,931	-4,499	-7,012	-8,637
Mali	18	33	33	19	23	2	2	4	4	4	16	31	29	15	19
Malta	57	58	172	88	107	65	91	140	96	132	-8	-33	32	-8	-25
Marshall Islands	38	34	36	33	32	3	8	5	5	11	35	26	31	28	21
Martinique	36	33	33	31	38	1	2	2	3	2	35	31	31	28	36
Mauritania	22	59	20	14	43	11	8	7	3	5	11	51	13	11	38
Mauritius	15	22	18	24	25	132	136	198	217	230	-117	-113	-180	-193	-205
Mexico	33,277	40,592	41,581	50,840	46,292	31,130	35,211	39,917	49,493	61,685	2,147	5,381	1,664	1,348	-15,393
Moldova	(X)	9	6	23	10	(X)	(Z)	(Z)	18	25	(X)	9	6	5	-15
Monaco	7	9	6	6	10	14	15	16	18	12	-7	-6	-10	-12	-3
Morocco	403	496	600	405	517	154	178	185	192	239	249	318	415	213	278
Mozambique	101	59	59	39	49	23	19	9	15	28	78	130	50	24	22
Namibia	33	34	22	16	27	35	23	22	28	12	-2	11	-1	-12	15
Netherlands	13,511	13,752	12,839	13,591	16,558	4,811	5,300	5,443	6,015	6,405	8,700	8,452	7,395	7,576	10,153
Netherlands Antilles	627	478	519	520	504	647	644	397	425	288	-20	-166	123	96	216
New Caledonia	44	36	23	27	22	15	15	24	23	40	24	21	-2	5	-18
New Zealand	1,006	1,307	1,249	1,508	1,691	1,209	1,219	1,208	1,421	1,452	-203	88	41	88	240
Nicaragua	150	185	150	186	250	60	69	128	167	239	90	117	22	19	11
Niger	10	13	16	12	40	5	3	3	2	2	5	10	13	10	38
Nigeria	831	1,001	895	509	603	5,168	5,103	5,301	4,430	4,801	-4,337	-4,102	-4,407	-3,921	-4,198
Norway	1,489	1,279	1,212	1,268	1,293	1,624	1,969	1,958	2,373	3,087	-135	-690	-745	-1,105	-1,794
Oman	202	257	251	219	222	115	186	277	459	295	87	71	-26	-240	-73
Pakistan	950	881	811	719	941	663	865	897	1,012	1,197	288	16	-86	-293	-256
Panama	978	1,103	1,187	1,276	1,390	269	254	280	323	307	709	850	908	954	1,083
Papua New Guinea	96	72	50	65	51	34	64	98	108	50	62	8	-48	-43	1
Paraguay	374	415	521	794	992	43	35	50	80	55	331	380	472	713	937
Peru	840	1,005	1,072	1,408	1,775	776	739	754	840	1,035	64	267	318	568	741
Philippines	2,265	2,759	3,529	3,888	5,295	3,471	4,355	4,894	5,720	7,007	-1,206	-1,597	-1,364	-1,832	-1,712
Poland	459	641	912	625	776	357	375	454	651	664	102	266	458	-26	112
Portugal	792	1,024	727	1,055	898	695	664	785	898	1,057	97	360	-59	156	-158
Qatar	147	189	166	162	226	30	70	65	81	91	117	119	101	81	135
Romania	209	248	324	337	253	69	87	69	195	222	140	161	254	142	31

See footnotes at end of table.

No. 1305. U.S. Exports, Imports, and Merchandise Trade Balance, by Country: 1991 to 1995—Continued

[See headnote, page 801]

COUNTRY	EXPORTS, DOMESTIC AND FOREIGN					GENERAL IMPORTS [1]					MERCHANDISE TRADE BALANCE				
	1991	1992	1993	1994	1995	1991	1992	1993	1994	1995	1991	1992	1993	1994	1995
Russia	(X)	2,112	2,970	2,579	2,823	(X)	481	1,743	3,235	4,030	(X)	1,631	1,227	-656	-1,207
Saudi Arabia	6,557	7,167	6,661	6,011	6,155	10,900	10,371	7,708	7,687	8,237	-4,343	-3,204	-1,047	-1,676	-2,082
Senegal	76	80	70	43	68	10	8	8	11	5	66	70	63	31	63
Singapore	8,804	9,626	11,678	13,022	15,333	9,957	11,313	12,798	15,361	18,561	-1,153	-1,687	-1,120	-2,339	-3,227
Slovakia	(X)	21	34	43	61	(X)	(X)	65	129	130	(X)	(X)	-31	-86	-69
Somalia	7	5	46	30	8	3	2	(Z)	(Z)	(Z)	4	3	46	30	8
South Africa	2,113	2,434	2,188	2,173	2,751	1,728	1,727	1,845	2,030	2,208	385	707	344	142	543
South Korea	15,505	14,639	14,782	18,028	25,380	17,019	16,682	17,118	19,658	24,184	-1,514	-2,043	-2,336	-1,629	1,196
Spain	5,474	5,537	4,168	4,625	5,526	2,848	3,002	2,992	3,554	3,875	2,626	2,535	1,176	1,071	1,651
Sri Lanka	121	178	203	198	279	604	789	1,002	1,093	1,260	-483	-612	-799	-895	-981
Sudan	92	53	59	55	43	16	11	12	35	23	76	42	47	21	20
Suriname	134	142	114	122	190	52	46	58	43	100	82	96	56	79	89
Sweden	3,287	2,844	2,354	2,520	3,080	4,525	4,716	4,534	5,044	6,256	-1,238	-1,872	-2,180	-2,524	-3,177
Switzerland	5,557	4,540	6,807	5,614	6,228	5,576	5,645	5,973	6,376	7,594	-19	-1,105	834	-762	-1,366
Syria	209	165	187	199	223	25	42	130	64	56	184	123	56	134	168
Taiwan	13,182	15,250	16,168	17,078	19,290	23,023	24,596	25,102	26,711	28,972	-9,841	-9,346	-8,934	-9,633	-9,682
Tajikistan	(X)	9	12	15	18	(X)	2	18	60	41	(X)	7	-6	-44	-23
Tanzania	35	34	33	49	66	15	11	11	15	22	20	23	21	34	44
Thailand	3,753	3,989	3,766	4,861	6,665	6,122	7,529	8,542	10,307	11,348	-2,369	-3,540	-4,775	-5,446	-4,683
Togo	24	20	13	13	19	2	7	3	4	4	22	13	9	9	15
Trinidad and Tobago	468	447	529	541	689	866	848	803	1,109	968	-398	-401	-274	-569	-279
Tunisia	172	233	232	327	215	25	48	41	54	70	147	184	192	273	145
Turkey	2,468	2,735	3,429	2,754	2,768	1,006	1,110	1,198	1,575	1,798	1,462	1,625	2,231	1,178	970
Turkmenistan	(X)	35	46	137	34	(X)	1	2	2	1	(X)	34	44	136	33
Turks and Caicos Islands	40	38	29	28	34	4	6	4	4	13	36	32	25	24	21
Uganda	13	15	21	29	22	18	12	10	35	13	-5	3	11	-6	9
Ukraine	(X)	307	310	181	223	(X)	89	166	327	406	(X)	218	145	-146	-182
United Arab Emirates	1,455	1,553	1,811	1,593	2,007	713	812	727	449	453	742	741	1,084	1,144	1,553
United Kingdom	22,046	22,800	26,438	26,833	28,857	18,413	20,093	21,730	25,063	26,898	3,633	2,707	4,708	1,770	1,959
Uruguay	216	231	254	311	396	237	266	266	168	167	-21	-35	-12	143	229
U.S.S.R. (former)	3,579	1,036	(X)	(X)	(X)	802	187	(X)	(X)	(X)	2,777	849	(X)	(X)	(X)
Uzbekistan	(X)	51	73	90	63	(X)	(Z)	7	3	19	(X)	51	66	87	45
Venezuela	4,656	5,444	4,590	4,042	4,640	8,179	8,181	8,140	8,378	9,721	-3,523	-2,737	-3,550	-4,337	-5,080
Vietnam	4	7	7	172	253	(Z)	2	(Z)	50	199	4	5	7	122	54
Western Samoa	7	73	10	7	8	1	1	1	(Z)	1	6	72	9	7	7
Yemen, Republic of	192	321	322	178	186	152	41	225	183	42	40	281	98	-5	144
Yugoslavia (former) [3]	371	167	(X)	(X)	(X)	674	225	(X)	(X)	(X)	-303	-58	(X)	(X)	(X)
Yugoslavia, Fed. Rep. of [3]	(X)	6	2	1	2	(X)	39	(Z)	(Z)	(X)	(X)	-33	2	1	(X)
Zaire	62	33	35	40	77	294	250	238	188	261	-232	-218	-203	-148	-184
Zambia	24	68	42	33	49	42	70	68	64	33	-18	-2	-26	-31	16
Zimbabwe	53	144	84	93	122	90	106	110	102	98	-37	38	-26	-10	24

- Represents zero. Z Less than $500,000. X Not applicable. [3] Beginning June 1992 trade data were reported for the following countries which were formerly part of Yugoslavia — Croatia, Slovenia, Bosnia-Hercegovina, and Macedonia. The Federal Republic of Yugoslavia, which now includes only Serbia and Montenegro, will continue to be shown as "Yugoslavia." "Yugoslavia (former)" reflects data for the former country and includes data for the period of January through May 1992.

[1] Imports are on a customs value basis. Exports are f.a.s. value. [2] Includes revisions not carried to country values; therefore, country values will not add to total.

Source: U.S. Bureau of the Census, U.S. Merchandise Trade, series FT 900, monthly.

No. 1306. U.S. Exports and General Imports, by Selected Commodity Groups: 1992 to 1995

[In millions of dollars. N.e.s.=Not elsewhere specified]

COMMODITY GROUP	EXPORTS [1]				GENERAL IMPORTS [2]			
	1992	1993	1994	1995	1992	1993	1994	1995
Total..................	448,164	465,091	512,626	584,742	532,665	580,659	663,256	743,445
Agricultural commodities	**42,238**	**41,938**	**44,936**	**54,850**	**23,375**	**23,641**	**25,955**	**29,261**
Animal feeds	3,550	3,464	3,353	3,667	337	368	433	473
Bulbs	112	107	112	110	201	217	238	283
Cereal flour	924	1,099	1,159	1,163	724	802	970	1,084
Cocoa....................	31	39	34	39	774	739	698	723
Coffee....................	18	32	53	15	1,563	1,383	2,270	2,985
Corn.....................	4,966	4,504	4,197	7,521	69	61	85	66
Cotton, raw and linters..........	2,015	1,575	2,641	3,711	11	12	21	29
Dairy products; eggs	711	820	717	776	506	544	583	620
Furskins, raw...............	95	98	131	127	61	59	78	59
Grains, unmilled	894	683	695	721	122	157	181	176
Hides and skins	1,253	1,187	1,391	1,621	124	119	126	140
Live animals................	609	519	587	521	1,437	1,536	1,392	1,727
Meat and preparations..........	4,208	4,353	5,195	6,450	2,712	2,792	2,627	2,316
Oils/fats, animal	497	472	566	789	18	21	21	24
Oils/fats, vegetable	725	734	963	1,293	955	859	1,051	1,157
Plants....................	135	112	117	120	102	92	105	131
Rice.....................	726	791	1,009	994	92	106	130	121
Seeds....................	302	294	315	321	153	154	152	173
Soybeans	4,463	4,580	4,355	5,422	16	22	46	32
Sugar....................	6	2	5	5	662	606	552	679
Tobacco, unmanufactured........	1,649	1,299	1,304	1,397	951	942	697	555
Vegetables and fruit	5,736	6,008	6,757	7,098	5,698	5,665	6,075	6,581
Wheat....................	4,503	4,679	4,055	5,464	191	213	291	238
Other agricultural	4,112	4,489	5,225	5,504	5,898	6,172	7,134	8,889
Manufactured goods...........	**347,494**	**364,849**	**402,674**	**451,828**	**434,349**	**479,898**	**557,310**	**629,632**
ADP equipment, office machinery. . .	27,000	27,177	30,867	36,410	36,377	43,193	52,058	62,824
Airplanes..................	26,286	21,270	18,803	13,836	3,860	3,805	3,719	3,552
Airplane parts...............	9,366	9,487	9,824	10,349	3,358	2,613	2,727	2,615
Aluminum	2,667	2,310	2,787	3,775	2,540	3,277	4,943	5,819
Artwork/antiques.............	1,076	951	1,184	1,071	2,087	2,673	2,432	2,671
Basketware, etc	1,522	1,644	1,816	1,996	2,189	2,392	2,588	2,940
Chemicals, cosmetics	2,632	3,047	3,537	3,835	1,711	1,808	1,998	2,310
Chemicals, dyeing.............	1,871	2,014	2,330	2,585	1,623	1,700	1,869	2,080
Chemicals, fertilizers	2,371	1,798	2,703	3,219	952	1,136	1,298	1,392
Chemicals, inorganic	4,123	3,810	4,067	4,541	3,305	3,284	4,087	4,655
Chemicals, medicinal...........	5,357	5,751	6,096	6,434	3,810	4,135	4,674	5,544
Chemicals, organic	10,993	11,076	12,789	16,106	9,406	9,279	10,805	13,325
Chemicals, plastics	10,258	10,743	12,485	14,958	4,292	4,848	5,941	7,152
Chemicals, n.e.s.	6,265	6,835	7,657	9,131	2,622	2,941	3,235	3,922
Clothing	4,092	4,815	5,461	6,482	31,227	33,780	36,748	39,526
Copper	1,172	1,200	1,266	1,728	1,642	1,733	2,295	2,984
Electrical machinery	32,172	36,817	44,454	53,139	39,710	46,735	57,750	75,170
Footwear..................	603	605	646	671	10,163	11,173	11,712	12,106
Furniture and parts	2,553	2,948	3,131	3,125	5,503	6,249	7,565	8,339
Gem diamonds...............	369	153	184	171	4,148	5,103	5,756	5,971
General industrial machinery......	18,480	19,515	21,813	24,394	15,520	17,082	21,330	24,113
Glass	1,213	1,341	1,503	1,644	850	1,004	1,350	1,467
Glassware.................	496	502	560	630	1,015	1,031	1,158	1,335
Gold, nonmonetary	4,109	9,115	5,689	5,055	1,899	2,014	1,933	2,153
Iron and steel mill products......	3,606	3,330	3,554	5,349	8,328	9,027	12,896	12,296
Lighting, plumbing.............	977	1,097	1,249	1,293	1,547	1,762	2,024	2,282
Metal manufactures, n.e.s.......	5,513	5,975	7,034	8,060	6,727	7,647	8,847	10,009
Metalworking machinery.........	3,034	3,256	3,897	4,626	3,187	3,683	4,596	5,925
Motorcycles, bicycles..........	1,439	1,433	1,515	1,786	1,913	2,161	2,322	2,821
Nickel....................	196	199	210	284	797	686	735	1,196
Optical goods...............	766	797	965	1,113	1,645	1,683	1,817	2,148
Paper and paperboard..........	6,348	6,463	7,448	9,572	7,998	8,640	9,066	12,472
Photographic equipment.........	2,950	2,932	3,016	3,351	3,844	4,267	4,676	5,146
Plastic articles, n.e.s...........	2,777	2,988	3,574	3,847	3,572	3,937	4,517	5,103
Platinum	292	339	306	318	1,429	1,255	1,325	1,694
Pottery	103	110	104	99	1,404	1,436	1,555	1,666
Power generating machinery......	17,995	19,167	20,346	21,856	15,888	17,125	19,543	20,486
Printed materials.............	3,803	3,995	3,971	4,325	1,875	2,026	2,234	2,588
Records/magnetic media	4,846	5,317	5,864	6,263	3,106	3,443	3,612	3,892
Rubber articles, n.e.s.	622	679	795	888	878	1,014	1,253	1,417
Rubber tires and tubes	1,409	1,465	1,614	1,858	2,512	2,736	3,034	3,144

See footnotes at end of table.

No. 1306. U.S. Exports and General Imports, by Selected SITC Commodity Groups: 1992 to 1995—Continued

[In millions of dollars]

COMMODITY GROUP	EXPORTS [1]				GENERAL IMPORTS [2]			
	1992	1993	1994	1995	1992	1993	1994	1995
Manufactured goods—Continued								
Scientific instruments	14,375	15,223	16,475	18,616	7,602	8,457	9,963	11,572
Ships, boats	1,421	976	1,165	1,178	319	969	808	817
Silver and bullion	209	203	256	663	449	390	488	579
Spacecraft	270	393	444	655	92	-	219	169
Specialized industrial machinery . . .	16,689	17,626	19,677	23,311	11,814	13,565	16,733	18,990
Telecommunications equipment	11,248	13,122	15,872	19,005	25,803	27,297	32,418	34,384
Textile yarn, fabric	5,778	5,895	6,445	7,192	7,844	8,438	9,207	9,985
Toys/games/sporting goods	2,437	2,707	3,079	3,560	10,749	11,637	11,824	13,081
Travel goods	194	199	233	253	2,509	2,653	3,085	3,411
Vehicles/new cars, Canada	5,931	6,350	7,465	7,187	13,890	17,654	21,687	24,407
Vehicles/new cars, Japan	694	982	1,787	2,642	20,801	21,581	24,020	21,501
Vehicles/new cars, Other	5,095	4,914	5,824	5,100	11,561	12,022	13,470	18,029
Vehicles/trucks	3,706	4,144	5,126	5,646	9,772	10,109	10,355	11,259
Vehicles/chassis/bodies	310	370	427	441	338	406	429	435
Vehicles/parts	16,753	19,307	21,314	23,354	15,838	17,653	19,609	20,070
Watches/clocks/parts	208	236	276	248	2,320	2,546	2,641	2,785
Wood manufactures	1,389	1,475	1,543	1,633	2,410	2,869	3,390	3,687
Zinc	38	40	47	58	855	736	787	924
Other manufactured goods	27,031	26,220	28,102	30,911	32,924	35,397	42,156	45,301
Mineral fuel	11,254	9,756	8,911	10,358	55,256	55,900	56,391	59,206
Coal	4,427	3,197	2,966	3,714	419	514	646	703
Crude oil	32	20	49	6	38,553	38,469	38,479	42,799
Petroleum preparations	4,011	3,920	3,167	3,244	11,277	10,789	10,270	9,118
Liquified propane/butane	257	229	195	316	707	951	873	852
Natural gas	353	241	254	266	3,030	3,678	3,937	3,275
Electricity	63	102	31	57	590	662	973	856
Other mineral fuels	2,111	2,046	2,248	2,755	680	836	1,213	1,605
Selected commodities:								
Fish and preparations	3,383	2,991	3,036	3,177	5,657	5,820	6,590	6,741
Cork, wood, lumber	5,314	5,786	5,572	5,637	3,970	5,633	6,680	6,153
Pulp and waste paper	3,859	2,978	3,794	6,206	2,129	1,886	2,315	3,827
Metal ores; scrap	3,470	3,227	3,713	5,564	3,340	3,030	3,262	4,000
Crude fertilizers	1,388	1,345	1,446	1,525	894	936	1,026	1,174
Cigarettes	4,193	3,919	4,965	4,770	271	491	70	64
Alcoholic bev. distilled	344	343	355	390	1,827	1,737	1,826	1,842
All other	2,801	2,716	3,243	3,857	1,597	1,687	1,831	1,607
Re-exports	22,427	25,244	29,981	36,581	(X)	(X)	(X)	(X)
Agricultural commodities	893	889	987	1,174	(X)	(X)	(X)	(X)
Manufactured goods	20,977	23,832	28,383	34,848	(X)	(X)	(X)	(X)
Mineral fuels	76	107	78	120	(X)	(X)	(X)	(X)
Other, re-exports	481	416	532	439	(X)	(X)	(X)	(X)
Timing adjustment	(X)	(X)	(X)	(X)	(X)	(X)	(X)	-75

X Not applicable.　[1] F.A.S. basis.　[2] Customs value basis.
Source: U.S. Bureau of the Census, *U.S. Merchandise Trade,* series FT 900, Final Reports.

No. 1307. Imports for Consumption—Values and Duties: 1980 to 1995

[Imports are on customs value basis. Beginning 1970, includes silver ores and bullion, and beginning 1980, includes trade of Virgin Islands with foreign countries. For basis of dollar values for area coverage, see text, section 28. See also *Historical Statistics, Colonial Times to 1970,* series U 207-212]

YEAR	VALUES				Duties calculated [1] (mil. dol.)	RATIO OF DUTIES TO VALUES		Duties per capita [2] (dollar)
	Total (mil. dol.)	Free (mil. dol.)	Dutiable (mil. dol.)	Percent free		Total imports (percent)	Dutiable imports (percent)	
1980	[3]244,007	106,992	132,951	45	7,535	3.1	5.7	33.09
1981	259,012	76,338	182,674	29	8,893	3.4	4.9	38.67
1982	242,340	75,856	166,484	31	8,688	3.6	5.2	37.40
1983	256,679	83,397	173,283	32	9,430	3.7	5.4	40.21
1984	322,989	102,977	220,012	32	12,042	3.7	5.5	50.90
1985	343,553	106,035	237,518	31	13,067	3.8	5.5	54.73
1986	368,657	121,742	246,915	33	13,312	3.6	5.4	55.10
1987	402,066	132,152	269,914	33	13,923	3.5	5.2	57.08
1988	437,140	151,693	285,447	35	15,054	3.4	5.3	61.12
1989	468,012	156,365	311,647	33	16,096	3.4	5.2	64.70
1990	490,554	161,108	329,446	33	16,339	3.3	5.0	65.38
1991	483,028	167,641	315,386	35	16,197	3.4	5.1	64.10
1992	525,091	194,583	330,508	37	17,164	3.3	5.2	67.12
1993	574,863	236,007	338,856	41	18,334	3.2	5.4	70.99
1994	657,885	292,257	365,628	44	19,846	3.0	5.6	73.64
1995	739,660	373,948	365,713	51	18,597	2.5	5.1	64.70

[1] Customs duties (including import excise taxes) calculated on the basis of reports of quantity and value of imports of merchandise entered directly for consumption or withdrawn from bonded customs warehouses.　[2] Based on estimated population including Armed Forces abroad as of July 1.　[3] Total includes revisions not carried to free and dutiable values.
Source: U.S. Bureau of the Census, 1970-1988, *Highlights of U.S. Export and Import Trade,* series FT 990, monthly; beginning 1989, *U.S. Merchandise Trade: Selected Highlights,* series FT 920, and unpublished data.

No. 1308. Domestic Exports and Imports for Consumption of Merchandise, by Selected SIC-Based Product Category: 1985 to 1995

[In millions of dollars. Includes nonmonetary gold]

SIC-BASED PRODUCT CATEGORY	SIC [1] code	1985	1990	1991	1992	1993	1994	1995
Domestic exports, total [2]	(X)	212,961	374,537	400,842	425,377	439,282	482,141	547,300
Agricultural, forestry and fishery products	(X)	20,074	26,225	25,052	26,785	25,324	26,102	33,418
Agricultural products	01	19,199	22,597	21,075	22,633	21,615	22,189	29,391
Livestock and livestock products	02	735	829	970	871	836	973	920
Forestry products	08	122	281	306	324	276	263	272
Fish, fresh or chilled; and other marine products [3]	09	18	2,518	2,701	2,959	2,596	2,677	2,836
Mineral commodities	(X)	6,394	7,335	7,442	7,210	5,584	5,650	7,159
Metallic ores and concentrates	10	686	1,137	1,014	1,084	799	1,018	1,562
Bituminous, lignite and anthracite coal	11,12	4,465	4,513	4,623	4,241	3,090	2,858	3,572
Crude petroleum and natural gas	13	476	638	675	737	588	576	729
Nonmetallic minerals, exc. fuels	14	767	1,047	1,130	1,148	1,107	1,199	1,296
Manufactured commodities	(X)	175,752	330,403	359,635	383,082	400,721	441,501	496,421
Food and kindred products	20	10,055	16,160	17,492	19,761	20,509	23,094	26,021
Tobacco manufactures	21	1,268	5,040	4,574	4,509	4,253	5,367	5,222
Textile mill products	22	1,462	3,635	4,108	4,473	4,687	5,151	5,696
Apparel and related products	23	1,019	2,848	3,679	4,599	5,433	6,145	7,190
Lumber and related products	24	2,668	6,523	6,477	6,802	7,361	7,252	7,424
Furniture and fixtures	25	483	1,589	2,086	2,518	2,818	3,030	2,953
Paper and allied products	26	3,886	8,631	9,214	9,969	9,457	11,000	14,943
Printing and publishing	27	1,250	3,150	3,590	3,808	4,057	4,070	4,471
Chemicals and allied products	28	21,797	37,806	41,483	41,953	42,742	48,950	57,897
Petroleum and coal products	29	5,433	6,794	7,026	6,403	6,163	5,510	6,014
Rubber and misc. plastics products	30	2,765	6,398	7,049	7,872	8,554	9,942	11,025
Leather and leather products	31	478	1,388	1,413	1,541	1,536	1,539	1,565
Stone, clay, and glass products	32	1,792	3,295	3,533	3,855	3,844	4,215	4,796
Primary metal products	33	4,747	13,116	15,243	15,105	18,669	16,327	20,191
Fabricated metal products	34	5,765	11,138	11,962	13,265	13,497	13,395	15,161
Machinery, except electrical	35	37,478	61,229	65,300	68,554	72,279	82,120	95,909
Electric and electronic machinery	36	18,908	39,807	42,330	45,992	52,947	63,839	76,235
Transportation equipment	37	38,024	68,113	76,172	82,862	80,196	85,068	82,699
Instruments and related products	38	8,623	19,524	21,699	22,815	24,699	26,560	29,581
Misc. manufactured commodities	39	1,773	4,296	4,621	5,446	5,288	5,813	7,383
Imports for consumption, total [2]	(X)	343,553	490,554	483,028	525,091	574,863	657,884	739,661
Agricultural, forestry and fishery products	(X)	12,805	12,750	13,148	14,216	15,866	17,427	19,799
Agricultural products	01	7,483	5,925	6,107	6,716	7,839	8,657	9,803
Livestock and livestock products	02	933	1,453	1,501	1,873	2,161	2,047	2,450
Forestry products	08	830	1,015	978	1,088	1,068	1,208	1,932
Fish, fresh or chilled; and other marine products [3]	09	3,559	4,357	4,562	4,540	4,798	5,515	5,614
Mineral commodities	(X)	39,011	51,391	44,581	44,823	45,965	47,300	51,050
Metallic ores and concentrates	10	1,265	1,500	1,244	1,167	1,108	1,283	1,413
Bituminous, lignite and anthracite coal	11,12	70	93	112	127	218	229	248
Crude petroleum and natural gas	13	35,872	48,917	42,415	42,796	43,871	44,949	48,495
Nonmetallic minerals, exc. fuels	14	1,804	881	810	734	767	839	894
Manufactured commodities	(X)	280,089	407,043	406,550	445,127	490,289	567,052	639,729
Food and kindred products	20	12,521	16,564	16,298	17,445	16,090	17,342	18,326
Tobacco manufactures	21	78	94	199	285	467	163	169
Textile mill products	22	3,616	6,807	7,132	7,808	6,161	6,534	6,965
Apparel and related products	23	15,710	24,644	25,497	30,533	35,475	38,561	41,208
Lumber and related products	24	5,105	5,446	5,229	6,700	8,901	10,528	10,406
Furniture and fixtures	25	3,220	5,235	5,130	5,601	6,242	7,522	8,303
Paper and allied products	26	7,493	11,669	10,431	10,382	10,891	11,772	16,757
Printing and publishing	27	1,200	1,849	1,878	2,046	2,211	2,422	2,902
Chemicals and allied products	28	12,790	21,611	22,999	25,849	27,259	31,697	38,079
Petroleum and coal products	29	18,282	14,472	11,097	10,410	9,906	9,504	8,971
Rubber and misc. plastics products	30	4,721	9,731	9,855	11,287	13,053	14,393	15,973
Leather and leather products	31	7,724	10,944	10,714	11,342	11,692	12,977	13,628
Stone, clay, and glass products	32	4,296	5,845	5,558	5,951	6,431	7,594	8,498
Primary metal products	33	20,439	23,232	22,262	22,891	22,772	30,106	33,519
Fabricated metal products	34	7,754	11,608	11,396	12,436	12,941	14,664	16,213
Machinery, except electrical	35	31,310	55,021	55,578	62,274	73,370	89,705	106,391
Electric and electronic machinery	36	37,951	55,736	58,610	65,596	76,869	94,332	114,912
Transportation equipment	37	65,944	89,599	88,000	92,930	102,259	115,998	122,344
Instruments and related products	38	8,805	16,846	18,668	20,338	22,080	24,410	27,473
Misc. manufactured commodities	39	11,130	20,090	20,015	23,025	25,219	26,830	28,694

X Not applicable.   [1] Standard Industrial Classification.   [2] Includes scrap and waste, used or secondhand merchandise, manufactured commodities not identified by kind, and timing adjustments.   [3] Includes frozen and packaged fish.

Source: U.S. Bureau of the Census, 1985 and 1988, *Highlights of U.S. Export and Import Trade,* series FT 990; beginning 1990, *U.S. Merchandise Trade,* series FT 900, December issues.

Figure 29.1
Selected Outlying Areas of the United States

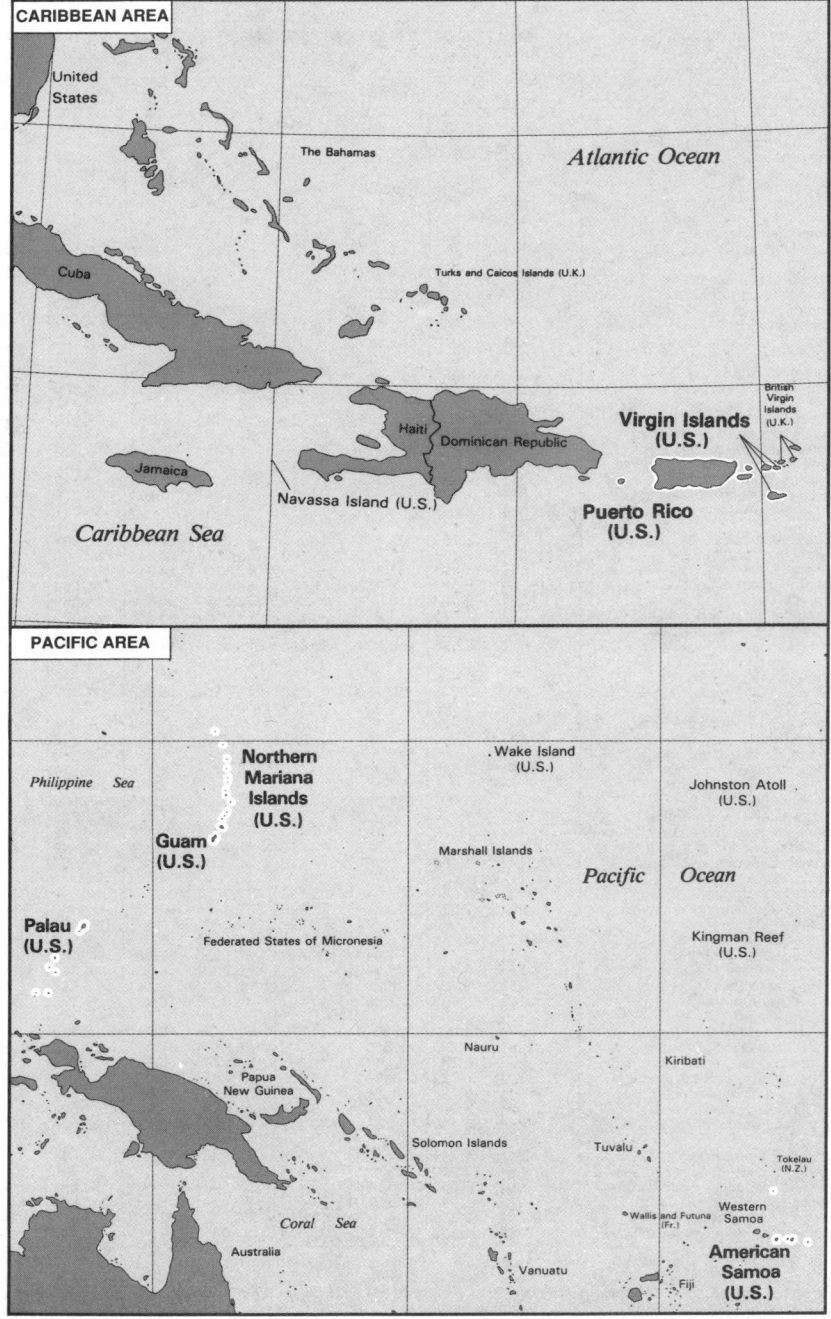

Outlying Areas

This section presents summary economic and social statistics for Puerto Rico, Virgin Islands, Guam, American Samoa, and the Northern Mariana Islands.

Primary sources are the decennial censuses of population and housing, and the censuses of agriculture, business, manufactures, and construction (taken every 5 years) conducted by the Bureau of the Census; the annual *Vital Statistics of the United States,* issued by the National Center for Health Statistics; and the annual *Income and Product* of the Puerto Rico Planning Board, San Juan.

Jurisdiction—The United States gained jurisdiction over these areas as follows:

The islands of *Puerto Rico* and *Guam,* surrendered by Spain to the United States in October 1898, were ceded to the United States by the Treaty of Paris, ratified in 1899. Puerto Rico became a commonwealth on July 25, 1952, thereby achieving a high degree of local autonomy under its own constitution. The *Virgin Islands,* comprising 50 islands and cays, was purchased by the United States from Denmark in 1917. *American Samoa,* a group of seven islands, was acquired by the United States in accordance with a convention among the United States, Great Britain, and Germany, ratified in 1900 (Swains Island was annexed in 1925).

By an agreement approved by the Security Council and the United States, the Northern Mariana Islands, previously under Japanese mandate, was administered by the United States between 1947 and 1986 under the United Nations trusteeship system. The Northern Mariana Islands became a commonwealth in 1986.

Censuses—Because characteristics of the outlying areas differ, the presentation of census data for them is not uniform. The 1960 Census of Population covered all of the places listed above except the Northern Mariana Islands (their census was conducted in April 1958 by the

In Brief

Persons per household, 1990:

Puerto Rico	*3.3*
Virgin Islands	*3.1*
Guam	*4.0*
American Samoa	*7.0*
Northern Mariana Islands	*4.6*

Office of the High Commissioner), while the 1960 Census of Housing also excluded American Samoa. The 1970, 1980, and 1990 Censuses of Population and Housing covered all five areas. The 1959, 1969, and 1978 Censuses of Agriculture covered Puerto Rico, American Samoa, Guam, and the Virgin Islands; the 1964, 1974, and 1982 censuses covered the same areas except American Samoa; and the 1969, 1978, 1987, and 1992 censuses included the Northern Mariana Islands. Beginning in 1967, Congress authorized the economic censuses, to be taken at 5-year intervals, for years ending in "2" and "7." Prior economic censuses were conducted in Puerto Rico for 1949, 1954, 1958, and 1963 and in Guam and the Virgin Islands for 1958 and 1963. In 1967, the census of construction industries was added for the first time in Puerto Rico; in 1972, Virgin Islands and Guam were covered. For 1982, 1987, and 1992 the economic censuses covered the Northern Mariana Islands.

Information in other sections—In addition to the statistics presented in this section, other data are included as integral parts of many tables showing distribution by States in various sections of the *Abstract.* See "Outlying areas of the United States" in the index. For definition and explanation of terms used, see section 1, Population; section 4, Education; section 23, Agriculture; section 25, Construction and Housing; section 26, Manufactures; and section 27, Domestic Trade and Services.

No. 1309. Estimated Resident Population With Projections: 1960 to 2020

[In thousands. Population data generally are de facto figures for the present territory. Population estimates were derived from information available as of early 1996. See text, section 30, for general comments regarding the data. For details of methodology, coverage, and reliability, see source]

AREA	1960	1970	1980	1990	1995	1996	2000, proj.	2010, proj.	2020, proj.
Puerto Rico................	2,358	2,716	3,206	3,605	3,813	3,819	3,850	4,017	4,227
American Samoa............	20	27	32	47	57	60	69	85	86
Guam	67	86	107	134	153	157	171	202	230
Virgin Islands................	33	63	98	101	97	97	99	107	111
Northern Mariana Islands.......	9	12	17	44	51	52	57	71	86

Source: U.S. Bureau of the Census, International Data Base.

No. 1310. Vital Statistics—Specified Areas: 1960 to 1992

[Births, deaths, and infant deaths by place of residence; marriages and divorces by place of occurrence. Rates for 1960, 1970, 1980, and 1990 based on population enumerated as of **April 1;** for other years, on population estimated as of **July 1**]

AREA AND YEAR	BIRTHS Number	BIRTHS Rate [1]	DEATHS Number	DEATHS Rate [1]	INFANT DEATHS Number	INFANT DEATHS Rate [2]	MARRIAGES Number	MARRIAGES Rate [1]	DIVORCES [3] Number	DIVORCES [3] Rate [1]
Puerto Rico: 1960	76,314	32.5	15,791	6.7	3,307	43.3	[4]20,212	[4]8.6	5,218	2.2
1970.............	67,628	24.8	18,080	6.7	1,930	28.6	29,905	11.0	9,688	3.6
1980.............	72,986	22.8	20,413	6.4	1,351	18.5	33,167	10.4	15,276	4.8
1985.............	63,547	19.4	23,071	7.0	944	14.9	30,355	9.2	14,686	4.5
1990.............	66,417	18.9	25,957	7.4	888	13.4	33,080	11.0	13,695	3.8
1992.............	(NA)	(NA)	27,229	7.6	816	(NA)	(NA)	(NA)	(NA)	(NA)
Guam: 1965	2,523	32.8	336	4.4	82	32.5	471	6.2	53	0.7
1970.............	2,842	28.8	355	5.8	62	21.6	874	9.9	84	1.0
1980.............	2,945	27.8	393	3.7	43	14.6	(NA)	(NA)	(NA)	(NA)
1985.............	3,049	24.6	415	3.4	35	11.5	(NA)	(NA)	(NA)	(NA)
1990.............	3,839	28.8	520	3.9	31	8.1	(NA)	(NA)	(NA)	(NA)
1992.............	(NA)	(NA)	560	3.9	42	(NA)	(NA)	(NA)	(NA)	(NA)
Virgin Islands: 1960	1,180	36.8	332	10.3	42	35.6	359	11.1	135	4.2
1970.............	2,898	46.8	469	7.9	72	24.6	1,149	18.4	270	4.3
1980.............	2,504	25.9	504	5.2	61	24.4	1,112	11.5	478	4.9
1985.............	2,375	21.4	506	4.6	42	17.7	1,448	13.1	363	3.3
1990.............	2,267	22.3	480	4.7	33	14.6	2,377	23.4	(NA)	(NA)
1992.............	(NA)	(NA)	496	5.0	35	(NA)	(NA)	(NA)	(NA)	(NA)

NA Not available.   [1] Per 1,000 population.   [2] Per 1,000 live births.   [3] Includes reported annulments.   [4] Data are incomplete.

Source: U.S. National Center for Health Statistics, *Vital Statistics of the United States,* annual.

No. 1311. Land Area and Population Characteristics, by Area: 1990

[As of **April 1.** For definition of median, see Guide to Tabular Presentation]

ITEM	United States	Puerto Rico	Virgin Islands	Guam	American Samoa	Northern Mariana Islands
Land area (sq. miles)	3,536,278	3,427	134	210	77	179
Total resident population......	248,709,873	3,522,037	101,809	133,152	46,773	43,345
Per square mile...........	70.3	1,027.9	760.9	634.1	607.4	242.2
Percent increase, 1980-90 ..	9.8	10.2	5.4	25.6	44.8	158.3
Urban..................	187,053,487	2,508,346	37,885	50,801	15,599	12,151
Rural	61,656,386	1,013,691	63,924	82,351	31,174	31,194
Male	121,239,418	1,705,642	49,210	70,945	24,023	22,802
Female	127,470,455	1,816,395	52,599	62,207	22,750	20,543
Males per 100 females.....	95.1	93.9	93.6	114.0	105.6	111.0
Median age (years).........	32.9	28.4	28.2	25.0	20.9	27.4
Male (years)............	31.7	27.2	27.1	25.2	20.6	29.9
Female (years)...........	34.1	29.6	29.2	24.9	21.2	24.9
Marital status, persons						
15 years old and over	195,142,002	2,563,818	72,365	93,200	28,952	33,030
Never married	52,559,853	711,470	27,539	30,759	11,412	13,810
Married [1]	111,498,578	1,499,449	35,199	54,717	15,958	17,869
Widowed or divorced........	31,083,571	352,899	9,627	7,724	1,582	1,351
Households and families:						
Households	91,947,410	1,054,924	32,020	31,373	6,607	6,873
Persons in households	242,012,129	3,487,667	100,488	124,596	46,267	31,856
Persons per household.....	2.63	3.31	3.14	3.97	7.00	4.63
Families	64,517,947	886,339	23,012	27,313	6,301	5,312
Husband-wife families......	50,708,322	634,872	13,197	21,342	5,153	3,947
Children ever born per						
1,000 females 15 to 44 years ..	1,223	1,512	1,662	1,523	1,757	1,226

[1] For Puerto Rico, includes consensually married couples and for all areas, includes separated couples.

Source: U.S. Bureau of the Census, *1990 Census of Population,* CP-1 parts 1, (United States), 53 (Puerto Rico), 55 (Virgin Islands); *1990 Census of Population and Housing,* CPH-1, parts 53A and 55; CPH-6, parts G (Guam), AS (American Samoa), and CNMI (Commonwealth of the Northern Mariana Islands); and Summary Tape File, parts 3C, (United States), 3A (Puerto Rico), and 3 (Virgin Islands).

No. 1312. Selected Social and Economic Characteristics, by Area: 1990

[As of **April 1**]

CHARACTERISTIC	United States	Puerto Rico	Virgin Islands	Guam	American Samoa	Northern Mariana Islands
EDUCATIONAL ATTAINMENT						
Persons 25 years and over	158,868,436	1,952,297	55,639	66,700	19,570	24,633
Less than 9th grade	16,502,211	691,835	12,908	9,238	3,664	4,285
9th to 12th grade, no diploma	22,841,507	290,173	11,278	8,602	5,239	4,016
High school graduate	47,642,763	410,559	14,021	22,220	6,253	8,659
Some college or associate degree	39,571,702	281,248	9,011	14,984	3,062	3,818
Bachelor's degree or higher	32,310,253	278,482	8,421	11,656	1,352	3,855
EMPLOYMENT STATUS						
Total persons, 16 years old and over	191,829,271	2,497,078	70,323	90,990	27,991	32,522
In labor force	125,182,378	1,180,162	47,553	66,138	14,198	26,589
Percent of total	65.3	47.3	67.6	72.7	50.7	81.8
Armed forces	1,708,928	5,486	110	11,952	11	8
Civilian labor force	123,473,450	1,174,676	47,443	54,186	14,187	26,581
Employed	115,681,202	934,736	44,267	52,144	13,461	25,965
Unemployed	7,792,248	239,940	3,176	2,042	726	616
Percent of civilian labor force	6.3	20.4	6.7	3.8	5.1	2.3
Not in labor force	66,646,893	1,316,916	22,770	24,852	13,793	5,933
FAMILY INCOME IN 1989						
Families, census year	65,049,428	889,998	23,012	27,313	6,301	5,312
Percent distribution by income class	100.0	100.0	100.0	100.0	100.0	100.0
Less than $5,000	4.0	25.1	8.8	4.0	11.0	8.2
$5,000 to $9,999	5.6	24.9	9.5	4.7	19.2	13.9
$10,000 to $14,999	7.2	16.5	12.8	8.3	17.0	13.1
$15,000 to $24,999	16.4	17.5	20.6	21.1	23.6	21.6
$25,000 or more	66.9	16.0	48.3	61.9	29.1	43.2
Median income (dollars)	35,225	9,988	24,036	31,178	15,979	21,275
RESIDENCE IN 1985						
Persons 5 years and over	230,445,777	3,219,765	92,579	118,055	39,821	39,206
Same house	122,796,970	2,190,479	56,098	54,665	30,759	11,479
Different house in this area	102,540,097	879,691	25,003	24,763	2,763	6,870
Outside area	5,108,710	149,595	11,478	38,627	6,299	20,857
LANGUAGE SPOKEN AT HOME						
Persons 5 years and over	230,445,777	3,219,765	92,579	118,055	39,821	39,206
Speak only English at home	198,600,798	(NA)	70,442	44,048	1,203	1,878

NA Not available.

Source: U.S. Bureau of the Census, *1990 Census of Population and Housing,* Summary Tape File, parts 3C, (United States), 3A, and unpublished data, (Puerto Rico), and 3 (Virgin Islands); CPH-L-98, *The Foreign Born Population in the United States: 1990; 1990 Census of Population and Housing,* CPH-6, parts G (Guam), AS (American Samoa), and CNMI (Commonwealth of the Northern Mariana Islands).

No. 1313. Federal Direct Payments for Individuals: 1994 and 1995

[**In thousands of dollars.** For fiscal years ending **September 30**]

PROGRAM PAYMENTS	1994				1995			
	Puerto Rico	Guam	Virgin Islands	American Samoa	Puerto Rico	Guam	Virgin Islands	American Samoa
Total	4,743,891	146,208	137,337	23,846	5,142,735	139,287	160,136	29,584
Pell Grants	352,878	1,411	1,279	1,114	289,526	1,389	1,142	2,139
Medicare: Hospital Insurance	330,739	4,022	8,805	-	388,081	402	6,755	-
Supplemental medical insurance	291,071	3,094	5,170	-	421,016	828	5,288	-
Social Security:								
Disability insurance	764,742	5,335	9,163	4,070	872,817	5,388	10,272	4,611
Retirement insurance	1,386,927	28,422	43,532	5,724	1,459,956	29,914	46,853	5,954
Survivors insurance	610,065	15,652	14,807	5,803	643,835	15,920	15,582	6,024
Veterans:								
Pension and disability	358,035	4,932	1,902	2,010	357,528	5,435	1,949	2,383
Education assistance	2,468	78	23	29	5,157	497	106	362
Federal retirement and disability	162,788	52,644	7,291	1,839	198,542	65,926	14,786	1,874
Food Stamps	[1]1,083,040	21,815	22,547	-	[1]1,110,885	24,280	27,544	-
Other	484,178	8,803	22,818	3,257	506,277	[2]-10,692	29,859	6,237

- Represents or rounds to zero.   [1] Food stamp program in Puerto Rico was replaced by the Nutritional Assistance Grant Program. Figures shown represent grants to State and local governments, not included in totals.   [2] Reflect deobligated funds awarded in an earlier period.

Source: U.S. Bureau of the Census, *Federal Expenditures by State for Fiscal Year,* annual.

No. 1314. Public Elementary and Secondary Schools, by Areas: 1994

[For school year ending in year shown, unless otherwise indicated]

ITEM	Puerto Rico	Guam	Virgin Islands	American Samoa	ITEM	Puerto Rico	Guam	Virgin Islands	American Samoa
PUBLIC EL/SEC					Teachers	39,816	1,644	1,570	656
Enrollment, fall	631,460	30,920	22,752	14,484	Other support				
Elementary					services staff.	17,919	1,135	379	366
(kindergarten-					Current expenditures [1]				
grade 8)	464,931	23,153	16,706	10,974	($1,000)	1,500,440	150,035	130,379	29,397
Secondary (grades					Per pupil [2] (dol.) . . .	2,376	4,852	5,730	2,030
9-12 and post									
graduates)	166,529	7,767	6,046	3,510	HIGHER				
Staff, fall	68,005	3,839	3,328	1,339	EDUCATION				
School district staff .	1,058	131	411	105	Enrollment, fall	159,709	5,843	2,942	1,264
School staff	46,970	2,465	2,213	828					

[1] Public elementary and secondary day schools.   [2] Annual expenditures per pupil enrolled.

Source: U.S. National Center for Education Statistics, unpublished data.

No. 1315. Puerto Rico—Summary: 1970 to 1995

ITEM	Unit	1970	1980	1985	1990	1992	1993	1994	1995
POPULATION									
Total [1]	1,000	2,722	3,184	3,378	3,527	3,580	3,622	3,686	3,720
Persons per family	Number. . .	4.6	4.3	3.9	3.7	3.6	3.6	3.6	3.6
EDUCATION [2]									
Enrollment, total.	1,000	922.6	1,090.9	1,107.9	777.9	768.7	724.3	767.0	(NA)
Public day school	1,000	672.3	716.1	692.9	644.7	637.0	631.5	621.1	(NA)
Other public.	1,000	103.9	149.5	152.0	(NA)	(NA)	(NA)	(NA)	(NA)
Private schools.	1,000	89.1	95.2	107.3	133.2	131.7	95.9	145.9	(NA)
College and university	1,000	57.3	130.1	155.7	156.1	157.1	161.1	161.3	131.9
Expenses	Mil. dol. . . .	288.8	825.0	1,171.8	1,686.4	2,039.0	2,214.0	2,270.4	2,527.0
As percent of GNP	Percent . . .	6.2	7.5	7.8	7.8	8.6	8.8	8.5	8.9
Public	Mil. dol. . . .	254.6	612.2	810.2	1,054.2	1,328.0	1,456.8	1,482.9	1,725.3
Private	Mil. dol. . . .	34.2	212.8	361.6	644.2	711.0	757.2	787.5	801.7
LABOR FORCE [3]									
Total [4]	1,000	765	907	985	1,124	1,170	1,201	1,203	1,219
Employed [5]	1,000	686	753	774	963	977	999	1,011	1,051
Agriculture [6]	1,000	68	38	39	36	34	34	34	34
Manufacturing.	1,000	132	143	141	168	164	168	165	172
Trade	1,000	128	138	150	185	193	201	201	211
Government	1,000	106	184	183	222	219	217	224	233
Unemployed . . . . [7]	1,000	79	154	211	161	193	202	192	168
Unemployment rate [7]	Rate	10	17	21	14	17	17	16	14
Compensation of employees	Mil. dol. . . .	2,800	7,200	9,442	13,639	14,997	16,042	16,721	17,595
Avg. compensation	Dollar	4,082	9,563	12,456	14,854	15,350	16,058	16,539	16,741
Salary and wages	Mil. dol. . . .	2,555	6,290	8,137	11,681	12,831	13,737	14,320	15,079
INCOME [8]									
Personal income:									
Current dollars	Mil. dol. . . .	3,753	11,002	14,588	21,105	22,911	24,612	25,609	27,017
Constant (1954) dollars	Mil. dol. . . .	2,654	3,985	4,274	5,551	5,694	6,056	6,220	6,510
Disposable personal income:									
Current dollars	Mil. dol. . . .	3,565	10,403	13,760	19,914	21,537	23,195	24,022	25,291
Constant (1954) dollars	Mil. dol. . . .	2,521	3,768	4,032	5,238	5,352	5,708	5,835	6,094
Average family income:									
Current dollars	Dollar	6,366	14,858	16,914	22,231	23,142	24,613	25,232	26,266
Constant (1954) dollars	Dollar	4,503	5,381	4,957	5,847	5,751	6,055	6,127	6,329
BANKING [9]									
Assets	Mil. dol. . . .	3,322	10,223	21,209	27,902	31,564	31,636	32,778	40,341
TOURISM [8]									
Number of visitors	1,000	1,225.0	2,140.0	2,061.6	3,425.8	3,730.0	3,869.0	4,022.6	4,085.8
Visitor expenditures	Mil. dol. . . .	235.4	618.7	757.7	1,366.4	1,519.7	1,628.1	1,728.3	1,826.1
Average per visitor	Dollar	192	289	368	399	407	421	430	447
Net income from tourism	Mil. dol. . . .	89.8	202.2	223.1	383.3	429.6	441.3	462.5	504.1

NA Not available.   [1] 1970, 1980, and 1990 enumerated as of April 1; all other years estimated as of July 1.   [2] Enrollment for the first school month. Expenses for school year ending in year shown.   [3] Annual average of monthly figures. For fiscal years.   [4] Beginning 1980, for population 16 years old and over; 1970, for population 14 years and over.   [5] Includes other employment not shown separately.   [6] Includes forestry and fisheries.   [7] Percent unemployed of the labor force.   [8] For fiscal years.   [9] As of June 30.

Source: Puerto Rico Planning Board, San Juan, PR, *Income and Product,* annual; and *Socioeconomics Statistics,* annual.

No. 1316. Puerto Rico—Gross Product and Net Income: 1980 to 1995

[In millions of dollars. For fiscal years ending June 30. Data for 1995 are preliminary]

ITEM	1980	1985	1990	1991	1992	1993	1994	1995
Gross product	**11,065**	**15,002**	**21,619**	**22,809**	**23,696**	**25,133**	**26,592**	**28,371**
Agriculture	380	357	434	449	420	411	377	366
Manufacturing	5,306	7,909	12,126	12,661	14,183	15,428	16,584	17,719
Contract construction and mining [1]	369	334	720	770	798	874	907	959
Transportation [2]	1,279	1,709	2,468	2,671	2,830	3,009	3,115	3,264
Trade	2,273	3,160	4,728	4,832	4,990	5,303	5,642	5,895
Finance, insurance, real estate	1,486	2,547	3,896	4,308	4,596	4,897	5,160	5,451
Services	1,279	1,837	3,015	3,322	3,582	3,909	4,284	4,546
Government	1,897	2,346	3,337	3,522	3,672	3,881	4,071	4,471
Commonwealth	1,574	1,996	2,884	3,044	3,154	3,327	3,476	3,842
Municipalities	323	350	453	478	518	555	596	629
Rest of the world	-3,372	-5,287	-8,985	-9,478	-10,934	-11,790	-12,945	-13,992
Statistical discrepancy	166	91	-121	-248	-439	-789	-605	-306
Net income	**9,007**	**12,182**	**17,941**	**18,927**	**19,631**	**21,185**	**22,096**	**23,231**
Agriculture	435	410	486	503	476	469	424	425
Manufacturing	4,756	7,117	11,277	11,732	13,215	14,462	15,605	16,614
Mining	9	10	26	26	28	25	25	28
Contract construction	337	309	679	728	753	805	814	837
Transportation [2]	1,022	1,248	1,778	1,900	1,943	2,132	2,186	2,297
Trade	1,609	2,285	3,420	3,485	3,538	3,712	3,878	4,045
Finance, insurance, and real estate	1,200	2,141	3,280	3,609	3,814	4,073	4,318	4,563
Services	1,114	1,606	2,643	2,901	3,125	3,415	3,720	3,943
Commonwealth government [3]	1,897	2,346	3,337	3,522	3,672	3,881	4,071	4,471
Rest of the world	-3,372	-5,287	-8,985	-9,478	-10,934	-11,790	-12,945	-13,992

[1] Mining includes only quarries. [2] Includes other public utilities, and radio and television broadcasting. [3] Includes public enterprises not elsewhere classified.

Source: Puerto Rico Planning Board, San Juan, PR, *Economic Report of the Governor, 1994-95.*

No. 1317. Puerto Rico—Transfer Payments: 1985 to 1995

[In millions of dollars. Data represent transfer payments between Federal and State governments and other nonresidents. See headnote, table 1316]

ITEM	1985	1990	1991	1992	1993	1994	1995
Total receipts	**3,531**	**4,871**	**4,973**	**5,108**	**5,478**	**5,954**	**6,348**
Federal government	3,348	4,649	4,708	4,903	5,279	5,628	6,020
Transfers to individuals [1]	3,283	4,577	4,633	4,818	5,186	5,532	5,936
Veterans benefits	317	349	370	383	405	414	439
Medicare	220	368	415	487	517	570	661
Old age, disability, survivors	1,581	2,055	2,243	2,315	2,463	2,722	2,912
Nutritional assistance	780	880	916	957	975	995	1,063
Industry subsidies	65	72	75	86	93	96	84
U.S. State governments	17	18	18	29	33	23	21
Other nonresidents	166	205	247	175	166	304	307
Total payments	**1,180**	**1,801**	**1,857**	**1,982**	**2,089**	**2,270**	**2,236**
Federal government	1,145	1,756	1,839	1,912	2,021	2,115	2,217
Transfers from individuals	508	817	864	918	980	1,032	1,097
Contribution to Medicare	44	97	101	108	122	142	162
Employee contribution for Social Security	463	720	762	809	856	889	933
Transfers from industries	13	16	19	24	26	32	49
Unemployment insurance	189	247	243	209	208	211	184
Employer contribution for Social Security	435	675	714	761	807	840	886
Other nonresidents	35	45	17	69	69	155	19
Net balance	**2,351**	**3,070**	**3,117**	**3,126**	**3,389**	**3,684**	**4,112**
Federal government	2,203	2,893	2,869	2,991	3,258	3,513	3,803
U.S. State governments	14	16	15	25	27	16	16
Other nonresidents	134	162	232	110	104	155	293

[1] Includes other receipts and payments not shown separately.

Source: Puerto Rico Planning Board, San Juan, PR, *Economic Report of the Governor, 1994-95.*

No. 1318. Puerto Rico—Merchandise Imports and Exports: 1980 to 1994

[In millions of dollars. Imports are imports for consumption; see text, section 28]

ITEM	1980	1984	1985	1986	1987	1988	1989	1990	1991	1992	1993	1994
Imports	9,018	10,116	10,162	10,321	11,308	13,096	15,010	16,200	15,079	16,476	16,124	17,152
From U.S	5,345	5,738	6,130	6,467	7,307	8,788	10,193	10,792	10,306	11,463	11,179	11,455
From other	3,673	4,378	4,032	3,854	4,001	4,308	4,817	5,408	4,773	5,013	4,945	5,697
Exports	6,576	9,426	11,087	11,854	12,508	14,436	17,455	20,402	21,128	20,455	20,351	22,711
To U.S.	5,643	8,074	9,873	10,524	11,153	12,756	15,334	18,729	18,729	17,990	17,613	20,098
To other	933	1,352	1,214	1,330	1,355	1,680	2,121	2,487	2,399	2,465	2,738	2,613

Source: U.S. Bureau of the Census, *Foreign Commerce and Navigation of the United States,* annual; *U.S. Trade with Puerto Rico and U.S. Possessions, FT 895;* and, through 1988, *Highlights of U.S. Export and Import Trade, FT990;* thereafter, *FT920* supplement.

No. 1319. Puerto Rico—Economic Summary, by Industry: 1993

[Covers establishments with payroll. Employees are for the week including March 12. Most government employees are excluded. For statement on methodology see Appendix III]

INDUSTRY	1987 SIC code [1]	Total estab-lish-ments	Employment-size class					Em-ploy-ees	Annual payroll (mil. dol.)
			1 to 4	5 to 9	10 to 19	20 to 49	50 or more		
Total [2]	(X)	36,996	21,879	6,065	4,121	2,929	2,002	589,568	8,452.9
Agricultural services, forestry, and fishing	A	83	61	13	5	4	-	405	3.2
Mining	B	36	10	9	5	8	4	842	10.2
Nonmetallic minerals, except fuels	14	28	8	6	4	7	3	567	7.6
Construction [2]	C	1,447	569	257	206	220	195	44,175	475.0
General contractors and operative builders	15	552	188	103	79	95	87	20,007	212.7
Special trade contractors	17	728	334	134	103	88	69	16,253	169.9
Manufacturing [2]	D	2,146	604	252	344	381	565	156,194	2,790.2
Food and kindred products	20	304	100	43	47	56	58	18,456	307.1
Textile mill products	22	23	6	3	3	2	9	3,407	37.1
Apparel and other textile products	23	271	45	25	29	46	126	30,979	300.4
Furniture and fixtures	25	133	51	27	22	25	8	2,202	20.9
Paper and allied products	26	46	4	5	12	11	14	2,244	38.5
Printing and publishing	27	192	83	26	44	25	14	4,932	89.0
Chemicals and allied products	28	196	30	17	24	32	93	30,616	913.3
Petroleum and coal products	29	26	2	2	7	6	9	1,684	46.4
Rubber and misc. plastic products	30	88	21	8	15	21	23	3,930	65.6
Leather and leather products	31	28	7	3	1	1	16	6,689	74.0
Stone, clay, and glass products	32	165	45	17	47	41	15	4,322	76.8
Fabricated metal products	34	197	72	21	39	43	22	4,415	60.9
Industrial machinery and equip	35	72	29	11	6	9	17	4,416	79.9
Electronic and other electronic equip	36	103	6	9	9	13	66	16,730	291.6
Instruments and related products	38	68	5	6	3	9	45	13,256	243.4
Transportation and public utilities [2]	E	1,033	611	173	102	80	67	27,164	522.0
Trucking and warehousing	42	302	179	57	30	25	11	3,137	55.6
Water transportation	44	56	17	8	8	9	14	7,011	103.1
Air transportation	45	66	17	14	10	12	13	2,427	44.4
Transportation services	47	415	320	58	18	13	6	2,694	38.3
Communication	48	106	24	21	26	20	15	10,786	262.3
Electric, gas, and sanitary services	49	20	12	1	1	-	6	656	11.7
Wholesale trade [2]	F	2,507	1,132	507	423	299	146	35,831	682.0
Durable goods	50	1,302	585	275	229	164	49	15,266	280.7
Nondurable goods	51	1,187	546	226	191	130	94	20,073	388.3
Retail trade [2]	G	12,889	7,336	2,545	1,556	1,042	410	126,984	1,206.2
Building materials, garden supplies	52	913	577	179	92	50	15	6,185	64.8
General merchandise stores	53	446	194	53	51	70	78	15,229	148.9
Food stores	54	1,889	1,140	310	157	135	147	26,503	219.1
Automotive dealers and service stations	55	2,028	1,328	443	151	84	22	11,573	130.2
Apparel and accessory stores	56	1,887	833	496	363	166	29	16,793	133.3
Furniture and home furnishings	57	978	543	244	133	53	5	6,351	77.5
Eating and drinking places	58	2,353	1,265	336	342	344	66	25,557	201.6
Finance, insurance, and real estate [2]	H	1,785	842	343	324	181	95	35,226	688.7
Depository institutions	60	320	61	53	123	59	24	14,309	264.8
Nondepository institutions	61	377	104	109	94	47	23	7,264	136.1
Insurance carriers	63	75	19	10	10	22	14	3,937	93.2
Insurance agents, brokers, and service	64	233	124	38	31	24	16	3,704	82.6
Real estate	65	721	499	122	62	25	13	4,902	60.1
Services [2]	I	10,336	6,826	1,513	931	584	482	144,491	1,839.7
Personal services	72	808	573	126	76	30	3	4,051	40.1
Business services	73	1,312	643	213	187	125	144	38,153	436.4
Auto repair, services, and parking	75	924	673	149	65	28	9	4,621	55.7
Motion pictures	78	133	61	20	34	15	3	1,354	11.6
Amusement and recreation services	79	217	131	33	32	15	6	2,178	22.1
Health services	80	2,987	2,343	370	126	66	82	31,795	397.6
Legal services	81	1,093	922	80	65	20	6	3,947	71.8
Education services	82	445	100	72	62	98	113	22,142	277.0
Social services	83	274	129	52	47	20	26	4,796	50.5
Membership organizations	86	517	326	82	46	40	23	5,926	58.6
Engineering and management services	87	913	554	170	97	61	31	8,719	169.6

- Represents or rounds to zero.   X Not applicable.   [1] 1987 Standard Industrial Classification (SIC) code; see text, section 13.   [2] Includes other establishments not shown separately.

Source: U.S. Bureau of the Census, *County Business Patterns,* 1993.

No. 1320. Puerto Rico—Agriculture: 1987 and 1992

[1 cuerda=.97 acre]

ITEM	1987	1992	ITEM	1987	1992
Farms	20,245	22,350	Tenants	84.0	63.4
Percent—			SALES ($1,000)		
Less than 10 cuerdas	48.7	46.6	Sugarcane	26,643	24,739
10 to 19 cuerdas	19.5	20.0	Coffee	41,786	56,802
20 to 49 cuerdas	16.7	17.7	Pineapples	15,495	11,254
50 to 99 cuerdas	6.7	7.7	Plantains	(NA)	23,227
100 to 174 cuerdas.	3.7	3.7	Bananas	(NA)	5,695
175 or more cuerdas.	4.7	4.3	Grains	7,263	9,767
Cuerdas in farms	886,846	826,893	Fruits/nuts [1]	20,645	11,277
Tenure of operator:			Vegetables and melons [2]	8,236	16,214
Percent—			Horticulture specialities	14,489	28,364
Full owners	79.8	79.5	Cattle and calves.	30,206	51,616
Part owners.	13.1	9.9	Poultry.	70,560	98,939
Tenants	7.1	10.6	Dairy products.	157,864	197,703
Avg. farm size—cuerdas:			Hogs and pigs.	9,525	11,633
Full owners	33.4	26.6	Sheep and goats	437	522
Part owners.	85.7	92.3	Fish and aquaculture	(NA)	628

NA Not available. [1] 1987 data include plantains and bananas. [2] 1987 data exclude melons.

Source: U.S. Bureau of the Census, *1992 Census of Agriculture,* vol. 1, part 52.

No. 1321. Virgin Islands—Agriculture: 1987 and 1992

[1 cuerda=.97 acre]

ITEM	1987	1992	ITEM	1987	1992
Farms	267	202	Tenants	8.6	15.3
Percent—			SALES ($1,000)		
Less than 3 acres.	30.0	35.1	Vegetables	355	429
3 to 9 acres.	30.3	29.7	Fruits and nuts	147	142
10 to 19 acres	12.0	13.9	Horticulture specialities	241	1,093
20 or more acres	27.7	21.3	Cattle and calves.	613	501
Acres in farms.	17,785	13,666	Hogs and pigs.	125	291
Tenure of operator:			Livestock	839	844
Percent—			Poultry.	3	9
Full owners	77.9	60.9	Chicken eggs	14	23
Part owners.	13.5	23.8	Milk.	1,043	780

Source: U.S. Bureau of the Census, *1992 Census of Agriculture,* vol. 1, part 54.

No. 1322. Guam, Virgin Islands, and Northern Mariana Islands— Economic Summary: 1992

[Sales and payroll in millions of dollars]

ITEM	Guam	Virgin Islands	No. Mariana Islands	ITEM	Guam	Virgin Islands	No. Mariana Islands
Total:				Wholesale trade:			
Establishments	1,955	2,932	1,266	Establishments	154	114	60
Sales.	3,018	2,281	1,132	Sales.	428	414	132
Annual payroll	567	338	161	Annual payroll	32	21	6
Paid employees [1]	33,057	20,968	20,105	Paid employees [1]	1,715	1,030	534
Unpaid family workers [2] . . .	337	330	268	Unpaid family workers [2] . . .	4	1	3
Construction:				Retail trade:			
Establishments	240	147	103	Establishments	886	1,339	616
Sales.	709	169	88	Sales.	1,114	881	384
Annual payroll	178	44	18	Annual payroll	141	120	38
Paid employees [1]	9,131	2,224	3,036	Paid employees [1]	9,565	8,859	4,715
Unpaid family workers [2] . . .	17	3	20	Unpaid family workers [2] . . .	237	239	157
Manufacturing:				Services:			
Establishments	48	78	73	Establishments	627	1,254	414
Sales.	110	134	264	Sales.	656	682	264
Annual payroll	23	23	49	Annual payroll	193	130	51
Paid employees [1]	1,130	1,196	6,267	Paid employees [1]	11,516	7,659	5,553
Unpaid family workers [2] . . .	8	3	4	Unpaid family workers [2] . . .	71	84	84

[1] For pay period including March 12. [2] Includes those who worked 15 hours or more during the week including March 12.

Source: U.S. Bureau of the Census, *1992 Economic Census of Outlying Areas,* OA92-E-5 to OA92-E-7.

Comparative International Statistics

This section presents statistics for the world as a whole and for many countries on a comparative basis with the United States. Data are shown for population, births and deaths, social and industrial indicators, finances, agriculture, communication, and military affairs.

Statistics of the individual nations may be found primarily in official national publications, generally in the form of yearbooks, issued by most of the nations at various intervals in their own national languages and expressed in their own or customary units of measure. (For a listing of selected publications, see Guide to Sources.) For handier reference, especially for international comparisons, the Statistical Office of the United Nations compiles data as submitted by member countries and issues a number of international summary publications, generally in English and French. Among these are the *Statistical Yearbook;* the *Demographic Yearbook*; the *Yearbook of International Trade Statistics*; the *Yearbook of National Accounts Statistics: Vol. II, International Tables; Population and Vital Statistics Reports* (quarterly); the *Monthly Bulletin of Statistics*; and the *Energy Statistics Yearbook*. Specialized agencies of the United Nations also issue international summary publications on agricultural, labor, health, and education statistics. Among these are the *Production Yearbook* and *Trade Yearbook* issued by the Food and Agriculture Organization, the *Yearbook of Labour Statistics* issued by the International Labour Office, *World Health Statistics* issued by World Health Organization, and the *Statistical Yearbook* issued by the Educational, Scientific, and Cultural Organization.

The Bureau of the Census presents estimates of basic demographic measures for countries and regions of the world in the *World Population Profile* series. The *International Population Reports* (series P95), *International Briefs* (series IB), and *Population Trends* (series PPT) also present population figures for many foreign countries. Detailed population statistics are also available from the Bureau of the Census' International Data Base.

In Brief

Ten most populous countries in 1996:

	(million persons)
China	1,210
India	952
United States	266
Indonesia	207
Brazil	163
Russia	148
Pakistan	129
Japan	125
Bangladesh	123
Nigeria	104

The U.S. Arms Control and Disarmament Agency and the International Monetary Fund (IMF) also compile data on international statistics. In its annual *World Military Expenditures and Arms Transfers*, the Arms Control and Disarmament Agency presents data on various economic indicators, as well as basic military data. Among the topics presented have been military expenditures, gross national product, imports and exports, and armed forces. The IMF publishes a series of reports relating to financial data. These include *International Financial Statistics, Direction of Trade,* and *Balance of Payments Yearbook*, published in English, French, and Spanish.

Statistical coverage, country names, and classifications— Problems of space and availability of data limit the number of countries and the extent of statistical coverage shown. The list of countries included and the spelling of country names are based almost entirely on the list of sovereign nations, dependencies, and areas of special sovereignty provided by the U.S. Department of State.

In recent years, several important changes took place in the status of the world's nations. In 1990, a unified Germany was formed from the Federal Republic of Germany (West) and the German Democratic Republic (East). The Republic of Yemen was formed by union of the Yemen Arab Republic and the People's Democratic Republic of Yemen. Also in 1990, Namibia, once a United Nations mandate, realized its independence from South Africa.

In 1991, the Soviet Union broke up into 15 independent countries: Armenia, Azerbaijan, Belarus, Estonia, Georgia, Kazakstan, Kyrgyzstan, Latvia, Lithuania, Moldova, Russia, Tajikistan, Turkmenistan, Ukraine, and Uzbekistan.

In 1992, the Socialist Federal Republic of Yugoslavia dissolved; none of the successor states has been recognized as its continuation. The United States recognizes Bosnia and Herzegovina, Croatia, Slovenia, and The Former Yugoslav Republic of Macedonia as independent countries. Serbia and Montenegro have asserted the formation of a joint independent state, but this entity has not been formally recognized as a state by the United States.

On January 1, 1993, Czechoslovakia was succeeded by two independent countries: the Czech Republic and Slovakia. Eritrea announced its independence from Ethiopia in April 1993, and was subsequently recognized as an independent nation by the United States.

The population estimates and projections used in tables 1325-1327 were prepared by the Census Bureau. For each country, the data on population, by age and sex, fertility, mortality, and international migration were evaluated and, where necessary, adjusted for inconsistencies and errors in the data. In most instances, comprehensive projections were made by the component method, resulting in distributions of the population by age and sex, and requiring an assessment of probable future trends of fertility, mortality, and international migration.

Economic associations—The Organization for European Economic Cooperation (OEEC), a regional grouping of Western European countries established in 1948 for the purpose of harmonizing national economic policies and conditions, was succeeded on September 30, 1961, by the Organization for Economic Cooperation and Development (OECD). The member nations of the OECD are Australia, Austria, Belgium, Canada, Czech Republic, Denmark, Finland, France, Germany, Greece, Hungary, Iceland, Ireland, Italy, Japan, Luxembourg, Mexico, the Netherlands, New Zealand, Norway, Portugal, Spain,

Sweden, Switzerland, Turkey, the United Kingdom, and the United States.

Quality and comparability of the data—The quality and comparability of the data presented here are affected by a number of factors:

(1) The year for which data are presented may not be the same for all subjects for a particular country, or for a given subject for different countries, though the data shown are the most recent available. All such variations have been noted. The data shown are for calendar years except as otherwise specified.

(2) The bases, methods of estimating, methods of data collection, extent of coverage, precision of definition, scope of territory, and margins of error may vary for different items within a particular country, and for like items for different countries.

Footnotes and headnotes to the tables give a few of the major time-period and coverage qualifications attached to the figures; considerably more detail is presented in the source publications. Many of the measures shown are, at best, merely rough indicators of magnitude.

(3) Figures shown in this section for the United States may not always agree with figures shown in the preceding sections. Disagreements may be attributable to the use of differing original sources, a difference in the definition of geographic limits (the 50 States, conterminous United States only, or the United States including certain outlying areas and possessions), or to possible adjustments made in the United States figures by the United Nations or other sources in order to make them more comparable with figures from other countries.

International comparisons of national accounts data—In order to compare national accounts data for different countries, it is necessary to convert each country's data into a common unit of currency, usually the U.S. dollar. The market exchange rates which are often used in converting national currencies do not necessarily reflect the relative purchasing power in the various countries. It is necessary that the goods and services produced in different countries be valued consistently if the differences observed are meant to reflect real differences in the volumes of goods and services produced. The use of purchasing power parities (see table 1335) instead of exchange rates is intended to achieve this objective.

The method used to present the data shown in table 1335 is to construct volume measures directly by revaluing the goods and services sold in different countries at a common set of international prices. By dividing the ratio of the gross domestic products of two countries expressed in their own national currencies by the corresponding ratio calculated at constant international prices, it is possible to derive the implied purchasing power parity (PPP) between the two currencies concerned. PPP's show how many units of currency are needed in one country to buy the same amount of goods and services which one unit of currency will buy in the other country. For further information, see *National Accounts, Main Aggregates*, volume I, issued annually by the Organization for Economic Cooperation and Development, Paris, France.

International Standard Industrial Classification—The original version of the International Standard Industrial Classification of All Economic Activities (ISIC) was adopted in 1948. Wide use has been made both nationally and internationally in classifying data according to kind of economic activity in the fields of production, employment, national income, and other economic statistics. A number of countries have utilized the ISIC as the basis for devising their industrial classification scheme.

Substantial comparability has been attained between the industrial classifications of many other countries, including the United States, and the ISIC by ensuring, as far as practicable, that the categories at detailed levels of classification in national schemes fitted into only one category of the ISIC. For more detail, see Bureau of the Census, The *International Standard Industrial Classification and the U.S. Standard Industrial Classification*, Technical Paper No. 14 and text, section 27. The United Nations, the International Labour Organisation, the Food and Agriculture Organization, and other international bodies have utilized the ISIC in publishing and analyzing statistical data. Revisions of the ISIC were issued in 1958, 1968, and 1989.

International maps—A series of regional world maps is provided on pages 816 and 820-825. References are included in table 1325 for easy location of individual countries on the maps. The Robinson map projection is used for this series of maps. A map projection is used to portray all or part of the round Earth on a flat surface, but this cannot be done without some distortion. For the Robinson projection, distortion is very low along the Equator and within 45 degrees of the center but is greatest near the poles. For additional information on map projections and maps, please contact the Earth Science Information Center, U.S. Geological Survey, 507 National Center, Reston, VA 22092.

Spain
Morocco
Tunisia
Malta
Greece
Cyprus
Lebanon
West Bank
Gaza Strip
Syria
Iraq
Iran
Afghanistan
Western Sahara
Algeria
Israel
Libya
Egypt
Jordan
Kuwait
Bahrain
Qatar
United Arab Emirates
Pakistan
Mauritania
Mali
Saudi Arabia
Oman
N'ger
Chad
Yemen
Nigeria
Sudan
Eritrea
Djibouti
Ethiopia
Somalia
See Inset
Central African Republic
Cameroon
Sao Tome & Principe
Uganda
Kenya
Indian Ocean
Gabon
Congo
Rwanda
Equatorial Guinea
Zaire
Burundi
Tanzania
Seychelles
Comoros
Mayotte
St. Helena
Angola
Zambia
Madagascar
Mauritius
Malawi
Namibia
Zimbabwe
Mozambique
Reunion
Atlantic Ocean
Botswana
Swaziland
South Africa
Lesotho

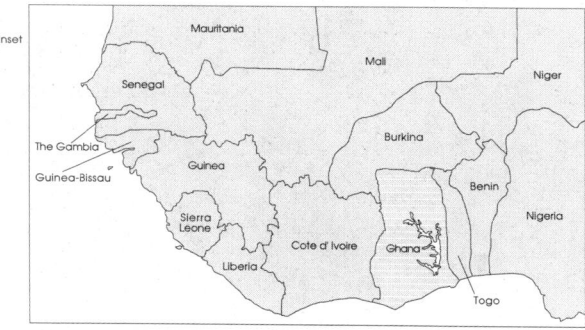

Inset
Mauritania
Mali
Niger
Senegal
The Gambia
Guinea-Bissau
Guinea
Burkina
Benin
Nigeria
Sierra Leone
Cote d'Ivoire
Ghana
Liberia
Togo

Nepal   Bhutan   China
                          Hong
                   Macau Kong
        Burma   Taiwan
                                                              Pacific Ocean
Bangladesh
India
                              see inset

                                                    Marshall Islands

                                        Federated States of Micronesia
                                                                Kiribati
                                        Papua New Guinea   Nauru

                                                    Solomon Islands
Indian Ocean   Tuvalu

                                                    Vanuatu   Wallis & Futuna
                                             New Caledonia   Fiji

                                Australia

                                                    New Zealand

inset   Pacific Ocean
                    Thailand   Vietnam   Philippines   Mariana Islands

                                                                    Guam
                        Cambodia
                              Brunei   Trust Ter. of the
                          Malaysia   Pac. Isl. (Palau)
                        Singapore

                                    Indonesia

Indian Ocean

Comparative International Statistics

No. 1323. World Summary: 1980 to 1994

[See text, section 30, for general comments concerning quality of the data]

ITEM	Unit	1980	1985	1988	1989	1990	1991	1992	1993	1994
Population [1]	Millions	4,458	4,855	5,109	5,194	5,282	5,366	5,448	5,529	5,610
Agriculture, forestry, fishing production: [2]										
Barley	Mil. metric tons .	156.7	172.7	163.1	164.0	177.6	168.2	164.6	169.1	160.8
Coffee	Mil. metric tons .	4.8	5.8	5.7	6.0	6.1	6.1	6.0	5.9	5.4
Corn	Mil. metric tons .	397.5	484.9	398.6	472.9	477.1	488.1	528.0	470.4	569.6
Cotton (lint)	Mil. metric tons .	13.8	17.3	18.3	17.1	18.5	20.6	18.1	16.7	18.4
Meats	Mil. metric tons .	135.9	152.6	169.1	171.8	177.5	181.3	184.3	188.4	194.7
Peanuts (groundnuts).	Mil. metric tons .	16.9	20.8	25.4	23.1	23.1	23.5	24.4	25.7	28.5
Rice	Mil. metric tons .	398.9	469.3	488.6	515.5	519.4	517.3	526.6	527.1	534.7
Tobacco.	Mil. metric tons .	5.3	7.0	6.8	7.0	7.0	7.5	8.3	8.3	6.5
Wheat	Mil. metric tons .	440.1	499.5	500.6	538.3	592.6	546.8	564.8	564.1	528.0
Wool, greasy	Mil. metric tons .	2.8	3.0	3.1	3.0	3.1	3.0	2.9	2.7	2.7
Roundwood	Mil. cubic meters	2,932	3,189	3,413	3,472	3,521	3,414	3,416	3,404	(NA)
Fish catches.	Mil. metric tons .	72.0	86.3	98.9	100.1	97.4	97.4	98.8	101.4	(NA)
Industrial production:										
Wine [2]	Mil. metric tons .	35.3	29.5	27.5	28.8	28.6	25.8	29.2	26.2	25.7
Sugar [2]	Mil. metric tons .	84.4	98.5	104.3	106.1	111.3	112.6	117.2	111.1	110.0
Wheat flour [2]	Mil. metric tons .	237.2	267.6	290.1	295.9	293.1	308.6	315.1	306.9	300.5
Coal	Mil. metric tons .	2,728	3,161	3,488	3,584	3,517	3,463	3,527	3,655	(NA)
Lignite and brown coal	Mil. metric tons .	1,042	1,202	1,261	1,282	1,218	1,081	1,033	944	(NA)
Crude petroleum [3]	Bil. bbl.	21.8	19.7	21.4	21.8	22.1	21.9	22.0	21.9	22.1
Natural gas (dry) [3]	Trl. cu. ft	53.1	61.8	69.7	72.1	73.7	74.8	74.5	76.0	(NA)
Electricity	Bil. kWh.	8,247	9,747	11,059	11,505	11,774	11,989	12,027	12,003	(NA)
Iron ore	Mil. metric tons .	841	862	916	920	921	922	930	940	(NA)
Pig iron and ferroalloys.	Mil. metric tons .	542	507	504	570	543	505	530	535	(NA)
Tin [4]	1,000 metric tons	231	196	210	242	237	214	230	220	(NA)
Crude steel	Mil. metric tons .	699	685	685	777	762	687	700	710	(NA)
Cement.	Mil. metric tons .	872	949	1,109	1,144	1,154	1,148	1,160	1,180	(NA)
Non-cellulosic fibers [4].	Mil. metric tons .	10.0	11.5	13.2	13.3	13.3	12.6	11.2	11.3	(NA)
Sawnwood	Mil. cubic meters	451	468	508	507	505	456	437	432	(NA)
Woodpulp	Mil. metric tons .	125.8	141.8	162.6	166.9	165.8	167.1	165.8	167.2	(NA)
Newsprint.	Mil. metric tons .	25.4	28.3	31.7	32.1	32.8	32.5	32.1	32.5	(NA)
Merchant vessels, launched [4]	Mil. gross tons .	13.9	17.3	11.8	12.7	14.7	16.7	20.5	18.7	(NA)
Motor vehicles	Millions	38.9	44.8	48.1	48.9	48.1	46.4	47.4	(NA)	(NA)
External trade:										
Imports, c.i.f	Bil. U.S. dollars.	2,047	2,028	2,915	3,162	3,567	3,546	3,805	3,717	(NA)
Exports, f.o.b	Bil. U.S. dollars.	1,998	1,927	2,827	3,044	3,437	3,421	3,656	3,632	(NA)
Transport:										
Civil aviation, kilometers flown [5]	Millions	9,362	10,565	13,020	13,570	14,350	14,240	15,310	(NA)	(NA)

NA Not available.   [1] Source: U.S. Bureau of the Census, unpublished data.   [2] Source: U.S. Department of Agriculture, Economic Research Service, *World Agriculture-Trends and Indicators.*   [3] Source: U.S. Energy Information Administration, *International Energy Annual* and *Annual Energy Review.*   [4] Excludes China. Tin and merchant vessels exclude Soviet Republics. For other exclusions, see source.   [5] Scheduled services of members of International Civil Aviation Organization. Excludes Soviet Republics.
Source: Except as noted, Statistical Division of the United Nations, New York, NY, *Monthly Bulletin of Statistics,* (copyright).

No. 1324. Religious Population of the World: 1995

[**In thousands, except percent.** Refers to adherents of all religions as defined and enumerated for each of the world's countries in *World Encyclopedia (1982),* projected to mid-1995, adjusted for recent data]

RELIGION	Total	Percent distri- bution	Africa	Asia	Latin America	Northern America	Europe [1]	Oceania
Total population. . .	**5,716,425**	**100.0**	**728,074**	**3,457,957**	**482,005**	**292,841**	**726,999**	**28,549**
Christians	1,927,953	33.7	348,176	306,762	448,006	249,277	551,892	23,840
Roman Catholics	968,025	16.9	122,108	90,041	402,691	74,243	270,677	8,265
Protestants	395,867	6.9	109,726	42,836	31,684	123,257	80,000	8,364
Orthodox.	217,948	3.8	29,645	14,881	481	6,480	165,795	666
Anglicans	70,530	1.2	25,362	707	1,153	6,819	30,625	5,864
Other Christians	275,583	4.8	61,335	158,297	11,997	38,478	4,795	681
Muslims	1,099,634	19.2	300,317	760,181	1,329	5,450	31,975	382
Nonreligious [2]	841,549	14.7	2,573	701,175	15,551	25,050	94,330	2,870
Hindus	780,547	13.7	1,535	775,252	748	1,185	1,522	305
Buddhists	323,894	5.7	38	320,691	569	920	1,478	200
Atheists	219,925	3.8	427	174,174	2,977	1,670	40,085	592
Chinese folk-religionists [3]	225,137	3.9	12	224,828	66	98	118	17
New-religionists [4]	121,297	2.1	19	118,591	913	956	808	10
Ethnic religionists	111,777	2.0	72,777	36,579	1,061	47	1,200	113
Sikhs	19,161	0.3	36	18,130	5	490	490	7
Jews	14,117	0.2	163	4,294	1,096	5,942	2,529	91
Spiritists	10,190	0.2	4	1,100	8,768	300	17	1
Baha'is.	6,104	0.1	1,851	3,010	719	356	93	75
Confucians	5,254	0.1	1	5,220	2	25	4	1
Jains	4,886	0.1	58	4,804	4	4	15	1
Shintoists	2,844	-	-	2,840	1	1	1	1
Other religionists	2,156	-	88	326	184	1,068	443	42

- Represents or rounds to zero.   [1] Includes Russia.   [2] Persons professing no religion, nonbelievers, agnostics, freethinkers, and dereligionized secularists indifferent to all religion.   [3] Followers of traditional Chinese religion (local deities, ancestor veneration, Confucian ethics, Taoism, etc.).   [4] Followers of Asiatic 20th-century New Religions, New Religious movements, radical new crisis religions, and non-Christian syncretistic mass religions.
Source: Encyclopædia Britannica, Inc., Chicago, IL, *Britannica Book of the Year.* Reprinted with permission from *Britannica Book of the Year,* 1996 © 1996 Encyclopædia Britannica, Inc.

No. 1325. Population, by Country: 1980 to 2000

[Population data generally are de facto figures for the present territory. Population estimates were derived from information available as of early 1996. See text, section 31, for general comments concerning the data. For details of methodology, coverage, and reliability, see source. Minus sign (-) indicates decrease]

COUNTRY OR AREA	Map refer- ence	MIDYEAR POPULATION (1,000)				Popu- lation rank, 1996	ANNUAL RATE OF GROWTH [1] (percent)		Population per sq. mile, 1996
		1980	1990	1996	2000, proj.	1996	1980- 1990	1990- 2000	1996
World	S0	4,457,593	5,281,673	5,771,939	6,090,914	(X)	1.7	1.4	114
Afghanistan.	S5	14,985	14,767	22,664	26,668	41	-0.1	5.9	91
Albania.	S3	2,699	3,273	3,249	3,427	128	1.9	0.5	307
Algeria	S4	18,862	25,352	29,183	31,788	34	3.0	2.3	32
Andorra	S3	34	53	73	80	202	4.5	4.2	418
Angola	S4	6,794	8,430	10,343	11,513	70	2.2	3.1	21
Antigua and Barbuda	S1	69	64	66	68	204	-0.7	0.7	386
Argentina	S2	28,237	32,386	34,673	36,202	31	1.4	1.1	33
Armenia	S5	3,115	3,366	3,464	3,481	123	0.8	0.3	301
Aruba.	S1	60	67	68	69	203	1.0	0.4	910
Australia	S6	14,616	17,033	18,261	18,950	51	1.5	1.1	6
Austria	S3	7,549	7,718	8,023	8,124	66	0.2	0.5	251
Azerbaijan.	S5	6,173	7,200	7,677	7,902	87	1.5	0.9	230
Bahamas, The	S1	210	241	259	269	177	1.4	1.1	67
Bahrain	S4	348	502	590	642	161	3.7	2.5	2,469
Bangladesh.	S5	88,077	110,118	123,063	132,081	9	2.2	1.8	2,380
Barbados	S1	252	254	257	260	179	0.1	0.2	1,548
Belarus.	S3	9,644	10,215	10,416	10,545	69	0.6	0.3	130
Belgium	S3	9,847	9,962	10,170	10,286	72	0.1	0.3	871
Belize.	S1	144	190	219	242	182	2.7	2.4	25
Benin	S4	3,444	4,676	5,710	6,517	98	3.1	3.3	134
Bhutan	S5	1,281	1,585	1,823	1,996	144	2.1	2.3	100
Bolivia	S2	5,296	6,388	7,165	7,680	90	1.9	1.8	17
Bosnia and Herzegovina	S3	4,092	4,360	2,656	2,618	131	0.6	-5.1	135
Botswana	S4	903	1,304	1,478	1,557	146	3.7	1.8	7
Brazil	S2	122,830	150,062	162,661	169,545	5	2.0	1.2	50
Brunei	S6	185	254	300	331	174	3.2	2.6	147
Bulgaria	S3	8,844	8,966	8,613	8,769	84	0.1	-0.2	202
Burkina	S4	6,939	9,033	10,623	11,684	67	2.6	2.6	100
Burma	S5	33,766	41,078	45,976	49,388	25	2.0	1.8	181
Burundi	S4	4,138	5,633	5,943	6,493	95	3.1	1.4	600
Cambodia	S5	6,499	8,731	10,861	12,098	66	3.0	3.3	159
Cameroon.	S4	8,761	11,905	14,262	15,966	59	3.1	2.9	79
Canada	S1	24,070	26,620	28,821	29,989	36	1.0	1.2	8
Cape Verde.	S1	296	375	449	503	165	2.4	2.9	289
Central African Republic	S4	2,244	2,806	3,274	3,539	127	2.2	2.3	14
Chad	S4	4,507	5,889	6,977	7,760	91	2.7	2.8	14
Chile	S2	11,094	13,121	14,333	14,996	58	1.7	1.3	50
China [2].	S5	984,736	1,133,710	1,210,005	1,253,438	1	1.4	1.0	336
Colombia	S2	26,580	32,983	36,813	39,172	30	2.2	1.7	92
Comoros.	S4	334	460	569	656	162	3.2	3.5	679
Congo	S4	1,620	2,204	2,528	2,750	134	3.1	2.2	19
Costa Rica	S2	2,307	3,022	3,463	3,744	124	2.7	2.1	177
Cote d'Ivoire	S4	8,276	11,926	14,762	16,172	57	3.7	3.0	120
Croatia.	S3	4,593	4,754	5,004	5,044	107	0.3	0.6	229
Cuba	S1	9,653	10,545	10,951	11,131	65	0.9	0.5	256
Cyprus	S5	627	681	745	777	157	0.8	1.3	209
Czech Republic	S3	10,289	10,310	10,321	10,358	71	-	-	213
Denmark.	S3	5,123	5,141	5,250	5,320	104	-	0.3	321
Djibouti.	S4	279	370	428	454	168	2.8	2.0	50
Dominica	S1	75	81	83	84	198	0.7	0.4	286
Dominican Republic	S1	5,697	7,213	8,089	8,635	85	2.4	1.8	433
Ecuador	S2	8,315	10,116	11,466	12,360	62	2.0	2.0	107
Egypt	S4	42,441	56,106	63,575	68,437	16	2.8	2.0	165
El Salvador.	S1	4,602	5,219	5,829	6,252	97	1.3	1.8	729
Equatorial Guinea	S4	256	369	431	478	167	3.7	2.6	40
Eritrea	S4	2,555	2,896	3,428	4,461	125	1.3	4.3	73
Estonia.	S3	1,482	1,573	1,459	1,422	147	0.6	-1.0	84
Ethiopia	S4	36,413	48,242	57,172	63,514	22	2.8	2.8	132
Fiji.	S6	635	738	782	823	156	1.5	1.1	111
Finland.	S3	4,780	4,986	5,105	5,115	106	0.4	0.3	43
France	S3	53,618	56,484	58,041	58,816	20	0.5	0.4	280
Gabon	S4	808	1,078	1,173	1,244	151	2.9	1.4	12
Gambia, The	S4	676	964	1,205	1,381	150	3.5	3.6	312
Georgia	S5	5,048	5,457	5,220	5,132	105	0.8	-0.6	194
Germany	S3	78,298	79,357	83,536	85,684	12	0.1	0.8	618
Ghana	S4	10,880	15,190	17,698	19,272	53	3.3	2.4	199
Greece.	S3	9,643	10,123	10,539	10,735	68	0.5	0.6	209
Grenada	S2	90	94	95	98	196	0.4	0.4	726
Guatemala	S1	7,232	9,633	11,278	12,408	63	2.9	2.5	269
Guinea	S4	4,320	5,936	7,412	7,640	88	3.2	2.5	78
Guinea-Bissau	S4	789	998	1,151	1,263	152	2.3	2.4	106
Guyana	S2	759	747	712	693	158	-0.2	-0.7	9
Haiti.	S1	5,068	6,060	6,732	7,223	93	1.8	1.8	633
Honduras	S1	3,625	4,741	5,605	6,192	99	2.7	2.7	130
Hungary.	S3	10,711	10,352	10,003	9,795	73	-0.3	-0.6	281
Iceland.	S1	228	255	270	280	176	1.1	0.9	7
India	S5	692,394	855,591	952,108	1,012,909	2	2.1	1.7	829
Indonesia	S6	154,936	187,728	206,612	219,267	4	1.9	1.6	293
Iran	S5	39,274	56,946	66,094	71,879	15	3.7	2.3	105

See footnotes at end of table.

No. 1325. Population, by Country: 1980 to 2000—Continued

[See headnote, page 827]

COUNTRY OR AREA	Map refer- ence	MIDYEAR POPULATION (1,000)				Popu- lation rank, 1996	ANNUAL RATE OF GROWTH [1] (percent)		Popula- tion per sq. mile, 1996
		1980	1990	1996	2000, proj.		1980- 1990	1990- 2000	
Iraq	S5	13,233	18,425	21,422	24,731	46	3.3	2.9	128
Ireland	S3	3,401	3,508	3,567	3,493	121	0.3	-	134
Israel	S4	3,737	4,512	5,422	5,852	102	1.9	2.6	691
Italy	S3	56,451	57,661	57,460	57,807	21	0.2	-	506
Jamaica	S1	2,229	2,466	2,595	2,669	133	1.0	0.8	621
Japan	S5	116,807	123,537	125,450	126,582	8	0.6	0.2	823
Jordan	S4	2,168	3,277	4,212	4,704	116	4.1	3.6	119
Kazakstan	S5	14,994	16,708	16,916	16,943	54	1.1	0.1	16
Kenya	S4	16,685	23,896	28,177	30,490	37	3.6	2.4	128
Kiribati	S6	58	72	81	87	199	2.1	1.9	292
Korea, North	S5	17,999	21,412	23,904	25,491	39	1.7	1.7	514
Korea, South	S5	38,124	42,869	45,482	47,351	26	1.2	1.0	1,200
Kuwait	S5	1,370	2,128	1,950	2,420	143	4.4	1.3	283
Kyrgyzstan	S5	3,623	4,390	4,530	4,664	111	1.9	0.6	59
Laos	S5	3,293	4,191	4,976	5,557	108	2.4	2.8	56
Latvia	S3	2,525	2,672	2,469	2,380	136	0.6	-1.2	99
Lebanon	S4	3,137	3,367	3,776	4,115	119	0.7	2.0	956
Lesotho	S4	1,346	1,735	1,971	2,114	141	2.5	2.0	168
Liberia	S4	1,900	2,265	2,110	3,048	139	1.8	3.0	57
Libya	S4	3,119	4,355	5,445	6,294	101	3.3	3.7	8
Liechtenstein	S3	25	29	31	33	215	1.3	1.3	501
Lithuania	S5	3,436	3,702	3,646	3,629	120	0.7	-0.2	145
Luxembourg	S3	364	382	416	442	169	0.5	1.5	417
Macedonia, The Former Yugoslav Republic of [3]	S3	1,893	2,031	2,104	2,152	140	0.7	0.6	212
Madagascar	S4	8,678	11,525	13,671	15,295	60	2.8	2.8	61
Malawi	S4	6,129	9,136	9,453	10,011	78	4.0	0.9	260
Malaysia	S6	13,764	17,507	19,963	21,610	48	2.4	2.1	157
Maldives	S5	154	218	271	310	175	3.5	3.5	2,338
Mali	S4	6,728	8,234	9,653	10,911	76	2.0	2.8	20
Malta	S4	364	354	376	391	173	-0.3	1.0	3,030
Marshall Islands	S6	31	46	58	68	208	4.1	3.9	835
Mauritania	S4	1,456	1,935	2,336	2,653	137	2.8	3.2	6
Mauritius	S4	964	1,074	1,140	1,196	153	1.1	1.1	1,597
Mexico	S1	68,686	85,121	95,772	102,912	11	2.1	1.9	129
Micronesia, Federated States of	S6	77	109	125	133	191	3.4	2.0	463
Moldova	S5	3,996	4,398	4,464	4,543	112	1.0	0.3	343
Monaco	S3	27	30	32	32	214	1.2	0.7	41,076
Mongolia	S5	1,662	2,216	2,497	2,655	135	2.9	1.8	4
Montenegro [3]	S3	579	616	635	647	160	0.6	0.5	119
Morocco	S4	20,457	26,164	29,779	32,229	33	2.5	2.1	173
Mozambique	S4	12,103	14,056	17,878	19,829	52	1.5	3.4	59
Namibia	S4	975	1,409	1,677	1,886	145	3.7	2.9	5
Nauru	S6	8	9	10	11	225	2.0	1.3	1,267
Nepal	S5	15,001	19,104	22,094	24,364	42	2.4	2.4	418
Netherlands	S3	14,144	14,952	15,568	15,893	56	0.6	0.6	1,188
New Zealand	S6	3,113	3,299	3,548	3,698	122	0.6	1.1	34
Nicaragua	S2	2,776	3,591	4,272	4,729	115	2.6	2.8	92
Niger	S4	5,629	7,644	9,113	10,260	80	3.1	2.9	19
Nigeria	S4	65,699	86,488	103,912	117,328	10	2.7	3.0	296
Norway	S3	4,086	4,242	4,384	4,461	114	0.4	0.5	37
Oman	S5	1,164	1,751	2,187	2,512	138	4.1	3.6	27
Pakistan	S5	85,219	113,914	129,276	141,145	7	2.9	2.1	430
Palau	S6	13	15	17	18	219	1.3	1.7	96
Panama	S2	1,956	2,387	2,655	2,828	132	2.0	1.7	90
Papua New Guinea	S6	2,991	3,823	4,395	4,812	113	2.5	2.3	25
Paraguay	S2	3,379	4,651	5,504	6,104	100	3.2	2.7	36
Peru	S2	17,295	21,841	24,523	26,198	38	2.3	1.8	50
Philippines	S6	51,092	65,037	74,481	80,961	13	2.4	2.2	647
Poland	S3	35,578	38,109	38,643	39,010	29	0.7	0.2	329
Portugal	S3	9,778	9,871	9,865	9,906	75	0.1	-	279
Qatar	S5	231	452	548	587	163	6.7	2.6	129
Romania	S5	22,109	22,775	21,657	20,996	44	0.3	-0.8	244
Russia	S5	139,045	148,081	148,178	147,938	6	0.6	-	22
Rwanda	S4	5,170	7,145	6,853	8,900	92	3.2	2.2	711
St. Kitts and Nevis	S1	44	40	41	43	212	-1.0	0.8	298
St. Lucia	S1	122	146	158	165	187	1.8	1.2	669
St. Vincent and the Grenadines	S1	98	113	118	121	192	1.4	0.7	904
San Marino	S3	21	23	25	25	217	0.8	0.9	1,058
Sao Tome and Principe	S4	94	123	144	159	190	2.7	2.6	389
Saudi Arabia	S4	9,949	15,871	19,409	22,246	49	4.7	3.4	23
Senegal	S4	5,640	7,408	9,093	10,390	81	2.7	3.4	123
Serbia [3]	S3	9,262	9,705	9,979	10,140	74	0.5	0.4	293
Seychelles	S4	66	73	78	80	200	1.0	0.8	441
Sierra Leone	S4	3,333	4,283	4,793	5,580	109	2.5	2.6	173
Singapore	S6	2,414	3,039	3,397	3,620	126	2.3	1.8	14,099
Slovakia	S3	4,966	5,263	5,374	5,472	103	0.6	0.4	111
Slovenia	S3	1,885	1,969	1,951	1,937	142	0.4	-0.2	250
Solomon Islands	S6	233	336	413	470	170	3.7	3.4	39
Somalia	S4	6,865	8,334	9,639	10,880	77	1.9	2.7	40

See footnotes at end of table.

No. 1325. Population, by Country: 1980 to 2000—Continued

[See headnote, page 827]

COUNTRY OR AREA	Map reference	MIDYEAR POPULATION (1,000)				Population rank, 1996	ANNUAL RATE OF GROWTH [1] (percent)		Population per sq. mile, 1996
		1980	1990	1996	2000, proj.		1980-1990	1990-2000	
South Africa	S4	29,252	37,191	41,743	44,462	27	2.4	1.8	89
Spain	S3	37,488	38,793	39,181	39,545	28	0.3	0.2	203
Sri Lanka	S5	14,900	17,227	18,553	19,377	50	1.5	1.2	742
Sudan	S4	19,064	26,628	31,548	35,530	32	3.3	2.9	34
Suriname	S2	355	398	436	465	166	1.2	1.6	7
Swaziland	S4	607	853	999	1,137	154	3.4	2.9	150
Sweden	S3	8,310	8,559	8,901	9,052	83	0.3	0.6	56
Switzerland	S3	6,385	6,779	7,207	7,374	89	0.6	0.8	469
Syria	S4	8,692	12,620	15,609	17,759	55	3.7	3.4	220
Tajikistan	S5	3,969	5,332	5,916	6,384	96	3.0	1.8	107
Tanzania	S4	18,689	24,826	29,058	31,045	35	2.8	2.2	85
Thailand	S5	47,026	55,052	58,851	61,164	18	1.6	1.1	298
Togo	S4	2,596	3,680	4,571	5,263	110	3.5	3.6	218
Tonga	S0	93	101	106	110	193	0.9	0.8	385
Trinidad and Tobago	S2	1,091	1,256	1,272	1,273	149	1.4	0.1	642
Tunisia	S4	6,443	8,048	9,020	9,671	82	2.2	1.8	150
Turkey	S5	45,121	56,123	62,484	66,618	17	2.2	1.7	210
Turkmenistan	S5	2,875	3,668	4,149	4,466	117	2.4	2.0	22
Tuvalu	S6	7	9	10	11	226	2.0	1.6	1,011
Uganda	S4	12,252	17,040	20,158	21,891	47	3.3	2.5	261
Ukraine	S5	50,047	51,592	50,864	50,380	23	0.3	-0.2	218
United Arab Emirates	S5	1,000	2,252	3,057	3,582	130	8.1	4.6	95
United Kingdom	S3	56,314	57,418	58,490	58,894	19	0.2	0.3	627
United States	S1	227,726	249,913	265,563	274,943	3	0.9	1.0	75
Uruguay	S2	2,920	3,106	3,239	3,333	129	0.6	0.7	48
Uzbekistan	S5	16,000	20,624	23,418	25,245	40	2.5	2.0	136
Vanuatu	S6	117	154	178	193	186	2.8	2.2	31
Venezuela	S2	14,768	19,325	21,983	23,596	43	2.7	2.0	65
Vietnam	S5	54,234	66,314	73,977	78,350	14	2.0	1.7	589
Western Samoa	S0	155	186	214	235	183	1.8	2.3	195
Yemen	S5	7,439	10,489	13,483	15,547	61	3.4	3.9	66
Zaire	S4	27,954	37,831	46,499	51,374	24	3.0	3.1	53
Zambia	S4	5,638	8,019	9,159	9,899	79	3.5	2.1	32
Zimbabwe	S4	7,298	10,121	11,271	11,777	64	3.3	1.5	75
Taiwan [2]	S5	17,848	20,279	21,466	22,214	45	1.3	0.9	1,723
AREAS OF SPECIAL SOVEREIGNTY AND DEPENDENCIES									
American Samoa	S0	32	47	60	69	207	3.8	3.8	775
Anguilla	S1	7	8	10	12	224	2.5	3.5	297
Bermuda	S1	55	59	62	64	206	0.8	0.8	3,282
Cayman Islands	S1	17	27	35	41	213	4.4	4.3	345
Cook Islands	S0	18	18	20	20	218	0.1	1.1	210
Faroe Islands	S3	43	47	44	41	211	0.9	-1.6	81
French Guiana	S2	68	116	151	173	189	5.4	4.0	4
French Polynesia	S0	151	196	225	245	180	2.6	2.2	159
Gaza Strip	S4	453	635	924	1,163	155	3.4	6.0	6,281
Gibraltar	S3	29	31	29	29	216	0.6	-0.6	12,417
Greenland	S1	50	56	58	60	209	1.0	0.8	(Z)
Guadeloupe	S1	337	378	408	426	171	1.1	1.2	600
Guam	S6	107	134	157	171	188	2.3	2.4	752
Guernsey	S3	53	61	63	66	205	1.4	0.8	840
Hong Kong	S5	5,063	5,688	6,305	6,685	94	1.2	1.6	16,513
Jersey	S3	76	84	88	90	197	1.0	0.8	1,945
Macau	S6	318	456	497	516	164	3.6	1.2	80,426
Man, Isle of	S3	64	69	74	76	201	0.7	1.0	325
Martinique	S1	339	374	399	416	172	1.0	1.1	976
Mayotte	S4	52	80	101	117	194	4.3	3.8	695
Montserrat	S1	12	13	13	13	223	0.6	0.3	331
Netherlands Antilles	S2	173	195	209	217	184	1.2	1.1	563
New Caledonia	S6	139	168	188	200	185	1.9	1.7	26
Northern Mariana Islands	S6	17	44	52	57	210	9.7	2.6	284
Puerto Rico	S1	3,206	3,605	3,819	3,850	118	1.2	0.7	1,104
Reunion	S4	507	600	679	730	159	1.7	2.0	704
St. Helena	S4	6	7	7	7	228	0.3	0.3	43
St. Pierre and Miquelon	S1	6	6	7	7	227	0.8	0.8	73
Turks and Caicos Islands	S1	7	12	14	15	221	4.5	2.7	86
Virgin Islands	S1	98	101	97	99	195	0.4	-0.2	719
Virgin Islands, British	S1	11	12	13	14	222	1.1	1.3	228
Wallis and Futuna	S6	11	14	15	15	220	2.4	1.1	139
West Bank	S4	833	1,080	1,428	1,662	148	2.6	4.3	656
Western Sahara	S4	126	191	223	245	181	4.2	2.5	2

- Represents or rounds to zero.   X Not applicable.   Z Less than one person per square mile.   [1] Computed by the exponential method. For explanation of average annual percent change, see Guide to Tabular Presentation.   [2] With the establishment of diplomatic relations with China on January 1, 1979, the U.S. government recognized the People's Republic of China as the sole legal government of China and acknowledged the Chinese position that there is only one China and that Taiwan is part of China.   [3] The U.S. view is that the Socialist Federal Republic of Yugoslavia has dissolved and no successor state represents its continuation. Macedonia has proclaimed independent statehood, but has not been recognized as a state by the United States. Serbia and Montenegro have asserted the formation of a joint independent state, but this entity has not been recognized by the United States.

Source: U.S. Bureau of the Census, unpublished data.

No. 1326. Age Distribution, by Country: 1996 and 2000

[In percent. Covers countries with 10 million or more population in 1996]

COUNTRY OR AREA	1996				2000, proj.			
	Under 5 years old	5 to 14 years old	15 to 64 years old	65 years old and over	Under 5 years old	5 to 14 years old	15 to 64 years old	65 years old and over
World.................	10.7	20.4	62.4	6.5	10.2	19.8	63.2	6.8
Afghanistan................	16.7	26.3	54.2	2.7	16.5	26.2	54.5	2.8
Algeria	13.4	26.4	56.5	3.7	12.5	23.9	59.7	3.9
Angola	17.8	26.9	52.7	2.6	17.4	27.4	52.4	2.8
Argentina.................	9.3	18.4	62.5	9.7	9.1	17.6	63.3	10.0
Australia	7.2	14.3	66.3	12.2	6.7	14.1	66.6	12.6
Bangladesh	13.5	25.4	57.9	3.2	12.4	23.6	60.7	3.3
Belarus..................	5.9	15.4	66.0	12.7	6.4	13.8	66.9	13.0
Belgium..................	6.0	11.9	65.9	16.2	5.8	11.9	65.4	16.8
Brazil	9.7	20.8	64.8	4.7	9.3	19.2	66.4	5.2
Burkina	19.1	29.0	48.8	3.1	18.5	29.5	49.0	3.0
Burma...................	13.4	23.5	59.0	4.1	12.8	23.1	59.9	4.2
Cambodia	18.1	27.3	51.4	3.1	17.2	27.7	52.1	3.0
Cameroon	18.1	27.9	50.7	3.3	17.8	28.0	50.9	3.3
Canada..................	6.9	13.6	67.1	12.4	6.3	13.6	67.2	12.9
Chile.	9.5	19.2	64.5	6.8	8.3	18.6	65.8	7.3
China [1]	8.3	18.0	67.4	6.2	7.6	17.4	68.1	6.9
Colombia.................	10.7	21.3	63.5	4.5	9.6	20.3	65.2	5.0
Cote d'Ivoire..............	18.2	29.3	50.3	2.2	17.6	29.2	51.0	2.2
Cuba	6.9	15.4	68.4	9.3	6.4	14.9	68.9	9.7
Czech Republic............	5.5	12.8	68.3	13.5	5.6	11.9	68.7	13.8
Ecuador	12.0	23.4	60.1	4.5	11.2	21.9	62.3	4.6
Egypt	12.9	24.0	59.6	3.6	12.1	23.1	61.1	3.7
Ethiopia.................	18.5	27.4	51.4	2.7	18.2	27.9	51.2	2.7
France	5.9	13.1	65.6	15.4	5.6	12.6	65.7	16.2
Germany.................	5.0	11.2	68.5	15.3	4.9	10.9	68.4	15.7
Ghana...................	16.0	27.4	53.5	3.1	14.3	27.4	55.1	3.2
Greece	4.9	11.5	67.5	16.0	5.0	10.5	67.1	17.5
Guatemala................	15.6	27.2	53.7	3.5	14.6	26.6	55.2	3.7
Hungary	5.5	12.2	67.9	14.4	5.7	11.9	67.8	14.7
India	11.9	22.5	61.6	4.1	11.0	21.6	63.1	4.4
Indonesia................	10.8	21.0	64.5	3.7	10.4	19.7	65.6	4.3
Iran	15.9	28.7	51.5	3.9	14.1	27.6	54.1	4.2
Iraq	18.7	28.8	49.3	3.1	18.2	28.8	50.2	2.9
Italy	4.9	10.0	68.4	16.7	5.1	9.8	67.4	17.8
Japan	4.8	10.9	69.3	14.9	5.1	9.9	68.1	16.9
Kazakstan	9.1	20.8	63.0	7.1	8.7	19.4	64.8	7.2
Kenya...................	15.4	29.2	52.7	2.6	14.1	27.7	55.5	2.8
Korea, North..............	11.0	18.5	66.2	4.2	10.2	19.2	65.9	4.7
Korea, South	7.8	15.3	71.0	5.9	7.8	14.2	71.1	6.9
Madagascar..............	17.8	27.1	51.7	3.4	17.4	27.1	52.3	3.3
Malaysia.................	12.6	23.3	60.2	3.9	11.8	22.5	61.6	4.1
Mexico	12.6	23.7	59.2	4.4	11.9	22.8	60.5	4.8
Morocco	12.9	24.8	58.0	4.3	12.1	23.3	60.1	4.6
Mozambique	18.4	27.7	51.4	2.4	17.8	27.8	52.0	2.4
Nepal	15.9	26.4	54.8	2.9	15.5	25.7	55.7	3.0
Netherlands	6.2	12.1	68.4	13.3	5.9	12.3	68.1	13.7
Nigeria	18.0	27.0	52.2	2.9	17.8	27.1	52.2	3.0
Pakistan	15.8	26.7	53.5	4.0	14.5	26.4	55.0	4.1
Peru....................	11.8	23.2	60.6	4.5	10.6	21.8	62.7	4.9
Philippines...............	13.9	24.3	58.2	3.5	13.1	24.0	59.3	3.6
Poland	6.2	16.0	66.5	11.3	6.2	13.9	68.0	11.9
Romania	5.1	14.6	67.7	12.6	5.4	13.0	67.8	13.9
Russia..................	5.2	15.7	67.0	12.1	5.7	13.6	68.6	12.1
Saudi Arabia	17.0	25.9	54.8	2.3	16.6	26.3	54.4	2.6
South Africa	13.1	22.8	59.6	4.5	12.2	22.7	60.4	4.6
Spain	4.9	11.1	68.2	15.7	5.3	10.0	67.8	16.9
Sri Lanka................	8.8	19.4	65.7	6.1	8.3	17.3	67.8	6.6
Sudan...................	17.8	28.0	52.0	2.2	17.0	27.8	53.0	2.3
Syria.	18.0	28.8	50.3	2.9	16.9	28.4	51.7	2.9
Taiwan [1]	7.5	16.0	68.7	7.8	7.2	14.4	69.9	8.6
Tanzania	17.2	27.9	52.0	2.9	16.8	27.7	52.6	3.0
Thailand	8.3	17.1	68.9	5.6	7.9	15.5	70.1	6.5
Turkey.	10.6	21.4	62.5	5.5	9.9	19.9	64.1	6.0
Uganda..................	19.6	29.9	48.2	2.3	18.5	31.0	48.2	2.3
Ukraine..................	5.4	14.4	66.0	14.2	5.9	12.9	67.3	13.9
United Kingdom	6.6	12.9	64.7	15.8	6.3	13.1	64.9	15.6
United States	7.3	14.6	65.4	12.8	6.9	14.5	65.9	12.6
Uzbekistan...............	13.7	26.2	55.4	4.6	12.8	25.3	57.2	4.7
Venezuela	12.2	22.6	60.8	4.4	10.8	22.0	62.6	4.6
Vietnam.................	11.8	24.4	58.7	5.2	10.1	22.6	62.0	5.4
Yemen	19.3	28.4	49.6	2.7	18.9	28.7	49.7	2.7
Zaire....................	19.3	28.6	49.4	2.6	19.3	28.9	49.2	2.6
Zimbabwe	14.9	29.4	52.9	2.8	13.7	28.3	55.1	2.9

[1] See footnote 2, table 1325.

Source: U.S. Bureau of the Census, unpublished data.

No. 1327. Vital Statistics, by Country: 1996 and 2000

[Covers countries with 5 million or more population in 1996]

COUNTRY OR AREA	CRUDE BIRTH RATE [1]		CRUDE DEATH RATE [2]		EXPECTATION OF LIFE AT BIRTH (years)		INFANT MORTALITY RATE [3]		TOTAL FERTILITY RATE [4]	
	1996	2000, proj.	1996	2000, proj.	1996	2000, proj.	1996	2000, proj.	1996	2000, proj.
United States	14.8	14.2	8.8	8.8	76.0	76.3	6.7	6.2	2.06	2.07
Afghanistan	43.0	41.6	18.2	16.6	45.9	47.8	149.7	137.5	6.14	5.87
Algeria	28.5	26.5	5.9	5.4	68.3	69.6	48.7	42.2	3.59	3.16
Angola	44.6	42.6	17.7	15.9	46.8	48.9	138.9	125.9	6.35	6.05
Argentina	19.4	19.1	8.6	8.6	71.7	72.3	28.3	26.1	2.62	2.50
Australia	14.0	13.0	6.9	6.9	79.4	80.4	5.5	5.0	1.84	1.80
Austria	11.2	10.3	10.4	10.3	76.5	77.3	6.2	5.8	1.49	1.52
Azerbaijan	22.3	21.1	8.7	8.6	64.8	65.4	74.5	72.3	2.64	2.61
Bangladesh	30.5	27.4	11.2	10.1	55.9	57.5	102.3	93.0	3.57	3.08
Belarus	12.2	14.0	13.6	12.9	68.6	69.4	13.4	12.0	1.69	1.92
Belgium	12.0	11.2	10.3	10.4	77.1	77.7	6.4	6.1	1.69	1.69
Benin	46.8	44.9	13.5	12.0	52.7	54.6	105.1	95.3	6.64	6.32
Bolivia	32.4	29.3	10.8	9.6	59.8	62.0	67.5	60.2	4.25	3.75
Brazil	20.8	19.2	9.2	10.1	61.6	60.9	55.3	47.7	2.34	2.14
Bulgaria	8.3	12.5	13.6	13.6	71.0	71.6	15.7	14.8	1.17	1.74
Burkina	47.0	44.9	20.0	21.4	43.2	39.8	117.8	112.8	6.80	6.48
Burma	30.0	28.1	11.7	10.7	56.1	58.1	80.7	71.8	3.83	3.57
Burundi	43.0	41.0	15.2	15.3	49.3	48.1	102.2	95.2	6.55	6.25
Cambodia	43.5	41.0	15.8	14.3	49.9	51.5	107.8	100.5	5.81	5.81
Cameroon	42.5	41.4	13.6	13.9	52.6	51.3	78.7	74.1	5.99	5.73
Canada	13.3	12.3	7.2	7.2	79.1	80.0	6.1	5.5	1.81	1.80
Chad	44.3	42.8	17.4	16.3	47.6	48.9	120.4	113.6	5.84	5.64
Chile [5]	18.1	15.9	5.7	5.7	74.5	75.5	13.6	11.9	2.23	2.00
China [5]	17.0	15.0	6.9	6.8	69.6	71.1	39.6	32.6	1.81	1.81
Colombia	21.3	19.0	4.7	4.6	72.8	74.2	25.8	21.3	2.35	2.17
Cote d'Ivoire	42.5	40.9	15.7	16.4	46.7	45.1	82.4	77.6	6.15	5.80
Croatia	9.8	11.8	11.3	11.6	72.8	73.3	10.2	9.7	1.40	1.69
Cuba	13.4	12.7	7.4	7.5	75.1	75.6	9.0	8.6	1.52	1.60
Czech Republic	10.4	13.3	10.9	11.0	73.8	74.2	8.4	8.0	1.38	1.74
Denmark	12.2	11.3	10.4	10.4	77.3	77.8	4.8	4.7	1.67	1.63
Dominican Republic	23.5	21.1	5.7	5.4	69.1	70.4	47.7	40.8	2.66	2.42
Ecuador	25.1	23.0	5.5	5.1	71.1	72.5	34.8	29.3	2.89	2.59
Egypt	28.2	26.2	8.7	8.1	61.4	62.7	72.8	65.7	3.58	3.24
El Salvador	28.3	26.5	5.8	5.5	68.9	70.5	31.9	27.2	3.20	2.92
Ethiopia	46.1	44.3	17.5	17.6	46.9	46.0	122.8	117.7	7.00	6.75
Finland	11.3	10.3	10.9	10.6	75.5	76.1	4.9	4.8	1.68	1.62
France	10.9	12.2	9.0	9.0	78.4	79.2	6.2	5.7	1.49	1.73
Georgia	12.8	16.7	12.2	12.5	68.1	68.6	22.5	22.2	1.69	2.22
Germany	9.7	10.5	11.2	10.8	76.0	76.7	6.0	5.7	1.30	1.56
Ghana	35.0	30.8	11.2	10.2	56.2	57.5	80.3	74.8	4.59	3.95
Greece	9.8	10.7	9.5	9.5	78.1	79.0	7.4	6.6	1.37	1.52
Guatemala	34.0	31.2	7.2	6.5	65.2	66.9	50.7	44.6	4.50	4.00
Guinea	42.6	40.0	18.7	16.8	45.1	47.0	134.1	123.7	5.72	5.46
Haiti	38.2	35.5	16.0	14.8	49.3	50.2	103.8	98.4	5.69	5.16
Honduras	33.4	30.3	5.8	5.2	68.4	70.0	41.8	35.4	4.41	3.83
Hong Kong	10.5	10.2	5.2	5.6	82.2	82.8	5.1	4.5	1.30	1.42
Hungary	10.7	13.1	15.1	14.8	69.0	69.6	12.3	11.7	1.51	1.78
India	25.9	23.5	9.6	8.9	59.7	61.5	71.1	63.5	3.20	2.90
Indonesia	23.7	22.4	8.4	8.1	61.6	63.4	63.1	55.4	2.70	2.53
Iran	33.7	29.2	6.6	5.8	67.4	69.1	52.7	45.1	4.72	3.90
Iraq	43.1	40.8	6.6	5.6	67.0	68.7	60.0	50.1	6.41	5.81
Israel	20.3	19.6	6.3	6.1	78.0	78.8	8.5	7.5	2.77	2.65
Italy	9.9	11.4	9.8	10.1	78.1	78.6	6.9	6.4	1.27	1.55
Japan	10.2	10.7	7.7	8.4	79.6	80.0	4.4	4.3	1.46	1.50
Kazakhstan	19.0	18.8	9.7	9.8	64.1	64.7	63.2	59.6	2.36	2.29
Kenya	33.4	29.5	10.3	12.6	55.6	51.1	55.3	54.9	4.45	3.69
Korea, North	22.9	19.9	5.5	5.4	70.3	71.5	25.9	22.2	2.31	2.21
Korea, South	16.2	15.8	5.7	5.7	73.3	74.7	8.2	7.4	1.77	1.80
Libya	44.4	42.6	7.7	6.9	64.7	66.2	59.5	52.1	6.26	6.00
Madagascar	42.6	41.2	14.4	13.3	54.2	53.6	93.5	87.6	5.89	5.64
Malawi	41.6	38.7	24.5	27.1	36.2	33.0	139.9	135.8	5.91	5.33
Malaysia	26.2	24.1	5.5	5.2	69.8	71.0	24.0	20.9	3.27	3.10
Mali	51.4	49.3	19.5	17.5	46.8	48.8	102.7	95.6	7.25	6.91
Mexico	26.2	24.3	4.6	4.4	73.7	75.0	25.0	20.7	3.03	2.79
Morocco	27.4	25.1	5.8	5.1	69.5	71.8	43.2	32.9	3.58	3.13
Mozambique	45.5	42.3	19.0	17.0	44.3	46.4	125.6	114.9	6.23	5.76
Nepal	37.0	35.6	12.6	11.2	53.6	55.9	79.0	70.1	5.06	4.68
Netherlands	12.1	11.5	8.7	8.7	77.7	78.2	4.9	4.7	1.51	1.53
Niger	54.5	51.6	24.6	22.2	40.7	42.4	117.6	111.2	7.44	7.17
Nigeria	42.9	41.5	12.7	11.7	54.3	55.6	72.4	63.7	6.24	5.95
Pakistan	36.2	32.6	11.2	10.2	58.5	59.7	96.8	90.3	5.25	4.56
Paraguay	31.0	29.1	4.3	4.1	73.8	74.9	23.2	19.6	4.15	3.86
Peru	24.3	21.8	6.1	5.8	69.1	70.8	52.2	44.4	3.04	2.66
Philippines	29.5	27.3	6.7	6.4	65.9	66.8	35.9	33.2	3.69	3.38
Poland	11.9	14.2	10.1	10.2	72.1	72.6	12.4	11.8	1.69	1.93
Portugal	10.5	11.9	10.2	10.3	75.3	76.1	7.6	7.1	1.36	1.53
Romania	9.8	14.3	12.3	12.7	69.4	70.0	23.2	21.7	1.25	1.83
Russia	10.2	14.5	16.3	14.8	62.3	65.4	24.7	21.6	1.42	1.95
Rwanda	38.8	38.5	20.3	23.5	40.1	36.5	118.8	118.8	5.99	5.73
Saudi Arabia	38.3	37.2	5.4	4.7	69.0	71.1	46.4	36.3	6.45	6.30
Senegal	45.5	43.4	11.8	10.4	56.5	58.3	64.0	58.4	6.31	6.04
Serbia [6]	14.0	14.8	10.3	10.5	72.0	72.5	22.9	21.3	2.00	2.10

See footnotes at end of table.

No. 1327. Vital Statistics, by Country: 1996 and 2000—Continued

[See headnote, page 831]

COUNTRY OR AREA	CRUDE BIRTH RATE [1]		CRUDE DEATH RATE [2]		EXPECTATION OF LIFE AT BIRTH (years)		INFANT MORTALITY RATE [3]		TOTAL FERTILITY RATE [4]	
	1996	2000, proj.	1996	2000, proj.	1996	2000, proj.	1996	2000, proj.	1996	2000, proj.
Slovakia	12.6	15.5	9.4	9.5	73.0	73.5	10.7	10.2	1.65	1.95
Somalia	44.2	41.7	13.2	12.0	55.5	57.0	121.1	111.6	7.01	6.53
South Africa	27.9	25.5	10.3	11.6	59.5	57.2	48.8	46.6	3.43	3.13
Spain	10.0	12.0	8.9	9.1	78.3	79.1	6.3	5.7	1.26	1.51
Sri Lanka	17.9	16.9	5.8	5.9	72.4	73.2	20.8	18.7	2.05	1.95
Sudan	41.1	38.8	11.5	10.3	55.1	56.8	76.0	69.2	5.89	5.47
Sweden	11.6	10.5	11.4	11.1	78.1	78.5	4.5	4.4	1.72	1.60
Switzerland	11.4	11.2	9.6	9.5	77.6	78.1	5.4	5.2	1.47	1.59
Syria	39.6	36.1	5.9	5.3	67.1	68.4	40.0	35.2	5.91	5.19
Taiwan [5]	15.0	14.4	5.5	5.7	76.0	77.3	7.0	6.3	1.76	1.75
Tajikistan	33.8	34.5	8.4	8.3	64.5	65.1	113.1	104.1	4.38	4.47
Tanzania	41.3	39.8	19.5	20.9	42.3	40.0	105.9	101.4	5.67	5.31
Thailand	17.3	16.2	7.0	7.2	68.6	69.4	33.4	28.3	1.89	1.80
Tunisia	24.0	22.5	5.2	5.1	72.6	73.6	35.1	30.1	2.92	2.68
Turkey	22.3	20.4	5.5	5.2	71.9	73.8	43.2	33.3	2.58	2.35
Uganda	45.9	43.1	20.7	21.8	40.3	38.1	99.4	95.6	6.61	6.24
Ukraine	11.2	13.2	15.2	14.9	66.8	67.8	22.5	21.2	1.60	1.87
United Kingdom	13.1	12.1	11.2	10.9	76.4	77.1	6.4	6.0	1.82	1.79
Uzbekistan	29.9	28.9	8.0	7.7	64.6	65.2	79.6	77.5	3.69	3.56
Venezuela	24.4	21.5	5.1	4.9	72.1	73.3	29.5	25.5	2.87	2.53
Vietnam	23.0	20.0	7.0	6.5	67.0	68.5	38.4	33.7	2.69	2.31
Yemen	45.2	43.3	9.6	7.9	59.6	62.6	71.5	57.9	7.29	6.86
Zaire	48.1	46.5	16.9	15.6	46.7	48.1	108.0	98.9	6.64	6.39
Zambia	44.7	43.8	23.7	25.8	36.3	33.7	96.1	97.6	6.55	6.28
Zimbabwe	32.3	29.3	18.2	21.6	41.9	38.2	72.8	72.2	4.09	3.50

[1] Number of births during 1 year per 1,000 persons (based on midyear population).   [2] Number of deaths during 1 year per 1,000 persons (based on midyear population).   [3] Number of deaths of children under 1 year of age per 1,000 live births in a calendar year.   [4] Average number of children that would be born if all women lived to the end of their childbearing years and, at each year of age, they experienced the birth rates occurring in the specified year.   [5] See footnote 2, table 1325.   [6] Serbia and Montenegro have asserted the formation of a joint independent state, but this entity has not been recognized by the United States. Data in this table are for Serbia alone.

Source: U.S. Bureau of the Census, unpublished data.

No. 1328. Death Rates, by Cause and Country

[**Age-standardized death rate per 100,000 population.** For explanation of age-adjustment, see text, section 2. The standard population for this table is the old European standard; see source for details. Deaths classified to ninth revision of *International Classification of Diseases*; see text, section 2]

COUNTRY	Year	Ischemic heart disease	Cerebro-vascular disease	CANCER OF —			Bronchi-tis, [1] emphy-sema, asthma	Chronic liver disease and cirrhosis	Motor vehicle traffic acci-dents	Suicide and self-inflicted injury
				Lung, trachea, bron-chus	Stomach	Female breast				
United States	1991	169.9	48.3	57.5	5.4	31.6	9.2	10.8	16.3	12.1
Australia	1992	175.8	65.9	38.1	7.2	27.7	12.1	6.8	11.1	12.7
Austria	1993	152.3	86.4	35.6	16.6	31.4	15.5	25.9	14.0	19.5
Belgium	1989	90.5	72.3	52.7	11.3	37.9	12.8	11.3	17.4	17.9
Bulgaria	1993	237.8	241.8	32.8	19.9	20.6	10.3	17.8	11.8	16.0
Canada	1992	147.0	47.1	53.0	7.4	32.4	6.8	8.1	11.2	12.8
Czech Republic	1993	276.6	168.0	53.1	17.4	31.2	19.6	16.5	13.6	18.1
Denmark	1992	190.3	72.0	51.1	7.8	40.6	36.5	13.5	10.2	20.4
Finland	1993	224.4	97.0	32.5	12.0	23.6	16.5	9.9	8.4	26.6
France	1992	58.6	51.1	35.0	8.1	28.1	9.5	15.5	14.6	19.1
Germany	1993	157.7	84.9	36.2	14.8	32.1	18.5	21.5	11.4	13.8
Hungary	1993	260.5	169.9	65.7	22.9	35.0	41.0	78.8	16.9	34.2
Italy	1991	94.7	91.1	42.7	18.2	29.8	22.9	22.0	15.1	6.9
Japan	1993	34.0	77.9	27.6	31.8	9.2	10.3	11.8	10.3	15.0
Netherlands	1992	118.2	67.6	52.0	12.2	38.5	14.5	5.1	7.9	9.9
New Zealand	1992	206.3	76.4	42.9	9.4	34.1	11.9	3.6	18.0	14.6
Norway	1992	169.1	78.5	28.9	11.1	27.2	12.3	4.5	6.8	13.9
Poland	1993	118.2	81.3	52.3	19.0	22.1	20.7	12.6	17.8	15.3
Portugal	1993	85.0	204.8	23.1	24.1	24.9	11.0	26.4	23.2	7.4
Spain	1991	75.0	89.3	33.4	14.7	24.3	8.2	18.7	18.5	7.0
Sweden	1992	173.3	67.3	24.3	8.9	25.7	10.6	6.4	7.3	14.5
Switzerland	1993	104.1	50.0	34.9	8.4	34.7	17.4	8.3	9.2	18.8
United Kingdom:										
England and Wales	1992	199.7	82.3	51.0	11.7	39.5	10.9	5.5	7.4	7.4
Scotland	1992	246.4	108.1	68.6	12.6	37.9	7.6	8.4	8.6	10.8

[1] Chronic and unspecified.

Source: World Health Organization, Geneva, Switzerland, *World Health Statistics Annual*.

No. 1329. Marriage and Divorce Rates, by Country: 1970 to 1994

COUNTRY	MARRIAGE RATE PER 1,000 POPULATION, 15 TO 64 YEARS OLD						DIVORCE RATE PER 1,000 MARRIED WOMEN					
	1970	1980	1990	1992	1993	1994	1970	1980	1990	1992	1993	1994
United States [1]	17	16	15	14	14	14	15	23	21	21	21	21
Canada	14	12	10	9	8	8	6	10	11	11	11	11
Denmark	12	8	9	9	9	10	8	11	13	13	13	13
France	12	10	8	7	7	7	3	6	8	(NA)	(NA)	(NA)
Germany [2]	12	9	9	8	9	8	5	6	8	7	7	(NA)
Italy	11	9	8	8	8	7	1	1	2	2	(NA)	(NA)
Japan	14	10	8	9	9	(NA)	4	5	5	6	6	(NA)
Netherlands	15	10	9	9	8	7	3	8	8	9	9	(NA)
Sweden	8	7	7	7	6	6	7	11	12	13	13	(NA)
United Kingdom	14	12	10	9	9	(NA)	[3]5	[3]12	13	13	13	(NA)

NA Not available. [1] Beginning 1980, includes unlicensed marriages registered in California. [2] Prior to 1991, data are for former West Germany. [3] England and Wales only.

No. 1330. Births to Unmarried Women, by Country: 1970 to 1993

[For U.S. figures, beginning 1980, marital status is inferred from a comparison of the child's and parents' surnames on the birth certificate for those States that do not report on marital status. No estimates are included for misstatements on birth records or failures to register births]

COUNTRY	1970		1980		1990		1993	
	Total live births (1,000)	Percent born to unmarried women	Total live births (1,000)	Percent born to unmarried women	Total live births (1,000)	Percent born to unmarried women	Total live births (1,000)	Percent born to unmarried women
United States	3,731	11	3,612	18	4,158	28	4,000	31
Canada [1]	372	10	360	13	398	24	388	27
Denmark	71	11	57	33	63	46	67	47
France [2]	850	7	800	11	762	30	(NA)	35
Germany [2]	811	6	621	8	727	11	798	15
Italy	902	2	640	4	554	6	538	7
Japan	1,932	1	1,616	1	1,240	1	1,204	1
Netherlands	239	2	181	4	198	11	196	13
Sweden	110	18	97	40	124	47	118	50
United Kingdom	904	8	754	12	799	28	762	32

NA Not available. [1] 1980 through 1990 excludes Newfoundland. After 1990, a significant number of births are not allocated according to marital status, resulting in an understatement of the proportion of births to unmarried women. [2] Prior to 1991, data are for former West Germany.
Source of tables 1329 and 1330: U.S. Bureau of Labor Statistics, *Monthly Labor Review*, 1990; and unpublished data.

No. 1331. Foreign or Immigrant Population, 1982 and 1993, and Foreign Labor Force, 1991, by Country

[In Australia, Canada, and the United States the data refer to people present in the country who are foreign born. In the European countries and Japan they generally refer to foreigners and represent the nationalities of residents; as a result, persons born in these countries may be counted among the foreign population, whereas others, who are foreign born, may have acquired the host-country nationality. Except as noted, data are from population registers. Data for foreign labor in European Union (EU) countries are taken from the EU labor force survey. For the other European countries data are based on population registers]

COUNTRY	FOREIGNERS				FOREIGN LABOR FORCE, 1991	
	Number (1,000)		Percent of total population		Number (1,000)	Percent of total labor force
	1982	1993	1982	1993		
United States [1]	[2]14,080	[3]19,767	[2]4.7	[3]7.9	[3]11,636	[3]9.3
Australia [4]	3,004	[5]4,125	20.6	[5]22.7	[5]2,164	[5]24.8
Austria	303	[6]562	4.0	[6]7.1	[6]296	[6]8.9
Belgium	891	[6]909	9.0	[6]9.0	297	7.4
Canada [1]	3,843	4,343	16.1	15.6	[6]2,681	[6]18.5
Denmark	103	189	2.0	3.6	74	2.5
Finland	14	56	0.3	1.1	(NA)	(NA)
France [1]	3,714	[3]3,597	6.8	[3]6.3	1,505	6.2
Germany	4,667	[7]6,878	7.6	8.5	[7]2,703	8.9
Italy	359	987	0.6	1.7	(NA)	(NA)
Japan [8]	802	1,321	0.7	1.1	[6]590	[9]0.9
Luxembourg	96	[6]120	26.2	[6]30.3	55	33.3
Netherlands	547	[6]757	3.8	[6]5.0	269	3.9
Norway	91	162	2.2	3.8	[6][9]47	[6]4.4
Spain	200	[6]393	0.5	[6]1.0	59	0.4
Sweden	406	[6]499	4.9	[6]5.7	[6]244	[6]5.5
Switzerland	926	1,260	14.4	18.1	[6]717	[6]20.1
United Kingdom [4]	1,601	2,001	2.8	3.5	960	3.3

NA Not available. [1] Census data. [2] 1980 data. [3] 1990 data. [4] Labor force survey. [5] 1994 data. [6] 1992 data. [7] Western Germany only. [8] Residence permits. [9] Excludes unemployed.
Source: Organization for Economic Cooperation and Development, Paris, France, *The OECD Observer*, No. 192, February/March 1995, (copyright.)

No. 1332. Health Expenditures, by Country: 1980 to 1994

[G.D.P.=gross domestic product; for explanation, see text, section 14. For explanation of purchasing power parities, see text, section 30]

COUNTRY	TOTAL HEALTH EXPENDITURES							PUBLIC HEALTH EXPENDITURES		
	Percent of gross domestic product					Per capita on basis of G.D.P. purchasing power parities		Percent of gross domestic product		
	1980	1985	1990	1991	1994	1991	1994	1980	1991	1994
United States	9.2	10.5	12.4	13.4	14.2	$2,867	$3,498	3.9	5.9	6.7
Australia	7.3	7.7	8.2	8.6	8.5	1,411	1,606	4.6	5.8	5.8
Austria	7.9	8.1	8.4	8.6	9.7	1,492	1,965	5.4	5.7	6.2
Belgium	6.6	7.4	7.6	7.9	8.2	1,354	1,653	5.5	7.0	7.2
Canada	7.4	8.5	9.5	10.0	9.8	1,917	2,010	5.5	7.2	7.0
Czech Republic	(NA)	(NA)	(NA)	(NA)	7.6	(NA)	662	(NA)	(NA)	(NA)
Denmark.	6.8	6.3	6.3	6.5	6.6	1,151	1,362	5.8	5.4	5.4
Finland.	6.5	7.3	8.0	9.1	8.3	1,420	1,357	5.1	7.4	6.2
France . . , ...	7.6	8.5	8.9	9.1	[2]9.7	1,656	[2]1,866	6.0	6.8	[2]7.6
Germany [1]	8.4	8.7	8.3	8.4	[2]8.6	1,663	[2,1]1,816	6.3	6.0	[2]6.0
Greece.	(NA)	(NA)	(NA)	(NA)	[2]3.6	404	[2]500	(NA)	(NA)	[2]2.8
Iceland.	6.4	7.1	8.3	8.4	8.1	1,476	1,598	5.7	7.2	[2]6.8
Ireland	9.2	8.2	7.0	7.3	[2]7.3	844	1,107	7.5	5.6	[2]5.7
Italy	6.9	7.0	8.1	8.3	[2]8.6	1,408	[2,1]1,522	5.6	6.5	[2]6.3
Japan	6.6	6.5	6.7	6.8	[2]7.3	1,307	[2,1]1,484	4.6	4.8	[2]5.3
Luxembourg	(NA)	(NA)	(NA)	(NA)	3.1	(NA)	1,697	(NA)	(NA)	[2]3.3
Mexico.	(NA)	(NA)	(NA)	[3]4.9	(NA)	[3]350	(NA)	(NA)	[3]2.9	3.1
Netherlands	8.0	8.0	8.2	8.4	[2]8.8	1,366	1,641	6.0	6.1	[2]6.9
New Zealand.	7.2	6.5	7.3	7.7	[2]7.7	1,047	[2,1]1,185	6.0	6.1	[2]6.0
Norway.	(NA)	(NA)	(NA)	(NA)	[2]5.5	1,305	[2,1]1,558	(NA)	(NA)	[2]5.2
Portugal	5.9	7.0	6.7	6.8	[2]7.4	624	[2]874	4.3	[4]4.1	[2]4.1
Spain.	5.6	5.7	6.6	6.7	[2]7.3	848	[2]971	4.5	5.5	[2]5.7
Sweden	9.4	8.8	8.6	8.6	7.7	1,443	1,348	8.7	6.7	[2]6.4
Switzerland	7.3	7.6	7.8	7.9	9.6	1,730	2,294	4.9	5.4	[2]6.8
Turkey	4.0	2.8	4.0	4.0	[2]2.6	142	[2]146	1.1	[4]1.4	[2]1.4
United Kingdom	5.8	6.0	6.2	6.6	6.9	1,033	1,211	5.2	5.5	5.8

NA Not available.   [1] Former West Germany.   [2] 1993 data.   [3] 1992 data.   [4] 1990 data.

Source: Organization for Economic Cooperation and Development, Paris, France, *OECD Health Data*, 1995; *OECD Health Systems: Facts and Trends*, 1993; *OECD in Figures, 1996 Edition*, and unpublished data.

No. 1333. Educational Attainment, by Country: 1992

[Percent of persons 25 to 64 years old]

COUNTRY	Total	Early childhood, primary, and lower secondary education only	Upper secondary education only	Non-university tertiary education only	University education only
Australia	100	47	30	11	12
Austria	100	32	61	([1])	[1]7
Belgium	100	55	25	11	9
Canada	100	29	30	26	15
Denmark.	100	41	40	6	13
Finland.	100	39	43	8	10
France	100	48	36	6	10
Germany	100	18	60	10	12
Greece.	100	66	21	3	10
Ireland	100	58	25	9	8
Italy	100	72	22	([1])	[1]6
Netherlands	100	42	37	([1])	[1]21
New Zealand.	100	43	33	13	11
Norway.	100	21	54	13	12
Portugal	100	86	7	2	5
Spain.	100	77	10	3	10
Sweden	100	30	46	12	12
Switzerland	100	19	60	13	8
Turkey	100	86	9	([1])	[1]5
United Kingdom	100	32	49	8	11
United States	100	16	53	7	24

[1] Non-university tertiary education included in University education only.

Source: Organization for Economic Cooperation and Development, Paris, France, *Education at a Glance*, annual, (copyright).

No. 1334. Gross National Product, by Country: 1985 to 1994

[In billions of dollars, except per capita. For most countries, data for GNP are based on local currencies which are deflated to constant 1994 local currency values before conversion to U.S. dollar equivalents. In general, rates used for conversion are the 1994 average par/market exchange rates as supplied by the International Bank for Reconstruction and Development]

COUNTRY	CURRENT DOLLARS				CONSTANT (1994) DOLLARS				Per capita (dollars)		
	1985	1990	1993	1994	1985	1990	1993	1994	1985	1990	1994
United States	4,054	5,568	6,348	6,727	5,413	6,197	6,479	6,727	22,700	24,790	25,810
Algeria	31	37	40	41	42	42	41	41	1,882	1,644	1,452
Argentina	145	178	254	278	194	200	260	278	6,377	6,181	8,205
Australia	183	250	298	320	245	278	304	320	15,500	16,270	17,720
Austria	117	163	187	196	157	181	191	196	20,750	23,490	24,600
Bangladesh	13	20	24	26	18	22	25	26	175	191	206
Belgium	139	194	220	229	185	216	224	229	18,770	21,630	22,800
Brazil	351	478	547	580	469	532	559	580	3,424	3,546	3,655
Bulgaria	41	45	32	37	55	50	32	37	6,154	5,622	4,239
Canada	323	444	490	523	432	494	500	523	17,150	18,570	18,600
Chile	19	33	46	50	25	37	47	50	2,072	2,799	3,609
China	777	1,351	2,047	2,214	1,037	1,504	2,089	2,214	984	1,323	1,860
Colombia	31	46	56	62	41	51	58	62	1,395	1,553	1,753
Croatia	(NA)	(NA)	11	12	(NA)	(NA)	11	12	(NA)	(NA)	2,660
Cuba [1]	30	34	21	22	39	37	22	22	3,911	3,556	2,025
Czech Republic	(NA)	(NA)	79	81	(NA)	(NA)	81	81	(NA)	(NA)	7,824
Denmark	90	116	133	141	121	129	135	141	23,600	25,080	27,210
Egypt	23	35	40	42	31	39	41	42	627	694	689
El Salvador	5	6	8	9	6	7	8	9	1,357	1,350	1,532
Ethiopia	3	4	5	5	4	5	5	5	93	101	91
Finland	66	93	88	93	89	104	90	93	18,090	20,850	18,390
France	823	1,146	1,256	1,316	1,100	1,275	1,282	1,316	19,930	22,480	22,760
Germany [2]	990	1,385	1,947	2,045	1,321	1,542	1,987	2,045	21,650	24,420	25,220
Ghana	3	4	5	5	4	4	5	5	273	294	309
Greece	50	65	75	78	67	73	77	78	6,754	7,195	7,398
Hungary	53	63	64	64	70	70	66	64	6,593	6,721	6,213
India	139	226	267	287	186	252	273	287	241	295	312
Indonesia	65	111	153	168	87	124	156	168	505	660	838
Iran [1]	88	107	140	125	118	119	143	125	2,477	2,092	1,981
Iraq [1]	31	23	(NA)	(NA)	41	26	(NA)	(NA)	2,618	1,400	(NA)
Israel	36	53	70	77	48	59	72	77	12,110	13,780	15,210
Italy	634	879	966	1,008	847	978	986	1,008	14,830	16,960	17,330
Japan	2,615	3,921	4,509	4,630	3,492	4,364	4,602	4,630	28,920	35,320	37,000
Kenya	4	6	6	7	5	6	6	7	243	262	232
Korea, North [1]	26	30	21	21	35	33	21	21	1,792	1,544	906
Korea, South	123	244	322	356	165	272	329	356	4,039	6,284	7,896
Kuwait [3]	26	25	28	28	35	28	28	28	20,500	13,050	16,600
Malaysia	25	44	60	67	34	49	62	67	2,186	2,786	3,483
Mexico	223	294	344	363	297	327	351	363	3,877	3,837	3,940
Morocco	16	24	26	30	22	27	27	30	928	1,036	1,057
Netherlands	199	278	315	331	266	309	321	331	18,370	20,670	21,540
Nigeria	24	32	39	41	31	36	40	41	420	412	421
Norway	66	85	101	108	88	95	103	108	21,270	22,390	25,030
Pakistan	26	40	49	51	35	44	50	51	352	387	399
Peru	32	35	42	49	42	39	43	49	2,148	1,804	2,071
Philippines	35	54	62	66	46	60	63	66	802	924	926
Poland	144	163	193	206	193	182	197	206	5,182	4,769	5,336
Portugal	47	76	84	87	63	84	86	87	6,162	8,125	8,280
Romania	99	105	66	66	133	117	68	66	5,839	5,035	2,864
Russia	(NA)	(NA)	777	780	(NA)	(NA)	793	780	(NA)	(NA)	5,216
Saudi Arabia	94	113	123	121	126	125	125	121	9,519	7,900	6,725
Serbia and Montenegro	(NA)	(NA)	10	10	(NA)	(NA)	10	10	(NA)	(NA)	967
Slovakia	(NA)	(NA)	34	36	(NA)	(NA)	35	36	(NA)	(NA)	6,573
Slovenia	(NA)	(NA)	15	16	(NA)	(NA)	15	16	(NA)	(NA)	7,819
South Africa	80	105	114	120	107	117	116	120	3,078	2,954	2,720
Spain	276	414	459	478	369	461	468	478	9,587	11,830	12,150
Sri Lanka	6	8	11	12	8	9	11	12	494	544	637
Sweden	132	176	181	189	176	196	185	189	21,110	22,930	21,490
Switzerland	175	238	256	267	234	265	262	267	35,840	39,140	37,960
Syria	42	51	(NA)	(NA)	56	57	(NA)	(NA)	5,352	4,481	(NA)
Taiwan	91	167	219	238	121	186	224	238	6,273	9,087	11,180
Tanzania	1	2	2	2	1	2	2	2	67	73	74
Thailand	47	92	128	142	63	103	130	142	1,207	1,830	2,378
Turkey	67	107	134	129	89	119	137	129	1,751	2,080	2,075
United Kingdom	635	883	970	1,027	848	983	990	1,027	14,970	17,120	17,670
Venezuela	33	46	58	58	45	51	59	58	2,693	2,715	2,807
Zaire	6	8	6	6	8	9	6	6	247	230	133

NA Not available.   [1] Estimated.   [2] Prior to 1991, data are for former West Germany.   [3] Constant dollars are estimated.

Source: U.S. Arms Control and Disarmament Agency, *World Military Expenditures and Arms Transfers*, annual. Data from International Bank for Reconstruction and Development and U.S. Central Intelligence Agency.

No. 1335. Gross Domestic Product, by Country: 1980 to 1994

COUNTRY	PURCHASING POWER PARITY BASIS [1]												CONSTANT (1990) PRICE LEVELS AND EXCHANGE RATES [2]								
	Amount (bil. dol.)						Per capita (dollars)						Amount (bil. dol.)						Annual growth rate [3] (percent)		
	1980	1985	1990	1992	1993	1994	1980	1985	1990	1992	1993	1994	1980	1985	1990	1992	1993	1994	1992	1993	1994
OECD, total [4]	7,373	10,798	15,041	16,838	17,260	18,130	8,501	11,963	16,003	17,604	17,890	18,646	12,764	14,361	16,800	17,240	17,423	17,921	1.6	1.1	2.9
OECD Europe [4]	3,087	4,368	6,106	6,921	6,917	7,232	7,517	10,391	14,130	15,808	15,694	16,321	5,714	6,200	7,229	7,386	7,357	7,548	1.1	-0.4	2.6
European Union [4]	2,870	4,035	5,620	6,368	6,328	6,645	8,079	11,244	15,427	17,307	17,116	17,914	5,344	5,776	6,730	6,871	6,828	7,019	1.0	-0.6	2.8
Australia	128	194	272	289	306	328	8,678	12,303	15,941	16,541	17,332	18,382	214	251	295	297	308	323	2.5	3.8	5.0
Austria	67	93	128	148	153	162	8,850	12,278	16,623	18,827	19,167	20,210	128	137	158	166	167	172	2.0	0.4	3.0
Belgium	87	118	163	190	195	204	8,820	11,933	16,318	18,953	19,323	20,166	159	166	192	200	197	201	1.8	-1.6	2.2
Canada	246	370	509	536	559	597	10,020	14,262	18,304	18,782	19,314	20,401	427	493	568	562	575	601	0.8	2.3	4.6
Denmark	45	67	85	94	99	107	8,746	12,997	16,548	18,241	19,154	20,546	106	120	129	132	134	140	0.8	1.5	4.4
Finland	38	57	81	76	79	83	8,004	11,682	16,193	15,083	15,646	16,208	99	114	135	121	119	124	-3.6	-1.2	4.1
France	507	712	984	1,107	1,078	1,112	9,414	12,872	17,347	19,294	18,690	19,201	957	1,031	1,195	1,221	1,203	1,235	1.3	-1.5	2.7
Germany	658	921	1,269	1,509	1,500	1,602	8,410	11,870	15,991	18,721	18,479	19,675	1,321	1,421	1,640	1,724	1,704	1,753	2.2	-1.2	2.9
Greece	51	71	92	109	112	118	5,283	7,131	9,133	10,537	10,783	11,315	70	75	82	85	84	85	0.4	-0.9	1.5
Iceland	2	3	4	5	5	5	9,495	13,104	17,267	18,348	18,696	19,271	5	5	6	6	6	6	-3.2	1.0	2.8
Ireland	18	27	39	48	49	54	5,291	7,501	11,245	13,416	13,791	15,212	32	36	45	48	49	53	3.9	3.1	6.7
Italy	478	666	923	1,045	1,011	1,068	8,464	11,756	16,274	18,377	17,709	18,681	880	943	1,095	1,116	1,103	1,127	0.7	-1.2	2.2
Japan	936	1,463	2,174	2,485	2,528	2,594	8,011	12,112	17,596	19,986	20,279	20,756	1,960	2,354	2,932	3,091	3,084	3,100	1.1	-0.2	0.5
Luxembourg [4]	4	6	9	10	11	12	10,852	15,855	22,929	26,752	28,135	29,454	7	8	10	11	11	11	1.9	(Z)	3.3
Mexico	244	349	446	621	637	673	3,499	4,479	5,180	6,939	6,987	7,239	207	228	244	260	262	271	2.8	0.6	3.5
Netherlands	124	172	239	269	271	286	8,750	11,839	15,958	17,693	17,743	18,589	229	243	284	296	297	305	2.0	0.2	3.5
New Zealand	24	37	45	49	53	57	7,711	11,185	13,484	14,307	15,206	16,248	36	42	44	44	47	49	3.0	5.4	6.1
Norway	38	58	74	88	92	95	9,205	13,898	17,497	20,612	21,328	21,968	91	107	115	123	125	132	3.3	2.1	5.7
Portugal	44	60	92	113	117	122	4,548	6,035	9,371	11,407	11,796	12,335	50	52	67	69	69	69	1.1	-1.2	0.8
Spain	219	308	458	522	521	532	5,868	8,018	11,787	13,374	13,323	13,581	366	395	492	506	501	511	0.7	-1.2	2.1
Sweden	77	109	146	149	147	153	9,250	13,057	17,004	17,205	16,823	17,422	188	205	230	224	218	223	-1.4	-2.6	2.2
Switzerland	75	104	143	159	161	167	11,720	15,969	21,283	23,088	23,183	23,942	184	197	226	225	218	226	-0.3	-0.8	1.2
Turkey	102	169	264	300	331	319	2,284	3,327	4,660	5,143	5,562	5,271	91	115	151	161	174	165	6.0	8.0	-5.5
United Kingdom	453	649	912	980	986	1,030	8,039	11,449	15,874	16,890	16,943	17,650	752	828	976	951	972	1,010	-0.5	2.2	3.8
United States	2,708	4,017	5,490	5,937	6,260	6,650	11,892	16,844	21,966	23,246	24,252	25,512	4,205	4,793	5,490	5,600	5,791	6,027	2.5	3.4	4.1

Z Less than 0.05 percent.   [1] The goods and services produced in different countries should be valued consistently if the differences observed are meant to reflect real differences in the volumes of goods and services produced. The use of purchasing power parities (PPP) instead of exchange rates is intended to achieve this objective. PPP's show how many units of currency are needed in one country to buy the same amount of goods and services which one unit of currency will buy in the other country. See text, section 30.   [2] Based on constant (1990) price data converted to U.S. dollars using 1990 exchange rates.   [3] Percent change from immediate prior year. Minus sign (-) indicates decrease.   [4] For countries, see text, section 30.

Source: Organization for Economic Cooperation and Development, Paris, France, National Accounts, Main Aggregates, vol. I, annual (copyright).

No. 1336. Selected International Economic Indicators, by Country: 1980 to 1995

[Data cover gross domestic product (GDP) at market prices. Gross fixed capital formation covers private and government sectors except military. Savings data are calculated by deducting outlays—such as personal consumption expenditures, interest paid, and transfer payments to foreigners—from disposable personal income]

YEAR	United States	France	Germany	Italy	Netherlands	United Kingdom	Japan	Canada
Ratio of gross fixed capital formation to GDP (current prices):								
1980	19.6	23.0	22.6	24.3	21.6	17.9	31.6	23.3
1990	16.2	21.4	20.9	20.3	20.9	19.5	31.7	21.1
1992	15.0	20.1	23.1	19.2	20.0	15.7	30.4	18.7
1993	15.4	18.5	21.8	16.9	19.3	15.0	29.5	18.1
1994	16.2	18.0	22.0	16.6	19.3	14.9	28.7	18.6
1995	16.7	18.0	21.7	17.0	19.7	14.9	28.4	17.6
Ratio of savings to disposable personal income:								
1980	8.2	17.6	14.2	21.6	11.0	13.4	17.9	13.3
1990	5.0	12.5	14.7	18.2	15.6	8.1	12.1	9.5
1992	5.9	13.6	13.9	17.7	13.0	12.2	13.1	10.2
1993	4.5	14.1	12.9	15.8	12.0	11.4	13.4	9.4
1994	3.8	13.6	12.2	14.8	11.3	9.6	12.8	7.8
1995	4.5	14.3	12.3	13.1	(NA)	10.1	13.4	7.3

NA Not available.

Source: U.S. Dept. of Commerce, International Trade Administration, Office of Trade and Economic Analysis, based on official statistics of listed countries.

No. 1337. At-Home Food and Beverage Expenditures, by Country: 1992

[Percent of total personal consumption expenditures. Expenditures spent on food and alcoholic beverages that were consumed at home]

COUNTRY	Food [1]	Alcoholic beverages	COUNTRY	Food [1]	Alcoholic beverages
United States	7.8	1.1	Korea, South	[3]33.6	(NA)
Australia	14.5	4.2	Mexico	[3]33.7	(NA)
Canada	10.5	2.7	Netherlands	12.5	1.5
Colombia	29.6	3.7	Norway	19.8	3.1
Denmark	15.7	3.4	Russia [4]	38.4	3.9
France	15.5	2.0	Singapore	17.0	2.0
Germany	[2]18.3	(NA)	South Africa	30.3	5.1
Greece	30.7	3.0	Spain	[3]21.3	(NA)
India	50.8	0.5	Sweden	14.3	2.9
Ireland	20.6	11.5	Switzerland	[2]25.1	(NA)
Israel	22.1	0.7	Thailand	26.3	4.1
Italy	17.6	1.0	United Kingdom	11.9	6.2
Japan	[3]20.8	(NA)	Venezuela	[2]37.1	(NA)

NA Not available. [1] Food expenditures include nonalcoholic beverages. [2] Food expenditures include all beverages. [3] Food expenditures include all beverages and tobacco. [4] This data was published by the Statistical Committee of the Commonwealth of Independent States (CIS), Moscow, 1995.

Source: U.S. Dept. of Agriculture, Economic Research Service, Food Consumption, Prices, and Expenditures, 1996: Annual Data, 1970-94.

No. 1338. Per Capita Consumption of Meat and Poultry: 1994

[Preliminary. In pounds per capita. Beef, veal, and pork quantities are as of September and in carcass-weight equivalents; poultry quantities are as of July and are on ready-to-cook basis]

COUNTRY	PORK Quantity	PORK Rank	COUNTRY	POULTRY Quantity	POULTRY Rank	COUNTRY	BEEF AND VEAL Quantity	BEEF AND VEAL Rank
Denmark	147	1	Israel	98	1	Uruguay	189	1
Spain	118	2	United States	92	2	Argentina	144	2
Belgium-Luxembourg	116	3	Hong Kong	90	3	United States	98	3
Austria	113	4	Singapore	85	4	Australia	82	4
Germany	107	5	Canada	69	5	Canada	78	5
Netherlands	103	6	Saudi Arabia	67	6	New Zealand	64	6
Taiwan	89	7	Taiwan	61	7	France	61	7
Switzerland	86	8	Australia	59	8	Italy	58	8
France	85	9	Spain	53	9	Brazil	56	9
Singapore	84	10	United Kingdom	51	10	Kazakstan	54	10
United States	68	18						

Source: U.S. Department of Agriculture, Foreign Agricultural Service, World Poultry Situation and World Livestock Situation, annual.

No. 1339. Percent of Households Owning Selected Appliances, by Country: 1990-1991

APPLIANCE	United States [1][2]	Bel-gium	Den-mark	France	Ger-many [3]	Italy	Nether-lands	Spain	Sweden	Swit-zerland	United King-dom
Cassette recorder. . .	(NA)	75	82	76	74	64	81	67	88	82	82
Clothes washer	77	88	[2]74	88	88	96	89	87	72	78	[4]88
Dishwasher.	45	26	[2]36	32	34	18	11	11	31	32	11
Food processor	(NA)	91	83	83	92	48	84	50	77	91	80
Microwave oven. . . .	84	21	[2]31	19	36	6	22	9	37	15	48
Radio.	(NA)	90	98	98	84	92	99	95	93	99	90
Television set, color/mono	98	97	98	95	97	98	95	98	97	93	[4]98
Tumbledrier.	72	39	[2]30	12	17	10	27	5	18	27	32
Vacuum cleaner. . . .	(NA)	92	96	89	96	56	98	29	97	93	98
Video recorder. . . .	(NA)	42	63	35	42	25	50	40	48	41	69

NA Not available.　[1] Represents appliances possessed and generally used by the household (as of November). Source: U.S. Energy Information Administration, *Annual Energy Review*.　[2] 1993 data.　[3] Former West Germany.　[4] 1992 data.

Source: Except as noted, Euromonitor PLC, London, England, *European Marketing Data and Statistics*, annual, (copyright).

No. 1340. Motor Vehicle Registrations, by Country: 1993

COUNTRY	ALL VEHICLES		PASSENGER CARS		COUNTRY	ALL VEHICLES		PASSENGER CARS	
	Number (mil.)	Persons per vehicle	Number (mil.)	Persons per car		Number (mil.)	Persons per vehicle	Number (mil.)	Persons per car
Argentina	6.5	5	4.9	7	Israel	1.2	4	1.0	5
Australia	10.5	2	8.3	2	Italy	32.3	2	29.6	2
Austria	4.1	2	3.4	2	Japan.	63.4	2	40.8	3
Belgium	4.6	2	4.1	2	Kuwait	0.7	3	0.5	3
Bulgaria	1.5	6	1.4	6	Netherlands. . .	6.4	2	5.8	3
Canada.	17.2	2	13.5	2	New Zealand . .	2.3	1	1.6	2
Chile	1.0	13	0.7	19	Norway	2.0	2	1.6	3
Costa Rica . . .	0.3	12	0.1	23	Panama	0.2	11	0.2	16
Denmark.	1.9	3	1.6	3	Paraguay	0.1	48	0.1	79
Dominican					Poland	7.9	5	6.5	6
Republic	0.2	40	0.1	66	Portugal	3.0	4	2.2	5
Ecuador	0.5	22	0.2	56	Puerto Rico . . .	1.6	2	1.4	2
Finland	2.1	2	1.9	3	Singapore	0.4	6	0.3	9
France	29.5	2	24.4	2	Sweden	3.9	2	3.6	2
Germany.	42.0	2	39.2	2	Switzerland . . .	3.4	2	3.1	2
Greece	2.8	4	2.0	5	Syria	0.3	55	0.1	126
Hong Kong . . .	0.5	12	0.3	18	Thailand	2.8	21	1.0	57
Hungary	2.3	4	2.1	5	**United States .**	194.0	1	146.3	2
Ireland	1.1	3	0.9	4	Uruguay	0.3	11	0.2	16

Source: American Automobile Manufactures Association, Inc., Detroit, MI, *AAMA Motor Vehicle Facts & Figures*, annual, (copyright).

No. 1341. Motor Vehicle Miles of Travel for Selected Countries

COUNTRY	Year	TOTAL VEHICLE MILES (billions)				AVERAGE VEHICLE MILES PER—			
		Auto-mobile	Motor-cycle	Bus	Truck	Auto-mobile	Motor-cycle	Bus	Truck
Canada.	1990	138.2	0.7	1.3	48.3	10,371	2,184	19,823	7,001
France	1993	213.1	3.7	2.5	65.9	8,740	1,247	32,704	13,202
Germany.	1991	288.4	7.0	2.7	26.9	7,674	2,955	31,706	16,208
Japan.	1992	252.1	(NA)	4.4	164.9	6,183	(NA)	17,724	7,380
Mexico	1991	22.7	0.7	0.3	9.7	3,027	2,532	3,141	2,765
Sweden	1993	26.6	(NA)	(NA)	(NA)	7,456	(NA)	(NA)	(NA)
United Kingdom	1993	207.2	2.8	2.9	39.9	10,186	3,922	26,713	10,271
United States	**1993**	**1,624.0**	**9.9**	**6.1**	**656.6**	**11,099**	**2,486**	**9,353**	**13,942**

NA Not available.

Source: U.S. Federal Highway Administration, *Highway Statistics, 1994*.

No. 1342. Telephones, Newspapers, Television, and Radio, by Country

[See text, section 30, for general comments about the data. For data qualifications for countries, see source]

COUNTRY	Telephone main lines per 100 people, [1] 1994	Cellular telephone subscribers per 100,000 people, [1] 1992	Daily newspaper circulation per 1,000 people, [2] 1992	Television receivers per 1,000 people, [3] 1993	Radio receivers per 1,000 people, [4] 1993
Algeria	4	18	38	79	236
Argentina	14	136	143	220	672
Australia	50	2,510	265	489	1,290
Austria	47	2,188	398	479	618
Belgium	45	615	310	453	771
Brazil	7	20	55	209	390
Bulgaria	34	-	164	260	450
Canada	58	3,727	204	618	992
Chile	11	474	147	211	345
China	2	15	43	38	184
Colombia	9	25	63	118	177
Costa Rica	13	-	101	142	258
Cuba	3	2	122	170	346
Cyprus	45	1,353	107	152	296
Czech Republic	21	(NA)	583	476	631
Denmark	60	3,993	332	538	1,035
Dominican Republic .	8	94	36	90	172
Ecuador	5	-	64	88	326
Egypt	4	13	41	113	307
Finland	55	7,028	512	504	996
France	55	568	205	412	890
Germany	48	958	323	559	890
Ghana	-	5	18	16	269
Greece	48	-	135	202	416
Guatemala	2	(NA)	18	53	68
Honduras	2	-	31	78	408
Hungary	17	226	282	427	617
Iceland	56	5,866	519	335	791
India	1	-	31	40	80
Indonesia	1	19	24	62	148
Iran	7	-	20	63	230
Iraq	3	-	35	75	217
Ireland	33	1,239	186	301	636
Israel	37	696	246	272	478
Italy	43	1,355	106	429	802
Jamaica	10	320	67	141	433
Japan	48	1,260	577	618	911
Korea, South	40	623	412	215	1,013
Kuwait	23	2,589	248	346	408
Lebanon	9	134	185	346	887
Luxembourg	54	287	372	261	633
Malaysia	15	442	117	151	430
Mexico	9	298	116	150	255
Morocco	4	12	13	79	219
Netherlands	51	1,097	275	333	907
New Zealand	47	2,938	305	451	935
Norway	55	6,527	607	427	798
Pakistan	1	12	6	18	88
Panama	11	-	90	169	227
Paraguay	3	33	37	83	170
Peru	4	121	71	99	253
Philippines	2	17	50	47	143
Poland	13	7	159	298	439
Portugal	35	378	47	190	232
Puerto Rico	33	1,428	141	267	712
Romania	12	-	324	200	202
Russia	16	4	387	372	338
Saudi Arabia	10	99	43	255	293
Singapore	47	4,270	336	381	644
South Africa	9	31	32	101	314
Spain	37	461	104	400	311
Sweden	68	7,558	511	470	879
Switzerland	60	3,231	377	400	832
Syria	5	-	22	62	257
Taiwan	40	1,850	[5]174	(NA)	(NA)
Thailand	4	431	85	113	189
Trinidad and Tobago .	16	101	138	317	489
Tunisia	5	22	49	81	198
Turkey	20	104	(NA)	176	162
United Kingdom	47	2,595	383	435	1,146
United States	**59**	**4,326**	**236**	**816**	**2,120**
Uruguay	17	55	240	232	604
Venezuela	11	101	205	163	443

- Represents or rounds to zero.   NA Not available.   [1] As of December 31.   [2] Publications containing general news and appearing at least 4 times a week; may range in size from a single sheet to 50 or more pages. Circulation data refer to average circulation per issue or number of printed copies per issue and include copies sold outside the country.   [3] Estimated number of sets in use.   [4] Data cover estimated number of receivers in use and apply to all types of receivers for radio broadcasts to the public, including receivers connected to a radio "redistribution system" but excluding television sets.   [5] For 1990. Source: U.S. Bureau of the Census. Data from Republic of China publications.

Source: Except as noted, International Telecommunications Union, Geneva, Switzerland, *World Telecom Indicators*, (copyright); and United Nations Educational, Scientific, and Cultural Organization, Paris, France, *Statistical Yearbook*, (copyright).

No. 1343. Tax Revenues, by Country: 1980 to 1993

[Covers national and local taxes and Social Security contributions. Minus sign (-) indicates decrease]

COUNTRY	TAX REVENUES, 1993		PERCENT CHANGE IN TOTAL TAX REVENUE AS EXPRESSED IN NATIONAL CURRENCY [1]					TAX REVENUES AS PERCENT OF GROSS DOMESTIC PRODUCT				
	Total (bil. dol.)	Per capita (dol.)	1989	1990	1991	1992	1993	1980	1985	1990	1992	1993
Australia	83.8	4,745	8.8	3.0	-3.4	2.8	6.6	28.4	30.1	30.7	28.6	28.7
Austria	79.4	9,933	4.3	8.4	8.5	9.7	4.3	41.2	43.1	41.3	43.3	43.6
Belgium	96.1	9,604	4.6	7.3	5.0	5.3	3.9	44.4	47.9	45.1	45.1	45.7
Canada.	198.8	6,915	10.2	5.5	2.5	0.6	2.0	31.6	33.1	36.5	36.2	35.6
Denmark.	67.3	12,961	2.8	0.2	3.8	4.0	3.7	45.5	49.0	48.7	49.4	49.9
Finland	38.4	7,580	12.4	10.7	-1.7	-2.9	-1.8	36.9	40.8	45.4	46.8	45.7
France	548.8	9,516	7.1	5.7	4.6	2.7	1.7	41.7	44.5	43.7	43.6	43.9
Germany [2].	745.7	11,379	7.7	4.5	22.3	10.1	3.0	38.2	38.1	36.7	38.9	39.0
Greece	30.1	2,909	15.0	30.1	27.0	20.4	14.1	29.4	35.1	37.5	40.8	41.2
Iceland	1.9	7,315	23.6	14.3	8.9	2.7	0.5	30.2	28.6	31.4	32.2	31.3
Ireland	17.3	4,857	1.7	6.3	5.6	7.3	7.9	33.8	36.4	35.3	36.2	36.3
Italy	470.7	8,247	12.8	13.6	10.4	11.7	17.0	30.2	34.5	39.1	42.1	47.8
Japan.	1,228.9	9,858	8.4	9.6	3.6	-3.3	0.6	25.4	27.6	31.3	29.2	29.1
Luxembourg	5.6	14,478	11.0	9.2	5.0	8.0	13.3	46.0	47.4	42.5	41.9	44.6
Netherlands.	148.4	9,701	-0.2	5.9	11.2	3.4	4.1	44.7	44.1	44.6	47.0	48.0
New Zealand. . . .	16.2	4,674	14.2	-1.1	-3.6	5.0	8.0	32.9	33.5	37.4	36.4	35.7
Norway.	47.3	10,978	2.5	7.1	5.7	1.1	2.7	47.1	47.6	46.3	46.5	45.7
Portugal	26.6	2,701	20.7	18.7	19.3	20.5	0.1	28.7	31.6	31.0	33.4	31.4
Spain	167.8	4,287	18.5	10.7	10.6	11.5	0.4	24.1	28.8	34.4	36.0	35.1
Sweden	92.5	10,611	12.0	10.6	0.8	-5.6	0.1	48.8	50.0	55.6	49.9	49.9
Switzerland	77.1	11,103	5.4	7.3	4.4	4.6	5.5	30.8	32.0	31.5	31.9	33.2
Turkey	40.9	688	84.6	85.4	68.0	85.4	83.2	18.1	15.3	20.0	22.4	23.5
United Kingdom . .	316.3	5,470	8.0	7.4	2.5	2.5	0.1	35.3	37.9	36.4	35.4	33.6
United States . . .	**1,836.0**	**7,128**	**8.2**	**5.0**	**3.6**	**4.3**	**6.4**	**29.3**	**28.7**	**29.4**	**29.5**	**29.7**

[1] Change from previous year.   [2] Prior to 1991, data are for former West Germany.

Source: Organization for Economic Cooperation and Development, Paris, France, *Revenue Statistics of OECD Member Countries*, annual (copyright).

No. 1344. Percent Distribution of Tax Receipts, by Country: 1980 to 1993

COUNTRY	Total [1]	INCOME AND PROFITS TAXES [2]			SOCIAL SECURITY CONTRIBUTIONS			TAXES ON GOODS AND SERVICES [5]		
		Total [3]	Individual	Corporate	Total [4]	Employees	Employers	Total [3]	General consumption taxes [6]	Taxes on specific goods, services [7]
United States: 1980	100.0	47.0	36.9	10.2	26.2	10.0	15.5	16.6	6.6	7.8
1990	100.0	43.2	35.8	7.4	29.5	11.6	16.6	16.5	7.6	6.8
1993	100.0	42.4	34.5	7.9	29.2	11.5	16.5	17.2	7.6	7.4
Canada: 1980.	100.0	46.6	34.1	11.6	10.5	3.7	6.6	32.6	11.5	13.0
1990.	100.0	48.8	41.0	7.2	14.4	4.4	9.7	26.0	14.5	9.6
1993.	100.0	44.1	37.9	5.7	16.6	5.4	11.0	26.6	14.9	9.6
France: 1980	100.0	18.1	12.9	5.1	42.7	11.1	28.4	30.4	21.1	8.4
1990	100.0	17.2	11.8	5.3	44.1	13.2	27.2	28.4	18.8	8.7
1993	100.0	17.4	13.9	3.4	44.6	13.6	27.3	26.7	17.1	8.7
Germany [8]: 1980.	100.0	35.1	29.6	5.5	34.3	15.3	18.4	27.1	16.6	9.3
1990	100.0	32.4	27.6	4.8	37.5	16.2	19.1	26.7	16.6	9.2
1993	100.0	30.7	27.1	3.6	38.7	16.9	19.7	27.8	17.5	9.1
Italy: 1980	100.0	31.1	23.1	7.8	38.0	6.9	28.4	26.5	15.6	9.7
1990	100.0	36.5	26.3	10.0	32.9	6.3	23.6	28.0	14.7	10.6
1993	100.0	34.0	24.9	8.5	37.1	6.0	27.4	23.7	11.7	9.4
Japan: 1980	100.0	46.1	24.3	21.8	29.1	10.2	14.8	16.3	-	14.1
1990.	100.0	48.3	26.8	21.5	29.2	10.9	15.0	13.2	4.2	7.3
1993.	100.0	40.6	25.6	14.9	33.6	12.7	17.4	14.4	5.1	7.5
Netherlands: 1980	100.0	32.8	26.3	6.6	38.1	15.7	17.8	25.2	15.8	7.3
1990.	100.0	32.2	24.7	7.5	37.4	23.1	7.5	26.4	16.5	7.5
1993.	100.0	32.4	25.4	7.0	38.2	24.0	6.9	25.3	14.5	8.2
Sweden: 1980	100.0	43.5	41.0	2.5	28.8	0.1	27.6	24.0	13.4	9.2
1990	100.0	41.6	38.5	3.1	27.2	0.1	26.0	25.0	14.9	9.2
1993	100.0	41.3	36.8	4.5	27.6	0.2	26.3	27.4	17.0	9.4
United Kingdom: 1980	100.0	38.2	29.8	8.3	16.6	6.7	9.5	29.2	14.4	13.1
1990	100.0	39.3	28.5	10.8	17.1	6.5	9.9	30.9	16.6	12.8
1993	100.0	35.0	27.8	7.2	17.8	6.6	10.5	35.3	19.5	14.1

- Represents zero.   [1] Includes property taxes, employer payroll taxes other than Social Security contributions, and miscellaneous taxes, not shown separately.   [2] Includes taxes on capital gains.   [3] Includes other taxes not shown separately.   [4] Includes contributions of self-employed not shown separately.   [5] Taxes on the production, sales, transfer, leasing, and delivery of goods and services and rendering of services.   [6] Primary value-added and sales taxes.   [7] For example, excise taxes on alcohol, tobacco, and gasoline.   [8] Prior to 1990, data are for former West Germany.

Source: Organization for Economic Cooperation and Development, Paris, France, *Revenue Statistics of OECD Member Countries,* annual (copyright).

No. 1345. Employee-Employer Payroll Tax Rates for Social Security Programs, by Country: 1981 to 1995

[In percent. Covers old-age, disability and survivors insurance, public health or sickness insurance, workers' compensation, unemployment insurance, and family allowance programs]

COUNTRY	ALL SOCIAL SECURITY PROGRAMS					OLD-AGE, DISABILITY, SURVIVORS INSURANCE				
	1981	1991	1995			1981	1991	1995		
			Total	Employer	Employee			Total	Employer	Employee
United States....	17.60	20.50	21.00	13.35	7.65	10.70	12.40	12.40	6.20	6.20
Austria	35.80	[1]39.40	[2]42.50	25.30	17.20	21.10	22.80	22.80	12.55	10.25
Belgium	34.70	39.33	40.51	27.44	13.07	15.11	16.36	16.36	8.86	7.50
Canada.........	[2]7.92	[2]10.00	[2][3]14.10	8.40	5.70	3.60	4.60	5.40	2.70	2.70
France	47.55	54.41	52.58	34.31	18.27	13.00	17.00	16.25	8.20	8.05
Germany [4]......	34.80	36.16	[3]34.54	17.99	16.55	18.50	17.70	18.60	9.30	9.30
Ireland	14.95	21.70	[3][5]19.95	[5]12.20	[5]7.75	12.00	18.70	[5][6]19.95	[5][6]12.20	[5][6]7.75
Italy	54.30	55.72	56.96	47.62	9.34	24.46	27.42	29.64	21.30	8.34
Japan.........	21.41	24.86	26.62	14.38	12.24	10.60	[7]14.50	16.50	8.25	8.25
Netherlands.....	54.85	43.73	[3]49.68	10.75	38.93	32.45	20.25	25.78	-	25.78
Norway........	(NA)	(NA)	[3]22.00	14.20	7.80	(NA)	(NA)	[6]22.00	[6]14.20	[6]7.80
Spain	(NA)	(NA)	38.30	32.00	6.30	(NA)	(NA)	[8]28.30	[8]23.60	[8]4.70
Sweden	32.65	34.11	[3]34.91	30.96	[9]3.95	21.15	20.95	20.03	19.03	1.00
Switzerland	11.90	12.00	14.14	7.74	6.40	9.40	9.60	9.80	4.90	4.90
United Kingdom ..	21.45	21.45	[3][5]22.20	[5]10.20	[5]12.00	(NA)	(NA)	[5][6]22.20	[5][6]10.20	[5][6]12.00

- Represents zero.   NA Not available.   [1] Sickness and maternity refers to wage earners.   [2] Excludes work-injury.   [3] The central government pays the whole cost of family allowances.   [4] Prior to 1991, data are for former West Germany.   [5] Range according to earnings brackets. Higher rate is shown, which applies to highest earnings class.   [6] Includes rate for public health or sickness insurance, workers' compensation, and unemployment insurance.   [7] OASDI rate refers to male employees and contributions for employee pension insurance only.   [8] Includes rate for public health or sickness insurace and family allowance programs.   [9] Plus flat amount for unemployment insurance.

Source: U.S. Social Security Administration, Office of Research and Statistics, *Social Security Programs Throughout the World*, biannual.

No. 1346. Annual Percent Change in Consumer Prices, by Country: 1991 to 1995

[Change from previous year. See text, section 30, for general comments concerning the data. For additional qualifications of the data for individual countries, see source]

COUNTRY	1991	1992	1993	1994	1995	COUNTRY	1991	1992	1993	1994	1995
United States.........	4	3	3	3	3	Korea, South	9	6	5	6	5
Argentina	172	25	11	4	3	Malaysia	4	5	4	4	5
Australia	3	1	2	2	5	Mexico	23	16	10	7	35
Belgium	3	2	3	2	2	Netherlands..........	3	1	2	2	3
Brazil	441	1,009	2,148	2,669	84	Nigeria	13	45	57	57	73
Canada.............	6	2	2	-	2	Norway	3	2	2	1	3
Chile	22	15	13	11	8	Pakistan	12	10	10	12	12
Colombia............	30	27	23	24	21	Philippines...........	19	9	8	9	8
France	3	2	2	2	2	Romania	231	211	255	137	32
Germany	4	4	4	3	2	South Africa..........	15	14	10	9	9
India...............	14	12	6	10	10	Spain	6	6	5	5	5
Indonesia	9	8	10	9	9	Sweden	9	2	5	2	3
Iran	17	26	21	32	50	Switzerland	6	4	3	1	2
Israel	19	12	11	12	10	Turkey	66	70	66	106	94
Italy	6	5	5	4	5	United Kingdom	6	4	2	3	3
Japan..............	3	2	1	1	-	Venezuela...........	34	31	38	61	60

- Represents or rounds to zero.

Source: International Monetary Fund, Washington, DC, *International Financial Statistics*, monthly (copyright).

No. 1347. Civilian Employment-Population Ratio and Females as Percent of Total Civilian Employment, by Country: 1980 to 1994

[See headnote, table 1348]

COUNTRY	CIVILIAN EMPLOYMENT-POPULATION RATIO [1]								CIVILIAN EMPLOYMENT, PERCENT FEMALE			
	Women				Men							
	1980	1990	1993	1994	1980	1990	1993	1994	1980	1990	1993	1994
United States ..	47.7	54.3	54.1	[2]55.3	72.0	72.0	70.0	[2]70.4	42.4	45.2	45.7	[2]46.0
Australia......	41.9	49.3	47.6	48.6	75.1	71.2	65.9	67.0	36.4	41.5	42.4	42.6
Canada	46.2	54.0	51.7	51.9	73.0	70.1	64.9	65.4	39.7	44.4	45.2	45.2
France	40.3	41.5	40.8	[3]40.6	68.6	61.3	58.4	[3]58.1	39.5	43.0	43.7	43.7
Germany [4]	38.9	40.9	[3]41.4	[3]41.2	69.9	65.6	[3]61.7	[3]60.0	39.2	41.0	[3]42.3	[3]42.8
Italy	27.9	29.2	[2][3]28.7	[3]28.3	66.0	60.0	[2][3]58.8	[3]57.2	31.7	34.7	[2][3]34.8	[3]35.1
Japan	45.7	48.0	48.3	48.0	77.9	75.4	75.9	75.4	38.4	40.3	40.3	40.3
Sweden	58.0	61.8	55.5	[3]54.5	73.6	70.6	61.6	[3]61.1	45.2	47.8	48.7	48.4
United Kingdom.	44.8	49.6	48.8	[3]49.0	72.8	69.7	64.2	[3]64.7	40.4	43.5	45.1	[3]45.0

[1] Civilian employment as a percent of the civilian working age population.   [2] Break in series. Data not comparable with prior years.   [3] Preliminary.   [4] Former West Germany.

Source: U.S. Bureau of Labor Statistics, *Comparative Labor Force Statistics for Ten Countries, 1959-1995*, June 1996.

No. 1348. Civilian Labor Force, Employment, and Unemployment, by Country: 1980 to 1994

[Data based on U.S. labor force definitions (see source) except that minimum age for population base varies as follows: United States, France, Sweden, and United Kingdom, 16 years; Australia, Canada, Japan, Netherlands, Germany, and Italy (beginning 1993), 15 years; and Italy (prior to 1993) 14 years]

YEAR	United States	Aus- tralia	Canada	France	Ger- many [1]	Italy	Japan	Nether- lands	Sweden	United King- dom
Civilian labor force (mil.):										
1980	106.9	6.7	12.0	22.9	27.3	21.1	55.7	5.9	4.3	26.5
1985	115.5	7.3	13.1	23.6	28.0	21.8	58.8	6.2	4.4	27.2
1990	[2]125.8	8.4	14.3	24.3	29.4	22.7	63.0	6.8	4.6	28.5
1992	128.1	8.6	14.5	24.6	[3]30.0	[3]22.9	65.0	[3]7.0	4.5	28.4
1993	129.2	8.6	14.7	24.7	[3]30.0	[2][3]22.8	65.5	[3]7.1	4.4	28.3
1994	[2]131.1	8.8	14.8	25.0	[3]29.8	[3]22.6	65.8	[3]7.3	4.4	[3]28.3
Labor force participation rate: [4]										
1980	63.8	62.1	64.6	57.5	54.7	48.2	62.6	55.4	66.9	62.5
1985	64.8	61.6	65.8	56.8	54.7	47.2	62.3	55.5	66.9	62.1
1990	[2]66.5	64.6	67.3	55.6	55.3	47.2	62.6	56.8	67.4	63.7
1992	66.4	63.9	65.9	55.9	[3]55.1	[3]47.5	63.4	[3]57.9	65.7	62.9
1993	66.3	63.6	65.5	55.7	[3]54.2	[2][3]48.1	63.3	[3]58.4	64.5	62.8
1994	[2]66.6	63.9	65.3	[3]56.0	[3]53.7	[3]47.5	63.1	[3]59.6	63.9	[3]62.6
Civilian employment (mil.):										
1980	99.3	6.3	11.1	21.4	26.5	20.2	54.6	5.5	4.2	24.7
1985	107.2	6.7	11.7	21.2	26.0	20.5	57.3	5.6	4.3	24.2
1990	[2]118.8	7.9	13.2	22.1	28.0	21.1	61.7	6.3	4.5	26.6
1992	118.5	7.6	12.8	22.0	[3]28.7	[3]21.2	63.6	[3]6.5	4.3	25.5
1993	120.3	7.7	13.0	21.8	[3]28.2	[2][3]20.4	63.8	[3]6.5	4.0	25.3
1994	[2]123.1	7.9	13.3	21.8	[3]27.9	[3]20.1	63.9	[3]6.6	4.0	[3]25.6
Employment-population ratio: [5]										
1980	59.2	58.3	59.7	53.8	53.1	46.1	61.3	52.1	65.6	58.1
1985	60.1	56.5	58.9	50.9	50.7	44.4	60.6	50.1	65.0	55.1
1990	[2]62.8	60.1	61.9	50.5	52.6	43.9	61.3	52.5	66.1	59.2
1992	61.5	57.0	58.4	50.0	[3]52.6	[3]44.0	62.0	[3]53.8	62.0	56.5
1993	61.7	56.6	58.2	49.1	[3]51.1	[2][3]43.1	61.7	[3]53.2	58.5	56.2
1994	[2]62.5	57.7	58.5	[3]48.9	[3]50.2	[3]42.1	61.3	[3]53.8	57.7	[3]56.5
Unemployment rate:										
1980	7.1	6.1	7.5	6.5	2.8	4.4	2.0	6.0	2.0	7.0
1985	7.2	8.3	10.5	10.5	7.2	6.0	2.6	9.6	2.8	11.2
1990	[2]5.6	6.9	8.1	9.1	5.0	7.0	2.1	7.5	1.8	7.0
1992	7.5	10.8	11.3	10.5	[3]4.6	[3]7.3	2.2	[3]7.2	5.6	10.1
1993	6.9	10.9	11.2	11.9	[3]5.7	[2][3]10.2	2.5	[3]8.8	9.3	10.5
1994	[2]6.1	9.7	10.4	12.7	[3]6.5	[3]11.3	2.9	[3]9.6	9.6	[3]9.6
Under 25 years old	12.5	17.3	16.5	[6]27.8	(NA)	32.4	5.5	(NA)	23.0	[6]16.2
Teenagers [7]	17.6	23.0	18.9	[6]26.4	(NA)	37.0	7.7	(NA)	25.0	[6]18.6
20 to 24 years old	9.7	13.8	15.0	[6]28.0	(NA)	30.8	5.0	(NA)	22.4	[6]14.9
25 years old and over	4.8	7.6	9.2	[6]10.9	(NA)	7.8	2.5	(NA)	7.8	[6]8.3

NA Not available.   [1] Former West Germany.   [2] Break in series. Data not comparable with prior years.   [3] Preliminary.
[4] Civilian labor force as a percent of the civilian working age population. Germany and Japan include the institutionalized population as part of the working age population.   [5] Civilian employment as a percent of the civilian working age population. Germany and Japan include the institutionalized population as part of the working age population.   [6] French data are for March and United Kingdom data are for the Spring quarter.   [7] 16 to 19 years old in the United States, France, Sweden, and the United Kingdom; 15 to 19 years old in Canada, Australia, Italy, and Japan.

Source: U.S. Bureau of Labor Statistics, *Comparative Labor Force Statistics for Ten Countries, 1959-1995*, June 1996, and *Monthly Labor Review*.

No. 1349. Female Labor Force Participation Rates, by Country: 1984 and 1994

[**In percent**. Female labor force of all ages divided by female population 15-64 years old]

COUNTRY	1984	1994	COUNTRY	1984	1994
United States	**62.8**	**63.7**	Japan	57.2	62.1
Australia	[1]52.7	63.2	Luxembourg	[1]41.7	47.3
Austria	51.5	62.1	Mexico	(NA)	40.0
Belgium	[1]48.7	56.1	Netherlands	40.7	57.1
Canada	63.5	67.8	New Zealand	46.0	65.0
Denmark	73.8	73.8	Norway	[1]65.5	71.3
Finland	72.9	69.9	Portugal	56.0	62.2
France	[1]54.3	59.5	Spain	33.2	44.1
Germany	[2]52.3	61.8	Sweden	77.3	74.4
Greece	[1]40.4	44.6	Switzerland	[1]55.2	67.5
Iceland	62.7	80.0	Turkey	(NA)	33.7
Ireland	[1]37.8	47.6	United Kingdom	[1]57.2	65.4
Italy	[1]40.3	43.2			

NA Not available.   [1] 1983 data.   [2] Former West Germany.

Source: Organization for Economic Cooperation and Development, Paris, France, *OECD in Figures, Statistics on the Member Countries*, annual.

No. 1350. Civilian Employment, by Industry and Country: 1980 and 1993

[Data based on U.S. labor force definitions except that minimum age for population base varies as follows: United States, France, Sweden, and United Kingdom, 16 years; Australia, Canada, Germany, Italy (beginning 1993), Japan and Netherlands, 15 years; and Italy (prior to 1993), 14 years. For the United States, Germany, Italy, Netherlands, and Sweden the data are not comparable between 1980 and 1993. Industries based on International Standard Industrial Classification; see text, section 31]

INDUSTRY	United States	Aus-tralia	Canada	France	Ger-many [1]	Italy	Japan	Nether-lands	Sweden	United Kingdom
TOTAL EMPLOYMENT (1,000)										
1980, ...	99,303	6,284	11,082	21,443	26,486	20,195	54,600	5,520	4,214	25,004
Agriculture, forestry, fishing	3,529	410	597	1,821	1,373	2,870	5,510	285	237	654
Industry [2]	29,136	1,798	3,033	7,523	11,373	[3]7,694	19,180	1,642	1,327	9,059
Manufacturing	21,942	1,222	2,187	5,530	8,998	5,433	13,630	1,176	1,025	7,081
Services	66,638	4,072	7,452	12,099	13,740	9,631	29,910	3,593	2,650	15,291
Public utilities	1,179	130	(NA)	190	215	(³)	300	50	36	353
Wholesale and retail trade, restaurants and hotels.	21,339	1,494	(NA)	3,440	4,079	3,765	12,980	985	582	4,818
Transport and communication . .	5,619	458	(NA)	1,329	1,572	1,124	3,500	328	295	1,580
Finance, insurance, real estate, and business.	8,351	578	(NA)	1,603	1,540	518	3,170	435	283	1,837
Community, social, personal [4] . .	30,148	1,405	(NA)	5,536	6,335	4,224	9,920	1,794	1,454	6,703
1993, total	120,259	7,680	13,015	21,777	28,227	20,242	63,810	[5]6,576	4,015	25,129
Agriculture, forestry, fishing	3,300	411	558	1,101	830	1,657	3,650	267	159	545
Industry [2]	27,659	1,715	2,739	5,826	10,131	[3]6,718	21,670	[5]1,609	982	6,434
Manufacturing	19,711	1,073	1,893	4,276	8,209	4,731	15,260	[5]1,199	734	(NA)
Services	89,300	5,554	9,718	14,850	17,266	11,868	38,490	[5]4,700	2,875	18,150
Public utilities	1,248	96	(NA)	205	348	(³)	350	[5]46	35	(NA)
Wholesale and retail trade, restaurants and hotels.	26,615	1,960	(NA)	3,676	4,835	4,270	15,200	[5]1,166	576	(NA)
Transport and communication . .	6,531	487	(NA)	1,479	1,636	1,147	3,960	[5]426	279	(NA)
Finance, insurance, real estate, and business.	12,706	957	(NA)	2,202	2,534	706	5,210	[5]727	378	(NA)
Community, social, personal [4] . .	42,200	2,055	(NA)	7,288	7,912	5,743	13,750	[5]2,335	1,606	(NA)
PERCENT DISTRIBUTION										
1980, ...	100	100	100	100	100	100	100	100	100	100
Agriculture, forestry, fishing	4	6	5	9	5	14	10	5	6	3
Industry [2]	29	29	27	35	43	[3]38	35	30	32	36
Services	67	65	67	56	52	48	55	65	63	61
1993, total	100	100	100	100	100	100	100	[5]100	100	100
Agriculture, forestry, fishing	3	5	4	5	3	8	6	[5]4	4	2
Industry [2]	23	22	21	27	36	[3]33	34	[5]24	25	26
Services	74	72	75	68	61	59	60	[5]72	72	72

NA Not available. [1] 1980 data for former West Germany. [2] Includes mining and construction. [3] Public utilities included in industry. [4] Includes public administration, education, health, and recreation services. [5] 1992 data.

Source: U.S. Bureau of Labor Statistics, Office of Productivity and Technology, *Monthly Labor Review*, October 1993 and unpublished data.

No. 1351. Index of Industrial Production, by Country: 1980 to 1995

[Industrial production index measures output in the manufacturing, mining, and electric and gas utilities industries. Minus sign (-) indicates decrease]

COUNTRY	INDEX (1990=100)							ANNUAL PERCENT CHANGE					
	1980	1985	1991	1992	1993	1994	1995	1980-81	1985-86	1991-92	1992-93	1993-94	1994-95
OECD, total.	78.9	86.3	99.6	99.4	98.9	103.6	106.5	0.3	1.2	-0.2	-0.5	4.8	2.8
Australia [1]	73.7	86.6	98.0	99.0	103.5	111.6	112.9	3.1	-0.2	1.0	4.5	7.8	1.2
Austria	76.1	82.5	101.9	100.5	99.0	102.4	107.9	-1.6	1.1	-1.4	-1.5	3.4	5.4
Belgium [2]	82.1	85.5	98.0	98.0	92.9	94.6	98.6	-2.7	0.8	-	-5.2	1.8	4.2
Canada [2]	81.5	94.5	95.8	96.9	101.2	107.8	112.0	2.0	-0.7	1.1	4.4	6.5	3.9
Finland.	75.3	87.8	90.3	92.4	97.2	108.3	115.8	2.5	1.6	2.3	5.2	11.4	6.9
France	89.2	89.3	98.9	98.9	93.9	97.4	99.0	-1.0	0.8	-	-5.1	3.7	1.6
Germany [3]	83.0	85.6	103.6	101.0	93.6	96.9	97.7	-1.8	1.8	-2.5	-7.3	3.5	0.8
Greece.	90.8	98.2	98.6	97.4	95.4	96.3	98.5	0.9	-1.0	-1.2	-2.1	0.9	2.3
Ireland	54.2	69.5	103.3	112.7	119.0	133.2	158.3	5.4	2.3	9.1	5.6	11.9	18.8
Italy	87.5	84.8	99.1	97.8	95.7	102.2	107.8	-2.2	4.1	-1.3	-2.1	6.8	5.5
Japan	67.3	79.8	101.9	96.0	92.0	93.1	96.2	1.0	-0.3	-5.8	-4.2	1.2	3.3
Luxembourg	69.7	84.7	100.1	99.3	96.8	102.5	103.3	-5.6	1.9	-0.8	-2.5	5.9	0.8
Mexico	(NA)	(NA)	(NA)	106.5	106.8	111.9	103.5	(NA)	(NA)	(NA)	0.3	4.8	-7.5
Netherlands	86.8	91.7	101.7	101.6	100.3	103.2	105.6	-1.8	0.2	-0.1	-1.3	2.9	2.3
Norway.	58.3	79.0	102.1	108.6	112.1	120.0	127.1	-0.9	3.3	6.4	3.2	7.0	5.9
Portugal	62.8	73.9	100.0	97.7	95.2	95.0	99.4	2.2	7.3	-2.3	-2.6	-0.2	4.6
Spain	83.3	86.1	99.3	96.5	91.9	98.6	103.2	-1.1	3.1	-2.8	-4.8	7.3	4.7
Sweden [4]	82.0	84.8	100.8	100.1	100.1	108.0	111.2	-	3.5	-0.7	-	7.9	3.0
Switzerland	82.5	91.5	94.9	93.5	93.3	103.1	114.0	-1.7	0.4	-1.5	-0.2	10.5	10.6
United Kingdom	81.6	88.2	96.4	96.3	98.4	103.2	105.5	-3.1	2.4	-0.1	2.2	4.9	2.2
United States	**79.3**	**89.0**	**98.2**	**101.6**	**105.2**	**111.4**	**115.0**	**1.9**	**1.0**	**3.5**	**3.5**	**5.9**	**3.2**

- Represents or rounds to zero. NA Not available. [1] Index of Real Gross Product in industry. [2] Gross domestic product in industry at factor cost and 1986 prices. [3] Former West Germany. [4] Mining and manufacturing. [5] Excludes mining and quarrying.

Source: Organization for Economic Cooperation and Development, Paris, France, *Main Economic Indicators, Historical Statistics, 1969-1988*, 1990; and *Main Economic Indicators*, monthly (copyright).

No. 1352. International Economic Composite Indexes, by Country: 1980 to 1995

[Average annual percent change from previous year; derived from indexes with base 1980=100. The coincident index changes are for calendar years and the leading index changes are for years ending June 30 because they lead the coincident indexes by about 6 months, on average. The G-7 countries are United States, Canada, France, Germany, Italy, United Kingdom, and Japan. Minus sign (-) indicates decrease]

COUNTRY	1980	1985	1986	1987	1988	1989	1990	1991	1992	1993	1994	1995
LEADING INDEX												
Total, 11 countries	2.4	3.1	2.0	4.3	8.0	5.0	2.3	-1.1	0.6	0.9	4.8	6.5
10 countries, excluding U.S.	6.6	4.4	1.6	5.2	8.2	5.9	3.3	-0.9	-1.8	-1.8	3.1	5.9
G-7 countries	2.3	2.9	1.9	4.2	7.8	4.9	2.3	-1.1	0.4	1.1	4.6	6.5
North America	-2.8	1.3	2.7	3.2	7.3	3.5	0.7	-1.6	4.1	5.4	7.1	7.2
United States	-3.3	1.0	2.7	3.2	7.5	3.7	0.9	-1.3	4.3	5.4	7.0	7.2
Canada	3.2	4.3	3.0	2.7	6.1	1.0	-2.5	-5.2	1.2	5.2	8.0	7.3
Four European countries	2.8	2.3	2.2	3.6	3.1	4.2	1.5	1.1	1.0	0.2	3.7	4.8
France.	4.5	2.6	1.9	6.1	5.1	6.0	0.5	1.2	2.5	0.3	4.0	6.3
Germany [1]	2.4	2.0	3.0	1.6	3.4	5.2	4.7	4.2	0.6	-1.8	3.6	5.0
Italy.	3.0	2.7	4.0	4.3	0.6	2.1	0.3	-1.3	0.8	2.0	3.9	3.8
United Kingdom.	1.0	2.2	0.2	3.4	1.9	2.4	-0.9	-2.0	0.1	1.9	3.1	3.2
Five Pacific region countries . .	14.4	7.8	0.6	7.9	16.1	8.6	6.1	-2.7	-5.7	-5.5	1.5	7.3
Australia	5.2	6.5	2.1	3.2	7.6	5.2	-3.3	-3.9	3.1	5.4	6.3	2.6
Taiwan.	4.7	6.5	8.1	13.6	14.9	12.3	7.0	1.2	8.0	6.0	8.2	8.1
Japan	17.2	8.3	-0.4	7.6	17.6	8.9	7.2	-3.2	-8.0	-8.3	-0.6	7.6
Korea, South	-2.6	4.7	9.8	17.2	13.7	10.0	4.5	3.7	4.6	3.7	12.0	10.7
New Zealand	1.8	5.4	-1.2	2.8	-1.5	0.8	1.2	-2.8	1.9	3.7	2.7	1.9
COINCIDENT INDEX												
Total, 11 countries	0.3	3.7	3.2	4.1	6.1	4.8	3.6	0.3	0.9	-	3.0	3.2
10 countries, excluding U.S.	2.5	4.0	3.5	4.5	6.9	6.4	5.8	2.7	1.0	-0.9	2.4	3.2
G-7 countries	0.2	3.6	2.9	4.0	6.0	4.6	3.6	0.3	0.9	-0.2	2.7	2.9
North America	-2.4	3.6	2.6	3.8	4.8	2.4	-0.1	-3.7	0.9	2.4	4.7	3.1
United States	-2.8	3.4	2.5	3.7	4.7	2.3	-	-3.7	1.1	2.6	4.9	3.3
Canada	2.0	5.3	3.5	4.8	5.8	2.8	-	-3.9	0.4	2.1	4.5	2.9
Four European countries	1.4	2.9	3.7	3.8	6.1	6.0	5.6	2.0	0.2	-3.0	1.5	3.7
France.	1.3	1.4	3.9	5.0	8.0	8.7	7.1	2.5	0.8	-1.7	4.1	6.3
Germany [1]	2.5	3.5	4.3	3.0	3.6	5.4	7.2	5.7	1.6	-4.1	-0.8	2.0
Italy.	5.2	2.5	1.7	1.5	5.3	2.0	4.7	2.1	-0.4	-7.6	-0.9	1.9
United Kingdom.	-2.1	4.3	3.6	5.2	8.0	5.9	2.3	-4.4	-2.5	-	3.7	3.8
Five Pacific region countries . .	4.2	5.0	3.5	5.2	8.2	7.5	6.8	4.6	1.9	0.5	2.2	2.7
Australia	4.8	7.6	4.9	4.3	8.5	9.9	0.9	-7.4	-1.3	2.3	9.4	8.9
Taiwan.	7.1	3.7	10.1	11.9	8.0	7.3	2.8	5.8	6.2	5.2	5.8	2.5
Japan	4.5	4.7	2.6	4.6	8.3	7.3	7.6	5.8	1.8	-0.2	0.8	1.4
Korea, South	-4.3	5.5	11.7	13.5	10.6	6.2	9.5	7.9	4.7	3.8	8.8	9.1
New Zealand	1.9	1.8	1.5	1.4	-0.8	-0.7	1.2	-1.1	1.2	3.8	5.3	4.6

- Represents or rounds to zero. [1] Former West Germany.
Source: Center for International Business Cycle Research, Columbia Business School, New York, NY, *International Economic Indicators*, monthly.

No. 1353. Patents, by Country: 1993

[Includes only U.S. patents granted to residents of areas outside of the United States and its territories]

COUNTRY	Total [1]	Inventions	Designs	COUNTRY	Total [1]	Inventions	Designs
Total	**48,652**	**45,107**	**3,214**	Netherlands	945	801	78
				Korea, South	830	779	50
Japan	23,398	22,292	1,037	Sweden	741	635	102
Germany	7,183	6,890	228	Australia	470	378	88
France.	3,154	2,908	215	Belgium	377	350	25
United Kingdom.	2,520	2,294	197	Israel.	358	314	22
Canada	2,229	1,943	275	Austria	341	313	26
Italy.	1,454	1,286	165	Finland	311	293	17
Taiwan.	1,510	1,189	320	Denmark	261	197	60
Switzerland.	1,197	1,126	69	Other countries	1,373	1,119	240

[1] Includes patents for botanical plants and reissues, not shown separately.
Source: U.S. Patent and Trademark Office, Technology Assessment and Forecast Data Base.

No. 1354. World's 500 Largest Corporations, by Country: 1995

[For company's fiscal year ended on or before March 31, 1996. All companies on the list must publish financial data and report part or all of their figures to a government agency. Includes revenues from discontinued operations and consolidated subsidiaries; excludes excise taxes. Profits are shown after taxes, after extraordinary credits or charges, and after cumulative effects of accounting changes. Minus sign (-) indicates loss]

COUNTRY	Number of companies	Revenues (bil. dol.)	Profits (bil. dol.)	COUNTRY	Number of companies	Revenues (bil. dol.)	Profits (bil. dol.)	COUNTRY	Number of companies	Revenues (bil. dol.)	Profits (bil. dol.)
Total [1]	500	11,378	323	Switzerland . .	16	345	18	Spain	6	81	4
Japan	141	3,985	30	Korea, South .	12	263	7	Canada	6	66	6
U.S.	**153**	**3,221**	**158**	Italy	12	255	7	Belgium	5	56	2
Germany	40	1,017	17	Netherlands . .	8	171	9	Sweden	3	54	2
France	42	880	3	Britain/Nether-				Brazil	4	54	-3
U.K.	32	516	38	lands.	2	160	9	Australia	4	45	4

[1] Includes other countries not shown separately.
Source: Time Warner, New York, NY, *Fortune*, August 5, 1996, (copyright).

No. 1355. Selected Indexes of Manufacturing Activity, by Country: 1970 to 1994

[1982=100. Data relate to all employed persons in the United States, Canada, France, Germany, Japan, and Sweden; all employees (wage and salary workers) in other countries. Minus sign (-) indicates decrease. For explanation of average annual percent change, see Guide to Tabular Presentation]

INDEX	United States	Cana-da	Japan	Bel-gium	Den-mark	France	Ger-many [1]	Italy	Neth-erlands	Swe-den	United King-dom
Output per hour:											
1970.	(NA)	76.9	50.3	47.9	57.2	58.6	66.4	54.9	54.4	68.9	72.1
1980.	92.9	99.9	91.1	86.9	98.0	90.8	98.5	95.5	96.1	96.6	91.0
1985.	106.7	119.8	114.9	119.6	105.0	107.9	113.4	122.3	123.4	113.8	116.4
1990.	122.1	122.0	149.1	134.1	105.5	127.6	125.6	139.3	135.4	124.0	140.1
1993.	132.0	130.9	159.5	149.5	111.2	132.3	130.5	158.0	140.0	139.2	159.2
1994.	137.4	136.2	164.2	(NA)	119.5	142.4	140.0	163.8	150.2	146.3	165.7
Average annual percent change:											
1979-85.	2.0	2.4	4.6	5.1	2.1	3.0	2.1	5.0	4.4	3.0	4.1
1985-90.	2.7	0.4	5.4	2.3	0.1	3.4	2.1	2.6	1.9	1.7	3.8
1990-94.	3.0	2.8	2.4	(NA)	3.2	2.8	2.8	4.1	2.6	4.2	4.3
Compensation per hour, national currency basis: [2]											
1970.	(NA)	28.7	25.0	23.2	22.3	18.5	34.5	11.6	28.5	24.4	14.7
1980.	83.3	78.6	89.0	86.3	83.4	72.7	89.2	70.2	90.2	84.5	78.9
1985.	111.3	116.8	110.1	122.0	120.6	129.6	116.3	150.9	114.1	131.8	125.1
1990.	134.7	143.0	138.3	147.5	156.5	161.3	147.9	210.8	126.4	197.5	180.6
1993.	152.0	158.7	159.3	171.2	175.7	181.5	178.5	267.1	145.6	221.6	235.6
1994.	154.5	163.5	162.3	(NA)	181.0	186.2	185.8	270.0	147.7	232.8	245.0
Average annual percent change:											
1979-85.	6.9	8.7	4.7	7.8	8.1	12.7	5.9	16.7	4.9	9.6	11.5
1985-90.	3.9	4.1	4.7	3.9	5.4	4.5	4.9	6.9	2.1	8.4	7.6
1990-94.	3.5	3.4	4.1	(NA)	3.7	3.7	5.9	6.4	4.0	4.2	7.9
Real hourly compensation: [2][3]											
1970.	(NA)	77.4	63.6	55.1	70.1	59.4	62.6	60.3	65.5	72.6	65.3
1980.	97.5	97.9	96.0	101.0	102.6	92.2	99.9	96.9	102.0	103.0	96.1
1985.	99.8	101.8	103.6	101.6	101.4	103.9	107.9	109.3	105.2	102.6	107.3
1990.	99.5	100.1	121.7	110.6	108.6	111.2	128.6	115.9	112.0	114.4	116.1
1993.	101.5	101.8	131.7	118.1	115.1	115.9	138.8	125.4	117.3	112.0	135.8
1994.	100.6	104.7	133.3	(NA)	116.2	117.0	140.3	122.1	115.1	115.1	137.8
Average annual percent change:											
1979-85.	0.2	0.7	1.1	0.7	-0.5	2.3	1.8	1.5	0.3	-0.5	2.3
1985-90.	-0.1	-0.3	3.3	1.7	1.4	1.4	3.6	1.2	1.3	2.2	1.6
1990-94.	0.3	1.1	2.3	(NA)	1.7	1.3	2.2	1.3	0.7	0.2	4.4
Unit labor costs, national currency:											
1970.	(NA)	37.3	49.7	48.4	39.0	31.5	51.9	21.1	52.5	35.4	20.4
1980.	89.7	78.7	97.8	99.4	85.1	80.1	90.6	73.5	93.8	87.5	86.7
1985.	104.2	97.6	95.8	102.0	114.9	120.2	102.6	123.4	92.5	115.8	107.5
1990.	110.4	117.2	92.7	110.0	148.3	126.4	117.8	151.3	93.3	159.2	128.9
1993.	115.1	121.2	99.8	114.5	158.0	137.2	136.8	169.0	104.0	159.3	148.0
1994.	112.5	120.1	98.8	(NA)	151.4	130.8	132.7	164.9	98.3	159.2	147.8
Average annual percent change:											
1979-85.	4.9	6.1	0.1	5.9	5.9	9.5	3.8	11.1	0.5	6.4	7.1
1985-90.	1.1	3.7	-0.7	5.2	5.2	1.0	2.8	4.2	0.2	6.6	3.7
1990-94.	0.5	0.6	1.6	(NA)	0.5	0.9	3.0	2.2	1.3	-	3.5
Unit labor costs, U.S. dollar basis: [4]											
1970.	(NA)	44.1	34.6	44.6	43.4	37.5	34.6	45.7	38.8	42.9	28.0
1980.	89.7	83.1	107.9	155.8	126.2	124.9	121.1	116.3	126.3	130.0	115.4
1985.	104.2	88.2	100.1	78.7	90.4	88.0	84.7	87.5	74.5	84.6	79.8
1990.	110.4	124.0	159.3	150.6	200.0	152.7	176.9	170.9	136.9	168.9	131.6
1993.	115.1	116.0	223.8	151.6	203.3	159.3	200.8	145.4	149.5	128.4	127.1
1994.	112.5	108.5	240.8	(NA)	198.8	155.1	198.7	138.5	144.4	129.6	129.6
Average annual percent change:											
1979-85.	4.9	3.4	-1.4	-8.8	-5.8	-3.4	-4.1	-3.3	-7.6	-5.3	-1.3
1985-90.	1.1	7.1	9.7	13.9	17.2	11.6	15.9	14.3	12.9	14.8	10.5
1990-94.	0.5	-3.3	10.9	(NA)	-0.1	0.4	2.9	-5.1	1.3	-6.4	-0.4
Employment:											
1970.	102.6	96.3	102.8	137.7	119.6	106.9	116.7	97.6	134.1	114.9	140.3
1980.	107.8	108.4	99.5	109.9	103.9	104.9	104.9	107.8	106.9	106.9	116.7
1985.	102.4	103.6	104.6	95.1	112.4	92.6	97.4	89.8	94.4	99.6	92.5
1990.	101.9	109.4	108.6	92.9	111.7	88.5	103.0	91.0	101.0	95.7	90.9
1993.	96.7	98.7	111.2	83.8	103.8	80.2	96.6	80.9	95.8	75.7	77.9
1994.	97.8	100.6	108.8	(NA)	104.8	78.1	91.7	80.0	92.6	76.5	77.4
Average annual percent change:											
1979-85.	-1.4	-0.8	1.2	-2.7	1.0	-2.3	-1.1	-2.9	-2.3	-1.2	-4.6
1985-90.	-0.1	1.1	0.8	-0.5	-0.1	-0.9	1.1	0.3	1.4	-0.8	-0.4
1990-94.	-1.0	-2.1	0.1	(NA)	-1.6	-3.1	-2.9	-3.2	-2.1	-5.5	-3.9
Aggregate hours:											
1970.	106.5	102.1	109.6	159.9	132.3	123.9	131.1	107.0	148.1	132.0	153.3
1980.	109.8	110.8	100.5	110.1	103.7	110.8	106.3	108.0	105.3	105.9	117.3
1985.	106.8	106.0	105.5	93.5	109.8	91.8	95.6	89.0	90.8	101.9	93.5
1990.	107.0	112.2	107.7	94.3	106.6	88.1	96.9	95.0	96.3	99.4	92.0
1993.	103.5	102.9	102.3	82.3	98.8	79.5	87.3	81.7	91.0	81.4	77.1
1994.	105.8	105.6	100.1	(NA)	99.7	77.4	83.4	83.0	88.0	85.7	77.1
Average annual percent change:											
1979-85.	-1.2	-0.9	1.1	-3.3	0.8	-3.3	-1.8	-3.1	-2.5	-0.8	-5.0
1985-90.	-	1.1	0.4	0.2	-0.6	-0.8	0.3	1.3	1.2	-0.5	-0.3
1990-94.	-0.3	-1.5	-1.8	(NA)	-1.6	-3.2	-3.7	-3.3	-2.2	-3.7	-4.3

- Represents or rounds to zero. NA Not available. [1] Former West Germany. [2] Compensation includes, but real hourly compensation excludes, adjustments for payroll and employment taxes that are not compensation to employees, but are labor costs to employers. [3] Index of hourly compensation divided by the index of consumer prices to adjust for changes in purchasing power. [4] Indexes in national currency adjusted for changes in prevailing exchange rates.

Source: Bureau of Labor Statistics, *News Release* USDL 95-342, September 8, 1995.

No. 1356. Indexes of Hourly Compensation Costs for Production Workers in Manufacturing, by Country: 1980 to 1994

[United States=100. Compensation costs include all pay made directly to the worker—pay for time worked and not worked (eg. leave, except sick leave), other direct pay, employer expenditures for legally required insurance programs and contractual and private benefit plans, and for some countries, other labor taxes. Data adjusted for exchange rates. Area averages are trade-weighted to account for difference in countries' relative importance to U.S. trade in manufactured goods. The trade weights used are the sum of U.S. imports of manufactured products for consumption (customs value) and U.S. domestic exports of manufactured products (f.a.s. value) in 1992; see source for detail]

AREA OR COUNTRY	1980	1990	1991	1992	1993	1994	AREA OR COUNTRY	1980	1990	1991	1992	1993	1994
United States	100	100	100	100	100	100	Austria [6]	90	119	116	126	122	127
Total [1]	67	83	86	88	86	88	Belgium.	133	129	127	138	129	134
OECD [2]	77	94	97	99	96	99	Denmark	110	120	117	124	114	120
Europe	102	118	117	123	112	115	Finland [7]	83	141	136	123	99	110
Asian newly industrial-							France	91	102	98	105	97	100
izing economies [3] . . .	12	25	28	30	31	34	Germany [6 8]	125	147	146	157	154	160
Canada.	88	106	110	105	98	92	Greece	38	45	44	46	41	(NA)
Mexico	22	11	12	14	15	15	Ireland	60	79	78	83	73	(NA)
Australia [4]	86	88	87	81	75	80	Italy	83	119	119	121	96	95
Hong Kong [5]	15	21	23	24	26	28	Luxembourg.	121	110	108	117	111	(NA)
Israel	38	57	56	56	53	53	Netherlands	122	123	117	126	119	122
Japan	56	86	94	101	114	125	Norway	117	144	139	143	121	122
Korea, South	10	25	30	32	33	37	Portugal	21	25	27	32	27	27
New Zealand	54	56	54	49	48	52	Spain	60	76	78	83	69	67
Singapore	15	25	28	31	31	37	Sweden.	127	140	142	152	106	110
Sri Lanka.	2	2	3	2	3	(NA)	Switzerland	112	140	139	144	135	145
Taiwan	10	26	28	32	31	32	United Kingdom	77	85	88	89	76	80

NA Not available. [1] The 24 foreign economies for which 1994 data are available. [2] Canada, Mexico, Australia, Japan, New Zealand, and the European countries. [3] Hong Kong, South Korea, Singapore, and Taiwan. [4] Includes non-production workers, except in managerial, executive, professional, and higher supervisory positions. [5] Average of selected manufacturing industries. [6] Excludes workers in establishments considered handicraft manufactures (including all printing and publishing and miscellaneous manufacturing in Austria). [7] Includes workers in mining and electrical power plants. [8] Former West Germany.

Source: U.S. Bureau of Labor Statistics, International Comparisons of Hourly Compensation Costs for Production Workers in Manufacturing, 1975-1994, June 1995.

No. 1357. World Production of Major Mineral Commodities: 1990 to 1994

COUNTRY	Unit	1990	1992	1993, est.	1994, est.	Leading producers, 1993
MINERAL FUELS [1]						
Coal.	Mil. metric tons .	4,856	4,546	4,446	(NA)	China, United States, Russia
Dry natural gas	Tril. cu. ft. . . .	73.7	74.5	76.0	(NA)	Russia, United States, Canada
Natural gas plant liquids [2] . . .	Mil. barrels [3] . .	1,690	1,808	1,882	(NA)	United States, Saudi Arabia, Canada
Petroleum, crude	Mil. barrels [3] . . .	22,107	21,978	22,134	(NA)	Saudi Arabia, Russia, United States
Petroleum, refined	Mil. barrels [3] . . .	23,791	23,959	(NA)	(NA)	United States, Russia, Japan (for 1992)
NONMETALLIC MINERALS						
Cement, hydraulic	Mil. metric tons .	1,148	1,254	1,300	1,300	China, Japan, United States
Diamond, gem and industrial .	1,000 carats . . .	110,919	105,521	107,620	(NA)	Australia, Botswana, Zaire
Nitrogen in ammonia.	Mil. metric tons .	97.1	92.5	92.0	92.0	United States, India, Canada
Phosphate rock	Mil. metric tons .	162	144	120	130	United States, China, Morocco
Potash, marketable.	Mil. metric tons .	27.8	24.3	21.0	22.0	Canada, Germany, Russia
Salt	Mil. metric tons .	184	185	190	190	United States, China, Germany
Sulfur, elemental basis	Mil. metric tons .	58.1	52.4	52.0	52.0	United States, Canada, China
METALS						
Aluminum [4]	Mil. metric tons .	19.3	19.2	20.0	19.0	United States, Russia, Canada
Bauxite, gross weight	Mil. metric tons .	108.6	103.6	110.0	110.0	Australia, Guinea, Jamaica
Chromite, gross weight [2]	1,000 metric tons	12,968	10,993	10,001	10,000	Kazakstan, South Africa, India
Copper, metal content [5]	1,000 metric tons	9,017	9,290	9,400	9,300	Chile, United States, Canada
Gold, metal content	Metric tons. . . .	2,133	2,248	2,300	2,300	South Africa, United States, Australia
Iron ore, gross weight [6]	Mil. metric tons .	982	930	1,000	1,000	China, Brazil, Australia
Lead, metal content [5]	1,000 metric tons	3,353	3,242	2,900	2,900	Australia, United States, China
Manganese ore, gross weight.	Mil. metric tons .	25.3	21.6	21.8	21.0	Ukraine, China, South Africa
Nickel, metal content [5]	1,000 metric tons	965	922	900	850	Russia, Canada, New Caledonia
Steel, crude	Mil. metric tons .	771	721	730	720	Japan, United States, China
Tin, metal content [5]	1,000 metric tons	222	179	180	180	China, Brazil, Indonesia
Zinc, metal content [5].	1,000 metric tons	7,184	7,137	6,900	6,700	Canada, Australia, China

NA Not available. [1] Source: Energy Information Administration, International Energy Annual. 1993 data preliminary. [2] Excludes China. [3] 42-gallon barrels. [4] Unalloyed ingot metal. [5] Mine output. [6] Includes iron ore concentrates and iron ore agglomerates.

Source: Except as noted, U.S. Bureau of Mines, Minerals Yearbook, 1993; Annual Reports, 1993; and Mineral Commodity Summaries, 1995.

No. 1358. Energy Consumption and Production, by Country: 1990 and 1994

[See text, section 30, for general comments about the data. For data qualifications for countries, see source]

COUNTRY	ENERGY CONSUMED [1] (coal equiv.) Total (mil. metric tons)		Per capita (kilograms)		ELECTRIC ENERGY PRODUCTION [2] (bil. kWh)		CRUDE PETROLEUM PRODUCTION [3] (mil. metric tons)		COAL PRODUCTION [4] (mil. metric tons)	
	1990	1994	1990	1994	1990	1994	1990	1994	1990	1994
World	10,826	11,258	2,004	1,993	11,774	12,681	3,003	3,032	3,517	3,580
United States	2,687	2,969	10,749	11,391	[5]3,012	[5]3,268	371	336	854	858
Algeria	40	43	1,586	1,583	16	20	37	35	[6](Z)	[6](Z)
Argentina	61	74	1,895	2,150	51	66	25	34	(Z)	(Z)
Australia	127	136	7,442	7,614	155	167	25	20	159	176
Austria	32	33	4,128	4,162	50	53	1	1	-	-
Bahrain [7]	8	10	16,231	17,745	3	5	2	2	(NA)	(NA)
Bangladesh [7]	8	11	75	94	8	10	[6](Z)	(Z)	(NA)	(NA)
Belgium	67	69	6,686	6,861	71	72	(X)	(X)	[8]1	(NA)
Brazil	117	135	785	850	223	261	32	33	5	5
Bulgaria	37	29	4,170	3,257	42	38	(Z)	(Z)	[6](Z)	(Z)
Burma [9]	2	15	59	4,263	3	(NA)	[6]1	1	[6](Z)	(Z)
Canada	292	327	10,957	11,209	482	554	76	86	38	37
Chile	17	(NA)	1,328	(NA)	18	(NA)	1	1	2	1
China	893	1,093	788	920	621	928	138	146	[10]1,080	1,240
Colombia	27	34	821	995	35	43	22	23	20	23
Cuba	15	(NA)	1,391	(NA)	15	(NA)	[6]1	1	(X)	(X)
Denmark	24	27	4,642	5,151	26	41	6	9	(X)	(X)
Ecuador	8	9	728	772	6	8	15	17	(X)	(X)
Egypt	37	41	697	658	39	48	44	45	(X)	(X)
Ethiopia	1	2	30	29	1	1	(X)	(X)	(NA)	(NA)
Finland	34	38	6,877	7,401	[5]54	[5]66	4	(NA)	(X)	(X)
France [11]	295	298	5,191	5,151	[5]420	[5]476	(Z)	3	[8]10	8
Germany [12]	383	445	6,241	5,475	452	528	[13]4	3	[6]77	58
Greece	31	34	3,085	3,224	35	41	[13]1	1	(X)	(X)
Hong Kong	10	14	1,769	2,358	29	27	(NA)	(NA)	(X)	(X)
Hungary	39	(NA)	3,670	(NA)	28	(NA)	2	2	[8]2	1
India [9]	269	344	318	374	289	384	33	31	202	255
Indonesia	58	90	312	465	44	61	72	74	7	29
Iran [14]	93	124	1,596	1,879	51	79	159	179	[6]1	[6](Z)
Iraq	16	35	887	1,761	29	27	101	37	(NA)	(NA)
Ireland	13	15	3,755	4,306	15	17	(X)	(X)	(Z)	(Z)
Israel [15]	15	18	3,149	3,261	21	28	(Z)	(Z)	(X)	(X)
Italy [15]	224	226	3,878	3,949	217	232	5	5	(Z)	-
Japan	564	621	4,567	4,978	857	964	1	1	8	7
Korea, North	94	99	4,322	4,208	54	37	(X)	(X)	[6]68	[6]72
Korea, South	119	168	2,743	3,772	119	186	(X)	(X)	17	7
Kuwait [16]	15	16	6,895	9,846	19	23	60	101	(NA)	(NA)
Libya	16	(NA)	3,508	(NA)	17	(NA)	67	67	(X)	(X)
Malaysia	27	45	1,490	2,291	23	40	30	31	(Z)	(Z)
Mexico	157	187	1,863	2,031	[5]122	[5]144	132	140	[6]7	9
Morocco	9	(NA)	378	(NA)	10	(NA)	(Z)	(Z)	1	1
Netherlands	109	111	7,286	7,217	72	80	(X)	(X)	-	-
New Zealand [17]	18	19	5,411	5,466	30	32	2	2	2	3
Nigeria	23	23	212	209	12	15	86	91	[6](Z)	[6](Z)
Norway [18]	29	32	6,803	7,441	122	113	80	125	(Z)	(Z)
Pakistan [7]	34	45	292	332	44	57	3	3	3	4
Peru	11	11	495	456	14	15	7	6	[6](Z)	(Z)
Philippines	25	28	398	426	26	26	(Z)	(Z)	1	[6]2
Poland	137	134	3,590	3,507	136	135	(Z)	(Z)	[6]148	[6]134
Portugal	19	21	1,947	2,134	29	31	(X)	(X)	(Z)	(Z)
Romania	80	58	3,445	2,544	64	55	8	7	[6]4	[6]1
Russia	(NA)	884	(NA)	5,996	(NA)	876	(NA)	316	(NA)	177
Saudi Arabia [16]	87	(NA)	5,859	(NA)	47	(NA)	320	401	(NA)	(NA)
South Africa [19]	112	(NA)	2,608	(NA)	167	184	(X)	(X)	176	184
Spain	115	119	2,961	3,013	152	162	1	1	[8]15	14
Sudan	2	2	64	60	1	1	(X)	(X)	(NA)	(NA)
Sweden	57	59	6,707	6,794	146	143	(Z)	(Z)	(Z)	-
Switzerland [20]	32	32	4,765	4,499	56	[5]66	(X)	(X)	(X)	(X)
Syria [21]	15	18	1,227	1,278	11	15	23	29	(NA)	(NA)
Taiwan [21]	69	87	3,285	4,139	90	126	(Z)	(Z)	(NA)	(NA)
Tanzania	1	(NA)	39	(NA)	1	1	(X)	(X)	[6](Z)	[6](Z)
Thailand	42	62	765	1,073	46	74	1	1	-	(Z)
Trinidad and Tobago	10	10	7,946	7,530	4	4	8	7	(NA)	(NA)
Tunisia	6	7	791	750	6	6	5	4	(X)	(Z)
Turkey	59	70	1,052	1,156	58	78	4	4	3	3
Ukraine	(X)	226	(X)	4,394	(X)	209	(X)	4	(X)	92
United Arab Emirates	35	39	21,980	21,025	17	19	102	104	(NA)	(NA)

See footnotes at end of table.

No. 1358. Energy Consumption and Production, by Country: 1990 and 1994—Continued

[See text, section 30, for general comments about the data. For additional data qualifications for countries, see source]

COUNTRY	ENERGY CONSUMED [1] (coal equiv.)				ELECTRIC ENERGY PRODUCTION [2] (bil. kWh)		CRUDE PETROLEUM PRODUCTION [3] (mil. metric tons)		COAL PRODUCTION [4] (mil. metric tons)	
	Total (mil. metric tons)		Per capita (kilograms)							
	1990	1994	1990	1994	1990	1994	1990	1994	1990	1994
United Kingdom	307	311	5,335	5,333	319	325	88	119	[8]94	48
Venezuela	65	80	3,352	3,746	60	73	112	143	2	5
Vietnam	9	12	137	158	9	12	3	(Z)	5	[6]6
Zaire	2	2	66	55	6	6	[6]1	(Z)	[6](Z)	[6](Z)
Zambia	2	2	209	187	8	8	(X)	(X)	[6](Z)	[6](Z)

- Represents zero.   NA Not available.   X Not applicable.   Z Less than 500,000 metric tons.   [1] Based on apparent consumption of coal, lignite, petroleum products, natural gas, and hydro, nuclear, and geothermal electricity.   [2] Comprises production by utilities generating primarily for public use, and production by industrial establishments generating primarily for own use. Relates to production at generating centers, including station use and transmission losses.   [3] Includes shale oil, but excludes natural gasoline.   [4] Excludes lignite and brown coal, except as noted.   [5] Net production, i.e. excluding station use.   [6] Provisional.   [7] For year ending June of year shown.   [8] Includes recovered slurries.   [9] For year ending April of year shown.   [10] Includes lignite.   [11] Includes Monaco.   [12] Prior to 1991, data for former West Germany.   [13] Includes inputs other than crude petroleum and natural gas liquids.   [14] For year ending March 20 of year shown.   [15] Includes San Marino.   [16] Includes share of production and consumption in the Neutral Zone.   [17] For year ending March 31 of year shown.   [18] Includes Svalbard and Jan Mayen Islands.   [19] Includes Botswana, Lesotho, Namibia, and Swaziland.   [20] Includes Liechtenstein.   [21] Source: U.S. Bureau of the Census. Data from Republic of China publications.

Source: Except as noted, Statistical Office of the United Nations, New York, NY, *Energy Statistics Yearbook*, annual (copyright).

No. 1359. Selected Petroleum Product Prices, by Country: 1994

[As of January. Includes taxes]

COUNTRY	AUTOMOTIVE FUELS (U.S. dollars per gallon)		RESIDENTIAL (U.S. dollars per gallon)			INDUSTRIAL (U.S. dollars per barrel)	
	Premium gasoline	Diesel fuel	Light fuel oil	Kerosene	Liquified petroleum gases	Light fuel oil	Heavy fuel oil
United States [1]	1.24	0.96	0.90	0.80	0.55	25.87	13.65
Argentina	2.65	(NA)	1.02	1.02	(NA)	(NA)	(NA)
Australia [1]	1.74	1.70	(NA)	(NA)	(NA)	(NA)	(NA)
Austria	3.13	2.03	1.30	(NA)	(NA)	32.74	14.24
Belgium [1]	3.15	2.14	0.78	(NA)	(NA)	27.31	15.99
Bolivia	2.28	1.30	1.22	0.80	0.53	51.41	(NA)
Brazil	1.88	1.09	(NA)	1.49	0.62	19.29	10.07
Canada [1]	1.57	1.47	1.09	(NA)	(NA)	24.14	17.74
Chile	1.46	1.16	(NA)	1.01	(NA)	(NA)	20.38
Denmark [1]	3.00	1.74	2.25	(NA)	(NA)	38.77	18.52
El Salvador [1]	1.75	0.88	(NA)	0.92	0.62	38.53	19.27
Finland [1]	3.12	2.15	1.11	(NA)	(NA)	38.25	20.14
France [1]	3.31	2.10	1.34	(NA)	(NA)	38.51	19.34
Germany [1]	3.34	2.16	0.93	(NA)	(NA)	34.15	16.10
Greece [1]	2.78	1.66	1.35	(NA)	(NA)	48.20	21.80
India	2.28	0.74	(NA)	0.31	0.66	28.08	25.29
Indonesia	1.26	0.68	0.43	0.72	(NA)	18.06	18.06
Ireland [1]	2.96	2.89	1.31	(NA)	(NA)	42.08	18.44
Italy [1]	3.46	2.31	2.76	(NA)	(NA)	97.59	20.63
Japan	4.14	2.48	1.71	1.83	(NA)	45.53	29.69
Korea, South	2.90	0.99	(NA)	(NA)	(NA)	(NA)	15.37
Lebanon	1.19	(NA)	0.85	0.90	0.90	30.10	17.15
Luxembourg [1]	2.36	1.81	0.84	(NA)	(NA)	31.66	15.43
Mexico [1]	1.60	1.02	(NA)	(NA)	(NA)	43.03	9.25
Netherlands [1]	3.66	2.61	1.06	(NA)	(NA)	(NA)	22.91
New Zealand	1.88	0.97	(NA)	(NA)	(NA)	35.09	29.51
Norway [1]	3.79	2.68	1.52	(NA)	(NA)	52.29	45.90
Pakistan	1.79	0.77	0.61	0.75	1.10	25.47	14.13
Panama	1.43	0.99	(NA)	0.97	0.83	42.30	29.93
Peru	2.03	1.18	(NA)	1.18	(NA)	(NA)	19.69
Philippines	1.37	0.96	(NA)	0.96	0.72	(NA)	15.21
Portugal [1]	3.12	2.15	2.26	(NA)	(NA)	90.26	21.62
Russia [1]	0.41	0.45	(NA)	(NA)	(NA)	(NA)	5.10
Spain [1]	2.75	1.91	1.18	(NA)	(NA)	43.19	17.11
Sweden [1]	3.44	2.44	1.78	(NA)	(NA)	33.21	21.61
Switzerland [1]	2.93	3.17	0.71	(NA)	(NA)	26.17	20.75
Taiwan [1]	2.23	1.59	(NA)	(NA)	(NA)	32.26	20.90
Turkey [1]	2.39	1.58	1.69	(NA)	(NA)	(NA)	19.93
United Kingdom [1]	2.86	2.46	0.71	0.71	(NA)	26.65	14.67
Venezuela	0.18	0.16	(NA)	0.12	(NA)	(NA)	5.06

NA Not available.   [1] Average for January.

Source: Energy Information Administration, *International Energy Annual*.

No. 1360. World Food Production, by Commodity: 1990 to 1995

[In millions of metric tons]

COMMODITY	1990	1991	1992	1993	1994	1995, prel.
Grains, total.	1,766.7	1,705.9	1,786.0	1,711.3	1,756.4	1,696.5
Wheat.	588.0	542.1	561.8	559.2	525.1	534.7
Coarse grains.	826.5	809.0	868.8	796.5	866.7	787.4
Rice, milled	352.2	354.8	355.4	355.6	364.6	374.4
Pulses [1] [2]	57.8	56.0	54.3	57.1	58.6	(NA)
Vegetables and melons [1]	460.4	464.3	470.2	474.0	485.6	(NA)
Fruits [1]	354.3	353.7	380.7	384.3	387.9	(NA)
Nuts [1]	4.5	4.7	5.0	4.7	4.7	(NA)
Red meat	113.3	115.8	116.4	117.2	122.0	126.1
Poultry	33.8	35.6	37.5	39.7	43.1	44.7
Milk	395.0	385.2	379.4	379.7	382.1	382.7

NA Not available.   [1] Data from Food and Agriculture Organization of the United Nations.   [2] Edible seeds of peas, beans, lentils and similar crops.

Source: U.S. Department of Agriculture, Economic Research Service, *Agricultural Outlook*, monthly.

No. 1361. Fisheries—Commercial Catch, by Country: 1989 to 1992

[In thousands of metric tons, live weight. Catch of fish, crustaceans, mollusks (including weight of shells). Does not include marine mammals and aquatic plants. Countries shown had a commercial catch of 1,000,000 metric tons or more in 1992]

COUNTRY	1989	1990	1991	1992	COUNTRY	1989	1990	1991	1992
World [1]	100,311	97,556	97,051	98,112	Korea, South	2,840	2,843	2,521	2,695
Canada.	1,572	1,624	1,534	1,251	Mexico	1,469	1,400	1,453	1,247
Chile	6,454	5,195	6,002	6,501	Norway	1,908	1,711	2,095	2,549
China	11,219	12,095	13,134	15,007	Peru.	6,853	6,875	6,949	6,842
Denmark	1,929	1,518	1,795	1,995	Philippines.	2,098	2,208	2,311	2,271
Iceland	1,502	1,508	1,050	1,577	Russia	(X)	(X)	6,894	5,611
India	3,640	3,794	4,044	4,175	Spain	1,560	1,400	1,320	1,330
Indonesia	2,948	3,044	3,251	3,357	Thailand	2,699	2,786	2,967	2,855
Japan.	11,173	10,354	9,301	8,460	United States	5,778	5,870	5,488	5,602
Korea, North (est.) .	1,700	1,750	1,700	1,750	Vietnam	930	960	1,020	1,080

X Not applicable.   [1] Includes other countries, not shown separately.

Source: U.S. National Oceanic and Atmospheric Administration, National Marine Fisheries Service, *Fisheries of the United States,* annual. Data from Food and Agricultural Organization of the United Nations, Rome, Italy.

No. 1362. Meat Production, by Country: 1990 to 1994

[In thousands of metric tons, carcass weight. Covers beef and veal (incl. buffalo meat), pork (incl. bacon and ham), mutton and lamb (incl. goat meat), horsemeat, and poultry. Refers to meat from animals slaughtered within the national boundaries irrespective of origin of animals, and relates to commercial and farm slaughter. Excludes lard, tallow, and edible offals. See text, section 30, for general comments concerning the data]

COUNTRY	1990	1993	1994	COUNTRY	1990	1993	1994
World [1]	177,464	188,431	194,657	Italy	3,950	4,051	3,997
Argentina	3,374	3,485	3,557	Japan	3,503	3,395	3,303
Brazil	7,294	9,213	9,434	Mexico	2,801	3,309	3,475
China	30,073	40,175	46,720	Russia	10,112	7,518	6,871
France	5,744	6,213	6,296	Spain	3,467	3,771	3,816
Germany.	7,259	6,162	5,757	United Kingdom	3,319	3,291	3,394
India.	3,751	4,033	4,083	United States	28,610	31,180	32,847

[1] Includes other countries, not shown separately.

Source: Food and Agriculture Organization of the United Nations, Rome, Italy, FAO AGRISTAT database.

No. 1363. Wheat, Rice, and Corn Production, by Country: 1990 to 1994

[In thousands of metric tons. Rice data cover paddy. Data for each country pertain to the calendar year in which all or most of the crop was harvested. See text, section 30, for general comments concerning quality of the data]

COUNTRY	WHEAT			RICE			CORN		
	1990	1993	1994	1990	1993	1994	1990	1993	1994
World	592,589	564,065	527,982	519,407	527,103	534,701	477,090	470,354	569,557
Argentina	10,992	9,604	10,680	428	593	606	5,047	10,901	10,246
Australia...........	15,066	16,877	8,803	846	858	1,017	219	199	256
Bangladesh..........	890	1,176	1,131	26,778	26,925	27,537	3	3	3
Brazil..............	3,094	2,153	2,276	7,421	10,143	10,582	21,348	30,004	32,305
Burma	124	139	109	13,969	16,760	19,057	187	205	271
Canada	32,098	27,232	23,350	(X)	(X)	(X)	7,066	6,501	7,043
China..............	98,232	106,395	101,205	191,589	179,975	178,251	97,158	103,046	103,550
Egypt..............	4,268	4,833	4,437	3,167	4,161	4,582	4,799	5,039	4,883
France	33,346	29,252	30,652	121	128	124	9,401	14,843	13,040
Germany	15,242	15,767	16,429	(X)	(X)	(X)	1,552	2,656	2,357
Hungary	6,198	3,021	4,900	39	13	14	4,500	4,044	4,920
India	49,850	56,762	59,131	111,517	117,052	118,400	8,962	9,653	10,500
Indonesia	(X)	(X)	(X)	45,179	48,181	46,245	6,734	6,460	6,617
Iran	8,012	10,732	11,500	1,981	2,281	2,700	130	210	210
Italy..............	8,109	8,126	7,805	1,291	1,286	1,324	5,864	8,029	7,661
Japan	952	638	565	13,124	9,793	14,976	1	1	-
Kazakstan...........	16,197	11,585	9,052	579	403	283	442	355	233
Korea, South........	1	1	2	7,722	6,597	7,056	120	82	75
Mexico	3,931	3,582	3,589	394	388	375	14,635	18,648	19,193
Nigeria	50	30	30	2,500	3,759	3,857	1,832	2,300	2,000
Pakistan...........	14,316	16,157	15,114	4,891	5,992	5,269	1,185	1,215	1,288
Philippines	-	-	-	9,885	9,534	10,150	4,854	4,798	5,400
Romania...........	7,289	5,314	5,991	67	36	14	6,810	7,987	9,300
Russia	49,596	43,500	32,094	896	688	522	2,451	2,441	879
South Africa	1,730	1,984	1,850	3	3	3	8,709	9,663	11,811
Thailand...........	-	1	1	17,193	19,917	18,447	3,722	3,328	3,800
Turkey	20,022	21,016	17,500	230	225	200	2,100	2,500	1,850
Ukraine	30,374	21,831	13,857	118	68	79	4,737	3,786	1,539
United Kingdom	14,033	12,900	13,100	(X)	(X)	(X)	-	-	-
United States	74,473	65,210	63,141	7,080	7,081	8,972	201,534	160,954	256,629

- Represents or rounds to zero. X Not applicable.

No. 1364. Wheat, Rice, and Corn—Exports and Imports of 10 Leading Countries: 1990 to 1994

[In thousands of metric tons. Countries listed are the ten leading exporters or importers in 1993]

LEADING EXPORTERS	EXPORTS			LEADING IMPORTERS	IMPORTS		
	1990	1993	1994		1990	1993	1994
WHEAT				WHEAT			
United States	28,749	37,141	32,110	China	13,487	7,368	8,120
France	19,337	20,954	15,033	Japan	5,474	5,814	6,353
Canada	18,166	18,415	21,683	Russia..............	(X)	5,774	2,285
Australia...........	11,629	9,582	12,823	Brazil	1,962	5,671	6,322
Argentina	6,041	6,019	5,572	Italy	4,705	5,066	4,904
Germany	2,829	4,640	6,148	Egypt	6,439	5,038	7,125
United Kingdom	4,561	4,014	3,616	Korea, South	2,516	4,939	6,057
Italy..............	1,777	1,902	1,823	Algeria	3,604	4,244	5,585
Belgium-Luxembourg ...	1,367	1,797	1,888	Uzbekistan..........	(X)	4,100	-
Saudi Arabia	1,267	1,569	895	Pakistan	2,047	2,890	1,902
RICE				RICE			
Thailand............	4,017	4,989	4,859	Iran	620	1,159	475
United States	2,474	2,680	2,822	Brazil	414	701	987
Vietnam	1,624	1,765	1,970	Iraq	380	655	200
China..............	405	1,507	1,630	Saudi Arabia	280	577	434
Pakistan............	744	1,032	984	Malaysia	330	389	341
India	505	768	891	South Africa.........	306	385	431
Italy...............	577	574	619	Hong Kong	374	373	358
Uruguay	290	505	408	Cuba	235	370	255
Australia...........	424	482	585	United Arab Emirates...	309	370	350
Indonesia	2	351	169	Senegal............	392	363	348
CORN				CORN			
United States	52,172	40,365	35,877	Japan	16,008	16,863	15,930
China..............	3,405	11,098	8,740	Korea, South	6,158	6,207	5,749
France	7,195	7,758	8,013	China	5,440	5,466	5,601
Argentina	2,998	4,871	4,154	Russia..............	(X)	4,391	901
Belgium-Luxembourg ...	20	414	489	Spain	1,810	2,401	2,339
Canada	122	357	381	Egypt	1,900	2,148	2,021
Germany	226	219	308	Malaysia	1,480	2,058	1,969
South Africa	2,001	216	4,000	United Kingdom	1,627	1,508	1,602
Zimbabwe...........	742	216	150	Brazil	699	1,323	1,409
Italy..............	80	213	16	Belgium-Luxembourg ...	1,035	1,284	1,557

- Represents or rounds to zero. X Not applicable.

Source of tables 1363 and 1364: Food and Agriculture Organization of the United Nations, Rome, Italy, FAO AGRISTAT database.

No. 1365. United States and Foreign Stock Markets—Market Capitalization and Value of Shares Traded: 1985 to 1994

[In millions of U.S. dollars. Market capitalization is the total amount of the various securities (bonds, debentures, and stock) issued by corporations]

COUNTRY	MARKET CAPITALIZATION				VALUE OF SHARES TRADED			
	1985	1990	1993	1994	1985	1990	1993	1994
United States	2,324,646	3,089,651	5,223,768	5,081,810	997,189	1,815,476	3,507,223	3,592,668
Argentina	2,037	3,268	43,967	36,864	631	852	10,339	11,372
Australia.	60,163	107,611	203,964	219,188	15,736	39,333	67,711	94,726
Austria	4,602	11,476	28,437	30,272	686	18,609	6,561	16,380
Belgium	20,871	65,449	78,067	84,103	1,876	6,425	11,199	12,820
Brazil	42,768	16,354	99,430	189,281	21,484	5,598	57,409	109,498
Canada	147,000	241,920	326,524	315,009	39,905	71,278	142,222	161,058
Chile	2,012	13,645	44,622	68,195	57	783	2,797	5,263
China	(NA)	(NA)	40,567	43,521	(NA)	(NA)	43,395	97,526
Colombia	416	1,416	9,237	14,028	30	71	732	2,191
Czech Republic	(NA)	(NA)	(NA)	5,938	(NA)	(NA)	(NA)	1,480
Denmark.	15,096	39,063	41,785	54,399	1,274	11,105	20,989	27,421
Finland.	5,855	22,721	23,562	38,278	502	3,933	8,112	13,194
France	79,000	314,384	456,111	451,263	14,672	116,893	174,283	615,371
Germany	183,765	355,073	463,476	470,519	71,572	501,805	302,985	460,617
Greece.	765	15,228	12,319	14,921	17	3,924	2,713	5,145
Hong Kong	34,504	83,397	385,247	269,508	9,732	34,633	131,550	147,158
India	14,364	38,567	97,976	127,515	4,959	21,918	21,879	27,290
Indonesia	117	8,081	32,953	47,241	3	3,992	9,158	11,801
Italy.	58,502	148,766	136,153	180,135	13,782	42,566	65,770	117,894
Japan	978,663	2,917,679	2,999,756	3,719,914	329,970	1,602,388	954,341	1,121,438
Korea, South	7,381	110,594	139,420	191,778	4,162	75,949	211,710	286,056
Luxembourg	12,658	10,456	19,337	28,511	36	87	1,104	269
Malaysia.	16,229	48,611	220,328	199,276	2,335	10,871	153,661	126,458
Mexico	3,815	32,725	200,671	130,246	2,360	12,212	62,454	82,964
Netherlands	59,363	119,825	181,876	283,251	16,864	40,199	67,185	170,596
New Zealand.	8,761	8,835	25,597	27,217	935	1,933	6,785	7,162
Norway.	10,063	26,130	27,380	36,469	1,877	13,996	8,751	8,817
Pakistan	1,370	2,850	11,602	12,263	236	231	1,844	3,198
Peru	760	812	5,113	8,178	38	99	1,672	3,080
Philippines	669	5,927	40,327	55,519	111	1,216	6,785	13,949
Portugal	192	9,201	12,417	16,249	5	1,687	4,835	5,275
South Africa	55,439	137,540	171,942	225,718	2,836	8,158	13,049	15,954
Spain	19,000	111,404	119,264	154,858	3,382	40,967	47,156	61,452
Sweden	37,296	92,102	107,376	130,939	9,644	15,718	43,593	85,407
Switzerland	90,000	160,044	271,713	284,092	(NA)	(NA)	167,880	226,723
Taiwan	10,432	100,710	195,198	247,325	4,899	715,005	346,487	711,346
Thailand.	1,856	23,896	130,510	131,479	568	22,894	86,934	80,188
Turkey	(NA)	19,065	37,496	21,605	(NA)	5,841	23,242	21,692
United Kingdom	328,000	848,866	1,151,646	1,210,245	68,417	278,740	423,526	928,171

NA Not available.

Source: International Finance Corporation, Washington, DC, *Emerging Stock Markets Factbook, 1995*, (copyright).

No. 1366. Dow-Jones World Stock Index, by Country and Industry: 1992 to 1995

[Index figures shown are as of **December 31. Indexes based on June 30, 1982=100 for United States; December 31, 1991=100 for World**. Based on share prices denominated in U.S. dollars. Stocks in countries that impose significant restrictions on foreign ownership are included in the world index in the same proportion that shares are available to foreign investors]

INDUSTRY	1992	1993	1994	1995	INDUSTRY	1992	1993	1994	1995
World, total	92.83	111.08	113.91	133.46	Asia/Pacific	79.42	106.76	119.39	119.80
					Australia	84.66	113.29	114.89	127.90
Americas.	104.37	112.18	108.53	143.61	Hong Kong.	125.44	270.36	184.08	223.67
United States	413.29	442.19	433.07	581.43	Indonesia.	112.32	233.92	176.25	172.48
Canada	84.65	100.36	95.23	108.25	Japan	76.89	95.71	116.21	114.08
Mexico	123.13	182.88	107.06	77.96	Malaysia.	128.80	269.99	216.69	223.08
Europe	93.66	116.08	115.70	136.54	New Zealand	95.89	151.52	155.86	176.17
Austria	81.30	104.82	104.36	101.29	Singapore	103.07	179.22	178.06	195.91
Belgium	90.06	111.55	115.75	142.56	Thailand	116.82	243.90	207.44	196.76
Denmark	71.95	95.73	98.16	112.42					
Finland	79.59	138.66	205.90	202.88					
France	97.86	117.78	109.17	120.03	Basic materials.	91.88	109.04	124.40	130.91
Germany	88.76	118.94	122.57	138.24	Conglomerate	93.90	129.80	127.47	146.57
Ireland.	80.72	111.95	122.90	152.83	Consumer, cyclical	98.88	123.24	124.27	135.13
Italy	77.92	99.11	109.54	103.51	Consumer, noncyclical . .	92.51	93.01	98.64	130.19
Netherlands	98.07	125.74	133.88	167.30	Energy	93.28	107.82	110.23	132.32
Norway	78.47	103.12	122.41	129.21	Financial services	90.75	114.97	112.75	134.62
Spain	78.10	94.89	89.33	114.31	Industrial	86.34	106.00	112.24	118.38
Sweden	83.07	104.06	119.43	163.14	Technology	94.63	114.61	134.91	168.07
Switzerland	111.46	158.28	162.99	232.62	Utilities	92.52	114.42	101.12	118.44
United Kingdom	94.32	112.30	107.34	124.49					

Source: Dow Jones & Company, Inc., New York, NY, *Wall Street Journal*, selected issues (copyright).

No. 1367. Foreign Stock Market Activity—Morgan Stanley Capital International Indexes: 1990 to 1995

[Index figures shown are as of **December 31. January 1, 1970=100, except as noted.** Based on share prices denominated in U.S. dollars. EMG=Emerging Markets Global. GDP=Gross Domestic Product]

INDEX AND COUNTRY	INDEX			PERCENT CHANGE [1]		INDEX AND COUNTRY	INDEX			PERCENT CHANGE [1]	
	1990	1994	1995	1994	1995		1990	1994	1995	1994	1995
All Country World index [2]	114.3	157.2	182.0	3.2	15.7	Sweden	915	1,363	1,796	17.3	31.7
						Switzerland	567	1,102	1,569	2.4	42.4
DEVELOPED MARKETS						United Kingdom	514	611	716	-4.7	17.2
						Hong Kong	1,547	4,076	4,818	-31.0	18.2
World index [3]	462	619	734	3.4	18.7	Japan	2,638	3,347	3,348	20.7	(Z)
EAFE index [4]	789	1,038	1,136	6.2	9.4	Singapore	1,166	2,604	2,735	5.4	5.0
Europe index	479	617	733	0.1	18.9						
Pacific index	1,735	2,321	2,362	11.8	1.8	EMERGING MARKETS					
Far East index	2,514	3,340	3,384	12.4	1.3	EMG Far East index	168.2	294.5	263.7	-0.1	-10.5
						India [6]	(NA)	145.1	98.8	9.1	-31.9
GDP-weighted indexes:						Indonesia	610.8	472.8	508.2	-27.0	7.5
World index	540	739	874	4.0	18.2	Korea, South	139.4	182.3	173.8	22.1	-4.6
EAFE index [4]	817	1,100	1,205	6.3	9.5	Malaysia	170.4	333.8	347.0	-20.7	4.0
						Pakistan [6]	(NA)	148.2	91.5	-8.2	-38.3
United States	306.9	431.3	581.1	-0.9	34.7	Philippines	94.1	523.2	442.5	0.3	-15.4
Canada	341.9	347.9	403.9	-4.9	16.1	Sri Lanka [6]	(NA)	156.9	105.6	-3.9	-32.7
						Taiwan	177.7	326.7	227.9	19.7	-30.2
Australia	184.6	281.0	304.2	2.9	8.3	Thailand	205.0	554.7	523.3	-11.1	-5.7
New Zealand [5]	53.0	97.4	114.2	5.8	17.3						
						EMG Latin America	236.7	928.3	781.8	-5.3	-15.8
Austria	1,052	945	890	-7.1	-5.8	Argentina	318	1,140	1,239	-25.0	8.7
Belgium	568	736	897	4.9	21.8	Brazil	89.2	734.5	578.1	63.8	-21.3
Denmark	867	958	1,124	2.6	17.3	Chile	214	962	903	41.2	-6.2
Finland [5]	66.3	124.6	128.8	51.3	3.4	Colombia [6]	(NA)	152.6	110.2	18.9	-27.8
France	461	599	672	-6.6	12.2	Mexico	424	969	744	-44.4	-23.2
Germany	551	713	818	3.3	14.8	Peru [6]	(NA)	181.3	221.3	44.5	22.1
Ireland [5]	138.4	180.7	215.7	11.9	19.4						
Italy	205.2	209.1	208.6	10.4	-0.2	Greece [5]	321.9	216.2	238.2	-1.9	10.2
Netherlands	594	959	1,192	8.9	24.3	Jordan	55.3	91.2	96.1	-9.1	5.4
Norway	896	978	1,023	22.1	4.6	Portugal [5]	66.8	70.1	68.4	8.2	-2.5
Spain	132.0	128.9	162.3	-7.4	26.0	Turkey	195.2	109.6	103.1	-52.6	-5.9

NA Not available.   Z Less than 0.05 percent.   [1] Percent change during calendar year (e.g. December 31, 1993, through December 31, 1994). Adjusted for foreign exchange fluctuations relative to U.S. dollar.   [2] Comprises World index, all emerging markets, and Luxembourg.   [3] Includes South African gold mines quoted in London.   [4] Europe, Australasia, Far East Index. Comprises all European and Far East countries listed under developed markets plus Malaysia, Australia, and New Zealand.   [5] January 1, 1988=100.   [6] December 1992=100.

Source: Morgan Stanley Capital International, New York, NY, unpublished data (copyright).

No. 1368. Central Bank Discount Rates, Money Market Rates, and Government Bond Yields, by Country: 1990 to 1996

[**In percent per annum. Central bank discount rates** refer to the rate at which the monetary authority lends or discounts eligible paper for deposit money banks. **Money market rates** refer to the rate at which short-term borrowings are effected between financial institutions. **Government bond yields** refer to one or more series representing average yields to maturity of government bonds or other bonds that would be indicative of longer term rates]

NATIONAL INTEREST RATE AND YEAR	United States	Canada	Japan	France	Ger-many	Italy	Nether-lands	Sweden	Switzer-land	United King-dom
Central bank discount rates: [1]										
1990	6.50	11.78	6.00	9.50	6.00	12.50	7.25	11.50	6.00	(2)
1992	3.00	7.36	3.25	9.50	8.25	12.00	7.75	[3]10.00	6.00	(2)
1993	3.00	4.11	1.75	9.50	5.75	8.00	5.00	5.00	4.00	(2)
1994	4.75	7.43	1.75	9.50	4.50	7.50	(NA)	7.00	3.50	(2)
1995	5.25	5.79	0.50	(NA)	3.00	9.00	(NA)	7.00	1.50	(2)
1996, May	5.00	5.00	(NA)	(NA)	2.50	(NA)	(NA)	5.50	1.50	(2)
Money market rates: [4]										
1990	8.10	11.62	7.24	9.85	7.92	12.38	8.29	13.45	8.33	14.64
1992	3.52	6.79	4.58	10.35	9.42	14.02	9.27	18.42	7.47	9.39
1993	3.02	3.79	[3]3.06	8.75	7.49	10.20	7.10	9.08	4.94	5.46
1994	4.20	5.54	2.20	5.69	5.35	8.51	5.14	7.36	3.85	4.76
1995	5.84	5.71	1.21	6.35	4.50	10.46	4.22	8.54	2.89	5.98
1996, May	5.24	4.77	(NA)	3.75	3.33	(NA)	2.67	6.70	2.23	6.13
Government bond yields:										
1990	8.55	10.85	7.36	9.96	8.88	11.51	8.92	13.08	[3]6.68	11.08
1992	7.01	8.77	4.94	8.60	7.96	13.27	8.10	10.02	5.48	9.12
1993	5.82	7.85	3.69	6.91	6.28	11.31	6.51	8.54	4.05	7.87
1994	7.11	8.63	3.71	7.35	6.67	10.56	7.20	[3]9.41	5.23	8.05
1995	6.58	8.28	2.53	7.59	6.50	12.21	7.20	(NA)	3.73	8.26
1996, May	6.74	7.92	(NA)	6.57	5.81	(NA)	6.67	(NA)	4.33	8.35

NA Not available.   [1] End of period.   [2] Minimum lending rate suspended as of August 20, 1981.   [3] Beginning in year shown, data not comparable with previous years.   [4] Period averages.

Source: International Monetary Fund, Washington, DC, *International Financial Statistics*, monthly (copyright).

No. 1369. Reserve Assets and International Transaction Balances, by Country: 1990 to 1994

[**In millions of U.S. dollars.** Assets include holdings of convertible foreign currencies, special drawing rights, and reserve position in International Monetary Fund and exclude gold holdings. Minus sign (-) indicates decrease]

COUNTRY	TOTAL RESERVE ASSETS				CURRENT ACCOUNT BALANCE			MERCHANDISE TRADE BALANCE		
	1990	1993	1994 Total	1994 Cur-rency hold-ings [1]	1990	1993	1994	1990	1993	1994
United States	72,260	62,350	63,280	41,220	-91,740	-103,930	-155,680	-109,020	-132,570	-166,360
Algeria	725	1,475	2,674	2,651	1,420	(NA)	(NA)	4,187	(NA)	(NA)
Argentina	4,592	13,791	14,327	13,764	4,552	-7,452	(NA)	8,628	-2,428	(NA)
Australia	16,265	11,102	11,285	10,706	-14,849	-10,369	(NA)	368	-123	(NA)
Austria	9,376	14,611	16,822	16,008	1,174	-875	(NA)	-7,012	-7,825	-9,210
Bangladesh.	629	2,411	3,139	3,103	-398	197	(NA)	-1,587	-1,283	(NA)
Belgium	12,151	11,415	13,876	12,884	4,950	12,588	(NA)	590	3,933	(NA)
Brazil	7,441	30,604	37,070	37,069	-3,788	-637	(NA)	10,747	13,072	(NA)
Burma	313	303	(NA)	(NA)	(NA)	(NA)	(NA)	(NA)	(NA)	(NA)
Cameroon.	26	2	2	2	-467	-742	(NA)	778	217	(NA)
Canada	17,845	12,481	12,286	10,219	-21,548	-23,869	-18,171	8,330	7,612	12,787
Chile	6,069	9,640	13,088	13,087	-648	-2,093	(NA)	1,273	-979	(NA)
China.	29,586	22,387	52,914	51,620	11,997	-11,609	(NA)	9,165	-10,654	(NA)
Colombia	4,212	7,552	7,750	7,453	542	(NA)	(NA)	1,971	(NA)	(NA)
Cote d'Ivoire	4	2	185	185	-1,210	-1,229	(NA)	1,327	1,072	(NA)
Denmark.	10,591	10,301	9,056	8,444	1,372	4,711	(NA)	4,875	7,812	(NA)
Ecuador	839	1,380	1,841	1,812	-166	-360	(NA)	1,003	578	(NA)
Egypt.	2,684	12,904	13,481	13,316	185	2,299	(NA)	-6,699	-6,680	(NA)
Finland.	9,644	5,411	10,662	10,051	-6,961	-980	1,068	725	6,392	7,660
France	36,778	22,649	26,257	23,520	-15,236	10,201	4,899	-13,671	6,997	8,660
Germany [2]	67,902	77,640	77,363	72,219	46	-15	-23	71	45	56
Ghana	219	410	584	554	-229	(NA)	(NA)	-308	(NA)	(NA)
Greece.	3,412	7,790	14,488	14,322	-3,537	-747	(NA)	-10,178	-10,557	(NA)
Hungary	1,070	6,771	(NA)	(NA)	379	-4,262	(NA)	534	-4,021	(NA)
India	1,521	10,199	19,698	19,386	-7,037	(NA)	(NA)	-5,151	(NA)	(NA)
Indonesia	7,459	11,263	12,133	11,820	-2,988	-2,016	(NA)	5,352	8,231	(NA)
Ireland	5,223	5,925	6,115	5,745	45	3,646	(NA)	3,969	8,172	(NA)
Israel	6,275	6,383	6,792	6,792	558	-1,373	-2,757	-2,981	-5,607	-6,096
Italy.	62,927	27,545	32,265	30,107	-16,827	11,176	(NA)	1,373	32,278	(NA)
Japan	78,501	98,524	125,860	115,146	35,870	131,150	(NA)	63,580	141,570	(NA)
Kenya	205	406	558	539	-520	153	(NA)	-995	-307	(NA)
Korea, South	14,793	20,228	25,639	25,032	-2,172	384	(NA)	-2,004	1,860	(NA)
Kuwait	1,952	4,214	3,501	3,212	4,164	6,344	(NA)	3,578	4,373	(NA)
Libya	5,839	(NA)	(NA)	(NA)	2,201	(NA)	(NA)	3,777	(NA)	(NA)
Malaysia.	9,754	27,249	(NA)	(NA)	-918	-2,466	(NA)	2,622	3,183	(NA)
Mexico.	9,863	25,110	6,278	6,101	-7,451	-23,391	(NA)	-4,433	-18,891	(NA)
Morocco.	2,066	3,655	4,352	4,281	-200	-525	(NA)	-2,071	-2,380	(NA)
Nepal.	295	640	694	685	-289	-223	(NA)	-449	-462	(NA)
Netherlands	17,484	31,344	34,532	32,716	8,930	9,371	(NA)	10,330	12,915	(NA)
Nigeria	3,864	1,372	1,386	1,386	4,988	(NA)	(NA)	8,653	(NA)	(NA)
Norway.	15,332	19,622	19,026	17,992	4,023	2,453	(NA)	7,761	8,016	(NA)
Pakistan	296	1,197	2,929	2,929	-1,654	-2,936	(NA)	-2,714	-2,552	(NA)
Peru	1,040	3,408	(NA)	(NA)	-901	-1,800	(NA)	339	-580	(NA)
Philippines	924	4,676	6,017	5,866	-2,695	-3,289	(NA)	-4,020	-6,222	(NA)
Poland	4,492	4,092	5,842	5,728	3,067	-5,788	(NA)	3,589	-3,505	(NA)
Portugal	14,485	15,840	(NA)	(NA)	-181	947	(NA)	-6,831	-6,886	(NA)
Romania.	373	995	2,086	2,031	-3,254	-1,162	(NA)	-3,344	-1,128	(NA)
Saudi Arabia	11,668	7,428	7,378	5,888	-4,117	-14,218	(NA)	22,756	19,020	(NA)
Singapore	27,748	48,361	58,177	57,890	2,094	2,039	(NA)	-4,718	-8,065	(NA)
South Africa	1,008	1,020	1,685	1,684	2,077	1,805	(NA)	6,783	5,781	(NA)
Spain	51,228	41,045	41,569	40,205	-16,819	-4,640	-5,173	-29,566	-15,718	-15,335
Sri Lanka	423	1,629	2,046	2,016	-298	-381	(NA)	-473	-742	(NA)
Sudan	11	38	(NA)	(NA)	-372	(NA)	(NA)	-322	(NA)	(NA)
Sweden	17,988	19,050	23,254	22,527	-6,693	-4,057	(NA)	3,402	7,669	(NA)
Switzerland	29,223	32,635	34,729	33,554	6,942	16,696	(NA)	-6,391	2,237	(NA)
Syria	(NA)	(NA)	(NA)	(NA)	1,762	-607	(NA)	2,094	-322	(NA)
Thailand	13,305	24,473	29,332	28,884	-7,282	-6,928	(NA)	-6,751	-4,146	(NA)
Trinidad and Tobago .	492	206	352	352	440	102	(NA)	988	524	(NA)
Turkey	6,050	6,272	7,169	7,121	-2,625	-6,380	(NA)	-9,555	-14,162	(NA)
United Kingdom	35,850	36,780	41,010	38,530	-33,037	-16,842	(NA)	-32,742	-19,869	(NA)
Venezuela.	8,321	9,216	8,067	7,393	8,279	-2,223	(NA)	10,637	2,902	(NA)
Zaire	219	46	121	121	-643	(NA)	(NA)	600	(NA)	(NA)

NA Not available.   [1] Holdings of convertible foreign currencies.   [2] Prior to July 1990, data for former West Germany.

Source: International Monetary Fund, Washington, DC, *International Financial Statistics*, monthly (copyright).

No. 1370. Foreign Trade—Source of Imports and Destination of Exports, by Country: 1994

[**In billions of dollars.** All exports are f.o.b. (free on board) and all imports are c.i.f. (cost insurance freight) except for United States, Australian, and Canadian imports, which are f.o.b.]

COUNTRY	Total [1]	O.E.C.D. [2] Total	O.E.C.D. [2] E.U. [3]	C.E.E.C. [4]	China, Vietnam, North Korea	O.P.E.C. [5]	Other developing countries [6]	Africa	America [7]	Middle East [8]	Far East [9]
IMPORTS											
Value (bil. dol.):											
Australia	49.9	35.9	11.8	0.6	2.6	1.8	9.2	0.6	0.5	1.2	8.3
Austria	55.3	48.0	37.8	1.3	0.8	1.0	4.0	0.7	0.5	0.5	2.0
Belgium-Luxembourg. . . .	122.0	105.8	91.1	0.8	1.3	1.3	10.8	3.6	1.7	1.3	4.1
Canada.	147.8	128.9	14.4	0.2	2.9	2.0	11.0	0.8	2.5	0.6	8.5
France	230.4	186.5	144.6	2.2	4.3	8.4	25.1	10.4	4.3	5.2	10.4
Germany.	378.1	299.0	209.6	12.0	10.0	8.2	47.3	8.8	8.3	3.7	25.1
Italy	166.7	127.0	101.2	3.6	3.1	8.8	21.6	11.5	4.1	3.6	6.0
Japan.	274.8	132.6	38.9	0.2	29.3	38.0	72.4	4.1	7.9	27.8	67.8
Netherlands	122.8	96.5	74.2	1.7	2.0	6.4	16.0	3.0	4.6	4.3	9.4
Spain	92.5	73.6	59.3	0.5	1.9	5.6	10.2	5.9	3.1	2.3	3.8
Sweden	51.7	44.4	32.5	1.1	1.1	0.8	4.2	0.4	0.8	0.6	2.3
Switzerland	67.7	61.7	53.8	0.2	0.8	0.8	4.0	0.1	0.7	0.7	2.3
United Kingdom . .	229.0	189.4	127.7	2.0	2.6	4.2	28.6	4.9	3.8	3.4	20.2
United States	663.8	433.2	119.5	1.6	38.9	33.4	149.5	14.2	38.5	15.8	117.5
Percent distribution:											
Australia	100.0	71.9	23.6	1.2	5.3	3.6	18.5	1.2	1.0	2.4	16.6
Austria	100.0	86.8	68.3	2.4	1.5	1.7	7.2	1.3	0.9	0.9	3.7
Belgium-Luxembourg. . . .	100.0	86.7	74.6	0.7	1.1	1.1	8.9	3.0	1.4	1.1	3.3
Canada.	100.0	87.2	9.7	0.2	2.0	1.4	7.5	0.6	1.7	0.4	5.8
France	100.0	80.9	62.8	0.9	1.9	3.7	10.9	4.5	1.9	2.2	4.5
Germany.	100.0	79.1	55.4	3.2	2.6	2.2	12.5	2.3	2.2	1.0	6.6
Italy	100.0	76.2	60.7	2.2	1.9	5.3	13.0	6.9	2.5	2.2	3.6
Japan.	100.0	48.3	14.2	0.1	10.7	13.8	26.3	1.5	2.9	10.1	24.7
Netherlands	100.0	78.6	60.4	1.4	1.7	5.2	13.0	2.4	3.7	3.5	7.6
Spain	100.0	79.5	64.1	0.5	2.1	6.1	11.0	6.4	3.4	2.5	4.2
Sweden	100.0	85.9	62.9	2.1	2.1	1.6	8.1	0.7	1.6	1.2	4.4
Switzerland	100.0	91.1	79.4	0.4	1.2	1.2	5.9	0.2	1.1	1.1	3.4
United Kingdom . .	100.0	82.7	55.8	0.9	1.2	1.8	12.5	2.2	1.7	1.5	8.8
United States	100.0	65.3	18.0	0.2	5.9	5.0	22.5	2.1	5.8	2.4	17.7
EXPORTS											
Value (bil. dol.):											
Australia	47.4	24.6	5.3	0.1	2.2	2.5	16.4	0.7	0.5	1.2	15.4
Austria	45.0	38.3	29.2	1.9	0.4	1.0	3.4	0.7	0.4	0.7	1.3
Belgium-Luxembourg. . . .	134.3	115.4	100.3	1.1	1.0	2.2	13.6	2.9	1.2	4.4	6.5
Canada.	165.8	154.4	9.0	0.1	1.7	2.0	7.3	0.8	2.5	1.1	4.9
France	234.2	186.1	148.6	2.3	2.5	8.0	34.2	14.3	7.3	6.4	11.9
Germany.	424.1	339.0	244.8	12.4	6.5	11.0	51.5	9.0	7.7	10.4	26.3
Italy	188.5	142.9	108.6	5.0	2.4	7.2	29.5	6.8	6.1	7.6	10.9
Japan.	395.6	205.1	61.3	0.2	19.4	16.4	150.8	6.8	13.4	9.8	138.4
Netherlands	134.9	116.8	102.7	1.9	0.6	2.6	11.4	2.5	1.9	2.5	5.4
Spain	73.3	60.4	51.7	0.6	0.8	2.4	8.9	3.0	3.2	1.7	2.5
Sweden	61.3	51.8	36.4	1.2	1.1	1.1	6.0	1.0	1.1	1.2	3.5
Switzerland	70.1	55.7	43.4	0.7	0.6	2.2	10.4	1.3	1.7	2.6	6.7
United Kingdom . .	206.5	165.4	118.1	1.7	1.4	7.2	27.8	6.4	3.4	8.2	16.7
United States	512.4	348.0	107.8	1.4	9.5	19.1	132.0	9.2	41.8	16.1	82.0
Percent distribution:											
Australia	100.0	51.9	11.1	0.3	4.6	5.3	34.7	1.5	1.0	2.5	32.4
Austria	100.0	85.1	64.8	4.3	0.8	2.1	7.5	1.6	0.8	1.6	2.9
Belgium-Luxembourg. . . .	100.0	86.0	74.7	0.8	0.7	1.6	10.1	2.1	0.9	3.3	4.8
Canada.	100.0	93.1	5.4	0.1	1.0	1.2	4.4	0.5	1.5	0.7	3.0
France	100.0	79.5	63.4	1.0	1.1	3.4	14.6	6.1	3.1	2.7	5.1
Germany.	100.0	79.9	57.7	2.9	1.5	2.6	12.1	2.1	1.8	2.5	6.2
Italy	100.0	75.8	57.6	2.7	1.3	3.8	15.7	3.6	3.3	4.0	5.8
Japan.	100.0	51.8	15.5	0.1	4.9	4.2	38.1	1.7	3.4	2.5	35.0
Netherlands	100.0	86.6	76.2	1.4	0.4	2.0	8.5	1.9	1.4	1.9	4.0
Spain	100.0	82.3	70.5	0.8	1.2	3.3	12.1	4.1	4.4	2.3	3.4
Sweden	100.0	84.5	59.3	2.0	1.8	1.8	9.8	1.6	1.8	2.0	5.7
Switzerland	100.0	79.5	62.0	1.0	0.9	3.1	14.9	1.9	2.4	3.8	9.6
United Kingdom . .	100.0	80.1	57.2	0.8	0.7	3.5	13.5	3.1	1.6	4.0	8.1
United States	100.0	67.9	21.0	0.3	1.9	3.7	25.8	1.8	8.2	3.1	16.0

[1] Includes other areas not shown separately. [2] Organization for Economic Cooperation and Development. For member countries, see text, section 30. [3] European Union comprises Austria, Belgium-Luxembourg, Denmark, Finland, France, Germany, Greece, Ireland, Italy, Netherlands, Portugal, Spain, Sweden, and United Kingdom. [4] Central and Eastern European countries comprises Albania, the Baltic States (Estonia, Latvia, Lithuania), Bulgaria, Poland, Romania, Slovakia and Slovenia. [5] Organization of Petroleum Exporting Countries comprises Algeria, Ecuador, Gabon, Iran, Iraq, Kuwait, Libya, Nigeria, Qatar, Saudi Arabia, United Arab Emirates, and Venezuela. [6] Comprises trade with all countries other than China, North Korea, Vietnam, South Africa, Eastern Europe, and members of OPEC and OECD. [7] All countries comprising the continent except Canada, Mexico, and the United States. [8] Comprises Syria, Lebanon, Israel, Gaza Strip, Jordan, Iraq, Saudi Arabia, Yemen, Kuwait, Bahrain, United Arab Emirates, Qatar, Oman, and Iran. [9] All countries comprising the continent of Asia except Japan, China, North Korea, Vietnam, and those countries listed under Middle East.

Source: Organization for Economic Cooperation and Development, Paris, France. Data derived from *Monthly Statistics of Foreign Trade* (copyright).

No. 1371. Foreign Exchange Rates: 1980 to 1995

[National currency units per dollar, except as noted. Data are averages of certified noon buying rates for cable transfers]

YEAR	Australia [1] (dollar)	Austria (schilling)	Belgium (franc)	Canada (dollar)	Denmark (krone)	France (franc)	Germany (deutsche mark)	Greece (drachma)	Hong Kong (dollar)
1980	114.00	12.945	29.237	1.1693	5.6345	4.2250	1.8175	42.62	4.9760
1985	70.03	20.676	59.336	1.3658	10.5980	8.9799	2.9420	138.40	7.7911
1986	67.09	15.260	44.662	1.3896	8.0954	6.9256	2.1705	139.93	7.8037
1987	70.14	12.649	37.357	1.3259	6.8477	6.0121	1.7981	135.47	7.7985
1988	78.41	12.357	36.783	1.2306	6.7411	5.9594	1.7570	142.00	7.8071
1989	79.19	13.236	39.409	1.1842	7.3210	6.3802	1.8808	162.60	7.8008
1990	78.07	11.331	33.424	1.1668	6.1899	5.4467	1.6166	158.59	7.7899
1991	75.93	11.686	34.195	1.1460	6.4038	5.6468	1.6610	182.63	7.7712
1992	73.52	10.992	32.148	1.2085	6.0372	5.2935	1.5618	190.81	7.7402
1993	67.99	11.639	34.581	1.2902	6.4863	5.6669	1.6545	229.64	7.7357
1994	73.16	11.409	33.426	1.3664	6.3561	5.5459	1.6216	242.50	7.7290
1995	74.07	10.076	29.472	1.3725	5.5999	4.9864	1.4321	231.68	7.7357

	India (rupee)	Ireland [1] (pound)	Italy (lira)	Japan (yen)	Malaysia (ringgit)	Netherlands (guilder)	New Zealand[1] (dollar)	Norway (krone)	Portugal (escudo)
1980	7.887	205.77	856.20	226.63	2.1767	1.9875	97.34	4.9381	50.08
1985	12.332	106.62	1,908.90	238.47	2.4806	3.3184	49.75	8.5933	172.07
1986	12.597	134.14	1,491.16	168.35	2.5830	2.4484	52.46	7.3984	149.80
1987	12.943	148.79	1,297.03	144.60	2.5185	2.0263	59.33	6.7408	141.20
1988	13.899	152.49	1,302.39	128.17	2.6189	1.9778	65.56	6.5242	144.26
1989	16.213	141.80	1,372.28	138.07	2.7079	2.1219	59.35	6.9131	157.53
1990	17.492	165.76	1,198.27	145.00	2.7057	1.8215	59.62	6.2541	142.70
1991	22.712	174.70	1,241.28	134.59	2.7503	1.8720	54.03	6.4912	144.77
1992	28.156	170.42	1,232.17	126.78	2.5463	1.7587	53.79	6.2142	135.07
1993	31.291	146.47	1,573.41	111.08	2.5738	1.8585	54.13	7.0979	161.08
1994	31.394	149.69	1,611.49	102.18	2.6237	1.8190	59.36	7.0553	165.93
1995	32.418	160.35	1,629.45	93.96	2.5073	1.6044	65.62	6.3355	149.88

	Singapore (dollar)	South Africa (rand)	South Korea (won)	Spain (peseta)	Sweden (krona)	Switzerland (franc)	Taiwan (dollar)	Thailand (baht)	United Kingdom[1] (pound)
1980	2.1412	0.7796	607.43	71.76	4.2309	1.6772	36.015	20.476	232.43
1985	2.2008	2.2344	861.89	169.98	8.6031	2.4551	39.889	27.193	129.74
1986	2.1782	2.2919	884.61	140.04	7.1272	1.7979	37.837	26.314	146.77
1987	2.1059	2.0385	825.93	123.54	6.3468	1.4918	31.756	25.774	163.98
1988	2.0132	2.2770	734.51	116.52	6.1369	1.4642	28.636	25.312	178.13
1989	1.9511	2.6214	674.29	118.44	6.4559	1.6369	26.407	25.725	163.82
1990	1.8134	2.5885	710.64	101.96	5.9231	1.3901	26.918	25.609	178.41
1991	1.7283	2.7633	736.73	104.01	6.0521	1.4356	26.759	25.528	176.74
1992	1.6294	2.8524	784.58	102.38	5.8258	1.4064	25.160	25.411	176.63
1993	1.6158	3.2729	805.75	127.48	7.7956	1.4781	26.416	25.333	150.16
1994	1.5275	3.5526	806.93	133.88	7.7161	1.3667	26.465	25.161	153.19
1995	1.4171	3.6286	772.82	124.64	7.1406	1.1812	26.495	24.921	157.85

[1] Value is U.S. cents per unit of foreign currency.

Source: Board of Governors of the Federal Reserve System, *Federal Reserve Bulletin,* monthly.

No. 1372. External Debt of Eastern European Countries: 1990 to 1994

[In billions of dollars. Gross debt: total amount owed. Commercial debt: money owed to private institutions or individuals. Official debt: money owed to or guaranteed by a foreign government]

ITEM	1990	1993	1994	ITEM	1990	1993	1994
Bulgaria: Gross debt	10.6	12.5	12.9	Commercial debt	14.4	12.7	(NA)
Commercial debt	8.6	(NA)	(NA)	Official debt	32.8	29.6	(NA)
Official debt	2.0	(NA)	(NA)	Multilateral institutions	1.3	6.1	(NA)
Czech Republic: Gross debt	(X)	8.5	9.0	Romania: Gross debt	0.9	3.4	4.4
Commercial debt	(X)	6.5	7.5	Commercial debt	0.4	(NA)	(NA)
Official debt	(X)	0.2	0.3	Official debt	0.1	(NA)	(NA)
Multilateral institutions	(X)	1.8	1.2	Multilateral institutions	0.4	(NA)	(NA)
Hungary: Gross debt	21.3	24.6	28.5	Russia: [1] Gross debt	53.6	95.0	110.0
Commercial debt	18.2	18.4	21.3	Commercial debt	35.6	50.0	35.0
Official debt	1.4	2.8	2.2	Official debt	18.0	30.0	60.0
Multilateral institutions	1.7	3.4	5.0	Other	(NA)	15.0	15.0
Poland: Gross debt	48.5	48.4	42.2	Slovakia: Gross debt	(X)	3.7	4.3

NA Not available.   X Not applicable.   [1] The debt of the former Soviet Union was assumed by Russia.

Source: U.S. Central Intelligence Agency, *Handbook of International Economic Statistics, 1995;* and unpublished data.

No. 1373. External Public Debt, by Country: 1990 to 1994

[External public debt is defined as debt repayable to external creditors in foreign currency, goods, or services, with an original or extended maturity of more than 1 year, which is a direct obligation of, or has repayment guaranteed by, a public body in the borrowing country. Excludes undisbursed debt (amounts not yet drawn by recipient) and unguaranteed private debt, which for some countries is substantial. Debt contracted for the purchase of military equipment is not usually reported. **Debt service payments** represent the sum of interest payments and repayments of principal on external public debt]

COUNTRY	TOTAL EXTERNAL PUBLIC DEBT (mil. dol.)							DEBT SERVICE PAYMENTS (mil. dol.)			DEBT SERVICE RATIO [2] (percent)		
				1994									
	1990	1992	1993	Total [1]	Bilateral official	Banks	International organizations	1990	1993	1994	1990	1993	1994
Argentina	46,906	47,605	52,024	55,785	11,070	918	7,695	4,812	5,137	4,522	32	29	22
Bangladesh	12,289	13,203	14,107	15,713	6,203	5	9,261	547	470	582	20	12	14
Bolivia	3,690	3,674	3,695	4,113	1,755	23	2,275	275	273	285	28	30	24
Brazil	89,187	91,988	92,968	94,512	20,304	6,514	9,272	5,670	5,143	8,792	16	12	17
Bulgaria	9,834	10,034	9,819	9,013	1,463	485	1,390	1,317	238	634	29	5	12
Cameroon	4,709	5,595	5,602	5,970	3,699	208	1,620	244	278	286	11	12	13
Chile	10,426	9,578	8,868	8,947	727	3,740	4,369	1,612	1,533	1,250	15	12	8
China	45,515	58,462	70,076	84,554	15,385	22,723	13,588	5,853	9,347	10,161	10	10	8
Colombia	14,671	13,238	12,865	13,604	1,886	4,623	5,379	3,115	2,756	3,232	33	26	26
Congo	4,208	3,877	4,117	4,667	2,982	846	697	475	95	532	32	8	49
Costa Rica	3,063	3,180	3,118	3,155	1,242	6	1,292	433	445	381	21	15	11
Cote d'Ivoire	9,849	10,528	10,430	11,271	5,195	2,553	3,367	473	457	657	13	14	21
Croatia	(X)	(X)	870	902	255	55	529	(X)	170	165	(X)	3	2
Dominican Republic	3,442	3,725	3,763	3,681	1,917	26	937	145	275	454	7	11	18
Ecuador	9,867	9,831	9,935	10,384	2,352	5,160	2,412	875	762	856	27	20	19
Egypt	26,976	28,254	28,404	30,538	24,268	553	4,161	2,487	1,862	1,857	18	12	12
Ethiopia	3,634	4,188	4,503	4,815	2,258	94	2,124	201	84	88	24	11	11
Gabon	3,135	3,002	2,891	3,483	2,752	188	454	102	61	182	4	2	8
Ghana	2,757	3,289	3,584	4,074	1,055	22	2,670	183	193	217	18	16	16
Guatemala	2,241	2,109	2,238	2,368	1,104	143	854	164	225	231	10	11	9
Honduras	3,425	3,232	3,650	3,884	1,492	96	2,062	307	331	380	29	29	31
Hungary	18,006	17,843	19,777	22,091	823	3,930	3,465	3,750	3,891	4,638	33	36	43
India [3]	69,328	77,479	81,668	87,880	31,067	18,455	31,485	5,677	7,047	8,131	22	22	20
Indonesia	48,066	53,958	57,461	63,848	30,589	7,553	19,146	7,371	9,102	9,319	23	22	19
Jamaica	3,934	3,567	3,460	3,440	1,911	265	1,183	481	425	469	20	16	16
Jordan	7,050	6,924	6,770	6,847	2,819	435	1,008	550	507	463	19	13	11
Kenya	4,760	5,157	5,254	5,651	2,151	664	2,754	502	404	709	23	19	27
Korea, South	18,787	24,051	24,567	27,103	6,313	4,734	3,100	4,770	6,214	4,462	6	6	4
Macedonia, The Former Yugoslav Republic of	(X)	(X)	528	529	113	108	218	(X)	8	137	(X)	1	11
Madagascar	3,360	3,496	3,357	3,565	1,879	39	1,597	147	58	46	28	12	6
Malaysia	12,684	13,469	13,829	13,751	3,432	2,342	1,721	2,828	3,307	4,015	8	6	6
Mali	2,345	2,474	2,499	2,623	1,389	2	1,232	40	28	119	8	5	25
Mexico	75,981	71,068	74,892	79,097	10,361	8,630	17,075	7,843	10,615	11,711	18	21	21
Morocco	22,143	20,510	20,311	21,560	10,466	3,274	6,178	1,432	2,374	2,736	19	28	30
Nicaragua	8,245	8,999	8,770	9,006	5,801	1,298	1,312	10	111	172	2	30	36
Oman	2,400	2,340	2,315	2,608	439	1,521	162	714	583	525	12	10	10
Pakistan	16,503	18,551	20,429	22,993	10,345	410	11,494	1,388	1,914	2,804	17	19	28
Panama	3,988	3,771	3,799	3,923	674	2,599	583	141	215	303	3	3	4
Papua New Guinea	1,501	1,543	1,572	1,622	466	148	902	274	251	303	18	9	10
Philippines	24,076	25,607	27,473	29,577	14,212	413	8,346	2,899	4,243	3,519	22	22	14
Poland	39,059	42,896	41,447	39,110	29,228	362	1,957	838	1,306	2,473	5	8	13
Senegal	2,939	2,961	3,009	3,070	1,188	66	1,775	211	71	142	13	5	10
Slovenia	(X)	(X)	1,256	1,358	250	578	494	(X)	187	207	(X)	2	2
Sri Lanka	4,934	5,625	5,946	6,597	3,487	253	2,653	285	372	372	10	9	9
Sudan	9,155	8,984	8,994	9,372	5,701	1,631	2,036	23	17	-	3	4	-
Syria	14,917	15,913	16,235	16,539	14,452	-	918	1,191	174	229	22	3	4
Tanzania	5,822	5,884	5,897	6,232	3,199	63	2,643	135	209	153	25	28	18
Thailand	12,550	13,427	14,553	16,672	7,539	2,808	3,121	3,270	2,175	2,650	10	4	4
Tunisia	6,662	7,202	7,424	7,914	3,303	612	3,504	1,221	1,218	1,314	21	19	17
Turkey	38,684	40,360	44,259	48,519	8,587	13,306	9,286	6,480	6,991	7,609	26	23	23
Uganda	2,236	2,517	2,685	2,955	831	27	2,028	87	151	123	35	62	36
Uruguay	3,045	3,139	3,368	3,774	325	261	1,218	711	510	420	29	18	12
Venezuela	24,509	25,830	26,855	28,039	1,411	585	3,133	4,168	2,300	2,125	19	13	11
Yemen	5,154	5,253	5,341	5,306	2,379	80	1,207	108	99	120	4	4	4
Yugoslavia [4]	12,986	11,117	8,656	8,963	3,118	4,127	1,711	2,719	14	(NA)	9	-	(NA)
Zaire	9,006	8,948	8,769	9,281	6,095	518	2,326	137	12	1	6	1	-
Zambia	4,852	4,744	4,668	4,858	2,674	7	1,989	173	237	305	13	22	26
Zimbabwe	2,464	2,788	3,012	3,253	1,115	81	1,489	370	476	442	18	23	19

- Represents or rounds to zero.   NA Not available.   X Not applicable.   [1] Includes other types of creditors not shown separately.   [2] Debt service payments as percent of exports.   [3] Fiscal year basis.   [4] The bulk of the debt of Yugoslavian enterprises is reported as nonguaranteed.

Source: The World Bank, Washington, DC, *World Debt Tables*, periodic.

No. 1374. Net Flow of Financial Resources to Developing Countries: 1980 to 1993

[In billions of U.S. dollars. Net flow covers loans, grants, and grant-like flows minus amortization on loans. Military flows are excluded. Developing countries cover countries designated by Development Assistance Committee (DAC) as developing. Official development assistance covers all flows to developing countries and multilateral institutions provided by official agencies, including State and local governments, or by their executive agencies, which are administered with the promotion of economic development and welfare of developing countries as their main objective and whose financial terms are intended to be concessional in character with grant element of at least 25 percent. Other official flows cover export credits and portfolio investment from the official sector]

ORIGIN AND TYPE OF RESOURCE	1980	1985	1986	1987	1988	1989	1990	1991	1992	1993
DAC countries [1]	75.4	45.2	68.8	66.4	85.6	84.4	76.4	94.7	115.8	(NA)
Official development assistance .	27.3	29.4	36.7	41.6	48.1	45.7	53.0	56.7	60.9	56.0
Bilateral grants [2]	14.1	17.8	21.1	23.4	26.0	25.9	30.8	34.6	32.9	33.1
Bilateral loans	4.0	4.1	5.2	6.6	7.1	7.1	6.4	6.6	8.3	5.9
Multilateral contributions [3] . . .	9.2	7.5	10.4	11.6	15.0	12.8	15.8	15.4	19.6	17.0
Other official flows	5.3	3.4	2.1	2.0	4.9	5.8	8.6	7.1	8.9	7.5
Private flows at market terms. . .	40.4	9.4	26.7	18.8	28.3	28.8	9.8	25.5	40.1	62.0
Direct investment	10.1	6.5	11.0	21.0	25.1	30.1	26.3	22.6	28.1	34.9
Private export credits	11.5	0.8	-1.7	-2.4	-1.3	5.7	-0.4	1.1	0.6	1.4
Portfolio investment	18.7	2.1	17.4	0.3	4.4	-7.0	-16.2	1.8	11.2	25.7
Private voluntary agencies.	2.4	2.9	3.3	4.0	4.2	4.0	5.1	5.4	6.0	5.6
OPEC [4]	10.8	4.1	(NA)	(NA)	(NA)	(NA)	(NA)	(NA)	(NA)	(NA)
Official development assistance .	9.7	3.6	4.7	3.3	2.4	1.7	6.0	2.7	1.2	(NA)
Other official flows	1.1	0.5	(NA)	(NA)	(NA)	(NA)	(NA)	(NA)	(NA)	(NA)
Total net flow to developing countries, by DAC country [1]	75.4	45.2	68.8	66.4	85.6	84.4	76.4	94.7	115.8	(NA)
United States	13.9	1.8	18.2	13.8	17.5	16.4	11.1	20.8	33.5	58.3
Official development assistance	7.1	9.4	9.6	8.9	10.1	7.7	11.4	11.3	11.7	10.1
Bilateral grants [2]	3.0	7.3	7.0	6.7	6.5	6.8	8.5	12.1	8.7	8.5
Bilateral loans.	1.4	0.9	0.6	0.3	0.3	(Z)	-0.2	-2.7	-0.8	-1.2
Multilateral contributions [3] . .	2.8	1.2	2.0	1.9	3.4	0.9	3.0	1.9	3.9	2.8
Other official flows	1.1	0.2	-0.6	-1.8	1.9	-0.5	-0.4	-0.8	1.3	0.1
Private flows at market terms .	4.3	-9.3	7.5	4.4	3.2	7.3	-2.4	7.6	17.7	45.4
Direct investment	3.4	0.9	3.1	8.0	4.2	7.1	7.8	10.5	14.0	20.6
Private export credits and portfolio investment	0.9	-10.2	4.4	-3.6	-1.0	-0.3	-10.1	-2.9	3.7	24.8
Private voluntary agencies . . .	1.3	1.5	1.7	1.6	2.3	1.9	2.5	2.7	2.8	2.6
Australia.	0.9	1.2	1.1	0.9	3.6	1.5	1.5	-2.1	4.2	2.1
Austria.	0.3	0.2	0.1	0.2	0.3	0.2	0.6	0.7	0.8	0.7
Belgium	2.9	1.3	-0.8	-0.3	1.8	1.5	0.1	1.5	2.2	(NA)
Canada	3.2	1.7	1.6	2.5	3.0	2.7	3.5	4.0	4.2	5.3
Denmark	0.8	0.4	0.5	0.9	0.7	0.9	1.1	1.1	1.6	1.4
Finland	0.2	0.3	0.4	0.6	0.8	0.9	1.0	1.0	0.8	0.3
France.	11.6	8.9	9.2	8.7	5.4	5.3	5.7	6.5	10.8	(NA)
Germany [5]	10.6	5.8	7.9	8.8	11.8	12.1	13.6	13.1	8.9	15.3
Ireland.	(Z)	0.1	0.1	0.1	0.1	0.1	0.2	0.1	0.2	0.1
Italy.	4.0	2.2	2.6	2.0	5.1	5.8	3.2	7.5	6.2	2.4
Japan	6.8	11.6	14.6	20.3	18.9	22.0	17.2	24.5	16.2	15.9
Luxembourg	(NA)	(NA)	(NA)	(NA)	(NA)	(NA)	(NA)	(Z)	5.9	(NA)
Netherlands	2.4	2.6	2.8	3.2	2.7	2.5	4.0	4.4	3.4	5.6
New Zealand	0.1	0.1	0.1	0.1	0.1	0.1	0.1	0.1	0.1	0.1
Norway	0.9	0.6	0.7	0.9	0.9	0.9	1.2	1.4	1.4	1.2
Portugal.	(NA)	(NA)	(NA)	(NA)	0.1	0.1	0.3	0.2	0.4	0.3
Spain.	(NA)	(NA)	0.2	1.2	0.6	0.4	1.0	1.3	1.6	1.3
Sweden	1.9	1.4	1.7	1.8	2.3	2.3	2.8	1.8	3.0	2.5
Switzerland.	2.7	2.5	1.4	1.6	1.4	1.8	3.4	3.0	3.1	0.9
United Kingdom.	12.2	2.5	6.7	3.5	4.3	9.5	6.5	5.6	9.3	8.8

NA Not available. Z Less than $50 million. [1] Includes flows to OPEC countries (see footnote 4). DAC countries listed below. Country totals may not add to DAC total because debt forgiveness of non-official development assistance claims is not included in DAC totals. [2] Includes "grant-like" flows (i.e., loans repayable in recipients' currencies). [3] Includes capital subscriptions to multilateral organizations in the form of demand instruments as of date of issue. [4] Organization of Petroleum Exporting Countries: Algeria, Ecuador, Gabon, Iran, Iraq, Kuwait, Libya, Nigeria, Qatar, Saudi Arabia, United Arab Emirates, and Venezuela. [5] Former West Germany.

No. 1375. Per Capita Public and Private Aid to Developing Countries: 1990 to 1993

[In dollars. See headnote, table 1374. Private aid figures exclude government subsidies to voluntary agencies]

COUNTRY	OFFICIAL DEVELOPMENT ASSISTANCE			PRIVATE VOLUNTARY AID			COUNTRY	OFFICIAL DEVELOPMENT ASSISTANCE			PRIVATE VOLUNTARY AID		
	1990	1992	1993	1990	1992	1993		1990	1992	1993	1990	1992	1993
Australia.	56	58	54	3	4	5	Luxembourg	(NA)	98	129	(NA)	10	13
Austria.	51	71	68	4	10	9	Netherlands	170	181	165	16	17	18
Belgium	89	87	80	6	3	13	New Zealand . . .	28	28	28	4	3	4
Canada	93	92	83	10	10	10	Norway	284	296	234	31	30	30
Denmark	228	270	258	6	9	9	Portugal.	14	30	25	(NA)	(Z)	(NA)
Finland	170	127	70	7	2	1	Spain	25	39	30	2	2	2
France.	127	144	137	3	5	3	Sweden	235	283	203	16	15	15
Germany [1]	100	94	86	12	11	10	Switzerland.	111	165	115	17	24	21
Ireland.	16	20	23	7	8	7	United Kingdom. .	46	56	50	6	8	8
Italy.	59	71	52	(NA)	2	1	**United States. . .**	**45**	**46**	**38**	**10**	**11**	**10**
Japan	73	90	90	1	2	1							

NA Not available. Z Less than 50 cents. [1] Former West Germany.

Source of tables 1374 and 1375: Organization for Economic Cooperation and Development, Paris, France, unpublished data.

No. 1376. Military Expenditures, by Country: 1980 to 1993

[In millions of dollars, except as indicated. See also table 548. For most countries, data for expenditures and for GNP were based on local currencies which were deflated to constant 1993 local currency values before conversion to U.S. dollar equivalents. In general, the rates used for conversion are the 1993 average par/market exchange rates as supplied by the International Bank for Reconstruction and Development]

| COUNTRY | CURRENT DOLLARS | | | | CONSTANT (1993) DOLLARS | | | | |
| | | | | | | | 1993 | | |
	1980	1990	1992	1993	1990	1992	Total	Per capita (dollars)	Percent of GNP
United States......	144,000	306,200	305,100	297,600	333,900	311,800	297,600	1,153	5
Algeria [1].........	940	845	910	1,360	922	930	1,360	50	3
Argentina.........	1,559	3,386	4,447	4,251	3,692	4,544	4,251	127	2
Australia.........	3,226	5,489	6,616	7,441	5,986	6,760	7,441	417	3
Austria...........	820	1,704	1,702	1,730	1,858	1,739	1,730	219	1
Belgium..........	2,951	4,492	3,863	3,746	4,899	3,947	3,746	373	2
Brazil...........	1,899	8,084	5,653	5,852	8,816	5,776	5,852	37	1
Bulgaria [1]........	3,993	3,887	935	1,010	4,239	955	1,010	114	3
Canada..........	5,176	9,990	10,020	10,300	10,890	10,240	10,300	371	2
Chile [2]...........	449	[1]999	992	1,002	[1]1,090	1,013	1,002	73	2
China...........	16,370	49,620	53,700	56,170	54,110	54,870	56,170	48	3
Cuba [2]...........	1,140	1,400	500	426	1,527	511	426	39	2
Czech Republic.....	(NA)	(NA)	(NA)	2,040	(NA)	(NA)	2,040	196	3
Denmark.........	1,454	2,464	2,629	2,682	2,687	2,686	2,682	518	2
Egypt [1]..........	2,923	1,541	1,578	1,670	1,680	1,612	1,670	28	4
El Salvador [1]......	120	197	120	100	215	122	100	18	1
Finland..........	909	1,376	1,758	1,710	1,500	1,796	1,710	339	2
France...........	21,230	40,490	42,230	42,590	44,150	43,150	42,590	740	3
Germany [3]........	22,400	[1]39,370	39,890	36,650	[1]42,930	40,760	36,650	454	2
Greece	1,779	3,776	4,071	4,070	4,118	4,159	4,070	389	6
Hungary [1]........	2,832	1,277	1,387	1,261	1,393	1,417	1,261	122	2
India............	3,608	6,398	7,500	8,471	6,977	7,663	8,471	9	3
Indonesia........	1,093	1,657	1,833	2,031	1,807	1,872	2,031	10	2
Iran [1]..........	2,624	6,308	3,853	4,857	6,878	3,937	4,857	78	4
Iraq [1]...........	(NA)	11,340	(NA)	(NA)	12,370	(NA)	(NA)	(NA)	(NA)
Israel...........	6,654	6,562	6,493	6,290	7,155	6,634	6,290	1,279	9
Italy............	10,110	19,110	19,950	20,570	20,840	20,380	20,570	354	2
Japan...........	12,330	35,880	40,450	41,730	39,130	41,330	41,730	335	1
Korea, North [1].....	4,380	5,940	5,500	(NA)	6,477	5,620	(NA)	(NA)	23
Korea, South	3,821	10,390	11,390	11,930	11,330	11,640	11,930	267	4
Kuwait..........	892	[1]13,020	18,780	3,545	[1]14,200	19,190	3,545	2,088	13
Malaysia	664	1,189	2,403	2,642	1,297	2,456	2,642	140	4
Mexico..........	456	[1]1,329	1,629	1,656	1,450	1,664	1,656	18	1
Morocco [1]	763	1,251	1,514	1,193	1,364	1,547	1,193	43	5
Netherlands	4,048	6,917	7,206	7,055	7,543	7,363	7,055	462	2
Nicaragua [1]	53	(NA)	42	37	(NA)	43	37	9	3
Nigeria..........	447	214	189	210	233	193	210	2	1
Norway	1,320	2,837	3,335	3,232	3,094	3,407	3,232	752	3
Oman	1,059	1,707	1,767	1,638	1,861	1,806	1,638	997	22
Pakistan.........	777	2,716	2,867	3,111	2,962	2,929	3,111	25	6
Peru [1]	1,457	664	675	696	724	689	696	30	2
Philippines	501	1,058	1,012	1,200	1,153	1,034	1,200	17	2
Poland [1].........	9,644	8,752	4,152	4,334	9,544	4,242	4,334	113	2
Portugal.........	858	2,099	2,214	2,192	2,289	2,262	2,192	209	3
Romania [1]	4,587	3,869	2,824	1,676	4,219	2,885	1,676	72	3
Russia..........	(NA)	(NA)	142,300	113,800	(NA)	145,400	113,800	762	15
Saudi Arabia......	14,990	[1]22,870	34,550	20,480	[1]24,930	35,310	20,480	1,163	16
Singapore	533	1,766	2,543	2,700	1,926	2,599	2,700	955	5
Slovakia.........	(NA)	(NA)	(NA)	843	(NA)	(NA)	843	157	2
Slovenia.........	(NA)	(NA)	341	195	(NA)	348	195	99	1
South Africa	2,563	[1]4,446	3,236	2,896	[1]4,848	3,306	2,896	68	3
Spain	4,560	7,924	7,458	8,289	8,641	7,621	8,289	211	2
Sweden	3,257	4,661	4,708	5,011	5,083	4,810	5,011	574	3
Switzerland.......	2,461	4,674	4,224	4,061	5,097	4,316	4,061	581	2
Syria [1] [2]........	1,936	4,435	(NA)	(NA)	4,836	(NA)	(NA)	(NA)	(NA)
Taiwan..........	3,222	9,052	10,450	10,420	[1]9,870	10,680	10,420	494	5
Thailand.........	1,011	2,197	2,907	3,511	2,396	2,971	3,511	60	3
Turkey..........	1,635	4,866	6,094	7,075	5,306	6,227	7,075	116	6
United Arab Emirates .	1,724	[1]2,590	2,098	1,771	[1]2,824	2,143	1,771	666	5
United Kingdom.....	22,080	35,240	34,680	34,020	38,420	35,430	34,020	587	4
Venezuela ·.......	317	927	1,475	1,029	[1]1,011	1,507	1,029	51	2

NA Not available.   [1] Estimated.   [2] Data probably omit a major share of total military expenditures, probably including most arms acquisitions.   [3] Prior to 1991, data for former West Germany.

Source: U.S. Arms Control and Disarmament Agency, *World Military Expenditures and Arms Transfers*, annual.

No. 1377. Armed Forces Personnel, by Country: 1980 to 1993

[**Personnel data as of July.** Armed Forces refer to active-duty military personnel, including paramilitary forces where those forces resemble regular units in their organization, equipment, training, or mission. Reserve forces are not included]

COUNTRY	ARMED FORCES PERSONNEL (1,000)						ARMED FORCES PER 1,000 POPULATION					
	1980	1985	1990	1991	1992	1993	1980	1985	1990	1991	1992	1993
United States	2,050	2,244	2,181	2,115	1,919	1,815	9.0	9.4	8.7	8.4	7.5	7.0
Algeria	101	170	126	126	139	139	5.4	7.7	5.0	4.8	5.2	5.1
Argentina.	155	129	85	70	65	65	5.5	4.2	2.6	2.1	2.0	1.9
Australia	71	70	68	66	68	68	4.9	4.4	4.0	3.9	3.9	3.8
Austria	40	40	43	44	52	(NA)	5.3	5.3	5.6	5.6	6.6	(NA)
Belgium.	108	107	106	101	79	70	11.0	10.9	10.6	10.1	7.9	7.0
Brazil	450	496	295	295	296	296	3.7	3.6	2.0	1.9	1.9	1.9
Bulgaria	188	189	129	107	99	52	21.2	21.2	14.4	12.0	11.2	5.9
Canada.	82	83	87	86	82	76	3.4	3.3	3.3	3.2	3.0	2.7
Chile.	116	124	95	90	92	92	10.5	10.3	7.2	6.8	6.8	6.7
China	4,650	4,100	3,500	3,200	3,160	3,031	4.7	3.9	3.1	2.8	2.7	2.6
Cuba	220	297	297	297	175	175	22.8	29.4	27.9	27.6	16.1	16.0
Czech Republic	(NA)	(NA)	(NA)	(NA)	(NA)	107	(NA)	(NA)	(NA)	(NA)	(NA)	10.3
Denmark.	33	29	31	30	28	27	6.4	5.7	6.0	5.8	5.4	5.2
Egypt	447	466	434	434	424	424	10.7	9.5	7.8	7.6	7.3	7.1
El Salvador	16	48	55	60	49	49	3.4	10.0	10.4	11.1	8.9	8.7
Finland	36	40	31	32	33	31	7.5	8.2	6.2	6.4	6.5	6.1
France	575	563	542	542	522	506	10.7	10.2	9.7	9.5	9.1	8.8
Germany [1]	490	495	2545	2457	442	398	8.0	8.1	8.6	5.7	5.5	4.9
Greece	186	201	201	205	208	213	19.3	20.2	19.9	20.0	20.1	20.3
Honduras	14	21	18	17	17	17	3.9	5.0	3.8	3.5	3.4	3.3
Hungary	120	117	94	87	78	(NA)	11.2	11.0	9.1	8.4	7.5	(NA)
India.	1,104	1,260	1,262	1,265	1,265	1,265	1.6	1.6	1.5	1.5	1.4	1.4
Indonesia	250	278	283	278	283	271	1.6	1.6	1.5	1.5	1.5	1.4
Iran	305	345	440	465	528	528	7.8	7.5	7.7	7.9	8.7	8.5
Iraq	430	788	1,390	475	407	407	32.5	50.2	75.4	26.5	22.0	21.2
Israel	196	195	190	190	181	181	52.4	49.6	44.2	41.9	38.1	36.8
Italy	500	504	493	473	471	450	8.9	8.8	8.5	8.2	8.1	7.8
Japan.	242	241	250	250	242	242	2.1	2.0	2.0	2.0	1.9	1.9
Korea, North	700	784	1,200	1,200	1,200	1,200	38.9	40.0	56.0	55.0	54.0	53.0
Korea, South	600	600	650	750	750	750	15.7	14.7	15.0	17.2	17.0	16.8
Kuwait	12	16	7	10	12	12	8.8	9.3	3.3	11.9	8.7	7.1
Malaysia	83	2110	130	128	128	115	6.0	27.1	7.4	7.1	7.0	6.1
Mexico	120	140	175	175	175	175	1.7	1.8	2.1	2.0	2.0	1.9
Morocco	117	165	195	195	195	195	5.7	7.1	7.5	7.3	7.1	7.0
Netherlands.	107	103	104	104	90	86	7.6	7.1	7.0	6.9	5.9	5.6
Nicaragua	24	74	28	20	15	15	8.6	23.5	7.7	5.3	3.9	3.8
Nigeria	150	134	94	94	76	76	1.7	1.8	1.1	1.1	0.8	0.8
Norway	40	36	51	41	42	42	8.7	8.7	12.0	9.6	9.8	9.8
Oman.	15	25	32	29	35	35	15.2	20.2	21.6	18.9	22.0	21.3
Pakistan	467	483	550	565	580	580	5.5	4.9	4.8	4.8	4.8	4.6
Peru	151	128	125	123	112	112	8.7	6.5	5.7	5.5	4.9	4.8
Philippines.	155	115	109	107	107	107	3.0	2.0	1.7	1.6	1.6	1.5
Poland	408	439	313	305	270	180	11.5	11.8	8.2	8.0	7.0	4.7
Portugal	88	102	87	86	80	68	9.0	10.0	8.4	8.3	7.7	6.5
Qatar	6	27	11	11	8	8	26.0	220.3	24.4	23.5	16.5	16.0
Romania	211	237	126	201	172	167	9.5	10.4	5.4	8.7	7.4	7.2
Russia	(NA)	(NA)	(NA)	(NA)	2,030	2,250	(NA)	(NA)	(NA)	(NA)	13.6	15.1
Saudi Arabia	79	280	146	191	172	172	7.8	25.9	9.0	11.6	10.1	9.8
Singapore	50	56	56	56	56	56	20.7	21.9	20.6	20.3	20.1	19.8
Slovakia	(NA)	(NA)	(NA)	(NA)	(NA)	33	(NA)	(NA)	(NA)	(NA)	(NA)	6.1
Slovenia	(NA)	(NA)	(NA)	(NA)	15	12	(NA)	(NA)	(NA)	(NA)	7.6	6.1
South Africa.	70	95	85	80	72	72	2.3	2.7	2.1	2.0	1.7	1.7
Spain	356	314	263	246	198	204	9.5	8.2	6.7	6.3	5.1	5.2
Sweden.	70	269	65	63	45	44	8.4	28.3	7.6	7.3	5.2	5.0
Switzerland	23	223	22	22	31	31	3.6	23.5	3.2	3.2	4.5	4.4
Syria	250	402	408	408	408	408	28.8	38.2	32.0	30.7	29.5	28.5
Taiwan	465	444	370	370	360	442	26.1	23.0	18.1	17.9	17.2	21.0
Thailand	234	235	283	283	283	295	5.0	4.5	5.0	5.0	4.9	5.0
Turkey	717	814	769	804	704	686	15.9	16.0	13.5	13.8	11.8	11.3
United Arab Emirates.	44	44	66	66	55	55	44.0	28.0	29.3	27.6	21.8	20.7
United Kingdom	330	334	308	301	293	271	5.9	5.9	5.4	5.2	5.1	4.7
Venezuela	55	71	75	73	75	75	3.7	4.3	4.0	3.8	3.8	3.7
Vietnam	900	1,027	1,052	1,041	857	857	16.9	16.9	15.5	15.1	12.2	11.9

NA Not available. [1] Prior to 1991, data for former West Germany. [2] Estimated.

Source: U.S. Arms Control and Disarmament Agency, *World Military Expenditures and Arms Transfers*, annual.

Figure 31.1
**Value of Shipments—
Selected Industries: 1995**

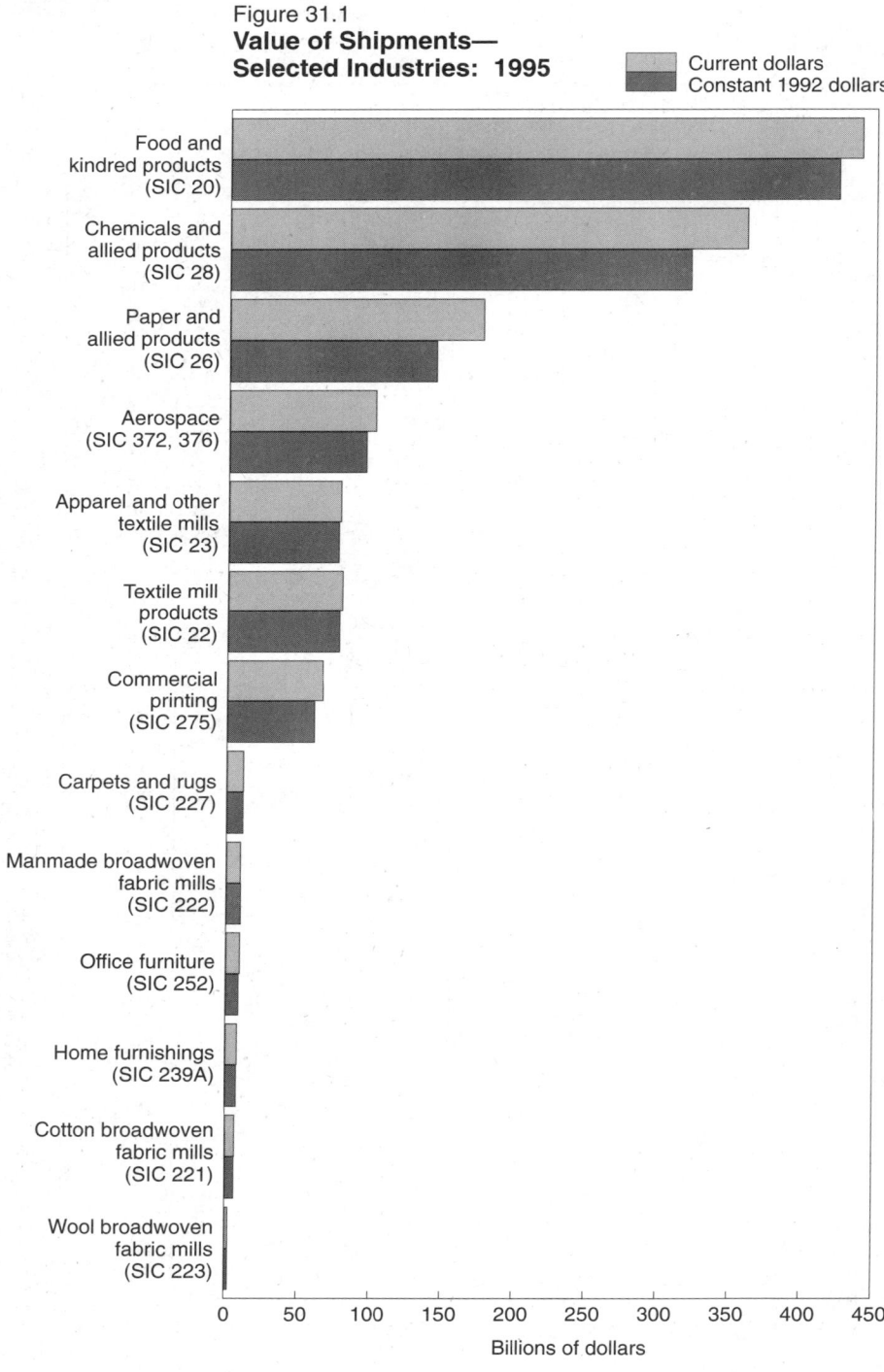

Current dollars
Constant 1992 dollars

Source: Chart prepared by U.S. Bureau of the Census. For data, see section 31.

Industrial Outlook

This new section presents statistics for major manufacturing groups and selected products. The 199 industries covered were among those featured in the *U.S. Industrial Outlook* published by the Department of Commerce's International Trade Administration (ITA) for many years. The 1994 edition of the *U.S. Industrial Outlook* was the last volume published in that series of publications.

The 92 tables combine industry and product shipments data from the *1992 Census of Manufactures* and estimates for 1993 and 1994 by ITA's analysts. The estimates were prepared in the spring of 1995 prior to the release of *1993 Annual Survey of Manufactures* results. The tables also contain employment, wages, capital expenditures, import and export data.

The value of shipments shown in these tables are expressed both in "current" and "constant" dollars. Current dollars show the value of the goods produced in the particular year referred to. Constant dollars, or sometimes referred to as changes in real dollars, show the value of a year's output in the prices of a base year so you can accurately compare real changes in output levels over time. In these tables the base year was 1987. ITA uses the Producer Price Index (for more information, see text, section 15) from the Bureau of Labor Statistics at the product level to deflate the current dollar shipments.

The tables distinguish between industry and product shipments. Shipments data are collected separately for individual factories, or establishments, and not at the company level. Most factories make a variety of products. For statistical purposes, each is an establishment classified in the industry identified with its major product. For instance, the total output of a plant may consist of 80 percent tires and 20 percent hose and belting. In this case, the total output of the plant would be credited to the tire industry. The total output of all plants so classified would make up the "industry shipments" of the tire industry in this case. The value of all tires shipped by all establishments is aggregated to derive "product shipments."

Trade data shown in the tables were tabulated following the Bureau of the Census' trade concordance, as adjusted by the ITA's analyst, to approximate the Standard Industrial Classification (SIC) industry grouping. The trade figures reflect final 1993 estimates and preliminary 1994 data. Exports are limited to domestic exports and are valued "free alongside ship" or f.a.s. Imports are restricted to goods imported for consumption and are on a customs value basis.

No. 1378. Recent Trends in Food and Kindred Products (SIC 20): 1989 to 1995

ITEM	Unit	1989	1990	1991	1992	1993	1994	1995 [1]
INDUSTRY DATA								
Value of shipments [2]	Mil. dol. . .	364,403	384,009	387,601	407,157	422,216	430,994	439,793
Value of shipments (1992 dollars)	Mil. dol. . .	375,914	383,126	388,301	407,157	415,101	419,195	423,802
Total employment	1,000. . . .	1,459	1,470	1,475	1,505	1,520	1,511	1,515
Production workers	1,000. . . .	1,049	1,061	1,070	1,101	1,118	1,112	1,118
Average hourly earnings	Dollar . . .	9.68	9.82	10.10	10.40	10.58	10.74	11.02
Capital expenditures	Mil. dol. . .	8,330	8,858	9,362	9,899	9,389	10,094	(NA)
PRODUCT DATA								
Value of shipments [3]	Mil. dol. . .	340,733	359,713	363,943	382,889	397,633	405,521	413,853
Value of shipments (1992 dollars)	Mil. dol. . .	351,223	358,812	364,419	382,889	391,063	394,445	398,780
TRADE DATA								
Value of imports	Mil. dol. . .	18,744	19,834	19,779	20,869	20,859	22,802	23,273
Value of exports	Mil. dol. . .	17,070	18,473	19,918	22,504	22,937	25,587	28,123

NA Not available. [1] Estimate, except exports and imports. [2] Value of all products and services sold by establishments in the food and kindred products industry. [3] Value of products classified in the food and kindred products industry produced by all industries.

Source: U.S. Department of Commerce, Bureau of the Census, International Trade Administration (ITA). Estimates by ITA.

No. 1379. Recent Trends in Higher Value Added Foods and Beverages and Lower Value Foods and Feeds: 1989 to 1995

ITEM	Unit	1989	1990	1991	1992	1993	1994	1995 [1]
HIGHER VALUE ADDED FOODS AND BEVERAGES [2]								
Industry data:								
Value of shipments [3]	Mil. dol. . .	176,415	185,953	192,654	201,198	209,323	216,731	223,113
Value of shipments (1992 dollars)	Mil. dol. . .	189,215	192,460	195,556	201,198	206,662	210,096	211,376
Total employment	1,000. . .	820	816	814	828	836	827	819
Production workers	1,000. . .	558	556	557	572	578	572	567
Average hourly earnings	Dollar . . .	10.71	10.95	11.27	11.55	11.83	12.08	12.37
Capital expenditures	Mil. dol. . .	5,236	5,474	5,969	6,385	5,935	6,247	(NA)
Product data:								
Value of shipments [4]	Mil. dol. . .	167,143	175,899	182,570	191,278	197,567	204,419	210,694
Value of shipments (1992 dollars)	Mil. dol. . .	179,165	181,908	185,227	191,278	195,237	198,401	199,610
Trade data:								
Value of imports	Mil. dol. . .	8,430	9,075	8,719	9,724	9,456	10,356	11,328
Value of exports	Mil. dol. . .	4,044	4,852	5,725	6,660	7,501	8,632	9,162
LOWER VALUE ADDED FOODS AND FEEDS [5]								
Industry data:								
Value of shipments [3]	Mil. dol. . .	187,988	198,056	194,947	205,959	212,894	214,263	216,680
Value of shipments (1992 dollars)	Mil. dol. . .	186,700	190,666	192,745	205,959	208,438	209,099	212,426
Total employment	1,000. . .	639	654	662	677	684	685	697
Production workers	1,000. . .	491	505	513	529	540	540	551
Average hourly earnings	Dollar . . .	8.56	8.63	8.86	9.22	9.29	9.39	9.67
Capital expenditures	Mil. dol. . .	3,094	3,384	3,393	3,514	3,454	3,848	(NA)
Product data:								
Value of shipments [4]	Mil. dol. . .	173,590	183,814	181,373	191,611	200,065	201,102	203,159
Value of shipments (1992 dollars)	Mil. dol. . .	172,059	176,904	179,192	191,611	195,826	196,043	199,170
Trade data:								
Value of imports	Mil. dol. . .	10,314	10,759	11,060	11,145	11,403	12,446	11,945
Value of exports	Mil. dol. . .	13,025	13,621	14,193	15,844	15,436	16,956	18,961

NA Not available. [1] Estimate, except exports and imports. [2] SIC's 2023, 24, 32-38, 43, 45, 47, 51-53, 64-68, 82, 84-86, 95, 96, 98, and 99. This aggregation includes those industries defined as higher value added. [3] Value of all products and services sold by establishments in this industry. [4] Value of products classified in this industry produced by all industries. [5] SIC 20 excluding 2023, 24, 32-38, 43, 45, 47, 51-53, 64-68, 82, 84-86, 95, 96, 98, and 99. This aggregation includes those industries defined as lower value added.

Source: U.S. Department of Commerce, Bureau of the Census, International Trade Administration (ITA). Estimates by ITA.

No. 1380. Recent Trends in Red Meat and Poultry Slaughtering and Processing: 1989 to 1995

ITEM	Unit	1989	1990	1991	1992	1993	1994	1995 [1]
RED MEAT (SIC 2011, 2013)								
Industry data:								
Value of shipments [2]	Mil. dol. . .	64,058	69,849	67,687	70,407	73,941	70,701	69,621
Value of shipments (1992 dollars) . . .	Mil. dol. . .	65,043	64,208	64,304	70,407	71,389	71,609	72,038
Total employment	1,000. . . .	199	200	200	208	209	204	210
Production workers	1,000. . . .	160	161	162	171	173	169	173
Average hourly earnings	Dollar . . .	8.44	8.58	8.68	8.98	9.06	9.43	9.71
Capital expenditures	Mil. dol. . .	670	758	749	723	703	699	(NA)
Product data:								
Value of shipments [3]	Mil. dol. . .	58,343	64,079	62,676	64,351	68,216	64,839	63,856
Value of shipments (1992 dollars) . . .	Mil. dol. . .	59,214	58,874	59,535	64,351	65,856	65,679	66,073
Trade data:								
Value of imports	Mil. dol. . .	2,775	3,162	3,138	2,924	3,067	2,979	2,657
Value of exports	Mil. dol. . .	4,078	4,364	4,348	4,807	4,698	5,273	6,303
POULTRY SLAUGHTERING AND PROCESSING (SIC 2015)								
Industry data:								
Value of shipments [2]	Mil. dol. . .	20,283	20,928	21,703	23,757	25,501	27,415	28,513
Value of shipments (1992 dollars) . . .	Mil. dol. . .	18,422	19,931	21,404	23,757	24,783	25,912	27,104
Total employment	1,000. . . .	164	177	190	194	205	216	224
Production workers	1,000. . . .	147	158	168	173	184	193	201
Average hourly earnings	Dollar . . .	6.53	6.63	6.96	7.37	7.40	7.49	7.64
Capital expenditures	Mil. dol. . .	500	498	587	466	555	594	(NA)
Product data:								
Value of shipments [3]	Mil. dol. . .	19,718	20,353	21,246	23,592	24,983	27,027	28,110
Value of shipments (1992 dollars) . . .	Mil. dol. . .	17,909	19,383	20,953	23,592	24,279	25,546	26,721
Trade data:								
Value of imports	Mil. dol. . .	42.7	31.8	37.3	27.4	31.8	27.2	32.5
Value of exports	Mil. dol. . .	555	717	879	990	1,157	1,633	2,097

NA Not available. [1] Estimate, except exports and imports. [2] Value of all products and services sold by establishments in this industry. [3] Value of products classified in this industry produced by all industries.
Source: U.S. Department of Commerce, Bureau of the Census, International Trade Administration (ITA). Estimates by ITA.

No. 1381. Recent Trends in Alcoholic Beverages (SIC 2082, 2084, 2085): 1989 to 1995

ITEM	Unit	1989	1990	1991	1992	1993	1994	1995 [1]
INDUSTRY DATA								
Value of shipments [2]	Mil. dol. . .	21,462	22,318	23,167	25,035	24,739	24,983	26,061
2082 Malt beverages	Mil. dol. . .	14,321	15,186	15,925	17,340	16,656	16,795	17,427
2084 Wines & brandy	Mil. dol. . .	3,539	3,658	3,586	4,301	4,514	4,301	4,530
2085 Distilled liquor	Mil. dol. . .	3,602	3,474	3,656	3,394	3,569	3,888	4,104
Value of shipments (1992 dollars)	Mil. dol. . .	23,538	23,986	23,602	25,035	24,734	25,315	25,599
2082 Malt beverages	Mil. dol. . .	15,333	16,259	16,217	17,340	16,791	17,314	17,340
2084 Wines & brandy	Mil. dol. . .	3,932	3,863	3,666	4,301	4,465	4,267	4,459
2085 Distilled liquor	Mil. dol. . .	4,273	3,864	3,719	3,394	3,478	3,734	3,800
Total employment	1,000. . . .	53.4	54.4	53.7	55.6	56.4	53.8	53.0
2082 Malt beverages	1,000. . . .	32.0	32.6	32.4	34.5	35.3	33.5	32.6
2084 Wines & brandy	1,000. . . .	13.9	14.4	13.9	14.0	14.1	13.7	13.8
2085 Distilled liquor	1,000. . . .	7.5	7.4	7.4	7.1	7.0	6.6	6.6
Production workers	1,000. . . .	35.7	35.8	35.5	36.7	37.0	34.9	34.6
2082 Malt beverages	1,000. . . .	23.3	23.5	23.5	25.1	25.3	23.6	23.2
2084 Wines & brandy	1,000. . . .	7.1	7.1	6.8	6.5	6.6	6.6	6.7
2085 Distilled liquor	1,000. . . .	5.3	5.2	5.2	5.1	5.1	4.7	4.7
Average hourly earnings	Dollar . . .	18.26	18.33	19.06	19.83	19.81	20.15	20.65
2082 Malt beverages	Dollar . . .	21.26	21.34	22.30	22.89	22.71	23.01	23.57
2084 Wines & brandy	Dollar . . .	11.97	11.95	12.13	12.68	12.80	13.53	13.86
2085 Distilled liquor	Dollar . . .	13.74	13.78	14.23	15.05	15.49	15.43	15.81
Capital expenditures	Mil. dol. . .	763	687	805	736	668	754	(NA)
2082 Malt beverages	Mil. dol. . .	602	543	649	565	479	564	(NA)
2084 Wines & brandy	Mil. dol. . .	123	108	97	115	146	151	(NA)
2085 Distilled liquor	Mil. dol. . .	37.6	36.4	59.1	56.3	42.1	39.7	(NA)
PRODUCT DATA								
Value of shipments [3]	Mil. dol. . .	20,961	21,864	22,758	24,607	24,324	24,370	25,417
2082 Malt beverages	Mil. dol. . .	14,195	15,111	15,887	17,302	16,629	16,714	17,343
2084 Wines & brandy	Mil. dol. . .	3,301	3,505	3,467	4,050	4,355	4,196	4,420
2085 Distilled liquor	Mil. dol. . .	3,465	3,248	3,404	3,255	3,340	3,460	3,654
Value of shipments (1992 dollars)	Mil. dol. . .	22,976	23,493	23,186	24,607	24,326	24,718	24,990
2082 Malt beverages	Mil. dol. . .	15,198	16,179	16,178	17,302	16,763	17,231	17,257
2084 Wines & brandy	Mil. dol. . .	3,668	3,701	3,545	4,050	4,308	4,163	4,350
2085 Distilled liquor	Mil. dol. . .	4,111	3,613	3,463	3,255	3,255	3,324	3,383
TRADE DATA								
Value of imports	Mil. dol. . .	3,165	3,374	3,065	3,527	3,387	3,668	3,980
2082 Malt beverages	Mil. dol. . .	870	939	840	881	961	1,072	1,192
2084 Wines & brandy	Mil. dol. . .	1,130	1,129	1,094	1,347	1,152	1,268	1,402
2085 Distilled liquor	Mil. dol. . .	1,165	1,305	1,131	1,299	1,274	1,328	1,386
Value of exports	Mil. dol. . .	516	585	661	751	777	983	1,250
2082 Malt beverages	Mil. dol. . .	174	178	207	221	234	391	526
2084 Wines & brandy	Mil. dol. . .	104	134	155	182	184	201	246
2085 Distilled liquor	Mil. dol. . .	238	273	300	347	359	390	478

NA Not available. [1] Estimate, except exports and imports. [2] Value of all products and services sold by establishments in the alcoholic beverages industry. [3] Value of products classified in the alcoholic beverages industry produced by all industries.
Source: U.S. Department of Commerce, Bureau of the Census, International Trade Administration (ITA). Estimates by ITA.

No. 1382. Recent Trends in Textile Mill Products (SIC 22): 1989 to 1995

ITEM	Unit	1989	1990	1991	1992	1993	1994	1995 [1]
INDUSTRY DATA								
Value of shipments [2]	Mil. dol.	67,321	65,951	65,706	70,518	73,955	78,267	79,250
Value of shipments (1992 dollars)	Mil. dol.	69,796	67,076	66,256	70,518	74,409	78,669	77,276
Total employment	1,000.	653	633	598	614	610	625	615
Production workers	1,000.	566	548	515	527	524	534	528
Average hourly earnings	Dollar	7.93	7.93	8.08	8.59	8.92	9.27	9.55
PRODUCT DATA								
Value of shipments [3]	Mil. dol.	65,747	64,986	65,266	70,008	73,216	77,632	78,607
Value of shipments (1992 dollars)	Mil. dol.	68,213	66,125	65,807	70,008	73,662	78,060	76,675
TRADE DATA								
Value of imports	Mil. dol.	4,786	4,888	5,375	5,843	6,161	6,534	6,965
Value of exports	Mil. dol.	2,803	3,636	4,101	4,467	4,687	5,151	5,696

[1] Estimate, except exports and imports. [2] Value of all products and services sold by establishments in the textile mill products industry. [3] Value of products classified in the textile mill products industry produced by all industries.

Source: U.S. Department of Commerce, Bureau of the Census, International Trade Administration (ITA). Estimates by ITA.

No. 1383. Recent Trends in Cotton, Manmade, and Wool Broadwoven Fabric Mills: 1989 to 1995

ITEM	Unit	1989	1990	1991	1992	1993	1994	1995 [1]
COTTON BROADWOVEN FABRIC MILLS (SIC 221)								
Industry data:								
Value of shipments [2]	Mil. dol.	5,457	5,325	5,695	5,814	5,990	6,262	6,375
Value of shipments (1992 dollars)	Mil. dol.	5,780	5,558	5,871	5,814	5,925	6,116	5,986
Total employment	1,000.	67.2	62.5	65.9	55.9	55.0	55.7	55.0
Production workers	1,000.	60.3	55.6	58.8	50.2	49.9	50.6	49.5
Average hourly earnings	Dollar	8.17	8.19	8.35	8.92	9.38	9.83	10.15
Product data:								
Value of shipments [3]	Mil. dol.	5,337	5,286	5,498	5,708	5,863	6,005	6,113
Value of shipments (1992 dollars)	Mil. dol.	5,653	5,518	5,668	5,708	5,799	5,864	5,740
Trade data:								
Value of imports	Mil. dol.	1,063	1,120	1,277	1,475	1,525	1,482	1,614
Value of exports	Mil. dol.	369	503	542	579	621	704	813
MANMADE BROADWOVEN FABRIC MILLS (SIC 222)								
Industry data:								
Value of shipments [2]	Mil. dol.	8,690	8,578	8,315	8,794	9,145	9,424	9,485
Value of shipments (1992 dollars)	Mil. dol.	8,996	8,735	8,511	8,794	9,303	9,816	9,679
Total employment	1,000.	88.4	85.3	78.3	87.4	85.8	80.7	80.0
Production workers	1,000.	77.6	74.6	68.5	76.9	75.0	70.6	70.2
Average hourly earnings	Dollar	8.45	8.55	8.68	9.21	9.46	9.88	10.20
Product data:								
Value of shipments [3]	Mil. dol.	8,434	8,133	7,898	8,500	8,853	9,431	9,492
Value of shipments (1992 dollars)	Mil. dol.	8,731	8,282	8,084	8,500	9,006	9,824	9,686
Trade data:								
Value of imports	Mil. dol.	1,247	1,241	1,381	1,468	1,541	1,586	1,550
Value of exports	Mil. dol.	658	756	790	891	974	1,049	1,099
WOOL BROADWOVEN FABRIC MILLS (SIC 223)								
Industry data:								
Value of shipments [2]	Mil. dol.	2,068	1,798	1,804	1,612	1,681	1,810	1,828
Value of shipments (1992 dollars)	Mil. dol.	1,996	1,724	1,747	1,612	1,683	1,810	1,764
Total employment	1,000.	17.2	15.7	15.3	13.7	13.8	14.6	14.0
Production workers	1,000.	14.8	13.5	13.2	11.8	11.9	12.6	12.1
Average hourly earnings	Dollar	8.19	8.09	8.03	8.46	8.87	9.70	9.98
Product data:								
Value of shipments [3]	Mil. dol.	1,658	1,443	1,492	1,388	1,502	1,462	1,476
Value of shipments (1992 dollars)	Mil. dol.	1,600	1,383	1,444	1,388	1,504	1,462	1,425
Trade data:								
Value of imports	Mil. dol.	237	241	247	240	230	242	252
Value of exports	Mil. dol.	39.2	49.0	62.4	99.3	84.6	87.2	114.0

[1] Estimate, except exports and imports. [2] Value of all products and services sold by establishments in this industry. [3] Value of products classified in this industry produced by all industries.

Source: U.S. Department of Commerce, Bureau of the Census, International Trade Administration (ITA). Estimates by ITA.

No. 1384. Recent Trends in Broadwoven Fabric Mills (SIC 221, 222, 223): 1989 to 1995

ITEM	Unit	1989	1990	1991	1992	1993	1994	1995 [1]
INDUSTRY DATA								
Value of shipments [2]	Mil. dol. . .	16,215	15,701	15,814	16,220	16,816	17,496	17,688
Value of shipments (1992 dollars)	Mil. dol. . .	16,773	16,017	16,128	16,220	16,911	17,742	17,429
Total employment	1,000. . . .	173	164	160	157	155	151	149
Production workers	1,000. . . .	153	144	141	139	137	134	132
Average hourly earnings	Dollar . . .	8.31	8.37	8.48	9.04	9.38	9.85	10.16
PRODUCT DATA								
Value of shipments [3]	Mil. dol. . .	15,429	14,862	14,888	15,596	16,218	16,898	17,082
Value of shipments (1992 dollars)	Mil. dol. . .	15,985	15,184	15,196	15,596	16,309	17,150	16,851
TRADE DATA								
Value of imports	Mil. dol. . .	2,547	2,602	2,905	3,183	3,295	3,310	3,417
Value of exports	Mil. dol. . .	1,066	1,308	1,395	1,569	1,680	1,840	2,026

[1] Estimate, except exports and imports.   [2] Value of all products and services sold by establishments in the food and kindred products industry.   [3] Value of products classified in the food and kindred products industry produced by all industries.

Source: U.S. Department of Commerce, Bureau of the Census, International Trade Administration (ITA). Estimates by ITA.

No. 1385. Recent Trends in Carpets and Rugs, Weft, Lace, and Knit, and Yarn Spinning Mills: 1989 to 1995

ITEM	Unit	1989	1990	1991	1992	1993	1994	1995 [1]
CARPETS AND RUGS (SIC 227)								
Industry data:								
Value of shipments [2]	Mil. dol. . .	10,220	10,038	8,988	9,831	10,234	10,961	11,110
Value of shipments (1992 dollars)	Mil. dol. . .	10,344	10,059	8,952	9,831	10,286	10,896	10,903
Total employment	1,000. . . .	54.5	51.8	48.5	49.4	50.6	55.2	55.5
Production workers	1,000. . . .	43.4	41.0	37.8	38.9	39.6	43.0	43.6
Average hourly earnings	Dollar . . .	7.97	7.95	8.26	8.83	9.17	9.54	9.85
Product data:								
Value of shipments [3]	Mil. dol. . .	9,826	9,611	8,555	9,518	9,953	10,538	10,681
Value of shipments (1992 dollars)	Mil. dol. . .	9,945	9,630	8,521	9,518	10,003	10,475	10,482
Trade data:								
Value of imports	Mil. dol. . .	604	590	584	700	660	736	843
Value of exports	Mil. dol. . .	366	534	683	705	698	667	632
WEFT, LACE, AND WARP KNIT FABRIC MILLS (SIC 2257, 2258)								
Industry data:								
Value of shipments [2]	Mil. dol. . .	6,576	5,887	6,399	7,234	7,526	8,166	8,825
Value of shipments (1992 dollars)	Mil. dol. . .	6,726	5,912	6,414	7,234	7,644	8,335	8,817
Total employment	1,000. . . .	56.0	53.0	53.2	61.7	60.6	62.3	62.9
Production workers	1,000. . . .	47.8	44.7	44.8	51.8	50.6	52.3	52.9
Average hourly earnings	Dollar . . .	8.22	8.09	8.08	8.42	8.90	9.46	9.75
Product data:								
Value of shipments [3]	Mil. dol. . .	6,575	5,923	6,542	7,436	7,478	8,109	8,763
Value of shipments (1992 dollars)	Mil. dol. . .	6,730	5,949	6,558	7,436	7,589	8,274	8,753
Trade data:								
Value of imports	Mil. dol. . .	139	164	200	233	302	354	356
Value of exports	Mil. dol. . .	153	253	334	377	375	400	495
YARN SPINNING MILLS (SIC 2281)								
Industry data:								
Value of shipments [2]	Mil. dol. . .	7,327	7,259	7,265	7,669	7,618	8,006	8,125
Value of shipments (1992 dollars)	Mil. dol. . .	7,546	7,347	7,251	7,669	7,960	8,296	7,997
Total employment	1,000. . . .	77.2	75.0	69.8	68.7	65.6	65.4	62.5
Production workers	1,000. . . .	71.0	68.8	63.6	62.6	59.7	59.6	56.7
Average hourly earnings	Dollar . . .	7.93	8.02	8.28	8.48	8.62	8.95	9.27
Product data:								
Value of shipments [3]	Mil. dol. . .	7,662	7,551	7,519	7,756	7,696	8,183	8,305
Value of shipments (1992 dollars)	Mil. dol. . .	7,890	7,643	7,504	7,756	8,041	8,479	8,174
Trade data:								
Value of imports	Mil. dol. . .	291	234	264	321	337	388	400
Value of exports	Mil. dol. . .	126	175	202	169	146	209	299

[1] Estimate, except exports and imports.   [2] Value of all products and services sold by establishments in this industry.   [3] Value of products classified in this industry produced by all industries.

Source: U.S. Department of Commerce, Bureau of the Census, International Trade Administration (ITA). Estimates by ITA.

No. 1386. Recent Trends in Apparel and Other Textile Products (SIC 23): 1989 to 1995

ITEM	Unit	1989	1990	1991	1992	1993	1994	1995 [1]
INDUSTRY DATA								
Value of shipments [2]	Mil. dol.	63,398	64,414	65,345	71,546	74,010	76,898	77,800
Value of shipments (1992 dollars)	Mil. dol.	67,821	67,059	66,561	71,546	73,323	75,929	76,387
Total employment	1,000.	1,018	993	960	985	980	953	901
Production workers	1,000.	865	845	815	824	825	798	748
Average hourly earnings	Dollar	6.46	6.54	6.73	7.15	7.34	7.44	7.73
PRODUCT DATA								
Value of shipments [3]	Mil. dol.	61,447	61,962	62,649	68,844	70,986	73,141	73,999
Value of shipments (1992 dollars)	Mil. dol.	65,733	64,468	63,780	68,844	70,329	72,214	72,655
TRADE DATA								
Value of imports	Mil. dol.	25,372	26,602	27,230	32,462	35,278	38,343	40,998
Value of exports	Mil. dol.	2,362	2,864	3,708	4,625	5,405	6,117	7,157

[1] Estimate, except exports and imports. [2] Value of all products and services sold by establishments in the apparel and other textile products industry. [3] Value of products classified in the apparel and other textile products industry produced by all industries.

Source: U.S. Department of Commerce, Bureau of the Census, International Trade Administration (ITA). Estimates by ITA.

No. 1387. Recent Trends in Selected Men's and Boys' Apparel (SIC 231, 2321, -3, -5, -6): 1989 to 1995

ITEM	Unit	1989	1990	1991	1992	1993	1994	1995 [1]
INDUSTRY DATA								
Value of shipments [2]	Mil. dol.	14,772	14,484	15,386	17,022	16,819	17,094	17,430
2311 Men/boys' suits/coats	Mil. dol.	2,918	2,622	2,467	2,426	2,463	2,362	2,292
2321 Men's and boys' shirts	Mil. dol.	3,873	4,243	4,494	5,916	5,012	5,088	5,378
2323 Men's and boys' neckwear	Mil. dol.	534	500	532	618	619	705	729
2325 Men/boys' trousers	Mil. dol.	5,983	5,657	6,467	6,490	7,055	7,226	7,295
2326 Men/boys' work clothing	Mil. dol.	1,464	1,462	1,426	1,573	1,670	1,714	1,735
Value of shipments (1992 dollars)	Mil. dol.	16,110	15,381	15,918	17,022	16,526	16,677	16,851
2311 Men/boys' suits/coats	Mil. dol.	3,172	2,755	2,525	2,426	2,458	2,340	2,251
2321 Men's and boys' shirts	Mil. dol.	4,298	4,567	4,676	5,916	4,938	5,023	5,294
2323 Men's and boys' neckwear	Mil. dol.	576	520	540	618	611	695	710
2325 Men/boys' trousers	Mil. dol.	6,503	6,018	6,736	6,490	6,889	6,975	6,968
2326 Men/boys' work clothing	Mil. dol.	1,561	1,521	1,441	1,573	1,629	1,644	1,628
Total employment	1,000.	258.0	239.0	230.0	247.0	229.0	225.0	211.0
2311 Men/boys' suits/coats	1,000.	54.5	48.4	43.6	43.8	41.2	34.0	30.5
2321 Men's and boys' shirts	1,000.	73.7	69.7	68.8	84.4	72.7	73.6	68.6
2323 Men's and boys' neckwear	1,000.	8.0	7.4	6.4	7.5	6.3	6.2	5.9
2325 Men/boys' trousers	1,000.	88.0	81.7	80.5	78.3	78.5	82.2	79.1
2326 Men/boys' work clothing	1,000.	34.0	31.5	30.8	32.6	30.0	28.5	26.5
Production workers	1,000.	225	208	201	215	199	196	183
2311 Men/boys' suits/coats	1,000.	47.0	41.3	36.5	37.2	34.7	28.7	25.3
2321 Men's and boys' shirts	1,000.	65.1	61.7	60.9	74.3	64.1	66.8	61.8
2323 Men's and boys' neckwear	1,000.	6.6	6.0	5.1	5.8	4.8	4.6	4.3
2325 Men/boys' trousers	1,000.	76.7	71.6	70.8	69.2	68.4	71.9	68.5
2326 Men/boys' work clothing	1,000.	30.0	27.8	27.2	28.4	26.5	24.4	22.6
Average hourly earnings	Dollar	6.42	6.61	6.79	6.94	7.21	7.18	7.48
2311 Men/boys' suits/coats	Dollar	7.58	7.84	8.14	7.97	8.32	8.35	8.55
2321 Men's and boys' shirts	Dollar	6.29	6.46	6.87	6.84	6.90	6.95	7.16
2323 Men's/boys' neckwear	Dollar	7.04	7.28	8.02	7.39	8.43	9.21	8.84
2325 Men/boys' trousers	Dollar	6.17	6.43	6.36	6.86	7.15	7.03	7.30
2326 Men/boys' work clothing	Dollar	5.41	5.46	5.68	5.97	6.47	6.49	6.91
PRODUCT DATA								
Value of shipments [3]	Mil. dol.	14,383	13,771	14,143	15,810	15,405	16,134	16,439
2311 Men/boys' suits/coats	Mil. dol.	2,915	2,633	2,450	2,387	2,257	2,417	2,345
2321 Men's and boys' shirts	Mil. dol.	3,681	3,740	3,915	5,318	4,632	4,715	4,984
2323 Men's and boys' neckwear	Mil. dol.	526	498	525	544	529	594	614
2325 Men/boys' trousers	Mil. dol.	5,889	5,544	5,911	6,065	6,338	6,636	6,700
2326 Men/boys' work clothing	Mil. dol.	1,372	1,355	1,341	1,495	1,650	1,773	1,795
Value of shipments (1992 dollars)	Mil. dol.	15,685	14,618	14,628	15,810	15,136	15,741	15,891
2311 Men/boys' suits/coats	Mil. dol.	3,168	2,766	2,508	2,387	2,252	2,395	2,304
2321 Men's and boys' shirts	Mil. dol.	4,085	4,026	4,074	5,318	4,563	4,654	4,906
2323 Men's and boys' neckwear	Mil. dol.	568	518	533	544	521	586	598
2325 Men/boys' trousers	Mil. dol.	6,401	5,898	6,158	6,065	6,190	6,405	6,399
2326 Men/boys' work clothing	Mil. dol.	1,463	1,410	1,355	1,495	1,609	1,700	1,684
TRADE DATA								
Value of imports	Mil. dol.	5,566	5,716	6,167	7,624	8,281	9,178	10,873
2311 Men/boys' suits/coats	Mil. dol.	745	650	678	789	824	954	1,042
2321 Men's and boys' shirts	Mil. dol.	2,749	2,792	3,039	4,028	4,519	4,917	5,875
2323 Men's and boys' neckwear	Mil. dol.	100	110	140	151	158	156	167
2325 Men/boys' trousers	Mil. dol.	1,971	2,164	2,310	2,657	2,780	3,151	3,789
2326 Men/boys' work clothing	Mil. dol.	(NA)	(NA)	(NA)	(NA)	(NA)	(NA)	(NA)
Value of exports	Mil. dol.	713	906	1,140	1,478	1,795	2,036	2,158
2311 Men/boys' suits/coats	Mil. dol.	84	129	161	197	237	292	269
2321 Men's and boys' shirts	Mil. dol.	217	268	333	457	595	721	842
2323 Men's and boys' neckwear	Mil. dol.	10.1	9.8	14.5	15.5	21.1	17.9	18.4
2325 Men/boys' trousers	Mil. dol.	402	500	631	809	942	1,005	1,029
2326 Men/boys' work clothing	Mil. dol.	(NA)	(NA)	(NA)	(NA)	(NA)	(NA)	(NA)

NA Not available. [1] Estimate, except exports and imports. [2] Value of all products and services sold by establishments in the selected men's and boys' apparel industry. [3] Value of products classified in the selected men's and boys' apparel industry produced by all industries.

Source: U.S. Department of Commerce, Bureau of the Census, International Trade Administration (ITA). Estimates by ITA.

No. 1388. Recent Trends in Men's and Boys' Underwear and Nightwear (SIC 2322): 1989 to 1995

ITEM	Unit	1989	1990	1991	1992	1993	1994	1995 [1]
INDUSTRY DATA								
Value of shipments [2]	Mil. dol. . .	828	725	710	749	581	664	692
Value of shipments (1992 dollars)	Mil. dol. . .	860	738	722	749	578	660	686
Total employment	1,000. . .	16.2	15.3	11.8	12.8	11.3	10.5	9.9
Production workers	1,000. . . .	15.3	14.4	10.9	11.8	10.5	10.1	9.4
Average hourly earnings	Dollar . . .	6.21	6.07	7.42	6.72	6.48	7.03	7.26
PRODUCT DATA								
Value of shipments [3]	Mil. dol. . .	779	738	744	808	689	743	775
Value of shipments (1992 dollars)	Mil. dol. . .	809	752	757	808	685	738	768
TRADE DATA								
Value of imports	Mil. dol. . .	226	251	289	396	528	652	963
Value of exports	Mil. dol. . .	53	95	157	218	314	331	431

[1] Estimate, except exports and imports.   [2] Value of all products and services sold by establishments in the men's and boys' underwear and nightwear industry.   [3] Value of products classified in the men's and boys' underwear and nightwear industry produced by all industries.

Source: U.S. Department of Commerce, Bureau of the Census, International Trade Administration (ITA). Estimates by ITA.

No. 1389. Recent Trends in Selected Women's Outerwear (SIC 2331, 2335, 2337): 1989 to 1995

ITEM	Unit	1989	1990	1991	1992	1993	1994	1995 [1]
INDUSTRY DATA								
Value of shipments [2]	Mil. dol. . .	13,009	13,810	13,790	13,700	14,123	14,598	14,734
2331 Women's/misses' blouses	Mil. dol. . .	3,402	3,733	3,801	3,978	4,012	4,147	4,161
2335 Women's/misses' dresses	Mil. dol. . .	5,366	5,915	5,665	5,352	5,602	6,396	6,529
2337 Women's suits and coats	Mil. dol. . .	4,241	4,163	4,324	4,370	4,509	4,055	4,044
Value of shipments (1992 dollars)	Mil. dol. . .	13,881	14,369	13,976	13,700	14,063	14,599	14,899
2331 Women's/misses' blouses	Mil. dol. . .	3,768	3,963	3,918	3,978	3,976	4,053	4,052
2335 Women's/misses' dresses	Mil. dol. . .	5,714	6,110	5,699	5,352	5,597	6,507	6,738
2337 Women's suits and coats	Mil. dol. . .	4,399	4,296	4,359	4,370	4,491	4,039	4,109
Total employment	1,000. . . .	215.0	217.0	210.0	188.0	190.0	182.0	166.0
2331 Women's/misses' blouses	1,000. . . .	64.6	64.4	59.5	56.2	52.9	51.8	46.0
2335 Women's/misses' dresses	1,000. . . .	105.0	106.0	102.0	83.3	87.1	87.5	80.0
2337 Women's suits and coats	1,000. . . .	46.1	45.9	47.9	48.6	49.6	43.1	40.4
Production workers	1,000. . . .	180.0	184.0	178.0	156.0	159.0	151.0	137.0
2331 Women's/misses' blouses	1,000. . . .	55.2	54.3	49.4	47.2	44.7	42.2	36.7
2335 Women's/misses' dresses	1,000. . . .	89.2	93.3	89.6	71.0	74.5	74.8	68.9
2337 Women's suits and coats	1,000. . . .	36.0	36.6	39.3	38.0	40.0	34.1	30.9
Average hourly earnings	Dollar . . .	6.16	6.13	6.38	6.87	7.02	7.09	7.48
2331 Women's/misses' blouses	Dollar . . .	5.70	5.85	5.93	6.44	6.96	6.61	6.74
2335 Women's/misses' dresses	Dollar . . .	6.10	5.93	6.30	6.81	6.71	7.10	7.53
2337 Women's suits and coats	Dollar . . .	7.02	7.00	7.09	7.53	7.64	7.68	8.09
PRODUCT DATA								
Value of shipments [3]	Mil. dol. . .	12,500	12,817	12,805	13,581	14,275	14,405	14,534
2331 Women's/misses' blouses	Mil. dol. . .	3,635	3,660	3,618	4,195	4,580	4,425	4,440
2335 Women's/misses' dresses	Mil. dol. . .	5,245	5,746	5,443	5,278	5,431	6,047	6,172
2337 Women's suits and coats	Mil. dol. . .	3,620	3,410	3,745	4,108	4,264	3,933	3,922
Value of shipments (1992 dollars)	Mil. dol. . .	13,366	13,341	12,980	13,581	14,211	14,394	14,680
2331 Women's/misses' blouses	Mil. dol. . .	4,025	3,886	3,730	4,195	4,539	4,325	4,324
2335 Women's/misses' dresses	Mil. dol. . .	5,586	5,936	5,475	5,278	5,426	6,151	6,370
2337 Women's suits and coats	Mil. dol. . .	3,755	3,519	3,775	4,108	4,247	3,918	3,986
TRADE DATA								
Value of imports	Mil. dol. . .	5,881	6,190	6,119	7,073	7,718	7,960	8,430
2331 Women's/misses' blouses	Mil. dol. . .	2,983	3,005	2,923	3,501	3,864	3,948	3,906
2335 Women's/misses' dresses	Mil. dol. . .	937	1,028	981	1,054	1,130	1,339	1,688
2337 Women's suits and coats	Mil. dol. . .	1,962	2,157	2,215	2,518	2,724	2,673	2,836
Value of exports	Mil. dol. . .	235	291	362	519	590	591	713
2331 Women's/misses' blouses	Mil. dol. . .	77.2	80.6	100.0	171.0	213.0	243.0	342.0
2335 Women's/misses' dresses	Mil. dol. . .	42.3	50.9	65.0	98.3	105.0	103.0	112.0
2337 Women's suits and coats	Mil. dol. . .	116	159	197	250	272	245	259

[1] Estimate, except exports and imports.   [2] Value of all products and services sold by establishments in the selected women's outerwear industry.   [3] Value of products classified in the selected women's outerwear industry produced by all industries.

Source: U.S. Department of Commerce, Bureau of the Census, International Trade Administration (ITA). Estimates by ITA.

No. 1390. Recent Trends in Women's and Children's Undergarments (SIC 234): 1989 to 1995

ITEM	Unit	1989	1990	1991	1992	1993	1994	1995 [1]
INDUSTRY DATA								
Value of shipments [2].	Mil. dol. . .	3,366	3,424	3,683	3,944	3,943	4,245	4,435
2341 Women/child's underwear	Mil. dol. . .	2,301	2,337	2,386	2,365	2,155	2,438	2,528
2342 Bras and allied garments	Mil. dol. . .	1,064	1,087	1,297	1,579	1,789	1,807	1,907
Value of shipments (1992 dollars)	Mil. dol. . .	3,556	3,563	3,776	3,944	3,884	4,129	4,282
2341 Women/child's underwear	Mil. dol. . .	2,443	2,430	2,450	2,365	2,135	2,390	2,464
2342 Bras and allied garments	Mil. dol. . .	1,113	1,133	1,326	1,579	1,748	1,739	1,818
Total employment	1,000. . . .	61.2	60.3	57.5	53.6	52.1	47.1	45.3
2341 Women/child's underwear	1,000. . . .	49.4	48.7	46.9	41.5	38.0	33.5	31.2
2342 Bras and allied garments	1,000. . . .	11.8	11.6	10.6	12.1	14.1	13.6	14.1
Production workers	1,000. . . .	51.6	50.8	48.5	45.5	43.7	39.4	37.6
2341 Women/child's underwear	1,000. . . .	43.2	42.3	40.7	35.8	33.0	29.0	27.1
2342 Bras and allied garments	1,000. . . .	8.4	8.5	7.8	9.7	10.7	10.4	10.5
Average hourly earnings	Dollar . . .	5.75	6.02	6.24	6.74	6.89	6.70	7.35
2341 Women/child's underwear	Dollar . . .	5.68	5.96	6.10	6.46	6.54	6.51	6.75
2342 Bras and allied garments.	Dollar . . .	6.16	6.34	7.01	7.79	7.93	7.22	8.15
PRODUCT DATA								
Value of shipments [3]	Mil. dol. . .	3,365	3,322	3,660	3,821	3,587	3,917	4,094
2341 Women/child's underwear	Mil. dol. . .	2,303	2,119	2,260	2,237	1,928	2,128	2,206
2342 Bras and allied garments	Mil. dol. . .	1,062	1,203	1,400	1,584	1,659	1,789	1,888
Value of shipments (1992 dollars)	Mil. dol. . .	3,555	3,457	3,752	3,821	3,532	3,808	3,950
2341 Women/child's underwear	Mil. dol. . .	2,445	2,202	2,320	2,237	1,911	2,086	2,150
2342 Bras and allied garments	Mil. dol. . .	1,111	1,254	1,431	1,584	1,621	1,722	1,800
TRADE DATA								
Value of imports	Mil. dol. . .	928	1,079	1,256	1,519	1,787	2,067	2,443
2341 Women/child's underwear	Mil. dol. . .	601	727	829	985	1,168	1,342	1,540
2342 Bras and allied garments	Mil. dol. . .	327	352	427	534	619	725	902
Value of exports	Mil. dol. . .	254	266	355	407	466	521	654
2341 Women/child's underwear	Mil. dol. . .	88.4	95.9	136.0	155.0	186.0	222.0	267.0
2342 Bras and allied garments	Mil. dol. . .	165	170	219	252	280	299	387

[1] Estimate, except exports and imports. [2] Value of all products and services sold by establishments in the women's and children's undergarments industry. [3] Value of products classified in the women's and children's undergarments industry produced by all industries.

Source: U.S. Department of Commerce, Bureau of the Census, International Trade Administration (ITA). Estimates by ITA.

No. 1391. Recent Trends in Girls' and Children's Outerwear (SIC 236): 1989 to 1995

ITEM	Unit	1989	1990	1991	1992	1993	1994	1995 [1]
INDUSTRY DATA								
Value of shipments [2]	Mil. dol. . .	3,691	3,698	3,579	3,159	3,221	3,926	4,103
2361 Child's dresses/blouses	Mil. dol. . .	1,671	1,725	1,800	1,626	1,567	1,716	1,835
2369 Children's outerwear n.e.c.	Mil. dol. . .	2,020	1,973	1,779	1,534	1,655	2,210	2,268
Value of shipments (1992 dollars)	Mil. dol. . .	4,015	3,829	3,621	3,159	3,203	3,932	4,092
2361 Child's dresses/blouses	Mil. dol. . .	1,810	1,789	1,829	1,626	1,570	1,728	1,768
2369 Children's outerwear n.e.c.	Mil. dol. . .	2,205	2,041	1,792	1,534	1,633	2,203	2,324
Total employment	1,000. . . .	66.7	60.9	58.8	53.7	49.2	48	44.9
2361 Child's dresses/blouses	1,000. . . .	30.6	29.0	30.2	24.2	23.1	19.5	18.1
2369 Children's outerwear n.e.c.	1,000. . . .	36.1	31.9	28.6	29.5	26.1	28.5	26.8
Production workers	1,000. . . .	56.5	50.7	49.7	44.0	39.8	38.4	35.6
2361 Child's dresses/blouses	1,000. . . .	25.6	24.2	25.6	19.4	18.6	15.2	14.1
2369 Children's outerwear n.e.c.	1,000. . . .	30.9	26.5	24.1	24.6	21.2	23.2	21.5
Average hourly earnings	Dollar . . .	5.65	5.52	5.72	6.36	6.63	6.78	7.04
2361 Child's dresses/blouses	Dollar . . .	5.64	5.80	5.94	6.49	6.24	6.53	6.70
2369 Children's outerwear n.e.c.	Dollar . . .	5.65	5.31	5.51	6.26	6.97	6.96	7.38
PRODUCT DATA								
Value of shipments [3]	Mil. dol. . .	3,607	3,648	3,592	3,503	3,452	3,636	3,805
2361 Child's dresses/blouses	Mil. dol. . .	1,765	1,812	1,812	1,719	1,626	1,680	1,796
2369 Children's outerwear n.e.c.	Mil. dol. . .	1,842	1,835	1,780	1,784	1,826	1,957	2,008
Value of shipments (1992 dollars)	Mil. dol. . .	3,923	3,778	3,634	3,503	3,432	3,642	3,789
2361 Child's dresses/blouses	Mil. dol. . .	1,912	1,880	1,841	1,719	1,629	1,692	1,731
2369 Children's outerwear n.e.c.	Mil. dol. . .	2,011	1,898	1,792	1,784	1,803	1,951	2,058
TRADE DATA								
Value of imports	Mil. dol. . .	6,360	6,487	6,694	8,016	8,196	8,926	8,890
2361 Child's dresses/blouses	Mil. dol. . .	-	-	-	-	-	-	-
2369 Children's outerwear n.e.c.	Mil. dol. . .	6,360	6,487	6,694	8,016	8,196	8,926	8,890
Value of exports	Mil. dol. . .	282	341	458	625	703	920	1,273
2361 Child's dresses/blouses	Mil. dol. . .	-	-	-	-	-	-	-
2369 Children's outerwear n.e.c.	Mil. dol. . .	282	341	458	625	703	920	1,273

- Represents or rounds to zero. [1] Estimate, except exports and imports. [2] Value of all products and services sold by establishments in the girls' and children's outerwear industry. [3] Value of products classified in the girls' and children's outerwear industry produced by all industries.

Source: U.S. Department of Commerce, Bureau of the Census, International Trade Administration (ITA). Estimates by ITA.

No. 1392. Recent Trends in Misc. Fabricated Textile Products (SIC 239): 1989 to 1995

ITEM	Unit	1989	1990	1991	1992	1993	1994	1995 [1]
INDUSTRY DATA								
Value of shipments [2]	Mil. dol. . . .	16,339	17,086	16,894	19,111	20,264	21,644	22,640
239A Homefurnishings	Mil. dol. . . .	6,168	6,371	6,483	6,898	7,154	7,425	7,698
239B Misc. textile products	Mil. dol. . . .	10,171	10,715	10,411	12,212	13,110	14,219	14,942
Value of shipments (1992 dollars)	Mil. dol. . . .	17,372	17,690	17,130	19,111	20,022	21,207	22,002
239A Homefurnishings	Mil. dol. . . .	6,604	6,647	6,572	6,898	7,011	7,220	7,338
239B Misc. textile products	Mil. dol. . . .	10,768	11,043	10,558	12,212	13,012	13,987	14,664
Total employment	1,000. . . .	188.0	190.0	186.0	211.0	212.0	221.0	217.0
239A Homefurnishings	1,000. . . .	69.6	68.2	67.1	73.8	72.1	71.5	69.2
239B Misc. textile products	1,000. . . .	119.0	121.0	119.0	137.0	140.0	149.0	148.0
Production workers	1,000. . . .	155.0	155.0	152.0	168.0	171.0	177.0	174.0
239A Homefurnishings	1,000. . . .	57.6	56.2	55.3	61.0	59.5	59.2	57.2
239B Misc. textile products	1,000. . . .	97.1	98.7	96.4	107.0	112.0	118.0	116.0
Average hourly earnings	Dollar . . .	7.92	8.06	8.19	8.34	8.61	8.79	9.08
239A Homefurnishings	Dollar . . .	6.36	6.43	6.64	7.25	7.79	7.90	8.25
239B Misc. textile products	Dollar . . .	8.90	9.04	9.12	8.98	9.06	9.23	9.51
PRODUCT DATA								
Value of shipments [3]	Mil. dol. . .	15,703	16,397	16,207	18,220	19,555	20,610	21,644
239A Homefurnishings	Mil. dol. . .	5,892	6,013	6,100	6,540	6,980	7,209	7,425
239B Misc. textile products	Mil. dol. . .	9,811	10,385	10,107	11,680	12,575	13,402	14,219
Value of shipments (1992 dollars)	Mil. dol. . .	16,673	16,956	16,423	18,220	19,320	20,195	21,032
239A Homefurnishings	Mil. dol. . .	6,307	6,275	6,184	6,540	6,840	7,010	7,078
239B Misc. textile products	Mil. dol. . .	10,366	10,682	10,240	11,680	12,480	13,185	13,954
TRADE DATA								
Value of imports	Mil. dol. . .	1,854	2,138	2,316	2,698	3,116	3,428	3,556
239A Homefurnishings	Mil. dol. . .	922	976	1,000	1,178	1,334	1,553	1,736
239B Misc. textile products	Mil. dol. . .	932	1,162	1,315	1,520	1,782	1,875	1,820
Value of exports	Mil. dol. . .	520	622	780	862	971	1,079	1,151
239A Homefurnishings	Mil. dol. . .	202	245	317	338	349	362	350
239B Misc. textile products	Mil. dol. . .	318	377	463	523	623	718	801

[1] Estimate, except exports and imports.   [2] Value of all products and services sold by establishments in the misc. fabricated textile products industry. The designation 239A represents SIC's 2391 and 2392; 239B represents SIC 239 less SIC's 2391 and 2392.   [3] Value of products classified in the misc. fabricated textile products industry produced by all industries.

Source: U.S. Department of Commerce, Bureau of the Census, International Trade Administration (ITA). Estimates by ITA.

No. 1393. Recent Trends in Logging and Sawmills and Planing Mills, General: 1989 to 1995

ITEM	Unit	1989	1990	1991	1992	1993	1994	1995 [1]
LOGGING (SIC 2411)								
Industry data:								
Value of shipments [2]	Mil. dol. . .	12,017	12,229	11,434	13,845	15,976	16,818	16,588
Value of shipments (1992 dollars)	Mil. dol. . .	14,427	13,710	12,649	13,845	13,085	13,369	13,092
Total employment	1,000. . . .	81.7	83.4	78.1	83.6	86.2	87.2	85.2
Production workers	1,000. . . .	68.0	68.9	65.4	69.4	71.6	71.7	71.1
Average hourly earnings	Dollar . . .	9.50	9.55	9.80	9.96	9.86	9.96	9.92
Capital expenditures	Mil. dol. . .	354	406	293	376	366	469	(NA)
Product data:								
Value of shipments [3]	Mil. dol. . .	11,360	11,572	10,728	12,962	15,362	16,001	15,508
Value of shipments (1992 dollars)	Mil. dol. . .	13,637	12,973	11,868	12,962	12,581	12,719	12,240
Trade data:								
Value of imports	Mil. dol. . .	248	210	199	219	265	273	293
Value of exports	Mil. dol. . .	2,836	2,930	2,715	2,749	3,077	2,915	3,026
SAWMILLS AND PLANING MILLS, GENERAL (SIC 2421)								
Industry data:								
Value of shipments [2]	Mil. dol. . .	18,479	17,923	17,485	21,066	24,460	26,761	24,555
Value of shipments (1992 dollars)	Mil. dol. . .	21,192	20,889	20,075	21,066	19,662	21,022	20,600
Total employment	1,000. . . .	144	139	130	138	142	142	139
Production workers	1,000. . . .	126	125	116	118	122	122	119
Average hourly earnings	Dollar . . .	8.94	9.23	9.33	9.63	9.83	9.99	(NA)
Capital expenditures	Mil. dol. . .	573	522	464	457	548	695	(NA)
Product data:								
Value of shipments [3]	Mil. dol. . .	18,439	17,862	17,515	20,347	23,641	25,738	23,617
Value of shipments (1992 dollars)	Mil. dol. . .	21,145	20,818	20,109	20,347	19,004	20,218	19,613
Trade data:								
Value of imports	Mil. dol. . .	3,016	2,659	2,638	3,472	5,022	6,039	5,505
Value of exports	Mil. dol. . .	2,034	2,128	2,203	2,322	2,450	2,428	2,412

NA Not available.   [1] Estimate, except exports and imports.   [2] Value of all products and services sold by establishments in this industry.   [3] Value of products classified in this industry produced by all industries.

Source: U.S. Department of Commerce, Bureau of the Census, International Trade Administration (ITA). Estimates by ITA.

No. 1394. Recent Trends in Hardwood Veneer and Softwood Veneer: 1989 to 1995

ITEM	Unit	1989	1990	1991	1992	1993	1994	1995 [1]
HARDWOOD VENEER AND PLYWOOD (SIC 2435)								
Industry data:								
Value of shipments [2]	Mil. dol.	2,185	2,052	1,897	2,248	2,537	2,599	2,645
Value of shipments (1992 dollars)	Mil. dol.	2,344	2,117	1,978	2,248	2,369	2,288	2,276
Total employment	1,000.	20.1	18.7	17.3	20.1	19.8	21.9	22.2
Production workers	1,000.	17.0	15.7	14.8	17.0	16.8	18.7	18.8
Average hourly earnings	Dollar	7.58	7.83	8.03	8.12	8.55	8.21	(NA)
Capital expenditures	Mil. dol.	47.2	40.8	45.5	47.0	46.6	52.3	(NA)
Product data:								
Value of shipments [3]	Mil. dol.	1,937	1,879	1,743	2,023	2,305	2,435	2,477
Value of shipments (1992 dollars)	Mil. dol.	2,078	1,939	1,817	2,023	2,152	2,143	2,132
Trade data:								
Value of imports	Mil. dol.	660	688	588	729	857	890	924
Value of exports	Mil. dol.	181	230	248	278	297	348	376
SOFTWOOD VENEER AND PLYWOOD (SIC 2436)								
Industry data:								
Value of shipments [2]	Mil. dol.	5,310	5,030	4,592	5,447	6,035	6,553	6,728
Value of shipments (1992 dollars)	Mil. dol.	5,887	5,444	5,019	5,447	5,721	5,830	5,750
Total employment	1,000.	36.5	35.6	31.7	31.3	30.7	30.3	30.0
Production workers	1,000.	32.9	32.2	28.6	28.0	27.7	27.2	26.9
Average hourly earnings	Dollar	10.34	10.44	10.78	11.1	11.42	11.83	(NA)
Capital expenditures	Mil. dol.	140	103	86.7	98.7	118	150	(NA)
Product data:								
Value of shipments [3]	Mil. dol.	4,605	4,412	3,972	4,778	5,321	5,712	5,863
Value of shipments (1992 dollars)	Mil. dol.	5,105	4,775	4,341	4,778	5,044	5,081	5,011
Trade data:								
Value of imports	Mil. dol.	52.5	44.3	35.5	59.0	76.9	96.4	99.4
Value of exports	Mil. dol.	292	326	275	336	369	323	334

NA Not available.   [1] Estimate, except exports and imports.   [2] Value of all products and services sold by establishments in this industry.   [3] Value of products classified in this industry produced by all industries.

Source: U.S. Department of Commerce, Bureau of the Census, International Trade Administration (ITA). Estimates by ITA.

No. 1395. Recent Trends in Reconstituted Wood Products (SIC 2493): 1989 to 1995

ITEM	Unit	1989	1990	1991	1992	1993	1994	1995 [1]
INDUSTRY DATA								
Value of shipments [2]	Mil. dol.	3,199	3,043	3,041	3,981	4,669	5,358	5,163
Value of shipments (1992 dollars)	Mil. dol.	3,281	3,199	3,181	3,981	4,180	4,367	4,225
Total employment	1,000.	22.2	22.3	21.0	22.8	23.5	24.1	(NA)
Production workers	1,000.	18.2	18.2	17.1	18.5	19.2	19.5	(NA)
Average hourly earnings	Dollar	10.15	10.41	10.73	11.5	11.72	11.84	(NA)
Capital expenditures	Mil. dol.	133	130	187	143	171	333	(NA)
PRODUCT DATA								
Value of shipments [3]	Mil. dol.	3,240	3,050	3,046	3,987	4,658	5,352	5,156
Value of shipments (1992 dollars)	Mil. dol.	3,323	3,207	3,186	3,987	4,170	4,361	4,219
TRADE DATA								
Value of imports	Mil. dol.	298	262	234	402	581	834	963
Value of exports	Mil. dol.	169	214	225	244	256	292	307

NA Not available.   [1] Estimate, except exports and imports.   [2] Value of all products and services sold by establishments in the reconstituted wood products industry.   [3] Value of products classified in the reconstituted wood products industry produced by all industries.

Source: U.S. Department of Commerce, Bureau of the Census, International Trade Administration (ITA). Estimates by ITA.

No. 1396. Recent Trends in Household Furniture (SIC 251): 1989 to 1995

ITEM	Unit	1989	1990	1991	1992	1993	1994	1995 [1]
INDUSTRY DATA								
Value of shipments [2]	Mil. dol. . .	19,955	19,913	19,499	20,693	21,906	23,663	24,188
2511 Wood furniture, house	Mil. dol. . .	8,461	8,303	7,980	8,737	9,267	9,919	10,019
2512 Upholstered furniture, house . . .	Mil. dol. . .	5,618	5,815	5,859	6,223	6,690	7,445	7,648
2514 Metal furniture, house.	Mil. dol. . .	2,229	2,184	2,090	2,112	2,141	2,191	2,205
2515 Mattresses and bedsprings	Mil. dol. . .	2,893	2,905	2,923	2,843	3,001	3,267	3,463
2517 Wood TV & radio cabinets	Mil. dol. . .	281	247	235	328	315	391	385
2519 Other furniture	Mil. dol. . .	473	459	412	451	493	451	468
Value of shipments (1992 dollars)	Mil. dol. . .	21,262	20,693	19,802	20,693	21,376	22,413	22,297
2511 Wood furniture, house	Mil. dol. . .	9,196	8,758	8,184	8,737	8,911	9,133	8,914
2512 Upholstered furniture, house . . .	Mil. dol. . .	5,901	6,008	5,907	6,223	6,591	7,193	7,222
2514 Metal furniture, house.	Mil. dol. . .	2,378	2,268	2,128	2,112	2,118	2,133	2,088
2515 Mattresses and bedsprings	Mil. dol. . .	2,998	2,940	2,935	2,843	2,953	3,126	3,264
2517 Wood TV & radio cabinets	Mil. dol. . .	291	250	236	328	311	381	372
2519 Other furniture	Mil. dol. . .	496	469	412	451	492	446	437
Total employment	1,000. . . .	280	275	259	257	255	267	262
Production workers	1,000. . . .	236	231	217	216	217	229	225
Average hourly earnings.	Dollar . . .	7.46	7.58	7.96	8.34	8.77	8.82	9.10
Capital expenditures	Mil. dol. . .	414	347	297	354	393	437	(NA)
2511 Wood furniture, house	Mil. dol. . .	264	185	166	197	238	257	(NA)
2512 Upholstered furniture, house . . .	Mil. dol. . .	56.3	73	49.9	73.6	70.2	79.6	(NA)
2514 Metal furniture, house.	Mil. dol. . .	33.6	35.7	34.1	36.8	27.1	50.7	(NA)
2515 Mattresses and bedsprings	Mil. dol. . .	30.6	28.2	35.5	31.2	38.6	29.6	(NA)
2517 Wood TV & radio cabinets	Mil. dol. . .	10.3	6.2	3.8	3.9	5.8	6.4	(NA)
2519 Other furniture	Mil. dol. . .	19.7	18.8	7.6	10.8	13.9	13.7	(NA)
PRODUCT DATA								
Value of shipments [3]	Mil. dol. . .	19,208	19,232	18,842	19,516	20,825	22,637	23,158
2511 Wood furniture, house	Mil. dol. . .	7,853	7,847	7,592	7,976	8,398	9,184	9,277
2512 Upholstered furniture, house . . .	Mil. dol. . .	5,324	5,392	5,402	5,811	6,235	7,113	7,307
2514 Metal furniture, house.	Mil. dol. . .	2,049	2,054	1,982	1,792	1,957	1,902	1,915
2515 Mattresses and bedsprings	Mil. dol. . .	3,135	3,185	3,182	3,079	3,282	3,539	3,751
2517 Wood TV & radio cabinets	Mil. dol. . .	353	313	292	376	435	468	462
2519 Other furniture	Mil. dol. . .	494	442	392	483	520	431	446
Value of shipments (1992 dollars)	Mil. dol. . .	20,447	19,973	19,130	19,516	20,331	21,450	21,365
2511 Wood furniture, house	Mil. dol. . .	8,536	8,278	7,787	7,976	8,075	8,456	8,254
2512 Upholstered furniture, house . . .	Mil. dol. . .	5,592	5,570	5,446	5,811	6,143	6,872	6,900
2514 Metal furniture, house.	Mil. dol. . .	2,186	2,133	2,019	1,792	1,936	1,852	1,813
2515 Mattresses and bedsprings	Mil. dol. . .	3,249	3,224	3,195	3,079	3,230	3,387	3,536
2517 Wood TV & radio cabinets	Mil. dol. . .	365	316	293	376	429	457	446
2519 Other furniture	Mil. dol. . .	518	452	392	483	519	426	417
TRADE DATA								
Value of imports	Mil. dol. . .	2,742	2,738	2,729	2,995	3,397	3,965	4,448
Value of exports	Mil. dol. . .	[4]633	756	955	1,113	1,183	1,307	1,320

NA Not available. [1] Estimate, except exports and imports. [2] Value of all products and services sold by establishments in the household furniture industry. [3] Value of products classified in the household furniture industry produced by all industries. [4] Exports for 1989 have been adjusted by the U.S. dollar value of Canadian imports.

Source: U.S. Department of Commerce, Bureau of the Census, International Trade Administration (ITA). Estimates by ITA.

No. 1397. Recent Trends in Office Furniture (SIC 252): 1989 to 1995

ITEM	Unit	1989	1990	1991	1992	1993	1994	1995 [1]
INDUSTRY DATA								
Value of shipments [2]	Mil. dol. . .	8,257	8,030	7,263	8,008	8,265	8,663	9,357
Value of shipments (1992 dollars)	Mil. dol. . .	8,737	8,179	7,245	8,008	8,142	8,168	8,583
Total employment	1,000. . . .	79.6	74.9	66.1	67.9	69.5	70.2	70.1
Production workers	1,000. . . .	59.4	55.5	47.8	50.4	52.2	53.3	54.0
Average hourly earnings.	Dollar . . .	10.49	10.69	10.91	10.83	11.19	11.16	11.37
Capital expenditures	Mil. dol. . .	302	292	173	202	235	243	(NA)
PRODUCT DATA								
Value of shipments [3]	Mil. dol. . .	8,051	7,880	7,130	7,676	7,885	8,428	9,105
Value of shipments (1992 dollars)	Mil. dol. . .	8,524	8,034	7,116	7,676	7,766	7,948	8,351
TRADE DATA								
Value of imports	Mil. dol. . .	627	631	609	652	777	953	1,129
Value of exports	Mil. dol. . .	286	365	419	509	567	637	556

NA Not available. [1] Estimate, except exports and imports. [2] Value of all products and services sold by establishments in the office furniture industry. [3] Value of products classified in the office furniture industry produced by all industries.

Source: U.S. Department of Commerce, Bureau of the Census, International Trade Administration (ITA). Estimates by ITA.

Industrial Outlook

No. 1398. Recent Trends in Household Consumer Durables (SIC 251, 3524, 363, 3651): 1989 to 1995

ITEM	Unit	1989	1990	1991	1992	1993	1994	1995 [1]
INDUSTRY DATA								
Value of shipments [2]	Mil. dol. . . .	50,227	50,412	50,004	53,114	57,329	63,562	64,820
Value of shipments (1992 dollars)	Mil. dol. . . .	52,226	51,482	50,322	53,114	56,702	62,028	62,794
Total employment	1,000. . . .	453	441	419	416	416	436	430
Production workers	1,000. . . .	372	361	341	342	345	365	361
Average hourly earnings	Dollar . . .	8.46	8.64	8.96	9.29	9.69	9.72	10.04
Capital expenditures	Mil. dol. . . .	1,166	1,075	1,162	1,288	1,178	1,305	(NA)
PRODUCT DATA								
Value of shipments [3]	Mil. dol. . . .	47,080	47,167	46,353	48,314	51,650	56,880	58,125
Value of shipments (1992 dollars)	Mil. dol. . . .	48,872	48,137	46,640	48,314	51,066	55,442	56,236
TRADE DATA								
Value of imports	Mil. dol. . . .	19,888	18,786	19,738	21,647	23,205	25,069	27,266
Value of exports	Mil. dol. . . .	4,275	5,124	5,872	6,508	7,100	7,787	8,098

NA Not available. [1] Estimate, except exports and imports. [2] Value of all products and services sold by establishments in the household consumer durables industry. [3] Value of products classified in the household consumer durables industry produced by all industries.
Source: U.S. Department of Commerce, Bureau of the Census, International Trade Administration (ITA). Estimates by ITA.

No. 1399. Recent Trends in Paper and Allied Products (SIC 26): 1989 to 1995

ITEM	Unit	1989	1990	1991	1992	1993	1994	1995 [1]
INDUSTRY DATA								
Value of shipments [2]	Mil. dol. . . .	131,366	131,444	128,824	133,062	133,262	143,762	176,483
Value of shipments (1992 dollars)	Mil. dol. . . .	128,262	128,062	127,988	133,062	135,076	141,401	143,903
Total employment	1,000. . . .	630	628	621	626	626	621	618
Production workers	1,000. . . .	484	480	477	478	479	479	478
Average hourly earnings	Dollar . . .	12.65	12.93	13.34	13.80	14.09	14.33	14.82
Capital expenditures	Mil. dol. . . .	10,067	10,809	9,009	7,950	7,370	7,312	7,568
PRODUCT DATA								
Value of shipments [3]	Mil. dol. . . .	127,266	127,528	124,658	128,941	128,695	138,381	170,079
Value of shipments (1992 dollars)	Mil. dol. . . .	123,886	124,086	123,908	128,941	130,568	136,229	138,681
TRADE DATA								
Value of imports	Mil. dol. . . .	11,894	11,702	10,473	10,424	10,948	11,842	16,862
Value of exports	Mil. dol. . . .	8,193	8,726	9,332	10,122	9,547	11,100	15,059

[1] Estimate, except exports and imports. [2] Value of all products and services sold by establishments in the paper and allied products industry. [3] Value of products classified in the paper and allied products produced by all industries.
Source: U.S. Department of Commerce, Bureau of the Census, International Trade Administration (ITA). Estimates by ITA.

No. 1400. Recent Trends in Pulp Mills and Paper and Paperboard Mills: 1989 to 1995

ITEM	Unit	1989	1990	1991	1992	1993	1994	1995 [1]
PULP MILLS (SIC 2611)								
Industry data:								
Value of shipments [2]	Mil. dol. . . .	6,416	6,239	5,329	5,466	4,282	4,424	7,165
Value of shipments (1992 dollars)	Mil. dol. . . .	4,735	4,792	5,210	5,466	4,899	4,711	4,720
Total employment	1,000. . . .	15.2	16.1	16.8	15.9	14.2	12.3	13.1
Production workers	1,000. . . .	11.7	12.3	12.8	12.1	10.8	9.4	9.7
Average hourly earnings	Dollar . . .	17.43	17.48	18.36	19.07	19.49	19.98	20.65
Capital expenditures	Mil. dol. . . .	697	1,054	991	772	426	259	313
Product data:								
Value of shipments [3]	Mil. dol. . . .	7,719	6,917	5,741	6,104	4,995	5,941	9,624
Value of shipments (1992 dollars)	Mil. dol. . . .	5,697	5,313	5,612	6,104	5,715	6,327	6,340
Trade data:								
Value of imports	Mil. dol. . . .	3,051	2,851	2,142	2,104	1,868	2,285	3,745
Value of exports	Mil. dol. . . .	3,643	3,288	2,920	3,236	2,482	2,954	4,698
PAPER AND PAPERBOARD MILLS (SIC 262, 263)								
Industry data:								
Value of shipments [2]	Mil. dol. . . .	51,706	51,241	48,357	48,926	48,267	53,820	68,873
Value of shipments (1992 dollars)	Mil. dol. . . .	48,811	48,943	47,539	48,926	48,625	52,614	52,877
Total employment	1,000. . . .	182	183	181	182	180	178	181
Production workers	1,000. . . .	141	139	138	140	138	136	138
Average hourly earnings	Dollar . . .	16.75	17.13	17.55	17.96	18.22	18.88	19.54
Capital expenditures	Mil. dol. . . .	6,890	7,254	5,790	4,952	4,507	4,570	4,821
Product data:								
Value of shipments [3]	Mil. dol. . . .	49,756	49,701	47,148	47,232	46,513	51,036	65,284
Value of shipments (1992 dollars)	Mil. dol. . . .	46,985	47,499	46,414	47,232	46,866	49,872	50,121
Trade data:								
Value of imports	Mil. dol. . . .	7,377	7,411	6,949	6,774	7,269	7,418	10,289
Value of exports	Mil. dol. . . .	3,082	3,523	4,135	4,349	4,284	4,917	6,555

[1] Estimate, except exports and imports. [2] Value of all products and services sold by establishments in this industry. [3] Value of products classified in this industry produced by all industries.
Source: U.S. Department of Commerce, Bureau of the Census, International Trade Administration (ITA). Estimates by ITA.

No. 1401. Recent Trends in Printing and Publishing (SIC 27): 1989 to 1995

ITEM	Unit	1989	1990	1991	1992	1993	1994	1995 [1]
INDUSTRY DATA								
Value of shipments [2]	Mil. dol. . .	149,912	157,060	156,685	166,797	172,633	176,382	190,849
2711 Newspapers	Mil. dol. . .	34,146	34,642	33,702	34,124	34,651	35,837	38,589
2721 Periodicals	Mil. dol. . .	19,787	20,397	20,345	22,034	22,653	21,723	22,772
2731 Book publishing	Mil. dol. . .	14,074	15,318	16,596	16,731	18,616	19,419	20,973
2732 Book printing	Mil. dol. . .	3,839	4,132	4,140	4,688	4,810	4,699	5,139
2741 Misc publishing	Mil. dol. . .	8,021	8,875	9,762	10,977	11,807	12,332	13,321
275 Commercial printing	Mil. dol. . .	50,312	52,904	51,948	56,439	58,173	60,527	65,995
2761 Manifold business forms	Mil. dol. . .	7,553	7,808	7,234	7,436	7,491	6,982	8,211
2771 Greeting cards	Mil. dol. . .	3,449	3,721	3,810	4,196	4,275	4,507	4,860
2782 Blankbooks and binders	Mil. dol. . .	3,058	3,186	3,243	3,788	3,771	3,984	4,345
2789 Bookbinding	Mil. dol. . .	1,240	1,363	1,328	1,321	1,258	1,379	1,454
279 Printing trade services	Mil. dol. . .	4,432	4,715	4,577	5,063	5,129	4,994	5,190
Value of shipments (1992 dollars)	Mil. dol. . .	168,067	168,572	161,528	166,797	167,488	166,827	170,818
2711 Newspapers	Mil. dol. . .	40,991	39,099	35,626	34,124	33,222	33,060	33,556
2721 Periodicals	Mil. dol. . .	23,840	23,021	21,506	22,034	22,122	20,848	21,223
2731 Book publishing	Mil. dol. . .	16,103	16,542	17,127	16,731	18,197	18,217	18,709
2732 Book printing	Mil. dol. . .	4,347	4,551	4,485	4,688	4,753	4,579	4,780
2741 Misc publishing	Mil. dol. . .	9,273	9,806	10,179	10,977	11,309	11,387	11,820
275 Commercial printing	Mil. dol. . .	52,864	54,195	52,281	56,439	56,774	58,372	60,234
2761 Manifold business forms	Mil. dol. . .	7,376	7,639	7,099	7,436	7,027	6,262	6,011
2771 Greeting cards	Mil. dol. . .	3,915	4,049	3,940	4,196	4,040	3,982	4,101
2782 Blankbooks and binders	Mil. dol. . .	3,447	3,448	3,316	3,788	3,697	3,816	3,900
2789 Bookbinding	Mil. dol. . .	1,305	1,401	1,334	1,321	1,249	1,354	1,378
279 Printing trade services	Mil. dol. . .	4,605	4,821	4,635	5,063	5,096	4,951	5,106

[1] Estimate. [2] Value of all products and services sold by establishments in the printing and publishing industry.
Source: U.S. Department of Commerce, Bureau of the Census, International Trade Administration (ITA). Estimates by ITA.

No. 1402. Recent Trends in Periodicals, Book Publishing, and Commercial Printing: 1989 to 1995

ITEM	Unit	1989	1990	1991	1992	1993	1994	1995 [1]
PERIODICALS (SIC 2721)								
Industry data:								
Value of shipments [2]	Mil. dol. . .	19,787	20,397	20,345	22,034	22,653	21,723	22,772
Value of shipments (1992 dollars) . . .	Mil. dol. . .	23,840	23,021	21,506	22,034	22,122	20,848	21,223
Total employment	1,000	116	115	111	116	117	116	117
Production workers	1,000	20.7	21.6	20.7	20.1	19.7	18.3	18.1
Average hourly earnings	Dollar . . .	12.45	13.09	13.21	13.40	12.51	12.97	12.93
Capital expenditures	Mil. dol. . .	272	275	223	234	290	307	(NA)
Product data:								
Value of shipments [3]	Mil. dol. . .	18,748	19,256	19,424	20,942	21,692	21,600	22,732
Value of shipments (1992 dollars) . . .	Mil. dol. . .	22,588	21,733	20,533	20,942	21,183	20,729	21,185
Trade data:								
Value of imports	Mil. dol. . .	140	122	121	136	195	212	228
Value of exports	Mil. dol. . .	448	666	705	731	737	788	825
BOOK PUBLISHING (SIC 2731)								
Industry data:								
Value of shipments [2]	Mil. dol. . .	14,074	15,318	16,596	16,731	18,616	19,419	20,973
Value of shipments (1992 dollars) . . .	Mil. dol. . .	16,103	16,542	17,127	16,731	18,197	18,217	18,709
Total employment	1,000	73.9	73.5	77.3	79.6	83.2	87.1	87.9
Production workers	1,000	17.1	17.3	17.1	18.6	18.2	18.7	18.8
Average hourly earnings	Dollar . . .	11.56	11.68	12.72	12.49	12.90	13.27	13.65
Capital expenditures	Mil. dol. . .	319	329	331	327	282	283	(NA)
Product data:								
Value of shipments [3]	Mil. dol. . .	12,981	14,267	15,215	14,761	16,596	17,128	18,427
Value of shipments (1992 dollars) . . .	Mil. dol. . .	14,852	15,407	15,701	14,761	16,223	16,068	16,438
Trade data:								
Value of imports	Mil. dol. . .	746	845	878	990	1,007	1,093	1,252
Value of exports	Mil. dol. . .	1,123	1,428	1,498	1,636	1,659	1,697	1,766
COMMERCIAL PRINTING (SIC 275)								
Industry data:								
Value of shipments [2]	Mil. dol. . .	50,312	52,904	51,948	56,439	58,173	60,527	65,995
Value of shipments (1992 dollars) . . .	Mil. dol. . .	52,864	54,195	52,281	56,439	56,774	58,372	60,234
Total employment	1,000	569	580	556	569	572	579	591
Production workers	1,000	414	421	401	409	415	418	425
Average hourly earnings	Dollar . . .	10.34	10.47	10.75	11.47	11.69	11.74	11.91
Capital expenditures	Mil. dol. . .	2,135	2,220	2,051	2,144	2,238	2,716	(NA)
Product data:								
Value of shipments [3]	Mil. dol. . .	49,621	52,572	51,761	54,902	56,960	58,971	64,050
Value of shipments (1992 dollars) . . .	Mil. dol. . .	52,154	53,862	52,096	54,902	55,587	56,867	58,459
Trade data:								
Value of imports	Mil. dol. . .	371	393	420	442	505	584	756
Value of exports	Mil. dol. . .	811	772	1,026	1,056	1,201	1,061	1,197

NA Not available. [1] Estimate, except exports and imports. [2] Value of all products and services sold by establishments in this industry. [3] Value of products classified in this industry produced by all industries.
Source: U.S. Department of Commerce, Bureau of the Census, International Trade Administration (ITA). Estimates by ITA.

No. 1403. Recent Trends in Chemicals and Allied Products (SIC 28): 1989 to 1995

ITEM	Unit	1989	1990	1991	1992	1993	1994	1995 [1]
INDUSTRY DATA								
Value of shipments [2]	Mil. dol. . .	278,085	288,184	292,326	305,371	314,907	333,259	360,026
Value of shipments (1992 dollars)	Mil. dol. . .	293,527	300,444	295,758	305,371	307,610	316,914	320,550
Total employment	1,000. . . .	848	853	846	848	838	824	812
Production workers	1,000. . . .	484	484	477	479	474	471	467
Average hourly earnings	Dollar . . .	13.82	14.40	14.98	15.27	15.62	16.21	16.93
Capital expenditures	Mil. dol. . .	13,480	15,202	16,009	16,384	15,690	15,455	17,634
PRODUCT DATA								
Value of shipments [3]	Mil. dol. . .	260,649	268,505	268,934	282,242	292,416	309,480	333,450
Value of shipments (1992 dollars)	Mil. dol. . .	273,211	278,546	271,466	282,242	285,755	294,459	296,748
TRADE DATA [4]								
Value of imports	Mil. dol. . .	20,519	22,173	23,808	27,213	28,502	33,407	40,260
Value of exports	Mil. dol. . .	36,489	38,989	42,974	43,964	45,065	51,599	60,761

[1] Estimate, except exports and imports.   [2] Value of all products and services sold by establishments in the chemicals and allied products industry.   [3] Value of products classified in the chemicals and allied products industry produced by all industries. [4] Trade data corresponds to SITC 5 (Standard International Trade Classification, rev. 3) rather than SIC 28.

Source: U.S. Department of Commerce, Bureau of the Census, International Trade Administration (ITA). Estimates by ITA.

No. 1404. Recent Trends in Industrial Inorganic Chemicals, Except Pigments (SIC 2812, 2813, 2819): 1989 to 1995

ITEM	Unit	1989	1990	1991	1992	1993	1994	1995 [1]
INDUSTRY DATA								
Value of shipments [2]	Mil. dol. . .	21,085	23,487	23,572	24,052	23,063	21,619	23,348
Value of shipments (1992 dollars)	Mil. dol. . .	21,915	23,758	23,433	24,052	22,771	20,873	21,008
Total employment	1,000. . . .	88.4	92.4	95.6	94.8	85.0	78.8	(NA)
Production workers	1,000. . . .	48.4	49.5	51.1	49.4	44.1	41.1	(NA)
Average hourly earnings	Dollar . . .	15.21	15.75	16.14	16.59	16.90	17.64	
PRODUCT DATA								
Value of shipments [3]	Mil. dol. . .	17,700	19,448	19,083	18,607	18,425	17,757	19,484
Value of shipments (1992 dollars)	Mil. dol. . .	18,345	19,638	18,944	18,607	18,202	17,107	17,203
TRADE DATA								
Value of imports	Mil. dol. . .	4,229	4,324	4,284	4,166	4,039	4,707	5,607
Value of exports	Mil. dol. . .	4,801	4,662	4,990	5,130	4,822	5,215	6,178

NA Not available.   [1] Estimate, except exports and imports.   [2] Value of all products and services sold by establishments in the industrial inorganic chemicals., except pigments industry.   [3] Value of products classified in the industrial inorganic chemicals, except pigments industry produced by all industries.

Source: U.S. Department of Commerce, Bureau of the Census, International Trade Administration (ITA). Estimates by ITA.

No. 1405. Recent Trends in Petrochemicals (SIC 2821, 2822, 2824, 2843, 2865, 2869, 2873): 1989 to 1995

ITEM	Unit	1989	1990	1991	1992	1993	1994	1995 [1]
INDUSTRY DATA								
Value of shipments [2]	Mil. dol. . .	120,851	118,989	115,600	117,074	119,225	131,712	146,314
Value of shipments (1992 dollars)	Mil. dol. . .	119,248	119,933	114,821	117,074	115,945	124,150	124,221
Total employment	1,000. . . .	260	264	262	256	255	252	(NA)
Production workers	1,000. . . .	164	165	162	158	158	156	(NA)
Average hourly earnings	Dollar . . .	15.89	16.50	17.05	17.63	17.93	18.57	(NA)
Capital expenditures	Mil. dol. . .	7,294	9,065	9,104	7,834	7,554	7,297	(NA)
PRODUCT DATA								
Value of shipments [3]	Mil. dol. . .	117,634	115,972	112,464	113,476	115,268	126,285	141,223
Value of shipments (1992 dollars)	Mil. dol. . .	115,363	116,260	111,539	113,476	112,236	119,154	119,875
TRADE DATA								
Value of imports	Mil. dol. . .	8,927	9,667	9,941	11,084	12,099	14,599	17,671
Value of exports	Mil. dol. . .	20,601	21,173	23,103	22,150	22,047	26,555	32,763

NA Not available.   [1] Estimate, except exports and imports.   [2] Value of all products and services sold by establishments in the petrochemicals industry.   [3] Value of products classified in the petrochemicals industry produced by all industries.

Source: U.S. Department of Commerce, Bureau of the Census, International Trade Administration (ITA). Estimates by ITA.

No. 1406. Recent Trends in Plastics Materials and Resins and Synthetic Rubber: 1989 to 1995

ITEM	Unit	1989	1990	1991	1992	1993	1994	1995 [1]
PLASTIC MATERIALS AND RESINS (SIC 2821)								
Industry data:								
Value of shipments [2]	Mil. dol. . .	33,257	31,326	29,566	31,304	31,546	36,965	43,503
Value of shipments (1992 dollars) . . .	Mil. dol. . .	29,250	29,497	28,677	31,304	31,172	35,004	35,140
Total employment	1,000. . . .	62.0	62.4	60.5	60.4	62.2	69.2	68.6
Production workers	1,000. . . .	37.8	37.9	36.7	35.9	36.6	40.6	40
Average hourly earnings	Dollars. . .	15.92	16.88	17.25	18.71	18.75	19.37	20.24
Capital expenditures	Mil. dol. . .	1,966	2,437	2,252	1,707	1,926	2,555	2,915
Product data:								
Value of shipments [3]	Mil. dol. . .	34,692	33,038	31,723	33,299	33,589	37,710	44,380
Value of shipments (1992 dollars) . . .	Mil. dol. . .	30,512	31,109	30,769	33,299	33,191	35,710	35,848
Trade data:								
Value of imports	Mil. dol. . .	1,554	1,811	1,776	2,063	2,520	3,281	4,086
Value of exports	Mil. dol. . .	5,590	6,316	7,447	7,052	7,225	8,478	10,350
SYNTHETIC RUBBER (SIC 2822)								
Industry data:								
Value of shipments [2]	Mil. dol. . .	4,008	4,210	4,088	4,184	4,739	4,984	5,752
Value of shipments (1992 dollars) . . .	Mil. dol. . .	3,910	3,979	4,060	4,184	4,623	4,774	4,774
Total employment	1,000. . . .	11.2	11.4	11.5	11.7	12.2	11.9	11.7
Production workers	1,000. . . .	7.1	7.2	7.4	7.5	7.7	7.7	7.6
Average hourly earnings	Dollar . . .	16.78	17.91	17.79	18.74	19.27	19.62	20.5
Capital expenditures	Mil. dol. . .	266	379	360	318	256	230	262
Product data:								
Value of shipments [3]	Mil. dol. . .	4,070	4,219	3,939	4,318	4,643	4,990	5,771
Value of shipments (1992 dollars) . . .	Mil. dol. . .	3,970	3,988	3,912	4,318	4,530	4,779	4,789
Trade data:								
Value of imports	Mil. dol. . .	514	514	466	530	555	624	691
Value of exports	Mil. dol. . .	869	885	900	1,010	947	1,081	1,264

[1] Estimate, except exports and imports.   [2] Value of all products and services sold by establishments in this industry.   [3] Value of products classified in this industry produced by all industries.

Source: U.S. Department of Commerce, Bureau of the Census, International Trade Administration (ITA). Estimates by ITA.

No. 1407. Recent Trends in Man-Made Fibers (SIC 2823, 2824): 1989 to 1995

ITEM	Unit	1989	1990	1991	1992	1993	1994	1995 [1]
INDUSTRY DATA								
Value of shipments [2]	Mil. dol. . .	13,266	12,884	12,581	12,862	13,293	13,366	13,495
Value of shipments (1992 dollars)	Mil. dol. . .	13,835	13,171	12,595	12,862	13,198	13,112	13,062
Total employment	1,000. . . .	58.1	57.8	57.4	55.4	51.6	46.9	46.0
Production workers	1,000. . . .	43.9	43.3	42.7	41.7	39.8	36.6	36.1
Average hourly earnings	Dollar . . .	13.45	13.62	14.46	14.22	14.63	14.04	14.65
PRODUCT DATA								
Value of shipments [3]	Mil. dol. . .	11,687	11,191	10,930	10,924	11,092	11,777	11,892
Value of shipments (1992 dollars)	Mil. dol. . .	12,190	11,438	10,938	10,924	11,017	11,620	11,576
TRADE DATA								
Value of imports	Mil. dol. . .	584	703	784	907	1,127	1,302	1,384
Value of exports	Mil. dol. . .	1,455	1,627	1,694	1,473	1,407	1,594	2,078

[1] Estimate, except exports and imports.   [2] Value of all products and services sold by establishments in the man-made fibers industry.   [3] Value of products classified in the man-made fibers industry produced by all industries.

Source: U.S. Department of Commerce, Bureau of the Census, International Trade Administration (ITA). Estimates by ITA.

No. 1408. Recent Trends in Drugs (SIC 283): 1989 to 1995

ITEM	Unit	1989	1990	1991	1992	1993	1994	1995 [1]
INDUSTRY DATA								
Value of shipments [2]	Mil. dol. . .	49,114	53,720	60,835	67,668	70,985	76,238	79,136
2833 Medicinals and botanicals	Mil. dol. . .	4,753	4,919	6,308	6,439	5,926	6,189	6,386
2834 Pharmaceutical preps.	Mil. dol. . .	40,028	44,182	47,376	50,418	53,281	56,961	59,268
2835 Diagnostic substances	Mil. dol. . .	2,325	2,462	4,746	6,838	6,864	7,778	7,981
2836 Bio. prod. exc. diagnostic	Mil. dol. . .	2,008	2,156	2,406	3,974	4,914	5,310	5,500
Value of shipments (1992 dollars)	Mil. dol. . .	60,453	61,534	64,565	67,668	68,216	71,475	72,065
2833 Medicinals and botanicals	Mil. dol. . .	5,275	5,359	6,444	6,439	5,523	5,546	5,607
2834 Pharmaceutical preps.	Mil. dol. . .	50,477	51,315	50,778	50,418	51,084	52,937	53,299
2835 Diagnostic substances	Mil. dol. . .	2,572	2,581	4,838	6,838	6,796	7,754	7,840
2836 Bio. prod. exc. diagnostic	Mil. dol. . .	2,130	2,279	2,506	3,974	4,813	5,237	5,319
Total employment	1,000. . . .	184.0	183.0	184.0	194.0	200.0	206.0	203.0
2833 Medicinals and botanicals	1,000. . . .	11.4	10.9	12.5	13.0	13.0	13.9	13.7
2834 Pharmaceutical preps.	1,000. . . .	142.0	144.0	129.0	123.0	128.0	134.0	132.0
2835 Diagnostic substances	1,000. . . .	16.1	14.9	30.5	39.8	39.3	38.4	37.8
2836 Bio. prod. exc. diagnostic	1,000. . . .	14.5	13.3	12.1	18.4	19.0	19.8	19.5
Production workers	1,000. . . .	82.8	81.4	82.7	92.5	94.6	102.0	106.0
2833 Medicinals and botanicals	1,000. . . .	6.6	6.5	7.2	7.4	7.7	7.8	7.7
2834 Pharmaceutical preps.	1,000. . . .	62.4	61.5	59.2	62.5	62.8	68.6	72.9
2835 Diagnostic substances	1,000. . . .	6.8	6.6	9.9	14.6	14.9	15.6	15.4
2836 Bio prod ex diagnostic	1,000. . . .	7.0	6.8	6.4	8.0	9.2	9.9	9.8
Average hourly earnings	Dollar . . .	13.48	14.22	15.36	14.76	15.8	16.25	17.36
2833 Medicinals and botanicals	Dollar . . .	16.29	17.35	20.06	18.91	19.62	19.71	20.59
2834 Pharmaceutical preps	Dollar . . .	13.83	14.71	14.77	14.71	15.81	16.04	16.76
2835 Diagnostic substances	Dollar . . .	11.54	11.80	18.17	14.03	15.64	16.9	17.66
2836 Bio. prod. exc. diagnostic	Dollar . . .	9.30	9.15	11.00	12.48	12.57	13.81	14.43
Capital expenditures	Mil. dol. . .	2,392	2,280	2,669	3,882	4,047	4,140	4,723
2833 Medicinals and botanicals	Mil. dol. . .	219	195	487	551	482	505	576
2834 Pharmaceutical preps.	Mil. dol. . .	1,933	1,809	1,772	2,450	2,493	2,714	3,096
2835 Diagnostic substances	Mil. dol. . .	117	147	302	587	667	561	640
2836 Bio. prod. exc. diagnostic	Mil. dol. . .	124	130	108	294	405	361	411
PRODUCT DATA								
Value of shipments [3]	Mil. dol. . .	43,796	47,832	51,880	60,793	63,970	68,289	70,867
2833 Medicinals and botanicals	Mil. dol. . .	5,393	5,789	6,647	7,002	6,749	6,683	6,896
2834 Pharmaceutical preps.	Mil. dol. . .	32,713	35,280	37,416	43,082	45,522	48,714	50,688
2835 Diagnostic substances	Mil. dol. . .	3,471	4,234	4,973	6,196	6,453	7,177	7,365
2836 Bio. prod. exc. diagnostic	Mil. dol. . .	2,220	2,529	2,844	4,512	5,246	5,715	5,919
Value of shipments (1992 dollars)	Mil. dol. . .	53,430	54,393	54,924	60,793	61,462	64,053	64,596
2833 Medicinals and botanicals	Mil. dol. . .	5,985	6,306	6,790	7,002	6,290	5,989	6,054
2834 Pharmaceutical preps.	Mil. dol. . .	41,252	40,975	40,102	43,082	43,645	45,273	45,583
2835 Diagnostic substances	Mil. dol. . .	3,839	4,438	5,070	6,196	6,389	7,156	7,235
2836 Bio. prod. exc. diagnostic	Mil. dol. . .	2,354	2,673	2,963	4,512	5,138	5,636	5,725
TRADE DATA								
Value of imports	Mil. dol. . .	3,531	3,884	4,812	5,958	6,094	6,966	8,582
2833 Medicinals and botanicals	Mil. dol. . .	2,354	2,303	2,854	3,277	3,101	3,366	4,632
2834 Pharmaceutical preps.	Mil. dol. . .	868	1,103	1,442	1,859	2,096	2,517	2,877
2835 Diagnostic substances	Mil. dol. . .	118	207	191	336	379	530	465
2836 Bio. prod. exc. diagnostic	Mil. dol. . .	191	271	325	486	518	553	608
Value of exports	Mil. dol. . .	4,345	5,050	5,731	6,774	7,222	7,565	7,996
2833 Medicinals and botanicals	Mil. dol. . .	1,794	1,908	2,064	2,444	2,401	2,281	2,445
2834 Pharmaceutical preps.	Mil. dol. . .	974	1,258	1,478	1,818	2,027	2,315	2,247
2835 Diagnostic substances	Mil. dol. . .	739	909	1,160	1,370	1,485	1,507	1,741
2836 Bio. prod. exc. diagnostic	Mil. dol. . .	839	974	1,028	1,142	1,309	1,462	1,562

[1] Estimate, except exports and imports. [2] Value of all products and services sold by establishments in the drugs industry. [3] Value of products classified in the drugs industry produced by all industries.

Source: U.S. Department of Commerce, Bureau of the Census, International Trade Administration (ITA). Estimates by ITA.

No. 1409. Recent Trends in Soap, Cleaners, and Toilet Goods (SIC 284): 1989 to 1995

ITEM	Unit	1989	1990	1991	1992	1993	1994	1995 [1]
INDUSTRY DATA								
Value of shipments [2]	Mil. dol.	38,869	41,438	41,854	43,055	46,903	46,314	47,474
2841 Soap and other detergents	Mil. dol.	13,281	15,373	15,299	14,761	15,458	14,528	14,865
2842 Polishes/sanitation goods	Mil. dol.	5,987	5,848	6,172	6,676	8,079	8,372	8,652
2843 Surface active agents	Mil. dol.	2,959	3,168	3,299	2,864	3,661	3,678	3,891
2844 Toilet preparations	Mil. dol.	16,642	17,048	17,085	18,754	19,706	19,736	20,066
Value of shipments (1992 dollars)	Mil. dol.	40,821	42,982	42,704	43,055	46,174	45,642	46,204
2841 Soap and other detergents	Mil. dol.	13,401	15,751	15,707	14,761	15,259	14,455	14,617
2842 Polishes/sanitation goods	Mil. dol.	6,376	6,066	6,265	6,676	8,014	8,232	8,327
2843 Surface active agents	Mil. dol.	3,206	3,293	3,315	2,864	3,599	3,568	3,626
2844 Toilet preparations	Mil. dol.	17,837	17,870	17,416	18,754	19,301	19,387	19,634
Total employment	1,000	129.0	126.0	123.0	123.0	124.0	118.0	116.0
2841 Soap and other detergents	1,000	34.8	36.3	36.6	32.9	31.2	31.3	30.8
2842 Polishes/sanitation goods	1,000	21.2	19.6	19.6	22.0	22.8	21.2	20.9
2843 Surface active agents	1,000	9.0	9.1	9.3	8.2	8.6	8.0	7.9
2844 Toilet preparations	1,000	63.8	61.1	57.4	60.1	61.7	57.6	56.8
Production workers	1,000	79.4	77.8	75.7	74.8	74.6	70.6	69.9
2841 Soap and other detergents	1,000	22.0	22.8	23.1	20.0	17.9	18.5	18.3
2842 Polishes/sanitation goods	1,000	13.4	12.3	12.2	13.4	13.8	12.9	12.8
2843 Surface active agents	1,000	4.6	4.6	4.8	4.2	4.3	3.9	3.9
2844 Toilet preparations	1,000	39.4	38.1	35.6	37.2	38.6	35.3	34.9
Average hourly earnings	Dollars	11.25	11.73	12.25	12.32	12.26	12.37	12.93
2841 Soap and other detergents	Dollars	14.36	14.65	14.67	14.85	15.06	14.92	15.59
2842 Polishes/sanitation goods	Dollars	10.24	10.63	11.09	11.84	11.94	11.17	11.67
2843 Surface active agents	Dollars	13.32	13.71	14.28	14.94	15.95	16.57	17.31
2844 Toilet preparations	Dollars	9.69	10.14	10.81	10.82	10.59	10.93	11.42
Capital expenditures	Mil. dol.	980	1,016	1,225	1,293	1,320	1,273	1,453
2841 Soap and other detergents	Mil. dol.	396	476	631	571	514	454	519
2842 Polishes/sanitation goods	Mil. dol.	141	95	137	122	130	124	141
2843 Surface active agents	Mil. dol.	129	165	157	92	203	205	233
2844 Toilet preparations	Mil. dol.	314	280	300	507	473	491	560
PRODUCT DATA								
Value of shipments [3]	Mil. dol.	36,764	38,634	38,695	39,999	43,293	42,711	43,776
2841 Soap and other detergents	Mil. dol.	10,916	11,860	11,785	11,022	11,594	11,086	11,344
2842 Polishes/sanitation goods	Mil. dol.	5,306	5,531	5,546	6,477	7,492	7,728	7,987
2843 Surface active agents	Mil. dol.	3,671	3,877	3,975	3,776	4,032	3,635	3,845
2844 Toilet preparations	Mil. dol.	16,872	17,366	17,390	18,724	20,175	20,262	20,601
Value of shipments (1992 dollars)	Mil. dol.	38,726	40,123	39,450	39,999	42,603	42,059	42,582
2841 Soap and other detergents	Mil. dol.	11,015	12,152	12,099	11,022	11,445	11,031	11,154
2842 Polishes/sanitation goods	Mil. dol.	5,650	5,737	5,630	6,477	7,433	7,599	7,687
2843 Surface active agents	Mil. dol.	3,977	4,030	3,995	3,776	3,965	3,525	3,583
2844 Toilet preparations	Mil. dol.	18,083	18,203	17,726	18,724	19,760	19,904	20,157
TRADE DATA								
Value of imports	Mil. dol.	893	1,000	1,076	1,308	1,463	1,689	1,936
2841 Soap and other detergents	Mil. dol.	148	196	178	213	254	335	421
2842 Polishes/sanitation goods	Mil. dol.	30.9	36.6	33.5	46.0	49.8	56.3	61.6
2843 Surface active agents	Mil. dol.	120	134	152	158	204	263	296
2844 Toilet preparations	Mil. dol.	594	634	712	892	956	1,035	1,156
Value of exports	Mil. dol.	1,421	1,853	2,235	2,529	2,853	3,358	3,710
2841 Soap and other detergents	Mil. dol.	271	390	510	583	644	716	828
2842 Polishes/sanitation goods	Mil. dol.	77	112	130	144	170	174	205
2843 Surface active agents	Mil. dol.	379	465	477	548	604	734	790
2844 Toilet preparations	Mil. dol.	694	886	1,118	1,254	1,437	1,733	1,887

[1] Estimate, except exports and imports.   [2] Value of all products and services sold by establishments in the soap, cleaners, and toilet goods industry.   [3] Value of products classified in the soap, cleaners, and toilet goods industry produced by all industries.

Source: U.S. Department of Commerce, Bureau of the Census, International Trade Administration (ITA). Estimates by ITA.

No. 1410. Recent Trends in Paints and Allied Products (SIC 2851): 1989 to 1995

ITEM	Unit	1989	1990	1991	1992	1993	1994	1995 [1]
INDUSTRY DATA								
Value of shipments [2]	Mil. dol. . .	13,656	14,239	14,255	14,974	16,030	17,544	18,651
Value of shipments (1992 dollars)	Mil. dol. . .	15,107	15,067	14,472	14,974	15,825	17,033	17,174
Total employment	1,000. . . .	55.0	53.9	51.1	51.2	50.3	50.1	49.4
Production workers	1,000. . . .	27.7	27.2	25.2	25.7	25.9	27.0	26.7
Average hourly earnings	Dollar	11.69	11.89	12.09	12.72	13.00	13.98	14.61
Capital expenditures	Mil. dol. . .	241	271	256	290	256	280	319
PRODUCT DATA								
Value of shipments [3]	Mil. dol. . .	13,185	13,681	13,722	14,283	15,356	16,617	17,665
Value of shipments (1992 dollars)	Mil. dol. . .	14,585	14,477	13,931	14,283	15,159	16,133	16,266
TRADE DATA								
Value of imports	Mil. dol. . .	106	137	141	184	197	261	343
Value of exports	Mil. dol. . .	422	570	686	754	811	936	1,009

[1] Estimate, except exports and imports.   [2] Value of all products and services sold by establishments in the paints and allied products industry.   [3] Value of products classified in the paints and allied products industry produced by all industries.

Source: U.S. Department of Commerce, Bureau of the Census, International Trade Administration (ITA). Estimates by ITA.

No. 1411. Recent Trends in Organic Chemicals, Except Gum and Wood (SIC 2865, 2869): 1989 to 1995

ITEM	Unit	1989	1990	1991	1992	1993	1994	1995 [1]
INDUSTRY DATA								
Value of shipments [2]	Mil. dol. . .	65,324	65,053	63,721	63,827	63,541	68,822	75,505
Value of shipments (1992 dollars)	Mil. dol. . .	67,052	67,615	63,893	63,827	61,162	64,658	65,066
Total employment	1,000. . . .	121	123	125	122	121	112	111
Production workers	1,000. . . .	72.2	72.7	72.5	70.6	70.9	65.7	67.0
Average hourly earnings	Dollar	17.01	17.73	18.29	18.70	18.88	20.23	(NA)
Capital expenditures	Mil. dol. . .	4,069	5,111	5,252	4,757	4,028	3,524	(NA)
PRODUCT DATA								
Value of shipments [3]	Mil. dol. . .	61,187	61,044	59,326	58,655	59,135	64,660	70,922
Value of shipments (1992 dollars)	Mil. dol. . .	62,426	63,059	59,427	58,655	57,017	60,933	61,338
TRADE DATA								
Value of imports	Mil. dol. . .	5,815	6,272	6,583	7,242	7,330	8,654	10,566
Value of exports	Mil. dol. . .	9,834	9,738	10,063	10,036	10,409	12,336	15,606

NA Not available.   [1] Estimate, except exports and imports.   [2] Value of all products and services sold by establishments in the organic chemicals, except gum and wood industry.   [3] Value of products classified in the organic chemicals, except gum and wood industry produced by all industries.

Source: U.S. Department of Commerce, Bureau of the Census, International Trade Administration (ITA). Estimates by ITA.

No. 1412. Recent Trends in Nitrogenous Fertilizers and Phosphatic Fertilizers: 1989 to 1995

ITEM	Unit	1989	1990	1991	1992	1993	1994	1995 [1]
NITROGENOUS FERTILIZERS (SIC 2873)								
Industry data:								
Value of shipments [2]	Mil. dol. . .	2,866	3,113	3,238	3,175	3,467	4,246	4,953
Value of shipments (1992 dollars)	Mil. dol. . .	2,878	3,170	3,117	3,175	3,340	3,614	3,639
Total employment	1,000. . . .	7.0	7.5	7.3	7.0	7.0	8.0	8.0
Production workers	1,000. . . .	4.4	4.8	4.7	4.7	4.7	5.4	5.3
Average hourly earnings	Dollar	14.03	13.80	14.77	15.65	16.11	16.69	17.45
Capital expenditures	Mil. dol. . .	123	99	220	209	186	175	199
Product data:								
Value of shipments [3]	Mil. dol. . .	3,147	3,357	3,438	3,589	3,737	4,428	5,165
Value of shipments (1992 dollars)	Mil. dol. . .	3,160	3,418	3,309	3,589	3,600	3,769	3,795
PHOSPHATIC FERTILIZERS (SIC 2874)								
Industry data:								
Value of shipments [2]	Mil. dol. . .	4,187	4,636	4,984	4,333	3,648	4,597	5,495
Value of shipments (1992 dollars)	Mil. dol. . .	3,522	4,177	4,360	4,333	4,155	4,152	4,163
Total employment	1,000. . . .	10.8	10.5	10.3	9.5	9.4	8.5	8.4
Production workers	1,000. . . .	7.4	7.5	7.3	6.7	6.7	6.2	6.1
Average hourly earnings	Dollar	13.55	13.70	14.65	13.82	14.70	16.69	17.45
Capital expenditures	Mil. dol. . .	132	138	197	308	150	159	182
Product data:								
Value of shipments [3]	Mil. dol. . .	4,285	4,462	4,572	3,929	3,397	4,272	5,107
Value of shipments (1992 dollars)	Mil. dol. . .	3,603	4,020	4,000	3,929	3,869	3,859	3,869

[1] Estimate.   [2] Value of all products and services sold by establishments in this industry.   [3] Value of products classified in this industry produced by all industries.

Source: U.S. Department of Commerce, Bureau of the Census, International Trade Administration (ITA). Estimates by ITA.

No. 1413. Recent Trends in Agricultural Chemicals, n.e.c. (SIC 2879): 1989 to 1995

ITEM	Unit	1989	1990	1991	1992	1993	1994	1995 [1]
INDUSTRY DATA								
Value of shipments [2]	Mil. dol. . .	8,327	8,539	8,346	9,151	9,554	9,636	9,958
Value of shipments (1992 dollars)	Mil. dol. . .	9,304	9,172	8,559	9,151	9,142	8,800	8,859
Total employment	1,000. . . .	17.4	17.7	16.4	16.9	16.3	15.3	15.1
Production workers	1,000. . . .	9.8	10.2	9.1	9.6	9.2	8.8	8.7
Average hourly earnings	Dollar . . .	15.08	16.27	15.15	15.59	16.41	18.40	19.23
Capital expenditures	Mil. dol. . .	503	558	481	428	356	299	342
PRODUCT DATA								
Value of shipments [3]	Mil. dol. . .	7,277	7,280	7,448	8,225	8,737	8,846	9,141
Value of shipments (1992 dollars)	Mil. dol. . .	8,130	7,820	7,639	8,225	8,361	8,078	8,133

[1] Estimate.   [2] Value of all products and services sold by establishments in the agricultural chemicals, n.e.c. industry.
[3] Value of products classified in the agricultural chemicals, n.e.c. industry produced by all industries.

Source: U.S. Department of Commerce, Bureau of the Census, International Trade Administration (ITA). Estimates by ITA.

No. 1414. Recent Trends in Adhesives and Sealants (SIC 2891): 1989 to 1995

ITEM	Unit	1989	1990	1991	1992	1993	1994	1995 [1]
INDUSTRY DATA								
Value of shipments [2]	Mil. dol. . .	5,286	5,485	5,483	5,659	5,859	5,849	6,284
Value of shipments (1992 dollars)	Mil. dol. . .	5,541	5,750	5,522	5,659	5,711	5,528	5,596
Total employment	1,000. . . .	21.9	21.4	20.9	21.1	20.9	19.2	18.9
Production workers	1,000. . . .	12.3	11.9	11.7	11.6	11.5	11.3	11.2
Average hourly earnings	Dollar . . .	11.02	11.5	11.43	12.41	12.57	13.41	14.02
Capital expenditures	Mil. dol. . .	136	127	139	190	183	204	233
PRODUCT DATA								
Value of shipments [3]	Mil. dol. . .	5,134	5,403	5,382	5,415	5,807	5,422	5,826
Value of shipments (1992 dollars)	Mil. dol. . .	5,382	5,663	5,420	5,415	5,660	5,125	5,188
TRADE DATA								
Value of imports	Mil. dol. . .	70	90	94	112	119	135	140
Value of exports	Mil. dol. . .	123	159	169	202	241	283	315

[1] Estimate, except exports and imports.   [2] Value of all products and services sold by establishments in the adhesives and
sealants industry.   [3] Value of products classified in the adhesives and sealants industry produced by all industries.

Source: U.S. Department of Commerce, Bureau of the Census, International Trade Administration (ITA). Estimates by ITA.

No. 1415. Recent Trends in Petroleum Refining (SIC 2911): 1989 to 1995

ITEM	Unit	1989	1990	1991	1992	1993	1994	1995 [1]
INDUSTRY DATA								
Value of shipments [2]	Mil. dol. . .	131,192	159,411	145,392	136,239	129,961	128,236	134,198
Value of shipments (1992 dollars)	Mil. dol. . .	139,270	138,258	140,475	136,239	135,376	138,783	141,113
Total employment	1,000. . . .	72.4	71.9	73.9	74.8	73.1	71.7	(NA)
Production workers	1,000. . . .	47.9	47.3	47.6	47.9	47.3	46.3	(NA)
Average hourly earnings	Dollar . . .	17.77	18.56	19.46	19.74	21.04	21.64	(NA)
Capital expenditures	Mil. dol. . .	2,987	3,819	5,601	6,140	5,986	5,215	(NA)
PRODUCT DATA								
Value of shipments [3]	Mil. dol. . .	124,452	151,559	138,322	131,640	125,456	123,184	128,912
Value of shipments (1992 dollars)	Mil. dol. . .	132,115	131,447	133,645	131,640	130,683	133,316	135,554
TRADE DATA								
Value of imports	Mil. dol. . .	11,797	14,269	10,890	10,185	9,742	9,274	8,765
Value of exports	Mil. dol. . .	4,318	5,988	6,356	5,759	5,641	4,958	5,333

NA Not available.   [1] Estimate, except exports and imports.   [2] Value of all products and services sold by establishments in
the petroleum refining industry.   [3] Value of products classified in the petroleum refining industry produced by all industries.

Source: U.S. Department of Commerce, Bureau of the Census; U.S. Department of Energy, Energy Information Administration
(EIA). Estimates by EIA.

No. 1416. Recent Trends in Tires and Inner Tubes (SIC 3011): 1989 to 1995

ITEM	Unit	1989	1990	1991	1992	1993	1994	1995 [1]
INDUSTRY DATA								
Value of shipments [2]	Mil. dol. . .	11,680	11,861	11,883	11,810	12,601	12,883	13,273
Value of shipments (1992 dollars)	Mil. dol. . .	11,907	12,152	12,015	11,810	12,614	12,935	13,194
Total employment	1,000. . . .	68.0	67.7	65.5	64.6	65.1	63.7	66.2
Production workers	1,000. . . .	54.6	54.7	52.4	52.8	53.3	52.7	54.9
Average hourly earnings	Dollar . . .	16.57	16.84	17.70	18.56	18.63	18.99	18.81
Capital expenditures	Mil. dol. . .	785	652	506	506	490	515	535
PRODUCT DATA								
Value of shipments [3]	Mil. dol. . .	11,256	11,340	11,303	11,316	12,241	12,516	12,894
Value of shipments (1992 dollars)	Mil. dol. . .	11,474	11,619	11,428	11,316	12,253	12,566	12,817
TRADE DATA								
Value of imports	Mil. dol. . .	2,667	2,553	2,271	2,463	2,680	2,979	3,089
Value of exports	Mil. dol. . .	854	1,140	1,262	1,395	1,453	1,598	1,856

[1] Estimate, except exports and imports.   [2] Value of all products and services sold by establishments in the tires and inner tubes industry.   [3] Value of products classified in the tires and inner tubes industry produced by all industries.

Source: U.S. Department of Commerce, Bureau of the Census, International Trade Administration (ITA). Estimates by ITA.

No. 1417. Recent Trends in Fabricated Rubber Products, n.e.c. (SIC 3069): 1989 to 1995

ITEM	Unit	1989	1990	1991	1992	1993	1994	1995 [1]
INDUSTRY DATA								
Value of shipments [2]	Mil. dol. . .	6,343	6,629	6,644	6,934	7,608	7,729	8,271
Value of shipments (1992 dollars)	Mil. dol. . .	6,755	6,877	6,684	6,934	7,474	7,425	7,574
Total employment	1,000. . . .	57.1	56.6	55.8	57.3	58.4	57.8	58.5
Production workers	1,000. . . .	44.0	43.6	42.6	42.1	43.4	43.2	44.1
Average hourly earnings	Dollar . . .	9.15	9.30	9.84	10.08	10.33	10.30	10.52
Capital expenditures	Mil. dol. . .	212	182	160	204	222	227	239
PRODUCT DATA								
Value of shipments [3]	Mil. dol. . .	6,193	6,462	6,490	6,600	7,179	7,341	7,855
Value of shipments (1992 dollars)	Mil. dol. . .	6,596	6,704	6,530	6,600	7,052	7,052	7,193
TRADE DATA								
Value of imports	Mil. dol. . .	755	733	847	1,090	1,303	1,528	1,779
Value of exports	Mil. dol. . .	483	660	716	735	786	930	993

[1] Estimate, except exports and imports.   [2] Value of all products and services sold by establishments in the fabricated rubber products, n.e.c. industry.   [3] Value of products classified in the fabricated rubber products, n.e.c., industry produced by all industries.

Source: U.S. Department of Commerce, Bureau of the Census, International Trade Administration (ITA). Estimates by ITA.

No. 1418. Recent Trends in Miscellaneous Plastic Products Excluding Bottles and Plumbing (SIC 3081-4, -6, -7, -9): 1989 to 1995

ITEM	Unit	1989	1990	1991	1992	1993	1994	1995 [1]
INDUSTRY DATA								
Value of shipments [2]	Mil. dol. . .	65,746	68,064	67,545	77,957	84,160	93,504	100,575
Value of shipments (1992 dollars)	Mil. dol. . .	66,470	68,085	67,304	77,957	83,479	91,245	92,431
Total employment	1,000. . . .	597	595	575	627	650	679	678
Production workers	1,000. . . .	460	457	440	479	504	531	530
Average hourly earnings	Dollar . . .	8.74	9.22	9.54	9.96	10.23	10.35	10.95
Capital expenditures	Mil. dol. . .	2,929	2,891	3,012	3,454	3,465	4,014	4,308
PRODUCT DATA								
Value of shipments [3]	Mil. dol. . .	65,219	67,410	66,669	75,532	81,512	90,389	97,429
Value of shipments (1992 dollars)	Mil. dol. . .	65,948	67,473	66,453	75,532	80,851	88,217	89,540
TRADE DATA								
Value of imports	Mil. dol. . .	3,535	3,677	3,751	4,330	4,693	5,300	6,084
Value of exports	Mil. dol. . .	2,837	3,519	3,858	4,471	5,029	5,933	6,489

[1] Estimate, except exports and imports.   [2] Value of all products and services sold by establishments in the miscellaneous plastic products excluding bottles and plumbing industry.   [3] Value of products classified in the miscellaneous plastic products excluding bottles and plumbing industry produced by all industries.

Source: U.S. Department of Commerce, Bureau of the Census, International Trade Administration (ITA). Estimates by ITA.

No. 1419. Recent Trends in Footwear, Except Rubber (SIC 314): 1989 to 1995

ITEM	Unit	1989	1990	1991	1992	1993	1994	1995 [1]
INDUSTRY DATA								
Value of shipments [2]	Mil. dol.	4,262	4,232	3,775	3,898	3,974	3,923	3,794
3142 House slippers	Mil. dol.	287	276	277	285	302	204	223
3143 Men's footwear	Mil. dol.	2,228	2,149	2,064	2,210	2,351	2,461	2,349
3144 Women's footwear	Mil. dol.	1,351	1,393	1,154	1,095	1,010	950	933
3149 Footwear n.e.c.	Mil. dol.	396	414	280	309	310	309	290
Value of shipments (1992 dollars)	Mil. dol.	4,664	4,446	3,872	3,898	3,907	3,816	3,584
3142 House slippers	Mil. dol.	278	267	271	285	310	205	216
3143 Men's footwear	Mil. dol.	2,479	2,276	2,121	2,210	2,305	2,382	2,191
3144 Women's footwear	Mil. dol.	1,482	1,470	1,194	1,095	987	927	899
3149 Footwear n.e.c.	Mil. dol.	426	433	285	309	305	302	278
Total employment	1,000.	66.0	62.1	53.1	49.0	48.5	46.8	43.5
Production workers	1,000.	57.5	53.5	46.0	41.4	41.3	40.3	37.2
Average hourly earnings	Dollar	6.38	6.50	6.83	7.29	7.43	7.44	(NA)
Capital expenditures	Mil. dol.	40.7	42.1	31.5	51.2	40.3	58.8	(NA)
3142 House slippers	Mil. dol.	3.8	3.3	2.4	2.1	2.5	4.8	(NA)
3143 Men's footwear	Mil. dol.	21.2	22.8	18.1	32.8	26.1	43.3	(NA)
3144 Women's footwear	Mil. dol.	11.1	13.4	9.1	10.5	6.8	7.6	(NA)
3149 Footwear n.e.c.	Mil. dol.	4.6	2.6	1.9	5.8	4.9	3.1	(NA)
PRODUCT DATA								
Value of shipments [3]	Mil. dol.	3,908	3,780	3,495	3,608	3,707	3,739	3,626
3142 House slippers	Mil. dol.	233	257	256	259	256	208	228
3143 Men's footwear	Mil. dol.	1,940	1,839	1,763	1,807	1,970	2,040	1,948
3144 Women's footwear	Mil. dol.	1,339	1,311	1,186	1,229	1,188	1,190	1,169
3149 Footwear n.e.c.	Mil. dol.	396	373	289	314	293	301	281
Value of shipments (1992 dollars)	Mil. dol.	4,278	3,970	3,586	3,608	3,643	3,639	3,434
3142 House slippers	Mil. dol.	225	249	251	259	263	209	221
3143 Men's footwear	Mil. dol.	2,158	1,948	1,812	1,807	1,931	1,975	1,817
3144 Women's footwear	Mil. dol.	1,468	1,382	1,228	1,229	1,160	1,161	1,126
3149 Footwear n.e.c.	Mil. dol.	426	390	295	314	289	294	270
TRADE DATA								
Value of imports	Mil. dol.	7,462	8,431	8,337	8,616	9,290	9,698	9,984
Value of exports	Mil. dol.	179	254	306	342	331	379	367

NA Not available. [1] Estimate, except exports and imports. [2] Value of all products and services sold by establishments in the footwear, except rubber industry. [3] Value of products classified in the footwear, except rubber industry produced by all industries.

Source: U.S. Department of Commerce, Bureau of the Census, International Trade Administration (ITA). Estimates by ITA.

No. 1420. Recent Trends in Leather Tanning and Finishing (SIC 3111): 1989 to 1995

ITEM	Unit	1989	1990	1991	1992	1993	1994	1995 [1]
INDUSTRY DATA								
Value of shipments [2]	Mil. dol.	2,501	2,411	2,183	2,910	3,198	3,038	3,105
Value of shipments (1992 dollars)	Mil. dol.	2,486	2,305	2,174	2,910	3,096	2,805	2,707
Total employment	1,000.	12.3	12.1	11.5	16.6	16.9	14.7	14.7
Production workers	1,000.	10.6	10.3	9.8	13.3	13.8	13.4	12.3
Average hourly earnings	Dollar	9.67	9.58	10.62	10.52	10.65	10.61	(NA)
Capital expenditures	Mil. dol.	47.9	39.0	41.4	48.5	52.2	45.5	(NA)
PRODUCT DATA								
Value of shipments [3]	Mil. dol.	2,525	2,458	2,226	2,952	3,218	3,055	3,122
Value of shipments (1992 dollars)	Mil. dol.	2,510	2,350	2,217	2,952	3,115	2,821	2,722
TRADE DATA								
Value of imports	Mil. dol.	744	683	571	631	736	960	1,089
Value of exports	Mil. dol.	625	751	680	705	764	812	870

NA Not available. [1] Estimate, except exports and imports. [2] Value of all products and services sold by establishments in the leather tanning and finishing industry. [3] Value of products classified in the leather tanning and finishing industry produced by all industries.

Source: U.S. Department of Commerce, Bureau of the Census, International Trade Administration (ITA). Estimates by ITA.

No. 1421. Recent Trends in Luggage and Personal Leather Goods (SIC 2386, 315, 316, 317): 1989 to 1995

ITEM	Unit	1989	1990	1991	1992	1993	1994	1995 [1]
INDUSTRY DATA								
Value of shipments [2]	Mil. dol.	2,340	2,403	2,354	2,180	2,106	2,068	1,956
2386 Leather and sheep-lined clothing	Mil. dol.	163	167	159	209	224	238	201
3151 Leather gloves/mittens	Mil. dol.	149	155	141	137	169	143	155
3161 Luggage	Mil. dol.	1,121	1,169	1,148	944	930	991	960
3171 Women's handbags/purses	Mil. dol.	544	547	545	463	387	304	269
3172 Personal leather goods	Mil. dol.	363	365	362	428	395	393	371
Value of shipments (1992 dollars)	Mil. dol.	2,538	2,505	2,393	2,180	2,090	2,062	1,948
2386 Leather and sheep-lined clothing	Mil. dol.	168	168	158	209	225	247	213
3151 Leather gloves/mittens	Mil. dol.	159	158	143	137	168	135	141
3161 Luggage	Mil. dol.	1,228	1,228	1,173	944	922	979	956
3171 Women's handbags/purses	Mil. dol.	583	566	549	463	385	313	271
3172 Personal leather goods	Mil. dol.	400	386	369	428	389	388	367
Total employment	1,000.	31.7	31.9	29.3	26.2	24.3	21.9	20.9
Production workers	1,000.	24.8	25.3	23.0	20.7	19.0	17.6	16.7
Average hourly earnings	Dollar	6.6	7.23	7.34	7.39	7.41	7.56	(NA)
Capital expenditures	Mil. dol.	28.2	24.4	18.2	26.5	28.2	26.8	(NA)
2386 Leather and sheep-lined clothing	Mil. dol.	0.8	0.4	0.3	1.3	1.6	0.1	(NA)
3151 Leather gloves/mittens	Mil. dol.	0.5	0.5	0.2	0.5	0.3	12.2	(NA)
3161 Luggage	Mil. dol.	15.0	11.5	9.6	14.5	16.4	9.5	(NA)
3171 Women's handbags/purses	Mil. dol.	6.3	6.8	3.1	3.4	4.2	3.1	(NA)
3172 Personal leather goods	Mil. dol.	5.6	5.2	5.0	6.8	5.7	1.9	(NA)
PRODUCT DATA								
Value of shipments [3]	Mil. dol.	2,126	2,170	2,164	2,109	2,013	2,047	1,930
2386 Leather and sheep-lined clothing	Mil. dol.	158	161	201	199	216	223	189
3151 Leather gloves/mittens	Mil. dol.	117	113	127	114	115	112	123
3161 Luggage	Mil. dol.	1,001	1,064	1,028	864	814	880	851
3171 Women's handbags/purses	Mil. dol.	462	453	432	411	366	328	290
3172 Personal leather goods	Mil. dol.	388	379	375	522	503	505	477
Value of shipments (1992 dollars)	Mil. dol.	2,307	2,264	2,199	2,109	1,997	2,043	1,924
2386 Leather and sheep-lined clothing	Mil. dol.	163	162	201	199	217	232	200
3151 Leather gloves/mittens	Mil. dol.	124	115	129	114	114	107	112
3161 Luggage	Mil. dol.	1,097	1,118	1,052	864	807	869	848
3171 Women's handbags/purses	Mil. dol.	496	468	436	411	364	338	293
3172 Personal leather goods	Mil. dol.	428	400	383	522	495	498	471
TRADE DATA								
Value of imports	Mil. dol.	3,410	3,545	3,498	3,820	3,990	4,460	4,543
2386 Leather and sheep-lined clothing	Mil. dol.	1,173	1,209	1,079	1,229	1,221	1,238	989
3151 Leather gloves/mittens	Mil. dol.	170	181	158	171	214	261	291
3161 Luggage	Mil. dol.	977	1,058	1,103	1,247	1,367	1,649	1,893
3171 Women's handbags/purses	Mil. dol.	832	842	893	883	902	949	959
3172 Personal leather goods	Mil. dol.	258	255	266	289	286	363	411
Value of exports	Mil. dol.	164	204	234	277	290	321	364
2386 Leather and sheep-lined clothing	Mil. dol.	45.8	51.9	57.3	65.5	69.5	64.9	88.7
3151 Leather gloves/mittens	Mil. dol.	11.5	14.0	13.1	12.2	14.0	13.8	13.4
3161 Luggage	Mil. dol.	68.4	95.2	115.0	143.0	146.0	177.0	187.0
3171 Women's handbags/purses	Mil. dol.	27.1	25.0	28.1	34.5	40.3	41.2	48.2
3172 Personal leather goods	Mil. dol.	11.5	17.8	21.3	22.8	20.0	23.9	27.2

Not available.   [1] Estimate, except exports and imports.   [2] Value of all products and services sold by establishments in the luggage and personal leather goods industry.   [3] Value of products classified in the luggage and personal leather goods industry produced by all industries.

Source: U.S. Department of Commerce, Bureau of the Census, International Trade Administration (ITA). Estimates by ITA.

No. 1422. Recent Trends in Flat Glass (SIC 3211): 1989 to 1995

ITEM	Unit	1989	1990	1991	1992	1993	1994	1995 [1]
INDUSTRY DATA								
Value of shipments [2]	Mil. dol.	2,477	2,279	2,104	2,078	2,283	2,600	2,630
Value of shipments (1992 dollars)	Mil. dol.	2,283	2,196	2,096	2,078	2,234	2,346	2,252
Total employment	1,000.	15	14.6	13.2	11.9	11.3	11.2	(NA)
Production workers	1,000.	12.1	11.9	10.7	9.7	9.2	9.2	(NA)
Average hourly earnings	Dollar	16.47	16.19	16.77	17.39	18.03	19.01	(NA)
Capital expenditures	Mil. dol.	144	127	112	148	159	137	(NA)
PRODUCT DATA								
Value of shipments [3]	Mil. dol.	2,442	2,241	2,089	1,994	2,151	2,474	2,503
Value of shipments (1992 dollars)	Mil. dol.	2,251	2,159	2,081	1,994	2,105	2,233	2,143
TRADE DATA								
Value of imports	Mil. dol.	481	328	324	319	392	488	476
Value of exports	Mil. dol.	497	665	692	723	833	895	970

NA Not available.   [1] Estimate, except exports and imports.   [2] Value of all products and services sold by establishments in the flat glass industry.   [3] Value of products classified in the flat glass industry produced by all industries.

Source: U.S. Department of Commerce, Bureau of the Census, International Trade Administration (ITA). Estimates by ITA.

No. 1423. Recent Trends in Hydraulic Cement, Ceramic Tile, and Gypsum Products: 1989 to 1995

ITEM	Unit	1989	1990	1991	1992	1993	1994	1995 [1]
HYDRAULIC CEMENT (SIC 3241)								
Industry data:								
Value of shipments [2]	Mil. dol.	4,129	4,251	3,778	4,051	4,187	4,808	5,041
Value of shipments (1992 dollars)	Mil. dol.	4,301	4,364	3,763	4,051	3,987	4,278	4,190
Total employment	1,000.	16.9	17.6	16.4	17.0	16.6	16.7	16.8
Production workers	1,000.	13.0	13.4	12.2	12.8	12.5	12.4	12.5
Average hourly earnings	Dollar	14.53	15.16	14.86	15.15	15.48	15.83	16.27
Capital expenditures	Mil. dol.	263	265	225	226	227	280	316
Product data:								
Value of shipments [3]	Mil. dol.	3,898	4,113	3,701	3,929	4,051	4,683	4,908
Value of shipments (1992 dollars)	Mil. dol.	4,061	4,223	3,686	3,929	3,858	4,166	4,080
Trade data:								
Value of imports	Mil. dol.	492	444	333	250	283	443	541
Value of exports	Mil. dol.	25.4	38.3	45.8	48.7	47.8	45.2	53.0
CERAMIC WALL AND FLOOR TILE (SIC 3253)								
Industry data:								
Value of shipments [2]	Mil. dol.	793	845	751	731	811	847	867
Value of shipments (1992 dollars)	Mil. dol.	807	846	759	731	806	829	834
Total employment	1,000.	10	9.8	9.5	8.9	8.7	8.6	8.4
Production workers	1,000.	8.4	8.1	7.7	7.3	7.3	7.1	7.0
Average hourly earnings	Dollar	8.98	9.57	8.94	9.50	10.41	9.85	10.05
Capital expenditures	Mil. dol.	32.3	68.8	22.1	48.9	68.0	73.1	65.0
Product data:								
Value of shipments [3]	Mil. dol.	681	696	683	678	739	735	752
Value of shipments (1992 dollars)	Mil. dol.	694	697	690	678	734	719	723
Trade data:								
Value of imports	Mil. dol.	431	421	365	419	472	519	562
Value of exports	Mil. dol.	17.9	20.5	21.0	19.3	22.6	23.5	26.1
GYPSUM PRODUCTS (SIC 3275)								
Industry data:								
Value of shipments [2]	Mil. dol.	2,408	2,375	2,008	2,076	2,290	2,849	3,212
Value of shipments (1992 dollars)	Mil. dol.	2,088	2,195	2,002	2,076	2,067	2,071	2,063
Total employment	1,000.	11.3	11.5	10.3	10.5	10.4	10.7	10.7
Production workers	1,000.	9.0	9.1	8.1	8.3	8.3	8.6	8.6
Average hourly earnings	Dollar	12.00	12.27	12.83	12.74	13.06	13.53	13.9
Capital expenditures	Mil. dol.	53.6	68.1	34.2	43.8	39.8	74.2	66.0
Product data:								
Value of shipments [3]	Mil. dol.	2,238	2,258	1,899	1,948	2,133	2,653	2,989
Value of shipments (1992 dollars)	Mil. dol.	1,941	2,087	1,893	1,948	1,925	1,928	1,920
Trade data:								
Value of imports	Mil. dol.	32.2	25.8	12.8	13.2	24.5	50.6	75.2
Value of exports	Mil. dol.	51.5	67.0	65.6	71.2	55.3	50.5	52.9

[1] Estimate, except exports and imports. [2] Value of all products and services sold by establishments in this industry. [3] Value of products classified in this industry produced by all industries.

Source: U.S. Department of Commerce, Bureau of the Census, International Trade Administration (ITA). Estimates by ITA.

No. 1424. Recent Trends in Steel Mill Products (SIC 3312, 3315, 3316, 3317): 1989 to 1995

ITEM	Unit	1989	1990	1991	1992	1993	1994	1995 [1]
INDUSTRY DATA								
Value of shipments [2]	Mil. dol.	63,054	60,941	55,182	57,183	61,301	68,531	74,404
Value of shipments (1992 dollars)	Mil. dol.	59,535	58,591	54,063	57,183	60,320	64,460	66,200
Total employment	1,000.	256	254	241	234	225	221	(NA)
Production workers	1,000.	199	196	184	179	173	171	(NA)
Capital expenditures	Mil. dol.	2,961	3,011	3,337	2,565	2,166	3,131	(NA)
PRODUCT DATA								
Value of shipments [3]	Mil. dol.	62,105	60,065	53,968	56,132	60,199	67,473	73,265
Value of shipments (1992 dollars)	Mil. dol.	58,639	57,727	52,866	56,132	59,247	63,474	65,187
TRADE DATA								
Value of imports	Mil. dol.	9,599	8,911	8,339	8,499	9,290	13,431	12,894
Value of exports	Mil. dol.	2,953	2,921	3,819	3,167	2,953	3,170	4,851

NA Not available. [1] Estimate, except exports and imports. [2] Value of all products and services sold by establishments in the steel mill products industry. [3] Value of products classified in the steel mill products industry produced by all industries.

Source: U.S. Department of Commerce, Bureau of the Census, International Trade Administration (ITA). Estimates by ITA.

No. 1425. Recent Trends in General Components (SIC 345, 3491, 3494, 3562): 1989 to 1995

[The code 349A in the table represents an aggregation of SIC's 3491 and 3494]

ITEM	Unit	1989	1990	1991	1992	1993	1994	1995 [1]
INDUSTRY DATA								
Value of shipments [2]	Mil. dol.	21,130	21,699	21,310	22,055	23,202	25,156	27,089
3451 Screw machine products	Mil. dol.	3,124	3,034	2,975	3,830	4,170	4,669	4,942
3452 Industrial fasteners	Mil. dol.	5,606	5,689	5,509	5,183	5,373	5,794	6,108
349A Valves and pipe fittings	Mil. dol.	8,073	8,669	8,776	8,754	9,102	9,803	10,743
3562 Ball and roller bearings	Mil. dol.	4,327	4,306	4,051	4,288	4,557	4,891	5,296
Value of shipments (1992 dollars)	Mil. dol.	23,041	22,604	21,464	22,055	22,806	24,213	25,182
3451 Screw machine products	Mil. dol.	3,272	3,096	2,990	3,830	4,137	4,582	4,747
3452 Industrial fasteners	Mil. dol.	5,970	5,823	5,525	5,183	5,320	5,675	5,879
349A Valves and pipe fittings	Mil. dol.	8,937	9,090	8,828	8,754	8,869	9,254	9,661
3562 Ball and roller bearings	Mil. dol.	4,862	4,596	4,121	4,288	4,481	4,702	4,895
Total employment	1,000	212.0	207.0	198.0	193.0	194.0	196.0	201.0
3451 Screw machine products	1,000	44.8	42.4	40.6	46.4	47.1	51.8	54.5
3452 Industrial fasteners	1,000	54.9	52.8	50.0	44.0	43.7	43.4	44.2
349A Valves and pipe fittings	1,000	73.3	72.4	70.9	68.0	69.0	67.5	68.2
3562 Ball and roller bearings	1,000	39.1	39.0	36.6	34.9	33.8	33.4	34.0
Production workers	1,000	158.0	154.0	146.0	142.0	144.0	148.0	152.0
3451 Screw machine products	1,000	35.8	34.3	32.3	36.5	38.5	41.9	44.3
3452 Industrial fasteners	1,000	40.7	39.0	36.3	31.8	32.0	31.9	33.0
349A Valves and pipe fittings	1,000	49.2	49.0	47.7	45.6	46.6	46.5	47.0
3562 Ball and roller bearings	1,000	32.1	32.1	29.8	28.2	27.3	27.2	27.8
Average hourly earnings	Dollar	11.19	11.53	11.92	12.56	12.7	12.92	(NA)
3451 Screw machine products	Dollar	9.77	10.13	10.23	11.29	11.36	11.25	11.34
3452 Industrial fasteners	Dollar	11.34	11.39	11.83	12.8	12.74	12.76	12.86
349A Valves and pipe fittings	Dollar	11.13	11.66	12.08	12.37	12.76	12.71	12.92
3562 Ball and roller bearings	Dollar	12.7	13.14	13.85	14.34	14.48	16.17	16.3
Capital expenditures	Mil. dol.	808	949	828	751	778	824	(NA)
3451 Screw machine products	Mil. dol.	129	125	101	135	152	225	(NA)
3452 Industrial fasteners	Mil. dol.	181	167	175	151	163	157	(NA)
349A Valves and pipe fittings	Mil. dol.	226	293	247	258	257	269	(NA)
3562 Ball and roller bearings	Mil. dol.	271	364	306	207	206	173	(NA)
PRODUCT DATA								
Value of shipments [3]	Mil. dol.	20,326	21,106	20,407	20,754	21,930	23,786	25,611
3451 Screw machine products	Mil. dol.	3,130	3,034	2,926	3,660	3,986	4,608	4,877
3452 Industrial fasteners	Mil. dol.	5,391	5,529	5,275	4,854	5,043	5,443	5,738
349A Valves and pipe fittings	Mil. dol.	7,644	8,301	8,313	8,100	8,461	8,942	9,805
3562 Ball and roller bearings	Mil. dol.	4,161	4,242	3,893	4,140	4,440	4,794	5,191
Value of shipments (1992 dollars)	Mil. dol.	22,155	21,978	20,544	20,754	21,561	22,907	23,824
3451 Screw machine products	Mil. dol.	3,277	3,096	2,941	3,660	3,954	4,522	4,685
3452 Industrial fasteners	Mil. dol.	5,741	5,660	5,291	4,854	4,993	5,331	5,523
349A Valves and pipe fittings	Mil. dol.	8,461	8,696	8,353	8,100	8,248	8,446	8,818
3562 Ball and roller bearings	Mil. dol.	4,676	4,527	3,960	4,140	4,366	4,609	4,798
TRADE DATA								
Value of imports	Mil. dol.	3,816	3,922	3,863	4,221	4,630	5,490	6,263
3451 Screw machine products	Mil. dol.	(NA)	(NA)	(NA)	(NA)	(NA)	(NA)	(NA)
3452 Industrial fasteners	Mil. dol.	1,234	1,213	1,121	1,231	1,386	1,666	1,894
349A Valves and pipe fittings	Mil. dol.	1,651	1,836	1,931	2,096	2,240	2,652	2,988
3562 Ball and roller bearings	Mil. dol.	932	873	812	895	1,004	1,171	1,381
Value of exports	Mil. dol.	1,989	2,794	2,970	3,149	3,327	3,842	4,562
3451 Screw machine products	Mil. dol.	(NA)	(NA)	(NA)	(NA)	(NA)	(NA)	(NA)
3452 Industrial fasteners	Mil. dol.	357	621	634	685	710	905	1,061
349A Valves and pipe fittings	Mil. dol.	1,158	1,485	1,662	1,805	1,960	2,204	2,612
3562 Ball and roller bearings	Mil. dol.	474	689	674	659	658	733	889

NA Not available.   [1] Estimate, except exports and imports.   [2] Value of all products and services sold by establishments in the general components industry.   [3] Value of products classified in the general components industry produced by all industries.

Source: U.S. Department of Commerce, Bureau of the Census, International Trade Administration (ITA). Estimates by ITA.

No. 1426. Recent Trends in Automotive Parts and Accessories (SIC 3465, 3592, 3647, 3691, 3694, 3714): 1989 to 1995

ITEM	Unit	1989	1990	1991	1992	1993	1994	1995 [1]
INDUSTRY DATA								
Value of shipments [2]	Mil. dol. . . .	97,629	93,020	90,711	105,886	119,678	138,600	135,424
Value of shipments (1992 dollar)	Mil. dol. . . .	100,213	94,114	91,113	105,886	119,264	137,455	132,919
Total employment	1,000. . . .	630	604	567	610	633	676	711
Production workers	1,000. . . .	506	482	448	482	506	546	573
Average hourly earnings	Dollar . . .	14.99	15.35	15.7	15.85	16.22	16.58	16.91
Capital expenditures	Mil. dol. . . .	4,334	4,874	4,548	4,593	5,308	6,007	(NA)
PRODUCT DATA								
Value of shipments [3]	Mil. dol. . . .	94,379	89,444	88,768	104,109	118,292	134,194	131,145
Value of shipments (1992 dollar)	Mil. dol. . . .	96,802	90,472	89,150	104,109	117,882	133,095	128,719
TRADE DATA [4]								
Value of imports [5]	Mil. dol. . . .	31,995	31,682	29,836	33,525	38,306	44,854	46,355
Value of exports [6]	Mil. dol. . . .	17,457	22,856	24,130	28,484	33,457	37,135	39,829

NA Not available.   [1] Estimate, except exports and imports.   [2] Value of all products and services in the automotive parts and accessories industry.   [3] Value of products classified in the automotive parts and accessories industry produced by all industries.   [4] Trade data encompasses more than is indicated by the SIC's cited.   [5] General imports, customs value.   [6] Total exports, f.a.s. value.

Source: U.S. Department of Commerce, Bureau of the Census, International Trade Administration (ITA). Estimates by ITA.

No. 1427. Recent Trends in Farm Machinery and Equipment (SIC 3523): 1989 to 1995

ITEM	Unit	1989	1990	1991	1992	1993	1994	1995 [1]
INDUSTRY DATA								
Value of shipments [2]	Mil. dol. . . .	10,419	11,546	10,347	9,617	11,190	13,218	13,977
Value of shipments (1992 dollars)	Mil. dol. . . .	11,538	12,336	10,689	9,617	10,938	12,600	12,978
Total employment	1,000. . . .	67.8	69.6	65.1	61.4	63.5	67.1	67.3
Production workers	1,000. . . .	48.9	49.9	45.4	42.5	45.8	48.1	48.1
Average hourly earnings	Dollar . . .	11.9	12.31	12.65	13.18	13.18	13.81	14.22
Capital expenditures	Mil. dol. . . .	183	210	205	196	229	260	(NA)
PRODUCT DATA								
Value of shipments [3]	Mil. dol. . . .	9,578	10,871	9,724	8,940	10,340	12,320	13,027
Value of shipments (1992 dollars)	Mil. dol. . . .	10,606	11,615	10,045	8,940	10,108	11,744	12,096
TRADE DATA								
Value of imports	Mil. dol. . . .	2,222	2,475	1,911	2,022	2,148	2,917	3,089
Value of exports	Mil. dol. . . .	2,219	2,298	2,130	2,176	2,473	2,647	3,119

NA Not available.   [1] Estimate, except exports and imports.   [2] Value of all products and services sold by establishments in the farm machinery and equipment industry.   [3] Value of products classified in the farm machinery and equipment industry produced by all industries.

Source: U.S. Department of Commerce, Bureau of the Census, International Trade Administration (ITA). Estimates by ITA.

No. 1428. Recent Trends in Lawn and Garden Equipment (SIC 3524): 1989 to 1995

ITEM	Unit	1989	1990	1991	1992	1993	1994	1995 [1]
INDUSTRY DATA								
Value of shipments [2]	Mil. dol. . . .	4,578	4,910	4,820	5,169	5,828	6,819	7,238
Value of shipments (1992 dollars)	Mil. dol. . . .	4,870	5,062	4,863	5,169	5,782	6,633	6,940
Total employment	1,000. . . .	25.7	24.5	24.4	24.8	25.7	27.8	27.3
Production workers	1,000. . . .	19.4	18.3	18.9	19.8	20.5	22.4	22.0
Average hourly earnings	Dollar . . .	8.86	9.82	9.88	10.71	10.88	10.64	10.84
Capital expenditures	Mil. dol. . . .	127	82.2	91.3	125	92.1	125	(NA)
PRODUCT DATA								
Value of shipments [3]	Mil. dol. . . .	4,044	4,343	4,267	4,344	4,884	5,716	6,068
Value of shipments (1992 dollars)	Mil. dol. . . .	4,302	4,477	4,306	4,344	4,845	5,561	5,818
TRADE DATA								
Value of imports	Mil. dol. . . .	174	177	118	134	162	175	172
Value of exports	Mil. dol. . . .	457	495	562	612	686	740	765

NA Not available.   [1] Estimate, except exports and imports.   [2] Value of all products and services sold by establishments in the lawn and garden equipment industry.   [3] Value of products classified in the lawn and garden equipment industry produced by all industries.

Source: U.S. Department of Commerce, Bureau of the Census, International Trade Administration (ITA). Estimates by ITA.

No. 1429. Recent Trends in Construction Machinery (SIC 3531): 1989 to 1995

ITEM	Unit	1989	1990	1991	1992	1993	1994	1995 [1]
INDUSTRY DATA								
Value of shipments [2]	Mil. dol. . .	15,349	16,070	13,351	13,452	15,444	17,697	19,030
Value of shipments (1992 dollars)	Mil. dol. . .	16,794	16,969	13,708	13,452	15,053	17,066	17,919
Total employment	1,000. . . .	87.7	89.9	81.0	77.1	74.7	77.9	79.3
Production workers	1,000. . . .	60.6	60.7	52.8	49.6	49.1	52.9	56.4
Average hourly earnings	Dollar . . .	14.46	14.96	15.21	15.41	15.33	14.84	(NA)
Capital expenditures	Mil. dol. . .	633	638	462	425	346	359	(NA)
PRODUCT DATA								
Value of shipments [3]	Mil. dol. . .	14,206	14,888	12,297	12,001	14,122	16,422	17,659
Value of shipments (1992 dollars)	Mil. dol. . .	15,542	15,721	12,626	12,001	13,764	15,836	16,628
TRADE DATA								
Value of imports	Mil. dol. . .	2,958	3,071	2,102	2,571	3,397	4,277	4,452
Value of exports	Mil. dol. . .	3,992	4,546	4,379	4,246	4,328	5,179	5,437

NA Not available.   [1] Estimate, except exports and imports.   [2] Value of all products and services sold by establishments in the construction machinery industry.   [3] Value of products classified in the construction machinery industry produced by all industries.

Source: U.S. Department of Commerce, Bureau of the Census, International Trade Administration (ITA). Estimates by ITA.

No. 1430. Recent Trends in Mining Machinery (SIC 3532): 1989 to 1995

ITEM	Unit	1989	1990	1991	1992	1993	1994	1995 [1]
INDUSTRY DATA								
Value of shipments [2]	Mil. dol. . .	1,806	1,866	1,643	1,558	1,881	1,695	1,810
Value of shipments (1992 dollars)	Mil. dol. . .	1,976	1,960	1,670	1,558	1,844	1,639	1,688
Total employment	1,000. . . .	15.7	15.5	14.5	12.6	12.6	12.8	13.7
Production workers	1,000. . . .	9.8	9.7	8.5	7.4	7.7	8.1	8.9
Average hourly earnings	Dollar . . .	11.05	10.92	10.9	11.89	12.21	12.96	(NA)
Capital expenditures	Mil. dol. . .	31.9	38.2	32.5	33.0	58.9	29.5	(NA)
PRODUCT DATA								
Value of shipments [3]	Mil. dol. . .	1,677	1,754	1,584	1,417	1,745	1,608	1,717
Value of shipments (1992 dollars)	Mil. dol. . .	1,835	1,843	1,610	1,417	1,711	1,555	1,602
TRADE DATA								
Value of imports	Mil. dol. . .	399	361	328	275	316	384	477
Value of exports	Mil. dol. . .	594	741	782	832	864	1,004	1,133

NA Not available.   [1] Estimate, except exports and imports.   [2] Value of all products and services sold by establishments in the mining machinery industry.   [3] Value of products classified in the mining machinery industry produced by all industries.

Source: U.S. Department of Commerce, Bureau of the Census, International Trade Administration (ITA). Estimates by ITA.

No. 1431. Recent Trends in Oil and Gas Field Machinery (SIC 3533): 1989 to 1995

ITEM	Unit	1989	1990	1991	1992	1993	1994	1995 [1]
INDUSTRY DATA								
Value of shipments [2]	Mil. dol. . .	3,314	3,635	4,073	3,918	3,740	3,753	4,109
Value of shipments (1992 dollars)	Mil. dol. . .	3,521	3,763	4,001	3,918	3,762	3,672	3,913
Total employment	1,000. . . .	26.1	27.2	28.7	27.0	24.5	25.4	24.5
Production workers	1,000. . . .	14.7	15.3	16.0	15.4	13.8	14.7	14.5
Average hourly earnings	Dollar . . .	12.99	13.11	13.51	13.62	14.22	15.59	(NA)
Capital expenditures	Mil. dol. . .	77.1	72.2	99.7	105.0	79.8	77.6	(NA)
PRODUCT DATA								
Value of shipments [3]	Mil. dol. . .	2,829	3,013	3,400	2,981	2,939	2,884	3,157
Value of shipments (1992 dollars)	Mil. dol. . .	3,007	3,119	3,339	2,981	2,956	2,822	3,007
TRADE DATA								
Value of imports	Mil. dol. . .	35.5	52.4	64.4	36.2	47.8	67.9	93.4
Value of exports	Mil. dol. . .	2,409	2,709	3,946	4,000	3,761	3,560	4,180

NA Not available.   [1] Estimate, except exports and imports.   [2] Value of all products and services sold by establishments in the oil and gas field machinery industry.   [3] Value of products classified in the oil and gas field machinery industry produced by all industries.

Source: U.S. Department of Commerce, Bureau of the Census, International Trade Administration (ITA). Estimates by ITA.

No. 1432. Recent Trends in Machine Tools (SIC 3541, 3542): 1989 to 1995

ITEM	Unit	1989	1990	1991	1992	1993	1994	1995 [1]
INDUSTRY DATA								
Value of shipments [2]	Mil. dol. . .	5,353	5,260	4,875	5,019	5,231	5,352	6,427
3541 Metal cutting machines	Mil. dol. . .	3,623	3,607	3,370	3,568	3,518	3,658	4,465
3542 Metal forming machines	Mil. dol. . .	1,730	1,653	1,506	1,451	1,713	1,694	1,962
Value of shipments (1992 dollars)	Mil. dol. . .	6,027	5,611	5,009	5,019	5,154	5,182	6,003
3541 Metal cutting machines	Mil. dol. . .	4,075	3,866	3,474	3,568	3,476	3,565	4,185
3542 Metal forming machines	Mil. dol. . .	1,952	1,745	1,535	1,451	1,677	1,617	1,818
Total employment	1,000. . . .	46.0	44.9	41.5	39.2	38.0	37.1	40.1
3541 Metal cutting machines	1,000. . . .	31.0	30.3	28.0	27.0	25.3	24.0	25.8
3542 Metal forming machines	1,000. . . .	15.0	14.6	13.5	12.2	12.7	13.1	14.3
Production workers	1,000. . . .	28.0	27.5	25.0	23.0	22.3	22.0	24.1
3541 Metal cutting machines	1,000. . . .	18.4	18.2	16.5	15.2	14.5	13.7	14.8
3542 Metal forming machines	1,000. . . .	9.6	9.3	8.5	7.8	7.8	8.3	9.3
Average hourly earnings	Dollar . . .	13.97	14.19	14.44	15.32	15.72	16.16	16.51
3541 Metal cutting machines	Dollar . . .	14.06	14.13	14.51	15.48	15.75	16.31	(NA)
3542 Metal forming machines	Dollar . . .	13.82	14.3	14.3	14.99	15.68	15.91	16.51
Capital expenditures	Mil. dol. . .	134.0	118.0	98.0	123.0	95.7	131.0	(NA)
3541 Metal cutting machines	Mil. dol. . .	94.6	84.2	66.4	82.4	63.0	106.0	(NA)
3542 Metal forming machines	Mil. dol. . .	39.4	33.3	31.6	40.4	32.7	25.4	(NA)
PRODUCT DATA								
Value of shipments [3]	Mil. dol. . .	4,857	4,806	4,291	4,521	4,524	5,096	6,116
3541 Metal cutting machines	Mil. dol. . .	3,172	3,249	2,838	3,093	2,915	3,440	4,200
3542 Metal forming machines	Mil. dol. . .	1,685	1,557	1,453	1,428	1,609	1,656	1,916
Value of shipments (1992 dollars)	Mil. dol. . .	5,469	5,127	4,407	4,521	4,456	4,933	5,712
3541 Metal cutting machines	Mil. dol. . .	3,568	3,483	2,926	3,093	2,881	3,353	3,936
3542 Metal forming machines	Mil. dol. . .	1,902	1,644	1,481	1,428	1,576	1,580	1,776
TRADE DATA								
Value of imports	Mil. dol. . .	3,003	2,801	2,596	2,319	2,599	3,403	4,383
3541 Metal cutting machines	Mil. dol. . .	2,246	2,062	1,935	1,689	1,885	2,398	3,104
3542 Metal forming machines	Mil. dol. . .	757	740	661	630	714	1,004	1,279
Value of exports	Mil. dol. . .	1,574	1,600	1,555	1,836	1,744	2,179	2,265
3541 Metal cutting machines	Mil. dol. . .	893	913	877	1,017	975	1,353	1,350
3542 Metal forming machines	Mil. dol. . .	680	687	677	819	769	825	914

NA Not available.   [1] Estimate, except exports and imports.   [2] Value of all products and services sold by establishments in the machine tools industry.   [3] Value of products classified in the machine tools industry produced by all industries.

Source: U.S. Department of Commerce, Bureau of the Census, International Trade Administration (ITA). Estimates by ITA.

No. 1433. Recent Trends in Special Dies, Tools, Jigs and Fixtures (SIC 3544): 1989 to 1995

ITEM	Unit	1989	1990	1991	1992	1993	1994	1995 [1]
INDUSTRY DATA								
Value of shipments [2]	Mil. dol. . .	9,236	9,487	8,890	9,310	9,951	11,195	12,092
Value of shipments (1992 dollars)	Mil. dol. . .	10,072	10,039	9,026	9,310	9,708	10,652	11,301
Total employment	1,000. . . .	122	120	114	111	118	120	125
Production workers	1,000. . . .	94.7	92.2	87.5	85.3	90.7	92.4	96.5
Average hourly earnings	Dollar . . .	13.20	13.56	13.59	14.57	14.70	15.00	15.40
Capital expenditures	Mil. dol. . .	386	413	386	370	532	541	(NA)
PRODUCT DATA								
Value of shipments [3]	Mil. dol. . .	9,911	10,055	9,692	10,230	10,990	12,290	13,275
Value of shipments (1992 dollars)	Mil. dol. . .	10,808	10,640	9,839	10,230	10,722	11,694	12,407
TRADE DATA								
Value of imports	Mil. dol. . .	952	852	1,325	1,039	1,632	2,375	2,672
Value of exports	Mil. dol. . .	455	542	543	667	1,082	1,144	1,285

NA Not available.   [1] Estimate, except exports and imports.   [2] Value of all products and services sold by establishments in the special dies, tools, jigs and fixtures industry.   [3] Value of products classified in the special dies, tools, jigs and fixtures industry produced by all industries.

Source: U.S. Department of Commerce, Bureau of the Census, International Trade Administration (ITA). Estimates by ITA.

No. 1434. Recent Trends in Power-Driven Handtools and Welding Apparatus: 1989 to 1995

ITEM	Unit	1989	1990	1991	1992	1993	1994	1995 [1]
POWER-DRIVEN HANDTOOLS (SIC 3546)								
Industry data:								
Value of shipments [2]	Mil. dol. . .	2,618	2,806	2,581	2,873	3,480	3,495	3,607
Value of shipments (1992 dollars)	Mil. dol. . .	2,873	2,969	2,650	2,873	3,405	3,341	3,390
Total employment	1,000. . . .	17.5	18.3	17.5	16.1	17.0	15.6	16.0
Production workers	1,000. . . .	12.3	12.6	11.4	10.6	11.7	10.9	11.4
Average hourly earnings	Dollar . . .	10.03	10.18	10.86	11.08	10.98	11.19	(NA)
Capital expenditures	Mil. dol. . .	66.2	98.4	74.7	72.3	112.0	104.0	(NA)
Product data:								
Value of shipments [3]	Mil. dol. . .	2,281	2,365	2,239	2,415	3,074	3,220	3,323
Value of shipments (1992 dollars)	Mil. dol. . .	2,504	2,503	2,298	2,415	3,008	3,078	3,123
Trade data:								
Value of imports	Mil. dol. . .	780	716	689	766	823	952	1,084
Value of exports	Mil. dol. . .	476	521	550	568	600	699	738
WELDING APPARATUS (SIC 3548)								
Industry data:								
Value of shipments [2]	Mil. dol. . .	2,521	2,684	2,651	2,764	3,101	3,075	3,230
Value of shipments (1992 dollars)	Mil. dol. . .	2,829	2,892	2,747	2,764	2,984	2,860	2,894
Total employment	1,000. . . .	19.0	19.2	19.5	19.8	20.3	18.5	(NA)
Production workers	1,000. . . .	11.6	12.0	11.8	11.9	13.1	12.0	(NA)
Average hourly earnings	Dollar . . .	12.67	13.15	13.07	13.87	14.76	15.28	(NA)
Capital expenditures	Mil. dol. . .	59.1	67.7	50.5	65.8	80.6	73.0	(NA)
Product data:								
Value of shipments [3]	Mil. dol. . .	2,298	2,475	2,434	2,391	2,717	2,831	2,981
Value of shipments (1992 dollars)	Mil. dol. . .	2,579	2,667	2,523	2,391	2,615	2,633	2,671
Trade data:								
Value of imports	Mil. dol. . .	480	365	478	381	533	528	657
Value of exports	Mil. dol. . .	491	566	597	621	651	681	768

NA Not available. [1] Estimate, except exports and imports. [2] Value of all products and services sold by establishments in this industry. [3] Value of products classified in this industry produced by all industries.

Source: U.S. Department of Commerce, Bureau of the Census, International Trade Administration (ITA). Estimates by ITA.

No. 1435. Recent Trends in Textile Machinery and Paper Industries Machinery: 1989 to 1995

ITEM	Unit	1989	1990	1991	1992	1993	1994	1995 [1]
TEXTILE MACHINERY (SIC 3552)								
Industry data:								
Value of shipments [2]	Mil. dol. . .	1,561	1,505	1,396	1,565	1,853	1,908	2,017
Value of shipments (1992 dollars)	Mil. dol. . .	1,760	1,629	1,440	1,565	1,792	1,837	1,923
Total employment	1,000. . . .	16.4	16.0	14.9	15.0	16.5	16.7	16.8
Production workers	1,000. . . .	11.5	11.0	10.1	9.6	10.1	10.6	10.8
Average hourly earnings	Dollar . . .	10.26	10.85	11.42	11.04	10.96	11.92	(NA)
Capital expenditures	Mil. dol. . .	37.4	46.6	32.9	39.5	46.9	71.4	(NA)
Product data:								
Value of shipments [3]	Mil. dol. . .	1,338	1,325	1,235	1,334	1,612	1,615	1,707
Value of shipments (1992 dollars)	Mil. dol. . .	1,509	1,434	1,274	1,334	1,559	1,554	1,627
Trade data:								
Value of imports	Mil. dol. . .	1,388	1,449	1,165	1,464	1,781	1,772	1,687
Value of exports	Mil. dol. . .	514	580	534	547	553	567	602
PAPER INDUSTRIES MACHINERY (SIC 3554)								
Industry data:								
Value of shipments [2]	Mil. dol. . .	2,580	2,770	2,206	2,524	2,529	2,813	2,968
Value of shipments (1992 dollars)	Mil. dol. . .	2,789	2,901	2,247	2,524	2,506	2,744	2,851
Total employment	1,000. . . .	19.9	20.3	17.8	18.2	18.1	17.4	(NA)
Production workers	1,000. . . .	11.7	12.2	9.6	10.2	9.8	9.7	(NA)
Average hourly earnings	Dollar . . .	13.74	13.19	14.83	14.76	15.24	16.11	(NA)
Capital expenditures	Mil. dol. . .	84.6	72	62.6	65.4	55.9	49.3	(NA)
Product data:								
Value of shipments [3]	Mil. dol. . .	2,238	2,453	2,061	2,225	2,253	2,463	2,587
Value of shipments (1992 dollars)	Mil. dol. . .	2,419	2,569	2,099	2,225	2,233	2,403	2,485
Trade data:								
Value of imports	Mil. dol. . .	962	880	694	637	709	907	981
Value of exports	Mil. dol. . .	494	599	637	583	652	653	862

NA Not available. [1] Estimate, except exports and imports. [2] Value of all products and services sold by establishments in this industry. [3] Value of products classified in this industry produced by all industries.

Source: U.S. Department of Commerce, Bureau of the Census, International Trade Administration (ITA). Estimates by ITA.

No. 1436. Recent Trends in Printing Trades Machinery, Food Products Machinery, and Packaging Machinery: 1989 to 1995

ITEM	Unit	1989	1990	1991	1992	1993	1994	1995 [1]
PRINTING TRADES MACHINERY (SIC 3555)								
Industry data:								
Value of shipments [2]	Mil. dol. . .	3,692	3,538	3,538	2,592	2,727	3,015	3,078
Value of shipments (1992 dollars) . . .	Mil. dol. . .	3,850	3,629	3,559	2,592	2,663	2,908	2,912
Total employment	1,000. . . .	26.4	25.0	24.0	18.7	18.9	21.1	21.9
Production workers	1,000. . . .	13.6	12.9	12.1	10.3	10.3	11.3	12.0
Average hourly earnings	Dollar . . .	12.77	13.07	13.29	13.65	14.59	14.27	14.29
Capital expenditures	Mil. dol. . .	99.5	89.6	74.7	59.6	52.9	70.7	70.8
Product data:								
Value of shipments [3]	Mil. dol. . .	3,303	3,141	3,171	2,342	2,345	2,750	2,802
Value of shipments (1992 dollars) . . .	Mil. dol. . .	3,444	3,222	3,190	2,342	2,290	2,652	2,651
Trade data:								
Value of imports	Mil. dol. . .	1,177	1,127	1,146	1,220	1,350	1,558	1,995
Value of exports	Mil. dol. . .	845	1,081	1,072	1,054	1,064	1,029	1,215
FOOD PRODUCTS MACHINERY (SIC 3556)								
Industry data:								
Value of shipments [2]	Mil. dol. . .	2,126	2,261	2,193	2,407	2,630	2,674	3,136
Value of shipments (1992 dollars) . . .	Mil. dol. . .	2,391	2,436	2,261	2,407	2,564	2,520	2,869
Total employment	1,000. . . .	19.0	19.0	17.9	18.8	18.8	19.8	21.0
Production workers	1,000. . . .	11.1	11.2	10.5	11.1	11.3	12.0	12.8
Average hourly earnings	Dollar . . .	11.5	12.07	12.7	13.06	13.23	13.05	(NA)
Capital expenditures	Mil. dol. . .	63.6	45.8	42.1	46.8	48.8	48.5	(NA)
Product data:								
Value of shipments [3]	Mil. dol. . .	1,881	1,954	1,970	2,102	2,311	2,266	2,552
Value of shipments (1992 dollars) . . .	Mil. dol. . .	2,116	2,105	2,030	2,102	2,252	2,136	2,335
Trade data:								
Value of imports	Mil. dol. . .	374	452	427	474	439	481	640
Value of exports	Mil. dol. . .	523	551	621	687	696	734	909
PACKAGING MACHINERY (SIC 3565)								
Industry data:								
Value of shipments [2]	Mil. dol. . .	2,498	2,762	2,880	3,127	3,418	3,621	4,017
Value of shipments (1992 dollars) . . .	Mil. dol. . .	2,718	2,898	2,942	3,127	3,322	3,426	3,706
Total employment	1,000. . . .	23.5	23.5	23.9	26.2	24.9	24.8	(NA)
Production workers	1,000. . . .	14.0	13.3	13.7	15.4	14.2	14.9	(NA)
Average hourly earnings	Dollar . . .	12.65	13.61	13.99	13.79	14.29	14.52	(NA)
Capital expenditures	Mil. dol. . .	67.1	73.5	68.4	70.1	90.2	98.6	(NA)
Product data:								
Value of shipments [3]	Mil. dol. . .	2,343	2,680	2,767	2,861	3,098	3,272	3,587
Value of shipments (1992 dollars) . . .	Mil. dol. . .	2,549	2,812	2,826	2,861	3,011	3,095	3,309
Trade data:								
Value of imports	Mil. dol. . .	597	621	643	699	719	842	930
Value of exports	Mil. dol. . .	486	579	611	606	672	841	888

NA Not available.   [1] Estimate, except exports and imports.   [2] Value of all products and services sold by establishments in this industry.   [3] Value of products classified in this industry produced by all industries.

Source: U.S. Department of Commerce, Bureau of the Census, International Trade Administration (ITA). Estimates by ITA.

No. 1437. Recent Trends in Computers and Peripherals (SIC 3571,2,5,7): 1989 to 1995

[Census reclassified some parts for electronic computers (3571) to component industries (367) for 1989-1990]

ITEM	Unit	1989	1990	1991	1992	1993	1994	1995 [1]
INDUSTRY DATA								
Value of shipments [2]	Mil. dol. . .	59,758	58,981	54,703	61,977	64,374	74,645	86,000
Total employment	1,000. . . .	263	248	227	220	211	213	207
Production workers	1,000. . . .	96.8	89.6	76.2	74.1	73.9	75.9	73.6
Average hourly earnings	Dollar . . .	11.68	11.72	12.52	12.28	12.77	13.68	14.27
Capital expenditures	Mil. dol. . .	2,148	1,993	1,813	2,135	2,045	1,907	1,800
PRODUCT DATA								
Value of shipments [3]	Mil. dol. . .	54,891	52,628	49,144	54,722	57,928	66,304	77,000
TRADE DATA								
Value of imports	Mil. dol. . .	21,714	22,900	26,000	31,600	37,900	46,100	55,400
Value of exports	Mil. dol. . .	22,360	23,000	24,000	25,000	25,400	29,100	33,500

[1] Estimate, except exports and imports.   [2] Value of all products and services sold by establishments in the computers and peripherals industry.   [3] Value of products classified in the computers and peripherals industry produced by all industries.

Source: U.S. Department of Commerce, Bureau of the Census, International Trade Administration (ITA). Estimates by ITA.

No. 1438. Recent Trends in Electrical Equipment (SIC 361, 3621, 3625): 1989 to 1995

ITEM	Unit	1989	1990	1991	1992	1993	1994	1995 [1]
INDUSTRY								
Value of shipments (1992 dollars)	Mil. dol. . .	26,780	26,234	24,555	25,237	27,337	29,038	30,940
3612 Transformers	Mil. dol. . .	4,252	4,216	3,875	4,096	4,028	4,783	5,680
3613 Switchgear and apparatus.	Mil. dol. . .	5,942	5,776	5,361	5,528	5,723	5,859	5,998
3621 Motors and generators	Mil. dol. . .	8,534	7,869	7,759	8,040	9,064	9,199	9,336
3625 Relays and controls.	Mil. dol. . .	8,052	8,373	7,560	7,573	8,522	9,197	9,926

[1] Estimate.

Source: U.S. Department of Commerce, Bureau of the Census, International Trade Administration (ITA). Estimates by ITA.

No. 1439. Recent Trends in Transformers, Except Electronic (SIC 3612): 1989 to 1995

ITEM	Unit	1989	1990	1991	1992	1993	1994	1995 [1]
INDUSTRY DATA								
Value of shipments [2].	Mil. dol. . .	3,934	4,178	3,995	4,096	3,940	4,673	5,737
Value of shipments (1992 dollars)	Mil. dol. . .	4,252	4,216	3,875	4,096	4,028	4,783	5,680
Total employment	1,000. . . .	33.5	32.8	30.6	28.9	27.9	30.7	30.4
Production workers	1,000. . . .	25.8	24.8	23.2	21.9	21.1	21.7	21.3
Average hourly earnings.	Dollar . . .	10.16	10.89	11.17	11.64	12.00	11.80	12.26
Capital expenditures	Mil. dol. . .	78.0	109.0	115.0	85.1	77.8	166.0	(NA)
PRODUCT DATA								
Value of shipments [3]	Mil. dol. . .	3,811	4,032	3,956	4,066	3,906	4,485	5,330
Value of shipments (1992 dollars)	Mil. dol. . .	4,120	4,069	3,837	4,066	3,994	4,591	5,277
TRADE DATA								
Value of imports	Mil. dol. . .	290	359	435	500	608	592	815
Value of exports	Mil. dol. . .	234	261	301	338	359	384	469

NA Not available. [1] Estimate, except exports and imports. [2] Value of all products and services sold by establishments in the transformers, except electronic industry. [3] Value of products classified in the transformers, except electronic industry produced by all industries.

Source: U.S. Department of Commerce, Bureau of the Census, International Trade Administration (ITA). Estimates by ITA.

No. 1440. Recent Trends in Household Appliances (SIC 363): 1989 to 1995

ITEM	Unit	1989	1990	1991	1992	1993	1994	1995 [1]
INDUSTRY DATA								
Value of shipments [2]	Mil. dol. . .	18,335	18,069	17,692	18,483	20,435	22,794	22,593
3631 Household cooking equipment . .	Mil. dol. . .	3,095	2,994	2,891	2,950	3,010	3,814	3,657
3632 Household refrigerators	Mil. dol. . .	4,015	3,800	3,721	4,232	4,463	5,149	5,117
3633 Household laundry equipment . .	Mil. dol. . .	3,104	3,234	3,206	3,329	3,871	4,612	4,505
3634 Electric housewares and fans . .	Mil. dol. . .	3,078	3,056	3,112	2,898	3,106	3,053	3,023
3635 Household vacuums.	Mil. dol. . .	1,605	1,860	1,805	1,905	2,096	1,933	1,994
3639 Home appliances, n.e.c.	Mil. dol. . .	3,438	3,125	2,958	3,169	3,889	4,233	4,298
Value of shipments (1992 dollars)	Mil. dol. . .	18,836	18,252	17,766	18,483	20,199	22,486	22,295
3631 Household cooking equipment . .	Mil. dol. . .	3,101	2,982	2,891	2,950	2,931	3,728	3,610
3632 Household refrigerators	Mil. dol. . .	3,925	3,729	3,725	4,232	4,436	5,068	5,076
3633 Household laundry equipment . .	Mil. dol. . .	3,154	3,199	3,168	3,329	3,887	4,668	4,574
3634 Electric housewares and fans . .	Mil. dol. . .	3,223	3,154	3,153	2,898	3,087	3,065	3,050
3635 Household vacuums.	Mil. dol. . .	1,704	1,916	1,796	1,905	2,037	1,843	1,892
3639 Home appliances, n.e.c.	Mil. dol. . .	3,729	3,272	3,034	3,169	3,820	4,114	4,093
Total employment	1,000. . . .	114	110	104	103	105	110	110
Production workers	1,000. . . .	91.8	88.3	83.8	83.2	85.0	90.5	90.0
Average hourly earnings.	Dollar . . .	10.92	11.09	11.20	11.34	11.72	11.74	12.25
Capital expenditures	Mil. dol. . .	485	390	496	556	481	517	(NA)
PRODUCT DATA								
Value of shipments [3]	Mil. dol. . .	16,688	16,500	16,089	16,789	18,026	19,808	19,611
3631 Household cooking equipment . .	Mil. dol. . .	3,136	3,027	2,942	3,007	3,162	3,788	3,632
3632 Household refrigerators	Mil. dol. . .	3,895	3,711	3,621	4,048	4,309	4,995	4,963
3633 Household laundry equipment . .	Mil. dol. . .	2,913	2,906	2,860	2,995	3,299	3,671	3,585
3634 Electric housewares and fans . .	Mil. dol. . .	2,847	2,684	2,608	2,653	2,710	2,651	2,625
3635 Household vacuums.	Mil. dol. . .	1,626	1,876	1,834	1,809	2,015	1,788	1,845
3639 Home appliances, n.e.c.	Mil. dol. . .	2,271	2,296	2,224	2,279	2,531	2,916	2,961
Value of shipments (1992 dollars)	Mil. dol. . .	17,081	16,637	16,141	16,789	17,813	19,534	19,368
3631 Household cooking equipment . .	Mil. dol. . .	3,142	3,015	2,942	3,007	3,079	3,702	3,585
3632 Household refrigerators	Mil. dol. . .	3,807	3,642	3,625	4,048	4,283	4,916	4,924
3633 Household laundry equipment . .	Mil. dol. . .	2,961	2,874	2,826	2,995	3,312	3,715	3,640
3634 Electric housewares and fans . .	Mil. dol. . .	2,981	2,769	2,642	2,653	2,694	2,662	2,649
3635 Household vacuums.	Mil. dol. . .	1,726	1,932	1,825	1,809	1,958	1,705	1,750
3639 Home appliances, n.e.c.	Mil. dol. . .	2,463	2,405	2,281	2,279	2,486	2,834	2,820
TRADE DATA								
Value of imports	Mil. dol. . .	3,439	3,356	3,631	4,275	4,480	4,869	5,091
Value of exports	Mil. dol. . .	1,545	1,828	2,120	2,353	2,540	2,624	2,679

NA Not available. [1] Estimate, except exports and imports. [2] Value of all products and services sold by establishments in the household appliances industry. [3] Value of products classified in the household appliances industry produced by all industries.

Source: U.S. Department of Commerce, Bureau of the Census, International Trade Administration (ITA). Estimates by ITA.

No. 1441. Recent Trends in Lighting Fixtures and Wiring Devices: 1989 to 1995

ITEM	Unit	1989	1990	1991	1992	1993	1994	1995 [1]
LIGHTING FIXTURES (SIC 3645, 3646, 3648)								
Industry data:								
Value of shipments [2]	Mil. dol. . .	6,699	6,620	6,212	6,718	7,075	7,935	9,104
Value of shipments (1992 dollars) . . .	Mil. dol. . .	7,097	6,802	6,267	6,718	7,041	7,833	8,714
Total employment	1,000. . . .	59.0	55.3	52.1	51.6	52.4	54.3	(NA)
Production workers	1,000. . . .	41.6	38.8	36.5	35.9	36.5	38.4	39.6
Average hourly earnings	Dollar . . .	8.58	8.84	9.11	9.34	9.5	10.12	10.43
Product data:								
Value of shipments [3]	Mil. dol. . .	6,687	6,621	6,194	6,720	7,150	7,686	8,442
3645 Residential lighting fixtures. . .	Mil. dol. . .	1,777	1,586	1,409	1,681	1,896	1,982	(NA)
3646 Commercial lighting fixtures . .	Mil. dol. . .	3,056	3,196	2,955	3,047	3,122	3,291	(NA)
3648 Lighting equipment, n.e.c. . . .	Mil. dol. . .	1,854	1,838	1,830	1,993	2,132	2,413	(NA)
Value of shipments (1992 dollars) . . .	Mil. dol. . .	7,084	6,803	6,249	6,720	7,111	7,580	8,080
3645 Residential lighting fixtures. . .	Mil. dol. . .	1,880	1,618	1,423	1,681	1,861	1,921	(NA)
3646 Commercial lighting fixtures . .	Mil. dol. . .	3,279	3,309	2,984	3,047	3,110	3,239	(NA)
3648 Lighting equipment, n.e.c. . . .	Mil. dol. . .	1,925	1,876	1,841	1,993	2,141	2,420	(NA)
WIRING DEVICES (SIC 3643, 3644)								
Industry data:								
Value of shipments (1992 dollars) . . .	Mil. dol. . .	8,143	7,958	7,175	7,892	7,896	8,206	8,528
3643 Wiring devices, current	Mil. dol. . .	4,653	4,554	4,316	4,668	4,576	4,714	(NA)
3644 Wiring goods, noncurrent. . . .	Mil. dol. . .	3,490	3,404	2,859	3,224	3,320	3,491	(NA)

NA Not available.   [1] Estimate.   [2] Value of all products and services sold by establishments in this industry.   [3] Value of products classified in this industry produced by all industries.

Source: U.S. Department of Commerce, Bureau of the Census, International Trade Administration (ITA). Estimates by ITA.

No. 1442. Recent Trends in Household Audio and Video Equipment (SIC 3651): 1989 to 1995

ITEM	Unit	1989	1990	1991	1992	1993	1994	1995 [1]
INDUSTRY DATA								
Value of shipments [2]	Mil. dol. . .	7,360	7,521	7,994	8,769	9,159	10,286	10,800
Value of shipments (1992 dollars)	Mil. dol. . .	7,259	7,476	7,891	8,769	9,346	10,496	11,262
Total employment	1,000. . . .	33.2	30.8	31.1	31.2	31.2	30.5	30.9
Production workers	1,000. . . .	24.9	22.5	21.7	22.3	22.6	23.3	23.6
Average hourly earnings	Dollar . . .	8.54	9.00	9.36	9.52	9.60	9.64	(NA)
Capital expenditures	Mil. dol. . .	139	256	278	253	212	226	(NA)
PRODUCT DATA								
Value of shipments [3]	Mil. dol. . .	7,141	7,092	7,154	7,664	7,915	8,719	9,288
Value of shipments (1992 dollars)	Mil. dol. . .	7,042	7,050	7,062	7,664	8,076	8,897	9,685
TRADE DATA								
Value of imports	Mil. dol. . .	13,533	12,515	13,260	14,243	15,166	16,060	17,555
Value of exports	Mil. dol. . .	1,640	2,045	2,235	2,430	2,691	3,116	3,334

NA Not available.   [1] Estimate, except exports and imports.   [2] Value of all products and services sold by establishments in the household audio and video equipment industry.   [3] Value of products classified in the household audio and video equipment industry produced by all industries.

Source: U.S. Department of Commerce, Bureau of the Census, International Trade Administration (ITA). Estimates by ITA.

No. 1443. Recent Trends in Telecommunications Equipment (SIC 3661, 3663): 1989 to 1995

ITEM	Unit	1989	1990	1991	1992	1993	1994	1995 [1]
INDUSTRY DATA								
Value of shipments [2]	Mil. dol. . .	32,754	36,057	35,590	39,971	42,190	44,349	46,087
Value of shipments (1992 dollars)	Mil. dol. . .	33,399	36,882	36,048	39,971	41,736	43,726	45,600
Total employment	1,000. . . .	232	228	218	215	208	206	218
Production workers	1,000. . . .	111	109	101	103	94.5	95.7	99.2
Average hourly earnings	Dollar . . .	13.13	12.99	13.39	14.30	14.35	14.56	14.27
Capital expenditures	Mil. dol. . .	1,271	1,345	1,051	1,315	1,445	1,581	(NA)
PRODUCT DATA								
Value of shipments [3]	Mil. dol. . .	31,014	33,772	32,531	36,106	38,151	40,799	42,691
Value of shipments (1992 dollars)	Mil. dol. . .	31,624	34,553	32,973	36,106	37,742	40,235	42,250
TRADE DATA [4]								
Value of imports [5]	Mil. dol. . .	7,016	7,126	7,231	8,323	9,111	11,359	12,289
Value of exports	Mil. dol. . .	5,081	6,374	6,717	6,717	7,827	9,689	15,524

NA Not available.   [1] Estimate, except exports and imports.   [2] Value of all products and services sold by establishments in the telecommunications equipment industry.   [3] Value of products classified in the telecommunications equipment industry produced by all industries.   [4] Data deviates from the SIC's cited: includes coaxial and fiber optic cable; excludes CB radios, low power radio transceivers and TV cameras.   [5] Imports are on a c.i.f. valuation.

Source: U.S. Department of Commerce, Bureau of the Census, International Trade Administration (ITA). Estimates by ITA.

No. 1444. Recent Trends in Telephone and Telegraph Apparatus, and Radio and TV Communications Equipment: 1989 to 1995

ITEM	Unit	1989	1990	1991	1992	1993	1994	1995 [1]
TELEPHONE AND TELEGRAPH APPARATUS (SIC 3661)								
Industry data:								
Value of shipments [2]	Mil. dol. . .	15,467	17,297	17,425	20,498	21,540	23,472	24,625
Value of shipments (1992 dollars) . . .	Mil. dol. . .	15,467	17,280	17,321	20,498	21,411	23,378	24,600
Total employment	1,000. . . .	96	93	94	91	85	86	87
Production workers	1,000. . . .	49.0	46.5	46.9	44.7	38.5	41.2	40.4
Average hourly earnings	Dollar . . .	14.51	14.48	14.47	14.95	15.34	15.46	(NA)
Capital expenditures	Mil. dol. . .	573	593	459	615	595	781	(NA)
Product data:								
Value of shipments [3]	Mil. dol. . .	14,679	16,037	15,284	18,328	19,589	22,028	23,273
Value of shipments (1992 dollars) . . .	Mil. dol. . .	14,679	16,021	15,193	18,328	19,472	21,940	23,250
Trade data:								
Value of imports	Mil. dol. . .	(NA)	(NA)	(NA)	(NA)	(NA)	(NA)	(NA)
Value of exports	Mil. dol. . .	(NA)	(NA)	(NA)	(NA)	(NA)	(NA)	(NA)
RADIO AND TV COMMUNICATIONS EQUIPMENT (SIC 3663)								
Industry data:								
Value of shipments [2]	Mil. dol. . .	17,287	18,759	18,165	19,472	20,650	20,877	21,462
Value of shipments (1992 dollars) . . .	Mil. dol. . .	17,932	19,602	18,727	19,472	20,325	20,348	21,000
Total employment	1,000. . . .	135	135	123	124	123	120	131
Production workers	1,000. . . .	62.1	62.4	53.7	58.3	56.0	54.5	58.8
Average hourly earnings	Dollar . . .	12.10	11.90	12.51	13.81	13.66	13.91	13.72
Capital expenditures	Mil. dol. . .	698	752	592	700	851	800	(NA)
Product data:								
Value of shipments [3]	Mil. dol. . .	16,335	17,735	17,247	17,778	18,562	18,771	19,418
Value of shipments (1992 dollars) . . .	Mil. dol. . .	16,945	18,532	17,781	17,778	18,269	18,296	19,000
Trade data:								
Value of imports	Mil. dol. . .	(NA)	(NA)	(NA)	(NA)	(NA)	(NA)	(NA)
Value of exports	Mil. dol. . .	(NA)	(NA)	(NA)	(NA)	(NA)	(NA)	(NA)

NA Not available. [1] Estimate, except exports and imports. [2] Value of all products and services sold by establishments in this industry. [3] Value of products classified in this industry produced by all industries.
Source: U.S. Department of Commerce, Bureau of the Census, International Trade Administration (ITA). Estimates by ITA.

No. 1445. Recent Trends in Electronic Components and Accessories (SIC 367): 1989 to 1995

ITEM	Unit	1989	1990	1991	1992	1993	1994	1995 [1]
INDUSTRY DATA								
Value of shipments [2]	Mil. dol. . .	59,913	60,844	65,233	73,848	81,236	93,635	110,930
Value of shipments (1992 dollars)	Mil. dol. . .	58,310	59,930	64,277	73,848	81,048	93,934	115,673
Total employment	1,000. . . .	551	536	519	532	531	546	(NA)
Production workers	1,000. . . .	339	325	314	318	321	336	(NA)
Average hourly earnings	Dollar . . .	9.96	10.22	10.34	10.83	10.98	11.13	(NA)
PRODUCT DATA								
Value of shipments [3]	Mil. dol. . .	57,009	59,307	62,766	71,372	77,840	89,430	105,866
Value of shipments (1992 dollars)	Mil. dol. . .	55,649	58,549	61,920	71,372	77,661	89,658	110,236
TRADE DATA								
Value of imports	Mil. dol. . .	18,342	19,111	20,409	22,842	27,532	36,092	51,373
Value of exports	Mil. dol. . .	12,630	15,581	15,498	16,192	18,867	24,525	31,252

NA Not available. [1] Estimate, except exports and imports. [2] Value of all products and services sold by establishments in the electronic components and accessories industry. [3] Value of products classified in the electronic components and accessories industry produced by all industries.
Source: U.S. Department of Commerce, Bureau of the Census, International Trade Administration (ITA). Estimates by ITA.

No. 1446. Recent Trends in Electron Tubes (SIC 3671): 1989 to 1995

ITEM	Unit	1989	1990	1991	1992	1993	1994	1995 [1]
INDUSTRY DATA								
Value of shipments [2]	Mil. dol. . .	3,039	2,570	2,568	3,145	3,052	3,148	3,274
Value of shipments (1992 dollars)	Mil. dol. . .	3,073	2,568	2,528	3,145	3,085	3,126	3,210
Total employment	1,000. . . .	27.8	23.4	22.1	22.2	20.2	20.4	20.6
Production workers	1,000. . . .	20.0	17.5	16.3	16.8	15.3	15.8	16.0
Average hourly earnings	Dollar . . .	12.53	12.58	12.9	13.21	13.73	13.25	(NA)
Capital expenditures	Mil. dol. . .	202.0	170.0	77.3	61.7	85.5	132.0	(NA)
PRODUCT DATA								
Value of shipments [3]	Mil. dol. . .	2,638	2,650	2,659	3,357	3,330	3,579	3,865
Value of shipments (1992 dollars)	Mil. dol. . .	2,668	2,647	2,617	3,357	3,367	3,554	3,789
TRADE DATA								
Value of imports	Mil. dol. . .	818	782	817	928	990	1,218	1,390
Value of exports	Mil. dol. . .	537	640	759	771	929	1,232	1,541

NA Not available. [1] Estimate, except exports and imports. [2] Value of all products and services sold by establishments in the electron tubes industry. [3] Value of products classified in the electron tubes industry produced by all industries.
Source: U.S. Department of Commerce, Bureau of the Census, International Trade Administration (ITA). Estimates by ITA.

No. 1447. Recent Trends in Printed Circuit Boards and Semiconductors and Related Devices: 1989 to 1995

ITEM	Unit	1989	1990	1991	1992	1993	1994	1995 [1]
PRINTED CIRCUIT BOARDS (SIC 3672)								
Industry data:								
Value of shipments [2]	Mil. dol. . .	7,354	7,844	6,353	7,312	7,378	8,262	9,687
Value of shipments (1992 dollars) . . .	Mil. dol. . .	7,246	7,766	6,309	7,312	7,551	8,643	10,112
Total employment	1,000. . . .	79.0	76.7	69.9	75.8	73.6	75.7	79.5
Production workers	1,000. . . .	52.4	51.0	47.1	50.8	50.5	53.1	57.3
Average hourly earnings	Dollar . . .	9.44	9.68	9.92	10.17	10.58	10.49	10.81
Capital expenditures	Mil. dol. . .	373	405	311	317	283	366	421
Product data:								
Value of shipments [3]	Mil. dol. . .	7,338	7,617	5,899	6,293	6,930	7,545	8,846
Value of shipments (1992 dollars) . . .	Mil. dol. . .	7,229	7,541	5,858	6,293	7,093	7,892	9,234
Trade data:								
Value of imports	Mil. dol. . .	1,751	2,601	2,712	2,097	2,141	2,384	2,741
Value of exports	Mil. dol. . .	799	1,818	1,374	1,092	973	1,377	1,651
SEMICONDUCTORS AND RELATED DEVICES (SIC 3674)								
Industry data:								
Value of shipments [2]	Mil. dol. . .	25,708	25,977	29,668	32,157	35,152	42,252	52,922
Value of shipments (1992 dollars) . . .	Mil. dol. . .	22,531	24,120	28,228	32,157	35,222	42,722	57,461
Total employment	1,000. . . .	184	182	175	172	163	174	189
Production workers	1,000. . . .	90.5	87.7	86.2	84.7	82.2	89.1	98.3
Average hourly earnings	Dollar . . .	12.02	12.58	12.69	13.55	14.08	14.48	(NA)
Product data:								
Value of shipments [3]	Mil. dol. . .	23,488	23,978	27,438	29,391	33,689	39,204	49,103
Value of shipments (1992 dollars) . . .	Mil. dol. . .	20,586	22,263	26,106	29,391	33,757	39,640	53,315
Trade data:								
Value of imports	Mil. dol. . .	12,172	12,023	12,928	15,275	19,244	25,670	38,618
Value of exports	Mil. dol. . .	9,531	10,710	10,831	11,465	13,744	17,991	23,189

NA Not available.   [1] Estimate, except exports and imports.   [2] Value of all products and services sold by establishments in this industry.   [3] Value of products classified in this industry produced by all industries.
Source: U.S. Department of Commerce, Bureau of the Census, International Trade Administration (ITA). Estimates by ITA.

No. 1448. Recent Trends in Passive Components (SIC 3675-9): 1989 to 1995

ITEM	Unit	1989	1990	1991	1992	1993	1994	1995 [1]
INDUSTRY DATA								
Value of shipments [2]	Mil. dol. . .	23,813	24,452	26,644	31,235	35,656	39,972	45,047
Value of shipments (1992 dollars)	Mil. dol. . .	25,461	25,476	27,212	31,235	35,189	39,443	44,890
Total employment	1,000. . . .	260	254	252	262	275	277	(NA)
Production workers	1,000. . . .	176	169	164	166	173	178	(NA)
Average hourly earnings	Dollar . . .	8.77	8.93	8.99	9.47	9.48	9.59	(NA)
Capital expenditures	Mil. dol. . .	826	789	794	991	1,314	1,354	(NA)
PRODUCT DATA								
Value of shipments [3]	Mil. dol. . .	23,545	25,063	26,771	32,330	33,892	39,102	44,052
Value of shipments (1992 dollars)	Mil. dol. . .	25,166	26,098	27,339	32,330	33,445	38,571	43,898
TRADE DATA								
Value of imports	Mil. dol. . .	3,602	3,705	3,952	4,543	5,157	6,820	8,624
Value of exports	Mil. dol. . .	1,763	2,413	2,534	2,863	3,221	3,926	4,872

NA Not available.   [1] Estimate, except exports and imports.   [2] Value of all products and services sold by establishments in the passive components industry.   [3] Value of products classified in the passive components industry produced by all industries.
Source: U.S. Department of Commerce, Bureau of the Census, International Trade Administration (ITA). Estimates by ITA.

No. 1449. Recent Trends in Motor Vehicles and Car Bodies (SIC 3711): 1989 to 1995

ITEM	Unit	1989	1990	1991	1992	1993	1994	1995 [1]
INDUSTRY DATA								
Value of shipments [2]	Mil. dol. . .	149,315	140,417	133,861	152,949	167,826	197,554	196,386
Value of shipments (1992 dollars)	Mil. dol. . .	164,263	151,638	138,144	152,949	162,151	183,942	181,671
Total employment	1,000. . . .	250	240	218	228	224	234	245
Production workers	1,000. . . .	213	200	179	193	191	203	220
Average hourly earnings	Dollar . . .	19.40	20.31	21.32	21.66	22.61	23.35	24.05
Capital expenditures	Mil. dol. . .	2,374	3,004	3,262	2,990	4,034	4,246	(NA)
PRODUCT DATA								
Value of shipments [3]	Mil. dol. . .	144,448	135,741	128,754	147,447	163,324	195,010	192,970
Value of shipments (1992 dollars)	Mil. dol. . .	158,909	146,588	132,873	147,447	157,801	181,573	178,511
TRADE DATA								
Value of imports	Mil. dol. . .	58,729	60,568	59,131	60,398	68,521	79,367	84,426
Value of exports	Mil. dol. . .	12,479	12,838	15,180	17,628	18,437	21,132	21,592

NA Not available.   [1] Estimate, except exports and imports.   [2] Value of all products and services sold by establishments in the motor vehicles and car bodies industry.   [3] Value of products classified in the motor vehicles and car bodies industry produced by all industries.
Source: U.S. Department of Commerce, Bureau of the Census, International Trade Administration (ITA). Estimates by ITA.

No. 1450. Recent Trends in Aerospace (SIC 372, 376): 1989 to 1995

ITEM	Unit	1989	1990	1991	1992	1993	1994	1995 [1]
INDUSTRY DATA								
Value of shipments [2]	Mil. dol.	113,477	125,194	131,345	131,858	116,346	105,002	101,749
Value of shipments (1992 dollars)	Mil. dol.	128,096	135,839	136,638	131,858	113,891	100,413	95,064
Total employment	1,000.	823	816	746	697	612	535	495
Production workers	1,000.	400	396	362	333	279	243	224
Average hourly earnings	Dollar	15.84	16.36	16.73	18.58	19.05	19.82	19.93
Capital expenditures	Mil. dol.	3,921	3,490	3,407	3,860	2,725	2,402	(NA)
PRODUCT DATA								
Value of shipments [3]	Mil. dol.	106,320	118,141	124,109	122,800	110,312	98,819	95,172
Value of shipments (1992 dollars)	Mil. dol.	119,628	127,856	129,081	122,800	107,971	94,487	88,933
TRADE DATA								
Value of imports	Mil. dol.	9,672	10,985	12,422	12,914	11,527	11,642	10,869
Value of exports	Mil. dol.	30,688	37,304	42,343	43,562	37,901	35,761	31,304

NA Not available.   [1] Estimate, except exports and imports.   [2] Value of all products and services sold by establishments in the aerospace industry.   [3] Value of products classified in the aerospace industry produced by all industries.
Source: U.S. Department of Commerce, Bureau of the Census, International Trade Administration (ITA). Estimates by ITA.

No. 1451. Recent Trends in Aircraft and Aircraft Engines and Engine Parts: 1989 to 1995

ITEM	Unit	1989	1990	1991	1992	1993	1994	1995 [1]
AIRCRAFT (SIC 3721)								
Industry data:								
Value of shipments [2]	Mil. dol.	43,339	51,370	58,090	62,981	55,120	50,944	48,500
Value of shipments (1992 dollars)	Mil. dol.	49,987	56,203	60,385	62,981	53,775	48,197	44,373
Total employment	1,000.	278	289	258	265	241	218	195
Production workers	1,000.	140	140	140	125	122	104	80
Average hourly earnings	Dollar	16.40	17.02	17.82	19.98	19.90	20.77	21.27
Capital expenditures	Mil. dol.	1,270	1,021	1,046	1,661	1,154	872	(NA)
Product data:								
Value of shipments [3]	Mil. dol.	39,531	46,885	52,514	56,569	51,006	46,878	44,300
Value of shipments (1992 dollars)	Mil. dol.	45,595	51,297	54,588	56,569	49,762	44,350	40,531
Trade data:								
Value of imports	Mil. dol.	2,805	2,838	3,438	3,921	3,738	3,809	3,557
Value of exports	Mil. dol.	14,339	19,631	24,173	26,419	21,306	18,831	13,605
AIRCRAFT ENGINES AND ENGINE PARTS (SIC 3724)								
Industry data:								
Value of shipments [2]	Mil. dol.	21,566	22,813	22,746	21,969	18,946	16,664	16,720
Value of shipments (1992 dollars)	Mil. dol.	25,194	25,348	23,994	21,969	18,575	15,931	15,774
Total employment	1,000.	132	129	122	117	103	86.9	82.3
Production workers	1,000.	76.2	72.6	67.3	64.2	53.6	46.4	44.2
Average hourly earnings	Dollar	14.81	15.68	15.56	16.97	17.15	18.02	17.83
Capital expenditures	Mil. dol.	718	785	771	590	440	438	(NA)
Product data:								
Value of shipments [3]	Mil. dol.	19,904	21,580	21,315	20,933	17,995	15,280	15,302
Value of shipments (1992 dollars)	Mil. dol.	23,252	23,978	22,484	20,933	17,642	14,608	14,436
Trade data:								
Value of imports	Mil. dol.	3,897	4,739	4,990	5,752	5,245	5,270	4,699
Value of exports	Mil. dol.	6,578	6,833	6,994	6,642	6,209	6,423	6,104

NA Not available.   [1] Estimate, except exports and imports.   [2] Value of all products and services sold by establishments in this industry.   [3] Value of products classified in this industry produced by all industries.
Source: U.S. Department of Commerce, Bureau of the Census, International Trade Administration (ITA). Estimates by ITA.

No. 1452. Recent Trends in Aircraft Parts and Equipment, n.e.c. (SIC 3728): 1989 to 1995

ITEM	Unit	1989	1990	1991	1992	1993	1994	1995 [1]
INDUSTRY DATA								
Value of shipments [2]	Mil. dol.	19,075	20,458	21,544	19,835	18,264	16,679	16,001
Value of shipments (1992 dollars)	Mil. dol.	21,218	22,141	22,560	19,835	17,750	15,855	15,152
Total employment	1,000.	193	198	187	165	139	120	116
Production workers	1,000.	103.0	111.0	108.0	93.6	78.4	65.4	64.4
Average hourly earnings	Dollar	14.55	14.89	15.05	16.44	18.37	19.12	19.06
Capital expenditures	Mil. dol.	813	815	1,006	1,132	713	656	(NA)
PRODUCT DATA								
Value of shipments [3]	Mil. dol.	21,295	23,082	25,288	21,940	18,684	17,647	16,950
Value of shipments (1992 dollars)	Mil. dol.	23,687	24,980	26,480	21,940	18,157	16,775	16,051
TRADE DATA								
Value of imports	Mil. dol.	2,852	3,324	3,888	3,132	2,437	2,476	2,515
Value of exports	Mil. dol.	8,708	9,517	9,953	9,050	9,133	9,472	10,079

NA Not available.   [1] Estimate, except exports and imports.   [2] Value of all products and services sold by establishments in the aircraft parts and equipment, n.e.c. industry.   [3] Value of products classified in the aircraft parts and equipment, n.e.c. industry produced by all industries.
Source: U.S. Department of Commerce, Bureau of the Census, International Trade Administration (ITA). Estimates by ITA.

No. 1453. Recent Trends in Ship Building and Repairing (SIC 3731): 1989 to 1995

ITEM	Unit	1989	1990	1991	1992	1993	1994	1995 [1]
INDUSTRY DATA								
Value of shipments [2]	Mil. dol. . .	9,640	10,856	10,849	10,608	9,964	9,864	10,012
Value of shipments (1992 dollars)	Mil. dol. . .	10,277	11,249	10,981	10,608	9,454	9,016	9,185
Total employment	1,000. . . .	119	121	121	118	112	102	100
Production workers	1,000. . . .	87.9	91.0	90.1	87.1	81.9	75.6	74.2
Average hourly earnings	Dollar . . .	12.31	12.59	12.97	12.98	13.45	13.98	(NA)
Capital expenditures [3]	Mil. dol. . .	193	227	172	128	156	141	(NA)
PRODUCT DATA								
Value of shipments [4]	Mil. dol. . .	9,530	10,741	10,700	10,381	9,801	9,876	9,951
Value of shipments (1992 dollars)	Mil. dol. . .	10,160	11,131	10,830	10,381	9,299	9,027	9,129
TRADE DATA								
Value of imports	Mil. dol. . .	145	15	14	51	517	12	29
Value of exports	Mil. dol. . .	313	434	321	652	379	595	483

NA Not available.   [1] Estimate, except exports and imports.   [2] Value of all products and services sold by establishments in the ship building and repairing industry.   [3] Capital expenditures, 1991 and 1992, supplied by U.S. Department of Transportation.   [4] Value of products classified in the ship building and repairing industry produced by all industries.

Source: U.S. Department of Commerce, Bureau of the Census, International Trade Administration (ITA). Estimates by U.S. Department of Transportation.

No. 1454. Recent Trends in Boat Building and Repairing (SIC 3732): 1989 to 1995

ITEM	Unit	1989	1990	1991	1992	1993	1994	1995 [1]
INDUSTRY DATA								
Value of shipments [2]	Mil. dol. . .	5,739	4,998	3,676	4,599	4,975	5,425	6,085
Value of shipments (1992 dollars)	Mil. dol. . .	6,286	5,267	3,770	4,599	4,887	5,242	5,714
Total employment	1,000. . . .	60.4	54.1	40.8	44.5	47.0	48.1	52.3
Production workers	1,000. . . .	49.2	42.7	31.7	34.4	36.8	38.9	42.3
Average hourly earnings	Dollar . . .	8.44	8.68	9.17	9.62	9.57	9.77	10.0
Capital expenditures	Mil. dol. . .	120	83	39	63	83	99	(NA)
PRODUCT DATA								
Value of shipments [3]	Mil. dol. . .	5,613	4,877	3,518	4,331	4,632	4,977	5,583
Value of shipments (1992 dollars)	Mil. dol. . .	6,148	5,140	3,608	4,331	4,550	4,809	5,242
TRADE DATA								
Value of imports	Mil. dol. . .	404	279	207	257	425	564	807
Value of exports	Mil. dol. . .	615	793	774	714	534	507	658

NA Not available.   [1] Estimate, except exports and imports.   [2] Value of all products and services sold by establishments in the boat building and repairing industry.   [3] Value of products classified in the boat building and repairing industry produced by all industries.

Source: U.S. Department of Commerce, Bureau of the Census, International Trade Administration (ITA). Estimates by ITA.

No. 1455. Recent Trends in Motorcycles, Bicycles, and Parts (SIC 3751): 1989 to 1995

ITEM	Unit	1989	1990	1991	1992	1993	1994	1995 [1]
INDUSTRY DATA								
Value of shipments [2]	Mil. dol. . .	1,370	1,476	1,914	1,878	2,566	2,632	2,758
Value of shipments (1992 dollars)	Mil. dol. . .	1,465	1,539	1,953	1,878	2,513	2,546	2,602
Total employment	1,000. . . .	8.4	9.4	10.8	11.7	14.1	15.7	16.0
Production workers	1,000. . . .	6.7	7.6	8.5	9.0	10.5	11.7	11.9
Average hourly earnings	Dollar . . .	10.13	10.26	11.69	11.58	13.53	14.71	15.00
Capital expenditures	Mil. dol. . .	26	24	62	46	51	92	(NA)
PRODUCT DATA								
Value of shipments [3]	Mil. dol. . .	1,515	1,799	2,112	2,153	2,640	2,549	2,671
Value of shipments (1992 dollars)	Mil. dol. . .	1,620	1,876	2,155	2,153	2,585	2,465	2,520
TRADE DATA								
Value of imports	Mil. dol. . .	1,318	1,199	1,329	1,537	1,717	1,763	2,130
Value of exports	Mil. dol. . .	245	420	615	671	703	711	850

NA Not available.   [1] Estimate, except exports and imports.   [2] Value of all products and services sold by establishments in the motorcycles, bicycles, and parts industry.   [3] Value of products classified in the motorcycles, bicycles, and parts industry produced by all industries.

Source: U.S. Department of Commerce, Bureau of the Census, International Trade Administration (ITA). Estimates by ITA.

No. 1456. Recent Trends in Guided Missiles and Space Vehicles and Space Propulsion Units and Parts: 1989 to 1995

ITEM	Unit	1989	1990	1991	1992	1993	1994	1995 [1]
GUIDED MISSILES AND SPACE VEHICLES (SIC 3761)								
Industry data:								
Value of shipments [2]	Mil. dol. . .	23,983	25,083	23,399	19,675	15,800	15,397	15,259
Value of shipments (1992 dollars) . . .	Mil. dol. . .	26,011	26,542	24,049	19,675	15,659	15,184	14,700
Total employment	1,000. . . .	173.0	156.0	136.0	100.0	86.6	76.8	71.0
Production workers	1,000. . . .	60.1	54.2	45.0	31.5	27.6	25.0	22.8
Average hourly earnings	Dollar . . .	17.53	18.25	19.07	22.23	20.88	21.02	21.36
Capital expenditures	Mil. dol. . .	795	659	450	307	308	329	(NA)
Product data:								
Value of shipments [3]	Mil. dol. . .	17,049	16,907	16,075	13,972	13,452	12,353	12,100
Value of shipments (1992 dollars) . . .	Mil. dol. . .	18,491	17,891	16,521	13,972	13,332	12,183	11,657
Trade data:								
Value of imports	Mil. dol. . .	6.9	4.2	1.8	4.1	5.2	1.6	2.7
Value of exports	Mil. dol. . .	396	568	318	599	507	364	718
SPACE PROPULSION UNITS AND PARTS (SIC 3764)								
Industry data:								
Value of shipments [2]	Mil. dol. . .	3,747	3,756	3,658	5,328	6,201	3,374	3,343
Value of shipments (1992 dollars) . . .	Mil. dol. . .	4,064	3,974	3,759	5,328	6,146	3,327	3,230
Total employment	1,000. . . .	30.0	29.7	27.7	32.3	29.2	22.8	20.5
Production workers	1,000. . . .	10.6	10.6	9.5	13.4	8.9	7.8	7.0
Average hourly earnings	Dollar . . .	19.51	18.87	19.05	23.74	22.03	22.1	22.52
Capital expenditures	Mil. dol. . .	262	182	102	128	85	69	(NA)
Product data:								
Value of shipments [3]	Mil. dol. . .	4,584	4,662	4,530	5,207	5,862	3,563	3,520
Value of shipments (1992 dollars) . . .	Mil. dol. . .	4,971	4,934	4,656	5,207	5,810	3,513	3,401
Trade data:								
Value of imports	Mil. dol. . .	1.2	0.1	0.5	0.4	0.2	(NA)	0.1
Value of exports	Mil. dol. . .	11.0	30.7	6.7	12.6	1.1	1.6	40.1

NA Not available.   [1] Estimate, except exports and imports.   [2] Value of all products and services sold by establishments in this industry.   [3] Value of products classified in this industry produced by all industries.
Source: U.S. Department of Commerce, Bureau of the Census, International Trade Administration (ITA). Estimates by ITA.

No. 1457. Recent Trends in Space Vehicle Equipment, n.e.c. (SIC 3769): 1989 to 1995

ITEM	Unit	1989	1990	1991	1992	1993	1994	1995 [1]
INDUSTRY DATA								
Value of shipments [2]	Mil. dol. . .	1,768	1,716	1,907	2,071	2,015	1,944	1,927
Value of shipments (1992 dollars)	Mil. dol. . .	1,622	1,631	1,892	2,071	1,987	1,919	1,835
Total employment	1,000. . . .	18.4	14.4	14.2	17.2	12.3	11.1	10.0
Production workers	1,000. . . .	9.1	8.0	7.7	7.7	5.6	5.5	5.0
Average hourly earnings	Dollar . . .	16.56	16.61	18.36	18.09	19.95	20.48	20.87
Capital expenditures	Mil. dol. . .	64.2	28.0	31.4	41.0	25.3	38.3	(NA)
PRODUCT DATA								
Value of shipments [3]	Mil. dol. . .	3,958	5,024	4,387	4,179	3,313	3,097	3,000
Value of shipments (1992 dollars)	Mil. dol. . .	3,631	4,776	4,352	4,179	3,267	3,057	2,857
TRADE DATA								
Value of imports	Mil. dol. . .	110	79	103	104	102	86	96
Value of exports	Mil. dol. . .	656	724	899	839	745	669	759

NA Not available.   [1] Estimate, except exports and imports.   [2] Value of all products and services sold by establishments in the space vehicle equipment, n.e.c. industry.   [3] Value of products classified in the space vehicle equipment, n.e.c., industry produced by all industries.
Source: U.S. Department of Commerce, Bureau of the Census, International Trade Administration (ITA). Estimates by ITA.

No. 1458. Recent Trends in Search and Navigation Equipment (SIC 3812): 1989 to 1995

ITEM	Unit	1989	1990	1991	1992	1993	1994	1995 [1]
INDUSTRY DATA								
Value of shipments [2]	Mil. dol. . .	35,295	36,734	36,213	35,266	33,546	30,103	28,598
Value of shipments (1992 dollars)	Mil. dol. . .	38,034	38,185	36,915	35,266	32,824	29,170	27,236
Total employment	1,000. . . .	340	314	280	255	225	199	(NA)
Production workers	1,000. . . .	141	130	112	104	89	80	(NA)
Average hourly earnings	Dollar . . .	14.99	14.49	14.08	17.29	18.79	18.86	(NA)
Capital expenditures	Mil. dol. . .	1,367	1,125	830	859	706	649	(NA)
PRODUCT DATA								
Value of shipments [3]	Mil. dol. . .	33,608	35,250	34,173	34,171	31,203	28,962	27,514
Value of shipments (1992 dollars)	Mil. dol. . .	36,216	36,642	34,835	34,171	30,532	28,064	26,204
TRADE DATA								
Value of imports	Mil. dol. . .	766	781	858	881	750	863	994
Value of exports	Mil. dol. . .	2,106	2,159	2,241	2,133	2,105	2,031	1,978

NA Not available.   [1] Estimate, except exports and imports.   [2] Value of all products and services sold by establishments in the search and navigation equipment industry.   [3] Value of products classified in the search and navigation equipment industry produced by all industries.
Source: U.S. Department of Commerce, Bureau of the Census, International Trade Administration (ITA). Estimates by ITA.

No. 1459. Recent Trends in Laboratory Instruments (SIC 3821, 3826, 3827): 1989 to 1995

ITEM	Unit	1989	1990	1991	1992	1993	1994	1995 [1]
INDUSTRY DATA								
Value of shipments [2]	Mil. dol. . .	8,193	9,041	9,234	9,560	10,384	10,967	11,492
3821 Lab apparatus and furniture. . . .	Mil. dol. . .	1,970	1,917	1,783	2,106	2,173	2,361	2,479
3826 Analytical instruments.	Mil. dol. . .	4,306	4,906	5,071	5,191	5,657	5,973	6,302
3827 Optical instruments	Mil. dol. . .	1,918	2,218	2,380	2,263	2,554	2,633	2,712
Value of shipments (1992 dollars)	Mil. dol. . .	8,952	9,688	9,479	9,560	10,221	10,702	11,027
3821 Lab apparatus and furniture. . . .	Mil. dol. . .	2,158	2,048	1,868	2,106	2,081	2,223	2,272
3826 Analytical instruments.	Mil. dol. . .	4,635	5,137	5,174	5,191	5,596	5,839	6,065
3827 Optical instruments	Mil. dol. . .	2,159	2,503	2,436	2,263	2,544	2,641	2,690
Total employment	1,000. . . .	75.2	77.6	74.2	76.3	78	75.5	(NA)
3821 Lab apparatus and furniture. . . .	1,000. . . .	18.2	17.8	14.8	17.7	16.9	17.8	(NA)
3826 Analytical instruments.	1,000. . . .	35.9	37.8	37	39.7	40.3	38.4	(NA)
3827 Optical instruments	1,000. . . .	21.1	22	22.4	18.9	20.8	19.3	(NA)
Production workers	1,000. . . .	37.0	36.8	32.7	33.6	34.0	34.7	(NA)
3821 Lab apparatus and furniture. . . .	1,000. . . .	9.8	9.1	6.9	9.0	8.2	8.8	(NA)
3826 Analytical instruments.	1,000. . . .	15.3	15.1	14.7	15.2	15.5	15.1	(NA)
3827 Optical instruments	1,000. . . .	11.9	12.6	11.1	9.4	10.3	10.8	(NA)
Average hourly earnings	Dollar . . .	11.51	11.86	12.38	12.76	13.06	13.36	(NA)
3821 Lab apparatus and furniture . .	Dollar . . .	10.57	10.80	11.41	11.63	11.86	11.89	(NA)
3826 Analytical instruments	Dollar . . .	11.51	11.79	12.30	13.32	13.51	14.09	(NA)
3827 Optical instruments.	Dollar . . .	12.34	12.71	13.1	12.96	13.35	13.52	(NA)
Capital expenditures	Mil. dol. . .	294	289	326	348	330	321	(NA)
3821 Lab apparatus and furniture. . . .	Mil. dol. . .	58.1	59.5	52.7	55.4	42.9	39.7	(NA)
3826 Analytical instruments.	Mil. dol. . .	163	152	195	228	213	176	(NA)
3827 Optical instruments	Mil. dol. . .	72.4	77.2	77.6	65	74.5	105	(NA)
PRODUCT DATA								
Value of shipments [3]	Mil. dol. . .	7,790	8,251	8,464	9,481	9,654	9,967	10,404
3821 Lab apparatus and furniture. . . .	Mil. dol. . .	1,794	1,779	1,673	1,846	1,833	1,943	2,021
3826 Analytical instruments.	Mil. dol. . .	4,020	4,461	4,763	5,126	5,267	5,599	5,934
3827 Optical instruments	Mil. dol. . .	1,977	2,011	2,029	2,509	2,554	2,425	2,449
Value of shipments (1992 dollars)	Mil. dol. . .	8,518	8,841	8,690	9,481	9,509	9,735	9,993
3821 Lab apparatus and furniture. . . .	Mil. dol. . .	1,965	1,901	1,754	1,846	1,755	1,830	1,852
3826 Analytical instruments.	Mil. dol. . .	4,327	4,671	4,860	5,126	5,210	5,473	5,711
3827 Optical instruments	Mil. dol. . .	2,226	2,269	2,077	2,509	2,544	2,432	2,430
TRADE DATA								
Value of imports	Mil. dol. . .	1,631	1,730	1,838	1,998	2,063	2,317	2,668
3821 Lab apparatus and furniture. . . .	Mil. dol. . .	124	121	121	116	126	148	126
3826 Analytical instruments.	Mil. dol. . .	669	755	794	891	890	988	1,122
3827 Optical instruments	Mil. dol. . .	839	855	922	992	1,047	1,181	1,421
Value of exports	Mil. dol. . .	2,333	2,493	2,793	2,939	3,036	3,327	3,779
3821 Lab apparatus and furniture. . . .	Mil. dol. . .	215	215	186	170	195	243	278
3826 Analytical instruments.	Mil. dol. . .	1,424	1,594	1,779	1,923	2,090	2,223	2,523
3827 Optical instruments	Mil. dol. . .	694	684	828	846	750	861	978

NA Not available.   [1] Estimate, except exports and imports.   [2] Value of all products and services sold by establishments in the laboratory instruments industry.   [3] Value of products classified in the laboratory instruments industry produced by all industries.

Source: U.S. Department of Commerce, Bureau of the Census, International Trade Administration (ITA). Estimates by ITA.

No. 1460. Recent Trends in Measuring and Controlling Instruments (SIC 3822, 3823, 3824, 3829): 1989 to 1995

ITEM	Unit	1989	1990	1991	1992	1993	1994	1995 [1]
INDUSTRY DATA								
Value of shipments [2]	Mil. dol.	13,515	14,026	14,789	15,969	16,279	17,735	18,890
3822 Environmental controls	Mil. dol.	2,336	2,396	2,244	2,607	2,813	2,968	3,160
3823 Process controls	Mil. dol.	5,693	5,924	5,904	6,360	6,356	7,012	7,398
3824 Fluid meters and devices	Mil. dol.	1,657	1,666	2,247	2,602	2,824	3,300	3,564
3829 Instruments, n.e.c.	Mil. dol.	3,829	4,040	4,395	4,400	4,287	4,456	4,768
Value of shipments (1992 dollars)	Mil. dol.	14,741	14,759	15,126	15,969	15,876	17,021	17,992
3822 Environmental controls	Mil. dol.	2,496	2,501	2,283	2,607	2,614	2,696	2,852
3823 Process controls	Mil. dol.	6,202	6,229	6,042	6,360	6,219	6,775	7,127
3824 Fluid meters and devices	Mil. dol.	1,868	1,799	2,297	2,602	2,815	3,204	3,437
3829 Instruments, n.e.c.	Mil. dol.	4,175	4,230	4,503	4,400	4,227	4,347	4,576
Total employment	1,000	130	128	124	129	126	126	(NA)
3822 Environmental controls	1,000	25.4	26.1	22.5	25.0	24.4	24.5	24.8
3823 Process controls	1,000	55.0	54.7	50.4	50.1	50.0	50.4	51.1
3824 Fluid meters and devices	1,000	10.7	10.4	12.8	16.2	15.8	16.6	(NA)
3829 Instruments, n.e.c.	1,000	38.4	36.3	38.7	38.1	35.7	34.5	(NA)
Production workers	1,000	73.4	69.0	66.4	71.4	69.4	71.2	(NA)
3822 Environmental controls	1,000	18.2	18.2	14.9	16.8	17.2	17.2	17.5
3823 Process controls	1,000	28.0	26.1	23.7	24.0	23.6	24.3	25.7
3824 Fluid meters and devices	1,000	6.8	6.6	8.3	11.3	10.7	11.8	(NA)
3829 Instruments, n.e.c.	1,000	20.4	18.1	19.5	19.3	17.9	17.9	(NA)
Average hourly earnings	Dollar	10.76	11.2	11.75	12.61	12.91	12.98	(NA)
3822 Environmental controls	Dollar	10.21	10.42	11.29	11.09	11.29	11.30	(NA)
3823 Process controls	Dollar	11.18	11.38	11.39	12.32	12.32	12.31	(NA)
3824 Fluid meters and devices	Dollar	10.43	10.74	13.13	15.36	15.55	16.70	(NA)
3829 Instruments, n.e.c.	Dollar	10.78	11.86	11.95	12.69	13.56	12.92	(NA)
Capital expenditures	Mil. dol.	388	396	616	494	420	497	(NA)
3822 Environmental controls	Mil. dol.	66.3	61.2	56.0	81.3	87.6	75.9	(NA)
3823 Process controls	Mil. dol.	136	151	347	158	133	227	(NA)
3824 Fluid meters and devices	Mil. dol.	38.2	57.0	81.8	74.1	76.1	92.3	(NA)
3829 Instruments, n.e.c.	Mil. dol.	147	127	132	180	123	102	(NA)
PRODUCT DATA								
Value of shipments [3]	Mil. dol.	12,912	14,221	14,121	15,448	16,071	17,159	18,436
3822 Environmental controls	Mil. dol.	2,353	2,312	2,164	2,370	2,433	2,755	2,949
3823 Process controls	Mil. dol.	5,218	5,515	5,304	5,997	6,213	6,578	7,010
3824 Fluid meters and devices	Mil. dol.	1,563	2,470	2,300	2,731	3,066	3,509	3,827
3829 Instruments, n.e.c.	Mil. dol.	3,778	3,924	4,353	4,350	4,359	4,318	4,650
Value of shipments (1992 dollars)	Mil. dol.	14,080	14,989	14,442	15,448	15,696	16,477	17,568
3822 Environmental controls	Mil. dol.	2,513	2,413	2,202	2,370	2,261	2,502	2,662
3823 Process controls	Mil. dol.	5,684	5,799	5,429	5,997	6,079	6,356	6,753
3824 Fluid meters and devices	Mil. dol.	1,762	2,668	2,352	2,731	3,056	3,407	3,690
3829 Instruments, n.e.c.	Mil. dol.	4,120	4,109	4,460	4,350	4,299	4,212	4,463
TRADE DATA								
Value of imports	Mil. dol.	1,772	1,904	2,044	2,372	2,772	3,696	4,208
3822 Environmental controls	Mil. dol.	317	378	399	511	611	897	992
3823 Process controls	Mil. dol.	716	683	755	856	866	966	1,239
3824 Fluid meters and devices	Mil. dol.	159	196	208	296	554	954	974
3829 Instruments, n.e.c.	Mil. dol.	580	647	682	708	742	878	1,002
Value of exports	Mil. dol.	2,960	3,519	3,919	4,007	4,607	5,108	5,543
3822 Environmental controls	Mil. dol.	240	397	447	488	718	905	1,035
3823 Process controls	Mil. dol.	1,086	1,363	1,557	1,610	1,748	1,811	1,889
3824 Fluid meters and devices	Mil. dol.	116	136	159	170	272	427	406
3829 Instruments, n.e.c.	Mil. dol.	1,518	1,622	1,757	1,738	1,869	1,964	2,213

NA Not available.   [1] Estimate, except exports and imports.   [2] Value of all products and services sold by establishments in the measuring and controlling instruments industry.   [3] Value of products classified in the measuring and controlling instruments industry produced by all industries.

Source: U.S. Department of Commerce, Bureau of the Census, International Trade Administration (ITA). Estimates by ITA.

No. 1461. Recent Trends in Instruments to Measure Electricity (SIC 3825): 1989 to 1995

ITEM	Unit	1989	1990	1991	1992	1993	1994	1995 [1]
INDUSTRY DATA								
Value of shipments [2]	Mil. dol. . .	7,920	8,390	8,240	8,873	8,746	10,098	11,185
Value of shipments (1992 dollars)	Mil. dol. . .	8,889	8,897	8,451	8,873	8,608	9,775	10,673
Total employment	1,000. . . .	78.4	78.4	69.3	68.7	64.9	62.6	62.4
Production workers	1,000. . . .	39.6	38.7	34.0	32.3	30.5	31.8	31.1
Average hourly earnings	Dollar . . .	12.24	12.88	12.47	14.15	14.56	14.85	15.05
Capital expenditures	Mil. dol. . .	305	293	257	325	402	333	360
PRODUCT DATA								
Value of shipments [3]	Mil. dol. . .	7,623	7,943	7,804	7,985	8,180	8,999	9,767
Value of shipments (1992 dollars)	Mil. dol. . .	8,556	8,423	8,004	7,985	8,051	8,711	9,320
TRADE DATA								
Value of imports	Mil. dol. . .	555	587	633	651	751	868	1,135
Value of exports	Mil. dol. . .	2,237	2,186	2,400	2,568	2,640	2,944	3,619

[1] Estimate, except exports and imports. [2] Value of all products and services sold by establishments in the instruments to measure electricity industry. [3] Value of products classified in the instruments to measure electricity industry produced by all industries.
Source: U.S. Department of Commerce, Bureau of the Census, International Trade Administration (ITA). Estimates by ITA.

No. 1462. Recent Trends in Surgical and Medical Instruments and Surgical Appliances and Supplies: 1989 to 1995

ITEM	Unit	1989	1990	1991	1992	1993	1994	1995 [1]
SURGICAL AND MEDICAL INSTRUMENTS (SIC 3841)								
Industry data:								
Value of shipments [2]	Mil. dol. . .	8,972	10,262	10,710	13,385	15,113	14,812	15,404
Value of shipments (1992 dollars)	Mil. dol. . .	9,554	10,656	10,962	13,385	14,860	14,450	14,869
Total employment	1,000. . . .	83.9	88.9	87.7	98.2	103.0	101.0	99.2
Production workers	1,000. . . .	50.7	53.8	53.1	58.5	61.4	60.0	60.2
Average hourly earnings	Dollar	9.58	9.81	10.59	10.86	11.32	11.52	12.07
Capital expenditures	Mil. dol. . .	403	469	536	689	809	624	(NA)
Product data:								
Value of shipments [3]	Mil. dol. . .	8,655	9,857	10,474	13,276	14,759	14,219	14,789
Value of shipments (1992 dollars)	Mil. dol. . .	9,217	10,236	10,720	13,276	14,512	13,873	14,275
Trade data:								
Value of imports	Mil. dol. . .	654	800	996	1,111	1,307	1,349	1,573
Value of exports	Mil. dol. . .	1,497	1,854	2,173	2,445	2,539	2,487	2,800
SURGICAL APPLIANCES AND SUPPLIES (SIC 3842)								
Industry data:								
Value of shipments [2]	Mil. dol. . .	10,187	11,128	12,555	13,843	14,553	14,573	15,011
Value of shipments (1992 dollars)	Mil. dol. . .	11,395	11,901	12,930	13,843	14,034	13,619	14,055
Total employment	1,000. . . .	84.4	86.6	93.3	96.8	98.0	96.1	94.4
Production workers	1,000. . . .	54.3	55.8	60.6	61.6	61.9	59.4	58.1
Average hourly earnings	Dollar	9.35	9.60	10.12	10.83	10.93	11.21	11.45
Capital expenditures	Mil. dol. . .	240	266	425	504	433	374	(NA)
Product data:								
Value of shipments [3]	Mil. dol. . .	9,474	10,355	11,514	12,438	13,285	13,132	13,527
Value of shipments (1992 dollars)	Mil. dol. . .	10,598	11,075	11,858	12,438	12,811	12,273	12,666
Trade data:								
Value of imports	Mil. dol. . .	394	554	645	892	899	1,004	1,178
Value of exports	Mil. dol. . .	965	1,226	1,450	1,693	1,834	2,030	2,262

NA Not available. [1] Estimate, except exports and imports. [2] Value of all products and services sold by establishments in this industry. [3] Value of products classified in this industry produced by all industries.
Source: U.S. Department of Commerce, Bureau of the Census, International Trade Administration (ITA). Estimates by ITA.

No. 1463. Recent Trends in Dental Equipment and Supplies (SIC 3843): 1989 to 1995

ITEM	Unit	1989	1990	1991	1992	1993	1994	1995 [1]
INDUSTRY DATA								
Value of shipments [2]	Mil. dol. . .	1,277	1,365	1,576	1,910	2,012	2,274	2,604
Value of shipments (1992 dollars)	Mil. dol. . .	1,252	1,335	1,587	1,910	1,912	2,084	2,344
Total employment	1,000. . . .	12.9	12.9	13.8	15.1	15.4	15.5	(NA)
Production workers	1,000. . . .	8.4	8.4	8.6	8.9	9.2	9.8	(NA)
Average hourly earnings	Dollar . . .	10.31	11.34	11.23	11.5	11.89	11.43	(NA)
Capital expenditures	Mil. dol. . .	27.3	24.4	32.2	48.6	58.5	52.0	(NA)
PRODUCT DATA								
Value of shipments [3]	Mil. dol. . .	1,177	1,265	1,397	1,621	1,664	1,978	2,076
Value of shipments (1992 dollars)	Mil. dol. . .	1,154	1,238	1,407	1,621	1,582	1,813	1,869
TRADE DATA								
Value of imports	Mil. dol. . .	138	168	183	230	226	221	262
Value of exports	Mil. dol. . .	265	312	376	448	498	512	574

NA Not available. [1] Estimate, except exports and imports. [2] Value of all products and services sold by establishments in the dental equipment and supplies industry. [3] Value of products classified in the dental equipment and supplies industry produced by all industries.
Source: U.S. Department of Commerce, Bureau of the Census, International Trade Administration (ITA). Estimates by ITA.

No. 1464. Recent Trends in X-Ray Apparatus and Tubes and Electromedical Equipment: 1989 to 1995

ITEM	Unit	1989	1990	1991	1992	1993	1994	1995[1]
X-RAY APPARATUS AND TUBES (SIC 3844)								
Industry data:								
Value of shipments [2]	Mil. dol. . .	1,926	2,577	3,011	3,235	3,372	3,373	3,448
Value of shipments (1992 dollars)	Mil. dol. . .	1,947	2,706	3,039	3,235	3,352	3,330	3,380
Total employment	1,000. . . .	9.4	12.6	13.0	14.3	14.2	14.0	13.9
Production workers	1,000. . . .	5.5	6.8	6.6	7.1	6.9	6.6	6.5
Average hourly earnings	Dollar	12.93	13.79	14.37	14.79	15.44	15.28	15.35
Capital expenditures	Mil. dol. . .	56.9	91.5	65.3	63.6	85.6	84.8	(NA)
Product data:								
Value of shipments [3]	Mil. dol. . .	1,690	1,854	2,201	2,360	2,510	2,566	2,622
Value of shipments (1992 dollars)	Mil. dol. . .	1,709	1,947	2,221	2,360	2,495	2,533	2,571
Trade data:								
Value of imports	Mil. dol. . .	878	997	1,117	1,155	1,236	1,131	1,226
Value of exports	Mil. dol. . .	527	605	753	791	850	987	1,171
ELECTROMEDICAL EQUIPMENT (SIC 3845)								
Industry data:								
Value of shipments [2]	Mil. dol. . .	4,821	5,604	5,743	7,175	7,186	7,746	8,125
Value of shipments (1992 dollars)	Mil. dol. . .	4,971	5,742	5,836	7,175	7,193	7,952	8,437
Total employment	1,000. . . .	31.8	33.6	33.2	40.0	39.9	40.0	40.3
Production workers	1,000. . . .	14.1	13.8	14.5	18.0	17.6	17.8	18.0
Average hourly earnings	Dollar	10.91	11.49	11.74	11.95	12.12	11.83	11.95
Capital expenditures	Mil. dol. . .	174	174	181	254	241	309	(NA)
Product data:								
Value of shipments [3]	Mil. dol. . .	4,658	4,808	5,194	6,306	6,515	7,011	7,354
Value of shipments (1992 dollars)	Mil. dol. . .	4,802	4,926	5,278	6,306	6,521	7,198	7,637
Trade data:								
Value of imports	Mil. dol. . .	978	1,156	1,286	1,277	1,303	1,308	1,420
Value of exports	Mil. dol. . .	1,610	1,796	2,043	2,255	2,396	2,820	3,092

NA Not available.   [1] Estimate, except exports and imports.   [2] Value of all products and services sold by establishments in this industry.   [3] Value of products classified in this industry produced by all industries.
Source: U.S. Department of Commerce, Bureau of the Census, International Trade Administration (ITA). Estimates by ITA.

No. 1465. Recent Trends in Photographic Equipment and Supplies (SIC 3861): 1989 to 1995

ITEM	Unit	1989	1990	1991	1992	1993	1994	1995[1]
INDUSTRY DATA								
Value of shipments [2]	Mil. dol. . .	22,738	21,018	21,398	22,150	22,368	23,368	22,000
Value of shipments (1992 dollars)	Mil. dol. . .	21,512	19,336	21,186	22,150	23,276	24,939	23,355
Total employment	1,000. . . .	87.0	79.3	78.0	77.5	75.7	64.8	61.6
Production workers	1,000. . . .	43.9	41.2	40.0	39.4	38.0	34.8	31.4
Average hourly earnings	Dollar . . .	13.41	13.69	14.73	14.65	14.64	15.80	16.12
Capital expenditures	Mil. dol. . .	1,008	1,009	1,089	808	775	755	(NA)
PRODUCT DATA								
Value of shipments [3]	Mil. dol. . .	17,894	17,854	18,518	18,861	19,686	20,234	19,000
Value of shipments (1992 dollars)	Mil. dol. . .	16,929	16,425	18,334	18,861	20,485	21,594	20,170
TRADE DATA								
Value of imports	Mil. dol. . .	5,549	5,431	5,804	6,409	7,026	7,711	8,409
Value of exports	Mil. dol. . .	3,044	3,458	3,785	3,763	3,635	3,706	4,083

NA Not available.   [1] Estimate, except exports and imports.   [2] Value of all products and services sold by establishments in the photographic equipment and supplies industry.   [3] Value of products classified in the photographic equipment and supplies industry produced by all industries.
Source: U.S. Department of Commerce, Bureau of the Census, International Trade Administration (ITA). Estimates by ITA.

No. 1466. Recent Trends in Jewelry, Precious Metal (SIC 3911): 1989 to 1995

ITEM	Unit	1989	1990	1991	1992	1993	1994	1995[1]
INDUSTRY DATA								
Value of shipments [2]	Mil. dol. . .	4,227	4,180	3,733	4,164	4,278	4,459	4,588
Value of shipments (1992 dollars)	Mil. dol. . .	4,431	4,214	3,726	4,164	4,215	4,350	4,437
Total employment	1,000. . . .	35.5	35.6	32.6	32.3	34.0	31.1	30.8
Production workers	1,000. . . .	24.1	24.6	22.2	22.3	23.6	20.1	19.7
Average hourly earnings	Dollar . . .	8.39	8.80	8.76	9.41	9.53	9.78	10.17
Capital expenditures	Mil. dol. . .	29.8	43.2	40.5	36.5	45.3	49.2	(NA)
PRODUCT DATA								
Value of shipments [3]	Mil. dol. . .	3,988	3,959	3,502	3,739	4,006	4,063	4,180
Value of shipments (1992 dollars)	Mil. dol. . .	4,180	3,991	3,495	3,739	3,947	3,964	4,043
TRADE DATA								
Value of imports	Mil. dol. . .	2,562	2,448	2,451	2,710	3,141	3,438	3,573
Value of exports	Mil. dol. . .	398	407	414	476	388	366	375

NA Not available.   [1] Estimate, except exports and imports.   [2] Value of all products and services sold by establishments in the jewelry, precious metal industry.   [3] Value of products classified in the jewelry, precious metal industry produced by all industries.
Source: U.S. Department of Commerce, Bureau of the Census, International Trade Administration (ITA). Estimates by ITA.

No. 1467. Recent Trends in Dolls, Toys, and Games (SIC 3942, 3944): 1989 to 1995

ITEM	Unit	1989	1990	1991	1992	1993	1994	1995 [1]
INDUSTRY DATA								
Value of shipments [2]	Mil. dol. . . .	4,125	4,003	4,307	4,437	4,968	4,553	(NA)
3942 Dolls and stuffed toys	Mil. dol. . . .	323	380	420	251	273	239	(NA)
3944 Games and toys	Mil. dol. . . .	3,803	3,623	3,887	4,186	4,696	4,313	(NA)
Value of shipments (1992 dollars)	Mil. dol. . . .	4,309	4,118	4,381	4,437	4,968	4,526	(NA)
3942 Dolls and stuffed toys	Mil. dol. . . .	360	398	426	251	268	234	(NA)
3944 Games and toys	Mil. dol. . . .	3,949	3,720	3,954	4,186	4,700	4,292	(NA)
Total employment	1,000. . . .	36.5	32.8	32.0	34.2	39.0	35.3	(NA)
3942 Dolls and stuffed toys	1,000. . . .	4.4	4.9	5.0	3.6	4.2	3.2	(NA)
3944 Games and toys	1,000. . . .	32.1	27.9	27.0	30.6	34.8	32.1	(NA)
Production workers	1,000. . . .	27.8	23.7	23.2	25.8	28.8	27.6	(NA)
3942 Dolls and stuffed toys	1,000. . . .	3.4	3.8	3.8	2.8	3.1	2.5	(NA)
3944 Games and toys	1,000. . . .	24.4	19.9	19.4	23.0	25.7	25.1	(NA)
Average hourly earnings	Dollar . . .	7.22	7.71	8.31	8.34	9.03	9.31	(NA)
3942 Dolls and stuffed toys	Dollar . . .	5.73	6.28	8.71	6.88	6.73	7.66	(NA)
3944 Games and toys	Dollar . . .	7.41	7.94	8.24	8.5	9.31	9.45	(NA)
Capital expenditures	Mil. dol. . . .	128.0	90.5	104.0	140.0	142.0	140.0	(NA)
3942 Dolls and stuffed toys	Mil. dol. . . .	10.4	11.8	11.4	3.0	2.7	1.7	(NA)
3944 Games and toys	Mil. dol. . . .	118.0	78.7	92.1	137.0	139.0	139.0	(NA)
PRODUCT DATA								
Value of shipments [3]	Mil. dol. . . .	3,732	3,666	3,840	3,983	4,248	4,172	(NA)
3942 Dolls and stuffed toys	Mil. dol. . . .	313	395	399	291	294	290	(NA)
3944 Games and toys	Mil. dol. . . .	3,419	3,271	3,440	3,693	3,955	3,883	(NA)
Value of shipments (1992 dollars)	Mil. dol. . . .	3,899	3,771	3,905	3,983	4,247	4,146	(NA)
3942 Dolls and stuffed toys	Mil. dol. . . .	349	413	405	291	289	283	(NA)
3944 Games and toys	Mil. dol. . . .	3,551	3,358	3,500	3,693	3,959	3,863	(NA)
TRADE DATA								
Value of imports	Mil. dol. . . .	5,488	6,117	5,653	6,979	7,744	7,247	7,813
3942 Dolls and stuffed toys	Mil. dol. . . .	1,193	1,384	1,466	1,661	1,687	1,711	2,034
3944 Games and toys	Mil. dol. . . .	4,294	4,733	4,187	5,318	6,057	5,536	5,779
Value of exports	Mil. dol. . . .	386	527	549	692	720	844	897
3942 Dolls and stuffed toys	Mil. dol. . . .	31.5	33.9	39.3	54.5	45.1	56.1	59.0
3944 Games and toys	Mil. dol. . . .	354	493	510	637	675	788	838

NA Not available.   [1] Estimate, except exports and imports.   [2] Value of all products and services sold by establishments in the dolls, toys, and games industry.   [3] Value of products classified in the dolls, toys, and games industry produced by all industries.

Source: U.S. Department of Commerce, Bureau of the Census, International Trade Administration (ITA). Estimates by ITA.

No. 1468. Recent Trends in Sporting and Athletic Goods, n.e.c. and Costume Jewelry: 1989 to 1995

ITEM	Unit	1989	1990	1991	1992	1993	1994	1995 [1]
SPORTING AND ATHLETIC GOODS, n.e.c. (SIC 3949)								
Industry data:								
Value of shipments [2]	Mil. dol. . . .	6,510	7,040	7,036	7,566	8,459	8,936	9,300
Value of shipments (1992 dollars)	Mil. dol. . . .	7,083	7,458	7,238	7,566	8,359	8,592	8,807
Total employment	1,000. . . .	59.3	65.8	61.3	61.7	64.4	68.1	69.7
Production workers	1,000. . . .	45.4	49.5	45.4	44.0	46.8	49.6	50.7
Average hourly earnings	Dollar . . .	8.26	8.20	8.20	8.52	8.74	8.66	8.97
Capital expenditures	Mil. dol. . . .	166	170	138	177	218	192	(NA)
Product data:								
Value of shipments [3]	Mil. dol. . . .	5,640	6,202	6,504	6,994	7,865	8,269	8,606
Value of shipments (1992 dollars)	Mil. dol. . . .	6,137	6,570	6,691	6,994	7,772	7,951	8,150
Trade data:								
Value of imports	Mil. dol. . . .	1,868	1,933	2,111	2,554	2,587	3,188	3,469
Value of exports	Mil. dol. . . .	942	1,023	1,148	1,289	1,490	1,758	2,171
COSTUME JEWELRY (SIC 3961)								
Industry data:								
Value of shipments [2]	Mil. dol. . . .	1,306	1,416	1,371	1,449	1,429	1,627	1,523
Value of shipments (1992 dollars)	Mil. dol. . . .	1,411	1,492	1,399	1,449	1,417	1,603	1,490
Total employment	1,000. . . .	19.2	19.2	17.6	17.5	17.1	18.8	17.0
Production workers	1,000. . . .	13.5	13.1	12.4	12.6	12.0	14.3	12.3
Average hourly earnings	Dollar . . .	6.37	6.65	6.93	7.25	7.50	8.06	8.48
Capital expenditures	Mil. dol. . . .	13.2	11.5	9.4	12.8	9.7	13.6	(NA)
Product data:								
Value of shipments [3]	Mil. dol. . . .	1,315	1,417	1,399	1,532	1,556	1,678	1,571
Value of shipments (1992 dollars)	Mil. dol. . . .	1,421	1,493	1,428	1,532	1,542	1,653	1,537
Trade data:								
Value of imports	Mil. dol. . . .	457	483	514	550	561	586	513
Value of exports	Mil. dol. . . .	92	115	128	121	135	148	150

NA Not available.   [1] Estimate, except exports and imports.   [2] Value of all products and services sold by establishments in this industry.   [3] Value of products classified in this industry produced by all industries.

Source: U.S. Department of Commerce, Bureau of the Census, International Trade Administration (ITA). Estimates by ITA.

Guide to—Sources of Statistics, State Statistical Abstracts, and Foreign Statistical Abstracts

Alphabetically arranged by subject, this guide contains references to the important primary sources of statistical information for the United States published since 1990. Secondary sources have been included if the information contained in them is presented in a particularly convenient form or if primary sources are not readily available. Nonrecurrent publications presenting compilations or estimates for years later than 1990 or types of data not available in regular series are also included.

Much valuable information may also be found in State reports (see pp. 931-934) and foreign statistical abstracts (see pp. 935 and 936) and in reports for particular commodities, industries, or similar segments of our economic and social structures, many of which are not included here.

Publications listed under each subject are divided into two main groups: "U.S. Government" and "Other." The location of the publisher of each report is given except for Federal agencies located in Washington, DC. Most Federal publications may be purchased from the Superintendent of Documents, U.S. Government Printing Office, Washington, DC 20402, tel. 202-512-1800, or from Government Printing Office bookstores in certain major cities. In some cases, Federal publications may be obtained from the issuing agency.

Major reports, such as the Census of Population, which consist of many volumes, are listed by their general, all-inclusive titles.

Bureau of the Census Publications

In most cases, separate reports of the most recent censuses are available for each State, subject, industry, etc. Complete information on publications of all the censuses and current surveys conducted by the Bureau of the Census appears in the *Bureau of the Census Catalog,* published annually and available from the Superintendent of Documents.

Abortions—*see* Vital Statistics.

Accidents —*see also* Health; Insurance; and Vital Statistics

  U.S. Government

    Bureau of Labor Statistics

      Evaluating Your Firm's Injury and Illness Record, Construction Industries, Report 776 (1990).

      Heatburn Injuries, Bulletin 2358 (1990).

      Occupational Injuries and Illnesses in the United States by Industry. Annual.

    Department of Transportation

      Transportation Safety Information Report. Quarterly.

    Federal Railroad Administration

      Accident/Incident Bulletin. Summary, statistics, and analysis of accidents on railroads in the United States. Annual.

      Rail-Highway Crossing Accident/Incident and Inventory Bulletin. Annual.

    Mine Safety and Health Administration

Accidents —Con.

  U.S. Government —Con.

      Informational Reports by Mining Industry: Coal; Metallic Minerals; Nonmetallic Minerals (except stone and coal); Stone, Sand, and Gravel. Annual.

      Mine Injuries and Worktime. (Some preliminary data.) Quarterly.

    National Center for Health Statistics

      Vital Statistics of the United States. Annual.

        Volume I, Natality

        Volume II, Mortality

        Volume III, Marriage and Divorce

    National Transportation Safety Board

      Accidents; Air Carriers. Annual.

      Accidents; General Aviation. Annual.

  Other

    Metropolitan Life Insurance Company, New York, NY

      Health and Safety Education.

Accidents —Con.
  Other —Con.
    Statistical Bulletin. Quarterly.
    National Fire Protection Association, Quincy, MA
      NFPA Journal. Bimonthly.
    National Safety Council, Itasca, IL
      Accident Facts. Annual.

Agriculture —*see also* Food; Foreign Commerce; Labor; Money and Banking; *and* Population
  U.S. Government
    Bureau of the Census
      Census of Agriculture. Quinquennial. (1992, most recent.)
      U.S. Commodity Exports and Imports as Related to Output. Annual. (Series ES2.)
    Bureau of Reclamation
      Summary Statistics:
        Vol. I, Water, Land, and Related Data.
    Commodity Futures Trading Commission
      Annual Report.
      Commitments of Traders in Commodity Futures. Every two weeks.
    Department of Agriculture
      Agricultural Income and Finance. Situation and Outlook Report. Quarterly.
      Agricultural Outlook. 11 issues per year.
      Agricultural Price Reports. Reports on prices received for farm commodities, prices paid for farm supplies, indexes and parity ratios. Monthly and annual.
      Agriculture and Trade Reports (five per year).
        Western Europe
        Pacific Rim
        Developing Economies
        China
        USSR
      Crop Production Reports. Acreage, yield, and production of various commodities. Monthly and annual.
      Crop Values Report. Price and value of various commodities. Annual.
      Economic Indicators of the Farm Sector. A series of five annual issues.
      Farmline. 11 issues per year.
      Financial Characteristics of U.S. Farms, January 1, 1989. (Agriculture Information Bulletin. No. 569.) Annual.
      Food Consumption, Prices, and Expenditures, 1968-89. (Statistical Bulletin No. 825.) Revised annually.
      Food Marketing Review, 1989-1990. (Agricultural Economic Report No. 639). Revised annually.
      Food Spending in American Households. (Statistical Bulletin No. 824.) Annual.
      Foreign Agricultural Trade of the United States (FATUS) six issues with annual supplements on calendar year and fiscal year trade data.

Agriculture —Con.
  U.S. Government —Con.
      Fruit and Vegetable Reports. Acreage, yield, production, value, and utilization of various fruits and vegetables. Periodic.
      Journal of Agricultural Economics Research. Quarterly.
      Livestock and Meat Statistics, 1984–88. (Statistical Bulletin No. 784.) Annual.
      Milk and Dairy Products Reports. Milk cows, milk production, and dairy products. Monthly and Annual.
      Other Reports. Reports on varied items including cold storage, farm employment and wages, farm production expenditures, mink, mushrooms, and floriculture crops. Monthly and annual.
      Poultry and Egg Reports. Reports covering eggs, chickens, turkeys, hatcheries, egg products, and poultry slaughter. Weekly, monthly, annual.
      Rural Development Perspectives. Three issues per year.
      Rural Conditions and Trends. Quarterly.
      Situation and Outlook Reports. Issued for agricultural exports, cotton and wool, dairy, feed, fruit and tree nuts, agricultural resources, livestock and poultry, oil crops, rice, aquaculture, sugar and sweeteners, tobacco, vegetables, wheat, and world agriculture. Periodic.
      Stock Reports. Stocks of grain, hops, peanuts, potatoes, rice, and soybeans. Quarterly, annual, periodic.
      U.S. Egg and Poultry Statistical Series, 1960–89. (Statistical Bulletin No. 816.) Periodic.
      U.S. Rice Distribution Patterns, 1986/87. (Statistical Bulletin No.776.) Periodic.
      Weekly Weather and Crop Bulletin. Report summarizing weather and its effect on crops the previous week. Weekly.
    Farm Credit Administration. Annual Report.
      Loans and Discounts of Farm Credit Banks and Associations. Annual.
    National Oceanic and Atmospheric Administration
      Weekly Weather and Crop Bulletin. National summary.
    Soil Conservation Service
      National Resources Inventory, 1982. Periodic.
      Report of Administrator of Soil Conservation Service. Annual.

Air Force —*see* National Defense.

Air Pollution —*see* Environment.

Aliens —*see* Immigration.

American Samoa —*see* Outlying Areas.

Area —*see* Geography.

Army— *see* National Defense.

Aviation— *see* Transportation.

Banks and Banking— *see* Money.

Births— *see* Vital Statistics.

Broadcasting— *see* Communications.

Building Permits— *see* Construction.

Business —*see also* Economic Indexes; Investments; Manufactures; Retail and Wholesale Trade; Science Resources; *and* Service Establishments

U.S. Government

Administrative Office of the United States Courts

Annual Report of the Director.

Federal Court Management Statistics

Board of Governors of the Federal Reserve System

Annual Statistical Digest.

Federal Reserve Bulletin. Monthly.

Bureau of the Census

Census of Finance, Insurance, and Real Estate Industries. Quinquennial. (1992, most recent.)

Census of Retail Trade. Quinquennial. (1992, most recent.)

Census of Service Industries. Quinquennial. (1992, most recent.)

Census of Transportation, Communications, and Utilities. Quinquennial. (1992, most recent.)

Census of Wholesale Trade. Quinquennial. (1992, most recent.)

County Business Patterns. Annual.

Current Business Reports. Retail Trade, Sales, and Inventories, BR; and Wholesale Trade, Sales, and Inventories, BW.

Minority-Owned Businesses. Quinquennial. (1992, most recent.)

Quarterly Financial Report for Manufacturing, Mining, and Trade Corporations.

Bureau of Economic Analysis

Business Statistics, 1963-91. 1992. (Discontinued.)

The Detailed Input-Output Structure of the U.S. Economy, 1982. 1991.

Fixed Reproducible Tangible Wealth in the United States, 1925-89. 1993.

The National Income and Product Accounts of the United States, 1929-1988: Statistical Tables. Volume I, 1993 and Volume II, 1992.

Summary Input-Output Tables of the U.S. Economy: 1966-87, 1992.

Survey of Current Business. Monthly.

U.S. Direct Investment Abroad: 1989 Benchmark Survey, 1992.

U.S. Direct Investment Abroad: Operations of U.S. Parent Companies and their Foreign Affiliates, Revised 1990 Estimates, and Preliminary 1991 Estimates, 1993.

Council of Economic Advisers

Economic Indicators. Monthly.

Economic Report of the President. Annual.

Internal Revenue Service

Statistics of Income Division.

Business —Con.

U.S. Government —Con.

Corporation Income Tax Returns. Annual.

Statistics of Income Bulletin. Quarterly.

International Trade Administration

U.S. Industrial Outlook. Annual.

Patent and Trademark Office

Commissioner of Patents and Trademarks Annual Report.

Technology Assessment and Forecast Report - "All Technologies." Annual.

Securities and Exchange Commission

Annual Report.

Small Business Administration

Annual Report.

Other

The Dun & Bradstreet Corporation, Wilton, CT.

The Business Failure Record. Annual.

Monthly Business Failure Report.

Monthly New Business Incorporations Report.

Quarterly Survey of Business Expectations.

Fortune (Time Warner), New York, NY

The Fortune Directory of the 500 Largest Industrial Corporations.

The Fortune Directory of the 500 Global Industrial Corporations.

Child Welfare —*see* Education; *and* Social Insurance.

City Government —*see* State and Local Government.

Civil Service —*see* Federal Government; *and* State and Local Government.

Climate —*see also* Agriculture

U.S. Government

National Oceanic and Atmospheric Administration

Climatography of the United States, No. 20, Supplement No. 1, Freeze/Frost Data.

Climatography of the United States, No. 81: Monthly Normals of Temperature, Precipitation, and Heating and Cooling Degree Days 1961-90. 1992. Issued by State.

Climatological Data. Issued in sections for States and outlying areas. Monthly with annual summary.

Comparative Climatic Data Through 1992.

General Summary of Tornadoes. Annual.

Hourly Precipitation Data. Monthly with annual summary; for each State.

Local Climatological Data. Monthly with annual summary; for major cities.

Storm Data. Monthly.

Weekly Weather and Crop Bulletin. National summary.

Commerce —*see* Foreign Commerce; Retail and Wholesale Trade; *and* Transportation.

Commodity Prices —*see also* Economic Indexes

U.S. Government

Board of Governors of the Federal Reserve System

Annual Statistical Digest.

Federal Reserve Bulletin. Monthly.

Bureau of Labor Statistics

Consumer Prices: Energy and Food. Monthly.

CPI Detailed Report. Monthly.

Monthly Labor Review.

Producer Price Indexes. Monthly, with annual supplement.

Relative Importance of Components in the Consumer Price Indexes. Annual.

U.S. Import and Export Price Indexes. Monthly.

Department of Agriculture

Agricultural Price Reports. Monthly and annual.

Other

Commodity Research Bureau, a Knight-Ridder Business Information Service, Chicago, IL.

Commodity Year Book Statistical Abstract Service. (Three editions annually.)

CRB Commodity Index Report. Weekly.

CRB Commodity Year Book. Annual.

CRB Futures Chart Service. Weekly.

CRB Infotech.

Electronic Futures Trend Analyzer. Daily.

Final Markets. End of day.

Futures Market Service. Weekly.

Futures Market Service Fundamental & Technical Commentary. Daily and weekly.

Knight-Ridder News Summaries. Daily

Price Service. Daily

The Blue Line. Daily

Wall Street Journal. (Dow Jones & Co., New York, NY.) Daily except Saturdays, Sundays, and holidays.

Communications —*see also* Newspapers

U.S. Government

Bureau of the Census

Census of Transportation, Communications, and Utilities. Quinquennial. (1992, most recent.)

Federal Communications Commission

Annual Report.

Statistics of Communications Common Carriers. Annual.

Rural Electrification Administration

Annual Statistical Report—Rural Telephone Borrowers.

Communications —Con.

U.S. Government —Con.

U.S. Postal Service

Annual Report of the Postmaster General.

Cost and Revenue Analysis. Annual.

Other

John Blair & Company, New York, NY

Statistical Trends in Broadcasting. Annual.

Book Industry Study Group, Inc., New York, NY

Book Industry Trends. Annual.

Reed Publishing USA, Newton, MA

Broadcasting & Cable Market Place. Annual.

Broadcasting Magazine. Weekly.

Corporation for Public Broadcasting, Washington, DC

Average Revenue Profiles for Public Broadcasting Grantees. Annual.

Frequently asked Questions About Public Broadcasting Periodic.

Public Broadcasting Stations' Income from State Governments and State Colleges & Universities Ranked State-By-State. Annual.

Public Radio and Television Programming Content by Category. Biennial.

Editor & Publisher Co., New York, NY

International Year Book. Annual.

Market Guide. Annual.

Electronic Industries Association, Washington, DC

Electronic Market Data Book. Annual.

Electronic Market Trends. Monthly.

Electronics Foreign Trade. Monthly.

Radio Advertising Bureau, New York, NY

Radio Facts. Annual.

United States Telephone Association, Washington, DC

Statistics of the Independent Telephone Industry. Annual.

Warren Publishing, Inc., Washington, DC

Cable Action Update. Weekly.

Cable and Station Coverage Atlas. Annual.

Television Action Update. Weekly.

Television and Cable Factbook. Annual.

TV Station & Cable Ownership Directory. Semi-annual.

Construction, Housing, and Real Estate —*see also* Money *and* Transportation

U.S. Government

Board of Governors of the Federal Reserve System

Annual Statistical Digest.

Federal Reserve Bulletin. Monthly.

Bureau of Census

Census of Construction Industries. Quinquennial. (1992, most recent.)

Construction, Housing, and Real Estate —Con.

U.S. Government —Con.

Census of Housing. Decennial. (1990, most recent.)

Current Construction Reports: Housing Starts, C20 (monthly); New Residential Construction in Selected Metropolitan Statistical Areas, C21 (quarterly); Housing Completions, C22 (monthly); New One-Family Houses Sold and for Sale, C25 (monthly with annual report, Characteristics of New Housing); Price Index of New One-Family Houses Sold, C27 (quarterly); Value of New Construction Put in Place, C30 (monthly with occasional historical supplement); Housing Units Authorized by Building Permits, C40 (monthly and annual); Residential Alterations and Repairs, C50 (quarterly and annual).

Current Housing Reports: Housing Vacancies, H-111 (quarterly and annual); Market Absorption of Apartments, H-130 (quarterly and annual); Characteristics of Apartments Completed, H-131 (annual); Annual Housing Survey, H-150 (series of six biennial reports—Annual Housing Survey—Housing Characteristics for Selected Metropolitan Areas, H-170.

Bureau of Economic Analysis

Business Statistics, 1963-91. 1992. (Discontinued.)

Fixed Reproducible Tangible Wealth in the United States, 1925-89. 1993.

The National Income and Product Accounts of the United States, 1929-88: Volume I, 1993 and Volume II, 1992.

Survey of Current Business. Monthly.

Bureau of Labor Statistics

Compensation and Working Conditions. Quarterly.

Employment and Earnings. Monthly.

Employment, Hours, and Earnings, United States, 1909-94. 1994. (Bulletin 2445.)

Employment, Hours, and Earnings, United States, 1988-96. 1996. (Bulletin 2481.)

Evaluating Your Firm's Injury and Illness Record, Construction Industries Report 812, (1991).

Monthly Labor Review.

Occupational Employment in Mining, Construction, Finance, and Services. 1995. (Bulletin 2460.)

Occupational Injuries and Illnesses in the United States by Industry. Annual.

Department of Housing and Urban Development

Survey of Mortgage Lending Activity. Monthly and quarterly press releases.

Department of Veterans Affairs

Loan Guaranty Highlights. Quarterly.

Energy Information Administration

Residential Energy Consumption Survey: Housing Characteristics. Triennial.

Construction, Housing, and Real Estate —Con.

U.S. Government —Con.

International Trade Administration

Construction Review. Bimonthly.

Office of Thrift Supervision

Annual Report.

Other

Dodge, F.W., National Information Services Division, McGraw-Hill Information Systems Co., New York, NY

Dodge Construction Potentials. Monthly.

NATIONAL ASSOCIATION OF REALTORS, Washington, DC

Real Estate Outlook: Market Trends & Insights, Monthly.

Consumer Income and Expenditures, and Personal Income —see also Agriculture; Economic Indexes; Investments; *and* National Income

U.S. Government

Board of Governors of the Federal Reserve System

Annual Statistical Digest.

Federal Reserve Bulletin. Monthly.

Bureau of the Census

Census of Population. Decennial. (1990, most recent.)

Current Population Reports. (Series on Consumer Income, P60.)

Current Population Reports. (Series on Household Economic Studies, P70.)

Special Studies Reports. (Series on Special Studies, P23.)

Bureau of Economic Analysis

Business Statistics, 1963-91. 1992. (Discontinued.)

Survey of Current Business. Monthly.

Bureau of Labor Statistics

Consumer Expenditure Survey, integrated Diary and Interview Survey data.

Annual press releases and reports, biannual bulletins.

Consumer Expenditure Survey: 1988-89. 1991. (Bulletin 2383.)

Consumer Expenditure Interview Survey. Quarterly.

Congressional Budget Office

The Changing Distribution of Federal Taxes: 1975-1990. October 1987.

Internal Revenue Service

Statistics of Income Division.

Individual Income Tax Returns. Annual.

Statistics of Income Bulletin. Quarterly.

National Science Foundation

Characteristics of Recent Science/Engineering Graduates. Detailed Statistical Tables. Biennial.

Science Resources Studies. Data Brief. Frequent.

Education —Con.
  U.S. Government —Con.
    Characteristics of Doctoral Scientists and
      Engineers in the United States. Detailed
      Statistical Tables. Biennial.
    Characteristics of Recent
      Science/Engineering Graduates.
      Detailed Statistical Tables. Biennial.
    Characteristics of Science/Engineering
      Equipment in Academic Settings: 1989-
      90. Report.
    Federal Support to Universities, Colleges,
      and Nonprofit Institutions. A report to
      the President and Congress. Detailed
      Statistical Tables. Annual.
    International Science and Technology
      Data Update. Report. Annual.
    National Patterns of R&D Resources.
      Report. Annual.
    Science and Engineering Degrees. A
      Source Book. Detailed Statistical
      Tables. Annual.
    Science and Engineering Degrees, by
      Race/Ethnicity of Recipients: 1977-90.
      Detailed Statistical Tables. Biennial.
    Science and Engineering Doctorates.
      Detailed Statistical Tables. Annual.
    Science and Engineering Indicators.
      Report. Biennial.
    Science and Engineering Personnel: A
      National Overview. Report. Biennial.
    Science and Technology Pocket Data
      Book. Report. Annual.
    Scientific and Engineering Research
      Facilities at Universities and Colleges.
      Report. Biennial.
    Undergraduate Origins of Recent Science
      and Engineering Doctorate Recipients.
      Special Report (NSF 92-332.)
    U.S. Universities and Colleges Report a
      9-percent Net Increase in Research
      Space Since 1988, the Majority of it
      Within Doctorate-Granting Institutions
      (NSF 92-333.)
    Women and Minorities in Science and
      Engineering. Report. Biennial.
  Other
    American Council on Education, Washing-
      ton, DC
      A Fact Book on Higher Education. Quar-
        terly.
      National Norms for Entering College
        Freshmen. Annual.
    Bowker (R.R.) Company, New Providence,
      NJ
      American Library Directory. Annual.
      Bowker Annual Library and Book Trade
        Almanac.
    Chronicle of Higher Education, Inc., Wash-
      ington, DC
      Almanac. Annual.
    College Entrance Examination Board, New
      York, NY
      National Report on College-Bound
        Seniors. Annual.

Education —Con.
  Other —Con.
    National Catholic Educational Association,
      Washington, DC
      Catholic Schools in America. Annual.
      United States Catholic Elementary and
        Secondary Schools. Staffing and Enroll-
        ment. Annual.
      U.S. Catholic Elementary Schools and
        their Finances. Biennial.
      U.S. Catholic Secondary Schools and
        their Finances. Biennial.
    National Education Association, Washington,
      DC
      Estimates of School Statistics. Annual.
      Rankings of the States. Annual.
      Status of the American Public School
        Teacher, 1990-91. Quinquennial.
    Research Associates of Washington, Wash-
      ington, DC
      Inflation Measures for Schools, Colleges,
        and Libraries. Annual.
      State Profiles: Financing Public Higher
        Education. Annual.
      Wages and Cost of Living: 508 County
        Indexes. (1995, most recent.)

Elections

  U.S. Government
    Bureau of the Census
      Congressional District Data:
        1990 Census of Population and
          Housing, 1990 CPH-4, Congres-
          sional Districts of the 103rd Con-
          gress.
        Current Population Reports. (Series P20,
          Voting and Registration in the Election
          of November 19—. Biennial survey; and
          P25, Projections of the Population of
          Voting Age for States: November 19—,
          Biennial projection.)
    Congress. Clerk of the House
      Statistics of the Presidential and Con-
        gressional Election Years. Biennial.
    Congress. Joint Committee on Printing
      Congressional Directory. Biennial.
  Other
    The Council of State Governments, Lexing-
      ton, KY
      The Book of the States. Biennial.
      State Elective Officials and the Legisla-
        tures. Biennial.
      State Legislative Leadership, Commit-
        tees, and Staff. Biennial.
    Elections Research Center, Chevy Chase
      MD
      America Votes. A handbook of contempo-
        rary American election statistics, com-
        piled and edited by Richard M.
        Scammon and Alice V. McGillivray.
        Biennial.
    Joint Center for Political and Economic
      Studies, Washington, DC

Environment

U.S. Government

Bureau of the Census

Current Industrial Report, Survey of Pollution Abatement Costs and Expenditures, series MA-200.

Council on Environmental Quality

Environmental Quality. Annual.

Environmental Protection Agency

Air Quality Data. Annual.

Cost of Clean Water. Annual.

Federal Certification Test Results for Motor Vehicles. Annual.

Municipal Water Facilities Inventory. Quinquennial.

National Air Pollutant Emission Trends, 1900-92.

National Air Quality and Emissions Trends Report. 1993.

Needs Survey, Conveyance and Treatment of Municipal Wastewater Summaries of Technical Data. Biennial.

Pesticides Monitoring Journal. Quarterly.

Radiation Data and Reports. Monthly.

Sewage Facility Construction. Annual.

Summary of Water Enforcement Actions Pursued by EPA since December 3, 1970. (Updated continuously.)

Geological Survey

A Statistical Summary of Data from the U.S. Geological Survey's National Water Quality Networks. (Open-File Report 83-533.)

Other

American Petroleum Institute, Washington, DC

Petroleum Industry Environmental Report. Annual.

Executions —*see* Law Enforcement.

Exports —*see* Foreign Commerce.

Family Characteristics —*see* Population.

Farms and Farm Characteristics —*see* Agriculture.

Federal Government Finances and Employment

—*see also* Elections; Science Resources; *and* State and Local Government

U.S. Government

Board of Governors of the Federal Reserve System

Annual Statistical Digest.

Federal Reserve Bulletin. Monthly.

Bureau of the Census

Federal Expenditures by State for Fiscal Year. Annual.

Bureau of Economic Analysis

Business Statistics, 1963-91. 1992. (Discontinued.)

Survey of Current Business. Monthly.

Council of Economic Advisers

Economic Indicators. Monthly.

Economic Report of the President. Annual.

Federal Government Finances and Employment —Con.

U.S. Government —Con.

Council on Environmental Quality

Environmental Quality. Annual.

Department of Labor

Annual Report of the Secretary.

Department of the Treasury

Consolidated Financial Statements of the United States Government. (Prototype.)

Daily Treasury Statement.

Monthly Statement of the Public Debt of the United States.

Monthly Treasury Statement of Receipts and Outlays of the United States Government.

Treasury Bulletin. Quarterly.

United States Government Annual Report and Appendix.

Internal Revenue Service

IRS Data Book.

Statistics of Income Division.

Corporation Income Tax Returns. Annual.

Statistics of Income Bulletin. Quarterly.

National Science Foundation

Federal Funds for Research and Development. Detailed Statistical Tables. Annual.

Federal R&D Funding by Budget Function. Report. Annual.

Federal Scientists and Engineers. Detailed Statistical Tables. Annual.

Federal Support to Universities, Colleges, and Nonprofit Institutions. Detailed Statistical Tables. Annual.

International Science and Technology Data Update. Report. Annual.

National Patterns of R&D Resources. Report. Annual.

Science and Engineering Indicators. Report. Biennial.

Science and Engineering Personnel: A National Overview. Report. Biennial.

Science and Technology Pocket Data Book. Report. Annual.

SRS (Science Resources Studies) Data Briefs.

Federal Academic R&D Support Increased by 6 Percent Between FYs 1989 and 1990. (NSF 92-328.)

Office of Management and Budget

The Budget of the United States Government. Annual.

Office of Personnel Management

Civil Service Retirement and Disability Fund. Report. Annual.

Demographic Profile of the Federal Workforce. Biennial. (Even years.)

Employment by Geographic Area. Biennial. (Even years.)

International Statistics —Con.
Other —Con.

Latest Information on National Accounts of Developing Countries. Annual.

Main Economic Indicators. Monthly.

Main Science and Technology Indicators. Biennial.

Maritime Transport. Annual.

Meat Balances in OECD Countries. Annual.

Milk and Milk Products Balances in OECD Countries. Annual.

National Accounts of OECD Countries. Annual.

Vol. I: Main Aggregates.

Vol. II: Detailed Tables.

OECD Economic Outlook. Bi-annual. Historical Statistics. Annual.

OECD Economic Studies. Annual for member countries.

OECD Employment Outlook. Annual.

OECD Financial Statistics. Annual (three vols.) and monthly supplements.

OECD Health Data (Diskette)

OECD Health Systems: Facts and Trends.

OECD Microtables on Foreign Trade by Commodities covering Series B (individual reporting countries) and Series C (total reporting countries). Annual from 1977.

Oil and Gas Information. Annual.

The Pulp and Paper Industry. Annual.

Quarterly Labor Force Statistics.

Quarterly National Accounts.

Quarterly Oil Statistics and Energy Balances.

Revenue Statistics of OECD Member Countries. Annual.

Review of Fisheries in OECD Member Countries. Annual.

Statistical Trends in Transport (ECMT.)

Statistics of Area Production and Field of Crop Products in OECD Member Countries.

Statistics of Foreign Trade:

Monthly Statistics of Foreign Trade. (Series A.)

Foreign Trade by Commodities. (Series C.) Annual.

Tourism Policy and International Tourism in OECD Member Countries. Annual.

Uranium Resources Production and Demand. Biennial.

World Energy Statistics and Balances.

Pan American Health Organization, Washington DC

Health Conditions in the Americas. 1990 Edition. Quadrennial.

Health Statistics from the Americas, 1991 Edition. PAHO Scientific Publication No. 537. 1991.

International Statistics —Con.
Other —Con.

Health Statistics from the Americas, 1992 Edition. PAHO Scientific Publication No. 542. 1992.

United Nations Educational, Scientific and Cultural Organization, Paris, France

Statistical Yearbook.

United Nations Statistics Division, New York, NY

Compendium of Human Settlements Statistics. (Series N.)

Demographic Yearbook. (Series R.)

Energy Balances and Electricity Profiles. (Series W.)

Energy Statistics Yearbook. (Series J.)

Industrial Statistics Yearbook: (Series P.)

Commodity Production Statistics.

International Trade Statistics Yearbook. (Series G.)

Monthly Bulletin of Statistics. (Series Q.)

National Accounts Statistics: (Series X, Annually.)

Main Aggregates and Detailed Tables.

Analysis of Main Aggregates.

Population and Vital Statistics Report. (Series A, Quarterly.)

Social Statistics and Indicators: (Series K, Occasional.)

The World's Women: Trends and Statistics.

Women's Indicators and Statistics Database (CD and diskette only.)

Statistical Yearbook. (Series; also available in CD-ROM, Series S/CD)

World Statistics Pocketbook. (Series V, Annually.)

World Health Organization, Geneva, Switzerland

1993 World Health Statistics Annual.

International Trade —see Foreign Commerce; and International Statistics.

Investments and Securities —see also Business; Construction; Insurance; International Accounts; and Money
U.S. Government

Board of Governors of the Federal Reserve System

Annual Statistical Digest.

Federal Reserve Bulletin. Monthly.

Commodity Futures Trading Commission

Annual Report.

Commitments of Traders in Commodity Futures. (Every two weeks.)

Securities and Exchange Commission

Annual Report.

Other

William B. Dana Co., New York, NY

Commercial and Financial Chronicle. Semi-weekly.

Labor —Con.
U.S. Government —Con.

Monthly Report of Class I Railroad Employees, by Group. (Statement No. 350.)

Wage Statistics of Class I Railroads in the United States. Annual. (Statement No. 300.)

Maritime Administration

Employment Report of United States Flag Merchant Fleet Ocean-going Vessels 1,000 Gross Tons and Over. Quarterly.

Seafaring Wage Rates. Biennial.

National Science Foundation

Characteristics of Doctoral Scientists and Engineers in the United States. Detailed Statistical Tables. Biennial.

Characteristics of Recent Science and Engineering Graduates. Detailed Statistical Tables. Biennial.

Immigrant Scientists and Engineers. Detailed Statistical Tables. Annual.

U.S. Scientists and Engineers. Detailed Statistical Tables. Biennial.

Woman and Minorities in Science and Engineering. Report. Biennial.

Office of Personnel Management

Demographic Profile of the Federal Workforce. Biennial. (Even years.)

Occupations of Federal White-Collar and Blue-Collar Workers. Biennial. (Odd years.)

Women's Bureau

Handbook on Women Workers. Periodic.

Other

Aerospace Industries Association of America, Washington, DC

Employment in the Aerospace Industry. Monthly.

Survey of Aerospace Employment. Annual.

The Bureau of National Affairs, Inc., Washington, DC

Basic Patterns in Union Contracts. Annual.

BNA's Employment Outlook. Quarterly.

BNA's Job Absence and Turnover. Quarterly.

Briefing Sessions on Employee Relations Workbook. Annual.

Calendar of Negotiations. Annual.

Directory of U.S. Labor Organizations. Annual.

National Labor Relations Board Election Statistics. Annual.

NLRB Representation and Decertification Elections Statistics. Quarterly.

101 Key Statistics on Work and Family for the 1990's. (The BNA Special Report Series on Work and Family. Special Report No. 21, September 21, 1989.)

Labor —Con.
Other —Con.

PPF Survey (Personnel Policies Forum.) Three times a year.

Law Enforcement, Courts, and Prisons

U.S. Government

Administrative Office of the United States Courts

Annual Report of the Director ... with, as issued, Reports of the Proceedings of the Judicial Conference of the United States. Includes statistics on Federal Courts.

Calendar Year Reports on Authorized Wiretaps. (State and Federal.)

Federal Court Management Statistics. Annual.

Federal Judicial Workload Statistics. Quarterly.

Bureau of the Census

Census of Population. Decennial. (1990, most recent.)

Bureau of Justice Statistics

American Response to Crime: An Overview of Criminal Justice Systems. December 1983.

Black Victims. April 1990.

Capital Punishment 1991, October 1992.

Census of Local Jails, 1988. February 1990.

Census of State and Federal correctional facilities 1990, June 1992.

Compendium of Federal justice statistics: 1989, May 1992.

Correctional Populations in the United States 1989, October 1991.

Correctional Populations in the United States 1990, July 1992.

Crime and the Nation's households, 1990. July 1992.

Criminal Victimization. Annual.

Criminal Victimization in the United States. Annual.

Drug enforcement and treatment in prisons 1990, July 1992.

Drug enforcement by police and sheriffs' departments, 1990. May 1992.

Drugs and crime facts: 1991. September 1992.

Drugs and jail inmates. August 1991.

Drunk driving: 1989 Survey of Inmates of Local Jails. September 1992.

Elderly Victims. October 1992.

Expenditure and Employment Data for the Criminal Justice System. Annual.

Federal Criminal Cases, 1980-1990, with preliminary data for 1991. September 1991.

Felony Case Processing in State Courts, 1986. February 1990.

Female Victims of violent crime. January 1991.

Handgun crime victims. July 1990.

Manufactures —Con.
  U.S. Government —Con.
    Productivity Measures for Selected Industries and Government Services. Annual.
    White-Collar Pay: Private Goods-Producing Industries, March 1990. 1990. (Bulletin 2374.)
  International Trade Administration
    U.S. Industrial Outlook. Annual.
  International Trade Commission
    Synthetic Organic Chemicals, U.S. Production and Sales. Annual.
  National Science Foundation
    International Science and Technology Data Update. Report. Annual.
    Planned R&D Expenditures of Major U.S. Firms. Special Report. (NSF 91-306.)
    Research and Development in Industry. Detailed Statistical Tables. Annual.
    Science and Engineering Indicators. Report. Biennial.
    Science and Engineering Personnel: A National Overview, Report. Biennial.
    Scientists, Engineers, and Technicians in Manufacturing Industries. Detailed Statistical Tables. Triennial.
    Scientists, Engineers, and Technicians in Nonmanufacturing Industries. Detailed Statistical Tables. Triennial.
    Scientists, Engineers, and Technicians in Trade and Regulated Industries. Detailed Statistical Tables. Triennial.

  Other
    Aerospace Industries Association of America, Washington, DC
      Aerospace Facts and Figures. Annual.
      Aerospace Industry Year-End Review and Forecast. Annual.
      AIA Survey of Aerospace Employment. Annual.
      Commercial Helicopter Shipments. Quarterly.
      Manufacturing Production, Capacity, and Utilization in Aerospace and Aircraft and Parts. Monthly.
      Orders, Shipments, Backlog and Inventories for Aircraft, Missiles, & Parts. Monthly.
    American Automobile Manufacturers Association of the United States, Inc., Detroit MI
      Motor Vehicle Facts and Figures. Annual.
    American Frozen Food Institute, Burlingame, CA
      Frozen Food Pack Statistics. Annual.
    American Iron and Steel Institute, Washington, DC
      Annual Statistical Report.
      Commodity Research Bureau, New York, NY
      Commodity Yearbook. Annual.
    Dataquest Inc., San Jose, CA
      Consolidated Data Base.

Manufactures —Con.
  Other —Con.
    Dealerscope Merchandising, Philadelphia, PA
      Merchandising. Annual.
    Electronic Industries Association, Washington, DC
      Electronic Market Data Book. Annual.
      Electronic Market Trends. Monthly.
      Electronics Foreign Trade. Monthly.
    National Association of Hosiery Manufacturers, Charlotte, NC
      Hosiery Statistics. Annual.
    National Food Processors Association, Washington, DC
      Canned Fruit and Vegetable Pack and Stock Situation Reports. Quarterly.
Marine Corps —*see* National Defense.
Marriage —*see* Vital Statistics.
Medical Care; Mental Health —*see* Health.
Merchant Vessels —*see* Transportation
Military Services —see National Defense.
Minerals and Metals —*see also* Economic Indexes; Energy; Foreign Commerce; *and* Manufactures
  U.S. Government
    Bureau of the Census
      Census of Mineral Industries. Quinquennial.(1992, most recent.)
    U.S. Geological Survey
      Mineral Commodity Summaries. Annual.
      Mineral Industry Surveys. (Monthly, quarterly, or annual report.)
      Minerals Yearbook. Annual.
    Department of the Treasury
      Treasury Bulletin. Quarterly.
    Energy Information Administration
      Annual Energy Review.
      Coal Industry. Annual.
      International Energy Annual.
      Monthly Energy Review.
      Natural Gas Annual.
      Petroleum Supply Annual.
      Quarterly Coal Report.
      U.S. Crude Oil, Natural Gas, and Natural Gas Liquids Reserves. Annual.

  Other
    American Bureau of Metal Statistics, Inc., Secaucus, NJ
      Non-Ferrous Metal Data.
    American Gas Association, Arlington, VA
      Gas Facts. Annual.
      Year Book.
    American Metal Market, New York, NY
      Daily Newspapers.
      Metal Statistics. Annual.
    American Petroleum Institute, Washington, DC
      Quarterly Well Completion Report.

Recreation —Con.
U.S. Government —Con.
Department of Transportation
U.S. International Air Travel Statistics.
Annual.
Fish and Wildlife Service
Federal Aid in Fish and Wildlife Restoration. Annual.
National Survey of Fishing, Hunting, and Wildlife-Associated Recreation. Quinquennial. (1991, most recent.)
National Park Service
Federal Recreation Fee Report. Annual.
National Park Statistical Abstract. Annual.
Other
Association of Racing Commissioners International, Inc., Lexington, KY
Statistical Reports on Greyhound Racing in the United States. Annual.
Statistical Reports on Horse Racing in the United States. Annual.
Statistical Reports on Jai Alai in the United States. Annual.
National Golf Foundation, Jupiter, FL
Americans' Attitudes Toward Golf in Their Community.
An Operational Profile of Canadian Golf Facilities.
Commercial Golf Ranges in the U.S.
Golf Consumer Spending and Facility Fees.
Golf Course Operations.
Golf Facilities in Canada.
Golf Facilities in the United States. 1994.
Golf Participation in Canada.
Golf Participation in the United States. 1994.
Golf Travel in the United States.
Trends in the Golf Industry 1989-1993.
Women in Golf.
National Marine Manufacturers Association, Chicago, IL
Boating. (A Statistical Report on America's Top Family Sport.) Annual.
State Boat Registration. Annual.
National Sporting Goods Association, Mt. Prospect, IL
The Sporting Goods Market in 1995. Annual.
Sports Participation in 1994. Annual.

Religious Bodies
Other
American Jewish Committee. New York, NY
American Jewish Year Book.
Glenmary Research Center, Atlanta, GA
Churches and Church Membership in the United States 1990 by M. Bradley; N.Green, Jr; D. Jones; M.Lynn; and L. McNeil. 1992.
National Council of the Churches of Christ in the U.S.A., New York, NY

Religious Bodies —Con.
Other —Con.
Yearbook of American and Canadian Churches. Annual.
Research and Development —*see* Science Resources.
Retail and Wholesale Trade —*see also* Commodity Prices; Economic Indexes; *and* Service Establishments
U.S. Government
Board of Governors of the Federal Reserve System
Annual Statistical Digest
Federal Reserve Bulletin. Monthly.
Bureau of the Census
Combined Annual and Revised Monthly Retail Trade.
Combined Annual and Revised Monthly Wholesale Trade.
Census of Retail Trade. Quinquennial. (1992, most recent.)
Census of Wholesale Trade. Quinquennial. (1992, most recent.)
County Business Patterns. Annual.
Merchant Wholesalers Measures of Value Produced, Capital Expenditures, Depreciable Assets, and Operating Expenses. (1992, most recent.)
Monthly Retail Trade Report. Sales and Inventories.
Monthly Wholesale Trade Report. Sales and Inventories.
Selected Characteristics of Retail Trade-Measures of Value Produced, Capital Expenditures, Depreciable Assets, and Operating Expenses. (1992, most recent.)
Bureau of Economic Analysis
Business Statistics, 1963-91. 1992. (Discontinued.)
Survey of Current Business. Monthly.
Bureau of Labor Statistics
Compensation and Working Conditions. Quarterly.
CPI Detailed Report. Monthly.
Employment and Earnings. Monthly.
Employment, Hours, and Earnings, United States, 1909-94. 1994. (Bulletin 2445.)
Employment, Hours, and Earnings, United States, 1988-96. 1996. (Bulletin 2481.)
Monthly Labor Review.
Occupational Employment Statistics, 1994. 1996. (Bulletin 2468.)
Occupational Injuries and Illnesses in the United States by Industry. Annual.
Producer Price Indexes. Monthly, with annual supplement.
Productivity Measures for Selected Industries and Government Services. Annual.

Retail and Wholesale Trade —Con.

U.S. Government —Con.

Technology and Labor in Three Service Industries: Utilities, Retail Trade, and Lodging. 1990. (Bulletin 2367.)

Other

Dealerscope Merchandising, Philadelphia, PA

Merchandising. Annual.

Lebhar-Friedman, Inc., New York, NY

Accounting Today. Biweekly.

Apparel Merchandising. Monthly.

Market Statistics, New York, NY

The Survey of Buying Power Data Service. Annual.

National Restaurant Association, Washington, DC

Foodservice Industry Forecast. Annual.

Foodservice Industry in Review. Annual.

Foodservice Market Measure. Monthly in Restaurants USA.

Foodservice Numbers: A Statistical Digest for the Foodservice Industry. 1992.

Restaurant Industry Operations Report. Annual.

Restaurants USA. Monthly.

Survey of Wage Rates for Hourly Employees. Biennial.

Compensation for Salaried Personnel in Foodservice. Triennial.

Roads —*see* Transportation.

Sales —*see* Retail and Wholesale Trade.

Savings Institutions —*see* Money.

Science Resources

U.S. Government

Bureau of the Census

Current Industrial Reports, MA37D. Annual.

Energy Research and Development Administration

The Nuclear Industry. Annual.

National Aeronautics and Space Administration

Annual Procurement Report.
The Civil Service Work Force.
Pocket Statistics. Annual.

National Science Foundation

Academic Research Equipment and Equipment needs in Selected Science/Engineering Fields: 1989-90.

Academic Research and Equipment Needs in the Physical Sciences: 1989.

Academic Science and Engineering: Graduate Enrollment and Support. Detailed Statistical Tables. Annual.

Academic Science and Engineering: R&D Expenditures. Detailed Statistical Tables. Annual.

Blacks in Undergraduate Science and Engineering Education, April 1992. Special Report. (NSF 92-305.)

Science Resources —Con.

U.S. Government —Con.

Characteristics of Doctoral Scientists and Engineers in the United States. Detailed Statistical Tables. Biennial.

Characteristics of Recent Grads.

Characteristics of Recent Scientists and Engineers. Detailed Statistical Tables. Biennial.

Characteristics of Science and Engineering Equipment in Academic Settings: 1989-90.

Federal R&D Funding by Budget Function. Report. Annual.

Federal Funds for Research and Development. Detailed Statistical Tables. Annual.

Federal Academic R&D Support Increased by 6 Percent Between FYs 1989 and 1990. (NSF 92-328.)

Federal Support to Universities, Colleges, and Nonprofit Institutions. Detailed Statistical Tables. Annual.

Immigrant Scientists and Engineers. Detailed Statistical Tables. Annual.

International Science and Technology Data Update. Report. Annual.

National Patterns of R&D Resources. Report. Annual.

Planned R&D Expenditures of Major U.S. firms: 1990-91. Special Report. (NSF 91-306.)

Research and Development Expenditures of State Government Agencies: Fiscal Years 1987 and 1988. Special Report. (NSF 90-309.)

Research and Development in Industry. Detailed Statistical Tables. Annual.

Science and Engineering Degrees. Detailed Statistical Tables. Annual.

Science and Engineering Degrees, by Race/Ethnicity of Recipients: 1977-90. Detailed Statistical Tables. Annual.

Science and Engineering Doctorates. Detailed Statistical Tables. Annual.

Science and Engineering Indicators. Report. Biennial.

Science and Engineering Personnel: A National Overview. Report. Biennial.

Science and Technology Pocket Data Book. Report. Annual.

Scientific and Engineering Research Facilities at Universities and Colleges. Report. Biennial.

Scientists, Engineers, and Technicians in Manufacturing are Concentrated in High Technology Industries. (NSF 91-321.)

Scientists, Engineers, and Technicians in Manufacturing Industries. Detailed Statistical Tables. Triennial.

Scientists, Engineers, and Technicians in Nonmanufacturing Industries. Detailed Statistical Tables. Triennial.

State and Local Government —Con.

U.S. Government —Con.

Quarterly Summary of Federal, State, and Local Tax Revenue. (GT Nos. 1-4.)

State Government Finances. Annual. (GF No. 3.)

State Government Tax Collections. Annual. (GF No. 1.)

Bureau of Labor Statistics

Employee Benefits in State and Local Governments. Biennial.

Employment and Earnings. Monthly.

Employment, Hours, and Earnings, United States, 1909-94. 1994. (Bulletin 2445.)

Employment, Hours, and Earnings, United States, 1988-96. 1996. (Bulletin 2481.)

Occupational Employment Statistics, 1994. 1996. (Bulletin 2468.)

Federal Highway Administration

Highway Statistics. Annual.

Office of Management and Budget

The Budget of the United States Government. Annual.

Social Security Administration

Benefits and Beneficiaries Under Public Employee Retirement Systems, Fiscal Year 1991, Social Security Bulletin, Spring 1995.

Other

Advisory Commission on Intergovernmental Relations,Washington, DC

1991: State Revenue Capacity and Effort.

Significant Features of Fiscal Federalism. Annual.

The Council of State Governments, Lexington, KY

The Book of the States. Biennial.

State Administrative Officials Classified by Function. Biennial.

International City Management Association, Washington, DC

Baseline Data Reports. Bimonthly.

Compensation: An Annual Report on Local Government Executive Salaries and Fringe Benefits.

Municipal Year Book. Annual.

Special Data Issues. Periodical.

National Governors' Association, Washington, DC

Directory of Governors of the American States, Commonwealths & Territories. Annual.

Governors' Staff Directory. Biannual.

National Governors' Association and National Association of State Budget Officers, Washington, DC

The Fiscal Survey of States. Biannual.

Tax Foundation, Washington, DC

Facts and Figures on Government Finance. Annual.

Stocks and Bonds —*see* Investments.

Stores —*see* Retail and Wholesale Trade *and* Service Establishments.

Tax Collections —*see* Federal Government; *and* State and Local Government.

Telephone and Telegraph Systems —*see* Communications.

Television —*see* Communications.

Trade —*see* Foreign Commerce; Retail and Wholesale Trade; *and* Service Establishments.

Transportation —*see also* Foreign Commerce.

U.S. Government

Army, Corps of Engineers

Waterborne Commerce of the United States (in five parts). Annual.

Bureau of the Census

Census of Transportation, Communications and Utilities. Quinquennial. (1992, most recent.)

Commodity Flow Survey. 1993.

Transportation Annual Survey. Annual.

Truck Inventory and Use Survey. Quinquennial. (1992, most recent.)

Vessel Entrances and Clearances. Annual. (FT 975.)

Bureau of Economic Analysis

Business Statistics, 1963-91. 1992. (Discontinued.)

Survey of Current Business. Monthly.

Coast Guard

Annual Report of the Secretary of Transportation.

Marine Casualty Statistics. Annual.

Polluting Incidents In And Around U.S. Waters. Annual.

Department of State, Bureau of Consular Affairs

Summary of Passport Statistics. Annual.

Department of Transportation

National Transportation Statistics. Annual.

Transportation Safety Information Report. Quarterly.

U.S. International Air Travel Statistics. Annual.

Federal Aviation Administration and Bureau of Transportation Statistics

Census of U.S. Civil Aircraft. Annual.

FAA Air Traffic Activity. Annual, for fiscal years.

FAA Aviation Forecasts. Annual.

FAA Statistical Handbook of Aviation. Annual.

General Aviation Activity and Avionics Survey. Annual.

U.S. Civil Airman Statistics. Annual.

Federal Aviation Administration and Bureau of Transportation Statistics

Airport Activity Statistics of Certificated Route Air Carriers. Annual.

Federal Highway Administration

Drivers Licenses. Annual.

Transportation —Con.
U.S. Government —Con.
Highway Statistics. Annual.
Highway Statistics, Summary to 1985. (Published every 10 years.)
Selected Highway Statistics and Charts. Annual.
Interstate Commerce Commission
Class I Freight Railroads Selected Earnings Data. Quarterly.
Large Class I Household Goods Carriers Selected Earnings Data. Quarterly.
Large Class I Motor Carriers of Passengers Selected Earnings Data. Quarterly.
Large Class I Motor Carriers of Property Selected Earnings Data. Quarterly.
Quarterly Report.
Transport Statistics in the United States. Issued annually in two separate parts:
Part 1: Railroads
Part 2: Motor Carriers
Maritime Administration
Annual Report.
Employment Report of United States Flag Merchant Fleet Ocean-going Vessels 1,000 Gross Tons and Over. Quarterly.
Foreign Flag Merchant Ships Owned by U.S. Parent Companies. Annual.
Maritime Manpower Report. Quarterly.
Research and Special Programs Administration
Air Carrier Financial Statistics. Quarterly.
Air Carrier Industry Scheduled Service Traffic Statistics. Quarterly.
Air Carrier Traffic Statistics. Monthly.
Other
Aerospace Industries Association of America, Washington, DC
Aerospace Facts and Figures. Annual.
Commercial Helicopter Shipments. Quarterly.
Air Transport Association of America, Washington, DC
Air Transport Facts and Figures. Annual.
American Automobile Manufacturers Association, Detroit, MI.
Motor Vehicle Facts and Figures. Annual.
World Motor Vehicle Data. Annual.
American Bureau of Shipping, Paramus, NJ
The Record. Annual with one supplement.
American Public Transit Association, Washington, DC
Transit Fact Book. Annual.
Association of American Railroads, Washington, DC
Analysis of Class I Railroads. Annual.
Cars of Revenue Freight Loaded. Weekly with annual summary.
Freight Commodity Statistics, Class I Railroads in the United States. Annual.
Yearbook of Railroad Facts.

Transportation —Con.
Other —Con.
ENO Transportation Foundation, Leesburg, VA
Transportation in America. mid-year, annually with periodic supplements.
General Aviation Manufacturers Association, Washington, DC
Shipment Report. Quarterly and Annual.
Statistical Databook. Annual.
Lake Carriers' Association, Cleveland, OH
Annual Report.
Monthly Bulk Commodities Report.
Lloyd's Register of Shipping, London, England
Casualty Return. (Annual statistical summary of all merchant ships totally lost or reported broken up during year.)
Merchant Shipbuilding Returns. (Quarterly Statistical summary of world shipbuilding.)
World Fleet Statistics. (An end-year analysis of world merchant fleet.)
National Air Carrier Association, Washington, DC
Annual Report.
Regional Airline Association, Washington, DC
Statistical Reports.
Shipbuilders Council of America, Arlington, VA
Annual Report.
Tanker Advisory Center, Inc., New York, NY
Worldwide Tanker Casualty Returns. Annual.
Travel —*see* Recreation *and* Transportation.
Unemployment Insurance —*see* Labor; *and* Social Insurance.
Utilities, Public—*see* Communications; Energy; Public Utilities *and* Transportation.
Veterans —*see* National Defense; *and* Population.
Virgin Islands of the United States —*see* Outlying Areas.
Vital Statistics —*see also* Accidents; *and* Health
U.S. Government
Centers for Disease Control and Prevention, Atlanta, GA
Morbidity and Mortality Weekly Report. Annual summary also.
National Center for Health Statistics
Monthly Vital Statistics Report. Provisional statistics. Annual summary also.
Vital and Health Statistics. (A series of statistical reports covering health-related topics.)
Series 20: Mortality Data. Irregular.
Series 21: Natality, Marriage, and Divorce Data. Irregular.
Series 23: National Survey of Family Growth Statistics. Irregular.
Vital Statistics of the United States. Annual.
Other
The Alan Guttmacher Institute, New York, NY

Guide to State Statistical Abstracts

This bibliography includes the most recent statistical abstracts for States and Puerto Rico published since 1986 plus those that will be issued in late 1996 or early 1997. For some States, a near equivalent has been listed in substitution for, or in addition to, a statistical abstract. All sources contain statistical tables on a variety of subjects for the State as a whole, its component parts, or both. The page counts given for publications are approximate.

Alabama

University of Alabama, Center for Business and Economic Research, Box 870221, Tuscaloosa 35487.   205-348-6191
*Economic Abstract of Alabama.*1995. 620 pp.

Alaska

Department of Commerce and Economic Development, Division of Trade & Development, P.O. Box 110804, Juneau 99811-0804 907-465-2017
The Alaska Economy Performance Report. 1994

Arizona

University of Arizona, Economic and Business Research, College of Business and Public Administration, McClelland Hall 204 Tucson, Arizona 85721-0001 520-621-2155 Fax 520-621-2150
Arizona Statistical Abstract: A 1993 Data Handbook. 616 pp.
Arizona Economic Indicators. 52 pp. Biennial.
Arizona's Economy. 20 pp. (Quarterly newsletter and data.)

Arkansas

University of Arkansas at Little Rock, Institute for Economic Advancement, Economic Research, 2801 South University, Little Rock 72204 501-569-8550
Arkansas State and County Economic Data. 9 pp. (Revised annually.)
University of Arkansas at Little Rock, Institute for Economic Advancement, Census State Data Center, Little Rock 72204 501-569-8530
Arkansas Statistical Abstract, 1996. 688 pp. (Revised biennially.)

California

Department of Finance, 915 L Street, 8th Floor, Sacramento 95814   916-322-2263
California Statistical Abstract, 1995.
Pacific Data Resources, P.O. Box 1922, Santa Barbara, CA 93116-1922 800-422-2546
California Almanac, 6th ed. Biennial. 275 pp.

Colorado

University of Colorado, Business Research Division, Campus Box 420, Boulder 80309 303-492-8227
Statistical Abstract of Colorado, 1987. 600 pp.

Connecticut

Connecticut Department of Economic & Community Development, 865 Brook St., Rocky Hill 06067-3405 1-800-392-2122
Connecticut Market Data. 1995, 140 pp. (Diskette also available.)
Connecticut Town Profiles, 1996-97. 340 pp.

Delaware

Delaware Economic Development Office, P.O. Box 1401, 99 Kings Highway, Dover 19903.   302-739-4271
Delaware Statistical Overview, 1995. 141 pp.
University of Delaware, Bureau of Economic Research, College of Business and Economics, Newark 19716-2730 302-831-8401
*Delaware Economic Report 1994-95.*200 pp. (Last edition. Bureau of Economic Research no longer exists.)

District of Columbia

Office of Planning, Data Management Division, Presidential Bldg., Suite 500, 415 12th St., N.W. Washington 20004 202-727-6533
1990 Census, Population and Housing for the District of Columbia 72 pp.
1990 Census: Social, Economic and Housing Characteristics.(44 pp. for each of nine volumes).
Socio-Economic Indicators by Census Tract. 221 pp.
Socio-Economic Indicators of Change by Census Tract, 1980-1990. 146 pp.
Office of Policy and Evaluation, Executive Office of the Mayor, 1 Judiciary Square, Suite 1000, 441 4th St., N.W., Washington 20001 202-727-6979
Indices—A Statistical Index to DC Services, Dec. 1995. 370 pp.

Florida

University of Florida, Bureau of Economic and Business Research, Box 117145, Gainesville 32611-7145.   352-392-0171
Florida Statistical Abstract, 1995. 29th ed. 800 pp. Also available on diskette.
Florida County Perspectives, 1995. One profile for each county. Annual.
Florida County Rankings, 1995.

Georgia

University of Georgia, Selig Center for
Economic Growth, Terry College of Business,
Athens 30602-6269.   706-542-4085
  Georgia Statistical Abstract, 1994-95. 1994.
  521 pp. 1996-1997 edition will be released
  in December 1996.

University of Georgia, College of Agricultural
and Environmental Sciences, Cooperative
Extension Service, Athens 30602-4356
706-542-8938 Fax 706-542-8934
  The Georgia County Guide. 1996. 15th ed.
  Annual. 195 pp.

Office of Planning and Budget,
254 Washington St., S.W., Atlanta 30334-
8501.   404-656-0911
  Georgia Descriptions in Data. 1990-91.
  249 pp.

Hawaii

Hawaii State Department of Business, and
Economic Development & Tourism, Research
and Economic Analysis Division, Statistics
Branch P.O. Box 2359, Honolulu 96804
Inquiries 808-586-2481;
Copies 808-586-2424
  *The State of Hawaii Data Book 1995: A
  Statistical Abstract.* 28th ed. 629 pp.

Idaho

Department of Commerce, 700 West State St.,
Boise 83720.   208-334-2470
  County Profiles of Idaho, 1995
  Idaho Community Profiles, 1995.
  Idaho Facts, 1994.
  Idaho Facts Data Book, 1995.
  Profile of Rural Idaho 1993.

Illinois

University of Illinois, Bureau of Economic and
Business Research, 428 Commerce West,
1206 South 6th Street, Champaign 61820
217-333-2332
  Illinois Statistical Abstract. 1995. 856 pages

Indiana

Indiana University, Indiana Business Research
Center, School of Business, 801 W. Michigan
BS4015 Indianapolis 46202-5151
317-274-2204
  Indiana Factbook, 1994-95. 413 pages.

Iowa

Public Interest Institute cø Iowa Wesleyan
College, 600 N. Jackson Street,
Mount Pleasant, IA 52641
319-385-3462
  1996 Statistical Profile of Iowa.

Kansas

University of Kansas, Institute for Public Policy
and Business Research, 607 Blake Hall,
Lawrence 66045-2960.   913-864-3701
  Kansas Statistical Abstract, 1993-94.
  29th ed. 1995.

Kentucky

Kentucky Cabinet for Economic Development,
Division of Research, 500 Mero Street,
Capital Plaza Tower, Frankfort 40601
502-564-4886
  Kentucky Deskbook of Economic Statistics.
  32nd ed. 1996.

Louisiana

University of New Orleans, Division of Business
and Economic Research, New Orleans 70148
504-286-6248
  Statistical Abstract of Louisiana. 9th ed.
  1994.

Maine

Maine Department of Economic and
Community Development, State House
Station 59, Augusta 04333
207-287-2656
  Maine: A Statistical Summary. (Updated
  periodically.)

Maryland

Regional Economic Studies Institute, Towson
State University, Towson 21204-7097
410-830-3765
  Maryland Statistical Abstract. 1993-94.
  274 pp.

Massachusetts

Massachusetts Institute for Social and
Economic Research, 128 Thompson Hall,
University of Massachusetts at
Amherst 01003
413-545-3460 Fax 413-545-3686
  *Projected Total Population and Age
  Distribution for 2000 and 2005:
  Massachusetts Cities and Towns.*
  Dec. 1994.
  *Projection of the Population, Mass.,
  Cities and Towns, Years 2000-2010.*

Minnesota

Department of Trade and Economic
Development, Business and Community
Development Division, 500 Metro Square
Building, St. Paul 55101.   612-296-8283
  *Compare Minnesota: An Economic and
  Statistical Factbook, 1994-95.* 165 pp.
  *Economic Report to the Governor: State of
  Minnesota, 1992.*148 pp.

Office of State Demographer, Minnesota
Planning, 300 Centennial Bldg.,
St. Paul 55155.   612-296-2557
  *Minnesota Population and Household
  Estimates, 1995.* Available diskette in
  Lotus, dBase or ASCII formats.
  Minnesota Population Projections, 1990.

Mississippi

Mississippi State University, College of Business and Industry, Division of Research, Mississippi State 39762.   601-325-3817

Mississippi Statistical Abstract. 1995. 553 pp.

Missouri

University of Missouri, Business and Public Administration Research Center, Columbia 65211.   573-882-4805

Statistical Abstract for Missouri, 1995 Biennial. 256 pp.

Montana

Montana Department of Commerce, Census and Economic Information Center, 1424 9th Ave., Helena 59620.   406-444-2896

Statistical Reports from the Montana County Database. (Separate county and State reports; available by subject section as well as complete reports by county and State, updated periodically.)

Nebraska

Department of Economic Development, Division of Research, Box 94666, Lincoln 68509 402-471-3784

Nebraska Statistical Handbook. 1995-1996. 300+ pp.

Nevada

Department of Administration, Budget and Planning Division, Capitol Complex, Carson City 89710.   702-687-4065

Nevada Statistical Abstract. 1996. Biennial. 225 pp.

New Hampshire

Office of State Planning, 2 1/2 Beacon St., Concord 0330.   1 603-271-2155

Current Estimates and Trends in New Hampshire's Housing Supply. Update: 1994. 32 pp.

1994 Population Estimates for New Hampshire Cities and Towns, New Hampshire Population Projections for Cities and Towns 1990-2015.

New Jersey

New Jersey State Data Center, NJ Department of Labor, CN 388, Trenton 08625-0388 609-984-2593

New Jersey Source Book, 1993. 156 pp.

New Mexico

University of New Mexico, Bureau of Business and Economic Research, 1920 Lomas N.E. Albuquerque 87131-6021.   505-277-6626 Fax 505-277-2773

County Profiles. *1994. 72 pp.*

Community Profiles for Selected New Mexico cities.

New York

Nelson A. Rockefeller Institute of Government, 411 State Street, Albany 12203-1003 518-443-5522

New York State Statistical Yearbook, 1995. 20th ed. 590 pp.

North Carolina

Office of Governor Office of State Planning, 116 West Jones Street, Raleigh 27603-8003 919-733-4131

Statistical Abstract of North Carolina Counties, 1991. 6th edition. (No longer being published.)

North Dakota

University of North Dakota, Box 8369, Bureau of Business and Economic Research, Grand Forks 58202.   701-777-2637

The Statistical Abstract of North Dakota. 1988. 700 pp.

North Dakots Department of Economic Development & Finance, 1833 E. Bismark Expressway, Bismark 58504-6708 701-328-5300

State of North Dakota Economic, Demographic, Public Services, and Fiscal Condition. Sept. 1995. 155 pp.

Ohio

Department of Development, Office of Strategic Research, P.O. Box 1001, Columbus 43216-1001.   614-466-2115

Research products and services. (Updated continuously.)

The Ohio State University, School of Public Policy and Management, 1775 College Road, Columbus 43210-1399.   614-292-7731

Benchmark Ohio, 1993. Biennial. 300 pp.

Oklahoma

University of Oklahoma, Center for Economic and Management Research, 307 West Brooks Street, Room 4, Norman 73019 405-325-2931

Statistical Abstract of Oklahoma, 1995. Annual. 469 pp.

Oregon

Secretary of State, Room 136, State Capitol, Salem 97310

Oregon Blue Book. 1995-1996. Biennial. 441 pp. $12.

Pennsylvania

Pennsylvania State Data Center, Institute of State and Regional Affairs, Penn State Harrisburg, 777 West Harrisburg Pike, Middletown Pennsylvania 17057-4898 717-948-6336

Pennsylvania Statistical Abstract, 1996. 301 pp.

Rhode Island

Rhode Island Economic Development Corporation, 1 West Exchange Street, Providence 02903.   401-277-2601 Fax 401-277-2102

Rhode Island 1990 Census of Population and Housing Summary. May 1994.

The Rhode Island Economy. April 1996.

South Carolina

Budget and Control Board, Office of Research and Statistical Services, R. C. Dennis Building, Room 425, Columbia 29201
803-734-3781

South Carolina Statistical Abstract: 1996. 440 pp.

South Dakota

University of South Dakota, State Data Center, Vermillion 57069.   605-677-5287

Selected Social and Economic Characteristics. 550 pp.

1995 South Dakota Community Abstracts. 400 pp.

Tennessee

University of Tennessee, Center for Business and Economic Research, Knoxville 37996-4170.   615-974-5441

Tennessee Statistical Abstract, 1994-95. 15th ed. 800 pp. Biennial. (1996-97 edition available early 1997)

Texas

Dallas Morning News, Communications Center, P.O. Box 655237, Dallas 75265
214-977-8261

Texas Almanac, 1996-97. 1995. 672 pp. Will be available on CD-ROM in 1996.

University of Texas, Bureau of Business Research, Austin 78713.   512-471-5180

Texas Fact Book, 1989. 6th ed. 250 pp.

Utah

University of Utah, Bureau of Economic and Business Research, 401 Kendall D. Garff Building, Salt Lake City 84112
801-581-6333

Statistical Abstract of Utah. 1993. (Triennial.)

Utah Foundation, 10 West 100 South, Suite 323, Salt Lake City 84101-1544
801-364-1837

Statistical Review of Government in Utah. 1995. 160 pp.

Vermont

Labor Market Information, Department of Employment and Training, 5 Green Mountain Drive, P.O. Box 488, Montpelier 05601-0488
802-828-4202

Demographic and Economic Profiles. Annual. Regional county reports also available.

Virginia

University of Virginia, Weldon Cooper Center for Public Service, 918 Emmet Street, North Suite 300, Charlottesville 22903
804-982-5585

Virginia Statistical Abstract, 1996-97. Biennial. 950 pp.

Washington

Washington State Office of Financial Management, Forecasting Division
P.O. Box 43113 Olympia 98504-3113
360-753-5617

Washington State Abstract, 1995. 300 pp.

Population Trends for Washington State. Annual. 48 pages.

West Virginia

West Virginia University, College of Business and Economics, Center for Economic Research, P.O. Box 6025, Morgantown 26506-6026
304-293-7835

West Virginia Statistical Abstract, 1995, Biennial. 400 pp.

County Data Profiles. Annual. 50 pp.

Census Data Profiles. Decennial. 30 pp.

West Virginia Economic Outlook. Annual. 50 pp.

West Virginia Research League, Inc., 405 Capitol Street, Suite 414, Charleston 25301-1721
304-346-9451

Economic Indicators. 1995. 215 pp.

The 1995 Statistical Handbook. 94 pp.

Wisconsin

Wisconsin Legislative Reference Bureau, P.O. Box 2037, Madison 53701-2037
608-266-7098

1995-1996 Wisconsin Blue Book. 980 pp. Biennial.

Wyoming

Department of Administration and Information, Division of Economic Analysis, 327 E. Emerson Building, Cheyenne 82002
307-777-7504

The Equality State Almanac 1995. 146 pp.

Puerto Rico

Planning Board, Area of Economic and Social Planning, Bureau of Economic Analysis and Bureau of Statistics, Santurce 00940
809-722-2070

Monthly Economic Indicators. December 1993.

Historic Series of Employment, Unemployment and Labor Force, 1992.

Social Statistics Abstract. 1990.

Socioeconomic Statistics of Puerto Rico. 1992.

Guide to Foreign Statistical Abstracts

This bibliography presents recent statistical abstracts for Mexico, Russia, and member nations of the Organization for Economic Cooperation and Development. All sources contain statistical tables on a variety of subjects for the individual countries. Many of the following publications provide text in English as well as in the national language(s). For further information on these publications, contact the named statistical agency which is responsible for editing the publication.

Austria

Osterreichisches Statistisches Zentralamt, P.O. Box 9000, A-1033 Vienna

Statistisches Jahrbuch for die Republik Osterreich. Annual. 1995 522 pp. (In German.)

Australia

Australian Bureau of Statistics, Canberra

Yearbook Australia. Annual. 1996 729 pp. (In English.)

Belgium

Institut National de Statistique, 44 rue de Louvain, 1000 Brussels

Annuaire statistique de la Belgique. Annual. 1994 822 pp. (In French and Dutch.)

Canada

Statistics Canada, Ottawa, Ontario, KIA OT6

Canada Yearbook: A review of economic, social and political developments in Canada. 1994 707 pp. Irregular. (In English and French.)

Croatia

Republika Hrvatska, Republicki Zavod Za Statistiku

Statisticki ljetopis 1995 644 pp. (In English and Serbo-Croatian.)

Czech Republic

Czech Statistical Office, Sokolovska 142, 186 04 Praha 8

Statisticka Rocenka Ceske Rpubliky 1995 626 pp. (In English and Czech.)

Denmark

Danmarks Statistik, Postboks 2550 Sejrogade 11, DK 2100, Copenhagen

Statistical Yearbook. 1995. Annual. 559 pp. (In Danish with English translations of table headings.)

Finland

Central Statistical Office of Finland, Box 504 SF-00101 Helsinki

Statistical Yearbook of Finland. Annual. 1995 454 pp. (In English, Finnish, and Swedish.)

France

Institut National de la Statistique et des Etudes Economiques, Paris 18, Bld. Adolphe Pinard, 75675 Paris (Cedex 14)

Annuaire Statistique de la France. Annual. 1996 925 pp. (In French.)

Greece

National Statistical Office, 14-16 Lycourgou St., 101-66 Athens

Concise Statistical Yearbook 1994 254 pp. (In English.)

Statistical Yearbook of Greece. Annual. 1990-1991 567 pp. (plus 7 pages of diagrams). (In English and Greek.)

Iceland

Hagstofa Islands/Statistical Bureau, Hverfisgata 8-10, Reykjavik.

Statistical Abstract of Iceland. 1994. Irregular. 303 pp. (In English and Icelandic.)

Ireland

Central Statistics Office, Earlsfort Terrace, Dublin 2

Statistical Abstract. Annual. 1995 440 pp. (In English.)

Italy

ISTAT (Istituto Centrale di Statistica), Via Cesare Balbo 16, 00100 Rome

Annuario Statistico Italiano. Annual. 1995 567 pp. (In Italian.)

Japan

Statistics Bureau, Management & Coordination Agency, 19-1 Wakamatsucho, Shinjuku Tokyo 162

Japan Statistical Yearbook. Annual. 1996 914 pp. (In English and Japanese.)

Luxembourg

STATEC (Service Central de la Statistique et des Etudes), P.O. Box 304, L-2013, Luxembourg

Annuaire Statistique. Annual. 1995. (In French.)

Mexico

Instituto Nacional de Estadistica Geografia e Informatica, Avda. Insurgentes Sur No. 795-PH Col. Napoles, Del. Benito Juarez 03810 Mexico, D.F.

Anuario estadistico de los Estados Unidos Mexicanos. Annual. 1993 610 pp. Also on disc. (In Spanish.)

Netherlands

Centraal Bureau voor de Statistiek. 428 Prinses Beatrixlaan P.O. Box 959, 2270 AZ Voorburg

Statistisch Yearbook 1995. 580 pp. (In Dutch.)

New Zealand
Department of Statistics, Wellington
New Zealand Official Yearbook. Annual.
1995 632 pp. (In English.)

Norway
Central Bureau of Statistics, Skippergate 15,
P.B. 8131 Dep. N-Oslo 1
Statistical Yearbook. Annual. 1995 493 pp.
(In English and Norwegian.)

Portugal
INE (Instituto Nacional de Estatistica), Avenida
Antonio Jose de Almeida, P-1078 Lisbon
Codex
Anuario Estatistico: de Portugal. 1994
337 pp. (In Portugese.)

Russia
State Committee of Statistics of Russia,
Moscow
*Russian Federation in the Year 1993.
Statistical Yearbook.* 1993 383 pp.
(In Russian.)

Slovakia
Statistical Office of the Slovak Republic,
Mileticova 3, 824 67 Bratislava
Statisticka Rocenka Slovensak 1991.
514 pp. (In English and Slovak)

Slovenia
Statistical Office of the Republic of Slovenia,
Vozarski Pot 12, 61000 Ljubljana
Statisticni Letopis Republike Slovenije 1992.
530 pp. (In Slovenian.)

Spain
INE (Instituto Nacional de Estadistica),
Paseo de la Castellana, 183, Madrid 16
Anuario Estadistico de Espana. Annual.
1994 890 pp. (In Spanish.)
Anuario Estadistico. 1988. (Edicion Manual.)
976 pp.

Sweden
Statistics Sweden, S-11581 Stockholm
Statistical Yearbook of Sweden. Annual.
1996 569 pp.
(In English and Swedish.)

Switzerland
Bundesamt fur Statistik, Hallwylstrasse 15,
CH-3003, Bern
Statistisches Jahrbuch der Schweiz. Annual.
1996 464 pp.
(In French and German.)

Turkey
State Institute of Statistics, Prime Ministry,
114 Necatibey Caddesi, Bakanliklar,
Yenisehir, Ankara
Statistical Yearbook of Turkey.
Published on odd numbered years. 1993
716 pp.
(In English and Turkish.)
Statistical Pocketbook of Turkey.
Published on even numbered years. 1990
312 pp.
(In English and Turkish.)

United Kingdom
Central Statistical Office,
Great George Street,
London SW1P 3AQ
Annual Abstract of Statistics. Annual. 1991
349 pp. (In English.)

West Germany
Statistische Bundesamt, Postfach 5528,
6200 Wiesbaden
*Statistisches Jahrbuch fur die
Bundesrepublic Deutschland.* Annual. 1995
771 pp. (In German.)
*Statistisches Jahrbuch fur das Ausland.
1995. 399 pp.*

Metropolitan Areas: Concepts, Components, and Population

Statistics for metropolitan areas (MA's) shown in the *Statistical Abstract* represent areas designated by the U.S. Office of Management and Budget (OMB) as metropolitan statistical areas (MSA's), consolidated metropolitan statistical areas (CMSA's), and primary metropolitan statistical areas (PMSA's).

The general concept of an MA is that of a core area containing a large population nucleus, together with adjacent communities having a high degree of economic and social integration with that core. Currently defined MA's are based on application of 1990 standards (which appeared in the *Federal Register* on March 30, 1990) to 1990 decennial census data. These MA definitions were announced by OMB effective June 30, 1995.

In this appendix, tables A, B, and C present historical summary information for MA's and nonmetropolitan areas as defined on certain dates. Table E presents geographic components and 1995 population estimates for each MSA, CMSA, and PMSA outside of New England. As of the June 1995 OMB announcement, there were 253 MSA's, and 18 CMSA's comprising 73 PMSA's in the United States. (In addition, there were three MSA's, one CMSA, and three PMSA's in Puerto Rico; MA's in Puerto Rico do not appear in these tables.) Table D presents definitions and data for New England county metropolitan areas (NECMA's), the county-based alternative metropolitan areas for the city- and town-based MSA's and CMSA's of the six New England States.

Standard definitions of metropolitan areas were first issued in 1949 by the then Bureau of the Budget (predecessor of OMB), under the designation "standard metropolitan area" (SMA). The term was changed to "standard metropolitan statistical area" (SMSA) in 1959, and to "metropolitan statistical area" (MSA) in 1983. The current collective term "metropolitan area" (MA) became effective in 1990. OMB has been responsible for the official metropolitan areas since they were first defined, except for the period 1977 to 1981, when they were the responsibility of the Office of Federal Statistical Policy and Standards, Department of Commerce.

The standards for defining metropolitan areas were modified in 1958, 1971, 1975, 1980, and 1990.

Defining MSA's, CMSA's, and PMSA's—The current standards provide that each MSA must include at least: (a) One city with 50,000 or more inhabitants, or (b) A Census Bureau-defined urbanized area (of at least 50,000 inhabitants) and a total metropolitan population of at least 100,000 (75,000 in New England).

Under the standards the county (or counties) that contains the largest city becomes the central county (counties), along with any adjacent counties that have at least 50 percent of their population in the urbanized area surrounding the largest city. Additional "outlying counties" are included in the MSA if they meet specified requirements of commuting to the central counties and other selected requirements of metropolitan character (such as population density and percent urban). In New England, the MSA's are defined in terms of cities and towns rather than counties.

An area that meets these requirements for recognition as an MSA and also has a population of one million or more may be recognized as a CMSA if: (1) separate component areas can be identified within the entire area by meeting statistical criteria specified in the standards, and (2) local opinion indicates there is support for the component areas. If recognized, the component areas are designated PMSA's, and the entire area becomes a CMSA. (PMSA's, like the CMSA's that contain them, are composed of individual or groups of counties outside New England, and cities and towns within New England.) If no PMSA's are recognized, the entire area is designated as an MSA.

The largest city in each MSA/CMSA is designated a "central city," and additional cities qualify if specified requirements are met concerning population size and commuting patterns. The title of each MSA consists of the names of up to three of its central cities and the name of each State into which the MSA extends. However, a central city with less than one-third the population of the area's largest city is not included in an MSA title unless local opinion desires its inclusion. Titles of PMSA's also typically are based on central city names but in certain cases consist of county names. Generally, titles of CMSA's are based on the names of their component PMSA's.

A 1990 census list, CPH-L-145, showing 1990 and 1980 populations for current MA's and their component counties or New England subcounty areas is available through the Statistical Information Office, Population Division, 301-457-2422. A 1990 census Supplementary Report, 1990 CPH-S-1-1, *Metropolitan Areas as Defined by the Office of Management and Budget, June 30, 1993*, contains extensive population and housing statistics for the current then MA's and is available from the U.S. Government Printing Office (GPO) (stock number 003-024-08738-3). Also available from the GPO is the Census Bureau's wall map for the 1994 MA's (stock number 003-024-08768-5).

Defining NECMA's—The OMB defines NECMA's as a county-based alternative for the city- and town-based New England MSA's and CMSA's. The NECMA for an MSA or CMSA includes: (1) the county containing the first-named city in that MSA/CMSA title (this county may include the first-named cities of other MSA's/CMSA's as well), and (2) each additional county having at least half its population in the MSA's/CMSA's whose first-named cities are in the previously identified county. NECMA's are not identified for individual PMSA's. There are twelve NECMA's, including one for the Boston-Worcester-Lawrence CMSA and one for the portion of the New York-Northern New Jersey-Long Island CMSA in Connecticut.

Central cities of a NECMA are those cities in the NECMA that qualify as central cities of an MSA or a CMSA. NECMA titles derive from names of central cities of MSA's/CMSA's.

Changes in MA definitions over time— Changes in the definitions of MA's since the 1950 census have consisted chiefly of (1) recognition of new areas as they reached the minimum required city or area population;

and (2) the addition of counties or New England cities and towns to existing areas as new census data showed them to qualify. Also, former separate MA's have been merged with other areas, and occasionally territory has been transferred from one MA to another or from an MA to nonmetropolitan territory. The large majority of changes have taken place on the basis of decennial census data, although the MA standards specify the bases for intercensal updates.

Because of these changes in definition, users must be cautious in comparing MA data from different dates. For some purposes, comparisons of data for MA's as defined at given dates may be appropriate. To facilitate constant-area comparisons, data for earlier dates have been revised in tables where possible to reflect the MA boundaries of the more recent date.

In tables A, B, and C below, data are given for MA's as defined for specific dates, thereby indicating the extent of change in population and land area resulting from revisions in definitions.

Table A. Number, Population, and Land Area of MA's as Defined at Specified Dates From 1960 to 1993

[The differences in population shown here for each year within each column of the table result entirely from net expansion of metropolitan territory through changes in the MA definitions. The differences in population over time shown for each MA definition (on the successive lines of the table) result entirely from population changes within that territory, unaffected by changes in MA definitions. The changes in 1990 land area result entirely from net change in MA territory. All data include Alaska and Hawaii and exclude Puerto Rico. Subtraction of any line of the table from the line below will show the net effect of change in population and land area undergone by the MA's as the result of changes in definitions between the specified dates. Such changes may have occurred throughout the period, not on any single date, and may have included reductions in, as well as additions to, MA territory. Census population data through 1980 include corrections made since publication. The area data for the 1960, 1970, and 1980 census definitions of MA's differ from the data published in those censuses because of subsequent remeasurement of land areas and changes in inland water area occurring for the 1990 census]

| MA DEFINITION AS OF— | Number of MA's | POPULATION | | | | | Land area, 1990 (sq. mi.) |
		1960 (April 1)	1970 (April 1)	1980 (April 1)	1990 (April 1)	1992 (July 1)	
1960 census (Nov. 1960)	212	[1]112,885,139	130,982,661	140,793,427	155,088,626	(NA)	308,742
1964 (Aug. 31) [2]	217	115,876,343	134,700,911	145,503,863	160,500,956	(NA)	348,400
1968 (Jan. 31) [3]	230	118,413,604	137,976,252	149,811,057	165,707,672	(NA)	377,042
1970 census (Feb. 28, 1971)	243	[4]119,593,498	[5]139,479,806	151,662,221	167,896,646	(NA)	386,241
1974 (Apr. 30) [6]	265	[7]126,613,710	148,198,993	162,753,335	181,125,276	(NA)	490,551
1977 (Dec. 31) [8]	277	127,674,818	149,482,664	164,383,496	182,989,860	(NA)	509,841
1980 census (June 30, 1981) [9]	318	131,318,714	153,693,767	169,430,623	188,759,597	(NA)	565,288
1983 (June 30)	[10]275	132,633,988	155,411,328	171,776,970	191,634,355	(NA)	559,752
1984 (June 30)	[10]277	132,707,748	155,519,340	171,955,900	191,903,497	(NA)	563,796
1985 (June 30)	[10]280	132,887,134	155,700,823	172,169,456	192,135,964	(NA)	569,816
1986 (June 30)	[10]281	132,977,580	155,805,452	172,304,016	192,314,367	(NA)	571,745
1987 (June 30) [11]	[10]281	133,003,445	155,832,688	172,334,547	192,345,395	(NA)	572,284
1988 (June 30) [12]	[10]282	133,088,400	155,937,275	172,454,948	192,476,951	(NA)	573,560
1989 (June 30) [12]	[10]283	133,233,777	156,084,580	172,601,873	192,618,846	(NA)	574,622
1990 census (June 30, 1990) [12]	[10]284	133,275,412	156,137,337	172,679,870	192,725,741	(NA)	580,136
1992 (Dec. 31) [12]	[10]268	(NA)	(NA)	176,662,797	197,466,567	202,903,519	669,927
1993 (June 30) [12] [13]	[10]268	(NA)	(NA)	176,892,735	197,724,892	203,172,185	673,057

NA Not available. [1] Corresponds to total MA population for 1960 published in 1960 census (112,885,178), corrected by subtracting population (39) erroneously included in Franklin County, Ohio (Columbus metropolitan area). [2] MA's as defined for the 1963 economic censuses. [3] MA's as defined for the 1967 economic censuses. [4] Corresponds to total 1960 population for 1970 MA's published in 1970 census (119,594,754), corrected by subtracting 1,256 population from Lawrence-Haverhill metropolitan area; this represented an addition to the 1960 population of Andover town made subsequent to the original census tabulations, and therefore not reflected in State or national totals. [5] Corresponds to total MA population for 1970 published in 1970 census (139,418,811), plus net corrections made subsequent to publication. [6] MA's as defined for the 1972 economic censuses. [7] Includes 1960 population (82,833) of Anchorage Census Division, as defined in 1970. [8] MA's as defined for the 1977 economic censuses. [9] MA's as defined for the 1982 economic censuses. [10] MSA's and CMSA's. [11] MA's as defined for the 1987 economic censuses. [12] Data exclude the portion of Sullivan city in Crawford County, MO (1990 population 1,116) added to the St. Louis, MO-IL MSA by congressional action effective Dec. 22, 1987. [13] MA's as defined for the 1992 economic censuses.

Source: U.S. Bureau of the Census, 1960-70, *U.S. Census of Population*, vol. 1; *1980 Census of Population*, vol. 1, chapters A and B and *Supplementary Report, Metropolitan Statistical Areas* (PC80-S1-18); *1990 Census of Population and Housing Data Paper Listing* (CPH-L-10 and CPH-L-118); *1990 Census of Population and Housing, Supplementary Reports, Metropolitan Areas as Defined by the Office of Management and Budget, June 30, 1993*, (1990 CPH-S-1-1); and *Population Paper Listing* (PPL-2).

Table B. Nonmetropolitan Population and Land Area as Defined at Specified Dates From 1960 to 1993

[See headnote for table A. Nonmetropolitan population and land area are equivalent to that portion of the total national population and land area not included within MA's at the dates specified]

METROPOLITAN AREA DEFINITION AS OF—	POPULATION					Land area, 1990 (sq. mi.)
	1960 (April 1)	1970 (April 1)	1980 (April 1)	1990 (April 1)	1992 (July 1)	
1960 census (Nov. 1960)	66,438,036	72,319,370	85,752,378	93,621,247	(NA)	3,231,027
1964 (Aug. 31).	63,446,832	68,601,120	81,041,942	88,208,917	(NA)	3,191,368
1968 (Jan. 31).	60,909,571	65,325,779	76,734,748	83,002,201	(NA)	3,162,726
1970 census (Feb. 28, 1971)	59,729,677	63,822,225	74,883,584	80,813,227	(NA)	3,153,527
1974 (Apr. 30).	52,709,465	55,103,038	63,792,470	67,584,597	(NA)	3,049,218
1977 (Dec. 31).	51,648,357	53,819,367	62,162,309	65,720,013	(NA)	3,029,928
1980 census (June 30, 1981)	48,004,461	49,608,264	57,115,182	59,950,276	(NA)	2,974,481
1983 (June 30).	46,689,187	47,890,703	54,768,835	57,075,518	(NA)	2,980,016
1984 (June 30).	46,615,427	47,782,691	54,589,905	56,806,376	(NA)	2,975,972
1985 (June 30).	46,436,041	47,601,208	54,376,349	56,573,909	(NA)	2,969,952
1986 (June 30).	46,345,595	47,496,579	54,241,789	56,395,506	(NA)	2,968,023
1987 (June 30).	46,319,730	47,469,343	54,211,258	56,364,478	(NA)	2,967,484
1988 (June 30).	46,234,775	47,364,756	54,090,857	56,232,922	(NA)	2,966,208
1989 (June 30).	46,089,398	47,217,451	53,943,932	56,091,027	(NA)	2,965,146
1990 census (June 30, 1990)	46,047,763	47,164,694	53,865,935	55,984,132	(NA)	2,959,632
1992 (Dec. 31).	(NA)	(NA)	49,883,008	51,243,306	52,174,017	2,866,411
1993 (June 30).	(NA)	(NA)	49,649,464	50,984,981	51,905,351	2,863,281

NA Not available.

Table C. Percent of Total U.S. Population and Percent of Land Area Inside MA's as Defined at Specified Dates From 1960 to 1993

[See headnote for table A]

METROPOLITAN AREA DEFINITION AS OF—	PERCENT OF POPULATION					Percent of land area, 1990
	1960 (April 1)	1970 (April 1)	1980 (April 1)	1990 (April 1)	1992 (July 1)	
1960 census (Nov. 1960)	63.0	64.4	62.1	62.4	(NA)	8.7
1964 (Aug. 31).	64.6	66.3	64.2	64.5	(NA)	9.8
1968 (Jan. 31)	66.0	67.9	66.1	66.6	(NA)	10.7
1970 census (Feb. 28, 1971)	66.7	68.6	66.9	67.5	(NA)	10.9
1974 (Apr. 30)	70.6	72.9	71.8	72.8	(NA)	13.9
1977 (Dec. 31)	71.2	73.5	72.6	73.6	(NA)	14.4
1980 census (June 30, 1981)	73.2	75.6	74.8	75.9	(NA)	16.0
1983 (June 30).	74.0	76.4	75.8	77.1	(NA)	15.8
1984 (June 30).	74.0	76.5	75.9	77.2	(NA)	15.9
1985 (June 30).	74.1	76.6	76.0	77.3	(NA)	16.1
1986 (June 30).	74.2	76.6	76.1	77.3	(NA)	16.2
1987 (June 30).	74.2	76.7	76.1	77.3	(NA)	16.2
1988 (June 30).	74.2	76.7	76.1	77.4	(NA)	16.2
1989 (June 30).	74.3	76.8	76.2	77.4	(NA)	16.2
1990 census (June 30, 1990)	74.3	76.8	76.2	77.5	(NA)	16.4
1992 (Dec. 31).	(NA)	(NA)	78.0	79.4	79.5	18.9
1993 (June 30).	(NA)	(NA)	78.1	79.5	79.7	19.0

NA Not available.

Source: U.S. Bureau of the Census, 1960-70, *U.S. Census of Population*, vol. 1; *1980 Census of Population*, vol. 1, chapters A and B and *Supplementary Report, Metropolitan Statistical Areas* (PC80-S1-18); *1990 Census of Population and Housing Data Paper Listing* (CPH-L-10 and CPH-L-118); *1990 Census of Population and Housing, Supplementary Reports, Metropolitan Areas as Defined by the Office of Management and Budget, June 30, 1993*, (1990 CPH-S-1-1); and *Population Paper Listing* (PPL-2).

Table D. New England County Metropolitan Areas (NECMA's)

[In thousands. As of July 1]

NECMA	Population, 1995	NECMA	Population, 1995	NECMA	Population, 1995
Bangor, ME	146	Burlington, VT	188	New London-Norwich, CT . . .	250
Penobscot County.	146	Chittenden County	139	New London County	250
Barnstable-Yarmouth, MA . . .	200	Franklin County	43	Pittsfield, MA	136
Barnstable County.	200	Grand Isle County.	6	Berkshire County	136
Boston-Worcester-Lawrence-		Hartford, CT.	1,115	Portland, ME	249
Lowell-Brockton, MA-NH . . .	5,769	Hartford County	836	Cumberland County.	249
Bristol County, MA	513	Middlesex County	148	Providence-Warwick-	
Essex County, MA.	684	Tolland County	132	Pawtucket, RI	908
Middlesex County, MA	1,408	Lewiston-Auburn, ME	104	Bristol County.	49
Norfolk County, MA	636	Androscoggin County.	104	Kent County.	162
Plymouth County, MA	454	New Haven-Bridgeport-		Providence County	580
Suffolk County, MA	641	Stamford-Waterbury-		Washington County	117
Worcester County, MA.	719	Danbury, CT	1,626	Springfield, MA.	593
Hillsborough County, NH . . .	350	Fairfield County	831	Hampden County	443
Rockingham County, NH . . .	258	New Haven County	795	Hampshire County	149
Strafford County, NH	107				

Source: U.S. Bureau of the Census, Internet site http://www.census.gov/population/estimates/metro-city/necal95.txt (accessed August 1, 1996).

Table E. Metropolitan Areas Outside of New England and Their Components as of June 30, 1995

[Population estimated as of **July 1, 1995**. All metropolitan areas are arranged alphabetically. PMSA's are included under their respective CMSA's, see CMSA entry. This table presents data for MAs outside New England only]

	Popu-lation, 1995 (1,000)		Popu-lation, 1995 (1,000)		Popu-lation, 1995 (1,000)
Abilene, TX MSA	123	Henry County	85	**Boise City, ID MSA**	360
Taylor County	123	Newton County	51	Ada County	252
		Paulding County	60	Canyon County	109
Albany, GA MSA	117	Pickens County	17		
Dougherty County	98	Rockdale County	64	**Brownsville-Harlingen, TX**	
Lee County	20	Spalding County	57	**MSA**	310
		Walton County	47	Cameron County	310
Albany-Schenectady-Troy,					
NY MSA	873	**Augusta-Aiken, GA-SC MSA**	453	**Bryan-College Station, TX**	
Albany County	290	Columbia County, GA	84	**MSA**	130
Montgomery County	52	McDuffie County, GA	22	Brazos County	130
Rensselaer County	156	Richmond County, GA	196		
Saratoga County	194	Aiken County, SC	133	**Buffalo-Niagara Falls, NY**	
Schenectady County	149	Edgefield County, SC	19	**MSA**	1,184
Schoharie County	33			Erie County	962
		Austin-San Marcos, TX MSA.	1,000	Niagara County	222
Albuquerque, NM MSA	660	Bastrop County	44		
Bernalillo County	522	Caldwell County	29	**Canton-Massillon, OH MSA**	404
Sandoval County	80	Hays County	78	Carroll County	28
Valencia County	58	Travis County	665	Stark County	376
		Williamson County	184		
Alexandria, LA MSA	127			**Casper, WY MSA**	64
Rapides Parish	127	**Bakersfield, CA MSA**	618	Natrona County	64
		Kern County	618		
Allentown-Bethlehem-				**Cedar Rapids, IA MSA**	179
Easton, PA MSA	613	**Baton Rouge, LA MSA**	564	Linn County	179
Carbon County	59	Ascension Parish	66		
Lehigh County	298	East Baton Rouge Parish	397	**Champaign-Urbana,**	
Northampton County	257	Livingston Parish	81	**IL MSA**	169
		West Baton Rouge Parish	20	Champaign County	169
Altoona, PA MSA	132				
Blair County	132	**Beaumont-Port Arthur, TX**		**Charleston-North Charleston,**	
		MSA	375	**SC MSA**	506
Amarillo, TX MSA	201	Hardin County	47	Berkeley County	135
Potter County	105	Jefferson County	243	Charleston County	282
Randall County	96	Orange County	85	Dorchester County	89
Anchorage, AK MSA	251	**Bellingham, WA MSA**	149	**Charleston, WV MSA**	255
Anchorage Borough	251	Whatcom County	149	Kanawha County	206
				Putnam County	49
Anniston, AL MSA	117	**Benton Harbor, MI MSA**	163		
Calhoun County	117	Berrien County	163	**Charlotte-Gastonia-Rock**	
				Hill, NC-SC MSA	1,289
Appleton-Oshkosh-Neenah,		**Billings, MT MSA**	125	Cabarrus County, NC	110
WI MSA	336	Yellowstone County	125	Gaston County, NC	181
Calumet County	37			Lincoln County, NC	56
Outagamie County	149	**Biloxi-Gulfport-Pascagoula, MS**		Mecklenburg County, NC	579
Winnebago County	149	**MSA**	342	Rowan County, NC	119
		Hancock County	38	Union County, NC	99
Asheville, NC MSA	207	Harrison County	175	York County, SC	144
Buncombe County	190	Jackson County	128		
Madison County	18			**Charlottesville, VA MSA**	142
		Binghamton, NY MSA	257	Albemarle County	73
Athens, GA MSA	135	Broome County	204	Fluvanna County	16
Clarke County	90	Tioga County	53	Greene County	13
Madison County	23			Charlottesville city	40
Oconee County	21	**Birmingham, AL MSA**	882		
		Blount County	43	**Chattanooga, TN-GA MSA**	443
Atlanta, GA MSA	3,432	Jefferson County	658	Hamilton County, TN	294
Barrow County	36	St. Clair County	58	Marion County, TN	26
Bartow County	64	Shelby County	124	Catoosa County, GA	48
Carroll County	78			Dade County, GA	14
Cherokee County	115	**Bismarck, ND MSA**	89	Walker County, GA	61
Clayton County	199	Burleigh County	65		
Cobb County	525	Morton County	25	**Cheyenne, WY MSA**	78
Coweta County	72			Laramie County	78
DeKalb County	582	**Bloomington, IN MSA**	115		
Douglas County	82	Monroe County	115	**Chicago-Gary-Kenosha,**	
Fayette County	79			**IL-IN-WI CMSA**	8,590
Forsyth County	62	**Bloomington-Normal, IL**		**Chicago, IL PMSA**	7,725
Fulton County	701	**MSA**	139	Cook County, IL	5,137
Gwinnett County	457	McLean County	139	DeKalb County, IL	83

	Popu-lation, 1995 (1,000)		Popu-lation, 1995 (1,000)		Popu-lation, 1995 (1,000)
DuPage County, IL	853	**Cumberland, MD-WV MSA**	101	**Dothan, AL MSA**	134
Grundy County, IL	35	Allegany County, MD	74	Dale County	50
Kane County, IL	360	Mineral County, WV	27	Houston County	84
Kendall County, IL	45				
Lake County, IL	572	**Dallas-Fort Worth, TX**		**Dover, DE MSA**	122
McHenry County, IL	225	**CMSA**	4,450	Kent County	122
Will County, IL	413	**Dallas, TX PMSA**	2,958		
Gary, IN PMSA	623	Collin County	346	**Dubuque, IA MSA**	89
Lake County, IN	483	Dallas County	1,959	Dubuque County	89
Porter County, IN	140	Denton County	334		
Kankakee, IL PMSA	102	Ellis County	94	**Duluth, MN-WI MSA**	240
Kankakee County, IL	102	Henderson County	64	St. Louis County, MN	197
Kenosha, WI PMSA	140	Hunt County	67	Douglas County, WI	43
Kenosha County, WI	140	Kaufman County	60		
		Rockwall County	33	**Eau Claire, WI MSA**	143
Chico-Paradise, CA MSA	193	**Fort Worth-Arlington, TX**		Chippewa County	54
Butte County	193	**PMSA**	1,492	Eau Claire County	88
		Hood County	33		
Cincinnati-Hamilton, OH-		Johnson County	106	**El Paso, TX MSA**	678
KY-IN CMSA	1,907	Parker County	74	El Paso County	678
Cincinnati, OH-KY-IN		Tarrant County	1,279		
PMSA	1,592			**Elkhart-Goshen, IN MSA**	167
Brown County, OH	39	**Danville, VA MSA**	110	Elkhart County	167
Clermont County, OH	167	Pittsylvania County	56		
Hamilton County, OH	864	Danville city	54	**Elmira, NY MSA**	94
Warren County, OH	131			Chemung County	94
Boone County, KY	70	**Davenport-Moline-**			
Campbell County, KY	87	**Rock Island, IA-IL MSA**	358	**Enid, OK MSA**	57
Gallatin County, KY	6	Scott County, IA	157	Garfield County	57
Grant County, KY	19	Henry County, IL	52		
Kenton County, KY	145	Rock Island County, IL	150	**Erie, PA MSA**	280
Pendleton County, KY	13			Erie County	280
Dearborn County, IN	44	**Dayton-Springfield, OH**			
Ohio County, IN	5	**MSA**	956	**Eugene-Springfield, OR**	
Hamilton-Middletown,		Clark County	148	**MSA**	303
OH PMSA	316	Greene County	141	Lane County	303
Butler County, OH	316	Miami County	97		
		Montgomery County	570	**Evansville-Henderson, IN-KY**	
Clarksville-Hopkinsville,				**MSA**	288
TN-KY MSA	189	**Daytona Beach, FL MSA**	449	Posey County, IN	26
Montgomery County, TN	124	Flagler County	41	Vanderburgh County, IN	168
Christian County, KY	66	Volusia County	408	Warrick County, IN	49
				Henderson County, KY	44
Cleveland-Akron, OH		**Decatur, AL MSA**	140		
CMSA	2,904	Lawrence County	33	**Fargo-Moorhead, ND-MN**	
Akron, OH PMSA	679	Morgan County	107	**MSA**	164
Portage County	149			Cass County, ND	111
Summit County	530	**Decatur, IL MSA**	116	Clay County, MN	52
Cleveland-Lorain-Elyria,		Macon County	116		
OH PMSA	2,225			**Fayetteville, NC MSA**	286
Ashtabula County	102	**Denver-Boulder-Greeley, CO**		Cumberland County	286
Cuyahoga County	1,398	**CMSA**	2,233		
Geauga County	84	**Boulder-Longmont, CO**		**Fayetteville-Springdale-**	
Lake County	223	**PMSA**	254	**Rogers, AR MSA**	253
Lorain County	281	Boulder County	254	Benton County	121
Medina County	136	**Denver, CO PMSA**	1,831	Washington County	132
		Adams County	303		
Colorado Springs, CO MSA.	466	Arapahoe County	449	**Flagstaff, AZ-UT MSA**	116
El Paso County	466	Denver County	494	Coconino County, AZ	110
		Douglas County	100	Kane County, UT	6
Columbia, MO MSA	124	Jefferson County	485		
Boone County	124	**Greeley, CO PMSA**	148	**Florence, AL MSA**	136
		Weld County	148	Colbert County	53
Columbia, SC MSA	482			Lauderdale County	84
Lexington County	192	**Des Moines, IA MSA**	421		
Richland County	290	Dallas County	33	**Florence, SC MSA**	123
		Polk County	350	Florence County	123
Columbus, GA-AL MSA	272	Warren County	39		
Chattahoochee County, GA.	16			**Fort Collins-Loveland, CO**	
Harris County, GA	20	**Detroit-Ann Arbor-Flint, MI**		**MSA**	217
Muscogee County, GA	185	**CMSA**	5,280	Larimer County	217
Russell County, AL	51	**Ann Arbor, MI PMSA**	523		
		Lenawee County	97	**Fort Myers-Cape Coral, FL**	
Columbus, OH MSA	1,438	Livingston County	134	**MSA**	375
Delaware County	79	Washtenaw County	293	Lee County	375
Fairfield County	118	**Detroit, MI PMSA**	4,320		
Franklin County	1,011	Lapeer County	84	**Fort Pierce-Port St. Lucie,**	
Licking County	137	Macomb County	734	**FL MSA**	284
Madison County	41	Monroe County	140	Martin County	111
Pickaway County	53	Oakland County	1,153	St. Lucie County	172
		St. Clair County	154		
Corpus Christi, TX MSA	379	Wayne County	2,056	**Fort Smith, AR-OK MSA**	189
Nueces County	313	**Flint, MI PMSA**	436	Crawford County, AR	48
San Patricio County	66	Genesee County	436	Sebastian County, AR	104
				Sequoyah County, OK	36

Appendix II

	Popu-lation, 1995 (1,000)
Fort Walton Beach, FL MSA	**164**
Okaloosa County	164
Fort Wayne, IN MSA	**472**
Adams County	32
Allen County	309
De Kalb County	38
Huntington County	37
Wells County	27
Whitley County	29
Fresno, CA MSA	**844**
Fresno County	737
Madera County	107
Gadsden, AL MSA	**100**
Etowah County	100
Gainesville, FL MSA	**196**
Alachua County	196
Glens Falls, NY MSA	**123**
Warren County	62
Washington County	61
Goldsboro, NC MSA	**110**
Wayne County	110
Grand Forks, ND-MN MSA	**105**
Grand Forks County, ND	72
Polk County, MN	33
Grand Junction, CO MSA	**107**
Mesa County	107
Grand Rapids-Muskegon-Holland, MI MSA	**998**
Allegan County	98
Kent County	525
Muskegon County	164
Ottawa County	210
Great Falls, MT MSA	**81**
Cascade County	81
Green Bay, WI MSA	**210**
Brown County	210
Greensboro-Winston- Salem-High Point, NC MSA	**1,124**
Alamance County	115
Davidson County	135
Davie County	30
Forsyth County	281
Guilford County	374
Randolph County	115
Stokes County	41
Yadkin County	33
Greenville, NC MSA	**118**
Pitt County	118
Greenville-Spartanburg-Anderson, SC MSA	**884**
Anderson County	154
Cherokee County	47
Greenville County	340
Pickens County	102
Spartanburg County	240
Harrisburg-Lebanon-Carlisle, PA MSA	**613**
Cumberland County	206
Dauphin County	246
Lebanon County	117
Perry County	44
Hattiesburg, MS MSA	**106**
Forrest County	73
Lamar County	34
Hickory-Morganton, NC MSA	**310**
Alexander County	30

	Popu-lation, 1995 (1,000)
Burke County	80
Caldwell County	74
Catawba County	126
Honolulu, HI MSA	**877**
Honolulu County	877
Houma, LA MSA	**189**
Lafourche Parish	88
Terrebonne Parish	101
Houston-Galveston-Brazoria, TX CMSA	**4,164**
Brazoria, TX PMSA	**216**
Brazoria County	216
Galveston-Texas City, TX PMSA	**238**
Galveston County	238
Houston, TX PMSA	**3,711**
Chambers County	22
Fort Bend County	293
Harris County	3,077
Liberty County	59
Montgomery County	234
Waller County	26
Huntington-Ashland, WV-KY-OH MSA	**317**
Cabell County, WV	97
Wayne County, WV	43
Boyd County, KY	51
Carter County, KY	26
Greenup County, KY	37
Lawrence County, OH	64
Huntsville, AL MSA	**318**
Limestone County	59
Madison County	258
Indianapolis, IN MSA	**1,477**
Boone County	42
Hamilton County	141
Hancock County	51
Hendricks County	87
Johnson County	102
Madison County	133
Marion County	818
Morgan County	62
Shelby County	43
Iowa City, IA MSA	**101**
Johnson County	101
Jackson, MI MSA	**154**
Jackson County	154
Jackson, MS MSA	**416**
Hinds County	251
Madison County	66
Rankin County	99
Jackson, TN MSA	**84**
Madison County	84
Jacksonville, FL MSA	**979**
Clay County	124
Duval County	702
Nassau County	51
St. Johns County	102
Jacksonville, NC MSA	**143**
Onslow County	143
Jamestown, NY MSA	**142**
Chautauqua County	142
Janesville-Beloit, WI MSA	**148**
Rock County	148
Johnson City-Kingsport-Bristol, TN-VA MSA	**454**
Carter County, TN	53
Hawkins County, TN	48
Sullivan County, TN	149

	Popu-lation, 1995 (1,000)
Unicoi County, TN	17
Washington County, TN	98
Scott County, VA	23
Washington County, VA	48
Bristol city, VA	18
Johnstown, PA MSA	**241**
Cambria County	161
Somerset County	80
Joplin, MO MSA	**144**
Jasper County	96
Newton County	48
Kalamazoo-Battle Creek, MI MSA	**443**
Calhoun County	141
Kalamazoo County	228
Van Buren County	75
Kansas City, MO-KS MSA	**1,663**
Cass County, MO	74
Clay County, MO	166
Clinton County, MO	18
Jackson County, MO	636
Lafayette County, MO	32
Platte County, MO	67
Ray County, MO	22
Johnson County, KS	401
Leavenworth County, KS	69
Miami County, KS	25
Wyandotte County, KS	154
Killeen-Temple, TX MSA	**290**
Bell County	218
Coryell County	72
Knoxville, TN MSA	**641**
Anderson County	72
Blount County	97
Knox County	361
Loudon County	36
Sevier County	60
Union County	15
Kokomo, IN MSA	**100**
Howard County	84
Tipton County	16
La Crosse, WI-MN MSA	**121**
La Crosse County, WI	102
Houston County, MN	19
Lafayette, LA MSA	**366**
Acadia Parish	57
Lafayette Parish	180
St. Landry Parish	83
St. Martin Parish	46
Lafayette, IN MSA	**168**
Clinton County	33
Tippecanoe County	135
Lake Charles, LA MSA	**176**
Calcasieu Parish	176
Lakeland-Winter Haven, FL MSA	**437**
Polk County	437
Lancaster, PA MSA	**448**
Lancaster County	448
Lansing-East Lansing, MI MSA	**438**
Clinton County	62
Eaton County	98
Ingham County	278
Laredo, TX MSA	**171**
Webb County	171
Las Cruces, NM MSA	**159**
Dona Ana County	159

	Popu-lation, 1995 (1,000)

Las Vegas, NV-AZ MSA	**1,139**
Clark County, NV	993
Nye County, NV	25
Mohave County, AZ	122
Lawrence, KS MSA	**88**
Douglas County	88
Lawton, OK MSA	**116**
Comanche County	116
Lexington, KY MSA	**436**
Bourbon County	19
Clark County	31
Fayette County	239
Jessamine County	34
Madison County	63
Scott County	28
Woodford County	22
Lima, OH MSA	**156**
Allen County	109
Auglaize County	47
Lincoln, NE MSA	**229**
Lancaster County	229
Little Rock-North Little Rock, AR MSA	**544**
Faulkner County	72
Lonoke County	46
Pulaski County	352
Saline County	74
Longview-Marshall, TX MSA	**204**
Gregg County	111
Harrison County	59
Upshur County	35
Los Angeles-Riverside-Orange County, CA CMSA	**15,362**
Los Angeles-Long Beach, CA PMSA	**9,139**
Los Angeles County	9,139
Orange County, CA PMSA	**2,564**
Orange County	2,564
Riverside-San Bernardino, CA PMSA	**2,949**
Riverside County	1,380
San Bernardino County	1,570
Ventura, CA PMSA	**710**
Ventura County	710
Louisville, KY-IN MSA	**987**
Bullitt County, KY	56
Jefferson County, KY	673
Oldham County, KY	41
Clark County, IN	92
Floyd County, IN	70
Harrison County, IN	33
Scott County, IN	23
Lubbock, TX MSA	**232**
Lubbock County	232
Lynchburg, VA MSA	**204**
Amherst County	30
Bedford County	52
Campbell County	49
Bedford city	6
Lynchburg city	67
Macon, GA MSA	**310**
Bibb County	155
Houston County	100
Jones County	22
Peach County	23
Twiggs County	10
Madison, WI MSA	**393**
Dane County	393
Mansfield, OH MSA	**176**
Crawford County	48
Richland County	128

McAllen-Edinburg-Mission, TX MSA	**480**
Hidalgo County	480
Medford-Ashland, OR MSA	**166**
Jackson County	166
Melbourne-Titusville-Palm Bay, FL MSA	**451**
Brevard County	451
Memphis, TN-AR-MS MSA	**1,069**
Fayette County, TN	27
Shelby County, TN	865
Tipton County, TN	43
Crittenden County, AR	50
DeSoto County, MS	84
Merced, CA MSA	**194**
Merced County	194
Miami-Fort Lauderdale, FL CMSA	**3,444**
Fort Lauderdale, FL PMSA	**1,412**
Broward County	1,412
Miami, FL PMSA	**2,031**
Dade County	2,031
Milwaukee-Racine, WI CMSA	**1,641**
Milwaukee-Waukesha, WI PMSA	**1,458**
Milwaukee County	931
Ozaukee County	79
Washington County	110
Waukesha County	338
Racine, WI PMSA	**183**
Racine County	183
Minneapolis-St. Paul, MN-WI MSA	**2,723**
Anoka County, MN	276
Carver County, MN	59
Chisago County, MN	37
Dakota County, MN	316
Hennepin County, MN	1,053
Isanti County, MN	28
Ramsey County, MN	482
Scott County, MN	70
Sherburne County, MN	53
Washington County, MN	180
Wright County, MN	79
Pierce County, WI	35
St. Croix County, WI	55
Mobile, AL MSA	**518**
Baldwin County	120
Mobile County	397
Modesto, CA MSA	**411**
Stanislaus County	411
Monroe, LA MSA	**147**
Ouachita Parish	147
Montgomery, AL MSA	**315**
Autauga County	39
Elmore County	57
Montgomery County	219
Muncie, IN MSA	**119**
Delaware County	119
Myrtle Beach, SC MSA	**158**
Horry County	158
Naples, FL MSA	**181**
Collier County	181
Nashville, TN MSA	**1,094**
Cheatham County	32
Davidson County	531
Dickson County	39
Robertson County	48
Rutherford County	148
Sumner County	117
Williamson County	102
Wilson County	77

New Orleans, LA MSA	**1,315**
Jefferson Parish	457
Orleans Parish	482
Plaquemines Parish	26
St. Bernard Parish	67
St. Charles Parish	47
St. James Parish	21
St. John the Baptist Parish	42
St. Tammany Parish	173
New York-Northern New Jersey-Long Island, NY-NJ-CT-PA CMSA (pt.) [1]	**18,107**
Bergen-Passaic, NJ PMSA	**1,309**
Bergen County, NJ	845
Passaic County, NJ	463
Dutchess County, NY PMSA	**262**
Dutchess County, NY	262
Jersey City, NJ PMSA	**550**
Hudson County, NJ	550
Middlesex-Somerset-Hunterdon, NJ PMSA	**1,080**
Hunterdon County, NJ	117
Middlesex County, NJ	698
Somerset County, NJ	265
Monmouth-Ocean, NJ PMSA	**1,050**
Monmouth County, NJ	585
Ocean County, NJ	465
Nassau-Suffolk, NY PMSA	**2,659**
Nassau County, NY	1,306
Suffolk County, NY	1,354
New York, NY PMSA	**8,570**
Bronx County, NY	1,188
Kings County, NY	2,244
New York County, NY	1,519
Putnam County, NY	90
Queens County, NY	1,964
Richmond County, NY	398
Rockland County, NY	277
Westchester County, NY	891
Newark, NJ PMSA	**1,936**
Essex County, NJ	759
Morris County, NJ	444
Sussex County, NJ	140
Union County, NJ	496
Warren County, NJ	97
Newburgh, NY-PA PMSA	**360**
Orange County, NY	323
Pike County, PA	37
Trenton, NJ PMSA	**330**
Mercer County, NJ	330
Norfolk-Virginia Beach-Newport News, VA-NC MSA	**1,540**
Gloucester County, VA	33
Isle of Wight County, VA	28
James City County, VA	40
Mathews County, VA	9
York County, VA	54
Chesapeake city, VA	188
Hampton city, VA	139
Newport News city, VA	180
Norfolk city, VA	238
Poquoson city, VA	12
Portsmouth city, VA	103
Suffolk city, VA	57
Virginia Beach city, VA	431
Williamsburg city, VA	13
Currituck County, NC	16
Ocala, FL MSA	**227**
Marion County	227
Odessa-Midland, TX MSA	**239**
Ector County	123
Midland County	116
Oklahoma City, OK MSA	**1,015**
Canadian County	82
Cleveland County	191
Logan County	31
McClain County	25
Oklahoma County	625
Pottawatomie County	61

	Popu-lation, 1995 (1,000)

Omaha, NE-IA MSA......	670
Cass County, NE......	23
Douglas County, NE.....	434
Sarpy County, NE......	112
Washington County, NE...	18
Pottawattamie County, IA..	84
Orlando, FL MSA........	1,391
Lake County...........	180
Orange County.........	750
Osceola County........	131
Seminole County.......	330
Owensboro, KY MSA......	91
Daviess County........	91
Panama City, FL MSA.....	143
Bay County...........	143
Parkersburg-Marietta, WV-OH MSA...........	152
Wood County, WV......	88
Washington County, OH...	64
Pensacola, FL MSA.......	378
Escambia County.......	274
Santa Rosa County.....	104
Peoria-Pekin, IL MSA.....	346
Peoria County.........	183
Tazewell County.......	128
Woodford County.......	35
Philadelphia-Wilmington-Atlantic City, PA-NJ-DE-MD CMSA...............	5,967
Atlantic-Cape May, NJ PMSA	332
Atlantic County, NJ.....	234
Cape May County, NJ....	98
Philadelphia, PA-NJ PMSA.	4,951
Bucks County, PA......	574
Chester County, PA.....	405
Delaware County, PA....	549
Montgomery County, PA..	705
Philadelphia County, PA...	1,499
Burlington County, NJ....	403
Camden County, NJ.....	507
Gloucester County, NJ....	244
Salem County, NJ.......	65
Vineland-Millville-Bridgeton, NJ PMSA....	138
Cumberland County, NJ...	138
Wilmington-Newark, DE-MD PMSA...............	546
New Castle County, DE...	468
Cecil County, MD......	78
Phoenix-Mesa, AZ MSA....	2,564
Maricopa County........	2,432
Pinal County..........	131
Pine Bluff, AR MSA.......	84
Jefferson County.......	84
Pittsburgh, PA MSA......	2,395
Allegheny County.......	1,310
Beaver County........	188
Butler County.........	166
Fayette County........	147
Washington County.....	208
Westmoreland County....	377
Portland-Salem, OR-WA CMSA...............	2,022
Portland-Vancouver, OR-WA PMSA...............	1,710
Clackamas County, OR...	316
Columbia County, OR...	42
Multnomah County, OR...	614
Washington County, OR...	370
Yamhill County, OR......	75
Clark County, WA......	292
Salem, OR PMSA.......	312
Marion County, OR......	255
Polk County, OR........	57

Provo-Orem, UT MSA.....	299
Utah County...........	299
Pueblo, CO MSA.........	130
Pueblo County........	130
Punta Gorda, FL MSA.....	129
Charlotte County.......	129
Raleigh-Durham-Chapel Hill, NC MSA..............	995
Chatham County........	43
Durham County........	195
Franklin County........	41
Johnston County.......	95
Orange County.........	108
Wake County..........	514
Rapid City, SD MSA......	87
Pennington County.....	87
Reading, PA MSA........	350
Berks County..........	350
Redding, CA MSA........	161
Shasta County........	161
Reno, NV MSA.........	291
Washoe County........	291
Richland-Kennewick-Pasco, WA MSA..............	178
Benton County........	133
Franklin County.......	44
Richmond-Petersburg, VA MSA................	927
Charles City County.....	7
Chesterfield County.....	240
Dinwiddie County......	23
Goochland County......	16
Hanover County.......	75
Henrico County........	233
New Kent County......	12
Powhatan County......	19
Prince George County...	28
Colonial Heights city.....	17
Hopewell city.........	23
Petersburg city........	38
Richmond city.........	198
Roanoke, VA MSA........	229
Botetourt County......	27
Roanoke County.......	82
Roanoke city.........	96
Salem city...........	24
Rochester, MN MSA......	113
Olmsted County........	113
Rochester, NY MSA.......	1,089
Genesee County........	61
Livingston County......	66
Monroe County........	723
Ontario County........	99
Orleans County........	45
Wayne County.........	94
Rockford, IL MSA........	351
Boone County.........	36
Ogle County..........	49
Winnebago County.....	265
Rocky Mount, NC MSA....	142
Edgecombe County.....	56
Nash County..........	86
Sacramento-Yolo, CA CMSA	1,605
Sacramento, CA PMSA...	1,457
El Dorado County......	148
Placer County.........	205
Sacramento County.....	1,103
Yolo, CA PMSA.........	148
Yolo County..........	148

Saginaw-Bay City-Midland, MI MSA........	404
Bay County...........	112
Midland County........	80
Saginaw County.......	212
St. Cloud, MN MSA......	159
Benton County........	33
Stearns County.......	126
St. Joseph, MO MSA.....	98
Andrew County........	15
Buchanan County......	82
St. Louis, MO-IL MSA.....	2,548
Franklin County, MO....	88
Jefferson County, MO....	186
Lincoln County, MO.....	33
St. Charles County, MO...	248
St. Louis County, MO....	1,008
Warren County, MO.....	23
St. Louis city, MO......	359
Clinton County, IL......	35
Jersey County, IL.......	21
Madison County, IL......	256
Monroe County, IL......	25
St. Clair County, IL......	265
Salinas, CA MSA.........	349
Monterey County......	349
Salt Lake City-Ogden, UT MSA.................	1,199
Davis County..........	215
Salt Lake County......	808
Weber County........	176
San Angelo, TX MSA......	102
Tom Green County.....	102
San Antonio, TX MSA.....	1,461
Bexar County..........	1,297
Comal County.........	64
Guadalupe County.....	73
Wilson County........	27
San Diego, CA MSA......	2,644
San Diego County......	2,644
San Francisco-Oakland-San Jose, CA CMSA.........	6,540
Oakland, CA PMSA.....	2,195
Alameda County......	1,323
Contra Costa County.....	872
San Francisco, CA PMSA..	1,646
Marin County.........	234
San Francisco County....	731
San Mateo County.....	681
San Jose, CA PMSA.....	1,565
Santa Clara County.....	1,565
Santa Cruz-Watsonville, CA PMSA...............	237
Santa Cruz County.....	237
Santa Rosa, CA PMSA....	415
Sonoma County.......	415
Vallejo-Fairfield-Napa, CA PMSA...............	482
Napa County..........	116
Solano County........	366
San Luis Obispo-Atascadero-Paso Robles, CA MSA....	226
San Luis Obispo County...	226
Santa Barbara-Santa Maria-Lompoc, CA MSA.......	381
Santa Barbara County...	381
Santa Fe, NM MSA.......	135
Los Alamos County.....	19
Santa Fe County.......	116
Sarasota-Bradenton, FL MSA	526
Manatee County.......	230
Sarasota County......	296

	Popu-lation, 1995 (1,000)

Savannah, GA MSA......	279
Bryan County..........	21
Chatham County........	226
Effingham County.......	32
Scranton-Wilkes-Barre-	
Hazleton, PA MSA.......	**636**
Columbia County.......	64
Lackawanna County.....	216
Luzerne County........	326
Wyoming County.......	29
Seattle-Tacoma-Bremerton,	
WA CMSA............	**3,265**
Bremerton, WA PMSA....	**227**
Kitsap County..........	227
Olympia, WA PMSA......	**192**
Thurston County.......	192
Seattle-Bellevue-Everett, WA	
PMSA..............	**2,197**
Island County.........	69
King County...........	1,595
Snohomish County.....	534
Tacoma, WA PMSA......	**649**
Pierce County.........	649
Sharon, PA MSA.........	**122**
Mercer County........	122
Sheboygan, WI MSA......	**108**
Sheboygan County.....	108
Sherman-Denison, TX	
MSA.................	**98**
Grayson County........	98
Shreveport-Bossier City, LA	
MSA................	**380**
Bossier Parish........	91
Caddo Parish..........	247
Webster Parish........	42
Sioux City, IA-NE MSA....	**120**
Woodbury County, IA....	102
Dakota County, NE......	18
Sioux Falls, SD MSA......	**153**
Lincoln County........	18
Minnehaha County......	136
South Bend, IN MSA......	**258**
St. Joseph County.......	258
Spokane, WA MSA.......	**401**
Spokane County.......	401
Springfield, IL MSA.......	**197**
Menard County........	12
Sangamon County......	185
Springfield, MO MSA......	**295**
Christian County.......	43
Greene County........	225
Webster County.......	27
State College, PA MSA....	**132**
Centre County........	132
Steubenville-Weirton, OH-	
WV MSA..............	**140**
Jefferson County, OH....	78
Brooke County, WV.....	27
Hancock County, WV.....	35
Stockton-Lodi, CA MSA....	**524**
San Joaquin County.....	524
Sumter, SC MSA.........	**107**
Sumter County........	107

Syracuse, NY MSA.......	750
Cayuga County.........	83
Madison County.......	71
Onondaga County.......	470
Oswego County.......	126
Tallahassee, FL MSA.....	**257**
Gadsden County........	43
Leon County..........	214
Tampa-St. Petersburg-	
Clearwater, FL MSA......	**2,180**
Hernando County......	120
Hillsborough County.....	885
Pasco County..........	305
Pinellas County.......	871
Terre Haute, IN MSA......	**150**
Clay County..........	26
Vermillion County......	17
Vigo County..........	107
Texarkana, TX-Texarkana,	
AR MSA.............	**123**
Bowie County, TX.......	84
Miller County, AR.......	39
Toledo, OH MSA.........	**613**
Fulton County..........	41
Lucas County..........	455
Wood County.........	117
Topeka, KS MSA.........	**165**
Shawnee County.......	165
Tucson, AZ MSA.........	**752**
Pima County..........	752
Tulsa, OK MSA..........	**747**
Creek County..........	64
Osage County.........	43
Rogers County........	62
Tulsa County.........	525
Wagoner County........	52
Tuscaloosa, AL MSA......	**159**
Tuscaloosa County.....	159
Tyler, TX MSA...........	**162**
Smith County.........	162
Utica-Rome, NY MSA.....	**309**
Herkimer County........	66
Oneida County........	242
Victoria, TX MSA.........	**80**
Victoria County.......	80
Visalia-Tulare-Porterville,	
CA MSA..............	**347**
Tulare County.........	347
Waco, TX MSA..........	**200**
McLennan County......	200
Washington-Baltimore, DC-MD-	
VA-WV CMSA..........	**7,107**
Baltimore, MD PMSA.....	**2,470**
Anne Arundel County, MD.	462
Baltimore County, MD...	715
Carroll County, MD......	140
Harford County, MD.....	205
Howard County, MD.....	219
Queen Anne's County, MD.	37
Baltimore city, MD.......	691
Hagerstown, MD PMSA...	**127**
Washington County, MD..	127

Washington, DC-MD-VA-WV	
PMSA...............	**4,510**
District of Columbia, DC...	554
Calvert County, MD......	65
Charles County, MD.....	112
Frederick County, MD....	175
Montgomery County, MD..	810
Prince George's County, MD	767
Arlington County, VA.....	173
Clarke County, VA......	12
Culpeper County, VA.....	31
Fairfax County, VA......	887
Fauquier County, VA.....	51
King George County, VA...	16
Loudoun County, VA.....	116
Prince William County, VA..	245
Spotsylvania County, VA...	72
Stafford County, VA......	80
Warren County, VA......	29
Alexandria city, VA......	116
Fairfax city, VA........	21
Falls Church city, VA.....	10
Fredericksburg city, VA...	22
Manassas city, VA......	33
Manassas Park city, VA...	7
Berkeley County, WV.....	67
Jefferson County, WV....	39
Waterloo-Cedar Falls, IA	
MSA...............	**123**
Black Hawk County......	123
Wausau, WI MSA........	**121**
Marathon County.......	121
West Palm Beach-Boca	
Raton, FL MSA........	**972**
Palm Beach County.....	972
Wheeling, WV-OH MSA....	**157**
Marshall County, WV.....	37
Ohio County, WV......	50
Belmont County, OH.....	70
Wichita, KS MSA.........	**508**
Butler County.........	58
Harvey County........	31
Sedgwick County......	419
Wichita Falls, TX MSA.....	**133**
Archer County........	8
Wichita County.......	125
Williamsport, PA MSA.....	**120**
Lycoming County.......	120
Wilmington, NC MSA.....	**201**
Brunswick County.......	61
New Hanover County....	140
Yakima, WA MSA........	**212**
Yakima County.......	212
York, PA MSA...........	**363**
York County.........	363
Youngstown-Warren, OH	
MSA...............	**603**
Columbiana County.....	112
Mahoning County......	262
Trumbull County........	228
Yuba City, CA MSA.......	**136**
Sutter County.........	75
Yuba County........	61
Yuma, AZ MSA.........	**133**
Yuma County.........	133

[1] Five PMSA's of the New York-Northern New Jersey-Long Island, NY-NJ-CTPA CMSA are in Connecticut and therefore do not appear in this table; also, the CMSA's population shown here reflects the absence of those PMSA's.

Source: U.S. Bureau of the Census, Internet site http://www.census.gov/population/estimates/metro-city/metal95.txt (accessed August 1, 1996).

Limitations of the Data

Introduction.—The data presented in this *Statistical Abstract* came from many sources. The sources include not only Federal statistical bureaus and other organizations that collect and issue statistics as their principal activity, but also governmental administrative and regulatory agencies, private research bodies, trade associations, insurance companies, health associations, and private organizations such as the National Education Association and philanthropic foundations. Consequently, the data vary considerably as to reference periods, definitions of terms and, for ongoing series, the number and frequency of time periods for which data are available.

The statistics presented were obtained and tabulated by various means. Some statistics are based on complete enumerations or censuses while others are based on samples. Some information is extracted from records kept for administrative or regulatory purposes (school enrollment, hospital records, securities registration, financial accounts, social security records, income tax returns, etc.), while other information is obtained explicitly for statistical purposes through interviews or by mail. The estimation procedures used vary from highly sophisticated scientific techniques, to crude "informed guesses."

Each set of data relates to a group of individuals or units of interest referred to as the *target universe* or *target population,* or simply as the *universe* or *population.* Prior to data collection the target universe should be clearly defined. For example, if data are to be collected for the universe of households in the United States, it is necessary to define a "household." The target universe may not be completely tractable. Cost and other considerations may restrict data collection to a *survey universe* based on some available list, such list may be inaccurate and out of date. This list is called a *survey frame* or *sampling frame.*

The data in many tables are based on data obtained for all population units, *a census,* or on data obtained for only a portion, or *sample,* of the population units. When the data presented are based on a sample, the sample is usually a scientifically selected *probability sample.* This is a sample selected from a list or sampling frame in such a way that every possible sample has a known chance of selection and usually each unit selected can be assigned a number, greater than zero and less than or equal to one, representing its likelihood or probability of selection.

For large-scale sample surveys, the probability sample of units is often selected as a multistage sample. The first stage of a multistage sample is the selection of a probability sample of large groups of population members, referred to as primary sampling units (PSU's). For example, in a national multistage household sample, PSU's are often counties or groups of counties. The second stage of a multistage sample is the selection, within each PSU selected at the first stage, of smaller groups of population units, referred to as secondary sampling units. In subsequent stages of selection, smaller and smaller nested groups are chosen until the ultimate sample of population units is obtained. To qualify a multistage sample as a probability sample, all stages of sampling must be carried out using probability sampling methods.

Prior to selection at each stage of a multistage (or a single stage) sample, a list of the sampling units or sampling frame for that stage must be obtained. For example, for the first stage of selection of a national household sample, a list of the counties and county groups that form the PSU's must be obtained. For the final stage of selection, lists of households, and sometimes persons within the households, have to be compiled in the field. For surveys of economic entities and for the economic census, the Census Bureau generally uses a frame constructed from the Bureau's Standard Statistical Establishment List (SSEL). The SSEL contains all establishments with payroll in the United States including small single establishment firms as well as large multi-establishment firms.

Wherever the quantities in a table refer to an entire universe, but are constructed from data collected in a sample survey, the table quantities are referred to as *sample estimates*. In constructing a sample estimate, an attempt is made to come as close as is feasible to the corresponding universe quantity that would be obtained from a complete census of the universe. Estimates based on a sample will, however, generally differ from the hypothetical census figures. Two classifications of errors are associated with estimates based on sample surveys: (1) *sampling error*—the error arising from the use of a sample, rather than a census, to estimate population quantities and (2) *nonsampling error*—those errors arising from nonsampling sources. As discussed below, the magnitude of the sampling error for an estimate can usually be estimated from the sample data. However, the magnitude of the nonsampling error for an estimate can rarely be estimated. Consequently, actual error in an estimate exceeds the error that can be estimated.

The particular sample used in a survey is only one of a large number of possible samples of the same size which could have been selected using the same sampling procedure. Estimates derived from the different samples would, in general, differ from each other. The *standard error* (SE) is a measure of the variation among the estimates derived from all possible samples. The standard error is the most commonly used measure of the sampling error of an estimate. Valid estimates of the standard errors of survey estimates can usually be calculated from the data collected in a probability sample. For convenience, the standard error is sometimes expressed as a percent of the estimate and is called the relative standard error or *coefficient of variation* (CV). For example, an estimate of 200 units with an estimated standard error of 10 units has an estimated CV of 5 percent.

A sample estimate and an estimate of its standard error or CV can be used to construct interval estimates that have a prescribed confidence that the interval includes the average of the estimates derived from all possible samples with a known probability. To illustrate, if all possible samples were selected under essentially the same general conditions, and

using the same sample design, and if an estimate and its estimated standard error were calculated from each sample, then: 1) Approximately 68 percent of the intervals from one standard error below the estimate to one standard error above the estimate would include the average estimate derived from all possible samples; 2) approximately 90 percent of the intervals from 1.6 standard errors below the estimate to 1.6 standard errors above the estimate would include the average estimate derived from all possible samples; and 3) approximately 95 percent of the intervals from two standard errors below the estimate to two standard errors above the estimate would include the average estimate derived from all possible samples.

Thus, for a particular sample, one can say with the appropriate level of confidence (e.g., 90 or 95 percent) that the average of all possible samples is included in the constructed interval. Example of a confidence interval: An estimate is 200 units with a standard error of 10 units. An approximately 90 percent confidence interval (plus or minus 1.6 standard errors) is from 184 to 216.

All surveys and censuses are subject to nonsampling errors. Nonsampling errors are of two kinds—*random* and *nonrandom*. Random nonsampling errors arise because of the varying interpretation of questions (by respondents or interviewers) and varying actions of coders, keyers, and other processors. Some randomness is also introduced when respondents must estimate values. These same errors usually have a nonrandom component. Nonrandom nonsampling errors result from total nonresponse (no usable data obtained for a sampled unit), partial or item nonresponse (only a portion of a response may be usable), inability or unwillingness on the part of respondents to provide correct information, difficulty interpreting questions, mistakes in recording or keying data, errors of collection or processing, and coverage problems (overcoverage and undercoverage of the target universe). Random nonresponse errors usually, but not always, result in an understatement of sampling errors and thus an overstatement of the precision of survey estimates. Estimating the magnitude of nonsampling errors would require special experiments or access to independent data and, consequently, the magnitudes are seldom available.

Nearly all types of nonsampling errors that affect surveys also occur in complete censuses. Since surveys can be conducted on a smaller scale than censuses, non-sampling errors can presumably be controlled more tightly. Relatively more funds and effort can perhaps be expended toward eliciting responses, detecting and correcting response error, and reducing processing errors. As a result, survey results can sometimes be more accurate than census results.

To compensate for suspected nonrandom errors, adjustments of the sample estimates are often made. For example, adjustments are frequently made for nonresponse, both total and partial. Adjustments made for either type of non-response are often referred to as *imputations*. Imputation for total nonresponse is usually made by substituting for the questionnaire responses of the nonrespondents the "average" questionnaire responses of the respondents. These imputations usually are made separately within various groups of sample members, formed by attempting to place respondents and non-respondents together that have "similar" design or ancillary characteristics. Imputation for item nonresponse is usually made by substituting for a missing item the response to that item of a respondent having characteristics that are "similar" to those of the nonrespondent.

For an estimate calculated from a sample survey, the *total error* in the estimate is composed of the sampling error, which can usually be estimated from the sample, and the nonsampling error, which usually cannot be estimated from the sample. The total error present in a population quantity obtained from a complete census is composed of only nonsampling errors. Ideally, estimates of the total error associated with data given in the *Statistical Abstract* tables should be given. However, due to the unavailability of estimates of nonsampling errors, only estimates of the levels of sampling errors, in terms of estimated standard errors or coefficients of variation, are

available. To obtain estimates of the estimated standard errors from the sample of interest, obtain a copy of the referenced report which appears at the end of each table.

Principal data bases.—Beginning below are brief descriptions of 37 of the sample surveys and censuses that provide a substantial portion of the data contained in this *Abstract.*

SECTION 1. POPULATION

Source and Title: Bureau of the Census, *Census of Population*

Tables: See tables citing *Census of Population* in section 1 and also in sections 2, 4, 6, 8, 13, 14, 21, 25, and 29.

Universe, Frequency, and Types of Data: Complete count of U.S. population conducted every 10 years since 1790. Data obtained on number and characteristics of inhabitants.

Type of Data Collection Operation: In 1970, 1980, and 1990 complete census for some items—age, sex, race, marital status, and relationship to household head. In 1970, other items collected from a 5% and a 15% probability (systematic) sample of the population. In 1980, approximately 19% of the housing units were included in the sample; in 1990, approximately 17%.

Data Collection and Imputation Procedures: In 1970, extensive use of mail questionnaires in urban areas; personal interviews in most rural areas. In 1980 and 1990, mail questionnaires were used in even more areas than in 1970, with personal interviews in the remainder. Extensive telephone and personal followup for nonrespondents was done in the censuses. Imputations were made for missing characteristics.

Estimates of Sampling Error: Sampling errors for data are estimated for all items collected by sample and vary by characteristic and geographic area. The CV's for national and State estimates are generally very small.

Other (nonsampling) Errors: Since 1950, evaluation programs have been conducted to provide information on the magnitude of some sources of nonsampling errors such as response bias and undercoverage in each census. Results from the evaluation program for the 1990 census indicate that the net under coverage amounted to about 1.5 to 2 % of the total resident population.

Sources of Additional Material: U.S. Bureau of the Census, *The Coverage of Population in the 1980 Census,* PHC80-E4; *Content Reinterview Study: Accuracy of*

Data for Selected Population and Housing Characteristics as Measured by Reinterview, PHC80-E2; 1980 Census of Population, vol. 1., (PC80-1), appendixes B, C, and D.

Source and Title: U.S. Bureau of the Census, Current Population Survey (CPS)

Tables: See tables citing Current Population Reports primarily in section 1, but also in sections 2, 3, 4, 8, 12, 13, 14, 18, 23, and 29. Many Bureau of Labor Statistics' (BLS) tables in section 13 are CPS based.

Universe, Frequency, and Types of Data: Nationwide monthly sample survey of civilian noninstitutional population, 15 years old or over, to obtain data on employment, unemployment, and a number of other characteristics.

Type of Data Collection Operation: Multistage probability sample of about 60,000 households in 729 PSU's in 1993. Oversampling in some States and the largest MSA's to improve reliability for those areas of employment data on annual average basis. A continual sample rotation system is used. Households are in sample 4 months, out for 8 months, and in for 4 more. Month-to-month overlap is 75%; year-to-year overlap is 50%.

Data Collection and Imputation Procedures: For first and fifth months that a household is in sample, personal interviews; other months, approximately, 85% of the data collected by phone. Imputation is done for both item and total nonresponse. Adjustment for total nonresponse is done by a predefined cluster of units, by MSA size and residence; for item nonresponse imputation varies by subject matter.

Estimates of Sampling Error: Estimated CV's on national annual averages for labor force, total employment, and nonagricultural employment, 0.2%; for total unemployment and agricultural employment, 1.0% to 2.5%. The estimated CV's for family income and poverty rate for all persons in 1986 are 0.5% and 1.5%, respectively. CV's for subnational areas, such as States, would be larger and would vary by area.

Other (nonsampling) Errors: Estimates of response bias on unemployment are not available, but estimates of unemployment are usually 5% to 9% lower than estimates from reinterviews. Four to 5.0% of sample households unavailable for interviews.

Sources of Additional Material: U.S. Bureau of the Census and Bureau of Labor Statistics, Concepts and Methods Used in Labor Force Statistics from Current Population Survey (Census series P-23, No. 62; BLS Report No. 463) and Bureau of the Census, Current Population Survey (Tech.

Paper 40) and Bureau of Labor Statistics, Employment and Earnings, monthly, Explanatory Notes and Estimates of Error, tables 1-A through 1-H and BLS Handbook of Methods, Chapter 1 (Bulletin 2414.)

SECTION 2. VITAL STATISTICS

Source and Title: U.S. National Center for Health Statistics (NCHS), Vital Registration System

Tables: See tables citing Vital Statistics of the United States; 316 in section 5; and 1310 in section 29.

Universe, Frequency, and Types of Data: Annual data on births and deaths in the United States.

Type of Data Collection Operation: Mortality data based on complete file of death records, except 1972, based on 50% sample. Natality statistics 1951-71, based on 50% sample of birth certificates, except a 20% to 50% in 1967, received by NCHS. Beginning 1972, data from some States received through Vital Statistics Cooperative Program (VSCP) and complete file used; data from other States based on 50% sample. Beginning 1986, all reporting areas participated in the VSCP.

Data Collection and Imputation Procedures: Reports based on records from registration offices of all States, District of Columbia, New York City, Puerto Rico, Virgin Islands, and Guam.

Estimates of Sampling Error: For recent years, CV's for births are small due to large portion of total file in sample (except for very small estimated totals).

Other (nonsampling) Errors: Data on births and deaths believed to be at least 99% complete.

Sources of Additional Material: U.S. National Center for Health Statistics, Vital Statistics of the United States, vol. I and vol. II, annual, and Monthly Vital Statistics Report.

(See section 1 above for information pertaining to tables 103-108.)

SECTION 3. HEALTH AND NUTRITION

Source and Title: U.S. National Center for Health Statistics, National Health Interview Survey (NHIS)

Tables: 182, 183, 208, 211, 212, 214, 218, 219, 222,and 224.

Universe, Frequency, and Types of Data: Continuous data collection covering the civilian noninstitutional population to obtain information on personal and demographic characteristics, illnesses, injuries, impairments, and other health topics.

Type of Data Collection Operation: Multistage probability sample of 42,000 households (in 376 PSU's) selected in groups of about four adjacent households.

Data Collection and Imputation Procedures: Personal household interviews with extensive followup of nonrespondents. Data are adjusted for nonresponse by imputation procedure based on "average" characteristics of persons in interviewed households in the same geographic area.

Estimates of Sampling Error: Estimated CV's: For physician visits by males, 1.5%; for workdays lost by males, 3.5%; for persons injured at home, 4.7%.

Other (nonsampling) Errors: Response rate was 95.7% in 1985 for the NHIS.

Sources of Additional Material: U.S. National Center for Health Statistics, "Current Estimates from the National Health Interview Survey, U.S., 1983," Vital and Health Statistics, series 10.

(See section 13 for information pertaining to table 177, section 15 for table 171, and section 27 for table 178.)

SECTION 4. EDUCATION

Source and Title: U.S. Department of Education, National Center for Education Statistics, *Higher Education General Information Survey (HEGIS), Fall Enrollment in Institutions of Higher Education;* beginning 1986, *Integrated Postsecondary Education Data Survey (IPEDS), Fall Enrollment*

Tables: 280, 281, 284 and 285.

Universe, Frequency, and Types of Data: Annual survey of all institutions and branches listed in the *Directory* to obtain data on total enrollment by sex, level of enrollment, type of program, racial/ethnic characteristics (in alternate years) and attendance status of student, and on first-time students.

Type of Data Collection Operation: Complete census.

Data Collection and Imputation Procedures: Survey package is usually mailed in the spring with surveys due at varying dates in the summer and fall; mail and phone followup procedures for nonrespondents. Missing data are imputed by using data of similar institutions.

Estimates of Sampling Error: Not applicable.

Other (nonsampling) Errors: Approximately 87% response rate.

Sources of Additional Material: U.S. Department of Education, National Center for Education Statistics, *Fall Enrollment in Higher Education,* annual.

Source and Title: U.S. Department of Education, National Center for Education Statistics, *Higher Education General Information Survey (HEGIS), Financial Statistics of Institutions of Higher Education;* beginning 1986, *Integrated Postsecondary Education Data Survey (IPEDS), Financial Statistics of Institutions of Higher Education*

Tables: 232, 235, 284, and 287.

Universe, Frequency, and Types of Data: Annual survey of all institutions and branches listed in the *Education Directory, Colleges and Universities* to obtain data on financial status and operations, including current funds revenues, current funds expenditures, and physical plant assets.

Type of Data Collection Operation: Complete census.

Data Collection and Imputation Procedures: Survey package is usually mailed in the spring with surveys due at varying dates in the summer and fall; mail and phone followup procedures for nonrespondents. Missing data are imputed by using data of similar institutions.

Estimates of Sampling Error: Not applicable.

Other (nonsampling) Errors: For 1990, a 87% response rate. Imputed expenditures amounted to about 2.8% of total expenditures.

Sources of Additional Material: U.S. Department of Education, National Center for Education Statistics, *Financial Statistics of Institutions of Higher Education,* annual.

Source and Title: U.S. Department of Education, National Center for Education Statistics, *Higher Education General Information Survey (HEGIS), Degrees and Other Formal Awards Conferred.* Beginning 1986, *Integrated Postsecondary Education Data Survey (IPEDS), Degrees and Other Formal Awards Conferred.*

Tables: 300-305.

Universe, Frequency, and Types of Data: Annual survey of all institutions and branches listed in the *Education Directory, Colleges and Universities* to obtain data on earned degrees and other formal awards, conferred by field of study, level of degree, sex, and by racial/ethnic characteristics (in alternate years).

Type of Data Collection Operation: Complete census.

Data Collection and Imputation Procedures: Survey package is usually mailed in the spring with surveys due at varying dates in the summer and fall; mail and phone followup procedures for nonrespondents. Missing data are imputed by using data of similar institutions.

Estimates of Sampling Error: Not applicable.

Other (nonsampling) Errors: For 1989-90, approximately 92.3% response rate.

Sources of Additional Material: U.S. Department of Education, National Center for Education Statistics, *Earned Degrees Conferred,* annual.

(See sections 1 and 9 for information pertaining to the Bureau of the Census and section 3 above for the National Center for Health Statistics.)

SECTION 5. LAW ENFORCEMENT, COURTS, AND PRISONS

Source and Title: U.S. Federal Bureau of Investigation, *Uniform Crime Reporting (UCR) Program*

Tables: 310-315, 317, 318, 323-325, and 327.

Universe, Frequency, and Types of Data: Monthly reports on the number of criminal offenses that become known to law enforcement agencies. Data are collected on crimes cleared by arrest, by age, sex, and race of offender, and on assaults on law enforcement officers.

Type of Data Collection Operation: Crime statistics are based on reports of crime data submitted either directly to the FBI by contributing law enforcement agencies or through cooperating State UCR programs.

Data Collection and Imputation Procedures: States with UCR programs collect data directly from individual law enforcement agencies and forward reports, prepared in accordance with UCR standards, to FBI. Accuracy and consistency edits are performed by FBI.

Estimates of Sampling Error: Not applicable.

Other (nonsampling) Errors: Coverage of 96% of the population (97.4% in MSA's, 90.6% in "other cities," and 87.8% in rural areas) by UCR program, though varying number of agencies report. Some error may be present through incorrect reporting.

Sources of Additional Material: U.S. Federal Bureau of Investigation, *Crime in the United States.*

Source and Title: U.S. Bureau of Justice Statistics (BJS), *National Crime Victimization Survey*

Tables: 319-322.

Universe, Frequency, and Types of Data: Monthly survey of individuals and households in the United States to obtain data on criminal victimization of those units for compilation of annual estimates.

Type of Data Collection Operation: National probability sample survey of about 50,000 interviewed households in 376

PSU's selected from a list of addresses from the 1980 census, supplemented by new construction permits and an area sample where permits are not required.

Data Collection and Imputation Procedures: Interviews are conducted every 6 months for 3 years for each household in the sample; 8,000 households are interviewed monthly. Personal interviews are used in the first and fifth interviews; the intervening interviews are conducted by telephone whenever possible.

Estimates of Sampling Error: CV's in 1994: 2.7% for crimes of violence; 8.5% for estimate of rape/sexual assault counts; 5.5% for robbery counts; 2.8% for assault counts; 8.0% for personal theft counts; 1.9% for property crimes; 3.0% for burglary counts; 2.0% for theft; and 4.4% for motor vehicle theft counts.

Other (nonsampling) Errors: Respondent recall errors which may include reporting incidents for other than the reference period; interviewer coding and processing errors; and possible mistaken reporting or classifying of events. Adjustment is made for a household noninterview rate of about 4% and for a within-household noninterview rate of 7%.

Sources of Additional Material: U.S. Bureau of Justice Statistics, *Criminal Victimization in the United States,* annual.

(See section 2 for details on table 316.)

SECTION 7. PARKS AND RECREATION

(See section 27 for details on table 403 and 425.)

SECTION 8. ELECTIONS

(See section 1 above for information pertaining to tables 456 and 457 and section 9 for information pertaining to tables 450.)

SECTION 9. STATE AND LOCAL GOVERNMENT FINANCES AND EMPLOYMENT

Source and Title: U.S. Bureau of the Census, *Census of Governments*

Tables: See tables in section 9 citing *Census of Governments* and table 450 in section 8.

Universe, Frequency, and Types of Data: Survey of all governmental units in the United States conducted every 5 years to obtain data on government revenue, expenditures, debt, assets, employment and employee retirement systems, property values, public school systems, and number, size, and structure of governments.

Type of Data Collection Operation: Complete census. List of units derived through classification of government units recently authorized in each State and identification, counting, and classification of existing local governments and public school systems.

Data Collection and Imputation Procedures: Data collected through field and office compilation of financial data from official records and reports for States and large local governments; mail canvass of selected data items, like State tax revenue and employee retirement systems; and collection of local government statistics through central collection arrangements with State governments.

Estimates of Sampling Error: Not applicable.

Other (nonsampling) Errors: Some nonsampling errors may arise due to possible inaccuracies in classification, response, and processing.

Sources of Additional Material: U.S. Bureau of the Census, *Census of Governments, 1987,* various reports, and *State Government Finances in 1990,* GF 90, No. 3.

Source and Title: U.S. Bureau of the Census, *Annual Surveys of State and Local Government*

Tables: See tables citing *Public Employment* and *Governmental Finances* in section 9; table 259 in section 4; and table 586 in section 12.

Universe, Frequency, and Types of Data: Sample survey conducted annually to obtain data on revenue, expenditure, debt, and employment of State and local governments. Universe is all governmental units in the United States (about 83,000).

Type of Data Collection Operation: Sample of about 22,000 units includes all State governments, county governments with 50,000+ population, municipalities and townships with 25,000+ population, all school districts with 10,000+ enrollment in October 1986, and other governments meeting certain criteria; probability sample for remaining units.

Data Collection and Imputation Procedures: Field and office compilation of data from official records and reports for States and large local governments; central collection of local governmental financial data through cooperative agreements with a number of State governments; mail canvass of other units with mail and telephone followups of nonrespondents. Data for nonresponses are imputed from previous year data or obtained from secondary sources, if available.

Estimates of Sampling Error: CV's for estimates of major employment and financial items are generally less than 2% for most States and less than 1.2% for the majority of States.

Other (nonsampling) Errors: Nonresponse rate is less than 15% for number of units. Other possible errors may result from undetected inaccuracies in classification, response, and processing.

Sources of Additional Material: U.S. Bureau of the Census, *Public Employment in 1990,* GE 90, No. 1, *Governmental Finances in 1989-90,* GF 90, No. 5, and *Census of Governments, 1987,* various reports.

SECTION 10. FEDERAL GOVERNMENT

Source and Title: U.S. Internal Revenue Service, *Statistics of Income, Individual Income Tax Returns*

Tables: 524-528.

Universe, Frequency, and Types of Data: Annual study of unaudited individual income tax returns, forms 1040, 1040A, and 1040EZ, filed by U.S. citizens and residents. Data provided on various financial characteristics by size of adjusted gross income, marital status, and by taxable and nontaxable returns. Data by State, based on 100% file, also include returns from 1040NR, filed by nonresident aliens plus certain self-employment tax returns.

Type of Data Collection Operation: Annual stratified probability sample of approximately 125,000 returns broken into sample strata based on the larger of total income or total loss amounts as well as the size of business plus farm receipts. Sampling rates for sample strata varied from .025% to 100%.

Data Collection and Imputation Procedures: Computer selection of sample of tax return records. Data adjusted during editing for incorrect, missing, or inconsistent entries to ensure consistency with other entries on return.

Estimates of Sampling Error: Estimated CV's for tax year 1987: Adjusted gross income less deficit .13%; salaries and wages .20%; and tax-exempt interest received 4.51%. (State data not subject to sampling error.)

Other (nonsampling) Errors: Processing errors and errors arising from the use of tolerance checks for the data.

Sources of Additional Material: U.S. Internal Revenue Service, *Statistics of Income, Individual Income Tax Returns,* annual.

SECTION 12. SOCIAL INSURANCE AND HUMAN SERVICES

Source and Title: U.S. Social Security Administration, *Benefit Data*

Tables: 582 and 583.

Universe, Frequency, and Types of Data: All persons receiving monthly benefits under Title II of Social Security Act. Data on number and amount of benefits paid by type and State.

Type of Data Collection Operation: Data based on administrative records. Data based on 100% files, as well as 10% and 1% sample files.

Data Collection and Imputation Procedures: Records used consist of actions pursuant to applications for benefits, updated by subsequent post-entitlement actions.

Estimates of Sampling Error: Varies by size of estimate and sample file size.

Other (nonsampling) Errors: Processing errors, which are believed to be small.

Sources of Additional Material: U.S. Social Security Administration, *Annual Statistical Supplement to the Social Security Bulletin.*

Source and Title: U.S. Social Security Administration, *Supplemental Security Income (SSI) Program*

Tables: 597-600.

Universe, Frequency, and Types of Data: All eligible aged, blind, or disabled persons receiving SSI benefit payments under SSI program. Data include number of persons receiving federally administered SSI, amounts paid, and State administered supplementation.

Type of Data Collection Operation: Data based on administrative records.

Data Collection and Imputation Procedures: Data adjusted to reflect returned checks and overpayment refunds. For federally administered payments, actual adjusted amounts are used.

Estimates of Sampling Error: Not applicable.

Other (nonsampling) Errors: Processing errors, which are believed to be small.

Sources of Additional Material: U.S. Social Security Administration, *Annual Statistical Supplement to the Social Security Bulletin.*

(See section 1 above for information pertaining to the Current Population Survey, section 3 for information pertaining to the National Center for Health Statistics, and section 9 for information pertaining to Annual Surveys of State and Local Government.)

SECTION 13. LABOR FORCE, EMPLOYMENT, AND EARNINGS

Source and Title: U.S. Bureau of Labor Statistics (BLS), *Current Employment Statistics (CES)* Program

Tables: 652-654, 659; in section 3, table 177; in section 21, table 985; and in section 22, table 1052.

Universe, Frequency, and Types of Data: Monthly survey covering about 6 million nonagricultural establishments to obtain data on employment, hours, and earnings, by industry.

Type of Data Collection Operation: Sample survey of over 390,000 establishments in March 1993.

Data Collection and Imputation Procedures: Cooperating State agencies mail questionnaires to sample establishments to develop State and local estimates; information is forwarded to BLS where national estimates are prepared.

Estimates of Sampling Error: Estimated CV's for employment, 0.1%, for average weekly hours paid, 0.1% and for average hourly earnings, 0.2%.

Other (nonsampling) Errors: Estimates of employment adjusted annually to reflect complete universe. Average adjustment is 0.2%.

Sources of Additional Material: U.S. Bureau of Labor Statistics, *Employment and Earnings,* monthly, Explanatory Notes and Estimates of Error, tables 2-A through 2-G.

(See section 1 above for information pertaining to the Current Population Survey.)

SECTION 14. INCOME, EXPENDITURES, AND WEALTH

Source and Title: Board of Governors of the Federal Reserve System, *Survey of Consumer Finances*

Tables: 741 and 742, and in section 16, 772-774, and 792.

Universe, Frequency, and Types of Data: Periodic sample survey of families. In this survey a given household is divided into a primary economic unit and other economic units. The primary economic unity, which may be a single individual, is generally chosen as the unit that contains the person who either holds the title to the home or is the first person listed on the lease. The primary unit is used as the reference family. The survey collects detailed data on the composition of family balance sheets, the terms of loans, and relationships with financial institutions. It also gathered information on the employment history and pension rights of the survey respondent and the spouse or partner of the respondent.

Type of Data Collection Operation: The survey employs a two-part strategy for sampling families. Some families were selected by standard multistage area-probability sampling methods from the forty-eight contiguous states. The remaining families in the survey were selected using tax data under the strict rules governing confidentiality and the rights of potential respondents to refuse participation.

Data Collection and Imputation Procedures: The Survey Research Center at the University of Michigan collected the 1989 survey data between August 1989 and March 1990. Adjustments for nonresponse errors are made through systematic imputation of unanswered questions and through weighting adjustments based on data used in the sample design for families that refused participation.

Estimates of Sampling Error: Because of the complex design of the survey, the estimation of potential sampling errors is not straightforward.

Other (nonsampling) Errors: The achieved sample of 3,143 families represents a response rate of about 69 % in the area-probability sample and a rate of about 34% in the tax-data sample. Proper training of interviewers and careful design of questionnaires were used to control inaccurate survey responses.

Sources of Additional Material: Board of Governors of the Federal Reserve System, "Changes in Family Finances from 1983 to 1989: Evidence from the Survey of Consumer Finances", *Federal Reserve Bulletin,* January 1992.

(See section 1 above for information pertaining to the Bureau of the Census.)

SECTION 15. PRICES

Source and Title: U.S. Bureau of Labor Statistics (BLS), *Consumer Price Index (CPI)*
Tables: 744-748, 761, 762, and in section 3, table 171.
Universe, Frequency, and Types of Data: Monthly survey of price changes of all types of consumer goods and services purchased by urban wage earners and clerical workers prior to 1978, and urban consumers thereafter. Both indexes continue to be published.
Type of Data Collection Operation: Prior to 1978, sample of various consumer items in 56 urban areas; thereafter, in 85 PSU's, except from January 1987 through March 1988, when 91 areas were sampled.
Data Collection and Imputation Procedures: Prices of consumer items are obtained from about 57,000 housing units, and 19,000 other reporters in 85 areas.

Prices of food, fuel, and a few other items are obtained monthly; prices of most other commodities and services are collected every month in the five largest geographic areas and every other month in others.
Estimates of Sampling Error: Estimates of standard errors are not available at present.
Other (nonsampling) Errors: Errors result from inaccurate reporting, difficulties in defining concepts and their operational implementation, and introduction of product quality changes and new products.
Sources of Additional Material: U.S. Bureau of Labor Statistics, *The Consumer Price Index:* 1987 Revision, Report 736, and *BLS Handbook of Methods,* Chapter19, Bulletin 2414.

Source and Title: U.S. Bureau of Labor Statistics, *Producer Price Index (PPI)*
Tables: 744, 751-753, and in section 21, table 1035; in section 24, table 1129; and in section 25, table 1170.
Universe, Frequency, and Types of Data: Monthly survey of producing companies to determine price changes of all commodities produced in the United States for sale in commercial transactions. Data on agriculture, forestry, fishing, manufacturing, mining, gas, electricity, public utilities, and a few services.
Type of Data Collection Operation: Probability sample of approximately 3,100 commodities and about 75,000 quotations per month.
Data Collection and Imputation Procedures: Data are collected by mail. If transaction prices are not supplied, list prices are used. Some prices are obtained from trade publications, organized exchanges, and government agencies. To calculate index, price changes are multiplied by their relative weights based on total net selling value of all commodities in 1982.
Estimates of Sampling Error: Not applicable.
Other (nonsampling) Errors: Not available at present.
Sources of Additional Material: U.S. Bureau of Labor Statistics, *BLS Handbook of Methods,* Chapter 16, Bulletin 2414.

SECTION 16. BANKING

(See section 14 for information pertaining to tables 772-774 and 792, and section 17 for information pertaining to table 767.)

SECTION 17. BUSINESS ENTERPRISE

Source and Title: U.S. Bureau of the Census, *County Business Patterns*
Tables: 838-840, and in section 16, table 767; in section 27 tables 1254 and 1280; and in section 29 table 1319.

Universe, Frequency, and Types of Data:
Annual tabulation of basic data items
extracted from the Standard Statistical
Establishment List, a file of all known single
and multiestablishment companies maintained and updated by the Bureau of the
Census. Data include number of establishments, number of employees, first-quarter
and annual payrolls, and number of establishments by employment size class. Data
are excluded for self-employed persons,
domestic service workers, railroad employees, agricultural production workers, and
most government employees.

Type of Data Collection Operation: The
annual Company Organization Survey provides individual establishment data for multiestablishment companies. Data for single
establishment companies are obtained from
various Census Bureau programs, such as
the Annual Survey of Manufactures and
Current Business Surveys, as well as from
administrative records of the Internal Revenue Service and the Social Security
Administration.

Estimates of Sampling Error: Not Applicable.

Other (nonsampling) Error: Response rates
of greater than 90% for the 1993 Company
Organization Survey.

Sources of Additional Materials: U.S.
Bureau of the Census, *General Explanation
of County Business Patterns.*

Source and Title: U.S. Internal Revenue
Service, *Statistics of Income, Sole Propri-
etorship Returns* and *Statistics of Income
Bulletin*

Tables: 827-830.

Universe, Frequency, and Types of Data:
Annual study of unaudited income tax
returns of nonfarm sole proprietorships,
form 1040 with business schedules. Data
provided on various financial characteristics
by industry.

Type of Data Collection Operation:
Stratified probability sample of approximately 31,000 sole proprietorships for tax
year 1990. The sample is classified based
on presence or absence of certain business
schedules; the larger of total income or
loss; and size of business plus farm
receipts. Sampling rates vary from .043% to
100%.

**Data Collection and Imputation Proce-
dures:** Computer selection of sample of tax
return records. Data adjusted during editing
for incorrect, missing, or inconsistent entries
to ensure consistency with other entries on
return.

Estimates of Sampling Error: Estimated
CV's for tax year 1990 are not available; for
1987 (the latest available): For sole proprietorships, business receipts, 1.66%; net
income, (less loss), 1.33%; depreciation
2.17%; interest expense 2.80%; and
employee benefit programs 7.55%.

Other (nonsampling) Errors: Processing
errors and errors arising from the use of tolerance checks for the data.

Sources of Additional Material: U.S. Internal Revenue Service, *Statistics of Income,
Sole Proprietorship Returns* (for years
through 1980) and *Statistics of Income Bulletin,* vol. 10, No. 1 (summer 1990).

Source and Title: U.S. Internal Revenue
Service, *Statistics of Income, Partnership
Returns* and *Statistics of Income Bulletin*

Tables: 827-829, 831, and 832.

Universe, Frequency, and Types of Data:
Annual study of unaudited income tax
returns of partnerships, Form 1065. Data
provided on various financial characteristics
by industry.

Type of Data Collection Operation:
Stratified probability sample of approximately 28,000 partnership returns from a
population of 1,660,000 filed during calendar year 1990. The sample is classified
based on combinations of gross receipts,
net income or loss, and total assets, and on
industry. Sampling rates vary from .04% to
100%.

**Data Collection and Imputation Proce-
dures:** Computer selection of sample of tax
return records. Data are adjusted during
editing for incorrect, missing, or inconsistent
entries to ensure consistency with other
entries on return. Data not available due to
regulations are not imputed.

Estimates of Sampling Error: Estimated
CV's for tax year 1988 (latest available):
For number of partnerships, .51%; business
receipts, .78%; net income, 3.03%; net loss,
2.21% and total assets, 1.22%.

Other (nonsampling) Errors: Processing
errors and errors arising from the use of tolerance checks for the data.

Sources of Additional Material: U.S. Internal Revenue Service, *Statistics of Income,
Partnership Returns* and *Statistics of
Income Bulletin,* vol. 10, No. 1 (summer
1990).

Source and Title: U.S. Internal Revenue
Service, *Corporation Income Tax Returns*

Tables: 827-829 and 835-837.

Universe, Frequency, and Types of Data:
Annual study of unaudited corporation
income tax returns, Forms 1120 and 1120
(A, F, L, PC, REIT, RIC, and S), filed by
corporations or businesses legally defined

as corporations. Data provided on various financial characteristics by industry and size of total assets, and business receipts.

Type of Data Collection Operation: Stratified probability sample of approximately 85,000 returns for 1987, distributed by sample classes generally based on type of return, size of total assets, size of net income or deficit, and selected business activity. Sampling rates for sample strata varied from .25% to 100%.

Data Collection and Imputation Procedures: Computer selection of sample of tax return records. Data adjusted during editing for incorrect, missing, or inconsistent entries to ensure consistency with other entries on return and to achieve statistical definitions.

Estimates of Sampling Error: Estimated CV's for 1988: Number of returns in subgroups ranged from 1.4% with assets under $100,000, to 0% with assets over $100 mil.; for amount of net income and amount of income tax, .18%

Other (nonsampling) Errors: Processing errors and errors arising from the use of tolerance checks for the data.

Sources of Additional Material: U.S. Internal Revenue Service, *Statistics of Income, Corporation Income Tax Returns,* annual.

SECTION 18. COMMUNICATIONS

(See section 1 for information pertaining to table 883, and section 26 for table 895.)

SECTION 19. ENERGY

Source and Title: U.S. Energy Information Administration, *Residential Energy Consumption Survey*

Tables: 920, 921 and table 1197 in section 25.

Universe, Frequency, and Types of Data: Triennial survey of households and fuel suppliers. Data are obtained on energy-related household characteristics, housing unit characteristics, use of fuels, and energy consumption and expenditures by fuel type.

Type of Data Collection Operation: Probability sample of 7,183 eligible units in 129 PSU's. For responding units, fuel consumption and expenditure data obtained from fuel suppliers to those households.

Data Collection and Imputation Procedures: Personal interviews. Extensive followup of nonrespondents including mail questionnaires for some households. Adjustments for nonrespondents were made in weighting for respondents. Most item nonresponses were imputed.

Estimates of Sampling Error: Estimated CV's for household averages: For consumption, 1.3%; for expenditures, 1.0%; for various fuels, values ranged from 1.4% for electricity to 5.9% for LPG.

Other (nonsampling) Errors: Household response rate of 86.7%. Nonconsumption data were mostly imputed for mail respondents (5.2% of eligible units). Usable responses from fuel suppliers for various fuels ranged from 82.8% for electricity to 55.7% for fuel oil.

Sources of Additional Material: U.S. Energy Information Administration, *Household Energy Consumption and Expenditures, 1990* and *Housing Characteristics, 1990.*

SECTION 21. TRANSPORTATION—LAND

(See section 1 for information pertaining to table 1007, section 13 for table 985, section 15 for table 1035, and section 27 for table 1026.)

SECTION 22. TRANSPORTATION—AIR AND WATER

Source and Title: U.S. Bureau of the Census, *Foreign Trade—Export Statistics*

Tables: See Bureau of the Census citations for export statistics in source notes in sections 22 and 28 and also table 1152 in section 24; and 1318 in section 29.

Universe, Frequency, and Types of Data: The export declarations collected by Customs are processed each month to obtain data on the movement of U.S. merchandise exports to foreign countries. Data obtained include value, quantity, and shipping weight of exports by commodity, country of destination, Customs district of exportation, and mode of transportation.

Type of Data Collection Operation: Shipper's Export Declarations are required to be filed for the exportation of merchandise valued over $1,500. Customs officials collect and transmit the documents to the Bureau of the Census on a flow basis for data compilation. Value data for shipments valued under $1,501 are estimated, based on established percentages of individual country totals.

Data Collection and Imputation Procedures: Statistical copies of Shipper's Export Declarations are received on a daily basis from Customs ports throughout the country and subjected to a monthly processing cycle. They are fully processed to the extent they reflect items valued over

$1,500. Estimates for shipments valued at $1,500 or less are made, based on established percentages of individual country totals.

Estimates of Sampling Error: Not applicable.

Other (nonsampling) Errors: Clerical and complex computer checks intercept most processing errors and minimize otherwise significant reporting errors; other nonsampling errors are caused by undercounting of exports to Canada due to the nonreceipt of some Shipper's Export Declarations.

Sources of Additional Material: U.S. Bureau of the Census, *U.S. Merchandise Trade: Exports, General Imports, and Imports for Consumption, SITC, Commodity by Country*, FT 925.

Source and Title: U.S. Bureau of the Census, *Foreign Trade—Import Statistics*

Tables: See Bureau of the Census citations for import statistics in source notes in sections 22 and 28 and also table 1152 in section 24; and 1318 in section 29.

Universe, Frequency, and Types of Data: The import entry documents collected by Customs are processed each month to obtain data on the movement of merchandise imported into the United States. Data obtained include value, quantity, and shipping weight by commodity, country of origin, Customs district of entry, and mode of transportation.

Type of Data Collection Operation: Import entry documents are required to be filed for the importation of goods into the United States valued over $1,000 or for articles which must be reported on formal entries. Customs officials collect and transmit statistical copies of the documents to the Bureau of the Census on a flow basis for data compilation. Estimates for shipments valued under $1,001 and not reported on formal entries are based on established percentages of individual country totals.

Data Collection and Imputation Procedures: Statistical copies of import entry documents, received on a daily basis from Customs ports of entry throughout the country, are subjected to a monthly processing cycle. They are fully processed to the extent they reflect items valued at $1,001 and over or items which must be reported on formal entries.

Estimates of Sampling Error: Not applicable.

Other (nonsampling) Errors: Verification of statistical data reporting by Customs officials prior to transmittal and a subsequent program of clerical and computer checks are utilized to hold nonsampling errors arising from reporting and/or processing errors to a minimum.

Sources of Additional Material: U.S. Bureau of the Census, *U.S. Merchandise Trade: Exports, General Imports and Imports for Consumption, SITC, Commodity by Country*, FT 925.

(See section 13 for information pertaining to table 1052.)

SECTION 23. AGRICULTURE

Source and Title: U.S. Bureau of the Census, *Census of Agriculture*.

Tables: 1073-1080.

Universe, Frequency, and Types of Data: Complete count of U.S. farms and ranches conducted once every five years with data at the national, state, and county level. Data published on farm numbers and related items/characteristics.

Type of Data Collection Operation: Complete census for—number of farms; land in farms; estimated market value of land and buildings, machinery and equipment, agriculture products sold; total cropland; irrigated land; total farm production expenses; farm operator characteristics; livestock and poultry inventory and sales; and selected crops harvested.

Data Collection and Imputation Procedures: Data collection is by mailing questionnaires to all farmers and ranchers. Nonrespondents are conducted by telephone and correspondence followups. Imputations were made for all nonresponse item/characteristics.

Estimates of Sampling Error: Variability in the estimates is due to the sample selection and estimation for items collected by sample and census nonresponse estimation procedures. The CV's for national and state estimates are generally very small. Approximately 85% response rate.

Other (nonsampling) Errors: Nonsampling errors are due to incompleteness of the census mailing list, duplications on the list, respondent reporting errors, errors in editing reported data, and in imputation for missing data. Evaluation studies are conducted to measure certain nonsampling errors such as list coverage and classification error. Results from the evaluation program for the 1987 census indicate the net under coverage amounted to about 7.2% of the nations total farms.

Sources of Additional Material: U.S. Bureau of the Census, *1992 Census of Agriculture*, Volume 2, Subject Series—Part 1, *Agriculture Atlas of the U.S.*, Part 2, *Coverage Evaluation*, Part 3, *Rankings of*

States and Counties, Part 4, *History,* Part 5, *ZIP Code Tabulation of Selected Items,* ; and Volume 4 *Farm and Ranch Irrigation Survey.*

Source and Title: U.S. Department of Agriculture, National Agricultural Statistics Service (NASS), *Basic Area Frame Sample*

Tables: See tables citing NASS in source notes in section 23, which pertain to this or the following two surveys.

Universe, Frequency, and Types of Data: Two annual area sample surveys of U.S. farm operators: June agricultural survey collects data on planted acreage and livestock inventories; and a February Farm Costs and Returns survey that collects data on total farm production, expenses and specific commodity costs of production.

Type of Data Collection Operation: Stratified probability sample of about 16,000 land area units of about 1 sq. mile (range from 0.1 sq. mile in cities to several sq. miles in open grazing areas). Sample includes 60,000 parcels of agricultural land. About 20% of the sample replaced annually.

Data Collection and Imputation Procedures: Data collection is by personal enumeration. Imputation is based on enumerator observation or data reported by respondents having similar agricultural characteristics.

Estimates of Sampling Error: Estimated CV's range from 1% to 2% for regional estimates to 3% to 6% for State estimates of livestock inventories.

Other (nonsampling) Errors: Minimized through rigid quality controls on the collection process and careful review of all reported data.

Sources of Additional Material: U.S. Department of Agriculture, SRS, *Scope and Methods of the Statistical Reporting Service,* (name changed to National Agricultural Statistics Service), Miscellaneous Publication No. 1308, September 1983 (revised).

Source and Title: U.S. Department of Agriculture, National Agricultural Statistics Service (NASS), *Multiple Frame Surveys*

Tables: See tables citing NASS in source notes in section 23, which pertain to this or the following survey.

Universe, Frequency, and Types of Data: Surveys of U.S. farm operators to obtain data on major livestock inventories, selected crop acreages and production, grain stocks, and farm labor characteristics; and to obtain farm economic data for price indexing.

Type of Data Collection Operation: Primary frame is obtained from general or special purpose lists, supplemented by a probability sample of land areas used to estimate for list incompleteness.

Data Collection and Imputation Procedures: Mail, telephone, or personal interviews used for initial data collection. Mail nonrespondent followup by phone and personal interviews. Imputation based on average of respondents.

Estimates of Sampling Error: Estimated CV for number of hired farm workers is about 3%. Estimated CV's range from 1% to 2% for regional estimates to 3% to 6% for State estimates of livestock inventories.

Other (nonsampling) Errors: In addition to above, replicated sampling procedures used to monitor effects of changes in survey procedures.

Sources of Additional Material: U.S. Department of Agriculture, SRS, *Scope and Methods of the Statistical Reporting Service,* (name changed to National Agricultural Statistics Service), Miscellaneous Publication No. 1308, September 1983 (revised).

Source and Title: U.S. Department of Agriculture, National Agricultural Statistics Service (NASS), *Objective Yield Surveys*

Tables: See tables citing NASS in source notes in section 23, which pertain to this or the preceding survey.

Universe, Frequency, and Types of Data: Surveys for data on corn, cotton, potatoes, soybeans, wheat, and rice to forecast and estimate yields.

Type of Data Collection Operation: Random location of plots in probability sample of fields. Fields selected in June from Basic Area Frame Sample (see above).

Data Collection and Imputation Procedures: Enumerators count and measure plant characteristics in sample fields. Production measured from plots at harvest. Harvest loss measured from post harvest gleanings.

Estimates of Sampling Error: CV's for national estimates of production are about 2-3%.

Other (nonsampling) Errors: In addition to above, replicated sampling procedures used to monitor effects of changes in survey procedures.

Sources of Additional Material: U.S. Department of Agriculture, SRS, *Scope and Methods of the Statistical Reporting Service,* (name changed to National Agricultural Statistics Service), Miscellaneous Publication No. 1308, September 1983 (revised).

(See section 1 above for information pertaining to the Census of Population and Current Population Survey.)

SECTION 24. NATURAL RESOURCES

(See section 15 for table 1129, and section 22 for table 1152.)

SECTION 25. CONSTRUCTION AND HOUSING

Source and Title: U.S. Bureau of the Census, *Monthly Survey of Construction*
Tables: 1178 and 1180-1183.
Universe, Frequency, and Types of Data: Survey conducted monthly of newly constructed housing units (excluding mobile homes). Data are collected on the start, completion, and sale of housing. (Annual figures are aggregates of monthly estimates.)
Type of Data Collection Operation: Probability sample of housing units obtained from building permits selected from 17,000 places. For nonpermit places, multistage probability sample of new housing units selected in 169 PSU's. In those areas, all roads are canvassed in selected enumeration districts.
Data Collection and Imputation Procedures: Data are obtained by telephone inquiry and field visit.
Estimates of Sampling Error: Estimated CV of 3% to 4% for estimates of national totals, but are as high as 20% for estimated totals of more detailed characteristics, such as housing units in multiunit structures.
Other (nonsampling) Errors: Response rate is over 90% for most items. Nonsampling errors are attributed to definitional problems, differences in interpretation of questions, incorrect reporting, inability to obtain information about all cases in the sample, and processing errors.
Sources of Additional Material: U.S. Bureau of the Census, *Construction Reports,* series C20, *Housing Starts;* C22, *Housing Completions;* and C25, *New One-Family Houses Sold and For Sale.*

Source and Title: U.S. Bureau of the Census, *Value of New Construction Put in Place*
Tables: 1172-1174.
Universe, Frequency, and Types of Data: Survey conducted monthly on total value of all construction put in place in the current month, both public and private projects. Construction values include costs of materials and labor, contractors' profits, overhead costs, cost of architectural and engineering work, and miscellaneous project costs. (Annual figures are aggregates of monthly estimates.)
Type of Data Collection Operation: Varies by type of activity: Total cost of private one-family houses started each month is distributed into value put in place using fixed

patterns of monthly construction progress; using a multistage probability sample, data for private multifamily housing are obtained by mail from owners of multiunit projects. Data for residential additions and alterations are obtained in a quarterly survey measuring expenditures; monthly estimates are interpolated from quarterly data. Estimates of value of private nonresidential buildings, and State and local government construction are obtained by mail from owners (or agents) for a probability sample of projects. Estimates of farm nonresidential construction expenditures are based on U.S. Department of Agriculture annual estimates of construction; public utility estimates are obtained from reports submitted to Federal regulatory agencies and from private utility companies; estimates for all other private construction (nonbuilding) are obtained by phasing F. W. Dodge contract award data; estimates of Federal construction are based on monthly data supplied by Federal agencies.
Data Collection and Imputation Procedures: See "Type of Data Collection Operation." Imputation accounts for approximately 20% of estimated value of construction each month.
Estimates of Sampling Error: CV estimates for private nonresidential building construction range from 3% for estimated value of industrial buildings to 9% for religious buildings. CV is approximately 2% for total new private nonresidential buildings.
Other (nonsampling) Errors: For directly measured data series based on samples, some nonsampling errors may arise from processing errors, imputations, and misunderstanding of questions. Indirect data series are dependent on the validity of the underlying assumptions and procedures.
Sources of Additional Material: U.S. Bureau of the Census, *Construction Reports,* series C30, *Value of New Construction Put in Place.*

Source and Title: U.S. Bureau of the Census, *Census of Housing*
Tables: See tables citing *Census of Housing* in source notes in section 25.
Universe, Frequency, and Types of Data: Census of all occupied and vacant housing, excluding group quarters, conducted every 10 years as part of the decennial census (see section 1 above) to determine characteristics of U.S. housing.
Type of Data Collection Operation: For 1970, 1980, and 1990, a complete count of some housing items (e.g. Owned or rented, and value). In 1970, other items collected from 5% and 15% probability samples selected from two sets of detailed questions

on housing (these two sets having some common items). In 1980, approximately 19% of the housing units were included in the sample; in 1990, approximately 17%.

Data Collection and Imputation Procedures: In 1970, a self-enumeration census using a mail-out/mail-back procedure was used in most areas. In 1980 and 1990, mail questionnaires were used in even more areas than in 1970, with personal interviews in the remainder. Followup for nonrespondents and identification of vacant units done by phone and personal visit.

Estimates of Sampling Error: Sampling errors for data are estimated for all items collected by sample and vary by characteristic and geographic area.

Other (nonsampling) Errors: Evaluation studies for 1980 estimated the underenumeration of occupied housing units at 1.5%. The missed rate in 1980 for all units was 2.6% or approximately 2.3 million units, 1 million of which were vacant housing units.

Sources of Additional Material: U.S. Bureau of the Census, *1980 Census of Population and Housing, The Coverage of Housing in the 1980 Census*, PHC80-E1, July 1985.

Source and Title: U.S. Bureau of the Census, *American Housing Survey*

Tables: See tables citing *American Housing Survey* in source notes.

Universe, Frequency, and Types of Data: Conducted nationally in the fall in odd numbered years to obtain data on the approximately 103 million occupied or vacant housing units in the United States (group quarters are excluded). Data include characteristics of occupied housing units, vacant units, new housing and mobile home units, financial characteristics, recent mover households, housing and neighborhood quality indicators, and energy characteristics.

Type of Data Collection Operation: The national sample was a multistage probability sample with about 51,300 units eligible for interview in 1987. Sample units, selected within 394 PSU's, were surveyed over a 5-month period.

Data Collection and Imputation Procedures: For 1987, the survey was conducted by personal interviews. The interviewers obtained the information from the occupants or, if the unit was vacant, from informed persons such as landlords, rental agents, or knowledgeable neighbors.

Estimates of Sampling Error: For the national sample, illustrations of the S.E. of the estimates are provided in the appendix

B of the 1987 report. As an example, the estimated CV is about 0.5% for the estimated percentage of owner occupied units with two persons.

Other (nonsampling) Errors: Response rate was about 97%. Nonsampling errors may result from incorrect or incomplete responses, errors in coding and recording, and processing errors. For the 1985 national sample, approximately 6% of the total housing inventory was not adequately represented by the AHS sample.

Sources of Additional Material: U.S. Bureau of the Census, *Current Housing Reports*, series H-150 and H-170, *American Housing Survey*.

(See section 1 above for information pertaining to the Census of Population, section 15 pertaining to table 1170, and section 19 for table 1197.)

Section 26. MANUFACTURES

Source and Title: U.S. Bureau of the Census, *Census of Manufactures*

Tables: See tables citing *Census of Manufactures* in source notes in section 26 and also table 895 in section 18 and table 1322 in section 29.

Universe, Frequency, and Types of Data: Conducted every 5 years to obtain information on labor, materials, capital input and output characteristics, plant location, and legal form of organization for all plants in the United States with one or more paid employees. Universe was 350,000 manufacturing establishments in 1987.

Type of Data Collection Operation: Complete enumeration of data items obtained from 200,000 firms. Administrative records from Internal Revenue Service and Social Security Administration are used for 150,000 smaller single-location firms, which were determined by various cutoffs based on size and industry.

Data Collection and Imputation Procedures: Five mail and telephone followups for larger nonrespondents. Data for small single-location firms (generally those with fewer than 10 employees) not mailed census questionnaires were estimated from administrative records of IRS and SSA. Data for nonrespondents were imputed from related responses or administrative records from IRS and SSA. Approximately 8% of total value of shipments was represented by fully imputed records in 1987.

Estimates of Sampling Error: Not applicable.

Other (nonsampling) Errors: Based on evaluation studies, estimates of nonsampling errors for 1972 were about 1.3% for estimated total payroll; 2% for total employment; and 1% for value of shipments. Estimates for later years are not available.

Sources of Additional Material: U.S. Bureau of the Census, *1987 Census of Manufactures, Industry Series, Geographic Area Series, and Subject Series.*

Source and Title: U.S. Bureau of the Census, *Annual Survey of Manufactures*

Tables: See tables citing *Annual Survey of Manufactures* in source notes.

Universe, Frequency, and Types of Data: Conducted annually to provide basic measures of manufacturing activity for intercensal years for all manufacturing establishments having one or more paid employees.

Type of Data Collection Operation: Sampling frame is 350,000 establishments in the 1987 Census of Manufactures (see above), supplemented by Social Security Administration lists of new manufacturers and new manufacturing establishments of multi-establishment companies identified annually by the Census Bureau's Company Organization Survey. A probability sample of about 55,000 establishments is selected. All establishments of companies with more than $500 million of manufacturing shipments in 1987 are included with certainty. All establishments with 250+ employees are also included with certainty along with a probability sample of smaller establishments.

Data Collection and Imputation Procedures: Survey is conducted by mail with phone and mail followups of nonrespondents. Imputation (for all nonresponse items) is based on previous year reports, or for new establishments in survey, on industry averages.

Estimates of Sampling Error: Estimated standard errors for number of employees, new expenditure, and for value added totals are given in annual publications. For U.S. level industry statistics, most estimated standard errors are 2% or less, but vary considerably for detailed characteristics.

Other (nonsampling) Errors: Response rate is about 85%. Nonsampling errors include those due to collection, reporting, and transcription errors, many of which are corrected through computer and clerical checks.

Sources of Additional Material: U.S. Bureau of the Census, *Annual Survey of Manufactures,* and Technical Paper 24.

Section 27. DOMESTIC TRADE AND SERVICES

Source and Title: U.S. Bureau of the Census, *Census of Wholesale Trade, Census of Retail Trade, Census of Service Industries*

Tables: See tables citing the above censuses in source notes in section 27 and table 1322 in section 29.

Universe, Frequency, and Types of Data: Conducted every 5 years to obtain data on number of establishments, number of employees, total payroll size, total sales, and other industry-specific statistics. In 1987, the universe was all employer establishments primarily engaged in wholesale trade, and employer and nonemployer establishments in retail trade or service industries.

Type of Data Collection Operation: All wholesale firms with paid employees surveyed; all retail and service large employer firms surveyed (i.e. all employer firms above the payroll size cutoff established to separate large from small employers) plus a 10-percent sample of smaller employer firms. Firms with no employees were not required to file a census return.

Data Collection and Imputation Procedures: Mail questionnaire is utilized with both mail and telephone followups for non-respondents. Data for nonrespondents and "nonselected" small employer firms in retail trade and service industries are obtained from administrative records of IRS and the Social Security Administration.

Estimates of Sampling Error: Not applicable.

Other (nonsampling) Errors: Response rate in 1987 of 80% for single establishment firms; 83% for multi-establishment firms. Item response ranged from 60% to 90% with higher rates for less detailed questions.

Sources of Additional Material: U.S. Bureau of the Census, Appendix A of *Census of Retail Trade; Census of Service Industries; Census of Wholesale Trade;* and *History of the 1987 Economic Censuses,* April 1992.

Source and Title: U.S. Bureau of the Census, *Current Business Surveys*

Tables: 1257-1260, 1272, 1277, 1281, and table 178 in section 3, tables 403 and 425 in section 7, and table 1026 in section 21.

Universe, Frequency, and Types of Data: Provides monthly estimates of retail sales by kind of business and geographic area, and end-of-month inventories of retail stores; wholesale sales and end-of-month inventories; and annual receipts of selected service industries.

Type of Data Collection Operation: Probability sample of all firms from a list frame and, additionally, for retail and service an area frame. The list frame is the Bureau's Standard Statistical Establishment List (SSEL) updated quarterly for recent birth Employer Identification (EI) Numbers issued by the Internal Revenue Service and assigned a kind-of-business code by the Social Security Administration. The largest firms are included monthly; a sample of others is included every three months on a rotating basis. The area frame covers businesses not subjected to sampling on the list frame.

Data Collection and Imputation Procedures: Data are collected by mail questionnaire with telephone followups for nonrespondents. Imputation made for each nonresponse item and each item failing edit checks.

Estimates of Sampling Error: For the 1989 monthly surveys, CV's are about 0.6% for estimated total retail sales, 1.7% for wholesale sales, 1.3% for wholesale inventories.

For dollar volume of receipts, CV's from the *Service Annual Survey* vary by kind of business and range between 1.5% to 15.0%. Sampling errors are shown in monthly publications.

Other (nonsampling) Errors: Imputation rates are about 18% to 23% for monthly retail sales, 20% to 25% for wholesale sales, about 25% to 30% for monthly wholesale inventories and 14% for the *Service Annual Survey.*

Sources of Additional Material: U.S. Bureau of the Census, *Current Business Reports, Monthly Retail Trade, Monthly Wholesale Trade,* and *Service Annual Survey.*

(See section 17 for information pertaining to tables 1254 and 1280.)

Section 29. OUTLYING AREAS

(See section 1 for information pertaining to tables 1311 and 1312, section 2 for table 1310, section 17 for table 1319, section 22 for table 1318, sections 26 and 27 for table 1322.)

Index to Tables Having Historical Statistics, Colonial Times to 1970 Series

[The most recent historical supplement to the *Statistical Abstract* is the bicentennial edition, *Historical Statistics of the United States, Colonial Times to 1970* (see inside back cover). Listed below are statistical time series (identified by number) appearing in this edition, for which tables in the *Statistical Abstract* present comparable figures. Historical series are listed only where related or comparable data are available for one or more years later than 1970. In a few instances, it may be necessary to combine figures shown in the *Abstract* to obtain totals comparable to the series shown in *Historical Statistics*]

Historical Statistics series	1996 Abstract table number	Historical Statistics series	1996 Abstract table number	Historical Statistics series	1996 Abstract table number	Historical Statistics series	1996 Abstract table number
N		**Q—Con.**		**T—Con.**		**X—Con.**	
N 1-29	1173	Q 414-416	1068	T 391-443	1279	X 444-453	801
N 66-69	1173	Q 438-448	1064	T 444-471	908	X 454-455	800
N 78-100	1175	Q 449-458	1066	T 472-484	907	X 474-491	804
N 118-137	1171	Q 473-480	1070			X 492-498	802
N 140-155	1170	Q 487-502	1065	**U**		X 517-530	809
N 156-163	1178	Q 507-517	1063			X 536-539	818
N 170	1178	Q 604-623	1049	U 1-25	1283	X 551-560	791
N 186-191	1203			U 26-39	1286	X 588-609	778
N 238-245	1190	**R**		U 41-46	1293	X 716-724	776
N 249-258	1201			U 47-74	1288	X 821; 835	768
N 273, 276	786	R 1-12	882	U 75-186	1294	X 864-878	783
		R 31-45	882	U 190-195	1299	X 879-889	824
P		R 46-70	880	U 207-212	1307	X 890-917	826
		R 75-88	880	U 264-273	1300		
P 1-12	1210	R 106-109	908	U 317-352	1305	**Y**	
P 13	1218	R 123-126	908				
P 18-39	1218	R 140-148	885	**V**		Y 79-83	431
P 58-67	1211	R 163-171	903			Y 84-134	434
P 74-92	1216	R 172-186	904	V 1-12	827	Y 135-186	435
P 93-106	872	R 188-191	905	V 20-30	843	Y 189-198	443
P 235, 236a	1227	R 191-216	900	V 42-53	829	Y 199-203	444
P 239-241	1228	R 224-231	897	V 167-183	837	Y 204-210	439
P 265-269	1232	R 232-243	896	V 193-196	837	Y 211-214	437
				V 197-212	948	Y 272-307	501
Q		**S**				Y 308-317	532
				W		Y 318-331	535
Q 36-42	985	S 32-52	939			Y 339-342	512
Q 50-51, 55	987	S 78-82	939	W 14, 17, 19	655	Y 343-351	513
Q 69-75	1025	S 86-107	939	W 22-25	656	Y 358-373	523
Q 90-94	993	S 133-146	948	W 30-54	655	Y 381-392	835
Q 136-147	996	S 160-175	950	W 62-65	655	Y 393-411	524
Q 148; 150	1261	S 190-204	954	W 82-95	887	Y 412-439	529
Q 156-162	1019	S 205-218	953	W 96-108	852	Y 458-460	541
Q 199-207	1022			W 109-125	958	Y 472-487	513
Q 208	1010	**T**		W 126	961	Y 505-637	471
Q 224-232	1010			W 142	960	Y 638-651	476
Q 233-234	995	T 43-47	1253	W 167	969	Y 652-848	471
Q 238-250	1023	T 79-196	1255			Y 710-782	487
Q 284-312	1032	T 197-219	1259	**X**		Y 787-788	473
Q 319, 330	1032	T 245-246	1257			Y 794	482
Q 332	1034	T 245-271	1258	X 114-147	771	Y 856-903	557
Q 356-378	1032	T 274-287	1273	X 192, 229	768	Y 904-916	552
Q 400-401	1032	T 280-371	1275	X 410-417	796	Y 943-956	565
						Y 998-999	568

Tables Deleted From the 1995 Edition of the Statistical Abstract

Index

NOTE: Index citations refer to table numbers, not page numbers.

NOTE: Index citations refer to table numbers, not page numbers.

NOTE: Index citations refer to table numbers, not page numbers.

NOTE: Index citations refer to table numbers, not page numbers.

NOTE: Index citations refer to table numbers, not page numbers.

NOTE: Index citations refer to table numbers, not page numbers.

NOTE: Index citations refer to table numbers, not page numbers.

NOTE: Index citations refer to table numbers, not page numbers.

NOTE: Index citations refer to table numbers, not page numbers.

NOTE: Index citations refer to table numbers, not page numbers.

NOTE: Index citations refer to table numbers, not page numbers.

NOTE: Index citations refer to table numbers, not page numbers.

NOTE: Index citations refer to table numbers, not page numbers.

NOTE: Index citations refer to table numbers, not page numbers.

NOTE: Index citations refer to table numbers, not page numbers.

NOTE: Index citations refer to table numbers, not page numbers.

NOTE: Index citations refer to table numbers, not page numbers.

NOTE: Index citations refer to table numbers, not page numbers.

NOTE: Index citations refer to table numbers, not page numbers.

NOTE: Index citations refer to table numbers, not page numbers.

NOTE: Index citations refer to table numbers, not page numbers.

NOTE: Index citations refer to table numbers, not page numbers.

NOTE: Index citations refer to table numbers, not page numbers.

NOTE: Index citations refer to table numbers, not page numbers.

NOTE: Index citations refer to table numbers, not page numbers.

NOTE: Index citations refer to table numbers, not page numbers.

NOTE: Index citations refer to table numbers, not page numbers.

998   Index

NOTE: Index citations refer to table numbers, not page numbers.

Index

NOTE: Index citations refer to table numbers, not page numbers.

NOTE: Index citations refer to table numbers, not page numbers.

NOTE: Index citations refer to table numbers, not page numbers.

NOTE: Index citations refer to table numbers, not page numbers.

NOTE: Index citations refer to table numbers, not page numbers.

NOTE: Index citations refer to table numbers, not page numbers.

NOTE: Index citations refer to table numbers, not page numbers.

NOTE: Index citations refer to table numbers, not page numbers.

1008 Index

NOTE: Index citations refer to table numbers, not page numbers.

NOTE: Index citations refer to table numbers, not page numbers.

NOTE: Index citations refer to table numbers, not page numbers.

NOTE: Index citations refer to table numbers, not page numbers.

NOTE: Index citations refer to table numbers, not page numbers.

NOTE: Index citations refer to table numbers, not page numbers.

NOTE: Index citations refer to table numbers, not page numbers.

NOTE: Index citations refer to table numbers, not page numbers.

NOTE: Index citations refer to table numbers, not page numbers.

NOTE: Index citations refer to table numbers, not page numbers.

NOTE: Index citations refer to table numbers, not page numbers.

NOTE: Index citations refer to table numbers, not page numbers.

NOTE: Index citations refer to table numbers, not page numbers.

U.S. Census Bureau Announces

Census Catalog and Guide: 1996

Helps you select from all the products

Covers every Census Bureau product issued from mid-1993 through 1995:

- *Reports*
- *Computer tapes*
- *CD-ROM*
- *Floppy disks*
- *Online access*
- *Maps*

And

Describes many statistical products from other Federal agencies

Features facts about each product

Topics covered	Timeliness
Areas reported	Cost

Makes finding the right product easy

Guides to statistics from all censuses and surveys, covering population, housing, business, construction, and more.

Information about the Census Bureau's site on the Internet (http://census.gov/)

Title index and detailed subject index

Identifies sources of assistance

1,800 data center organizations
200 Census Bureau data specialists
1,500 depository libraries
Other Federal statistical agencies
3 other directory lists